Luis Jaramillo
1995

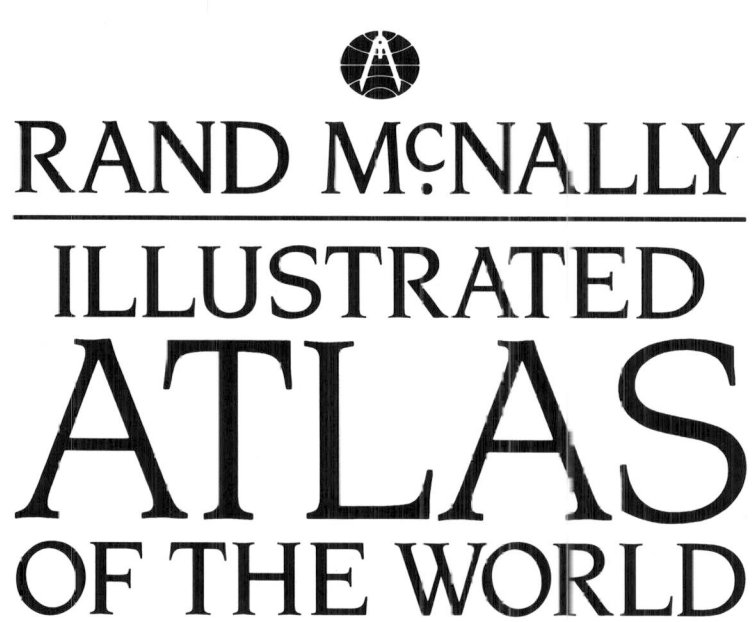

RAND McNALLY

ILLUSTRATED ATLAS OF THE WORLD

ILLUSTRATED
ATLAS
OF THE WORLD

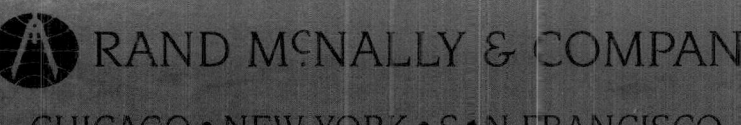

RAND McNALLY & COMPANY

CHICAGO • NEW YORK • SAN FRANCISCO

CONTENTS

Pages 1 through 240 and
A·1 through A·144 from
The Great Geographical Atlas
Copyright © 1992 Instituto Geografico De Agostini

Library of Congress Cataloging-in-Publication Data
Rand McNally and Company.
    Illustrated atlas of the world. — 1993 rev. ed.
        p.   cm.
    Shows changes to Czechoslovakia, Yugoslavia, and Eritrea.
    Title on added t.p.: Rand McNally illustrated atlas of the world.
    Includes indexes.
    ISBN 0-528-83492-4
    1. Atlases.   I. Title.   II. Title: Rand McNally illustrated atlas
of the world.   III. Title: Atlas of the world.
G1021.R185   1993   < G&M >
912—dc20   93-504
                                    CIP
                                    MAP

Printed in the United States of America by
Rand McNally & Company

Jacket photo Comstock/Hartman-Dewitt
Title page photo by Ray Atkeson

Our Planet Earth Section

Maps

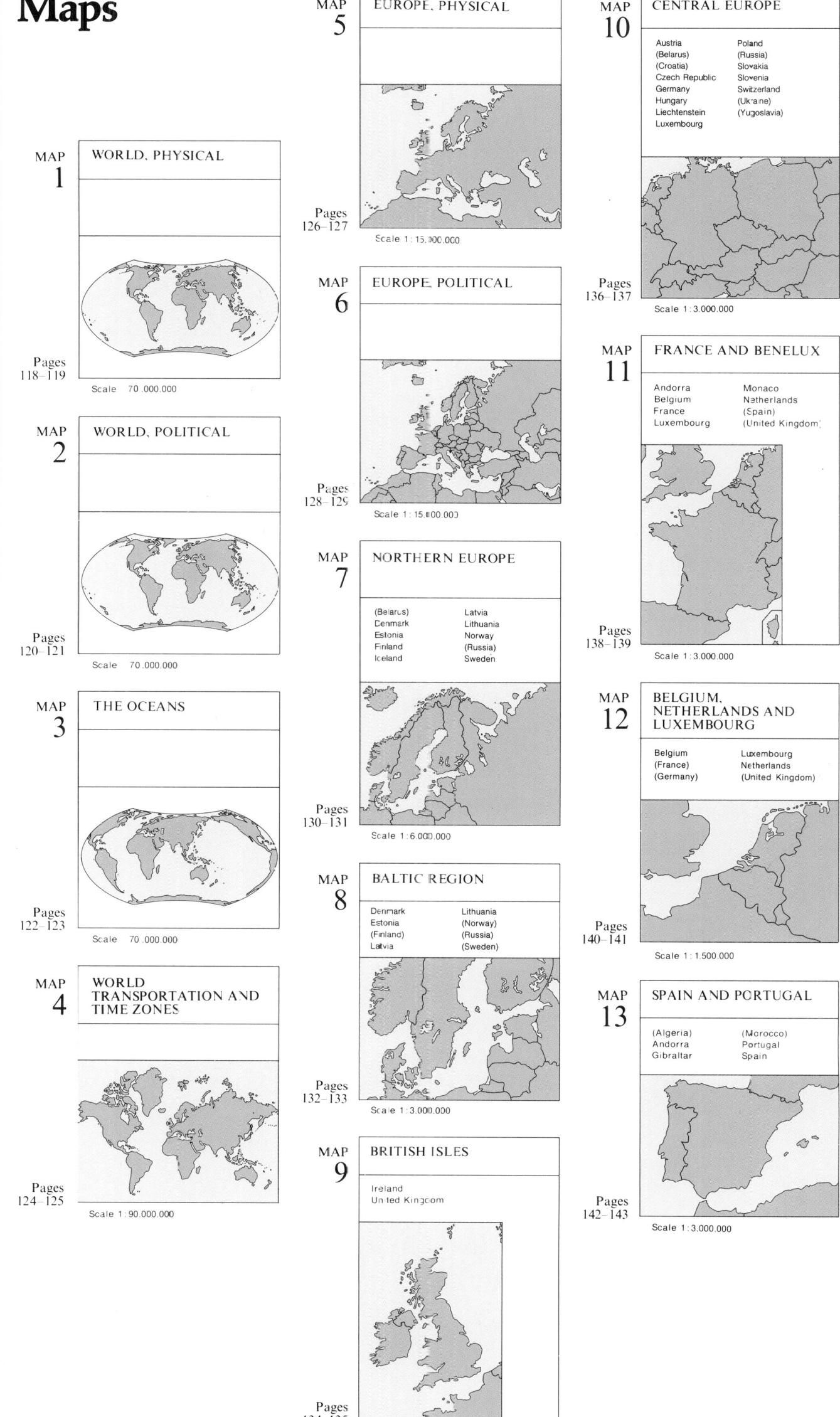

MAP **1** WORLD, PHYSICAL
Pages 118–119
Scale 70 .000.000

MAP **2** WORLD, POLITICAL
Pages 120–121
Scale 70 .000.000

MAP **3** THE OCEANS
Pages 122–123
Scale 70 .000.000

MAP **4** WORLD TRANSPORTATION AND TIME ZONES
Pages 124–125
Scale 1 : 90.000.000

MAP **5** EUROPE, PHYSICAL
Pages 126–127
Scale 1 : 15.000.000

MAP **6** EUROPE, POLITICAL
Pages 128–129
Scale 1 : 15.000.000

MAP **7** NORTHERN EUROPE

(Belarus)   Latvia
Denmark   Lithuania
Estonia   Norway
Finland   (Russia)
Iceland   Sweden

Pages 130–131
Scale 1 : 6.000.000

MAP **8** BALTIC REGION

Denmark   Lithuania
Estonia   (Norway)
(Finland)   (Russia)
Latvia   (Sweden)

Pages 132–133
Scale 1 : 3.000.000

MAP **9** BRITISH ISLES

Ireland
United Kingdom

Pages 134–135
Scale 1 : 3.000.000

MAP **10** CENTRAL EUROPE

Austria   Poland
(Belarus)   (Russia)
(Croatia)   Slovakia
Czech Republic   Slovenia
Germany   Switzerland
Hungary   (Ukraine)
Liechtenstein   (Yugoslavia)
Luxembourg

Pages 136–137
Scale 1 : 3.000.000

MAP **11** FRANCE AND BENELUX

Andorra   Monaco
Belgium   Netherlands
France   (Spain)
Luxembourg   (United Kingdom)

Pages 138–139
Scale 1 : 3.000.000

MAP **12** BELGIUM, NETHERLANDS AND LUXEMBOURG

Belgium   Luxembourg
(France)   Netherlands
(Germany)   (United Kingdom)

Pages 140–141
Scale 1 : 1.500.000

MAP **13** SPAIN AND PORTUGAL

(Algeria)   (Morocco)
Andorra   Portugal
Gibraltar   Spain

Pages 142–143
Scale 1 : 3.000.000

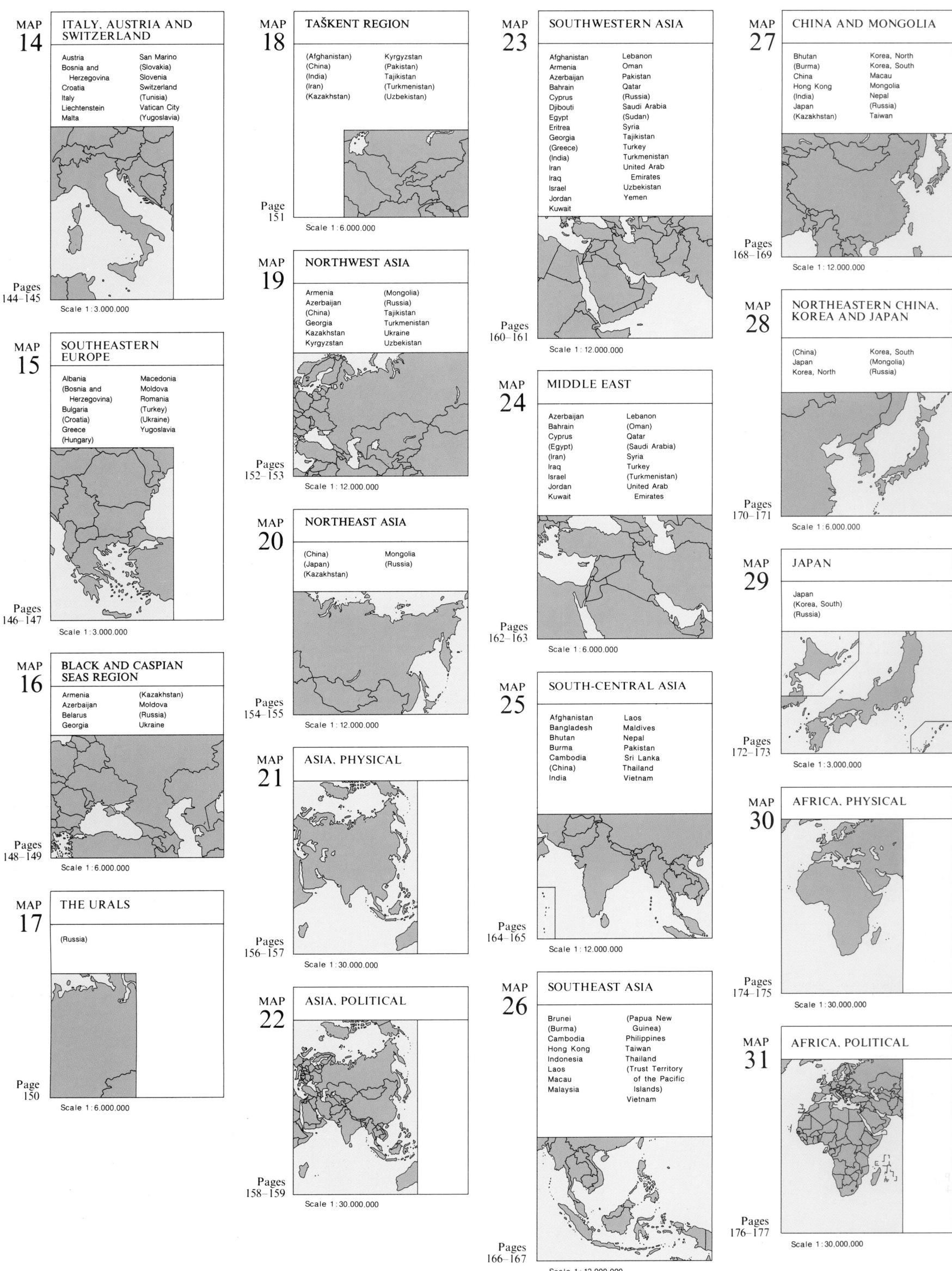

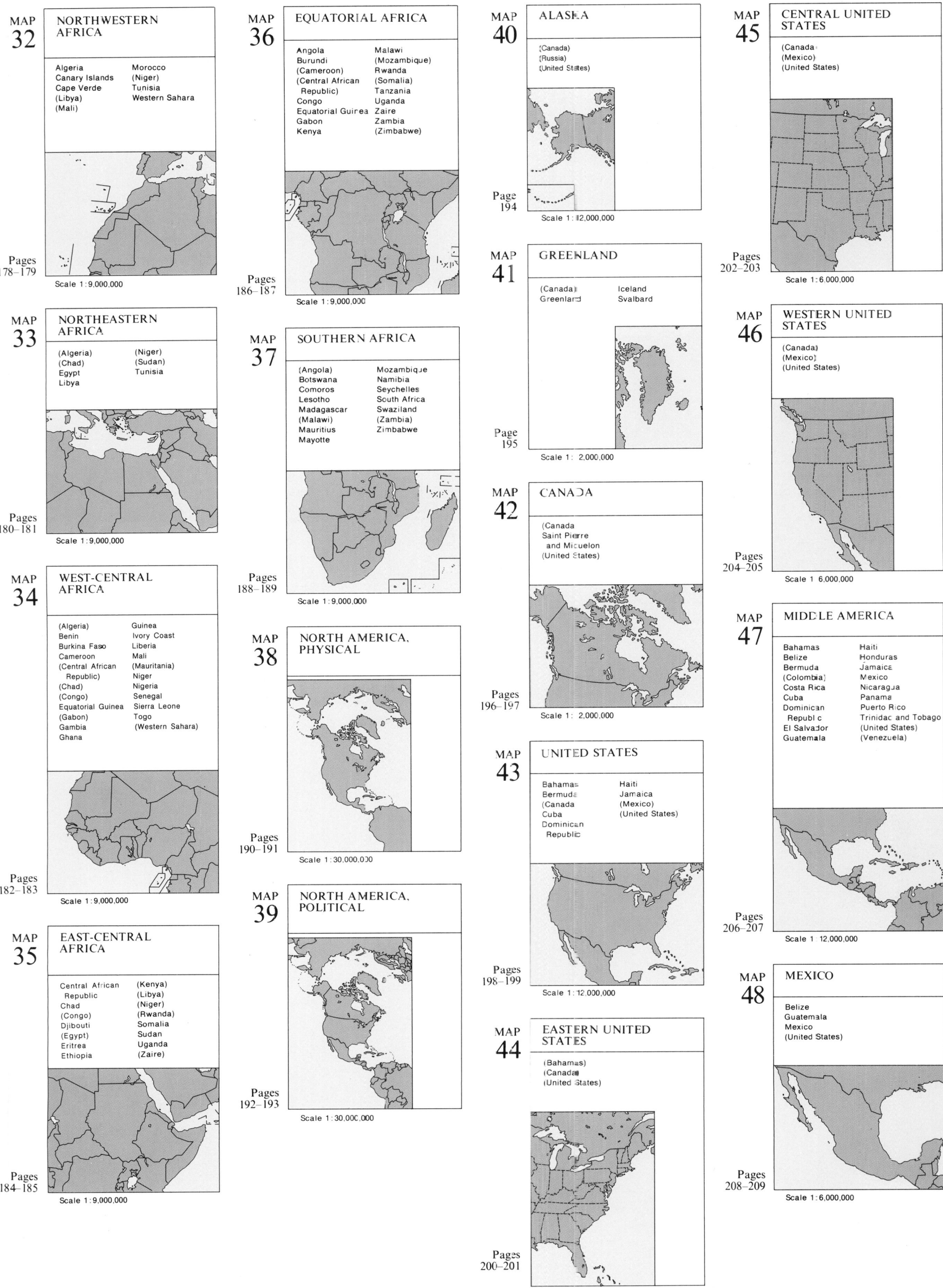

MAP 32   NORTHWESTERN AFRICA

Algeria
Canary Islands
Cape Verde
(Libya)
(Mali)

Morocco
(Niger)
Tunisia
Western Sahara

Pages 178–179

Scale 1:9,000,000

MAP 33   NORTHEASTERN AFRICA

(Algeria)
(Chad)
Egypt
Libya

(Niger)
(Sudan)
Tunisia

Pages 180–181

Scale 1:9,000,000

MAP 34   WEST-CENTRAL AFRICA

(Algeria)
Benin
Burkina Faso
Cameroon
(Central African
  Republic)
(Chad)
(Congo)
Equatorial Guinea
(Gabon)
Gambia
Ghana

Guinea
Ivory Coast
Liberia
Mali
(Mauritania)
Niger
Nigeria
Senegal
Sierra Leone
Togo
(Western Sahara)

Pages 182–183

Scale 1:9,000,000

MAP 35   EAST-CENTRAL AFRICA

Central African
  Republic
Chad
(Congo)
Djibouti
(Egypt)
Eritrea
Ethiopia

(Kenya)
(Libya)
(Niger)
(Rwanda)
Somalia
Sudan
Uganda
(Zaire)

Pages 184–185

Scale 1:9,000,000

MAP 36   EQUATORIAL AFRICA

Angola
Burundi
(Cameroon)
(Central African
  Republic)
Congo
Equatorial Guinea
Gabon
Kenya

Malawi
(Mozambique)
Rwanda
(Somalia)
Tanzania
Uganda
Zaire
Zambia
(Zimbabwe)

Pages 186–187

Scale 1:9,000,000

MAP 37   SOUTHERN AFRICA

(Angola)
Botswana
Comoros
Lesotho
Madagascar
(Malawi)
Mauritius
Mayotte

Mozambique
Namibia
Seychelles
South Africa
Swaziland
(Zambia)
Zimbabwe

Pages 188–189

Scale 1:9,000,000

MAP 38   NORTH AMERICA, PHYSICAL

Pages 190–191

Scale 1:30,000,000

MAP 39   NORTH AMERICA, POLITICAL

Pages 192–193

Scale 1:30,000,000

MAP 40   ALASKA

(Canada)
(Russia)
(United States)

Page 194

Scale 1:12,000,000

MAP 41   GREENLAND

(Canada)
Greenland

Iceland
Svalbard

Page 195

Scale 1:12,000,000

MAP 42   CANADA

(Canada
Saint Pierre
 and Miquelon
(United States)

Pages 196–197

Scale 1:12,000,000

MAP 43   UNITED STATES

Bahamas
Bermuda
(Canada)
Cuba
Dominican
  Republic

Haiti
Jamaica
(Mexico)
(United States)

Pages 198–199

Scale 1:12,000,000

MAP 44   EASTERN UNITED STATES

(Bahamas)
(Canada)
(United States)

Pages 200–201

Scale 1:6,000,000

MAP 45   CENTRAL UNITED STATES

(Canada)
(Mexico)
(United States)

Pages 202–203

Scale 1:6,000,000

MAP 46   WESTERN UNITED STATES

(Canada)
(Mexico)
(United States)

Pages 204–205

Scale 1:6,000,000

MAP 47   MIDDLE AMERICA

Bahamas
Belize
Bermuda
(Colombia)
Costa Rica
Cuba
Dominican
  Republic
El Salvador
Guatemala

Haiti
Honduras
Jamaica
Mexico
Nicaragua
Panama
Puerto Rico
Trinidad and Tobago
(United States)
(Venezuela)

Pages 206–207

Scale 1:12,000,000

MAP 48   MEXICO

Belize
Guatemala
Mexico
(United States)

Pages 208–209

Scale 1:6,000,000

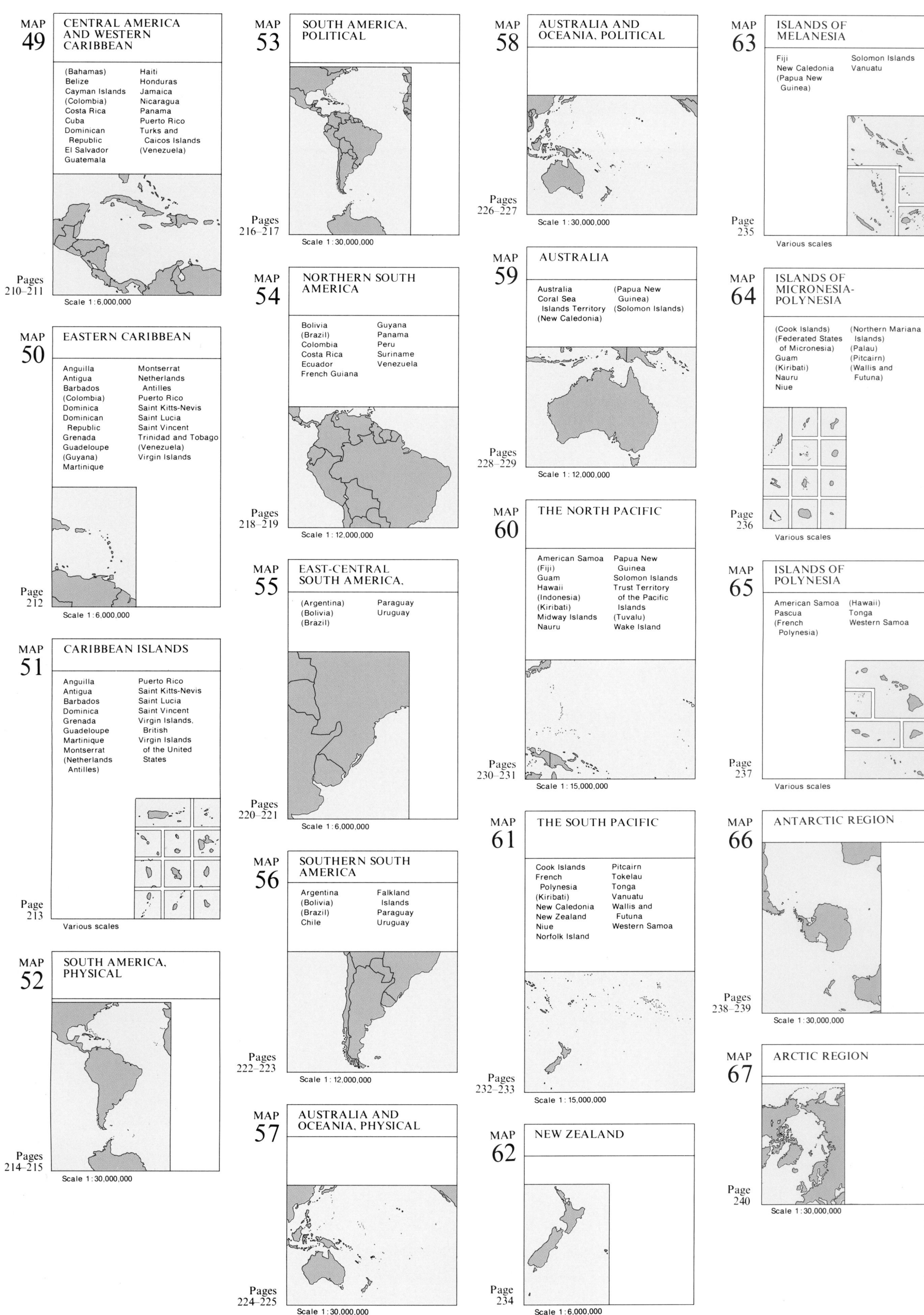

OUR PLANET EARTH SECTION

Part 1

THE EARTH AND THE UNIVERSE

How the universe began · Earth's place in the Solar System
How the Earth became fit for life
Man looks at Earth from outer space

CREATION AND DESTRUCTION

Violent activity pervades our universe and has done so ever since the primordial fireball of creation. Evidence of violence comes from radio telescopes scanning the farthest reaches: entire galaxies may be exploding, torn apart by gravitational forces of unimaginable power. Some very large stars may burst apart in supernovas, spraying interstellar space with cosmic debris. From this violence new stars and new planets are constantly being formed throughout the universe.

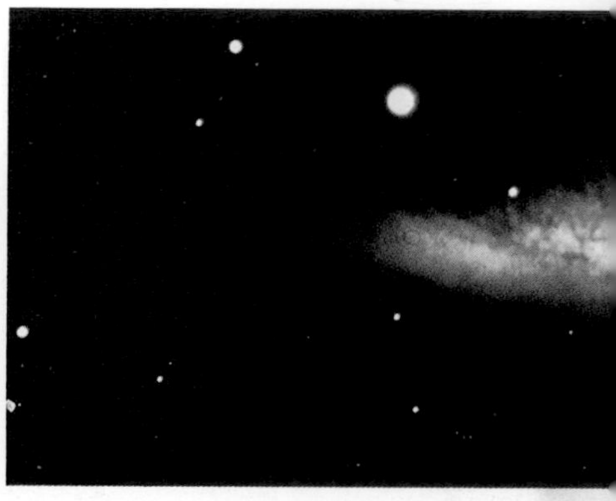

The Big Bang theory (left) of the origin of the universe envisages all matter originating from one point in time and space—a point of infinite density. In the intensely hot Big Bang all the material that goes to make up the planets, stars and galaxies that we see now began to expand outward in all directions. This expansion has been likened to someone blowing up a balloon on which spots have been painted. As the air fills and expands the balloon, the spots get farther away from each other. Likewise, clusters of galaxies that formed from the original superdense matter began, and continue, to move away from neighboring clusters. The Big Bang generated enormous temperatures and the remnants of the event still linger throughout space. A leftover, background radiation provides a uniform and measurable temperature of 3°C. It is generally believed that the universe will continue to expand into complete nothingness.

Stars vary enormously in size, temperature and luminosity. The largest, so-called red giants like Antares (1)—the biggest yet known—or Aldebaran (2), are nearing the end of their lives: diminishing nuclear "fuel" causes their thinning envelopes to expand. Rigel (3) is many times brighter than our Sun (4)—a middle-aged star—but both are so-called main-sequence stars. Epsilon Eridani (5) is rather like the Sun. Wolf 359 (6) is a red dwarf.

Our Solar System was formed from a collapsing cloud of gas and dust (A). Collapse made the center hotter and denser (B) until nuclear reactions started. Heat blew matter from the heart of the now flattened, spinning disc (C). Heavier materials condensed closest to the young Sun, now a hot star, eventually forming the inner ring of planets; the lighter ones accumulated farther out, making up the atmosphere and composition of the giant outer planets (D).

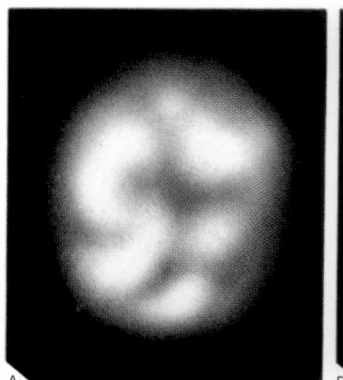

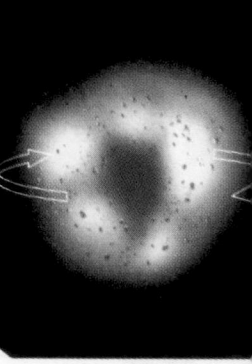

Billions of galaxies exist outside our own Milky Way, each thousands of light-years across and filled with millions of stars. Found in clusters, they are either elliptical or spiral in form. The clusters recede from each other following the space-time geometry, as established by Hubble in 1929, proving that the universe is expanding.

The "exploding" galaxy M82 may be an example of the violence of our universe. Clouds of hydrogen gas, equivalent in mass to 5,000,000 suns, have been ejected from the nucleus at 160 km (100 miles) per second. Black holes may cause the explosions, when gravity sucks in all matter, so that even light cannot escape.

Our own cluster of galaxies (below), the Local Group (A), consists of about 30 members, weakly linked by the force of gravity. Earth lies in the second-largest galaxy, the Milky Way (B)—here shown edge-on and at an angle—which is a spiral galaxy of about 100,000 million stars. Its rotating "arms" are great masses of clouds, dust and stars that sweep around a dense nucleus. In the course of this new stars are regularly created from dust and gas. Our Sun (S) lies 33,000 light-years from the nucleus and takes 225 million years to complete an orbit. The Andromeda Galaxy (C), known to astronomers as M31, is the largest of our Local Group. It too is a spiral, and lies about two million light-years away. Roughly 130,000 light-years in diameter, it appears as a flattened disc, and indicates how our galaxy would look if viewed from outside. Two smaller elliptical galaxies, M32 and NGC 205, can also be seen.

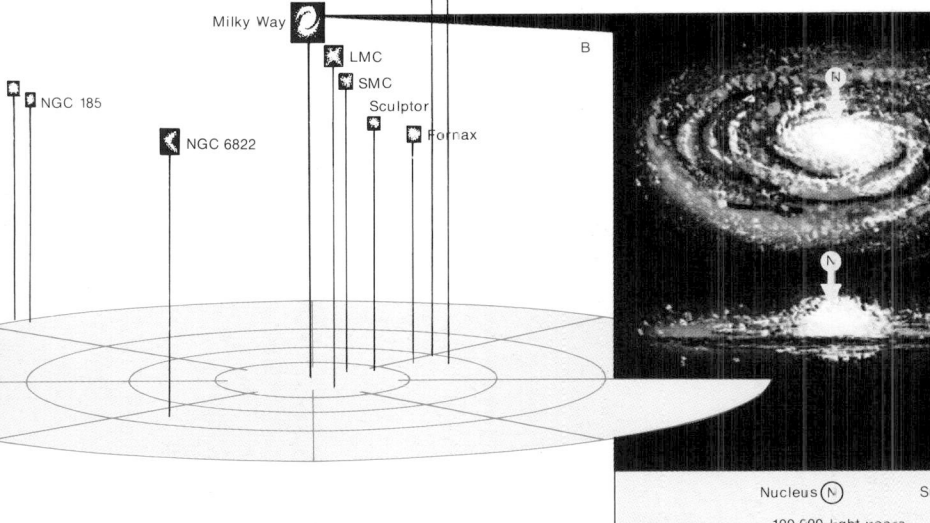

Nucleus (N)   Sun (S)

100,000 light-years

Stars are being born (left) in the Great Nebula of Orion, visible from Earth. The brilliant light comes from a cluster of very hot young stars, the Trapezium, surrounded by a glowing aura of hydrogen gas. Behind the visible nebula there is known to be a dense cloud where radio astronomers have detected emissions from interstellar molecules, and have identified high-density globules. These probably indicate that stars are starting to form.

The Making of the Universe

Most astronomers believe that the universe began in a great explosion of matter and energy – the "Big Bang" – about 15,000 million years ago. This event was implied by Einstein's theory of general relativity, as well as by more recent astronomical observations and calculations. But the clinching evidence came in 1965, when two American radio astronomers discovered a faint, uniform, background radiation which permeated all space. This they identified as the remnants of the primordial Big Bang.

The generally accepted explanation for the so-called "cosmic microwave" background, detected by American astronomers Arno Penzias and Robert Wilson, is indeed that it is the echo of the Big Bang itself, the radio noise left over from the fireball of creation. In recognition of their discovery, Penzias and Wilson shared a Nobel Prize in 1978.

The Big Bang has also been identified by astronomers in other ways. All the evidence shows that the universe is expanding, and its constituent parts—clusters of galaxies, each containing thousands of millions of stars like our Sun—are moving away from each other at great speeds. From this and other evidence scientists deduce that long ago the galaxies must have been closer together, in a superdense phase, and that at some time in the remote past all the material in the universe must have started spreading out from a single point. But this "single point" includes not only all three-dimensional matter and space but also the dimension of time, as envisioned in Einstein's revolutionary concept of space-time. Einstein's theory of relativity describes the phenomenon, not in terms of galaxies moving through space in the expansion, but as being carried apart by the expansion of space-time itself. Space-time may be imagined as a rubber sheet speckled with paint blobs (galaxies), which move apart as the rubber sheet expands.

Galaxies consist of star systems, dust clouds and gases formed from the hot material exploding outward from the original cosmic fireball. Our own Milky Way system, the band of light that stretches across the night sky, is typical of many galaxies, containing millions of stars slowly rotating around a central nucleus.

Exploding space

The original material of the universe was hydrogen, the simplest of all elements. Nuclear reactions that occurred during the superdense phase of the Big Bang converted about 20 percent of the original hydrogen into helium, the next simplest element. So the first stars were formed from a mixture of about 80 percent hydrogen and 20 percent helium. All other matter in the universe, including the atoms of heavier elements such as carbon and oxygen—which help to make up the human body or the pages of this book—has been processed in further nuclear reactions. The explosion of a star—a relatively rare event called a supernova—scatters material across space, briefly radiating more energy than a trillion suns and ejecting matter into the cosmic reservoir of interstellar space. This is then reused to form new stars and planets.

Thus, from the debris of such explosions new stars can form to repeat the creative cycle, and at each stage more of the heavy elements are produced. Today's heavenly bodies are very much the products of stellar violence in the universe, and indeed the universe itself is now seen to be an area of violent activity. During the past two decades the old idea of the universe as a place of quiet stability has been increasingly superseded by evidence of intense activity on all scales. Astronomers have identified what appear to be vast explosions involving whole galaxies, as well as those of individual stars.

Black holes

The evidence of just why these huge explosions occur is often hard to obtain, because the exploding galaxies may be so far away that light from them takes millions of years to reach telescopes on Earth. But it is becoming increasingly accepted by astronomers that such violent events may be associated with the presence of black holes at the centers of some galaxies.

These black holes are regions in which matter has become so concentrated that the force of gravity makes it impossible for anything—even light itself—to escape. As stars are pulled into super-massive black holes they are torn apart by gravitational forces, and their material forms into a swirling maelstrom from which huge explosions can occur. Collapse into black holes, accompanied by violent outbursts from the maelstrom, may be the ultimate fate of all matter in the universe. For our own Solar System, however, such a fate is far in the future: the Sun in its present form is believed to have enough "fuel" to keep it going for at least another 5,000 million years.

A star is born

The origins of the Earth and the Solar System are intimately connected with the structure of our own galaxy, the Milky Way. There are two main types of galaxies: flattened, disc-shaped spiral galaxies (like the Milky Way), and the more rounded elliptical galaxies, which range in form from near spheres to cigar shapes. The most important feature of a spiral galaxy is that it is rotating, a great mass of stars sweeping around a common center. In our galaxy the Sun, located some way out from the galaxy's center, takes about 225 million years to complete one circuit, called a cosmic year.

New stars are born out of the twisting arms of a spiral galaxy, with each arm marking a region of debris left over from previous stellar explosions. These arms are in fact clouds of dust and gas, including nitrogen and oxygen. As the spiral galaxy rotates over a period of millions of years, the twisting arms are squeezed by a high-density pressure wave as they pass through the cycle of the cosmic year. With two main spiral arms twining around a galaxy such as our own, large, diffuse clouds get squeezed twice during each orbit around the center of the galaxy.

Even if one orbit takes as long as hundreds of millions of years, a score or more squeezes have probably occurred since the Milky Way was first formed thousands of millions of years ago. At a critical point, such repeated squeezing increases the density of a gas cloud so much that it begins to collapse rapidly under the inward pull of its own gravity. A typical cloud of this kind contains enough material to make many stars. As it breaks up it collapses into smaller clouds—which are also collapsing—and these become stars in their own right.

Our own Solar System may have been formed in this way from such a collapsing gas cloud, which went on to evolve into the system of planets that we know today.

Earth in the Solar System

The Sun is an ordinary, medium-sized star located some two-thirds of the way from the center of our galaxy, the Milky Way. Yet it comprises more than 99 percent of the Solar System's total mass and provides all the light and heat that make life possible on Earth. This energy comes from nuclear reactions that take place in the Sun's hot, dense interior. The reactions convert hydrogen into helium, with the release of vast amounts of energy – the energy that keeps the Sun shining.

Nuclear reactions in the Sun's core maintain a temperature of some 15,000,000°C and this heat prevents the star from shrinking. The surface temperature is comparatively much lower —a mere 6,000°C. Thermonuclear energy-generating processes cause the Sun to "lose" mass from the center at the rate of four million tonnes of hydrogen every second. This mass is turned into energy (heat), and each gram of matter "burnt" produces the heat equivalent of 100 trillion electric fires. The Sun's total mass is so great, however, that it contains enough matter to continue radiating at its present rate for several thousand million years before it runs out of "fuel."

The Sun's retinue

The Solar System emerged from a collapsing gas cloud. In addition to the Sun there are at least nine planets, their satellites, thousands of minor planets (asteroids), comets and meteors. Most stars occur in pairs, triplets or in even more complicated systems, and the Sun is among a minority of stars in being alone except for its planetary companions. It does seem, however, that a single star with a planetary system offers the greatest potential for the development of life. When there are two or more stars in the same system, any planets are likely to have unstable orbits and to suffer from wide extremes of temperature.

The Solar System's structure is thought to be typical of a star that formed in isolation. As the hot young Sun threw material outward, inner planets (Mercury, Venus, Earth and Mars) were left as small rocky bodies, whereas outer planets (Jupiter, Saturn, Uranus and Neptune) kept their lighter gases and became huge "gas giants." Jupiter has two and a half times the mass of all the other planets put together. Pluto, a small object with a strange orbit, which sometimes carries it within the orbit of Neptune, is usually regarded as a ninth planet, but some astronomers consider it to be an escaped moon of Neptune or a large asteroid.

Planetary relations

Several planets are accompanied by smaller bodies called moons or satellites. Jupiter and Saturn have at least 17 and 22 respectively, whereas Earth has its solitary Moon. Sizes vary enormously, from Ganymede, one of Jupiter's large, so-called Galilean satellites, which has a diameter of 5,000 km (3,100 miles), to Mars' tiny Deimos, which is only 8 km (5 miles) across.

The Earth's Moon is at an average distance of 384,000 km (239,000 miles) and has a diameter of 3,476 km (2,160 miles). Its mass is $\frac{1}{81}$ of the Earth's. Although it is referred to as the Earth's satellite, the Moon is large for a secondary body. Some astronomers have suggested that the Earth/Moon system is a double planet. Certain theories of the origins of the Moon propose that it was formed from the solar nebula in the same way as the Earth was and very close to it. The Moon takes 27.3 days to orbit the Earth—exactly the same time that it takes to rotate once on its axis. As a result, it presents the same face to the Earth all the time.

Our planet's orbit around the Sun is not a perfect circle but an ellipse and so its distance from the Sun varies slightly. More importantly, the Earth is tilted, so that at different times of the year one pole or another "leans" toward the Sun. Without this tilt there would be no seasons. The angle of tilt is not constant: over tens of thousands of years the axis of the Earth "wobbles" like a slowly spinning top, so that the pattern of the seasons varies over the ages. These changes have been linked to recent ice ages, which seem to occur when the northern hemisphere has relatively cool summers.

Patterns of time

The Earth's movements on its axis and around the Sun give us our basic measurements of time—the day and the year—as well as setting the rhythm of the seasons and the ice ages. One rotation of the Earth on its axis—the time from one sunrise to the next—originally defined the day, and the time taken for one complete orbit around the Sun defined the year. Today, however, scientists define both the day and the year in terms of time units "counted" by precision instruments called atomic clocks.

A third basic rhythm is set not by the Sun but by the Moon, which runs through a cycle of phases $29\frac{1}{2}$ days long. This is the basis of the calendar month. But just as the modern calendar cannot cope with months $29\frac{1}{2}$ days long, so too it would have trouble with the precise year, which is, inconveniently, just less than $365\frac{1}{4}$ days long. This is the reason for leap years, by means of which an extra day is added to the month of February every fourth year.

Even this system does not keep the calendar exactly in step with the Sun. Accordingly, the leap year is left out in the years which complete centuries, such as 1900, but retained when they divide exactly by 400. The year 2000 will, therefore, be a leap year. With all these corrections, the average length of the calendar year is within 26 seconds of the year defined by the Earth's movements around the Sun. Thus the calendar will be one day out of step with the heavens in the year 4906.

Cosmic rubble

The other planets are too small and too far away to produce noticeable effects on the Earth, but the smallest members of the Sun's family, the asteroids, can affect us directly. Some of them have orbits that cross the orbit of the Earth around the Sun. From time to time they penetrate the Earth's atmosphere: small fragments burn up high in the atmosphere as meteors, whereas larger pieces may survive to strike the ground as meteorites. These in fact provide an echo of times gone by. All the planets, as the battered face of the Moon shows, suffered collisions from many smaller bodies in the course of their evolution from the collapsing pre-solar gas cloud.

Eclipses occur because the Moon, smaller than the Sun, is closer to Earth and looks just as big. This means that when all three are lined up the Moon can blot out the Sun, causing a solar eclipse. When the Earth passes through the main shadow cone, or umbra, the eclipse is total; in the area of partial shadow, or penumbra, a partial eclipse is seen. A similar effect is produced when Earth passes between the Moon and the Sun, causing a lunar eclipse. At most full moons, eclipses do not occur; the Moon passes either above or below the Earth's shadow, because the Moon's orbit is inclined at an angle of 5° to the orbit of the Earth.

JUPITER
Mean distance from Sun: 778,340,000 km
Orbital inclination: 1.3°
Eccentricity: 0.048
Sidereal period: 11.8 Earth years
Rotation period: 9.8 Earth hours
Diameter: 142,800 km
Mass (Earth = 1): 317.89
Volume (Earth = 1): 1,318.7
Specific gravity: 1.3
Number of satellites: at least 17

MARS
Mean distance from Sun: 227,940,000 km
Orbital inclination: 1.8°
Eccentricity: 0.093
Sidereal period: 686.9 Earth days
Rotation period: 24.6 Earth hours
Diameter: 6,790 km
Mass (Earth = 1): 0.10
Volume (Earth = 1): 0.15
Specific gravity: 3.9
Number of satellites: 2

EARTH
Mean distance from Sun: 149,600,000 km
Orbital inclination: —
Eccentricity: 0.016
Sidereal period: 365.2 days
Rotation period: 23.9 hours
Diameter: 12,756 km
Mass: 1.00
Volume: 1.00
Specific gravity: 5.5
Number of satellites: 1

VENUS
Mean distance from Sun: 108,210,000 km
Orbital inclination: 3.3°
Eccentricity: 0.006
Sidereal period: 224.7 Earth days
Rotation period: 243 Earth days
Diameter: 12,100 km
Mass (Earth = 1): 0.81
Volume (Earth = 1): 0.85
Specific gravity: 5.2
Number of satellites: 0

MEMBERS OF THE SOLAR SYSTEM

The Sun has nine planetary attendants. They are best compared in terms of orbital data (distance from the Sun, inclination of orbit to the Earth's orbit, and eccentricity, which means the departure of a planet's orbit from circularity); planetary periods (the time for a planet to go around the Sun—sidereal periods, and the time it takes for one axial revolution—the rotation period); and physical data (equatorial diameter, mass, volume and density or specific gravity—the weight of a substance compared with the weight of an equal volume of water).

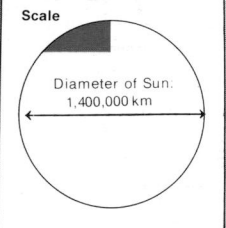

Scale
Diameter of Sun:
1,400,000 km

MERCURY
Mean distance from Sun: 57,910,000 km
Orbital inclination: 7°
Eccentricity: 0.205
Sidereal period: 87.9 Earth days
Rotation period: 58.7 Earth days
Diameter: 4,870 km
Mass (Earth = 1): 0.05
Volume (Earth = 1): 0.05
Specific gravity: 5.5
Number of satellites: 0

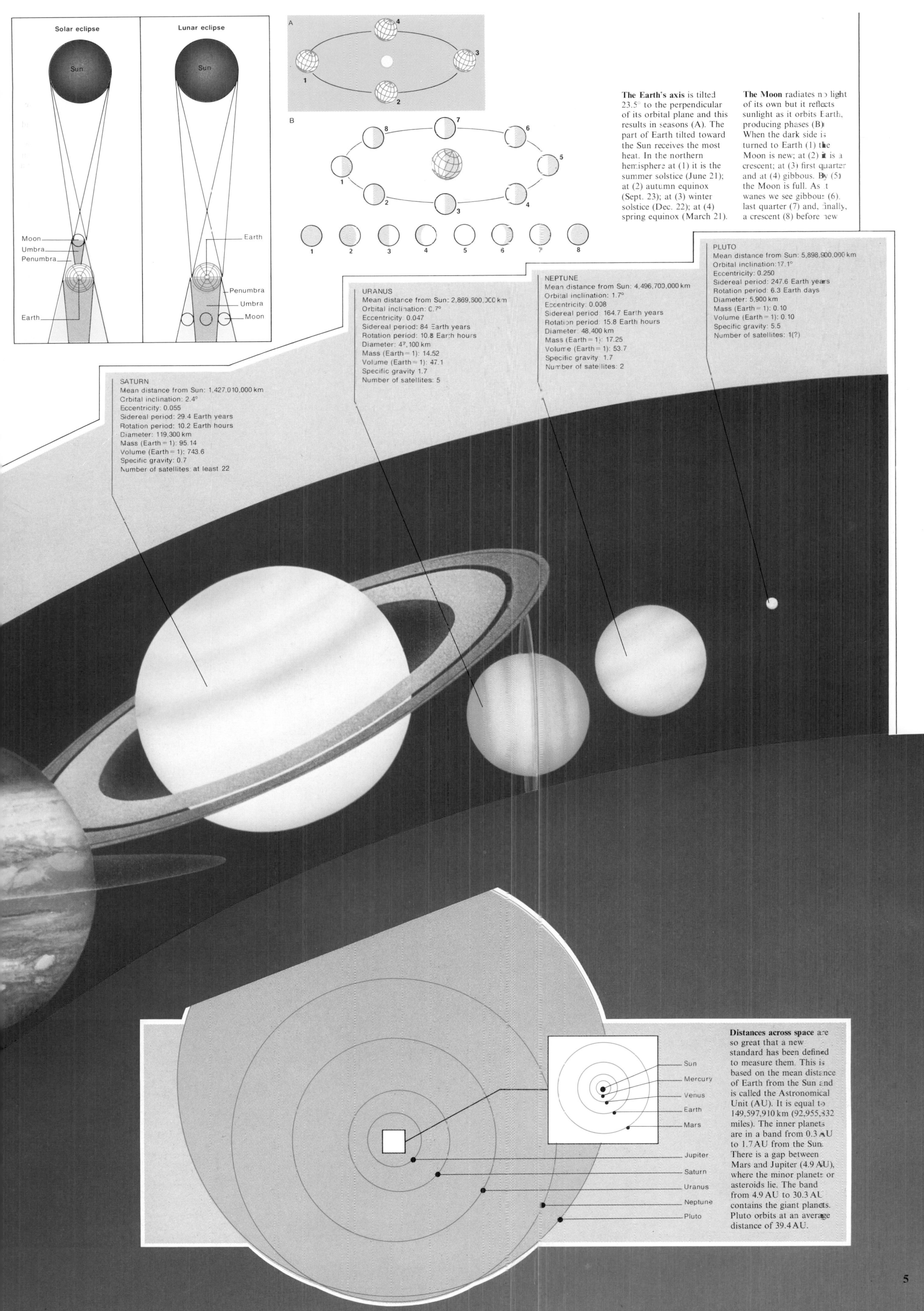

Solar eclipse

Lunar eclipse

Sun

Sun

Moon
Umbra
Penumbra

Earth

Earth

Penumbra
Umbra
Moon

A

1 2 3 4

B

1 2 3 4 5 6 7 8

1 2 3 4 5 6 7 8

The Earth's axis is tilted 23.5° to the perpendicular of its orbital plane and this results in seasons (A). The part of Earth tilted toward the Sun receives the most heat. In the northern hemisphere at (1) it is the summer solstice (June 21); at (2) autumn equinox (Sept. 23); at (3) winter solstice (Dec. 22); at (4) spring equinox (March 21).

The Moon radiates no light of its own but it reflects sunlight as it orbits Earth, producing phases (B). When the dark side is turned to Earth (1) the Moon is new; at (2) it is a crescent; at (3) first quarter and at (4) gibbous. By (5) the Moon is full. As it wanes we see gibbous (6), last quarter (7) and, finally, a crescent (8) before new.

PLUTO
Mean distance from Sun: 5,898,900,000 km
Orbital inclination: 17.1°
Eccentricity: 0.250
Sidereal period: 247.6 Earth years
Rotation period: 6.3 Earth days
Diameter: 5,900 km
Mass (Earth = 1): 0.10
Volume (Earth = 1): 0.10
Specific gravity: 5.5
Number of satellites: 1(?)

NEPTUNE
Mean distance from Sun: 4,496,700,000 km
Orbital inclination: 1.7°
Eccentricity: 0.008
Sidereal period: 164.7 Earth years
Rotation period: 15.8 Earth hours
Diameter: 48,400 km
Mass (Earth = 1): 17.25
Volume (Earth = 1): 53.7
Specific gravity: 1.7
Number of satellites: 2

URANUS
Mean distance from Sun: 2,869,600,000 km
Orbital inclination: 0.7°
Eccentricity: 0.047
Sidereal period: 84 Earth years
Rotation period: 10.8 Earth hours
Diameter: 47,100 km
Mass (Earth = 1): 14.52
Volume (Earth = 1): 47.1
Specific gravity: 1.7
Number of satellites: 5

SATURN
Mean distance from Sun: 1,427,010,000 km
Orbital inclination: 2.4°
Eccentricity: 0.055
Sidereal period: 29.4 Earth years
Rotation period: 10.2 Earth hours
Diameter: 119,300 km
Mass (Earth = 1): 95.14
Volume (Earth = 1): 743.6
Specific gravity: 0.7
Number of satellites: at least 22

Sun
Mercury
Venus
Earth
Mars

Jupiter
Saturn
Uranus
Neptune
Pluto

Distances across space are so great that a new standard has been defined to measure them. This is based on the mean distance of Earth from the Sun and is called the Astronomical Unit (AU). It is equal to 149,597,910 km (92,955,332 miles). The inner planets are in a band from 0.3 AU to 1.7 AU from the Sun. There is a gap between Mars and Jupiter (4.9 AU), where the minor planets or asteroids lie. The band from 4.9 AU to 30.3 AU contains the giant planets. Pluto orbits at an average distance of 39.4 AU.

5

Earth as a Planet

Viewed from space, the Earth appears to be an ordinary member of the group of inner planets orbiting the Sun. But the Earth is unique in the Solar System because it has an atmosphere that contains oxygen. It is the nature of this surrounding blanket of air that has allowed higher life forms to evolve on Earth and provides their life-support system. At the same time the atmosphere acts as a shield to protect living things from the damaging effects of radiation from the Sun.

Any traces of gas that may have clung to the newly formed Earth were soon swept away into space by the heat of the Sun before it attained a stable state powered by nuclear fusion. Farther out in the Solar System, the Sun's heat was never strong enough to blow these gases away into space, so that even today the giant planets retain atmospheres composed of these primordial gases—mostly methane and ammonia.

The evolution of air

Until the Sun "settled down," Earth was a hot, airless ball of rock. The atmosphere and oceans—like the atmospheres of Venus and Mars—were produced by the "outgassing" of material from the hot interior of the planet as the crust cooled. Volcanoes erupted constantly and produced millions of tonnes of ash and lava. They also probably yielded, as they do today, great quantities of gas, chiefly carbon dioxide, and water vapor. A little nitrogen and various sulphur compounds were also released. Other things being equal, we would expect rocky planets, like the young Earth, to have atmospheres rich in carbon dioxide and water vapor. Venus and Mars do indeed have carbon dioxide atmospheres today, but the Earth now has a nitrogen/oxygen atmosphere. This results from the fact that life evolved on Earth, converting the carbon dioxide to oxygen and storing carbon in organic remains such as coal. Some carbon dioxide was also dissolved in the oceans. The Earth's oxygen atmosphere is a clear sign of life; the carbon dioxide atmospheres of Venus and Mars suggest the absence of life. Why did the Earth begin to evolve in a different way from the other inner planets?

When the Sun stabilized, Earth, Venus and Mars started off down the same evolutionary road, and carbon dioxide and water vapor were the chief constituents of the original atmospheres. On Venus the temperature was hot enough for the water to remain in a gaseous form, and both the water vapor and carbon dioxide in the Venusian atmosphere trapped heat by means of the so-called "greenhouse effect." In this process, radiant energy from the Sun passes through the atmospheric gases and warms the ground. The warmed ground re-radiates heat energy, but at infrared wavelengths, with the result that carbon dioxide and water molecules absorb it and stop it escaping from the planet. Instead of acting like a window, the atmosphere acts like a mirror for outgoing energy. As a result, the surface of Venus became hotter still. Today the surface temperature has stabilized at more than 500°C.

Mars, farther out from the Sun than Earth, was never hot enough for the greenhouse effect to dominate. The red planet once had a much thicker atmosphere than it does today, but, being smaller than the Earth, its gravity is too weak to retain a thick atmosphere. As a result, the planet cooled into a frozen desert as atmospheric gases escaped into space. Mars then, in fact, suffered a climatic change. At one time—hundreds of millions of years ago—there must have been running water because traces of old riverbeds still scar the Martian surface. Today, however, Mars has a thin atmosphere of carbon dioxide and surface temperatures below zero.

Earth—the ideal home

On Earth conditions were just right. Water stayed as a liquid and formed the oceans, while some carbon dioxide from outgassing went into the atmosphere, and some dissolved in the oceans. The resulting modest greenhouse effect

The thermosphere extends from 80 km (50 miles) up to 400 km (250 miles). Within this zone temperatures rise steadily with height to as much as 1,650°C (3,000°F), but the air is so thin that temperature is not a meaningful concept. At this height the air is mostly composed of nitrogen molecules to a height of 200 km (125 miles), when oxygen molecules become the dominant constituent.

The mesosphere is between 50 and 80 km (30 and 50 miles) above ground level. The stratopause is its lower limit and the mesopause its upper. This zone of the atmosphere is mainly distinguished by its ever decreasing temperatures and, unlike the stratosphere, it does not absorb solar energy.

The stratosphere is the level above the troposphere and extends as far as 50 km (30 miles). The chemical composition of the air up to this height is nearly constant and, in terms of volume, it is composed of nitrogen (78%) and oxygen (20%). The rest is mostly argon and other trace elements. The percentage of carbon dioxide (0.003) is small but crucial because this gas absorbs heat. There is virtually no water vapor or dust in this region of the atmosphere, but it does include the ozone layer, which is strongest between 20 km (12 miles) and 40 km (24 miles) high.

The troposphere extends from ground level to a height of between 10 and 15 km (6 and 9 miles). This height varies with latitude and season of the year: it is greater at the Equator than at the poles. Most weather phenomena occur in this zone. Mixed with the gases of the troposphere is water vapor and millions of tiny dust particles, around which vapor condenses to form clouds. The upper limit of this zone is called the tropopause.

EARTH'S OUTER SKIN

The Earth's atmosphere is wafer thin when compared with the size of the planet. Half of the atmosphere's mass lies in the 5.5 km (3½ miles) nearest the ground and more than 99 percent of it lies within 40 km (24 miles) of the Earth.

Scale

Atmosphere
Earth

Earth's radius: 6,378 km

Earth reduced by 90% in proportion to this scale

Stratosphere and Mesosphere
Troposphere

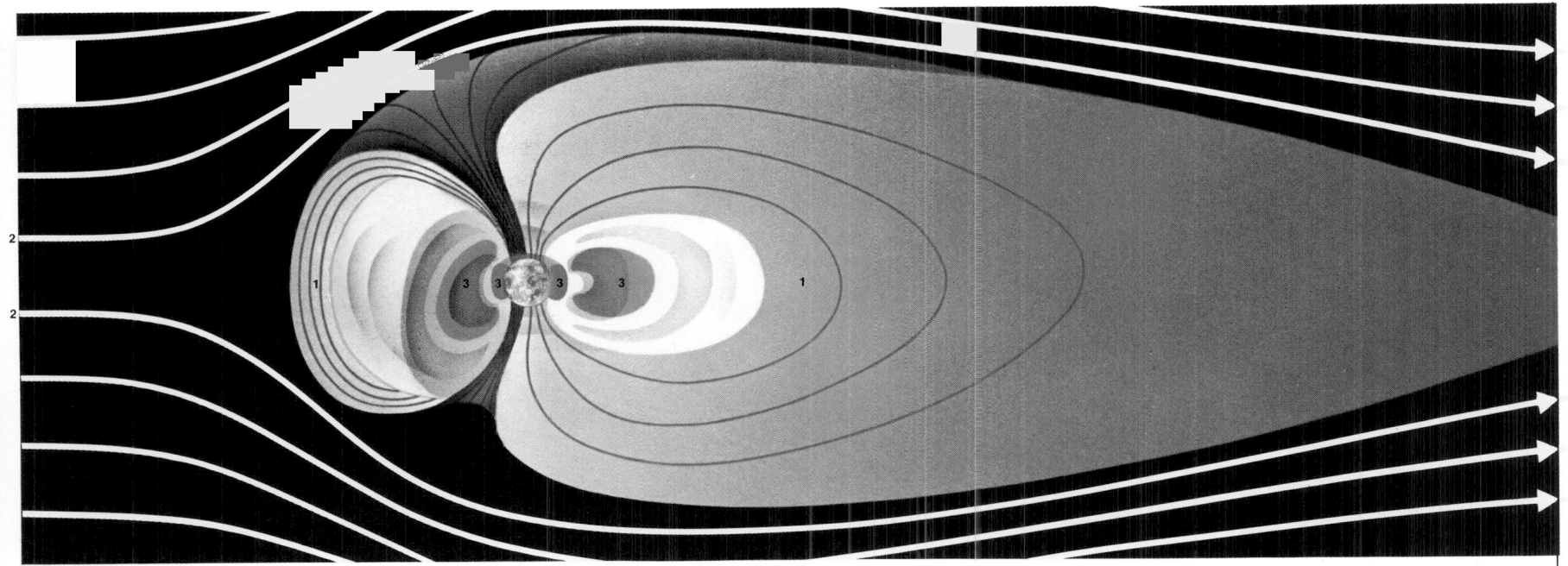

was compensated for by the formation of shiny white clouds of water droplets which reflected some of the Sun's radiation back into space. Our planet stabilized with an average temperature of 15°C. This proved ideal for the emergence of life, which evolved first in the seas and then moved onto land, converting carbon dioxide into oxygen as it did so.

In any view from space, planet Earth is dominated by water—in blue oceans and white clouds—and water is the key to life as we know it. Animal life—oxygen-breathing life—could only evolve after earlier forms of life had converted the atmosphere to an oxygen-rich state. The nature of the air today is a product of life as well as being vital to its existence.

An atmospheric layer cake

Starting at ground level, the first zone of the atmosphere is the troposphere, kept warm near the ground by the greenhouse effect but cooling to a chilly −60°C at an altitude of 15 km (9 miles). Above the troposphere is a warming layer, the stratosphere, in which energy from the Sun is absorbed and temperatures increase to reach 0°C at an altitude of 50 km (30 miles). The energy—in the form of ultraviolet radiation—is absorbed by molecules of ozone, a form of oxygen. Without the ozone layer in the atmosphere, ultraviolet rays would penetrate the

The Earth's magnetic field behaves as if there were a huge bar magnet placed inside the globe, with its magnetic axis tilted at a slight angle to the geographical north–south axis. The speed of rotation of the liquid core differs from that of the mantle, producing an effect like a dynamo (below). The region in which the magnetic field extends beyond the Earth is the magnetosphere (1). Streams of charged particles (2) from the Sun distort its shape into that of a teardrop. Zones of the magnetosphere include the Van Allen Belts (3), which are regions of intense radioactivity where magnetic particles are "trapped."

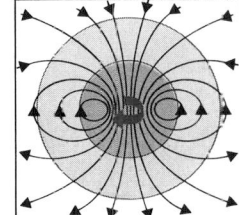

ground and sterilize the land surface: without life, there would be no oxygen from which an ozone layer could form.

Above the stratosphere, another cooling layer, the mesosphere, extends up to 80 km (50 miles), at which point the temperature has fallen to about −100°C. Above this level the gases of the atmosphere are so thin that the standard concept of temperature is no real guide to their behavior, and from the mesosphere outwards the atmosphere is best described in terms of its electrical properties.

In the outer layers of the atmosphere, the Sun's energy is absorbed by individual atoms in such a way that it strips electrons off them, leaving behind positively charged ions, which give the region its name—the ionosphere. A few hundred kilometers above the Earth's surface, gravity is so feeble that electromagnetic forces begin to determine the behavior of the charged particles, which are shepherded along the lines of force in the Earth's magnetic field. Above 500 km (300 miles), the magnetic field is so dominant that yet another region, the magnetosphere, is distinguished. This is the true boundary between Earth and interplanetary space.

The magnetosphere has been likened to the hull of "spaceship Earth." Charged particles (the solar wind) streaming out from the Sun are deflected around Earth by the magnetosphere

like water around a moving ship, while the region of the Earth's magnetic influence in space trails "downstream" away from the Sun like the wake of a ship. The Van Allen Belts, at altitudes of 3,000 and 15,000 km (1,850 and 9,300 miles) are regions of space high above the Equator where particles are trapped by the magnetic field. Particles spilling out of the belts spiral towards the polar regions of Earth, producing the spectacle of the auroras—the northern and southern lights. The Earth and Mercury are the only inner planets with magnetospheres such as this. The cause of the Earth's magnetism is almost certainly the planet's heavy molten core, which is composed of magnetic materials.

The Earth's atmosphere exhibits a great variety of characteristics on a vertical scale. As well as variations of temperature and the electrical properties of the air, there are differences in chemical composition—in the mixture of gases and water vapor—according to altitude. The Earth's gravitational pull means that air density and pressure decrease with altitude. Pressure of about 1,000 millibars at sea level falls to virtually nothing (10^{-42} millibars) by a height of 700 km (435 miles) above the Earth. All these factors, and their interrelationships, help to maintain the Earth's atmosphere as a protective outer covering or radiation shield and an essential life-support system.

The ionosphere is another name for the atmospheric layer beyond 80 km (50 miles). The region is best described in terms of the electrical properties of its constituents rather than by temperature. It is here that ionization occurs. Gamma and X-rays from the Sun are absorbed by atoms and molecules of nitrogen and oxygen and, as a result, each molecule or atom gives up one or more of its electrons, thus becoming a positively charged ion. These ions reflect radio waves and are used to bounce back radio waves transmitted from the surface of the Earth.

The exosphere is the layer above the thermosphere and it extends from 400 km (250 miles) up to about 700 km (435 miles), the point at which, it may be said, space begins. It is almost a complete vacuum because most of its atoms and molecules of oxygen escape the Earth's gravity.

The magnetosphere includes the exosphere, but it extends far beyond the atmosphere—to a distance of between 64,000 and 130,000 km (40,000 and 80,000 miles) above the Earth. It represents the Earth's external magnetic field and its outer limit is called the magnetopause.

The atmosphere protects the Earth from harmful solar radiation and also from bombardment by small particles from space. Most meteors (particles orbiting the Sun) burn up in the atmosphere, but meteorites (debris of minor planets) reach the ground. Of all incoming solar radiation, only visible light, radio waves and infrared rays reach the surface of Earth. X-rays are removed in the ionosphere, and ultraviolet and some infrared radiations are filtered out in the stratosphere. Studies of such radiations have, therefore, to be made from observatories in space.

Man Looks at the Earth

Orbiting satellites keep a detailed watch on the Earth's land surface, oceans and atmosphere, feeding streams of data to meteorologists, geologists, oceanographers, farmers, fishermen and many others. Some information would be unobtainable by any other means. Surveys from orbit are quicker and less expensive than from aircraft, for example, because a satellite can scan a much larger area. And, surprisingly enough, certain features on the ground are easier to see from space.

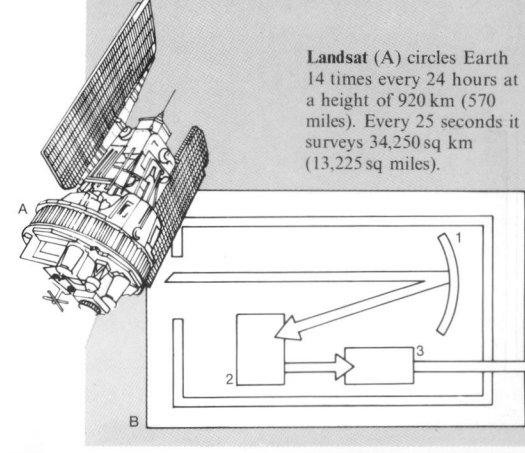

Landsat (A) circles Earth 14 times every 24 hours at a height of 920 km (570 miles). Every 25 seconds it surveys 34,250 sq km (13,225 sq miles).

MAPPING AND MEASURING
Man has been looking at Earth from satellites since the beginning of the 1960s, and has firmly established the value of surveys from space to those engaged in a variety of earthly pursuits. Chief of these activities are resource management, ranging from monitoring the spread of deserts and river silting to locating likely mineral deposits; environmental protection, which includes observing delicate ecosystems and natural disasters; and a whole range of mapping and land-use planning.

Satellites give us a greater overview of numerous aspects of life on Earth than any earthbound eye could see.

Of all the information gleaned from satellites, accurate weather forecasts are of particular social and economic value. The first weather satellite was Tiros 1 (Television and Infrared Observation Satellite), launched by the United States in 1960. By the time Tiros 10 ceased operations in 1967, the series had sent back more than half a million photographs, firmly establishing the value of satellite imagery.

Tiros was superseded by the ESSA (Environmental Science Services Administration) and the NOAA (National Oceanic and Atmospheric Administration) satellites. These orbited the Earth from pole to pole, and they covered the entire globe during the course of a day. Other weather satellites, such as the European Meteosat, are placed in geostationary orbit over the Equator, which means they stay in one place and continually monitor a single large region.

Watching the weather
In addition to photographing clouds, weather satellites monitor the extent of snow and ice cover, and they measure the temperature of the oceans and the composition of the atmosphere. Information about the overall heat balance of our planet gives clues to long-term climatic change, and includes the effects on climate of human activities such as the burning of fossil fuels and deforestation.

Infrared sensors allow pictures to be taken at night as well as during the day. The temperature of cloud tops, measured by infrared devices, is a guide to the height of the clouds. In a typical infrared image, high clouds appear white because they are the coldest, lower clouds and land areas appear gray, and oceans and lakes are black. Information on humidity in the atmosphere is provided by sensors tuned to wavelengths between 5.5 and 7 micrometers, at which water vapor strongly absorbs the radiation.

To "see" inside clouds, where infrared and visible light cannot penetrate, satellites use sensors tuned to short-wavelength radio waves (microwaves) around the 1.5 centimeter wavelength. These sensors can reveal whether or not clouds will give rise to heavy rainfall, snow or hail. Microwave sensors are also useful for locating ice floes in polar regions, making use of the different microwave reflections from land ice, sea ice and open water.

Satellites that send out such pictures are in relatively low orbits, at a height of about 1,000 km (620 miles), and they pass over each part of the Earth once every 12 hours. But to build up a global model of the Earth's weather and climate, meteorologists need continual information on wind speed and direction at

various levels in the atmosphere, together with temperature and humidity profiles. This data is provided by geostationary satellites. Cloud photographs taken every half-hour give information on winds, and computers combine this with temperature and humidity soundings to give as complete a model as is possible of the Earth's atmosphere.

Increasing attention is also being paid to the Earth's surface, notably by means of a series of satellites called Landsat (originally ERTS or Earth Resource Technology Satellites), the first of which was launched by the United States in 1972. The third and current Landsat is in a similar pole-to-pole orbit as the weather satellites, but its cameras are more powerful and they make more detailed surveys of the Earth. Landsat rephotographs each part of the Earth's surface every 18 days.

How to map resources
The satellite has two sensor systems: a television camera, which takes pictures of the Earth using visible light; and a device called a multispectral scanner, which scans the Earth at several distinct wavelengths, including visible light and infrared. Data from the various channels of the multispectral scanner can be combined to produce so-called false-color images, in which each wavelength band is assigned a color (not necessarily its real one) to emphasize features of interest.

An important use of Landsat photographs is for making maps, particularly of large countries with remote areas that have never been adequately surveyed from the ground. Several countries, including Brazil, Canada and China, have set up ground stations to receive Landsat data directly. Features previously unknown or incorrectly mapped, including rivers, lakes and glaciers, show up readily on Landsat images. Urban mapping and hence planning are aided by satellite pictures that can distinguish areas of industry, housing and open parkland.

Landsat photographs have also proved invaluable for agricultural land-use planning.

They are used for estimates of soil types and for determining land-use patterns. Areas of crop disease or dying vegetation are detectable by their different colors. Yields of certain crops such as wheat can now be accurately predicted from satellite imagery, so that at last it is becoming possible to keep track of the worldwide production of vital food crops. Fresh water, too, is one of our most valuable resources, and knowing its sources and seasonal variation is vital to irrigation projects.

Finally, the geologist and mineral prospector have benefited from remote sensing. Features such as fault lines and different types of sediments and rocks show up clearly on Landsat pictures. This allows geologists to select promising areas in which the prospector can look for mineral deposits.

Another way to study the Earth is by bouncing radar beams off it. Radar sensing indicates the nature of soil or rock on land and movement of water at sea, for example. This was not done by Landsat, but by equipment aboard the United States' Skylab and by a short-lived American satellite called Seasat. The former Soviet Union included Earth surveying in its Salyut program, and resource mapping is also a feature of the spacelab aboard the American space shuttle. All these activities help man to manage the limited resources on our planet and to preserve the environment.

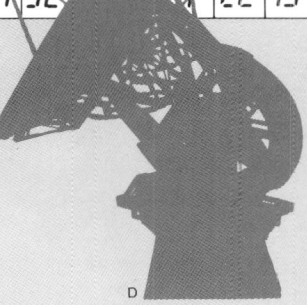
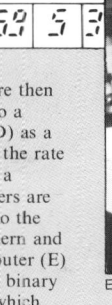

A **multispectral scanner** (B) has an oscillating mirror (1) that focuses visible and near infrared radiation on to a detector (2). This converts the intensity of the radiation into a voltage. An electronics unit (3) turns the voltage pattern into a series of digitized numbers that can be fed into a computer.

The numbers (C) are then transmitted back to a receiving station (D) as a radio frequency at the rate of 15 million units a second. The numbers are translated back into the digital voltage pattern and converted by computer (E) into the equivalent binary numbers, each of which represents a color.

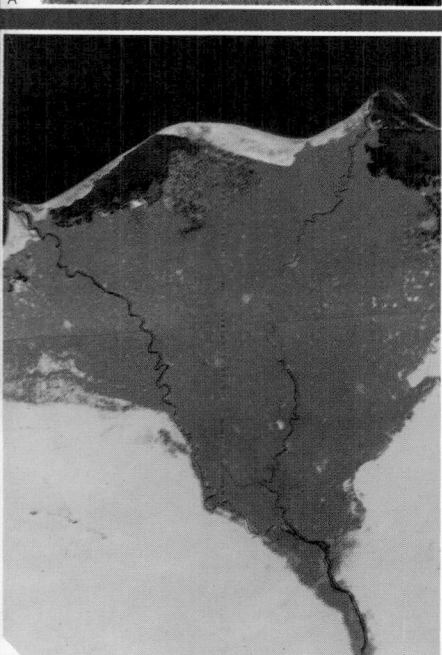

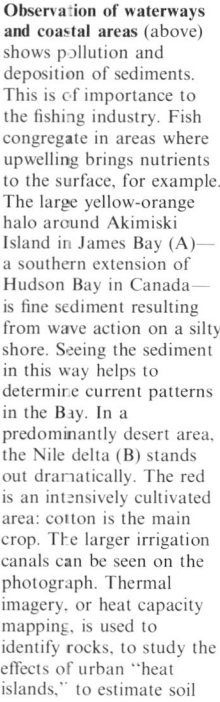

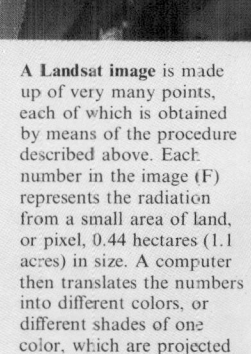

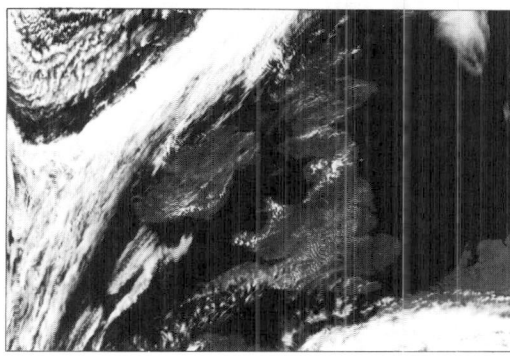
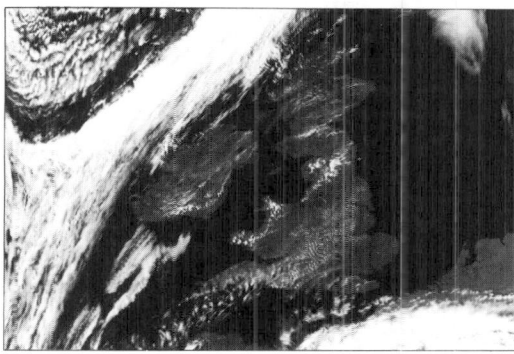

A Landsat image is made up of very many points, each of which is obtained by means of the procedure described above. Each number in the image (F) represents the radiation from a small area of land, or pixel, 0.44 hectares (1.1 acres) in size. A computer then translates the numbers into different colors, or different shades of one color, which are projected on to a TV screen (G) and the image is seen for the first time. Finally, photographs of this false-color image are produced (H). This picture, showing a forest fire in the Upper Peninsula, Michigan, is of use to those engaged in forest management. Other satellite data of use in forestry include types of trees, patterns of growth and the spread of disease.

Observation of waterways and coastal areas (above) shows pollution and deposition of sediments. This is of importance to the fishing industry. Fish congregate in areas where upwelling brings nutrients to the surface, for example. The large yellow-orange halo around Akimiski Island in James Bay (A)— a southern extension of Hudson Bay in Canada— is fine sediment resulting from wave action on a silty shore. Seeing the sediment in this way helps to determine current patterns in the Bay. In a predominantly desert area, the Nile delta (B) stands out dramatically. The red is an intensively cultivated area: cotton is the main crop. The larger irrigation canals can be seen on the photograph. Thermal imagery, or heat capacity mapping, is used to identify rocks, to study the effects of urban "heat islands," to estimate soil moisture and snow melt,

and to map shallow ground water. In this photograph of the northeast coast of North America (C) purple represents the coldest temperatures—in Lakes Erie and Ontario. The coldest parts of the Atlantic Ocean are deep blue, whereas warmer waters near the coast are light blue. Green is the warmer land, but also the Gulf Stream in the lower right part of the image. Brown, yellow and orange represent successively warmer land surface areas. Red is hot regions around cities and coal-mining regions found in eastern Pennsylvania (to the upper left of center in the picture); and, finally, gray and white are the very hottest areas—the urban heat islands of Baltimore, Philadelphia and New York City. Black areas in the upper left are cold clouds. The temperature range of the image is about 30°C (55°F).

Weather satellite imagery can save lives and property by giving advance warning of bad weather conditions, as well as providing day-to-day forecasts. This Tiros image (left) shows a cold front moving west of Ireland with low-level wave clouds over southern and central England. There are low-pressure systems over northern France and to the northwest of Ireland.

The Earth seen from space shows phases just like the Moon, Mercury and Venus do to us. These dramatic photographs were taken from a satellite moving at 35,885 km (22,300 miles) above South America at 7.30 am (1), 10.30 am (2), noon (3), 3.30 pm (4) and at 10.30 pm (5), and clearly show the Earth in phase.

LANDSAT AND THE FARMER

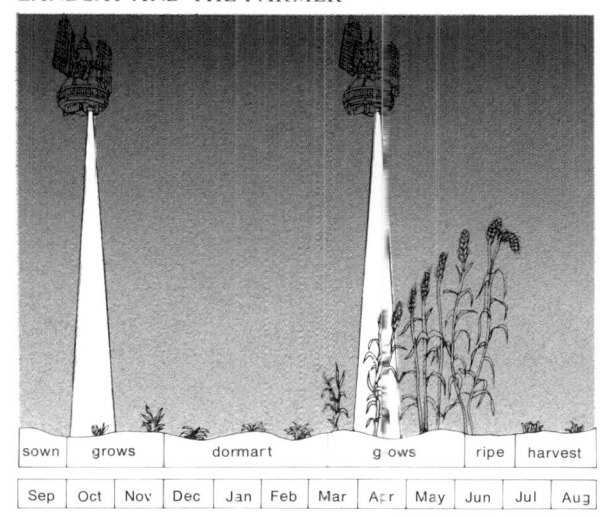

sown	grows	dormant	grows	ripe	harvest
Sep	Oct	Nov	Dec	Jan	Feb	Mar	Apr	May	Jun	Jul	Aug

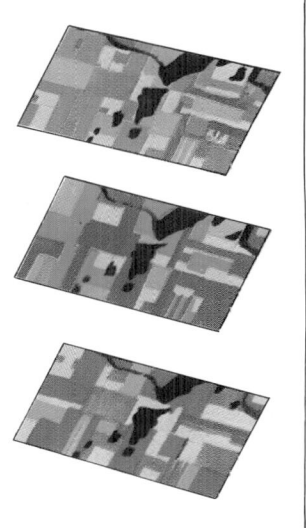

Agriculturists benefit from "multitemporal analysis" by satellites (left). This is the comparison of data from the same field recorded on two or more dates. It is also able to differentiate crops, which may have an identical appearance, or signature, on one day, but on another occasion exhibit different rates of growth. The pattern of growth is different for small grains than most other crops. A "biowindow" is the period of time in which vegetation is observed. These three biowindows (right) show the emergence and ripening (light blue to red to dark blue) of wheat in May, July and August.

Part 2

MAKING AND SHAPING THE EARTH

The structure and substance of the Earth
Forces that move continents · Forces that fashion Earth's landscapes
How man has changed the face of the Earth

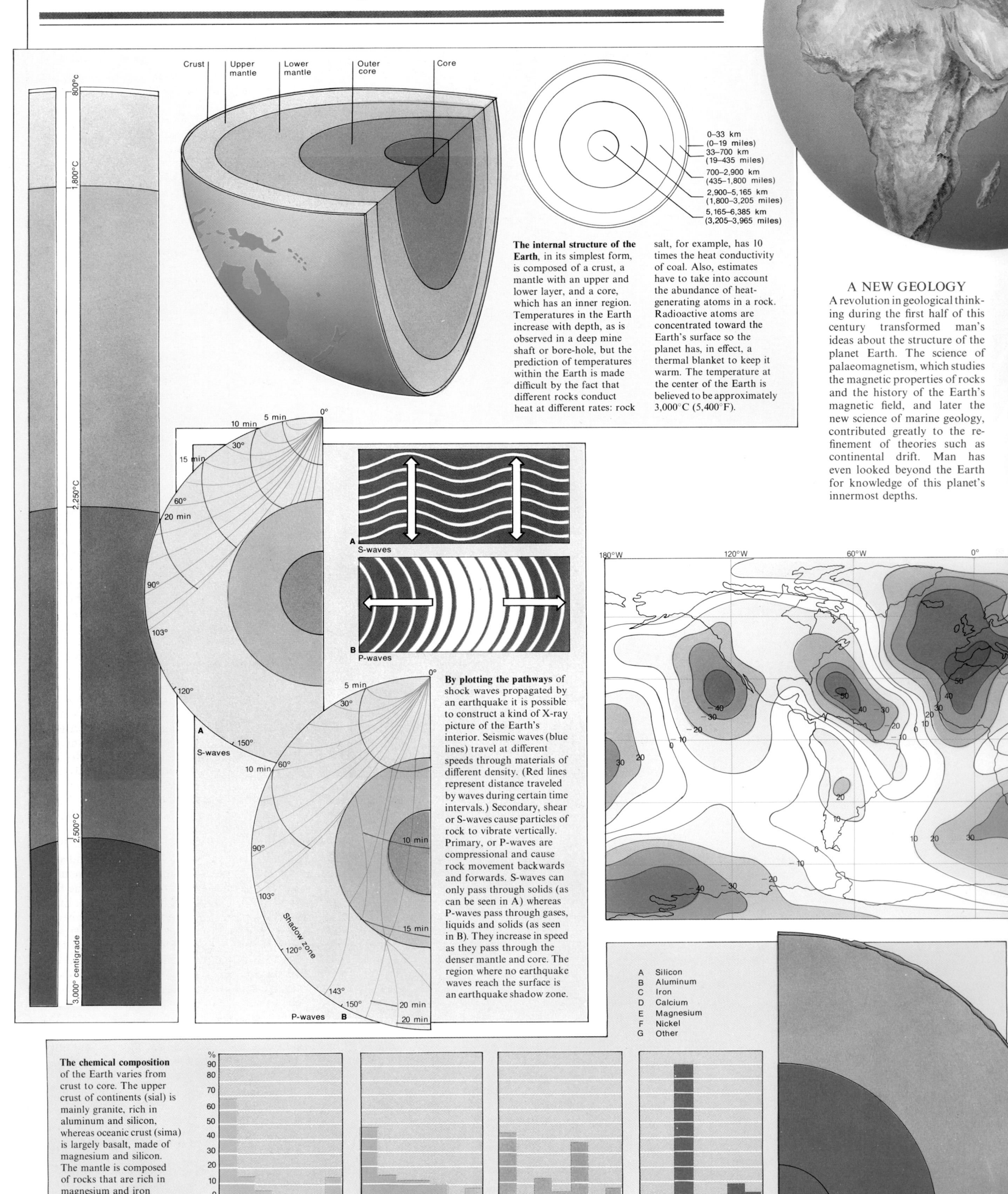

0–33 km
(0–19 miles)
33–700 km
(19–435 miles)
700–2,900 km
(435–1,800 miles)
2,900–5,165 km
(1,800–3,205 miles)
5,165–6,385 km
(3,205–3,965 miles)

The internal structure of the Earth, in its simplest form, is composed of a crust, a mantle with an upper and lower layer, and a core, which has an inner region. Temperatures in the Earth increase with depth, as is observed in a deep mine shaft or bore-hole, but the prediction of temperatures within the Earth is made difficult by the fact that different rocks conduct heat at different rates: rock salt, for example, has 10 times the heat conductivity of coal. Also, estimates have to take into account the abundance of heat-generating atoms in a rock. Radioactive atoms are concentrated toward the Earth's surface so the planet has, in effect, a thermal blanket to keep it warm. The temperature at the center of the Earth is believed to be approximately 3,000°C (5,400°F).

A NEW GEOLOGY

A revolution in geological thinking during the first half of this century transformed man's ideas about the structure of the planet Earth. The science of palaeomagnetism, which studies the magnetic properties of rocks and the history of the Earth's magnetic field, and later the new science of marine geology, contributed greatly to the refinement of theories such as continental drift. Man has even looked beyond the Earth for knowledge of this planet's innermost depths.

By plotting the pathways of shock waves propagated by an earthquake it is possible to construct a kind of X-ray picture of the Earth's interior. Seismic waves (blue lines) travel at different speeds through materials of different density. (Red lines represent distance traveled by waves during certain time intervals.) Secondary, shear or S-waves cause particles of rock to vibrate vertically. Primary, or P-waves are compressional and cause rock movement backwards and forwards. S-waves can only pass through solids (as can be seen in A) whereas P-waves pass through gases, liquids and solids (as seen in B). They increase in speed as they pass through the denser mantle and core. The region where no earthquake waves reach the surface is an earthquake shadow zone.

A   Silicon
B   Aluminum
C   Iron
D   Calcium
E   Magnesium
F   Nickel
G   Other

The chemical composition of the Earth varies from crust to core. The upper crust of continents (sial) is mainly granite, rich in aluminum and silicon, whereas oceanic crust (sima) is largely basalt, made of magnesium and silicon. The mantle is composed of rocks that are rich in magnesium and iron silicates, whereas the core, it is believed, is made of iron and nickel oxides.

Sial

Sima

Mantle

Core

Earth's Structure

The Earth is made up of concentric shells of different kinds of material. Immediately beneath us is the crust; below that is the mantle; and at the center of the globe is the core. Knowledge of the internal structure of Earth is the key to an understanding of the substances of Earth and an appreciation of the forces at work, not only deep in the center of the planet but also affecting the formation of surface features and large-scale landscapes. The workings of all these elements are inextricably linked.

A 17th-century diagram of the Earth shows an internal structure of fire and subterranean rivers.

Our knowledge of the Earth is largely restricted to the outer crust. The deepest hole that man has drilled reaches only 10 km (6 miles)—less than 1/600th of the planet's radius—and so our knowledge about the rest of the Earth has had to come via indirect means: by the study of earthquake waves, and a comparison between rocks on Earth and those that make up meteorites—small fragments of asteroids and other minor planetary bodies that originated from similar materials to the Earth.

The Earth's crust
The outermost layer of the Earth is called the crust. The crust beneath the oceans is different from the material that makes up continental crust. Ocean crust is formed at mid-ocean ridges where melted rocks (magma) from the mantle rise up in great quantities and solidify to form a layer a few kilometers thick over the mantle. As this ocean crust spreads out from the ridge it becomes covered with deep-ocean sediments. The ocean crust was initially called "sima," a word made up from the first two letters of the characteristic elements—silicon and magnesium. Sima has a density of 2.9 gm/cc (1 gm/cc is the density of water).

Continental crust was named "sial"—from silicon and aluminum, the most abundant elements. Sial is lighter than sima with a density of 2.7 gm/cc. The continental crust is like a series of giant rafts, 17 to 70 km (9–43 miles) thick. As a result of numerous collisions and breakages, these continental rafts have been bulldozed into their present shape, but they have been forming for at least 4,000 million years. The oldest known rocks, in Greenland, are 3,750 million years old, which is only about 800 million years younger than the Earth itself. The complex history of the continents' evolution over this vast time span makes construction of an ideal cross section difficult, but the rocks of the lower two-thirds of the crust appear to be denser (2.9 gm/cc) than the upper levels.

The Moho, or Mohorovičić discontinuity, discovered in 1909, marks the base of the crust and the beginning of the mantle rocks, where the density increases from 2.9 to 3.3 gm/cc. The Moho is at an average depth of 10 km (6 miles) under the sea and 35 km (20 miles) below land.

The mantle
Our knowledge of the mantle comes from mantle rocks that are sometimes brought to the surface. These are even more enriched in magnesium oxides than the sima, with lesser amounts of iron and calcium oxides. The uppermost mantle to a depth of between 60 and 100 km (40–60 miles), together with the overlying crust, forms the rigid lithosphere, which is divided into plates. Below this is a pasty layer, or asthenosphere, extending to a depth of 700 km (435 miles). The upper mantle is separated from the lower mantle by another discontinuity where the density of the rock increases from 3.3 to 4.3 gm/cc.

Scientists now believe that the mantle is the planetary motor force behind the movements of the continents. By studying in detail the chemistry of the volcanic rocks that have come directly from the mantle, they have gathered much information about this mantle motor. The rocks that come up along oceanic ridges and form new oceanic crust reveal by their chemical composition that they have formed from mantle that has undergone previous melting. By contrast, islands such as Hawaii and Iceland have formed from mantle material that, for the most part, has never been melted before. One explanation for these chemical observations is that, while the top 700 km (435 miles) of the mantle region is moving in accordance with movement of the plates, the mantle beneath it is moving independently and sending occasional rivers of unaltered material through the surface to form islands like volcanic Hawaii.

The core
Structurally, the most important boundary in the Earth lies at a depth of 2,900 km (1,800 miles) below the surface, where the rock density almost doubles from about 5.5 to 9.9 gm/cc. This is known as the Gutenberg discontinuity and was discovered in 1914. Below this level the material must have the properties of a liquid since certain earthquake waves cannot penetrate it. Scientists infer from the composition of meteorites, some of which are composed of iron and nickel, that this deep core material is composed largely of iron, with some nickel and perhaps lighter elements such as silicon. The processes involved in the formation of a planet have been compared to the separation of the metals (the core) from the slag (the mantle and crust) in a blast furnace.

The core has a radius of 3,485 km (2,165 miles) and makes up only one-sixth of the Earth's volume, yet it has one-third of its mass. In the middle of the liquid outer core there is an even denser ball with a radius of 1,220 km (760 miles)—two-thirds the size of the Moon—where, under intense pressure, the metals have solidified. The inner core is believed to be solid iron and nickel and is 20 percent denser (12–13 gm/cc) than the surrounding liquid.

Electric currents in the core are the only possible source of the Earth's magnetic field. This drifts and alters in a way which could arise only from some deeply buried fluid movement. At the top of the core, the pattern of the field moves about 100 m (330 ft) west each day. Every million years or so during the Earth's history, the north–south magnetic poles have switched so that compasses pointed south, not north.

The dynamo that generates magnetism and its strange variations is still not fully understood. Motion in the core may be powered by giant slabs of metal that crystallize out from the liquid and sink to join the inner core. Our knowledge of the Earth's structure has increased greatly over the last 50 years, but many intriguing questions remain to be answered.

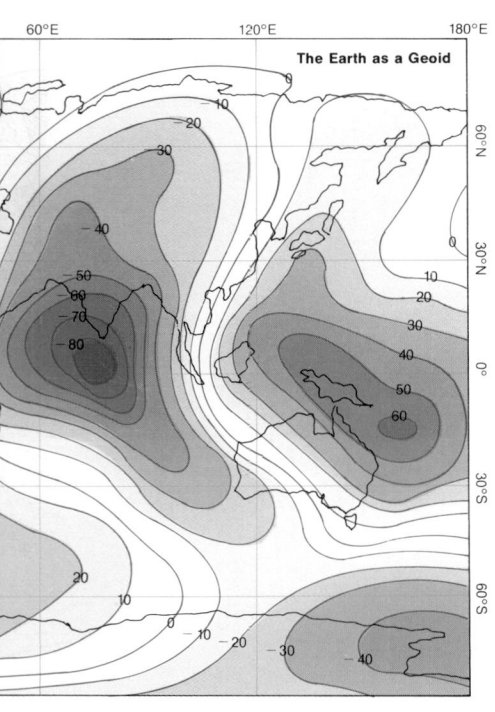

The Earth is not a sphere but an ellipsoid (below) that is flattened at the poles, where the radius is 6,378 km (3,960 miles), and bulging at the Equator, where the radius is 6,536 km (4,060 miles). This results from the Earth's rapid rotation. But, rather than a perfect ellipsoid, the true shape is a "geoid"—the actual shape of sea level—which is lumpy, with variations away from ellipsoid of up to 80 m (260 ft) (left). This reflects major variations in density in Earth's outer layers.

The Earth as a Geoid

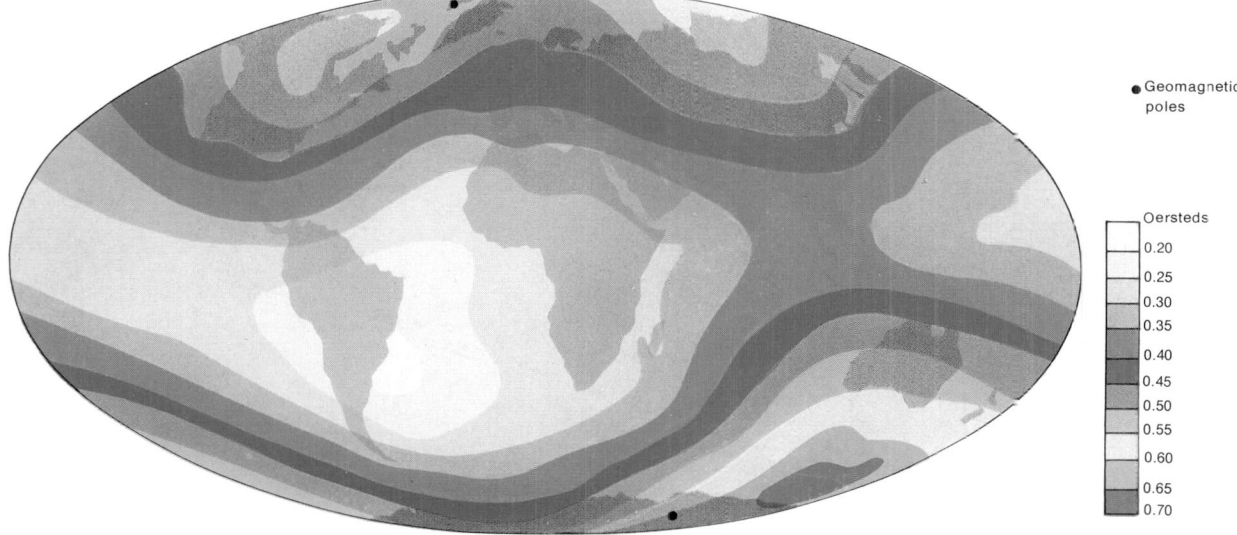

● Geomagnetic poles

Oersteds
0.20
0.25
0.30
0.35
0.40
0.45
0.50
0.55
0.60
0.65
0.70

The Earth's magnetic field is strongest at the poles and weakest in equatorial regions. If the field were simply like a bar magnet inside the globe, lines of intensity would mirror lines of latitude; but the field is inclined at an angle of 11° to the Earth's axis. The geomagnetic poles are similarly inclined and they do not coincide with the geographic poles. In reality, the field is much more complex than that of a bar magnet. In addition, over long periods of time, the magnetic poles and the north–south orientation of the field change slowly. The strength of the Earth's magnetic field is measured in units called oersteds.

Earth's Moving Crust

The top layer of the Earth is known as the lithosphere and is composed of the crust and the uppermost mantle. It is divided into six major rigid plates and several smaller platelets that move relative to each other, driven by movements that lie deep in the Earth's liquid mantle. The plate boundaries correspond to the zones of earthquakes and the sites of active volcanoes. The concept of plate tectonics – that the Earth's crust is mobile despite being rigid – emerged in the 1960s and helped to confirm the early twentieth-century theory of continental drift proposed by Alfred Wegener.

THE DYNAMIC EARTH

As early as the 17th century, the English philosopher Francis Bacon noted that the coasts on either side of the Atlantic were similar and could be fitted together like pieces of a jigsaw puzzle. Three hundred years later Alfred Wegener proposed the theory of continental drift, but no one would believe the Earth's rigid crust could move. Today, geological evidence has provided the basis for the theory of plate tectonics, which demonstrates that the Earth's crust is slowly but continually moving.

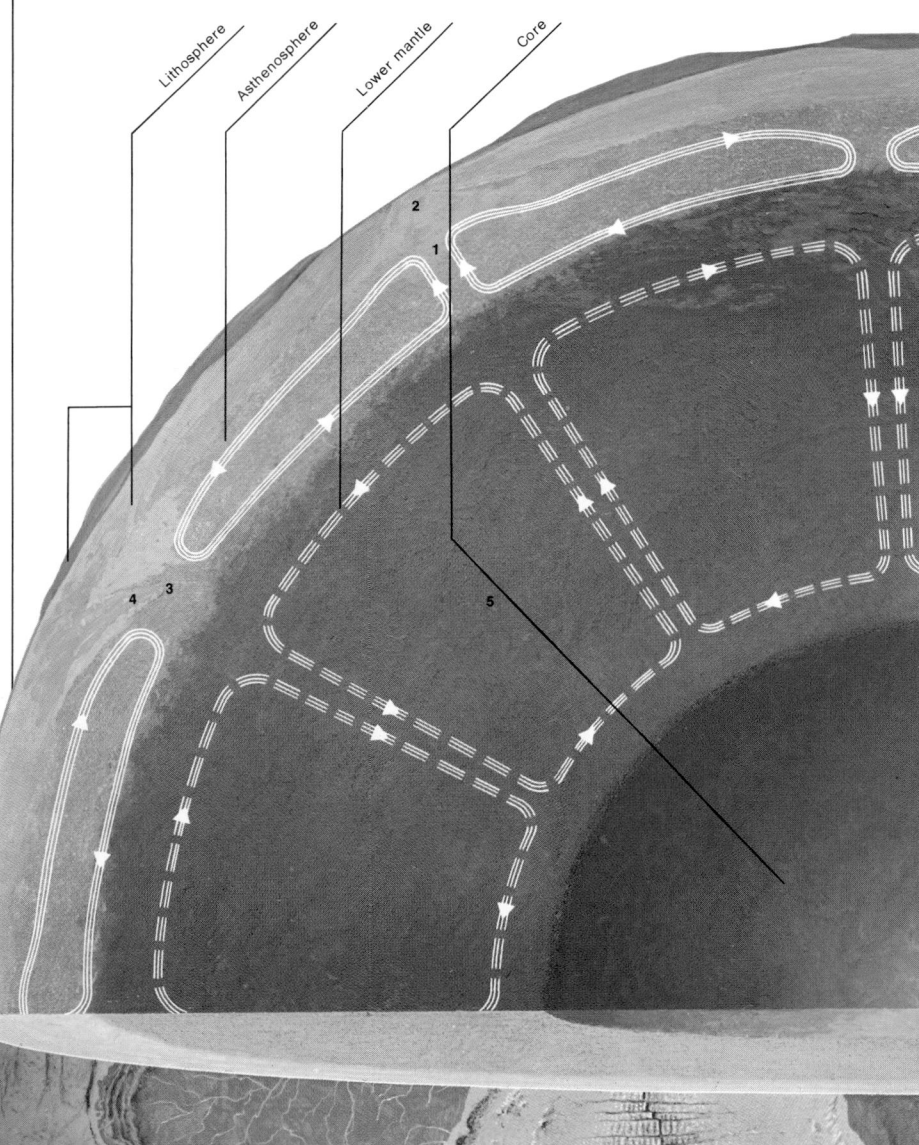

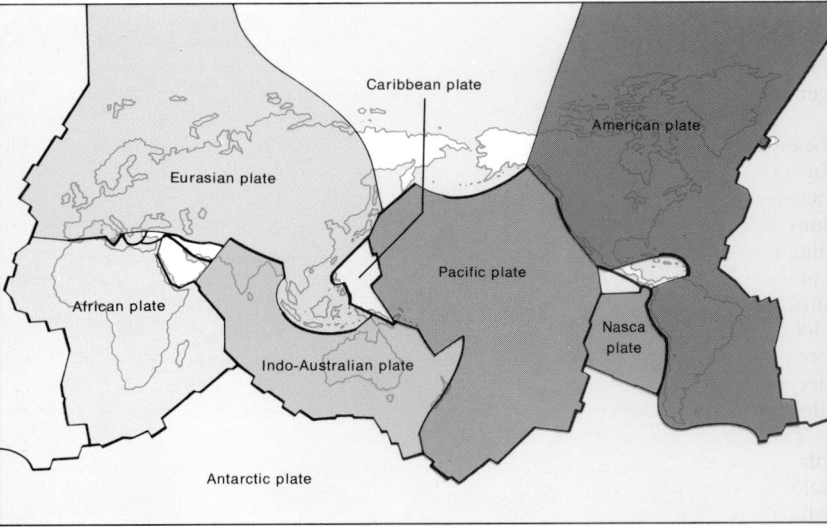

Earth's lithosphere—the rocky shell, or crust—is made up of six major plates and several smaller platelets, each separated from each other by ridges, subduction zones or transcurrent faults. The plates grow bigger by accretion along the mid-ocean ridges, are destroyed at subduction zones beneath the trenches, and slide beside each other along the transcurrent faults. The African and Antarctic plates have no trenches along their borders to destroy any of their crust, so they are growing bigger. This growth is compensated by the subduction zone that is developing to the north of the Tonga Islands and subduction zones in the Pacific. Conversely, the Pacific and Indo-Australian plates are shrinking. Along the plate boundaries magma wells up from the mantle to form volcanoes. Here, too, are the origins of earthquakes as the plates collide or slide slowly past each other.

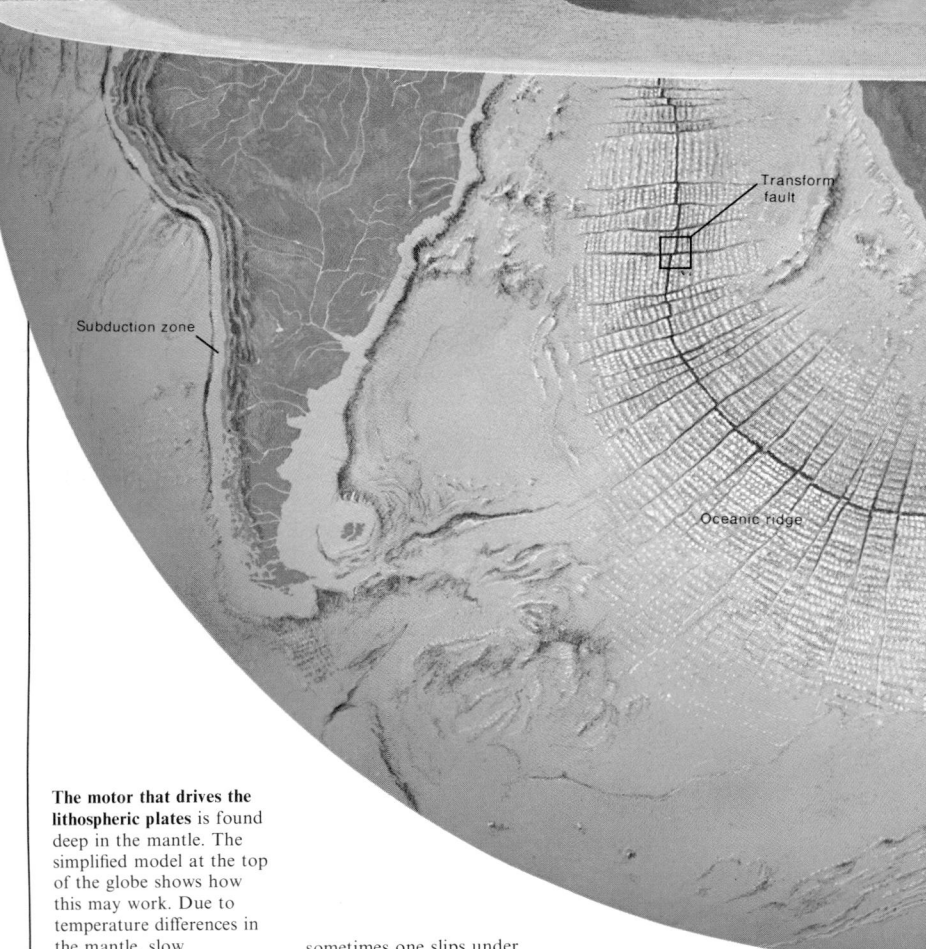

The motor that drives the lithospheric plates is found deep in the mantle. The simplified model at the top of the globe shows how this may work. Due to temperature differences in the mantle, slow convection currents circulate. Where two current cycles move upwards together and separate (1), the plates bulge and move apart along mid-ocean ridges (2). Where there is a downward moving current (3), the plates move together and sometimes one slips under the other to form a subduction zone (4). Another model proposes that the convection currents are found deep in the mantle (5). Only time and more research, however, will reveal the true mechanism of plate movement.

Subduction zones are the sites of destruction of the ocean crust. As one plate passes beneath another down into the mantle, the ocean floor is pulled downward and a deep ocean trench is formed. The movement taking place along the length of the subduction zone causes earthquakes, while melting of the rock at depth produces magma that rises to create the volcanoes that form island arcs.

An oceanic ridge is formed when two plates move away from each other. As they move, molten magma from the mantle forces its way to the surface. This magma cools and is in turn injected with new magma. Thus the oceanic ridge is gradually forming the newest part of Earth's crust.

Transform, or transcurrent, faults are found where two plates slide past each other. They may, for example, link two parts of a ridge (A, B). A study of the magnetic properties of the seabed may suggest a motion shown by the white arrows, but the true movements of the plates are shown by the red arrows. The transform fault is active only between points (2) and (3). Between points (1) and (2) and between (3) and (4) the scar of the fault is healed and the line of the fault is no longer a plate boundary.

The early evidence for continental drift was gathered by Alfred Wegener, a German meteorologist. He noticed that the coastlines on each side of the Atlantic Ocean could be made to fit together, and that much of the geological history of the flanking continents—shown by fossils, structures and past climates—also seemed to match. Wegener compared the two sides of the Atlantic with a sheet of torn newspaper and reasoned that if not just one line of print but 10 lines match then there is a good case for arguing that the two sides were once joined. Yet for 50 years continental drift was generally considered to be a fanciful dream.

Seafloor spreading
In the 1950s the first geological surveys of the oceans began, and a 60,000 km (37,200 mile) long chain of mountains was discovered running down the center of the Atlantic Ocean, all round the Antarctic, up to the Indian Ocean, into the Red Sea and up the Eastern Pacific Ocean into Alaska. Along the axis of this mid-ocean ridge system there was often a narrow, deep rift valley. In places this ridge was offset along sharp fractures in the ocean floor.

The breakthrough in developing the global plate tectonic theory came with the first large-scale survey of the ocean floor. Magnetometers, which were developed during World War II for tracking submarines, showed the ocean floor to be magnetically striped. The ocean floor reveals magnetic characteristics because the ocean crust basalts are full of tiny crystals of the magnetic mineral magnetite. As the basalt cooled, the magnetic field of these crystals aligned itself with the Earth's magnetic field. This would be insignificant if it were not for the fact that the magnetic pole of the Earth has switched from north to south at different times in the past. Half the magnetite compasses of the ocean floor point south rather than north.

In the middle 1960s, two Cambridge geophysicists, Drummond Matthews and Fred Vine, noticed that the pattern of stripes was symmetrical around the mid-ocean ridge. Such an extraordinary and unlikely symmetry could mean only one thing—any two matching stripes must originally have been formed together at the mid-ocean ridge and then moved away from each other as newer crust formed between them to create new stripes. It was soon calculated that the North Atlantic Ocean was growing wider by about 2 cm ($\frac{3}{4}$ in) a year. At last, drifting continents was accepted.

Consumption of the seafloor
Seafloor spreading soon became included in an even more sensational model—plate tectonics. If the oceans are growing wider, then either the whole planet is expanding or the spreading ocean floor is consumed elsewhere. In the late 1950s a global network of seismic stations had been set up to monitor nuclear explosions and earthquakes. For the first time the positions of all earthquakes could be accurately defined.

It was found that the zones of earthquake activity were predominantly narrow, following the mid-ocean ridges and extending along the rim of the Pacific, beneath the island arcs of the

West Pacific and beneath the continental margins in the East Pacific as well as underlying the Alpine-Himalayan Mountain Belt. The seismic zones around the Pacific dipped away from the ocean and continued to depths as great as 700 km (430 miles). They intercepted the surface at the curious arc-shaped deep-ocean trenches. It had been known for 20 years that the pull of gravity over these trenches is strangely reduced, so to survive they must continually be dragged downwards. Here was the site of ocean-floor consumption—now known as a subduction zone. Subduction zones must be efficient at consuming ocean crust because no known ocean crust is older than 200 million years—less than five percent of Earth's lifetime.

The oceanic lithosphere (the Earth's rocky crust) is extraordinarily rigid. Even where the oceanic lithosphere becomes consumed within subduction zones it still maintains its rigidity. As it bends down into the Earth it tends to corrugate, forming very long folds. These corrugations give rise to the pattern of chains of deep-ocean trenches and chains of volcanic islands formed above the subduction zone.

As oceanic lithosphere grows older it cools, contracts and sinks. From the depth of the ocean floor it is possible to make an accurate estimate of the age of the crust beneath. Even the steepness of the subduction zone is a function of the age, and therefore the density, of the lithosphere. The oldest crust provides the strongest downward pull and hence the steepest angle of dip of the subduction zone.

As well as the spreading ridges (constructive margins) and the subduction zones (destructive margins) there is another kind of plate boundary (conservative margins), where the plates slip past one another along a major fault such as the San Andreas Fault of California.

The past positions of the continents
Continental drift is thus the result of the creation and destruction of oceanic lithosphere, but only the continents can record the oceanic plate motions taking place more than 200 million years ago. The discovery of ancient lines of subduction zone volcanoes can testify to the destruction of long-gone oceans. One particularly important technique for finding the positions of the continents is to study the magnetism of certain rocks, particularly lavas, that record the position of the north–south magnetic poles at the time when the rock cooled. If the rock "compass" points, for example, west, then the continent must have rotated by 90°. The vertical dip of the rock compass can reveal the approximate latitude of the rock at its formation (the dip increases from horizontal at the Equator to vertical at the magnetic poles).

As longitude is entirely arbitrary (defined on the position of Greenwich) one can only hope to gain the relative positions of the continents with regard to one another. The best additional information is provided by studies of fossils—if the remains of shallow-water marine organisms are very different they must have been separated by an ocean. The full impact of continental drift on the development of land animals and plants is only beginning to be realized.

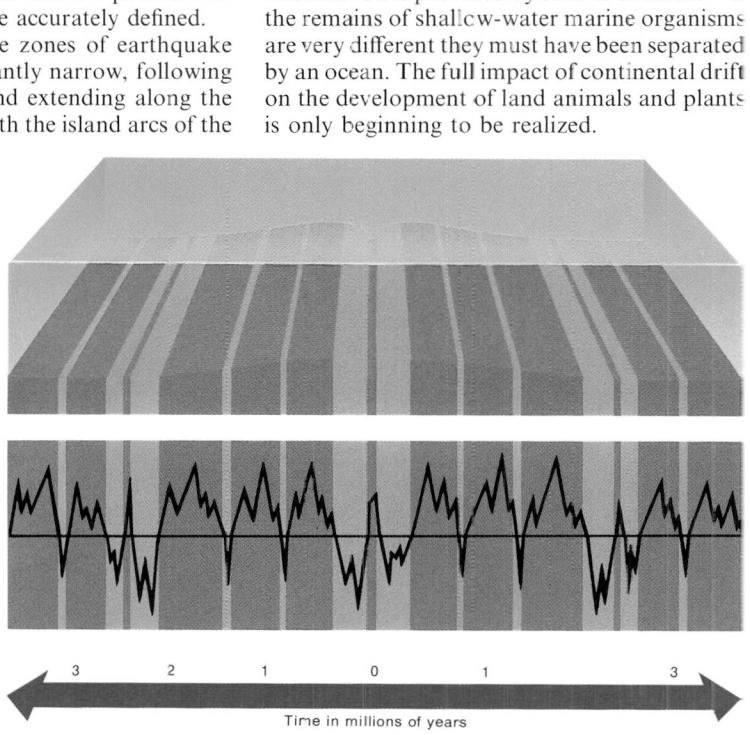

Magnetic surveys of the seabed helped build the plate tectonics theory. Research vessels equipped with magnetometers sailed back and forth over a mid-ocean ridge and recorded the varying magnetism of the seabed. The Earth's magnetic pole has switched from north to south at different times in the past, and this mapping revealed a striped magnetic pattern on the seabed. It was noticed that the stripes on either side of the ridge were symmetrical. The explanation was that the matching stripes must have formed together and moved apart as more crust was injected between them—a notion that was subsequently supported by dating of the seafloor.

Time in millions of years

THE DRIFTING CONTINENTS
It is now accepted that the continents have changed their positions during the past millions of years, and by studying the magnetism preserved in the rocks the configuration of the continents has been plotted for various geological times. The sequence of continental drifting, illustrated below, begins with one single landmass—the so-called supercontinent Pangaea—and the ancestral Pacific Ocean, called the Panthalassa Ocean. Pangaea first split into a northern landmass called Laurasia and a southern landmass called Gondwanaland, and subsequently into the continents we see today. The maps illustrate the positions of the continents in the past, where they are now and their predicted positions in 50 million years' time.

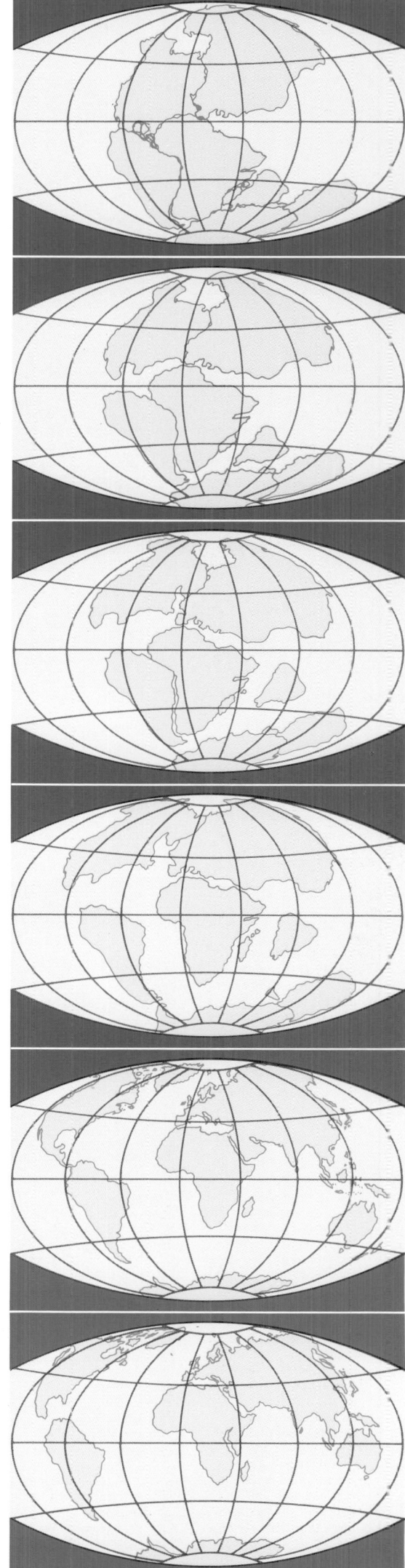

225 million years ago one large landmass, the supercontinent Pangaea, exists and Panthalassa forms the ancestral Pacific Ocean. The Tethys Sea separates Eurasia and Africa and forms an ancestor of the Mediterranean Sea.

180 million years ago Pangaea splits up, the northern block of continents, Laurasia, drifts northwards and the southern block, Gondwanaland, begins to break up. India separates and the South American–African block divides from Australia-Antarctica. New ocean floor is created between the continents.

135 million years ago the Indian plate continues its northward drift and Eurasia rotates to begin to close the eastern end of the Tethys Sea. The North Atlantic and the Indian Ocean have opened up and the South Atlantic is just beginning to form.

65 million years ago Madagascar has split from Africa and the Tethys Sea has closed, with the Mediterranean Sea opening behind it. The South Atlantic Ocean has opened up considerably, but Australia is still joined to the Antarctic and India is about to collide with Asia.

The present day: India has completed its northward migration and collided with Asia, Australia has set itself free from Antarctica, and North America has freed itself from Eurasia to leave Greenland between them. During the past 65 million years (a relatively short geological span of time) nearly half of the present-day ocean floor has been created.

50 million years in the future, Australia may continue its northward drift, part of East Africa will separate from the mainland, and California west of the San Andreas Fault will separate from North America and move northwards. The Pacific Ocean will become smaller, compensating for the increase in size of both the Atlantic and Indian oceans. The Mediterranean Sea will disappear as Africa moves to the north.

Folds, Faults and Mountain Chains

The continents are great rafts of lighter rock that float in the mantle of the Earth. When drifting continents collide, great mountain chains are thrown up as the continental crust is forced to thicken to absorb the impact of the collision. The highest mountains are formed out of thick piles of sediment that are built up from the debris of erosion constantly washed off the land and deposited on the continental margins. Through the massive deformations of rock faults and folds these remains of old mountains become recycled, thus building new mountains from the remains of old ones.

For the formation of mountain ranges such as the Appalachians or the Himalayas, or the Caledonian mountain chain of Norway, Scotland and Newfoundland, the pattern of development is very much the same. First, a widening ocean with passive margins is located between two continents.

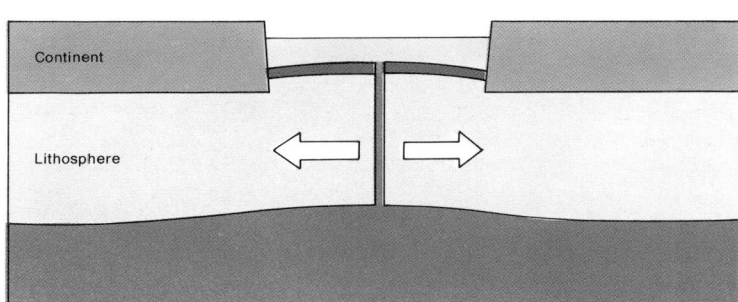

As more ocean floor is created the continents move farther apart, and at the edge of each continent sediment accumulates from the debris of erosion. These piles of thick sediment are known as sedimentary basins.

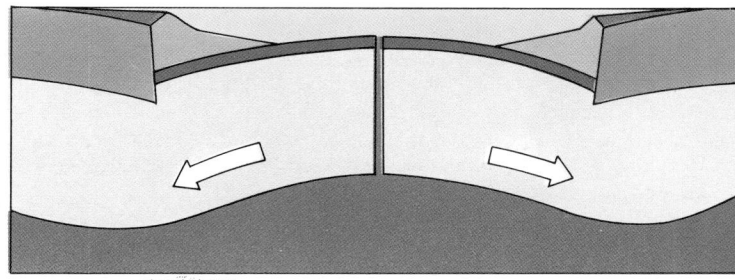

For the formation of the Appalachians, the ancestral Atlantic Ocean began to close, a subduction zone was formed at the ocean–continent boundary, and the oceanic lithosphere began to be absorbed into the mantle. Magma intruded to form granite "plutons" and volcanoes, and much of the sedimentary basin was metamorphosed.

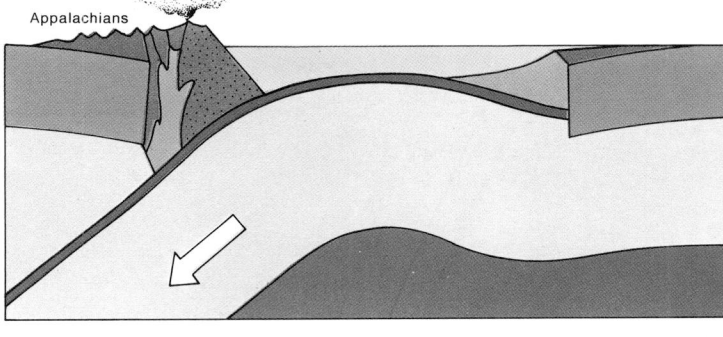

The ocean continued to close until North America and Africa were joined together, further compressing the sediments in the sedimentary basin at the passive ocean margin. The two continents were joined like this between 350 and 225 million years ago.

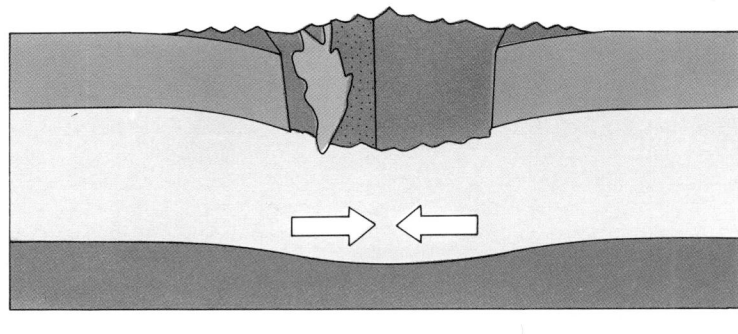

About 180 million years ago, after the original Appalachians had been worn down in size, the present Atlantic Ocean opened along a new break in the continental crust, offset from the line of the original mountains. As the continents split, so the crust became stretched along great curved faults.

Parts of the ancient Appalachian mountains have been eroded to sea level, leaving the Appalachians, that formed on the edge of the old continent, inland.

 Continental shelf
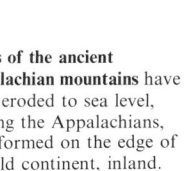 Granite
Metamorphic rock
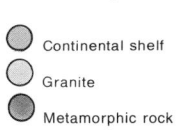 Sediment
Ocean crust

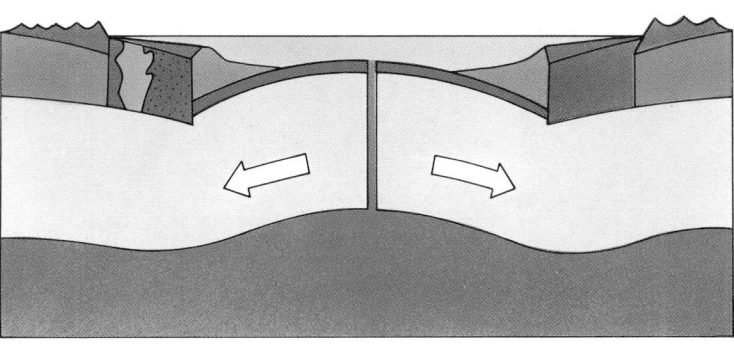

BIRTH AND DEATH OF A MOUNTAIN

Mountains are thrust upward by the pressure exerted by the moving plates of the Earth's crust, and are formed out of the sediments that have been eroded from the continental masses. Young mountains are lofty and much folded, but the agents of erosion and weathering soon begin to reduce their height, and over many millions of years the mountain range is eroded to sea level. This eroded material accumulates in the sea at the edge of the continents and becomes the building material for another phase of mountain building.

ISOSTASY

The continents float in the Earth's mantle, and because they are only slightly less dense (2.67 g/cc compared to 3.27 g/cc), 85% of their bulk lies below sea level. Thus the higher the mountain the deeper the mountain root. And as the crust can exist only to a maximum depth of about 70 km (43 miles) before it is liquefied in the mantle, mountains can never rise above a maximum of 10 km (6 miles) above sea level.

Folds are generally related to underlying faults. The commonest simple folds are monoclines, formed when a single fault exhibits underlying movement. With continued movement a simple symmetrical anticline (1) may fold unevenly to form an asymmetric anticline (2). More movement bends the strata further into a recumbent fold (3) and eventually the strata break to form an overthrust fold (4). Over a long period an overthrust fold may be pushed many kilometers from its original position to form a nappe (5). Faults are generally of three kinds: faults of tension known as normal faults, when one block drops down (6); faults of horizontal shear (7), known as strike-slip faults; and faults of compression (8), known as thrust faults.

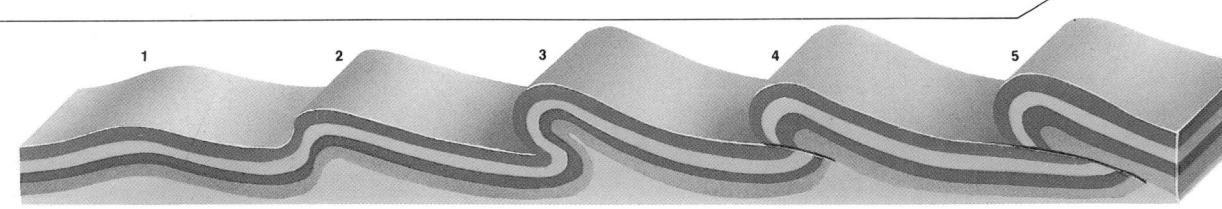

Continents float in the Earth's mantle like icebergs in the sea—more than four-fifths of their bulk lies beneath the surface. The continental crust is 28 km (17 miles) thick at sea level, and where mountains rise above this level there is a corresponding thickening in the crust beneath. The maximum thickness of crust is 70 km (43 miles), so mountains can only ever rise to a maximum height of approximately 10 km (6 miles) above sea level. This relation between upper and underlying crust is known as isostasy, or state of equal pressure.

As mountains become eroded, the process of isostatic rebound allows them to recover about 85 cm (34 in) for every 1 meter (40 in) removed. When, after about 100 million years, a major mountain range has been eroded down to sea level, the rocks exposed at the surface are those that were 15–25 km (9–15 miles) underground when the mountains were at their highest. Such rocks are coarsely crystalline, and make up the fabric of the old, tough continental crust.

Sedimentary basins

As early as the nineteenth century it was noticed that the biggest mountains formed where there had previously been the thickest pile of sediments. According to the principle of isostasy, a thick pile of sediments can form only where the Earth's crust is thin and sinking. The Aegean Sea in the eastern Mediterranean, for example, is at present being pulled apart, and therefore becoming thinner. Over the next few million years, as the Aegean crust sinks, a thick pile of sediments—a sedimentary basin—will accumulate. Most sedimentary basins are at present shallow seas, and form the continental shelves. The depth of water over these shelf seas has been determined by the erosion that accompanied the lowest sea levels of the past 100 million years—about 140 m (460 ft) below the present sea level.

Mountain building

When continents collide, it is the regions of stretched crust that are the first to absorb some of the impact. Such a former sedimentary basin is being turned into the Zagros Mountains of southwestern Iran as Arabia advances northeastward into Asia. The individual blocks of continental crust appear to be sliding back along curved faults, and the sediments that have built up over the thinned crust are now being forced into folds.

Early in the life of such a sedimentary basin sea water may become cut off from the ocean and evaporate to form extensive deposits of salt. Such salt deposits reduce friction and allow the folded pile of sediments overlying the continental blocks to become disconnected and to slide up to 100 km (62 miles) away from the collision zone. In the Zagros Mountains this process has only just begun, but in older mountain ranges, such as the Canadian Rockies or the European Alps, the formation of nappes—disconnected sediment piles forced ahead of the main compression zone—has been widespread.

As mountain ranges often form out of the sedimentary basins along the boundaries between a continent and the ocean, new mountains tend to add on to the fringes of the continents. In North America, for example, the oldest remnants of ranges that make up large tracts of the Canadian shield are found in the center of the continent, while the process of mountain building is continuing in the west.

Other continents show a more complex pattern of mountain ranges through subsequent phases of splitting and amalgamation, and the Himalayas and the Urals have formed where smaller continents have come together to make up the continent of Asia.

The boundary between the continent and the ocean along the western coast of the Atlantic Ocean is not a plate boundary and is therefore termed passive, in contrast to active boundaries such as the eastern coast of the Pacific Ocean, where the ocean plate is moving down into the mantle at a subduction zone beneath the Andean mountain chain. The highest Andean mountains are tall volcanoes of andesite (formed from magmas pouring off the underlying subduction zone). The bulk of the mountain range consists of enormous underground batholiths, in which the magma has solidified before being able to erupt, and compressed and uplifted sedimentary basins formed along the continental margin.

The crustal region immediately beyond the volcanoes that form above subduction zones, however, is very often in tension and in the process of being pulled apart. This appears to be caused by mantle material being dragged down with the oceanic lithosphere. Small ocean basins, such as the Sea of Japan, may open up under such conditions.

Folds and faults

When movement of the Earth's crust has taken place along a planar fracture through sedimentary rocks, it can be easily identified by the breaks in the layers, and such planes of movement are known as faults. Folds form where rock layers bend rather than break. Generally, faults form when rocks are brittle, and folds are found when rocks are plastic.

Sediments close to the surface are often so soft that they behave plastically, as do rocks at depths greater than 15–20 km (9–12 miles), where the continental crust is of sufficiently high temperature and pressure for slow rock flow to take place. Thus most continental faults are found between these levels. All major folds found in soft sediments apparently have a fault of some kind beneath them, and it is the failure of the fault to pass right through to the surface that creates the fold.

Folds are often extremely complicated and some geologists have tended to describe them in extraordinary detail, but in fact they are little more than brush strokes in the overall picture. Pre-existing faults beneath the folds tend to determine the folds' orientation. Once a continental fault has formed, it provides a plane of weakness wherever the continental crust is subject to stress. Many faults around the Mediterranean Sea came into existence during a period of tension, and these are now being reactivated and produce the large earthquakes associated with the continuing collision of Africa with Europe.

At the end of all the complications and intricacies of continental collision, the final phase of mountain building—that involving uplift—remains perhaps the least understood. In the last two million years, for example, while man has been increasingly active on Earth, 2,500,000 sq km (almost 1,000,000 sq miles) of Tibet has risen 4,000 m (2 miles). But the origin of such gigantic and rapid movement lies within the Earth's mantle.

The highest mountains are the product of continental collisions. As the rocks are squeezed, folded and faulted, the original continental crust becomes shortened and thickened. Although the overall extent and height of mountain chains is controlled by mountain building, the whole range can only be viewed from a spacecraft. For the earthbound mountain visitor the familiar shapes of peaks and valleys are those formed by mountain destruction (1). Snow at high altitudes consolidates to form ice that moves slowly downhill in the form of glaciers. To wear away a mountain range at an average of 5 km (3 miles) above sea level requires the removal of more than 20 km (12 miles) of rock, as the thick continental crust that floats in the underlying mantle rises to compensate for the loss of surface mass. Half-eroded mountains (2), such as the Appalachians, pictured above, may linger on for tens of millions of years until, like large regions of the Canadian interior, the mountains are all eroded away and only the hard crystalline surface rocks that were once buried 20 km (12 miles) underground remain (3).

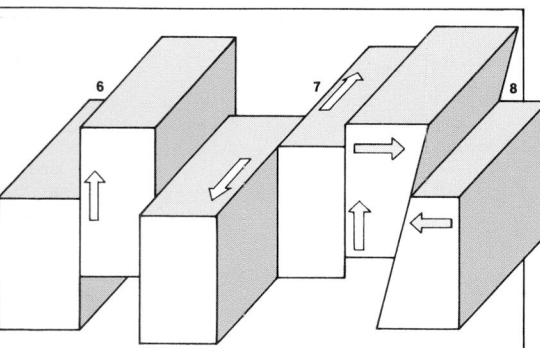

Rock Formation and History

All the rocks on Earth are interrelated through the rock cycle – a never-ending chain of processes that forms and modifies rocks and minerals on the Earth's surface, in its crust and in the mantle. These events are powered both by energy from the Sun and the heat of the Earth itself, and the processes include the forces of nature – from wind and water to the movements of the continents. This geological cycle of creation and destruction is one of the most distinctive features of our planet. Each feature of geological activity, each agent of landscape-making is but a stage of the continuing rock cycle.

CONSTANT CHANGE

The processes of formation and destruction of the three basic rock types—igneous, sedimentary and metamorphic—are linked in an interminable cycle of change. Igneous rocks are thrown up from inside the Earth, are eroded and eventually laid down as sediments. As accumulated sediments sink into the Earth, they are changed by heat and pressure—metamorphosed—before surfacing again in the processes of mountain building.

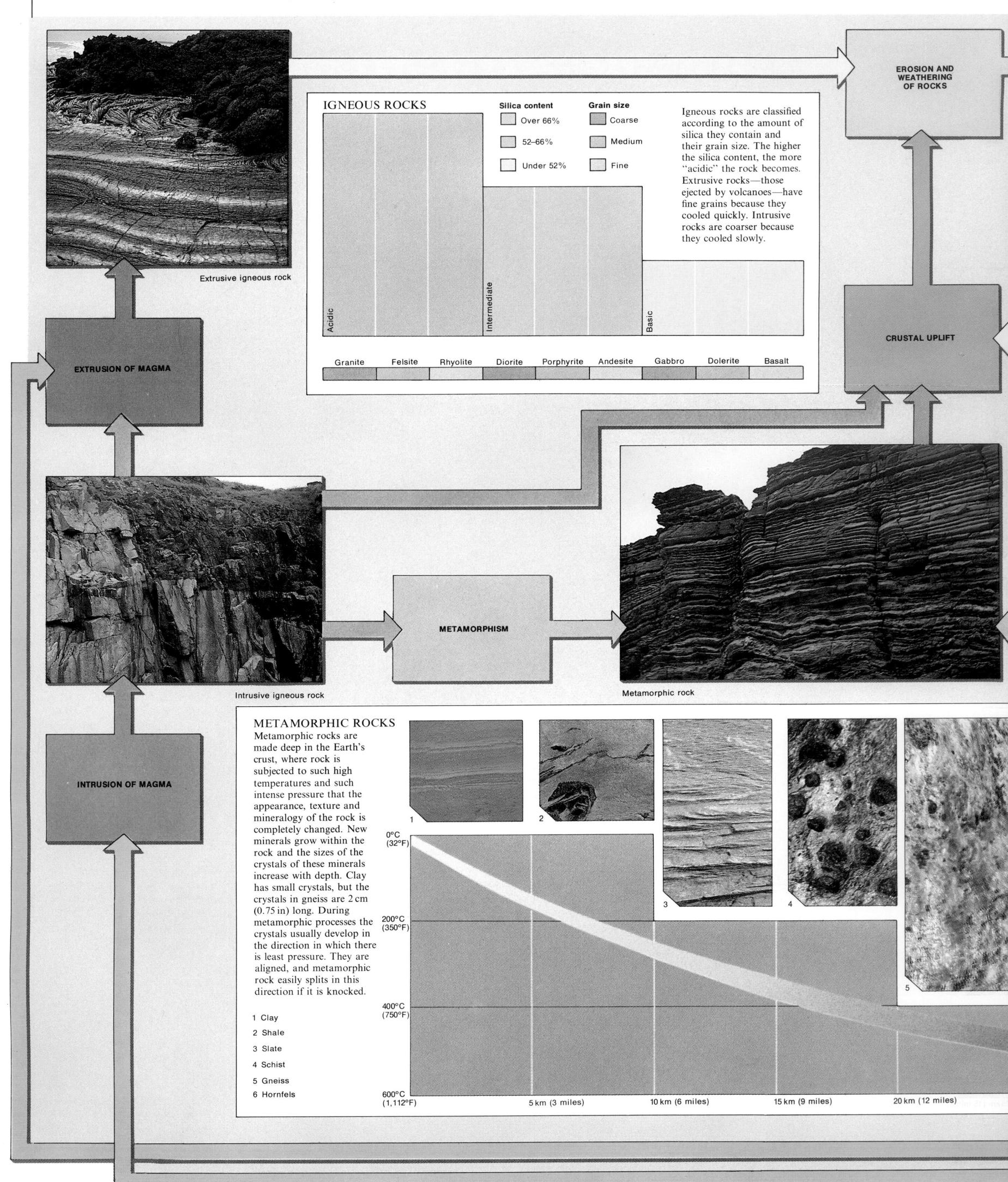

Extrusive igneous rock

EROSION AND WEATHERING OF ROCKS

IGNEOUS ROCKS

Silica content
- Over 66%
- 52–66%
- Under 52%

Grain size
- Coarse
- Medium
- Fine

Igneous rocks are classified according to the amount of silica they contain and their grain size. The higher the silica content, the more "acidic" the rock becomes. Extrusive rocks—those ejected by volcanoes—have fine grains because they cooled quickly. Intrusive rocks are coarser because they cooled slowly.

Acidic — Intermediate — Basic

Granite | Felsite | Rhyolite | Diorite | Porphyrite | Andesite | Gabbro | Dolerite | Basalt

EXTRUSION OF MAGMA

CRUSTAL UPLIFT

INTRUSION OF MAGMA

METAMORPHISM

Intrusive igneous rock

Metamorphic rock

METAMORPHIC ROCKS

Metamorphic rocks are made deep in the Earth's crust, where rock is subjected to such high temperatures and such intense pressure that the appearance, texture and mineralogy of the rock is completely changed. New minerals grow within the rock and the sizes of the crystals of these minerals increase with depth. Clay has small crystals, but the crystals in gneiss are 2 cm (0.75 in) long. During metamorphic processes the crystals usually develop in the direction in which there is least pressure. They are aligned, and metamorphic rock easily splits in this direction if it is knocked.

1 Clay
2 Shale
3 Slate
4 Schist
5 Gneiss
6 Hornfels

0°C (32°F)
200°C (350°F)
400°C (750°F)
600°C (1,112°F)

5 km (3 miles) | 10 km (6 miles) | 15 km (9 miles) | 20 km (12 miles)

SEDIMENTARY ROCKS

Sediments can be turned into rock by means of three main processes. Cementation is the term used when water percolates between grains of sand. As it does so, any iron oxide, silica or calcium carbonate that were in solution are deposited in thin layers around the grains, thus cementing them into a hard sandstone (1). As more sediment is laid down, the increasing weight of the sediments on top exerts pressure on the underlying layers. Water is squeezed out and a dense rock is formed (2) by the process of compaction. This is the way clay becomes mudstone. Finally, during mountain-building processes forces are exerted on rock minerals that cause them to recrystallize into a solid mass of rock (3) that has no spaces between its mineral constituents.

TRANSPORTATION AND DEPOSITION OF SEDIMENTS

BURIAL AND FORMATION OF ROCK FROM SEDIMENTS (LITHIFICATION)

Sedimentary rock

METAMORPHISM

MELTING

25 km (15 miles)   30 km (18 miles)

All the rocks on Earth are formed at one stage or another in what is known as the rock cycle. All high ground on the continents suffers erosion; the eroded material is transported and deposited on lower ground; in time, these sediments may be elevated by mountain-building processes and so, in turn, become eroded. If, between their formation and destruction, sediments pass deep into the Earth's crust, they may be transformed by heat or pressure into metamorphic rock; or, at even greater depths, they may melt to form yet another kind of rock—igneous rock.

Materials at the bottom of a thick pile of sediments may be heated enough to melt. If this material then cools and solidifies underground, it is called plutonic rock. Sometimes, however, it escapes to the surface by means of a short cut— a volcano—to become part of the rock cycle. On the other hand, some sediments are lost off the edge of the continents on to the deep ocean floor, and they disappear into the mantle of the Earth by means of the downward movements of the oceanic crust. A measure of the difference between the input and the output of the continental rock cycle is a measure of how fast the continental crust is increasing or decreasing. Scientists believe it is increasing—at a rate of between 0.1 and 1.0 cu km a year.

Types of rock

The range of rock types found on the continents has been classified under three headings: sedimentary, igneous and metamorphic. Sedimentary rocks include all those formed at low temperatures on the Earth's surface; igneous rocks have all solidified from molten rock, or magma; and metamorphic rocks are sedimentary or igneous rocks that have changed their nature under conditions of high temperature and pressure.

There is a certain amount of difficulty in defining the boundaries between the different types. Ash formed from solidified magma falling out of the air after a volcanic eruption is igneous, but what if it should move downhill in a mudslide? If a metamorphic rock is deeply buried it may start to melt and form a "migmatite," which is part liquid and part solid. Is this igneous? And where does the boundary lie between a deeply buried sediment and a metamorphic rock? Coal seams that have been thoroughly metamorphosed from their original peat deposits are found as layers in unaltered sandstones. This classification does, however, provide a useful preliminary guide to understanding the nature of different types of rock.

Rock types are defined by studying their texture, the way they were formed, and their composition. There are interesting textural similarities between evaporites—salt deposits formed as an inland sea dries up—and some plutonic igneous rocks. Both have crystallized

directly from a liquid. There are similarities between sandstones and plutonic "cumulates," which form at the base of enormous magma reservoirs where strong magma currents deposit thick layers of crystals. So rock types must be defined in terms of more than just texture.

Rock formation

The simplest sedimentary rocks are those made up of whole fragments of eroded material. "Scree" deposits that accumulate at the base of a cliff or a steep valley side from angular rock fragments that have broken off the rock face above can make a sedimentary "breccia." A rock made from rounded stream pebbles is a "conglomerate." Further erosion reduces the rock into three components: dissolved ions (atoms with an electrical charge) such as those of calcium or magnesium; mineral grains (sand) that cannot be broken down chemically, such as quartz; and a variety of minerals containing sheet-like layers of silicate and alumina (silicon and aluminum oxides)—the minerals that are often the main constituents of clays.

A river carrying these minerals first deposits the sand, and then the clay, while the dissolved ions pass out into the sea, where some are absorbed by living organisms and used to construct protective shells and rigid skeletons. When the creatures die, the shells and bones again become part of the rock cycle, building up great thicknesses of limestone.

Igneous rocks are chemically far more complex than are sedimentary rocks, but are texturally simpler. The slower the magma cools, the larger are the crystals that form within it. If it cools too quickly it may not crystallize at all, forming instead a super-cooled liquid, or glass. A plutonic igneous rock—one cooled deep underground—is coarse grained; a volcanic rock is fine grained. A rock can, however, have both large and small crystals, testifying to a more complex history.

The most striking feature of Earth magmas is their uniformity. With few exceptions, they are all rich in silica. The greater the silica content, the higher their viscosity (resistance to flowing). Those rich in silica tend to solidify underground. The complex chemistry of magmas comes from the melting of the variety of minerals making up the mantle.

The chemistry of metamorphic rocks is like that of their igneous or sedimentary starting materials. As these become more deeply buried and heated, the constituent minerals grow larger. A mudstone metamorphoses to a slate, then to a schist and finally a gneiss. The "slateness" or "schistosity" of these rocks is provided by micas and other sheet-shaped mineral grains. Such minerals require abundant alumina to form. If this is not present in the starting rock, it will be metamorphosed into more granular material.

A record in the rocks

Rocks contain an unwritten history of the Earth. Sedimentary rocks hold information about climates of the past and fossil relics of organisms that lived when the sediments were laid down. Igneous rocks record periods of crustal activity that relate to the movements of the continents; and metamorphic rocks indicate periods of uplift that exposed previously buried rock. From such information it is possible to construct a geological time scale. Although fossils are a useful means of correlating one pile of sediment with another, good fossils go back only 600 million years. Earlier organisms are believed to have been soft bodied and were not easily fossilized.

The only complete time scale comes from the radioactive "clocks" in many igneous and metamorphic rocks. Certain forms of natural elements, or isotopes, are unstable and emit energy. By measuring the amount of "daughter" atoms that have been formed by the radioactive decay of a larger "parent" atom, it is possible to determine the age of a rock and events in the history of its formation. The dating of rocks from radioactive decay has thus enabled a true time scale for the history of the Earth to be constructed.

Earth's Minerals

Minerals are the basic ingredients of the Earth, from crust to core. They make up not only the ores on which man has based much of his technology, and the gemstones which he values for their beauty or rarity, but also the components of rocks, pebbles and sands. Two million years ago minerals – in the form of stones – provided early man with his first tools. Today, man's use of minerals, such as uranium for nuclear power or silicon for microcomputers, is revolutionizing our lives.

Minerals, and the metals derived from them, have always had an inherent fascination for man, as well as providing the basis for his technology. Gold in particular, which was worked in Egypt as early as 5000 BC, still retains its mysterious attraction. Because of its chemical inactivity it is imperishable, immutable and nontarnishing, and has served as the basis of world trade for almost 2,000 years. Copper has been smelted since the early part of the third millennium BC, to be replaced eventually by harder alloys. Arsenical bronze, for instance, bridged the gap between the Copper and Bronze ages (bronze is an alloy of copper and tin). More complex technology was needed for the working of iron, which began c.1100 BC, whereas brass (an alloy of copper and zinc) did not appear until Roman times.

Although the steel-making process had its roots in antiquity, it was not until the nineteenth century that new techniques changed man's attitude to minerals. Before the modern age of plastics, the capacity to produce steel was the hallmark of industrial development, and together with coal it formed the linchpin of western industrial progress. Today minerals have come to assume their greatest importance as exploitable—but nonrenewable—resources.

Components of the Earth

The terms "mineral," "rock" and "stone" are often used interchangeably, but in fact all rocks are made up of minerals, which are natural and usually inorganic substances with a particular chemical makeup and crystal structure.

Certain stones have properties that satisfy basic human needs for beauty and color. Some possess a flashing sparkle, others have special optical characteristics such as refraction and dispersion ("fire"), or contain inclusions that give rise to phenomena like the "asterism" found in sapphires. About 100 such minerals are classified as gemstones and valued for their beauty, durability or rarity.

Most minerals occur as either pure (ore) deposits or mixed with other minerals in rocks—an economically important difference. Their exploitation has been vastly extended in recent decades through our greater understanding of the mineral-forming processes that take place in the Earth's crust. All mineral ores result from a separation process in which a mineral-rich solution separates into its various components according to the temperature, pressure and composition of the original mixture. Precipitation is the simplest kind of separation, as when calcium salts separate from circulating groundwater to yield stalactites and stalagmites in caves, in the form of calcite crystals.

Mineral formation

Most deposits of metallic ores originate in the intense physicochemical activity that takes place at the boundaries between the Earth's huge crustal plates. Very high concentrations of minerals occur in association with warm solutions coming from springs in the seabed, notably along the spreading zones in the southeastern Pacific Ocean, the Red Sea, the African Rift Valley and the Gulf of Aden. This process also occurs in shallow-water volcanic areas, as near the Mediterranean island of Thira and the submarine volcano of Bahu Wuhu, Indonesia. Cold seawater penetrates the crust and leaches out minerals from the basalts of these "hot spots," returning to the surface of the seabed as hot springs. The minerals then precipitate in the cold, oxygen-rich seawater.

Mineral separation may also occur when part of the deep-seated magma forces its way into the upper layers of the Earth's crust and begins to cool. The great plugs of magma that form the

rock kimberlite, in which diamonds are found, must have come from a depth of at least 100 km (62 miles). If the magma reaches the surface through fissures as extrusive rocks, the pattern of minerals in the surrounding rocks is also changed by a process called contact metamorphism, with various bands or zones of minerals occurring at various distances from the contact boundary.

As rocks become weathered, mineral concentrations that resist weathering may be left. Alternatively, all the weathered materials may be transported by running water, becoming concentrated as they are sorted out according to their different densities. Gold is the best-known example of this alluvial type of mineral deposit—known as a placer deposit. If the minerals are washed into the sea, they may be distributed over deltas or over the seafloor, but when this happens the concentrations of minerals are usually very low.

Mineral energy

Fossil fuels such as coal and petroleum are major mineral sources of energy. But with the twentieth-century discovery of nuclear fission, uranium also became an important energy resource. The richest deposits occur, as with other minerals, as veins deposited in fractures by hot-water movements. These deposits, consisting of a uranium oxide called pitchblende were the first to be mined, for example at Joachimstal (Czech Republic), Great Bear Lake (Canada) and Katanga (Zaire). Weathered products of such rocks, redeposited as sandstones, also contain uranium, as in Wyoming (USA) and in the Niger basin. In many respects uranium is similar to silver: both occur with similar geological abundance, their ores are enriched about 2,000 times during processing, and the metals are recovered by using chemicals to dissolve the metal selectively and then by "stripping" the metal from the solution.

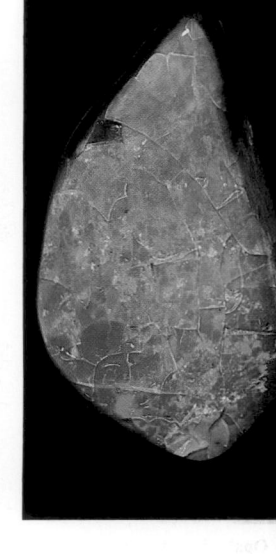

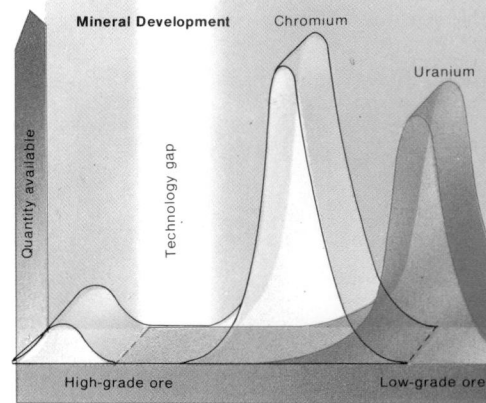

MINERALS FROM THE OCEAN
Ocean sediments that originally came from land contain organic matter that absorbs the oxygen in the sediments. As a result, solutions of minerals such as manganese and iron are released, seeping upwards through the debris. When they come in contact with the oxygen in seawater they are precipitated, condensing into so-called "manganese" nodules in amounts that may eventually prove to be a valuable source of mineral wealth. Metallic elements also accumulate very slowly from the seawater itself.

METAL-RICH BRINES
Scientists have recently discovered deep hollows on the floor of the Red Sea and other similar enclosed basins connected with rift valleys. These prevent normal circulation of water and form undersea pools of hot, high-density brines. The brines contain sulphur and other minerals in very high concentrations, and overlie sediments rich in metals such as zinc, copper, lead, silver and gold. Hot springs in fissures below the pools escape into them, carrying up solutions of the metallic minerals which combine with sulphur to create a concentrated broth rich in metals.

METALS FROM THE INTERIOR
Rift zones on the bed of the Pacific Ocean, where the Earth's crustal plates are slowly separating, provide sensational visual evidence of metallic ores in the actual process of creation. Seawater percolates through the fractured surface to the molten rock below, where it leaches out the soluble metallic components, erupting in superheated hydrothermal springs to form geysers of mineral-rich water. Oxygen in the cold water of the sea-floor causes the minerals to condense out, precipitating in plumes of dark powder. Continental drift, collision and sedimentation over millions of years will eventually incorporate these deposits into the landmasses.

Uranium, chromium and many other minerals are widely distributed through the Earth's crust, but they are valuable as a resource only if the technology exists to extract them economically. In mineral development, the high-grade ores are worked out first, followed by the poorer deposits if demand remains or increases. With uranium, the low-grade deposits contain far more of the total quantity of the mineral, but these are worth exploiting because of uranium's importance and because the technology exists. Chromium, on the other hand, is currently extracted only from high-grade ores. Large deposits of low-grade ores do exist, but technology for exploiting them economically has not yet been developed.

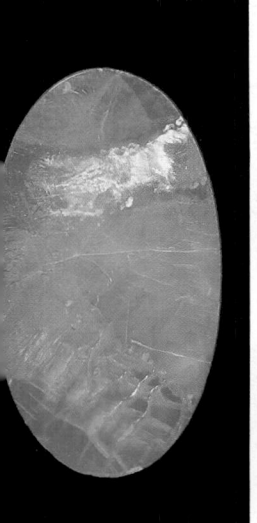

Opal (above), a silica mineral, often contains impurities which give it a range of colors. These flash and change according to the angle of vision, a result of the interference of light along minute internal cracks in the stone.

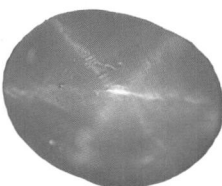

Sapphire gemstone (left), a form of the dull gray mineral corundum (below), owes its color to inclusions of titanium and iron.

MINERALS IN THE SERVICE OF MAN

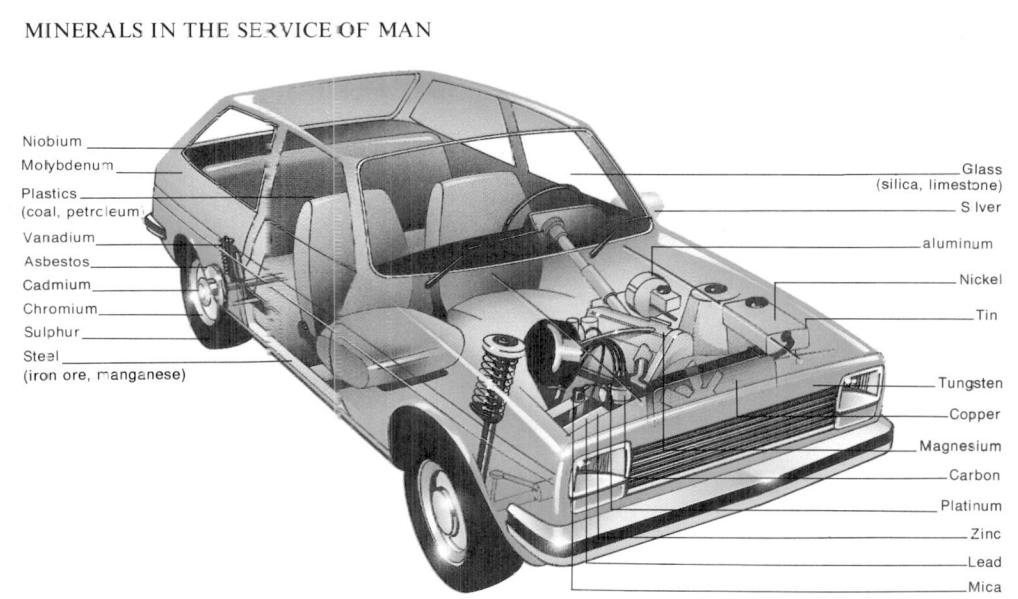

Niobium
Molybdenum
Plastics (coal, petroleum)
Vanadium
Asbestos
Cadmium
Chromium
Sulphur
Steel (iron ore, manganese)

Glass (silica, limestone)
Silver
aluminum
Nickel
Tin
Tungsten
Copper
Magnesium
Carbon
Platinum
Zinc
Lead
Mica

The modern automobile makes use of a whole alphabet of minerals in its composition, from aluminum to zinc. The importance of plastics, made from petroleum and coal, is constantly increasing, but the need for specialist metals is as great as ever. Cadmium, for example, is used in electroplating; carbon goes into making electrodes and graphite seals; transistors and electric contact points require platinum; sulphur is present in vulcanizing rubber and lubricants; lamp filaments contain tungsten. Of basic metals, iron and steel still account for almost three-quarters of the total quantity of the metals used; lead for 1.19 percent and copper for only 0.94 percent. But the amount of useful metal is often a small fraction of the rock that has to be mined and processed. A copper ore, for instance, only yields about 0.7 percent of metal, so to equip a single car's radiator with copper well over one and a half tonnes of rock will have to be excavated, of which 99.3 percent will simply be discarded.

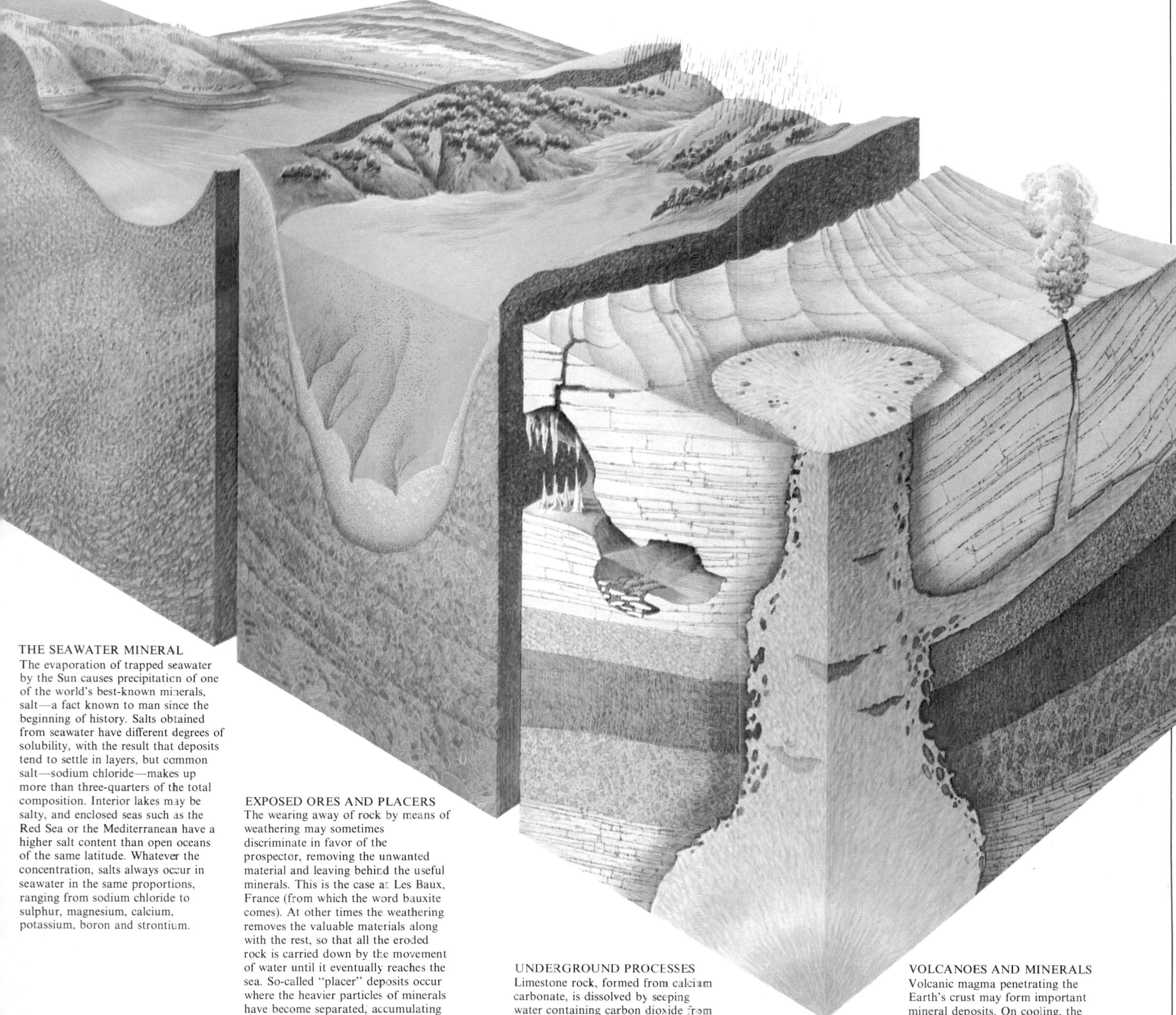

THE SEAWATER MINERAL
The evaporation of trapped seawater by the Sun causes precipitation of one of the world's best-known minerals, salt—a fact known to man since the beginning of history. Salts obtained from seawater have different degrees of solubility, with the result that deposits tend to settle in layers, but common salt—sodium chloride—makes up more than three-quarters of the total composition. Interior lakes may be salty, and enclosed seas such as the Red Sea or the Mediterranean have a higher salt content than open oceans of the same latitude. Whatever the concentration, salts always occur in seawater in the same proportions, ranging from sodium chloride to sulphur, magnesium, calcium, potassium, boron and strontium.

EXPOSED ORES AND PLACERS
The wearing away of rock by means of weathering may sometimes discriminate in favor of the prospector, removing the unwanted material and leaving behind the useful minerals. This is the case at Les Baux, France (from which the word bauxite comes). At other times the weathering removes the valuable materials along with the rest, so that all the eroded rock is carried down by the movement of water until it eventually reaches the sea. So-called "placer" deposits occur where the heavier particles of minerals have become separated, accumulating as deposits of mineral sand and concentrating in riverbeds or estuaries. Gold is the best-known example of this alluvial type of deposit, but tin and other minerals are also found as placers in many parts of the world.

UNDERGROUND PROCESSES
Limestone rock, formed from calcium carbonate, is dissolved by seeping water containing carbon dioxide from the air and the soil. The subsurface water may create vast networks of underground caverns in the limestone, and as the water slowly evaporates it leaves deposits of calcium carbonate, forming stalactites and stalagmites.

VOLCANOES AND MINERALS
Volcanic magma penetrating the Earth's crust may form important mineral deposits. On cooling, the heavy or "basic" minerals are the first to crystallize and sink to the bottom. The minerals may also separate out chemically. The intense heat affects surrounding rocks, causing mineral changes in banded zones.

Earthquakes and Volcanoes

Earthquakes and volcanic eruptions challenge man's faith in the stability of the world, but these violent releases of energy testify to our planet's ever-dynamic activity. Earthquakes are caused when the rigid crust is driven past or over itself by underlying movements that extend deep into the Earth's mantle. Stress builds up until it exceeds the strength of the rocks, when there follows a sudden movement. Volcanoes occur where molten rock, or magma, from the mantle forces its way to the surface through lines of weakness in the crust, often at the lithospheric plate boundaries.

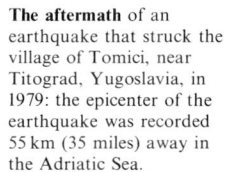

MODIFIED MERCALLI SCALE

I Earthquake not felt, except by a few.

II Felt on upper floors by few at rest. Swinging of suspended objects.

III Quite noticeable indoors, especially on upper floors. Standing cars may sway.

IV Felt indoors. Dishes and windows rattle, standing cars rock. Like a heavy truck hitting a building.

V Felt by nearly all, many wakened. Fragile objects broken, plaster cracked, trees and poles disturbed.

VI Felt by all, many run outdoors. Slight damage, heavy furniture moved, some fallen plaster.

VII People run outdoors. Average homes slightly damaged, substandard ones badly damaged. Noticed by car drivers.

VIII Well-built structures slightly damaged, others badly damaged. Chimneys and monuments collapse. Car drivers disturbed.

IX Well-designed buildings badly damaged, substantial ones greatly damaged, shifted off foundations. Conspicuous ground cracks open up.

X Well-built wood-structures destroyed, masonry structures destroyed. Rails bent, ground cracked, landslides. Rivers overflow.

XI Few masonry structures left standing. Bridges and underground pipes destroyed. Broad cracks in ground. Earth slumps.

XII Damage total. Ground waves seem like sea waves. Line of sight disturbed, objects thrown into the air.

The Earth's crust generally breaks along pre-existing planes of weakness, or faults. Such breakages give rise to an "explosive" release of stress that is familiar to surface dwellers as the vibrations of an earthquake.

Not all earthquakes, however, take place along pre-existing faults, otherwise no new faults would be generated. Many recent large earthquakes have been located immediately north of the Tonga Islands because a giant rent is developing through previously unbroken ocean crust. The crust to the south is being swallowed down into the mantle and that to the north continues at the surface to be subducted farther to the west. Once a fault has formed, however, it remains a plane of weakness even though the two sides tend to become partly resealed, so that when movement does occur there is a considerable release of energy.

Measuring earthquakes

Earthquakes are quantified in two ways. The actual energy release (magnitude) at the source of the earthquake (the focus) is measured on the Richter scale, a log scale where every unit of increase represents approximately 24 times the energy release. A magnitude 7 earthquake is roughly equivalent to the explosion of a one megaton nuclear bomb (one million tonnes of TNT). The strongest earthquake recorded this century was a magnitude 8.5 event in Alaska in 1964. Earthquakes as they are perceived are measured on the Modified Mercalli scale by their impact in terms of the amount of surface destruction. A medium-size earthquake under a town, such as that beneath Tangshan, China, in 1976 which killed more than a quarter of a million people, might record higher on the Mercalli scale than the Alaska event, which affected a large but sparsely populated region.

The magnitude of the earthquake depends on the frictional resistance that has to be overcome before movement can take place. This total frictional resistance, therefore, increases with the area of the fault plane. So the bigger the fault plane that moves, the bigger the earthquake. The largest earthquakes occur on wide fault planes that dip at a very shallow angle and can pass through a great deal of relatively shallow crust that will not deform plastically.

Earthquakes are unlikely to occur where rocks are plastic and can flow to accommodate the buildup of stress. Some faults, such as the San Andreas Fault in the western United States, pass from brittle rocks into a plastic zone at depths of only a few kilometers. Therefore, the next San Francisco earthquake cannot be as great as the 1964 Alaskan one, although this may be of little comfort to the potential victims. Along some sections of the San Andreas Fault the plastic zone comes directly to the surface, and motion occurs without large earthquakes.

Earthquake prediction is still in its infancy, although it is recognized that a number of phenomena may occur before a major earthquake—the ground may swell, the electrical conductivity of groundwater may change, and the water height of wells may rapidly alter.

How volcanoes are formed

Volcanoes, although spectacular, are safer than earthquakes. While an average of 20,000 people are killed each year in earthquakes, only about 400 are killed by volcanoes; and many of the victims die from starvation due to crop failure after heavy ash falls.

Volcanoes are formed when molten rock (magma) escapes through the Earth's crust to the Earth's surface. Most of this magma forms within the upper mantle between 30 and 100 km (20–60 miles) underground. The temperature increases with depth between 20° and 50°C per

The aftermath of an earthquake that struck the village of Tomici, near Titograd, Yugoslavia, in 1979: the epicenter of the earthquake was recorded 55 km (35 miles) away in the Adriatic Sea.

Earthquakes occur when slabs of the Earth's crust move in relation to each other. The focus of the earthquake is the point where movement occurs (1), and the epicenter is the point on the surface directly above it (2). Blue lines represent zones of surface damage as measured on the Modified Mercalli scale.

km (35°–90°F per 3,250 ft) from the crust to the mantle, but even so the rocks are normally not hot enough to melt.

Basaltic magmas, found along mid-ocean spreading ridges and oceanic islands, are formed when hot, deep mantle rises and, on reduction of pressure, begins to melt. Such "basic" magmas generally have low silica and water content, a high temperature and flow easily—often, as in Hawaii, "quietly erupting" to form volcanoes with very gentle gradients known as shield volcanoes. Silica-rich magma forms under continental crust. Ocean crust sucks up water after it has formed at the oceanic spreading ridges and much of this water later becomes taken with the crust down a subduction zone, where it helps to lower the melting point of both mantle and ocean-crust rocks.

By the time these magmas reach the surface they are cooler and have a higher water content than basalts. These "intermediate" or andesite magmas are also more viscous (less willing to

flow) because they contain more silica. The eruptions are more explosive as the water and other gases dissolve out of the magma as it approaches the surface, and the lava remains close to the volcanic vent, building up the archetypal steep-sided conical stratified volcano, such as Mount Fujiyama in Japan. Sometimes the conical form may be destroyed in catastrophic eruptions, as has happened at Mount St Helens in the United States.

The most violent of all eruptions are found where magmas from the mantle have penetrated and melted a great thickness of continental rocks, so as to create highly viscous silica- and water-rich "acid" magmas. As such magmas approach the surface they may turn into a red-hot froth that blasts out from fissures to cover enormous areas in a volcanic material known as ignimbrite. The most extensive eruption known to have occurred in the past 2,000 years was probably on Mount Taupo, on North Island, New Zealand. In AD 150 it discharged some

THE VIOLENT EARTH

Large, destructive earthquakes occur somewhere in the world approximately every two weeks, but fortunately most take place under the sea, where they cause little harm. Most of the millions of small earthquakes that occur on Earth pass unnoticed. Volcanoes are the most impressive display of the Earth's dynamic activity and are also responsible for forming the starting materials of the Earth's crust.

ASH FALLOUT

Some volcanic eruptions are so violent that ash is thrown high into the atmosphere to be carried away on the prevailing winds. Krakatoa in 1883 distributed ash around the world. The map shows the limits of airborne ash deposited by the eruption of Quizapu in Chile in 1932, the bulk of which fell within 10 km (6 miles).

Volcanoes are fed by magma, or molten rock, that wells up from deep in the Earth's mantle. The magma can either rise directly to the surface through fissures in the Earth's crust (1) and pour forth gently and continuously to form a shield volcano, or lava plateau, or be stored in a magma chamber (2) that swells up before erupting to the surface. To form the traditional cone-shaped stratified volcano, magma reaches the surface through a vent (3) and spews forth as gases, ash and lava (4, 5). Eventually the conical shape is made up of alternate layers of ash consolidated by lava. As rock and other debris build up around the main vent, and pressure increases, flank vents (6) open up other pathways to the surface, thereby creating parasitic cones (7).

When a volcano erupts violently the surrounding countryside can be devastated. The power of the blast flattens trees, poisonous gases kill all forms of wildlife, ash falls damage property and crops and can create mudflows and avalanches, and lava pouring from the vent can dam rivers to create floods.

Other special features of a volcanic landscape include extinct craters, which sometimes fill with water to form lakes, and calderas (8). Calderas are created either by vast explosions or when the magma chamber and vent are emptied of magma and the volcano collapses in on itself. Magma may later force itself through the collapsed debris so as to form new active cones on the floor of the caldera.

In volcanic regions there are other forms of volcanic activity. Water may seep down to be heated by the hot magma and reach the surface some distance away as a geyser (9) or hot spring, or be mixed with soil and ejected as a mud volcano. Some vents emit gases and steam, and these are called fumaroles. Geysers are created when water is heated in underground passageways or caverns (10). Water is periodically converted to superheated steam, which builds up pressure until it is able to rush up a vent and throw steam and water great distances into the air.

Not all magma reaches the surface: some cools and solidifies underground to form volcanic intrusions. Dykes (11) are sheets of cooled magma that have cut through strata of overlying rock, sills (12) are magma sheets injected between strata, and laccoliths (13) are large lens-shaped pools of solidified magma. Years later, when weathering and erosion have removed the overlying rock, these intrusions become features of the landscape.

10 cu km (2½ cu miles) of ignimbrite in about 15 minutes—spreading across the landscape at more than 100 m (330 ft) per second.

Other more explosive eruptions, such as that of Krakatoa in 1883, or Santorini more than 3,000 years ago, can result in the collapse of the volcano into the underlying magma chamber after it has become partly emptied during an eruption to create a caldera. Many of the largest explosions are caused by the mixing of water with magma—at Krakatoa the cataclysm probably resulted from seawater breaking into the magma and flashing straight to steam, thereby allowing more seawater to enter until the chain reaction could set off more energy than the most powerful nuclear bomb.

Predicting at least the approximate time of an eruption is relatively easy. Small earthquakes indicate that a new batch of magma is rising toward the surface. Many volcanoes also swell prior to an eruption and release gases that indicate the arrival of new magma.

The Oceans

Earth is the water planet. Of all the planets of the solar system only the Earth has abundant liquid water, and 97 percent of this surface water is found in the seas and oceans. The water of the oceans appears to be passive and unchanging, whereas the rain and rivers seem active, but this is far from true. In reality the oceans are a turmoil of giant sluggish rivers – far larger than any of the land rivers – and of circulating surface currents that are driven by the prevailing winds.

No topographic map of the Earth can be drawn unless there is some kind of base line from which to measure depths and heights. This base line has always been taken as the level of the sea, yet the sea is perpetually changing level. One can choose some kind of average to call "sea level," but even today different countries have defined that base line in different ways. The currents found within the sea itself can also give the water surface a slope—the calm Sargasso Sea off the northern coast of South America is, for example, about 1.5 m (5 ft) higher than the water to the west adjacent to the Gulf Stream.

Waves
The changes in the level of the sea, at its surface, provide the most familiar image of motion within the waters. Various changes take place over many different time periods, but the most rapid are those that we call waves.

Waves are produced by the wind moving over the water and catching on the surface. They can move at between 15 and 100 km/hr (10–60 mph) and wave crests may be separated by up to 300 m (1,000 ft) in the open ocean. In general, the greater the wavelength, the faster the wave's speed and the farther the distance traveled by the wave. Waves that have traveled a long way from the winds that created them are known as swell. Without the wind continually pushing them they become symmetrical and smooth. Wind waves produce spilling breakers more like the rapids of a mountain torrent, whereas swell produces giant plunging breakers.

A combination of strong winds and low atmospheric pressure associated with storms can cause yet another kind of wave, known as a storm surge. A storm surge is formed by the water being driven ahead of the wind, and rising as the atmospheric pressure weighing down on the water decreases. Where storms drive water into funnel-shaped coasts, the water can rise more than 10 m (33 ft) above normal sea level, flooding large areas of low-lying land at the head of the bay. Venice, the Netherlands and Bangladesh have been particularly subject to destructive storm surges. Other catastrophic changes in sea level have their origins in the seabed. These are tsunamis (Japanese for "high-water in the harbor") and are generally triggered by underwater earthquakes that suddenly raise or lower large areas of the seafloor.

Tides
As the Earth orbits around the Sun the water in the oceans experiences a changing pull of gravity from both the Moon and the Sun. The Sun is overhead once a day, and because the Moon is itself orbiting the Earth, it is overhead once every 24 hours 50 minutes. The pull of gravity from the Sun is less than half that from the Moon, and so it is the Moon that sets the rhythm of the water movements we call tides. The variation in gravitational pull from the Moon is extremely small, however, and even if the whole of the Earth were covered with deep water a tide of only about 30 cm (12 in) would be produced, rushing around the world keeping pace with the circling Moon. Yet the tides in shallow coastal regions are often very much higher than this—for example, up to 18 m (60 ft) in the Bay of Fundy, Canada. The seas and bays with the highest tides are located where the whole mass of water is resonating—rebounding backwards and forwards like water in a bath, as the smaller tides in the outlying oceans push it twice each day.

The Bay of Fundy experiences a particularly high tidal range because it happens to have a resonant frequency—a range of movement—very close to the 12½-hour frequency between tides. Large enclosed seas such as the Mediterranean have very small tides because there is no outside push from an ocean to set them resonating. In contrast, where water movement associated with the tides passes through a narrow channel it can produce tidal currents of up to 30 km/hr (19 mph), such as the famous maelstrom of northern Norway.

After these relatively short-lived disturbances the sea returns to its normal, or at least to its average, level again. When the total volume of free water at the Earth's surface alters, or when the shapes of the ocean basins vary, the sea level itself may start to wander.

How does the volume of water vary? It can be buried in rocks—but the steam clouds above volcanoes return such water so it is normally recycled rather than lost. Some vapor can be broken down through radiation in the upper atmosphere and the hydrogen lost to outer space, but this is relatively insignificant. Or it can be frozen and stacked up on land in the form of ice—this is significant as we are still living in an ice age. The lowest ice-age sea levels produced beaches at about 130 m (430 ft) below present sea level, and the low-lying coastal regions of that period have now become flooded to form the continental shelves.

The salt content of the oceans
Average ocean water contains about 35 parts per 1,000 of salts which include 14 elements in concentrations greater than 1 part per million—the most abundant being sodium and chlorine. Where there is considerable surface evaporation, for example in enclosed seas such as the Dead Sea, the salt concentration builds up and the water becomes denser. Where the sea-surface is turning to ice the salt also becomes concentrated in the water.

The coldest, saltiest ocean water comes from the Antarctic. As it is also the densest it hugs the ocean bottom as it flows northwards, reaching as far as the latitudes of Spain. A similar current from the Arctic is slightly lighter and therefore rides above it—but traveling southwards, as far as the southern Atlantic. A second slightly lighter body of Antarctic water rides above the Arctic water—again traveling northwards. Where these water movements meet each other they rise up, bringing to the surface oxygenated water that can support a profusion of life in oceans that have been compared to a desert because of their lack of biological activity. Unlikely as it seems, it is the icy, stormy, polar waters that provide the lungs of the oceans.

Depth in meters
0 1 2 3 4 5 6 7 8

Earth
Sun
Moon
1
Neap tide

Moon
Earth
2
Sun
Spring tide

Moon
Earth
3
Sun
Neap tide

Moon
Earth
4
Sun
Spring tide

Both the Sun and the Moon exert gravitational pull on the water in the oceans, but the pull of the Sun is less than half that of the Moon. It is the Moon, therefore, that sets the rhythm of the tides. Because the Moon orbits the Earth every 24 hours and 50 minutes, the time of high or low tide advances approximately an hour each day. When the Moon is in its first and last quarters (1, 3) it forms a right angle with the Earth and the Sun and the gravitational fields are opposed, thus causing only a small difference between high and low tide. These are called neap tides. When the Sun, Moon and Earth lie in a straight line (2, 4), at the full and the new Moon, then the high tides become higher and the low tides lower. These are the spring tides. The graph illustrates tidal range over a period of a month.

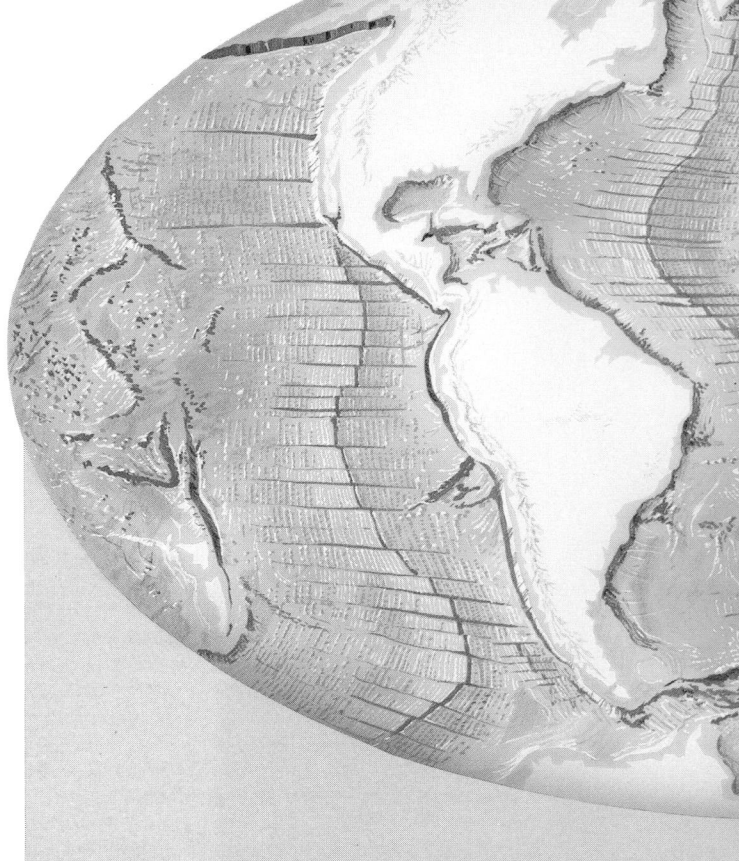

Depth in meters
0
1,000
2,000
3,000
4,000
5,000
6,000
7,000
8,000

1 Continent
2 Continental shelf
3 Continental slope
4 Continental rise
5 Submarine canyon
6 Abyssal plain
7 Abyssal hills
8 Mid-ocean ridge
9 Oceanic trench
10 Island arc
11 Continental sea

THE CHANGING OCEANS

Nearly two-thirds of the Earth's surface is covered by the seas and oceans and this great expanse of water is continually in movement. The most familiar movements are waves formed by the wind and the rising and falling tides that respond to the position of the Moon. But even greater movements take place. Currents driven by prevailing winds form whirlpools an ocean in width, and below the surface flow great rivers of colder water. Sea level is also rising as ice melts from the polar caps.

Cl	55.0%
Na	30.6%
SO₄	7.7%
Mg	3.7%
Ca	1.5%
K	1.5%

Seawater is about 96% pure water and the rest is made up of dissolved salts. Many elements are present in minute quantities, but only chlorine (Cl), sodium (Na), sulphate (SO₄), magnesium (Mg), calcium (Ca) and potassium (K) appear in concentrations of more than 1% of the total dissolved salts.

The surface currents of the world's oceans (A) are driven by the prevailing winds (B). The winds and the spinning motion of the Earth drive the currents into gyres—massive whirlpools the width of an ocean. These gyres draw warm water away from the Equator and pull cold polar waters towards it. The centers of gyres are characterized by areas of high pressure, around which winds circulate. Because the Earth is spinning, gyres formed in the northern hemisphere rotate in a clockwise direction, whereas those of the southern hemisphere turn anticlockwise. In all, there are five major gyres, made up of the 38 major named currents. The formation of warm (red) and cold (blue) surface currents is not difficult to understand, given the regions from which they flow. However, even in temperate and subtropical regions, the warm waters of the oceans' surfaces have a permanent layer of cold water beneath them. This cold layer has been formed in the polar regions, where, as the ocean waters have been chilled, they have sunk and then spread out into all the other major ocean basins of the world. The warm subtropical and temperate waters float like an oil slick, from 10 m to 550 m (33–1,900 ft) thick, on top of this cold layer. There is very little mixing between the two layers because the warm water is lighter than the cold water.

Much of the Earth's water is locked up as ice and stacked on the land. As the ice melts the sea level rises. Only 20,000 years ago the sea level was a full 100 m (330 ft) lower than it is today, and the continental shelves were dry land. About 10,000 years ago the sea level was rising as fast as 3 cm (1 in) each year. Today the melting ice is causing the sea level to rise about 1 mm (0.04 in) each year: only a small increment, but if all the ice melted, the sea level would rise by about 60 m (197 ft) and would flood many of the world's major cities

●	< 60 m
●	> 60 m
•	Major cities

The seabed, more uniform than the land surface, also contains a landscape of underwater features that resemble the plains, valleys and mountains of the continents. Off the edge of continents lie the flat, shallow continental shelves, which are bounded by the steeper incline of the continental slope, which meets the true ocean floor at the continental rise.

Here deep submarine canyons may be found. These seem to be in a process of continual erosion from turbidity currents. River water pouring into major estuaries and carrying sediment can also scour out the slope—especially during periods of low sea level. The abyssal plain is rarely interrupted by volcanic hills and

mountains. The largest chains are at the mid-ocean ridge, where two crustal plates are moving apart and new ocean floor is being created. At some ocean margins deep trough-shaped valleys or trenches are the sites of ocean floor consumption at a subduction zone. The volcanic island arcs that form behind it sometimes isolate a continental sea.

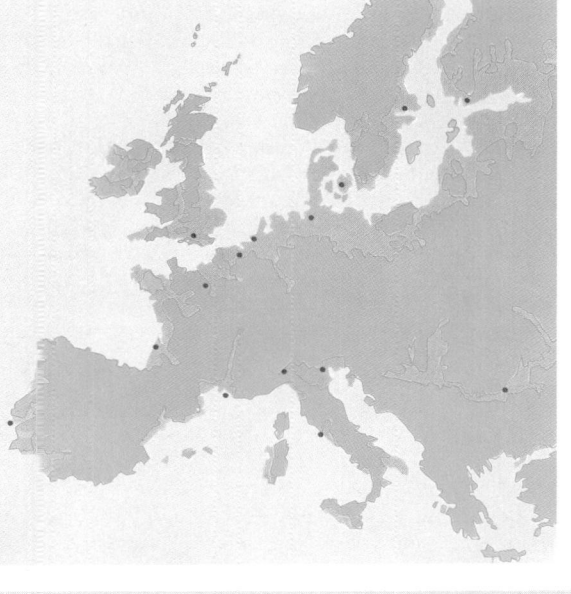

TSUNAMIS

Tsunamis are generated by massive underwater earthquakes (A) and are common around the Pacific. They can travel at more than 700 km/hr (435 mph) and individual waves may occur at intervals of 15 minutes, or 200 km (125 miles). Low-lying atolls of the Pacific have extremely steep sides underwater, and are generally unharmed, but the gently shelving islands such as Hawaii slow down the tsunami and build it into a giant wave 30 m (100 ft) or more in height. This map plots the hourly position of a tsunami that originated south of Alaska.

Landscape-makers: Water

Of all the natural agents of erosion at work on the Earth's surface, water is probably the most powerful. Many of the finer details of the landscape, from the contouring of hills and valleys to the broad spread of plains, are the work of water. In recent years we have come to understand more fully the subtle factors at work in a river, for example, as it deepens mountain gorges or builds up sedimentary layers in its approach to the sea. The full force of a waterfall, the instability of a meandering stream, the multiple layering of river terraces – all are features of this most versatile landscape-maker.

Ninety-seven percent of the world's water is in the oceans, another two percent is locked up in the ice caps of Greenland and Antarctica, which leaves one percent only on the surface of Earth, under the ground and in the air. The importance of this one percent is, however, inestimable: most life forms could not exist without it, and yet at the same time many are threatened by it, in the form of flood and storm.

The Sun's energy "powers" the evaporation of water from the oceans. Water vapor then circulates in the atmosphere and is precipitated as rain or snow over land, from which it eventually drains back to the oceans. This is the vast, never-ending water cycle. Water in the air that falls as, for example, rain is replaced on average every 12 days. The total water supply remains constant and is believed to be exactly the same as it was 3,000 million years ago.

From raindrops to rivers

Rain falling on to the surface of the land has a great deal of energy: large drops may hit the ground with a terminal velocity of about 35 km/hr (20 mph). If the rain falls on bare soil, it splashes upwards, breaking off and transporting tiny fragments of soil, which come to rest downhill. Vegetation-covered soil breaks the impact and some of the rain may evaporate without ever reaching the ground.

Soil is rather like a sponge. If the holes or pores are very small, rain finds it difficult to penetrate and water runs over the surface of the soil. If the pores are large, rain infiltrates, filling up the pore spaces. Soils that are thin, have low infiltration rates, or already have a lot of water in them, are very susceptible to overland flow. The water may then concentrate into a channel called a gully, and this can have a dramatic effect upon the landscape. The creation of gullies, together with the splash effect, leads to soil erosion. The problem is particularly severe in semiarid regions, where rainfall is sporadic but intense, vegetation is sparse and overgrazing is common. In extreme cases, badlands are formed and by this time recuperation of the land is impossible or is prohibitively expensive.

Where the infiltration rate is high, water percolates through the soil and eventually into the bedrock. There are two well-defined regions, the saturated and the unsaturated. The upper limit of the saturated zone is the water table. Beneath this, water moves at a rate of a few meters a day, but in rocks such as limestone it can move much more quickly along cracks and joints. In most rock types there are some soluble components which are removed as water continually flows through. In limestone regions, the dissolution of calcium salts results in spectacular cave formations.

Groundwater often provides a vital source for domestic consumption. In porous materials, especially chalk, water is stored in large quantities. Such strata are called aquifers and in some areas, notably North Africa, it is believed that water being pumped up now resulted from rainfall when the climate was wetter tens of thousands of years ago.

Water from a number of sources—from overland flow, soil seepage and springs draining aquifers—produces the flow in rivers. Groundwater appears days or even weeks after a heavy rainfall, but overland flow reaches the channel in hours, producing the sudden peak in flow that may cause flooding and occasionally great damage farther downstream. Flood waves usually rise quickly in mountain areas and the wave moves downstream as the river collects more and more water from its tributaries. Eventually, although the volume continues to increase downstream, the flood wave becomes broader and flatter, so it moves more slowly and causes less damage. The most serious floods occur after intense rainfall on already saturated soils where upland rivers issue on to plains.

Rivers at work

The work of a river from its source to its mouth involves three processes, the first of which is erosion. This includes corrasion, or abrasion—the grinding of rocks and stones against the river's banks and bed—which produces both

A RIVER SYSTEM

Rivers form by the accumulation of runoff water, groundwater and from springs and small streams. Few rivers reach the sea without gaining tributaries, thus forming a river system. Highland regions at source are called catchment areas and the total area drained by a river system is the drainage basin.

The course of a river from source to mouth includes distinctive stages and land forms. All rivers flow from high ground to lower ground. Many rise in an upland area where precipitation is heavy. The upper course is where vertical erosion is dominant and the resulting valley is narrow, deep and V-shaped. A gorge is formed if this downcutting is particularly rapid. If the river has a winding course, the valley walls project to produce interlocking spurs. In the middle course erosion is lateral rather than vertical and the valley takes a more open V-shape. The river may start to meander and bluffs are formed as interlocking spurs are eroded. In the lower course the river deposits much material as it meanders across an almost flat flood plain. The bed is sometimes higher than the plain and the river has raised banks, or levées, formed from material deposited when the river is in flood. Ox-bow lakes are common, as is a delta where the slow-flowing river enters the sea.

The hydrological cycle involves a vast transfer of water from sea to air to land, and back to sea again. Water evaporates from the world's oceans and is carried by maritime air masses towards land, where it condenses and is precipitated in the form of rain or snow. This water then evaporates from the ground surface; drains off the surface into lakes, rivers or seas; seeps as groundwater into rivers, lakes or seas; or is taken in by vegetation from the soil and then transpired.

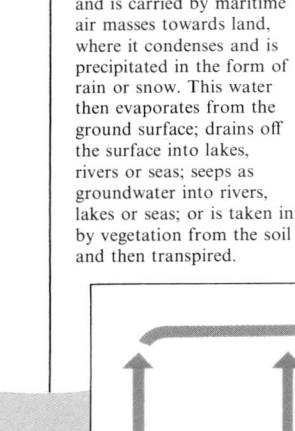

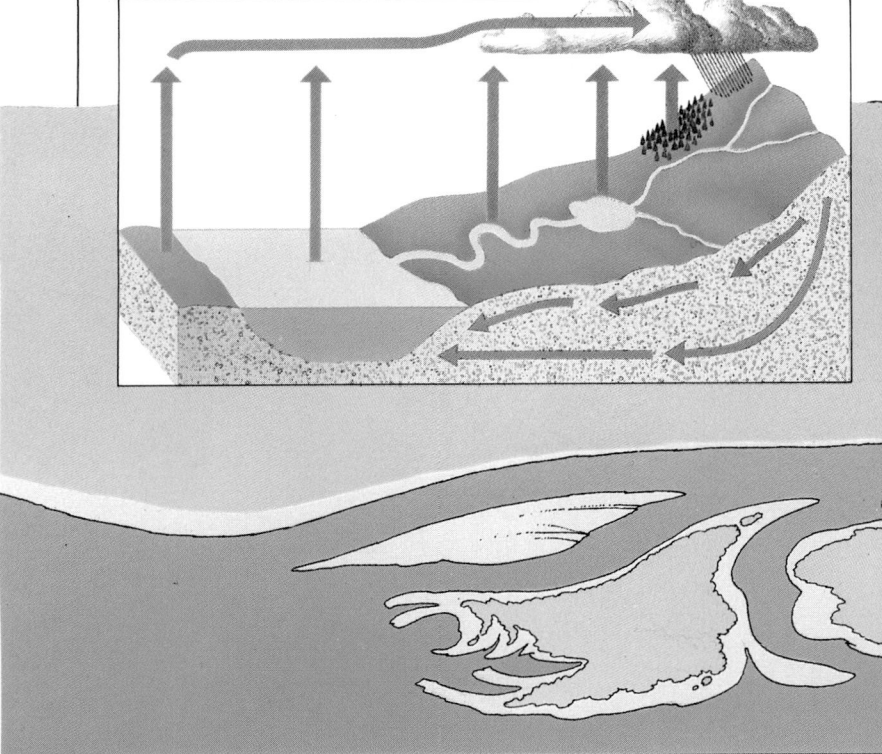

When a river reaches the sea, providing the coast is sheltered and the sea is shallow with no strong currents, its speed is checked and material is deposited (1). The river then forms distributaries (2) in order to continue its flow to the sea. A delta forms its characteristic fan shape (3) as it grows sideways and seawards. A river needs active erosion in its upper course in order to form a delta.

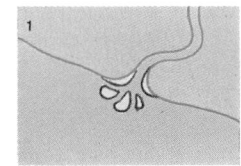
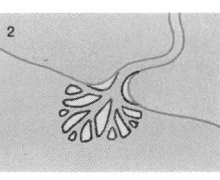
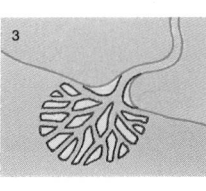

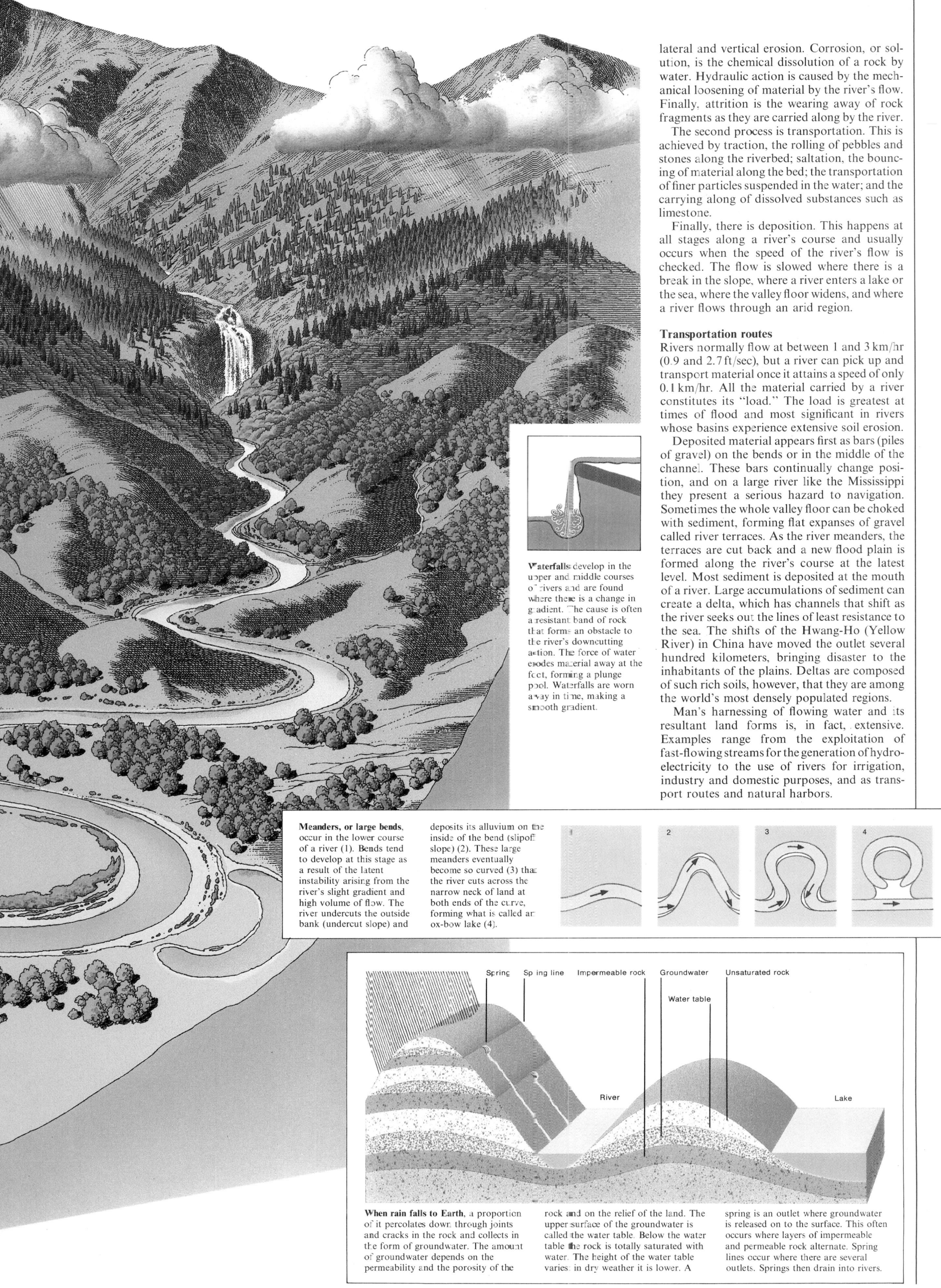

lateral and vertical erosion. Corrosion, or solution, is the chemical dissolution of a rock by water. Hydraulic action is caused by the mechanical loosening of material by the river's flow. Finally, attrition is the wearing away of rock fragments as they are carried along by the river.

The second process is transportation. This is achieved by traction, the rolling of pebbles and stones along the riverbed; saltation, the bouncing of material along the bed; the transportation of finer particles suspended in the water; and the carrying along of dissolved substances such as limestone.

Finally, there is deposition. This happens at all stages along a river's course and usually occurs when the speed of the river's flow is checked. The flow is slowed where there is a break in the slope, where a river enters a lake or the sea, where the valley floor widens, and where a river flows through an arid region.

Transportation routes

Rivers normally flow at between 1 and 3 km/hr (0.9 and 2.7 ft/sec), but a river can pick up and transport material once it attains a speed of only 0.1 km/hr. All the material carried by a river constitutes its "load." The load is greatest at times of flood and most significant in rivers whose basins experience extensive soil erosion.

Deposited material appears first as bars (piles of gravel) on the bends or in the middle of the channel. These bars continually change position, and on a large river like the Mississippi they present a serious hazard to navigation. Sometimes the whole valley floor can be choked with sediment, forming flat expanses of gravel called river terraces. As the river meanders, the terraces are cut back and a new flood plain is formed along the river's course at the latest level. Most sediment is deposited at the mouth of a river. Large accumulations of sediment can create a delta, which has channels that shift as the river seeks out the lines of least resistance to the sea. The shifts of the Hwang-Ho (Yellow River) in China have moved the outlet several hundred kilometers, bringing disaster to the inhabitants of the plains. Deltas are composed of such rich soils, however, that they are among the world's most densely populated regions.

Man's harnessing of flowing water and its resultant land forms is, in fact, extensive. Examples range from the exploitation of fast-flowing streams for the generation of hydroelectricity to the use of rivers for irrigation, industry and domestic purposes, and as transport routes and natural harbors.

Waterfalls develop in the upper and middle courses of rivers and are found where there is a change in gradient. The cause is often a resistant band of rock that forms an obstacle to the river's downcutting action. The force of water erodes material away at the foot, forming a plunge pool. Waterfalls are worn away in time, making a smooth gradient.

Meanders, or large bends, occur in the lower course of a river (1). Bends tend to develop at this stage as a result of the latent instability arising from the river's slight gradient and high volume of flow. The river undercuts the outside bank (undercut slope) and deposits its alluvium on the inside of the bend (slipoff slope) (2). These large meanders eventually become so curved (3) that the river cuts across the narrow neck of land at both ends of the curve, forming what is called an ox-bow lake (4).

When rain falls to Earth, a proportion of it percolates down through joints and cracks in the rock and collects in the form of groundwater. The amount of groundwater depends on the permeability and the porosity of the rock and on the relief of the land. The upper surface of the groundwater is called the water table. Below the water table the rock is totally saturated with water. The height of the water table varies: in dry weather it is lower. A spring is an outlet where groundwater is released on to the surface. This often occurs where layers of impermeable and permeable rock alternate. Spring lines occur where there are several outlets. Springs then drain into rivers.

Landscape-makers: Ice and Snow

A series of glacial periods has punctuated the Earth's history for the last two million years. During the last glacial, the ice covered an area nearly three times larger than that covered by ice sheets and glaciers today. Its remnants are still found in the ice caps of the world: most present-day glacial ice is in Antarctica and Greenland in two great ice sheets which together contain about 97 percent of all the Earth's ice. The rest is in glaciers in Iceland, the Alps and other high mountain chains.

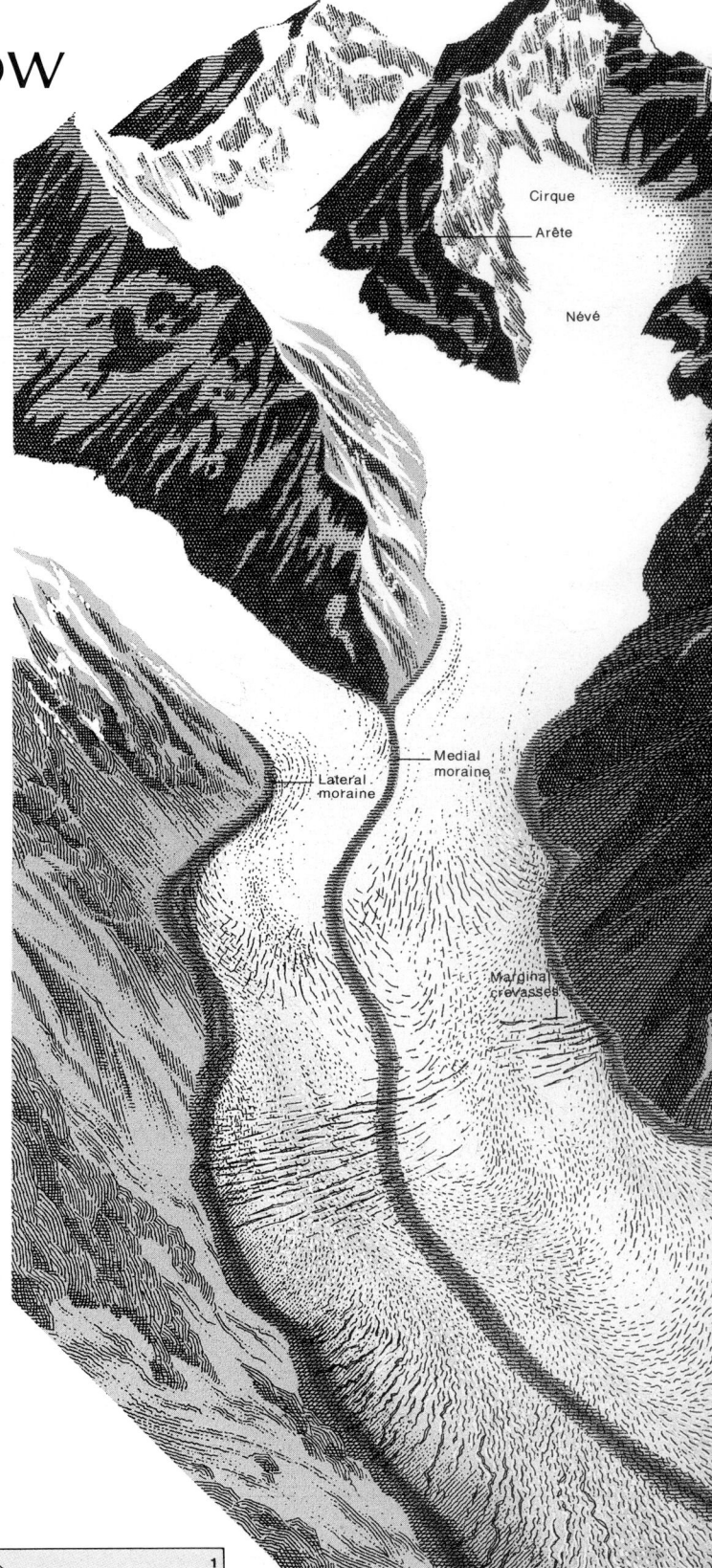

During the Earth's major glacial periods, ice sheets almost as big as that of present-day Antarctica spread over the northern part of North America, reaching as far south as the Ohio River, and over northern Europe as far south as southern England, the Netherlands and southern Poland. Today glacial activity is more restricted, but the mechanisms by which it carves dramatic features of the Earth's landscape remain the same.

Types of glacier
There are six main types of ice mass: cirque glaciers, which occupy basin-shaped depressions in mountain areas; valley glaciers; piedmont glaciers, in which the ice spreads in a lobe over a lowland; floating ice tongues and ice shelves; mountain ice caps; and ice sheets. Climate and relief are responsible for these differences, but glaciers can also be classified according to their internal temperatures.

Cold glaciers are those in which the ice temperature is below freezing point and they are frozen to the rock beneath. This condition, which hinders the movement of glaciers, exists in many parts of Antarctica and Greenland, where air temperatures are low, as well as at high altitudes in some lower-latitude mountain regions. Temperate glaciers, on the other hand, show internal temperatures at or close to the melting point of ice. Unlike cold glaciers, they are not frozen to the rock beneath and can therefore slide over it. Ice melts on the surface of the glacier when the weather is warm, and underneath the glacier as it is warmed by geothermal heat from inside the Earth. Streams collecting meltwater may flow over, through or under the ice and emerge at the ice edge. In other glaciers, cold ice may overlie temperate ice.

Glaciers are formed from snow that, as it accumulates year after year, becomes compacted, turning first into "névé" or "firn" and eventually, after several years or even decades, into glacial ice. This process of accumulation is offset by ablation, through which ice is lost by

melting, evaporation or, in glaciers that end in the sea or in lakes, by calving. If accumulation exceeds ablation, the glacier increases in size; conversely, if ablation is higher, the glacier shrinks and eventually disappears.

Glaciers move because of the force of gravity. The fastest-moving glaciers, for example those of coastal Greenland which descend steeply from areas of great accumulation, move at speeds of more than 20 m (65 ft) a day. A few meters a day is more common, however. Some glaciers move exceptionally quickly in surges, which usually last for a few weeks; rates of more than 100 m (330 ft) a day have been recorded. At the other extreme, some glaciers or parts of glaciers—the central zones of ice sheets and ice caps for example—are virtually motionless. When the ice in a glacier is subject to pressure or tension—as it flows down a valley, for example—it behaves rather like a plastic substance and changes its shape to fit the contours of the valley. Part or all of the movement of a glacier is accomplished by means of this internal deformation. In temperate glaciers, or glaciers whose lower layers are temperate, there is also basal sliding. Movement of a glacier produces cracks or crevasses in areas where stress exceeds the strength of the ice.

The work of glaciers
Glaciers and ice sheets can profoundly modify the landscape by both erosion and deposition. Measured rates of erosion of bedrock may be as much as several millimeters a year. Rock surfaces are scratched, or striated, and worn down by the constant grinding action (abrasion) of rock fragments embedded in the base of the ice. The extreme pressure of thick glacial ice on a basal boulder has been known to rupture solid bedrock beneath it.

The products of bedrock erosion range from fine clays and silts produced by abrasion, to large boulders picked up and transported by the ice. Some rocks have been carried hundreds of kilometers, from southern Scandinavia to

A U-shaped valley, such as Langdale (below) in the English Lake District, is a clear indication of a glaciated past. The floor is quite flat and the valley sides rise steeply from it.

A crevasse (below left) is created by stress within a glacier. Internally, the ice is rather like plastic but its surface is rigid and brittle. This causes tension and cracking on the surface.

This erratic (below right) is made of Silurian grit, yet it sits on a limestone perch. Ice left Yorkshire 20,000 years ago, since when the limestone surface has been lowered by solution.

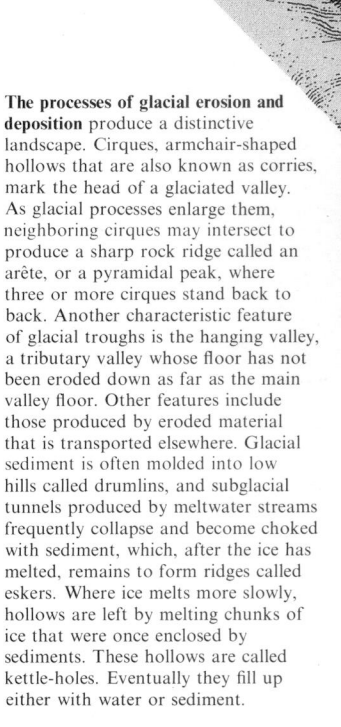

Before the onset of glaciation a mountain region is often sculpted largely by the work of rivers and the processes of weathering. The hills are rounded and the valleys are V-shaped (1). During a period of glacial activity, valleys become filled with snow and eventually

glaciers and, after thousands of years, the region shows a typically glaciated landscape (2). When the ice has finally disappeared there remains a glacial trough (3) with hanging valleys, truncated spurs, waterfalls and all the landforms associated with deposition of material.

The processes of glacial erosion and deposition produce a distinctive landscape. Cirques, armchair-shaped hollows that are also known as corries, mark the head of a glaciated valley. As glacial processes enlarge them, neighboring cirques may intersect to produce a sharp rock ridge called an arête, or a pyramidal peak, where three or more cirques stand back to back. Another characteristic feature of glacial troughs is the hanging valley, a tributary valley whose floor has not been eroded down as far as the main valley floor. Other features include those produced by eroded material that is transported elsewhere. Glacial sediment is often molded into low hills called drumlins, and subglacial tunnels produced by meltwater streams frequently collapse and become choked with sediment, which, after the ice has melted, remains to form ridges called eskers. Where ice melts more slowly, hollows are left by melting chunks of ice that were once enclosed by sediments. These hollows are called kettle-holes. Eventually they fill up either with water or sediment.

THE SNOW LINE

Glaciation is still evident today in regions that are above the snow line—the lowest limit of perpetual snow cover. The height of the snow line varies with latitude: from about 5,200 m (17,000 ft) at the Equator, to 2,700 m (9,000 ft) in the Alps, to 1,200 m (4,000 ft) in Scandinavia and sea level nearer the north and south polar regions.

eastern England, for example, and such far-traveled rocks are termed erratics. The finer sediments, compacted at the base of the glacier by the weight of the overlying ice, form till or boulder clay.

The surface of a glacier is often strewn with rock debris, which either rests on the ice or is within the glacier and revealed as the ice melts. Lateral moraines consist of rock debris that has accumulated along the sides of the glacier as a result of rockfall from, and erosion of, the valley sides. Where two glaciers join, the inner lateral moraines merge to form a medial moraine. In the ablation zone, the surface of the glacier becomes increasingly laden with debris "melting out" so that the ice may become completely buried. At the end of the glacier all rock debris is dumped, forming a terminal moraine.

Meltwater streams pouring out from glaciers or flowing in tunnels beneath them can be powerful agents of erosion and can transport large quantities of sediment. Bedrock surfaces become potholed and carved by channels that are eroded with great speed. As the streams emerge from the edge of the ice, they carry with them and deposit vast quantities of sand and gravel which form flood plains (outwash plains). Alternatively, meltwater streams may deposit sediment between the edge of the glacier and valley side, leaving a "kame terrace" when the ice finally melts. Meltwater streams feeding glacial lakes that are dammed by a glacier or moraine, for example, construct deltas of sand and gravel and lay down finer sediments (varved clays) on the lake floor.

Snow processes

Snow plays a smaller part than glacial ice in landform sculpture. Its most important role is in avalanches, which, in mountain regions, regularly bring down thousands of tonnes of rock debris. The mixture of snow, rock and other debris forms avalanche boulder tongues on the flat ground where the avalanche comes to rest and the snow melts. Gullies (avalanche chutes) on mountain slopes are swept clean of loose debris several times a year and they are gradually enlarged. Snow patches that remain stationary on more gentle slopes or in hollows encourage rock weathering under and around them. Such a process, termed nivation, may lead to deepening and enlargement of hollows and further snow accumulation. This is one way in which new glaciers are formed.

A glaciated valley exhibits a distinctive shape and profile. A cross section shows a U-shape, while longitudinally the valley floor is marked by a series of rocky steps and basins. The zone of accumulation is characterized by a cirque, in which snow collects to produce a firn field. A bergschrund is a type of crevasse that opens up near the top of the firn field where the head of the glacier is pulled away from the cirque walls. A rock step is where the gradient becomes much steeper. The speed of the ice flow is accelerated and consequent tension within the ice creates a number of deep crevasses called an ice fall. The zone of ablation has large accumulations of various kinds of rock debris.

Glacial erosion of rock surfaces is typified by a roche moutonnée, a resistant rock hummock that lies in the path of the ice. The upstream side is smooth as a result of abrasion by rock debris that is frozen into the base of the glacier. This debris scratches and scrapes rock, producing striations. The downstream side is rough as a result of ice plucking. Meltwater removes the small blocks of rock.

A great variety of material arrives at the terminus or snout of a glacier—ranging from large blocks of rock and boulders to very finely ground rock "flour." All the material is dropped in a haphazard way as the ice melts. The mixture of clay and boulders is termed glacial till. If the ice margin remains stationary, till accumulates to form a terminal moraine. If the snout recedes continuously, no ridge forms.

Landscape-makers: The Seas

The coastline is both the birthplace and the graveyard of the land. Over tens of thousands of years, geological uplift of a continent, or a fall in sea level, may create an emerging fringe of new land, whereas a period of submergence drowns the coasts and floods the adjacent river valleys, destroying land but producing some of the most attractive coastal landscapes. More rapid are the changes brought about by the sea itself. Erosion of coastal rocks or beaches can cut back the coastline at a rate of several meters a year, whereas other coastlines are built up at a comparable rate from marine sediments.

Changing coastlines are apparent on a human time scale. In temperate latitudes, beaches tend to be combed down and narrowed by winter waves, only to be restored during the calmer weather of summer. They may be lost one week and replenished the next, demonstrating an invaluable ability to recover from the wounds of all but the most devastating storms. Cliffs are generally much less dynamic, particularly if composed of resistant rock, but any loss that they suffer is permanent because there is no process that is capable of rebuilding them.

Coasts vary greatly around the world. Tropical areas often have wide beaches made up of fine material which in many cases forms broad mangrove swamps that collect sediment and build up the coast. In more exposed tropical zones coral reefs are common, either fringing the shore or (particularly where the sea level is rising) separated from the shore by a lagoon to give a barrier reef. Continued submergence of a small island surrounded by such a reef may produce an atoll. In contrast, Arctic beaches are narrow and coarse, and may be icebound for up to 10 months each year. Recession of soft rock cliffs results more from melting of ice in the ground than from wave erosion.

Waves at work
Across great expanses of open ocean energy is transferred from the wind to the sea surface to produce waves, thus fueling the machine that ultimately creates the coast. Originating as waves with heights of up to 20 or even 30 m (65–100 ft), they lose part of their energy quite rapidly as they travel, and once they have been reduced in height to the lower but more widely spaced ocean swell, they continue to travel across enormous distances.

The coasts of western Europe receive waves produced almost 10,000 km (6,200 miles) away off Cape Horn, and swell reaching California has sometimes crossed more than 11,000 km

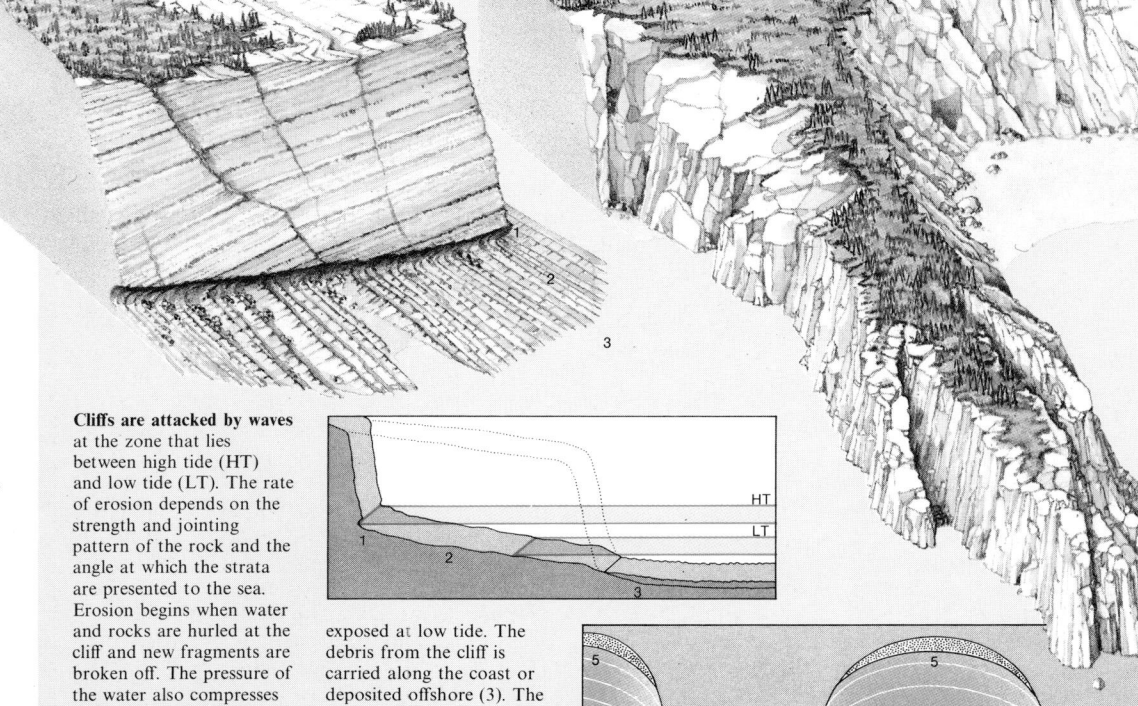

Cliffs are attacked by waves at the zone that lies between high tide (HT) and low tide (LT). The rate of erosion depends on the strength and jointing pattern of the rock and the angle at which the strata are presented to the sea. Erosion begins when water and rocks are hurled at the cliff and new fragments are broken off. The pressure of the water also compresses air in joints and cracks to shatter the rock face. As the base of the cliff is attacked, a notch (1) may be cut, and as this is made deeper the cliff above collapses. Eventually a wave-cut platform (2) is created, the top of which is

exposed at low tide. The debris from the cliff is carried along the coast or deposited offshore (3). The shallow seabed now slows down incoming waves: they attack the cliff (4), but their energy is reduced. In calm water, for example at the head of a bay (5), wave energy is diffused and light material such as sand is deposited as beaches.

THE SEA COAST
The coastline is continually changing, whether day by day as the tides sift and sort the sand and shingle on the beaches, or over tens of thousands of years as the erosive power of waves carves out headlands and bays. And over millions of years the coastline is subjected to major changes of sea level, whether it is the land uplifting or sinking, or the sea itself rising or receding. Today, interference by man can damage the coast. Dam building and river-channel engineering drastically reduce the amount of sediment reaching the coast; and sea walls built to protect the coast and groynes constructed to retard sand removal both pose a long-term threat to adjacent coasts, which become starved of the sediment that previously supplied their beaches.

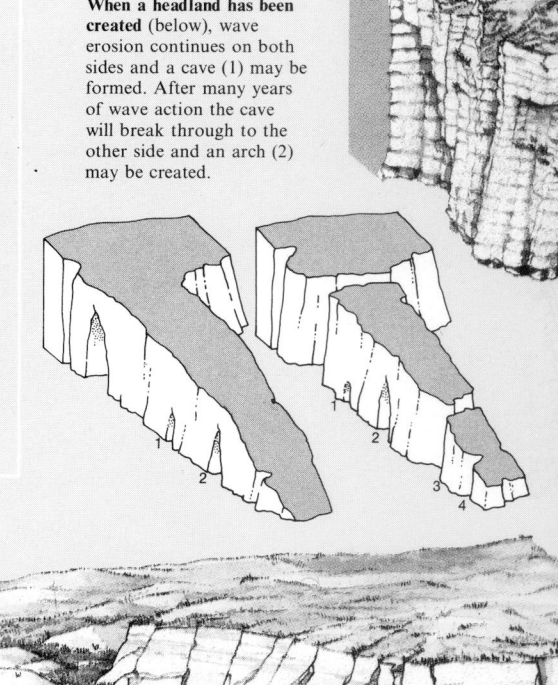

When a headland has been created (below), wave erosion continues on both sides and a cave (1) may be formed. After many years of wave action the cave will break through to the other side and an arch (2) may be created.

Light material such as mud, sand and shingle is carried by the sea. Waves tend to push the particles obliquely up a beach (right), but the backwash moves the material down again at right-angles to the shore. Thus the materials move in a zigzag fashion along the beach (1). This is known as longshore drift. When the load-carrying capacity of the waves is reduced for any reason, the material is deposited and forms a variety of features. The largest beaches (2) are found in the calmest waters such as in bays or at river mouths, with the finest grains sorted out nearest to the sea and larger pebbles

stranded higher up. Spits (3) and bars (4) are sand ridges deposited across a bay or river mouth. When one end of the ridge is attached to the land it is called a spit. Spits are very often shaped like a hook as waves are refracted around the tip of land. Bars are formed where sand is deposited in shallow water offshore across the entrances to bays and run parallel to the coastline. Dunes, pictured above, are formed when sand on the beach is driven inland by onshore winds. Very often they isolate flooded land behind them to form coastal features such as salt marshes and mud flats.

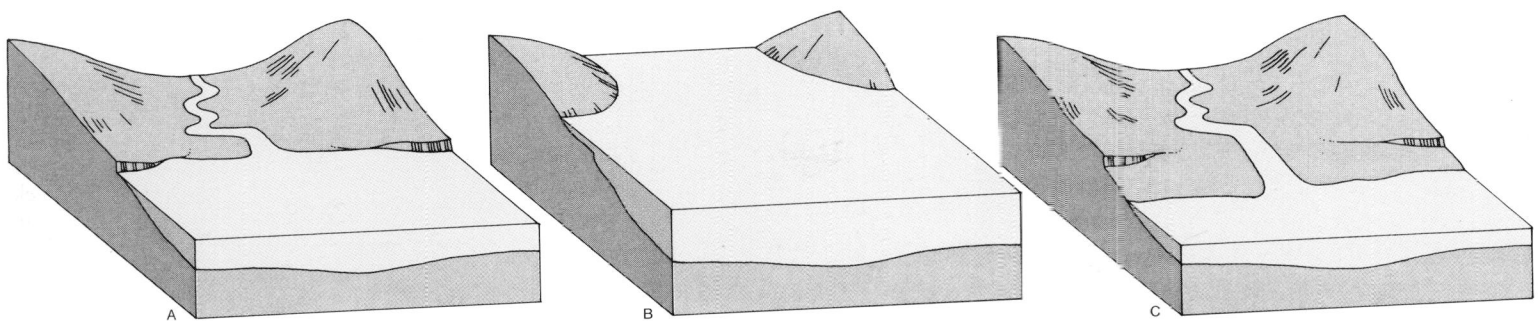

There are two major kinds of coastline—coastlines of submergence and coastlines of emergence. They are created by either a sinking or an uplift of the land, or by a change in sea level. A coastline with wave-cut cliffs and a river valley (A), for example, that experiences a rise in sea level will produce a new coastline (B) with a drowned estuary, coastal uplands isolated as islands, and a submerged coastal plain. The same coastline subjected to a drop in sea level (C) results in an extended river, abandoned cliffs far inland, and a raised beach that forms a new coastal plain.

(6,800 miles) of the Pacific from the storm belt south of New Zealand. The waves thus act as a giant conveyor for the energy that is finally used up in a few seconds of intense activity. Few other natural systems gather their energy so widely and then concentrate it so effectively.

A ball floating on the sea surface shows that, although a passing wave form moves forward, the water (and ball) follow a near-circular path and end up almost where they started. Beneath the surface the water follows similar orbits, but the amount of movement becomes progressively less with depth, until it dies out altogether. The greater the wavelength (the distance between crests) the greater is the depth of disturbance.

Long-swell waves approaching a gentle shore start disturbing the seabed far from the coast and these waves slow up, pack closer together and increase in height until they become unstable, thus producing the spilling white surf that carries much sediment to build up wide sandy beaches. Shorter local storm waves disturb the water to less depth, and thus reach much closer inshore before they interact with the seabed. Such waves do not therefore break until they plunge directly down on to the beach, leading to severe erosion, which results in the production of steep pebble beaches.

Waves slow up in shallow water, and so an undulating seabed causes their crests to bend and change their direction of approach. As a result, waves converge toward headlands (where their erosional attack is concentrated),

but they diverge as they enter bays, spreading out their energy and encouraging the deposition of the sediment they carry across the seabed close inshore. The high-energy waves at the headlands remove any rock fragments that become detached and transport them to the beaches that form at the bayheads.

Erosional coasts

Much of the local variability of coastal scenery results from differing rates of erosion on different types of rock. Bays are cut back rapidly into soft rocks such as clay, sand or gravel. Headlands are evidence that the sea takes longer to remove higher areas of harder rock such as granite or limestone. Despite the enormous power of storm waves, erosion of resistant rocks is slow and relies on any weakness that the sea can exploit.

Joints, faults and bedding planes are etched out by the water and by rock fragments hurled against them by breaking waves. Air compressed into such crevices by water pressure widens and deepens them into cracks and then into caves. In this way a solid cliff face can be eroded to form the great variety of features.

Resistant rocks can form steep simple cliffs of great height—more than 600 m (2,000 ft) in some places—and the sea may have to undercut them to produce collapse and retreat. Cliffs of weaker rocks rarely reach 100 m (330 ft) in height and are more rapidly eroded by atmospheric processes, by running water and by

landslips. There the role of the sea is largely confined to removing the rock debris from the foot of the cliff. Soft rock cliffs are gently sloping but complex in form.

Coasts of deposition

Although waves bend as they approach the shore, they rarely become completely parallel to the coastline. Wave crests drive sediment obliquely toward the beach, whereas the troughs carry it back directly offshore down the beach slope. In this way, sand and pebbles are transported in a zigzag motion, called longshore drift, away from the areas where they are produced. One such source of material is cliff erosion, but on average about 95 percent of the material moving on to beaches was originally carried to the coast by rivers.

Beaches are built up wherever longshore drift is impeded (for example, by a headland) or where wave and current energy is reduced (as at the head of a bay). An abundant supply of sediment may build a sandbar across the mouth of a bay or in shallow water offshore. Where the coast changes direction, longshore drift may continue in its original direction and build a spit out from the land. Depositional features may become strengthened by vegetation. Plants may take root and bind together newly deposited sediments, but they constitute relatively delicate coasts that are vulnerable to erosion if for any reason they are not continually supplied with fresh deposits of sediment.

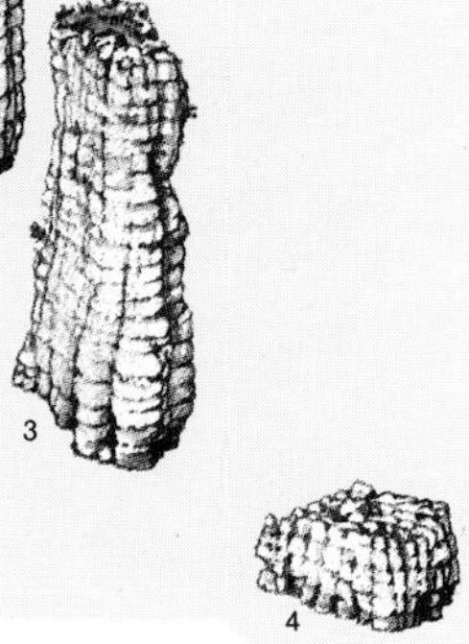

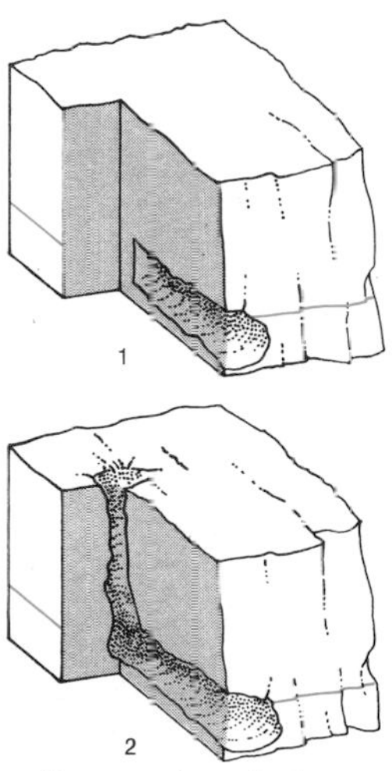

Further wave erosion (above) causes the roof of the arch to collapse, leaving an isolated column of rock called a stack (3). Another cave, and then an arch, may be formed behind the stack, which itself may be eroded to a short stump (4).

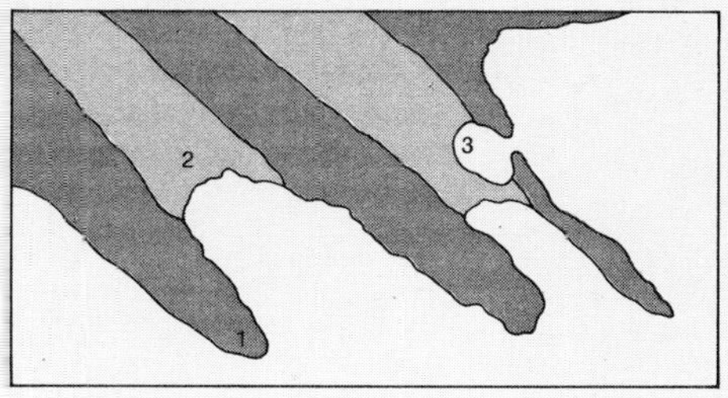

Headlands alternating with bays are found where bands of strong (1) and weak (2) rocks meet the coast at an angle and there is a varied resistance to erosion. The bays are first carved out of the softer rock, leaving the waves to attack the headlands of hard rock. If, in contrast, the strata lie parallel to the coast, then the hard rock has few irregular indentations except where the sea has broken through to the soft rock behind and has scoured out a cove (3).

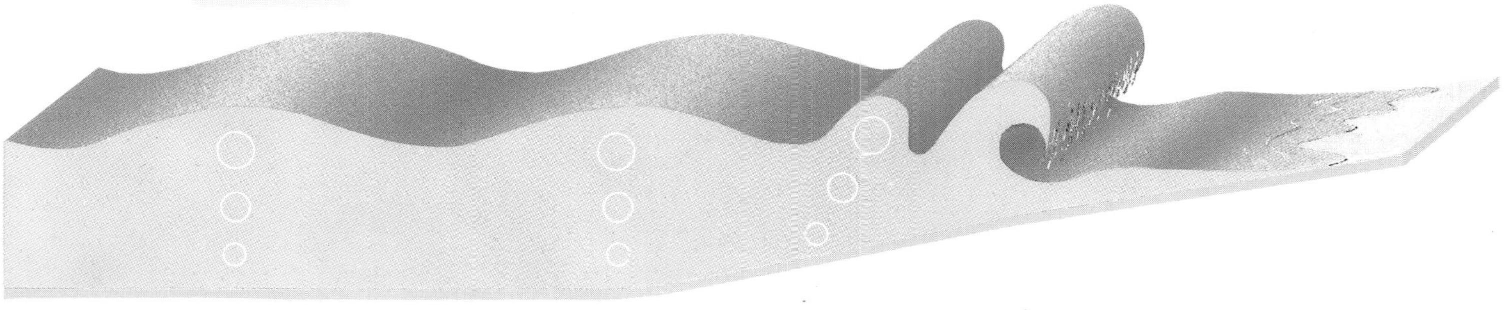

Gloups are formed when waves first erode a cave, then extend it backward as a long shaft running into the cliff (1). If the roof collapses at one point, a blowhole, or gloup (2), is formed. If the whole roof collapses, a deep cleft called a geo is created.

Waves are generated by wind on the surface of the sea. It is the shape of the wave that travels forward—the individual water particles move in near-circular orbits. Disturbance diminishes with depth to about half a wavelength. Waves break when they strike a sloping shore, and the wave height is about the same as the depth of the water.

Landscape-makers: Wind and Weathering

Winds are part of the global circulation of air and they can affect landforms wherever surface material is loose and unprotected by vegetation. The effects of a strong wind are a familiar sight—whether in the dust clouds that rise from a plowed field after a dry spell, or in the sand swept along the beach on a windy day. Weathering is the disintegration and decomposition of rocks through their exposure to the atmosphere. It includes the changes that destroy the original structure of rocks, and few on the Earth's surface have not been weathered at one time or another in the history of our evolving landscape.

Active and fixed dunes in Africa and western Asia

Sand dunes cover only 20 percent of the world's deserts, and tend to be concentrated in a small number of sand seas, or ergs, such as the Erg Bourharet in Algeria (above).

Longitudinal, or seif, dunes (below) are long, narrow ridges that lie parallel to the direction of prevailing winds. Surface heating and wind flow produce vertical spiraling motions of air.

Most sand seas today are being actively molded by winds. The landscape has long been shaped by wind, and some dune fields produced in dry climates in the distant past may be "fossilized" now by soils and vegetation cover. Desertification often occurs where this vegetation is disturbed by man.

☐ Fixed sand dunes

▨ Active sand dunes

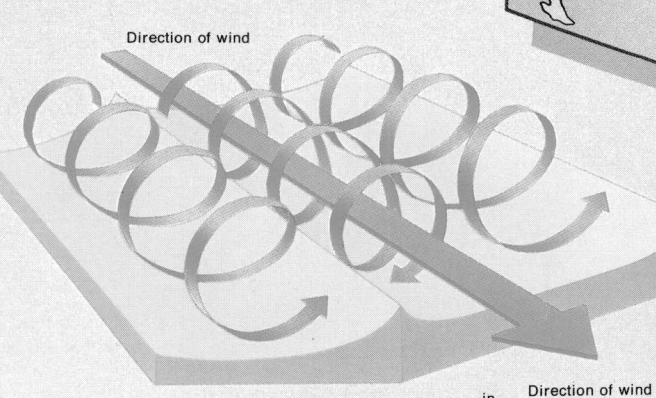

Direction of wind

EROSION AND WEATHERING

Winds result from the differential heating of regions of the globe. They act indirectly as agents of erosion through water or waves, but they also directly affect the surface of the Earth, molding landforms either by erosion or deposition. The nature of weathering processes and the rate at which they operate depend upon climate, the properties of the rock and the conditions of the biosphere. Both wind erosion and the various weathering processes are significant landscape-makers.

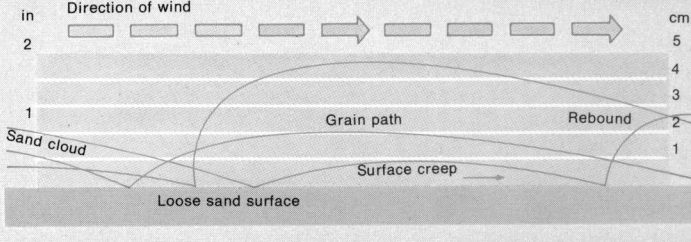

in 2 / 1 — Direction of wind — cm 5 4 3 2 1

Sand cloud / Grain path / Rebound / Surface creep / Loose sand surface

Many rocks are formed deep in the Earth, where they are in equilibrium with the forces that created them. If they become exposed at the surface, they are in disequilibrium with atmospheric forces. This brings about the changes —adjustments to atmospheric and organic agents—that we call weathering. Products of weathering are moved by agents of erosion, one of which is the wind. Where the surface is protected, for example by vegetation, the wind has little effect, but where strong winds attack loose surface material that is unprotected, erosion, abrasion and deposition may occur, producing characteristic landforms.

How wind shapes the surface

Strong winds occur in many places, but nowhere are they more effective in forming the surface of the land than in deserts, where their work is largely unhindered by vegetation. There the wind can pick up material and then, charged with sand particles, blast away at the ground, carrying away the debris and depositing it. Many notorious desert winds are associated with sand movement and dust storms—the harmattan of West Africa and the sirocco of the Middle East, for example.

Wind erosion occurs where winds charged with sand attack soils or rock. Dry soils may be broken up and the resulting debris, which includes soil nutrients, is carried away as dust. This poses a serious problem, especially when arid and semiarid lands experience drought. Wind erosion involving the lifting and blowing away of loose material from the ground surface is called deflation.

Erosion by sand and rock fragments carried by winds is called abrasion. In this way winds erode individual surface pebbles into distinctive shapes known as ventifacts. They can also mold larger rock masses into aerodynamic shapes known as yardangs—features that often look rather like upturned rowing boats. Some of these features are so large that they have been identified only since satellite photographs have become available. Finally, winds erode by attrition, which involves the mutual wearing down of particles as they are carried along.

Winds can transport material in three different ways. They can lift loose, sand-sized particles into the air and carry them downwind along trajectories that resemble those of ballistic missiles: the particles rise steeply and descend along gentle flight paths. This produces a bouncing movement known as saltation in a layer extending approximately 1 m (3 ft) above the

Sand particles move in a series of long jumps—a process called saltation. Particles describe a curved path (above), the height and length of which depends upon the mass of the grain, the wind velocity and the number of other particles moving around. Saltation only occurs in a layer extending up to approximately 1 m (3 ft) above the ground surface. Sand grains moving in this way are also responsible for the abraded base of features such as pedestal rocks (right). These landforms are weathered first—for example by the crystallization of salts—and are then eroded by the sand-laden winds.

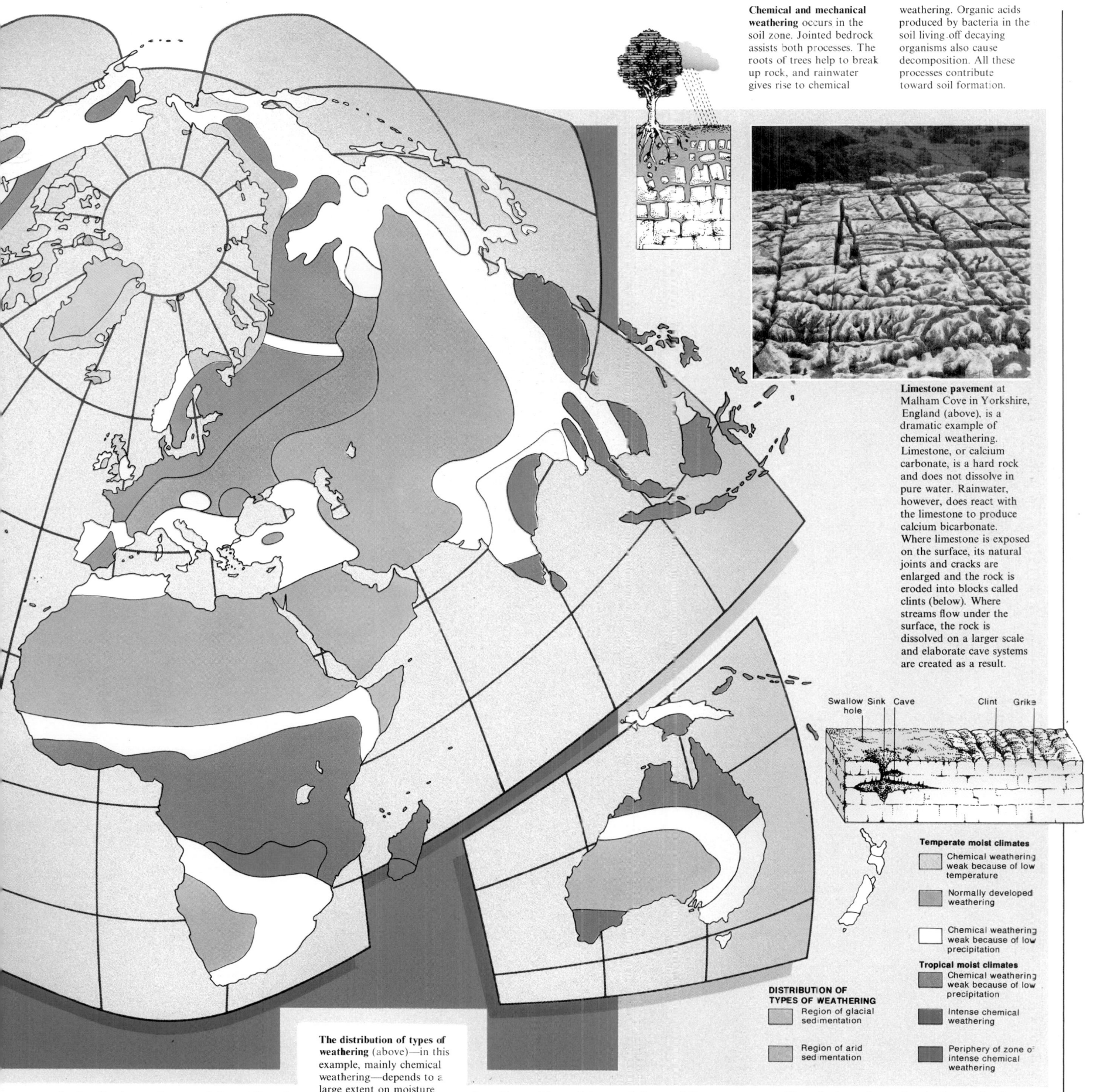

Limestone pavement at Malham Cove in Yorkshire, England (above), is a dramatic example of chemical weathering. Limestone, or calcium carbonate, is a hard rock and does not dissolve in pure water. Rainwater, however, does react with the limestone to produce calcium bicarbonate. Where limestone is exposed on the surface, its natural joints and cracks are enlarged and the rock is eroded into blocks called clints (below). Where streams flow under the surface, the rock is dissolved on a larger scale and elaborate cave systems are created as a result.

Swallow Sink Cave   Clint   Grike
hole

Temperate moist climates

Chemical weathering weak because of low temperature

Normally developed weathering

Chemical weathering weak because of low precipitation

Tropical moist climates

Chemical weathering weak because of low precipitation

Intense chemical weathering

Periphery of zone of intense chemical weathering

DISTRIBUTION OF TYPES OF WEATHERING

Region of glacial sedimentation

Region of arid sedimentation

The distribution of types of weathering (above)—in this example, mainly chemical weathering—depends to a large extent on moisture and temperature. When classifying regions with different rates of chemical weathering in terms of climatic zones, many areas of the world can be placed into one of two principal categories: tropical moist climates and temperate moist climates. The white areas on the map are mountain ranges or regions of tectonic activity where there is no appreciable weathering mantle.

ground. As the bouncing particles strike the surface, they push other particles along the ground (creep or drift). Fine particles that are disturbed by saltation rise up into the airflow and are carried away as dust (suspension).

The materials eroded and transported by winds must eventually come to rest in features of deposition, the most extensive of which are sand dunes. Sand seas at first sight appear to be random and complex, rather like a choppy ocean, but their features generally fall into three size groups: small ripples, which have a wavelength of up to 3 m (10 ft) and a height of 20 cm (8 in); dunes, with a wavelength of 20–300 m (65–1,000 ft) and a height of up to 30 m (68 ft); and sand mountains or "draa," which have a wavelength of 1–3 km (0.6–1.5 miles) and rise to a height of up to 200 m (650 ft). Within each size group various forms can be explained in terms of the nature of the sand and the kinds of winds that blow over it. Where winds blow consistently from one direction, long linear dunes form parallel or transverse to the wind direction. Where sand supply is limited, horned "barchan" dunes may form. If winds blow from several directions during a year, then star-shaped dunes and other complex patterns appear. Sand dunes are also common along the

shorelines of large lakes and the world's oceans, where onshore winds can pile quite extensive areas of loose drifting sand.

Agents of weathering

Weathering takes two forms: mechanical weathering breaks up rock without altering its mineral constituents, whereas chemical weathering changes in some way the nature of mineral crystals. One agent of mechanical weathering is temperature change. It used to be thought that rocks disintegrated as a result of a huge daily range of temperature (thermal weathering). Despite travelers' tales of rocks splitting in the desert night with cracks like pistol shots, there is little evidence to support this view. In the presence of water, however, alternate heating and cooling of rocks does result in fracture. Frost is also an effective rock breaker. The freezing of water and expansion of ice in the cracks and pores of rocks create disruptive pressures; alternate freezing and thawing eventually causes pieces of rock to break off in angular fragments. Finally the roots of plants and trees grow into the joints of rock and widen them, thus loosening the structure of the rock. Animals burrowing through the soil can have a similar effect on rocks.

Chemical and mechanical weathering can work hand in hand. In arid regions, for example, the crystallization of salts results in the weathering of rock. As water evaporates from the rock surface, salt crystals grow (from minerals dissolved in the water) in small openings in the rock. In time these crystals bring to bear enough pressure to break off rock fragments from the parent block.

Chemical weathering is most effective in humid tropical climates, however, and it usually involves the decomposition of rocks as a result of their exposure to air and rainwater, which contains dissolved chemicals. Carbon dioxide from the air, for example, becomes dissolved in rainwater, making it into weak carbonic acid. This reacts with minerals such as calcite, which is found in many rocks. Similarly, rocks can be oxidized by oxygen in the air. This happens to rocks that contain iron, for example, if they are exposed on the surface: a reddish iron oxide is produced which causes the rocks to crumble.

Over many thousands, even millions, of years, the processes of mechanical and chemical weathering have affected many of the rocks on the Earth's surface. When rocks are weakened in such a way, they then fall prey to the agents of erosion—water, ice, winds and waves.

Landscape-makers: Man

Man has done much to reshape the face of the planet since his first appearance on Earth more than two million years ago. Early man did little to harm the environment but, with the rise of agriculture, the landscape began to change. An increasing population and the growth of urban settlements gradually created greater demands for agricultural land and living space. But industrialization during the last 200 years has had the biggest impact. Man's search for and exploitation of the Earth's resources has to a large extent transformed the natural landscape and at the same time created totally artificial man-made environments.

MAN THE GEOLOGICAL AGENT

In 1864 a conservationist named George Perkins Marsh introduced the thesis that "man in fact made the Earth" rather than the converse. The idea of man as a geological agent was further developed in the 1920s. Man modifies the landscape in many ways; sometimes he transforms the Earth completely—he even creates land where no land was before.

Man's major impact on the landscape has been through forest clearance. He made the first attack on natural forests about 8,000 years ago in Neolithic times in northern and western Europe, as revealed by the changing composition of tree pollen deposited in bogs. After Roman times, especially in the Mediterranean region, there was another spate of forest clearance, so that by the Middle Ages little original forest survived in the Old World. As population and emigration increased, it was the turn of trees in the New World and Africa to fall before the axe and plow. Man's present voracious appetite for timber and its products could, if unchecked, clear most of the Earth's great forests by the end of this century.

Forest clearance not only changes the appearance of the landscape but can alter the balance of nature within a region. The hydrological cycle may be affected, and soil erosion may be increased, which in turn chokes rivers with sediment and leads to the silting up of harbors and estuaries. The coastal area of Valencia in Spain, for example, has widened by nearly 4 km (2.5 miles) since Roman times, much of which can be accounted for by forest clearance, and subsequent soil erosion and the deposition of the material by rivers as they near the sea. Reafforestation of an area can reduce soil erosion and the threat of flooding. Landscape management can reduce wind speeds: for example, shelter belts in the Russian steppes have been planted over distances of more than 100 km (62 miles).

Water management

The second great impact of man has been on the waterways of the world. The most spectacular changes are caused by the construction of dams to make vast new lakes. Such projects have frequently had effects far beyond those originally anticipated. The Aswan High Dam on the River Nile was completed in 1970, creating Lake Nasser and making possible the irrigation of an additional 550,000 hectares (1,358,000 acres) in upper Egypt. But some would argue that the dam holds back silt from the rivers and stores it in the lake, a fact that has seriously reduced the rate of silting in the Nile delta. This has resulted in increased salinity and some loss of fertility of the soil, as well as changes to the delta's coastline. The storage of silt in Lake Nasser has caused increased erosion of the riverbed downstream and the undermining of the foundations of bridges and barrages.

Other man-made changes to rivers include straightening and canalization, usually for

Massive power plants (left) symbolize man's modifications to the landscape in modern, industrialized society. Demand for energy and mineral resources has led to the creation of huge holes in the ground like this borax mine (below left) in the Mojave desert in California. The open pit is 100 m (330 ft) deep, 1,460 m (4,800 ft) long and 915 m (3,000 ft) wide. In opening up resource areas in Brazil, the Trans-Amazonian highway has disturbed the forest (below).

Hong Kong's bustling waterfront (below) captures the true essence of urban man. If space is in short supply, he expands his world vertically and maximizes his use of every square meter. Central business districts in the world's major cities reflect this concern with space.

flood protection, but also to prevent the channel from shifting. As long ago as the third millennium BC, during the reign of Emperor Yao, a hydraulic engineer was apparently appointed to control the wandering course of the Hwang-Ho (Yellow River), and the system he devised survived for at least 1,500 years. Even so, over the centuries, the river has changed course radically, and today measures are still being taken to control the fine sediment that the river carries and the flooding caused by its deposition. The Missouri River in the United States is estimated to erode material from an area of about 3,680 hectares (9,000 acres) annually over a length of 1,220 km (758 miles). It is little wonder that engineers attempt to control rivers by means of realignment or try to "train" a river's flow by using concrete stays.

New land from old

The continuing pressure of population on food resources and the need to create new agricultural land illustrate still further the impact of man as a landscape shaper. As part of irrigation projects land is often leveled and new waterways are created in the form of canals. Pakistan has one of the most extensive man-made irrigation systems in the world. It controls almost completely the flow of the Indus, Sutlej and Punjab rivers through some 640 km (400 miles) of linking canals.

A huge demand for rice in many parts of southeastern Asia has led to farmers terracing steep slopes on many mountainous islands. In the Netherlands, about one-third of the entire cultivated area of the country is land that has been reclaimed from the sea. In the future more grandiose schemes are likely. Any large-scale expansion of agricultural land in the former Soviet Union will be mainly dependent on water supply. There have been plans since the 1930s to divert northward-flowing rivers to irrigated areas in the south and west. This idea, which might become a reality by the turn of the century, could have serious implications for the waters of the Arctic Ocean. If the amount of fresh water flowing into the ocean is reduced, salinity will increase, thus affecting the melting of ice floes and, consequently, sea level.

Man has also made his mark along the coastlines, from small-scale measures, such as

the construction of groynes—wooden piles that reduce the amount of sand that is transported along the beach by wave action—to large-scale man-made harbors.

Modern man, the urban dweller of the machine age, has brought great changes to the face of the landscape. The need for materials for the construction of the urban fabric has led to the creation of huge quarries, in which building stone and road-building materials are extracted from the ground. Demand for energy and minerals leads to extensive modification of the landscape, especially where mineral deposits are near the surface and can be extracted by open-cast mining. The largest holes on Earth (excluding ocean basins) are those that result from the extraction of fuel (coal) and minerals.

The side effects of mining can be detrimental to the environment. Land may subside and despoliation of the landscape by slag heaps, for example, is considerable. Escaping coal dust can suffocate vegetation in a mining area, and gases given off during some mining operations can also damage plant and animal life.

Reclamation of spoiled areas is obligatory in many countries. Old open-cast workings are often filled with water to be used for recreational facilities, and slag heaps are treated and planted with vegetation: research has produced certain strains of plants that will grow even in the most acidic soils.

The true impact of man

During the last hundred years or so man has become much more aware of his role as an agent of landscape creation and destruction. The significance of man the landscape-maker, in comparison with slow, natural changes, is the speed with which he effects transformation, the sheer amount of energy which he can apply to a relatively small area, and the selectiveness and determination with which he applies that energy. Man's increased impact has not been a smooth and continuous process: it has occurred at different rates in different places and at different times. While it can be argued that some landscapes have been constructed which themselves conserve and often beautify the natural environment, man's active role has primarily been destructive: he has transformed the Earth's surface, perhaps irreversibly.

THE DUTCH POLDERS

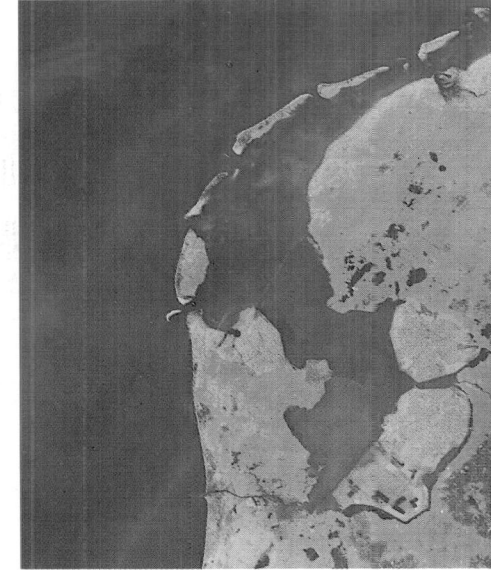

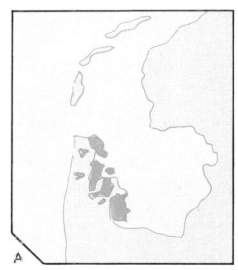
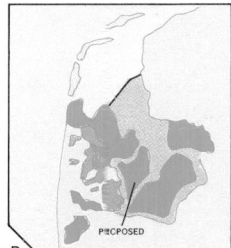

Reclamation of the Dutch polders from the North Sea is an example of man creating land. Many centuries ago a large part of what is now the western Netherlands was beneath the sea. From the 15th to the 17th centuries (A) dykes were constructed to enclose land and protect it against inundation from the sea, and enable it to be farmed. Later, windmills were used to drain away sea water. Further reclamation in the 19th and 20th centuries (B) has brought the total area to

165,000 hectares (408,000 acres). In 1932 a 40 km (25 mile) dam was completed, enclosing the Zuider Zee—which is now a freshwater lake that was renamed the IJsselmeer—and reducing Holland's vulnerable coastline by 320 km (200 miles). To create a polder, a dyke is built and the water pumped out. Reeds are grown to help dry out the soil. After a few years drains are put in to remove water remaining. Newly created polders (light blue) show up well on this satellite image (top).

Man-made environments have become increasingly complex and large scale. Highway construction—this vast interchange (left) is in Chicago—is typical of the extensive use of land for modern transport systems alone. The acreage of land use classified as urban continues to increase. Man's endeavors to make still more land available for his many purposes have extended to cultivating previously inhospitable desert lands (above). More than half the land in Israel is

naturally unproductive because of its aridity. By means of elaborate water carriage and storage schemes and scientifically researched irrigation projects, the desert has been totally transformed from a barren wasteland into intensively cultivated fields. Output from agriculture can also be increased by terracing. In densely populated areas, or mountainous regions, as in Luzon in the Philippines (right), man's skillful landscaping has completely reshaped the topography.

Part 3

THE EMERGENCE OF LIFE

How life on Earth began and developed
How life has evolved and spread over the planet
How man came to inherit the Earth

THE STAGES OF LIFE

Simple organic molecules, the precursors of life, could certainly have evolved in Earth's primitive atmosphere. Energy from the Sun, volcanoes and electric storms had the power to combine the basic chemicals into the amino acids and other molecules that are the constituents of living matter, forming droplets of "pre-life" in pools and on shorelines. Concentrations of droplets collected around some minerals, coagulating in a "soup" of long-chain polymers—proteins and nucleic acids which together form the living cell. Thus far have scientists re-created life's origins, but the combining of proteins and nucleic acids into a living unit remains to be achieved.

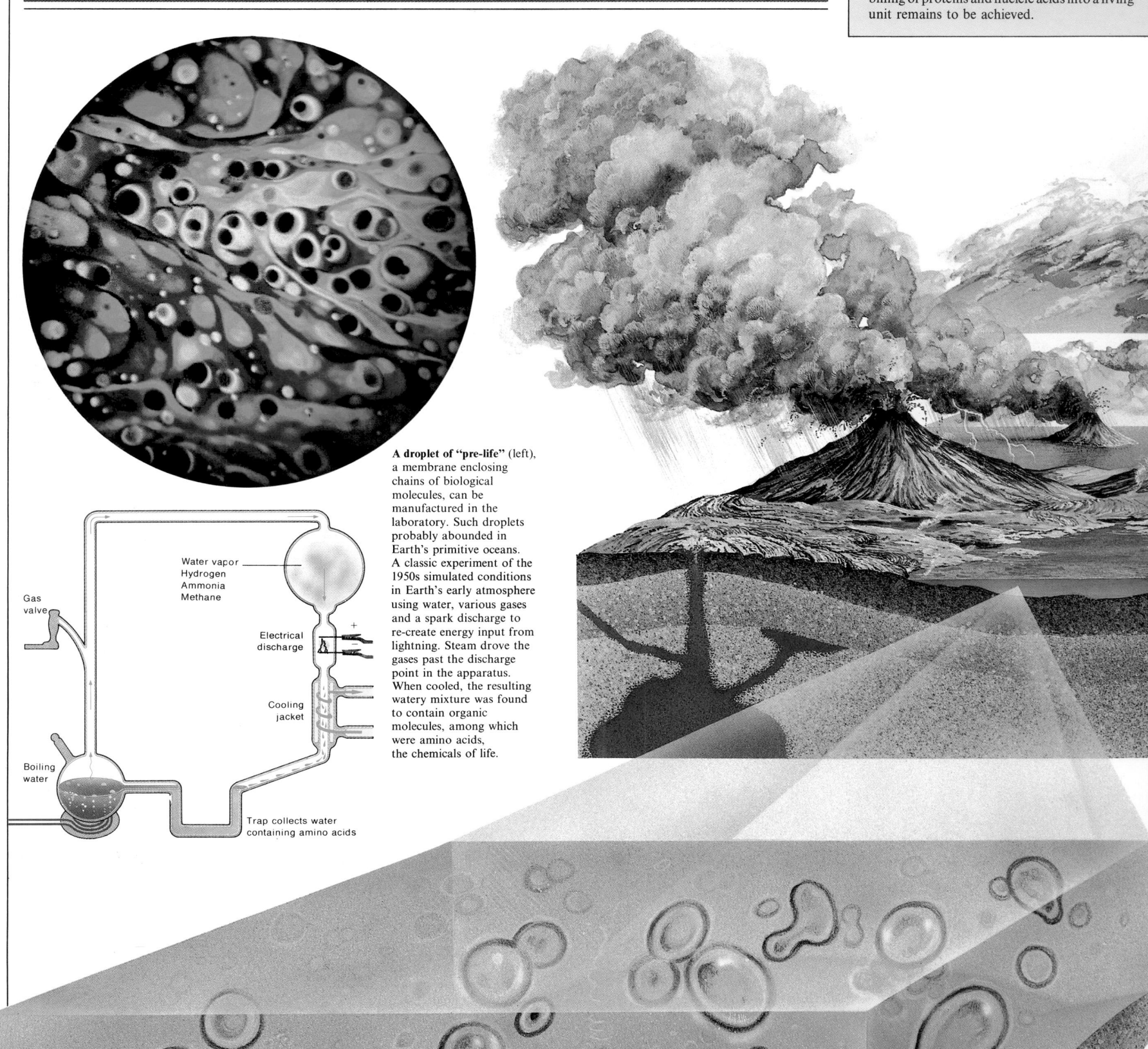

A droplet of "pre-life" (left), a membrane enclosing chains of biological molecules, can be manufactured in the laboratory. Such droplets probably abounded in Earth's primitive oceans. A classic experiment of the 1950s simulated conditions in Earth's early atmosphere using water, various gases and a spark discharge to re-create energy input from lightning. Steam drove the gases past the discharge point in the apparatus. When cooled, the resulting watery mixture was found to contain organic molecules, among which were amino acids, the chemicals of life.

Gas valve

Water vapor
Hydrogen
Ammonia
Methane

Electrical discharge

Cooling jacket

Boiling water

Trap collects water containing amino acids

LIFE BEGINS

A "primordial soup" of organic molecules, each separated from the water by a membrane, formed thick concentrations in Earth's shallow pools. From these evolved the long-chain polymers that form proteins and nucleic acids in every living cell.

The Source of Life

Life may have come to Earth from outer space – some meteorites contain life-like organic molecules – but the basic constituents of life, the biochemical structures called proteins and nucleic acids, could just as well have formed on Earth itself. By simulating possible primitive conditions on Earth, and applying a likely energy source, American scientists of the 1950s manufactured, from inorganic substances, the amino acids that form the subunits of all living things.

THE RADIANT SUN
A dense atmosphere of water vapor and various gases—but not oxygen—formed round the cooling planet Earth after its creation 4,600 million years ago. Oxygen in the atmosphere would have prevented the evolution of life from nonliving organic matter by blocking the Sun's ultraviolet radiation (which may have provided energy for the forming of organic compounds), and free oxygen would also have destroyed such compounds as they began to accumulate.

THE PRIMITIVE ATMOSPHERE
Volcanic eruptions drove water vapor and gases into the atmosphere of the young Earth; lightning and other discharges of atmospheric electricity accompanied the torrential rain; dissolved minerals collected in the pools. These were some of the preconditions for life on Earth, whereby mixtures of organic compounds in water may have combined to form more complex units essential for life.

Water played a key part in the creation of life on Earth. At first the temperature of the newly formed planet was far too high for water to exist in a liquid state. Instead, it formed a dense atmosphere of steam, which, as the Earth cooled, condensed into droplets of rain that poured down for perhaps thousands of years. This torrential, thundery rain eroded the land and dissolved the minerals, which collected in pools on the surface.

Earth's original atmosphere was also very different from today's. Most importantly, it contained no free oxygen, the gas which makes air-breathing life possible; the primitive atmosphere was composed of carbon monoxide, carbon dioxide, hydrogen and nitrogen. But the absence of oxygen created two conditions that are essential if life is to evolve. First, without oxygen the atmosphere could have no layer of ozone (an oxygen compound), which now acts as a barrier to most of the Sun's high-energy radiation (mainly ultraviolet light). Second, the absence of free oxygen meant that any complex chemicals that might be formed would not immediately break down again. Thus the molecules of life could form.

The chemistry of life

Life may be distinguished from nonlife in three ways: living organisms are able to increase the complexity of their parts through synthetic, self-building reactions; they obtain and use energy by breaking down chemical compounds; and they can make new copies of themselves.

It is the combined properties of the chemicals

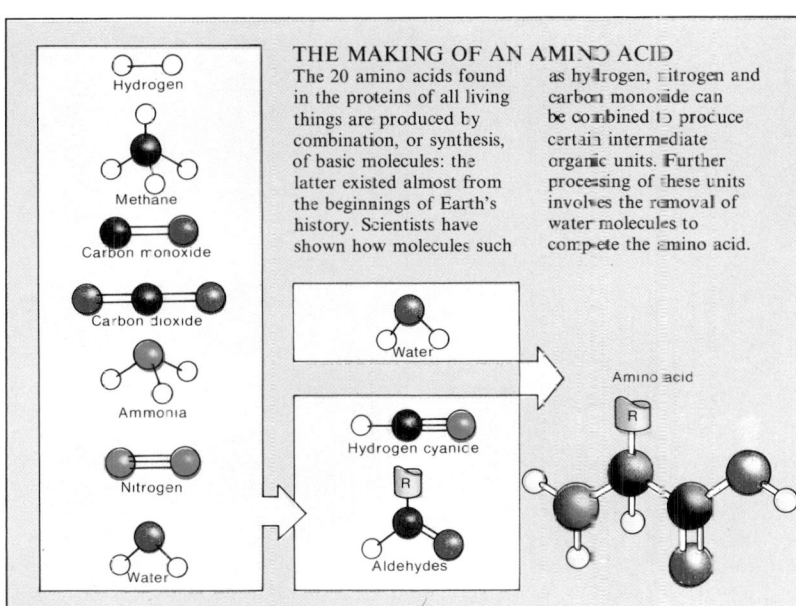

THE MAKING OF AN AMINO ACID
The 20 amino acids found in the proteins of all living things are produced by combination, or synthesis, of basic molecules: the latter existed almost from the beginnings of Earth's history. Scientists have shown how molecules such as hydrogen, nitrogen and carbon monoxide can be combined to produce certain intermediate organic units. Further processing of these units involves the removal of water molecules to complete the amino acid.

of life that make them so special, not just the chemicals themselves. Experiments in the last few decades have given us a very good idea of how life could have arisen from the simple, nonliving chemicals which compose it. In the early 1950s, Harold Urey and Stanley Miller simulated the atmosphere of a primitive world by filling a flask with water, ammonia, methane and hydrogen. They supplied it with energy in the form of heat and an electric spark—to simulate lightning—and the experiment was left to run for a week.

Analyzing the mixture formed, they found it contained many chemicals that are associated with living things, particularly nitrogen compounds called amino acids—the really important chemicals of life. Further experiments brought together other gas mixtures, including the one that is now thought to have covered the young Earth, and these gave similar results, as long as there was no free oxygen present. The resulting mixture of organic compounds in water came to be known as the "primordial

soup," and it is from this "soup" that life may have emerged.

Miller and Urey had shown that the basic substances of life can be derived from a primitive atmosphere. But there are still large gaps in our understanding of how these substances became more organized and self-regulating: in other words, how they became alive. More complex molecular structures somehow developed through the linking up of the basic units to form long, chain-like sequences of larger units, called polymers. But how this happened is still not fully understood.

The two most important classes of biological molecules are proteins and nucleic acids, both of which are polymers. Proteins are the building materials of living matter, the chief components of muscles, skin and hair. They also form enzymes—the chemicals that control biochemical reaction in living cells. Nucleic acids—DNA (deoxyribonucleic acid) and RNA (ribonucleic acid)—are so called because they are found in the central nuclei of cells. They are the cell's genetic material, the raw stuff of heredity. They act as the memories and the messengers of life, storing information in units called genes, and releasing that information to the cells when it is needed. Nucleic acids can reproduce themselves and, without this ability, life would not exist or continue.

The basic units that link together to form proteins are amino acids, and all proteins in living organisms are made up of just 20 different amino acids. In chemical terms, a protein molecule is a polymer consisting of a long chain of amino acid units joined together in a particular sequence, and the code to this sequence is held by DNA.

How living chemicals joined

Experiments with simulated primordial conditions have produced many amino acids other than the 20 commonly found in proteins. All amino acids (and other types of chemicals) tend to "stick" onto the surface of clay, but those 20 found in proteins stick particularly well to clays rich in the metal nickel. This suggests that the first proteins may have been formed in pools or on the fringes of seas, where the primordial soup was in contact with nickel-rich clays. There heat from the Sun or a volcano could have combined the amino acids to form a primitive protein.

The four classes of chemicals that form the basic components of nucleic acids have also, like the amino acids, been "cooked" up in a primordial soup, and they too will stick to clay to form long-chain polymers. And, just as nickel-rich clays are best at absorbing the amino acid constituents of protein, so clays rich in zinc absorb the building blocks of nucleic acids. This suggests that such clays could have been the birthplace of genes, which are the "messengers" of inheritance.

However, the coupling of proteins and nucleic acids, which together form the living cell, has yet to be explained, and it is improbable that proteins or nucleic acids alone could have provided the basis for life.

The Russian biochemist I. A. Oparin has shown that, in water, solutions of polymers (such as proteins) have a tendency to form droplets surrounded by an outer membrane very like that which encloses living cells. As these droplets grow by absorbing more polymers, some split in two when they become too large for stability. If such a droplet had protein enzymes to harness energy and make more polymers, and if it had nucleic acids with instructions for making those proteins, and if each new droplet received a complete copy of the nucleic acid instructions, the droplet would be alive—it would be a living cell.

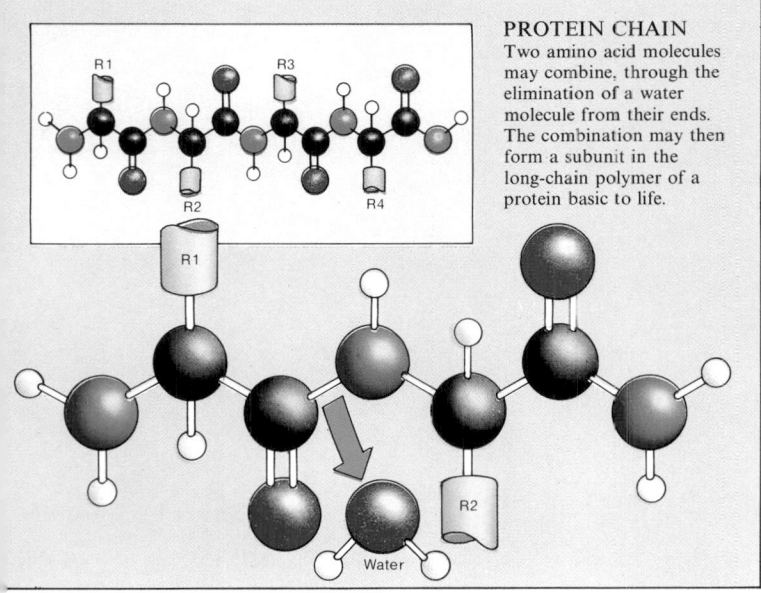

PROTEIN CHAIN
Two amino acid molecules may combine, through the elimination of a water molecule from their ends. The combination may then form a subunit in the long-chain polymer of a protein basic to life.

The Structure of Life

All life forms stem from a single cell, and every cell contains in its nucleus instructions for the re-creation of the organism of which it forms a part. These are encoded in chromosomes, which contain the miraculous molecular substance of DNA, sectioned into units of heredity called genes. The genetic code determines in detail the physical characteristics of an individual creature, so that variations in DNA cause variations in the individual. Scientists believe that it is the interaction of the individual variation with the environment that ultimately leads to the evolution of the similar, interbreeding groups of creatures that are known as species.

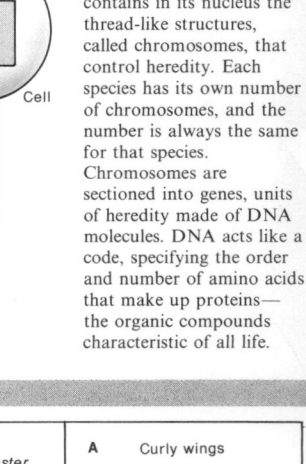

THE HIDDEN SECRET

Dramatic discoveries in recent decades have revolutionized biology, the primary life science. Scientists can now trace parts of the genetic blueprint that lays down the pattern for every form of life, linking the large-scale unfolding of species that we know as evolution with the ultramicroscopic activity of the molecules within the nucleus of every cell. This may be the secret behind the rich diversity of life on Earth.

Deoxyribonucleic acid (DNA) consists of a "backbone" of alternating sugar and phosphate molecules, and to each sugar is attached one of four nitrogenous bases (adenine, guanine, thymine and cytosine, or A, G, T, C). A single gene might contain 2,000 of these bases, and in the body cell of a human being the 46 chromosomes (thread-like bodies of DNA and protein) run to 3,000 million bases. The sequence of these bases stores the information for making amino acids into proteins, just as the sequence of letters in this sentence stores the information for making a particular verbal structure. But the DNA alphabet has only four letters (A, G, T, C).

The thread of life

DNA is a double molecule, resembling a twisted ladder, its two main strands twining around each other to form the famous double helix. The strands are linked by pairs of bases—A and T, or G and C—whose shape is such that each pair fits together neatly, like pieces of a jigsaw, to form the rungs of the DNA ladder. As a result, the information on the strands can be duplicated by "unzipping" the double helix and making new strands by using the old ones as templates. DNA stores, duplicates and passes on the information that makes life alive.

Cells multiply by splitting in two, and each newly made cell thus gets instructions for its existence by the mechanism of heredity, the gene. But heredity is a word more often applied to the passing on of DNA from an organism to its offspring. In sexual reproduction the offspring gets some of the DNA (usually half) from one parent, and the rest from the other, ending up with a unique mix all of its own.

The laws of heredity

Man has long known that characteristics can be passed on from one generation to the next, for he has been selectively breeding crops and animals for thousands of years. However, it was not until the mid-nineteenth century that an obscure Austrian monk, Gregor Mendel (1822–84), discovered the laws that govern inheritance, and his work was ignored until the beginning of the twentieth century, when more powerful microscopes made possible the direct observation of the cell.

Mendel experimented with pea plants because they had easily recognizable traits, and because, although normally self-fertilizing, they could be cross-fertilized with pollen from a different plant. Mendel made many crosses between different pure-bred plants and found that in the offspring, or hybrids, some characters always prevailed over others: red flowers over white, tall plants over short, and so on. He called the prevailing characters dominant, and the nonprevailing characters recessive. He then let the first-generation hybrids self-fertilize, and found not only that the recessive traits reappeared in the hybrids' offspring, but also that they reappeared in a constant proportion of three dominant to one recessive; the second generation contained three times as many red-flowered peas as white-flowered peas.

To explain his results, Mendel proposed that each plant had two hereditary "factors"— today called alleles—for each character, and that the dominant factor suppressed the recessive factor. If a plant inherited both a dominant and a recessive factor, the dominant one would prevail. Only if both factors were recessive would the recessive character be apparent. Mendel found many other pairs of traits where one form was dominant and the other recessive. He established that permutations arising from the crossing of the two first-generation hybrids allows the dominant gene to be present in three out of four crosses in the second generation; but

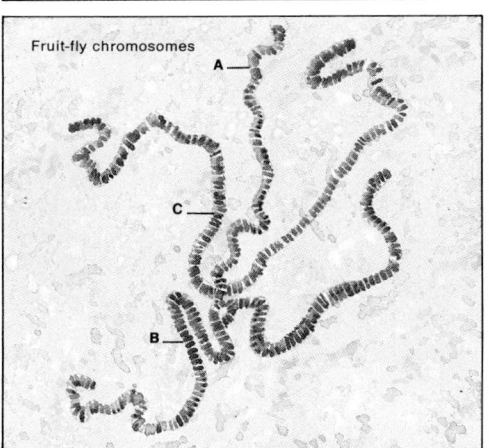

Genes

Chromosomes

Cell

Protein (myoglobin)   Amino acids

Fruit-fly chromosomes

A

C

B

The cell is the basic unit of all life, and every cell contains in its nucleus the thread-like structures, called chromosomes, that control heredity. Each species has its own number of chromosomes, and the number is always the same for that species. Chromosomes are sectioned into genes, units of heredity made of DNA molecules. DNA acts like a code, specifying the order and number of amino acids that make up proteins— the organic compounds characteristic of all life.

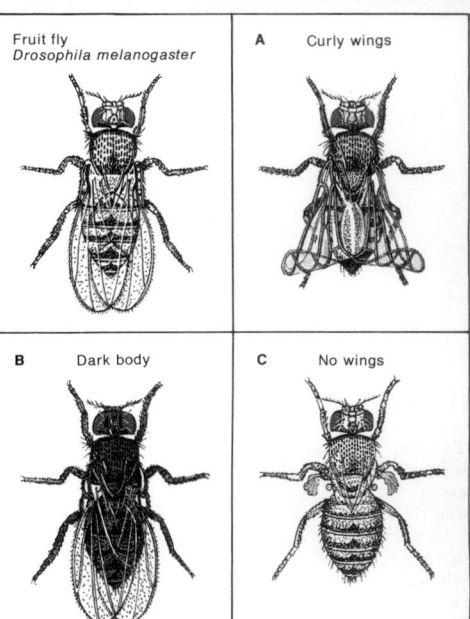

Chromosomes (below left) of the fruit fly, much magnified, show bands of DNA arranged in sections that correspond exactly with specific genes, the chemical units of heredity. The proof of this correspondence came when the American geneticist Hermann Muller introduced the use of ionizing radiation to damage the fruit flies' chromosomes at ultra-microscopic points, causing precise point mutations in offspring of parents whose DNA had been damaged at the places indicated. Random mutations may occur in any organism, and not only as a result of radiation. A gradual accumulation of minor mutations may lead to evolutionary change.

Fruit fly
Drosophila melanogaster

A   Curly wings

B   Dark body

C   No wings

in the fourth cross, only the two recessive alleles of the genes are present. So there is always a three-to-one ratio of dominant to recessive.

Theories of evolution

Mendel's work was of course unknown to his contemporaries, Charles Darwin and Alfred Russel Wallace, who even then were providing solutions to the major mystery of biology—the way that species evolve, change and develop over time. Evolution was not a new idea in Darwin's day. In 1809 the French naturalist Jean-Baptiste Lamarck had proposed a theory of the inheritance of acquired characteristics, suggesting that new habits learned by an organism in response to environmental change may become physically incorporated in the animal's descendants. For instance, the fact that the ancestral giraffe had to stretch its neck to reach food might give its offspring long necks to enable them to reach food more easily. Less satisfactory than the "natural selection" theory of Darwin and Wallace (who independently reached the same conclusion), Lamarckism founders on the fact that there is no genetic mechanism enabling acquired characters to pass on in this way.

Darwin's theory of natural selection has three key elements: all individuals vary, and some variations are passed on to the next generation; the gap between the potential and the actual number of offspring reproduced by organisms is very wide and implies that not all will survive; organisms best adapted to the environment will survive, their offspring will have been selected, and the favorable variation

will spread through the population, perhaps eventually changing it.

Genetic variation, the mainspring of natural selection, is reflected in variations of DNA, the material substance of heredity. Changes in the order of DNA's nitrogenous bases—called mutations—produce changes in the proteins which are usually, but not always, harmful. More important than these is the effect of genes recombining in sexually reproduced offspring.

Sexual reproduction provides the offspring with two sets of DNA, one from each parent. The processes that give rise to a half-set of chromosomes in a sperm or egg shuffle and recombine the genes on each chromosome to provide new combinations. Then, when sperm and egg fuse together at fertilization, the half-sets come together and even more combinations are produced. The world's enormous diversity of life can be explained in terms of a struggle that favors certain genetic combinations.

Iiwi
Vestiaria coccinea

Apapane
Himatione sanguinea

Laysan finch
Psittirostra cantans

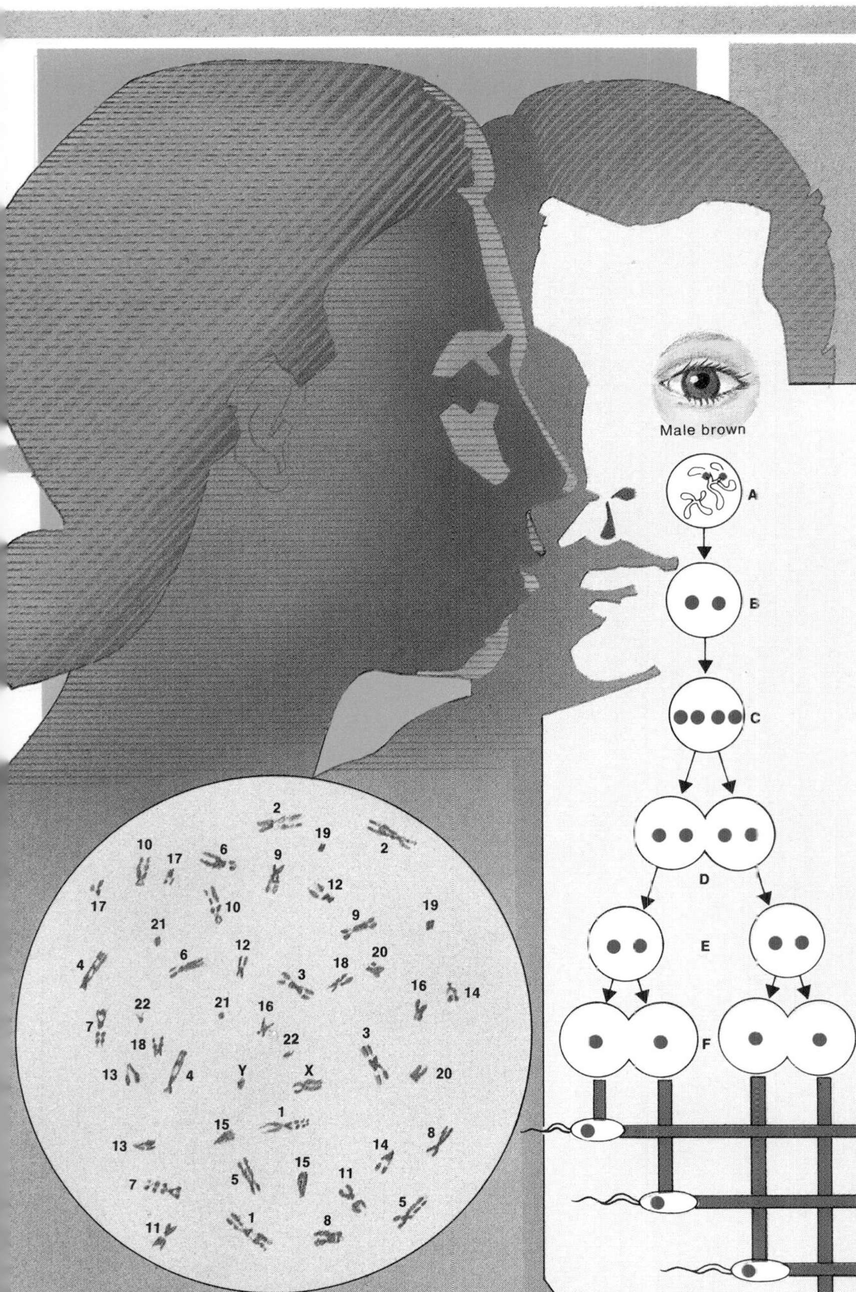

Some human traits, such as eye color, are inherited as single factors (below). In such cases one gene is dominant over the other, recessive, gene, and the gene giving a brown eye color is always dominant over that which gives a blue eye color. The chromosomes carrying eye-color genes (A) pair (B) and duplicate (C, D)

before dividing twice (E, F) in the process known as meiosis, or reduction division. This ensures that the offspring gets half the chromosomes from the male and half from the female parent, so each new cell gets both genes when sperm and egg unite. But because brown-eye genes are dominant over blue, all offspring have brown eyes,

with the blue-eye gene hidden. But if two brown-eyed parents carry recessive blue-eye genes, half the male sperm cells have blue-eye genes, and the female eggs carry a gene for either blue or brown eyes. So the two recessive genes have a one-in-four chance of being combined to produce a blue-eyed child, no brown-eye genes being present.

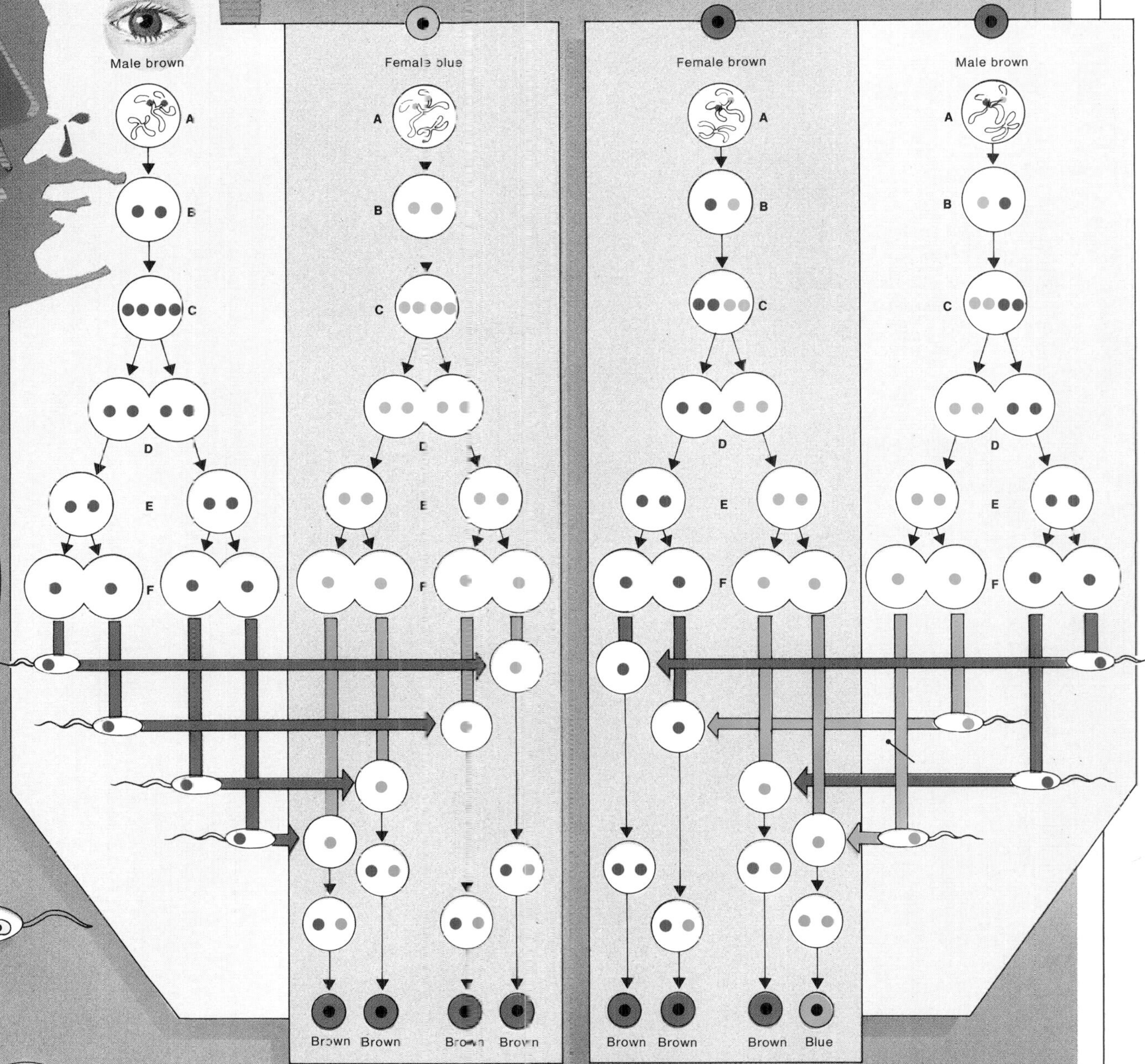

Male brown   Female blue   Female brown   Male brown

Brown   Brown   Brown   Brown   Brown   Brown   Brown   Blue

A human body cell (above) contains 46 chromosomes— 22 matching pairs and the chromosomes (X, Y) which determine sex. Males have X and Y, females X and X. In sexual reproduction (right) traits carried by the male sperm and the female egg combine in the zygote, the fertilized egg from which new life starts. All growth is the result of repeated cell division, or mitosis, where the nucleus forms paired chromosomes that duplicate themselves; the cell splits, and the chromosomes re-form in the nucleus of the new cells. Sex cells are produced by reduction division, or meiosis, with each cell taking only one from each pair of chromosomes, which exchange corresponding segments in the process called recombination. The genes are thus reshuffled at each generation, so that new combinations of gene traits are available for selection each time meiosis takes place. The result is genetic diversity, with many possibilities for the species to adapt to a changing environment.

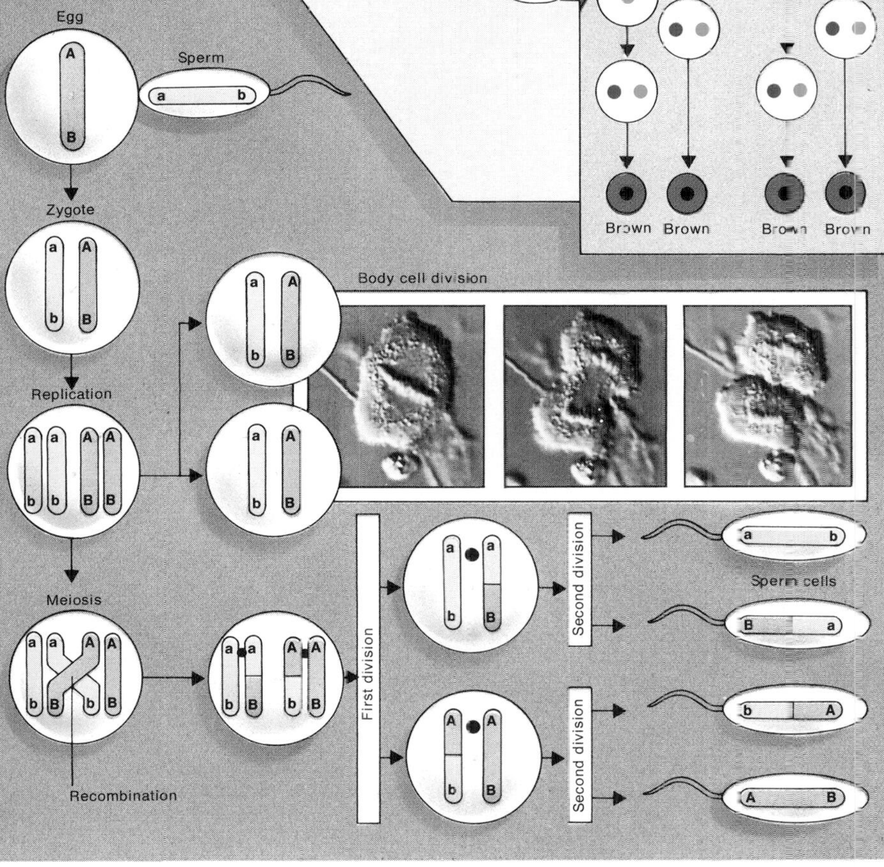

Egg   Sperm   Zygote   Replication   Meiosis   Recombination

Body cell division   First division   Second division   Sperm cells

A diversity of forms (left) has stemmed from a single ancestor of the Hawaiian honeycreeper, which now numbers 14 species. These have adapted in their mid-Pacific isolation to fill niches usually taken by other birds, ranging from the nectar-feeding iiwi to the Laysan finch with its thick beak for cracking seeds, and the short-billed apapane, which includes insects in its diet. But the honeycreepers' success in divergence may have led to overspecialization, with at least eight species now extinct. The Australian marsupial mouse and the Indian spiny mouse (right) look very similar, due to the fact that they fill similar ecological niches, but they belong to groups evolving separately for almost 100 million years.

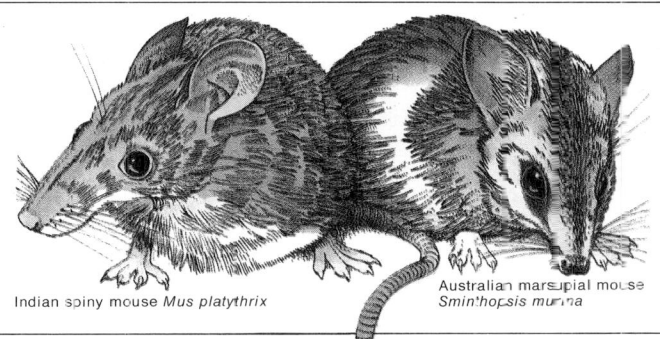

Indian spiny mouse *Mus platythrix*

Australian marsupial mouse *Sminthopsis murina*

VARIANT FORMS

Dark forms of many insects, such as the peppered moth *Biston betularia*, have developed widely in industrial areas of the world since the industrial age. The dark variant, resulting from a single genetic mutation, escapes the eye of predators against the black, lichen-free bark of soot-darkened trees (top), whereas the typical pale form is very conspicuous. In rural, unpolluted areas where tree trunks are light and lichen covered (bottom) the well-concealed pale form is much commoner. *Biston's* rapid evolutionary response is remarkable: in 1849 only one dark example was recorded at Manchester, England, but by 1900 98% of the moths caught in the area were of the dark type. A similar change occurred in other industrial areas, during the period when the most coal was being burned and the population was most rapidly expanding. But with today's clean-air laws the number of pale moths in these areas is once again on the increase.

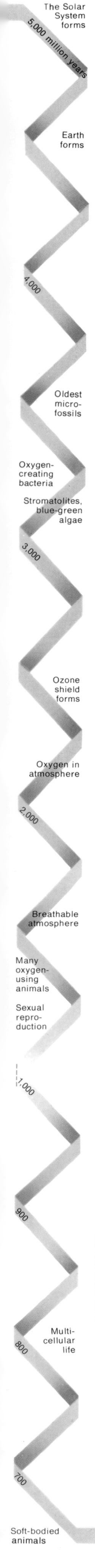

Earliest Life Forms

Earth's original atmosphere lacked oxygen, without which there could be no survival for air-breathing creatures. This vital gas was supplied by life itself, in the form of microscopic organisms that flourished in the atmosphere of the time and emitted oxygen as "waste." In this way a breathable atmosphere built up; increasingly complex life forms were able to develop in the seas; early plants and insects gained a foothold on the shores; and, finally, larger animals could survive on land.

A BREATHABLE ATMOSPHERE

Without oxygen, life as we know it could not exist; yet Earth's original atmosphere contained practically none. The oxygenation of the atmosphere was the work of the planet's first life—primeval bacteria and algae. Of these, some released oxygen as waste while consuming carbon dioxide or nitrogen in photosynthesis. Colonies of algae forming stromatolites ("stony carpets") generated even more oxygen, but this was first taken up by ocean rocks, visible today as "banded iron formations." Once all the ocean rocks were oxidized, an oxygen-rich atmosphere could develop, with an ozone layer to filter out harmful radiation from the Sun.

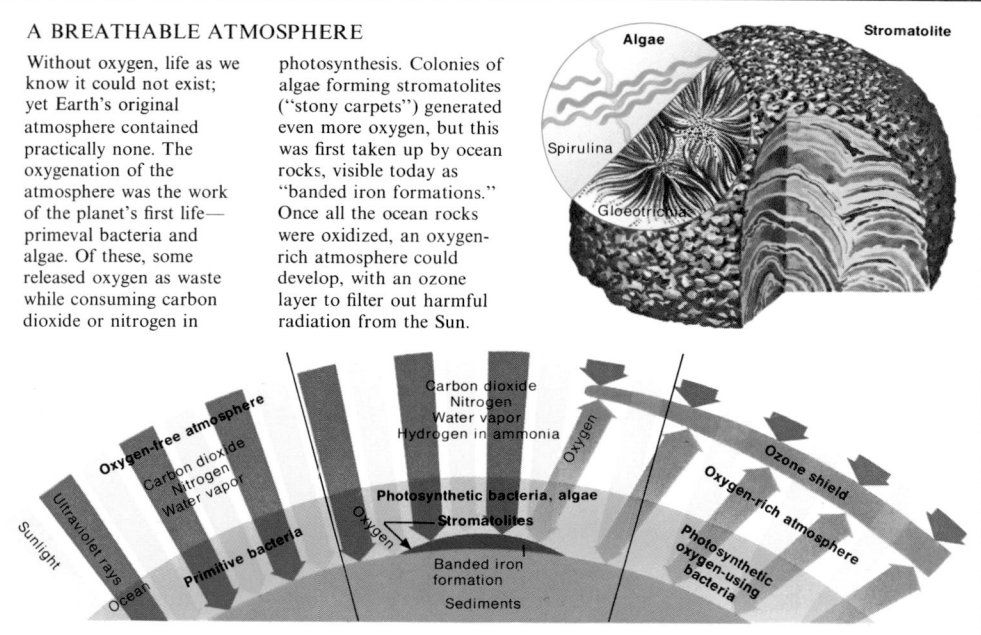

Scientists have identified bacteria-like microfossils in the rocks that were formed more than 3,500 million years ago. Some of these organisms appear to have been capable of photosynthesis—the process of utilizing sunlight, water and carbon dioxide for "food," with release of oxygen as the vitally important by-product. As a result, surplus oxygen very gradually accumulated in the Earth's atmosphere, forming an upper-atmosphere shield of ozone (which kept out damaging ultraviolet radiation from the Sun) and providing an oxygen-rich atmosphere in which breathing life could develop.

At least five types of microfossil have been found in ancient sediments of Western Australia, aged about 3,560 million years, and these provide the earliest evidence of life so far discovered. Other early proof of life comes from the so-called "stromatolites," some of which may date back as far as 3,400 million years. These curious columns, growing in warm, shallow waters, are formed of blue-green algae which have entrapped chalky sediments, bacteria and other microfossils. Their study is made easier by the fact that similar structures have developed at later geological times, and some are even being formed at the present day.

Living below the surface of the water and not initially reliant on oxygen for life, such bacteria and algae were shielded from the Sun's ultraviolet rays as they imperceptibly altered the Earth's atmosphere. For hundreds of millions of years life of this kind persisted, with few obvious developments or changes.

Breathing life

About 1,800 million years ago, the effects of these microscopic photosynthesizers became dramatically apparent in the "rusting" of the ocean sediments, when the red color of the rocks being formed at that time indicates that there was enough free oxygen on Earth to bring about the process known as oxidation. Once the ocean rocks capable of absorbing oxygen had done so, forming the red "banded iron formations" known to geologists, oxygen could enter the atmosphere in ever greater quantities.

It has been estimated that a breathable atmosphere existed on Earth about 1,700 million years ago, and aerobic (oxygen-using) organisms first became abundant not very long afterwards. These organisms were single celled, and it may have been almost 1,000 million years before multicellular animals evolved. The fossilized remains of animals alive 800 million years ago have been found in many parts of the world, but it is not yet known whether multicellular animals had a long history before these earliest known forms, or whether they had developed and radiated rapidly from a creature capable of feeding as well as photosynthesizing.

One of the earliest collections of animals of this type was discovered in the Ediacara Sandstones of the Flinders Range in Australia, where some 650 million years ago the rocks once formed part of an ancient beach. Here a spectacular collection of soft-bodied animals, similar to today's coelenterates (such as jellyfish) and worms, was washed ashore and preserved in silt from the nearby shallow sea. Comparable, mainly floating forms have been found in other parts of the world in rocks dating from between 650 and 580 million years ago.

The first vertebrates

One of the most important changes in animal life seems to have occurred about 580 million years ago. At that date many creatures evolved hard, protective shells, which also acted as areas of muscle attachment and as support for their bodies—in other words, as external skeletons. Hard shells were more easily preserved as fossils than the soft bodies of earlier animals, so rich collections have been recovered from rocks of the Cambrian Period, beginning 580 million years ago, as well as from later strata.

The first fish-like animals—the earliest true vertebrates—are found in rocks of the Ordovician Period, from about 500 million years ago, and these were in many ways very similar to the lampreys and hagfishes of today. But unlike them, these ancient creatures were heavily armored with external bone. They must have been poor swimmers, living mainly on the seabed and filtering edible particles from the sediments, which they sucked into their jawless mouths. From them arose true fishes, with backbones, jaws and teeth, and they came to replace the less efficient earlier forms.

During the Devonian Period, about 400 million years ago, the fishes diversified greatly, adapting to fit all kinds of aquatic environments. Some grew to a huge size, such as *Dunkleosteus*, which achieved a length of up to 9 m (29 ft 7 in), although it belonged to a group of fishes that retained heavy armor. Some of these curious creatures probably used their stilt-like pectoral fins to hitch themselves across the beds of the pools in which they lived.

From water to land

The fishes that teemed in the seas and fresh waters of the Devonian world found their way into difficult environments such as swamps and oasis pools, where there was a danger of drying out in the warmer weather. Many of these fishes had rudimentary lungs, and one group developed powerful jointed fins.

Such marginal habitats were not ideal for fishes, but they were nevertheless rich in species, and it is from them that the first land vertebrates developed. When the water dried up they survived, for their strong fins held them up so that they did not flop over helplessly.

They found themselves in a new, dry world, but one which was already inhabited, at least round the water's edges, with plants related to modern liverworts, mosses and club mosses. There were also numerous invertebrate animals such as millipedes, spiders and wingless insects. These plants and animals provided shelter and food, so that the environment was not wholly hostile to larger animals.

The first steps on land probably took the form of strong flexions of the body—desperate swimming movements which swung the fins forward, pegging the animal's position in the drying mud. But in a very short time geologically, animals had evolved in which the rays of the lobe fins had vanished, leaving stubby legs with which the animals—no longer fishes but amphibians—could haul themselves over land. But they still had to return to water to breed and lay eggs.

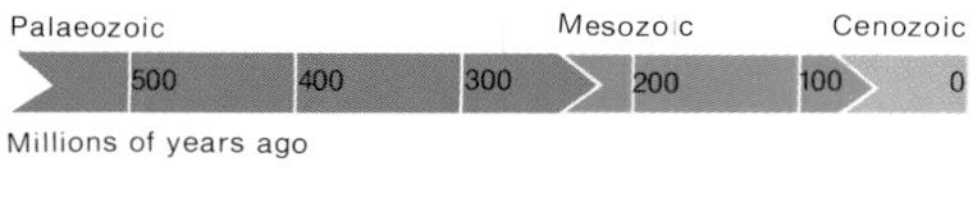

THE FIRST SHELLED CREATURES

These evolved (right) in the seas when conditions allowed soft-bodied life to form protective casings. In the fossil record of 550 million years ago, soft and shelled forms are found. The trilobites (1, 2, 3)—a now extinct order of woodlouse-like animals—dominated the scene, but other early arthropods (4) included a possible insect ancestor (5), and there may even have been an ancestor to fish (6). Sponges (7), crinoids (8), early moluscs (9), bristleworms (10) and lampshells (11) were plentiful, but other creatures (12) are bewilderingly strange.

THE FIRST AMPHIBIANS

Amphibians (1) emerged some 345 million years ago (right), inhabiting swampy environments with luxuriant vegetation—club mosses and ferns (2, 3) that made up the early coal forests. Lungfish (4) were well adapted to life in oxygen-poor waters, but the move to land was probably made by related fish with a passage linking nostrils to throat—*Eusthenopteron* (5). Land offered food (6, 7, 8) and suitably damp conditions for a possibly stranded aquatic animal.

Palaeozoic			Mesozoic		Cenozoic	
500	400	300	200	100	0	

Millions of years ago

A timescale of life on Earth emerges from the record of fossils embedded in rock strata. Major breaks in faunas (animal assemblages) separate eras coinciding roughly with periods of intense mountain-building activity. These eras are broken down into geological periods, which are separated by lesser faunal breaks and which are generally named from the area where rocks of that age were first discovered. The geological eras and periods do not imply particular rock types.

Left margin timeline:
The Solar System forms — 5,000 million years — Earth forms — 4,000 — Oldest micro-fossils — Oxygen-creating bacteria — Stromatolites, blue-green algae — 3,000 — Ozone shield forms — Oxygen in atmosphere — 2,000 — Breathable atmosphere — Many oxygen-using animals — Sexual reproduction — 1,000 — 900 — Multi-cellular life — 800 — 700 — Soft-bodied animals

Bottom timeline: 600 — Shelled/skeletal animals — CAMBRIAN — 550 — First fishes — ORDOVICIAN

LIFE ON SEA AND LAND

For more than half the Earth's existence, its atmosphere has been hostile to air-breathing life. Then, about 1,600 million years ago, the photosynthesizing action of minute organisms built up enough free oxygen in the atmosphere for more complex oxygen-dependent forms to develop. The first multicellular life led to the soft-bodied animals of the pre-Cambrian time—worms, jellyfish and sea pens. About 580 million years ago many animals developed hard parts, including shells. Over 1,200 new marine species date from this period, and the evolutionary explosion came to fill the Earth's seas with fishes. Some of these had powerful jointed fins and rudimentary lungs, and lived in swamps where primitive plants and insects had already made the move to land. As the pools dwindled the stranded animals could survive by breathing air.

THE AGE OF JELLYFISH

Jellyfish (left) and other soft-bodied animals flourished in the pre-Cambrian seas, more than 600 million years ago. The forms of one group, imprinted on sand, have been preserved as fossils in the Australian Ediacara Sandstones. They include varieties similar to modern jellyfish (1, 2); worm-like crawlers (3); sea pens (4) very like modern types; segmented worms (5); "three-legged" creatures like no known animal (6); and sand casts of burrowing worms (7).

LIVING FOSSILS

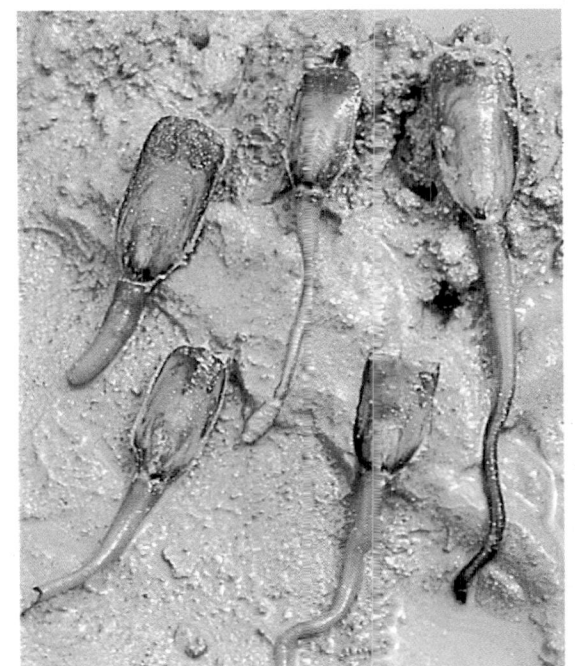
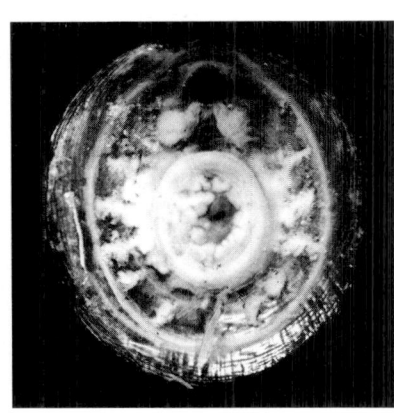

Some life forms that emerged 570 million years ago have survived virtually unchanged to the present day. These "living fossils" include *Lingula* (left), today found in warm, brackish coastal waters, poor in oxygen and unsuited to most life, off the Pacific and Indian oceans. *Neopilina* (below), a primitive marine mollusc first found alive in 1952, has features unlike other molluscs but suggesting much closer affinities with the annelids (worms) and arthropods (insects, crabs, etc.).

THE AGE OF JELLYFISH

1 Jellyfish (*Ediacaria*)
2 Jellyfish (*Medusina*)
3 Flatworm (*Dicxinsonia costata*)
4 Sea pens (*Rangea, Charnia*)
5 Segmented worms (*Spriggina floundersi*)
6 Unknown animal (*Tribrachidium*)
7 Burrowing worm (fossil casts)
8 Sponges and algae (hypothetical)

THE FIRST SHELLED CREATURES

1 Trilobites (*Waptia*)
2 Trilobites (*Marella splendens*)
3 Trilobite (*Oleroides serratus*)
4 Primitive arthropod (*Perspicaris dictynna*)
5 Primitive arthropod (*Aysheaia pedunculata*)
6 Ancestral lancelet fish (*Branchiostoma*)
7 Sponge (*Vauxia*)
8 Crinoids (*Echinatocrinus*)
9 Mollusc (*Wiwaxia*)
10 Bristleworm (*Nereis*)
11 Brachiopod (*Lingulella*)
12 Unknown animal (*Hallucigenia sparsa*)

THE AGE OF FISHES

1 Primitive plant (*Nematophyton*)
2 Psilophite plant (*Asteroxylon*)
3 Psilophite plant (*Rhynia*)
4 Primitive insect (*Rhyniella*)
5 Placoderm fish (*Bothriolepis*)
6 Placoderm fish (*Phyliolepis*)
7 Placoderm fish (*Dunkleosteus*)
8 Early shark (*Cladoselache*)
9 Lungfish (*Dipterus*)
10 Lobe-fin fish (*Osteolepis*)
11 Crustacean (*Montecaris*)

THE FIRST AMPHIBIANS

1 Amphibian (*Ichthyostega*)
2 Club moss (*Cyclostigma*)
3 Fern (*Pseudosporochnus*)
4 Lungfish (*Scaumenacia*)
5 Rhipidistian fish (*Eusthenopteron*)
6 Millipede (*Acantherpestes ornatus*)
7 Early scorpion (*Palaeophonus*)
8 Spider-like creature (*Palaeocharinoides*)
9 Small plant (*Sciadophyton*)

THE AGE OF FISHES

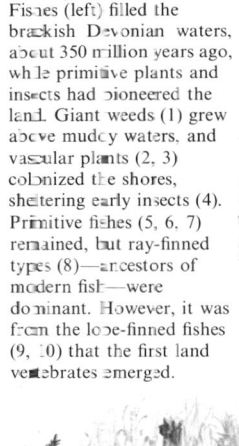

Fishes (left) filled the brackish Devonian waters, about 350 million years ago, while primitive plants and insects had pioneered the land. Giant weeds (1) grew above muddy waters, and vascular plants (2, 3) colonized the shores, sheltering early insects (4). Primitive fishes (5, 6, 7) remained, but ray-finned types (8)—ancestors of modern fish—were dominant. However, it was from the lobe-finned fishes (9, 10) that the first land vertebrates emerged.

The Age of Reptiles

When the Carboniferous Period began, the world was already populated with animals and plants of many kinds. The oceans were full of fishes, invertebrates and aquatic plants. The land, meanwhile, was producing dramatic new species: giant mosses and ferns, spiders and insects and, most important of all, the rapidly evolving amphibians. These creatures were taking the first evolutionary steps on a path that would lead to some of the most remarkable creatures ever to live – the dinosaurs.

The broad, low-lying, swampy plains of the late Carboniferous provided ideal conditions for the world's early plants. They spread and diversified, and some of them grew to enormous size. Giant club mosses, huge horsetails and luxuriant tree ferns took on the proportions of modern-day trees and formed the world's first forests. These new forests were full of animal life: primitive spiders and scorpions hunting their prey, giant dragonflies hovering over the marshy waters and other insects scavenging or hunting on the mossy forest floor or in the branches of the "trees." In the huge coal-forest swamps, the most advanced of all animals, the amphibians, were rapidly evolving. Some of these would ultimately return to life in the water. But others were developing stronger legs and were becoming better able to cope with an existence on dry land.

It was from this second group that the reptiles evolved—the first animals to be equipped with waterproof skins. Unlike their amphibian ancestors, they could stay out of the water indefinitely without losing their body fluids through their skins. They were no longer tied to the water's edge and the pattern of life was revolutionized. The world was soon inhabited by the first wave of land vertebrates—reptiles, which then rapidly diversified.

Included among these first reptiles were creatures known as sailbacks. They had a row of long, bony spines that supported a great fin running down from the back of their heads to the base of their tails. This whole apparatus functioned as a heat-exchange organ: the fin absorbed heat from the atmosphere in the early, cooler parts of the day, when the animal was cold, and blushed off warmth later, when it became overheated. Unlike the cold-blooded reptiles, sailbacked reptiles could, to a certain extent, regulate their body temperatures.

Mammal-like reptiles
It was only about 50 million years later, however, that animals skeletally identical to mammals were found throughout the world. Almost certainly these creatures had a degree of warm-bloodedness. But they were all rather small—the biggest was no larger than a domestic cat—and this may account for their decline. They were destined to be overshadowed for many millions of years by the dinosaurs.

The late Triassic Period, about 200 million years ago, is marked by a sudden decline in the

THE RULING REPTILES
Seymouria and other advanced amphibians evolved to form the first reptiles, such as *Scutosaurus*. From these a multitude of adaptations evolved. Some herbivores, such as *Corythosaurus*, developed 2,000 or more teeth, to help them consume tough, fibrous food plants. Another herbivorous group attained enormous size—*Brachiosaurus* weighed as much as 80 tonnes—and this may have been an adaptation to regulate body temperature (large objects lose and gain heat more slowly than small objects). Another adaptation, but one that developed mainly in the carnivores, was that of offensive weaponry: *Deinonychus* had a huge sickle-shaped claw on each hind foot and the later *Tyrannosaurus* combined a massive body with a jagged mouthful of 60 teeth. Armor plating was a defensive adaptation, produced by herbivores such as *Triceratops*, whereas speed of movement was developed both by some herbivores and by small carnivores such as *Struthiomimus*.

Corythosaurus

Deinonychus

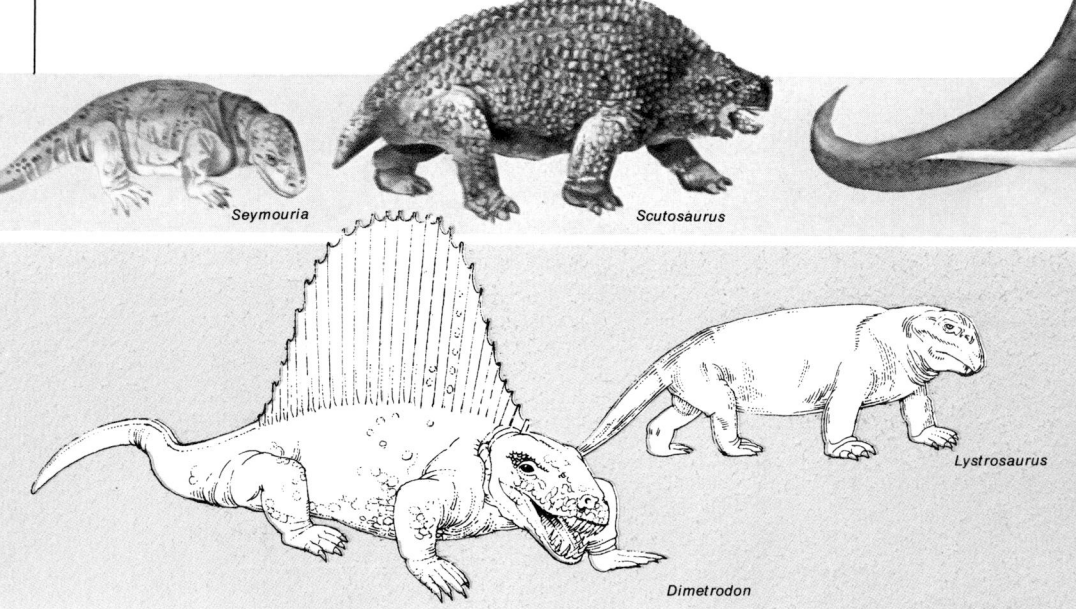

Seymouria

Scutosaurus

Lystrosaurus

Dimetrodon

THE MAMMAL LINE
Sailbacks such as *Dimetrodon* mark the beginning of mammal history. These reptiles had developed the first method of regulating body temperature—each was equipped with a large fin on its back which acted as a heat-exchange organ, a living solar panel. From these strange creatures, para-mammals such as *Lystrosaurus* evolved, animals with many mammal-like features. Some of the later members of this group, such as *Thrinaxodon*, probably even had fur on their bodies. Then, about 200 million years ago, the first true warm-blooded mammals, such as *Morganucodon*, developed. But by this time the group as a whole was declining in response to reptilian competition. Mammals would have to wait 140 million years before becoming successful again.

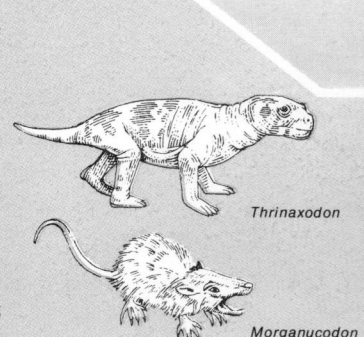

Thrinaxodon

Morganucodon

COAL FORMATION
Coal consists of carbon from plant remains and most of it was formed in the swamp-forests from which reptiles emerged. First, peat formed from rotted vegetation. Sea levels rose, ocean covered the peat bogs and marine sediments were laid down. The resulting pressure converted peat to coal. The cycle recurred and the deepest coal seams were compressed and hardened.

Coal-forming forest swamp
Peat layer
Lignite seam
Bituminous seam
Anthracite seam

Palaeozoic — Mesozoic — Cenozoic
500 400 300 200 100 0
Millions of years ago

Three geological eras mark the evolution of life on Earth. It was the Mesozoic era, beginning 230 million years ago, that spanned the age of reptiles. Until then, throughout the Palaeozoic era, life had been slowly evolving from the primitive organisms that appeared 400 million years earlier.

By the Mesozoic, the earliest reptiles had developed. Among their descendants were dinosaurs and early representatives of the mammalian line. Mammals, however, would have to wait another 165 million years, until the Cenozoic, before they achieved dominance.

Cycadale

Gingko biloba

The plant communities underwent as many developments in the course of the Mesozoic era as did the reptiles. The end of the Palaeozoic saw changes in climate—the Permian Period was much drier than the Carboniferous. Giant horsetails, ferns and club mosses that had formed the world's first forests gave way to other types of plant: early conifers and their relatives

(the gymnosperms) came to the fore. These new species, such as the Cycadales, had evolved a new, improved method of reproduction—using seeds not spores. By Jurassic times, the climate had changed again and the moist conditions supported dense forests of ferns and of conifers. The final major Mesozoic development took place in Cretaceous times, when the flowering plants evolved.

CARBONIFEROUS | 300 | Earliest reptiles ▶ PERMIN Early conifers | 250 | First radiation of reptiles ▶ TRIASSIC | First mammals

EVOLUTION AND ADAPTATION

Once their amphibian ancestors had crawled from the swamps, reptiles rapidly evolved and developed a remarkable range of adaptations: they took to the air, invaded the seas and held dominion over the land. By early Jurassic times, they had firmly established their claim to the title Ruling Reptiles. Another group of early reptile descendants led to the mammals, and although these were long overshadowed by the dinosaurs, they were destined to rise to dominance.

mammal-like reptiles and by the extraordinary evolutionary radiation of the so-called Archosaurs ("ruling reptiles"). These began to fill every available ecological niche. They evolved into carnivores, herbivores and omnivores. They included the Crocodilians, which adapted to a life in the water; the flying pterosaurs, which were the first vertebrates to fly, and, most important of all, the dinosaurs, whose evolutionary reign over the land was to endure for the next 140 million years.

Dinosaurs adapted well to life on the land. They developed "fully erect" limbs (not unlike those of the later higher mammals) rather than the splayed legs found in most other reptiles. The new position of their limbs, which gave them the necessary mobility on dry land, was also accompanied by a general increase in size. But the dinosaurs were not the only land reptiles of the time; many other forms, including tortoises, snakes and lizards, were also carving their niches during the Mesozoic era.

Similarly, the pterosaurs did not remain the only creatures of the sky. By 170 million years ago, birds in the form of claw-winged *Archaeopteryx* had evolved, and these were to prove a serious challenge to the primitive winged reptiles which had poor flying abilities.

Aquatic reptiles

Just as the land and the air were rapidly inhabited by newly evolving forms, so the water produced many new developments. Several of the Mesozoic reptiles began to adapt to aquatic life in ways often parallel to present-day mammals: the long-necked, fish-eating plesiosaurs led a life much like that of seals; the larger

pliosaurs had a streamlined shape similar to that of certain whales; some mollusc-eating placodonts could be likened to the walrus; and the elegant icthyosaurs were in many ways like dolphins. Large invertebrates were also found in the seas. The most dramatic of these were the ammonites—shelled relatives of the octopus—some of which grew to more than 2 m (6 ft) in size. Among fishes a new type emerged, the Teleosts, and these were destined to become the dominant fishes of the modern world.

Wholesale extinction

At the end of the Cretaceous Period, the reptiles were flourishing. Then suddenly, 65 million years ago, a catastrophe occurred. Virtually every species, including all the large animals, were wiped out. Throughout the Mesozoic, a series of dinosaurs and other reptiles had been evolving and slowly becoming extinct, but they were always replaced by other species. This wholesale extinction was unprecedented.

The cause of the catastrophe is unknown, but since the nature of the Earth itself was unchanged, it seems likely that some outside phenomenon was responsible. One theory suggests that a large meteorite collided with the Earth, throwing enough dust into the atmosphere to blot out the sun for several years—long enough to kill almost all the green plants on land and in the sea. If this was the case, only small animals that fed on carrion, decaying vegetation, seeds or nuts could hope to survive. Whatever the cause, the reign of the reptiles was at an end, leaving the small, adaptable mammals and birds to recolonize the virtually empty planet during the Cenozoic era.

Brachiosaurus

Tyrannosaurus rex

Struthiomimus

Rhamphorhynchus

Triceratops

Archaeopteryx

Plesiosaurus

Ichthyornis

Plesiosaurs evolved at the same time as the dinosaurs and were as successful in their marine environment as were the dinosaurs on land. They were most common in Jurassic times.

Pterosaurs such as *Rhamphorhynchus* were the first vertebrates to take to the sky. They were not strong fliers and probably glided on air currents much of the time.

Birds are relatives of the reptiles. The first bird, *Archaeopteryx*, evolving in Jurassic times, had many reptilian features—a long bony tail, toothed mouth and clawed wings. By Cretaceous times, birds such as *Ichthyornis* had a more familiar form.

Norfolk Island pine
Araucaria heterophylla

Williamsonia

Common oak
Quercus robur

Fig tree
Ficus sp

Plane tree
Platanus sp

liation of reptiles **JURASSIC** First birds | 150 | **CRETACEOUS** First flowering plants | 100 First modern fishes | Extinction of dinosaurs

The Age of Mammals

After the time of the great dying, 65 million years ago, reptiles never regained the importance they had achieved during the Mesozoic era. A new era, the Cenozoic, had begun. On the continental landmasses, mammals and birds, newly released from 160 million years of reptilian domination, began to occupy their niches in the rich, empty habitats. They flourished and diversified, and the cold-blooded reptiles became second-class citizens in a world of warm-blooded animals.

While reptiles still dominated the world, during the late Mesozoic, a new group of mammals had arisen. These were the first creatures on Earth to give birth to fully formed, live young. Until this time, the most advanced of the mammals had been marsupials whose young were still virtually embryos at birth and had to develop in the mother's pouch, or marsupium. The new mammals had evolved a more sophisticated system—the mother retained the fetus safely inside her body until it was fully formed, nourishing it during this time through a special organ, the placenta, developed during pregnancy. These mammals, the placentals, were destined to become the major mammalian group.

Although all the Mesozoic placentals were small, they had already evolved into a number of different forms that existed alongside the dinosaurs. Besides the insectivores, which were the ancestral type, they included early representatives of the Primates (precursors of modern monkeys and apes), the Carnivores, and the now extinct Condylarthrans (primitive hoofed mammals). When suddenly, 65 million years ago, there was no longer competition from the large land reptiles, these early groups rapidly evolved and extravagant forms developed.

But just as the first reptiles had passed through an early evolution, largely to be replaced by a second evolutionary wave, so the first large mammals were, in many cases, superseded by other, more successful lines. In the earliest part of the Cenozoic era, the different groups of placentals, although not closely related, all tended to be heavy limbed and heavy tailed and to walk on the whole length of their feet (as do modern bears) or on thick, stubby toes. These ungainly, thickset mammals soon died out. Some became extinct because their descendants, more efficiently adapted to their environment, overtook and replaced them. Others, such as the powerful taeniodonts and the large rodent-like tillodonts, seem to have been evolutionary blind alleys.

Spectacular developments

It was the Oligocene Period, 36 million years ago, that saw the end of most of these early essays in mammalian gigantism, but, in many parts of the world, they were replaced by others just as spectacular. In South America, the giant sloths and glyptodonts (massive relatives of the armadillos) survived until comparatively recently. The ground sloths, at least, were contemporaries of the first men on the continent.

As each group of early mammals evolved, during the early and middle part of the Cenozoic era, many of their developments closely reflected changes taking place in their environment. The first horse-like creature, for example, was *Hyracotherium*, also called *Eohippus* or "dawn horse." It lived 54 million years ago and was a small, multi-toed creature, well adapted to its densely forested habitat. The teeth of its descendants gradually changed in size and complexity, but it was not until the Miocene Period, nearly 20 million years later, that any radical alterations took place. This was the time when grasses (the Gramineae), until then a rare family of plants, came to the fore. The world's plains suddenly became clothed in a food plant very suitable for the attention of grazing creatures such as the early horses.

Animals of the grasslands

Horses and many other animals moved from the forests to make use of this new and abundant food supply. Once on the plains, different adaptations for survival were required: high-crowned teeth to deal with tough grasses; limbs enabling the animal to run tirelessly without extra, unwanted weight from supporting side toes (which were lost); large eyes capable of seeing for long distances and placed far back on the head for detecting predators approaching from any direction (as a result of which, however, the ability to judge distances ahead had to be sacrificed). Thus, the modern horses are plains-dwelling animals, perfectly adapted to their present way of life.

Mammals reached the climax of diversity during the Pliocene Period, 10 million years ago. But in the following period, the Pleistocene, ice sheets swept down from the polar regions and from the high mountains of the north, bringing massive and sudden changes to the ecology of virtually every region in the world. This dramatic disturbance to the environment brought extinction to an enormous number of species.

The survivors consisted mainly of the smaller species. Unfortunately for many of them, however, they included *Homo sapiens*. Man rose to success at the end of the Pleistocene and has, in the last 10,000 years, taken dominion over virtually every part of the world. During this time, he has proved far more destructive to other animal species than any natural force has ever been. More than 5,000 years ago, the giant sloths may have been a dying species, but there is no doubt that early human hunters hurried on their extinction. Since then, the list of species eliminated by man has grown ever longer. Today the human race is causing the extinction of both animals and plants at a rate comparable to that of 65 million years ago, when some dramatic natural catastrophe swept the dinosaurs from the face of the world. Unless man, the super-efficient species, can curb his numbers and his destructive activities, a new age of dying may soon be upon the world.

By early Cenozoic times, many forms had evolved from the insectivorous mammals of the Mesozoic Period. *Miacis*, *Hyaenodon* and *Oxyaena* were flesh eaters. Plant-eating mammals, such as Taeniodonts, *Arsinoitherium* and *Phenacodus* (one of the first hoofed mammals), had also evolved, while other early forms, such as *Andrewsarchus*, were omnivorous. The early Primates, however, remained insect eaters for millions of years.

EARLY STAGES

Miacis

Andrewsarchus

Hyaenodon

Ars

Diatryma

Euryapteryx

CENOZOIC BIRDS
Giant flightless birds came to the fore more than once during the Cenozoic era. *Diatryma*, a massive, flesh-eating bird, ruled the North American grasslands in early Cenozoic times, while mammals were still small, fairly primitive and easily dominated. *Euryapteryx* and its relatives (the moas) evolved in New Zealand, where, because there were no mammals, they filled an empty ecological niche.

The Carnivores diversified into two major types—the cats and their kin (Aeluroidea), and the dogs and their relatives (Arctoidea). During the Oligocene Period, about 36 million years ago, Aeluroidea gave rise not only to early relatives of modern cats, such as sabre-toothed *Hoplophoneus*, but also to two other families, the civets and the hyenas. At the same time, Arctoidea also diversified and produced the dogs, weasels, bears and racoons. It was a complex group, with many forms that were later to become extinct—the massive bear-dogs, such as *Daphoenus*, for example, which lived during the Miocene Period. Cats and dogs evolved to exploit different habitats. The cats adapted to life in forests, and learned to hide and then stalk and ambush their prey. Dogs evolved as plains animals, and used pack-hunting techniques to catch fleet-footed, grassland animals.

Perissodactyls and Artiodactyls were two important groups that evolved from the primitive hoofed mammals; Perissodactyls had an odd number of toes on each foot, Artiodactyls had an even number. These two groups suffered very different fortunes. Artiodactyls are still at the height of their success; the early stock produced the modern pig, camel, deer, giraffe, hippopotamus, antelope, sheep, goat and cow. Perissodactyls, however, are in decline and the only survivors are the horse, rhinoceros and tapir. But they were once important and many, now-extinct, kinds such as *Moropus* and *Brontotherium* existed alongside more familiar types such as *Hyracotherium*. Few remained after the Pliocene Period, however. This was when the Artiodactyls came to the fore. They, too, had had casualties—the pig-like *Archaeotherium* was by then extinct—but many other Artiodactyls, such as the early giraffe, *Palaeotragus*, were evolving. Most important, however, was small *Archaeomeryx*, for it had developed the key to Artiodactyl success—it was a ruminant and this enabled it to make the best possible use of the world's new grasslands.

Palaeozoic			Mesozoic		Cenozoic
500	400	300	200	100	0

Millions of years ago

Three geological eras mark the slow evolution of life on Earth. The Palaeozoic era, 570 million years ago, saw the appearance of the first primitive life forms. By the end of the era, 340 million years later, the reptiles had evolved and the following Mesozoic era was the age of reptilian domination. This reign over the land ended 65 million years ago as the Cenozoic era began. Then mammals came to the fore and the age of mammalian dominance of the world had dawned.

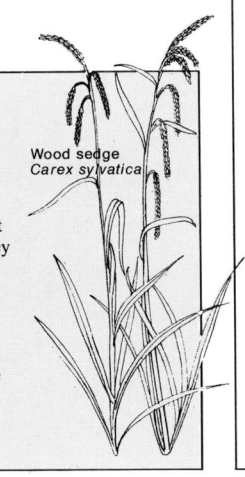

EARLY GRASSES
Grasses first appeared in the densely forested lands of 60 million years ago. Probably similar to the sedges (right) found in wet woodland areas today, they offered an attractive meal to many mammals. But it was not until the Miocene Period, when a change in climate reduced forest cover, that grasses became widespread. Then many forest creatures migrated to grassland areas.

Wood sedge
Carex sylvatica

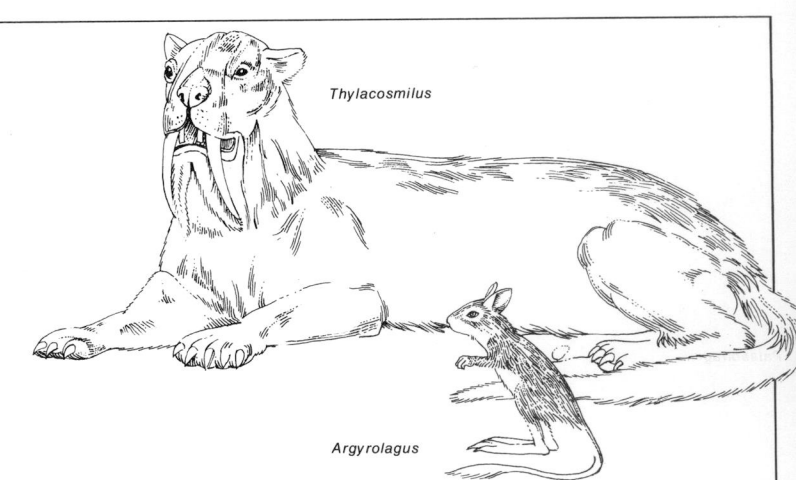

THE MARSUPIALS
Thylacosmilus and mouse-like *Argyrolagus* were two of the many forms of marsupial mammal that evolved in Cenozoic times in South America. Almost everywhere else, the marsupials, unable to compete with their more efficient placental cousins, met with an early extinction. But in two remote regions—South America (then separate from North America) and Australia—there was no competition from placentals, and there the marsupials flourished.

Thylacosmilus

Argyrolagus

TERTIARY	First radiation of mammals and birds		Forest horses			Second radiation of mammals
Palaeocene	60	**Eocene**	50	40	**Oligocene**

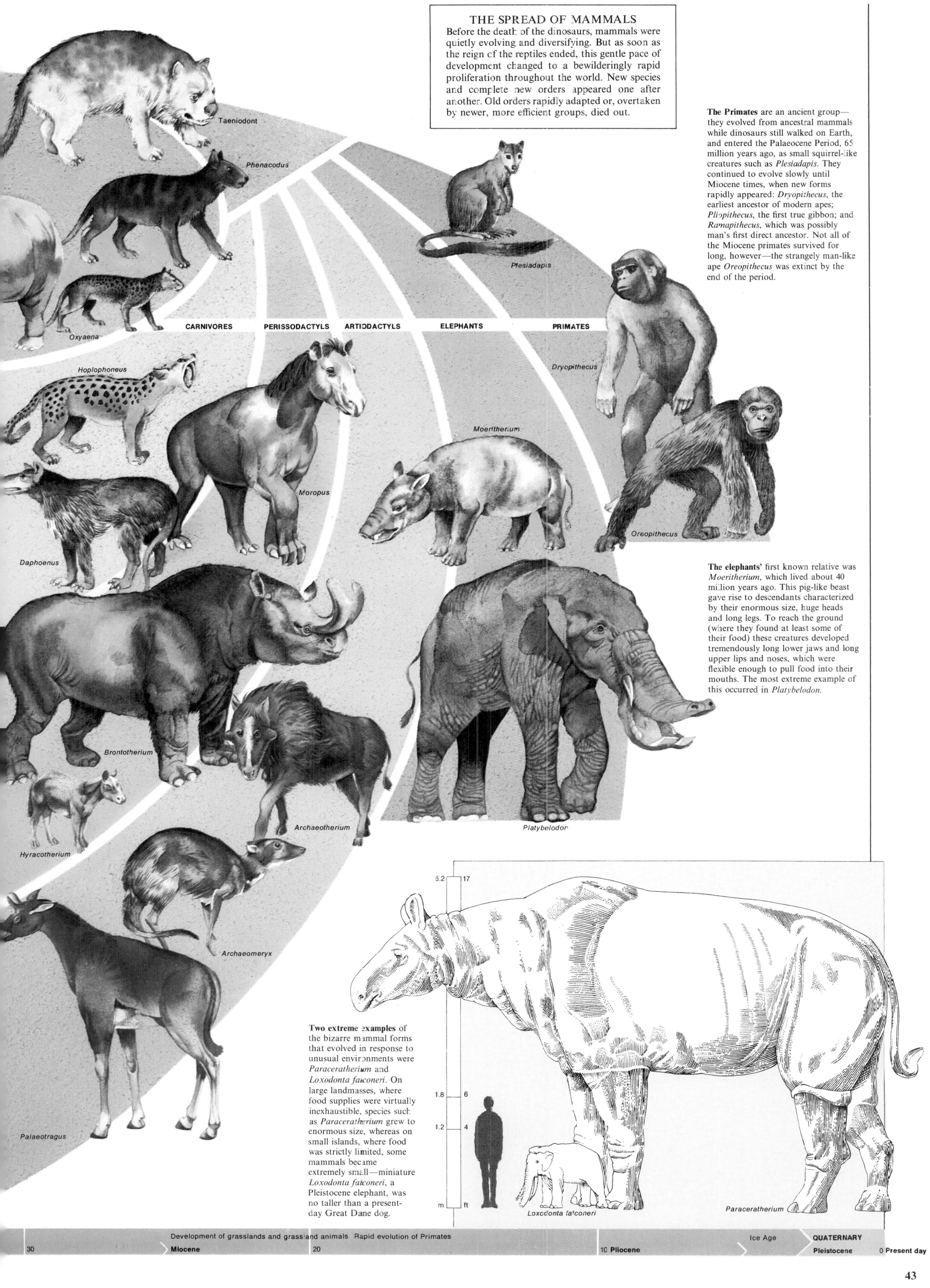

THE SPREAD OF MAMMALS

Before the death of the dinosaurs, mammals were quietly evolving and diversifying. But as soon as the reign of the reptiles ended, this gentle pace of development changed to a bewilderingly rapid proliferation throughout the world. New species and complete new orders appeared one after another. Old orders rapidly adapted or, overtaken by newer, more efficient groups, died out.

The Primates are an ancient group—they evolved from ancestral mammals while dinosaurs still walked on Earth, and entered the Palaeocene Period, 65 million years ago, as small squirrel-like creatures such as *Plesiadapis*. They continued to evolve slowly until Miocene times, when new forms rapidly appeared: *Dryopithecus*, the earliest ancestor of modern apes; *Pliopithecus*, the first true gibbon; and *Ramapithecus*, which was possibly man's first direct ancestor. Not all of the Miocene primates survived for long, however—the strangely man-like ape *Oreopithecus* was extinct by the end of the period.

The elephants' first known relative was *Moeritherium*, which lived about 40 million years ago. This pig-like beast gave rise to descendants characterized by their enormous size, huge heads and long legs. To reach the ground (where they found at least some of their food) these creatures developed tremendously long lower jaws and long upper lips and noses, which were flexible enough to pull food into their mouths. The most extreme example of this occurred in *Platybelodon*.

Taeniodont

Phenacodus

Oxyaena

Plesiadapis

CARNIVORES   PERISSODACTYLS   ARTIODACTYLS   ELEPHANTS   PRIMATES

Hoplophoneus

Dryopithecus

Moropus

Moeritherium

Oreopithecus

Daphoenus

Brontotherium

Platybelodon

Hyracotherium

Archaeotherium

Archaeomeryx

Palaeotragus

Two extreme examples of the bizarre mammal forms that evolved in response to unusual environments were *Paraceratherium* and *Loxodonta falconeri*. On large landmasses, where food supplies were virtually inexhaustible, species such as *Paraceratherium* grew to enormous size, whereas on small islands, where food was strictly limited, some mammals became extremely small—miniature *Loxodonta falconeri*, a Pleistocene elephant, was no taller than a present-day Great Dane dog.

5.2   17

1.8   6

1.2   4

m   ft

Loxodonta falconeri

Paraceratherium

Spread of Life

Different parts of the Earth have their own characteristic groups of animals, and this pattern of distribution caused nineteenth-century zoologists to divide the world into zoogeographical regions. Charles Darwin suggested how these assemblages of animals may have come about by the process of evolution. But we now know that movements of the Earth's land surfaces are also responsible for the present-day distribution of many of the world's animal species and groups.

The evolution of a major group of animals, such as the reptiles or the mammals, tends to follow a set pattern in five stages. First the original ancestral group spreads out, with each subgroup adapting to its environment. This process, called adaptive radiation, results in a variety of different kinds of animals, each suited to life in a particular niche or habitat—determined largely by food supply and environmental conditions. The different kinds then move into all of the areas they can reach in which the environment is right, producing the second stage of widespread distribution.

Competition for food or living space, or changes in climate may then cause some forms to decline and disappear from parts of the range, resulting in a third stage of discontinuous distribution. Any further reduction leads to isolated relict populations—the fourth stage—in which the animal exists only in one or two limited areas. The final stage is extinction.

In all distribution patterns, however, there is not only an ecological element but also a historical one, with past events determining where animals are and where they are not. There are thus two basic types of distribution: continuous, where the area is not interrupted by an insurmountable barrier (such as a mountain range), and discontinuous, where the area of distribution is subdivided and there is no way that members of one group can interchange with members of another.

One of these factors—the earliest and most important—is the (continuing) movement of the Earth's tectonic plates. This caused the supercontinent Pangaea to break up, probably in the Triassic Period (225–180 million years ago), and the continental masses to drift apart to their present positions. New oceans developed, separating the Americas from the Euro-African block and splitting both from Antarctica. Madagascar and Australia became islands, India moved north from Africa to join the Asian block, and mountain ranges such as the Alps, Andes, Rockies and Himalayas were thrown up. As a result, animal types that had already evolved on Pangaea or its fragments before they had significantly separated (i.e. all the major invertebrate groups and most of the earlier vertebrates) can be expected to exist on all the present-day continents.

Bridging the continents

Independently of these activities, ice ages occurred from time to time, resulting in the vast accumulations of ice at the poles and a consequent general lowering of the sea level by as much as 100 m (330 ft). This temporarily exposed the previously submerged continental shelves, providing additional land for colonization, and new corridors that linked existing areas, such as the land bridge that appeared between Alaska and Siberia.

Groups that had evolved after the breakup of Pangaea, e.g. the hare, squirrel and dog families, made use of land bridges as the climate allowed, and came to occupy more than one continent. Flying animals—birds and bats—also made intercontinental crossings and established themselves on both sides of oceans, although a surprising number of these have remained very restricted in distribution. But most animals have to stay where they are because of special dietary or environmental requirements, or because they are "trapped" on islands, such as Madagascar and Australia, and cannot get off. These areas have the most distinctive faunas in the world.

Barriers and corridors

The extent to which an expanding group can spread from its original area depends on whether there are barriers, such as mountain ranges, deserts or seas, or corridors that link major areas in which the animals can live. Different animals have different environmental requirements, and so a topographical feature that is a barrier for one may be a corridor for another.

The dispersal of many animals is achieved by "hopping" from lake to lake across a continent, or from island to island across a sea. Some, such as insects, are good at this, whereas others, such as land mammals, are bad. Thus a considerable range of weevils (Curculionidae) are found on islands from New Caledonia to the Marquesas, some 6,500 km (4,000 miles) across the southern Pacific Ocean, whereas the marsupials of the region are concentrated in Australia, Papua New Guinea and a few adjacent islands, with only one genus reaching the Celebes and none crossing Wallace's Line into Borneo.

An example of colonization by "hopping" is seen on the volcanic island of Krakatoa near Java, which exploded in 1883 destroying all life. Within 25 years there were 263 species of animals on the island. Most were insects, but there were three species of land snails, two species of reptiles and 16 of birds. In another 22 years, 46 species of vertebrates had arrived, including two species of rats.

The effect of man

Animal distribution cannot be considered merely as a natural phenomenon, because it has been greatly and increasingly modified by man's impact on the environment. Agricultural practice has made large sections of the land area unsuitable for many of the animals that originally lived there, notably through the clearing of forests and the draining of marshes.

Man has also introduced animals, either deliberately or accidentally, to regions where they were not endemic. The rabbit in Australia and the deer in New Zealand were both deliberately introduced, but rats, cockroaches and many other animals have been accidentally transported throughout the world on ships and aircraft. The enormous growth in human population has driven many animals from their natural homes and into more remote environments, such as mountains. Indeed, in the past century human interference has altered the pattern of animal distribution more drastically than any topographic or climatic change.

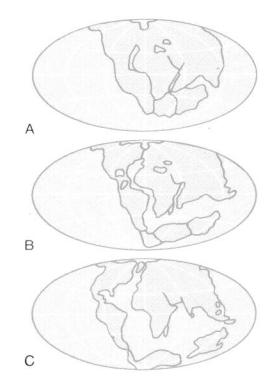

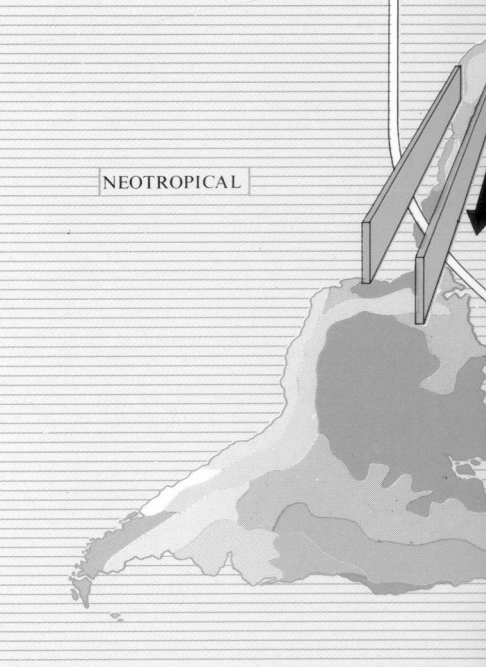

Earth's original single landmass, Pangaea (A), probably began to break up more than 200 million years ago. Species that had already evolved diversified on the Noah's Arks of the drifting supercontinents (B), called Laurasia and Gondwanaland. As the process continued (C), related animals flourished in the separated continents of the southern hemisphere.

NEOTROPICAL

PATTERNS OF ANIMALS

Over the ages the shape of the Earth has changed. Whole continents have moved; mountains and deserts have grown; land bridges between continents have opened and closed. These events, together with food supply, climate and other animals, account for the present natural pattern of life in the six zoogeographical regions, each containing a unique mix of animals. But man's activities have drastically affected this natural distribution in all parts of the world.

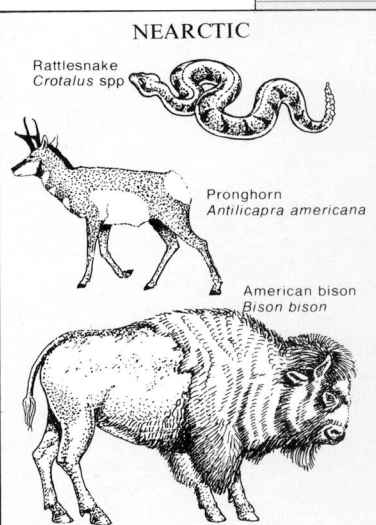

NEARCTIC

Rattlesnake
Crotalus spp

Pronghorn
Antilicapra americana

American bison
Bison bison

The Nearctic or "New North" region covers all of North America, from the highlands of Mexico in the south to Greenland and the Aleutian Islands in the north. Its climate and vegetation resemble that of the Palearctic region, and many of its mammals crossed over from the Palearctic via the Bering land bridge, which linked Siberia and Alaska when the sea level was lower. Animals unique to the Nearctic group include the pronghorn, an antelope-like mammal that inhabits the grasslands and plains of western and central America, and the bison, another large mammal that inhabits the prairies. Several species of rattlesnakes also belong to the Nearctic group, although they are not exclusive to this region.

NEOTROPICAL

Two-toed sloth
Choloepus didactylus

Marmoset
Callithrix jacchus

Crested seriema
Cariama cristata

The Neotropical or "New Tropical" region consists of South America, the West Indies and most of Mexico. The climate and vegetation are mostly tropical—only the southern tip is in the temperate zone—and it is linked to the Nearctic by the Central American corridor. The Neotropical region has more distinctive families than any other. These include, among mammals, the sloth, which inhabits the tropical forests and has adapted to an upside-down existence. Among birds, the long-legged crested seriema is also unique to the region. Neotropical monkeys, such as the marmoset, have lateral-facing nostrils, which distinguish them from their downward-nosed relatives found in the Old World.

Land routes around the world have altered with the ages, sometimes allowing invaders to penetrate new lands, or closing to form natural sanctuaries for less efficient animals. The Central American isthmus (A) opened South America to placental mammals from the north. The Sahara desert closed most of Africa (B) to Eurasian species. Asia and Australia (C) share "island hoppers" in the transitional zones, but sea barriers have kept the regions separate.

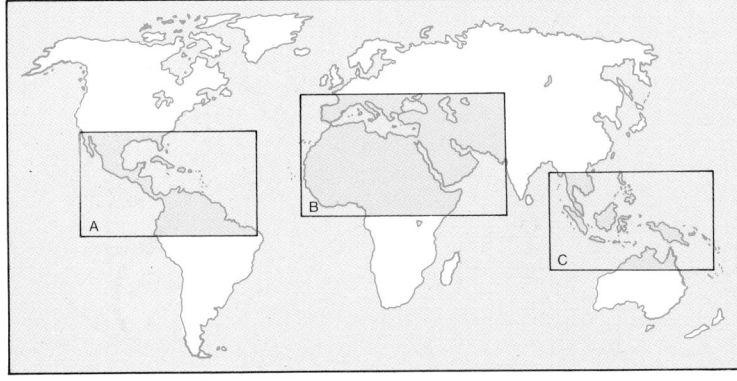

A land bridge between the Americas emerged about three million years ago, breaking the long isolation of the south. The primitive pouched mammals which had developed there were now threatened by more advanced mammals from the north, and many extinctions followed. Northern invaders included peccaries, raccoons and a llama-like camelid. But members of the armadillo and opossum families were successful in making their way to the northern region.

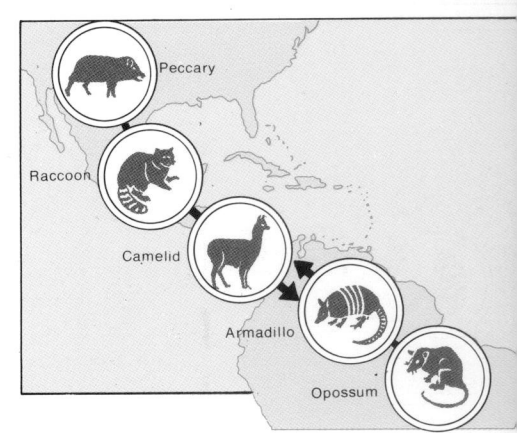

Peccary

Raccoon

Camelid

Armadillo

Opossum

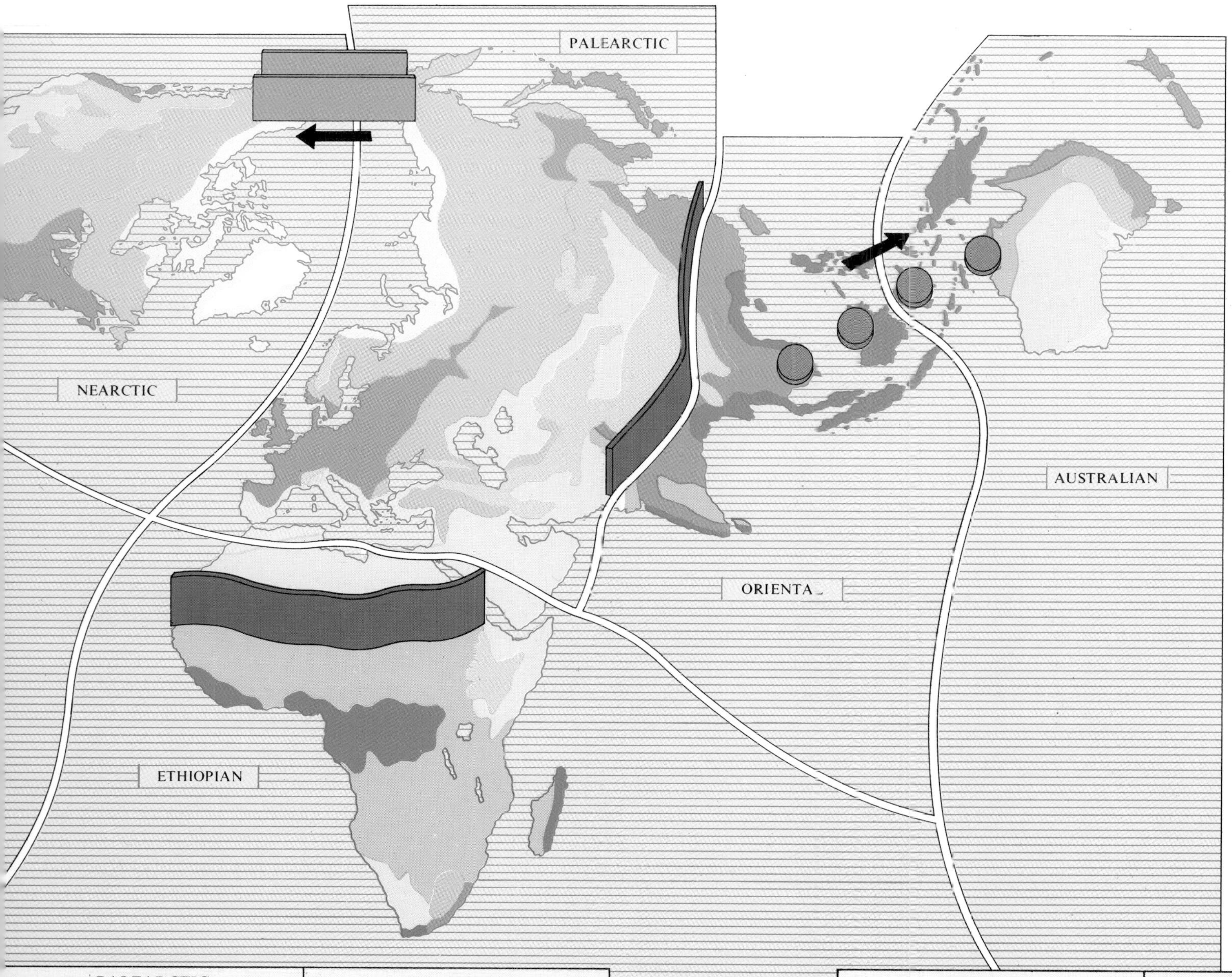

PALEARCTIC

NEARCTIC

ORIENTAL

AUSTRALIAN

ETHIOPIAN

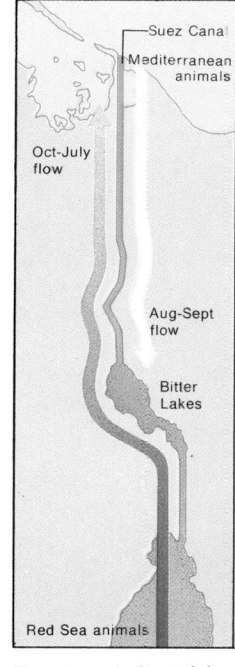

Suez Canal
Mediterranean animals

Oct-July flow

Aug-Sept flow

Bitter Lakes

Red Sea animals

The man-made filter of the Suez Canal, cut in 1869, is an animal corridor between the Mediterranean and Red Sea. But movement is mainly from the latter, for the channel passes through the hot, salty Bitter Lakes, favoring animals adapted to these conditions, and the current flows northwards for 10 months of the year. However, not all the 130 invading species are likely to survive Mediterranean conditions.

PALEARCTIC

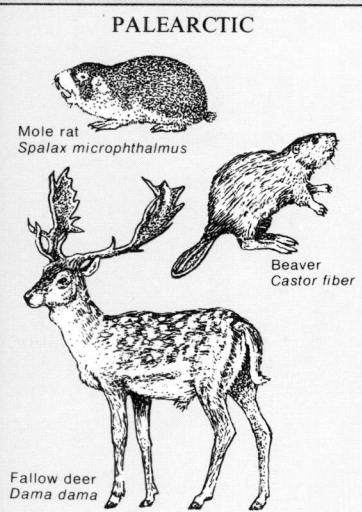

Mole rat
Spalax microphthalmus

Beaver
Castor fiber

Fallow deer
Dama dama

The Palearctic or "Old North" region covers the entire northerly part of the Old World, with seas to the north, east and west. To the south, the Sahara desert and the Himalaya mountains form barriers that separate the Palearctic from the Ethiopian and Oriental regions, although these regions are all part of the same landmass. One of the few species of mammals unique to the Palearctic is the Mediterranean mole rat, a thick-furred rodent. Another Palearctic rodent, the beaver, is shared with the Nearctic region. Fallow deer occur throughout Europe. They have been introduced by man into many other parts of the world, but their origin is almost certainly Mediterranean.

ETHIOPIAN

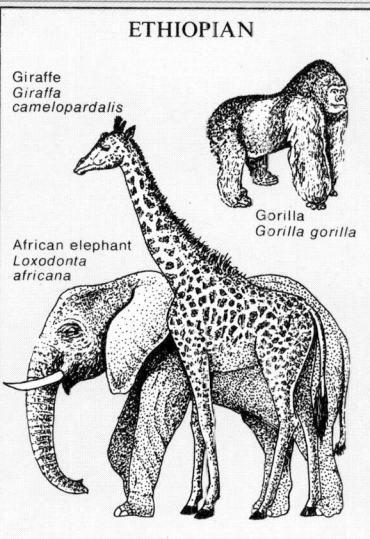

Giraffe
Giraffa camelopardalis

Gorilla
Gorilla gorilla

African elephant
Loxodonta africana

The Ethiopian region includes southern Arabia as well as all Africa south of the Sahara. It resembles in many ways the Neotropical region and is almost as rich in unique families. Its fauna also has much in common with the Oriental region. Unique mammals include the giraffe, at 5.5 m (18 ft) the tallest of living land animals, which inhabits the savanna. The region also supports two of the world's four great apes, the gorilla and the chimpanzee, which are found in the forests of western and central Africa. (The other great apes, the orangutan and the gibbon, are Oriental.) The African elephant is distinguished from its Indian relative by its greater size and by its huge ears and massive tusks.

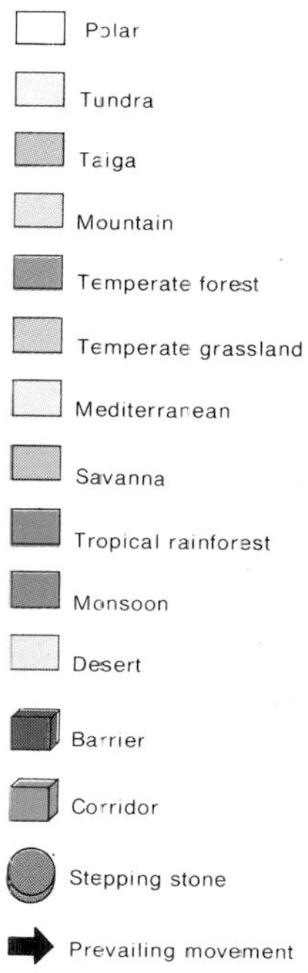

☐ Polar
☐ Tundra
☐ Taiga
☐ Mountain
☐ Temperate forest
☐ Temperate grassland
☐ Mediterranean
☐ Savanna
☐ Tropical rainforest
☐ Monsoon
☐ Desert
☐ Barrier
☐ Corridor
◯ Stepping stone
→ Prevailing movement

ORIENTAL

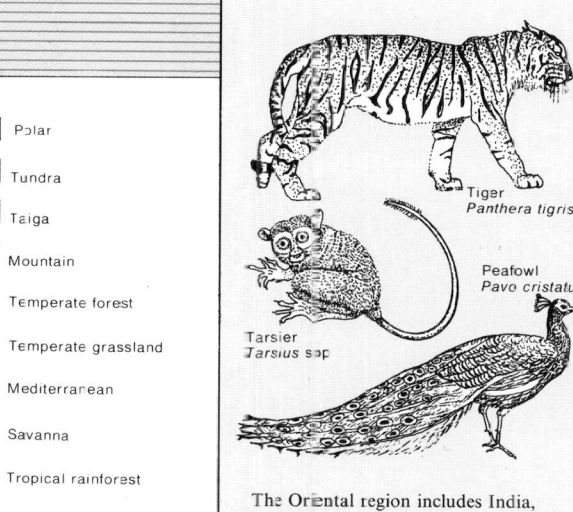

Tiger
Panthera tigris

Peafowl
Pavo cristatus

Tarsier
Tarsius sap

The Oriental region includes India, southern China, southeastern Asia and part of Malaysia. It is bounded to the north by the Himalayas and on either side by ocean, and is separated from the Australian region by a line known as Wallace's Line. It shares a quarter of its mammal families with Africa, but has more primates than any other region. The tarsier, a small relative of the monkey, is unique to southeastern Asia and represents an important early stage of primate evolution. The tiger was once widespread, but its natural habitats are steadily diminishing and the tiger itself is in danger of extinction by man. The peacock is one of the region's many brilliantly colored birds.

AUSTRALIAN

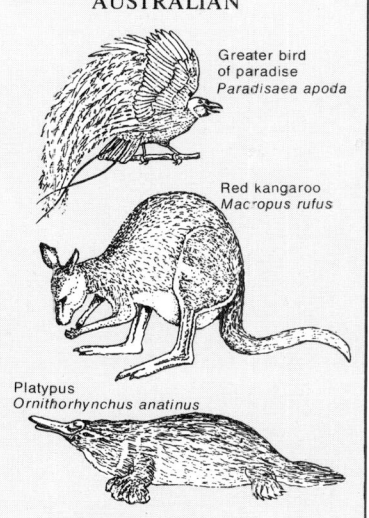

Greater bird of paradise
Paradisaea apoda

Red kangaroo
Macropus rufus

Platypus
Ornithorhynchus anatinus

The Australian region is unique in having no land connection with any other region. Its native fauna has developed in isolation from the rest of the world for at least 50 million years. Most of the mammals are marsupial—animals such as the kangaroo that carry their young in a pouch. Even more of a biological curiosity than the marsupials is the duckbilled platypus, a monotreme or egg-laying mammal. It lives along the banks of streams in Australia and Tasmania, and lays small, leathery eggs like those of snakes and turtles, but it is a true mammal and nurses its young with milk. Some 13 bird families are unique to the region, including the magnificent bird of paradise.

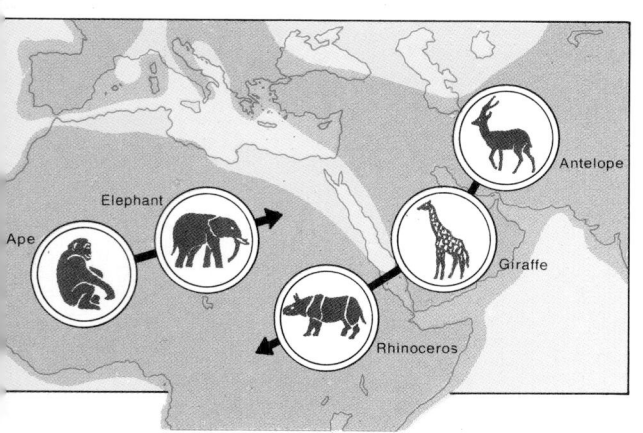

Ape
Elephant
Antelope
Giraffe
Rhinoceros

A desert barrier gradually began to form in northern Africa about nine million years ago, replacing the forest corridor between the Ethiopian and Palearctic regions. During the change, many animals typical of the African plains moved in from the north, including ancestors of today's antelopes, giraffes and rhinoceroses. But African animals also moved up north: early elephants and, much later, apes, which may have been precursors of modern man.

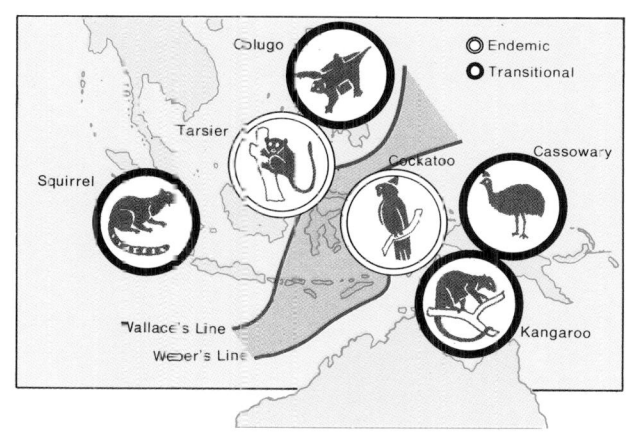

Colugo
Tarsier
Squirrel
Cockatoo
Cassowary
Kangaroo

◉ Endemic
◎ Transitional

Wallace's Line
Weber's Line

The transitional area of "Wallacea" contains animals from both the Oriental and Australian regions, bounded by Wallace's and Weber's Lines, but few have crossed to the other region. Some Oriental mammals, such as tarsiers, are found in Wallacea, but the gliding colugo and varieties of squirrel are not. The Australian cockatoo has reached the transition area, but the flightless cassowary and the tree kangaroo have not.

Spread of Man

Modern Man, *Homo sapiens sapiens*, has proved a highly successful animal since his emergence some 50,000 years ago: today more than 4,000 million members of this subspecies of the *Homo* (Man) group occupy the Earth, living in even the most inhospitable regions. But the fossil record shows that man's lineage goes back millions of years, with different stages of development leading to a greater control of the environment, and with climate itself helping man's ultimate domination of Earth.

Man's lineage may go back at least 14 million years to a small woodland creature known as *Ramapithecus* (Rama's ape). Since the first discoveries of *Ramapithecus* in the Indian sub-continent, its fossils have come to light in many parts of the world, including China, eastern Europe, Turkey and eastern Africa. Fossil remains show that it survived for several million years until, about eight million years ago, there is a tantalizing gap in the fossil record. Then, about four and a half million years later (according to recent discoveries in eastern Africa), we have solid evidence of an upright hominid—a member of man's zoological family. This is "Lucy," a fossil skeleton found in 1973 by Donald Johanson and Tom Gray, and subsequently classified with many other finds as *Australopithecus afarensis*.

This may be man's ancestral "rootstock," but a little later there existed two kinds of "ape-man" (*Australopithecus*), and our own direct ancestor Handy Man (*Homo habilis*). Datable volcanic ash found with the fossils provides a time scale and indicates that, about two million years ago, ape-man and "true" man lived side by side in the lush grassland that then covered the eastern African plains.

One and a half million years ago, according to the fossil evidence, there was again only one hominid species. The varieties of australopithe-cines had died out, and Handy Man (*Homo habilis*) had apparently evolved into Upright Man (*Homo erectus*). Remains of Upright Man have been found in many regions of the world, from various parts of Africa and Europe to China and Indonesia, although not in the Americas. But there is reason to believe that it was in Africa, well over one million years ago, that he evolved from his ancestor, and began a very gradual expansion out of the continent.

Upright Man had about one million years to spread across the Old World, adapting as he did so to local conditions, just as people of today are adapted in their various ways. He was a nomadic hunter gatherer, socially organized in groups. His skills included the use of fire and cooking, as well as the making of quite large structures out of wood. Recent discoveries suggest that, during the million years of his existence, *Homo erectus* gradually evolved into the next stage of man – *Homo sapiens*.

The next step is revealed most clearly in fossils from more than 100,000 to less than 50,000 years ago. Called Neanderthal Man in Europe, Solo Man in Indonesia, and Rhodesian Man in southern Africa, these types of human being were all descendants of *Homo erectus*.

Variable in brain size, but with prominent eyebrow ridges and receding jaws, they may have been dead ends on the evolutionary road; or some may have led to, or been incorporated in, Modern Man (*Homo sapiens sapiens*).

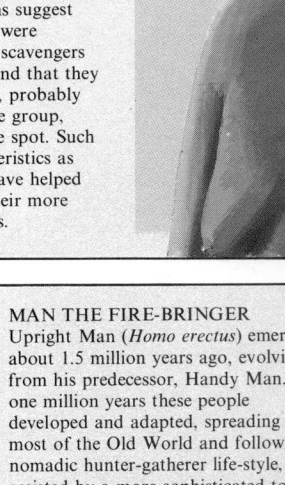

THE AFRICAN CRADLE
Handy Man (*Homo habilis*), who shared the East African grasslands two million years ago with a related "ape-man" species, was a slender and agile creature with a human way of walking and a capacity for conceptual thought, as evidenced in systematic making of tools. Handy Man collected stones, often from far away, and reshaped them into purpose-made tools, using other stones. Fossil remains suggest that these earliest humans were efficient hunters as well as scavengers of larger predators' kills, and that they brought food to campsites, probably sharing it among the whole group, rather than eating it on the spot. Such specifically human characteristics as the sharing of food may have helped our ancestors to survive their more primitive hominid relations.

MAN THE FIRE-BRINGER
Upright Man (*Homo erectus*) emerged about 1.5 million years ago, evolving from his predecessor, Handy Man. For one million years these people developed and adapted, spreading over most of the Old World and following a nomadic hunter-gatherer life-style, assisted by a more sophisticated tool technology. The cooler climates of northern Asia and Europe may have encouraged their most impressive innovation—the use of fire for warmth, cooking and hunting game—and also their ability to construct quite elaborate shelters. It seems likely that they possessed language; and traces of ocher lumps at a campsite perhaps 400,000 years old suggest the possibility of ritual adornment or some kind of body painting.

THE HUMANIZING OF MAN
Modern man's predecessor, although called Wise Man (*Homo sapiens*), was long regarded as more brutish than human. But widespread finds have now changed this image, as can be seen in an old and an updated reconstruction of the same Neanderthal skull (right). Many scientists believe that these people showed a human concern for each other, burying their dead with ceremonial reverence, and looking after disabled members of the group. In their Neanderthal form they inhabited Europe and the Middle East from about 100,000 to 40,000 years ago, and were perhaps adapted to ice-age conditions. *Homo sapiens* counterparts of Neanderthal Man also occur in Africa and southeastern Asia.

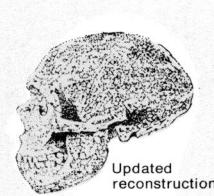
Updated reconstruction

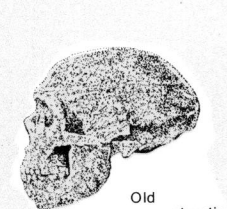
Old reconstruction

The burial of a Neanderthal man took place 60,000 years ago at Shanidar in the Iraq highlands. Fossil traces suggest that the body was laid on a bed of branches, and that flowers were brought to the grave and placed deliberately around the body. The flowers included many varieties still known locally for their medicinal properties. Ritual burials occur at many Neanderthal sites, from the Pyrenees to northern Asia, and indicate a sensitivity that contradicts Neanderthal man's traditional image.

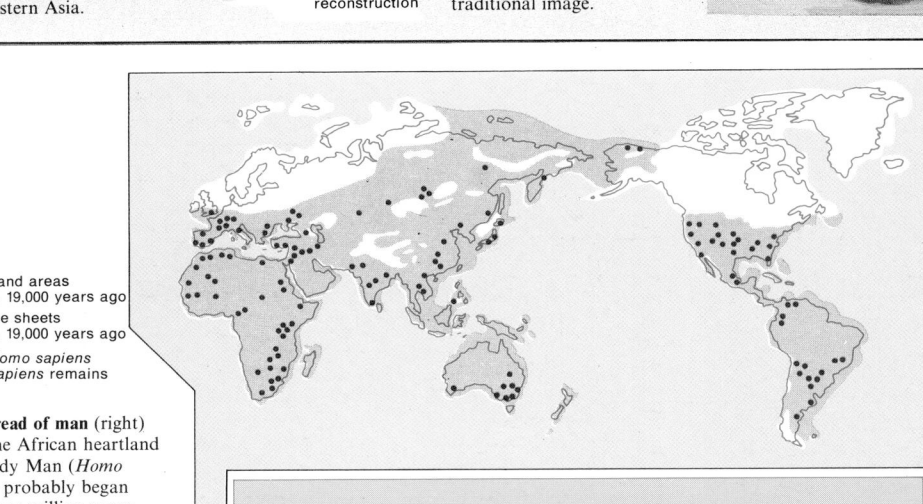

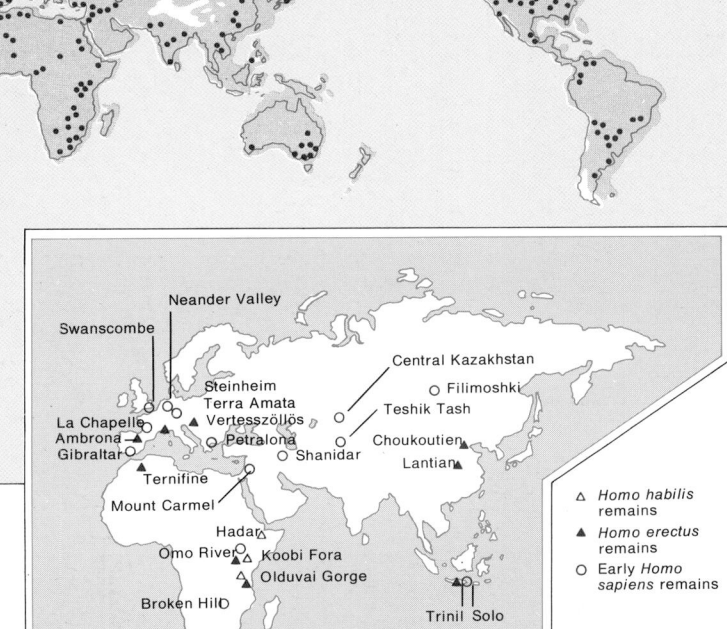

The spread of man (right) from the African heartland of Handy Man (*Homo habilis*) probably began about one million years ago. Remains of Upright Man (*Homo erectus*) have been found all over the Old World, and show a gradual physical and cultural evolution toward a later *Homo sapiens* ancestor, beginning about 350,000 years ago. Between 70,000 and 12,000 years ago, glacial periods locked up the sea water as ice (top), lowering sea levels and opening a land bridge to America that was used by later nomadic peoples. But they had to cross open sea to reach Australia.

Land areas
c. 19,000 years ago

Ice sheets
c. 19,000 years ago

Homo sapiens sapiens remains

Neander Valley
Swanscombe
Steinheim
Terra Amata
La Chapelle
Ambrona
Gibraltar
Vertesszöllös
Petralona
Ternifine
Mount Carmel
Hadar
Omo River
Koobi Fora
Olduvai Gorge
Broken Hill
Central Kazakhstan
Filimoshki
Teshik Tash
Choukoutien
Lantian
Shanidar
Trinil
Solo

△ *Homo habilis* remains
▲ *Homo erectus* remains
○ Early *Homo sapiens* remains

THE AGE OF ART
Toward the end of the last Ice Age, from about 35,000 years ago, truly modern humans began to depict their world in wonderfully vivid terms. The age of art may have reached its peak at Lascaux, France, some 15,000 years ago, but less well-preserved cave paintings from Africa show that the artistic impulse was equally present elsewhere. Called Cro-Magnon Man in Europe, these people spread to all parts of the world, crossing to the Americas by way of the Bering land bridge (when ice locked up the water of the straits), and even venturing over the seas to Australia. Physically these people were just like present-day humans. They led a nomadic, hunter-gathering life, living in large, organized groups, hunting such animals as mammoths, reindeer, bison and horses, and using a technology, as well as an artistry, far in advance of anything previously developed.

Fossils almost four million years old, found since 1973, may mark the ancestral "rootstock" of humanity, but the earliest form of true man is thought to be *Homo habilis*, who shared his African habitat with "ape-man" relatives some two million years ago. His successor, *Homo erectus*, spread over Asia and Europe, evolving gradually into modern man's predecessors, creatures whose large brow ridges belie many typically human characteristics. These were replaced by Modern Man.

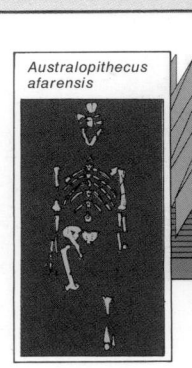
Australopithecus afarensis

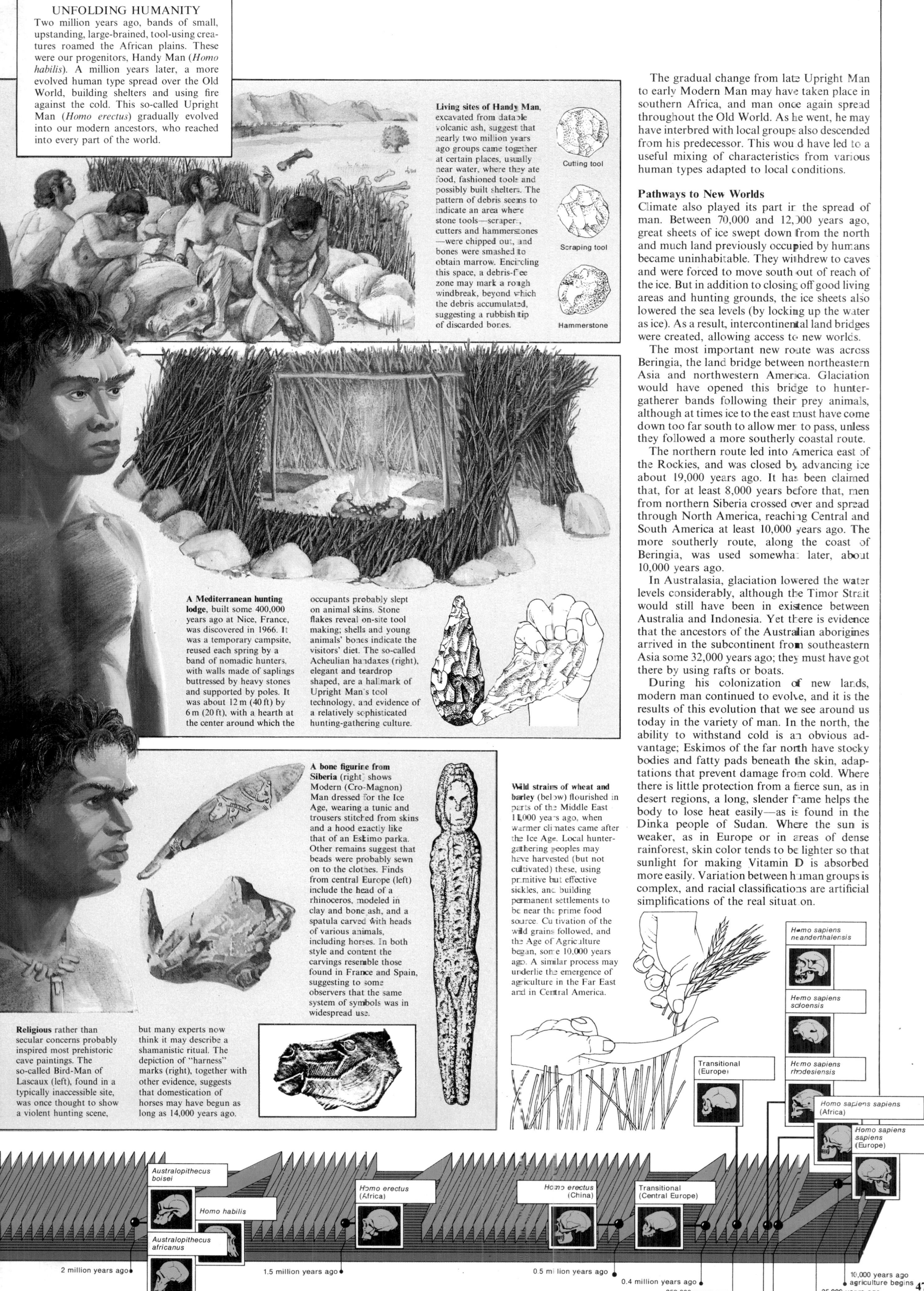

UNFOLDING HUMANITY

Two million years ago, bands of small, upstanding, large-brained, tool-using creatures roamed the African plains. These were our progenitors, Handy Man (*Homo habilis*). A million years later, a more evolved human type spread over the Old World, building shelters and using fire against the cold. This so-called Upright Man (*Homo erectus*) gradually evolved into our modern ancestors, who reached into every part of the world.

Living sites of Handy Man, excavated from datable volcanic ash, suggest that nearly two million years ago groups came together at certain places, usually near water, where they ate food, fashioned tools and possibly built shelters. The pattern of debris seems to indicate an area where stone tools—scrapers, cutters and hammerstones —were chipped out, and bones were smashed to obtain marrow. Encircling this space, a debris-free zone may mark a rough windbreak, beyond which the debris accumulated, suggesting a rubbish tip of discarded bones.

Cutting tool

Scraping tool

Hammerstone

A Mediterranean hunting lodge, built some 400,000 years ago at Nice, France, was discovered in 1966. It was a temporary campsite, reused each spring by a band of nomadic hunters, with walls made of saplings buttressed by heavy stones and supported by poles. It was about 12 m (40 ft) by 6 m (20 ft), with a hearth at the center around which the occupants probably slept on animal skins. Stone flakes reveal on-site tool making; shells and young animals' bones indicate the visitors' diet. The so-called Acheulian handaxes (right), elegant and teardrop shaped, are a hallmark of Upright Man's tool technology, and evidence of a relatively sophisticated hunting-gathering culture.

A bone figurine from Siberia (right) shows Modern (Cro-Magnon) Man dressed for the Ice Age, wearing a tunic and trousers stitched from skins and a hood exactly like that of an Eskimo parka. Other remains suggest that beads were probably sewn on to the clothes. Finds from central Europe (left) include the head of a rhinoceros, modeled in clay and bone ash, and a spatula carved with heads of various animals, including horses. In both style and content the carvings resemble those found in France and Spain, suggesting to some observers that the same system of symbols was in widespread use.

Wild strains of wheat and barley (below) flourished in parts of the Middle East 11,000 years ago, when warmer climates came after the Ice Age. Local hunter-gathering peoples may have harvested (but not cultivated) these, using primitive but effective sickles, and building permanent settlements to be near the prime food source. Cultivation of the wild grains followed, and the Age of Agriculture began, some 10,000 years ago. A similar process may underlie the emergence of agriculture in the Far East and in Central America.

Religious rather than secular concerns probably inspired most prehistoric cave paintings. The so-called Bird-Man of Lascaux (left), found in a typically inaccessible site, was once thought to show a violent hunting scene, but many experts now think it may describe a shamanistic ritual. The depiction of "harness" marks (right), together with other evidence, suggests that domestication of horses may have begun as long as 14,000 years ago.

The gradual change from late Upright Man to early Modern Man may have taken place in southern Africa, and man once again spread throughout the Old World. As he went, he may have interbred with local groups also descended from his predecessor. This would have led to a useful mixing of characteristics from various human types adapted to local conditions.

Pathways to New Worlds

Climate also played its part in the spread of man. Between 70,000 and 12,000 years ago, great sheets of ice swept down from the north and much land previously occupied by humans became uninhabitable. They withdrew to caves and were forced to move south out of reach of the ice. But in addition to closing off good living areas and hunting grounds, the ice sheets also lowered the sea levels (by locking up the water as ice). As a result, intercontinental land bridges were created, allowing access to new worlds.

The most important new route was across Beringia, the land bridge between northeastern Asia and northwestern America. Glaciation would have opened this bridge to hunter-gatherer bands following their prey animals, although at times ice to the east must have come down too far south to allow men to pass, unless they followed a more southerly coastal route.

The northern route led into America east of the Rockies, and was closed by advancing ice about 19,000 years ago. It has been claimed that, for at least 8,000 years before that, men from northern Siberia crossed over and spread through North America, reaching Central and South America at least 10,000 years ago. The more southerly route, along the coast of Beringia, was used somewhat later, about 10,000 years ago.

In Australasia, glaciation lowered the water levels considerably, although the Timor Strait would still have been in existence between Australia and Indonesia. Yet there is evidence that the ancestors of the Australian aborigines arrived in the subcontinent from southeastern Asia some 32,000 years ago; they must have got there by using rafts or boats.

During his colonization of new lands, modern man continued to evolve, and it is the results of this evolution that we see around us today in the variety of man. In the north, the ability to withstand cold is an obvious advantage; Eskimos of the far north have stocky bodies and fatty pads beneath the skin, adaptations that prevent damage from cold. Where there is little protection from a fierce sun, as in desert regions, a long, slender frame helps the body to lose heat easily—as is found in the Dinka people of Sudan. Where the sun is weaker, as in Europe or in areas of dense rainforest, skin color tends to be lighter so that sunlight for making Vitamin D is absorbed more easily. Variation between human groups is complex, and racial classifications are artificial simplifications of the real situation.

Homo sapiens neanderthalensis

Homo sapiens soloensis

Homo sapiens rhodesiensis

Transitional (Europe)

Homo sapiens sapiens (Africa)

Homo sapiens sapiens (Europe)

Australopithecus boisei

Homo habilis

Australopithecus africanus

Homo erectus (Africa)

Homo erectus (China)

Transitional (Central Europe)

2 million years ago

1.5 million years ago

0.5 million years ago

0.4 million years ago

250,000 years ago

100,000 years ago

50,000 years ago

35,000 years ago

10,000 years ago agriculture begins

Part 4

THE DIVERSITY OF LIFE

Earth's habitats from the Poles to the Equator
Plants and animals of the Earth's natural regions
Man the preserver and man the destroyer

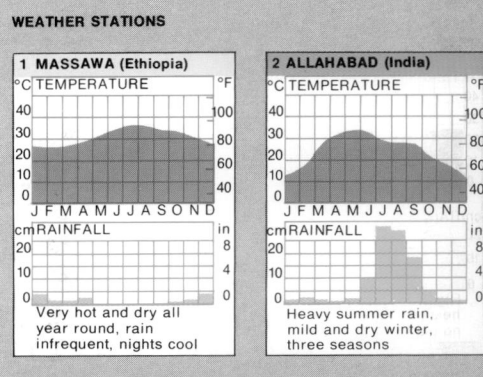

WEATHER STATIONS
1 MASSAWA (Ethiopia)
°C TEMPERATURE °F
J F M A M J J A S O N D
cm RAINFALL in
Very hot and dry all year round, rain infrequent, nights cool
2 ALLAHABAD (India)
°C TEMPERATURE °F
J F M A M J J A S O N D
cm RAINFALL in
Heavy summer rain, mild and dry winter, three seasons

Arctic Circle
Tropic of Cancer
Equator
Tropic of Capricorn
Antarctic Circle
The Natural Regions
Desert
Monsoon
Tropical rainforest
Savanna
Mediterranean
Temperate grassland
Temperate forest
Mountain
Taiga
Tundra
Polar
CLIMATE, RAINFALL AND THE BIOMES
Tundra
Taiga
Temperate grassland
Mediterranean
Temperate forest
Desert
Savanna
Monsoon
Tropical rainforest
–10/26
0°C/32°F
10/37.5
20/68
0 cm/0 in
100/39
200/78
300/117

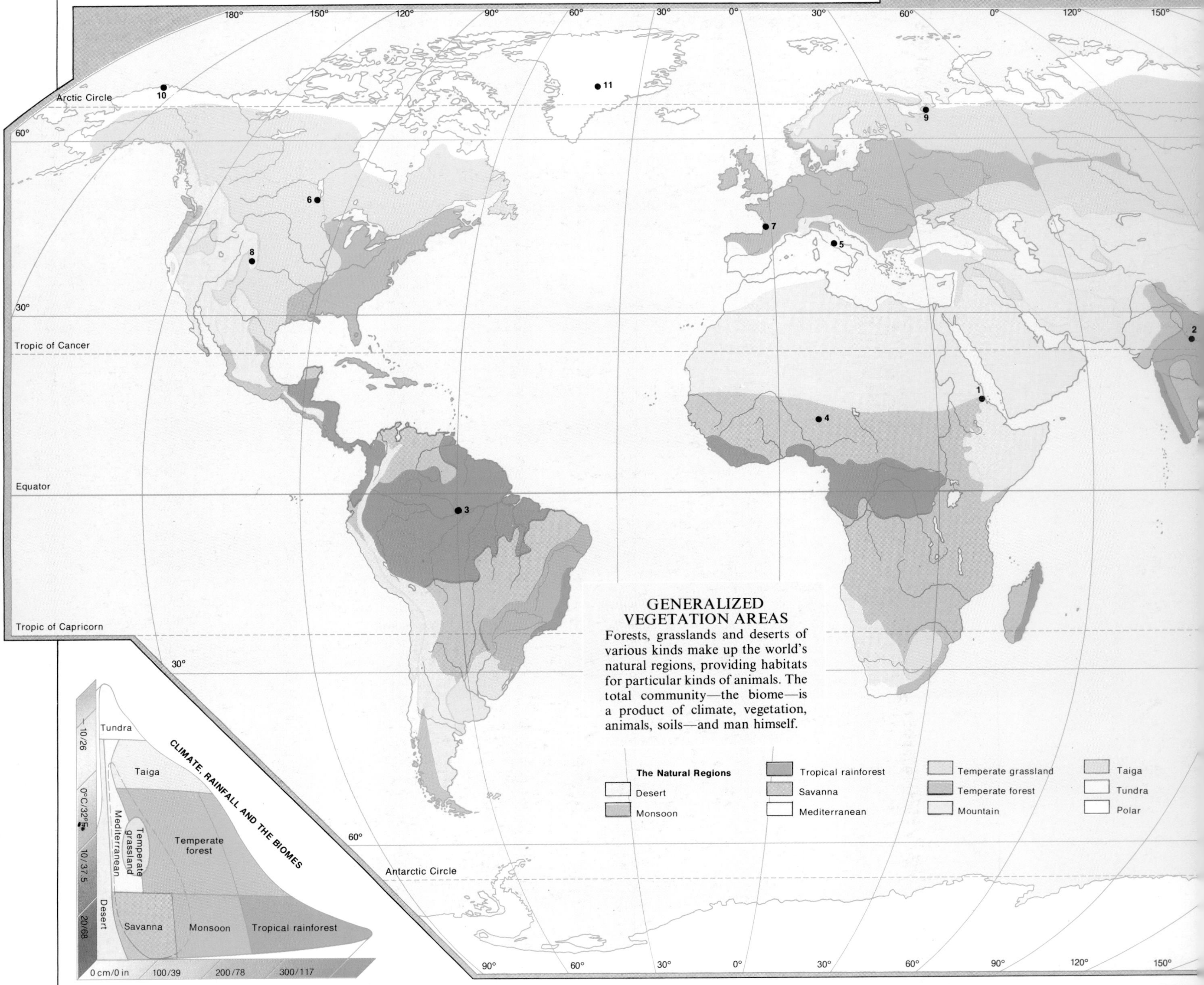

GENERALIZED VEGETATION AREAS

Forests, grasslands and deserts of various kinds make up the world's natural regions, providing habitats for particular kinds of animals. The total community—the biome—is a product of climate, vegetation, animals, soils—and man himself.

Temperature and rainfall (above) govern the world's zones of plant and animal life. Dryness prevents tree growth both in icy tundra and in hot deserts. Wetter conditions cause savannas and grasslands to yield to forest biomes, tropical or temperate (the dotted line indicates zones within which variations occur).

A broad correlation (below) between soil types, climate and vegetation areas shows the interconnections that define the biomes. The soil of the biome is related to climatic conditions and is also modified by plant and animal activity, but soil types are not necessarily confined to any one particular biome.

SOIL AND THE BIOMES

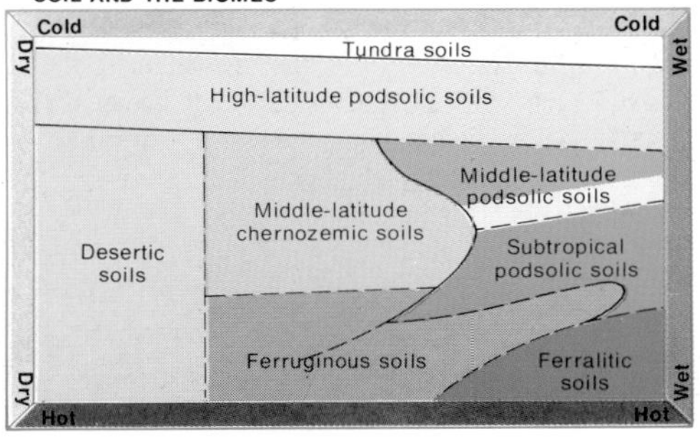

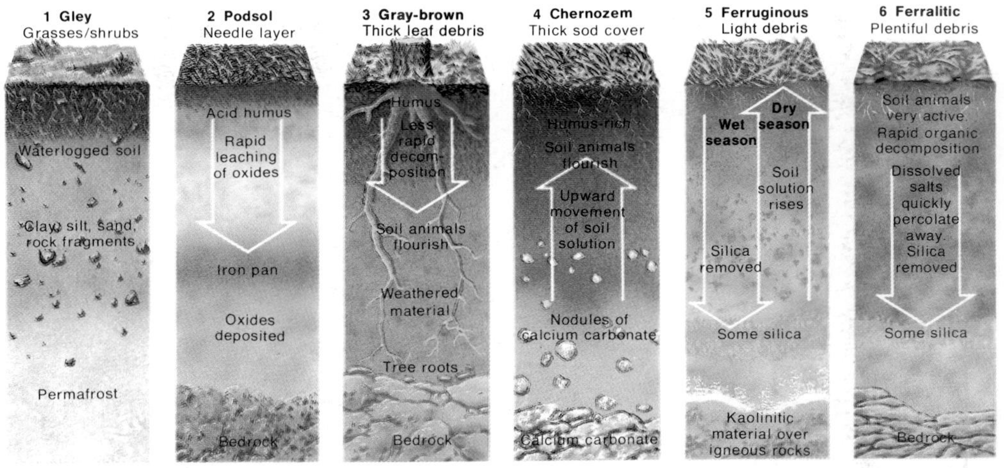

Cold
Cold
Dry
Wet
Tundra soils
High-latitude podsolic soils
Middle-latitude podsolic soils
Middle-latitude chernozemic soils
Desertic soils
Subtropical podsolic soils
Ferruginous soils
Ferralitic soils
Dry
Wet
Hot
Hot

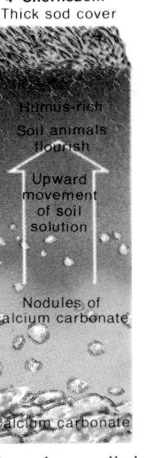

1 Gley
Grasses/shrubs
Waterlogged soil
Clay, silt, sand, rock fragments
Permafrost
2 Podsol
Needle layer
Acid humus
Rapid leaching of oxides
Iron pan
Oxides deposited
Bedrock
3 Gray-brown
Thick leaf debris
Humus
Less rapid decom-position
Soil animals flourish
Weathered material
Tree roots
Bedrock
4 Chernozem
Thick sod cover
Humus-rich
Soil animals flourish
Upward movement of soil solution
Nodules of calcium carbonate
Calcium carbonate
5 Ferruginous
Light debris
Wet season
Dry season
Soil solution rises
Silica removed
Some silica
Kaolinitic material over igneous rocks
6 Ferralitic
Plentiful debris
Soil animals very active
Rapid organic decomposition
Dissolved salts quickly percolate away
Silica removed
Some silica
Bedrock

Soil profiles (above) from surface to bedrock reflect the influence of climate and vegetation on the rock. Depths vary from 1 m in the tundra to 30–40 m at the Equator. Waterlogged gley (1) may form above tundra permafrost. Podsol (2) is typical of taiga forests, where spring snow-melt is heavily leached through a needle layer, sometimes forming an iron "pan." Gray-brown forest soil (3) has rich, organic humus, as has chernozem (4), the typical temperate grassland soil. Ferruginous soils (5) occur in dry-season tropical climates (monsoon, savanna), and ferralitic soils (6) where there is constant rainfall.

ECOSYSTEM DYNAMICS

An ecosystem consists of a group of organisms and its physical environment. A marshland ecosystem from North America (right) shows the dynamic interactions between plant and animal communities and their habitats, which include climate, soil and water. The energy and food in the system initially derive from the Sun—the main energy source for living things, notably plants. Plants are food for herbivores, on land and in water; herbivores are food for carnivores; decomposers (bacteria and fungi) nourish plants, breaking down dead bodie into compounds.

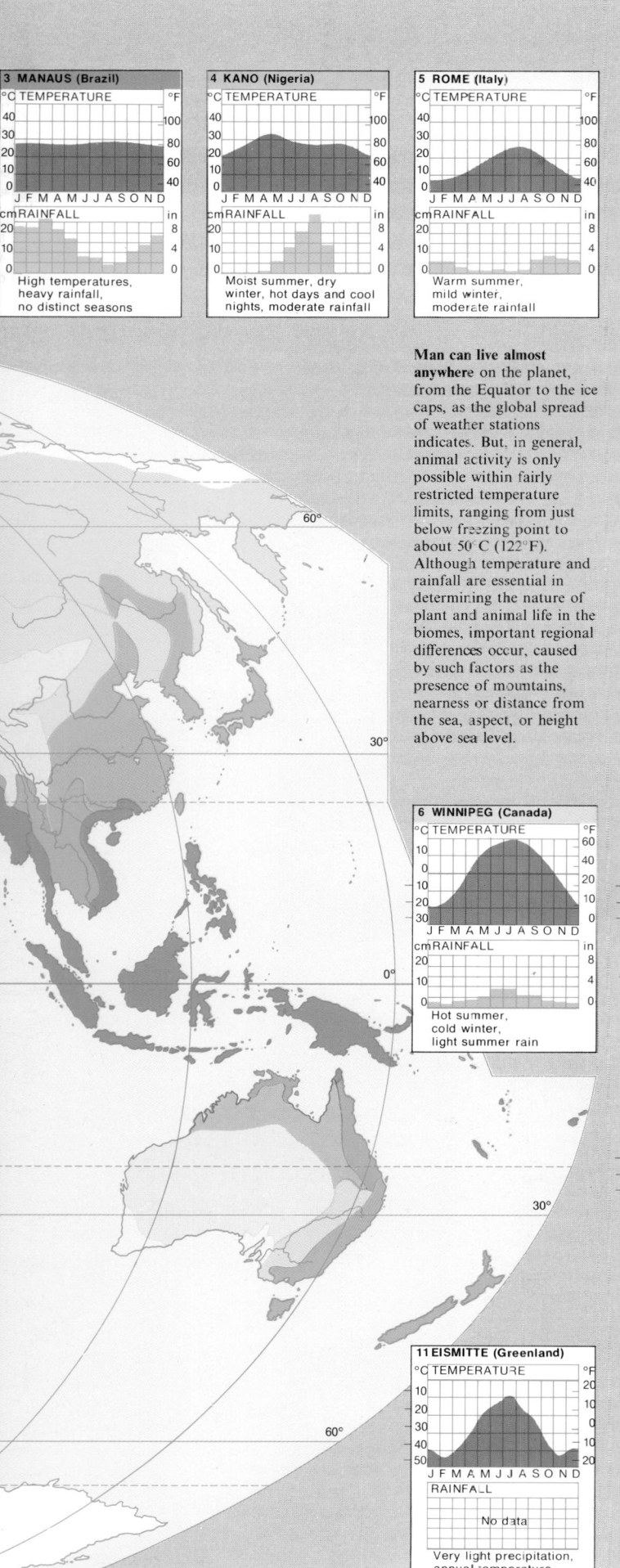

3 MANAUS (Brazil)
°C TEMPERATURE °F

High temperatures, heavy rainfall, no distinct seasons

4 KANO (Nigeria)
°C TEMPERATURE °F

Moist summer, dry winter, hot days and cool nights, moderate rainfall

5 ROME (Italy)
°C TEMPERATURE °F

Warm summer, mild winter, moderate rainfall

Man can live almost anywhere on the planet, from the Equator to the ice caps, as the global spread of weather stations indicates. But, in general, animal activity is only possible within fairly restricted temperature limits, ranging from just below freezing point to about 50°C (122°F). Although temperature and rainfall are essential in determining the nature of plant and animal life in the biomes, important regional differences occur, caused by such factors as the presence of mountains, nearness or distance from the sea, aspect, or height above sea level.

6 WINNIPEG (Canada)
°C TEMPERATURE °F

Hot summer, cold winter, light summer rain

7 BORDEAUX (France)
°C TEMPERATURE °F

Warm summer, mild winter, four distinct seasons

8 PIKE'S PEAK (USA)
°C TEMPERATURE °F

4,300 m (14,111ft) Temperature decreases with increasing altitude

9 ARKHANGELSK (RUSSIA)
°C TEMPERATURE °F

Short summer, long and cold winter, light summer rain

10 BARROW (Alaska)
°C TEMPERATURE °F

Brief summer, very long and cold winter, very light rainfall

11 EISMITTE (Greenland)
°C TEMPERATURE °F
RAINFALL

No data

Very light precipitation, annual temperature variation 15.3°C/27.5°F

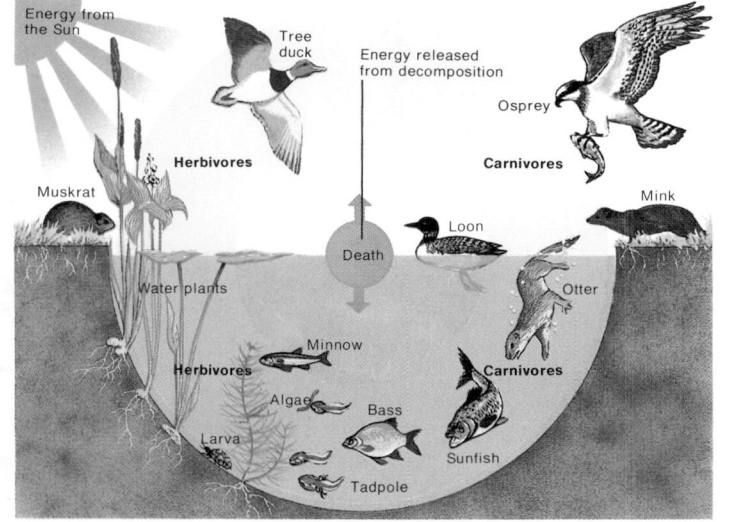

Energy from the Sun
Tree duck
Energy released from decomposition
Osprey
Herbivores
Carnivores
Muskrat
Mink
Death
Loon
Water plants
Otter
Herbivores
Minnow
Carnivores
Algae
Bass
Larva
Sunfish
Tadpole

Earth's Natural Regions

Geographers have long looked for ways of classifying conditions such as climate, soil and vegetation to describe the general similarities and differences from area to area throughout the world. By identifying distinctive patterns of climate and vegetation they have provided a convenient global division into natural regions or biomes. And recent developments in ecology – the study of plants and animals in relation to their environments – have given such divisions a greater depth.

Divisions according to climate were first suggested by the Greek philosopher Aristotle, and his ideas were still in use until about 100 years ago. Aristotle posited a number of climatic zones—called torrid, temperate and frigid —defined by latitude. But with time it became increasingly apparent that the complex distribution of atmospheric pressure, winds, rainfall and temperature could not be related to such a simple frame. Nineteenth-century scientists divided the world into 35 climatic provinces. Then in 1900 the German meteorologist Wladimir Köppen produced a more sophisticated climatic classification based on temperature and moisture conditions related to the needs of plants. At about the same time other scientists studied the distribution of vegetation types throughout the world. These studies together provided the basis for much of the later work on climatic regions.

An important step forward was made in 1904 by the British geographer A. J. Herbertson. He argued that subdivision of physical environments should take into account the distribution of the various phenomena as they related to each other. He conceived the idea of *natural regions*, each with "a certain unity of configuration (relief), climate and vegetation." His final classification contained four groups or regions: Polar Types, Cool Temperate Types, Warm Temperate Types and Tropical Hot Lands. Herbertson's scheme, controversial at first, was later much used for teaching geography.

Ecology

Meanwhile the study of environmental problems had been advanced by the idea of *ecology*, the relationship of living things between each other and their surroundings. The term was first used in 1868 by Ernst Haeckel, the German biologist, but it was not until the end of the nineteenth century that scientists really began to study life forms in relation to their habitat. In addition to the central ideas of interdependence between the members of plant and animal communities and between the community and the physical environment, there now came the suggestion that communities develop in a sequence that leads to a "climax"—a final step of equilibrium or balance. Their climax stage depends on conditions of climate or soil.

Later the British botanist A. G. Tansley, a leading exponent of ecological thinking, introduced the term *ecosystem* to describe a group of living organisms and its effective environment. Tansley's definition of 1935 referred to the whole system, including "not only the organism complex, but also the whole complex of physical factors forming what we call the environment of the biome." The idea became very influential and has been used in the social sciences as well as in the natural ones. But it is difficult to apply in practice, partly because of the highly complex and often diverse interactions that take place in different parts of the ecosystem.

Ecologists have developed special methods and have given particular attention to the ways in which energy is transferred within the system. The term *biome* refers to the whole complex of organisms, both animals and plants, that live together naturally as a society. By *environment* is meant all the external conditions that affect the life and development of an organism.

Biomes

The biomes shown on the map are broadly drawn generalizations. They should be regarded as idealized regions, within which many local variations may exist—for example, of climate or soil conditions. On a larger scale such features as mountain ranges may cause variations at a regional level. Scientists have tried to work out "hierarchies" that include many levels or orders of scale leading to the major climatic-vegetation realms or biomes. These realms give a broad picture that is useful at the world level of scale, and which forms a starting point for further analysis. Any map of the biomes has to have lines to indicate the boundaries of each region, but these too are generalizations. Although climate and vegetation do sometimes change abruptly from place to place, more often there are transitional zones, and the boundaries on the maps give the broad locations of these.

Herbertson's concept of natural regions attempted also to take account of the influence of man as an important factor in the environment. But he was not totally successful in including man in his analysis, no doubt because of the complexity of the problems involved and because of the immense influence that man has had upon the natural vegetation of the world. The cutting of forests, the drainage and reclamation of land, the introduction, use and spread of cultivated plants, the domestication of animals, the development of sophisticated systems of agriculture and many other actions all create, over large areas of the biomes, landscapes that are more man-made than natural.

Resource systems

An idea that clarifies the study of the interrelations of societies and environments, and the ways in which these change with the passage of time, is that of the *resource system*. This is a model of a population of human beings and their social and economic characteristics, including their technical skills and resources, together with those aspects of the natural environment that affect them and which they influence. The model includes the sequences by which natural materials are obtained, transformed and used. It tries to show how societies are organized according to their natural resources, the effects of that use, and the ways in which natural conditions limit or expand the life and work of the society. But it is easier to apply such a model to societies that have direct relations with natural conditions, through farming, fishing or forestry, than to great urban–industrial complexes.

The sections that follow present a picture of the diversity of habitats from ice caps to equatorial forests, the principal ways man has modified the environment and the problems of maintaining healthy resource systems.

Climate and Weather

The pattern of world climates depends largely on great circulations of air in the atmosphere. These movements of air are driven by energy from the Sun, and they transfer surplus heat from the tropics to the polar regions. Over a long period of time – such as months, seasons or years – they create the climate. Over a short period – day by day, or week by week – they form the weather. Together, climate and weather are among the most significant natural components of the world's diverse environments.

The world's tropical zones receive more heat from the Sun than they re-emit into space, and so their land and sea surfaces become warm. The polar regions, on the other hand, emit more radiation than they receive, and so they become cold. Warm air is less dense than cold air, and this means that atmospheric pressure becomes low at the Equator and high at the poles. As a result, a circulation of air—both vertical and horizontal—is set up. But because of the Earth's rotation and the distribution of land and sea there is not a simple air circulation pattern in each hemisphere; winds are deflected to the right in the northern hemisphere and to the left in the southern hemisphere, a phenomenon known as the Coriolis effect.

A climatic patchwork

When warm air rises it expands and cools and the water vapor it is carrying condenses to form clouds. For this reason heavy, showery rain is frequent in the belt of rising air near the Equator. In the subtropical zones (where the air is sinking), clouds evaporate and the weather is fine. Air moves out of the subtropical high-pressure belts in the lower atmosphere. Some of it flows towards the poles and meets colder air, flowing out of the polar high-pressure region, in a narrow zone called the polar front. This convergence of air is concentrated around low-pressure systems known as depressions.

The pattern of climates does not remain constant throughout the year because of seasonal changes in the amount of radiation from the Sun—the "fuel" of the atmospheric engine. In June, when the northern hemisphere is tilted towards the Sun, the radiation is at a maximum at latitude 23°N and all the climatic belts shift northwards. In December it is summer in the southern hemisphere and all the belts move southwards.

Climate is also affected by the distribution of land and sea across the globe. The temperature of the land changes more quickly than that of

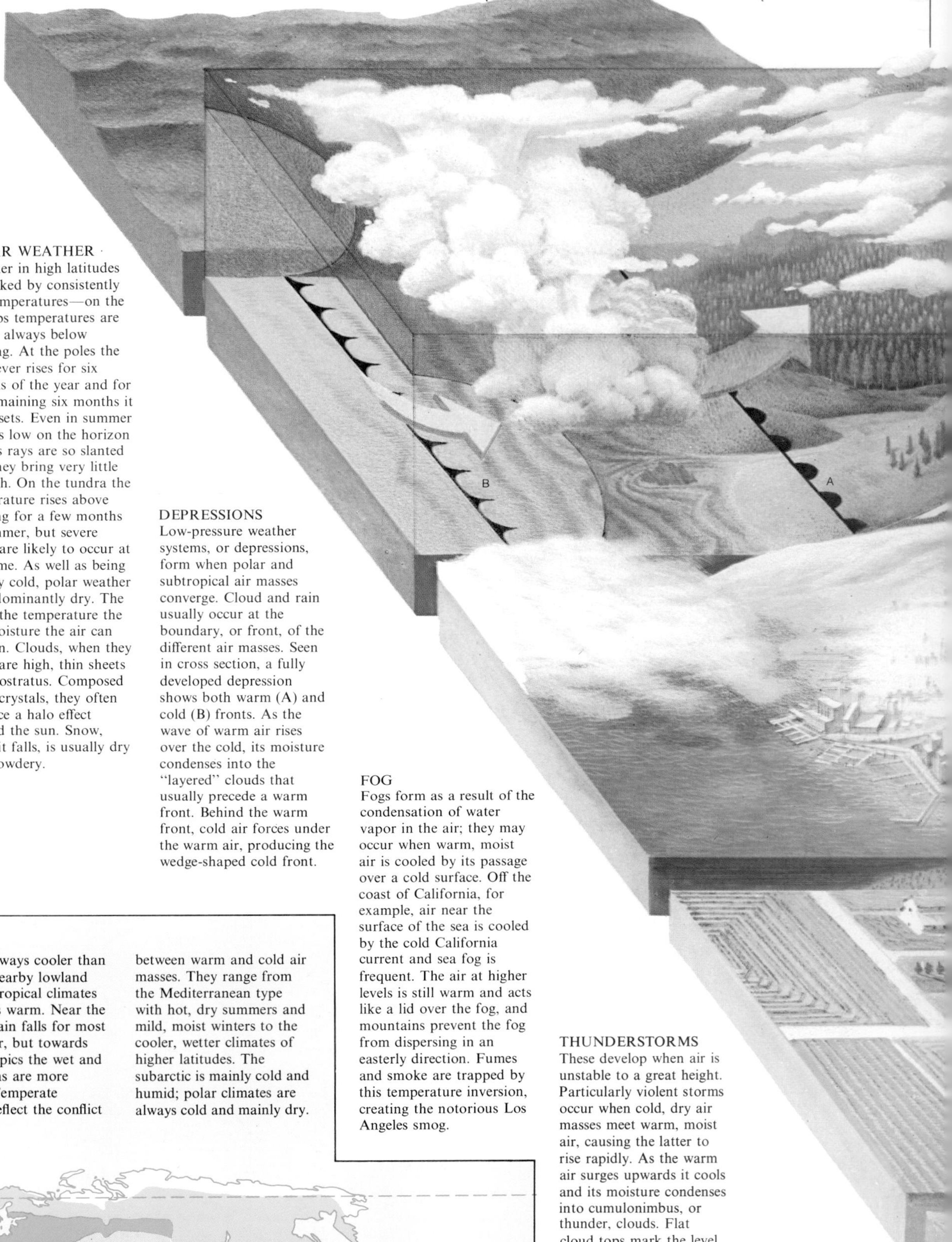

POLAR WEATHER
Weather in high latitudes is marked by consistently low temperatures—on the ice caps temperatures are nearly always below freezing. At the poles the sun never rises for six months of the year and for the remaining six months it never sets. Even in summer it stays low on the horizon and its rays are so slanted that they bring very little warmth. On the tundra the temperature rises above freezing for a few months in summer, but severe frosts are likely to occur at any time. As well as being bitterly cold, polar weather is predominantly dry. The lower the temperature the less moisture the air can contain. Clouds, when they form, are high, thin sheets of cirrostratus. Composed of ice crystals, they often produce a halo effect around the sun. Snow, when it falls, is usually dry and powdery.

DEPRESSIONS
Low-pressure weather systems, or depressions, form when polar and subtropical air masses converge. Cloud and rain usually occur at the boundary, or front, of the different air masses. Seen in cross section, a fully developed depression shows both warm (A) and cold (B) fronts. As the wave of warm air rises over the cold, its moisture condenses into the "layered" clouds that usually precede a warm front. Behind the warm front, cold air forces under the warm air, producing the wedge-shaped cold front.

FOG
Fogs form as a result of the condensation of water vapor in the air; they may occur when warm, moist air is cooled by its passage over a cold surface. Off the coast of California, for example, air near the surface of the sea is cooled by the cold California current and sea fog is frequent. The air at higher levels is still warm and acts like a lid over the fog, and mountains prevent the fog from dispersing in an easterly direction. Fumes and smoke are trapped by this temperature inversion, creating the notorious Los Angeles smog.

THUNDERSTORMS
These develop when air is unstable to a great height. Particularly violent storms occur when cold, dry air masses meet warm, moist air, causing the latter to rise rapidly. As the warm air surges upwards it cools and its moisture condenses into cumulonimbus, or thunder, clouds. Flat cloud tops mark the level where stable air occurs again. Quickly moving raindrops and hail in the clouds become electrically charged and cause lightning, and the explosion of heated air along the path of the flash creates the sound wave that is heard as thunder.

HURRICANES
These are tropical storms on a vast scale that build up over warm oceans. Their core is an area of low pressure around which large quantities of warm, moist air are carried to the high atmosphere at great speed. The Earth's rotation is responsible for the huge swirling movement: in the northern hemisphere the movement is anticlockwise, in the southern hemisphere it is clockwise. Towering bands of clouds produce torrential rain. The central region, or "eye," of a hurricane, however, has light winds, clear skies and no rainfall.

THE WORLD'S CLIMATIC REGIONS
Climate is the characteristic weather of a region over a long period of time. It is often described in terms of average monthly and yearly temperatures and rainfall. These in turn depend largely on latitude, which determines whether a region is basically hot or cold and whether it has pronounced seasonal changes. Climate is also influenced by prevailing winds, by ocean currents and by geographical features such as the distribution of land and water. Highland climates are influenced by altitude and are always cooler than those of nearby lowland regions. Tropical climates are always warm. Near the Equator rain falls for most of the year, but towards the subtropics the wet and dry seasons are more marked. Temperate climates reflect the conflict between warm and cold air masses. They range from the Mediterranean type with hot, dry summers and mild, moist winters to the cooler, wetter climates of higher latitudes. The subarctic is mainly cold and humid; polar climates are always cold and mainly dry.

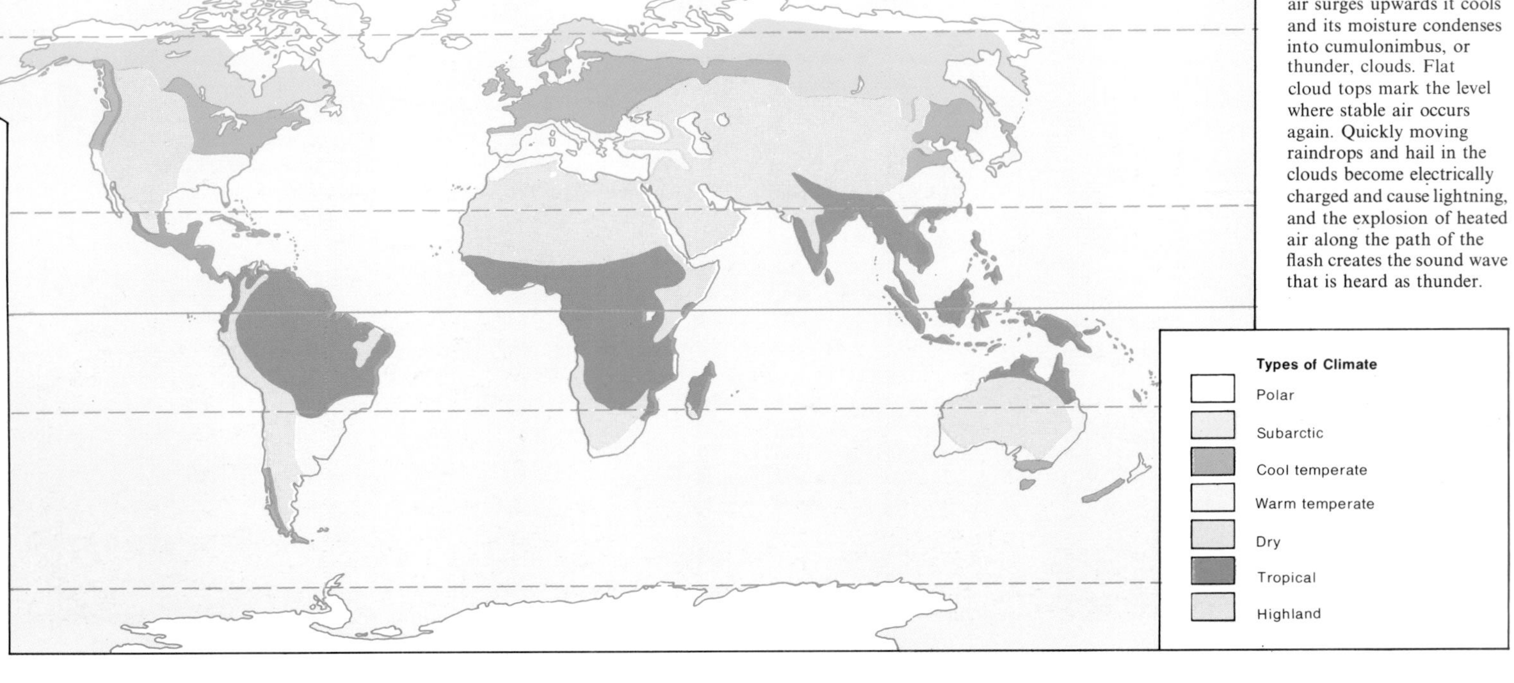

Types of Climate
- Polar
- Subarctic
- Cool temperate
- Warm temperate
- Dry
- Tropical
- Highland

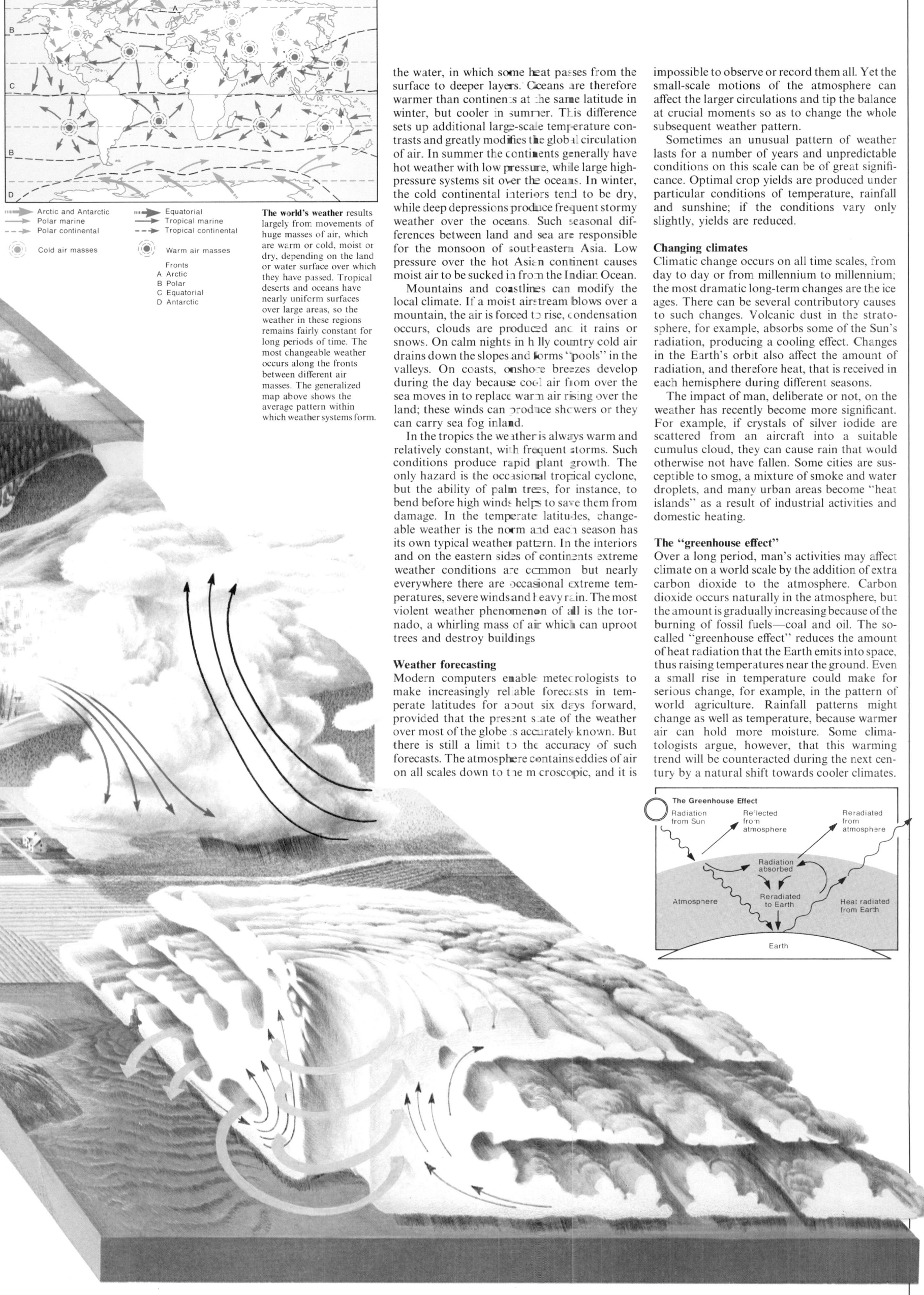

The world's weather results largely from movements of huge masses of air, which are warm or cold, moist or dry, depending on the land or water surface over which they have passed. Tropical deserts and oceans have nearly uniform surfaces over large areas, so the weather in these regions remains fairly constant for long periods of time. The most changeable weather occurs along the fronts between different air masses. The generalized map above shows the average pattern within which weather systems form.

the water, in which some heat passes from the surface to deeper layers. Oceans are therefore warmer than continents at the same latitude in winter, but cooler in summer. This difference sets up additional large-scale temperature contrasts and greatly modifies the global circulation of air. In summer the continents generally have hot weather with low pressure, while large high-pressure systems sit over the oceans. In winter, the cold continental interiors tend to be dry, while deep depressions produce frequent stormy weather over the oceans. Such seasonal differences between land and sea are responsible for the monsoon of southeastern Asia. Low pressure over the hot Asian continent causes moist air to be sucked in from the Indian Ocean.

Mountains and coastlines can modify the local climate. If a moist airstream blows over a mountain, the air is forced to rise, condensation occurs, clouds are produced and it rains or snows. On calm nights in hilly country cold air drains down the slopes and forms "pools" in the valleys. On coasts, onshore breezes develop during the day because cool air from over the sea moves in to replace warm air rising over the land; these winds can produce showers or they can carry sea fog inland.

In the tropics the weather is always warm and relatively constant, with frequent storms. Such conditions produce rapid plant growth. The only hazard is the occasional tropical cyclone, but the ability of palm trees, for instance, to bend before high winds helps to save them from damage. In the temperate latitudes, changeable weather is the norm and each season has its own typical weather pattern. In the interiors and on the eastern sides of continents extreme weather conditions are common but nearly everywhere there are occasional extreme temperatures, severe winds and heavy rain. The most violent weather phenomenon of all is the tornado, a whirling mass of air which can uproot trees and destroy buildings

Weather forecasting
Modern computers enable meteorologists to make increasingly reliable forecasts in temperate latitudes for about six days forward, provided that the present state of the weather over most of the globe is accurately known. But there is still a limit to the accuracy of such forecasts. The atmosphere contains eddies of air on all scales down to the microscopic, and it is impossible to observe or record them all. Yet the small-scale motions of the atmosphere can affect the larger circulations and tip the balance at crucial moments so as to change the whole subsequent weather pattern.

Sometimes an unusual pattern of weather lasts for a number of years and unpredictable conditions on this scale can be of great significance. Optimal crop yields are produced under particular conditions of temperature, rainfall and sunshine; if the conditions vary only slightly, yields are reduced.

Changing climates
Climatic change occurs on all time scales, from day to day or from millennium to millennium; the most dramatic long-term changes are the ice ages. There can be several contributory causes to such changes. Volcanic dust in the stratosphere, for example, absorbs some of the Sun's radiation, producing a cooling effect. Changes in the Earth's orbit also affect the amount of radiation, and therefore heat, that is received in each hemisphere during different seasons.

The impact of man, deliberate or not, on the weather has recently become more significant. For example, if crystals of silver iodide are scattered from an aircraft into a suitable cumulus cloud, they can cause rain that would otherwise not have fallen. Some cities are susceptible to smog, a mixture of smoke and water droplets, and many urban areas become "heat islands" as a result of industrial activities and domestic heating.

The "greenhouse effect"
Over a long period, man's activities may affect climate on a world scale by the addition of extra carbon dioxide to the atmosphere. Carbon dioxide occurs naturally in the atmosphere, but the amount is gradually increasing because of the burning of fossil fuels—coal and oil. The so-called "greenhouse effect" reduces the amount of heat radiation that the Earth emits into space, thus raising temperatures near the ground. Even a small rise in temperature could make for serious change, for example, in the pattern of world agriculture. Rainfall patterns might change as well as temperature, because warmer air can hold more moisture. Some climatologists argue, however, that this warming trend will be counteracted during the next century by a natural shift towards cooler climates.

Resources and Energy

Resources, it has been said, comprise mankind's varying needs from generation to generation and are valued because of the uses societies can make of them. They represent human appraisals and are the products of man's ingenuity and experience. While natural resources remain vitally important in themselves, they must always be regarded as the rewards of human skill in locating, extracting and exploiting them. The development of resources depends on many factors, including the existence of a demand, adequate transport facilities, the availability of capital and the accessibility, quality and quantity of the resource itself.

The world's extraction of its resources highlights the inequality of their distribution. Each resource shown on the map is attributed to the three countries with the largest production percentages of that commodity. So, in 1976, the three leading bauxite producers were Australia (26.69%), Jamaica (14.19%) and Rep. of Guinea (13.9%). Usually, the larger and more wealthy a state the greater its monopoly of resources—although the tiny Pacific island of New Caledonia produces more than 14% of the world's nickel. China is reputed to mine 75% of the world's tungsten and to be increasing its oil supply rapidly. Energy consumption figures are for the year 1976, since when there have been some outstanding changes to patterns of availability, perhaps most noticeably in Britain's new-found oil and gas surplus. Bahrain and Tobago, too small to be shown on this map, also have surpluses of energy production.

A dictionary defines the term "resource" as "a means of aid or support," implying anything that lends support to life or activity. Man has always assessed nature with an eye to his own needs, and it is these varying needs that endow resources with their usefulness. Fossil fuels such as oil have lain long in the Earth, but it was not until about 1900 that the large-scale needs fostered by the rising demands of motor vehicles led to the development of new techniques for locating and extracting this raw material. Today oil has also become precious in the manufacture of a wide variety of industrial products, which themselves are resources that are much used by other industries.

The nature of resources

Resources can be most usefully classified in two groups: "renewable" and "nonrenewable." The latter is composed of materials found at or near the Earth's surface, which are sometimes known as "physical" resources. They include such essential minerals as uranium, iron, copper, nickel, bauxite, gold, silver, lead, mercury and tungsten. Oil, coal and natural gas are the principal nonrenewable fuel and energy resources, but after they have been used for producing heat or power their utility is lost and part of the geological capital of 325 million years of history is gone for ever. Some minerals such as iron and its product, steel, can be recycled and renewed, however. "Renewable" resources are basically biological, being the food and other vegetable matter which life needs to sustain human needs. Provided soil quality is maintained, their productivity may even be increased as better strains of plants and breeds of animals are developed.

Work has long been in progress to improve renewable resources, and has moved forward to manufacturing vegetable-flavored protein (VFP) from soybeans as a meat substitute and to viable experiments to extract protein from leaves. In Brazil, many cars have been converted to run successfully on alcohol extracted from sugar. One renewable resource—the tree—can be closely related to other resources: some conservationists are alarmed at the overuse of firewood as a source of fuel and energy in the semiarid areas of Africa. This may be an important factor in increasing the tendency for the deserts to spread in that continent, and in such a situation there is a new realization of the concept of closely managing resources such as soil, timber and fisheries. This is partly because we have a clearer understanding of the ecology of vegetation and the important interdependence of climate, soil, plants and animal life. Much, however, remains to be done.

The politics of nonrenewable resources

Today we are naturally troubled about the availability of natural resources. Oil is a prime cause for concern. Although many believe that production will grow until the mid-2020s and that new oil reserves will be discovered, oil's scarcity, based on a growing rate of demand and increasingly wasteful use, is now widely accepted. Because, like many resources, it is unevenly distributed, those countries with large and accessible supplies—such as the members of OPEC—have used their political power on a number of occasions to raise oil's price, with adverse effects on the economies of most importers. Ironically, these substantial price rises have had the effect of stimulating exploration and development in many new areas; there are already signs of increased production in China.

Other nonrenewable resources are also distributed unevenly, but have not been mined on any scale comparable with their availability; vast reserves of coal in the former Soviet Union and China have not been worked on any scale resembling their known extent.

New energy sources

As resources such as oil become less available and more expensive, the renewable resources of power such as water, wind, waves and solar energy, all of which are currently under study or development, will receive new injections of capital. Attention will also have to be paid to more widespread nuclear energy production. Energy has been called "the ultimate resource," and it is imperative that we make wise provisions for its future availability.

Future resources

It has been calculated that within four years of the launch of Sputnik I, more than 3,000 products resulting from space research were put into commercial production. These included new alloys, ceramics, plastics, fabrics and chemical compounds. Satellite developments have meant that land use can now be measured quickly and potential mineral sources closely identified. A satellite capable of converting solar power to electricity and contributing to the Earth's energy deficit has been widely discussed, while the Moon and planets have been mooted as future possible sources of minerals.

Conclusions

Resources are, in the main, the products of man's skill, ingenuity and expertise, and their widespread use, as in the case of timber and iron for shipbuilding, became apparent only as man's needs for them became clear. Our forebears were once concerned about the availability of flint, seaweed, charcoal and natural rubber; countries even went to war over supplies of spices. Today our requirements are slightly different—we no longer depend only on local sites for resources, and improved transport facilities and appropriate technologies have lowered the costs of obtaining materials for manufacture.

Nevertheless, the principles remain the same. A continual search for new resources capable of exploitation and wide application must be maintained, together with a close regard for the value of the renewable resources such as animal and vegetable products required to support man in his search for new resources. Perhaps the most vital consideration is the need for wise policies of conservation relating to the proven reserves of nonrenewable resources still in the ground, and the careful future use of such valuable deposits known or thought to exist.

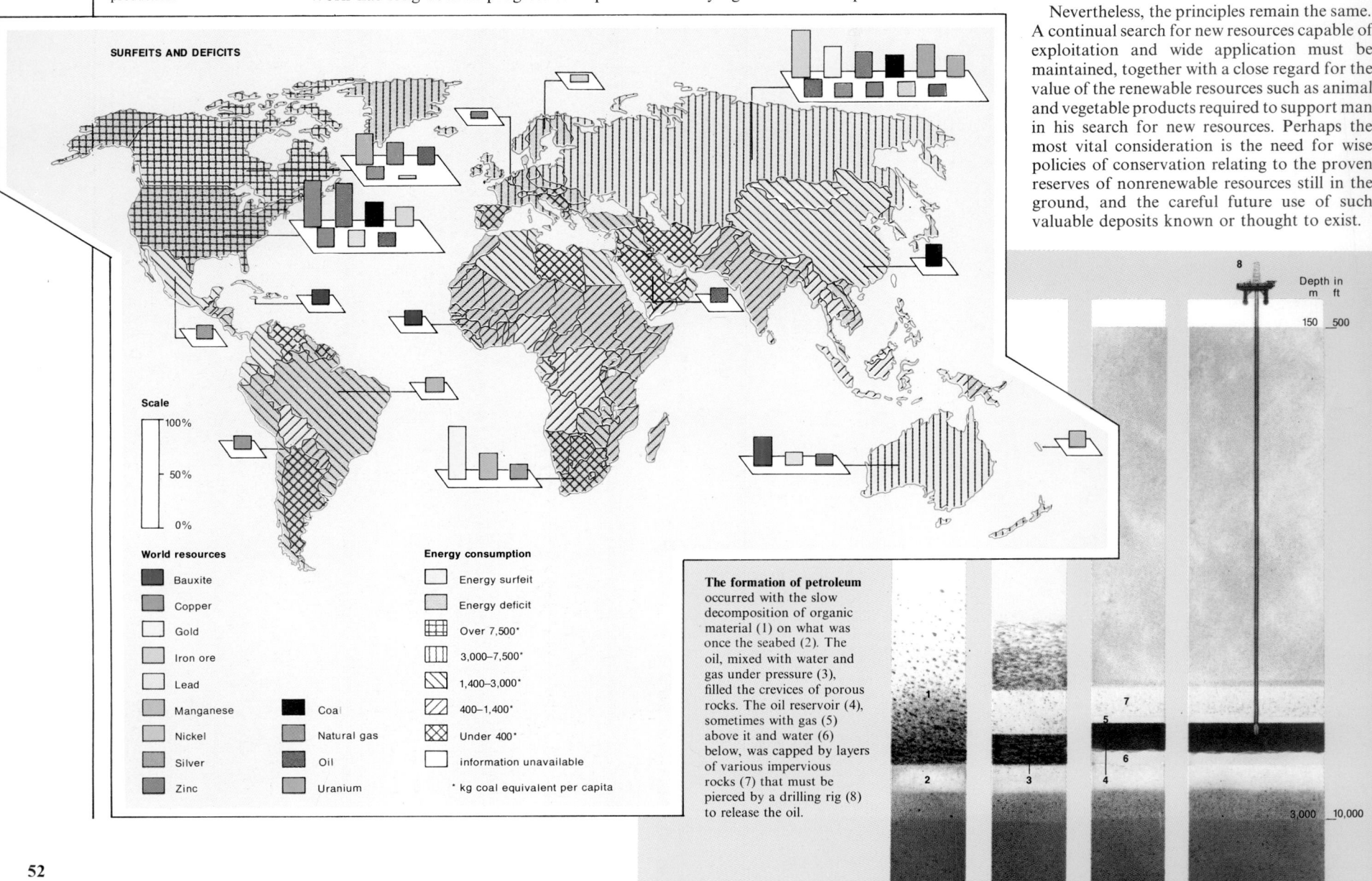

SURFEITS AND DEFICITS

Scale
100%
50%
0%

World resources
- Bauxite
- Copper
- Gold
- Iron ore
- Lead
- Manganese
- Nickel
- Silver
- Zinc
- Coal
- Natural gas
- Oil
- Uranium

Energy consumption
- Energy surfeit
- Energy deficit
- Over 7,500*
- 3,000–7,500*
- 1,400–3,000*
- 400–1,400*
- Under 400*
- information unavailable

* kg coal equivalent per capita

The formation of petroleum occurred with the slow decomposition of organic material (1) on what was once the seabed (2). The oil, mixed with water and gas under pressure (3), filled the crevices of porous rocks. The oil reservoir (4), sometimes with gas (5) above it and water (6) below, was capped by layers of various impervious rocks (7) that must be pierced by a drilling rig (8) to release the oil.

Depth in
m   ft
150   500

3,000   10,000

MAN'S ENDURING INGENUITY

A continuing search for new energy supplies has led man to explore potential oil sources in the offshore waters of the main continental land-masses. A firmly anchored production platform exemplifies the many new sites from which oil is being extracted, in an attempt to reduce reliance on the monopoly of reserves held by powerful organizations such as OPEC.

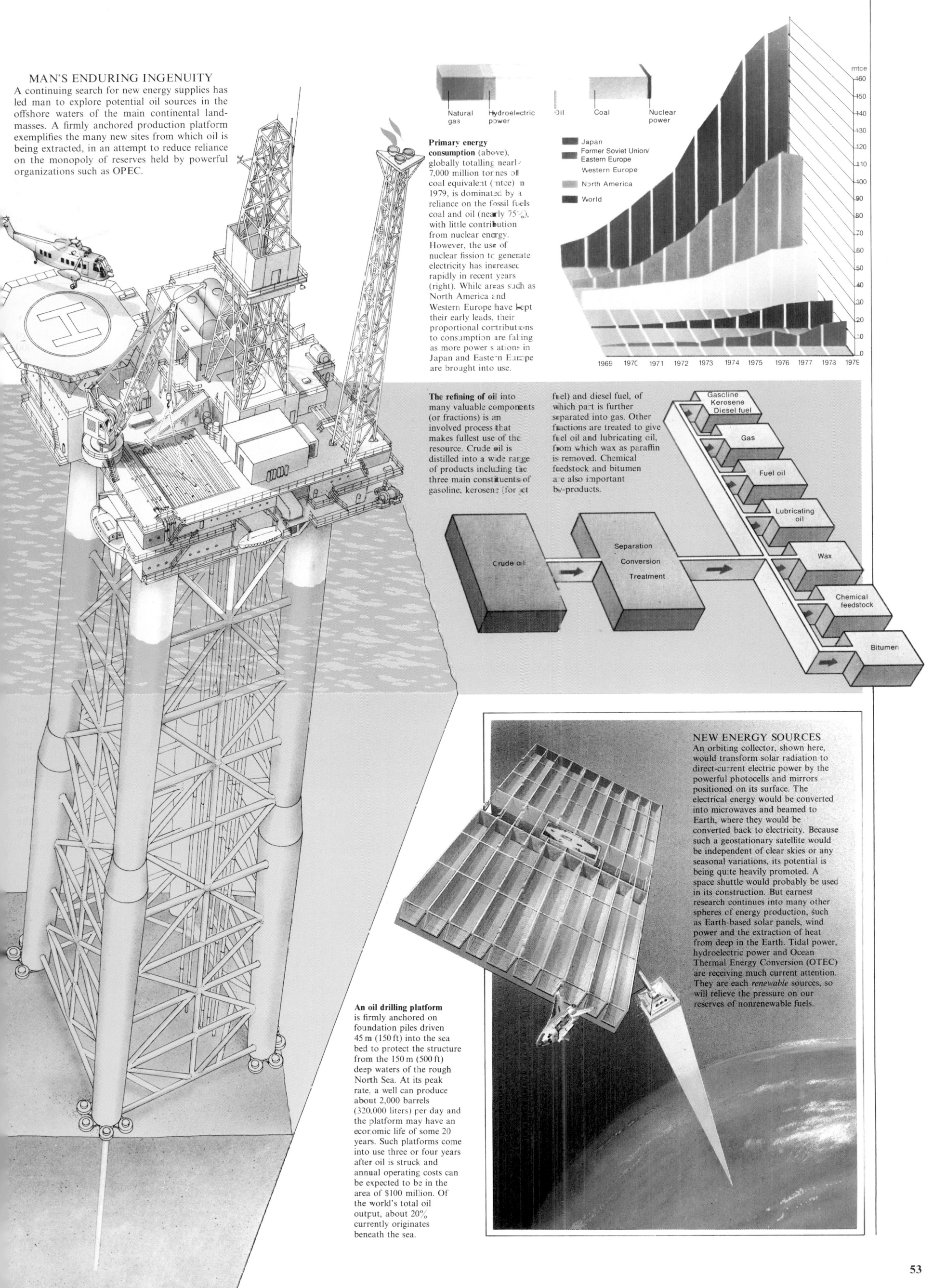

Natural gas   Hydroelectric power   Oil   Coal   Nuclear power

Japan
Former Soviet Union/ Eastern Europe
Western Europe
North America
World

mtce

Primary energy consumption (above), globally totalling nearly 7,000 million tonnes of coal equivalent (mtce) in 1979, is dominated by a reliance on the fossil fuels coal and oil (nearly 75%), with little contribution from nuclear energy. However, the use of nuclear fission to generate electricity has increased rapidly in recent years (right). While areas such as North America and Western Europe have kept their early leads, their proportional contributions to consumption are falling as more power stations in Japan and Eastern Europe are brought into use.

The refining of oil into many valuable components (or fractions) is an involved process that makes fullest use of the resource. Crude oil is distilled into a wide range of products including the three main constituents of gasoline, kerosene (for jet fuel) and diesel fuel, of which part is further separated into gas. Other fractions are treated to give fuel oil and lubricating oil, from which wax as paraffin is removed. Chemical feedstock and bitumen are also important by-products.

Crude oil → Separation Conversion Treatment →

Gasoline Kerosene Diesel fuel
Gas
Fuel oil
Lubricating oil
Wax
Chemical feedstock
Bitumen

An oil drilling platform is firmly anchored on foundation piles driven 45 m (150 ft) into the sea bed to protect the structure from the 150 m (500 ft) deep waters of the rough North Sea. At its peak rate, a well can produce about 2,000 barrels (320,000 liters) per day and the platform may have an economic life of some 20 years. Such platforms come into use three or four years after oil is struck and annual operating costs can be expected to be in the area of $100 million. Of the world's total oil output, about 20% currently originates beneath the sea.

NEW ENERGY SOURCES

An orbiting collector, shown here, would transform solar radiation to direct-current electric power by the powerful photocells and mirrors positioned on its surface. The electrical energy would be converted into microwaves and beamed to Earth, where they would be converted back to electricity. Because such a geostationary satellite would be independent of clear skies or any seasonal variations, its potential is being quite heavily promoted. A space shuttle would probably be used in its construction. But earnest research continues into many other spheres of energy production, such as Earth-based solar panels, wind power and the extraction of heat from deep in the Earth. Tidal power, hydroelectric power and Ocean Thermal Energy Conversion (OTEC) are receiving much current attention. They are each *renewable* sources, so will relieve the pressure on our reserves of nonrenewable fuels.

Population Growth

Every minute of every day, more than 250 children are born into the world. The Earth's population now stands at about 4,300 million and is continuing to grow extremely rapidly. The problems associated with such growth are enormous – already, about two-thirds of the world's people are underfed, according to United Nations' recommended standards of nutrition. And an even greater number live in very poor housing conditions, have inadequate access to medical facilities, receive little or no education and, at present, have no hope of improving their lot. As yet, there are no simple or immediate solutions.

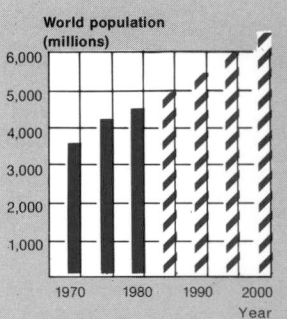

World population (millions)

If the world's population continues to grow at its present rate, by the year 2000 there could be more than 6,400 million people on Earth (above). Such growth rates are only a recent phenomenon—for most of mankind's existence on Earth the numbers grew slowly (right). Then in the late 18th century, scientific and industrial developments and the discovery of new food sources (the prairies of the New World) raised living standards. Death rates declined and populations grew rapidly.

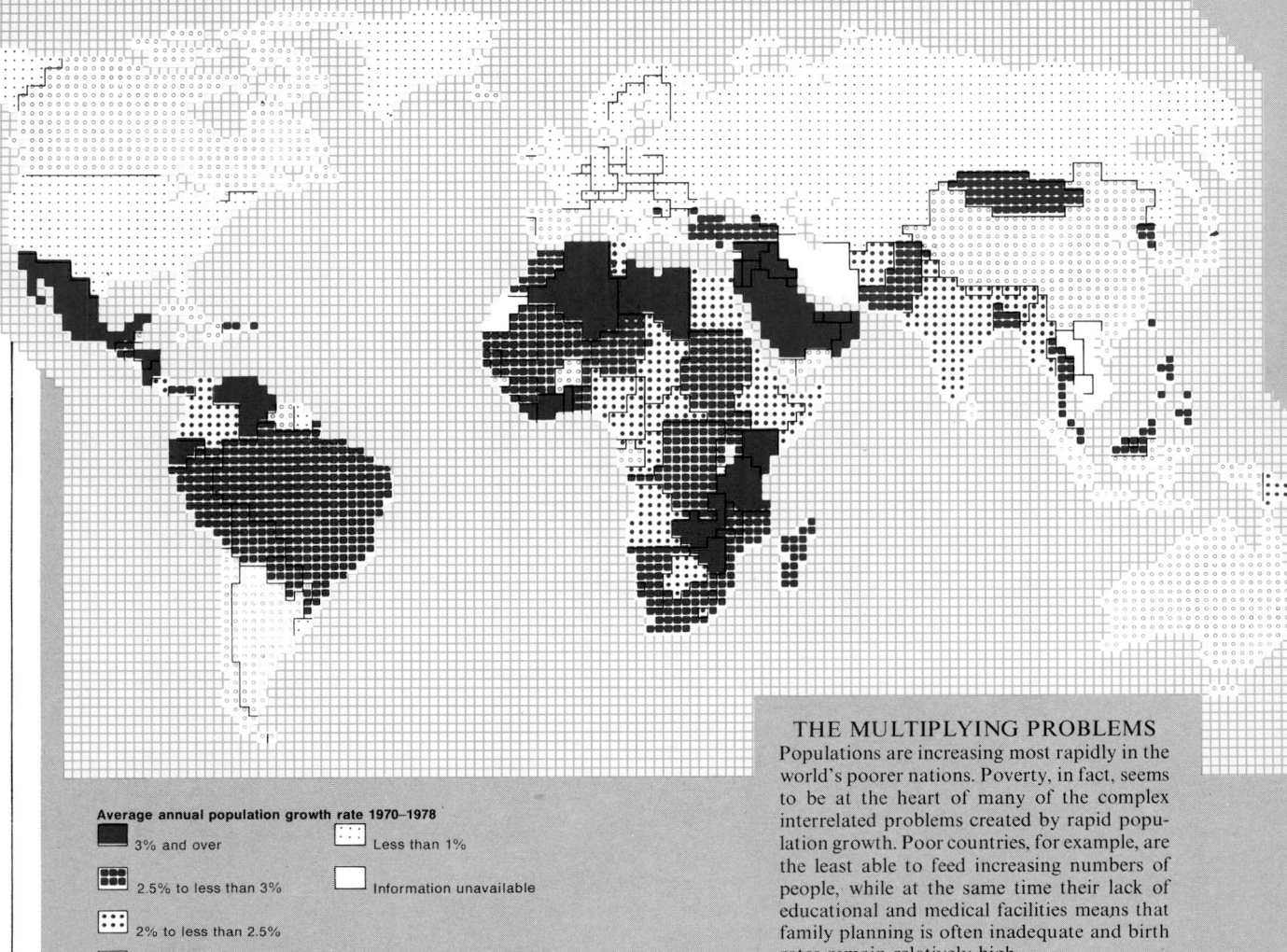

Average annual population growth rate 1970–1978

- ■ 3% and over
- ▦ 2.5% to less than 3%
- ▤ 2% to less than 2.5%
- ▢ 1.0% to less than 2%
- ⋯ Less than 1%
- □ Information unavailable

THE MULTIPLYING PROBLEMS

Populations are increasing most rapidly in the world's poorer nations. Poverty, in fact, seems to be at the heart of many of the complex interrelated problems created by rapid population growth. Poor countries, for example, are the least able to feed increasing numbers of people, while at the same time their lack of educational and medical facilities means that family planning is often inadequate and birth rates remain relatively high.

In 1830, there were only about 1,000 million people on Earth. By 1930, this figure had doubled. And by 1975, it had doubled again. If the present rate of increase continues, it will have doubled again by the year 2020.

This may not happen—it is extremely difficult to predict how world population will behave. What is certain is that it will continue to increase and, moreover, that this increase will not be evenly distributed. Since more than 50 percent of the human race lives in Asia, it is inevitable that the largest population increases will take place there. In fact, by the year 2000, the population of Asia may well have grown from about 2,000 million to more than 3,600 million. Substantial increases, of 400 million or more, will probably also occur in Africa, and Latin America is growing equally quickly.

In more prosperous North America and Europe, however, population growth seems to be stabilizing as women have fewer children and families become smaller—several countries, such as West Germany, now record a zero population growth rate. The poorer countries, the so-called Third World, are therefore gaining, and will probably continue to gain, an increasing share of the world's people. In 1930, about 64 percent of the human race lived in the poor countries of Asia, Africa and Latin America. By 1980, this proportion had increased to more than 75 percent. Population growth in these regions is creating enormous problems. It is estimated that there are now

more than 800 million people living in absolute poverty in the developing world, and these numbers can but increase as populations swell.

An obvious solution is to reduce birth rates, but this cannot be achieved quickly. In much of Africa and Asia, a very high proportion of the population is made up of young people who are, or soon will be, of childbearing age. Population increases are therefore inevitable. This will probably change as family planning becomes more widespread and women have fewer children, but such relief lies in the future and is likely to affect the poorest countries last. The most pressing problem for the growing numbers of impoverished people today is that of hunger.

Food – the fundamental problem

In theory, no food supply problem should exist—already enough food is produced in the world to feed a population of 5,500 million people. In fact, however, two-thirds of this food is consumed by the rich industrialized nations, and supplies are not reaching many of those in need. The developed nations dominate world food markets because developing nations, and people within those nations, are too poor to buy food, and are themselves unable to produce sufficient quantities to feed their growing populations. The answer to undernutrition and malnutrition lies largely in raising the incomes of poor peoples and improving distribution of supplies of food.

At a local level, food produced or imported

by developing countries must reach those in need at a price they can afford. One way of doing this is to encourage the rural poor to produce their own food. Small-scale, intensively farmed plots often prove to be the most efficient form of agriculture in areas where labor is plentiful. At present, many of the rural poor are either without land, or hold plots on extremely unfavorable terms of tenancy. By providing land, appropriate technology (small-scale, inexpensive farming equipment such as windpumps to draw water for irrigation), financial aid and information and education, small farmers could be helped to farm their land as effectively and efficiently as possible.

At a national level, too, developing countries must become more self-sufficient in food. This has already been achieved in some countries. India, although at one time heavily dependent upon imports of one of its staple foodstuffs—rice—has now increased production on such a scale that imports are no longer necessary. Unfortunately, for many developing countries this is not the case. Zaire, for example, was once an exporter of food. Today the country can no longer produce enough to keep pace with the demands of its own expanding population. At a world level, food production must be maintained as well, for unless production is kept high, prices are unstable and at times of bad harvests the poorer nations cannot afford to import essential supplies.

Food alone, however, is not enough to solve

FEEDING THE WORLD

How are the growing numbers of people on Earth to be fed when millions are already undernourished? In the short term, the food problem could be solved by improving distribution of supplies that are already available. But the world can also be made to produce more food. Fertilizers and pest control can make land more productive and genetic engineering could produce higher-yielding and more nutritious crops.

The world will have to produce more food than it does today (below) if future populations are to be fed. At present, large areas of the Earth's land surface cannot be farmed—they are either too cold, dry, marshy, mountainous or forested. Cultivatable areas could be extended, given the necessary investment.

THE HEALTH OF NATIONS

Many developing nations are severely short of medical and welfare facilities for their growing populations. Yet these are the very countries with high incidences of disease—mainly because of malnutrition, lack of clean water supplies, and inadequate and overcrowded housing. Furthermore, without health services family planning facilities are not widely available, and expanding populations continue to strain existing resources.

Birth and Death Rates
- High birth rate/ High death rate
- High birth rate/ Moderate or low death rate
- Low birth rate/ Low death rate
- Information unavailable

THE NONPRODUCTIVE LANDS

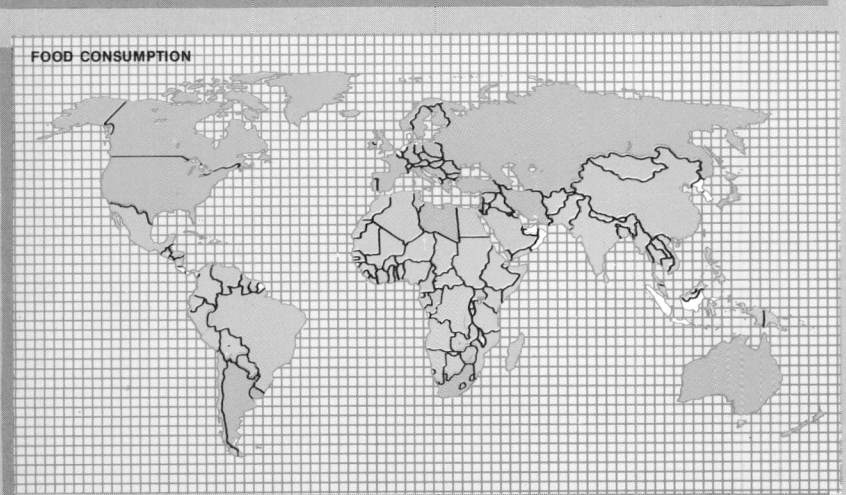

- Areas with no agricultural activity

PATTERNS OF POPULATION GROWTH

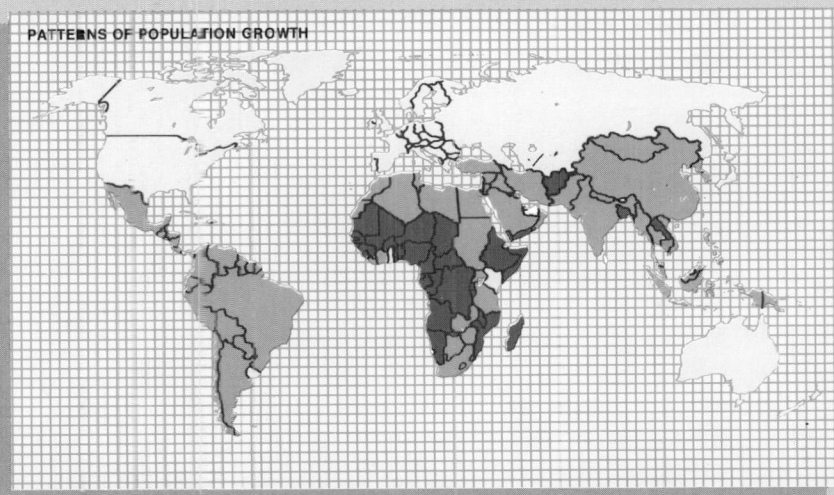

FOOD CONSUMPTION

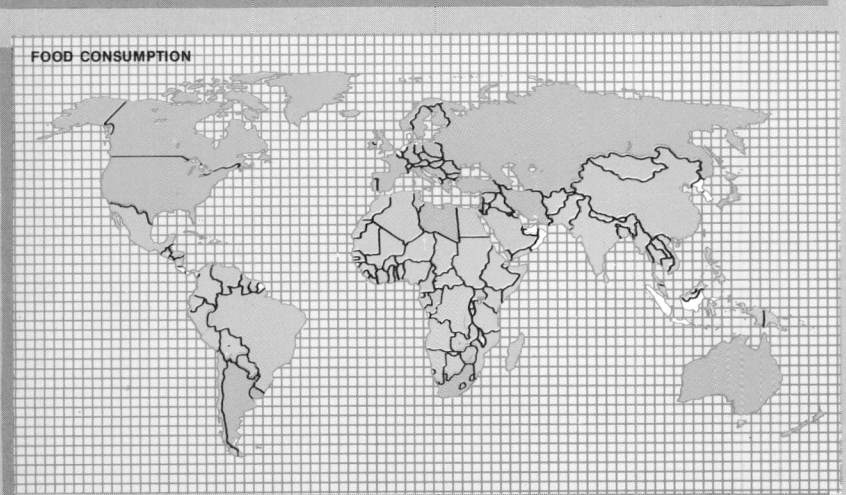

As a country's health facilities improve, its mortality rates decline. Birth rates, however, do not immediately fall (above). Thus, ironically, an improvement in facilities at first exacerbates the problem of rapid growth in population. A country with a declining death rate and a high birth rate gains an increasing percentage of young people who are, or will be, of child-bearing age. Population pyramids (right) plot the percentage balance between age and youth in a nation.

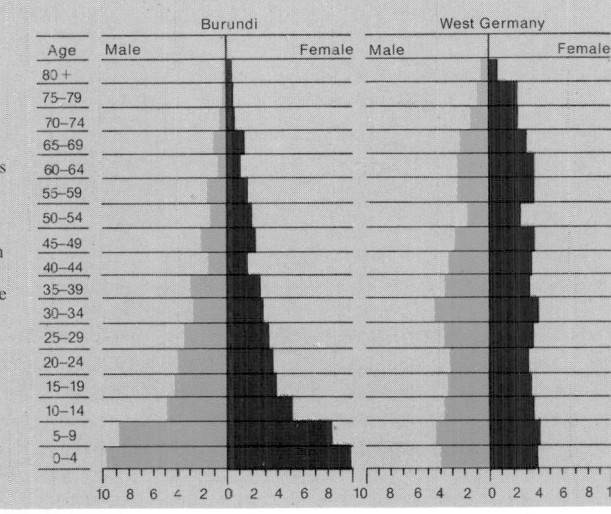

Calories per capita
- Less than 95% of needs
- 95% to 115% of needs
- More than 115% of needs
- Information unavailable

Malnutrition is widespread throughout the developing nations of Africa, Asia and South America. The problem is made worse by the fact that populations in these countries are growing more rapidly than anywhere else in the world.

the problems created by population growth. Broadly based economic development, such as in manufacturing and industry, is essential if developing countries are to have the income and other resources to enable them to cope with their evergrowing numbers of people.

Economic growth

To achieve economic development, certain obstacles must be overcome. First, the Third World needs energy supplies at a price it can afford, for, with the exception of Nigeria and the now-rich Middle East, most developing regions are woefully short of the energy resources needed to fuel growth. Second, for sustained economic development a skilled labor force is required, as are educational facilities to provide the necessary skills from within the nations themselves. Third, investment is required to enable developing nations to exploit the resources they do have—minerals, for example. And this investment must be on terms that are as beneficial to the developing nations as they are to powerful multinational organizations that frequently fund such projects. Finally, and most important, more enlightened social and political outlooks are needed within many countries if their growing populations of impoverished people are to benefit from any economic development and consequent increase in national wealth.

It has been said that wealth is the best method of contraception and, judging by the history of population growth in the rich industrialized nations, this seems to be the case. If it is, economic development of the Third World may well alleviate many of the problems created by population growth.

INCOME

When the income level of a population is raised sufficiently, it seems that birth rates ultimately decline. This has been the pattern that has emerged in the Western world. If this is the case, then economic development of the Third World countries could eventually help to stabilize world population growth, as well as provide nations with the means to cope. It could also help provide for their growing numbers.

POVERTY AND WEALTH

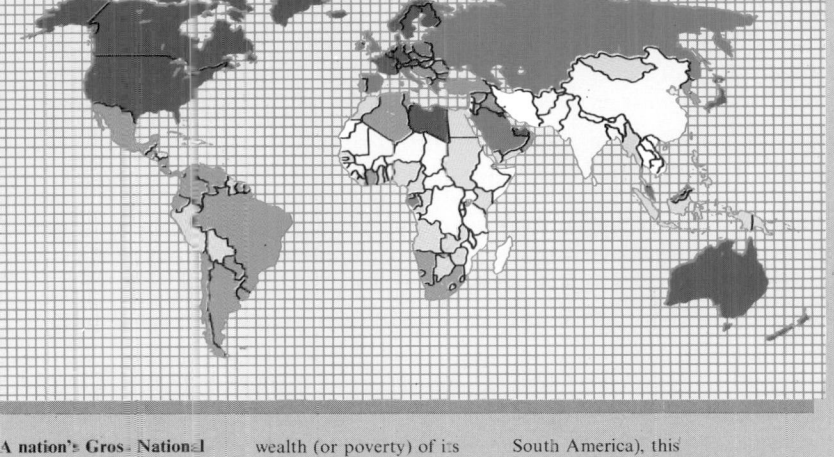

Gross National Product per capita 1978 ($US)
- Less than $300
- $300 to $699
- $700 to $2,999
- $3,000 to $6,999
- $7,000 and over
- Information unavailable

A nation's Gross National Product (GNP), when divided by the number of its population, gives some indication of the relative wealth (or poverty) of its people. But because national wealth is not evenly distributed in many countries (particularly in South America), this figure can conceal the extreme poverty of very large numbers of a nation's people.

EDUCATIONAL RESOURCES

Education is essential if the people of the developing world are to be equipped to improve their lot. Basic education on health and hygiene could dramatically reduce the incidence of disease; education about birth control would help lower birth rates; agricultural advice could help the rural poor to produce more food. Finally, general schooling is required to provide skilled labor.

ILLITERACY

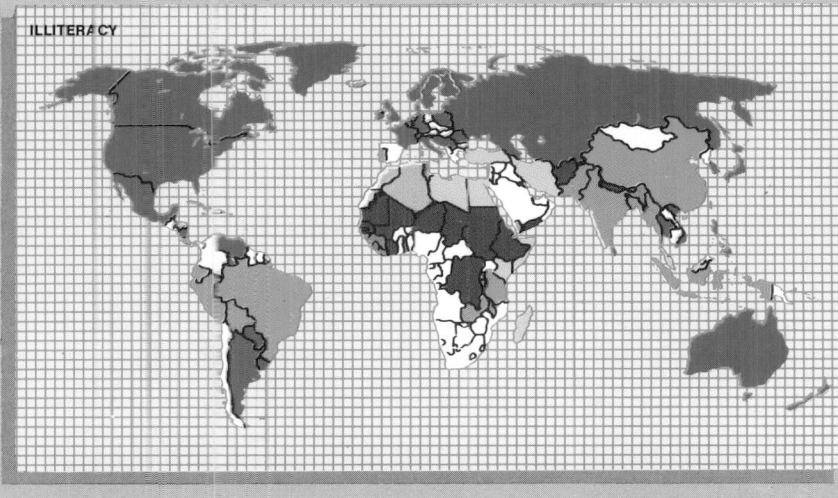

Illiteracy rate
- 80% and over
- 60% to less than 80%
- 40% to less than 60%
- 20% to less than 40%
- Less than 20%
- Information unavailable

Literacy rates are in fact improving in developing countries and national expenditure on schools is growing more quickly than is population. Two major problems are, first, the social traditions that severely restrict the number of girls attending school and, second, the reluctance of many rural poor to send to school children who provide valuable manual labor on the land.

Human Settlement

Man is naturally a gregarious animal. As an agriculturist he first settled in small communities, but it was not long before the emergence of towns and cities. Now nearly half the world's people live in these larger settlements, and by the year 2000, for the first time in history, more people will live in cities than in the countryside. Cities have grown up for various reasons, and are unevenly distributed across the world; but it is in the developing countries that the most rapid rates of urban growth are today taking place.

City life has a long and varied history going back to the early population centers of the Tigris–Euphrates, Indus and Nile valleys. Administrative and political needs led to the development of capital cities. Some, like London and Paris, evolved on conveniently located river crossings; others, such as Canberra, Islamabad and Brasilia, have locations that were deliberately planned.

Types of towns and cities
Market towns were established to exchange produce and, as trade expanded, hierarchies of service centers became established. These ranged from small "central places" that supplied rural areas with simple goods and services from elsewhere, to large cities that provided highly specialized services. Through such centrally placed systems, rural areas became connected with major industrialized areas. Mining towns such as Johannesburg, South Africa, and Broken Hill, Australia, sprang up as man began to exploit the Earth's mineral resources, their locations determined by the presence of rich ore deposits. Fishing ports and settlements dependent on forestry fall into the same group.

Increasing specialization, exemplified by the Black Country, England, and the Ruhr, West Germany, was a feature of European industrial development in the eighteenth and nineteenth centuries, and was based on the availability of capital investment and the presence of sources of fuel and power, especially water and steam power. Such industrialized cities relied on newly developed forms of transport to bring in new materials and to carry away manufactured products. Chicago is a good example of the relationship between the development of rail and water routes and the growth of a city as a market, agricultural processing and manufacturing center. As transport developed, further specialized centers concentrated on locomotive, ship or aircraft construction.

Uneven settlement patterns
Across the world, density and distribution of population are uneven. The land surface of the Earth as a whole has a density of 28 people per sq km (73 per sq mile) although Manhattan, for example, has 26,000 per sq km (63,340 per sq mile) and Australia has only 1.5 per sq km (4 per sq mile). In Brazil, towns and cities are mostly sited in the rich southeast, in contrast to a sparseness of settlement in its interior. Contrasts also occur between Mediterranean North Africa and the deserted Sahara to the south; or Canada of the St. Lawrence and the Canadian Shield to the north. Here the causes are not hard to find: extremes of climate, terrain and vegetation form effective barriers to settlement. Geographers estimate that two-thirds of the world's population lives within 500 km (310 miles) of the sea.

Any true consideration of human settlements must, however, be placed within the context of the economic, political and social systems in which they have evolved. Physical considerations alone cannot fully explain the urban concentrations of Western Europe, Japan or the northeastern USA, or the comparative absence of cities elsewhere. Only 5 percent of Malawi's and 4.7 percent of New Guinea's populations live in towns; in Belgium the percentage is 87, in Australia 86, in the UK 78 and in the USA 73.5. The figure for Norway is only 42 percent. Urbanization is a varied phenomenon and cities grow for many reasons.

The attractions of the city
Cities have always acted as magnets to poor or unemployed rural populations, and migrations from the countryside have assisted high rates of

THE DISTRIBUTION OF POPULATION
Human settlement is highly uneven because it is related to many social and topographical factors. At first, man was tied to the sites of his crops and the grazing land of his cattle; life in nonrural centers only became a typical feature of population development as specialized services came into demand and towns and cities arose to support these needs. But during the 20th century there has been a vast increase in urban populations, particularly in Third World countries.

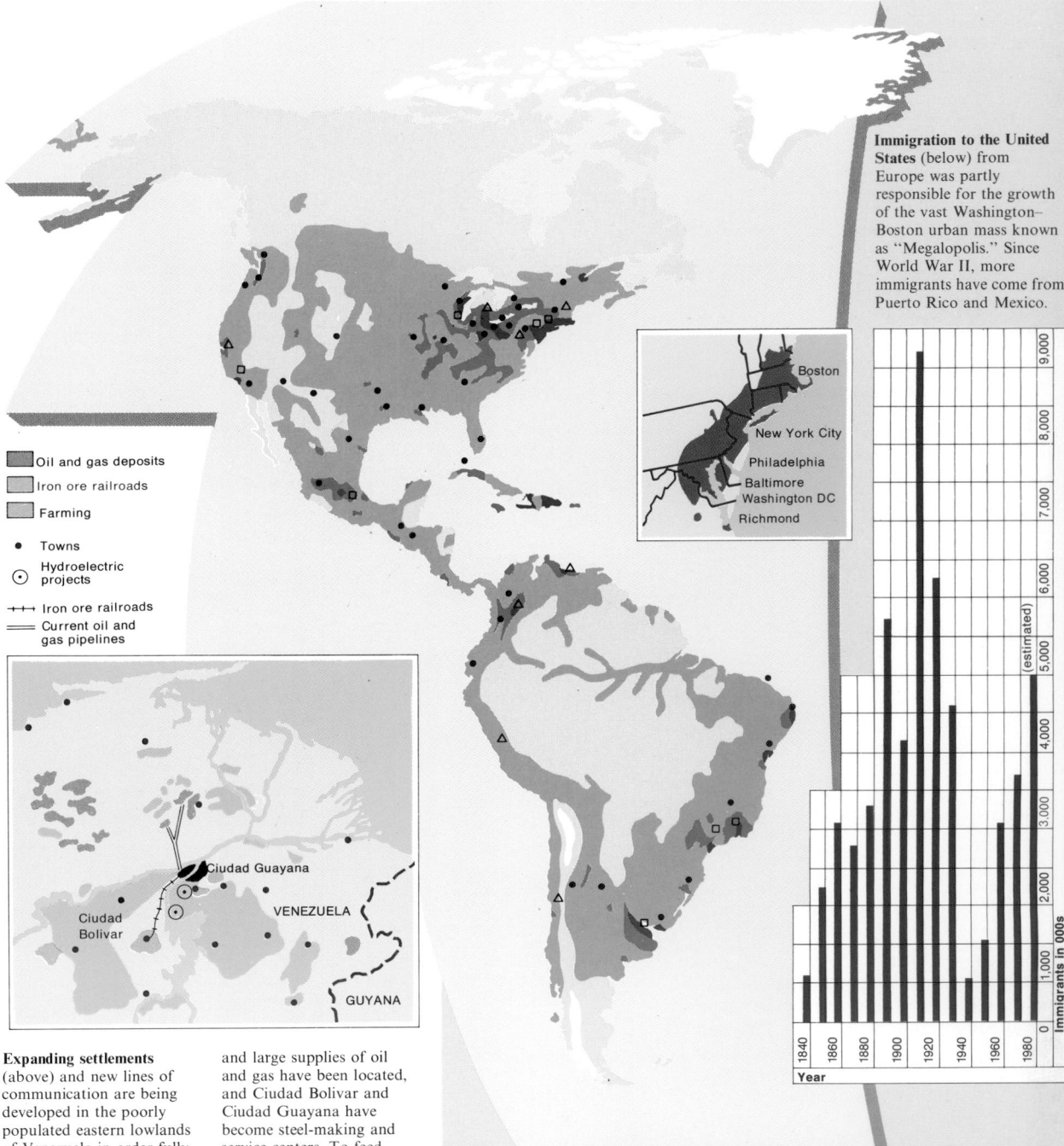

Immigration to the United States (below) from Europe was partly responsible for the growth of the vast Washington–Boston urban mass known as "Megalopolis." Since World War II, more immigrants have come from Puerto Rico and Mexico.

Oil and gas deposits
Iron ore railroads
Farming
• Towns
⊙ Hydroelectric projects
+++ Iron ore railroads
═ Current oil and gas pipelines

Expanding settlements (above) and new lines of communication are being developed in the poorly populated eastern lowlands of Venezuela in order fully to exploit the resources being discovered there. Huge deposits of iron ore and large supplies of oil and gas have been located, and Ciudad Bolivar and Ciudad Guayana have become steel-making and service centers. To feed the people of these new settlements, agriculture has been greatly expanded.

city growth. Very large cities—Tokyo, New York and Los Angeles—are still found in the northern world, but many cities with far faster growth rates are sited in the Third World, especially in Asia. There the total number of inhabitants living in towns and cities is still much lower than in Europe, but centers such as Shanghai, Karachi, Bandung, New Delhi, Seoul, Jakarta and Manila are among the world's most rapidly expanding urban centers. Perhaps as many as a third of these city dwellers in Asia, Africa and Latin America put up with makeshift housing in shanty towns that present enormous problems of health, sanitation, education and unemployment: city growth in the developing world is a daunting prospect.

People on the move
In the past, one solution to population pressure on the land could be found in the migrations which occurred on a large scale from Asia into Europe, from Europe to the Americas and Australasia, and from China into southeastern Asia. But as claims are being made on almost every habitable area of the Earth, mass migrations have largely declined in importance. Many nations restrict movement to or from

their countries. Australia has strict immigration quotas; Vietnam restricts emigration for largely ideological reasons. Large movements of labor still take place, however, from the poorer regions of the Mediterranean to the industrial cities of France and Germany. Migrant workers from neighboring countries in Africa also play an essential part in the mining economy of South Africa.

New trends in urbanization
In many industrialized countries, a strong process of decentralization is leading to reductions in the populations of cities and corresponding increases in those of the suburbs and beyond. In 1951 the geographer Jean Gottman showed how groups of city regions tend to form chains of functionally linked cities, to which he gave the term "megalopolis." His prime example was Megalopolis, USA, stretching from north of Boston to south of Washington DC. Similar settlements occur in the Tokyo–Yokohama–Osaka area of Japan and the Ruhr megalopolis of northwestern Europe. Ultimately, equally drastic and large-scale patterns are likely to emerge in the already overcrowded human settlements of the Third World.

Migrating refugees, the world total of which increases on average by 2,000–3,000 every day, can affect settlement patterns. The Ugandan children (below) fled to the northern province of Karamoja in the wake of the 1979 war with Tanzania and the resultant famine that occurred in much of Uganda.

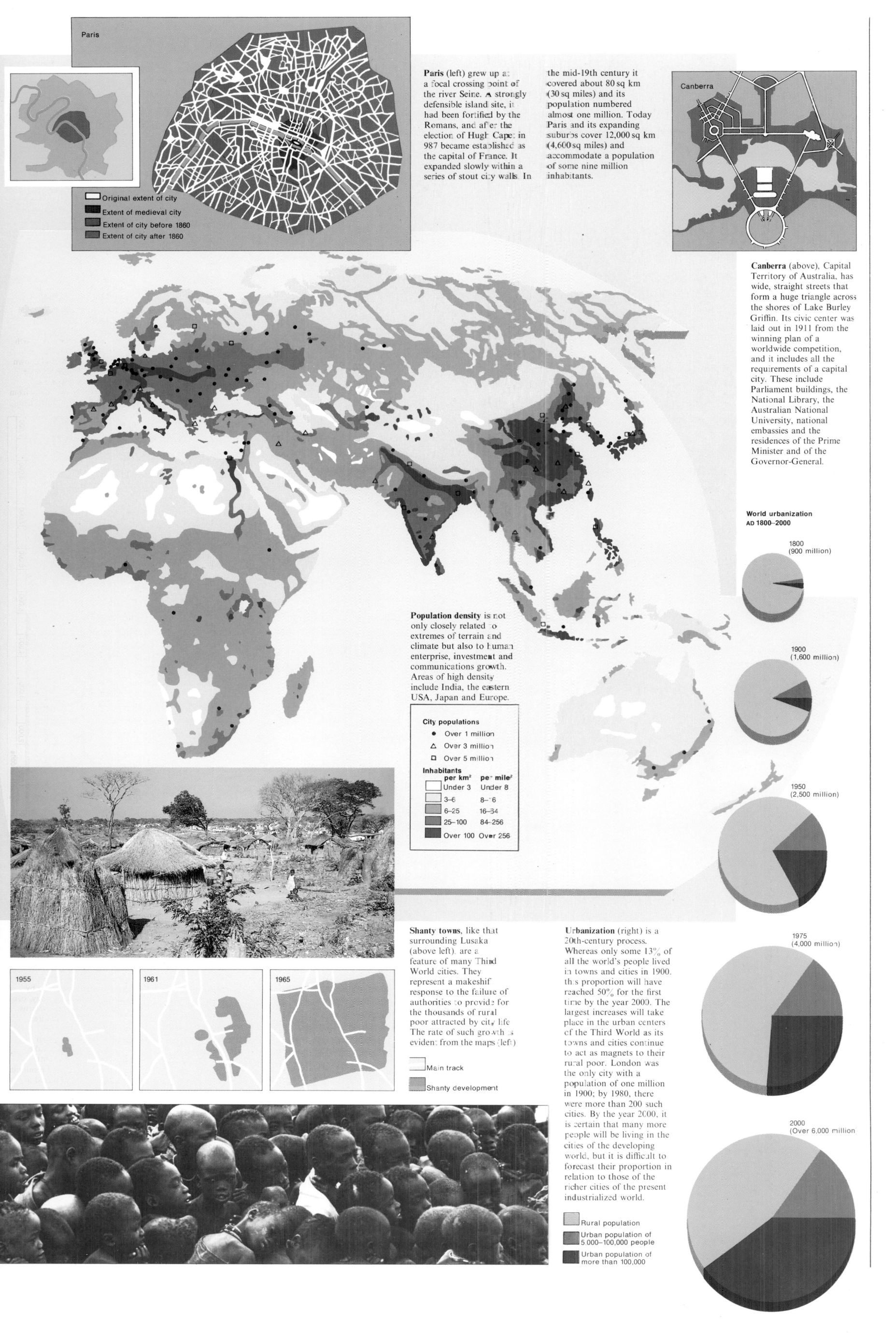

Paris

Paris (left) grew up at a focal crossing point of the river Seine. A strongly defensible island site, it had been fortified by the Romans, and after the election of Hugh Capet in 987 became established as the capital of France. It expanded slowly within a series of stout city walls. In the mid-19th century it covered about 80 sq km (30 sq miles) and its population numbered almost one million. Today Paris and its expanding suburbs cover 12,000 sq km (4,600 sq miles) and accommodate a population of some nine million inhabitants.

☐ Original extent of city
■ Extent of medieval city
■ Extent of city before 1860
■ Extent of city after 1860

Canberra

Canberra (above), Capital Territory of Australia, has wide, straight streets that form a huge triangle across the shores of Lake Burley Griffin. Its civic center was laid out in 1911 from the winning plan of a worldwide competition, and it includes all the requirements of a capital city. These include Parliament buildings, the National Library, the Australian National University, national embassies and the residences of the Prime Minister and of the Governor-General.

World urbanization
AD 1800–2000

1800
(900 million)

1900
(1,600 million)

1950
(2,500 million)

Population density is not only closely related to extremes of terrain and climate but also to human enterprise, investment and communications growth. Areas of high density include India, the eastern USA, Japan and Europe.

City populations
● Over 1 million
△ Over 3 million
☐ Over 5 million

Inhabitants

	per km²	per mile²
☐	Under 3	Under 8
	3–6	8–16
	6–25	16–64
	25–100	84–256
	Over 100	Over 256

Shanty towns, like that surrounding Lusaka (above left), are a feature of many Third World cities. They represent a makeshift response to the failure of authorities to provide for the thousands of rural poor attracted by city life. The rate of such growth is evident from the maps (left)

1955   1961   1965

Main track
Shanty development

Urbanization (right) is a 20th-century process. Whereas only some 13% of all the world's people lived in towns and cities in 1900, this proportion will have reached 50% for the first time by the year 2000. The largest increases will take place in the urban centers of the Third World as its towns and cities continue to act as magnets to their rural poor. London was the only city with a population of one million in 1900; by 1980, there were more than 200 such cities. By the year 2000, it is certain that many more people will be living in the cities of the developing world, but it is difficult to forecast their proportion in relation to those of the richer cities of the present industrialized world.

1975
(4,000 million)

2000
(Over 6,000 million)

☐ Rural population
■ Urban population of 5,000–100,000 people
■ Urban population of more than 100,000

57

Trade and Transport

It is a commonplace that we live in a "shrinking" world. During the last century the development of communications has been so rapid that man appears almost to have conquered the challenge of distance; but such a concept depends on the kind of area to be covered and the cost of transporting goods in relation to their value, bulk and perishability. People, goods and services become accessible by trade. Transport makes trade possible: trade's demands lead to improvements in transport.

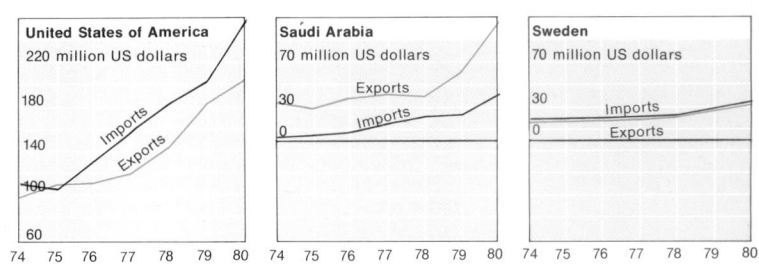

Exports in millions of US dollars (A)

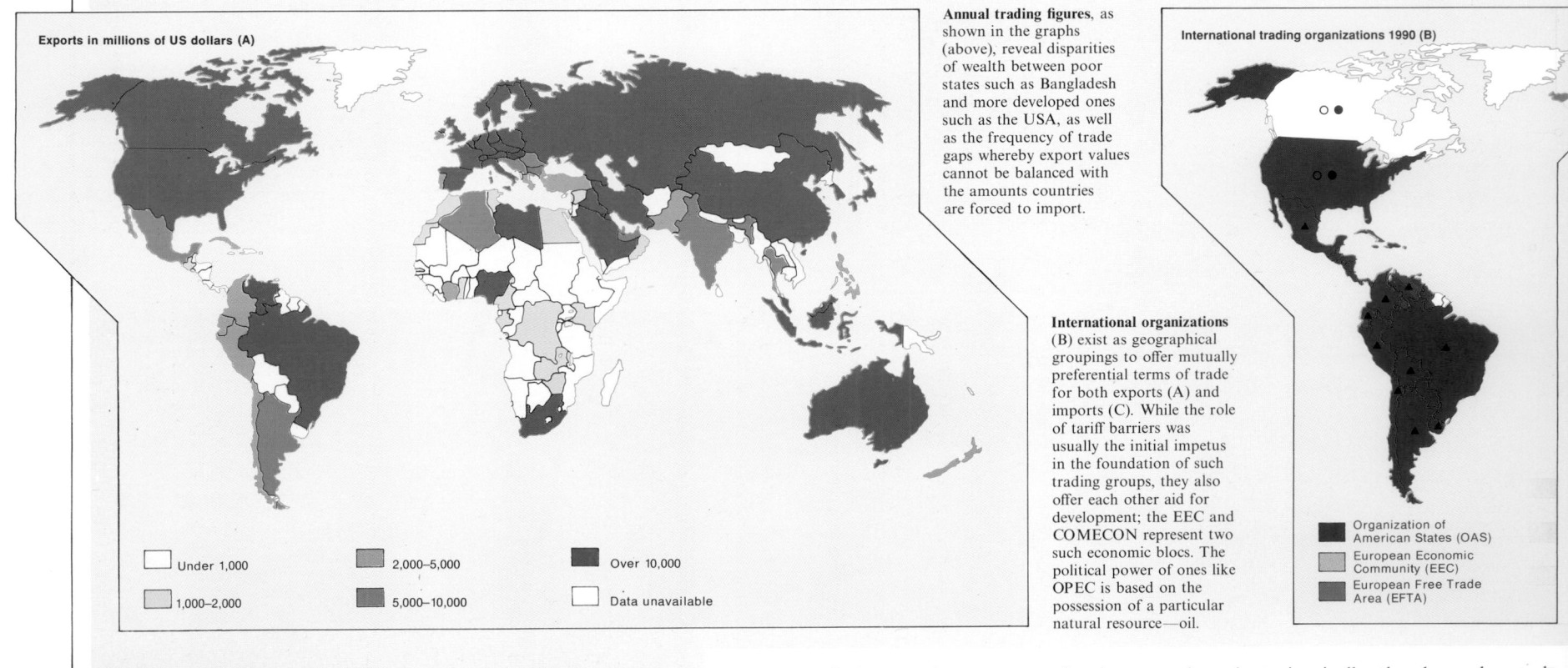

Annual trading figures, as shown in the graphs (above), reveal disparities of wealth between poor states such as Bangladesh and more developed ones such as the USA, as well as the frequency of trade gaps whereby export values cannot be balanced with the amounts countries are forced to import.

International trading organizations 1990 (B)

International organizations (B) exist as geographical groupings to offer mutually preferential terms of trade for both exports (A) and imports (C). While the role of tariff barriers was usually the initial impetus in the foundation of such trading groups, they also offer each other aid for development; the EEC and COMECON represent two such economic blocs. The political power of ones like OPEC is based on the possession of a particular natural resource—oil.

Under 1,000   2,000–5,000   Over 10,000
1,000–2,000   5,000–10,000   Data unavailable

Organization of American States (OAS)
European Economic Community (EEC)
European Free Trade Area (EFTA)

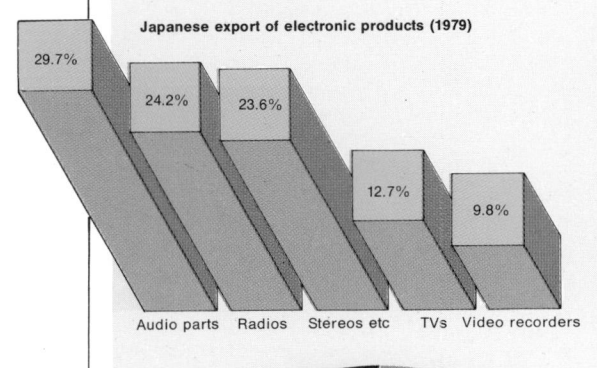

Japanese export of electronic products (1979)

29.7% — Audio parts
24.2% — Radios
23.6% — Stereos etc
12.7% — TVs
9.8% — Video recorders

Electronic products comprise only one-sixth of Japanese exports (left); their high export value and reputation for quality make their sales abroad vital to Japan's economy. Trading links (below) with industrialized countries are very well established; now Japan is mounting new export drives to sell its products to much less traditional markets.

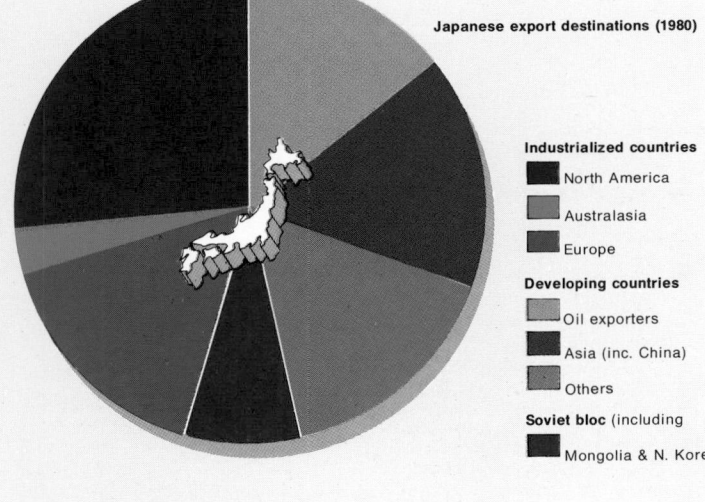

Japanese export destinations (1980)

Industrialized countries
North America
Australasia
Europe

Developing countries
Oil exporters
Asia (inc. China)
Others

Soviet bloc (including Mongolia & N. Korea)

It is only a little more than two centuries since navigators completed the mapping of the world's major landmasses and much less since the mapping of the continental interiors was completed—even today some gaps still remain. Canals like the Suez (1869) and Panama (1915) reduced the extent of long sea voyages—the Suez Canal shortened the distance from northwestern Europe to India by 15,000 km (9,300 miles)—so that in transport terms, the various parts of the world became more accessible, especially as steamships and motor vessels replaced sailing ships, and time distances were reduced still further by the airplane.

Locational advantages

Inland waterways, roads and railroads opened up new areas for mining or specialized agriculture, and created opportunities for the manufacture of goods and for the distribution of the finished products. The contrast, however, between locations such as London, Tokyo or Chicago (which are accessible to all forms of transport) and parts of South America where modern transport hardly penetrates, has become much more marked over the years. New transport developments tend to connect major centers first of all, and thus increase their already high locational status.

Such developments must nevertheless be seen in the light of the demand for communications and trade between different points, the nature of the goods being carried and the actual cost of transport. Transport improvements have allowed different parts of the world to share ideas

and products; ironically, they have also made such places more dissimilar, since each area of the Earth has had the chance to specialize in the services it can provide most efficiently.

Specialization of area

Before the widespread development of canals and railroads, road transport was expensive and towns and villages tended to be more self-sufficient. Railroads played a vital role in reducing transport costs in relation to distance and in providing an opportunity for different areas to specialize. After the emergence of railroad networks in North America, specialized areas of agricultural production quickly developed because they were well adjusted to the climatic conditions needed for growing maize (corn), cotton, fruit and fresh vegetables for the new urban markets. In the southern hemisphere, steamships and the introduction of refrigeration enabled meat, butter and cheese to be kept fresh on their journeys to the north.

This concept of specialization of area is basic to world trading patterns, since regions tend to concentrate on commodities and services that they can exchange for other specialized goods and products from other regional or world markets. Countries and areas do best when they concentrate on products for which they have comparative cost advantages in terms of the presence of natural resources, the availability of the skills to develop them, and a demand for the products. Enterprise in adapting natural conditions for the production of goods at competitive price levels is also important. Settlers in New

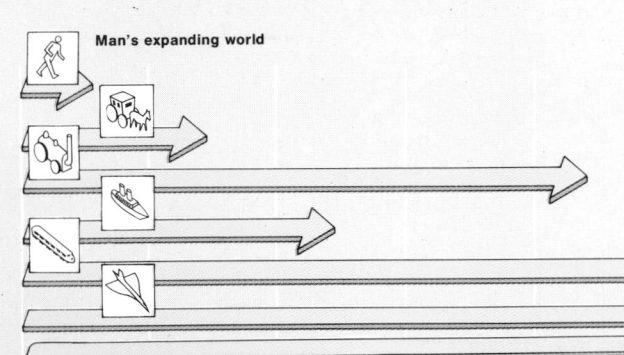

Man's expanding world

Technological change in transport has resulted in important reductions in the cost of trade. A man trading on foot might travel half the area a

draft horse could cover in a 12-hour day, but it was the acceptance of steam after *The Rocket* (1829) that made trade more reliable and greatly

expanded the potential for international commerce. Modern jet airliners can easily fly thousands of kilometers in half a day, and while they are being

used more and more for freight, most bulk freight is still carried by train or by specialized cargo vessel. The graph below plots changing transport technology.

0   120   240   360   480   600   720   840   960   1,080   1,200   1,320   1,440   1,560
Kilometers traveled in 12 hours

THE WEALTH OF NATIONS

Economists measure a country's richness in terms of Gross National Product (GNP), the value of the goods and services available for consumption and for adding to its wealth. The difference in value between its exported and imported goods is often an important aspect of a nation's economy, and effective systems to transport such goods must play a major role in overseas trade. The 1980 Brandt Report highlighted the huge gap between the income of the rich world and the poverty of many developing states, but solutions to such problems of inequality will be difficult to obtain.

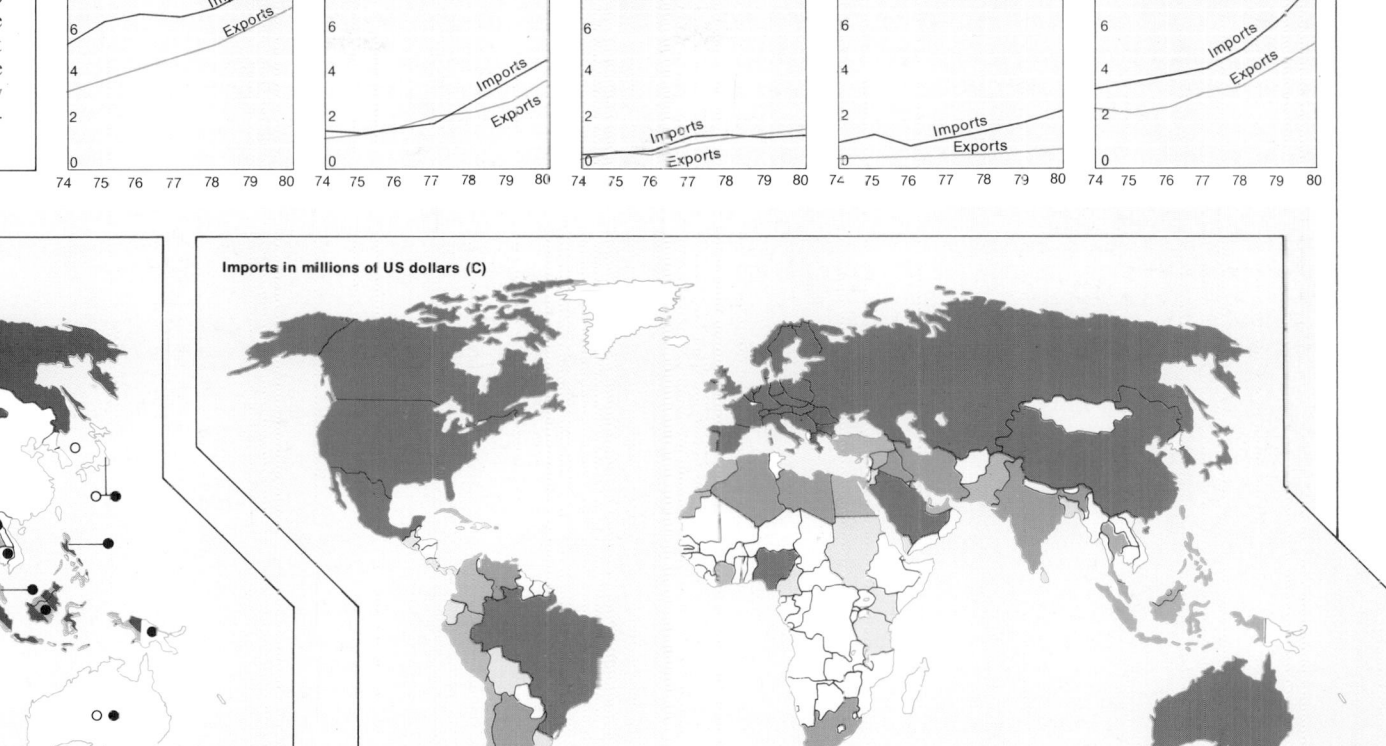

Imports in millions of US dollars (C)

Council for Mutual Economic Aid (COMECON)

Organization of Petroleum Exporting Countries (OPEC)

Association of South-East Asian Nations (ASEAN)

Organization for African Unity (OAU)

▲ Latin American Free Trade Association (LAFTA)

■ Arab League (AL)

○ Colombo Plan

● Organization for Economic Cooperation and Development (OECD)

Under 1,000

1,000–2,000

2,000–5,000

5,000–10,000

Over 10,000

Data unavailable

Zealand, for example, had little hesitation in clearing the prevailing tussock grass to create a new pastoral environment for their large-scale production of sheep and dairy products.

In the real world, however, there are many impediments to the operation of a free market system, and it is unwise for states like New Zealand to assume that they will always dominate Commonwealth dairy trade.

Impediments to free markets

Countries erect protectionist tariff barriers to assist their home industries and/or to obtain extra revenue. Import or export quotas may be imposed, and trade agreements with other countries give special preference to certain commodities. Problems arise from the exchange of currencies and their fluctuations in value. Tariff barriers may be erected for political, welfare or defense reasons. Sometimes special measures may be adopted to encourage the internal production of certain goods rather than obtaining them more cheaply from abroad, and such methods may be economically important to a new country that has always relied on the export of raw materials for its income but now wishes domestically to manufacture previously imported goods.

Political ties are vital to the groupings of certain countries. For reasons of international politics, countries such as those of the Soviet bloc trade with each other rather than with the outside world; and historical links, as between the UK and the Commonwealth, France and her ex-colonies, and Spain and Portugal with

Latin America, are also influential. The European Economic Community (EEC) is composed of countries that have formed a strong bloc among the developed countries.

Rich man, poor man

The developed countries of "the North" have more than 80 percent of the world's manufacturing income but only a quarter of its population, whereas the poorer peoples of "the South" number 3,000 million and receive only a fifth of world income. Attempts have been made to obtain a better economic balance. The 1948 General Agreement on Tariffs and Trade (GATT) and the United Nations Conference on Trade and Development (UNCTAD) provided mechanisms for multinational trade negotiations, and the World Bank and the International Monetary Fund (IMF) together with the 1960 International Development Association (IDA) have all provided easier loans for less developed states.

The widening gap between rich and poor countries has led to understandable demands for a new international order calling for basic changes in the structure of world production, aid and trade, and the transfer of resources. The 1980 Independent Commission on International Development Issues (The Brandt Commission) advocated just such a transfer to the Third World. But during a major world recession there seems little sign of any international political will strong enough to take action on the scale needed to solve the problems that contrasts in wealth and poverty involve.

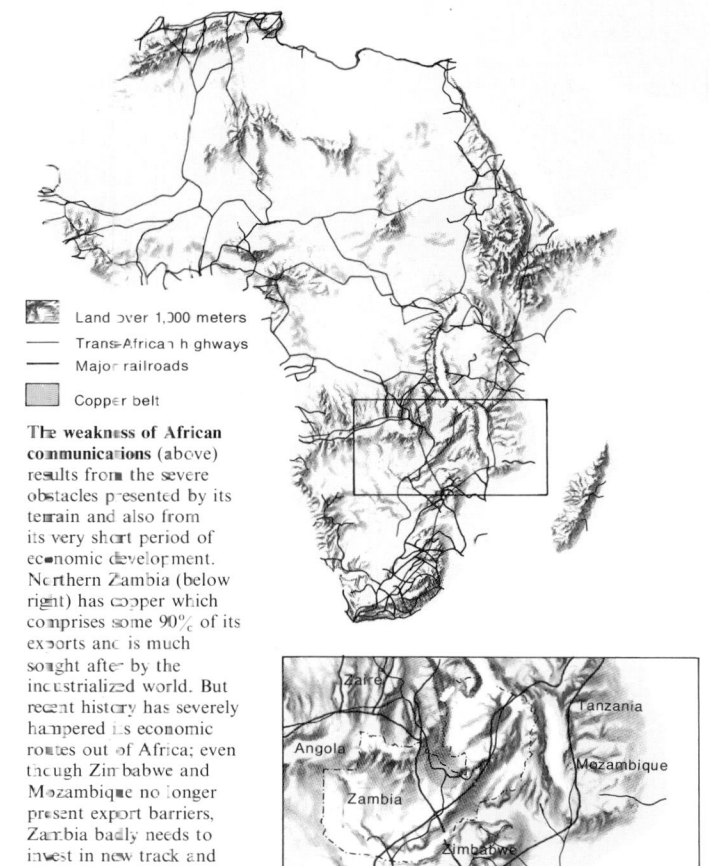

Land over 1,000 meters

Trans-African highways

Major railroads

Copper belt

The weakness of African communications (above) results from the severe obstacles presented by its terrain and also from its very short period of economic development. Northern Zambia (below right) has copper which comprises some 90% of its exports and is much sought after by the industrialized world. But recent history has severely hampered its economic routes out of Africa; even though Zimbabwe and Mozambique no longer present export barriers, Zambia badly needs to invest in new track and rolling stock.

Zaire · Tanzania · Angola · Mozambique · Zambia · Zimbabwe

1,800 · 1,920 · 2,040 · 2,160 · 2,280 · 2,400 · 2,520 · 2,640 · 2,760 · 2,880 · 3,000 · 3,120 · 3,240 · 3,360

Polar Regions

Sunless in winter, and capped with permanent land ice and shifting sea ice, the world's polar regions present an image of intense and everlasting cold. But permanent ice caps have been the exception rather than the rule in the 4,600 million years of Earth's history. The most recent intensification of the present ice age (which began at least two million years ago) reached its maximum about 20,000 years ago and still continues to fluctuate. Polar conditions preclude all but the toughest life forms on land, but the plankton-rich waters attract many animals, and man is beginning to exploit the polar regions' potential.

There have been about a dozen ice ages since the world began. During the intervening periods there was still a zonal pattern of world temperatures, with hot equatorial regions and cooler poles. But the ice caps, which are both chilling and self-sustaining, were absent altogether—the poles being cold temperate rather than icebound. The shiny ice surfaces of today's poles reflect more than 90 percent of the solar radiation which reaches them from the low-angled summer sun, while in winter the sun never rises at all. Thus the regions are now permanently ice capped.

Antarctica, the great southern polar continent, lies under an ice mantle 14 million sq km (5.4 million sq miles) in area, and sometimes more than 4,000 m (13,000 ft) thick. Many of its neighboring islands also carry permanent ice. In the Arctic, the three islands of Greenland lie under a pall of ice of subcontinental size, more than 1.8 million sq km (700,000 sq miles) in area and up to 3,000 m (9,800 ft) thick.

The ice cover of polar seas varies. The central core of the Arctic Ocean carries a mass of permanent pack ice, slowly circulating within the polar basin, which is added to each winter by a belt of ice forming over the open sea. Currents and winds break this up to form pack ice that also circulates, gradually melting in summer or drifting south. Antarctica too is surrounded by fast ice, which breaks up in spring to form a broad belt of persistent pack ice. Circulating slowly about the continent, the pack ice forms huge gyres spreading far to the north, dotted with tabular bergs that have broken away from the continental ice sheet.

The frozen land
In the present glacial phase, the ice caps reached their farthest spread about 20,000 years ago, and then began the retreat which brought them, some 10,000 to 12,000 years ago, to their current position and size. Since then the climate of the polar regions has been both warmer and colder than it is at the present time.

The fluctuating nature of the polar climates creates very difficult conditions for plants and animals. Very little will grow on the terrestrial ice caps, but water scarcity rather than cold is the most important factor inhibiting plant growth: the small patches of lichens, algae and mosses that occur on rock faces and nunataks (points of rock jutting above the land ice) are usually in the path of a snowmelt runnel. Vegetation patches sometimes contain tiny populations of insects and mites, which may be active for only a few days each year when the sun warms them from a state of dormancy.

However, these tiny scattered plant communities appear all over Antarctica wherever rock surfaces break through the ice cap, and have been seen less than 300 km (190 miles) from the South Pole, and on peaks 2,000 m (6,600 ft) above sea level. Insects and mites occur within 600 km (380 miles) of the Pole itself. In specially favored positions on the Antarctic Peninsula and the offshore islands, carpets of moss and grasses may be seen. Conditions around the northern terrestrial ice cap are similar, with aridity, strong winds and cold discouraging all but the hardiest plants and the smallest, toughest animal colonies.

The frozen seas
The marine ice caps, by contrast, are relatively lively places, especially during summer, when days are long and the sea ice is patchy. Water-lanes between floes are often rich in microscopic algae and the minute zooplanktonic animals

that feed on them. These animals in turn attract fish, sea birds and seals in their thousands, as well as whales—including the largest baleen species. Some of the richest patches of sea are close to islands where strong currents stir the water and bring nutrients to the surface, and these attract semipermanent populations of seals and birds. The birds breed on the island cliffs and feed in the sheltered waters among the ice; the seals may breed on the ice itself, producing their pups on a floating nursery where food is close at hand.

Different species of seals are found on inshore and offshore ice environments. In the Arctic, bearded and ringed seals, which produce their young in spring as the inshore ice begins to break up, are often preyed upon by floe-riding polar bears; Eskimos too prize both species for their meat, blubber and skins. Farther out on the offshore pack ice live hooded and harp seals, where their pups are safe from all but the ship-borne commercial hunters. In the Antarctic, Weddell seals are the inshore species, whereas crabeater and Ross seals prefer the distant pack ice. Crabeaters, which feed largely on planktonic krill (once thought to be crab larvae), are probably the most numerous of all seal species, with a population estimated at 10 to 15 million.

Sea ice in the north provides a precarious platform on which coastal human populations of the Arctic, such as Eskimos, can extend their winter hunting range. When the land is snow-bound and animals are scarce, the sea may still provide food for hunters skilled in fishing, and in stalking seals to their breathing holes.

Nonindigenous inhabitants of the ice caps have greatly increased in recent years, following the discovery and exploitation of oil in the north, as well as other valuable minerals in both the regions. Scientists and technicians today occupy bases and weather stations which in some cases, such as the Amundsen-Scott at the South Pole, are several decades old and have to be maintained by means of aircraft.

The coldness of the poles is caused by the tilt of the Earth's axis, which prevents sunlight from reaching them at all in the winter. Even in summer, little heat is received from the sun because of the low angle at which its rays reach the surface; much even of this is reflected away by the ice.

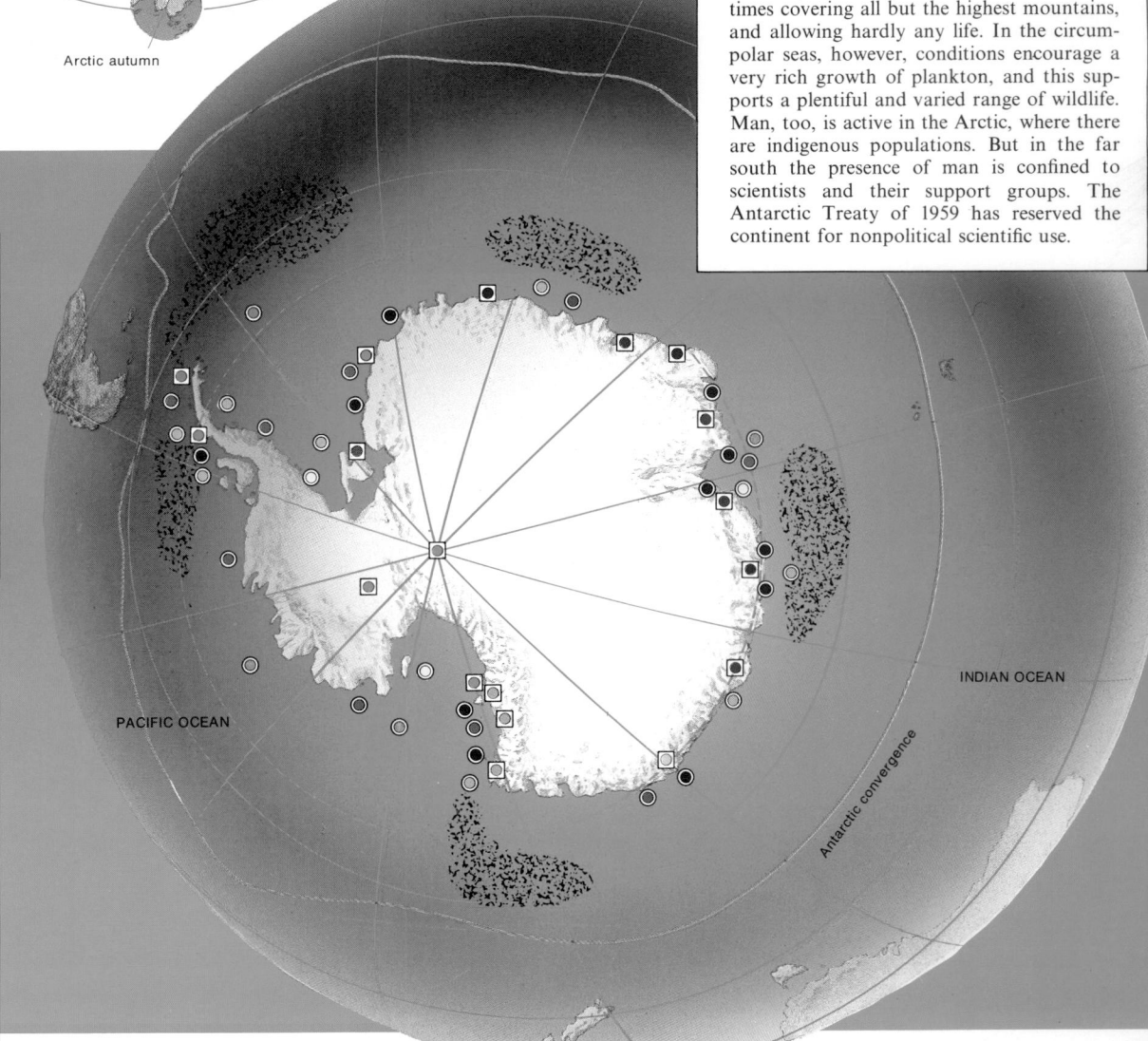

Arctic spring

Arctic summer

Arctic winter

ATLANTIC OCEAN

Arctic autumn

EARTH'S FROZEN LIMITS
The permanent ice around Earth's poles covers whole oceans, as well as landmasses of immense size. These ice sheets fluctuate, and on land may be thousands of meters thick, sometimes covering all but the highest mountains, and allowing hardly any life. In the circumpolar seas, however, conditions encourage a very rich growth of plankton, and this supports a plentiful and varied range of wildlife. Man, too, is active in the Arctic, where there are indigenous populations. But in the far south the presence of man is confined to scientists and their support groups. The Antarctic Treaty of 1959 has reserved the continent for nonpolitical scientific use.

THE FAR SOUTH

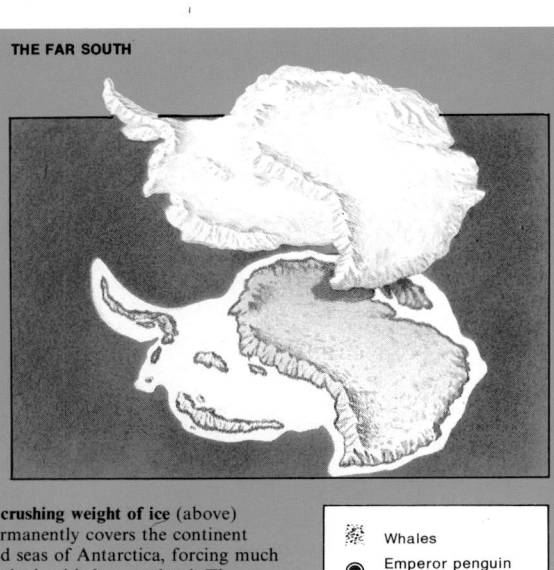

INDIAN OCEAN

PACIFIC OCEAN

Antarctic convergence

A crushing weight of ice (above) permanently covers the continent and seas of Antarctica, forcing much of the land below sea level. The Antarctic convergence (right), the line at which northern and southern water masses meet, marks a sharp change in temperature and marine life. Especially in areas of upwelling, nutrients make these waters rich in plankton. This feeds a multitude of shrimp-like krill that provide food for a huge number of other animals—fish, penguins, flying birds, seals and whales. The Antarctic landmass allows little natural life, but since the 1959 Antarctic Treaty it has proved to be an area of international scientific cooperation.

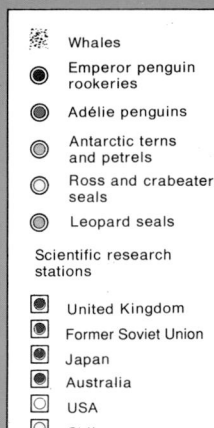

Whales

Emperor penguin rookeries

Adélie penguins

Antarctic terns and petrels

Ross and crabeater seals

Leopard seals

Scientific research stations

United Kingdom
Former Soviet Union
Japan
Australia
USA
Chile
France
New Zealand
Argentina

Pleistocene ice sheet — Iceberg tracks — Limit of pack ice
Iceberg source — Approx. iceberg limit

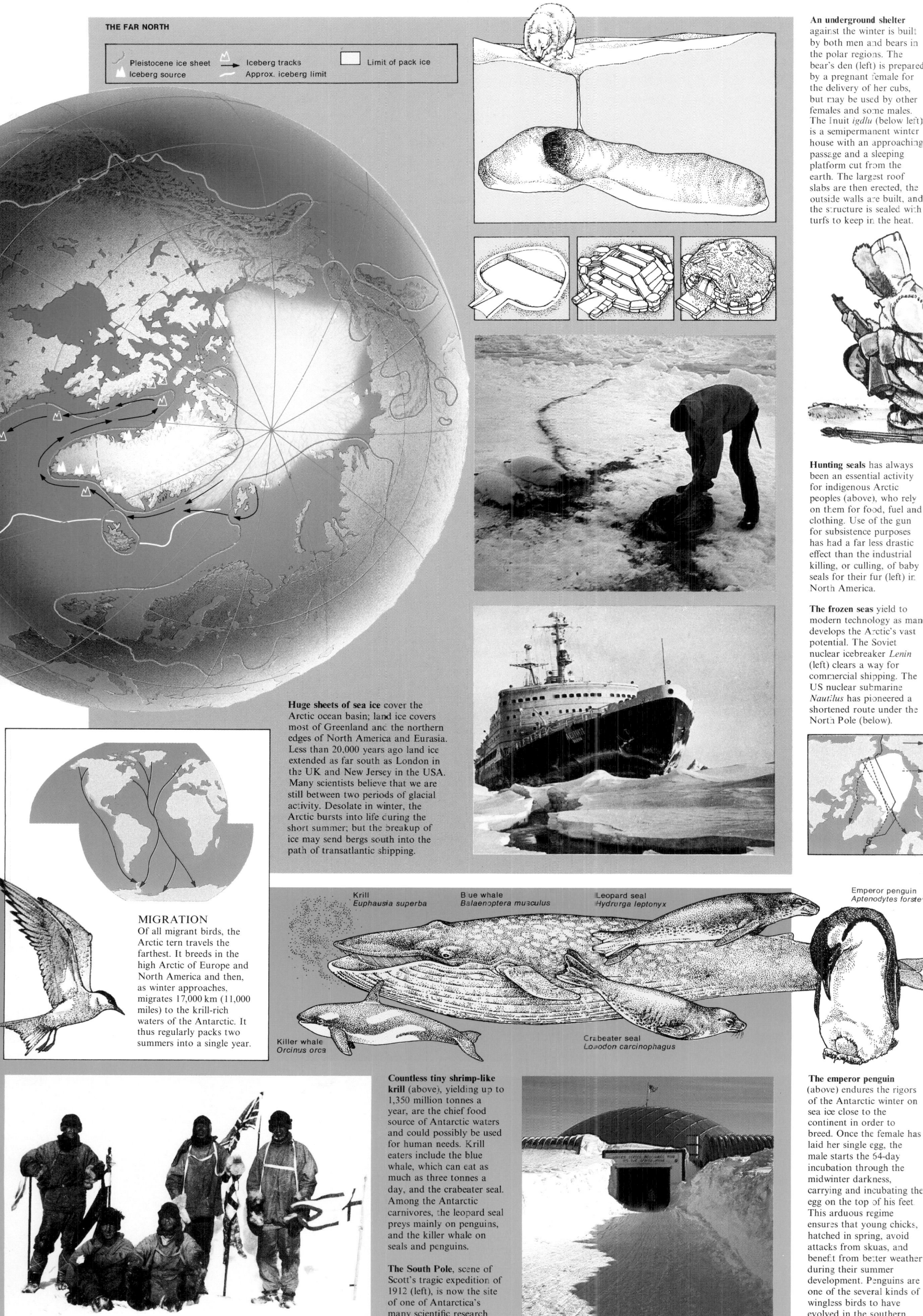

An underground shelter against the winter is built by both men and bears in the polar regions. The bear's den (left) is prepared by a pregnant female for the delivery of her cubs, but may be used by other females and some males. The Inuit *igdlu* (below left) is a semipermanent winter house with an approaching passage and a sleeping platform cut from the earth. The largest roof slabs are then erected, the outside walls are built, and the structure is sealed with turfs to keep in the heat.

Hunting seals has always been an essential activity for indigenous Arctic peoples (above), who rely on them for food, fuel and clothing. Use of the gun for subsistence purposes has had a far less drastic effect than the industrial killing, or culling, of baby seals for their fur (left) in North America.

The frozen seas yield to modern technology as man develops the Arctic's vast potential. The Soviet nuclear icebreaker *Lenin* (left) clears a way for commercial shipping. The US nuclear submarine *Nautilus* has pioneered a shortened route under the North Pole (below).

Route of *Nautilus* 1958
Proposed submarine tanker routes

Huge sheets of sea ice cover the Arctic ocean basin; land ice covers most of Greenland and the northern edges of North America and Eurasia. Less than 20,000 years ago land ice extended as far south as London in the UK and New Jersey in the USA. Many scientists believe that we are still between two periods of glacial activity. Desolate in winter, the Arctic bursts into life during the short summer; but the breakup of ice may send bergs south into the path of transatlantic shipping.

MIGRATION
Of all migrant birds, the Arctic tern travels the farthest. It breeds in the high Arctic of Europe and North America and then, as winter approaches, migrates 17,000 km (11,000 miles) to the krill-rich waters of the Antarctic. It thus regularly packs two summers into a single year.

Krill
Euphausia superba

Blue whale
Balaenoptera musculus

Leopard seal
Hydrurga leptonyx

Emperor penguin
Aptenodytes forsteri

Killer whale
Orcinus orca

Crabeater seal
Lobodon carcinophagus

Countless tiny shrimp-like krill (above), yielding up to 1,350 million tonnes a year, are the chief food source of Antarctic waters and could possibly be used for human needs. Krill eaters include the blue whale, which can eat as much as three tonnes a day, and the crabeater seal. Among the Antarctic carnivores, the leopard seal preys mainly on penguins, and the killer whale on seals and penguins.

The South Pole, scene of Scott's tragic expedition of 1912 (left), is now the site of one of Antarctica's many scientific research stations (right). The bleak region may eventually yield a vast supply of mineral and other resources.

The emperor penguin (above) endures the rigors of the Antarctic winter on sea ice close to the continent in order to breed. Once the female has laid her single egg, the male starts the 64-day incubation through the midwinter darkness, carrying and incubating the egg on the top of his feet. This arduous regime ensures that young chicks, hatched in spring, avoid attacks from skuas, and benefit from better weather during their summer development. Penguins are one of the several kinds of wingless birds to have evolved in the southern hemisphere; but of all birds the emperor penguin is best adapted to the harsh polar environment of the Antarctic region.

Tundra and Taiga

Tundra is land that has been exposed for only about 8,000 years, since the retreat of the ice caps, and only relatively recently occupied by plants. In consequence, few plants and animals have yet had time to adapt to the virtually soilless and treeless environment. The less rigorous conditions of neighboring taiga forest allow a longer growing season and a somewhat wider range of species. The delicately balanced ecology of both areas is being increasingly threatened, however, by the activities of man.

"Tundra," from a Lapp word meaning "rolling, treeless plain," defines the narrow band of open, low ground that surrounds the Arctic Ocean. It lies north of the line beyond which the temperature of the warmest month usually fails to reach 10°C (50°F). North of this trees do not generally grow well, so the line forms a natural frontier between tundra and the broad band of coniferous forest that circles the northern hemisphere to its south between about 60°N and 48°N. This forest, forming the world's largest and most uninterrupted area of vegetation, is usually referred to by its Russian name of "taiga."

Cheerless landscapes

The tundra presents a desolate and restrictive environment for most of the year: in winter there are several months of semidarkness. While there is considerable variation in the climates of places at the same latitude, temperatures average only −5°C (23°F) and are well below freezing for many months of the year. Frost-free days are restricted to a few weeks in midsummer and even then, although days are warmer, the sun is never high in the sky. Nearly all tundra has been free from ice for only a few thousand years. As a result, it either has no soil at all or has developed only a thin covering of

sandy, muddy or peaty soil, successfully colonized by only a few types of plants.

Trimmed by such grazing animals as hares, musk oxen and reindeer or caribou, and by strong winds carrying abrasive rock dust and ice particles, typical tundra vegetation forms a low, patchy mat a few centimeters deep. Much of it grows on permafrost — ground that thaws superficially in summer but remains perennially frozen beneath the surface. Here drainage is poor, shallow ponds are frequent and the scanty soils tend to be waterlogged and acidic. Nevertheless, a small number of grasses, sedges, mosses and marsh plants may grow well and the summer tundra in flower can be an impressive sight. Knee-high forests of dwarf birch, willow and alder grow in valleys sheltered from the strong and biting wind.

The taiga also is a dark and monotonous habitat. Again, while there is a good deal of variation in climatic conditions, on average the region has somewhat milder summers than the tundra with mean average temperatures of 2–6°C (34–42°F), less wind and a slightly longer growing season. The taiga is mostly older than the tundra, and its soils have had longer to mature. They support a small number of tree species, with coniferous spruce, pine, fir and

larch predominating. Short-season broadleaves such as willows, alders, birches and poplars tend to occur on the better soils of river valleys and the edges of forest lakes.

Animals of the far north

The number of animal species supported throughout the year by tundra and taiga is also comparatively small, with interdependent populations that may fluctuate wildly from season to season. In winter both tundra and taiga are silent, although far from deserted. Mice, voles and lemmings remain active, living in tunnels under the snow, which keeps them well insulated from the wind and subzero temperatures. Above the snow Arctic hares forage; they tend to gather in snow-free areas where food can still be found. Arctic foxes are mainly tundra animals and the musk oxen, too, winter on high, exposed tundra where their dense, shaggy coats protect them from the worst

The circumpolar north that surrounds the permanently frozen ice cap is dominated by tundra—open plain that remains snowfree for only several months in the summer—and taiga, the vast coniferous forest stretching right round the northern hemisphere. The Siberian taiga, for example, is one-third larger than the entire United States.

Tundra ☐   Taiga ☐

Producers
■ USSR
■ USA

Man's pursuit of resources has accelerated in the past two decades, with the former Soviet Union drastically increasing its outflow of both oil and gas since 1970. North American output has lagged far behind, mainly because the need for exploration and exploitation has only recently become important. In all tundra and taiga areas, gas did not start flowing until the early 1960s. The former Soviet Union's coal output has been rising steadily while that of North America has fluctuated. (In these figures, North America is composed of Alaska and the Yukon and Northwest territories. The former Soviet Union is more loosely defined as "regions of the far north".)

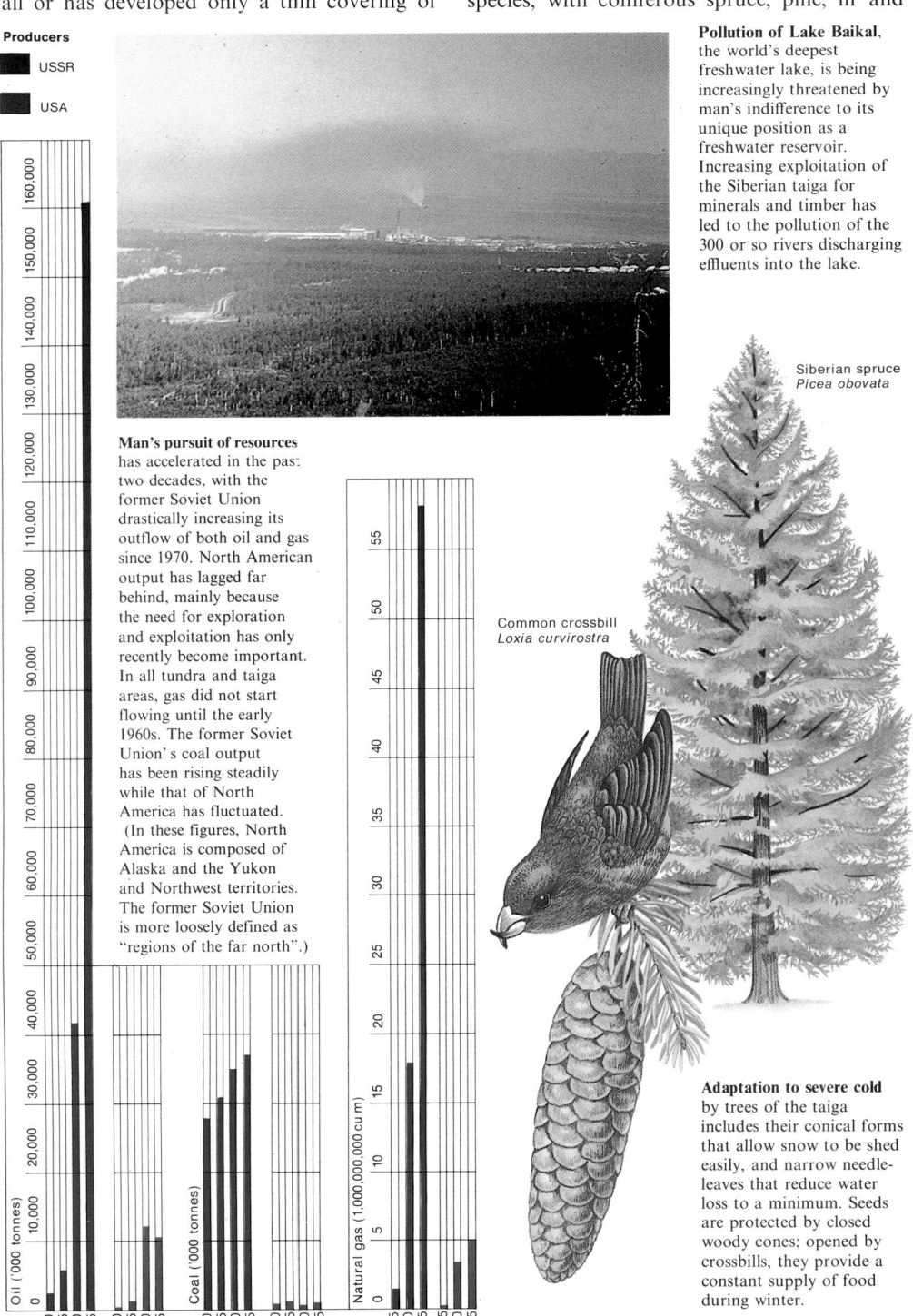

Oil ('000 tonnes)
Coal ('000 tonnes)
Natural gas (1,000,000,000 cu m)
1960 1965 1970 1975

Pollution of Lake Baikal, the world's deepest freshwater lake, is being increasingly threatened by man's indifference to its unique position as a freshwater reservoir. Increasing exploitation of the Siberian taiga for minerals and timber has led to the pollution of the 300 or so rivers discharging effluents into the lake.

Common crossbill
Loxia curvirostra

Siberian spruce
Picea obovata

Adaptation to severe cold by trees of the taiga includes their conical forms that allow snow to be shed easily, and narrow needle-leaves that reduce water loss to a minimum. Seeds are protected by closed woody cones; opened by crossbills, they provide a constant supply of food during winter.

Reindeer or caribou
Rangifer tarandus

Raven
Corvus corax

Arctic fox
Alopex lagopus

Capercaillie
Tetrao urogallus

Snowy owl
Nyctea scandiaca

Brown lemming
Lemmus lemmus

Arctic skua
Stercorarius parasiticus

January February March April May June

Movement in these regions takes many directions. The capercaillie spends all winter in the taiga, where it thrives on the abundant conifer needles, buds and shoots. Some move southward into deciduous woods during the summer months. The Arctic skua breeds on the tundra but moves to the warmer oceans in winter, while the tundra movements of the all-scavenging raven and the snowy owl are governed by those of their

prey. The raven picks clean the carcasses left by other predators; the snowy owl feeds on small rodents such as mice and lemmings, as does the Arctic fox. Lemmings remain static and inconspicuous in normal years but some populations expand rapidly every third or fourth year, leading to mass local migration in every direction, possibly caused by an abundance of vegetation that encourages more frequent breeding.

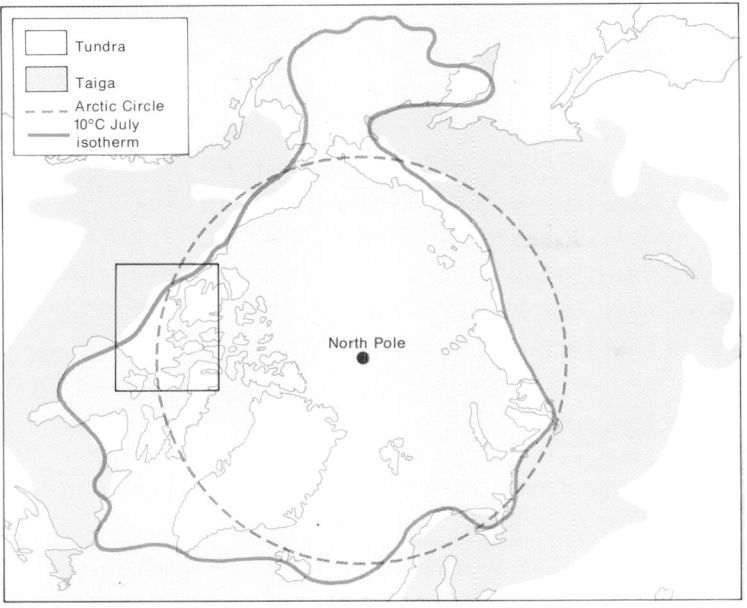

Tundra
Taiga
Arctic Circle
10°C July isotherm

North Pole

The rough boundary between the tundra and taiga—the tree line—approximates to the 10°C July isotherm, the climatic point north of which trees fail to grow successfully. Seasonal caribou migration in the Canadian barren grounds (boxed) is shown in the main diagram (below). Such migration is also undertaken by reindeer in northern Eurasia.

The summer tundra—seen here in Swedish Lapland—provides a wide cover of low plants including "reindeer mosses" and other lichens. Grazing reindeer return minerals to the soil. Shallow ponds form as the frozen ground thaws for a few months in summer. Mountains stay partly snow covered in the warmest weather and are a prominent physical feature of the tundra.

weather. Bears, badgers, beavers and squirrels are common taiga mammals. Elk and reindeer (in North America, moose and caribou) winter in the shelter of the taiga; wolves are mostly woodland animals in winter, following their prey to the open tundra in spring. Red foxes, coyotes, mink and wolverines also move to the tundra in summer.

Snow buntings, ptarmigans and snowy owls live on the tundra throughout the coldest months and are fully adapted to life there. Crossbills and capercaillies are among taiga residents, equipped to live on its abundant conifer buds, seeds and needles. Enormous populations of migrant birds, especially water birds and waders, fly north to both tundra and taiga with the spring thaw. Waxwings, bramblings, siskins and redpolls leave their temperate latitudes to feed on the lush and fast-growing vegetation and the profusion of insects that appear as soon as the snows begin to melt.

Man in the northlands

These circumpolar regions separate the world's greatest centers of population. They are now crisscrossed with air routes. A total population of about nine million people currently inhabits the tundra and taiga. Numbers have been increased by the immigration of technicians and administrators during the last few decades; oil prospecting and mining, forest exploitation and other activities of these newcomers is altering the seminomadic lives of the million or so aboriginal peoples such as the Khanty (Ostyaks) and Nentsy (Samoyeds) of Russia, the Samer (Lapps) of Scandinavia and Russia, and the Inuit (formerly Eskimos) of North America. New roads, exploitation of minerals and forests, and pipeline construction have disrupted the migration of their reindeer (caribou) and their land has been appropriated for hydroelectric schemes.

In the taiga, Russia is constructing railroads and towns and extracting huge amounts of timber; they have prospected widely and successfully for gold, nickel, iron, tin, mica, diamonds and tungsten, and have discovered vast reserves of oil and natural gas in western Siberia. Alaskan oil, discovered in 1968, now flows across the state at 54–62°C (130–145°F), and to protect the permafrost from this heat the pipeline has had to be elevated for half its 1,300 km (800 mile) length. The pipe's route to the ice-free port of Valdez has interfered with the migration of caribou; hunting and other pressures have led to a drop in their population from three million to some 200,000 in about 30 years. Only official protection has saved the musk ox from a similar fate. These bleak areas are so vast and inhospitable that living space there will never be threatened. However, if only on a local scale, their ecologies are under increasing pressure from man.

Many Norwegian Lapps (or Samer) derive their income from reindeer, which they domesticated many centuries ago to provide meat, milk and skins. Now they follow them through the seasons along well-worn and familiar routes. Such nomadic life styles are becoming rarer as Samer settle down.

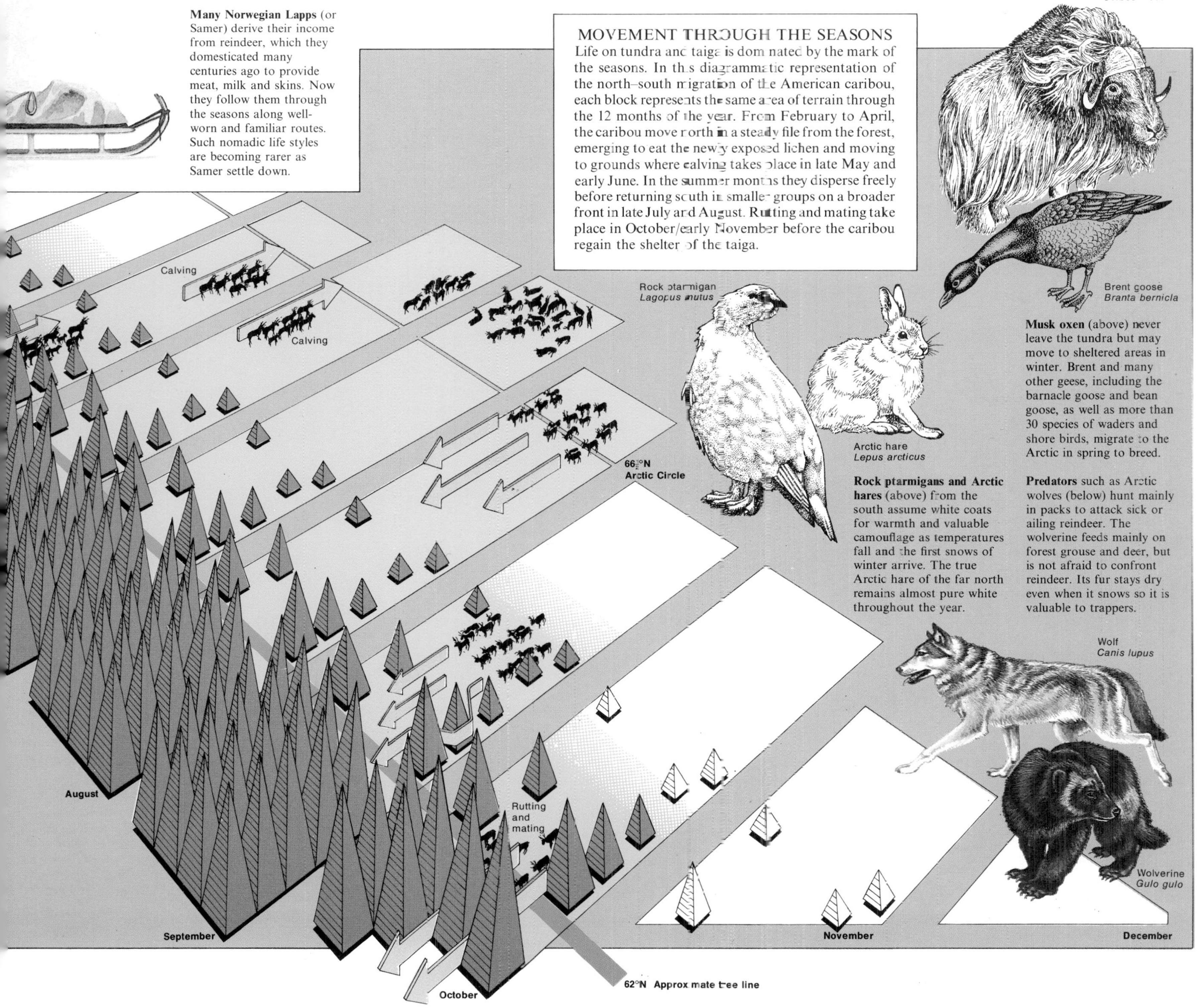

MOVEMENT THROUGH THE SEASONS

Life on tundra and taiga is dominated by the mark of the seasons. In this diagrammatic representation of the north–south migration of the American caribou, each block represents the same area of terrain through the 12 months of the year. From February to April, the caribou move north in a steady file from the forest, emerging to eat the newly exposed lichen and moving to grounds where calving takes place in late May and early June. In the summer months they disperse freely before returning south in smaller groups on a broader front in late July and August. Rutting and mating take place in October/early November before the caribou regain the shelter of the taiga.

Calving

Calving

66°N Arctic Circle

August

September

Rutting and mating

October

62°N Approximate tree line

Musk ox *Ovibos moschatus*

Brent goose *Branta bernicla*

Rock ptarmigan *Lagopus mutus*

Arctic hare *Lepus arcticus*

Musk oxen (above) never leave the tundra but may move to sheltered areas in winter. Brent and many other geese, including the barnacle goose and bean goose, as well as more than 30 species of waders and shore birds, migrate to the Arctic in spring to breed.

Rock ptarmigans and Arctic hares (above) from the south assume white coats for warmth and valuable camouflage as temperatures fall and the first snows of winter arrive. The true Arctic hare of the far north remains almost pure white throughout the year.

Predators such as Arctic wolves (below) hunt mainly in packs to attack sick or ailing reindeer. The wolverine feeds mainly on forest grouse and deer, but is not afraid to confront reindeer. Its fur stays dry even when it snows so it is valuable to trappers.

Wolf *Canis lupus*

Wolverine *Gulo gulo*

November

December

Temperate Forests

At one time, dense, primeval forests blanketed large areas of North America, Europe and eastern Asia. Almost all of the trees that flourished in these temperate regions were deciduous – they shed their leaves in autumn, stood bare branched through winter and produced new foliage every spring. Little of this forest now exists. The few remaining pockets, however, still provide habitats for a large range of shade-loving plants: lichens and fungi, tree-hugging mosses, scrambling creepers and shrubs. And this vegetation in turn provides sanctuary for a surprisingly wide variety of forest creatures.

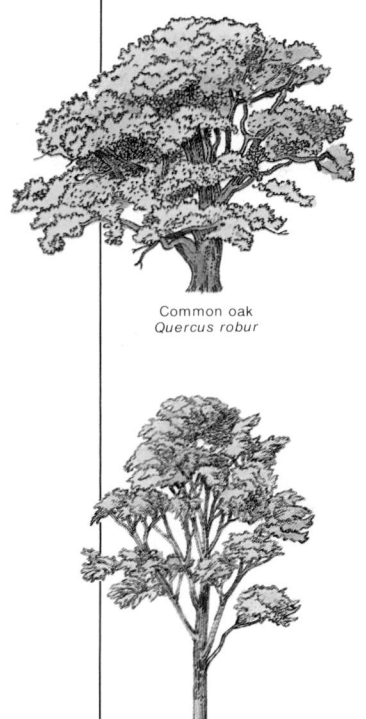

Common oak
Quercus robur

Silver beech
Nothofagus menziesii

Deciduous trees such as the oak (top) make up the temperate forests in cooler temperate regions. In milder, wetter climates, where the seasons are less distinct, evergreens such as southern beech (above) are typical temperate species.

The greater part of the temperate forest zone lies in the northern hemisphere, where winter soil temperatures reduce the ability of plants to absorb water. Hence the trees tend to shed their leaves, which use up moisture through evaporation. In the southern hemisphere, however, the temperate latitudes encourage a type of rainforest in such areas as southern Chile, Tasmania, New Zealand and parts of southeastern Australia. Here the climate is maritime, often with high rainfall and frequent fogs, and evergreen rather than deciduous types of trees grow. Temperate rainforests also occur in the northern hemisphere, in China and in northwestern and northeastern North America.

Deciduous forest consists of a mixture of trees, sometimes with one variety predominant. In central Europe, beech is the leading—and sometimes the only—tree species, whereas oaks mixed with other species made up the forest farther west and east. In North America, beech and maple were once extensive.

The climate in temperate forest zones varies sharply according to seasons—summers tend to be warm, winters moderately cold, and rainfall fairly regular. In fact, the seasonal rhythm is a central feature of temperate forests, and it affects the entire ecosystem—the whole community of plants and animals found there. Soils are generally of the fertile "brown earth" type: the leaf litter of deciduous forests in particular breaks down easily, and is quickly worked into the soil by burrowing animals such as earthworms. In wetter or rockier regions, the soil is more "podsolic"—bleached, sandy and less fertile than the true brown earths.

After the ice

Two million years ago, a series of ice sheets began to extend into the temperate latitudes. In Europe, species moving south before the advancing cold were cut off from the warmer climates by the east–west run of mountains. As a result, many varieties of plants and animals

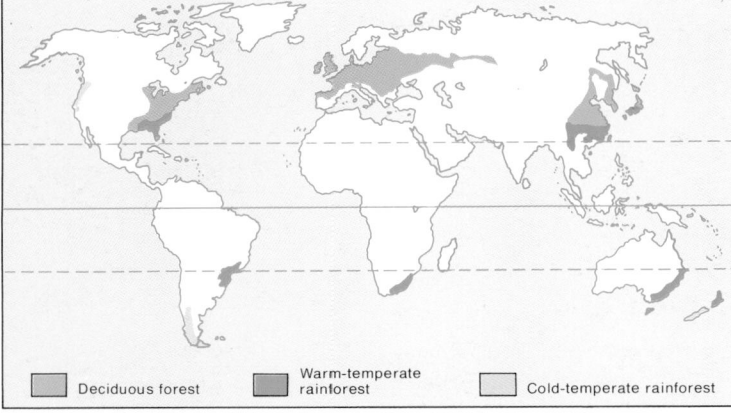

Deciduous forest

Warm-temperate rainforest

Cold-temperate rainforest

Natural distribution: in the northern hemisphere's temperate zone deciduous forests occur in the cooler areas—in eastern USA, northeastern China, Korea, the northern parts of Japan's Honshu island and western Europe. These forests only give way to evergreens in the warmer and wetter parts of the zone. In the southern hemisphere, the climate is generally rather milder throughout the temperate zone and so there are virtually no deciduous forests. Evergreen forests, however, can be found in southeastern South Africa, Chile, New Zealand, Australia and Tasmania.

were killed off. Species were reduced still further in islands such as Britain, where the newly formed barriers of the English Channel, Irish Sea and North Sea made recolonization even more difficult after the ice had retreated.

Eastern Asia was one of the few areas in the world that escaped the extreme climatic changes of the ice ages and therefore its temperate forests, unlike those of Europe, still contain an enormous variety of tree species. North America also fared better than Europe, for although glaciers at one time extended deep into the continent, the north–south direction of the mountain ranges allowed relatively easy migration of trees southwards as the climate worsened. Hence most species survived and were able to reoccupy their former territories when the ice retreated. As a result, some 40 species of deciduous trees occur in the North American forests, and contribute to the spectacular display of color during the autumn, notably in

the eastern USA. But a combination of climatic change and, more recently and importantly, of intense human activity, has meant that the remnants of temperate forest seen today differ greatly from the original forest in both composition and form. Only in remote regions such as the southern Appalachian Mountains do substantial areas of the original forest survive. Elsewhere, regrowth has occurred, but much of this is essentially scrub woodland.

The forest structure

Mature temperate deciduous forest is made up of distinct horizontal layers, particularly where the dominant tree is the oak, which allows enough light for a rich shrub layer to grow beneath it. The largest trees, such as oak, maple or ash, may be 25–50 m (80–160 ft) tall, and beneath them grows a prominent layer of smaller trees such as hazel, hornbeam or yew. Lower down again, a varied ground cover of perennial herbs, ferns, lichens and mosses flourishes in the comparative dampness of the forest floor. Because the trees are bare of leaves in winter, many of the plants growing on the forest floor take advantage of the warmth and light of spring to flower early in the year before the main trees come into full leaf and prevent the sun from reaching them. Various woody climbers, such as ivy and honeysuckle, are also present, growing over the trees and shrubs.

Much of the food supply in temperate forests is locked up in the trees themselves, but the annual fall of leaves in the deciduous forests produces a soil rich in nourishment. This supports a vast quantity of life, ranging in size from earthworms and insects to microscopic bacteria of the soil. The death of individual trees and branches also releases the food supply back to the earth. In shady, damp locations, insects, fungi, bacteria and other decomposing agents break down the leaves and other plant and animal debris more quickly, returning them to the soil as food for new plants.

Creatures of the forest

Temperate forests once contained many varieties of animal life, including several species of large animals. Herbivores such as wild oxen, wood bison, elk and moose ate grass and leaves; scavengers such as wild pigs rooted in the forest floor; predators such as wolves preyed on the other animals. Most of these have now been hunted to extinction by man or are extremely rare. Smaller animals still survive in comparatively large numbers, and include squirrels, chipmunks and raccoons, hedgehogs, wood mice, badgers and foxes.

The bird life of temperate forests is very diverse. Some species are insect eaters, exploring the bark and crevices for insects and grubs. Others, such as the wood pigeon, concentrate on seeds. Yet others, like the tawny owl, are predators. Complex interactions between predators and prey have developed at all levels of the forest, from the high canopy to the rotting ground litter, with each group evolving more efficient techniques of capture or escape in a kind of evolutionary race for survival.

The invertebrate insect life is also extremely varied and numerous, and forms a key component of the ecosystem. Oaks are particularly rich in insect life, and more than 100 species of moths feed on their leaves.

The plant and animal life of the temperate forest is remarkably rich and plentiful. And yet it is only a fraction of what once existed. Ever since man has occupied these regions he has found them so suited to his needs that he has long since cleared most of the original tree cover, replaced it with "civilization" and, in the process, destroyed innumerable species of forest wildlife.

THE SEASONAL CYCLE

It is the cycle of the four seasons that gives the temperate deciduous forest its distinctive character. All animals and plants have adapted their ways of life to cope with the seasonal changes in heat, light, moisture and food. The yearly shedding and regrowth of the forest's leaves is one of the most striking and important of adaptations to the seasonal cycle and one that affects all other life in the forest. In summer the leafy canopy of the trees blocks out the sunlight from the forest floor and creates unsuitable conditions for many other plants to flourish. When the leaves fall they form a layer over the soil and provide winter protection for the plant roots and hibernating animals beneath the ground. Finally, once the dead leaves have been broken down, they give fertility to the soil and provide food for future generations of plants.

SPRING

Between February and April, the low spring sun climbs steadily higher in the sky and, streaming through the still leafless branches of the trees, falls more directly on the forest floor, warming the soil and melting the last frosts. As soon as the days become warmer the sluggish sap in the trees begins to flow more quickly, carrying nutrients to the branches, where leaf buds start to form.

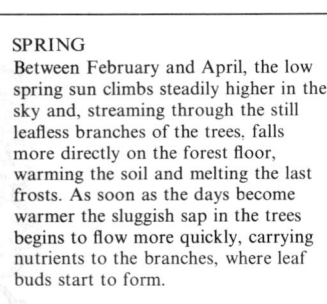

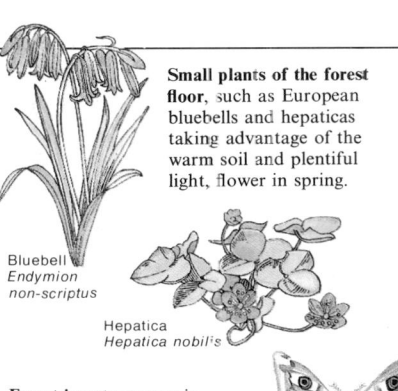

Bluebell *Endymion non-scriptus*

Hepatica *Hepatica nobilis*

Small plants of the forest floor, such as European bluebells and hepaticas taking advantage of the warm soil and plentiful light, flower in spring.

Small emperor moth *Saturnia pavonia*

Forest insects emerge in spring, some, such as the emperor moth, from their winter cocoons, some from hibernation and some newly hatched from eggs

European blackbird *Turdus merula*

Birds building nests in early spring make use of the forest's winter litter—broken twigs, dead leaves and dried grasses all serve as construction materials.

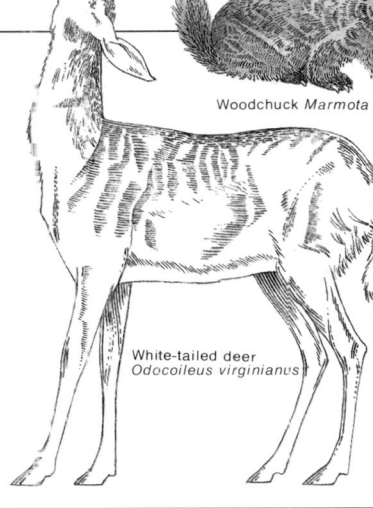

Woodchuck *Marmota monax*

Western European hedgehog *Erinaceus europaeus*

White-tailed deer *Odocoileus virginianus*

New plant growth and the increase in insects provide food for such animals as the North American woodchuck and the European hedgehog that wake thin and hungry from months of hibernation. Deer and other non-hibernating animals are also weak and thin—indeed many may have died during the harsh weather. The spring birth of young, however, soon restores their numbers.

SUMMER

By early summer the leaves of the trees are fully grown. They form a dense canopy, blocking out the sun and cooling the soil of the forest floor. Most of the small ground plants have long since finished flowering, but their leaves remain green and they continue actively storing food in their roots ready for their rapid spring growth.

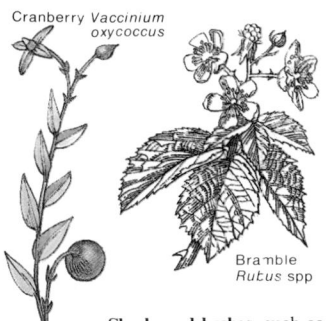

Cranberry *Vaccinium oxycoccus*

Bramble *Rubus* spp

Shrubs and bushes, such as bramble and cranberry, form tangled flowering masses wherever sunlight manages to filter through the forest's gloomy canopy.

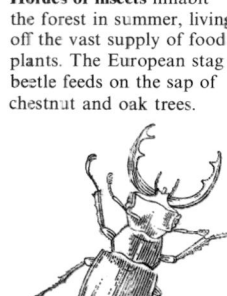

Stag beetle *Lucanus cervus*

Hordes of insects inhabit the forest in summer, living off the vast supply of food plants. The European stag beetle feeds on the sap of chestnut and oak trees.

Willow warbler *Phylloscopus trochilus*

The North American pewee and the willow warbler are two of the forest's many summer visitors that feed on the insect population. Some seed-eating birds, finches for example, also take advantage of this summer food supply.

Eastern wood pewee *Contopus virens*

Hazel mouse *Muscardinus avellanarius*

The hazel mouse protects its young by raising them in a summer nest, which it builds in a tree: almost every creature in the forest is viewed as a source of food by some other animal and the young litters are particularly at risk.

AUTUMN

As the autumn days grow shorter and cooler the forest foliage begins to turn color; the trees are responding to the drop in temperature and are cutting off the food supply to their leaves, which lose their green color and fall to the ground, forming a thick carpet on the forest's floor. Rain, frost, insects, earthworms and fungi then break down the leaves, making them part of the fertile forest soil.

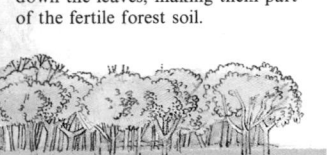

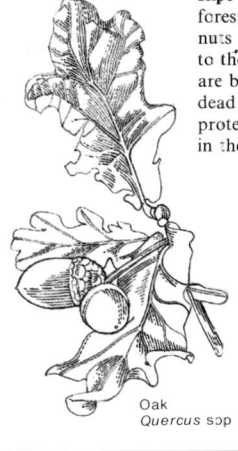

Oak *Quercus* spp

Ripe fruits and seeds of the forest trees—acorns, beech nuts and hazel nuts—drop to the ground, where a few are buried in the layers of dead leaves and remain protected until they sprout in the early spring.

Common hazel *Corylus avellana*

Acorn woodpecker *Melanerpes formicivorus*

Preparing for winter, the acorn woodpecker stores seeds in holes that it drills in tree trunks. Chipmunks hide supplies of nuts in their winter nests.

Eastern chipmunk *Tamias striatus*

American black bear *Ursus americanus*

The black bear of North America, like other winter hibernators, consumes vast quantities of food during autumn to build up its winter stores of food in the form of body fat.

WINTER

By winter, only evergreen shrubs and a few small hardy plants remain green. Many of the plants of the forest floor lose their green leaves during the first deep frost. The leaves of the trees still lie rotting on the bare ground, but within the soil, beneath the protective layers of leaf litter, plants are growing and spring flowers are developing buds.

Holly *Ilex* spp

Late-fruiting plants, such as holly, mistletoe and dog rose, provide food for winter residents of the temperate forest such as the European hawfinch.

Hawfinch *Coccothraustes coccothraustes*

European woodcock *Scolopax rusticola*

Woodcocks are insect-eaters. They can survive winter by prizing insects from the soil with their long beaks, providing that the ground is not too deeply frozen.

North American screech owl *Otus asio*

Owls and foxes remain fairly active in winter, regularly leaving their nests or lairs to catch small animals or birds that are also in search of food.

European badger *Meles meles*

Red fox *Vulpes vulpes*

European badgers, like racoons, opossums, bears and skunks, are "shallow" hibernators. On mild winter days they wake and go to search for food.

THE EVERGREEN TEMPERATE RAINFORESTS

There are two main kinds of temperate rainforest, the warm temperate, such as can still be found on North Island, New Zealand (left), and the cold temperate, such as that of the Chilean coast. Both of these kinds of forest have one major feature in common: they have enough water for even the most moisture-greedy plants, such as mosses and ferns, to grow throughout the year. The animal life of the forest is also affected by the abundance of rain, so that snails, slugs, frogs and other water-loving creatures flourish. Most temperate rainforest is of the warm-temperate kind, normally found on the edges of subtropical regions, and the vegetation, with palms, lianas, bamboos, as well as ferns and mosses, is similar to, although less rich than, the tropical rainforest's vegetation. The cold-temperate rainforests grow in cooler regions but their coastal position means that the climate is milder and wetter than inland (where deciduous trees dominate). Their vegetation is less lush and less varied than the warm-temperate forests, but mosses and ferns grow in abundance. Broad-leaved evergreens, such as New Zealand's southern beech, are the most common trees of these forests, although on the northwestern coast of North America Douglas firs and other conifers outnumber the broad-leaved evergreen species.

Man and the Temperate Forests

Temperate forests have suffered enormously at the hands of man. For the great civilizations of China, Europe and, later, North America the forests not only yielded cropland for expanding populations but also contributed materials and fuel for early technologies. More recently the demands of industry have reduced the forests still further. But today, scientists believe that this depleted resource could again play an important role in providing energy, food and materials for future generations.

PERMANENT SETTLEMENT
The Bronze Age and, later, the Iron Age laid the foundations of Chinese and Western civilizations. The forest shrank as permanent settlements grew (3) and, with the use of metals and improved technology, agricultural land was extended (4). But the forest was recognized as an important resource and areas were protected. Management techniques were introduced that, especially in medieval Europe, changed dense forest to coppice woods (5).

EARLY INDUSTRIAL TIMES
Sources of cropland and timber had been discovered in the New World, but in the Far East and Europe forests were drastically reduced. Virtually no Chinese forest remained, and in Europe nations began importing timber to serve growing industrial needs (6). To help solve shortages, plantations were established on country estates (7), which were often landscaped into parkland and planted with introduced species of trees (8).

PREHISTORIC FORESTS
Hunter gatherers made clearings in the forest when they cut brushwood for building shelters and for fuel (1): human impact on the temperate forest was small. But 7,000 years ago in Europe, 6,000 years ago in eastern Asia and 1,000 years ago in eastern North America, the first farming communities of the temperate forest (2) began to clear larger pockets of forest to provide land for crops and timber for houses and tools.

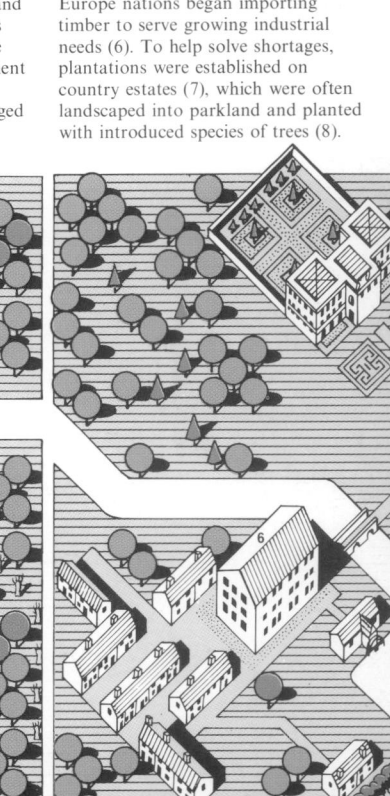

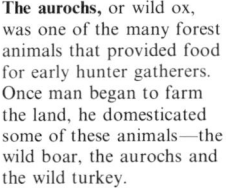
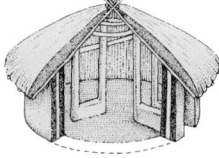

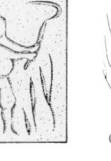

The aurochs, or wild ox, was one of the many forest animals that provided food for early hunter gatherers. Once man began to farm the land, he domesticated some of these animals—the wild boar, the aurochs and the wild turkey.

The dwellings of the late Neolithic Chinese were relatively sophisticated, reflecting an increasingly settled way of life that was soon to alter the landscape as forests were felled to provide building materials and land to plant crops.

The fortified villages and the farms of the Eastern Woodland Indians were set in semipermanent clearings cut in the North American forest. Before European settlement, however, human populations were small and deforestation was negligible.

Grain harvesting is depicted in a Chinese tomb image. By the 1st century AD, China contained nearly 60 million people, and agriculture, along with stock raising and metal mining, was drastically depleting the tree cover.

Coppicing and pollarding allowed continual cropping of forests. Branches were cut from trees, the bases of which were left to regrow shoots. This technique reduced the density of tree cover, encouraging a richer growth of ground plants.

Coppicing

Pollarding

Production of charcoal (below), which was a basic raw material for smelting in early industrial times, was responsible for much deforestation of the land.

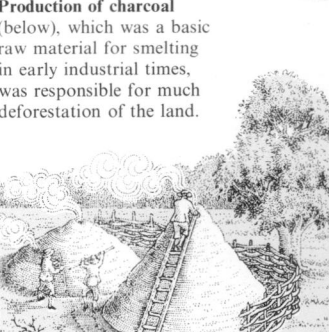

Human interference with the forests goes back deep into prehistory. There is evidence that fire was used to stampede hunted animals in southern Europe as long as 400,000 years ago. Human populations, while they remained small, had only a slight effect on the vast stretches of primeval forest. Even so, hunting practices and the use of fire to clear land reduced some of the forests of Europe and Asia even before the invention of agriculture. In the New World, too, Eastern Woodland Indians had already affected the North American forests, and early Maori hunters had burned much of the tree cover of New Zealand by the time Europeans arrived.

Nevertheless it was the development of agriculture in Neolithic (New Stone Age) times that had the first really destructive effect on the temperate forests. Clearings were made for crops and the felled trees provided fuel and building material for the new communities. Large forest animals suffered as well, some (such as deer) being hunted for food and others (such as wolves) because they threatened grazing animals. But it was the population increase resulting from the new, settled way of life that caused the extension of man-made cropland deep into former forests.

With man's development of metals, more forests were destroyed: wood and charcoal were used for smelting and the new iron tools made tree clearance easier and more thorough. Firing of forests was also a familiar military ploy, used by such warriors as the Romans.

Medieval woodlands
By medieval times, large tracts of forest had been cleared in Europe and in the Far East, although in the former area there remained extensive royal hunting forest reserves. Local woodlands were carefully managed to serve the needs of the community; the techniques used included pollarding and coppicing.

Pollarding involved the cropping of main branches at a certain height above ground. In coppicing, the "coppice with standards" method was used to harvest the smaller species, such as hazel and hornbeam, whereas the standards (such as oaks) were cut on a longer rotation of 100 years or so. Alternatively, the oak itself could be part of the coppice crop, its stems being cut near ground level so that shoots arose from the stump, to be cut 10 to 20 years later. For local communities, industries and cities, forests provided a variety of materials for building, tanning and fencing, as well as dye-stuffs, charcoal and domestic fuel.

The growth of the iron and shipbuilding industries in the sixteenth century devastated so much woodland and forest that in many regions good timber became scarce and had to be imported from considerable distances. The pressure on woodland continued until the production of coke and cheap coal brought some relaxation, but by the early twentieth century the coppice system had broken down and management of Europe's woodlands had largely been abandoned. In Europe the poor state of the deciduous forests was further worsened by two world wars. Many countries have since set up organizations with the specific task of building reserves of timber. Economic pressures, however, have led to the planting mainly of quick-growing conifers, rather than typical trees of the temperate deciduous forest.

New World forests
The migrants who settled in the New World were the descendants of the people who had largely destroyed the forests of Europe. Confronted by the temperate deciduous forests of eastern North America, they virtually continued where they had left off. Tracts were cleared to create arable and range land and to provide the massive amounts of timber needed for the colonization, industrialization and urbanization of North America. With the opening of the prairie lands for agriculture, however,

Disturbance to the natural vegetation has occurred throughout the temperate forest zone. Exploitation of this biome's greatest resource, its agricultural potential, has been one of the major causes of deforestation. The only forests that have escaped major disturbance are in remote areas, too rocky or too steep for cultivation. Today, intensive farming is still a major economic activity of the temperate forest regions. But farmland is not the only important resource to have disturbed the forests. Mining for key minerals such as copper, iron and coal, all of which made possible the development of Western and Chinese civilization, has also contributed to destruction of the forest cover. For centuries the forests provided man with food, fuel and materials, but, ironically, it has been the removal of the forest that has enabled man to exploit the most important of these regions' resources.

THE 19TH CENTURY

The Industrial Revolution developed in Europe and the New World, large towns and cities sprang up (9), pushing back the woodlands and forests still farther. This process was aided by the spreading network of railroads (10). Coke, iron and other minerals were replacing timber products as raw materials for growing industries (11), but demands were still made on the forests to provide, for example, railway sleepers and mine pit props.

FORESTS TODAY

The 20th century has seen an increasing trend towards urbanization in areas that were once temperate forest. Housing complexes (12) and new factory sites (13) cover large areas, while roadbuilding (14), industrial agriculture (15) and open-cast mining (16) destroy remaining woodland. Leisure areas (17) and nature reserves protect some woods, but plantations of exotic conifers (18) do not always provide suitable wildlife habitats.

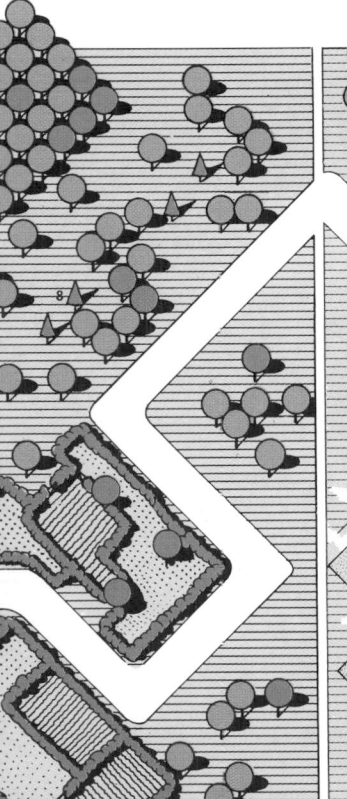
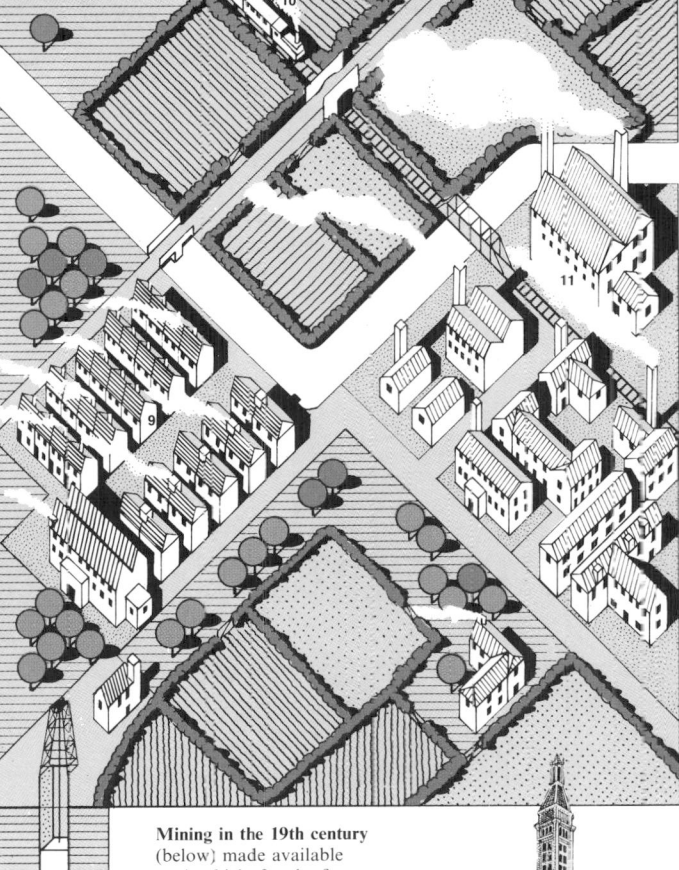
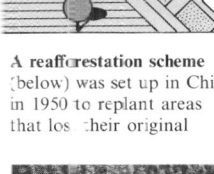

Early pioneers in the USA (below) transformed forestland as they moved west. By 1830 most of the eastern forests had been felled for settlement.

Mining in the 19th century (below) made available coal, which, for the first time, was being converted to coke and iron makers no longer needed charcoal.

Large department stores appeared in 19th-century Chicago, a town that, within 100 years, had been transformed from a remote fort to a city. This rapid growth reflected the huge population increase in many 19th-century towns.

A reafforestation scheme (below) was set up in China in 1950 to replant areas that lost their original forest cover many centuries ago. Similar projects are under way in many other temperate forest regions.

The European wood bison has escaped extinction because one herd of the animals has lived, for centuries, in a royal hunting reserve. Today, wildlife parks throughout temperate regions protect endangered forest species.

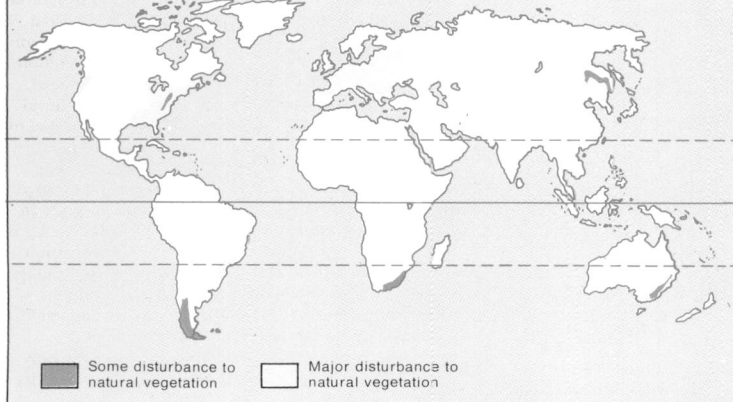

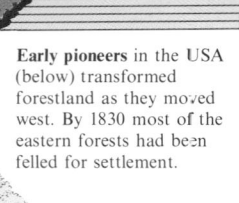
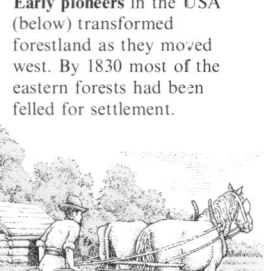

Some disturbance to natural vegetation

Major disturbance to natural vegetation

the pressures shifted, some of the east coast deciduous forest grew up again, and it is possible that parts of the eastern USA may have nearly as much forest cover now as when the settlers first arrived. Nevertheless, other areas of forestland have been destroyed in recent decades by strip mining and the creation of a vast road and rail network. In the southern hemisphere, especially in the last 200 years, the temperate rainforests of Australia and New Zealand have been subjected to much the same pattern of events, although on a smaller and somewhat less devastating scale.

Conservation

Today the general need to preserve and extend the woodlands is clearly recognized, but great uncertainty exists about their future. The demand for hardwoods for veneers, quality papermaking and furniture still exceeds supply. Oak is still the preferred material for some types of boat building and, especially in Europe, for joinery work. But one of the major difficulties with forestry as a land use is forecasting future trends within the industry, largely as a result of the long-term nature of the crop—hardwood trees planted today will not yield their timber until well into the next century. Government tax policies can be all important in deciding whether the majority of woodlands are, or will

continue to be, sound economic investments.

Temperate forests and woodlands still exist in sizeable quantities in central Europe and the USA, but many of today's plots, particularly in western Europe, are far too small for efficient conservation of plant and animal life, and are isolated from other woods. As a result, successful breeding and exchange of genetic material is very difficult, especially when modern agriculture is rapidly destroying the linking corridors of hedgerows. The use of woodlands for recreation is also presenting considerable problems. Controlling agencies have been formed to cope with leisure demands, and a start has been made in the multiple use of forests for recreation, conservation and timber felling, but progress still needs to be made in harmonizing these potentially conflicting interests. Meanwhile, natural expanses of woodland and forest are still being lost to agricultural and urban expansion and to plantations of nonnative conifers.

Temperate forests are a biologically efficient form of land use. In terms of biomass—the amount of living material (animal and plant) in any one area—they could still play an important role in the provision of food, materials and even renewable energy. Thus on scientific, economic and aesthetic grounds a strong case can be made for immediate conservation measures.

Mediterranean Regions

Forests of evergreen trees once covered much of the Mediterranean regions. They flourished in spite of the hot, rainless summer months – as the original plant life, they had evolved to survive such harsh conditions. Man, however, has proved to be a greater threat than the climate. He introduced domestic animals and cleared the land to grow crops; the natural vegetation was burned, browsed and plowed into nonexistence. Man's activities left behind tracts of impoverished soil which rapidly became scrubland. Today, scrub is the most typical vegetation in all the Mediterranean climate zones throughout the world.

CONVERGENCE

Isolated from each other by enormous areas of land and ocean, regions with a Mediterranean type of climate rarely have any plant species in common. But, by a process known as "convergent evolution," the plant communities in each of these areas have produced remarkably similar responses to their similar environments. This can be seen in the conifer communities, the broad-leaved evergreen trees, and in the various hardy shrubs and ground plants typical of each of the regions.

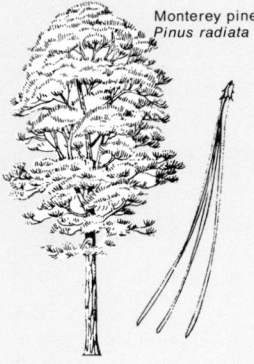

Monterey pine
Pinus radiata

California's Monterey pine and other Mediterranean conifers—South African podocarps and Chile pines, for example—have needle-shaped leaves that prevent rapid loss of water from such trees during drought.

Bailey's mimosa
Acacia baileyana

Nonconiferous evergreens such as Australia's acacias and eucalypts, Chile's *quillajas* and California's evergreen oaks are typical Mediterranean trees. Their leathery leaves limit summer moisture loss.

Giant protea
Protea cynaroides

Shrubs and ground plants show various adaptations to drought. South African proteas and Europe's laurel have thick evergreen leaves. Narrow leaves and water-storing roots are other common adaptations.

Long, hot, dry summers and warm, moist winters form the seasonal rhythm of the "Mediterranean" year. This climatic pattern can be found in small areas of nearly every continent in the world, typically on the western side of landmasses and in the mild, temperate latitudes. North America's "Mediterranean" is in California, South America's occurs in Chile and Africa's lies at the southern tip of Cape Province. Australia has two small "Mediterranean" areas, one on the southern coast and one on the western. Europe's Mediterranean region, which has given its name to this climate, covers much of the southern part of the continent and extends into northern Africa.

Wherever Mediterranean conditions prevail, the native plant life has adapted to survive the scanty annual rainfall and the long summer droughts. Some species have developed deep root systems that can tap low summer water tables, and many of the ground plants—such as bulbs and aromatic herbs—grow vigorously only in early summer while rain still moistens the soil. But it is the broad-leaved evergreens with their drought-resistant leaves that are the most typical of the Mediterranean areas.

This natural pattern of vegetation has been drastically altered by man. In southern Europe in particular, almost all the original evergreen forests have long since been destroyed and thickets of fast-growing, tough scrub plants have grown up in their place. This scrub, which once probably covered only small areas, is now so widespread that it is considered the most typically Mediterranean of all kinds of vegetation. It is the *maquis* of France, the *macchia* of Italy and the *mattoral* of Spain. A similar type of vegetation (although containing different species) can also be found in South Africa's fynbos, in California's chaparral, and in Australia's tracts of natural mallee scrub.

Classical land use

Southern Europe, with its long history of human settlement, farming and pastoralism, is the most altered of all the Mediterranean regions. Over the centuries vast tracts of original vegetation have been removed, either by farmers (for crop growing) or by grazing animals. And, particularly on the steep slopes and rocky outcrops, this has resulted in extensive deterioration and erosion of the soil. Agriculture generally has less serious effects upon the vegetation than animal grazing. Mankind has learned, over many hundreds of years, which are the most suitable crops for the various soils, terrain and climatic conditions of the region. The Mediterranean "triad" of wheat on the lowlands and olives and vines on the hills has been a successful combination since Classical times.

Pastoral plundering of the land, however, has more serious consequences. The virtually omnivorous goat is particularly damaging and can strip a whole forest of its foliage, bark, shrubs, ground plants and grass. After such an assault

the vegetation rarely returns to its former condition; normally, a scrubby growth of kermes oak and shrubs springs up to form a typical maquis-type vegetation.

The rise and fall of each great Mediterranean civilization has seen forests destroyed in one area after another. The Greek colonization of southern Italy was provoked by deforestation and soil erosion in Attica. The Romans extended clearance north to the Po valley and into eastern Tunisia. From the seventh century onwards, Muslims made great inroads into the forests of North Africa as well as southern and eastern Spain; and in the north of Spain and southern France, medieval monks cleared forested valleys. During the seventeenth and eighteenth centuries large areas of Provence and Italy were cleared to plant vines and this process continued in the 1800s, when the great wine-producing areas of Languedoc and Algeria were established. During this time the iron industries of Spain and northern Italy, with their growing need for charcoal, were adding to the destruction. Recent reafforestation efforts have been puny compared to past degradation.

Protected species

But throughout this history of forest removal some tree species have been protected. These have been the natural tree crops that have, at times, supported complete peasant economies. The chestnut forests of Corsica, for example, sustained a large rural population until this century; the chestnuts provided flour for bread and fodder for pigs. In Portugal and Sardinia the cork-oak forests are still important today.

It is the olive, however, symbol of peace and of New Testament landscapes, that is the Mediterranean's most characteristic tree crop. Of all the Mediterranean plants, it is the most perfectly adapted to its environment, with its deep roots to search out scarce water and its hard, shiny leaves to conserve what it finds. In fact, the summer drought is essential to olive growers for it encourages the build-up of oil in the fruit. Paradoxically, however, the olive—like the vine, the fig and many other "Mediterranean" crops—did not originate in the Mediterranean but was introduced from Asia Minor.

In spite of massive destruction of the natural landscape, mankind has learned many valuable lessons during his occupation of this region. Ideas that were to become important in laying the foundations of sound land management policy were developed in the Mediterranean area. Hillside terracing, irrigation, crop rotation and manuring were all, from necessity, practiced from early times. The flourishing agricultural industries of the world's other Mediterranean regions—the wine industry of California, the vast soft-fruit plantations of Australia and the citrus industry of South Africa—all owe a considerable debt to the generations of farmers who learned to exploit the red soils of the Mediterranean basin.

The Mediterranean regions occur between the latitudes 30° and 40°, on the western and southwestern sides of the continents. These areas are affected in summer by the high-pressure systems of nearby desert regions, and in winter by wet, low-pressure systems brought in from the oceans and over the land by the prevailing Westerlies. This distinct seasonal shifting of major influences on the climate produces the hot, waterless summers and warm, moist, sometimes stormy winters typical of the Mediterranean climate.

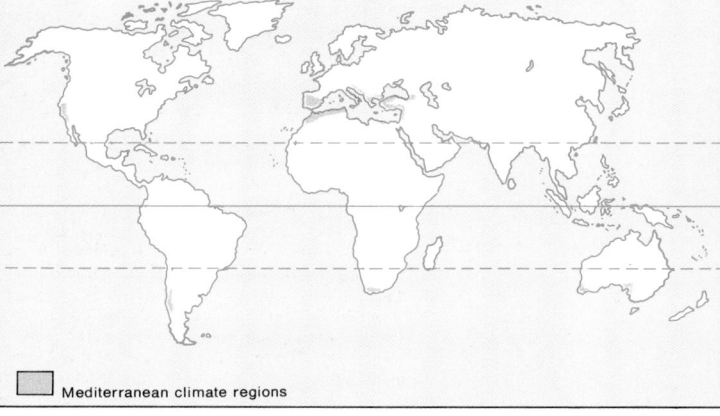

Mediterranean climate regions

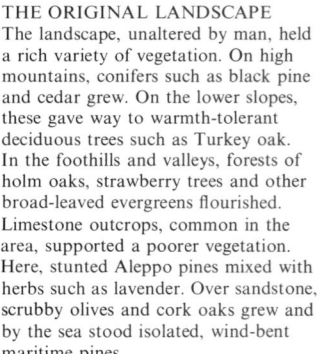
6

THE ORIGINAL LANDSCAPE

The landscape, unaltered by man, held a rich variety of vegetation. On high mountains, conifers such as black pine and cedar grew. On the lower slopes, these gave way to warmth-tolerant deciduous trees such as Turkey oak. In the foothills and valleys, forests of holm oaks, strawberry trees and other broad-leaved evergreens flourished. Limestone outcrops, common in the area, supported a poorer vegetation. Here, stunted Aleppo pines mixed with herbs such as lavender. Over sandstone, scrubby olives and cork oaks grew and by the sea stood isolated, wind-bent maritime pines.

THE CLASSICAL AGE

Civilizations followed one after another, each taking its toll of the environment. In the mountains, forests were felled, the tall, straight conifers sought after by shipbuilders such as the Phoenicians, and deciduous hardwood timber in demand for charcoal to fuel growing industries. Some replanting did take place, especially as groves of crop trees such as chestnuts. Below in the foothills, agriculture and the grazing of animals had destroyed vast areas of natural forest. Terracing techniques, however, helped to stop soil erosion, and irrigation reached the height of its Classical art with Roman aqueducts and canals. Tree crops, such as olives, were found best suited to the thin hill soils. On the plains, especially where alluvial soils had been deposited, cereals were grown. Meanwhile, towns sprang up and the coastline became densely populated as ships and ports were built and sea trade increased. Exotic food plants, such as pomegranate trees, citron trees and vines, were brought into the region by merchant seamen.

THE MEDITERRANEAN TODAY

The region today bears the scars of many centuries of human activity. The once-forested mountains will never return to their former state, although some regrowth and some replanting (mostly with introduced tree species) has occurred. As in Classical times, hillsides are terraced and planted with vines and fruit trees. But with modern irrigation and fertilizing, land is less readily exhausted and abandoned now. On the plains, native shrubs, such as lavender, are commercially cultivated and grain is widely grown, particularly durum wheat used for making pasta. Cork oaks are planted, especially over dry sandstone areas, but indigenous vegetation has not suffered by this—scrubby woodland is more widespread than ever and can be found throughout the landscape. Perhaps the single most important part of the Mediterranean basin today is the coastline, for this has produced the region's major modern industry—tourism.

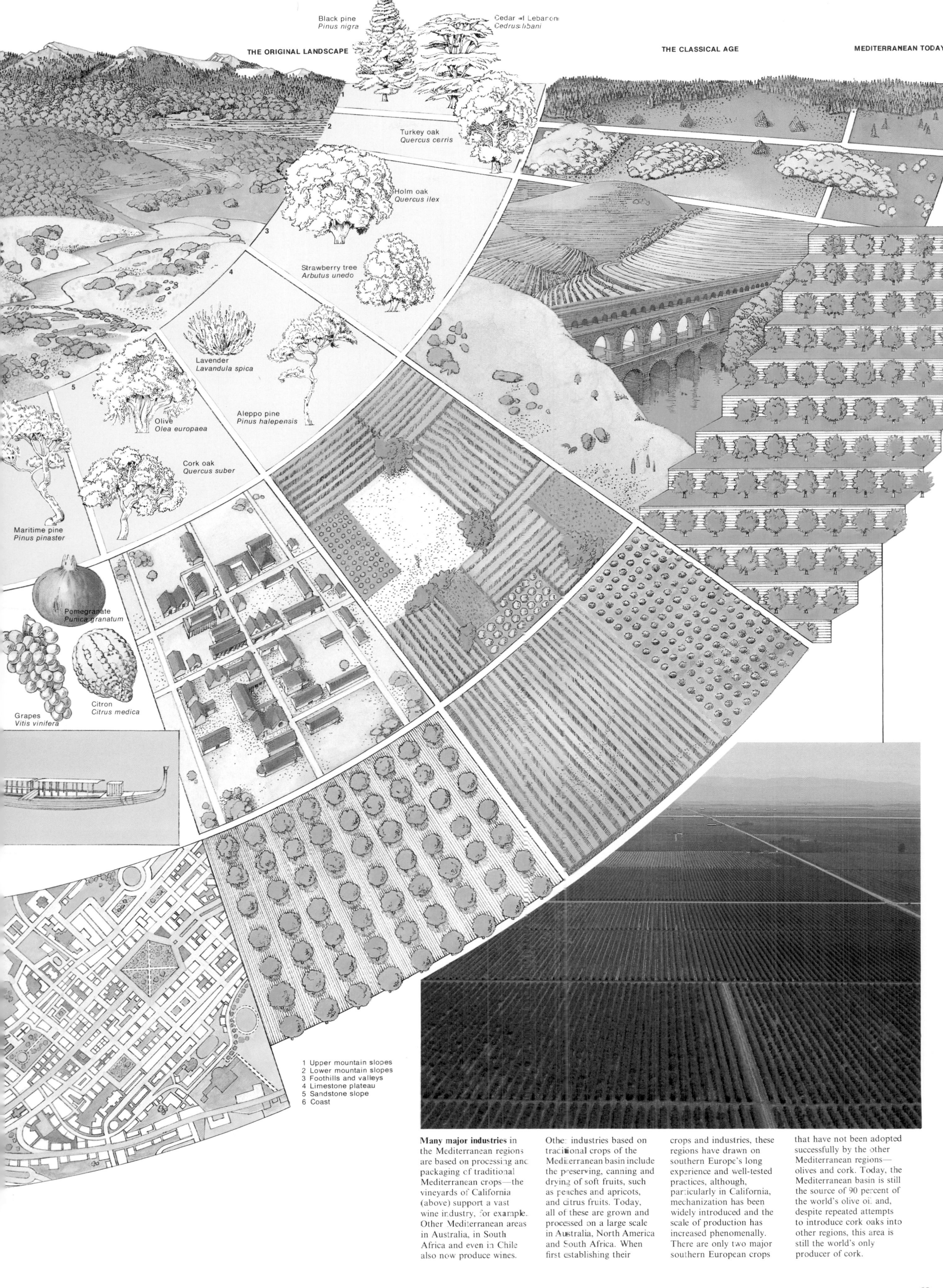

Black pine
Pinus nigra

Cedar of Lebanon
Cedrus libani

Turkey oak
Quercus cerris

Holm oak
Quercus ilex

Strawberry tree
Arbutus unedo

Lavender
Lavandula spica

Olive
Olea europaea

Aleppo pine
Pinus halepensis

Cork oak
Quercus suber

Maritime pine
Pinus pinaster

Pomegranate
Punica granatum

Citron
Citrus medica

Grapes
Vitis vinifera

1 Upper mountain slopes
2 Lower mountain slopes
3 Foothills and valleys
4 Limestone plateau
5 Sandstone slope
6 Coast

Many major industries in the Mediterranean regions are based on processing and packaging of traditional Mediterranean crops—the vineyards of California (above) support a vast wine industry, for example. Other Mediterranean areas in Australia, in South Africa and even in Chile also now produce wines.

Other industries based on traditional crops of the Mediterranean basin include the preserving, canning and drying of soft fruits, such as peaches and apricots, and citrus fruits. Today, all of these are grown and processed on a large scale in Australia, North America and South Africa. When first establishing their crops and industries, these regions have drawn on southern Europe's long experience and well-tested practices, although, particularly in California, mechanization has been widely introduced and the scale of production has increased phenomenally. There are only two major southern European crops that have not been adopted successfully by the other Mediterranean regions—olives and cork. Today, the Mediterranean basin is still the source of 90 percent of the world's olive oil and, despite repeated attempts to introduce cork oaks into other regions, this area is still the world's only producer of cork.

Temperate Grasslands

Compared with other flowering plants, grasses are newcomers to the Earth. They appeared only 60 million years ago, but since then they have proved to be an extremely successful family of plants. Today, the grasses dominate large areas of the world's natural vegetation and play a vital part in the intricate balance of plant and animal life in these regions. In spite of the inroads made by man, vast stretches of original grassland still cover the interiors of the North American and Eurasian landmasses.

Saiga
Saiga tatarica

American bison
Bison bison

European hare
Lepus europaeus

Guanaco
Lama guanicoë

Springhaas
Pedetes cafer

RUNNING AND LEAPING HERBIVORES

The prairies of North America and the steppes of Eurasia extend far into the interiors of the northern continents. These are the best known and the most extensive of the world's temperate grasslands. The southern hemisphere, however, has examples in the veld of South Africa and the pampas of South America. Extensive grasslands also occur in southern Australia, although these are sometimes described as semiarid scrub because of the high average temperatures and the prolonged droughts in the region.

Temperate grasslands probably developed wherever the rainfall was too low to support forest and too high to result in semiarid regions, conditions found typically in the interiors of large continents. Continental interiors tend to be somewhat drier than coastal regions, but they are also characterized by extreme changes in temperature from one season to the next. In the North American grasslands, for example, winter temperatures may fall well below freezing whereas summer temperatures of 38°C (100°F) are not unusual. And these sharp fluctuations in seasonal temperature greatly influence how much of the rainfall is made available to plants. In summer particularly, when most of the rain falls, high temperatures, strong winds and lack of protective tree cover cause much of the moisture to evaporate before it can be absorbed into the soil.

Climatic conditions are not the only factor responsible for the distribution and form of the temperate grasslands. There are many pointers that indicate the importance of fire in determining their continuing existence and their extent. Natural fires, caused by lightning and fueled by the dry summer grasses, have always been a feature of these regions, but more recently,

man-made fires have been crucial in fixing the boundary between forest and grassland.

Trees and shrubs frequently invade the margins of grasslands, but whenever there is a fire few of them survive. Grasses, however, have certain characteristics that enable them to withstand the potentially destructive impact of fire. The growing point of grasses is at the base of the leaves, close to the ground, and so destruction of the leaves above this point does not interrupt growth—in fact it may stimulate it. These same characteristics also serve to protect grasses from destruction by grazing animals. The large animals of these lands, such as the North American bison and the Eurasian horse, are able to crop the grasses without permanently damaging their food supply.

Grazers and predators

Large migrating herbivores with a strong herd instinct characterize one of the major types of temperate grassland animal. In the North American grasslands the bison (which may have numbered 60 million before being virtually exterminated by settlers) and the antelope-like pronghorn were the major examples of large herbivores. In Eurasia large herds of saiga antelopes, wild horses and asses at one time roamed the steppes, although they too have suffered from human activities, as has South America's largest grassland herd animal, the pampas deer. As these herds of grazing animals have been reduced, so have the carnivorous animals of the grasslands that preyed upon them. At one time, however, these predators played an important part in protecting the grasslands by continually keeping the numbers of grazing herd animals in check.

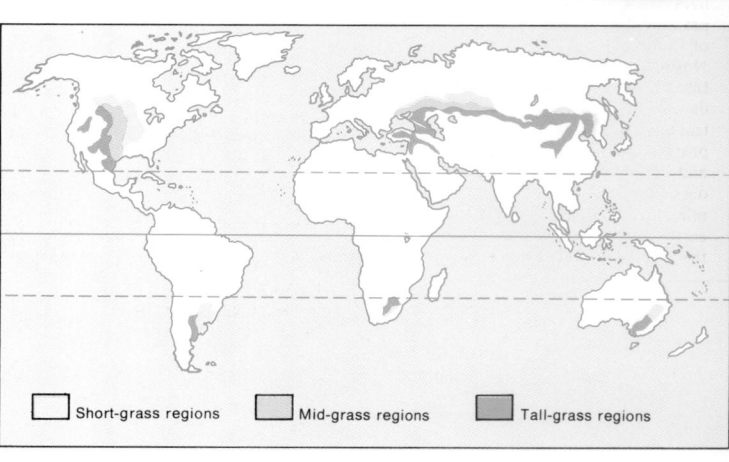

Maned wolf
Chrysocyon brachyurus

Plains wolf
Canis lupus nubilus

Coyote
Canis latrans

RUNNING CARNIVORES

Prairie dog
Cynomys ludovicianus

European souslik
Citellus citellus

Viscacha
Lagostomus maximus

Marsupial mole
Notoryctes typhlops

SMALL BURROWING ANIMALS

Pampas cat
Lynchailurus pajeros

Black-footed ferret
Mustela nigripes

Marbled polecat
Vormela peregusna

Gopher snake
Pituophis melanoleucus

SMALL CARNIVORES

The dominant native species of grass varies from area to area. In the undisturbed prairies, for example, tall bluestem and Indian grass grow in the east and in wet central lowlands and mix with switch grass in drier parts. Farther west and on high land in the east, little bluestem and also western wheatgrass grow. June grass grows in the north, and buffalo grass and blue grama grow farthest west.

Many flowering herbs grow in the grasslands and have developed resistance to summer droughts: Russian tarragon has narrow leaves to help prevent moisture evaporation; rhizomes and bulbs, such as Eurasia's iris and anemone, store water in their specialized "root" systems.

Russian tarragon
Artemisia dracunculoides

Iris
Iris sibirica

Anemone
Anemone patens

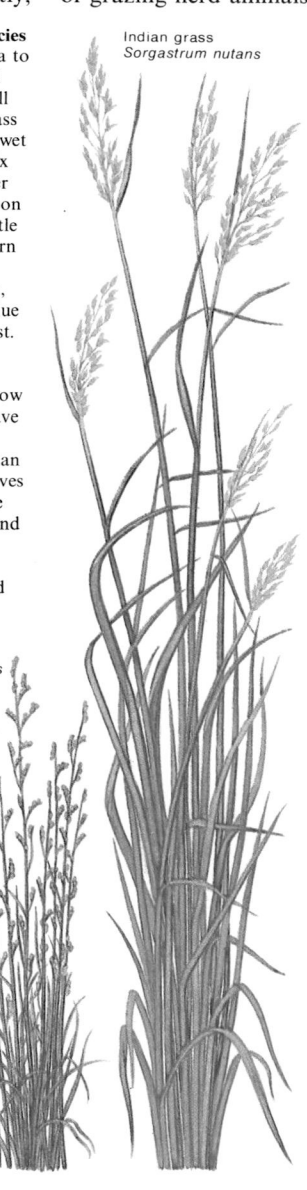

Indian grass
Sorgastrum nutans

Little bluestem
Andropogon scoparius

Blue grama grass
Bouteloua gracilis

The natural distribution of the temperate grasslands is dictated mainly by rainfall: most occur in continental interiors where there is too little rain for forest but enough to prevent desert from forming. Between these limits the large range in rainfall allows three main types of grassland: tall grass in wetter areas, mid-grass, and short grass in drier parts. The largest grasslands exist in North America, Eurasia, South America, in Australia's Murray–Darling river basin and on the South African plateau.

☐ Short-grass regions   ☐ Mid-grass regions   ☐ Tall-grass regions

Mid-grass prairies

Short-grass prairies

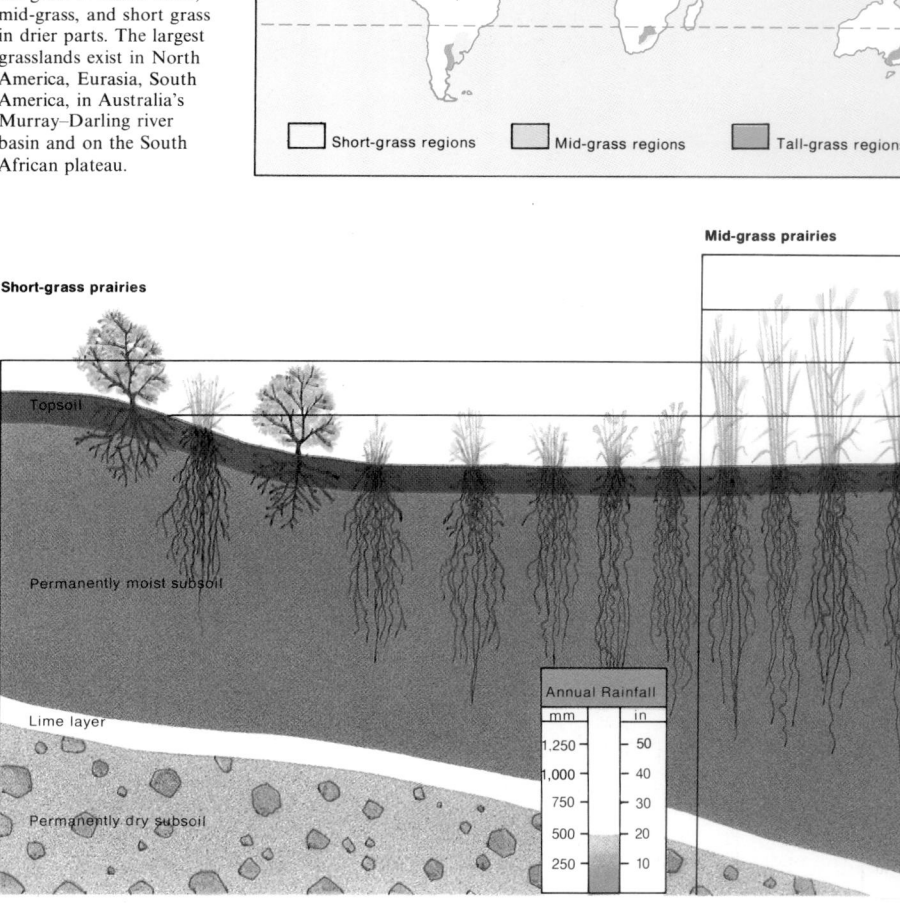

Topsoil

Permanently moist subsoil

Lime layer

Permanently dry subsoil

Annual Rainfall	
mm	in
1,250	50
1,000	40
750	30
500	20
250	10

GRASSLAND ADAPTATION

Animals of these regions have had to adapt to a difficult environment: vast, treeless expanses of grass offer little protection from harsh weather or predators. Different animals have found various answers to the problem and a clearly defined pattern of these adaptations can be traced throughout the grasslands.

Running and leaping herbivores survive because of their ability to move faster than a pursuer. The larger animals such as the Eurasian saiga, North America's bison and pronghorn and the guanaco of South America are runners. The leaping herbivores are usually smaller creatures that escape danger by bounding away to bolt-holes. They include the European hare and the African springhaas.
Running carnivores follow, and prey on, running and leaping herbivores. These animals, such as the coyote and the now extinct plains wolf of North America, and South America's maned wolf, also depend on speed—to enable them to catch their prey.
Small burrowing animals hide from predators by digging under the ground. Some, such as Australia's marsupial mole, spend most of their lives below ground. Others, such as the European souslik, South America's viscacha and North America's prairie dog, live and sleep under the ground but come to the surface to find food.
Small carnivores concentrate on the burrowers as their main source of food. They either, like the pampas cat, rely on surprise attack of their prey, or, like Eurasia's marbled polecat and the grasslands' many kinds of snake, depend on their long, lithe shape to follow creatures into their burrows.

Two distinctive types of grassland bird can be distinguished: the sky birds, which spend long periods of time on the wing, and the ground birds.
Birds of the sky include songbirds such as the skylark which, having no perch from which to proclaim its territory, sings in the sky, and birds of prey such as Eurasia's tawny eagle and North America's red-tailed hawk and prairie falcon, which ride the thermals scanning the ground for their prey.
Ground birds rarely take to the wing, although none has actually lost the ability to fly when necessary. They include birds such as the New World sage grouse and burrowing owl (which lives below ground in abandoned prairie dog burrows), the black grouse of Eurasia and songbirds such as North America's meadowlark.
Insects and other invertebrates have developed many different survival techniques. Some use camouflage: the praying mantis resembles a leaf bud and the tumble bug is the color of the dark grassland soil. Grasshoppers are miniature leaping herbivores and earthworms are small-scale versions of the grassland burrowers.

Skylark
Alauda arvensis

Tawny eagle
Aquila rapax

Red-tailed hawk
Buteo jamaicensis

Prairie falcon
Falco mexicanus

BIRDS OF THE SKY

Western meadowlark
Sturnella neglecta

Burrowing owl
Speotyto cunicularia

Sage grouse
Centrocercus urophasianus

Black grouse
Lyrurus tetrix

GROUND BIRDS

Lubber grasshopper
Romalea microptera

Tumble bug
Canthonlaevis drury

Common earthworm
Lumbricus terrestris

Praying mantis
Mantis religiosa

INSECTS AND OTHER INVERTEBRATES

A typical cross section, based on the North American prairies, shows temperate grasslands in relation to rainfall. Annual rainfall determines the depth of the permanently moist subsoil, which in turn dictates the length to which grass roots can grow. Tall grasses have deep root systems and need a considerable depth of moist subsoil. As the rainfall decreases, they gradually give way to shorter grass species. Short grasses require less water and their shallower roots are well suited to drier regions. On dry margins, desert plants start to dominate, and on the wet margins, trees appear.

Another major type of animal found in the temperate grasslands, and one that is better adapted to survive man's activities, is the small, burrowing animal, for example the prairie dog and the gopher of North America, the viscacha of South America and the little ground squirrel known as the souslik in Eurasia.

Unlike the large herd animals, these creatures tend not to migrate. Many of them live together in complex, permanent, underground communities. The colonial "townships" of the prairie dog, for example, may house more than one million individuals, which each year excavate vast quantities of the grassland soil. This has considerable effect upon the structure of the soil. By bringing up earth from lower layers to the surface, these animals are responsible for changing the mineral content of certain areas of topsoil. This then encourages isolated pockets of different plant species to flourish.

A third group of grassland animals, consisting of insects and other invertebrates such as earthworms, has an even more important effect upon the soil. They live in or on the soil and play a vital role in maintaining grassland fertility. These creatures may be herbivores, carnivores or primary (first stage) decomposers (which break down such material as dead grass and animal remains). These three types of activity allow a complete range of organic matter to be processed and incorporated into the earth, where it is further broken down by the second-stage decomposers, the countless millions of soil bacteria. In this way nutrients continuously flow back to the earth and restore its fertility.

Fertile black earths

The topsoil of temperate grassland regions, therefore, contains large amounts of organic material, which is produced every year and is quickly incorporated into the soil. The low and intermittent rainfall and the protective cover of grasses mean that the topsoil undergoes little chemical leaching, a process in which minerals are removed and carried down to lower layers by rainfall percolating through the earth. The soils are thus dark in color, generally fertile and of the "black earth" type ("chernozem" in Russian) which is, at least at first, capable of producing high yields of crops.

The most suitable and most widely grown crops are, predictably, the cultivated grasses, and it is these grasses that provide more food for mankind (either directly as grain or indirectly as animal fodder) than any other source. The temperate grassland biome is therefore an important agricultural resource. Undisturbed natural grasslands, however, are also valuable resources. They need to be preserved both for the information that they can provide about how complex communities of wildlife function efficiently, and because, as a rich source of genetic material, they hold many of the answers to the major agricultural problems that probably lie ahead for the human race.

Tall-grass prairies

cm ft
215 7
180 6
150 5
120 4
90 3
60 2
30 1
0 0

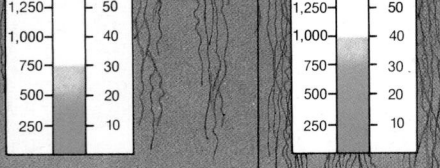

Annual Rainfall	
mm	in
1,250	50
1,000	40
750	30
500	20
250	10

Annual Rainfall	
mm	in
1,250	50
1,000	40
750	30
500	20
250	10

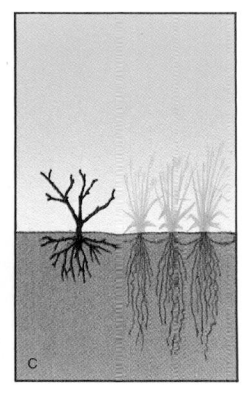

Fire plays a major part in fixing and maintaining the natural boundaries of the temperate grasslands, where tree saplings and shrubs are continually attempting to invade (A). Man-made fires are recent phenomena, natural fires have always occurred. In summer, low-pressure systems build up in continental interiors, causing violent electrical storms. The dry sward of summer grass is easily ignited by lightning and fire is quickly spread by wind. Shrubs and saplings are killed or badly damaged by fire, but grasses, with their growing points close to the soil, remain unharmed (B). They may even benefit from this "pruning" and grow more quickly. Some species grow new buds from their underground shoots. Removal of the main shoot may encourage growth of "tillers" (shoots growing out sideways), which then increase the spread of the grasses as they begin to invade the area left vacant by the dead, or slowly recuperating shrubs (C).

Man and the Temperate Grasslands

The vast areas of temperate grassland lay virtually empty until the end of the eighteenth century. Over the next 125 years they were occupied by millions of people, most of them migrants from overcrowded Europe. By 1914, the grasslands had become the granaries and the stockyards of the world. Today, they are still the most important food-producing regions on Earth and their riches, properly distributed, are the world's first reserve against the possibility of a hungry future for the human race.

The great nineteenth-century migration to the grasslands proved of immense significance to the human race. It meant that, within a single century, the area of productive land available was suddenly enlarged by thousands of millions of hectares. In all of mankind's history, such a thing had never happened before.

But before the grasslands could be occupied a number of major problems had to be solved. First, in order to reach these regions it was almost always necessary to travel deep into the continental interiors, and there were few navigable rivers and no mechanized forms of transportation for early pioneers. Second, with virtually no indigenous population, newcomers had to learn by their mistakes how best to exploit the new and unfamiliar environment. Third, even if settlers succeeded in using the land, they still had to find markets for their produce.

A number of technological developments, however, that took place in the nineteenth century provided the right combination of circumstances for the opening up of the grasslands. The Industrial Revolution in Europe produced the steamship and the railway locomotive, which created both a means of travel to and from these distant parts and an internal transport system for moving produce to ports and markets. It also produced the kind of machinery needed to plow and farm the great new open spaces; it made it possible for one family to cultivate an area 50 times as large as that which most farmers had known in Europe. Industrialization also threw thousands of Europeans out of work, and therefore provided a large supply of eager migrants. And it crowded further thousands into cities, thus creating vast markets for the settlers' produce.

It was the coming together of these various circumstances that acted as the catalyst and converted, for example, the Russian penetration of the Eurasian steppes in the late eighteenth

THE CRADLE OF AGRICULTURE

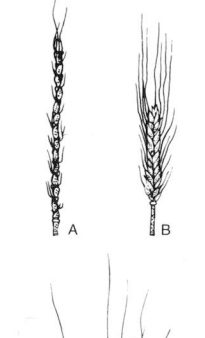
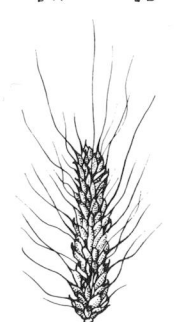

Stands of wild einkorn (A), emmer wheat (B) and wild barleys can be seen today in the grassy foothills that flank the Taurus and the Zagros mountains, and the uplands of northern Israel. It was in this region 10,000 years ago that the world's earliest farmers gathered seeds from these species and sowed the first crops. Wild einkorn is probably the oldest of all wheats and the parent of every modern variety—including the most important and most widely grown kind of grain in the world today, common bread wheat (C).

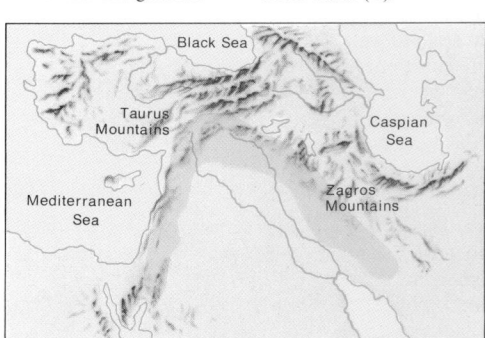

GRASSLAND EXPLOITATION

Today, temperate grasslands provide mankind with a superabundance of food. But the vast potential of these regions was not exploited until the mid-19th century, when mass migration by Europeans, combined with new technology, allowed full-scale development and settlement.

BEFORE EUROPEAN SETTLEMENT
The grasslands were sparsely populated. Most of the indigenous tribespeoples were nomadic hunters and gatherers. They wandered widely over the regions, making temporary camps (1) as they followed the movement of their quarry—the plentiful herds of grazing animals (2). These peoples made little impact on the natural grasslands.

GRASSLAND SETTLERS
Early pioneers relied on animal-drawn transport (3), primitive farm tools (4) and unpredictable free-range livestock grazing (5). During the 19th century, farming became more productive: better equipment cultivated larger areas (6); barbed wire made stock raising efficient (7); railways and the telegraph improved communication (8).

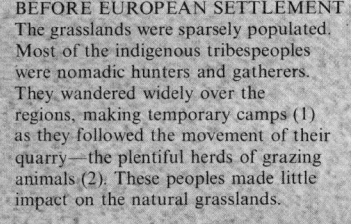

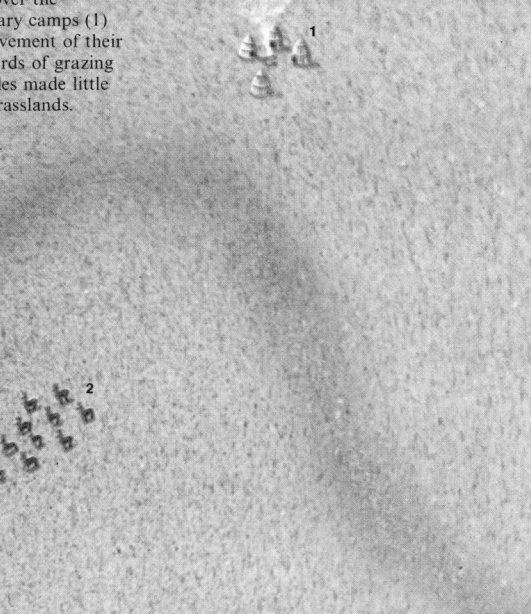

Tehuelche Indians (above) adopted horses for hunting from early Spanish settlers to the pampas. In South Africa and North America, too, the introduced horse became a valued asset for grassland hunters. For people of the Eurasian steppes, for example the Mongols (right), native horses have always been culturally important.

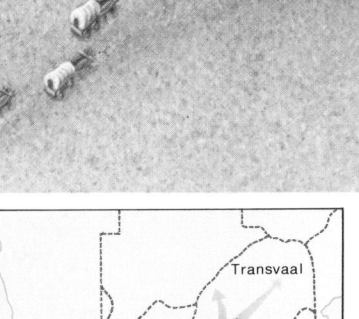

The **South African veld** was first settled by Europeans after 1836 (left). Dutch farmers (Boers), rejecting British rule of the Cape Colony, trekked north in search of new land. Moving into the Transvaal they discovered rich grassland, recently emptied of its original inhabitants, who had fled to escape the aggressive attentions of neighboring Zulus.

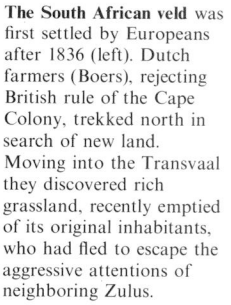

Vaqueros were the original cowboys (left). Tending herds of cattle for the missionaries in 18th-century California, they developed techniques and traditions that served hundreds of later cowboys working the prairie ranges. In other grassland regions, as free-range stock raising became important, similar "cowboy" professions evolved—the Australian stockman and the gaucho of South America.

century into the explosive movement of hundreds of thousands of settlers a few years later. In the USA, too, by the year 1850, settlement had reached and then rapidly crossed the Mississippi. In the Argentine, genuine colonization of the pampas had begun, in South Africa, the Boers had reached the high veld, and in Australia pioneer settlers were moving outwards from the various areas of coastal settlement into the scrub grasslands of the interior.

Farmers or ranchers?

The fundamental question posed for these settlers was whether their newly found land should be used for crops or for livestock. Most grasslands have a dry edge and a wet edge, and it was therefore sensible to use the drier parts for stock raising and the wetter parts for cultivation. But the question was complicated by the fact that most of the newcomers were cultivators, and also that the line dividing dry from wet was vague—worse, it shifted from year to year.

Early attempts to define the dividing line tended to be ignored by the settlers themselves, and they pushed the limit of cultivation into areas where plowing the soil led to its destruction. Several generations of farmers had to learn this bitter lesson, and they learned only slowly: the worst disasters on the American grasslands occurred in the 1930s and created the infamous

Dust Bowl region in the dry grasslands of the Midwest. Similarly, the Soviet Virgin Lands Program for growing cereal crops on the dry steppes was established in 1954 and is still experiencing difficulties.

Special methods are required both for farming and for ranching the grasslands successfully. Farming has to take account of the open, treeless surface, the scanty and variable rainfall and the comparatively shallow topsoil. To minimize the risk of soil erosion, farmers plant windbreaks, plow fields along the contour, and protect the soil with a covering of the previous year's stubble and by planting cover crops in rotation with cereals. Ranchers, too, have learned to live with variable rainfall. They build stock ponds, irrigate areas of fodder crops to be used as a reserve in dry years and avoid overstocking and consequent overgrazing, which destroys the quality of the grass.

Food for the world

Today, the world's principal trading supplies of cereals and meat flow from these lands, over the networks of railway which link the grasslands to mill towns, slaughter yards and ports of shipment such as Adelaide in Australia, Buenos Aires in Argentina and Montreal in Canada. Without these links to large towns, the grasslands would be of little value, for even

today their populations are sparse and the local markets are relatively insignificant.

Throughout most of the world, however, the human population continues to soar and it remains to be seen whether the grasslands can continue to supply these growing numbers with food. Undoubtedly, the output of cereals and meat can be increased, although at considerable cost in fertilizers, new crop strains, more irrigation and more machines. On the other hand, the problem at present is not mainly one of production, nor will it be in the near future. The land can produce more, but there is no point in doing so unless the yields can be made available where they are most needed.

The world's hungry people live in other regions, many of them in countries that are unable to afford imported food supplies, particularly during those years when prices are high. The major importers of temperate grassland produce are the rich industrialized nations, such as those of western Europe. Furthermore, much of the grain imported by those countries is not consumed by humans but used to feed stalled, beef-producing cattle—a highly inefficient way of using these supplies. Consequently, unless producer nations and wealthy importing nations can create a system for produce to reach those in need of it, extra output from the grasslands will be irrelevant.

MODERN-DAY FARMING
Livestock feed on carefully selected grasses, which are sown and fertilized by aircraft (9). Fodder crops are grown as reserve animal feed (10), and stock ponds ensure against drought (11). Feedlots (12) fatten stock on grain (13). Cereal farms (14) are highly mechanized, and road and rail serve even the remotest regions (15).

The steam-driven plow (below) went through many developments to reduce its unwieldiness and heaviness. The version produced in 1858 used a traction engine and pulley wheel system. The plow was drawn back and forth between these by a power-driven cable. This design was, however, superseded by the steam tractor, which, although unsuited to small European fields, was ideal for drawing multifurrow plows across the grasslands.

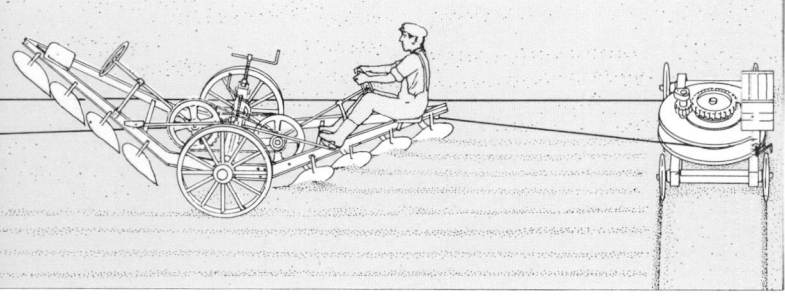

Sand-smothered farms in the heart of the Dust Bowl were rapidly abandoned during the 1930s and 40s (above). This was one costly lesson that man had to learn in the process of developing the grasslands. Traditionally grazing land, the western part of the prairies was first plowed this century. Years of drought arrived, crops died and the desert encroached.

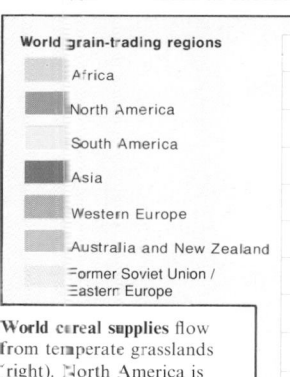

World cereal supplies flow from temperate grasslands (right). North America is the most important producing region, for although almost all nations produce grain, few can grow enough to feed their populations and even fewer have any surplus to export or hold in reserve against poor harvests. But North America, with its prairie cornfields and its small population, exports many millions of tonnes.

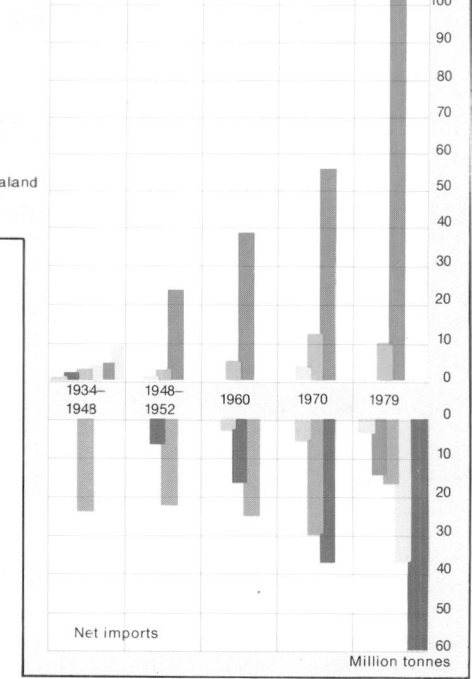

World grain-trading regions

- Africa
- North America
- South America
- Asia
- Western Europe
- Australia and New Zealand
- Former Soviet Union / Eastern Europe

Net exports

1934–1948 1948–1952 1960 1970 1979

Net imports

Million tonnes

Deserts

Much of the Earth's land surface is so short of water that it is defined as desert. Not all deserts are hot, sandy wastelands; some are cold, some are rocky, but all lack moisture for most of the year. Even so, a surprising variety of plants and animals have adapted to these hostile environments. Plants have developed ingenious ways of surviving long periods of drought, and many desert animals shelter during the intense heat of the day, emerging only at night to feed.

LIFE IN THE DESERT
The overriding need to obtain and conserve water dictates the pattern of desert life. Many plants close their pores during the day and most daytime creatures limit their activity to early morning and late afternoon. At night the temperature drops sharply and dew provides welcome moisture. Some plants bloom at night, and the desert is alive with insects, night-hunting birds, reptiles and small mammals.

DESERTS BY DAY

Many birds are at home in the desert. The lanner falcon of Africa and Asia gets all the moisture it needs from its diet of small birds and rodents. Sandgrouse live in the open deserts of Eurasia and North Africa; mainly seed eaters, they must make long flights each day to find water. Roadrunners, in American deserts, hunt insects, lizards and small rattlesnakes.

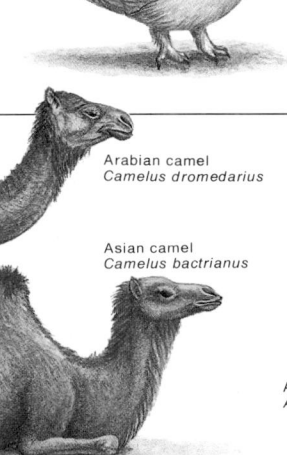

Lanner falcon
Falco biarmicus

Pallas's sandgrouse
Syrrhaptes paradoxus

Roadrunner
Geococcyx californianus

Large mammals are nomadic and obtain most of the moisture they need from plants. Camels can go for long periods without food or water because their humped back stores fat which can be drawn on when food is scarce, and water stored in their body tissues prevents dehydration. Addax antelopes survive entirely on plants. They roam remote parts of the Sahara, their broad hooves enabling them to travel easily over soft sand. Gazelles rely on speed. Small and fleet footed, they are able to disperse quickly over great distances to find food and water.

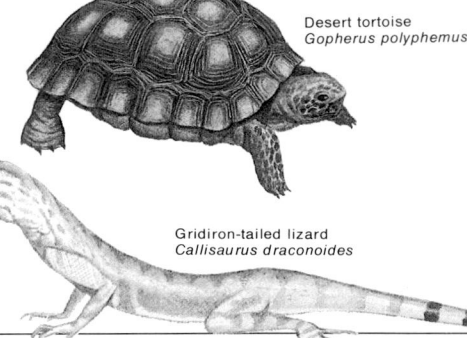
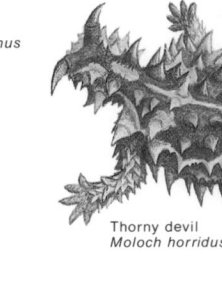

Arabian camel
Camelus dromedarius

Asian camel
Camelus bactrianus

Addax antelope
Addax nasomaculatus

Dorcas gazelle
Gazella dorcas

Insects and reptiles are well adapted to desert life. Desert locusts, when overpopulation threatens their food supply, change from a solitary to a swarming migratory form. Harvester ants store seeds against times of drought; desert tortoises withstand drought by becoming torpid. Lizards are cold blooded and need the sun to warm them, but must shelter from the intense heat of midday. The thorny devil, a small Australian ant-eating lizard, is protected from potential predators by its prickly scales.

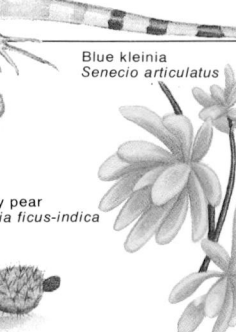

Desert locust
Schistocerca gregaria

swarming adult

solitary hopper

Harvester ants
Pogonomyrmex sp

Desert tortoise
Gopherus polyphemus

Gridiron-tailed lizard
Callisaurus draconoides

Thorny devil
Moloch horridus

Desert plants have evolved various ways of coping successfully with drought. The ocotillo of southwestern America sheds its leaves, reducing its need for water. Euphorbias, and cacti such as the prickly pear, store water in their stems. Blue kleinia, a South African succulent, has a waxy coating that limits water loss. Agaves mature very slowly, building up reserves of food and water in their leaves before they flower. Esparto, a needlegrass, is typical of many desert grasses.

Ocotillo
Fouquieria splendens

Euphorbia
Euphorbia obesa

Prickly pear
Opuntia ficus-indica

Blue kleinia
Senecio articulatus

Agave
Agave americana

Deserts occur where rainfall is low and infrequent and where any moisture quickly evaporates or disappears instantly into the parched ground. In the driest deserts, rainfall rarely exceeds 100 mm (4 in) a year, and is so unreliable that some places may have no rain for 10 years or more. These are deserts in the truest sense of the word: harsh wildernesses that are almost totally without life. Regions with less than 255 mm (10 in) of rain a year are generally classified as arid and those with less than 380 mm (15 in) as semiarid.

Hot deserts have very high daytime temperatures in summer, although they drop sharply at night, and the winters are relatively mild. In the so-called cold deserts the summers are hot but the winters are so cold that temperatures may fall as low as −30°C (−22°F).

Desert climates and landscapes
In the subtropical latitudes, swept by hot, drying winds, high-pressure weather systems prevent rain clouds from forming. In these regions, rain comes only from local storms or follows low-pressure weather systems (often seasonal) when they move in across the desert. Large areas of central Asia have become desert because they are so far from the sea that clouds have shed all their rain before they reach them. Other deserts occur because mountains cut them off from moisture-bearing winds. The Andes, for example, shelter the drylands of Argentina, and a high sierra stops rain from reaching the Mojave and Great Basin deserts of North America. Rain is also rare on the western sides of continents where cold ocean currents flow from the polar regions towards the Equator.

Desert climates vary not only from place to place but also with time. Over short periods rainfall is much less predictable than it is in temperate regions and droughts are frequent. Some droughts, such as those that occur along the southern fringe of the Sahara, are so severe that it may seem that the climate has changed permanently. But most droughts are short-lived and are followed by years of normal (although sparse) rainfall. Over longer periods of time, however, desert climates do change. Prehistoric cave drawings in the Saharan highlands, for example, show that elephants, rhinoceroses and even hippopotamuses—animals that are at home in wetter climates—lived in these now dry, barren uplands in a more moist period between 7,000 and 4,000 years ago.

Desert landscapes also vary enormously. They are as contrasted as the Colorado canyon country of the United States and the sandy wastes of the Middle East, but most include one or more of several basic features: steep, rocky mountain slopes, broad plains, basin floors dominated by dry lake beds or sand seas, and canyon-like valleys. In low-lying areas, evaporation sometimes leaves a glistening residue of salt. Where there is soil, it is often sandy or consists of little more than fragmented rock, and because plant life is usually sparse there is little or no humus to enrich the ground.

Where water is life
Plant growth depends on water, and desert plants are usually widely spaced to reduce competition for what little moisture is available. Many plants rely on short, sharp rainstorms; others make use of dew and grow in locations, such as crevices in rocks, where water can accumulate. Some complete their life cycle in a single wet season, producing seeds that lie dormant during the following drought and germinate only when enough moisture is available for them to grow. These are the ephemerals that carpet the desert with a brief but brilliant display of flowers shortly after rain has fallen.

Most desert plants, however, are able to tolerate or resist drought. These are the xerophytes ("dry plants") and phreatophytes ("deep-water plants"). Xerophytic trees and shrubs have a wide-spreading network of shallow roots that take in water from a large area of ground. Many xerophytes also limit the amount of water

Esparto grass
Stipa tenacissima

Adaptations to desert life: kangaroo rats, jerboas and gerbils (A) make prodigious leaps with their long back legs to escape predators, and some desert lizards (B) run at high speed on their hind legs when pursued, using their tail for balance. Spadefoot toads have scoop-like hind feet with which they dig burrows to avoid the intense heat of day. Skinks use flattened toes fringed with scales to "swim" through the sand. Fan-toed geckos have toes that spread into fans at the tips, enabling them to walk easily on sand dunes, and the Namib palmate gecko has webbed feet that support it on loose sand.

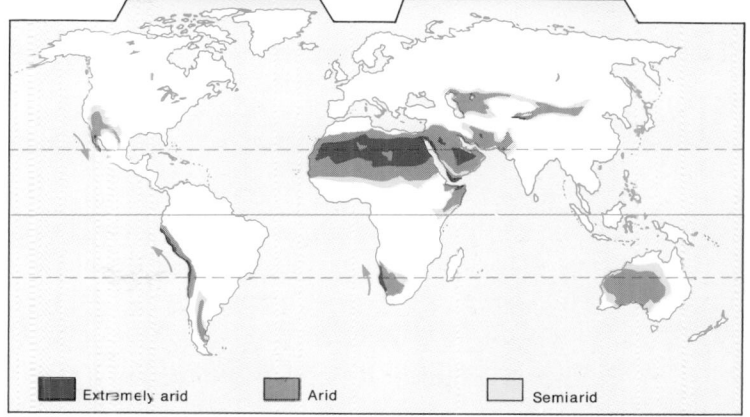

The saguaro dominates the desert landscapes of Mexico and southern America. Immensely slow growing, it can take 200 years to reach its full height, and more than four-fifths of its weight may be water stored in its stem to be used in times of drought. To minimize water loss, it opens its pores only at night to absorb carbon dioxide and to help radiate heat accumulated by day.

Five great arid regions are bordered by semi-arid steppe and scrub. Cold deserts—the Gobi in central Asia, the Great Basin in North America and the Patagonian Desert in South America—lie in the higher latitudes. Cold ocean currents also affect climate, causing fogs to form over coastal deserts in southwest Africa, South America and Baja California, Mexico.

Extremely arid   Arid   Semiarid

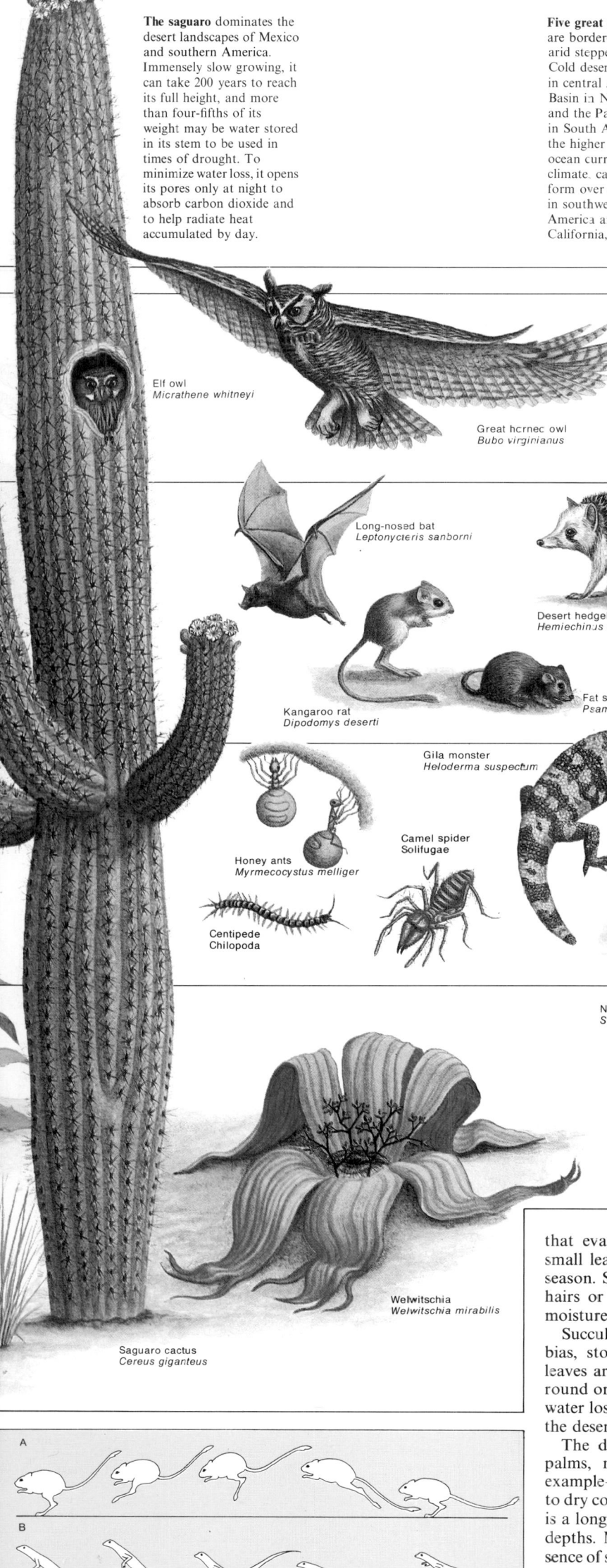

White-throated poorwill
Phalaenoptilus nuttallii

Elf owl
Micrathene whitneyi

Great horned owl
Bubo virginianus

Long-nosed bat
Leptonycteris sanborni

Desert hedgehog
Hemiechinus auritus

Fennec fox
Fennecus zerda

Kangaroo rat
Dipodomys deserti

Fat sand rat
Psammomys obesus

Gila monster
Heloderma suspectum

Scorpion
Buthus occitanus

Honey ants
Myrmecocystus melliger

Camel spider
Solifugae

Centipede
Chilopoda

Sidewinder rattlesnake
Crotalus cerastes

Darkling beetle
Tenebrionidae

Night-blooming cereus
Selenicereus spp

Welwitschia
Welwitschia mirabilis

Saguaro cactus
Cereus giganteus

A

B

Skink
Scincus scincus

Fan-toed gecko
Ptyodactylus hasselquistii

Palmate gecko
Palmatogecko rangei

Spadefoot toad
Scaphiopus couchi

Owls and nightjars hunt under cover of darkness. Elf owls shelter by day, emerging at dusk to catch insects, and great horned owls often come into the desert at night to hunt. The poorwill, a small desert nightjar, is known to American Indians as "the sleeper." An insect eater, it sometimes survives the rigors of winter, when food is scarce, by hibernating.

Most small animals are active at night. Nectar-eating bats visit plants that blossom at night, pollinating the flowers while they feed. American kangaroo rats obtain water from a dry diet of seeds and conserve moisture by producing very concentrated urine. The sand rat of North Africa feeds on salty succulents and excretes great quantities of extremely salty urine. Hedgehogs are mainly insect eaters; the long ears of desert species help to disperse body heat. The Saharan fennec, the smallest type of desert fox, hunts lizards, rodents and locusts.

Among insects and other invertebrates the hunt for food intensifies at night. Honey ants gather nectar; centipedes and camel spiders hunt insects. The gila monster, a poisonous American lizard, eats centipedes, eggs and sometimes other lizards, and uses its tail to store fat. The sidewinder, a small rattlesnake, is active mainly at night, leaving its distinctive parallel tracks in the sand. Scorpions emerge from their burrows to stalk insects and spiders, and darkling beetles feed on dry, decomposing vegetation.

Some desert plants are nocturnal, in the sense that they bloom only at night or make use of the dew that forms when the temperature falls. The welwitschia, unique to the Namib Desert in southwest Africa, has broad, sprawling leaves on which moisture condenses at night. The night-blooming cereus of the American deserts flowers for a single night in summer. Like other nocturnal plants, its flowers are luminously pale and strongly scented to attract pollinating night insects.

that evaporates from their leaves by having small leaves, or by shedding them in the dry season. Some produce a protective covering of hairs or a coating of wax to prevent loss of moisture and to help to withstand heat.

Succulent plants, such as cacti and euphorbias, store water in their thick stems. Their leaves are usually reduced to spines, and their round or cylindrical shape also helps to reduce water loss. Spines have the added advantage in the desert of discouraging foraging animals.

The drought-resisting phreatophytes—date palms, mesquite and cottonwood trees, for example—have a similar variety of adaptations to dry conditions, but their most typical feature is a long tap root that draws water from great depths. Many plants can also tolerate the presence of salt in the soil. These are the halophytes ("salt plants") such as saltbush and other small shrubs that grow in and around salt pans.

The struggle to survive

Animals, too, need to obtain and conserve water at all costs and to be able to adjust to extremes of temperature. Most are small enough to shelter under stones or in burrows during the intense heat of day; others survive adverse conditions by becoming dormant or by migrating. For most desert creatures it is also an advantage to be inconspicuous, and many are

pale in color so that they are hard to see against their light background of sand or stones.

Many animals, especially those that are active by day, show adaptations that are strikingly similar to those of desert plants. Frogs and toads are activated by rain, emerging from dormancy to feed and mate in temporary pools and then quickly burying themselves until the next rain falls. Mammals have hairy coats that reduce water loss and also help to keep their body temperature at a tolerable level. Most desert insects have a waxy coating that serves much the same purpose.

Some geckos and other lizards store food, in the form of fat, in their tails, and camels store fat in their humped backs to sustain them when food is scarce. Honey ants force-feed nectar to some members of the colony, creating living "honey pots" for the rest of the community to feed from in times of drought. Many creatures are able to survive on the moisture contained in their food, and rarely need to drink. Most desert dwellers also have extremely efficient kidneys that produce very concentrated urine, so that little or no moisture is lost in the process.

Man enjoys no such advantages. Nevertheless, he still seeks to live in deserts, as he has for thousands of years, and the pressures he exerts on the environment may well have irrevocably changed much of the world's desert landscapes.

Man and the Deserts

Water is the key to man's survival in deserts: where water has been available, great civilizations have flourished, and man's dream of making the desert bloom has become a reality. More recently, discoveries of great mineral wealth have spurred the opening up of some of Earth's most inhospitable regions. But while man's ingenuity has made many deserts both habitable and productive, the human tendency to increase the extent of deserts has become a problem of international proportions.

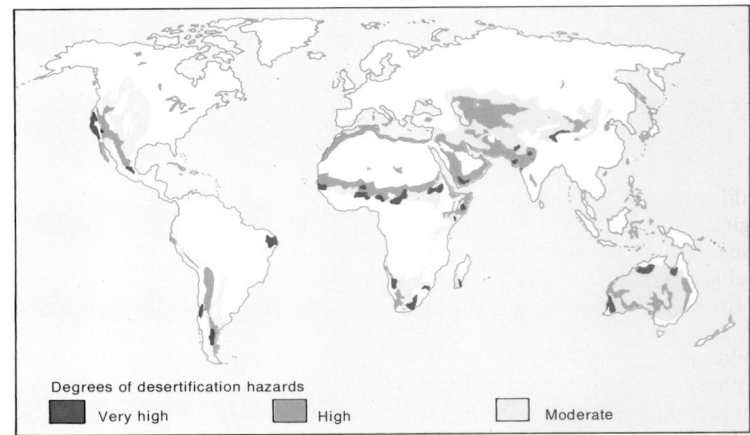

Degrees of desertification hazards

Very high   High   Moderate

Given water, much is possible, and not surprisingly man has tended to settle where water is most readily available: along the courses of rivers (such as the Nile) that rise outside the desert, and around oases fed by springs or by wells that tap groundwater supplies. But desert rainfall is so unreliable that often runoff and spring flow are uncertain in quantity and timing. Much groundwater is either also unreliable or it is fossil water that has accumulated in the geological past and is not being replenished by today's rainfall. Thus in areas such as southern Libya and some of the oasis settlements of the Arabian Gulf, and in America's arid west, groundwater is a nonrenewable resource that is being rapidly depleted.

Making water go farther

Man has also used great ingenuity to secure water supplies and to transport them to where they are needed. Runoff from flash floods that follow rare desert storms may be collected in channels and distributed to crops in nearby fields, and terracing slopes to trap runoff is a traditional way of obtaining the maximum benefit from limited rainfall. Reservoirs, ranging from the small night tanks of the southern Atacama desert in Chile to the massive artificial lakes along the Colorado river in the United States, store seasonally or perennially unreliable runoff. Also, surface runoff may be increased by reducing the permeability of runoff surfaces, a

solution engineered by the Nabataeans in the Negev desert more than 2,000 years ago and being reemployed by the Israelis today.

The transport of water is a fundamental desert activity. Open canals are typical, usually carrying water to irrigated fields—a practice used throughout the fertile crescent of Mesopotamia more than 8,000 years ago and still widespread today. A striking alternative are the ancient qanats, which limit the evaporation of water while it is in transit. Qanats are still found in the Middle East, although today pipelines are increasingly used.

Ultimately the conversion of salt water to fresh water may ensure plentiful supplies for many desert regions. The process is expensive, but large-scale desalination has already become a reality in some affluent communities such as oil-rich Saudi Arabia and Kuwait. Increasing emphasis is also being placed on more efficient use of existing freshwater supplies: in Egypt and Israel, waste water from towns is being purified and recycled for use in agriculture.

Cultivating the desert

The successful control of water has enabled large areas of otherwise arid and semiarid land to be made productive. The Egyptian civilization along the Nile depended, and still depends, on the management of seasonal floodwaters. In North America, the large-scale, long-distance piping of water has made central

Desertification—the advance of desert areas across the Earth—now affects more than 30 million sq km (12 million sq miles) and deserts are continuing to expand at an alarming rate. In recent years, on the southern edge

of the Sahara alone, as much as 650,000 sq km (250,900 sq miles) of land that was once productive have been lost, and in places there is little left to show where the Sahara ends and the Sahel–Sudan region begins. Intense and

often inappropriate human pressures are major causes, frequently aggravated by drought: overcultivating vulnerable land, chopping down trees for fuelwood and grazing too many livestock, especially on the margins of arid lands.

THE SHIFTING SANDS

Recent decades have seen unprecedented changes in the world's deserts. Increasing pressure on the environment, especially from pastoralists and farmers, has caused extensive damage and a rapid expansion of barren land. In many desert regions, nomadism has long been the only way in which man could survive, except in oases. Today, even these traditional ways of life are changing as the exploitation of oil and other mineral resources, and the introduction of new agricultural techniques, are drawing many of the deserts into a spectacular new age of development.

The traditional pastoral response to limited water supplies and forage in desert regions is nomadic livestock herding, still practiced by the Tuareg of the northern Sahara (right) and by tribal groupings in Mongolia (left). The nomadic way of life has, however, become severely restricted in recent years. Long-distance migrations are often incompatible with the requirements of the modern state, and the poor rewards no longer match the incentives to settle in towns and cities.

Oases have provided welcome refuges in deserts since ancient times. Secure water supplies from wells or springs make settled life possible in the midst of the most arid landscapes. Many oases are intensively cultivated with three tiers of vegetation: tall date palms shade orchards of citrus fruits, apricots, peaches, pomegranates and figs, and both palms and orchard trees shade the ground crops of vegetables and cereals. Irrigation channels distribute water to the desert soils, which are frequently rich in plant foods although they lack humus. Windbreaks help to protect cultivated land from erosion and from migrating dunes, although many oases are losing the battle with encroaching sands and the oasis people are leaving to find work in the oil fields.

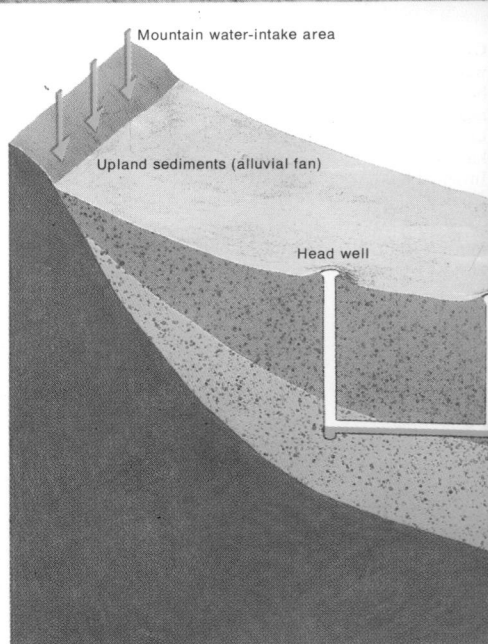

Mountain water-intake area

Upland sediments (alluvial fan)

Head well

California the most productive agricultural region in the world. But while irrigation can bring enormous benefits, it can also create problems. Too much water causes waterlogging of the land, and where water evaporates in the dry desert air, concentrations of dissolved salts build up in the soil.

Farming without irrigation is possible only where rainfall, although meager, is sufficient to sustain crops with a short growing season. Soil moisture is conserved by using dry surface mulches, by fallowing and crop rotation, by planting seeds sparsely and by controlling weeds. Geneticists are also producing new varieties of cereal crops that can survive for weeks without water. Dry farming, however, is precarious. Especially at times of drought it can cause serious problems of soil erosion, chiefly by the action of wind.

Man the desert maker
The extension of dry farming into unsuitable regions, and waterlogging and the accumulation of salts in irrigated areas, are major causes of desertification—the spread of deserts into formerly habitable land. Other major causes are the overgrazing of livestock on land with too little forage and the removal of trees and shrubs for firewood by communities that have no alternative fuel supply. A sequence of drier than normal years does the rest.

Many scientists believe that desertification can be reversed, provided the pressures on the land are reduced sufficiently to allow vegetation to recover. But desertification affects such huge areas, often crossing national frontiers, that broad-scale, international cooperation is needed to coordinate reductions in population and livestock pressures and to improve understanding of drought.

In some countries the battle against desertification has already begun. In China, extensive

planting of drought-tolerant trees has created windbreaks to control sand movement and to protect farmland. In Algeria, a broad belt of trees has been planted to keep the Sahara at bay, and in Iran, advancing dunes have been halted by spraying them with petroleum residue: when the spray dries it forms a mulch that retains moisture and allows vegetation to grow, and much desert land has been reclaimed.

The deserts' riches
The exploitation of resources has also led to an "opening up" of many deserts. The rushes for precious metals in Arizona, Australia and South Africa started man's development of these regions in the nineteenth century. Some minerals, such as the evaporite deposits of Searles Basin in California and the nitrates of the Atacama desert in Chile, are actually products of the arid environment.

A resource that deserts also possess in abundance is solar power, and in many hot, dry regions the heat of the sun is used to evaporate mineral-rich solutions of salts, as well as being harnessed as a source of energy. Sunshine and the dry, clear air are also drawing ever-increasing numbers of tourists to the "sun cities" of the western United States and to Saharan oases, which were, until recently, only remote desert outposts.

No resource, however, has created as much attention or wealth as has oil. Oil has transformed the fortunes of several desert nations and provided an economic boom that has led to rapid industrialization and spectacular urban growth. The benefits of such growth in terms of affluence are substantial. The problems—the weakening of traditional desert societies, the submerging of traditional cities in the concrete labyrinths of modern complexes, and the precariousness of prosperity that is based on finite resources—are also clear.

Mineral wealth provides a powerful incentive for man's development of arid lands, and today the flow of oil rather than water is often a measure of a desert nation's prosperity. In some of the world's most desolate regions, flares signal the presence of modern "oases" where fossil fuels are being extracted—products, like the fossil waters that are sometimes trapped in the same sedimentary rocks, of the desert's geological past. Uranium, another mineral "fuel," also often lies beneath desert sands. Arid environments may also provide a rich harvest of other minerals: potash, phosphates and nitrates, valuable sources of commercial fertilizers; gypsum, manganese and salt; and borax, source of the element boron, used in nuclear reactors.

A "plastic" revolution has helped transform much of Israel's desert hinterland into productive farmland. Plastic cloches, plastic mulches and greenhouses trap moisture and reduce evaporation, and water trickled through thin plastic tubes irrigates the plants' roots with a minimum of wastage. Such innovative agricultural techniques enable Israel to produce most of its own food requirements, and fruit and vegetables grown in the relatively mild desert winters are also exported to Europe, where they command high prices.

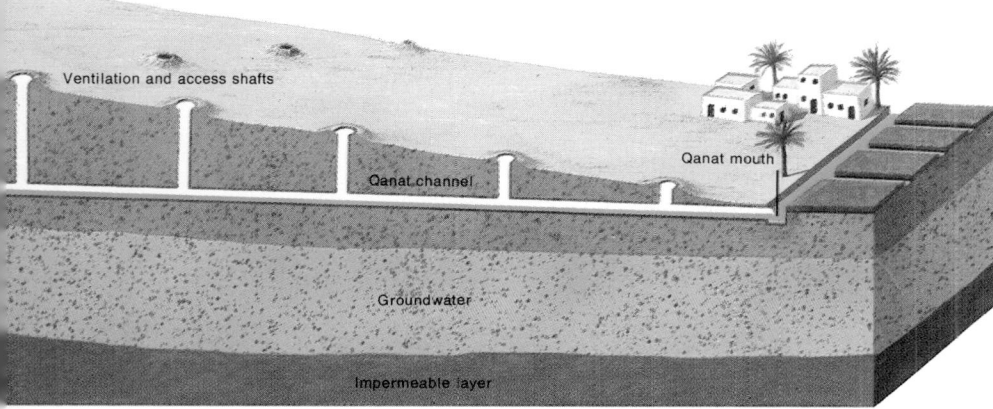

One of the most ingenious ways man has devised of bringing water to desert regions is by the ancient underground system known as the qanat. Invented by the Persians in the first millennium BC, qanats tap groundwater in upland sediments and carry it by gravity to the surface on lower land. The head well is dug first, sometimes to a depth of 100 m (330 ft), until water is reached. A line of shafts is then sunk to provide ventilation and to give access to the channel being tunneled below. Work begins at the mouth end, and a typical channel is 10–20 km (6–12 miles) long when completed, depending on the depth of the head well and the slope of the land. Its slight gradient ensures that water flows freely but gently down to ground level. Surface canals then divert the water to where it is needed. Thousands of such qanats are still in use, their routes marked by mounds of excavated debris.

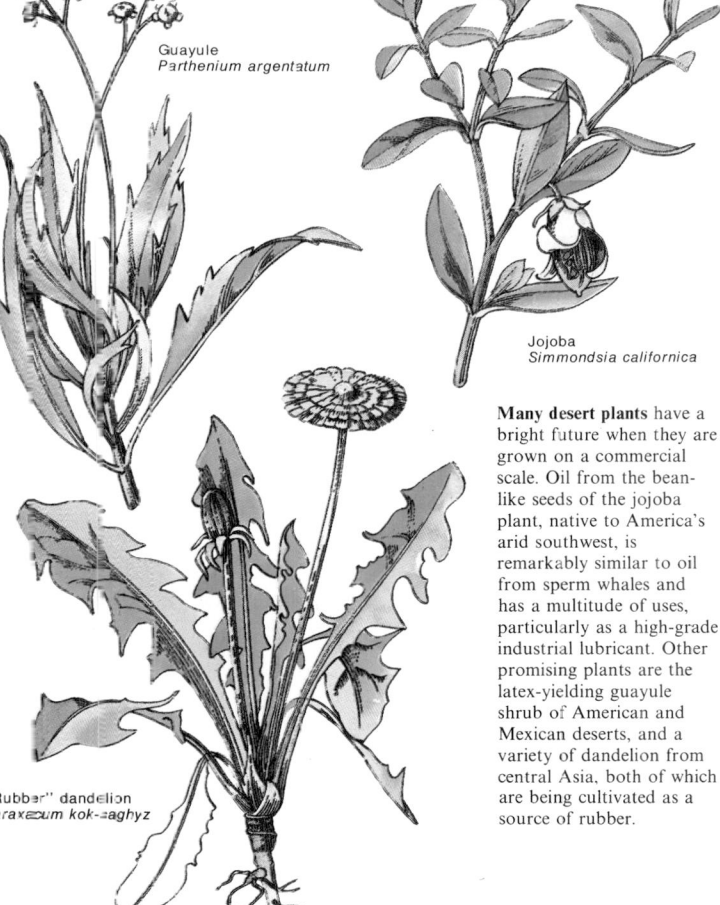

Guayule
Parthenium argentatum

Jojoba
Simmondsia californica

"Rubber" dandelion
Taraxacum kok-saghyz

Many desert plants have a bright future when they are grown on a commercial scale. Oil from the bean-like seeds of the jojoba plant, native to America's arid southwest, is remarkably similar to oil from sperm whales and has a multitude of uses, particularly as a high-grade industrial lubricant. Other promising plants are the latex-yielding guayule shrub of American and Mexican deserts, and a variety of dandelion from central Asia, both of which are being cultivated as a source of rubber.

Ventilation and access shafts

Qanat channel

Qanat mouth

Groundwater

Impermeable layer

Savannas

Between the tropical rainforest and desert regions lie large stretches of savanna, which are characterized by seasonal rainfall and long periods of drought. Those nearest to the forests usually take the form of open woodland, whereas those nearest to the deserts consist of widely scattered thorn scrub or tufts of grass. Unlike temperate grasslands, where the summers are hot but the winters are cold, savanna regions are always warm and in the wet season rain falls in heavy tropical downpours.

The most extensive areas of savanna are in Africa, north and south of the rainforest, and in South America, where the two main regions are the *llanos* of Venezuela, north of the Amazon rainforest, and the *campos* of Brazil in the south. Smaller areas of savanna also occur in Australia, India and southeastern Asia.

Savannas range from thickly wooded grasslands to almost treeless plains. Some are the result of man's destruction of the forest, and most are maintained in their present state by the high incidence of fire, both natural and manmade. The grasses tend to be taller and coarser than their temperate counterparts and they grow in tufts rather than as a uniform ground cover. In areas of high rainfall some grasses grow up to 4.5 m (15 ft) tall. Trees and bushes are usually widely spaced so that they do not compete with each other for water in the dry season. Humid, or moist, savannas experience 3 to 5 dry months a year, dry savannas 6 to 7 months, and thornbush savannas 8 to 10 months. Rainfall also varies widely, from more than 1,200 mm (47 in) a year in humid savannas to as little as 200 mm (8 in) where the savanna merges into desert.

Types of savannas

Humid woodland savanna presents an abrupt contrast to the rainforest. Trees tend to be scattered and some are so low growing that they are dwarfed by the tall grass that springs up during the summer rains. In the dry season the grass fuels fierce fires, which destroy all except thick-barked, large-leaved deciduous trees. Consequently, the proportion of fire-resistant trees and shrubs is large, and the grass quickly regenerates with the coming of the next rains.

In Africa this type of savanna is known as Guinea savanna north of the rainforest and as miombo savanna south of the rainforest. In South America it is known as *campo cerrado*, from the Portuguese words meaning field (*campo*) and dense. (*Campos sujos* are *campos* in which stretches of open grassland predominate and *campos limpos* are grasslands from which trees are entirely absent.) The *llanos*, or plains, of northern South America are grasslands interspersed with forests and swamps.

North of the Guinea savanna in Africa lies a belt known as Sudan savanna. The annual rainfall is in the range 500 to 1,000 mm (20–40 in) and the dry season lasts from October to April. This is typical dry savanna. Tall grasses between 1 and 1.5 m (3–5 ft) form an almost continuous ground cover and acacias and other thorny trees dot the landscape, together with branching dôm palms and massive water-storing baobab trees. Because of the interrupted tree cover the old name given to many savannas of this type was orchard steppe, and this description gives a good idea of the countryside. Like the humid woodland savannas it is maintained by regular burning of the grass in the dry season, and there is a delicate balance and interaction between climate, soil, vegetation, animals and fire. On the desert margins the grasses grow in short tufts and the scattered acacias are seldom more than 3 m (10 ft) tall. The scrub and grasses are too widely dispersed for fires to spread, and this type of savanna is modified not by fire but by aridity and blistering heat.

Thorn-scrub and thorn-forest savannas frequently form transitional zones between tropical forests and grasslands. The *caatinga*, or "light forest," of northeastern Brazil is a typical thorn-forest savanna. Long, hot, dry seasons alternate with erratic downpours of rain, and the rate of evaporation is high. Drought-resisting trees and thorny shrubs mix with bromeliads, cacti and palm trees.

Abundance of life

No other environment supports animals so spectacular in size and so immense in numbers as do the African savannas. In spite of the concentration of animal life, however, competition for food is not severe. Each species has its own preferences and feeds from different levels of the vegetation. Giraffes and elephants can easily reach the upper branches of trees, antelopes feed on bushes at different heights from the ground, zebras and impalas eat the grasses and warthogs root for the underground parts of plants. With the onset of the dry season, massed herds assemble for the great migrations that are a major part of savanna life, moving to areas where rain has recently fallen and new grass is plentiful.

Following the grazing animals are the large predators: the lions, leopards and cheetahs. Wild dogs hunt in packs, and the scavengers—jackals, hyenas and vultures—move in to dispose of the remains of the kill.

The savannas of South America and Australia are much poorer in animal species. The only mammal of any size on the South American savanna is the elusive, nocturnal maned wolf, which eats almost anything from small animals to wild fruit. On the Australian savanna the largest inhabitant is the kangaroo, and the prime predator—apart from man—is the dingo, or native dog.

Many of the resident savanna birds are ground-living species such as the ostrich in Africa and its counterparts, the rhea in South America and the emu in Australia. The warm African climate attracts large numbers of visiting birds, which migrate each year across the Sahara to escape from the severe winter of the northern hemisphere.

For many thousands of years man has lived in harmony with the savanna. Within the last century, however, and in recent decades in particular, the savanna has come under increasing pressure. Inevitably, there is competition between the needs of the environment and those of the human population, and the future of the savanna is very much in the balance.

On each side of the Equator are broad tracts of tropical grassland known as savannas. In these regions there are distinct wet and dry seasons and temperatures are high all the year round, seldom falling below 21°C (70°F). Rain falls mainly in the hottest months, whereas the cooler months are generally dry. Thorn-scrub and thorn-forest savannas occur where the rainfall is more erratic; they have relatively little grass cover, and trees and bushes can tolerate long periods of drought.

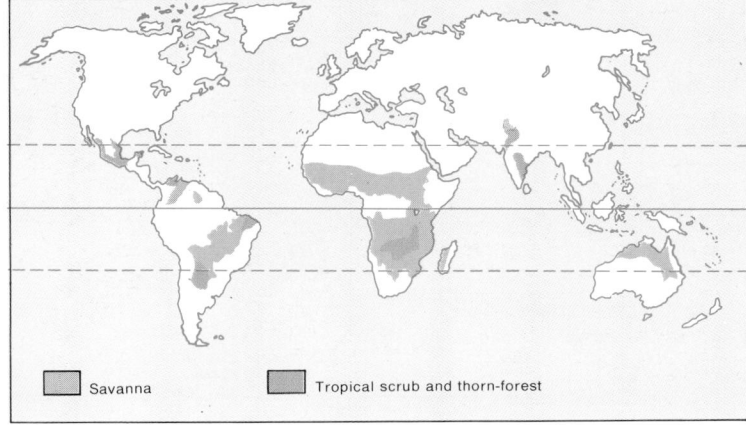

Savanna | Tropical scrub and thorn-forest

THE AFRICAN SAVANNA

More than a third of Africa is savanna, the vast parklike plains and gently rolling foothills providing the setting for a supreme wildlife spectacle. Vegetation is the basis of the immense wealth of animal life. It supports the large herds of grazing animals, and they return nutrients to the grassland in their droppings. The plant eaters, in turn, provide food for the hunters and for the scavengers that play an indispensable role by keeping the savanna free from carrion. Most of the plant-eating animals are agile and swift-footed, which enables them to escape from their enemies, and live in herds, which also provides some protection in the open habitat. Many of the animals, both predators and prey, are camouflaged: stripes or spots, at a distance, help to break up their outline; dappled markings merge with the pattern of sunlight and shade in the undergrowth; and tawny colors make them difficult to see against a background of dry grass.

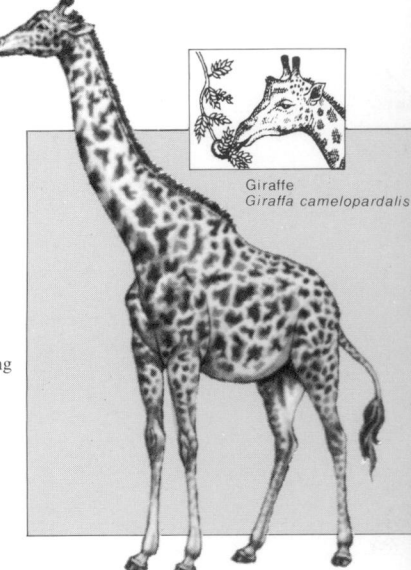

THE PLANT EATERS
Most plant eaters have adapted to feeding at a particular level of the vegetation. Giraffes browse on acacia tips that other animals cannot reach and elephants use their trunks to tear down succulent branches and leaves, although both feed on low-growing vegetation when it is easily available. Elephants will also uproot trees to gather leaves that are otherwise out of reach. The black rhinoceros plucks low-growing twigs and leaves by grasping them with its upper lip (the white rhinoceros has a broad, square mouth for grazing on grass). Eland often use their horns to collect twigs by twisting and breaking them. Zebra, wildebeest, topi and gazelle all graze on the same grasses, but at different stages of the plants' growth.

Giraffe
Giraffa camelopardalis

HUNTERS OF THE PLAINS
The plant eaters provide rich hunting for the carnivores. Lions kill the largest prey and hunt in family groups; the lioness usually makes the kill but the male is the first to eat. The leopard is a solitary hunter. It lies in ambush or stalks its prey, mainly at night, in brush country where it has ground cover. Cheetahs are the swiftest of all the hunters. They usually hunt in pairs in open grassland, stalking their prey and then charging in a lightning-fast sprint. Hunting dogs travel in well-organized packs. They exhaust their quarry by chasing it to a standstill and attacking as a team. Whereas lions, leopards and cheetahs usually kill by leaping for the neck or throat, packs of hunting dogs characteristically attack from the rear.

Lion
Panthera leo

THE SCAVENGERS
When the hunters have eaten, the scavengers move in. Jackals, small and quick, make darting runs to snatch titbits while packs of hyenas use their powerful bone-crushing jaws to demolish the bulk of the carcass. Hyenas are the most voracious of the carnivores, often driving the primary predator from its kill. Vultures are frequently the first to see a kill as they circle high in the sky, but must await their turn to feed on the skin and scraps because their descent attracts the more aggressive scavengers. Carrion beetles, carrion flies and the larvae of the horn-boring moth dispose of what is left. Most of the large scavengers, particularly the hyenas, also do their own hunting, singling out prey that is small, weak or sickly.

Jackal
Canis aureus

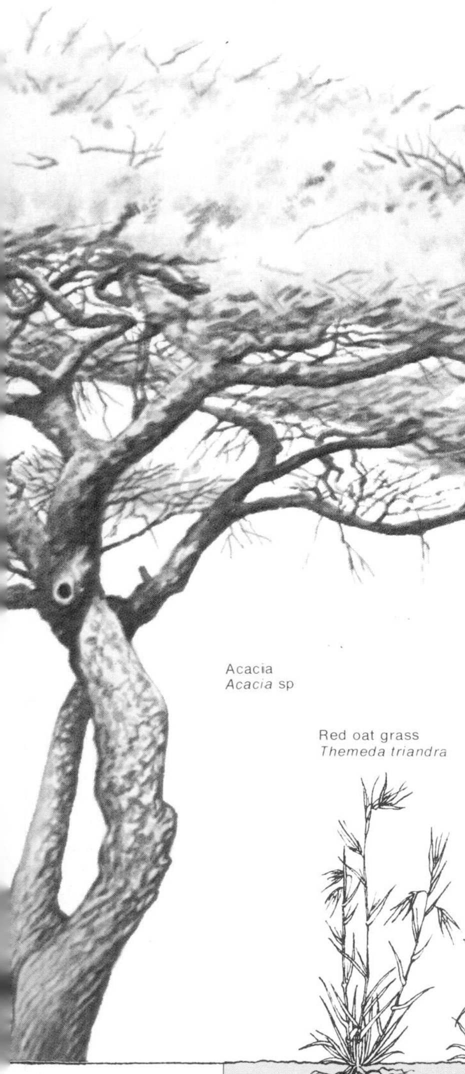

Plants in the savanna are remarkably well adapted to withstand drought, fire and the onslaughts of the animals that eat them. Acacias tolerate both drought and fire, and are armed with sharp thorns—although many animals do feed on them, thorns and all. Red oat grass survives fire because its seeds twist deep into the ground. Bermuda, or sawtooth, grass is a favorite food of many grazers, but it recovers quickly from close cropping because its growing point lies too flat against the ground to be eaten.

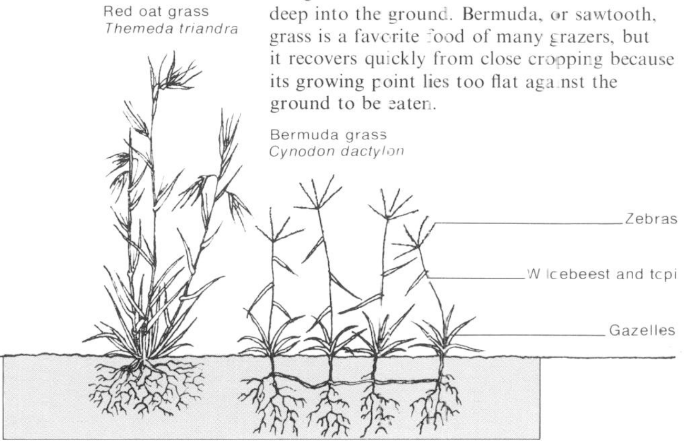

Acacia
Acacia sp

Red oat grass
Themeda triandra

Bermuda grass
Cynodon dactylon

Zebras

Wildebeest and topi

Gazelles

SAVANNA SWAMPS, LAKES AND MARSHES

Swamps, lakes and marshes are especially characteristic of the African savanna. Many are fringed with papyrus, the paper reed, *Cyperus papyrus* (1) which grows to a height of 3.5 m (12 ft) or more, and most are rich in microscopic organisms that play the same role in the water as grass does on the plains, supporting large numbers of birds and animals. Swamps and marshes also act as natural reservoirs, which collect and hold excess water during the rainy season, and provide welcome dry-season grazing for plains animals when other savanna productivity is at its lowest. The lakes of the Great Rift Valley, which form a chain down the northeastern side of the continent, are also rich with life. Many provide a refuge for crocodiles, their numbers seriously depleted by systematic hunting, and for multitudes of birds, including huge flocks of flamingos.

Many birds and animals have adapted to a semiaquatic way of life. The shoebill stork *Balaeniceps rex* (2) uses its feet and the hooked tip of its beak to stir up mud and dislodge the frogs, fish and soft-shelled turtles that form the bulk of its diet. The goliath heron *Ardea goliath* (3) is a shallow-water fisher. The sitatunga *Tragelaphus speki* (4) has long, splayed hooves that support its weight on soft mud. It hides by day among reeds on the edge of the swamp and moves to dry ground at night to feed. The jacana, or lily trotter, *Actophilornis africanus* (5) relies on long toes and constant motion to walk on floating plants. The hippopotamus *Hippopotamus amphibius* (6) wallows in the water for most of the day and leaves the swamp at dusk to graze. It helps to fertilize the swamp with the enormous amounts of waste matter it excretes.

Elephant
Loxodonta africana

Black rhinoceros
Diceros bicornis

Eland
Taurotragus oryx

Wildebeest
Connochaetes taurinus

Grant's zebra
Equus quagga boehmi

Topi
Damaliscus lunatus topi

Thomson's gazelle
Gazella thomsoni

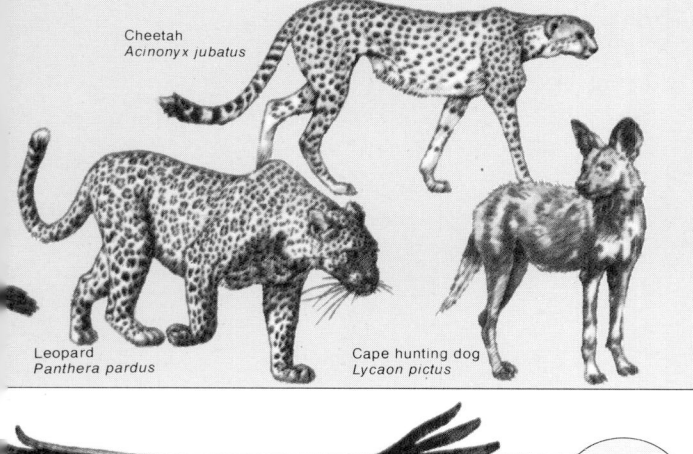

Cheetah
Acinonyx jubatus

Leopard
Panthera pardus

Cape hunting dog
Lycaon pictus

Ostrich
Struthio camelus

Secretary bird
Sagittarius serpentarius

LONG-LEGGED BIRDS

The ostrich, up to 2.4 m (8 ft) tall, can see for great distances across the plains and can outrun most of its enemies. Its territory is often shared with grazing animals, such as wildebeest, which take advantage of the ostrich's keen sight to alert them to danger. The secretary bird (so-called because of its quill-like crest) strides through the grass hunting small mammals, insects and snakes; it kills snakes by battering them with its powerful, long-clawed feet.

Large termite mounds
are a distinctive feature of many savanna landscapes. The mounds, or termitaria, are made of soil excavated by the termites and bound with their saliva. Thick walls help to keep the interior at a constant temperature, and some species of termite cultivate fungus "gardens" as a source of food. The royal chamber deep inside the mound is occupied by the colony's queen, grossly distended with eggs, and her consort. Predators include the aardwolf and the aardvark. The aardwolf is related to the hyena but is smaller and has weak jaws; it digs the termites out of their mound and scoops them up with its long sticky tongue. The aardvark, distantly related to the elephant, uses its powerful hoof-like claws to break into termite nests.

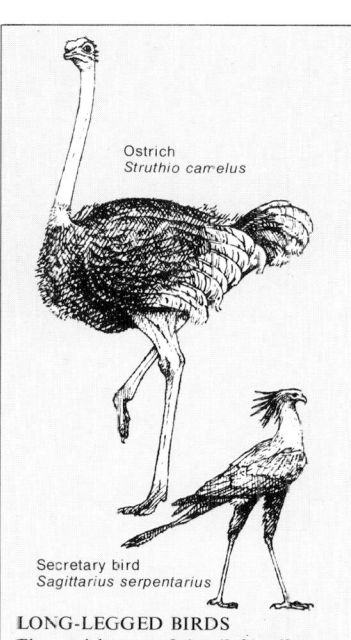

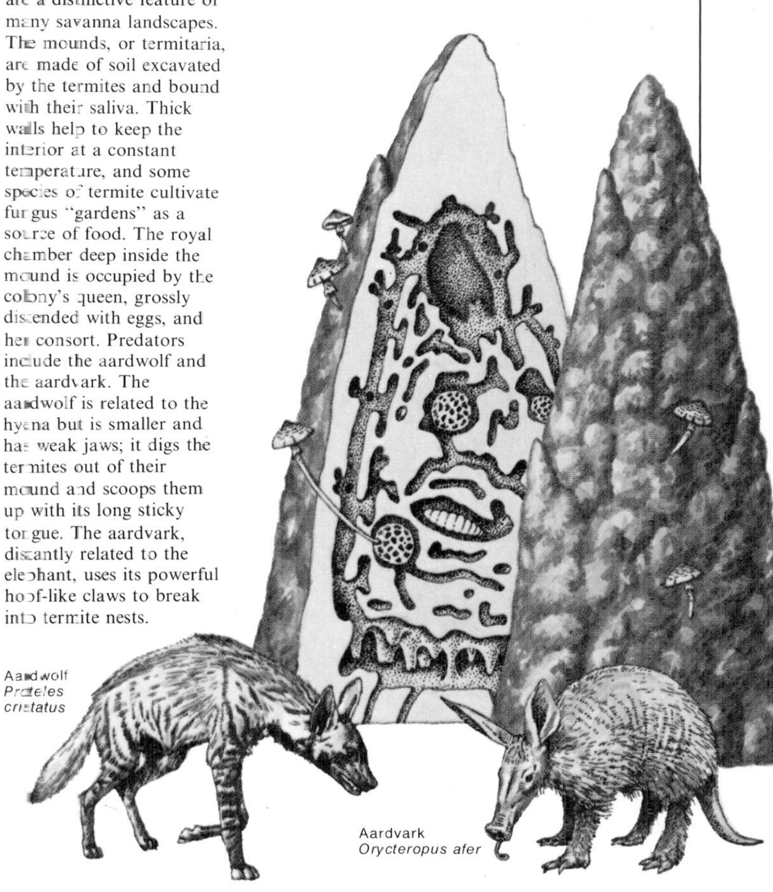

Aardwolf
Proteles cristatus

Aardvark
Orycteropus afer

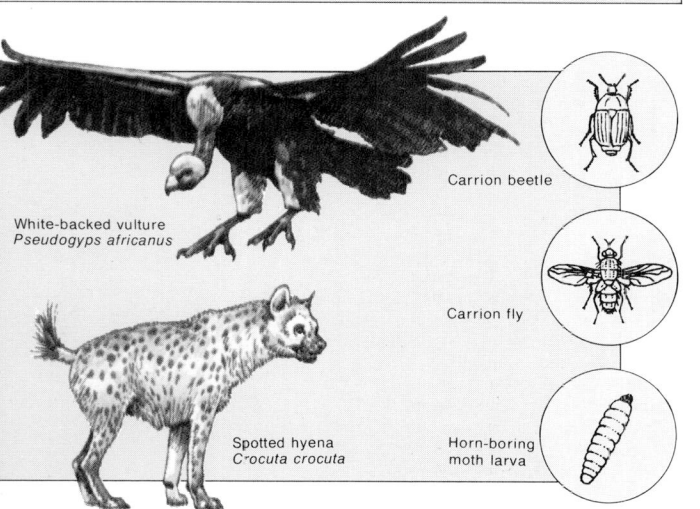

White-backed vulture
Pseudogyps africanus

Carrion beetle

Carrion fly

Spotted hyena
Crocuta crocuta

Horn-boring moth larva

Man and the Savannas

In their natural state, savannas are among the most strikingly productive of all Earth's regions. Before the coming of man they supported a wealth of animal life that has seldom been surpassed. As yet they are relatively undeveloped, but many of them lie in areas where the pressures of population growth are becoming increasingly acute. Wisely used, they offer great hope for the future, both as cattle lands and for the cultivation of food crops. But without proper management savannas can rapidly turn into wasteland, and man will be the poorer for the loss of such a great natural resource.

Throughout much of the savannas the climate is semiarid and the soils tend to be poor: stripped of their plant cover, they bake hard and crack during the long months of hot sunshine, and during the wet season they often become waterlogged or are washed away by the rains. Man's indiscriminate use of fire, unwise agricultural methods and the unrestricted grazing of domestic animals have already led to much soil loss, and erosion is widespread in tropical Africa, Asia, South America and Australia.

Systematic burning has long been practiced by the people of the savannas. Large areas are burned each year to clear land for agriculture or to remove dead grass and encourage a fresh growth to feed livestock. The resulting ash provides much-needed nutrients for crops, and the grasses rapidly produce new green shoots that provide a rich pasture for domestic herds. But although the short-term effects may be beneficial, repeated burning is harmful to the vegetation, the animals and the soil.

Trees are always more or less damaged by fire. Their trunks become twisted and gnarled, fresh shoots are killed and young trees are prevented from growing. Constant burning can destroy some species altogether, and when they disappear so too does the wildlife that depends on them for food and shelter.

Grasses, on the other hand, may be encouraged by burning, and the lush new growth that springs up when the first rains break the long dry season provides welcome nourishment for domestic herds and game animals alike. But whereas game animals move freely over the range, cropping grasses at various stages of growth, cattle tend to feed on grass only in the neighborhood of wells and other sources of drinking water. They may trample the soil and continue to graze the same area until the grass is completely suppressed.

The hazards of large projects

Cultivation in marginal areas that are unsuited to intensive agriculture also contributes to the impoverishment of the savanna. The Sahel and Sudan savannas on the fringes of the Sahara are particularly vulnerable to large-scale development projects that fail to take account of local climate and soil. Mechanized agriculture in fragile areas bordering the desert may well lead to soil erosion and dustbowl conditions, and large-scale irrigation schemes often result in waterlogging and an accumulation of salts in the soil. Cultivation in the savannas requires understanding and care. Many smaller schemes are safer—and usually more productive—than a few large ones, but not all planners yet realize that agricultural methods that are effective in temperate regions seldom come up to expectations in tropical climates.

Man first inhabited the savannas, as he did many other regions of the world, as a hunter and gatherer. He took from the land only what he needed from day to day, and although he used fire as a hunting tool, his impact was little more than that of any other savanna inhabitant. In East Africa, groups of nomadic Hadza (left) still hunt game and collect roots, fruit and the honey of wild bees, building grass huts as temporary shelters.

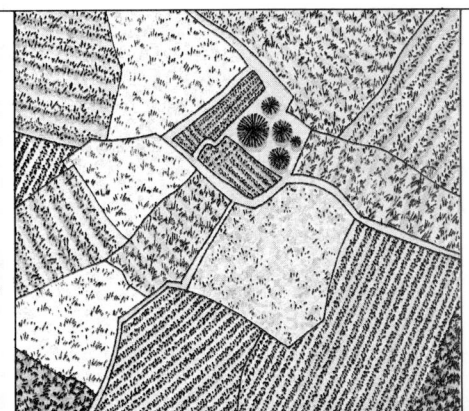

Small farms are scattered over much of the savannas. Plots close to houses are farmed continuously; beyond them lie the main fields, where periods of cultivation are usually followed by periods of fallow. Maize, millet and peanuts are the main food crops, and early and late crops are sometimes sown on the same plot to extend the growing season. Most of the work is done by hand, and any surplus to a family's needs is sold.

THE VULNERABLE WILDERNESS

Nowhere has man's impact on the tropical grasslands been felt more keenly than in Africa, although much of what is happening in Africa is happening also in savannas elsewhere. The majority of the people still live on the land, where the determining factor is the length and severity of the annual dry season. In the moister savannas the people are primarily cultivators, while in savannas that are too dry to sustain agriculture the main occupation is raising livestock. Most of the savannas are as yet sparsely settled, but competition is inevitably growing between man and wildlife, particularly in Africa, for the remaining tracts of relatively untouched wilderness.

The development of mineral resources and industries has led to an increasing movement of people—mainly young adults—from rural areas to towns and mining centers, attracted by opportunities for work—often at the expense of agriculture, since the heavy work of farming is left to the women, old people and children. Mining enterprises such as those in the Zambian Copper Belt (above), may recruit large labor forces from the surrounding countryside. Mining also dramatically alters the landscape, especially where the bedrock containing the ore reaches the surface and is quarried in huge terraces. The need for electricity to power mining and other industries leads, in turn, to the development of hydroelectric schemes, many of which entail resettling people whose villages are flooded by the creation of large artificial lakes.

Large areas of savanna have been set aside in East and Central Africa, and to a lesser extent in South America and Australia, as national parks and reserves where the landscape is kept intact and animals can be studied in their natural habitats. In Africa, observation platforms are frequently built close to waterholes where animals congregate to drink, and wardens use light aircraft to patrol the vast areas involved. Camel units are also used to patrol near-desert regions where much of the wildlife flourishes. Animals, such as elephants, whose numbers can grow out of control in the protected environment of the reserves are culled by licensed hunters to prevent the vegetation being destroyed. Culling maintains the health of the community as a whole and is also an economic source of meat in many countries where the people are short of protein foods.

Similarly, the introduction of European breeds of cattle into the savannas has not been an unqualified success. Not only are these breeds more susceptible to tropical pests and diseases than are the local varieties, but they are also adversely affected by the hot climate and their productivity is greatly reduced. In Africa and Brazil, native breeds are replacing more recent importations, and their productivity is being enhanced by selective breeding. In Australia, where most of the cattle are of British stock, tropical zebu, or humped cattle, are being introduced into the herds.

In the future, much more of the savanna may be developed as ranch lands, because the temperate grasslands will become less able to support enough animals to satisfy the world demand for meat. The *llanos* of Venezuela, the *campos* of Brazil and the tropical grasslands of Argentina and Australia already carry large herds of beef cattle. Throughout the savannas, however, ranching is still hampered by lack of water, poor natural pasture and remoteness from markets. In Africa, where herding is mainly nomadic, the sinking of wells by government organizations is changing the traditional ways of life, and cattle raising on a commercial

scale is likely to become increasingly important. In Africa, too, the conservation and controlled cropping of game animals could become one of the most productive—and constructive—forms of land use.

Game as a resource
The value of game animals as a source of food is considerable. Buffaloes, for example, and kangaroos in Australia, can thrive on natural grasses that will not even maintain the weight of domestic stock, and they show greater gains in weight than African and European cattle on most forms of vegetation, while several species of antelopes can survive on a water ration that is wholly inadequate for cattle.

In recent years attention has been directed toward the economics of controlled cropping of wild game, and of ranching animals such as eland, which can be kept as if they were domesticated stock and can convert poor pasture into excellent meat. Game animals are also more resistant than cattle to the tsetse fly, which infests large areas of Africa and transmits the disease trypanosomiasis (known as nagana in cattle and as sleeping sickness in man).

But for the most part game animals are still

considered to be a nuisance by man, and it is perhaps fortunate that by denying much of the savanna to domestic animals—and to man—the tsetse fly has preserved these regions from exploitation at the expense of the game. Many countries have also set aside large tracts of savanna as national parks and game reserves, where the natural environment is preserved and the wildlife can thrive.

Safeguarding the savanna
At a time when the pressure of the expanding human population calls for the development of areas hitherto uninhabited or only sparsely populated, it may seem paradoxical to maintain that the development of national parks and nature reserves is essential to the welfare of mankind. The aim of game conservation, however, is not simply to preserve rare or unusual animals for the enjoyment of posterity, or even for their scientific interest. It is to ensure that the land is put to its most economic and efficient use. The next few decades will show whether the savannas of the world will be developed into major sources of food and revenue for the countries that own them, or whether they will be misused and degraded into desert.

Commercial agriculture is important to the economies of many savanna countries. Cotton and coffee are major cash crops in Africa and Brazil, together with maize, tobacco, sisal and peanuts—crops that need a cycle of wet and dry seasons and year-round warmth. But large-scale cultivation of one crop tends to attract pests and diseases, and dependence on a single crop makes the economy vulnerable to fluctuating world prices.

Cattle rearing takes the place of cultivation in areas that are too dry to be cropped successfully. In Africa, people such as the Masai are nomadic herders, moving their cattle long distances in search of pasture. Wealth is counted in terms of the numbers rather than the quality of the cattle they own, but improved management of their herds and better control of animal diseases are now making their cattle much more productive.

SAVANNA FIRES
Fires have been sweeping the savannas for thousands of years. Hunters set fires to flush game from cover, farmers use fire to clear land for crops, and cattle owners burn off parched, unpalatable grasses to make way for a fresh new growth for their stock. At the end of the dry season, when fires are particularly fierce, large areas of savanna lie under a thin haze of smoke.

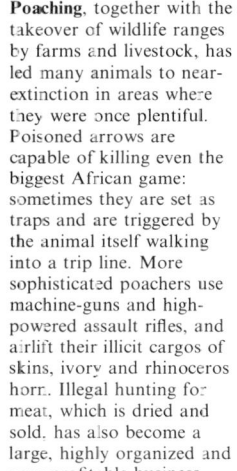

Poaching, together with the takeover of wildlife ranges by farms and livestock, has led many animals to near-extinction in areas where they were once plentiful. Poisoned arrows are capable of killing even the biggest African game: sometimes they are set as traps and are triggered by the animal itself walking into a trip line. More sophisticated poachers use machine-guns and high-powered assault rifles, and airlift their illicit cargos of skins, ivory and rhinoceros horn. Illegal hunting for meat, which is dried and sold, has also become a large, highly organized and very profitable business in many areas.

Game animals also provide the spectacular displays that attract tourists and make tourism an important source of income for many developing nations. Today, most tourists pursue game with cameras instead of guns. The hunting that led to the wholesale slaughter of wildlife in previous years is banned, and so is the traffic in trophies, although even in the sanctuary provided by parks and reserves animals still fall prey to poachers.

Animals are frequently transferred from areas where they are at risk to safer areas such as game parks and reserves. In Kenya, helicopters came to the rescue of a herd of rare antelopes when their range was threatened by a proposed irrigation scheme and moved them to Tsavo National Park. Animals are also moved to introduce new blood to small, isolated herds or to restock areas from which they have been lost.

Tropical Rainforests

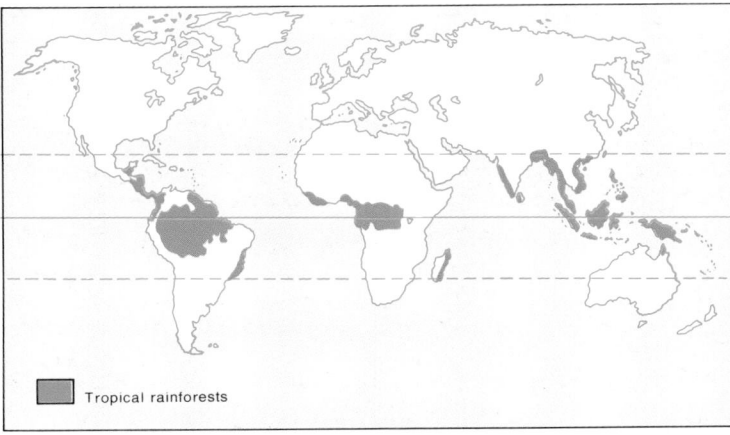

Crested tree swift
Hemiprocne longipennis

Crowned eagle
Stephanoaetus coronatus

Tropical rainforests, extremely rich in both plant and animal life, consist of a series of layered or stratified habitats. These range from the dark and humid forest floor through a layer of shrubs to the emerging tops of the scattered giant trees towering above the dense main canopy of the forest. Each layer of vegetation is a miniature life zone containing a wide selection of animal species. These can be divided into a number of ecological groups according to their various ways of life, and many have evolved special adaptations to enable them to make maximum use of the plentiful food supply surrounding them.

Tropical rainforests occur only in the regions close to the Equator; they have a heavy rainfall and a uniformly hot and moist climate. There are slightly more of these forests in the northern half of the world than in the southern half and they occur at altitudes of up to 1,500 m (5,000 ft). Temperatures are normally between 24°C and 30°C (77°–86°F) and rarely fall below 21°C (70°F) or rise above 32°C (90°F). The skies are often cloudy and the rain falls more or less evenly throughout the year. Rainfall is usually more than 2,000 mm (78 in) a year and is never less than 1,500 mm (59 in). A distinctive feature of this tropical, humid climate is that the average daily temperature range is much greater than the range between the hottest and coolest months.

A stratified habitat

There are usually three to five overlapping layers in the mature tropical rainforest. The tallest trees (called "emergents") rise above a closed, dense canopy formed by the crowns of less tall trees, which nevertheless can reach more than 40 m (130 ft) tall. Below this canopy is a third or middle layer of trees—the understory; their crowns do not meet but they still form a dense layer of growth about 5–20 m (16–65 ft) tall. The fourth layer consists of woody shrubs of varying heights between 1–5 m (3–16 ft). The bottom layer comprises decomposers (fungi) that rarely reach 50 cm (20 in) in height.

Although the trees are so tall, few of them have really thick trunks. Nearly all are evergreens, shedding their dark, leathery leaves and growing new ones continuously. Many of the larger species grow buttresses—thin, triangular slabs of hardwood that spread out from the bases of their trunks. These support the trees, so removing the need for a heavy outlay of energy and resources on deep root systems. Hanging lianas (vines), thin and strong as rope, vanish like cables into the mass of foliage. They are especially abundant on riverbanks, where the canopy of trees is thinner; their leaves and flowers appear only among the treetops.

Epiphytes—plants that grow on other plants but do not take their nourishment from them—festoon the trunks and branches of trees, and up to 80 may grow on a single tree. They include many kinds of orchid and bromeliad. Their aerial roots make use of a humus substitute derived from the remains of other plants, often

Moth orchid
Phalaenopsis sanderana

Flowering plants of the forest include epiphytes such as bromeliads and orchids like the species of *Phalaenopsis* illustrated here. Epiphytes grow on other plants such as trees where they can receive sunlight and are nourished by humus in the bark. Many epiphytic orchids have swellings in their roots or at the bases of their leaves where water can be stored. Seventy species of *Phalaenopsis* grow in southeast Asian forests and *P. sanderana*, one of the most beautiful, was first discovered in the Philippines in 1882.

Tropical rainforests are located in the hot and wet equatorial lands of Latin America, West Africa, Madagascar and Asia. These areas have consistently high temperatures throughout the year and receive high rainfall from the moist and unstable winds blowing in from the oceans.

The hummingbird numbers about 300 species, most of which are confined to the forests of South America. It is renowned for its ability to hover while gathering nectar, a feat achieved by the almost 180° rotations of its wings, which beat rapidly more than 80 times per second.

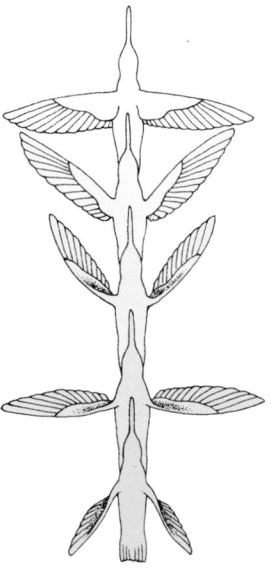

Tropical rainforests

brought together by ants. The bases of their leaves may be broad and bowl shaped and collect and hold water; they also provide homes for a variety of insects and reptiles.

Rainforest soils are not as fertile as might be supposed by the luxuriance of their vegetation. On the contrary, the silicates and compounds necessary for plant growth are leached away by the rain to leave red or yellow soils of poor quality. This process, known as laterization, is widespread in the humid tropics. Humus is rapidly broken down by bacteria, fungi and termites, while earthworms, which in more temperate regions normally contribute to the mixing of humus with mineral particles, are usually absent.

In rainforests there are often up to 25 different tree species on a single hectare of land (60 species to the acre). Most temperate forests have only a fifth of this number, with nothing like the abundance of plants that grow in the tropics. This incredible variety supports—directly or indirectly—a corresponding variety of animal species which has an abundant food supply because the forest never ceases to be productive. This is why most mammals do not move far; they stay where their food grows.

Life in the canopy

The dense leaves and branches of the canopy provide the most food and so support the greatest number of species. Macaws and toucans (from the American tropics) and parrots and trogons (which live in forests throughout the tropics) eat the fruit growing in the

THE LAYERS OF THE FOREST

Stratification—the existence of distinct layers of forest vegetation—is especially pronounced in the tropics, where there are usually five main storys. These can overlap greatly and may vary in height from area to area. The large differences between the layers present many varied habitats and ecological niches for a very wide range of animals.

CANOPY LAYER

This dense story exerts a powerful influence on the levels below since its trees, which grow between 20 m (65 ft) and 40 m (130 ft) tall, form such a thick layer of vegetation that they cut off sunlight from the forest below. The canopy is noted for the diversity of its fauna. Many birds and animals are adapted to running along branches to get the flowers, fruits or nuts that form their diets. The pointed tips of canopy leaves encourage rapid drainage.

Sacred langur
Presbytis entellu

Tree shrew
Tupaia glis

MIDDLE LAYER

This understory comprises trees from 5 m (16 ft) to 20 m (65 ft) tall whose long, narrow crowns do not become quite so dense as those of the canopy. There is very often no clear distinction, however, between this level and the canopy. Middle-layer trees are strong enough to bear large animals such as leopards that spend part of their lives on the ground. Epiphytes are plentiful in this layer.

Leopard
Panthera pardus

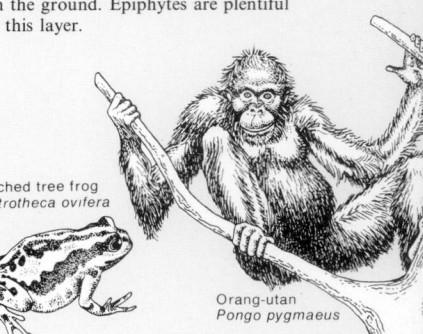

Pouched tree frog
Gastrotheca ovifera

Orang-utan
Pongo pygmaeus

SHRUB LAYER

The vegetation of this level is sparse in comparison with that above it and consists of treelets and woody shrubs that rarely reach 5 m (16 ft). These grow up in any available space between the abundant boles of large trees. Life in this story exists equally well at ground level.

Four-striped squirrel
Funisciurus lemniscatus

Oriental civet
Viverra tangalunga

Tree pangolin
Manis tricuspis

GROUND LAYER

Shade-tolerant herbs, ferns and tree seedlings represent the only flora at ground level; there is no grass there. Light is less than one percent of full daylight so that many mammals are well camouflaged in the gloom, whereas others have compact bodies to facilitate movement through the undergrowth. Ants and termites are well adapted to the high humidity and darkness of the forest floor. Fungi and a host of invertebrates quickly break down the litter of rotting leaves, fruit and fallen branches to provide vital nutrients for the fast-growing trees of the tropical rainforest.

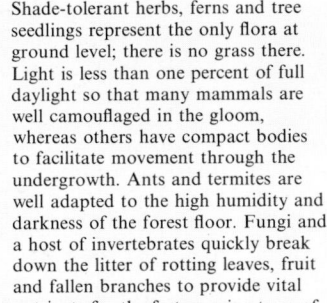

Okapi
Okapia johnstoni

Forest buffalo
Syncerus caffer nanus

Indian tiger
Panthera tigris tigris

Malayan tapir
Tapirus indicus

Congo forest mouse
Deomys ferrugineus

Short-eared elephant shrew
Macroscelides proboscideus

Orange-rumped agouti
Dasyprocta aguti

Mandrill
Mandrillus sphinx

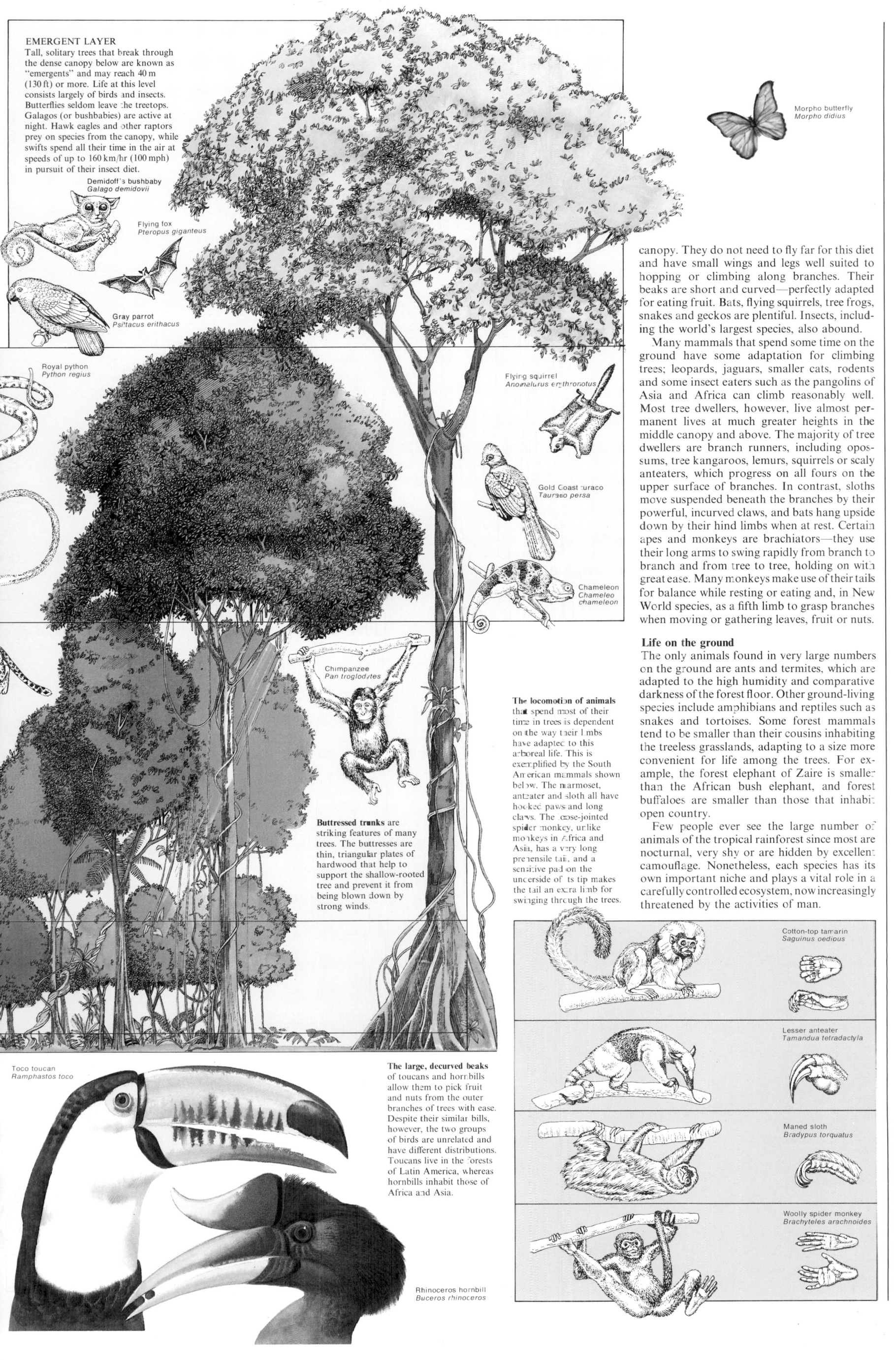

Tall, solitary trees that break through the dense canopy below are known as "emergents" and may reach 40 m (130 ft) or more. Life at this level consists largely of birds and insects. Butterflies seldom leave the treetops. Galagos (or bushbabies) are active at night. Hawk eagles and other raptors prey on species from the canopy, while swifts spend all their time in the air at speeds of up to 160 km/hr (100 mph) in pursuit of their insect diet.

Demidoff's bushbaby
Galago demidovii

Flying fox
Pteropus giganteus

Gray parrot
Psittacus erithacus

Morpho butterfly
Morpho didius

Royal python
Python regius

Flying squirrel
Anomalurus erythronotus

Gold Coast turaco
Tauraco persa

Chameleon
Chameleo chameleon

Chimpanzee
Pan troglodytes

Buttressed trunks are striking features of many trees. The buttresses are thin, triangular plates of hardwood that help to support the shallow-rooted tree and prevent it from being blown down by strong winds.

The locomotion of animals that spend most of their time in trees is dependent on the way their limbs have adapted to this arboreal life. This is exemplified by the South American mammals shown below. The marmoset, anteater and sloth all have hooked paws and long claws. The loose-jointed spider monkey, unlike monkeys in Africa and Asia, has a very long prehensile tail, and a sensitive pad on the underside of its tip makes the tail an extra limb for swinging through the trees.

canopy. They do not need to fly far for this diet and have small wings and legs well suited to hopping or climbing along branches. Their beaks are short and curved—perfectly adapted for eating fruit. Bats, flying squirrels, tree frogs, snakes and geckos are plentiful. Insects, including the world's largest species, also abound.

Many mammals that spend some time on the ground have some adaptation for climbing trees; leopards, jaguars, smaller cats, rodents and some insect eaters such as the pangolins of Asia and Africa can climb reasonably well. Most tree dwellers, however, live almost permanent lives at much greater heights in the middle canopy and above. The majority of tree dwellers are branch runners, including opossums, tree kangaroos, lemurs, squirrels or scaly anteaters, which progress on all fours on the upper surface of branches. In contrast, sloths move suspended beneath the branches by their powerful, incurved claws, and bats hang upside down by their hind limbs when at rest. Certain apes and monkeys are brachiators—they use their long arms to swing rapidly from branch to branch and from tree to tree, holding on with great ease. Many monkeys make use of their tails for balance while resting or eating and, in New World species, as a fifth limb to grasp branches when moving or gathering leaves, fruit or nuts.

Life on the ground
The only animals found in very large numbers on the ground are ants and termites, which are adapted to the high humidity and comparative darkness of the forest floor. Other ground-living species include amphibians and reptiles such as snakes and tortoises. Some forest mammals tend to be smaller than their cousins inhabiting the treeless grasslands, adapting to a size more convenient for life among the trees. For example, the forest elephant of Zaire is smaller than the African bush elephant, and forest buffaloes are smaller than those that inhabit open country.

Few people ever see the large number of animals of the tropical rainforest since most are nocturnal, very shy or are hidden by excellent camouflage. Nonetheless, each species has its own important niche and plays a vital role in a carefully controlled ecosystem, now increasingly threatened by the activities of man.

Cotton-top tamarin
Saguinus oedious

Lesser anteater
Tamandua tetradactyla

Maned sloth
Bradypus torquatus

Woolly spider monkey
Brachyteles arachnoides

Toco toucan
Ramphastos toco

The large, decurved beaks of toucans and hornbills allow them to pick fruit and nuts from the outer branches of trees with ease. Despite their similar bills, however, the two groups of birds are unrelated and have different distributions. Toucans live in the forests of Latin America, whereas hornbills inhabit those of Africa and Asia.

Rhinoceros hornbill
Buceros rhinoceros

Man and the Tropical Rainforests

Every three seconds a portion of original rainforest the size of a football field disappears as man fells the trees and extends his cultivation. Although tropical conditions allow rapid regrowth of secondary forest, the loss of primary forest is destroying thousands of plant and animal species that will never again be seen on Earth. Even by conservative estimates, it is likely that all the world's primary tropical forest will have disappeared within 85 years unless the trend is reversed.

The activities of man have only recently begun to threaten the tropical rainforest. Since prehistoric times, forests have offered shelter to people who, lacking any knowledge of agriculture, have existed as hunters and gatherers. They used only stone and wooden weapons such as bows and arrows to kill their animal prey, and collected berries, fruit and honey from their surroundings. Their influence on the forest environment was minimal and today a few races such as African pygmies and the Punans of Borneo still live in such a simple state of balance with nature. The Punans, for example, have no permanent homes, but use leaves and branches to construct temporary shelters that are used for only a few weeks before being abandoned. The pygmies build similar homes.

Shifting agriculture

Most forest dwellers, however, live in more permanent settlements and grow most of their food in forest clearings they have made. Such people are expert at chopping down trees in order to set fire to them, and this "slash-and-burn" farming results in small areas littered with charred logs and stumps whose ashes enrich the ground. Crops such as wild tapioca (cassava or manioc) are widely grown, but after a year or two the soil loses the little fertility it once had so that a new tract of forest has to be cleared and burned. Such shifting agriculture provides food for more than 200 million inhabitants of the Third World. As a farming system it has been used throughout the world for more than 2,000 years. When there were few farmers per kilometer the land was allowed to lie fallow for at least 10 years so that the soil could recover. Today, however, population pressures are so great that fallow periods have been drastically reduced and a swift repetition of slash-and-burn degrades and removes nutrients from the soil.

Effects on world climate

Tropical forest floors seldom have deep layers of humus so that, once trees are removed, the shallow topsoil is exposed and soon becomes eroded. In turn, this reduces the capacity of the ground to retain moisture, and without this sponge-like effect runoff can become very erratic and lead to floods, such as those that frequently occur in India and Bangladesh. Estuary sedimentation is often greatly increased

Living in harmony with the forest are small groups of hunter gatherers who mainly live on a flesh diet, killing their prey with bows and arrows. Nuts and berries supplement this diet, and leaves gathered from the immediate jungle cover their temporary dome-shaped shelters. These are abandoned as an area becomes exhausted and the tribe moves on. Twenty or so pygmies need about 500 sq km (200 sq miles) to support themselves.

Selective logging by gangs of men seeking out the straightest and most valuable hardwood species has been the most common form of tree extraction, even though 75 percent of the canopy might have to be destroyed to remove just a few important trees. Today heavy axes are being replaced by power saws that have no difficulty in cutting down the large buttresses that were once left behind.

Plantation forestry has made increasing inroads into the forests over the decades. The commercial advantage of products that can be cropped several times during the hardwoods' maturation period is becoming increasingly apparent to farmers in the regions. Many rubber plantations in southeastern Asia consist of small holdings that have tended to encroach upon the forest, and intercropping now takes place between the long-established trees.

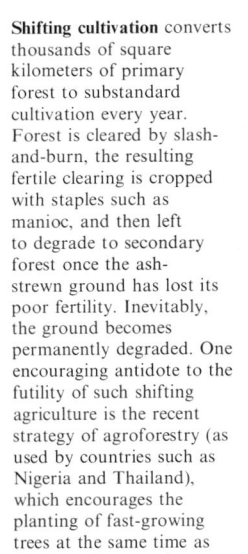

Shifting cultivation converts thousands of square kilometers of primary forest to substandard cultivation every year. Forest is cleared by slash-and-burn, the resulting fertile clearing is cropped with staples such as manioc, and then left to degrade to secondary forest once the ash-strewn ground has lost its poor fertility. Inevitably, the ground becomes permanently degraded. One encouraging antidote to the futility of such shifting agriculture is the recent strategy of agroforestry (as used by countries such as Nigeria and Thailand), which encourages the planting of fast-growing trees at the same time as the farmer's normal crops. Such intercropping offers considerable financial incentives to the small itinerant farmer.

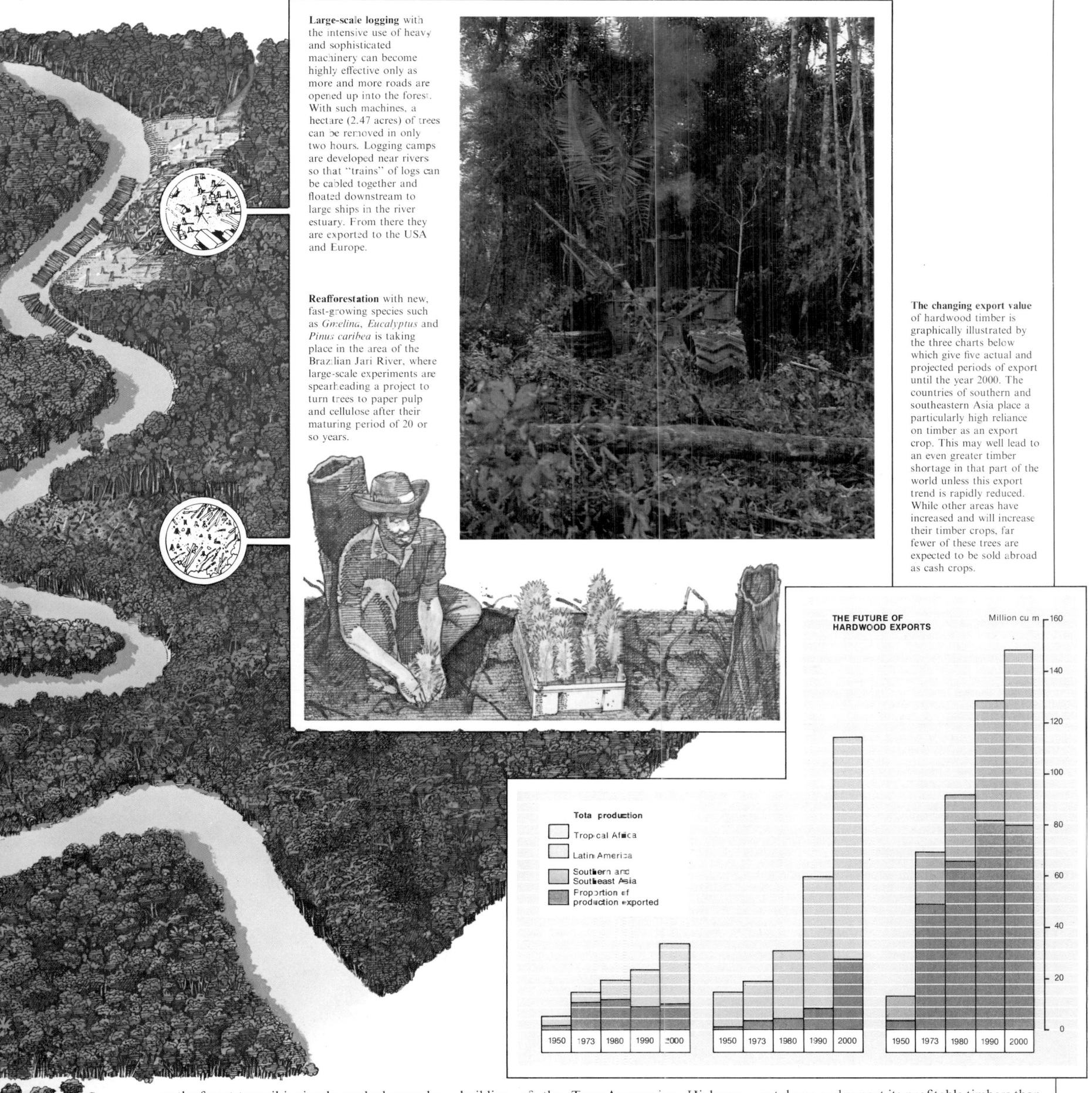

Large-scale logging with the intensive use of heavy and sophisticated machinery can become highly effective only as more and more roads are opened up into the forest. With such machines, a hectare (2.47 acres) of trees can be removed in only two hours. Logging camps are developed near rivers so that "trains" of logs can be cabled together and floated downstream to large ships in the river estuary. From there they are exported to the USA and Europe.

Reafforestation with new, fast-growing species such as *Gmelina*, *Eucalyptus* and *Pinus caribea* is taking place in the area of the Brazilian Jari River, where large-scale experiments are spearheading a project to turn trees to paper pulp and cellulose after their maturing period of 20 or so years.

The changing export value of hardwood timber is graphically illustrated by the three charts below which give five actual and projected periods of export until the year 2000. The countries of southern and southeastern Asia place a particularly high reliance on timber as an export crop. This may well lead to an even greater timber shortage in that part of the world unless this export trend is rapidly reduced. While other areas have increased and will increase their timber crops, far fewer of these trees are expected to be sold abroad as cash crops.

THE FUTURE OF HARDWOOD EXPORTS — Million cu m

Total production
- Tropical Africa
- Latin America
- Southern and Southeast Asia
- Proportion of production exported

as the forest topsoil is simply washed away by torrential rain. In parts of Asia, deforestation has caused changes in water flow that have interfered with the production of new high-yield rice crops.

Tropical forests contain an enormous store of carbon, and some authorities believe that its release into the air (as carbon dioxide) when the forest is burned down may be as great in volume as that released by the rest of the world's fossil fuels. The higher proportion of carbon dioxide in the atmosphere may lead to an increase in global temperatures, especially at the poles. Trees also release oxygen into the air through photosynthesis, and some scientists have estimated that half of the world's oxygen is derived from this source. Others estimate that half of the rainfall of the Amazon basin is generated by the forest itself, so that any great reduction in tree cover would turn Amazonia into a much drier region.

Threats to Amazonia
Much attention has been paid to the situation of Amazonia, covering as it does some 6.5 million sq km (2½ million sq miles). In an attempt to give better access to timber and mineral reserves, the Brazilian government's building of the TransAmazonian Highway (3,000 km or 1,860 miles long) has opened the way to deforestation, and settlers have been encouraged to make small holdings on the cleared forest beside the road. Between 1966 and 1978, the government calculated that farmers and big business interests had turned 80,000 sq km (31,000 sq miles) of forest into grazing land for 6 million cattle intended for hamburgers. However, like the wholesale extraction of timber, this has proved to be of doubtful economic value. Because costs rise steeply as less accessible areas are tapped, expenses tend to eliminate logging profits.

Threats in Africa
Even greater threats to tropical forest land have come from less cautious and realistic governments, such as that of Ivory Coast. There neither shifting agriculture nor excessive logging for valuable export sales appear to be under any sort of control. Accordingly, between 1966 and 1974, the area of forest declined from 156,000 sq km (60,000 sq miles) to 54,000 sq km (20,000 sq miles), much of the latter being secondary forest that can never be returned to its original status. Like many other developing countries, Ivory Coast has been more keen to cut down and export its profitable timbers than to think about protecting its invaluable forest environment. Inevitably, forest farmers move into cleared areas and often establish plantation cash crops such as coffee, cocoa and rubber, while the establishment of national parks to curtail depletion has often had very little profitable effect. The Malaysian rainforest is also disappearing rapidly, through widescale logging and open-cast mining for bauxite (aluminum ore).

A large proportion of the world's rainforest occurs in tropical countries faced with severe problems of population control. It is therefore inevitable that the pressures on such forests will be great. Human interference does more than merely destroy the primary forest, to be replaced in time by secondary growth; more importantly, the wholesale removal of trees also drastically reduces the vast genetic reservoir contained in the number of plant and animal species the forests harbor. This in itself is a sound ecological argument for preserving forests and for reversing current trends towards monoculture in the tropics. All the warnings about forest depletion appear to be clear, yet there seems little hope that man will heed them until it is too late.

Monsoon Regions

The word monsoon often conjures up the image of torrential rain and steaming tropical jungles. Yet such a view is misleading, for very great contrasts occur in the regions of the tropical world with a monsoon climate. What distinguishes monsoon regions is not so much the amount of rainfall or the permanently high temperatures, but the dramatic contrast between seasons, with an extended dry season as an essential feature. And in fact the word monsoon derives from the Arabic word for season.

THE SEASON OF RAIN
Life in the monsoon regions balances on the expectation of seasonal heavy rain. In much of India, for instance, 85 percent of the annual rainfall occurs during the limited monsoon periods, and humans as well as plants and animals depend on it wholly. About half the world's people live in these regions, in communities whose rhythm of life necessarily reflects the rains' seasonal nature.

This contrast between wet and dry seasons reflects the reversals of winds over sea and land, which in the northern hemisphere blow from the northeast in the dry winter season, and from the southwest in the wet summer periods.

The monsoon regions occur most widely in southern, southeastern and eastern Asia to the south of latitude 25°N, and in western and central Africa north of the Equator, but there are also smaller regions with a characteristically monsoon climate in eastern Africa, northern Australia and central America. Despite the similar overall climatic pattern, however, the monsoon regions are otherwise very diverse.

Before human settlement the original vegetation of the monsoon regions reflected the dominance of an extended dry season followed by a period of violent rainfall. Typical forest cover was provided by the sal (*Shorea robusta*) deciduous forest, which adjusts to extended periods of moisture deficiency by shedding its leaves. However, within the monsoon region rainfall varies from 200 mm (8 in) a year to more than 20,000 mm (800 in), and the rainy periods may vary between three and nine months.

The range of vegetation found in the monsoon regions reflects this diversity. Where tropical rainforest alters to monsoon forest, as in eastern Java, there is a sharp fall in the total number of plant and animal species, and species adapted to endure seasonal drought begin to be seen. At the other extreme of rainfall the forest thins and shades into semidesert vegetation in India's northwest. But if there is a "type" of monsoon vegetation it is tropical deciduous forest, with sal as the dominant species.

As well as contrasts in climate, the monsoon regions also exhibit pronounced changes in temperature and vegetation as a result of variations in altitude. The Western Ghats of India and the foothills of the Himalayas in Assam both rise to more than 2,500 m (8,200 ft). Temperatures decrease sharply at such altitudes with corresponding changes in vegetation. In southern India on the Nilgiri Hills a wet temperate forest is characteristic, with an intermingling of temperate and tropical species. Magnolias, planes and elms all grow there.

Agriculture in monsoon regions
Despite its extensive area there is no part of the monsoon world that is untouched by man and by man's activities. In southern Asia, agricultural activity can be traced back at least 5,000 years, and there have been agricultural settlements throughout the monsoon regions for at least 1,500 years. Man's activity and the grazing of domesticated animals have interfered with, and progressively modified, the natural vegetation. The range of species indicates that, in the whole of the monsoon biome, there is now virtually no primary forest left. The pace of man's interference has speeded up considerably over the last 100 years. As a result, less than 10 percent of the land in southern Asia is now forested, and other parts of the monsoon

regions are similarly losing their forest cover.

Many of today's farming methods incorporate traditional cultivation practices, but there have also been very significant changes in recent decades. Traditional agriculture in the monsoon regions has been developed to take into account the seasonal nature of its rainfall pattern and the total rainfall received. The fundamental role of water throughout the region and the absence of low temperatures have placed great importance on either cultivating crops that can tolerate the seasonal rainfall pattern, or on providing irrigation.

Through most of southern Asia, overwhelmingly the most populous of the monsoon regions, the most important single crop is rice, which covers about one-third of the total cultivated area. Rice needs a great deal of water and for this reason is grown mainly in areas of high irrigation, such as the delta lands of the southern and eastern coasts of India, and in areas where rainfall is more than 1,500 mm (59 in) a year. Its cultivation creates a very distinctive landscape as a result of the fact that rice must spend much of its growing period with a few centimeters of water over the soil.

Rice cultivation gives the monsoon regions their characteristic pattern of paddy fields, but other cereal crops such as wheat, the millets and sorghum are also very important. These can tolerate far drier conditions than can rice and occur in areas such as central India or upland Thailand, where uncertain and less abundant rainfall puts a premium on drought tolerance.

Even with traditional crops, man has often interfered extensively with the environment in order to increase yields and attempt to guarantee successful cropping. Traditional irrigation schemes range from diverting rivers at times of flood, in order to lead water to dry land, to digging wells and building small reservoirs. But recent technological developments have brought a new dimension to agricultural activity in the monsoon regions. Large-scale dam and irrigation canal schemes have become important in Africa as well as in monsoon Asia. The introduction and speed of electric or diesel "pumpsets" have transformed well irrigation in regions with extensive groundwater. The

reliable water supply that irrigation can give has brought in its train the opportunity for farmers to adopt a wide range of new farming practices. Chemical fertilizers and new strains of seed have made possible great increases in the productivity of the land in many parts of the monsoon regions, but their use is generally restricted to areas of reliable water supply.

Subsistence cultivation over thousands of years has been by far the most important element in the transformation of the landscape and vegetation of the monsoon world, but the introduction of plantation cultivation during the last centuries has also had a major effect. Tea plantations, for instance, have led to the almost total replacement of natural vegetation in the hills of southern India and Sri Lanka.

Populations in all the countries of the monsoon regions are rapidly increasing, and demands for economic development are constantly growing, placing increasing pressures on the environment, pressures which to date have seemed almost irresistible.

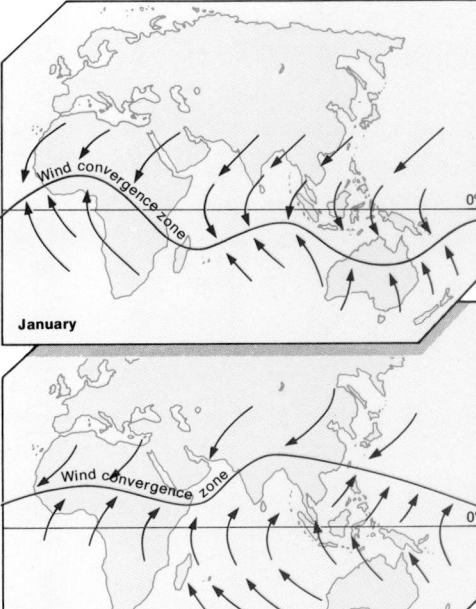

Many parts of the world experience "monsoon" winds, blowing from sea to land in summer, and from land to sea in winter; but typical monsoon vegetation is most clearly seen in the regions of southeastern Asia and the Indian subcontinent. In climatic terms, however, the monsoon circulation of seasonal wind reversals, with wetter summers and dry winters, also affects considerable areas of Africa, South America and northern Australia.

☐ Annual rainfall more than 500 mm (20 in), with wet and dry seasons

January

July

Heat differences in the atmosphere cause the seasonal wind reversals (left) characteristic of monsoon circulation. In January the northern hemisphere is tilted away from the sun, and cold, dry winds blow from the central Asian landmass toward the Equator. Here they change direction (an effect of the Earth's rotation), converge with other winds, and drop their rain. In July the situation is reversed when the heated Asian landmass attracts a flow of cooler air from the equatorial oceans, which moves northward with the sun. The moist air condenses on reaching land, and the monsoon rains descend.

DISAPPEARING ANIMALS
The dwindling wildlife of southeastern Asia includes species that may be regarded locally as pests—a fact that makes their protection difficult outside game reserves. Animals such as the tiger and the wild pig are doubly threatened as human cultivation spreads into the natural habitat: their hunting and foraging grounds are reduced, and their destruction of crops or livestock provides villagers with an obvious incentive for killing them in order to protect their own livelihoods.

Tiger
Panthera tigris

Wild pig
Sus scrofa

SELF-SUFFICIENCY IN CHINA
Local materials are turned into saleable products at a ratan factory in southern China. This factory is not owned by the state but by the village-sized brigade responsible for the manufacturing. The brigade functions as a smaller economic unit within the Ting Chow people's commune of 20 to 30 villages, but is encouraged to act independently, owning what it creates. The commune takes care of such matters as waterways—it contains 82 km (51 miles) of canals.

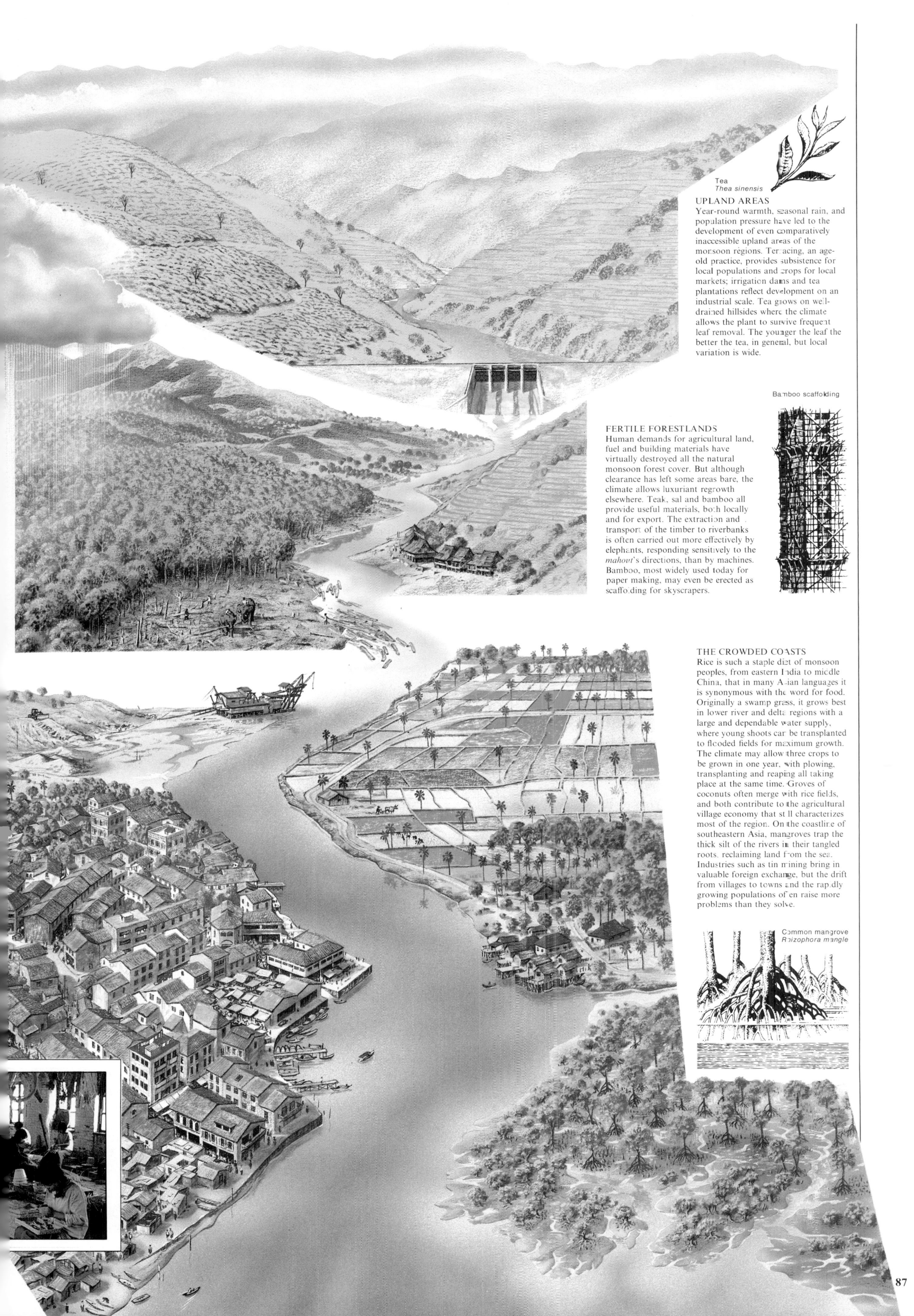

UPLAND AREAS

Year-round warmth, seasonal rain, and population pressure have led to the development of even comparatively inaccessible upland areas of the monsoon regions. Terracing, an age-old practice, provides subsistence for local populations and crops for local markets; irrigation dams and tea plantations reflect development on an industrial scale. Tea grows on well-drained hillsides where the climate allows the plant to survive frequent leaf removal. The younger the leaf the better the tea, in general, but local variation is wide.

Tea
Thea sinensis

Bamboo scaffolding

FERTILE FORESTLANDS

Human demands for agricultural land, fuel and building materials have virtually destroyed all the natural monsoon forest cover. But although clearance has left some areas bare, the climate allows luxuriant regrowth elsewhere. Teak, sal and bamboo all provide useful materials, both locally and for export. The extraction and transport of the timber to riverbanks is often carried out more effectively by elephants, responding sensitively to the *mahout*'s directions, than by machines. Bamboo, most widely used today for paper making, may even be erected as scaffolding for skyscrapers.

THE CROWDED COASTS

Rice is such a staple diet of monsoon peoples, from eastern India to middle China, that in many Asian languages it is synonymous with the word for food. Originally a swamp grass, it grows best in lower river and delta regions with a large and dependable water supply, where young shoots can be transplanted to flooded fields for maximum growth. The climate may allow three crops to be grown in one year, with plowing, transplanting and reaping all taking place at the same time. Groves of coconuts often merge with rice fields, and both contribute to the agricultural village economy that still characterizes most of the region. On the coastline of southeastern Asia, mangroves trap the thick silt of the rivers in their tangled roots, reclaiming land from the sea. Industries such as tin mining bring in valuable foreign exchange, but the drift from villages to towns and the rapidly growing populations often raise more problems than they solve.

Common mangrove
Rhizophora mangle

Mountain Regions

A quarter of Earth's land surface lies at heights of 1,000 m (3,300 ft) or more above sea level. But the highland regions are thinly populated by man, who is, generally speaking, a lowland dweller (most major population centers are less than 100 m (330 ft) above sea level). Some formerly lowland animals have fled from man to the harsh refuge of the mountains, joining with specially adapted plants and wildlife, but today man himself is finding the highland regions increasingly useful and desirable.

The world's highest mountain peaks rise to almost 9.6 km (6 miles) above sea level, but these heights are small compared to the total diameter of the Earth. The rough surface of an orange would have mountains higher than the Himalayas if scaled up to world size. But mountain environments, although they vary enormously from system to system, all tend to demand remarkable endurance and adaptability from the plants and animals that inhabit them.

Altitude rather than geological variation determines conditions of life on mountains. The temperature falls by 2°C with every 300 m (3.4°F every 1,000 ft)—hence the snowcapped beauty of the heights—and life forms must be adapted to increasingly harsh conditions as height increases. As a result, zones of different life occur at different levels, from tropical forests (at the base of low-latitude mountains) to arctic-type life in the zone of ice and snow at the summit. The latitude of the mountain affects the heights to which these zones extend: trees occur at 2,300 m (7,500 ft) in the southern Alps, whereas farther north, in central Sweden, trees cannot survive above 1,000 m (3,300 ft).

Life at the top
The specially adapted plant and animal life of the mountains occurs above the tree line, for here the variations in living conditions reach their greatest extremes. A plant that has found a foothold on a bare rock face may have to endure intense heat, even where the average temperature is low, when the summer sun blazing through the clear air warms the slabs to tropical temperatures. But when that part of the mountain falls into shadow, the temperature decreases very rapidly, often assisted by the high winds that blow almost constantly throughout the year in many mountain areas.

Soil necessary for plant life develops with the breakdown of the rock through the agency of water, frost and ice. Lichens, whose acids may aid in this destruction, can survive at very high levels, and as they die may add some humus to the newly forming soil. This may first accumulate in sheltered places where plants requiring high humidity, such as mosses and filmy ferns, are found. Flowering plants follow where a greater depth of soil has formed, although some grow in cracks between rocks.

Flowering plants of the mountains all tend to be small (to avoid harsh, drying winds), deep rooted (to anchor the plant firmly), and abundantly flowering (to benefit from the short growing season). Many unrelated species have independently developed a similar cushion form. This enables them to shed excess rainwater easily and to retain heat better in a tight tangle of stems and leaves, where the temperature may be more than 10°C (18°F) higher than that of the outside air. Insects sheltering there are well placed to perform the vital task of pollination. But pollinating insects are relatively rare at high altitudes, and some mountain plants are wind pollinated. The brilliant color of many others may be to increase their attractiveness for the insects. Nearly all upland plants are very slow-growing perennials, and many are evergreen, with leaves that exploit all available light.

Some large animals, such as the ibex or the Rocky Mountain goat, are adapted to spend their lives among the rocks and slopes. These stocky creatures, with hooves that act rather like suction cups, produce their summer young in the security of the heights, although in winter they descend to the shelter of the upper forests. Among smaller mammals, most of which are rodents, some dig burrows in which they hibernate through the winter. Others have very thick insulating coats, and may stay awake through the coldest weather in burrows under the snow.

Refugees from the lowlands
Some mountain animals, particularly carnivorous mammals and birds, have been driven by human persecution into remote mountain fastnesses. Many birds of prey, which could otherwise survive well in lowland areas, have their last strongholds among the mountains. They survive by feeding on small rodents, many of which are extremely wary. Some upland birds feed on insects or on seeds, but their number is comparatively small. The Alpine chough is one of the most interesting of mountain birds, for it has learned to find food among the scraps provided by climbers and skiers, whom it often follows to very high altitudes.

Insects and other small invertebrates, like their Arctic counterparts, may take several years to mature. Some are wingless, and many tend to fly low in order not to be blown away from their home range. Jumping spiders have been seen at heights of 6,700 m (22,000 ft) on the slopes of Mount Everest, where they exist on small flies and springtails, but even above this level springtails and glacier "fleas" occur where there are no plants, apparently surviving on wind-blown insects and pollen grains.

Man and the mountains
The remote beauty of the mountains has led many peoples to identify them as the abode of the gods, but man himself prefers to live in the more convenient lowlands. The rarefied atmosphere of the heights makes physical work difficult, although some mountain-dwelling peoples have developed adaptations of the blood system to enable them to carry scarce oxygen more efficiently. The short growing season prevents cultivation of all but the hardiest cereal crops, and most uplanders rely on their livestock—cattle, sheep, llamas or yaks—for their existence. The animals are often driven to high pasture during the summer, descending to the valleys in the winter.

Modern, urbanized man finds the beauty and freshness of mountains increasingly attractive. Climbers have invaded most of the world's mountain regions, and in winter hosts of skiers flock to the resorts. Many important wildlife sanctuaries and national parks, particularly in the United States, are in mountain areas.

Lowland populations often rely on the pure mountain streams for both water and energy. Whole upland valleys are sometimes flooded to store water for distant conurbations. And the forceful flow of the water as it descends from the snow-fed heights is frequently harnessed to produce electricity for entire regions hundreds of kilometers away. The clear mountain air also offers the best conditions for astronomical observation, and most observatories today are built in dry, cloudless mountain areas.

LIFE ON THE HEIGHTS
Mountain climates become colder the higher one goes. This change in conditions creates distinctive horizontal zones of plant and animal life, although the pattern may vary according to the latitude and aspect of a mountain. Some life forms manage to eke out a precarious existence even on the roof of the world. Lower down, the brief growing season encourages a short burst of plant and animal activity above the timber line, conspicuous for the brightly colored summer flowers. Man mainly inhabits the lower slopes and valleys. He exploits mountain resources but rarely lives on the inhospitable heights.

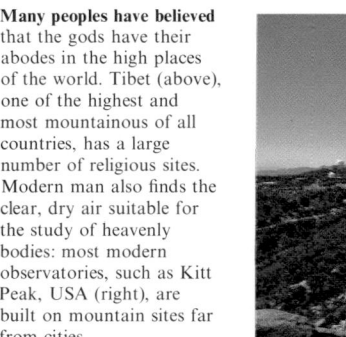

Many peoples have believed that the gods have their abodes in the high places of the world. Tibet (above), one of the highest and most mountainous of all countries, has a large number of religious sites. Modern man also finds the clear, dry air suitable for the study of heavenly bodies: most modern observatories, such as Kitt Peak, USA (right), are built on mountain sites far from cities.

Activity in Earth's crust has produced mountains in every continent (left). Some thrust up sharply, while older mountains have been eroded to rounded shapes. The Scottish Highlands were made by mountain-building forces 400 million years ago (170 million years before the Appalachians and the Urals). The Rockies are 70 million years old and the Alps 15 million years old.

☐ Ancient mountains (Caledonian orogenesis)   ☐ Intermediate mountains (Hercynian orogenesis)   ☐ Recent mountains (Alpine orogenesis)

MOUNTAIN ADAPTATIONS
Saussurea
Saussurea tridactyla

Alpine soldanella
Soldanella alpina

Ingenious adaptations to harsh mountain conditions have been evolved by many plants, most of which have tiny cells with thick sap that does not freeze easily. Saussurea masks itself with white hair to reduce evaporation from the leaf surface. Alpine soldanellas are active even under snow, pushing up their flowers before the thaw.

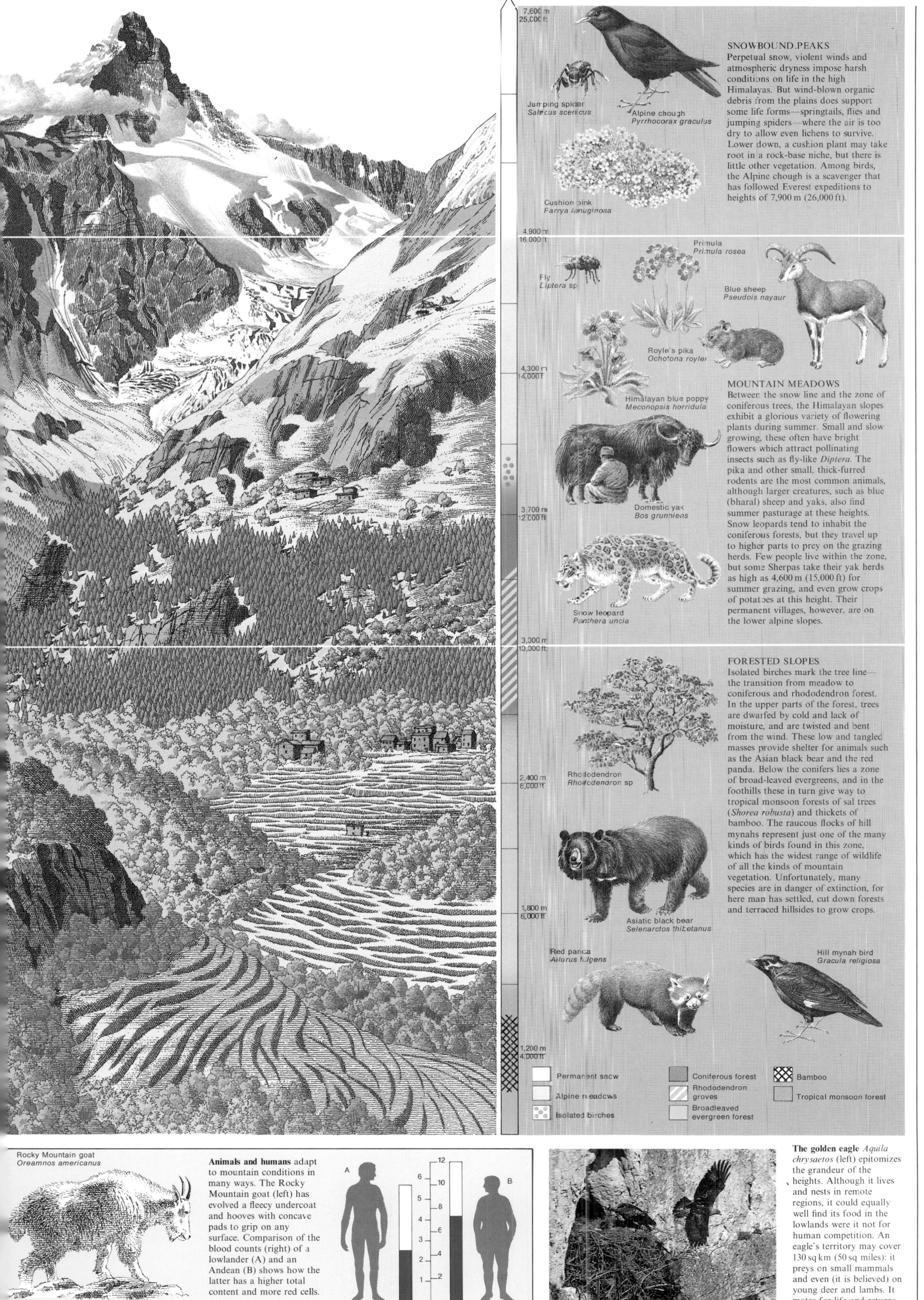

7,600 m 25,000 ft	

SNOWBOUND PEAKS

Perpetual snow, violent winds and atmospheric dryness impose harsh conditions on life in the high Himalayas. But wind-blown organic debris from the plains does support some life forms—springtails, flies and jumping spiders—where the air is too dry to allow even lichens to survive. Lower down, a cushion plant may take root in a rock-base niche, but there is little other vegetation. Among birds, the Alpine chough is a scavenger that has followed Everest expeditions to heights of 7,900 m (26,000 ft).

Jumping spider
Salticus scenicus

Alpine chough
Pyrrhocorax graculus

Cushion pink
Farrya lanuginosa

4,900 m
16,000 ft

Primula
Primula rosea

Fly
Diptera sp.

Blue sheep
Pseudois nayaur

Royle's pika
Ochotona royler

4,300 m
14,000 ft

Himalayan blue poppy
Meconopsis horridula

MOUNTAIN MEADOWS

Between the snow line and the zone of coniferous trees, the Himalayan slopes exhibit a glorious variety of flowering plants during summer. Small and slow growing, these often have bright flowers which attract pollinating insects such as fly-like *Diptera*. The pika and other small, thick-furred rodents are the most common animals, although larger creatures, such as blue (bharal) sheep and yaks, also find summer pasturage at these heights. Snow leopards tend to inhabit the coniferous forests, but they travel up to higher parts to prey on the grazing herds. Few people live within the zone, but some Sherpas take their yak herds as high as 4,600 m (15,000 ft) for summer grazing, and even grow crops of potatoes at this height. Their permanent villages, however, are on the lower alpine slopes.

Domestic yak
Bos grunniens

3,700 m
12,000 ft

Snow leopard
Panthera uncia

3,300 m
10,000 ft

FORESTED SLOPES

Isolated birches mark the tree line— the transition from meadow to coniferous and rhododendron forest. In the upper parts of the forest, trees are dwarfed by cold and lack of moisture, and are twisted and bent from the wind. These low and tangled masses provide shelter for animals such as the Asian black bear and the red panda. Below the conifers lies a zone of broad-leaved evergreens, and in the foothills these in turn give way to tropical monsoon forests of sal trees (*Shorea robusta*) and thickets of bamboo. The raucous flocks of hill mynahs represent just one of the many kinds of birds found in this zone, which has the widest range of wildlife of all the kinds of mountain vegetation. Unfortunately, many species are in danger of extinction, for here man has settled, cut down forests and terraced hillsides to grow crops.

Rhododendron
Rhododendron sp.

2,400 m
8,000 ft

Asiatic black bear
Selenarctos thibetanus

1,800 m
6,000 ft

Red panda
Ailurus fulgens

Hill mynah bird
Gracula religiosa

1,200 m
4,000 ft

☐ Permanent snow	▨ Coniferous forest	▨ Bamboo
☐ Alpine meadows	▨ Rhododendron groves	☐ Tropical monsoon forest
▨ Isolated birches	☐ Broadleaved evergreen forest	

Rocky Mountain goat
Oreamnos americanus

Animals and humans adapt to mountain conditions in many ways. The Rocky Mountain goat (left) has evolved a fleecy undercoat and hooves with concave pads to grip on any surface. Comparison of the blood counts (right) of a lowlander (A) and an Andean (B) shows how the latter has a higher total content and more red cells.

liters pints

The golden eagle *Aquila chrysaetos* (left) epitomizes the grandeur of the heights. Although it lives and nests in remote regions, it could equally well find its food in the lowlands were it not for human competition. An eagle's territory may cover 130 sq km (50 sq miles): it preys on small mammals and even (it is believed) on young deer and lambs. It mates for life and returns each year to the same nest.

Freshwater Environments

Broad, muddy rivers, fast-running streams, miniature ponds and deep, ancient lakes all provide their own distinctive environments for populations of animals and colonies of aquatic plants. And in spite of the fact that these, the world's freshwater systems, contain only a minute proportion of the Earth's total supplies of water, the remarkable variety and richness of the wildlife they support make them among the most valuable and significant of all the world's natural habitats.

Fresh water is never really pure for, like sea water, and indeed like all other natural waters, it contains various dissolved minerals. Fresh water differs from seawater only in the relatively low concentrations of the minerals it contains. But these mineral traces are extremely important; they provide essential nutrients without which freshwater plants could not exist. And without plant life, there would be virtually no animal life either.

Not all parts of every freshwater system are rich in both plants and animals. Large, deep lakes are very similar to oceans—no light can penetrate their gloomy depths, and few plants can live in these conditions. The surface waters, on the other hand, where light is plentiful, teem with microscopic floating plants, mainly single-celled algae such as desmids and diatoms. The edges of lakes provide a different set of conditions again, for here the water is shallow and light can penetrate right through it. Plants can take root in the silt on the bottom, grow up through the water and thrust their leaves out into the light and air. Edges of lakes and, for the same reasons, the waters of small ponds are usually full of such plant life, which in turn supports many freshwater animals.

Running waters
Just as the still waters of lakes and ponds offer a variety of habitats, so the running waters of rivers support many different forms of life, each adapted to the particular conditions of its environment. In the upper reaches, where rivers are scarcely more than upland streams, water is fast flowing and clear of silt. Few plants, except close-clinging mosses, can gain a hold on the bare stony bottom and most of the fish are well muscled and strong bodied to enable them to withstand the constant tug of the current. As a river swells to form a mature lowland water course, however, it becomes slower moving and the water is warmer and richer in nutrients. Plants grow readily in these lower reaches and provide a supply of food for aquatic animals.

With such a wide range of conditions, freshwater environments support an enormous variety of animal life—insects, fishes, amphibians, reptiles, mammals and birds. In some ways insects are the most important of all these creatures: freshwater systems contain more insects and other invertebrates, representing a greater variety of species, than any other kind of animal. Furthermore, these, the smallest representatives of the freshwater animal world, provide one of the most important links in the complex freshwater food chain.

Insects may be the most numerous, but fishes are probably the most familiar of all freshwater creatures, and they certainly show some of the greatest varieties of adaptations to the many different habitats. Their sizes vary from the tiny, 14 mm ($\frac{1}{2}$ in) of the virtually transparent dwarf goby fish found in small streams and lakes in the Philippines to the 4 m (14 ft) of the arapaima found in deep rivers in tropical South America. Their feeding habits vary from those of the ferocious carnivorous piranha of South America to those of the North American paddle fish which, although more than three times the size of the largest piranha, feed solely on microscopic organisms which they filter from the water with their specially adapted throats.

The breeding habits of freshwater fish also vary widely, from the carefully maternal instincts of the African mouthbreeding cichlids—these retain the developing eggs safely in their mouths until the offspring hatch—to the rather more common ejection of eggs into the water, where their fertilization and survival is simply left to chance. Other adaptations include the ability to breathe air (as does the African lungfish), to leap waterfalls (a common practice among migrating salmon) and to emit an electric shock of up to 600 volts (an adaptation of the South American electric eel).

Creatures of the water's edge
Of all the other major groups of animals, amphibians (such as frogs and toads) are probably the most reliant on freshwater habitats. Because their skins must not dry out and they have to lay their eggs in water, few amphibians can venture far from the water's edge. And because they cannot tolerate the salt in seawater (it causes them to lose their body fluids through their skins) they are totally dependent upon fresh water for their existence. Reptiles, rather less typical of freshwater environments, range in size from miniature North American terrapins to the giant crocodiles that live along the banks of the Nile. Freshwater mammals, on the other hand, with the considerable exception of the hippopotamus, all tend to be rather small creatures such as otters, beavers, coypus, aquatic moles and water shrews.

Birds are another important group of freshwater creatures. Although few birds are truly aquatic an enormous number of species live in or near freshwater systems and take advantage of the various food supplies: the plants and fish within the waters; the bankside vegetation and small animal life; and the many forms of freshwater insects. Marshes and swamps, for example, provide some of the richest bird habitats in the world.

Also numbered among the species dependent on Earth's freshwater systems is man. And although strictly a nonaquatic, land-living animal, man uses more fresh water than any other creature. His needs seem to be inexhaustible as he harnesses, channels, diverts and often pollutes freshwater systems throughout the world. Unfortunately, the vast requirements of the human race are not always compatible with the rather more humble needs of all other species that depend upon fresh water.

Volume of Lakes in cu km (cu miles)	Discharge of Rivers in cu m (cu ft) per second
Huron, North America 3,447 (827)	Ganges, Asia 18,689 (660,000)
Nyasa, Africa 8,373 (2,009)	Brahmaputra, Asia 19,822 (700,000)
Superior, North America 12,153 (2,916)	Yangtze, Asia 21,804 (770,000)
Tanganyika, Africa 19,418 (4,659)	Congo, Africa 39,644 (1,400,000)
Baikal, Asia 23,260 (5,581)	Amazon, South America 212,376 (7,500,000)

The five largest lakes in the world hold more than 53% of all fresh water that flows over the land. The rest of the world's lakes account for another 45%.

The world's largest river, the Amazon, discharges more than one-fifth of all fresh water that flows from the mouths of the world's rivers into the oceans.

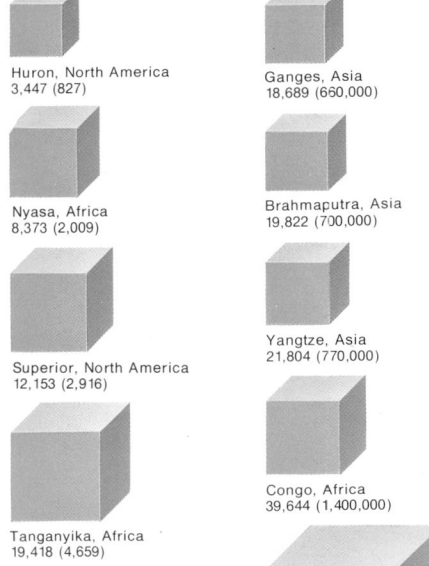

THE UPPER REACHES Here, water flows rapidly. Tumbling over bare rocks and stones, it is chilly, oxygen-rich and free of silt. Bird life attracted to these reaches includes the sure-footed dipper, which walks the stream bed hunting for caddis larvae. Slightly farther downstream, but where the river is still narrow and easily dammed, beavers are found. Few plants can live within the water, but river crowfoot has feathery underwater leaves that remain intact where most other plants would be shredded by the current. Many fish, such as trout, have streamlined bodies to offer the least resistance to the stream's pull, while others survive on the bottom by bracing against the rocks—the bullhead, for example. Insects have various means of anchoring themselves to the stream bed—blackfly larvae have hooks to fix themselves to pebbles.

Dipper
Cinclus cinclus

Beaver
Castor fiber

River crowfoot
Ranunculus fluitans

Brown trout
Salmo trutta

Bullhead
Cottus bairdi

Blackfly larvae
Simulium spp

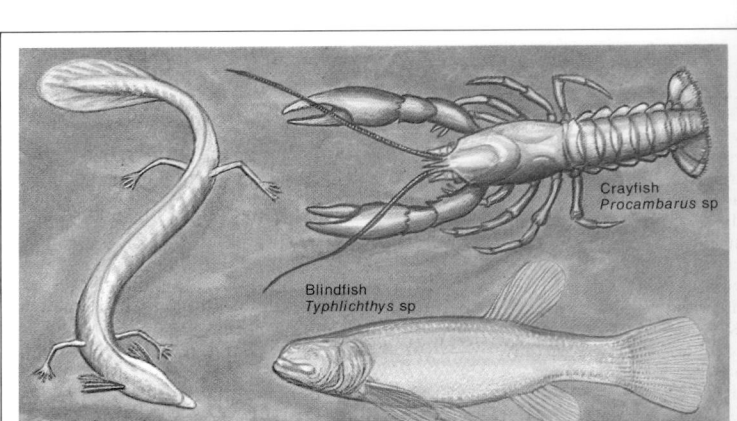

Crayfish
Procambarus sp

Blindfish
Typhlichthys sp

Cave salamander
Proteus anguinus

THE LIFE OF A RIVER

As a river makes its way from its upland source to the sea, it gradually changes its character. And at every stage in its progress, the animals and plants that inhabit the riverbanks and the waters reflect these changes by their adaptations to their environments. Most distinctive and dramatic are those adaptations produced in the wildlife of the upper and lower river reaches.

African spoonbill
Platalea alba

Southern painted turtle
Chrysemys picta dorsalis

THE LOWER REACHES
The slowly flowing river and its muddy banks are rich in animals and plants. Many birds live along the water's edge; spoonbills wade in the shallows, filtering food from the water with their beaks. The banks, fringed with reedmaces and other plants, provide habitats for many reptiles, such as the American painted turtle, and mammals, such as the platypus. Plants also grow on the water—they range from large waterlilies to tiny algae that are food for river fishes: Africa's upside-down-feeding catfish, for example. In these waters, mammals as well as fish are to be found—Amazonian manatees live entirely aquatic lives. The plentiful river plants, such as curled pondweed, provide food for water snails and other herbivores, and cover for predators such as pike. Crustacea and insects living in the silt of the riverbed are food for bottom-feeding fish such as the strange-looking North American paddle fish.

LAKES: CHANGE AND EVOLUTION
No two lakes are alike: each is virtually a self-contained world for its population of aquatic animals and plants. Furthermore, no individual lake remains the same for long: in every lake, slow, inexorable changes in conditions are gradually but constantly changing the balance of species inhabiting the lake bed, the bankside and the water.

Changing conditions may be caused by one of several processes. Accumulating sediments, one of the most common of these processes, may eliminate a lake altogether. The water becomes shallower as sediments thicken (1) and these sediments are then added to and consolidated by water plants taking root. Ultimately, land plants (2) invade the area.

Lakes develop their own peculiar species when the aquatic wildlife that evolves within them has no means of migrating to other freshwater systems to interbreed. The world's only existing species of freshwater seal, for example, is found in just one lake—isolated Lake Baikal in Asia.

Baikal seal
Phoca sibirica

Reedmace
Typha sp

Platypus
Ornithorhynchus anatinus

Waterlily
Nymphaea sp

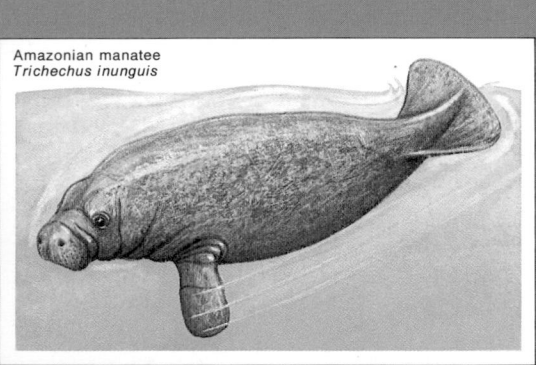

Amazonian manatee
Trichechus inunguis

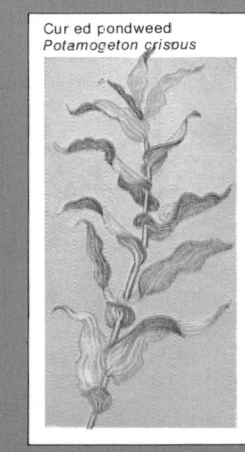

Curled pondweed
Potamogeton crispus

African catfish
Synocontis batensoda

White ramshorn snail
Planorbis albus

Pike
Esox lucius

DARK WATERS
Underground rivers that flow through many of the world's cave systems support surprising numbers of creatures that have adapted to the permanent darkness. Many of these, such as the American cave crayfish, have lost the coloration of their surface-living kin. Some, such as Kentucky blind fishes, no longer possess eyes. Some salamanders are sighted and black when born, but become blind and colorless by adulthood.

Paddle fish
Polydon spathula

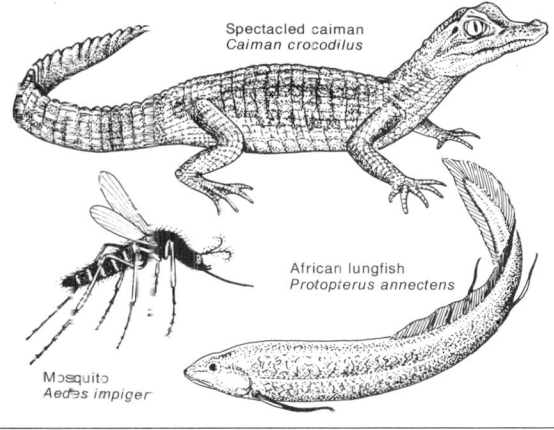

Spectacled caiman
Caiman crocodilus

African lungfish
Protopterus annectens

Mosquito
Aedes impiger

WETLANDS
Marshes and swamps are the richest of freshwater habitats. Wading birds, such as Asia's painted stork *Ibis leucocephalus* (above), are particularly common. Reptiles include caimans, which lay their eggs in swamps' warm, rotting vegetation. Of the many insects, mosquitoes are probably the most numerous, and of the many fishes, African lungfish are perhaps best adapted to life in wetlands. They survive drought, when marshes dry up, by their ability to breathe air.

Man and the Freshwater Environments

From earliest times, man has been finding new uses for and making new demands upon the world's freshwater resources. Today, the whole of modern society depends upon a vast supply to serve its agricultural, industrial, domestic and other needs. To meet the ever-growing demand for water, man has performed remarkable engineering feats: altering the courses of rivers, creating and destroying lakes, drowning valleys and tapping water sources that lie deep within the Earth.

Water is essential to human life. Simply to remain alive, an active adult living in a temperate climate needs a liquid intake of about two liters (3½ pints) every day. In warmer climates, the body's fluid requirements are even greater. Consequently, man has always been tied to reliable sources of drinking water—rivers, springs, lakes and ponds—and the availability of these, until very recently, has dictated the routes of all his wanderings and determined the sites of all his settlements.

From the time of the earliest human settlements, however, man has looked upon freshwater systems not simply as a source of drinking water but also as an increasingly useful resource for a multitude of other purposes. Today, water enters into virtually every aspect of modern life, and enormous quantities are used in agriculture, in industry, in the home, in the production of energy, for transport and for recreation.

The farmer's resource

Of all the major activities that rely on fresh water, agriculture is by far the world's largest consumer. In much of Europe and North America, rainfall is usually plentiful and lack of sufficient water for crops is rarely a problem. But in other parts of the world the climate simply does not produce enough rainfall and water shortages are a perennial problem. There, irrigation is not just a sophisticated technique to improve the yields and increase the varieties of crops grown; it is, and always has been, an essential element of agriculture.

Methods of irrigation range from small-scale devices—such as miniature windpumps—used in many developing countries simply to lift water from rivers for bankside crops, to vast dams, reservoirs and canal systems such as the Indus River project in Pakistan, which irrigates 10 million hectares (25 million acres) of land.

Traditional irrigation techniques usually involve using open channels or furrows for conducting water to fields. But one of the major problems with these, particularly in hot climates, is that much of the water evaporates and is lost before it can be used. Several new techniques, such as sprinklers and drip-feed systems, have recently been developed, however, to help make more efficient use of available supplies.

Although the most severe water deficiencies are experienced in the dry subtropical and tropical regions of the world, the temperate regions of North America and Europe, in spite of their relatively wet climates, do suffer shortages. Large towns and cities rarely have enough locally available rainfall or river flow to satisfy both domestic demand and the insatiable needs of industry. In the developed nations, industry consumes more water than any other activity.

Industrial demands

Fresh water is not only an integral part of almost every manufacturing process, it has other important industrial uses. As a source of power, it has been used since the early days of civilization—water wheels were one of man's first industrial inventions. Today, these simple devices are rarely seen in industrial societies, but water power is more important than ever before. Giant dams allow enormous volumes of water to be controlled and the power harnessed to drive turbines and generate electricity.

Freshwater systems have also, for centuries, provided industry with an important means of transporting its goods, and canal systems are still an essential part of industrial infrastructure in many countries of the world: the Europa Canal, when completed, will link three of Europe's major rivers, the Rhine, Main and Danube, and so form a continuous waterway running east–west across the breadth of Europe.

Man obtains fresh water by trapping it as it passes through one of the stages in the hydrological cycle—the never-ending circulation of Earth's waters from the ocean, to the atmosphere, to land. This cycle can be traced from the point at which water evaporates from the sea. The water vapor is blown across the land and falls as rain, hail or snow. Some then evaporates, but the rest completes the cycle by flowing over the land or through the soil or rocks back to the sea. It is at this point in its journey that man obtains his water supplies—from lakes (1), boreholes and wells (2) and dammed rivers (3). These supplies are then either used locally, or are transported by pipe or canal (4) to reservoirs (5) where they are stored ready for distribution.

➤ Movement of water in the hydrological cycle

▨ Water-bearing rock

Already, the finished sections of the canal are carrying oil, chemicals, fertilizers, coal, coke and building materials to and from some of Europe's major industrial regions.

Many of Europe's waterways date back to the great canal-building days of the Industrial Revolution. Although a few of these are still used for commerce, many are today considered too narrow to transport economical quantities of goods. Some, however, are now finding a role to play in one of the world's fastest-growing new industries—the leisure market. Today, canals provide a wide range of aquatic activities for holiday makers, tourists and sportsmen.

Recreation and sport

Freshwater systems throughout the world, in fact, are rapidly being recognized and developed as major recreational resources. Lakes and reservoirs are stocked with fish for anglers, silted waterways are dredged to provide sailing and swimming facilities, and old quarries and open-cast workings are landscaped and flooded to provide entirely new freshwater systems purely for leisure pursuits. The projects not only help to rejuvenate previously misused land, they also provide significant incomes to otherwise underdeveloped areas, especially highland regions that are too remote to attract other industries, and are unsuitable for farming.

Unfortunately, however, few of the world's freshwater systems can continue indefinitely to absorb the ever-growing demands that are being made upon them. Overuse of water resources is already a problem and has led to the pollution and destruction of many water systems—in some places overtapping has lowered water tables so drastically that rivers and lakes have been permanently destroyed. Although steps have been taken to protect certain waterways, legislation to guard against misuse and overuse is costly, time consuming and, inevitably, comes up against vested interests. Nevertheless, stringent conservation measures are becoming increasingly necessary if society is to maintain one of its most precious resources.

RESERVOIRS

About 70 trillion liters (15 trillion gallons) of fresh water are held in storage during any one year. Reservoirs ensure a continuous supply of water in spite of the inevitable seasonal fluctuations in demand and in the natural supply from rivers and rainfall. And where reservoirs are formed by damming rivers, there are additional benefits—the vast quantities of water held can be controlled and the power used to generate electricity. The Kariba Dam in Zimbabwe (right) has the potential for producing 8,500 million kilowatt hours of electrical power every year.

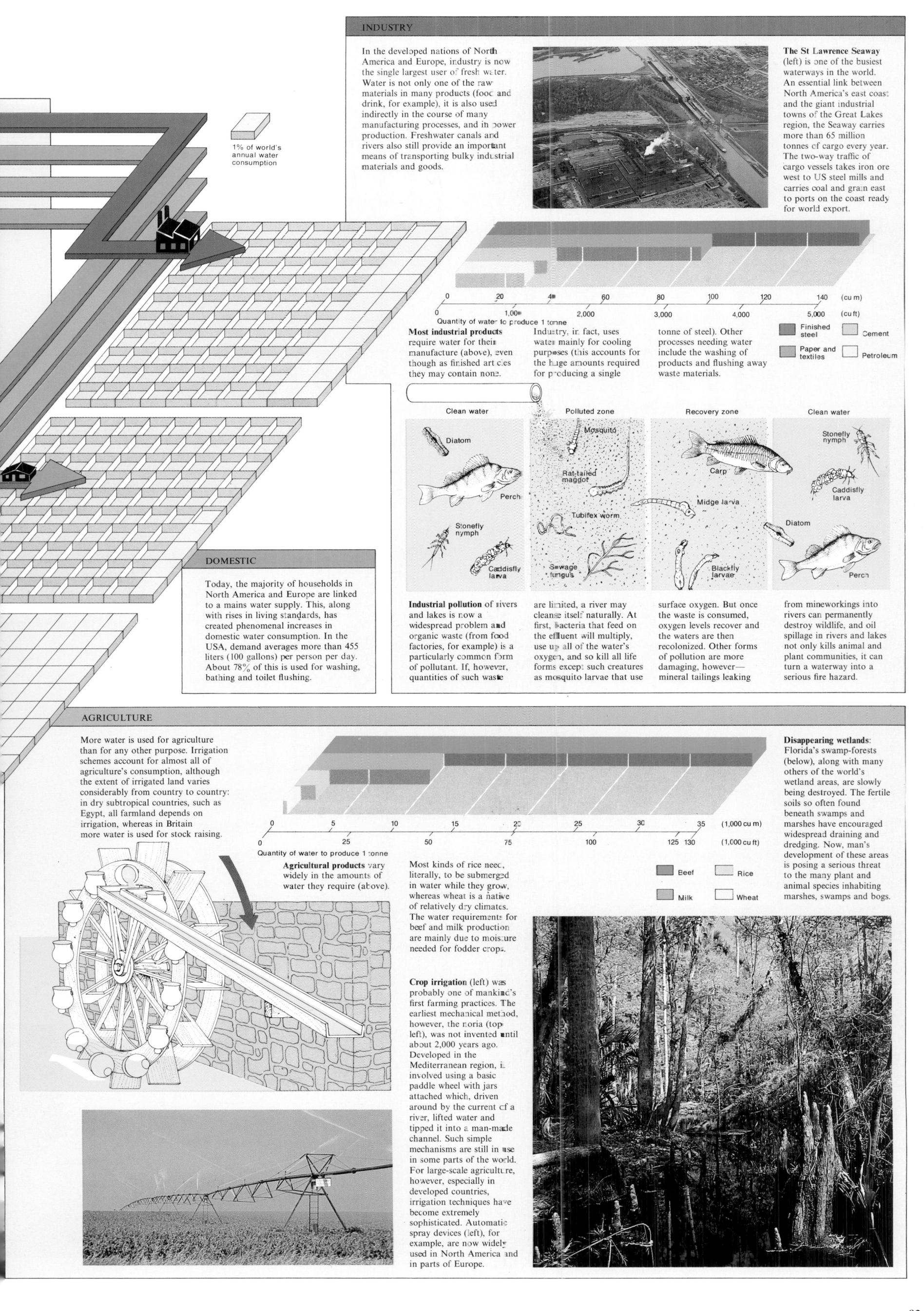

INDUSTRY

In the developed nations of North America and Europe, industry is now the single largest user of fresh water. Water is not only one of the raw materials in many products (food and drink, for example), it is also used indirectly in the course of many manufacturing processes, and in power production. Freshwater canals and rivers also still provide an important means of transporting bulky industrial materials and goods.

The St Lawrence Seaway (left) is one of the busiest waterways in the world. An essential link between North America's east coast and the giant industrial towns of the Great Lakes region, the Seaway carries more than 65 million tonnes of cargo every year. The two-way traffic of cargo vessels takes iron ore west to US steel mills and carries coal and grain east to ports on the coast ready for world export.

1% of world's annual water consumption

Quantity of water to produce 1 tonne

0   20   40   60   80   100   120   140   (cu m)
0   1,000   2,000   3,000   4,000   5,000   (cu ft)

- Finished steel
- Paper and textiles
- Cement
- Petroleum

Most industrial products require water for their manufacture (above), even though as finished articles they may contain none.

Industry, in fact, uses water mainly for cooling purposes (this accounts for the huge amounts required for producing a single tonne of steel). Other processes needing water include the washing of products and flushing away waste materials.

Clean water — Polluted zone — Recovery zone — Clean water

Diatom, Perch, Stonefly nymph, Caddisfly larva

Mosquito, Rat-tailed maggot, Tubifex worm, Sewage fungus

Carp, Midge larva, Blackfly larvae

Stonefly nymph, Caddisfly larva, Diatom, Perch

Industrial pollution of rivers and lakes is now a widespread problem and organic waste (from food factories, for example) is a particularly common form of pollutant. If, however, quantities of such waste are limited, a river may cleanse itself naturally. At first, bacteria that feed on the effluent will multiply, use up all of the water's oxygen, and so kill all life forms except such creatures as mosquito larvae that use surface oxygen. But once the waste is consumed, oxygen levels recover and the waters are then recolonized. Other forms of pollution are more damaging, however—mineral tailings leaking from mineworkings into rivers can permanently destroy wildlife, and oil spillage in rivers and lakes not only kills animal and plant communities, it can turn a waterway into a serious fire hazard.

DOMESTIC

Today, the majority of households in North America and Europe are linked to a mains water supply. This, along with rises in living standards, has created phenomenal increases in domestic water consumption. In the USA, demand averages more than 455 liters (100 gallons) per person per day. About 78% of this is used for washing, bathing and toilet flushing.

AGRICULTURE

More water is used for agriculture than for any other purpose. Irrigation schemes account for almost all of agriculture's consumption, although the extent of irrigated land varies considerably from country to country: in dry subtropical countries, such as Egypt, all farmland depends on irrigation, whereas in Britain more water is used for stock raising.

Quantity of water to produce 1 tonne

0   5   10   15   20   25   30   35   (1,000 cu m)
0   25   50   75   100   125   130   (1,000 cu ft)

Agricultural products vary widely in the amounts of water they require (above).

Most kinds of rice need, literally, to be submerged in water while they grow, whereas wheat is a native of relatively dry climates. The water requirements for beef and milk production are mainly due to moisture needed for fodder crops.

- Beef
- Milk
- Rice
- Wheat

Disappearing wetlands: Florida's swamp-forests (below), along with many others of the world's wetland areas, are slowly being destroyed. The fertile soils so often found beneath swamps and marshes have encouraged widespread draining and dredging. Now, man's development of these areas is posing a serious threat to the many plant and animal species inhabiting marshes, swamps and bogs.

Crop irrigation (left) was probably one of mankind's first farming practices. The earliest mechanical method, however, the noria (top left), was not invented until about 2,000 years ago. Developed in the Mediterranean region, it involved using a basic paddle wheel with jars attached which, driven around by the current of a river, lifted water and tipped it into a man-made channel. Such simple mechanisms are still in use in some parts of the world. For large-scale agriculture, however, especially in developed countries, irrigation techniques have become extremely sophisticated. Automatic spray devices (left), for example, are now widely used in North America and in parts of Europe.

Seawater Environments

The oceans form by far the largest of the world's habitable environments, covering almost three-quarters of the Earth's surface at an average depth of more than 3,500 m (11,500 ft). Little more than a century ago, scientists believed that the deep sea's low temperatures, perpetual darkness and immense pressures made life in these regions completely untenable. But we now know that animals live at all depths in the ocean, even at the bottom of trenches more than 11,000 m (36,000 ft) deep.

THE PATTERN OF MARINE LIFE

The distribution of life in the seas is like an inverted pyramid whose broad base is formed by billions of minute single-celled plants—the phytoplankton. Plants need sunlight and nutrient salts, so phytoplankton occurs only in the upper, sunlit layers and where salts are present. Elsewhere, the distribution of marine life thins out rapidly.

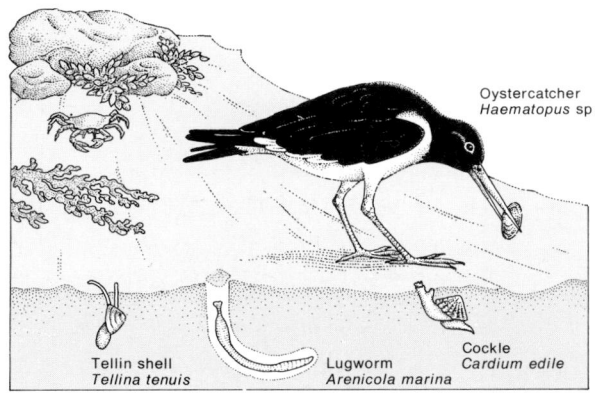

Shore life belongs to both land and sea, and thus has to cope with a wide range of conditions. Seaweeds get all their food from the sea and are quite unlike land plants. Many animals take refuge below the surface: tellin shell molluscs sift food particles through special "lips"; lugworms swallow sand, digesting any organic matter; cockles take in food and eject waste through two siphons. Some birds have bills adapted for opening bivalve molluscs.

Oystercatcher
Haematopus sp

Tellin shell
Tellina tenuis

Lugworm
Arenicola marina

Cockle
Cardium edile

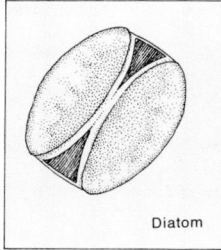
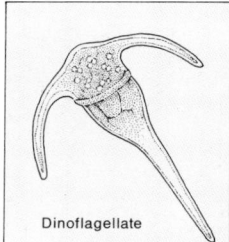
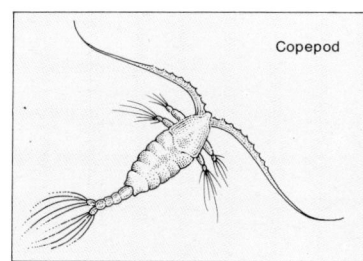

Marine plant life consists largely of diatoms—minute single-celled specks, each enclosed in a lidded box of silicon. Dinoflagellates, classed as plants but able to swim, dominate warmer waters. Both are food for copepods, the flea-sized grazers whose total weight, in the North Sea alone, is some seven million tonnes.

Diatom

Dinoflagellate

Copepod

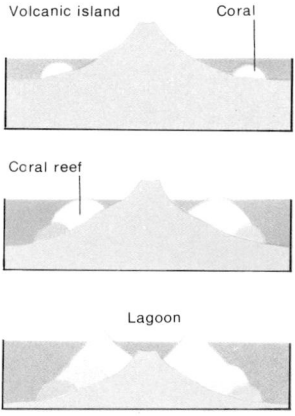

A coral atoll, forming in warm shallow water round an extinct volcano, makes up a living aquarium for thousands of tropical marine life forms. Countless billions of tiny polyps, each secreting a hard, calcareous skeleton, form the first layer of the reef, but die as the volcano gradually sinks. Their skeletons provide a base for further layers of corals, which enclose the sinking island to create a shallow, salt water lagoon. Different coral species in the same reef provide homes for a great variety of life.

Volcanic island   Coral

Coral reef

Lagoon

Life is by no means evenly distributed throughout the oceans, either vertically or horizontally. The great majority of marine creatures are concentrated in the upper few hundred meters, for the biological organization of life in the seas, as on land, depends on photosynthesis (the process by which plants use the Sun's energy to combine carbon dioxide and water to produce more complex compounds). This near-surface layer is the euphotic ("well-lighted") zone.

Some of the Sun's rays are reflected from the surface of the sea, and those that penetrate are scattered and absorbed as they pass through the water, so that even in the clearest oceanic water there is insufficient light to support photosynthesis at depths greater than about 100 m (330 ft). In turbid inshore regions, where the water is less clear, this near-surface layer may be reduced to a very few meters. So the large seaweeds that anchor themselves to the seabed are restricted to the small areas of the sea where the water is sufficiently shallow to allow them to photosynthesize. Of much greater importance over most of the oceans are the tiny floating plants of the phytoplankton, which live suspended in the sunlit surface layers.

Pastures of the sea

Phytoplankton, like all plant life, requires not only sunlight for survival but also adequate supplies of nutrient salts and chemical trace elements. River waters carry down considerable quantities of dissolved mineral salts and other matter, so that high levels of phytoplankton production may occur locally around major estuaries. But a far more important source of nutrient supply to the euphotic zone is the recycling of salts that have sunk into the deeper layers, locked up in the bodies of plants and animals or in their fecal pellets.

In those areas of the oceans that overlie the continental shelves (about six percent of the total), the depth is nowhere more than about 200 m (650 ft), and the nutrient-rich bottom water is fairly readily brought back to the surface by currents and the stirring effect of storms. This stirring can reach much greater depths in near-polar latitudes, where the "water column" is not layered by temperature but remains more or less uniformly cold from top to bottom. In the Antarctic, cold (and therefore heavy) surface water sinks and is replaced by nutrient-rich water that may surface from depths of 1,000 m (3,300 ft).

In subtropical and tropical regions of the open ocean, where the warm surface layer is only a few tens of meters deep, the temperature falls rapidly with depth. There is little exchange between deep and shallow layers, and the euphotic zone receives an adequate supply of nutrient salts only in certain areas. These occur between westward-flowing and eastward-flowing currents in each of the major oceans. The Earth's rotation causes these currents to diverge so as to create an upwelling of nutrient-rich water along their common boundaries.

Finally, in restricted coastal regions of the tropics and subtropics the local climatic conditions cause an offshore movement of surface water, which is again replaced by upwelling nutrient-rich deep water. The central oceanic regions, including the deep blue subtropical waters, are in effect the deserts of the sea.

Sea grazers and carnivores

The abundance of animals in the oceans closely follows that of the plants. But very few of the larger marine animals can feed directly on the phytoplankton because the individual plants are so small—often only a fraction of a millimeter across. Instead, the phytoplankton supports an amazingly diverse community of planktonic animals, which also spend their lives in mid-water and are swept along by the ocean currents. This community, the zooplankton, includes many different protozoans (single-celled animals), crustaceans, worms and molluscs, and also the juvenile stages of fishes and of many invertebrate animals that live as adults on the seabed. Most members of the zooplankton are very small and many of them graze on the phytoplankton. But some planktonic animals, particularly among the jellyfish and salps, may be a meter or more across and are voracious carnivores feeding on their planktonic neighbors. In turn, the zooplankton provides food for many of the active swimmers such as the fishes and baleen whales, while at the top of the food chain are larger carnivores including

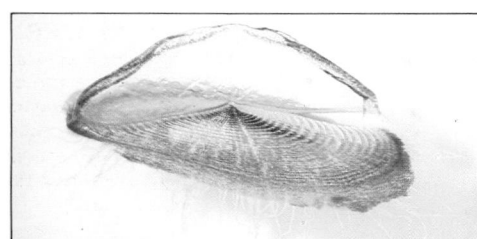

The by-the-wind sailor, *Velella,* is a so-called colonial animal, consisting of a whole collection of animals that function as a single individual. The gas-filled float of its body carries a vertical sail to catch the wind, and below dangle a group of modified polyps specialized for particular roles such as deterrence, reproduction, feeding and digesting.

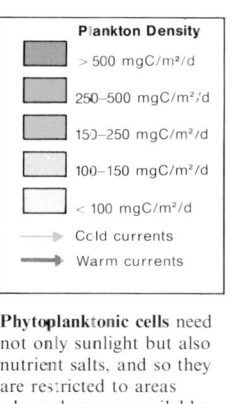

Plankton Density

	> 500 mgC/m²/d
	250–500 mgC/m²/d
	150–250 mgC/m²/d
	100–150 mgC/m²/d
	< 100 mgC/m²/d
→	Cold currents
→	Warm currents

Phytoplanktonic cells need not only sunlight but also nutrient salts, and so they are restricted to areas where these are available: coastal regions, high latitudes (particularly the Antarctic), narrow tongues extending across the tropical regions of the main ocean basins, and a number of subtropical upwelling regions.

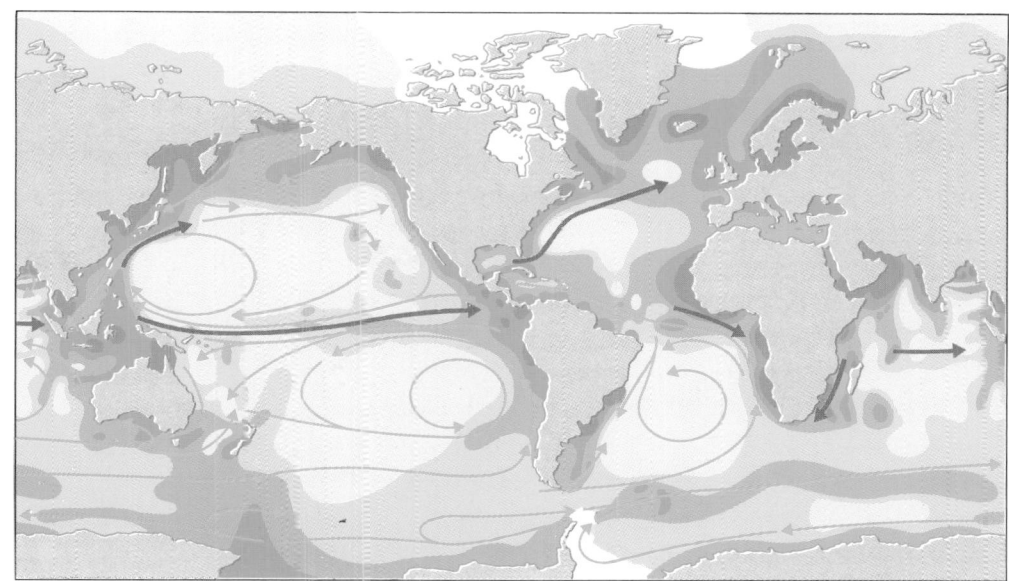

Zones of life (below) extend from the teeming euphotic ("well-lighted") layer to the sparsely populated bathypelagic ("deep-sea") depths, while benthic ("bottom") life occurs at all seabed levels. Phytoplankton (plant life) (1) dictates the pattern of the rest, flourishing where surface conditions allow nutrient salts to well up from lower depths. Herbivores such as minute zooplankton (2) provide food for a host of surface-layer life, which in turn feeds larger predators. Dead animals and fecal pellets fall to lower levels, where they sustain life, but in far smaller quantity.

1 Phytoplankton
2 Zooplankton
3 Blue whale *Balaenoptera musculus*
4 Herring *Clupea harengus*
5 Gray seal *Halichoerus grypus*
6 Bluefin tuna *Thunnus thynnus*
7 Bottlenosed dolphin *Tursiops truncatus*
8 Mackerel *Scomber scomber*
9 Common squid *Loligo* spp
10 White shark *Carcharodon carcharias*
11 Hatchet fish *Argyropelecus hemigymnus*
12 Giant squid *Architeuthis* spp
13 Sea anemone *Cerianthus orientalis*
14 Tripod fish *Benthosaurus grallator*
15 Scarlet shrimp *Notostomus longirostris*
16 Angler fish *Linophryne bicornis*
17 Brittle star *Ophiothrix fragilis*
18 Sea cucumber class Holothuroidea

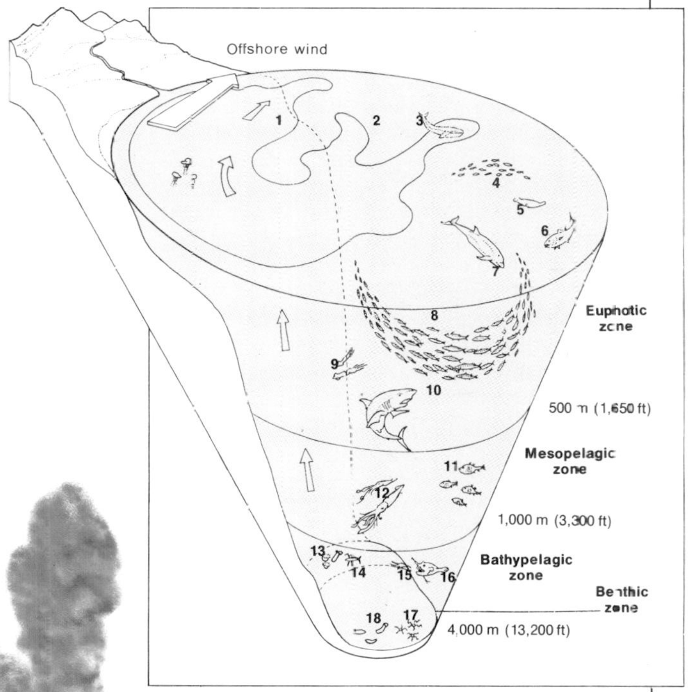

Bizarre life forms new to science live in the sunless depths, where plumes of hot mineral-rich water gush through deep-sea vents in the Earth's crust. These oases of life support huge, gutless tubeworms more than 1.5 m (5 ft) long, which appear to take food particles from the hot vents through blood-red tentacles. Other creatures include blind crabs and large white clams.

sharks, tuna-like fishes and toothed whales.

Beneath the euphotic zone, of course, there can be no herbivores at all, although some animals that spend the daylight hours in the deeper layers move upwards at night to feed in the plankton-rich surface waters. All of the permanent members of the deep-living communities are dependent for food upon material that sinks or is carried downwards from the euphotic zone. Many of them feed on dead animal remains and fecal material as it sinks through the water column or after it reaches the seabed. These detritus eaters in turn support the predatory carnivores that feed upon the detritivores or upon each other.

In shallow areas the food material that reaches the bottom supports complex communities, notably the rich and varied groups of invertebrates and fishes associated with coral reefs. In the deep sea, however, where the euphotic zone is separated from the seabed by several kilometers of water, much of the sinking material is recycled within the water column and relatively little reaches the bottom. Life on the deep-sea floor therefore becomes more and more sparse with increasing depth, but in recent years scientists have discovered that this community includes a surprising number of fishes, some many meters in length. So far man's knowledge of these deep-sea communities is relatively meager, but with our increasing use of the deep oceans we may need to know much more about the life in this environment.

Man and the Seawater Environments

For thousands of years man has used the oceans as a source of food and other materials, and as a repository for wastes. But only in the last 100 years have technological advances and fast-growing human populations had a significant effect, to a point where overfishing and pollution are becoming a cause for concern. Harvesting of krill and seaweeds may ease the pressure on traditional seafoods, but legal restrictions on dumping of wastes or on overfishing are notoriously hard to enforce.

Until about the middle of the nineteenth century the seas had always seemed to be a boundless source of food and of income for fishermen who were brave enough to face the elements with their relatively small sailing ships and primitive gear. But once fishing vessels began to be fitted with steam engines in the 1880s they became relatively independent of the weather, while improvements in the fishing gear itself, such as steam-powered winches in trawling and harpoon guns in whaling, made the whole business of fishing much more efficient.

At first these advances resulted in enormous increases in catches, but in many fisheries this was rapidly followed by a distressing fall in the catch per unit of effort—that is, it was becoming more and more difficult in successive years to catch the same amount of fish as before. In most fisheries the initial response to this situation was to increase the size and number of fishing vessels and to search for new fishing grounds. But as the fishing pressure on the stocks increased, with smaller fish being captured, often before they were able to reproduce, the catch per unit of effort frequently continued to fall.

In many cases attempts were made to counter the effects of overfishing by introducing regulations to control the mesh size of the nets, so allowing the small fish to escape; by establishing closed seasons or quotas of fish which might legitimately be taken from a particular fishing ground in any one year; or even, as in the case of the British herring fishery in the late 1970s, by imposing a complete ban on fishing. Moral questions also sometimes intervene, as in whaling operations, which, many conservationists believe, have driven some species close to extinction despite attempts to rationalize the fisheries.

Fisheries in decline
The North Sea trawl fishery, the first to be affected by the new technology in the nineteenth century, has been declining in terms of catch per unit of effort since the early decades of this century. Dramatic but short-lived improvements after the "closed seasons" of the two world wars proved that fishing pressure had a serious effect on stocks, but by the 1970s many North Sea fishing ports had become almost deserted. This decline put pressure on more distant fishing grounds used by European fishermen, and recent decades have been marked by a series of fishing disputes, with nations fighting for the continued existence of their fisheries despite clear evidence that there are not enough catchable fish to satisfy everyone.

A similar story of declining catches during the present century could be told of many of the old-established fisheries around the world, but at the same time the demand for fish in a protein-hungry world has increased. To satisfy this demand the total annual world catch increased by about seven percent from the end of World War II until the early 1970s, by this time reaching a figure of around 60–70 million tonnes. But this increase was achieved only by exploiting previously unfished stocks or new geographical areas. Such an increase cannot go on indefinitely, for we are rapidly running out of "new" areas and some of the new fisheries have already shown the same symptoms of overfishing as the older ones—and sometimes even more dramatically.

New foods from the sea
The indications are that the present total catch is close to the maximum that can be obtained from relatively conventional fisheries even with careful management, and that. to increase the total, or even to sustain it, we must look to completely new sources such as krill, the shrimp-like food of the whalebone whales.

Estimates of the sustainable annual catch of krill in the Antarctic range from about 50 to 500 million tonnes, that is up to about seven times as much as the current total from all other fisheries put together. Of course, the use of such an enormous quantity of small crustaceans would present considerable problems. Part of it might be converted into a protein-rich paste for human consumption, but much would be used indirectly as a feed for farm animals.

Many larger seaweeds are already cropped in several parts of the world, particularly in Japan, and are used not only for human food but also for animal food and in many industrial processes. About one million tonnes of seaweed are taken each year, but because seaweeds grow naturally only in relatively shallow areas of the oceans this figure could probably not be significantly increased using natural populations. However, seaweeds can be grown artificially on frames floating over deep water. Experiments suggest that, by enriching the surface layers through artificial upwelling of nutrient-rich deep water, each square kilometer of such a floating seaweed farm could produce enough food to feed 1,000–2,000 people, and enough energy and other products to satisfy the needs of a further 1,000. With an estimated 260 million sq km (100 million sq miles) of "arable" surface, the seas might thus support up to 10 times the present world population.

Polluted waters
Of course, the present century has seen an increase not only in what man takes out of the sea but also in the harmful substances that he throws into it. Not only oil but many other substances are dumped into the seas accidentally or intentionally, usually either in the discharged effluent from industrial plant or as a result of agricultural chemicals being leached into rivers and thence into the ocean. In many cases the amounts are very small compared with the amounts present in the oceans as a whole; the problem is that they are usually released, and accumulate, in restricted inshore areas near which we live and from which we obtain most of our sea-caught food.

Since the 1930s there have been both national and international attempts to control pollution by legislation, and since 1958 a series of United Nations conferences has sought agreement on many aspects of international maritime law, including pollution. Despite many prophecies of imminent doom, it does not seem that marine pollution yet poses any general threat to humanity. Nevertheless, with ever-increasing industrialization and the production of more and more toxic materials, including radioactive wastes, it is essential that we monitor the effects of man's activities on the ocean.

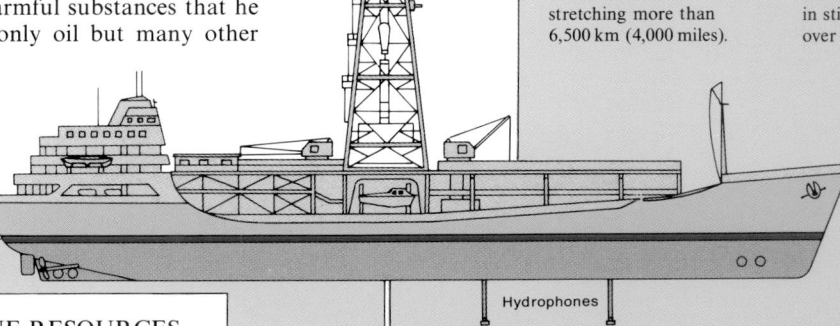

The ocean is home to the **Bajau** (above), the "sea gypsies" of southeastern Asia, who inhabit a tract of sea and islands stretching more than 6,500 km (4,000 miles).

Each group has its own clan pattern, blazoned on the sails of their *praus*. The Bajau may live on the open sea in clusters of boats, or in stilt-house villages built over estuaries.

Drilling derrick

Hydrophones

THE MARINE RESOURCES
Modern technology has enabled man to expand his age-old exploitation of the seas to the limit in some areas, and a need for the careful management of our marine resource is imperative. But in some fields, such as energy and the extraction of fresh water, the seas may yield inexhaustible riches.

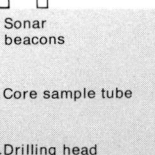

Sonar beacons

Core sample tube

Drilling head

The deep-sea drilling ship *Glomar Challenger* (above) plays an important role in surveying and prospecting the oceans. It can drill in water depths of 7,000 m (23,000 ft) and obtain core samples 1,200 m (4,000 ft) below the ocean bed. The ship is positioned over the drill hole through signals from a sonar beacon to hydrophones in the hull.

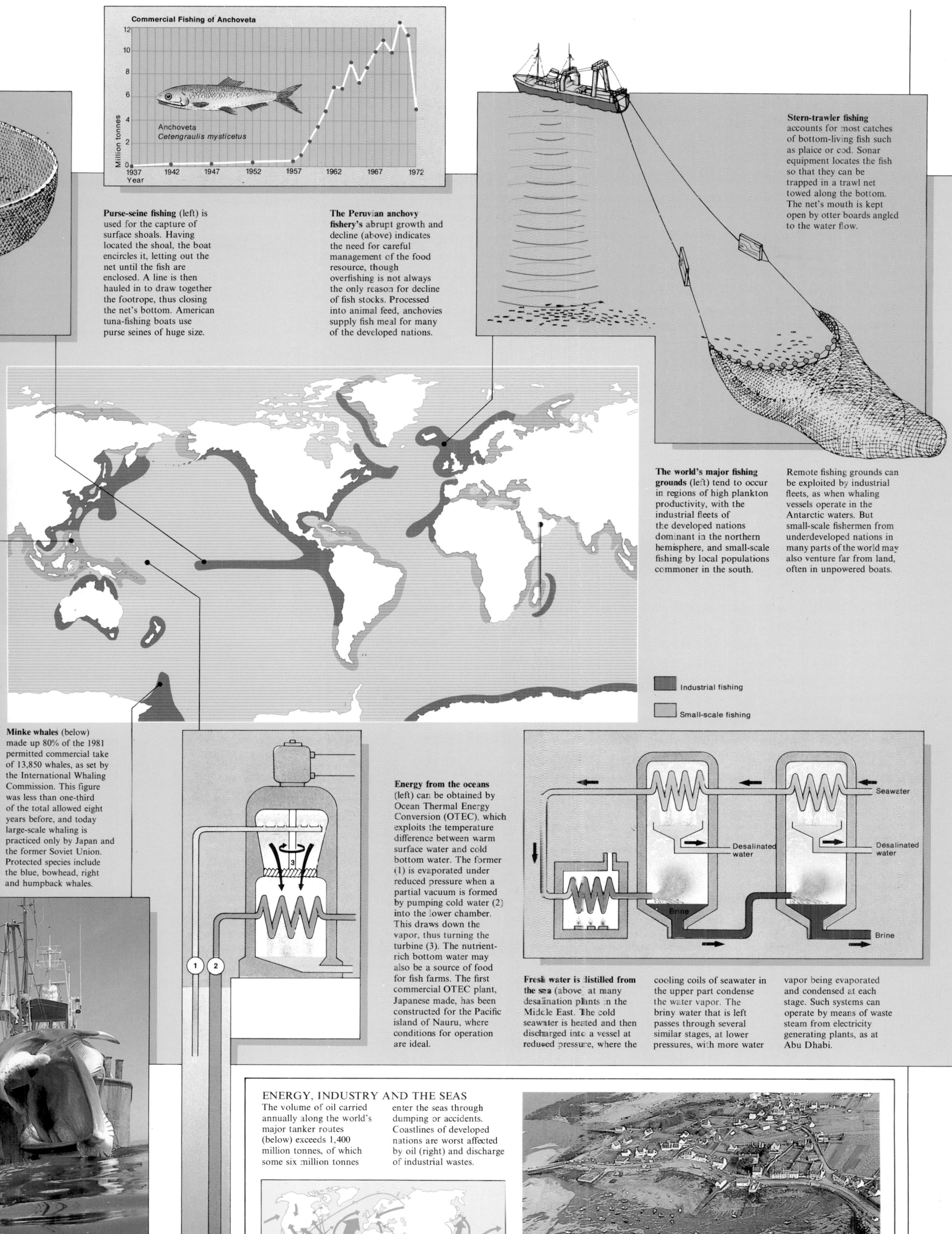

Commercial Fishing of Anchoveta

Anchoveta
Cetengraulis mysticetus

Purse-seine fishing (left) is used for the capture of surface shoals. Having located the shoal, the boat encircles it, letting out the net until the fish are enclosed. A line is then hauled in to draw together the footrope, thus closing the net's bottom. American tuna-fishing boats use purse seines of huge size.

The Peruvian anchovy fishery's abrupt growth and decline (above) indicates the need for careful management of the food resource, though overfishing is not always the only reason for decline of fish stocks. Processed into animal feed, anchovies supply fish meal for many of the developed nations.

Stern-trawler fishing accounts for most catches of bottom-living fish such as plaice or cod. Sonar equipment locates the fish so that they can be trapped in a trawl net towed along the bottom. The net's mouth is kept open by otter boards angled to the water flow.

The world's major fishing grounds (left) tend to occur in regions of high plankton productivity, with the industrial fleets of the developed nations dominant in the northern hemisphere, and small-scale fishing by local populations commoner in the south.

Remote fishing grounds can be exploited by industrial fleets, as when whaling vessels operate in the Antarctic waters. But small-scale fishermen from underdeveloped nations in many parts of the world may also venture far from land, often in unpowered boats.

■ Industrial fishing
□ Small-scale fishing

Minke whales (below) made up 80% of the 1981 permitted commercial take of 13,850 whales, as set by the International Whaling Commission. This figure was less than one-third of the total allowed eight years before, and today large-scale whaling is practiced only by Japan and the former Soviet Union. Protected species include the blue, bowhead, right and humpback whales.

Energy from the oceans (left) can be obtained by Ocean Thermal Energy Conversion (OTEC), which exploits the temperature difference between warm surface water and cold bottom water. The former (1) is evaporated under reduced pressure when a partial vacuum is formed (2) by pumping cold water (2) into the lower chamber. This draws down the vapor, thus turning the turbine (3). The nutrient-rich bottom water may also be a source of food for fish farms. The first commercial OTEC plant, Japanese made, has been constructed for the Pacific island of Nauru, where conditions for operation are ideal.

Fresh water is distilled from the sea (above at many desalination plants in the Middle East. The cold seawater is heated and then discharged into a vessel at reduced pressure, where the cooling coils of seawater in the upper part condense the water vapor. The briny water that is left passes through several similar stages, at lower pressures, with more water vapor being evaporated and condensed at each stage. Such systems can operate by means of waste steam from electricity generating plants, as at Abu Dhabi.

Seawater

Desalinated water

Desalinated water

Brine

Brine

ENERGY, INDUSTRY AND THE SEAS

The volume of oil carried annually along the world's major tanker routes (below) exceeds 1,400 million tonnes, of which some six million tonnes enter the seas through dumping or accidents. Coastlines of developed nations are worst affected by oil (right) and discharge of industrial wastes.

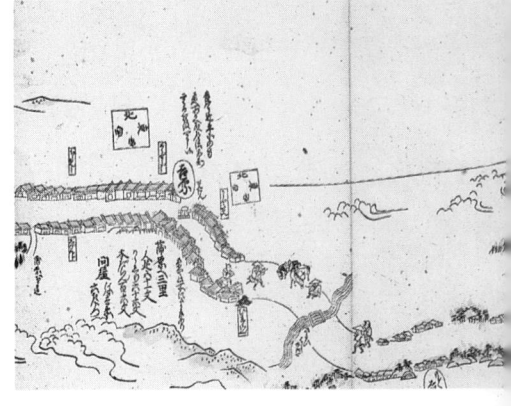

Part 5

UNDERSTANDING MAPS
What maps are and how they are made
New horizons and latest developments in maps and mapmaking
How to read the language of maps

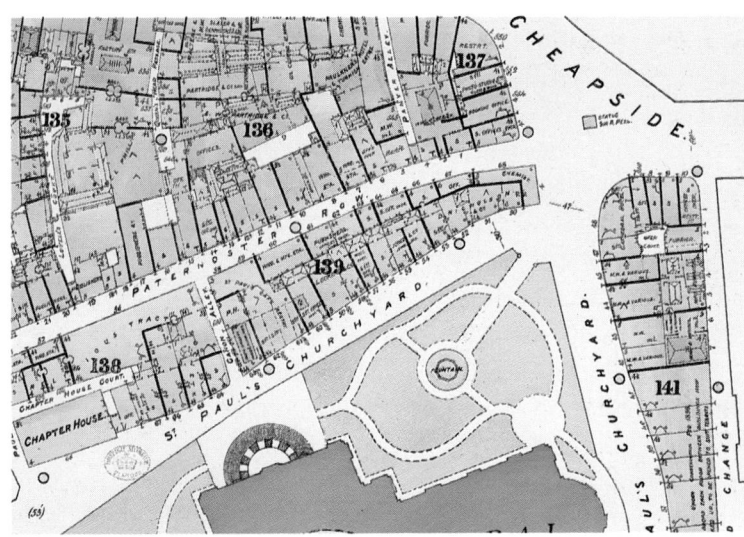

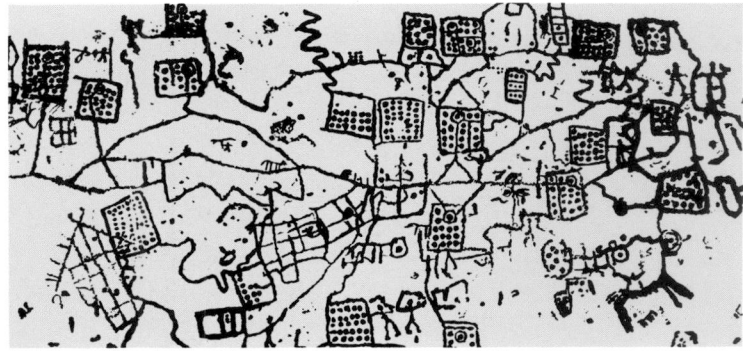

Maps defining territory and ownership are almost as old as the human territorial instinct itself. The rock-carving maps of the Val Camonica, Italy (above), dating from the second and first millennia BC, show stippled square fields, paths, river lines, houses, and even humans and animals. It is uncertain whether their purpose was legal, but the need to establish ownership is a basic function of many maps, as seen in a detail from Goad's 19th-century insurance map of London (left), where every occupation is recorded.

Elegant road maps with pictorial and geographical features have been produced by many different cultures. The woodcut map of the Tōkaidō (detail above), the great Japanese highway, 555 km (345 miles) long, between Edo (Tokyo) and Kyoto, was drawn as a panorama by the famous artist Moronobu in 1690. Its pictorial details do not prevent it being an accurate representation of the road's track. A Mexican map of the Tepetlaoztoc valley (right) drawn in 1583 marks roads with footprints between parallel lines, and hill ranges with wavy lines. Symbols in panels represent place-names.

America first appears as a separate continent (below) in an inset to Martin Waldseemüller's world map of 1507, with the two hemispheres facing each other. Presiding over the Old World is Claudius Ptolemy, the 2nd-century geographer whose remarkably scientific maps, copied and recopied over a thousand years, were revised and emended by Waldseemüller to show some of the results of Portuguese exploration. His New World counterpart is the Italian Amerigo Vespucci, one of the early explorers of the continent, after whom it was named. This is the first map to show the Pacific (not yet named) as an ocean between America and Asia. The west coast of South America, still to be explored by Europeans, seems to be inspired guesswork. The island between the landmasses is Cipango (Japan) known from Marco Polo.

The earliest surviving Chinese globe (above) was made in 1623 by two Jesuit missionaries, probably for the emperor of China. The long legend in Chinese expresses terms and ideas derived from early Chinese cosmology. It describes the Earth as "floating in the Heavens like the yolk of an egg . . . with all objects having mass tending toward its center"—one of the first known references to gravity.

High-altitude photography (left) allows accurate updating of topographic maps (right), while data gathering by satellites (above) expands the range. Landsat satellites carry electronic remote-sensing equipment that detects the energy emitted by surface materials and translates it into images. Healthy plants may show as bright red, sparse vegetation as pink, barren lands as light gray, and urban areas as green or dark gray. The folded shape of the Appalachians (1) is clearly seen; the Canada–US border (2) is revealed by land-use patterns; silt from the Mississippi (3) builds up the delta. Sudan irrigation (4) shows up as brilliant red.

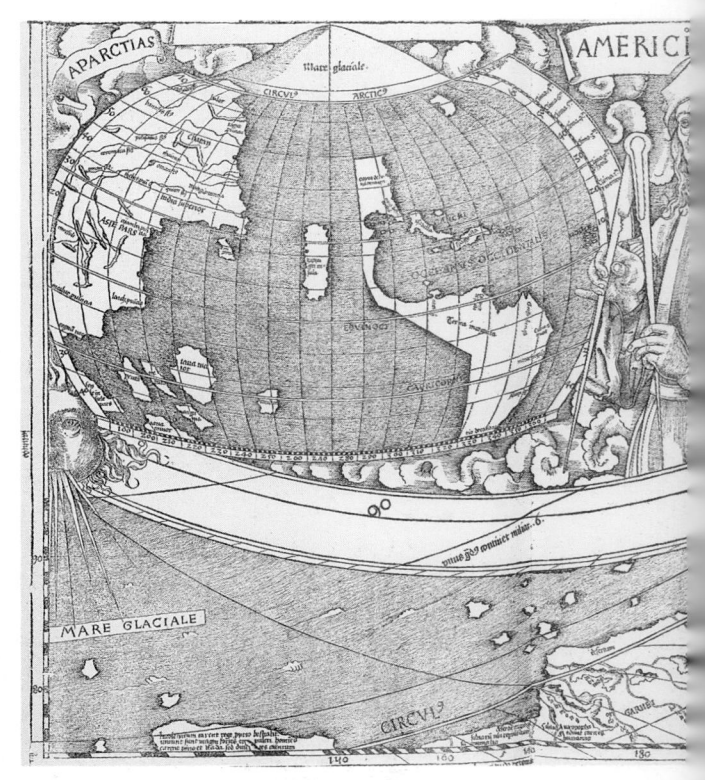

Mapping, Old and New

Mapmaking must have its origins in the earliest ages of human history, since people of preliterate as well as literate cultures possess an innate skill in map drawing. This innate capacity is further indicated by the ease with which almost anyone can sketch in the sand or on paper simple directions for showing the way. But maps may also define territory and express man's idea of the world in graphic representation. Today, modern technology has vastly extended the scope of cartography.

Many non-European cultures developed ingenious route-map techniques: the North American Indians, for example, made sketch maps of routes on birch bark. These were diagrammatic maps in which directions and distances were not accurate but relationships were true, as in New York Subway or London Underground maps. The people of the Marshall Islands in the western Pacific made route maps over the seas, depicting the direction of the main seasonal wave swells in relation to the islands.

Although maps of routes are the simplest type of map in concept, they developed complex forms as cartography progressed. A road map of the whole Roman Empire, drawn about AD 280, survives today in a thirteenth-century copy known as the Peutinger Table. Hernando Cortes, the Spanish conqueror, made his way across Mexico in the 1520s with the help of pre-conquest Mexican maps painted on cloth. These showed roads with double lines or colored bands marked with footprints. Another type of map is the strip map depicting a single road along its entire length. Pictorial maps of the Tōkaidō highway from Edo to Kyoto in Japan, made from a survey of 1651, were popular in the Edo period of Japanese history.

Nautical charts evolved as a special type of direction-finding map to meet the needs of seamen. Those of the late Middle Ages came to be known as "portolan" charts, from the word "portolani," or sailing directions. They showed the sea and adjacent coasts superimposed on a network of radiating compass lines.

Territorial maps

Another basic type of map derives from man's sense of territorial possession. The earliest example of a "cadastral" plan (a map showing land parcels and property boundaries) appears to be that preserved as rock carvings at Bedolina in Val Camonica in northern Italy. However, in the ancient civilizations of Mesopotamia and Egypt, land surveying had become an established profession by 2000 BC. An idea of what Egyptian surveyors' plans of 1000 BC were like can be seen from the "Fields of the Dead" representing the Egyptians' idea of life after death. These show plots of land surrounded by water and intersected by canals. The Romans used cadastral surveys to determine land ownership and assess tax liability.

Another form of map showing territorial demarcations is the map of administrative units. The Chinese in the thirteenth century AD were making official district maps to help in the organization of grain supplies and the collection of taxes. Many of their gazetteers (*fang chih*), written in the form of local geographies and

histories from the eleventh century onward, were illustrated with maps. Political maps showing the boundaries of states were increasingly significant in European cartography from the sixteenth century onward.

A third major class of map is the general or topographical map expressing man's perception of the world, its regions and its place in the universe. A Babylonian world map of the seventh century BC is drawn on a clay tablet and shows the Earth as a circular disc surrounded by the Earthly Ocean. With the ancient Greeks, geography developed on scientific principles. The treatise on mapmaking by Claudius Ptolemy (AD 87–150), later known as the *Geographia*, was the most famous cartographic text of the period. It influenced the Arabic geographers of the Middle Ages, notably Muhammad Ibn Muhammad, Al-Idrisi (1099–1164), and with the revival of Ptolemy in fifteenth-century Europe became one of the major works of the Renaissance. Published, with engraved maps, at Bologna in 1477, the *Geographic* ranks as the first printed atlas in the western world. The invention of techniques of engraving in wood and copper facilitated a wide diffusion of geographical knowledge through the map-publishing trade. The first atlas made up of modern maps to a uniform design was Abraham Ortelius's *Theatrum Orbis Terrarum* published at Antwerp in 1570. From 1492, when Martin Behaim made his "Erdapfel" at Nürnberg, globes also became popular, and globemakers vied with each other to make larger and more elaborate ones to keep pace with the growth of knowledge about the world.

Over the last two hundred years cartography has made rapid and remarkable advances. Observatories built in Paris in 1671 and at Greenwich in 1675 enabled the location of places to be established more exactly with the use of astronomical tables. Improvements in surveying instruments facilitated more accurate and rapid land survey. France was the pioneer in establishing (from 1679 onward) a national survey on a geometrical basis of triangulation. By the end of the eighteenth century national surveys on small and medium scales had been begun by most European countries. In the United States the Geological Survey was set up in 1879 to undertake the topographical and geological mapping of the country.

Mapping today

Since World War II cartographic techniques have undergone a revolution. The use of air survey and photogrammetry has made it possible to map most of the Earth's surface. Electronic distance measurement by laser or light beams in surveying, and digital computers in mapping, are among the most recent advances in methods. Mosaics or air photography are used to produce orthophoto maps which can supplement or substitute for the conventional topographic map. Artificial satellites and manned space craft make it possible to provide a world-wide framework of geodetic networks.

Earth Resource Technology Satellites (ERTS) imagery has made it possible to map mountain ranges in Africa and features on the surface of Antarctica that were hitherto unknown. The imagery is made available by means of remote-sensing instruments, carried by the satellites, that are sensitive to invisible portions of the electromagnetic spectrum—longer and shorter wavelengths than can be sensed by the human eye. Remote-sensing instruments usually work in the infrared bands. They can also pick up the energy emitted by all types of surface material—rocks, soils, vegetation, water and man-made structures—and produce photographs or images from it.

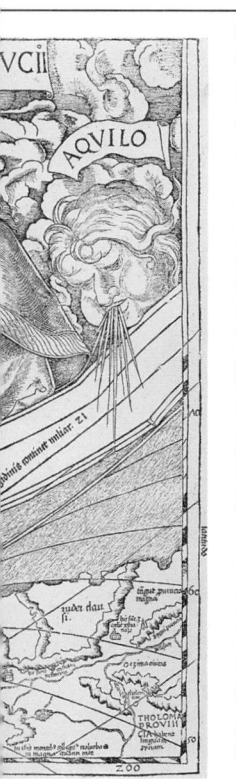

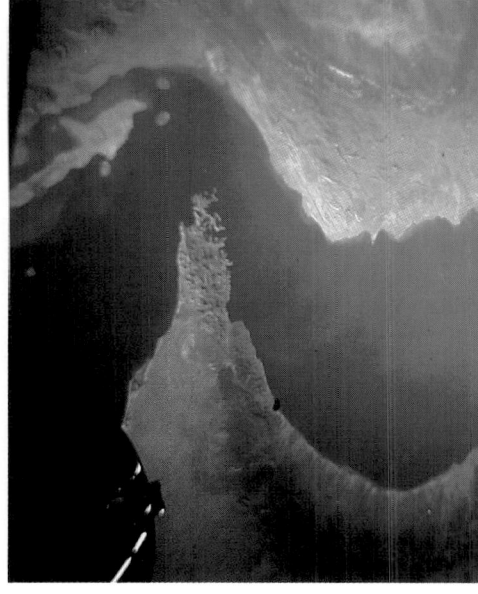

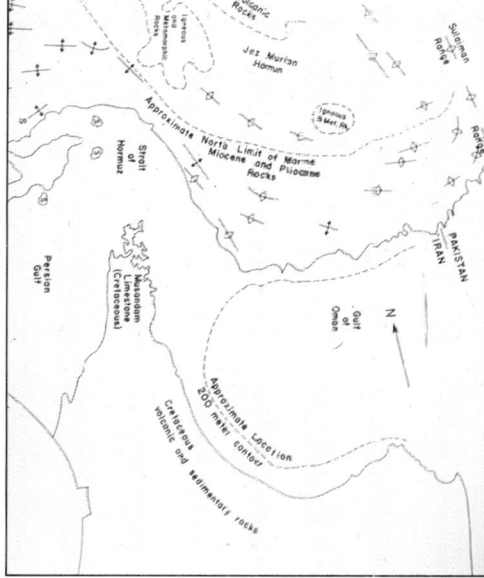

Space technology helps cartographers to map even interior details of the planet: its geology and mineral wealth. A photo (below) taken from Gemini 12 at an altitude of 272 km (168 miles) forms the basis of a geologic sketch map of SW Asia (below right), showing the oil-rich area around the region between the Persian Gulf and the Gulf of Oman. The symbol S on the map indicates salt plugs; diamonds show fold trends; double-headed arrows anticlines.

The Language of Maps

Mapmakers for more than 4,000 years have tried to find the best way to represent the shape and features of the three-dimensional Earth on two-dimensional paper, parchment and cloth. The measurement of distance and direction is a basic requirement for accurate surveys, but until about 1800 theoretical understanding of the method was well in advance of the technical equipment available. Today the use of lasers and light beams sometimes takes the place of direct measurement on the ground.

A reference system must be used to show distance and direction correctly in the construction of maps. The simplest type is the rectangular or square grid. The Chinese mapmaker Pei Xin made a map with a grid in about AD 270, and this system remained in continuous use in China until modern times. The Roman system of centuriation, a form of division of public lands on a square or rectangular basis, was also a "coordinate" system starting from a point of origin at the intersection of two perpendicular axes. Roman surveyors' maps, dating from the first century AD, are the earliest known European maps based on a grid system.

Latitude and longitude
Makers of small-scale regional maps and of world maps in early times also had to take account of the fact that the Earth is a sphere. The Greeks derived from the Babylonians the idea of dividing a circle into 360 degrees. In the second century BC the Greek geographer Eratosthenes (c. 276–194 BC) was the first to calculate the circumference of the globe and was reported to have made a world map based on the concept of the Earth's sphericity. From this the Greeks went on to develop the system of spherical coordinates which remains in use today. The poles at each end of the Earth's axis provide reference points for the Earth in its rotation in relation to the celestial sphere. Parallel circles around the Earth are degrees of latitude and express the idea of distance north or south of the Equator. Lines of longitude running north and south through the poles express east–west distances. One meridian is chosen as the meridian of origin, known as the prime meridian.

Whereas latitude from early times could be observed from the height of the Sun or (in the northern hemisphere) from the position of the Pole Star at night, accurate observations of longitude were not possible until the middle of the eighteenth century, when the chronometer was invented and more accurate astronomical tables were provided. In 1884 most countries agreed, at an international conference in Washington DC, to adopt the prime meridian through the Royal Greenwich Observatory in England and to calculate longitude to 180 degrees east and west of Greenwich.

Projection and distortion
The mathematical system by which the spherical surface of the Earth is transferred to the plane surface of a map is called a map projection. The Greek geographer Ptolemy gave instructions in his geographical treatise of AD 150 for the construction of two projections. When the *Geographia* was revised in Europe in the fifteenth century, and navigators began sailing across the oceans, mapmakers devised new projections more appropriate to the expanding geographical knowledge of the world. The Dutch geographer Gerard Mercator invented the projection named after him, applying it to his world chart of 1569. This cylindrical projection, in which all points are at true compass courses from each other, was of great benefit to navigators and is still one of the most commonly used projections. Another advance was made when Johann Heinrich Lambert of Alsace (1728–1777) invented the azimuthal equal-area projection, in which the sizes of all areas are represented on the projection in correct proportion to one another, and the conformal projection, in which at any point on the map the scale is constant in all directions.

Since all projections involve deformation of the geometry of the globe, the cartographer has to choose the one that best suits the purpose of his map. "Conformal" or "orthomorphic" projections, in which angular relations (or shape) are preserved, are widely used for the construction of topographical maps. "Equivalent" or "equal-area" projections retain relative sizes and are particularly useful for general reference maps displaying economic, historical, political and other geographical phenomena.

Since the mid-fifteenth century, European mapmakers have generally arranged their maps with north at the top of the sheet. Earlier maps, however, were not standardized in this way. The circular world maps of the Middle Ages were orientated with east at the top, because this was where the terrestrial paradise was traditionally sited. Indeed, the word "orientation" originally meant the arrangement of something so as to face east.

Map scale
Scale is another basic property of a map. The scale of a map is the ratio of the distance on the map to the actual distance represented. Whereas the Babylonians, Egyptians, Greeks and Romans drew surveys to scale, in medieval Europe mapmakers used customary methods of estimating. The earliest known local map since Roman times which is drawn to scale (it displays a scale bar) is a plan of Vienna, 1422.

Projection, grid, orientation and scale form the framework of a map. The language of maps in concept and content is much more complex. To represent the surface of the Earth on a map, the cartographer must select and generalize from a vast quantity of material, using symbols and conventional signs as codes.

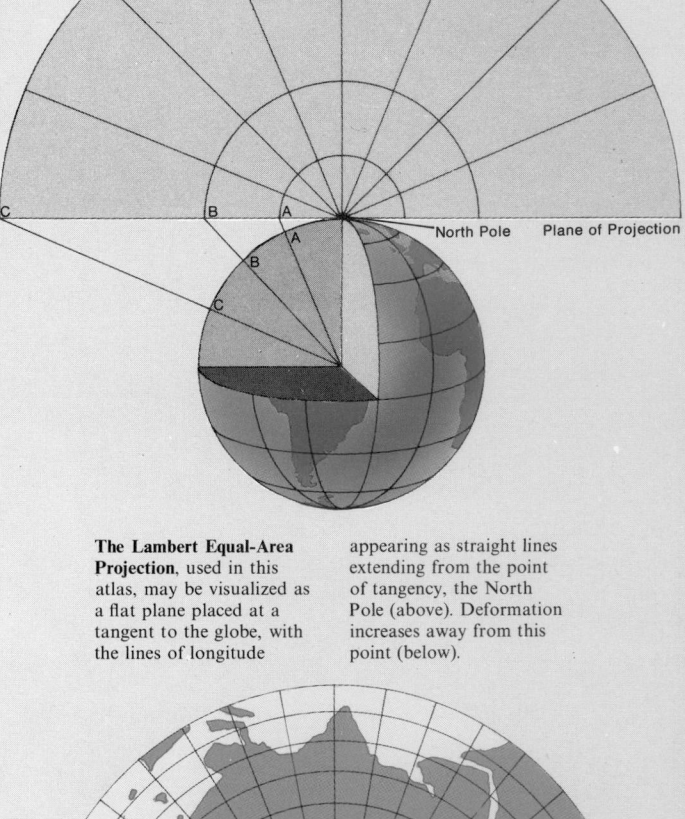

MAP PROJECTIONS

The Lambert Equal-Area Projection, used in this atlas, may be visualized as a flat plane placed at a tangent to the globe, with the lines of longitude appearing as straight lines extending from the point of tangency, the North Pole (above). Deformation increases away from this point (below).

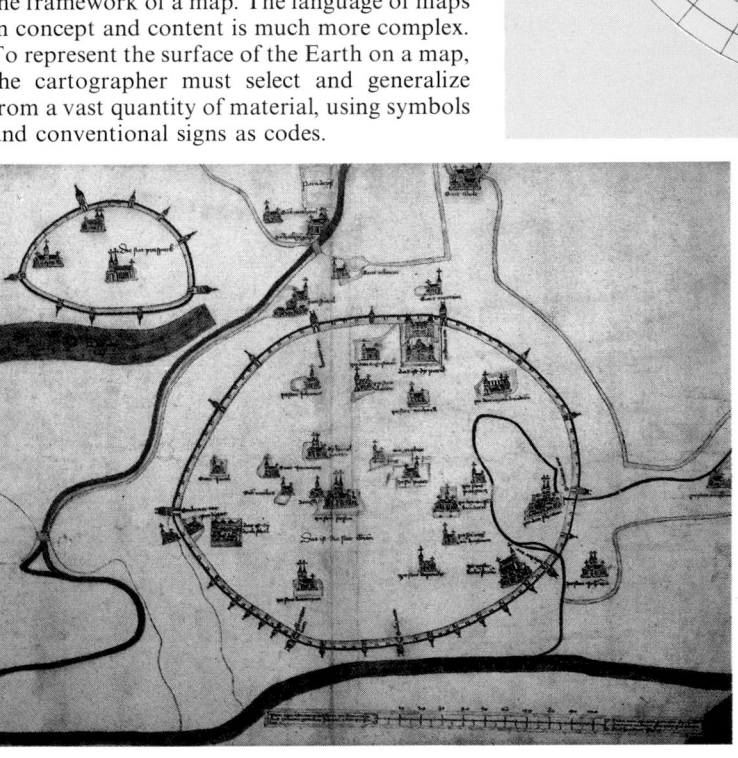

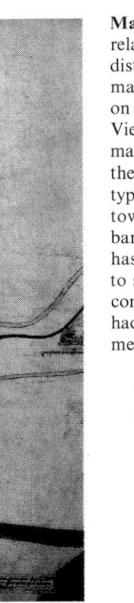

Map scales express the relationship between a distance measured on the map and the true distance on the ground. A plan of Vienna (left), originally made in 1422, is drawn in the bird's-eye-view style typical of early medieval town plans. But the scale bar at its foot shows that it has been explicitly drawn to scale, indicating that the concept of a uniform scale had been grasped in medieval Europe.

Direction and distance are concepts used in the relative location of two or more points (below). These concepts are organized according to a general frame of reference, with direction following the grid system of coordinates. Thus places shown in (A) can be precisely located in terms of longitude and of latitude (B), with the degrees further subdivided into one-sixtieths of minutes.

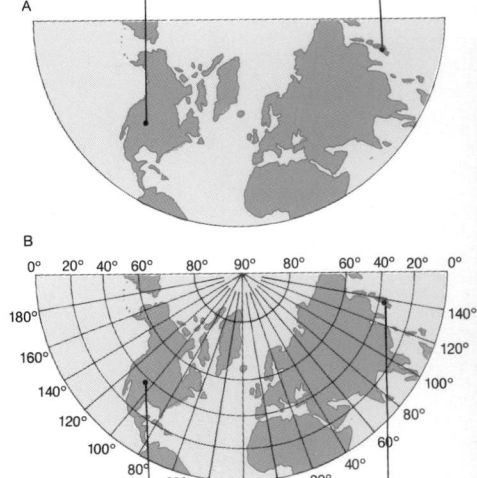

Superimposed on the globe (left), lines of latitude (A) and longitude (B) allow every place to be exactly located in terms of a coordinate system (C). The parallels of latitude measure distance from 0° to 90° north and south of the Equator. The meridians of longitude measure distance from 0° to 180° east and west of a "prime meridian" at Greenwich.

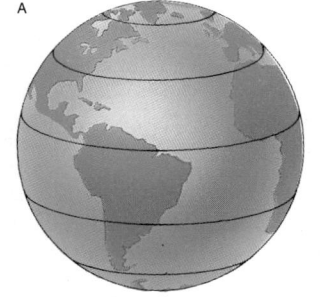

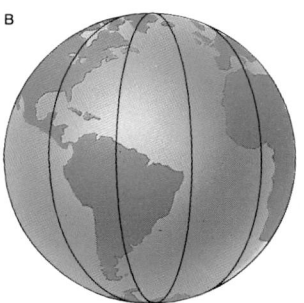

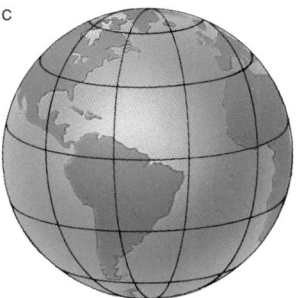

The Hammer Projection
(far right), developed from the Lambert Projection of one hemisphere (right), is designed to show the whole world in a single view, and is used in this atlas in a version modified by Wagner and known as the Hammer-Wagner Projection. The Earth appears as an ellipse because the lines of longitude are plotted at twice their horizontal distance from the center line, and numbered at twice their previous values. The central meridian is half the length of the Equator.

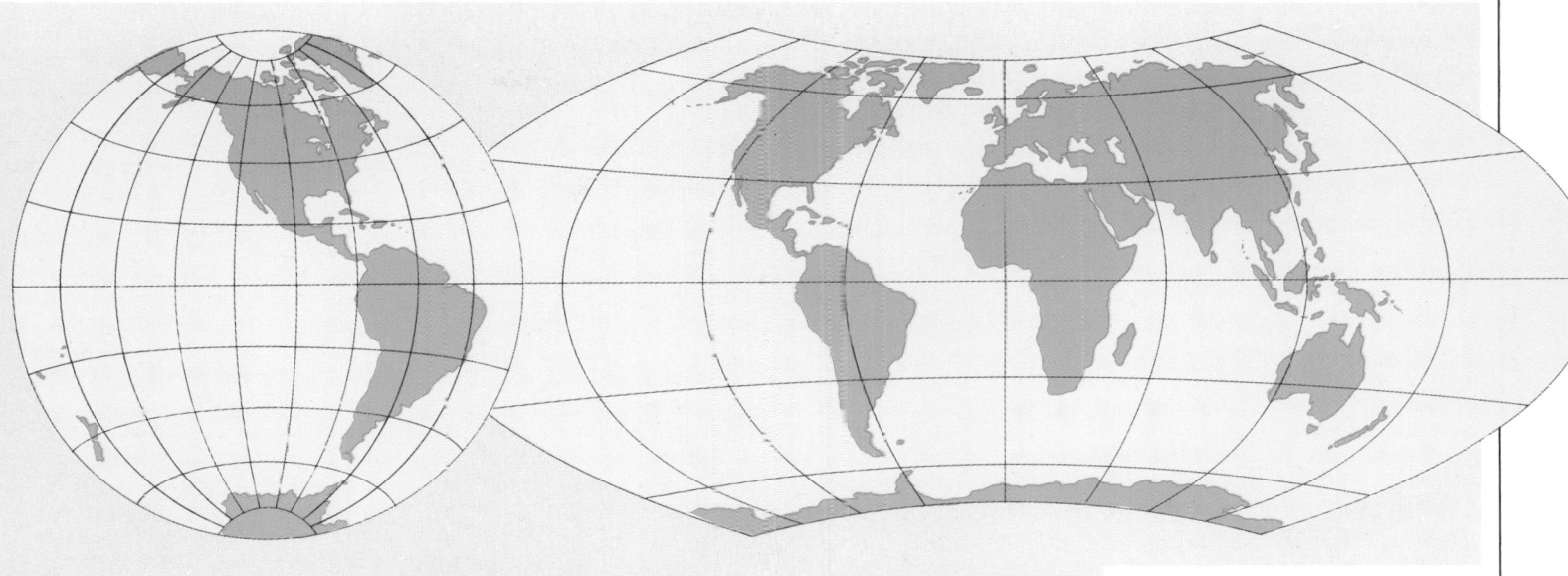

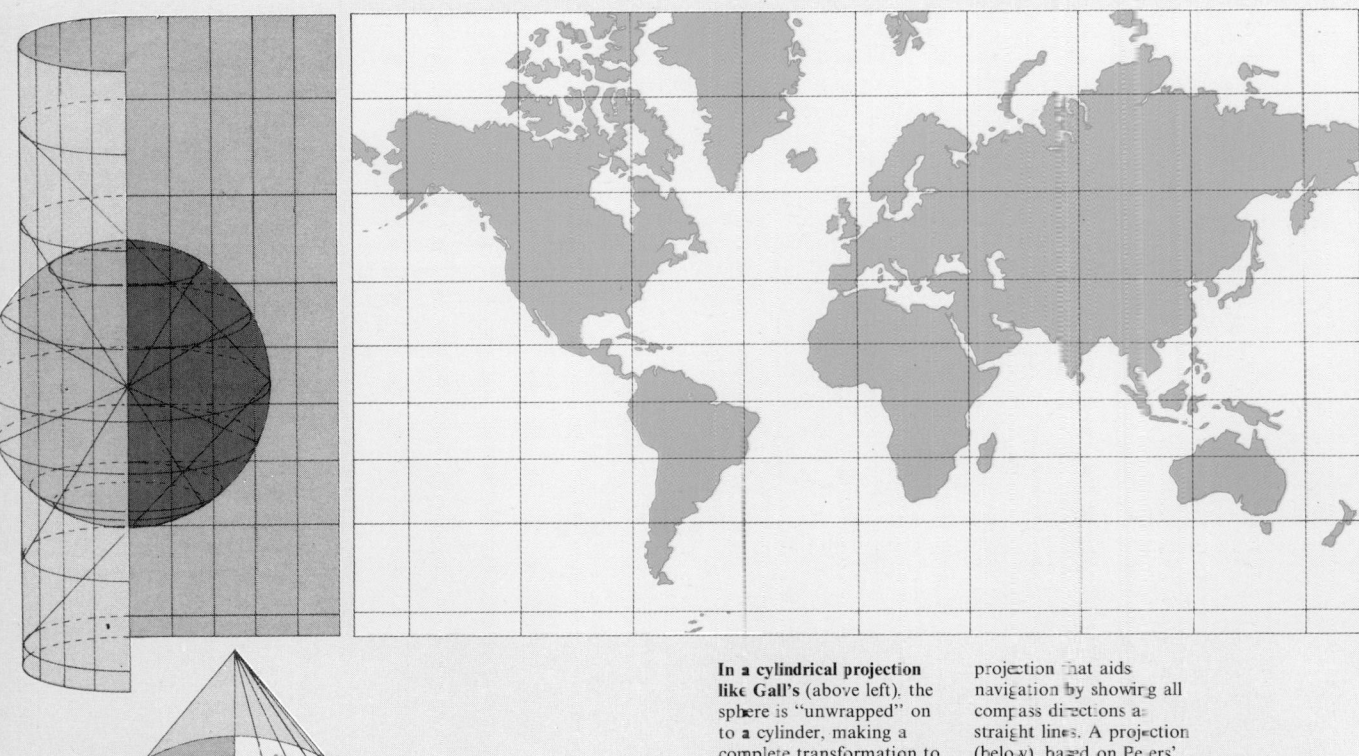

Photogrammetric plotting instruments (above) are now used in the preparation of large-scale accurate topographic maps. These are sophisticated machines that provide very precise measurements, plotting the map data in orthogonal projection.

In a cylindrical projection like Gall's (above left), the sphere is "unwrapped" on to a cylinder, making a complete transformation to a flat surface. Mercator's Projection (above), devised in 1569, is a cylindrical projection that aids navigation by showing all compass directions as straight lines. A projection (below), based on Peters', distorts shape to show land surface area ratios, emphasizing the Third World.

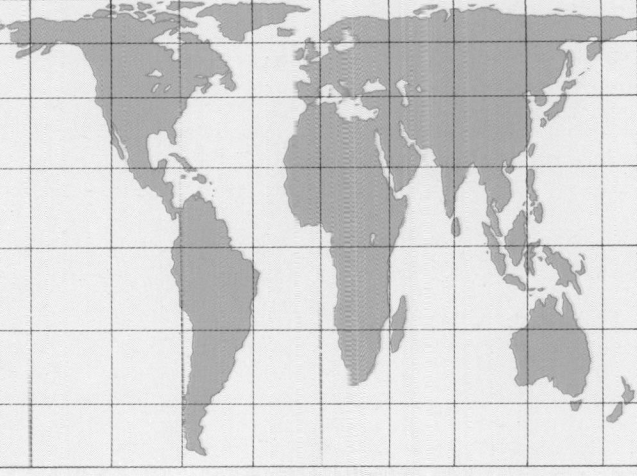

Delisle's Conic Projection
(right), used in this atlas, intersects the globe at two points (above). Distortion is least at the parallels where the cone "touches" the globe, increasing with distance from them. Thus it is good for mid-latitudes.

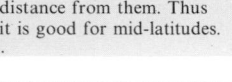

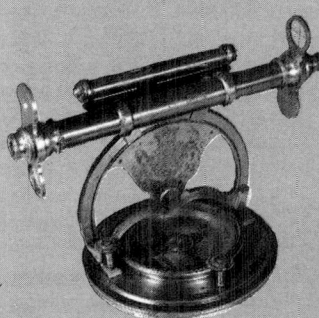

The theodolite (above), a basic surveying instrument dating back to the 16th century, can measure angles and directions horizontally and vertically. A swivel telescope with cross-hairs inside it permits accurate alignment, and it may be used in the field.

EARTH MEASUREMENT THROUGH THE AGES

Surveying—the technique of making accurate measurements of the Earth's surface—is as old as civilization and has been an essential element in mankind's development of his environment. The need to establish land boundaries arose at least 3,500 years ago in the fertile valleys of the Nile, Tigris and Euphrates rivers. Man's urge to explore and to describe the world also led to the development of instruments determining position, distance and direction. The astrolabe, sometimes called the world's oldest scientific instrument (right), may date to the 3rd century BC. Today's techniques make increasing use of computers.

An Egyptian wall painting (left) from the middle of the second millennium BC shows what appears to be the measurement of a grain field by means of a rope with knots at regular intervals on its length.

The astrolabe (right), used in classical times to observe the positions of celestial bodies, became a navigational instrument in the Middle Ages, when it was developed to permit establishment of latitude.

How to Use Maps

Today maps play a role more important than ever before in increasing our knowledge of the Earth, its regions and peoples. How maps communicate knowledge is now a subject of scientific study. The process comprises the collection and mapping of the data and the reading of the map. In this final stage the map user is all important. Through him the map is transformed into an image in the mind, and the effectiveness of the map depends on the reader being able to understand it.

The cartographer's map has to convey an objective picture of reality. To compile the map the cartographer selects and generalizes information, taking into account the purpose of his map. If he is making a topographical reference map, he has to reduce the three-dimensional landforms of the Earth on to the flat surface of the map. He adds cultural detail such as towns, roads and railroads, and features not apparent to the eye, such as administrative boundaries. On the topographical base map he adds appropriate place-names, using typefaces which reflect their class and significance. All this requires the classification of phenomena, with emphasis to direct the reader's attention.

Themes and symbolization
The cartographer who seeks not merely to represent visible features but to convey geographical ideas about specific phenomena uses the techniques of thematic cartography, where the emphasis is on one or two elements, or themes. Maps today provide one of the most effective means of communicating many kinds of data and ideas relating to the world and its peoples. Their extensive use makes them an important force in education, planning, recreation and in many other human affairs.

The map is designed in code, with symbols to represent features, and a legend, or key, to explain them. There are three types of symbol: point, line and area. Point symbols usually denote places, which may be distinguished into classes by the shape, color and size of the symbol. Line symbols express connections, such as roads or traffic flow, and they may also define and distinguish areas. Area symbols in which variations of color are often combined with patterns of lines or dots are used to depict spatial phenomena, such as types of soil, vegetation and density of population.

How much detail can be shown on a map will depend on its scale, which controls the process of generalization. Scale expresses the relationship of the distance on the map to the distance on the Earth, with the distance on the map always given as the unit 1. It is denoted in various ways: as a representative fraction such as 1:1,000,000; as a written statement; or by means of a graph or bar. Some map scales have become widely used and are generally familiar to map users. The scale 1:25,000 is ideal for walkers and relief can be shown in detail. That of 1:50,000 is a typical medium scale for national surveys. The publication of an international map of the world on a scale of one to

one million (1:1,000,000) has been in progress since 1909. On this scale 1 mm represents 1 km on the ground. The regional maps of countries in this atlas are drawn on scales of 1:6,000,000, 1:3,000,000 and 1:1,500,000; those of the continents are at 1:30,000,000 and 1:15,000,000. The Map Section index maps show the arrangement.

Terrain depiction
Since the early days of map making in ancient Chinese and classical Greek and Roman civilizations, map makers have been concerned to show the configuration of the land. For many centuries they symbolized mountains and hills by pictorial features often looking like caterpillars or sugar loaves. As topographical mapping developed in Europe from the seventeenth century onward, new techniques were devised to improve the visual impression of the features and to depict them accurately in terms of height and location. The system of hachuring (shading with fine parallel or crossed lines), first used in 1674, gives a good idea of relief but not of height. The use of contours, which became general from the nineteenth century onward, is more exact in representing actual elevation, but for many regions, especially those of irregular relief, the appearance of the land is lost.

The addition of hypsometric tints (tints between contours which show elevation) helps clarify the elevation. Applying shadows to the form of the land through the process called hill shading or relief shading creates a visual impression of the configuration of the land surface. Hypsometric tints combined with hill shading gives both elevation information and surface form of the area being depicted, leading to an almost three-dimensional effect.

Maps are classed (right) as either general (A) or thematic (B,C). The purpose of a general reference map is to provide locational information, showing how the positions of various geographical phenomena relate to each other. Thematic maps concentrate on a particular type of information, or theme, such as the distribution of people (B) or rainfall (C), and are generally based on statistical data.

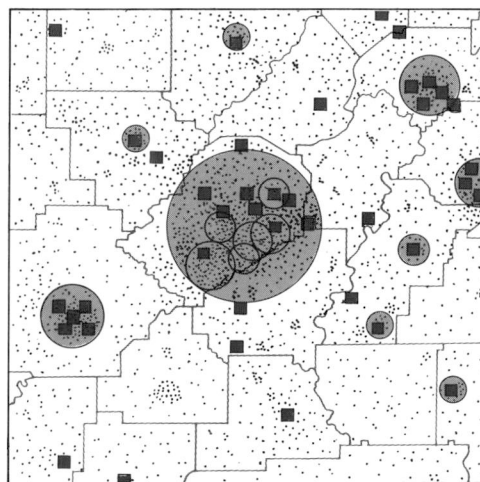

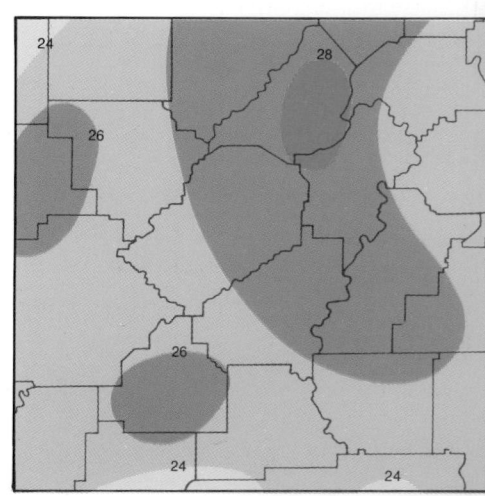

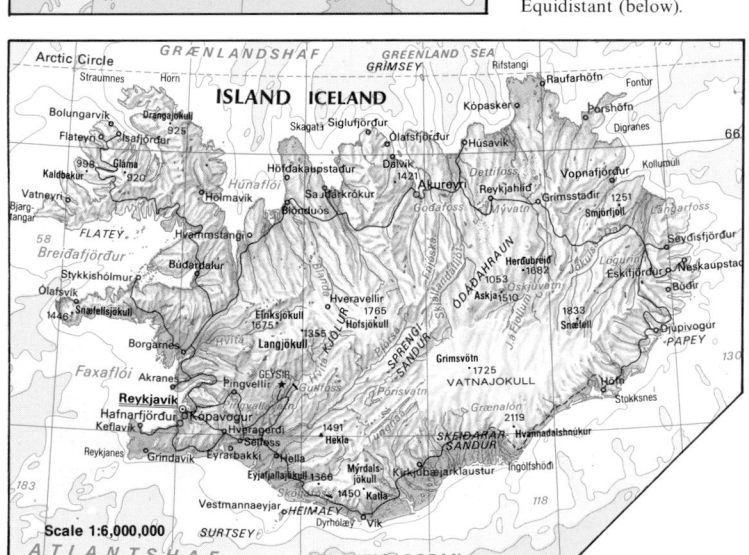

The ratio between a map's dimensions and those of the physical world is defined by the map scale (left and below), with the map distance always given as the unit 1. The larger the reduction, the smaller the scale, so that a scale of 1:6,000,000—1 mm (.04 in) to 6 km (3.74 miles)—is twice that of 1:12,000,000 (.04 in to 7.5 miles). The size of the scale reflects the amount of detail that needs to be shown. The projections are the Lambert Azimuthal Equal-Area (left) and Delisle Conic Equidistant (below).

Scale 1:12,000,000

Scale 1:6,000,000

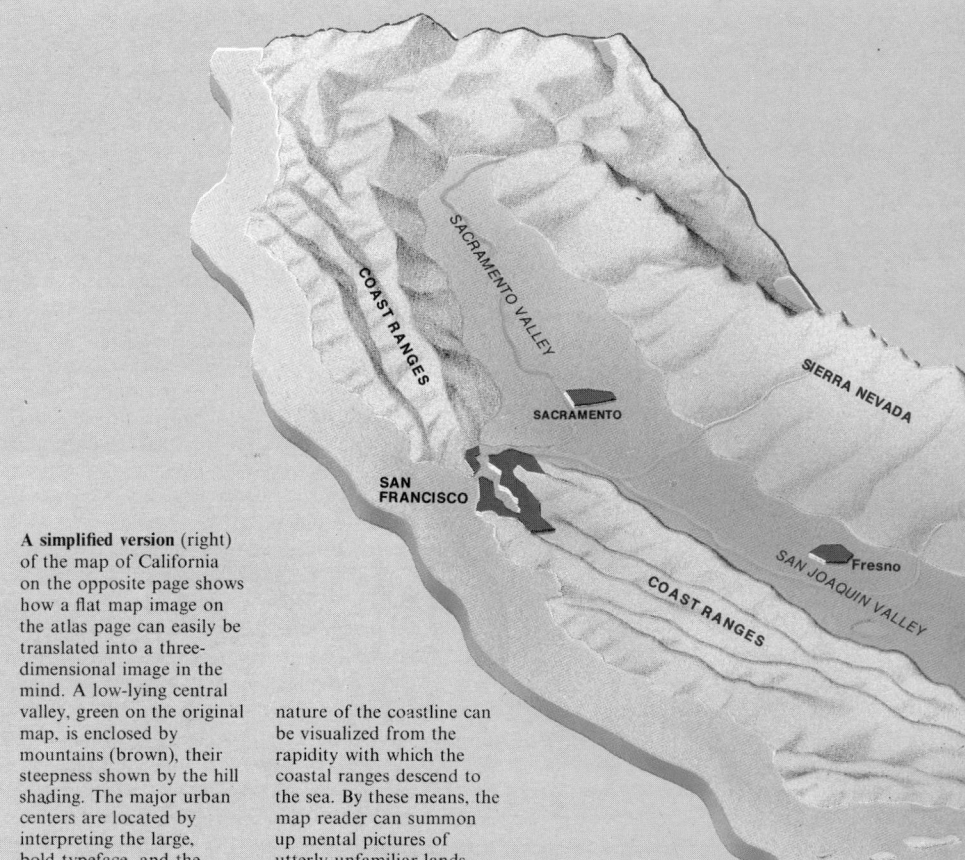

A simplified version (right) of the map of California on the opposite page shows how a flat map image on the atlas page can easily be translated into a three-dimensional image in the mind. A low-lying central valley, green on the original map, is enclosed by mountains (brown), their steepness shown by the hill shading. The major urban centers are located by interpreting the large, bold typeface, and the nature of the coastline can be visualized from the rapidity with which the coastal ranges descend to the sea. By these means, the map reader can summon up mental pictures of utterly unfamiliar lands.

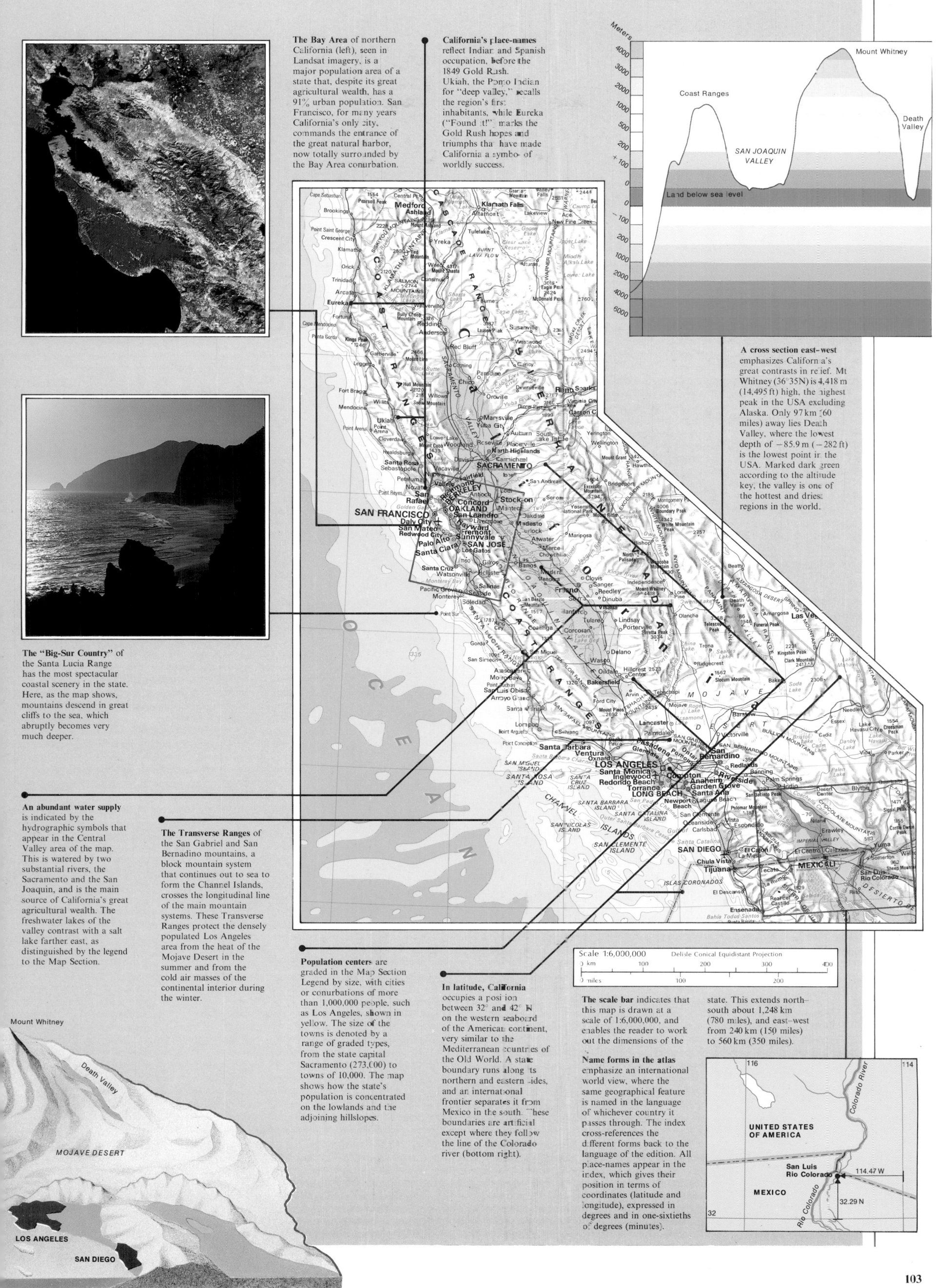

The Bay Area of northern California (left), seen in Landsat imagery, is a major population area of a state that, despite its great agricultural wealth, has a 91% urban population. San Francisco, for many years California's only city, commands the entrance of the great natural harbor, now totally surrounded by the Bay Area conurbation.

California's place-names reflect Indian and Spanish occupation, before the 1849 Gold Rush. Ukiah, the Pomo Indian for "deep valley," recalls the region's first inhabitants, while Eureka ("Found it!") marks the Gold Rush hopes and triumphs that have made California a symbol of worldly success.

A cross section east–west emphasizes California's great contrasts in relief. Mt Whitney (36°35N) is 4,418 m (14,495 ft) high, the highest peak in the USA excluding Alaska. Only 97 km (60 miles) away lies Death Valley, where the lowest depth of −85.9 m (−282 ft) is the lowest point in the USA. Marked dark green according to the altitude key, the valley is one of the hottest and driest regions in the world.

The **"Big-Sur Country"** of the Santa Lucia Range has the most spectacular coastal scenery in the state. Here, as the map shows, mountains descend in great cliffs to the sea, which abruptly becomes very much deeper.

An abundant water supply is indicated by the hydrographic symbols that appear in the Central Valley area of the map. This is watered by two substantial rivers, the Sacramento and the San Joaquin, and is the main source of California's great agricultural wealth. The freshwater lakes of the valley contrast with a salt lake farther east, as distinguished by the legend to the Map Section.

The Transverse Ranges of the San Gabriel and San Bernadino mountains, a block mountain system that continues out to sea to form the Channel Islands, crosses the longitudinal line of the main mountain systems. These Transverse Ranges protect the densely populated Los Angeles area from the heat of the Mojave Desert in the summer and from the cold air masses of the continental interior during the winter.

Population centers are graded in the Map Section Legend by size, with cities or conurbations of more than 1,000,000 people, such as Los Angeles, shown in yellow. The size of the towns is denoted by a range of graded types, from the state capital Sacramento (273,000) to towns of 10,000. The map shows how the state's population is concentrated on the lowlands and the adjoining hillslopes.

In latitude, California occupies a position between 32° and 42° N on the western seaboard of the American continent, very similar to the Mediterranean countries of the Old World. A state boundary runs along its northern and eastern sides, and an international frontier separates it from Mexico in the south. These boundaries are artificial except where they follow the line of the Colorado river (bottom right).

The scale bar indicates that this map is drawn at a scale of 1:6,000,000, and enables the reader to work out the dimensions of the state. This extends north–south about 1,248 km (780 miles), and east–west from 240 km (150 miles) to 560 km (350 miles).

Name forms in the atlas emphasize an international world view, where the same geographical feature is named in the language of whichever country it passes through. The index cross-references the different forms back to the language of the edition. All place-names appear in the index, which gives their position in terms of coordinates (latitude and longitude), expressed in degrees and in one-sixtieths of degrees (minutes).

Mount Whitney

Scale 1:6,000,000 — Delisle Conical Equidistant Projection

ACKNOWLEDGMENTS

Senior Executive Art Editor
Michael McGuinness

Executive Editor
James Hughes

Coordinating Editor
Dian Taylor

Editors
Lesley Ellis
Judy Garlick
Ken Hewis

Art Editor
Mike Brown

Designers
Sue Rawkins
Lisa Tai

Picture Researcher
Flavia Howard

Researchers
Nicholas Law
Nigel Morrison
Alicia Smith

Editorial Assistant
Barbara Gish

Proofreader
Kathie Gill

Indexers
Hilary and Richard Bird

Production Controller
Barry Baker

Typesetting by Servis Filmsetting
Limited, Manchester, England

Reproduction by Gilchrist
Brothers Limited, Leeds, England

CONTRIBUTORS AND CONSULTANTS

GENERAL CONSULTANT
Professor Michael Wise, CBE, MC, BA, PhD, D.Univ, Professor of
Geography, London School of Economics and Political Science

EDITORIAL CONSULTANT
John Clark

Frances Atkinson, BSc

British Museum (Natural History), Botany Library

Robert W. Bradnock, MA, PhD, Lecturer in Geography with special
reference to South Asia at the School of Oriental and African
Studies, University of London

Michael J. Bradshaw, MA, Principal Lecturer in Geography, College
of St Mark and St John, Plymouth

Dr J. M. Chapman, BSc, ARCS, PhD, MIBiol, Lecturer in Biology,
Queen Elizabeth College, University of London

Dr Jeremy Cherfas, Departmental Demonstrator in Zoology, Oxford
University

Dr M. J. Clark, Senior Lecturer in Geomorphology, Geography
Department, Southampton University

J. L. Cloudsley-Thompson, MA, PhD(Cantab), DSc(Lond),
Hon DSc(Khartoum), Professor of Zoology, Birkbeck College,
University of London

Professor R. U. Cooke, Department of Geography, University
College, London

Professor Clifford Embleton, MA, PhD, Department of Geography,
King's College, University of London

Dr John Gribbin, Physics Consultant to *New Scientist* magazine

Dr John M. Hellawell, BSc, PhD, FIBiol, MIWES, Principal,
Environmental Aspects, Severn Trent Water Authority, Birmingham

Dr Garry E. Hunt, BSc, PhD, DSc, FRAS, FRMetS, FIMA, MBCS,
Head of Atmospheric Physics, Imperial College, London

David K. C. Jones, Lecturer in Geography, London School of
Economics and Political Science

Dr Russell King, Department of Geography, University of Leicester

Dr D. McNally, Assistant Director, University of London
Observatory

Meteorological Office, Berkshire

Dr Robert Muir Wood, PhD

Dr B. O'Connor, Department of Geography, University of London

J. H. Paterson, MA, Professor of Geography in the University of
Leicester

Dr Nigel Pears, Department of Geography, University of Leicester

Joyce Pope, BA

Dr A. L. Rice, Institute of Oceanographic Sciences, Wormley, Surrey

Ian Ridpath, science writer and broadcaster

Royal Geographical Society

Helen Scoging, BSc, Department of Geography, London School of
Economics and Political Science

Bernard Stonehouse, DPhil, MA, BSc, Chairman, Post-Graduate
School of Environmental Science, University of Bradford

Dr Christopher B. Stringer, PhD, Senior Scientific Officer,
Palaeontology Department, British Museum (Natural History)

J. B. Thornes, Professor of Physical Geography and Head of
Department, Bedford College, University of London

UN Information Office and Library

Professor J. E. Webb, DSc, *Emeritus*, Department of Zoology,
Westfield College, University of London

Peter B. Wright, BSc, MPhil

UNDERSTANDING MAPS
Helen Wallis, MA, DPhil, FSA, The Map Librarian, British Library

A great many other individuals, organizations, and institutions have
given invaluable advice and assistance during the preparation of this
Our Planet Earth Section and the publishers wish to extend their
thanks to them all.

ILLUSTRATION CREDITS

Maps in the Our Planet Earth Section by Creative Cartography Limited
unless otherwise specified. Map of the world's climatic regions, page 50,
adapted from *An Introduction to Climate* 4th edition by Trewartha/
Elements of Geography by G. T. Trewartha, A. H. Robinson and
E. H. Hammond © McGraw-Hill Book Co., N.Y., 1967. Used with
permission of McGraw-Hill Book Co. Map diagram page 101 (bottom)
courtesy Doctor Arno Peters.

2–3 *Exploding universe* Product Support (Graphics); *others* Quill.
4–5 Bob Chapman. 6–7 Bob Chapman. 8–9 Mick Saunders;
Landsat diagrams Gary Marsh; *biowindows* Chris Forsey. 10–11
Mick Saunders. 12–13 Bob Chapman. 14–15 *Diagrams* Chris Forsey;
mountain sequence Donald Myall. 16–17 Colin Salmon. 18–19 Peter
Morter; *graph* Mick Saunders; *car* Peter Owen. 20–21 Bob
Chapman; *diagram* Chris Forsey; *map* Colin Salmon. 22–23 Chris
Forsey (*including maps*). 24–25 Brian Delf. 26–27 Brian Delf.
28–29 Dave Etchell/John Ridyard. 30–31 Creative Cartography Ltd.
32–33 Mick Saunders. 34–35 Chris Forsey; *experiment* Gary Hincks;
others Mick Saunders. 36–37 Chris Forsey; *fruit flies, birds and mice*
Donald Myall. 38–39 Chris Forsey; *time scale* Mick Saunders;
stromatolite and diagram Garry Hincks. 40–41 Donald Myall;
time scale Mick Saunders. 42–43 Donald Myall; *time scale* Mick
Saunders. 44–45 Creative Cartography Ltd. 46–47 Donald Myall;
diagram Kai Choi; *skulls* Jim Robins. 48–49 Creative Cartography
Ltd. 50–51 Peter Morter; *diagram* Marilyn Clark. 52–53 Kai Choi.
54–55 Creative Cartography Ltd. 56–57 Creative Cartography Ltd.
58–59 Creative Cartography Ltd. 60–61 Creative Cartography Ltd;
illustrations Jim Robins. 62–63 *Migration diagram and graph* Kai
Choi; *illustrations* Coral Mula. 64–65 Donald Myall. 66–67
Landscape diagram Bill le Fever; *illustrations* Russell Barnett. 68–69
Donald Myall. 70–71 Jim Robins; *plants, bottom left* Andrew
Macdonald. 72–73 Rory Kee; *bottom left* Russell Barnett; *plow*
Kai Choi; *grains and graph* Creative Cartography Ltd. 74–75 Bob
Bampton/The Garden Studio; *animal adaptations* Russell Barnett.
76–77 Donald Myall; *qanat* Bob Chapman. 78–79 David Ashby.
80–81 David Ashby. 82–83 Coral Mula; *trees, orchid, toucan and
hornbill* Donald Myall. 84–85 Jim Robins. 86–87 Creative
Cartography Ltd. 88–89 Brian Delf; *blood counts diagram* Colin
Salmon. 90–91 Bob Chapman; *animals and plants* Rod Sutterby.
92–93 Kai Choi; *hydrological cycle* Bob Chapman. 94–95 Andy
Farmer; *shore and plant life* Russell Barnett; *coral atoll* Colin
Salmon. 96–97 Creative Cartography Ltd. 98–99 *Topographic maps*
Rand McNally; *sketch map* Space Frontiers Ltd. 100–101 *Diagrams*
Creative Cartography Ltd. 102–103 *Maps* Istituto Geografico De
Agostini; Rand McNally; *diagrams* Creative Cartography Ltd.

PICTURE CREDITS

Credits read from top to bottom and from left to right on each page. Images that extend over two pages are credited to the left-hand page only.

2 US Naval Observatory; California Institute of Technology and Carnegie Institution of Washington. **3** Both pictures from Royal Observatory, Edinburgh. **8** All pictures from NASA. **9** All pictures from NASA except top and top right, courtesy of Garry Hunt, Laboratory of Planetary Atmospheres, University College, London. **14–15** Maurice and Sally Landre/Colorific! **16–17** All pictures courtesy of Dr Basil Booth, Geoscience Features. **18** Institute of Geological Sciences. **19** Paul Brierley; Institute of Geological Sciences. **20** Camera Press, London. **26** Barnaby's Picture Library; Barnaby's Picture Library; Institute of Geological Sciences. **28** Dr Alan Beaumont. **30** Tom Sheppard/Robert Harding Picture Library; Professor Ronald Cooke. **31** Institute of Geological Sciences. **32** Stuart Windsor; Sefton Photo Library, Manchester; Rio Tinto Zinc; Douglas Botting; Aspect Picture Library. **33** NASA; Mireille Vautier; Explorer/Vision International. **34** Paul Brierley. **37** Paediatric Research Unit, Guy's Hospital Medical School; Dr Laurence Cook, Zoology Department, University of Manchester. **39** Both pictures from British Museum (Natural History). **46** Colophoto Hans Hinz. **47** Dr P. G. Bahn, School of Archaeology and Oriental Studies, University of Liverpool/Musée des Antiquités Nationales. St. Germain-en-Laye. **56** UNICEF (Photo no. 8675 by H. Dalrymple). **57** Dr A. M. O'Connor, Department of Geography, University College, London. **61** International Fund for Animal Welfare; K. Kunov/Novosti Press Agency; Popperfoto; Charles Swithinbank. **62** Alan Robson. **63** Gösta Hakansson/Frank Lane Agency. **65** G. R. Roberts. **67** Anglo-Chinese Educational Trust; Aerofilms. **69** Ted Streshinsky. **72** Engraving from *At Home with the Patagonians*. **73** The Mansell Collection. **76** J. Bitsch/Zefa; Penny Tweedie/Colorific! **77** Alan Hutchison Library; Bill Holden/Zefa. **80** Syndication International; Gerald Cubitt/Bruce Coleman Ltd; Bruce Coleman Ltd. **81** Alan Hutchison Library; R. and M. Borland/Bruce Coleman Ltd; M. P. Kahl/Bruce Coleman Ltd; Jan and Des Bartlett/Bruce Coleman Ltd. **84** J. von Puttkamer/Alan Hutchison Library. **85** Marion Morrison. **86–87** Richard and Sally Greenhill. **88** Alan Hutchison Library; The Association of Universities for Research in Astronomy, Inc. **89** Gunter Ziesler/Bruce Coleman Ltd. **91** Mike Price/Bruce Coleman Ltd. **92** Ian Murphy. **93** Paolo Koch/Vision International; J. Allan Cash; M. Timothy O'Keefe/Bruce Coleman Ltd. **94** Heather Angel. **95** Institute of Oceanographic Sciences. **96** Fritz Prenzel/Bruce Coleman Ltd; Gordon Williamson/Bruce Coleman Ltd. **97** Martin Rogers/Susan Griggs Agency. **98** British Library; British Museum; Centro Camuno di Studi Preistorici; British Library; NASA; NASA; Rand McNally; British Museum; British Museum. **99** British Museum; NASA; NASA; Rand McNally; Space Frontiers Ltd; Paul G. Lowman/NASA Goddard SFC/Space Frontiers Ltd. **100** Historisches Museum, Vienna. **101** Hunting Surveys Ltd; Michael Holford/Science Museum, London; Michael Holford; Michael Holford/Science Museum, London. **103** Space Frontiers Ltd; F. Damm/Zefa.

INTERNATIONAL MAP SECTION

Hydrographic and Topographic Features
Symboles hydrographiques et morphologiques
Gewässer- und Geländeformen
Idrografia, Morfologia
Hidrografía y morfología

River, Stream
Cours d'eau permanent
Ständig wasserführender Fluß
Corso d'acqua perenne
Corriente de agua de régimen permanente

Lake
Lac d'eau douce
Süßwassersee
Lago d'acqua dolce
Lago de agua dulce

Rocks
Ecueils, Roches
Klippen, Felsriffe
Scogli, Rocce
Escollos, Rocas

Summer Limit of Pack-Ice
Limite du pack en été
Packeisgrenze im Sommer
Limite estivo del pack ghiacciato
Límite estival de banco de hielo

Intermittent Stream
Cours d'eau intermittent
Zeitweilig wasserführender Fluß
Corso d'acqua periodico
Corriente de agua intermitente

Intermittent Lake
Lac d'eau douce temporaire
Zeitweiliger Süßwassersee
Lago d'acqua dolce periodico
Lago de agua dulce intermitente

Reef, Atoll
Barrière, Atoll
Riff, Atoll
Barriera, Atollo
Barrera de arrecifes

Winter Limit of Pack-Ice
Limite du pack en hiver
Packeisgrenze im Winter
Limite invernale del pack ghiacciato
Límite invernal de banco de hielo

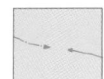
Disappearing Stream
Perte de cours d'eau
Versickernder Fluß
Corso d'acqua che si inabissa
Corriente de agua que desaparece

Salt Lake
Lac d'eau salée
Salzsee
Lago d'acqua salata
Lago de agua salada

Mangrove
Mangrove
Mangrove
Mangrovie
Manglar

Limit of Icebergs
Limite des glaces flottantes
Treibeisgrenze
Limite dei ghiacci alla deriva
Límite de hielo a la deriva

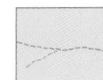
Undefined or Fluctuating River Course
Cours d'eau incertain
Fluß mit veränderlichem Lauf
Fiume dal corso incerto
Corriente de agua incerta

Intermittent Salt Lake
Lac d'eau salée temporaire
Zeitweiliger Salzsee
Lago d'acqua salata periodico
Lago de agua salada intermitente

Continental Ice-cap
Glacier continental
Inlandeis, Gletscher
Ghiacciaio continentale
Glaciar continental

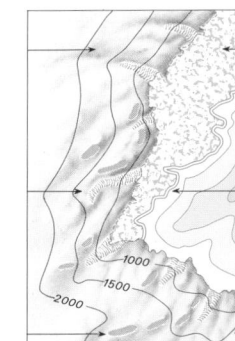

Ice Shelf
Banquise
Schelfeis oder Eisschelf
Banchisa polare (Ice-shelf)
Banquisa

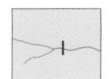
Waterfall, Rapids, Cataract
Chute, Rapide, Cataracte
Wasserfall, Stromschnelle, Katarakt
Cascata, Rapida, Cateratta
Cascada, Rapido, Catarata

Dry Lake Bed
Lac asséché
Trockener Seeboden
Alveo di lago asciutto
Lecho de lago seco

Glacial Tongue
Langue glaciaire
Gletscherzunge
Lingua di ghiaccio
Lengua de glaciar

Limit of Ice Shelf
Limite de la banquise
Schelfeisgrenze
Limite della banchisa
Límite de la banquisa

Canal
Canal
Kanal
Canale
Canal

Lake Surface Elevation
Cote du lac au-dessus du niveau de la mer
Höhe des Seespiegels
Altitudine del lago
Elevación de lago sobre el nivel del mar

Rocky Areas (Antarctica)
Région de roches (Antarctique)
Eisfreie Gebiete, Gebirge (Antarktika)
Aree rocciose (Antartide)
Área rocosa (Antártida)

Contour Lines in Continental Ice
Courbes de niveau dans les régions glaciaires
Höhenlinien auf vergletschertem Gebiet
Curve altimetriche nelle aree ghiacciate
Curvas de nivel en áreas heladas

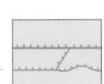
Navigable Canal
Canal navigable
Schiffbarer Kanal
Canale navigabile
Canal navegable

Lake Depth
Profondeur du lac
Seetiefe
Profondità del lago
Profundidad del lago

Defined Shoreline
Trait de côte définie
Küsten- oder Uferlinie
Linea di costa definita
Línea de costa definida

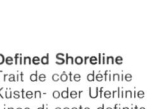

Bathymetric Contour
Courbe bathymétrique
Tiefenlinie
Curva batimetrica
Curva batimétrica

Swamp
Marais
Sumpf
Palude d'acqua dolce
Pantano

Sand Area
Région de sable, Désert
Sandgebiet, Sandwüste
Area sabbiosa, Deserto
Zona arenosa, desierto

Undefined or Fluctuating Shoreline
Trait de côte indéfinie
Unbestimmte oder veränderliche Uferlinie
Linea di costa indefinita
Línea de costa indefinida

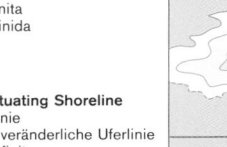

Depth of Water
Valeur de sonde
Tiefenzahl
Quota batimetrica
Cota batimétrica

Salt Marsh
Marais d'eau salée
Salzsumpf
Palude d'acqua salata
Pantano de agua salada

Sandbank, Sandbar
Banc de sable
Sandbank
Bassofondo sabbioso
Banco submarino de arena

Mountain Range
Chaine de montagnes
Bergkette
Catena di monti
Cadena montañosa

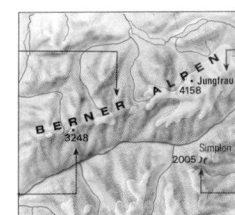

Mountain
Mont
Berg, Bergmassiv
Monte
Monte

Salt Pan
Marais salant
Salzpfanne
Salina
Salina

Port Facilities
Installations portuaires
Hafenanlagen
Impianti portuali
Instalaciones portuarias

Elevation
Cote, Altitude
Höhenzahl
Quota altimetrica
Cota altimétrica

Mountain Pass, Gap
Passage, Col, Port
Paß, Joch, Sattel
Passo, Colle, Valico
Paso, Collado, Puerto de montaña

Key to Elevation and Depth Tints
Hypsométrie, Bathymétrie
Höhenstufen, Tiefenstufen
Altimetria, Batimetria
Altimetría, Batimetría

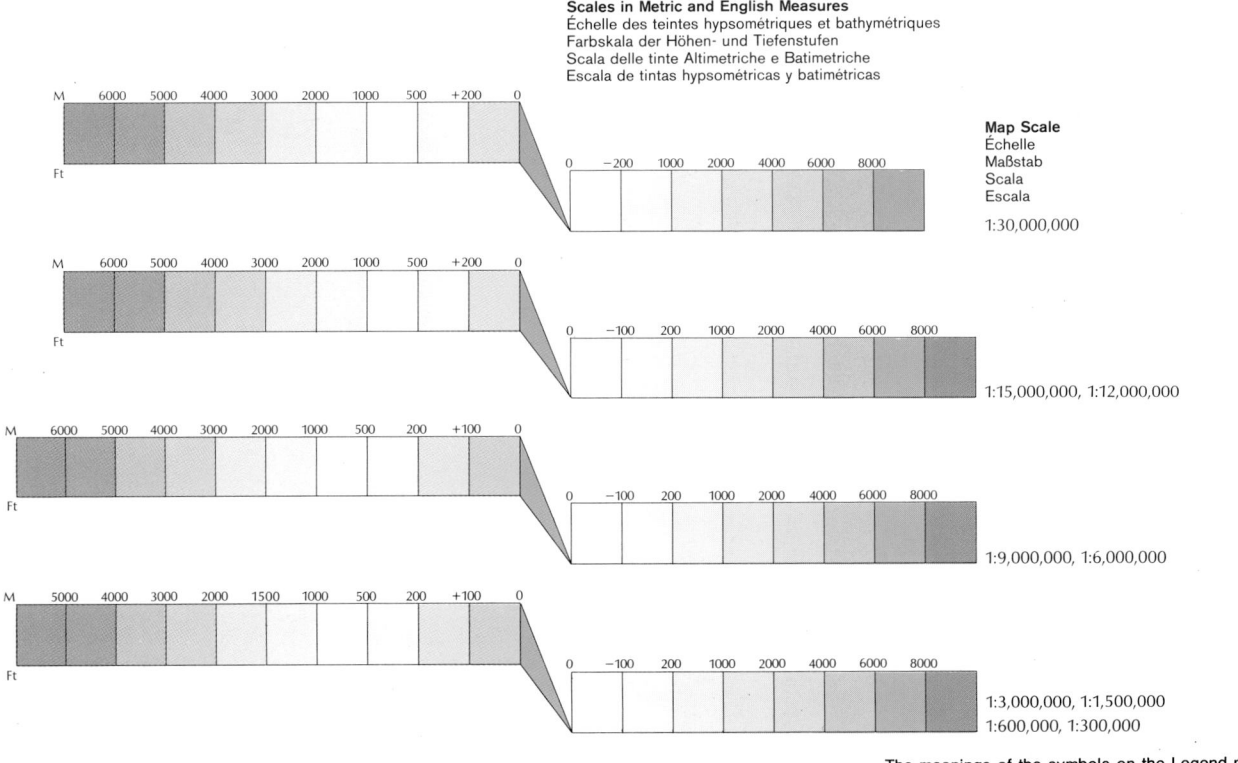

Scales in Metric and English Measures
Échelle des teintes hypsométriques et bathymétriques
Farbskala der Höhen- und Tiefenstufen
Scala delle tinte Altimetriche e Batimetriche
Escala de tintas hipsométricas y batimétricas

Land Elevation Below Sea Level
Dépression et cote au-dessous du niveau de la mer
Senke mit Tiefenzahl unter dem Meeresspiegel
Depressione e quota sotto il livello del mare
Depresión y elevación bajo el nivel del mar

Map Scale
Échelle
Maßstab
Scala
Escala

1:30,000,000

1:15,000,000, 1:12,000,000

1:9,000,000, 1:6,000,000

1:3,000,000, 1:1,500,000
1:600,000, 1:300,000

Map Projections
Projections cartographiques
Kartennetzentwürfe
Proiezioni cartografiche
Proyecciones cartográficas

The projections appearing in this atlas have been plotted by computer

Les réseaux des projections ont été obtenus par élaboration automatique à partir de formules mathématiques

Die Kartennetze aller im Atlas vorkommenden Abbildungen wurden mit Hilfe der Datenverarbeitung (EDV) völlig neu errechnet

I disegni delle proiezioni presenti in quest'opera sono stati realizzati interamente ex-novo con l'uso del computer e del plotter a partire dalle formule matematiche

El reticulado de las proyecciones (redes geográficas) incluidas en esta obra han sido obtenidas por proceso automático a partir de las formulas matemáticas

The meanings of the symbols on the Legend pages are in English, French, German, Italian, and Spanish languages to permit the interpretation of the maps by a broad readership.

Boundaries, Capitals
Frontières, Soulignements   Confini, Sottolineature
Grenzen, Unterstreichungen   Límites, Subrayados

 **Defined International Boundary**
Frontière internationale définie
Staatsgrenze
Confine di Stato definito
Límite de Nación definido

 **International Boundary (Continent Maps)**
Frontière internationale (Continents)
Staatsgrenze (Erdteilkarten)
Confine di Stato (Carte dei Continenti)
Límite de Nación (Continentes)

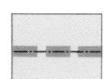 **Undefined International Boundary**
Frontière internationale indéfinie
Nicht genau festgelegte Staatsgrenze
Confine di Stato indefinito
Límite de Nación indefinido

International Ocean Floor Boundary Defined by Treaty or Bilateral Agreement
Frontière d'état en mer définie par traités et conventions bilatéraux
Durch Verträge festgelegte Staatsgrenze im Meeresgebiet
Confine di Stato nel mare definito da trattati e convenzioni bilaterali
Límite de Nación en el Mar definido por los tratados bilaterales

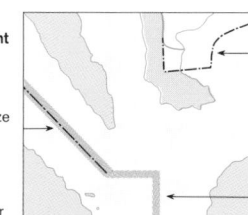

National Capital
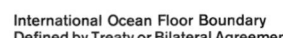 ROMA
Capitale d'État
Hauptstadt eines unabhängigen Staates
Capitale di Stato
Capital de Nación

Dependency or Second-order Capital
LYON
Capitale d'État fédéré, Région
Bundesstaats-, Regionshauptstadt
Capitale di Stato federato, Regione
Capital de Estado federado, Región

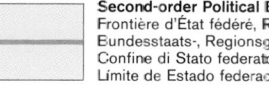 **Second-order Political Boundary**
Frontière d'État fédéré, Région
Bundesstaats-, Regionsgrenze
Confine di Stato federato, Regione
Límite de Estado federado, Región

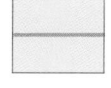 **Third-order Political Boundary**
Frontière de Province, Comte, Bezirk
Provinz-, Grafschafts-, Bezirksgrenze
Confine di Provincia, Contea, Bezirk
Límite de Provincia, Condado. Bezirk

 **Administrative District Boundary**
Frontière de Circonscription
Kreisgrenze
Confine di Circondario
Límite de Circunscripción administrativa

International Ocean Floor Boundary
Frontière d'état en mer
Staatsgrenze im Meeresgebiet
Confine di Stato nel mare
Límite de Nación en el mar

Undefined Ocean Floor Boundary
Frontière indéfinie d'état tracée en mer
Unbstimmte Staatsgrenze im Meeresgebiet
Confine di Stato indefinito ne mare
Límite indefinido de Nación en el mar

Third - order Capital
Kristiansand
Capitale de Province, Comté, Bezirk
Provinz-, Grafschafts-, Bezirkshauptstadt
Capoluogo di Provincia, Contea, Bezirk
Capital de Provincia, Condado, Bezirk

Administrative District Capital
Anadyr
Capitale de Circonscription
Kreishauptstadt
Capoluogo di Circondario
Capital de Circunscripción administrativa

Other Symbols
Symboles divers   Simboli vari
Sonstige Zeichen   Signos varios

 International Airport
Aéroport international
Internationaler Flughafen
Aeroporto internazionale
Aeropuerto internacional

 **Lighthouse**
Phare
Leuchtturm
Faro
Faro

 Dam
Barrage
Staudamm, Staumauer
Diga artificiale, Sbarramento
Presa

 Section of a City
Faubourg
Stadt- oder Ortsteil
Sobborgo urbano
Suburbio

 **Uninhabited Locality, Hamlet**
Ville inhabitée, Ferme. Hameau
Unbewohnte Stadt, Gehöft, Weiler
Città disabitata, Fattoria, Nucleo di case
Ciudad despoblada, Granja, Casar

 Periodically Inhabited Oasis
Oasis habitées périodiquement
Zeitweilig bewohnte Oase
Oasi periodicamente abitate
Oasis periodicamente habitados

 Scientific Station
Base géophysique
Geophysikalische Beobachtungsstation
Base geofisica
Base geofisica

 **Church, Monastery, Abbey**
Monastère, Église, Abbaye
Kloster, Kirche, Abtei
Monastero, Chiesa, Abbazia
Monasterio, Iglesia, Abadía

 Castle
Château
Burg, Schloß
Castello
Castillo

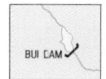 **Ruin, Archeological Site**
Ruine, Centre archéologique
Ruine, Archäologisches Zentrum
Rovina, Zona archeologica
Ruina, Zona arqueológica

 Monument, Historic Site, etc.
Monument
Denkmal
Monumento
Monumento

 **Wall**
Muraille
Wall, Mauer
Vallo, Muraglia
Muralla

 Point of Interest
Curiosité
Sehenswürdigkeit
Curiosità
Curiosidad

 Cave
Grotte, Caverne
Höhle
Grotta, Caverna
Cueva, Gruta

Populated Places
Population   Popolazione
Bevölkerung   Población

Continent Maps
Cartes des Continents   Carte dei Continenti
Erdteilkarten   Mapas de Continentes

< 25 000
25 000-100 000
100 000-250 000
250 000-1 000 000
> 1 000 000

Regional Maps
Cartes à plus grande échelle   Carte di sviluppo
Karten größeren Maßstabs   Mapas a gran escala
< 10 000
10 000-25 000
25 000-100 000
100 000-250 000
250 000-1 000 000
> 1 000 000

Symbols represent population of inhabited localities
Les symboles représentent le nombre d'habitants des localités
Die Signaturen entsprechen der Einwohnerzahl des Ortes
I simboli sono relativi al valore demografico dei centri abitati
Los símbolos son proporcionales a la población del lugar

Town area symbol represents the shape of the urban area
Le petit plan de la ville reproduit la configuration de l'aire urbaine
Die Plansignatur stellt die Gestalt des Stadtgebietes dar
La piantina della città rappresenta la configurazione dell'area urbana
El pequeño plano de la ciudad representa la forma del área urbana

Transportation
Communications   Comunicazioni
Verkehrsnetz   Comunicaciones

Primary Railway
Chemin de fer principal
Hauptbahn
Ferrovia principale
Ferrocarril principal

Secondary Railway
Chemin de fer secondaire
Sonstige Bahn
Ferrovia secondaria
Ferrocarril secundario

Motorway, Expressway
Autoroute
Autobahn
Autostrada
Autopista

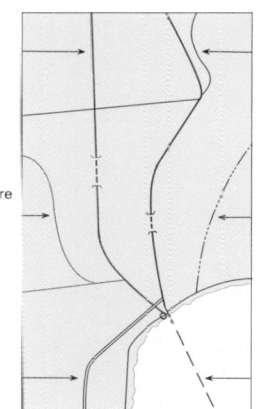

Road
Route de grande communication, Autres Routes
Fernverkehrsstraße, andere Straßen
Strada principale, Altre Strade
Carretera principal, Otras Carreteras

Trail, Caravan Route
Piste, Voie caravanière
Wüstenpiste, Karawanenweg
Pista nel deserto, Carovaniera
Pista en el desierto, Vía de Caravanas

Ferry, Shipping Lane
Bac, Ligne maritime
Fähre, Schiffahrtslinie
Traghetto, Linea di navigazione
Transbordador (Ferry), Línea de navegación

Type Styles
Caractères utilisés pour la toponymie   Caratteri usati per la toponomastica
Zur Namenschreibung verwendete Schriftarten   Caracteres utilizados para la toponimia

ITALY
Hessen RIBE
Political Units
Etat, Dépendance, Division administrative
Staat, abhängiges Gebiet, Verwaltungsgliederung
Stato, Dipendenza, Divisione amministrativa
Nación, Dependencia, Division administrativa

SAXONY
THRACE SUSSEX
Historical or Cultural Region
Région historique ou culturelle
Historische oder Kulturlandschaft
Regione storico - culturale
Región histórica y cultural

PATAGONIA
BASSIN DE RENNES
PENÍNSULA DE YUCATÁN
Physical Region (plain, peninsula)
Région physique (plaine, péninsule)
Landschaft (Ebene, Halbinsel)
Regione fisica (pianura, penisola)
Región natural (llanura, península)

PYRENEES
CUMBRIAN MOUNTAINS
SIERRA DE GÁDOR   LA SILA
Mountain Range
Chaîne de montagnes
Bergkette, Gebirge
Catena di monti
Cadena montañosa

Ankaratra   Monte Bianco
Tsafajavona   Ngorongoro Crater
Nevado del Tolima   Kings Peak
Small Mountain Range, Mountain, Peak
Petit massif, Mont, Cime
Bergmassiv, Berg, Gipfel
Piccolo gruppo montuoso, Monte, Vetta
Macizo pequeño, Monte, Cima

Cabo de São Vicente   Land's End
Mizen Head   Point Conception
Col de la Perche   Passo della Cisa
Cape, Point, Pass
Cap, Pointe, Passe
Kap, Landspitze, Paß
Capo, Punta, Passo
Cabo, Punta, Paso

MAHÉ   ALDABRA ISLANDS
CORSE   CHANNEL ISLANDS
SULU ARCHIPELAGO
Island, Archipelago
Ile, Archipel
Insel, Archipel
Isola, Arcipelago
Isla, Archipiélago

Thames   Po   Victoria Falls
Lotagipi Swamp   Gota kanal
Lago Maggiore
River, Waterfall, Cataract, Canal, Lake
Fleuve, Chute d'eau, Cataracte, Canal, Lac
Fluß, Wasserfall, Katarakt, Kanal, See
Fiume, Cascata, Cateratta, Canale, Lago
Río, Cascada, Catarata, Canal, Lago

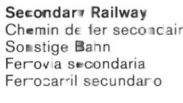 *LABRADOR SEA*
Gulf of Alaska   Hudson Bay
Estrecho de Magallanes
Sea, Gulf, Bay, Strait
Mer, Golfe, Baie, Détroit
Meer, Golf, Bucht, Meeresstraße
Mare, Golfo, Baia, Stretto
Mar, Golfo, Bahía, Estrecho

West Mariana Basin
Galapagos Fracture Zone
Mid-Atlantic Ridge
Undersea Features
Formes du relief sous-marin
Formen des Meeresbodens
Forme del rilievo sottomarino
Formas del relieve submarino

Tarfaya
Tombouctou
Agadir
Nouakchott
BRAZZAVILLE
CASABLANCA
Size of type indicates relative importance of inhabited localities
La dimension des caractères indique l'importance d'une localité
Die Schriftgröße entspricht der Gesamtbedeutung des Ortes
La grandezza del carattere è proporzionale all'importanza della località
La dimensión de los caracteres de imprenta indica la importancia de la localidad

INDEX MAPS

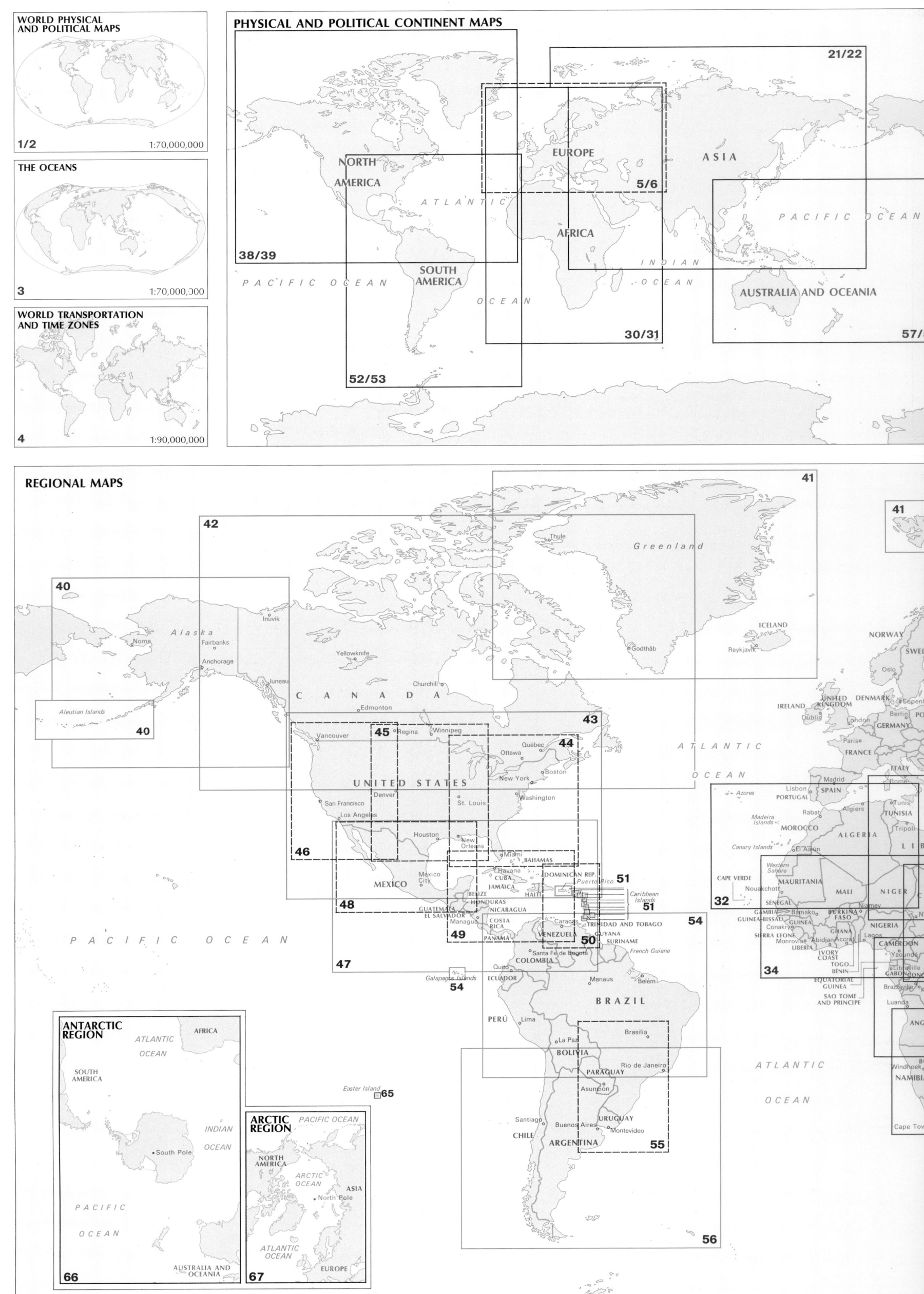

WORLD PHYSICAL AND POLITICAL MAPS

1/2   1:70,000,000

THE OCEANS

3   1:70,000,000

WORLD TRANSPORTATION AND TIME ZONES

4   1:90,000,000

PHYSICAL AND POLITICAL CONTINENT MAPS

21/22

NORTH AMERICA

EUROPE

ASIA

5/6

AFRICA

38/39

SOUTH AMERICA

ATLANTIC

PACIFIC OCEAN

INDIAN OCEAN

PACIFIC OCEAN

AUSTRALIA AND OCEANIA

52/53

30/31

57/58

REGIONAL MAPS

41

42

40

Greenland

Thule

ICELAND

Godthåb

Reykjavik

NORWAY

SWEDEN

FINLAND

41

40

Alaska

Nome

Fairbanks

Anchorage

Juneau

Inuvik

Yellowknife

CANADA

Churchill

Edmonton

Aleutian Islands

40

45

Regina

Winnipeg

Vancouver

Québec

Ottawa

43

44

Boston

New York

OSLO

Copenhagen

IRELAND

UNITED KINGDOM

DENMARK

Berlin

POLAND

Dublin

London

GERMANY

Paris

FRANCE

ATLANTIC OCEAN

UNITED STATES

Denver

St. Louis

Washington

San Francisco

Los Angeles

Houston

New Orleans

Miami

46

Madrid

SPAIN

Lisbon

PORTUGAL

Azores

ITALY

Rome

Tunis

TUNISIA

Algiers

Madeira Islands

Rabat

MOROCCO

ALGERIA

LIBYA

BAHAMAS

Mexico City

Havana

CUBA

JAMAICA

DOMINICAN REP.

Puerto Rico

51

Caribbean Islands

51

Canary Islands

El Aaiún

Western Sahara

CAPE VERDE

MAURITANIA

MALI

NIGER

32

MEXICO

BELIZE

HONDURAS

HAITI

Nouakchott

48

GUATEMALA

EL SALVADOR

NICARAGUA

Managua

COSTA RICA

49

PANAMA

Caracas

VENEZUELA

TRINIDAD AND TOBAGO

GUYANA

SURINAME

50

54

SENEGAL

GAMBIA

Bamako

BURKINA FASO

GUINEA-BISSAU

Conakry

GUINEA

SIERRA LEONE

Monrovia

LIBERIA

IVORY COAST

Abidjan

GHANA

Accra

TOGO

BÉNIN

Lagos

NIGERIA

Niamey

N'D

CAMEROON

PACIFIC OCEAN

COLOMBIA

Santa Fé de Bogotá

French Guiana

Quito

ECUADOR

47

Galapagos Islands

54

Manaus

Belém

BRAZIL

34

Yaoundé

Libreville

GABON

CONGO

EQUATORIAL GUINEA

SAO TOME AND PRINCIPE

Brazzaville

Kin

Luanda

ANGO

PERÚ

Lima

BOLIVIA

La Paz

Brasília

Rio de Janeiro

PARAGUAY

Asunción

ATLANTIC OCEAN

BO

Windhoek

NAMIBIA

ANTARCTIC REGION

AFRICA

ATLANTIC OCEAN

SOUTH AMERICA

INDIAN OCEAN

South Pole

PACIFIC OCEAN

66

Easter Island

65

ARCTIC REGION

PACIFIC OCEAN

NORTH AMERICA

ARCTIC OCEAN

ASIA

North Pole

ATLANTIC OCEAN

EUROPE

AUSTRALIA AND OCEANIA

67

Santiago

CHILE

Buenos Aires

URUGUAY

Montevideo

ARGENTINA

55

Cape Town

56

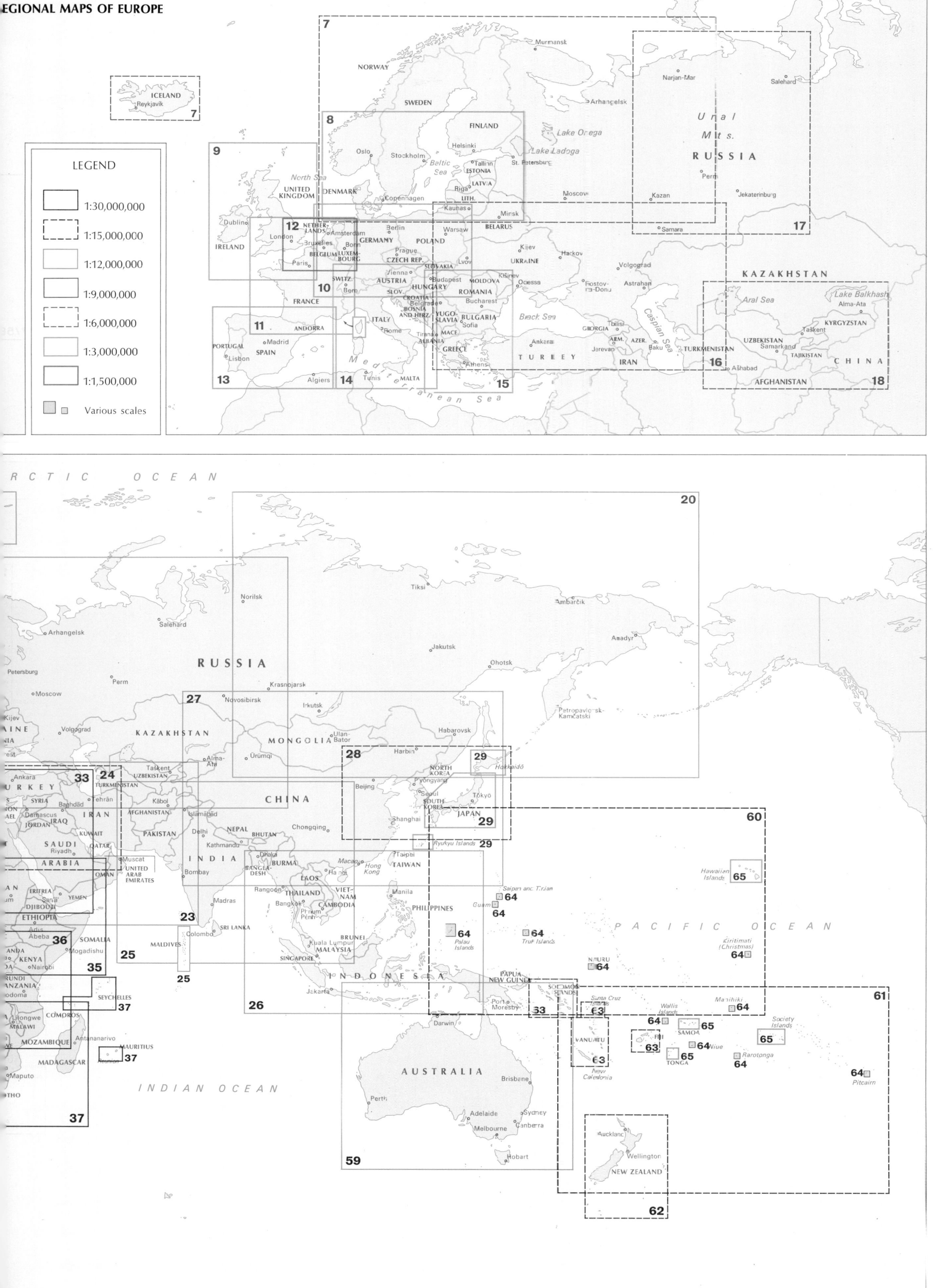

REGIONAL MAPS OF EUROPE

LEGEND

	1:30,000,000
	1:15,000,000
	1:12,000,000
	1:9,000,000
	1:6,000,000
	1:3,000,000
	1:1,500,000
	Various scales

Map 1 **WORLD, PHYSICAL**

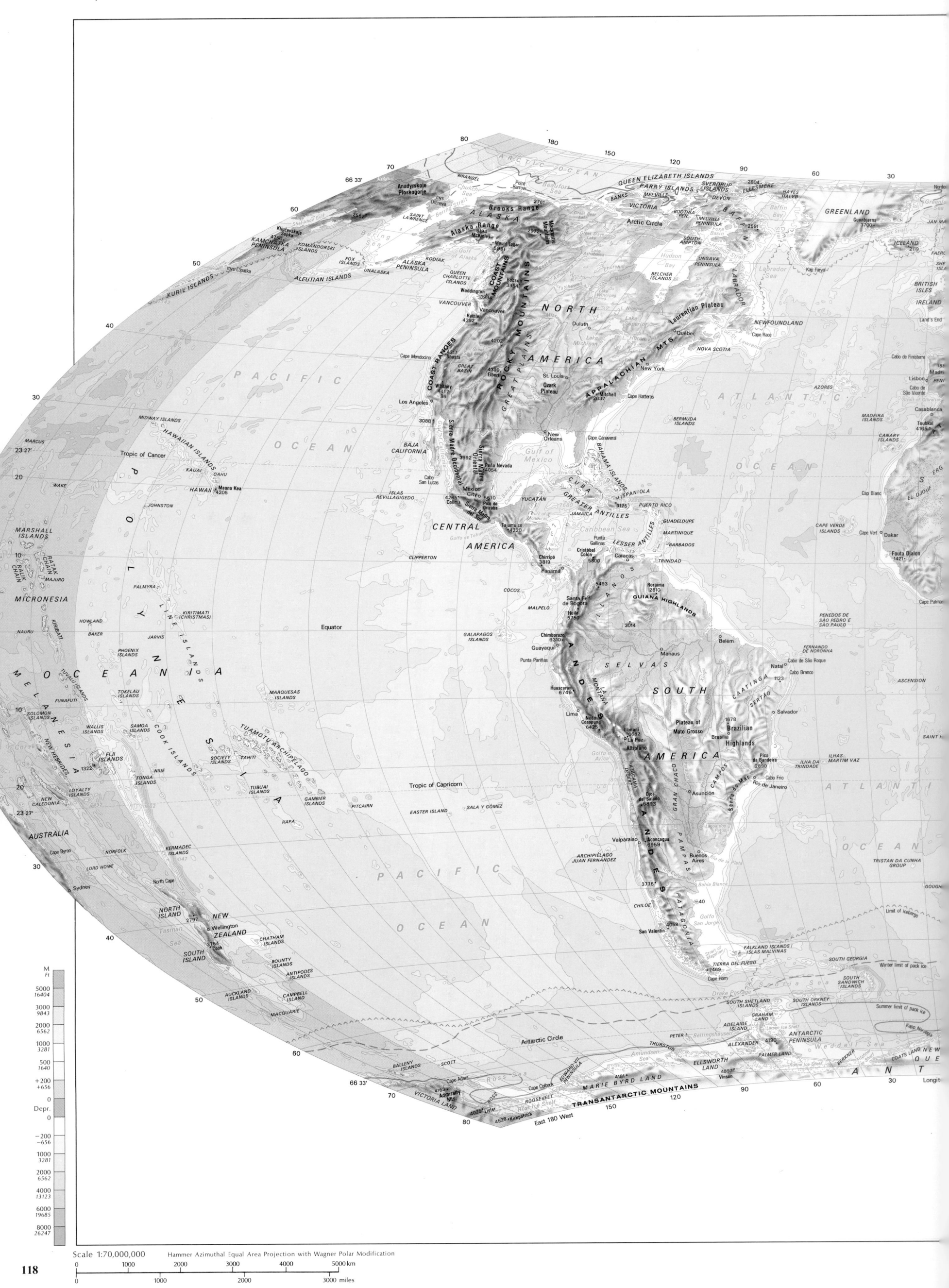

Scale 1:70,000,000   Hammer Azimuthal Equal Area Projection with Wagner Polar Modification

0   1000   2000   3000   4000   5000 km

0   1000   2000   3000 miles

M
Ft

5000
16404

3000
9843

2000
6562

1000
3281

500
1640

+200
+656

0
Depr.
0

−200
−656

1000
3281

2000
6562

4000
13123

6000
19685

8000
26247

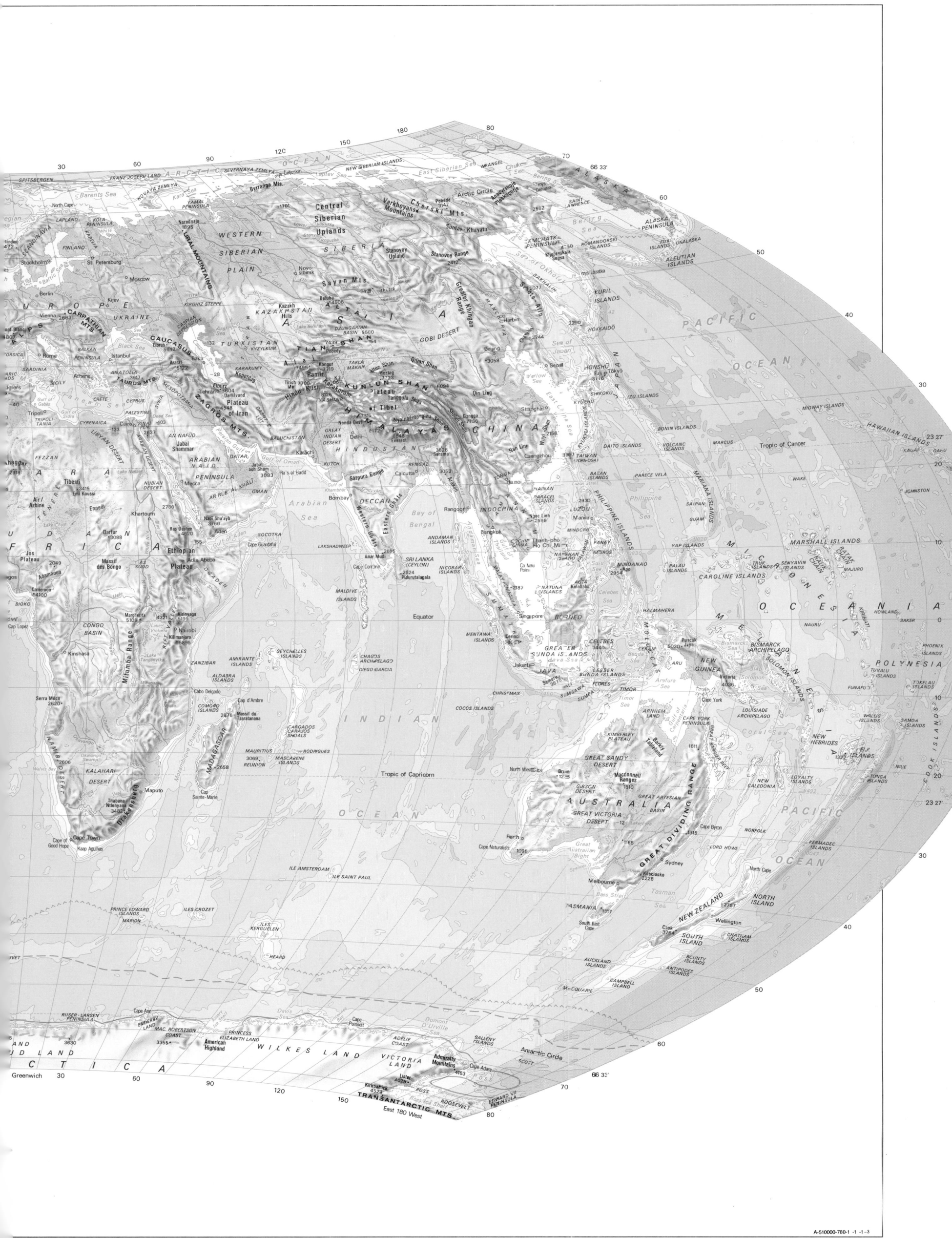

Map 2 **WORLD, POLITICAL**

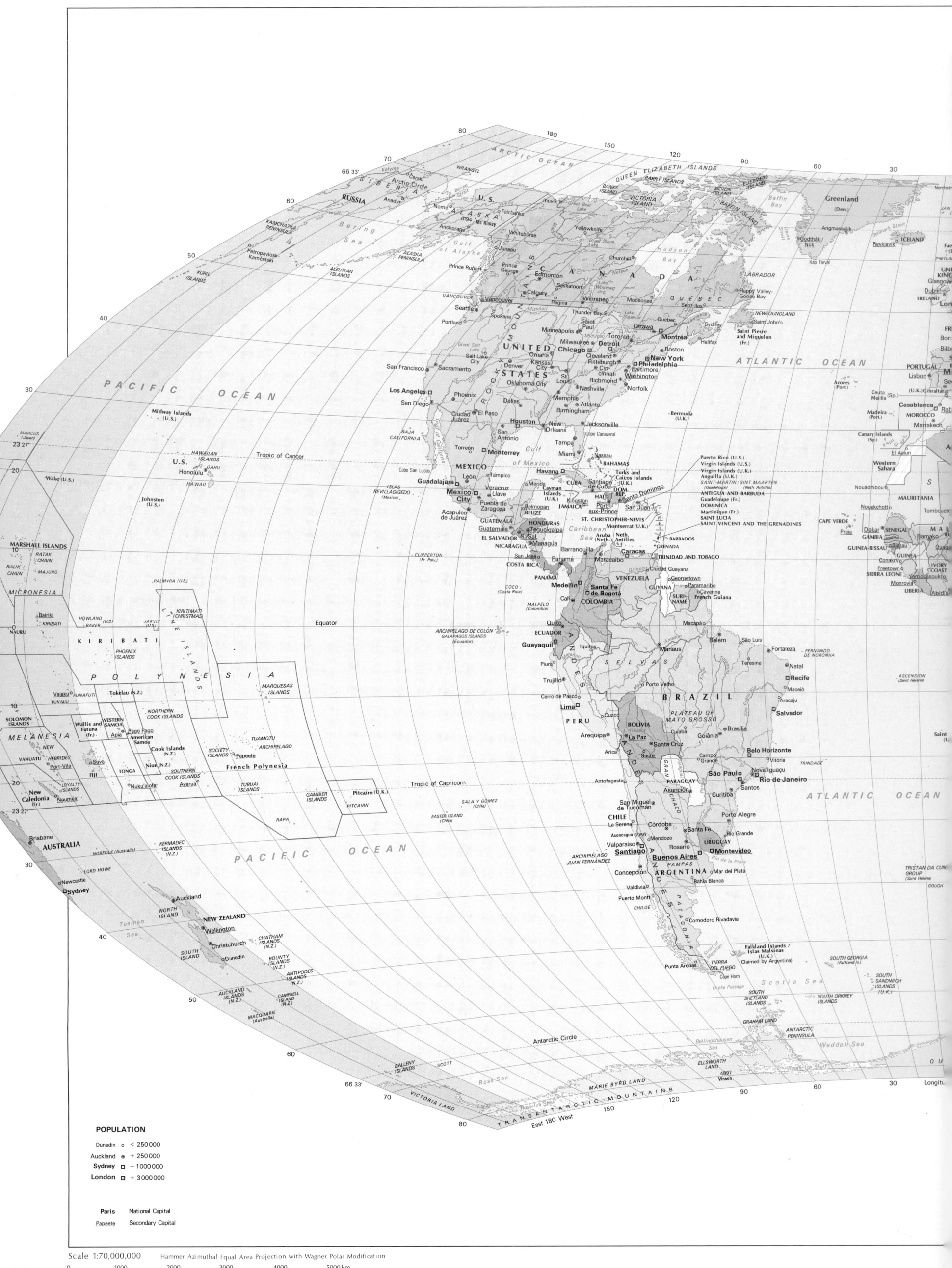

POPULATION

Dunedin	∘ < 250 000
Auckland	• + 250 000
Sydney	▫ + 1 000 000
London	◻ + 3 000 000

Paris   National Capital

Papeete   Secondary Capital

Scale 1:70,000,000   Hammer Azimuthal Equal Area Projection with Wagner Polar Modification

0	1000	2000	3000	4000	5000 km
0		1000		2000	3000 miles

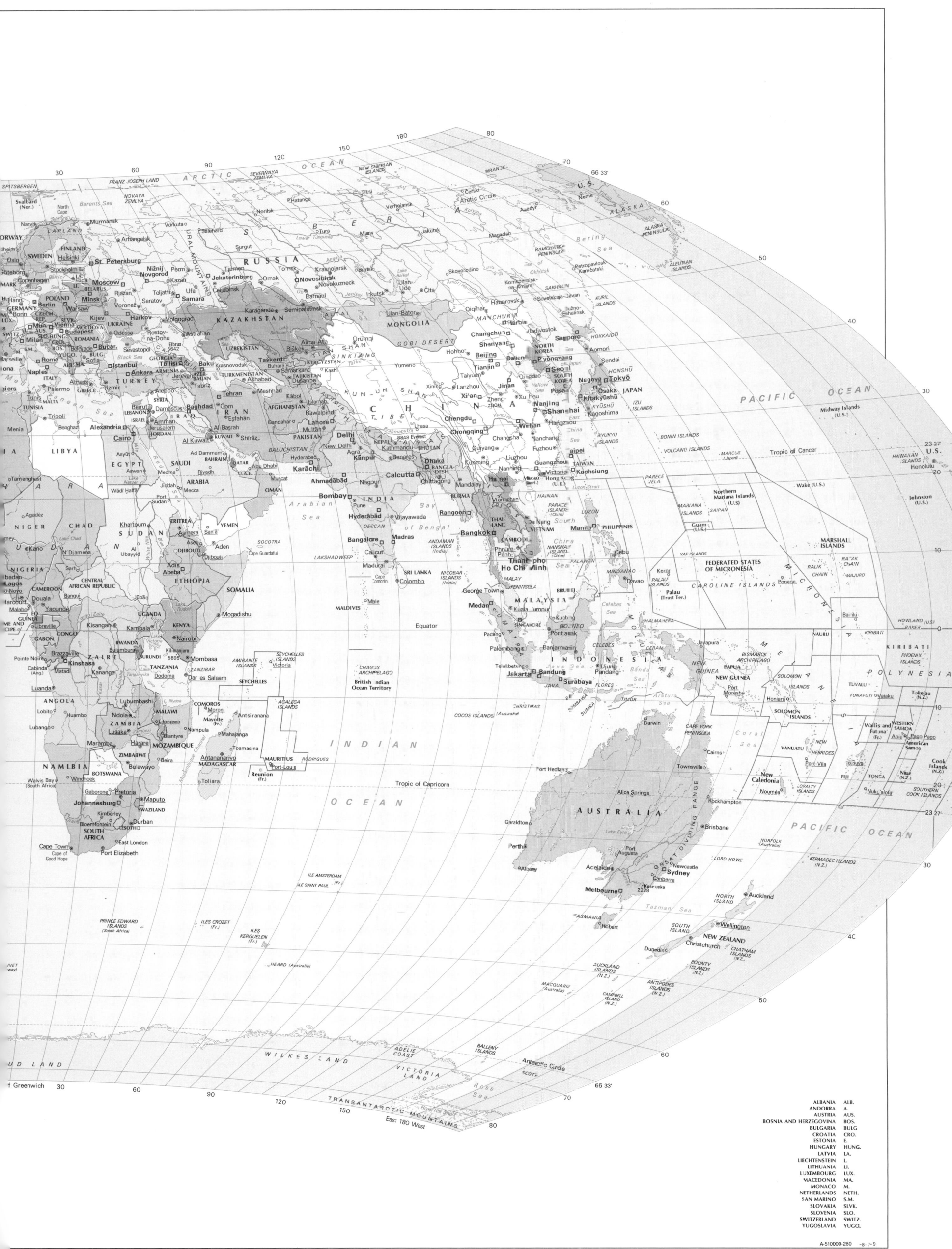

A-510000-280   -8-   -9

Map 3 THE OCEANS

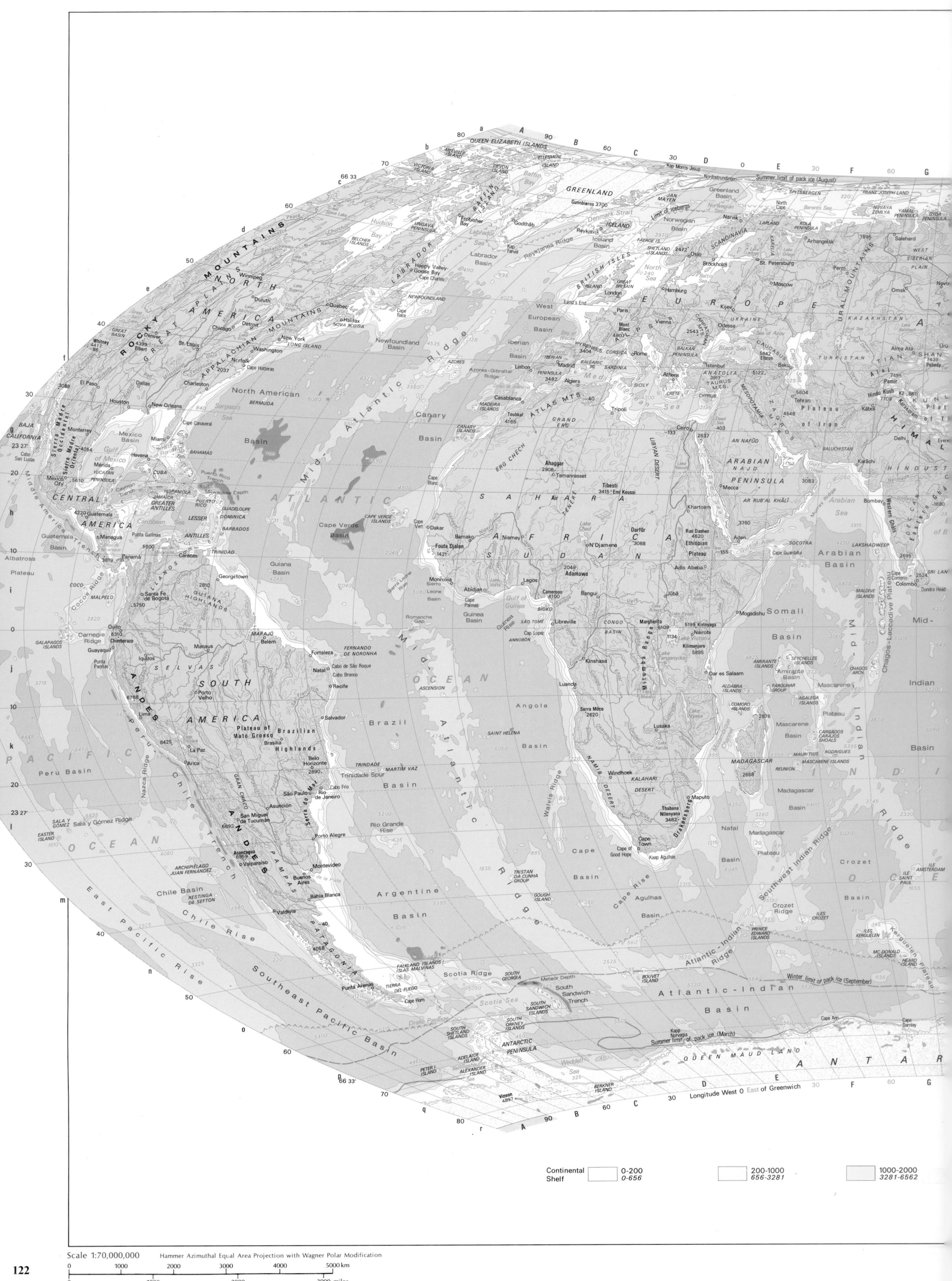

Continental Shelf
| 0-200 | 200-1000 | 1000-2000 |
| 0-656 | 656-3281 | 3281-6562 |

Scale 1:70,000,000   Hammer Azimuthal Equal Area Projection with Wagner Polar Modification

0   1000   2000   3000   4000   5000 km
0   1000   2000   3000 miles

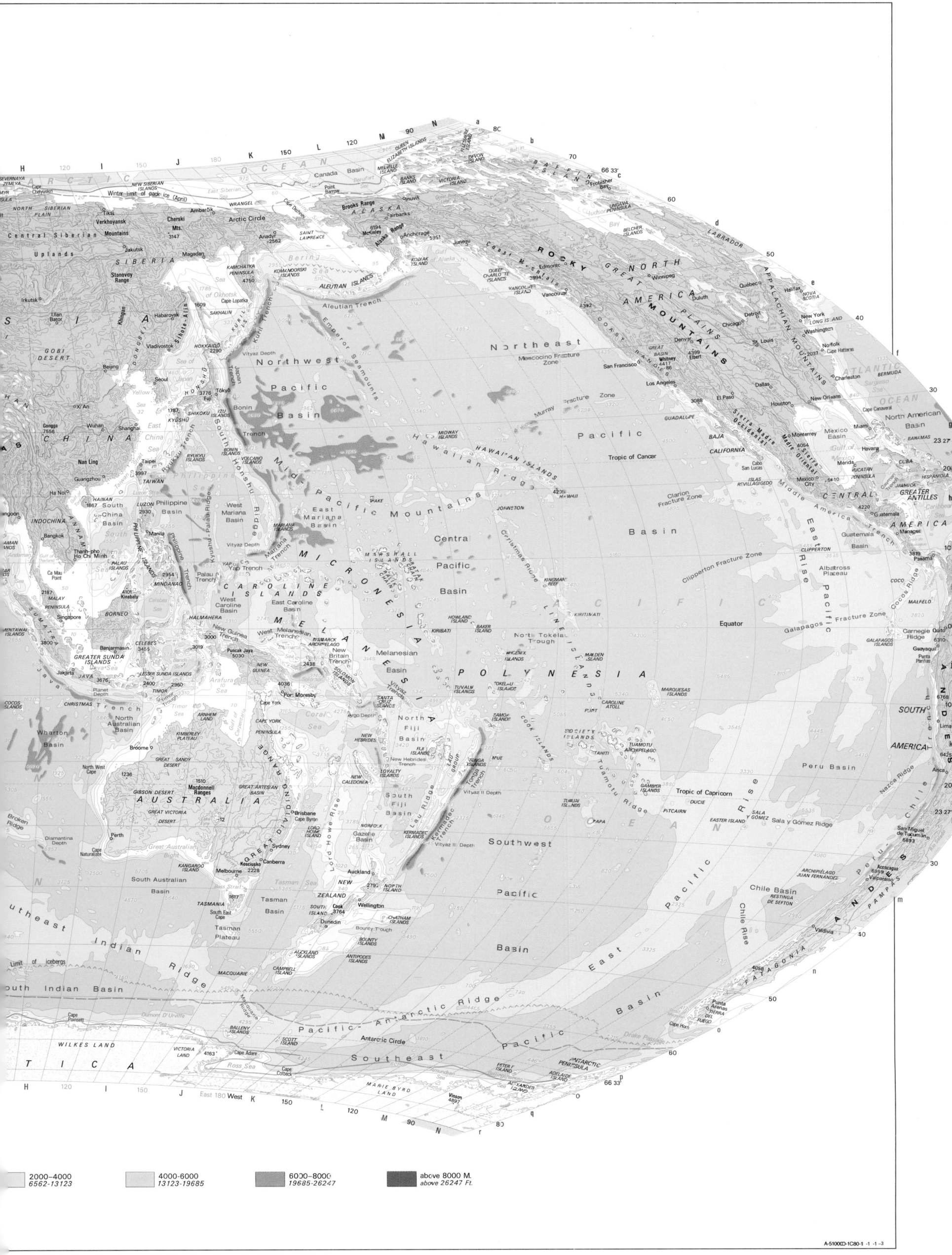

	2000–4000		4000–6000		6000–8000		above 8000 M.
	6562–13123		13123–19685		19685–26247		above 26247 Ft.

A-5100D-1C80-1 -1 -1 –3

Map 4 **WORLD TRANSPORTATION AND TIME ZONES**

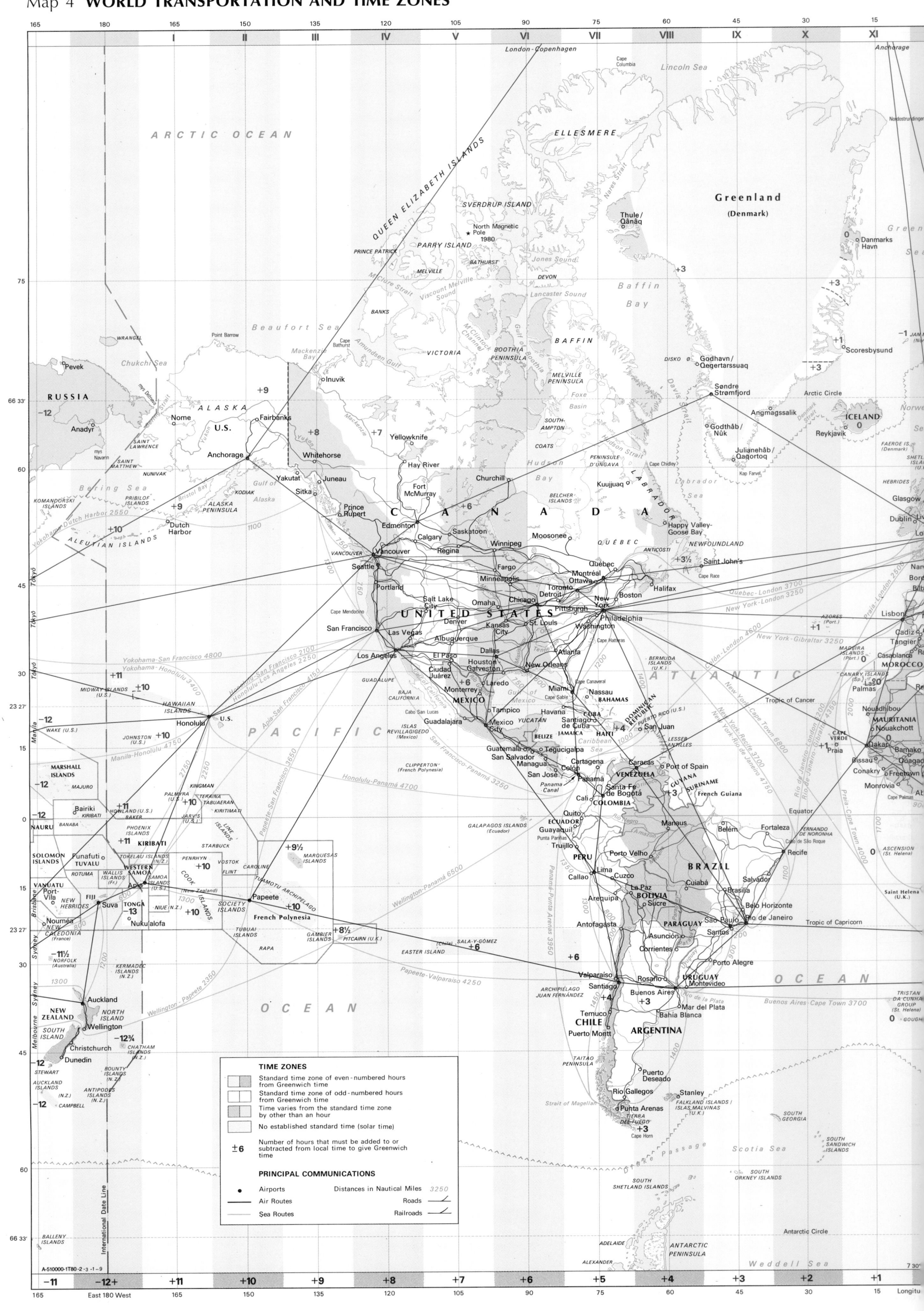

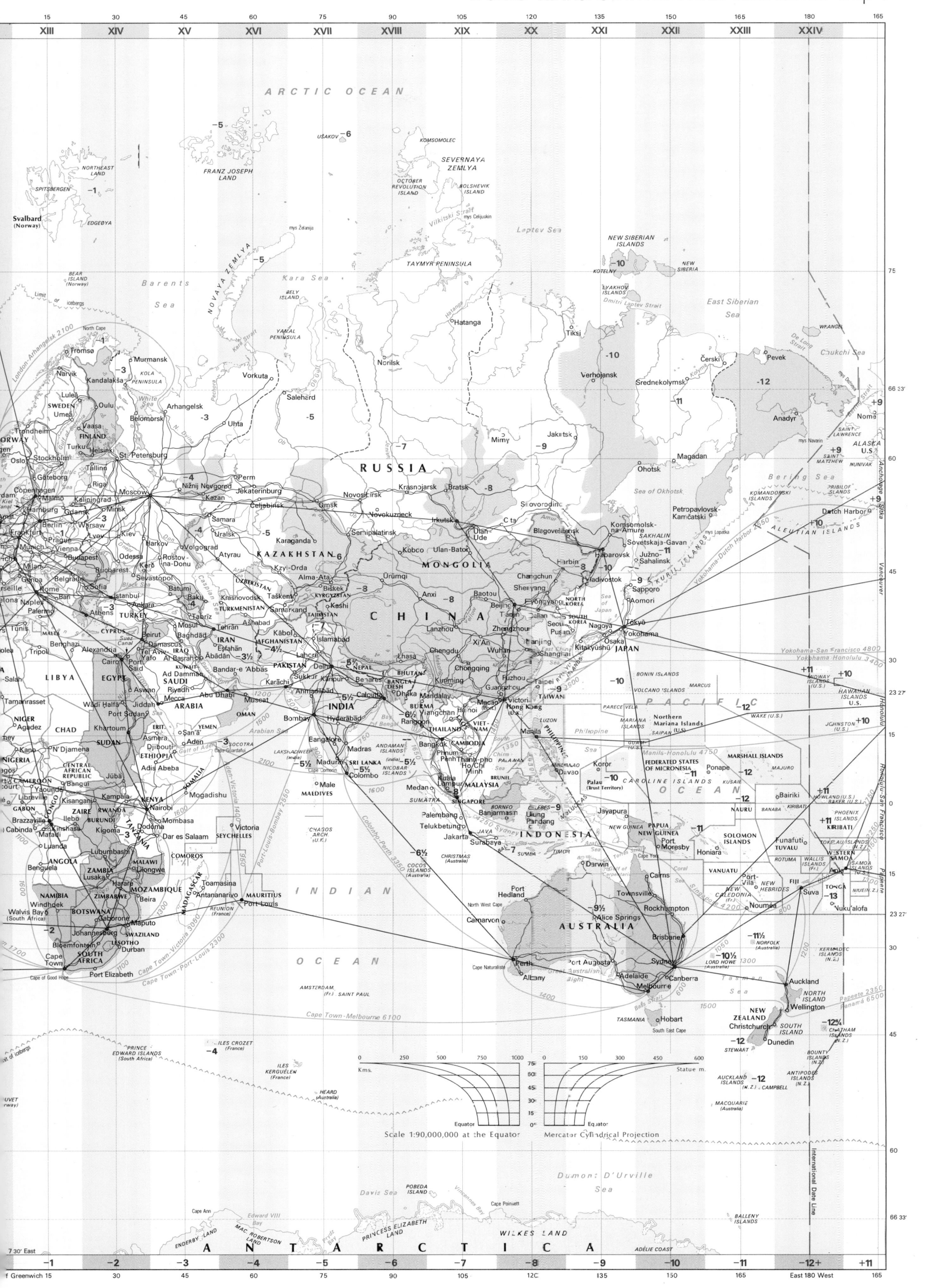

Map 5 **EUROPE, PHYSICAL**

GREENLAND

KING FREDERIK VI COAST

KING CHRISTIAN IX LAND

GREENLAND SEA

Denmark Strait

ICELAND

Reykjavík

VATNAJÖKULL

Arctic Circle

Mohns Ridge

JAN MAYEN

NORWEGIAN SEA

Norwegian Basin

Reykjanes Ridge

Iceland Basin

Faeroe-Iceland Ridge

FAEROE ISLANDS

Faraday Seamounts

ATLANTIC OCEAN

Mid-Atlantic Ridge

West European Basin

Rockall Rise

Rockall

Ireland Trough

Porcupine Bank

BRITISH ISLES

HEBRIDES

SHETLAND ISLANDS

ORKNEY ISLANDS

MAINLAND

North West Highlands

GRAMPIAN MTS.

Glasgow Edinburgh

Southern Uplands

GREAT BRITAIN

NORTH SEA

SCANDINAVIA

Trondheim

Bergen Oslo

SVEALAND

Stockholm

GÖTALAND

VESTERÅLEN

LOFOTEN

IRELAND

Dublin

Cork

IRISH SEA

MAN

ANGLESEY

Liverpool

PENNINES

ENGLAND

Birmingham

WALES

CAMBRIAN MTS.

Bristol

London

CELTIC SEA

CORNWALL

LAND'S END

ISLES OF SCILLY

ENGLISH CHANNEL

Dover Strait of Dover

Calais

CHANNEL ISLANDS

BRITTANY

Armorican Massif

Normandy Hills

NORMANDY

Le Havre

Brest

ILE DE RÉ

ILE D'OLÉRON

FLANDERS

Brussels

PARIS

FRENCH BASIN

CHAMPAGNE

ARDENNES

Luxembourg

RHENISH SLATE MOUNTAINS

Frankfurt

BAVARIA

Munich

BAVARIAN PLATEAU

BLACK FOREST

SWABIAN JURA

VOSGES

GERMAN PLAIN

Hamburg

Berlin

HARZ

BOHEMIA

Prague

FRISIAN ISLANDS

FRIESLAND

Amsterdam

Rotterdam

Cologne

Düsseldorf

BALTIC

JYLLAND

København Copenhagen

SJÆLLAND

FYN

LOLLAND

BORNHOLM

RÜGEN

POMERANIA

Gdańsk (Danzig)

SILESIA

Wrocław Breslau

ÖLAND

GOTLAND

SKÅNE

Malmö

Kiel

BORDEAUX

AQUITAINE BASIN

Toulouse

PYRENEES

MASSIF CENTRAL

Lyon

PROVENCE

Marseille

GULF OF LION

JURA

ALPS

Bern

Geneva

Mont Blanc

Torino

Milano

PO VALLEY

Genova

Venezia

LIGURIAN SEA

CORSICA

Ajaccio

TUSCAN ARCHIPELAGO

ELBA

APENNINES

Roma Rome

Napoli

VESUVIUS

TYRRHENIAN SEA

TYRRHENIAN BASIN

SARDINIA

Cagliari

ASINARA

ADRIATIC SEA

DALMATIA

SLAVONIA

BOSNIA

HERZEGOVINA

GALICIA

La Coruña

CANTABRIAN MTS.

Bilbao

IBERIAN PENINSULA

SUBMESETA NORTE

IBERIAN MTS.

Madrid

SISTEMA CENTRAL

SUBMESETA SUR

Serra da Estrela

Lisboa Lisbon

Porto

ARAGON

CATALONIA

Barcelona

Catalan Coastal Range

LA MANCHA

Valencia

BALEARIC ISLANDS

MINORCA

MAJORCA

IBIZA

FORMENTERA

SIERRA MORENA

ANDALUSIA

Sevilla Seville

SISTEMAS BÉTICOS

SIERRA NEVADA

Málaga

Gulf of Cádiz

Cádiz

ALGARVE

Tangier

Gibraltar

SEA OF ALBORAN

RIF

Rabat

Casablanca

Marrakech

MIDDLE ATLAS

HIGH ATLAS

ANTI-ATLAS

ATLAS MOUNTAINS

SAHARAN ATLAS

TELL ATLAS

Oran

Constantine

HAUTS PLATEAUX

Tunis

SICILY

Palermo

Messina

LIPARI ISLANDS

EGADI ISLANDS

USTICA

PANTELLERIA

PELAGIE ISLANDS

MALTA

GOZO

IONIAN SEA

JABAL NAFŪSAH

TRIPOLITANIA

Tarābulus Tripoli

Gulf of Sidra

Gulf of Gabès

DJERBA

KERKENNAH ISLANDS

JBEL OUARKZIZ

HAMADA DU DRAA

HAMADA DU GUIR

GRAND ERG OCCIDENTAL

GRAND ERG ORIENTAL

AL ḤAMĀDAH AL ḤAMRĀ

AZORES

GRACIOSA

SÃO JORGE

PICO

TERCEIRA

SÃO MIGUEL

SANTA MARIA

Azores-Gibraltar Ridge

Iberian Basin

Josephine Seamount

Ampère Seamount

Seine Seamount

MADEIRA ISLANDS

Funchal

PORTO SANTO

ILHAS DESERTAS

CANARY ISLANDS

LA PALMA

HIERRO

GOMERA

TENERIFE

Santa Cruz de Tenerife

GRAN CANARIA

FUERTEVENTURA

LANZAROTE

ILHAS SELVAGENS

Dacia Seamount

MEDITERRANEAN SEA

ALGERIAN BASIN

Scale 1:15,000,000   Lambert Azimuthal Equal Area Projection

0   200   400   600   800   1000 km

0   250   500 miles

Longitude East 10 of Greenwich

Map 6 **EUROPE, POLITICAL**

Greenland (Den.)

KING FREDERIK VI COAST

KING CHRISTIAN IX LAND

Greenland Sea

Denmark Strait

Scoresby Sund

Norwegian Sea

JAN MAYEN (Norway)

ICELAND

Reykjavik

Arctic Circle

VATNAJÖKULL

VESTERÅLEN

LOFOTEN

NORWAY

Namsos

Kristiansund

Ålesund

Molde

Trondheim

Östersund

SWEDEN

Dombås

Gjøvik

Oslo

Bergen

Haugesund

Stavanger

Skien

Kristiansand

Göteborg

Falun

Västerås

Örebro

Stockholm

Norrköping

Linköping

Jönköping

Faeroe Islands (Den.)

FØROYAR / FÆRØENE

SHETLAND ISLANDS

ORKNEY ISLANDS

HEBRIDES

ROCKALL

Thurso

Inverness

Aberdeen

Dundee

Glasgow

Edinburgh

Londonderry

Sligo

Belfast

North Sea

DENMARK

Ålborg

Frederikshavn

Herning

Esbjerg

Århus

København Copenhagen

Kolding

Odense

Flensburg

Kiel

Helsingborg

Halmstad

Malmö

Karlskrona

Trelleborg

BORNHOLM (Den.)

ÖLAND

GOTLAND

Gdynia

Gdańsk (Danzig)

Szczecin Stettin

IRELAND

Galway

Limerick

Waterford

Cork

Mizen Head

Irish Sea

Dublin

Carlisle

Newcastle upon Tyne

Middlesbrough

UNITED KINGDOM

Manchester

Liverpool

Leeds

Sheffield

Kingston-upon-Hull

Nottingham

Leicester

Birmingham

Norwich

Ipswich

Celtic Sea

Swansea

Cardiff

Oxford

London

Bristol

Exeter

Plymouth

Penzance

Land's End

ISLES OF SCILLY

English Channel

CHANNEL ISLANDS (U.K.)

Brighton

Dover

Calais

Amsterdam

Groningen

Den Haag

's-Gravenhage

Rotterdam

Antwerpen

Bremerhaven

Bremen

Hamburg

Lübeck

Rostock

Stralsund

RÜGEN

Berlin

Magdeburg

GERMANY

Hannover

Osnabrück

Dortmund

Essen

Düsseldorf

Köln Cologne

Bonn

Leipzig

Dresden

Wrocław Breslau

POLAND

Poznań

Bydgoszcz

BELGIUM

Bruxelles Brussel

Liège

Luxembourg

LUXEMBOURG

Frankfurt

Wiesbaden

Mannheim

Würzburg

Nürnberg

Erfurt

Chemnitz

Praha Prague

CZECH REP.

Wałbrzych

Katowice

Ostrava

Brno

Brest

Pointe de Saint-Mathieu

Saint-Malo

Caen

Rouen

Amiens

Reims

Metz

Saarbrücken

Nancy

Strasbourg

Stuttgart

Augsburg

Freiburg

München Munich

Regensburg

Linz

Salzburg

Wien Vienna

AUSTRIA

Graz

Győr

Székesfehérvár

HUNGARY

Lorient

Rennes

Angers

Nantes

Le Mans

Tours

Orléans

Paris

Troyes

Dijon

Mulhouse

Besançon

Basel

Bern

Zürich

SWITZERLAND

LIECHTENSTEIN

Innsbruck

Bolzano

Klagenfurt

SLOVENIA

Ljubljana

Zagreb

Trieste

Pécs

La Rochelle

Poitiers

Limoges

FRANCE

Bourges

Clermont-Ferrand

Monts Dore

Saint-Étienne

Lyon

Genève

Lausanne

Mont Blanc 4807

Grenoble

Torino

Milano Milan

Brescia

Verona

Venezia Venice

Parma

Bologna

Genova Genoa

CROATIA

Rijeka

Osijek

BOSNIA AND HERZEGOVINA

Zadar

Split

Dubrovnik

Bordeaux

Cabo de Finisterre

A Coruña

Gijón

Oviedo

Santander

San Sebastián

Bayonne

Toulouse

Montpellier

Nîmes

Avignon

Marseille

Nice

MONACO

Toulon

Cabo de Creus

Perpignan

ANDORRA

Vella

PYRENEES

Pamplona

Bilbao

León

Burgos

Zaragoza Saragossa

La Spezia

Livorno Leghorn

Firenze Florence

SAN MARINO

Ligurian Sea

CORSICA (Fr.)

Bastia

Ajaccio

Perugia

Ancona

ITALY

Pescara

Vigo

Braga

Porto

Coimbra

Valladolid

Salamanca

Douro

Duero

Madrid

Tarragona

Barcelona

Castellón de la Plana

VATICAN CITY

Roma Rome

Napoli Naples

Foggia

Bari

Salerno

Brindisi

Taranto

Lecce

ALBANIA

PORTUGAL

Lisboa Lisbon

Setúbal

Toledo

Cáceres

Badajoz

Évora

SPAIN

Albacete

Valencia

Alicante

BALEARIC ISLANDS

MINORCA

MAJORCA

Palma

IBIZA

SARDINIA

Sassari

Olbia

Nuoro

Cagliari

Tyrrhenian Sea

Ionian Sea

Cosenza

Catanzaro

Cabo de São Vicente

Faro

Huelva

Córdoba

Murcia

Cartagena

Almería

Cádiz

Sevilla

Granada

Málaga

Algeciras

Gibraltar (U.K.)

Ceuta (Spain)

ISLA DE ALBORÁN (Spain)

MEDITERRANEAN SEA

Palermo

Trapani

SICILY

Messina

Reggio di Calabria

Mt. Etna

Catania

Siracusa

Capo delle Correnti

PANTELLERIA (Italy)

MALTA

Valletta

ISOLE PELAGIE

KERKENNAH ISLANDS

DJERBA

ATLANTIC OCEAN

AZORES

GRACIOSA

SÃO JORGE

TERCEIRA

Angra do Heroísmo

PICO

FAIAL

SÃO MIGUEL

Ponta Delgada

SANTA MARIA

Azores (Portugal)

Tangier

Tétouan

Melilla (Spain)

Oujda

Oran

Mostaganem

Tlemcen

Sidi Bel Abbès

Relizane

Chélif

Blida

Al Jazā'ir Algiers

Tizi Ouzou

Bejaïa

Jijel

Skikda

Constantine

Annaba

Sétif

Batna

Biskra

Tébessa

Tūnis

Bizerte

Sūsah Sousse

Şafāqis Sfax

TUNISIA

Tarābulus Tripoli

Al Khums

Ra's Mişrātah

Mişrātah

MADEIRA ISLANDS

Funchal

Madeira (Portugal)

PORTO SANTO

ILHAS DESERTAS

ILHAS SELVAGENS

LA PALMA

TENERIFE

Santa Cruz de Tenerife

Canary Islands (Spain)

GOMERA

HIERRO

GRAN CANARIA

Las Palmas de Gran Canaria

LANZAROTE

FUERTEVENTURA

Casablanca

Rabat

Kenitra

Ksar el Kebir

Larache

El Jadida

Safi

Essaouira

Meknès

Fès

MOROCCO

Marrakech

Agadir

Sidi Ifni

Tiznit

Goulimine

Tan-Tan

ATLAS MOUNTAINS

Er Rachidia

Béchar

Oued Zem

ALGERIA

Ghardaïa

Touggourt

Ouargla

GRAND ERG OCCIDENTAL

GRAND ERG ORIENTAL

El Goléa

Timimoun

Adrar

Hassi Messaoud

Ghadāmis

El Aaiún

Western Sahara

Dakhla

LIBYA

TRIPOLITANIA

Gulf of Sidra

Scale 1:15,000,000   Lambert Azimuthal Equal Area Projection

0 200 400 600 800 1000 km

0 250 500 miles

Longitude East 0 of Greenwich

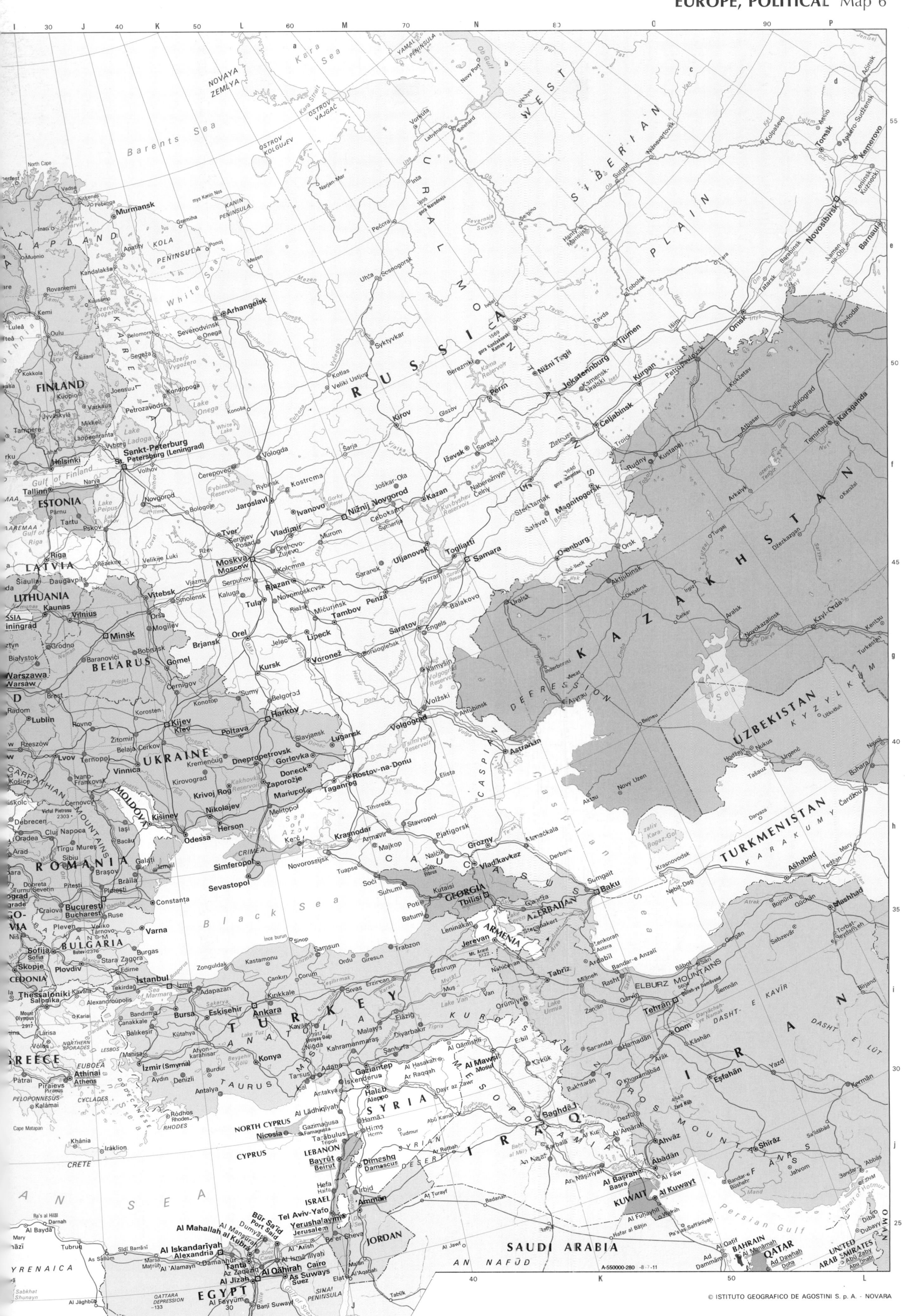

Map 7 **NORTHERN EUROPE**

Scale 1:6,000,000   Delisle Conic Equidistant Projection

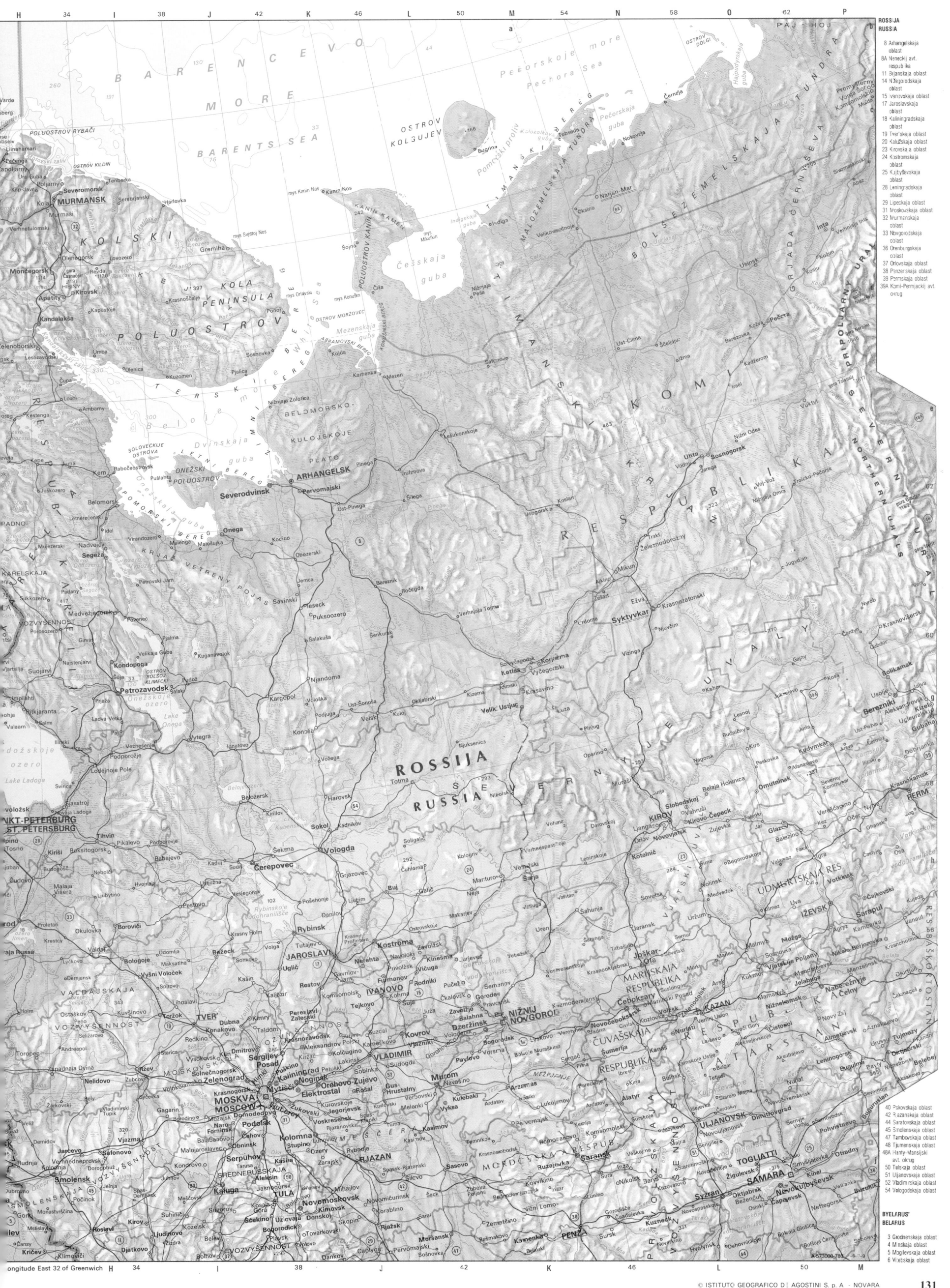

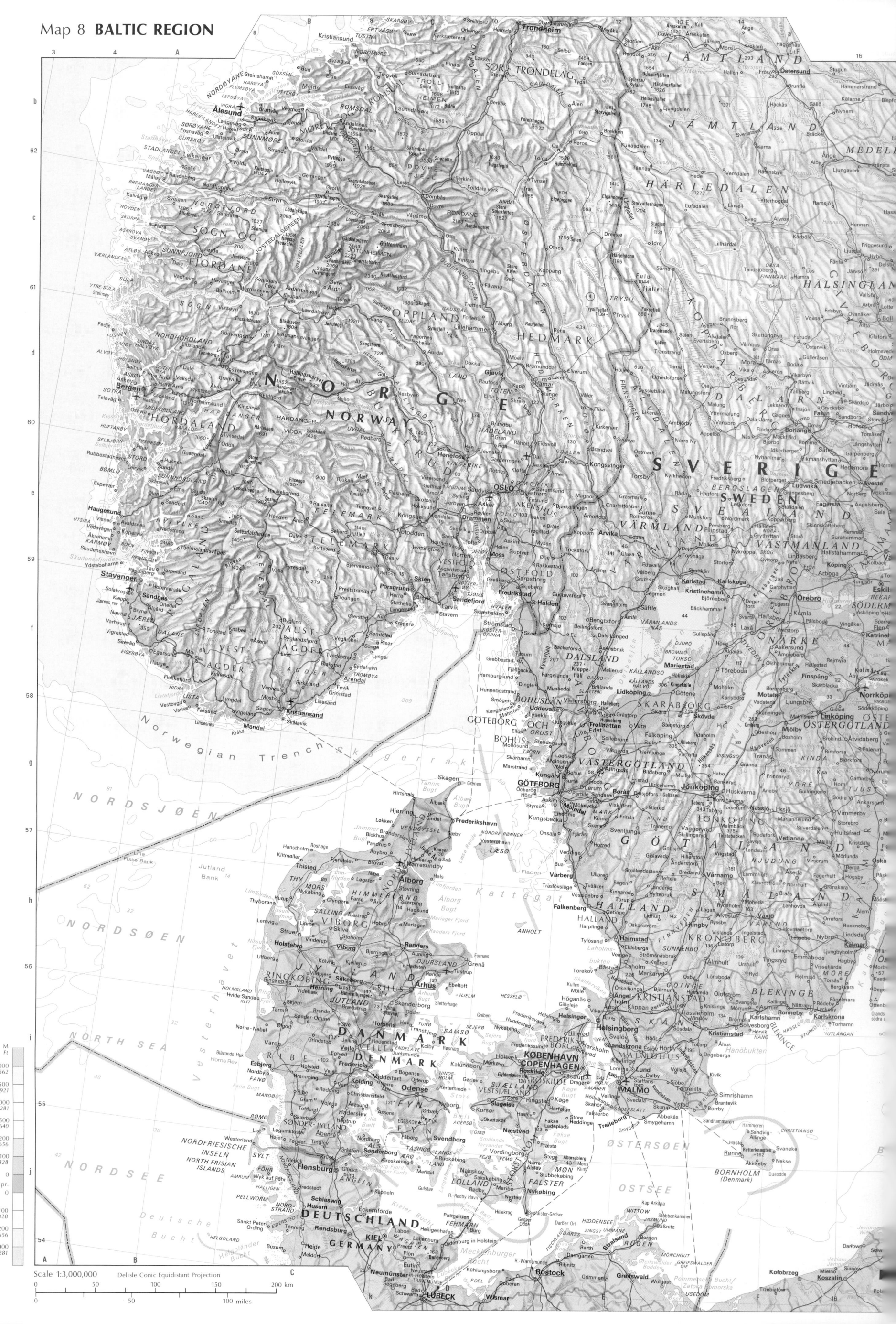

Map 8 **BALTIC REGION**

Scale 1:3,000,000   Delisle Conic Equidistant Projection

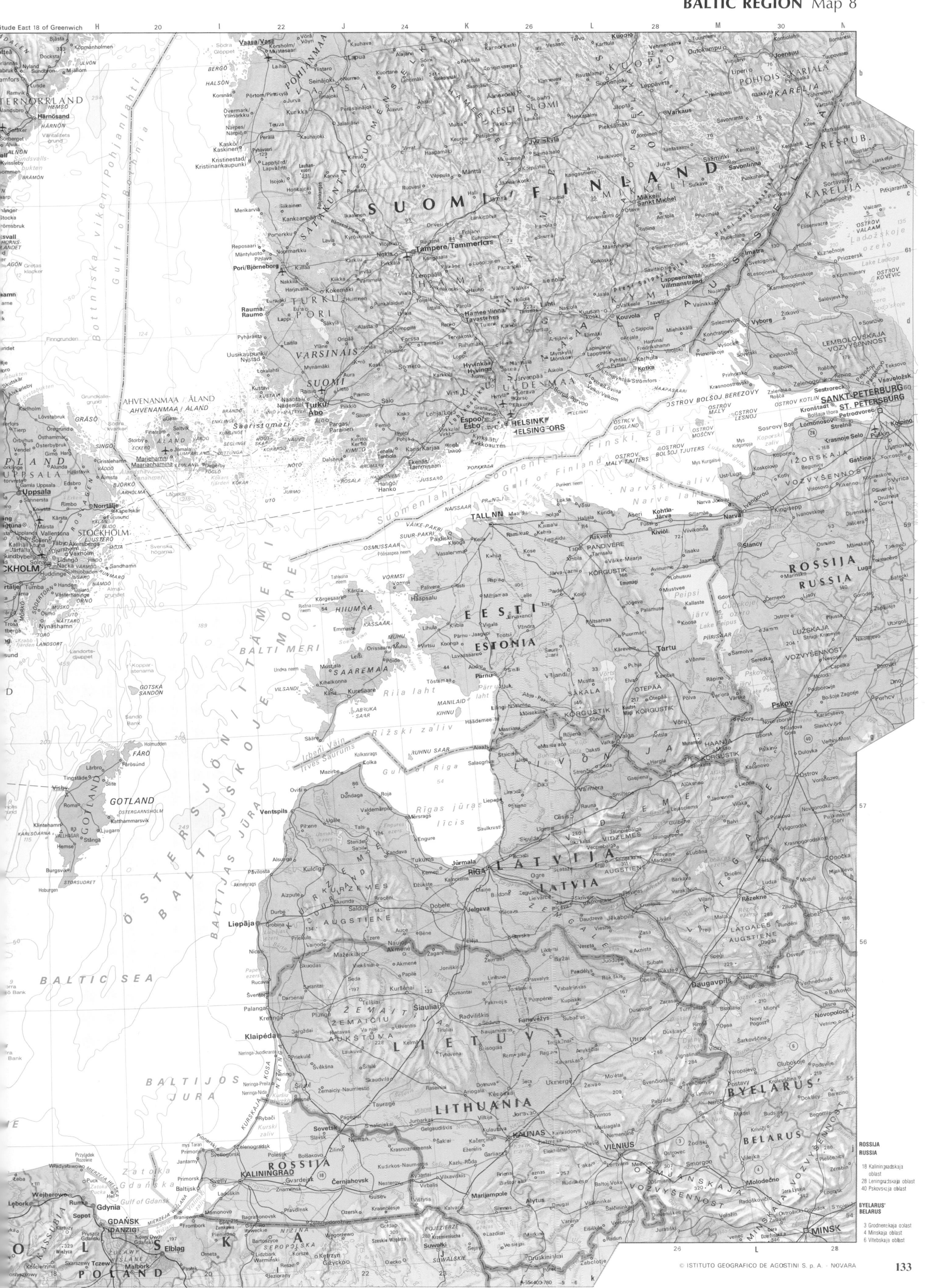

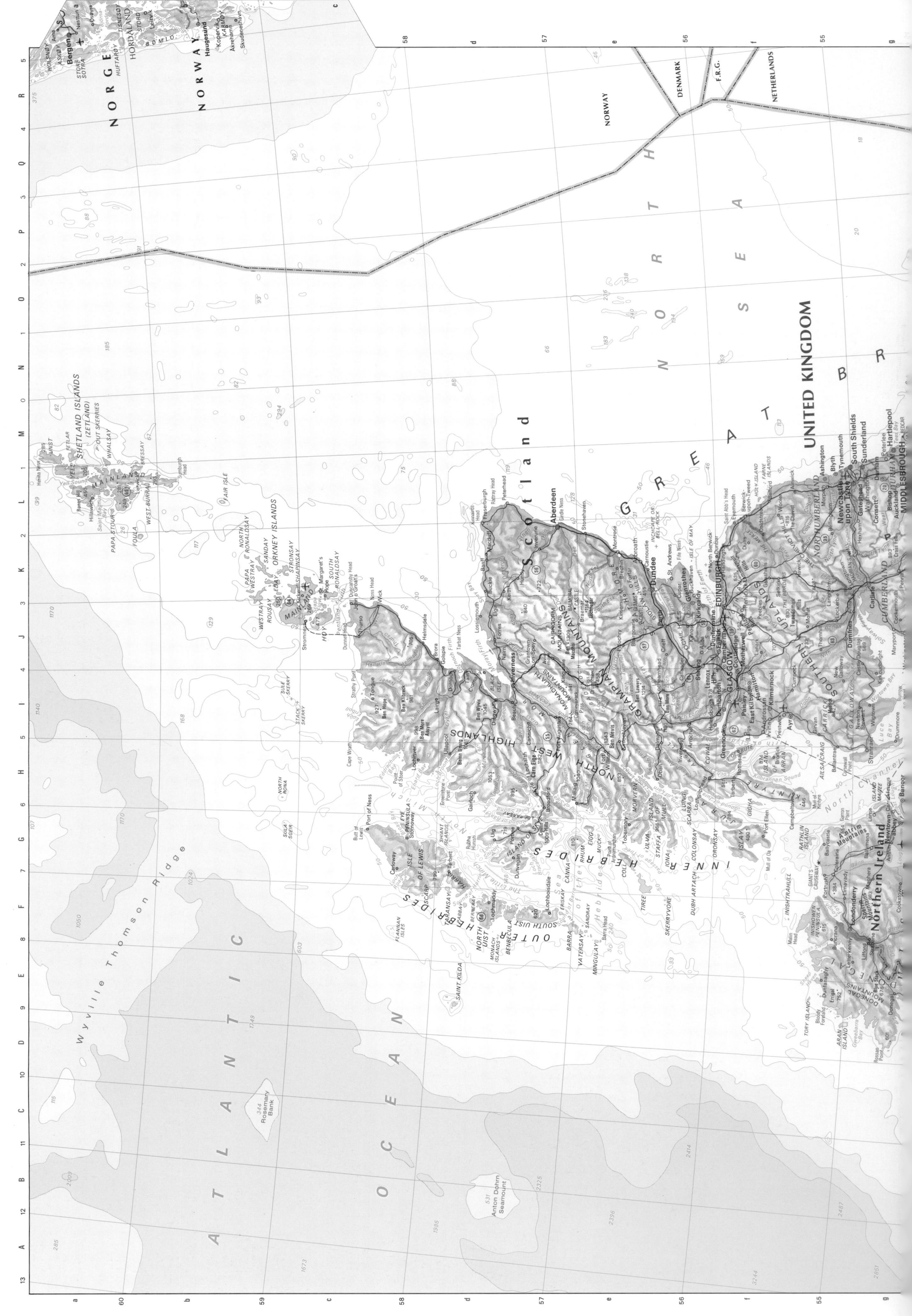

© ISTITUTO GEOGRAFICO DE AGOSTINI S.p.A. - NOVARA

A N G L I A

England

N O R T H   S E A

E N G L I S H   C H A N N E L

L A   M A N C H E

F R A N C E

P I C A R D I A

N O R M A N D I E

PARIS

BELGIQUE
BELGIE
BELGIUM

LONDON

Wales

C A M B R I A N   M O U N T A I N S

Cardigan
Bay

Bristol Channel

S a i n t   G e o r g e ' s   C h a n n e l

I R I S H   S E A

I R E L A N D
E I R E

DUBLIN
BAILE ÁTHA CLIATH

C O N N A U G H T

L E I N S T E R

M U N S T E R

C E L T I C   S E A

A T L A N T I C
O C E A N

CHANNEL
ISLANDS

JERSEY
GUERNSEY

B R I T T A N Y

KINGSTON-UPON-HULL
LEEDS
BRADFORD
SHEFFIELD
MANCHESTER
LIVERPOOL
STOKE-ON-TRENT
NOTTINGHAM
LEICESTER
BIRMINGHAM
COVENTRY
CARDIFF
BRISTOL
SOUTHAMPTON
PORTSMOUTH
PLYMOUTH
EXETER
Brighton
Southend-on-Sea

Le Havre
Caen
Rennes
Le Mans
Brest

Longitude West 0 East of Greenwich

Scale 1:3,000,000

Delisle Conic Equidistant Projection

UNITED KINGDOM OF GREAT BRITAIN
AND NORTHERN IRELAND

England
METROPOLITAN COUNTIES
1 Greater London
2 Greater Manchester
3 Merseyside
4 South Yorkshire
5 Tyne and Wear
6 West Midlands
7 West Yorkshire

NON METROPOLITAN COUNTIES
8 Avon
9 Bedfordshire
10 Berkshire
11 Buckinghamshire
12 Cambridgeshire
13 Cheshire
14 Cleveland
15 Cornwall/Isles of Scilly
16 Cumbria
17 Derbyshire
18 Devon
19 Dorset
20 Durham
21 East Sussex
22 Essex
23 Gloucestershire
24 Hampshire
25 Hereford & Worcester
26 Hertfordshire
27 Humberside
28 Isle of Wight
29 Kent
30 Lancashire
31 Leicestershire
32 Lincolnshire
33 Norfolk
34 Northamptonshire
35 Northumberland
36 North Yorkshire
37 Nottinghamshire
38 Oxfordshire
39 Salop
40 Somerset
41 Staffordshire
42 Suffolk
43 Surrey
44 Warwickshire
45 West Sussex
46 Wiltshire

Scotland
REGIONS
55 Highland
56 Grampian
57 Tayside
58 Fife
59 Lothian
60 Borders
61 Central
62 Strathclyde
63 Dumfries and Galloway

ISLANDS AREA
64 Orkney
65 Shetland
66 Western Isles

Wales
COUNTIES
47 Clwyd
48 Dyfed
49 Gwent
50 Gwynedd
51 Mid Glamorgan
52 Powys
53 South Glamorgan
54 West Glamorgan

CROWN DEPENDENCY

200 km
100 miles

M ft
1000 3281
500 1640
200 656
+100 +328
Depr. 0
-100 -328
1000 3281
2000 6562
4000 13123

Map 10 CENTRAL EUROPE

Scale 1:3,000,000   Delisle Conic Equidistant Projection

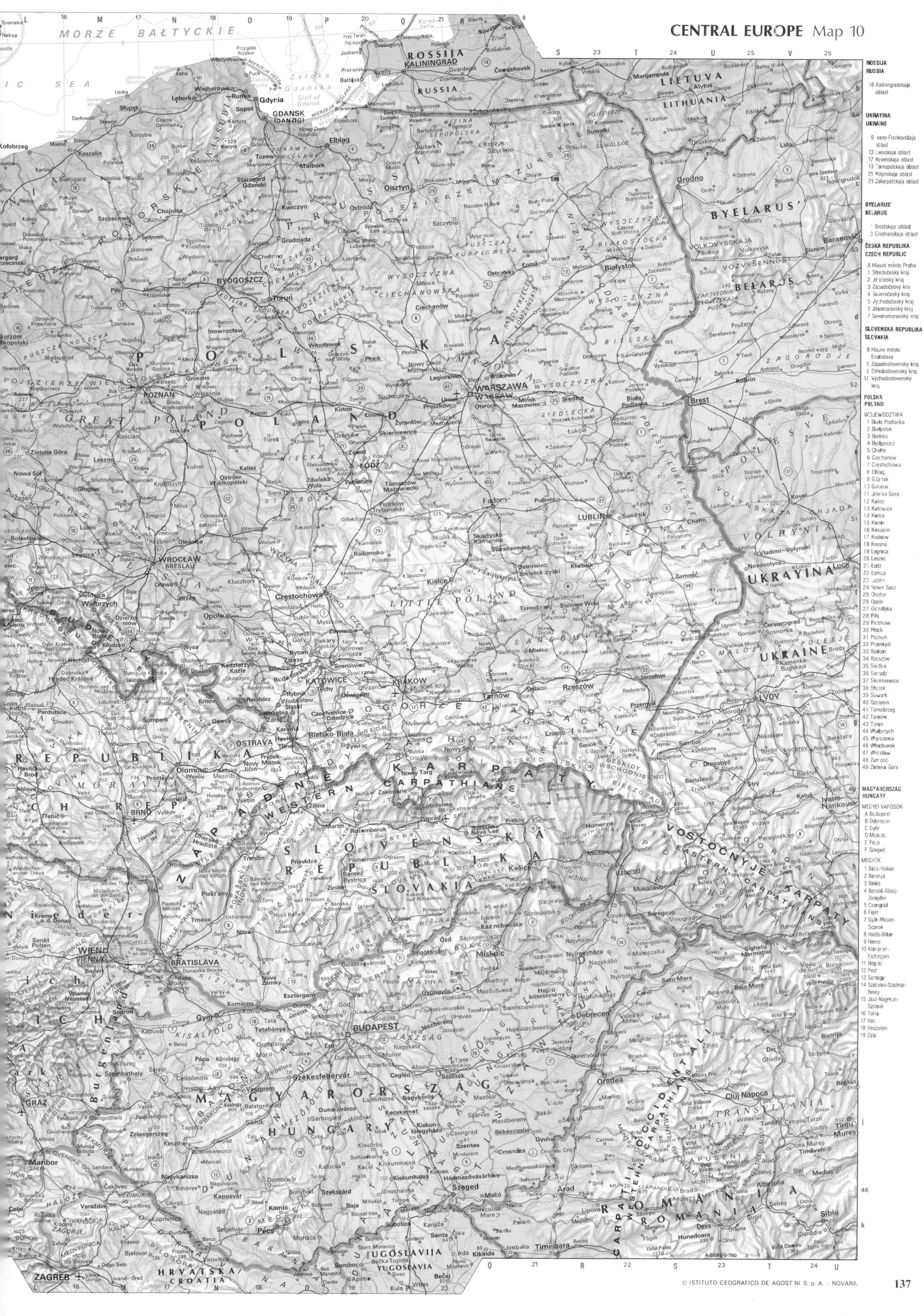

Map 11 FRANCE AND BENELUX

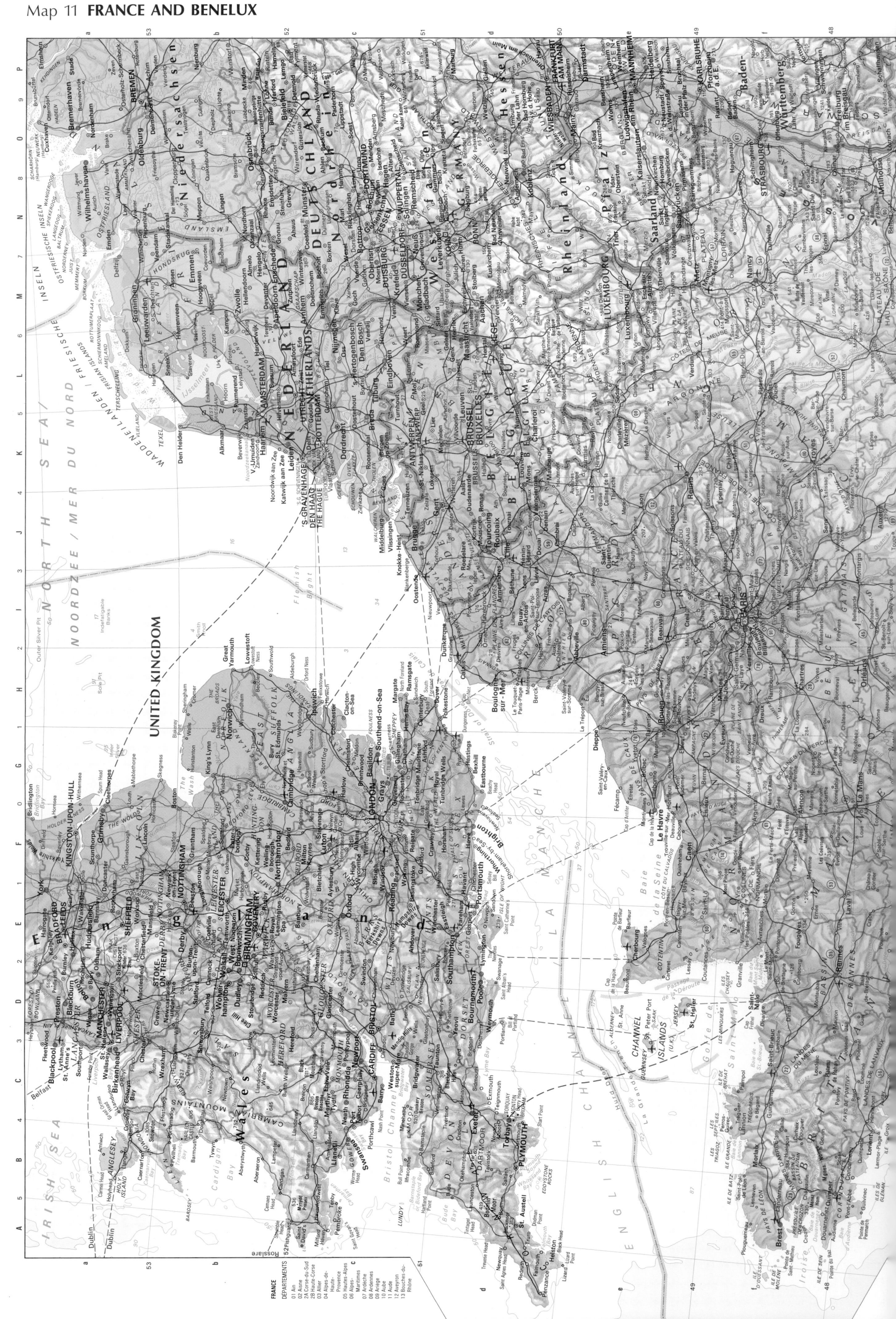

FRANCE
DÉPARTEMENTS
01 Ain
02 Aisne
2A Corse-du-Sud
2B Haute-Corse
04 Alpes-de-
   Haute-
   Provence
05 Alpes-
   Maritimes
07 Ardèche
08 Ardennes
11 Aude
12 Aveyron
13 Bouches-du-
   Rhône

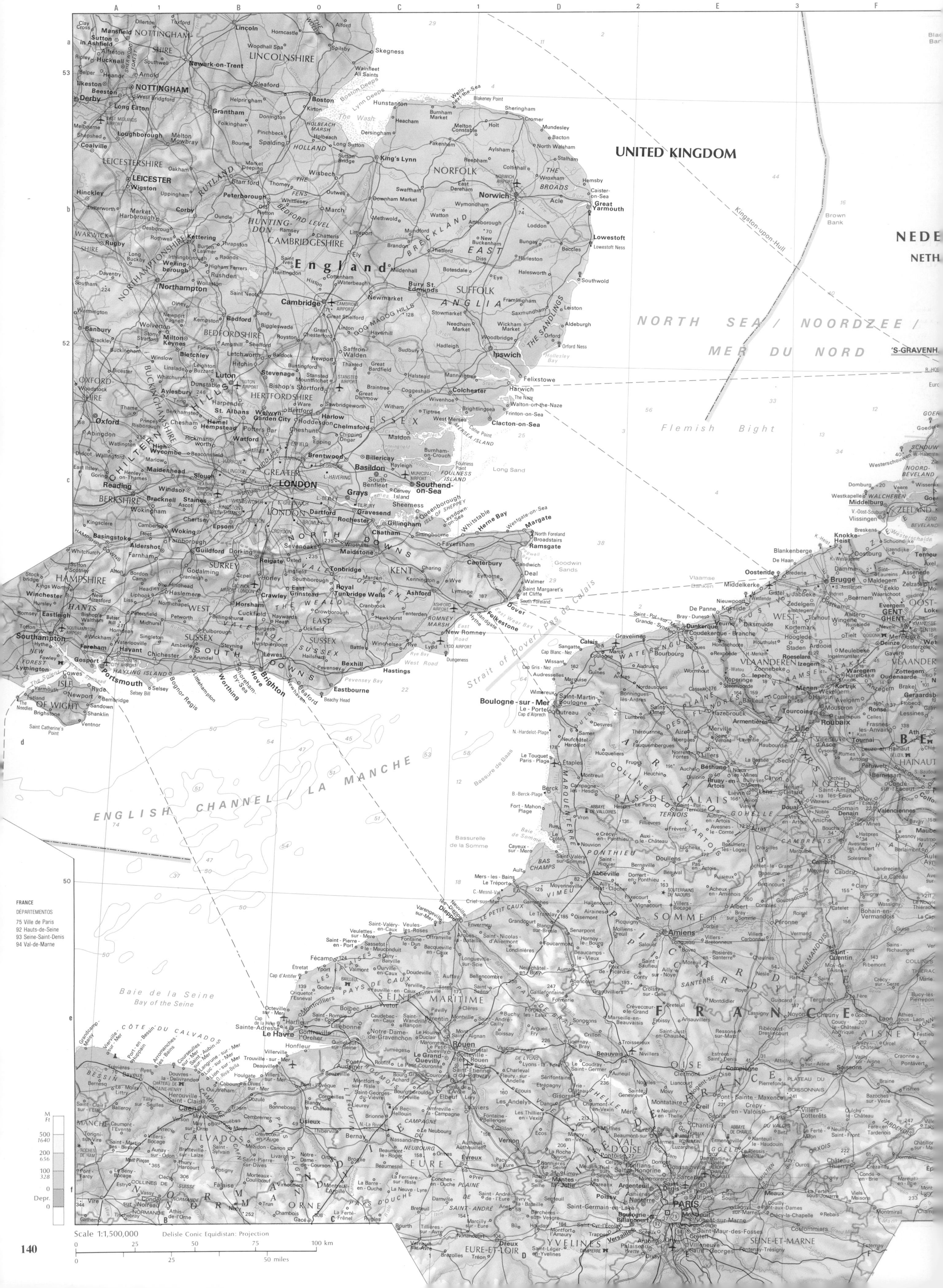

Map 12 **BELGIUM, NETHERLANDS AND LUXEMBOURG**

UNITED KINGDOM

NEDE
NETH
'S-GRAVENH

NORTH SEA / NOORDZEE /
MER DU NORD

Flemish Bight

ENGLAND

NORFOLK

SUFFOLK

EAST
ANGLIA

ESSEX

KENT

SURREY

SUSSEX

LONDON

ENGLISH CHANNEL / LA MANCHE

Strait of Dover / Pas de Calais

Baie de la Seine
Bay of the Seine

CÔTE DU CALVADOS

NORMANDIE

FRANCE

VLAANDEREN
WEST-VLAANDEREN
OOST-GENT
HAINAUT
NORD
PAS DE CALAIS
SOMME
PICARDIE
AISNE
OISE
EURE
SEINE-MARITIME
CALVADOS
ORNE
EURE-ET-LOIR
YVELINES
SEINE-ET-MARNE
PARIS

Brugge
Oostende
Calais
Boulogne-sur-Mer
Dunkerque
Lille
Roubaix
Tourcoing
Amiens
Abbeville
Rouen
Le Havre
Caen
Dieppe
Saint-Quentin

FRANCE
DÉPARTEMENTOS
75 Ville de Paris
92 Hauts-de-Seine
93 Seine-Saint-Denis
94 Val-de-Marne

M
Ft
500 1640
200 656
100 328
0
Depr
0

Scale 1:1,500,000   Delisle Conic Equidistan: Projection

0 ___ 25 ___ 50 ___ 75 ___ 100 km
0 ___ 25 ___ 50 miles

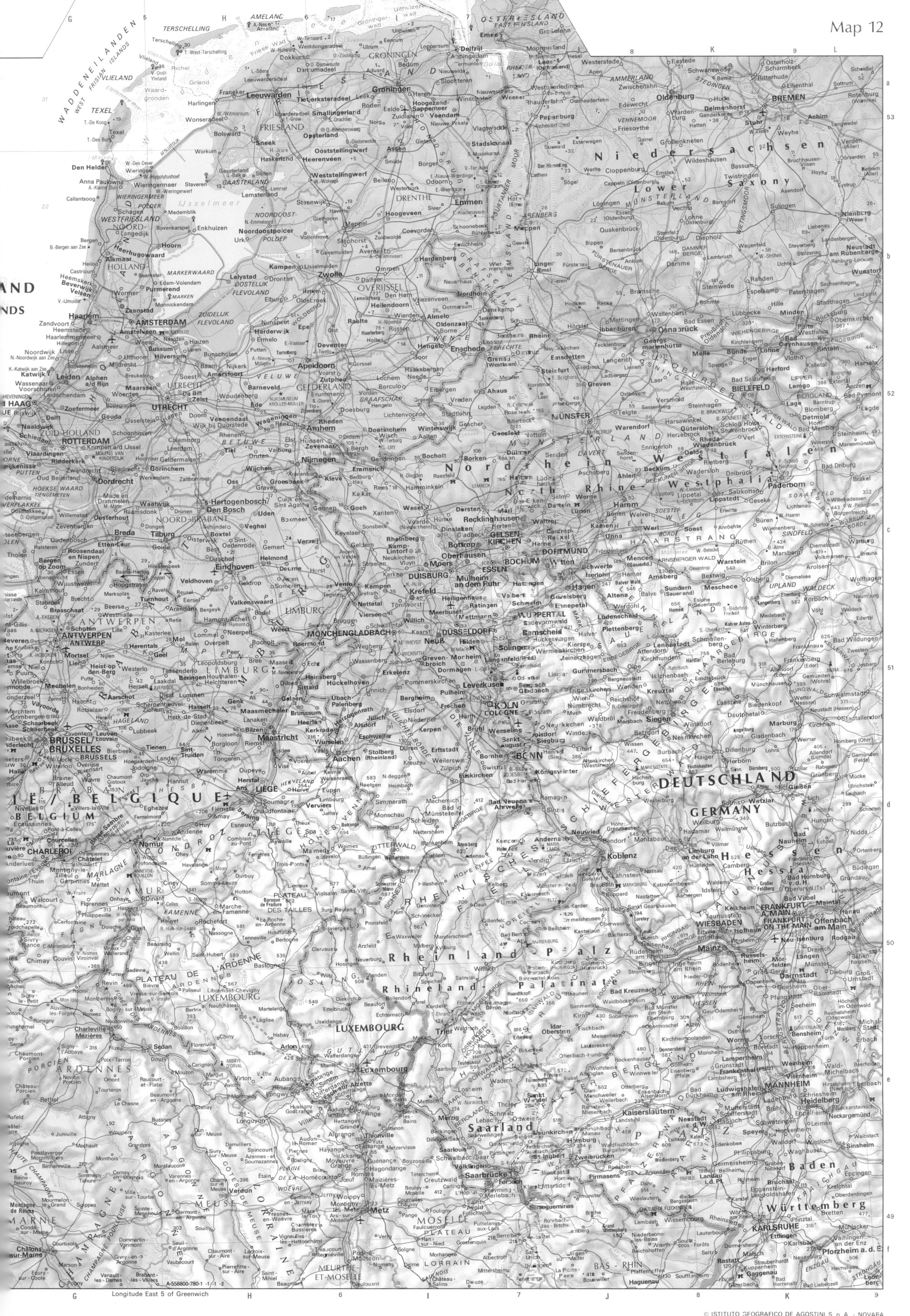

Map 12

Map 13 SPAIN AND PORTUGAL

Scale 1:3,000,000   Delisle Conic Equidistant Projection

Map 14 **ITALY, AUSTRIA AND SWITZERLAND**

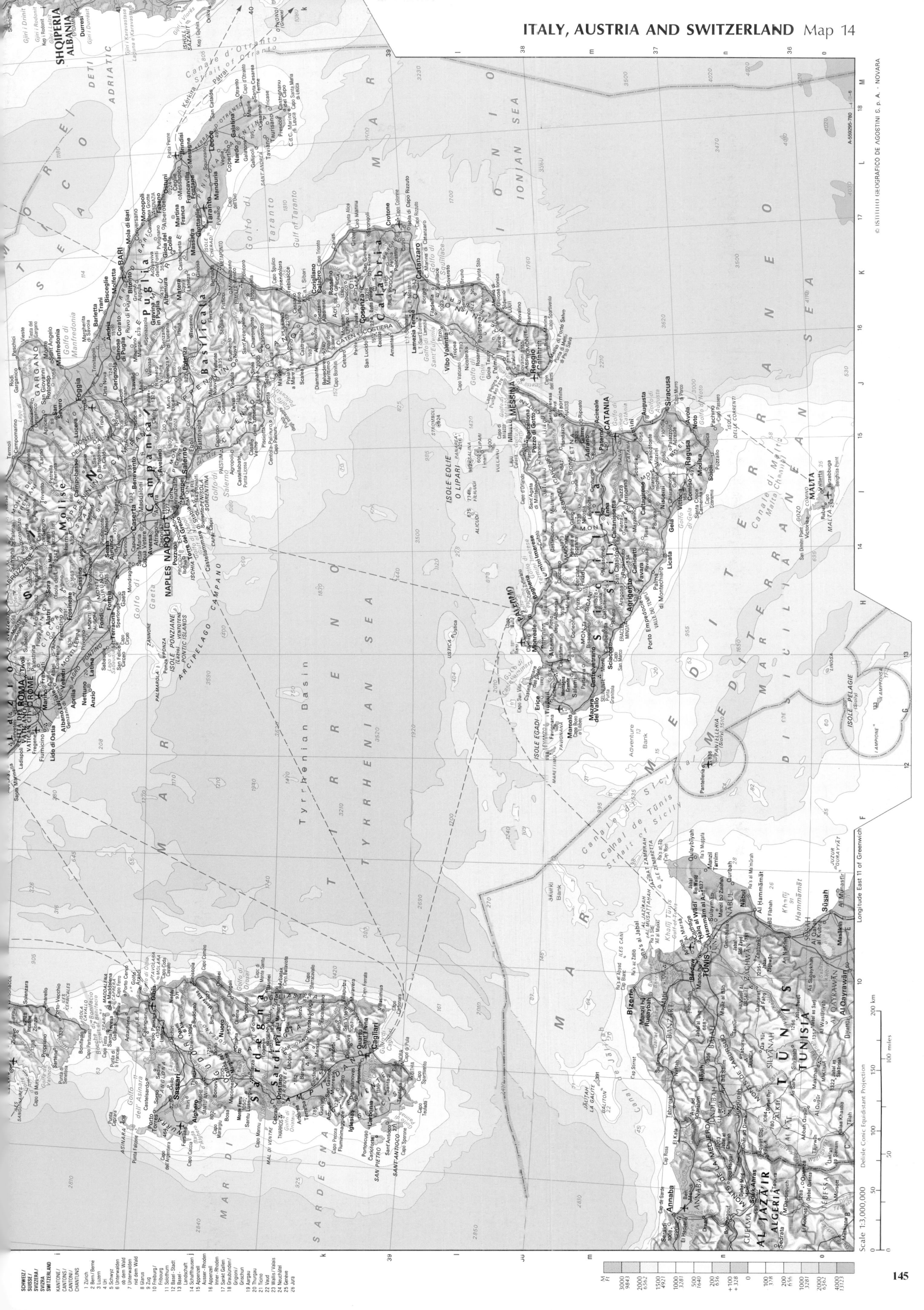

Map 15 **SOUTHEASTERN EUROPE**

Map 15

Map 16 **BLACK AND CASPIAN SEAS REGION**

Scale 1:6,000,000   Delisle Conic Equidistant Projection

Map 17 THE URALS

ROSSIJA
RUSSIA

8 Arhangelskaja oblast
8A Neneckij avt. respublika
12 Čeljabinskaja oblast
14 Gorkovskaja oblast
23 Kirovskaja oblast
24 Kostromskaja oblast
25 Kujbiševskaja oblast
26 Kurganskaja oblast
35 Omskaja oblast
36 Orenburgskaja oblast
39 Permskaja oblast
39A Komi-Permjackij avt. okrug
44 Saratovskaja oblast
46 Jekaterinburgskaja oblast
48 Tjumenskaja oblast
48A Hanty-Mansijskij avt. okrug
48B Jamalo-Neneckij respublika
51 Uljanovskaja oblast
54 Vologodskaja oblast

QAZAQSTAN
KAZAKHSTAN

3 Celinogradskaja oblast
10 Kokčetavskaja oblast
11 Kustanajskaja oblast
15 Severo-Kazahstanskaja oblast
17 Turgajskaja oblast

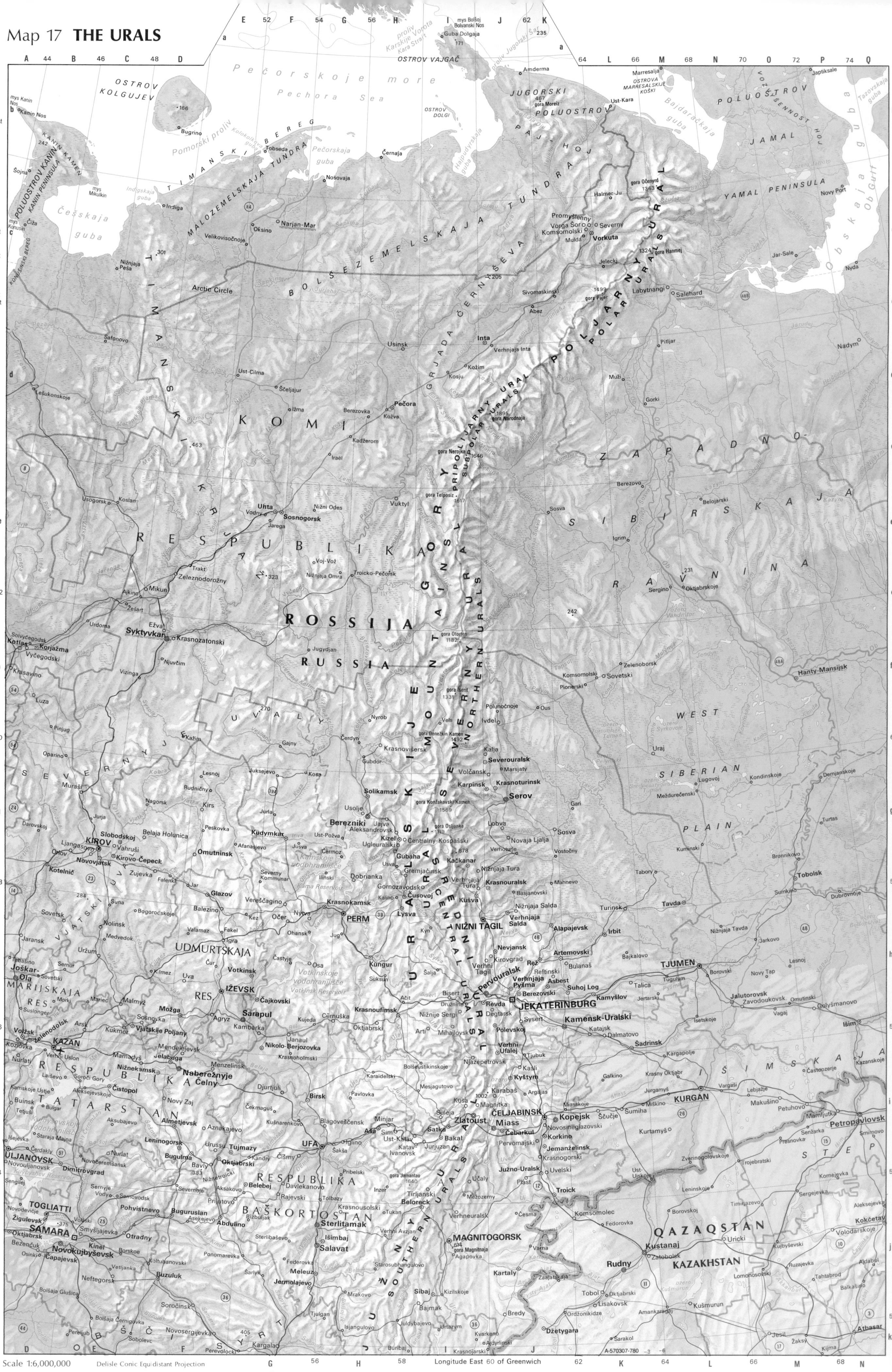

Scale 1:6,000,000   Delisle Conic Equidistant Projection

Longitude East 60 of Greenwich

© ISTITUTO GEOGRAFICO DE AGOSTINI S. p. A. - NOVARA

0   100   200   300   400 km
0   100   200 miles

M   ft
1000 3281
500   1640
200   656
+100 +328
0   0
−100 −328
−200 −656

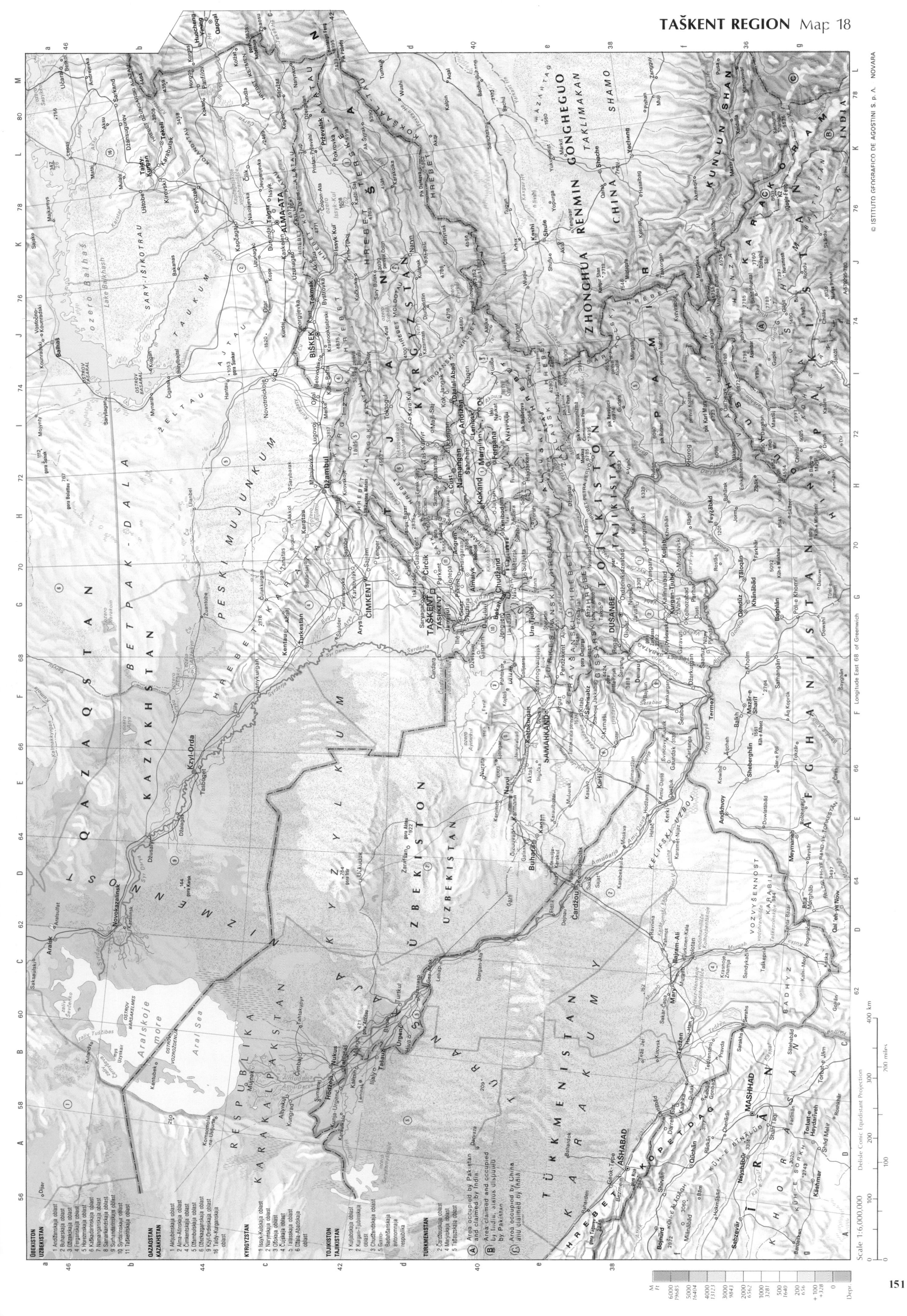

© ISTITUTO GEOGRAFICO DE AGOSTINI S.p.A. NOVARA

Scale 1:6,000,000

DeLisle Conic Equidistant Projection

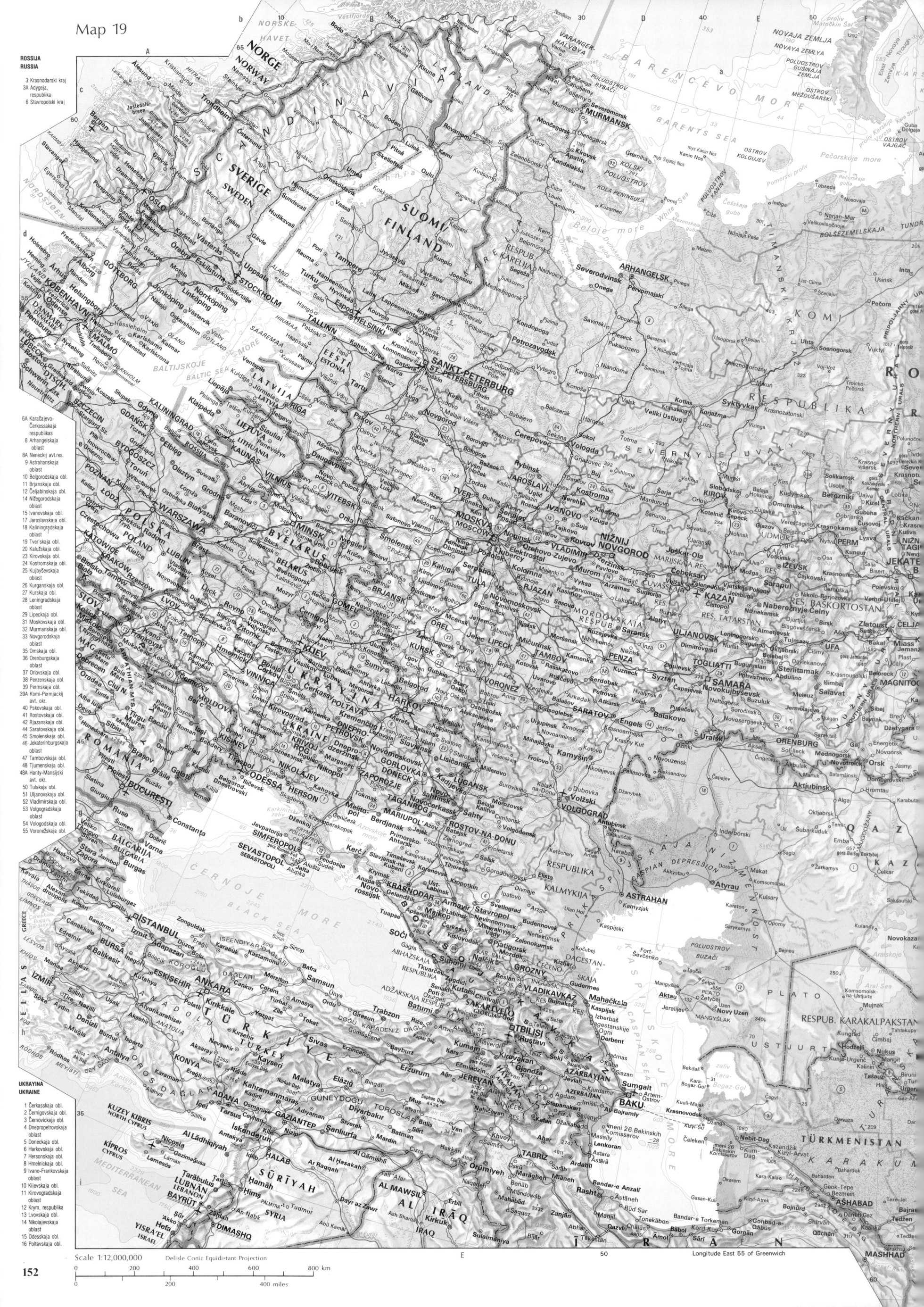

The Commonwealth of Independent States (CIS) was created by republics of the former Soviet Union.

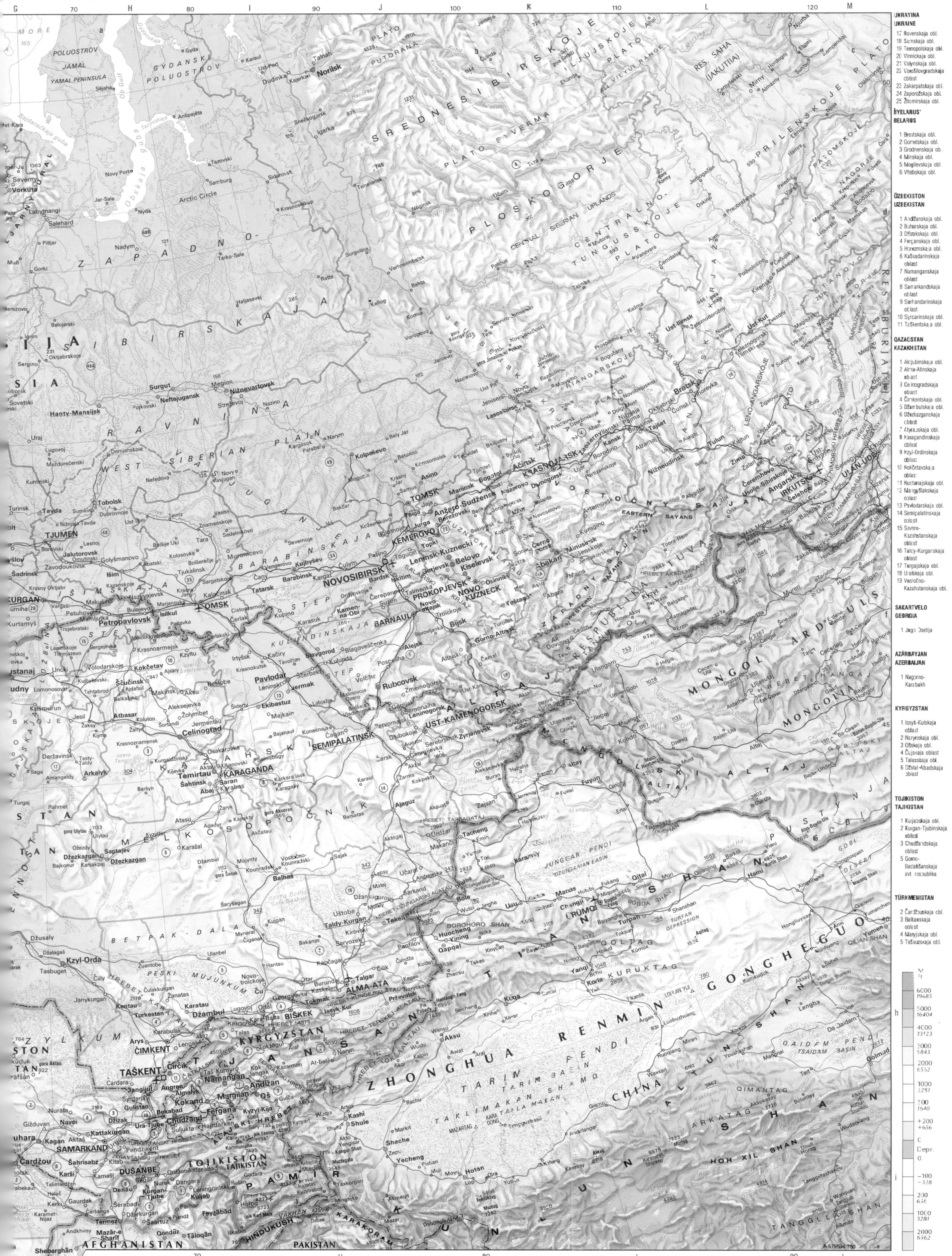

UKRAYINA
UKRAINE
17 Rovenskaja obl.
18 Sumskaja obl.
19 Ternopolskaja obl.
20 Vinnickaja obl.
21 Volynskaja obl.
22 Vorošilovgradskaja oblast
23 Zakarpatskaja obl.
24 Zaporožskaja obl.
25 Žitomirskaja obl.
BYELARUS' BELARUS
1 Brestskaja obl.
2 Gomelskaja obl.
3 Grodnenskaja obl.
4 Minskaja obl.
5 Mogilevskaja obl.
6 Vitebskaja obl.
ÜZBEKISTON UZBEKISTAN
1 Andižanskaja obl.
2 Buharskaja obl.
3 Džizakskaja obl.
4 Ferganskaja obl.
5 Horezmskaja obl.
6 Kaškadarinskaja oblast
7 Namanganskaja oblast
8 Samarkandskaja oblast
9 Surhandarinskaja oblast
10 Syrdarinskaja obl.
11 Taškentskaja obl.
QAZAQSTAN KAZAKHSTAN
1 Aktjubinskaja obl.
2 Alma-Atinskaja oblast
3 Celinogradskaja oblast
4 Čimkentskaja obl.
5 Džambulskaja obl.
6 Džezkazganskaja oblast
7 Atyrauskaja obl.
8 Karagandinskaja oblast
9 Kzyl-Ordinskaja oblast
10 Kokčetavskaja oblast
11 Kustanajskaja obl.
12 Mangyšlakskaja oblast
13 Pavlodarskaja obl.
14 Semipalatinskaja oblast
15 Severo-Kazahstanskaja oblast
16 Talcy-Kurganskaja oblast
17 Turgajskaja obl.
18 Uralskaja obl.
19 Vostočno-Kazahstanskaja obl.
SAKARTVELO GEORGIA
1 Jugo Osetija
AZÄRBAYJAN AZERBAIJAN
1 Nagorno-Karabakh
KYRGYZSTAN
1 Issyk-Kulskaja oblast
2 Narynskaja obl.
3 Ošskaja obl.
4 Čujskaja oblast
5 Talasskaja obl.
6 Džalal-Abadskaja oblast
TOJIKISTON TAJIKISTAN
1 Kuljabskaja obl.
2 Kurgan-Tjubinskaja oblast
3 Chudžandskaja oblast
4 Gorno-Badahšanskaja avt. respublika
TÜRKMENISTAN
2 Čardžouskaja obl.
3 Balkanskaja oblast
4 Maryjskaja obl.
5 Tašauzskaja obl.
M Ft
6000 19685
5000 16404
4000 13123
3000 9843
2000 6562
1000 3281
500 1640
+200 +656
0
Depr.
0
-100 -328
200 656
1000 3281
2000 6562
ZAPADNO-SIBIRSKAJA RAVNINA
WEST SIBERIAN PLAIN
SREDNESIBIRSKOJE PLOSKOGORJE
CENTRAL SIBERIAN UPLANDS
KAZAHSKIJ MELKOSOPOČNIK
ZHONGHUA RENMIN GONGHEGUO
CHINA
MONGOLIA
TARIM PENDI
TARIM BASIN
TAKLIMAKAN SHAMO
KYRGYZSTAN
TOJIKISTON TAJIKISTAN
AFGHANISTAN
PAKISTAN

Map 20

Scale 1:12,000,000   Delisle Conic Equidistant Projection

0   200   400   600   800 km

0   200   400 miles

154

ZHONGHUA RENMIN GONGHEGUO   CHI

The Commonwealth of Independent States (CIS) was created by republics of the former Soviet Union.

ARCTIC OCEAN

SEVERNYJ LEDOVITYJE OKEAN

NEW SIBERIAN ISLANDS
NOVOSIBIRSKIJE OSTROVA
OSTROVA ANŽU
ANJOU ISLANDS
OSTROVA DE-LONGA
DE LONG ISLANDS

ČUKOTSKOJE MORE
CHUKCHI SEA

ČUKOTSKI POLUOSTROV
CHUCH PENINSULA

Alaska U.S.

OSTROV WRANGEL

VOSTOČNO-SIBIRSKOJE MORE
EAST SIBERIAN SEA

ANADYRSKOJE PLOSKOGORJE

KORJAKSKOJE NAGORJE

KOLYMSKAJA NIZMENNOST

JANO-INDIGIRSKAJA NIZMENNOST

VERHOJANSKIJ HREBET

CHERSKOGO

Jakutsk

JUGOSLOVSKAJA

Magadan

OHOTSKOJE MORE

POLUOSTROV KAMČATKA
KAMCHATKA PENINSULA

SREDINNYJ HREBET

BERINGOVO MORE
BERING SEA

Petropavlovsk-Kamčatski

Aleutian Trench

Obruchev Rise

KOMANDORSKIJE OSTROVA
KOMANDORSKI ISLANDS

OSTROV SACHALIN

SAKHALIN

KURILSKIJE OSTROVA
KURIL ISLANDS

Južno-Sahalinsk

Komsomolsk-na-Amure

HABAROVSK

Birobidžan

Blagoveščensk

STANOVOJ HREBET
STANOVOY RANGE

HREBET DZUGDZUR

HARBIN

QIQIHAR

MUDANJIANG

VLADIVOSTOK

Ussurijsk

Nahodka

MANCHURIA

CHANGCHUN

SEA OF JAPAN

JAPONSKOJE MORE

HOKKAIDO

SAPPORO

ASAHIKAWA

HAKODATE

NIPPON JAPAN

HONSHŪ

PACIFIC OCEAN

VELIKIJ (TICHIJ) OKEAN

Ostrov Kunašir, ostrov Šikotan, ostrov Iturup and Malaja Kurilskaja Grjada, occupied since 1945, are claimed by Japan pending a final peace treaty.

Longitude East 150 of Greenwich

Map 21 **ASIA, PHYSICAL**

PACIFIC

Aleutian Trench

ALEUTIAN ISLANDS

FOX ISLANDS

ANDREANOF ISLANDS

ALASKA PENINSULA

ALASKA RANGE

ALASKA

BROOKS RANGE

Bering Sea

Seward Peninsula

Chukchi Sea

Anadyr Gulf

KORJAKSKOJE NAGORJE

KOLYMA RANGE

KAMCHATKA PENINSULA

SREDINNY HREBET

SIHOTE-ALIN

EASTERN SIBERIA

CHERSKIJ MOUNTAINS

VERKHOYANSK MOUNTAINS

STANOVOY RANGE

ALDAN PLATEAU

LENA MOUNTAINS

CENTRAL SIBERIAN PLAIN

MANCHURIA

GREATER KHINGAN RANGE

LESSER KHINGAN RANGE

STANOVOY UPLAND

NORTH SIBERIAN PLAIN

WEST SIBERIAN PLAIN

YENISEY RIDGE

CENTRAL SIBERIAN UPLAND

Arctic Circle

SAYAN

EASTERN SAYANS

KHANGAI

ALTAI

MONGOLIAN ALTAI

DZUNGARIAN BASIN

GOBI DESERT

TIAN SHAN

TARIM BASIN

TAYMYR PENINSULA

BYRRANGA MOUNTAINS

SEVERNAYA ZEMLYA

NOVAYA ZEMLYA

YAMAL PENINSULA

KAZAKHSTAN

KAZAKH HILLS

URAL MOUNTAINS

TIMAN RIDGE

NORTHERN URALS

KARELIA

SCANDINAVIA

Gulf of Bothnia

KOLA PENINSULA

White Sea

VALDAI HILLS

CENTRAL RUSSIAN UPLAND

UKRAINE

VOLGA BASIN

KIRGHIZ STEPPE

CASPIAN DEPRESSION

Caspian Sea

CAUCASUS

CISCAUCASIA

TRANSCAUCASIA

ARMENIA

MESOPOTAMIA

ZAGROS

GREENLAND

ARCTIC OCEAN

North Pole

Lomonosov Ridge

Eurasia Basin

Makarov Basin

Canada Basin

BAFFIN

ELLESMERE

DEVON

QUEEN ELIZABETH ISLANDS

VICTORIA

BANKS

MELVILLE

PRINCE OF WALES

SVERDRUP ISLANDS

AXEL HEIBERG

KNUD RASMUSSEN LAND

Fram Basin

SPITSBERGEN

FRANZ JOSEPH LAND

Barents Sea

Kara Sea

BEAR ISLAND

EDGEØYA

Greenland Sea

Norwegian Sea

Greenland Basin

Mohns Ridge

Denmark Strait

JAN MAYEN

ICELAND

Reykjanes Ridge

Iceland Basin

ATLANTIC OCEAN

FAEROE ISLANDS

SHETLAND ISLANDS

ORKNEY ISLANDS

BRITISH ISLES

GREAT BRITAIN

IRELAND

North Sea

Celtic Sea

Land's End

BRITTANY

MASSIF CENTRAL

ALPS

JURA

VOSGES

POLAND

SILESIA

BOHEMIA

BOHEMIAN FOREST

CARPATHIAN MTS

BALKAN MTS

BALKAN PENINSULA

PINDUS MTS

APENNINES

CORSICA

SARDINIA

Mediterranean Sea

ANATOLIA

TAURUS MTS

CYPRUS

CRETE

KURIL ISLANDS

Kuril Trench

HOKKAIDO

SAKHALIN

Sea of Okhotsk

KAMCHATKA

Tatar Strait

BUREYA RANGE

Yellow Sea

SHANDONG

ORDOS

Map 22 **ASIA, POLITICAL**

Scale 1:30,000,000   Lambert Azimuthal Equal Area Projection

Map 23 **SOUTHWESTERN ASIA**

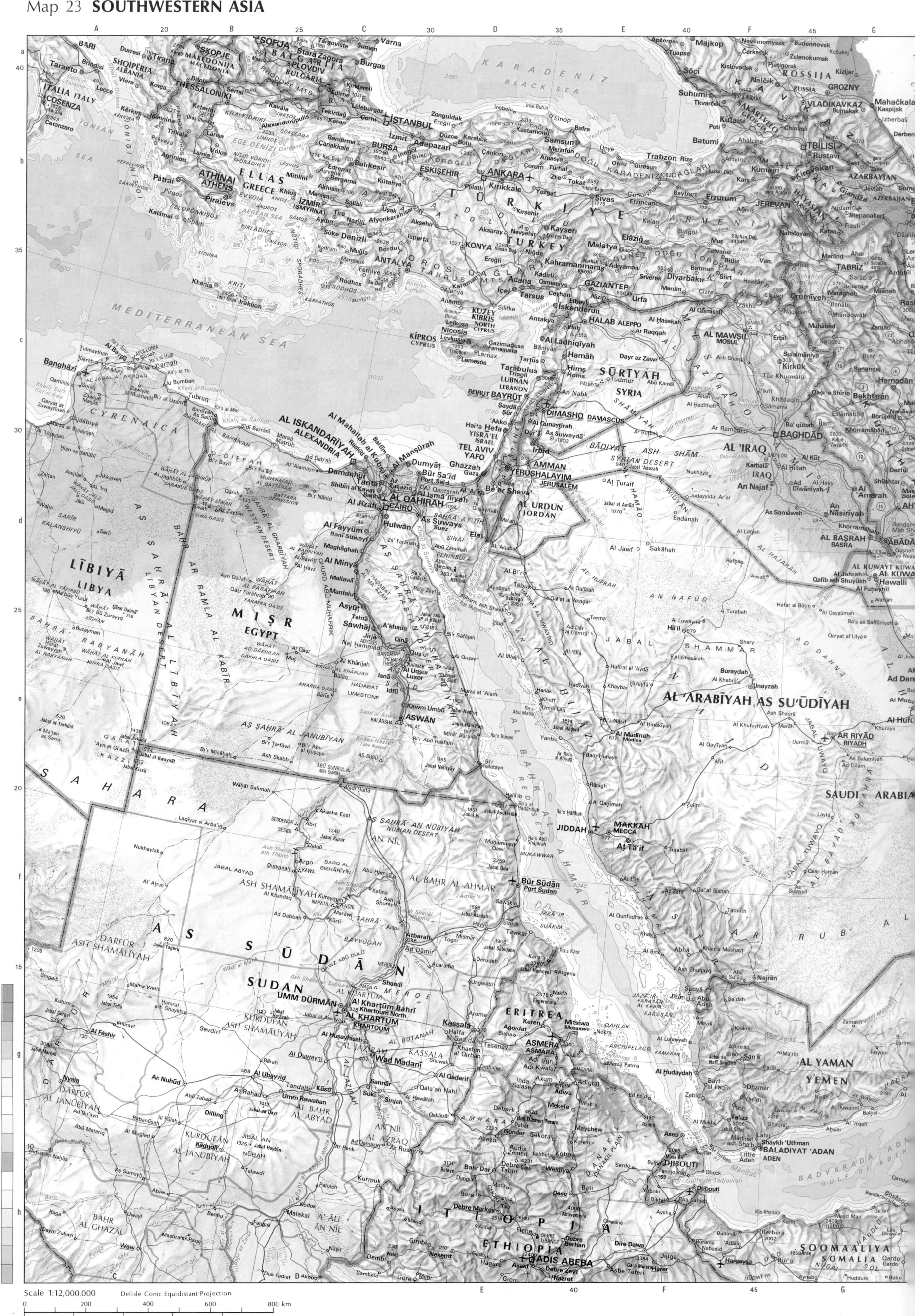

Scale 1:12,000,000   Delisle Conic Equidistant Projection

A Area occupied by Pakistan and claimed by India.
B Area claimed and occupied by India; status disputed by Pakistan.
C Area occupied by China and claimed by India.

A-569900-780

© ISTITUTO GEOGRAFICO DE AGOSTINI S.P.A. - NOVARA

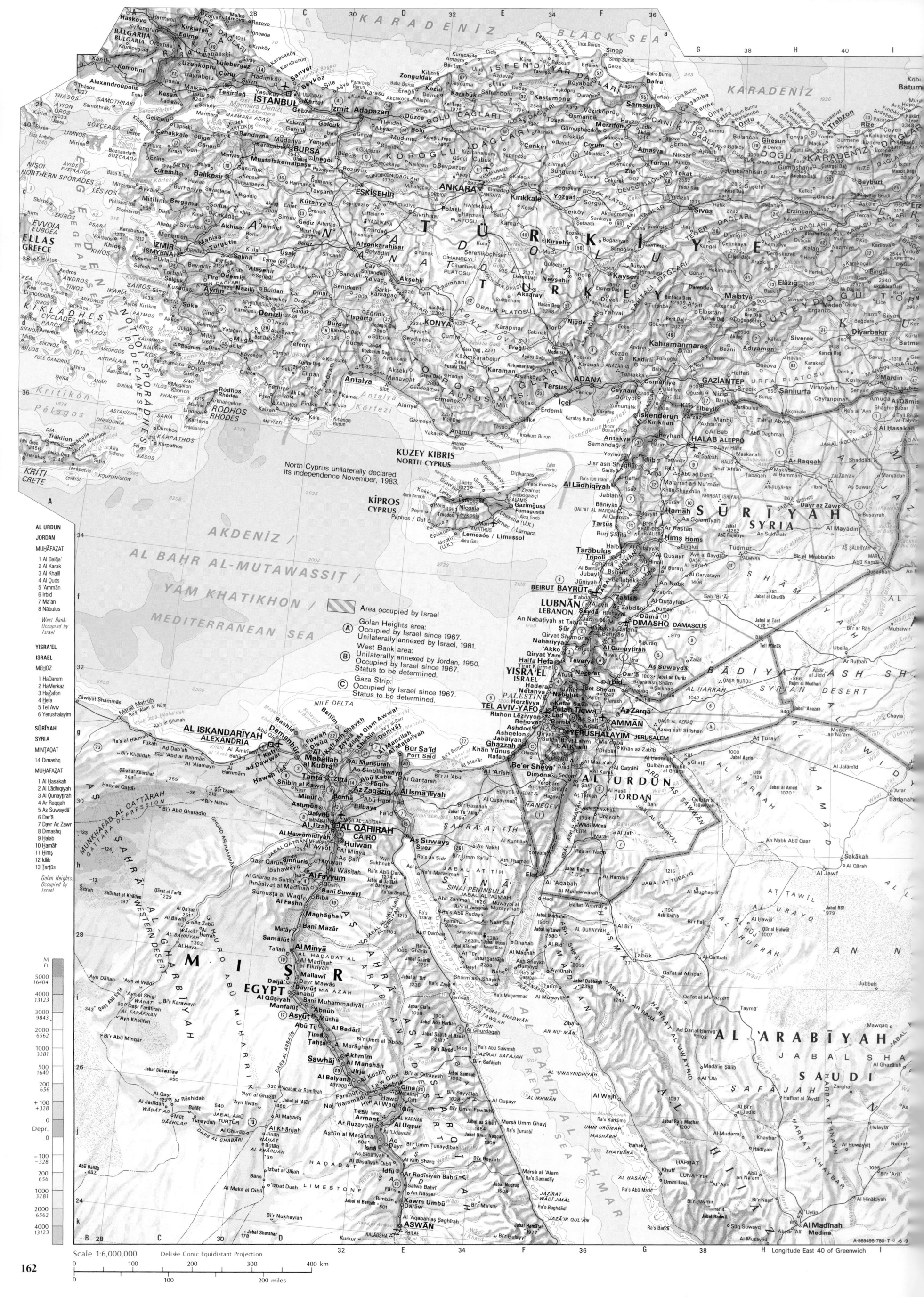

Scale 1:6,000,000   Delisle Conic Equidistant Projection   Longitude East 40 of Greenwich

A-569495-780-7

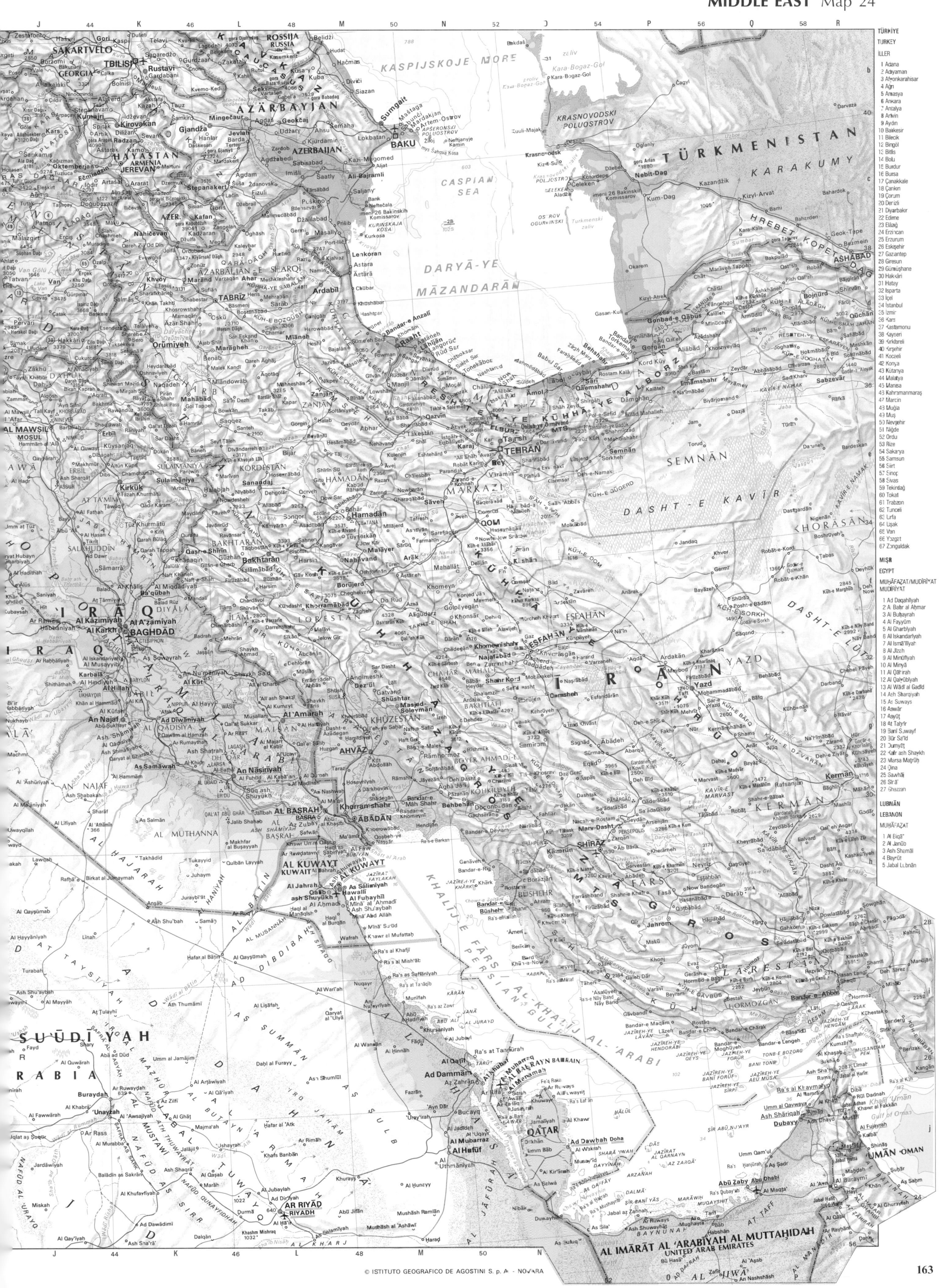

TÜRKIYE
TURKEY
İLLER

1 Adana
2 Adıyaman
3 Afyonkarahisar
4 Ağrı
5 Amasya
6 Ankara
7 Antalya
8 Artvin
9 Aydın
10 Balıkesir
11 Bilecik
12 Bitlis
13 Bingöl
14 Bolu
15 Burdur
16 Bursa
17 Çanakkale
18 Çankırı
19 Çorum
20 Denizli
21 Diyarbakır
22 Edirne
23 Elazığ
24 Erzincan
25 Erzurum
26 Eskişehir
27 Gaziantep
28 Giresun
29 Gümüşhane
30 Hakkari
31 Hatay
32 Isparta
33 İçel
34 İstanbul
35 İzmir
36 Kars
37 Kastamonu
38 Kayseri
39 Kırklareli
40 Kırşehir
41 Kocaeli
42 Konya
43 Kütahya
44 Malatya
45 Manisa
46 Kahramanmaraş
47 Mardin
48 Muğla
49 Muş
50 Nevşehir
51 Niğde
52 Ordu
53 Rize
54 Sakarya
55 Samsun
56 Siirt
57 Sinop
58 Sivas
59 Tekirdağ
60 Tokat
61 Trabzon
62 Tunceli
63 Urfa
64 Uşak
65 Van
66 Yozgat
67 Zonguldak

MIŞR
EGYPT
MUḨĀFAZAT/MUDĪRĪYAT
MUDĪRYAT

1 Ad Daqahlīyah
2 A. Baḩr al Aḩmar
3 Al Buḩayrah
4 Al Fayyūm
5 Al Gharbīyah
6 Al Iskandarīyah
7 Al Ismāʿīlīyah
8 Al Jīzah
9 Al Minūfīyah
10 Al Minyā
11 Al Qāhirah
12 Al Qalyūbīyah
13 Al Wādī al Gadīd
14 Ash Sharqīyah
15 As Suways
16 Aswān
17 Asyūţ
18 At Taḩrīr
19 Banī Suwayf
20 Būr Saʿīd
21 Dumyāţ
22 Kafr ash Shaykh
23 Marsa Maţrūḩ
24 Qinā
25 Saʿawhāj
26 Shamāl Sīnāʾ
27 Ghazzan

LUBNĀN
LEBANON
MUḨĀFAZAT

1 Al Biqāʿ
2 Al Janūb
3 Ash Shamāl
4 Bayrūt
5 Jabal Lubnān

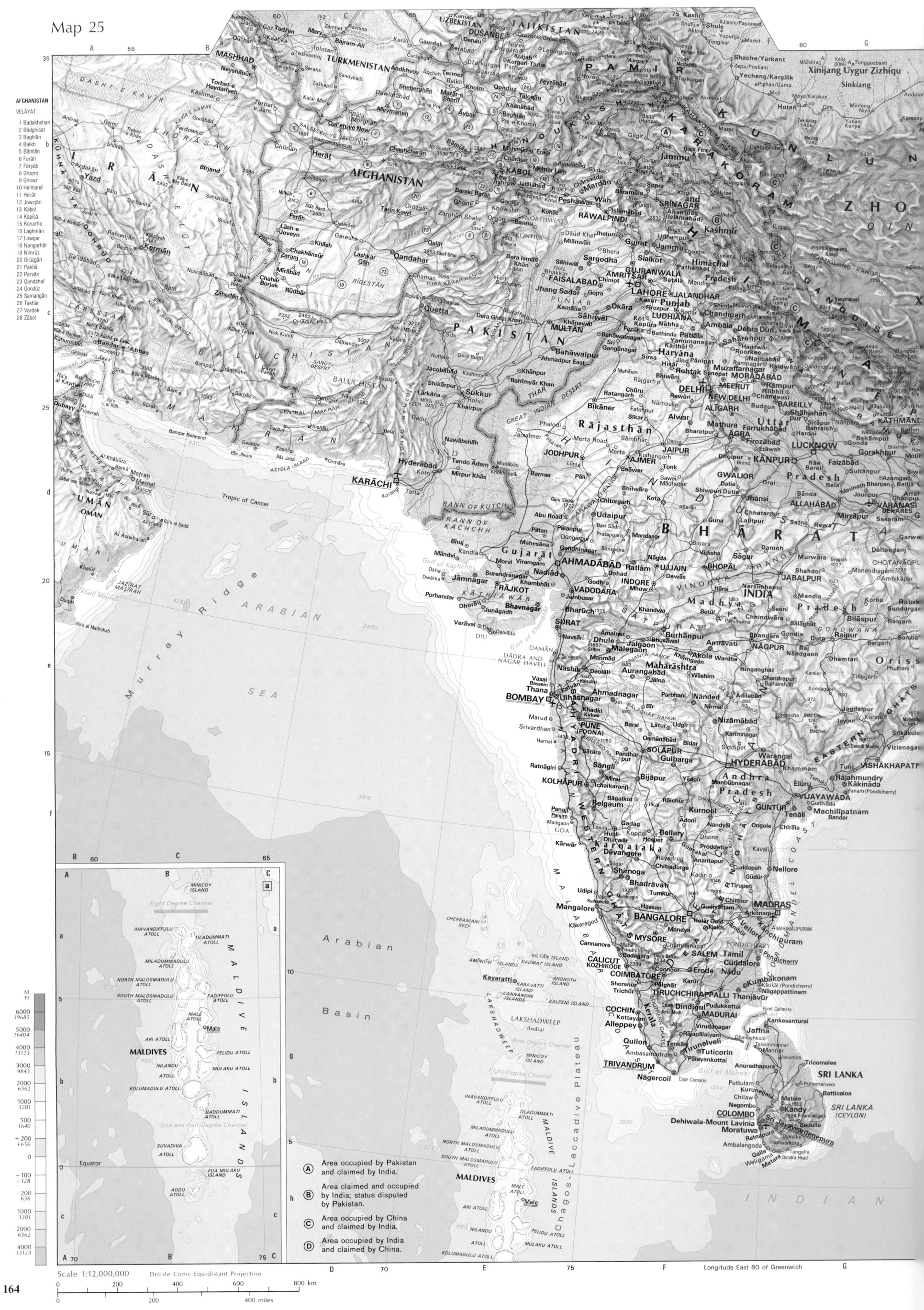

Map 25

Scale 1:12,000,000   Delisle Conic Equidistant Projection

Longitude East 80 of Greenwich

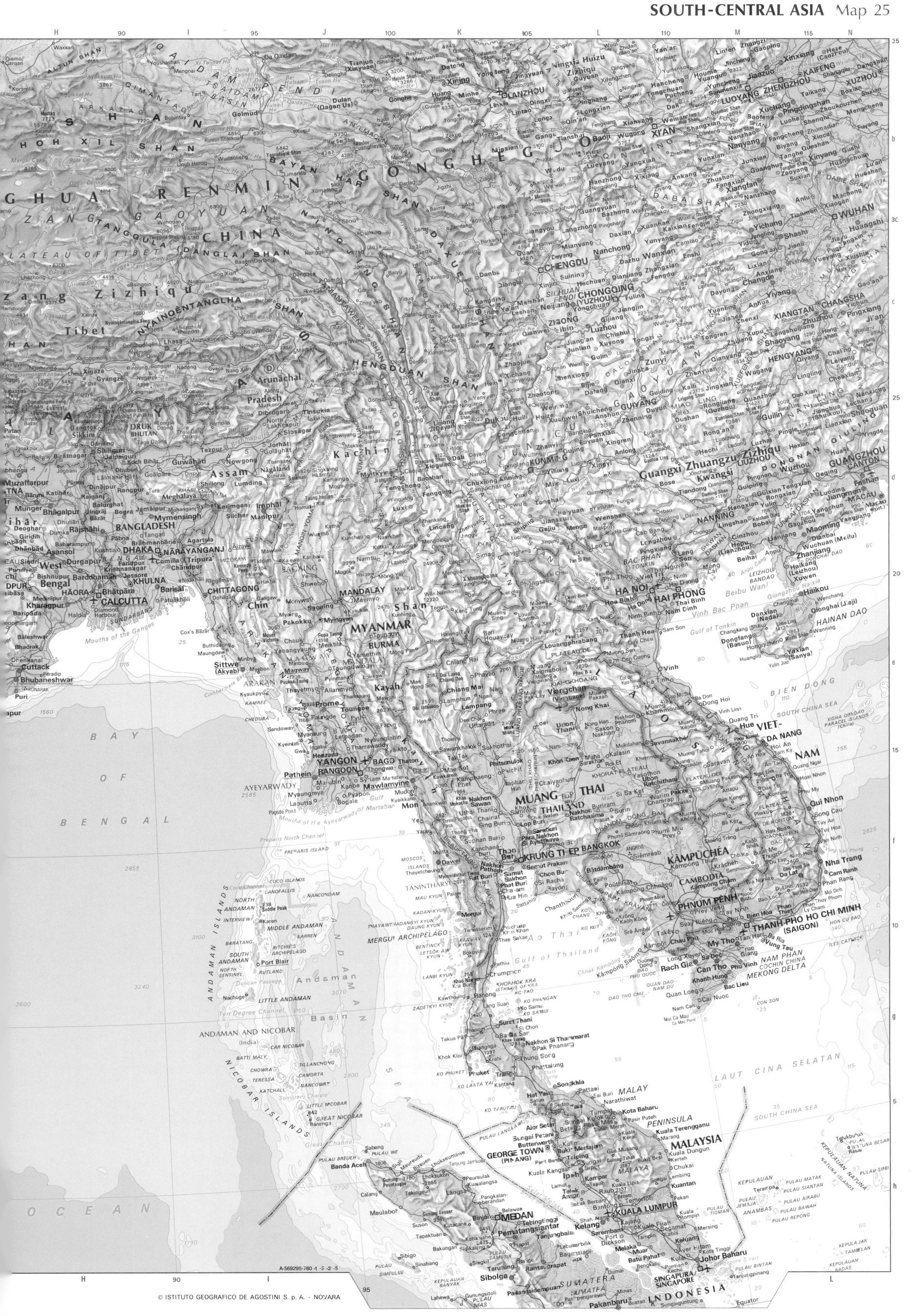

Map 26 **SOUTHEAST ASIA**

MALAYSIA
Semenanjung
Malaysia

WILAYAH
PERSEKUTUAN

A Kuala Lumpur

NEGERI

1 Johor
2 Kedah
3 Kelatan
4 Melaka
5 Negeri Sembilan
6 Pahang
7 Perak
8 Perlis
9 Pulau Pinang
10 Selangor
11 Terengganu

M ft
5000 16404
4000 13123
3000 9843
2000 6562
1000 3281
500 1640
+ 200 + 656
0 0
− 100 − 328
200 656
2000 6562
4000 13123
6000 19685
8000 26247

Scale 1:12,000,000 at the Equator

Mercator Cylindrical Projection

Longitude East 110 of Greenwich

0   200   400   600   800 km

0   200   400 miles

A-569800-780-2 -2 -2 -2

© ISTITUTO GEOGRAFICO DE AGOSTINI S. p. A. - NOVARA

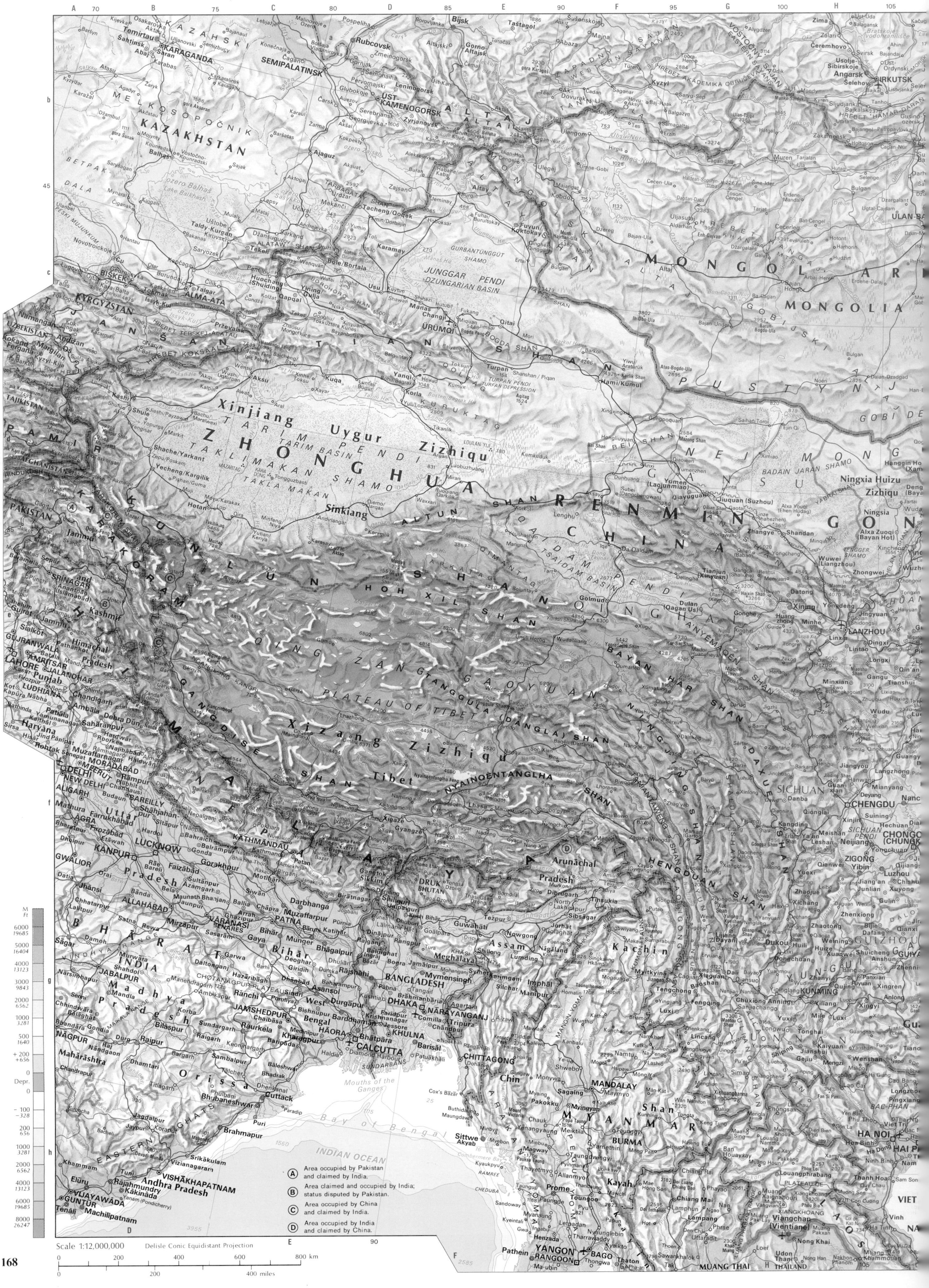

Map 27 **CHINA AND MONGOLIA**

M Ft
6000 19685
5000 16404
4000 13123
3000 9843
2000 6562
1000 3281
500 1640
+ 200 +656
0 0
Depr.
0 0
— 100 —328
200 656
1000 3281
2000 6562
4000 13123
6000 19685
8000 26247

Ⓐ Area occupied by Pakistan and claimed by India.
Ⓑ Area claimed and occupied by India; status disputed by Pakistan.
Ⓒ Area occupied by China and claimed by India.
Ⓓ Area occupied by India and claimed by China.

Scale 1:12,000,000   Delisle Conic Equidistant Projection

0   200   400   600   800 km
0   200   400 miles

Longitude East 120 of Greenwich

© ISTITUTO GEOGRAFICO DE AGOSTINI S.p.A. - NOVARA

Map 28 **NORTHEASTERN CHINA, KOREA AND JAPAN**

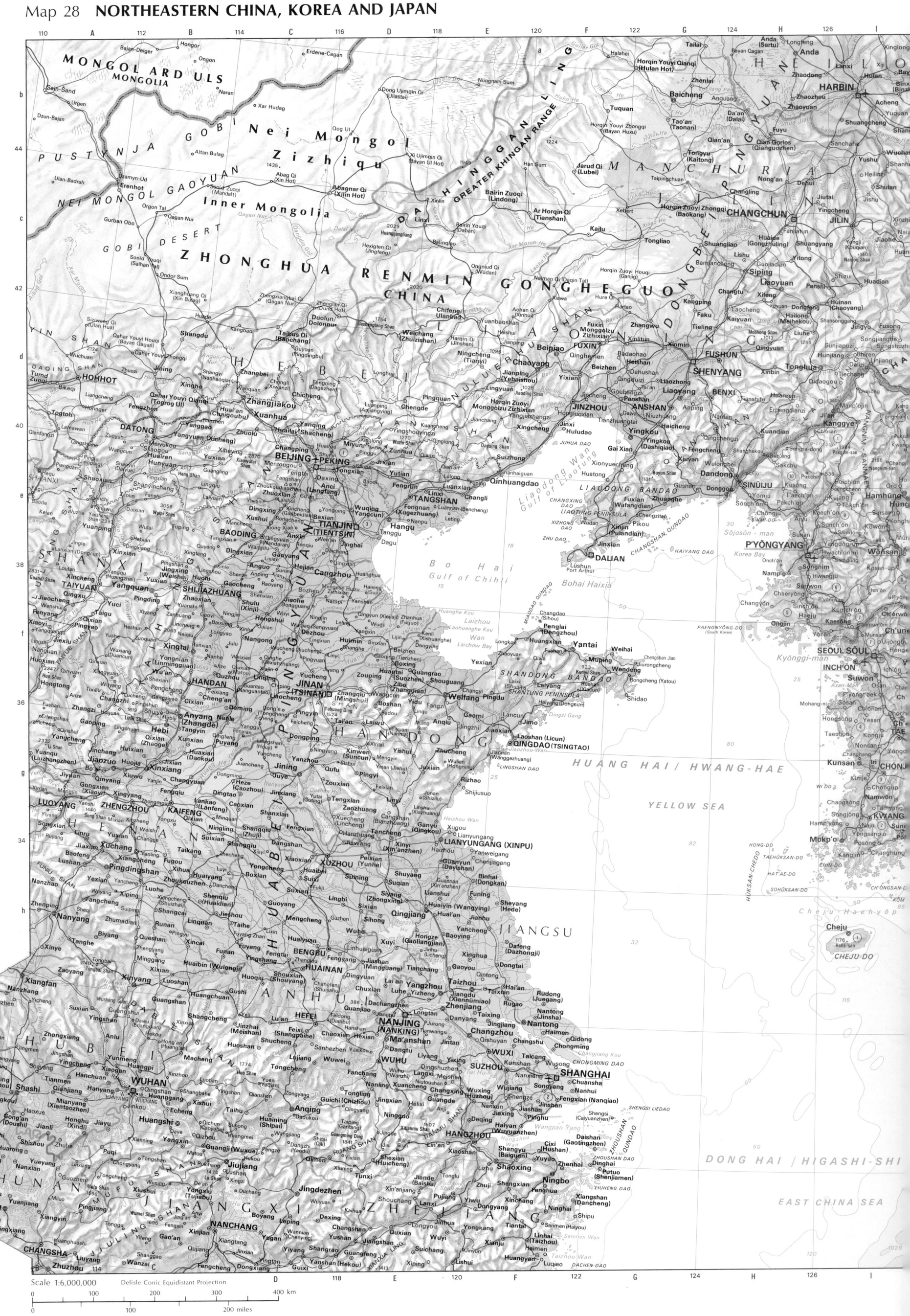

Scale 1:6,000,000   Delisle Conic Equidistant Projection

Map 29 **JAPAN**

Longitude East 144 of Greenwich

Ostrov Kunasir, ostrov Sikotan, ostrov Iturup, and Malaja Kurilskaja Grjada, occupied since 1945, are claimed by Japan pending a final peace treaty.

KURILSKIJE OSTROVA/
CHISHIMA-RETTŌ
KURIL ISLANDS

ROSSIJA
RUSSIA

OSTROV KUNAŠIR/
KUNASHIRI-TŌ
Južno-Kurilsk

MALAJA KURILSKAJA
GRJADA/
HABOMAI-SHOTŌ

NIPPON-KAI

SEA OF
JAPAN

OHOTSKOJE MORE
HOK-KAI

SEA OF OKHOTSK

HOKKAIDŌ

SAPPORO

HAKODATE

KITA - TAIHEIYŌ

PACIFIC OCEAN

HONSHŪ

HONSHŪ

TAEHAN - MIN'GUK

SOUTH KOREA

PUSAN

TSUSHIMA

HIROSHIMA

OKAYAMA

KŌBE

OSAKA

KYŌTO

HIMEJI

KURASHIKI

FUKUYAMA

TAKAMATSU

MATSUYAMA

KŌCHI

SHIKOKU

KITAKYŪSHŪ

FUKUOKA

SHIMONOSEKI

YAMAGUCHI

SASEBO

NAGASAKI

KUMAMOTO

ŌITA

KYŪSHŪ

MIYAZAKI

KAGOSHIMA

HIGASHI-SHINA KAI

EAST CHINA
SEA

Scale 1:3,000,000   Delisle Conic Equidistant Projection

0   50   100   150   200 km

0   50   100 miles

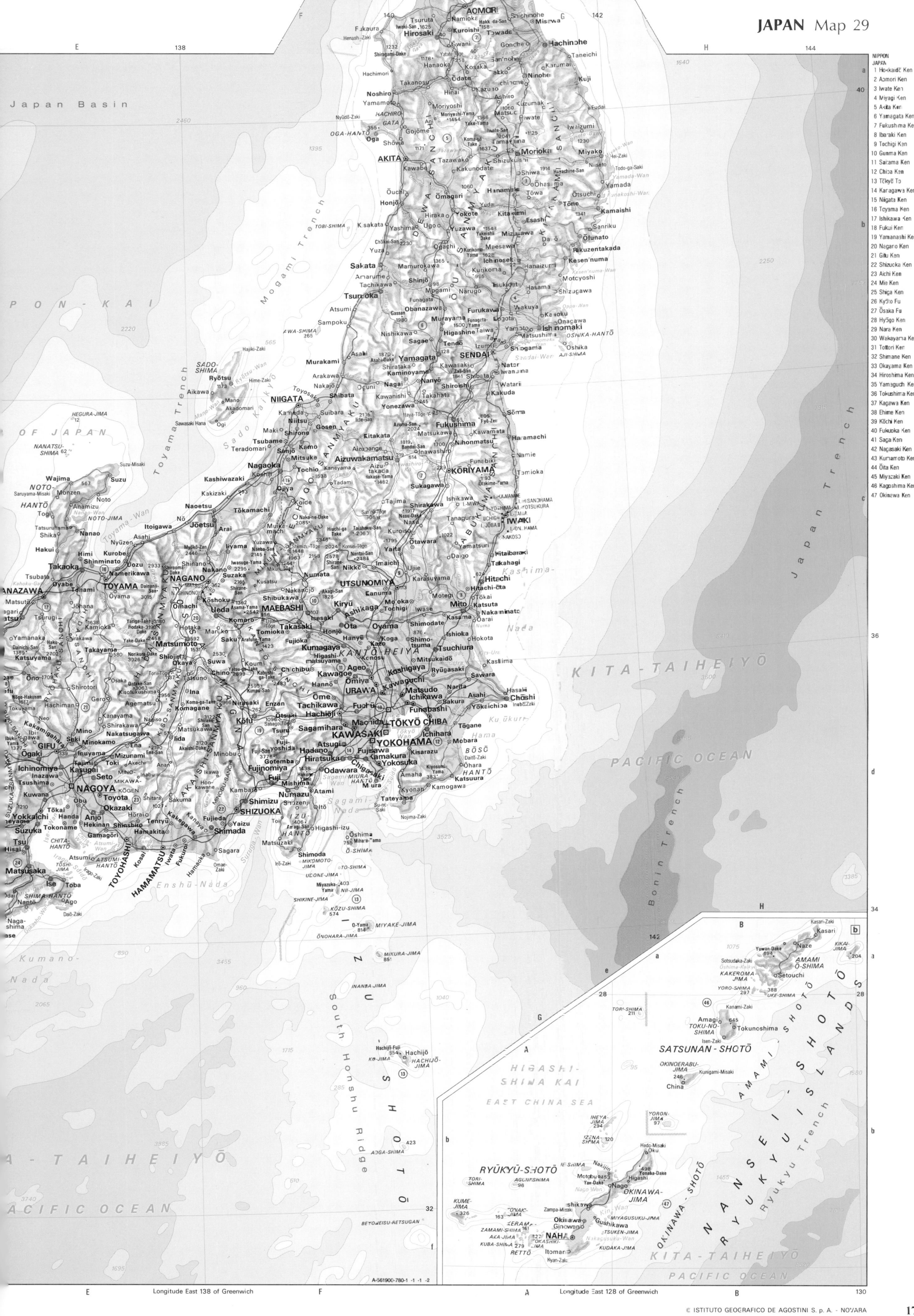

NIPPON
JAPAN
1 Hokkaidō Ken
2 Aomori Ken
3 Iwate Ken
4 Miyagi Ken
5 Akita Ken
6 Yamagata Ken
7 Fukushima Ken
8 Ibaraki Ken
9 Tochigi Ken
10 Gunma Ken
11 Saitama Ken
12 Chiba Ken
13 Tōkyō To
14 Kanagawa Ken
15 Niigata Ken
16 Toyama Ken
17 Ishikawa Ken
18 Fukui Ken
19 Yamanashi Ken
20 Nagano Ken
21 Gifu Ken
22 Shizuoka Ken
23 Aichi Ken
24 Mie Ken
25 Shiga Ken
26 Kyōto Fu
27 Ōsaka Fu
28 Hyōgo Ken
29 Nara Ken
30 Wakayama Ken
31 Tottori Ken
32 Shimane Ken
33 Okayama Ken
34 Hiroshima Ken
35 Yamaguchi Ken
36 Tokushima Ken
37 Kagawa Ken
38 Ehime Ken
39 Kōchi Ken
40 Fukuoka Ken
41 Saga Ken
42 Nagasaki Ken
43 Kumamoto Ken
44 Ōita Ken
45 Miyazaki Ken
46 Kagoshima Ken
47 Okinawa Ken

© ISTITUTO GEOGRAFICO DE AGOSTINI S.p.A. - NOVARA

Map 30 **AFRICA, PHYSICAL**

Map 30

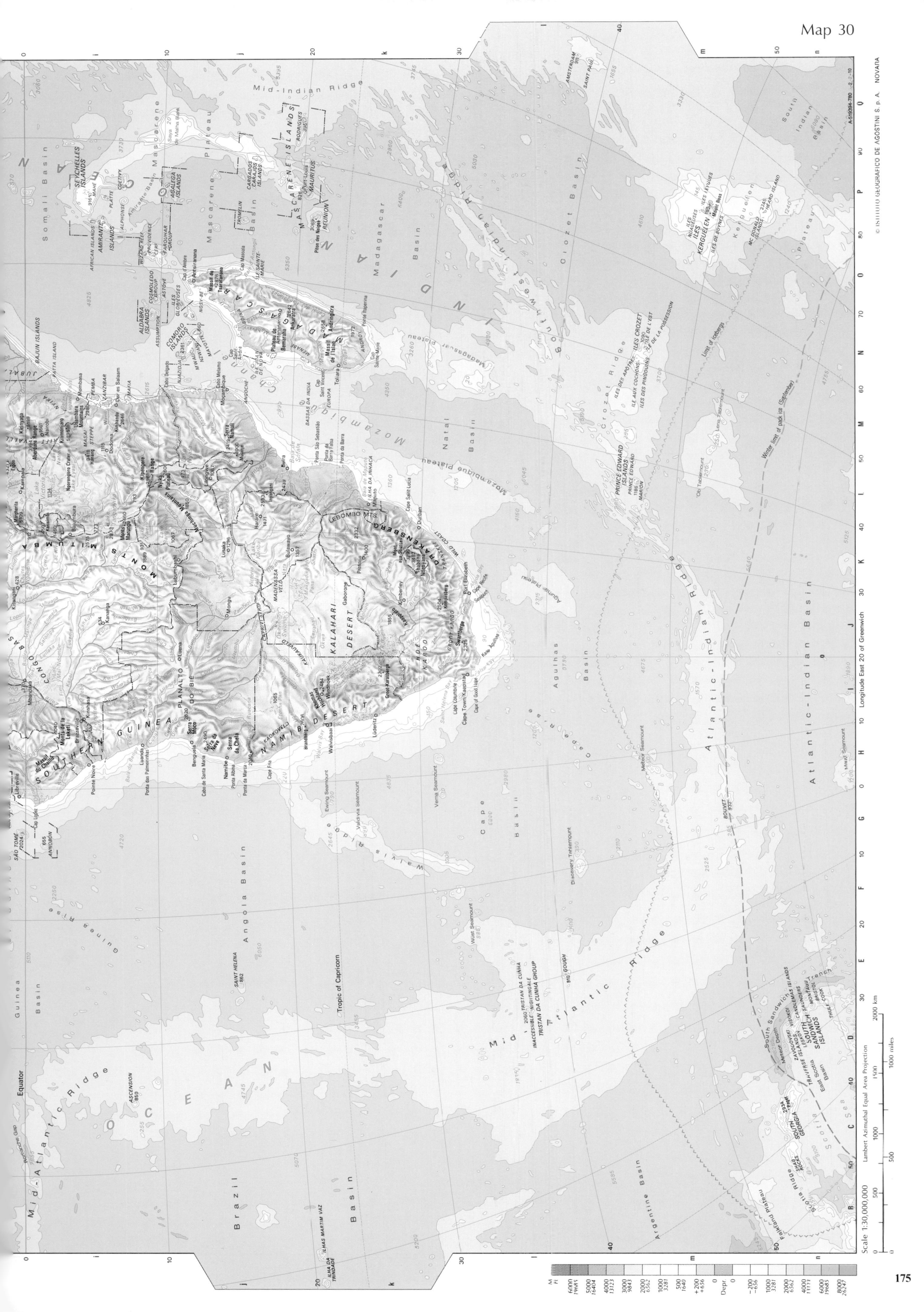

Scale 1:30,000,000   Lambert Azimuthal Equal Area Projection   Longitude East 20 of Greenwich

Map 31 **AFRICA, POLITICAL**

Map 31

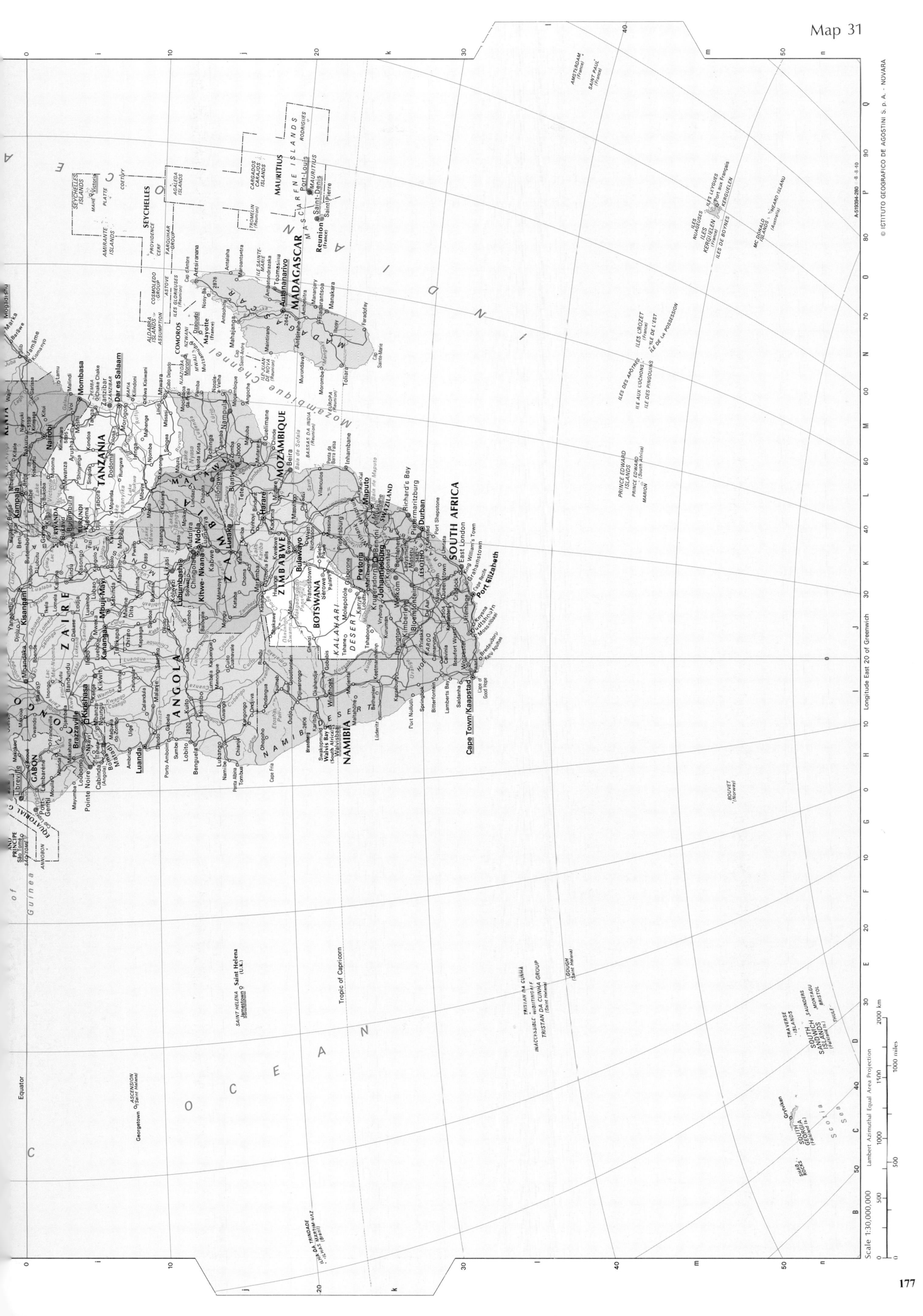

Map 32

**AL JAZĀ'IR
ALGERIA**

WILĀYATE
1 Adrar
2 Al Jazā'ir
3 Annaba
4 Batna
5 Béchar
6 Bejaia
7 Biskra
8 Blida
9 Bouira
10 Cheliff
11 Constantine
12 Djelfa
13 Guelma
14 Jijel
15 Laghouat
16 Mascara
17 Médéa
18 Mostaganem
19 M'Sila
20 Oran
21 Ouargla
22 Oum el Bouaghi
23 Saida
24 Sétif
25 Sidi Bel Abbes
26 Skikda
27 Tamanrasset
28 Tebessa
29 Tiaret
30 Tizi Ouzou
31 Tlemcen

**AL MAGHRIB
MOROCCO**

PRÉFECTURES
A Casablanca
B Rabat-Salé

PROVINCES
1 Agadir
2 Al Hoceima
3 Ar Rachidiya
4 Azilal
5 Beni Mellal
6 Boulemane
7 Chechaouene
8 El Jadida
9 El Kelaa des Srarhna
10 Essaouira
11 Fès
12 Figuig
13 Kenitra
14 Khemisset
15 Khenifra
16 Khouribga
17 Marrakech
18 Meknès
19 Nador
20 Ouarzazate
21 Oujda
22 Safi
23 Settat
24 Tanger
25 Tan Tan
26 Taounate
27 Tata
28 Taza
29 Tétouan
30 Tiznit

**TŪNIS
TUNISIA**

WILĀYATE
1 Al Kāf
2 Al Mahdiyah
3 Al Munastir
4 Al Qaṣrayn
5 Al Qayrawān
6 Bajah
7 Banzart
8 Jundubah
9 Madanīyin
10 Nābul
11 Qābis
12 Qafṣah
13 Qamūdah
14 Ṣafāqis
15 Silyānah
16 Sūsah
17 Tūnis
18 Zaghwān

Scale 1:9,000,000   Lambert Azimuthal Equal Area Projection

Ⓐ Western Sahara is occupied by Morocco.

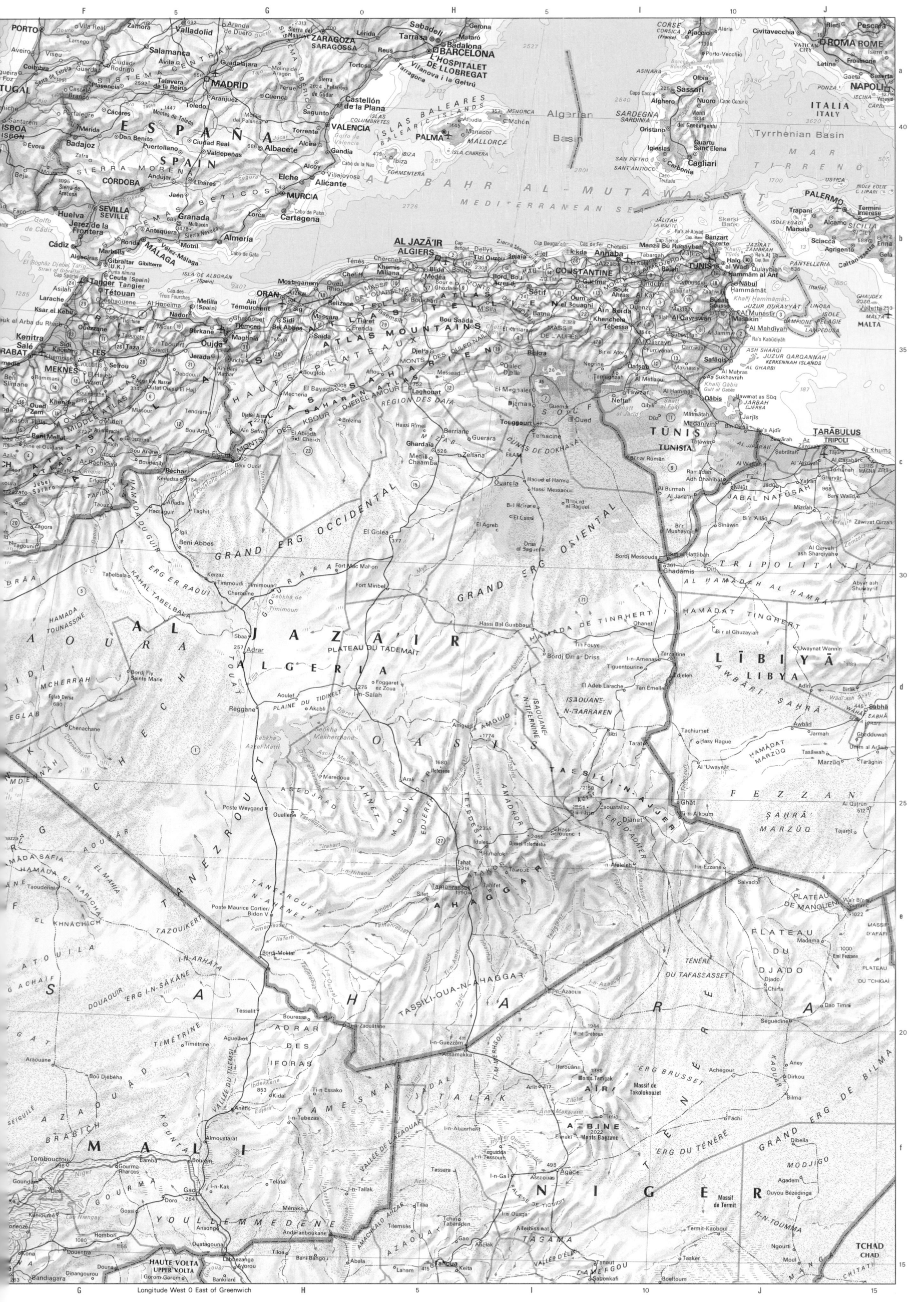

© ISTITUTO GEOGRAFICO DE AGOSTINI S. p. A. - NOVARA

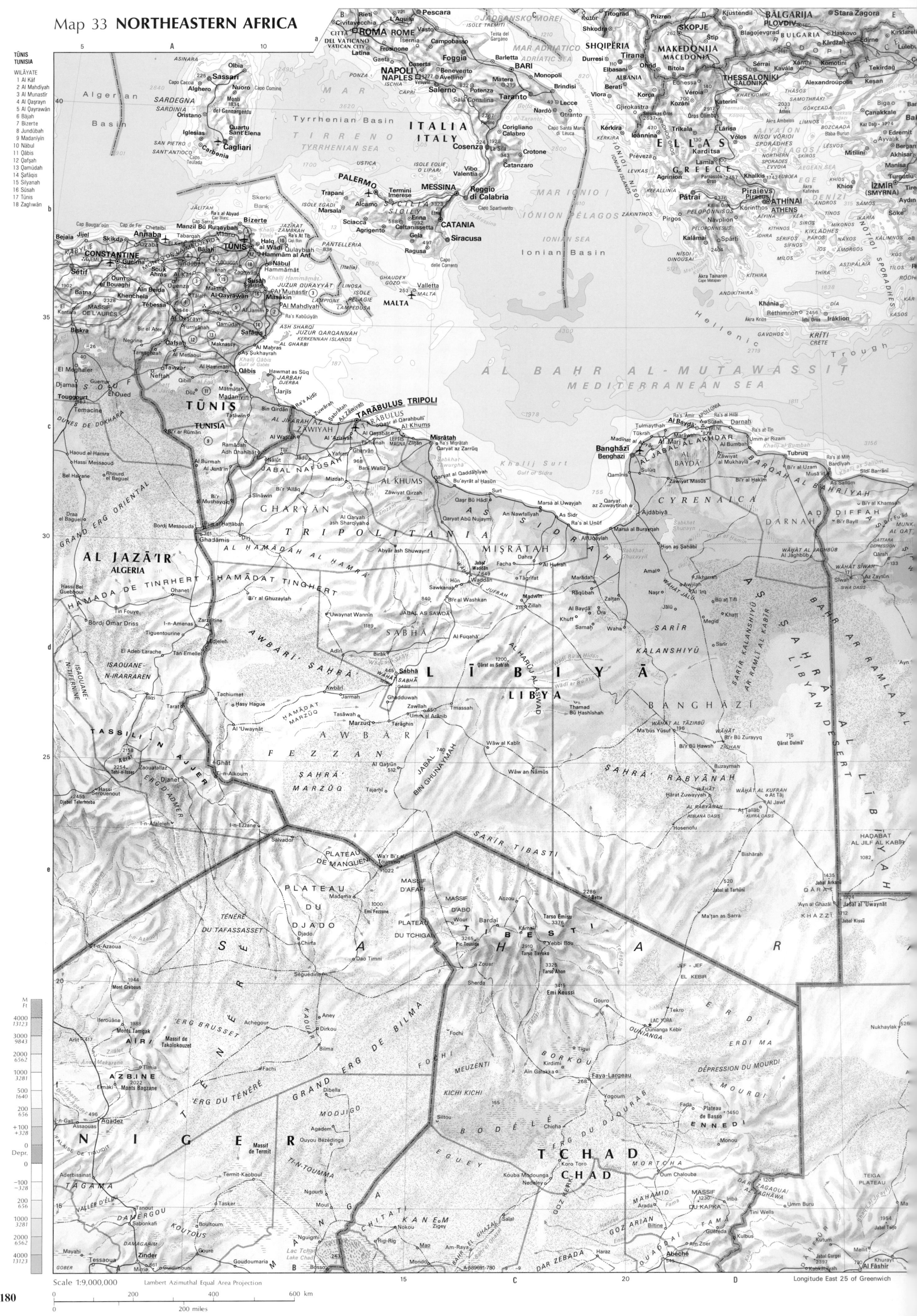

Map 33 **NORTHEASTERN AFRICA**

Scale 1:9,000,000   Lambert Azimuthal Equal Area Projection   Longitude East 25 of Greenwich

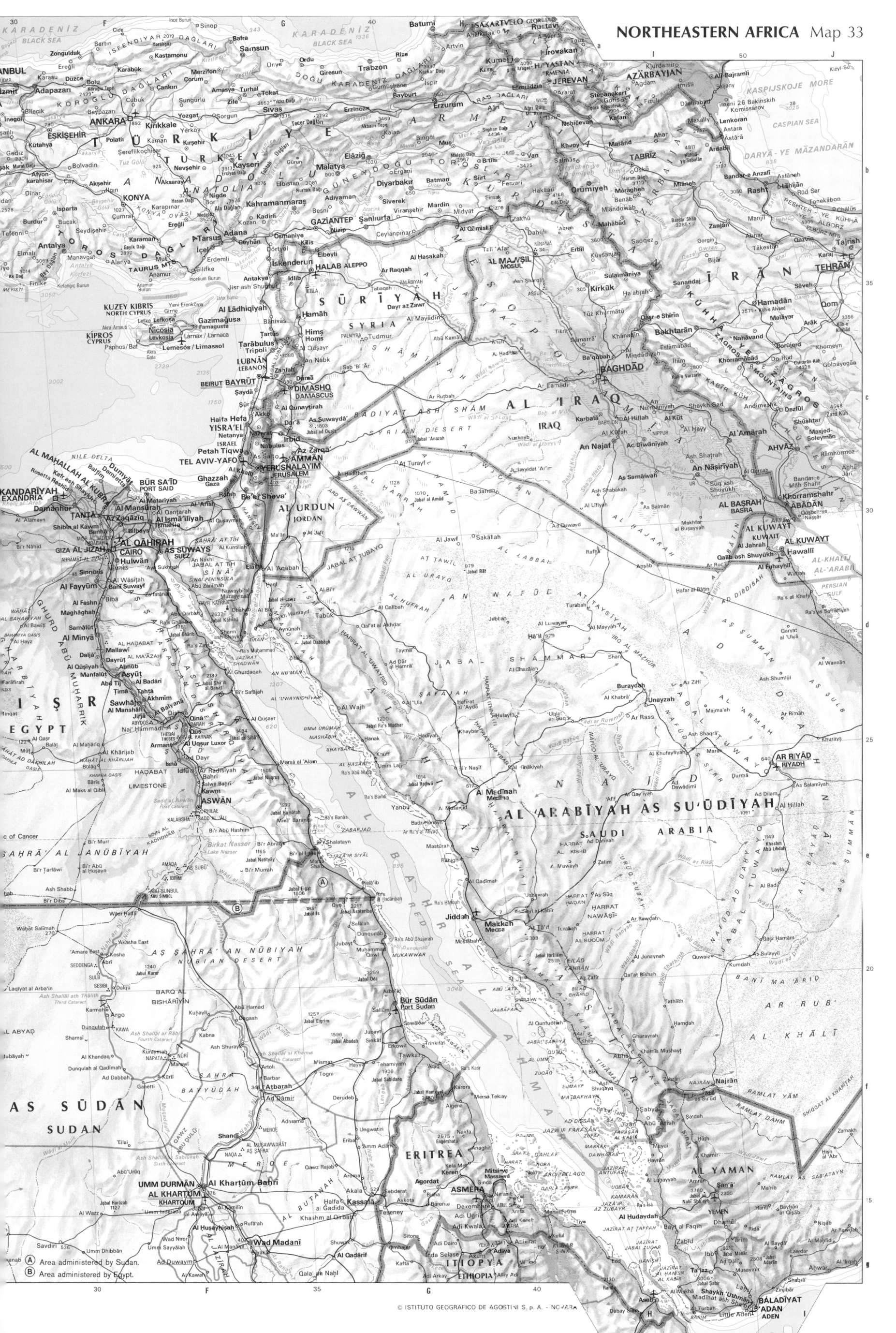

Ⓐ Area administered by Sudan.
Ⓑ Area administered by Egypt.

© ISTITUTO GEOGRAFICO DE AGOSTINI S.p.A. - NOVARA

Map 34 **WEST-CENTRAL AFRICA**

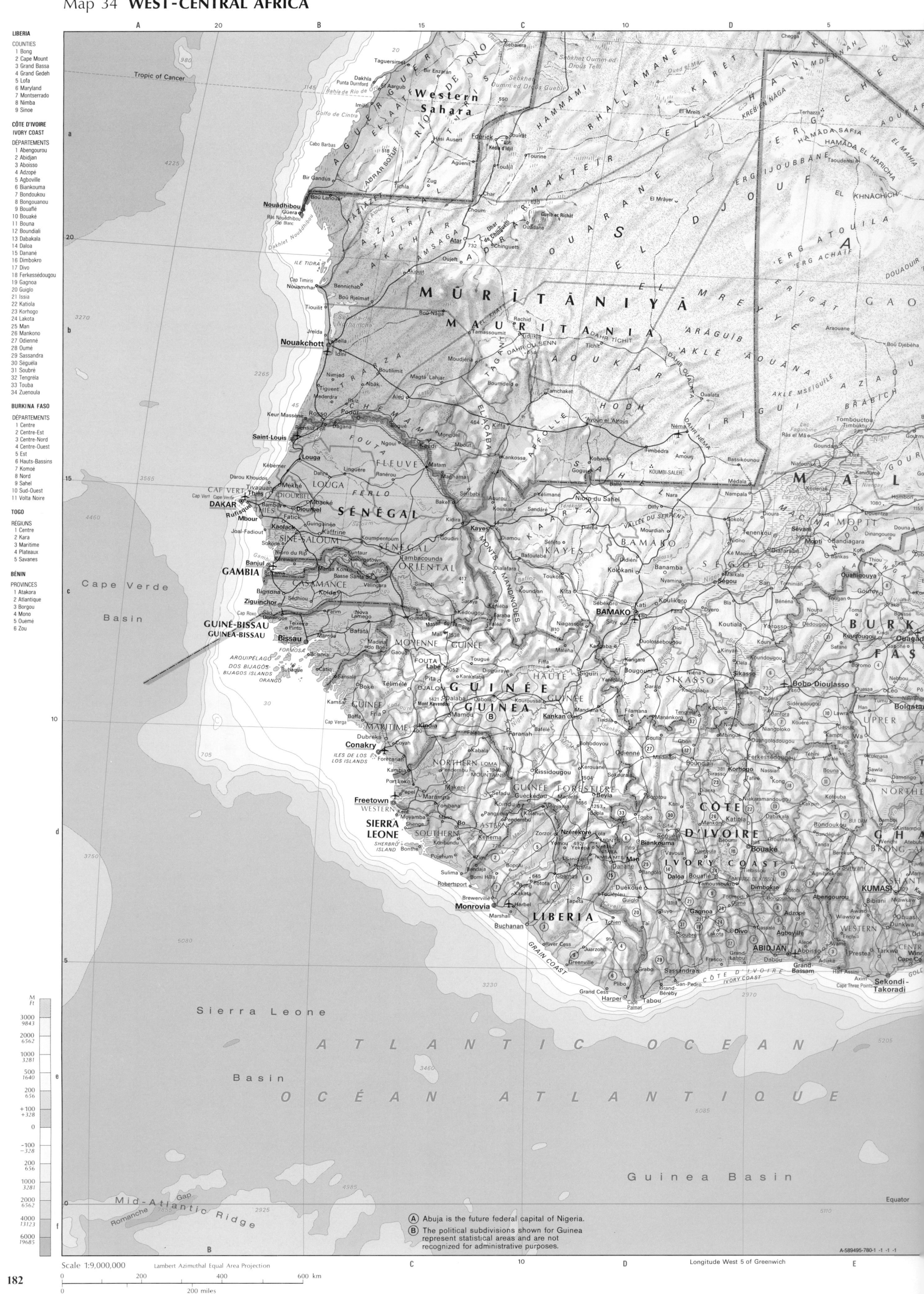

Scale 1:9,000,000 Lambert Azimuthal Equal Area Projection

Longitude West 5 of Greenwich

A-589495-780-1 -1 -1 -1

(A) Abuja is the future federal capital of Nigeria.

(B) The political subdivisions shown for Guinea represent statistical areas and are not recognized for administrative purposes.

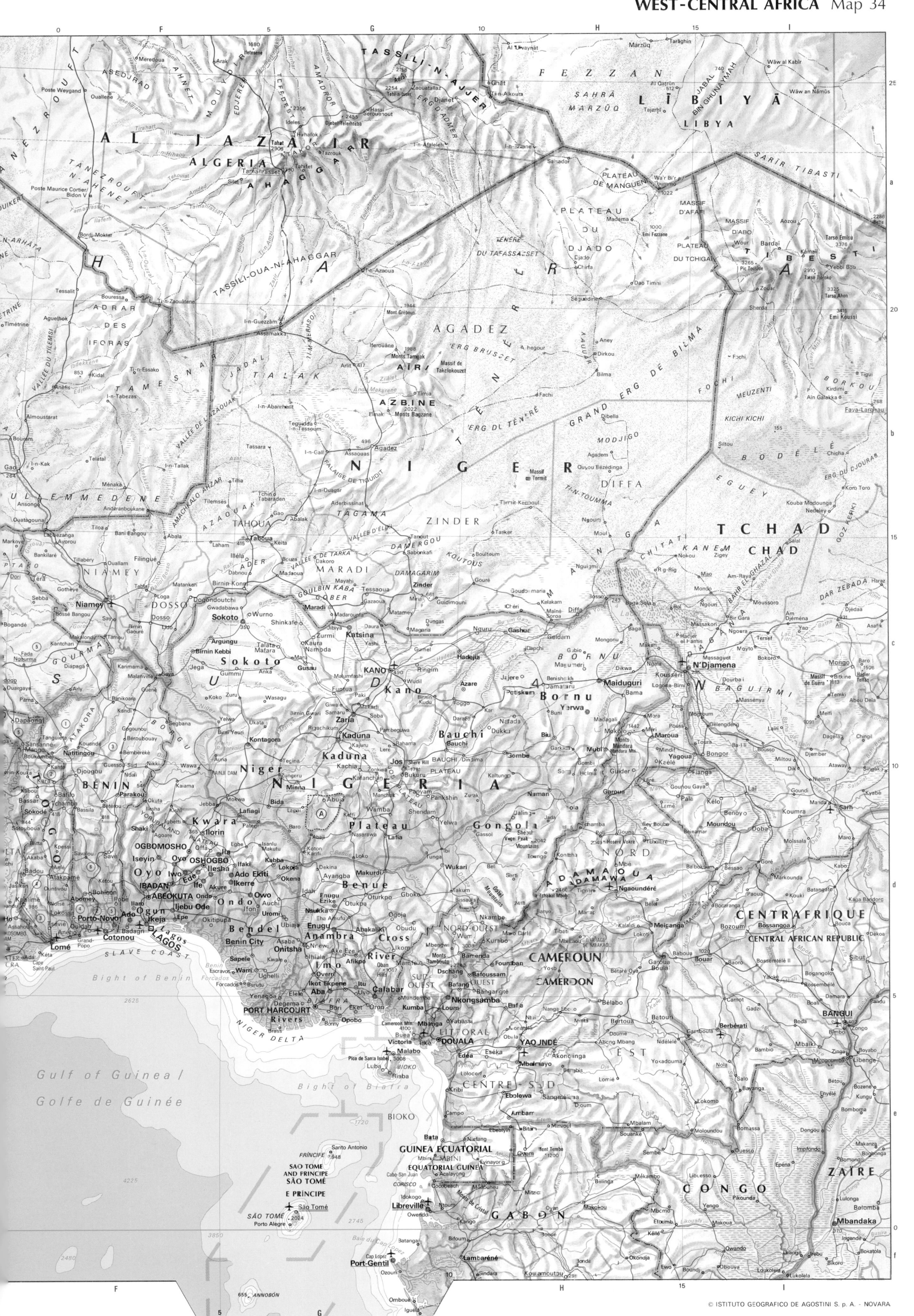

Map 35 **EAST-CENTRAL AFRICA**

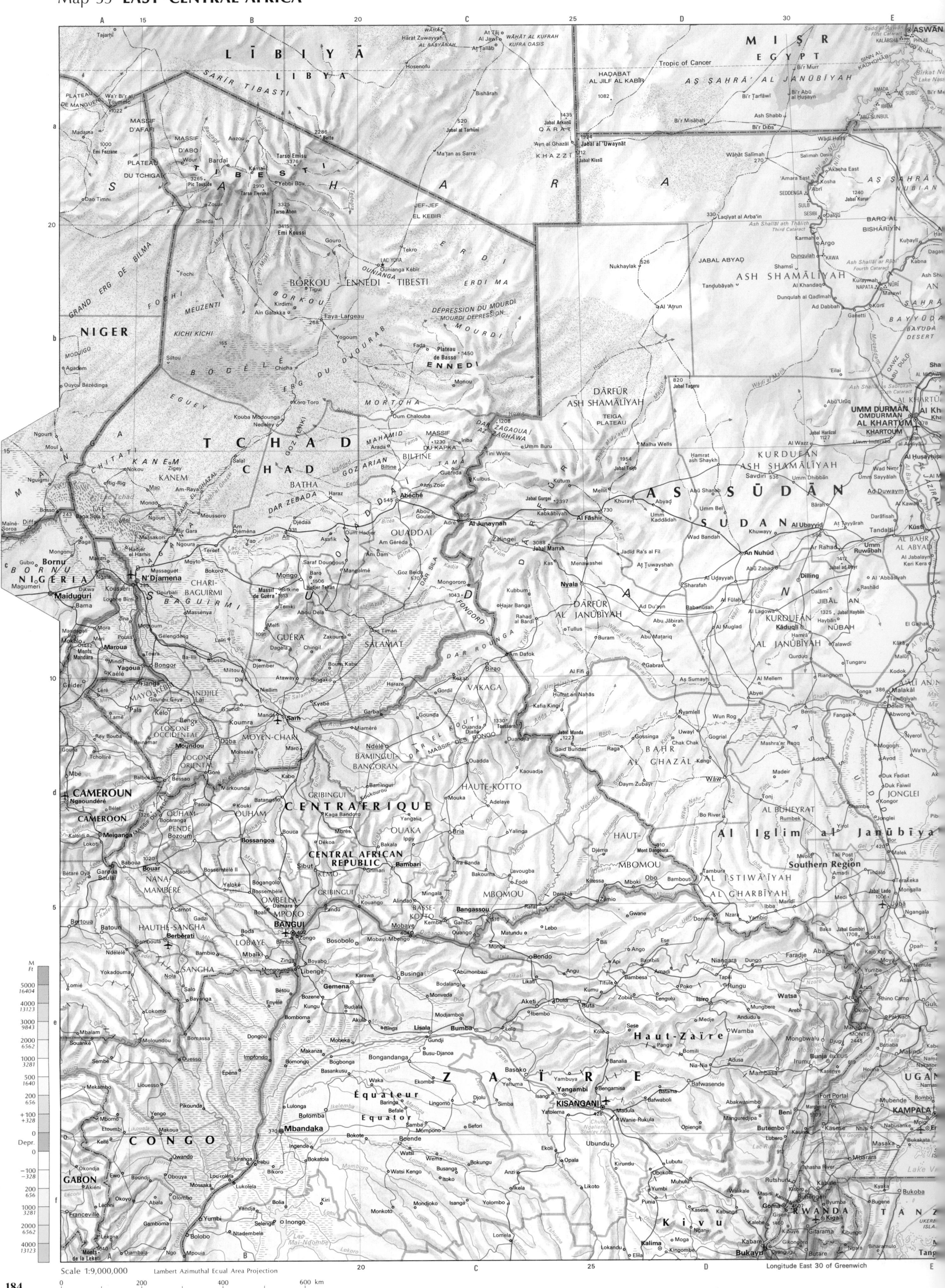

Scale 1:9,000,000   Lambert Azimuthal Equal Area Projection

Longitude East 30 of Greenwich

A Area administered by Sudan
B Area administered by Egypt

© ISTITUTO GEOGRAFICO DE AGOSTINI S.p.A. - NOVARA

Map 36 **EQUATORIAL AFRICA**

Scale 1:9,000,000   Lambert Azimuthal Equal Area Projection

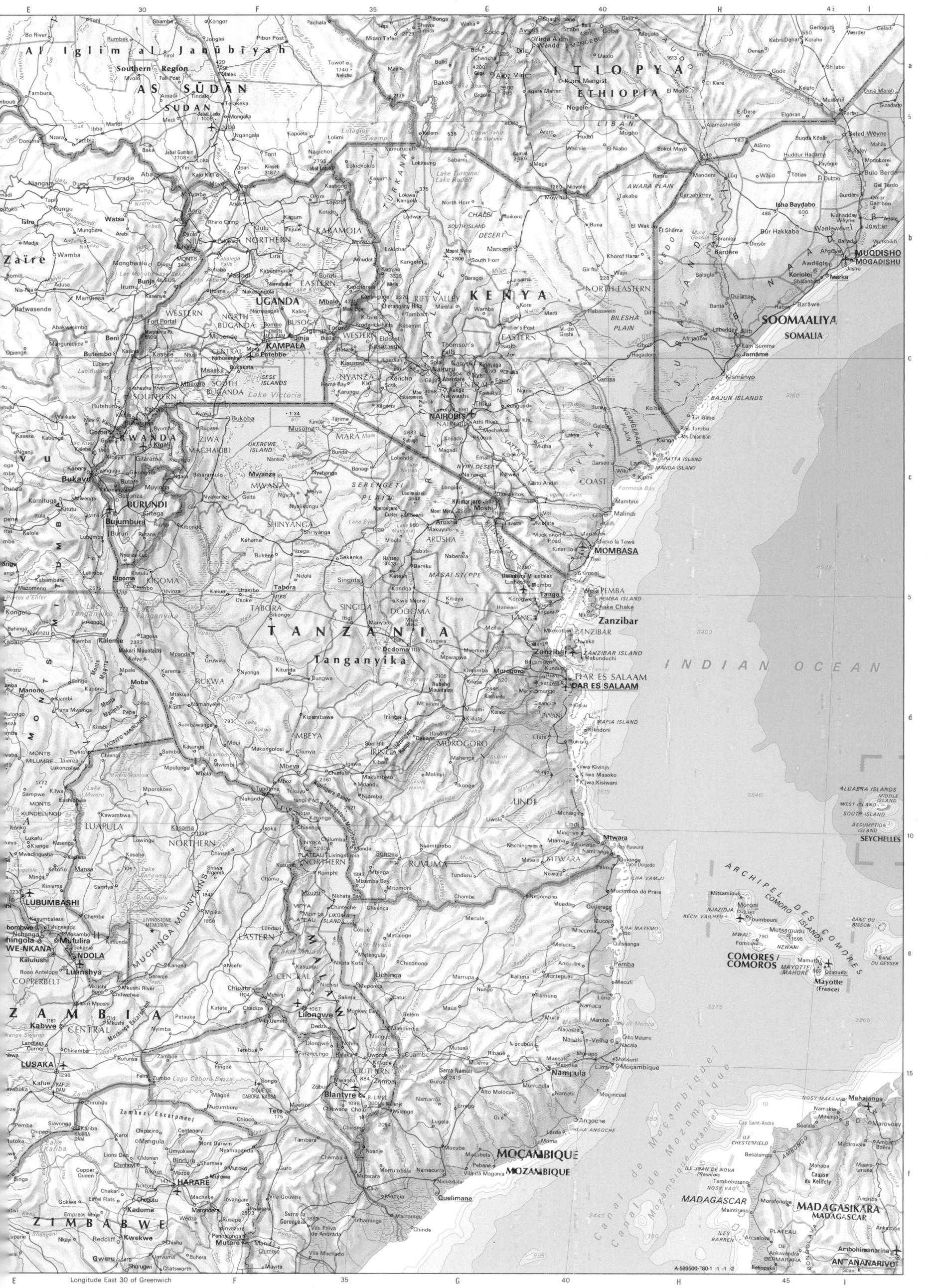

Map 37 **SOUTHERN AFRICA**

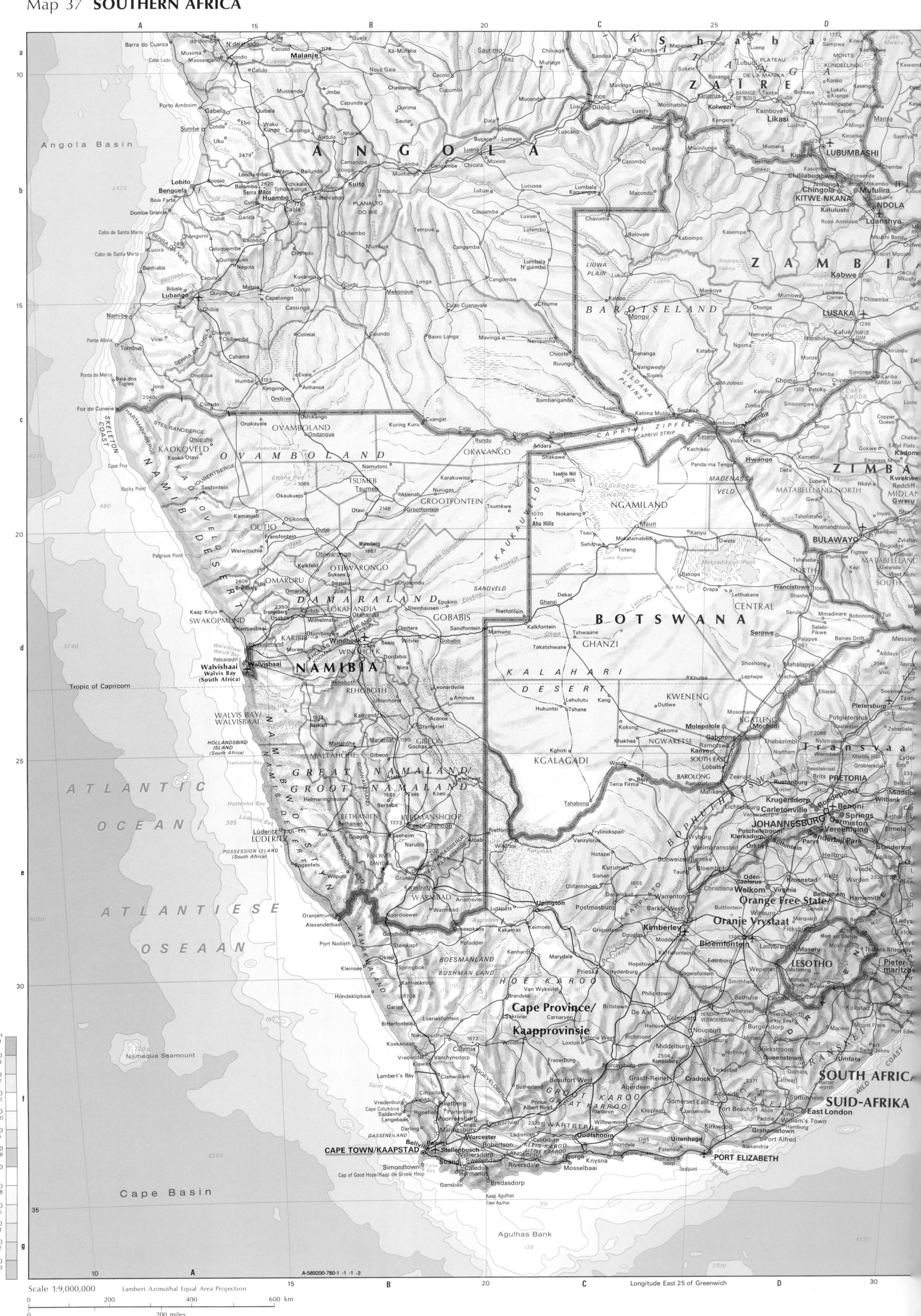

Scale 1:9,000,000   Lambert Azimuthal Equal Area Projection

Longitude East 25 of Greenwich

Map 38 **NORTH AMERICA, PHYSICAL**

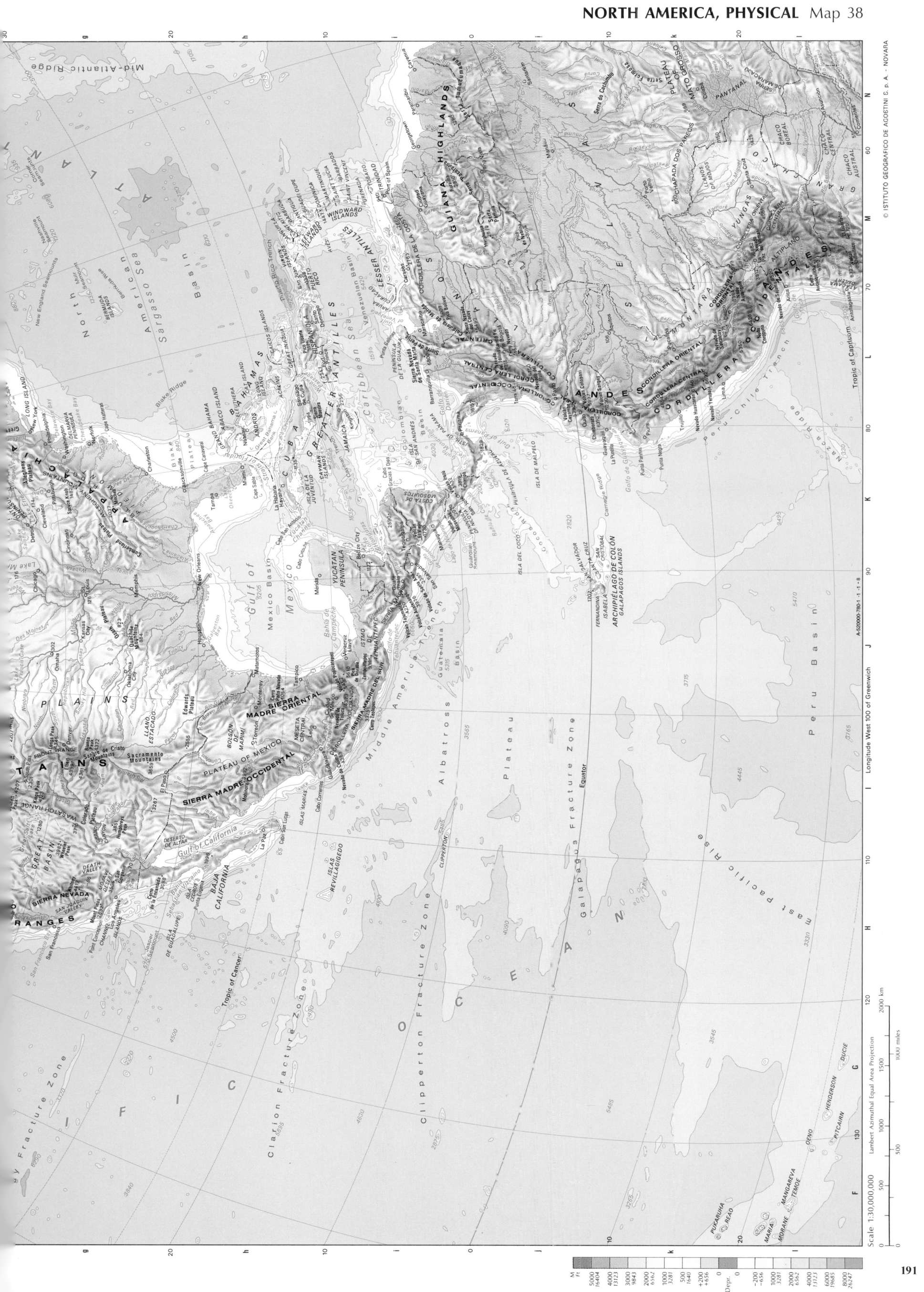

© ISTITUTO GEOGRAFICO DE AGOSTINI S. p. A. - NOVARA

Scale 1:30,000,000   Lambert Azimuthal Equal Area Projection

A-5200000-780-1 -1 -1 - 8

Map 39 **NORTH AMERICA, POLITICAL**

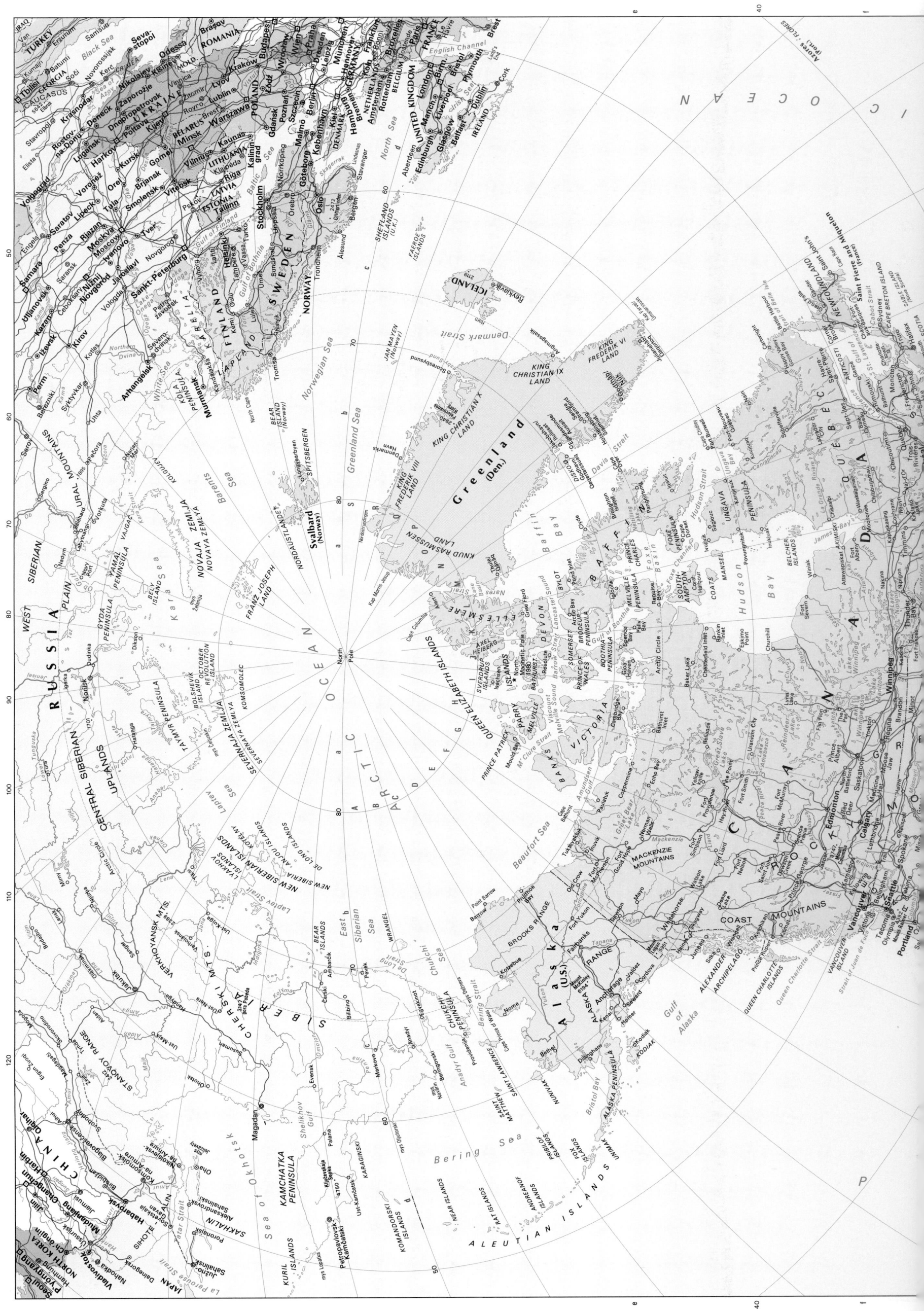

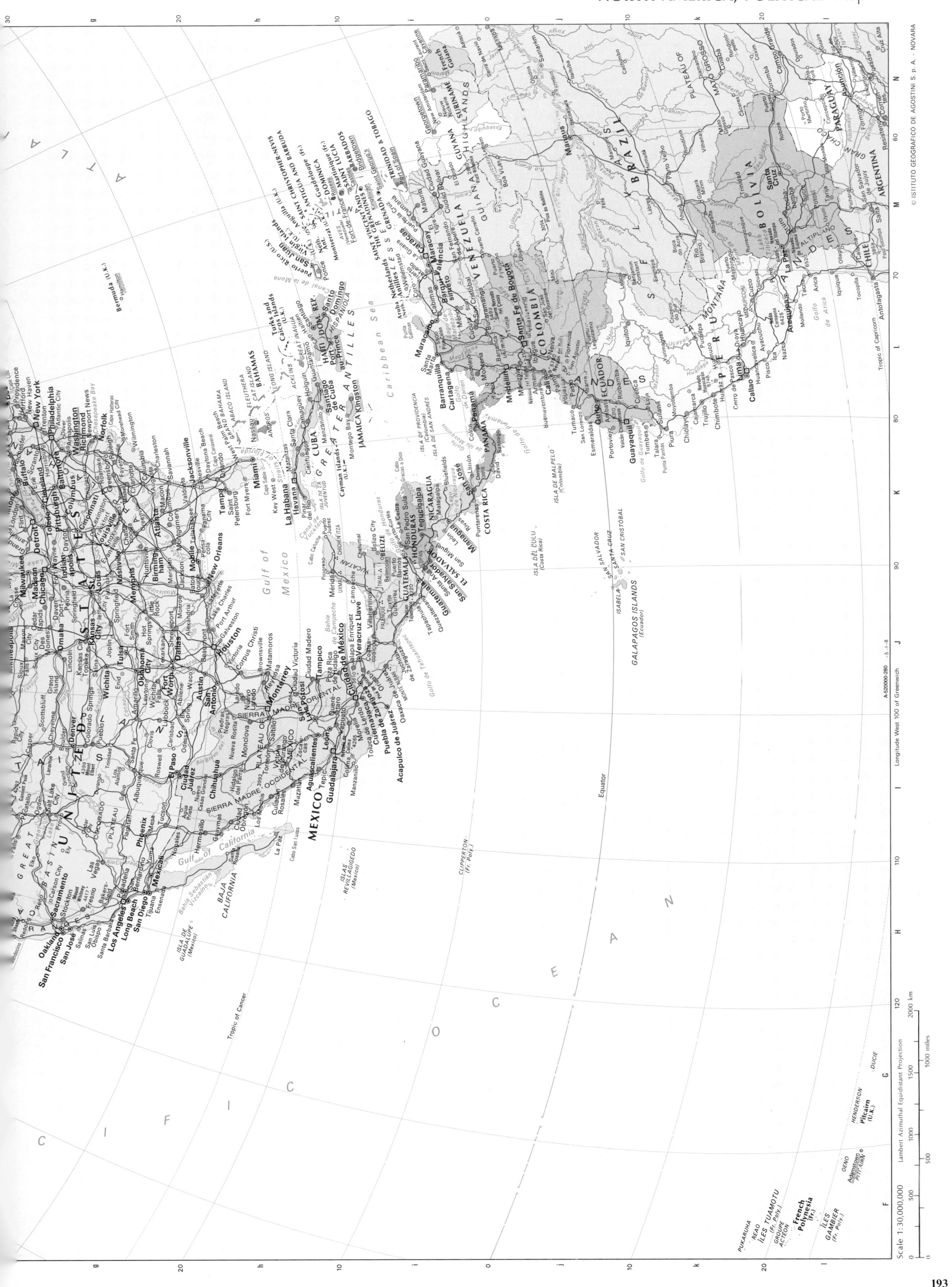

Scale 1:30,000,000

Lambert Azimuthal Equidistant Projection

Map 40 **ALASKA**

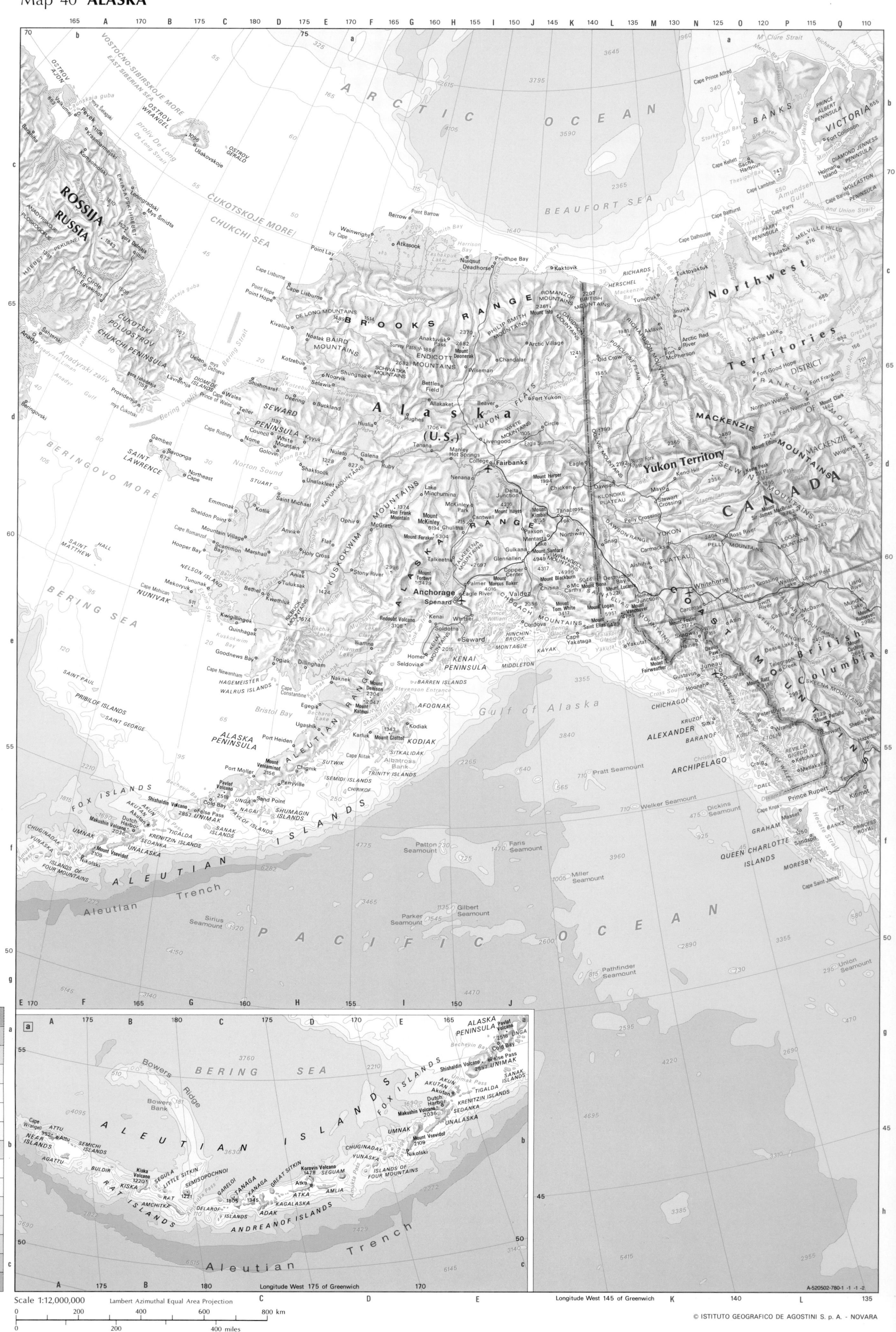

Scale 1:12,000,000   Lambert Azimuthal Equal Area Projection

© ISTITUTO GEOGRAFICO DE AGOSTINI S. p. A. - NOVARA

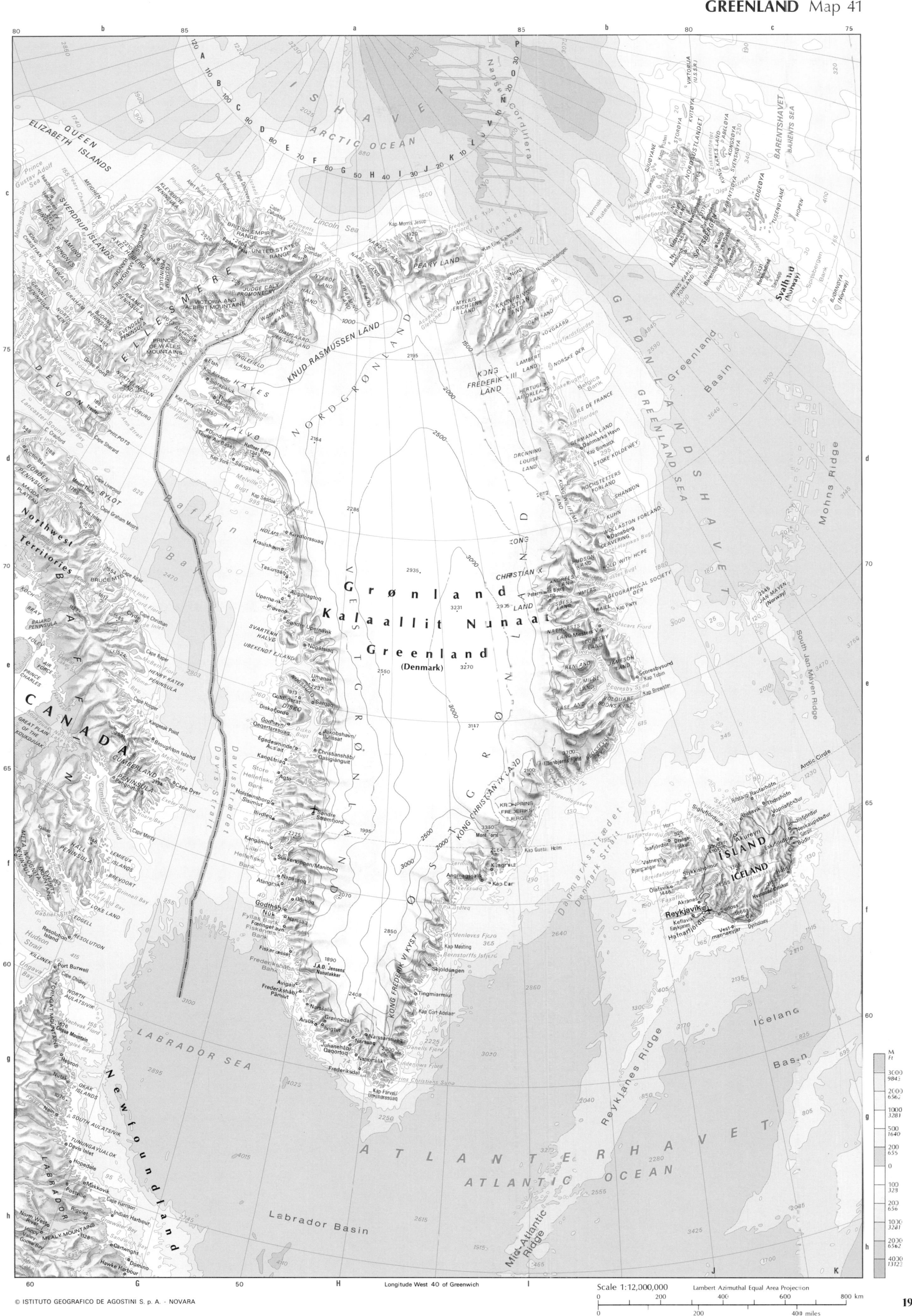

Grønland
Kalaallit Nunaat
Greenland
(Denmark)

Longitude West 40 of Greenwich

Scale 1:12,000,000

Lambert Azimuthal Equal Area Projection

0   200   400   600   800 km

0   200   400 miles

Map 42 **CANADA**

Scale 1:12,000,000   Lambert Azimuthal Equal Area Projection

Longitude West 100 of Greenwich

0   200   400   600   800 km

0   200   400 miles

Map 43 **UNITED STATES**

Scale 1:12,000,000

Lambert Azimuthal Equidistant Projection

Longitude West 100 of Greenwich

M Ft	
5000 16404	
4000 13123	
3000 9843	
2000 6562	
1000 3281	
500 1640	
+ 200 +656	
0	
Depr.	
0	
− 100 −328	
− 200 −656	
1000 3281	
2000 6562	
4000 13123	
6000 19685	
8000 26247	

0   200   400   600   800 km

0   200   400 miles

Map 44

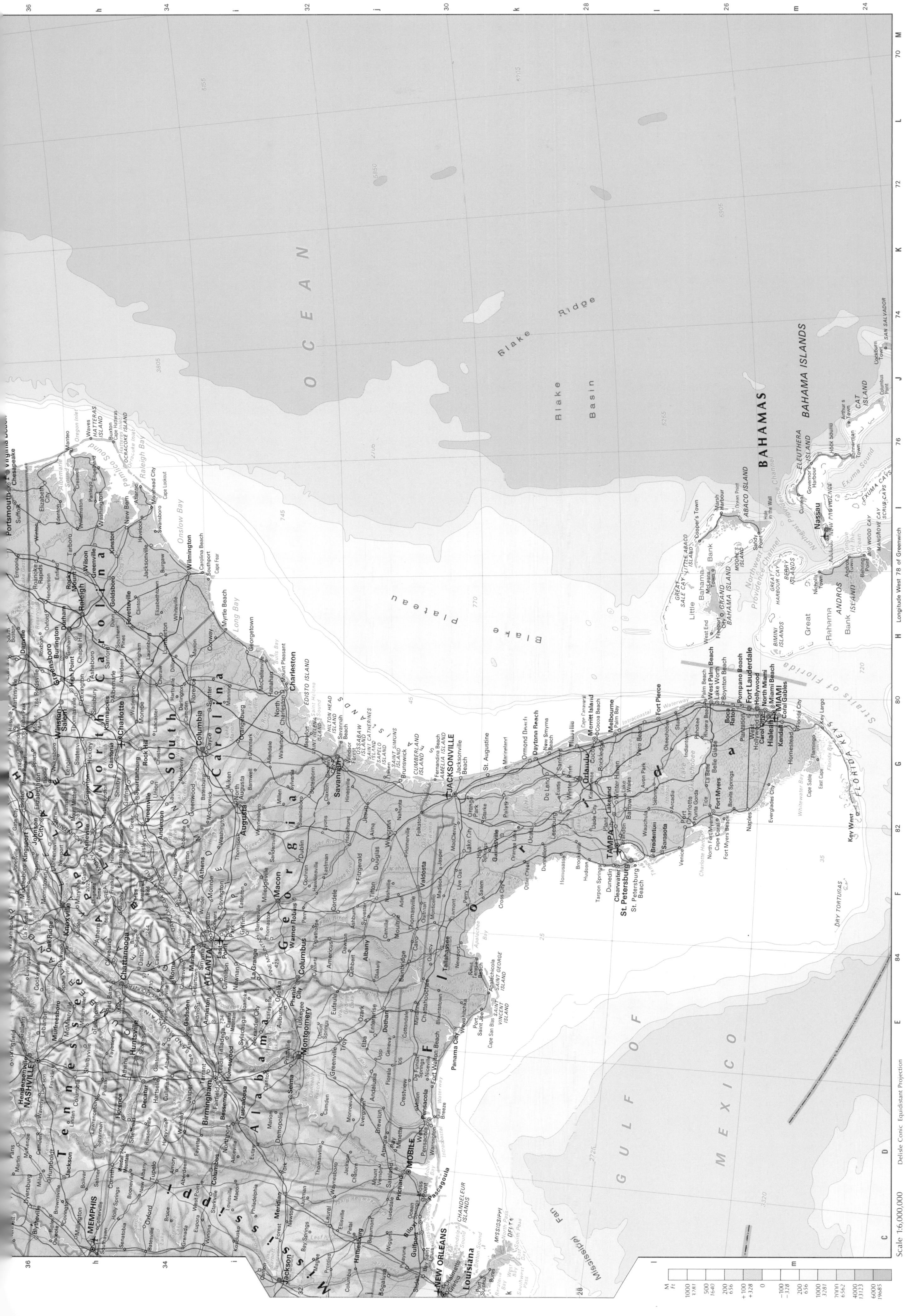

OCEAN

ATLANTIC OCEAN

BAHAMAS

BAHAMA ISLANDS

Blake Ridge

Blake Basin

Blake Plateau

GULF OF MEXICO

Straits of Florida

FLORIDA KEYS

Tennessee
NASHVILLE
MEMPHIS
Mississippi
NEW ORLEANS
Louisiana
Alabama
BIRMINGHAM
Montgomery
MOBILE
Georgia
ATLANTA
Columbus
Macon
Savannah
Augusta
South Carolina
Columbia
Charleston
Charlotte
North Carolina
Raleigh
Wilmington
Florida
JACKSONVILLE
ORLANDO
TAMPA
St. Petersburg
MIAMI
Fort Lauderdale
Key West
Nassau
ANDROS ISLAND
ABACO ISLAND
ELEUTHERA
CAT ISLAND
SAN SALVADOR

Scale 1:6,000,000

Delisle Conic Equidistant Projection

Longitude West 78 of Greenwich

© ISTITUTO GEOGRAFICO DE AGOSTINI S. p. A. - NOVARA

Map 45

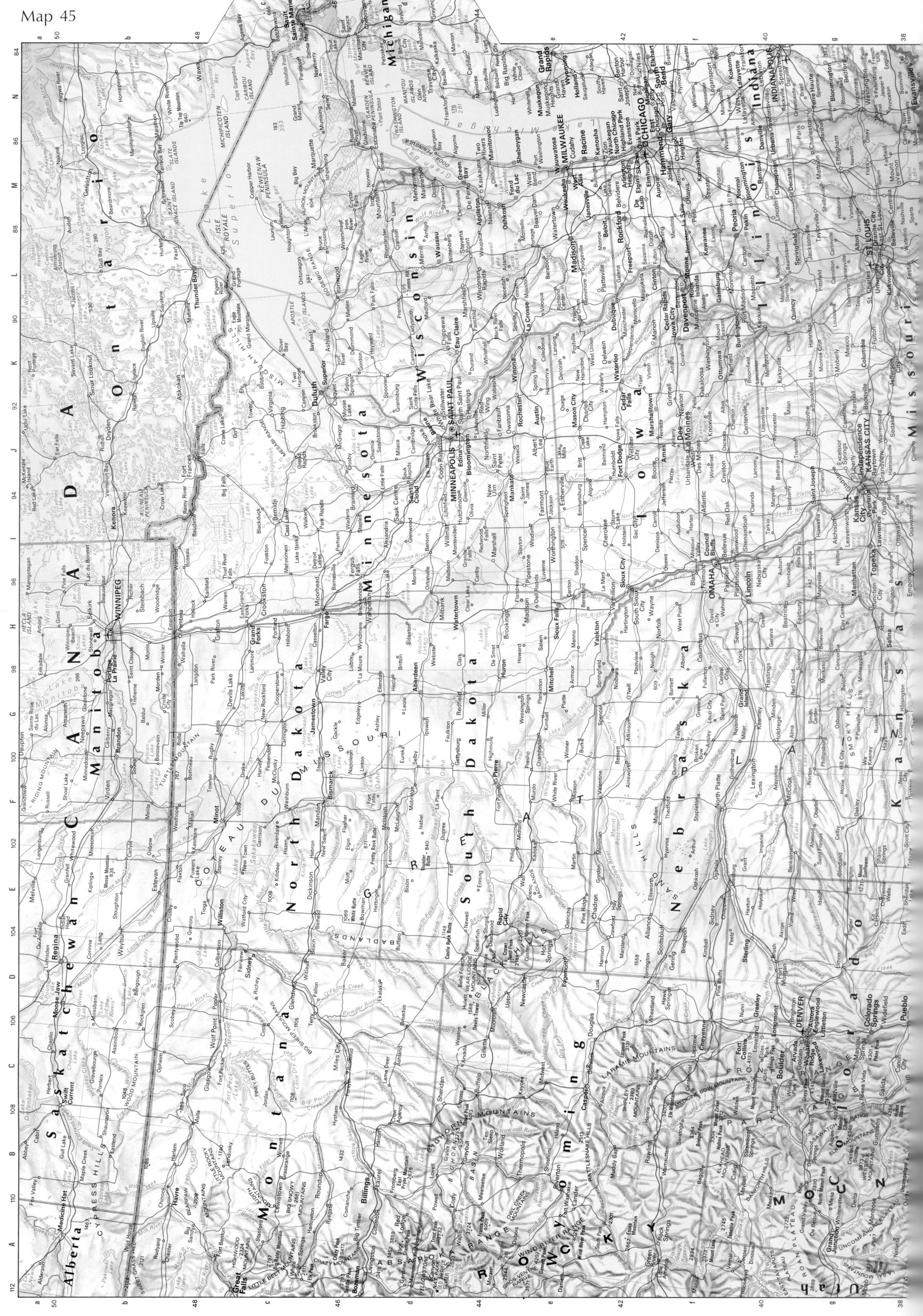

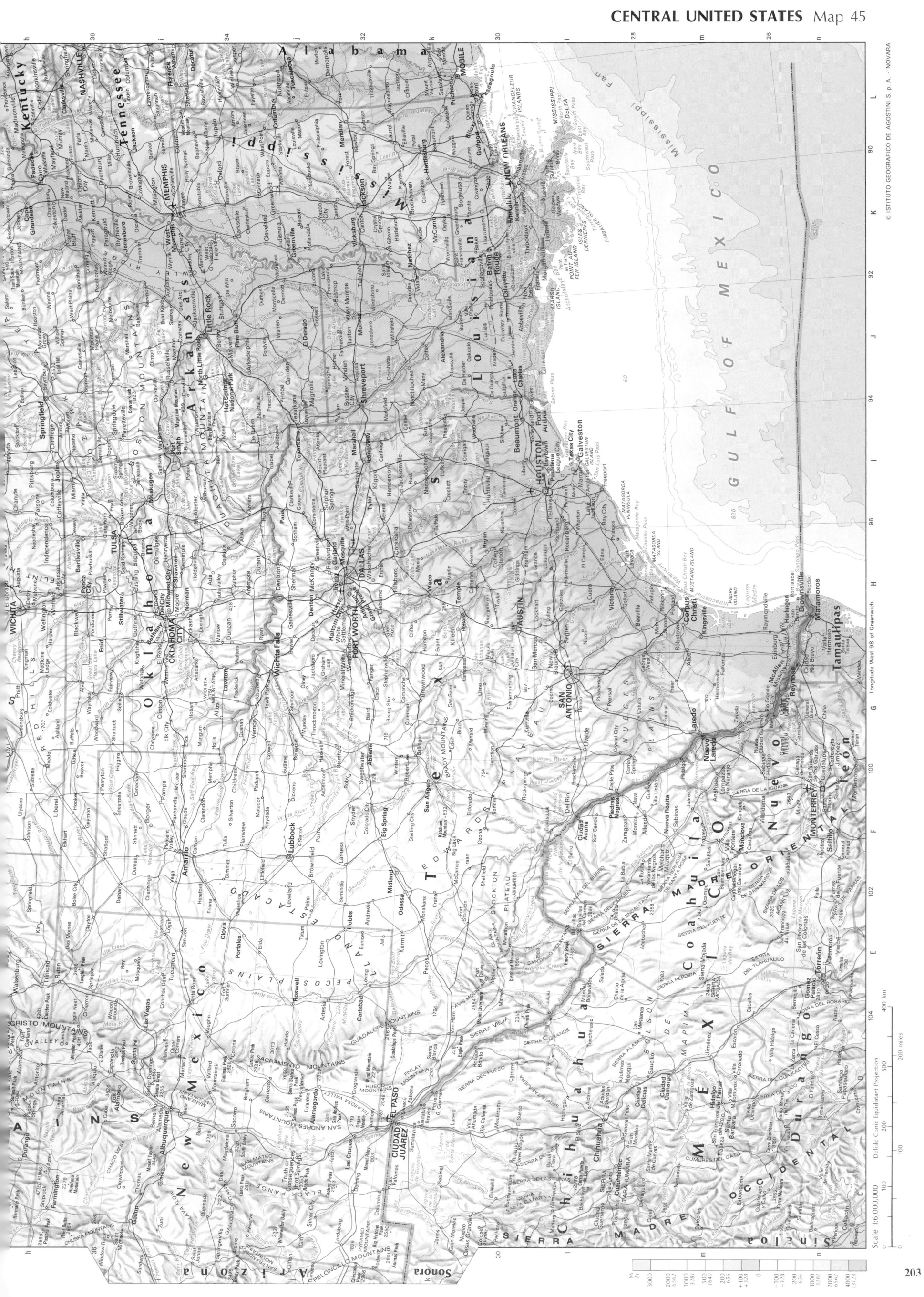

Scale 1:6,000,000

Delisle Conic Equidistant Projection

203

Map 46 **WESTERN UNITED STATES**

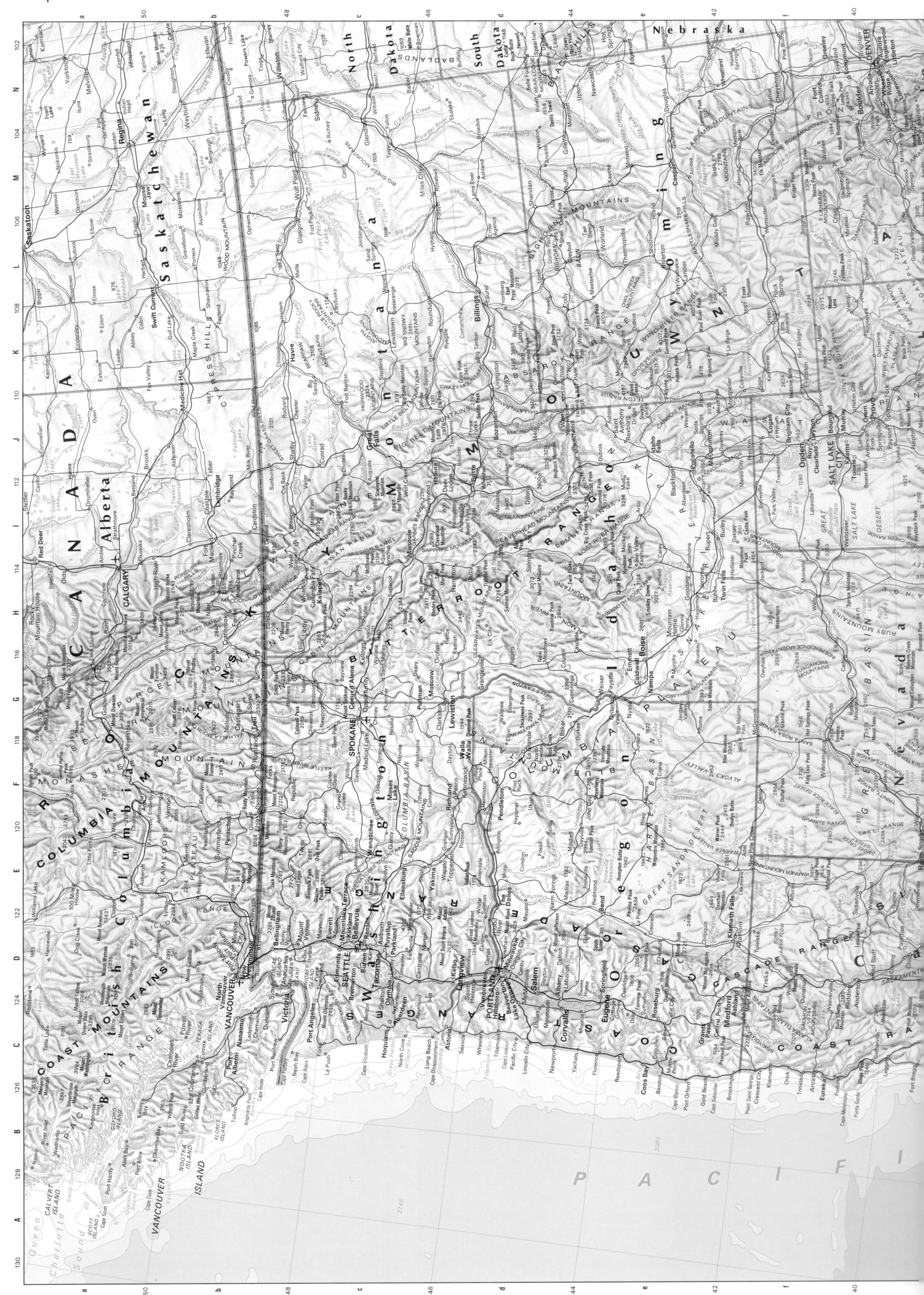

Map 47 **MIDDLE AMERICA**

MÉXICO

ESTADOS

D.F. Distrito Federal
1 Aguascalientes
2 Baja California Norte
3 Baja California Sur
4 Campeche
5 Coahuila
6 Colima
7 Chiapas
8 Chihuahua
9 Durango
10 Guanajuato
11 Guerrero
12 Hidalgo
13 Jalisco
14 México
15 Michoacán
16 Morelos
17 Nayarit
18 Nuevo León
19 Oaxaca
20 Puebla
21 Querétaro
22 Quintana Roo
23 San Luis Potosí
24 Sinaloa
25 Sonora
26 Tabasco
27 Tamaulipas
28 Tlaxcala
29 Veracruz
30 Yucatán
31 Zacatecas

M
Ft
5000 / 16404
4000 / 13123
3000 / 9843
2000 / 6562
1000 / 3281
500 / 1640
+200 / +656
Depr.
0
−100 / −328
200 / 656
1000 / 3281
2000 / 6562
4000 / 13123
6000 / 19685
8000 / 26247

Scale 1:12,000,000   Lambert Azimuthal Equal Area Projection

0   200   400   600   800 km
0   200   400 miles

A-530000-780-1 -1 -1 -3

Longitude West 90 of Greenwich

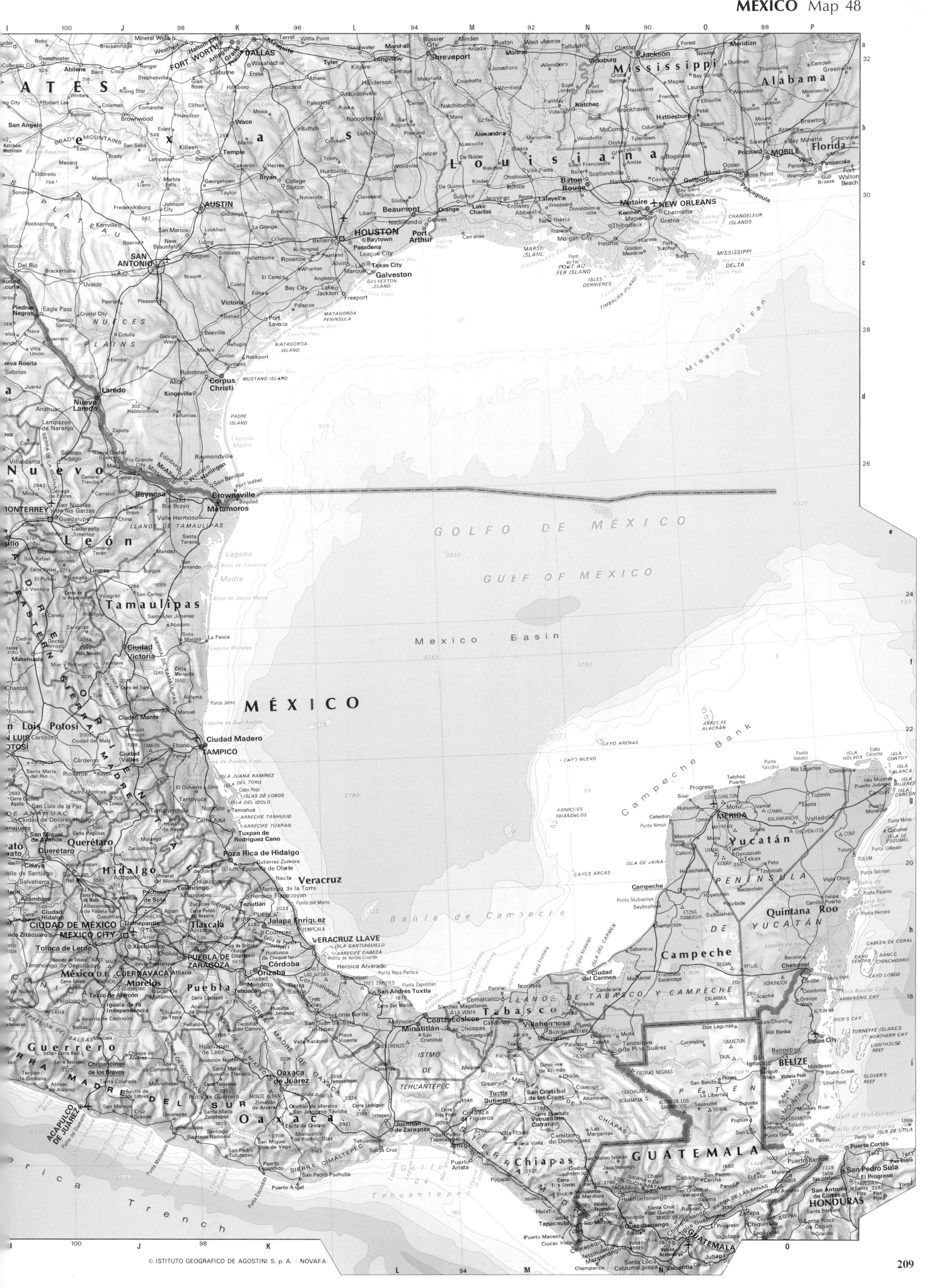

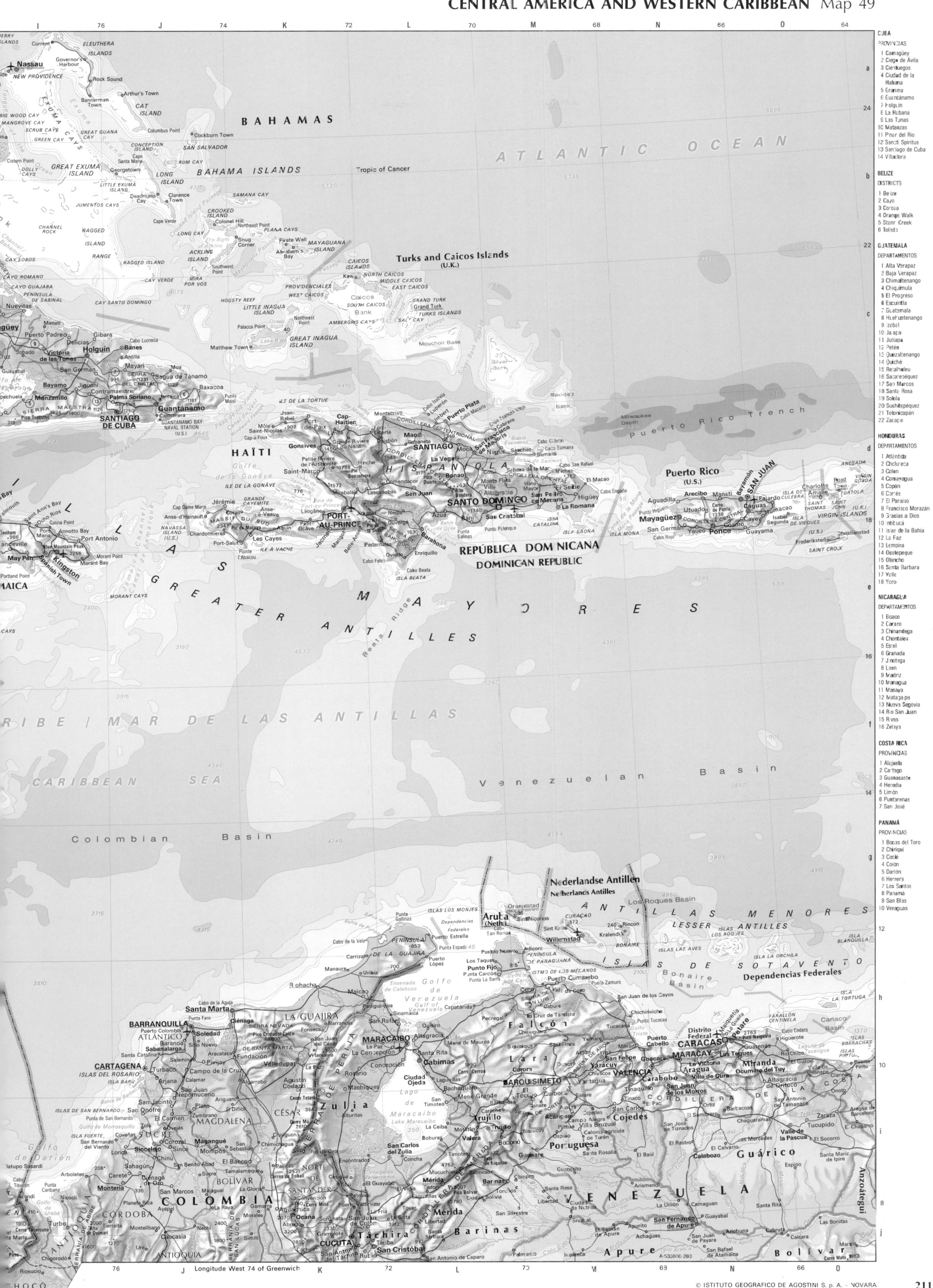

Map 50 **EASTERN CARIBBEAN**

ATLANTIC OCEAN

Tropic of Cancer

Mouchoir Bank

Silver Bank

Navidad Bank

PUERTO RICO TRENCH

Milwaukee Depth

Puerto Plata
SANTIAGO
Moca
San Francisco de Macorís
La Vega
Bonao
CORDILLERA
SANTO DOMINGO
San Cristóbal
Baní

LA ESPAÑOLA
HISPANIOLA

REPÚBLICA
DOMINICANA
DOMINICAN
REPUBLIC

ANTILLAS MAYORES
GREATER ANTILLES

Virgin Islands
(U.S.-U.K.)

Puerto Rico
(U.S.)

Aguadilla
Arecibo
Manatí
SAN JUAN
Mayagüez
Utuado
San Germán
Yauco Ponce
Guayama

Charlotte Amalie
Road Town

VIRGIN ISLANDS
(U.K.)

Anguilla (U.K.)
The Valley
SAINT-MARTIN
Marigot
Philipsburg
SINT MAARTEN
SAINT-BARTHÉLEMY

Nederlandse Antillen
Netherlands Antilles

Christiansted
Frederiksted
SAINT CROIX

SABA
The Bottom
SINT EUSTATIUS
Oranjestad
Sandy Point Town
SAINT KITTS/
SAINT CHRISTOPHER
Basseterre
NEVIS
Charlestown
SAINT CHRISTOPHER-NEVIS
REDONDA

Codrington
BARBUDA

Saint John's
ANTIGUA

Plymouth
Montserrat
(U.K.)

Port Louis
GRANDE-TERRE
Moule
LA DÉSIRADE
Baie-Mahault
Pointe-à-Pitre
Guadeloupe
(Fr.)
BASSE-TERRE
Soufrière
Basse-Terre
Capesterre-Belle-Eau
Grand-Bourg
MARIE-GALANTE
ÎLES DES SAINTES

ISLA DE AVES
(Dependencias Federales
Venezolanas)

Portsmouth
Marigot
Morne Diablotin
Roseau
DOMINICA
Berekua

MAR CARIBE / MAR DE LAS ANTILLAS

CARIBBEAN SEA

Montagne
Saint-Pierre
Fort-de-France
Martinique (Fr.)
Lamentin
La Trinité

Venezuelan Basin

Pointe d'Enfer

Cap Point
Castries
SAINT LUCIA
Soufrière
Mount Gimie
Vieux Fort

Soufrière
SAINT VINCENT
Kingstown
Georgetown

BEQUIA ISLAND
MUSTIQUE ISLAND
CANOUAN ISLAND
UNION ISLAND
CARRIACOU
RONDE ISLAND

Tobago
Speightstown
Bathsheba
Mount Hillaby
Bridgetown
BARBADOS

Victoria
Grenville
Saint George's
GRENADA
Point Saline

ISLAS
LOS TESTIGOS

Speyside
Canaan
Scarborough
TOBAGO

TRINIDAD
AND
TOBAGO

Aruba
(Neth.)
Oranjestad
Sint Nicolaas

Nederlandse Antillen
Netherlands Antilles

Los Roques
Basin

CURAÇAO
Sint Kruis
Kralendijk
Willemstad
BONAIRE

Pueblo Nuevo
Los Taques
Adícora
PENÍNSULA
DE PARAGUANÁ
Punto Fijo
Punta
Cardón
Coro

ISLAS LAS AVES

Dependencias Federales

ISLAS
LOS ROQUES

ISLA LA ORCHILA

ISLA
BLANQUILLA

ISLAS
LOS HERMANOS

ISLA LA SOLA

ISLAS LOS FRAILES

Nueva Esparta
Juangriego
La Asunción
ISLA DE MARGARITA
Porlamar
ISLA COCHE
ISLA CUBAGUA

Río Caribe
PENÍNSULA
DE PARIA
Macuro

Port of Spain
TRINIDAD
Arima
San Fernando
Siparia
Galeota Point

Falcón
Lara
BARQUISIMETO
VALENCIA
Carabobo
Yaracuy
MARACAY
CARACAS
Distrito
Federal
La Guaira
Aragua
Miranda
Ocumare del Tuy
Cumaná
Araya
Carúpano
Guiria

Sucre
Güiria

San Juan de los Cayos
Chichiriviche
Puerto Cabello

Guárico
Calabozo

Cojedes
San Carlos
San José de Tiznados

Valle de
la Pascua

Barcelona
Puerto la Cruz

El Tigre
Anaco

Maturín

Monagas

DELTA
DEL ORINOCO

Portuguesa

Guanare

Anzoátegui

Ciudad
Guayana
Ciudad
Bolívar

Delta Amacuro

VENEZUELA

Apure
San Fernando
de Apure

Georgetown

Bolívar

GUYANA

COLOMBIA

Scale 1:6,000,000   Delisle Conic Equidistant Projection

Longitude West 64 of Greenwich

© ISTITUTO GEOGRAFICO DE AGOSTINI S. p. A. - NOVARA

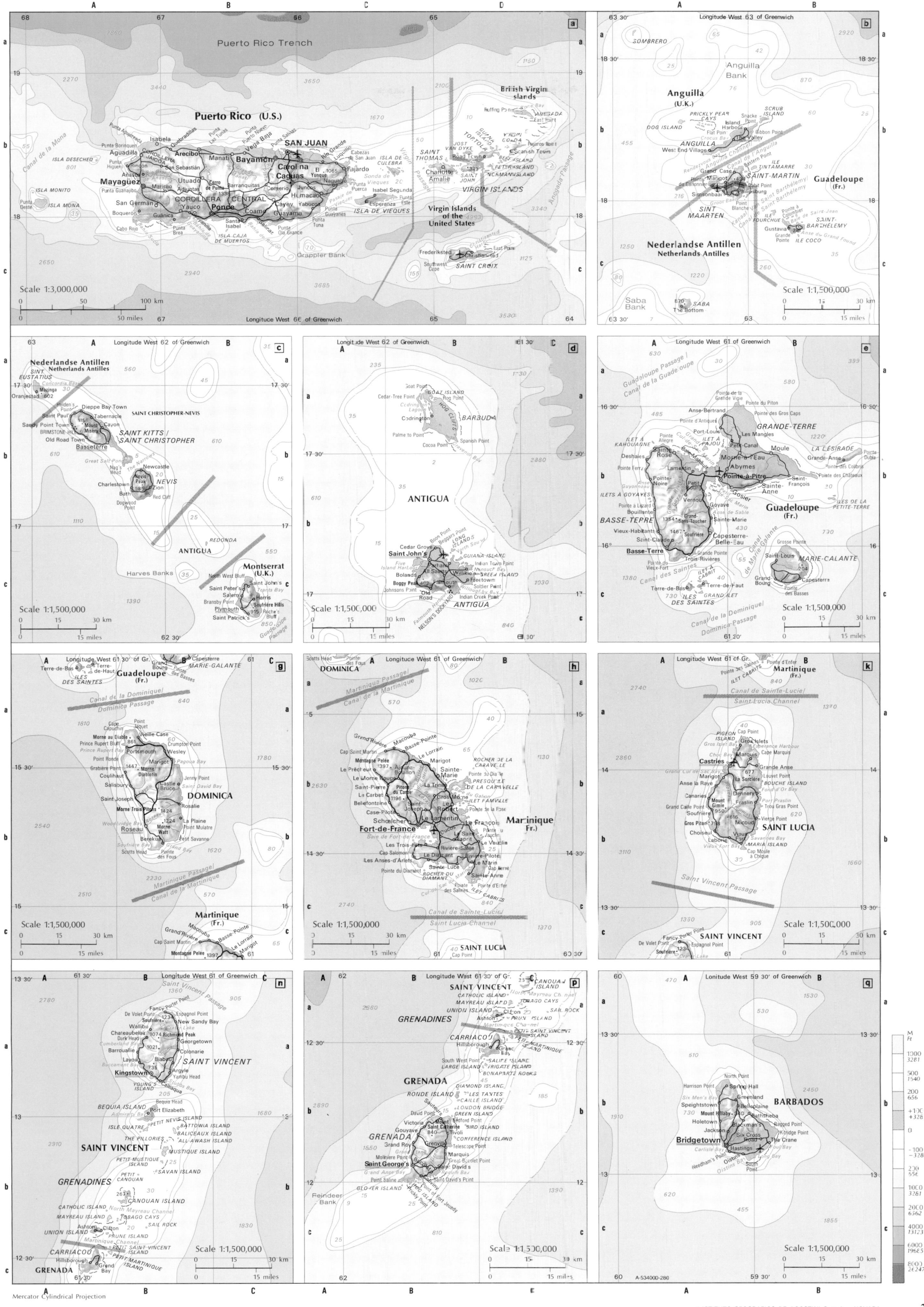

Map 52

SOUTH AMERICA, PHYSICAL

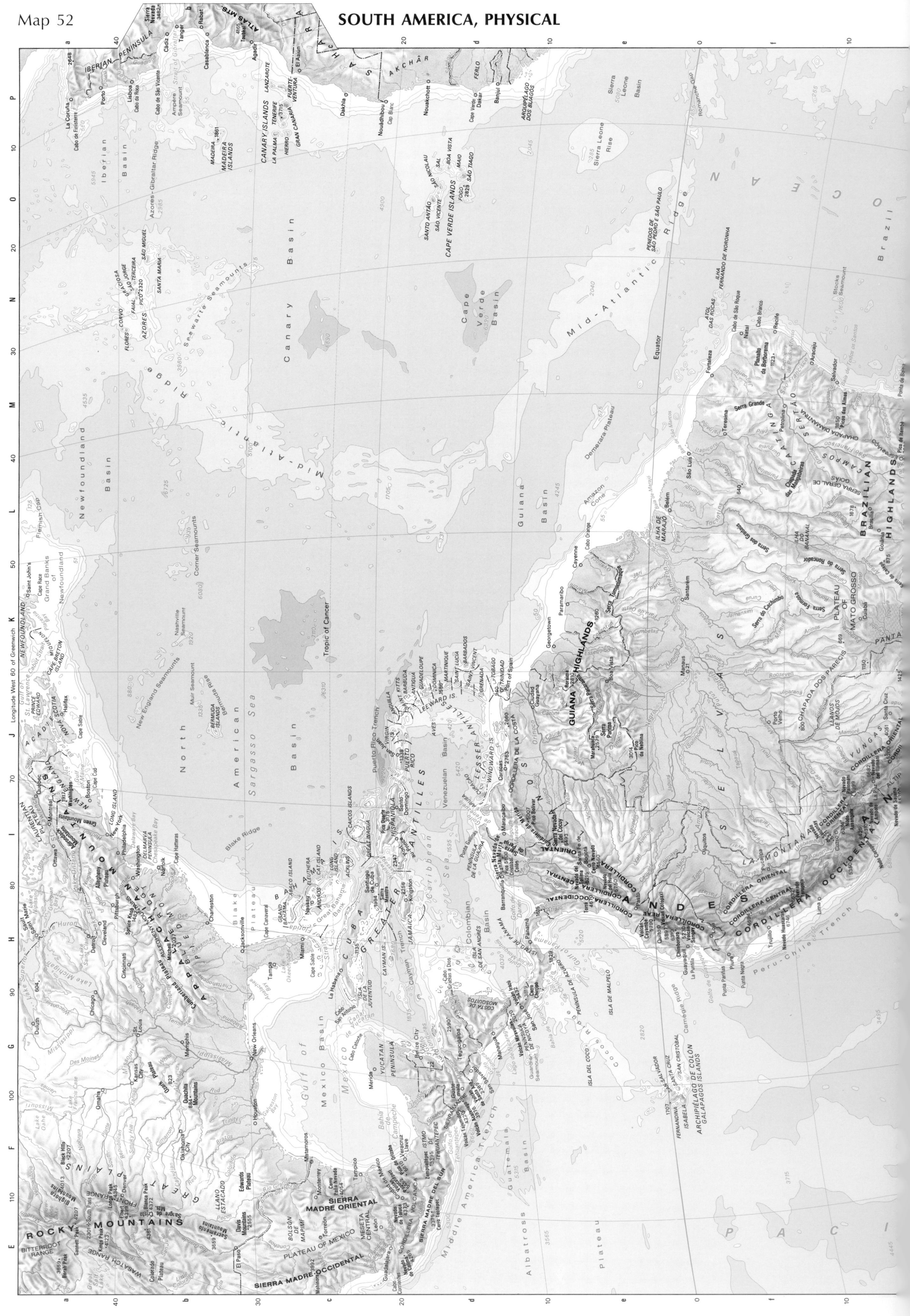

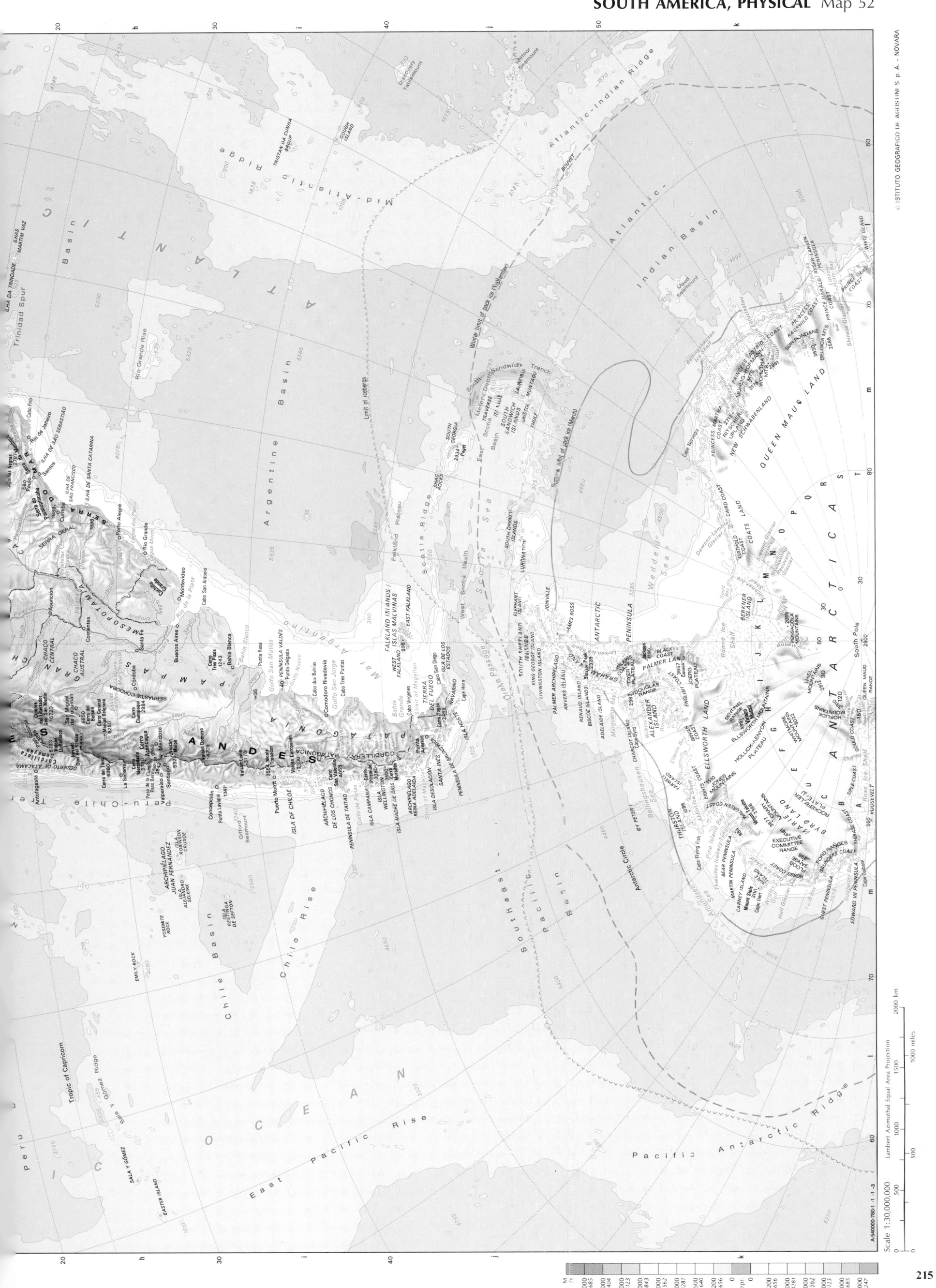

Map 53

SOUTH AMERICA, POLITICAL

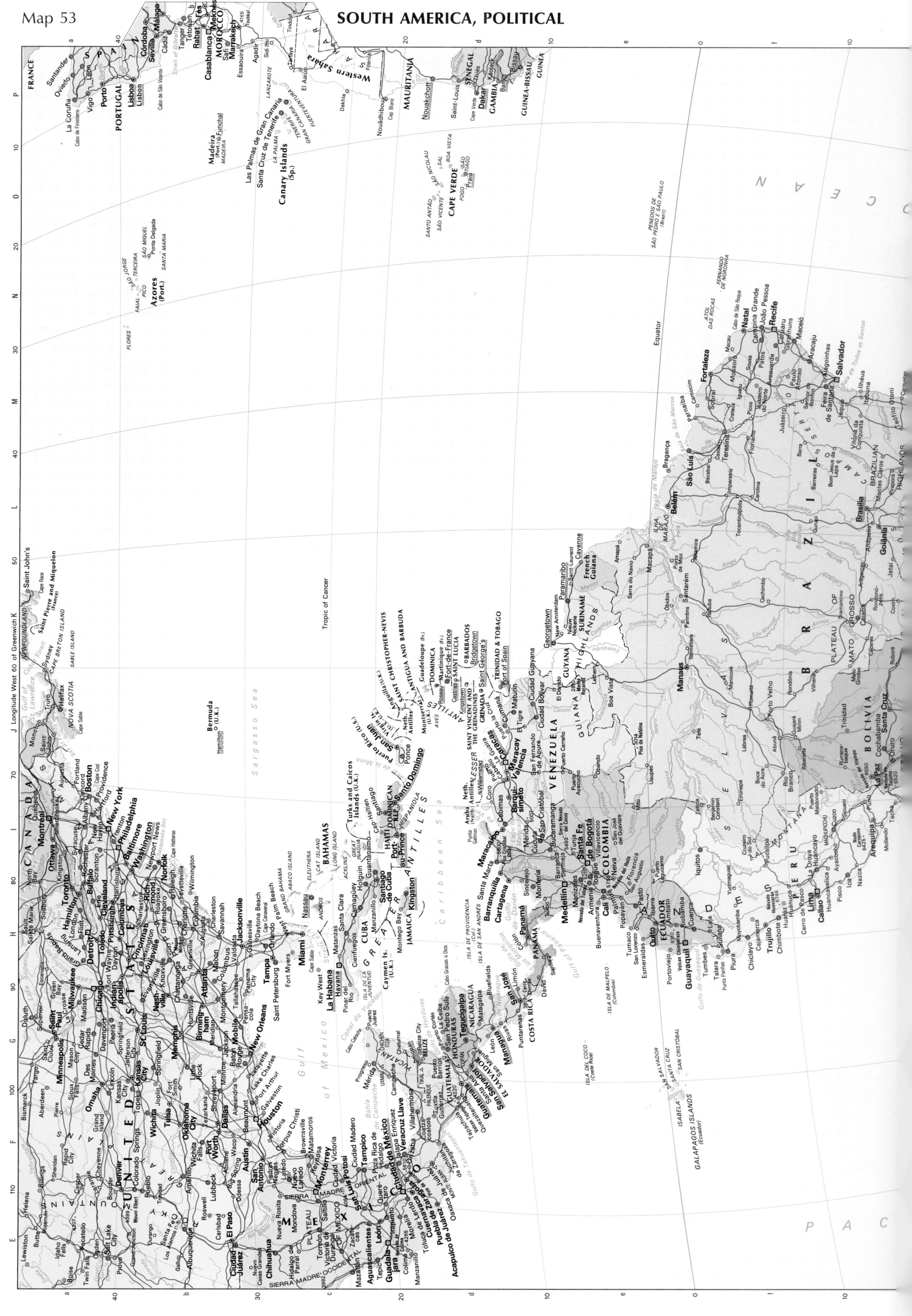

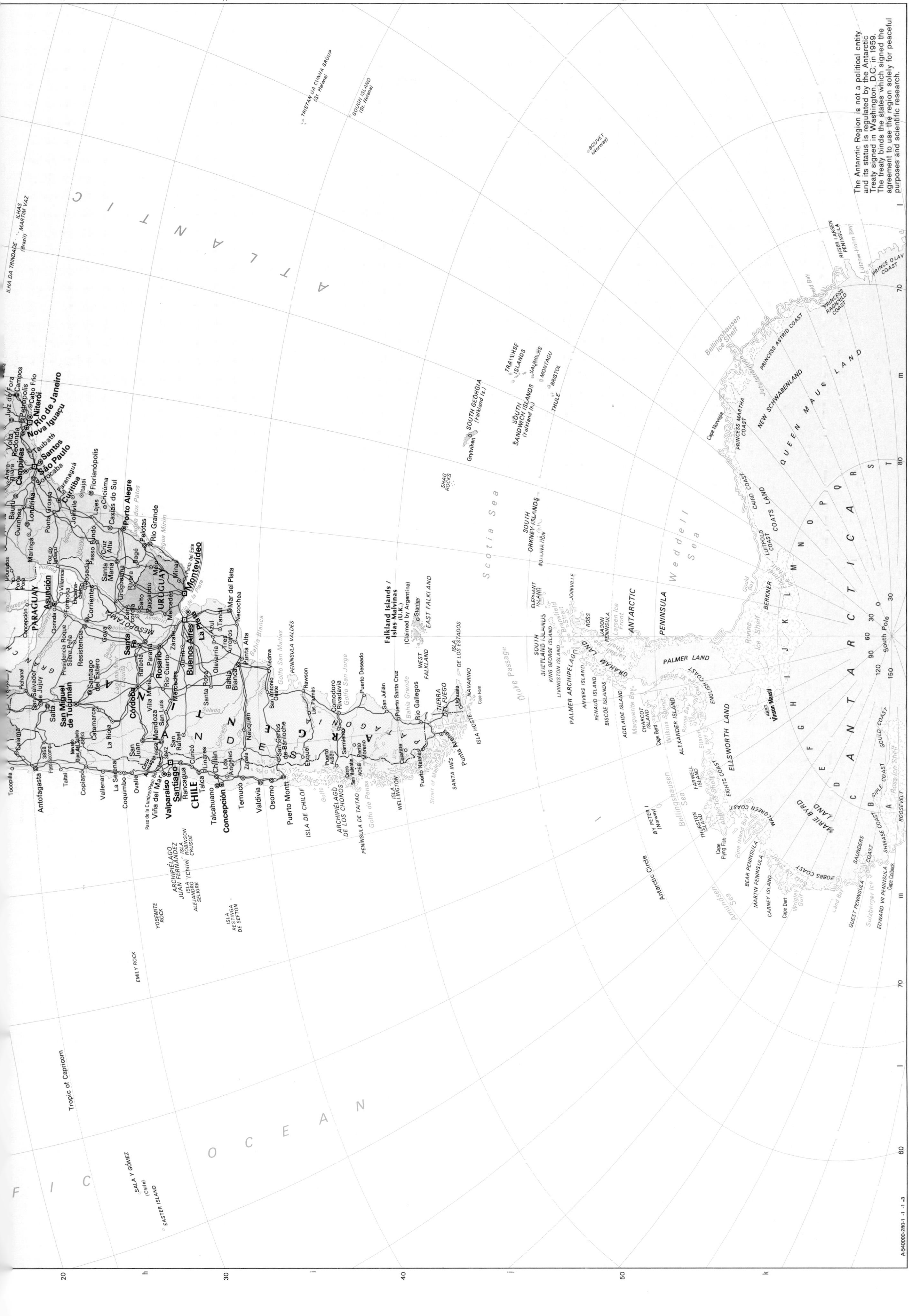

The Antarctic Region is not a political entity and its status is regulated by the Antarctic Treaty signed in Washington, D.C. in 1959. The treaty binds the states which signed the agreement to use the region solely for peaceful purposes and scientific research.

© ISTITUTO GEOGRAFICO DE AGOSTINI S. p. A. - NOVARA.

ATLANTIC

PACIFIC OCEAN

Tropic of Capricorn

Antarctic Circle

BRAZIL

PARAGUAY

URUGUAY

Montevideo

Buenos Aires

La Plata

CHILE

Santiago

Valparaíso

Concepción

ARGENTINA

PATAGONIA

Rio de Janeiro

Niterói

Nova Iguaçu

São Paulo

Santos

Curitiba

Porto Alegre

Pelotas

Rio Grande

Asunción

Córdoba

Rosario

Santa Fe

Mendoza

San Miguel de Tucumán

Salta

San Juan

La Rioja

Catamarca

Antofagasta

Coquimbo

La Serena

Talca

Talcahuano

Temuco

Valdivia

Osorno

Puerto Montt

San Carlos de Bariloche

Neuquén

Bahía Blanca

Mar del Plata

Necochea

Tandil

Azul

Comodoro Rivadavia

Puerto Deseado

Puerto Santa Cruz

Río Gallegos

TIERRA DEL FUEGO

Cape Horn

Punta Arenas

Falkland Islands / Islas Malvinas (U.K.) (Claimed by Argentina)

Stanley

WEST FALKLAND

EAST FALKLAND

Scotia Sea

SOUTH GEORGIA (Falkland Is.)

Grytviken

SOUTH ORKNEY ISLANDS

SOUTH SANDWICH ISLANDS (Falkland Is.)

SHAG ROCKS

Drake Passage

SOUTH SHETLAND ISLANDS

ANTARCTIC PENINSULA

GRAHAM LAND

PALMER LAND

ELLSWORTH LAND

MARIE BYRD LAND

Weddell Sea

Bellingshausen Sea

Ross Ice Shelf

South Pole

ANTARCTICA

QUEEN MAUD LAND

NEW SCHWABENLAND

COATS LAND

EASTER ISLAND (Chile)

SALA Y GÓMEZ (Chile)

ARCHIPIÉLAGO JUAN FERNÁNDEZ

TRISTAN DA CUNHA GROUP (St. Helena)

GOUGH ISLAND (St. Helena)

BOUVET (Norway)

ILHA DA TRINDADE (Brazil)

Scale 1:30,000,000

Lambert Azimuthal Equal Area Projection

2000 km

1000 miles

217

Map 54 **NORTHERN SOUTH AMERICA**

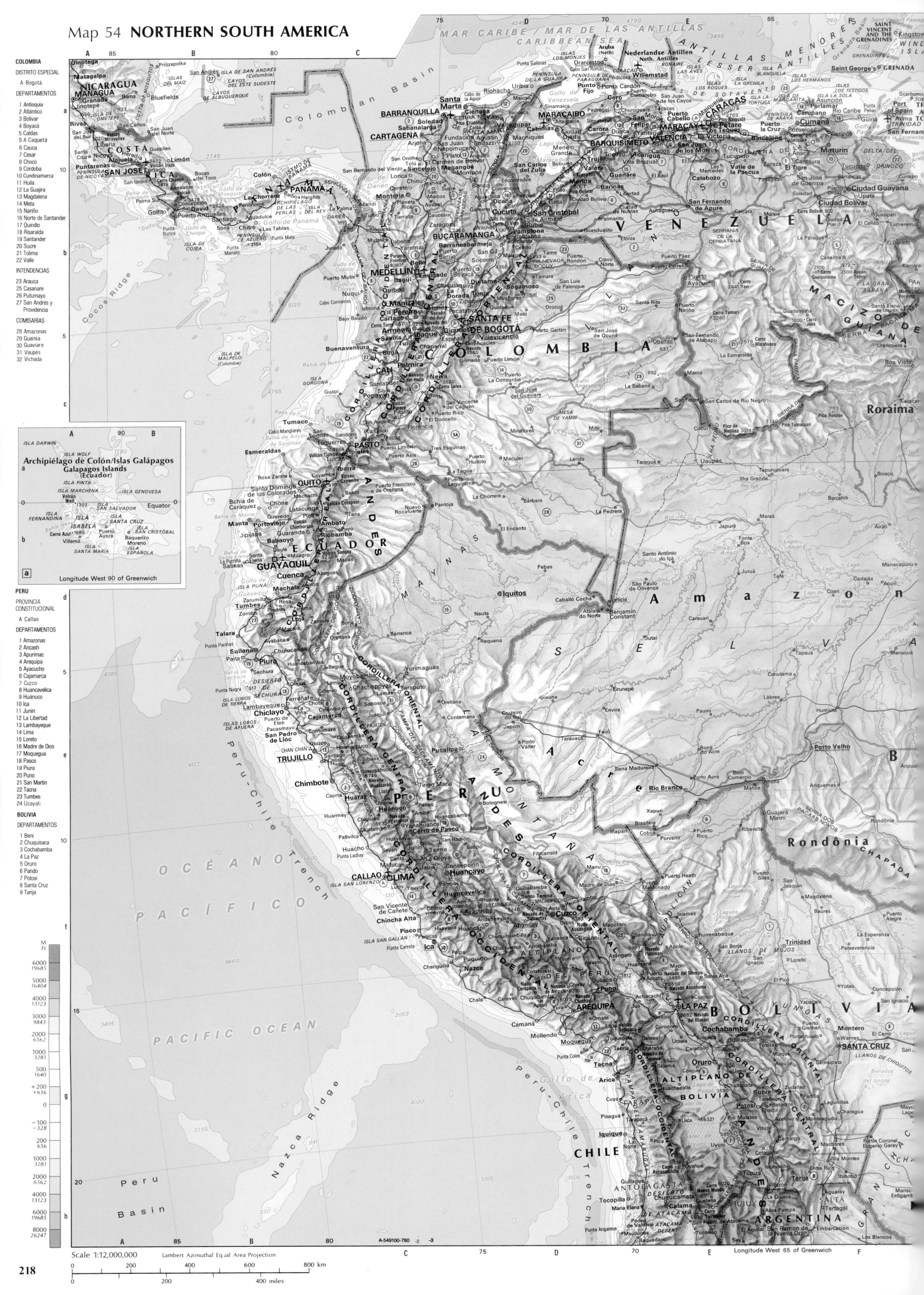

COLOMBIA

DISTRITO ESPECIAL
A Bogotá

DEPARTAMENTOS
1 Antioquia
2 Atlántico
3 Bolívar
4 Boyacá
5 Caldas
5 A Caquetá
6 Cauca
7 Cesar
8 Chocó
9 Córdoba
10 Cundinamarca
11 Huila
12 La Guajira
13 Magdalena
14 Meta
15 Nariño
16 Norte de Santander
17 Quindío
18 Risaralda
19 Santander
20 Sucre
21 Tolima
22 Valle

INTENDENCIAS
23 Arauca
25 Casanare
26 Putumayo
27 San Andrés y
   Providencia

COMISARÍAS
28 Amazonas
29 Guainía
30 Guaviare
31 Vaupés
32 Vichada

PERU

**PROVINCIA
CONSTITUCIONAL**
A Callao

DEPARTAMENTOS
1 Amazonas
2 Ancash
3 Apurímac
4 Arequipa
5 Ayacucho
6 Cajamarca
7 Cuzco
8 Huancavelica
9 Huánuco
10 Ica
11 Junín
12 La Libertad
13 Lambayeque
14 Lima
15 Loreto
16 Madre de Dios
17 Moquegua
18 Pasco
19 Piura
20 Puno
21 San Martín
22 Tacna
23 Tumbes
24 Ucayali

BOLIVIA

DEPARTAMENTOS
1 Beni
2 Chuquisaca
3 Cochabamba
4 La Paz
5 Oruro
6 Pando
7 Potosí
8 Santa Cruz
9 Tarija

Scale 1:12,000,000   Lambert Azimuthal Equal Area Projection

Mid-Atlantic Ridge

Guiana Basin

OCEANO ATLÂNTICO

ATLANTIC OCEAN

OCEANO ATLÂNTICO

BRASIL

BRAZIL

Mato Grosso

Pará

Maranhão

Piauí

Bahia

Goiás

Tocantins

Minas Gerais

SÃO PAULO

RIO DE JANEIRO

Map 55 **EAST-CENTRAL SOUTH AMERICA**

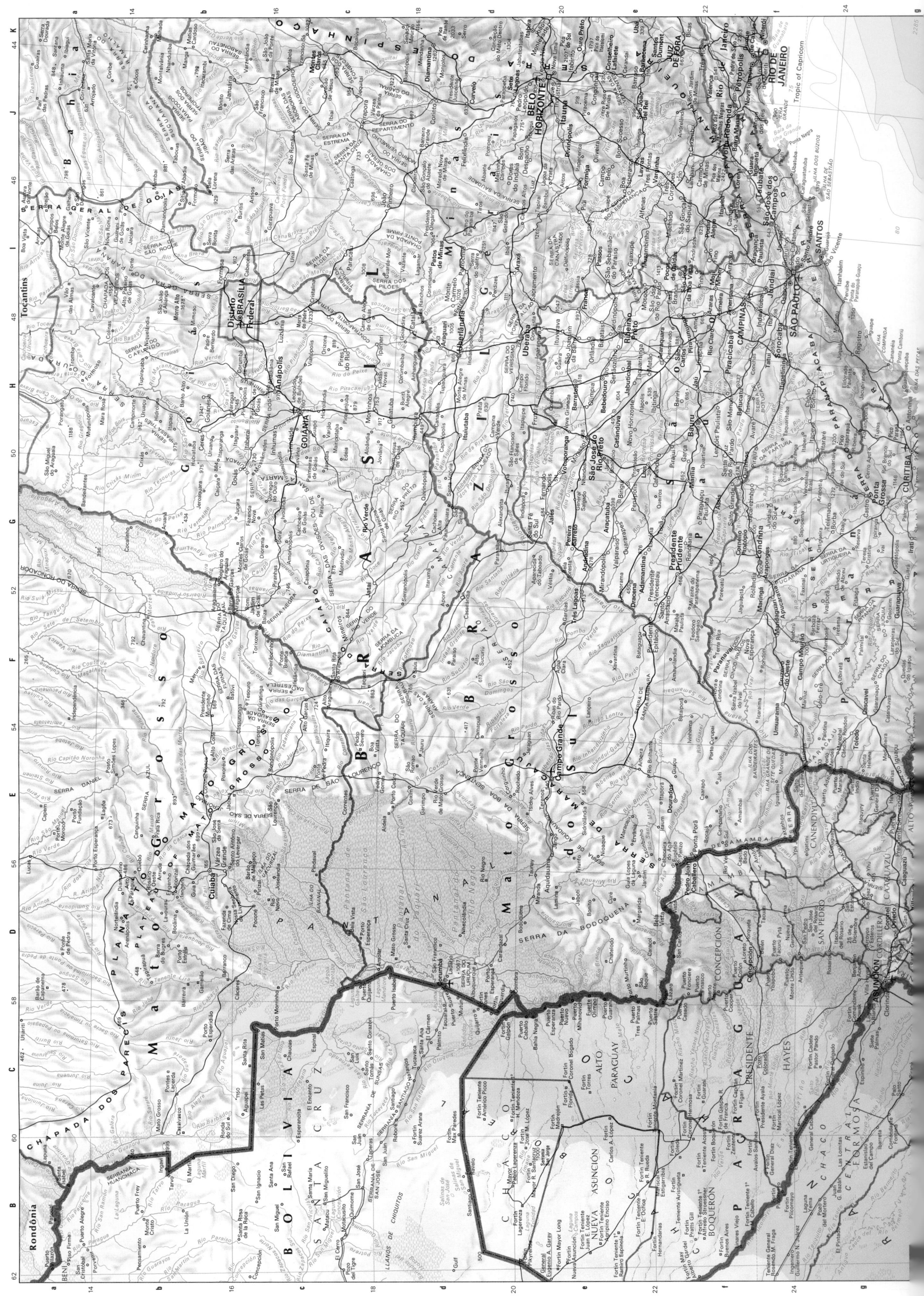

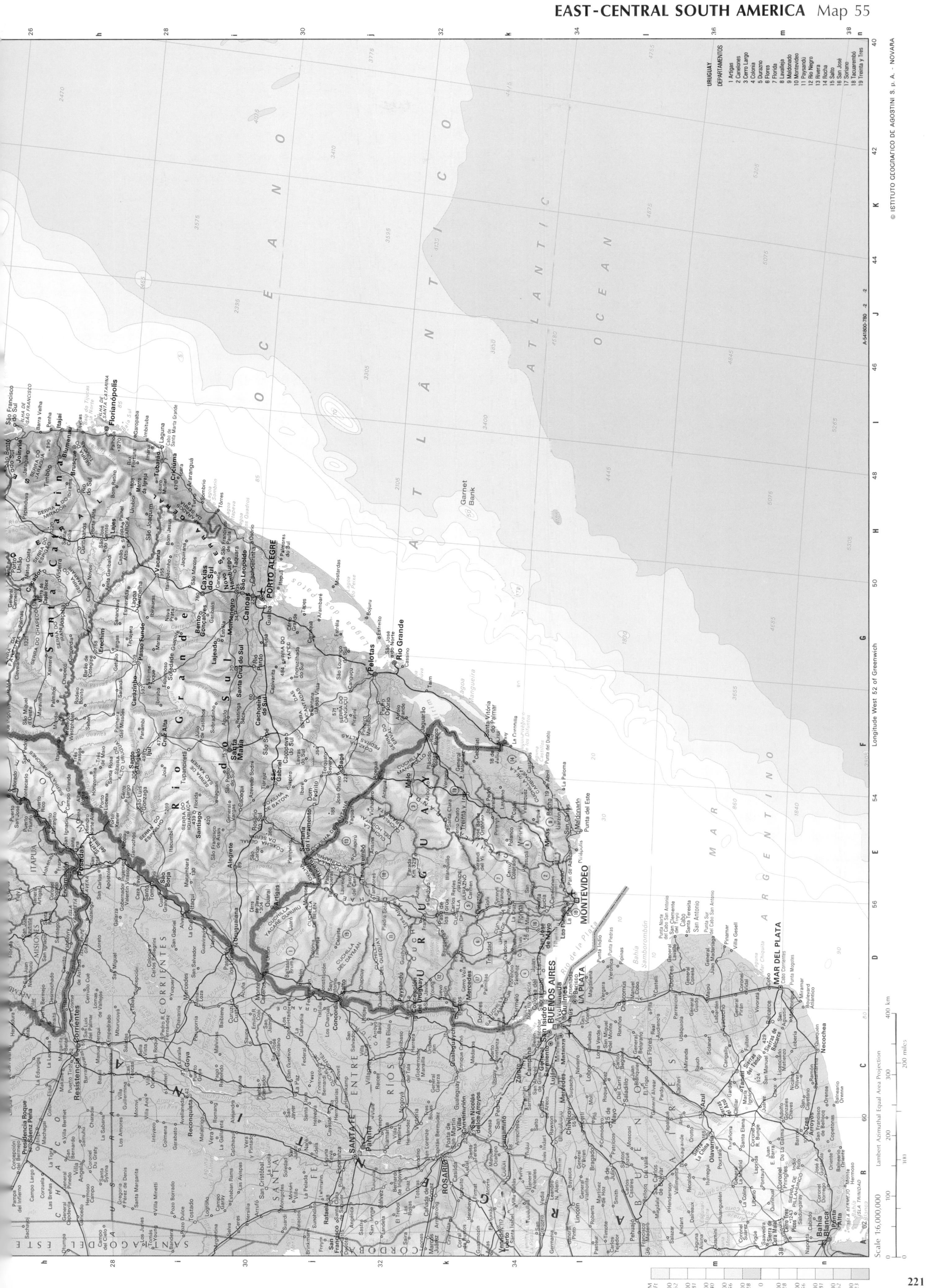

© ISTITUTO GEOGRAFICO DE AGOSTINI S. p. A. - NOVARA

URUGUAY
DEPARTAMENTOS

1 Artigas
2 Canelones
3 Cerro Largo
4 Colonia
5 Durazno
6 Flores
7 Florida
8 Lavalleja
9 Maldonado
10 Montevideo
11 Paysandú
12 Río Negro
13 Rivera
14 Rocha
15 Salto
16 San José
17 Soriano
18 Tacuarembó
19 Treinta y Tres

Scale 1:6,000,000

Lambert Azimuthal Equal Area Projection

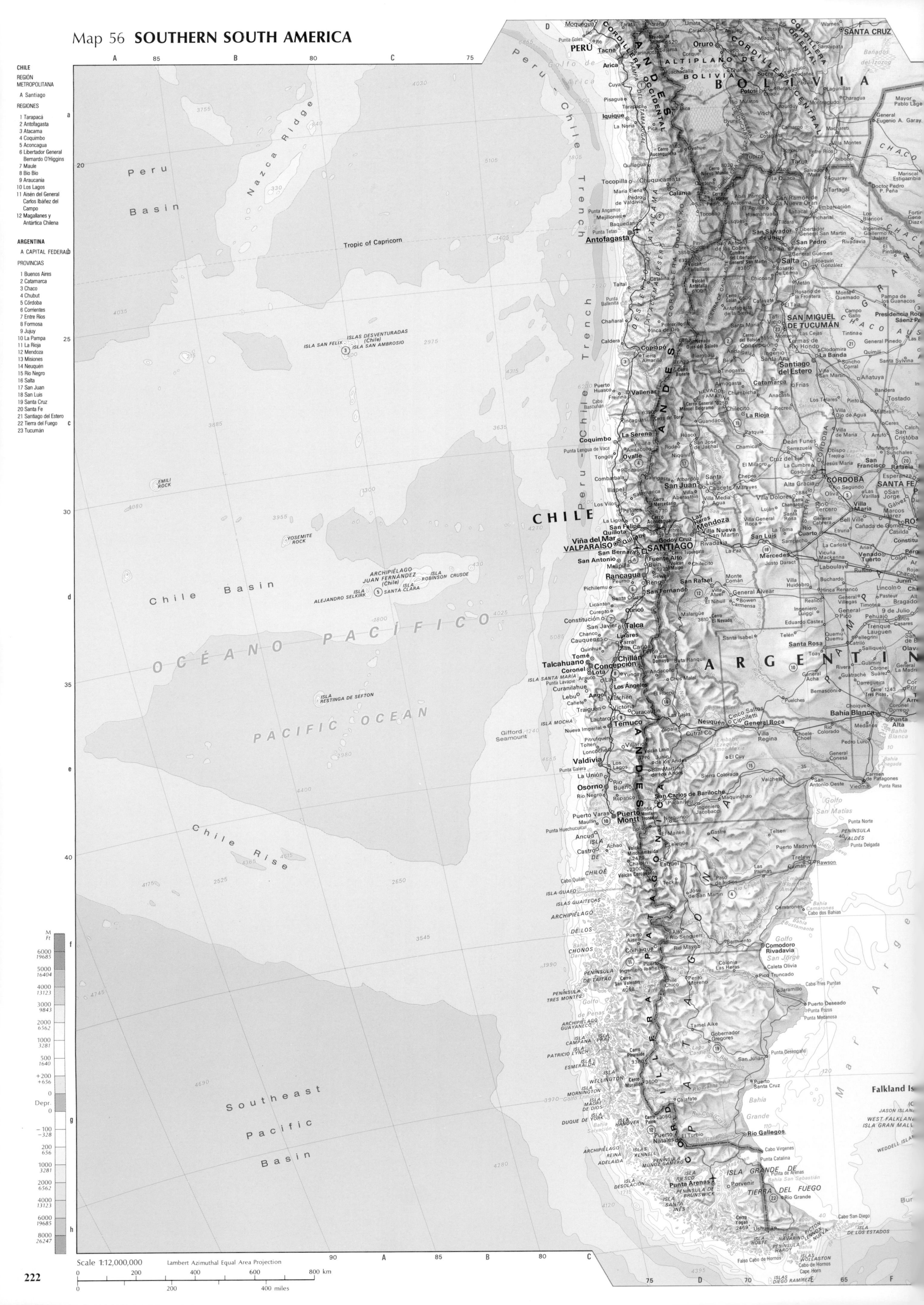

Map 56 **SOUTHERN SOUTH AMERICA**

CHILE

REGIÓN
METROPOLITANA

A Santiago

REGIONES

1 Tarapacá
2 Antofagasta
3 Atacama
4 Coquimbo
5 Aconcagua
6 Libertador General
  Bernardo O'Higgins
7 Maule
8 Bío Bío
9 Araucanía
10 Los Lagos
11 Aisén del General
   Carlos Ibáñez del
   Campo
12 Magallanes y
   Antártica Chilena

ARGENTINA

A CAPITAL FEDERAL

PROVINCIAS

1 Buenos Aires
2 Catamarca
3 Chaco
4 Chubut
5 Córdoba
6 Corrientes
7 Entre Ríos
8 Formosa
9 Jujuy
10 La Pampa
11 La Rioja
12 Mendoza
13 Misiones
14 Neuquén
15 Río Negro
16 Salta
17 San Juan
18 San Luis
19 Santa Cruz
20 Santa Fe
21 Santiago del Estero
22 Tierra del Fuego
23 Tucumán

M
Ft

6000
19685

5000
16404

4000
13123

3000
9843

2000
6562

1000
3281

500
1640

+200
+656

0

Depr.
0

−100
−328

200
656

1000
3281

2000
6562

4000
13123

6000
19685

8000
26247

Scale 1:12,000,000

Lambert Azimuthal Equal Area Projection

0   200   400   600   800 km

0   200   400 miles

Map 57 **AUSTRALIA AND OCEANIA, PHYSICAL**

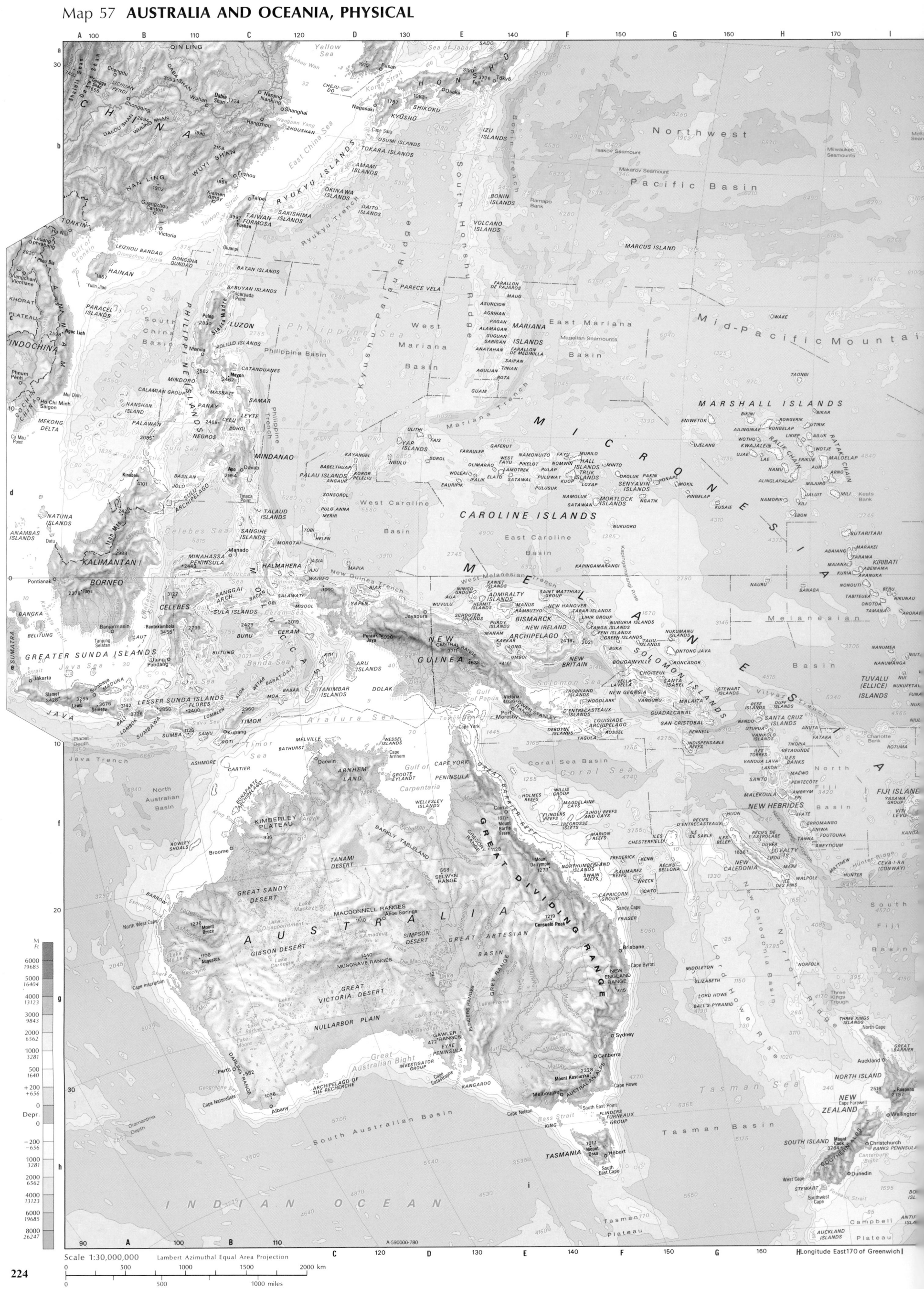

Scale 1:30,000,000 Lambert Azimuthal Equal Area Projection

Map 58 **AUSTRALIA AND OCEANIA, POLITICAL**

CHINA

JAPAN

SOUTH KOREA

Chengdu Nanchong Xuzhou Kaifeng
Zigong Chongqing Wuhan Nanjing Nanking
Kunming Guiyang Changsha Hangzhou Shanghai
Guilin Liuzhou Ganzhou Fuzhou
Nanning Guangzhou Canton Shantou Taipei
Hai phong Hong Kong Macao (Port.) Kaohsiung TAIWAN
HAINAN

Tōkyō Yokohama Nagoya Kyōto Ōsaka
Kōbe Hiroshima Fukuoka Nagasaki Kagoshima
KYŪSHŪ SHIKOKU Sendai

THAILAND LAOS VIET-NAM CAMBODIA
Phnum Penh Ho Chi Minh (Saigon) Nha Trang
Da Nang Qui Nhon Hue

PHILIPPINES
LUZON Manila Quezon City Baguio
MINDORO PANAY NEGROS SAMAR LEYTE
Cebu Bacolod Iloilo PALAWAN
MINDANAO Davao Zamboanga General Santos

MALAYSIA BRUNEI
KALIMANTAN (BORNEO) Kuching Pontianak
Balikpapan Banjarmasin

INDONESIA
SUMATRA Jakarta Bandung Semarang Surabaya Yogyakarta
CELEBES Ujung Pandang Makassar
Manado HALMAHERA CERAM TIMOR FLORES
MOLUCCAS

South China Sea Philippine Sea Celebes Sea Banda Sea Arafura Sea Timor Sea

Northern Mariana Islands (U.S.)
MARIANA ISLANDS Saipan TINIAN ROTA Agana
Guam (U.S.)

MARSHALL ISLANDS
Wake (U.S.) BIKINI ENEWETAK KWAJALEIN MAJURO

FEDERATED STATES OF MICRONESIA
CAROLINE ISLANDS YAP ISLANDS Palau Belau (Trust Territory) Koror
TRUK ISLANDS Ponape KOSRAE (KUSAIE)

MICRONESIA

NAURU / NAOERO Banaba

KIRIBATI

MELANESIA

PAPUA NEW GUINEA
NEW GUINEA Puncak Jaya Jayapura Madang Lae Port Moresby
BISMARCK ARCHIPELAGO NEW BRITAIN NEW IRELAND Rabaul
Gulf of Papua Solomon Sea

SOLOMON ISLANDS
BOUGAINVILLE CHOISEUL NEW GEORGIA GUADALCANAL Honiara SAN CRISTOBAL

TUVALU

VANUATU
NEW HEBRIDES ESPIRITU SANTO Luganville ÉFATÉ Port-Vila

NEW CALEDONIA (France) Nouméa LOYALTY ISLANDS ILE DES PINS

FIJI ISLANDS VITI LEVU KANDAVU

ROTUMA

Norfolk (Australia) Kingston
LORD HOWE (Australia) BALL'S PYRAMID

AUSTRALIA
Darwin ARNHEM LAND Katherine GULF OF CARPENTARIA
CAPE YORK PENINSULA Cooktown Cairns Townsville Mackay Rockhampton Gladstone
KIMBERLEY Wyndham Broome Derby Halls Creek
GREAT SANDY DESERT Port Hedland Karratha Dampier Onslow
Carnarvon Shark Bay Geraldton GIBSON DESERT GREAT VICTORIA DESERT
Perth Bunbury Albany Esperance NULLARBOR PLAIN Eucla
Alice Springs SIMPSON DESERT TANAMI DESERT Mount Isa Cloncurry
Coober Pedy Oodnadatta Port Augusta Port Pirie
Adelaide Kangaroo Broken Hill Mildura
Melbourne Geelong Ballarat Bendigo Shepparton
Great Australian Bight
Brisbane Gold Coast Ipswich Toowoomba Bundaberg Maryborough Gympie
Charleville Roma Dalby Charters Towers Longreach Barcaldine Blackall
Dubbo Tamworth Armidale Newcastle Sydney Wollongong
Canberra Wagga Wagga Albury Goulburn Bourke Cobar
TASMANIA Hobart Launceston Devonport Bass Strait

NEW ZEALAND
NORTH ISLAND Auckland Manukau Hamilton Wellington New Plymouth
SOUTH ISLAND Christchurch Dunedin Invercargill Timaru Nelson Blenheim
STEWART ISLAND

Coral Sea Tasman Sea INDIAN OCEAN

Scale 1:30,000,000   Lambert Azimuthal Equal Area Projection

0 500 1000 1500 2000 km
0 500 1000 miles

Longitude East 170 of Greenwich

J   170   K   160   L   150   M   140   N   130   O   120   P   110   Q   10C   R

San Luis
Obispo
Santa Barbara
Los Angeles
Long Beach
San Bernardino
San Diego
Ensenada
Tijuana
Mexicali

UNITED STATES

Bakersfield
Pasadena
Phoenix
Yuma
Tucson
Nogales
Agua Prieta

Odessa

El Paso
Ciudad Juárez

ISLA DE
GUADALUPE
(Mexico)

BAJA
CALIFORNIA

Hermosillo
Guaymas

Ciudad
Obregón

Santa
Rosalía

La Paz

Cabo San Lucas

MEXICO

Chihuahua

Hidalgo
del Parral

Culiacán
Rosales
Mazatlán

Tropic of Cancer

Midway Islands
(U.S.)
PEARL AND HERMES

LISIANSKI
LAYSAN
MARO
GARDNER
PINNACLES

FRENCH FRIGATE
SHOALS
NECKER
NIHOA

Hawaii
(U.S.)

KAUAI
NIHAU
OAHU
KAULA
LANAI
MOLOKA'I
MAUI
Hawi
KAHOOLAWE
Honolulu
Hilo
HAWAII

ISLAS
REVILLAGIGEDO
(Mexico)

HAWAIIAN ISLANDS

Johnston
(U.S.)

P A C I F I C   O C E A N

CLIPPERTON
(French Polynesia)

KINGMAN
(U.S.)
PALMYRA
(U.S.)
TERAINA
(WASHINGTON)
TABUAERAN
(FANNING)

KIRITIMATI
(CHRISTMAS)

Equator

OWLAND
(U.S.)
BAKER
(U.S.)

JARVIS
(U.S.)

WINSLOW
PHOENIX ISLANDS
KANTON
ENDERBURY
MCKEAN
BIRNIE
RAWAKI
(PHOENIX)
NIKUMARORO
(GARDNER)
ORONA
(HULL)
MANRA
(SYDNEY)
CARONDELET

K I R I B A T I

MALDEN

STARBUCK

P O L Y N E S I A

LINE ISLANDS

Tokelau (New Zealand)
ATAFU
TOKELAU
ISLANDS
NUKUNONU
FAKAOFO
SWAINS

PENRHYN

RAKAHANGA
MANIHIKI

EIAA

NUKU FIVA
U.S. HUKA
MARQUESAS
UA POU
NIVA OA
UA HUKA
ISLANDS
FATU HIVA

**WESTERN
SAMOA**
SAMOA ISLANDS
SAVAI'I
Apia
UPOLU
TUTUILA
MANUA
ISLANDS

PUKAPUKA
**NORTHERN
COOK ISLANDS**
NASSAU
SUWARROW

VOSTOK
CAROLINE

FLINT

Futuna
Mata-Utu
WALLIS
UVEA
FUTUNA
ALOFI
Pago Pago
**American
Samoa**
(U.S.)

Cook Islands
(New Zealand)

TUAMOTU ARCHIPELAGO

RANGIROA
ILES DU
ROI GEORGES
ILES DU
DÉSAPPOINTEMENT
MATAIVA
MANIHI
MOTU
ONE
MAUPITI
APATAKI
ARATIKA
TAKUME
FANGATAU
PUKAPUKA
**LEEWARD
ISLANDS**
KAUKURA
MANUAE
BORA-BORA
HUAHINE
FAKARAVA
MAKEMO
TAKAROA
MAUFIHAA
RAIATEA
TETIAROA
TAHANEA
MARUTEA
HAO
TAKOTO
NIUAFO'OU
NIUATO PUTAPU
TONGA
FONUALEI
ANTIOPE
MOOREA
Papeete
TAHITI
MOTUTUNGA
PUKARUHA
RAVAHERE
VAHITAHI
REAO
VAVA'U
GROUP
**TONGA
ISLANDS**
PALMERSTON
MANUAE
AITUTAKI
MANUAE
TAKUTEA
MITIARO
AHUNUI
HA'APAI GROUP
KOTU GROUP
Niue
(New Zealand)
Alofi
ATIU
MAUKE
HEREHERETUE
ILES DU DUC
DE GLOUCESTER
TUREIA
GROUPE
ACTEON
NOMUKA GROUP
BEVERIDGE
**SOUTHERN
COOK
ISLANDS**
RAROTONGA
Avarua
MARIA
RURUTU
MANUANGI
MURUROA
MARUTEA
NUKU'alofa
TONGATAPU
GROUP
MANGAIA
**French
Polynesia**
TEMATANGI
MARIA
ATA
RIMATARA
FAGATAUFA
MORANE
NERVA REEFS
**TUBUAI
ISLANDS**
TUBUAI
RAEVAVAE
GAMBIER TEMOE
ISLANDS
MANGAREVA
OENO
HENDERSON
DUCIE
Tropic of Capricorn
RAPA
ILOTS
DE BASS
Adamstown
PITCAIRN
Pitcairn
(U.K.)

RAOUL
KEY KERMADEC
ISLANDS
(New Zealand)
PERANCE ROCK

SALA Y GOMEZ
(Chile)
EASTER ISLAND
(Chile)

ERNEST
LEGOUVÉ

MARIA THERESA

CHATHAM ISLANDS
(New Zealand)
PITT

i

J   170   K   160   L   150   M   140   N   130   O   120   P   1'0   Q   100   90

A—90000-280-2-2 -2 -3

Map 59 **AUSTRALIA**

Scale 1:12,000,000   Delisle Conic Equidistant Projection

0   200   400   600   800 km

0   200   400 miles

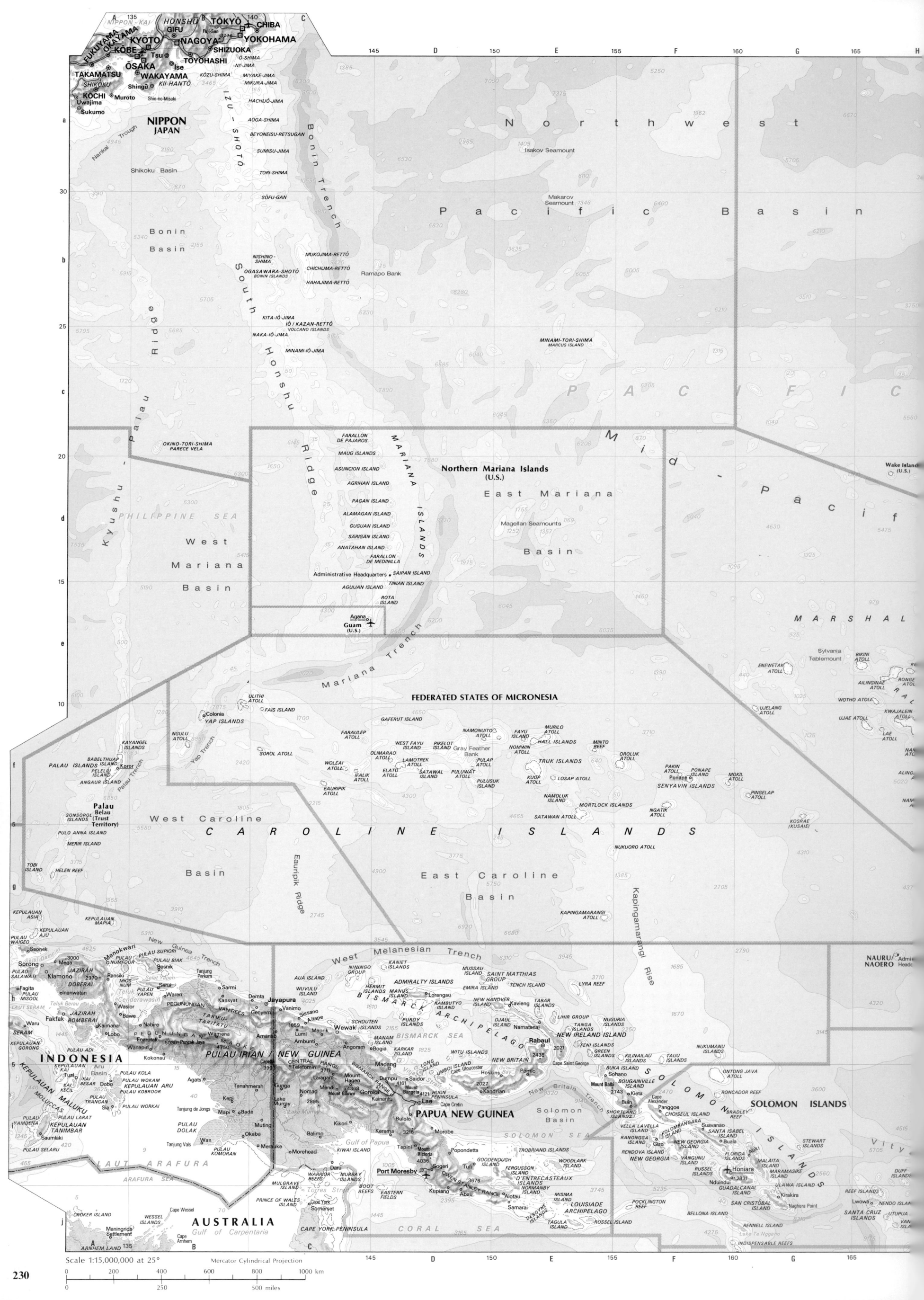

Scale 1:15,000,000 at 25°

Mercator Cylindrical Projection

0   200   400   600   800   1000 km

0   250   500 miles

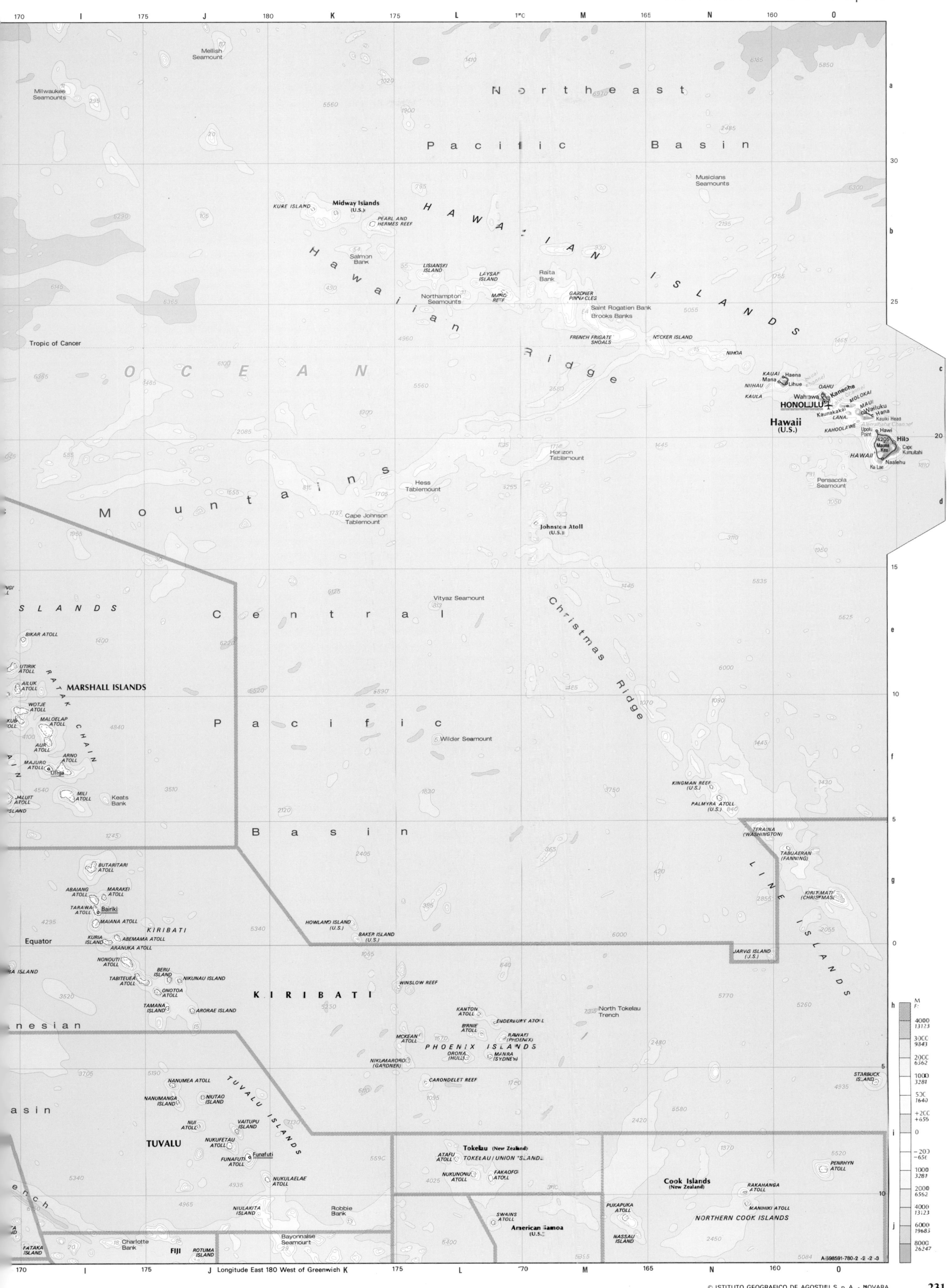

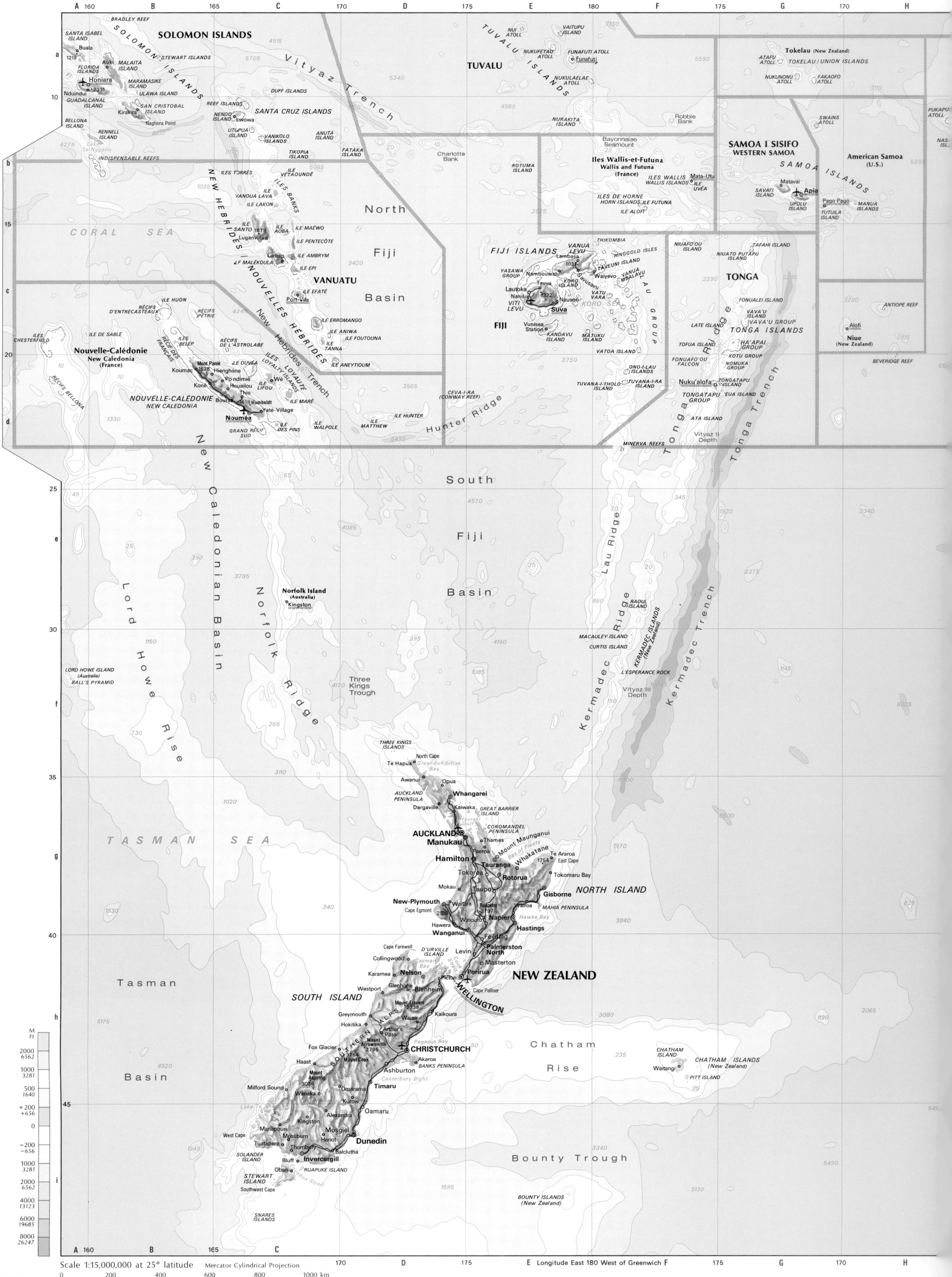

Map 61 THE SOUTH PACIFIC

SOLOMON ISLANDS

SANTA ISABEL ISLAND
Buala
STEWART ISLANDS
Auki MALAITA ISLAND
FLORIDA ISLANDS
Honiara
Nduindui
MARAMASIKE ISLAND
SAN CRISTOBAL ISLAND
ULAWA ISLAND
GUADALCANAL
Kirakira
BELLONA ISLAND
RENNELL ISLAND
Naghora Point
REEF ISLANDS
NENDO ISLAND Lwowa
UTUPUA ISLANDS
SANTA CRUZ ISLANDS
VANIKOLO ISLANDS
TIKOPIA ISLAND
ANUTA ISLAND
FATAKA ISLAND
INDISPENSABLE REEFS
Te Nggano

DUFF ISLANDS

Vityaz Trench

TUVALU

NUI ATOLL
NUKUFETAU ATOLL
FUNAFUTI ATOLL
Funafuti
NUKULAELAE ATOLL
TUVALU ISLANDS
NURAKITA ISLAND

VAITUPU ISLAND

Tokelau (New Zealand)
ATAFU ATOLL
TOKELAU / UNION ISLANDS
NUKUNONU ATOLL
FAKAOFO ATOLL
SWAINS ATOLL
PUKAPUKA ATOLL

Robbie Bank

CHARLOTTE BANK
Bayonnaise Seamount

ROTUMA ISLAND

Iles Wallis-et-Futuna
Wallis and Futuna (France)
ILES WALLIS Mata-Utu
WALLIS ISLANDS UVEA
ILES DE HORNE
HORN ISLANDS ILE FUTUNA
ILE ALOFI

SAMOA I SISIFO
WESTERN SAMOA
SAVAII ISLAND Matavai
Apia
UPOLU ISLAND
TUTUILA ISLAND

American Samoa (U.S.)
Pago Pago
MANUA ISLANDS

CORAL SEA

New Hebrides
ILES TORRES
ILE VETAOUNDE
ILES BANKS
VANUA LAVA
ILE LAKON
ILE SANTO
Luganville
ILE MAEWO
ILE AOBA
ILE PENTECOTE
Lamap ILE AMBRYM
ILE MALEKOULA
ILE EPI
Port-Vila
ILE EFATE
VANUATU
ILE ERROMANGO
ILE ANIWA
ILE TANNA
ILE FOUTOUNA
ILE ANEYTIOUM

North Fiji Basin

FIJI ISLANDS
VANUA LEVU
THIKOMBIA
RINGGOLD ISLES
Lambasa
TAVEUNI ISLAND
YASAWA GROUP
VANUA MBALAVU
KORO ISLAND Waiyevo
Lautoka KORO SEA
Nambouwalu
VATU VARA
Nandi VITI LEVU
Nausori
VUNISEA STATION
Suva
FIJI
VUNISEA
KANDAVU ISLAND
MATUKU ISLAND
VATOA ISLAND
ONO-I-LAU ISLANDS
CEVA-I-RA (CONWAY REEF)
TUVANA-I-THOLO ISLAND
TUVANA-I-RA ISLAND

KORO SEA
LAU GROUP

NIUAFO'OU ISLAND
TAFAHI ISLAND
NIUATO PUTAPU ISLAND

TONGA

FONUALEI ISLAND
VAVA'U ISLAND
VAVA'U GROUP
LATE ISLAND
TONGA ISLANDS
TOFUA ISLAND
HA'APAI GROUP
FONUAFO'OU OR FALCON
KOTU GROUP
NOMUKA GROUP
Nuku'alofa
TONGATAPU GROUP
TONGATAPU 'EUA ISLAND
ATA ISLAND

Niue (New Zealand)
ANTIOPE REEF
Alofi
BEVERIDGE REEF

RECIFS D'ENTRECASTEAUX
ILE HUON
RECIFS PETRIE
ILE BELEP
RECIFS DE L'ASTROLABE
ILES CHESTERFIELD
ILE DE SABLE
RECIFS FRANCAIS
Koumac Mont Panie Hienghene
Pondimie
Kone Houailou
Thio
Boulouparis
Poya
Nouvelle-Calédonie
New Caledonia (France)
NOUVELLE-CALEDONIE
NEW CALEDONIA
ILE OUVEA
We LOYALTY ISLANDS
ILE LIFOU
ILES LOYAUTE
ILE MARE
Nouméa
Paté-Village
GRAND RECIF SUD
ILE DES PINS
ILE WALPOLE
ILE HUNTER
ILE MATTHEW

RECIFS BELLONA

Hunter Ridge

MINERVA REEFS
VITYAZ II DEPTH

Tonga Trench

New Caledonian Basin

South Fiji Basin

Lord Howe Rise

Norfolk Ridge

Norfolk Island (Australia)
Kingston

LORD HOWE ISLAND (Australia)
BALL'S PYRAMID

Three Kings Trough

Lau Ridge

Kermadec Ridge

RAOUL ISLAND
KERMADEC ISLANDS (New Zealand)
MACAULEY ISLAND
CURTIS ISLAND
L'ESPERANCE ROCK
VITYAZ III DEPTH

Kermadec Trench

TASMAN SEA

THREE KINGS ISLANDS
North Cape
Te Hapua Great Exhibition Bay
Awanui Opua
AUCKLAND PENINSULA
Whangarei
Dargaville Kaiwaka
GREAT BARRIER ISLAND
COROMANDEL PENINSULA
AUCKLAND
Manukau Thames
Paeroa Mount Maunganui
Hamilton Tauranga BAY OF PLENTY
Tokoroa Whakatane Te Araroa
Rotorua East Cape
Mokau Taupo Tokomaru Bay
NORTH ISLAND
New-Plymouth Gisborne
Cape Egmont Waitara
Hawera Wairoa MAHIA PENINSULA
Wanganui Napier
Feilding Hastings
Levin Palmerston North
Masterton
Karamea Nelson
Collingwood Porirua
Cape Farewell D'URVILLE ISLAND
Tasman Bay WELLINGTON
Glenhope Picton Cape Palliser
Westport Blenheim NEW ZEALAND
SOUTH ISLAND
Greymouth Kaikoura
Hokitika Waiau
Arthur's Pass
SOUTHERN ALPS
Fox Glacier Mount Arrowsmith
Haast Mount Cook
CHRISTCHURCH
Akaroa BANKS PENINSULA
Ashburton Canterbury Bight
Milford Sound Timaru
Mount Aspiring
Wanaka Omarama
Kurow Oamaru
West Cape Alexandra
Manapouri Mosgiel
Tuatapere Heriot Dunedin
Thornbury Balclutha
Invercargill
Bluff RUAPUKE ISLAND
Oban
STEWART ISLAND
Southwest Cape
SNARES ISLANDS
SOLANDER ISLAND

Pegasus Bay

Chatham Rise

CHATHAM ISLAND
CHATHAM ISLANDS (New Zealand)
Waitangi
PITT ISLAND

Bounty Trough

BOUNTY ISLANDS (New Zealand)

South Fiji Basin

Tasman Basin

Scale 1:15,000,000 at 25° latitude   Mercator Cylindrical Projection

M Ft
2000 6562
1000 3281
500 1640
+200 +656
0
−200 −656
1000 3281
2000 6562
4000 13123
6000 19685
8000 26247

0 200 400 600 800 1000 km
0 250 500 miles

Longitude East 180 West of Greenwich

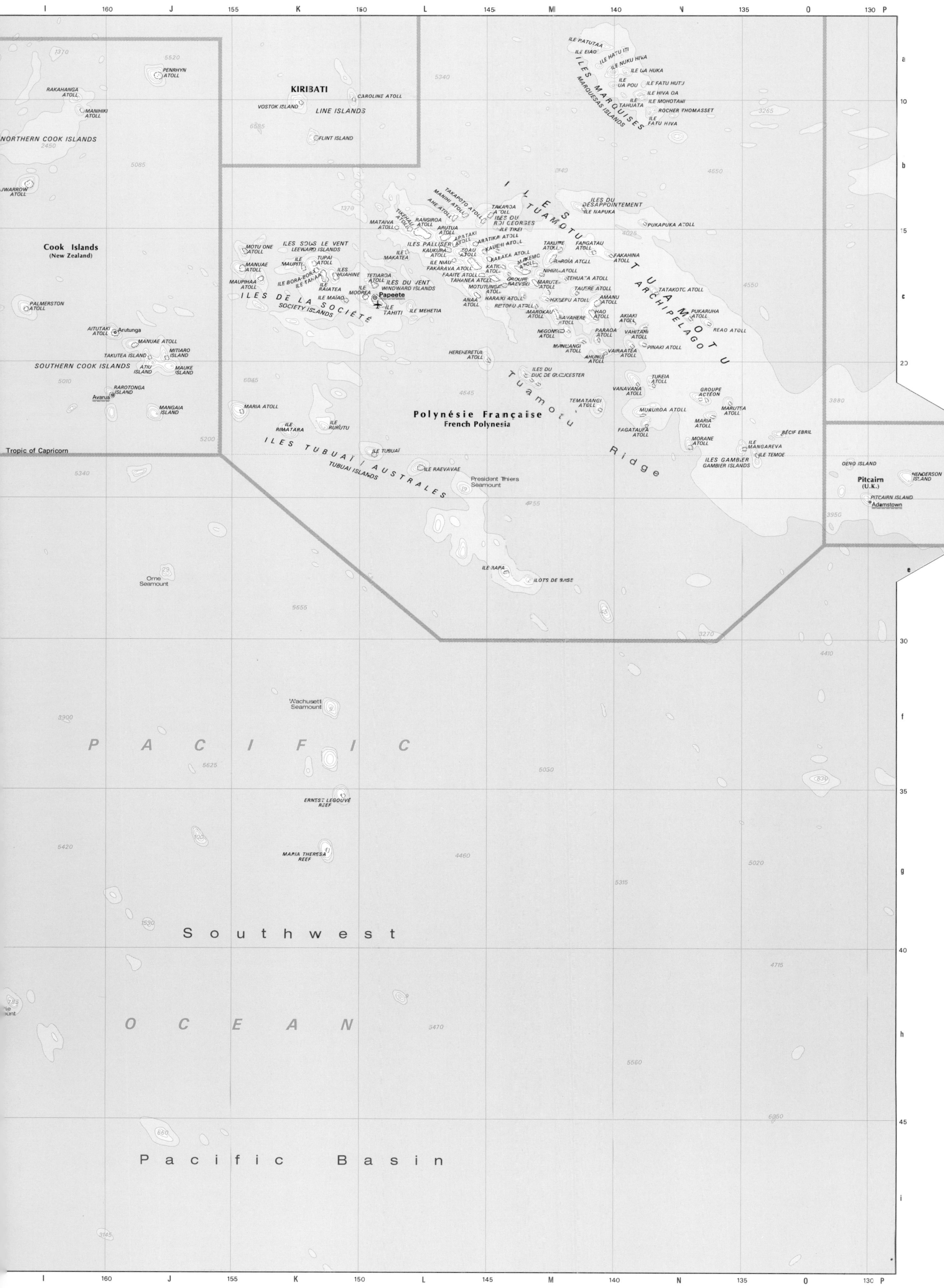

Map 62 **NEW ZEALAND**

NORTH ISLAND

NEW ZEALAND

Northland
Central
Auckland
South Auckland-
Bay of Plenty
Taranaki
Wanganui
Wellington
Palmerston North
Hawke's Bay
East Coast
Coromandel
Peninsula
New Plymouth

TASMAN SEA

Nelson
Marlborough
Westland
Canterbury
CHRISTCHURCH
Timaru

SOUTH ISLAND

PACIFIC

OCEAN

Chatham Rise

CHATHAM ISLANDS
(New Zealand)

Otago
Southland
Dunedin
Invercargill

STEWART ISLAND

Bounty Trough

BOUNTY ISLANDS
(New Zealand)

ANTIPODES ISLANDS
(New Zealand)

Campbell Plateau

AUCKLAND ISLANDS
(New Zealand)

CAMPBELL ISLAND
(New Zealand)

Longitude East 174 of Greenwich

Scale 1:6,000,000

Delisle Conic Equidistant Projection

The political subdivisions shown
for New Zealand represent statistical
areas and are not recognized for
administrative purposes.

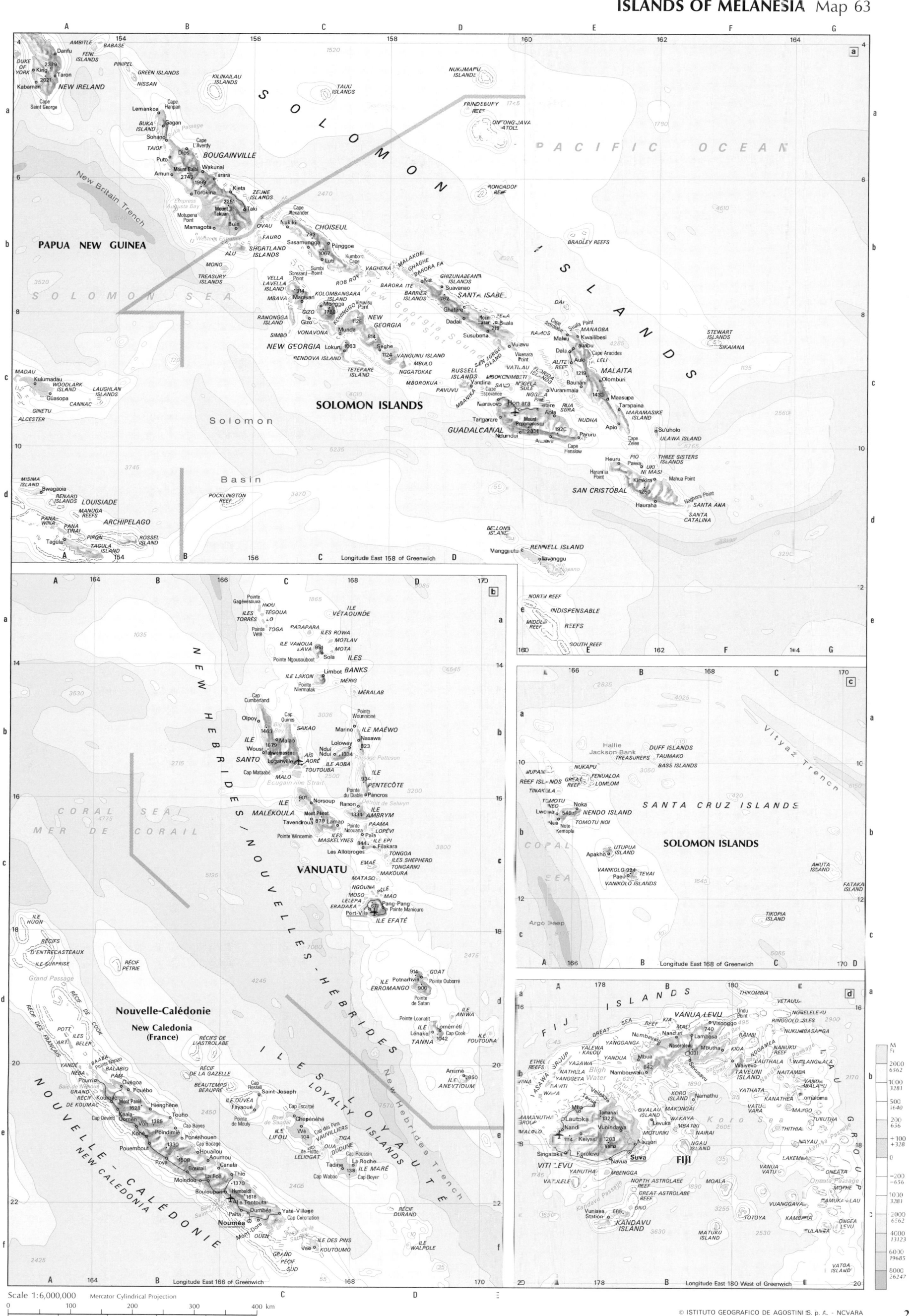

Scale 1:6,000,000   Mercator Cylindrical Projection

0   100   200   300   400 km

0   100   200 miles

Map 64 **ISLANDS OF MICRONESIA-POLYNESIA**

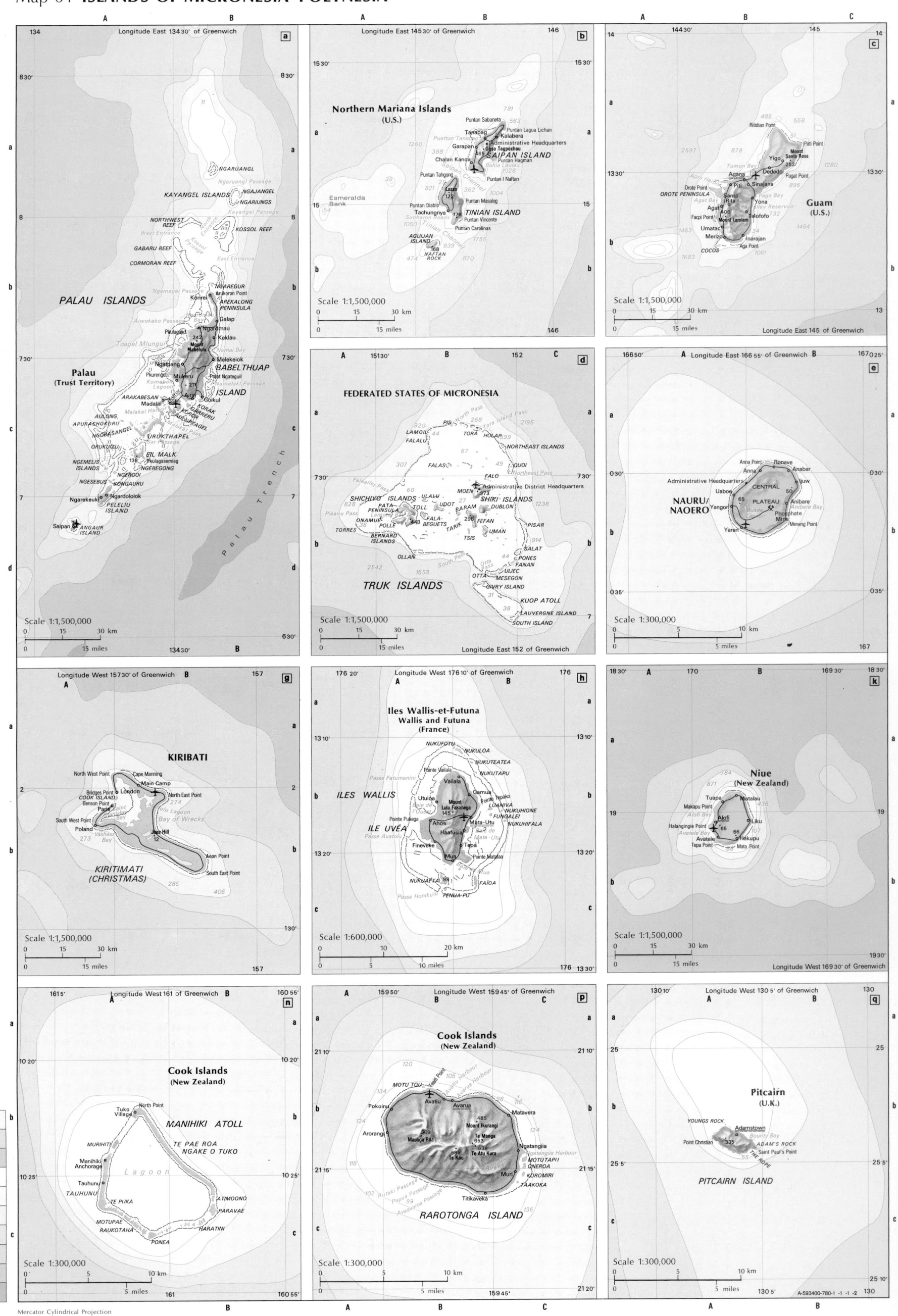

© ISTITUTO GEOGRAFICO DE AGOSTINI S. p. A. ~ NOVARA

Mercator Cylindrical Projection

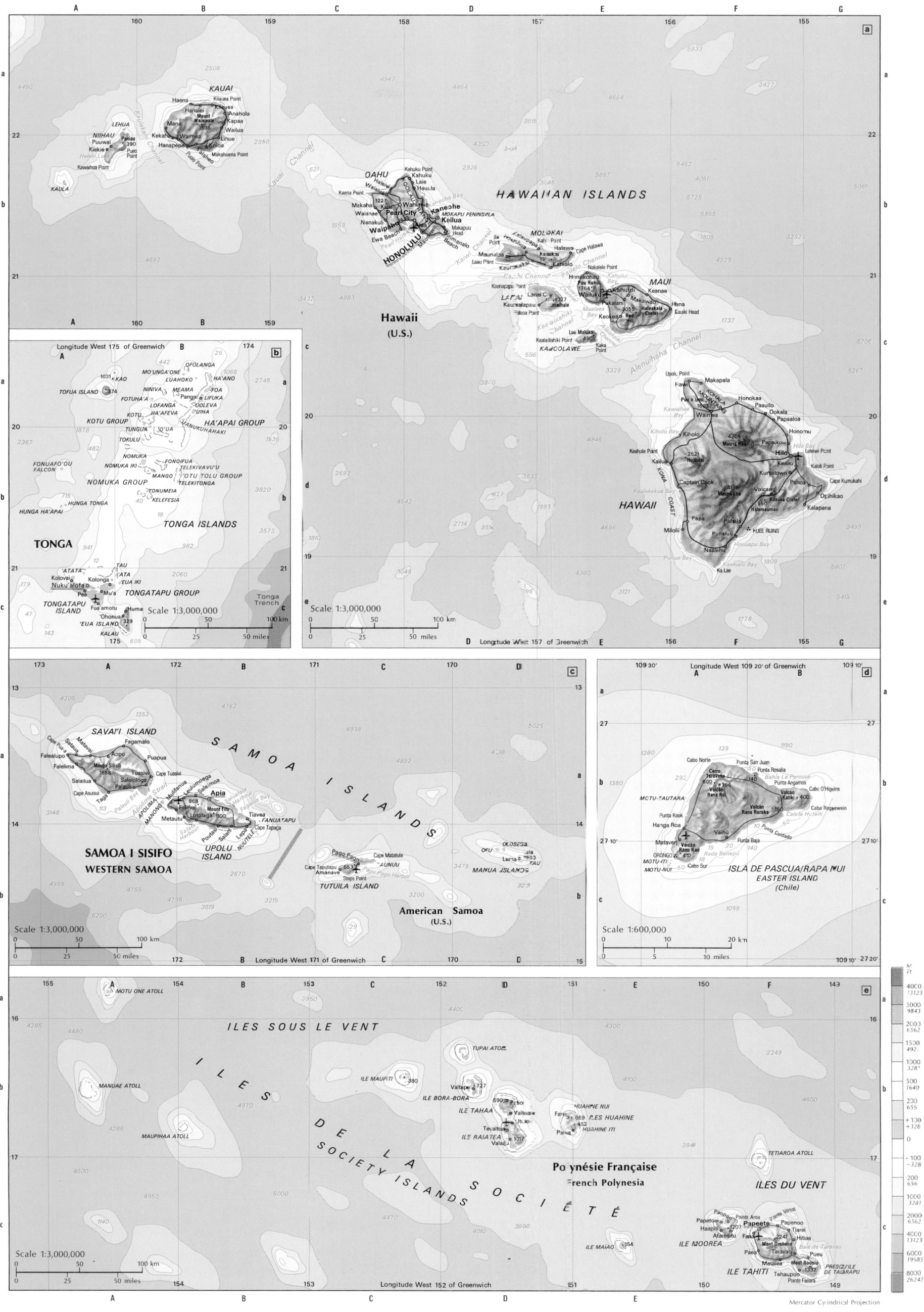

HAWAIIAN ISLANDS

KAUAI

Haena, Kilauea Point, Kilauea, Anahola, Kapaa, Wailua, Hanalei, Mount Waialeale 1606, Lihue, Koloa, Makahuena Point, Mana, Kekaha, Waimea, Hanapepe, Puolo Point, Puu Point, Puali Point

NIIHAU Puuwai, Puhui, Kiekie, 390, Pueo Point

LEHUA

KAULA

Kawaihoa Point, Halalii Lake

Kauai Channel

OAHU, Kahuku Point, Kahuku, Laie, Hauula, Haleiwa, Waialua, Wahiawa 1227, Makaha, Kailua, Kaneohe, Keilua, Waianae, Nanakuli, Waipahu, PEARL CITY, Pearl Harbor, Ewa Beach, HONOLULU, Makapuu Head, Waimanalo Beach, MOKAPU PENINSULA, Koko Head

Kaiwi Channel

MOLOKAI, Kalaupapa, Kahi Point, Halawa, Cape Halawa, Maunaloa, Kaunakakai, Kamalo, Nakalele Point, Laau Point

Pailolo Channel

LANAI, Lanai City, 1327, Lahaina, Kaunakakai, Shaloa Point

MAUI, Kahului, Wailuku, Keanae, Makawao, Haleakala Crater, Hana, Kauiki Head, Paia, 3055, Kihei, Maalaea, Keokea, Ulupalakua Hill, 1764

Kealaikahiki Channel, Maalaea Bay

Alalakeiki Channel

KAHOOLAWE, Kealaikahiki Point, Lua Makika 450, Kaka Point

Alenuihaha Channel

Hawaii (U.S.)

HAWAII

Upolu Point, Makapala, Hawi, Honokaa, Honokohau, Paauilo, Ookala, Paauhau, Kawaihae Bay, Kawaihae, Waimea, Honomu, Kailua, Kihola, 4205, Papaikou, Hilo, Hilo Bay, Keahole Point, Mauna Kea 13784, Keaau, 2521, Hualalai, Kaloli Point, Captain Cook, Kurtistown, Pahoa, Mauna Loa 13675, Volcano, Kilauea Crater, Ojikhalo, Kekaha, Kealakekua Bay, Cape Kumukahi, Kalapana, Papa, Pahala, Honuapo, Kalapana, Milolii, Punaluu, KUEE RUINS, Honuapo Bay, Naalehu, Ka Lae, Pohue Bay, Kaalualu Bay

Scale 1:3,000,000
0 — 50 — 100 km
0 — 25 — 50 miles

Longitude West 157 of Greenwich

TONGA

Longitude West 175 of Greenwich

OFOLANGA, MO'UNGA'ONE, HA'ANO, LUAHOKO, MEAMA, FOA, TOFUA ISLAND 374, KAO 1031, NINIVA, PANGAI, LIFUKA, UOLEVA, FOTUHA'A, LOFANGA, KOTU, HA'AFEVA, UIHA, KOTU GROUP, TUNGUA, O'UA, TOKULU, HA'APAI GROUP, NUKUNAMO, FONUAFO'OU FALCON, NOMUKA, FONOIFUA, TELEKIVAVU'U, NOMUKA IKI, MANGO, OTU TOLU GROUP, HUNGA HA'APAI, NOMUKA GROUP, TONUMEIA, KELEFESIA, TELEKITONGA, HUNGA TONGA

TONGA ISLANDS

'ATATA, TAU, ATA, Kolovai, Kolonga, 'EUA IKI, Nuku'alofa, Pea, Mu'a, TONGATAPU GROUP, TONGATAPU ISLAND, Fua'amotu, Huma, 'Ohonua, 'EUA ISLAND 329, KALAU 605

Tonga Trench

Scale 1:3,000,000
0 — 50 — 100 km
0 — 25 — 50 miles

SAMOA ISLANDS

SAVAI'I ISLAND, Matautu, Cape Puava, Safotu, Fagamalo, Aopo, Puapua, Falealupo, Faletima, Mauga Silisili 1858, Tuasivi, Cape Tuasivi, Salailua, Saleilogaa, Palauli, Cape Asuisu, Taga

Apolima Strait, *APOLIMA*, *MANONO*

UPOLU ISLAND, Aufaituai, Salelologa, **Apia**, 868, Mount Fito 1100, Lotofaga, Faleolo, Metautu, Poutasi, Saluafata, Tiavea, Lepa, Cape Tapaga, NUUTELE, FANUATAPU

SAMOA I SISIFO / WESTERN SAMOA

OFU, *OLOSEGA*, *MANUA ISLANDS*, Luma 633, TAU

TUTUILA ISLAND, Cape Taputapu, 653, Pago Pago, Cape Matatula, Amanave, Steps Point, Pago Pago Harbor, AUNUU

American Samoa (U.S.)

Scale 1:3,000,000
0 — 50 — 100 km
0 — 25 — 50 miles

Longitude West 171 of Greenwich

ISLA DE PASCUA/RAPA NUI EASTER ISLAND (Chile)

Longitude West 109 20' of Greenwich

Cabo Norte, Punta San Juan, Cerro Terevaka, Punta Rosalia, 396, Vulcan Rano Roi, Punta Angamos, MOTU-TAUTARA, Cabo O'Higgins, Volcan Katiki 400, Vulcan Rano Roraka, Cabo Roggewein, Hanga Roa, Mataveri, Vulcan Rana Kao, Vaihu, Punta Baja, Punta Cuidado, ORONGO, MOTU-ITI, MOTU-NUI, Cabo Sur, Rada Benepu, Caleta Hotuiti

Scale 1:600,000
0 — 10 — 20 km
0 — 5 — 10 miles

ÎLES SOUS LE VENT / ÎLES DE LA SOCIÉTÉ / SOCIETY ISLANDS

MOTU ONE ATOLL, *MANUAE ATOLL*, *MAUPIHAA ATOLL*, *TUPAI ATOLL*, *ÎLE MAUPITI* 380, Vaitape 727, *ÎLE BORA-BORA*, *ÎLE TAHAA*, Vaitoare, Uturoa, Faanui, 869, *ÎLES HUAHINE*, *HUAHINE NUI*, Fare, Tehaitoo, 482, *HUAHINE ITI*, *ÎLE RAIATEA* 1017, Valaea, Paino

Polynésie Française / French Polynesia

TETIAROA ATOLL, *ÎLES DU VENT*

ÎLE MAIAO 154, *ÎLE MOOREA*, Mont Orohena 2241, Paopao, Pointe Aroa, Papenoo, Papeari, Haapiti, Afareaitu, 1207, **Papeete**, Faaa, Tiarei, Hitiaa, Taravao, Mataiea, Mont Roonui 1332, Pueu, Tautira, Tehaupoo, Pointe Faiara, Baie de Taravao, PRESQU'ÎLE DE TAIARAPU, *ÎLE TAHITI*

Scale 1:3,000,000
0 — 50 — 100 km
0 — 25 — 50 miles

Longitude West 152 of Greenwich

Mercator Cylindrical Projection

© ISTITUTO GEOGRAFICO DE AGOSTINI S.p.A. - NOVARA

m/ft
4000 / 13123
3000 / 9843
2000 / 6562
1500 / 4921
1000 / 3281
500 / 1640
200 / 656
+100 / +328
0
−100 / −328
200 / 656
1000 / 3281
2000 / 6562
4000 / 13123
6000 / 19685
8000 / 26247

Map 66 **ANTARCTIC REGION**

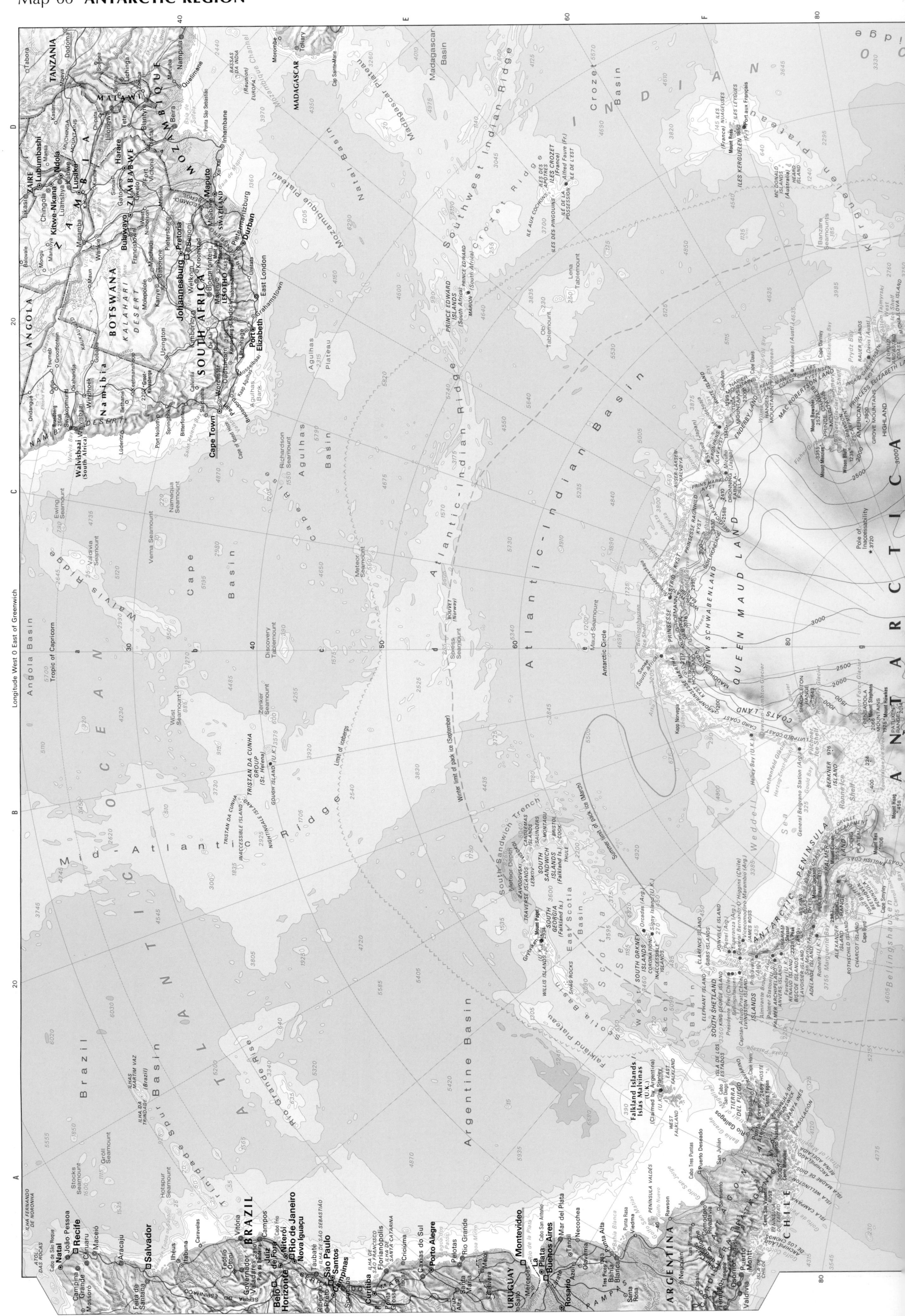

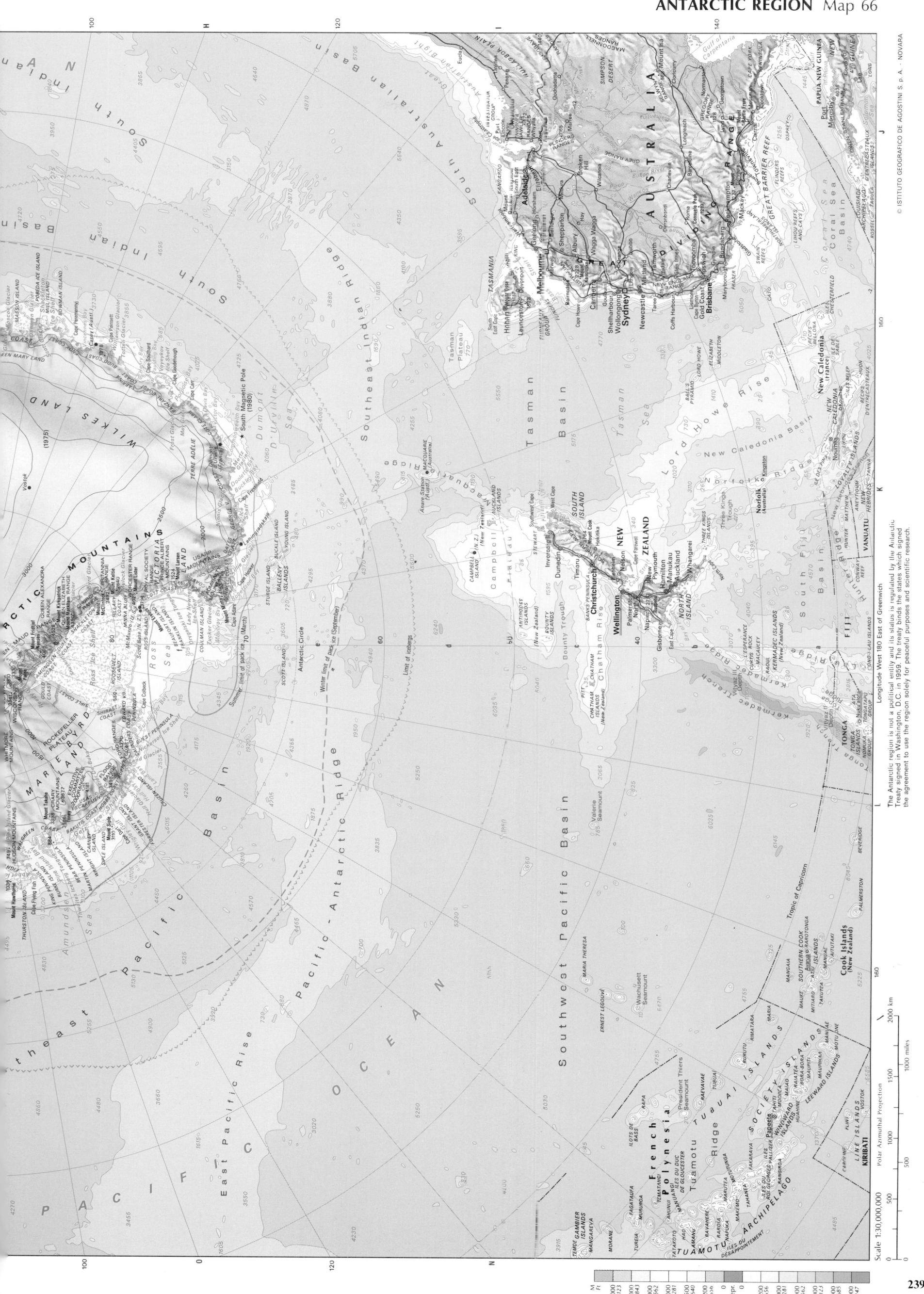

The Antarctic region is not a political entity and its status is regulated by the Antarctic Treaty signed in Washington, D.C. in 1959. The treaty binds the states which signed the agreement to use the region solely for peaceful purposes and scientific research.

Longitude West 180 East of Greenwich

Scale 1:30,000,000

Polar Azimuthal Projection

Map 67 **ARCTIC REGION**

Scale 1:30,000,000   Polar Azimuthal Projection

Longitude West 0 East of Greenwich

A-514000-780-1 -4 -1 -4

© ISTITUTO GEOGRAFICO DE AGOSTINI S. p. A. - NOVARA

GEOGRAPHICAL INFORMATION AND INTERNATIONAL MAP INDEX

World Nations

This table gives the area, population, population density, form of government, capital and location of every country in the world.

Area figures include inland water.

The populations are estimates made by Rand McNally on the basis of official data, United Nations estimates and other available information.

Besides specifying the form of government for all political areas, the table classifies them into five groups according to their political status. Units labeled *A* are independent sovereign nations. Units labeled *B* are independent as regards internal affairs, but for purposes of foreign affairs they are under the protection of another country. Units labeled *C* are colonies, overseas territories, dependencies, etc. of other countries. Units labeled *D* are states, provinces or other major administrative subdivisions of important countries. Units in the table with no letter designations are regions, islands or other areas that do not constitute separate political units by themselves.

Map Plate numbers refer to the International Map section of the atlas.

Country, Division, or Region: English (Conventional)	Local Name	Area km²	Area sq mi	Population 1/1/93	Population Density per km²	Population Density per sq mi	Form of Government and Political Status		Capital	Continent and Map Plate
Afars and Issas, see Djibouti	. . .	. . .	. . .	. . .	. . .	. . .			. . .	
† AFGHANISTAN	Afghānestān	652,225	*251,826*	16,290,000	25	*65*	Islamic republic	*A*	Kābol	Asia 23
Africa	. . .	30,300,000	*11,700,000*	668,700,000	22	*57*			. . .	Africa 30-31
Alabama	Alabama	135,775	*52,423*	4,128,000	30	*79*	State (U.S.)	*D*	Montgomery	N. Amer. 44
Alaska	Alaska	1,700,139	*656,424*	564,000	0.3	*0.9*	State (U.S.)	*D*	Juneau	N. Amer. 40
† ALBANIA	Shqipëria	28,748	*11,100*	3,305,000	115	*298*	Republic	*A*	Tirana	Europe 15
Alberta	Alberta	661,190	*255,287*	2,839,000	4.3	*11*	Province (Canada)	*D*	Edmonton	N. Amer. 42
† ALGERIA	Al Jazā'ir	2,381,741	*919,595*	26,925,000	11	*29*	Provisional military government	*A*	Al Jazā'ir (Algiers)	Africa 32
American Samoa	American Samoa (English) / Amerika Samoa (Samoan)	199	*77*	52,000	261	*675*	Unincorporated territory (U.S.)	*C*	Pago Pago	Oceania 65
Andaman and Nicobar Islands	Andaman and Nicobar Islands	8,293	*3,202*	302,000	36	*94*	Territory (India)	*D*	Port Blair	Asia 25
ANDORRA	Andorra	453	*175*	56,000	124	*320*	Coprincipality (Spanish and French protection)	*B*	Andorra la Vella	Europe 13
† ANGOLA	Angola	1,246,700	*481,354*	10,735,000	8.6	*22*	Republic	*A*	Luanda	Africa 36
ANGUILLA	Anguilla	91	*35*	7,000	77	*200*	Dependent territory (U.K. protection)	*B*	The Valley	N. Amer. 51
Anhui	Anhui	139,000	*53,668*	58,440,000	420	*1,089*	Province (China)	*D*	Hefei	Asia 28
Antarctica	. . .	14,000,000	*5,400,000*	[1]	. . .	. . .			. . .	Antarctica 66
† ANTIGUA AND BARBUDA	Antigua and Barbuda	442	*171*	77,000	174	*450*	Parliamentary state	*A*	St. John's	N. Amer. 51
Arabian Peninsula	. . .	3,010,000	*1,160,000*	35,848,000	12	*31*			. . .	Asia 23
† ARGENTINA	Argentina	2,780,400	*1,073,519*	32,950,000	12	*31*	Republic	*A*	Buenos Aires and Viedma [2]	S. Amer. 56
Arizona	Arizona	295,276	*114,006*	3,872,000	13	*34*	State (U.S.)	*D*	Phoenix	N. Amer. 46
Arkansas	Arkansas	137,742	*53,182*	2,410,000	17	*45*	State (U.S.)	*D*	Little Rock	N. Amer. 45
† ARMENIA	Hayastan	29,800	*11,506*	3,429,000	115	*298*	Republic	*A*	Jerevan	Asia 16
ARUBA	Aruba	193	*75*	65,000	337	*867*	Self-governing territory (Netherlands protection)	*B*	Oranjestad	N. Amer. 49
Ascension	Ascension	88	*34*	1,200	14	*35*	Dependency (St. Helena)	*C*	Georgetown	Africa 30-31
Asia	. . .	44,900,000	*17,300,000*	3,337,800,000	74	*193*			. . .	Asia 21-22
† AUSTRALIA	Australia	7,682,300	*2,966,155*	16,965,000	2.2	*5.7*	Federal parliamentary state	*A*	Canberra	Oceania 59
Australian Capital Territory	Australian Capital Territory	2,400	*927*	282,000	118	*304*	Territory (Australia)	*D*	Canberra	Oceania 59
† AUSTRIA	Österreich	83,856	*32,377*	7,899,000	94	*244*	Federal republic	*A*	Wien (Vienna)	Europe 14
† AZERBAIJAN	Azărbayjan	86,600	*33,436*	7,510,000	87	*225*	Republic	*A*	Baku	Asia 16
Azores	Açores	2,247	*868*	252,000	116	*301*	Autonomous region	*D*	Ponta Delgada	Europe 32
Baden-Wurttemberg	Baden-Württemberg	35,751	*13,804*	9,798,000	274	*710*	State (Germany)	*D*	Stuttgart	Europe 10
† BAHAMAS	Bahamas	13,939	*5,382*	265,000	19	*49*	Parliamentary state	*A*	Nassau	N. Amer. 47
† BAHRAIN	Al Baḩrayn	691	*267*	561,000	812	*2,101*	Monarchy	*A*	Al Manāmah (Manama)	Asia 24
Balearic Islands	Islas Baleares	5,014	*1,936*	743,000	148	*384*	Province (Spain)	*D*	Palma	Europe 13
Baltic Republics	. . .	174,000	*67,182*	8,154,000	47	*121*			. . .	Europe 8
† BANGLADESH	Bangladesh	143,998	*55,598*	120,850,000	839	*2,174*	Republic	*A*	Dhaka	Asia 25
† BARBADOS	Barbados	430	*166*	258,000	600	*1,554*	Parliamentary state	*A*	Bridgetown	N. Amer. 51
Bavaria	Bayern	70,554	*27,241*	11,430,000	162	*420*	State (Germany)	*D*	München (Munich)	Europe 10
† BELARUS	Byelarus'	207,600	*80,155*	10,400,000	50	*130*	Republic	*A*	Minsk	Europe 16
† BELGIUM	Belgique (French) / België (Flemish)	30,518	*11,783*	10,030,000	329	*851*	Constitutional monarchy	*A*	Bruxelles (Brussels)	Europe 12
† BELIZE	Belize	22,963	*8,866*	186,000	8.1	*21*	Parliamentary state	*A*	Belmopan	N. Amer. 49
Benelux	. . .	74,968	*28,945*	25,612,000	342	*885*	Economic union		. . .	Europe 12
† BENIN	Bénin	112,600	*43,475*	5,083,000	45	*117*	Republic	*A*	Porto-Novo and Cotonou	Africa 34
Berlin	Berlin	883	*341*	3,475,000	3,935	*10,191*	State	*D*	Berlin	Europe 10
Bermuda	Bermuda	54	*21*	60,000	1,111	*2,857*	Dependent territory (U.K.)	*C*	Hamilton	N. Amer. 47
† BHUTAN	Druk	46,500	*17,954*	1,680,000	36	*94*	Monarchy (Indian protection)	*B*	Thimphu	Asia 25
Bioko	Bioko	2,017	*779*	75,000	37	*96*	Province of Equatorial Guinea	*D*	Malabo	Africa 34
† BOLIVIA	Bolivia	1,098,581	*424,165*	7,411,000	6.7	*17*	Republic	*A*	La Paz and Sucre	S. Amer. 54
BOPHUTHATSWANA [3]	Bophuthatswana	40,509	*15,641*	2,525,000	62	*161*	National state (South African protection)	*B*	Mmabatho	Africa 37
Borneo, Indonesian	Kalimantan	539,460	*208,287*	9,458,000	18	*45*	Part of Indonesia (4 provinces)		. . .	Asia 26
† BOSNIA AND HERZEGOVINA	Bosna i Hercegovina	51,129	*19,741*	4,375,000	86	*222*	Republic	*A*	Sarajevo	Europe 14
† BOTSWANA	Botswana	582,000	*224,711*	1,379,000	2.4	*6.1*	Republic	*A*	Gaborone	Africa 37
Brandenburg	Brandenburg	29,060	*11,220*	2,690,000	93	*240*	State (Germany)	*D*	Potsdam	Europe 10
† BRAZIL	Brasil	8,511,996	*3,286,500*	159,630,000	19	*49*	Federal republic	*A*	Brasília	S. Amer. 54-56
Bremen	Bremen	404	*156*	687,000	1,700	*4,404*	State (Germany)	*D*	Bremen	Europe 10
British Columbia	British Columbia (English) / Colombie-Britannique (French)	947,800	*365,948*	3,665,000	3.9	*10*	Province (Canada)	*D*	Victoria	N. Amer. 42
British Indian Ocean Territory	British Indian Ocean Territory	60	*23*	[1]	. . .	. . .	Dependent territory (U.K.)	*C*	. . .	Africa 22
† BRUNEI	Brunei	5,765	*2,226*	273,000	47	*123*	Monarchy	*A*	Bandar Seri Begawan	Asia 26
† BULGARIA	Bălgarija	110,912	*42,823*	8,842,000	80	*206*	Republic	*A*	Sofija (Sofia)	Europe 15
† BURKINA FASO	Burkina Faso	274,200	*105,869*	9,808,000	36	*93*	Provisional military government	*A*	Ouagadougou	Africa 34
† BURMA	Myanmar	676,577	*261,228*	43,070,000	64	*165*	Provisional military government	*A*	Yangon (Rangoon)	Asia 25
† BURUNDI	Burundi	27,830	*10,745*	6,118,000	220	*569*	Republic	*A*	Bujumbura	Africa 36
California	California	424,002	*163,707*	31,310,000	74	*191*	State (U.S.)	*D*	Sacramento	N. Amer. 46
† CAMBODIA	Kâmpŭchéa	181,035	*69,898*	8,928,000	49	*128*	Transitional government	*A*	Phnum Pénh (Phnom Penh)	Asia 26
† CAMEROON	Cameroon (English) / Cameroun (French)	475,442	*183,569*	12,875,000	27	*70*	Republic	*A*	Yaoundé	Africa 34
† CANADA	Canada	9,970,610	*3,849,674*	30,530,000	3.1	*7.9*	Federal parliamentary state	*A*	Ottawa	N. Amer. 42
Canary Islands	Islas Canarias	7,273	*2,808*	1,613,000	222	*574*	Part of Spain (2 provinces)		. . .	Africa 32
† CAPE VERDE	Cabo Verde	4,033	*1,557*	404,000	100	*259*	Republic	*A*	Praia	Africa 32
Cayman Islands	Cayman Islands	259	*100*	29,000	112	*290*	Dependent territory (U.K.)	*C*	Georgetown	N. Amer. 49
Celebes	Sulawesi	189,216	*73,057*	12,995,000	69	*178*	Part of Indonesia (4 provinces)		. . .	Asia 26
† CENTRAL AFRICAN REPUBLIC	Centrafrique	622,984	*240,535*	3,068,000	4.9	*13*	Republic	*A*	Bangui	Africa 35
Central America	. . .	520,000	*200,000*	30,402,000	58	*152*			. . .	N. Amer. 49

Country, Division, or Region English (Conventional)	Local Name	Area km²	Area sq mi	Population 1/1/93	Population Density per km²	Population Density per sq mi	Form of Government and Political Status	Capital	Continent and Map Plate
Ceylon, see Sri Lanka	...	...	...	...	...	...			....
† CHAD	Tchad	1,284,000	495,755	5,297,000	4.1	11	Republic	A N'Djamena	Africa 35
CHANNEL ISLANDS	...	194	75	143,000	737	1,907	Dependent territory (U.K.)	B ...	Europe 9
† CHILE	Chile	756,626	292,135	13,635,000	18	47	Republic	A Santiago	S. Amer. 56
† CHINA (excl. Taiwan)	Zhongguo Renmin Gongheguo	9,556,100	3,689,631	1,179,030,000	123	320	Socialist republic	A Beijing (Peking)	Asia 27
China (Nationalist), see Taiwan	...	...	...	...	...	...			
Christmas Island	Christmas Island	135	52	900	6.7	17	External territory (Australia)	C Flying Fish Cove	Oceania 26
CISKEI (3)	Ciskei	7,760	2,996	1,105,000	142	369	National state (South African protection)	B Bisho	Africa 37
Cocos (Keeling) Islands	Cocos (Keeling) Islands	14	5.4	500	36	93	Territory (Australia)	C ...	Oceania 22
† COLOMBIA	Colombia	1,141,748	440,831	34,640,000	30	79	Republic	A Santa Fe de Bogotá	S. Amer. 54
Colorado	Colorado	269,620	104,100	3,410,000	13	33	State (U.S.)	D Denver	N. Amer. 45
Commonwealth of Independent States	...	22,031,200	8,506,294	281,640,000	13	33	Alliance of sovereign states	... Minsk	Eur.-Asia ....
Commonwealth of Nations	...	29,230,000	11,320,000	1,498,930,000	51	132	....	London	....
† COMOROS (excl. Mayotte)	Al-Qumur (Arabic) / Comores (French)	2,235	863	503,000	225	583	Federal Islamic republic	A Moroni	Africa 37
† CONGO	Congo	342,000	132,047	2,413,000	7.1	18	Republic	A Brazzaville	Africa 36
Connecticut	Connecticut	14,358	5,544	3,358,000	234	606	State (U.S.)	D Hartford	N. Amer. 44
COOK ISLANDS	Cook Islands	236	91	18,000	76	198	Self-governing territory (New Zealand protection)	B Avarua	Oceania 61
Coral Sea Islands Territory	Coral Sea Islands Territory	2.6	1.0	(1)	...	...	External territory (Australia)	C ...	Oceania 59
Corsica	Corse	8,720	3,367	255,000	29	76	Part of France	D ...	Europe 11
† COSTA RICA	Costa Rica	51,100	19,730	3,225,000	63	163	Republic	A San José	N. Amer. 49
Côte d'Ivoire, see Ivory Coast	...	...	...	...	...	...			....
† CROATIA	Hrvatska	56,538	21,829	4,793,000	85	220	Republic	A Zagreb	Europe 14
† CUBA	Cuba	110,861	42,804	10,900,000	98	255	Socialist republic	A La Habana (Havana)	N. Amer. 49
Curacao	Curaçao	444	171	146,000	329	854	Division of Netherlands Antilles (Neth.)	D Willemstad	N. Amer. 49
† CYPRUS	Kípros (Greek) / Kıbrıs (Turkish)	5,896	2,276	527,000	89	232	Republic	A Nicosia (Levkosía)	Asia 24
CYPRUS, NORTH	Kuzey Kıbrıs	3,355	1,295	193,000	58	149	Republic	A Nicosia (Lefkoşa)	Asia 24
† CZECH REPUBLIC	Česká Republika	78,864	30,450	10,335,000	131	339	Republic	A Praha (Prague)	Europe 10
Delaware	Delaware	6,447	2,489	692,000	107	278	State (U.S.)	D Dover	N. Amer. 44
† DENMARK	Danmark	43,093	16,638	5,169,000	120	311	Constitutional monarchy	A København (Copenhagen)	Europe 8
Denmark and Possessions	...	2,220,092	857,182	5,275,000	2.4	6.2	....		....
District of Columbia	District of Columbia	177	68	590,000	3,333	8,676	Federal district (U.S.)	D Washington	N. Amer. 44
† DJIBOUTI	Djibouti	23,200	8,958	396,000	17	44	Republic	A Djibouti	Africa 35
† DOMINICA	Dominica	790	305	88,000	111	289	Republic	A Roseau	N. Amer. 51
† DOMINICAN REPUBLIC	República Dominicana	48,442	18,704	7,591,000	157	406	Republic	A Santo Domingo	N. Amer. 49
† ECUADOR	Ecuador	283,561	109,484	11,055,000	39	101	Republic	A Quito	S. Amer. 54
† EGYPT	Mişr	1,001,449	386,662	57,050,000	57	148	Socialist republic	A Al Qāhirah (Cairo)	Africa 33
Ellis Islands, see Tuvalu	...	...	...	...	...	...			
† EL SALVADOR	El Salvador	21,041	8,124	5,635,000	268	694	Republic	A San Salvador	N. Amer. 49
England	England	130,478	50,378	48,235,000	370	957	Administrative division (U.K.)	D London	Europe 9
† EQUATORIAL GUINEA	Guinea Ecuatorial	28,051	10,831	394,000	14	36	Republic	A Malabo	Africa 36
ERITREA	Eritrea	93,679	36,170	3,425,000	37	95	Republic	A Asmera	Africa 35
† ESTONIA	Eesti	45,100	17,413	1,613,000	36	93	Republic	A Tallinn	Europe 8
† ETHIOPIA	Itiopya	1,157,603	446,953	51,715,000	45	116	Transitional military government	A Ādīs Ābeba (Addis Ababa)	Africa 35
Eurasia	...	54,800,000	21,100,000	4,032,700,000	74	191	....		....
Europe	...	9,900,000	3,800,000	694,900,000	70	183			Europe 5-6
European Community	...	4,070,000	1,570,000	346,800,000	85	221	....	Brussels (Bruxelles)	Europe 5-6
FAEROE ISLANDS	Føroyar	1,399	540	49,000	35	91	Self-governing territory (Danish protection)	B Thorshavn	Europe 6
Falkland Islands (4)	Falkland Islands (English) / Islas Malvinas (Spanish)	12,173	4,700	2,100	0.2	0.4	Dependent territory (U.K.)	C Stanley	S. Amer. 56
† FIJI	Fiji (French) / Viti (Fijian)	18,274	7,056	754,000	41	107	Republic	A Suva	Oceania 63
† FINLAND	Suomi (Finnish) / Finland (Swedish)	338,145	130,559	5,074,000	15	39	Republic	A Helsinki (Helsingfors)	Europe 7
Florida	Florida	170,313	65,758	13,630,000	80	207	State (U.S.)	D Tallahassee	N. Amer. 44
† FRANCE (excl. Overseas Departments)	France	547,026	211,208	57,570,000	105	273	Republic	A Paris	Europe 11
France and Possessions	...	666,866	257,476	59,617,000	89	232	....	Paris	....
French Guiana	Guyane Française	91,000	35,135	131,000	1.4	3.7	Overseas department (France)	C Cayenne	S. Amer. 54
French Polynesia	Polynésie Française	3,521	1,359	208,000	59	153	Overseas territory (France)	C Papeete	Oceania 61
French West Indies	...	2,880	1,112	785,000	273	706	....		N. Amer. 50
Fujian	Fujian	120,000	46,332	31,160,000	260	673	Province (China)	D Fuzhou	Asia 27
† GABON	Gabon	267,667	103,347	1,115,000	4.2	11	Republic	A Libreville	Africa 36
Galapagos Islands	Archipiélago de Colón (Islas Galápagos)	7,964	3,075	8,500	1.1	2.8	Province (Ecuador)	D Baquerizo Moreno	S. Amer. 54
† GAMBIA	Gambia	10,689	4,127	916,000	86	222	Republic	A Banjul	Africa 34
Gansu	Gansu	450,000	173,746	23,280,000	52	134	Province (China)	D Lanzhou	Asia 27
Georgia	Georgia	153,953	59,441	6,795,000	44	114	State (U.S.)	D Atlanta	N. Amer. 44
GEORGIA	Sakartvelo	69,700	26,911	5,593,000	80	208	Provisional military government	A Tbilisi	Asia 16
† GERMANY	Deutschland	356,955	137,822	80,590,000	226	585	Federal republic	A Berlin and Bonn	Europe 10
† GHANA	Ghana	238,533	92,098	16,445,000	69	179	Provisional military government	A Accra	Africa 34
Gibraltar	Gibraltar	6.0	2.3	32,000	5,333	13,913	Dependent territory (U.K.)	C Gibraltar	Europe 13
Gilbert Islands, see Tuvalu	...	...	...	...	...	...			....
Great Britain, see United Kingdom	...	...	...	...	...	...			....
† GREECE	Ellas	131,957	50,949	10,075,000	76	198	Republic	A Athínai (Athens)	Europe 15
GREENLAND	Kalaallit Nunaat (Inuit) / Grønland (Danish)	2,175,600	840,004	57,000	...	0.1	Self-governing territory (Danish protection)	B Godthåb (Nûk)	N. Amer. 41
† GRENADA	Grenada	344	133	97,000	282	729	Parliamentary state	A St. George's	N. Amer. 51
Guadeloupe (incl. Dependencies)	Guadeloupe	1,780	687	413,000	232	601	Overseas department (France)	C Basse-Terre	N. Amer. 51
Guam	Guam	541	209	143,000	264	684	Unincorporated territory (U.S.)	C Agana	Oceania 64
Guangdong	Guangdong	178,000	68,726	65,380,000	367	951	Province (China)	D Guangzhou (Canton)	Asia 27
† GUATEMALA	Guatemala	108,889	42,042	9,705,000	89	231	Republic	A Guatemala	N. Amer. 49
GUERNSEY (incl. Dependencies)	Guernsey	78	30	58,000	744	1,933	Crown dependency (U.K. protection)	B St. Peter Port	Europe 9
† GUINEA	Guinée	245,857	94,926	7,726,000	31	81	Provisional military government	A Conakry	Africa 34
† GUINEA-BISSAU	Guiné-Bissau	36,125	13,948	1,060,000	29	76	Republic	A Bissau	Africa 34
Guizhou	Guizhou	170,000	65,637	33,745,000	199	514	Province (China)	D Guiyang	Asia 27
† GUYANA	Guyana	214,969	83,000	737,000	3.4	8.9	Republic	A Georgetown	S. Amer. 54
Hainan	Hainan	34,000	13,127	6,820,000	201	520	Province (China)	D Haikou	Asia 27
† HAITI	Haïti	27,750	10,714	6,509,000	235	608	Provisional military government	A Port-au-Prince	N. Amer. 49
Hamburg	Hamburg	755	292	1,657,000	2,195	5,675	State (Germany)	D Hamburg	Europe 10
Hawaii	Hawaii	28,313	10,932	1,159,000	41	106	State (U.S.)	D Honolulu	N. Amer. 60
Hebei	Hebei	190,000	73,359	63,500,000	334	866	Province (China)	D Shijiazhuang	Asia 28

Country, Division, or Region English (Conventional)	Local Name	Area km²	sq mi	Population 1/1/93	Population Density per km²	sq mi	Form of Government and Political Status		Capital	Continent and Map Plate	
Heilongjiang	Heilongjiang	469,000	181,082	36,685,000	78	203	Province (China)	D	Harbin	Asia	27
Henan	Henan	167,000	64,479	88,890,000	532	1,379	Province (China)	D	Zhengzhou	Asia	27
Hessia	Hessen	21,114	8,152	5,766,000	273	707	State (Germany)	D	Wiesbaden	Europe	10
Hispaniola	La Española	76,192	29,418	14,100,000	185	479			. . . .	N. Amer.	49
Holland, see Netherlands		. . .	. . .	. . .	. . .	. . .			. . . .	. . . .	
† HONDURAS	Honduras	112,088	43,277	5,164,000	46	119	Republic	A	Tegucigalpa	N. Amer.	49
Hong Kong	Hong Kong (English) / Xianggang (Chinese)	1,072	414	5,580,000	5,205	13,478	Chinese territory under British administration	C	Victoria (Hong Kong)	Asia	27
Hubei	Hubei	187,400	72,356	56,090,000	299	775	Province (China)	D	Wuhan	Asia	27
Hunan	Hunan	210,000	81,081	63,140,000	301	779	Province (China)	D	Changsha	Asia	27
† HUNGARY	Magyarország	93,033	35,920	10,305,000	111	287	Republic	A	Budapest	Europe	10
† ICELAND	Ísland	103,000	39,769	260,000	2.5	6.5	Republic	A	Reykjavík	Europe	7
Idaho	Idaho	216,456	83,574	1,026,000	4.7	12	State (U.S.)	D	Boise	N. Amer.	46
Illinois	Illinois	150,007	57,918	11,640,000	78	201	State (U.S.)	D	Springfield	N. Amer.	45
† INDIA (incl. part of Jammu and Kashmir)	India (English) / Bhārat (Hindi)	3,203,975	1,237,062	873,850,000	273	706	Federal republic	A	New Delhi	Asia	25
Indiana	Indiana	94,328	36,420	5,667,000	60	156	State (U.S.)	D	Indianapolis	N. Amer.	44
† INDONESIA	Indonesia	1,948,732	752,410	186,180,000	96	247	Republic	A	Jakarta	Asia	26
Inner Mongolia	Nei Mongol Gaoyuan	1,183,000	456,759	22,340,000	19	49	Autonomous region (China)	D	Hohhot	Asia	27
Iowa	Iowa	145,754	56,276	2,821,000	19	50	State (U.S.)	D	Des Moines	N. Amer.	45
† IRAN	Īrān	1,638,057	632,457	60,500,000	37	96	Islamic republic	A	Tehrān	Asia	23
† IRAQ	Al 'Irāq	438,317	169,235	18,815,000	43	111	Republic	A	Baghdād	Asia	24
† IRELAND	Ireland (English) / Éire (Gaelic)	70,285	27,137	3,525,000	50	130	Republic	A	Dublin (Baile Átha Cliath)	Europe	9
ISLE OF MAN	Isle of Man	572	221	70,000	122	317	Crown dependency (U.K. protection)	B	Douglas	Europe	9
† ISRAEL (excl. Occupied Areas)	Yisra'el (Hebrew) / Isrā'īl (Arabic)	20,770	8,019	4,593,000	221	573	Republic	A	Yerushalayim (Jerusalem)	Asia	24
Israeli Occupied Areas [5]	. . .	7,632	2,947	2,461,000	322	835	None		. . . .	Asia	24
† ITALY	Italia	301,277	116,324	56,550,000	188	486	Republic	A	Roma (Rome)	Europe	14
† IVORY COAST	Côte d'Ivoire	322,500	124,518	13,765,000	43	111	Republic	A	Abidjan and Yamoussoukro [2]	Africa	34
† JAMAICA	Jamaica	10,991	4,244	2,412,000	219	568	Parliamentary state	A	Kingston	N. Amer.	49
† JAPAN	Nippon	377,801	145,870	124,710,000	330	855	Constitutional monarchy	A	Tōkyō	Asia	29
Java	Jawa	132,187	51,038	107,580,000	814	2,108	Part of Indonesia (5 provinces)		. . . .	Asia	26
JERSEY	Jersey	116	45	85,000	733	1,889	Crown dependency (U.K. protection)	B	St. Helier	Europe	9
Jiangsu	Jiangsu	102,600	39,614	69,730,000	680	1,760	Province (China)	D	Nanjing (Nanking)	Asia	28
Jiangxi	Jiangxi	166,600	64,325	39,270,000	236	610	Province (China)	D	Nanchang	Asia	27
Jilin	Jilin	187,000	72,201	25,630,000	137	355	Province (China)	D	Changchun	Asia	27
Johnston Atoll	Johnston Atoll	1.3	0.5	1,400	1,077	2,800	Unincorporated territory (U.S.)	C	. . . .	Oceania	60
† JORDAN (excl. West Bank)	Al Urdun	91,000	35,135	3,632,000	40	103	Constitutional monarchy	A	'Ammān	Asia	24
Kansas	Kansas	213,110	82,282	2,539,000	12	31	State (U.S.)	D	Topeka	N. Amer.	45
Kashmir, Jammu and	Jammu and Kashmir	222,236	85,806	11,565,000	52	135	Disputed territory (India and Pakistan)	D	. . . .	Asia	25
† KAZAKHSTAN	Qazaqstan	2,717,300	1,049,156	17,190,000	6.3	16	Republic	A	Alma-Ata	Asia	19
Kentucky	Kentucky	104,665	40,411	3,745,000	36	93	State (U.S.)	D	Frankfort	N. Amer.	44
† KENYA	Kenya	582,646	224,961	26,635,000	46	118	Republic	A	Nairobi	Africa	36
Kerguelen Islands	Iles Kerguélen	6,993	2,700	200	. . .	0.1	Territory (France)	C	. . . .	S. Amer.	30-31
KIRIBATI	Kiribati	811	313	76,000	94	243	Republic	A	Bairiki	Oceania	60
† KOREA, NORTH	Chosŏn Minjujuŭi Inmīn Konghwaguk	120,538	46,540	22,450,000	186	482	Socialist republic	A	P'yŏngyang	Asia	28
† KOREA, SOUTH	Taehan-min'guk	99,016	38,230	43,660,000	441	1,142	Republic	A	Sŏul (Seoul)	Asia	28
Korea (entire)	. . .	219,554	84,770	66,110,000	301	780			. . . .	Asia	28
† KUWAIT	Al Kuwayt	17,818	6,880	2,388,000	134	347	Constitutional monarchy	A	Al Kuwayt (Kuwait)	Asia	24
Kwangsi	Guangxi Zhuangzu Zizhiqu	236,300	91,236	43,975,000	186	482	Autonomous region (China)	D	Nanning	Asia	27
† KYRGYZSTAN	Kyrgyzstan	198,500	76,641	4,613,000	23	60	Republic	A	Bishkek	Asia	18
Labrador	Labrador	292,218	112,826	36,000	0.1	0.3	Part of Newfoundland province (Canada)		. . . .	N. Amer.	42
† LAOS	Lao	236,800	91,429	4,507,000	19	49	Socialist republic	A	Viangchan (Vientiane)	Asia	26
Latin America	. . .	20,500,000	7,900,000	461,900,000	23	58			. . . .	N.A.,S.A.	52-53
† LATVIA	Latvija	63,700	24,595	2,737,000	43	111	Republic	A	Rīga	Europe	8
† LEBANON	Lubnān	10,400	4,015	3,467,000	333	864	Republic	A	Bayrūt (Beirut)	Asia	24
† LESOTHO	Lesotho	30,355	11,720	1,873,000	62	160	Constitutional monarchy under military rule	A	Maseru	Africa	37
Liaoning	Liaoning	145,700	56,255	41,035,000	282	729	Province (China)	D	Shenyang (Mukden)	Asia	28
† LIBERIA	Liberia	99,067	38,250	2,869,000	29	75	Republic	A	Monrovia	Africa	34
† LIBYA	Lībiyā	1,759,540	679,362	4,552,000	2.6	6.7	Socialist republic	A	Ṭarābulus (Tripoli)	Africa	33
† LIECHTENSTEIN	Liechtenstein	160	62	30,000	188	484	Constitutional monarchy	A	Vaduz	Europe	14
† LITHUANIA	Lietuva	65,200	25,174	3,804,000	58	151	Republic	A	Vilnius	Europe	8
Louisiana	Louisiana	134,275	51,843	4,282,000	32	83	State (U.S.)	D	Baton Rouge	N. Amer.	45
Lower Saxony	Niedersachsen	47,349	18,282	7,420,000	157	406	State (Germany)	D	Hannover	Europe	10
† LUXEMBOURG	Luxembourg (French) / Lezebuurg (Luxembourgish)	2,586	998	392,000	152	393	Constitutional monarchy	A	Luxembourg	Europe	12
Macao	Macau	17	6.6	477,000	28,059	72,273	Chinese territory under Portuguese administration	C	Macau	Asia	27
MACEDONIA	Makedonija	25,713	9,928	2,179,000	85	219	Republic	A	Skopje	Europe	15
† MADAGASCAR	Madagasikara	587,041	226,658	12,800,000	22	56	Republic	A	Antananarivo	Africa	37
Madeira	Madeira	794	307	284,000	358	925	Autonomous region (Portugal)	D	Funchal	Europe	32
Maine	Maine	91,653	35,387	1,257,000	14	36	State (U.S.)	D	Augusta	N. Amer.	44
† MALAWI	Malaŵi	118,484	45,747	9,691,000	82	212	Republic	A	Lilongwe	Africa	36
Malaya	Semenanjung Malaysia	131,598	50,810	15,335,000	117	302	Part of Malaysia (11 states)	D	. . . .	Asia	26
† MALAYSIA	Malaysia	334,758	129,251	18,630,000	56	144	Federal constitutional monarchy	A	Kuala Lumpur	Asia	26
† MALDIVES	Maldives	298	115	235,000	789	2,043	Republic	A	Male	Asia	25
† MALI	Mali	1,248,574	482,077	8,754,000	7.0	18	Republic	A	Bamako	Africa	34
† MALTA	Malta	316	122	360,000	1,139	2,951	Republic	A	Valletta	Europe	14
Manitoba	Manitoba	649,950	250,947	1,221,000	1.9	4.9	Province (Canada)	D	Winnipeg	N. Amer.	42
Maritime Provinces	. . .	134,560	51,965	1,983,000	15	38			. . . .	N. Amer.	42
† MARSHALL ISLANDS	Marshall Islands	181	70	51,000	282	729	Republic (U.S. protection)	A	Uliga	Oceania	60
Martinique	Martinique	1,100	425	372,000	338	875	Overseas department (France)	C	Fort-de-France	N. Amer.	51
Maryland	Maryland	32,135	12,407	4,975,000	155	401	State (U.S.)	D	Annapolis	N. Amer.	44
Massachusetts	Massachusetts	27,337	10,555	6,103,000	223	578	State (U.S.)	D	Boston	N. Amer.	44
† MAURITANIA	Mūritāniyā (Arabic) / Mauritanie (French)	1,025,520	395,956	2,092,000	2.0	5.3	Republic	A	Nouakchott	Africa	32
† MAURITIUS (incl. Dependencies)	Mauritius	2,040	788	1,096,000	537	1,391	Republic	A	Port-Louis	Africa	37
Mayotte [6]	Mayotte	374	144	89,000	238	618	Territorial collectivity (France)	C	Dzaoudzi and Mamoudzou [2]	Africa	37
Mecklenburg-Vorpommern	Mecklenburg-Vorpommern	23,835	9,203	2,000,000	84	217	State (Germany)	D	Schwerin	Europe	10
† MEXICO	México	1,967,183	759,534	86,170,000	44	113	Federal republic	A	Ciudad de México (Mexico City)	N. Amer.	48
Michigan	Michigan	250,738	96,810	9,488,000	38	98	State (U.S.)	D	Lansing	N. Amer.	44
† MICRONESIA, FEDERATED STATES OF	Federated States of Micronesia	702	271	117,000	167	432	Republic (U.S. protection)	A	Ponape	Oceania	60
Middle America	. . .	2,710,000	1,050,000	151,200,000	56	144			. . . .	N. Amer.	47

Country, Division, or Region English (Conventional)	Local Name	Area km²	sq mi	Population 1/1/93	Population Density per km²	sq mi	Form of Government and Political Status		Capital	Continent and Map Plate	
Midway Islands	Midway Islands	5.2	2.0	500	96	250	Unincorporated territory (U.S.)	C	. . .	Oceania	60
Minnesota	Minnesota	225,182	86,943	4,513,000	20	52	State (U.S.)	D	St. Paul	N. Amer.	45
Mississippi	Mississippi	125,443	48,434	2,616,000	21	54	State (U.S.)	D	Jackson	N. Amer.	45
Missouri	Missouri	180,546	69,709	5,231,000	29	75	State (U.S.)	D	Jefferson City	N. Amer.	45
† MOLDOVA	Moldova	33,700	13,012	4,474,000	133	344	Republic	A	Kišnev (Kishinev)	Europe	16
MONACO	Monaco	1.9	0.7	31,000	16,316	44,286	Constitutional monarchy	A	Monaco	Europe	11
† MONGOLIA	Mongol Ard Uls	1,566,500	604,829	2,336,000	1.5	3.9	Republic	A	Ulan-Bator (Ulaanbaatar)	Asia	27
Montana	Montana	380,850	147,046	821,000	2.2	5.6	State (U.S.)	D	Helena	N. Amer.	46
Montenegro	Crna Gora	13,812	5,333	650,000	47	122	Republic (Yugoslavia)	D	Titograd	Europe	15
Montserrat	Montserrat	102	39	13,000	127	333	Dependent territory (U.K.)	C	Plymouth	N. Amer.	51
† MOROCCO (excl. Western Sahara)	Al Maghrib	446,550	172,414	27,005,000	60	157	Constitutional monarchy	A	Rabat	Africa	32
† MOZAMBIQUE	Moçambique	799,380	308,642	15,795,000	20	51	Republic	A	Maputo	Africa	37
† NAMIBIA (excl. Walvis Bay)	Namibia	823,144	317,818	1,603,000	1.9	5.0	Republic	A	Windhoek	Africa	37
NAURU	Nauru (English) / Naoero (Nauruan)	21	8.1	10,000	476	1,235	Republic	A	Domaneab	Oceania	64
Navassa Island	Navassa Island	4.9	1.9	(1)	. . .	. . .	Unincorporated territory (U.S.)	C	. . .	N. Amer.	49
Nebraska	Nebraska	200,358	77,358	1,615,000	8.1	21	State (U.S.)	D	Lincoln	N. Amer.	45
† NEPAL	Nepal	147,181	56,827	20,325,000	138	358	Constitutional monarchy	A	Kathmandu	Asia	25
† NETHERLANDS	Nederland	41,864	16,164	15,190,000	363	940	Constitutional monarchy	A	Amsterdam and 's-Gravenhage (The Hague)	Europe	12
NETHERLANDS ANTILLES	Nederlandse Antillen	800	309	191,000	239	618	Self-governing territory (Netherlands protection)	B	Willemstad	N. Amer.	50
Nevada	Nevada	286,368	110,567	1,308,000	4.6	12	State (U.S.)	D	Carson City	N. Amer.	46
New Brunswick	New Brunswick (English) / Nouveau-Brunswick (French)	73,440	28,355	824,000	11	29	Province (Canada)	D	Fredericton	N. Amer.	42
New Caledonia	Nouvelle-Calédonie	19,058	7,358	177,000	9.3	24	Overseas territory (France)	C	Nouméa	Oceania	63
New England	New England	186,472	71,997	13,488,000	72	187	Part of U.S. (6 states)		. . .	N. Amer.	43
Newfoundland	Newfoundland (English) / Terre-Neuve (French)	405,720	156,649	641,000	1.6	4.1	Province (Canada)	D	St. John's	N. Amer.	42
Newfoundland (island)	Newfoundland (English) / Terre-Neuve (French)	108,860	42,031	605,000	5.6	14	Part of Newfoundland province (Canada)		. . .	N. Amer.	42
New Hampshire	New Hampshire	24,219	9,351	1,154,000	48	123	State (U.S.)	D	Concord	N. Amer.	44
New Hebrides, see Vanuatu	. . .	. . .	. . .	. . .	. . .	. . .	. . .		. . .	. . .	. . .
New Jersey	New Jersey	22,590	8,722	7,898,000	350	906	State (U.S.)	D	Trenton	N. Amer.	44
New Mexico	New Mexico	314,939	121,598	1,590,000	5.0	13	State (U.S.)	D	Santa Fe	N. Amer.	45
New South Wales	New South Wales	801,600	309,500	5,770,000	7.2	19	State (Australia)	D	Sydney	Oceania	59
New York	New York	141,089	54,475	18,350,000	130	337	State (U.S.)	D	Albany	N. Amer.	44
† NEW ZEALAND	New Zealand	270,534	104,454	3,477,000	13	33	Parliamentary state	A	Wellington	Oceania	62
† NICARAGUA	Nicaragua	129,640	50,054	3,932,000	30	79	Republic	A	Managua	N. Amer.	49
† NIGER	Niger	1,267,000	489,191	8,198,000	6.5	17	Provisional military government	A	Niamey	Africa	34
† NIGERIA	Nigeria	923,768	356,669	91,700,000	99	257	Provisional military government	A	Lagos and Abuja (2)	Africa	34
Ningsia	Ningxia Huizu Zizhiqu	66,400	25,637	4,820,000	73	189	Autonomous region (China)	D	Yinchuan	Asia	27
NIUE	Niue	258	100	1,700	6.6	17	Self-governing territory (New Zealand protection)	B	Alofi	Oceania	64
Norfolk Island	Norfolk Island	36	14	2,600	72	186	External territory (Australia)	C	Kingston	Oceania	61
North America	. . .	24,700,000	9,500,000	438,200,000	18	46	. . .		. . .	N. Amer.	38-39
North Borneo, see Sabah	. . .	. . .	. . .	. . .	. . .	. . .	. . .		. . .	. . .	. . .
North Carolina	North Carolina	139,397	53,821	6,846,000	49	127	State (U.S.)	D	Raleigh	N. Amer.	44
North Dakota	North Dakota	183,123	70,704	632,000	3.5	8.9	State (U.S.)	D	Bismarck	N. Amer.	45
Northern Ireland	Northern Ireland	14,121	5,452	1,604,000	114	294	Administrative division (U.K.)	D	Belfast	Europe	9
NORTHERN MARIANA ISLANDS	Northern Mariana Islands	477	184	48,000	101	261	Commonwealth (U.S. protection)	B	Saipan (island)	Oceania	60
Northern Territory	Northern Territory	1,346,200	519,771	176,000	0.1	0.3	Territory (Australia)	D	Darwin	Oceania	59
North Rhine-Westphalia	Nordrhein-Westfalen	34,068	13,154	17,420,000	511	1,324	State (Germany)	D	Düsseldorf	Europe	10
Northwest Territories	Northwest Territories (English) / Territoires du Nord-Ouest (French)	3,426,320	1,322,910	61,000	. . .	. . .	Territory (Canada)	D	Yellowknife	N. Amer.	42
† NORWAY (incl. Svalbard and Jan Mayen)	Norge	386,975	149,412	4,308,000	11	29	Constitutional monarchy	A	Oslo	Europe	7
Nova Scotia	Nova Scotia (English) / Nouvelle-Écosse (French)	55,490	21,425	1,007,000	18	47	Province (Canada)	D	Halifax	N. Amer.	42
Oceania (incl. Australia)	. . .	8,500,000	3,300,000	26,700,000	3.1	8.1	. . .		. . .	Oceania	57-53
Ohio	Ohio	116,103	44,828	11,025,000	95	246	State (U.S.)	D	Columbus	N. Amer.	44
Oklahoma	Oklahoma	181,049	69,903	3,205,000	18	46	State (U.S.)	D	Oklahoma City	N. Amer.	45
† OMAN	'Uman	212,457	82,030	1,617,000	7.6	20	Monarchy	A	Masqaţ (Muscat)	Asia	23
Ontario	Ontario	1,068,580	412,581	11,265,000	11	27	Province (Canada)	D	Toronto	N. Amer.	42
Oregon	Oregon	254,819	98,386	2,949,000	12	30	State (U.S.)	D	Salem	N. Amer.	46
Orkney Islands	Orkney Islands	976	377	20,000	20	53	Part of Scotland (U.K.)	D	Kirkwall	Europe	9
Pacific Islands, Trust Territory of the, see Palau	. . .	. . .	. . .	. . .	. . .	. . .	. . .		. . .	. . .	. . .
† PAKISTAN (incl. part of Jammu and Kashmir)	Pakistan	879,902	339,732	123,490,000	140	363	Federal Islamic republic	A	Islamabad	Asia	25
PALAU	Palau (English) / Belau (Palauan)	508	196	16,000	31	82	Under U.S. administration	B	Koror	Oceania	60
† PANAMA	Panamá	75,517	29,157	2,555,000	34	88	Republic	A	Panamá	N. Amer.	49
† PAPUA NEW GUINEA	Papua New Guinea	462,340	178,704	3,737,000	8.1	21	Parliamentary state	A	Port Moresby	Oceania	60
† PARAGUAY	Paraguay	406,752	157,048	5,003,000	12	32	Republic	A	Asunción	S. Amer.	56
Peking	Beijing	16,800	6,487	11,290,000	672	1,740	Autonomous city (China)	D	Beijing (Peking)	Asia	28
Pennsylvania	Pennsylvania	119,291	46,058	12,105,000	101	263	State (U.S.)	D	Harrisburg	N. Amer.	44
† PERU	Perú	1,285,216	496,225	22,995,000	18	46	Republic	A	Lima	S. Amer.	54
† PHILIPPINES	Pilipinas (Pilipino) / Philippines (English)	300,000	115,831	65,500,000	218	565	Republic	A	Manila	Asia	26
Pitcairn (incl. Dependencies)	Pitcairn	49	19	50	1.0	2.6	Dependent territory (U.K.)	C	Adamstown	Oceania	61
† POLAND	Polska	312,683	120,728	38,330,000	123	317	Republic	A	Warszawa (Warsaw)	Europe	10
† PORTUGAL	Portugal	91,985	35,516	10,660,000	116	300	Republic	A	Lisboa (Lisbon)	Europe	13
Prairie Provinces	Prairie Provinces	1,963,470	758,100	5,159,000	2.6	6.8	Part of Canada (3 provinces)		. . .	N. Amer.	42
Prince Edward Island	Prince Edward Island (English) / Île-du Prince-Édouard (French)	5,660	2,185	152,000	27	70	Province (Canada)	D	Charlottetown	N. Amer.	42
PUERTO RICO	Puerto Rico	9,104	3,515	3,594,000	395	1,022	Commonwealth (U.S. protection)	B	San Juan	N. Amer.	51
† QATAR	Qaţar	11,427	4,412	492,000	43	112	Monarchy	A	Ad Dawḩah (Doha)	Asia	24
Qinghai	Qinghai	720,000	277,994	4,585,000	6.4	16	Province (China)	D	Xining	Asia	27
Quebec	Québec	1,540,680	594,860	7,725,000	5.0	13	Province (Canada)	D	Québec	N. Amer.	42
Queensland	Queensland	1,727,200	666,876	3,000,000	1.7	4.5	State (Australia)	D	Brisbane	Oceania	59
Reunion	Réunion	2,510	969	633,000	252	653	Overseas department (France)	C	Saint-Denis	Africa	37
Rhineland-Palatinate	Rheinland-Pfalz	19,849	7,664	3,771,000	190	492	State (Germany)	D	Mainz	Europe	10
Rhode Island	Rhode Island	4,002	1,545	1,026,000	256	664	State (U.S.)	D	Providence	N. Amer.	44
Rhodesia, see Zimbabwe	. . .	. . .	. . .	. . .	. . .	. . .	. . .		. . .	. . .	. . .

A • 5

Country, Division, or Region English (Conventional)	Local Name	Area km²	Area sq mi	Population 1/1/93	Population Density per km²	Population Density per sq mi	Form of Government and Political Status	Capital	Continent and Map Plate
Rodrigues	Rodrigues	104	*40*	40,000	385	*1,000*	Part of Mauritius	. . .	Africa 30-31
†ROMANIA	România	237,500	*91,699*	23,200,000	98	*253*	Republic	*A* Bucureşti (Bucharest)	Europe 15
†RUSSIA	Rossija	17,075,400	*6,592,849*	150,500,000	8.8	*23*	Republic	*A* Moskva (Moscow)	Eur., Asia 19-20
Russia in Europe	. . .	3,955,818	*1,527,350*	106,980,000	27	*70*	. . .	. . .	Europe 19
†RWANDA	Rwanda	26,338	*10,169*	7,573,000	288	*745*	Provisional military government	*A* Kigali	Africa 36
Saarland	Saar	2,570	*992*	1,085,000	422	*1,094*	State (Germany)	*D* Saarbrücken	Europe 10
Sabah	Sabah	73,711	*28,460*	1,544,000	21	*54*	State (Malaysia)	*D* Kota Kinabalu	Asia 26
†ST. CHRISTOPHER-NEVIS	St. Christopher-Nevis	269	*104*	40,000	149	*385*	Parliamentary state	*A* Basseterre	N. Amer. 51
St. Helena (incl. Dependencies)	St. Helena	314	*121*	7,000	22	*58*	Dependent territory (U.K.)	*C* Jamestown	Africa 31
†ST. LUCIA	St. Lucia	616	*238*	153,000	248	*643*	Parliamentary state	*A* Castries	N. Amer. 51
St. Pierre and Miquelon	St.-Pierre et Miquelon	242	*93*	7,000	29	*75*	Territorial collectivity (France)	*C* Saint-Pierre	N. Amer. 42
†ST. VINCENT AND THE GRENADINES	St. Vincent and the Grenadines	388	*150*	116,000	299	*773*	Parliamentary state	*A* Kingstown	N. Amer. 51
†SAN MARINO	San Marino	61	*24*	23,000	377	*958*	Republic	*A* San Marino	Europe 14
†SAO TOME AND PRINCIPE	São Tomé e Príncipe	964	*372*	134,000	139	*360*	Republic	*A* São Tomé	Africa 34
Sarawak	Sarawak	129,449	*49,981*	1,751,000	14	*35*	State (Malaysia)	*D* Kuching	Asia 26
Sardinia	Sardegna	24,090	*9,301*	1,681,000	70	*181*	Autonomous region (Italy)	*D* Cagliari	Europe 14
Saskatchewan	Saskatchewan	652,330	*251,866*	1,099,000	1.7	*4.4*	Province (Canada)	*D* Regina	N. Amer. 42
†SAUDI ARABIA	Al 'Arabīyah as Su'ūdīyah	2,149,690	*830,000*	15,985,000	7.4	*19*	Monarchy	*A* Ar Riyāḍ (Riyadh)	Asia 23
Saxony	Sachsen	18,338	*7,080*	4,993,000	272	*705*	State (Germany)	*D* Dresden	Europe 10
Saxony-Anhalt	Sachsen-Anhalt	20,444	*7,893*	3,021,000	148	*383*	State (Germany)	*D* Magdeburg	Europe 10
Scandinavia	. . .	1,320,000	*510,000*	23,479,000	18	*46*	. . .	. . .	Europe 7
Schleswig-Holstein	Schleswig-Holstein	15,730	*6,073*	2,643,000	168	*435*	State (Germany)	*D* Kiel	Europe 10
Scotland	Scotland	78,789	*30,421*	5,145,000	65	*169*	Administrative division (U.K.)	*D* Edinburgh	Europe 9
†SENEGAL	Sénégal	196,712	*75,951*	7,849,000	40	*103*	Republic	*A* Dakar	Africa 34
Serbia	Srbija	88,361	*34,116*	10,020,000	113	*294*	Republic (Yugoslavia)	*D* Belgrade (Beograd)	Europe 15
†SEYCHELLES	Seychelles	453	*175*	70,000	155	*400*	Republic	*A* Victoria	Africa 37
Shaanxi	Shaanxi	205,000	*79,151*	34,215,000	167	*432*	Province (China)	*D* Xi'an (Sian)	Asia 27
Shandong	Shandong	153,000	*59,074*	87,840,000	574	*1,487*	Province (China)	*D* Jinan	Asia 27
Shanghai	Shanghai	6,200	*2,394*	13,875,000	2,238	*5,796*	Autonomous city (China)	*D* Shanghai	Asia 28
Shanxi	Shanxi	156,000	*60,232*	29,865,000	191	*496*	Province (China)	*D* Taiyuan	Asia 27
Shetland Islands	Shetland Islands	1,433	*553*	22,000	15	*40*	Part of Scotland (U.K.)	*D* Lerwick	Europe 9
Sichuan	Sichuan	570,000	*220,078*	111,470,000	196	*507*	Province (China)	*D* Chengdu	Asia 27
Sicily	Sicilia	25,709	*9,926*	5,270,000	205	*531*	Autonomous region (Italy)	*D* Palermo	Europe 14
†SIERRA LEONE	Sierra Leone	72,325	*27,925*	4,424,000	61	*158*	Transitional military government	*A* Freetown	Africa 34
†SINGAPORE	Singapore (English) / Singapura (Malay)	636	*246*	2,812,000	4,421	*11,431*	Republic	*A* Singapore	Asia 26
Sinkiang	Xingiang Uygur Zizhiqu	1,600,000	*617,764*	15,755,000	9.8	*26*	Autonomous region (China)	*D* Ürümqi	Asia 27
†SLOVAKIA	Slovenská Republika	49,035	*18,933*	5,287,000	108	*279*	Republic	*A* Bratislava	Europe 10
†SLOVENIA	Slovenija	20,251	*7,819*	1,965,000	97	*251*	Republic	*A* Ljubljana	Europe 14
†SOLOMON ISLANDS	Solomon Islands	28,370	*10,954*	366,000	13	*33*	Parliamentary state	*A* Honiara	Oceania 63
†SOMALIA	Soomaaliya	637,657	*246,201*	6,000,000	9.4	*24*	None	*A* Muqdisho (Mogadishu)	Africa 35
†SOUTH AFRICA (incl. Walvis Bay)	South Africa (English) / Suid-Afrika (Afrikaans)	1,123,226	*433,680*	33,040,000	29	*76*	Republic	*A* Pretoria, Cape Town, and Bloemfontein	Africa 37
South America	. . .	17,800,000	*6,900,000*	310,700,000	17	*45*	. . .	. . .	S. Amer. 52-53
South Australia	South Australia	984,000	*379,925*	1,410,000	1.4	*3.7*	State (Australia)	*D* Adelaide	Oceania 59
South Carolina	South Carolina	82,898	*32,007*	3,616,000	44	*113*	State (U.S.)	*D* Columbia	N. Amer. 44
South Dakota	South Dakota	199,745	*77,121*	718,000	3.6	*9.3*	State (U.S.)	*D* Pierre	N. Amer. 45
South Georgia (incl. Dependencies)	South Georgia	3,755	*1,450*	[1]	. . .	. . .	Dependent territory (U.K.)	*C* . . .	S. Amer. 56
South West Africa, see Namibia	. . .	. . .	. . .	. . .	. . .	. . .	. . .	. . .	. . .
†SPAIN	España	504,750	*194,885*	39,155,000	78	*201*	Constitutional monarchy	*A* Madrid	Europe 13
Spanish North Africa [7]	Plazas de Soberanía en el Norte de África	32	*12*	144,000	4,500	*12,000*	Five possessions (Spain)	*C* . . .	Africa 13
Spanish Sahara, see Western Sahara	. . .	. . .	. . .	. . .	. . .	. . .	. . .	. . .	. . .
†SRI LANKA	Sri Lanka	64,652	*24,962*	17,740,000	274	*711*	Socialist republic	*A* Colombo and Sri Jayawardenapura	Asia 25
†SUDAN	As Sūdān	2,505,813	*967,500*	28,760,000	11	*30*	Provisional military government	*A* Al Kharṭūm (Khartoum)	Africa 35
Sumatra	Sumatera	473,606	*182,860*	36,455,000	77	*199*	Part of Indonesia (7 provinces)	. . .	Asia 26
†SURINAME	Suriname	163,820	*63,251*	413,000	2.5	*6.5*	Republic	*A* Paramaribo	S. Amer. 54
†SWAZILAND	Swaziland	17,364	*6,704*	925,000	53	*138*	Monarchy	*A* Mbabane and Lobamba	Africa 37
†SWEDEN	Sverige	449,964	*173,732*	8,619,000	19	*50*	Constitutional monarchy	*A* Stockholm	Europe 7
SWITZERLAND	Schweiz (German) / Suisse (French) / Svizzera (Italian)	41,293	*15,943*	6,848,000	166	*430*	Federal republic	*A* Bern (Berne)	Europe 14
†SYRIA	Sūrīyah	185,180	*71,498*	14,070,000	76	*197*	Socialist republic	*A* Dimashq (Damascus)	Asia 24
TAIWAN	Taiwan	36,002	*13,900*	20,985,000	583	*1,510*	Republic	*A* Taipei	Asia 27
†TAJIKISTAN	Tojikiston	143,100	*55,251*	5,765,000	40	*104*	Republic	*A* Dušanbe (Dushanbe)	Asia 18
†TANZANIA	Tanzania	945,087	*364,900*	28,265,000	30	*77*	Republic	*A* Dar es Salaam and Dodoma [2]	Africa 36
Tasmania	Tasmania	67,800	*26,178*	456,000	6.7	*17*	State (Australia)	*D* Hobart	Oceania 59
Tennessee	Tennessee	109,158	*42,146*	5,026,000	46	*119*	State (U.S.)	*D* Nashville	N. Amer. 44
Texas	Texas	695,676	*268,601*	17,610,000	25	*66*	State (U.S.)	*D* Austin	N. Amer. 45
†THAILAND	Muang Thai	513,115	*198,115*	58,030,000	113	*293*	Constitutional monarchy	*A* Krung Thep (Bangkok)	Asia 26
Thuringia	Thüringen	16,251	*6,275*	2,734,000	168	*436*	State (Germany)	*D* Erfurt	Europe 10
Tibet	Xizang Zizhiqu	1,220,000	*471,045*	2,235,000	1.8	*4.7*	Autonomous region (China)	*D* Lhasa	Asia 27
Tientsin	Tianjin	11,300	*4,363*	9,170,000	812	*2,102*	Autonomous city (China)	*D* Tianjin (Tientsin)	Asia 28
†TOGO	Togo	56,785	*21,925*	4,030,000	71	*184*	Provisional military government	*A* Lomé	Africa 34
Tokelau	Tokelau	12	*4.6*	1,800	150	*391*	Island territory (New Zealand)	*C* . . .	Oceania 61
TONGA	Tonga	747	*288*	103,000	138	*358*	Constitutional monarchy	*A* Nuku'alofa	Oceania 61
TRANSKEI [3]	Transkei	43,553	*16,816*	4,845,000	111	*288*	National state (South African protection)	*B* Umtata	Africa 37
†TRINIDAD AND TOBAGO	Trinidad and Tobago	5,128	*1,980*	1,307,000	255	*660*	Republic	*A* Port of Spain	N. Amer. 50
Tristan da Cunha	Tristan da Cunha	104	*40*	300	2.9	*7.5*	Dependency (St. Helena)	*C* Edinburgh	Africa 30-31
†TUNISIA	Tunisie (French) / Tūnis (Arabic)	163,610	*63,170*	8,495,000	52	*134*	Republic	*A* Tūnis	Africa 32
†TURKEY	Türkiye	779,452	*300,948*	58,620,000	75	*195*	Republic	*A* Ankara	Eur.,Asia 24
Turkey in Europe	. . .	23,764	*9,175*	8,805,000	371	*960*	. . .	. . .	Europe 24
†TURKMENISTAN	Turkmenistan	488,100	*188,456*	3,884,000	8.0	*21*	Republic	*A* Ašhabad	Asia 19
Turks and Caicos Islands	Turks and Caicos Islands	500	*193*	13,000	26	*67*	Dependent territory (U.K.)	*C* Grand Turk	N. Amer. 49
TUVALU	Tuvalu	26	*10*	10,000	385	*1,000*	Parliamentary state	*A* Funafuti	Oceania 60
†UGANDA	Uganda	241,139	*93,104*	17,410,000	72	*187*	Republic	*A* Kampala	Africa 36
†UKRAINE	Ukrayina	603,700	*233,090*	51,990,000	86	*223*	Republic	*A* Kijev (Kiev)	Europe 16
†UNITED ARAB EMIRATES	Al Imārāt al 'Arabīyah al Muttaḥidah	83,600	*32,278*	2,590,000	31	*80*	Federation of monarchs	*A* Abū Ẓaby (Abu Dhabi)	Asia 23
†UNITED KINGDOM	United Kingdom	244,154	*94,269*	57,890,000	237	*614*	Constitutional monarchy	*A* London	Europe 9
United Kingdom and Possessions	. . .	259,753	*100,291*	63,860,000	246	*637*	. . .	. . .	. . .
†UNITED STATES	United States	9,809,431	*3,787,425*	256,420,000	26	*68*	Federal republic	*A* Washington	N. Amer. 43

Country, Division, or Region English (Conventional)	Local Name	Area km²	Area sq mi	Population 1/1/93	Population Density per km²	Population Density per sq mi	Form of Government and Political Status		Capital	Continent and Map Plate	
United States and Possessions	. . .	9,820,617	3,791,744	260,380,000	27	69	. . . .		. . .	. . . .	. . .
Upper Volta, see Burkina Faso	. . .	. . .	. . .	. . .	. . .	. .				. . . .	. . .
† URUGUAY	Uruguay	177,414	68,500	3,151,000	18	46	Republic	A	Montevideo	S. Amer.	55
Utah	Utah	219,902	84,904	1,795,000	8.2	21	State (U.S.)	D	Salt Lake City	N. Amer.	46
† UZBEKISTAN	Üzbekiston	447,400	172,742	21,885,000	49	127	Republic	A	Taškent (Tashkent)	Asia	19
† VANUATU	Vanuatu	12,190	4,707	157,000	13	33	Republic	A	Port-Vila	Oceania	63
VATICAN CITY	Città del Vaticano	0.4	0.2	800	2,000	4,000	Monarchical-sacerdotal state	A	Vatican City	Europe	14
VENDA (3)	Venda	6,198	2,393	732,000	118	306	National state (South African protection)	B	Thohoyandou	Africa	37
† VENEZUELA	Venezuela	912,050	352,145	19,085,000	21	54	Federal republic	A	Caracas	S. Amer.	54
Vermont	Vermont	24,903	9,615	590,000	24	61	State (U.S.)	D	Montpelier	N. Amer.	44
Victoria	Victoria	227,600	87,877	4,273,000	19	49	State (Australia)	D	Melbourne	Oceania	59
† VIETNAM	Viet Nam	330,036	127,428	69,650,000	211	547	Socialist republic	A	Ha Noi	Asia	26
Virginia	Virginia	110,771	42,769	6,411,000	58	150	State (U.S.)	D	Richmond	N. Amer.	44
Virgin Islands of the United States	Virgin Islands	344	133	104,000	302	782	Unincorporated territory (U.S.)	C	Charlotte Amalie	N. Amer.	51
Virgin Islands, British	British Virgin Islands	153	59	13,000	85	220	Dependent territory (U.K.)	C	Road Town	N. Amer.	51
Wake Island	Wake Island	7.8	3.0	200	26	67	Unincorporated territory (U.S.)	C	. . .	Oceania	60
Wales	Wales	20,766	8,018	2,906,000	140	362	Administrative division (U.K.)	D	Cardiff	Europe	9
Wallis and Futuna	Îles Wallis et Futuna	255	98	17,000	67	173	Overseas territory (France)	C	Mata-Utu	Oceania	61
Washington	Washington	184,674	71,303	5,052,000	27	71	State (U.S.)	D	Olympia	N. Amer.	46
Western Australia	Western Australia	2,525,500	975,101	1,598,000	0.6	1.6	State (Australia)	D	Perth	Oceania	59
Western Sahara	. . .	266,000	102,703	200,000	0.8	1.9	Occupied by Morocco	C	El Aaiún	Africa	32
† WESTERN SAMOA	Western Samoa (English) / Samoa i Sisifo (Samoan)	2,831	1,093	197,000	70	180	Constitutional monarchy	A	Apia	Oceania	65
West Indies	West Indies (English) / Indias Occidentales (Spanish)	235,000	91,000	34,627,000	147	381	. . . .		. . . . .	N. Amer. . . .	47
West Virginia	West Virginia	62,759	24,231	1,795,000	29	74	State (U.S.)	D	Charleston	N. Amer. . . .	44
Wisconsin	Wisconsin	169,653	65,503	5,000,000	29	76	State (U.S.)	D	Madison	N. Amer. . . .	45
Wyoming	Wyoming	253,349	97,818	462,000	1.8	4.7	State (U.S.)	D	Cheyenne	N. Amer. . . .	46
† YEMEN	Al Yaman	527,968	203,850	12,215,000	23	60	Republic	A	San'a'	Asia	23
YUGOSLAVIA	Jugoslavija	102,173	39,449	10,670,000	104	270	Republic	A	Beograd (Belgrade)	Europe	14-15
Yukon Territory	Yukon Territory	483,450	186,661	31,000	0.1	0.2	Territory (Canada)	D	Whitehorse	N. Amer.	42
Yunnan	Yunnan	394,000	152,124	38,450,000	98	253	Province (China)	D	Kunming	Asia	27
† ZAIRE	Zaïre	2,345,095	905,446	39,750,000	17	44	Republic	A	Kinshasa	Africa	36
† ZAMBIA	Zambia	752,614	290,586	8,475,000	11	29	Republic	A	Lusaka	Africa	36
Zanzibar	Zanzibar	2,461	950	434,000	176	457	Part of Tanzania	. .	Zanzibar	Africa	36
Zhejiang	Zhejiang	101,800	39,305	43,150,000	424	1,098	Province (China)	D	Hangzhou	Asia	27
† ZIMBABWE	Zimbabwe	390,759	150,873	10,000,000	26	66	Republic	A	Harare	Africa	37
WORLD	. . .	150,100,000	57,900,000	5,477,000,000	36	95	. . . .		. . . . .	. . . .	1-2

† Member of the United Nations (1992).
. . . None, or not applicable.
(1) No permanent population.
(2) Future capital.
(3) Bophuthatswana, Ciskei, Transkei, and Venda are not recognized by the United Nations.
(4) Claimed by Argentina.
(5) Includes West Bank, Golan Heights, and Gaza Strip.
(6) Claimed by Comoros.
(7) Comprises Ceuta, Melilla, and several small islands.

World Geographical Tables

The Earth: Land and Water

	Total Area km²	Total Area sq mi	Area of Land km²	Area of Land sq mi	%	Area of Oceans and Seas km²	Area of Oceans and Seas sq mi	%
Earth	510,100,000	197,100,000	150,100,000	57,900,000	29.4	360,200,000	139,100,000	70.6
N. Hemisphere	255,050,000	98,500,000	106,571,000	41,109,000	41.6	148,762,600	57,448,300	58.4
S. Hemisphere	255,050,000	98,500,000	43,529,000	16,791,000	17.0	211,437,400	81,651,700	83.0

The Continents

Continent	Area km² / sq mi	Population Estimate (1/1/93)	Population per km² / sq mi	Mean Elevation m / ft	Highest Elevation m/ft	Lowest Elevation m/ft (below sea level)	Highest Recorded Temperature °C/°F	Lowest Recorded Temperature °C/°F
Europe	9,900,000 / 3,800,000	694,700,000	70 / 183	300 / 980	gora Elbrus, Russia 5,642/18,510	Caspian Sea, Asia-Europe −28/−92	Sevilla, Spain 50°/122°	Ust-Ščugor, Russia −55°/−67°
Asia	44,900,000 / 17,300,000	3,337,800,000	74 / 193	910 / 3,000	Everest, China-Nepal 8,848/29,028	Dead Sea, Israel-Jordan −403/−1,322	Tirat Zevi, Israel 54°/129°	Ojmjakon and Verkhoyansk, Russia −68°/−90°
Africa	30,300,000 / 11,700,000	668,700,000	22 / 57	580 / 1,900	Kilimanjaro, Tanzania 5,895/19,340	Lac Assal, Djibouti −157/−515	Al 'Azīzīyah, Libya 58°/136°	Ifrane, Morocco −24°/−11°
North America	24,700,000 / 9,500,000	438,200,000	18 / 46	610 / 2,000	Mt. McKinley, U.S. 6,194/20,320	Death Valley, U.S. −86/−282	Death Valley, U.S. 57°/134°	Northice, Greenland −66°/−87°
South America	17,800,000 / 6,900,000	310,700,000	17 / 45	550 / 1,800	Cerro Aconcagua, Argentina 6,960/22,835	Salinas Chicas −42/−138	Rivadavia, Argentina 49°/120°	Sarmiento, Argentina −33°/−27°
Oceania, incl. Australia	8,500,000 / 3,300,000	26,700,000	3 / 8	.... /	Mt. Wilhelm, Papua New Guinea 4,509/14,793	Lake Eyre, Australia −12/−39	Cloncurry, Australia 53°/128°	Charlotte Pass, Australia −22°/−8°
Australia	7,682,300 / 2,966,155	16,965,000	2 / 6	300 / 1,000	Mt. Kosciusko, Australia 2,228/7,310	Lake Eyre, Austraila −12/−39	Cloncurry, Australia 53°/128°	Charlotte Pass, Australia −22°/−8°
Antarctica	14,000,000 / 5,400,000	....	... / ...	1,830 / 6,000	Vinson Massif 4,897/116,06	sea level	Vanda Station 15°/59°	Vostok −89°/−129°
World	150,100,000 / 57,900,000	5,477,000,000	36 / 95	.... /	Everest, China-Nepal 8,848/29,028	Dead Sea, Israel-Jordan −403/−1,322	Al 'Azīzīyah, Libya 58°/136°	Vostok −89°/−129°

Principal Mountains

Mountain	Country	Height m	Height ft
Europe			
Elbrus, gora	△Russia	5,642	18,510
Dyhtau, gora	Russia	5,204	17,073
Blanc, Mont	△France-△Italy	4,807	15,771
Rosa, Monte	Italy-△Switzerland	4,634	15,203
Matterhorn	Italy-Switzerland	4,478	14,692
Grossglockner	△Austria	3,797	12,457
Teide, Pico de	△Spain (Canary Is.)	3,718	12,198
Aneto, Pico de	Spain	3,404	11,168
Etna	Italy	3,323	10,902
Zugspitze	Austria-△Germany	2,963	9,721
Ólimbos, Óros	△Greece	2,917	9,570
Corno Grande	Italy	2,912	9,554
Gerlachovský štít	△Slovakia	2,663	8,737
Glittertind	△Norway	2,472	8,110
Kebnekaise	△Sweden	2,111	6,926
Narodnaja, gora	Russia	1,895	6,217
Nevis, Ben	△United Kingdom	1,343	4,406
Asia			
Everest	△China-△Nepal	8,848	29,028
K2 (Qogir Feng)	China-△Pakistan	8,611	28,250
Kānchenjunga	△India-Nepal	8,598	28,208
Makālu	China-Nepal	8,481	27,825
Dhaulāgiri	Nepal	8,172	26,810
Annapurna	Nepal	8,078	26,504
Muztag	China	7,723	25,338
Tirich Mīr	Pakistan	7,690	25,230
Kommunizma, pik (Communism Peak)	△Tajikistan	7,495	24,590
Pobedy, pik	China-Russia	7,439	24,406
Damāvand, Qolleh-ye	△Iran	5,604	18,386
Ağrı Dağı, Büyük (Mt. Ararat)	△Turkey	5,122	16,804
Jaya, Puncak	△Indonesia	5,030	16,503
Ključevskaja Sopka, vulkan	Russia	4,750	15,584
Kinabalu, Gunong	△Malaysia	4,101	13,455
Yushan	△Taiwan	3,997	13,114
Fuji-San	△Japan	3,776	12,388
Nabī Shu'ayb, Jabal an	△Yemen	3,760	12,336
Apo, Mt.	△Philippines	2,954	9,692
Shaykh, Jabal ash- (Mt. Hermon)	Lebanon-△Syria	2,814	9,232
Mayon, Mt.	Philippines	2,462	8,077
Chili-san	△South Korea	1,915	6,283
Meron, Hare	△Israel	1,208	3,963

Mountain	Country	Height m	Height ft
Africa			
Kilimanjaro	△Tanzania	5,895	19,340
Kirinyaga (Mt. Kenya)	△Kenya	5,199	17,058
Margherita	△Uganda-△Zaire	5,109	16,762
Ras Dashan Terara	△Ethiopia	4,620	15,158
Toubkal, Jebel	△Morocco	4,165	13,665
Cameroon, Mt.	△Cameroon	4,100	13,451
North America			
McKinley, Mt.	△United States	6,194	20,320
Logan, Mt.	△Canada	5,951	19,524
Orizaba, Pico de	△Mexico	5,610	18,406
Popocatépetl, Volcán	Mexico	5,452	17,887
Whitney, Mt.	United States	4,417	14,491
Elbert, Mt.	United States	4,399	14,433
Rainier, Mt.	United States	4,392	14,410
Shasta, Mt.	United States	4,317	14,162
Pikes Pk.	United States	4,301	14,110
Tajumulco, Volcán	△Guatemala	4,220	13,845
Mauna Kea	United States	4,205	13,796
Grand Teton	United States	4,197	13,770
Waddington, Mt.	Canada	3,994	13,104
Robson, Mt.	Canada	3,954	12,972
Chirripó, Cerro	△Costa Rica	3,819	12,530
Gunnbjørns Fjeld	△Greenland	3,700	12,139
Duarte, Pico	△Dominican Rep.	3,175	10,417
Mitchell, Mt.	United States	2,037	6,684
Marcy, Mt.	United States	1,629	5,344
South America			
Aconcagua, Cerro	△Argentina	6,960	22,835
Ojos del Salado, Nevado	Argentina-△Chile	6,863	22,516
Huascarán, Nevado	△Peru	6,746	22,133
Illimani, Nevado del	△Bolivia	6,682	21,923
Chimborazo, Volcán	△Ecuador	6,310	20,702
Cristóbal Colón, Pico	△Colombia	5,800	19,029
Neblina, Pico da	△Brazil-Venezuela	3,014	9,888
Oceania			
Wilhelm, Mt.	△Papua New Guinea	4,509	14,793
Cook, Mt.	△New Zealand	3,764	12,349
Kosciusko, Mt.	△Australia	2,228	7,310
Antarctica			
Vinson Massif	△Antarctica	4,897	16,066
Kirkpatrick, Mt.	Antarctica	4,528	14,856

△ Highest mountain in country.

Oceans, Seas, and Gulfs

Name	Area km²	sq mi	Greatest Depth m	ft
Pacific Ocean	165,200,000	63,800,000	11,020	36,155
Atlantic Ocean	82,400,000	31,800,000	9,220	30,249
Indian Ocean	74,900,000	28,900,000	7,450	24,442
Arctic Ocean	14,000,000	5,400,000	5,450	17,881
Arabian Sea	3,864,000	1,492,000	5,800	19,029
South China Sea	3,447,000	1,331,000	5,560	18,241
Caribbean Sea	2,753,000	1,063,000	7,680	25,197
Mediterranean Sea	2,505,000	967,000	5,020	16,470
Bering Sea	2,269,000	876,000	4,096	13,438
Bengal, Bay of	2,173,000	839,000	5,258	17,251
Okhotsk, Sea of	1,603,000	619,000	3,372	11,063
Norwegian Sea	1,546,000	597,000	4,020	13,189
Mexico, Gulf of	1,544,000	596,000	4,380	14,370
East China Sea	1,248,000	482,000	4,424	14,514
Hudson Bay	1,230,000	475,000	259	850

Waterfalls

Waterfall	Country	River	Height m	ft
Angel	Venezuela	Churún	972	3,189
Tugela	South Africa	Tugela	948	3,110
Yosemite	United States	Yosemite Creek	739	2,425
Sutherland	New Zealand	Arthur	579	1,900
Gavarnie	France	Gave de Pau	421	1,381
Lofoi	Zaire	Lofoi	384	1,260
Krimml	Austria	Krimml	381	1,250
Takakkaw	Canada	Yoho	380	1,248
Staubbach	Switzerland	Staubbach	305	1,091
Mardalsfoss	Norway	. . .	297	974
Gersoppa	India	Sharavati	253	830
Kaieteur	Guyana	Potaro	247	810

Principal Rivers

River	Continent	Length km	mi
Nile	Africa	6,671	4,145
Amazon-Ucayali	South America	6,400	4,000
Yangtze (Chang Jiang)	Asia	6,300	3,900
Yellow (Huang He)	Asia	5,464	3,395
Ob-Irtyš	Asia	5,410	3,362
Río de la Plata-Paraná	South America	4,876	3,030
Congo (Zaïre)	Africa	4,700	2,900
Paraná	South America	4,500	2,800
Amur (Heilong Jiang)	Asia	4,416	2,744
Lena	Asia	4,400	2,700
Mekong	Asia	4,200	2,600
Niger	Africa	4,200	2,600
Jenisej	Asia	4,092	2,543
Mississippi	North America	3,779	2,348
Missouri	North America	3,726	2,315
Volga	Europe	3,531	2,194
São Francisco	South America	3,199	1,988
Rio Grande	North America	3,034	1,885
Indus	Asia	2,900	1,800
Danube	Europe	2,858	1,776
Yukon	North America	2,849	1,770
Brahmaputra	Asia	2,849	1,770
Salween (Thanlwin)	Asia	2,816	1,750
Zambezi	Africa	2,700	1,700
Tocantins	South America	2,639	1,640
Orinoco	South America	2,600	1,600
Paraguay	South America	2,591	1,610
Amudarja	Asia	2,540	1,578
Murray	Australia	2,520	1,566
Ganges	Asia	2,511	1,560
Euphrates	Asia	2,430	1,510
Ural	Asia	2,428	1,509
Arkansas	North America	2,348	1,459
Colorado	North America (U.S.-Mex.)	2,334	1,450
Syrdarja	Asia	2,205	1,370
Tarim	Asia	2,137	1,328
Orange	Africa	2,100	1,300
Negro	South America	2,100	1,300
Irrawaddy (Ayeyarwady)	Asia	2,100	1,300
Red	North America	2,044	1,270
Columbia	North America	2,000	1,200
Xingu	South America	1,979	1,230
Ucayali	South America	1,963	1,220
Saskatchewan-Bow	North America	1,939	1,205
Peace	North America	1,923	1,195
Tigris	Asia	1,899	1,180
Sungari	Asia	1,835	1,140
Pechora	Europe	1,809	1,124
Limpopo	Africa	1,800	1,100
Snake	North America	1,670	1,038

Principal Islands

Island	Area km²	sq mi	Highest Point Name	m	ft
Grønland (Greenland)	2,175,600	840,000	Gunnbjørns Fjeld	3,700	12,139
New Guinea	800,000	309,000	Puncak Jaya	5,030	16,503
Borneo	744,100	287,300	Gunong Kinabalu	4,101	13,455
Madagascar	587,000	227,000	Maromokotro	2,876	9,436
Baffin Island	507,451	195,928	Unnamed	2,591	8,501
Sumatera (Sumatra)	473,606	182,860	Gunung Kerinci	3,800	12,467
Honshū	230,966	89,176	Fuji-San	3,776	12,388
Great Britain	229,978	88,795	Ben Nevis	1,343	4,406
Victoria Island	217,291	83,897	Mt. Bumpus	655	2,149
Ellesmere Island	196,236	75,767	Barbeau Peak	2,604	8,543
Sulawesi (Celebes)	189,216	73,057	Bulu Rantekombola	3,455	11,335
South Island	149,883	57,970	Mt. Cook	3,764	12,349
Jawa (Java)	132,187	51,038	Gunung Semeru	3,676	12,060
North Island	114,669	44,274	Mt. Ruapehu	2,797	9,177
Cuba	110,800	42,800	Pico Turquino	1,994	6,542
Newfoundland	108,860	42,031	Unnamed	814	2,670
Luzon	104,688	40,420	Mt. Pulog	2,930	9,613
Ísland (Iceland)	103,000	39,800	Hvannadalshnúkur	2,119	6,952
Mindanao	94,630	36,537	Mt. Apo	2,954	9,692
Ireland	84,400	32,600	Carrauntoohil	1,038	3,406
Hokkaidō	83,515	32,245	Taisetsu-Zan	2,290	7,513
Novaja Zemlja (Novaya Zemlya)	82,600	31,900	Unnamed	1,547	5,075
Sahalin, ostrov (Sakhalin)	76,400	29,500	gora Lopatina	1,609	5,279
Hispaniola	76,000	29,300	Pico Duarte	3,175	10,417
Banks Island	70,028	27,038	Unnamed	747	2,451
Tasmania	67,800	26,200	Mt. Ossa	1,617	5,305
Sri Lanka	64,600	24,900	Pidurutalagala	2,524	8,281
Devon Island	55,247	21,331	Unnamed	1,887	6,191
Tierra del Fuego, Isla Grande de	48,200	18,600	Cerro Yogan	2,469	8,100

Major Lakes

Lake	Location	Area km²	sq mi	Depth m	ft
Caspian Sea	Asia-Europe	370,990	143,240	1,025	3,363
Superior, L.	Canada-U.S.	82,100	31,700	406	1,332
Victoria, L.	Africa	69,463	26,820	85	279
Aral'skoje more (Aral Sea)	Asia	64,100	24,700	68	223
Huron, L.	Canada-U.S.	60,000	23,000	229	750
Michigan, L.	U.S.	57,800	22,300	282	924
Tanganyika, L.	Africa	31,986	12,350	1,463	4,800
Bajkal, ozero (L. Baikal)	Russia	31,500	12,200	1,620	5,315
Great Bear Lake	Canada	31,326	12,095	413	1,356
Nyasa, L.	Africa	28,878	11,150	695	2,280
Great Slave Lake	Canada	28,568	11,030	614	2,015
Erie, L.	Canada-U.S.	25,667	9,910	62	204
Winnipeg, L.	Canada	24,387	9,416	28	92
Ontario, L.	Canada-U.S.	19,529	7,540	243	798
Balhaš, ozero (L. Balkhash)	Kazakhstan	18,300	7,100	26	85
Chad, L.	Africa	16,300	6,300	7	24
Onežskoje ozero (L. Onega)	Russia	9,720	3,753	127	417
Eyre, L.	Australia	9,500	3,700	1	4
Titicaca, Lago	Bolivia-Peru	8,300	3,200	302	990
Nicaragua, Lago de	Nicaragua	8,158	3,150	70	230
Mai-Ndombe, Lac	Zaire	8,000	3,100	11	36
Athabasca, L.	Canada	7,935	3,064	124	407
Reindeer Lake	Canada	6,650	2,568	219	720
Tônlé Sab, Bœng	Cambodia	6,500	2,500	12	39
Rudolf, L.	Ethiopia-Kenya	6,405	2,473	219	720
Torrens, L.	Australia	5,900	2,300	*	*
Albert, L.	Uganda-Zaire	5,594	2,160	51	168
Vänern	Sweden	5,584	2,156	99	325

* Intermittently dry lake

Drainage Basins

Name	Continent	Area km²	sq mi
Amazon	South America	6,151,000	2,375,000
Congo (Zaïre)	Africa	3,823,000	1,476,000
Mississippi-Missouri	North America	3,230,000	1,247,000
Río de la Plata-Paraná	South America	3,100,000	1,197,000
Ob'-Irtyš	Asia	2,989,000	1,154,000
Nile	Africa	2,802,000	1,082,000
Lena	Asia	2,489,000	961,000
Amur-Argun	Asia	2,051,000	792,000
Niger	Africa	1,891,000	730,000
Yangtze (Chang Jiang)	Asia	1,826,000	705,000
Mackenzie	North America	1,572,000	607,000
Volga	Europe	1,360,000	525,000
Zambezi	Africa	1,331,000	514,000
St. Lawrence	North America	1,303,000	503,000

World Geographical Tables

Historical Population of the World

AREA	1650	1750	1800	1850	1900	1914	1920	1939	1950	1993
Europe	*100,000,000*	*140,000,000*	*190,000,000*	265,000,000	400,000,000	470,000,000	453,000,000	526,000,000	530,000,000	694,700,000
Asia	*335,000,000*	*476,000,000*	*593,000,000*	754,000,000	*932,000,000*	1,006,000,000	1,000,000,000	1,247,000,000	1,418,000,000	3,337,800,000
Africa	*100,000,000*	*95,000,000*	*90,000,000*	*95,000,000*	*118,000,000*	*130,000,000*	*140,000,000*	170,000,000	199,000,000	668,700,000
North America	*5,000,000*	*5,000,000*	*13,000,000*	39,000,000	106,000,000	141,000,000	147,000,000	186,000,000	219,000,000	438,200,000
South America	*8,000,000*	*7,000,000*	*12,000,000*	20,000,000	38,000,000	55,000,000	61,000,000	90,000,000	111,000,000	310,700,000
Oceania, incl. Australia	*2,000,000*	*2,000,000*	*2,000,000*	*2,000,000*	6,000,000	8,000,000	9,000,000	11,000,000	13,000,000	26,700,000
Australia					4,000,000	5,000,000	6,000,000	7,000,000	8,000,000	16,965,000
World	*550,000,000*	*725,000,000*	*900,000,000*	1,175,000,000	1,600,000,000	1,810,000,000	1,810,000,000	2,230,000,000	2,490,000,000	5,477,000,000

Figures in italics represent very rough estimates.

Largest Countries: Population

Country	Population 1/1/93
1. China	1,179,030,000
2. India	873,850,000
3. United States	256,420,000
4. Indonesia	186,180,000
5. Brazil	159,630,000
6. Russia	150,500,000
7. Japan	124,710,000
8. Pakistan	123,490,000
9. Bangladesh	120,850,000
10. Nigeria	91,700,000
11. Mexico	86,170,000
12. Germany	80,590,000
13. Vietnam	69,650,000
14. Philippines	65,500,000
15. Iran	60,500,000
16. Turkey	58,620,000
17. Thailand	58,030,000
18. United Kingdom	57,890,000
19. France	57,570,000
20. Egypt	57,050,000
21. Italy	56,550,000
22. Ukraine	51,990,000
23. Ethiopia	51,715,000
24. South Korea	43,660,000
25. Burma	43,070,000
26. Zaire	39,750,000
27. Spain	39,155,000
28. Poland	38,330,000
29. Colombia	34,640,000
30. South Africa	33,040,000
31. Argentina	32,950,000
32. Canada	30,530,000
33. Sudan	28,760,000
34. Tanzania	28,265,000
35. Morocco	27,005,000
36. Algeria	26,925,000
37. Kenya	26,635,000
38. Romania	23,200,000
39. Peru	22,995,000
40. North Korea	22,450,000
41. Uzbekistan	21,885,000
42. Taiwan	20,985,000
43. Nepal	20,325,000
44. Venezuela	19,085,000
45. Iraq	18,815,000

Largest Countries: Area

Country	Area km²	sq mi
1. Russia	17,075,400	6,592,849
2. Canada	9,970,610	3,849,674
3. United States	9,809,431	3,787,425
4. China	9,556,100	3,689,631
5. Brazil	8,511,996	3,286,500
6. Australia	7,682,300	2,966,155
7. India	3,203,975	1,237,062
8. Argentina	2,780,400	1,073,519
9. Kazakhstan	2,717,300	1,049,156
10. Sudan	2,505,813	967,500
11. Algeria	2,381,741	919,595
12. Zaire	2,345,095	905,446
13. Greenland	2,175,600	840,004
14. Saudi Arabia	2,149,690	830,000
15. Mexico	1,967,183	759,534
16. Indonesia	1,948,732	752,410
17. Libya	1,759,540	679,362
18. Iran	1,638,057	632,457
19. Mongolia	1,566,500	604,829
20. Peru	1,285,216	496,225
21. Chad	1,284,000	495,755
22. Niger	1,267,000	489,191
23. Mali	1,248,574	482,077
24. Angola	1,246,700	481,354
25. Ethiopia	1,157,603	446,953
26. Colombia	1,141,748	440,831
27. South Africa	1,123,226	433,680
28. Bolivia	1,098,581	424,165
29. Mauritania	1,025,520	395,956
30. Egypt	1,001,449	386,662
31. Tanzania	945,087	364,900
32. Nigeria	923,768	356,669
33. Venezuela	912,050	352,145
34. Pakistan	879,902	339,732
35. Namibia	823,144	317,818
36. Mozambique	799,380	308,642
37. Turkey	779,452	300,948
38. Chile	756,626	292,135
39. Zambia	752,614	290,586
40. Burma	676,577	261,228
41. Afghanistan	652,225	251,826
42. Somalia	637,657	246,201
43. Central African Republic	622,984	240,535
44. Ukraine	603,700	233,090
45. Madagascar	587,041	226,658

Smallest Countries: Population

Country	Population 1/1/93
1. Vatican City	800
2. Niue	1,700
3. Anguilla	7,000
4. Nauru	10,000
Tuvalu	10,000
5. Palau	16,000
6. Cook Islands	18,000
7. San Marino	23,000
8. Liechtenstein	30,000
9. Monaco	31,000
10. St. Christopher-Nevis	40,000
11. Northern Mariana Islands	48,000
12. Faeroe Islands	49,000
13. Marshall Islands	51,000
14. Andorra	56,000
15. Greenland	57,000
16. Guernsey	58,000
17. Aruba	65,000
18. Isle of Man	70,000
Seychelles	70,000
19. Kiribati	76,000
20. Antigua and Barbuda	77,000
21. Jersey	85,000
22. Dominica	88,000
23. Grenada	97,000
24. Tonga	103,000
25. St. Vincent and the Grenadines	116,000
26. Micronesia, Federated States of	117,000
27. Sao Tome and Principe	134,000
28. St. Lucia	153,000
29. Vanuatu	157,000
30. Belize	186,000
31. Netherlands Antilles	191,000
32. Cyprus, North	193,000
33. Western Samoa	197,000
34. Maldives	235,000
35. Barbados	258,000
36. Iceland	260,000
37. Bahamas	265,000
38. Brunei	273,000
39. Malta	360,000
40. Solomon Islands	366,000
41. Luxembourg	392,000
42. Equatorial Guinea	394,000
43. Djibouti	396,000

Smallest Countries: Area

Country	Area km²	sq mi
1. Vatican City	0.4	0.2
2. Monaco	1.9	0.7
3. Nauru	21	8.1
4. Tuvalu	26	10
5. San Marino	61	24
6. Guernsey	78	30
7. Anguilla	91	35
8. Jersey	116	45
9. Liechtenstein	160	62
10. Marshall Islands	181	70
11. Aruba	193	75
12. Cook Islands	236	91
13. Niue	258	100
14. St. Christopher-Nevis	269	104
15. Maldives	298	115
16. Malta	316	122
17. Grenada	344	133
18. St. Vincent and the Grenadines	388	150
19. Barbados	430	166
20. Antigua and Barbuda	442	171
21. Andorra	453	175
Seychelles	453	175
22. Northern Mariana Islands	477	184
23. Palau	508	196
24. Isle of Man	572	221
25. St. Lucia	616	238
26. Singapore	636	246
27. Bahrain	691	267
28. Micronesia, Federated States of	702	271
29. Tonga	747	288
30. Dominica	790	305
31. Netherlands Antilles	800	309
32. Kiribati	811	313
33. Sao Tome and Principe	964	372
34. Faeroe Islands	1,399	540
35. Mauritius	2,040	788
36. Comoros	2,235	863
37. Luxembourg	2,586	998
38. Western Samoa	2,831	1,093
39. Cyprus, North	3,355	1,295
40. Cape Verde	4,033	1,557
41. Trinidad and Tobago	5,128	1,980
42. Brunei	5,765	2,226
43. Cyprus	5,896	2,276
44. Venda	6,198	2,393

Highest Population Densities

Country	Density per km²	sq mi	Country	Density per km²	sq mi
1. Monaco	16,316	44,286	16. Tuvalu	385	1,000
2. Singapore	4,421	11,431	17. San Marino	377	958
3. Vatican City	2,000	4,000	18. Netherlands	363	940
4. Malta	1,139	2,951	19. Aruba	337	867
5. Bangladesh	839	2,174	20. Lebanon	333	864
6. Bahrain	812	2,101	21. Japan	330	855
7. Maldives	789	2,043	22. Belgium	329	851
8. Guernsey	744	1,933	23. St. Vincent and the Grenadines	299	773
9. Jersey	733	1,889	24. Rwanda	288	745
10. Barbados	600	1,554	25. Grenada	282	729
11. Taiwan	583	1,510	Marshall Islands	282	729
12. Mauritius	537	1,391	26. Sri Lanka	274	711
13. Nauru	476	1,235	27. India	273	706
14. Korea, South	441	1,142	28. El Salvador	268	694
15. Puerto Rico	395	1,022	29. Trinidad and Tobago	255	660

Lowest Population Densities

Country	Density per km²	sq mi	Country	Density per km²	sq mi
1. Greenland	...	0.1	16. Niue	6.6	17
2. Mongolia	1.5	3.9	17. Bolivia	6.7	17
3. Namibia	1.9	5.0	18. Mali	7.0	18
4. Mauritania	2.0	5.3	19. Congo	7.1	18
5. Australia	2.2	5.7	20. Saudi Arabia	7.4	19
6. Botswana	2.4	6.1	21. Oman	7.6	20
7. Iceland	2.5	6.5	22. Turkmenistan	8.0	21
Suriname	2.5	6.5	23. Belize	8.1	21
8. Libya	2.6	6.7	Papua New Guinea	8.1	21
9. Canada	3.1	7.9	24. Angola	8.6	22
10. Guyana	3.4	8.9	25. Russia	8.8	23
11. Chad	4.1	11	26. Somalia	9.4	24
12. Gabon	4.2	11	27. Algeria	11	29
13. Central African Republic	4.9	13	28. Norway	11	29
14. Kazakhstan	6.3	16	29. Zambia	11	29
15. Niger	6.5	17			

... Less than 0.1

Major Metropolitan Areas of the World

This table lists the major metropolitan areas of the world according to their estimated population on January 1, 1993. For convenience in reference, the areas are grouped by major region with the total for each region given. The number of areas by population classification is given in parentheses with each size group.

For ease of comparison, each metropolitan area has been defined by Rand McNally according to consistent rules. A metropolitan area includes a central city, neighboring communities linked to it by continuous built-up areas, and more distant communities if the bulk of their population is supported by commuters to the central city. Some metropolitan areas have more than one central city; in such cases each central city is listed.

SIZE	ANGLO AMERICA	LATIN AMERICA	WESTERN EUROPE	EASTERN EUROPE/ RUSSIA	WEST ASIA	EAST ASIA	AFRICA/OCEANIA
Over 15,000,000 (6)	New York	Ciudad de México (Mexico City) São Paulo				Ōsaka-Kōbe-Kyōto Sŏul (Seoul) Tōkyō-Yokohama	
10,000,000- 15,000,000 (13)	Los Angeles	Buenos Aires Rio de Janeiro	London Paris	Moskva (Moscow)	Bombay Calcutta Delhi-New Delhi	Jakarta Manila Shanghai	Al-Qāhirah (Cairo)
5,000,000- 10,000,000 (21)	Chicago Philadelphia-Trenton- Wilmington San Francisco- Oakland-San Jose	Lima Santa Fe de Bogotá Santiago	Essen-Dortmund- Duisburg (Ruhr Area)	Sankt-Peterburg (St. Petersburg)	Dhaka (Dacca) İstanbul Karāchi Madras Tehrān	Beijing (Peking) Krung Thep (Bangkok) Nagoya Tianjin (Tientsin) T'aipei Victoria (Hong Kong)	Johannesburg Lagos
3,000,000- 5,000,000 (37)	Boston Dallas-Fort Worth Detroit-Windsor Houston Miami-Fort Lauderdale Montréal San Diego-Tijuana Toronto Washington	Belo Horizonte Caracas Guadalajara Porto Alegre	Barcelona Berlin Madrid Milano (Milan) Roma (Rome)	Athínai (Athens) Kijev (Kiev)	Ahmadābād Baghdād Bangalore Hyderābād Lahore	Guangzhou (Canton) Pusan Shenyang (Mukden) Singapore Thanh Pho Ho Chi Minh (Saigon) Wuhan Yangon (Rangoon)	Al-Iskandarīyah (Alexandria) Casablanca Kinshasa Melbourne Sydney
2,000,000- 3,000,000 (64)	Atlanta Baltimore Cleveland Minneapolis-St. Paul Phoenix Pittsburgh St. Louis Seattle-Tacoma	Fortaleza La Habana (Havana) Medellín Monterrey Recife Salvador San Juan Santo Domingo	Amsterdam Birmingham Bruxelles (Brussels) Frankfurt am Main Hamburg Leeds-Bradford Lisboa (Lisbon) Liverpool Manchester München (Munich) Napoli (Naples) Stuttgart Wien (Vienna)	București (Bucharest) Budapest Char'kov (Kharkov) Doneck-Makejevka Katowice-Bytom- Gliwice Nižnij Novgorod (Gorkiy) Warszawa (Warsaw)	Ankara Baku Colombo Dimashq (Damascus) İzmir Kānpur Pune (Poona) Taškent	Bandung Changchun Chengdu (Chengtu) Chongqing (Chungking) Dalian (Dairen) Fukuoka Harbin Kuala Lumpur Nanjing (Nanking) P'yongyang Sapporo-Otaru Surabaya Taegu Xi'an (Sian)	Abidjan Adis Abeba Al-Khartūm-Umm Durmān (Khartoum- Omdurman) Cape Town Durban El Djazaïr (Algiers)
1,500,000- 2,000,000 (48)	Cincinnati Denver El Paso-Ciudad Juárez Portland Vancouver	Brasília Cali Curitiba Guatemala Guayaquil Montevideo San José	Glasgow København (Copenhagen) Köln (Cologne) Mannheim Stockholm	Beograd (Belgrade) Dnepropetrovsk Jekaterinburg (Sverdlovsk) Minsk Novosibirsk	'Amman Ar-Riyad (Riyadh) Bayrūt (Beirut) Chittagong Faisalabad Halab (Aleppo) Jaipur Jiddah Kābol (Kabul) Lucknow Mashhad Nāgpur Rāwalpindi- Islāmābād Surat Tbilisi Tel Aviv-Yafo	Hiroshima-Kure Jinan (Tsinan) Kaohsiung Kitakyūshū- Shimonoseki Medan Qingdao (Tsingtao) Taiyuan	Accra Dakar Rabat-Salé
1,000,000- 1,500,000 (119)	Buffalo-Niagara Falls- St. Catharines Columbus Hartford-New Britain Indianapolis Kansas City Milwaukee New Orleans Norfolk-Newport News Sacramento St. Petersburg- Clearwater San Antonio	Asunción Barranquilla Belém Campinas Córdoba Goiânia La Paz Manaus Maracaibo Puebla Quito Rosario San Salvador Santos Valencia Vitória	Antwerpen (Antwerp) Dublin (Baile Átha Cliath) Düsseldorf Hannover Helsinki Lille-Roubaix Lyon Marseille Newcastle-Sunderland Nürnberg Porto Rotterdam Sevilla Torino (Turin) Valencia	Čel'abinsk (Chelyabinsk) Łódź Kazan' Kraków Krasnojarsk Odessa Omsk Perm Praha (Prague) Rīga Rostov-na-Donu Samara (Kuybyshev) Saratov Sofija (Sofia) Ufa Volgograd Voronež	Adana Agra Allahābād Al-Kuwayt (Kuwait) Alma-Ata Asansol Bhopāl Cochin Coimbatore Esfahān Indore Jerevan Ludhiāna Madurai Patna Shīrāz Tabrīz Vadodara Vārānasi (Benares) Vishākhapatnam	Anshan Baotou Changsha Fushun Guiyang Hangzhou Ha Noi Jilin (Kirin) Kunming Kwangju Lanzhou Nanchang Palembang Qiqihar (Tsitsihar) Semarang Sendai Shijiazhuang Shizuoka-Shimizu Taejŏn Tangshan Ujung Pandang Ürümqi Zhengzhou Zibo	Adelaide Antananarivo Brisbane Dar es Salaam Douala Harare Ibadan Kampala Luanda Lusaka Maputo Nairobi Perth Pretoria Ţarābulus (Tripoli) Tunis
Total by region (308)	38	42	41	33	57	64	33

A 11

Populations of Major Cities

The largest and most important of the world's major cities are listed in the following table. Also included are some smaller cities because of their regional significance.

Local official name forms have been used throughout the table. When a commonly used "conventional" name form exists, it has been featured within parentheses, following the official name. Each city name is followed by the English name of its country. Names in the United States, the United Kingdom, and Canada are further distinguished by the name of the state, region, or province in which they are located.

Many cities have population figures within parentheses following the country name. These are metropolitan populations, comprising the central city and its suburbs. When a city is within the metropolitan area of another city the name of the metropolitan central city is specified in parentheses preceded by a *. The symbol † identifies a political district population which includes some rural population. For these cities the estimated city population has been based upon the district figure.

The population of each city has been dated for ease of comparison. The date is followed by a letter designating: Census (C) or Official Estimate (E).

City and Country	Population	Date
Aachen, Germany (535,000) . . .	233,255	89E
Ābādān, Iran	296,081	76C
Abidjan, Ivory Coast	1,950,000	83E
Abū Ẓaby (Abu Dhabi), United Arab Emirates	242,975	80C
Acapulco [de Juárez], Mexico	301,902	80C
Accra, Ghana (1,250,000)	949,113	87C
Adana, Turkey	931,555	90C
Ad Dawḥah (Doha), Qatar (310,000)	217,294	86E
Addis Ababa, see Ādīs Ābeba		
Adelaide, Australia (1,036,747)	12,340	89E
Aden, see Baladiyad ʿAdan		
Ādīs Ābeba (Addis Ababa), Ethiopia (1,760,000)	1,686,300	88E
Agana, Guam (44,000)	896	80C
Āgra, India (955,684)	899,195	91C
Aguascalientes, Mexico	293,152	80C
Ahmadābād, India (3,297,655)	2,872,865	91C
Ahvāz, Iran	579,826	86C
Akita, Japan	302,359	90C
Akron, Oh., U.S. (*Cleveland)	223,019	90C
Albany, N.Y., U.S. (874,304) . . .	101,082	90C
Al Baṣrah, Iraq	616,700	85E
Albuquerque, N.M., U.S. (480,557)	384,736	90C
Aleppo, see Halab		
Alexandria, see Al Iskandarīyah		
Algiers, see Al Jazāʾir		
Al Iskandarīyah (Alexandria), Egypt (3,350,000)	2,917,327	86C
Al Jazāʾir (Algiers), Algeria (2,547,983)	1,507,241	87E
Al Jīzah (Giza), Egypt (*Al Qāhirah)	1,870,508	86C
Al Kharṭūm (Khartoum), Sudan (1,450,000)	476,218	83C
Al Kuwayt (Kuwait), Kuwait (1,375,000)	44,335	85C
Allahābād, India (858,213)	806,447	91C
Alma-Ata, Kazakhstan (1,190,000)	1,128,000	89C
Al Madīnah (Medina), Saudi Arabia	290,000	80E
Al Maḥallah al Kubrā, Egypt	358,844	86C
Al Manāmah (Manama), Bahrain (224,643)	115,054	81C
Al Manṣūrah, Egypt (375,000)	316,870	86C
Al Mawṣil (Mosul), Iraq	570,926	85E
Al Qāhirah (Cairo), Egypt (9,300,000)	6,052,836	86C
Amagasaki, Japan (*Ōsaka) . . .	498,998	90C
ʿAmmān, Jordan (1,450,000) . . .	936,300	89E
Amritsar, India	709,456	91C
Amsterdam, Netherlands (1,860,000)	696,500	89E
Anchorage, Ak., U.S.	226,338	90C
Andorra la Vella, Andorra	20,437	91E
Ankara, Turkey (2,650,000) . . .	2,553,209	90C
Annaba (Bône), Algeria	305,526	87C
Anshan, China	1,330,000	88E
Antananarivo, Madagascar . . .	663,000	85E
Antwerpen (Antwerp), Belgium (1,100,000)	479,748	87E
Apia, Western Samoa	33,170	81C
Arequipa, Peru (446,942)	108,023	81C
Arhangelsk, Russia	416,000	89C
Arnhem, Netherlands (296,362)	129,000	89E
Ar Riyāḍ (Riyadh), Saudi Arabia	1,250,000	80E
Asansol, India (763,845)	261,836	91C
Ašhabad, Turkmenistan	398,000	89C
As Suways (Suez), Egypt	326,820	86C
Astrahan, Russia	509,000	89C

City and Country	Population	Date
Asunción, Paraguay (700,000)	477,100	85E
Athínai (Athens), Greece (3,027,331)	885,737	81C
Atlanta, Ga., U.S. (2,833,511)	394,017	90C
Auckland, New Zealand (850,000)	149,046	86C
Augsburg, Germany (405,000)	247,731	89E
Austin, Tx., U.S. (781,572)	465,622	90C
Baghdād, Iraq	3,841,268	87C
Bakhtarān, Iran	560,514	86C
Baku, Azerbaijan (2,020,000)	1,150,000	89C
Baladiyat ʿAdan (Aden), Yemen (318,000)	176,100	84E
Balikpapan, Indonesia (†279,852)	208,040	80C
Baltimore, Md., U.S. (2,382,172)	736,014	90C
Bamako, Mali	646,163	87C
Bandar Seri Begawan, Brunei (64,000)	22,777	81C
Bandung, Indonesia (1,800,000)	1,633,000	85E
Bangalore, India (4,086,548) . . .	2,650,659	91C
Banghāzī (Benghazi), Libya . . .	466,250	88E
Bangkok, see Krung Thep		
Bangui, Cen. Afr. Rep.	473,817	84E
Banjul, Gambia (95,000)	44,188	83C
Barcelona, Spain (4,040,000)	1,714,355	88E
Barnaul, Russia (665,000)	602,000	89C
Barquisimeto, Venezuela	497,635	81C
Barranquilla, Colombia (1,140,000)	899,781	85C
Basel, Switzerland (575,000) . . .	169,587	90E
Basse-Terre, Guadeloupe (26,000)	13,656	82C
Basseterre, St. Chris.-Nevis . . .	14,725	80C
Baton Rouge, La., U.S. (528,264)	219,531	90C
Bayrūt (Beirut), Lebanon (1,675,000)	509,000	82E
Beijing (Peking), China (7,320,000)	6,710,000	88E
Beirut, see Bayrūt		
Belém, Brazil (1,200,000)	1,116,578	85E
Belfast, N. Ire., U.K. (685,000)	303,800	87E
Belgrade, see Beograd		
Belize City, Belize	47,000	85E
Belmopan, Belize	4,500	85E
Belo Horizonte, Brazil (2,950,000)	2,114,429	85E
Benares, see Vārānasi		
Bengbu, China (†612,600)	403,900	86E
Benxi, China	860,000	88E
Beograd (Belgrade), Yugoslavia (1,400,000)	1,130,000	87E
Bergamo, Italy (345,000)	118,959	87E
Berlin, Germany (3,825,000) . . .	3,352,848	89E
Bern (Berne), Switzerland (298,363)	134,393	90E
Bhopāl, India	1,063,662	91C
Bielefeld, Germany (515,000)	311,946	89E
Bilbao, Spain (985,000)	384,733	88E
Billings, Mt., U.S. (113,419) . . .	81,151	90C
Birmingham, Eng., U.K. (2,675,000)	1,013,995	81C
Birmingham, Al., U.S. (907,810)	265,968	90C
Biškek Kirghizia	616,000	89C
Bissau, Guinea-Bissau	125,000	88E
Blackpool, Eng., U.K. (280,000)	146,297	81C
Bloemfontein, South Africa (235,000)	104,381	85C
Bogor, Indonesia (560,000) . . .	246,946	80C
Boise, Id., U.S. (205,775)	125,738	90C
Bologna, Italy (525,000)	432,406	87E
Bombay, India (12,571,720) . . .	9,909,547	91C
Bonn, Germany (570,000)	282,190	89E
Bordeaux, France (640,012) . . .	208,159	82C

City and Country	Population	Date
Boston, Ma., U.S. (4,171,643)	574,283	90C
Brasília, Brazil	1,567,709	85E
Bratislava, Slovakia	442,999	90E
Braunschweig, Germany (330,000)	253,794	89E
Brazzaville, Congo	585,812	84C
Bremen, Germany (800,000) . . .	5,325,058	89E
Brest, France (201,145)	156,060	82C
Bridgetown, Barbados (115,000)	7,466	80C
Brighton, Eng., U.K. (420,000)	134,581	81C
Brisbane, Australia (1,273,511)	744,828	89E
Bristol, Eng., U.K. (630,000) . . .	413,861	81C
Bruxelles / Brussel (Brussels), Belgium (2,385,000)	136,920	87E
Bucaramanga, Colombia (550,000)	352,326	85C
Bucureşti (Bucharest), Romania (2,275,000)	1,989,823	86E
Budapest, Hungary (2,565,000)	2,016,132	90E
Buenos Aires, Argentina (10,750,000)	2,922,829	80C
Buffalo, N.Y., U.S. (1,189,288)	328,123	90C
Bujumbura, Burundi	273,000	86E
Bulawayo, Zimbabwe	429,000	83E
Burlington, Vt., U.S. (131,439)	39,127	90C
Bursa, Turkey	838,323	90C
Būr Saʿīd (Port Said), Egypt . . .	399,793	86C
Cádiz, Spain (240,000)	156,591	88E
Cagliari, Italy (305,000)	220,574	87E
Cairo, see Al Qāhirah		
Calcutta, India (11,605,833) . . .	4,388,262	91C
Calgary, Alta., Can. (671,326)	636,104	86C
Cali, Colombia (1,400,000) . . .	1,350,565	85C
Calicut (Kozhikode), India (800,913)	419,531	91C
Callao, Peru (*Lima)	264,133	81C
Campinas, Brazil (1,125,000)	841,016	85E
Canberra, Australia (271,362)	247,194	86C
Cannes, France (295,525)	72,259	82C
Canton, see Guangzhou		
Cape Town, South Africa (1,790,000)	776,617	85C
Caracas, Venezuela (3,600,000)	1,816,901	81C
Cardiff, Wales, U.K. (625,000)	262,313	81C
Cartagena, Colombia	531,426	85C
Casablanca, Morocco (2,475,000)	2,139,204	82C
Castries, St. Lucia	53,933	87E
Catania, Italy (550,000)	372,486	87E
Cayenne, French Guiana	38,091	82C
Cebu, Philippines (720,000) . . .	610,000	90C
Čeljabinsk (Chelyabinsk), Russia (1,325,000)	1,143,000	89C
Chandīgarh, India (574,646) . . .	502,992	91C
Changchun, China (†2,000,000)	1,822,000	88E
Changshu, China (†998,000) . . .	281,300	86E
Changzhou, China	522,700	86E
Chaoʿan, China (†1,214,500) . . .	265,400	86E
Charleston, W.V., U.S. (250,454)	57,287	90C
Charlotte, N.C., U.S. (1,162,093)	395,934	90C
Chattanooga, Tn., U.S. (433,210)	152,466	90C
Chengdu, China (†2,960,000)	1,884,000	88E
Chiba, Japan (*Tōkyō)	829,467	90C
Chicago, Il., U.S. (8,065,633)	2,783,726	90C
Chiclayo, Peru (279,527)	213,095	81C
Chihuahua, Mexico	385,603	80C
Chittagong, Bangladesh (1,391,877)	980,000	81C
Chʿŏngjin, N. Korea	490,000	81E
Chongqing (Chungking), China (†2,890,000)	2,502,000	88E
Chŏnju, S. Korea	426,473	85C

City and Country	Population	Date
Christchurch, New Zealand (320,000)	168,200	86C
Chungking, see Chongqing		
Cincinnati, Oh., U.S. (1,744,124)	364,040	90C
Ciudad de México, Mexico (14,100,000)	8,831,079	80C
Ciudad Juárez, Mexico (*El Paso)	544,496	80C
Clermont-Ferrand, France (256,189)	147,361	82C
Cleveland, Oh., U.S. (2,759,823)	505,616	90C
Cochin, India (1,139,543)	564,038	91C
Coimbatore, India (1,135,549)	853,402	91C
Cologne, see Köln		
Colombo, Sri Lanka (2,050,000)	683,000	86E
Columbia, S.C., U.S. (453,331)	98,052	90C
Columbus, Oh., U.S. (1,377,419)	632,910	90C
Conakry, Guinea	800,000	86E
Concepción, Chile (675,000)	267,891	82C
Constanța, Romania	327,676	86E
Constantine, Algeria	440,842	87C
Córdoba, Argentina (1,070,000)	993,055	80C
Córdoba, Spain	302,301	88E
Cotonou, Benin	478,000	84E
Coventry, Eng., U.K. (645,000)	318,718	81C
Cúcuta, Colombia (445,000)	379,478	85C
Cuernavaca, Mexico	192,770	80C
Curitiba, Brazil (1,700,000)	1,279,205	85E
Cusco, Peru (184,550)	89,563	81C
Dakar, Senegal	1,447,642	88C
Dalian (Lüda), China	2,280,000	88E
Dallas, Tx., U.S. (3,885,415)	1,006,877	90C
Dandong, China	579,800	86E
Danzig, see Gdańsk		
Daqing, China (†880,000)	640,000	88E
Dar es Salaam, Tanzania	1,300,000	84E
Darmstadt, Germany (305,000)	136,067	89E
Datong, China (†1,040,000)	810,000	88E
Davao, Philippines (*850,000)	569,300	90C
Dayton, Oh., U.S. (951,270)	182,044	90C
Delhi, India (8,375,188)	7,174,755	91C
Denver, Co., U.S. (1,848,319)	467,610	90C
Des Moines, Ia., U.S. (392,928)	193,187	90C
Detroit, Mi., U.S. (4,665,236)	1,027,974	90C
Dhaka, Bangladesh (3,430,312)	2,365,695	81C
Dhānbād, India (817,549)	151,334	91C
Dimashq (Damascus), Syria (1,950,000)	1,326,000	88E
Djibouti, Djibouti	120,000	76E
Dnepropetrovsk, Ukraine (1,600,000)	1,179,000	89C
Doneck, Ukraine (2,200,000)	1,110,000	89C
Dongguan, China (†1,208,500)	254,900	86E
Dortmund, Germany (*Essen)	587,328	89E
Douala, Cameroon	1,029,731	86E
Dresden, Germany (670,000)	518,057	89E
Dublin (Baile Átha Cliath), Ireland (1,140,000)	502,749	86C
Duisburg, Germany (*Essen)	527,447	89E
Durban, South Africa (1,550,000)	634,301	85C
Dušanbe, Tajikistan	595,000	89C
Düsseldorf, Germany (1,190,000)	569,641	89E
Ecatepec de Morelos, Mexico (*Ciudad de México)	741,821	80C
Edinburgh, Scot., U.K. (630,000)	433,200	89E
Edmonton, Alta., Can. (785,465)	573,982	86C
El Paso, Tx., U.S. (1,211,300)	515,342	90C
Enschede, Netherlands (288,000)	145,200	89E
Erbīl, Iraq	333,903	85E
Eṣfahān (Isfahan), Iran (1,175,000)	986,753	86C
Essen, Germany (4,950,000)	620,594	89E
Faisalabad, Pakistan	1,104,209	81C
Fargo, N.D., U.S (153,296)	74,111	90C
Fès, Morocco (535,000)	488,823	82C
Firenze (Florence), Italy (640,000)	425,835	87E
Florianópolis, Brazil (365,000)	178,400	85E
Fortaleza, Brazil (1,825,000)	1,582,414	85E
Fort-de-France, Martinique (116,017)	99,844	82C
Fort Worth, Tx., U.S. (*Dallas)	447,619	90C
Frankfurt am Main, Germany (1,855,000)	625,258	89E
Freetown, Sierra Leone (525,000)	469,776	85C
Fukuoka, Japan (1,750,000)	1,237,107	90C
Funabashi, Japan (*Tōkyō)	533,273	90C
Funafuti, Tuvalu	2,191	79C
Fushun, China	1,290,000	88E

City and Country	Population	Date
Fuxian, China (†960,700)	246,200	86E
Fuxin, China	700,000	88E
Fuzhou, China (†1,240,000)	910,000	88E
Gaborone, Botswana	107,677	87E
Gdańsk (Danzig), Poland (909,000)	461,500	89E
General Sarmiento, Argentina (*Buenos Aires)	502,926	80C
Genève (Geneva), Switzerland (470,000)	165,404	90E
Genova (Genoa), Italy (805,000)	727,427	87E
Gent (Ghent), Belgium (465,000)	233,856	87E
Georgetown, Cayman Islands	13,700	88E
Georgetown, Guyana (188,000)	78,500	83E
George Town (Pinang), Malaysia (495,000)	248,241	80C
Gifu, Japan	410,318	90C
Giza, see Al Jīzah		
Glasgow, Scot., U.K. (1,800,000)	695,630	89E
Godthåb (Nûk), Greenland	12,217	90E
Goiânia, Brazil (990,000)	923,333	85E
Gorki, see Nižnij Novgorod		
Göteborg, Sweden (710,894)	431,840	90E
Granada, Spain	263,334	88E
Graz, Austria (325,000)	243,166	81C
Grenoble, France (392,021)	156,637	82C
Guadalajara, Mexico (2,325,000)	1,626,152	80C
Guadalupe, Mexico (*Monterrey)	370,524	80C
Guangzhou (Canton), China (†3,420,000)	3,100,000	88E
Guarulhos, Brazil (*São Paulo)	571,700	86E
Guatemala, Guatemala (1,400,000)	1,057,210	89E
Guayaquil, Ecuador (1,580,000)	1,572,615	87C
Guilin, China (†457,500)	342,200	86E
Guiyang, China (†1,430,000)	1,030,000	88E
Gujranwala, Pakistan (658,753)	600,993	81C
Gwalior, India (720,068)	692,982	91C
Haicheng, China (†984,800)	210,700	86E
Haikou, China (†289,600)	209,200	86E
Hai Phong, Vietnam (†1,447,523)	351,919	89C
Halab (Aleppo), Syria (1,261,000)	1,261,000	88E
Halifax, N.S., Can. (295,990)	113,577	86C
Hamamatsu, Japan	534,624	90C
Hamburg, Germany (2,225,000)	1,603,070	89E
Hamilton, Bermuda (15,000)	1,676	85E
Hamilton, Ont., Can. (557,029)	306,728	86C
Handan, China (†1,030,000)	870,000	88E
Hannover, Germany (1,000,000)	498,495	89E
Ha Noi (Hanoi), Vietnam (1,275,000)	905,939	89C
Hāora (Howrah), India (*Calcutta)	946,732	91C
Harare, Zimbabwe (890,000)	681,000	83E
Harbin, China	2,710,000	88E
Harkov, Ukraine (1,940,000)	1,611,000	89C
Hartford, Ct., U.S. (1,085,837)	139,739	90C
Havana, see La Habana		
Hefa (Haifa), Israel (435,000)	222,600	89E
Hefei, China (†930,000)	740,000	88E
Hegang, China	588,300	86E
Helsinki, Finland (1,040,000)	490,034	88E
Hibli, India	647,640	91C
Ḥims (Homs), Syria	447,000	88E
Hiroshima, Japan (1,575,000)	1,085,677	90C
Hohhot, China (†830,000)	670,000	88E
Hong Kong, see Victoria		
Honiara, Solomon Is.	30,413	86C
Honolulu, Ha., U.S. (836,231)	365,272	90C
Houston, Tx., U.S. (3,711,043)	1,630,553	90C
Huainan, China (†1,110,000)	700,000	83E
Hyderābād, India (4,280,261)	2,991,864	91C
Ibadan, Nigeria	1,144,000	87E
Ilorin, Nigeria	380,000	87E
Inch'ŏn, S. Korea (*Seoul)	1,628,000	89E
Indianapolis, In., U.S. (1,249,822)	731,327	90C
Indore, India (1,104,065)	1,086,673	91C
Irkutsk, Russia	626,000	89C
Isfahan, see Eṣfahān		
Islāmābād, Pakistan (*Rāwalpindi)	204,364	81C
Istanbul, Turkey (7,550,000)	6,748,435	90C
Iževsk, Russia	635,000	89C
İzmir, Turkey (1,900,000)	1,762,849	90C
Jabalpur, India (887,188)	739,961	91C
Jackson, Ms., U.S. (395,396)	196,637	90C
Jacksonville, Fl., U.S. (906,727)	635,230	90C
Jaipur, India (1,514,425)	1,454,678	91C

City and Country	Population	Date
Jakarta, Indonesia (10,000,000)	9,200,000	89E
Jamshedpur, India (834,535)	461,212	91C
Jaroslavl, Russia (1,620,000)	633,000	89C
Jekaterinburg, Russia (1,620,000)	1,367,000	89C
Jerevan, Armenia (1,315,000)	1,199,000	89C
Jiaozuo, China (†509,900)	335,400	86E
Jīddah, Saudi Arabia	1,300,000	80E
Jinan, China (†2,140,000)	1,546,000	88E
Jinzhou, China (†810,000)	710,000	88E
Jixi, China (†820,000)	700,000	88E
João Pessoa, Brazil (550,000)	348,500	85E
Jodhpur, India	648,621	91C
Johannesburg, South Africa (3,650,000)	632,369	85C
Kābol, Afghanistan	1,424,400	88E
Kagoshima, Japan	536,385	90C
Kaifeng, China (†629,100)	458,300	86E
Kaliningrad, Russia	401,000	89C
Kampala, Uganda	1,008,707	90E
Kano, Nigeria	538,300	87E
Kānpur, India (2,111,284)	1,958,282	91C
Kansas City, Mo., U.S. (1,566,280)	435,146	90C
Kaohsiung, Taiwan (1,845,000)	1,342,797	88E
Karāchi, Pakistan (5,300,000)	4,901,627	81C
Karaganda, Kazakhstan	614,000	89C
Karl-Marx-Stadt, Germany (450,000)	311,765	89E
Kāthmāndau, Nepal (320,000)	235,160	81C
Katowice, Poland (2,778,000)	365,800	88E
Kawasaki, Japan (*Tōkyō)	1,173,606	60C
Kayseri, Turkey	416,276	90C
Kazan, Russia (1,140,000)	1,094,000	89C
Keelung (Chilung), Taiwan	348,541	88E
Kemerovo, Russia	520,000	89C
Khartoum, see Al Kharṭum		
Khulna, Bangladesh	648,359	81C
Kiel, Germany (335,000)	240,675	89E
Kigali, Rwanda	181,600	83E
Kijev (Kiev), Ukraine (2,900,000)	2,587,000	89C
Kingston, Jamaica (770,000)	646,400	87E
Kingston-upon-Hull, Eng., U.K. (350,000)	322,144	81C
Kingstown, St. Vin. and the Gren. (28,936)	19,028	87E
Kinshasa, Zaire	3,000,000	86E
Kisangani (Stanleyville), Zaire	282,650	84C
Kišinev, Moldavia	665,000	89C
Kitakyūshū, Japan (1,525,000)	1,026,467	90C
Kitchener, Ont., Can. (311,195)	150,604	86C
Kitwe-Nkana, Zambia (283,962)	207,500	80C
Knoxville, Tn., U.S. (604,816)	165,121	90C
Kōbe, Japan (*Ōsaka)	1,477,423	90C
København (Copenhagen), Denmark (1,685,000)	466,723	90E
Köln (Cologne), Germany (1,760,000)	937,482	89E
Kowloon, Hong Kong (*Victoria)	774,781	88C
Kraków, Poland (828,000)	743,700	89E
Krasnodar, Russia	620,000	89C
Krasnojarsk, Russia	912,000	89C
Krivoj Rog, Ukraine	713,000	89C
Krung Thep (Bangkok), Thailand (7,025,000)	5,845,152	89E
Kuala Lumpur, Malaysia (1,475,000)	919,610	80C
Kujbyšev, see Samara		
Kumamoto, Japan	579,305	90C
Kumasi, Ghana (600,000)	385,192	87C
Kunming, China (†1,550,000)	1,310,000	88E
Kuwait, see Al Kuwayt		
Kwangju, S. Korea (975,000)	1,165,000	89E
Kyōto, Japan (*Ōsaka)	1,461,140	90C
Lagos, Nigeria (3,800,000)	1,213,000	87E
La Habana (Havana), Cuba (2,125,000)	2,036,800	87E
Lahore, Pakistan (3,025,000)	2,707,215	81C
Lansing, Mi., U.S. (432,674)	127,321	90C
Lanzhou, China (†1,420,000)	1,297,000	88E
La Paz, Bolivia	1,057,200	88E
La Plata, Argentina (*Buenos Aires)	477,175	80C
Las Palmas de Gran Canaria, Spain (†366,347)	319,000	88E
Las Vegas, Nv., U.S. (741,459)	258,295	90C
Lausanne, Switzerland (263,442)	122,600	90E
Leeds, Eng., U.K. (1,540,000)	445,242	81C
Le Havre, France (254,595)	199,388	82C

politan area populations are shown in parentheses.
s located within the metropolitan area of another city; for example, Kyōto, Japan is located in the Ōsaka metropolitan area
ation of entire municipality or district, including rural area.

C Census
E Official estimate

A • 13

City and Country	Population	Date
Leicester, Eng., U.K. (495,000)	324,394	81C
Leipzig, Germany (700,000)	545,307	89E
Leningrad, see Sankt-Peterburg		
León, Mexico	593,002	80C
Leshan, China (†972,300)	307,300	86E
Lexington, Ky., U.S. (348,428)	225,366	90C
Libreville, Gabon	235,700	85E
Liège, Belgium (750,000)	200,891	87E
Lille, France (1,020,000)	168,424	82C
Lilongwe, Malawi	233,973	87C
Lima, Peru (4,608,010)	371,122	81C
Linyi, China (†1,365,000)	190,000	86E
Linz, Austria (355,000)	199,910	81C
Lisboa (Lisbon), Portugal (2,250,000)	807,167	81C
Little Rock, Ar., U.S. (513,117)	175,795	90C
Liuzhou, China	680,000	88E
Liverpool, Eng., U.K. (1,525,000)	538,809	81C
Ljubljana, Slovenia (†316,607)	233,200	87E
Łódź, Poland (1,061,000)	851,500	89E
Lomas de Zamora, Argentina (*Buenos Aires)	510,130	80C
Lomé, Togo	400,000	81C
London, Ont., Can. (342,302)	269,140	86C
London, Eng., U.K. (11,100,000)	6,574,009	81C
Los Angeles, Ca., U.S. (14,531,529)	3,485,398	90C
Louisville, Ky., U.S. (952,662)	269,063	90C
Luanda, Angola	1,459,900	89E
Lubumbashi, Zaire	543,268	84C
Lucknow, India (1,642,134)	1,592,010	91C
Ludhiāna, India	1,012,062	91C
Luoyang, China (1,090,000)	760,000	88E
Lusaka, Zambia	535,830	80C
Luxembourg, Luxembourg (136,000)	76,130	85E
Lvov, Ukraine	790,000	89C
Lyon, France (1,275,000)	413,095	82C
Madison, Wi., U.S. (367,085)	191,262	90C
Madras, India (5,361,468)	3,795,028	91C
Madrid, Spain (4,650,000)	3,102,846	88E
Madurai, India (1,093,702)	951,696	91C
Magdeburg, Germany (400,000)	290,579	89E
Magnitogorsk, Russia	440,000	89C
Makkah (Mecca), Saudi Arabia	550,000	80E
Malabo, Equatorial Guinea	31,630	83C
Málaga, Spain	574,456	88E
Malang, Indonesia	547,000	83E
Male, Maldives	46,334	85E
Malmö, Sweden (445,000)	232,908	90E
Managua, Nicaragua	682,000	85E
Manama, see Al Manāmah		
Manaus, Brazil	809,914	85E
Manchester, Eng., U.K. (2,775,000)	437,612	81C
Manchester, N.H., U.S. (147,809)	99,567	90C
Mandalay, Burma	532,949	83E
Manila, Philippines (6,800,000)	1,587,000	90C
Manizales, Colombia (330,000)	299,352	85C
Mannheim, Germany (1,400,000)	300,468	89E
Maputo, Mozambique	1,069,727	89E
Maracaibo, Venezuela	890,643	81C
Mar del Plata, Argentina	414,696	80C
Mariupol', Ukraine	517,000	89C
Marrakech, Morocco (535,000)	439,728	82C
Marseille, France (1,225,000)	874,436	82C
Maseru, Lesotho	109,382	86C
Masqaṭ (Muscat), Oman	50,000	81E
Mbabane, Swaziland	38,290	86C
Mbuji-Mayi, Zaire	423,363	84C
Medan, Indonesia	2,110,000	85E
Medellín, Colombia (2,095,000)	1,468,089	85C
Medina, see Al Madīnah		
Meknès, Morocco (375,000)	319,783	82C
Melbourne, Australia (3,039,100)	55,300	89E
Memphis, Tn., U.S. (981,747)	610,337	90C
Mendoza, Argentina (650,000)	119,088	80C
Mexicali, Mexico (365,000)	341,559	80C
Mexico City, see Ciudad de México		
Miami, Fl., U.S. (3,192,582)	358,548	90C
Middlesbrough (Teesside), Eng., U.K. (580,000)	158,516	81C
Milano (Milan), Italy (3,750,000)	1,495,260	87E
Milwaukee, Wi., U.S. (1,607,183)	628,088	90C
Minneapolis, Mn., U.S. (2,464,124)	368,383	90C
Minsk, Byelorussia (1,650,000)	1,589,000	89C
Mobile, Al., U.S. (476,923)	196,278	90C
Mombasa, Kenya	537,000	90E

City and Country	Population	Date
Mönchengladbach, Germany (410,000)	252,910	89E
Monrovia, Liberia	465,000	86E
Monterrey, Mexico (2,015,000)	1,090,009	80C
Montevideo, Uruguay (1,550,000)	1,251,647	85C
Montgomery, Al., U.S. (292,517)	187,106	90C
Montréal, Que., Can. (2,921,357)	1,015,420	86C
Morón, Argentina (*Buenos Aires)	598,420	80C
Moroni, Comoros	23,432	90C
Moskva (Moscow), Russia (13,100,000)	8,769,000	89C
Mudanjiang, China	650,000	88E
Multān, Pakistan (732,070)	696,316	81C
München (Munich), Germany (1,955,000)	1,211,617	89E
Münster, Germany	248,919	89E
Muqdisho (Mogadishu), Somalia	600,000	84E
Murcia, Spain (†314,124)	149,800	88E
Murmansk, Russia	468,000	89C
Mysore, India (652,246)	480,006	91C
Naberežnyje Čelny (Brežnev), Russia	501,000	89C
Nagasaki, Japan	444,616	90C
Nagoya, Japan (4,800,000)	2,154,664	90C
Nāgpur, India (1,661,409)	1,622,225	91C
Nairobi, Kenya	1,505,000	90E
Nanchang, China (†1,260,000)	1,090,000	88E
Nancy, France (306,982)	96,317	82C
Nanjing (Nanking), China	2,390,000	88E
Nanning, China (†1,000,000)	720,000	88E
Nantes, France (464,857)	240,539	82C
Napoli (Naples), Italy (2,875,000)	1,204,211	87E
Nashville, Tn., U.S. (985,026)	487,969	90C
Nassau, Bahamas	135,000	82E
Natal, Brazil	510,106	85E
N'Djamena, Chad	500,000	88E
Netzahualcóyotl, Mexico (*Ciudad de México)	1,341,230	80C
Newark, N.J., U.S. (*New York)	275,221	91C
Newcastle, Australia (425,610)	130,940	89E
Newcastle upon Tyne, Eng., U.K. (1,300,000)	199,064	81C
New Delhi, India (*Delhi)	294,149	91C
New Kowloon, Hong Kong (*Victoria)	1,526,910	88C
New Orleans, La., U.S. (1,238,816)	496,938	90C
Newport, Wales, U.K. (310,000)	115,896	81C
New York, N.Y., U.S. (18,087,251)	7,322,564	90C
Niamey, Niger	398,265	88C
Nice, France (449,496)	337,085	82C
Nicosia, Cyprus (185,000)	48,221	82E
Nikolajev, Ukraine	503,000	89C
Ningbo, China (†1,050,000)	570,000	88E
Niterói, Brazil (*Rio de Janeiro)	441,684	85E
Nižnij Novgorod, Russia (2,025,000)	1,438,000	89C
Norfolk, Va., U.S. (1,396,107)	261,229	90C
North York, Ont., Can. (*Toronto)	556,297	86C
Nottingham, Eng., U.K. (655,000)	273,300	81C
Nouakchott, Mauritania	285,000	87E
Nouméa, New Caledonia (88,000)	65,110	89C
Nova Iguaçu, Brazil (*Rio de Janeiro)	592,800	85E
Novokuzneck, Russia	600,000	89C
Novosibirsk, Russia (1,600,000)	1,436,000	89C
Nuku'alofa, Tonga	21,265	86C
Nürnberg, Germany (1,030,000)	480,078	89E
Odessa, Ukraine (1,185,000)	1,115,000	89C
Ogbomosho, Nigeria	582,900	87E
Okayama, Japan	593,742	90C
Oklahoma City, Ok., U.S. (958,839)	444,719	90C
Omaha, Nb., U.S. (618,262)	335,796	90C
Omdurman, see Umm Durmān		
Omsk, Russia (1,175,000)	1,148,000	89C
Oran, Algeria	628,558	87C
Orenburg, Russia	547,000	89C
Orlando, Fl., U.S. (1,072,748)	164,693	91C
Orūmīyeh, Iran	300,746	86C
Ōsaka, Japan (16,450,000)	2,623,831	90C
Osasco, Brazil (*São Paulo)	591,568	85E
Oshogbo, Nigeria	380,800	87E
Oslo, Norway (720,000)	452,415	87E
Ostrava, Czechoslovakia (760,000)	331,557	90E
Ottawa, Ont., Can. (819,263)	300,763	86C
Ouagadougou, Burkina Faso	441,514	85C

City and Country	Population	Date
Palembang, Indonesia	874,000	83E
Palermo, Italy	723,732	87E
Palma, Spain (†314,608)	249,000	88E
Panamá, Panama (770,000)	411,549	90C
Papeete, French Polynesia (80,000)	23,555	88C
Paramaribo, Suriname (296,000)	241,000	88E
Paris, France (9,775,000)	2,078,900	87E
Patna, India (1,098,572)	916,980	91C
Peking, see Beijing		
Penza, Russia	543,000	89C
Perm, Russia (1,160,000)	1,091,000	89C
Perth, Australia (1,158,387)	82,413	89E
Peshāwar, Pakistan (566,248)	506,896	81C
Philadelphia, Pa., U.S. (5,899,345)	1,585,577	90C
Phnum Pénh, Cambodia	700,000	86E
Phoenix, Az., U.S. (2,122,101)	900,013	90C
Pingxiang, China (†1,286,700)	368,700	86E
Pittsburgh, Pa., U.S. (2,242,798)	369,879	90C
Ploiești, Romania (310,000)	234,886	86E
Plovdiv, Bulgaria	364,162	89E
Pointe-à-Pitre, Guadeloupe (83,000)	25,310	82C
Port-au-Prince, Haiti (880,000)	797,000	87E
Port Elizabeth, South Africa (690,000)	272,844	85C
Port Harcourt, Nigeria	327,300	87E
Portland, Me., U.S. (215,281)	64,358	90C
Portland, Or., U.S. (1,477,895)	437,319	90C
Port-Louis, Mauritius (420,000)	139,730	87E
Port Moresby, Papua New Guinea	152,100	87E
Porto (Oporto), Portugal (1,225,000)	327,368	81C
Porto Alegre, Brazil (2,600,000)	1,272,121	85E
Port of Spain, Trinidad and Tobago (370,000)	50,878	90C
Porto-Novo, Benin	164,000	84E
Port Said, see Būr Sa'īd		
Portsmouth, Eng., U.K. (485,000)	174,218	81C
Port-Vila, Vanuatu (23,000)	18,905	89C
Poznań, Poland (672,000)	586,500	89E
Praha (Prague), Czech Republic (1,325,000)	1,215,656	90E
Praia, Cape Verde	61,797	90C
Pretoria, South Africa (960,000)	443,059	85C
Providence, R.I., U.S. (1,141,510)	160,728	90C
Puebla [de Zaragoza], Mexico (1,055,000)	835,759	90C
Pune, India (2,485,014)	1,559,558	91C
Pusan, S. Korea (3,800,000)	3,773,000	89E
P'yŏngyang, N. Korea (1,600,000)	1,283,000	80E
Qingdao, China	1,300,000	88E
Qiqihar, China (†1,330,000)	1,180,000	88E
Qom, Iran	543,139	86C
Québec, Que., Can. (603,267)	164,580	86C
Quetta, Pakistan (285,719)	244,842	81C
Quezon City, Philippines (*Manila)	1,632,000	90C
Quilmes, Argentina (*Buenos Aires)	446,587	80C
Quito, Ecuador (1,300,000)	1,137,705	87C
Rabat, Morocco (980,000)	518,616	82C
Rājkot, India (651,007)	556,137	91C
Raleigh, N.C., U.S. (735,480)	207,951	90C
Rānchī, India (614,454)	598,498	91C
Rangoon, see Yangon		
Rāwalpindi, Pakistan (1,040,000)	457,091	81C
Recife, Brazil (2,625,000)	1,287,623	85E
Reno, Nv., U.S. (254,667)	133,850	90C
Reykjavík, Iceland (137,941)	93,425	87E
Ribeirão Prêto, Brazil	383,125	85E
Richmond, Va., U.S. (865,640)	203,056	90C
Rīga, Latvia (1,005,000)	915,000	89C
Rio de Janeiro, Brazil (10,150,000)	5,603,388	85E
Riverside, Ca., U.S. (*Los Angeles)	226,505	90C
Riyadh, see Ar Riyāḍ		
Rjazan, Russia	515,000	89C
Rochester, N.Y., U.S. (1,002,410)	231,636	90C
Roma (Rome), Italy (3,175,000)	2,815,457	87E
Rosario, Argentina (1,045,000)	938,120	80C
Rostov-na-Donu, Russia (1,165,000)	1,020,000	89C
Rotterdam, Netherlands (1,110,000)	576,300	89E
Rouen, France (379,879)	101,945	82C
Rouseau, Dominica	9,348	84E

City and Country	Population	Date
Sacramento, Ca., U.S. (1,481,102)	369,365	90C
Safāqis, Tunisia (310,000)	231,911	84C
Saigon, see Ho Chi Minh		
St. Catharines, Ont., Can. (343,258)	123,455	86C
St.-Étienne, France (317,228)	204,955	82C
St. George's, Grenada (25,000)	4,788	81C
St. John's, Antigua and Barbuda	24,359	77E
St. Louis, Mo., U.S. (2,444,099)	396,685	90C
St. Paul, Mn., U.S. (*Minneapolis)	272,235	90C
St. Petersburg, Fl., U.S. (*Tampa)	238,629	90C
Sakai, Japan (*Ōsaka)	807,859	90C
Salem, India (573,685)	363,934	91C
Salt Lake City, Ut., U.S. (1,072,227)	159,936	90C
Salvador, Brazil (2,050,000)	1,804,438	85E
Samara, Russia (1,505,000)	1,257,000	89C
Samarkand, Uzbekistan	366,000	89C
Şan'ā', Yemen	427,150	90E
San Antonio, Tx., U.S. (1,302,099)	935,933	90C
San Diego, Ca., U.S. (2,949,000)	1,110,549	90C
San Francisco, Ca., U.S. (6,253,311)	723,959	90C
San José, Costa Rica (670,000)	278,600	88C
San Jose, Ca., U.S. (*San Francisco)	782,248	90C
San Juan, Puerto Rico (1,775,260)	424,600	80C
Sankt-Peterburg, Russia (5,825,000)	4,456,000	89C
San Luis Potosí, Mexico (470,000)	362,371	80C
San Miguel de Tucumán, Argentina (525,000)	392,888	80C
San Salvador, El Salvador (920,000)	462,652	85E
San Sebastián, Spain (285,000)	177,622	88E
Santa Fe de Bogotá, Colombia (4,260,000)	3,982,941	85C
Santiago, Chile (4,100,000)	232,667	82C
Santo André, Brazil (São Paulo)	635,129	85E
Santo Domingo, Dominican Rep.	1,313,172	81C
Santos, Brazil (1,065,000)	460,100	85E
São Bernardo do Campo, Brazil (*São Paulo)	562,485	85E
São Luís, Brazil (600,000)	227,900	85E
São Paulo, Brazil (15,175,000)	10,063,110	85E
São Tomé, Sao Tome and Prin.	17,380	70C
Sapporo, Japan (1,900,000)	1,671,765	90C
Sarajevo, Bosnia and Herzegovina (†479,688)	341,200	87E
Saratov, Russia (1,155,000)	905,000	89C
Sargodha, Pakistan (291,362)	231,895	81C
Savannah, Ga., U.S. (242,622)	137,560	90C
Scarborough, Ont., Can. (*Toronto)	484,676	86C
Seattle, Wa., U.S. (2,559,164)	516,259	90C
Semarang, Indonesia	1,206,000	83E
Semipalatinsk, Kazakhstan	334,000	89C
Sendai, Japan (1,175,000)	918,378	90C
Seoul, see Sŏul		
Sevilla (Seville), Spain (945,000)	663,132	88E
's-Gravenhage (The Hague), Netherlands (770,000)	443,900	89E
Shanghai, China (9,300,000)	7,220,000	88E
Shantou, China (†790,000)	560,000	88E
Sheffield, Eng., U.K. (710,000)	470,685	81C
Shenyang (Mukden), China (†4,370,000)	3,910,000	88E
Shīrāz, Iran	848,289	86C
Shizuoka, Japan (975,000)	472,199	90C
Shubrā al Khaymah, Egypt (*Al Qāhirah)	710,794	86C
Sialkot, Pakistan (302,009)	258,147	81C
Singapore, Singapore (3,025,000)	2,685,400	89E
Sioux Falls, S.D., U.S. (123,809)	100,814	90C
Sofija (Sofia), Bulgaria (1,205,000)	1,136,875	89E
Solāpur, India (620,499)	603,870	91C
Sŏul (Seoul), S. Korea (15,850,000)	10,522,000	89E
Southampton, Eng., U.K. (415,000)	211,321	81C
Soweto, South Africa (*Johannesburg)	521,948	85C
Springfield, Il., U.S. (189,550)	105,227	90C
Springfield, Ma., U.S. (529,519)	156,983	90C
Srīnagar, India (606,002)	594,775	81C
Stalingrad, see Volgograd		
Stockholm, Sweden (1,449,972)	672,187	90E
Stoke-on-Trent, Eng., U.K. (440,000)	272,446	81C
Strasbourg, France (400,000)	248,712	82C
Stuttgart, Germany (1,925,000)	562,658	89E
Suez, see As Suways		
Suichang, China (†2,216,500)	363,500	86E
Suixian, China (†1,281,600)	187,700	86E
Surabaya, Indonesia	2,345,000	85E
Surakarta, Indonesia (575,000)	491,000	83E
Surat, India (1,517,076)	149,643	91C
Suva, Fiji (141,273)	69,665	86C
Suzhou, China	740,000	88E
Swansea, Wales, U.K. (275,000)	172,433	81C
Sydney, Australia (3,623,550)	9,800	89E
Syracuse, N.Y., U.S. (659,864)	163,860	90C
Szczecin, Poland (449,000)	409,500	89E
Tabrīz, Iran	971,482	86C
Tacoma, Wa., U.S. (*Seattle)	176,664	90C
Taegu, S. Korea	2,207,000	89E
Taejŏn, S. Korea	1,041,000	89E
Tai'an, China (†1,325,400)	215,900	86E
Taichung, Taiwan	715,107	85E
Tainan, Taiwan	656,927	85E
Taipei, Taiwan (6,130,000)	2,637,100	88E
Taiyuan, China (†1,980,000)	1,700,000	88E
Tallinn, Estonia	482,000	89C
Tampa, Fl., U.S. (2,067,959)	280,015	90C
Tampico, Mexico (435,000)	267,957	80C
Tanger (Tangier), Morocco (370,000)	266,346	82C
Tangshan, China (†1,440,000)	1,080,000	88E
Ţanţā, Egypt	334,505	86C
Ţarābulus (Tripoli), Libya	591,062	88E
Taškent (Tashkent), Uzbekistan (2,325,000)	2,073,000	89C
Tbilisi, Georgia (1,460,000)	1,260,000	89C
Tegucigalpa, Honduras	551,606	88C
Tehrān, Iran (7,500,000)	6,042,584	86C
Tel Aviv-Yafo, Israel (1,735,000)	317,800	89E
Teresina, Brazil (525,000)	425,300	85E
Thanh Pho Ho Chi Minh (Saigon), Vietnam (3,300,000)	2,796,229	89C
The Hague, see 's-Gravenhage		
Thessaloníki, Greece (706,180)	406,413	81C
Thimphu, Bhutan	12,000	82E
Thunder Bay, Ont., Can. (122,217)	112,272	86C
Tianjin (Tientsin), China (†5,540,000)	4,950,000	88E
Tianshui, China (†953,200)	209,500	86E
Tijuana, Mexico (*San Diego)	429,500	80C
Tirana, Albania	238,100	89C
Tiruchchirāppalli, India (711,120)	386,628	91C
Tlalnepantla, Mexico (*Ciudad de México)	778,173	80C
Togliatti (Stavropol), Russia	630,000	89C
Tōkyō, Japan (27,700,000)	8,163,127	90C
Tomsk, Russia	502,000	89C
Torino (Turin), Italy (1,550,000)	1,035,565	87E
Toronto, Ont., Can. (3,427,168)	612,289	86C
Torreón, Mexico (575,000)	328,086	80C
Toulon, France (410,393)	179,423	82C
Toulouse, France (541,271)	347,995	82C
Tours, France (262,786)	132,209	82C
Tripoli, see Ţarābulus		
Trivandrum, India (825,682)	523,733	91C
Trujillo, Peru (354,301)	202,469	81C
Tsun Wan, Hong Kong (*Victoria)	514,241	88C
Tucson, Az., U.S. (666,880)	405,390	90C
Tula, Russia (640,000)	540,000	89C
Tulsa, Ok., U.S. (708,954)	367,302	90C
Tūnis, Tunisia (1,225,000)	596,654	84C
Tver', Russia	451,000	89C
Ufa, Russia (1,100,000)	1,083,000	89C
Ujung Pandang (Makasar), Indonesia	841,000	83E
Ulan-Bator, Mongolia	548,400	89E
Ulsan, S. Korea	551,014	85C
Umm Durmān (Omdurman), Sudan (*Khartoum)	526,287	83C
Utrecht, Netherlands (518,779)	230,700	89E
Vadodara (Baroda), India (1,115,390)	1,021,084	91C
Vaduz, Liechtenstein	4,874	90E
Valencia, Spain (1,270,000)	743,933	88E
Valletta, Malta (215,000)	9,210	89E
Valparaíso, Chile (675,000)	265,355	82C
Vancouver, B.C., Can. (1,380,729)	431,147	86C
Vārānasi (Benares), India (1,026,467)	925,962	91C
Venezia (Venice), Italy (420,000)	88,700	87E
Veracruz [Llave], Mexico (385,000)	284,822	80C
Vereeniging, South Africa (525,000)	60,584	85C
Verona, Italy	259,151	87E
Viangchan (Vientiane), Laos	377,409	85C
Victoria, B.C., Can. (255,547)	66,303	86C
Victoria, Hong Kong (4,770,000)	1,175,860	88C
Victoria, Seychelles	23,000	84E
Vienna, see Wien		
Vientiane, see Viangchan		
Vilnius, Lithuania	582,000	89C
Vishākhapatnam, India (1,051,918)	750,024	91C
Vitória, Brazil (735,000)	201,500	85E
Vladivostok, Russia	648,000	89C
Volgograd (Stalingrad), Russia (1,360,000)	999,000	89C
Volta Redonda, Brazil (375,000)	219,267	85E
Voronež, Russia	837,000	89C
Vorošilovgrad, Ukraine	497,000	89C
Warszawa (Warsaw), Poland (2,323,000)	1,651,200	89E
Washington, D.C., U.S. (3,923,574)	606,900	90C
Weifang, China (†1,042,200)	372,500	86E
Wellington, New Zealand (350,000)	137,495	86C
Wichita, Ks., U.S. (485,270)	304,011	90C
Wien (Vienna), Austria (1,875,000)	1,482,800	88E
Wiesbaden, Germany (795,000)	254,209	89E
Willemstad, Netherlands Antilles (130,000)	31,883	81C
Wilmington, De., U.S. (*Philadelphia)	71,529	90C
Windhoek, Namibia	114,500	88E
Windsor, Ont., Can. (253,988)	193,111	86C
Winnipeg, Man., Can. (625,304)	594,551	86C
Wrocław, Poland	637,400	89E
Wuhan, China	3,570,000	88E
Wuppertal, Germany (830,000)	371,283	89E
Wuxi, China	880,000	88E
Wuxing (Huzhou), China (†964,400)	208,500	86E
Xiamen, China (†546,400)	343,700	86E
Xi'an, China (†2,580,000)	2,210,000	88E
Xiaogan, China (†1,204,400)	125,500	86E
Xining, China	620,000	88E
Xuzhou, China	860,000	88E
Yancheng, China (†1,251,400)	256,400	86E
Yangon, Burma (2,800,000)	2,705,039	83C
Yaoundé, Cameroon	653,670	86E
Yerushalayim (Jerusalem), Israel (530,000)	493,500	87E
Yichun, China	840,000	88E
Yokohama, Japan (*Tōkyō)	3,220,350	90C
Yulin, China (†1,228,800)	115,600	86E
Zagreb, Croatia	697,925	87E
Zanzibar, Tanzania	133,000	84E
Zaozhuang, China (†1,592,000)	292,200	86E
Zaporožje, Ukraine	884,000	89C
Zaragoza (Saragossa), Spain	582,239	88E
Zhangjiakou, China (†640,000)	500,000	88E
Zhengzhou, China (†1,580,000)	1,150,000	88E
Zhongshan, China (†1,059,700)	238,700	86E
Zibo, China (†2,370,000)	840,000	88E
Zurich, Switzerland (870,000)	342,361	90E

litan area populations are shown in parentheses.
s located within the metropolitan area of another city; for example, Kyōto, Japan is located in the Ōsaka metropolitan area.
tion of entire municipality or district, including rural area.

C Census
E Official estimate

A • 15

Transliteration Systems

Toponymy: Criteria Used for the Writing of Names on the Maps

The language of geography is a language which defines geographic features in universally recognized terms. In creating this language, toponymy experts and cartographers have confronted complex problems in finding terms which are universally acceptable. So that the reader can fully understand the maps in this atlas, here is a brief explanation of how the toponyms (place-names for geographic features) have been written, particularly those relating to regions or countries where the Roman alphabet is not used. Among these are the Slavic-speaking nations such as Russia, Yugoslavia and Bulgaria; and China and Japan, which use ideographic characters. Of the European countries, Greece has its own alphabet, which is totally different from the Roman alphabet. Many of the Islamic countries use Arabic, with variations derived from local dialects.

There are two basic systems for Romanizing writing. The first is by phonetic transcription, using combinations of different alphabetical signs for each language when the phonetic sound in other languages should be maintained. For example, the Italian sound "sc" (which must be followed by an "e" or "i" to remain soft) in French is "ch," in English is "sh," and in German is "sch."

The second system is transliteration, in which the words, letters or characters of one language are represented or spelled in the letters or characters of another language.

Chinese, Japanese and Arabic Languages

Various Asian and African countries use non-Roman forms in their writing. For example, the Chinese and Japanese languages use ideographic characters instead of an alphabet, and these ideographic characters are transformed into the Roman alphabet through phonetic transcription. Until recently, one of the methods used for transforming Chinese was the Wade-Giles system, named for its English authors. Used in this atlas is the Pinyin system, which was approved by the Chinese government in 1958 and has been incorporated into the official maps of the People's Republic of China. The Pinyin system also has been adopted by the United States Board on Geographic Names and is used in official United Nations documents. The Pinyin names, however, often are accompanied by the Wade-Giles form, as the latter was widely known.

In Japan, ideographic characters are used, although the Roman alphabet is used in many Japanese scientific works. Japan uses two principal systems for standardizing names. They are the Kunreisiki, used by the government in official publications, and the Hepburn method. Adopted for this atlas is the Hepburn method, the system used in international English-language publications and by the United States Board on Geographic Names.

Romanization of the Arabic alphabet, which is used in many Islamic countries, is by transliteration. Since English and French are still used as international languages in many Arab countries, the name forms proposed by the major English and French sources have been taken into consideration. Generally, the systems proposed by the United States Board on Geographic Names and the Permanent Committee on Geographical Names have been used for most Asian countries and Arab-speaking countries.

Greek, Russian and Other Slavic Languages

Practically all written languages in Europe use the Roman alphabet. The differences in phonetics and grammar are shown by the use of diacritical marks and by groupings of consonants, vocals and syllables which give meaning to the various tones in the language. According to a centuries-old tradition, each written language maintains its formal characters, using the translated form rather than the phonetic transcription when a geographical term must be given in another language. This system, therefore, makes it more a translation than a transliteration.

In the Aegean area, Greek and the Greek alphabet are particularly significant because of historical links to the beginning of European civilization. The 1962 United States Board on Geographic Names and the Permanent Committee on Geographical Names systems, based on modern Greek pronunciation, have been used in transcribing toponyms from official sources for these maps. (The table that follows has an example indicating essential norms for Romanizing the modern Greek alphabet.)

A different situation arises in countries using the Cyrillic alphabet. Six principal Slavic languages using this alphabet are Russian, Byelorussian, Ukrainian, Bulgarian, Serbian, and Macedonian. The Cyrillic alphabet also is used by some non-Slavic people of the former Soviet Union. The nomenclature of these regions has been transliterated in accordance with the system proposed by the International Organization for Standardization, taking into consideration sounds and letters and uses of the diacritical marks normal in Slavic languages. The International Organization for Standardization method is accepted and used in bibliographical works and international documents. (The table which follows gives the relationship between the letters of the Cyrillic and Roman alphabets for the above six languages.)

Special Cases: Conventional Forms and Multilinguals

Cartographic nomenclature generally derives from the official nomenclature of the sovereign and nonsovereign countries, although a number of cases need explanation.

In numerous situations, English conventional forms are used along with the local or conventional name in referring to a geographical entity used outside the official English language area. For example, Vienna, Prague, Copenhagen and Moscow are English forms for Wien, Praha, København and Moskva, respectively. There are cases, however, where the conventional or historical form commonly used in English cartography has been applied with the same meaning. Thus, Peking and Nanking are the English conventional forms for Beijing and Nanjing, while Tsinan, Tientsin and Mukden are the former conventional spellings or names for Jinan, Tianjin and Shenyang, respectively. Other examples are Saigon, the former name for Ho Chi Minh, Vietnam; and Bangkok, the name for Krung Thep, which is used in Thailand.

The lack of reliable data for countries, especially ex-colonies without a firm national cartographic tradition, has made it necessary to utilize mapping skills of former colonial nations such as France, the United Kingdom and Belgium. A lack of data has led to the adoption of French and British forms in many areas, as these two languages are widely used for official purposes.

Another special case is that of the multilingual areas. Many countries and areas officially recognize two or more written and spoken languages; therefore, all of the principal written forms appear on the maps. This is true, for example, of Belgium where the official languages are French and Dutch (e.g. Bruxelles/Brussel) and of Italian regions such as Valle d'Aosta and Alto Adige, where French, German and Italian are used (e.g. Aosta/Aoste) (Bolzano/Bozen).

In preparing this atlas, each of these special cases has been taken into full consideration within the limits of the scale, space and readability of the maps.

Transliteration of the Cyrillic Alphabet
(International System—ISO)

Cyrillic Letter		Roman Letter		Cyrillic Letter		Roman Letter	
А	а	a		О	о	o	
Б	б	b		П	п	p	
В	в	v		Р	р	r	
Г	г	g		С	с	s	
Д	д	d		Т	т	t	
Е	е	e	initially, after a vowel or after the mute sign "Ъ", becomes "je"	У	у	u	
				Ф	ф	f	
				Х	х	h	
Ё	ё	ë		Ц	ц	c	
Ж	ж	ž		Ч	ч	č	
З	з	z		Ш	ш	š	
И	и	i		Щ	щ	šč	
Й	й	j	not written if preceded by "И" or "Ы"	Ъ	ъ	—	not written
				Ы	ы	y	
К	к	k		Ь	ь	—	not written
Л	л	l		Э	э	e	
М	м	m		Ю	ю	ju	
Н	н	n		Я	я	ja	

Transcription of Modern Greek
(U.S. B. G. N./P.C.G.N.)

Greek Letter (or combination)		Roman Letter (or combination)		Greek Letter (or combination)		Roman Letter (or combination)	
Α	α	a			μπ	b	beginning a word
	αι	ai				mb	within a word
	αυ	av		Ν	ν	n	
Β	β	v			ντ	d	beginning a word
Γ	γ	g				nd	within a word
	γγ	ng		Ξ	ξ	x	
	γκ	g	beginning a word	Ο	ο	o	
					οι	oi	
		ng	within a word		ου	ou	
Δ	δ	d		Π	π	p	
Ε	ε	e		Ρ	ρ	r	
	ει	i		Σ	σ	s	
	ευ	ev			ς	s	ending a word
Ζ	ζ	z		Τ	τ	t	
Η	η	i			τζ	tz	
	ηυ	iv		Υ	υ	i	
Θ	θ	th			υι	i	
Ι	ι	i			φ	f	
Κ	κ	k		Χ	χ	kh	
Λ	λ	l		Ψ	ψ	ps	
Μ	μ	m		Ω	ω	o	

The "Geographical Glossary" lists the principal geographical terms used on the maps. All of these terms, including abbreviations, prefixes and suffixes, appear in the cartographic table as they appear on the maps. Terms are listed in accordance with the English alphabet, without consideration of diacritical marks on letters or of particular groups of letters.

Prefixes and suffixes relating to principal names or forming part of geographical toponyms are followed or preceded by a dash and the language to which they refer: e.g. Chi-/Dan. (Chi, a Danish prefix, means large); -bor/Slvn. (-bor, a Slovakian suffix, means city). Suffixes can also appear as words in themselves. In this case, the suffix and primary word are coupled together: e.g. Berg, -berg (Berg, which means mountain, can be used alone or as part of another word, such as Hapsberg).

Certain terms are followed or preceded by the r abbreviation used on the maps. Both instances are listed: e.g. Fjord, Fj. and Fj., Fjord.

All geographical terms are identified by the language or languages to which each belongs. The language or languages in italics follows the term: e.g. Abbey/Eng.; -bad/Nor., Dut., Swed., Germ. Each term is translated into a corresponding English term or terms.

Below is a table identifying the abbreviations of various language names used on the maps. Note that certain abbreviations represent a group of languages, instead of one language: e.g. Ural. is the abbreviation for Uralic, a group word for Udmurt, Komi, and Nenets.

Alt. = Altaic (Turkmen, Tatar, Bashkir, Kazakh, Karalpak, Nogai, Kirghiz, Uzbek, Uigur, Altaic, Yakut, Khakass)

Ban. = Bantu (KiSwahili, ChiLuba, Lingala, KiKongo)

Cauc. = Caucasian (Chechen, Ingush, Kalmuck, Georgian)
Iran. = Iranian (Baluchi, Tagus)
Mel. = Melanesian (Fijian, New Caledonian, Micronesian, Nauruan)
Mong. = Mongolian (Buryat, Khalka Mongol)
Poly. = Polynesian (Maori, Samoan, Tongan, Tahitian, Hawaiian)
Sah. = Saharan (Kanuri, Tubu)
Som. = Somalian (Somali, Galla)
Sud. = Sudanese (Peul, Ehoué, Mossi, Yoruba, Ibo)
Ural. = Uralic (Udmurt, Komi, Nenets).

Because of their technical application to geography, some geographical terms may not fully correspond with the meaning given for them in some dictionaries.

Abbreviations of Language Names

Abbreviations in English	English	Abbreviations in English	English	Abbreviations in English	English	Abbreviations in English	English	Abbreviations in English	English	Abbreviations in English	English
Afr.	Afrikaans	Bulg.	Bulgarian	Fr.	French	Khm.	Khmer	Pers.	Persian	Som.	Somalian
A.I.	American Indian	Burm.	Burmese	Gae.	Gaelic	Kor.	Korean	Pol.	Polish	Sp.	Spanish
Alb.	Albanian	Cat.	Catalan	Georg.	Georgian	K.S.	Khoi-San	Poly.	Polynesian	Sud.	Sudanese
Alt.	Altaic	Cauc.	Caucasian	Germ.	German	Laot.	Laotian	Port.	Portuguese	Swa.	Swahili
Amh.	Amharic	Chin.	Chinese	Gr.	Greek	Lapp.	Lappish	Prov.	Provençal	Swed.	Swedish
Ar.	Arabic	Cz.	Czech	Hebr.	Hebrew	Latv.	Latvian	Rmsh.	Romansh	Tam.	Tamil
Arm.	Armenian	Dan.	Danish	Hin.	Hindi	Lith.	Lithuanian	Rom.	Romanian	Thai	Thai
Az.	Azerbaidzhani	Dut.	Dutch	Hung.	Hungarian	Mal.	Malay	Rus.	Russian	Tib.	Tibetan
Ban.	Bantu	Eng.	English	Icel.	Icelandic	Malag.	Malagasy	Sah.	Saharan	Tur.	Turkish
Bas.	Basque	Esk.	Eskimo	Indon.	Indonesian	Mel.	Melanesian	S.C.	Serbo-Croatian	Ural.	Uralic
Beng.	Bengali	Est.	Estonian	Ir.	Irish	Mong.	Mongolian	Sin.	Sinhalese	Urdu	Urdu
Ber.	Berber	Far.	Faroese	It.	Italian	Nep.	Nepalese	Slvk.	Slovak	Viet.	Vietnamese
Br.	Breton	Finn.	Finnish	Jap.	Japanese	Nor.	Norwegian	Slvn.	Slovene	Wall.	Walloon
		Fle.	Flemish			Pash.	Pashto			Wel.	Welsh

Glossary of Geographical Terms

Local Form	English
A	
A- / Ban.	people
A' / Icel.	river
Å / Dan.; Nor.; Swed.	stream
a., an / Germ.	on
Aa / Germ.	stream
Aache / Germ.	stream
Aaiún / Ar.	springs
Aan / Dut.; Fle.	on
Āb / Pers.	stream
Ābād / Pers.	city, town
Abad, -abad / Pers.	city, town
Ābār / Ar.	spring
Abbadia / It.	abbey
Abbaye / Fr.	abbey
Abbazia / It.	abbey
Abbi / Amh.	great
Abd / Ar.	servant
Abeba / Amh.	flower
Aber / Br.; Wel.	estuary
Abhang / Germ.	slope
Abū / Ar.	father, master
Abyad / Ar.	white
Abyaḍ / Ar.	white
Abyār / Ar.	well
Abyss / Eng.	ocean depth, deep
Ach / Germ.	stream
Achaïf / Ar.	dunes
Ache / Germ.	stream
Achter / Afr.; Dut.; Fle.	back
Acqua / It.	water
Açu / A.I.	great
Açude / Port.	reservoir, dam
Ada / Tur.	island
Adalar / Tur.	archipelago
Adasr / Tur.	island
Addis / Amh.	new
Adi / Amh.	village
Adrar / Ber.	mount, mountains
Aéroport / Fr.	airport
Aeroporto / It.; Port.	airport
Aeropuerto / Sp.	airport
Af / Som.	mouth, gorge
Afsluitdijk / Dut.	dam
Agadir / Ber.	castle
Ağız / Tur.	mouth
Agro / Sp.; It.	plain
Agua / Sp.	water
Aguja / Sp.	needle
Agulha / Port.	needle, promontory
Ahal / Georg.	new
Aḥmar / Ar.	red
Ahrāmāt / Ar.	pyramids
Ahzar / Ber.	wadi
Aigialós / Gr.	coast
Aigue / Prov.	water
Aiguille / Fr.	needle
Ain / Ar.	spring
Ait / Ar.; Ber.	sons
Aivi, -aivi / Lapp.	mountain
Ak / Tur.	white
'Aklé / Ar.	dunes
Akmens / Latv.	stone
Ákra / Gr.	point
Akti / Gr.	coast
Ala / Malag.	forest
Ala / Finn.	low, lower
Alan / Tur.	field
Alb / Rom.	white
Albo / Sp.	white
Albufera / Sp.	lagoon
Alcalá / Sp.	castle
Alcázar / Sp.	castle
Aldea / Sp.	village
Alföld / Hung.	lowland
Ali / Amh.	mountain
Alia / Poly.	stream
Alin / Mong.	range
Alm / Germ.	mountain pasture
Alor / Mal.	river
Alp / Germ.	mountain pasture
Alpe / Germ.; Fr.; It.	mountain pasture
Alps / Eng.	mountains
Alsó / Hung.	low, lower
Alt / Germ.	old
Altin / Tur.	lower
Altiplano / Sp.	plateau
Alto / Sp.; It.; Port.	high
Altopiano / It.	plateau
Älv / Swed.	river
Am / Kor.	mountain, peak
Amane / Ber.	water
Amba / Amh.	mountain
Ambato / Malag.	rock
An / Gae.	of
An, a. / Germ.	on
Ana / Poly.	grotto
Anatolikós / Gr.	eastern
Äng / Swed.	meadow
Angra / Port.	bay, anchorage
Ani- / Malag.	center
Áno / Gr.	upper
Ânou / Ber.	well
Anse / Fr.	inlet
Ant- / Malag.	center
Ao / Chin.; Khm.; Thai	gulf
'Âouâna / Ar.	well
Apá / Rom.	water
'Aqabat / Ar.	pass
Aqueduc / Fr.	aqueduct
Ar / Mong.	north
Ar / Sin.; Tam.	river
'Arâguïb / Ar.	hills
Arba / Amh.	mount
Arbore / Rom.	tree
Archipiélago / Sp.	archipelago
Arcipelago / It.	archipelago
Arḍ / Ar.	region
Ard- / Gae.	high
Areg / Ar.	dune
Areia / Por.	beach
Arena / Sp.	beach
Argent / Fr.	silver
Arhipelag / Rus.	archipelago
Arkhaios / Gr.	old, antique
Arm / Eng.; Germ.	branch
Arquipélago / Port.	archipelago
Arr., Arroyo / Sp.	stream
Arrecife / Sp.	reef
Arroio / Por.	stream
Art / Tur.	pass, watershed
Aru / Sin.; Tam.	river
Ås / Dan., Nor.; Swed.	hills
Asfar / Ar.	yellow
Asif / Ber.	river
Asky / Alt.	lower
Áspres / Gr.	white
Assa / Ber.	wadi
Atalaia / Sp.	frontier
Áth / Gae.	ford
Átha / Gae.	ford
Atol / Port.	atoll
Au / Germ.	meadow
Aue / Germ.	irrigated field
Aust / Nor.	east
Austur / Icel.	east
Ava / Poly.	canal
Aven / Fr.	doline, sink
Awa / Poly.	bay
Áyios / Gr.	saint
'Ayn / Ar.	spring, well
'Ayoûn / Ar.	springs, wells
'Ayoûn / Ar.	spring
Aza / Ber.	wadi
Azraq / Ar.	light blue
Azul / Port.; Sp.	light blue
Azur / Fr.	light blue
B	
B., Bay / Eng.	bay
b., bei / Germ.	by
B., Bucht / Germ.	bay
Ba / Sud.	river
Ba- / Ban.	people
Ba / Mel.	hill, mountain
Baai / Afr.	bay
Bab / Ar.	gate
Bac / Viet.	north
Bach / Germ.	brook, torrent
Bacino / It.	reservoir
Back / Eng.	ridge
Bäck / Swed.	brook
Backe / Swed.	brook
Bad, -bad / Dan.; Germ.; Nor.; Swed.	thermal springs
Baden, -baden / Germ.	thermal springs
Bādiyat / Ar.	desert
Badwéynta / Som.	ocean
Badyarada / Som.	gulf
Baeg / Kor.	white
Bæk / Dan.	brook
Bælt / Dan.	strait
Bagni / It.	thermal springs
Baharu / Mal.	new
Bahia / Port.	bay
Bahía / Sp.	bay
Bahir / Ar.	river, lake, sea
Bahnhof / Germ.	railway station
Bahr / Ar.	wadi
Bahr / Ar.	river, lake, sea
Baḥrat / Ar.	lake
Baḥri / Ar.	north, northern
Bahrī / Ar.	north
Bahrīyah / Ar.	northern
Bai / Chin.	white
Băi / Rom.	thermal springs
Baia / Port.	bay
Baie / Fr.	bay
Baigne / Fr.	seaside resort
Baile / Gae.	city, town
Bain / Fr.	thermal springs
Bains / Fr.	thermal springs
Baixo / Port.	low, lower
Bajan / Mong.	rich
Bajo / Sp.	low
Bajrak / Alb.	tribe
Bakhtiyārī / Pers.	western
Bakki / Icel.	hill
Bālā / Pers.	high
Bald / Eng.	peak
Balka / Rus.	gorge
Balkan / Bulg.; Tur.	mountain range
Ballin / Gae.	mouth
Ballon / Fr.	dome
Bally / Gae.	city, town
Balta / Rom.	marsh
Báltos / Gr.	marsh
Ban / Laot.	village
Bana / Jap.	promontory
Baña / Slvk.	mine
Bañados / Sp.	marsh
Banc / Fr.	bank
Banco / It.; Sp.	bank
Band / Pers.	dam, mountain range
Bandao / Chin.	peninsula
Bandar / Ar.; Mal.; Pers.	port, market
Bang / Indon.; Mal.	stream
Bangou / Sah.	well
Banhado / Port.	marsh
Bani / Ar.	sons
Banja / Bulg.; S.C.; Slvn.	thermal springs
Banjaran / Mal.	mountain range
Banka / Rus.	sandbank
Banke / Dan.	bank
Baño / Sp.	thermal springs
Banský / Cz.	upper
Bánya / Hung.	mine
Bar / Gae.	peak
Bar / Eng.	sandbar

Geographical Glossary

Local Form	English
Bar / Hin.	great
Bāra / Hin.	great
Bara / S.C.	pond
Barã / Urdu	great
Baraji / Tur.	dam
Barat / Indon.; Mal.	west, western
Barkas / Lith.	castle, city, town
Barlovento / Sp.	windward
Barq / Ar.	hill
Barra / Port.; Sp.	bar, bank
Barrage / Fr.	dam
Barragem / Port.	reservoir
Barranca / Sp.	gorge
Barranco / Port.; Sp.	gorge
Barre / Fr.	bar
Barun / Mong.	western
Bas / Fr.	low
-bas / Rus.	reservoir
Bassa / Port.	flat
Bassejn / Rus.	reservoir
Bassin / Fr.	basin
Bassure / Fr.	flat
Bassurelle / Fr.	flat
Bašta / S.C.	garden
Bataille / Fr.	battle
Batalha / Port.	battle
Batang / Indon.; Mal.	river
Batha / Sah.	stream
Batın / Ar.	depression
Bătlăq / Pers.	marsh
Batu / Mal.	rock
Bayan / Mong.	rich
Bayır / Tur.	mountain, slope
Bayou / Fr.	branch, stream
Bayt / Ar.	house
Bazar / Pers.	market
Be / Malag.	great
Beau / Fr.	beautiful
Becken / Germ.	basin
Bed / Eng.	river bed
Beek / Dut.	creek
Be'er / Hebr.	spring
Bei / Chin.	north
Bei, b. / Germ.	by
Beida / Ar.	white
Beinn / Gae.	mount
Bel / Ar.	son
Bel / Bulg.	white
Bel / Tur.	pass
Beled / Ar.	village
Belen / Tur.	mount
Belet / Ar.	village
Beli / S.C.; Slvn.	white
Beli / Tur.	pass
Bellah / Sah.	well
Belogorje / Rus.	mountains
Belt / Dan.; Germ.	strait
Bely / Rus.	white
Bělý / Cz.	white
Ben / Ar.	son
Ben / Gae.	mount
Bender / Pers.	port, market
Bendi / Tur.	dam
Beni / Ar.	son
Beo / S.C.	white
Bereg / Rus.	bank
Berg, -berg / Afr.; Dut.; Fle.; Germ.; Nor.; Swed.	mount
Berge / Afr.	mountain
Bergen / Dut.; Fle.	dunes
Bergland / Germ.	upland
Bermejo / Sp.	red
Besar / Mal.	great
Betsu / Jap.	river
Betta / Tam.	mountain
Bhani / Hin.	community
Bharu / Mal.	new
Bheag / Gae.	little
Bīābān / Pers.	desert
Biały / Pol.	white
Bianco / It.	white
Bien / Viet.	lake
Bight / Eng.	bay
Bijeli / S.C.	white
Bill / Eng.	promontory
Bilo / S.C.	range
Bilý / Cz.	white
Binnen / Dut.; Fle.; Germ.	inner
Biqā' / Ar.	valley
Bir / Ar.	well
Bi'r / Ar.	well
Birkat / Ar.	pond
Bistrica / Bulg.; S.C.; Slvn.	stream
Bjarg / Icel.	rock
Bjerg / Dan.	mount
Bjeshkët / Alb.	mountain pasture
Blaauw / Afr.	blue
Blanc / Fr.	white
Blanco / Sp.	white
Blau / Germ.	blue
Bleu / Fr.	blue
Bluff / Eng.	cliff
Bo- / Ban.	people
Bo / Chin.	white
Bo / Swed.	habitation
Boca / Sp.	gap, mouth
Bôca / Port.	gap, mouth
Bocage / Fr.	forest
Bocca / It.	gap, pass
Bocchetta / It.	gap, pass
Bodden / Germ.	bay, lagoon
Boden / Germ.	soil
Běng / Khm.	lake, marsh
Bog / Eng.	marsh
Bogaz / Alt.; Az.; Tur.	strait
Bogăzi / Tur.	strait
Bogdo / Mong.	high
Bogen / Nor.	bay
Bois / Fr.	forest
Boka / S.C.	channel
Boloto / Rus.	marsh
Bolšoj / Rus.	great
Bolsón / Sp.	basin
Bom / Port.	good
Bong / Kor.	peak
Bongo / Malag.	upland
Bor / Cz.; Rus.	coniferous forest
Bór / Pol.	forest
-bor / Slvn.	city, town
Bóras / Gr.	north
Börde / Germ.	fertile plain
Bordj / Ar.	fort
Bóreios / Gr.	northern
Borg, -borg / Dan.; Nor.; Swed.	castle
Borgo / It.	village
Born / Germ.	spring
Bory / Pol.	forest
Bosch / Dut.; Fle.	forest
Bosco / It.	wood
Bosque / Sp.	forest
Bosse / Fr.	hill
Botn / Nor.	bay
Bou / Ar.	father, master
Bouche / Fr.	mouth
Boula / Sud.	well
Bourg / Fr.	city, town
Bourne, - bourne / Eng.	frontier
Boven / Afr.	upper
Boz / Tur.	grey
Bozorg / Pers.	great
Brána / Cz.	gate
Braña / Sp.	mountain pasture
Branche / Fr.	branch
Branco / Port.	white
Braţul / Rom.	branch
Bravo / Sp.	wild
Brazo / Sp.	branch
Brdo / Cz.; S.C.	hill
Bre / Nor.	glacier
Bredning / Dan.	bay
Breg / Alb.; Bulg.; S.C.	hill, coast
Brjag / Bulg.	bank
Bro / Dan.; Nor.; Swed.	bridge
Brod / Bulg.; Cz.; Rus.; S.C.; Slvk.; Slvn.	ford
Bród / Pol.	ford
Bron / Afr.	spring
Bronn / Germ.	spring
Bru / Nor.	bridge
Bruch / Germ.	peat-bog
Bruchzone / Germ.	fracture zone
Bruck, -bruck / Germ.	bridge
Brücke / Germ.	bridge
Brug / Dut.; Fle.	bridge
Brugge / Dut.; Fle.	bridge
Bruk / Nor.	factory
Brunn / Swed.	spring
-brunn / Swed.	spring
Brunnen / Germ.	spring
Brygg / Swed.	bridge
Brzeg / Pol.	coast
Bü / Ar.	father, master
Bucht, B. / Germ.	bay
Bugt / Dan.	bay
Buḥayrat / Ar.	lake, lagoon
Bühel / Germ.	hill
Bühl / Germ.	hill
Buhta / Rus.	bay
Bukit / Mal.	mountain, peak
Bukt / Nor.; Swed.	bay
Buku / Indon.	hill, mountain
Bulag / Mong.; Tur.	spring
Bulak / Mong.; Tur.	spring
Bülāq / Tur.	spring
Bult / Afr.	hill
Bulu / Indon.	mountain
Bur / Som.	mount
Bür / Ar.	port
Burg, - burg / Afr.; Ar.; Dut.; Eng.; Germ.	castle
Burgh / Eng.	city, town
Burgo / Sp.	village
Burha / Hin.	old
Buri / Thai	city, town
Burj / Ar.	village
Burn / Eng.	stream
Burnu / Tur.	promontory
Burqat / Ar.	mount, marsh
Burun / Tur.	cape
Busen / Germ.	bay
Busu / Ban.	land
Būtat / Ar.	lake, pond
Butte / Eng.; Fr.	flat-topped hill
Büyük / Tur.	great
By / Eng.	near
By, -by / Dan.; Nor.; Swed.	city, town
Bystrica / Cz.; Slvk.	stream
Bystrzyca / Pol.	stream

C

Local Form	English
C., Cap / Cat.; Fr.; Rom.	cape
C., Cape / Eng.	cape
C., Colle / It.	pass
Caatinga / A.I.	forest
Cabeça / Port.	peak
Cabeço / Port.	peak
Cabeza / Sp.	peak
Cabezo / Sp.	peak, mountain
Cabo / Port.; Sp.	cape
Cachoeira / Port.	waterfall, rapids
Cachopo / Port.	reef
Cadena / Sp.	range
Caer / Wel.	castle
Cagan / Cauc.; Mong.	white
Cairn / Gae.	hill
Čáj / Az.; Tur.	river
Cajdam / Mong.	salt marsh
Caka / Chin.	lake
Cala / Sp.; It.	inlet
Calar / Sp.	plateau
Caldas / Sp.; Port.	thermal springs
Caleta / Sp.	inlet
Camp / Cat.; Fr.; Eng.	field
Campagna / It.	plain
Campagne / Fr.	plain
Campo / Sp.; It.; Port.	field
Cañada / Sp.	gorge, ravine
Canale / It.	canal, channel
Caño / Sp.	branch
Cañón / Sp.	gorge
Canyon / Eng.	gorge
Cao / Viet.	mountain
Cap, C. / Cat.; Fr.; Rom.	cape
Car / Gae.	castle
Càrn / Gae.	peak
Carrera / Sp.	road
Carrick / Gae.	rock
Casale / It.	hamlet
Cascada / Sp.	waterfall
Cascata / It.	waterfall
Castel / It.	castle
Castell / Cat.	castle
Castello / It.	castle
Castelo / Port.	castle
Castillo / Sp.	castle
Castro / Sp.; It.	village
Catarata / Sp.	cataract
Catena / It.	mountain range
Catinga / Port.	degraded forest
Cauce / Sp.	river bed
Causse / Fr.	highland
Cava / It.	stone quarry
Çay / Tur.	river
Cay / Eng.	islet, island
Caye / Fr.	island
Cayo / Sp.	islet, island
Ceann / Gae.	promontory
Centralny / Rus.	middle
Čeren / Alb.	black
Černi / Bulg.	black
Černý / Cz.	black
Čërny / Rus.	black
Cerrillo / Sp.	hill
Cerrito / Sp.	hill
Cerro / Sp.; Port.	hill, mountain
Cêrro / Port.	hill, mountain
Červen / Bulg.	red
Červony / Rus.	red
Cetate / Rom.	city, town
Chaco / Sp.	scrubland
Chāh / Pers.	well
Chaïf / Ar.	dunes
Chaîne / Fr.	mountain range
Champ / Fr.	field
Chang / Chin.	highland
Chapada / Port.	highland
Chapadão / Port.	highland
Château / Fr.	castle
Châtel / Fr.	castle
Chăy / Tur.	river
Chedo / Kor.	archipelago
Chenal / Fr.	canal
Cheng / Chin.	city, town, wall
Cheon / Kor.	city, river
Chergui / Ar.	eastern
Cherry, -cherry / Hin.; Tam.	city, town
Chew / Amh.	salt mine, salt
Chhâk / Khm.	bay
Chhotla / Hin.	little
Chi- / Ban.	great
Chi / Chin.	marsh, lake
Chi / Kor.	lake, pond
Chi- / Swa.	land
Chiang / Thai	city, town
Chico / Sp.	little
Chine / Eng.	ridge
Ch'on / Kor.	station
Ch'ŏn / Kor.	river
Chŏsuji / Kor.	reservoir
Chott / Ar.	salt marsh
Chu / Chin.; Viet.	mountain, hill
Chuŏr phnum / Khm.	mountain range
Chute / Fr.	waterfall
Chutes / Fr.	waterfalls
Cidade / Port.	city, town
Ciems / Latv.	village
Čierny / Slvk.	black
Cime / Fr.	peak
Cimp / Rom.	field
Cimpie / Rom.	plain
Cinco / Sp.; Port.	five
Citeli / Georg.	red
Città / It.	city, town
Ciudad / Sp.	city, town
Ckali / Georg.	water
Ckaro / Georg.	spring
Co / Chin.	lake
Col / Cat.; Fr.	pass
Colina / Port.; Sp.	hill
Coll / Cat.	hill
Collado / Sp.	pass
Colle, C. / It.	pass
Collina / It.	hill
Colline / Fr.	hill
Colonia / Sp.; It.	colony
Coma / Sp.	hill country
Comb / Eng.	basin
Comba / Sp.	basin
Combe / Fr.	basin
Comté / Fr.	county, shire
Con / Viet.	island
Conca / It.	depression
Condado / Sp.	county, shire
Cone / Eng.	volcanic cone
Cône / Fr.	volcanic cone
Contraforte / Port.	front range
Cordal / Sp.	crest
Cordilheira / Port.	mountain range
Cordillera / Sp.	mountain range
Coring / Chin.	lake
Corixa / A.I.	stream
Corno / It.	peak
Cornone / It.	peak
Corrente / It.; Port.	stream
Corriente / Sp.	stream
Costa / Sp.; It.; Port.	coast
Côte / Fr.	coast
Coteau / Fr.	height, slope
Coxilha / Port.	ridge
Craig / Gae.	rock
Cratère / Fr.	crater
Cresta / Sp.; It.	crest
Crêt / Fr.	crest
Crête / Fr.	crest
Crkva / S.C.	church
Crni / S.C.; Slvn.	black
Crven / S.C.	red
Csatorna / Hung.	canal
Cuchilla / Sp.	ridge
Cuenca / Sp.	basin
Cuesta / Sp.	escarpment
Cueva / Sp.	cave
Čuka / Bulg.; S.C.	peak
Çukur / Tur.	well
Cu Lao / Viet.	island
Cumbre / Sp.	peak
Cun / Chin.	village
Cura / A.I.	stone
Curr / Alb.	rock
Cy., City / Eng.	city, town
Czarny / Pol.	black

D

Local Form	English
Da / Chin.	great
Da / Viet.	mountain, peak
Daal / Dut.; Fle.	valley
Daba / Mong.	pass
Daba / Som.	hill
Daban / Chin.; Mong.	pass
Dae / Kor.	great
Dağ / Tur.	mountain
Dağı, Dağı / Tur.	mountain
Dāgh / Pers.; Tur.	mountain
Daği, Dağı / Tur.	mountain
Dağları / Tur.	mountain range
Dahar / Ar.	hill
Dahr / Ar.	plateau, escarpment
Dai / Chin.; Jap.	great
Daiet / Ar.	marsh
Dak / Viet.	stream
Dake / Jap.	mountain
Dakhla / Ar.	depression
Dakhlet / Ar.	depression, bay
Dal, -dal / Afr.; Dan.; Dut.; Fle.; Nor.; Swed.	valley
Dala / Alt.	steppe, plain
Dalaj / Mong.	lake, sea
Dalan / Mong.	wall
Dallol / Sud.	valley, torrent
Dalur / Icel.	valley
Damm / Germ.	dam
Dan / Kor.	point

Local Form	English
Danau / Indon.	lake
Danda / Nep.	mountains
Dao / Chin.	island, peninsula
Dao / Viet.	island
Dar / Ar.	house, region
Dar / Swa.	port
Dara / Tur.	torrent, valley
Darb / Ar.	track
Darja / Alt.	river, sea
Darya, Daryā / Pers.	river, sea
Daryācheh / Pers.	lake, sea
Daš / Alt.; Az.	rock
Dasht / Pers.	desert, plain
Dawhat / Ar.	bay
Dayr / Ar.	convent
De / Sp.; Fr.	of
Deal / Rom.	hill
Dearg / Gae.	red
Debre / Amh.	hill, monastery
Dega / Som.	stone
Deh / Pers.	village
Dēh / Som.	stream
Deich / Germ.	dike
Dél / Hung.	south
Delft / Dut.; Fle.	deep
Delger / Mong.	wide, market
-den / Eng.	city, town
Deniz / Tur.	sea
Denizi / Tur.	sea
Dent / Fr.	peak
Deo / Laot.; Viet.	pass
Dépression / Fr.	depression
Depressione / It.	depression
Der / Som.	high
Dera / Hin.; Urdu	temple
Derbent / Tur.	gorge, pass
Dere / Tur.	river, valley
Désert / Fr.	desert
Desfiladero / Sp.	pass
Desh / Hin.	land, country
Desierto / Sp.	desert
Det / Alb.	sea
Détroit / Fr.	strait
Deux / Fr.	two
Dezh / Pers.	castle
Dhar / Ar.	heights, hills
Dhār / Hin.; Urdu	mountain
Dhitikós / Gr.	western
Dien / Khm.; Viet.	rice-field
Diep / Dut.; Fle.	deep, strait
Dijk, -dijk / Dut.; Fle.	dam
Ding / Chin.	mountain, peak
Dique / Sp.	dam
Di Sopra / It.	upper
Di Sotto / It.	lower
Distrito / Sp.; Port.	district
Diu / Hin.	island
Diz / Pers.	castle
Djebel / Ar.	mountain
Dji / Ban.	water
Djup / Swed.	deep
Do / Kor.	Island
Do / S.C.	valley
Dō / Jap.	island, administrative division
Dōho / Som.	valley
Doi / Thai	mountain, peak
Dol / Bulg.; Cz.; Rus.; S.C.	valley
Dol / Pol.	valley
Dolen / Bulg.	low
Dolgi / Rus.	long
Dolina / Bulg.; Cz.; Pol.; Rus.; S.C.; Slvn.	valley
Dolni / Bulg.	low
Dolni / Pol.	lower
Dolny / Pol.	lower
Domb / Hung.	hill
Dôme / Fr.	dome
Dong / Chin.; Viet.	east
Dong / Kor.	city, town
Dong / Thai	mountain
Dong / Viet.	marsh, plain
Donji / S.C.	low, lower
Dorf, -dorf / Germ.	village
Doroga / Rus.	road
Dorp, -dorp / Afr.; Dut.; Fle.	village
Dos / Rom.	ridge
Dos / Sp.	two
Douarn / Br.	land
Dougou / Sud.	settlement
Doukou / Sud.	settlement
Down / Eng.	hill
Drâa / Ar.	dunes, hills
Dracht / Germ.	sandbank
Draw / Eng.	ravine, valley
Drif / Afr.	ford
Drift / Afr.	ford
Droichead / Gae.	bridge
Droûs / Ar.	crest
Dry / Pash.	river
Dubh / Gae.	black
Dugi / S.C.	long
Dugu / Sud.	settlement
Dun / Gae.	castle
Duna / Sp.; It.	dune
Düne / Germ.	dune
Dungar / Hin.	mountain
Düngar / Hin.	mountain
Duong / Viet.	stream
Durchbruch / Germ.	gorge
Durg / Hin.	castle
-durga / Hin.	castle
Duży / Pol.	great
Dvor / Cz.	court
Dvorec / Rus.	castle
Dvůr / Cz.	castle
Dwór / Pol.	court
Džebel / Bulg.	mountain
Dzong / Tib.	fort, monastery

E

Local Form	English
Ea / Thai	river
Eau / Fr.	water
Ebe / Ban.	forest
Ebene / Germ.	plain
Eck / Germ.	point
Eclusa / Sp.	lock
Écluse / Fr.	lock
Écueil / Fr.	cliff
Edeien / Ber.	sand desert
Edjérir / Ber.	wadi
Egg / Germ.; Nor.	crest, point
Eglab / Ar.	hills
Ehi / Sah.	mountain
Eid / Nor.	isthmus
Eiland / Afr.	island
Eisen / Germ.	iron
Eisenerz / Germ.	iron ore
El / Amh.	well
Elv, -elv / Nor.	river
Embalse / Sp.	reservoir
Embouchure / Fr.	mouth
Emi / Sah.	mountain
En / Fr.	in
Ende / Germ.	end
Enneri / Sah.	stream
Ennis / Gae.	island
Enseada / Port.	Bay, inlet
Ensenada / Sp.	bay, inlet
Ér / Hung.	stream
Erdő / Hung.	forest
Erg / Ar.	sand desert
Erz / Germ.	ore
Espigão / Port.	plateau
Estān / Pers.	land
Este / Sp.	east
Estero / So.	estuary, marsh
Estrecho / Sp.	strait
Estreito / Port.	strait
Estuaire / Fr.	estuary
Estuário / Port.	estuary
Estuario / Sp.; It.	estuary
Észak / Hung.	north
Étang / Fr.	pond
Ewaso / Ban.	river
Ey / Icel.	island
Eyja / Icel.	island
Eyjar / Icel.	islands
Eylandt / Dut.	island
Ežeras / Lith.	lake
Ezers / Latv.	lake

F

Local Form	English
Fa / Mel.	stream
Falaise / Fr.	cliff
Fall, -fall / Germ.; Eng.; Swed.	waterfall
Falls / Eng.	waterfall
Falu / Hung.	village
-falva / Hung.	village
Fan / Eng.	village
Faraglione / It.	cliff
Farallón / Sp.	cliff
Faro / Sp.; It.	lighthouse
Farvand / Dan.	strait
Fehér / Hung.	white
Fehn / Germ.	peat fen, peat-bog
Fekete / Hung.	black
Feld / Dan.; Germ.	field
Fell / Eng.	upland moor
Fell / Icel.	mountain
Fels / Germ.	rock
Fen / Eng.	marsh, peat-bog
Feng / Chin.	mountain, peak
Feste / Germ.	fort
Festung / Germ.	fort
Fier / Rom.	iron
Firn / Germ.	snow-field
Firth / Eng.	estuary, fjord
Fiume / It.	river
Fjäll / Swed.	mountain
Fjärd / Swed.	fjord
Fjell / Nor.	mountain
Fjöll / Icel.	mountain
Fjord, Fj. / Dan.; Nor.; Swed.	fjord
Fjörður / Icel.	fjord, bay
Fleuve / Fr.	river
Fließ / Germ.	torrent
Fjót / Icel.	river
Fój / Icel.	bay, gulf
Floresta / Sp.; Por.	forest
Flow / Eng.	strait
Flughafen / Germ.	airport
Fluß / Germ.	river
Fo / Mel.	stream
Foa / Mel.	stream
Foa / Poly.	cove
Foce / It.	mouth
Föld / Hung.	plain
Fonn / Nor.	glacier
Fontaine / Fr.	fountain
Fonte / It.; Port.	spring
Fontein / Afr.; Dut.	spring
Foort / Afr.; Dut.	ford
Forca / It.	pass
Forcella / It.	defile
Ford / Rus.	fjord
Förde / Germ.	fjord, gulf
Foreland / Eng.	promontory
Foresta / It.	forest
Forêt / Fr.	forest
Fors / Swed.	rapids, waterfall
Forst / Germ.; Dut.	forest
Forte / It.; Port.	fort
Fortin / Sp.	fort
Fosa / Sp.	trench
Foss / Icel.; Nor.	rapids, waterfall
Fossé / Fr.	trench
Foum / Ar.	pass
Fourche / Fr.	pass
Foz / Sp.; Port.	mouth
Fre / Germ.	free
Fronteira / Port.	frontier
Frontera / Sp.	frontier
Frontón / Sp.	promontory
Fuente / Sp.	spring
Fuerte / Sp.	fort
Fuji / Jap.	mountain
Fület / Av.	marsh
Furt / Germ.	ford
Fushë / Alb.	plain

G

Local Form	English
G., Gora / Bulg.; Rus.; S.C.	mountain, hill
G., Gunung / Indon.	mountain
Ga / Jap.	bay
Ga / Mel.	mountain, peak
Gabel / Germ.	pass
Gaissa / Lapp.	mountain
Gala / Sin.; Tam.	mountain
Gam / Hin.; Urdu	village
Gamle / Nor.; Swed.	old
Gana / Sud.	little
Gang / Germ.	passage
Gang / Chin.	port, bay
Gang / Kor.	stream, bay
Gang / Tib.	glacier
Ganga / Hin.	river
Ganj / Hin.; Urdu	market
-gaon / Hin.	city, town
Gaoyuan / Chin.	plateau
Gap / Kor.	point
Gar / Hin.	house
Gara / Bulg.	station
Gara / Ar.	hills, range
Gară / Rom.	station
Garaet / Ar.	marsh, intermittent lake
Garam / Beng.; Hin.; Urdu	village
-gard / Pol.	city, town
Gård, -gård / Dan.; Nor.; Swed.	farmhouse
Gardaneh / Pers.	pass
Gare / Fr.	railway station
Garet / Ar.	hill
Garh, -garh / Hin.; Urdu	castle
Garhi / Hin.; Nep.; Urdu	fort
Garten / Germ.	garden
Gat / Dan.; Fle.; Dut.	strait
Gata / Jap.	bay, lake
Gau, -gau / Germ.	district
Gäu, -gäu / Germ.	district
Gavan / Rus.	port
Gave / Bas.	torrent
Gawa / Jap.	river
Geb., Gebirge / Germ.	mountain range
Gebergte / Afr.; Dut.	mountain range
Gebirge, Geb. / Germ.	mountain range
Geç., Geçit / Tur.	pass
Geçidi / Tur.	pass
Geçit, Geç. / Tur.	pass
Geysir / Icel.	geyser
Ghar / Hin.; Urdu	house
Ghar / Pash.	mountain, mountain range
Gharbīyah / Ar.	western
Ghat / Hin.; Nep.; Urdu	pass
Ghubbat / Ar.	bay
Ghurd / Ar.	dune
Gi / Kor.	peninsula
Giang / Viet.	stream
Giri / Hin.; Urdu	mountain, hill
Girlo / Rus.	branch
Gjebel / Ar.	mountain
Gji / Alb.	bay
Glace / Fr.	ice
Glaciar / Sp.	glacier
Glacier / Eng.; Fr.	glacier
Glen / Gae.	valley
Gletscher / Germ.	glacier
Gobi / Mong.	desert
Godār / Ar.	ford
Gok / Kor.	river
Gök / Tur.	blue
Gol / Cauc.; Mong.	river
Göl / Tur.	lake
Gola / It.	gorge
Gold / Germ.; Eng.	gold
Golet / S.C.	mountain
Golf / Germ.	gulf
Golfe / Fr.	gulf
Golfete / Sp.	inlet
Golfo / Sp.; It.; Port.	gulf
Goljam / Bulg.	great
Gölü / Tur.	lake
Gong / Tib.	high
Gonggar / Tib.	mountain
Gongo / Ban.	mountain
Góra / Pol.	mountain
Gora, G. / Bulg.; Rus.; S.C.	mountain, hill
Gorica / S.C.; Slvn.	hill
Gorje / S.C.	mountain range
Gorlo / Rus.	gorge
Gorm / Gae.	blue
Gorni / Bulg.; S.C.; Slvn.	upper
Gornji / S.C.; Slvn.	upper
Górny / Pol.	high
Gorod / Rus.	city, town
Gorodok / Rus.	village
Gorski / Bulg.	upper
Gory / Rus.	mountains
-gou / Chin.	river
Goulbi / Sud.	river, lake
Goulbin / Sud.	wadi
Goulet / Fr.	gap
Gour / Ar.	hills, range
Goureu / Sud.	wadi
Goz / Sah.	dune
Graafschap / Dut.	county, shire
Graben / Germ.	ditch, canal
Gracht / Dut.	canal
Grad, -grad / Bulg.; Rus.; S.C.; Slvn.	city, town, castle
Gradac / S.C.	castle
Gradec / Bulg.	village
Gradec / Slvn.	castle
Gran / Icel.	green
Gran / S.C.	great
Grande / Sp.; It.; Port.	great
Grao / Cat.; Sp.	gap
Grat / Germ.	crest
Grève / Fr.	beach
Grind / Germ.	peak
Grjada / Rus.	range
Gród, -gród / Pol.	castle, city, town
Grön / Icel.	green
Grond / Afr.	soil
Gronden / Dut.; Fle.	flat
Groot / Afr.; Dut.; Fle.	great
Groß / Germ.	great
Grotta / It.	grotto
Grotte / Fr.; Germ.	grotto
Grube / Germ.	mine
Grün / Germ.	green
Grunn / Nor.	ground
Gruppe / Germ.	mountain system
Gruppo / It.	mountain system
Gua / Mal.	cave
Guaçu / A.I.	great
Guan / Chin.	pass
Guazú / A.I.	great
Guba / Rus.	bay
Guchi / Jap.	strait
Guelb / Ar.	hill, mountain
Guelta / Ar.	well
Guic / Br.	village
Güney / Tur.	south, southern
Gunong / Mal.	mountain
Guntō / Jap.	archipelago
Gunung, G. / Indon.	mountain
Guo / Chin.	state, land
Gur / Rom.	mountain
Guri / Jap.	cliff
Gurud / Ar.	hills, dunes
Gyár / Hung.	factory

H

Local Form	English
Haag / Dut.; Fle.	hedge
-hâb / Dan.	port
Hadabat / Ar.	highland
Hadd / Ar.	point
Hadjer / Ar.	hill, mountain
Hae / Kor.	bay, sea
Haehyeop / Kor.	strait

Geographical Glossary

Local Form	English
Haf / Icel.	sea
Ḩafar / Ar.	well
Hafen / Germ.	port
Haff / Germ.	lagoon
Hafir / Ar.	spring, ditch
Hafnar / Icel.	port
Hāfūn / Som.	bay
Hage / Dan.	point
Hage / Dut.; Fle.	hedge
Hågna / Swed.	peak
Hai / Chin.	sea, lake, bay
Hain / Germ.	forest
Haixia / Chin.	strait
Ḩajar / Ar.	hill, mountain
Hajar / Ar.	hill country
Halbinsel / Germ.	peninsula
Halma / Hung.	hill
Halom / Hung.	hill
Halq / Ar.	gap
Hals / Nor.	peninsula
Halvø / Dan.	peninsula
Halvøy / Nor.	peninsula
Hama / Jap.	beach
Hamāda / Ar.	rocky desert
Ḩamādah / Ar.	plateau
Ḩamādat / Ar.	plateau
Hammam / Ar.	thermal springs
Ḩammām / Ar.	well
Hamn / Nor.; Swed.	port
Hamrā' / Ar.	red
Hāmūn / Jap.	salt lake
Hana / Jap.	cape
Hana / Poly.	bay
Hane / Tur.	house
Hang / Kor.	port
Hank / Ar.	escarpment, plateau
Hantō / Jap.	peninsula
Har / Hebr.	mountain
Hara / Mong.	black
Harar / Swa.	well
Ḩarrah / Ar.	lava field
Ḩarrat / Ar.	lava field
Hasi / Ar.	well
Ḩasi / Ar.	well
Hassi / Ar.	well
Ḩasy / Ar.	well
Haug / Nor.	hill
Haupt- / Germ.	principal
Haure / Lapp.	lake
Haus / Germ.	house
Hausen / Germ.	village
Haut / Fr.	high
Hauteur / Fr.	hill
Hauts Plateaux / Fr.	highlands
Hauz / Pers.	reservoir
Hav / Dan.; Nor.; Swed.	sea, gulf
Haven / Eng.; Fle.; Dut.	port
Havn / Dan.; Nor.	port
Havre / Fr.	port
Hawr / Ar.	lake, marsh
Ház / Hung.	house
-háza / Hung.	house
Hazm / Ar.	height, mountain range
He / Chin.	river
Head / Eng.	headland
Hed / Dan.; Swed.	heath
Hegy / Hung.	mountain
Hegység / Hung.	mountain
Hei / Nor.	heath
Heide / Germ.	heath
Heijde / Dut.; Fle.	heath
Heilig / Germ.	saint
Heim, -heim / Germ.; Nor.	house
Heiya / Jap.	plain
-hely / Hung.	locality
Hem / Swed.	home
Hen / Br.	old
Higashi / Jap.	east, eastern
Hima / Hin.	ice
Himal / Nep.	peak
Hisar / Tur.	castle
Ho / Chin.	reservoir, river
Ho / Kor.	river, reservoir
Hō / Jap.	mountain
Hoch / Germ.	high, upper
Hochland / Germ.	highland
Hochplato / Afr.	highland
Hodna / Ar.	highland
Hoek / Dut.; Fle.	cape
Hof / Dut.; Germ.	court
Höfn / Icel.	port
Høg / Nor.	peak
Hög / Swed.	mountain
Hogna / Nor.	peak
Höhe / Germ.	peak
Høj / Dan.	hill
Hoj / Ural.	mountain range
Hok / Jap.	north
Hoku / Jap.	north, northern
Holm / Dan.; Nor.; Swed.	island
Holz / Germ.	forest
Hon / Viet.	island, point
Hong / Chin.; Viet.	red
Hono / Poly.	bay, anchorage
Hoog / Afr.; Dut.; Fle.	high
Hook / Eng.	point
Hoorn / Afr.; Dut.; Fle.	cape, point

Local Form	English
Hora / Cz.; Slvk.	point
Horn / Eng.; Germ.; Icel.; Nor.; Swed.	point
Horní / Cz.	high
Horný / Slvk.	upper
Horst / Germ.	mountain
Horvot / Hebr.	ruins
Hory / Cz.; Slvk.	mountain range
Hout / Dut.; Fle.	forest
Hovd, -hovd / Dan.; Nor.	cape
Ḩowz / Pers.	basin
Hrad / Cz.; Slvk.	castle, city, town
Hradiště / Cz.	citadel
Hřeben / Cz.	crest
Hrebet / Rus.	mountain range
Hu / Rmsh.	lake
Huang / Chin.	yellow
Hude / Germ.	pasture
Huerta / Sp.	market garden
Hügel / Germ.	hill
Hügelland / Germ.	hill country
Huis, -huis / Afr.; Dut.; Fle.	house
Huisie / Afr.	house
Huizen, -huizen / Dut.	houses
Huk / Afr.; Dan.; Swed.	cape
Hum / S.C.	hill
Hurst / Eng.	grove
Hus / Dut.; Nor.; Swed.	house
Huta / Pol.; Slvk.	hut
Hütte / Germ.	hut
Hver / Icel.	crater
Hvit / Icel.	white
Hvost / Rus.	spit

I

Local Form	English
I., Island / Eng.	island
Ierós / Gr.	holy
Igarapé / A.I.	river
Ighazer / Ber.	torrent
Ighil / Ber.	hill
Iguidi / Ber.	dunes
Ih / Mong.	great
Ike / Jap.	pond
Ile / Fr.	island
Ilha / Port.	island
Iller / Tur.	administrative division
Ilot / Fr.	islet
Imi / Ar.	spring
I-n / Ber.	well
Inch / Gae.	island
Inder / Dan.; Nor.	inner
Indre / Nor.	inner
Inferiore / It.	lower
Inish / Gae.	island
Insel / Germ.	island
Insulă / Rom.	island
Inver / Gae.	mouth
Irhazér / Ber.	wadi
Irmak / Tur.	river
'Irq / Ar.	dunes
Is / Nor.	glacier
Ís / Icel.	ice
Isblink / Dan.	glacier
Ishi / Jap.	rock
Iske / Alt.	old
Isla / Sp.	island
Iso / Finn.	great
Iso / Jap.	cliff
Isola / It.	island
Isthmós / Gr.	isthmus
Istmo / Sp.; It.	isthmus
Ita / A.I.	stone
Itä / Finn.	east
Itivdleq / Esk.	isthmus
Iwa / Jap.	rock, cliff
Iztočni / Bulg.	eastern
Izvor / Bulg.; Rom.; S.C.; Slvn.	spring

J

Local Form	English
J., Jazīrat / Ar.	island
J., Jiang / Chin.	river
Jabal / Ar.	mountain
Jaha / Ural.	river
Jam / Ural.	lake, river
Jama / Rus.	cave
Jan / Alt.	great
Janga / Tur.	north
Jangi / Alt.; Iran.	new
Janūbīyah / Ar.	southern
Jar / Rus.	bank
Järv / Est.	lake
Järve / Finn.	lake
Järvi / Finn.	lake
Jasirēd / Som.	island
Jaun / Latv.	new
Jaur / Lapp.	lake
Jaure / Lapp.	lake
Javr / Lapp.	lake
Javrre / Lapp.	lake

Local Form	English
Jazā'ir / Ar.	islands
Jazīrat, J. / Ar.	island
Jazovir / Bulg.	reservoir
Jbel / Ar.	mountain
Jebel / Ar.	mountain
Jedid / Ar.	new
Jedo / Kor.	archipelago
Jezero / S.C.; Slvn.	lake
Jezioro / Pol.	lake
Jhil / Hin.; Urdu	lake
Jian / Chin.	mountain
Jiang, J. / Chin.	river
Jiao / Chin.	cape, cliff
Jibāl / Ar.	mountain
Jih / Cz.	south
Jima / Jap.	island
Jin / Kor.	cove
Jing / Chin.	spring
Jisr / Ar.	bridge
Joch / Germ.	pass
Jõgi / Est.	river
Jøkel / Nor.	glacier
Joki / Finn.	river
Jokka / Lapp.	river
Jökull / Icel.	glacier
Jord, -jord / Nor.	earth
Ju / Ural.	river
Judeţ / Rom.	district
Jugan / Ural.	river
Jura / Lith.	sea
Jūra / Latv.	sea
Jūras Līcis / Latv.	bay
Jūrmala / Latv.	beach
Jurt / Cauc.	village
Južni / Bulg.; S.C.; Slvn.	southern
Južny / Rus.	southern
Juzur / Ar.	islands

K

Local Form	English
Ka / Poly.	lake
Kaap / Afr.	cape
Kabīr / Ar.	great
Kae / Kor.	inlet
Kāf / Ar.	peak, mountain
Kafr / Ar.	village
Kaga / Ban.	hills, mountain range
Kahal / Ar.	plateau, escarpment
Kai / Jap.	sea
Kaikyō / Jap.	strait
Kaise / Lapp.	mountain
Kal / Pers.	stream
Kala / Az.; Kor.	fort
Kala / Finn.	river
Kala / Hin.	black
Kala / Tur.	castle
Kalaa / Ar.	castle
Kalaki / Georg.	city, town
Kale / Tur.	castle
Kali / Hin.	black
Kali / Indon.; Mal.	bay, river
Kallio / Finn.	rock
Kaln / Latv.	mountain
Kalós / Gr.	beautiful, good
Kamen / Bulg.; Rus.; S.C.; Slvn.	mountain, peak
Kámen / Cz.	rock
Kameň / Slvk.	rock
Kami / Jap.	upper
Kamień / Pol.	rock
Kamm / Germ.	crest
Kamp / Germ.	field
Kâmpóng / Khm.	village
Kámpos / Gr.	field
Kampung / Indon.; Mal.	village
Kan., Kanal / Alb.; Dan.; Germ.; Nor.; Rus.; S.C.; Slvn.; Swed.; Tur.	canal, channel
Kanaal / Dut.; Fle.	canal
Kanał / Pol.	canal
Kanal, Kan. / Alb.; Dan.; Germ.; Nor.; Rus.; S.C.; Slvn.; Swed.; Tur.	canal, channel
Kand, -kand / Pers.; Tur.	city, town
Kang / Chin.; Kor.	bay, river
Kangas / Fle.	heath
Kange / Esk.	east
Kangri / Tib.	snow-capped mountain
Kantara / Ar.	bridge
Kaôh / Khm.	island
Kap / Dan.; Germ.	cape
Kapija / S.C.	gate, gorge
Kapp / Nor.	cape
Kar / Tib.	white
Kar / Ural.	city, town
Kara / Tur.	black
Karang / Indon.; Mal.	sandbank, cliff
Kari / Finn.	cliff
Kariba / Ban.	gorge
Kariet / Ar.	village
Karki / Finn.	peninsula
Kastel / Germ.	castle
Kástron / Gr.	fort, city, town
Káto / Gr.	lower

Local Form	English
Kaupstadur / Icel.	city, town
Kaupunki / Finn.	city, town
Kavīr / Pers.	salt desert
Kawa / Jap.	river
Kawm / Ar.	hill
Kebir / Ar.	great
Kedi / Georg.	mountain range
Kédia / Ar.	mountain, plateau
Kedim / Ar.	old
Kef / Ar.	mountain
Kefála / Gr.	mountain, peak
Kefar / Hebr.	village
Kei / Jap.	river
Kelet / Hung.	east
Ken / Gae.	cape
Kent / Alt.; Iran.; Tur.	city, town
Kenya / Swa.	fog
Kep / Alb.	cape
Kep., Kepulauan / Mal.	archipelago
Kepulauan, Kep. / Mal.	archipelago
Kereszt / Hung.	cross
Kerk / Dut.; Fle.	church
Keski / Finn.	middle
Kette / Germ.	mountain range
Keur / Sud.	village
Key / Eng.	coral island
Kha / Tib.	valley
Khal / Hin.	canal
Khalīj / Ar.	gulf
Khand / Hin.	district
Khao / Thai	hill, mountain
Kharābeh / Pers.	ruins
Khashm / Ar.	promontory
Khatt / Ar.	wadi
Khawr / Ar.	mouth, bay
Khazzān / Ar.	dam
Khemis / Ar.	fifth
Khersónisos / Gr.	peninsula
Khirbat / Ar.	ruins
Khlong / Thai	stream, mouth
Khokhok / Thai	isthmus
Khor / Ar.	mouth, bay
Khóra / Gr.	land
Khorion / Gr.	village
Khowr / Pers.	bay
Khrisós / Gr.	gold
Ki- / Ban.	little
Kibali / Sud.	river
Kil / Gae.	church
Kilde / Dan.	spring
Kilima / Swa.	mountain
Kill / Gae.	strait
Kilwa / Ban.	lake
Kin / Gae.	cape
Kinn / Nor.	cape, point
Kirche / Germ.	church
Kirk / Eng.	church
Kis / Hung.	little
Kisiwa / Swa.	island
Kita / Jap.	north, northern
Kızıl / Tur.	red
Klein / Afr.; Dut.; Germ.	little
Kliff / Germ.	cliff
Klint / Dan.	reef
Klip / Afr.; Dut.	rock, cliff
Klit / Dan.	dune
Kloof / Afr.; Dut.	gorge
Kloster / Dan.; Germ.; Nor.; Swed.	convent
Knob / Eng.	mountain
Knock / Gae.	mountain, hill
Ko / Jap.	bay, lake, little
Ko / Sud.	stream
Ko / Thai	island, point
Købing / Dan.	town
Kogel / Germ.	dome
Kōgen / Jap.	plateau
Koh / Hin.; Pers.	mountain, mountain range
Kol / Alt.	river, valley
Kol / Alt.; Tur.	lake
Koll / Nor.	peak
Kólpos / Gr.	gulf
Kong / Dan.; Nor.; Swed.	king
Kong / Indon.; Mal.	mountain
Kong / Viet.	mountain, hill
Konge / Ban.	river
König / Germ.	king
Koog / Germ.	polder
Kop / Afr.	hill
Kopec / Cz.; Slvk.	hill
Kopf / Germ.	peak
Köping / Swed.	town
Köprü / Tur.	bridge
Körfezi / Tur.	gulf
Korfi / Gr.	rock
Koro / Mel.	mountain, island
Koro / Sud.	old
Koru / Tur.	forest
Kosa / Rus.	spit
Koška / Rus.	cliff
Koski / Finn.	rapids
Kosui / Jap.	lake
Kot / Urdu	castle
Kota / Mal.	city, town
Kotal / Pash.; Pers.	pass
Kotar / S.C.	cultivated area
Kotlina / Pol.	basin

Local Form	English	Local Form	English	Local Form	English	Local Form	English
Kotlovina / Rus.	basin, plain	Les / Bulg.; Cz.; Rus.; Slvk.	forest	Marisma / Sp.	marsh	Most / Bulg.; Cz.; Pol.; Rus.; S.C.; Slvn.	bridge
Kou / Chin.	mouth, pass	Leso / Rus.	forested	Mark / Dan.; Nor.; Swed.	land		
Kourou / Sud.	well	Levante / It.; Sp.	eastern	Markt / Germ.	market	Moto / Jap.	spring
Kowr / Pers.	river	Levkós / Gr.	white	Marsa / Ar.	anchorage, bay	Motte / Fr.	hill
Kowtal / Pers.	pass	Levy / Rus.	left	Marsch / Germ.	marsh	Motu / Mel.; Poly.	island, rock
Koy / Tur.	bay	Lha / Tib.	temple	Maru / Jap.	mountain	Moutier / Fr.	monastery
Köy / Tur.	village	Lhari / Hin.; Nep.	mountain	Mas / Prov.	farmhouse	Movilă / Rom.	hill
Kraal / Afr.	village	Lho / Tib.	south	Maşabb / Ar.	mouth	Moyen / Fr.	central
Kraina / Pol.	land	Lido / It.	sandbar	Mashra' / Ar.	landing, pier	Mta / Georg.	mountain
Kraj / Rus.; S.C.	land	Liedao / Chin.	archipelago	Masivul / Rom.	massif	Mts., Monts, Mountains / Eng.; Fr.	mountains
Kraj / Rus.	administrative division	Liehtao / Chin.	archipelago	Massiv / Germ.; Rus.	massif	Muang / Laot.; Thai	city, town, land
		Liels / Latv.	great	Mata / Poly.	point		
Krajina / S.C.	land	Lilla / Swed.	little	Mata / Port.; Sp.	forest	Muara / Indon.; Mal.	mouth
Krak / Ar.	hill, castle	Lille / Dan.; Nor.	little	Mata / Sum.	waterfall	Muela / Sp.	mountain
Krans / Afr.	mountain	Liman / Alb.; Rus.; Tur.	lagoon, bay	Mato / Port.; Sp.	forest	Mühle / Germ.	mill
Kras / S.C.; Slvn.	karst landscape	Liman / Tur.	bay, port	Matsu / Jap.	point	Mui / Mel.	point
Krasny / Rus.	red	Limin / Gr.	port	Mauna / Poly.	mountain	Mui / Viet.	point, cape
Kreb / Ar.	hills, mountain range	Limni / Gr.	lake	Mèvros / Gr.	black	Muiden / Dut.; Fle.	mouth
Kriaž / Ar.	mountain range	Ling / Chin.	mountain range, peak	Mayo / Sud.	river	Muir / Gae.	sea
Krš / S.C.	karst area, limestone area	Linna / Finn.	castle	Maza / Lith.	little	Mukh / Hin.	mouth
		Liqen / Alb.	lake	Mazar / Pers.; Tur.	sanctuary	Mull / Gae.	promontory
Krung / Thai	city, town	Lithos / Gr.	stone	Mazs / Latv.	little	Münde / Germ.	mouth
Ksar / Ar.	castle	Litoral / Port.; Sp.	littoral	Me / Khm.	river	Mündung / Germ.	mouth
Ksour / Ar.	fortified village	Litorale / It.	littoral	Me / Mel.	hill, mountain	Municipiul / Rom.	commune
Ku- / Ban.	river branch	Llan / Wel.	church	Me / Thai	great	Munkhafaḍ / Ar.	depression
Kuala / Mal.	river, mouth	Llano / Sp.	plain	Medina / Ar.	city, town	Münster / Germ.	monastery
Kubra / Ar.	bridge	Llanura / Sp.	plain	Medjez / Ar.	ford	Munte / Rom.	mountain
Küçük / Tur.	little	Lo- / Ban.	river	Meer / Dut.; Fle.	lake	Muntelé / Rom.	mountain
Kuduk / Ar.	spring	Loch / Gae.	lake, inlet	Meer / Germ.	lake, sea	Munţii / Rom.	mountain range
Küh / Pers.	mountain	Loch / Germ.	grotto	Megálos / Gr.	great	Muren / Mong.	river
Kühhä / Pers.	mountain range	Loka / Slvn.	forest	Mégas / Gr.	great	Mushāsh / Ar.	spring
Kul / Alt.; Iran.; Tur.	lake	Loma / Sp.	hill	Megye / Hung.	district	Muz / Tur.	ice
Kulam, -kulam / Hin.; Tam.	pond	Long / Indon.	stream	Mélas / Gr.	black	Muztagh / Tur.	snow-capped mountain
		Loo / Dut.; Fle.	clearing	Melkosopeinik / Rus.	hill country		
Kulle / Swed.	hill	Lough / Gae.	lake	Mellan / Swed.	central	Mwambo / Ban.	rock, cliff
Kulm / Germ.	peak	Loutrá / Gr.	thermal springs	Mer / Chin.	gate, channel	Myit / Burm.	stream
Kultuk / Rus.	bay	Ložbina / Rus.	depression	Ménez / Br.	mountain	Mynydd / Wel.	mountain
Kum / Tur.	dunes, sand desert	Lu- / Ban.	river	Merzel / Ar.	bivouac	Myo / Burm.	city, town
		Lua / Ban.	river	Meos / Indon.	island	Mýri / Icel.	marsh
Kuppe / Germ.	dome, seamount	Lua / Mel.	island, reef	Mer / Fr.	sea	Mys / Rus.	cape
		Lua / Poly.	crater	Mercato / It.	market		
Kurayb / Ar.	hill	Luang / Thai	yellow	Merilja / Al.	lagoon, marsh		
Kurgan / Alt.	hill	Luch / Germ.	peat-bog	Meri / Est.; Finn.	sea		
Kurgan / Rus.	fort	Lücke / Germ.	pass	Meridional / Pom.; Sp.	southern	**N**	
Kuro / Jap.	black	Lug / Rus.	meadow	Merin / A.I.	little		
Kurort / Bulg.; Germ.; Rus.	spa	Luka / S.C.; Slvn.	port	Merja / Ar.	lagoon, marsh	Na / Cz.; Pol.; Rus.; S.C.; Slvn.	on
		Lule / Lapp.	east, eastern	Mers / Ar.	port		
Kust / Dut.; Fle.	coast	Lum / Alb.	river	Mersa / Ar.	port	Nab / Ar.	spring
Kust- / Swed.	coast	Lund / Dan.; Swed.	forest	Mesa / Sp.	mesa, tableland	Nad / Cz.; Pol.; Rus.	on
Küste / Germ.	coast	Lung / Rom.	long			Nada / Jap.	bay, sea
Kút / Hung.	spring	Lung / Tib.	valley	Meseta / Sp.	plateau	Nadi, -nadi / Hin.; Urdu	river
Kuyu / Tur.	spring	Luoto / Finn.	shoal	Méses / Gr.	central	Næs / Dan.	point
Kvemo / Georg.	low, lower	Lurg / Pers.	salt flat	Mesto / Bulg.; S.C.; Slvk.; Slvn.	city, town	Nafūd / Ar.	dunes
Kwa / Ban.	village	Lut / Pers.	desert			Nag / Tib.	black
Kylä / Finn.	village			Město / Cz.	city, town	Nagar, -nagar / Hin.; Tib.	city, town
Kyle / Gae.	strait, channel			Mestre / Port.	principal	Nagaram / Hin.; Tam.	city, town
Kyō / Jap.	strait	**M**		Meydan / Tur.	square	Nagorje / Rus.	plateau, mountains
Kyrka / Swed.	church			Mezad / Hebr.	castle		
Kyst / Dan.; Nor.	coast	M., Monte / It.; Port.; Sp.	mountain	Mező / Hung.	field	Nagy / Hung.	great
Kyun / Burm.	island	Ma / Ar.	water	Mgne., Montagne / Fr.	mountain	Nahr / Ar.	river
Kyūryō / Jap.	hills, mountains	Ma- / Ban.	people	Mgnes., Montagnes / Fr.	mountains	Naikai / Jap.	sea
Kyzyl / Tur.	red	Maa / Est.; Finn.	island, land	Miao / Chin.	temple	Naka / Jap.	central
Kzyl / Tur.	red	Ma'arrat / Ar.	height	Miasto / Pol.	city, town	Nakhon / Thai	city, town
		Machi / Jap.	district	Mic / Rom.	little	Nam / Burm.; Laot.; Thai	river
		Macizo / Sp.	massif	Middel / Afr.; Dut.; Fle.	middle	Nam / Kor.	south
L		Madhya / Hin.	central	Midi / Fr.	noon, south	Namakzar / Pers.	salt desert
		Madīnah / Ar.	city, town	Między / Pol.	central	Nan / Chin.	south
L., Lake, Lago / Eng.; It.; Port.; Sp.	lake	Madīq / Ar.	strait	Miedzyrzecze / Pol.	interfluve	Narrows / Eng.	strait
		Mado / Swa.	well	Mierzeja / Pol.	sand spit	Narssaq / Esk.	plain, valley
La / Tib.	pass	Madu / Tam.	pond	Mifraz / Hebr.	bay, gulf	Näs / Swed.	cape
Laagte / Afr.	stream, valley	Mae / Thai	stream	Miftah / Ar.	gorge	Nationalpark / Swed.; Germ.	national park
Labuan / Indon.; Mal.	bay, port	Mae nam / Thai	stream, mouth	Mikrós / Gr.	little		
Lac / Fr.	lake	Magh / Gae.	plain	Mina / Port.; Sp.	mine	Nau / Lith.	new
Lach / Som.	stream, wadi	Mägi / Est	mountain	Minā' / Ar.	port	Nauja / Lith.	new
Lacul / Rom.	lake	Măgura / Rom.	height	Minami / Jap.	south, southern	Navolok / Rus.	cape, promontory
Lae / Poly.	cape, point	Mahā / Hin.	great	Minamoto / Jap.	spring		
Laem / Thai	bay, port	Mahal / Hin.; Urdu	palace	Minate / Jap.	port	Ne / Jap.	cliff
Låg / Nor.; Swed.	low, lower	Mai / Amh.; Ban.	stream	Mine / Jap.	peak	Neder / Fle.; Dut.	low
Lag / Swed.	stream, wadi	Majdan / S.C.	quarry	Mirim / A.I.	little	Neem / Est.	cape
Läge / Swed.	beach	Mäki / Finn.	mountain, hill	Misaki / Jap.	cape	Negro / Port.; Sp.	black
Lagh / Som.	stream, wadi	Makrós / Gr.	long	Mittel- / Germ.	middle	Negru / Rom.	black
Lago, L. / It.; Port.; Sp.	lake	Mala / Hin.; Tam.	mountain	Mo / Chin.	sand desert	Nehir / Tur.	river
Lagoa / Port.	lagoon	Malai / Hin.; Tam	mountain	Mo / Nor.; Swed.	heath	Nei / Chin.	inner
Laguna / Alb.; It.; Rus.; Sp.	lagoon, lake	Malal / A.I.	fence	Moana / Poly.	lake	Nene, -nene / Ban.	great
		Malhão / Port.	dome	Mogila / Bulg.; Rus.	hill	Néos / Gr.	new
Lagune / Fr.	lagoon	Mali / Alb.	mountain	Moku / Poly.	island	Nero / It.	black
Laht / Est.	bay	Mali / S.C.; Slvn.	little	Melle / Dan.	mill	Nes / Icel.; Nor.	cape
Lahti / Finn.	bay, gulf	Malki / Bulg.	little	Monasterio / Sp.	monastery	Ness / Gae.	promontory
Laks / Finn.	bay	Malla / Tam.	mountain	Mond / Afr.; Dut.; Fle.	mouth	Neu / Germ.	new
Lalla / Ar.	saint	Maly / Rus.	little	Mong / Burm.; Thai; Viet.	city, town	Neuf / Fr.	new
Lampi / Finn.	pond	Malý / Cz.; Slvk.	little	Moni / Gr.	monastery	Nevado / Sp.	snow-capped mountain
Lande / Fr.	heath	Mały / Pol.	little	Mont / Cat.; Fr.	mountain		
Lang / Afr.; Dut.; Germ.	long	Man / Kor.	bay	Montagna / It.	mountain	Nez / Fr.	cape
Lang / Viet.	village	Manastir / Bulg.; S.C.	monastery	Montagne, Mgne. / Fr.	mountain	Ngok / Viet.	mountain, peak
Lao / Chin.	old	Manche / Fr.	channel	Montagnes, Mgnes. / Fr.	mountains	Ngolo / Ber.	great
Lapa / Poly.	mountain range, peak	Mar / It.; Port.; Sp.	sea	Montaña / Sp.	mountain	Ni / Fr.	village
		Mar / Tib.	red	Monte, M. / It.; Port.; Sp.	mountain	Niecka / Pol.	basin
Largo / Port.; Sp.	basin	Mar / Ural.	city, town	Monts, Mts. / Fr.	mountains	Niemi / Finn.	peninsula
Las / Pol.	forest	Marais / Fr.	marsh	Moos / Germ.	moor	Nieuw / Fle.; Dut.	new
Las, Läs / Som.	well	Marché / Fr.	market	Mór / Gae.	great	Nij / Dut.	new
Laut / Mal.	sea	Mare / Fr.	pond	More / Bulg.; Rus.; S.C.	sea	Nīl / Hin.	blue
Law / Gae.	hill, mountain	Mare / It.; Rom.	sea	Mòrë / Gae.	great	Nishi / Jap.	west
Lázně / Cz.	thermal springs	Mare / Rom.	great	Mori / Jap.	mountain, forest	Niski / Pol.	lower
Lednik / Rus.	glacier	Marea / Rom.	sea			Nisko / S.C.	low
Leite / Germ.	coast	Marécage / Fr.	marsh	Morne / Fr.	mountain	Nisoi / Gr.	islands
Lekh / Nep.	mountain range	Marios / Lith.	reservoir	Moron / Mong.	river	Nisos / Gr.	island
				Morro / Port.; Germ.	hill, peak	Nizina / Pol.	lowland
				Morrón / Sp.	mountain	Nižina / Cz.	depression
				Morze / Pol.	sea	Nizký / Cz.	low, lower

Geographical Glossary

Local Form	English
Nizmennost / Rus.	lowland, depression
Nižni / Rus.	low, lower
Nižný / Slvk.	low, lower
No / Mel.	stream
Nock / Gae.	ridge
Noir / Fr.	black
Non / Thai	hill
Nong / Thai	lake, marsh
Noord / Afr.; Fle.; Dut.	north
Noordoost / Afr.; Fle.; Dut.	northeast
Nor / Arm.	new
Nord / Fr.; It.; Germ.	north
Nördlich / Germ.	northern
Nørdre / Dan.; Nor.	northern
Norra / Swed.	northern
Nørre / Dan.	northern
Norte / Sp.	north
Nos / Bulg.; Rus.; S.C.; Slvn.	cape
Nosy / Malag.	island
Nótios / Gr.	southern
Nou / Rom.	new
Novi / Bulg.; S.C.; Slvn.	new
Novo / Port.	new
Novy / Rus.	new
Nový / Cz.; Slvk.	new
Now / Pers.	new
Nowy / Pol.	new
Nudo / Sp.	mountain
Nuevo / Sp.	new
Nui / Viet.	mountain
Numa / Jap.	marsh, lake
Nummi / Finn.	heath
Nunatak / Esk.	peak
Nuovo / It.	new
Nur / Chin.	lake
Nusa / Mal.	island
Nut, -nut / Nor.	peak
Nuwara / Sin.; Tam.	city, town
Nuwe / Afr.	new
Nyanza / Ban.	water, river, lake
Nyasa / Ban.	lake
Nyeong / Kor.	pass
Nyika / Ban.	upland
Nyöng / Kor.	mount, pass
Nyugat / Hung.	west

O

Local Form	English
Ō / Jap.	great
Ó / Hung.	old
Ö / Swed.	island
Ø, -ø / Dan.; Nor.	island
Öar / Swed.	islands
Ober / Germ.	upper
Oblast / Rus.	province
Obo / Mong.	mountain, hill
Occidental / Fr.; Rom.; Sp.	western
Océan / Fr.	ocean
Océano / Sp.	ocean
Oceano / It.; Port.	ocean
Ocnă / Rom.	salt mine
Odde / Dan.; Nor.	promontory
Oeste / Port.; Sp.	west
Oever / Fle.; Dut.	bank
Oewer / Afr.	bank
Oie / Germ.	islet
Ojos / Sp.	spring
Oka / Jap.	coast
Oke / Sud.	height
Okean / Rus.	ocean
Oki / Jap.	bay
Okrug / Rus.	district
Ola / Alt.	city, town
Omuramba / K.S.	stream
Onder / Afr.	under
Oni / Malag.	river
Oos / Afr.	east
Oost / Fle.; Dut.	east
Oostelijk / Dut.	eastern
Opatija / Slvn.	abbey
Or / Fr.	gold
Oraş / Rom.	city, town
Óri / Gr.	mountains
Oriental / Fr.; Port.; Rom.; Sp.	eastern
Orientale / It.	eastern
Orilla / Sp.	bank
Órmos / Gr.	bay
Óros / Gr.	mountain
Ország / Hung.	land
Ort / Germ.	cape
Orta / Tur.	central
Orto / Alt.	central
Oseaan / Afr.	ocean
Ōshima / Jap.	large island
Ost / Dan.; Germ.	east
Öst / Swed.	east
Ostān, -ostān / Pers.	province
Øster / Dan.; Nor.	east, eastern
Öster / Swed.	east, eastern
Östlich / Germ.	eastern
Ostrog / Rus.	castle

Local Form	English
Ostrov / Rus.	island
Ostrovul / Rom.	island
Ostrów / Pol.	island
Ostrvo / S.C.	island
Otok / S.C.; Slvn.	island
Otrog / Rus.	front range (mountains)
Oua / Mel.	stream
Ouar / Ar.	rocky desert
Oud / Fle.; Dut.	old
Oued / Ar.	wadi
Ouest / Fr.	west
Ouled / Ar.	son
Oum / Ar.	mother
Ouro / Port.	gold
Outu / Poly.	cape
Ova / Ban.	people
Ova / Tur.	plain
Ovasi / Tur.	plain
Øver / Nor.	over
Över / Swed.	over
Övre / Swed.	over
Øy / Dan.; Nor.	island
oz., Ozero / Rus.	lake
Ozek / Alt.	hollow
Ozera / Rus.	lakes
Ozero, oz. / Rus.	lake

P

Local Form	English
P., Pulau / Mal.; Indon.	island
Pää / Finn.	principal
Pad / Rus.	valley
Padang / Indon.	plain
Padiş / Rom.	upland
Padół / Pol.	valley
Pădure / Rom.	forest
Pahorek / Cz.	hill
Pahorkatina / Cz.	plateau, hills
Pais / Port.; Sp.	land, country
Pak / Thai	mouth
Pala / It.	peak
Palaiós / Gr.	old
Palanka / S.C.	village
Pali / Poly.	cliff
-palli / Hin.	village
Pampa / Sp.	plain, prairie
Panda / Swa.	junction
Panev / Cz.	basin
Pantanal / Sp.	swamp
Pantano / Sp.	swamp, lake
Pao / Mel.	hill
Pará / A.I.	river
Paramera / Sp.	desert highland
Páramo / Sp.	moor
Paraná / A.I.	river
Parbat / Hin.; Urdu	mountain
Parc / Fr.	park
Parco / It.	park
Parco Nazionale / It.	national park
Pardo / Port.	grey
Parque / Sp.	park
Parque Nacional / Sp.; Port.	national park
Pas / Fr.; Rom.	pass, strait
Pasaje / Sp.	passage
Pasir / Mal.	sand, beach
Paso / Sp.	pass
Passágem / Port.	passage
Passe / Fr.	pass
Passo / It.; Port.	pass
Pasul / Rom.	pass
Patak / Hung.	stream
Patam, -patam / Hin.	city, town
Patnă / Hin.	city, town
Patnam, -patnam / Hin.	city, town
Pattinam, -pattinam / Hin.	city, town
Pays / Fr.	land, country
Pazar / Tur.	market
Pea / Est.	cape
Pech / Cat.	hill
Pedhiás / Gr.	plain
Pedra / Port.	rock, mountain
Peg., Pegunungan / Mal.; Indon.	mountain range
Pegunungan, Peg. / Mal.; Indon.	mountain range
Pélagos / Gr.	sea
Pele / Poly.	peak, hill
Pen / Br.	principal
Pen / Br.; Gae.	cape, mountain
Peña / Sp.	peak
Pendi / Chin.	basin
Pendiente / Sp.	slope
Penha / Port.	peak
Peninsula / Port.; Sp.	peninsula
Péninsule / Fr.	peninsula
Penisola / It.	peninsula
Peñon / Sp.	rock, island
Pente / Fr.	slope
Perekop / Rus.	channel
Pereval / Rus.	pass
Perevoz / Rus.	ford
Pertuis / Fr.	strait
Peščara / S.C.	sandy soil
Peski / Rus.	sand desert

Local Form	English
Petit / Fr.	little
Pétra / Gr.	rock
Phanom / Thai; Khm.	mountain range, mountain
Phau / Laot.	mountain
Phnum / Khm.	hill, mountain
Phu / Viet.	mountain, hill
Phum / Thai	forest
Phumĭ / Khm.	village
Pi / Chin.	cape
Piana, Pianura / It.	plain
Piano / It.	plain
Piatră / Rom.	stone
Pic / Cat.; Fr.	peak
Picacho / Sp.	peak
Piccolo / It.	little
Pico / Port.; Sp.	peak
Piedra / Sp.	rock, cliff
Pietra / It.	stone
Pieve / It.	parish
Pik / Rus.	peak
Pils / Latv.	city, town
Pinar / Sp.	pine forest
Pingyuan / Chin.	plain
Pioda / It.	crest
Pirgos / Gr.	tower, peak
Pĭsh / Pers.	anterior, before
Pitkä / Finn.	great
Piton / Fr.	mountain, peak
Piz / Rmsh.	peak
Pizzo / It.	peak
Pjasăci / Bulg.	beach
Plaat / Fle.; Dut.	sandbank
Plage / Fr.	beach
Plaine / Fr.	plain
Plan / Fr.	plain
Planalto / Port.	plateau
Planina / Bulg.	mountain
Plano / Sp.	plain
Plas / Dut.; Fle.	lake, marsh
Plato / Bulg.; Rus.	plateau
Platosu / Tur.	plateau
Platte / Germ.	plain, plateau
Plav / S.C.	blue
Plavnja / Rus.	marsh
Playa / Sp.	beach
Ploskogorje / Rus.	plateau
Plou / Br.	church
Po / Kor.	port
Po / Chin.	lake, white
P'o / Kor.	bay, lake
Poa / Mel.	hill
Poarta / Rom.	pass
Poartă / Rom.	gate
Pobla / Cat.	village
Pobrzeże / Pol.	littoral, coast
Poço / Port.	well
Poço / Port.	point
Pod / Cz.; Pol.; Rus.; S.C.; Slvn.	bridge
Podkamenny / Rus.	stony
Poggio / It.	hill
Pohja / Finn.	north, northern
Pohjois- / Finn.	north
Pojezierze / Pol.	lake region
Pol / Pers.	bridge
Pol, -pol / Rus.	city, town
Pola / Port.; Sp.	village
Polder / Fle.; Dut.	reclaimed land
Pole / Pol.	field
Pólis / Gr.	city, town
Poljana / Bulg.; Rus.; S.C.; Slvn.	field, terrace
Poljarny / Rus.	polar
Polje / S.C.; Slvn.	valley, field, basin
Poluostrov / Rus.	peninsula
Pomorije / Bulg.	littoral
Pomorze / Pol.	littoral
Ponente / It.	western
Pont / Cat.; Fr.	bridge
Ponta / Port.	point
Ponte / It.; Port.	bridge
Póntos / Gr.	sea
Poort / Afr.; Fle.; Dut.	pass
Pore, -pore / Hin.; Urdu	city, town
Porog / Rus.	rapids
Porte / Fr.	gate
Portile / Rom.	gorge
Portillo / Sp.	pass
Portiţa / Rom.	small gate
Porto / It.	port
Pôrto / Port.	port
Posht / Pers.	back, posterior
Potjo / Indon.	peak
Potok / Bulg.; Cz.; Pol.; Rus.; S.C.; Slvn.	stream
Póvoa / Port.	village
Pozo / Sp.	well
Pozzo / It.	well
Pradesh / Hin.	region, state
Prado / Sp.	meadow
Praia / Port.	beach
Prato / It.	meadow
Pré / Fr.	meadow
Prealpi / It.	prealps
Presa / Sp.	reservoir
Presqu'île / Fr.	peninsula
Prêto / Port.	black

Local Form	English
Priehradní nádrž / Cz.	reservoir
Pripoljarny / Rus.	subpolar
Pristan / Rus.	port
Prohod / Bulg.	pass
Proliv / Rus.	strait
Promontoire / Fr.	promontory
Průchod / Cz.	pass
Przedgorze / Pol.	front range (mountains)
Przełęcz / Pol.	pass
Przemyst / Pol.	industry
Przylądek / Pol.	cape
Pua / Mel.	hill
Puebla / Sp.	village
Puente / Sp.	bridge
Puerto / Sp.	port, pass
Puig / Cat.	peak
Puits / Fr.	well
Pul / Pash.	bridge
Pulau, P. / Mal.; Indon.	island
Pulau Pulau / Mal.	islands
Pulo / Mal.; Indon.	island
Puna / Sp.	upland
Puncak / Indon.	mountain
Punjung / Mal.; Indon.	mountain
Punt / Afr.	point
Punta / It.; Sp.	point
Pur, -pur / Hin.; Urdu	city, town
-pura / Hin.; Urdu	city, town
Pura / Indon.	city, town, temple
Puri, -puri / Hin.; Urdu	city, town
Pus / Alb.	spring
Pušča / Rus.	forest
Pustynja / Rus.	desert
Puszcza / Pol.	heath
Puszta / Hung.	lowland
Put / Afr.	well
Put / Rus.; S.C.	road
Putra, -putra / Hin.	son
Puu / Poly.	mountain, volcano
Puy / Fr.	peak
Pwell / Wel.	pond
Pyeong / Kor.	plain
Pyhä / Finn.	saint

Q

Local Form	English
Qagan / Mong.	white
Qala / Pash.	fortified town
Qal'at / Ar.	castle
Qalb / Ar.	hill
Qalīb / Ar.	spring
Qalīq / Ar.	spring
Qanāt / Ar.	canal
Qantara / Ar.	bridge
Qaqortoq / Esk.	white
Qar / Som.	mountain
Qara / Pers.	black
Qarah / Tur.	black
Qārat / Ar.	height, mountain
Qāret / Ar.	village, hill
Qaryah / Ar.	village
Qaryat / Ar.	village
Qaşr / Ar.	castle
Qawz / Ar.	dunes
Qeqertarssuaq / Esk.	peninsula
Qezel / Tur.	red
Qi / Chin.	river
Qing / Chin.	blue, green
Qiryat / Hebr.	city, town
Qolleh / Pers.	mountain, peak
Qu / Chin.	river, canal
Quan dao / Viet.	islands
Quebracho / Sp.	stream
Quebrada / Sp.	gorge, stream
Quedas / Port.	waterfalls
Qulbān / Ar.	well
Qundao / Chin.	archipelago
Qūr / Ar.	height, hill
Qytet / Alb.	city, town
Qyteti / Alb.	city, town

R

Local Form	English
R., Rio, River / Eng.; Sp.	river
Rada / It.; Sp.	anchorage
Rade / Fr.	anchorage
Rags / Latv.	cape
Rahad / Ar.	lake, pond
Rajon / Rus.	district
Rak / Fle.; Dut.	strait
Rakai / Poly.	reef
Ramla / Ar.	sand
Rancho / Port.; Sp.	farm, ranch
Rand / Afr.; Germ.	escarpment
Range / Eng.	mountain range
Rann / Urdu	marsh
Rano / Malag.	water
Ranta / Finn.	bank, beach
Rapide / Fr.	rapids
Ras / Amh.	peak
Rãs / Ar.	point, cape

Local Form	English
Ras, Ràs / Ar.	promontory, peak
Rãsiga / Som.	promontory
Rass / Ar.	promontory, peak
Rassa / Lapp.	mountain
Ráth / Gae.	castle
Raunina / Bulg.; Rus.	plain
Raz / Fr.	strait
Razliv / Rus.	flood plain
Récif / Fr.	reef
Recife / Port.	reef
Reede / Germ.; Dut.; Slvn.	anchorage
Reek / Afr.; Gae.	mountain range
Reg / Pash.	dunes
Région / Fr.	region
Rei / Port.	king
Reka / Bulg.; Rus.; S.C.; Slvn.	river
Řeka / Cz.	river
Réma / Gr.	torrent
Renne / Dan.; Nor.	deep
Reprêsa / Port.	dam, reservoir
Represa / Sp.	dam, reservoir
República / Port.; Sp.	republic
République / Fr.	republic
Rés., Réservoir / Fr.	reservoir
Res., Reservoir / Eng.	reservoir
Réservoir, Rés. / Fr.	reservoir
Reshteh / Pers.	mountain range
Respublika / Rus.	republic
Restinga / Port.	cliff, sandbank
Retsugan / Jap.	reef
Rettö / Jap.	archipelago
Rev / Dan.; Nor.; Swed.	reef
Rey / Sp.	king
Ri / Tib.	mountain
Ria / Sp.	estuary
Riacho / Port.	stream
Rialto / It.	plateau
Rialto / It.	rise
Riba / Port.	bank
Ribeira / Port.	river
Ribeirão / Port.	stream
Ribeiro / Port.	stream
Ribera / Sp.	coast
Ribnik / Slvn.	pond
Rid / Bulg.	mountain range
Rif / Icel.	cliff
Riff / Germ.	reef
Rïg / Pash.	dunes
Rijeka / S.C.	river
Rimâl / Ar.	sand desert
Rincón / Sp.	peninsula between two rivers
Ring / Tib.	long
Rinne / Germ.	trench
Rio / Port.	river
Rio, R. / Sp.	river
Riu / Rom.	river
Riva / It.	bank
Rive / Fr.	bank
Rivera / Sp.	brook, stream
Rivier, -rivier / Afr.; Dut.; Fle.	river
Riviera / It.	coast
Rivière / Fr.	river
Roads / Eng.	anchorage
Roc / Fr.	rock
Roca / Port.; Sp.	rock
Rocca / It.	castle
Roche / Fr.	rock
Rocher / Fr.	rock
Rock / Eng.	rock
Rod / Pash.	river
Rode / Germ.	tilled soil
Rodnik / Rus.	spring
Rog / Rus.; S.C.; Slvn.	peak
Roi / Fr.	king
Rojo / Sp.	red
Roque / Sp.	rock
Rot / Germ.	red
Roto / Poly.	lake
Rouge / Fr.	red
Równina / Pol.	plain
Rt / S.C.; Slvn.	cape
Ru / Tib.	mountain
Ruck / Germ.	ridge
Rücken / Germ.	ridge
Rud / Pers.	river
Ruda / Cz.; Slvk.	mine
Ruda / Pol.	ore
Rûdbâr / Pers.	river
Rudha / Gae.	point
Rudnik / Rus.; S.C.; Slvn.	mine
Rug / Fle.; Dut.	ridge
Ruggen / Afr.	ridge
Ruina / Sp.	ruins
Ruine / Fr.; Dut.; Germ.	ruins
Rujm / Ar.	hill
Run / Eng.	stream

S

Local Form	English
S., See / Germ.	lake, sea
Saar / Est.	island
Saari / Finn.	island
Sabbia / It.	sand
Sabkhat / Ar.	salt flat, salt marsh
Sable / Fr.; Eng.	beach
Sacca / It.	anchorage
Saco / Port.	bay
Sad / Cz.; Slvk.	park
Sad / Pers.	wall
Sadd / Ar.; Pers.	cataract, dam
Safid / Pash.; Urdu; Hin.	white
Şafrâ' / Ar.	desert
Sâgar / Hin.	reservoir
Saguia / Ar.	irrigation canal
Sahara / Ar.	desert
Sahel / Ar.	plain, coast
Sahr / Iran.	city, town
Şahrâ' / Ar.	desert
Said / Ar.	sweet
Saj / Ait.	stream, valley
Saki / Jap.	point
Sala / Latv.; Lith.	island
Saladillo / Sp.	salt desert
Salar / Sp.	salt lake
Sale / Ural.	village
Salina / It.; Sp.	salt flat, salt marsh
Saline / Dut.; Fr.; Germ.	salt flat, salt marsh
Salmi / Finn.	strait
Salseleh-ye Küh / Pers.	mountain range
Salto / Port.; Sp.	waterfall, rapids
Salz / Germ.	salt
Samudera / Indon.	ocean
Samudra / Hin.	lake
Samut / Thai	sea
San / Jap.; Kor.	mountain
San / It., Sp.	saint
Sanchi / Jap.	mountain range
Sand / Dan.; Eng.; Nor.; Swed.; Germ.	beach
Šand / Mong.	spring
Sandur / Icel.	sand
Sank / Pers.	rock
Sankt, St. / Germ.; Swed.	saint
Sanmaeg / Kor.	mountain range
Sanmyaku / Jap.	mountain range
Sansanné / Sud.	campsite
Santo / It.; Port.; Sp.	saint
Santuario / It.	sanctuary
São / Port.	saint
Sar / Pers.	cape; peak
Šar / Rus.; Tur.	strait
Saraf / Ar.	well
Sari / Finn.	island
Sari / Tur.	yellow
Sarïr / Ar.	rocky desert
Sary / Tur.	yellow
Sasso / It.	stone
Sat / Rom.	village
Sattel / Germ.	pass
Saurum / Latv.	strait
Schleuse / Germ.	lock
Schloß / Germ.	castle
Schlucht / Germ.	gorge
Schnee / Germ.	snow
Schwarz / Germ.	black
Scoglio / It.	cliff
Se / Jap.	bank, shoal
Sebkha / Ar.	salt flat
Sebkhet / Ar.	salt flat
Sed / Ar.	dam
Seda / Ural.	mountain
See, S. / Germ.	lake, sea
Sefra / Ar.	yellow
Segara / Indon.	lagoon
Şehir / Tur.	city, town
Seki / Jap.	dam
Selat / Mal.; Indon.	strait
Selatan / Indon.	southern
Selkä / Finn.	ridge, lake
Sella / It.	pass
Selo / Bulg.; Rus.; S.C.; Slvn.	village
Selsela Kohe / Pers.	mountain range
Selva / It.; Sp.	forest
Semenanjung / Mal.	peninsula
Sen / Jap.	mountain
Seong / Kor.	castle
Sep / Alt.	canal
Serïr / Ar.	rocky desert
Serra / Cat.; Port.	mountain range
Serra / It.	mountain
Serrania / Sp.	mountain range
Sertão / Port.	steppe
Seto / Jap.	strait
Sett., Settentrionale / It.	northern
Settentrionale, Sett. / It.	northern
Seuil / Fr.	sill
Sev / Arm.	black
Sever / Rus.	north
Severny / Rus.	northern
Sfint / Rom.	saint
Sfintu / Rom.	saint
Sgeir / Gae.	cliff
Sha'b / Ar.	cliff
Shahr / Pers.; Hin.	city, town
Sha'ib / Ar.	stream
Shallâl / Ar.	cataract
Shâm / Ar.	north; northern
Shamo / Chin.	sand desert
Shan / Chin.	mountain, mountain range
Shan / Gae.	old
Shand / Mong.	spring
Shankou / Chin.	pass
Shaqq / Ar.	wadi
Sharm / Ar.	bay
Sharqï / Ar.	east, eastern
Sharqïyah / Ar.	eastern
Shatt / Ar.	river, salt lake
Shatt / Tur.	stream
Shên / Alb.	saint
Sheng / Chin.	province
Shi / Chin.	city, town
Shibïn / A..	village
Shïn / Chin.	rock
Shima / Jap.	island
Shimo / Jap.	lower
Shin / Jap.	new
Shê / Jap.	island
Shotö / Jap.	archipelago
Shü / Jap.	administrative division
Shui / Chin.	river
Shuiku / Chin.	reservoir
Shu' / Pers.	salt
Sidhïros / Gr.	iron
Sidi / Ar.	master
Sieben / Germ.	seven
Sierra / Sp.	mountain range
Sikt / Ural.	village
Sillon / Fr.	furrow
Šine / Mong.	new
Sink / Eng.	depression
Sinn / Ar.	point
Sint / Dut.; Fle.	saint
Sirt / Tur.	mountain range
Sirtlar / Tur.	mountain range
Sistema / It.; Sp.	mountain system
Sïyâh / Pers.	black
Sjø / Nor.	lake
Sjö / Swed.	lake, sea
Skag / Icel.	peninsula
Skala / Bulg.; Rus.	rock
Skála / Slvk.	rock
Skar / Nor.	pass
Skär / Swed.	cliff
Skeir / Gae.	cliff
Skerry / Gae.	cliff
Skog / Nor.; Swed.	forest
Skóg / Icel.	forest
Skov / Dan.; Nor.	forest
Slatina / S.C.; Slvn.	mineral water
Slätt / Swed.	plain
Slieve / Gae.	mountain
Slot / Dut.; Fle.	castle
Slott / Nor.; Swed.	castle
Slough / Eng.	creek, pond, marsh
Sluis / Dut.; Fle.	sluice
Små / Swed.	little
Sne / Nor.	snow
Sneeuw / Afr.; Dut.	snow
Snežny / Rus.	snowy
Sne / Nor.	snow
So / Kor.	little
Sø / Dan.; Nor.	lake; sea
So / Ural.	passage
Söder / Swed.	south
Södra / Swed.	southern
Solončak / Rus.	salt flat
Sommet / Fr.	peak
Son / Viet.	mountain
Sønder / Dan. Nor.	southern
Søndre / Dan.	southern
Sone / Jap.	bank
Song / Viet.	river
Sopka / Rus.	volcano
Sopočnik / Pus.	mountain system
Soprana / It.	upper
Šor, Sor / Alt.	salt marsh
Sos / So.	upon
Sotavento / Sp.	leeward
Sotoviento / Sp.	leeward
Sottana / It.	lower
Souk / Ar.	market
Souq / Ar.	market
Sour / Ar.	rampart
Source / Eng.; Fr.	spring
Souto / Port.	forest
Spitze / Germ.	peak
Spruit / Afr.	current
Sreden / Bulg.	central
Sredni / Rus.	central
Sredni / Pol.	central
Srednji / S.C.; Slvn.	central
St., Sain-, Sankt / Eng.; Fr.; Germ.; Swed.	saint
Stadhur / Icel.	city, town
Stadt, -stadt / Germ.	city, town
Stag / Eng.	city, town
Stagno / It.	pond
-stan / Hin.; Pers.; Urdu	land
Star / Belg.	old
Stari / S.C.; Slvn.	old
Stary / Pol.; Rus.	old
Starý / Cz.; Slvk.	old
Stat / Afr.; Dan.; Fle.; Nor.; Dut.; Swed.	city, town
Stathmós / Gr.	railway station
Stausee / Germ.	reservoir
Stavrós / Gr.	cross
Sted / Dan.; Nor.	place
Stedt / Germ.	place
Stein, -stein / Nor., Germ.	stone
Sten / Nor.; Swed.	stone
Stena / Rus.; S.C.; Slvn.	rock
Stěna / Cz.	mountain range
Stenón / Gr.	strait, pass
Step / Rus.	steppe
-sthãn / Hin.; Pers.; Urdu	land
Stift / Germ.	foundation
Štit / Cz.; Slvk.	peak
Stock / Germ.	massif
Stok / Pol.	slope
Stor / Dan.; Nor.; Swed.	great
Store / Dan.	great
Stræde / Dan.	strait
Strana / Rus.	land
Strand / Germ.; Nor.; Swed.; Afr.; Dan.	beach
Straße / Germ.	street, road
Strath / Gae.	valley
Straum / Nor.; Swed.	stream
Středni / Cz.	central
Stredný / Slvk.	central
Strelka / Rus.	spit
Stret / Nor.	strait
Stretto / It.	strait
Strom / Germ.	stream
Strøm / Nor.	stream
Ström / Swed.	stream
Stroom / Dut.	stream
Su / Jap.	sandbank
Su / Tur.	river
Suando / Finn.	pond
Suid / Afr.	south
Suidô / Jap.	strait
Sul / Port.	south
Sund / Dan.; Nor.; Swed.; Germ.	strait
Sungai / Mal.	river
Sunn / Nor.	south
Süq / Ar.	market
Sur / Fr.	on
Sur / Sp.	south
Surkh / Pers.	red
Suu / Finn.	mouth, river mouth
Suur / Cat.	great
Svart / Nor.; Swed.	black
Sveti / S.C.; Slvn.	saint
Swa / Ban.	great
Swart / Afr.	black
Świety / Pol.	saint
Syrt / Alt.	ridge
Szállás / Hung.	village
Szczyt / Pol.	peak
Szeg / Hung.	bend
Székes / Hung.	residence
Szent / Hung.	saint
Sziget / Hung.	river island

T

Local Form	English
Tadi / Ban.	rock, cliff
Tae / Kor.	great
Tafua / Poly.	mountain
Tag / Alt.; Tur.	mountain
Tahta / Ar.	lower
Tahti / Ar.	lower
Tai / Chin.; Jap.	great
Taipale / Finn.	isthmus
Tajga / Rus.	forest
Take / Jap.	mountain
Tal / Germ.	valley
Tala / Mong.	plain, steppe
Tala / Ber.	spring
Tall / Ar.	hill
Talsperre / Germ.	dam
Tam / Viet.	stream
Tamgout / Ber.	peak
Tan / Chin.; Kor.	sandbank
Tana / Malag.	city, town
Tanana / Malag.	city, town
Tandjung / Mal.	cape, point
Tanezrouft / Ber.	desert
Tang / Tib.	upland
Tangeh / Pers.	strait
Tanjong / Mal.	cape, point
Tanjung, Tg. / Indon.	cape, point
Tanout / Ber.	well
Tao / Chin.	island
Taourirt / Ber.	peak
Targ / Pol.	market
Târg / Bulg.	market
Tarn / Eng.	glacial lake
Tarso / Sah.	crater
Taš / Alt.	stone

Geographical Glossary

Local Form	English
Tassili / Ber.	upland
Tau / Tur.	mountain
Taung / Burm.	mountain
Ṭawīl / Ar.	hill
Tégi / Sah.	hill
Teguidda / Ber.	well
Tehi / Ber.	pass, mountain
Teich / Germ.	pond
Tell / Tur.	hill
Telok / Mal.	bay, port
Teluk / Mal.	bay, port
Tempio / It.	temple
Ténéré / Ber.	rocky desert
Tengah / Indon.; Mal.	central
Tepe / Tur.	hill
Tepesi / Tur.	hill
Termas / Sp.	thermal springs
Terme / It.	thermal springs
Terra / It.; Dut.	land, earth
Terrazzo / It.	guyot, tablemount
Terre / Fr.	land, earth
Teso / Cat.	hill
Téssa / Ber.	wadi, depression
Testa / It.	point
Tête / Fr.	peak
Tetri / Georg.	white
Teu / Poly.	reef
Teze / Alt.	new
Tg., Tanjung / Indon.	cape, point
Thaba / Ban.	mountain
Thabana / Ban.	mountain
Thal / Germ.	valley
Thálassa / Gr.	sea
Thale / Thai	lagoon
Thamad / Ar.	well
Theós / Gr.	god
Thermes / Fr.	thermal springs
Thog / Tib.	high, upper
Tian / Chin.	field
Tiefe / Germ.	deep
Tierra / Sp.	land, earth
Timur / Indon.; Mal.	eastern
Tind / Nor.	mountain
Tinto / Sp.	black
Tirg / Rom.	market
Tis / Amh.	new
Tizgui / Ber.	forest
Tizi / Ber.	pass
Tjåkko / Lapp.	mountain
Tjärn / Swed.	tarn, glacial lake
Tji / Mal.	stream
To / Kor.	island
To / Mel.	stream
Tō / Jap.	island
Tó / Hung.	lake
To / Ural.	lake
Tobe / Tur.	hill
Tofua / Poly.	mountain
Tog / Som.	valley
Tōge / Jap.	pass
Tokoj / Alt.	forest
Tônle / Khm.	stream, lake
Tope / Dut.	peak
Toplice / S.C.; Slvn.	thermal springs
Topp / Nor.	peak
Tor / Gae.	rock
Tor / Germ.	gate
Torbat / Pers.	tomb
Törl / Germ.	pass
Torp / Swed.	hut
Torre / Cat.; It.; Sp.; Port.	tower
Torrente / It.; Sp.	torrent, stream
Tossa / Cat.	mountain, peak
Tota / Sin.	port
Tour / Fr.	tower
Traforo / It.	tunnel
Träsk / Swed.	lake
Trg / S.C.	market
Trog / Germ.	trough, trench
Trois / Fr.	three
Trung / Viet.	central
Tse / Tib.	peak, point
Tsi / Chin.	pond
Tskali / Georg.	river
Tsu / Jap.	bay
Tulül / Ar.	hills
Túnel / Pers.	tunnel
Tunturi / Lapp.	mountain, tundra
Tur'ah / Ar.	irrigation canal
Turm / Germ.	tower
Turn / Rom.	tower
Turó / Cat.	dome
Tuz / Tur.	salt
Týn / Cz.	fortress

U

Local Form	English
U., Unter-, Upon / Eng.; Germ.	under, lower
Uaimh / Gae.	cave
Uchi / Jap.	bay
Udde / Swed.	cape
Údolní nádrž / Cz.	reservoir
Uebi / Som.	river
Új- / Hung.	new
Ujście / Pol.	mouth
Ujung / Indon.	point, cape
Ul / Chin.; Mong.	mountain, mountain range
Ula / Mong.	mountain range
Ulan / Mong.	red
Uls / Mong.	state
Umi / Jap.	bay
Umm / Ar.	mother, spring
Umne / Mong.	south
Under / Mong.	mountain, peak
Ungur / Alt.	cave
Unter-, U. / Germ.	under, lower
Upar / Hin.	river
'Uqlat / Ar.	well
Ür / Tam.	city, town
Ura / Jap.	bay, coast
Ura / Alt.	depression
Urd / Mong.	south
Uru / Tam.	city, town
Ušće / S.C.	mouth
Uske / Alt.	upper
Ust / Rus.	mouth
Ústí / Cz.	mouth
Ustup / Rus.	terrace
Utan / Indon.; Mal.	forest
Utara / Indon.	north, northern
Uusi / Finn.	new
Uval / Rus.	height
Úval / Cz.	mountain
'Uwaynāt / Ar.	well
Uzboj / Alt.	river bed
Uzun / Tur.	long
Užūrekis / Lith.	gulf

V

Local Form	English
Va / Alb.	ford
Va / Ural.	water, river
Vaara / Finn.	mountain
Väärti / Finn.	bay
Vad / Rom.	ford
Vær / Nor.	port
Våg / Nor.	bay
Vähä / Finn.	little
Väike / Est.	little
Väin / Est.	strait
Val / Fr.; It.	valley
Val / Rom.; Rus.	wall
Valico / It.	pass
Vall / Cat.	valley
Vall / Swed.	pasture
Valle / It.; Sp.	valley
Vallée / Fr.	valley
Vallei / Afr.	valley
Vallo / It.	wall
Valta / Finn.	cape
Váltos / Gr.	marsh
Valul / Rom.	wall
Vann / Dan.; Nor.	water, lake
Vanua / Mel.	land
Vár / Hung.	fort
Vara / Finn.	mountain
Varoš / S.C.	city, town
Város / Hung.	city, town
Varre / Lapp.	mountain
Vary / Cz.	spring
Vas / S.C.; Slvn.	village
Vásár / Hung.	market
Väst / Swed.	west
Väster / Swed.	western
Vatn / Icel.; Nor.	lake
Vatten / Swed.	water, lake
Vatu / Mel.; Poly.	island, reef
Vdhr., Vodohranilišče / Rus.	reservoir
Vechiu / Rom.	old
Vecs / Latv.	old
Veen / Dut.; Fle.	moor
Vega / Sp.	irrigated crops
Veld / Afr.; Dut.; Fle.	field
Veli / S.C.; Slvn.	great
Velik / Bulg.	great
Veliki / Rus.; S.C.; Slvn.	great
Veliký / Cz.	great
Vel'ky / Slvk.	great
Vella / Cat.	old
Ver / Ural.	forest
Verde / It.; Sp.	green
Verh / Rus.	peak
Verhni / Rus.	upper
Verk / Swed.	factory
Vermelho / Port.	red
Vert / Fr.	green
Ves / Cz.	village
Vesi / Finn.	water, lake
Vest / Dan.; Nor.	west
Vester / Dan.; Nor.	western
Vestur / Icel.	west
Vetta / It.	summit
Viaduc / Fr.	viaduct
Vidda / Nor.	upland
Vidde / Nor.	upland
Viejo / Sp.	old
Vier / Germ.	four
Viertel / Germ.	quarter
Vieux / Fr.	old
Vig / Dan.	bay
Vik / Icel.; Nor.; Swed.	gulf, bay
Vila / Port.	city, town
Villa / Sp.	city, town
Ville, -ville / Eng.; Fr.	city, town
Vinh / Viet.	bay
Virful / Rom.	peak, mountain
Virta / Finn.	river
Višni / Rus.	high
Visok / S.C.	high
Viz / Hung.	water
Viztároló / Hung.	reservoir
Vlakte / Dut.; Fle.	plain
Vlei / Afr.	pond
Vliet / Dut.; Fle.	river
Vloer / Afr.	depression
Voda / Bulg.; Cz.; Rus.; S.C.; Slvn.	water
Vodny put / Rus.	stream, canal
Vodohranilišče, vdhr. / Rus.	reservoir
Vodopad / Rus.	waterfall
Volcan / Fr.	volcano
Volcán / Sp.	volcano
Voll / Nor.	meadow
Vórios / Gr.	northern
Vorota / Rus.	gate
Vorrás / Gr.	north
Vostočny / Rus.	eastern
Vostok / Rus.	east
Vötn / Icel.	lake, water
Vož / Ural.	mouth
Vozvyšennost / Rus.	upland
Vpadina / Rus.	depression
Vrah / Bulg.	peak
Vrata / Bulg.; S.C.; Slvn.	pass
Vrch / Cz.; Slvk.	mountain
Vrch / S.C.; Slvn.	peak
Vrchni- / Cz.	upper
Vrchovina / Cz.	upland
Vulcan / Rom.; Rus.	volcano
Vulcano / It.	volcano
Vulkan / Germ.; Rus.	volcano
Vuopio / Lapp.	bend
Vuori / Finn.	rock
Východný / Cz.	eastern
Vyšný / Slvk.	upper
Vysoki / Rus.	high
Vysoky / Cz.; Slvk.	high
Vyšši / Cz.	high

W

Local Form	English
W., Wādī / Ar.	wadi
Wa / Ban.	people
Wabe / Amh.	stream
Wad / Ar.	wadi
Wad / Dut.	tidal flat
Wādī, W. / Ar.	wadi
Wāḥāt / Ar.	oasis
Wai / Mel.; Poly.	stream
Wal / Afr.	wall
Wala / Hin.	mountain range
Wald / Germ.	forest
Wan / Burm.	village
Wan / Chin.; Jap.	bay
Wand / Germ.	bluff
War / Som.	pond
Wār / Ar.	desert
-waram / Hin.; Tam.	village
Wasser / Germ.	water
Wat / Pol.	wall
Wat / Thai	church
Waterval / Afr.; Dut.	waterfall
Watt / Germ.	tidal flat
Wāw / Ar.	oasis
Weald / Eng.	wooded country
Webi / Som.	stream
Weg / Germ.	way, road
Wei / Chin.	cape, point
Weide / Germ.	pasture
Weiler / Germ.	village
Weiß / Germ.	white
Weon / Kor.	field
Wer / Som.	pond
Werder / Germ.	river island
Werk / Germ.	factory
Wes / Afr.	west
Westlich / Germ.	western
Westr- / Sca.	western
Wëyn / Som.	great
Wëyne / Som.	great
Wick / Eng.	village
Wiek / Germ.	bay
Wielki / Pol.	great
Wieś / Pol.	village
Wijk / Dut.; Fle.	quarter, district
-willer / Germ.	village
Woda / Pol.	water
Woestyn / Afr.	desert
Wold / Dut.; Fle.; Eng.	forest
Wörth / Germ.	river island
Woud / Dut.; Fle.	forest
Wschodni / Pol.	eastern
Wysoczyzna / Pol.	upland
Wysoki / Pol.	upper
Wyspa / Pol.	island
Wyżyna / Pol.	highland
Wzgórze / Pol.	hill

X

Local Form	English
Xi / Chin.	west
Xia / Chin.	gorge, strait
Xian / Chin.	county, shire
Xiang / Chin.	village
Xiao / Chin.	little
Xin / Chin.	new
Xu / Chin.	island

Y

Local Form	English
Yam / Hebr.	lake, sea
Yama / Jap.	mountain
Yan / Chin.	mountain
Yang / Chin.	strait, ocean
Yani / Tur.	new
Yar / Tur.	gorge
Yarimada / Tur.	peninsula
Yazı / Tur.	plain
Yegge / Sah.	well
Yeni / Tur.	new
Yeon / Kor.	sea
Yeong / Kor.	mountain
Yeşil / Tur.	green
Ylä / Finn.	upper
Yli- / Finn.	upper
Yō / Jap.	ocean
Yobe / Sud.	great
Yōm / Kor.	island
Yoma / Burm.	mountain range
Yön / Kor.	lake, pond
Yŏng / Kor.	mountain, peak
Ytter / Nor.; Swed.	outer
Yttre / Swed.	outer
Yu / Chin.	old
Yu / Chin.	island
Yu / Jap.	thermal spring
Yüan / Chin.	spring, river
Yunhe / Chin.	canal

Z

Local Form	English
Zāb / Ar.	river
Zachodni / Pol.	western
Zaki / Jap.	cape
Zalew / Pol.	gulf
Zaliv / Bulg.; Rus.; S.C.; Slvn.	gulf
Zaljev / Slvn.	bay
Zámek / Cz.	castle
Zan / Jap.	mountain
Zand / Dut.; Fle.	sand
Zandt / Dut.; Fle.	sand
Zangbo / Chin.	river
Zapad / Rus.	west
Zapaden / Bulg.	western
Zapadni / S.C.; Slvn.	western
Západní / Cz.	western
Zapadny / Rus.	western
Zapovednik / Rus.	reserve
Zatoka / Pol.	gulf
Zavod / Rus.	roadstead
Zāwiyat / Ar.	monastery
Zdrój / Pol.	thermal springs
Ze / Jap.	islet
Zee / Dut.; Fle.	sea
Zelëny / Rus.	green
Žem / Lith.	land, country
Zemé / Cz.; Slvk.	land, country
Zemlja / Rus.	land
Zen / Jap.	mountain
Zhan / Chin.	mountain
Zhen / Chin.	market
Zhong / Chin.	central
Zhou / Chin.	quarter, district
Zhuang / Chin.	village
Ziemia / Pol.	land
Zigos / Gr.	pass
Zipfel / Germ.	tip, point
Ziwa / Swa.	marsh
Zizhiqu / Chin.	autonomous region
Zlato / Bulg.	gold
Zuid / Dut.; Fle.	south
Zuidelijk / Dut.	southern
Żuława / Pol.	marsh
Zun / Mong.	east
Zwart / Dut.	black
Zwei / Germ.	two

International Map Index

All of the toponyms (place-names) which appear on the maps are listed in the International Map Index. Each entry includes the following: Place-name and, where applicable, other forms by which it is written or known; a symbol, where applicable, indicating what kind of feature it is; the number of the map on which it appears; and the map-reference letters and geographical coordinates indicating its location on the map.

Toponyms

Each toponym, or place-name, is written in full, with accents and diacritical marks. Since many countries have more than one official language, many of these forms are included on the maps. For example, many Belgian place-names are listed as follows: Bruxelles/Brussel; Antwerpen/Anvers, and vice versa, Brussel/Bruxelles; Anvers/Antwerpen. In Italy, certain regions have a special status—they are largely autonomous and officially bilingual. As a result, Index listings appear as follows: Aosta/Aoste; Alto Adige/Sud Tirol, and vice versa. One name, however, may be the only name on the map.

In China, the written forms of commonly used regional languages have been taken into account. These forms are enclosed in parenthesis following the official name: e.g. Xiangshan (Dancheng). However, when the regional is listed first, it is linked to the official name with an →: e.g. Dancheng→Xiangshan. The same style is used for former or historical name forms: e.g. Rhodesia→Zimbabwe and Zimbabwe (Rhodesia).

Place-names for major features (countries, major cities, and large physical features), where applicable, include the English conventional form identified by (EN) and linked in the local name or names with an = sign: e.g. Italia = Italy (EN), and vice versa, Italy (EN) = Italia. Former English names are linked in the Index to the conventional form by an →.

Symbols

The last component with the place-name is a symbol, where applicable, specifying the broad category of the feature named. A table preceding the Index lists all of the symbols used and their meanings; this information also appears as a footnote on each page of the Index. Place-names without symbols are cities and towns.

Alphabetization

Place-names are listed in English alphabetical order—26 letters, from A to Z—because of its international usage. Names including two or more words are listed alphabetically according to the first letter of the word: e.g. De Ruyter is listed under D; Le Havre is listed under L. Names with the prefix Mc are listed as if spelled Mac. The generic portion of a name (lake, sierra, mountain, etc.) is placed after the name: e.g. Lake Erie is listed as Erie, Lake; Sierra Morena is listed as Morena, Sierra. In Spanish, "ch" and "ll" groups and the letter "ñ" are included respectively under C, L, and N, without any distinction.

The same place-name sometimes is listed in the Index several times. It may because of the various translations of a name, or it may be that several places have the same name.

Various translations of a name appear as follows:

| Danube (EN) = Dunav | Danube (EN) = Donau |
| Danube (EN) = Dunărea | Danube (EN) = Dunaj |

Several places with the same name appear as follows; however, only in these cases is the location—abbreviated and enclosed in brackets—included. A table of these abbreviations precedes the Index.

Abbeville [U.S.]	Aberdeen [Scot.-U.K.]
Abbeville [Fr.]	Aberdeen [N.C.-U.S.]
Abberdeen [S. Afr.]	

Map Number

Each map in the atlas is identified by a number. Where multiple maps are on one page, each map is additionally identified by a boxed letter in the upper-right-hand corner of the map. In the Index listing following the place-name and its variations in language and spelling, where applicable, is the number of the map on which it appears. If the map is one of several on a page, the Index listing includes the map number and letter.

Although a place-name may appear on one or more maps, it is indexed to only one map. Most places are indexed to the regional maps. However, if a place-name appears on either the physical or political continental maps, it is indexed to one of the two types of map. For example, a river or mountain would be indexed to a physical continental map; a city or state would be indexed to a political continental map.

Map-Reference Letters and Geographical Coordinates

The next elements in the Index listing are the map-reference letters and the geographical coordinates, respectively, locating the place on the map.

Map-reference letters consist of a capital and a lowercase letter. Capital letters are across the top and bottom of the maps; lowercase letters are down the sides. The map-reference letters assigned to each place-name refer to the location of the name within the area formed by grid lines connecting the geographical coordinates on either sides of the letters.

Geographical coordinates are the latitude (N for North, S for South) and longitude (E for East, W for West) expressed in degrees and minutes and based on the prime meridian, Greenwich.

Map-reference letters and coordinates for extensive geographical features, such as mountain ranges and countries, are given for the approximate central point of the area. Those for waterways, such as canals and rivers, are given for the mouth of the river, the point where it enters another river or where the feature reaches the map margin. On this page are sample maps showing points to which features are indexed according to map-reference letters and coordinates.

On most maps there is not enough space to place all of the names of administrative subdivisions. In these cases the location of the place is shown on the map by a circled letter or number and the place-name and circled letter or number are listed in the map margin. The map-reference numbers and coordinates for these places refer to the location of the circled letter or number on the map.

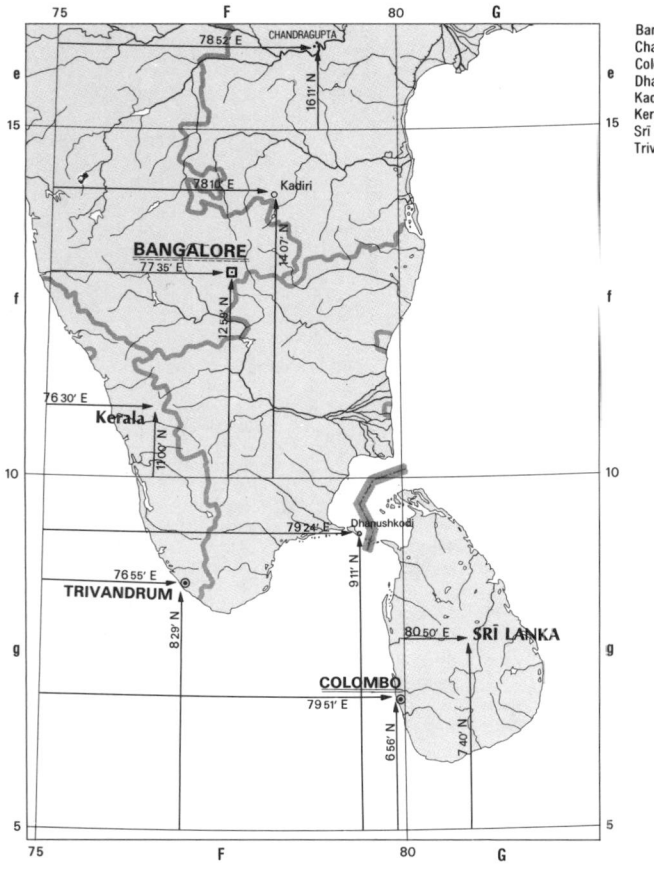

Bangalore		25	Ff	12°59'N	77°35'E
Chandragupta		35	Fe	16°11'N	78°52'E
Colombo		25	Fg	6°56'N	79°51'E
Dhanushkodi		25	Fg	9°11'N	79°24'E
Kadiri		25	Ff	14°07'N	78°10'E
Kerala		25	Ff	11°00'N	76°30'E
Sri Lanka		25	Gg	7°40'N	80°50'E
Trivandrum		25	Fg	8°29'N	76°55'E

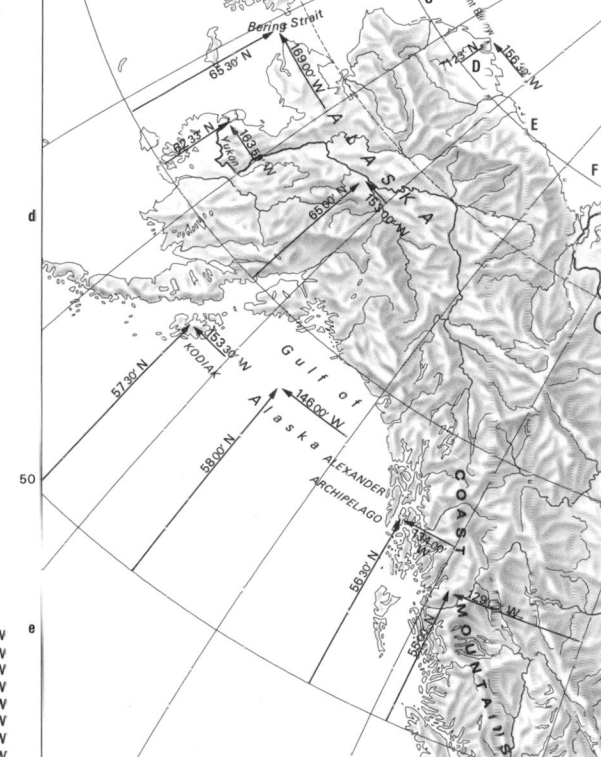

Alaska		38	Dc	65°00'N	153°00'W
Alaska, Gulf of-		38	Ed	58°00'N	146°00'W
Alexander Archipelago		38	Fd	56°00'N	134°00'W
Barrow, Point-		38	Db	71°23'N	156°30'W
Bering Strait		38	Cc	65°30'N	169°00'W
Coast Mountains		38	Gd	55°00'N	129°00'W
Kodiak		38	Dd	57°30'N	153°30'W
Yukon		38	Cc	62°33'N	163°59'W

List of Abbreviations

Afg.	Afghanistan	D.C.-U.S.	District of Columbia, U.S.	Kir.	Kiribati
Afr.	Africa	De.-U.S.	Delaware, U.S.	Ks.-U.S.	Kansas, U.S.
Agl.	Anguilla	Den.	Denmark	Kuw.	Kuwait
Ak.-U.S.	Alaska, U.S.	Dji.	Djibouti	Ky.-U.S.	Kentucky, U.S.
Al.-U.S.	Alabama, U.S.	Dom.	Dominica	La.-U.S.	Louisiana, U.S.
Alb.	Albania	Dom. Rep.	Dominican Republic	Laos	Laos

Afg.   Afghanistan
Afr.   Africa
Agl.   Anguilla
Ak.-U.S.   Alaska, U.S.
Al.-U.S.   Alabama, U.S.
Alb.   Albania
Alg.   Algeria
Alta.-Can. Alberta, Canada
Am. Sam.   American Samoa
And.   Andorra
Ang.   Angola
Ant.   Antarctica
Ar.-U.S.   Arkansas, U.S.
Arg.   Argentina
Asia   Asia
Atg.   Antigua and Barbuda
Aus.   Austria
Austl.   Australia
Az.-U.S.   Arizona, U.S.
Azr.   Azores
Bah.   Bahamas
Bar.   Barbados
B.A.T.   British Antarctic Territory
B.C.-Can.   British Columbia, Canada
Bel.   Belgium
Ben.   Benin
Ber.   Bermuda
Bhr.   Bahrain
Bhu.   Bhutan
Blz.   Belize
Bnd.   Burundi
Bngl.   Bangladesh
Bol.   Bolivia
Bots.   Botswana
Braz.   Brazil
Bru.   Brunei
Bul.   Bulgaria
Bur.   Burma
Burkina   Burkina Faso
B.V.I.   British Virgin Islands
Ca.-U.S.   California, U.S.
Cam.   Cameroon
C. Amer.   Central America
Can.   Canada
Can. Is.   Canary Islands
C.A.R.   Central African Republic
Cay. Is   Cayman Islands
Chad   Chad
Chan. Is.   Channel Islands
Chile   Chile
China   China
Co.-U.S.   Colorado, U.S.
Cocos Is.   Cocos Islands
Col.   Colombia
Con.   Congo
Cook   Cook Islands
Cor. Sea Is. Coral Sea Islands
C.R.   Costa Rica
Ct.-U.S.   Connecticut, U.S.
Cuba   Cuba
C.V.   Cape Verde
Cyp.   Cyprus
Czech.   Czech Republic

D.C.-U.S.   District of Columbia, U.S.
De.-U.S.   Delaware, U.S.
Den.   Denmark
Dji.   Djibouti
Dom.   Dominica
Dom. Rep.   Dominican Republic
Ec.   Ecuador
Eg.   Egypt
El Sal.   El Salvador
Eng.-U.K.   England, U.K.
Eq. Gui.   Equatorial Guinea
Est.   Estonia
Eth.   Ethiopia
Eur.   Europe
Falk. Is.   Falkland Islands
Far. Is.   Faeroe Islands
Fiji   Fiji
Fin.   Finland
Fl.-U.S.   Florida, U.S.
Fr.   France
Fr. Gui.   French Guiana
Fr. Poly.   French Polynesia
F.S.M.   Federated States of Micronesia
Ga.-U.S.   Georgia, U.S.
Gabon   Gabon
Gam.   Gambia
Geor.   Georgia
Ger.   Germany
Ghana   Ghana
Gib.   Gibraltar
Grc.   Greece
Gren.   Grenada
Grld.   Greenland
Guad.   Guadeloupe
Guam   Guam
Guat.   Guatemala
Gui.   Guinea
Gui. Bis.   Guinea Bissau
Guy.   Guyana
Haiti   Haiti
Hi.-U.S.   Hawaii, U.S.
H.K.   Hong Kong
Hond.   Honduras
Hun.   Hungary
Ia.-U.S.   Iowa, U.S.
I.C.   Ivory Coast
Ice.   Iceland
Id.-U.S.   Idaho, U.S.
Il.-U.S.   Illinois, U.S.
In.-U.S.   Indiana, U.S.
India   India
Indon.   Indonesia
I. of M.   Isle of Man
Iran   Iran
Iraq   Iraq
Ire.   Ireland
Isr.   Israel
It.   Italy
Jam.   Jamaica
Jap.   Japan
Jor.   Jordan
Kam.   Cambodia
Kenya   Kenya
Ker. Is.   Kermadec Islands

Kir.   Kiribati
Ks.-U.S.   Kansas, U.S.
Kuw.   Kuwait
Ky.-U.S.   Kentucky, U.S.
La.-U.S.   Louisiana, U.S.
Laos   Laos
Lat.   Latvia
Lbr.   Liberia
Leb.   Lebanon
Les.   Lesotho
Lib.   Libya
Liech.   Liechtenstein
Lith.   Lithuania
Lux.   Luxembourg
Ma.-U.S.   Massachusetts, U.S.
Mac.   Macao
Mad.   Madagascar
Mala.   Malaysia
Mald.   Maldives
Mali   Mali
Malta   Malta
Man.-Can.   Manitoba, Canada
Mar. Is.   Marshall Islands
Mart.   Martinique
Maur.   Mauritius
May.   Mayotte
Mco.   Monaco
Md.-U.S.   Maryland, U.S.
Me.-U.S.   Maine, U.S.
Mex.   Mexico
Mi.-U.S.   Michigan, U.S.
Mid. Is.   Midway Islands
Mn.-U.S.   Minnesota, U.S.
Mo.-U.S.   Missouri, U.S.
Mong.   Mongolia
Mont.   Montserrat
Mor.   Morocco
Moz.   Mozambique
Ms.-U.S.   Mississippi, U.S.
Mt.-U.S.   Montana, U.S.
Mtna.   Mauritania
Mwi.   Malawi
Nam.   Namibia
N. Amer.   North America
Nauru   Nauru
N.B.-Can.   New Brunswick, Canada
Nb.-U.S.   Nebraska, U.S.
N.C.-U.S.   North Carolina, U.S.
N. Cal.   New Caledonia
N.D.-U.S.   North Dakota, U.S.
Nep.   Nepal
Neth.   Netherlands
Neth. Ant. Netherlands Antilles
Newf.-Can. Newfoundland, Canada
N.H.-U.S.   New Hampshire, U.S.
Nic.   Nicaragua
Nig.   Nigeria
Niger   Niger

N. Ire.-U.K. Northern Ireland, U.K.
N.J.-U.S.   New Jersey, U.S.
N. Kor.   North Korea
N.M.-U.S.   New Mexico, U.S.
N. M. Is.   Northern Mariana Islands
Nor.   Norway
Nor. I.   Norfolk Island
N.S.-Canada Nova Scotia, Canada
Nv.-U.S.   Nevada, U.S.
N.W.T.-Can. Northwest Territories, Canada
N.Y.-U.S.   New York, U.S.
N.Z.   New Zealand
Ocn.   Oceania
Oh.-U.S.   Ohio, U.S.
Ok.-U.S.   Oklahoma, U.S.
Oman   Oman
Ont.-Ont.   Ontario, Canada
Or.-U.S.   Oregon, U.S.
Pa.-U.S.   Pennsylvania, U.S.
Pak.   Pakistan
Pal.   Palau
Pan.   Panama
Pap. N. Gui. Papua New Guinea
Par.   Paraguay
Pas.   Pascua
P.E.I.-Can. Prince Edward Island, Canada
Peru   Peru
Phil.   Philippines
Pit.   Pitcairn
Pol.   Poland
Port.   Portugal
P.R.   Puerto Rico
Qatar   Qatar
Que.-Can.   Quebec, Canada
Reu.   Reunion
R.I.-U.S.   Rhode Island, U.S.
Rom.   Romania
Rwn.   Rwanda
S. Afr.   South Africa
S. Amer.   South America
Sao T.P.   Sao Tome and Principe
Sask.-Can. Saskatchewan, Canada
Sau. Ar.   Saudi Arabia
S.C.-U.S.   South Carolina, U.S.
Scot.-U.K. Scotland, U.K.
S.D.-U.S.   South Dakota, U.S.
Sen.   Senegal
Sey.   Seychelles
Sing.   Singapore
S. Kor.   South Korea
S.L.   Sierra Leone
S. Lan.   Sri Lanka
S.M.   San Marino
S.N.A.   Spanish North Africa
Sol. Is.   Solomon Islands
Som.   Somalia
Sp.   Spain

St. C.N.   Saint Christopher-Nevis
St. Hel.   Saint Helena
St. Luc.   Saint Lucia
St. P.M.   Saint Pierre and Miquelon
St. Vin.   Saint Vincent and the Grenadines
Sud.   Sudan
Sur.   Suriname
Sval.   Svalbard
Swe.   Sweden
Switz.   Switzerland
Syr.   Syria
Tai.   Taiwan
Tan.   Tanzania
T.C. Is.   Turks and Caicos Islands
Thai.   Thailand
Tn.-U.S.   Tennessee, U.S.
Togo   Togo
Ton.   Tonga
Trin.   Trinidad and Tobago
T.T.P.I.   Trust Territory of the Pacific Islands
Tun.   Tunisia
Tur.   Turkey
Tuv.   Tuvalu
Tx.-U.S.   Texas, U.S.
U.A.E.   United Arab Emirates
Ug.   Uganda
U.K.   United Kingdom
Ukr.   Ukraine
Ur.   Uruguay
U.S.   United States
Ut.-U.S.   Utah, U.S.
Va.-U.S.   Virginia, U.S.
Van.   Vanuatu
V.C.   Vatican City
Ven.   Venezuela
Viet.   Vietnam
V.I.U.S.   Virgin Islands of the U.S.
Vt.-U.S.   Vermont, U.S.
Wa.-U.S.   Washington, U.S.
Wake   Wake Island
Wales-U.K. Wales, U.K.
W.F.   Wallis and Futuna
Wi.-U.S.   Wisconsin, U.S.
W. Sah.   Western Sahara
W. Sam.   Western Samoa
W.V.-U.S.   West Virginia, U.S.
Wy.-U.S.   Wyoming, U.S.
Yem.   Yemen
Yugo.   Yugoslavia
Yuk.-Can.   Yukon, Canada
Zaire   Zaire
Zam.   Zambia
Zimb.   Zimbabwe

List of Symbols

Plains and Associated Features
- Plain, Basin, Lowland
- Delta
- Salt Flat

Valleys and Depressions
- Valley, Gorge, Ravine, Canyon
- Cave, Crater, Quarry
- Karst Features
- Depression
- Polder, Reclaimed Marsh

Vegetational Features
- Desert, Dunes
- Forest, Woods
- Heath, Steppe, Tundra, Moor
- Oasis

Political/Administrative Units
- [1] Independent Nation
- [2] State, Canton, Region
- [3] Province, Department, County, Territory, District
- [4] Municipality
- [5] Colony, Dependency, Administered Territory

Geographical Regions
- Continent
- Physical Region
- Historical or Cultural Region

Mountain Features
- Mount, Mountain, Peak
- Volcano
- Hill
- Mountains, Mountain Range
- Hills, Escarpment
- Plateau, Highland, Upland
- Pass, Gap

Coastal Features
- Cape, Point
- Coast, Beach
- Cliff
- Peninsula, Promontory
- Isthmus
- Sandbank, Tombolo, Sandbar

Islands Rocks, Reefs
- Island
- Atoll
- Rock, Reef
- Islands, Archipelago
- Rocks, Reefs
- Coral Reef

Hydrographic Features
- Well, Spring
- Geyser, Fumarole
- River, Stream, Brook
- Waterfall, Rapids, Cataract
- River Mouth, Estuary
- Lake
- Salt Lake
- Intermittent Lake, Dry Lake Bed
- Reservoir, Artificial Lake
- Swamp, Marsh, Pond
- Irrigation Canal, Navigable Canal, Ditch, Aqueduct

Ice Features
- Glacier, Snowfield
- Ice Shelf, Pack Ice

Marine Features
- Ocean
- Sea
- Gulf, Bay
- Strait, Fjord, Sea Channel
- Lagoon, Anchorage

Submarine Features
- Bank, Shoal
- Seamount
- Rise, Plateau, Tablemount
- Seamount Chain, Ridge
- Platform, Shelf
- Basin, Depression
- Escarpment, Slope, Sea Scarp
- Fracture
- Trench, Abyss, Valley, Canyon

Other Features
- National Park, Nature Reserve
- Scenic Area, Point of Interest
- Recreation Site, Sports Arena
- Cave, Cavern
- Historic Site, Memorial, Mausoleum, Museum
- Ruins
- Wall, Walls, Tower, Castle, Fortress
- Church, Abbey, Cathedral, Sanctuary
- Temple, Synagogue, Mosque
- Research or Scientific Station
- Airport, Heliport
- Port, Dock
- Lighthouse
- Mine
- Tunnel
- Dam, Bridge

A

Å	7	Cc	67.53N	12.59 E
Aa [Eur.]	12	Ic	51.50N	6.25 E
Aa [Fr.]	11	Ic	51.01N	2.06 E
Aa [Fr.]	12	Dd	50.44N	2.18 E
Aa [Ger.]	12	Kb	52.07N	8.41 E
Aa [Ger.]	12	Jb	52.15N	7.18 E
Aachen	10	Cf	50.46N	6.06 E
Aalen	10	Gh	48.50N	10.06 E
A'ālī an Nīl	35	Ed	9.15N	33.00 E
Aalsmeer	12	Gb	52.15N	4.45 E
Aalst/Alost	11	Kd	50.56N	4.02 E
Aalten	12	Ic	51.55N	6.35 E
Aalter	12	Fc	51.05N	3.27 E
Äänekoski	7	Fe	62.36N	25.44 E
Aa of Weerijs	12	Gc	51.35N	4.46 E
Aar	12	Kd	50.23N	8.00 E
Aarau	14	Cc	47.25N	8.02 E
Aarbergen	12	Kd	50.13N	8.03 E
Aare	14	Cc	47.37N	8.13 E
Aargau	14	Cc	47.30N	8.10 E
Aarlen/Arlon	11	Le	49.41N	5.49 E
Aarschot	11	Kd	50.59N	4.50 E
Aat/Ath	11	Jd	50.38N	3.47 E
Aazanèn	13	Ii	35.06N	3.02W
Āb	24	Md	36.00N	48.05 E
Aba [Nig.]	31	Hh	5.07N	7.22 E
Aba [Zaire]	31	Hk	3.52N	30.14 E
Aba/Ngawa	27	He	32.55N	101.45 E
Abā ad Dūd	24	Ki	27.02N	44.04 E
Abā as Su'ūd	23	Ff	17.28N	44.06 E
Abacaxis, Rio-	54	Gd	3.54S	58.50W
Abaco Island	38	Lg	26.25N	77.10W
Abacou, Pointe l'-	49	Kd	18.03N	73.47W
Abadab. Jabal-	35	Fb	18.53N	35.59 E
Ābādān	22	Gf	30.10N	48.50 E
Ābādeh [Iran]	23	Hc	31.10N	52.37 E
Ābādeh [Iran]	24	Oh	29.08N	52.52 E
Abadiânia	55	Hc	16.06S	48.48W
Abadla	31	Ge	31.01N	2.43W
Abaeté	55	Jd	19.09S	45.27W
Abaeté, Rio-	55	Jd	18.02S	45.12W
Abaetetuba	54	Id	1.42S	48.54W
Abagnar Qi (Xilin Hot)	22	Ne	43.58N	116.08 E
Abag Qi (Xin Hot)	27	Jc	44.01N	114.59 E
Abai	55	Eh	26.01S	55.57W
Abaiang Atoll	57	Id	1.51N	172.58 E
Abaj	19	Hf	49.38N	72.50 E
Abaji	34	Gd	8.28N	6.57 E
Abajo Mountains	46	Kh	37.50N	109.25W
Abakaliki	34	Gd	6.20N	8.03 E
Abakan	20	Ef	53.43N	91.30 E
Abakan	22	Ld	53.43N	91.26 E
Abakwasimbo	36	Eb	0.36N	28.43 E
Abala [Con.]	36	Cc	1.21S	15.30 E
Abala [Niger]	34	Fc	14.56N	3.26 E
Abalak	34	Gb	15.27N	6.17 E
Aban	20	Ee	56.40N	96.10 E
Abancay	54	Df	13.35S	72.55W
Abancourt	12	De	49.42N	1.46 E
Abanga	36	Bb	0.13N	10.28 E
Abano Terme	14	Fe	45.21N	11.47 E
Ābār al Jidd	24	Hf	32.50N	39.50 E
Abarqū	23	Hc	31.08N	53.17 E
Abarqu, Kavīr-e-	24	Og	31.00N	53.50 E
Abashiri	27	Pc	44.01N	144.17 E
Abashiri-Gawa	29a	Db	43.56N	144.09 E
Abashiri-Ko	29a	Da	44.00N	144.10 E
Abashiri-Wan	29a	Da	44.00N	144.35 E
Abasolo	48	Je	24.04N	98.22W
Abatski	19	Hd	56.18N	70.28 E
Abau	60	Dj	10.11S	148.42 E
Abava	7	Eh	57.06N	21.54 E
Abay=Blue Nile (EN)	30	Kg	15.38N	32.31 E
Abaya, Lake-	30	Kh	6.20N	37.55 E
Abaza	20	Ef	52.39N	90.06 E
Abbadia San Salvatore	14	Fh	42.53N	11.41 E
Abbah Quşūr	14	Co	35.57N	8.50 E
Āb Bārīk	24	Oh	29.45N	52.37 E
'Abbāsābād	24	Qd	36.20N	56.25 E
Abbekås	8	Ei	55.24N	13.36 E
Abberton Reservoir	12	Cc	51.50N	0.55 E
Abbeville [Fr.]	11	Hd	50.06N	1.50 E
Abbeville [La.-U.S.]	45	Jl	29.58N	92.08W
Abbeville [S.C.-U.S.]	44	Fh	34.10N	82.23W
Abbey	46	Ka	50.43N	108.45W
Abbeyfeale/Mainistir na Féile	9	Di	52.24N	9.18W
Abbiategrasso	14	Ce	45.24N	8.54 E
Abbot, Mount-	59	Jd	20.03S	147.45 E
Abbot Ice Shelf	66	Pf	72.45S	96.00W
'Abd Al 'Azīz, Jabal-	24	Id	36.25N	40.20 E
'Abd al Kūrī	21	Hh	12.12N	52.13 E
Ābdānān	24	Lf	32.57N	47.26 E
Abdul Ghadir	35	Gc	10.42N	42.59 E
Abdulino	19	Fe	53.42N	53.38 E
Abe, Lake-	35	Gc	11.10N	41.45 E
Abéché	31	Jg	13.49N	20.49 E
Abeek	12	Hc	51.15N	6.00 E
Abe-Gawa	29	Fd	34.55N	138.22 E
Abeløya	41	Pc	79.00N	30.15 E
Abelvær	7	Cd	64.44N	11.11 E
Abemama Atoll	57	Id	0.21N	173.51 E
Abenab	37	Bc	19.12S	18.06 E
Abengourou	34	Ed	6.35N	3.25W
Abengourou	31	Gh	6.44N	3.29W
Åbenrå	7	Bi	55.02N	9.26 E
Åbenrå Fjord	8	Ci	55.05N	9.35 E
Abeokuta	31	Hh	7.09N	3.21 E
Āb-e-Pany	23	If	37.06N	68.20 E
Aberayron	9	Ii	52.15N	4.15W
Aberdare Range	30	Ki	0.25S	36.38 E
Aberdeen [Id.-U.S.]	46	Ie	42.57N	112.50W
Aberdeen [Md.-U.S.]	44	If	39.30N	76.14W
Aberdeen [Ms.-U.S.]	45	Lj	33.49N	88.33W
Aberdeen [N.C.-U.S.]	44	Hh	35.08N	79.26W
Aberdeen [S.Afr.]	37	Cf	32.29S	24.03 E
Aberdeen [Scot.-U.K.]	6	Fd	57.10N	2.04W
Aberdeen [S.D.-U.S.]	39	Je	45.28N	98.29W
Aberdeen [Wa.-U.S.]	43	Cb	46.59N	123.50W
Aberdeen Lake	42	Hd	64.28N	99.00W
Abergavenny	9	Kj	51.50N	3.00W
Aberystwyth	9	Ii	52.25N	4.05W
Abetone	14	Ef	44.08N	10.40 E
Abez	19	Gb	66.32N	61.46 E
Abhā	22	Gh	18.13N	42.30 E
Abhainn an Chláir/Clare	9	Dh	53.20N	9.03W
Abhainn an Lagáin/Lagan	9	Hg	54.37N	5.53W
Abhainn na Bandan/Bandon	9	Ej	51.40N	8.30W
Abhainn na Deirge/Derg	9	Fg	54.40N	7.25W
Abhar	24	Md	36.02N	49.45 E
Abhar	23	Gb	36.09N	49.13 E
Abhazskaja respublika	19	Eg	43.00N	41.10 E
Abibe, Serrania de-	54	Cb	8.00N	76.30W
Abidjan	31	Gh	5.19N	4.02W
Abidjan	34	Ed	5.30N	4.30W
Abilene [Ks.-U.S.]	45	Hg	38.55N	97.13W
Abilene [Tx.-U.S.]	39	Jf	32.27N	99.44W
Abingdon	9	Lj	51.41N	1.17W
Abinsk	16	Kg	44.52N	38.10 E
Abiquiu	45	Ch	36.12N	106.19W
Abiquiu Reservoir	45	Ch	36.18N	106.32W
Abisko	7	Eb	68.20N	18.51 E
Abitibi	42	Jf	51.04N	80.55W
Abitibi, Lake-	38	Le	48.42N	79.45W
Abiy Adi	35	Fc	13.37N	39.01 E
Abiyata, Lake-	35	Fd	7.38N	38.36 E
Abja-Paluoja	8	Kf	58.02N	25.14 E
Abnūb	33	Fd	27.16N	31.09 E
Åbo/Turku	6	Ic	60.27N	22.17 E
Abo, Massif d'-	35	Ba	21.41N	16.08 E
Abóboras, Serra das-	55	Jc	16.12S	44.35W
Abodo	35	Ed	7.50N	34.25 E
Aboisso	34	Ed	5.28N	3.02W
Aboisso	34	Ed	5.28N	3.12W
Abomey	31	Hh	7.11N	1.59 E
Abong Mbang	34	He	3.59N	13.11 E
Abony	10	Pi	47.11N	20.00 E
Aborigen, Pik-	20	Jd	62.05N	149.10 E
Aborlar	26	Ge	9.26N	118.33 E
Aborrebierg	8	Ej	54.59N	12.32 E
Abou Deïa	35	Bc	11.27N	19.17 E
Abou Goulem	35	Cc	13.37N	21.38 E
Abovjan	16	Ni	40.14N	44.37 E
Abrād, Wādī-	23	Gf	15.51N	46.05 E
Abraham's Bay	49	Kb	22.21N	72.55W
Abramovski Bereg	7	Kc	66.25N	43.05 E
Abrántes	13	De	39.28N	8.12W
Abra Pampa	56	Gb	22.43S	65.42W
Abrego	49	Ki	8.04N	73.14W
Abreojos, Punta-	47	Bc	26.42N	113.35W
'Abrī	35	Ea	20.48N	30.20 E
Abrolhos, Arquipélago dos-	54	Kg	18.00S	38.40W
Abrud	15	Gc	46.16N	23.04 E
Abruka, Ostrov-/Abruka Saar	8	Jf	58.08N	22.25 E
Abruka Saar/Abruka, Ostrov-	8	Jf	58.08N	22.25 E
Abruzzi	14	Hh	42.20N	13.45 E
Absaroka Range	43	Fc	44.45N	109.50W
Abtenau	14	Hc	47.33N	13.21 E
Abū, Ḥād, Wādī-	24	Ei	27.46N	33.30 E
Abū ad Duhūr	24	Ge	35.44N	37.02 E
Abū 'Alī	24	Mi	27.20N	49.33 E
Abū al Khaşīb	24	Lg	30.27N	47.59 E
Abū an Na'am	24	Hj	25.14N	38.49 E
Abū 'Arīsh	23	Ff	16.58N	42.50 E
Abū Ballaş	33	Ee	24.26N	27.39 E
Abū Daghmah	24	Hd	36.25N	38.15 E
Abū Darbah	33	Fd	28.29N	33.20 E
Abu Dhabi (EN)=Abū Ẓaby	22	Hg	24.28N	54.22 E
Abū Ḥadrīyah	24	Mi	27.20N	48.58 E
Abū Ḥamad	31	Kg	19.32N	33.19 E
Abū Ḥammād	24	Dg	30.32N	31.40 E
Abū Ḥarbah, Jabal-	24	Ei	27.17N	33.13 E
Abū Ḥashā'ifah, Khalīj-	24	Bg	31.16N	27.25 E
Abuja	31	Hh	9.10N	7.11 E
Abu Jābirah	35	Dc	11.04N	26.51 E
Abū Jifān	24	Lj	24.31N	47.43 E
Abū Kabīr	24	Dg	30.44N	31.40 E
Abū Kamāl	23	Fc	34.27N	40.55 E
Abukuma-Gawa	29	Gb	38.06N	140.52 E
Abukuma-Sanchi	29	Gc	37.20N	140.45 E
Abū Latt	33	Hf	19.58N	40.08 E
Abū Libdah, Khashm-	33	Ie	22.58N	46.13 E
Abū Maţāriq	35	Dc	10.58N	26.17 E
Abu Mendi	35	Fc	11.47N	35.42 E
Abumonbazi	36	Db	3.42N	22.10 E
Abū Muḥarrik, Ghurd-	33	Ed	27.00N	30.00 E
Abū Musā, Jazīreh-ye-	23	Id	25.52N	55.03 E
Abunā	53	Jf	9.42S	65.23W
Abuná, Rio-	52	Jf	9.41S	65.23W
Abune Yosef	35	Fc	12.09N	39.12 E
Abū Qīr	24	Dg	31.19N	30.04 E
Abū Qīr, Khalīj-	24	Dg	31.20N	30.15 E
Abū Qumayyis, Ra's-	24	Nj	24.34N	51.30 E
Abu Road	25	Ed	24.29N	72.47 E
Abū Sawmah, Ra's-	24	Ei	26.51N	33.59 E
Abū Shanab	35	Dc	13.57N	27.47 E
Abu Simbel (EN)=Abū Sumbul	33	Fe	22.22N	31.38 E
Abū Şukhayr	24	Kg	31.52N	44.27 E
Abū Sumbul=Abu Simbel (EN)	33	Fe	22.22N	31.38 E
Abuta	28	Pc	42.31N	140.46 E
Abut Head	62	De	43.06S	170.15 E
Abū Tij	33	Fd	27.02N	31.19 E
Abū Ţurţūr, Jabal-	24	Cj	25.20N	30.00 E
Abū'Urūq	35	Eb	15.54N	30.27 E
Abuyemeda	35	Fc	10.38N	39.43 E
Abū Zabad	35	Dc	12.21N	29.15 E
Abū Ẓaby=Abu Dhabi (EN)	22	Hg	24.28N	54.22 E
Abū Zanīmah	33	Fd	29.03N	33.06 E
Abwong	35	Ed	9.07N	32.12 E
Åby	8	Gf	58.40N	16.11 E
Abyaḍ	35	Dc	13.46N	25.23 E
Abyaḍ, Al Baḥr al-=White Nile (EN)	30	Kg	15.38N	32.31 E
Abyaḍ, Al Baḥr al-=White Nile (EN)	35	Ec	12.40N	32.30 E
Abyaḍ, Ar Ra's al-	23	Ee	23.32N	38.32 E
Abyaḍ, Jabal-	35	Db	18.55N	28.40 E
Abyaḍ, Ra's al-=Blanc, Cape- (EN)	30	He	37.20N	9.50 E
Abyār Alī	24	Hj	24.25N	39.33 E
Abyār ash Shuwayrif	33	Bd	29.59N	14.16 E
Åbybro	7	Bh	57.09N	9.45 E
Abydos	33	Fd	26.11N	31.55 E
Abyei	35	Dd	9.36N	28.26 E
Ābyek	24	Nd	36.02N	50.31 E
Abymes	51e	Ab	16.16N	61.31W
Acacías	54	Dc	3.59N	73.47W
Academy Gletscher	41	Ib	81.45N	33.35W
Acadie	38	Me	46.00N	65.00W
Acaill/Achill	9	Dh	54.00N	10.00W
Acajutla	49	Cg	13.36N	89.50W
Acalayong	34	Ge	1.05N	9.40 E
Acámbaro	47	Dd	20.02N	100.44W
Acandí	54	Cb	8.31N	77.17W
Acaponeta	47	Cd	22.30N	105.22W
Acaponeta, Río-	48	Gf	22.20N	105.37W
Acapulco de Juárez	39	Jh	16.51N	99.55W
Acará	54	Id	1.57S	48.11W
Acarai, Serra-	54	Gc	1.50N	57.40W
Acaraú	54	Jd	2.53S	40.07W
Acaray, Río-	55	Eg	25.29S	54.42W
Acari, Rio- [Braz.]	54	Ge	5.18S	59.42W
Acari, Rio- [Braz.]	55	Jb	16.00S	45.03W
Acarigua	54	Eb	9.33N	69.12W
Acatenango, Volcán-	38	Jh	14.30N	91.40W
Acatlán de Osorio	48	Jh	18.12N	98.03W
Acayucan	47	Fe	17.57N	94.55W
Accéglio	14	Af	44.28N	7.00 E
Aččitau, Gora-	18	Cc	42.07N	60.31 E
Accomac	44	Jg	37.43N	75.40W
Accra	31	Gh	5.33N	0.13W
Acebal	55	Bk	33.14S	60.50W
Acebuches	48	Hc	28.15N	102.43W
Aceguá [Braz.]	55	Ej	31.52S	54.09W
Aceguá [Ur.]	55	Ej	31.52S	54.12W
Aceh	26	Cf	4.10N	96.50 E
Acerenza	14	Jj	40.48N	15.56 E
Acerra	14	Ij	40.57N	14.22 E
Achacachi	54	Eg	16.03S	68.43W
Achaguas	54	Eb	7.46N	68.14W
Achaïf, 'Erg-	34	Ea	20.45N	4.24W
Achao	56	Ff	42.28S	73.30W
Achegour	34	Hb	19.02N	11.53 E
Acheng	27	Mb	45.32N	126.56 E
Acheux-en-Amiénois	12	Ed	50.04N	2.32 E
Achiet-le-Grand	12	Ed	50.08N	2.47 E
Achill/Acaill	9	Dh	54.00N	10.00W
Achilleion	15	Cj	39.34N	19.55 E
Achill Head/Ceann Acla	9	Ch	53.59N	10.13W
Achim	10	Fc	53.02N	9.02 E
Achim	35	Bb	15.53N	19.32 E
Achterwasser	10	Jb	54.00N	13.57 E
Acı Gölü	24	Cd	37.50N	29.54 E
Ačinsk	22	Ld	56.17N	90.30 E
Acıpayam	24	Cd	37.25N	29.22 E
Acireale	14	Jm	37.37N	15.10 E
Acîş	15	Fb	47.32N	22.47 E
Ačisaj	18	Gc	43.33N	68.54 E
Ačit	17	Hh	56.48N	57.54 E
Ačit-Nur	27	Fb	49.30N	90.30 E
Acklins	38	Lg	22.25N	74.00W
Acklins, The Bight of-	49	Jb	22.30N	74.15W
Acle	12	Db	52.38N	1.33 E
Acobamba	54	Df	12.48S	74.34W
Acolin	11	Jh	46.49N	3.22 E
Aconcagua	56	Fd	32.15S	70.50W
Aconcagua, Cerro-	52	Ji	32.39S	70.00W
Açor, Serra do-	13	Ed	40.13N	7.48W
Açores=Azores (EN)	31	Ee	38.30N	28.00W
Açores, Arquipélago dos-=Azores (EN)	30	Ee	38.30N	28.00W
Acorizal	55	Db	15.12S	56.22W
Acoyapa	49	Eh	11.58N	85.10W
Acquapendente	14	Fh	42.44N	11.52 E
Acquasanta Terme	14	Hh	42.46N	13.24 E
Acquasparta	14	Gh	42.41N	12.33 E
Acquaviva delle Fonti	14	Kj	40.54N	16.50 E
Acqui Terme	14	Cf	44.41N	8.28 E
Acraman, Lake-	59	Hf	32.05S	135.25 E
Acre	54	Ee	9.00S	70.00W
Acre, Rio-	52	Jf	8.45S	67.22W
Acri	14	Kk	39.29N	16.23 E
Actéon, Groupe-	57	Ng	21.20S	136.30W
Actopan	48	Jg	20.16N	98.56W
Açu	54	Ke	5.34S	36.54W
Acuña	55	Di	29.55S	57.58W
Ada [Ghana]	34	Fd	5.47N	0.38 E
Ada [Ok.-U.S.]	43	He	34.46N	96.41W
Ada [Yugo.]	15	Dd	45.48N	20.08 E
Adaba	35	Fd	7.03N	39.31 E
'Adād	35	Hb	8.23N	46.48 E
'Adādle	35	Gd	9.45N	44.41 E
Adair, Bahía-	48	Cb	31.30N	113.50W
Adair, Cape -	42	Kb	71.31N	71.24W
Adaja	13	Hc	41.32N	4.52W
Adak	40a	Cb	51.45N	176.40W
Adalar	15	Mi	40.52N	29.07 E
'Adale	35	He	2.46N	46.20 E
Ådalen	8	Ga	63.20N	17.30 E
Adalselv	8	Dd	60.04N	10.11 E
Adam, Mount-	56	Hh	51.34S	60.04W
Adamantina	55	Ge	21.42S	51.04W
Adamaoua=Adamawa (EN)	30	Ih	7.00N	15.00 E
Adamawa (EN)=Adamaoua	30	Ih	7.00N	15.00 E
Adamello	14	Ed	46.09N	10.30 E
Adamovka	16	Ud	51.32N	59.59 E
Adams	45	Le	43.58N	89.49W
Adams, Mount-	43	Cb	46.12N	121.28W
Adams Lake	46	Fa	51.13N	119.33W
Adams River	42	Ff	50.54N	119.33W
Adam's Rock	64q	Ab	25.04S	130.05W
Adamstown	58	Ng	25.04S	130.05W
Adamuz	13	Hf	38.02N	4.31W
Adana	22	Ff	37.01N	35.18 E
Adapazarı	24	Db	40.46N	30.24 E
Adarama	35	Eb	17.05N	34.54 E
Adarān, Jabal-	33	Ig	13.46N	45.08 E
Adare, Cape-	66	Kf	71.17S	170.14 E
Adavale	59	Ie	25.55S	144.36 E
Adda [It.]	5	Gf	45.08N	9.53 E
Adda [Sud.]	35	Cd	9.51N	24.50 E
Ad Ḍab'ah	33	Ec	31.02N	28.26 E
Ad Dabbah	35	Eb	18.03N	30.57 E
Ad Dafīnah	33	He	23.18N	41.58 E
Aḍ Ḍafrah	24	Ok	23.25N	53.25 E
Ad Dahnā'	21	Gg	24.30N	48.10 E
Addala-Šuhgelmeer, Gora-	16	Oh	42.20N	46.15 E
Aḍ Ḍāli'	33	Hg	13.42N	44.44 E
Ad Damazin	35	Ec	11.49N	34.23 E
Ad Dāmir	35	Eb	17.35N	33.58 E
Ad Dammām	22	Hg	26.26N	50.07 E
Ad Dār al Ḥamrā'	23	Ed	27.19N	37.44 E
Ad Dawādimī	23	Fe	24.28N	44.18 E
Ad Dawḥah=Doha (EN)	22	Hg	25.17N	51.32 E
Ad Dawr	24	Je	34.27N	43.47 E
Ad Dayr	33	Fd	25.20N	32.35 E
Ad Dibdibah	24	Lh	28.00N	46.30 E
Aḍ Ḍiffah	33	Ec	30.30N	25.30 E
Ad Dikākah	35	Ib	19.25N	51.30 E
Ad Dilam	23	Ge	23.59N	47.10 E
Ad Dindar	35	Ec	13.20N	34.05 E
Ad Dir'īyah	24	Lj	24.48N	46.32 E
Ad Dissān	33	Hf	16.56N	41.41 E
Addis Zemen	35	Fc	12.05N	37.44 E
Ad Dīwānīya	23	Fc	31.59N	44.56 E
Addu Atoll	21	Jj	0.25S	73.10 E
Ad Du'ayn	35	Dc	11.26N	26.09 E
Ad Duwayd	24	Jg	30.13N	42.18 E
Ad Duwaym	35	Ec	14.00N	32.19 E
Adel [Ga.-U.S.]	44	Fj	31.18N	83.25W
Adel [Or.-U.S.]	46	Fe	42.11N	119.54W
Adelaide [Austl.]	58	Eh	34.56S	138.36 E
Adelaide [Bah.]	44	Im	25.00N	77.31W
Adelaide [S.Afr.]	37	Df	32.42S	26.20 E
Adelaide Island	66	Qe	67.15S	68.30W
Adelaide Peninsula	42	Hc	68.05N	97.50W
Adelaide River	58	Ef	13.15S	131.06 E
Adelaye	35	Cd	7.07N	22.49 E
Adelboden	14	Bd	46.30N	7.33 E
Adele Island	59	Ec	15.30S	123.10 E
Adélie, Terre-	66	Ie	67.00S	139.00 E
Ademuz	13	Kd	40.04N	1.17W
Aden (EN)=Baladiyat 'Adan	22	Gh	12.46N	45.01 E
Aden, Gulf of-	30	Lg	12.00N	48.00 E
Aden, Gulf of- (EN)='Admēd, Badyarada-	30	Lg	12.00N	48.00 E
Adenau	12	Id	50.23N	6.56 E
Ader	30	Hg	14.10N	5.05 E
Aderbissinat	34	Gb	15.37N	7.52 E
Adhan, Jabal-	24	Qj	25.27N	56.13 E
Adh Dhahībāt	32	Jc	32.01N	10.42 E
Adh Dhayd	24	Pj	25.17N	55.53 E
Adhélfi	15	Gj	39.08N	23.59 E
Adhelfoi	15	Jm	36.25N	26.37 E
'Adhirīyāt, Jibāl- al-	24	Gg	30.25N	36.48 E
Adi, Pulau-	26	Jg	4.18S	133.26 E
Adiaké	34	Ed	5.16N	3.17W
Adi Arkay	35	Fc	13.31N	38.00 E
Adicora	54	Ea	11.57N	69.48W
Adi Dairo	35	Fc	14.21N	38.12 E
Adigala	35	Gc	10.24N	42.18 E
Adige/Etsch	5	Hf	45.10N	12.20 E
Adigrat	35	Fc	14.16N	39.28 E
Adi Keyeh	35	Fc	14.48N	39.23 E
Adi Kwala	35	Fc	14.37N	38.51 E
Ādilābād	25	Fe	19.40N	78.32 E
Adīrī	31	If	27.30N	13.16 E
Adirondack Mountains	38	Le	44.00N	74.00W
Adis Abeba	31	Kh	9.01N	38.46 E
Adis Alem	35	Fd	9.03N	38.24 E
Adi Ugri	35	Fc	14.53N	38.49 E
Adıyaman	23	Eb	37.46N	38.17 E
Adjud	15	Kc	46.06N	27.10 E
Adjuntas	51a	Bb	18.09N	66.43W
'Admēd, Badyarada-=Aden, Gulf of- (EN)	30	Lg	12.00N	48.00 E
Admer, Erg d'-	32	Ie	24.12N	9.10 E
Admiralty	40	Me	57.50N	134.30W
Admiralty Bay	51n	Ba	13.00N	61.16W
Admiralty Gulf	59	Fb	14.20S	125.50 E
Admiralty Inlet	42	Ib	72.30N	86.00W
Admiralty Islands	57	Fe	2.10S	147.00 E
Admiralty Mountains	66	Kf	71.45S	168.30 E
Admont	14	Ic	47.34N	14.27 E
Ado	34	Fd	6.36N	2.56 E
Ado Ekiti	34	Gd	7.38N	5.13 E
Adok	35	Ed	8.11N	30.19 E
Adolfo Gonzales Chaves	55	Bn	38.02S	60.06W
Adolfo López Mateos, Presa-	48	Fe	25.05N	107.20W
Adonara, Pulau-	26	Hh	8.20S	123.10 E
Ādoni	25	Fe	15.38N	77.17 E
Adra	13	Ih	36.44N	3.01W
Adrano	14	Im	37.40N	14.50 E
Adrar	30	Ff	20.30N	13.30W
Adrar	31	Gf	27.54N	0.17W
Adrar	30	Hf	25.12N	8.10 E
Adrar [Alg.]	32	Gd	27.00N	1.00W
Adrar [Mtna.]	32	Ee	21.00N	11.00W
Adré	35	Cc	13.28N	22.12 E
Adria	14	Ge	45.03N	12.03 E
Adrian	44	Ee	41.54N	84.02W
Adrianópolis	55	Hg	24.41S	48.50W
Adriatic, Deti-=Adriatic Sea (EN)	5	Hg	43.00N	16.00 E
Adriatico, Mar-=Adriatic Sea (EN)	5	Hg	43.00N	16.00 E
Adriatic Sea (EN)=Adriatic, Deti-	5	Hg	43.00N	16.00 E
Adriatic Sea (EN)=Adriatico, Mar-	5	Hg	43.00N	16.00 E
Adriatic Sea (EN)=Jadransko More	5	Hg	43.00N	16.00 E
Aduard	12	Ia	53.15N	6.25 E
Adula	14	Dd	46.30N	9.05 E
Adulis	35	Fb	15.15N	39.37 E
Adur	12	Bd	50.49N	0.16W
Adusa	36	Eb	1.23N	28.01 E
Adventure Bank (EN)	14	Gm	37.20N	12.10 E
Adwa	31	Kg	14.10N	38.55 E
Adyča	21	Pc	68.13N	135.03 E
Adygalah	20	Jd	62.57N	146.25 E
Adygeja, respublika	19	Eg	44.30N	40.05 E
Adžarskaja respublika	19	Eg	41.40N	42.10 E
Adzopé	34	Ed	6.15N	3.45W
Adzopé	34	Ed	6.06N	3.52W
Adzva	17	Ic	66.36N	59.28 E
Aegean Sea (EN)=Aiyaion Pélagos	5	Ih	39.00N	25.00 E
Aegean Sea (EN)=Ege Denizi	5	Ih	39.00N	25.00 E
Aegina (EN) = Aíyina	15	Gl	37.40N	23.30 E
Aegviidu	8	Ke	59.17N	25.37 E
Aeon Point	64g	Bb	1.46N	157.11W
Aerfort na Sionainne/Shannon	9	Ei	52.42N	8.57W
Ærø	8	Dj	54.55N	10.20 E
Ærøskøbing	8	Dj	54.53N	10.25 E
Aerzen	12	Lb	52.02N	9.16 E
Afafi, Massif d'-	34	Ha	22.15N	15.00 E
'Afak	24	Kf	32.04N	45.15 E
Afanasjevo	7	Mg	58.54N	53.16 E
Afareaitu	65e	Fc	17.33S	149.47W
Afars and Issas→Djibouti	31	Lg	11.30N	43.00 E
Aff	11	Dg	47.43N	2.07W
Affollé	30	Fg	16.55N	10.25W
Affrica, Scoglio d'-	14	Eh	42.20N	10.05 E
Afghanistan	22	If	33.00N	65.00 E
Afgōye	35	He	2.09N	45.07 E
'Afīf	23	Fe	23.55N	42.56 E
Afikpo	34	Gd	5.53N	7.55 E
Afipski	16	Kg	44.52N	38.50 E
Aflou	32	Hc	34.07N	2.06 E
Afmadōw	35	Ge	0.29N	42.06 E
Afognak	40	Ie	58.15N	152.30W
Afonso Cláudio	54	Jh	20.05S	41.08W
Afon Teifi	9	Ii	52.06N	4.43W
Afon Tywi	9	Ij	51.40N	4.15W
Afragola	14	Ij	40.55N	14.18 E
Afrērā, Lake-	35	Gc	13.20N	41.03 E
Africa	30	Jh	10.00N	22.00 E
African Islands	30	Mi	4.53S	43.24 E
Afşin	24	Gc	38.36N	36.55 E
Afsluitdijk	11	La	53.00N	5.15 E
Afton	46	Je	42.44N	110.56W
Afuá	54	Hd	0.10S	50.23W
'Afula	24	Ff	32.36N	35.17 E
Afyonkarahisar	22	Ff	38.45N	30.40 E
Agadem	31	Ig	16.50N	13.17 E
Agadez	31	Hg	16.58N	7.59 E
Agadez	34	Hb	19.45N	10.15 E
Agadir	31	Ge	30.25N	9.37W
Agadir	32	Fc	30.00N	9.00W
Agadyr	19	Hf	48.17N	72.53 E
Agalega Islands	30	Mj	10.24S	56.30 E
Agalta, Sierra de-	47	Ge	15.00N	85.53W
Agan	19	Hc	61.23N	74.35 E
Agana	58	Fc	13.28N	144.45 E
Agano-Gawa	28	Of	37.57N	139.07 E
Aga Point	64c	Bb	13.14N	144.43 E
Agapovka	17	Ij	53.18N	59.10 E
Agaro	35	Fd	7.53N	36.36 E
Agartala	22	Lg	23.49N	91.16 E
Agassiz Pool	45	Ib	48.20N	95.58W
Agat	64c	Bb	13.23N	144.39 E
Agat Bay	64c	Bb	13.24N	144.39 E
Agats	58	Ee	5.33S	138.08 E
Agattu	40a	Ab	52.25N	173.35 E
Agawa Bay	44	Eb	47.22N	84.33W
Agawa Bay	44	Eb	47.20N	84.42W
Agboville	34	Ed	5.56N	4.13W
Agboville	34	Ed	6.00N	4.15W
Agdam	19	Eh	39.58N	46.57 E
Agdaš	16	Oi	40.38N	47.29 E
Agde	11	Jk	43.19N	3.28 E
Agde, Cap d'-	11	Jk	43.16N	3.30 E
Agder	8	Cf	58.25N	8.15 E
Agdz	32	Fc	30.27N	7.56W
Agdžabedi	16	Oi	40.03N	47.28 E
Agematsu	29	Ed	35.47N	137.41 E
Agen	11	Gj	44.12N	0.38 E
Ageo	29	Fd	35.58N	139.35 E
Agepsta, Gora-	16	Lh	43.32N	40.30 E
Ager	14	Hb	48.05N	13.51 E
Agere Mariam	35	Fd	5.39N	38.15 E
Agersø	8	Di	55.10N	11.10 E
Agger	12	Jd	50.48N	7.11 E
Āghā Jārī	23	Gc	30.42N	49.50 E
Aghireşu	15	Gc	46.53N	23.15 E
Agiabampo, Estero de-	48	Ed	26.15N	109.15W
Ağır	24	Hc	38.57N	38.43 E

Index Symbols

1 Independent Nation
2 State, Region
3 District, County
4 Municipality
5 Colony, Dependency
Continent
Physical Region

Historical or Cultural Region
Mount, Mountain
Volcano
Hill
Mountains, Mountain Range
Hills, Escarpment
Plateau, Upland

Pass, Gap
Plain, Lowland
Delta
Salt Flat
Valley, Canyon
Crater, Cave
Karst Features

Depression
Polder
Desert, Dunes
Forest, Woods
Heath, Steppe
Oasis
Cape, Point

Coast, Beach
Cliff
Peninsula
Isthmus
Sandbank
Island
Atoll

Rock, Reef
Islands, Archipelago
Rocks, Reefs
Coral Reef
Well, Spring
Geyser
River, Stream

Waterfall, Rapids
River Mouth, Estuary
Lake
Salt Lake
Intermittent Lake
Reservoir
Swamp, Pond

Canal
Glacier
Ice Shelf, Pack Ice
Ocean
Sea
Gulf, Bay
Strait, Fjord

Lagoon
Bank
Seamount
Tablemount
Ridge
Shelf
Basin

Escarpment, Sea Scarp
Fracture
Trench, Abyss
National Park, Reserve
Point of Interest
Recreation Site
Cave, Cavern

Historic Site
Ruins
Wall, Walls
Church, Abbey
Temple
Scientific Station
Airport

Port
Lighthouse
Mine
Tunnel
Dam, Bridge

Aginskoje 20 Gf 51.03N 114.33 E
Agnew 59 Ee 28.01S 120.30 E
Agnibilékrou 34 Ed 7.08N 3.12W
Agnita 15 Hd 45.58N 24.37 E
Agno 14 Fe 45.32N 11.21 E
Agnone 14 Ii 41.48N 14.22 E
Ago 29 Ed 34.19N 136.50 E
Agoare 34 Fd 8.30N 3.25 E
Agogna 14 Ce 45.04N 8.54 E
Agön 8 Gc 61.35N 17.25 E
Agordat 31 Kg 15.32N 37.53 E
Agordo 14 Gd 46.17N 12.02 E
Agout 11 Hk 43.47N 1.41 E
Āgra 22 Jg 27.11N 78.01 E
Agrahanski Poluostrov 16 Oh 43.45N 47.35 E
Agramunt 13 Nc 41.47N 1.06 E
Agreda 13 Kc 41.51N 1.56W
Ağrı 23 Fb 39.44N 43.03 E
Ağrı Dağı = Mount Ararat (EN) 21 Gf 39.40N 44.24 E
Agričaj 16 Oi 41.17N 46.43 E
Agrigento 6 Hh 37.19N 13.34 E
Agrihan Island 57 Fc 18.46N 145.40 E
Agrij 15 Gb 47.15N 23.16 E
Agrínion 15 Ek 38.38N 21.25 E
Agropoli 14 Ij 40.21N 14.59 E
Agro Pontino 14 Gi 41.25N 12.55 E
Agryz 7 Mh 56.31N 53.01 E
Agto 41 Ge 67.37N 53.49W
Agua Brava, Laguna- 48 Gf 22.10N 105.32W
Agua Caliente, Cerro- 47 Cc 26.27N 106.12W
Aguachica 54 Db 8.18N 73.38W
Agua Clara 55 Fe 20.27S 52.52W
Aguada de Pasajeros 49 Gb 22.23N 80.51W
Aguadez, Irhazer Oua-n- 34 Gb 17.28N 6.26 E
Aguadilla 49 Nd 18.26N 67.09W
Aguadulce 49 Gi 8.15N 80.33W
Agua Fria River 46 Ij 33.23N 112.21W
Agua Limpa, Rio- 55 Gb 14.58S 51.20W
Aguán, Río- 49 Ef 15.57N 85.44W
Aguanaval, Río- 48 Hf 25.28N 102.53W
Aguapeí 55 Cc 16.12S 59.43W
Aguapei, Rio- 56 Jb 21.03S 51.47W
Aguapeí, Rio- 55 Cb 15.53S 58.25W
Agua Prieta 39 If 31.18N 109.34W
Aguaray 56 Hb 22.16S 63.44W
Aguaray Guazú, Río- [Par.] 55 Dg 24.05S 56.40W
Aguaray Guazú, Río- [Par.] 55 Dg 24.47S 57.19W
Aguasay 50 Eh 9.25N 63.44W
Aguascalientes 39 Ig 21.53N 102.18W
Aguascalientes [2] 47 Dd 22.00N 102.30W
Aguasvivas 13 Lc 41.20N 0.25W
Água Verde, Rio- 55 Da 13.42S 56.43W
Agua Vermelha, Représa- 56 Ja 19.53S 50.17W
Agudo [Braz.] 55 Fi 29.38S 53.15W
Agudo [Sp.] 13 Hf 38.59N 4.52W
Agueda 13 Fc 41.02N 6.56W
Águeda 13 Dd 40.34N 8.27W
Aguelhok 34 Fb 19.28N 0.51 E
Agüenit 32 Ee 22.11N 13.08W
Aguerguer 30 Ff 23.09N 16.01W
Aguijan Island 57 Fc 14.51N 145.34 E
Aguilar de Campóo 13 Hb 42.48N 4.16W
Aguilar de la Frontera 13 Hg 37.31N 4.39W
Aguilas 13 Kg 37.24N 1.35W
Aguilila 48 Hh 18.44N 102.44W
Aguirre, Río- 50 Fh 8.28N 61.02W
Aguja, Cabo de la- 54 Da 11.21N 73.59W
Agujereada, Punta- 51a Ab 18.31N 67.08W
Agul 20 Ee 55.40N 95.45 E
Agulhas, Cape-(EN)= Agulhas, Kaap- 30 Jl 34.50S 20.00 E
Agulhas, Kaap-=Agulhas, Cape-(EN) 30 Jl 34.50S 20.00 E
Agulhas Negras, Pico das- 52 Lh 22.23S 44.38W
Agulhas Plateau (EN) 30 Jm 40.00S 26.00 E
Agung, Gunung- 26 Gh 8.21S 115.30 E
Aguni-Shima 27 Mf 26.35N 127.15 E
Agupey, Río- 55 Di 29.07S 56.36W
Agustin Codazzi 54 Da 10.02N 73.15W
Ağva 24 Cb 41.05N 29.50 E
Ahaggar 30 Hf 23.10N 5.50 E
Ahaggar, Tassili-oua-n- 30 Hf 20.30N 5.00 E
Aha Hills 37 Cc 19.45S 21.10 E
Ahalcihe 19 Eg 41.38N 42.59 E
Ahalkalaki 19 Eg 41.25N 43.29 E
Ahangaran 18 Gd 40.57N 69.37 E
Ahar 23 Gb 38.28N 47.04 E
Ahat 15 Mk 38.39N 29.47 E
Ahaus 10 Cd 52.04N 7.00 E
Ahe Atoll 57 Mf 14.30S 146.18W
Ahenet, Tanezrouft-n- 32 He 22.00N 1.00 E
Ahini 20 Ff 53.18N 105.01 E
Ahipara 62 Ea 35.10S 173.09 E
Ahja Jõgi 8 Lf 58.19N 27.15 E
Ahlat 24 Jc 38.45N 42.29 E
Ahlen 10 De 51.45N 7.55 E
Ahmadābād 22 Jg 23.02N 72.37 E
Aḥmadī 24 Qi 27.56N 56.42 E
Ahmadnagar 25 Ee 19.05N 74.44 E
Ahmadpur East 25 Ec 29.09N 71.16 E
Ahmar 30 Lh 9.23N 41.13 E
Aḥmar, Al Baḥr al-=Red Sea (EN) 30 Kf 25.00N 38.00 E
Ahmeta 16 Nh 42.02N 45.11 E
Ahmetli 15 Kk 38.31N 27.57 E
Ahnet 32 He 24.35N 3.15 E
Ahoa 64h Ab 13.17S 176.12W
Ahome 48 Ee 25.55N 109.11W
Ahon, Tarso- 35 Ba 20.23N 18.18 E
Ahr 10 Df 50.33N 7.17 E
Ahram 24 Nh 28.52N 51.16 E
Ahrāmāt al Jīzah 33 Fd 29.55N 31.05 E
Ahrensburg 10 Gc 53.41N 10.15 E
Ahrgebirge 12 Id 50.31N 6.54 E
Ahse 12 Jc 51.42N 7.51 E
Ahsu 16 Pi 40.35N 48.26 E
Ähtäri 7 Ee 62.02N 21.20 E
Ahtärinjarvi 8 Kb 62.40N 24.05 E
Ähtävänjoki 7 Fe 63.38N 22.48 E
Ahtopol 15 Kg 42.06N 27.57 E
Ahtuba 5 Kf 46.42N 48.00 E
Ahtubinsk 6 Kf 48.14N 46.14 E
Ahtyrka 19 De 50.19N 34.55 E
Ahuacapán 49 Cg 13.55N 89.51W
Ahuazotepec 48 Jg 20.03N 98.09W
Ahunui Atoll 57 Mf 19.35S 140.28W
Åhus 7 Di 55.55N 14.17 E
Ahvāz 22 Gf 31.19N 48.42 E
Ahvenanmaa/Åland [2] 7 Ef 60.15N 20.00 E
Ahvenanmaa/Åland=Aland Islands (EN) 5 Hc 60.15N 20.00 E
Ahvenanmeri 8 Hd 60.00N 19.30 E
Aḥwar 23 Gg 13.31N 46.42 E
Aibag Gol 28 Ad 41.42N 110.24 E
Aibetsu 29a Cb 43.55N 142.33 E
Aichach 10 Hh 48.28N 11.08 E
Aichi Ken [2] 28 Ng 35.00N 137.07 E
Aiea 65a Db 21.23N 157.56W
Aigle 14 Ad 46.20N 6.59 E
Aigoual, Mont- 11 Jj 44.07N 3.35 E
Aiguá 55 El 34.12S 54.45W
Aigues 11 Kj 44.07N 4.43 E
Aigues-Mortes 11 Kk 43.34N 4.11 E
Aiguilles 11 Mj 44.47N 6.52 E
Aiguillon 11 Gj 44.18N 0.21 E
Aigurande 11 Hh 46.26N 1.50 E
Ai He 28 Hd 40.13N 124.30 E
Aihui (Heihe) 22 Od 50.13N 127.26 E
Aikawa 29 Fb 38.02N 138.14 E
Aiken 43 Ke 33.34N 81.44W
Ailao Shan 27 Hg 23.15N 102.20 E
Ailette 12 Fe 49.35N 3.10 E
Ailinginae Atoll 57 Hc 11.08N 166.24 E
Aillte an Mhothair/Moher, Cliffs of- 9 Di 52.58N 9.27W
Ailly-le-Haut-Clocher 12 Dd 50.05N 1.59 E
Ailly-sur-Noye 12 Ee 49.45N 2.22 E
Ailsa Craig 9 Hf 55.16N 5.07W
Ailuk Atoll 57 Hc 10.20N 169.56 E
Aim 20 Ie 58.48N 134.12 E
Aimogasta 56 Gc 28.33S 66.49W
Aimorés 54 Jg 19.30S 41.04W
Ain [3] 11 Lh 46.10N 5.20 E
Ain 11 Li 45.48N 5.10 E
Ainazi/Ajnazi 7 Fh 57.52N 24.25 E
Aïn Beïda 32 Ib 35.48N 7.24 E
Aïn Beni Mathar 32 Gc 34.01N 2.01W
Aïn Bessem 13 Ph 36.18N 3.40 E
Aïn Boucif 13 Pi 35.53N 3.09 E
Aïn Defla 13 Nh 36.16N 1.58 E
Aïn el Berd 13 Li 35.21N 0.31W
Aïn el Hammam 13 Qh 36.34N 4.19 E
Aïn el Turck 13 Li 35.44N 0.46W
Aïn Galakka 35 Bb 18.05N 18.31 E
Ainos Óros 15 Dk 38.07N 20.40 E
Aïn Oulmene 13 Ri 35.55N 5.18 E
Aïn Oussera 13 Oi 35.27N 2.54 E
Aïn Sefra 31 Ge 32.45N 0.35W
Ainsworth 45 Ge 42.33N 99.52W
Aïn Taghrout 13 Rh 36.08N 5.05 E
Aïn Tedeles 13 Mh 36.00N 0.18 E
Ain Témouchent 32 Gb 35.18N 1.08W
Aïn Tolba 13 Ki 35.15N 1.15W
Aioi 29 Dd 34.49N 134.28 E
Aiquile 54 Eg 18.10S 65.10W
Aïr/Azbine 30 Hg 18.00N 8.30 E
Airabu, Pulau- 26 Ef 2.46N 106.14 E
Airai 64a Bc 7.21N 134.34 E
Airaines 12 De 49.58N 1.57 E
Airão 54 Fd 1.56S 61.22W
Airbangis 26 Cf 0.12N 99.23 E
Airdrie 46 Ha 51.18N 114.02W
Aire 11 Id 50.38N 2.24 E
Aire [Eng.-U.K.] 9 Mh 53.44N 0.54W
Aire [Fr.] 11 Ke 49.19N 4.49 E
Aire, Canal d'- 11 Id 50.38N 2.25 E
Aire, Isla del- 13 Qe 39.47N 4.16 E
Aire-sur-l'Adour 11 Fk 43.42N 0.16W
Air Force 42 Kc 67.55N 74.05W
Airolo 14 Cd 46.33N 8.35 E
Aïs 63b Cb 15.26S 167.15 E
Aisch 10 Hg 49.46N 11.01 E
Aisén del General Carlos Ibàñez del Çampo [2] 56 Fg 46.00S 73.00W
Aishihik 42 Dd 61.34N 137.30W
Ai-Shima 29 Bd 34.30N 131.18 E
Aisne [3] 11 Je 49.30N 3.30 E
Aisne 11 Ie 49.26N 2.50 E
Aisne à la Marne, Canal de l'- 11 Je 49.24N 3.55 E
Aïssa, Djebel- 32 Gc 32.51N 0.30W
Aitana, Pico- 13 Lf 38.39N 0.16W
Aitape 60 Ch 3.08S 142.21 E
Aitolikón 15 Ek 38.26N 21.21 E
Aitutaki Atoll 57 Lf 18.52S 159.45W
Ait Youssef ou Ali 13 Ii 35.09N 3.55W
Aiud 15 Gc 46.18N 23.43 E
Aiviekste 7 Fh 56.36N 25.44 E
Aiviekste/Ajviekste 7 Fh 56.36N 25.44 E
Aiwokako Passage 64a Bb 7.39N 134.33 E
Aix, Ile d'- 11 Eh 46.01N 1.10W
Aix-en-Provence 11 Lk 43.32N 5.26 E
Aixe-sur-Vienne 11 Hi 45.48N 1.08 E
Aix-les-Bains 11 Li 45.42N 5.55 E
Aiyaíon Pélagos=Aegean Sea (EN) 5 Ih 39.00N 25.00 E
Aiyina 15 Gl 37.45N 23.26 E
Aiyina = Aegina (EN) 15 Gl 37.40N 23.30 E
Aiyínion 15 Fi 40.30N 22.33 E
Aiyion 15 Fk 38.15N 22.05 E
Aizawl 25 Id 23.44N 92.43 E
Aizenay 11 Eh 46.44N 1.37W
Aizpute/Ajzpute 7 Eh 56.45N 21.39 E
Aizubange 29 Fc 37.34N 139.49 E
Aizutakada 29 Fc 37.29N 139.48 E
Aizuwakamatsu 28 Of 37.30N 139.56 E
Ajā', Jabal- 24 Ii 27.30N 41.30 E
'Ajab Shīr 24 Kd 37.28N 45.54 E
Ajaccio 6 Gg 41.55N 8.44 E
Ajaccio, Golfe d'- 11a Ab 41.50N 8.41 E
Ajaguz 22 Ke 47.58N 80.27 E
Ajakli 20 Eb 70.13N 95.55 E
Ajan 20 Fe 59.38N 106.45 E
Ajan 20 Ie 56.27N 138.10 E
Ajanka 20 Ld 63.40N 167.30 E
Ajanta Range 25 Fd 20.30N 76.00 E
Ajat 17 Kj 52.54N 62.50 E
Ajax Peak 46 Id 45.20N 113.40W
Ajdābiyā 31 Je 30.46N 20.14 E
Ajdabul 19 Ge 52.42N 69.01 E
Ajdar 16 Ke 48.42N 39.13 E
Ajdar, Soloncak- 18 Fd 40.50N 66.50 E
Ajdovščina 14 He 45.53N 13.53 E
Ajdyrlinski 17 Ij 52.03N 59.50 E
Ajhal 20 Gc 66.00N 111.32 E
Ajigasawa 28 Pd 40.47N 140.12 E
Aji-Shima 29 Gb 38.15N 141.30 E
Ajjer, Tassili-n- 30 Hf 25.30N 9.00 E
Ajka 10 Ni 47.06N 17.34 E
Ajke, Ozero- 16 Vd 50.55N 61.35 E
Ajkino 17 De 62.15N 49.56 E
'Ajlūn 24 Ff 32.20N 35.45 E
'Ajmah, Jabal al- 24 Fh 29.12N 34.02 E
'Ajmān 23 Id 25.25N 55.27 E
Ajmer 22 Jg 26.27N 74.38 E
Ajnaži/Ainaži 7 Fh 57.52N 24.25 E
Ajni 18 Ge 39.23N 68.36 E
Ajo 43 Ee 32.22N 112.52W
Ajo, Cabo de- 13 Ia 43.31N 3.35W
Ajon, Ostrov- 21 Sc 69.50N 168.40 E
Ajoupa-Bouillon 51h Ab 14.50N 61.08W
Ajsary 19 He 53.05N 71.00 E
Ajtos 15 Kg 42.42N 27.15 E
Aju, Kepulauan- 26 Jf 0.28N 131.03 E
'Ajūz, Jabal al- 24 Dj 25.49N 30.43 E
Ajviekste 7 Fh 56.36N 25.44 E
Ajviekste 7 Fh 56.36N 25.44 E
Ajzkraukle (Stučka) 7 Fh 56.36N 25.17 E
Ajzpute/Aizpute 7 Eh 56.45N 21.39 E
Akaba 34 Fd 7.57N 1.03 E
Akabira 28 Qc 43.30N 142.04 E
Akabli 32 Hd 26.42N 1.22 E
Akademika Obručeva, Hrebet- 20 Ef 51.30N 96.45 E
Akadomari 29 Fc 37.54N 138.24 E
Aka-Gawa 29 Fb 38.54N 139.50 E
Akagi-San 29 Fc 36.33N 139.11 E
Akaishi-Dake 29 Fd 35.27N 138.09 E
Akaishi-Sanmyaku 29 Fd 35.25N 138.10 E
Akajaure 7 Dc 67.42N 17.30 E
Aka-Jima 29b Ab 26.14N 127.17 E
Akaki 35 Fd 8.51N 38.48 E
Akala 35 Fb 15.38N 36.12 E
Akan 29a Db 43.08N 144.07 E
Akan-Gawa 29a Db 43.00N 144.16 E
Akar 24 Dc 38.38N 31.06 E
Akarnaniká Óri 15 Dk 38.45N 21.00 E
Akaroa 61 Dh 43.48S 172.59 E
Akasaki 29 Cd 35.31N 133.38 E
'Akasha East 35 Ea 21.05N 30.43 E
Akashi 28 Mg 34.38N 134.59 E
Akbaba Tepe 24 Hc 39.32N 39.33 E
Akbajtal, Pereval- 19 Hh 38.31N 73.41 E
Akbou 13 Qh 36.28N 4.32 E
Akbulak 19 Fe 51.03N 55.37 E
Akbura 18 Id 40.34N 72.45 E
Akçaabat 24 Hb 40.59N 39.34 E
Akçadağ 24 Gc 38.21N 37.59 E
Akçakale 24 Hd 36.41N 38.56 E
Akçakara Dağı 24 Ic 38.40N 40.52 E
Akçakoca 24 Db 41.05N 31.09 E
Akçaova [Tur.] 15 Mh 41.03N 29.57 E
Akçaova [Tur.] 15 Ll 37.30N 28.02 E
Akčatau 19 Hf 47.59N 74.02 E
Akçay 15 Ll 37.50N 28.15 E
Akçay 15 Mm 36.36N 29.45 E
Akchâr 30 Ff 20.20N 14.28W
Ak Dağ [Tur.] 24 Ib 40.35N 41.46 E
Ak Dağ [Tur.] 23 Cb 36.32N 29.34 E
Akdağ [Tur.] 24 Gd 37.53N 37.56 E
Akdağ [Tur.] 24 Fb 40.57N 35.55 E
Akdağ [Tur.] 24 Cc 39.15N 28.49 E
Akdağ [Tur.] 15 Ll 37.42N 28.56 E
Akdağ [Tur.] 15 Mk 38.18N 29.58 E
Akdağ [Tur.] 15 Jk 38.33N 26.30 E
Ak Dağlar 24 Gc 39.30N 36.00 E
Ak Dağları 24 Ic 38.40N 40.12 E
Akdağmadeni 24 Fc 39.40N 35.54 E
Akdeniz=Mediterranean Sea (EN) 5 Hh 35.00N 20.00 E
Ak-Dovurak 20 Ef 51.10N 90.40 E
Akechi 29 Ed 35.18N 137.22 E
Ake Eze 34 Gd 5.55N 7.40 E
Akera 16 Oj 39.09N 46.48 E
Åkersberga 8 He 59.29N 18.18 E
Akershus [2] 7 Cf 60.00N 11.10 E
Aketi 31 Jh 2.44N 23.46 E
Akharnai 15 Gk 38.05N 23.44 E
Akhdar, al Jabal al- 21 Hg 23.30N 57.00 E
Akhḑar, Al Jabal al- 30 Je 32.30N 21.30 E
Akhḑar, Wādī al- 24 Gh 28.35N 36.35 E
Akhelóös 15 Ej 38.18N 21.10 E
Akhisar 23 Cb 38.55N 27.51 E
Akhmīm 33 Fd 26.34N 31.44 E
Akhtarīn 24 Gd 36.31N 37.20 E
Aki 29 Ce 33.30N 133.53 E
Akiaki Atoll 61 Nc 18.30S 139.12W
Akiéni 36 Bc 1.11S 13.53 E
Akimiski 38 Kd 53.00N 81.20W
Akimovka 16 If 46.42N 35.09 E
Aki-Nada 29 Cd 34.05N 132.40 E
Åkirkeby 8 Fi 55.04N 14.56 E
Akita 22 Qf 39.43N 140.07 E
Akita Ken [2] 28 Pe 39.45N 140.20 E
Akjoujt 31 Fg 19.44N 14.22W
Akka 32 Fd 29.25N 8.15W
Akkanburluk 17 Mj 52.46N 66.35 E
'Akko 23 Ec 32.55N 35.05 E
Akkol 18 Hc 43.25N 70.47 E
Akköy 24 Bd 37.29N 27.15 E
Akkystau 19 Ff 47.17N 51.03 E
Aklavik 42 Dc 68.14N 135.02W
Aklé Mseïguîlé 34 Eb 16.20N 4.45W
Akmenė/Akmene 8 Jh 56.14N 22.43 E
Akmenrags/Akmeņrags 8 Ih 56.54N 20.55 E
Akmeņrags/Akmenrags 8 Ih 56.54N 20.55 E
Akmeqit 27 Cd 37.05N 76.55 E
Akniste 8 Kh 56.10N 25.54 E
Akō 29 Dd 34.45N 134.23 E
Akobo 30 Kh 7.48N 33.03 E
Akobo 31 Kh 7.47N 33.01 E
Akola 22 Jg 20.44N 77.00 E
Akonolinga 34 He 3.46N 12.15 E
Akosombo Dam 34 Fd 6.16N 0.03 E
Akpatok 42 Kd 60.24N 68.05W
Akqi 27 Cc 40.50N 78.01 E
Ákra Ámbelos 15 Gj 39.56N 23.56 E
Ákra Kambanós 15 Hl 37.59N 24.45 E
Akranes 7a Ab 64.19N 22.06W
Ákra Spathí 15 Gl 37.27N 23.31 E
Åkrehamn 7 Ag 59.16N 5.11 E
Akrítas, Ákra- = Akritas, Cape- (EN) 15 Em 36.43N 21.53 E
Akritas Cape- (EN) = Akrítas, Ákra- 15 Em 36.43N 21.53 E
Akron [Co.-U.S.] 45 Ef 40.10N 103.13W
Akron [Oh.-U.S.] 43 Kc 41.04N 81.31W
Akrotiri 24 Ee 34.36N 32.57 E
Akša 20 Gf 50.17N 113.17 E
Aksaj 16 Oh 43.32N 46.55 E
Aksaj 19 Fe 51.13N 53.01 E
Aksaj 16 Kf 47.15N 39.52 E
Aksakal 15 Li 40.09N 28.07 E
Aksakovo 17 Gi 54.02N 54.09 E
Aksaray 23 Db 38.23N 34.03 E
Aksay 27 Fd 39.28N 94.15 E
Akşehir 23 Db 38.21N 31.25 E
Aksehir Gölü 24 Dc 38.30N 31.28 E
Akseki 24 Dd 37.02N 31.48 E
Aksenovo-Zilovskoje 20 Gf 53.00N 117.35 E
'Aks-e Rostam 24 Ph 28.23N 54.52 E
Aksoran, Gora 19 Hf 48.25N 75.30 E
Akstafa 16 Ni 41.13N 45.27 E
Akstafa 16 Ni 41.06N 45.28 E
Aksu [China] 22 Ke 41.09N 80.15 E
Aksu 19 He 52.28N 71.59 E
Aksu 18 Lb 45.34N 79.30 E
Aksu 19 Hf 46.20N 78.15 E
Aksu [Tur.] 15 Ll 37.56N 28.56 E
Aksu [Tur.] 24 Dd 36.51N 30.54 E
Aksuat 19 If 47.48N 82.50 E
Aksubajevo 7 Mi 54.52N 50.50 E
Aksu He 21 Ke 40.28N 80.52 E
Aksum 35 Fc 14.07N 38.44 E
Ak-Šyjrak 18 Ld 41.49N 78.44 E
Aktag 27 Dd 36.45N 84.40 E
Aktaš 20 Df 50.18N 87.44 E
Aktaš 19 Gh 39.55N 65.53 E
Aktau 19 He 50.16N 73.07 E
Aktau (Ševčenko) 22 He 43.35N 51.05 E
Aktau, Gora- 19 Gg 41.45N 64.30 E
Aktjubinsk 6 Le 50.17N 57.10 E
Aktjubinskaja Oblast [3] 19 Ff 48.00N 58.00 E
Ak-Tjuz 18 Kc 42.50N 76.07 E
Akto 27 Cd 39.05N 76.02 E
Aktogaj 19 Hf 47.01N 79.40 E
Akula 36 Db 2.22N 20.11 E
Akun 40a Eb 54.12N 165.35W
Akune 28 Kh 32.01N 130.11 E
Akure 34 Gd 7.15N 5.12 E
Akureyri 6 Eb 65.40N 18.06W
Akuseki-Jima 28 Jj 29.28N 129.33 E
Akutan 40a Eb 54.10N 165.55W
Akutan 40a Eb 54.08N 165.46W
Akyab → Sittwe 22 Lg 20.09N 92.54 E
Akyazı 24 Db 40.41N 30.37 E
Akžajkyn, Ozero- 18 Fb 44.55N 67.45 E
Akzăl 19 If 49.13N 81.30 E
Ål 8 Cd 60.38N 8.34 E
Alà, Monti di- 14 Dj 40.35N 9.16 E
Alabama 38 Kf 31.08N 87.57W
Alabama [2] 43 Je 32.50N 87.30W
Al'Abbāsīyah 35 Ec 12.10N 31.18 E
Alaca 24 Fb 40.10N 34.51 E
Alaçam Dağlari 15 Lj 39.20N 28.32 E
Alaçan 24 Fb 41.37N 35.37 E
Alaçati 15 Jk 38.16N 26.23 E
Aladağ 24 Jc 43.35N 39.20 E
Ala Dağ [Tur.] 24 Jb 40.11N 42.49 E
Ala Dağ [Tur.] 24 Ed 37.58N 32.04 E
Alādāgh, Kūh-e- 24 Qd 37.13N 57.30 E
Ala Dağları 24 Fd 37.55N 35.13 E
Aladža 16 Rj 39.21N 53.12 E
Aladža Manastir 15 Lf 43.17N 28.01 E
Alagir 16 Nh 43.01N 44.12 E
Alagna Valsesia 14 Be 45.51N 7.56 E
Alagnon 11 Ji 45.27N 3.19 E
Alagoas [2] 54 Ke 9.30S 36.30W
Alagoinhas 53 Mg 12.07S 38.26W
Alagón 13 Kc 41.46N 1.07W
Alagón 13 Fe 39.44N 6.53W
Ala Gou 27 Ec 42.42N 89.12 E
Alahanpanjang 26 Dg 1.05S 100.47 E
Alahärmä 7 Fe 63.14N 22.51 E
Al Aḥmadī 24 Mh 29.05N 48.04 E
Alaid, Vulkan 20 Kf 50.50N 155.33 E
Alajärvi 7 Fe 63.00N 23.49 E
Alajku 19 Hg 40.18N 74.29 E
Alajski Hrebet 21 Jf 39.45N 72.30 E
Alajuela [3] 49 Eh 10.30N 84.30W
Alajuela 47 Hf 10.01N 84.13W
Alajuela, Lago- 49 Hi 9.05N 79.24W
Alakol, Ozero- 21 Ke 46.05N 81.50 E
Alakurtti 7 Hc 66.59N 30.20 E
Alalakeiki Channel 65a Ec 20.35N 156.30W
Al 'Alamayn 31 Je 30.49N 28.57 E
Alalau, Rio- 54 Fd 0.30S 61.10W
Al Amādīyah 24 Jd 37.06N 43.29 E
Alamagan Island 57 Fc 17.36N 145.50 E
Al 'Amārah 23 Gc 31.50N 47.09 E
'Alam ar Rūm, Ra's- 24 Bg 31.22N 27.21 E
Alāmarvdasht 24 Oi 27.52N 52.34 E
Alamashindo 35 Ge 4.51N 42.04 E
Alamata 35 Fc 12.25N 39.37 E
Alameda 45 Ci 35.11N 106.37W
Alaminos 26 Gc 16.10N 119.59 E
Al 'Āmirīyah 24 Cg 31.01N 29.48 E
Alamito Creek 45 Dl 29.31N 104.17W
Alamitos, Sierra de los- 48 Hd 26.20N 102.15W
'Alāmo 35 Ge 4.23N 43.09 E
Alamo 46 Hh 37.22N 115.10W
Alamogordo 43 Fe 32.54N 105.57W
Alamos 47 Cc 27.01N 108.56W
Alamos, Sierra- 48 Gc 28.25N 105.00W
Alamosa 43 Fd 37.28N 105.52W
Al Anbār [3] 24 If 34.00N 42.00 E
Åland/Ahvenanmaa [2] 7 Ef 60.15N 20.00 E
Åland/Ahvenanmaa=Aland Islands (EN) 5 Hc 60.15N 20.00 E
Aland Islands (EN)= Ahvenanmaa/Åland 5 Hc 60.15N 20.00 E
Aland Islands (EN)=Åland/ Ahvenanmaa 5 Hc 60.15N 20.00 E
Älandsbro 8 Gb 62.40N 17.50 E
Ålandshav 8 Hd 60.00N 19.30 E
Alange 13 Ff 38.47N 6.15W
Alanje 49 Fi 8.24N 82.33W
Alanya 23 Db 36.33N 32.01 E
Alaotra, Lac- 37 Hc 17.30S 48.30 E
Alapaha River 44 Fj 30.26N 83.06W
Alapajevsk 19 Gd 57.52N 61.42 E
Alaplı 24 Db 41.08N 31.25 E
Al 'Aqabah=Àqaba (EN) 23 Dd 29.31N 35.00 E
Al 'Aqabah aş Şaghīrah 24 Ej 24.14N 32.53 E
Al 'Arabīyah As-Su'ūdīyah= Saudi Arabia (EN) [1] 22 Gg 25.00N 45.00 E
Alarcón, Embalse de- 13 Je 39.45N 2.20W
Al 'Arīsh 33 Fc 31.08N 33.48 E
Al 'Armah 24 Lj 25.30N 46.30 E
Al Arţāwīyah 24 Ki 26.30N 45.20 E
Alas, Selat- 26 Gh 8.40S 116.40 E
Al 'Aşab 24 Pk 23.20N 54.10 E
Alaşehir 24 Cc 38.21N 28.32 E
Al Ashkharah 23 Ie 21.47N 59.30 E
Al 'Āshūrīyah 24 Jg 31.02N 43.05 E
Alaska [2] 40 Ic 65.00N 153.00W
Alaska 38 Dc 65.00N 153.00W
Alaska, Gulf of- 38 Ed 58.00N 146.00W
Alaska Peninsula 38 Dd 57.00N 158.00W
Alaska Range 38 Ec 62.30N 150.00W
Alassio 14 Cf 44.00N 8.10 E
Alastaro 8 Jd 60.57N 22.51 E
Alat 18 De 39.26N 63.48 E
Alataw Shan 27 Cb 45.00N 80.00 E
Alataw Shankou= Dzungarian Gate (EN) 21 Ke 45.25N 82.25 E
Al 'Athāmīn 24 Jg 30.35N 43.40 E
Alatri 14 Hi 41.43N 13.21 E
Al 'Aţrun 31 Jg 18.11N 26.36 E
Alatyr 7 Li 54.52N 46.36 E
Alatyr 19 Ee 54.50N 46.36 E
Álava [3] 13 Jb 42.50N 2.45W
Alava, Cape- 46 Cb 48.10N 124.43W
Alaverdi 19 Eg 41.08N 44.37 E
Alavījeh 24 Nf 33.03N 51.05 E
Alavo/Alavus 7 Fe 62.35N 23.37 E
Alavus/Alavo 7 Fe 62.35N 23.37 E
Al 'Awāliq 23 Gg 14.15N 46.30 E
Al 'Awāriq 35 Ha 20.25N 48.40 E
Al 'Awsajīyah 24 Ki 26.04N 44.08 E
'Ālayh 24 Ff 33.48N 35.36 E
Al 'Ayn [Sau.Ar.] 24 Hj 25.04N 38.06 E
Al 'Ayn [U.A.E.] 24 Pj 24.13N 55.45 E
Alayor 13 Qe 39.56N 4.08 E
Al 'Ayyōţ 24 Dh 29.37N 31.15 E
Al A'ẓamīyah 24 Kf 33.23N 44.22 E
Alazani 16 Oi 41.03N 46.40 E
Alazeja 20 Kb 70.55N 153.40 E
Al'Azīzīyah 33 Bc 32.32N 13.01 E
Alazores, Puerto de los- 13 Hg 37.05N 4.15W
Alb [Ger.] 12 Ke 49.04N 8.20 E
Alb [Ger.] 10 Ei 47.35N 8.08 E
Alba 15 Gc 46.08N 23.30 E
Alba 14 Cf 44.42N 8.02 E
Alba Adriatica 14 Hh 42.50N 13.56 E
Al Bāb 24 Gd 36.22N 37.31 E
Albac 15 Fc 46.27N 22.58 E
Albacete 6 Fh 38.59N 1.51W
Albacete [3] 13 Kf 38.50N 2.00W
Al Badārī 33 Fd 26.59N 31.25 E
Alba de Tormes 13 Gd 40.49N 5.31W
Al Badi 33 Ie 22.02N 46.34 E
Al Bādi 24 Ie 35.56N 41.32 E
Ålbæk 8 Dg 57.36N 10.25 E
Ålbæk Bugt 8 Dg 57.35N 10.30 E
Al Bahrah 24 Lh 29.40N 47.52 E
Al Baḥr al Aḥmar [3] 35 Fb 19.50N 35.30 E
Al Baḩrayn 21 Hg 26.00N 50.30 E

Index Symbols

[1] Independent Nation
[2] State, Region
[3] District, County
[4] Municipality
[5] Colony, Dependency
Continent
Physical Region
Historical or Cultural Region
Mount, Mountain
Volcano
Hill
Mountains, Mountain Range
Hills, Escarpment
Plateau, Upland
Pass, Gap
Plain, Lowland
Delta
Salt Flat
Valley, Canyon
Crater, Cave
Karst Features
Depression
Polder
Desert, Dunes
Forest, Woods
Heath, Steppe
Oasis
Cape, Point
Coast, Beach
Cliff
Peninsula
Isthmus
Sandbank
Island
Atoll
Rock, Reef
Islands, Archipelago
Rocks, Reefs
Coral Reef
Well, Spring
Geyser
River, Stream
Waterfall Rapids
River Mouth, Estuary
Lake
Salt Lake
Intermittent Lake
Reservoir
Swamp, Pond
Canal
Glacier
Ice Shelf, Pack Ice
Ocean
Sea
Gulf, Bay
Strait, Fjord
Lagoon
Bank
Seamount
Tablemount
Ridge
Shelf
Basin
Escarpment, Sea Scarp
Fracture
Trench, Abyss
National Park, Reserve
Point of Interest
Recreation Site
Cave, Cavern
Historic Site
Ruins
Wall, Walls
Church, Abbey
Temple
Scientific Station
Airport
Port
Lighthouse
Mine
Tunnel
Dam, Bridge

Al Baḩrayn=Bahrain (EN) [1] 22 Hg 26.00N 50.29 E
Albaida 13 Lf 38.51N 0.31W
Alba Iulia 15 Gc 46.04N 23.35 E
Albalate del Arzobispo 13 Lc 41.07N 0.31W
Al Balyanā 33 Fd 26.14N 32.00 E
Alban 11 Ik 43.54N 2.28 E
Albanel, Lac- 42 Kf 51.05N 73.05W
Albani, Colli- 14 Gi 41.45N 12.45 E
Albania (EN)=Shqiperia [1] 6 Hg 41.00N 20.00 E
Albano, Lago- 14 Gi 41.45N 12.40 E
Albano Laziale 14 Gi 41.44N 12.39 E
Albany 38 Kd 52.17N 81.31W
Albany [Austl.] 58 Ch 35.02S 117.53 E
Albany [Ga.-U.S.] 43 Ke 31.35N 84.10W
Albany [Ky.-U.S.] 44 Eg 36.42N 85.08W
Albany [N.Y.-U.S.] 39 Le 42.39N 73.45W
Albany [Or.-U.S.] 43 Cc 44.38N 123.06W
Alba Posse 55 Eh 27.33S 54.42W
Albarche 13 He 39.58N 4.46W
Albardón 56 Gd 31.26S 68.32W
Albarracín 13 Kd 40.25N 1.26W
Albarracín, Sierra de- 13 Kd 40.30N 1.30W
Al Başalīyah Qiblī 24 Ej 25.06N 32.47 E
Al Başrah [3] 24 Lg 30.30N 47.27 E
Al Başrah=Basra (EN) 22 Gf 30.30N 47.47 E
Al Baţḩā' 24 Kg 31.07N 45.54 E
Al Bātin 24 Lh 29.00N 46.35 E
Al Bāţinah 21 Hg 23.45N 57.20 E
Albatross Bank (EN) 40 Ie 56.10N 152.20W
Albatross Bay 59 Ib 12.45S 141.43 E
Albatross Plateau (EN) 3 Mi 10.00N 103.00W
Albatross Point 62 Fc 38.07S 174.40 E
Al Batrūn 24 Fe 34.15N 35.39 E
Al Bawīţī 33 Ed 28.21N 28.52 E
Al Bayāḑ 21 Gg 22.00N 47.00 E
Al Bayḑā' [3] 33 Dc 32.00N 21.30 E
Al Bayḑā' 33 Cd 28.21N 18.58 E
Al Bayḑā' 31 Je 32.46N 21.43 E
Al Bayḑā' 33 Ig 13.58N 45.35 E
Albegna 14 Fh 42.30N 11.11 E
Albemarle 44 Gh 35.21N 80.12W
Albemarle Sound 43 Ld 36.03N 76.12W
Albenga 14 Cf 44.03N 8.13 E
Alberdi 56 Ic 26.10S 58.09W
Albères, Chaîne des- 11 Il 42.28N 2.56 E
Albères, Montes-/Les Alberes 11 Il 42.28N 2.56 E
Albergaria-a-Velha 13 Dd 40.42N 8.29W
Alberique 13 Le 39.07N 0.31W
Alberobello 14 Lj 40.47N 17.16 E
Albert 11 Id 50.00N 2.39 E
Albert, Canal-/Albert Kanaal =Albert Canal (EN) 11 Ld 50.39N 5.37 E
Albert, Lake- [Afr.] 30 Kh 1.40N 31.00 E
Albert, Lake- [Or.-U.S.] 46 Ee 42.38N 120.13W
Albert, Lake- (EN)=Mobuto Sese Seko, Lac- 30 Kh 1.40N 31.00 E
Alberta [3] 42 Gf 55.00N 115.00W
Albert Canal (EN)=Albert, Canal-/Albert Kanaal 11 Ld 50.39N 5.37 E
Albert Canal (EN)=Albert Kanaal/Albert, Canal- 11 Ld 50.39N 5.37 E
Albert Edward, Mount- 59 Ja 8.23S 147.27 E
Albert Edward Bay 42 Hc 69.35N 103.10W
Alberti 56 He 35.02S 60.16W
Albertirsa 10 Pi 47.15N 19.37 E
Albert Kanaal/Albert, Canal- =Albert Canal (EN) 11 Ld 50.39N 5.37 E
Albert Lea 43 Ic 43.39N 93.22W
Albert Nile 30 Kh 3.36N 32.02 E
Albertville [Al.-U.S.] 44 Dh 34.16N 86.12W
Albertville [Fr.] 11 Mi 45.41N 6.23 E
Albestroff 12 If 48.56N 6.51 E
Albi 11 Ik 43.56N 2.09 E
Albia 45 Jf 41.02N 92.48W
Al Bid' 24 Fh 28.28N 35.01 E
Albina 54 Hb 5.30N 54.03W
Albina, Ponta- 30 Ij 15.51S 11.44 E
Albino 14 De 45.46N 9.47 E
Albion [Mi.-U.S.] 44 Ed 42.15N 84.45W
Albion [Nb.-U.S.] 45 Hf 41.42N 98.00W
Albion [N.Y.-U.S.] 44 Hd 43.15N 78.12W
Al Biqa' 24 Ge 34.10N 36.10 E
Al Bi'r 23 Ed 28.51N 36.15 E
Al Bi'r al Jadīd 23 Ed 26.01N 38.29 E
Al Birk 23 Ff 18.13N 41.33 E
Albis 14 Cc 47.20N 8.30 E
Albo, Monte- 14 Dj 40.32N 9.35 E
Albocácer/Albocasser 13 Md 40.21N 0.02 E
Albocasser/Albocácer 13 Md 40.21N 0.02 E
Alborán, Isla de- 5 Fh 35.58N 3.02W
Alboran Basin (EN) 13 Ii 36.00N 4.00W
Ålborg 6 Gd 57.03N 9.56 E
Ålborg Bugt 7 Ch 56.45N 10.30 E
Alborz, Reshteh-ye Kūhhā-ye-=Elburz Mountains (EN) 21 Hf 36.00N 53.00 E
Albox 13 Jg 37.23N 2.08W
Albret, Pays d'- 11 Fj 44.10N 0.20W
Ālbū 'Alī 24 Je 34.49N 43.35 E
Albufeira 13 Dg 37.05N 8.15W
Albū Gharz, Sabkhat- 24 Ie 34.45N 41.15 E
Al Buheyrat [3] 35 Dd 7.00N 29.30 E
Al Bumbah 33 Dc 32.13N 23.00 E
Albuñol 13 Ih 36.47N 3.12W
Albuquerque [Braz.] 55 Dd 19.23S 57.26W
Albuquerque [N.M.-U.S.] 39 If 35.05N 106.40W
Albuquerque, Cayos de- 47 Hf 12.10N 81.50W
Al Burayj 24 Ge 34.15N 36.46 E
Al Buraymī 23 Ie 24.15N 55.45 E
Al Burmah 32 Ic 31.45N 9.02 E
Alburquerque 13 Fe 39.13N 7.00W
Albury [Austl.] 58 Fh 36.05S 146.55 E
Albury [N.Z.] 62 Df 44.14S 170.53 E
Al Buţanah 30 Kg 15.00N 35.00 E
Al Buţayn 24 Kj 25.52N 45.50 E
Alby 8 Fb 62.30N 15.28 E
Alcácer do Sal 13 Df 38.22N 8.30W
Alcáçovar 13 Df 38.25N 8.13W
Alcalá de Chivert 13 Md 40.18N 0.14 E
Alcalá de Guadaira 13 Gg 37.20N 5.50W
Alcalá de Henares 13 Id 40.29N 3.22W
Alcalá del Júcar 13 Ke 39.12N 1.26W
Alcalá de los Gazules 13 Gh 36.28N 5.44W
Alcalá del Río 13 Gg 37.31N 5.59W
Alcalá la Real 13 Ig 37.28N 3.56W
Alcamo 14 Gm 37.59N 12.58 E
Alcanandre 13 Mc 41.37N 0.12 E
Alcañices 13 Fc 41.42N 6.21W
Alcañiz 13 Lc 41.03N 0.08W
Alcántara 13 Fe 39.43N 6.53W
Alcântara 54 Jd 2.24S 44.24W
Alcantara 14 Jm 37.49N 15.16 E
Alcántara, Embalse de- 13 Fe 39.45N 6.48W
Alcantarilla 13 Kg 37.58N 1.13W
Alcaraz 13 Jf 38.40N 2.29W
Alcaraz, Sierra de- 13 Jf 38.35N 2.25W
Alcaudete 13 Hg 37.36N 4.05W
Alcázar de San Juan 13 Ie 39.24N 3.12W
Alcester 63a Ac 9.33S 152.25 E
Alčevsk (Kommunarsk) 16 Ke 48.27N 38.52 E
Alcira/Alzira 13 Le 39.09N 0.26W
Alcobaça [Braz.] 54 Kg 17.30S 39.13W
Alcobaça [Port.] 13 De 39.33N 8.59W
Alcobendas 13 Id 40.32N 3.38W
Alcoi/Alcoy 13 Lf 38.42N 0.28W
Alcolea del Pinar 13 Jc 41.02N 2.28W
Alcorta 55 Bk 33.32S 61.07W
Alcoutim 13 Eg 37.28N 7.28W
Alcova 46 Le 42.37N 106.36W
Alcoy/Alcoi 13 Lf 38.42N 0.28W
Alcubierre, Sierra de- 13 Lc 41.44N 0.29W
Alcudia 13 Pe 39.52N 3.07 E
Alcudia, Bahía de-/Alcúdia, Badia d'- 13 Pe 39.48N 3.13 E
Alcudia, Sierra de- 13 Hf 38.35N 4.35W
Aldabra Group 37b Ab 9.25S 46.22 E
Aldabra Islands 30 Li 9.25S 46.22 E
Aldama [Mex.] 48 Jf 22.55N 98.04W
Aldama [Mex.] 47 Cc 28.51N 105.54W
Aldan 22 Od 58.37N 125.24 E
Aldan 20 Hd 63.20N 129.25 E
Aldan 21 Oc 63.28N 129.35 E
Aldan Plateau (EN)= Aldanskoje Nagorje 21 Od 57.30N 127.30 E
Aldanskoje Nagorje=Aldan Plateau (EN) 21 Od 57.30N 127.30 E
Aldarhan 27 Gb 47.42N 96.36 E
Alde 12 Db 52.10N 1.32 E
Aldeburgh 9 Oi 52.09N 1.35 E
Aldeia 55 Ed 13.12S 55.10W
Aldeia, Serra da- 55 Ic 17.00S 46.50W
Alderney 9 Kl 49.43N 2.12W
Aldershot 12 Bc 51.15N 0.46W
Alderson 46 Ja 50.13N 111.26W
Aledo 45 Kf 41.12N 90.45W
Aleg 31 Fg 17.03N 13.53W
Alegranza 32 Ed 29.23N 13.30W
Alegre 54 Jh 20.46S 41.32W
Alegre, Rio- 55 Cb 15.14S 59.58W
Alegrete 56 Ic 29.46S 55.46W
Alej 20 Df 52.50N 83.35 E
Alejandra 55 Ci 29.54S 59.50W
Alejandro Selkirk, Isla- 52 Hi 33.45S 80.46W
Alejsk 20 Df 52.28N 82.45 E
Aleksandrija 16 He 48.40N 33.07 E
Aleksandrov 19 Dd 56.25N 38.42 E
Aleksandrov Gaj 19 Ee 50.08N 48.32 E
Aleksandrovka 16 He 48.59N 32.13 E
Aleksandrovsk 17 Hg 59.10N 57.35 E
Aleksandrovskoje 16 Mg 44.39N 43.00 E
Aleksandrovsk-Sahalinsk 22 Qd 50.54N 142.10 E
Aleksandrów Kujawski 10 Od 52.52N 18.42 E
Aleksandrów Łódzki 10 Pe 51.49N 19.19 E
Aleksandry, Zemlja- 21 Ga 80.45N 46.00 E
Aleksejevka 19 If 48.26N 85.40 E
Aleksejevka 19 He 51.58N 70.59 E
Aleksejevka 17 Nj 53.31N 69.28 E
Aleksejevka 19 De 50.39N 38.42 E
Aleksejevsk 20 Fe 57.50N 108.23 E
Aleksejevskoje 7 Mi 55.19N 50.03 E
Aleksin 16 Jb 54.31N 37.07 E
Aleksinac 15 Ef 43.32N 21.43 E
Alem 56 Ic 27.31S 55.15W
Ålem 7 Dh 56.57N 16.23 E
Alem Maya 35 Gd 9.27N 41.58 E
Ålen 8 Db 62.51N 11.17 E
Alençon 11 Gf 48.26N 0.05 E
Alenquer 54 Hd 1.56S 54.46W
Alenuihaha Channel 60 Oc 20.26N 156.00W
Alépé 34 Ed 5.30N 3.39W
Aleppo (EN)=Ḩalab 22 Ff 36.12N 37.10 E
Aléria 11a Ba 42.06N 9.31 E
Aléria, Plaine d'- 11a Ba 42.05N 9.30 E
Alert 39 Ma 82.30N 62.00W
Alert Bay 46 Ba 50.35N 126.55W
Alès 11 Kj 44.08N 4.05 E
Aleşd 15 Fb 47.04N 22.25 E
Alessandria 14 Cf 44.54N 8.37 E
Ålestrup 8 Ch 56.42N 9.30 E
Ålesund 6 Gc 62.28N 6.09 E
Aleutian Basin (EN) 38 Ad 57.00N 177.00 E
Aleutian Islands 38 Bd 52.00N 176.00W
Aleutian Range 38 Dd 59.00N 155.00W
Aleutian Trench (EN) 3 Je 51.00N 179.00 E
Alexander, Cape- 60 Fi 6.35S 156.30 E
Alexander, Kap- 41 Ec 78.10N 72.45W
Alexander Archipelago 38 Fd 56.30N 134.00W
Alexanderbaai 37 Be 28.40S 16.30 E
Alexander City 43 Je 32.56N 85.57W
Alexander Island 66 Qe 71.00S 70.00W
Alexandra 61 Ci 45.15S 169.24 E
Alexandra Fiord 42 Ka 79.17N 75.00W
Alexandretta (EN)= İskenderun 22 Ff 36.37N 36.07 E
Alexandretta, Gulf of- (EN) =İskenderun Körfezi 23 Eb 36.30N 35.40 E
Alexándria 15 Fi 40.38N 22.27 E
Alexandria [Austl.] 59 Hc 19.05S 136.40 E
Alexandria [La.-U.S.] 39 Jf 31.18N 92.27W
Alexandria [Mn.-U.S.] 43 Hb 45.53N 95.22W
Alexandria [Rom.] 15 If 43.59N 25.20 E
Alexandria [S.Afr.] 37 Df 33.39S 26.24 E
Alexandria [Va.-U.S.] 44 If 38.49N 77.06W
Alexandria (EN)=Al Iskandarīyah [Eg.] 31 Je 31.12N 29.54 E
Alexandria Bay 44 Jc 44.20N 75.55W
Alexandrina, Lake- 59 Hg 35.25S 139.10 E
Alexandrita 54 Hg 19.42S 50.27W
Alexandroúpolis 6 Ig 40.51N 25.52 E
'Aleyak, Godār-e- 24 Qd 36.30N 57.45 E
Alf 10 Df 50.03N 7.07 E
Alfabia, Sierra de- 13 Oe 39.45N 2.48 E
Alfambra 13 Kd 40.21N 1.07W
Al Fardah 35 Hc 14.51N 48.26 E
Alfaro 13 Kb 42.11N 1.45W
Al Fāshir 31 Jg 13.38N 25.21 E
Al Fashn 33 Fd 28.49N 30.54 E
Alfatar 15 Kf 43.57N 27.17 E
Al Fathah 24 Je 35.04N 43.34 E
Al Fāw 23 Gd 29.58N 48.29 E
Al Fawwārah 24 Ji 26.03N 43.05 E
Al Fayyūm 31 Kf 29.19N 30.58 E
Alfbach 12 Jd 50.03N 7.08 E
Alfeld 10 Fe 51.59N 9.50 E
Alfenas 54 Ih 21.26S 45.57W
Al Fifi 35 Dc 10.03N 25.01 E
Alfiós 15 El 37.37N 21.27 E
Alföld 5 If 47.15N 20.25 E
Alfonsine 14 Gf 44.30N 12.03 E
Alford 12 Ca 53.15N 0.11 E
Ålfotbreen 8 Ac 61.45N 5.30 E
Alfreton 12 Aa 53.06N 1.23W
Alfta 7 Df 61.21N 16.05 E
Al Fuḩayḩīl 23 Gd 29.05N 48.08 E
Al Fuhūd 24 Lg 30.58N 46.43 E
Al Fujayrah 23 Id 25.06N 56.21 E
Al Fūlah 35 Dc 11.44N 28.24 E
Al Fuqahā' 33 Cd 27.50N 16.21 E
Al Furāt=Euphrates (EN) 21 Gf 31.00N 47.25 E
Al Fuwayriţ 24 Ni 26.02N 51.22 E
Alga 19 Ff 49.53N 57.20 E
Algador 13 Ie 39.55N 3.53W
Al Gārah 24 Ih 29.52N 40.15 E
Algarås 8 Ff 58.48N 14.14 E
Ålgård 8 Af 58.46N 5.51 E
Algarrobo 49 Jh 10.12N 74.04W
Algarve 13 Dg 37.10N 8.15W
Algarve 5 Fh 37.10N 8.15W
Algeciras 6 Fh 36.08N 5.30W
Algeciras, Bahía de- 13 Gh 36.09N 5.25W
Algena 35 Fb 17.20N 38.34 E
Algeria (EN)=Al Jazā'ir [1] 31 Hf 28.00N 3.00 E
Algerian Basin (EN) 5 Gh 39.00N 5.00 E
Al Gharaq as Sulţānī 24 Dh 29.08N 30.42 E
Al Gharbi 32 Jc 34.40N 11.13 E
Al Ghāţ 24 Ki 26.00N 45.03 E
Al Ghaydah 23 Hf 16.12N 52.15 E
Alghero 14 Cj 40.33N 8.19 E
Alghero, Rada d'- 14 Cj 40.35N 8.20 E
Älghult 8 Fg 57.01N 15.34 E
Al Ghurāb 24 Dj 25.20N 30.20 E
Al Ghurayfah 24 Qk 23.59N 56.29 E
Al Ghurdaqah 33 Fd 27.14N 33.50 E
Algiers (EN)=Al Jazā'ir 31 He 36.47N 3.03 E
Algiers (EN)=Al Jazā'ir [3] 32 Hb 36.35N 3.00 E
Algoa Bay 30 Jl 33.50S 25.50 E
Algodoeiro, Serra do- 55 Jc 16.30S 44.45W
Algoma 45 Md 44.36N 87.27W
Algoma Uplands 44 Fb 47.00N 83.35W
Algona 45 Ie 43.04N 94.14W
Algonquin Park 44 Hc 45.27N 78.26W
Algrange 12 Ie 49.21N 6.03 E
Al Ḩabakah 24 Jh 29.51N 42.16 E
Al Ḩadd 23 Ie 22.29N 59.58 E
Al Ḩadīdah 35 Ia 21.31N 50.28 E
Al Ḩadīthah 23 Fc 34.07N 42.23 E
Al Ḩadithah 24 Gg 31.28N 37.08 E
Al Ḩaḑr 24 Je 35.35N 42.44 E
Al Haffah 24 Ge 35.35N 36.02 E
Al Ḩahjarah 23 Fc 30.25N 44.30 E
Al Ḩā'ır 24 Lj 24.23N 46.50 E
Al Ḩajar 35 Hb 16.08N 47.50 E
Al Hajar 23 Ie 23.15N 57.30 E
Al Halfāyah 24 Lg 31.49N 47.26 E
Alhama 13 Kb 42.11N 1.45W
Al Ḩamād 21 Ff 32.00N 39.30 E
Alhama de Granada 13 Ih 37.00N 3.59W
Alhama de Murcia 13 Kg 37.51N 1.25W
Alhamilla, Sierra- 13 Jh 36.58N 2.20W
Al Ḩammāh 32 Ic 33.54N 9.43 E
Al Ḩammām [Eg.] 24 Cg 30.50N 29.23 E
Al Ḩammām [Iraq] 24 Kg 31.08N 44.04 E
Al Ḩamrā 24 Pj 25.42N 55.47 E
Al Hanīyah 24 Kh 29.10N 45.50 E
Al Ḩarrah 24 Ch 28.20N 29.07 E
Al Ḩarrah 24 Hg 31.00N 38.40 E
Al Harūj al Aswad 30 If 27.00N 17.10 E
Al Ḩasā 24 Fg 30.49N 35.59 E
Al Hasā' 21 Gg 26.35N 48.10 E
Al Ḩasakah 23 Fb 36.29N 40.45 E
Al Ḩasan 24 Je 34.39N 43.43 E
Al Ḩasānī 24 Gj 24.58N 37.05 E
Alhaurín el Grande 13 Hh 36.38N 4.41W
Al Ḩawāmidīyah 24 Dh 29.54N 31.15 E
Al Ḩawātah 35 Ec 13.25N 34.38 E
Al Ḩawjā' 24 Hh 28.59N 38.34 E
Al Hawrah 35 Hc 13.49N 47.35 E
Al Ḩayy 23 Gc 32.10N 46.03 E
Al Ḩayz 33 Ed 28.02N 28.39 E
Al Hibāk 23 He 20.20N 53.10 E
Al Ḩijāz 21 Fg 24.30N 38.30 E
Al Hillah 33 Ie 23.50N 46.51 E
Al Ḩillah 23 Fc 32.29N 44.25 E
Al Ḩinākīyah 23 Fe 24.51N 40.31 E
Al Hindīyah 24 Kf 32.32N 44.13 E
Al Ḩinnāh 24 Mi 26.56N 48.45 E
al Hirmil 24 Ge 34.23N 36.23 E
Al Hoceima 32 Gb 35.15N 3.55W
Al Hoceima [3] 32 Gb 35.00N 4.15W
Alhucemas, Peñón de- 13 Ii 35.13N 3.53W
Al Ḩudaydah 22 Gh 14.48N 42.57 E
Al Ḩufrah 33 Cd 29.30N 17.55 E
Al Ḩufrah 23 Ed 28.49N 38.15 E
Al Hufūf 22 Gg 25.22N 49.34 E
Al Hūj 24 Hh 29.00N 38.25 E
Al Ḩunayy 24 Mj 24.48N 48.45 E
Al Ḩuşayḩişah 35 Ec 14.44N 33.18 E
Al Ḩuwaimī 23 Fg 13.58N 47.40 E
Al Ḩuwayyiţ 24 Ij 25.36N 40.23 E
Al Ḩyyānīyah 24 Jh 28.42N 42.18 E
'Alīābād [Iran] 23 Id 28.37N 55.51 E
'Alīābād [Iran] 24 Le 35.04N 46.58 E
'Alīābād [Iran] 24 Nd 36.37N 51.33 E
Alīābād 24 Pd 36.56N 54.50 E
Alīābād, Kūh-e- 23 Hc 34.13N 50.46 E
Aliaga 13 Ld 40.40N 0.42W
Aliağa 24 Bc 38.48N 26.59 E
Aliákmon 15 Fi 40.30N 22.40 E
'Alī al Gharbī 24 Lf 32.27N 46.41 E
'Alī ash Sharqī 24 Lf 32.07N 46.44 E
Ali-Bajramly 19 Eh 39.55N 48.57 E
Alibej, Ozero- 15 Nd 45.50N 30.00 E
Alibey Adasi 15 Jj 39.20N 26.38 E
Alibo 35 Fd 9.53N 37.05 E
Alibori 34 Fc 11.56N 3.17 E
Alibunar 15 Dd 45.04N 20.58 E
Alicante 6 Fh 38.21N 0.29W
Alicante [3] 13 Lf 38.30N 0.30W
Alicante, Golfo de- 13 Lf 38.20N 0.15W
Alice [S.Afr.] 37 Df 32.47S 26.50 E
Alice [Tx.-U.S.] 43 Hf 27.45N 98.04W
Alice, Punta- 14 Lk 39.12N 17.09 E
Alice Springs 58 Eg 23.42S 133.53 E
Aliceville 44 Ci 33.08N 88.09W
Alicudi 14 Il 38.30N 14.20 E
Aligarh 22 Jg 28.02N 78.17 E
Alīgūdarz 24 Mf 33.24N 49.41 E
Alihe→Oroqen Zizhiqi 27 La 50.35N 123.42 E
Alijó 13 Ec 41.16N 7.28W
Alijos, Rocas- 47 Ad 24.57N 115.44W
'Alī Ījūq, Kūh-e- 24 Ng 31.30N 51.45 E
Al Ikhwān 21 Hh 12.08N 53.10 E
Al Ikhwān 24 Fi 26.19N 34.52 E
Alima 30 Ii 1.36S 16.36 E
Al Imārāt al 'Arabīyah al Muttaḩidah=United Arab Emirates (EN) [1] 22 Hg 24.00N 54.00 E
Alimiá 15 Km 36.16N 27.43 E
Alindao 35 Cd 5.02N 21.13 E
Alinglapalap Atoll 57 Hd 7.08N 168.16 E
Alingsås 7 Ch 57.56N 12.31 E
Aliquippa 44 Ge 40.38N 80.16W
Al 'Irāq=Iraq (EN) [1] 22 Gf 33.00N 44.00 E
Al'Irq 33 Dd 29.01N 21.31 E
Al 'Irqah 23 Gg 13.40N 47.18 E
Ali-Sabjeh 35 Gc 11.08N 42.43 E
'Alī Shāh 'Avaz 24 Ne 35.39N 51.04 E
Al Iskandarīyah [Eg.] = Alexandria (EN) 31 Je 31.12N 29.54 E
Al Iskandarīyah [Iraq] 24 Kf 32.53N 44.21 E
Aliskerovo 20 Lc 67.52N 167.40 E
Al Ismā'īlīyah=Ismailia (EN) 33 Fc 30.35N 32.16 E
Al Istiwā'īyah al Gharbīyah [3] 35 Dd 5.20N 28.30 E
Al Istiwā'īyah al Sharqīyah [3] 35 Ed 5.20N 33.50 E
Alistráti 15 Gh 41.04N 23.58 E
Alitak, Cape- 40 Ie 56.51N 154.21W
Alite Reef 63a Ec 8.53S 160.38 E
Alitus/Alytus 19 Ce 54.25N 24.08 E
Alivérion 15 Hk 38.25N 24.02 E
Aliwal North 31 Jl 30.44S 26.40 E
Al Jabalayn 35 Ec 12.36N 32.48 E
Al Jadīdah [Eg.] 24 Cj 25.34N 28.51 E
Al Jadīdah [Sau.Ar.] 24 Mj 25.39N 49.32 E
Al Jafr 24 Gg 30.18N 36.13 E
Al Jāfūrah 35 Ia 23.25N 50.17 E
Al Jāfūrah 24 Nj 25.00N 50.15 E
Al Jaghbūb 31 Jf 29.45N 24.31 E
Al Jahrah 23 Gc 29.20N 47.40 E
Al Jalāmīd 24 Ig 31.17N 40.06 E
Al Jamalīyah 24 Nj 25.37N 51.05 E
Al Jamm 32 Jb 35.18N 10.43 E
Al Jarā'in 32 Jc 31.44N 10.09 E
Aljat 16 Pj 39.58N 49.27 E
Al Jawf [Lib.] 31 Jf 24.12N 23.18 E
Al Jawf [Sau.Ar.] 22 Fg 29.50N 39.52 E
Al Jazā'ir=Algeria (EN) [1] 31 Hf 28.00N 3.00 E
Al Jazā'ir=Algiers (EN) [3] 32 Hb 36.35N 3.00 E
Al Jazā'ir=Algiers (EN) 31 He 36.47N 3.03 E
Al Jazā'ir-El Harrach 13 Ph 36.43N 3.08 E
Al Jazīrah [3] 35 Ec 14.40N 33.30 E
Al Jazīrah [Asia] 21 Gf 35.10N 42.00 E
Al Jazīrah [Sud.] 30 Kg 14.25N 33.00 E
Aljezur 13 Dg 37.19N 8.48W
Aljibe 13 Gh 36.31N 5.37W
Al Jifārah 30 Ie 32.30N 11.45 E
Al Jiwā' 23 He 23.00N 54.00 E
Al Jīzah=Giza (EN) 31 Ke 30.01N 31.13 E
Al Jubayl 23 Gd 27.01N 49.40 E
Al Jubaylah 24 Lj 24.54N 46.27 E
Al Junaynah [Sau.Ar.] 33 He 20.17N 42.48 E
Al Junaynah [Sud.] 31 Jg 13.27N 22.27 E
Al Jurayd 24 Mi 27.11N 49.52 E
Aljustrel 13 Dg 37.52N 8.10W
Alka 40a Db 52.15N 174.30W
Al Kaba'ish 24 Lg 30.58N 47.00 E
Al Kāf [3] 32 Ib 36.00N 9.00 E
Al Kāf 32 Ib 36.11N 8.43 E
Alkali Lake 46 Fe 41.42N 119.50W
Al Kamāsin 23 Fe 20.25N 44.48 E
Al Kāmilīn 35 Eb 15.05N 33.11 E
Al Karak 24 Fg 31.11N 35.42 E
Al Karkh 24 Kf 33.20N 44.20 E
Al Karnak 33 Fd 25.43N 32.39 E
Al Kawah 35 Ec 13.44N 32.30 E
Al Kāẓimīyah 24 Kf 33.22N 44.20 E
Alken 12 Hd 50.52N 5.18 E
Al Khabrā' 23 Fc 26.04N 43.33 E
Al Khābūra 23 Ie 23.50N 57.18 E
Al-Khalīj al- 'Arabi=Persian Gulf (EN) 21 Hg 27.00N 51.00 E
Al Khalīl 24 Fg 31.32N 35.06 E
Al Khālis 24 Kf 33.51N 44.32 E
Al Khandaq 35 Eb 18.36N 30.34 E
Al Khārijah 31 Kf 25.26N 30.33 E
Al Kharj 24 Lj 24.10N 47.30 E
Al Kharţūm=Khartoum (EN) [3] 35 Eb 15.50N 33.00 E
Al Kharţūm=Khartoum (EN) 31 Kg 15.36N 32.32 E
Al Kharţūm Baḩrī= Khartoum North (EN) 31 Kg 15.38N 32.33 E
Al Khaşab 24 Qi 26.12N 56.15 E
Al Khaţţ 24 Qk 25.37N 56.01 E
Al Khawr 23 Hd 25.40N 51.30 E
Al Khidr 24 Kg 31.12N 45.33 E
Al Khubar 23 Hd 26.17N 50.12 E
Al Khufayfīyah 23 Fe 24.55N 44.42 E
Al Khums [3] 33 Bc 31.20N 14.10 E
Al Khums 31 Ie 32.39N 14.16 E
Al Khunn 35 Ha 23.18N 49.15 E
Al Khuwayr 24 Ni 26.04N 51.05 E
Al Kidn 35 Ia 22.30N 54.00 E
Al Kilḩ Sharq 24 Ej 25.03N 32.52 E
Alkionídhon, Kólpos- 15 Fk 38.05N 23.00 E
Al Kır'ānah 24 Nj 25.00N 51.03 E
Alkmaar 11 Kb 52.37N 4.44 E
Al Kūfah 24 Kf 32.02N 44.24 E
Al Kumayt 24 Lf 32.02N 46.52 E
Al Kuntillah 33 Fc 30.00N 34.41 E
Al Kushḩ 24 Ei 26.14N 32.05 E
Al Kut 23 Gc 32.30N 45.49 E
Al Kuwayt=Kuwait (EN) [1] 22 Gg 29.30N 47.45 E
Al Kuwayt=Kuwait (EN) 22 Gg 29.20N 47.59 E
Al Labbah 24 Ih 29.20N 41.30 E
Al Lādhiqīyah=Latakia (EN) 22 Ff 35.31N 35.07 E
Allagash River 44 Mb 47.05N 69.20W
Al Lagowa 35 Dc 11.24N 29.08 E
Allahābād 22 Kg 25.27N 81.51 E
Allah-Jun 20 Id 60.27N 134.57 E
Allah-Jun 20 Id 61.08N 137.59 E
Allahüekber DaGı 24 Jb 40.35N 42.32 E
Allakaket 40 Ic 66.34N 152.41W
Allanmyo 25 Je 19.22N 95.13 E
Allariz 13 Eb 42.11N 7.48W
All-Awash Island 51n Bb 12.55N 61.10W
Alldays 37 Dd 22.41S 29.06 E
Ålleberg 8 Ef 58.08N 13.36 E
Allegan 44 Ed 42.32N 85.51W
Allegheny Mountains 38 Lf 38.30N 80.00W
Allegheny Plateau 38 Le 41.30N 78.00W
Allegheny Reservoir 44 He 42.00N 78.56W
Allegheny River 43 Lc 40.27N 80.00W
Allègre, Pointe- 51e Ab 16.22N 61.45W
Allen 26 Hd 12.30N 124.17 E
Allen, Bog of- 9 Gh 53.20N 7.00W
Allen, Lough-/Loch Aillionn 9 Eg 54.08N 8.08W
Allendale 44 Gi 33.01N 81.19W
Allende 47 Dc 28.20N 100.51W
Allendorf (Eder) 12 Kc 51.02N 8.40 E
Allendorf (Lumda) 12 Kd 50.41N 8.50 E
Allentown 43 Lc 40.37N 75.30W
Alleppey 22 Ji 9.29N 76.19 E
Aller 10 Fd 52.57N 9.11 E
Allevard 11 Mi 45.24N 6.04 E
Allgäuer Alpen 10 Gi 47.20N 10.25 E
Alliance [Nb.-U.S.] 43 Gc 42.06N 102.52W
Alliance [Oh.-U.S.] 44 Ge 40.56N 81.06W
Allier [3] 11 Ih 46.30N 3.00 E
Allier 5 Gf 46.57N 3.05 E
Al Lifiyah 23 Fc 30.35N 43.09 E
Al Lişāfah 24 Li 27.37N 46.52 E
Alliston 44 Hc 44.09N 79.52W
Al Lith 23 Fe 20.09N 40.16 E
Alloa 9 Je 56.07N 3.49W
Allonnes 11 Gg 47.58N 0.09 E
Allos 11 Mj 44.14N 6.38 E
All Saints 51d Bb 17.03N 61.48W
Al Luḩayyah 23 Ff 15.43N 42.42 E
Al Luwaymī 23 Fd 27.54N 42.22 E
Alm 14 Hb 48.05N 13.55 E
Alma [Ga.-U.S.] 44 Fj 31.33N 82.28W
Alma [Mi.-U.S.] 44 Ed 43.23N 84.39W
Alma [Nb.-U.S.] 45 Gf 40.06N 99.22W
Alma [Que.-Can.] 42 Kg 48.32N 71.40W
Alma-Ata 22 Je 43.15N 76.57 E
Alma-Atinskaja Oblast [3] 19 Hg 44.00N 77.00 E
Almada 13 Cf 38.41N 9.09W
Almadén 13 Hf 38.46N 4.50W
Al Madīnah [Iraq] 24 Lg 30.57N 47.16 E
Al Madīnah [Sau.Ar.] = Medina (EN) 22 Fg 24.28N 39.36 E
Al Madīnah al Fikrīyah 24 Di 27.56N 30.49 E
'Al Madōw 35 Hc 10.59N 48.42 E
Al Mafraq 24 Gf 32.21N 36.12 E
Al Maghrib=Morocco (EN) [1] 31 Ge 32.00N 5.50W
Almagro 13 If 38.53N 3.43W
Almagrundet 8 He 59.06N 19.00 E

Index Symbols

[1] Independent Nation · [2] State, Region · [3] District, County · [4] Municipality · [5] Colony, Dependency · Continent · Physical Region · Historical or Cultural Region · Mount, Mountain · Volcano · Hill · Mountains, Mountain Range · Hills, Escarpment · Plateau, Upland · Pass, Gap · Plain, Lowland · Delta · Salt Flat · Valley, Canyon · Crater, Cave · Karst Features · Depression · Polder · Desert, Dunes · Forest, Woods · Heath, Steppe · Oasis · Cape, Point · Coast, Beach · Cliff · Peninsula · Isthmus · Sandbank · Island · Atoll · Rock, Reef · Islands, Archipelago · Rocks, Reefs · Coral Reef · Well, Spring · Geyser · River, Stream · Waterfall Rapids · River Mouth, Estuary · Lake · Salt Lake · Intermittent Lake · Reservoir · Swamp, Pond · Canal · Glacier · Ice Shelf, Pack Ice · Ocean · Sea · Gulf, Bay · Strait, Fjord · Lagoon · Bank · Seamount · Tablemount · Ridge · Shelf · Basin · Escarpment, Sea Scarp · Fracture · Trench, Abyss · National Park, Reserve · Point of Interest · Recreation Site · Cave, Cavern · Historic Site · Ruins · Wall, Walls · Church, Abbey · Temple · Scientific Station · Airport · Port · Lighthouse · Mine · Tunnel · Dam, Bridge

Index Symbols

[1] Independent Nation	■ Historical or Cultural Region	▱ Pass, Gap
[2] State, Region	▲ Mount, Mountain	▱ Plain, Lowland
[3] District, County	▲ Volcano	▱ Delta
[4] Municipality	▲ Hill	▱ Salt Flat
[5] Colony, Dependency	▲ Mountains, Mountain Range	▱ Valley, Canyon
■ Continent	▲ Hills, Escarpment	▱ Crater, Cave
■ Physical Region	▲ Plateau, Upland	▱ Karst Features

▱ Depression	▱ Coast, Beach	▱ Rock, Reef
▱ Polder	▱ Cliff	▱ Islands, Archipelago
▱ Desert, Dunes	▱ Peninsula	▱ Rocks, Reefs
▱ Forest, Woods	▱ Isthmus	▱ Coral Reef
▱ Heath, Steppe	▱ Sandbank	▱ Well, Spring
▱ Oasis	▱ Island	▱ Geyser
▱ Cape, Point	▱ Atoll	▱ River, Stream

▱ Waterfall Rapids	▱ Canal	▱ Lagoon
▱ River Mouth, Estuary	▱ Glacier	▱ Bank
▱ Lake	▱ Ice Shelf, Pack Ice	▱ Seamount
▱ Salt Lake	▱ Sea	▱ Tablemount
▱ Intermittent Lake	▱ Gulf, Bay	▱ Ocean
▱ Reservoir	▱ Strait, Fjord	▱ Ridge
▱ Swamp, Pond		▱ Shelf
		▱ Basin

▱ Escarpment, Sea Scarp	▱ Historic Site	▱ Port
▱ Fracture	▱ Ruins	▱ Lighthouse
▱ Trench, Abyss	▱ Wall, Walls	▱ Mine
▱ National Park, Reserve	▱ Church, Abbey	▱ Tunnel
▱ Point of Interest	▱ Temple	▱ Dam, Bridge
▱ Recreation Site	▱ Scientific Station	
▱ Cave, Cavern	▱ Airport	

'Amm Adām 35 Fb 16.22N 36.09 E
'Ammān 22 Ff 31.57N 35.56 E
Ammanford 9 Jj 51.48N 3.59W
Ammarnäs 7 Dd 65.58N 16.12 E
Åmmeberg 8 Ff 58.52N 15.00 E
Ammer 10 Hi 47.57N 11.08 E
Ammerån 8 Ga 63.09N 16.13 E
Ammerland 10 Dc 53.15N 8.00 E
Ammersee 10 Hi 48.00N 11.08 E
Ammi-Moussa 13 Ni 35.52N 1.07 E
Ammokhostos → Famagusta (EN) 23 Dc 35.07N 33.57 E
Amnja 17 Me 63.45N 67.07 E
Amnok-kang 27 Ld 39.55N 124.20 E
Āmol 23 Hb 36.23N 52.20 E
Amolar 55 Dd 18.01 S 57.30W
Amorgós 15 Im 36.50N 25.53 E
Amorgós 15 Im 36.50N 25.59 E
Amorinópolis 55 Gc 16.36 S 51.08W
Amory 45 Lj 33.59N 88.29W
Amos 42 Jg 48.34N 78.07W
Amot [Nor.] 8 Be 59.35N 8.00 E
Amot [Nor.] 7 Bg 59.54N 9.54 E
Amotfors 8 Ee 59.46N 12.22 E
Amoucha 13 Rh 36.23N 5.25 E
Amouliani 15 Gi 40.20N 23.55 E
Amour, Djebel- 32 Hc 33.45N 1.45 E
Amourj 32 Ff 16.10N 7.35W
Ampanihy 37 Gd 24.40 S 44.45 E
Amparafaravola 37 Hc 17.36 S 48.12 E
Amparo 55 If 22.42 S 46.47W
Amper 10 Hh 48.10N 11.50 E
Ampère Seamount (EN) 5 Eh 35.05N 12.13W
Amphitrite Point 46 Cb 48.56N 125.35W
Amposta 13 Md 40.43N 0.35 E
Ampthill 12 Bb 52.02N 0.29W
Ampurdán/L'Empordà 13 Ob 42.12N 2.45 E
Ampurias 13 Pb 42.10N 3.05 E
Amqui 44 Na 48.28N 67.26W
'Amrān 23 Ff 15.41N 43.55 E
Amrāvati 22 Jg 20.56N 77.45 E
Am-Raya 35 Bc 14.05N 16.30 E
Amritsar 22 Jf 31.35N 74.53 E
Amrum 8 Cj 54.40N 8.20 E
Amsaga 32 Ee 20.07N 14.10W
Amsittene, Jebel- 32 Fc 31.11N 9.40W
Amstel 12 Gb 52.22N 4.56 E
Amstelveen 12 Gb 52.18N 4.53 E
Amsterdam 30 Ol 37.57 S 77.40 E
Amsterdam [Neth.] 6 Ge 52.22N 4.54 E
Amsterdam [N.Y.-U.S.] 44 Jd 42.56N 74.12W
Amsterdam-Rijnkanaal 12 Hc 51.57N 5.25 E
Amstetten 14 Ib 48.07N 14.52 E
Am Timan 31 Jg 11.02N 20.17 E
Amūd, Jabal al- 23 Ec 30.59N 39.20 E
Āmūdā 24 Id 37.05N 40.54 E
Amu-Darja 18 Ef 37.57N 65.15 E
Amudarja = Amu Darya (EN) 21 He 43.40N 59.01 E
Āmū Daryā = Amu Darya (EN) 21 He 43.40N 59.01 E
Amu Darya (EN) = Amudarja 21 He 43.40N 59.01 E
Amu Darya (EN) = Āmū Daryā 21 He 43.40N 59.01 E
Amudat 36 Fb 1.58N 34.56 E
Amukta Pass 40a Db 52.25N 172.00W
Amun 63a Ba 5.57 S 154.45 E
Amund Ringnes 42 Ha 78.15N 97.00W
Amundsen Bay 66 Ee 66.55 S 50.00 E
Amundsen Coast 66 Mg 85.30 S 159.00W
Amundsen Glacier 66 Mg 85.35 S 159.00W
Amundsen Gulf 38 Gb 71.00N 124.00W
Amundsen-Scott Station 66 Bg 90.00 S 0.00
Amundsen Sea (EN) 66 Of 72.30 S 112.00W
Amungen 8 Fc 61.10N 15.40 E
Amuntai 22 Nj 2.26 S 115.15 E
Amur 21 Qd 52.56N 141.10 E
'Amūr, Wādī 35 Eb 18.56N 33.34 E
Amurang 26 Hf 1.11N 124.35 E
Amursk 20 If 50.16N 136.55 E
Amurskaja Oblast [3] 20 Hf 54.00N 128.00 E
Amurzet 20 Ig 47.41N 131.07 E
Amvrakia, Gulf of- (EN) = Amvrakikós Kólpos 15 Dk 39.00N 21.00 E
Amvrakikós Kólpos = Amvrakia, Gulf of- (EN) 15 Dk 39.00N 21.00 E
Amvrosijevka 16 Kf 47.44N 38.31 E
Am Zoer 35 Cc 14.13N 21.23 E
Anaa Atoll 61 Lc 17.25 S 145.30W
Anabar 64e Ba 0.29 S 166.57 E
Anabar 21 Nb 73.08N 113.36 E
Anabarskoje Ploskogorje 21 Mc 70.00N 108.00 E
An Abhainn Dubh/Blackwater 9 Gh 53.39N 6.43W
An Abhainn Mhór/Blackwater [Ire.] 9 Fj 51.51N 7.50W
An Abhainn Mhór/Blackwater [N.Ire.-U.K.] 9 Gg 54.30N 6.35W
Anabuki 29 Dd 34.02N 134.11 E
Anacasti 56 Gc 28.49 S 65.30W
Anaco 54 Fb 9.27N 64.28W
Anaconda 43 Eb 46.08N 112.57W
Anacortes 46 Db 48.30N 122.37W
Anadarko 45 Gi 35.04N 98.15W
Anadolu = Anatolia (EN) 21 Ff 39.00N 35.00 E
Anadyr 21 Tc 64.55N 176.05 E
Anadyr 22 Tc 64.45N 177.29 E
Anadyr Gulf (EN) = Anadyrski Zaliv 21 Uc 64.00N 179.00W
Anadyr Range (EN) = Anadyrskoje Ploskogorje 21 Tc 67.00N 174.00 E
Anadyrski Liman 20 Md 64.30N 178.00 E
Anadyrski Zaliv = Anadyr Gulf (EN) 21 Uc 64.00N 179.00W
Anadyrskoje Ploskogorje = Anadyr Range (EN) 21 Tc 67.00N 174.00 E
Anáfi 15 Im 36.22N 25.47 E
Anaghit 35 Fb 16.20N 38.39 E
Anagni 14 Hi 41.44N 13.09 E
'Ānah 23 Fc 34.28N 41.56 E
Anaheim 46 Gj 33.51N 117.57W
Anahola 65a Ba 22.09N 159.19W
Anáhuac 48 Id 27.14N 100.09W
Anahuac, Meseta de- 47 Dd 21.30N 101.00W
An Aird/Ards Peninsula 9 Hg 54.30N 5.30W
Anaj Mudi 21 Jh 10.10N 77.04 E
Anaktuvuk Pass 40 Ic 68.10N 151.50W
Analalava 37 Hb 14.38 S 47.45 E
Analavelona 37 Gd 22.37 S 44.10 E
Ana Maria, Golfo de- 49 Hc 21.25N 78.40W
Anambas, Kepulauan- = Anambas Islands (EN) 21 Mi 3.00N 106.00 E
Anambas Islands (EN) = Anambas, Kepulauan- 21 Mi 3.00N 106.00 E
Anambra [2] 34 Gd 6.30N 7.30 E
Anamé 63b De 20.08 S 169.49 E
Anamizu 28 Nf 37.14N 136.54 E
Anamur 23 Db 36.06N 32.50 E
Anamur Burun 23 Db 36.03N 32.48 E
Anan [Jap.] 28 Mh 33.55N 134.39 E
Anan [Jap.] 29 Ed 35.19N 137.48 E
Anane, Djebel- 13 Mi 35.12N 0.47 E
Anánes 15 Hm 36.31N 24.08 E
Ananjev 16 Ff 47.43N 29.59 E
Anankwin 25 Je 15.41N 97.59 E
Anantapur 25 Ff 14.41N 77.36 E
Anantnāg (Islāmābād) 25 Fb 33.44N 75.09 E
Anapa 19 Dg 44.53N 37.19 E
Anapo 14 Jm 37.03N 15.16 E
Anápolis 53 Lg 16.20 S 48.58W
Anapu, Rio- 54 Hd 2.15 S 51.30W
Anār 23 Ic 30.53N 55.18 E
Anārak 23 Hc 33.20N 53.42 E
Anare Station 66 Jd 54.30 S 158.55 E
Anaro, Río- 49 Lj 7.48N 70.12W
Añasco 51a Ab 18.17N 67.10W
Anatahan Island 57 Fc 16.22N 145.40 E
Anatolia (EN) = Anadolu 21 Ff 39.00N 35.00 E
Anatoliki Rodhópi 15 Ih 41.44N 25.31 E
Añatuya 56 Hc 28.28 S 62.50W
Anauá, Rio- 54 Fc 0.58N 61.21W
Anazarba 24 Fd 37.15N 35.45 E
An Baile Meánach/Ballymena 9 Gg 54.52N 6.17W
An Bhanna/Bann 9 Gf 55.10N 6.46W
An Bhearú/Barrow 9 Gi 52.10N 7.00W
An Bhinn Bhuí/Benwee Head 9 Dg 54.21N 9.48W
An Bhograch/Boggeragh Mountains 9 Ei 52.05N 9.00W
An Bhóinn/Boyne 9 Gh 53.43N 6.15W
An Bhrosnach/Brosna 9 Fh 53.13N 7.58W
An Blascaod Mór/Great Blasket 9 Ci 52.05N 10.32W
Anbyŏn 28 Ie 39.02N 127.32 E
An Cabhán/Cavan [2] 9 Fh 53.55N 7.30W
An Cabhán/Cavan 9 Fg 54.00N 7.21W
An Caisleán Nua/Newcastle 9 Hg 54.12N 5.54W
An Caisleán Nua/Newcastle West 9 Di 52.27N 9.03W
An Caisleán Riabhach/Castlerea 9 Eh 53.46N 8.29W
An Caoláire Rua/Killary Harbour 9 Dh 53.38N 9.55W
Ancares, Sierra de- 13 Fb 42.46N 6.54W
Ancash [2] 54 Ce 9.30 S 77.45W
Ancenis 11 Eg 47.22N 1.10W
An Chathair/Caher 9 Fi 52.22N 7.55W
An Cheacha/Caha Mountains 9 Dj 51.45N 9.45W
Anchorage 39 Ec 61.13N 149.53W
An Chorr Chríochach/Cookstown 9 Gg 54.39N 6.45W
Anci (Langfang) 27 Kd 39.29N 116.40 E
An Clár/Clare [2] 9 Ei 52.50N 9.00W
An Cóbh/Cóbh 9 Ej 51.51N 8.17W
Ancohuma, Nevado- 54 Eg 15.51 S 68.36W
Ancona 6 Hg 43.38N 13.30 E
Ancón de Sardinas, Bahía de- 54 Cc 1.30N 79.50W
Ancre 11 Ie 49.54N 2.28 E
Ancuabe 37 Fb 12.58 S 39.51 E
Ancud 56 Ff 41.52 S 73.50W
Ancud, Golfo de- 56 Ff 42.05 S 73.00W
Anda 27 Mb 46.24N 125.20 E
Anda (Sartu) 28 Ha 46.35N 125.00 E
Andacollo [Arg.] 56 Fe 37.11 S 70.41W
Andacollo [Chile] 56 Fd 30.14 S 71.06W
Andahuaylas 54 Df 13.39 S 73.23W
An Daingean/Dingle 9 Ci 52.03N 10.15W
Andalgalá 56 Gc 27.36 S 66.19W
Åndalsnes 7 Be 62.34N 7.42 E
Andalucía = Andalusia (EN) 13 Hg 37.30N 4.30W
Andalucía = Andalusia (EN) 5 Fh 37.30N 4.30W
Andalusia 43 Je 31.19N 86.29W
Andalusia (EN) = Andalucía 13 Hg 37.30N 4.30W
Andalusia (EN) = Andalucía 5 Fh 37.30N 4.30W
Andaman and Nicobar [3] 25 If 12.30N 92.45 E
Andaman Basin (EN) 21 Lh 10.00N 94.00 E
Andaman Islands 21 Lh 12.30N 92.43 E
Andaman Sea (EN) 21 Lh 10.00N 95.00 E
Andamooka 59 Hf 30.27 S 137.12 E
'Andān, Wādī- 23 Ie 21.05N 58.23 E
Andant 55 Am 36.34 S 62.07W
Andapa 37 Hb 14.38 S 49.33 E
Andara 37 Cc 18.03 S 21.27 E
Andelle 12 De 49.19N 1.14 E
Andenes 7 Db 69.19N 16.08 E
Andenne 12 Hd 50.29N 5.06 E
Andenne-Namêche 12 Hd 50.28N 5.00 E
Anderanboukane 34 Fb 15.26N 3.02 E
Anderlecht 12 Gd 50.50N 4.18 E
Anderlues 12 Gd 50.24N 4.16 E
Andermatt 14 Cd 46.38N 8.37 E
Andernach 10 Df 50.26N 7.24 E
Andernos-les-Bains 11 Ej 44.44N 1.06W
Anderson 42 Ec 69.42N 129.00W
Anderson [Ca.-U.S.] 46 Df 40.27N 122.18W
Anderson [In.-U.S.] 43 Jc 40.10N 85.41W
Anderson [S.C.-U.S.] 43 Ke 34.30N 82.39W
Anderstorp 8 Eg 57.17N 13.38 E
Andes (EN) = Andes, Cordillera de los- 52 Jh 20.00 S 67.00W
Andes, Cordillera de los- = Andes (EN) 52 Jh 20.00 S 67.00W
Andevoranto 37 Hc 18.58 S 49.02 E
Andfjorden 7 Db 69.10N 16.20 E
Andhra Pradesh [3] 25 Fe 16.00N 79.00 E
Andía, Sierra de- 13 Kb 42.45N 2.00W
Andikhásia Óri 15 Ej 39.47N 21.55 E
Andikira 15 Fk 38.23N 22.38 E
Andikithira = Andikithira (EN) 15 Gn 35.52N 23.18 E
Andikithira (EN) = Andikithira 15 Gn 35.52N 23.18 E
Andikíthiron, Stenón- 15 Gn 35.45N 23.25 E
Andilamena 37 Hc 17.01 S 48.32 E
Andilanatoby 37 Hc 17.56 S 48.14 E
Andīmeshk 24 Mf 32.27N 48.21 E
Andimilos 15 Hm 36.47N 24.14 E
Andiparos 15 Il 37.00N 25.03 E
Andipaxoi 15 Dj 39.08N 20.14 E
Andipsara 15 Ik 38.33N 25.24 E
Andir He 27 Dd 38.00N 83.36 E
Andirin 24 Gd 37.34N 36.20 E
Andirlangar 27 Dd 37.38N 83.50 E
Andírrion 15 Ek 38.20N 21.46 E
Andítilos 15 Km 36.22N 27.28 E
Andižan 22 Je 40.45N 72.22 E
Andižanskaja Oblast [3] 19 Hg 40.45N 72.20 E
Andkhvoy 23 Kb 36.56N 65.08 E
Andŏng 27 Md 36.36N 128.44 E
Andorra (Valls d'Andorra) [1] 6 Gg 42.30N 1.30 E
Andorra la Vella 6 Gg 42.31N 1.30 E
Andover 9 Lj 51.13N 1.28W
Andøya 7 Db 69.08N 15.54 E
Andradas 55 If 22.05 S 46.35W
Andradina 56 Jb 20.54 S 51.23W
Andraitx 13 Oe 39.35N 2.25 E
Andreanof Islands 38 Bd 52.00N 176.00W
Andreapol 7 Hh 56.39N 32.16 E
Andrées Land 41 Jd 73.20N 26.30W
Andrejevka 19 If 45.47N 80.35 E
Andrejevka 16 Je 49.32N 36.40 E
Andrejevo-Ivanovka 15 Nb 47.31N 30.27 E
Andrejevsk 20 Ge 58.10N 114.15 E
Andrelândia 55 Je 21.44 S 44.18W
Andresito 55 Dk 33.08 S 57.09W
Andrespol 10 Pe 51.43N 19.40 E
Andrews 45 Ej 32.19N 102.33W
Andria 14 Ki 41.13N 16.17 E
Andriamena 37 Hc 17.28 S 47.29 E
Andriba 37 Hc 17.36 S 46.53 E
Andrijevica 15 Cg 42.44N 19.48 E
Andringitra 30 Lk 22.20 S 46.55 E
Andrítsaina 15 El 37.29N 21.54 E
Androka 37 Gd 24.59 S 44.04 E
Andropov → Rybinsk 6 Jd 58.03N 38.52 E
Ándros 5 Ih 37.50N 24.50 E
Andros 38 Lg 24.25N 78.00W
Ándros 15 Hl 37.50N 24.56 E
Androscoggin River 44 Md 43.55N 69.55W
Androssan 9 If 55.40N 4.55W
Andros Town 47 Id 24.43N 77.47W
Androth Island 25 Ef 10.50N 73.41 E
Androy 30 Lk 25.00 S 45.40 E
Andruševka 16 Fe 49.59N 29.01 E
Andrychów 10 Pg 49.52N 19.21 E
Andselv 7 Eb 69.04N 18.30 E
Andudu 36 Eb 2.29N 28.41 E
Andújar 13 Hf 38.03N 4.04W
Andulo 36 Ce 11.28 S 16.43 E
Andu Tan 26 Fe 7.35N 114.15 E
Anduze 11 Jj 44.03N 3.59 E
An Earagail/Errigal 9 Ef 55.02N 8.07W
Aneby 8 Fg 57.50N 14.48 E
Anéfis 34 Fb 18.03N 0.36 E
Anegada 47 Le 18.45N 64.20W
Anegada, Bahía- 56 Hf 40.15 S 62.15W
Anegada Passage 47 Le 18.30N 63.40W
Aného 34 Fd 6.14N 1.36 E
An Éirne/Erne 9 Eg 54.30N 8.15W
An Eithne/Inny 9 Fh 53.35N 7.50W
An Eoghanach/Annalee 9 Fg 54.02N 7.25W
Anet 12 Df 48.51N 1.26 E
Aneto, Pico de- 5 Gg 42.38N 0.40 E
Aney 34 Hb 19.24N 12.56 E
Aneytioum, Ile- 57 Hg 20.12 S 169.49 E
An Feabhal 9 Ff 55.04N 7.15W
An Fhéil/Feale 9 Di 52.28N 9.40W
An Fheoir/Nore 9 Gi 52.25N 6.58W
Angamos, Punta- [Chile] 56 Fb 23.01 S 70.32W
Angamos, Punta- [Pas.] 65d Bb 27.04 S 109.17W
Angara 21 Ld 58.06N 93.00 E
Angarsk 22 Md 52.34N 103.54 E
Angarski, Pereval- 16 Ig 44.47N 34.25 E
Angarski Krjaž 20 Fe 57.30N 103.00 E
Angathonisi 15 Jl 37.28N 27.00 E
Angaur Island 57 Ed 6.54N 134.09 E
Ånge 7 De 62.31N 15.37 E
Änge 8 Fa 63.27N 14.03 E
An Gearran/Garron Point 9 Hf 55.05N 5.58W
Ángel, Cerro- 48 Hf 22.49N 102.34W
Ángel, Salto- = Angel Falls (EN) 52 Je 5.57N 62.30W
Angelburg 12 Kd 50.47N 8.25 E
Ángel de la Guarda, Isla- 47 Bc 29.20N 113.25W
Angeles 26 Hc 15.09N 120.35 E
Ángeles, Sierra de los- 48 Jf 23.10N 99.20W
Angel Falls (EN) = Ángel, Salto- 52 Je 5.57N 62.30W
Angel Falls (EN) = Churún Merú 52 Je 5.57N 62.30W
Ängelholm 7 Ch 56.15N 12.51 E
Angélica 55 Bj 31.33 S 61.33W
Angeln 10 Fb 54.40N 9.45 E
Ängelsberg 8 Ge 59.58N 16.02 E
Anger 35 Fd 9.40N 36.06 E
Angereb 35 Fc 13.44N 36.28 E
Ångermanälven 5 Hc 62.48N 17.56 E
Angermünde 10 Jc 53.02N 14.00 E
Angers 6 Ff 47.28N 0.33W
Angkor 25 Kf 13.26N 103.52 E
Angikuni Lake 42 Hd 62.10N 99.55W
Angistrion 15 Gl 37.40N 23.20 E
Anglem, Mount- 62 Bg 46.44 S 167.54 E
Anglés 13 Oc 41.57N 2.39 E
Anglesey 5 Fe 53.18N 4.20W
Anglet 11 Ek 43.29N 1.32W
Angleton 45 Il 29.10N 95.26W
Anglin 11 Gh 46.42N 0.52 E
Anglona 14 Cj 40.45N 8.45 E
Angmagssalik 67 Mc 65.45N 37.30W
Ango 36 Eb 4.02N 25.52 E
Angoche 31 Kj 16.12 S 39.54 E
Angoche, Ilha- 30 Kj 16.20 S 39.51 E
Angol 56 Fe 37.48 S 72.43W
Angola [1] 31 Ij 12.30 S 18.30 E
Angola 44 Ee 41.38N 85.00W
Angola Basin (EN) 3 Ek 15.00 S 3.00 E
Angoram 60 Ch 4.04 S 144.04 E
Angostura 48 Ee 25.22N 108.11W
Angostura, Presa de la- 48 Mi 16.30N 92.30W
Angostura, Salto- 54 Dc 2.43N 70.57W
Angostura Reservoir 45 Ee 43.18N 103.27W
Angoulême 11 Gi 45.39N 0.09 E
Angoumois 11 Fi 45.30N 0.10W
Angra do Heroísmo [3] 32 Bb 38.42N 27.15W
Angra do Heroísmo 31 Ee 38.39N 27.13W
Angra dos Reis 55 Jf 23.00 S 44.18W
Angren 19 Hg 41.03N 70.10 E
Angu 36 Db 3.33N 24.28 E
Anguang 28 Gb 45.36N 123.48 E
Anguilla [5] 39 Mh 18.15N 63.05W
Anguilla 38 Mh 18.15N 63.05W
Anguilla, Canal de l'- = Anguilla Channel (EN) 51b Ab 18.09N 63.04W
Anguilla Bank (EN) 51b Ab 18.30N 63.03W
Anguilla Cays 49 Hb 23.31N 78.33W
Anguilla Channel (EN) = Anguilla, Canal de l'- 51b Ab 18.09N 63.04W
Anguli Nur 28 Cd 41.23N 114.30 E
Anguo 28 Ce 38.25N 115.20 E
Anhanca 36 Cf 16.47 S 15.33 E
Anhanguera 55 Hd 18.21 S 48.17W
An Hoa 25 Le 15.46N 108.03 E
Anholt 7 Ch 56.40N 11.35 E
Anhua (Dongping) 27 Jf 28.27N 111.15 E
Anhui Sheng (An-hui Sheng) = Anhwei (EN) [2] 27 Ke 32.00N 117.00 E
An-hui Sheng → Anhui Sheng = Anhwei (EN) [2] 27 Ke 32.00N 117.00 E
Anhwei (EN) = Anhui Sheng (An-hui Sheng) [2] 27 Ke 32.00N 117.00 E
Anhwei (EN) = An-hui Sheng → Anhui Sheng [2] 27 Ke 32.00N 117.00 E
Ani 29 Gb 39.59N 140.25 E
Aniak 40 Hd 61.34N 159.30W
An Iarmhí/Westmeath [2] 9 Fh 53.30N 7.30W
Anibare 64e Bb 0.32 S 166.57 E
Anibare Bay 64e Bb 0.32 S 166.57 E
Aniche 12 Fd 50.20N 3.15 E
Ánidros 15 Im 36.37N 25.41 E
Anié 34 Fd 7.45N 1.12 E
Anie, Pic d'- 11 Fl 42.57N 0.43W
Aniene 14 Gi 41.56N 12.30 E
Anijiangying → Luanping 28 Dd 40.55N 117.19 E
Anikščiai/Anykščiai 7 Fi 55.31N 25.08 E
Animas Peak 45 Bk 31.35N 108.47W
Anina 15 Ed 45.05N 21.51 E
Anita Garibaldi 55 Gh 27.37 S 51.05W
Anittepe 15 Kh 41.21N 27.42 E
Aniva 20 Jg 46.41N 142.35 E
Aniva, Zaliv- 20 Jg 46.20N 142.40 E
Anivorano Nord 37 Hb 12.43 S 49.12 E
Aniwa, Ile- 57 Hf 19.16 S 169.35 E
Anizy-le-Château 12 Fe 49.30N 3.27 E
Anjala 7 Gf 60.41N 26.50 E
Anji 28 Ei 30.39N 119.41 E
Anjiang → Qianyang 27 Jf 27.19N 110.13 E
Anjō 29 Ed 34.57N 137.05 E
Anjou 11 Fg 47.20N 0.30W
Anjou, Ostrova- = Anjou Islands (EN) 21 Qb 75.30N 143.00 E
Anjouan → Nzwani 30 Lj 12.15 S 44.25 E
Anjou Islands (EN) = Anjou, Ostrova- 21 Qb 75.30N 143.00 E
Anjozorobe 37 Hc 18.24 S 47.52 E
Anju 27 Md 39.37N 125.40 E
Anjuj 20 Ig 49.20N 136.20 E
Anjujski Hrebet 20 Lc 67.20N 166.00 E
Anjuou, Val d'- 11 Fg 47.25N 0.15W
Anka 34 Gc 12.07N 5.55 E
Ankang (Xing'an) 22 Mf 32.37N 109.03 E
Ankara 22 Ff 39.56N 32.52 E
Ankaratra 30 Lj 19.25 S 47.12 E
Ankarsrum 7 Dh 57.42N 16.19 E
Ankavandra 37 Hc 18.45 S 45.18 E
Ankazoabo 37 Gd 22.18 S 44.30 E
Ankazobe 37 Hc 18.17 S 47.05 E
Ankeny 45 Jf 41.44N 93.36W
Ankhor 35 Hc 10.47N 46.18 E
Anklam 10 Jc 53.52N 13.42 E
Ankober 35 Fc 9.40N 39.44 E
Ankoro 36 Ec 6.45 S 26.57 E
Ankum 12 Jb 52.33N 7.53 E
An Laoi/Lee 9 Ej 51.55N 8.30W
Anlong 27 If 25.02N 105.30 E
An Longfort/Longford [2] 9 Fh 53.40N 7.40W
An Longfort/Longfort 9 Fh 53.44N 7.47W
An Lorgain/Lurgan 9 Gg 54.28N 6.20W
Anlu 27 Je 31.12N 113.46 E
An Mhí/Meath [2] 9 Gh 53.35N 6.40W
An Mhuaidh/Moy 9 Dg 54.12N 9.08W
An Mhuir Cheilteach = Celtic Sea (EN) 5 Fe 51.00N 7.00W
An Muileann gCearr/Mullingar 9 Fh 53.32N 7.20W
An Muirthead/Mullet Peninsula 9 Cg 54.15N 10.04W
Ånn 7 Ce 63.15N 12.35 E
Ånn 8 Ea 63.19N 12.33 E
Ann, Cape- [Ant.] 66 Ee 66.10 S 51.22 E
Ann, Cape- [Ma.-U.S.] 44 Ld 42.39N 70.38W
Anna [Il.-U.S.] 45 Lh 37.28N 89.15W
Anna [Nauru] 64e Ba 0.29 S 166.56 E
Anna 19 Ee 51.29N 40.26 E
Annaba 31 He 36.54N 7.46 E
Annaba [3] 32 Ib 35.35N 8.00 E
An Nabaţīyah at Taḩtā 24 Gf 33.23N 35.29 E
Annaberg-Buchholz 10 If 50.34N 13.00 E
An Nabī Şāliḩ 24 Eh 28.38N 33.59 E
An Nabk 23 Ec 34.01N 36.44 E
An Nabk Abū Gaşr 24 Hg 30.21N 38.34 E
An Nafīḑah 14 En 36.08N 10.23 E
An Nafūd 21 Gg 28.30N 41.00 E
An Najaf 22 Gf 31.59N 44.20 E
An Najaf [3] 24 Kg 31.20N 44.07 E
An Nakhl 33 Fd 29.55N 33.45 E
Annalee/An Eoghanach 9 Fg 54.02N 7.25W
Annam (EN) = Trung Phan 21 Me 15.00N 108.00 E
Annamitique, Chaîne- 25 Le 17.00N 106.00 E
Annan 9 Jg 54.59N 3.16W
Annan 9 Jg 55.00N 3.16W
Anna Paulowna 12 Gb 52.52N 4.52 E
Anna Paulowna-Kleine Sluis 12 Gb 52.52N 4.52 E
Anna Point 64e Ba 0.29 S 166.56 E
Annapolis 39 Lf 38.59N 76.30W
Annapolis Royal 44 Oc 44.45N 65.31W
Annapurna 21 Kg 28.34N 83.50 E
Ann Arbor 43 Kc 42.18N 83.45W
Anna Regina 50 Gi 7.16N 58.30W
An Nás/Naas 9 Gh 53.13N 6.39W
An Nashshāsh 24 Pk 23.05N 54.02 E
An Nashwah 24 Lg 30.49N 47.36 E
An Nāşirīyah 23 Gc 31.02N 46.16 E
An Nasser 24 Ej 24.36N 32.58 E
An Nawfalīyah 33 Cc 30.47N 17.50 E
Annecy 11 Mi 45.54N 6.07 E
Annecy, Lac d'- 11 Mi 45.51N 6.11 E
Annemasse 11 Mh 46.12N 6.15 E
Annevoie-Rouillon 12 Gd 50.21N 4.50 E
An Nīl [3] 35 Ea 20.10N 33.00 E
An Nīl al Azraq [3] 35 Ed 12.20N 34.15 E
Anning 27 Hg 24.58N 102.29 E
Anniston 43 Je 33.40N 85.50W
Annobón 30 Hi 1.32 S 5.38 E
Annonay 11 Ki 45.14N 4.40 E
Annotto Bay 49 Id 13.16N 76.46W
An Nu'ayrīyah 24 Mi 27.28N 48.27 E
An Nuhūd 31 Jg 12.42N 28.26 E
An Nu' Mān 24 Fi 27.06N 35.46 E
An Nu'mānīyah 24 Kf 32.32N 45.25 E
Annweiler am Trifels 12 Je 49.12N 7.58 E
Anoia/Noya 13 Nc 41.28N 1.56 E
Anoka 45 Jd 45.11N 93.23W
An Ómaigh/Omagh 9 Fg 54.36N 7.18W
Ancri 54 Fd 3.47 S 61.38W
Ancsyennes, Chaînes- 37 Hd 24.20 S 47.00 E
Ânou Makarene 34 Gb 18.07N 7.35 E
Áno Viánnos 15 In 35.03N 25.25 E
Anóyia 15 Hn 35.15N 24.54 E
Anping [China] 28 Ce 38.13N 115.32 E
Anping [China] 28 Gd 41.10N 123.25 E
An Pointe/Warrenpoint 9 Gg 54.06N 6.15W
Anpu 27 Ig 21.30N 110.00 E
Anpu Gang 27 Ig 21.25N 109.40 E
Anqing 22 Nf 30.32N 116.59 E
Anqiu 28 Ef 36.25N 119.12 E
An Ráth/Ráth Luirc 9 Ei 52.21N 8.41W
An Ribhéar/Kenmare River 9 Dj 51.50N 9.50W
Anröchte 12 Kc 51.34N 8.20 E
Ans 12 Hd 50.39N 5.32 E
Anşāb 23 Fd 29.11N 44.43 E
Ansauvillers 12 Ee 49.34N 2.24 E
Ansbach 10 Gg 49.18N 10.35 E
An Sciobairin/Skibbereen 9 Dj 51.33N 9.15W
An Seancheann/Kinsale, Old Head of- 9 Ej 51.36N 8.32W
Anse-à-Veau 49 Kd 18.30N 73.19W
Anse-Bertrand 51e Ab 16.29N 61.31W
Anse-d'Hainault 49 Jd 18.30N 74.27W
Anse la Raye 51k Ab 13.57N 61.03W
Anshan 22 Oe 41.08N 122.59 E
Anshun 22 Mg 26.15N 105.58 E
Ansina 56 Id 31.54 S 55.28W
Ansley 45 Gf 41.18N 99.23W
Anson Bay 59 Gb 13.20 S 130.05 E
Ansongo 34 Fb 15.40N 0.31 E
An Srath Bán/Strabane 9 Fg 54.49N 7.27W
Anta 54 Df 13.29 S 72.09W

Index Symbols

[1] Independent Nation
[2] State, Region
[3] District, County
[4] Municipality
[5] Colony, Dependency
Continent
Physical Region
Historical or Cultural Region
Mount, Mountain
Volcano
Hill
Mountains, Mountain Range
Hills, Escarpment
Plateau, Upland
Pass, Gap
Plain, Lowland
Delta
Salt Flat
Valley, Canyon
Crater, Cave
Karst Features
Depression
Polder
Desert, Dunes
Forest, Woods
Heath, Steppe
Oasis
Cape, Point
Coast, Beach
Cliff
Peninsula
Isthmus
Sandbank
Island
Atoll
Rock, Reef
Islands, Archipelago
Rocks, Reefs
Coral Reef
Well, Spring
Geyser
River, Stream
Waterfall Rapids
River Mouth, Estuary
Lake
Salt Lake
Intermittent Lake
Reservoir
Swamp, Pond
Canal
Glacier
Ice Shelf, Pack Ice
Ocean
Sea
Gulf, Bay
Strait, Fjord
Lagoon
Bank
Seamount
Tablemount
Ridge
Shelf
Basin
Escarpment, Sea Scarp
Fracture
Trench, Abyss
National Park, Reserve
Point of Interest
Recreation Site
Cave, Cavern
Historic Site
Ruins
Wall, Walls
Church, Abbey
Temple
Scientific Station
Airport
Port
Lighthouse
Mine
Tunnel
Dam, Bridge

Antabamba	54	Df	14.19S	72.55W
Antakya=Antioch (EN)	23	Eb	36.14N	36.07 E
Antalaha	31	Mj	14.55S	50.15 E
Antalya	22	Ff	36.53N	30.42 E
Antalya, Gulf of- (EN)=Antalya Körfezi	23	Db	36.30N	31.00 E
Antalya Körfezi=Antalya, Gulf of- (EN)	23	Db	36.30N	31.00 E
An Tan	25	Le	15.26N	108.39 E
Antananarivo	31	Lj	18.55S	47.30 E
Antananarivo [3]	37	Hc	19.00S	46.40 E
Antanimora	37	Hd	24.48S	45.39 E
An tAonach/Nenagh	9	Ei	52.52N	8.12W
Antarctica (EN)	66	Bg	90.00S	0.00
Antarctic Peninsula (EN)	66	Qe	69.30S	65.00W
Antas, Cachoeira das-	55	Ha	13.06S	48.09W
Antas, Rio das-	55	Gi	29.04S	51.21W
An Teampall Mór/Templemore	9	Fi	52.48N	7.50W
Antela, Laguna de-	13	Eb	42.07N	7.41W
Antelao	14	Gd	46.27N	12.16 E
Antelope Creek	46	Me	43.29N	105.23W
Anten	8	Ef	58.03N	12.30 E
Antequera [Par.]	55	Dg	24.08S	57.07W
Antequera [Sp.]	13	Hg	37.01N	4.33W
Anthony	45	Cj	32.00N	106.34W
Anti-Atlas	30	Ge	30.00N	8.30W
Antibes	11	Nk	43.35N	7.07 E
Antibes, Cap d'-	11	Nk	43.32N	7.07 E
Antica, Isla-	50	Eg	10.24N	62.43W
Anticosti, Ile d'-	38	Me	49.30N	63.00W
Antigo	45	Ld	45.09N	89.09W
Antigonish	42	Lg	45.37N	61.58W
Antigua	38	Mh	17.03N	61.48W
Antigua and Barbuda	39	Mh	17.03N	61.48W
Antigua Guatemala	47	Ff	14.34N	90.44W
Antiguo Cauce del Río Bermejo	56	Hc	25.39S	60.11W
Antiguo Morelos	48	Jf	22.30N	99.05W
Antilla	49	Jc	20.50N	75.45W
Antillas, Mar de las-/Caribe, Mar-=Caribbean Sea (EN)	38	Lh	15.00N	73.00W
Antillas Mayores=Greater Antilles (EN)	38	Lh	20.00N	74.00W
Antillas Menores=Lesser Antilles (EN)	38	Mh	15.00N	61.00W
Antilles, Mer des-/Caraïbe, Mer-=Caribbean Sea (EN)	38	Lh	15.00N	73.00W
An tInbhear Mór/Arklow	9	Gi	52.48N	6.09W
Antioch	46	Eg	38.00N	121.49W
Antioch (EN)=Antakya	23	Eb	36.14N	36.07 E
Antioche, Pertuis d'-	11	Eh	46.05N	1.20W
Antiope Reef	57	Kf	18.18S	168.40W
Antioquia [2]	54	Cb	7.00N	75.30W
Antipajëta	20	Cc	69.09N	77.00 E
Antipodes Islands	57	Ii	49.40S	178.50 E
Antiques, Pointe d'-	51e	Ab	16.26N	61.33W
An t-Iúr/Newry	9	Gg	54.11N	6.20W
Antler River	45	Fb	49.08N	101.00W
Antlers	45	Ii	34.14N	95.37W
Antofagasta [2]	56	Gb	23.30S	69.00W
Antofagasta	53	Ih	23.39S	70.24W
Antofagasta de la Sierra	56	Gc	26.04S	67.25W
Antofalla, Salar de-	56	Gc	25.44S	67.45W
Antofalla, Volcán-	56	Gc	25.34S	67.55W
Antoing	12	Fd	50.34N	3.27 E
Antón	49	Gi	8.24N	80.16W
Anton Dohrn Seamount (EN)	9	Cd	57.30N	11.00W
Antongil, Baie d'-	37	Lj	15.45S	49.50 E
Antonina	56	Kc	25.27S	48.43W
Antônio João	55	Ef	23.15S	55.31W
Antonito	45	Dh	37.05N	106.00W
Antón Lizardo, Punta de-	48	Lh	19.03N	95.58W
Antony	12	Ef	48.45N	2.18 E
Antopol	10	Ud	52.12N	24.53 E
Antracit	16	Ke	48.06N	39.06 E
Antreff	12	Ld	50.52N	9.15 E
Antrim/Aontroim	9	Gg	54.43N	6.13W
Antrim Mountains	9	Gf	55.00N	6.10W
Antrodoco	14	Hh	42.25N	13.05 E
Antsakabary	37	Hc	15.03S	48.56 E
Antsalova	37	Gc	18.42S	44.33 E
Antseranana [3]	37	Hb	13.40S	49.15 E
An tSionainn/Shannon	5	Fe	52.36N	9.41W
Antsirabe	31	Lj	19.51S	47.01 E
Antsiranana	31	Lj	12.17S	49.17 E
An tSiúir/Suir	9	Gi	52.15N	7.00W
Antsla	7	Gh	57.52N	26.33 E
An tSláine/Slaney	9	Gi	52.21N	6.30W
Antsohihy	31	Lj	14.52S	47.58 E
An tSuca/Suck	9	Eh	53.16N	8.03W
Anttola	8	Lc	61.35N	27.39 E
Antu (Songjiang)	28	Jc	42.33N	128.20 E
An Tuc	25	Lf	13.57N	108.39 E
Antufash, Jazīrat-	33	Hf	15.42N	42.25 E
An Tulach/Tullow	9	Gi	52.48N	6.44W
An Tulach Mhór/Tullamore	9	Fh	53.16N	7.30W
Antwerp (EN)=Antwerpen/Anvers	6	Ge	50.38N	5.34 E
Antwerp (EN)=Anvers/Antwerpen	6	Ge	50.38N	5.34 E
Antwerpen [3]	12	Gc	51.10N	4.30 E
Antwerpen/Anvers=Antwerp (EN)	6	Ge	50.38N	5.34 E
Antwerpen-Ekeren	11	Kc	51.17N	4.25 E
Antwerpen-Hoboken	12	Gc	51.10N	4.21 E
Antwerpen-Merksem	12	Gc	51.15N	4.27 E
Antykan	20	If	54.55N	135.13 E
An Uaimh/Navan	9	Gh	53.39N	6.41W
Anuradhapura	25	Gg	8.21N	80.23 E
Anuta Island	57	Hf	11.38S	169.50 E
Anvers/Antwerpen=Antwerp (EN)	6	Ge	50.38N	5.34 E
Anvers Island	66	Qe	64.33S	63.35W
Anvik	40	Gd	62.40N	160.12W
Anxi	22	Le	40.30N	96.00 E
Anxiang	27	Jf	29.26N	112.11 E
Anxin	28	Ce	38.55N	115.56 E
Anxious Bay	59	Gf	33.25S	134.35 E
Anyang (Zhangde)	22	Nf	36.01N	114.25 E
A'nyêmaqen Shan	21	Lf	34.30N	100.00 E
Anyi	28	Cj	28.50N	115.31 E
Anykščiai/Anikščjaj	7	Fi	55.31N	25.08 E
Anyva, Mys-	20	Jg	46.00N	143.25 E
Anza	14	Ce	46.00N	8.17 E
Anze	28	Bf	36.09N	112.14 E
Anzegem	12	Fd	50.50N	3.28 E
Anžero-Sudženskl	22	Kd	56.07N	86.00 E
Anzi	36	Dc	0.52S	23.24 E
Anzio	14	Gi	41.27N	12.37 E
Anzoátegui [2]	54	Fb	9.00N	64.30W
Anzob, Pereval-	18	Ge	39.07N	68.53 E
Aoba, Ile-	61	Cc	15.25S	167.50 E
Ao Ban Don	25	Jg	9.20N	99.25 E
Aoga-Shima	27	Oe	32.30N	139.50 E
Aohan Qi (Xinhui)	28	Ec	42.18N	119.53 E
Aoiz	13	Kb	42.47N	1.22W
Aoji	28	Kc	42.31N	130.24 E
Aola	63a	Ec	9.32S	160.29 E
Aomen/Macau=Macao (EN) [5]	22	Ng	22.10N	113.33 E
Aomen/Macau=Macao (EN)	27	Jg	22.12N	113.33 E
Aomori	22	Qe	40.49N	140.45 E
Aomori Ken [2]	28	Pd	40.40N	140.40 E
Aono-Yama	29	Bd	34.27N	131.48 E
Aontroim/Antrim	9	Gg	54.43N	6.13W
Aopo	65c	Aa	13.29S	172.30W
Aôral, Phnum-	25	Kf	12.02N	104.10 E
Aoré	63b	Cb	15.35S	167.10 E
Aosta / Aoste	14	Be	45.44N	7.20 E
Aosta, Val d'-	14	Be	45.45N	7.20 E
Aoste / Aosta	14	Be	45.44N	7.20 E
Aouk, Bahr-	30	Ih	8.51N	18.53 E
Aoukalé	35	Cd	9.10N	20.30 E
Aoukâr [Afr.]	32	Ge	24.00N	2.30W
Aoukâr [Mtna.]	30	Gg	17.30N	9.30W
Aoulef	32	Hd	26.58N	1.05 E
Aoumou	63b	Be	21.24S	165.49 E
Aourou	34	Cc	14.28N	11.34W
Aoya	29	Cd	35.32N	133.59 E
Aozou	31	If	21.49N	17.25 E
Apa, Rio-	56	Ib	22.06S	58.00W
Apaća	20	Kf	52.50N	157.10 E
Apache	46	Kk	31.44N	109.07W
Apache Junction	46	Jj	33.26N	111.32W
Apahida	15	Gc	46.49N	23.45 E
Apakho	63c	Bb	11.25S	166.32 E
Apalachee Bay	38	Kg	29.30N	84.00W
Apalachicola	44	Ek	29.44N	84.59W
Apalachicola River	44	Ek	29.44N	84.59W
Apan	48	Jh	19.43N	98.25W
Apaporis, Río-	52	Jf	1.23S	69.25W
Aparecida do Taboado	54	Hg	20.05S	51.05W
Aparri	22	Oh	18.22N	121.39 E
Apataki Atoll	57	Mf	15.26S	146.20W
Apatin	15	Bd	45.40N	18.59 E
Apatity	6	Jb	67.34N	33.18 E
Apatzingán de la Constitucion	47	De	19.05N	102.21W
Apaxtla de Castrejón	48	Jh	18.09N	99.52W
Ape	7	Gh	57.32N	26.42 E
Apeldoorn	11	Lb	52.13N	5.58 E
Apeldoorn-Nieuw Milligen	12	Hb	52.14N	5.45 E
Apen	12	Ja	53.13N	7.48 E
Apennines (EN) = Appennini	5	Hg	43.00N	13.00 E
Apere, Río-	54	Ef	13.44S	65.18W
Aphrodisias	24	Cd	37.45N	28.40 E
Api	21	Kf	30.00N	80.57 E
Api	36	Eb	3.40N	25.26 E
Apia	58	Jf	13.50S	171.44W
Apiacás, Serra dos-	54	Gf	10.15S	57.15W
Apio	63a	Ec	9.39S	161.23 E
Apipé Grande, Isla-	55	Di	27.30S	56.54W
Apizaco	48	Jh	19.25N	98.09W
Aplao	54	Dc	16.05S	72.31W
Apo, Mount-	21	Oi	6.59N	125.16 E
Apodi	54	Ke	5.39S	37.48W
Apolda	10	He	51.01N	11.30 E
Apolima	65c	Aa	13.49S	172.07W
Apolima Strait	65c	Aa	13.50S	172.10W
Apollo Bay	59	Ig	38.45S	143.40 E
Apollonia [Alb.]	15	Ci	40.43N	19.27 E
Apollonia [Lib.]	33	Dc	32.54N	21.58 E
Apolo	54	Ef	14.43S	68.31W
Apón, Río-	49	Kh	10.06N	72.23W
Apopka, Lake-	44	Gk	28.37N	81.38W
Aporé	55	Fd	18.58S	52.01W
Aporé, Rio-	52	Kg	19.27S	50.57W
Apostle Islands	43	Ib	46.50N	90.30W
Apostoles	56	Ic	27.55S	55.46W
Apostolovo	16	Hf	47.39N	33.43 E
Apoteri	54	Gc	4.02N	58.34W
Apôtres, Iles des-	30	Mm	45.40S	50.20 E
Appalachia	44	Fg	36.54N	82.48W
Appalachian Mountains	38	Lc	41.00N	77.00W
Äppelbo	8	Ed	60.30N	14.00 E
Appennini = Apennines (EN)	5	Hg	43.00N	13.00 E
Appennino Abruzzese	14	Hh	42.00N	13.55 E
Appennino Calabro	14	Kl	39.00N	16.30 E
Appennino Campano	14	Ii	40.50N	14.45 E
Appennino Ligure	14	Cf	44.30N	9.00 E
Appennino Lucano	14	Jj	40.30N	16.00 E
Appennino Tosco-Emiliano	14	Fg	44.00N	11.30 E
Appennino Umbro-Marchigiano	14	Gg	43.20N	12.55 E
Appenzell	14	Dc	47.20N	9.25 E
Appenzell Ausser-Rhoden [2]	14	Dc	47.20N	9.20 E
Appenzell Inner-Rhoden [2]	14	Dc	47.15N	9.25 E
Appingedam	12	Ia	53.19N	6.52 E
Appleby	9	Kg	54.36N	2.29W
Appleton	43	Jc	44.16N	88.25W
Appomattox	44	Hg	37.21N	78.51W
Apra Harbor	64c	Bb	13.27N	144.38 E
Apricena	14	Ji	41.47N	15.27 E
Aprilia	14	Gi	41.36N	12.39 E
Apšeronsk	19	Dg	44.27N	39.44 E
Apšeronskij Poluostrov=Apsheron Peninsula (EN)	5	Lg	41.00N	50.50 E
Apsheron Peninsula (EN)=Apšeronskij Poluostrov	5	Lg	41.00N	50.50 E
Apt	11	Lk	43.53N	5.24 E
Apucarana	56	Jb	23.33S	51.29W
Apuoarana, Serra da-	55	Gf	23.50S	51.20W
Apuka	20	Ld	60.23N	169.45 E
Apuka	20	Ld	60.25N	169.35 E
Apulia (EN) = Puglia [2]	14	Ki	41.15N	16.15 E
Apurashokoru	64a	Ac	7.17N	134.18 E
Apure [2]	54	Eb	7.10N	68.50W
Apure, Rio-	52	Je	7.37N	66.25W
Apurimac [2]	54	Df	14.00S	73.00W
Apurímac, Río-	52	Ig	12.17S	73.56W
Apurito	50	Bi	7.56N	68.27W
Apuseni, Munţii-=Apuseni Mountains (EN)	5	If	46.30N	22.30 E
Apuseni Mountains (EN)=Apuseni, Munţii-	5	If	46.30N	22.30 E
Āq	24	Kc	38.59N	45.27 E
Āqā	24	Me	35.00N	47.00 E
Aqaba (EN)=Al 'Aqabah	23	Dd	29.31N	35.00 E
Aqaba, Gulf of- (EN)='Aqabah, Khalīj al-	30	Kf	29.00N	34.40 E
Āqā Bāba	24	Md	36.20N	49.46 E
'Aqabah, Khalīj al-=Aqaba, Gulf of- (EN)	30	Kf	29.00N	34.40 E
Āqcheh	23	Kb	36.56N	66.11 E
'Aqdā	24	Of	32.26N	53.37 E
'Aqiq	35	Fb	18.14N	38.12 E
Aqitag	27	Fc	41.49N	90.38 E
Āqotāq	24	Ld	37.10N	47.05 E
Āq Qal'eh	24	Pd	37.01N	54.30 E
Aqqikkol Hu	27	Ed	37.00N	88.20 E
'Aqrah	24	Jd	36.45N	43.54 E
Aqrin, Jabal-	24	Hg	31.32N	38.18 E
Āq Şū	24	Ke	34.35N	44.31 E
Aquidabã, Rio-	55	De	20.58S	57.50W
Aquidabán, Río-	55	Df	23.11S	57.32W
Aquidauana	54	Gh	20.28S	55.48W
Aquidauana, Rio-	54	Gg	19.44S	56.50W
Aquidauna, Serra de-	55	Ee	20.50S	55.30W
Aquiles Serdán	48	Gc	28.36N	105.53W
Aquin	49	Kd	18.16N	73.24W
Aquitaine, Bassin d'-=Aquitaine Basin (EN)	5	Fg	44.00N	0.10W
Aquitaine Basin (EN)=Aquitaine, Bassin d'-	5	Fg	44.00N	0.10W
Ara	13	Mb	42.25N	0.08 E
'Arab, Baḩr al-	30	Jh	9.02N	29.28 E
'Arab, Khalīj al-	33	Ec	30.55N	29.05 E
'Arab, Shaṭṭ al-	21	Gf	30.28N	47.59 E
'Arabah, Wādī-	24	Eh	29.07N	32.39 E
'Arabah, Wādī al-	24	Fg	30.58N	32.24 E
Arabatskaja Strelka, Kosa-	16	Ig	45.40N	35.05 E
'Arabestān	24	Mg	30.30N	50.00 E
Arabian Basin (EN)	3	Gh	11.30N	65.00 E
Arabian Desert (EN)=Sharqīyah, Aş Şaḩrā' ash-	30	Kf	28.00N	32.00 E
Arabian Peninsula (EN)	21	Gg	25.00N	45.00 E
Arabian Sea (EN)	21	Ih	15.00N	65.00 E
Araç	24	Eb	41.15N	33.21 E
Aracá, Rio-	54	Fd	0.25S	62.55W
Aracaju	53	Mg	10.55S	37.04W
Aracataca	49	Jh	10.35N	74.13W
Aracati	54	Kd	4.34S	37.46W
Araçatuba	53	Kh	21.12S	50.25W
Aracena	13	Fg	37.53N	6.33W
Aracena, Sierra de-	13	Fg	37.56N	6.50W
Aracides, Cape-	63a	Ec	8.39S	161.01 E
Aracruz	54	Jg	19.49S	40.16W
Araçuai	54	Jg	16.52S	42.04W
Arad	6	If	46.11N	21.19 E
'Arad	24	Fg	31.15N	35.13 E
Arad [2]	15	Ec	46.11N	21.25 E
Arada	35	Cb	15.01N	20.40 E
'Arādah	35	Ia	22.59N	53.26 E
Arafali	35	Fb	15.04N	39.45 E
Ara Fana	35	Gd	6.01N	41.11 E
Arafune-Yama	29	Fc	36.12N	138.38 E
Arafura, Laut-=Arafura Sea (EN)	57	Ee	9.00S	133.00 E
Arafura Sea (EN)=Arafura, Laut-	57	Ee	9.00S	133.00 E
Aragac, Gora-	5	Kg	40.31N	44.10 E
Aragarças	53	Kg	15.55S	52.15W
Aragón	13	Kb	42.13N	1.44W
Aragón	5	Fg	41.00N	1.00W
Aragón	13	Lc	41.00N	1.00W
Aragona	14	Hm	37.24N	13.37 E
Aragua [2]	54	Eb	10.00N	67.10W
Araguacema	54	Ie	8.50S	49.34W
Aragua de Barcelona	50	Dh	9.28N	64.49W
Aragua de Maturin	50	Eh	9.58N	63.29W
Araguaia, Rio-	52	Lf	5.21S	48.41W
Araguaiana	55	Gb	16.49S	53.05W
Araguaina	54	Ie	7.12S	48.14W
Araguao, Boca-	54	Fb	9.17N	60.48W
Araguao, Caño-	50	Fh	9.15N	60.50W
Araguapiche, Punta-	50	Fh	9.29N	60.56W
Araguari	54	Ig	18.38S	48.11W
Araguari, Rio- [Braz.]	52	Le	1.15N	49.55W
Araguari, Rio- [Braz.]	55	Hd	18.21S	48.40W
Araguatins	54	Ie	5.38S	48.07W
'Arāgūib	32	Ff	18.50N	7.45W
Aragvi	16	Ni	41.50N	44.43 E
Arai	28	Of	37.09N	138.06 E
Árainn/Inishmore	9	Dh	53.07N	9.45W
Árainn Mhór/Aran Island	9	Ef	55.00N	8.30W
Araioses	54	Jd	2.53S	41.55W
Arāk	22	Gf	34.05N	49.41 E
Arak	32	Hd	25.18N	3.45 E
Arakabesan	64a	Ac	7.21N	134.27 E
Arakan [2]	25	Ie	19.00N	94.15 E
Arakan Yoma	21	Lh	19.00N	94.40 E
Arakawa	29	Fb	38.09N	139.25 E
Ara-Kawa [Jap.]	29	Fb	38.09N	139.23 E
Ara-Kawa [Jap.]	29	Fc	37.11N	138.15 E
Arákhthos	15	Ej	39.01N	21.03 E
Araks	21	Gf	39.56N	48.20 E
Aral [China]	27	Dc	40.38N	81.24 E
Aral	19	Hg	41.48N	74.25 E
Aral Sea (EN)=Aralskoje More	21	He	45.00N	60.00 E
Aralsk	22	Ie	46.48N	61.40 E
Aralskoje More=Aral Sea (EN)	21	He	45.00N	60.00 E
Aralsor, Ozero-	16	Pe	49.05N	48.15 E
Aralsulfat	19	Gf	46.50N	61.59 E
Aramac	59	Jd	22.59S	145.14 E
Arambaré	55	Gj	30.55S	51.29W
Ārān	24	Ne	34.03N	51.30 E
Aranda de Duero	13	Ic	41.41N	3.41W
Arandelovac	15	De	44.18N	20.35 E
Arandilla	13	Ic	41.40N	3.41W
Aran Island/Arainn Mhór	9	Dh	53.07N	9.43W
Aran Islands	9	Ef	55.00N	8.30W
Aranjunez	13	Id	40.02N	3.36W
Aranos	37	Bd	24.09S	19.09 E
Arañuelo, Campo-	13	Ge	39.55N	5.30W
Aranuka Atoll	57	Id	0.11N	173.36 E
Arao	29	Be	32.59N	130.27 E
Araouane	31	Gg	18.53N	3.35W
Arapahoe	45	Gf	40.18N	99.54W
Arapey Grande, Río-	55	Dj	30.55S	57.49W
Arapiraca	54	Ke	9.45S	36.39W
Arápis, Ákra-	15	Gi	40.27N	24.00 E
Arapkir	24	Hc	39.03N	38.30 E
Arapoim, Rio-	55	Kb	15.45S	43.39W
Arapongas	56	Jb	23.23S	51.27W
Arapoti	55	Hg	24.08S	49.50W
'Ar'ar	24	Ig	30.59N	41.02 E
'Ar'ar, Wādī	24	Ig	31.23N	42.26 E
Araranguá	56	Kc	28.56S	49.29W
Araraquara	53	Lh	21.47S	48.10W
Araras	55	If	22.22S	47.23W
Araras, Açude-	54	Jd	4.20S	40.30W
Araras, Serra das-	55	Fd	18.45S	53.30W
Ararat	19	Eh	39.50N	44.43 E
Ararat [Austl.]	59	Ig	37.17S	142.56 E
Ararat, Mount- (EN)=Büyük Ağri Daği	21	Gf	39.40N	44.24 E
Arari	54	Jd	3.28S	44.47W
Arari, Lago-	54	Id	0.37S	49.07W
Aras	21	Gf	39.56N	48.20 E
Aras Dağlari	24	Jc	40.00N	43.00 E
Aratika Atoll	57	Mf	15.32S	145.32W
Aratürük/Yiwu	27	Fc	43.15N	94.35 E
Arauca [2]	54	Db	6.30N	71.00W
Arauca	54	Db	7.03N	70.47W
Arauca, Río-	52	Je	7.24N	66.35W
Araucania [2]	56	Fe	37.50S	73.15W
Arauco	56	Fe	37.15S	73.19W
Araure	50	Bh	9.38N	69.15W
Aravaca, Madrid-	13	Id	40.27N	3.47W
Aravis	11	Mi	45.53N	6.28 E
Arawalli Range	21	Jg	25.00N	73.30 E
Araxá	54	Ig	19.35S	46.55W
Araxos, Ákra-	15	Ek	38.10N	21.23 E
Araya	50	Dg	10.34N	64.15W
Araya, Peninsula de-	54	Fa	10.35N	64.00W
Arba	13	Kc	41.52N	1.18W
Arba'āt	35	Fb	19.50N	37.03 E
Arba'în, Darb al-	24	Di	26.40N	30.50 E
Arbaj-Here	27	Hb	46.15N	102.48 E
Arba Minch	31	Kh	5.59N	37.38 E
'Arbat	24	Ke	35.25N	45.35 E
Arbatax	14	Dk	39.56N	9.42 E
Arboga	7	Dg	59.24N	15.50 E
Arbogaån	8	Ge	59.26N	16.04 E
Arbois	11	Lh	46.54N	5.46 E
Arboletes	49	Ii	8.52N	76.25W
Arbolito	55	Ek	32.39S	54.15W
Arbon	14	Dc	47.30N	9.25 E
Arbore	15	Ib	47.44N	25.56 E
Arborea	14	Ck	39.46N	8.35 E
Arborea	14	Ck	39.50N	8.50 E
Arborg	45	Ha	50.55N	97.15W
Arbrå	7	Dc	61.29N	16.23 E
Arbroath	9	Ke	56.34N	2.35W
Arbus	14	Ck	39.32N	8.36 E
Arc [Fr.]	11	Mi	45.34N	6.12 E
Arc [Fr.]	11	Lk	43.31N	5.07 E
Arcachon	11	Ej	44.39N	1.10W
Arcachon, Bassin d'-	11	Ej	44.42N	1.09W
Arcadia [Fl.-U.S.]	44	Gl	27.14N	81.52W
Arcadia [La.-U.S.]	45	Jj	32.33N	92.55W
Arcagly-Ajat	17	Jj	53.00N	61.50 E
Arcas, Cayos-	47	Fd	20.12N	91.58W
Arcata	46	Cf	40.52N	124.05W
Arcelia	48	Ih	18.17N	100.16W
Arcen, Areen en Velden-	12	Ic	51.28N	6.11 E
Arcevia	14	Gg	43.30N	12.56 E
Archangel (EN)=Arhangelsk	6	Kc	64.34N	40.32 E
Archaringa Creek	59	He	28.15S	135.15 E
Archer River	59	Ib	13.28S	141.41 E
Archer's Post	36	Gb	0.39N	37.41 E
Archidona	13	Hg	37.05N	4.23W
Arcidosso	14	Fh	42.52N	11.33 E
Arcipelago Campano	5	Hg	40.30N	13.20 E
Arcipelago Toscano=Tuscan Archipelago (EN)	5	Hg	42.45N	10.20 E
Arcis-sur-Aube	11	Kf	48.32N	4.08 E
Arciz	16	Fg	45.59N	29.27 E
Arco [Id.-U.S.]	46	Ie	43.38N	113.18W
Arco [It.]	14	Ee	45.55N	10.53 E
Arconce	11	Jh	46.27N	4.00 E
Arcos	55	Je	20.17S	45.32W
Arcos de Jalón	13	Jc	41.13N	2.16W
Arcos de la Frontera	13	Gh	36.45N	5.48W
Arcos de Valdevez	13	Dc	41.51N	8.25W
Arcoverde	53	Mf	8.25S	37.04W
Arctic Bay	39	Kb	73.02N	85.11W
Arctic Ocean	67	Be	85.00N	170.00 E
Arctic Ocean (EN)=Ishavet	67	Be	85.00N	170.00 E
Arctic Ocean (EN)=Severny Ledovity Okean	67	Be	85.00N	170.00 E
Arctic Red River	42	Ec	67.27N	133.45W
Arctic Red River	42	Ec	67.22N	133.30W
Arctic Village	40	Jc	68.08N	145.19W
Arda [Eur.]	15	Jh	41.39N	26.29 E
Arda [It.]	14	Ee	45.02N	10.02 E
Ardabīl [Iran]	22	Gf	38.15N	48.18 E
Ardabīl [Iraq]	24	Ie	34.24N	40.59 E
Ardahan	24	Jb	41.07N	42.41 E
Ardakāh	23	Hc	32.19N	53.59 E
Ardakān	24	Og	30.16N	52.01 E
Ardal	24	Ng	31.59N	50.39 E
Ardales	13	Hh	36.52N	4.51W
Ardalsfjorden	8	Bc	61.15N	7.30 E
Årdalstangen	7	Bf	61.14N	7.43 E
Ardanuç	24	Jb	41.08N	42.03 E
Ardatov	7	Ki	55.17N	43.12 E
Ardatov	7	Li	54.53N	46.13 E
'Arde	35	Hd	9.58N	46.04 E
Ardèche	11	Kj	44.16N	4.39 E
Ardèche [3]	11	Kj	44.40N	4.20 E
Ardee/Béal Átha Fhirdhia	9	Gh	53.52N	6.33W
Ardencaple Fjord	41	Jd	75.15N	20.10W
Ardenne, Plateau de l'-/Ardennen, Plateau van der-=Ardennes (EN)	5	Ge	50.10N	5.45 E
Ardennen, Plateau van der-/Ardenne, Plateau de l'-=Ardennes (EN)	5	Ge	50.10N	5.45 E
Ardennes [3]	11	Ke	49.40N	4.40 E
Ardennes (EN)=Ardenne, Plateau de l'-/Ardennen, Plateau van der-	5	Ge	50.10N	5.45 E
Ardennes (EN)=Ardennen, Plateau van der-/Ardenne, Plateau de l'-	5	Ge	50.10N	5.45 E
Ardennes, Canal des-	11	Ke	49.26N	4.02 E
Ardennes, Forêt des-	12	Ge	49.48N	4.50 E
Ardentes	11	Hh	46.45N	1.50 E
Ardeşen	24	Ib	41.12N	41.00 E
Ardestān	24	Of	33.22N	52.23 E
Árdhas	15	Jh	41.39N	26.29 E
Ardila	13	Ef	38.12N	7.28W
Ard Mhacha/Armagh	9	Gg	54.21N	6.39W
Ardmore	43	He	34.10N	97.08W
Ardnamurchan, Point of-	9	Ge	56.45N	6.30W
Ardon	16	Nh	43.07N	44.13 E
Ardooie	12	Fd	50.59N	3.12 E
Ardre	12	Fe	49.18N	3.40 E
Ardres	12	Dd	50.51N	1.59 E
Ards Peninsula/An Aird	9	Hg	54.30N	5.30W
Ar Dub'al Khālī	21	Hg	21.00N	51.00 E
Ardud	15	Fb	47.38N	22.53 E
Arebi	36	Eb	2.50N	29.38 E
Arecibo	47	Ke	18.28N	66.43W
Areen en Valden	12	Ic	51.28N	6.11 E
Areen en Velden-Arcen	12	Ic	51.28N	6.11 E
Arégala/Ariogala	8	Ji	55.13N	23.30 E
Areia, Ribeirão da-	55	Jc	16.07S	45.52W
Areia Branca	54	Kd	4.57S	37.08W
Arekalong Peninsula	64a	Bb	7.40N	134.38 E
Aremberg	12	Id	50.25N	6.49 E
Arena	26	He	9.14N	120.46 E
Arena, Point-	43	Cd	38.57N	123.44W
Arena, Punta-	47	Cd	23.30N	109.30W
Arena de la Ventana, Punta-	47	Cd	24.04N	109.52W
Arenápolis	54	Gf	14.26S	56.49W
Arenas, Cayo-	47	Fd	22.08N	91.24W
Arenas, Punta de-	56	Gh	53.09S	68.13W
Arenas de San Pedro	13	Gd	40.12N	5.05W
Arenberg	12	Jb	52.42N	7.20 E
Arendal	7	Bg	58.27N	8.48 E
Arendonk	12	Hc	51.19N	5.05 E
Arénys de Mar/Arenys de Mar	13	Oc	41.35N	2.33 E
Arenys de Mar/Arénys de Mar	13	Oc	41.35N	2.33 E
Areópolis	15	Fm	36.40N	22.23 E
Areq, Sebkha bou-	13	Ji	35.10N	2.45W
Arequipa	53	Ig	16.24S	71.33W
Arequipa [2]	54	Dg	16.00S	72.30W
Arequito	55	Bk	33.09S	61.28W
Arero	35	Fe	4.44N	38.50 E
Ares, Muela de-	13	Ld	40.28N	0.07W
Åreskutan	8	Ea	63.26N	13.06 E
Åreskutan	7	Ce	63.26N	13.06 E
Arévalo	13	Hc	41.04N	4.43W
Arezzo	14	Fg	43.25N	11.53 E
Arga	13	Kb	42.18N	1.47W
Argajas	17	Ji	55.31N	60.55 E
Argamasilla de Alba	13	Ie	39.07N	3.06W
Argan	27	Ec	40.09N	88.22 E
Arganda	13	Id	40.18N	3.26W
Arga-Sala	20	Gc	68.37N	112.05 E
Argelés-Gazost	11	Fk	43.01N	0.06W
Argelès-sur-Mer	11	Jl	42.33N	3.01 E
Argens	11	Mk	43.24N	6.44 E

Index Symbols

- [1] Independent Nation
- [2] State, Region
- [3] District, County
- [4] Municipality
- [5] Colony, Dependency
- Continent
- Physical Region
- Historical or Cultural Region
- Mount, Mountain
- Volcano
- Hill
- Mountains, Mountain Range
- Hills, Escarpment
- Plateau, Upland
- Pass, Gap
- Plain, Lowland
- Delta
- Salt Flat
- Valley, Canyon
- Crater, Cave
- Karst Features
- Depression
- Polder
- Desert, Dunes
- Forest, Woods
- Heath, Steppe
- Oasis
- Cape, Point
- Coast, Beach
- Cliff
- Peninsula
- Isthmus
- Sandbank
- Island
- Atoll
- Rock, Reef
- Islands, Archipelago
- Rocks, Reefs
- Coral Reef
- Well, Spring
- Geyser
- River, Stream
- Waterfall Rapids
- River Mouth, Estuary
- Lake
- Salt Lake
- Intermittent Lake
- Reservoir
- Swamp, Pond
- Canal
- Glacier
- Ice Shelf, Pack Ice
- Ocean
- Sea
- Gulf, Bay
- Strait, Fjord
- Lagoon
- Bank
- Seamount
- Tablemount
- Ridge
- Shelf
- Basin
- Escarpment, Sea Scarp
- Fracture
- Trench, Abyss
- National Park, Reserve
- Point of Interest
- Recreation Site
- Cave, Cavern
- Historic Site
- Ruins
- Wall, Walls
- Church, Abbey
- Temple
- Scientific Station
- Airport
- Port
- Lighthouse
- Mine
- Tunnel
- Dam, Bridge

Name	Map	Grid	Lat.	Long.
Assam	21	Lg	26.50N	94.00 E
Assam	25	Ic	26.00N	93.00 E
Assamakka	34	Gb	19.21N	5.38 E
As Samawah	23	Gc	31.18N	45.17 E
As Sanām	35	Ia	22.00N	51.10 E
Assaouas	34	Gb	16.52N	7.27 E
As Sars	14	Dn	36.05N	9.01 E
As Sayl al Kabīr	33	He	21.38N	40.25 E
Asse	12	Gd	50.56N	4.12 E
Asse	11	Lk	43.53N	5.53 E
Assebroek, Brugge-	12	Fc	51.12N	3.16 E
Assekkâraï	34	Fb	15.50N	2.52 E
Assemini	14	Dk	39.17N	9.01 E
Assen	11	Ma	53.00N	6.34 E
Assenede	12	Fc	51.14N	3.45 E
Assens	8	Ci	55.16N	9.55 E
As Sıbā'īyah	24	Ej	25.11N	32.41 E
As Sidr	31	Ie	30.39N	18.22 E
As Sidrah=Sirte Desert (EN)	30	Ie	30.30N	17.30 E
As Sila'	23	He	24.02N	51.46 E
As Simbillāwayn	24	Dg	30.53N	31.27 E
Assiniboia	42	Gg	49.38N	105.59W
Assiniboine	38	Je	49.53N	97.08W
Assiniboine, Mount-	38	Hd	50.52N	115.39W
Assis	56	Jb	22.40S	50.25W
Assisi	14	Gg	43.04N	12.37 E
Aßlar	12	Kd	50.36N	8.28 E
Assos	15	Jj	39.31N	26.20 E
As Sślimīyah	24	Mh	29.20N	48.04 E
As Subaykhah	14	Eo	35.56N	10.01 E
As Subū'	33	Fe	22.45N	32.34 E
As Sūdān=Sudan (EN)	31	Jg	15.00N	30.00 E
As Sudd	30	Kh	8.00N	31.00 E
As Sufāl	35	Hc	14.06N	48.43 E
Aş Şufuq	24	Nk	23.52N	51.45 E
Aş Şukhayrah	32	Jc	34.17N	10.06 E
As Sukhnah	24	He	34.52N	38.52 E
As Sulaymī	24	Ii	26.17N	41.21 E
As Sulayyil	23	Ge	20.27N	45.34 E
Aş Şulb	24	Mj	25.42N	48.25 E
Aş Sumayḩ	35	Dd	9.49N	27.39 E
Aş Şummān	33	Ie	23.00N	48.00 E
Aş Şummān	24	Li	27.00N	47.00 E
Assumption Island	30	Li	9.45S	46.30 E
As Sūq	33	He	21.54N	42.03 E
Assur	24	Je	35.25N	43.16 E
Aş Şuwār	24	Ie	35.30N	40.39 E
As Suwaydā'	23	Ec	32.42N	36.34 E
Aş Şuwayrah	24	Kf	32.55N	44.47 E
As Suways=Suez (EN)	31	Kf	29.58N	32.33 E
Astakídha	15	Jn	35.53N	26.50 E
Astakós	15	Ek	38.32N	21.05 E
Āstāneh [Iran]	24	Md	37.17N	49.59 E
Āstāneh [Iran]	24	Mf	33.53N	49.22 E
Āstārā	23	Gb	38.26N	48.52 E
Astara	6	Kh	38.28N	48.52 E
Aštarak	16	Ni	40.16N	44.18 E
Asten	12	Hc	51.24N	5.45 E
Asti	14	Cf	44.54N	8.12 E
Astico	14	Fe	45.37N	11.37 E
Astipálaia	15	Jm	36.33N	26.21 E
Astipálaia	15	Jm	36.35N	26.20 E
Asto, Monte-	11a	Ba	42.30N	9.15 E
Astola Island	25	Cc	25.07N	63.51 E
Astorga	13	Fb	42.27N	6.03W
Astoria	43	Cb	46.11N	123.50W
Åstorp	8	Eh	56.08N	12.57 E
Astove Island	30	Lj	10.06S	47.45 E
Astrahan	6	Kf	46.21N	48.03 E
Astrahanskaja Oblast	19	Ef	47.10N	47.30 E
Astrolabe, Cape-	63a	Ec	8.20S	160.34 E
Astrolabe, Récifs de l'-	57	Hf	19.49S	165.35 E
Astudillo	13	Hb	42.12N	4.18W
Asturias	13	Ga	43.20N	6.00W
Asuisui, Cape-	65c	Aa	13.47S	172.29W
Asunción	53	Kh	25.16S	57.40W
Asunción, Bahía-	48	Bd	27.05N	114.10W
Asunción, Cerro de la-	48	Je	24.15N	99.56W
Asuncion Island	57	Fc	19.40N	145.24 E
Asunción Mita	49	Cf	14.20N	89.43W
Asunción Nochixtlán	48	Ki	17.28N	97.14W
Asunden	8	Fg	58.00N	15.50 E
Åsunden	8	Eg	57.44N	13.22 E
Aswa	36	Fb	3.43N	31.55 E
Aswān	31	Kf	24.05N	32.53 E
Aswān, Sadd al-=First Cataract (EN)	30	Kf	24.01N	32.52 E
Asyūţ	31	Kf	27.11N	31.11 E
Asyūţī, Wādī al-	24	Di	27.10N	31.16 E
Aszód	10	Pi	47.39N	19.30 E
'Ata	65b	Bc	21.03S	174.59W
Atacama	56	Gc	27.30S	70.00W
Atacama, Desierto de-=Atacama Desert (EN)	52	Jh	22.30S	69.15W
Atacama, Salar de-	52	Jh	23.30S	68.15W
Atacama Desert (EN)=Atacama, Desierto de-	52	Jh	22.30S	69.15W
Atacama Trench (EN)	3	Nm	30.00S	73.00W
Atafu Atoll	57	Je	8.33S	172.30W
Atagaj	20	Ee	55.06N	99.25 E
Ata Island	57	Jg	21.03S	175.00W
Atakor	30	Hf	23.13N	5.40 E
Atakora	34	Fc	10.00N	1.35 E
Atakora	34	Fc	10.45N	1.30 E
Atakpamé	31	Hh	7.32N	1.08 E
Atalaia do Norte	54	Dd	4.20S	70.12W
Atalándi	15	Fk	38.39N	23.00 E
Atalaya	54	Df	10.44S	73.45W
Atalayasa	13	Nf	38.55N	1.15 E
Atambua	26	Hh	9.07S	124.54 E
Atami	29	Fd	35.05N	139.02 E
Atangmik	41	Gf	64.53N	52.00W
Aţâr	31	Ff	20.30N	13.03W
Atas-Bogdo-Ula	27	Gc	43.20N	96.30 E
Atascadero	46	Ei	35.29N	120.41W
Atasu	19	Hf	48.42N	71.38 E
'Atata	65b	Ac	21.03S	175.15W
Atatürk Barajı	24	Hd	37.30N	38.30 E
Atauro, Pulau	26	Ih	8.13S	125.35 E
Atáviros	15	Km	36.12N	27.52 E
Ataway	35	Bd	9.59N	18.38 E
Atbara	35	Eb	17.40N	33.56 E
'Aţbarah	30	Kg	17.40N	33.56 E
'Aţbarah	31	Kg	17.42N	33.59 E
Atbasar	22	Id	51.48N	68.20 E
At-Baši	19	Hg	41.08N	75.51 E
Atça	15	Ll	37.53N	28.13 E
Atchafalaya Bay	43	If	29.25N	91.20W
Atchison	43	Hd	39.34N	95.07W
Atebubu	34	Ed	7.45N	0.59W
Ateca	13	Kc	41.20N	1.47W
Aterno	14	Hh	42.11N	13.51 E
Atessa	14	Ih	42.04N	14.27 E
Ath/Aat	11	Jd	50.38N	3.47 E
Athabasca	38	Hd	58.40N	110.50W
Athabasca	42	Gf	54.43N	113.17W
Athabasca, Lake-	38	Id	59.07N	110.00W
Athamánon, Óri-	15	Ej	39.27N	21.08 E
Athamánon Óri	15	Ej	39.27N	21.08 E
Athens [Al.-U.S.]	44	Dh	34.48N	86.58W
Athens [Ga.-U.S.]	43	Ke	33.57N	83.23W
Athens [Oh.-U.S.]	44	Ff	39.20N	82.06W
Athens [Tn.-U.S.]	44	Eh	35.28N	84.35W
Athens [Tx.-U.S.]	45	Ij	32.12N	95.51W
Athens (EN) = Athínai	6	Ih	37.59N	23.44 E
Athéras	15	Jl	37.38N	26.15 E
Atherton	59	Jc	17.16S	145.29 E
Athi	36	Gc	2.59S	38.31 E
Athies-sous-Laon	12	Fe	49.34N	3.41 E
Athínai = Athens (EN)	6	Ih	37.59N	23.44 E
Athi River	36	Gc	1.27S	36.59 E
Athis-de-l'Orne	12	Bf	48.49N	0.30W
Athlone/Baile Átha Luain	9	Fh	53.25N	7.56W
Athol	44	Kd	42.36N	72.14W
Áthos	15	Hi	40.10N	24.20 E
Athos, Mount- (EN)=Áyion Óros	15	Hi	40.15N	24.15 E
Ath Thamad	24	Fh	29.41N	34.18 E
Ath Thumāmī	24	Ki	27.42N	44.59 E
Athus, Aubange-	12	He	49.34N	5.50 E
Athy	9	Gi	53.00N	7.00W
Ati	31	Ig	13.13N	18.20 E
Atiak	36	Fb	3.16N	32.07 E
Atiamuri	62	Gc	38.23S	176.02 E
Atibaia, Rio-	55	If	22.42S	47.17W
Atienza	13	Jc	41.12N	2.52W
Atikokan	42	Ig	48.45N	91.37W
Atikonak Lake	42	Lf	52.40N	64.35W
Atimoono	64n	Bc	10.26S	160.58W
Atitlán, Lago de-	49	Bf	14.42N	91.12W
Atitlán, Volcán-	47	Ff	14.35N	91.11W
Atiu Island	57	Lg	20.02S	158.07W
'Atk, Wādī al-	24	Li	26.03N	46.30 E
Atka	38	Bd	52.15N	174.30W
Atka [Ak.-U.S.]	40a	Db	52.12N	174.12W
Atka	20	Kd	60.49N	151.58 E
Atka Iceport	66	Bf	70.35S	7.45W
Atkarsk	19	Ee	51.52N	44.59 E
Atkasook	40	Hb	70.28N	157.24W
Atkinson	45	Ge	42.32N	98.59W
Atlacomulco de Fabela	48	Jh	19.48N	99.53W
Atlanta [Ga.-U.S.]	39	Kf	33.45N	84.23W
Atlanta [Mi.-U.S.]	44	Ec	45.00N	84.09W
Atlanta [Tx.-U.S.]	45	Ij	33.07N	94.10W
Atlanterhavet=Atlantic Ocean (EN)	3	Di	2.00N	25.00W
Atlantic [Ia.-U.S.]	45	If	41.24N	95.01W
Atlantic [N.C.-U.S.]	44	Ih	34.54N	76.20W
Atlantic City	39	Lf	39.27N	74.35W
Atlantic Coastal Plain	38	Lf	34.00N	79.00W
Atlantic-Indian Basin (EN)	3	Eo	60.00S	15.00 E
Atlantic-Indian Ridge (EN)	3	Eo	52.00S	25.00 E
Atlántico	54	Da	10.40N	75.00W
Atlántico, Océano-=Atlantic Ocean (EN)	3	Di	2.00N	25.00W
Atlântico, Oceano-=Atlantic Ocean (EN)	3	Di	2.00N	25.00W
Atlantic Ocean	3	Di	2.00N	25.00W
Atlantic Ocean (EN)=Atlanterhavet	3	Di	2.00N	25.00W
Atlantic Ocean (EN)=Atlântico, Oceano-	3	Di	2.00N	25.00W
Atlantic Ocean (EN)=Atlántico, Océano-	3	Di	2.00N	25.00W
Atlantic Ocean (EN)=Atlantiese Oseaan	3	Di	2.00N	25.00W
Atlantic Ocean (EN)=Atlantique, Océan-	3	Di	2.00N	25.00W
Atlantic Ocean (EN)=Atlantshaf	3	Di	2.00N	25.00W
Atlantic Ocean (EN)=Muhīt, Al Baḩr al-	3	Di	2.00N	25.00W
Atlántida	49	Df	15.30N	87.00W
Atlantiese Oseaan=Atlantic Ocean (EN)	3	Di	2.00N	25.00W
Atlantique	34	Fd	6.35N	2.15 E
Atlantique, Océan-=Atlantic Ocean (EN)	3	Di	2.00N	25.00W
Atlantshaf=Atlantic Ocean (EN)	3	Di	2.00N	25.00W
Atlas=Atlas Mountains (EN)	30	Ge	32.00N	2.00W
Atlas Mountains (EN)=Atlas	30	Ge	32.00N	2.00W
Atlasova, Ostrov-	20	Kf	50.50N	155.25 E
Atlasovo	20	Jg	46.00N	142.09 E
Atlas Saharien=Saharan Atlas (EN)	30	He	34.00N	2.00 E
Atlas Tellien=Tell Atlas (EN)	30	He	36.00N	2.00 E
Atlin	42	Ee	59.35N	133.42W
Atlin Lake	42	Ee	59.35N	133.43W
Atlixco	47	Ee	18.54N	98.26W
Atløy	8	Ac	61.20N	4.55 E
Atmore	44	Dj	31.02N	87.29W
Atna	8	Dc	61.44N	10.49 E
Atna Peak	42	Ef	53.57N	128.04W
Atō	29	Bd	34.24N	131.43 E
Atoka	45	Hi	34.23N	96.08W
Átokos	15	Dk	38.29N	20.49 E
Atotonilco el Alto	48	Hg	20.33N	102.31W
Atoui, Khatt-	32	De	20.04N	15.58W
Atouila, 'Erg-	30	Gf	21.15N	3.20W
Atoyac, Río-	48	Ki	16.30N	97.31W
Atoyac de Alvarez	48	Ii	17.12N	100.26W
Atrak	21	Hf	37.23N	53.57 E
Ätran	7	Ch	56.53N	12.30 E
Atrato, Río-	52	Ie	8.17N	76.58W
Atrek	21	Hf	37.23N	53.57 E
Atri	14	Hh	42.35N	13.59 E
Atsugi	29	Fd	35.26N	139.20 E
Atsukeshi	28	Rc	43.02N	144.51 E
Atsukeshi-Wan	29a	Db	43.00N	144.45 E
Aţsumi [Jap.]	28	Oe	38.37N	139.35 E
Atsumi [Jap.]	29	Ed	34.37N	137.05 E
Atsumi-Hantō	29	Ed	34.40N	137.15 E
Atsumi-Wan	29	Ed	34.45N	137.15 E
Atsuta	29a	Bb	43.24N	141.25 E
Atsutoko	29a	Db	43.15N	145.13 E
Aţ Ţaff	23	He	23.55N	54.25 E
Aţ Ţafīlah	24	Fg	30.50N	35.36 E
Aţ Ţā'if	22	Gg	21.16N	40.25 E
At Tāj	33	De	24.13N	23.18 E
Attalla	44	Dh	34.01N	86.05W
Aţ Ţallāb	33	De	24.01N	23.10 E
At Ta'mīm	24	Ke	36.00N	44.00 E
Attapu	25	Lf	14.48N	106.50 E
Aţ Ţārmīyah	24	Kf	33.40N	44.24 E
Attawapiskat	38	Kd	52.57N	82.18W
Attawapiskat	39	Kd	52.55N	82.26W
Attawapiskat Lake	42	If	52.15N	87.50W
Aţ Ţawīl	24	Hh	29.20N	39.35 E
At Taysīyaḩ	24	Jh	28.00N	44.00 E
Aţ Ţayyārah	35	Ec	13.12N	30.47 E
Attendorn	12	Jc	51.07N	7.54 E
Attersee	14	Hc	47.55N	13.33 E
Attert	12	Ie	49.49N	6.05 E
Attica	44	De	40.17N	87.15W
Attichy	12	Fe	49.25N	3.03 E
Attigny	12	Ge	49.29N	4.35 E
At Tīh Desert (EN)=Tīh, Şaḩrā' at-	33	Fc	30.05N	34.00 E
Attikamagen Lake	42	Ke	55.00N	66.30W
Attleboro	44	Le	41.56N	71.17W
Attleborough	12	Db	52.31N	1.01 E
Attre	12	Fd	50.37N	3.50 E
Attu	40a	Ab	52.56N	173.15 E
Attu	40a	Ab	52.55N	173.00 E
Aţ Ţulayhī	24	Ki	27.33N	44.08 E
Aţ Ţūr	24	Eh	28.14N	33.37 E
Aţ Ţurayf	23	Ec	31.44N	38.33 E
At Turbah	23	Fg	12.40N	43.30 E
Aţ Ţuwayshah	35	Dc	12.21N	26.32 E
Åtvidaberg	7	Dg	58.12N	16.00 E
Atwater	46	Eh	37.21N	120.36W
Atwood	45	Fg	39.45N	101.03W
Atyrau (Gurjev)	6	Lf	47.07N	51.56 E
Atyrauskaja oblast	19	Ff	47.30N	52.00 E
Auasbila	49	Ef	14.52N	84.40W
Auatu	35	Gd	7.17N	41.03 E
Auau Channel	65a	Ec	20.51N	156.45W
Aubagne	11	Lk	43.17N	5.34 E
Aubange	12	He	49.35N	5.48 E
Aubange-Athus	12	He	49.34N	5.50 E
Aube	11	Jf	48.34N	3.43 E
Aube	11	Kf	48.15N	4.05 E
Aubel	12	Hc	50.42N	5.51 E
Aubenas	11	Kj	44.37N	4.23 E
Aubenton	12	Ge	49.50N	4.12 E
Aubetin	12	Ff	48.49N	3.01 E
Aubigny-en-Artois	12	Ec	50.21N	2.35 E
Aubigny-sur-Nère	11	Ig	47.29N	2.26 E
Aubin	11	Ij	44.32N	2.15 E
Aubrac, Monts d'-	11	Ij	44.38N	3.00 E
Aubry, Lake -	42	Ec	67.25N	126.30W
Auburn [Al.-U.S.]	44	Ei	32.36N	85.29W
Auburn [Ca.-U.S.]	46	Eg	38.54N	121.04W
Auburn [In.-U.S.]	44	Ee	41.22N	85.04W
Auburn [Me.-U.S.]	44	Lc	44.06N	70.14W
Auburn [Nb.-U.S.]	45	If	40.23N	95.51W
Auburn [N.Y.-U.S.]	44	Ic	42.57N	76.34W
Auburn [Wa.-U.S.]	46	Dc	47.18N	122.13W
Auburn Range	59	Ke	25.10S	150.30 E
Aubusson	11	Ii	45.57N	2.10 E
Aucanquilcha, Cerro-	52	Jh	21.14S	68.28W
Auce	8	Jh	56.28N	22.50 E
Auch	11	Gk	43.39N	0.35 E
Auchel	12	Ed	50.30N	2.28 E
Auchi	34	Gd	7.04N	6.16 E
Auckland	58	Ih	36.52S	174.45 E
Auckland Islands	57	Hi	50.35S	166.00 E
Auckland Peninsula	62	Eb	36.15S	174.00 E
Aude	11	Jk	43.13N	3.14 E
Aude	11	Ik	43.05N	2.30 E
Auden	45	Ma	50.13N	87.47W
Audenarde/Oudenaarde	11	Jd	50.51N	3.36 E
Audierne	11	Bf	48.01N	4.32W
Audierne, Baie d'-	11	Bg	47.57N	4.28W
Audincourt	11	Mg	47.29N	6.50 E
Audo	35	Gd	6.09N	41.53 E
Audresselles	12	Dd	50.49N	1.35 E
Audru	8	Kf	58.20N	24.19 E
Audruicq	12	Ed	50.53N	2.05 E
Audubon	45	If	41.43N	94.55W
Audun-le-Roman	12	He	49.22N	5.53 E
Audun-le-Tiche	12	He	49.28N	5.57 E
Aue	10	If	50.35N	12.42 E
Aue [Ger.]	10	Fd	52.33N	9.05 E
Aue [Ger.]	12	Kb	52.16N	8.59 E
Auerbach	10	If	50.31N	12.24 E
Auezov	19	If	49.40N	81.40 E
Auffay	12	De	49.43N	1.06 E
Augathella	58	Fg	25.48S	146.35 E
Auge, Pays d'-	11	Ge	49.05N	0.10 E
Augpilagtoq	41	Gd	72.45N	55.35W
Augrabies Falls	30	Jk	28.35S	20.23 E
Augsburg	6	Hf	48.22N	10.53 E
Augusta [Ar.-U.S.]	45	Ki	35.17N	91.22W
Augusta [Austl.]	58	Ch	34.10S	115.10 E
Augusta [Ga.-U.S.]	39	Kf	33.29N	81.57W
Augusta [It.]	14	Jm	37.13N	15.13 E
Augusta [Ks.-U.S.]	45	Hh	37.41N	96.58W
Augusta [Me.-U.S.]	39	Me	44.19N	69.47W
Augusta [Mt.-U.S.]	46	Ic	47.30N	112.24W
Augusta, Golfo di-	14	Jm	37.10N	15.15 E
Augustów	10	Sc	53.51N	22.59 E
Augustowski, Kanał-	10	Tc	53.54N	23.26 E
Augustus, Mount-	57	Cg	24.20S	116.50 E
Auki	58	He	8.45S	160.42 E
Auld, Lake-	59	Ed	22.30S	123.45 E
Aulla	14	Df	44.12N	9.58 E
Aulne	11	Bf	48.17N	4.16W
Aulneau Peninsula	45	Ib	49.23N	94.29W
Aulnoye-Aymeries	12	Fd	50.12N	3.50 E
Aulong	64a	Ac	7.17N	134.17 E
Ault	12	Dd	50.06N	1.27 E
Auluptagel	64a	Ac	7.19N	134.29 E
Aulus-les-Bains	11	Hl	42.48N	1.20 E
Aumale	11	He	49.46N	1.45 E
Auna	34	Fc	10.11N	4.43 E
Aunay-sur-Odon	12	Be	49.01N	0.38W
Auneuil	12	Ee	49.22N	2.00 E
Auning	7	Ch	56.26N	10.23 E
Aunis	11	Fh	46.10N	1.00W
Aunuu	65c	Cb	14.17S	170.33W
Auob	30	Jk	26.27S	20.38 E
Aura	8	Jd	60.36N	22.34 E
Aurangābād	25	Fe	19.53N	75.20 E
Aurari Bay	59	Gb	11.40S	133.40 E
Aur Atoll	57	Id	8.16N	171.06 E
Auray	11	Dg	47.40N	2.59W
Aurdal	7	Bf	60.56N	9.24 E
Aure	11	Ee	49.20N	1.07W
Aure [Nor.]	7	Be	63.13N	8.32 E
Aure [Nor.]	8	Bb	62.24N	6.36 E
Aurejärvi	8	Jb	62.05N	23.25 E
Aurès, Massif de l'-	30	He	35.14N	6.10 E
Aurich	10	Dc	53.28N	7.29 E
Aurillac	11	Ij	44.55N	2.27 E
Aurlandsfjorden	8	Bc	61.05N	7.05 E
Aurlandsvangen	7	Bf	60.54N	7.11 E
Auron	11	Mj	44.12N	6.56 E
Auron	11	Ig	47.06N	2.24 E
Aurora [Co.-U.S.]	43	Gd	39.44N	104.52W
Aurora [Il.-U.S.]	43	Jc	42.46N	88.19W
Aurora [Mo.-U.S.]	45	Jh	36.58N	93.43W
Aurora [Phil.]	26	He	7.57N	123.36 E
Aurora do Norte	55	Ia	12.38S	46.23W
Aursjøen	8	Cb	62.20N	8.40 E
Aursunden	8	Db	62.40N	11.40 E
Aurukun Mission	59	Ib	13.19S	141.45 E
Aurunci, Monti-	14	Hi	41.20N	13.40 E
Aus	37	Be	26.40S	16.15 E
Au Sable River	44	Fc	44.25N	83.20W
Ausangate, Nudo-	52	Ig	13.47S	71.13W
Ausiait/Egedesminde	67	Nc	68.50N	52.45W
Ausoni, Monti-	14	Hi	41.25N	13.20 E
Aust-Agder	7	Bg	58.50N	8.00 E
Austfonna	41	Oc	79.55N	25.00 E
Austin [Mn.-U.S.]	43	Ic	43.40N	92.59W
Austin [Nv.-U.S.]	43	Dd	39.30N	117.04W
Austin [Tx.-U.S.]	39	Jf	30.16N	97.45W
Austin, Lake-	59	De	27.40S	118.00 E
Austral, Chaco-	52	Jh	25.00S	61.00W
Australes, Iles-/Tubuaï, Iles-=Tubuai Islands (EN)	57	Lg	23.00S	150.00W
Australia	57	Eg	25.00S	135.00 E
Australia	58	Eg	25.00S	135.00 E
Australian Alps	57	Fh	37.00S	148.00 E
Australian Capital Territory	59	Jg	35.30S	149.00 E
Austria (EN) = Österreich	6	Hf	47.30N	14.00 E
Austvågøy	7	Db	68.20N	14.36 E
Autazes	54	Gd	3.35S	59.08W
Autheuil-Authouillet	12	De	49.06N	1.17 E
Authie	11	Hd	50.21N	1.38 E
Autlán de Navarro	47	De	19.46N	104.22W
Autun	11	Kh	46.57N	4.18 E
Auve	12	Ge	49.02N	4.42 E
Auvergne	11	Ii	45.20N	3.00 E
Auvergne, Monts d'-	11	Ii	45.30N	2.45 E
Auvézère	11	Gi	45.12N	0.50 E
Auvillers-lès-Forges-Mon Idée	12	Ge	49.52N	4.21 E
Auxerre	11	Jg	47.48N	3.34 E
Auxi-le-Château	11	Id	50.14N	2.07 E
Auxois	11	Kg	47.20N	4.30 E
Auxonne	11	Lg	47.12N	5.23 E
Auyán-Tepuy	54	Fb	5.55N	62.32W
Auzances	11	Ih	46.01N	2.30 E
Avaavaroa Passage	64p	Bc	21.16S	159.47W
Availles-Limouzine	11	Gh	46.07N	0.39 E
Avala	15	De	44.42N	20.31 E
Avaldsnes	8	Ae	59.21N	5.16 E
Avallon	11	Jg	47.29N	3.54 E
Avalon Peninsula	42	Mg	47.30N	53.30W
Avana	64p	Cb	21.14S	159.41W
Avaré	55	Hf	23.05S	48.55W
Avarua	58	Lg	21.12S	159.46W
Avarua Harbour	64p	Bb	21.11S	159.46W
Avatele	64k	Bb	19.06S	169.55W
Avatele Bay	64k	Bb	19.05S	169.56W
Avatiu	64p	Bb	21.12S	159.47W
Avatiu Harbour	64p	Bb	21.11S	159.47W
Avatolu, Passe-	64h	Ab	13.19S	176.14W
Ávdhira	15	Hi	40.59N	24.57 E
Ave	13	Dc	41.20N	8.45W
Aveh	24	Ne	34.47N	50.25 E
Aveh, Gardaneh-ye-	24	Me	35.32N	49.09 E
Aveiro	13	Dd	40.45N	8.30W
Aveiro [Braz.]	54	Gd	3.15S	55.10W
Aveiro [Port.]	13	Dd	40.38N	8.39W
Āvej	24	Me	35.34N	49.13 E
Avelgem	12	Fd	50.46N	3.26 E
Avellaneda [Arg.]	56	Ic	29.07S	59.40W
Avellaneda [Arg.]	56	Id	34.39S	58.23W
Avellino	14	Ij	40.54N	14.47 E
Aven Armand	11	Jj	44.15N	3.22 E
Averbode	12	Gc	51.02N	4.59 E
Avereest	12	Ib	52.37N	6.27 E
Avereest-Dedemsvaart	12	Ib	52.37N	6.27 E
Averøya	7	Be	63.00N	7.35 E
Aversa	14	Ij	40.58N	14.12 E
Avesnes-le-Compte	12	Ed	50.17N	2.32 E
Avesnes-les-Aubert	12	Fd	50.12N	3.23 E
Avesnes-sur-Helpe	11	Jd	50.07N	3.56 E
Aves Ridge (EN)	47	Lf	14.00N	63.30W
Avesta	7	Df	60.09N	16.12 E
Aveyron	11	Hj	44.05N	1.16 E
Aveyron	11	Ij	44.15N	2.30 E
Avezzano	14	Hh	42.02N	13.25 E
Avgan	15	Mk	38.25N	29.24 E
Avgó [Grc.]	15	In	35.36N	25.34 E
Avgó [Grc.]	15	Jn	35.55N	26.30 E
Aviemore	9	Jd	57.12N	3.50W
Avigait	41	Gf	62.15N	50.00W
Avigliano	14	Jj	40.44N	15.43 E
Avignon	6	Gg	43.57N	4.49 E
Ávila	13	Hd	49.39N	4.42W
Ávila	13	Hd	40.35N	5.00W
Ávila, Sierra de-	13	Gd	40.35N	5.08W
Avilés	13	Ga	43.33N	5.55W
Avinurme	8	Lf	58.55N	26.50 E
Avion	12	Ed	50.24N	2.50 E
Ávios Theódhoros	15	Gn	35.32N	23.56 E
Avioth	12	He	49.34N	5.24 E
Avis	13	Ee	39.03N	7.53W
Avisio	14	Fd	46.07N	11.05 E
Avize	12	Gf	48.58N	4.01 E
Avlaka Burun	15	Ii	40.07N	25.40 E
Avola [B.C.-Can.]	46	Fa	51.47N	119.19W
Avola [It.]	14	Jn	36.54N	15.08 E
Avon	9	Kj	51.30N	2.30W
Avon [Eng.-U.K.]	9	Kj	51.59N	2.10W
Avon [Eng.-U.K.]	9	Kj	51.30N	2.43W
Avon [Eng.-U.K.]	9	Lk	50.43N	1.46W
Avon Downs	58	Eg	20.05S	137.30 E
Avon Park	44	Gl	27.36N	81.31W
Avon River	59	Df	31.40S	116.07 E
Avranches	11	Ef	48.41N	1.22W
Avre [Fr.]	11	Ie	49.53N	2.20 E
Avre [Fr.]	11	Hf	48.47N	1.22 E
Avrig	15	Hd	45.43N	24.23 E
Avron	11	Ki	45.15N	4.50 E
Avşa Adasi	15	Ki	40.30N	27.30 E
Avuavu	63a	Ec	9.50S	160.23 E
Awaji	28	Mg	34.35N	135.01 E
Awaji-Shima	28	Mg	34.25N	134.50 E
'Awālī	24	Ni	26.05N	50.33 E
Awanui	61	Dg	35.03S	173.15 E
Awara Plain	36	Hb	3.45N	41.07 E
Aware	35	Gd	8.14N	44.10 E
Awarua Bay	62	Cf	44.20S	168.05 E
Awasa	31	Kh	7.02N	38.29 E
Awash	30	Lg	11.12N	41.40 E
Awash	35	Gd	8.59N	40.10 E
Awa-Shima	28	Oe	38.27N	139.14 E
Awaso	34	Ed	6.14N	2.16W
Awat	27	Dc	40.38N	80.22 E
Awata	35	Fe	4.45N	39.26 E
Awatere	62	Fd	41.36S	174.10 E
Awbārī	31	If	26.35N	12.46 E
Awbārī	33	Bd	26.35N	12.46 E
Awbārī' Şaḩrā'	30	If	27.30N	11.30 E
Awdēgle	35	Ge	1.58N	44.51 E
Awe, Loch-	9	He	56.15N	5.15W
Awjilah	31	Jf	29.06N	21.17 E
Axel	12	Fc	51.16N	3.54 E
Axel Heiberg	38	Ja	80.30N	92.00W
Axim	34	Ee	4.52N	2.14W
Axiós	15	Fi	40.35N	22.50 E
Axixá	54	Jd	2.51S	44.04W
Ax-les-Thermes	11	Hl	42.43N	1.50 E
Ayabaca	54	Cd	4.38S	79.43W
Ayabe	28	Mg	35.18N	135.15 E
Ayachi, Ari n'-	32	Gc	32.30N	4.50W
Ayacucho	54	Df	14.00S	74.00W
Ayacucho [Arg.]	56	Ie	37.09S	58.29W
Ayacucho [Peru]	53	Ig	13.07S	74.13W
Ayakita-Gawa	29	Bf	31.58N	131.23 E
Ayakkum Hů	27	Ed	37.30N	89.20 E
Ayamé	34	Ed	5.37N	3.11W
Ayamonte	13	Eg	37.13N	7.24W
Ayancık	24	Fb	41.57N	34.36 E
Ayangba	34	Gd	7.31N	7.08 E
Ayapel	54	Cb	8.18N	75.08W
Ayas	24	Eb	40.01N	32.21 E
Ayaviri	54	Df	14.52S	70.35W
Āybak	23	Kb	36.16N	68.01 E
Aybastı	24	Gb	40.41N	37.24 E
Aycliffe	9	Lg	54.36N	1.34W
'Aydim, Wādī-	35	Ib	18.08N	53.08 E
Aydın	23	Cb	37.51N	27.51 E
Aydıncık	24	Ed	36.08N	33.17 E
Aydın Dağları	24	Bc	38.00N	28.00 E
Aydingkol Hu	27	Ec	42.40N	89.15 E
Aydinkent	24	Ed	37.06N	31.36 E
Aydos Dağı	24	Fd	37.21N	34.22 E
Ayerbe	13	Lb	42.17N	0.41W
Ayer Hitam	26	Df	1.55N	103.11 E

Index Symbols

- 1 Independent Nation
- 2 State, Region
- 3 District, County
- 4 Municipality
- 5 Colony, Dependency
- Continent
- Physical Region
- Historical or Cultural Region
- Mount, Mountain
- Volcano
- Hill
- Mountains, Mountain Range
- Hills, Escarpment
- Plateau, Upland
- Pass, Gap
- Plain, Lowland
- Delta
- Salt Flat
- Valley, Canyon
- Crater, Cave
- Karst Features
- Depression
- Polder
- Desert, Dunes
- Forest, Woods
- Heath, Steppe
- Oasis
- Cape, Point
- Coast, Beach
- Cliff
- Peninsula
- Isthmus
- Sandbank
- Island
- Atoll
- Rock, Reef
- Islands, Archipelago
- Rocks, Reefs
- Coral Reef
- Well, Spring
- Geyser
- River, Stream
- Waterfall Rapids
- River Mouth, Estuary
- Lake
- Salt Lake
- Intermittent Lake
- Reservoir
- Swamp, Pond
- Canal
- Glacier
- Ice Shelf, Pack Ice
- Ocean
- Sea
- Gulf, Bay
- Strait, Fjord
- Lagoon
- Bank
- Seamount
- Tablemount
- Ridge
- Shelf
- Basin
- Escarpment, Sea Scarp
- Fracture
- Trench, Abyss
- National Park, Reserve
- Point of Interest
- Recreation Site
- Cave, Cavern
- Historic Site
- Ruins
- Wall, Walls
- Church, Abbey
- Temple
- Scientific Station
- Airport
- Port
- Lighthouse
- Mine
- Tunnel
- Dam, Bridge

Ayeyarwady	25	Ie	17.00N	95.00 E
Ayeyarwady = Irrawaddy (EN)	21	Lg	15.50N	95.06 E
Ayiá	15	Fj	39.43N	22.46 E
Ayía Marína	15	Jl	37.09N	26.52 E
Ayiásos	15	Jj	39.06N	26.22 E
Áyion Óros = Athos, Mount- (EN) [2]	15	Hi	40.15N	24.15 E
Áyios Evstrátios	15	Hj	39.31N	25.00 E
Áyios Ioánnis, Ákra-	15	In	35.20N	25.46 E
Áyios Kírikos	15	Jl	37.35N	26.14 E
Áyios Minás	15	Jl	37.36N	26.34 E
Áyios Nikólaos	15	In	35.11N	25.43 E
Áyios Yeóryios	15	Gl	37.28N	23.56 E
Aykota	35	Fb	15.10N	37.03 E
Aylesbury	9	Mj	51.50N	0.50W
Ayllón, Sierra de-	13	Ic	41.15N	3.25W
Aylmer Lake	42	Gd	64.05N	108.30W
Aylsham	12	Db	52.47N	1.15 E
Ayna	13	Jf	38.33N	2.05W
'Aynabo	35	Hd	8.57N	46.30 E
'Ayn ad Darāhim	14	Cn	36.47N	8.42 E
'Ayn al Baydā	24	Ge	34.32N	37.55 E
'Ayn al Ghazāl [Eg.]	24	Dj	25.46N	30.38 E
'Ayn al Ghazāl [Lib.]	31	Jf	21.50N	24.55 E
'Ayn al Shigi	24	Ci	27.01N	28.02 E
'Ayn al Wādī	24	Ci	27.23N	28.13 E
'Ayn Bū Sālim	14	Cn	36.37N	8.59 E
'Ayn Dāllah	33	Ed	27.19N	27.20 E
'Ayn Dār	24	Mj	25.58N	49.14 E
'Ayn Dīwār	24	Jd	37.17N	42.11 E
'Ayn Ilwān	24	Dj	25.44N	30.25 E
'Ayn Khalīfah	24	Bi	26.46N	27.47 E
'Ayn Sifnī	24	Jd	36.42N	43.21 E
'Ayn Sukhnah	33	Fd	29.30N	32.10 E
'Aynūnah	23	Ed	28.05N	35.08 E
Ayod	35	Ed	8.08N	31.24 E
Ayora	13	Ke	39.04N	1.03W
Ayorou	34	Fc	14.44N	0.55 E
'Ayoûn el 'Atroûs	31	Gg	16.38N	9.36W
Ayr	9	If	55.29N	4.28W
Ayr [Austl.]	59	Jc	19.35 S	147.24 E
Ayr [Scot.-U.K.]	9	If	55.28N	4.38W
Ayre, Point of-	9	Ig	54.26N	4.22W
Ayrolle, Étang de l'-	11	Jk	43.16N	3.30 E
Aysha	35	Gc	10.45N	42.35 E
Aytré	11	Eh	46.08N	1.06W
Ayutla	48	Gg	20.07N	104.22W
Ayutla de los Libres	48	Ji	16.54N	99.13W
Ayvacık	24	Gb	41.00N	36.45 E
Ayvacik	15	Jj	39.36N	26.24 E
Ayvalık	23	Cb	39.18N	26.41 E
Aywaille	12	Hd	50.28N	5.40 E
Āzādshahr	24	Pd	37.05N	55.08 E
Azahar, Costa del-	13	Me	39.58N	0.01 E
Azaila	13	Lc	41.17N	0.29W
Azambuja	13	De	39.04N	8.52W
Azamgarh	25	Gc	26.04N	83.11 E
Azángaro	54	Df	14.55 S	70.13W
Azannes-et-Soumazannes	12	He	49.18N	5.28 E
Azaouâd = Azaouad (EN)	30	Gg	19.00N	3.00W
Azaouad (EN) = Azaouâd	30	Gg	19.00N	3.00W
Azaouak	34	Fb	15.30N	3.18 E
Azaouak	30	Hg	15.20N	4.55 E
Azaouak, Vallée de l'-	30	Hg	17.30N	3.40 E
Azar	34	Fb	16.02N	4.04 E
Āžarbāijān-e Gharbī [3]	23	Fb	37.00N	45.00 E
Āžarbāijān-e Sharqī [3]	23	Gb	37.00N	47.00 E
Azarbaijčan SSR → Azärbayjan	19	Eg	40.30N	47.30 E
Azärbayjan = Azerbaijan (EN)	19	Eg	40.30N	47.30 E
Azare	34	Hc	11.41N	10.12 E
Āzār Shahr	24	Kd	37.45N	45.59 E
Azay-le-Rideau	11	Gg	47.16N	0.28 E
A 'zāz	24	Gd	36.35N	37.03 E
Azazga	13	Qh	36.44N	4.22 E
Azbine/Aïr	30	Hg	18.00N	8.30 E
Azdaak, Gora-	16	Ni	40.13N	44.59 E
Azdavay	24	Eb	41.39N	33.18 E
Azefal	30	Ff	21.00N	14.45W
Azeffoun	13	Qh	36.53N	4.25 E
Azemmour	32	Fc	33.17N	8.21W
Azerbaijan (En) = Azärbayjan	19	Eg	40.30N	47.30 E
Azerbajdžanskaja Sovetskaja Socialističeskaja Respublika → Azärbayjan	19	Eg	40.30N	47.30 E
Azerbajdžanskaja SSR/Azarbaijčan Sovet Socialistik Respublicasy → Azärbayjan	19	Eg	40.30N	47.30 E
Azerbajdžanskaja SSR → Azärbayjan	19	Eg	40.30N	47.30 E
Azeri/Aseri	7	Gg	59.29N	26.51 E
Azevedo Sodré	55	Ej	30.04S	54.36W
Azezo	35	Fc	12.33N	37.25 E
Azilal [3]	32	Fc	32.09N	6.05W
Azilal	32	Fc	31.58N	6.35W
Aznā	24	Mf	33.56N	49.24 E
Aznakajevo	7	Mi	54.56N	53.04 E
Azogues	54	Cd	2.44 S	78.48W
Azores (EN) = Açores [5]	31	Ee	38.30N	28.00W
Azores (EN) = Açores, Arquipélago dos-	30	Ee	38.30N	28.00W
Azores-Gibraltar Ridge (EN)	3	Df	37.00N	16.00W
Azoum, Bahr-	30	Jg	10.53N	20.15 E
Azov	19	Df	47.05N	39.25 E
Azov, Sea of- (EN) = Azovskoje More	5	Jf	46.00N	36.00 E
Azovskoje More = Azov, Sea of- (EN)	5	Jf	46.00N	36.00 E
Azpeitia	13	Ja	43.11N	2.16W
Azrak, Bahr-	35	Bc	10.50N	19.50 E
Azraq, Al Baḩr al- = Blue Nile (EN)	30	Kg	15.38N	32.31 E
Azraq ash Shīshān	24	Gg	31.50N	36.49 E
Azrou	32	Fc	33.26N	5.13W
Aztec	45	Ch	36.49N	107.59W
Aztec Ruins	46	Kh	36.51N	108.10W
Azua	49	Ld	18.27N	70.44W
Azuaga	13	Gf	38.16N	5.41W
Azuar	13	Ie	39.08N	3.36W
Azuero, Península de- = Azuero Peninsula (EN)	38	Ki	7.40N	80.30W
Azuero Peninsula (EN) = Azuero, Península de-	38	Ki	7.40N	80.30W
Azul	53	Ki	36.45 S	59.50W
Azul, Arroyo del-	55	Cm	36.15 S	59.07W
Azul, Cerro-	54a	Ab	0.54 S	91.21W
Azul, Cordillera-	54	Ce	8.30 S	76.00W
Azul, Río-	48	Oi	17.54N	88.52W
Azul, Serra-	55	Eb	14.50 S	54.50W
Azul, Sierras del-	55	Cm	37.02 S	59.55W
Azūm	35	Cc	10.53N	20.15 E
Azuma-San	29	Gc	37.44N	140.08 E
Azur, Côte d'-	11	Mk	43.30N	7.00 E
Azurduy	54	Fg	19.59 S	64.29W
Azzaba	32	Ib	36.44N	7.06 E
Az Zāb al Kabīr	23	Fb	36.00N	43.21 E
Az Zāb aş Şaghīr	23	Fb	35.12N	43.25 E
Az Zabdānī	24	Gf	33.43N	36.05 E
Az Zabū	24	Ch	28.22N	28.56 E
Az Zafir	23	Ff	19.57N	41.30 E
Az Zaghāwa	35	Cb	15.15N	23.14 E
Az Zāhirah	24	Qk	23.30N	56.15 E
Az Zallāq	24	Ni	26.03N	50.29 E
Az Zaqāzīq	33	Fc	30.35N	31.31 E
Az Zarqā'	24	Oj	24.53N	53.04 E
Az Zarqā'	24	Gf	32.05N	36.06 E
Az Zāwiyah [3]	33	Bc	32.40N	12.10 E
Az Zāwiyah	33	Bc	32.45N	12.44 E
Az Zaytūn	33	Ed	29.09N	25.47 E
Azzel Matti, Sebkha-	30	Hf	26.00N	0.55 E
Az Zilfī	24	Ki	26.18N	44.48 E
Az Zubayr	24	Lg	30.23N	47.43 E

B

Baa	26	Hi	10.43 S	123.03 E
Baaba	63b	Ae	20.03 S	163.58 E
Ba'ādwēyn	35	Hd	7.12N	47.24 E
Bá an Daingin/Dingle Bay	9	Ci	52.05N	10.15W
Baar	10	Ei	48.00N	8.30 E
Baarle-Hertog	12	Gc	51.27N	4.56 E
Baarn	12	Hb	52.14N	5.17 E
Baas, Bassure de-	12	Dd	50.30N	1.15 E
Bāb	24	Ok	23.55N	53.45 E
Baba	35	Bd	6.25N	17.07 E
Baba	15	Ei	40.55N	21.10 E
Baba Burun [Tur.]	24	Db	41.18N	31.26 E
Baba Burun [Tur.]	24	Bc	39.29N	26.04 E
Babadağ	15	Ll	37.48N	28.52 E
Baba Dağ	15	Mm	36.32N	29.10 E
Babadag	15	Le	44.54N	28.43 E
Babadag, Gora-	16	Pi	41.01N	48.29 E
Babaeski	24	Bb	41.26N	27.06 E
Bābā-Ḩeydar	24	Nf	32.20N	50.28 E
Babajevo	19	Dd	59.24N	35.55 E
Babajtag, Gora-	18	Hd	41.13N	70.16 E
Babajurt	16	Oh	43.35N	46.47 E
Bāb al Māndab = Bab el Mandeb (EN)	30	Lg	12.35N	43.25 E
Babanūsah	35	Dc	11.20N	27.48 E
Babao → Qilian	27	Hd	38.14N	100.15 E
Babaoyo	54	Cd	1.50 S	79.30W
Babar, Kepulauan-	26	Ih	7.50 S	129.45 E
Babar, Pulau-	57	De	7.55 S	129.45 E
Babase	63a	Aa	4.01 S	153.42 E
Babatag, Hrebet-	18	Ge	38.00N	68.10 E
Babati	36	Gc	4.13 S	35.45 E
Babbitt	45	Kc	47.43N	91.57W
B'abdā	24	Ff	33.50N	35.32 E
Bab el Mandeb (EN) = Bāb al Māndab	30	Lg	12.35N	43.25 E
Babelthuap Island	57	Ed	7.30N	134.36 E
Babenhausen [Ger.]	10	Gh	48.09N	10.15 E
Babenhausen [Ger.]	12	Ke	49.58N	8.57 E
Babeni	15	He	44.59N	24.15 E
Baberton	44	Ge	41.02N	81.38W
Bá Bheanntrai/Bantry Bay	9	Dj	51.38N	9.48W
Babian Jiang = Black River (EN)	21	Mg	20.17N	106.34 E
Babil [3]	24	Kf	32.40N	44.50 E
Babine Lake	42	Ef	54.45N	126.00W
Babino Polje	14	Lh	42.43N	17.33 E
Babit Point	51b	Ab	18.03N	63.02W
Babo	26	Jg	2.33 S	133.25 E
Bābol	23	Hb	36.34N	52.42 E
Babol Sar	24	Od	36.43N	52.39 E
Baboquivari Peak	46	Jk	31.46N	111.35W
Babor, Djebel-	13	Rh	36.32N	5.28 E
Baborigame	48	Fd	26.27N	107.16W
Baboua	35	Ad	5.48N	14.49 E
Babozero, Ozero-	7	Ic	66.30N	37.25 E
Babu → Hexian	27	Jg	24.28N	111.34 E
Babuna	15	Eh	41.30N	21.40 E
Babuyan	26	Hc	19.32N	121.57 E
Babuyan	26	Gd	10.01N	118.58 E
Babuyan Channel	26	Hc	18.44N	121.40 E
Babuyan Islands	21	Oh	19.15N	121.40 E
Babylon	23	Fc	32.32N	44.25 E
Bač	15	Cd	45.23N	19.14 E
Bacabachi	48	Ed	26.55N	109.24W
Bacabal	53	Lf	4.14 S	44.47W
Ba-Cagan	27	Gb	45.40N	99.30 E
Bacajá, Rio-	54	Hd	3.25 S	51.50W
Bacalar	48	Oh	18.43N	88.27W
Bacalar, Laguna de-	48	Oh	18.43N	88.22W
Bacalar Chico, Boca-	49	Dd	18.12N	87.53W
Bacan, Kepulauan-	26	Ig	0.35 S	127.30 E
Bacan, Pulau-	26	Ig	0.35 S	127.30 E
Bacău [2]	15	Jc	46.36N	27.00 E
Bacău	6	If	46.34N	26.54 E
Baccarat	11	Mf	48.27N	6.45 E
Bacchiglione	14	Ge	45.11N	12.14 E
Baceşti	15	Kc	46.51N	27.14 E
Bachaquero	49	Li	9.56N	71.08W
Bacharach	12	Jd	50.04N	7.46 E
Bacheli	25	Ge	18.40N	81.15 E
Bachiniva	48	Fc	28.45N	107.15W
Bachu/Maralwexi	27	Cd	39.46N	78.15 E
Back	38	Jd	67.15N	95.15W
Bačka	15	Cd	45.50N	19.30 E
Bac Kan	25	Ld	22.08N	105.49 E
Bačka Palanka	15	Cd	45.15N	19.22 E
Bačka Topola	15	Cd	45.49N	19.39 E
Bäckefors	8	Ef	58.48N	12.10 E
Bäckhammar	8	Fe	59.10N	14.11 E
Backnang	10	Fh	48.57N	9.26 E
Bačkovski Manastir	15	Hh	41.56N	24.51 E
Bac Lieu	25	Lg	9.17N	105.43 E
Bac Ninh	25	Ld	21.11N	106.03 E
Bacolet	51p	Bb	12.02N	61.41W
Bacolod	22	Oh	10.40N	122.57 E
Bac-Phan = Tonkin (EN)	21	Mg	22.00N	105.00 E
Bacqueville, Lac-	42	Ke	58.00N	74.00W
Bacqueville-en Caux	12	Ce	49.47N	1.00 E
Bácsalmás	10	Pj	46.08N	19.20 E
Bács-Kiskun [2]	10	Pj	46.30N	19.25 E
Bacton	12	Db	52.51N	1.28 E
Bād	23	Hc	33.41N	52.01 E
Badagara	25	Ff	11.36N	75.35 E
Badagri	34	Fd	6.25N	2.53 E
Badain Jaran Shamo	21	Me	40.20N	101.40 E
Badajós, Lago-	54	Fd	3.15 S	62.45W
Badajoz	6	Fh	38.53N	6.58W
Badajoz [3]	13	Ff	38.40N	6.10W
Badakhshan [3]	23	Lb	36.45N	72.00 E
Badalona	13	Oc	41.27N	2.15 E
Badanah	23	Fc	30.59N	41.02 E
Badaohao	28	Fd	41.50N	121.59 E
Badas, Kepulauan-	26	Ef	0.35N	107.06 E
Bad Aussee	14	Hc	47.36N	13.47 E
Bad Axe	44	Fd	43.48N	83.00W
Bad Bergzabern	10	Dg	49.06N	8.00 E
Bad Berleburg	12	Kc	51.04N	8.24 E
Bad Bertrich	12	Jd	50.03N	7.02 E
Bad Bramstedt	10	Fc	53.55N	9.53 E
Bad Brückenau	10	Ff	50.18N	9.45 E
Badda	35	Fd	7.55N	39.23 E
Baddo	25	Cc	27.59N	64.21 E
Bad Doberan	10	Hb	54.06N	11.54 E
Bad Driburg	12	Lc	51.44N	9.01 E
Bad Düben	10	Ie	51.36N	12.35 E
Bad Dürkheim	12	Ke	49.28N	8.12 E
Bade	26	Kh	7.10 S	139.35 E
Bademli	15	Lk	38.04N	28.04 E
Baden [Aus.]	14	Kb	48.01N	16.14 E
Baden [Switz.]	14	Cc	47.28N	8.18 E
Baden-Baden	10	Eh	48.45N	8.15 E
Badenoch	9	Je	56.50N	4.00W
Baden-Württemberg [2]	10	Eh	48.30N	9.00 E
Bad Essen	12	Kb	52.19N	8.20 E
Bad Freienwalde	10	Kd	52.47N	14.02 E
Badgastein	14	Hc	47.07N	13.08 E
Bādghīsat [3]	23	Jc	35.00N	63.45 E
Bad Gleichenberg	14	Jd	46.52N	15.54 E
Bad Godesberg, Bonn-	10	Df	50.41N	7.09 E
Bad Hall	14	Ib	48.02N	14.12 E
Bad Harzburg	10	Ge	51.53N	10.34 E
Bad Herrenalb	12	Kf	48.48N	8.25 E
Bad Hersfeld	10	Ff	50.52N	9.42 E
Bad Homburg	10	Ef	50.13N	8.37 E
Bad Honnef	12	Jd	50.38N	7.13 E
Bá Dhún na nGall/Donegal Bay	5	Fe	54.30N	8.30W
Badhyz	18	Cg	35.50N	62.00 E
Badiraguato	48	Fe	25.22N	107.37W
Bad Ischl	14	Hc	47.43N	13.37 E
Bad Kissingen	10	Gf	50.12N	10.05 E
Bad Kreuznach	10	Dg	49.50N	7.52 E
Badlands [S.D.-U.S.]	45	Ee	43.30N	102.20W
Badlands [U.S.]	43	Gb	46.45N	103.30W
Bad Langensalza	10	Ge	51.06N	10.39 E
Bad Lautenberg am Harz	10	Ge	51.38N	10.28 E
Bad Liebenwerda	10	Je	51.31N	13.24 E
Bad Liebenzel	12	Kf	48.46N	8.44 E
Bad Mergentheim	10	Fg	49.29N	9.46 E
Bad Mondorf/Mondorf-les-Bains	12	Ie	49.30N	6.17 E
Bad Münster am Stein Ebernburg	12	Je	49.49N	7.51 E
Bad Münstereifel	12	Id	50.34N	6.45 E
Bad Muskau	10	Ke	51.33N	14.43 E
Bad Nauheim	12	Kd	50.22N	8.45 E
Bad Neuenahr-Ahrweiler	10	Df	50.33N	7.08 E
Bad Neustadt an der Saale	10	Gf	50.20N	10.13 E
Bad Oeynhausen	12	Kb	52.12N	8.48 E
Bad Oldesloe	10	Gc	53.49N	10.23 E
Ba Don	25	Le	17.45N	106.27 E
Badou [China]	28	Df	36.27N	117.56 E
Badou [Togo]	34	Fd	7.35N	0.36 E
Bad Pyrmont	10	Fe	51.59N	9.15 E
Bad Ragaz	14	Dc	47.00N	9.30 E
Badrah	24	Kf	33.06N	45.58 E
Bad Reichenhall	10	Ii	47.44N	12.53 E
Badr Ḩunayn	23	Ee	23.44N	38.46 E
Bad River	45	Fd	44.22N	100.22W
Bad Salzuflen	12	Kb	52.05N	8.45 E
Bad Salzungen	10	Gf	50.49N	10.14 E
Bad Schwartau	10	Gc	53.55N	10.42 E
Bad Segeberg	10	Gc	53.56N	10.19 E
Bad Tölz	10	Hi	47.46N	11.34 E
Badulla	25	Gg	6.59N	81.03 E
Bad Wildungen	10	Fe	51.07N	9.07 E
Bad Wimpfen	10	Fg	49.14N	9.08 E
Baena	13	Hg	37.37N	4.19W
Baeza [Ec.]	54	Cd	0.28 S	77.53W
Baeza [Sp.]	13	Ig	37.59N	3.28W
Baf/Paphos	24	Ee	34.50N	32.35 E
Bafang	34	Hd	5.09N	10.11 E
Bafatà	31	Fg	12.10N	14.40W
Bafélé	34	Cc	10.09N	10.08W
Baffin	38	Mc	68.00N	70.00W
Baffin Bay	38	Mb	73.00N	65.00W
Bafia	34	He	4.45N	11.14 E
Bafilo	34	Fd	9.21N	1.16 E
Bafing [Afr.]	30	Fg	13.49N	10.50W
Bafing [I.C.]	34	Dd	7.52N	7.07W
Bafoulabé	34	Cc	13.48N	10.50W
Bafoussam	31	Ih	5.28N	10.25 E
Bāfq	23	Ic	31.35N	55.24 E
Bāfq, Kūh-e-	24	Pg	31.20N	55.10 E
Bafra	23	Ea	41.34N	35.56 E
Bāft	24	Qh	29.14N	56.38 E
Bafwaboli	36	Eb	0.39N	26.10 E
Bafwasende	36	Eb	1.05N	27.16 E
Baga	34	Hc	13.06N	13.50 E
Bagaces	49	Eh	10.31N	85.15W
Bagagem, Rio-	55	Ha	13.58 S	48.21W
Bagajevski	16	Lf	47.19N	40.25 E
Bāgalkot	25	Fe	16.11N	75.42 E
Bagamoyo	36	Gd	6.26 S	38.54 E
Bagansiapi-Api	26	Df	2.09N	100.49 E
Bağarasi	15	Kl	37.42N	27.33 E
Baga Sola	35	Ac	13.32N	14.19 E
Bagata	36	Cc	3.44 S	17.57 E
Bagdad	48	Ke	25.57N	97.09W
Bagdarin	20	Gf	54.30N	113.36 E
Bagdati (Majakovski)	16	Mh	42.02N	42.47 E
Bağdere	24	Ic	38.10N	40.45 E
Bagé	53	Ki	31.20 S	54.06W
Bages et de Sigean, Étang de-	11	Jk	43.05N	3.01 E
Baggs	46	Lf	41.02N	107.39W
Bagh Baile na Sgealg/Ballinskelligs Bay	9	Cj	51.50N	10.15W
Baghdād [3]	24	Kf	33.18N	44.36 E
Baghdād	22	Gf	33.21N	44.23 E
Baghdādī, Ra's-	24	Fj	24.40N	35.06 E
Bāgh-e Chenār	24	Qh	28.11N	56.54 E
Bāgh-e Malek	24	Mg	31.32N	49.55 E
Bagheria	14	Hl	38.05N	13.30 E
Bāghīn	23	Ic	30.12N	56.48 E
Baghlān [3]	23	Kb	35.45N	69.00 E
Baghlān	23	Kb	36.13N	68.46 E
Bāglung	25	Gc	28.16N	83.36 E
Bagn	8	Cd	60.49N	9.34 E
Bagnara Calabra	14	Jl	38.17N	15.48 E
Bagnères-de-Bigorre	11	Gk	43.04N	0.09 E
Bagnères-de-Luchon	11	Gl	42.47N	0.36 E
Bagni di Lucca	14	Ef	44.01N	10.35 E
Bagno di Romagna	14	Fg	43.50N	11.57 E
Bagnolo Mella	14	Ee	45.26N	10.10 E
Bagnols-sur-Cèze	11	Kj	44.10N	4.37 E
Bago	22	Lh	17.30N	96.30 E
Bagoé	30	Gg	12.36N	6.34W
Bagolino	14	Ee	45.49N	10.28 E
Bagrationovsk	8	Ij	54.23N	20.40 E
Bagrax/Bohu	27	Ec	41.58N	86.29 E
Bagrax Hu/Bosten	21	Ke	42.00N	87.00 E
Bagua	54	Ce	5.40 S	78.31W
Baguio	22	Oh	16.25N	120.36 E
Baguirmi	30	Ig	11.40N	16.20 E
Bagzane, Monts-	30	Hg	17.43N	8.45 E
Bahama Islands	38	Lg	24.15N	76.00W
Bahamas [1]	39	Lg	24.15N	76.00W
Bahamas, Canal Viejo de- = Old Bahama Channel (EN)	49	Ib	22.30N	78.05W
Bahār	24	Me	34.54N	48.26 E
Baharampur	25	Hd	24.06N	88.15 E
Baharden	19	Fh	38.28N	57.28 E
Bahardok	19	Fh	38.51N	58.24 E
Baharīyah, Wāḩāt al-	33	Ed	28.10N	29.00 E
Bahariya Oasis (EN) = Baharīyah, Wāḩāt al-	33	Ed	28.15N	28.57 E
Bahau	26	Fg	3.20N	114.00 E
Bahawalnagar	25	Ec	29.59N	73.16 E
Bahawalpur	22	Jg	29.24N	71.41 E
Bahčisaraj	16	Hg	44.45N	33.51 E
Bahçe	24	Gd	37.14N	36.34 E
Bahi	36	Gd	5.39 S	35.19 E
Bahia [2]	54	Jf	12.00 S	42.00W
Bahía, Islas de la-	47	Ge	16.20N	86.30W
Bahía Blanca	53	Ji	38.44 S	62.16W
Bahía de Caráquez	54	Bd	0.37 S	80.25W
Bahía Kino	47	Bc	28.50N	111.55W
Bahía Negra	56	Ib	20.15 S	58.12W
Bahías, Cabo dos-	52	Jj	44.55 S	65.32W
Bahīj	24	Cg	30.56N	29.35 E
Bahinga	36	Ed	5.57 S	27.06 E
Bahi Swamp	36	Gd	6.05 S	35.10 E
Bahlui	15	Kb	47.08N	27.44 E
Bahmač	19	De	51.11N	32.50 E
Bahoruco, Sierra de-	49	Ld	18.10N	71.25W
Bahraich	25	Gc	27.35N	81.36 E
Bahrain (EN) = Al Baḩrayn [1]	22	Hg	26.00N	50.29 E
Baḩr al Ghazāl [3]	35	Dd	8.15N	26.50 E
Bahr ar Ramla al Kabīr	33	Ed	27.00N	26.00 E
Baḩrayn, Khalīj al-	24	Nj	25.45N	50.40 E
Bahr Dar	31	Kg	11.36N	37.22 E
Bahta	20	Dd	62.20N	89.15 E
Bahus	15	Jc	46.43N	26.42 E
Baia	15	Le	44.43N	28.40 E
Baia de Aramă	15	Fe	45.00N	22.50 E
Baia de Fier	15	Gd	45.10N	23.46 E
Baia dos Tigres	36	Bf	16.35 S	11.43 E
Baia Farta	36	Be	12.37 S	13.26 E
Baia Mare	15	Gb	47.40N	23.35 E
Baião	54	Id	2.41 S	49.41W
Baia Sprie	15	Gb	47.40N	23.42 E
Baibiene	55	Ci	29.36 S	58.10W
Baïbokoum	35	Bd	7.45N	15.41 E
Baicheng	22	Oe	45.34N	122.49 E
Baicheng/Bay	27	Dc	41.46N	81.52 E
Băicoi	15	Id	45.02N	25.51 E
Băiculeşti	15	Hd	45.04N	24.42 E
Baidoa (EN) = Isha Baydabo	31	Lh	3.04N	43.48 E
Baïdou	35	Cd	5.52N	20.41 E
Baie-Comeau	39	Me	49.13N	68.10W
Baie-Mahault	50	Fd	16.16N	61.35W
Baie-Saint-Paul	42	Kg	47.27N	70.30W
Baie-Trinité	44	Na	49.24N	67.19W
Baie Verte	42	Lg	49.55N	56.11W
Baiguan → Shangyu	28	Fi	30.01N	120.53 E
Baihe	27	Je	32.46N	110.06 E
Bai He [China]	28	Bh	32.10N	112.20 E
Bai He [China]	28	Dd	40.43N	116.33 E
Baikal, Lake- (EN) = Bajkal, Ozero-	21	Md	53.00N	107.40 E
Baikal Range (EN) = Bajkalski Hrebet	21	Md	55.00N	108.40 E
Baile an Chaistil/Ballycastle	18	Gf	55.12N	6.15W
Baile an Róba/Ballinrobe	18	Dh	53.37N	9.13W
Baile Átha Cliath/Dublin [2]	9	Gh	53.20N	6.15W
Baile Átha Cliath/Dublin	6	Fe	53.20N	6.15W
Baile Átha Luain/Athlone	9	Fh	53.25N	7.56W
Baile Átha Troim/Trim	9	Gh	53.34N	6.47W
Băile Borşa	15	Hb	47.41N	24.43 E
Baile Brigín/Balbriggan	9	Gh	53.37N	6.11W
Băile Govora	15	Hd	45.05N	24.11 E
Baile Locha Riach/Loughrea	9	Eh	53.12N	8.34W
Baile Mhistéala/Mitchelstown	9	Ei	52.16N	8.16W
Bailén	3	If	38.06N	3.46W
Baile na Mainistreach/Newtownabbey	9	Hg	54.42N	5.54W
Baile Nua na hArda/Newtownards	9	Hg	54.36N	5.41W
Băile Olăneşti	15	Hd	45.12N	24.14 E
Băileşti	15	Ge	44.01N	23.21 E
Bailleul	12	Ce	49.12N	0.26 E
Bailleul	12	Ed	50.44N	2.44 E
Ba Illi	35	Bc	10.31N	16.29 E
Bailong Jiang	27	Ie	32.42N	105.15 E
Bailundo	36	Ce	12.10 S	15.56 E
Baima	27	He	33.05N	100.29 E
Bain	12	Ba	53.04N	0.12W
Bainbridge	43	Ke	30.54N	84.34W
Bain-de-Bretagne	11	Eg	47.50N	1.41W
Baines Drift	37	Dd	22.30 S	28.43 E
Baing	26	Hi	10.14 S	120.34 E
Baingoin	27	Ee	31.36N	89.48 E
Baiquan	27	Mb	47.38N	126.04 E
Bā'ir	24	Gg	30.46N	36.41 E
Bā'ir, Wādī-	24	Gg	31.12N	37.31 E
Baird	45	Gj	32.24N	99.24W
Baird Inlet	40	Gd	60.45N	164.00W
Baird Mountains	40	Gc	67.35N	161.30W
Baird Peninsula	42	Jc	69.00N	75.15W
Bairiki	58	Id	1.20N	173.01 E
Bairin Youqi (Daban)	27	Kc	43.30N	118.37 E
Bairin Zuoqi (Lindong)	27	Kc	43.59N	119.22 E
Bairnsdale	58	Fh	37.50 S	147.38 E
Bais	26	He	9.35N	123.07 E
Bai Shan	27	Fc	40.53N	93.48 E
Baisogala/Bajsogala	8	Ji	55.35N	23.44 E
Baitou Shan	21	Oe	42.00N	128.00 E
Baitoushan Tian Chi	28	Jc	42.00N	128.03 E
Baixiang	28	Cf	37.29N	114.44 E
Baixo Alentejo	13	Dg	37.55N	8.10W
Baixo Guandu	54	Jg	19.31 S	41.01W
Baixo Longa	36	Cf	15.42 S	18.38 E
Baiyanghe	27	Ec	43.12N	88.28 E
Baiyü	27	Ge	31.13N	98.51 E
Baja	10	Oj	46.11N	18.58 E
Baja, Punta- [Mex.]	48	Dc	28.25N	111.45W
Baja, Punta- [Pas.]	65d	Ab	27.10 S	109.22W
Baja California = Lower California (EN)	38	Hg	28.00N	112.00W
Baja California Sur [2]	47	Bd	25.50N	111.50W
Bājah [3]	32	Ib	36.30N	9.30 E
Bājah	32	Ib	36.44N	9.11 E
Bajalān	24	Md	37.18N	48.47 E
Bajan	27	Jb	49.15N	111.58 E
Bajanaul	19	He	50.47N	75.42 E
Bajandaj	20	Ff	53.04N	105.30 E
Bajan-Delger	27	Jb	45.55N	112.15 E
Bajangol	20	Ff	50.40N	103.25 E
Bajan-Hongor	22	Me	46.20N	100.40 E
Bajan-Ula [Mong.]	27	Jb	49.07N	112.45 E
Bajan-Ula [Mong.]	27	Gb	47.05N	95.15 E
Bajan-Under	27	Gc	44.45N	98.45 E
Baja Verapaz [3]	49	Bf	15.05N	90.20W
Bajawa	26	Hh	8.47 S	120.59 E
Bajčunas	16	Rf	47.17N	53.03 E
Bajdarackaja Guba	20	Bc	69.00N	67.30 E
Bajdarata	17	Nb	68.12N	68.18 E
Bajdrag Gol	27	Hb	45.10N	100.45 E
Bājgīrān	24	Rd	37.36N	58.24 E
Baj-Haak	20	Ef	51.07N	94.34 E
Bajiazi	28	Jc	42.41N	129.13 E
Bajina Bašta	15	Cf	43.58N	19.34 E
Bajkal	20	Ff	51.53N	104.47 E
Bajkal, Ozero- = Baikal, Lake- (EN)	21	Md	53.00N	107.40 E
Bajkalovo	17	Kh	57.24N	63.40 E
Bajkalsk	20	Ff	51.30N	104.05 E
Bajkalski Hrebet = Baikal Range (EN)	21	Md	55.00N	108.40 E
Bajkit	20	Ed	61.41N	96.25 E
Bajkonur	19	Gf	47.50N	66.07 E
Bajmak	19	Fe	52.36N	58.19 E
Bajmba, Mount-	59	Ke	29.20 S	152.05 E
Bajmok	15	Cd	45.58N	19.26 E
Bajo Baudó	54	Cc	4.58N	77.22W

Index Symbols

[1] Independent Nation · [2] State, Region · [3] District, County · [4] Municipality · [5] Colony, Dependency · Continent · Physical Region · Historical or Cultural Region · Mount, Mountain · Volcano · Hill · Mountains, Mountain Range · Hills, Escarpment · Plateau, Upland · Pass, Gap · Plain, Lowland · Delta · Salt Flat · Valley, Canyon · Crater, Cave · Karst Features · Depression · Polder · Desert, Dunes · Forest, Woods · Heath, Steppe · Oasis · Cape, Point · Coast, Beach · Cliff · Peninsula · Isthmus · Sandbank · Island · Atoll · Rock, Reef · Islands, Archipelago · Rocks, Reefs · Coral Reef · Well, Spring · Geyser · River, Stream · Waterfall Rapids · River Mouth, Estuary · Lake · Salt Lake · Intermittent Lake · Reservoir · Swamp, Pond · Canal · Glacier · Ice Shelf, Pack Ice · Ocean · Sea · Gulf, Bay · Strait, Fjord · Lagoon · Bank · Seamount · Tablemount · Ridge · Shelf · Basin · Escarpment, Sea Scarp · Fracture · Trench, Abyss · National Park, Reserve · Point of Interest · Recreation Site · Cave, Cavern · Historic Site · Ruins · Wall, Walls · Church, Abbey · Temple · Scientific Station · Airport · Port · Lighthouse · Mine · Tunnel · Dam, Bridge

Bajo Boquete 49 Fi 8.46N 82.26W
Bajram-Ali 19 Gh 37.39N 62.12 E
Bajram Curri 15 Dg 42.21N 20.04 E
Bajsogala/Baisogala 8 Ji 55.35N 23.44 E
Bajsun 18 Fe 38.14N 67.12 E
Bajun Islands 30 Li 0.50S 42.15 E
Bajžansaj 18 Gc 43.13N 69.56 E
Baka 35 Ee 4.33N 30.05 E
Bakacak 15 Ki 40.12N 27.05 E
Bakadžicite 15 Jg 42.25N 26.43 E
Bakal 19 Fe 54.56N 58.48 E
Bakala 35 Cd 6.11N 20.22 E
Bakanas 19 Hg 44.48N 76.15 E
Bakar 14 Ie 45.18N 14.32 E
Bakčar 20 De 57.01N 82.10 E
Bake 26 Dg 3.03S 100.16 E
Bakel 34 Cc 14.54N 12.27W
Baker [Ca.-U.S.] 46 Gi 35.15N 116.02W
Baker [La.-U.S.] 45 Kk 30.35N 91.10W
Baker [Mt.-U.S.] 43 Gb 46.22N 104.17W
Baker [Or.-U.S.] 43 Dc 44.47N 117.50W
Baker, Mount- 43 Cb 48.47N 121.49W
Baker Island 57 Jd 0.15N 176.27W
Baker Lake 39 Jc 64.10N 95.30W
Baker Lake 38 Jc 64.10N 95.30W
Bakersfield 39 Hf 35.23N 119.01W
Bā Kēv 25 Lf 13.42N 107.12 E
Bakhma 24 Kd 36.38N 44.17 E
Bakhtarān (Kermānshāh) 22 Gf 34.19N 47.04 E
Bakhtarān [3] 23 Gc 34.15N 47.20 E
Bakhtegān, Daryāchech-ye 24 Ph 29.20N 54.05 E
Bakhūn, Kūh-e- 23 Id 27.56N 56.18 E
Bakır 24 Bc 38.55N 27.00 E
Bakırköy, İstanbul 15 Li 40.59N 28.52 E
Baklan 15 Ml 37.58N 29.36 E
Bako 35 Fd 7.19N 35.08 E
Bako [Eth.] 35 Fd 9.05N 37.07 E
Bako [Eth.] 35 Fd 5.50N 36.37 E
Bakony=Bakony Mountains (EN) 5 Hf 47.15N 17.50 E
Bakony Mountains (EN)=Bakony 5 Hf 47.15N 17.50 E
Bakool [3] 35 Ge 4.10N 43.50 E
Bakouma 35 Cd 5.42N 22.47 E
Bakoye 34 Cc 13.49N 10.50W
Bakpulád 24 Qc 38.10N 57.00 E
Baksan 16 Mh 43.40N 43.28 E
Baksan 16 Nh 43.42N 44.03 E
Baku 6 Kg 40.23N 49.51 E
Bakum 12 Kb 52.44N 8.11 E
Bakungan 26 Cf 2.56N 97.30 E
Bakuriani 16 Mi 41.43N 43.31 E
Bakutis Coast 66 Of 74.45S 120.00W
Balâ 24 Ec 39.34N 33.08 E
Bala, Cerros de- 54 Ef 14.30S 67.40W
Balabac 26 Ge 7.59N 117.04 E
Balabac 26 Ge 7.57N 117.01 E
Balabac, Selat-=Balabac Strait (EN) 21 Ni 7.40N 117.00 E
Balabac Strait (EN)=Balabac, Selat- 21 Ni 7.40N 117.00 E
Ba'labakk 24 Ge 34.00N 36.12 E
Balabalangan, Kepulauan- 26 Gg 2.20S 117.25 E
Balaban Dağı 24 Hb 40.28N 39.15 E
Balabanovo 16 Jb 55.11N 36.40 E
Balabio 63b Be 20.07S 164.11 E
Balaci 15 He 44.21N 24.55 E
Bal'ad 35 He 2.22N 45.24 E
Balad 24 Ke 34.01N 44.01 E
Balādīn as Sakrān 24 Kj 25.12N 44.37 E
Baladiyat 'Adan=Aden (EN) 22 Gh 12.46N 45.01 E
Balad Rūz 24 Kf 33.42N 45.05 E
Balagannoje 20 Je 59.43N 149.15 E
Balagansk 20 Ff 53.58N 103.02 E
Bālāghāt 25 Gd 21.48N 80.11 E
Bālāghāt Range 25 Fe 18.45N 76.30 E
Balagne 11a Aa 42.35N 8.50 E
Balaguer 13 Mc 41.47N 0.49 E
Balahna 7 Kh 56.31N 43.37 E
Balahta 20 Ee 55.24N 91.37 E
Balaka 36 Fe 14.59S 34.57 E
Balaklava 16 Hg 44.31N 33.34 E
Balakleja 19 Df 49.27N 36.52 E
Balakovo 6 Ke 52.02N 47.45 E
Balama 37 Fb 13.16S 38.36 E
Balambangam, Pulau- 26 Ge 7.17N 116.55 E
Bālā Morghāb 23 Jb 35.35N 63.20 E
Balan Dağı 15 Lm 36.52N 28.20 E
Balankanche 48 Og 20.45N 88.30W
Balasan 26 Hd 11.28N 123.05 E
Balasore → Bāleshwar 25 Hd 21.30N 86.56 E
Balašov 19 Ee 51.33N 43.10 E
Balassagyarmat 10 Ph 48.05N 19.18 E
Balāţ 33 Ed 25.33N 29.16 E
Balaton 5 Hf 46.50N 17.45 E
Balatonfüred 10 Nj 46.57N 17.53 E
Balatonkeresztúr 10 Nj 46.42N 17.23 E
Balaurin 26 Hh 8.15S 123.43 E
Bălăușeri 15 Hc 46.24N 24.41 E
Balayan 26 Hd 13.57N 120.44 E
Balazote 13 Jf 38.53N 2.08W
Balbi, Mount- 60 Ei 5.55S 154.59 E
Balboa Heights 47 Ig 8.57N 79.33W
Balbriggan/Baile Brigin 9 Gh 53.37N 6.11W
Balby 8 Ei 55.40N 13.20 E
Balcarce 56 Ie 37.50S 58.15W
Balcarce, Sierras de- 55 Cm 37.50S 58.40W
Bălcești 15 Ge 44.37N 23.57 E
Balčik 15 Lf 43.25N 28.10 E
Balclutha 61 Ci 46.14S 169.44 E
Bald Eagle Mountain 44 Ie 41.00N 77.45W
Bald Head 59 Dg 35.07S 118.01 E
Bald Knob 44 Hg 37.56N 79.51W
Bald Knob 45 Ki 35.19N 91.34W
Baldo, Monte- 14 Ee 45.40N 10.50 E
Baldock 12 Bc 51.59N 0.11W
Baldone 8 Kh 56.41N 24.22 E
Baldur 45 Gb 49.23N 99.15W
Baldwin 44 Ed 43.54N 85.51W
Baldy Peak 43 Fe 33.55N 109.35W
Bale [3] 35 Gd 6.00N 41.00 E
Bâle/Basel 6 Gf 47.30N 7.30 E
Baleares [3] 13 Oe 39.30N 3.00 E
Balearic Islands (EN)=Baleares, Islas-/Balears, Illes- 5 Gh 39.30N 3.00 E
Balearic Islands (EN)=Balears, Illes-/Baleares, Islas- 5 Gh 39.30N 3.00 E
Balears, Illes-/Baleares, Islas-=Balearic Islands (EN) 5 Gh 39.30N 3.00 E
Baleare, Gunung- 26 Hg 2.24S 120.33 E
Baleia, Ponta de- 52 Mg 17.40S 36.07W
Baleine, Rivière à la- 42 Ke 58.15N 67.38W
Balej 20 Gf 51.35N 116.38 E
Balen 12 Hc 51.10N 5.09 E
Baler 26 Hc 15.46N 121.34 E
Bāleshwar 25 Hd 21.30N 86.56 E
Balezino 19 Fd 57.59N 53.02 E
Balfate 49 Df 15.48N 86.25W
Bălgarija=Bulgaria (EN) [1] 6 Ig 43.00N 25.00 E
Balgazyn 20 Ef 50.58N 95.12 E
Balguntay 27 Ec 42.45N 86.18 E
Balḩāf 23 Fg 13.58N 48.11 E
Balhaš 22 Je 46.49N 74.59 E
Balhaš, Ozero-=Balkhash, Lake- (EN) 21 Je 46.00N 74.00 E
Balho 35 Gc 12.00N 42.10 E
Balholm 7 Bf 61.12N 6.33 E
Bali [3] 26 Gh 8.30S 115.00 E
Bali, Laut-=Bali Sea (EN) 21 Nj 7.45S 115.30 E
Bali, Pulau- 21 Nj 8.20S 115.00 E
Bali, Selat-=Bali Strait (EN) 26 Fh 8.18S 114.25 E
Baliceaux Island 51n Bb 12.57N 61.08W
Baliem 26 Kg 4.25S 138.59 E
Balige 26 Cf 2.20N 99.04 E
Balıkesir 23 Cb 39.39N 27.53 E
Balık Gölü 24 Jc 39.45N 43.36 E
Balikh, Nahr- 24 He 35.53N 39.10 E
Balikpapan 22 Nj 1.17S 116.50 E
Balimbing 26 Dh 5.55S 104.34 E
Balimo 60 Ci 8.03S 142.56 E
Balingen 10 Eh 48.17N 8.51 E
Ba inqiao 22 Ec 43.16N 118.38 E
Ba intang Channel 26 Hc 19.49N 121.40 E
Bali Sea (EN)=Bali, Laut- 21 Nj 7.45S 115.30 E
Bali Strait (EN)=Bali, Selat- 26 Fh 8.18S 114.25 E
Balitung, Palau- 21 Mj 2.50S 107.55 E
Baliza 55 Fc 16.15S 52.25W
Balk, Gaasterland- 12 Hb 52.54N 5.36 E
Balkan Mountains (EN)=Stara Planina 5 Ig 43.15N 25.00 E
Balkan Peninsula (EN) 5 Ig 41.30N 23.00 E
Balkanskaja oblast 19 Fh 39.50N 55.00 E
Balkašino 19 Ge 52.32N 68.46 E
Balkh 23 Kb 36.46N 66.54 E
Balkh [3] 23 Kb 36.30N 67.00 E
Balkhash, Lake- (EN)=Balhaš, Ozero- 21 Je 46.00N 74.00 E
Balladonia 59 Ef 32.27S 123.51 E
Ballagen 7 Db 68.20N 16.50 E
Ballaghaderreen/Bealach an Doirin 9 Eh 53.55N 8.35W
Ballantrae 9 If 55.06N 5.00W
Ballantyne Strait 42 Ga 77.30N 115.00W
Ballarat 58 Fh 37.34S 143.52 E
Ballard, Lake- 59 Ee 29.25S 120.55 E
Ballé 34 Db 15.20N 8.36W
Ballenas, Bahía- 48 Cd 26.45N 113.25W
Ballenas, Canal de- 48 Cc 29.10N 113.25W
Ballenero, Canal- 56 Fh 54.50S 71.00W
Ballenita, Punta- 56 Fc 25.46S 70.44W
Balleny Islands 66 Ke 66.35S 162.50 E
Balleroy 12 Be 49.11N 0.50W
Balleza 48 Fd 26.57N 106.21W
Balli 15 Ki 40.50N 27.03 E
Ballia 25 Gc 25.45N 84.10 E
Ballina 59 Ke 28.52S 153.33 E
Ballina/Béal an Átha 9 Dg 54.07N 9.09W
Ballinasloe/Béal Átha na Sluaighe 9 Eh 53.20N 8.13W
Ballinger 45 Gk 31.44N 99.57W
Ballinrobe/Baile an Róba 9 Dh 53.37N 9.13W
Ballinskelligs Bay/Bágh Baile na Sgealg 9 Cj 51.50N 10.15W
Ballshi 15 Ci 40.36N 19.44 E
Ball's Pyramid 57 Gh 31.45S 159.15 E
Ballycastle/Baile an Chaistil 9 Gf 55.12N 6.15W
Ballyhaunis/Béal Átha hAmhnais 9 Eh 53.46N 8.46W
Ballymena/An Baile Meánach 9 Gg 54.52N 6.17W
Ballyshannon/Béal Átha Seanaidh 9 Eg 54.30N 8.11W
Balmazújváros 10 Ri 47.37N 21.21 E
Balmoral Castle 9 Jd 57.02N 3.15W
Balneario Orense 55 Cn 38.49S 59.46W
Balneario Oriente 55 Bn 38.55S 60.32W
Balombo 36 Be 12.21S 14.43 E
Balonne River 57 Fg 28.47S 147.56 E
Balota, Virful- 15 Gd 45.18N 23.53 E
Balovale 31 Jj 13.33S 23.07 E
Balrāmpur 25 Gc 27.26N 82.11 E
Balranald 59 If 34.38S 143.33 E
Balş 15 He 44.21N 24.06 E
Balsas [Braz.] 54 Ie 7.31S 46.02W
Balsas [Mex.] 48 Jh 18.00N 99.47W
Balsas, Depresión del- 48 Ih 18.00N 100.10W
Balsas, Rio- [Mex.] 38 Ih 17.55N 102.10W
Balsas, Rio- [Pan.] 49 Ii 8.15N 77.59W
Balsas, Rio das- [Braz.] 54 Ie 9.58S 47.52W
Balsas, Rio das- [Braz.] 54 Je 7.14S 44.33W
Bålsta 8 Ge 59.35N 17.30 E
Balsthal 14 Bc 47.19N 7.42 E
Balta 16 Ff 47.57N 29.38 E
Baltanás 13 Hc 41.56N 4.15W
Baltasar Brum 56 Id 30.44S 57.19W
Baltaţi 15 Kb 47.13N 27.09 E
Baltic Sea (EN)=Baltijas Jūra 5 Hd 57.00N 19.00 E
Baltic Sea (EN)=Baltijos Jura 5 Hd 57.00N 19.00 E
Baltic Sea (EN)=Balti Meri 5 Hd 57.00N 19.00 E
Baltic Sea- (EN)=Baltiskoje More 5 Hd 57.00N 19.00 E
Baltic Sea (EN)=Bałtyckie, Morze- 5 Hd 57.00N 19.00 E
Baltic Sea (EN)=Itämeri 5 Hd 57.00N 19.00 E
Baltic Sea (EN)=Östersjön 5 Hd 57.00N 19.00 E
Baltic Sea (EN)=Østersøen 5 Hd 57.00N 19.00 E
Baltic Sea (EN)=Ostsee 5 Hd 57.00N 19.00 E
Baltijas Jūra=Baltic Sea (EN) 5 Hd 57.00N 19.00 E
Baltijos Jura=Baltic Sea (EN) 5 Hd 57.00N 19.00 E
Baltijsk 19 Be 54.40N 19.58 E
Baltijskaja Grjada 7 Fi 55.00N 25.00 E
Baltīm 33 Fc 31.33N 31.05 E
Balti Meri=Baltic Sea (EN) 5 Hd 57.00N 19.00 E
Baltimore 39 Lf 39.17N 76.37W
Baltiskoje More=Baltic Sea (EN) 5 Hd 57.00N 19.00 E
Baltit (Hunza) 25 Ea 36.20N 74.40 E
Baltoj Voke 8 Kj 54.24N 25.16 E
Baltrum 10 Dc 53.44N 7.23 E
Bałtyckie, Morze-=Baltic Sea (EN) 5 Hd 57.00N 19.00 E
Baluarte, Rio- 48 Ff 22.49N 106.02W
Baluchistān=Baluchistan (EN) 21 Ig 28.00N 63.00 E
Baluchistān=Baluchistan (EN) [3] 25 Cc 28.00N 63.00 E
Baluchistan (EN)=Baluchistān [3] 25 Cc 28.00N 63.00 E
Baluchistan (EN)=Baluchistān 21 Ig 28.00N 63.00 E
Balupe 8 Lh 56.54N 27.02 E
Balurghat 25 Hc 25.13N 88.46 E
Balvard 24 Qh 29.25N 56.06 E
Balve 12 Jc 51.20N 7.52 E
Balver Wald 12 Jc 51.21N 7.51 E
Balvi/Balvy 7 Gh 57.08N 27.20 E
Balvy/Balvi 7 Gh 57.08N 27.20 E
Balya 24 Bc 39.45N 27.35 E
Balygyčan 20 Kd 64.00N 154.10 E
Balykši 16 Qf 47.02N 51.55 E
Bām 24 Qd 36.58N 57.59 E
Bam 23 Id 29.06N 58.21 E
Bama 34 Hc 11.31N 13.41 E
Bamaji Lake 45 Ka 51.09N 91.25W
Bamako 31 Gg 12.38N 8.00W
Bamako [3] 34 Dc 13.00N 8.00W
Bamba 34 Eb 17.02N 1.24W
Bambama 36 Bc 2.32S 13.33 E
Bambana, Rio- 49 Fg 13.27N 83.50W
Bambangando 36 Df 16.59S 20.57 E
Bambari 31 Jh 5.45N 20.40 E
Bamberg 10 Gg 49.42N 10.52 E
Bambesa 36 Eb 3.28N 25.43 E
Bambesi 35 Ed 9.45N 34.44 E
Bambey 34 Bc 14.42N 16.28W
Bambezi 37 Dc 19.57S 28.55 E
Bambili 36 Eb 3.39N 26.07 E
Bambio 35 Be 3.54N 16.59 E
Bamboi 34 Ed 8.10N 2.02W
Bambouti 35 Dd 5.24N 27.12 E
Bambouto, Monts- 30 Ih 5.44N 10.04 E
Bambui 55 Je 20.01S 45.58W
Bam Co 27 Fe 31.15N 90.32 E
Bamenda 34 Hd 5.56N 10.10 E
Bāmīān [3] 23 Kc 34.45N 67.15 E
Bāmīān 23 Kc 34.50N 67.50 E
Bamiancheng 28 Gc 43.15N 124.00 E
Bamiantong → Muling 28 Kb 44.55N 130.32 E
Bamingui 35 Cd 7.34N 20.11 E
Bamingui 30 Ih 8.33N 19.05 E
Bamingui-Bangoran [3] 35 Cd 7.50N 20.15 E
Bampūr 23 Jd 27.12N 60.27 E
Bampūr 23 Id 27.18N 59.06 E
Banaadir 30 Lh 1.00N 44.00 E
Banaadir [3] 35 He 2.00N 45.15 E
Banaba Island 57 He 0.52S 169.35 E
Banabuiú, Açude- 54 Ke 5.20S 39.00W
Banagi 36 Fc 2.16S 34.51 E
Banalia 36 Eb 1.33N 25.20 E
Banamba 34 Dc 13.32N 7.27W
Bananal, Ilha do- [Braz.] 52 Kg 11.30S 50.15W
Bananal, Ilha do- [Braz.] 55 Dc 17.05S 56.25W
Bananga 25 Ig 6.57N 93.54 E
Banarli 15 Kh 41.04N 27.20 E
Banās 25 Fc 25.54N 76.45 E
Banās, Ra's- 30 Kf 23.54N 35.48 E
Banat 5 If 45.30N 21.00 E
Banat 15 Dd 45.30N 21.00 E
Banaz 24 Cc 38.46N 29.46 E
Banaz 24 Cc 38.12N 29.14 E
Banbar 27 Fe 30.48N 94.52 E
Banbridge/Droichead na Banna 9 Gg 54.21N 6.16W
Banbury 9 Li 52.04N 1.20W
Banco, Punta- 49 Fi 8.23N 83.09W
Bancroft 44 Ic 45.03N 77.51W
Bānda 25 Gc 25.29N 80.20 E
Banda, Kepulauan-=Banda Islands (EN) 26 Ig 4.35S 129.55 E
Banda, Laut-=Banda Sea (EN) 57 De 5.00S 128.00 E
Banda, Punta- 48 Ab 31.45N 116.45W
Banda Aceh 22 Li 5.34N 95.20 E
Bandai-San 29 Gc 37.38N 140.04 E
Banda Islands (EN)=Banda, Kepulauan- 26 Ig 4.35S 129.55 E
Bandak 8 Ce 59.25N 8.15 E
Bandama 30 Gh 5.10N 4.58W
Bandama Blanc 34 Dd 6.54N 5.31W
Bandar Beheštī 23 Jd 25.18N 60.37 E
Bandar-e 'Abbās 22 Hg 27.11N 56.17 E
Bandar-e Anzalī 23 Gb 37.28N 49.27 E
Bandar-e Būshehr 22 Hq 28.59N 50.50 E
Bandar-e Chīrū 24 Oi 26.43N 53.43 E
Bandar-e Deylam 23 Hg 30.05N 50.07 E
Bandar-e-Gaz 24 Od 36.47N 53.59 E
Bandar-e-Khomeynī 24 Mg 30.25N 49.08 E
Bandar-e Lengeh 23 Hd 26.33N 54.53 E
Bandar-e Māh Shahr 23 Gc 30.33N 49.12 E
Bandar-e Maqām 23 Hd 26.56N 53.29 E
Bandar-e Moghūyeh 24 Pi 26.35N 54.31 E
Bandar-e-Rīg 24 Nh 29.29N 50.38 E
Bandar-e-Torkeman 23 Hb 36.54N 54.05 E
Bandar Seri Begawan 22 Ni 4.53N 114.56 E
Banda Sea (EN)=Banda, Laut- 57 De 5.00S 128.00 E
Bande 13 Eb 42.02N 7.58W
Bandeira, Pico da- 52 Lh 20.26S 41.47W
Bandeirantes 55 Ga 13.41S 50.48W
Bandeirantes, Ilha dos- 55 Ff 23.22S 53.50W
Bandera 56 Hc 28.54S 62.16W
Bandera, Alto- 49 Ld 18.49N 70.37W
Banderas, Bahía de- 47 Cd 20.40N 105.25W
Bandiagara 34 Ec 14.20N 3.37W
Bandiat 11 Gi 45.46N 0.20 E
Bandırma 23 Ca 40.20N 27.58 E
Bandirma Körfezi 15 Ki 40.25N 28.00 E
Bandol 11 Lk 43.08N 5.45 E
Bandon 46 Ce 43.07N 124.25W
Bandon/Abhainn na Bandan 9 Ej 51.40N 8.30W
Bandon/Droichead na Bandan 9 Ej 51.45N 8.45W
Ban Don, Ao- 25 Jg 9.20N 99.25 E
Bandundu [2] 36 Cc 5.00S 17.00 E
Bandundu 31 Ii 3.18S 17.20 E
Bandung 22 Mj 6.54S 107.36 E
Bāneh 24 Ke 35.59N 45.53 E
Banes 47 Id 20.58N 75.43W
Banff [Alta.-Can.] 42 Ff 51.10N 115.34W
Banff [Scot.-U.K.] 9 Kd 57.40N 2.31W
Banfora 34 Ec 10.38N 4.46W
Banga 36 Dd 5.57S 20.28 E
Bangalore 22 Jh 12.59N 77.35 E
Bangangté 34 Hd 5.09N 10.31 E
Bangar 26 Gf 4.43N 115.04 E
Bangassou 31 Jh 4.44N 22.49 E
Bangeta, Mount- 60 Di 6.16S 147.04 E
Banggai 26 Hg 1.34S 123.30 E
Banggai, Kepulauan-=Banggai Archipelago (EN) 26 Hg 1.30S 123.15 E
Banggai, Selat- 26 Hg 1.55S 124.00 E
Banggai Archipelago (EN)=Banggai, Kepulauan- 26 Hg 1.30S 123.15 E
Banggi, Pulau- 26 Ge 7.17N 117.12 E
Banghāzī=Benghazi (EN) 31 Je 32.07N 20.04 E
Banghāzī=Benghazi (EN) [3] 33 Dd 27.00N 20.30 E
Bangka, Pulau- [Indon.] 26 If 1.48N 125.09 E
Bangka, Pulau- [Indon.] 21 Mj 2.15S 106.00 E
Bangka, Selat-=Bangka Strait (EN) 26 Eg 2.20S 105.45 E
Bangkalan 26 Fh 7.02S 112.44 E
Bangka Strait (EN)=Bangka, Selat- 26 Eg 2.20S 105.45 E
Bangkinang 26 Df 0.21N 101.02 E
Bangko 26 Dg 2.05S 102.17 E
Bangkok (EN)=Krung Thep 22 Mh 13.45N 100.31 E
Bangladesh [1] 22 Kg 24.00N 90.00 E
Bangli 26 Gh 8.27S 115.21 E
Bangolo 34 Dd 7.01N 7.09W
Bangong Co 27 Ce 33.45N 79.15 E
Bangor [Me.-U.S.] 43 Nc 44.49N 68.47W
Bangor [Wales-U.K.] 9 Ih 53.13N 4.08W
Bangor/Beannchar 9 Hg 54.40N 5.40W
Bangoran 35 Bd 8.42N 19.06 E
Bangsund 7 Cd 64.24N 11.24 E
Bangu 36 Dd 9.05S 23.44 E
Bangued 26 Hc 17.36N 120.37 E
Bangui [C.A.R.] 31 Ih 4.22N 18.35 E
Bangui [Phil.] 26 Hc 18.32N 120.46 E
Bangweulu, Lake- 30 Jj 11.05S 29.45 E
Bangweulu Swamps 36 Fe 11.30S 30.15 E
Banhā 33 Fc 30.28N 31.11 E
Ban Houayxay 25 Kd 20.18N 100.26 E
Bani 30 Gg 14.30N 4.12W
Bani 47 Je 18.17N 70.20W
Bani, Jbel- 30 Gf 28.30N 9.00W
Bani Bangou 34 Fb 15.03N 2.42 E
Banie 10 Kc 53.08N 14.38 E
Banifing 34 Dc 12.43N 6.25W
Banī Forūr, Jazīreh-ye- 24 Pi 26.07N 54.28 E
Banihal Pass 25 Fb 33.15N 75.09 E
Banija 14 Ke 45.10N 16.10 E
Banikoara 34 Fc 11.18N 2.26 E
Banī ma 'Ārid 33 Ie 20.42N 47.42 E
Banī Mazār 33 Fd 28.30N 30.48 E
Banī Muḥammadīyāt 24 Di 27.17N 31.05 E
Banī Suwayf 33 Fd 29.05N 31.05 E
Banī Tonb 24 Pi 26.12N 54.56 E
Banī Walīd 33 Bc 31.46N 13.59 E
Bāniyās 23 Ec 33.15N 35.41 E
Banja 15 Hg 42.33N 24.50 E
Banja Koviljača 15 Ce 44.30N 19.11 E
Banja Luka 14 Lf 44.46N 17.10 E
Banjarmarsin 22 Nj 3.20S 114.35 E
Banjul 31 Fg 13.27N 16.35W
Bank 16 Pj 39.27N 49.14 E
Bankas 34 Ec 14.05N 3.31W
Bankeryd 8 Fg 57.51N 14.07 E
Banket 37 Ec 17.23S 30.24 E
Bankhead Lake 44 Di 33.30N 87.15W
Bankilaré 34 Fc 14.35N 0.44 E
Bankja 15 Gg 42.42N 23.08 E
Ban Kongmi 25 Lf 14.31N 106.55 E
Banks [Can.] 38 Gb 73.15N 121.30W
Banks [Can.] 42 Ef 53.25N 130.10W
Banks, Iles-=Banks Islands (EN) 57 Hf 13.50S 167.35 E
Banks Island 59 Ib 10.10S 142.15 E
Banks Islands (EN)=Banks, Iles- 57 Hf 13.50S 167.35 E
Banks Lake 46 Fc 47.45N 119.15W
Banks Peninsula 57 Ii 43.40S 172.40 E
Banks Strait 59 Jh 40.40S 148.10 E
Bann/An Bhanna 9 Gf 55.10N 6.46W
Ban Na San 25 Jg 8.53N 99.17 E
Bannerman Town 44 Im 24.40N 76.09W
Banning 46 Gj 33.56N 116.52W
Bannock Range 46 Ie 42.30N 112.20W
Bannu 25 Eb 32.59N 70.36 E
Bañolas/Banyoles 13 Ob 42.07N 2.46 E
Bánovce nad Bebravou 10 Oh 48.44N 18.15 E
Banqiao 27 Hf 25.28N 104.02 E
Banská Bystrica 10 Ph 48.44N 19.09 E
Banská Štiavnica 10 Oh 48.27N 18.55 E
Bansko 15 Gh 41.50N 23.29 E
Bānswāra 25 Ed 23.33N 74.27 E
Banta 35 Ge 1.13N 42.30 E
Bantenan, Tanjung- 26 Fh 8.47S 114.33 E
Bantry/Beanntrai 9 Dj 51.41N 9.27W
Bantry Bay/Bá Bheanntraí 9 Dj 51.38N 9.48W
Bañuela 13 Hf 38.24N 4.11W
Banyak, Kepulauan-=Banyak Islands (EN) 26 Cf 2.10N 97.15 E
Banyak Islands (EN)=Banyak, Kepulauan- 26 Cf 2.10N 97.15 E
Banyo 34 Hd 6.45N 11.49 E
Banyoles/Bañolas 13 Ob 42.07N 2.46 E
Banyuls-sur-Mer 11 Jl 42.29N 3.08 E
Banyuwangi 22 Nj 8.12S 114.21 E
Banzare Coast 66 Ie 67.00S 126.00 E
Banzare Seamounts (EN) 66 Df 58.50S 77.44 E
Banzart [3] 32 Ib 37.00N 9.30 E
Banzart=Bizerte (EN) 31 He 37.17N 9.52 E
Banzart, Buḩayrat- 14 Dm 37.11N 9.52 E
Bao'an 27 Jg 22.35N 114.10 E
Bao'an → Zhidan 27 Id 36.48N 108.46 E
Baochang → Taibus Qi 27 Kc 41.55N 115.22 E
Baode 27 Jd 38.59N 111.07 E
Baodi 28 De 39.43N 117.18 E
Baoding 22 Nf 38.47N 115.30 E
Baofeng [China] 27 Je 33.48N 113.14 E
Baofeng [China] 28 Bh 33.52N 113.04 E
Baoji 22 Mf 34.26N 107.12 E
Baokang 27 Je 31.49N 111.13 E
Baokang → Horqin Zuoyi Zhongqi 27 Lc 44.06N 123.19 E
Bao Loc 25 Lf 11.32N 107.48 E
Baoqing 27 Nb 46.20N 132.11 E
Baoro 35 Bd 5.40N 15.58 E
Baoshan 22 Lg 25.09N 99.12 E
Baotou 22 Me 40.38N 110.00 E
Baoulé [Afr.] 30 Gg 12.35N 6.34W
Baoulé [Mali] 30 Gg 13.33N 9.54W
Baoying 28 Eh 33.15N 119.18 E
Bapaume 11 Id 50.06N 2.51 E
Baqên (Dartang) 27 Fe 31.58N 94.00 E
Bāqerābād 24 Ne 34.56N 50.50 E
Ba'qūbah 23 Fc 33.45N 44.38 E
Baquedano 56 Gb 23.20S 65.51W
Bar 12 Ge 49.42N 4.50 E
Bar 16 Ee 49.02N 27.40 E
Bar [Yugo.] 15 Cg 42.05N 19.06 E
Barabai 26 Gg 2.35S 115.23 E
Barabevú 55 Bk 33.20S 61.52W
Barabinsk 22 Jd 55.21N 78.21 E
Barabinskaja Step 20 Ce 55.00N 79.00 E
Baraboo 45 Le 43.28N 89.45W
Baracaldo 13 Ja 43.18N 2.59W
Baracoa 47 Jd 20.21N 74.30W
Bărăganului, Cîmpia- 15 Ke 44.55N 27.15 E
Baragoi 36 Gb 1.47N 36.47 E
Bārah 35 Ec 13.42N 30.22 E
Barahona 47 Je 18.12N 71.06W
Barak 24 Gd 36.51N 37.59 E
Baraka 35 Fb 18.13N 37.35 E
Barakah 35 Fb 18.13N 37.35 E
Barakāt 35 Ec 14.20N 33.36 E
Barakī Barak 23 Kc 33.58N 68.58 E
Baram 26 Ff 4.36N 113.59 E
Baram 26 Ff 4.36N 113.58 E
Baramanni 50 Gi 7.50N 59.13W
Barama River 50 Gi 7.40N 59.15W
Barāmūla 25 Eb 34.12N 74.21 E
Bāran 25 Fc 25.06N 76.31 E
Baran 7 Hi 54.29N 30.19 E
Baraniha 20 Lc 68.31N 168.25 E
Baranja 14 Me 46.00N 18.30 E
Baranoa 49 Jh 10.49N 75.03W
Baranof 40 Le 57.00N 135.00W

Index Symbols

[1] Independent Nation
[2] State, Region
[3] District, County
[4] Municipality
[5] Colony, Dependency
Continent
Physical Region
Historical or Cultural Region
Mount, Mountain
Volcano
Hill
Mountains, Mountain Range
Hills, Escarpment
Plateau, Upland
Pass, Gap
Plain, Lowland
Delta
Salt Flat
Valley, Canyon
Crater, Cave
Karst Features
Depression
Polder
Desert, Dunes
Forest, Woods
Heath, Steppe
Oasis
Cape, Point
Coast, Beach
Cliff
Peninsula
Isthmus
Sandbank
Island
Atoll
Rock, Reef
Islands, Archipelago
Rocks, Reefs
Coral Reef
Well, Spring
Geyser
River, Stream
Waterfall Rapids
River Mouth, Estuary
Lake
Salt Lake
Intermittent Lake
Reservoir
Swamp, Pond
Canal
Glacier
Ice Shelf, Pack Ice
Ocean
Sea
Gulf, Bay
Strait, Fjord
Lagoon
Bank
Seamount
Tablemount
Ridge
Shelf
Basin
Escarpment, Sea Scarp
Fracture
Trench, Abyss
National Park, Reserve
Point of Interest
Recreation Site
Cave, Cavern
Historic Site
Ruins
Wall, Walls
Church, Abbey
Temple
Scientific Station
Airport
Port
Lighthouse
Mine
Tunnel
Dam, Bridge

Baranoviči 6 Ie 53.08N 26.02 E
Baranovka 16 Ed 50.18N 27.41 E
Baranya [2] 10 Oj 46.05N 18.15 E
Barão de Capanema 55 Da 13.19S 57.52W
Barão de Cotegipe 55 Fh 27.37S 52.23W
Barão de Grajaú 54 Je 6.45S 43.01W
Barão de Melgaço 54 Gg 16.13S 55.58W
Baraque de Fraiture 11 Ld 50.15N 5.45 E
Baratang 25 If 12.13N 92.45 E
Barataria Bay 45 Ll 29.22N 89.57W
Barat Daya, Kepulauan- 21 Oj 7.25S 128.00 E
Barāwe 31 Lh 1.09N 44.03 E
Barbacena 53 Lh 21.14S 43.46 E
Barbacoas [Ven.] 49 Li 9.49N 70.03W
Barbacoas [Ven.] 50 Ch 9.29N 66.58W
Barbacoas, Bahía de- 49 Jh 10.10N 75.35W
Barbado, Rio- 55 Cb 15.12S 58.58W
Barbados [1] 39 Nh 13.10N 59.32W
Barbados 38 Nh 13.10N 59.32W
Barbados Ridge (EN) 50 Gf 12.45N 59.35W
Barbagia 14 Dj 40.10N 9.10 E
Barbar 35 Eb 18.01N 33.59 E
Bárbara 54 Dd 0.52S 72.30W
Barbaros 15 Ki 40.54N 27.27 E
Barbas, Cabo- 32 De 22.18N 16.41W
Barbastro 13 Mb 42.02N 0.08 E
Barbate de Franco 13 Gh 36.12N 5.55W
Barbeau Peak 38 La 81.54N 75.01W
Barbeton 37 Ee 25.48S 31.03 E
Barbezieux 11 Fi 45.28N 0.09W
Barbourville 44 Fg 36.52N 83.53W
Barboza Ferraz 55 Fg 24.04S 52.03W
Barbuda 38 Mh 17.38N 61.48W
Barcaldine 58 Fg 23.33S 145.17 E
Barcarrota 13 Ff 38.31N 6.51W
Barcău 15 Ec 46.59N 21.07 E
Barcellona Pozzo di Gotto 14 Jl 38.09N 15.13 E
Barcelona [3] 13 Nc 41.40N 2.00 E
Barcelona [Sp.] 6 Gg 41.23N 2.11 E
Barcelona [Ven.] 54 Fa 10.08N 64.42W
Barcelonnette 11 Mj 44.23N 6.39 E
Barcelos [Braz.] 54 Fd 0.58S 62.57W
Barcelos [Port.] 13 Dc 41.32N 8.37W
Barcin 10 Nd 52.52N 17.57 E
Barcoo River 59 Ie 25.30S 142.50 E
Barcs 10 Nk 45.58N 17.28 E
Barda 16 Oi 40.25N 47.05 E
Bardagé 35 Ba 22.06N 16.28 E
Bardaï 31 If 21.21N 16.59 E
Bardār Shāh 24 Ld 36.45N 47.15 E
Bārdaw 14 En 36.49N 10.08 E
Barddhamān 25 Hd 23.15N 87.51 E
Bardejov 10 Rg 49.18N 21.16 E
Bardēre 31 Lh 2.20N 42.20 E
Bardeskan 24 Qe 35.12N 57.58 E
Bardīyah 33 Ed 31.46N 25.06 E
Bardonecchia 14 Ae 45.05N 6.42 E
Bardsey 9 Ii 52.45N 4.45W
Bardstown 44 Eg 37.49N 85.28W
Barēda 31 Mg 11.52N 51.03 E
Bareilly 22 Jg 28.25N 79.23 E
Barencevo More=Barents Sea (EN) 67 Jd 74.00N 36.00 E
Barentin 11 Ge 49.33N 0.57 E
Barentsburg 67 Kd 78.04N 14.14 E
Barentshav=Barents Sea (EN) 67 Jd 74.00N 36.00 E
Barentsøya 41 Oc 78.27N 21.15 E
Barents Sea (EN)= Barencevo More 67 Jd 74.00N 36.00 E
Barents Sea (EN)= Barentshav 67 Jd 74.00N 36.00 E
Barents Trough (EN) 5 la 73.00N 29.00 E
Barentu 35 Fb 15.06N 37.36 E
Barfleur 11 Ee 49.40N 1.15W
Barfleur, Pointe de- 11 Ee 49.42N 1.16W
Barga 22 Kf 30.48N 81.17 E
Bārgāl 35 Ic 11.18N 51.07 E
Bargarh 25 Gd 21.20N 83.37 E
Barguelonne 11 Gj 44.07N 0.50 E
Barguzin 20 Ff 53.27N 108.58 E
Barguzinski Hrebet 20 Ff 54.30N 110.00 E
Bar Harbor 44 Mc 44.23N 68.13W
Barhi 25 Hd 24.18N 85.25 E
Bari [3] 35 Hd 10.00N 50.00 E
Bari 6 Hg 41.08N 16.51 E
Bari, Terra di- 14 Kj 41.05N 16.50 E
Ba Ria 25 Lf 10.30N 107.10 E
Barīdī, Ra's- 24 Gj 24.17N 37.31 E
Barika 13 Ri 35.22N 5.05 E
Barīm 33 Hg 12.39N 43.25 E
Barima, Rio- 50 Fh 8.35N 60.25W
Barima River 50 Fh 8.35N 60.25W
Barinas 54 Db 8.38N 70.12W
Barinas [2] 54 Eb 8.10N 70.00W
Baring, Cape- 42 Fb 70.01N 117.28W
Baringa 36 Db 0.45N 20.52 E
Barinitas 49 Li 8.45N 70.25W
Baripāda 25 Hd 21.56N 86.43 E
Bariri 55 Hf 22.04S 48.44W
Bariri, Reprêsa- 55 Hf 22.21S 48.39W
Bārīs 33 Fe 24.40N 30.36 E
Bari Sādri 25 Ed 24.25N 74.28 E
Barisāl 25 Id 22.42N 90.22 E
Barisan, Pegunungan-= Barisan Mountains (EN) 21 Mj 3.00S 102.15 E
Barisan Mountains (EN)= Barisan, Pegunungan- 21 Mj 3.00S 102.15 E
Barito 21 Nj 3.32S 114.29 E
Barjols 11 Lk 43.33N 6.00 E
Barkā' 23 Ie 23.35N 57.55 E
Barkam 27 He 31.45N 102.32 E
Barkan, Ra's-e- 24 Mg 30.01N 49.35 E
Barkava 8 Lh 56.40N 26.45 E
Barkley, Lake- 43 Jd 36.40N 87.55W
Barkley Sound 46 Cb 48.53N 125.20W
Barkly East 37 Df 30.58S 27.33 E
Barkly Tableland 57 Ef 19.00S 138.00 E
Barkly West 37 Ce 28.05S 24.31 E
Barkol 27 Fc 43.35N 92.51 E
Barkol Hu 27 Fc 43.40N 92.39 E
Barlavento [3] 32 Cf 16.10N 24.40W
Bar-le-Duc 11 Lf 48.47N 5.10 E
Barlee, Lake- 57 Cg 29.10S 119.30 E
Barlee Range 59 Dd 23.35S 116.00 E
Barletta 14 Ki 41.19N 16.17 E
Barlinek 10 Lc 53.00N 15.12 E
Barlovento, Islas de-= Windward Islands (EN) 38 Mh 15.00N 61.00W
Barma 26 Jg 1.54S 133.00 E
Barmer 25 Ec 25.45N 71.23 E
Barmera 59 If 34.15S 140.28 E
Barmouth 9 Ii 52.43N 4.03W
Barnard Castle 9 Lg 54.33N 1.55W
Barnaul 22 Kd 53.22N 83.45 E
Barnes Ice Cap 42 Kc 70.00N 73.30W
Barnesville [Ga.-U.S.] 44 Ei 33.04N 84.09W
Barnesville [Mn.-U.S.] 45 Hc 46.39N 96.25W
Barnet, London- 12 Bc 51.39N 0.12W
Barneveld 12 Hb 52.08N 5.34 E
Barnim 10 Jd 52.40N 13.45 E
Barnsley 9 Lh 53.34N 1.28W
Barnstaple 9 Ij 51.05N 4.04W
Barnstaple (Bideford Bay) 9 Ij 51.05N 4.20W
Barnstorf 12 Kb 52.43N 8.30 E
Barntrup 12 Lc 51.59N 9.07 E
Barnwell 44 Gi 33.14N 81.21W
Baro 30 Kh 8.26N 33.14 E
Baro [Chad] 35 Bc 12.12N 18.58 E
Baro [Nig.] 34 Gd 8.36N 6.25 E
Baronnies 11 Lj 44.15N 5.30 E
Barora Fa 63a Db 7.30S 158.20 E
Barora Ite 63a Db 7.36S 158.24 E
Barotseland 36 Df 15.05S 24.00 E
Barqah=Cyrenaica (EN) 33 Dc 31.00N 22.30 E
Barqah=Cyrenaica (EN) 30 Je 31.00N 23.00 E
Barqah, Jabal al- 24 Ej 24.24N 32.34 E
Barqah al Bahrīyah= Marmarica (EN) 30 Je 31.40N 24.30 E
Barqū, Jabal- 14 Dn 36.04N 9.37 E
Barques, Pointe aux- 44 Fc 44.04N 82.58W
Barquisimeto 53 Jd 10.04N 69.19W
Barr 11 Nf 48.24N 7.27 E
Barr, Ra's al- 24 Nj 25.47N 50.34 E
Barra 53 Lg 11.05S 43.10W
Barra 9 Fd 57.00N 7.30W
Barra, Ponta da- 30 Kk 23.47S 35.32 E
Barra, Sound of- 9 Fd 57.10N 7.20W
Barraba 59 Kf 30.22S 150.36 E
Barra Bonita, Reprêsa- 55 Hf 22.38S 48.20W
Barra de Navidad 47 De 19.12N 104.41W
Barra do Bugres 54 Gg 15.05S 57.11W
Barra do Corda 54 Ie 5.30S 45.15W
Barra do Cuanza 36 Bd 9.18S 13.09 E
Barra do Dande 36 Bd 8.28S 13.22 E
Barra do Garças 54 Hg 15.53S 52.15W
Barra Falsa, Ponta da- 30 Kk 22.55S 35.37 E
Barra Head 9 Fe 56.46N 7.36W
Barra Mansa 54 Jh 22.32S 44.11W
Barrāmīyah, Wādī al- 24 Ej 25.00N 33.23 E
Barranca 54 Cd 4.50S 76.42W
Barrancabermeja 53 Ie 7.03N 73.52W
Barrancas [Col.] 49 Kh 10.57N 72.50W
Barrancas [Ven.] 54 Fb 8.42N 62.11W
Barrancas, Arroyo- 55 Cj 30.19S 59.25W
Barranco 55 Db 15.56S 57.41W
Barrancos 13 Ff 38.08N 6.59W
Barranqueras 56 Ic 27.29S 58.56W
Barranquilla 53 Id 10.59N 74.48W
Barranquitas 51a Bb 18.12N 66.23W
Barra Patuca 49 Ef 15.50N 84.17W
Barras 54 Jd 4.15S 42.18W
Barra Velha 55 Hh 26.39S 48.43W
Barre 44 Kc 44.12N 72.30W
Barreira 55 Db 15.24S 57.52W
Barreiras 53 Lg 12.08S 45.00W
Barreirinha 54 Gd 2.47S 57.03W
Barreirinhas 54 Jd 2.45S 42.50W
Barreiro 13 Cf 38.40N 9.04W
Barreiro, Rio- 55 Fb 15.43S 52.45W
Barreiro Grande 55 Jd 18.12S 45.10W
Barreiros 54 Ke 8.49S 35.12W
Barren 55 If 12.16N 93.51 E
Barren, Iles- 37 Gc 18.25S 43.40 E
Barren Islands 40 Ie 58.55N 152.15W
Barretos 56 Kb 20.33S 48.33W
Barrie 44 Jh 44.24N 79.40W
Barrier Bay 66 Ge 67.45S 81.10 E
Barrier Islands 63a Db 7.44S 158.32 E
Barrington Tops 59 Kf 32.00S 151.28 E
Barro Alto 55 Hb 15.04S 48.58W
Barrois, Plateau du- 11 Kf 48.45N 5.00 E
Barros, Lagoa dos- 55 Gi 29.56S 50.23W
Barros, Tierra de- 13 Ff 38.40N 6.25W
Barroso 55 Ke 21.11S 43.58W
Barrouallie 51n Ba 13.14N 61.17W
Barrow [Ak.-U.S.] 39 Db 71.17N 156.47W
Barrow [Arg.] 55 Bn 38.18S 60.14W
Barrow/An Bhearú 9 Gi 52.10N 7.00W
Barrow, Point- 38 Db 71.23N 156.30W
Barrow Creek 58 Eg 21.33S 133.53 E
Barrow-in-Furness 9 Jg 54.07N 3.14W
Barrow Island 57 Cg 20.50S 115.25 E
Barrow Range 59 Fe 26.05S 127.30 E
Barrow Strait 38 Jb 74.21N 94.10W
Barru 26 Gg 4.25S 119.37 E
Barry 9 Jj 51.24N 3.18W
Barrytown 62 De 42.14S 171.20 E
Barsakelmes, Ostrov- 18 Bb 45.40N 59.55 E
Barsalogo 34 Ec 13.25N 1.03W
Barsatas 19 Hf 48.13N 78.33 E
Baršč/Forst 10 Ke 51.44N 14.38 E
Bārsi 25 Fe 18.14N 75.42 E
Barsinghausen 10 Fd 52.18N 9.27 E
Barstow 43 De 34.54N 117.01W
Bar-sur-Aube 11 Kf 48.14N 4.43 E
Bar-sur-Seine 11 Kf 48.07N 4.22 E
Baršyn 19 Gf 49.45N 69.36 E
Bārta/Barta 8 Ih 56.57N 20.57 E
Barta/Bārta 8 Ih 56.57N 20.57 E
Barţallah 24 Jd 36.23N 43.25 E
Bartang 18 Hf 37.55N 71.33 E
Barth 10 Ib 54.22N 12.44 E
Bartholomew, Bayou- 45 Jj 32.43N 92.04W
Bartica 54 Gb 6.24N 58.37W
Bartın 24 Eb 41.38N 32.21 E
Bartle Frere, Mount- 57 Ff 7.23S 145.49 E
Bartlesville 43 Hd 36.45N 95.59W
Bartlett 45 Gf 41.53N 98.33W
Bartoszyce 10 Qb 54.16N 20.49 E
Bartow 44 Gl 27.54N 81.50W
Barú, Isla- 49 Jh 10.26N 75.35W
Barú, Volcán 47 Hg 8.48N 82.33W
Bārūd, Ra's- 24 Ei 26.47N 33.39 E
Barumini 14 Dk 39.42N 9.01 E
Barun-Bogdo-Ula 27 Hb 45.00N 100.20 E
Bāruni 25 Hc 25.29N 85.59 E
Barun-Šabartuj, Gora- 20 Fg 49.43N 109.58 E
Barun-Urt 27 Jb 46.40N 113.12 E
Barwice 10 Mc 53.45N 16.22 E
Barwon River 57 Fg 30.00S 148.05 E
Barycz 10 Me 51.42N 16.15 E
Baryš 7 Lj 53.40N 47.08 E
Baryš 7 Li 54.35N 46.47 E
Bāsa'īdū 24 Pi 26.39N 55.17 E
Basail 55 Ch 27.52S 59.18W
Basankusu 36 Cb 1.14N 19.48 E
Basaral, Ostrov- 18 Ib 46.25N 73.45 E
Basauri 13 Ja 43.13N 2.53W
Basavilbaso 55 Ck 32.22S 58.53W
Bas Champs 12 Dd 50.20N 1.41 E
Basco 26 Hb 20.27N 121.58 E
Bascuñán, Cabo- 56 Fc 28.51S 71.30W
Base 11 Gj 44.17N 0.18 E
Basel [2] 14 Bc 47.35N 7.40 E
Basel/Bâle 6 Gf 47.30N 7.30 E
Baselland [2] 14 Bc 47.30N 7.45 E
Basentello 14 Kj 40.40N 16.23 E
Basento 14 Kj 40.20N 16.49 E
Başeu 15 Kb 47.44N 27.15 E
Basey 26 Id 11.17N 125.04 E
Bashi Channel (EN)=Bashi Haixia 27 Lg 22.00N 121.00 E
Bashi Haixia=Bashi Channel (EN) 27 Lg 22.00N 121.00 E
Bāsht 24 Ng 30.21N 51.09 E
Ba Shui 28 Ci 30.25N 115.02 E
Basilan 21 Oi 6.34N 122.03 E
Basilan City (Isabela) 22 Oi 6.42N 121.58 E
Basilan Strait 26 He 6.49N 122.05 E
Basildon 9 Nj 51.34N 0.25 E
Basilicata [2] 14 Kj 40.30N 16.30 E
Basingstoke 9 Lj 51.16N 1.05W
Basjanovski 17 Jg 58.19N 60.44 E
Başkale 24 Jc 38.02N 44.00 E
Baskatong, Réservoir- 42 Jg 46.47N 75.50W
Baškaus 20 Df 51.09N 87.43 E
Baskil 24 Hc 38.35N 38.40 E
Baškortostan respublika 19 Fe 55.00N 56.00 E
Baskunčak, ozero 16 Oe 48.10N 46.55 E
Bašmakovo 16 Mc 53.12N 43.03 E
Bāsmenj 24 Ld 37.59N 46.29 E
Basoko 36 Db 1.14N 23.36 E
Basongo 36 Dc 4.20S 20.24 E
Basque Provinces (EN)= Euzkadi/Vascongadas 13 Ja 43.00N 2.30W
Basque Provinces (EN)= Vascongadas/Euzkadi 13 Ja 43.00N 2.30W
Basra (EN)=Al Başrah 22 Gf 30.30N 47.47 E
Bas Rhin [3] 11 Nf 48.35N 7.40 E
Bass, Ilots de- 57 Mg 27.55S 143.26W
Bassano 46 Ia 50.47N 112.28W
Bassano del Grappa 14 Fe 45.46N 11.44 E
Bassar 34 Fd 9.15N 0.47 E
Bassas da India 30 Lk 21.25S 39.42 E
Bassein → Pathein 22 Lh 16.47N 94.44 E
Bassein → Vasai 25 Ee 19.21N 72.48 E
Basse-Kotto [3] 35 Ce 5.00N 21.30 E
Basse-Pointe 51h Ab 14.52N 61.07W
Basses, Pointe des- 51e Bc 15.52N 61.17W
Basse-Sambre 12 Gd 50.27N 4.37 E
Basse Santa Su 34 Cc 13.19N 14.13W
Basse-Terre 50 Fd 16.10N 61.40W
Basse-Terre 47 Le 16.00N 61.44W
Basseterre 47 Le 17.18N 62.43W
Bassett 45 Ge 42.35N 99.32W
Bassigny 11 Lf 48.00N 5.30 E
Bassikounou 32 Ff 15.52N 5.58W
Bassila 34 Fd 9.01N 1.40 E
Bass Islands 63c Ba 9.56S 167.17 E
Basso, Plateau de- 30 Jg 17.20N 22.40 E
Bass Strait 57 Fh 39.20S 145.30 E
Bassum 12 Kb 52.51N 8.44 E
Basswood Lake 45 Kb 48.05N 91.35W
Båstad 7 Ch 56.26N 12.51 E
Bastak 24 Pi 27.14N 54.22 E
Bastām 24 Pd 36.29N 55.04 E
Bastenaken/Bastogne 11 Le 50.00N 5.43 E
Bastia [Fr.] 6 Gg 42.42N 9.27 E
Bastia [It.] 14 Gg 43.04N 12.33 E
Bastogne/Bastenaken 11 Le 50.00N 5.43 E
Bastrop 45 Kj 32.47N 91.55W
Basudan Ula 27 Fe 33.05N 91.00 E
Basuo → Dongfang 27 Ih 19.14N 108.39 E
Basuto 37 Dc 19.52S 26.32 E
Bas-Zaïre [2] 36 Bd 5.30S 14.30 E
Bata 31 Hh 1.51N 9.45 E
Batabanó, Golfo de- 47 Hd 22.15N 82.30W
Batagaj 20 Ic 67.38N 134.38 E
Batagaj-Alyta 20 Ic 67.53N 130.31 E
Bataguaçu 54 Hh 21.42S 52.22W
Bataiporã 55 Ff 22.20S 53.17W
Batajnica 15 De 44.54N 20.17 E
Batajsk 19 Df 47.05N 39.46 E
Batak 15 Hh 41.57N 24.13 E
Bataklık Gölü 24 Ed 37.42N 33.07 E
Batala 25 Fb 31.48N 75.12 E
Batalha 13 De 39.39N 8.50W
Batama 36 Eb 0.56N 26.39 E
Batamaj 20 Hd 63.30N 129.25 E
Batamšinski 19 Fe 50.36N 58.17 E
Batan 26 Hb 20.30N 121.50 E
Batang 27 Ge 30.02N 99.10 E
Batanga 36 Ac 0.21S 9.18 E
Batangafo 35 Bd 7.18N 18.18 E
Batangas 22 Oh 13.45N 121.03 E
Batanghari 26 Mj 1.00S 104.00 E
Batan Islands 21 Og 20.30N 121.50 E
Batanta, Pulau- 26 Jg 0.50S 130.40 E
Bátaszék 10 Oj 46.11N 18.44 E
Batatais 55 Ie 20.53S 47.37W
Batavia 44 Hd 43.00N 78.11W
Bat-Cengel 27 Hb 47.47N 101.58 E
Batchawana 44 Eb 46.58N 84.34W
Batchelor 59 Gb 13.04S 131.01 E
Bātdâmbâng 22 Mh 13.06N 103.12 E
Batéké, Plateaux- 36 Cc 3.30S 15.45 E
Batel, Esteros del- 55 Ci 28.30S 58.20W
Batemans Bay 59 Kg 35.43S 150.11 E
Batesburg 44 Gi 33.56N 81.33W
Batesville [Ar.-U.S.] 45 Ki 35.46N 91.39W
Batesville [Ms.-U.S.] 45 Li 34.18N 90.00W
Bath [Eng.-U.K.] 9 Kj 51.23N 2.22W
Bath [Me.-U.S.] 44 Md 43.55N 69.49W
Bath [N.B.-Can.] 44 Nb 46.32N 67.33W
Bath [St.C.N.] 51c Ab 17.08N 62.37W
Batha 35 Bc 14.00N 19.00 E
Bathinda 25 Fb 30.12N 74.57 E
Bá Thrá Lí/Tralee Bay 9 Di 52.15N 9.59W
Bathsheba 50 Gf 13.13N 59.31W
Bá Thuath Reanna/ Liscannor Bay 9 Di 52.55N 9.25W
Bathurst 38 Ib 76.00N 100.30W
Bathurst [Austl.] 59 Jf 33.25S 149.35 E
Bathurst [N.B.-Can.] 39 Me 47.36N 65.39W
Bathurst, Cape- 38 Gb 70.35N 128.00W
Bathurst Inlet 38 Ic 68.10N 108.50W
Bathurst Inlet 39 Ic 66.50N 108.01W
Bathurst Island 57 Ef 11.35S 130.25 E
Bati 35 Gc 11.13N 40.01 E
Batié 34 Ed 9.53N 2.55W
Bāţin, Wādī al- 23 Gc 30.25N 47.35 E
Batman 23 Fb 37.52N 41.07 E
Batman 24 Id 37.45N 41.00 E
Batna [3] 32 Ib 35.10N 6.00 E
Batna 31 He 35.34N 6.11 E
Ba To 25 Lf 14.46N 108.44 E
Bato Bato 26 Ge 5.06N 119.50 E
Batoka 36 Ef 16.47S 27.15 E
Baton Rouge 39 Jf 30.23N 91.11W
Batopilas 48 Fd 27.01N 107.44W
Batouri 34 He 4.26N 14.22 E
Batovi 55 Fb 15.53S 53.24W
Batovi, Coxilha de- 55 Ej 30.33S 54.27W
Båtsfjord 7 Ga 70.33N 29.44 E
Bat-Sumber 27 Ib 48.25N 106.42 E
Batticaloa 25 Gg 7.43N 81.42 E
Batti Malv 25 Ig 8.50N 92.51 E
Battipaglia 14 Ij 40.37N 14.58 E
Battle 12 Cd 50.55N 0.30 E
Battle 42 Gf 52.42N 108.15W
Battle Creek 46 Kb 48.36N 109.11W
Battle Creek 43 Jc 42.19N 85.11W
Battle Harbour 39 Nd 52.17N 55.35W
Battle Mountain 43 Dc 40.38N 116.56W
Battonya 10 Rj 46.17N 21.01 E
Battowia Island 51n Bb 12.58N 61.09W
Batu 35 Fd 6.59N 39.37 E
Batu, Kepulauan-=Batu Islands (EN) 21 Lj 0.18S 98.28 E
Batuasa 26 Jg 3.32S 130.08 E
Batuata, Pulau- 26 Hh 6.12S 122.42 E
Batudaka, Pulau- 26 Hg 0.28S 121.48 E
Batui 26 Hg 1.17S 122.33 E
Batu Islands (EN)=Batu, Kepulauan- 21 Lj 0.18S 98.28 E
Batumi 6 Kg 41.38N 41.38 E
Batu Pahat 26 Df 1.51N 102.56 E
Baturaja 26 Dg 4.08S 104.10 E
Baturino 20 De 57.45N 85.12 E
Baturité 54 Kd 4.20S 38.53W
Batz, Île de- 11 Bf 48.45N 4.01W
Bau 26 Ff 1.25N 110.09 E
Baubau 22 Oj 5.28S 122.38 E
Baucau 26 Ih 8.27S 126.27 E
Bauchi 31 Hg 10.19N 9.50 E
Bauchi [2] 34 Hc 10.40N 10.00 E
Bauchi Plateau 34 Gc 10.00N 9.30 E
Baud 11 Cg 47.52N 3.01W
Baudette 45 Ib 48.43N 94.36W
Baudó, Serrania de- 54 Cb 6.00N 77.05W
Baudour, Saint-Ghislain- 12 Fd 50.29N 3.49 E
Baugé 11 Fg 47.33N 0.06W
Bauges 11 Mi 45.38N 6.10 E
Baúl, Cerro- 48 Ii 17.38N 100.19W
Baula 26 Hg 4.09S 121.41 E
Bauld, Cape- 38 Nd 51.38N 55.25W
Bauman Fiord 42 Ia 77.45N 86.00W
Baume-les-Dames 11 Mg 47.21N 6.22 E
Baunach 10 Gg 49.59N 10.51 E
Baunani 63a Ec 9.08S 160.51 E
Baunei 14 Dj 40.02N 9.40 E
Baures 54 Ff 13.35S 63.35W
Bauru 53 Lh 22.19S 49.04W
Baús 55 Fd 18.19S 53.10W
Baús, Serra dos- 55 Fd 18.20S 53.25W
Bauska 7 Fh 56.24N 24.13 E
Bautzen/Budyšin 10 Ke 51.11N 14.26 E
Bavaria (EN)=Bayern [2] 10 Hg 49.00N 11.30 E
Bavaria (EN)=Bayern 5 Hf 49.00N 11.30 E
Bavarian Forest (EN)= Bayerischer Wald 10 Ig 49.00N 12.55 E
Bavay 12 Fd 50.18N 3.47 E
Båven 8 Ge 59.00N 16.55 E
Bavispe 48 Eb 30.24N 108.50W
Bavispe, Rio de- 48 Ec 29.15N 109.11W
Bavly 7 Mi 54.26N 53.18 E
Bawah, Pulau- 26 Ef 2.31N 106.03 E
Bawal, Pulau- 26 Fg 2.44S 110.06 E
Bawe 58 Ee 2.59S 134.43 E
Bawean, Pulau- 26 Fh 5.46S 112.40 E
Bawku 34 Ec 11.03N 0.15W
Baxian 27 Kd 39.03N 116.24 E
Baxoi 27 Ge 30.07N 96.55 E
Bay [3] 35 Ge 2.50N 43.30 E
Bay/Baicheng 27 Dc 41.46N 81.52 E
Bayamo 47 Id 20.23N 76.39W
Bayamón 49 Nd 18.24N 66.09W
Bayan 28 Ia 46.05N 127.24 E
Bayanbulak 27 Dc 43.05N 84.05 E
Bayanga 35 Be 2.53N 16.19 E
Bayan Gol 27 Gd 37.18N 96.50 E
Bayan Gol → Dengkou 22 Me 40.25N 106.59 E
Bayan Har Shan 21 Lf 34.20N 97.00 E
Bayan Har Shankou 27 Ge 34.06N 97.36 E
Bayan Hot → Alxa Zuoqi 27 Id 38.50N 105.32 E
Bayan Hure → Chen Barag Qi 27 Kb 49.21N 119.25 E
Bayan Huxu → Horqin Youyi Zhongqi 27 Lb 45.04N 121.27 E
Bayano, Lago de- 49 Hi 9.00N 78.30W
Bayan Obo 27 Ic 41.50N 109.58 E
Bayan Qagan 28 Ga 46.11N 123.59 E
Bayan Qagan → Qaha Youyi Houqi 28 Ed 41.28N 113.10 E
Bayan Ul Hot → Xi Ujimqin Qi 27 Kc 44.31N 117.33 E
Bayas 48 Gf 23.32N 104.50W
Bayat 24 Fb 40.39N 34.15 E
Bayauca 55 Bl 34.51S 61.18W
Bayawan 26 He 9.20N 123.00 E
Bayāẓ 24 Pg 30.42N 55.28 E
Bayāzeh 24 Pf 30.42N 55.28 E
Baybay 26 Hd 10.41N 124.48 E
Bayburt 23 Fa 40.16N 40.15 E
Bay City [Mi.-U.S.] 43 Kc 43.36N 83.53W
Bay City [Tx.-U.S.] 43 Hf 29.09N 95.39W
Bayerische Alpen 10 H 47.30N 11.30 E
Bayerischer Wald=Bavarian Forest (EN) 10 Ig 49.00N 12.55 E
Bayern=Bavaria (EN) 5 Hf 49.00N 11.30 E
Bayern=Bavaria (EN) [2] 10 Hg 49.00N 11.30 E
Bayes, Cap- 63b Be 20.57S 165.25 E
Bayeux 11 Fe 49.16N 0.42W
Bayfield 45 Kc 46.49N 90.49W
Bay Fiord 42 Ja 79.00N 84.00W
Baygorria 55 Dk 32.52S 56.44W
Baygorria, Lago Artificial de- 55 Dk 33.05S 57.00W
Bayḩān al Qişāb 33 Ig 14.48N 45.44 E
Bayındır 24 Bc 38.13N 27.40 E
Bayjī 24 Je 34.56N 43.29 E
Bay Minette 44 Dj 30.53N 87.47W
Baynūnah 24 Ok 23.50N 52.50 E
Bayombong 26 Hc 16.29N 121.09 E
Bayona 13 Db 42.07N 8.51W
Bayonnaise Seamount (EN) 57 Jf 12.00S 179.30W
Bayonne 6 Fg 43.29N 1.29W
Bayou Bodcau Lake 45 Jj 32.58N 93.30W
Bayou D'Arbonne Lake 45 Jj 32.45N 92.27W
Bayramiç 15 Jj 39.48N 26.37 E
Bayreuth 10 Hg 49.57N 11.35 E
Bayrūt=Beirut (EN) 22 Ff 33.53N 35.30 E
Bay Saint Louis 45 Lk 30.19N 89.20W
Bay Springs 45 Lk 31.59N 89.17W
Bayt al Faqīh 23 Fg 14.31N 43.17 E
Baytik Shan 27 Fb 45.15N 90.50 E
Bayt Laḩm=Bethlehem (EN) 24 Fg 31.43N 35.12 E
Baytown 43 If 29.44N 94.58W
Bayuda Desert (EN)= Bayyūḑah, Şaḩrā'- 30 Kg 18.00N 33.00 E
Bayunglencir 26 Dg 2.03S 103.41 E
Bayview 46 Gc 48.00N 116.30W
Bay View 62 Gc 39.26S 176.52 E
Bayy al Kabīr 33 Cc 31.11N 15.53 E
Bayyūḑah, Şaḩrā'-=Bayuda Desert (EN) 30 Kg 18.00N 33.00 E
Baza 13 Jg 37.29N 2.46W
Baza, Sierra de- 13 Jg 37.15N 2.45W
Bazardjuzju, Gora- 5 Kg 41.13N 47.51 E
Bazaruto, Ilha do- 37 Fd 21.40S 35.25 E
Bazas 11 Fj 44.26N 0.13W
Bazhong 27 Ie 31.54N 106.42 E
Bazoches-sur-Vesle 12 Fe 49.19N 3.37 E
Baztán 13 Ka 43.09N 1.31W
Beach 43 Gb 46.55N 103.52W
Beachy Head 9 Nk 50.44N 0.16 E
Beacon 44 Ke 41.31N 73.59W
Beaconsfield [Austl.] 59 Jh 41.12S 146.48 E
Beaconsfield [Eng.-U.K.] 12 Bc 51.36N 0.38W
Beagle, Canal- 56 Gh 54.53S 68.10W
Beagle Gulf 59 Gb 12.00S 130.20 E
Bealach an Doirin/ Ballaghaderreen 9 Eh 53.55N 8.35W
Béalanana 37 Hb 14.33S 48.44 E
Béal an Átha/Ballina 9 Dg 54.07N 9.09W
Béal an Bheara/Gweebarra Bay 9 Eg 54.52N 8.20W
Béal Átha Fhirdhia/Ardee 9 Gh 53.52N 6.33W
Béal Átha hAmhnais/ Ballyhaunis 9 Eh 53.46N 8.46W

Index Symbols

[1] Independent Nation · [2] State, Region · [3] District, County · Municipality · Colony, Dependency · Continent · Physical Region · Historical or Cultural Region · Mount, Mountain · Volcano · Hill · Mountains, Mountain Range · Hills, Escarpment · Plateau, Upland · Pass, Gap · Plain, Lowland · Delta · Salt Flat · Valley, Canyon · Crater, Cave · Karst Features · Depression · Polder · Desert, Dunes · Forest, Woods · Heath, Steppe · Oasis · Cape, Point · Coast, Beach · Cliff · Peninsula · Isthmus · Sandbank · Island · Atoll · Rock, Reef · Islands, Archipelago · Rocks, Reefs · Coral Reef · Well, Spring · Geyser · River, Stream · Waterfall Rapids · River Mouth, Estuary · Lake · Salt Lake · Intermittent Lake · Reservoir · Swamp, Pond · Canal · Glacier · Ice Shelf, Pack Ice · Ocean · Sea · Gulf, Bay · Strait, Fjord · Lagoon · Bank · Seamount · Tablemount · Ridge · Shelf · Basin · Escarpment, Sea Scarp · Fracture · Trench, Abyss · National Park, Reserve · Point of Interest · Recreation Site · Cave, Cavern · Historic Site · Ruins · Wall, Walls · Church, Abbey · Temple · Scientific Station · Airport · Port · Lighthouse · Mine · Tunnel · Dam, Bridge

Béal Átha na Muice/ Swinford	9	Eh	53.57N	8.57W
Béal Átha na Sluaighe/ Ballinasloe	9	Eh	53.20N	8.13W
Béal Átha Seanaidh/ Ballyshannon	9	Eg	54.30N	8.11W
Beale, Cape-	46	Cb	48.44N	125.20W
Béal Easa/Foxford	9	Dh	53.59N	9.07W
Béal Feirste/Belfast	6	Fe	54.35N	5.55W
Beal Range	59	Ie	25.30S	141.30 E
Béal Tairbirt/Belturbet	9	Fg	54.06N	7.26W
Beanna Boirche/Mourne Mountains	9	Gg	54.10N	6.04W
Beannchar/Bangor	9	Hg	54.40N	5.40W
Beanntraí/Bantry	9	Dj	51.41N	9.27W
Bear Bay	42	Ia	75.45N	86.30W
Beardmore	45	Mb	49.36N	87.57W
Beardstown	45	Kg	39.59N	90.26W
Bear Island (EN)= Björnöya	5	Ha	74.30N	19.00 E
Bear Islands (EN)=Medveži, Ostrova-	21	Sb	70.52N	161.26 E
Bear Lake	43	Ec	42.00N	111.20W
Bear Lodge Mountains	45	Dd	44.35N	104.15W
Béarn	11	Fk	43.20N	0.45W
Bearpaw Mountains	46	Kb	48.15N	109.30W
Bear Peninsula	66	Of	74.36S	110.50W
Bear River	46	If	41.30N	112.08W
Bearskin Lake	42	If	53.57N	90.59W
Beās	25	Eb	31.10N	74.59 E
Beas de Segura	13	Jf	38.15N	2.53W
Beata, Cabo-	47	Je	17.36N	71.25W
Beata, Isla-	49	Le	17.35N	71.31W
Beata Ridge (EN)	47	Je	16.00N	72.30W
Beatrice	43	Hc	40.16N	96.44W
Beatrice, Cape-	59	Hb	14.15S	137.00 E
Beatton	42	Fe	56.06N	120.22W
Beatton River	42	Fe	56.10N	120.25W
Beatty	43	Dd	36.54N	116.46W
Beattyville	44	Ia	48.52N	77.10W
Beatys Butte	46	Fe	42.23N	119.20W
Beau-Bassin	37a	Bb	20.13S	57.27 E
Beaucaire	11	Kk	43.48N	4.38 E
Beaucamps-le-Vieux	12	De	49.50N	1.47 E
Beaucanton	44	Ha	49.05N	79.15W
Beauce	11	Hf	48.22N	1.50 E
Beaudesert	59	Ke	27.59S	153.00 E
Beaufort [Mala.]	26	Ge	5.20N	115.45 E
Beaufort [S.C.-U.S.]	44	Gi	32.26N	80.40W
Beaufort/Befort	12	Ie	49.50N	6.18 E
Beaufort, Massif de-	11	Mi	45.50N	6.40 E
Beaufort Island	66	Kf	76.57S	166.56 E
Beaufort Sea	67	Eb	73.00N	140.00W
Beaufort West	31	Jl	32.20S	22.33 E
Beaugency	11	Hg	47.47N	1.38 E
Beaujolais, Monts du-	11	Kh	46.00N	4.22 E
Beauly	9	Id	57.29N	4.29W
Beaumesnil	12	Ce	49.01N	0.43 E
Beaumetz-lès-Loges	12	Ed	50.14N	2.39 E
Beaumont [Bel.]	12	Gd	50.14N	4.14 E
Beaumont [Fr.]	11	Gj	44.46N	0.46 E
Beaumont [Fr.]	11	Ee	49.40N	1.51W
Beaumont [Fr.]	12	Hf	48.51N	5.47 E
Beaumont [Ms.-U.S.]	45	Lk	31.11N	88.55W
Beaumont [N.Z.]	62	Cf	45.49S	169.32 E
Beaumont [Tx.-U.S.]	39	Jf	30.05N	94.06W
Beaumont-de-Lomagne	11	Gk	43.53N	0.59 E
Beaumont-en-Argonne	12	He	49.32N	5.03 E
Beaumont-le-Roger	12	Ce	49.05N	0.47 E
Beaumont-sur-Oise	12	Ee	49.08N	2.17 E
Beaumont-sur-Sarthe	11	Gf	48.13N	0.08 E
Beaune	11	Kg	47.02N	4.50 E
Beaupré	44	Lb	47.03N	70.53W
Beauraing	12	Gd	50.07N	4.48 E
Beaurepaire	11	Li	45.20N	5.03 E
Beausejour	42	Hf	50.04N	96.33W
Beautemps Beaupré	63b	Ce	20.25S	166.08 E
Beauvais	11	Ie	49.26N	2.05 E
Beauval	12	Ed	50.06N	2.20 E
Beauvoir-sur-Mer	11	Dh	46.55N	2.03W
Beaver [Ak.-U.S.]	40	Jc	66.22N	147.24W
Beaver [Ok.-U.S.]	45	Fh	36.48N	100.30W
Beaver [Ut.-U.S.]	43	Ed	38.17N	112.38W
Beaver Creek [Co.-U.S.]	45	Ef	40.20N	103.33W
Beaver Creek [U.S.]	45	Ec	47.20N	103.39W
Beaver Creek [U.S.]	45	Gf	40.04N	99.20W
Beaver Creek [U.S.]	45	Ee	43.25N	103.59W
Beaver Dam	45	Le	43.28N	88.50W
Beaver Falls	44	Ge	40.45N	80.21W
Beaverhead Mountains	46	Id	45.00N	113.20W
Beaver Island	44	Ec	45.40N	85.31W
Beaver Lake	45	Jh	36.20N	93.55W
Beaver River [U.S.]	45	Gh	36.10N	98.45W
Beaver River [Ut.-U.S.]	46	Ig	39.10N	112.57W
Beaverton	46	Dd	45.29N	122.48W
Beāwar	25	Ec	26.06N	74.19 E
Bebedouro	56	Kb	20.56S	48.28W
Becan	48	Oh	18.37N	89.35W
Becanchén	48	Oh	19.50N	89.22W
Beccles	9	Oi	52.28N	1.34 E
Bečej	15	Dd	45.37N	20.03 E
Beceni	15	Jd	45.23N	26.47 E
Becerreá	13	Eb	42.51N	7.10W
Becerro, Cayos-	49	Ff	15.57N	83.17W
Béchar	31	Ge	31.37N	2.13W
Béchar [3]	32	Gd	30.00N	2.00W
Becharof Lake	40	He	58.00N	156.30W
Bechet	15	Gf	43.46N	23.57 E
Bechevin Bay	40	Ge	55.00N	163.27W
Bechyně	10	Kg	49.18N	14.28 E
Beckingen	12	Ie	49.24N	6.42 E
Beckley	43	Kd	37.46N	81.12W
Beckum	10	Ee	51.45N	8.02 E
Beckumer Berge	12	Kc	51.43N	8.10 E
Beclean	15	Hb	47.11N	24.11 E
Bédarieux	11	Jk	43.37N	3.09 E
Bedburg-Hau	12	Ic	51.46N	6.11 E
Bedele	35	Fd	8.27N	36.22 E
Bedesa	35	Gd	8.53N	40.46 E
Bedford	9	Mi	52.10N	0.50W
Bedford [Eng.-U.K.]	9	Mi	52.08N	0.29W
Bedford [In.-U.S.]	44	Df	38.52N	86.29W
Bedford [Pa.-U.S.]	44	He	40.00N	78.31W
Bedford [Va.-U.S.]	44	Hg	37.20N	79.31W
Bedford Level	9	Ni	52.30N	0.05 E
Bedford Point	51p	Bb	12.13N	61.36W
Bedfordshire [3]	9	Mi	52.05N	0.20W
Bednja	14	Kd	46.18N	16.45 E
Bednodemjanovsk	16	Mc	53.55N	43.12 E
Bedourie	59	Hd	24.21S	139.28 E
Bedum	12	Ia	53.18N	6.39 E
Beech Grove	44	Df	39.43N	86.03W
Beecroft Head	59	Kg	35.01S	150.50 E
Beef Island	51a	Db	18.27N	64.31W
Beelitz	10	Id	52.14N	12.58 E
Beemster	12	Gb	52.34N	4.56 E
Beerfelden	12	Ke	49.34N	8.59 E
Beernem	12	Fc	51.09N	3.20 E
Beerse	12	Gc	51.19N	4.52 E
Beersel	12	Gd	50.46N	4.18 E
Beersheba (EN)=Be'er Shevà	23	Dc	31.14N	34.47 E
Be'er Shevà=Beersheba (EN)	23	Dc	31.14N	34.47 E
Beerze	12	Hc	51.36N	5.19 E
Beeskow	10	Kd	52.10N	14.14 E
Beestekraal	37	De	25.23S	27.38 E
Beeston	9	Li	52.56N	1.12W
Beethoven Peninsula	66	Qf	71.40S	73.45W
Beetsterzwaag, Opsterland-	12	Ia	53.03N	6.04 E
Beeville	43	Hf	28.24N	97.45W
Befale	36	Db	0.28N	20.58 E
Befandriana Nord	37	Hc	15.15S	48.32 E
Befandriana Sud	37	Gd	22.06S	43.54 E
Befori	36	Db	0.06N	22.17 E
Befort/Beaufort	12	Ie	49.50N	6.18 E
Bega	15	Dd	45.13N	20.19 E
Bega	58	Fh	36.40S	149.50 E
Bégard	11	Cf	48.38N	3.18W
Begejski kanal	15	Dd	45.27N	20.27 E
Beggars Point	51d	Bb	17.10N	61.48W
Bègle	11	Fj	44.48N	0.32W
Begna	7	Bf	60.35N	10.00 E
Begoml	8	Mj	54.46N	28.14 E
Begunicy	8	Me	59.31N	29.30 E
Behābād	24	Pg	31.52N	55.57 E
Behbehān	23	Hc	30.35N	50.14 E
Behring Point	49	Ia	24.27N	77.43W
Behshahr	23	Hb	36.43N	53.34 E
Bei'an	22	Oe	48.16N	126.29 E
Beibu Wan=Tonkin, Gulf of- (EN)	21	Mh	20.00N	108.00 E
Beida He	27	Gc	40.18N	99.01 E
Beihai	22	Mg	21.31N	109.07 E
Bei Hulsan Hu	27	Gd	36.55N	95.55 E
Bei Jiang	27	Jg	23.02N	112.58 E
Beijing=Peking (EN)	22	Nf	39.55N	116.23 E
Beijing Shi (Pei-ching Shih) [4]	27	Kc	40.15N	116.30 E
Beïla	32	Df	18.10N	15.53W
Beilen	12	Ib	52.52N	6.32 E
Beiliutang He	28	Eg	34.12N	119.33 E
Beilrstroom	12	Ib	52.41N	6.12 E
Beilsteim	12	Jd	50.07N	7.15 E
Beilu He	27	Fe	34.34N	94.00 E
Beinamar	35	Bd	8.40N	15.23 E
Beine-Nauroy	12	Ge	49.15N	4.13 E
Beipiao	27	Lc	41.49N	120.45 E
Beira	31	Kj	19.50S	34.52 E
Beira Alta	13	Ed	40.40N	7.35W
Beira Baixa	13	Ee	39.55N	7.30W
Beira Litoral	13	Dd	40.15N	8.25W
Beiru He	28	Bh	33.40N	113.35 E
Beirut (EN)=Bayrūt	22	Ff	33.53N	35.30 E
Bei Shan	21	Le	41.30N	96.00 E
Beitstad	7	Cd	64.05N	11.22 E
Beiuş	15	Fc	46.40N	22.21 E
Beiwei Tan	27	Kg	21.10N	116.10 E
Beizhen [China]	27	Kd	37.24N	117.59 E
Beizhen [China]	28	Fd	41.36N	121.47 E
Beja	13	Ef	38.01N	7.52W
Beja [2]	13	Eg	37.58N	7.50W
Bejaïa [3]	32	Ib	36.40N	5.10 E
Bejaïa	31	He	36.45N	5.05 E
Bejaia, Golfe de-	13	Rh	36.45N	5.20 E
Béjar	13	Gd	40.23N	5.46W
Beji	25	Dc	29.47N	67.58 E
Bejneu	19	Ff	45.15N	55.05 E
Bejsug	16	Kf	46.02N	38.35 E
Bejsugski Liman	16	Kf	46.05N	38.25 E
Bekabad	19	Gg	40.13N	69.14 E
Bekasi	26	Eh	6.14S	106.59 E
Bekdaš	19	Fg	41.31N	52.40 E
Békés	10	Rj	46.46N	21.08 E
Békés [2]	10	Qj	46.45N	21.00 E
Békéscsaba	10	Rj	46.41N	21.06 E
Bekilli	15	Mk	38.14N	29.26 E
Bekily	37	Hd	24.12S	45.18 E
Bekkai	29a	Db	43.25N	145.07 E
Bekoji	35	Fd	7.32N	39.15 E
Bekopaka	37	Gc	19.08S	44.45 E
Bekovo	16	Mc	52.29N	43.45 E
Bela [India]	25	Gc	25.56N	81.59 E
Bela [Pak.]	25	Dc	26.14N	66.19 E
Bélabo	34	He	4.52N	13.10 E
Bela Crkva	15	Ee	44.54N	21.26 E
Bela Dila	25	Ge	18.40N	80.55 E
Bela Floresta	55	Ge	20.36S	51.16W
Belaga	26	Ff	2.42N	113.47 E
Belaja	20	Mc	65.30N	173.15 E
Belaja	5	Ld	56.00N	54.32 E
Belaja	16	Kg	45.03N	39.25 E
Belaja Cerkov	6	Jf	49.49N	30.07 E
Belaja Gora	20	Jc	68.30N	146.15 E
Belaja Holunica	19	Fd	58.53N	50.50 E
Belaja Kalitva	19	Ef	48.09N	40.49 E
Bela Krajina	14	Je	45.35N	15.15 E
Bela Lorena	55	Ib	15.13S	46.01W
Belang	26	Hf	0.57N	124.47 E
Bela Palanka	15	Ff	43.13N	22.19 E
Belarbi	13	Li	35.09N	0.27W
Belarus (EN) = Byelarus'	19	Ce	53.50N	28.00 E
Belasica	15	Fh	41.21N	22.50 E
Belau → Palau (EN)	58	Ed	7.30N	134.30 E
Bela Vista [Braz.]	54	Gh	22.06S	56.31W
Bela Vista [Braz.]	55	Dc	17.37S	57.01W
Bela Vista [Moz.]	37	Ee	26.20S	32.40 E
Belawan	26	Cf	3.47N	98.41 E
Běła Woda/Weißwasser	10	Ke	51.31N	14.38 E
Belayan	26	Gg	0.14S	116.36 E
Belbo	14	Cf	44.54N	8.31 E
Bel'c'	19	Cf	47.46N	27.55 E
Bełchatow	10	Pe	51.22N	19.21 E
Belcher Channel	42	Ia	77.20N	4.30W
Belcher Islands	38	Ld	56.20N	79.30W
Belchite	13	Lc	41.18N	0.45W
Bełczyna	10	Ne	51.25N	17.50 E
Belebej	19	Fe	54.10N	54.07 E
Belecke, Warstein-	12	Kc	51.29N	8.20 E
Beled	10	Ni	47.28N	17.06 E
Beled Wēyne	31	Lh	4.47N	45.12 E
Bélel	34	Hd	7.03N	14.26 E
Belém [Moz.]	37	Fb	14.08S	35.58 E
Belém [Braz.]	53	Lf	1.27S	48.29W
Belem [Mex.]	48	Dd	27.45N	110.28W
Belém de São Francisco	54	Ke	8.46S	38.58W
Belen	43	Fe	34.40N	106.46W
Belén [Arg.]	56	Gc	27.39S	67.02W
Belén [Nic.]	49	Eh	11.30N	85.53W
Belén [Par.]	55	Df	23.30S	57.06W
Belén [Ur.]	55	Dj	30.47S	57.47W
Belén, Cuchilla de-	55	Dj	30.55S	56.30W
Belén de Escobar	55	Cl	34.21S	58.47W
Belene	15	If	43.39N	25.07 E
Bélep, Iles-	57	Hf	19.45S	163.40 E
Beles	35	Fc	10.55N	35.10 E
Belev	16	Jc	53.50N	36.10 E
Beleye	35	Fc	11.24N	36.10 E
Belfast [Me.-U.S.]	44	Mc	44.27N	69.01W
Belfast [S.Afr.]	37	Ee	25.43S	30.03 E
Belfast/Béal Feirste	6	Fe	54.35N	5.55W
Belfast Lough/Loch Lao	9	Hg	54.40N	5.50W
Belfield	45	Ec	46.53N	103.12W
Belford	9	Lf	55.36N	1.49W
Belfort	11	Mg	47.45N	7.00 E
Belgaum	22	Jh	15.52N	74.30 E
Belgica Bank (EN)	67	Ld	78.28N	15.00W
Belgicafjella	66	Df	72.35S	31.10 E
België/Belgique=Belgium (EN) [1]	6	Ge	50.30N	4.30 E
Belgique/België=Belgium (EN) [1]	6	Ge	50.30N	4.30 E
Belgium (EN)=België/ Belgique [1]	6	Ge	50.30N	4.30 E
Belgium (EN)=Belgique/ België [1]	6	Ge	50.30N	4.30 E
Belgorod	6	Je	50.36N	36.35 E
Belgorod-Dnestrovski	19	Df	46.12N	30.17 E
Belgorodskaja Oblast [3]	19	De	50.45N	37.30 E
Belgrade (EN) = Beograd	6	Ig	44.50N	20.30 E
Bel Haïrane	32	Ic	31.17N	6.20 E
Beli	34	Hd	7.52N	10.58 E
Belice	14	Gm	37.35N	12.52 E
Beli Drim	15	Dg	42.05N	20.20 E
Belidži	16	Pi	41.53N	48.20 E
Beli Lom	15	If	43.41N	26.00 E
Beli Manastir	14	Me	45.46N	18.37 E
Belimbegovo	15	Eh	42.00N	21.35 E
Belin	11	Fj	44.30N	0.47W
Belinga	36	Bb	1.04N	13.12 E
Belinski	16	Mc	52.58N	43.29 E
Belinyu	26	Eg	1.38S	105.46 E
Beliş	15	Gc	46.39N	23.02 E
Beli Timok	15	Ff	43.55N	22.18 E
Belize [1]	39	Kh	17.15N	88.45W
Belize (British Honduras)	49	Ce	17.35N	88.35W
Belize City	39	Kh	17.30N	88.12W
Belize River	49	Ce	17.32N	88.14W
Beljajevka	16	Gf	46.29N	30.14 E
Beljanica	15	Ee	44.07N	21.43 E
Belka	8	Mg	57.40N	29.47 E
Belkovski, Ostrov-	20	Ia	75.30N	136.00 E
Bellac	11	Hh	46.07N	1.03 E
Bella Coola	42	Ef	52.22N	126.46W
Bellagio	14	De	45.59N	9.15 E
Bellaire [Oh.-U.S.]	44	Ge	40.02N	80.46W
Bellaire [Tx.-U.S.]	45	Il	29.43N	95.28W
Bellaria-Igea Marina	14	Gf	44.09N	12.28 E
Bellary	22	Jh	15.09N	76.56 E
Bella Unión	55	Dj	30.15S	57.35W
Bella Vista [Arg.]	56	Ic	28.30S	59.03W
Bella Vista [Par.]	55	Df	22.08S	56.31W
Bellavista, Capo-	14	Dk	39.56N	9.43 E
Bell Bay	42	Jb	71.10N	84.55W
Belle-Anse	49	Kd	18.14N	72.04W
Belledonne	11	Mi	45.18N	6.08 E
Bellefontaine [Mart.]	51h	Ab	14.40N	61.10W
Bellefontaine [Oh.-U.S.]	44	Fe	40.22N	83.45W
Belle Fourche	43	Gc	44.40N	103.51W
Belle Fourche River	45	Ed	44.26N	102.19W
Bellegarde	11	If	47.59N	2.26 E
Bellegarde-sur-Valserine	11	Lh	46.06N	5.49 E
Belle Glade	44	Gl	26.41N	80.40W
Belle Ile	5	Ff	47.19N	3.11W
Belle Isle	42	Lf	51.55N	55.20W
Belle Isle, Strait of-	38	Nd	51.35N	56.30W
Bellencombre	12	De	49.42N	1.14 E
Belleplaine	51q	Ab	13.15N	59.34W
Belleville [Fr.]	11	Kh	46.06N	4.45 E
Belleville [Il.-U.S.]	45	Lg	38.31N	90.00W
Belleville [Ks.-U.S.]	45	Hg	39.49N	97.38W
Belleville [Ont.-Can.]	42	Jh	44.10N	77.23W
Bellevue [Nb.-U.S.]	45	If	41.09N	95.54W
Bellevue [Wa.-U.S.]	46	Dc	47.37N	122.12W
Belley	11	Li	45.46N	5.41 E
Bellheim	12	Ke	49.12N	8.17 E
Bellin → Kangirsuk	39	Lc	60.00N	70.01W
Bellingham [Eng.-U.K.]	9	Kf	55.09N	2.16W
Bellingham [Wa.-U.S.]	39	Ge	48.46N	122.29W
Bellingsfors	8	Ef	58.59N	12.15 E
Bellingshausen	66	Re	62.12S	58.56W
Bellingshausen Ice Shelf	66	Ce	71.00S	89.00W
Bellingshausen Sea (EN)	66	Pf	71.00S	85.00W
Bellinzona	14	Dd	46.11N	9.02 E
Bello	54	Cb	6.19N	75.34W
Bellocq	55	Bl	35.55S	61.32W
Bellona, Récifs-	57	Gg	21.00S	159.00 E
Bellona Island	60	Fj	11.17S	159.47 E
Bellot Strait	42	Ib	72.00N	94.30W
Bellow Falls	44	Kd	43.08N	72.28W
Bell Peninsula	42	Jd	63.45N	81.30W
Bell River	42	Jg	49.49N	77.39W
Bell Rock → Inchcape	9	Ke	56.26N	2.24W
Bellsund	41	Nc	77.39N	14.15 E
Belluno	14	Gd	46.09N	12.13 E
Bell Ville	56	Hd	32.37S	62.42W
Bellville	37	Bf	33.53S	18.36 E
Belmond	45	Je	42.51N	93.37W
Belmont	44	Hd	42.14N	78.02W
Belmonte [Braz.]	54	Kg	15.51S	38.54W
Belmonte [Port.]	13	Ed	40.21N	7.21W
Belmonte [Sp.]	13	Je	39.34N	2.42W
Belmopan	39	Kh	17.15N	88.46W
Beloeil	12	Fd	50.35N	3.43 E
Belogorsk	22	Od	50.57N	128.25 E
Belogorsk	16	Ig	45.01N	34.33 E
Belogradčik	15	Ff	43.38N	22.41 E
Belogradčiški	15	Ff	43.38N	22.28 E
Belo Horizonte	53	Lg	19.55S	43.56W
Beloit [Ks.-U.S.]	45	Gg	39.28N	98.06W
Beloit [Wi.-U.S.]	43	Jc	42.31N	89.02W
Belojarovo	20	Hf	51.35N	128.55 E
Belojarski	19	Gc	63.40N	66.45 E
Beloje More=White Sea (EN)	5	Kb	66.00N	44.00 E
Beloje Ozero=White Lake (EN)	5	Jc	60.11N	37.35 E
Belokany	16	Oi	41.43N	46.28 E
Belomorsk	6	Jc	64.29N	34.43 E
Belomorsko-Baltijski Kanal =White Sea-Baltic Canal (EN)	5	Jc	63.30N	34.48 E
Belomorsko-Kulojskoje Plato	7	Jd	65.20N	41.50 E
Beloozersk	16	Dc	52.28N	25.13 E
Belopolje	19	De	51.09N	34.18 E
Belorečensk	16	Kg	44.43N	39.52 E
Beloreck	19	Fe	53.58N	58.24 E
Belorusskaja Grjada	16	Ec	53.50N	27.00 E
Belorusskaja Sovetskaja Socialističeskaja Respublika → Belarus	19	Ce	53.50N	28.00 E
Belorusskaja SSR/ Belaruskaja Sovetskaja Socialistyčnaja Respublika → Belarus	19	Ce	53.50N	28.00 E
Belorusskaja SSR → Belarus	19	Ce	53.50N	28.00 E
Belo-sur-Mer	37	Gd	20.44S	44.00 E
Belo-sur-Tsiribihina	37	Gc	19.39S	44.32 E
Belot, Lac -	42	Ec	66.50N	126.20W
Belovo	20	Df	54.25N	86.18 E
Belovodsk	16	Ke	49.10N	39.33 E
Belovodskoe	18	Jc	42.47N	74.13 E
Belozersk	19	Dd	60.03N	37.48 E
Belper	12	Aa	53.02N	1.28W
Belted Range	46	Gh	37.25N	116.10W
Belton [Mo.-U.S.]	45	Ig	38.49N	94.32W
Belton [Tx.-U.S.]	45	Hk	31.04N	97.28W
Belton Lake	45	Hk	31.08N	97.32W
Belturbet/Béal Tairbirt	9	Fg	54.06N	7.26W
Beluha	21	Ke	49.48N	86.35 E
Belvedere Marittimo	14	Jk	39.37N	15.52 E
Belvidere	45	Le	42.15N	88.50W
Bely	7	Hi	55.50N	32.58 E
Bely, Ostrov-=Bely Island (EN)	21	Jb	73.10N	70.45 E
Belyando River	59	Jd	21.38S	146.50 E
Bely Čeremoš	15	Ia	48.06N	25.04 E
Bely Island (EN)=Bely, Ostrov-	21	Jb	73.10N	70.45 E
Bely Jar	20	De	58.26N	85.03 E
Belyje Berega	16	Ic	53.12N	34.42 E
Belz	16	Dd	50.23N	24.03 E
Bełżec	10	Tf	50.24N	23.26 E
Belzoni	45	Kj	33.11N	90.29W
Bełżyce	10	Se	51.11N	22.18 E
Bemaraha, Plateau de-	30	Lj	19.00S	45.15 E
Bembe	36	Bd	7.02S	14.18 E
Bembéréké	34	Fc	10.13N	2.40 E
Bembézar	13	Gg	37.45N	5.13W
Bembridge	12	Ad	50.41N	1.05W
Bemidji	43	Ib	47.29N	94.53W
Ben	24	Nf	32.32N	50.45 E
Benāb	23	Gb	37.18N	46.05 E
Benabarre/Benavarn	13	Mb	42.07N	0.29 E
Bena Dibele	36	Dc	4.07S	22.50 E
Bénaize	11	Hh	46.34N	1.04 E
Benalla	59	Jg	36.33S	145.59 E
Benares → Vārānasi	22	Kg	25.20N	83.00 E
Benasc/Benasque	13	Mb	42.36N	0.32 E
Benasque/Benasc	13	Mb	42.36N	0.32 E
Benavarn/Benabarre	13	Mb	42.07N	0.29 E
Benavente	13	Gc	42.00N	5.41W
Benbecula	9	Fd	57.27N	7.20W
Bencheng → Luannan	28	Ee	39.30N	118.42 E
Ben-Chicao, Col de-	13	Oh	36.12N	2.51 E
Bend	43	Cc	44.03N	121.19W
Bendaja	34	Cd	7.10N	11.15W
Bendel [2]	34	Gd	6.00N	5.50 E
Bendela	36	Cc	3.18S	17.36 E
Bender Bäyla	31	Mh	9.30N	50.30 E
Bendersiyada	35	Hc	11.14N	48.57 E
Bendery	19	Cf	46.48N	29.22 E
Bendigo	58	Fh	36.46S	144.17 E
Bendorf	12	Jd	50.26N	7.34 E
Bēne/Bene	8	Jh	56.28N	23.01 E
Bene/Bēne	8	Jh	56.28N	23.01 E
Bénéna	34	Ec	13.06N	4.22W
Benepú, Rada-	65d	Ac	27.10S	109.25W
Benešov	10	Kg	49.47N	14.40 E
Benevento	14	Ii	41.08N	14.45 E
Bengal	21	Kg	24.00N	90.00 E
Bengal, Bay of- (EN)	21	Kh	15.00N	90.00 E
Bengamisa	36	Eb	0.57N	25.10 E
Bengbis	34	He	3.27N	12.27 E
Bengbu	22	Nf	32.47N	117.23 E
Benghazi (EN)=Banghāzī	31	Je	32.07N	20.04 E
Benghazi (EN)= Banghāzī [3]	33	Dd	27.00N	20.30 E
Benghisa Point	14	Io	35.50N	14.35 E
Bengkalis	26	Df	1.28N	102.08 E
Bengkulu [3]	26	Dg	3.48S	102.16 E
Bengkulu	22	Mj	3.48S	102.16 E
Bengo, Baía do-	30	Ii	8.43S	13.21 E
Bengo He	28	Eg	35.04N	118.22 E
Bengough	46	Mb	49.24N	105.08W
Bengtsfors	7	Cg	59.02N	12.13 E
Benguela	31	Ij	12.35S	13.26 E
Benguela [3]	36	Be	12.00S	15.00 E
Benguerir	32	Fc	32.14N	7.57W
Benguérua, Ilha-	37	Fd	21.53S	35.26 E
Bengue Viejo	49	Ce	17.05N	89.08W
Bengut, Cap-	32	Hb	36.55N	3.54 E
Beni	31	Jh	0.30N	29.28 E
Beni [2]	54	Ef	14.00S	65.30W
Beni, Rio-	52	Jg	10.23S	65.24W
Beni Abbes	32	Gc	30.08N	2.10W
Beni Baufrah	13	Hi	35.05N	4.18W
Benicarló	13	Md	40.25N	0.26 E
Benicasim	13	Md	40.03N	0.04 E
Beni Chougran, Monts des-	13	Mi	35.30N	0.15 E
Benidorm	13	Lf	38.32N	0.08W
Beni Enzar	13	Ji	35.14N	2.57W
Beni Haoua	13	Nh	36.32N	1.34 E
Beni Mellal	31	Ge	32.20N	6.21W
Beni Mellal [3]	32	Fc	32.30N	6.30W
Benin	34	Gd	5.45N	5.04 E
Bénin=Benin (EN) [1]	31	Hh	9.30N	2.15 E
Bénin (Dahomey) [1]	31	Hh	9.30N	2.15 E
Benin (EN)=Bénin [1]	31	Hh	9.30N	2.15 E
Benin, Bight of-	30	Hh	5.30N	4.00 E
Benin City	31	Hh	6.20N	5.38 E
Beni Ounif	32	Gc	32.03N	1.15W
Benisa	13	Mf	38.43N	0.03 E
Beni Saf	13	Ki	35.19N	1.23W
Benisheikh	34	Hc	11.48N	12.29 E
Benito Juárez	48	Mi	17.50N	92.32W
Benito Juárez, Presa-	48	Li	16.27N	95.30W
Benjamen Island	37b	Bb	5.27S	53.21 E
Benjamin	45	Gj	33.35N	99.48W
Benjamín Aceval	55	Dg	24.58S	57.34W
Benjamin Constant	53	If	4.22S	70.02W
Benjamin Hill	48	Db	30.10N	111.10W
Benkei-Misaki	29a	Bb	42.50N	140.11 E
Benkelman	45	Ff	40.03N	101.32W
Benkovac	14	Jf	44.02N	15.37 E
Ben Mehidi	14	Bn	36.46N	7.54 E
Bennett, Lake-	59	Gd	23.50S	131.00 E
Bennett, Ostrov-	20	Ja	76.45N	149.00 E
Benneydale	62	Fc	38.31S	175.21 E
Bennichab	32	Df	19.26N	15.21W
Bennington	44	Kd	42.53N	73.12W
Benom	26	Df	3.50N	102.06 E
Benoni	31	Jk	26.19S	28.27 E
Bénoué=Benue (EN)	30	Hh	7.48N	6.46 E
Benoy	35	Bd	8.59N	16.19 E
Benrath	12	Ic	51.10N	6.52 E
Bensekrane	13	Ki	35.04N	1.13W
Bensheim	10	Eg	49.41N	8.37 E
Ben Slimane	32	Fc	33.37N	7.07W
Benson [Az.-U.S.]	46	Jk	31.58N	110.18W
Benson [Mn.-U.S.]	45	Id	45.19N	95.36W
Benson Point	64g	Ab	1.56N	157.30W
Bent	23	Id	26.17N	59.31 E
Benteng [Indon.]	26	Hg	0.24S	121.59 E
Benteng [Indon.]	26	Hh	6.08N	120.27 E
Bentheim	10	Dd	52.19N	7.10 E
Bentiaba	36	Be	14.29S	12.50 E
Bentinck	25	Jf	11.45N	98.03 E
Bentinck Island	59	Hc	17.05S	139.30 E
Bentiu	35	Dd	9.14N	29.50 E
Bento Conçalves	56	Jc	29.10S	51.31W
Bento Gomes, Rio-	55	Dc	16.40S	57.12W
Benton [Ar.-U.S.]	45	Ji	34.34N	92.35W
Benton [Il.-U.S.]	45	Lg	38.01N	88.55W
Bentong	26	Df	3.32N	101.55 E
Benton Harbor	44	Dd	42.07N	86.27W
Bentonville	45	Ih	36.22N	94.13W
Benua, Pulau-	26	Ef	0.56N	107.27 E
Benue [2]	34	Gd	7.15N	8.20 E
Benue	30	Hh	7.48N	6.46 E
Benue (EN)=Bénoué	30	Hh	7.48N	6.46 E
Benwee Head/An Bhinn Bhuí	9	Dg	54.21N	9.48W
Benxi	22	Oe	41.16N	123.48 E
Beo	26	If	4.15N	126.48 E
Beograd = Belgrade (EN)	6	Ig	44.50N	20.30 E
Beograd-Krnjača	15	De	44.52N	20.28 E
Beograd-Zemun	15	De	44.53N	20.25 E
Béoumi	34	Dd	7.40N	5.34W

Index Symbols

[1] Independent Nation
[2] State, Region
[3] District, County
[4] Municipality
[5] Colony, Dependency
Continent
Physical Region
Historical or Cultural Region
Mount, Mountain
Volcano
Hill
Mountains, Mountain Range
Hills, Escarpment
Plateau, Upland
Pass, Gap
Plain, Lowland
Delta
Salt Flat
Valley, Canyon
Crater, Cave
Karst Features
Depression
Polder
Desert, Dunes
Forest, Woods
Heath, Steppe
Oasis
Cape, Point
Coast, Beach
Cliff
Peninsula
Isthmus
Sandbank
Island
Atoll
Rock, Reef
Islands, Archipelago
Rocks, Reefs
Coral Reef
Well, Spring
Geyser
River, Stream
Waterfall Rapids
River Mouth, Estuary
Lake
Salt Lake
Intermittent Lake
Reservoir
Swamp, Pond
Canal
Glacier
Ice Shelf, Pack Ice
Ocean
Sea
Gulf, Bay
Strait, Fjord
Lagoon
Bank
Seamount
Tablemount
Ridge
Shelf
Basin
Escarpment, Sea Scarp
Fracture
Trench, Abyss
National Park, Reserve
Point of Interest
Recreation Site
Cave, Cavern
Historic Site
Ruins
Wall, Walls
Church, Abbey
Temple
Scientific Station
Airport
Port
Lighthouse
Mine
Tunnel
Dam, Bridge

Beppu 27 Ne 33.17N 131.30 E
Beppu-Wan 29 Be 33.20N 131.35 E
Bequia Head 51n Ba 13.03N 61.12W
Bequia Island 50 Ff 13.01N 61.13W
Beraketa 37 Hd 24.11S 45.42 E
Berati 15 Ci 40.42N 19.57 E
Beratus, Gunung- 26 Gg 1.02S 116.20 E
Berau, Teluk-=McCluer Gulf (EN) 26 Jg 2.30S 132.30 E
Berberá 31 Lg 10.25N 45.02 E
Berbérati 31 Ih 4.16N 15.47 E
Berberia, Cabo- 13 Nf 38.38N 1.23 E
Berbice River 54 Gb 6.17N 57.32W
Berca 15 Jd 45.17N 26.41 E
Berchères-sur-Vesgre 12 Df 48.51N 1.33 E
Berchtesgaden 10 Ii 47.38N 13.00 E
Berck [Fr.] 12 Dd 50.24N 1.36 E
Berck [Fr.] 11 Hd 50.24N 1.34 E
Berck- Berck Plage 12 Dd 50.24N 1.34 E
Berck-Plage, Berck- 12 Dd 50.24N 1.34 E
Berda 16 Jf 46.47N 36.52 E
Berdāle 35 Hd 7.04N 47.51 E
Berdičev 19 Cf 49.53N 28.36 E
Berdigestjah 20 Hd 62.03N 126.50 E
Berdjansk 19 Df 46.43N 36.48 E
Berdsk 20 Df 54.47N 83.05 E
Beregomet 15 Ia 48.10N 25.24 E
Beregovo 19 Cf 48.13N 22.41 E
Bereku 36 Gc 4.27S 35.44 E
Berekua 50 Fe 15.14N 61.19W
Berekum 34 Ed 7.27N 2.35W
Berens 42 Hf 52.21N 97.01W
Berens River 42 Hf 52.22N 97.02W
Beresford 45 He 43.05N 96.47W
Berestečko 10 Vf 50.16N 25.14 E
Bereşti 15 Kc 46.06N 27.53 E
Berettyó 15 Ec 46.59N 21.07 E
Berettyóújfalu 10 Ri 47.13N 21.33 E
Bereza 19 Ce 52.33N 24.58 E
Berezan 16 Gd 50.19N 31.31 E
Berežany 16 De 49.29N 25.00 E
Berezina 16 Dc 53.48N 25.59 E
Berezina 5 Je 52.33N 30.14 E
Berezino 16 Fc 53.51N 29.00 E
Berezino 8 Mj 54.55N 28.16 E
Berezino 15 Mc 46.16N 29.11 E
Bereznegovatoje 16 Hf 47.20N 32.49 E
Bereznik 19 Ec 62.53N 42.42 E
Berezniki 6 Ld 59.24N 56.46 E
Berezno 16 Ed 51.01N 26.45 E
Berezovka 10 Vc 53.40N 25.37 E
Berezovka 17 Hd 64.59N 56.29 E
Berezovka 19 Df 47.12N 30.56 E
Berezovka Višerka 17 Hf 60.55N 56.50 E
Berezovo 19 Gc 63.58N 65.00 E
Berezovski 17 Jh 56.55N 60.50 E
Berezovski 20 De 55.39N 86.16 E
Berezovy 20 If 51.41N 135.52 E
Berga [Sp.] 13 Nb 42.06N 1.51 E
Berga [Swe.] 8 Gg 57.13N 16.02 E
Bergama 23 Cb 39.07N 27.10 E
Bergamo 14 De 45.41N 9.43 E
Bergantiños 13 Da 43.20N 8.45W
Bergby 7 Df 60.56N 17.02 E
Bergen [Ger.] 10 Jb 54.25N 13.26 E
Bergen [Neth.] 12 Gb 52.40N 4.42 E
Bergen [Nor.] 6 Gc 60.23N 5.20 E
Bergen/Mons 11 Jd 50.27N 3.56 E
Bergen aan Zee, Bergen- 12 Gb 52.40N 4.38 E
Bergen-Bergen aan Zee 12 Gb 52.40N 4.38 E
Bergen op Zoom 11 Kc 51.30N 4.17 E
Bergerac 11 Gj 44.51N 0.29 E
Bergeyk 12 Hc 51.19N 5.22 E
Bergh 12 Ic 51.53N 6.16 E
Bergheim 10 Cf 50.58N 6.39 E
Bergh-s'Heerenberg 12 Ic 51.53N 6.16 E
Bergisches Land 10 De 51.07N 7.10 E
Bergisch Gladbach 10 Df 50.59N 7.08 E
Bergkvara 8 Gh 56.23N 16.05 E
Bergneustadt 12 Jc 51.02N 7.39 E
Bergö 8 Ib 62.55N 21.10 E
Bergsjö 7 Df 61.59N 17.04 E
Bergslagen 8 Fd 60.05N 14.30 E
Bergstraße 12 Ke 49.40N 8.40 E
Bergues 12 Ed 50.58N 2.26 E
Bergum, Tietjerksteradeel- 12 Ha 53.12N 6.00 E
Bergviken 8 Gc 61.10N 16.45 E
Bergville 37 De 28.52S 29.18 E
Berh 27 Jb 47.45N 111.07 E
Berhala, Selat- 26 Dg 0.48S 104.25 E
Berici, Monti- 14 Fe 45.26N 11.31 E
Berīkān 24 Nh 28.17N 51.14 E
Berikulski 20 De 55.32N 88.08 E
Beringa, Ostrov-=Bering Island (EN) 20 Lf 55.00N 166.10 E
Beringen 12 Hc 51.03N 5.13 E
Bering Glacier 40 Kd 60.15N 143.30W
Bering Island (EN)= Beringa, Ostrov- 20 Lf 55.00N 166.10 E
Beringovo More=Bering Sea (EN) 38 Bd 60.00N 175.00W
Beringovski 22 Tc 63.07N 179.19 E
Bering Proliv=Bering Strait (EN) 38 Cc 65.30N 169.00W
Bering Sea 38 Bd 60.00N 175.00W
Bering Sea (EN)=Beringovo More 38 Bd 60.00N 175.00W
Bering Strait 38 Cc 65.30N 169.00W
Bering Strait (EN)=Bering Proliv 38 Cc 65.30N 169.00W
Berislav 16 Hf 46.51N 33.29 E
Berisso 55 Dl 34.52S 57.53W
Berit Dağı 24 Gc 38.01N 36.52 E
Berīzak 24 Qi 26.06N 57.15 E
Berja 13 Jh 36.51N 2.57W
Berkåk 7 Be 62.50N 10.00 E
Berkane 32 Gc 34.56N 2.20W
Berkel 10 Cd 52.09N 6.12 E
Berkeley 43 Cd 37.57N 122.18W
Berkhamsted 12 Bc 51.45N 0.33W
Berkner Island 66 Rf 79.30S 49.30W
Berkovica 15 Gf 43.14N 23.07 E
Berks 9 Lj 51.15N 1.20W
Berkshire [3] 9 Lj 51.30N 1.10W
Berkshire Downs 9 Lj 51.35N 1.25W
Berkshire Hills 44 Kd 42.20N 73.10W
Berlaimont 12 Fd 50.12N 3.49 E
Berlanga de Duero 13 Jc 41.28N 2.51W
Berlengas, Ilhas- 13 Ce 39.25N 9.30W
Berlevåg 7 Ga 70.51N 29.06 E
Berlin [N.H.-U.S.] 43 Mc 44.29N 71.10W
Berlin [Ger.] 6 He 52.31N 13.24 E
Berlin (Ost) = Berlin 6 He 52.31N 13.24 E
Berlin (West) = Berlin 6 He 52.31N 12.24 E
Berlin-Pankow 10 Jd 52.34N 13.24 E
Bermeja, Sierra- 13 Gh 36.30N 5.15W
Bermejillo 47 Dc 25.53N 103.37W
Bermejito, Río- 55 Bg 25.39S 60.11W
Bermejo, Isla- 55 An 39.01S 62.01W
Bermejo, Paso-/Cumbre, Paso de la- 52 Ii 32.50S 70.05W
Bermejo, Río- [Arg.] 52 Ji 31.52S 67.22W
Bermejo, Río- [S.Amer.] 52 Kh 26.52S 58.23W
Bermen, lac- 42 Kf 53.35N 68.55W
Bermeo 13 Ja 43.26N 2.43W
Bermillo de Sayago 13 Fc 41.22N 6.06W
Bermuda [5] 39 Mf 32.20N 64.45W
Bermuda Islands 39 Mf 32.20N 64.45W
Bermuda Rise (EN) 38 Mf 32.30N 65.00W
Bern [2] 14 Bd 46.55N 7.40 E
Bern/Berne 6 Gf 46.55N 7.30 E
Bernalda 14 Kj 40.24N 16.41 E
Bernalillo 45 Ci 35.18N 106.33W
Bernard Islands 64d Bb 7.18N 151.32 E
Bernardo de Irigoyen 55 Bk 32.10S 61.09W
Bernardo do Irigoyen 56 Jc 26.15S 53.39W
Bernasconi 56 He 37.54S 63.43W
Bernau bei Berlin 10 Jd 52.40N 13.35 E
Bernaville 12 Ed 50.08N 2.10 E
Bernay 11 Ge 49.06N 0.36 E
Bernburg 10 He 51.48N 11.44 E
Berndorf 14 Kc 47.57N 16.06 E
Berne [Ger.] 12 Ka 53.11N 8.29 E
Berne [In.-U.S.] 44 Ee 40.39N 84.57W
Berne/Bern 6 Gf 46.55N 7.30 E
Berner Alpen/Alpes Bernoises=Bernese Alps (EN) 14 Bd 46.25N 7.30 E
Berneray 9 Fd 57.43N 7.15W
Bernese Alps (EN)=Alpes Bernoises/Berner Alpen 14 Bd 46.25N 7.30 E
Bernese Alps (EN)=Berner Alpen/Alpes Bernoises 14 Bd 46.25N 7.30 E
Bernesga 13 Gb 42.28N 5.31W
Bernesq 12 Be 49.16N 0.56W
Bernier Bay 42 Ib 71.08N 88.00W
Bernier Island 59 Cd 24.50S 113.10 E
Bernina 14 Ed 46.25N 10.01 E
Bernina 5 Gf 46.22N 9.50 E
Berninapaß 14 Ed 46.25N 10.01 E
Bernissart 12 Fd 50.28N 3.38 E
Bernkastel-Kues 10 Dg 49.55N 7.04 E
Bernstorffs Isfjord 41 Hf 63.10N 40.45W
Berón de Astrada 55 Dh 27.33S 57.32W
Beroroha 37 Hd 21.39S 45.10 E
Beroubouay 34 Fc 10.32N 2.44 E
Beroun 10 Kg 49.58N 14.04 E
Berounka 10 Kg 50.00N 14.24 E
Berovo 15 Fh 41.43N 22.51 E
Berre, Étang de- 11 Lk 43.27N 5.08 E
Berriane 32 Hc 32.50N 3.46 E
Berrouaghia 13 Oh 36.08N 2.55 E
Berry 11 Hh 47.00N 2.00 E
Berry-au-Bac 12 Fe 49.24N 3.54 E
Berryessa, Lake- 46 Dg 38.37N 122.16W
Berry Head 9 Jk 50.24N 3.29W
Berry Islands 47 Ic 25.34N 77.45W
Berry River 46 Ja 50.50N 111.36W
Beršad 19 Cf 48.23N 29.33 E
Berseba 37 Be 26.01S 17.41 E
Bersenbrück 12 Jb 52.33N 7.56 E
Berthierville 44 Kb 46.05N 73.11W
Bertincourt 12 Ed 50.05N 2.59 E
Bertogne 12 Hd 50.05N 5.40 E
Bertolinia 54 Je 7.38S 43.57W
Bertoua 31 Ih 4.35N 13.41 E
Bertraghboy Bay 9 Dh 53.23N 9.50W
Bertrix 12 He 49.51N 5.15 E
Beru Island 57 Ie 1.20S 176.00 E
Berwick-upon-Tweed 9 Lf 55.46N 2.00W
Berwyn 9 Ji 52.53N 3.24W
Besalampy 37 Gc 16.44S 44.24 E
Besançon 6 Gf 47.15N 6.02 E
Besar, Gunung- 26 Gg 1.25S 115.39 E
Besbre 11 Jh 46.33N 3.44 E
Besed 16 Gc 52.38N 31.11 E
Besikama 26 Hh 9.36S 124.57 E
Beskid Mountains (EN) 10 Pg 49.40N 20.00 E
Beskid Niski 10 Rg 49.20N 21.30 E
Beskid Średni 10 Pg 49.45N 19.20 E
Beskid Wysoki 10 Pg 49.32N 20.00 E
Beskidy Wschodnie 10 Sg 49.20N 22.30 E
Beskidy Zachodnie 10 Pg 49.30N 19.30 E
Beskol 18 Ma 46.05N 81.01 E
Beslan 19 Eg 43.10N 44.35 E
Besna Kobila 15 Fg 42.32N 22.14 E
Besni 24 Gd 37.41N 37.52 E
Besparmak Dağ 15 Kl 37.30N 27.35 E
Bessao 35 Bd 7.53N 15.59 E
Bessarabia (EN)= Bessarabija 15 Lb 47.00N 28.30 E
Bessarabija=Bessarabia (EN) 15 Lb 47.00N 28.30 E
Bessarabka 16 Ff 46.20N 28.59 E
Bességes 11 Kj 44.17N 4.06 E
Bessemer 43 Je 33.25N 86.57W
Bessin 11 Fe 49.10N 1.00W
Bessines-sur-Gartempe 11 Hh 46.06N 1.22 E
Bessoki, Gora- 16 Rh 43.57N 52.30 E
Best 12 Hc 51.30N 5.24 E
Bestjah 20 Hc 66.00N 123.35 E
Bestjah 20 Hd 61.17N 123.50 E
Bestobe 19 He 52.30N 73.05 E
Bestwig 12 Kc 51.22N 8.24 E
Betafo 37 Hc 19.49S 46.50 E
Betanzos [Bol.] 54 Eg 19.34S 65.27W
Betanzos [Sp.] 13 Da 43.17N 8.12W
Betanzos, Ria de- 13 Da 43.23N 8.15W
Bétaré Oya 34 Hd 5.36N 14.05 E
Bétérou 34 Fd 9.12N 2.16 E
Beteta 13 Jd 40.34N 2.04W
Bethal 37 De 26.27S 29.28 E
Bethanien [3] 37 Be 26.30S 17.00 E
Bethanien 31 Ik 26.32S 17.11 E
Bethany [Mo.-U.S.] 45 If 40.16N 94.02W
Bethany [Ok.-U.S.] 45 Hi 35.31N 97.33W
Bethel 39 Cc 60.48N 161.46W
Bétheniville 12 Ge 49.18N 4.22 E
Bethlehem [Pa.-U.S.] 44 Je 40.36N 75.22W
Bethlehem [S.Afr.] 31 Jk 28.15S 28.15 E
Bethlehem (EN)=Bayt Laḩm 24 Fg 31.43N 35.12 E
Bethulie 37 Df 30.32S 25.59 E
Béthune 11 Id 50.32N 2.38 E
Béthune 11 He 49.53N 1.09 E
Betioky 37 Gd 23.42S 44.22 E
Betong 25 Kg 5.45N 101.05 E
Betor 35 Fc 11.37N 39.00 E
Bétou 36 Cb 3.03N 18.31 E
Betpak-Dala 21 Ie 46.00N 70.00 E
Betroka 37 Hd 23.15S 46.05 E
Bet She'an 24 Ff 32.30N 35.30 E
Betsiamites, Rivière- 42 Kg 48.56N 68.38W
Betsiboka 30 Lj 16.03S 46.36 E
Bette 30 If 22.00N 19.12 E
Bettembourg/Bettemburg 12 Ie 49.31N 6.06 E
Bettemburg/Bettembourg 12 Ie 49.31N 6.06 E
Bettendorf 45 Kf 41.32N 90.30W
Bettles Field 40 Ic 66.53N 151.51W
Bettna 8 Gf 58.55N 16.38 E
Bettola 14 Df 44.47N 9.36 E
Betūl 25 Fd 21.55N 77.54 E
Betuwe 11 Lc 51.55N 5.30 E
Betwa 25 Hc 25.55N 80.12 E
Betz 12 Ee 49.09N 2.57 E
Betzdorf 10 Df 50.47N 7.53 E
Beulah 44 Dc 44.33N 86.06W
Beult 12 Cc 51.13N 0.26 E
Beuvron 11 Hg 47.29N 1.15 E
Beuzeville 12 Ce 49.20N 0.21 E
Beveland 11 Jc 51.30N 3.40 E
Beveren 12 Gc 51.13N 4.15 E
Beveridge Reef 57 Kg 20.00S 168.00W
Beverley [Austl.] 59 Df 32.06S 116.56 E
Beverley [Eng.-U.K.] 9 Mh 53.51N 0.26W
Beverwijk 11 Kb 52.28N 4.40 E
Bewsher, Mount- 66 Ff 70.54S 66.23 E
Bexhill 9 Nk 50.50N 0.29 E
Bexley, London- 12 Cc 51.26N 0.09 E
Beyağaç 15 Ll 37.13N 28.57 E
Beyānlū 24 Ld 36.02N 47.53 E
Bey Dağı 24 Hc 38.15N 38.22 E
Bey Dağlari 23 Db 36.40N 30.15 E
Beykoz 24 Cb 41.08N 29.05 E
Beyla 34 Dd 8.41N 8.38W
Beyoğlu, İstanbul 15 Lh 41.02N 28.59 E
Beyoneisu-Retsugan 27 Oe 31.55N 139.55 E
Beypazari 24 Db 40.10N 31.55 E
Beyra 35 Hd 6.57N 47.19 E
Beyram 24 Oi 27.26N 53.31 E
Beyşehir 24 Dd 37.41N 31.43 E
Beyşehir Gölü 23 Db 37.40N 31.30 E
Bezaha 37 Gd 23.29S 44.30 E
Bežanickaja Vozvyšennost 7 Gh 56.45N 29.30 E
Bežanicy 7 Gh 56.58N 29.57 E
Bezdan 15 Bd 45.51N 18.56 E
Bezděz 10 Kf 50.32N 14.43 E
Bezdež 10 Vd 52.18N 25.20 E
Bežeck 19 Dd 57.50N 36.41 E
Bezenčuk 7 Lj 53.01N 49.24 E
Bezerra, Rio- 55 Ia 13.16S 47.31W
Bezerros 54 Ke 8.14S 35.45W
Beziers 11 Jk 43.21N 3.15 E
Bezmein 19 Fh 38.05N 58.12 E
Bežta 19 Eg 42.03N 46.08 E
Bhadrak 25 Hd 21.04N 86.30 E
Bhadrāvati 25 Ff 13.52N 75.43 E
Bhāgalpur 22 Kg 25.15N 87.00 E
Bhairawa 25 Gc 27.31N 83.24 E
Bhaironghati 25 Fb 31.01N 78.53 E
Bhakkar 25 Eb 31.38N 71.04 E
Bhamo 25 Jd 24.16N 97.14 E
Bhandāra 25 Fd 21.10N 79.39 E
Bhanjan 25 Gc 25.47N 83.26 E
Bhārat Juktarashtra=India (EN) [1] 22 Jh 20.00N 77.00 E
Bharatpur 25 Fc 27.13N 77.29 E
Bharūch 25 Ed 21.46N 72.54 E
Bhatinda → Bathinda 25 Eb 30.12N 74.57 E
Bhātpāra 25 Hd 22.52N 88.24 E
Bhavnagar 22 Jg 21.46N 72.09 E
Bhera 25 Eb 32.29N 72.55 E
Bheri 25 Gc 28.44N 81.16 E
Bhīlwāra 25 Ec 25.21N 74.38 E
Bhīma 21 Jh 16.25N 77.17 E
Bhind 25 Fc 26.34N 78.48 E
Bhiwāni 25 Fc 28.47N 76.08 E
Bhopāl 22 Jg 23.16N 77.24 E
Bhubaneshwar 22 Kg 20.14N 85.50 E
Bhuj 25 Dd 23.16N 69.40 E
Bhusāwal 25 Fd 21.03N 75.46 E
Bhutan (Druk-Yul) [1] 22 Lg 27.30N 90.30 E
Bia 34 Ed 5.21N 3.11W
Bia, Phou- 21 Mh 18.36N 103.01 E
Biá, Rio- 54 Ed 3.28S 67.23W
Bīābān, Kūh-e- 24 Qi 26.30N 57.25 E
Biabou 51n Ba 13.12N 61.09W
Biafra 30 Hh 5.00N 7.30 E
Biafra, Bight of- 30 Hh 3.20N 9.20 E
Biak 26 Kg 1.10S 136.06 E
Biak, Pulau- 57 Ee 1.00S 136.00 E
Biała Piska 10 Sc 53.37N 22.04 E
Biała Podlaska [2] 10 Td 52.00N 23.05 E
Biała Podlaska 10 Td 52.02N 23.06 E
Białobrzegi 10 Qe 51.40N 20.57 E
Białogard 10 Lb 54.01N 16.00 E
Białostocka, Wysoczyzna- 10 Tc 53.23N 23.10 E
Białowieża 10 Td 52.41N 23.50 E
Białystok 6 Ie 53.09N 23.09 E
Białystok [2] 10 Tc 53.10N 23.10 E
Biancavilla 14 Im 37.38N 14.52 E
Bianco 14 Kl 38.05N 16.09 E
Bianco, Monte- 5 Gf 45.50N 6.52 E
Biankouma 34 Dd 7.44N 7.37W
Biankouma [3] 34 Dd 7.43N 7.40W
Bianzhuang → Cangshan 28 Eg 34.51N 118.03 E
Biaro, Pulau- 26 If 2.05N 125.20 E
Biarritz 11 Ek 43.29N 1.34W
Biasca 14 Cd 46.22N 8.57 E
Bibā 33 Fd 28.55N 30.59 E
Bibai 27 Pc 43.19N 141.52 E
Bibala 36 Be 14.50S 13.30 E
Biban, Chaine des- 13 Qh 36.12N 4.25 E
Bibbiena 14 Fg 43.42N 11.49 E
Biberach an der Riß 10 Fh 48.06N 9.48 E
Bibiani 34 Ed 6.28N 2.20W
Bic 44 Ma 48.22N 68.42W
Bicaj 15 Dh 41.59N 20.25 E
Bicas 55 Ke 21.43S 43.04W
Bicaz 15 Jc 46.55N 26.04 E
Bicaz, Pasul- 15 Ic 46.49N 25.52 E
Bičenekski, Pereval- 16 Nj 39.33N 45.48 E
Bicester 9 Lj 51.54N 1.09W
Bichena 35 Fc 10.21N 38.14 E
Bickerton Island 59 Hb 13.45S 136.10 E
Bicske 10 Oi 47.29N 18.38 E
Bičura 20 Ff 50.36N 107.35 E
Bīd 24 Qd 36.33N 57.35 E
Bida 31 Hh 9.05N 6.01 E
Bīdar 25 Fe 17.54N 77.33 E
Bidasoa 13 Ka 43.22N 1.47W
Biddeford 43 Mc 43.30N 70.26W
Bideford 9 Ij 51.01N 4.13W
Bideford Bay → Barnstaple 9 Ij 51.05N 4.20W
Bidon V/Poste Maurice Cortier 32 He 22.18N 1.05 E
Bié [3] 36 Ce 13.00S 17.30 E
Bié, Planalto do- 30 Ij 13.30S 17.02 E
Biebrza 10 Sc 53.13N 22.28 E
Biecz 10 Rg 49.44N 21.14 E
Biedenkopf 10 Ef 50.55N 8.32 E
Biei 29a Cb 43.35N 142.28 E
Biel/Bienne 14 Bc 47.10N 7.15 E
Bielefeld 10 Ed 52.02N 8.32 E
Bielefeld-Brackwede 12 Kc 51.59N 8.31 E
Bielefeld-Sennestadt 12 Kc 51.57N 8.35 E
Biella 14 Ce 45.34N 8.03 E
Bielsk 10 Pd 52.40N 19.49 E
Bielska, Wysoczyzna- 10 Sd 52.35N 23.00 E
Bielsko [2] 10 Og 49.50N 19.00 E
Bielsko-Biała 10 Pg 49.49N 19.02 E
Bielsk Podlaski 10 Td 52.47N 23.12 E
Bien Dong=South China Sea (EN) 21 Ni 10.00N 113.00 E
Bien Hoa 25 Lf 10.57N 106.49 E
Bienne 11 Lh 46.20N 5.38 E
Bienne/Biel 14 Bc 47.10N 7.15 E
Bienvenida 13 Jd 40.30N 2.30W
Bienville, Lac - 42 Ke 55.20N 72.40W
Bierbeek 12 Gd 50.50N 4.46 E
Bieszczady 10 Sg 49.10N 22.35 E
Bièvre 12 He 49.56N 5.01 E
Biferno 14 Ji 41.59N 15.02 E
Bifoum 36 Bc 0.20S 10.23 E
Bifuka 28 Qb 44.29N 142.21 E
Biga 24 Bb 40.13N 27.14 E
Bigadiç 24 Cc 39.23N 28.08 E
Big Bald Mountain 44 Nb 47.37N 66.38W
Big Baldy Mountain 46 Jc 46.58N 110.37W
Big Bay [Mi.-U.S.] 44 Db 46.49N 87.44W
Big Bay [Van.] 63b Cb 15.05S 166.54 E
Big Beaver House 42 If 52.58N 89.57W
Big Belt Mountains 46 Jc 46.40N 111.25W
Big Black River 45 Kj 32.00N 91.05W
Big Blue River 43 Hd 39.11N 96.32W
Big Creek Peak 46 Id 44.28N 113.32W
Big Dry Creek 46 Lc 47.30N 106.19W
Big Falls 45 Jb 48.11N 93.46W
Biggar 42 Gf 52.04N 108.00W
Biggenden 59 Ke 25.30S 152.00 E
Biggleswade 9 Mi 52.05N 0.17W
Big Hatchet Peak 45 Bk 31.37N 108.20W
Big Hole River 46 Id 45.34N 112.20W
Bighorn Basin 43 Fc 44.15N 108.10W
Bighorn Lake 46 Kd 45.08N 108.10W
Bighorn Mountains 38 Ie 44.00N 107.30W
Bighorn River 43 Fb 46.09N 107.28W
Bight, Head of- 59 Gf 31.30S 131.10 E
Big Island 42 Kd 62.43N 70.40W
Big Lake 44 Nc 45.10N 67.40W
Big Lake 45 Fk 31.12N 101.28W
Big Lost River 46 Ie 43.50N 112.44W
Big Muddy Creek 46 Mb 48.08N 104.36W
Big Muddy Lake 46 Mb 49.08N 104.54W
Bignona 34 Bc 12.49N 16.14W
Bigorre 11 Gk 43.06N 0.05 E
Big Porcupine Creek 46 Lc 46.17N 106.47W
Big Quill Lake 42 Hf 51.51N 104.18W
Big Rapids 44 Ed 43.42N 85.29W
Big River 42 Gf 53.50N 107.01W
Big River 42 Fb 72.50N 125.00W
Big Sand Lake 42 He 57.45N 99.45W
Big Sandy 46 Jb 48.11N 110.07W
Big Sandy Creek 45 Eg 38.06N 102.29W
Big Sandy River [Az.-U.S.] 46 Ii 34.19N 113.31W
Big Sandy River [Wy.-U.S.] 46 Kf 41.50N 109.48W
Big Sheep Mountains 46 Mc 47.03N 105.43W
Big Sioux River 43 Hc 42.30N 96.25W
Big Smoky Valley 46 Dd 38.30N 117.15W
Big Snowy Mountain 46 Kc 46.50N 109.30W
Big Spring 39 If 32.15N 101.28W
Big Spruce Knob 44 Gf 38.16N 80.12W
Big Stone Lake 45 Hd 45.25N 96.40W
Big Timber 46 Kd 45.50N 109.57W
Big Trout Lake 42 If 53.45N 90.00W
Biguglia, Étang de- 11a Ba 42.33N 9.29 E
Big Wood Cay 49 Ia 24.21N 77.44W
Big Wood River 46 He 42.52N 114.55W
Bihać 14 Jf 44.49N 15.52 E
Bihār [3] 25 Hd 25.00N 86.00 E
Bihār 25 Hc 25.11N 85.31 E
Biharamulo 36 Fc 2.38S 31.20 E
Bihor [2] 15 Ec 47.00N 22.00 E
Bihoro 27 Pc 43.49N 144.07 E
Bihorului, Munţii- 15 Fc 46.40N 22.45 E
Bija 21 Kd 52.25N 85.05 E
Bijagós, Arquipélago dos-= Bijagós Islands (EN) 30 Fg 11.15N 16.05W
Bijagós Islands (EN)= Bijagós, Arquipélago dos- 30 Fg 11.15N 16.05W
Bijapur 25 Fe 16.50N 75.42 E
Bījār 23 Gb 35.52N 47.36 E
Bijeljina 14 Mf 44.45N 19.13 E
Bijelo Polje 15 Cf 43.02N 19.45 E
Bijiang (Zhiziluo) 27 Gf 26.39N 99.00 E
Bijie 27 If 27.15N 105.16 E
Bijlikol, Ozero- 18 Hc 43.05N 70.40 E
Bijou Creek 45 Ef 40.17N 103.52W
Bijoutier Island 37b Eb 7.04S 52.45 E
Bijsk 22 Kd 52.34N 85.15 E
Bīkāner 22 Jg 28.01N 73.18 E
Bikar Atoll 57 Ic 12.15N 170.06 E
Bikeqi 28 Ad 40.45N 111.17 E
Bikin 20 Ig 46.43N 134.02 E
Bikin 20 Ig 46.51N 134.02 E
Bikini Atoll 57 Hc 11.35N 165.23 E
Bikoro 31 Ii 0.45S 18.07 E
Bilād Ghāmid 33 Hf 19.58N 41.38 E
Bilād Zahrān 33 He 20.15N 41.15 E
Bilāspur 22 Kg 22.03N 82.10 E
Bilate 35 Fd 6.34N 38.04 E
Bilauktaung Range 21 Lh 13.00N 99.00 E
Bilbao 6 Fg 43.15N 2.58W
Bilbays 33 Fc 30.25N 31.34 E
Bileća 14 Mh 42.53N 18.26 E
Bilecik 23 Ca 40.09N 29.59 E
Bīlehsavār 24 Mc 39.28N 48.20 E
Bilé Karpaty=White Carpathians (EN) 10 Nh 48.55N 17.50 E
Bilesha Plain 36 Hb 0.35N 40.45 E
Biłgoraj 10 Sf 50.34N 22.43 E
Bili 36 Db 4.50N 22.29 E
Bili 36 Eb 4.09N 25.10 E
Bilibino 22 Sc 68.03N 166.20 E
Biliran 26 Hd 11.35N 124.28 E
Bilishti 15 Di 40.37N 20.59 E
Biliu He 28 Ge 39.30N 122.36 E
Bill Baileys Bank (EN) 9 Ca 60.40N 10.20W
Billerbeck 12 Jc 51.58N 7.18 E
Billericay 12 Cc 51.37N 0.35 E
Billingen 8 Ef 58.24N 13.45 E
Billings 39 Jf 37.04N 93.33W
Billings, Represa- 55 If 23.45S 46.40W
Billingshurst 12 Bc 51.01N 0.27W
Bill Williams River 46 Hi 34.17N 114.03W
Billy Chinook, Lake- 46 Ed 44.33N 121.20W
Bilma 31 Ig 18.41N 12.56 E
Biloela 59 Kd 24.24S 150.30 E
Bilo Gora 14 Le 45.50N 17.10 E
Biloku 54 Gc 1.46N 58.33W
Biloxi 43 Je 30.24N 88.53W
Bilqās Qism Awwal 24 Dg 31.13N 31.21 E
Bilteni 15 Ge 44.52N 23.17 E
Biltine 35 Cc 14.32N 20.55 E
Biltine [3] 35 Cc 15.00N 21.00 E
Bilzen 12 Hd 50.51N 5.31 E
Bima 36 Eb 3.23N 25.09 E
Bimbān 24 Ej 24.26N 32.53 E
Bimberi Peak 59 Jg 35.40S 148.47 E
Bimbila 34 Fd 8.51N 0.04 E
Bimbo 35 Be 4.18N 18.33 E
Bimini Islands 47 Ic 25.44N 79.15W
Bināb 24 Md 36.35N 48.41 E
Binačka Morava 15 Eg 42.27N 21.47 E
Binaiya, Gunung- 26 Ig 3.11S 129.26 E
Binatang 26 Ff 2.10N 111.38 E
Binboga Dağı 24 Gc 38.21N 36.32 E
Binche 12 Gd 50.24N 4.10 E
Binder 27 Jb 48.35N 110.36 E
Bindura 31 Kj 17.17S 31.20 E
Bine el Ouidane 32 Fc 32.08N 6.28W
Binéfar 13 Mc 41.51N 0.18 E
Binem 35 Bb 18.43N 19.40 E
Binga [Zaire] 36 Db 2.23N 20.30 E
Binga [Zimb.] 37 Dc 17.37S 27.20 E

Index Symbols

[1] Independent Nation
[2] State, Region
[3] District, County
[5] Municipality
[5] Colony, Dependency
Continent
Physical Region
Historical or Cultural Region
Mount, Mountain
Volcano
Hill
Mountains, Mountain Range
Hills, Escarpment
Plateau, Upland
Pass, Gap
Plain, Lowland
Delta
Salt Flat
Valley, Canyon
Crater, Cave
Karst Features
Depression
Polder
Desert, Dunes
Forest, Woods
Heath, Steppe
Oasis
Cape, Point
Coast, Beach
Cliff
Peninsula
Isthmus
Sandbank
Island
Atoll
Rock, Reef
Islands, Archipelago
Rocks, Reefs
Coral Reef
Well, Spring
Geyser
River, Stream
Waterfall Rapids
River Mouth, Estuary
Lake
Salt Lake
Intermittent Lake
Reservoir
Swamp, Pond
Canal
Glacier
Ice Shelf, Pack Ice
Ocean
Sea
Gulf, Bay
Strait, Fjord
Lagoon
Bank
Seamount
Tablemount
Ridge
Shelf
Basin
Escarpment, Sea Scarp
Fracture
Trench, Abyss
National Park, Reserve
Point of Interest
Recreation Site
Cave, Cavern
Historic Site
Ruins
Wall, Walls
Church, Abbey
Temple
Scientific Station
Airport
Port
Lighthouse
Mine
Tunnel
Dam, Bridge

Bingen 10 Dg 49.58N 7.54 E
Bingham [Me.-U.S.] 44 Mc 45.03N 69.53W
Bingham [N.M.-U.S.] 45 Cj 33.56N 106.17W
Binghamton 44 Je 42.06N 75.55W
Bin Ghunaymah, Jabal- 30 If 25.00N 15.30 E
Bing Inlet 44 Gc 45.13N 80.30W
Bingöl 23 Fb 38.53N 40.29 E
Bingöl Dağları 24 Ic 39.20N 41.20 E
Binhai (Dongkan) 27 Ke 34.00N 119.52 E
Binjai 26 Cf 3.36N 98.30 E
Binkiliç 15 Lh 41.25N 28.11 E
Binongko, Pulau- 26 Hh 5.57S 124.02 E
Bin Qirdān 32 Jc 33.08N 11.13 E
Bintan, Pulau- 26 Df 1.05N 104.30 E
Bintuhan 26 Dg 4.48S 103.22 E
Bintulu 26 Ff 3.10N 113.02 E
Bin Walīd, Jabal- 14 En 36.52N 10.47 E
Binxian 28 Df 37.22N 117.57 E
Binxian (Binzhou) [China] 27 Mb 45.45N 127.27 E
Binxian (Binzhou) [China] 27 Id 35.02N 108.06 E
Binzhou → Binxian [China] 27 Id 35.02N 108.06 E
Binzhou → Binxian [China] 27 Mb 45.45N 127.27 E
Bioara 25 Fd 23.58N 76.55 E
Biobío 56 Fe 36.49S 73.10W
Bio Bio [2] 56 Fe 37.45S 72.00W
Biograd na Moru 14 Jg 43.57N 15.27 E
Bioko [3] 34 Ge 3.00N 8.40 E
Bioko 30 Hh 4.30N 9.30 E
Biokovo 14 Lg 43.18N 17.02 E
Biorra/Birr 9 Fh 53.05N 7.54W
Bippen 12 Jb 52.35N 7.44 E
Bir 25 Fe 18.59N 75.46 E
Bira 20 Ig 49.03N 132.27 E
Bi'r Abraq 33 Fe 23.35N 34.48 E
Bi'r Abū al Ḩuşayn 33 Ee 22.53N 29.55 E
Bi'r Abū Gharādiq 24 Cg 30.06N 28.06 E
Bi'r Abū Hashim 33 Fe 23.42N 34.08 E
Bi'r Abū Minqat 33 Ed 26.30N 27.35 E
Birah Kaprah 24 Kd 36.52N 44.01 E
Birāk 33 Bd 27.39N 14.17 E
Birakan 20 Ig 49.02N 131.40 E
Bi'r al 'Abd 24 Eg 31.22N 32.58 E
Bi'r al Ghuzaylah 33 Bd 28.50N 10.45 E
Bi'r al Ḩakīm 33 Dc 31.36N 23.29 E
Bi'r al Hasa 35 Fa 22.58N 35.40 E
Bi'r al Khamsah 33 Ec 30.57N 25.46 E
Bi'r 'Allāq 33 Bc 31.10N 11.55 E
Bi'r al Mushayqiq 32 Jc 30.53N 10.18 E
Bi'r al Qurayyah 24 Ei 26.22N 33.01 E
Bi'r al Uzam 33 Dc 31.46N 23.59 E
Bi'r al Wa'r 31 Be 22.39N 14.10 E
Bi'r al Washkah 33 Cd 28.52N 15.35 E
Birao 31 Jg 10.17N 22.47 E
Bi'r 'Arjā' 24 Ij 25.17N 40.58 E
Bi'r ar Rāh 24 If 33.27N 40.25 E
Bi'r ar Rūmān 32 Ic 32.31N 8.21 E
Birātnagar 25 Hc 26.29N 87.17 E
Biratori 28 Qc 42.35N 142.12 E
Bi'r Baylī 33 Ec 30.32N 25.08 E
Bi'r Bayzaḩ 24 Fj 25.10N 34.05 E
Bi'r Bū Ḩawsh 33 Dd 24.34N 22.07 E
Bi'r Bū Zurayyq 33 Dd 24.32N 22.38 E
Bîrca 15 Gf 43.58N 23.37 E
Birch 42 Ge 58.28N 112.17W
Birch Mountains 42 Ge 57.20N 112.55W
Bird 42 Ie 56.30N 94.14W
Bi'r Dibs 33 Ee 22.12N 29.32 E
Bird Island [Gren.] 51p Bb 12.12N 61.33W
Bird Island [Sey.] 37b Ca 3.43S 55.12 E
Birdsville 59 He 25.54S 139.22 E
Birdum 59 Gc 15.39S 133.13 E
Birecik 24 Gd 37.02N 37.58 E
Bir El Ater 32 Ic 34.44N 8.03 E
Bir el Mrabba'ab 24 He 34.30N 39.07 E
Bir Enzarán 32 Ee 23.53N 14.32W
Bireuen 26 Ce 5.12N 96.41 E
Bi'r Fajr 24 Gh 28.54N 37.54 E
Bi'r Fu'ād 33 Ec 30.27N 26.27 E
Bir Gandús 32 De 21.36N 16.30W
Birganj 25 Gc 27.00N 84.52 E
Bir Gara 35 Bc 13.11N 15.58 E
Bir-Ghbalou 13 Ph 36.16N 3.35 E
Birgi 15 Lk 38.15N 28.05 E
Bi'r Ḩasanah 24 Eg 30.28N 33.47 E
Bi'r Ḩaymir 24 Hj 24.41N 38.04 E
Bi'r Ḩulayyī 24 Fj 24.06N 34.32 E
Birigui 55 Ge 21.18S 50.19W
Biriliussy 20 Ee 57.07N 90.42 E
Birīn 24 Ge 35.01N 36.40 E
Birine 13 Pi 35.37N 3.13 E
Birjand 23 Hf 32.53N 59.13 E
Birjusa 21 Ld 57.43N 95.24 E
Birjusinsk 20 Ee 55.55N 97.55 E
Bi'r Karawayn 24 Ci 27.06N 28.32 E
Birkeland 7 Bg 58.20N 8.14 E
Birkenfeld 10 Dg 49.39N 7.11 E
Birkenhead 9 Jh 53.24N 3.02W
Birkerød 8 Ei 55.50N 12.26 E
Bi'r Khālidah 24 Bg 30.50N 27.15 E
Birksgate Range 59 Fe 27.10S 129.45 E
Bîrlad 15 Kc 46.14N 27.40 E
Bîrlad 15 Kc 45.36N 27.31 E
Bir Lehlú 32 Fd 26.21N 9.34W
Bi'r Ma'sūr 24 Fj 24.31N 34.12 E
Birmingham [Al.-U.S.] 39 Kf 33.31N 86.49W
Birmingham [Eng.-U.K.] 6 Fe 52.30N 1.50W
Bi'r Misāḩah 33 Ee 22.12N 27.57 E
Bi'r Murr 33 Fe 23.21N 30.05 E
Bi'r Murrah 33 Fe 22.32N 33.54 E
Bi'r Nāhid 33 Ec 30.13N 28.52 E
Bi'r Naşīf 33 Ee 24.51N 39.11 E
Birnie Atoll [?] 57 Je 3.35S 171.31W
Birnin Gaouré 34 Fc 13.05N 2.54 E
Birnin Gwari 34 Gc 11.02N 6.47 E
Birnin Kebbi 34 Fc 12.28N 4.12 E
Birni Nkonni 31 Hg 13.48N 5.15 E
Birnin Kudu 34 Gc 11.27N 9.30 E
Birni Yauri 34 Fc 10.47N 4.49 E
Bi'r Nukhaylah 24 Dj 24.01N 30.52 E
Birobidžan 22 Pe 48.48N 132.57 E
Birr/Biorra 9 Fh 53.05N 7.54W
Birs 14 Bc 47.26N 7.33 E
Bi'r Şafājah 33 Fd 26.50N 34.54 E
Bi'r Sayyālah 24 Ei 26.07N 33.56 E
Bi'r Shalatayn 33 Ge 23.08N 35.36 E
Birsk 19 Fd 55.25N 55.32 E
Birštonas 8 Kj 54.33N 24.07 E
Bi'r Ţarfāwi 33 Ee 22.55N 28.53 E
Biru 27 Fe 31.30N 93.50 E
Bi'r Umm al 'Abbās 24 Ei 26.57N 32.34 E
Bi'r Umm Fawākhir 24 Ei 26.01N 33.38 E
Bi'r Umm Sa'īd 24 Eh 29.40N 33.34 E
Bi'r Umm Ţunaydibah 24 Ej 25.16N 33.06 E
Biruni 19 Gg 41.42N 60.45 E
Biržai/Biržaj 19 Cd 56.12N 24.48 E
Biržaj/Biržai 19 Cd 56.12N 24.48 E
Bîrzava 15 Ec 46.07N 21.59 E
Bîrzava 15 Dd 45.16N 20.49 E
Birzebbuga 14 Io 35.49N 14.32 E
Bisa, Pulau- 26 Ig 1.15S 127.28 E
Bisaccia 14 Ji 41.01N 15.22 E
Bisaccuino 14 Hm 37.42N 13.15 E
Bisbee 43 Fe 31.27N 109.55W
Biscarrosse, Étang de- 11 Ej 44.21N 1.10W
Biscay, Bay of- (EN)=
Gascogne, Golfe de- 5 Fg 44.00N 4.00W
Bisceglie 14 Ki 41.14N 16.30 E
Bischofslofen 10 Jc 47.25N 13.13 E
Bischofswerda/Biskopicy 10 Ke 51.07N 14.11 E
Biscoe Islands 66 Qe 66.00S 66.30W
Biscotasi Lake 44 Fb 47.20N 82.05W
Biscucuy 50 Bh 9.22N 69.59W
Bisert 17 Hh 56.39N 59.57 E
Bisert' 19 Fd 56.52N 59.03 E
Biševiski Kanal 14 Kg 43.00N 16.03 E
Biševo 14 Kh 42.59N 16.01 E
Bisha 35 Fb 15.28N 37.33 E
Bishārah 33 De 22.58N 22.39 E
Bishārīyīn, Barq al- 35 Eb 19.26N 32.22 E
Bishnupur 25 Hd 23.05N 87.19 E
Bishop 43 Dd 37.22N 118.24W
Bishop Auckland 9 Lg 54.40N 1.40W
Bishop Rock 9 Gl 49.53N 6.25W
Bishop's Falls 42 Lg 49.01N 55.30W
Bishop's Stortford 9 Nj 51.53N 0.09 E
Bishop's Waltham 12 Ad 50.57N 1.13W
Bishri, Jabal- 24 He 35.20N 39.20 E
Bishui 27 La 52.07N 123.43 E
Biškek (Frunze) 22 Je 42.54N 74.36 E
Biskra 31 He 34.51N 5.44 E
Biskra [3] 32 Ic 34.40N 6.00 E
Biskupiec 10 Qc 53.52N 20.27 E
Bislig 26 Ie 8.13N 126.19 E
Bismarck 39 Ie 46.48N 100.47W
Bismarck, Kap- 41 Kc 76.40N 18.40W
Bismarck Archipelago 57 Fe 5.00S 150.00 E
Bismarck Sea 60 Dh 4.00S 147.30 E
Bismarck Range 60 Ci 5.30S 144.45 E
Bismil 24 Id 37.51N 40.40 E
Bison 45 Ed 45.31N 102.28W
Bīsotūn 24 Le 34.23N 47.26 E
Bispfors 8 Ga 63.02N 16.37 E
Bissau 31 Fg 11.51N 15.35W
Bissaula 34 Hd 7.01N 10.27 E
Bissett 44 Hb 46.13N 78.02W
Bisson, Banc du- 37 Hb 12.00S 46.25 E
Bistcho Lake 42 Fe 59.45N 118.50W
Bistineau, Lake- 45 Jj 32.25N 93.22W
Bistra 15 Fd 45.29N 22.11 E
Bistra 15 Dh 41.37N 20.44 E
Bistreţ 15 Gf 43.54N 23.30 E
Bistrica 15 Dg 42.09N 20.59 E
Bistrica 15 Cf 43.28N 19.42 E
Bistriţa 15 Hb 47.08N 24.29 E
Bistriţa [Rom.] 15 Jc 46.30N 26.57 E
Bistriţa [Rom.] 15 Hb 47.04N 24.25 E
Bistriţa-Năsăud [2] 15 Hb 47.05N 24.35 E
Bitam 36 Bb 2.05N 11.29 E
Bitam 13 Ri 35.15N 5.11 E
Bitburg 10 Cg 49.58N 6.32 E
Bitche 11 Ne 49.03N 7.26 E
Bitéa 35 Cc 13.11N 20.10 E
Bithia 14 Cl 38.55N 8.52 E
Bithynia 15 Mi 40.20N 29.30 E
Bitjug 16 Kd 50.37N 39.55 E
Bitkine 35 Bc 11.59N 18.13 E
Bitlis 23 Fb 38.22N 42.06 E
Bitola 6 Ig 41.02N 21.20 E
Bitonto 14 Ki 41.06N 16.41 E
Bitterfeld 10 Ie 51.37N 12.19 E
Bitterfontein 31 Il 31.00S 18.32 E
Bitterroot Range 46 He 47.06N 115.10W
Bitterroot River 46 Hc 46.52N 114.06W
Bitti 14 Dj 40.29N 9.23 E
Bitung 26 If 1.27N 125.11 E
Biu 31 Ig 10.37N 12.12 E
Bivolari 15 Kb 47.32N 27.26 E
Bivolu, Vîrful- 15 Ib 47.15N 25.56 E
Bivona 14 Hm 37.37N 13.26 E
Biwa-ko 28 Ng 35.13N 136.05 E
Bixad [Rom.] 15 Ic 46.06N 25.52 E
Bixad [Rom.] 15 Gb 47.56N 23.24 E
Bixby 45 Ii 35.57N 95.53W
Biyalā 24 Dg 31.10N 31.13 E
Biyang 27 Je 32.40N 113.21 E
Biyārjomand 24 Pd 36.06N 55.53 E
Bizbuljak 17 Gj 53.43N 54.16 E
Bize 18 Kb 45.10N 77.58 E
Bizen 28 Mg 34.44N 134.09 E
Bizerte (EN)=Banzart 31 He 37.17N 9.52 E
Bjala 15 If 43.27N 25.44 E
Bjala Slatina 15 Gf 43.28N 23.56 E
Bjargtangar 5 Db 65.30N 24.32W
Bjärna/Perniö 7 Ff 60.12N 23.08 E
Bjärnum 8 Eh 56.17N 13.42 E
Bjästa 8 Ha 63.12N 18.30 E
Bjelašnica 14 Mg 43.43N 18.09 E
Bjelašnica 14 Mh 42.51N 18.09 E
Bjelašnica 14 Mg 43.09N 18.23 E
Bjelolasica 14 Ie 45.16N 14.58 E
Bjelovar 14 Ke 45.54N 16.51 E
Bjerkvik 7 Db 68.33N 17.34 E
Bjerringbro 8 Ch 56.23N 9.40 E
Bjervamoen 8 Ce 59.25N 9.04 E
Bjeshkët e Nemuna 15 Cg 42.30N 19.50 E
Björdo 8 Fd 60.28N 14.42 E
Bjørkelangen 8 De 59.53N 11.34 E
Björkfors 8 Ff 58.01N 15.54 E
Björklinge 8 Gd 60.02N 17.33 E
Björkö 7 Eg 59.55N 19.00 E
Björna 7 Ee 63.34N 18.33 E
Bjørnafjorden 8 Ad 60.05N 5.20 E
Björneborg 8 Fe 59.15N 14.15 E
Björneborg/Pori 6 Ic 61.29N 21.47 E
Bjorne Peninsula 42 Ia 77.30N 87.00W
Bjornesfjorden 8 Bd 60.10N 7.40 E
Bjørnevatn 7 Gb 69.40N 30.00 E
Bjørnøya 67 Kd 74.30N 19.00 E
Björnöya=Bear Island (EN)
5 Ha 74.30N 19.00 E
Bjurholm 7 Ee 63.56N 19.13 E
Bjuröklubb 7 Ed 64.28N 21.35 E
Bjuv 8 Eh 56.05N 12.54 E
Bla 34 Dc 12.56N 5.45W
Blace 15 Ef 43.18N 21.18 E
Blackall 58 Gf 24.25S 145.28 E
Black Bank (EN)=Zwarte
Bank 12 Fa 53.15N 3.55 E
Black Bay 45 Lb 48.40N 88.30W
Blackburn 9 Kh 53.45N 2.29W
Blackburn, Mount- 38 Ec 61.44N 143.26W
Black Butte Lake 46 Dg 39.45N 122.20W
Black Coast 66 Qf 71.45S 62.00W
Blackdown Hills 9 Jk 50.57N 3.09W
Blackduck 45 Ic 47.44N 94.33W
Blackfoot 43 Ec 43.11N 112.20W
Blackfoot Reservoir 46 Je 42.55N 111.35W
Black Forest (EN)=
Schwarzwald 5 Gf 48.00N 8.15 E
Black Head 9 Hk 50.01N 5.03W
Black Hills 38 Ie 44.00N 104.00W
Black Isle 9 Id 57.35N 4.20W
Black Lake 42 Ge 59.11N 105.20W
Blackman's 51q Ab 13.11N 59.32W
Black Mesa 46 Jh 36.35N 110.20W
Blackmoor 9 Ik 50.23N 4.50W
Black Mountain 43 Kd 36.54N 82.54W
Black Mountains [U.S.] 46 Hi 35.30N 114.30W
Black Mountains
[Wales-U.K.] 9 Jj 51.57N 3.08W
Blackpool 9 Jh 53.50N 3.03W
Black Range 43 Fe 33.20N 107.50W
Black River 49 Id 18.01N 77.51W
Black River [Az.-U.S.] 46 Jj 33.44N 110.13W
Black River [Mi.-U.S.] 44 Fd 43.00N 82.25W
Black River [N.Y.-U.S.] 44 Id 43.59N 76.04W
Black River [U.S.] 45 Ki 35.38N 91.19W
Black River [Wi.-U.S.] 45 Ke 43.57N 91.22W
Black River (EN)=Babian
Jiang 21 Mg 20.17N 106.34 E
Black River (EN)=Da, Sông-
21 Mg 20.17N 106.34 E
Black River Falls 45 Kd 44.16N 90.52W
Black Rock 56 Lh 53.39S 41.48W
Black Rock [Ire.] 9 Cg 54.05N 10.20W
Black Rock [Phil.] 26 Ge 8.48N 119.50 E
Black Rock Desert 43 Dc 41.10N 119.00W
Blacksburg 44 Gg 37.15N 80.25W
Black Sea (EN)=Černoje
More 5 Jg 43.00N 35.00 E
Black Sea (EN)=Černo
More 5 Jg 43.00N 35.00 E
Black Sea (EN)=
Karadeniz 5 Jg 43.00N 35.00 E
Black Sea (EN)=Neagră,
Marea- 5 Jg 43.00N 35.00 E
Blacksod Bay/Cuan an
Fhóid Duibh 9 Dg 54.08N 10.00W
Blackstairs Mountains/Na
Staighri Dubha 9 Gi 52.33N 6.49W
Blackstone 44 Hg 37.04N 78.01W
Blackville 44 Ob 46.47N 65.54W
Black Volta 30 Gh 8.38N 1.30W
Black Volta (EN)=Volta
Noire 30 Gh 8.38N 1.30W
Black Volta (EN)=Volta
Noire [3] 34 Ec 12.30N 4.00W
Blackwater 12 Cc 51.43N 0.28 E
Blackwater/An Abhainn
Dubh 9 Gh 53.39N 6.43W
Blackwater/An Abhainn
Mhór [Ire.] 9 Fj 51.51N 7.50W
Blackwater/An Abhainn
Mhór [N.Ire.-U.K.] 9 Gg 54.30N 6.35W
Blackwell 45 Hh 36.48N 97.17W
Blackwood River 59 Df 34.35S 115.02 E
Blagnac 11 Hk 43.38N 1.24 E
Blagodarny 16 Mg 45.04N 43.24 E
Blagojevgrad 15 Gg 42.01N 23.06 E
Blagojevgrad [2] 15 Gh 41.45N 23.25 E
Blagoveščenka 20 Cf 52.50N 79.55 E
Blagoveščensk 19 Fd 55.01N 55.59 E
Blagoveščensk 22 Od 50.17N 127.32 E
Blåhø 8 Cb 62.45N 9.19 E
Blain 11 Eg 47.29N 1.45W
Blaine [Mn.-U.S.] 45 Jd 45.11N 93.14W
Blaine [Wa.-U.S.] 46 Db 48.59N 122.44W
Blair 45 Hf 41.33N 96.08W
Blair Athol 59 Jd 22.42S 147.33 E
Blairgowrie 9 Je 56.36N 3.21W
Blairmore 46 Hb 49.36N 114.26W
Blaise 11 Kf 48.38N 4.43 E
Blaj 15 Gc 46.11N 23.55 E
Blake Basin (EN) 43 Mf 29.00N 76.00W
Blakely 44 Ej 31.23N 84.56W
Blakeney Point 9 Ni 52.59N 1.00 E
Blake Plateau (EN) 38 Lf 31.00N 79.00W
Blake Ridge (EN) 38 Lg 29.00N 73.30W
Blakstad 7 Bg 58.30N 8.39 E
Blanc, Cape- (EN)=Abyaḑ,
Ra's al- 30 He 37.20N 9.50 E
Blanc, Cape- (EN)=
Nouâdhibou, Râs- 30 Ff 20.46N 17.03W
Blanc, Lac- 44 Kb 47.45N 73.12W
Blanc, Mont- 5 Gf 45.50N 6.52 E
Blanca, Bahía- 52 Ji 38.55S 62.10W
Blanca, Cerro- 49 Gi 8.40N 80.35W
Blanca, Cordillera- 54 Ce 9.10S 77.35W
Blanca, Costa- 13 Lg 37.38N 0.40W
Blanca, Isla- 48 Pg 21.24N 86.50W
Blanca, Punta- 48 Bc 29.05N 114.45W
Blancagrande 55 Bm 36.32S 60.53W
Blanca Peak [Co.-U.S.] 43 Fd 37.34N 105.29W
Blanca Peak [U.S.] 38 If 37.35N 105.29W
Blanche, Lake- [Austl.] 59 Ed 22.25S 123.15 E
Blanche, Lake- [Austl.] 59 He 29.15S 139.40 E
Blanche, Point- 51b Ac 18.00N 63.03W
Blanche Channel 63a Cc 8.30S 157.30 E
Blanc-Nez, Cap- 12 Dd 50.56N 1.42 E
Blanco, Cabo- [C.R.] 47 Gg 9.33N 85.06W
Blanco, Cabo- [Sp.] 13 Oe 39.22N 2.46 E
Blanco, Cape- 43 Cc 42.50N 124.34W
Blanco, Cerro- 48 Fe 25.43N 107.39W
Blanco, Río- 54 Ff 12.30S 64.18W
Blanco del Sur, Cayo- 49 Gb 22.02N 81.24W
Blanda 7a Bb 65.39N 20.18W
Blanding 46 Kh 37.37N 109.29W
Blanes 13 Oc 41.41N 2.48 E
Blangy-le-Château 12 Ce 49.14N 0.17 E
Blangy-sur-Bresle 11 He 49.56N 1.38 E
Blanice [Czech.] 10 Kg 49.48N 14.58 E
Blanice [Czech.] 10 Kg 49.17N 14.09 E
Blankaholm 8 Gg 57.35N 16.31 E
Blankenberge 12 Jc 51.19N 3.08 E
Blankenheim 12 Id 50.26N 6.39 E
Blanquilla, Isla- 54 Fa 11.51N 64.37W
Blanquillo 55 Ek 32.55S 55.40W
Blansko 10 Mg 49.22N 16.39 E
Blantyre 31 Ki 15.47S 35.00 E
Blantyre-Limbe 36 Gf 15.49S 35.03 E
Blåskavlen 8 Bd 60.58N 7.18 E
Błaszki 10 Oe 51.39N 18.27 E
Blatná 10 Jg 49.26N 13.53 E
Blato 14 Kh 42.56N 16.48 E
Blåvands Huk 8 Ci 55.33N 8.05 E
Blavet [Fr.] 11 Cf 48.13N 3.10W
Blavet [Fr.] 11 Cg 47.46N 3.18W
Blaye 11 Fi 45.08N 0.40W
Blaye-les-Mines 11 Ij 44.01N 2.08 E
Bled 14 Id 46.22N 14.08 E
Blefjell 8 Ce 59.48N 9.10 E
Bleialf 12 Id 50.14N 6.17 E
Blekinge [2] 7 Dh 56.20N 15.20 E
Blenheim 58 Ii 41.31S 173.57 E
Bletchley 9 Mj 52.00N 0.46W
Bleus, Monts- 36 Fb 1.30N 30.30 E
Bhārshāh 25 Fe 19.50N 79.22 E
Blida [3] 32 Hb 36.35N 2.30 E
Blida 31 He 36.34N 2.55 E
Blidö 8 He 59.35N 18.55 E
Blidsberg 8 Eg 57.56N 13.29 E
Blies 12 Je 49.07N 7.04 E
Blieskastel 12 Je 49.14N 7.15 E
Bligh Water 63d Ab 17.00S 178.00 E
Blind River 42 Jg 46.10N 82.58W
Blitar 26 Fh 8.06S 112.09 E
Blitta 34 Fd 8.19N 0.59 E
Block Island 44 Le 41.11N 71.35W
Bloemfontein 31 Jk 29.12S 26.07 E
Bloemhof 37 De 27.38S 25.32 E
Blois 11 Hg 47.35N 1.20 E
Blokhus 8 Cg 57.15N 9.35 E
Blomberg 12 Lc 51.56N 9.05 E
Blönduós 7a Bb 65.40N 20.18W
Bloody Foreland/Cnoc
Fola 9 Ef 55.09N 8.17W
Bloomfield [Ia.-U.S.] 45 Jf 40.45N 92.25W
Bloomfield [In.-U.S.] 44 Df 39.01N 86.56W
Bloomington [Il.-U.S.] 43 Jc 40.29N 88.59W
Bloomington [In.-U.S.] 43 Jd 39.10N 86.32W
Bloomington [Mn.-U.S.] 45 Jd 44.50N 93.17W
Bloomsburg 44 Ie 41.01N 76.27W
Blosseville Kyst 41 Je 68.45N 27.25W
Blötberget 8 Fd 60.07N 15.04 E
Blountstown 44 Ej 30.29N 85.03W
Bludenz 14 Dc 47.09N 9.49 E
Blue Earth 45 Ie 43.38N 94.06W
Bluefield 43 Kd 37.14N 81.17W
Bluefields 39 Kh 12.00N 83.45W
Bluefields, Bahía de- 49 Fg 12.02N 83.44W
Blue Mesa Reservoir 45 Cg 38.28N 107.15W
Blue Mountain 44 Ie 40.15N 77.30W
Blue Mountain [Or.-U.S.] 46 Ge 42.25N 117.50W
Blue Mountain [U.S.] 45 Ii 34.41N 94.03W
Blue Mountain Lake 44 Jd 43.53N 74.26W
Blue Mountain Pass 46 Ge 42.18N 117.45W
Blue Mountain Peak 47 Ie 18.03N 76.35W
Blue Mountains [Austl.] 59 Kf 33.35S 150.15 E
Blue Mountains [U.S.] 43 Ec 44.35N 118.25W
Blue Mud Bay 59 Hb 13.25S 135.55 E
Blue Nile (EN)=Abay 30 Kg 15.38N 32.31 E
Blue Nile (EN)=Azraq, Al
Baḩr al- 30 Kg 15.38N 32.31 E
Bluenose Lake 42 Fc 68.30N 121.00W
Blue Ridge 44 Eh 34.52N 84.20W
Blue Ridge 38 Kf 37.00N 82.00W
Blue Stack/Na Cruacha 9 Eg 54.45N 8.06W
Bluestone Lake 44 Gg 37.30N 80.50W
Bluff [N.Z.] 61 Ci 46.36S 168.21 E
Bluff [Ut.-U.S.] 46 Kh 37.17N 109.33W
Bluff Point 59 Ce 27.50S 114.05 E
Bluffton 44 Ee 40.44N 85.11W
Blumberg 10 Ei 47.50N 8.32 E
Blumenau 56 Kc 26.56S 49.03W
Blyth 12 Db 52.19N 1.41 E
Blyth 9 Lf 55.07N 1.30W
Blythe 43 Ee 33.37N 114.36W
Blytheville 43 Jd 35.56N 89.55W
Bø 7 Bg 59.25N 9.04 E
Bo 31 Fh 7.58N 11.45W
Boa 34 Dd 8.26N 7.10W
Boac 26 Hd 12.28N 122.28 E
Boaco [3] 49 Eg 12.35N 85.25W
Boaco 49 Eg 12.28N 85.40W
Boa Esperança 55 Je 21.05S 45.34W
Boa Esperança, Represa- 54 Je 6.50S 44.00W
Boa Esperança, Serra da-
55 Je 20.57S 45.40W
Bo'ai 28 Bg 35.10N 113.03 E
Boal 13 Fa 43.26N 6.49W
Boali 35 Be 4.48N 18.07 E
Boano, Pulau- 26 Ig 2.56S 127.56 E
Boardman 46 Fd 45.51N 119.43W
Boa Sentença, Serra da- 55 Ed 19.13S 57.33W
Boa Vista 30 Eg 16.05N 22.50W
Boa Vista [Braz.] 55 Ec 17.51S 54.13W
Boa Vista [Braz.] 55 Ia 12.40S 46.51W
Boa Vista [Braz.] 53 Je 2.49N 60.40W
Bobai 27 Ig 22.15N 109.58 E
Bobali, Cerros de- 49 Ki 8.53N 73.28W
Bobali, Cerros de- 49 Ki 8.53N 73.28W
Bobbio 14 Df 44.46N 9.23 E
Bobigny 11 If 48.54N 2.27 E
Bobo Dioulasso 31 Gg 11.12N 4.18W
Bobojod, Gora- 18 Hd 40.50N 70.20 E
Bobolice 10 Mc 53.57N 16.36 E
Bobonong 37 Dd 21.58S 28.25 E
Bobovdol 15 Fg 42.22N 23.00 E
Bóbr 10 Ld 52.04N 15.04 E
Bobrik 16 Ec 52.08N 26.48 E
Bobrinec 16 He 48.04N 32.09 E
Bobrka 10 Ug 49.34N 24.20 E
Bobrov 19 Ee 51.06N 40.01 E
Bobrovica 16 Gd 50.43N 31.28 E
Bobrowniki 10 Tc 53.08N 23.50 E
Bobrujsk 6 Ie 53.09N 29.15 E
Bobures 54 Db 9.15N 71.11W
Boby, Pic- 37 Hd 22.12S 46.55 E
Boca del Rio 48 Ee 25.20N 108.25W
Boca de Pozo 50 Dg 11.00N 64.23W
Boca do Acre 53 Jf 8.45S 67.23W
Bocage, Cap- 63b Be 21.12S 165.37 E
Bocaina 55 Db 15.16S 56.45W
Bocaiúva 55 Kc 17.07S 43.49W
Bocajá 55 Ef 22.45S 55.13W
Bocaranga 35 Bd 6.59N 15.39 E
Boca Raton 43 Kf 26.21N 80.05W
Bocas del Toro 47 Hg 9.20N 82.15W
Bocas del Toro [3] 49 Fi 8.50N 82.10W
Bocas del Toro, Archipiélago
de- 49 Fi 9.20N 82.10W
Bocay 49 Ef 14.19N 85.10W
Bochaine 11 Lj 44.20N 5.50 E
Bochnia 10 Qg 49.58N 20.26 E
Bocholt [Bel.] 12 Hc 51.10N 5.35 E
Bocholt [Ger.] 10 Ce 51.50N 6.36 E
Bochum 10 De 51.29N 7.13 E
Bocognano 11a Ba 42.05N 9.04 E
Bocoio 36 Be 12.28S 14.08 E
Boconó 49 Li 9.15N 70.16W
Bocşa 15 Ed 45.23N 21.47 E
Boda 35 Be 4.19N 17.28 E
Boda 8 Fc 61.01N 15.13 E
Böda 8 Gg 57.15N 17.03 E
Bodafors 8 Fg 57.30N 14.42 E
Bodajbo 22 Nd 57.51N 114.10 E
Bodalangi 36 Db 3.14N 22.14 E
Bode 10 Hd 52.01N 11.12 E
Bödefeld-Freiheit,
Schmallenberg- 12 Kc 51.15N 8.24 E
Bodegraven 12 Gb 52.06N 4.44 E
Bodélé 30 Ig 16.30N 17.30 E
Boden 6 Ib 65.50N 21.42 E
Bodenheim 12 Ke 49.56N 8.18 E
Bodensee=Constance,
Lake- (EN) 5 Gf 47.35N 9.25 E
Boderg, Lough- 9 Fh 53.52N 8.00W
Bodmin 9 Ik 50.29N 4.43W
Bodmin Moor 9 Ik 50.35N 4.40W
Bodø 6 Hb 67.17N 14.23 E
Bodoquena 55 De 20.12S 56.48W
Bodoquena, Serra da- 54 Gh 21.00S 56.50W
Bodrog 10 Rh 48.07N 21.25 E
Bodrogköz 10 Rh 48.15N 21.45 E
Bodrum 23 Cb 37.02N 27.06 E
Bodrum Yarimadasi 15 Kl 37.05N 27.30 E
Bodva 10 Qh 48.12N 20.47 E
Boën 11 Ji 45.44N 4.00 E
Boende 31 Ji 0.13S 20.52 E
Boeo, Capo- (Lilibeo, Capo-)
14 Gm 37.34N 12.41 E
Boerne 45 Gl 29.47N 98.44W
Boesmanland=Bushman-
land (EN) 37 Be 29.30S 19.00 E
Boffa 34 Cc 10.10N 14.02W
Boga 15 Cg 42.24N 19.38 E
Bogale 25 Je 16.17N 95.24 E
Bogalusa 45 Lk 30.47N 89.52W
Bogandé 34 Ec 12.59N 0.08W
Bogangolo 35 Bd 5.34N 18.15 E
Bogatić 15 Ce 44.51N 19.29 E
Bogatynia 10 Kf 50.55N 14.59 E
Boğazkale 24 Fb 40.01N 34.35 E
Boğazlıyan 24 Fc 39.12N 35.15 E
Bogbonga 36 Cb 1.35N 19.25 E

Index Symbols

[1] Independent Nation
[2] State, Region
[3] District, County
[4] Municipality
[5] Colony, Dependency
Continent
Physical Region
Historical or Cultural Region
Mount, Mountain
Volcano
Hill
Mountains, Mountain Range
Hills, Escarpment
Plateau, Upland
Pass, Gap
Plain, Lowland
Delta
Salt Flat
Valley, Canyon
Crater, Cave
Karst Features
Depression
Polder
Desert, Dunes
Forest, Woods
Heath, Steppe
Oasis
Cape, Point
Coast, Beach
Cliff
Peninsula
Isthmus
Sandbank
Island
Atoll
Rock, Reef
Islands, Archipelago
Rocks, Reefs
Coral Reef
Well, Spring
Geyser
River, Stream
Waterfall Rapids
River Mouth, Estuary
Lake
Salt Lake
Intermittent Lake
Reservoir
Swamp, Pond
Canal
Glacier
Ice Shelf, Pack Ice
Ocean
Sea
Gulf, Bay
Strait, Fjord
Lagoon
Bank
Seamount
Tablemount
Ridge
Shelf
Basin
Escarpment, Sea Scarp
Fracture
Trench, Abyss
National Park, Reserve
Point of Interest
Recreation Site
Cave, Cavern
Historic Site
Ruins
Wall, Walls
Church, Abbey
Temple
Scientific Station
Airport
Port
Lighthouse
Mine
Tunnel
Dam, Bridge

Bogda Feng	27	Ec	43.45N	88.32 E
Bogdan	15	Hg	42.37N	24.28 E
Bogdanovka → Ninocminda	16	Mi	41.15N	43.36 E
Bogda Shan	21	Ke	43.35N	90.00 E
Bogen	7	Db	68.32N	17.00 E
Bogenfels	37	Be	27.23S	15.22 E
Bogense	8	Di	55.34N	10.06 E
Boggeragh Mountains/An Bhograch	9	Ei	52.05N	9.00W
Boggy Peak	51d	Bb	17.03N	61.51W
Boghar	13	Oi	35.55N	2.43 E
Boghni	13	Ph	36.32N	3.57 E
Bogia	60	Ch	4.16S	144.58 E
Bognor Regis	12	Bd	50.47N	0.39W
Bogny-sur-Meuse	12	Ge	49.54N	4.43 E
Bogoduhov	16	Id	50.12N	35.31 E
Bogomila	15	Eh	41.36N	21.28 E
Bogor	22	Mj	6.35S	106.47 E
Bogoridick	19	De	53.50N	38.08 E
Bogorodčany	10	Uh	48.45N	24.40 E
Bogorodsk	7	Kh	56.09N	43.32 E
Bogorodskoje	7	Mh	57.51N	50.48 E
Bogorodskoje	20	Jf	52.22N	140.30 E
Bogotá → Santa Fe de Bogotá	53	Ie	4.36N	74.05W
Bogotol	20	De	56.17N	89.43 E
Bogøy	7	Dc	67.54N	15.11 E
Bogra	25	Hd	24.51N	89.22 E
Bogučany	20	Ee	58.23N	97.39 E
Bogučar	16	Le	49.57N	40.33 E
Bogué	32	Ef	16.36N	14.15W
Boguševsk	7	Hi	54.50N	30.13 E
Boguslav	19	Df	49.33N	30.54 E
Bo Hai=Chihli, Gulf of- (EN)	21	Nf	38.30N	120.00 E
Bohai Haixia	27	Ld	38.00N	121.30 E
Bohain-en-Vermandois	12	Fe	49.59N	3.27 E
Bohemia (EN)=Čechy	5	Hf	50.00N	14.30 E
Bohemia (EN)=Čechy	10	Kf	50.00N	14.30 E
Bohemian Forest (EN)=Böhmerwald	5	Hf	49.00N	13.30 E
Bohemian Forest (EN)=Český Les	10	Ig	49.50N	12.30 E
Bohemian Forest (EN)=Oberpfälzer Wald	10	Ig	49.50N	12.30 E
Bohemian Forest (EN)=Šumava	5	Hf	49.00N	13.30 E
Bohicon	34	Fd	7.12N	2.04 E
Bohmte	12	Kb	52.22N	8.19 E
Bohodoyou	34	Dd	9.46N	9.04W
Bohol	21	Oi	9.50N	124.10 E
Böhönye	10	Nj	46.24N	17.24 E
Bohor	14	Jd	46.04N	15.26 E
Bohu/Bagrax	27	Ec	41.58N	86.29 E
Bohus	8	Eg	57.51N	12.01 E
Bohuslän	8	Df	58.15N	11.50 E
Boiaçu	54	Fd	0.27S	61.46W
Boiano	14	Ii	41.29N	14.29 E
Boina	30	Lj	16.00S	46.30 E
Bois, Lac des -	42	Ec	66.50N	125.15W
Bois, Rio dos- [Braz.]	55	Gd	18.35S	50.02W
Bois, Rio dos- [Braz.]	55	Ha	13.55S	49.51W
Bois Blanc Island	44	Ec	45.45N	84.28W
Boischaut	11	Hb	46.40N	1.45 E
Boise	39	He	43.37N	116.13W
Boise City	45	Eh	36.44N	102.31W
Boise River	46	Ge	43.49N	117.01W
Boissay	12	De	49.31N	1.21 E
Boissevain	42	Hg	49.14N	100.03W
Boizenburg	10	Gc	53.23N	10.43 E
Bojador, Cabo-	30	Ff	26.08N	14.30W
Bojana	15	Ch	41.52N	19.22 E
Bojanowo	10	Me	51.42N	16.44 E
Bojarka	19	De	50.19N	30.20 E
Bojčinovci	15	Gf	43.28N	23.20 E
Bojnūrd	23	Ib	37.28N	57.19 E
Bojonegoro	26	Fh	7.09S	111.52 E
Bojuru	55	Gj	31.38S	51.26W
Bokatola	36	Cc	0.38S	18.46 E
Boké	34	Cc	10.56N	14.13W
Bokhara River	59	Je	29.55S	146.42 E
Bokn	8	Ae	59.15N	5.25 E
Boknafjorden	5	Gd	59.10N	5.35 E
Boko	36	Bc	4.47S	14.38 E
Bokol Mayo	35	Ge	4.31N	41.32 E
Bokoro	35	Bc	12.23N	17.03 E
Bokote	36	Dc	0.05S	20.08 E
Bokpyin	25	Jf	11.16N	98.46 E
Boksitogorsk	19	Dd	59.29N	33.52 E
Bokungu	36	Dc	0.41S	22.19 E
Bol [Chad]	35	Ac	13.30N	14.41 E
Bol	14	Kg	43.16N	16.40 E
Bola, Bahr-	35	Bd	9.50N	18.59 E
Bolama	34	Bc	11.35N	15.28W
Bolands	51d	Bb	17.02N	61.53W
Bolaños, Río-	48	Gg	21.14N	104.08W
Bolattau, Gora-	18	Ha	46.44N	71.54 E
Bolayir	15	Ji	40.31N	26.45 E
Bolbec	11	Ge	49.34N	0.29 E
Bolda	16	Pg	45.58N	48.35 E
Bole [Eth.]	35	Fd	6.37N	37.22 E
Bole [Ghana]	34	Ed	9.02N	2.29W
Bole/Bortala	27	Dc	44.59N	81.57 E
Bolehov	16	Ce	49.03N	23.50 E
Bolesławiec	10	Le	51.16N	15.34 E
Bolgatanga	31	Gg	10.47N	0.51W
Bolgrad	16	Fg	45.40N	28.38 E
Bolhov	19	De	53.30N	36.01 E
Boli	27	Nb	45.46N	130.31 E
Bolia	36	Cc	1.36S	18.23 E
Boliden	7	Ed	64.52N	20.23 E
Bolinao, Cape-	26	Gc	16.22N	119.50 E
Bolintin Vale	15	Ie	44.27N	25.46 E
Bolívar [Col.]	54	Db	9.00N	74.40W
Bolivar [Mo.-U.S.]	45	Jh	37.37N	93.25W
Bolivar [Tn.-U.S.]	44	Ch	35.15N	88.59W
Bolívar [Ven.]	54	Fb	6.20N	63.30W
Bolívar, Cerro-	54	Fb	7.28N	63.25W
Bolívar, Pico-	52	Ie	8.30N	71.02W
Bolivia	53	Jg	17.00S	65.00W
Bolivia, Altiplano de-	52	Jg	18.00S	68.00W
Boljevac	15	Ef	43.50N	21.58 E
Bollendorf	12	Ie	49.51N	6.22 E
Bollène	11	Kj	44.17N	4.45 E
Bollnäs	7	Df	61.21N	16.25 E
Bollon	59	Je	28.02S	147.28 E
Bollstabruk	8	Ga	63.00N	17.41 E
Bollullos par del Condado	13	Fg	37.20N	6.32W
Bolmen	7	Ch	56.55N	13.40 E
Bolnisi	16	Ni	41.28N	44.31 E
Bolobo	36	Cc	2.10S	16.14 E
Bolodek	20	If	53.43N	133.09 E
Bologna	6	Hg	44.29N	11.20 E
Bolognesi	54	Df	10.01S	74.05W
Bologoje	6	Jd	57.54N	34.02 E
Bolohovo	16	Jb	54.05N	37.52 E
Bolomba	36	Cb	0.29N	19.12 E
Bolombo	36	Dc	3.59S	21.22 E
Bolon	20	Ig	49.58N	136.04 E
Bolotnoje	20	De	55.41N	84.33 E
Bolovens, Plateau des-	25	Le	15.20N	106.20 E
Bolšaja Balahnja	20	Fb	73.37N	107.05 E
Bolšaja Berestovica	10	Uc	53.09N	24.02 E
Bolšaja Černigovka	7	Mj	52.08N	50.48 E
Bolšaja Glušica	7	Mj	52.24N	50.29 E
Bolšaja Ižora	8	Me	59.55N	29.40 E
Bolšaja Kinel	7	Mj	53.14N	50.32 E
Bolšaja Koksaga	7	Lh	56.07N	47.48 E
Bolšaja Kuonamka	20	Gc	70.50N	113.20 E
Bolšaja Oju	17	Jb	69.42N	60.42 E
Bolšaja Rogovaja	17	Jc	66.30N	60.40 E
Bolšaja Synja	17	Id	65.58N	58.01 E
Bolšaja Tap	17	Lg	59.55N	65.42 E
Bolšaja Ussurka	20	Ig	46.00N	133.30 E
Bolšaja Vladimirovka	19	He	50.53N	79.30 E
Bolšakovo	8	Ij	54.50N	21.36 E
Bolsena	14	Fh	42.39N	11.59 E
Bolsena, Lago di-	14	Fh	42.35N	11.55 E
Bolšerečje	19	Hd	56.06N	74.38 E
Bolšereck	20	Kf	52.22N	156.24 E
Bolšeustikinskoje	17	Ii	55.57N	58.20 E
Bolševik	20	Jd	62.40N	147.30 E
Bolševik, Ostrov-=Bolshevik Island (EN)	21	Mb	78.40N	102.30 E
Bolšezemelskaja Tundra	19	Fb	67.30N	58.30 E
Bolshevik Island (EN)=Bolševik, Ostrov-	21	Mb	78.40N	102.30 E
Bolšije Uki	19	Hd	56.57N	72.37 E
Bolšoj Anjuj	20	Lc	68.30N	160.50 E
Bolšoj Begičev, Ostrov-	20	Gb	74.20N	112.30 E
Bolšoj Berezovy, Ostrov-	8	Md	60.15N	28.35 E
Bolšoj Boktybaj, Gora- [Kaz.-U.S.S.R.]	19	Ff	48.30N	58.20 E
Bolšoj Boktybaj, Gora- [U.S.S.R.]	16	Ue	48.30N	58.25 E
Bolšoj Bolvanski Nos, Mys-	17	Ia	70.27N	59.05 E
Bolšoj Čeremšan	7	Li	54.12N	49.40 E
Bolšoje Muraškino	7	Ki	55.47N	44.46 E
Bolšoje Vlasjevo	20	Jf	53.25N	140.55 E
Bolšoje Zagorje	8	Mg	57.47N	28.58 E
Bolšoj Gašun	16	Mf	47.22N	42.42 E
Bolšoj Ik	17	Hj	51.47N	56.20 E
Bolšoj Irgiz	19	Ee	52.01N	47.24 E
Bolšoj Jenisej	20	Ef	51.40N	94.26 E
Bolšoj Jugan	19	Hc	60.55N	73.40 E
Bolšoj Kamen	20	Ih	43.08N	132.28 E
Bolšoj Klimecki, Ostrov-	7	Ie	62.00N	35.15 E
Bolšoj Kujalnik	16	Gf	46.46N	30.38 E
Bolšoj Kumak	16	Ud	51.22N	58.55 E
Bolšoj Ljahovski, Ostrov-	20	Jb	73.35N	142.00 E
Bolšoj Murta	20	Ee	56.55N	93.10 E
Bolšoj Nimnyr	20	He	58.08N	125.45 E
Bolšoj Pit	20	Ee	59.02N	91.40 E
Bolšoj Tjuters, Ostrov-	8	Le	59.50N	27.10 E
Bolšoj Uluj	20	Ee	56.45N	90.46 E
Bolšoj Uvat, Ozero-	17	Oh	57.35N	70.30 E
Bolšoj Uzen	5	Kf	48.50N	49.40 E
Bolsón, Cerro del-	52	Jh	27.13S	66.06W
Bolšovcy	10	Ug	49.08N	24.47 E
Bolsward	12	Ha	53.04N	5.30 E
Boltaña	13	Mb	42.27N	0.04 E
Bolton	9	Kh	53.35N	2.26W
Bolu	23	Da	40.44N	31.37 E
Bolu Dağları	24	Eb	41.05N	32.05 E
Bolungarvík	7a	Aa	66.09N	23.15W
Boluntay	27	Fd	36.29N	92.18 E
Bolva	16	Ic	53.17N	34.20 E
Bolvadin	24	Dc	38.42N	31.04 E
Bolzano/Bozen	6	Hf	46.31N	11.22 E
Bom, Rio-	55	Gf	23.56S	51.44W
Boma	31	Ii	5.51S	13.03 E
Bomassa	36	Cb	2.12N	16.12 E
Bombala	59	Jg	36.54S	149.14 E
Bombarral	13	Ce	39.16N	9.09W
Bombay	22	Jh	18.58N	72.50 E
Bomberai, Jazirah-	26	Jg	3.00S	133.00 E
Bombo	36	Fb	0.35N	32.32 E
Bomboma	36	Cb	2.26N	18.57 E
Bom Comércio	54	Ee	9.45S	65.54W
Bom Conselho	54	Ke	9.10S	36.41W
Bom Despacho	54	Ig	19.43S	45.15W
Bomdila	25	Ic	27.16N	92.23 E
Bomi/Bowo	27	Ge	30.02N	95.39 E
Bomi Hills	31	Fh	6.52N	10.45W
Bomili	36	Eb	1.40N	27.01 E
Bom Jardim de Goiás	55	Fc	16.17S	52.07W
Bom Jardim de Minas	55	Je	21.57S	44.11W
Bom Jesus	55	Gi	28.42S	50.24W
Bom Jesus da Lapa	53	Lg	13.15S	43.25W
Bom Jesus de Goiás	55	Hd	18.12S	49.37W
Bømlafjorden	8	Ae	59.40N	5.20 E
Bømlo	7	Ag	59.45N	5.10 E
Bomokandi	36	Eb	3.30N	26.08 E
Bomongo	36	Cb	1.22N	18.21 E
Bom Retiro	55	Hh	27.48S	49.31W
Bom Sucesso	55	Je	21.02S	44.46W
Bomu	30	Jh	4.08N	22.26 E
Bomu (EN)=Mbomou	30	Jh	4.08N	22.26 E
Bomu (EN)=Mbomou	35	Cd	5.30N	23.30 E
Bon, Cape- (EN)=Ţīb, Ra's At-	30	Ie	37.05N	11.03 E
Bona, Mount-	40	Kd	61.20N	141.50W
Bonaire	54	Ea	12.10N	68.15W
Bonaire Basin (EN)	50	Cg	11.25N	67.30W
Bonampak	48	Ni	16.43N	91.05W
Bonanza	49	Ef	14.01N	84.35W
Bonanza Peak	46	Eb	48.14N	120.52W
Bonao	49	Ld	18.56N	70.25W
Bonaparte, Mount-	46	Fb	48.45N	119.08W
Bonaparte Archipelago	57	Df	14.20S	125.20 E
Bonaparte Lake	46	Ea	51.16N	120.35W
Bonaparte Rocks	51p	Cb	12.24N	61.30W
Bonasse	50	Fg	10.05N	61.52W
Bonavista	42	Mg	48.39N	53.07W
Bonavista Bay	42	Mg	49.00N	53.20W
Bon-Cagan-Nur	27	Gb	45.35N	99.15 E
Bondeno	14	Ff	44.53N	11.25 E
Bondo	31	Jh	3.49N	23.40 E
Bondoukou	34	Ed	8.02N	2.48W
Bondoukou	34	Ed	8.20N	2.55W
Bondowoso	26	Fh	7.55S	113.49 E
Bone, Gulf of- (EN)=Bone, Teluk-	21	Oj	4.00S	120.40 E
Bone, Teluk-=Bone, Gulf of- (EN)	21	Oj	4.00S	120.40 E
Bone Bay	51a	Db	18.45N	64.22W
Bonelohe	26	Hh	5.48S	120.27 E
Bönen	12	Jc	51.36N	7.46 E
Bone Rate, Kepulauan-	26	Hh	7.00S	121.00 E
Bone Rate, Pulau-	26	Hh	7.22S	121.08 E
Bonete, Cerro-	56	Gc	27.51S	68.47W
Bong	34	Cd	6.49N	10.19W
Bong	34	Dd	7.00N	9.40W
Bonga	35	Fd	7.16N	36.14 E
Bongabong	26	Hd	12.45N	121.29 E
Bongandanga	36	Db	1.30N	21.03 E
Bongo, Massif des-	30	Jh	8.40N	22.25 E
Bongolava	37	Hc	18.35S	45.20 E
Bongor	31	Ig	10.17N	15.22 E
Bongouanou	34	Ed	6.43N	4.12W
Bongouanou	34	Ed	6.39N	4.12W
Bonham	45	Hj	33.35N	96.11W
Bonheiden	12	Gc	51.02N	4.32 E
Bonhomme, Col du-	11	Nf	48.10N	7.06 E
Bonhomme, Pic-	49	Kd	19.05N	72.15W
Bonifacio	11a	Bb	41.23N	9.09 E
Bonifacio, Bocche di-=Bonifacio, Strait of- (EN)	5	Gg	41.13N	9.15 E
Bonifacio, Strait of- (EN)=Bonifacio, Bocche di-	5	Gg	41.13N	9.15 E
Bonifati, Capo-	14	Jk	39.33N	15.52 E
Bonin Basin (EN)	60	Bb	29.00N	137.00 E
Bonin Islands (EN)=Ogasawara-Shotō	21	Qg	27.00N	142.10 E
Bonin Trench (EN)	3	If	30.00N	145.00 E
Bonita Springs	44	Gl	26.2 N	81.47W
Bonito [Braz.]	55	Jb	15.2[illegible]S	44.46W
Bonito [Braz.]	55	De	21.0[illegible]S	56.28W
Bonito, Pico-	47	Ge	15.38N	86.55W
Bonito, Rio- [Braz.]	55	Hb	15.18S	49.36W
Bonito, Rio- [Braz.]	55	Gc	16.3[illegible]S	51.23W
Bonn	6	Ge	50.44N	7.06 E
Bonn-Bad Godesberg	10	Df	50.41N	7.09 E
Bonnebosq	12	Ce	49.12N	0.05 E
Bonnechère River	44	Ic	45.31N	76.33W
Bonners Ferry	46	Gb	48.41N	116.18W
Bonnet, Lac du-	45	Ia	50.22N	95.55W
Bonnétable	11	Gf	48.11N	0.26 E
Bonnet Plume	42	Ec	65.53N	134.58W
Bonneval	11	Hf	48.11N	1.24 E
Bonneville	11	Mh	46.05N	6.25 E
Bonneville Salt Flats	46	If	40.45N	113.50W
Bonnières-sur-Seine	12	De	49.02N	1.35 E
Bonningues-lès-Ardres	12	Ed	50.47N	2.01 E
Bonny	34	Ge	4.25N	7.10 E
Bono	14	Dj	40.25N	9.02 E
Bō-no-Misaki	29	Bf	31.15N	130.13 E
Bonorva	14	Cj	40.25N	8.46 E
Bontang	26	Gf	0.08N	117.30 E
Bonthain	26	Gh	5.32S	119.56 E
Bonthe	34	Cd	7.32N	12.30W
Bontoc	26	Hc	17.05N	120.58 E
Bonyhád	10	Oj	46.18N	18.32 E
Boo, Kepulauan-	26	Ig	1.12S	129.24 E
Boola	34	Dd	8.22N	8.43W
Booligal	59	If	33.52S	144.53 E
Boone [Ia.-U.S.]	45	Je	42.04N	93.53W
Boone [N.C.-U.S.]	44	Gg	36.13N	81.41W
Booneville [Ar.-U.S.]	45	Ji	35.08N	93.55W
Booneville [Ms.-U.S.]	45	Li	34.39N	88.34W
Boon Point	51d	Bb	17.10N	61.50W
Boonville [In.-U.S.]	44	Df	38.03N	87.16W
Boonville [Mo.-U.S.]	45	Jg	38.58N	92.44W
Boos	12	De	49.23N	1.12 E
Boothia, Gulf of-	38	Jb	71.00N	91.00W
Boothia Peninsula	38	Jb	70.30N	95.00W
Boot Reefs	60	Cj	10.00S	144.35 E
Booué	31	Ii	0.06S	11.56 E
Bophuthatswana	37	De	26.00S	25.30 E
Bopolu	34	Cd	7.04N	10.29W
Boppard	12	Jd	50.14N	7.36 E
Boquerón	55	Bf	23.00S	61.00W
Boquerón	51a	Ab	18.03N	67.09W
Boquilla, Presa de la-	48	Gd	27.30N	105.30W
Boquillas del Carmen	48	Hc	29.17N	102.53W
Bor [Czech.]	10	Ig	49.43N	12.47 E
Bor	7	Kh	56.23N	44.07 E
Bor [Sud.]	31	Kh	6.12N	31.33 E
Bor [Swe.]	8	Fg	57.07N	14.10 E
Bor [Tur.]	24	Fd	37.54N	34.34 E
Bor	15	Fe	44.06N	22.06 E
Bora-Bora, Ile-	57	Lf	16.30S	151.45W
Borah Peak	38	He	44.08N	113.14W
Boraldaj	18	Gc	42.30N	69.05 E
Bora Marina	14	Jm	37.56N	15.55 E
Bōramo	35	Gd	9.58N	43.07 E
Borås	7	Ch	57.43N	12.55 E
Borāzjān	24	Nh	29.16N	51.12 E
Borba [Braz.]	54	Gd	4.24S	59.35W
Borba [Port.]	13	Ef	38.48N	7.27W
Borborema, Planalto da-	52	Mf	7.00S	37.00W
Borca	15	Ib	47.11N	25.46 E
Borcea	15	Ke	44.20N	27.45 E
Borcea, Braţul-	15	Ke	44.40N	27.53 E
Borchgrevink Coast	66	Kf	73.00S	171.00 E
Borçka	24	Ib	41.22N	41.40 E
Borculo	12	Ib	52.07N	6.31 E
Borda da Mata, Serra-	55	Ie	21.18S	47.06W
Bordeaux	6	Fg	44.50N	0.34W
Borden	42	Ga	78.30N	110.30W
Borden Peninsula	38	Kb	73.00N	83.00W
Borders	9	Kf	55.35N	3.00W
Bordertown	58	Fh	36.19S	140.47 E
Bordighera	14	Bg	43.46N	7.39 E
Bordj Bou Arreridj	32	Hb	36.04N	4.46 E
Bordj el Emir Abdelkader	13	Oi	35.52N	2.16 E
Bordj Fly Sainte Marie	32	Gd	27.18N	2.59W
Bordj-Menaïel	13	Ph	36.44N	3.43 E
Bordj Messouda	32	Ic	30.12N	9.25 E
Bordj Moktar	31	Hf	21.20N	0.56 E
Bordj Omar Driss	31	Hf	28.09N	6.49 E
Bord Khūn-e Now	24	Nh	28.03N	51.28 E
Bordon Camp	12	Bc	51.07N	0.51W
Boreal, Chaco-	52	Kh	23.00S	60.00W
Boren	8	Ff	58.35N	15.10 E
Borensberg	8	Ff	58.34N	15.17 E
Borgå/Porvoo	7	Ff	60.24N	25.40 E
Borgarnes	7a	Bb	64.32N	21.55W
Børgefjell	7	Cd	65.23N	13.50 E
Borgentreich	12	Lc	51.34N	9.15 E
Borger [Neth.]	12	Ib	52.55N	6.48 E
Borger [Tx.-U.S.]	43	Gd	35.39N	101.24W
Borgholm	7	Dh	56.53N	16.39 E
Borghorst, Steinfurt-	12	Jb	52.08N	7.25 E
Borgia	14	Kl	38.49N	16.30 E
Borgloon	12	Hd	50.48N	5.20 E
Borgomanero	14	Ce	45.42N	8.28 E
Borgorose	14	Hh	42.11N	13.15 E
Borgo San Dalmazzo	14	Bf	44.20N	7.30 E
Borgo San Lorenzo	14	Fg	43.57N	11.23 E
Borgosesia	14	Ce	45.43N	8.16 E
Borgou	34	Fc	10.30N	2.50 E
Borgo Val di Taro	14	Df	44.29N	9.46 E
Borgo Valsugana	14	Fd	46.03N	11.27 E
Borgu	30	Hg	10.35N	3.40 E
Borgworm/Waremme	11	Ld	50.42N	5.15 E
Bori	34	Ge	4.42N	7.21 E
Borinquen, Punta-	51a	Ab	18.30N	67.10W
Borislav	19	Cf	49.18N	23.27 E
Borisoglebsk	6	Ke	51.23N	42.06 E
Borisov	19	Ce	54.15N	28.30 E
Borisovka	16	Jd	50.36N	36.06 E
Borispol	19	De	50.23N	30.59 E
Bo River	35	Dd	6.48N	27.55 E
Borja	14	Lf	44.31N	17.44 E
Borja [Peru]	54	Cd	4.26S	77.33W
Borja [Sp.]	13	Kc	41.50N	1.32W
Borjas Blancas/Les Borges Blanques	13	Mc	41.31N	0.52 E
Borken	10	Ce	51.51N	6.52 E
Borkou	30	Ig	18.15N	18.50 E
Borkou-Ennedi-Tibesti	35	Bb	18.00N	19.00 E
Borkoviči	8	Mi	55.38N	28.23 E
Borkum	10	Cc	53.35N	6.41 E
Borlänge	7	Df	60.29N	15.25 E
Borlu	24	Cc	38.44N	28.27 E
Bormida	14	Cf	44.56N	8.40 E
Bormio	14	Ed	46.28N	10.22 E
Born	11	Fj	44.30N	1.00W
Borna	10	Ie	51.07N	12.30 E
Borndiep	12	Ha	53.25N	5.35 E
Borne	12	Ib	52.18N	6.45 E
Borneo/Kalimantan	21	Ni	1.00N	114.00 E
Bornheim	12	Id	50.46N	7.00 E
Bornholm	5	Hd	55.10N	15.00 E
Bornholm	8	Fi	55.10N	15.00 E
Bornos	13	Gh	36.48N	5.44W
Bornova, İzmir-	24	Bc	38.27N	27.14 E
Bornu	34	Hc	12.00N	12.40 E
Bornu	30	Ig	12.30N	13.00 E
Boro	30	Jh	8.52N	26.11 E
Borodino	7	Ii	55.32N	35.49 E
Borodino	20	Ee	55.57N	95.03 E
Borodinskoje	8	Md	61.00N	29.29 E
Borogoncy	20	Id	62.39N	131.08 E
Borohoro Shan	21	Ke	42.00N	85.00 E
Boromo	34	Ec	11.45N	2.56W
Borongan	26	Id	11.37N	125.26 E
Borotou	34	Dd	8.44N	7.30W
Borovan	15	Gf	43.26N	23.45 E
Borovec	15	Gg	42.16N	23.35 E
Boroviči	19	Dd	58.24N	33.56 E
Borovici	8	Mg	57.58N	29.47 E
Borovljanka	20	Df	52.38N	84.35 E
Borovo	14	Me	45.24N	18.59 E
Borovski	19	Gd	57.03N	65.44 E
Borovskoj	19	Ge	53.48N	64.17 E
Borrachas, Islas-	50	Dg	10.18N	64.44W
Borān	35	Hc	10.11N	48.53 E
Borrby	8	Fi	55.27N	14.10 E
Borroloola	58	Ef	16.04S	136.17 E
Borş	15	Eb	47.07N	21.49 E
Borşa	15	Hb	47.39N	24.40 E
Borščovočny Hrebet=Borshchovochny Range (EN)	20	Gf	52.00N	118.30 E
Borsec	15	Ic	46.57N	25.34 E
Borshchovochny Range (EN)=Borščovočny Hrebet	20	Gf	52.00N	118.30 E
Borsod-Abaúj-Zemplén	10	Qh	48.15N	21.00 E
Bortala/Bole	27	Dc	44.59N	81.57 E
Bortala He	27	Dc	44.53N	82.45 E
Bort-les-Orgues	11	Ii	45.24N	2.30 E
Borūjen	24	Ng	31.59N	51.18 E
Borūjerd	23	Gc	33.54N	48.46 E
Borzja	22	Nd	50.24N	116.31 E
Borzna	16	Hd	51.15N	32.29 E
Boržomi	16	Mi	41.50N	43.25 E
Borzsöny	10	Oi	47.55N	19.00 E
Borzyszkowy	10	Nb	54.03N	17.22 E
Bosa	14	Cj	40.18N	8.30 E
Bosanska Dubica	14	Ke	45.11N	16.48 E
Bosanska Gradiška	14	Le	45.09N	17.15 E
Bosanska Krupa	14	Kf	44.53N	16.10 E
Bosanski Brod	14	Me	45.08N	18.01 E
Bosanski Novi	14	Ke	45.03N	16.22 E
Bosanski Petrovac	14	Kf	44.34N	16.21 E
Bosanski Šamac	14	Me	45.04N	18.28 E
Bosansko Grahovo	23	Ff	44.11N	16.22 E
Bōsāso	31	Lg	11.13N	49.08 E
Bosavi, Mount-	59	Ia	6.35S	142.50 E
Bosbeek	12	Hc	51.06N	5.48 E
Bose	22	Mg	24.01N	106.32 E
Boshan	27	Kd	36.30N	117.50 E
Boshrūyeh	24	Qf	33.53N	57.26 E
Bosilegrad	15	Fg	42.30N	22.28 E
Bosingfeld, Extertal-	12	Lb	52.04N	9.07 E
Bosna	14	Me	45.04N	18.28 E
Bosna	15	Kg	42.11N	27.27 E
Bosna=Bosnia (EN)	5	Hg	44.00N	18.00 E
Bosna = Bosnia (EN)	14	Lf	44.00N	18.00 E
Bosnia i Hercegovina = Bosnia and Herzegovina (EN)	14	Lf	44.15N	17.50 E
Bosnia (EN) = Bosna	14	Lf	44.00N	18.00 E
Bosnia (EN) = Bosna	5	Hg	44.00N	18.00 E
Bosnia and Herzegovina (EN) = Bosna i Hercegovina	14	Lf	44.15N	17.50 E
Bosnik	26	Kg	1.10S	136.14 E
Bošnjakovo	20	Jg	49.41N	142.10 E
Bosobolo	36	Cb	4.11N	19.54 E
Bōsō-Hantō	28	Pg	35.20N	140.10 E
Bosporus (EN)=İstanbul Boğazi	5	Ig	41.00N	29.00 E
Bosque Bonito	48	Gb	30.42N	105.06W
Bossangoa	31	Ih	6.29N	17.27 E
Bossé Bangou	34	Fc	13.21N	1.18 E
Bossembélé	35	Bd	5.16N	17.39 E
Bossemtélé II	35	Bd	5.41N	16.38 E
Bossier City	43	Ie	32.31N	93.43W
Bosso	34	Hc	13.42N	13.19 E
Bosso, Dallol-	30	Hg	12.25N	2.50 E
Bossut, Cape-	59	Ec	18.43S	121.38 E
Bostān	25	Db	30.26N	67.02 E
Bostānābād	24	Ld	37.50N	46.50 E
Bosten/Bagrax Hu	21	Ke	42.00N	87.00 E
Boston [Eng.-U.K.]	9	Mi	52.59N	0.01W
Boston [Ma.-U.S.]	39	Le	42.21N	71.04W
Boston Bar	46	Eb	49.52N	121.26W
Boston Deeps	12	Ca	53.00N	0.15 E
Boston Mountains	43	Id	35.50N	93.20W
Botan	24	Id	37.44N	41.48 E
Botas, Ribeirão das-	55	Fe	20.26S	53.43W
Botesdale	12	Db	52.20N	1.01 E
Botev	5	Ig	42.43N	24.55 E
Botevgrad	15	Gg	42.54N	23.47 E
Bothnia, Gulf of- (EN)=Bottniska viken	5	Hc	63.00N	20.00 E
Bothnia, Gulf of- (EN)=Pohjanlahti	5	Hc	63.00N	20.00 E
Boticas	13	Ec	41.41N	7.40W
Botletle	37	Cd	21.07S	24.42 E
Botlih	16	Oh	42.41N	46.13 E
Botna	15	Mc	46.48N	29.30 E
Botoşani	15	Jb	47.40N	26.43 E
Botoşani	15	Jb	47.45N	26.40 E
Botrange	11	Md	50.30N	6.08 E
Botswana	31	Jk	22.00S	24.00 E
Botte Donato	14	Kk	39.17N	16.27 E
Bottineau	43	Gb	48.50N	100.27W
Bottniska viken=Bothnia, Gulf of- (EN)	5	Hc	63.00N	20.00 E
Bottrop	10	Ce	51.31N	6.55 E
Botucatu	55	Kb	22.52S	48.26W
Botucatu, Serra de-	55	Hf	23.00S	48.20W
Botwood	42	Lg	49.08N	55.21W
Bouaflé	34	Dd	6.59N	5.45W
Bouaflé	34	Dd	7.03N	5.48W
Bouaké	31	Gh	7.41N	5.02W
Bouaké	34	Dd	7.45N	5.02W
Bou Anane	32	Gc	32.02N	3.03W
Bouar	31	Ih	5.57N	15.36 E
Bou Arfa	32	Gc	32.32N	1.57W
Boubín	10	Jh	43.58N	13.50 E
Bouca	31	Ih	6.30N	18.17 E
Bouchain	12	Fd	50.17N	3.19 E
Bouchegouf	14	Bn	36.28N	7.44 E
Bouche Island	51k	Bb	13.57N	60.53W
Bouches-du-Rhône	11	Kk	43.30N	5.00 E
Boudenib	32	Gc	31.57N	3.36W
Boudeuse Cay	37b	Bb	6.05S	52.51 E
Boû Djébéha	34	Eb	18.33N	2.45W
Bouenza	36	Bc	3.00S	13.00 E
Boufarik	13	Oh	36.34N	2.55 E
Bougaa	13	Rh	36.20N	5.05 E
Bougainville Island	57	Ge	6.00S	155.00 E
Bougainville Reef	59	Jc	15.30S	147.05 E
Bougainville Strait [Ocn.]	63a	Cb	6.40S	156.10 E
Bougainville Strait [Van.]	63b	Cb	15.50S	167.10 E
Bougouni	31	Gg	11.25N	7.28W

Index Symbols

1 Independent Nation
2 State, Region
3 District, County
4 Municipality
5 Colony, Dependency
Continent
Physical Region
Historical or Cultural Region
Mount, Mountain
Volcano
Hill
Mountains, Mountain Range
Hills, Escarpment
Plateau, Upland
Pass, Gap
Plain, Lowland
Delta
Salt Flat
Valley, Canyon
Crater, Cave
Karst Features
Depression
Polder
Desert, Dunes
Forest, Woods
Heath, Steppe
Oasis
Cape, Point
Coast, Beach
Cliff
Peninsula
Isthmus
Sandbank
Island
Atoll
Rock, Reef
Islands, Archipelago
Rocks, Reefs
Coral Reef
Well, Spring
Geyser
River, Stream
Waterfall Rapids
River Mouth, Estuary
Lake
Salt Lake
Intermittent Lake
Reservoir
Swamp, Pond
Canal
Glacier
Ice Shelf, Pack Ice
Ocean
Sea
Gulf, Bay
Strait, Fjord
Lagoon
Bank
Seamount
Tablemount
Ridge
Shelf
Basin
Escarpment, Sea Scarp
Fracture
Trench, Abyss
National Park, Reserve
Point of Interest
Recreation Site
Cave, Cavern
Historic Site
Ruins
Wall, Walls
Church, Abbey
Temple
Scientific Station
Airport
Port
Lighthouse
Mine
Tunnel
Dam, Bridge

Name	Map	Grid	Lat.	Long.
Bougtob	32	Hc	34.02N	0.05 E
Bouguenais	11	Eg	47.11N	1.37W
Bougzoul	13	Oi	35.42N	2.51 E
Bou Hadjar	14	Cn	36.30N	8.06 E
Bouhalla, Jbel-	13	Gi	35.06N	5.07W
Bou Hamed	13	Hi	35.19N	4.58W
Bouillante	51e	Ab	16.08N	61.46W
Bouillon	11	Le	49.48N	5.04 E
Bouira	32	Hb	36.23N	3.54 E
Bouira [3]	32	Hb	36.15N	4.10 E
Bou Ismail	13	Oh	36.38N	2.41 E
Bou Izakarn	32	Fd	29.10N	9.44W
Bou Kadir	13	Nh	36.04N	1.07 E
Boukombé	34	Fc	10.11N	1.06 E
Boû Lanouâr	32	De	21.16N	16.30W
Boulay-Moselle	12	Le	49.11N	6.30 E
Boulder [Co.-U.S.]	39	Ie	40.01N	105.17W
Boulder [Mt.-U.S.]	46	Ic	46.14N	112.07W
Boulder City	46	Hi	35.59N	114.50W
Boulemane	32	Gc	33.22N	4.45W
Boulemane [3]	32	Gc	33.02N	4.04W
Boulevard Atlántico	55	Dn	38.19S	57.59W
Boulia	59	Hd	22.54S	139.54 E
Bouligny	11	Le	49.17N	5.45 E
Boulogne	12	Gf	47.05N	1.40W
Boulogne-Billancourt	11	If	48.50N	2.15 E
Boulogne-sur-Mer	11	Hd	50.43N	1.37 E
Boulonnais	11	Hd	50.42N	1.40 E
Bouloupari	63b	Ce	21.52S	166.03 E
Boulsa	34	Ec	12.39N	0.34W
Boultoum	34	Hc	14.40N	10.18 E
Bou Maad, Djebel-	13	Oh	36.26N	2.08 E
Boumba	34	Ie	2.02N	15.12 E
Boumdeid	32	Ef	17.26N	11.21W
Boum Kabir	35	Bc	10.11N	19.24 E
Boumort	13	Nb	42.14N	1.08 E
Bouna	31	Gh	9.16N	3.00W
Bouna [3]	34	Ed	9.15N	3.20W
Boû Nâga	32	Ef	19.00N	13.13W
Bou Nasser, Adrar-	32	Gc	33.35N	3.53W
Boundary Peak	46	Fh	37.51N	118.21W
Boundiali [3]	34	Dd	9.23N	6.32W
Boundiali	34	Dd	9.31N	6.29W
Boundji	36	Cc	1.03S	15.22 E
Boungou	35	Ge	6.45N	22.06 E
Bountiful	43	Ec	40.53N	111.53W
Bounty Bay	64q	Ab	25.03S	130.05W
Bounty Islands	57	Ii	47.45S	179.05 E
Bounty Trough (EN)	3	Jn	46.00S	178.00 E
Bourail	61	Cd	21.34S	165.30 E
Bourbon-Lancy	11	Jh	46.37N	3.47 E
Bourbonnais	11	Ih	46.30N	3.00 E
Bourbonne-les-Bains	11	Lg	47.57N	5.45 E
Bourbourg	12	Ed	50.57N	2.12 E
Bourbre	11	Li	45.47N	5.11 E
Bourem	34	Fb	16.58N	0.21W
Bouressa	34	Fa	20.01N	2.18 E
Bourg-Achard	12	Ce	49.21N	0.49 E
Bourganeuf	11	Hi	45.57N	1.45 E
Bourg-de-Péage	11	Li	45.02N	5.03 E
Bourg-en-Bresse	11	Lh	46.12N	5.13 E
Bourges	6	Gf	47.05N	2.24 E
Bourget, Lac du-	11	Li	45.44N	5.52 E
Bourgneuf, Baie de-	11	Dg	47.05N	2.13W
Bourgogne	12	Ge	49.21N	4.04 E
Bourgogne = Burgundy (EN)	5	Gf	47.00N	4.30 E
Bourgogne = Burgundy (EN)	11	Kg	47.00N	4.30 E
Bourgogne, Canal de-	11	Jg	47.58N	3.30 E
Bourgogne, Porte de-	11	Mg	47.38N	6.52 E
Bourgoin-Jallieu	11	Li	45.35N	5.17 E
Bourgtheroulde-Infreville	12	Ce	49.18N	0.53 E
Bourguèbus	12	Be	49.07N	0.18W
Boû Rjeimat	32	Df	19.04N	15.08W
Bourke	58	Fh	30.05S	145.56 E
Bourne	12	Bb	52.46N	0.23W
Bournemouth	9	Lk	50.43N	1.54W
Bourtanger Moor	12	Jb	52.50N	7.06 E
Bourth	12	Cf	48.46N	0.49 E
Bou Saâda	32	Hb	35.12N	4.11 E
Bou Sellam	13	Oh	36.26N	4.34 E
Boussac	11	Hh	46.21N	2.13 E
Boussé	34	Ec	12.39N	1.53W
Boussens	11	Gk	43.11N	0.58 E
Bousso	35	Bc	10.29N	16.43 E
Bouthaleb, Djebel-	13	Ri	35.48N	5.12 E
Boutilimit	32	Ef	17.33N	14.42W
Bou-Tlélis	13	Li	35.34N	0.54W
Boutonne	11	Fi	45.55N	0.49W
Bouvet	66	Cd	54.26S	3.24 E
Bouxwiller	12	Jf	48.49N	7.29 E
Bouza	34	Gc	14.25N	6.02 E
Bouzanne	11	Hh	46.38N	1.28 E
Bouzghaïa	13	Nh	36.20N	1.15 E
Bouzonville	12	Jf	49.18N	6.32 E
Bovalino	14	Kl	38.09N	16.11 E
Bovec	14	Hd	46.20N	13.33 E
Bovenkarspel	12	Hb	52.42N	5.17 E
Boves	12	Ee	49.51N	2.23 E
Bovino	14	Ji	41.15N	15.20 E
Bovril	55	Cj	31.21S	59.26W
Bowa → Muli	27	Hf	27.56N	101.13 E
Bowen [Arg.]	56	Ge	35.02S	67.31W
Bowen [Austl.]	59	Jc	20.01S	148.15 E
Bowers Bank (EN)	40a	BB	54.00N	180.00
Bowers Ridge (EN)	40a	Bb	54.30N	180.00
Bowie	45	Hj	33.34N	97.51W
Bowkān	24	Ld	36.31N	46.12 E
Bowland, Forest of-	9	Kh	54.00N	2.30W
Bowling Green [Ky.-U.S.]	43	Jd	37.00N	86.27W
Bowling Green [Oh.-U.S.]	44	Fe	41.23N	83.40W
Bowman	43	Gb	46.11N	103.24W
Bowman Bay	42	Kc	65.33N	73.40W
Bowman Island	66	He	65.17S	103.08 E
Bowman, Mount-	46	Ea	51.10N	121.55W
Bowo/Bomi	27	Ge	30.02N	95.39 E
Bowokan, Kepulauan-	26	Hg	2.05S	123.35 E
Bowral	59	Kf	34.28S	150.25 E
Bow River	42	Gg	49.56N	111.42W
Box Elder Creek	46	Kc	46.57N	108.04W
Boxelder Creek	46	Md	45.59N	103.57W
Boxholm	7	Dg	58.12N	15.03 E
Boxian	27	Ke	33.46N	115.44 E
Boxing	27	Kd	37.07N	118.04 E
Boxmeer	12	Hc	51.39N	5.57 E
Boxtel	11	Lc	51.35N	5.20 E
Boyabat	24	Fb	41.28N	34.47 E
Boyabo	36	Cb	3.43N	18.46 E
Boyacá [2]	54	Db	5.30N	72.50W
Boyang	27	Kf	29.00N	116.41 E
Boyer, Cap-	63b	Be	21.37S	168.07 E
Boyer Ahmadi-e Kohkīlūyeh [3]	23	Hc	31.00N	50.30 E
Boyle/Mainistir na Búille	9	Eh	53.58N	8.18W
Boyne/An Bhóinn	9	Gh	53.43N	6.15W
Boyne City	44	Ec	45.13N	85.01W
Boynes, Iles de-	30	Nm	49.58S	69.93 E
Boynton Beach	42	Gl	26.32N	80.03W
Boysen Reservoir	46	Ke	43.19N	108.11W
Boz, Küh-e-	24	Pi	27.46N	55.54 E
Bozburun	15	Li	40.32N	28.46 E
Bozburun	15	Lm	36.41N	28.04 E
Bozburun Dağı	24	Dd	37.18N	31.03 E
Bozcaada	24	Bc	39.50N	26.04 E
Bozcaada	24	Bc	39.49N	26.03 E
Bozdağ	15	Lk	38.20N	28.06 E
Boz Dağı [Tur.]	24	Cd	37.18N	29.12 E
Boz Dağı [Tur.]	24	Cc	38.19N	28.08 E
Bozdoğan	15	Ll	37.40N	28.19 E
Bozeman	39	He	45.41N	111.02W
Bozen / Bolzano	6	Hf	46.31N	11.22 E
Bozene	36	Cb	2.56N	19.12 E
Bozhou	24	De	38.04N	116.34 E
Bozkol, Zaliv-	18	Cb	45.00N	61.45 E
Bozkurt	24	Fb	41.57N	34.01 E
Bozok Platosu	24	Fc	39.05N	35.05 E
Bozouls	11	Ij	44.28N	2.43 E
Bozoum	31	Ih	6.19N	16.23 E
Bozova	24	Hd	37.22N	38.31 E
Bozovici	14	Ee	44.56N	22.00 E
Bozqūsh, Kūh-e-	24	Ld	37.45N	47.40 E
Bra	14	Bf	44.42N	7.51 E
Braås	8	Fg	57.04N	15.03 E
Braathen, Cape-	66	Pf	71.48S	96.05W
Brabant	11	Lc	51.10N	5.05 E
Brabant	12	Gd	50.45N	4.30 E
Brabant-les-Villers	12	Gf	48.51N	4.59 E
Bräbích	34	Eb	17.30N	3.00W
Brač	14	Kg	43.19N	16.40 E
Bracadale, Loch-	9	Gd	57.20N	6.35W
Bracciano	14	Gh	42.06N	12.40 E
Bracciano, Lago di-	14	Gh	42.05N	12.15 E
Bräcke	7	De	62.43N	15.27 E
Brackettville	45	Fl	29.19N	100.24W
Brackley	12	Ab	52.02N	1.09W
Brački Kanal	14	Kg	43.24N	16.40 E
Bracknell	12	Mj	51.26N	0.46W
Brackwede, Bielefeld-	12	Kc	51.59N	8.31 E
Brad	15	Fc	46.08N	22.47 E
Bradano	14	Kj	40.23N	16.51 E
Bradenton	43	Kf	27.29N	82.34W
Bradford [Eng.-U.K.]	9	Lh	53.48N	1.45W
Bradford [Pa.-U.S.]	44	He	41.57N	78.39W
Bradley Reef	60	Gi	6.52S	160.48 E
Brady	43	He	31.08N	99.20W
Brady Mountains	45	Gk	31.20N	99.40W
Brædstrup	8	Ci	55.58N	9.37 E
Braemar	9	Jd	57.01N	3.24W
Braga [2]	13	Dc	41.35N	8.26W
Braga	6	Fj	41.33N	8.26W
Bragadiru	15	If	43.46N	25.31 E
Bragado	56	Hf	35.08S	60.30W
Bragança, Rio- [Braz.]	13	Fc	41.30N	6.45W
Bragança [Braz.]	53	Lf	1.03S	46.46W
Bragança [Port.]	13	Fc	41.49N	6.45W
Bragança Paulista	55	Jf	22.57S	46.34W
Brahestad/Raahe	7	Fd	64.41N	24.29 E
Brähmanbäria	25	Jd	23.59N	91.07 E
Brahmapur	22	Kh	19.19N	84.47 E
Brahmaputra	21	Lg	24.02N	90.59 E
Bräila [3]	15	Kd	45.13N	27.48 E
Bräila	6	If	45.16N	27.59 E
Brăilei, Balta-	15	Kd	45.00N	28.00 E
Braine	12	Fe	49.20N	3.32 E
Braine-l'Alleud/Eigenbrakel	12	Gd	50.41N	4.22 E
Brainerd	45	Ib	46.21N	94.12W
Braintree	12	Lc	51.53N	0.34 E
Braithwaite Point	59	Gb	11.58S	134.00 E
Brake (Unterweser)	10	Ec	53.20N	8.29 E
Brakel [Bel.]	12	Fd	50.47N	3.45 E
Brakel [Ger.]	12	Lc	51.43N	9.11 E
Brakna [3]	32	Ef	17.30N	13.30W
Brålanda	8	Ef	58.34N	12.22 E
Bralorne	46	Da	50.47N	122.49W
Bramming	8	Ci	55.28N	8.42 E
Brampton	42	Gi	62.10N	17.40 E
Bramön	44	Hd	43.41N	79.46W
Bramsche	12	Hc	52.06N	7.59 E
Bran, Pasul-	15	Id	45.26N	25.17 E
Branco	52	Cf	16.39N	24.41W
Branco, Cabo-	52	Mf	7.09S	34.47W
Branco, Rio- [Braz.]	51	Jf	1.24S	61.51W
Branco, Rio- [Braz.]	55	Jb	20.01S	57.48W
Branco ou Cabixi, Rio-	55	Ba	13.55S	60.10W
Brandberg	30	Jk	21.08S	14.35 E
Brandbu	7	Cf	60.26N	10.28 E
Brande	8	Ci	55.57N	9.08 E
Brandenburg	10	Fc	52.25N	12.33 E
Brandenburg	10	Gc	52.10N	13.00 E
Brandö	8	Id	60.25N	21.05 E
Brandon [Eng.-U.K.]	12	Cb	52.27N	0.37 E
Brandon [Fl.-U.S.]	44	Fl	27.56N	82.17W
Brandon [Man.-Can.]	39	Je	49.50N	99.57W
Brandon [Vt.-U.S.]	44	Kd	43.47N	73.05W
Brandon Head/Na Machairí	9	Ci	52.16N	10.15W
Brandon Mount/Cnoc Bréanainn	9	Ci	52.14N	10.15W
Brandval	27	Kd	33.46N	115.44 E
Brandvlei	37	Cf	30.25S	20.30 E
Brandýs nad Labem-Stará Boleslav	10	Kf	50.11N	14.40 E
Brăneşti	15	Je	44.27N	26.20 E
Braniewo	10	Pb	54.24N	19.50 E
Bransby Point	51c	Bc	15.43N	62.14W
Bransfield Strait	66	Re	63.00S	59.00W
Bránsk	10	Sd	52.45N	22.51 E
Branson	45	Jh	36.39N	93.13W
Brantevik	8	Fi	55.31N	14.21 E
Brantford	42	Jh	43.08N	80.16W
Brantôme	11	Gi	45.22N	0.39 E
Bras d'Or Lake	42	Lg	45.50N	60.50W
Brasil = Brazil [En]	53	Kf	9.00S	53.00W
Brasil, Planalto do- = Brazilian Highlands (EN)	52	Lg	17.00S	45.00W
Brasiléia	54	Ef	11.00S	68.44W
Brasilia	53	Lg	15.47S	47.55W
Brasilia de Minas	55	Jc	16.12S	44.26W
Brasla	8	Kg	57.08N	24.50 E
Braslaw	7	Gi	55.37N	27.05 E
Braşov [2]	15	Id	45.40N	25.10 E
Braşov	6	If	45.38N	25.35 E
Brass	34	Ge	4.19N	6.14 E
Brassac	11	Ik	43.38N	2.30 E
Brasschaat	12	Gc	51.17N	4.27 E
Brasstown Bald	44	Fh	34.52N	83.48W
Brastavăţu	14	Hf	43.55N	24.24 E
Braţul	15	Ci	40.16N	19.40 E
Bráte	8	De	59.43N	11.27 E
Bratea	15	Fc	46.56N	22.37 E
Bratislava	6	Hf	48.09N	17.07 E
Bratsk	22	Md	56.05N	101.48 E
Bratskoje Vodohranilišče = Bratsk Reservoir (EN)	20	Fe	56.30N	102.00 E
Bratsk Reservoir (EN) = Bratskoje Vodohranilišče	20	Fe	56.30N	102.00 E
Brattleboro	43	Mc	42.51N	72.36W
Brattvåg	8	Bb	62.36N	6.02 E
Braubach	12	Jd	50.17N	7.40 E
Braunau am Inn	14	Hb	48.16N	13.02 E
Braunschweig	10	Gd	52.16N	10.32 E
Brava	8	Jg	14.52N	24.43W
Brava, Costa-	13	Pc	41.45N	3.04 E
Bråviken	8	Gf	58.40N	16.30 E
Bravo del Norte, Rio- = Grande, Rio- (EN)	38	Jg	25.57N	97.09W
Brawley	43	De	32.59S	115.34W
Bray	9	Gh	53.12N	6.06W
Bray	42	Jc	69.20N	77.00W
Bray/Brè	9	Gh	53.12N	6.06W
Bray, Pays de-	11	Je	49.46N	1.26 E
Bray-Dunes	12	Ec	51.05N	2.31 E
Braye	11	Gg	47.45N	0.42 E
Bray Head	9	Cj	51.53N	10.26W
Bray-sur-Somme	12	Ee	49.56N	2.43 E
Brazi	15	Je	44.52N	26.01 E
Brazil	37	Jh	39.32N	87.08W
Brazil (EN) = Brasil	53	Kf	9.00S	53.00W
Brazil Basin (EN)	3	Dk	15.00S	25.00W
Brazilian Highlands (EN) = Brasil, Planalto do-	52	Lg	17.00S	45.00W
Brazos	38	Jg	28.53N	95.23W
Brazos Santiago Pass	45	Hm	26.05N	97.16W
Brazzaville	31	Ji	4.16S	15.17 E
Brčko	14	Mf	44.52N	18.49 E
Brda	10	Oc	53.07N	18.08 E
Brdy	10	Jj	49.35N	13.50 E
Bré/Bray	9	Gh	53.12N	6.06W
Brea, Punta-	51a	Bc	17.54N	66.55W
Breaden, Lake-	59	Ee	25.45S	125.40 E
Breaksea Sound	62	Mf	45.35S	166.40 E
Breaza [Rom.]	15	Id	45.11N	25.40 E
Breaza, Vîrful-	15	Hb	47.22N	24.02 E
Brebes	26	Eh	6.53S	109.03 E
Brèche	12	Ke	49.30N	2.33 E
Brechin	9	Ke	56.44N	2.40W
Brecht	12	Gc	51.21N	4.38 E
Brecht	12	Fe	49.20N	3.32 E
Breckenridge [Mn.-U.S.]	45	Hc	46.16N	96.35W
Breckenridge [Tx.-U.S.]	45	Gj	32.45N	98.54W
Breckland	12	Cb	52.30N	0.35 E
Břeclav	10	Mj	48.46N	16.53 E
Brecon	9	Jj	51.57N	3.24W
Brecon Beacons	9	Jj	51.53N	3.31W
Breda	11	Kc	51.35N	4.46 E
Bredaryd	8	Eg	57.10N	13.44 E
Bredasdorp	31	Jl	34.32S	20.02 E
Brede	12	Dc	50.55N	0.43 E
Bredstedt	10	Eb	54.37N	8.59 E
Bredy	19	Gc	52.26N	60.21 E
Bree	12	Hc	51.08N	5.36 E
Breg	10	Ei	47.57N	8.31 E
Bregalnica	15	Fi	41.36N	21.56 E
Bregenz	14	Dc	47.30N	9.46 E
Bréhat, Ile de-	11	Db	48.51N	3.00W
Breíðafjörður	7	Ab	65.15N	23.15W
Breimsvatnet	8	Bc	61.40N	6.25 E
Breisach am Rhein	10	Db	48.02N	6.00 E
Breisund	7	Ab	62.30N	6.00 E
Breivikbotn	7	Fa	70.37N	22.29 E
Brejão	55	Ce	12.59S	46.28W
Brekken	8	Id	60.25N	21.05 E
Brekstad	7	Be	63.41N	9.41 E
Bremangerlandet	7	Af	61.50N	5.00 E
Brembana, Val-	14	De	45.55N	9.40 E
Brembo	14	De	45.35N	9.32 E
Bremen [2]	10	Ec	53.05N	8.50 E
Bremen [Ger.]	6	Ge	53.05N	8.48 E
Bremen [In.-U.S.]	44	De	41.27N	86.09W
Bremerhaven	6	Ge	53.33N	8.35 E
Bremerton	43	Cb	47.34N	122.38W
Bremervörde	10	Ec	53.29N	9.08 E
Brendel	46	Kg	38.57N	109.50W
Brenham	45	Hk	30.10N	96.24W
Brenne	11	Hh	46.44N	1.14 E
Brennero, Passo del- = Brenner Pass (EN)	5	Hf	47.00N	11.30 E
Brennerpaß = Brenner Pass (EN)	5	Hf	47.00N	11.30 E
Brenner Pass (EN) = Brennero, Passo del-	5	Hf	47.00N	11.30 E
Brennerpaß	5	Hf	47.00N	11.30 E
Brenta	14	Ge	45.11N	12.18 E
Brentwood	9	Nj	51.38N	0.18 E
Brescia	6	Hf	45.33N	10.15 E
Breskens	12	Fc	51.24N	3.33 E
Breslau (EN) = Wrocław	5	Hf	51.06N	17.00 E
Bresle	11	Hd	50.04N	1.22 E
Bressanone / Brixen	14	Fd	46.43N	11.39 E
Bressay	9	La	60.08N	1.05W
Bresse	11	Lh	46.30N	5.15 E
Bressuire	11	Fh	46.51N	0.29W
Brest	6	Ie	52.06N	23.42 E
Brest [Fr.]	6	Ff	48.24N	4.29W
Brestova	14	Ie	45.08N	14.14 E
Brestskaja Oblast [3]	19	Df	52.20N	25.30 E
Bretagne = Brittany (EN)	11	Df	48.00N	3.00W
Bretagne = Brittany (EN)	5	Ff	48.00N	3.00W
Bretçu	15	Jc	46.03N	26.18 E
Breteuil [Fr.]	12	Cf	48.50N	0.55 E
Breteuil [Fr.]	11	Je	49.38N	2.18 E
Breton, Marais-	11	Dh	46.56N	2.00W
Breton, Pertuis-	11	Eh	46.16N	1.22W
Breton Sound	45	Ll	29.30N	89.30W
Brett	12	Cc	51.58N	0.57 E
Brett, Cape-	62	Fa	35.10S	174.20 E
Bretten	12	Ke	49.02N	8.42 E
Bretteville-sur-Laize	12	Be	49.03N	0.20W
Breueh, Pulau-	26	Be	5.41N	95.05 E
Breuil Cervinia	14	Bd	45.56N	7.38 E
Breukelen	12	Db	52.01N	5.01 E
Breuna	12	Lc	51.25N	9.11 E
Breves	54	Hd	1.40S	50.29W
Brevik	7	Cg	59.04N	9.42 E
Brevoort	42	Ld	63.30N	64.20W
Brewarrina	59	Je	29.57S	146.52 E
Brewerville	34	Cd	6.25N	10.47W
Brewster	44	Hf	40.06N	119.47W
Brewster, Kap-	67	Md	70.10N	21.30W
Brewton	43	Je	31.07N	87.04W
Brezičе	14	Je	45.54N	15.35 E
Brézina	32	Hc	33.05N	1.16 E
Březnice	10	Jj	49.33N	13.57 E
Breznik	15	Fg	42.44B	22.54 E
Brezno	10	Ph	48.49N	19.39 E
Brezoi	15	Hd	45.21N	24.15 E
Brezolles	12	Bf	48.41N	1.04 E
Brezovo	15	Ig	42.21N	25.05 E
Bria	31	Jh	6.32N	21.59 E
Briançe	11	Hi	45.47N	1.12 E
Briançon	11	Mj	44.54N	6.39 E
Brianza	12	De	45.45N	9.15 E
Briare, Canal de-	11	If	48.02N	2.43 E
Bribie Island	59	Ke	27.00S	153.05 E
Bričany	15	Ka	48.18N	27.04 E
Bride	9	Fi	52.05N	7.50W
Bridgend	9	Jj	51.31N	3.35W
Bridgeport [Ca.-U.S.]	46	Fg	38.10N	119.13W
Bridgeport [Ct.-U.S.]	43	Mc	41.11N	73.11W
Bridgeport [Nb.-U.S.]	45	Ef	41.40N	103.06W
Bridge River	46	Ea	50.45N	121.55W
Bridger Peak	46	Lf	41.12N	107.02W
Bridges Point	64g	Bb	1.58N	157.28W
Bridgeton	44	Je	39.26N	75.14W
Bridgetown [Austl.]	59	Df	33.57S	116.08 E
Bridgetown [Bar.]	39	Nh	13.06N	59.37W
Bridgewater	42	Lh	44.23N	64.31W
Bridgwater	9	Kj	51.08N	3.00W
Bridlington	9	Mg	54.05N	0.12W
Bridlington Bay	9	Mg	54.04N	0.08W
Bridport	9	Kk	50.44N	2.46W
Brie	11	Jf	48.40N	3.30 E
Brielle	12	Gc	51.54N	4.10 E
Brienne-le-Château	11	Kf	48.24N	4.32 E
Brienzer-See	14	Bd	46.45N	7.55 E
Briey	11	Lf	49.15N	5.56 E
Brig	14	Bd	46.20N	8.00 E
Brigach	12	Ke	48.05N	8.22 E
Brigg	9	Mh	53.34N	0.30W
Brigham City	43	Ec	41.31N	112.01W
Brighouse	9	Lh	53.42N	1.47W
Brighstone	9	Ja	50.38N	1.24W
Brightlingsea	12	Dc	51.48N	1.02 E
Brighton [Co.-U.S.]	45	Eg	39.59N	104.49W
Brighton [Eng.-U.K.]	6	Fe	50.50N	0.10W
Brignoles	11	Mk	43.24N	6.04 E
Brihuega	13	Jc	40.45N	2.52W
Brijuni	14	Hf	44.55N	13.46 E
Brikama	34	Bc	13.16N	16.39W
Brilhante, Rio-	54	Hc	21.58S	54.18W
Brilon	11	Db	51.24N	8.34 E
Brilon-Alme	12	Kc	51.27N	8.37 E
Brimstone Hill	51c	Ab	17.21N	62.49W
Brinkley	45	Ki	34.53N	91.12W
Brinkmann	55	Bi	30.52S	62.02W
Brioude	11	Ji	45.18N	3.23 E
Brisbane	58	Kf	27.28S	153.02 E
Brisighella	14	Ff	44.13N	11.46 E
Bristol	66	Ad	59.02S	26.31W
Bristol [Eng.-U.K.]	6	Fe	51.27N	2.35W
Bristol [Tn.-U.S.]	44	Fg	36.36N	82.11W
Bristol Bay	38	Dd	58.00N	159.00W
Bristol Channel	5	Fe	51.20N	4.00W
Bristol Lake	46	Hi	34.28N	115.41W
Bristow	45	Hi	35.50N	96.23W
Britannia Range	66	Jf	80.00S	158.00 E
British Columbia [3]	42	Fe	55.00N	125.00W
British Honduras = Belize	49	Ce	17.35N	88.35W
British Indian Ocean Territory [5]	22	Jj	7.00S	72.00 E
British Isles	5	Fd	54.00N	4.00W
British Mountains	40	Kc	69.20N	140.20W
British Solomon Islands = Solomon Islands	60	Ge	8.00S	159.00 E
British Virgin Islands [5]	39	Mh	18.20N	64.50W
Brits	37	De	25.40S	27.46 E
Britstown	37	Cf	30.37S	23.30 E
Britt	45	Ja	43.06N	93.48W
Brittany (EN) = Bretagne	5	Ff	48.00N	3.00W
Brittany (EN) = Bretagne	11	Df	48.00N	3.00W
Britton	45	Hd	45.48N	97.45W
Brive-la-Gaillarde	11	Hi	45.09N	1.32 E
Briviesca	13	Ib	42.33N	3.19W
Brixen / Bressanone	14	Fd	46.43N	11.39 E
Brixham	9	Jk	50.24N	3.30W
Brjansk	6	Je	53.15N	34.22 E
Brjanskaja Oblast [3]	19	De	52.50N	33.20 E
Brjuhoveckaja	16	Kg	45.46N	39.01 E
Brjukoviči	6	Hf	49.12N	16.37 E
Brno	6	Hf	49.12N	16.37 E
Broa, Ensenada de la-	49	Fb	22.35N	82.00W
Broad Bay	9	Gc	58.15N	6.15W
Broadford	9	Hd	57.14N	5.54W
Broad Sound	59	Jd	22.10S	149.45 E
Broadstairs	12	Dc	51.22N	1.27 E
Broadus	43	Fb	45.27N	105.25W
Brocēni/Broceny	8	Jh	56.41N	22.30 E
Broceny/Brocēni	8	Jh	56.41N	22.30 E
Brochet	42	Fe	57.53N	101.40W
Brochu, Lac-	44	Ja	48.26N	74.15W
Brock	42	Ga	77.55N	114.30W
Brocken	10	Ge	51.48N	10.36 E
Brockman, Mount-	59	Dd	22.28S	117.18 E
Brockton	44	Ld	42.05N	71.01W
Brockville	42	Jh	44.35N	75.41W
Brod	15	Eh	41.31N	21.14 E
Brodarevo	15	Cf	43.14N	19.43 E
Broderick Falls	36	Fb	0.37N	34.46 E
Brodeur Peninsula	38	Kb	73.00N	88.00W
Brodick	9	Hf	55.35N	5.09W
Brodnica	10	Pc	53.16N	19.23 E
Brody	16	Dd	50.04N	25.12 E
Broglie	12	Ce	49.01N	0.32 E
Brok	10	Rd	52.43N	21.52 E
Brok	10	Rd	52.38N	21.51 E
Broken Arrow	45	Ih	36.03N	95.48W
Broken Bow	45	Gf	41.24N	99.38W
Broken Bow Lake	45	Ii	34.10N	94.40W
Broken Hill	58	Fh	31.57S	141.27 E
Broken Ridge (EN)	3	Hm	31.30S	95.00 E
Brokind	8	Ff	58.13N	15.40 E
Brokopondo	54	Hb	5.05N	55.00W
Bromarv	8	Je	59.55N	23.00 E
Bromley, London-	12	Cc	51.25N	0.01 E
Bromölla	8	Fh	56.04N	14.28 E
Brønderslev	8	Cg	57.16N	9.58 E
Brong-Ahafo [3]	34	Ed	7.45N	1.30W
Bronnikovo	17	Ng	58.29N	68.27 E
Brønnøysund	7	Cd	65.28N	12.13 E
Bronte	14	Im	37.47N	14.50 E
Brooke's Point	26	Ge	8.47N	117.50 E
Brookfield	45	Jg	39.47N	93.04W
Brookhaven	45	Jk	31.35N	90.26W
Brookings [Or.-U.S.]	43	Cc	42.03N	124.17W
Brookings [S.D.-U.S.]	43	Hc	44.19N	96.48W
Brooks	42	Gg	50.35N	111.53W
Brooks Banks (EN)	60	Mc	24.05N	166.50W
Brooks Range	38	Dc	68.00N	154.00W
Brookston	45	Jc	46.52N	92.32W
Brooksville	44	Fk	28.33N	82.23W
Brookton	59	Df	32.22S	117.01 E
Brookville [In.-U.S.]	44	Ef	39.25N	85.01W
Brookville [Pa.-U.S.]	44	He	41.10N	79.06W
Broom, Loch-	9	Hd	57.55N	5.15W
Broome	58	Dc	17.58S	122.14 E
Brora	9	Jc	58.01N	3.51W
Brora	9	Jc	58.00N	3.50W
Brosna/An Bhrosnach	9	Fh	53.13N	7.58W
Broşteni	15	Ib	47.14N	25.42 E
Brou	11	Hf	48.13N	1.11 E
Brough	9	Kg	54.32N	2.19W
Broughton Island	39	Mc	67.35N	63.50W
Broussard	45	Kk	30.09N	91.58W
Brovary	16	Ee	50.30N	30.48 E
Brovst	8	Cg	57.06N	9.32 E
Brown Bank (EN) = Bruine Bank	12	Fb	52.35N	3.20 E
Brownfield	43	Gj	33.11N	102.16W
Browning	46	Ja	48.34N	113.01W
Browns Bank (EN)	42	Mh	43.00N	66.05W
Brownsville [Tn.-U.S.]	44	Ch	35.36N	89.15W
Brownsville [Tx.-U.S.]	43	Hf	25.56N	97.30W
Brownwood	43	He	31.43N	98.59W
Browse Island	58	Ec	14.05S	123.35 E
Broye	14	Bb	46.55N	7.02 E
Bruay-en-Artois	11	If	50.29N	2.33 E
Bruay-sur-l'Escaut	12	Fd	50.23N	3.32 E
Bruce	45	Lj	33.59N	89.21W
Bruce, Mount-	57	Df	22.37S	118.08 E
Bruce Crossing	44	Cb	46.32N	89.10W
Bruce Peninsula	42	Hh	45.00N	81.20W
Bruce Rock	59	Df	31.53S	118.09 E
Bruche	11	Nf	48.34N	7.43 E

Index Symbols

Independent Nation	Historical or Cultural Region	Pass, Gap	Depression
State, Region	Mount, Mountain	Plain, Lowland	Cliff
District, County	Volcano	Delta	Peninsula
Municipality	Hill	Salt Flat	Isthmus
Colony, Dependency	Mountains, Mountain Range	Valley, Canyon	Forest, Woods
Continent	Hills, Escarpment	Crater, Cave	Heath, Steppe
Physical Region	Plateau, Upland	Karst Features	Oasis
			Cape, Point

Coast, Beach	Rock, Reef	Waterfall Rapids	Canal
Islands, Archipelago	River Mouth, Estuary	Glacier	Bank
Rocks, Reefs	Ice Shelf, Pack Ice	Seamount	Trench, Abyss
Coral Reef	Lake	Ocean	Tablemount
Sandbank	Well, Spring	Salt Lake	Sea
Island	Geyser	Intermittent Lake	Gulf, Bay
Atoll	River, Stream	Reservoir	Swamp, Pond

Lagoon	Escarpment, Sea Scarp	Historic Site
Fracture	Ruins	Lighthouse
	Wall, Walls	Mine
National Park, Reserve	Church, Abbey	Tunnel
Ridge	Point of Interest	Temple
Shelf	Recreation Site	Scientific Station
Basin	Cave, Cavern	Airport
		Port
		Dam, Bridge

Bruchhausen Vilsen 12 Lb 52.50N 9.01 E
Bruchmühlbach Miesau 12 Je 49.23N 7.28 E
Bruchsal 10 Eg 49.08N 8.36 E
Bruck an der Leitha 14 Kb 48.01N 16.46 E
Bruck an der Mur 14 Jc 47.25N 15.17 E
Brue 9 Kj 51.13N 3.00W
Bruges/Brugge 11 Jc 51.13N 3.14 E
Brugg 14 Cc 47.29N 8.12 E
Brugge/Bruges 11 Jc 51.13N 3.14 E
Brugge-Assebroek 12 Fc 51.12N 3.16 E
Brüggen 12 Ic 51.15N 6.11 E
Brugge-Sint-Andries 12 Fc 51.12N 3.10 E
Brühl [Ger.] 12 Ke 49.24N 8.32 E
Brühl [Ger.] 12 Id 50.50N 6.54 E
Bruine Bank = Brown Bank (EN) 12 Fb 52.35N 3.20 E
Bruin Point 43 Ed 39.39N 110.22W
Brule River 44 Cc 45.57N 88.12W
Brumado 54 Jf 14.13S 41.40W
Brummen 12 Ib 52.06N 6.10 E
Brummo 8 Ef 58.50N 13.40 E
Brumunddal 7 Cf 60.53N 10.56 E
Bruna 14 Eh 42.45N 10.53 E
Brune 12 Fe 49.45N 3.47 E
Bruneau 46 He 42.53N 115.48W
Bruneau River 46 He 42.57N 115.58W
Bruneck / Brunico 14 Fd 46.48N 11.56 E
Brunehamel 12 Ge 49.46N 4.11 E
Brunei 22 Ni 4.30N 114.40 E
Brunei, Teluk- 21 Ni 5.05N 115.18 E
Brunette Downs 59 Hc 18.38S 135.57 E
Brunflo 8 Fa 63.05N 14.49 E
Brunico / Bruneck 14 Fd 46.48N 11.56 E
Brunna 8 Ge 59.52N 17.25 E
Brunner 62 De 42.26S 171.19 E
Brunner, Lake- 62 De 42.35S 171.25 E
Brunnsberg 8 Ec 61.17N 13.55 E
Brunsbüttel 10 Fc 53.54N 9.07 E
Brunssum 12 Hd 50.57N 5.57 E
Brunswick [Ga.-U.S.] 43 Ke 31.10N 81.29W
Brunswick [Me.-U.S.] 43 Nc 43.55N 69.58W
Brunswick, Península de- 52 Ik 53.30S 71.25W
Brunswick Lake 44 Fa 49.00N 83.23W
Bruntál 10 Ng 49.59N 17.28 E
Bruny Island 59 Jh 43.30S 147.05 E
Brus 15 Ef 43.23N 21.02 E
Brus, Laguna de- 49 Ef 15.50N 84.35W
Brush 43 Gc 40.15N 103.37W
Brus Laguna 49 Ef 15.47N 84.35W
Brusque 56 Kc 27.06S 48.56W
Brussel/Bruxelles=Brussels (EN) 6 Ge 50.50N 4.20 E
Brussels (EN)=Brussel/Bruxelles 6 Ge 50.50N 4.20 E
Brussels (EN)=Bruxelles/Brussel 6 Ge 50.50N 4.20 E
Brusset, 'Erg- 34 Hb 18.55N 10.30 E
Brusturi 15 Fb 47.09N 22.15 E
Brusy 10 Nc 53.53N 17.45 E
Bruxelles/Brussel=Brussels (EN) 6 Ge 50.50N 4.20 E
Bruzual 50 Bh 8.03N 69.19W
Bryan [Oh.-U.S.] 44 Ee 41.30N 84.34W
Bryan [Tx.-U.S.] 43 He 30.40N 96.22W
Bryan Coast 66 Pf 73.35S 84.00W
Bryne 7 Ag 58.44N 5.39 E
Brza Palanka 15 Fe 44.28N 22.27 E
Brzava kanal 15 Dd 45.16N 20.49 E
Brzeg 10 Nf 50.52N 17.27 E
Brzeg Dolny 10 Me 51.15N 16.40 E
Brzeziny 10 Pe 51.48N 19.46 E
Brzozów 10 Sg 49.42N 22.02 E
Bsharrī 24 Ge 34.15N 36.01 E
Bû 12 Df 48.48N 1.30 E
Bua 8 Eg 57.14N 12.07 E
Buada Lagoon 64e Ab 0.32S 166.54 E
Buala 58 Ge 8.10S 159.35 E
Bū al Ḩidān, Wādī- 33 Cd 27.25N 19.22 E
Buapinang 26 Hg 4.46S 121.34 E
Buatan 26 Df 0.44N 101.51 E
Bū aţ Tifl 33 Dd 28.54N 22.30 E
Bua Yai 25 Ke 15.34N 102.24 E
Bu'ayrāt al Ḩasūn 33 Cc 31.24N 15.44 E
Bubanza 36 Ec 3.06S 29.23 E
Bubaque 34 Bc 11.17N 15.50W
Būbīyan 24 Mh 29.45N 48.15 E
Bubu 36 Gd 6.03S 35.19 E
Bubye 37 Ed 22.20S 31.07 E
Buca 15 Kk 38.22N 27.11 E
Bučač 16 De 49.04N 25.23 E
Bucačača 20 Gf 52.59N 116.55 E
Bucak 24 Dd 37.28N 30.36 E
Bucaramanga 53 Ie 7.08N 73.09W
Bucas Grande 26 Ie 9.40N 125.58 E
Buccament Bay 51n Ba 13.12N 61:17W
Buccaneer Archipelago 59 Ec 16.17S 123.20 E
Bucecea 15 Jb 47.46N 26.26 E
Buchanan 31 Fh 5.53N 10.03W
Buchanan, Lake- [Austl.] 59 Jd 21.30S 145.50 E
Buchanan, Lake- [Tx.-U.S.] 45 Gk 30.48N 98.25W
Buchanan Bay 42 Ka 78.55N 75.00W
Buchan Gulf 42 Kb 71.48N 74.06W
Buchardo 56 Hd 34.43S 63.31W
Bucharest (EN)=Bucureşti 6 Ig 44.26N 26.06 E
Buchen 10 Fg 49.31N 9.20 E
Buchholz in der Nordheide 10 Fc 53.20N 9.52 E
Buchon, Point- 46 Ei 35.15N 120.54W
Buchs 14 Dc 47.10N 9.30 E
Buchy 12 De 49.35N 1.22 E
Bückeburg 12 Lb 52.16N 9.03 E
Buckeye 46 Ij 33.22N 112.35W
Buckhaven 9 Je 56.11N 3.03W
Buckie 9 Kd 57.40N 2.58W
Buckingham [Eng.-U.K.] 12 Bb 52.00N 0.59W
Buckingham [Que.-Can.] 44 Jc 45.35N 75.25W
Buckingham Bay 59 Hb 12.10S 135.46 E
Buckinghamshire 9 Mj 51.50N 0.55W
Buckland 40 Gc 66.16N 161.20W
Buckle Island 66 Ke 66.47S 163.14 E
Buckley Bay 66 Je 68.16S 148.12 E
Bucks 9 Mj 51.50N 0.55W
Bucksport 44 Mc 44.34N 68.48W
Buco Zau 36 Bc 4.50S 12.33 E
Bu Craa 32 Ed 26.17N 12.46W
Bucureşti 15 Je 44.30N 26.05 E
Bucureşti=Bucharest (EN) 6 Ig 44.26N 26.06 E
Bucy-lès-Pierrepont 12 Fe 49.39N 3.54 E
Bucyrus 44 Fe 40.47N 82.57W
Bud 7 Be 62.55N 6.55 E
Budacu, Vîrful- 15 Ib 47.07N 25.41 E
Buda-Koševelo 16 Gc 52.43N 30.39 E
Budapest 10 Pi 47.30N 19.05 E
Budapest 6 Hf 47.30N 19.05 E
Búdardalur 7a Bb 65.07N 21.46W
Budaun 25 Fc 28.03N 79.07 E
Budbud 35 He 4.13N 46.31 E
Budd Coast 66 He 66.30S 113.00 E
Buddusò 14 Di 40.35N 9.15 E
Bude [Eng.-U.K.] 9 Ik 50.50N 4.33W
Bude [Ms.-U.S.] 45 Kk 31.28N 90.51W
Bude Bay 9 Ik 50.50N 4.37W
Budel 12 Hc 51.16N 5.30 E
Budennovsk 19 Eg 44.45N 44.08 E
Budeşti 15 Je 44.14N 26.27 E
Budia 13 Jd 40.38N 2.45W
Büdingen 10 Ff 50.18N 9.07 E
Búdir 7a Cb 64.56N 14.01W
Budjala 36 Cb 2.39N 19.42 E
Budkowiczanka 10 Nf 50.52N 17.33 E
Budogošč 7 Hg 59.19N 32.29 E
Budrio 14 Ff 44.32N 11.32 E
Budslav 8 Lj 54.49N 27.32 E
Budva 15 Bg 42.17N 18.51 E
Budyšin/Bautzen 10 Ke 51.11N 14.26 E
Budžjak 15 Lc 46.15N 28.45 E
Buea 34 Ge 4.09N 9.14 E
Buech 11 Lj 44.12N 5.57 E
Buenaventura [Col.] 53 Ie 3.53N 77.04W
Buenaventura [Mex.] 47 Cc 29.51N 107.29W
Buenaventura, Bahía de- 54 Cc 3.45N 77.15W
Buenavista 48 Ef 23.39N 109.42W
Buena Vista [Co.-U.S.] 45 Cg 38.50N 106.08W
Buena Vista [Mex.] 48 Mi 16.05N 93.00W
Buena Vista [Mex.] 48 Bb 31.10N 115.40W
Buena Vista [Ven.] 50 Eh 9.02N 63.49W
Buenavista, Bahía de- 49 Hb 22.30N 79.08W
Buendia, Embalse de- 13 Jd 40.25N 2.43W
Buenópolis 55 Jc 17.54S 44.11W
Buenos Aires 56 Ie 36.00S 60.00W
Buenos Aires [Arg.] 53 Ki 34.36S 58.27W
Buenos Aires [C.R.] 49 Fi 10.04N 84.26W
Buenos Aires, Lago- 52 Ij 46.30S 72.00W
Buffalo 42 Fe 60.52N 115.03W
Buffalo [N.Y.-U.S.] 39 Le 42.54N 78.53W
Buffalo [Ok.-U.S.] 45 Gh 36.50N 99.38W
Buffalo [S.D.-U.S.] 43 Gb 45.35N 103.33W
Buffalo [Tx.-U.S.] 45 Hk 31.28N 96.04W
Buffalo [Wy.-U.S.] 43 Fc 44.21N 106.42W
Buffalo Bill Reservoir 46 Kd 44.29N 109.13W
Buffalo Lake 42 Fd 60.12N 115.25W
Buffalo Narrows 42 Ge 55.51N 108.30W
Buffalo Pound Lake 46 Ma 50.38N 105.20W
Buffels 37 Be 29.41S 17.04 E
Bū Fishah 14 En 36.18N 10.28 E
Buford 44 Fh 34.07N 84.00W
Buftea 15 Ie 44.34N 25.57 E
Bug 5 Ie 52.31N 21.05 E
Buga 54 Cc 3.55N 76.18W
Bugarach, Pech de- 11 Il 42.52N 2.23 E
Bugeat 11 Hi 45.36N 1.56 E
Bugene 36 Fc 1.35S 31.08 E
Bugey 11 Li 45.48N 5.30 E
Bugojno 23 Ff 44.03N 17.27 E
Bugøynes 7 Gb 69.58N 29.39 E
Bugrino 17 Db 68.48N 49.09 E
Bugsuk 26 Ge 8.15N 117.18 E
Bugt 27 Lb 48.47N 121.55 E
Bugulma 19 Fe 54.33N 52.48 E
Bugun 18 Hc 43.22N 70.10 E
Bugun 18 Gc 42.56N 68.36 E
Bügür/Luntai 27 Dc 41.46N 84.10 E
Buguruslan 19 Fe 53.39N 52.30 E
Buhara 22 If 39.49N 64.25 E
Buharskaja Oblast 19 Gg 41.20N 64.20 E
Bū Ḩaşā' 24 Ok 23.20N 53.20 E
Buhera 37 Ec 19.18S 31.29 E
Buh He 27 Gd 36.58N 99.48 E
Buhl 46 He 42.36N 114.46W
Bühl 10 Eh 48.42N 8.09 E
Bühödle 35 Hd 8.15N 46.20 E
Buhtarminskoje Vodohranilišče 19 If 49.10N 84.00 E
Bui Dam 34 Ed 8.22N 2.10W
Builth Wells 9 Ji 52.09N 3.24W
Buin [Chile] 56 Fd 33.44S 70.44W
Buin [Pap.N.Gui.] 60 Fi 6.50S 155.44 E
Buinsk 19 Ee 54.59N 48.17 E
Buir Nur 27 Kb 47.48N 117.42 E
Buitrago del Lozoya 13 Id 41.00N 3.38W
Buj 17 Gh 56.15N 54.12 E
Buj 19 Ed 58.29N 41.31 E
Bujalance 13 Hg 37.54N 4.22W
Bujanovac 15 Eg 42.28N 21.47 E
Bujaraloz 13 Lc 41.30N 0.09W
Buje 14 He 45.24N 13.40 E
Bujnaksk 19 Eg 42.49N 47.07 E
Bujukly 20 Jg 49.33N 142.55 E
Bujumbura 31 Ji 3.23S 29.22 E
Bujunda 20 Kd 62.00N 153.30 E
Buk 10 Md 52.22N 16.31 E
Bük 10 Mi 47.23N 16.45 E
Buk 10 Hb 54.10N 11.42 E
Buka Island 57 Ge 5.15S 154.35 E
Bukakata 36 Fc 0.18S 32.02 E
Bukama 31 Ji 9.12S 25.51 E
Buka Passage 63a Ba 5.25S 154.41 E
Bukavu 31 Ji 2.30S 28.52 E
Bukene 36 Fc 4.14S 32.53 E
Bukhā 24 Qi 26.10N 56.09 E
Bukit Besi 26 Df 4.46N 103.12 E
Bukit Mertajam 26 De 5.22N 100.28 E
Bukittinggi 22 Mj 0.19S 100.22 E
Bükk 10 Qh 48.05N 20.30 E
Bukoba 31 Ki 1.20S 31.49 E
Bukovina 15 Ia 48.00N 25.30 E
Bukowiec 10 Ld 52.23N 15.20 E
Bukuru 34 Gd 9.48N 8.52 E
Būl, Kūh-e- 23 Hc 30.48N 52.45 E
Bulajevo 19 He 54.53N 70.26 E
Bulan 26 Hd 12.40N 123.52 E
Bulanaš 17 Kh 57.16N 62.02 E
Bulancak 24 Hb 40.57N 38.14 E
Bulanık 24 Jc 39.05N 42.15 E
Būlāq 33 Fd 25.12N 30.32 E
Bulawayo 31 Jk 20.09S 28.34 E
Buldan 24 Cc 38.03N 28.51 E
Bulgan [Mong.] 27 Hc 44.05N 103.32 E
Bulgan [Mong.] 27 Hb 48.45N 103.34 E
Bulgan [Mong.] 27 Fb 46.05N 91.34 E
Bulgar (Kujbyšev) 7 Li 55.01N 49.06 E
Bulgaria (EN)=Bălgarija 6 Ig 43.00N 25.00 E
Buli 26 If 0.53N 128.18 E
Buli, Teluk- 26 If 0.45N 128.30 E
Buliluyan, Cape- 26 Ge 8.20N 117.11 E
Bulki 35 Fd 6.01N 36.36 E
Bullahār 35 Gc 10.23N 44.27 E
Bullange/Büllingen 12 Id 50.25N 6.16 E
Bullaque 13 Hf 38.59N 4.17W
Bulla Regia 14 Cn 36.33N 8.45 E
Bullas 13 Kf 38.03N 1.40W
Bulle 14 Bd 46.37N 7.04 E
Buller 62 Dd 41.44S 171.35 E
Bullfinch 59 Df 30.59S 119.06 E
Büllingen/Bullange 12 Id 50.25N 6.16 E
Bullion Mountains 46 Hi 34.25N 116.00W
Bulloo River 57 Fg 28.43S 142.30 E
Bull Point [Eng.-U.K.] 9 Ij 51.12N 4.10W
Bull Point [Falk.Is.] 56 Ih 52.19S 59.18W
Bulls 62 Fd 40.10S 175.23 E
Bulls Bay 44 Hi 32.59N 79.33W
Bull Shoals Lake 45 Jh 36.30N 92.50W
Bully Choop Mountain 46 Df 40.35N 122.45W
Bully-les-Mines 12 Ed 50.26N 2.43 E
Bulo Berde 35 He 3.52N 45.40 E
Bulolo 60 Di 7.12S 146.39 E
Bulqiza 15 Dh 41.30N 20.21 E
Bulter 45 Ig 38.16N 94.20W
Bultfontein 37 De 28.20S 26.05 E
Bulukumba 26 Hh 5.33S 120.11 E
Bulungu [Zaire] 36 Cc 4.33S 18.36 E
Bulungu [Zaire] 36 Dd 6.04S 21.54 E
Bumba 31 Jh 2.11N 22.28 E
Bumbah, Khalīj al- 33 Dc 32.25N 23.06 E
Buna 15 Ch 41.52N 19.22 E
Buna 36 Gb 2.47N 39.31 E
Bunbury 58 Ch 33.19S 115.38 E
Buncrana/Bun Cranncha 9 Ff 55.08N 7.27W
Bun Cranncha/Buncrana 9 Ff 55.08N 7.27W
Bunda 36 Fc 2.03S 33.52 E
Bundaberg 58 Gg 24.52S 152.21 E
Bünde 10 Ed 52.12N 8.35 E
Bundesrepublik Deutschland = Germany 6 Ge 51.00N 10.00 E
Bun Dobhráin/Bundoran 9 Eg 54.28N 8.17W
Bundoran/Bun Dobhráin 9 Eg 54.28N 8.17W
Bungay 12 Db 52.27N 1.27 E
Bungku 26 Hg 2.33S 121.58 E
Bungo 36 Cd 7.26S 15.24 E
Bungo Strait (EN)=Bungo-Suidō 28 Lh 32.40N 132.18 E
Bungo-Suidō=Bungo Strait (EN) 28 Lh 32.40N 132.18 E
Bungotakada 29 Be 33.33N 131.27 E
Bungsberg 10 Gb 54.12N 10.43 E
Buni 34 Hc 11.12N 12.02 E
Bunia 31 Kh 1.34N 30.15 E
Bunji 25 Ea 35.40N 74.36 E
Bunker 45 Kh 37.27N 91.13W
Bunker Group 59 Kd 23.50S 152.20 E
Bunkeya 36 Ee 10.24S 26.58 E
Bunkie 45 Jk 30.57N 92.11W
Bunnerfjällen 8 Ea 63.10N 12.34 E
Buñol 13 Le 39.25N 0.47W
Bunschoten 12 Hb 52.14N 5.24 E
Buntingford 12 Bc 51.57N 0.01W
Buntok 26 Fg 1.42S 114.48 E
Bünyan 24 Fc 38.51N 35.52 E
Bunyu, Pulau- 26 Gf 3.30N 117.50 E
Buon Me Thuot 25 Lf 12.40N 108.03 E
Buor-Haja, Guba- 20 Ib 71.00N 131.00 E
Buotama 20 Hd 61.17N 128.56 E
Buqayaq 23 Gd 25.56N 49.40 E
Buqda Kōsār 35 Ge 4.31N 44.40 E
Bur 20 Hb 71.40N 123.40 E
Bura 36 Gc 1.06S 39.57 E
Buram 31 Jg 10.49N 25.10 E
Buran 19 If 48.04N 85.15 E
Burang 27 De 30.18N 81.08 E
Burāq 24 Gf 33.10N 36.29 E
Buras 45 Ll 29.21N 89.32W
Buraydah 22 Gg 26.20N 43.59 E
Burbach 12 Kd 50.43N 8.03 E
Bürdab 35 Hd 9.05N 46.30 E
Burdekin River 59 Jc 19.39S 147.30 E
Burdēre 35 He 3.30N 45.37 E
Burdur 23 Db 37.43N 30.17 E
Burdur Gölü 24 Dd 37.44N 30.12 E
Burdwood Bank (EN) 56 Ih 54.15S 59.00W
Bure 12 Db 52.38N 1.45 E
Bure [Eth.] 35 Fd 8.20N 35.08 E
Bure [Eth.] 35 Fc 10.43N 37.03 E
Bureå 7 Ed 64.37N 21.12 E
Bureinski Hrebet=Bureya Range (EN) 21 Pd 50.40N 134.00 E
Bureja 20 Hg 49.43N 129.51 E
Bureja 21 Oe 49.25N 129.35 E
Büren 10 Ee 51.33N 8.34 E
Buren-Cogt 27 Jb 46.45N 111.30 E
Bureya Range (EN)=Bureinski Hrebet 21 Pd 50.40N 134.00 E
Burfjord 7 Fb 69.56N 22.03 E
Bür Gābo 35 Gf 1.10S 41.50 E
Burgas 6 Ig 42.30N 27.28 E
Burgas 15 Kg 42.30N 27.20 E
Burgas, Gulf of- (EN)=Burgaski Zaliv 15 Kg 42.30N 27.33 E
Burgaski Zaliv=Burgas, Gulf of- (EN) 15 Kg 42.30N 27.33 E
Burg auf Fehmarn 10 Hb 54.26N 11.12 E
Burg auf Fehmarn-Puttgarden 10 Hb 54.30N 11.13 E
Burgaw 44 Ih 34.33N 77.56W
Burgaz Daği 15 Mk 38.25N 29.46 E
Burg bei Magdeburg 10 Hd 52.16N 11.51 E
Burgdorf [Ger.] 10 Gd 52.27N 10.01 E
Burgdorf [Switz.] 14 Bc 47.04N 7.37 E
Burgenland 14 Kc 47.30N 16.25 E
Burgersdorp 37 Df 31.00S 26.20 E
Burgess Hill 12 Bd 50.58N 0.08W
Burgfjället 7 Dd 64.56N 15.03 E
Burghausen 10 Ih 48.10N 12.50 E
Burghūth, Sabkhat al- 24 Ie 34.58N 41.06 E
Burglengenfeld 10 Ig 49.12N 12.02 E
Burgos 13 Ib 42.20N 3.40W
Burgos [Mex.] 48 Je 24.57N 98.57W
Burgos [Sp.] 6 Fg 42.21N 3.42W
Burg-Reuland 12 Id 50.12N 6.09 E
Burgsvik 7 Eh 57.03N 18.16 E
Burguncy (EN)=Bourgogne 5 Gf 47.00N 4.30 E
Burguncy (EN)=Bourgogne 11 Kg 47.00N 4.30 E
Burgwald 12 Kd 50.57N 8.48 E
Bür Hakkaba 35 Ge 2.43N 44.10 E
Burhaniye 24 Bc 39.30N 26.58 E
Burhānpur 22 Jg 21.18N 76.14 E
Burias 26 Hd 12.57N 123.08 E
Buribaj 17 Ij 51.57N 58.11 E
Burica, Punta- 47 Hg 8.03N 82.53W
Burien 46 Dc 47.27N 122.21W
Burin Peninsula 42 Lg 47.00N 55.40W
Buriram 25 Kf 14.59N 103.08 E
Buriti, Rio- 55 Ca 12.50S 58.28W
Buriti Alegre 55 Hd 18.09S 49.03W
Buriti Bravo 54 Je 5.50S 43.50W
Buriti dos Lopes 54 Jd 3.10S 41.52W
Buritis 55 Ib 15.37S 46.26W
Burj al Ḩaţţābah 32 Ic 30.20N 9.30 E
Burjasot 13 Le 39.31N 0.25W
Burjatija, respublika 20 Ff 53.00N 110.00 E
Burj Şāfitā 24 Ge 34.49N 36.07 E
Burkandja 20 Jd 63.27N 147.27 E
Burkburnett 45 Gi 34.06N 98.34W
Burke 45 Ge 43.11N 99.18W
Burke, Mount- 46 Ha 50.13N 114.30W
Burke Island 66 Of 73.03S 105.06W
Burke River 59 Hd 23.12S 139.33 E
Burketown 58 Ef 17.44S 139.22 E
Burkina Faso 31 Gg 13.00N 2.00W
Burley 43 Ec 42.32N 113.48W
Burli 16 Rd 51.28N 52.44 E
Burlingame 45 Ig 38.45N 95.50W
Burlington [Co.-U.S.] 43 Gd 39.18N 102.16W
Burlington [Ia.-U.S.] 43 Ic 40.49N 91.07W
Burlington [Ks.-U.S.] 45 Ig 38.12N 95.45W
Burlington [N.C.-U.S.] 44 Hg 36.06N 79.26W
Burlington [Ont.-Can.] 44 Hd 43.19N 79.43W
Burlington [Vt.-U.S.] 43 Mc 44.28N 73.14W
Burlington [Wi.-U.S.] 45 Le 42.41N 88.17W
Burma 22 Lg 22.00N 98.00 E
Burma (Myanmar-Nainggan-Daw) 22 Lg 22.00N 98.00 E
Burnazului, Cîmpia- 15 Ie 44.10N 25.50 E
Burnett River 59 Kd 24.46S 152.25 E
Burney 46 Ef 40.53N 121.40W
Burnham Market 12 Cb 52.57N 0.44 E
Burnham-on-Crouch 12 Cc 51.37N 0.50 E
Burnie 59 Jh 41.04S 145.54 E
Burnley 9 Kh 53.48N 2.14W
Burns 43 Dc 43.35N 119.03W
Burnside 42 Gc 66.51N 108.04W
Burnside, Lake- 59 Ee 25.20S 123.10 E
Burns Lake 42 Ef 54.14N 125.46W
Burnsville 44 Fh 35.55N 82.18W
Burnt Lava Flow 46 Ef 41.35N 121.35W
Burnt River 44 Hc 44.35N 78.46W
Burntwood 42 He 56.08N 96.33W
Buro 31 Lh 9.30N 45.34 E
Burqin 27 Eb 47.43N 86.53 E
Burqin He 27 Eb 47.42N 86.50 E
Burqūm, Ḩarrat al- 33 He 20.54N 42.00 E
Burra 59 Hf 33.40S 138.56 E
Burragorang Lake 59 Kf 34.00S 150.25 E
Burreli 15 Ch 41.37N 20.00 E
Burrendong Reservoir 59 Jf 32.40S 149.10 E
Burriana 13 Le 39.53N 0.05W
Burro, Serranias del 48 Ic 28.50N 101.35W
Burrow Head 9 Ig 54.41N 4.24W
Bursa 22 Ee 40.11N 29.04 E
Būr Sa'īd=Port Said (EN) 31 Ke 31.16N 32.18 E
Burscheid 12 Jc 51.06N 7.07 E
Bürstadt 12 Ke 49.38N 8.27 E
Burštyn 16 De 49.16N 24.37 E
Būr Sūdān=Port Sudan (EN) 31 Kg 19.37N 37.14 E
Burt Lake 44 Ec 45.27N 84.40W
Burtnieku, Ozero- 8 Kg 57.35N 25.10 E
Burtnieku, Ozero-/Burtnieku Ezers 8 Kg 57.35N 25.10 E
Burtnieku Ezers 8 Kg 57.35N 25.10 E
Burtnieku Ezers/Burtnieku, Ozero- 8 Kg 57.35N 25.10 E
Burton 44 Fd 43.02N 83.36W
Burton Latimer 12 Bb 52.21N 0.40W
Burton-upon-Trent 9 Li 52.49N 1.36W
Burträsk 7 Ed 64.31N 20.39 E
Buru, Pulau- 57 De 3.24S 126.40 E
Burullus, Buḩayrat al- 24 Dg 31.30N 30.50 E
Burultokay/Fuhai 27 Eb 47.06N 87.23 E
Burum Gana 34 Hc 13.00N 11.57 E
Burūn, Ra's- 24 Eg 31.14N 33.04 E
Burundaj 19 Hg 43.20N 76.49 E
Burundi 31 Ki 3.15S 30.00 E
Bururi 36 Ec 3.57S 29.37 E
Burutu 34 Gd 5.21N 5.31 E
Bury 9 Kh 53.36N 2.17W
Burylbajtal 18 Ib 44.56N 73.59 E
Buryn 16 Hd 51.13N 33.48 E
Bury Saint Edmunds 9 Ni 52.15N 0.43 E
Burzil Pass 25 Ff 34.54N 75.06 E
Busalla 14 Cf 44.34N 8.57 E
Busanga [Zaire] 36 Ee 10.12S 25.23 E
Busanga [Zaire] 36 Dc 0.51S 22.04 E
Busanga Swamp 36 Ee 14.10S 25.50 E
Buşayrah 24 Ie 35.09N 40.26 E
Būsh 24 Dh 29.09N 31.08 E
Būshehr 23 Hd 28.00N 52.00 E
Būshgān 24 Nh 28.48N 51.42 E
Bushimaie 29 Ji 6.02S 23.45 E
Bushmanland (EN) = Boesmanland 37 Be 29.30S 19.00 E
Busia 36 Fb 0.28N 34.06 E
Busigny 12 Fd 50.02N 3.28 E
Businga 36 Db 3.20N 20.53 E
Busira 30 Ii 0.15S 18.59 E
Busk 16 Dd 50.01N 24.37 E
Buskerud 7 Bf 60.30N 9.10 E
Busko-Zdrój 10 Qf 50.28N 20.44 E
Busoga 36 Fb 0.45N 33.30 E
Buşrá ash Shām 24 Gf 32.31N 36.29 E
Busselton 59 Df 33.39S 115.20 E
Bussum 11 Lb 52.16N 5.10 E
Bustamante, Bahía- 56 Gg 45.07S 66.27W
Buşteni 15 Id 45.24N 25.32 E
Busto Arsizio 14 Ce 45.37N 8.51 E
Buštyna 10 Th 48.03N 23.28 E
Busuanga 26 Hd 12.05N 120.05 E
Busu-Djanoa 36 Db 1.43N 21.23 E
Büsum 10 Eb 54.08N 8.51 E
Buta 31 Jh 2.48N 24.44 E
Butajira 35 Fd 8.08N 38.27 E
Buta Ranquil 56 Ge 37.03S 69.50W
Butare 36 Ec 2.36S 29.44 E
Butaritari Atoll 57 Id 3.03N 172.49 E
Bute, Island of- 9 Hf 55.50N 5.05W
Bute Inlet 46 Ca 50.37N 124.53W
Butembo 31 Jh 0.09N 29.17 E
Butera 14 Im 37.11N 14.11 E
Butere 36 Fb 0.13N 34.30 E
Butha Qi (Zalantun) 27 Lb 48.02N 122.42 E
Buthidaung 25 Id 20.52N 92.32 E
Butiá 56 Jd 30.07S 51.58W
Butiaba 36 Fb 1.49N 31.19 E
Butler 44 He 40.51N 79.55W
Butser Hill 12 Bd 50.57N 0.59W
Butte 39 He 46.00N 112.32W
Butterworth [Malay.] 26 Df 5.25N 100.24 E
Butterworth [S.Afr.] 37 Df 32.23S 28.04 E
Button Bay 42 Ie 58.45N 94.25W
Butuan 22 Oi 8.57N 125.33 E
Butung, Palau- 21 Oj 5.00S 122.55 E
Buturlinovka 16 Ld 50.48N 40.45 E
Butzbach 12 Kd 50.26N 8.41 E
Bützow 10 Hc 53.50N 11.59 E
Buxtehude 10 Fc 53.27N 9.42 E
Buxton [Eng.-U.K.] 9 Lh 53.15N 1.55W
Buxton [N.C.-U.S.] 44 Jh 35.16N 75.32W
Buyo 34 Dd 6.16N 7.03W
Büyük Ağri Daği=Ararat, Mount- (EN) 21 Gf 39.40N 44.24 E
Büyükanafarta 15 Ji 40.17N 26.22 E
Büyükçekmece 15 Lh 41.01N 28.34 E
Büyükkarıştıran 15 Kh 41.18N 27.32 E
Büyük Kemikli Burun 15 Ji 40.18N 26.14 E
Büyük Mahya 15 Kh 41.47N 27.36 E
Büyük Menderes 23 Cb 37.57N 28.58 E
Büyükorhan 15 Lj 39.45N 28.55 E
Buyun Shan 27 Lc 40.06N 122.42 E
Buzači, Poluostrov- 19 Ff 45.00N 52.00 E
Buzan 16 Pf 46.18N 49.06 E
Buzançais 11 Hh 46.53N 1.25 E
Buzancy 12 Ge 49.25N 4.57 E
Buzău 15 Jd 45.09N 26.50 E
Buzău 15 Jd 45.09N 26.50 E
Buzău 15 Kd 45.26N 27.44 E
Buzaymah 33 De 24.55N 22.02 E
Buzen 29 Be 33.37N 131.08 E
Buzet 14 He 45.24N 13.59 E
Būzhān 24 Le 34.09N 47.05 E
Búzi 37 Ec 19.51S 34.30 E
Búzi 37 Ec 19.52S 34.46 E
Buziaş 15 Ed 45.39N 21.36 E
Búzios, Ilha dos- 55 Jf 23.48S 45.08W
Bužora, Gora- 10 Th 48.24N 23.15 E
Buzuluk 19 Fe 52.46N 52.17 E
Buzuluk 16 Md 50.13N 42.12 E
Buzuluk 16 Rc 52.47N 52.16 E
Buzzards Bay 44 Le 41.33N 70.47W

Index Symbols

[1] Independent Nation
[2] State, Region
[3] District, County
[4] Municipality
[5] Colony, Dependency
Continent
Physical Region
Historical or Cultural Region
Mount, Mountain
Volcano
Hill
Mountains, Mountain Range
Hills, Escarpment
Plateau, Upland
Pass, Gap
Plain, Lowland
Delta
Salt Flat
Valley, Canyon
Crater, Cave
Karst Features
Depression
Polder
Desert, Dunes
Forest, Woods
Heath, Steppe
Oasis
Cape, Point
Coast, Beach
Cliff
Peninsula
Isthmus
Sandbank
Island
Atoll
Rock, Reef
Islands, Archipelago
Rocks, Reefs
Coral Reef
Well, Spring
Geyser
River, Stream
Waterfall Rapids
River Mouth, Estuary
Lake
Salt Lake
Intermittent Lake
Reservoir
Swamp, Pond
Canal
Glacier
Ice Shelf, Pack Ice
Ocean
Sea
Gulf, Bay
Strait, Fjord
Lagoon
Bank
Seamount
Tablemount
Ridge
Shelf
Basin
Escarpment, Sea Scarp
Fracture
Trench, Abyss
National Park, Reserve
Point of Interest
Recreation Site
Cave, Cavern
Historic Site
Ruins
Wall, Walls
Church, Abbey
Temple
Scientific Station
Airport
Port
Lighthouse
Mine
Tunnel
Dam, Bridge

Bwagaoia 63a Ad 10.42S 152.50 E
Byälven 8 Ee 59.06N 12.54 E
Byam Martin 42 Ha 75.15N 104.15W
Byam Martin Channel 42 Ha 76.00N 105.00W
Bychawa 10 Se 51.01N 22.32 E
Byczyna 10 Oe 51.07N 18.11 E
Bydgoszcz [2] 10 Nc 53.10N 18.00 E
Bydgoszcz 6 He 53.08N 18.00 E
Byelarus' = Belarus (EN) 19 Ce 53.50N 28.00 E
Bygdin 8 Cc 61.20N 8.35 E
Bygland [Nor.] 7 Bg 58.51N 7.51 E
Bygland [Nor.] 8 Bf 58.41N 7.48 E
Byglandsfjorden 8 Bf 58.50N 7.50 E
Byhov 19 De 53.31N 30.15 E
Byk 15 Mc 46.55N 29.25 E
Bykovec 15 Lb 47.12N 28.18 E
Bykovo 16 Ne 49.47N 45.25 E
Bykovski 20 Hb 71.56N 129.05 E
Bylot 38 Lb 73.13N 78.34W
Byrd, Cape- 66 Qe 69.38S 76.07W
Byrdbreen 66 Df 71.35S 26.00 E
Byrd Glacier 66 Jg 80.15S 160.20 E
Byron, Cape- 57 Gg 28.39S 153.38 E
Byron Bay 42 Gc 68.55N 108.25W
Byron Bay 59 Ke 28.39S 153.37 E
Byrranga Gory = Byrranga Mountains (EN) 21 Mb 75.00N 104.00 E
Byrranga Mountains (EN) = Byrranga Gory 21 Mb 75.00N 104.00 E
Bystraja 20 Kf 52.40N 156.10 E
Bystreyca 10 Se 51.40N 22.33 E
Bystřice 10 Lf 50.11N 15.30 E
Bystrovka 18 Jc 42.45N 75.43 E
Bystrzyca [Pol.] 10 Se 51.16N 22.45 E
Bystrzyca [Pol.] 10 Me 51.13N 16.54 E
Bystrzyca Kłodzka 10 Mf 50.19N 16.39 E
Bytantaj 20 Ic 68.40N 134.50 E
Bytča 10 Og 49.14N 18.35 E
Byten 10 Vd 52.49N 25.33 E
Bytom 10 Of 50.22N 18.54 E
Bytów 10 Nb 54.11N 17.30 E
Byumba 36 Fc 1.35S 30.04 E
Byxelkrok 7 Dh 57.20N 17.00 E
Bzura 10 Qd 52.23N 20.09 E
Bzyb 16 Lh 43.12N 40.15 E

C

Cà, Sông- 25 Le 18.40N 105.40 E
Caacupé 56 Ic 25.23S 57.09W
Čaadajevka 16 Nc 53.09N 45.56 E
Caaguazú 56 Ic 25.26S 56.02W
Caaguazú [3] 55 Eg 25.00S 55.45W
Caála 36 Ce 12.55S 15.35 E
Caapucú 55 Dh 26.13S 57.12W
Caarapó 55 Ef 22.38S 54.48W
Caatinga 54 Ig 17.10S 45.53W
Caatinga 52 Lf 9.00S 42.00W
Caatinga, Rio- 55 Jc 17.10S 45.52W
Caazapá [3] 55 Dh 26.10S 56.00W
Caazapá 56 Ic 26.09S 56.24W
Cabaçal, Rio- 55 Db 16.00S 57.42W
Cabadbaran 26 Ie 9.10N 125.38 E
Cabaiguán 49 Hb 22.05N 79.30W
Caballeria, Cabo de- 13 Qd 40.05N 4.05 E
Caballo Cocha 54 Dd 3.54S 70.32W
Caballo Reservoir 45 Cj 32.58N 107.18W
Cabañas 13 Jg 37.40N 3.00W
Cabanatuan 22 Oh 15.29N 120.58 E
Cabano 44 Mb 47.41N 68.54W
Čabar 14 Ie 45.36N 14.39 E
Cabeceira do Apa 55 Ef 22.01S 55.46W
Cabeceiras 55 Ib 15.48S 46.59W
Cabeceiras de Basto 13 Ec 41.31N 7.59W
Cabeza, Arrecife- 48 Lh 19.04N 95.50W
Cabeza de Buey 13 Gf 38.43N 5.13W
Cabildo 55 Bn 38.29S 61.54W
Cabimas 53 Id 10.23N 71.28W
Cabinda 31 Ii 5.35S 12.13 E
Cabinda [3] 36 Bd 5.00S 12.30 E
Cabinet Mountains 46 Hb 48.08N 115.46W
Cabo Bojador 32 Ed 26.08N 14.30W
Cabo Frio 53 Lh 22.53S 42.01W
Cabo Gracias a Dios 49 Ff 14.59N 83.10W
Cabonga, Réservoir- 42 Jg 47.20N 76.35W
Caboolture 59 Ke 27.05S 152.50 E
Cabora Bassa, Dique de- 37 Ec 15.34S 32.42 E
Cabora Bassa, Lago- = Cabora Bassa, Lake-(EN) 30 Kj 15.40S 31.40 E
Cabora Bassa, Lake-(EN) = Cabora Bassa, Lago- 30 Kj 15.40S 31.40 E
Caborca 47 Bb 30.37N 112.06W
Cabot Strait 38 Ne 47.20N 59.30W
Cabourg 11 Fe 49.17N 0.08W
Cabo Verde = Cape Verde (EN) [1] 31 Eg 16.00N 24.00W
Cabo Verde, Ilhas do- = Cape Verde Islands (EN) 30 Eg 16.00N 24.10W
Cabra 13 Hg 37.28N 4.27W
Cabral, Serra do- 55 Jc 17.45S 44.22W
Cabras 14 Ck 39.56N 8.32 E
Cabras, Stagno di- 14 Ck 39.55N 8.30 E
Cabreira 13 Dc 41.39N 8.04W
Cabrejas, Puerto de- 13 Jd 40.08N 2.25W
Cabrera 49 Md 19.38N 69.54W
Cabrera, Isla- 13 Oe 39.09N 2.56 E
Cabrera, Sierra de la- 13 Fb 42.10N 6.25W
Cabri 46 Ka 50.37N 108.28W
Cabriel 13 Ke 39.14N 1.03W
Cabrit, Ilet 'a- 51e Ac 15.53N 61.36W
Cabrits, Ilet- 51h Bc 14.23N 60.52W
Cabrón, Cabo- 49 Md 19.22N 69.12W
Cabruta 50 Ci 7.38N 66.15W
Čabulja 14 Lg 43.30N 17.35 E
Cabure 49 Mh 11.08N 69.38W
Cacacas, Islas- 50 Dg 10.22N 64.26W
Caçador 56 Jc 26.47S 51.00W
Čačak 15 Df 43.54N 20.21 E
Caçapava dó Sul 56 Jd 30.30S 53.30W
Caccamo 14 Hm 37.56N 13.40 E
Caccia, Capo- 14 Cj 40.34N 8.09 E
Cacequi 55 Ei 29.53S 54.49W
Cáceres [3] 13 Ge 39.40N 6.00W
Cáceres [Braz.] 53 Kg 16.04S 57.41W
Cáceres [Sp.] 13 Fe 39.29N 6.22W
Cáceres, Laguna- 55 Dd 18.56S 57.48W
Cachari 55 Cn 36.24S 59.32W
Cache Peak 46 Ie 42.11N 113.40W
Cacheu 34 Bc 12.10N 16.21W
Cachimbo 53 Kf 9.08S 55.10W
Cachimbo, Serra do- 52 Kf 8.30S 55.50W
Cachimo 36 Dd 8.20S 21.21 E
Cáchira 49 Kj 7.46N 73.03W
Cáchira, Rio- 49 Kj 7.52N 73.40W
Cachoeira 54 Kf 12.36S 38.58W
Cachoeira Alta 55 Gd 18.48S 50.58W
Cachoeira de Goiás 55 Gc 16.44S 50.38W
Cachoeira do Arari 54 Id 1.01S 48.58W
Cachoeira do Sul 56 Jc 29.58S 52.54W
Cachoeira Dourada, Represa de- 54 Ig 18.30S 49.00W
Cachoeirinha 55 Gi 29.57S 51.05W
Cachoeiro de Itapemirim 54 Jh 20.51S 41.06W
Cacimbinho 55 Ee 21.50S 55.43W
Căciulaţi 15 Je 44.38N 26.10 E
Cacolo 36 Ce 10.08S 19.18 E
Caconda 36 Ce 13.45S 15.05 E
Cacuaco 36 Bd 8.47S 13.21 E
Cacuchi 36 Ce 14.23S 16.59 E
Cacula 36 Be 14.29S 14.10 E
Caculé 54 Jf 14.30S 42.13W
Caculuvar 36 Bf 16.46S 14.56 E
Cacuso 36 Cd 9.26S 15.45 E
Čadan 20 Ef 51.17N 91.40 E
Cadaqués 13 Pb 42.17N 3.17 E
Čadca 10 Og 49.26N 18.48 E
Caddo Lake 45 Ij 32.42N 94.01W
Cadena Costero Catalana/ Serralada Litoral Catalana = Catalan Coastal Range (EN) 5 Gg 41.35N 1.40 E
Cadereyta Jiménez 48 Ie 25.36N 100.00W
Cadi, Serra del-/Cadi, Sierra del- 13 Nb 42.17N 1.42 E
Cadibarrawirracanna, Lake- 59 He 28.50S 135.25 E
Cadibona, Colle di- 14 Cf 44.20N 8.22 E
Cadillac [Fr.] 11 Fj 44.38N 0.19W
Cadillac [Mi.-U.S.] 43 Jc 44.15N 85.24W
Cadi, Sierra del/Cadi, Serra del- 13 Nb 42.17N 1.42 E
Cadiz 26 Hd 10.57N 123.18 E
Cádiz [3] 13 Gh 36.30N 5.45W
Cádiz 6 Fh 36.32N 6.18W
Cadiz [Ca.-U.S.] 46 Hi 34.30N 115.30W
Cadiz [Ky.-U.S.] 44 Dg 36.52N 87.50W
Cádiz, Bahía de- 13 Fh 36.32N 6.16W
Cádiz, Golfo de- 5 Fh 36.50N 7.10W
Cadiz Lake 46 Hi 34.18N 115.24W
Cadore 14 Gd 46.30N 12.20 E
Cadwell 43 Dc 43.40N 116.41W
Čadyr-Lunga 16 Ff 46.04N 28.52 E
Caen 6 Ff 49.11N 0.21W
Caen, Campagne de- 11 Fe 49.05N 0.20W
Caernarvon 9 Ih 53.08N 4.16W
Caernarvon Bay 9 Ih 53.05N 4.30W
Caerphilly 9 Jj 51.35N 3.14W
Caetité 54 Jf 14.04S 42.29W
Cafayate 56 Gc 26.05S 65.58W
Cafelândia [Braz.] 55 Fc 16.40S 53.25W
Cafelândia [Braz.] 55 Ie 21.49S 49.35W
Cafundó, Serra do- 55 Hb 14.40S 48.23W
Čagan 55 He 50.30N 79.10 E
Cagan-Aman 19 Ef 47.32N 46.43 E
Cagan-Nur [Mong.] 27 Eb 49.40N 89.55 E
Cagan-Nur [Mong.] 27 Ia 50.25N 105.15 E
Cagan-Ula 27 Gb 49.35N 98.25 E
Cagatá, Arroyo- 55 Df 23.26S 56.36W
Cagayan 26 Hc 18.22N 121.37 E
Cagayan de Oro 22 Oi 8.29N 124.39 E
Cagayan Islands 26 He 9.40N 121.16 E
Cagayan Sulu 26 Ge 7.01N 118.30 E
Čagda 20 Ie 58.42N 130.37 E
Cageri 16 Mh 42.39N 42.42 E
Çağış 15 Lj 39.30N 28.01 E
Cagli 14 Gg 43.33N 12.39 E
Cagliari 6 Gh 39.13N 9.07 E
Cagliari, Golfo di- 14 Dk 39.10N 9.10 E
Cagliari, Stagno di- 14 Dk 39.15N 9.05 E
Čaglinka 17 Nj 53.59N 69.47 E
Cagnes-sur-Mer 11 Nk 43.40N 7.09 E
Čagoda 7 Ig 59.12N 35.13 E
Čagodošča 7 Ig 58.58N 36.37 E
Caguas 47 Ke 18.14N 66.02W
Čagyl 16 Fg 40.43N 55.25 E
Cahama 36 Bf 16.16S 14.17 E
Caha Mountains/An Cheacha 9 Dj 51.45N 9.45W
Caher/An Chathair 9 Fi 52.22N 7.55W
Cahersiveen/Cathair Saidhbhin 9 Cj 51.57N 10.13W
Cahore Point/Rinn Chathóir 9 Gi 52.34N 6.11W
Cahors 11 Hj 44.26N 1.26 E
Cai, Rio- 55 Gi 29.56S 51.16W
Caia 37 Fc 17.49S 35.20 E
Caia 13 Ef 38.50N 7.05W
Caiabis, Serra dos- 54 Gf 11.40S 56.30W
Caiapó, Rio- 55 Gb 15.49S 51.53W
Caiapó, Serra do- 52 Kg 17.00S 52.00W
Caiapônia 55 Gc 16.57S 51.49W
Caibarién 47 Id 22.31N 79.28W
Caiçara 55 Gb 15.34S 50.12W
Caicara 54 Eb 7.37N 66.10W
Caicara de Maturín 50 Eh 9.49N 63.36W
Caicó 54 Ke 6.27S 37.06W
Caicos Bank (EN) 47 Jd 21.35N 71.55W
Caicos Islands 38 Lg 21.45N 71.35W
Caicos Passage 47 Jd 22.00N 72.30W
Caille Island 51p Bb 12.17N 61.35W
Caimanera 49 Jd 19.59N 75.09W
Caine, Rio- 54 Eg 13.23S 65.21W
Cai Nuoc 25 Lg 8.56N 105.01 E
Caird Coast 66 Af 75.00S 24.30W
Cairngorms Mountains 9 Jd 57.06N 3.30W
Cairns 58 Ff 16.55S 145.46 E
Cairo [Ga.-U.S.] 44 Ej 30.53N 84.12W
Cairo [Il.-U.S.] 43 Jd 37.00N 89.11W
Cairo (EN) = Al Qāhirah 31 Ke 30.03N 31.15 E
Cairo Montenotte 14 Cf 44.24N 8.16 E
Caiseal/Cashel 9 Fi 52.31N 7.53W
Caisleán an Bharraigh/ Castlebar 9 Dh 53.52N 9.17W
Caister-on-Sea 12 Db 52.40N 1.45 E
Caiundo 36 Cf 15.42S 17.27 E
Caiúva, Lagoa- 55 Fk 32.24S 52.30W
Caiyuanzhen → Shengsi 28 Gi 30.42N 122.29 E
Caizi Hu 28 Di 30.48N 117.05 E
Čaja 20 De 58.17N 82.45 E
Cajabamba 54 Ce 7.58S 77.59W
Caja de Muertos, Isla- 51a Bc 17.53N 66.31W
Cajamarca 53 If 7.10S 78.31W
Cajamarca [2] 54 Ce 6.15S 78.50W
Cajapió 54 Jd 2.58S 44.48W
Cajarc 11 Hj 44.29N 1.51 E
Cajatambo 54 Cf 10.29S 77.02W
Čajkovski 19 Fd 56.47N 54.09 E
Çakırgöl Dağ 24 Hb 40.34N 39.42 E
Çakmak 24 Fd 37.37N 34.19 E
Çakmak Dağı 24 Jc 39.46N 42.12 E
Čakor 15 Dg 42.40N 20.02 E
Čakovec 14 Kd 46.23N 16.26 E
Cakrani 15 Ci 40.36N 19.37 E
Çal 24 Cc 38.05N 29.24 E
Cal, Rio de la- 55 Cc 17.27S 58.15W
Calabar 31 Hh 4.57N 8.19 E
Calabozo 54 Eb 8.56N 67.26W
Calabozo, Ensenada de- 49 Lh 11.30N 71.45W
Calabria [2] 14 Kl 39.00N 16.30 E
Calaburras, Punta de- 13 Hh 36.30N 4.38W
Calacoto 54 Eg 17.18S 68.39W
Calacuccia 11a Ba 42.20N 9.01 E
Calaf 13 Nc 41.44N 1.31 E
Calafat 15 Ff 43.59N 22.56 E
Calafate 53 Ik 50.20S 72.16W
Cala Figuera, Cabo de- 13 Oe 39.27N 2.31 E
Calagua Islands 26 Hd 14.27N 122.55 E
Calahorra 13 Kb 42.18N 1.58W
Calai 36 Cf 17.50S 19.20 E
Calais [Fr.] 6 Ge 50.57N 1.50 E
Calais [Me.-U.S.] 44 Nc 45.11N 67.17W
Calais, Pas de- = Dover, Strait of- (EN) 5 Ge 51.00N 1.30 E
Calakmul 48 Oh 18.05N 89.55W
Calalaste, Sierra de- 56 Gc 25.30S 67.30W
Calama 53 Jh 22.28S 68.56W
Calamar 49 Jh 10.14N 74.56W
Calamian Group 21 Nh 12.00N 120.00 E
Calamocha 13 Kd 40.55N 1.18W
Călan 15 Fd 45.44N 22.59 E
Calanda 13 Lc 40.56N 0.14W
Calang 26 C# 4.30N 95.40 E
Calangiánus 14 D 40.56N 9.11 E
Calapan 26 Hd 13.25N 121.10 E
Calar Alto 13 Jg 37.15N 2.25W
Călăraşi 15 Ke 44.12N 27.20 E
Cala Ratjada 13 Pe 39.42N 3.25 E
Calar del Mundo 13 J# 38.31N 2.28W
Calatañazor 13 Jc 41.42N 2.49W
Calatayud 13 Kc 41.21N 1.38W
Calatrava 13 If 38.35N 3.48W
Calatrava, Campo de- 13 Hf 38.50N 4.15W
Calavà, Capo- 14 Il 38.10N 14.55 E
Calavon 11 Kk 43.51N 5.00 E
Calayan 26 Hc 19.20N 121.27 E
Calbayog 22 Oh 12.04N 124.36 E
Calchaqui 56 Hc 29.54S 60.18W
Calçoene 54 Hc 2.30N 50.57W
Calcutta 22 Kg 22.32N 88.22 E
Caldaro / Kaltern 14 Fd 46.25N 11.14 E
Caldas [2] 54 Cb 5.15N 75.30W
Caldas da Rainha 13 Ce 39.24N 9.08W
Caldas Novas 55 Hc 17.45S 48.38W
Caldeirão, Serra de- 13 Dg 37.19N 8.04W
Calder 9 Jh 53.44N 1.21W
Caldera 56 Fc 27.04S 70.50W
Calderina, Sierra de la- 13 Ie 39.19N 3.48W
Caldes de Mombúy 13 Oc 41.38N 2.10 E
Caldwell 44 Gf 39.44N 81.32W
Caledon 37 Bf 34.12S 19.23 E
Caledon 30 Jl 30.32S 26.05 E
Caledonia [Blz.] 49 Cd 18.14N 88.29W
Caledonia [Mn.-U.S.] 45 Ke 43.38N 91.29W
Caledonian Canal 9 Id 57.20N 4.30W
Calella 13 Oc 41.37N 2.40 E
Caledonia Olivia 56 Gg 46.26S 67.32W
Calexico 46 Hj 32.40N 115.30W
Çalgal Dağı 24 Hc 39.06N 38.05 E
Calgary 39 Hd 51.03N 114.05W
Calhoun 44 Eh 34.30N 84.57W
Cali 53 Ie 3.27N 76.31W
Calicut (Kozhikode) 21 Jh 11.19N 75.46 E
Caliente 43 Ed 37.37N 114.31W
California [2] 43 Dd 37.30N 119.30W
California, Golfo de- = California, Gulf of- (EN) 38 Hg 28.00N 112.00W
California, Gulf of- (EN) = California, Golfo de- 38 Hg 28.00N 112.00W
Călimăn, Munții- 15 Ib 47.07N 25.03 E
Călimănești 15 Hd 45.14N 24.20 E
Calimere, Point- 25 Ff 10.18N 79.52 E
Calingasta 56 Gd 31.19S 69.25W
Calispell Peak 46 Gb 48.26N 117.30W
Calitri 14 Jj 40.54N 15.26 E
Calitzdorp 37 Cf 33.33S 21.42 E
Caliviny 51p Bb 12.01N 61.43W
Calixtlahuaca 48 Jh 19.15N 99.45W
Calka 16 Ni 41.35N 44.05 E
Calkini 48 Ng 20.22N 90.03W
Callabonna, Lake- 59 Ie 29.45S 140.05 E
Callac 11 Cf 48.24N 3.26W
Callaghan, Mount- 46 Gg 39.42N 116.57W
Callainn/Callan 9 Fi 52.33N 7.23W
Callan/Callainn 9 Fi 52.33N 7.23W
Callander [Ont.-Can.] 44 Hb 46.13N 79.23W
Callander [Scot.-U.K.] 9 Ie 56.15N 4.13W
Callantsoog 12 Gb 52.50N 4.41 E
Callao 53 Ig 12.02S 77.05W
Callao [2] 54 Cf 2.04S 77.09W
Calliaqua 51n Ba 13.08N 61.12W
Callosa de Ensarriá 13 Lf 38.39N 0.07W
Callosa de Segura 13 Lf 38.08N 0.52W
Calmalli 48 Cc 28.14N 113.33W
Călmăţui [Rom.] 15 If 43.46N 25.10 E
Călmăţui [Rom.] 15 Ke 44.50N 27.50 E
Calonne 12 Ce 49.17N 0.12 E
Calore 14 Ii 41.11N 14.28 E
Čalovo → Veľký Meder 10 Ni 47.52N 17.47 E
Calpe 13 Mf 38.39N 0.03 E
Caltabellotta 14 Hm 37.34N 13.13 E
Caltagirone 14 Im 37.14N 14.31 E
Caltanissetta 14 Im 37.29N 14.04 E
Caltilibük 15 Lj 39.57N 28.36 E
Čaltyr 16 Kf 47.17N 39.29 E
Caluango 36 Cd 8.15S 19.38 E
Calucinga 36 Ce 11.19S 16.13 E
Călugareni 15 Ie 44.11N 25.59 E
Calulo 36 Bd 9.59S 14.54 E
Caluquembe 36 Be 13.46S 14.41 E
Calvados [3] 11 Fe 49.10N 0.30W
Calvados, Côte du- 11 Fe 49.22N 0.30W
Calvert Island 46 Ba 51.35N 128.00W
Calvert River 59 Hc 16.17S 137.44 E
Calvi 11a Aa 42.34N 8.45 E
Calvillo 48 Hg 21.51N 102.43W
Calvinia 31 Il 31.25S 19.45 E
Calvitero 13 Gd 40.20N 5.43W
Cam 9 Ni 52.21N 0.15 E
Camabatela 36 Cd 8.13S 15.23 E
Camacá 54 Kg 15.24S 39.30W
Camacupa 36 Ce 12.01S 17.22 E
Camaguán 50 Ch 8.06N 67.36W
Camagüey [3] 49 Ic 21.30N 78.10W
Camagüey 39 Lg 21.23N 77.55W
Camagüey, Archipiélago de- 47 Id 22.18N 78.00W
Camaiore 14 Eg 43.56N 10.18 E
Camajuaní 49 Hb 22.28N 79.44W
Camamu 54 Kf 13.57S 39.07W
Camaná 54 Dg 16.37S 72.42W
Camapuã 55 Ed 19.30S 54.05W
Camapuã, Sertão de- 52 Kg 19.00S 51.30W
Camaquã 56 Jd 30.51S 51.49W
Camaquã, Rio- 55 Gj 31.17S 51.47W
Camarat, Cap- 11 Mk 43.12N 6.41 E
Camargo [Bol.] 54 Eh 20.39S 65.13W
Camargo [Sp.] 13 Ia 43.24N 3.54W
Camargos, Represa- 55 Je 21.20S 44.30W
Camargue 11 Kk 43.31N 4.34 E
Camariñas 13 Ca 43.07N 9.10W
Camarón, Cabo- 47 He 16.00N 85.04W
Camarones 56 Gf 44.48S 65.42W
Camarones, Bahía- 56 Gf 44.45S 65.34W
Camas [Sp.] 13 Fg 37.24N 6.02W
Camas [Wa.-U.S.] 46 Dd 45.35N 122.24W
Camatagua, Embalse de- 50 Ch 9.48N 66.55W
Ca Mau, Mui- = Ca Mau Point (EN) 21 Mi 8.38N 104.44 E
Ca Mau Point (EN) = Ca Mau, Mui- 21 Mi 8.38N 104.44 E
Cambados 13 Db 42.30N 8.48W
Camberg 12 Kd 50.18N 8.16 E
Camberley 12 Bc 51.21N 0.44W
Cambo 36 Cd 7.40S 17.17 E
Cambodia (EN) = Kampuchea 22 Mh 13.00N 105.00 E
Cambo-les-Bains 11 Ek 43.22N 1.24W
Cambrai 11 Jd 50.10N 3.14 E
Cambremer 12 Ce 49.09N 0.03 E
Cambrésis 12 Fd 50.15N 3.05 E
Cambrian Mountains 5 Fe 52.35N 3.35W
Cambridge 9 Ni 52.25N 0.10 E
Cambridge [Eng.-U.K.] 6 Ni 52.12N 0.07 E
Cambridge [Id.-U.S.] 46 Gd 44.34N 116.41W
Cambridge [Ma.-U.S.] 44 Ld 42.22N 71.06W
Cambridge [Md.-U.S.] 44 If 38.34N 76.04W
Cambridge [Mn.-U.S.] 45 Jd 45.31N 93.14W
Cambridge [N.Z.] 62 Fb 37.53S 175.28 E
Cambridge [Oh.-U.S.] 44 Ge 40.02N 81.36W
Cambridge Airport 12 Cb 52.10N 0.08 E
Cambridge Bay 39 Ic 69.03N 105.05W
Cambridge Gulf 59 Fb 14.55S 128.15 E
Cambridgeshire [3] 9 Mi 52.25N 0.05W
Cambutal, Cerro- 49 Gj 7.16N 80.36W
Camden [Al.-U.S.] 44 Dj 32.00N 87.17W
Camden [Ar.-U.S.] 43 Ie 33.35N 92.50W
Camden [N.J.-U.S.] 44 Jf 39.57N 75.07W
Camden [S.C.-U.S.] 44 Gh 34.16N 80.36W
Camden [Tn.-U.S.] 44 Cg 36.04N 88.06W
Camden Bay 40 Kb 70.00N 145.00W
Camdenton 45 Jg 38.00N 92.45W
Camel 9 Ik 50.33N 4.55W
Çameli 24 Cd 37.05N 29.20 E
Camerino 14 Hg 43.08N 13.04 E
Cameron 42 Ha 76.15N 104.00W
Cameron [Az.-U.S.] 46 Ji 35.51N 111.25W
Cameron [La.-U.S.] 45 Jl 29.48N 93.19W
Cameron [Mo.-U.S.] 45 Ig 39.44N 94.14W
Cameron [Tx.-U.S.] 45 Hk 30.51N 96.59W
Cameron [Wi.-U.S.] 45 Kd 45.25N 91.44W
Cameron Hills 42 Fe 60.00N 118.00W
Cameron Mountains 62 Bf 46.00S 166.55 E
Cameroon (EN) = Cameroun [1] 31 Ih 6.00N 12.00 E
Cameroon, Mount- (EN) = Cameroun 30 Hh 4.12N 9.11 E
Camerota 14 Jj 40.02N 15.22 E
Cameroun = Cameroon (EN) [1] 31 Ih 6.00N 12.00 E
Cameroun = Cameroon, Mount- (EN) 30 Hh 4.12N 9.11 E
Cametá 54 Id 2.15S 49.30W
Camiguin [Phil.] 26 Hc 18.56N 121.55 E
Camiling 26 He 15.42N 120.24 E
Camilla 44 Ej 31.14N 84.12W
Caminha 13 Dc 41.52N 8.50W
Camissombo 36 Dd 8.10S 20.39 E
Camoapa 49 Eg 12.23N 85.31W
Camocim 53 Lf 2.54S 40.50W
Camonica, Val- 14 Ed 46.00N 10.20 E
Camooweal 59 Hc 19.55S 138.07 E
Camopi 54 Hc 3.13N 52.28W
Camorta 25 Ig 8.08N 93.30 E
Campagne-lès-Hesdin 12 Dd 50.24N 1.52 E
Campana 55 Cl 34.10S 58.57W
Campana, Isla- 52 Ij 48.20S 75.15W
Campanario 13 Gf 38.52N 5.37W
Campanário 55 Ef 22.48S 55.03W
Campania [2] 14 Ii 41.00N 14.30 E
Campanquiz, Cerros- 54 Cd 4.30S 77.40W
Campbell, Cape- 62 Fd 41.44S 174.16 E
Campbell Island 62 Ci 52.30S 169.10 E
Campbell Plateau (EN) 57 Ij 51.00S 170.00 E
Campbell River 42 Ef 50.01N 125.15W
Campbellsville 44 Eg 37.21N 85.20W
Campbellton 42 Kg 48.00N 66.40W
Campbelltown, Sydney- 59 Kf 34.04S 150.49 E
Campbeltown 9 Hf 55.26N 5.36W
Campeche 39 Jh 19.51N 90.32W
Campeche [2] 47 Fe 19.00N 90.30W
Campeche, Bahía de- = Campeche, Gulf of- (EN) 38 Jg 20.00N 94.00W
Campeche, Gulf of- (EN) = Campeche, Bahía de- 38 Jg 20.00N 94.00W
Campeche Bank (EN) 47 Fd 22.00N 90.00W
Campechuela 49 Ic 20.14N 77.17W
Camperdown 59 Ig 38.14S 143.09 E
Campidano 14 Ck 39.30N 8.45 E
Campiglia Marittima 14 Eg 43.03N 10.37 E
Campillos 13 Hg 37.03N 4.51W
Campina Grande 53 Mf 7.13S 35.53W
Campinas 53 Lh 22.54S 47.05W
Campina Verde 55 Hd 19.31S 49.28W
Campine/Kempen 11 Lc 51.10N 5.20 E
Campinorte 55 Hb 14.20S 49.08W
Campione d'Italia 14 Ce 45.59N 8.59 E
Campo 34 Ge 2.22N 9.49 E
Campo Alegre 50 Bh 9.15N 68.25W
Campo Alegre de Goiás 55 Ic 17.36S 47.46W
Campobasso 14 Ii 41.34N 14.39 E
Campo Belo 55 Je 20.53S 45.16W
Campo de Criptana 13 Ie 39.24N 3.07W
Campo de la Cruz 49 Jh 10.23N 74.52W
Campo del Cielo 55 Bh 27.53S 61.49W
Campo Florido 55 Hd 19.46S 48.34W
Campo Formoso 54 Jf 10.31S 40.20W
Campo Gallo 56 Hc 26.35S 62.51W
Campo Garay 55 Bi 29.41S 61.37W
Campo Grande [Arg.] 55 Eh 27.13S 54.58W
Campo Grande [Braz.] 53 Kh 20.27S 54.37W
Campo Largo [Arg.] 55 Bh 26.48S 60.50W
Campo Largo [Braz.] 55 Hg 25.26S 49.32W
Campo Maior [Braz.] 54 Jd 4.49S 42.10W
Campo Maior [Port.] 13 Ee 39.01N 7.04W
Campomarino 14 Ji 41.57N 15.02 E
Campo Mourão 56 Jb 24.03S 52.22W
Campos 53 Lh 21.45S 41.18W
Campos [Braz.] 52 Lg 15.00S 44.30W
Campos [Braz.] 52 Kh 21.00S 51.00W
Campos, Laguna- 55 Be 20.50S 61.31W
Campos, Tierra de- 13 Hb 42.10N 4.50W
Campos Altos 55 Id 19.41S 46.10W
Campos Belos 55 Ia 13.03S 46.53W
Campos do Jordão 55 Jf 22.44S 45.35W
Campos Novos 55 Gh 27.24S 51.12W
Campos Sales 54 Je 7.04S 40.23W
Campo Tures / Sand in Taufers 14 Fd 46.55N 11.57 E
Camp Verde 43 Ee 34.34N 111.51W
Cam Ranh 25 Lf 11.54N 109.13 E
Camrose 42 Gf 53.01N 112.50W
Camsell 42 Fc 65.40N 118.07W
Camsell Portage 42 Ge 59.38N 109.42W
Çan 24 Bb 40.02N 27.03 E
Canaan [Ct.-U.S.] 44 Kd 42.02N 73.20W
Canaan [Trin.] 50 Fg 11.09N 60.49W
Canaan Mountain 46 Jh 37.45N 111.51W
Cana Brava, Ribeirão- 55 Ic 16.35S 46.34W
Cana Brava, Rio- [Braz.] 55 Ib 14.40S 47.07W
Cana Brava, Rio- [Braz.] 55 Ha 12.12S 48.40W
Cana Brava, Rio- [Braz.] 55 Ha 13.11S 48.11W
Canada [1] 39 Jc 60.00N 95.00W
Cañada 17 Fh 42.50N 6.05W
Canada Basin (EN) 67 Ad 80.00N 145.00W
Cañada de Gomez 56 Hd 32.49S 61.24W
Canadian 45 Fi 35.55N 100.23W
Canadian River 38 Jf 35.27N 95.03W
Canaguá, Rio- 49 Mj 7.57N 69.36W
Canaima 54 Db 9.49N 70.56W

Index Symbols

[1] Independent Nation
[2] State, Region
[3] District, County
[4] Municipality
[5] Colony, Dependency
Continent
Physical Region
Historical or Cultural Region
Mount, Mountain
Volcano
Hill
Mountains, Mountain Range
Hills, Escarpment
Plateau, Upland
Pass, Gap
Plain, Lowland
Delta
Salt Flat
Valley, Canyon
Crater, Cave
Karst Features
Depression
Polder
Desert, Dunes
Forest, Woods
Heath, Steppe
Oasis
Cape, Point
Coast, Beach
Cliff
Peninsula
Isthmus
Sandbank
Island
Atoll
Rock, Reef
Islands, Archipelago
Rocks, Reefs
Coral Reef
Well, Spring
Geyser
River, Stream
Waterfall Rapids
River Mouth, Estuary
Lake
Salt Lake
Intermittent Lake
Reservoir
Swamp, Pond
Canal
Glacier
Ice Shelf, Pack Ice
Ocean
Sea
Gulf, Bay
Strait, Fjord
Lagoon
Bank
Seamount
Tablemount
Ridge
Shelf
Basin
Escarpment, Sea Scarp
Fracture
Trench, Abyss
National Park, Reserve
Point of Interest
Recreation Site
Cave, Cavern
Historic Site
Ruins
Wall, Walls
Church, Abbey
Temple
Scientific Station
Airport
Port
Lighthouse
Mine
Tunnel
Dam, Bridge

Index Symbols

[1] Independent Nation	▣ Historical or Cultural Region	Pass, Gap	Depression
[2] State, Region	▲ Mount, Mountain	Plain, Lowland	Polder
[3] District, County	▲ Volcano	Delta	Desert, Dunes
[4] Municipality	△ Hill	Salt Flat	Forest, Woods
[5] Colony, Dependency	▲ Mountains, Mountain Range	Valley, Canyon	Heath, Steppe
■ Continent	◭ Hills, Escarpment	Crater, Cave	Oasis
◨ Physical Region	▦ Plateau, Upland	Karst Features	Cape, Point

Coast, Beach	Rock, Reef	Waterfall Rapids	Canal
Cliff	Islands, Archipelago	River Mouth, Estuary	Glacier
Peninsula	Rocks, Reefs	Lake	Ice Shelf, Pack Ice
Isthmus	Coral Reef	Salt Lake	Ocean
Sandbank	Well, Spring	Intermittent Lake	Sea
Island	Geyser	Reservoir	Gulf, Bay
Atoll	River, Stream	Swamp, Pond	Strait, Fjord

Lagoon	Escarpment, Sea Scarp	Historic Site
Bank	Fracture	Ruins
Seamount	Trench, Abyss	Wall, Walls
Tablemount	National Park, Reserve	Church, Abbey
Ridge	Point of Interest	Temple
Shelf	Recreation Site	Scientific Station
Basin	Cave, Cavern	Airport

Port
Lighthouse
Mine
Tunnel
Dam, Bridge

Name	Page	Grid	Lat.	Long.
Case-Pilote	51h	Ab	14.38N	61.08W
Caserta	14	Ii	41.04N	14.20 E
Casey	66	He	66.17S	110.32 E
Casey Bay	66	Ee	67.00S	48.00 E
Cashel/Caiseal	9	Fi	52.31N	7.53W
Casigua	49	Ki	8.46N	72.30W
Casilda	56	Hd	33.03S	61.10W
Casimcea	15	Le	44.24N	28.33 E
Casino	59	Ke	28.52S	153.03 E
Casiquiare, Brazo-	54	Ec	2.01N	67.07W
Čáslav	10	Lg	49.55N	15.25 E
Casma	54	Ce	9.28S	78.19W
Časnačorr, Gora-	7	Hc	67.45N	33.29 E
Čašniki	7	Gi	54.52N	29.08 E
Casoli	14	Ih	42.07N	14.18 E
Casoria	14	Ij	40.54N	14.17 E
Caspe	13	Lc	41.14N	0.02W
Casper	39	Ie	42.51N	106.19W
Caspian Depression (EN)= Prikaspijskaja Nizmennost	5	Lf	48.00N	52.00 E
Caspian Sea (EN)= Kaspijskoje More	5	Lg	42.00N	50.30 E
Caspian Sea (EN)= Māzandarān, Daryā-ye-	5	Lg	42.00N	50.30 E
Cassai	30	Ii	3.02S	16.57 E
Cassamba	36	De	13.04S	20.25 E
Cassange, Rio-	55	Dc	17.06S	57.23W
Cassano allo Ionio	14	Kk	39.47N	16.19 E
Cass City	44	Fd	43.36N	83.10W
Cassel	12	Ed	50.47N	2.29 E
Casselton	45	Hc	46.54N	97.13W
Cássia	55	Ie	20.36S	46.56W
Cassiar	42	Ee	59.16N	129.40W
Cassiar Mountains	38	Gd	59.00N	129.00W
Cassilândia	54	Hg	19.09S	51.45W
Cassino [Braz.]	55	Fk	32.11S	52.10W
Cassino [It.]	14	Hi	41.30N	13.49 E
Cassis	11	Lk	43.13N	5.32 E
Cass Lake	45	Ic	47.23N	94.36W
Cass River	44	Fd	43.23N	83.59W
Cassununga	55	Fc	16.03S	53.38W
Castagneto Carducci	14	Eg	43.10N	10.36 E
Castagniccia	11a	Ba	42.25N	9.30 E
Castañar, Sierra del-	13	He	39.35N	4.10W
Castanhal	54	Id	1.18S	47.55W
Castaños	48	Id	26.47N	101.25W
Castelbuono	14	Im	37.56N	14.05 E
Castel di Sangro	14	Ii	41.47N	14.06 E
Castelfidardo	14	Hg	43.28N	13.33 E
Castelfranco Veneto	14	Fe	45.40N	11.55 E
Casteljaloux	11	Gj	44.19N	0.06 E
Castellabate	14	Ij	40.17N	14.57 E
Castellammare, Golfo di-	14	Gl	38.10N	12.55 E
Castellammare del Golfo	14	Gl	38.01N	12.53 E
Castellammare di Stabia	14	Ij	40.42N	14.29 E
Castellana Grotte	14	Lj	40.53N	17.10 E
Castellane	11	Mk	43.51N	6.31 E
Castellaneta	14	Kj	40.38N	16.56 E
Castelldefels	13	Nc	41.17N	1.58 E
Castelli [Arg.]	56	Hc	25.57S	60.37W
Castelli [Arg.]	55	Dm	36.06S	57.47W
Castelló de la Plana/ Castellón de la Plana	6	Fh	39.59N	0.02W
Castellón	13	Ld	40.10N	0.10W
Castellón de la Plana/ Castelló de la Plana	6	Fh	39.59N	0.02W
Castellón de la Plana-El Grao	13	Me	39.58N	0.01 E
Castellote	13	Ld	40.48N	0.19W
Castelnaudary	11	Hk	43.19N	1.57 E
Castelnau-de-Médoc	11	Fi	45.02N	0.48W
Castelnovo ne' Monti	14	Ef	44.26N	10.24 E
Castelo Branco	13	Ee	40.00N	7.30W
Castelo Branco	13	Ee	39.49N	7.30W
Castelo de Vide	13	Ee	39.25N	7.27W
Castelo do Piauí	54	Je	5.20S	41.33W
Castel San Giovanni	14	De	45.04N	9.26 E
Castelsardo	14	Cj	40.55N	8.43 E
Castelsarrasin	11	Hj	44.02N	1.06 E
Casteltermini	14	Hm	37.32N	13.39 E
Castelvetrano	14	Gm	37.41N	12.47 E
Castets	11	Ek	43.53N	1.09W
Castiglione del Lago	14	Gg	43.07N	12.03 E
Castiglione della Pescaia	14	Eh	42.46N	10.53 E
Castiglion Fiorentino	14	Fg	43.20N	11.55 E
Castilla la Nueva=New Castile (EN)	13	Id	40.00N	3.45W
Castilla la Vieja=Old Castile (EN)	13	Ic	41.30N	4.00W
Castillejo	13	Gc	41.14N	5.30W
Castillon-la-Bataille	11	Fj	44.51N	0.02W
Castillonnès	11	Gj	44.39N	0.36 E
Castillos	56	Jd	34.12S	53.50W
Castillos, Laguna de-	55	Fl	34.20S	53.54W
Castlebar/Caisleán an Bharraigh	9	Dh	53.52N	9.17W
Castle Bruce	51g	Bb	15.26N	61.16W
Castle Dome Peak	46	Hj	33.05N	114.08W
Castle Douglas	9	Jg	54.57N	3.56W
Castlegar	42	Fg	49.19N	117.40W
Castleisland/Oileán Ciarraí	9	Di	52.14N	9.27W
Castlemaine	59	Ig	37.04S	144.13 E
Castle Peak	46	Hd	44.03N	114.32W
Castlepoint	62	Gd	40.55S	176.13 E
Castlepollard	9	Fh	53.41N	7.17W
Castlerea/An Caisleán Riabhach	9	Eh	53.46N	8.29W
Castlereagh Bay	59	Hb	12.10S	135.10 E
Castle Rock Butte	45	Ed	45.00N	103.27W
Castle Rock Lake	45	Le	43.56N	89.58W
Častoozerje	17	Mi	55.34N	67.53 E
Castor	46	Ja	52.13N	111.53W
Castres	11	Ik	43.36N	2.15 E
Castricum	12	Gb	52.33N	4.42 E
Castries	39	Mh	14.01N	61.00W
Castrignano del Capo	14	Mk	39.50N	18.20 E
Castro [Braz.]	56	Jb	24.47S	50.03W
Castro [Chile]	56	Ff	42.29S	73.46W
Castro Alves	54	Kf	12.45S	39.26W
Castrocaro Terme e Terra del Sole	14	Ff	44.10N	11.57 E
Castro Daire	13	Ed	40.54N	7.56W
Castro del Río	13	Hg	37.41N	4.28W
Castrojeriz	13	Hb	42.17N	4.08W
Castropol	13	Ea	43.32N	7.02W
Castrop-Rauxel	12	Jc	51.33N	7.19 E
Castro Urdiales	13	Ia	43.23N	3.13W
Castro Verde	13	Dg	37.42N	8.05W
Castrovillari	14	Kk	39.49N	16.12 E
Castrovirreyna	54	Cf	13.16S	75.19W
Castuera	13	Gf	38.43N	5.33W
Častyje	17	Gh	57.19N	54.59 E
Casupá	55	El	34.09S	55.38W
Caswell Sound	62	Bf	45.00S	167.10 E
Çat	24	Ic	39.40N	41.02 E
Čata	10	Oi	47.58N	18.40 E
Catacamas	49	Ef	14.54N	85.56W
Catahoula Lake	45	Jk	31.30N	92.06W
Çatak	24	Jc	38.01N	43.07 E
Çatak	24	Jd	37.53N	42.39 E
Catalan Coastal Range (EN) =Cadena Costero Catalana /Serralada Litoral Catalana	5	Gg	41.35N	1.40 E
Catalan Coastal Range (EN) =Serralada Litoral Catalana/Cadena Costero Catalana	5	Gg	41.35N	1.40 E
Catalão	54	Ig	18.10S	47.57W
Čatal Balkan	15	Jg	42.46N	27.00 E
Çatalca	15	Lh	41.09N	28.27 E
Çatal Dağ	15	Lj	39.51N	28.20 E
Catalina	56	Gc	25.13S	69.43W
Catalina, Isla-	49	Md	18.21N	69.00W
Catalina, Punta-	56	Gh	52.32S	68.47W
Catalonia (EN)=Cataluña/ Catalunya	5	Gg	42.00N	2.00 E
Catalonia (EN)=Cataluña/ Catalunya	13	Nc	42.00N	2.00 E
Catalonia (EN)=Catalunya/ Cataluña	5	Gg	42.00N	2.00 E
Catalonia (EN)=Catalunya/ Cataluña	13	Nc	42.00N	2.00 E
Cataluña/Catalunya= Catalonia (EN)	5	Gg	42.00N	2.00 E
Cataluña/Catalunya= Catalonia (EN)	13	Nc	42.00N	2.00 E
Catalunya/Cataluña= Catalonia (EN)	13	Nc	42.00N	2.00 E
Catalunya/Cataluña= Catalonia (EN)	5	Gg	42.00N	2.00 E
Çatalzeytin	24	Fb	41.57N	34.13 E
Catamarca	53	Jh	28.30S	65.45W
Catamarca	56	Gc	27.00S	67.00W
Catanduanes	21	Oh	13.45N	124.15 E
Catanduva	56	Kb	21.08S	48.58W
Catanduvas	55	Fg	25.12S	53.08W
Catania	6	Hh	37.30N	15.06 E
Catania, Golfo di-	14	Jm	37.25N	15.10 E
Catania, Piana di-	14	Im	37.25N	14.50 E
Catanzaro	6	Hh	38.54N	16.35 E
Catarman	26	Hd	12.30N	124.38 E
Catastrophe, Cape-	57	Eh	35.00S	136.00 E
Catatumbo, Río-	49	Li	9.21N	71.45W
Catbalogan	26	Hd	11.46N	124.53 E
Catemaco, Lago-	48	Lh	18.25N	95.05W
Catete	36	Bd	9.07S	13.41 E
Cathair na Mart/Westport	9	Dh	53.48N	9.32W
Cathair Saidhbhín/ Cahersiveen	9	Cj	51.57N	10.13W
Cathcart	37	Df	32.18S	27.09 E
Catherine, Mount-	46	Ig	39.05N	112.04W
Catholic Island	51n	Bb	12.40N	61.24W
Catio	34	Bc	11.17N	15.15W
Cat Island	38	Lg	24.30N	75.30W
Čatkal	18	Hd	41.36N	70.05 E
Čatkalski Hrebet	19	Hg	41.30N	70.50 E
Cat Lake	42	If	51.40N	91.52W
Catoche, Cabo-	38	Kg	21.36N	87.07W
Cato Island	57	Gg	23.15S	155.35 E
Catolé do Rocha	54	Ke	6.21S	37.45W
Catoute	13	Fb	42.45N	6.20W
Catria	14	Gg	43.28N	12.42 E
Catriló	56	He	36.26S	63.24W
Catrimani, Rio-	54	Fc	0.28N	61.44W
Catskill Mountains	44	Jd	42.10N	74.30W
Cattenom	12	Ie	49.25N	6.15 E
Cattolica	14	Gg	43.58N	12.44 E
Catu	54	Kf	12.21S	38.23W
Catuane	37	Ee	26.48S	32.14 E
Catumbela	36	Be	12.27S	13.29 E
Catur	37	Fb	13.45S	35.37 E
Catwick, Iles-	25	Lg	10.00N	109.00 E
Catwright	39	Nd	53.50N	56.45W
Catyrkël, Ozero-	18	Jd	40.35N	75.20 E
Catyrtaš	18	Kd	40.52N	76.23 E
Cauca	54	Cc	2.30N	77.00W
Cauca, Río-	52	Ie	8.54N	74.28W
Caucasia	54	Cb	7.59N	75.13W
Caucasus (EN)=Kavkaz, Bolšoj-	5	Kg	42.30N	45.00 E
Caucete	56	Gd	31.38S	68.16W
Caudebec-en-Caux	12	Ce	49.32N	0.44 E
Caudete	13	Lf	38.42N	0.59W
Caudry	11	Jd	50.08N	3.25 E
Caulonia	14	Kl	38.23N	16.24 E
Caumont-l'Eventé	12	Be	49.05N	0.48W
Caungula	31	Ii	8.26S	18.37 E
Čaunskaja Guba	20	Lc	69.30N	170.00 E
Caupolican	54	Ef	13.30S	68.30W
Cauquenes	56	Fe	35.58S	72.21W
Caura, Río-	52	Je	7.38N	64.53W
Causapscal	44	Na	48.22N	67.14W
Caussade	11	Hj	44.10N	1.32 E
Čausy	16	Gc	53.50N	30.59 E
Cauterets	11	Fl	42.53N	0.07W
Cauto, Río-	49	Ic	20.33N	77.15W
Cauvery	21	Jh	11.09N	78.52 E
Caux, Pays de-	11	Ge	49.40N	0.40 E
Cávado	13	Dc	41.32N	8.48W
Cavaillon	11	Lk	43.50N	5.02 E
Cavalcante	55	Ia	13.48S	47.30W
Cavalese	14	Fd	46.17N	11.27 E
Cavalli Islands	62	Ea	35.00S	173.55 E
Cavallo, Isola-	11a	Bb	41.22N	9.16 E
Cavallo Pass	45	Hl	28.25N	96.26W
Cavally	30	Gh	4.22N	7.32W
Cavan/An Cabhán	9	Fg	54.00N	7.21W
Cavan/An Cabhán	9	Fh	53.55N	7.30W
Cavarzere	14	Ge	45.08N	12.05 E
Çavdarhisar	15	Mj	39.12N	29.37 E
Çavdir	15	Ml	37.09N	29.42 E
Caviana, Ilha-	54	Hc	0.10N	50.05W
Cavili	26	He	9.17N	120.50 E
Cavour, Canale-	14	Be	45.11N	7.54 E
Cavtat	14	Mh	42.35N	18.13 E
Caxambu	55	Je	21.59S	44.56W
Caxias	53	Lf	4.50S	43.21W
Caxias do Sul	53	Kh	29.10S	51.11W
Caxito	36	Bd	8.34S	13.40 E
Çay	24	Dc	38.35N	31.02 E
Cayambe	54	Cc	0.05N	78.08W
Cayambe, Volcán-	52	Ie	0.02N	77.59W
Cayastá	55	Bj	31.12S	60.10W
Cayce	44	Gi	33.59N	81.04W
Çaycuma	24	Eb	41.25N	32.05 E
Çayeli	24	Ib	41.05N	40.44 E
Cayenne	53	Ke	4.56N	52.20W
Cayeux-Sur-Mer	12	Dd	50.11N	1.29 E
Cayey	49	Nd	18.07N	66.10W
Çayırlı	24	Ic	39.48N	40.01 E
Çaykara	24	Ib	40.45N	40.19 E
Caylus	11	Hj	44.14N	1.47 E
Cayman Brac	47	Ie	19.43N	79.49W
Cayman Islands	39	Kh	19.30N	80.30W
Cayman Islands	38	Kh	19.30N	80.30W
Cayman Ridge (EN)	47	He	19.30N	80.30W
Cayman Trench (EN)	3	Bh	19.00N	80.00W
Cayo	49	Ce	17.10N	88.50W
Cayon	51c	Ab	17.21N	62.43W
Cayones, Cayos-	49	Fe	16.05N	83.12W
Cay Sal Bank	47	Hd	23.45N	80.00W
Cayuga Lake	44	Id	42.45N	76.45W
Cazalla de la Sierra	13	Gg	37.56N	5.45W
Caza Pava	55	Di	28.17S	56.07W
Cazaux, Étang de-	11	Ej	44.29N	1.10W
Cazombo	31	Jj	11.54S	22.53 E
Cazorla	13	Jg	37.55N	3.00W
Cazorla, Sierra de-	13	Jf	37.55N	2.55W
Cea	13	Gb	42.00N	5.36W
Ceahlău	15	Ib	47.03N	25.58 E
Ceanannas Mór/Kells	9	Gh	53.44N	6.53W
Ceanna Caillighe/Hags Head	9	Di	52.57N	9.28W
Ceann Acla/Achill Head	9	Ch	53.59N	10.13W
Ceann an Chairn/Carnsore Point	9	Gi	52.10N	6.22W
Ceann Chill Mhantáin/ Wicklow Head	9	Hi	52.58N	6.00W
Ceann Gólaim/Slyne Head	9	Ch	53.24N	10.13W
Ceann Iorrais/Erris Head	5	Fe	54.19N	10.00W
Ceann Léime/Loop Head	9	Di	52.34N	9.56W
Ceann Ros Eoghain/Rossan Point	9	Eg	54.42N	8.48W
Ceann Sléibhe/Slea Head	9	Ci	52.06N	10.27W
Ceann Toirc/Kanturk	9	Ei	52.10N	8.55W
Ceará	54	Kd	5.00S	39.30W
Ceará-Mirim	54	Ke	5.38S	35.26W
Ceatharlach/Carlow	9	Gi	52.50N	7.00W
Ceatharlach/Carlow	9	Gi	52.50N	6.55W
Cébaco, Isla-	49	Gj	7.32N	81.09W
Ceballos	48	Gd	26.32N	104.09W
Čebarkul	17	Ji	54.58N	60.25 E
Čeboksary	6	Kd	56.09N	47.15 E
Cebollati	55	Fk	33.16S	53.47W
Cebollati, Río-	55	Fk	33.09S	53.38W
Cebollera, Sierra-	13	Jc	42.00N	2.40W
Ceboruco, Volcán-	48	Gg	21.09N	104.30W
Cebreros	13	Hd	40.27N	4.28W
Cebrikovo	15	Nb	47.09N	30.02 E
Cebu	21	Oh	10.20N	123.45 E
Cebu	22	Oh	10.18N	123.54 E
Cece	10	Oj	46.46N	18.39 E
Čečen, Ostrov-	16	Og	44.00N	47.45 E
Čečeno respublika	19	Eg	43.15N	45.30 E
Cecen-Ula	27	Gb	48.45N	95.55 E
Cecerleg	22	Me	47.30N	101.27 E
Čečersk	16	Gc	52.56N	30.58 E
Čechy=Bohemia (EN)	5	Hf	50.00N	14.30 E
Čechy=Bohemia (EN)	10	Kf	50.00N	14.30 E
Cecina	14	Eg	43.18N	10.29 E
Cecina	14	Eg	43.10N	10.31 E
Čečuisk	20	Fe	58.07N	108.32 E
Cedar City	39	Hf	37.41N	113.04W
Cedar Creek	45	Fc	46.07N	101.18W
Cedar Creek Reservoir	45	Hj	32.20N	96.10W
Cedar Falls	43	Ic	42.32N	92.27W
Cedar Grove	51d	Bb	17.10N	61.49W
Cedar Lake	42	Hf	53.25N	100.00W
Cedar Rapids	39	Je	41.59N	91.40W
Cedar River [Nb.-U.S.]	45	Hf	41.22N	97.57W
Cedar River [U.S.]	43	Ic	41.17N	91.20W
Cedartown	44	Eh	34.01N	85.15W
Cedar-Tree Point	51d	Ba	17.42N	61.53W
Cedeira	13	Da	43.39N	8.03W
Cedral	48	If	23.48N	100.44W
Cedrino	14	Dj	40.23N	9.44 E
Cedro	54	Ke	6.36S	39.03W
Cedrón	13	Ie	39.48N	3.33W
Cedros, Isla- [Mex.]	47	Ac	28.12N	115.15W
Cedros, Isla [Mex.] =Cedros Island (EN)	38	Hg	28.10N	115.15W
Cedros Island (EN)=Cedros, Isla [Mex.]	38	Hg	28.10N	115.15W
Cedros Trench (EN)	47	Ac	27.45N	115.45W
Ceduna	59	Gf	32.07S	133.40 E
Cedynia	10	Kd	52.50N	14.14 E
Cefalù	14	Il	38.02N	14.01 E
Cega	13	Hc	41.33N	4.46W
Čegdomyn	22	Pd	51.07N	133.05 E
Čegem	16	Mh	43.36N	43.48 E
Cegléd	10	Pi	47.10N	19.48 E
Ceglie Messapico	14	Lj	40.39N	17.31 E
Cehegín	13	Kf	38.06N	1.48W
Cehotina	15	Bf	43.31N	18.45 E
Čehov	7	Ii	55.11N	37.29 E
Čehov	20	Jg	47.24N	142.05 E
Ceica	15	Fc	46.51N	22.11 E
Çekerek	24	Fb	40.34N	35.46 E
Çekerek	24	Fb	40.04N	35.31 E
Čekmaguš	17	Gi	55.10N	54.40 E
Celano	14	Hh	42.05N	13.33 E
Celaya	47	Dd	20.31N	100.37W
Čelbas	16	Kf	46.06N	38.59 E
Célé	11	Hj	44.28N	1.38 E
Celebes/Sulawesi	21	Oj	2.00S	121.10 E
Celebes Basin (EN)	26	Hf	4.00N	122.00 E
Celebes Sea (EN)= Sulawesi, Laut-	21	Oj	3.00N	122.00 E
Čeleken	19	Fh	39.27N	53.10 E
Čeleken, Poluostrov-	16	Rj	39.25N	53.35 E
Celendín	54	Ce	6.52S	78.09W
Celerain, Punta-	48	Pg	20.16N	86.59W
Celeste	55	Dj	31.18S	57.04W
Celestún	48	Ng	20.52N	90.24W
Celinograd	22	Jd	51.10N	71.30 E
Celinogradskaja Oblast	19	Gh	51.00N	70.00 E
Čeljabinsk	22	Id	55.10N	61.24 E
Čeljabinskaja Oblast	19	Ge	54.00N	61.00 E
Celje	14	Jd	46.14N	15.16 E
Celjuskin, Mys-	21	Mb	77.45N	104.20 E
Čelkar	19	Ff	47.50N	59.29 E
Celldömölk	10	Ni	47.15N	17.09 E
Celle	10	Gd	52.37N	10.05 E
Celles	12	Fd	50.43N	3.27 E
Celles, Houyet-	12	Hd	50.19N	5.01 E
Cellina	14	Ge	46.02N	12.47 E
Celone	14	Ji	41.36N	15.41 E
Celorico da Beira	13	Ed	40.38N	7.23W
Celtic Sea	5	Fe	51.00N	7.00W
Celtic Sea (EN)=An Mhuir Cheilteach	5	Fe	51.00N	7.00W
Cemaes Head	9	Ii	52.07N	4.44W
Čemal	20	Df	51.25N	86.05 E
Čemdalsk	20	Fe	59.45N	103.18 E
Cemernica	14	Lf	44.30N	17.15 E
Cemerno	15	Df	43.36N	20.26 E
Çemişkezek	24	Hc	39.04N	38.55 E
Cenajo, Embalse de-	13	Kf	38.20N	1.55W
Cenderawasih, Teluk-	26	Kg	2.25S	135.10 E
Cengel	27	Eb	48.56N	89.10 E
Çengel Geçidi	24	Kc	39.45N	44.02 E
Ceno	14	Ef	44.41N	10.05 E
Centenary	37	Ec	16.44S	31.07 E
Centennial	46	Lf	41.51N	106.07W
Centennial Lake	44	Ic	45.15N	77.00W
Centennial Mountains	46	Jd	44.35N	111.55W
Center	45	Ik	31.48N	94.11W
Center Hill Lake	44	Eg	36.00N	85.45W
Centerville	45	Jf	40.43N	92.52W
Centinela, Farallón-	50	Cg	10.49N	66.05W
Centinela, Picacho del-	47	Dc	29.07N	102.27W
Cento	14	Ff	44.43N	11.17 E
Centrafrique=Central African Republic (EN)	31	Jh	7.00N	21.00 E
Central [Bots.]	37	Dd	21.30S	26.00 E
Central [Ghana]	34	Ed	5.30N	1.00W
Central [Kenya]	36	Gc	0.45S	37.00 E
Central [Mwi.]	36	Fe	13.30S	34.00 E
Central [Par.]	55	Dg	25.30S	57.30W
Central [Scot.-U.K.]	9	Ie	56.15N	4.10W
Central [Ug.]	36	Fb	0.10N	32.05 E
Central [Zam.]	36	Ee	15.00S	29.00 E
Central, Chaco-	52	Kh	25.00S	59.45W
Central, Cordillera- [Dom.Rep.]	47	Je	18.45N	70.30W
Central, Cordillera- [P.R.]	49	Nd	18.10N	66.35W
Central, Massif-	5	Gf	45.00N	3.10 E
Central, Meseta-	38	Ig	23.00N	103.00W
Central African Republic (EN)=Centrafrique	31	Jh	7.00N	21.00 E
Central Auckland	62	Fb	36.45S	174.40 E
Central Brāhui Range	25	Dc	29.20N	66.55 E
Central City	45	Hf	41.07N	98.00W
Centralia [Il.-U.S.]	45	Lg	38.31N	89.08W
Centralia [Wa.-U.S.]	43	Cb	46.43N	122.58W
Central Lowland	38	Ke	40.20N	90.00W
Central Makrān Range	21	Ig	26.40N	64.30 E
Centralno Tungusskoje Plato	20	Fd	61.15N	102.00 E
Centralny-Kospašski	17	Hg	59.03N	57.50 E
Central Pacific Basin (EN)	3	Ki	5.00N	175.00W
Central Plateau	64e	Bb	0.32S	166.56 E
Central Point	46	De	42.23N	122.57W
Central Range	57	Fe	5.00S	142.30 E
Central Russian Uplands (EN)=Srednerusskaja Vozvyšennost	5	Je	52.00N	38.00 E
Central Siberian Uplands (EN)=Srednesibirskoje Ploskogorje	21	Mc	65.00N	105.00 E
Central Urals (EN)=Sredni Ural	5	Ld	58.00N	59.00 E
Centre [Togo]	34	Fd	9.15N	1.00 E
Centre [U.V.]	34	Ec	12.00N	1.00W
Centre, Canal du-	11	Jh	46.28N	3.59 E
Centre-Est	34	Ec	11.30N	0.20W
Centre-Nord	34	Ec	13.20N	0.55W
Centre-Ouest	34	Ec	12.00N	2.20W
Centre-Sud	34	He	3.30N	11.50 E
Centro, Cayo-	48	Ph	18.35N	87.20W
Centuripe	14	Im	37.37N	14.44 E
Čepca	19	Fd	58.35N	50.05 E
Čepelare	15	Hh	41.44N	24.41 E
Cephalonia (EN)= Kefallinia	5	Ih	38.15N	20.35 E
Čepin	14	Me	45.32N	18.34 E
Cepleniţa	15	Jb	47.23N	26.58 E
Cepu	26	Fh	7.09S	111.35 E
Cer	15	Ce	44.37N	19.28 E
Ceram Sea (EN)=Seram, Laut-	57	De	2.30S	128.00 E
Cerbatana, Serranía de la-	54	Eb	6.50N	66.15W
Cerbicales, Iles-	11a	Bb	41.33N	9.22 E
Cercal	13	Dg	37.47N	8.42W
Čerchov	10	Rg	49.10N	21.05 E
Čerdakly	7	Li	54.23N	48.51 E
Čerdyn	17	Hf	60.25N	56.29 E
Cère	11	Hj	44.55N	1.49 E
Čereha	7	Gh	57.47N	28.22 E
Čeremhovo	22	Md	53.09N	103.05 E
Čerepanovo	20	Df	54.13N	83.32 E
Čerepovec	6	Jd	59.08N	37.54 E
Ceres [Arg.]	56	Hc	29.53S	61.57W
Ceres [Braz.]	54	Ig	15.17S	49.35W
Ceres [S.Afr.]	37	Bf	33.21S	19.18 E
Céret	11	Il	42.29N	2.45 E
Cereté	54	Cb	8.53N	75.47W
Cerf Island	30	Mi	9.31S	51.01 E
Cerfontaine	12	Gd	50.10N	4.25 E
Cergy	12	Ee	49.02N	2.04 E
Cerignola	14	Ji	41.16N	15.54 E
Čerikov	16	Gc	53.35N	31.25 E
Cérilly	11	Ih	46.37N	2.50 E
Čerkasskaja Oblast	19	Df	49.15N	31.15 E
Čerkassy	19	Df	49.26N	32.04 E
Çerkeş	24	Eb	40.50N	32.54 E
Čerkessk	19	Eg	44.14N	42.04 E
Čerkesskaja respublika	19	Eg	43.45N	41.45 E
Çerkezköy	15	Kh	41.17N	28.00 E
Čerlak	19	He	54.09N	74.58 E
Čerlakski	19	He	53.47N	74.31 E
Čermasàn	17	Gi	55.10N	55.20 E
Cermei	15	Ec	46.33N	21.51 E
Çermenika	15	Dh	41.03N	20.20 E
Čermoz	17	Hg	58.47N	56.10 E
Cerna [Rom.]	15	Ge	44.37N	23.57 E
Cerna [Rom.]	15	Fd	44.42N	22.25 E
Cerna [Rom.]	15	Fe	45.53N	22.58 E
Černaja	17	Hb	68.35N	56.31 E
Černaja	17	Hb	68.35N	56.30 E
Černaja	15	Mb	47.39N	29.11 E
Černa Skala, Prohod-	15	Fg	42.02N	22.47 E
Černatica	15	Hh	41.53N	24.33 E
Černavčicy	10	Td	52.11N	23.47 E
Cernavoda	15	Le	44.22N	28.01 E
Cernay	11	Ng	47.49N	7.10 E
Cernay-en-Dormois	12	Ge	49.13N	4.46 E
Černevo	8	Mf	58.35N	28.23 E
Černigov	6	Je	51.30N	31.18 E
Černigovskaja Oblast	19	De	51.20N	32.00 E
Černi Lom	15	If	43.33N	25.57 E
Černi vrăh	15	Gg	42.35N	23.15 E
Černjahovsk	19	Ce	54.38N	21.48 E
Černjanka	16	Jd	50.55N	37.49 E
Černobyl	19	De	51.17N	30.13 E
Černogorsk	20	Ef	53.45N	91.18 E
Černoje More=Black Sea (EN)	5	Jg	43.00N	35.00 E
Černo More=Black Sea (EN)	5	Jg	43.00N	35.00 E
Černomorskoje	16	Hg	45.31N	32.42 E
Černovcy	6	If	48.18N	25.56 E
Černovickaja Oblast	19	Cf	48.20N	26.10 E
Černuška	19	Fd	56.31N	56.03 E
Černy Jar	16	Oe	48.03N	46.05 E
Černyje Zemli	16	Nf	45.55N	46.00 E
Černyšëva, Grjada-	17	Ic	66.20N	59.45 E
Černyševa, Zaliv-	18	Bb	45.50N	59.10 E
Černyševsk	20	Gf	52.35N	117.02 E
Černyševski	20	Gd	62.58N	112.15 E
Černyškovski	16	Me	48.27N	42.14 E
Cérou	11	Hj	44.08N	1.52 E
Cerralvo	48	Jd	26.06N	99.37W
Cerralvo, Isla-	47	Cd	24.15N	109.55W
Cerredo, Torre de-	13	Ha	43.13N	4.50W
Cerriku	15	Ch	41.02N	19.57 E
Cerrito [Col.]	54	Db	6.51N	72.42W
Cerrito [Par.]	55	Dh	27.19S	57.40W
Cerritos	47	Dd	22.26N	100.17W
Cerro Azul	48	Kg	21.12N	97.44W
Cêrro Azul	56	Kb	24.50S	49.15W
Cerro Chato	55	Ek	33.06S	55.08W
Cerro Colorado	55	Ek	33.52S	55.33W
Cerro de las Mesas	48	Kh	18.47N	96.05W
Cerro de Pasco	53	Ig	10.41S	76.16W
Cêrro Grande	55	Gj	30.36S	51.45W
Cerro Largo	56	Jc	28.09S	54.45W
Cerro Largo	55	Ek	32.20S	54.20W
Cerron, Cerro-	49	Lh	10.19N	70.39W
Cerro San Valentín	52	Ij	46.36S	73.20W
Cerros Colorados, Embalse-	56	Ge	38.35S	68.40W
Cerro Vera	55	Dk	33.11S	57.28W
Cerrudo Cué	55	Dh	27.34S	57.57W
Čerski	22	Sc	68.45N	161.45 E
Čerskogo, hrebet-	20	Gf	52.00N	114.00 E
Čerskogo, hrebet- = Cherski Mountains	21	Qc	65.00N	145.00 E

Index Symbols

- 1 Independent Nation
- 2 State, Region
- 3 District, County
- 4 Municipality
- 5 Colony, Dependency
- Continent
- Physical Region
- Historical or Cultural Region
- Mount, Mountain
- Volcano
- Hill
- Mountains, Mountain Range
- Hills, Escarpment
- Plateau, Upland
- Pass, Gap
- Plain, Lowland
- Delta
- Salt Flat
- Valley, Canyon
- Crater, Cave
- Karst Features
- Depression
- Polder
- Desert, Dunes
- Forest, Woods
- Heath, Steppe
- Oasis
- Cape, Point
- Coast, Beach
- Cliff
- Peninsula
- Isthmus
- Sandbank
- Island
- Atoll
- Rock, Reef
- Islands, Archipelago
- Rocks, Reefs
- Coral Reef
- Well, Spring
- Geyser
- River, Stream
- Waterfall Rapids
- River Mouth, Estuary
- Lake
- Salt Lake
- Intermittent Lake
- Reservoir
- Swamp, Pond
- Canal
- Glacier
- Ice Shelf, Pack Ice
- Ocean
- Sea
- Gulf, Bay
- Strait, Fjord
- Lagoon
- Bank
- Seamount
- Tablemount
- Ridge
- Shelf
- Basin
- Escarpment, Sea Scarp
- Fracture
- Trench, Abyss
- National Park, Reserve
- Point of Interest
- Recreation Site
- Cave, Cavern
- Historic Site
- Ruins
- Wall, Walls
- Church, Abbey
- Temple
- Scientific Station
- Airport
- Port
- Lighthouse
- Mine
- Tunnel
- Dam, Bridge

Certaldo	14	Fg	43.33N	11.02 E
Čertkovo	16	Le	49.20N	40.12 E
Cervaro	14	Ji	41.30N	15.52 E
Cervati	14	Jj	40.17N	15.29 E
Červeh	15	Jf	43.37N	26.02 E
Červen	16	Fc	53.43N	28.29 E
Červen brjag	15	Hf	43.16N	24.06 E
Cervera	13	Nc	41.40N	1.17 E
Cervera del Río Alhama	13	Kb	42.01N	1.57W
Cervera de Pisuerga	13	Hb	42.52N	4.30W
Cerveteri	14	Gh	42.00N	12.06 E
Cervia	14	Gf	44.15N	12.22 E
Cervin/Cervino	14	Be	45.58N	7.39 E
Cervino/Cervin	14	Be	45.58N	7.39 E
Cervione	11a	Ba	42.20N	9.29 E
Červonoarmejsk	10	Vf	50.03N	25.18 E
Červonoarmejskoje	15	Ld	45.50N	28.38 E
Červonograd	19	Ce	50.24N	24.12 E
Cesano	14	Hg	43.45N	13.10 E
Cesar [2]	54	Db	9.50N	73.30W
César, Río-	49	Ki	9.00N	73.58W
Cesena	14	Gf	44.08N	12.15 E
Cesenatico	14	Gf	44.12N	12.24 E
Cēsis/Cesis	19	Cd	57.18N	25.18 E
Cesis/Cēsis	19	Cd	57.18N	25.18 E
Česká Lípa	10	Kf	50.42N	14.32 E
Česká Republika = Czech Republic (EN)	6	Hf	50.00N	13.00 E
Česká Třebová	10	Mg	49.54N	16.27 E
České Budějovice	10	Kh	48.58N	14.29 E
České středohoří	10	Jf	50.35N	14.00 E
České země [2]	10	Kg	49.45N	15.00 E
Českomoravská Vrchovina = Moravian Upland (EN)	5	Hf	49.20N	15.30 E
Český Krumlov	10	Kh	48.49N	14.19 E
Český Les = Bohemian Forest (EN)	10	Ig	49.50N	12.30 E
Cesma	14	Kf	45.35N	16.29 E
Česma	17	Jj	53.50N	60.40 E
Çeşme	24	Bc	38.18N	26.19 E
Çeşme Yarimadasi	15	Jk	38.30N	26.30 E
Češskaja Guba = Chesha Bay (EN)	5	Kb	67.20N	46.30 E
Cessnock	59	Kf	32.50S	151.21 E
Cestos	30	Gh	5.27N	9.35W
Cesvaine/Cesvajne	8	Lh	56.55N	26.20 E
Cesvajne/Cesvaine	8	Lh	56.55N	26.20 E
Cetate	15	Ge	44.06N	23.03 E
Cetina	14	Kg	43.27N	16.42 E
Cetinje	15	Bg	42.24N	18.55 E
Çetinkaya	24	Gc	39.15N	37.38 E
Cetraro	14	Jk	39.31N	15.56 E
Cetynia	10	Sd	52.33N	22.26 E
Ceuta [5]	31	Ge	35.53N	5.19W
Ceva-i-Ra (Conway Reef)	57	Ig	21.45S	174.35 E
Cevedale/Zufallspitze	14	Ed	46.27N	10.37 E
Cévennes	5	Gg	44.40N	4.00 E
Ceyhan	23	Eb	36.45N	35.42 E
Ceyhan	23	Eb	37.04N	35.47 E
Ceylanpınar	24	Id	36.51N	40.02 E
Ceylon → Srī Lanka [1]	22	Ki	7.40N	80.50 E
Cézallier	11	Ii	45.20N	3.00 E
Cèze	11	Kj	44.06N	4.42 E
Chaalis, Abbaye de-	12	Ee	49.10N	2.40 E
Cha-am	25	Jf	12.48N	99.58 E
Chabanais	11	Gi	45.52N	0.43 E
Chabjuwardoo Bay	59	Cd	22.55S	113.50 E
Chablais	11	Mh	46.20N	6.30 E
Chāboksar	24	Nd	36.58N	50.34 E
Chabówka	10	Pg	49.34N	19.58 E
Chacabuco	56	Hd	34.38S	60.29W
Chachan, Nevado-	54	Dg	16.12S	71.33W
Chachapoyas	54	Ce	6.13S	77.51W
Chachoengsao	25	Kf	13.41N	101.03 E
Chaco [2]	56	Hc	26.00S	60.30W
Chaco [3]	55	Bd	20.00S	60.30W
Chaco, Gran-	52	Jh	23.00S	60.00W
Chaco Mesa	45	Ci	35.50N	107.35W
Chaco River	45	Bh	36.46N	108.39W
Chad (EN) = Tchad [1]	31	Ig	15.00N	19.00 E
Chad, Lake- (EN) = Tchad, Lac-	30	Ig	13.20N	14.00 E
Chādegān	24	Nf	32.46N	50.38 E
Chadileuvú, Río-	56	Ee	38.49S	64.57W
Chadiza	36	Fe	14.04S	32.26 E
Chadron	43	Gc	42.50N	103.02W
Chaeryŏng	28	He	38.24N	125.37 E
Chafarinas, Islas-	13	Ji	35.11N	2.26W
Chāgai Hills	21	Ig	29.30N	64.15 E
Chagang-Do [2]	28	Ie	40.50N	126.30 E
Chaghcharān	22	If	34.31N	65.15 E
Chagny	11	Kh	46.55N	4.45 E
Chagos Archipelago	21	Jj	6.00S	72.00 E
Chagos-Laccadive Plateau (EN)	3	Gi	3.00N	73.00 E
Chagu, Serra do-	55	Fg	25.10S	52.40W
Chaguaramas	50	Ch	9.20N	66.16W
Chahār Borjak	23	Jc	30.17N	62.03 E
Chahār Mahāl-e Bakhtīārī [3]	23	Hc	32.00N	50.00 E
Chahbounia	13	Oi	35.33N	2.36 E
Ch'aho	28	Jd	40.12N	128.38 E
Chai Badan	25	Ke	15.05N	101.04 E
Chaibāsa	25	Hd	22.34N	85.49 E
Chaigoubu → Huai'an	28	Cd	40.40N	114.25 E
Chai He	28	Gc	42.20N	123.51 E
Chaillu, Massif du-	30	Ii	2.32S	11.10 E
Chainat	25	Ke	15.10N	100.10 E
Chaitén	56	Ff	42.55S	72.43W
Chaiyaphum	25	Ke	16.09N	102.02 E
Chajul	49	Bf	15.30N	91.02W
Chakari	37	Dc	18.09S	29.52 E
Chak Chak	35	Dd	8.40N	26.54 E
Chake Chake	31	Ki	5.15S	39.46 E
Chakhānsūr	23	Jc	31.10N	62.04 E
Chala	54	Dg	15.52S	74.16W
Chalais	11	Gi	45.17N	0.02 E
Chalaltenango	49	Cf	14.03N	88.56W
Chalan Kanoa	64b	Ba	15.08N	145.43 E
Chālūs	22	Gf	37.16N	49.36 E
Chalbi Desert	30	Kh	3.00N	37.20 E
Chalchuapa	49	Cg	13.59N	89.41W
Chalcidice (EN) = Khalkidhiki	5	Ig	40.25N	23.25 E
Chālesbān	24	Ne	35.18N	50.03 E
Chaleur Bay	42	Kg	47.50N	65.30W
Chalhuanca	54	Df	14.17S	73.15W
Chaling	27	Jf	26.47N	113.32 E
Chalky Inlet	62	Bg	46.05S	166.30 E
Challans	11	Eh	46.51N	1.53W
Challapata	54	Eg	18.54S	66.47W
Challis	46	Hd	44.30N	114.14W
Chalmette	45	Ll	29.56N	89.58W
Châlons-sur-Marne	11	Kf	48.57N	4.22 E
Châlon-sur-Saône	11	Kh	46.47N	4.51 E
Chaltubo	16	Mh	42.19N	42.34 E
Chālūs	23	Hb	36.38N	51.26 E
Châlus	11	Gi	45.39N	0.59 E
Cham	10	Ig	49.13N	12.40 E
Chama	36	Fe	11.12S	33.10 E
Chama, Río-	45	Ch	36.03N	106.05W
Chama, Río-	49	Li	9.03N	71.37W
Chaman	25	Db	30.55N	66.27 E
Chaman Bīd	24	Qd	37.25N	56.38 E
Chamba [India]	25	Fb	32.34N	76.08 E
Chamba [Tan.]	36	Ge	11.35S	36.58 E
Chambal	21	Jg	26.29N	79.15 E
Chambaran, Plateau de-	11	Li	45.10N	5.20 E
Chambas	49	Hb	22.12N	78.55W
Chamberlain	45	Ge	43.49N	99.20W
Chamberlain Lake	44	Mb	46.17N	69.20W
Chamberlain River	59	Fc	15.35S	127.51 E
Chambersburg	44	If	39.57N	77.40W
Chambéry	11	Li	45.34N	5.56 E
Chambeshi	30	Jj	11.53S	29.48 E
Chambley-Bussières	12	He	49.03N	5.54 E
Chambly	12	Ee	49.10N	2.15 E
Chambois	12	Cf	48.48N	0.07 E
Chambon, Lac de-	11	Ih	45.35N	2.55 E
Chambord	11	Hg	47.37N	1.31 E
Chamchamal	24	Ke	35.32N	44.50 E
Chame, Punta-	49	Hi	8.39N	79.42W
Chamela	48	Gh	19.32N	105.05W
Chamela, Bahía-	48	Gh	19.30N	105.10W
Chamelecón, Río-	49	Df	15.51N	87.49W
Chamical	56	Gd	30.21S	66.19W
Chamiss Bay	46	Ba	50.07N	127.22W
Chamoli	25	Fb	30.24N	79.21 E
Chamonix-Mont-Blanc	11	Mi	45.55N	6.52 E
Chamouchouane, Rivière-	44	Ka	48.40N	72.20W
Champagne	5	Gf	49.00N	4.30 E
Champagne	11	Kf	49.00N	4.30 E
Champagne Berrichonne	11	Hh	47.00N	2.00 E
Champagne Humide	11	Kf	48.20N	4.30 E
Champagne Pouilleuse	11	Kf	48.40N	4.20 E
Champagnole	11	Lh	46.45N	5.55 E
Champaign	43	Jc	40.07N	88.14W
Champaquí, Cerro-	52	Ji	31.59S	64.56W
Champasak	25	Lf	14.53N	105.52 E
Champaubert	12	Ff	48.53N	3.47 E
Champdoré, Lac-	42	Ke	55.55N	65.45W
Champeigne	11	Gg	47.15N	0.50 E
Champerico	49	Bf	14.18N	91.55W
Champlain, Lake-	43	Mc	44.45N	73.15W
Champlitte-et-le-Prélot	11	Lg	47.37N	5.31 E
Champotón	47	Fe	19.21N	90.43W
Champsaur	11	Mj	44.45N	6.10 E
Chāmrājnagar	25	Ff	11.55N	76.57 E
Chañaral	56	Fc	26.21S	70.37W
Chança	13	Eg	37.33N	7.31W
Chan Chan	54	Ce	8.07S	79.02W
Chanco	56	Fe	35.44S	72.32W
Chandalar	40	Jc	66.36N	145.48W
Chandalar	40	Jc	67.30N	148.30W
Chandausi	25	Fc	28.27N	78.46 E
Chandeleur Islands	43	Jf	29.48N	88.51W
Chandeleur Sound	45	Ll	29.55N	89.10W
Chandīgarh	22	Jf	30.44N	76.55 E
Chandler	42	Lg	48.21N	64.41W
Chandless, Rio	54	Ee	9.08S	69.51W
Chāndpur	25	Id	23.13N	90.39 E
Chandragupta	25	Fe	16.11N	78.52 E
Chandrapur	22	Jh	19.57N	79.18 E
Chang, Ko-	25	Kf	12.00N	102.23 E
Changajn Nuruu → Hangaj, Hrebet- = Khangai Mountains (EN)	21	Le	47.30N	100.00 E
Chang'an → Rong'an	27	If	25.16N	109.23 E
Changane	30	Kk	24.43S	33.32 E
Changbai	28	Jd	41.25N	128.11 E
Changbai Shan	21	Oe	42.00N	128.00 E
Changchun	22	Oe	43.51N	125.20 E
Changdao(Sihou)	28	Ff	37.56N	120.42 E
Changde	22	Ng	29.04N	111.42 E
Ch'angdo	28	Ie	38.30N	127.45 E
Changfeng (Shuijiahu)	28	Dh	32.29N	117.10 E
Changge	28	Bg	34.12N	113.45 E
Changhang	28	If	36.01N	126.42 E
Chang He	28	Ei	31.21N	118.21 E
Changhowŏn	28	If	37.07N	127.38 E
Changhua	27	Lg	24.05N	120.32 E
Changhŭng	28	Ig	34.40N	126.54 E
Changji	27	Ec	44.01N	87.16 E
Chang Jiang	28	Dj	28.59N	116.42 E
Changjiang (Shiliu)	27	Ih	19.20N	109.03 E
Chang Jiang (Yangtze Kiang)	21	Of	31.48N	121.10 E
Changjiang Kou	27	Le	31.24N	121.59 E
Changjin-gang	28	Id	40.30N	127.12 E
Changjin-ho	28	Id	40.30N	127.12 E
Changjin-ŭp	27	Mc	40.23N	127.15 E
Changli	28	Ee	39.43N	119.10 E
Changling	27	Lc	44.15N	123.58 E
Changlung	25	Fb	34.56N	77.29 E
Changping	28	Dd	40.14N	116.13 E
Changsha	22	Ng	28.12N	113.02 E
Changshan	28	Ej	28.55N	118.31 E
Changshan Qundao	28	Ge	39.10N	122.34 E
Changshu	28	Fi	31.38N	120.44 E
Changsŏng	28	Ig	35.19N	126.48 E
Changting	28	Jb	44.27N	128.50 E
Changtu	28	Hc	42.47N	124.08 E
Changuillo	54	Cf	14.40S	75.12W
Changuinola	49	Fi	9.26N	82.31W
Changwu	27	Id	35.17N	107.52 E
Changxing	28	Ei	31.01N	119.55 E
Changxing Dao	28	Fe	39.35N	121.42 E
Changyi	28	Ef	36.52N	119.25 E
Changyŏn	27	Md	38.15N	125.05 E
Changyuan	28	Cg	35.12N	114.40 E
Changzhi	27	Jd	36.07N	113.10 E
Changzhou	28	Ei	31.46N	119.56 E
Channel Islands [5]	9	Kl	49.20N	2.20W
Channel Islands [Chan.Is.]	5	Ff	49.20N	2.20W
Channel Islands [U.S.]	38	Hf	34.00N	120.00W
Channel Port-aux-Basques	39	Ne	47.35N	59.11W
Channel Rock	49	Ib	23.00N	77.55W
Channing	45	Ei	35.41N	102.20W
Chantada	13	Eb	42.37N	7.46W
Chantengo, Laguna-	48	Ji	16.35N	98.10W
Chanthaburi	25	Kf	12.35N	102.06 E
Chantilly	11	Ie	49.12N	2.28 E
Chantonnay	11	Eh	46.41N	1.03W
Chantrey Inlet	38	Jc	67.48N	96.20W
Chanute	45	Ih	37.41N	95.27W
Chanza	13	Eg	37.33N	7.31W
Chao'an (Chaozhou)	27	Kg	23.41N	116.37 E
Chaobai Xinhe	28	De	39.07N	117.41 E
Chao He	28	Dd	40.36N	117.08 E
Chao Hu	28	Di	31.31N	117.33 E
Chao Phraya	21	Mh	13.32N	100.36 E
Chaor He	27	Lb	46.49N	123.45 E
Chaoxian	27	Ke	31.37N	117.49 E
Chaoyang [China]	22	Oe	41.35N	120.26 E
Chaoyang [China]	27	Kg	23.17N	116.37 E
Chaoyang → Huinan	28	Ic	42.41N	126.03 E
Chaoyang → Jiayin	27	Nb	48.52N	130.21 E
Chaoyangchuan	28	Jc	42.53N	129.23 E
Chaoyangcun	27	La	50.01N	124.22 E
Chaozhong	27	La	50.53N	121.23 E
Chaozhou → Chao'an	27	Kg	23.41N	116.37 E
Chapada dos Guimarães	54	Gg	15.25S	55.45W
Chapadinha	54	Jd	3.44S	43.21W
Chapais	44	Ja	49.47N	74.56W
Chapala	48	Hg	20.18N	103.12W
Chapala, Lago de-	38	Ig	20.15N	103.00W
Chaparral	54	Cc	3.43N	75.28W
Chapecó	56	Jc	27.06S	52.36W
Chapecó, Rio-	55	Fh	27.06S	53.01W
Chapecó, Serra do-	55	Gh	26.44S	51.44W
Chapel Hill	44	Hh	35.55N	79.04W
Chapicuy	55	Dj	31.40S	57.55W
Chapleau	42	Jg	47.50N	83.24W
Chaplin	46	La	50.28N	106.40W
Chaplin Lake	46	La	50.18N	106.35W
Chapman, Cape -	42	Ic	69.15N	89.27W
Chappell	45	Ef	41.06N	102.28W
Chāpra	25	Gc	25.46N	84.45 E
Chapultepec	48	Hf	23.27N	103.04W
Chaqui	54	Eg	19.36S	65.32W
Char	32	Ee	21.31N	12.51W
Charadai	55	Ch	27.38S	59.54W
Charagua	54	Fg	19.48S	63.13W
Charām	24	Ng	30.45N	50.44 E
Charaña	54	Eg	17.36S	69.28W
Charcas	48	If	23.08N	101.07W
Charco de la Aguja	48	Gc	28.25N	104.0 W
Charcot Island	66	Qe	69.45S	75.1 W
Chard [Alta.-Can.]	42	Ge	55.48N	111.1 W
Chard [Eng.-U.K.]	9	Kk	50.53N	2.5 W
Chardāvol	24	Lf	33.45N	46.38 E
Chardonnières	49	Jd	18.16N	74.10W
Charente [3]	11	Gi	45.40N	0.05 E
Charente	11	Ei	45.57N	1.05W
Charente-Maritime [3]	11	Fi	45.30N	0.45W
Charentonne	12	Ce	49.07N	0.44 E
Chari	30	Ig	12.58N	14.31 E
Chari-Baguirmi [3]	35	Bc	12.00N	17.00 E
Chārīkār	23	Kb	35.01N	69.11 E
Charing	12	Cc	51.12N	0.48 E
Chariton	45	Jf	41.00N	93.19W
Chariton River	45	Jg	39.19N	92.57W
Charity	54	Gb	7.24N	58.36W
Charleroi	11	Kd	50.25N	4.26 E
Charleroi-Jumet	11	Kd	50.27N	4.26 E
Charleroi-Marcinelle	12	Gd	50.25N	4.28 E
Charles	42	Kd	62.38N	74.15W
Charles, Cape- [Can.]	38	Nd	52.13N	55.40W
Charles, Cape- [Va.-U.S.]	43	Ld	37.08N	75.53W
Charles, Peak-	59	Ef	32.52S	121.11 E
Charlesbourg	44	Lb	46.52N	71.16W
Charles City	43	Ic	43.04N	92.40W
Charles de Gaulle, Aéroport- = Charles de Gaulle Airport (EN)	12	Ee	49.02N	2.35 E
Charles de Gaulle Airport (EN) = Charles de Gaulle, Aéroport-	12	Ee	49.02N	2.35 E
Charleston [Il.-U.S.]	45	Lg	39.30N	88.10W
Charleston [Mo.-U.S.]	45	Lh	36.55N	89.21W
Charleston [Ms.-U.S.]	45	Ki	34.01N	90.04W
Charleston [N.Z.]	62	Dd	41.54S	171.27 E
Charleston [S.C.-U.S.]	39	Lf	32.48N	79.57W
Charleston [W.V.-U.S.]	39	Kf	38.21N	81.38W
Charleston Peak	43	Dd	36.16N	115.42W
Charles Town	44	If	39.18N	77.52W
Charlestown	50	Ed	17.12N	62.35W
Charleval	12	De	49.22N	1.23 E
Charleville	58	Fg	26.24S	146.15 E
Charleville-Mézières	11	Ke	49.46N	4.43 E
Charleville Mézières-Mohon	12	Ge	49.46N	4.43 E
Charlevoix	44	Ec	45.19N	85.16W
Charlieu	11	Kh	46.09N	4.11 E
Charlotte [Mi.-U.S.]	44	Ed	42.36N	84.50W
Charlotte [N.C.-U.S.]	39	Kf	35.14N	80.50W
Charlotte Amalie	47	Le	18.21N	64.56W
Charlotte Bank (EN)	57	If	11.47S	173.13 E
Charlotte Harbor	44	Fl	26.45N	82.12W
Charlottenberg	8	Ee	59.53N	12.17 E
Charlottesville	43	Ld	38.02N	78.29W
Charlottetown	39	Me	46.14N	63.08W
Charlton	59	Ig	36.16S	143.21 E
Charlton	42	Jf	52.00N	79.26W
Charly	12	Ff	48.58N	3.17 E
Charmes	11	Mf	48.22N	6.17 E
Charnley River	59	Ec	16.20S	124.53 E
Charny-sur-Meuse	12	He	49.12N	5.22 E
Charollais	11	Kh	46.26N	4.16 E
Charouïne	32	Gd	29.01N	0.16W
Charroux	11	Gh	46.09N	0.24 E
Chārsadda	25	Eb	34.09N	71.44 E
Charters Towers	58	Fg	20.05S	146.16 E
Chartres	11	Hf	48.27N	1.30 E
Charzykowskie, Jezioro-	10	Nc	53.47N	17.30 E
Chascomus	56	Ie	35.34S	58.01W
Chase	46	Fa	50.49N	119.41W
Chasŏng	28	Id	41.25N	126.35 E
Chassengue	36	Ce	10.26S	18.32 E
Chassezac	11	Kj	44.26N	4.19 E
Chassiron, Pointe de-	11	Eh	46.03N	1.24W
Chat	24	Pd	37.59N	55.16 E
Châtaigneraie	11	Ij	44.45N	2.20 E
Chātāl	24	Pd	37.40N	55.45 E
Château-Arnoux	11	Lj	44.06N	6.00 E
Chateaubelair	51n	Ba	13.17N	61.15W
Châteaubriant	11	Eg	47.43N	1.23W
Château-Chinon	11	Jg	47.04N	3.56 E
Château-du-Loir	11	Gg	47.42N	0.25 E
Châteaudun	11	Hf	48.05N	1.20 E
Château-Gontier	11	Fg	47.50N	0.42W
Châteaulin	11	Bf	48.12N	4.05W
Châteaulin, Bassin de-	11	Cf	48.18N	3.50W
Châteaumeillant	11	Ih	46.34N	2.12 E
Châteauneuf-de-Randon	11	Jj	44.39N	3.04 E
Châteauneuf-sur-Cher	11	Ih	46.5 N	2.19 E
Châteauneuf-sur-Loire	11	Ig	47.52N	2.14 E
Château-Porcien	12	Ge	49.32N	4.15 E
Châteaurenard	11	Kk	43.53N	4.51 E
Château-Renault	11	Gg	47.35N	0.54 E
Châteauroux	11	Hh	46.49N	1.42 E
Château-Salins	11	Mf	48.49N	6.30 E
Château-Thierry	11	Je	49.03N	3.24 E
Châteaux, Pointe des-	51e	Bb	16.15N	61.11W
Châtelaillon-Plage	11	Eh	46.04N	1.05W
Châtelet	12	Gd	50.24N	4.31 E
Châtelguyon	11	Ji	45.55N	3.04 E
Châtellerault	11	Gh	46.48N	0.32 E
Chatelodo	55	De	21.19S	57.28W
Chatham [Eng.-U.K.]	9	Nj	51.23N	0.32 E
Chatham [N.B.-Can.]	42	Kg	47.02N	65.26W
Chatham [Ont.-Can.]	42	Jh	42.24N	82.11W
Chatham [Va.-U.S.]	44	Hg	36.49N	79.26W
Chatham Island	57	Ji	44.00S	176.30W
Chatham Islands	57	Ji	44.00S	176.30W
Chatham Rise (EN)	57	Ii	43.30S	180.00
Chatham Strait	40	Me	57.30N	134.45W
Châtillon-en-Bazois	11	Jg	47.03N	3.40 E
Châtillon-sur-Indre	11	Hh	46.59N	1.10 E
Châtillon-sur-Marne	12	Fe	49.06N	3.45 E
Châtillon-sur-Seine	11	Kg	47.51N	4.33 E
Chatom	44	Cj	31.28N	88.16W
Chatsworth	37	Ec	19.38S	30.50 E
Chattahoochee	44	Ej	30.42N	84.51W
Chattahoochee	38	Kf	30.52N	84.57W
Chattanooga	39	Kf	35.03N	85.19W
Chatteris	12	Cb	52.27N	0.03 E
Chaucas	55	Cc	16.46S	58.44W
Chaudfontaine	12	Hd	50.35N	5.38 E
Chaudière, Rivière-	44	Lb	46.43N	71.17W
Chauk	25	Id	20.53N	94.49 E
Chaulnes	12	Ee	49.49N	2.48 E
Chaumont	11	Lf	48.07N	5.08 E
Chaumont-en-Vexin	12	De	49.16N	1.53 E
Chaumont-Gistoux	12	Gd	50.41N	4.44 E
Chaumont-Porcien	12	Ge	49.39N	4.15 E
Chaumont-sur-Aire	12	Hf	48.56N	5.15 E
Chaumont-sur-Loire	11	Hg	47.29N	1.11 E
Chauny	11	Je	49.37N	3.13 E
Chau Phu	25	Lf	10.42N	105.07 E
Chausey, Iles-	11	Ef	48.53N	1.50W
Chauvigny	11	Gh	46.34N	0.39 E
Chavantina	54	Hf	14.40S	52.21W
Chavarría	55	Ci	28.57S	58.35W
Chaves [Braz.]	54	Id	0.10S	49.55W
Chaves [Port.]	13	Ec	41.44N	7.28W
Chavigny, Lac -	42	Je	58.00N	75.05W
Chavuma	36	De	13.05S	22.42 E
Chazelles-sur-Lyon	11	Ki	45.38N	4.23 E
Chbar	25	Lf	12.46N	107.10 E
Cheaha Mountain	44	Ei	33.30N	85.47W
Cheat River	44	Hf	39.45N	79.55W
Cheb	10	If	50.04N	12.23 E
Cheboygan	43	Kb	45.39N	84.29W
Chech, Erg-	30	Gf	25.00N	3.00W
Chechaouene [3]	32	Fb	35.00N	5.00W
Chechaouene	32	Fb	35.10N	5.16W
Checheng	27	Lg	22.05N	120.42 E
Che-Chiang Sheng → Zhejiang Sheng [2]	27	Kf	29.00N	120.00 E
Chech'ŏn	28	Jf	37.08N	128.12 E
Chęciny	10	Qf	50.48N	20.28 E
Cheddar Gorge	9	Kj	51.13N	2.47W
Cheduba	25	Ie	18.48N	93.38 E
Chée	12	Gf	48.45N	4.39 E
Cheektowaga	44	Hd	42.57N	78.38W
Chefu	37	Ed	22.27S	32.45 E
Chegga	31	Gf	25.22N	5.49W
Cheghelvandī	24	Mf	33.42N	48.25 E
Chehel Pāyeh	24	Qg	31.54N	57.14 E
Cheju	27	Me	33.31N	126.32 E
Cheju-Do	21	Of	33.25N	126.30 E
Cheju-Do [2]	28	Ih	33.25N	126.30 E
Cheju-Haehyŏp	28	Ih	33.40N	126.28 E
Chela, Serra da-	30	Ij	16.00S	13.10 E
Chelan	46	Ec	47.51N	120.01W
Chelan, Lake-	46	Eb	48.05N	120.30W
Chelforó, Arroyo-	55	Cm	36.55S	58.12W
Cheliff [3]	32	Hb	36.10N	1.15 E
Cheliff	30	He	36.02N	0.08 E
Cheliff	32	Hb	36.10N	1.20 E
Cheliff, Plaine du-	13	Mi	35.57N	0.15 E
Chellalat el Adhaouara	13	Pi	35.56N	3.15 E
Chelleh Khāneh, Kūh-e-	24	Md	36.52N	48.36 E
Chełm [2]	10	Te	51.10N	23.30 E
Chełm	10	Te	51.10N	23.28 E
Chelmer	12	Cc	51.44N	0.42 E
Chełmińskie, Pojezierze-	10	Oc	53.20N	19.00 E
Chełmno	10	Oc	53.22N	18.26 E
Chelmsford	9	Nj	51.44N	0.28 E
Chełmża	10	Oc	53.12N	18.37 E
Cheltenham	9	Kj	51.54N	2.04W
Chelva	13	Le	39.45N	0.59W
Chemainus	46	Db	48.55N	123.43W
Chemâma	32	Ef	16.50N	14.00 E
Chemba	37	Ec	17.09S	34.53 E
Chembe	36	Ee	11.58S	28.45 E
Chemillé	11	Fg	47.13N	0.43W
Chemnitz = Karl-Marx-Stadt	6	He	50.50N	12.55 E
Chemult	46	Ee	43.13N	121.47W
Chenachane	32	Gd	26.00N	4.15W
Chenārbāshi	24	Lf	33.20N	46.29 E
Chen Barag Qi (Bayan Hure)	27	Kb	49.21N	119.25 E
Chencha	35	Fd	6.17N	37.44 E
Chencoyi	48	Nh	19.48N	90.14W
Cheney	46	Gc	47.29N	117.34W
Cheney Reservoir	45	Hh	37.45N	97.50W
Cheng'an	28	Cf	36.27N	114.4 E
Chengde	27	Kc	41.00N	117.57 E
Chengdu	22	Mf	30.45N	104.04 E
Chengkou	27	Ie	31.54N	108.37 E
Chengmai	27	Ih	19.50N	109.59 E
Chengshan Jiao	27	Ld	37.24N	122.42 E
Chengxi Hu	28	Dh	32.22N	116.12 E
Chengzitan	27	Ld	39.31N	122.26 E
Chehisckali	16	Mh	42.06N	42.16 E
Chenjiagang	28	Eg	34.22N	119.48 E
Chenonceaux	11	Hg	47.20N	1.04 E
Chenxi	27	Jf	28.02N	110.15 E
Chenxian	27	Jf	25.49N	113.05 E
Chenying → Wannian	28	Dj	28.42N	117.04 E
Chépénéhé	63b	Ce	20.47S	167.09 E
Chepes	56	Gd	31.21S	66.36W
Chepo	49	Hi	9.10N	79.06W
Cher [3]	11	Ig	47.00N	2.30 E
Cher	5	Gf	47.21N	0.29 E
Cheradi, Isole-	14	Lj	40.25N	17.10 E
Cherangany Hills	36	Gb	1.15N	35.27 E
Cheraw	44	Hh	34.42N	79.53W
Cherbaniani Reef	25	Ef	12.18N	71.53 E
Cherbourg	6	Ff	49.39N	1.39W
Cherchell	32	Hb	36.36N	2.12 E
Chère	11	Eg	47.42N	1.50W
Chergui, Chott Ech-	30	He	34.21N	0.30 E
Chéri	34	Hc	13.26N	11.21 E
Cherlen → Kerulen	21	Ne	48.48N	117.00 E
Cherokee	45	Ie	42.45N	95.33W
Cherokees, Lake O' the-	45	Ih	36.39N	94.49W
Cherksi Mountains (EN) = Čerskogo, hrebet-	21	Qc	65.00N	145.00 E
Chesterfield Inlet	39	Jc	63.21N	90.42W
Chertsey	12	Bc	51.23N	0.30W
Cherwell	9	Lj	51.44N	1.15W
Chesapeake	44	Ig	36.45N	76.15W
Chesapeake Bay	38	Lf	38.40N	76.25W
Chesapeake Bay Bridge-Tunnel	44	Ig	37.00N	76.02W
Chesha Bay (EN) = Češskaja Guba	5	Kb	67.20N	46.30 E
Chesham	12	Bc	51.42N	0.36W
Cheshire [3]	9	Kh	53.15N	2.30W
Cheshire Plain	9	Kh	53.20N	2.40W
Cheshunt	12	Bc	51.42N	0.02W
Chester	9	Kh	53.10N	2.55W
Chester [Eng.-U.K.]	9	Kh	53.12N	2.54W
Chester [Il.-U.S.]	45	Lh	37.55N	89.49W
Chester [Mt.-U.S.]	46	Jb	48.31N	110.58W
Chester [Pa.-U.S.]	44	Jf	39.50N	75.23W
Chester [S.C.-U.S.]	44	Gh	34.40N	81.12W
Chesterfield	9	Lh	53.15N	1.25W
Chesterfield, Ile-	37	Gc	16.20S	43.58 E
Chesterfield, Récifs et Iles- = Chesterfield Reefs and Islands (EN)	57	Gf	20.00S	159.00 E
Chesterfield Inlet	38	Jc	63.25N	90.45W
Chesterfield Reefs and Islands (EN) = Chesterfield, Récifs et Iles-	57	Gf	20.00S	159.00 E
Chesterton Range	59	Je	25.30S	147.30 E
Chestnut Ridge	44	He	40.10N	79.25W
Chesuncook Lake	44	Mb	46.00N	69.20W
Chetaibi	32	Ib	37.04N	7.23 E
Chetumal	39	Kh	18.35N	88.07W
Chetumal, Bahía de	47	Ge	18.20N	88.05W
Cheviot	62	Ee	42.49S	173.16 E
Chew Bahir = Stefanie, Lake- (EN)	30	Kh	4.38N	36.50 E
Chewelah	46	Gb	48.17N	117.43W
Cheyenne [Ok.-U.S.]	45	Gi	35.37N	99.40W

Index Symbols

[1] Independent Nation
[2] State, Region
[3] District, County
[4] Municipality
[5] Colony, Dependency
Continent
Physical Region
Historical or Cultural Region
Mount, Mountain
Volcano
Hill
Mountains, Mountain Range
Hills, Escarpment
Plateau, Upland
Pass, Gap
Plain, Lowland
Delta
Salt Flat
Valley, Canyon
Crater, Cave
Karst Features
Depression
Polder
Desert, Dunes
Forest, Woods
Heath, Steppe
Oasis
Cape, Point
Coast, Beach
Cliff
Peninsula
Isthmus
Sandbank
Island
Atoll
Rock, Reef
Islands, Archipelago
Rocks, Reefs
Coral Reef
Well, Spring
Geyser
River, Stream
Waterfall Rapids
River Mouth, Estuary
Lake
Salt Lake
Intermittent Lake
Reservoir
Swamp, Pond
Canal
Glacier
Ice Shelf, Pack Ice
Ocean
Sea
Gulf, Bay
Strait, Fjord
Lagoon
Bank
Seamount
Tablemount
Ridge
Shelf
Basin
Escarpment, Sea Scarp
Fracture
Trench, Abyss
National Park, Reserve
Point of Interest
Recreation Site
Cave, Cavern
Historic Site
Ruins
Wall, Walls
Church, Abbey
Temple
Scientific Station
Airport
Port
Lighthouse
Mine
Tunnel
Dam, Bridge

Cheyenne [Wy.-U.S.]	39	Ie	41.08N	104.49W
Cheyenne River	43	Gc	44.40N	101.15W
Cheyenne Wells	45	Eg	38.51N	102.11W
Cheyne Bay	59	Df	34.35S	118.50 E
Chhatarpur	25	Fd	24.54N	79.36 E
Chhindwāra	25	Fd	22.04N	78.56 E
Chi	25	Ke	15.11N	104.43 E
Chiamboni, Rās-	35	Gf	1.38S	41.36 E
Chiana, Val di-	14	Fg	43.15N	11.50 E
Chianciano Terme	14	Fg	43.02N	11.49 E
Chiang-hsi Sheng → Jangxi Sheng = Kiangsi (EN) [2]	27	Kf	28.00N	116.00 E
Chiang Mai	22	Lh	18.46N	98.58 E
Chiang Rai	22	Lh	19.54N	99.50 E
Chiang-su Sheng → Jiangsu Sheng = Kiangsu (EN) [2]	27	Ke	33.00N	120.00 E
Chiani	14	Gh	42.44N	12.07 E
Chianje	31	Ij	15.45S	13.54 E
Chianti	14	Fg	43.30N	11.25 E
Chiapa, Río-	48	Mj	16.30N	93.10W
Chiapas [2]	47	Fe	16.30N	92.30W
Chiapas, Meseta de-	47	Fe	16.30N	92.00W
Chiaramonte Gulfi	14	Im	37.02N	14.42 E
Chiaravalle	14	Hg	43.36N	13.19 E
Chiaromònte	14	Kj	40.07N	16.13 E
Chiautla de Tapia	48	Jh	18.17N	98.36W
Chiavari	14	Df	44.19N	9.19 E
Chiavenna	14	Dd	46.19N	9.24 E
Chiayi	27	Lg	23.29N	120.27 E
Chiba	27	Pd	35.36N	140.07 E
Chiba Ken [2]	28	Pg	35.40N	140.20 E
Chibemba	36	Bf	15.45S	14.06 E
Chibia	36	Bf	15.11S	13.41 E
Chibougamau	39	Le	49.53N	74.21W
Chibougamau, Lac-	44	Ja	49.50N	74.15W
Chibougamau, Rivière-	44	Ja	49.50N	74.25W
Chiburi-Jima	28	Lf	36.00N	133.02 E
Chibuto	37	Ed	24.42S	33.33 E
Chicago	39	Ke	41.53N	87.38W
Chicago Heights	45	Mf	41.30N	87.38W
Chicala	36	Ce	11.59S	19.30 E
Chicapa	30	Ji	6.25S	20.48 E
Chic-Chocs, Monts-	44	Na	48.55N	66.45W
Chicha	35	Bb	16.52N	18.33 E
Chichagof	40	Le	57.30N	135.30W
Chichancanab, Laguna de-	48	Oh	19.54N	88.46W
Chichaoua	32	Fc	31.32N	8.46W
Chichas, Cordillera de-	54	Eh	20.30S	66.30W
Chicheng	27	Kc	40.55N	115.47 E
Chichén Itzá	39	Kg	20.40N	88.35W
Chichester	9	Mk	50.50N	0.48W
Chichester Range	59	Dd	22.20S	119.20 E
Chichibu	28	Og	35.59N	139.05 E
Chichigalpa	49	Dg	12.34N	87.02W
Chichijma-Rettō	60	Cb	27.06N	142.12 E
Chichilla de Monte-Aragón	13	Kf	38.55N	1.43W
Chichiriviche	49	Mh	10.56N	68.16W
Chickasawhay River	45	Lk	31.00N	88.45W
Chickasha	43	Hd	35.02N	97.58W
Chicken	40	Kd	64.04N	141.56W
Chiclana de la Frontera	13	Fh	36.25N	6.08W
Chiclayo	53	If	6.46S	79.50W
Chico	43	Cd	39.44N	121.50W
Chico, Río- [Arg.]	52	Jj	43.48S	66.25W
Chico, Río- [Arg.]	52	Jj	49.56S	68.32W
Chicoana	56	Gc	25.06S	65.33W
Chicomo	37	Ed	24.31S	34.17 E
Chiconono	37	Fb	12.57S	35.45 E
Chicopee	44	Kd	42.10N	72.36W
Chicote	36	Df	16.01S	21.48 E
Chicoutimi	39	Le	48.26N	71.04W
Chicoutimi Nord	44	La	48.29N	71.02W
Chicualacuala	37	Ed	22.05S	31.42 E
Chidenguele	37	Ed	24.55S	34.10 E
Chidley, Cape-	38	Mc	60.25N	64.30W
Chiemsee	10	Ii	47.54N	12.29 E
Chiengi	36	Ed	8.39S	29.10 E
Chienti	14	Hg	43.18N	13.45 E
Chieri	14	Be	45.01N	7.49 E
Chiers	12	He	49.39N	5.00 E
Chiese	14	Ee	45.08N	10.25 E
Chieti	14	Ih	42.21N	14.10 E
Chièvres	12	Fd	50.35N	3.48 E
Chifeng/Ulanhad	27	Kc	42.16N	118.57 E
Chifumage	36	De	12.10S	22.30 E
Chifwefwe	36	Fe	13.35S	29.35 E
Chigasaki	29	Fd	35.19N	139.24 E
Chignik	40	He	56.18N	158.23W
Chigombe	37	Ed	23.26S	33.19 E
Chigorodó	49	Ij	7.41N	76.41W
Chigubo	37	Ed	22.50S	33.31 E
Chigu Co	27	Ff	28.40N	91.50 E
Chi He	28	Dh	32.51N	117.59 E
Chihli, Gulf of- (EN) = Bo Hai	21	Nf	38.30N	120.00 E
Chihuahua [2]	47	Cc	28.30N	106.00W
Chihuahua	39	Ig	28.38N	106.05W
Chii-san	28	Ig	35.20N	127.44 E
Chikaskia River	45	Hh	36.37N	97.15W
Chikugo	29	Be	33.13N	130.30 E
Chikugo-Gawa	29	Be	33.10N	130.21 E
Chikuma-Gawa	29	Fc	37.00N	138.35 E
Chikwana	36	Ff	16.03S	34.48 E
Chilapa de Alvarez	48	Ji	17.36N	99.10W
Chilās	25	Ea	35.26N	74.05 E
Chilaw	25	Fg	7.34N	79.47 E
Chilcotin	42	Ff	51.46N	122.22W
Childers	59	Ke	25.14S	152.17 E
Childress	43	Ge	34.25N	100.13W
Chile [1]	53	Ii	30.00S	71.00W
Chile Basin (EN)	3	Mm	33.00S	90.00W
Chile Chico	56	Fg	46.33S	71.44W
Chilecito [Arg.]	56	Gd	33.53S	69.03W
Chilecito [Arg.]	56	Gc	29.10S	67.30W
Chile Rise (EN)	3	Mm	40.00S	90.00W
Chili	35	Cb	16.44N	20.53 E
Chilia, Braţul-	15	Md	45.13N	29.43 E
Chililabombwe	36	Ee	12.22S	27.50 E
Chi-lin Sheng → Jilin Sheng = Kirin (EN) [2]	27	Mc	43.00N	126.00 E
Chilko Lake	46	Ca	51.20N	124.05W
Chilko River	46	Da	52.00N	123.40W
Chillán	53	Ii	36.36S	72.07W
Chillar	56	Ie	37.18S	59.59W
Chillicothe [Il.-U.S.]	45	Lf	40.55N	89.29W
Chillicothe [Mo.-U.S.]	45	Jg	39.48N	93.33W
Chillicothe [Oh.-U.S.]	43	Kd	38.20N	82.59W
Chilliwack	46	Eb	49.10N	121.57W
Chiloé, Isla de-	52	Ij	42.30S	73.55W
Chilón	48	Mi	17.14N	92.25W
Chiloquin	46	Ee	42.35N	121.52W
Chilpancingo de los Bravos	47	Ee	17.33N	99.30W
Chiltern Hills	9	Mj	51.42N	0.48W
Chilton	45	Ld	44.02N	88.10W
Chiluage	36	Dd	9.31S	21.46 E
Chiumba	36	Fe	10.27S	34.16 E
Chilwa, Lake-	36	Fc	15.12S	35.50 E
Chimala	36	Fd	8.51S	34.01 E
Chimaltenango	49	Bf	14.39N	90.49W
Chimaltenango [3]	49	Bf	14.40N	90.55W
Chimán	49	Hi	8.42N	78.37W
Chimanas, Islas-	50	Dg	10.17N	64.38W
Chimay	12	Gd	50.03N	4.19 E
Chimborazo, Volcán-	52	If	1.28S	78.48W
Chimbote	53	If	9.05S	78.36W
Chimichagua	49	Ki	9.16N	73.49W
Chimoio	37	Ec	19.00S	33.23 E
Chimorra	13	Hf	38.18N	4.53W
Chin [2]	25	Id	22.00N	93.30 E
China [Jap.]	29b	Bb	27.20N	128.36 E
China [Mex.]	48	Je	25.42N	99.14W
China (EN) = Zhonghua Renmin Gongheguo [1]	22	Mf	35.00N	105.00 E
Chinacates	48	Ge	25.00N	105.13W
China Lake	46	Gi	35.46N	117.39W
Chinandega	47	Gf	12.37N	87.09W
Chinandega [3]	49	Dg	12.45N	87.05W
Chinati Peak	45	Dl	29.57N	104.29W
Chincha Alta	54	Cf	13.27S	76.08W
Chinchaga	42	Fe	58.52N	118.19W
Chinchilla	59	Ke	26.45S	150.38 E
Chinchón	13	Id	40.08N	3.25W
Chinchorro, Banco-	47	Ge	18.35N	87.20W
Chincoteague	44	Jg	37.55N	75.23W
Chinde	31	Kj	18.34S	36.27 E
Chin-Do	28	Ig	34.25N	126.15 E
Chindu	27	Ge	33.30N	96.31 E
Chindwinn	21	Lg	21.26N	95.15 E
Ch'ing-hai Sheng → Qinghai Sheng = Tsinghai (EN) [2]	27	Gd	36.00N	96.00 E
Chingil	35	Bc	10.33N	18.57 E
Chingola	31	Jj	12.32S	27.52 E
Chinguar	36	Ce	12.33S	16.22 E
Chinguetti	32	Ee	20.27N	12.21W
Chinguetti, Dahr de-	32	Ee	20.43N	12.20W
Chinhae	28	Jg	35.08N	128.40 E
Chiniot	25	Eb	31.43N	72.59 E
Chínipas	48	Ed	27.23N	108.32W
Chinju	27	Md	35.11N	128.05 E
Chinko	30	Jh	4.50N	23.53 E
Chinle	46	Kh	36.09N	109.33W
Chinle Creek	46	Kh	37.12N	109.43W
Chinmen	27	Kg	24.25N	118.25 E
Chino	29	Fd	36.00N	138.09 E
Chinon	11	Gg	47.10N	0.15 E
Chinook	46	Kb	48.35N	109.14W
Chinquila	48	Pg	21.30N	87.25W
Chinsali	36	Fe	10.33S	32.04 E
Chinteche	36	Fe	11.50S	34.10 E
Chinú	54	Cb	9.06N	75.24W
Chinvali	19	Eg	42.13N	43.57 E
Chiny	12	He	49.44N	5.20 E
Chinyŏng	28	Jg	35.18N	128.44 E
Chioco	37	Ec	16.25S	32.50 E
Chioggia	14	Ge	45.13N	12.17 E
Chios (EN) = Khíos	5	Ih	38.22N	26.00 E
Chipata	31	Kj	13.39S	32.40 E
Chipepo	36	Ef	16.49S	27.50 E
Chipindo	36	Ce	13.48S	15.48 E
Chiping	28	Df	36.35N	116.16 E
Chipinge	37	Ed	20.12S	32.38 E
Chipman	44	Ob	46.11N	65.53W
Chippenham	9	Kj	51.28N	2.07W
Chippewa, Lake-	45	Kd	45.56N	91.13W
Chippewa Falls	43	Ic	44.56N	91.24W
Chippewa River [Wi.-U.S.]	45	Id	44.56N	95.44W
Chippewa River [U.S.]	45	Jd	44.25N	92.10W
Chipping Ongar	12	Cc	51.42N	0.15 E
Chiputneticook Lakes	44	Mc	45.45N	68.45W
Chiquián	54	Cf	10.09S	77.11W
Chiquimula [3]	49	Cf	14.40N	89.25W
Chiquimula	49	Cf	14.48N	89.33W
Chiquimulilla	49	Bf	14.05N	90.23W
Chiquinquirá	54	Db	5.37N	73.50W
Chiquitos, Llanos de-	54	Fg	18.00S	61.30W
Chīrāla	25	Ge	15.49N	80.21 E
Chiran	29	Bf	31.22N	130.27 E
Chiredzi	31	Kk	21.03S	31.45 E
Chirfa	34	Ha	20.57N	12.21 E
Chirgua, Río-	50	Bh	8.30N	68.01W
Chiricahua Peak	43	Fe	31.52N	109.20W
Chiriguaná	49	Ki	9.22N	73.37W
Chirikof	40	He	55.50N	155.35W
Chiriquí [3]	49	Fi	8.30N	82.00W
Chiriquí, Golfo de-	38	Ki	8.00N	82.20W
Chiriquí, Laguna de-	47	Hg	9.03N	82.00W
Chiriquí Grande	49	Fi	8.57N	82.07W
Chirnogi	15	Je	44.07N	26.84 E
Chiromo	36	Gf	16.33S	35.08 E
Chirripó, Cerro-	38	Ki	9.29N	83.29W
Chirripó, Río- [C.R.]	49	Fh	10.03N	83.16W
Chirripó, Río- [C.R.]	49	Fh	10.41N	83.41W
Chirundu	37	Dc	15.59S	28.54 E
Chisamba	36	Ee	14.59S	28.23 E
Chisāpāni Garhi	25	Hc	27.34N	85.08 E
Chisenga	36	Fd	9.56S	33.26 E
Chisasibi	39	Ld	53.50N	79.00W
Chishui	27	If	28.30N	105.44 E
Chişineu Criş	15	Ec	46.32N	21.31 E
Chisone	14	Bf	44.49N	7.25 E
Chitado	36	Bf	17.18S	13.54 E
Chita-Hantō	29	Ed	34.50N	136.50 E
Chitati	35	Ac	14.40N	14.30 E
Chitato	31	Jl	7.22S	20.49 E
Chita-Wan	29	Ed	34.50N	136.55 E
Chitembo	36	Ce	13.31S	16.45 E
Chitina	40	Kd	61.31N	144.27W
Chitipa	36	Fd	9.43S	33.16 E
Chitorgarh	25	Ed	24.53N	74.38 E
Chitose	28	Pc	42.49N	141.39 E
Chitradurga	25	Ff	14.14N	76.24 E
Chitrāl	25	Ea	35.51N	71.47 E
Chitré	47	Hg	7.58N	80.26W
Chittagong	22	Lg	22.20N	91.50 E
Chittoor	25	Ff	13.12N	79.07 E
Chiumbe	30	Ji	6.59S	21.12 E
Chiume	36	Df	15.08S	21.12 E
Chiusi	14	Fg	43.01N	11.57 E
Chiusi, Lago di-	14	Fg	43.05N	12.00 E
Chiva	13	Le	39.28N	0.43W
Chivacoa	50	Bg	10.10N	68.54W
Chivapuri, Rio-	50	Ci	6.25N	66.23W
Chivasso	14	Be	45.11N	7.53 E
Chivay	54	Dg	15.38S	71.36W
Chivilcoy	56	Hd	34.53S	60.01W
Chixoy o Negro, Río-	49	Be	16.28N	90.33W
Chizou → Guichi	27	Ke	30.38N	117.30 E
Chizu	29	Dd	35.15N	134.14 E
Chŏâm Khsant	25	Kf	14.13N	104.56 E
Choapa, Río-	56	Fd	31.38S	71.34W
Chobe	30	Jj	17.47S	25.10 E
Choc Bay	51k	Ba	14.03N	60.59W
Choch'iwŏn	28	If	36.36N	127.18 E
Chocó [2]	54	Cb	6.00N	77.00W
Chocolate Mountains	46	Hj	33.25N	114.10W
Chodecz	10	Pd	52.24N	19.01 E
Chodov	10	If	50.15N	12.45 E
Chodzież	10	Md	52.59N	16.56 E
Choele-Choel	56	Ge	39.16S	65.41W
Choique	56	He	38.28S	62.43W
Choiseul	51k	Ab	13.47N	61.03W
Choiseul Island	57	Ge	7.00S	157.00 E
Choix	48	Ed	26.43N	108.17W
Chojna	10	Kd	52.58N	14.28 E
Chojnice	10	Nc	53.42N	17.34 E
Chojnów	10	Le	51.17N	15.56 E
Chōkai-San	21	Q[illegible]	39.10N	140.02 E
Choke	30	Kg	10.45N	37.35 E
Chókué	37	Ed	24.27S	32.55 E
Cho La	27	Ge	31.52N	98.51 E
Cholet	11	Fg	47.04N	0.53W
Chŏlla-Namdo [2]	28	Ig	34.45N	127.00 E
Chŏlla-Pukto [2]	28	Ic	35.45N	127.15 E
Cholo	36	Gf	16.04S	35.08 E
Cholula	48	Jh	19.04N	98.18W
Choluteca	47	Gf	13.18N	87.12W
Choluteca [3]	49	Dg	13.20N	87.10W
Choluteca, Río-	49	Dg	13.07N	87.19W
Choma	31	Jj	16.49S	26.59 E
Chomo/Yadong	27	Ef	27.38N	89.03 E
Chomo Lhari	27	Ef	27.50N	89.16 E
Chomutov	10	Jf	50.28N	13.25 E
Ch'ŏnan	27	Md	36.48N	127.09 E
Chon Buri	25	Kf	13.22N	100.59 E
Chone	54	Bd	0.42S	80.07W
Ch'ŏngch'ŏn-gang	28	He	39.35N	125.28 E
Ch'ŏngjin	22	Oe	41.46N	129.49 E
Ch'ŏngjin Si [2]	28	Jd	41.45N	129.45 E
Chŏngju	27	Md	39.51N	125.15 E
Ch'ŏngju	27	Md	36.38N	127.30 E
Chongli (Xiwanzi)	28	Cd	40.57N	115.12 E
Chongming	28	Fi	31.38N	121.24 E
Chongming Dao	28	Fi	31.36N	121.33 E
Chongoroi	36	Be	13.34S	13.55 E
Chongqing (Yuzhou) = Chungking (EN)	22	Mg	29.34N	106.27 E
Chongqing → Yuzhou = Chungking (EN)	22	Mg	29.34N	106.27 E
Ch'ŏngsan-Do	28	Ig	34.11N	126.54 E
Chŏngŭp	28	Ig	35.34N	126.51 E
Chongyang	28	Cj	29.32N	114.02 E
Chongzuo	27	Ig	12.29N	107.22 E
Chŏnju	27	Md	35.49N	127.09 E
Choni (Culukidze)	16	Mh	42.18N	42.25 E
Chonos, Archipiélago de los-	52	Ij	45.00S	74.00W
Chontaleña, Cordillera-	49	Eh	11.50N	85.00W
Chontales [3]	49	Eg	12.05N	85.10W
Chopim, Rio-	55	Fg	25.35S	53.05W
Chopinzinho	55	Fg	25.51S	52.30W
Chorito, Sierra del-	13	He	39.25N	4.25W
Choroszcz	10	Sc	53.09N	22.59 E
Chorreras, Cerro-	48	Fd	26.02N	106.21W
Ch'ŏrwŏn	27	Md	38.15N	127.13 E
Chorzele	10	Qc	53.16N	20.55 E
Chorzów	10	Of	50.19N	18.57 E
Ch'osan	28	Hd	40.45N	125.50 E
Chośebuz/Cottbus	10	Ke	51.46N	14.20 E
Chōshi	28	Pg	35.44N	140.50 E
Chos Malal	56	Fe	37.23S	70.16W
Chosŏn M.I.K. = North Korea (EN) [1]	22	Oe	40.00N	127.30 E
Chosŏn Minjuju-Inmin-Konghwaguk = Chosŏn M.I.K. [1]	22	Oe	40.00N	127.30 E
Choszczno	10	Lc	53.10N	15.26 E
Chota	54	Ce	6.33S	78.39W
Chotanagpur Plateau	21	Kg	22.00N	86.00 E
Choteau	46	Ic	47.49N	112.11W
Chotla, Cerro de-	48	Ii	17.55N	101.31W
Choukchot, Djebel-	13	Qh	36.01N	4.11 E
Choum	32	Ee	21.18N	12.59W
Chovd → Kobdo	27	Fb	48.06N	92.11 E
Chövsgöl nuur → Hubsugul Nur	21	Md	51.00N	100.30 E
Chowchilla	46	Eh	37.07N	120.16W
Chowra	25	Ig	8.27N	93.02 E
Chréa	13	Oh	36.25N	2.53 E
Chřiby	10	Ng	49.10N	17.20 E
Christchurch	58	Ii	43.32S	172.37 E
Christian, Cape -	42	Kb	70.32N	68.18W
Christian, Point-	64q	Ab	25.04S	130.07W
Christiana	37	De	27.52S	25.08 E
Christian IV Gletscher	41	Ie	68.40N	30.20W
Christiansburg	44	Gg	37.07N	80.26W
Christiansfeld	8	Ci	55.21N	9.29 E
Christianshåb/Qasigiánguit	41	Ge	68.45N	51.30W
Christiansø	8	Fi	55.20N	15.10 E
Christian Sound	40	Me	55.56N	134.40W
Christiansted	50	Dd	17.45N	64.40W
Christiansted Harbor	51a	Dc	17.46N	64.42W
Christie Bay	42	Gd	62.45N	110.15W
Christmas → Kiritimati Atoll	57	Ld	1.52N	157.20W
Christmas Creek	59	Fc	18.29S	125.23 E
Christmas Creek	59	Fc	18.53S	125.55 E
Christmas Island [5]	22	Mk	10.30S	105.40 E
Christmas Ridge (EN)	3	Ki	10.00N	165.00W
Chrudim	10	Lg	49.57N	15.47 E
Chrzanów	10	Pf	50.09N	19.24 E
Chrząstowa	10	Mc	53.35N	16.58 E
Chuansha	28	Fi	31.11N	121.42 E
Chūbar	24	Mc	38.11N	48.51 E
Chubut [2]	56	Gf	44.00S	69.00W
Chubut, Rio-	52	Jj	43.20S	65.03W
Chugach Mountains	40	Jd	61.00N	145.00W
Chudžand (Leninabad)	22	Ie	40.17N	69.37 E
Chudžandskaja oblast	19	Gh	40.00N	69.10 E
Chu He	28	Eh	32.15N	119.03 E
Chuhuichupa	48	Ec	29.38N	108.22W
Chuí	55	Fk	33.41S	53.27W
Chuka	36	Gc	0.20S	37.39 E
Chukai	26	Df	4.15N	103.25 E
Chukchi Peninsula (EN) = Čukotski Poluostrov	21	Uc	66.00N	175.00W
Chukchi Plateau (EN)	67	Bd	78.00N	165.00W
Chukchi Sea	67	Bd	69.00N	171.00W
Chukchi Sea (EN) = Čukotskoje More	67	Bd	69.00N	171.00W
Chula Vista	46	Gj	32.39N	117.05W
Chulitna	40	Jd	62.55N	149.39W
Chullo	13	Jg	37.10N	2.57W
Chulucanas	54	Be	5.06S	80.10W
Chumbicha	56	Gc	28.52S	66.14W
Chumphon	25	Jf	10.32N	99.13 E
Chumunjin	28	Jf	37.53N	128.49 E
Ch'unch'ŏn	27	Md	37.52N	127.44 E
Chunga	36	Ef	15.03S	26.00 E
Ch'ungch'ŏng-Namdo [2]	28	If	36.30N	127.00 E
Ch'ungch'ŏng-Pukto [2]	28	Jf	36.45N	128.00 E
Ch'ungju	27	Md	36.58N	127.56 E
Chungking (EN) = Chongqing (Yuzhou)	22	Mg	29.34N	106.27 E
Chungking (EN) = Yuzhou → Chongqing	22	Mg	29.34N	106.27 E
Ch'ungmu	28	Jg	34.51N	128.26 E
Chunya	36	Fd	8.32S	33.25 E
Chuquibamba	54	Dg	15.50S	72.39W
Chuquibambilla	54	Df	14.07S	72.43W
Chuquicamata	56	Gb	22.19S	68.56W
Chuquisaca [2]	54	Fg	20.00S	64.20W
Chur/Cuera	14	Dd	46.50N	9.35 E
Churchill	39	Jd	58.46N	94.10W
Churchill [Can.]	38	Md	53.30N	60.10W
Churchill [Can.]	38	Jd	58.47N	94.12W
Churchill, Cape -	42	Ie	58.46N	93.12W
Churchill Falls	42	Lf	53.30N	64.10W
Churchill Lake	42	Ge	56.05N	108.15W
Churchill Peak	42	Ee	58.20N	125.02W
Churchill Range	66	Jg	81.30S	158.30 E
Chūru	25	Ec	28.18N	74.57 E
Churuguara	54	Ea	10.49N	69.32W
Churún Merú = Angel Falls (EN)	52	Je	5.57N	62.30W
Chuska Mountains	46	Kh	36.15N	108.50W
Chute-des Passes	42	Kg	49.50N	71.00W
Chuxian	27	Ke	32.16N	118.15 E
Chuxiong	27	Hf	25.02N	101.32 E
Chuy	55	Fk	33.41S	53.27W
Chynčešt'(Kotovsk)	16	Ff	46.49N	28.33 E
Ciamis	26	Eh	7.20S	108.21 E
Cianjur	26	Eh	6.49S	107.08 E
Ciarraí/Kerry [2]	9	Di	52.10N	9.30W
Čiatura	16	Mh	42.17N	43.15 E
Cibuta, Cerro-	48	Db	31.02N	110.58W
Ćićarija	14	He	45.28N	13.54 E
Ćićevac	15	Ef	43.43N	21.27 E
Cicicleja	15	Nb	47.23N	30.50 E
Cicolano	14	Hh	42.15N	13.10 E
Cidacos	13	Kb	42.19N	1.55W
Cide	24	Eb	41.54N	33.00 E
Cidlina	10	Lf	50.09N	15.12 E
Ciechanów	10	Qd	52.53N	20.38 E
Ciechanów [2]	10	Qd	52.55N	20.40 E
Ciechanowiec	10	Sd	52.42N	22.31 E
Ciechanowska, Wysoczyzna-	10	Qc	53.10N	20.30 E
Ciego de Ávila	47	Id	21.51N	78.46W
Ciego de Ávila [3]	49	Hb	22.00N	78.40W
Ciénaga	54	Da	11.00N	74.14W
Ciénaga de Flores	48	Ie	25.57N	100.11W
Ciénaga de Oro	49	Ji	8.53N	75.38W
Cieneguita	48	Fd	27.57N	106.59W
Cienfuegos [3]	49	Gb	22.15N	80.30W
Cienfuegos	39	Kg	22.09N	80.27W
Cíes, Islas de-	13	Db	42.13N	8.54W
Cieszanów	10	Tf	50.16N	23.08 E
Cieza	13	Kf	38.14N	1.25W
Çifteler	24	Dc	39.22N	31.03 E
Cifuentes	13	Jd	40.47N	2.37W
Čiganak	19	Hf	45.05N	73.58 E
Čigirin	16	He	49.03N	32.42 E
Cigüela	13	Ie	39.08N	3.44W
Cihanbeyli	24	Ec	38.40N	32.56 E
Cihanbeyli Platosu	24	Ec	38.40N	32.45 E
Čihareši	16	Mh	42.47N	43.02 E
Cihuatlán	48	Gh	19.14N	104.35W
Čiily	19	Gg	44.13N	66.46 E
Cijara, Embalse de-	13	He	39.18N	4.52W
Cijulang	26	Eh	7.44S	108.27 E
Čik	15	Dd	45.42N	20.04 E
Čikoj	20	Ff	51.02N	106.39 E
Cikurački, Vulkan-	20	Kf	50.15N	155.29 E
Cilacap	26	Eh	7.44S	109.00 E
Çıldır	24	Jb	41.08N	43.07 E
Çıldır Gölü	24	Jb	41.04N	43.15 E
Cilento	14	Jj	40.20N	15.20 E
Čilik	18	Lc	43.42N	78.14 E
Čilik	19	Hg	43.35N	78.12 E
Cill Airne/Killarney	9	Di	52.03N	9.30W
Cill Chainnigh/Kilkenny	9	Fi	52.39N	7.15W
Cill Chainnigh/Kilkenny [2]	9	Fi	52.40N	7.20W
Cill Chaoi/Kilkee	9	Di	52.41N	9.38W
Cill Dara/Kildare [2]	9	Gh	53.15N	6.45W
Cill Dara/Kildare	9	Gh	53.10N	6.55W
Cill Mhantáin/Wicklow	9	Gi	52.59N	6.03W
Cill Mhantain/Wicklow [2]	9	Gi	53.00N	6.30W
Cill Mocheallóg/Kilmallock	9	Ei	52.25N	8.35W
Cill Rois/Kilrush	9	Di	52.39N	9.29W
Cilma	17	Fd	65.25N	52.05 E
Cilo Dağı	24	Kd	37.30N	44.00 E
Cimaltepec, Sierra-	47	Ee	16.00N	96.40W
Cimarron	38	Jf	36.10N	96.17W
Cimarron	45	Dh	36.31N	104.55W
Čimbaj	19	Fg	42.59N	59.47 E
Cimini, Monti-	14	Gh	42.24N	12.12 E
Čimišlija	16	Ff	46.32N	28.46 E
Čimkent	22	Ie	42.18N	69.36 E
Čimkentskaja Oblast [3]	19	Gg	43.00N	68.40 E
Cimljansk	19	Ef	47.37N	42.04 E
Cimljanskoje Vodohranilišče = Tsimlyansk Reservoir (EN)	5	Kf	48.00N	43.00 E
Cimone	5	Hg	44.12N	10.40 E
Cîmpeni	15	Gc	46.22N	23.03 E
Cîmpia Turzii	15	Gc	46.33N	23.53 E
Cîmpina	15	Id	45.08N	25.44 E
Cîmpulung	15	Id	45.16N	25.03 E
Cîmpulung Moldovenesc	15	Ib	47.32N	25.34 E
Čimtarga, Gora-	18	Ge	39.14N	68.12 E
Cina, Tanjung-	26	Dh	5.55S	104.35 E
Çinar	24	Id	37.39N	40.06 E
Cinarcik	15	Mi	40.39N	29.06 E
Cinaruco, Río-	50	Ci	6.41N	67.07W
Cina Selatan, Laut- = South China Sea (EN)	21	Ni	10.00N	113.00 E
Cinaz	18	Gd	40.56N	68.45 E
Cinca	13	Mc	41.26N	0.21 E
Cincar	14	Lg	43.54N	17.04 E
Cincinnati	39	Kf	39.06N	84.31W
Cinco Irmãos, Serra dos-	55	Ff	22.55S	52.50W
Cinco Saltos	56	Ge	38.49S	68.04W
Cindrelu, Vîrful-	15	Gd	45.35N	23.48 E
Çine	24	Cd	37.36N	28.04 E
Çine	15	Kl	37.46N	27.49 E
Ciney	11	Ld	50.18N	5.06 E
Čingirlau	19	Fe	51.07N	54.05 E
Cingoli	14	Hg	43.22N	13.13 E
Cintalapa de Figueroa	48	Mi	16.44N	93.43W
Cinto, Monte-	5	Gg	42.23N	8.56 E
Cintra, Golfo de-	32	De	23.00N	16.15W
Cinzas, Rio das-	55	Gf	22.56S	50.32W
Ciociaria	14	Hi	41.45N	13.15 E
Cionn Mhálanna/Malin Head	5	Fd	55.23N	7.24W
Cionn tSáile/Kinsale	9	Ej	51.42N	8.32W
Ciorani	15	Je	44.49N	26.25 E
Čiovo	14	Kg	43.30N	16.18 E
Cipa	20	Ge	55.20N	115.55 E
Cipikan	20	Gf	54.58N	113.21 E
Cipó	54	Kf	11.06S	38.31W
Cipolletti	56	Ge	38.56S	67.59W
Čiprovci	15	Ff	43.23N	22.53 E
Čir	16	Me	48.35N	42.55 E
Circeo, Capo-	14	Hi	41.14N	13.03 E
Čirčik	19	Gg	41.28N	69.35 E
Circle [Ak.-U.S.]	40	Kc	65.50N	144.04W
Circle [Mt.-U.S.]	46	Mc	47.25N	105.35W
Circleville	44	Ff	39.36N	82.57W
Cirebon	22	Mj	6.44S	108.34 E
Cirencester	9	Lj	51.44N	1.59W
Cirié	14	Be	45.14N	7.36 E
Čirinda	20	Fc	67.30N	100.35 E
Čirip, Vulkan-	20	Jg	45.20N	147.58 E
Čirka-Kem	7	Hd	64.45N	32.10 E
Cirò	14	Lk	39.23N	17.04 E
Cirò Marina	14	Lk	39.22N	17.08 E
Ciron	11	Fj	44.36N	0.18W
Čirpan	15	Ig	42.12N	25.20 E
Cirque Mountain	42	Le	58.55N	63.33W
Cisa, Passo della-	14	Df	44.28N	9.55 E
Ciscaucasia (EN)	5	Kf	45.00N	43.00 E
Cisco	45	Gj	32.23N	98.59W
Ciskei	37	Df	31.30S	26.40 E
Čišmy	19	Fe	54.35N	55.25 E
Cisnădie	15	Hd	45.43N	24.09 E
Cisne, Islas del-	47	He	17.22N	83.51W
Cistern Point	49	Ib	24.40N	77.45W
Cistierna	13	Gb	42.48N	5.07W
Čistoozernoje	20	Cf	54.43N	76.43 E
Čistopol	19	Fd	55.23N	50.39 E
Čita	22	Nd	52.03N	113.30 E
Çitak	15	Mk	38.08N	29.39 E

Index Symbols

[1] Independent Nation · [2] State, Region · [3] District, County · [5] Municipality · [5] Colony, Dependency · Continent · Physical Region · Historical or Cultural Region · Mount, Mountain · Volcano · Hill · Mountains, Mountain Range · Hills, Escarpment · Plateau, Upland · Pass, Gap · Plain, Lowland · Delta · Salt Flat · Valley, Canyon · Crater, Cave · Karst Features · Depression · Polder · Desert, Dunes · Forest, Woods · Heath, Steppe · Oasis · Cape, Point · Coast, Beach · Cliff · Peninsula · Isthmus · Sandbank · Island · Atoll · Rock, Reef · Islands, Archipelago · Rocks, Reefs · Coral Reef · Well, Spring · Geyser · River, Stream · Waterfall Rapids · River Mouth, Estuary · Lake · Salt Lake · Intermittent Lake · Reservoir · Swamp, Pond · Canal · Glacier · Ice Shelf, Pack Ice · Ocean · Sea · Gulf, Bay · Strait, Fjord · Lagoon · Bank · Seamount · Tablemount · Ridge · Shelf · Basin · Escarpment, Sea Scarp · Fracture · Trench, Abyss · National Park, Reserve · Point of Interest · Recreation Site · Cave, Cavern · Historic Site · Ruins · Wall, Walls · Church, Abbey · Temple · Scientific Station · Airport · Port · Lighthouse · Mine · Tunnel · Dam, Bridge

Name	Map	Grid	Lat	Long
Čitinskaja Oblast [3]	20	Gf	52.30 N	117.30 E
Citlaltépetl, Volcán- → Orizaba, Pico de- [▲]	38	Jh	19.01 N	97.16 W
Citrusdale	37	Bf	32.36 S	19.00 E
Città del Vaticano = Vatican City (EN) [1]	6	Hg	41.54 N	12.27 E
Città di Castello	14	Gg	43.27 N	12.14 E
Cittanova	14	KI	38.21 N	16.05 E
Ciucașu, Vîrful- [▲]	15	Id	45.31 N	25.55 E
Ciucea	15	Fd	46.57 N	22.49 E
Ciudad	48	Gf	23.44 N	105.44 W
Ciudad Acuña	47	Dc	29.18 N	100.55 W
Ciudad Altamirano	48	Ih	18.20 N	100.40 W
Ciudad Bolívar	53	Je	8.08 N	63.33 W
Ciudad Bolivia	54	Bj	8.21 N	70.34 W
Ciudad Camargo [Mex.]	47	Ec	26.19 N	98.50 W
Ciudad Camargo [Mex.]	47	Cc	27.40 N	105.10 W
Ciudad Cuauhtémoc	48	Mj	15.37 N	92.00 W
Ciudad Darío	49	Dg	12.43 N	86.08 W
Ciudad de Areco	55	CI	34.18 S	59.46 W
Ciudad de Dolores Hidalgo	48	Ig	21.10 N	100.56 W
Ciudad de la Habana [3]	50	Bb	23.10 N	82.10 W
Ciudad del Carmen	47	Fe	18.38 N	91.50 W
Ciudad del Maíz	48	Jf	22.24 N	99.36 W
Ciudad de México = Mexico City (EN)	39	Jh	19.24 N	99.09 W
Ciudad de Nutrias	54	Bb	8.07 N	69.19 W
Ciudad de Río Grande	47	Dd	23.50 N	103.02 W
Ciudadela / Ciutadella	13	Pd	40.02 N	3.50 E
Ciudad Guayana	53	Je	8.22 N	62.40 W
Ciudad Guerrero	47	Cc	28.33 N	107.30 W
Ciudad Guzmán	48	In	19.41 N	103.29 W
Ciudad Hidalgo [Mex.]	48	Mj	14.41 N	92.09 W
Ciudad Hidalgo [Mex.]	48	Ih	19.41 N	100.34 W
Ciudad Juárez	39	If	31.44 N	106.29 W
Ciudad Lerdo	47	Dc	25.32 N	103.32 W
Ciudad Madero	39	Jg	22.16 N	97.50 W
Ciudad Mante	47	Ed	22.44 N	98.57 W
Ciudad Mendoza	48	Kh	18.48 N	97.11 E
Ciudad Obregón	39	Ig	27.59 N	109.56 W
Ciudad Ojeda	54	Da	10.12 N	71.19 W
Ciudad Piar	54	Fb	7.27 N	63.19 W
Ciudad Real [3]	13	If	38.59 N	3.56 W
Ciudad Real [3]	13	If	39.00 N	4.00 W
Ciudad Río Bravo	47	Ec	25.59 N	98.06 W
Ciudad-Rodrigo	13	Fd	40.36 N	6.32 W
Ciudad Valles	47	Ed	21.59 N	99.01 W
Ciudad Victoria	39	Jg	23.44 N	99.08 W
Ciutadella / Ciudadela	13	Pd	40.02 N	3.50 E
Civa Burnu [▶]	24	Gb	41.22 N	36.35 E
Cividale del Friuli	14	Hd	46.06 N	13.25 E
Civilsk	7	Li	55.53 N	47.29 E
Civita Castellana	14	Gg	42.17 N	12.25 E
Civitanova Marche	14	Hg	43.18 N	13.44 E
Civitavecchia	14	Fh	42.06 N	11.48 E
Civitella del Tronto	14	Hh	42.46 N	13.40 E
Çivril	24	Cc	38.56 N	35.29 E
Cixerri [S]	14	Ck	39.17 N	8.59 E
Cixi (Hushan)	28	Fi	30.10 N	121.14 E
Cixian	28	Cf	36.22 N	114.22 E
Čiža	19	Eb	67.06 N	44.19 E
Cizre	23	Fb	37.20 N	42.12 E
Cjurupinsk	16	Hf	46.37 N	32.43 E
Čkalovsk	7	Kh	56.47 N	43.17 E
Clacton-on-Sea	9	Oj	51.48 N	1.09 E
Clain [S]	11	Gh	46.47 N	0.33 E
Claire, Côte- [S]	66	Ie	66.30 S	133.00 E
Claire, Lake- [S]	42	Ge	58.30 N	112.00 W
Clair Engle Lake [S]	46	Df	40.52 N	122.43 W
Claise [S]	11	Gh	46.56 N	0.42 E
Clamecy	11	Jg	47.27 N	3.31 E
Clan Alpine Mountains [▲]	46	Gg	39.40 N	117.55 W
Clanton	44	Dj	32.50 N	86.38 W
Clanwilliam	37	Bf	32.11 S	18.54 E
Claraz	55	Cm	37.54 S	59.17 W
Clár Chlainne Mhuiris / Claremorris	9	Eh	53.44 N	9.00 W
Clare [Austl.]	59	Hf	33.50 S	138.36 E
Clare [Mi.-U.S.]	44	Ed	43.49 N	84.46 W
Clare / Abhainn an Chláir [S]	9	Dh	53.20 N	9.03 W
Clare / An Clár [3]	9	Ei	52.50 N	9.00 W
Clare / Cliara [S]	9	Dh	53.49 N	10.00 W
Claremont	44	Kd	43.23 N	72.21 W
Claremore	45	Ih	36.19 N	95.36 W
Claremorris / Clár Chlainne Mhuiris	9	Eh	53.44 N	9.00 W
Clarence [S]	62	Ee	42.10 S	173.57 E
Clarence	62	Ee	42.10 S	173.56 E
Clarence, Cape - [▶]	42	Ib	-73.55 N	90.12 W
Clarence Cannon Reservoir [S]	45	Kg	39.31 N	91.45 W
Clarence Island [S]	64	Re	61.12 S	54.00 W
Clarence River [S]	59	Ke	29.25 S	153.22 E
Clarence Strait [Ak.-U.S.] [S]	40	Me	55.25 N	132.00 W
Clarence Strait [Austl.] [S]	59	Gb	12.00 S	131.00 E
Clarence Town	50	Eb	23.06 N	74.59 W
Clarendon	45	Fi	34.56 N	100.53 W
Clarenville	42	Mg	48.09 N	53.58 W
Claresholm	42	Gd	50.03 N	113.35 W
Clarinda	45	If	40.44 N	95.02 W
Clarines	54	Fb	9.56 N	65.10 W
Clarion, Isla- [S]	47	Be	18.22 N	114.44 W
Clarion Fracture Zone (EN) [S]	3	Lh	18.00 N	130.00 W
Clarion River [S]	44	He	41.07 N	79.41 W
Clark	45	Hd	44.53 N	97.44 W
Clark, Lake- [S]	40	Id	60.15 N	154.15 W
Clark, Mount - [▲]	46	Ii	34.46 N	112.03 W
Clarkdale	46	Ii	34.46 N	112.03 W
Clarke Range [▲]	59	Jd	20.50 S	148.35 E
Clark Fork [S]	38	He	48.09 N	116.15 W
Clark Hill Lake [S]	44	Fi	33.50 N	82.20 W
Clark Mountain [▲]	46	Hi	35.32 N	115.35 W
Clarksburg	39	Kf	39.17 N	80.21 W
Clarksdale	43	Ie	34.12 N	90.34 W
Clarks Fork [S]	46	Ke	45.39 N	108.43 W

Name	Map	Grid	Lat	Long
Clark's Harbour	44	Od	43.26 N	65.38 W
Clarkston	46	Gc	46.30 N	117.03 W
Clarksville [Ar.-U.S.]	45	Ji	35.28 N	93.28 W
Clarksville [Tn.-U.S.]	43	Jd	36.32 N	87.21 W
Clarksville [Tx.-U.S.]	45	Ij	33.37 N	95.03 W
Claro, Rio- [Braz.] [S]	54	Hg	19.08 S	50.40 W
Claro, Rio- [Braz.] [S]	54	Hg	15.28 S	51.45 W
Clary	12	Fd	50.00 N	3.24 E
Claude	45	Fi	35.07 N	101.22 W
Claustra / Klosters	14	Dd	46.52 N	9.52 E
Clavering [S]	41	Jd	74.20 N	21.10 W
Claxton	44	Gi	32.10 N	81.55 W
Clay Belt [▶]	38	Kd	51.50 N	82.00 W
Clay Center	45	Hg	39.23 N	96.08 W
Clay Cross	12	Aa	53.09 N	1.25 W
Clayton	43	Gd	36.27 N	103.11 W
Clear, Cape- [▶]	9	Dj	51.26 N	9.31 W
Clear Boggy Creek [S]	45	Ii	34.03 N	95.47 W
Clear Creek [Az.-U.S.] [S]	46	Ji	33.59 N	110.38 W
Clear Creek [U.S.] [S]	46	Ld	44.53 N	106.04 W
Clearfield [Pa.-U.S.]	44	He	41.02 N	78.27 W
Clearfield [Ut.-U.S.]	46	If	41.07 N	112.01 W
Clear Fork Brazos [S]	45	Gj	33.01 N	98.40 W
Clear Lake [S]	43	Cd	39.02 N	122.50 W
Clear Lake [Ia.-U.S.]	45	Je	43.08 N	93.23 W
Clear Lake [S.D.-U.S.]	45	Hd	44.45 N	96.41 W
Clear Lake Reservoir [S]	46	Ef	41.52 N	121.08 W
Clearwater	42	Ge	56.45 N	111.22 W
Clearwater	43	Kf	27.58 N	82.48 W
Clearwater Mountains [▲]	43	Db	46.00 N	115.30 W
Clearwater River [Alta.-Can.] [S]	46	Ha	52.23 N	114.50 W
Clearwater River [U.S.] [S]	46	Gc	46.25 N	117.02 W
Cleburne	43	He	32.21 N	97.23 W
Clécy	12	Bf	48.55 N	0.29 W
Clee Hills [▲]	9	Ki	52.25 N	2.35 W
Cleethorpes	9	Mh	53.34 N	0.02 W
Clères	12	De	49.36 N	1.07 E
Clerf / Clervaux	12	Id	50.03 N	6.02 E
Clermont [Austl.]	59	Jd	22.49 S	147.39 E
Clermont [Fr.]	11	Ie	49.23 N	2.24 E
Clermont-en-Argonne	12	He	49.06 N	5.04 E
Clermont-Ferrand	6	Gf	45.47 N	3.05 E
Clermont-l'Hérault	11	Jk	43.37 N	3.26 E
Clervaux / Clerf	12	Id	50.03 N	6.02 E
Clervé [S]	12	Ie	49.57 N	6.01 E
Cles	14	Fd	46.22 N	11.02 E
Clevedon	9	Kj	51.27 N	2.51 W
Cleveland	9	Lg	54.25 N	1.05 W
Cleveland [Ms.-U.S.]	45	Kj	33.45 N	90.50 W
Cleveland [Oh.-U.S.]	39	Ke	41.30 N	81.41 W
Cleveland [Tn.-U.S.]	43	Kd	35.10 N	84.53 W
Cleveland [Tx.-U.S.]	45	Ik	30.21 N	95.05 W
Cleveland, Mount- [▲]	43	Eb	48.56 N	113.51 W
Clevelândia	55	Fh	26.24 S	52.21 W
Cleveland Heights	44	Ge	41.30 N	81.34 W
Cleveland Mountain [▲]	46	Ic	46.37 N	113.47 W
Clew Bay / Cuan Mó [S]	9	Dh	53.50 N	9.50 W
Cliara / Clare [S]	9	Dh	53.49 N	10.00 W
Cliff	45	Bj	32.59 N	108.36 W
Clifton [Az.-U.S.]	43	Fe	33.03 N	109.18 W
Clifton [St.Vin.]	51b Bb		12.36 N	61.26 W
Clifton [Tx.-U.S.]	45	Hk	31.47 N	97.35 W
Clinch River [S]	44	Eh	35.53 N	84.29 W
Cline, Mount- [▲]	46	Ga	52.10 N	116.40 W
Clines Corners	43	Di	35.01 N	105.34 W
Clingmans Dome [▲]	44	Fh	35.35 N	83.30 W
Clinton [Ar.-U.S.]	45	Ji	35.36 N	92.28 W
Clinton [B.C.-Can.]	42	Ef	51.05 N	121.35 W
Clinton [Ia.-U.S.]	43	Ic	41.51 N	90.12 W
Clinton [Il.-U.S.]	45	Lf	40.09 N	88.57 W
Clinton [Mo.-U.S.]	45	Jg	38.22 N	93.46 W
Clinton [Ms.-U.S.]	45	Kj	32.20 N	90.20 W
Clinton [N.C.-U.S.]	44	Hh	34.59 N	78.20 W
Clinton [N.Z.]	62	Cg	46.13 S	169.23 E
Clinton [Ok.-U.S.]	43	Hd	35.31 N	98.59 W
Clinton-Colden Lake [S]	42	Gd	63.55 N	107.30 W
Clintonville	45	Ld	44.37 N	88.46 W
Clipperton [S]	38	Ih	10.17 N	109.13 W
Clipperton, Fracture Zone (EN) [S]	3	Mi	10.00 N	115.00 W
Clisson	11	Eg	47.05 N	1.17 W
Cloates, Point- [▶]	59	Cd	22.45 S	113.40 E
Clochán an Aifir / Giant's Causeway	9	Gf	55.15 N	6.35 W
Clodomira	56	Hc	27.35 S	64.08 W
Cloich na Coillte / Clonakilty	9	Ej	51.37 N	8.54 W
Clonakilty / Cloich na Coillte	9	Ej	51.37 N	8.54 W
Cloncurry	58	Fg	20.42 S	140.30 E
Clones / Cluain Eois	9	Fg	54.11 N	7.14 W
Clonmel / Cluain Meala	9	Fi	52.21 N	7.42 W
Cloppenburg	10	Ed	52.51 N	8.02 E
Clorinda	53	Kh	25.20 S	57.40 W
Cloud Peak [▲]	43	Fc	44.25 N	107.10 W
Clouère [S]	11	Gh	46.26 N	0.17 E
Cloverdale	46	Dg	38.48 N	123.01 W
Clovis [Ca.-U.S.]	46	Fh	36.49 N	119.42 W
Clovis [N.M.-U.S.]	39	If	34.24 N	103.12 W
Cluain Meala / Clonmel	9	Fi	52.21 N	7.42 W
Cluan Eois / Clones	9	Fg	54.11 N	7.14 W
Cluj [2]	15	Gc	46.49 N	23.35 E
Cluj Napoca	17	Kf	46.46 N	23.36 E
Cluny	11	Kh	46.26 N	4.39 E
Cluses	11	Mh	46.04 N	6.36 E
Clusone	14	De	45.53 N	9.57 E
Clutha [S]	62	Cg	46.21 S	169.48 E
Clwyd [S]	9	Jh	53.20 N	3.30 W
Clwyd [3]	9	Jh	53.13 N	3.15 W
Clyde [N.W.T.-Can.]	39	Mb	70.25 N	68.30 W
Clyde [N.Z.]	62	Cf	45.11 S	169.19 E
Clyde, Firth of- [S]	9	Hf	55.42 N	5.00 W
Clyde Inlet [S]	42	Kb	70.20 N	68.20 W

Name	Map	Grid	Lat	Long
Cna [S]	5	Ke	54.32 N	42.05 E
Cnoc Bréanainn / Brandon Mount [▲]	9	Ci	52.14 N	10.15 W
Cnoc Fola / Bloody Foreland [▶]	9	Ef	55.09 N	8.17 W
Cnoc Mhaoldonn / Knockmealdown Mountains [▲]	9	Fi	52.15 N	8.00 W
Cnori	16	Ni	4.35 N	-5.59 E
Cnossus (EN) = Knosós [S]	15	Ih	18 N	25.10 E
Côa [S]	13	Ec	4.05 N	7.06 W
Coachella Canal [S]	46	Hj	33.34 N	116.00 W
Coahuayana	48	Hh	18.44 N	103.41 W
Coahuila [2]	47	Dc	27.20 N	102.00 W
Coalcomán, Sierra de- [▲]	48	Hh	18.30 N	102.55 W
Coalcomán de Matamoros	48	Hh	18.47 N	103.09 W
Coaldale	46	Jb	45.43 N	112.37 W
Coalgate	45	Hi	34.32 N	96.13 W
Coalinga	46	Eh	36.09 N	120.21 W
Coalville	9	Li	52.44 N	1.20 W
Coamo	49	Nd	18.05 N	66.22 W
Coari	54	Fd	4.05 S	63.08 W
Coari, Lago de- [S]	54	Fd	4.15 S	63.25 W
Coari, Rio- [S]	52	Jf	4.30 S	63.33 W
Coast [3]	36	Gc	3.00 S	39.30 E
Coast Mountains [▲]	38	Gd	55.00 N	129.00 W
Coast Plain (EN) = Kustvlakte [▶]	11	Ic	51.00 N	3.30 E
Coast Ranges [▲]	38	Ge	41.00 N	123.30 W
Coatbridge	9	If	55.52 N	4.01 W
Coatepec	48	Kh	19.27 N	96.58 W
Coatepec, Cerro- [▲]	48	Kh	18.25 N	99.35 W
Coatepeque	49	Bf	14.42 N	91.52 W
Coats [S]	38	Kc	62.30 N	83.00 W
Coats Land (EN) [▶]	66	Af	77.00 S	28.00 W
Coatzacoalcos	39	Jh	18.09 N	94.25 W
Coatzacoalcos, Bahía- [S]	48	Lh	18.10 N	94.25 W
Coatzacoalcos, Río- [S]	48	Lh	18.09 N	94.24 W
Coba [S]	47	Gd	20.36 N	87.25 W
Cobadin	15	Le	44.45 N	28.13 E
Cobalt	42	Jg	47.24 N	79.41 W
Cobán	47	Fs	15.29 N	90.19 W
Cobar	59	Jf	31.30 S	145.49 E
Cobb, Mount- [▲]	46	Dg	38.45 N	122.40 W
Cobb Seamount (EN) [S]	38	Fe	46.46 N	130.43 W
Cóbh / An Cóbh	9	Ej	51.51 N	8.17 W
Cobija	54	Ef	11.02 S	68.44 W
Cobo	55	Dm	37.48 S	57.38 W
Cobourg	42	Jh	43.58 N	78.10 W
Cobourg Peninsula [▶]	59	Gb	11.20 S	132.15 E
Côbué	37	Eb	12.07 S	34.52 E
Coburg	10	Ga	50.15 N	10.58 E
Coburn Mountain [▲]	44	Lc	45.29 N	70.06 W
Coca, Pizzo di- [▲]	14	Ed	46.04 N	10.01 E
Cocalinho	55	Gb	14.22 S	51.00 W
Cocentaina	13	Lf	38.45 N	0.26 W
Cochabamba [2]	54	Eg	17.30 S	65.00 W
Cochabamba	53	Jg	17.24 S	66.09 W
Coche, Isla- [S]	50	Eg	10.47 N	63.56 W
Cochem	10	Df	50.09 N	7.10 E
Cochin	22	Ji	9.54 N	76.14 E
Cochin China (EN) = Nam Phan [▶]	21	Mg	11.00 N	107.00 E
Cochinos, Bahía de- = Pigs, Bay of- (EN) [S]	49	Gb	22.07 N	81.10 W
Cochrane	39	Kd	49.03 N	81.00 W
Cochrane [Alta.-Can.]	46	Na	51.11 N	114.28 W
Cochrane [Ont.-Can.]	39	Ke	49.04 N	81.01 W
Cockburn, Canal- [S]	56	Gh	54.20 S	71.50 W
Cockburn, Mount- [▲]	59	Gd	22.46 S	130.36 E
Cockburn Bank [S]	9	Ei	49.40 N	8.50 W
Cockburn Island [S]	44	Fc	45.55 N	83.25 W
Cockburn Town	49	Ja	24.02 N	74.31 W
Cockermouth	9	Jg	54.40 N	3.20 W
Coclé [3]	49	Gi	8.30 N	80.30 W
Coco, Cayo- [S]	49	Hb	22.30 N	78.20 W
Coco, Ile- [S]	51b Bc		17.52 S	62.40 W
Coco, Isla del- [S]	38	Ki	5.32 N	87.00 W
Coco, Rio- o Segovia, Rio- [S]	38	Kh	15.00 N	83.00 W
Cocoa	43	Kf	28.21 N	80.43 W
Cocoa Beach	44	Gk	28.19 N	80.36 W
Cocoa Point [▶]	51d Ba		17.33 N	61.44 W
Cocobeach	36	Ab	0.59 N	9.36 E
Coco Channel [S]	25	If	14.00 N	93.00 E
Coco Islands [S]	25	If	14.05 N	93.31 E
Coconino Plateau [▲]	46	Ii	35.50 N	112.30 W
Cocorpuma, Cayos- [S]	49	Ff	15.05 N	82.30 W
Côcos	55	Jb	14.10 S	44.33 W
Cocos Islands (Keeling Islands) [S]	21	Lk	12.10 S	96.55 E
Cocos Islands (Keeling Islands) [3]	21	Lk	12.10 S	96.55 E
Cocos Ridge (EN) [S]	3	Ni	5.30 N	86.00 W
Cocula	48	Hg	20.23 N	103.50 W
Cocuzzo [▲]	14	Kk	39.13 N	16.08 E
Cod, Cape- [▶]	44	Me	41.42 N	70.15 W
Cod, Cape- [▶]	38	Me	42.00 N	70.00 W
Coda Cavallo, Capo- [▶]	14	Dj	40.51 N	9.43 E
Codaești	15	Kc	46.52 N	27.45 E
Codajás	54	Fd	3.50 S	62.05 W
Codera, Cabo- [▶]	50	Dg	10.35 N	66.04 W
Codfish Island [S]	62	Bg	46.45 S	167.40 E
Codigoro	14	Gf	44.49 N	12.08 E
Codlea	15	Id	45.42 N	25.27 E
Codó	54	Jd	4.30 S	43.53 W
Codogno	14	De	45.09 N	9.42 E
Codrington	51d Ba		17.38 N	61.50 W
Codrington Lagoon [S]	51d Ba		17.40 N	61.49 W
Codrului, Munții- [▲]	15	Fc	46.35 N	22.10 E
Cody	43	Fc	44.32 N	109.03 W
Coen	58	Ff	13.56 S	143.12 E
Coesfeld	10	De	51.56 N	7.10 E
Coetivy Island [S]	30	Mi	7.08 S	56.16 E
Coeur d'Alene	43	Db	47.41 N	116.46 W

Name	Map	Grid	Lat	Long
Coevorden	11	Mb	52.40 N	6.45 E
Coffeyville	45	Ih	37.02 N	95.37 W
Coffs Harbour	58	Gh	30.18 S	153.08 E
Cofre de Perote, Cerro- (Nauhcampatépetl) [▲]	48	Kh	19.29 N	97.08 W
Cofrentes	13	Ke	39.14 N	1.04 W
Coggeshall	12	Cc	51.52 N	0.41 E
Coghinas [S]	14	Cj	40.56 N	8.48 E
Coghinas, Lago del- [S]	14	Dj	40.45 N	9.05 E
Cognac	6	Gf	45.42 N	0.20 W
Cogne	14	Be	45.37 N	7.21 E
Cogolludo	13	Id	40.57 N	3.05 W
Cogrăjskoje Vodohranilišče [S]	16	Ng	45.30 N	44.30 E
Coiba, Isla de- [S]	47	Ng	7.27 N	81.45 W
Coig, Río- (Coyle) [S]	56	Gh	50.58 S	69.11 W
Coihaique	56	Fg	45.34 S	72.04 W
Coimbatore	22	Jh	11.00 N	76.58 E
Coimbra [3]	13	Dd	40.12 N	8.25 W
Coimbra [Braz.]	55	Dd	19.55 S	57.47 W
Coimbra [Port.]	6	Fg	40.12 N	8.25 W
Coín	13	Hh	36.40 N	4.45 W
Coipasa, Salar de- [S]	54	Eg	19.30 S	68.10 W
Cojbalsan	22	Ne	48.04 N	114.30 E
Cojedes [2]	50	Bh	9.37 N	68.55 W
Cojedes [3]	54	Bb	9.20 N	68.20 W
Cojedes, Río- [S]	50	Bh	8.44 N	68.15 W
Cojutepeque	49	Cg	13.43 N	88.56 W
Coka	15	Dc	45.56 N	20.09 E
Cokeville	46	Je	42.05 N	110.55 W
Cokox\over River [S]	38	Hd	54.00 N	121.45 E
Cokurdah	20	Jb	70.38 N	147.55 E
Colac [Austl.]	59	Ig	38.20 S	143.35 E
Colac [N.Z.]	62	Bg	46.22 S	167.53 E
Colatina	54	Lh	20.40 S	31.30 W
Colbeck, Cape- [▶]	30	Il	32.49 S	17.51 E
Golbitz-Letzlinger Heide [▲]	10	Hd	52.27 N	11.35 E
Colby	45	Fg	39.24 N	101.03 W
Colchester	9	Nj	51.54 N	0.54 E
Cold Bay	40	Ge	55.11 N	162.30 W
Cold Lake	42	Gd	54.27 N	110.10 W
Coldstream	9	Kf	55.39 N	2.15 W
Coldwater [Ks.-U.S.]	45	Gh	37.16 N	99.19 W
Coldwater [Mi.-U.S.]	44	Ee	41.57 N	85.00 W
Colebrook	44	Lc	44.53 N	71.30 W
Coleman	45	Gk	31.50 N	99.26 W
Coleman River [S]	59	Ic	15.06 S	141.38 E
Coleraine	9	Gf	55.08 N	6.40 W
Coleridge, Lake- [S]	62	De	43.20 S	171.30 E
Coles, Punta- [▶]	54	Dg	17.42 S	71.23 W
Colesberg	37	Df	30.45 S	25.05 E
Colfax [La.-U.S.]	45	Jk	31.31 N	92.42 W
Colfax [Wa.-U.S.]	46	Gc	46.53 N	117.22 W
Col Visentin [▲]	14	Gd	46.05 N	12.20 E
Colima [2]	48	Hh	19.10 N	103.45 W
Colima	39	Jh	19.14 N	103.43 W
Colima, Nevado de- [▲]	48	Hh	19.33 N	103.38 W
Colinas	55	Hb	14.12 S	48.03 W
Coll [S]	9	Ge	56.40 N	6.35 W
Collado Bajo [▲]	13	Kd	40.14 N	1.50 W
Collarada [▲]	13	La	42.43 N	0.29 W
Colle di Val d'Elsa	14	Fg	43.25 N	11.07 E
Colleferro	14	Gi	41.44 N	12.59 E
College	40	Jd	64.51 N	147.47 W
College Place	46	Hc	46.03 N	118.23 W
College Station	45	Hk	30.37 N	96.21 W
Collegno	14	Be	45.05 N	7.34 E
Collie	59	Df	33.21 S	116.09 E
Collier Bay [S]	58	Ec	16.10 S	124.15 E
Collierville	44	Ch	35.03 N	89.40 W
Collingwood [N.Z.]	61	Bo	40.41 S	172.41 E
Collingwood [Ont.-Can.]	44	Gc	44.29 N	80.13 W
Collinson Peninsula [▶]	42	Hb	70.00 N	101.00 W
Collinsville	59	Jd	20.34 S	147.51 E
Collmberg [▲]	10	Je	51.15 N	13.02 E
Collmenar	13	If	36.54 N	4.20 W
Collooney	9	Eg	54.11 N	8.29 W
Colmar	6	Gf	48.05 N	7.22 E
Colmenar	13	Hh	36.54 N	4.20 W
Colmenar Viejo	13	Id	40.40 N	3.46 W
Colne [S]	12	Cc	51.51 N	0.59 E
Colne Point [▶]	12	Dc	51.46 N	1.03 E
Colnett, Punta- [▶]	48	Ab	31.00 N	116.20 W
Cologne (EN) = Köln	6	Ge	50.56 N	6.57 E
Colomb-Béchar	35	Ie	4.00 N	72.00 W
Colombia	55	Gk	26.10 S	48.40 W
Colombia [3]	54	Cc	3.24 N	76.16 W
Colombian Basin (EN) [S]	38	Lh	13.00 N	76.00 W
Colombier, Pointe à- [▶]	51b Bc		17.55 S	62.53 W
Colombo	22	Ji	6.56 N	79.51 E
Colón [Arg.]	56	Hd	33.53 S	61.07 W
Colón [Arg.]	56	Id	32.13 S	58.08 W
Colón [Cuba]	47	Hd	22.43 N	80.54 W
Colón [Hond.] [3]	49	Ef	15.20 N	84.30 W
Colón [Pan.] [3]	49	Hi	9.20 N	79.15 W
Colón [Pan.]	38	Li	9.22 N	79.54 W
Colón [Ur.]	55	Ek	33.53 S	54.43 W
Colón, Archipiélago de- / Galápagos, Islas- [S]	38	Kh	0.00	91.00 W
Colón, Montañas de- [▲]	49	Ef	14.55 N	84.45 W
Colonarie	51b Ba		13.14 N	61.08 W
Colonarie [S]	51b Ba		13.14 N	61.08 W
Colonial Hill	49	Jb	22.52 N	74.15 W
Colonia [2]	56	Id	34.10 S	57.50 W
Colonia	56	Be	9.31 N	138.08 E
Colonia agrícola de Turén	50	Bh	9.23 N	69.05 W
Colonia Carlos Pellegrini	55	Di	28.32 S	57.10 W
Colonia del Sacramento	56	Id	34.28 S	57.51 W
Colonia Elisa	55	Eh	26.55 S	59.33 W
Colonia Juárez	48	Eb	30.19 N	108.05 W
Colonia Lavalleja	55	Di	31.06 S	57.01 W

Name	Map	Grid	Lat	Long
Colonia Morelos	48	Eb	30.50 N	109.10 W
Colonne, Capo- [▶]	14	Lk	39.02 N	17.12 E
Colonsay [S]	9	Ge	56.05 N	6.10 W
Colorado	49	Fh	10.46 N	83.35 W
Colorado, Cerro- [▲]	48	Bb	31.31 N	115.31 W
Colorado, Río- [Arg.] [S]	52	Ji	39.50 S	62.08 W
Colorado, Río- [N.Amer.] [S]	38	Hf	31.45 N	114.40 W
Colorado City	45	Fj	32.24 N	100.52 W
Colorado Plateau [▲]	38	Hf	36.30 N	118.00 W
Colorado River [N.Amer.] [S]	38	Hf	31.45 N	114.40 W
Colorado River [N.Amer.] [S]	38	Jg	28.36 N	95.58 W
Colorados, Archipiélago de los- [S]	49	Eb	22.36 N	84.20 W
Colorado Springs	39	If	38.50 N	104.49 W
Colotlán	48	If	22.03 N	103.16 W
Colpon-Ata	18	Kc	42.39 N	77.06 E
Colthshall	12	Db	52.44 N	1.22 E
Colui [S]	36	Cf	15.10 S	16.40 E
Columbia [Ky.-U.S.]	44	Eg	37.06 N	85.18 W
Columbia [Mo.-U.S.]	39	Jf	38.57 N	92.20 W
Columbia [Ms.-U.S.]	45	Lk	31.15 N	89.56 W
Columbia [Pa.-U.S.]	44	Ie	40.02 N	76.30 W
Columbia [S.C.-U.S.]	39	Kf	34.00 N	81.03 W
Columbia [Tn.-U.S.]	44	Dh	35.37 N	87.02 W
Columbia, Mount- [▲]	38	La	52.08 N	117.25 W
Columbia Basin [▶]	43	Db	46.45 N	119.05 W
Columbia Falls	46	Hb	48.23 N	114.11 W
Columbia Mountains [▲]	38	Hd	52.00 N	119.00 W
Columbia Plateau [▲]	38	Ge	44.00 N	117.30 W
Columbia Seamount (EN) [S]	54	Lh	20.40 S	31.30 W
Columbretes, Islas- / Columbrets, Els- [S]	13	Me	39.52 N	0.40 E
Columbrets, Els- / Columbretes, Islas- [S]	13	Me	39.52 N	0.40 E
Columbus [Ga.-U.S.]	39	Kf	32.29 N	84.59 W
Columbus [In.-U.S.]	43	Jd	39.13 N	85.55 W
Columbus [Ks.-U.S.]	45	Ih	37.10 N	94.50 W
Columbus [Ms.-U.S.]	44	Ci	33.30 N	88.25 W
Columbus [Mt.-U.S.]	46	Kd	45.38 N	109.15 W
Columbus [Nb.-U.S.]	43	Hc	41.26 N	97.22 W
Columbus [N.M.-U.S.]	45	Ck	31.50 N	107.38 W
Columbus [Tx.-U.S.]	45	Hl	29.42 N	96.33 W
Columbus Point [▶]	49	Ja	24.08 N	75.16 W
Colville	38	Dc	70.25 N	150.30 W
Colville, Cape- [▶]	62	Fb	36.28 S	175.21 E
Colville Channel [S]	62	Fb	36.25 S	175.30 E
Colville Lake [S]	42	Ec	67.10 N	126.00 W
Colville Lake	42	Ec	67.06 N	126.00 W
Colwyn Bay	9	Jh	53.18 N	3.43 W
Comacchio	14	Gf	44.42 N	12.11 E
Comacchio, Valli di- [S]	14	Gf	44.40 N	12.05 E
Comai (Damxoi)	27	Ff	28.26 N	91.32 E
Comala	48	Hh	19.19 N	103.45 W
Coman, Mount- [▲]	66	Qf	73.49 S	64.18 W
Comanche [Tx.-U.S.]	45	Gk	31.54 N	98.36 W
Comandante Fontana	55	Cg	25.20 S	59.41 W
Comandău	15	Jd	45.46 N	26.16 E
Comănești	15	Jc	46.25 N	26.26 E
Comayagua [3]	49	Df	14.30 N	87.40 W
Comayagua	47	Gf	14.25 N	87.37 W
Combahee [S]	44	Gi	32.30 N	80.31 W
Combeaufontaine	11	Lg	47.43 S	5.53 E
Combermere Bay [S]	25	Ie	19.37 N	93.34 E
Comblain-au-Pont	12	Hd	50.28 N	5.35 E
Combles	12	Ed	50.01 N	2.52 E
Combourg	11	Ef	48.25 N	1.45 W
Combraille [▶]	11	Jh	46.30 N	3.10 E
Combrailles [▶]	11	Jh	46.15 N	3.10 E
Comedero	55	Fe	24.37 N	106.46 W
Comendador	49	Ld	18.53 N	71.42 W
Comeragh Mountains / Na Comaraigh [▲]	9	Fi	52.13 N	7.35 W
Comerío	51a Bb		18.13 N	66.16 W
Comilla	25	Id	23.27 N	91.12 E
Comines	12	Fd	50.46 N	3.01 E
Comines / Komen	12	Fd	50.46 N	3.01 E
Comino, Cape- [▶]	14	Dj	40.32 N	9.49 E
Comiso	14	Jm	36.56 N	14.36 E
Comitán de Domínguez	47	Fe	16.15 N	92.08 W
Commentry	11	Jh	46.17 N	2.45 E
Commerce	45	Ij	33.15 N	95.54 W
Commercy	11	Lf	48.45 N	5.35 E
Committee Bay [S]	42	Ic	68.30 N	86.30 W
Commonwealth Bay [S]	66	Je	66.54 S	142.40 E
Communism Peak (EN) = Kommunizma, Pik- [▲]	21	Jf	38.57 N	72.08 E
Como [China]	27	Ee	33.26 N	85.21 E
Como [It.]	39	Sh	45.47 N	9.05 E
Como, Lago di- [S]	14	De	46.00 N	9.15 E
Comodoro	55	Bl	35.59 S	60.31 W
Comodoro Rivadavia	53	Jj	45.50 S	67.30 W
Comondú	47	Bc	26.03 N	111.46 W
Comores, Archipel des / Comoros [S]	31	Lj	12.10 S	44.10 E
Comores, Archipel des- = Comoros [3]	30	Lj	12.10 S	44.15 E
Comorin, Cape- [▶]	21	Ji	8.04 N	77.34 E
Comoros, Archipel des- / Comores [S]	30	Lj	12.10 S	44.15 E
Comoros (EN) [3]	30	Lj	13.00 S	44.15 E
Comoros / Comores [3]	31	Lj	12.10 S	44.10 E
Compiègne	11	Ie	49.25 N	2.50 E
Comprida, Ilha- [S]	55	Ig	24.50 S	47.42 W
Comstock	45	Fl	29.41 N	101.11 W
Comtal, Causse du- [▶]	11	Ij	44.26 N	2.38 E

Index Symbols

[1] Independent Nation	[▲] Historical or Cultural Region	[◊] Pass, Gap
[2] State, Region	[▲] Mount, Mountain	[▲] Plain, Lowland
[3] District, County	[▲] Volcano	[▲] Delta
[4] Municipality	[▲] Hill	[▲] Salt Flat
[5] Colony, Dependency	[▲] Mountains, Mountain Range	[▲] Valley, Canyon
[▲] Continent	[▲] Hills, Escarpment	[▲] Crater, Cave
[▲] Physical Region	[▲] Plateau, Upland	[▲] Karst Features

[▲] Depression	[▲] Coast, Beach	[▲] Rock, Reef
[▲] Polder	[▲] Cliff	[▲] Islands, Archipelago
[▲] Desert, Dunes	[▲] Peninsula	[▲] Rocks, Reefs
[▲] Forest, Woods	[▲] Isthmus	[▲] Coral Reef
[▲] Heath, Steppe	[▲] Sandbank	[▲] Well, Spring
[▲] Oasis	[▲] Island	[▲] Geyser
[▲] Cape, Point	[▲] Atoll	[▲] River, Stream

[▲] Waterfall Rapids	[▲] Canal	[▲] Lagoon
[▲] River Mouth, Estuary	[▲] Glacier	[▲] Bank
[▲] Lake	[▲] Ice Shelf, Pack Ice	[▲] Seamount
[▲] Salt Lake	[▲] Ocean	[▲] Tableland
[▲] Intermittent Lake	[▲] Sea	[▲] Ridge
[▲] Reservoir	[▲] Gulf, Bay	[▲] Shelf
[▲] Swamp, Pond	[▲] Strait, Fjord	[▲] Basin

[▲] Escarpment, Sea Scarp	[▲] Historic Site	[▲] Port
[▲] Fracture	[▲] Ruins	[▲] Lighthouse
[▲] Trench, Abyss	[▲] Wall, Walls	[▲] Mine
[▲] National Park, Reserve	[▲] Church, Abbey	[▲] Tunnel
[▲] Point of Interest	[▲] Temple	[▲] Dam, Bridge
[▲] Recreation Site	[▲] Scientific Station	
[▲] Cave, Cavern	[▲] Airport	

Index Symbols

	Independent Nation
	State, Region
	District, County
	Municipality
	Colony, Dependency
	Continent
	Physical Region
	Historical or Cultural Region
	Mount, Mountain
	Volcano
	Hill
	Mountains, Mountain Range
	Hills, Escarpment
	Plateau, Upland
	Pass, Gap
	Plain, Lowland
	Delta
	Salt Flat
	Valley, Canyon
	Crater, Cave
	Karst Features
	Depression
	Polder
	Desert, Dunes
	Forest, Woods
	Heath, Steppe
	Oasis
	Cape, Point
	Coast, Beach
	Cliff
	Peninsula
	Isthmus
	Sandbank
	Island
	Atoll
	Rock, Reef
	Islands, Archipelago
	Rocks, Reefs
	Coral Reef
	Well, Spring
	Geyser
	Waterfall Rapids
	River Mouth, Estuary
	Lake
	Salt Lake
	Intermittent Lake
	Sea
	Reservoir
	Canal
	Bank
	Ice Shelf, Pack Ice
	Ocean
	Ridge
	Gulf, Bay
	River, Stream
	Lagoon
	Glacier
	Seamount
	Tablemount
	Shelf
	Basin
	Escarpment, Sea Scarp
	Fracture
	Trench, Abyss
	National Park, Reserve
	Point of Interest
	Recreation Site
	Cave, Cavern
	Strait, Fjord
	Historic Site
	Ruins
	Wall, Walls
	Church, Abbey
	Temple
	Scientific Station
	Airport
	Port
	Lighthouse
	Mine
	Tunnel
	Dam, Bridge

D

Index Symbols

Dainanji-San 29 Ec 36.36N 137.42 E
Dainichi-San 29 Ec 36.09N 136.30 E
Dainkog 27 Ge 32.31N 97.59 E
Daiō-Zaki 28 Ng 34.22N 136.53 E
Dairan (EN)=Dalian (Lüda) 22 Of 38.55N 121.39 E
Dairan (EN) = Lüda→Dalian 22 Of 38.55N 121.39 E
Dairbhre/Valentia 9 Cj 51.55N 10.20W
Daireaux 55 Bm 36.36S 61.45W
Dai-Sen 29 Cd 35.24N 133.34 E
Daisengen-Dake 29a Bc 41.35N 140.09 E
Daishan (Gaotingzhen) 28 Gi 30.15N 122.13 E
Daitō [Jap.] 29 Cd 35.19N 132.58 E
Daitō [Jap.] 29 Gb 39.02N 141.22 E
Daito Islands (EN)=Daitō Shotō 21 Pg 25.00N 131.15 E
Daitō Shotō=Daito Islands (EN) 21 Pg 25.00N 131.15 E
Daitō-Zaki 29 Gd 35.18N 140.24 E
Daixian 28 Be 39.03N 112.57 E
Daiyue→Shanyin 28 Be 39.30N 112.48 E
Dajabón 49 Ld 19.33N 71.42W
Dajarra 58 Eg 21.42S 139.31 E
Dajtit, Mali i- 15 Ch 41.22N 19.55 E
Daka 34 Ed 8.19N 0.13W
Dakar 31 Fg 14.40N 17.26W
Dākhilah, Wāḥāt al-= Dakhla Oasis (EN) 30 Jf 25.30N 29.10 E
Dakhla Oasis (EN)= Dākhilah, Wāḥāt al- 30 Jf 25.30N 29.10 E
Dakhlet Nouâdhibou [3] 32 De 20.30N 16.00W
Dakla 31 Ff 23.42N 15.56W
Dakoro 34 Gc 14.30N 6.25 E
Đakovo 14 Me 45.19N 18.25 E
Daksti 8 Kg 57.38N 25.32 E
Dak To 25 Lf 14.42N 107.51 E
Dal 8 Dd 60.15N 11.12 E
Dal, Jökulsá á- 7a Cb 65.40N 14.20W
Đala 15 Dc 46.09N 20.07 E
Dala [Ang.] 36 De 11.03S 20.17 E
Dala [Sol.Is.] 63a c 8.36S 160.41 E
Dalaba 34 Cc 10.42N 12.15W
Dalai → Da'an 27 Lb 45.35N 124.16 E
Dalai Nur 27 Kc 43.18N 116.15 E
Dala-Järna 8 Fd 60.33N 14.21 E
Dālakī 24 Nh 29.19N 51.06 E
Dalälven 5 Hc 60.38N 17.27 E
Dalaman 24 Cd 36.48N 28.45 E
Dalaman 15 Lm 36.44N 28.49 E
Dalāmī 35 Ec 11.52N 30.28 E
Dalān 24 Kj 24.15N 45.47 E
Dalan-Dzadgad 22 Me 43.47N 104.29 E
Dalane 8 Bf 58.35N 6.20 E
Dalarna 8 Fd 61.00N 14.05 E
Dalarö 8 He 59.08N 18.24 E
Da Lat 22 Mh 11.56N 108.25 E
Dālbandin 25 Cc 28.53N 64.25 E
Dalbosjön 8 Ef 58.45N 12.50 E
Dalboslätten 8 Ef 58.35N 12.25 E
Dalby 59 Ke 27.11S 151.16 E
Dale [Nor.] 7 Af 60.35N 5.49 E
Dale [Nor.] 7 Af 61.22N 5.25 E
Dale Hollow Lake 44 Eg 36.36N 85.19W
Dalen 7 Bg 59.27N 8.00 E
Dalfsen 12 Ib 52.30N 6.14 E
Dalgaranger, Mount- 59 De 27.51S 117.06 E
Dălgopol 15 Kf 43.03N 27.21 E
Dalhart 43 Gd 36.04N 102.31W
Dalhousie 42 Kg 48.04N 66.23W
Dalhousie, Cape- 42 Eb 70.15N 129.41W
Dali [China] 22 Mg 25.43N 100.07 E
Dali [China] 27 Ie 34.55N 110.00 E
Dalian (Lüda) = Dairan (EN) 22 Of 38.55N 121.39 E
Dalias 13 Jh 36.49N 2.52W
Daling He 28 Fd 40.56N 121.44 E
Dalizi 27 Mc 41.45N 126.50 E
Dalj 14 Me 45.29N 18.59 E
Daljā' 33 Fd 27.39N 30.42 E
Dalkowskie, Wzgórza- 10 Le 51.35N 15.50 E
Dall [Ak.-U.S.] 40 Mf 54.50N 132.55W
Dall [Can.] 2 Ef 55.00N 133.00W
Dallas [Or.-U.S.] 46 Dd 44.55N 123.19W
Dallas [Tx.-U.S.] 39 Jf 32.47N 96.48W
Dalmā' 24 Oj 24.30N 52.20 E
Dalmā', Qārat- 33 Dd 25.32N 23.57 E
Dalmacija 14 Kg 43.00N 17.00 E
Dalmacija = Dalmatia (EN) 5 Hg 43.00N 17.00 E
Dalmaj, Hawr- 24 Kf 32.20N 45.28 E
Dalmally 9 Ie 56.24N 4.58W
Dalmatia (EN) = Dalmacija 5 Hg 43.00N 17.00 E
Dalmatovo 17 Kh 56.16N 63.00 E
Dalnegorsk 22 Pe 44.31N 135.31 E
Dalnerečensk 22 Pe 45.55N 133.45 E
Dalni 20 Kf 53.15N 157.30 E
Dalni 20 Ih 44.57N 135.03 E
Dalnjaja, Gora- 20 Mc 68.08N 179.53 E
Daloa [3] 34 Dd 6.58N 6.23W
Daloa 31 Gh 6.53N 6.27W
Dalou Shan 21 Mg 28.00N 106.40 E
Dalqū 35 Ea 20.07N 30.35 E
Dalrymple, Mount- 57 Fg 21.02S 148.38 E
Dalsbruk 8 Jd 60.02N 22.31 E
Dalsbruk/Taalintendas 8 Jd 60.02N 22.31 E
Dalsfjorden 8 Ac 61.20N 5.05 E
Dalsjöfors 8 Eg 57.43N 13.05 E
Dalsland 8 Ef 58.35N 12.55 E
Dalslands kanal 8 Ef 58.50N 12.25 E
Dals Långed 7 Cg 58.55N 12.18 E
Dalton 44 Eh 34.47N 84.58W
Daltonganj 25 Gd 24.02N 84.04 E
Dalul 35 Gc 14.22N 40.21 E
Daluo 27 Hg 21.38N 100.15 E
Dalupiri 26 Hc 19.05N 121.12 E
Dalvík 7a Bb 65.58N 18.32W
Dalwallinu 59 Df 30.17S 116.40 E
Dalyan 15 Lm 36.50N 28.39 E
Daly Bay 42 Id 64.00N 89.40W
Daly City 46 Dh 37.42N 122.29W
Daly River 57 Ef 13.20S 130.19 E
Daly Waters 59 Gc 16.15S 133.22 E
Damā, Wādī- 24 Fi 27.09N 35.47 E
Damagarim 34 Gc 13.42N 9.00 E
Damān [3] 25 Ed 20.10N 73.00 E
Damanhūr 33 Fc 31.02N 30.28 E
Damar, Pulau- 26 Ih 7.09S 128.40 E
Damara 35 Be 4.58N 18.42 E
Damaraland 37 Bd 21.00S 17.30 E
Damas Cays 49 Hb 23.58N 79.55W
Damascus (EN)=Dimashq 22 Ff 33.30N 36.15 E
Dāmāsh 24 Md 36.46N 49.46 E
Damaturu 34 Hc 11.45N 11.58 E
Damāvand 24 He 35.56N 52.08 E
Damāvand, Qolleh-ye- 21 Hf 35.56N 52.08 E
Damba 36 Cd 6.50S 15.07 E
Dambaslar 15 Kh 41.13N 27.14 E
Dame Marie, Cap- 47 Je 18.36N 74.26W
Damergou 30 Hg 15.00N 9.00 E
Dāmghān 24 Pd 36.09N 54.22 E
Damianópolis 55 Ib 14.33S 46.10W
Damiao 27 He 30.52N 104.38 E
Damietta (EN)=Dumyāṭ 31 Ke 31.25N 31.48 E
Daming 28 Cf 36.17N 115.09 E
Daming Shan 27 Ig 23.23N 108.30 E
Damīr Qābū 24 Id 36.54N 41.47 E
Dammartin en Goële 12 Ee 49.03N 2.41 E
Dammastock 14 Cd 46.38N 8.25 E
Damme [Bel.] 12 Fc 51.15N 3.17 E
Damme [Ger.] 12 Kb 52.31N 8.12 E
Dammer Berge 12 Kb 52.35N 8.17 E
Damoh 25 Fd 23.50N 79.27 E
Damongo 34 Ed 9.05N 1.49W
Damous 13 Nh 36.33N 1.42 E
Dampier 58 Cg 20.39S 116.45 E
Dampier, Selat-=Dampier Strait (EN) 26 Jg 0.40S 130.40 E
Dampier Archipelago 59 Dd 20.35S 116.35 E
Dampier Land 59 Ec 17.30S 122.55 E
Dampierre 12 Df 48.42N 1.59 E
Dampier Strait 59 Ja 5.36S 148.12 E
Dampier Strait (EN)= Dampier, Selat- 26 Jg 0.40S 130.40 E
Damqawt 23 Hf 16.34N 52.50 E
Damqog Kanbab/Maquan He 27 Df 29.36N 84.09 E
Dam Qu 27 Fe 33.56N 92.41 E
Damville 12 Df 48.52N 1.04 E
Damvillers 12 He 49.20N 5.24 E
Damwoude, Dantumadeel- 12 Ha 53.18N 5.59 E
Damxoi → Comai 27 Ff 28.26N 91.32 E
Damxung 27 Fe 30.34N 91.16 E
Danakil=Danakil Plain (EN) 30 Lg 12.25N 40.30 E
Danakil Plain (EN)= Danakil 30 Lg 12.25N 40.30 E
Danané [3] 34 Dd 7.25N 8.10W
Danané 34 Dd 7.16N 8.09W
Da Nang 22 Mh 16.04N 108.13 E
Danba/Rongzhag 27 He 30.48N 101.54 E
Danbury 44 Ke 41.23N 73.27W
Danby Lake 46 Hi 34.14N 115.07W
Dancheng 28 Ch 33.36N 115.14 E
Dancheng→Xiangshan 27 Lf 29.29N 121.52 E
Dandarah 33 Fd 26.10N 32.39 E
Dandeldhura 25 Gc 29.18N 80.35 E
Dandenong, Melbourne- 59 Jg 37.59S 145.12 E
Dandong 22 Oe 40.10N 124.15 E
Daneborg 41 Jd 74.25N 20.10W
Danells Fjord 41 Hf 60.45N 42.45W
Daneţi 15 Hf 43.59N 24.03 E
Danfeng (Longjuzhai) 27 Je 33.44N 110.22 E
Danforth Hills 45 Cf 40.15N 108.00W
Danfu 63a Aa 4.12S 153.04 E
Dangara 19 Gh 38.09N 69.22 E
Dangchengwan → Subei 27 Fd 39.36N 94.58 E
Dang He 27 Fc 40.30N 94.42 E
Dangjin Shankou 21 Lf 39.15N 94.30 E
Dangla 35 Fc 11.16N 36.50 E
Dangla Shan→ Tanggula Shan 21 Lf 33.00N 92.00 E
Dangoura, Mount- 35 Dd 6.12N 26.27 E
Dangrek Range (EN)=Dong Rak, Phanom- 21 Mh 14.25N 104.30 E
Dangshan 27 Ke 34.22N 116.21 E
Dangtu 28 Ei 31.33N 118.30 E
Dangu 12 De 49.15N 1.42 E
Dangyang 28 Ai 30.49N 111.47 E
Dan He 28 Bg 35.05N 112.59 E
Daniel 46 Je 42.52N 110.04W
Daniel, Serra- 55 Ea 13.40S 54.55W
Danielskuil 37 Ce 28.11S 23.33 E
Danilov 19 Ed 58.12N 40.13 E
Danilovgrad 15 Cg 42.33N 19.07 E
Danilovka 16 Nd 50.21N 44.06 E
Daning 27 Jd 36.31N 110.45 E
Danjiang → Junxian 27 Je 32.31N 111.32 E
Danjiangkou Shuiku 27 Je 32.37N 111.30 E
Danjo-Guntō 27 Me 32.00N 128.20 E
Dank 24 Qk 23.33N 56.16 E
Dankov 16 Kc 53.16N 39.07 E
Danli 49 Df 14.00N 86.35W
Danmark=Denmark (EN) [1] 6 Gd 56.00N 10.00 E
Danmark Fjord 67 Me 81.10N 23.20W
Danmarks Havn 67 Ld 76.50N 18.30W
Danmarksstraedet= Denmark Strait (EN) 38 Qc 67.00N 25.00W
Dannenberg 10 Hc 53.06N 11.06 E
Dannevirke 62 Gd 40.12S 176.06 E
Danot 35 Hd 7.33N 45.17 E
Dantumadeel 12 Ha 53.18N 5.59 E
Dantumadeel-Damwoude 12 Ha 53.18N 5.59 E
Danube (EN)=Donau 5 If 45.20N 29.40 E
Danube (EN)=Duna 5 If 45.20N 29.40 E
Danube (EN)=Dunaj 5 If 45.20N 29.40 E
Danube (EN)=Dunărea 5 If 45.20N 29.40 E
Danube (EN)=Dunav 5 If 45.20N 29.40 E
Danube, Mouths of the- (EN) = Dunării, Delta- 5 If 45.30N 29.45 E
Danville [Ar.-U.S.] 45 Ji 35.03N 93.24W
Danville [Il.-U.S.] 43 Jc 40.08N 87.37W
Danville [In.-U.S.] 44 Df 39.46N 86.32W
Danville [Ky.-U.S.] 43 Kd 37.39N 84.46W
Danville [Va.-U.S.] 43 Ld 36.34N 79.25W
Danxian (Nada) 27 Ih 19.38N 109.32 E
Danyang 28 Eh 32.00N 119.33 E
Danzig (EN)=Gdańsk 6 He 54.23N 18.40 E
Dao 26 Hd 10.31N 121.57 E
Dão 13 Dd 40.20N 8.11W
Daocheng/Dabba 27 Hf 29.01N 100.26 E
Daokou → Huaxian 28 Cg 35.33N 114.30 E
Daosa 25 Fc 26.53N 76.20 E
Dao Shui 28 Ci 30.42N 114.40 E
Dao Timni 34 Ha 20.38N 13.39 E
Daoura 32 Gd 29.03N 4.33W
Daoxian 27 Jf 25.37N 111.36 E
Dapaong 34 Fc 10.52N 0.12 E
Dapchi 34 Hc 12.29N 11.29 E
Daqing Shan 28 Ad 41.00N 111.00 E
Daqin Tal → Naiman Qi 27 Lc 42.49N 120.38 E
Daquing Shan 28 Ed 40.30N 119.38 E
Dar'ā 23 Ec 32.37N 36.06 E
Dārāb 24 Ph 28.45N 54.34 E
Darabani 15 Ja 48.11N 26.35 E
Daraçya Yarimadasi 15 Lm 36.40N 28.10 E
Darāfisah 35 Ec 13.23N 31.59 E
Dārān 24 Nf 32.59N 50.24 E
Darasun 20 Gf 51.39N 113.59 E
Daravica 15 Dg 42.32N 20.08 E
Darāw 24 Ej 24.25N 32.56 E
Darazo 34 Hc 11.00N 10.25 E
Darband 23 Ic 31.38N 57.02 E
Darband, Kūh-e- 24 Qg 31.34N 57.08 E
Darbandī Khān, Sad ad- 24 Ke 35.07N 45.50 E
Darbat Alī, Ra's- 23 Hf 16.43N 53.33 E
Darbėnai/Darbenaj 8 Ih 56.02N 21.08 E
Dar Ben Karriche el Bahri 13 Gi 35.51N 5.21W
Darbhanga 25 Hc 26.10N 85.54 E
Dārboruk 35 Gd 9.44N 44.31 E
Darby 46 He 46.01N 114.11W
Darchan → Darhan 22 Me 49.33N 106.21 E
Darda 14 Me 45.38N 18.42 E
Dardanelle Lake 45 Ji 35.25N 93.20W
Dardanelles (EN)= Çanakkale Boğazi 5 Ig 40.15N 26.25 E
Dardo/Kangding 27 He 30.01N 101.58 E
Dar el Kouti 30 Jh 8.50N 21.50 E
Darende 24 Gc 38.34N 37.30 E
Dar es Salaam [3] 36 Gd 6.50S 39.02 E
Dar es Salaam 31 Ki 6.48S 39.17 E
Darfield 62 Ee 43.29S 172.07 E
Darfo Boario Terme 14 Ee 45.53N 10.11 E
Dārfūr 30 Jg 12.40N 24.20 E
Dārfūr al Janūbīyah [3] 35 Dc 11.30N 25.10 E
Dārfūr ash Shamālīyah [3] 35 Db 16.00N 25.30 E
Dargan-Ata 19 Gg 40.29N 62.12 E
Dargaville 61 Dg 35.56S 173.52 E
Darhan (Darchan) 22 Me 49.33N 106.21 E
Darhan Muminggan Lianheqi 27 Jc 41.45N 110.24 E
Darica [Tur.] 15 Kj 40.00N 27.50 E
Darica [Tur.] 15 Mi 40.45N 29.23 E
Darién 47 Ig 8.30N 77.30W
Darien 44 Gj 31.22N 81.26W
Darién [3] 49 Ii 8.10N 77.45W
Darién, Golfo de- 52 Ie 8.25N 76.53W
Darién, Serrania del- 47 Ig 8.30N 77.30W
Dariense, Cordillera- 49 Eg 12.55N 85.30W
Darja 18 Ee 38.13N 65.46 E
Darjeeling → Dārjiling 25 Hc 27.02N 88.16 E
Dārjiling 25 Hc 27.02N 88.16 E
Dar-Kebdani 13 Ii 35.07N 3.21W
Dark Head 51n Ba 13.17N 61.17W
Dārkhovīn 24 Mg 30.45N 48.25 E
Darlag 27 Ge 33.49N 99.08 E
Darling 37 Bf 33.23S 18.23 E
Darling Downs 59 Ke 27.30S 150.30 E
Darling Range 57 Ch 32.00S 116.30 E
Darling River 57 Fh 34.07S 141.55 E
Darlington [Eng.-U.K.] 9 Lg 54.31N 1.34W
Darlington [S.C.-U.S.] 44 Hh 34.19N 79.53W
Darłowo 10 Mb 54.26N 16.23 E
Darmouth 9 Jk 50.21N 3.35W
Darmstadt 10 Eg 49.52N 8.39 E
Darnah 31 Je 32.46N 22.39 E
Darnah [3] 33 Dc 31.00N 23.40 E
Darnétal 12 De 49.27N 1.09 E
Darney 11 Mf 48.05N 6.03 E
Darnley, Cape- 66 Fe 67.43S 69.30 E
Darnley Bay 42 Fc 69.45N 123.45W
Daroca 13 Kc 41.07N 1.25W
Darou Khoudos 34 Bb 15.06N 16.50W
Darovskoj 7 Lg 58.47N 47.59 E
Darrah, Mount- 46 Hb 49.28N 114.35W
Darregueira 56 He 37.42S 63.10W
Darrehshahr 24 Lf 33.10N 47.18 E
D'Arros Island 37b Bb 5.24S 53.18 E
Dar Rounga 30 Jg 10.45N 22.20 E
Dar Sila 35 Cc 12.11N 21.21 E
Darss 10 Ib 54.25N 12.31 E
Darßer Ort 10 Ib 54.29N 12.31 E
Dart 9 Jk 50.20N 3.33W
Dart, Cape- 66 Nf 73.06S 126.20W
D'Artagnan Bank (EN) 59 Eb 13.00S 121.00 E
Dartang → Baqên 27 Fe 31.58N 94.00 E
Dartford 12 Cc 51.27N 0.13 E
Dartmoor 9 Jk 50.35N 4.00W
Dartmouth 42 Lh 44.40N 63.34W
Dartuch, Cabo- 13 Pe 39.56N 3.48 E
Daru 60 Ci 9.04S 143.12 E
Daruneh 24 Qe 35.10N 57.18 E
Daruvar 14 Le 45.35N 17.14 E
Darvaza 19 Fg 40.15N 58.24 E
Darvel, Teluk- 26 Gf 4.50N 118.30 E
Darwin 58 Ef 12.28S 130.50 E
Darwin, Bahía- 56 Fg 45.27S 74.40W
Darwin, Isla- 54a Aa 1.39N 92.00W
Darwin, Port- 59 Gb 12.20S 130.40 E
Dar Zagaoua 35 Cb 15.15N 23.14 E
Dar Zebada 35 Bc 13.45N 18.50 E
Dās 24 Oj 25.09N 52.53 E
Dašava 10 Ug 49.13N 24.05 E
Daš-Balbar 27 Jb 49.31N 114.21 E
Dasha He 28 Ce 38.27N 114.39 E
Dashengtang Shan 28 Dc 42.07N 117.12 E
Dashennongjia 27 Je 31.47N 114.12 E
Dashennongjia 27 Je 31.26N 110.18 E
Dashiqiao → Yingkou 28 Gd 40.39N 122.31 E
Dashitou 28 Jc 43.18N 128.29 E
Dasht 24 Qd 37.17N 56.04 E
Dasht Āb 24 Qh 28.59N 56.32 E
Dashtak 24 Og 30.23N 52.30 E
Dasht-e-Āzādegan 24 Mg 31.32N 48.10 E
Daškesan 16 Oi 40.30N 46.03 E
Dasseneiland 37 Bf 33.26S 18.05 E
Dastgardān 24 Qe 34.19N 56.51 E
Dastjerd-e Qaddādeh 24 Nf 32.44N 51.32 E
Datça 24 Bd 36.45N 27.40 E
Date 28 Pc 42.27N 140.51 E
Dāth, Sha'īb ad- 24 Jj 25.45N 43.10 E
Datia 25 Fc 25.40N 78.28 E
Datian Ding 27 Jg 22.17N 111.13 E
Datil 45 Ci 34.09N 107.47W
Datong [China] 27 Hd 36.56N 101.40 E
Datong [China] 22 Ne 40.09N 113.17 E
Datteln 12 Jc 51.40N 7.23 E
Datteln-Hamm Kanal 12 Jc 51.39N 7.21 E
Datu 21 Mi 2.05N 109.39 E
Datu, Teluk 21 Ni 2.00N 111.00 E
Datu Plang 26 He 6.58N 124.40 E
Dāūd Khel 25 Eb 32.53N 71.34 E
Daudzeva 8 Kh 56.28N 25.18 E
Daugaard-Jensen Land 41 Fb 80.10N 63.30W
Daugaj/Daugai 8 Kj 54.20N 24.28 E
Daugava=Dvina(EN) 19 Cd 57.04N 24.03 E
Daugavpils 6 Id 55.53N 26.32 E
Daule 54 Cd 1.50S 79.57W
Daun 10 Cf 50.12N 6.50 E
Daung Kyun 25 Jf 12.14N 98.05 E
Daunia, Monti della- 14 Ji 41.25N 15.05 E
Dauphin 42 Hf 51.09N 100.03W
Dauphiné 11 Lj 44.50N 6.00 E
Dauphin Lake 42 Hf 51.15N 99.45W
Daura 34 Gc 13.02N 8.18 E
Dautphetal 12 Kd 50.52N 8.33 E
Dāvangere 25 Ff 14.28N 75.55 E
Davao 22 Oi 7.04N 125.36 E
Davao Gulf 21 Oi 6.40N 125.55 E
Dāvarān, Kūh-e- 24 Qg 30.40N 56.15 E
Dāvar Panāh 23 Jd 27.21N 62.21 E
Dāvarzan 24 Qd 36.23N 56.50 E
Đavat 15 Eh 41.04N 21.06 E
Davenport [Ia.-U.S.] 39 Je 41.32N 90.41W
Davenport [Wa.-U.S.] 46 Fc 47.39N 118.09W
Davenport Range 59 Gd 20.45S 134.50 E
Daventry 12 Ab 52.15N 1.10W
Davert 12 Jc 51.51N 7.36 E
Davey, Port- 59 Jh 43.20S 145.55 E
David 39 Ki 8.25N 82.27W
David City 45 Hf 41.15N 97.08W
David-Gorodok 16 Ec 52.03N 27.13 E
David Point 51p Bb 12.14N 61.39W
Davidson 46 Ma 51.18N 105.59W
Davidson Mountains 40 Kc 68.45N 142.10W
Davies, Mount- 59 Fe 26.14S 129.16 E
Davis 43 Cd 38.33N 121.44W
Davis 66 Fe 68.35S 77.58 E
Davis, Cape- 66 Ee 66.24S 56.50 E
Davis, Mount- 44 Hf 39.47N 79.10W
Davis Bay 66 Ie 66.08S 134.05 E
Davis Inlet 42 Le 56.00N 61.30W
Davis Mountains 45 Ek 30.35N 104.00W
Davis Sea (EN) 66 Ge 66.00S 92.00 E
Davisstrædet = Davis Strait (EN) 38 Nc 68.00N 58.00W
Davis Strait 38 Nc 68.00N 58.00W
Davis Strait (EN) = Davisstrædet 38 Nc 68.00N 58.00W
Davlekanovo 19 Fe 54.13N 55.03 E
Davo 34 Dd 5.00N 6.08W
Davos/Tavau 14 Dd 46.47N 9.50 E
Davutlar 15 Kl 37.43N 27.17 E
Dawa 28 Gd 40.58N 122.01 E
Dawanlē 35 Gc 11.06N 42.38 E
Dawāsir, Wādī ad- 21 Gg 20.24N 46.29 E
Dawei 22 Lh 14.05N 98.12 E
Dawen He 28 Dg 35.37N 116.23 E
Dawes Range 59 Kd 24.30S 151.10 E
Dawḩarab 33 Hf 16.17N 41.57 E
Dawson [Ga.-U.S.] 44 Ej 31.47N 84.26W
Dawson [Yuk.-Can.] 39 Fc 64.04N 139.25W
Dawson, Mount- 46 Ga 51.09N 117.25W
Dawson Creek 39 Gd 55.45N 120.07W
Dawson-Lambton Glacier 66 Af 76.15S 27.30W
Dawson Range 42 Dd 65.15N 137.45W
Dawson River 59 Jd 23.38S 149.46 E
Dawu 27 He 30.45N 101.11 E
Dawu (Erlangdian) 28 Ci 31.33N 114.07 E
Dawu → Maqên 27 He 34.29N 100.01 E
Dawukou → Shizuishan 27 Id 39.03N 106.24 E
Dax 11 Ek 43.43N 1.03W
Da Xi 28 Ej 28.10N 120.14 E
Daxian 27 Ie 31.15N 107.28 E
Daxin 27 Ig 22.52N 107.14 E
Daxing 28 De 39.45N 116.19 E
Daxinggou 28 Jc 43.23N 129.39 E
Daxue Shan 21 Mf 30.30N 101.30 E
Dayan → Lijiang 22 Mg 26.56N 100.15 E
Dayang He 28 Ge 39.52N 123.40 E
Dayao 27 Hf 25.49N 101.18 E
Daye 28 Ci 30.05N 114.58 E
Dayishan → Guanyun 28 Eg 34.18N 119.14 E
Daymán, Cuchilla del- 55 Dj 31.38S 57.10W
Daymán, Río- 55 Dj 31.40S 58.02W
Daym Zubayr 35 Dd 7.43N 26.13 E
Dayong 27 Jf 29.09N 110.30 E
Dayr, Jabal ad- 35 Ec 12.27N 30.45 E
Dayr az Zawr 22 Gf 35.20N 40.09 E
Dayr Ḩāfir 24 Gd 36.09N 37.42 E
Dayr Kātrīnā = Saint Catherine Monastery of- (EN) 33 Fd 28.31N 33.57 E
Dayr Mawās 24 Di 27.38N 30.51 E
Dayrūṭ 33 Fd 27.33N 30.49 E
Dayton [Oh.-U.S.] 39 Kf 39.45N 84.15W
Dayton [Wa.-U.S.] 46 Gc 46.19N 117.59W
Daytona Beach 39 Kg 29.12N 80.59W
Dayu 27 Jf 25.29N 114.22 E
Da Yunhe=Grand Canal (EN) 21 Nf 39.54N 116.44 E
Dayville 46 Fd 44.28N 119.32W
Dayyīnah 24 Oj 24.57N 52.24 E
Dazhongji → Dafeng 28 Fh 33.11N 120.27 E
Dazhu 27 Ie 30.42N 107.12 E
Dazjā 24 Pe 35.50N 55.46 E
Dazkırı 24 Cd 37.54N 29.42 E
De Aar 31 Jl 30.39S 24.00 E
Dead 9 Ei 52.40N 8.30W
Deadhorse 40 Jb 70.11N 148.27W
Deadmans Cay 49 Jb 23.14N 75.14W
Dead Sea (EN)=Mayyit, Al Baḩr al- 21 Ff 31.30N 35.30 E
Deadwood 45 Ed 44.23N 103.44W
Deal 12 Dc 51.13N 1.24 E
Dealu Mare 15 Jb 47.27N 26.40 E
De'an 28 Cj 29.18N 115.45 E
Deán Funes 56 Hd 30.26S 64.21W
Dearborn 44 Fd 42.18N 83.10W
Dearg, Beinn- 9 Id 57.48N 4.57W
Deary 46 Gc 46.52N 116.31W
Dease 42 Ee 59.55N 128.29W
Dease Arm 42 Fc 66.50N 120.00W
Dease Lake 42 Ee 58.35N 130.02W
Dease Strait 42 Gc 69.00N 107.00W
Death Valley 38 Hf 36.30N 117.00W
Death Valley 46 Gh 36.20N 116.50W
Deauville 11 Ge 49.22N 0.04 E
Debak 26 Ff 1.34N 111.25 E
Debalcevo 16 Ke 48.20N 38.29 E
Debao 27 Ig 23.17N 106.21 E
Debar 15 Dh 41.32N 20.32 E
Debark 35 Fc 13.08N 37.53 E
Debdou 32 Gc 33.59N 3.03W
Debed 16 Ni 41.22N 44.58 E
Deben 12 Db 52.01N 1.22 E
De Beque 45 Bg 39.20N 108.13W
Dębica 10 Rf 50.04N 21.24 E
De Bilt 12 Hb 52.06N 5.11 E
Debin 20 Kd 62.18N 150.47 E
Dęblin 10 Re 51.35N 21.50 E
Dębno 10 Kd 52.45N 14.40 E
Débo, Lac- 34 Eb 15.18N 4.09W
Deborah East, Lake- 59 Df 30.45S 119.10 E
Deborah West, Lake- 59 Df 30.45S 119.05 E
Deboyne Islands 57 Gf 10.43S 152.22 E
Debrc 15 Ce 44.37N 19.54 E
Debre Berhan 35 Fd 9.41N 39.33 E
Debrecen 6 If 47.32N 21.38 E
Debrecen [2] 10 Ri 47.31N 21.40 E
Debre Libanos 35 Fd 9.43N 38.52 E
Debre Markós 31 Kg 10.10N 37.36 E
Debre Sina 35 Fd 9.51N 39.46 E
Debre Tabor 35 Fc 11.51N 38.00 E
Debre Zeyt 31 Kh 8.47N 39.00 E
De-Buka, Glacier- 66 Nf 76.00S 131.00W
Decatur [Al.-U.S.] 43 Je 34.36N 86.59W
Decatur [Ga.-U.S.] 44 Ei 33.46N 84.18W
Decatur [Il.-U.S.] 43 Jd 39.51N 89.32W
Decatur [In.-U.S.] 44 Ee 40.50N 84.56W
Decatur [Tx.-U.S.] 45 Hj 33.14N 97.35W
Decazeville 11 Ij 44.33N 2.15 E
Deccan 21 Jh 14.00N 77.00 E
Decelles, Reservoir- 44 Hb 47.40N 78.08W
Deception Bay 59 Ia 7.07S 144.05 E
Dechang 27 Hf 27.22N 102.12 E
Děčín 10 Kf 50.47N 14.13 E
Decize 11 Jh 46.50N 3.28 E
Decorah 45 Ke 43.18N 91.48W
Deda 15 Hc 46.56N 24.54 E
Dededo 64c Ba 13.31N 144.49 E
Dedemsvaart, Avereest- 12 Ib 52.37N 6.27 E
Dedopolis-Ckaro 16 Oi 41.28N 46.06 E
Dédougou 34 Ec 12.28N 3.28W
Dedoviči 7 Gh 57.33N 29.58 E
Dedza 36 Fe 14.22S 34.20 E
Dee [Eng.-U.K.] 9 Jh 53.19N 3.11W
Dee [Scot.-U.K.] 9 Kd 57.08N 2.04W
Dee [Scot.-U.K.] 9 Ig 54.50N 4.03W
Deep Creek Range 46 If 40.00N 113.57W
Deering 40 Gc 66.05N 162.43W
Deer Isle 44 Mc 44.13N 68.41W
Deer Lake [Newf.-Can.] 42 Lg 49.10N 57.25W
Deer Lake [Ont.-Can.] 42 If 52.40N 94.30W
Deer Park 46 Gc 47.57N 117.28W
Defiance 44 Ee 41.17N 84.21W
Defla 13 Oi 35.14N 4.26 E
De Funiak Springs 44 Dj 30.43N 86.07W
Dega Ahmedo 35 Gd 7.50N 42.53 E
Dêgê 27 Ge 31.52N 98.36 E
Degebe 13 Ef 38.13N 7.29W
Degeh Bur 35 Gd 8.13N 43.34 E
Degema 34 Ge 4.45N 6.46 E
Degerby 8 Id 60.02N 20.23 E
Degerfors 7 Dg 59.14N 14.26 E
Degerhamn 7 Dh 56.21N 16.24 E
Deggendorf 10 Ih 48.50N 12.58 E

Index Symbols

[1] Independent Nation
[2] State, Region
[3] District, County
[4] Municipality
[5] Colony, Dependency
Continent
Physical Region
Historical or Cultural Region
Mount, Mountain
Volcano
Hill
Mountains, Mountain Range
Hills, Escarpment
Plateau, Upland
Pass, Gap
Plain, Lowland
Delta
Salt Flat
Valley, Canyon
Crater, Cave
Karst Features
Depression
Polder
Desert, Dunes
Forest, Woods
Heath, Steppe
Oasis
Cape, Point
Coast, Beach
Cliff
Peninsula
Isthmus
Sandbank
Island
Atoll
Rock, Reef
Islands, Archipelago
Rocks, Reefs
Coral Reef
Well, Spring
Geyser
River, Stream
Waterfall Rapids
River Mouth, Estuary
Lake
Salt Lake
Intermittent Lake
Reservoir
Swamp, Pond
Canal
Glacier
Ice Shelf, Pack Ice
Ocean
Sea
Gulf, Bay
Strait, Fjord
Lagoon
Bank
Seamount
Tablemount
Ridge
Shelf
Basin
Escarpment, Sea Scarp
Fracture
Trench, Abyss
National Park, Reserve
Point of Interest
Recreation Site
Cave, Cavern
Historic Site
Ruins
Wall, Walls
Church, Abbey
Temple
Scientific Station
Airport
Port
Lighthouse
Mine
Tunnel
Dam, Bridge

Değirmendere 15 Kk 38.06N 27.09 E
De Gray Lake 45 Ji 34.15N 93.15W
De Grey River 59 Dd 20.12S 119.11 E
Degtarsk 17 Jh 56.42N 60.06 E
De Haan 12 Fc 51.16N 3.02 E
Dehaj 24 Pg 30.42N 54.53 E
Dehaq 24 Nf 32.55N 50.57 E
Deh Bārez 24 Qi 27.26N 57.12 E
Deh Bīd 24 Og 30.38N 53.13 E
Deh Dasht 24 Ng 30.47N 50.34 E
Dehdez 24 Ng 31.43N 50.17 E
Deh-e-Namak 24 Oe 35.25N 52.50 E
Deh-e Shīr 24 Og 31.29N 53.45 E
Deh-e Ziyār 24 Qg 30.40N 57.00 E
Dehgolān 24 Le 35.17N 47.25 E
Dehiwala-Mount Lavinia 25 Fg 6.50N 79.52 E
Dehlorān 24 Lf 32.41N 47.16 E
Deh Now 24 Qf 33.01N 57.41 E
Dehra Dūn 25 Fb 30.19N 78.02 E
Dehui 27 Mc 44.33N 125.38 E
Deinze 11 Jd 50.59N 3.32 E
Dej 15 Gb 47.09N 23.52 E
Deje 8 Ee 59.36N 13.28 E
Dejen 35 Fc 10.05N 38.11 E
Dejës, Mali i- 15 Dh 41.42N 20.10 E
Dejnau 19 Gh 39.18N 63.11 E
De Jongs, Tanjung- 26 Kh 6.56S 138.32 E
De Kalb 45 Lf 41.56N 88.45W
Dekar 37 Cd 21.30S 21.58 E
Dekese 31 Ji 3.27S 21.24 E
Dekina 34 Gd 7.42N 7.01 E
Dékoa 35 Bd 6.19N 19.04 E
De Koog, Texel- 12 Ga 53.07N 4.46 E
De La Garma 55 Bm 37.58S 60.25W
Delakhe 44 Gk 29.02N 81.18W
Delano 43 Dd 35.41N 119.15W
Delano Peak 43 Ed 38.22N 112.23W
Delārām 23 Jc 32.11N 63.25 E
Delarof Islands 40a Cb 51.30N 178.45W
Delaware 44 Fe 40.18N 83.06W
Delaware 45 Ek 32.00N 104.00W
Delaware [2] 43 Ld 39.10N 75.30W
Delaware Bay 38 Lc 39.05N 75.15W
Delaware River 43 Ld 39.20N 75.25W
Delbrück 12 Kc 51.46N 8.34 E
Del Carril 55 Cl 35.31S 59.30W
Delčevo 15 Fh 41.58N 22.47 E
Del City 45 Hi 35.27N 97.27W
Delegate 59 Jg 37.03S 148.58 E
Delémont/Delsberg 14 Bc 47.22N 7.21 E
Delet/Teili 8 Id 60.15N 20.35 E
Delfinópolis 55 Ie 20.20S 46.51W
Delft 11 Kb 52.00N 4.21 E
Delfzijl 11 Ma 53.19N 6.56 E
Delgada, Punta- 52 Jj 42.46S 63.38W
Delgado, Cabo-=Delgado, Cape-(EN) 30 Lj 10.40S 40.38 E
Delgado, Cabo-=Delgado, Cape-(EN) [3] 37 Fb 12.30S 39.00 E
Delgado, Cape-(EN)= Delgado, Cabo- 30 Lj 10.40S 40.38 E
Delgado, Cape-(EN)= Delgado, Cabo- [3] 37 Fb 12.30S 39.00 E
Delger Muren 27 Hb 49.17N 100.40 E
Delhi [Co.-U.S.] 45 Eh 37.42N 103.58W
Delhi [India] 25 Jg 28.40N 77.13 E
Delhi [N.Y.-U.S.] 44 Jd 42.17N 74.57W
Deliblatska Peščara 15 Dd 45.00N 21.00 E
Delice 24 Fc 39.58N 34.02 E
Deliceırmak 24 Fb 40.28N 34.10 E
Delicias [Cuba] 49 Ic 21.11N 76.34W
Delicias [Mex.] 47 Cc 28.13N 105.28W
Delījān 24 Nf 33.59N 50.40 E
Delingha 27 Gd 37.26N 97.25 E
Dēliņkalns/Delinkalns, Gora- 8 Lg 57.30N 27.02 E
Delinkalns, Gora-/ Dēliņkalns 8 Lg 57.30N 27.02 E
Delitzsch 10 Ie 51.32N 12.21 E
Deljatin 15 Ha 48.29N 24.45 E
Delle 11 Mg 47.30N 7.00 E
Dell Rapids 45 He 43.50N 96.43W
Dellys 32 Hb 36.55N 3.55 E
Delmarva Peninsula 38 Lf 38.50N 75.30W
Delme 12 Ka 53.05N 8.40 E
Delme 12 If 48.53N 6.24 E
Delmenhorst 10 Ec 53.03N 8.37 E
Delnice 14 Ie 45.24N 14.48 E
Delo 35 Fd 5.49N 37.57 E
De Long Strait (EN)= Longa, Proliv- 21 Tb 70.20N 178.00 E
De-Longa, Ostrova-=De Long Islands (EN) 21 Rb 76.30N 153.00 E
De Long Islands (EN)=De-Longa, Ostrova- 21 Rb 76.30N 153.00 E
De Long Mountains 40 Gc 68.20N 162.00W
Deloraine 59 Jh 41.31S 146.39 E
Delorme, Lac- 42 Kf 54.35N 69.55W
Delphi (EN) = Dhelfoi 15 Fk 38.29N 22.30 E
Del Rio 43 Gf 29.22N 100.54W
Delsberg/Delémont 14 Bc 47.22N 7.21 E
Delsbo 7 Dc 61.48N 16.35 E
Delta [Co.-U.S.] 43 Fd 38.44N 108.04W
Delta [Ut.-U.S.] 43 Ed 39.21N 112.35W
Delta Amacuro [2] 54 Fb 8.30N 61.30W
Delta Junction 40 Jd 64.02N 145.41W
Delvāda 25 Ed 20.46N 71.02 E
Del Valle 55 Bl 35.54S 60.43W
Delvina 15 Dj 39.57N 20.06 E
Dema 17 Gi 54.42N 55.58 E
Demanda, Sierra de la- 13 Ib 42.15N 3.05W
Demba 36 Dd 5.30S 22.16 E
Dembi 35 Fd 8.05N 36.28 E
Dembia 35 Cd 5.07N 24.25 E
Dembi Dolo 35 Ed 8.32N 34.49 E
De Medinilla, Farallon- 57 Fc 16.01N 146.04 E
Demer 11 Kd 50.58N 4.45 E
Demerara Plateau (EN) 52 Le 4.30N 44.00W
Demerara River 50 Gi 6.48N 58.10W
Demidov 16 Gb 55.15N 31.29 E
Demidovka 10 Vf 50.20N 25.27 E
Deming 43 Fe 32.16N 107.45W
Demini, Rio- 54 Fd 0.46S 62.56W
Demirci 24 Cc 39.03N 28.40 E
Demir Kapija 15 Fh 41.25N 22.15 E
Demirköy 15 Kh 41.49N 27.15 E
Demirtaş 15 Mi 40.16N 29.06 E
Demjanka 19 Gd 59.34N 69.20 E
Demjansk 7 Hh 57.38N 32.29 E
Demjanskoje 19 Gd 59.36N 69.18 E
Demmin 10 Jc 53.54N 13.02 E
Demopolis 44 Di 32.31N 87.50W
Dempo, Gunung- 21 Mj 4.02S 103.09 E
Demta 26 Lg 2.20S 140.08 E
Denain 11 Jd 50.20N 3.23 E
Denan 35 Gd 6.30N 43.30 E
Denau 19 Gh 38.18N 67.55 E
Den Bosch/'s-Hertogenbosch 11 Lc 51.41N 5.19 E
Den Burg, Texel- 12 Ga 53.03N 4.47 E
Den Chai 25 Ke 17.59N 100.04 E
Dendang 26 Eg 3.05S 107.54 E
Dender/Dendre 11 Kc 51.02N 4.06 E
Dendermonde/Termonde 12 Gc 51.02N 4.07 E
Dendre/Dender 11 Kc 51.02N 4.06 E
Dendtler Island 66 Pf 72.58S 89.57W
Denekamp 12 Jb 52.23N 7.00 E
Deneżkin Kamen, Gora- 19 Fc 60.25N 59.31 E
Dengarh 25 Hd 23.50N 81.42 E
Dêngkagoin → Têwo 27 He 34.03N 103.21 E
Dengkou (Bayan Gol) 22 Me 40.25N 106.59 E
Dêngqên 27 Ge 31.29N 95.32 E
Dengzhou → Penglai 27 Ld 37.44N 120.45 E
Den Haag/'s-Gravenhage= The Hague (EN) 6 Ge 52.06N 4.18 E
Den Ham 12 Ib 52.28N 6.32 E
Denham → Shak Bay 59 Ce 25.55S 113.32 E
Denham, Mount- 49 Id 18.13N 77.32W
Denham Range 59 Jd 21.55S 147.45 E
Denham Sound 59 Ce 25.40S 113.15 E
Den Helder 11 Kb 52.54N 4.45 E
Denia 13 Mf 38.51N 0.07 E
Deniliquin 59 Ig 35.32S 144.58 E
Denio 46 Ff 41.59N 118.39W
Denis Island 37b Ca 3.48S 55.40 E
Denison [Ia.-U.S.] 43 Hc 42.01N 95.20W
Denison [Tx.-U.S.] 43 He 33.45N 96.33W
Denison, Mount- 40 Ie 58.25N 154.27W
Denizli 23 Cb 37.46N 29.06 E
Denkiingen, Reichshoft- 12 Jd 50.55N 7.39 E
Denman Glacier 66 Ge 66.45S 99.25 E
Denmark [Austl.] 59 Df 34.57S 117.21 E
Denmark [S.C.-U.S.] 44 Gi 33.19N 81.09W
Denmark (EN)=Danmark [1] 6 Gd 56.00N 10.00 E
Denmark Strait (EN)= Danmarksstraedet 38 Qc 67.00N 25.00W
Dennery 51k Bb 13.55N 60.54W
Den Oever, Wieringen- 12 Hb 52.56N 5.02 E
Denpasar 22 Nj 8.39S 115.13 E
Denton 43 He 33.13N 97.08W
D'Entrecasteaux, Point- 59 Df 34.50S 116.00 E
D'Entrecasteaux Islands 57 Ge 9.35S 150.40 E
Denver 39 If 39.43N 105.01W
Deoghar 25 Hd 24.29N 86.42 E
Deolāli 25 Ee 19.54N 73.50 E
De Pajaros, Farallon- 57 Fb 20.32N 144.54 E
De Panne/La Panne 12 Ec 51.06N 2.35 E
De Pere 45 Ld 44.27N 88.04W
Deputatski 20 Ic 69.13N 139.55 E
Dêqên 27 Gf 28.32N 98.50 E
Deqing 27 Jg 23.14N 111.42 E
De Queen 45 Ii 34.02N 94.21W
De Quincy 45 Jk 30.27N 93.26W
Dequing 28 Fi 30.34N 120.05 E
Dera, Lach- 35 Ge 0.15N 42.17 E
Dera, Lagh- 30 Lh 0.15N 42.17 E
Dera Bugti 25 Dc 29.02N 69.09 E
Dera Ghāzi Khan 22 Jf 30.03N 70.38 E
Dera Ismāil Khan 25 Eb 31.50N 70.54 E
Derbent 6 Kg 42.03N 48.18 E
Derbent [Tur.] 15 Lk 38.11N 28.33 E
Derby 9 Lh 53.05N 1.40W
Derby [Austl.] 58 Df 17.18S 123.38 E
Derby [Eng.-U.K.] 9 Li 52.55N 1.30W
Derby [Ks.-U.S.] 45 Hh 37.33N 97.16W
Derbyshire [3] 9 Lh 53.10N 1.35W
Đerdap 15 Fe 44.41N 22.10 E
Derecske 10 Ri 47.21N 21.34 E
Dereköy 15 Kh 41.56N 27.21 E
Dereli 24 Hb 40.45N 38.27 E
Derg/Abhainn na Deirge 9 Fg 54.4?N 7.25W
Derg, Lough-/Loch Deirgeirt 9 Ei 53.0?N 8.20W
Dergači 16 Pd 51.13N 48.46 E
Dergači 16 Jd 50.09N 36.09 E
Der Grabow 10 Ib 54.23N 12.50 E
De Ridder 45 Jk 30.51N 93.17W
Derik 24 Id 37.22N 40.17 E
Derkul 16 Qd 51.17N 51.15 E
Dermott 45 Kj 33.32N 91.26W
Dernieres, Isles- 45 Kl 29.02N 90.47W
Derong 27 Gf 28.44N 99.18 E
De Rose Hill 59 Ge 26.25S 133.15 E
Déroute, Passage de la- 11 Ee 49.12N 1.51W
Dersa, Eglab- 32 Gd 26.45N 4.26W
Dersca 15 Jb 47.59N 26.12 E
Dersingham 12 Cb 52.51N 0.30 E
Derudeb 35 Fb 17.32N 36.06 E
Derventa 14 Lf 44.59N 17.55 E
Derwent [Eng.-U.K.] 9 Mg 54.10N 0.40W
Derwent [Eng.-U.K.] 12 Ab 52.53N 1.17W
Derwent River 59 Jh 43.03S 147.22 E
Derżavinsk 19 Ge 51.03N 66.19 E
Desaguadero, Rio- 52 Ji 34.13S 66.47W
Desappointement, Iles du- 57 Mf 14.10S 141.20W
Des Arc 45 Ki 34.58N 91.30W
Desborough 12 Eb 52.26N 0.49W
Descalvado 55 Ie 21.54S 47.37W
Descartes 11 Gh 46.58N 0.45 E
Deschambault Lake 42 Hf 54.50N 103.30W
Deschutes River 43 Cb 45.38N 120.54W
Descoberto, Rio- 55 Hc 14.20S 48.19W
Dese 31 Kg 11.07N 39.38 E
Deseado, Rio- 52 Jj 47.45S 65.54W
Desecheo, Isla- 51a Ab 18.25N 67.28W
Desengaño, Punta- 56 Gg 49.15S 67.37W
Desengano del Garda 14 Ee 45.23N 10.32 E
Desert Center 46 Hj 33.42N 115.26W
Desert Peak 46 If 40.23N 112.38W
Deshaies [Guad.] 51e Ab 16.13N 61.48W
Deshaies [Guad.] 51e Ab 16.18N 61.47W
Desiderio, Ric- 55 Ja 12.20S 44.50W
Desmaraisville 44 Ia 49.31N 75.10W
De Smet 45 Hd 44.23N 97.33W
Desmochado 55 Ch 27.07S 58.06W
Des Moines 38 Je 40.22N 91.26W
Des Moines [Ia.-U.S.] 39 Je 41.35N 93.37W
Des Moines [N.M.-U.S.] 45 Eh 36.46N 103.50W
Desmoronado, Cerro- 47 Dd 20.21N 105.01W
Desna 5 Je 50.33N 30.32 E
Desnățui 15 Ge 43.53N 23.35 E
Desolación, Isla- 52 Ik 53.05S 74.10W
De Soto 45 Kg 38.08N 90.33W
Despeñaperros, Desfiladero de- 13 If 38.24N 3.30W
Des Roches, Ile- 37b Bb 5.41S 53.41 E
Dessau 10 Ie 51.50N 12.15 E
Destruction Bay 42 Dd 61.20N 139.00W
Desvres 11 Hd 50.40N 1.50 E
Deta 15 Ed 45.24N 21.14 E
Dete 37 Dc 18.37S 26.51 E
Detmold 10 Ee 51.56N 8.53 E
Detour, Point- 44 Dc 45.36N 86.37W
Detroit [Mi.-U.S.] 39 Ke 42.20N 83.03W
Detroit [Or.-U.S.] 46 Dd 44.42N 122.10W
Detroit Lakes 45 Ic 46.49N 95.51W
Dettifoss 7a Cb 65.49N 16.24W
Detva 10 Ph 48.34N 19.25 E
Deûle 12 Ed 50.44N 2.56 E
Deurdeur 13 Oh 36.14N 2.16 E
Deurne 12 Hc 51.28N 5.48 E
Deutsche Bucht 10 Db 54.30N 7.30 E
Deutsche Demokratische Republik = Germany 6 Ge 51.00N 10.00 E
Deutschlandsberg 14 Jd 46.49N 15.13 E
Deux-Bassins, Col des- 13 Ph 36.27N 3.18 E
Deux Sèvres [3] 11 Fh 46.30N 0.15W
Deva 15 Fd 45.53N 22.54 E
Dévaványa 10 Qi 47.02N 20.58 E
Deveci Dağları 24 Gb 40.05N 36.00 E
Devecser 10 Ni 47.06N 17.26 E
Develi 24 Fc 38.22N 35.06 E
Deventer 11 Mb 52.15N 6.10 E
Deverd, Cap- 63b Be 20.45S 164.22 E
Deveron 9 Kd 57.40N 2.40W
Devès, Monts du- 11 Jj 44.57N 3.46 E
Devetak 14 Mg 43.54N 19.00 E
Devil River Peak 62 Ed 40.54S 172.39 E
Devil's Hole 9 Ne 56.34N 0.10 E
Devil's Island (EN)=Diable, Ile du- 54 Hb 5.17N 52.35W
Devils Lake 43 Hb 48.07N 98.59W
Devils Lake 45 Gb 48.07N 98.52W
Devils Paw 40 Me 58.44N 133.50W
Devils River 45 Fl 29.39N 100.58W
Devils Tower 46 Md 44.31N 104.57W
Devin 15 Hh 41.45N 24.24 E
Devizes 9 Lj 51.22N 1.59W
Devnja 15 Kf 43.13N 27.33 E
Devodi Munda 25 Ge 17.37N 82.57 E
De Volet Point 51n Ba 13.22N 61.13W
Devoll 15 Ci 40.49N 19.51 E
Devolli 15 Di 40.30N 20.50 E
Dévoluy 11 Lj 44.39N 5.53 E
Devon 9 Jk 50.50N 3.50W
Devon 9 Jk 50.50N 4.00W
Devon 38 Kb 75.00N 87.00W
Devon 9 Jk 53.04N 0.49W
Devonport 57 Fi 41.11S 146.21 E
Devoto 55 Aj 31.24S 62.18W
Devrek 24 Db 41.13N 31.57 E
Devrez 24 Fb 41.06N 34.25 E
Dewa 30 Lh 4.11N 42.06 E
Dewar Lakes 42 Kc 68.00N 72.00W
Dewās 25 Fd 22.58N 76.04 E
Dewa-Sanchi 29 Gb 39.30N 140.15 E
Dewey 45 Ih 36.48N 95.56W
De Witt 45 Ki 34.18N 91.20W
Dexemhare 35 Fb 15.04N 39.03 E
Dexing 28 Dj 28.55N 117.33 E
Dexter 45 Lh 36.48N 89.57W
Deyang 27 He 31.07N 104.25 E
Dey-Dey, Lake- 59 Ge 29.15S 131.05 E
Deyhūk 24 Qf 33.17N 57.30 E
Deyyer 23 Hd 27.50N 51.55 E
Dez 24 Mg 31.39N 48.52 E
Dezfūl 22 Gf 32.23N 48.24 E
Dez Gerd 24 Ng 30.45N 51.57 E
Dezhou 27 Kd 37.28N 116.18 E
Dháfni 15 Fl 37.48N 22.02 E
Dhahab 33 Fd 28.29N 34.32 E
Dhaka 22 Lg 23.43N 90.25 E
Dhamār 23 Fg 14.37N 44.23 E
Dhamtari 25 Gd 20.41N 81.34 E
Dhānbād 25 Hd 23.48N 86.27 E
Dhanushkodi 25 Fg 9.11N 79.24 E
Dhaulagiri 21 Kg 28.44N 83.25 E
Dhekelea 24 Ee 35.03N 33.40 E
Dhelfoi = Delphi (EN) 15 Fk 38.29N 22.30 E
Dhelvinákion 15 Dj 39.56N 20.28 E
Dhenkanal 25 Hd 20.40N 85.36 E
Dheskáti 15 Ej 39.55N 21.49 E
Dhespotikó 15 Hm 36.58N 25.00 E
Dhiapóndioi Nisoi 15 Cj 39.50N 19.25 E
Dhībān 24 Fg 31.30N 35.47 E
Dhidhimótikhon 15 Jh 41.21N 26.30 E
Dhíkti Óros 15 In 35.15N 25.30 E
Dhílos 15 Il 37.24N 25.16 E
Dhílos 15 Il 37.24N 25.16 E
Dhimitsána 15 Fl 37.36N 22.03 E
Dhionisiádhes, Nisoi- 15 Jn 35.21N 26.10 E
Dhiórix Potidhaia 15 Gi 40.10N 23.20 E
Dhī-Qār [3] 24 Lg 31.10N 46.10 E
Dhī-Qār 24 Kf 32.14N 44.22 E
Dhírfis Óros 15 Gk 38.38N 23.50 E
Dhísoros Óros 15 Fh 41.11N 22.57 E
Dhivoúnia 15 Jm 35.50N 26.28 E
Dhodhekánisos = Dodecanese (EN) 15 Jm 36.20N 27.00 E
Dhodhóni = Dodona (EN) 15 Dj 39.33N 20.46 E
Dholpur 25 Fc 26.42N 77.54 E
Dhomokos 15 Fj 39.08N 22.18 E
Dhone 25 Fe 15.25N 77.53 E
Dhonoúsa 15 Il 37.10N 25.50 E
Dhorāji 25 Ed 21.44N 70.27 E
Dhoxáton 15 Hh 41.06N 24.14 E
Dhragónisos 15 Il 37.27N 25.29 E
Dhubri 25 Hc 26.02N 89.58 E
Dhule 22 Jg 20.54N 74.47 E
Dhuliān 25 Hd 24.41N 87.58 E
Dia 15 In 35.27N 25.13 E
Diable, Ile du-=Devil's Island (EN) 54 Hb 5.17N 52.35W
Diable, Morne au- 51g Ba 15.37N 61.27W
Diable, Pointe du- [Mart.] 51h Bb 14.47N 60.54W
Diable, Pointe du- [Van.] 63b Dc 16.01S 168.12 E
Diablo, Punta del- 55 Fl 34.22S 53.46W
Diablo, Puntan- 64b Ba 15.00N 145.34 E
Diablo Range 46 Eh 36.45N 121.20W
Diafarabé 34 Ec 14.10N 5.00W
Dialafara 34 Cc 13.27N 11.23W
Diamant, Pointe du- 51h Ac 14.27N 61.04W
Diamant, Rocher du- 51h Ac 14.27N 61.03W
Diamante [Arg.] 56 Hd 32.04S 60.39W
Diamante [It.] 14 Jk 39.41N 15.49 E
Diamante, Punta del- 48 Ji 16.47N 99.52W
Diamantina 54 Jg 18.15S 43.36W
Diamantina, Chapada- 52 Lg 11.30S 41.10W
Diamantina, Rio- 55 Fc 16.42S 52.45W
Diamantina Depth (EN) 3 Hm 33.30S 102.00 E
Diamantina Lakes 59 Id 23.46S 141.09 E
Diamantina River 57 Eg 26.45S 139.10 E
Diamantina Trench (EN) 3 Hm 36.00S 104.00 E
Diamantino 53 Kg 14.25S 56.27W
Diamantino, Rio- 55 Fc 16.08S 52.28W
Diamond Harbour 25 Hd 22.12N 88.12 E
Diamond Island 51p Bb 12.20N 61.35W
Diamond Jenness Peninsula 42 Fb 71.00N 117.00W
Diamond Peak [Nv.-U.S.] 46 Hg 39.40N 115.48W
Diamond Peak [Or.-U.S.] 46 De 43.33N 122.09W
Diamond Peak [U.S.] 46 Id 44.09N 113.05W
Diamond Peak [U.S.] 46 Gc 46.07N 117.32W
Diamou 34 Cc 14.05N 11.16W
Diana, Baie- 42 Kd 61.00N 70.00W
Dianbai 27 Jg 21.33N 110.58 E
Dianbu → Feidong 23 Di 31.53N 117.29 E
Diancang Shan 27 Hf 25.42N 100.02 E
Dian Chi 27 Hg 24.50N 102.45 E
Diane, Étang de- 11a Ba 42.07N 9.32 E
Dianjiang 27 Ie 30.19N 107.25 E
Diane Marina 14 Cg 43.54N 8.05 E
Dianópolis 54 If 11.38S 46.50W
Dianra 34 Dd 8.45N 6.18W
Diapaga 34 Fc 12.04N 1.47 E
Diaz 55 Bk 32.22S 61.05W
Dibā, Dawḥat- 24 Qk 25.38N 56.18 E
Dibagah 24 Je 35.52N 43.49 E
Dibang 25 Jc 27.50N 95.32 E
Dibaya 36 Dd 6.30S 22.57 E
Dibaya-Lubue 36 Cc 4.09S 19.52 E
Dibella 34 Hb 17.31N 12.59 E
Dibrugarh 22 Lg 27.29N 94.54 E
Dibs 24 Ke 35.40N 44.04 E
Dibsi Afnān 24 Ee 35.55N 38.16 E
Dickens 45 Fj 33.37N 100.50W
Dickinson 43 Gb 46.53N 102.47W
Dickins Seamount (EN) 40 Lf 54.30N 137.00W
Dickson 44 Dg 36.05N 87.23W
Dicle 24 Ic 38.22N 40.04 E
Dicle=Tigris (EN) 21 Gf 31.00N 47.25 E
Didam 12 Ic 51.56N 6.09 E
Didao 28 Kb 45.22N 130.48 E
Didcot 12 Ac 51.36N 1.15W
Didesa 35 Fd 9.30N 35.32 E
Didieni 34 Dc 13.23N 8.05W
Didyma 15 Kl 37.21N 27.16 E
Die 11 Lj 44.45N 5.22 E
Dieburg 10 Eg 49.54N 8.51 E
Dieciocho de Abril 55 Ek 34.22S 54.04W
Dieciocho de Julio 55 Fk 33.41S 53.33W
Diefenbaker Lake 42 Gf 51.00N 107.00W
Dièges 11 Ii 45.36N 2.16 E
Diego Garcia 21 Jj 6.20S 72.20 E
Diego Ramirez, Islas 56 Gi 56.30S 68.44W
Diekirch 11 Me 49.53N 6.10 E
Die Leewitz 10 Hc 53.30N 11.30 E
Diéma 34 Dc 14.33N 9.11W
Diemel 10 Fe 51.39N 9.27 E
Diemelsee 12 Kc 51.19N 8.43 E
Diemelstadt 12 Lc 51.27N 9.01 E
Dien Bien Phu 25 Kd 21.23N 103.01 E
Diepenbeek 12 Hd 50.54N 5.24 E
Diepholz 10 Ed 52.36N 8.22 E
Dieppe 11 He 49.56N 1.05 E
Dieppe Bay Town 51c Ab 17.25N 62.48W
Dierdorf 12 Jd 50.33N 7.40 E
Dieren, Rheden- 12 Ib 52.03N 6.08 E
Di'er Songhua Jiang 27 Lc 45.26N 124.39 E
Diest 12 Hd 50.59N 5.03 E
Dieulefit 11 Lj 44.31N 5.04 E
Dieulouard 12 If 48.51N 6.04 E
Dieuze 11 Mf 48.49N 6.43 E
Dieveniškes 8 Kj 54.10N 25.44 E
Die Ville 12 Id 50.40N 6.55 E
Diez 12 Kd 50.22N 8.01 E
Dif 36 Hb 0.59N 40.57 E
Diffa [2] 34 Hb 16.00N 13.30 E
Diffa 34 Hc 13.19N 12.37 E
Differdange/Differdingen 11 Le 49.32N 5.52 E
Differdingen/Differdange 11 Le 49.32N 5.52 E
Digby 42 Kh 44.40N 65.50W
Dighton 45 Fg 38.29N 100.28W
Digne 11 Mj 44.06N 6.14 E
Digoin 11 Jh 46.29N 3.59 E
Digora 16 Nh 43.07N 44.06 E
Digos 26 Ie 6.45N 125.20 E
Digranes 7a Ca 66.02N 14.45W
Digul 26 Kh 7.07S 138.42 E
Dihang 25 Jc 27.48N 95.30 E
Dijar 16 Tf 46.33N 56.05 E
Dijlah=Tigris (EN) 21 Gf 31.00N 47.25 E
Dijle 11 Kd 50.53N 4.42 E
Dijon 6 Gf 47.19N 5.01 E
Dik 35 Bd 9.58N 17.31 E
Dikanäs 7 Dd 65.14N 16.00 E
Dikhil 35 Gc 11.06N 42.22 E
Dikili 24 Bc 39.04N 26.53 E
Dikli 8 Kg 57.30N 25.00 E
Diksmuide/Dixmude 11 Ic 51.02N 2.52 E
Dikson 22 Kb 73.30N 80.35 E
Dikwa 34 Hc 12.02N 13.55 E
Dila 35 Fc 6.23N 38.19 E
Dilbeek 12 Gd 50.51N 4.16 E
Dili 22 Oj 8.33S 125.34 E
Di Linh 25 Lf 11.35N 108.04 E
Dilizan 16 Ni 40.46N 44.55 E
Dilj 14 Me 45.16N 18.01 E
Dill 12 Kc 50.33N 8.29 E
Dillenburg 10 Ef 50.44N 8.17 E
Dillia 30 Ig 14.09N 12.50 E
Dilling 31 Jg 12.03N 29.39 E
Dillingen (Saar) 12 Ie 49.21N 6.44 E
Dillingham 39 Dd 59.02N 158.29W
Dillon [Mt.-U.S.] 43 Eb 45.13N 112.38W
Dillon [S.C.-U.S.] 44 Hh 34.25N 79.22W
Dilly 34 Dc 14.57N 7.43W
Dilolo 31 Jj 10.42S 22.20 E
Dilsen 12 Hc 51.02N 5.44 E
Dimashq=Damascus (EN) 22 Ff 33.30N 36.15 E
Dimbelenge 36 Dd 5.30S 23.53 E
Dimbokro [3] 34 Ed 6.50N 4.45W
Dimbokro 34 Ed 6.39N 4.42W
Dimboola 59 Ig 36.27S 142.02 E
Dîmbovița 15 Je 44.14N 26.27 E
Dîmbovița [2] 15 Ie 44.55N 25.30 E
Dîmbovnic 15 Ie 44.20N 25.40 E
Dimitrovgrad [Bul.] 15 Ig 42.03N 25.36 E
Dimitrovgrad 19 Ee 54.14N 49.42 E
Dimitrovgrad [Yugo.] 15 Fg 43.01N 22.47 E
Dimmitt 45 Ei 34.33N 102.19W
Dimona 24 Fg 31.04N 35.02 E
Dimovo 15 Ff 43.44N 22.44 E
Dinagat 26 Id 10.12N 125.35 E
Dinājpur 25 Hc 25.38N 88.38 E
Dinan 11 Df 48.27N 2.02W
Dinangourou 34 Ec 14.27N 2.14W
Dinant 11 Kd 50.16N 4.55 E
Dinar 24 Dc 38.04N 30.10 E
Dinar, Kūh-e- 24 Ng 30.50N 51.35 E
Dinara 14 Kf 44.04N 16.23 E
Dinara=Dinaric Alps (EN) 5 Hg 43.50N 16.35 E
Dinard 11 Df 48.38N 2.04W
Dinaric Alps (EN)= Dinara 5 Hg 43.50N 16.35 E
Dindar, Nahr ad- 35 Ec 14.06N 33.40 E
Dinder 35 Ec 14.06N 33.40 E
Dindigul 25 Ff 10.21N 77.57 E
Dindima 34 Hc 10.14N 10.09 E
Dinga 36 Cd 5.19S 16.34 E
Dingbian 27 Id 37.35N 107.37 E
Dingden, Hamminkeln- 12 Ic 51.46N 6.37 E
Dinggyê 27 Ef 28.25N 87.45 E
Dinghai 27 Le 30.05N 122.07 E
Dingle 8 Df 58.32N 11.34 E
Dingle/An Daingean 9 Ci 52.08N 10.15W
Dingle Bay/Bá an Daingin 9 Ci 52.05N 10.15W
Dingolfing 10 Ih 48.38N 12.30 E
Dingshuzhen 28 Ei 31.16N 119.50 E
Dingtao 28 Cg 35.04N 115.35 E
Dinguiraye 34 Cc 11.18N 10.43W
Dingwall 9 Id 57.35N 4.26W
Dingxi 27 Hd 35.33N 104.32 E
Dingxian 27 Jd 38.29N 115.00 E
Dingxiang 28 Be 38.32N 112.59 E
Dingxing 28 Kd 39.11N 115.48 E
Dingyuan 28 Dh 32.32N 117.41 E
Dingzi Gang 28 Ff 33.33N 120.59 E
Dinh, Mui- 21 Mh 11.22N 109.01 E
Dinkel 12 Ib 52.30N 6.58 E
Dinosaur 45 Bf 40.15N 109.01W
Dinskaja 16 Kg 45.09N 39.12 E
Dinslaken 12 Ic 51.34N 6.44 E
Dinsor 35 Ge 2.23N 42.58 E
Dintel 12 Gc 51.39N 4.24 E
Dinuba 46 Fh 36.36N 119.27W

Index Symbols

[1] Independent Nation
[2] State, Region
[3] District, County
[4] Municipality
[5] Colony, Dependency
Continent
Physical Region
Historical or Cultural Region
Mount, Mountain
Volcano
Hill
Mountains, Mountain Range
Hills, Escarpment
Plateau, Upland
Pass, Gap
Plain, Lowland
Delta
Salt Flat
Valley, Canyon
Crater, Cave
Karst Features
Depression
Polder
Desert, Dunes
Forest, Woods
Heath, Steppe
Oasis
Cape, Point
Coast, Beach
Cliff
Peninsula
Isthmus
Sandbank
Island
Atoll
Rock, Reef
Islands, Archipelago
Rocks, Reefs
Coral Reef
Well, Spring
Geyser
River, Stream
Waterfall Rapids
River Mouth, Estuary
Lake
Salt Lake
Intermittent Lake
Reservoir
Swamp, Pond
Canal
Glacier
Ice Shelf, Pack Ice
Ocean
Sea
Gulf, Bay
Strait, Fjord
Lagoon
Bank
Seamount
Tablemount
Ridge
Shelf
Basin
Escarpment, Sea Scarp
Fracture
Trench, Abyss
National Park, Reserve
Point of Interest
Recreation Site
Cave, Cavern
Historic Site
Ruins
Wall, Walls
Church, Abbey
Temple
Scientific Station
Airport
Port
Lighthouse
Mine
Tunnel
Dam, Bridge

Index Symbols

- Independent Nation
- State, Region
- District, County
- Municipality
- Colony, Dependency
- Continent
- Physical Region
- Historical or Cultural Region
- Mount, Mountain
- Volcano
- Hill
- Mountains, Mountain Range
- Hills, Escarpment
- Plateau, Upland
- Pass, Gap
- Plain, Lowland
- Delta
- Salt Flat
- Valley, Canyon
- Crater, Cave
- Karst Features
- Depression
- Polder
- Desert, Dunes
- Forest, Woods
- Heath, Steppe
- Oasis
- Cape, Point
- Coast, Beach
- Cliff
- Peninsula
- Isthmus
- Sandbank
- Island
- Cape, Point
- Rock, Reef
- Islands, Archipelago
- Rocks, Reefs
- Coral Reef
- Well, Spring
- Geyser
- River, Stream
- Atoll
- Waterfall Rapids
- River Mouth, Estuary
- Lake
- Salt Lake
- Ocean
- Sea
- Ridge
- Shelf
- Gulf, Bay
- Strait, Fjord
- Basin
- Lagoon
- Canal
- Glacier
- Ice Shelf, Pack Ice
- Bank
- Seamount
- Tablemount
- Point of Interest
- Recreation Site
- Escarpment, Sea Scarp
- Fracture
- Trench, Abyss
- National Park, Reserve
- Cave, Cavern
- Airport
- Historic Site
- Ruins
- Wall, Walls
- Church, Abbey
- Temple
- Scientific Station
- Port
- Lighthouse
- Mine
- Tunnel
- Dam, Bridge

Dragon's Mouths/Dragón, Bocas del-	54	Fa	10.45N	61.46W
Dragør	8	Ei	55.36N	12.41 E
Draguignan	11	Mk	43.32N	6.28 E
Drahanska vrchovina	10	Mg	49.30N	16.45 E
Drain	46	De	43.40N	123.19W
Drake	45	Fc	47.55N	100.23W
Drake, Estrecho de-=Drake Passage (EN)	52	Jk	58.00 S	70.00W
Drakensberg	30	Jk	29.00 S	29.00 E
Drake Passage (EN)=Drake, Estrecho de-	52	Jk	58.00 S	70.00W
Dráma	15	Hh	41.09N	24.09 E
Drammen	6	Hd	59.44N	10.15 E
Dramselva	8	De	59.44N	10.14 E
Drangajokull	7a	Aa	66.09N	22.15W
Dranse	11	Mh	46.24N	6.30 E
Drau=Drava (EN)	5	Hf	45.33N	18.55 E
Dráva=Drava (EN)	5	Hf	45.33N	18.55 E
Drava (EN)=Drau	5	Hf	45.33N	18.55 E
Drava (EN)=Drăva	5	Hf	45.33N	18.55 E
Dravograd	14	Jd	46.35N	15.01 E
Drawa	10	Ld	52.52N	15.59 E
Drawno	10	Lc	53.13N	15.45 E
Drawsko, Jezioro-	10	Mc	53.33N	16.10 E
Drawsko Pomorskie	10	Lc	53.32N	15.48 E
Drayton Valley	42	Gf	53.13N	115.00W
Drean	14	Bn	36.41N	7.45 E
Dreieich	12	Ke	50.01N	8.43 E
Drenovci	14	Mf	44.55N	18.55 E
Drenthe [3]	12	Ib	52.45N	6.30 E
Dresden	6	He	51.03N	13.45 E
Dreux	11	Hf	48.44N	1.22 E
Drevsjø	7	Cf	61.54N	12.02 E
Drezdenko	10	Ld	52.51N	15.50 E
Dricēni/Driceni	8	Lh	56.39N	27.11 E
Driceni/Dricēni	8	Lh	56.39N	27.11 E
Driffield	9	Mg	54.01N	0.26W
Driggs	46	Je	43.44N	111.14W
Drina	5	Hg	44.53N	19.21 E
Drincea	15	Fe	44.07N	22.59 E
Drin Gulf (EN)=Drinit, Gjiri i-	15	Ch	41.45N	19.28 E
Drini	5	Hg	41.45N	19.34 E
Drini i Zi	15	Dg	42.05N	20.23 E
Drinit, Gjiri i-=Drin Gulf (EN)	15	Ch	41.45N	19.28 E
Drinjača	14	Nf	44.17N	19.10 E
Drinosi	15	Di	40.17N	20.02 E
Drissa	7	Gi	55.47N	27.57 E
Drisvjaty, Ozero-/Drūkšiu Ežeras	8	Lj	55.37N	26.45 E
Driva	8	Cb	62.40N	8.34 E
Drjanovo	15	Ig	42.58N	25.28 E
Drniš	14	Kg	43.52N	16.09 E
Drøbak	7	Cg	59.39N	10.39 E
Drocea, Vîrful-	15	Fc	46.12N	22.14 E
Drogheda/Droichead Átha	9	Gh	53.43N	6.21W
Drogičin	16	Dc	52.13N	25.10 E
Drogobyč	16	Ce	49.22N	23.33 E
Drohiczyn	10	Sd	52.24N	22.41 E
Droichead Átha/Drogheda	9	Gh	53.43N	6.21W
Droichead na Bandan/Bandon	9	Ej	51.45N	8.45W
Droichead na Banna/Banbridge	9	Gg	54.21N	6.16W
Drokija	16	Ee	48.01N	27.53 E
Drôme	12	Be	49.19N	0.45W
Drôme [3]	11	Lj	44.35N	5.10 E
Drömling	10	Hd	52.29N	11.04 E
Dronero	14	Bf	44.28N	7.22 E
Dronne	11	Fi	45.02N	0.09W
Dronning Fabiola-Fjella	66	Df	71.30 S	35.40 E
Dronning Louise Land	41	Jc	76.45N	24.00W
Dronten	11	Lb	52.31N	5.42 E
Dropt	11	Fj	44.35N	0.06W
Drovjanoj	20	Cb	72.25N	72.45 E
Drowning River	45	Na	50.55N	84.35W
Druja	7	Gi	55.47N	27.29 E
Drūkšiu Ežeras/Drisvjaty, Ozero-	8	Lj	55.37N	26.45 E
Druk-Yul → Bhutan [1]	22	Lg	27.30N	90.30 E
Drulingen	12	Jf	48.52N	7.11 E
Drumheller	42	Gf	51.28N	112.42W
Drummond [Mt.-U.S.]	46	Ic	46.40N	113.09W
Drummond [Wi.-U.S.]	45	Kc	46.20N	91.15W
Drummond Island	44	Fb	46.00N	83.40W
Drummond Range	59	Jd	23.30 S	147.15 E
Drummondville	42	Kg	45.50N	72.20W
Drummore	9	Ig	54.42N	4.54W
Drumochter, Pass of-	9	Ie	56.50N	4.12W
Drunen	12	Hc	51.41N	5.10 E
Druskininkai/Druskininkaj	7	Fi	54.04N	24.06 E
Druskininkaj/Druskininkai	7	Fi	54.04N	24.06 E
Drut	16	Gc	53.04N	30.35 E
Druten	12	Hc	51.54N	5.38 E
Družba	16	Hc	52.02N	33.59 E
Druzba	19	If	45.18N	82.29 E
Družkovka	16	Je	48.36N	37.33 E
Družnaja Gorka	8	Ne	59.11N	30.10 E
Družnino	17	Ih	56.48N	59.29 E
Drużno, Jezioro-	10	Pb	54.08N	19.30 E
Drvar	14	Kf	44.22N	16.23 E
Drvenik	14	Lg	43.09N	17.15 E
Drwęca	10	Oc	53.00N	18.42 E
Dryden	42	Ig	49.47N	92.50W
Dry Fork	46	Me	43.30N	105.24W
Drygalski Ice Tongue	66	Kf	75.24 S	163.30 E
Drygalski Island	66	Ge	65.45 S	92.30 E
Drysdale River	59	Fb	13.59 S	126.51 E
Dry Tortugas	43	Kg	24.38N	82.55W
Drzewica	10	Qe	51.27N	20.28 E
Drzewiczka	10	Qe	51.33N	20.35 E
Dschang	34	Hd	5.27N	10.04 E
Dua	36	Db	3.20N	20.53 E
Duaca	54	Ea	10.18N	69.10W
Duancun → Wuxiang	28	Bf	36.50N	112.51 E
Duarte, Pico-	38	Lh	19.00 N	71.00 W
Duartina	55	Hf	22.24 S	49.25W
Dubawnt	42	Hd	64.30N	100.06W
Dubawnt Lake	38	Ic	63.08N	101.30W
Ḑubay'ah, Ra's-	24	Pj	24.20N	54.09 E
Dubayy	22	Hg	25.18N	55.18 E
Dubbo	58	Fh	32.15 S	148.36 E
Dübener Heide	10	Ie	51.40N	12.40 E
Dubenski	16	Td	51.29N	56.38 E
Dubesar'	16	Ff	47.17N	29.10 E
Dubh Artach	9	Ge	56.08N	6.39W
Dubica	14	Ke	45.13N	16.48 E
Dublin	43	Ke	32.32N	82.54W
Dublin/Baile Átha Cliath [2]	9	Gh	53.20N	6.15W
Dublin/Baile Átha Cliath	6	Fe	53.20N	6.15W
Dublin Bay/Cuan Bhaile Átha Cliath	9	Gh	53.20N	6.06W
Dubljany	10	Tg	49.26N	23.16 E
Dublon	64d	Bb	7.23N	151.53 E
Dubna	8	Lh	56.20N	26.31 E
Dubna	19	Dd	56.47N	37.10 E
Dubnica nad Vánom	10	Oh	48.58N	18.10 E
Dubno	19	Ce	50.29N	25.46 E
Du Bois	44	He	41.06N	78.46W
Dubois [Id.-U.S.]	46	Id	44.10N	112.14W
Dubois [Wy.-U.S.]	46	Ke	43.33N	109.38W
Dubovka	19	Ef	49.03N	44.50 E
Dubovoje	10	Ih	48.08N	23.59 E
Dubreka	34	Cd	9.48N	13.31W
Dubrovica	16	Ed	51.34N	26.34 E
Dubrovnik	6	Hg	42.39N	18.07 E
Dubrovno	7	Hi	54.33N	30.41 E
Dubrovnoje	19	Gd	57.58N	69.25 E
Dubuque	43	Ic	42.30N	90.41W
Dubysa	8	Ji	55.02N	23.27 E
Duc de Gloucester, Iles du-=Duke of Gloucester, Islands (En)	57	Mg	20.38 S	143.20W
Duchang	28	Dj	29.16N	116.11 E
Duchesne	46	Jf	40.10N	110.24W
Duchess	59	Hd	21.22 S	139.52 E
Ducie Atoll	57	Og	24.40 S	124.47W
Duck River	44	Dg	36.02N	87.52W
Duckwater Peak	46	Hg	38.58N	115.26W
Duclair	12	Ce	49.29N	0.53 E
Duc Lap	25	Lf	12.27N	107.38 E
Ducos	51h	Bb	14.34N	60.58W
Dudelange/Düdelingen	12	Ie	49.28N	6.06 E
Duderstadt	10	Ge	51.31N	10.16 E
Dudinka	22	Kc	69.25N	86.15 E
Dudley	9	Ki	52.30N	2.05W
Ḑūdo	35	Id	9.20N	50.14 E
Dudub	35	Hd	6.55N	46.42 E
Dudune	63b	Ce	21.21 S	167.44 E
Dudváh	10	Ni	47.58N	17.50 E
Dudweiler, Saarbrücken-	12	Je	49.17N	7.02 E
Dūdwēyn	35	Gd	9.19N	44.53 E
Dudypta	20	Db	70.55N	89.50 E
Duékoué	34	Dd	6.45N	7.21W
Dueodde	8	Fj	54.59N	15.05 E
Duerna	13	Gb	42.19N	5.54W
Duero	5	Fg	41.08N	8.40W
Dufek Coast	66	Lg	84.30 S	179.00W
Duffer Peak	46	Ff	41.40N	118.44W
Duff Islands	57	He	9.50 S	167.10 E
Dugi Otok	14	Ii	44.00N	15.00 E
Dugo Selo	14	Ke	45.48N	16.15 E
Du Gué, Rivière-	42	Ke	57.20N	70.46W
Duhovnickoje	16	Pc	52.29N	48.15 E
Duijan Yan	27	He	31.01N	103.28 E
Duiru → Wuchuan	27	If	28.28N	107.57 E
Duisburg	10	Ce	51.26N	6.45 E
Duitama	54	Db	5.50N	73.02W
Dujūma	35	Ge	1.14N	42.34 E
Dukagjini	15	Cg	42.18N	19.45 E
Dūkān	24	Ke	35.56N	44.58 E
Dukan, Sad ad-	24	Kd	36.10N	44.56 E
Dukat	15	Fg	42.26N	22.21 E
Duke of Gloucester Islands (EN)=Duc de Gloucester, Iles du-	57	Mg	20.38 S	143.20W
Duke of York	63a	Aa	4.10 S	152.28 E
Duke of York Bay	42	Jc	65.25N	84.50W
Duk Fadiat	35	Ed	7.45N	31.25 E
Duk Faiwil	35	Ed	7.30N	31.29 E
Dukhān	23	Hd	25.25N	50.48 E
Dukielska, Przełecz-	10	Rg	49.25N	21.42 E
Dukku	34	Hc	10.49N	10.46 E
Dukla	10	Rg	49.34N	21.41 E
Dukou	22	Mg	26.31N	101.44 E
Dūkštas/Dukštas	8	Li	55.32N	26.28 E
Dukštas/Dūkštas	8	Li	55.32N	26.28 E
Dulan (Qagan Us)	22	Lf	36.29N	98.29 E
Dulce, Bahía-	48	Ji	16.30N	98.50W
Dulce, Golfo-	47	Hg	8.36N	83.15W
Dulce, Rio-	52	Ji	30.31 S	62.32W
Dulce Nombre de Culmí	49	Ef	15.09N	85.37W
Duldurga	20	Gf	50.38N	113.35 E
Dulgalah	21	Pc	67.30N	133.20 E
Dulia	36	Db	2.57N	24.08 E
Dülmen	10	De	51.50N	7.18 E
Dulovka	8	Mg	57.27N	28.29 E
Dulovo	15	Kf	43.49N	27.09 E
Duluth	39	Je	46.47N	92.06W
Dūmā	24	Gf	33.35N	36.24 E
Dumaguete	26	He	9.18N	123.18 E
Dumai	26	Df	1.41N	101.27 E
Dumaran	26	Gd	10.33N	119.51 E
Dumaresq River	59	Ke	28.40 S	150.28 E
Dumas [Ar.-U.S.]	45	Kj	33.53N	91.29W
Dumas [Tx.-U.S.]	45	Fi	35.52N	101.58W
Dumayr	24	Gf	33.38N	36.40 E
Dumbarton	9	If	55.57N	4.35W
Dumbéa	63b	Cf	22.09 S	166.27 E
Dumbrăveni [Rom.]	15	Jb	47.39N	26.25 E
Dumbrăveni [Rom.]	15	Hc	46.14N	24.34 E
Dumfries	9	Jf	55.04N	3.37W
Dumfries and Galloway [3]	9	Jf	55.10N	3.35W
Dumka	25	Hd	24.16N	87.15 E
Dumlupinar	15	Mk	38.52N	30.00 E
Dümmer	10	Ed	52.31N	8.19 E
Dumoine, Lac-	44	Ib	46.52N	77.52W
Dumoine, Rivière-	44	Ib	46.13N	77.50W
Dumont d'Urville	66	Je	66.40 S	140.01 E
Dumont D'Urville Sea (EN)	66	Je	63.00 S	140.00 E
Dumpu	58	Fe	5.52 S	145.46 E
Dümrek	15	Lk	39.40N	28.24 E
Dumuhe	28	La	46.21N	133.33 E
Dumyāţ=Damietta (EN)	31	Ke	31.25N	31.48 E
Dumyāţ, Maşabb-	24	Dg	31.27N	31.51 E
Duna=Danube (EN)	5	If	45.20N	29.40 E
Dunaföldvár	10	Oi	46.48N	18.56 E
Dunaharaszti	10	Pi	47.21N	19.05 E
Dunaj	20	Ih	42.57N	132.20 E
Dunaj=Danube (EN)	5	If	45.20N	29.40 E
Dunajec	10	Qf	50.15N	20.44 E
Dunajevcy	16	Ee	48.51N	26.44 E
Dunajská Streda	10	Ni	48.01N	17.38 E
Dunakeszi	10	Pi	47.38N	19.08 E
Dunántúl	10	Nj	47.00N	18.00 E
Dunărea=Danube (EN)	5	If	45.20N	29.40 E
Dunărea Veche	15	Ld	45.17N	28.02 E
Dunării, Delta- = Danube, Mouths of the- (EN)	5	If	45.30N	29.45 E
Duna-Tisza Köze	10	Pj	46.45N	19.30 E
Dunaújváros	10	Oj	46.58N	18.56 E
Dunav=Danube (EN)	5	If	45.20N	29.40 E
Dunavăţu de Jos	15	Me	44.59N	29.13 E
Dunav-Tisa-Dunav kanal	15	Dd	45.10N	20.50 E
Dunback	62	Df	45.23 S	170.38 E
Dunbar	9	Kf	56.00N	2.31W
Duncan [Az.-U.S.]	46	Kj	32.43N	109.06W
Duncan [B.C.-Can.]	46	Db	48.47N	123.42W
Duncan [Ok.-U.S.]	43	He	34.30N	97.57W
Duncan Passage	25	If	11.00N	92.00 E
Duncansby Head	5	Fd	58.39N	3.01W
Dundaga	8	Jg	57.31N	22.14 E
Dundalk	44	If	39.15N	76.31W
Dundalk/Dún Dealgan	9	Gg	54.01N	6.25W
Dundalk Bay/Cuan Dhun Dealgan	9	Gh	53.57N	6.17W
Dundas [Grld.]	41	Fc	76.30N	68.00W
Dundas [Ont.-Can.]	44	Hd	43.16N	79.58W
Dundas, Lake-	59	Ef	32.35 S	121.50 E
Dundas Peninsula	42	Gb	74.40N	113.00W
Dundas Strait	59	Gb	11.20 S	131.35 E
Dún Dealgan/Dundalk	9	Gg	54.01N	6.25W
Dundee [S.Afr.]	37	Ee	28.12 S	30.16 E
Dundee [Scot.-U.K.]	6	Fd	56.28N	3.00W
Dund Hot → Zhenglan Qi	28	Cc	42.14N	115.59 E
Dundrum Bay/Cuan Dhún Droma	9	Hg	54.13N	5.45W
Dunedin [Fl.-U.S.]	44	Fk	28.02N	82.47W
Dunedin [N.Z.]	58	Ii	45.53 S	170.31 E
Dunfanaghy	9	Ff	55.11N	7.59W
Dunfermline	9	Je	56.04N	3.29W
Dungannon/Dún Geanainn	9	Gg	54.31N	6.46W
Dún Garbhán/Dungarvan	9	Fi	52.05N	7.37W
Dūngarpur	25	Ed	23.50N	73.43 E
Dungarvan/Dún Garbhán	9	Fi	52.05N	7.37W
Dungas	34	Gc	13.04N	9.20 E
Dungau	10	Ih	48.45N	12.30 E
Dún Geanainn/Dungannon	9	Gg	54.31N	6.46W
Dungeness	9	Nk	50.55N	0.58 E
Dungu	36	Eb	3.42N	28.40 E
Dungu	36	Eb	3.37N	28.34 E
Dunhua	27	Mc	43.22N	128.12 E
Dunhuang	27	Fc	40.10N	94.50 E
Dunkerque	11	Ic	51.03N	2.22 E
Dunkery Beacon	9	Jj	51.11N	3.35W
Dunkirk	43	Lc	42.29N	79.21W
Dunkwa	34	Ed	5.58N	1.47W
Dún Laoghaire	9	Gh	53.17N	6.08W
Dún Mánmhai/Dunmanway	9	Dj	51.43N	9.07W
Dunmanway/Dún Mánmhai	9	Dj	51.43N	9.07W
Dunn	44	Hh	35.19N	78.37W
Dún na nGall/Donegal [2]	9	Fg	54.50N	8.00W
Dún na nGall/Donegal	9	Eg	54.39N	8.06W
Dunnellon	44	Fk	29.03N	82.28W
Dunnet Head	9	Jc	58.39N	3.23W
Dunning	45	Ff	41.50N	100.06W
Dún Pádraig/Downpatrick	9	Hg	54.20N	5.43W
Dunqulah=Dongola (EN)	31	Kg	19.10N	30.29 E
Dunqulah al Qadīmah	35	Eb	18.13N	30.45 E
Dunqunāb	35	Fa	21.06N	37.05 E
Dunqunāb, Khalīj-	35	Fa	21.05N	37.05 E
Dunrankin	44	Fa	48.39N	83.04W
Duns	9	Kf	55.47N	2.20W
Dünsberg	12	Kd	50.39N	8.35 E
Dunsmuir	46	Df	41.13N	122.16W
Dunstable	12	Bc	51.53N	0.31W
Dunstan Mountains	62	Cf	44.55 S	169.30 E
Dun-sur-Auron	11	Ih	46.53N	2.34 E
Dun-sur-Meuse	12	He	49.23N	5.11 E
Duntroon	62	Df	44.51 S	170.41 E
Dunvegan	9	Gd	57.26N	6.35W
Duobukur	27	La	50.19N	124.57 E
Duolun/Dolonnur	27	Kc	42.10N	116.30 E
Duong Dong	25	Kf	10.13N	103.58 E
Dupree	45	Fd	45.03N	101.36W
Duqm	22	Hf	19.41N	57.32 E
Duque de Bragança, Quedas-	30	Ii	9.05 S	16.10 E
Duque de Caxias	54	Jh	22.47 S	43.18W
Duque de York, Isla-	56	Eh	50.40 S	75.20W
Du Quoin	45	Lg	38.01N	89.14W
Durack Range	59	Fc	17.00 S	128.00 E
Durack River	59	Fc	15.33 S	127.52 E
Durağan	24	Fb	41.25N	35.04 E
Durance	5	Gg	43.55N	4.44 E
Durand	45	Kd	44.38N	91.58W
Durand, Récif-	63b	Df	22.02 S	168.39 E
Durango [2]	47	Dd	24.50N	104.50W
Durango [Co.-U.S.]	39	If	37.16N	107.53W
Durango [Sp.]	13	Ja	43.10N	2.37W
Durañona	55	Bm	37.15 S	60.31W
Durant	43	He	33.59N	96.23W
Duras	11	Gj	44.40N	0.11 E
Duratón	13	Hc	41.37N	4.07W
Durazno	56	Id	33.22 S	56.31W
Durazno [2]	55	Dk	33.05 S	56.05W
Durazno, Cuchilla Grande del-	55	Dk	33.15 S	56.15W
Durazzo (EN)=Durresi	15	Ch	41.19N	19.26 E
Durban	31	Kk	29.55 S	30.56 E
Durbe	8	Ih	56.39N	21.14 E
Durbet-Daba, Pereval-	27	Eb	49.37N	89.25 E
Ḑurbo	35	Ic	11.30N	50.18 E
Durbuy	12	Hd	50.21N	5.28 E
Đurđevac	14	Ld	46.02N	17.04 E
Düren	10	Cf	50.48N	6.29 E
Durg	25	Gd	21.11N	81.17 E
Durgapur	25	Hd	23.30N	87.15 E
Durgen-Nur	27	Fb	47.40N	93.30 E
Durham	9	Lg	54.45N	1.45W
Durham [3]	9	Lg	54.45N	1.40W
Durham [Eng.-U.K.]	9	Lg	54.47N	1.34W
Durham [N.C.-U.S.]	43	Ld	35.59N	78.54W
Durkee	46	Gd	44.36N	117.28W
Durlas/Thurles	9	Fi	52.41N	7.49W
Durmā	23	Ge	24.37N	46.08 E
Durmersheim	12	Kf	48.56N	8.16 E
Durmitor	5	Hg	43.09N	19.02 E
Durnford, Punta-	32	De	23.37N	16.00W
Durresi=Durazzo (EN)	15	Ch	41.19N	19.26 E
Durrësit, Gjiri-	15	Ch	41.16N	19.28 E
Dursey/Oiléan Baoi	9	Cj	51.36N	10.12W
Dursunbey	24	Cc	39.35N	28.38 E
Durtal	11	Fg	47.40N	0.15W
Duru → Wuchuan	27	If	28.28N	107.57 E
Duruksi	35	Hd	8.29N	45.38 E
Durusu Gölü	15	Lh	41.20N	28.38 E
Durūz, Jabal ad-	24	Gf	32.40N	36.44 E
D'Urville Island	61	Dh	40.50 S	173.50 E
Dušak	18	Cf	37.15N	60.01 E
Dusa Mareb	35	Hd	5.31N	46.24 E
Dušanbe	22	If	38.35N	68.48 E
Dušeti	16	Nh	42.05N	44.42 E
Dusetos	8	Li	55.42N	26.02 E
Dushan	22	Mg	25.55N	107.36 E
Dushan Hu	28	Dg	35.06N	116.48 E
Dusios Ežeras/Dusja, Ozero-	8	Jj	54.15N	23.45 E
Dusja, Ozero-/Dusios Ežeras	8	Jj	54.15N	23.45 E
Dusky Sound	62	Bf	45.45 S	166.30 E
Düsseldorf	6	Ge	51.13N	6.46 E
Dusti	18	Gf	37.22N	68.43 E
Dutch Harbor	40a	Eb	53.53N	166.32W
Dutlwe	37	Cd	23.58 S	23.54 E
Dutton, Mount-	46	Jg	38.01N	112.13W
Duved	8	Ea	63.24N	12.52 E
Duvergé	49	Ld	18.22N	71.31W
Duvertepe	15	Lj	39.14N	28.27 E
Duvno	14	Lg	43.43N	17.14 E
Duwayhin	23	He	24.16N	51.20 E
Duwayhin, Khawr-	24	Nj	24.20N	51.25 E
Duyfken Point	59	Ib	12.35 S	141.40 E
Duyun	27	If	26.20N	107.28 E
Dūz	32	Ic	33.28N	9.01 E
Düzce	23	Da	40.50N	31.10 E
Dve Mogili	15	If	43.36N	25.52 E
Dvina (EN)=Daugava	19	Cd	57.04N	24.03 E
Dvina Gulf (EN)=Dvinskaja Guba	5	Jb	65.00N	39.45 E
Dvinskaja Guba=Dvina Gulf (EN)	5	Jb	65.00N	39.45 E
Dvor	14	Ke	45.04N	16.23 E
Dvuh Cirkov, Gora-	20	Lc	67.30N	168.20 E
Dvur Králové nad Labem	10	Lf	50.26N	15.48 E
Dwārka	25	Dd	22.14N	68.58 E
Dworshak Reservoir	46	Hc	46.45N	116.00W
Dyer, Cape-	38	Mc	66.37N	61.18W
Dyero	34	Dc	12.50N	6.30W
Dyer Plateau	66	Qf	70.45 S	65.30W
Dyersburg	43	Jd	36.03N	89.23W
Dyfed [3]	9	Ji	52.05N	4.00W
Dykhtau, Gora-	16	Mh	43.05N	43.12 E
Dyje	10	Mh	48.37N	16.56 E
Dyjsko-Svratecký úval	10	Mh	48.56N	16.25 E
Dyle	12	Gd	50.57N	4.40 E
Dylewska Góra	10	Pc	53.34N	19.57 E
Dynów	10	Sg	49.49N	22.14 E
Dyr, Djebel-	14	Cn	36.13N	8.46 E
Dyrhólaey	5	Ec	63.24N	19.08W
Dysnų Ežeras/Disnaj, Ozero-	7	Gi	55.35N	26.32 E
Dytiki Rodhopi	15	Hh	41.45N	24.05 E
Dzavhan	21	Le	48.54N	93.23 E
Džalagaš	19	Gf	45.05N	64.40 E
Džalal-Abad	18	Id	40.56N	73.05 E
Džalal-Abadskaja oblast	18	Hc	41.40N	71.50 E
Džalilabad	19	Eh	39.12N	48.31 E
Džalinda	20	Hf	53.31N	123.59 E
Džambejty	16	Rd	50.14N	52.38 E
Džambul	22	Je	42.54N	71.22 E
Džambul	19	Hf	47.17N	71.42 E
Džambulskaja Oblast [3]	19	Hg	44.30N	72.30 E
Dzamyn-Ud	27	Jb	43.50N	111.45 E
Džanak	16	Si	40.30N	55.35 E
Džanga	19	Fg	40.01N	53.10 E
Džankoj	19	Df	45.42N	34.22 E
Džansugurov	19	Hf	45.23N	79.29 E
Džanybek	19	Ef	49.24N	46.50 E
Dzaoudzi	31	Lj	12.47 S	45.17 E
Džardžan	20	Hc	68.55N	124.05 E
Džargalant	27	Gb	47.20N	99.35 E
Dzargalant	27	Ib	48.35N	105.50 E
Džarkurgan	19	Gh	37.29N	67.25 E
Džava	16	Mh	42.24N	43.53 E
Džebariki-Haja	20	Id	62.23N	135.50 E
Džebel [Bul.]	15	Ih	41.30N	25.18 E
Džebel	16	Sj	39.37N	54.18 E
Džebrail	16	Oj	39.23N	47.01 E
Dzereg	27	Fb	47.08N	92.50 E
Džergalan	18	Lc	42.33N	79.02 E
Dzermuk	16	Nj	39.48N	45.39 E
Dzeržinsk	16	Ec	53.44N	27.08 E
Dzeržinsk	19	Ed	56.16N	43.32 E
Dzeržinsk	16	Je	48.22N	37.50 E
Dzeržinskaja, Gora-	8	Lk	53.53N	27.10 E
Dzeržinskoje	20	Ee	56.49N	95.18 E
Džetygara	22	Id	52.11N	61.12 E
Džetysaj	18	Gd	40.49N	68.20 E
Džezkazgan	19	Gf	47.53N	67.27 E
Džezkazgan	22	Ie	47.47N	67.46 E
Džezkazganskaja Oblast [3]	19	Gf	47.30N	70.00 E
Dzhugdzhur Range (EN)=Džugdžur, Hrebet-	21	Pd	58.00N	136.00 E
Działdówka	10	Qd	52.58N	20.05 E
Działdowo	10	Qc	53.15N	20.10 E
Działoszyce	10	Qf	50.22N	20.21 E
Dzibalchén	48	Oh	19.31N	89.45W
Dzibilchaltún	48	Og	21.05N	89.36W
Dzierzgoń	10	Pc	53.56N	19.21 E
Dzierżoniów	10	Mf	50.44N	16.39 E
Džirgatal	18	He	39.13N	71.12 E
Džizak	19	Gg	40.07N	67.52 E
Džizakskaja Oblast [3]	19	Gg	40.20N	67.40 E
Džugdžur, Hrebet-=Dzhugdzhur Range (EN)	21	Pd	58.00N	136.00 E
Džūkste/Džukste	8	Jh	56.45N	23.10 E
Džukste/Džūkste	8	Jh	56.45N	23.10 E
Džulfa	16	Nj	38.59N	45.35 E
Džuma	18	Fe	39.44N	66.39 E
Dzun-Bajan	27	Jc	44.26N	110.03 E
Dzungarian Basin (EN)=Junggar Pendi	21	Ke	45.00N	88.00 E
Dzungarian Gate (EN)=Alataw Shankou	21	Ke	45.25N	82.25 E
Dzungarian Gate (EN)=Džungarskije Vorota	21	Ke	45.25N	82.25 E
Džungarski Alatau, Hrebet-	21	Ke	45.00N	81.00 E
Džungarskije Vorota=Dzungarian Gate (EN)	21	Ke	45.25N	82.25 E
Dzun-Hara	27	Ib	48.40N	106.40 E
Dzun-Mod	27	Ib	47.50N	106.57 E
Džurak-Sal	16	Mf	47.18N	43.36 E
Džusaly	19	Gf	45.29N	64.05 E
Džvari	16	Mh	42.42N	42.02 E

E

Éadan Doire/Edenderry	9	Fh	53.21N	7.03W
Eads	45	Eg	38.29N	102.47W
Eagle	40	Kd	64.46N	141.16W
Eagle	42	Lf	53.35N	57.25W
Eagle Creek	46	La	52.22N	107.24W
Eagle Lake	44	Mb	47.02N	68.36W
Eagle Lake [Ca.-U.S.]	46	Ef	40.39N	120.44W
Eagle Lake [Me.-U.S.]	44	Mb	46.20N	69.20W
Eagle Lake [Ont.-Can.]	45	Jb	49.42N	93.13W
Eagle Mountain	45	Kc	47.54N	90.33W
Eagle Nest	45	Dh	36.35N	105.14W
Eagle Pass	43	Gf	28.43N	100.30W
Eagle Peak [Ca.-U.S.]	43	Cc	41.17N	120.12W
Eagle Peak [Tx.-U.S.]	45	Dk	30.56N	105.01W
Eagle River [Ak.-U.S.]	40	Jd	61.19N	149.34W
Eagle River [Wi.-U.S.]	45	Ld	45.55N	89.15W
Eagle Summit	40	Jc	65.30N	145.38W
Ealing, London-	12	Bc	51.30N	0.19W
Ear Falls	45	Ja	50.38N	93.13W
Earn	9	Je	56.25N	3.30W
Earn, Loch-	9	Ie	56.28N	4.10W
Earnslaw, Mount-	62	Cf	44.37 S	168.25 E
Easley	44	Fh	34.50N	82.36W
East Alligator River	59	Gb	12.08 S	132.42 E
East Anglia	9	Ni	52.25N	1.00 E
East Angus	44	Lc	45.29N	71.40W
East Bay [Can.]	42	Jd	64.05N	81.30W
East Bay [U.S.]	45	Ll	29.05N	89.15W
East Berlin = Berlin	6	He	52.31N	13.24 E
Eastbourne [Eng.-U.K.]	9	Nk	50.46N	0.17 E
Eastbourne [N.Z.]	62	Fd	41.17 S	174.54 E
East Caicos	49	Lc	21.41N	71.30W
East Cape [Fl.-U.S.]	44	Gm	25.07N	81.05W
East Cape [N.Z.]	57	Ih	37.41 S	178.33 E
East Caroline Basin (EN)	3	Ii	4.00N	146.45 E
East Chicago	44	De	41.38N	87.27W
East China Sea (EN)=Dong Hai	21	Og	29.00N	125.00 E
East China Sea (EN)=Higashi-Shina-Kai	21	Og	29.00N	125.00 E
East Coast [2]	62	Gc	38.20 S	177.50 E
East Dereham	9	Ni	52.41N	0.56 E
Eastend	46	Kb	49.31N	108.48W
East Entrance	64a	Bb	7.50N	134.40 E
Easter Island (EN)=Pascua, Isla de-/Rapa Nui	57	Qg	27.07 S	109.22W
Easter Island (EN)=Rapa Nui/Pascua, Isla de-	57	Qg	27.07 S	109.22W
Eastern [Ghana] [3]	34	Ed	6.30N	0.30W
Eastern [Kenya] [3]	36	Gb	0.05N	38.00 E
Eastern [S.L.] [3]	34	Cd	8.15N	11.00W
Eastern [Ug.] [3]	36	Fb	1.30N	33.50 E
Eastern [Zam.] [3]	36	Fe	13.00 S	32.15 E
Eastern Fields	60	Dj	10.03 S	145.22 E

Index Symbols

- [1] Independent Nation
- [2] State, Region
- [3] District, County
- Municipality
- Colony, Dependency
- Continent
- Physical Region
- Historical or Cultural Region
- Mount, Mountain
- Volcano
- Hill
- Mountains, Mountain Range
- Hills, Escarpment
- Plateau, Upland
- Pass, Gap
- Plain, Lowland
- Delta
- Salt Flat
- Valley, Canyon
- Crater, Cave
- Karst Features
- Depression
- Polder
- Desert, Dunes
- Forest, Woods
- Heath, Steppe
- Oasis
- Cape, Point
- Coast, Beach
- Cliff
- Peninsula
- Isthmus
- Sandbank
- Island
- Atoll
- Rock, Reef
- Islands, Archipelago
- Rocks, Reefs
- Coral Reef
- Well, Spring
- Geyser
- River, Stream
- Waterfall Rapids
- River Mouth, Estuary
- Lake
- Salt Lake
- Intermittent Lake
- Reservoir
- Swamp, Pond
- Canal
- Glacier
- Ice Shelf, Pack Ice
- Ocean
- Sea
- Gulf, Bay
- Strait, Fjord
- Lagoon
- Bank
- Seamount
- Tablemount
- Ridge
- Shelf
- Basin
- Escarpment, Sea Scarp
- Fracture
- Trench, Abyss
- National Park, Reserve
- Point of Interest
- Recreation Site
- Cave, Cavern
- Historic Site
- Ruins
- Wall, Walls
- Church, Abbey
- Temple
- Scientific Station
- Airport
- Port
- Lighthouse
- Mine
- Tunnel
- Dam, Bridge

Name			Lat	Long
Eastern Ghats ▣	21	Jh	14.00N	78.50 E
Eastern Point ▣	51b Ab	18.07N	63.01W	
Eastern Sayans (EN) =				
Vostočny Sajan ▣	21	Ld	53.00N	97.00 E
Eastern Siberia (EN) ▣	21	Rc	65.00N	155.00 E
Eastern Sierra Madre (EN) =				
Madre Oriental, Sierra- ▣	38	Jg	22.00N	99.30W
Eastern Turkistan (EN) ▣	21	Jf	40.00N	80.00 E
East Falkland/Soledad, Isla-				
▣	52	Kk	51.45 S	58.50W
East Fork ⬅	45	Ie	42.41N	94.12W
East Friesland (EN) =				
Ostfriesland ▣	10	Dc	53.20N	7.40 E
East Frisian Islands (EN) =				
Ostfriesische Inseln ▣				
East Grand Forks	45	Hc	47.56N	97.01W
East Grand Rapids	44	Ed	42.56N	85.35W
East Greenland (EN) =				
Østgrønland ▣	41	Id	72.00N	35.00W
East Grinstead	9	Mj	51.08N	0.01W
East Ilsley	12	Ac	51.32N	1.17W
East Kilbride	9	If	55.46N	4.10W
East Lansing	44	Ed	42.44N	84.29W
East Las Vegas	46	Hh	36.07N	115.01W
Eastleigh	9	Lk	50.58N	1.22W
East London	31	Jl	33.00S	27.55 E
East Lynn Lake ▣	44	Ff	38.05N	82.20W
Eastmain ⬅	42	Jf	52.15N	78.34W
Eastmain	42	Jf	52.14N	78.31W
Eastman	44	Fi	32.12N	83.11W
East Mariana Basin (EN) ▣	3	Jh	12.00N	153.00 E
East Midlands Airport ▣	12	Ab	52.50N	1.20W
East Novaya Zemlya Trough				
(EN) ▣	67	Hd	73.30N	61.00 E
Easton	44	Ae	40.41N	75.13W
East Pacific Rise (EN) ▣	3	Mi	20.00S	110.00W
East Point	44	Ei	33.40N	84.27W
East Point [B.V.I.] ▣	51a Db	18.43N	64.16W
East Point [V.I.U.S.] ▣	51a Dc	17.46N	64.33W
Eastport	44	Nc	44.54N	67.00W
East Pryor Mountain ▣	46	Kd	45.14N	108.30W
East Retford	9	Mh	53.19N	0.56W
East Road ▣	12	Cd	51.00N	1.02 E
East Schelde (EN) =				
Oosterschelde ▣	11	Jc	51.30N	4.00 E
East Scotia Basin (EN) ▣	52	Mk	57.00 S	35.00W
East Siberian Sea (EN) =				
Vostočno Sibirskoje				
More	67	Cd	74.00N	166.00 E
East St. Louis	43	Id	38.38N	90.05W
East Sussex ▣	9	Nk	50.55N	0.15 E
East Tavaputs Plateau ▣	46	Kg	39.45N	109.30W
East Wear Bay ▣	12	Dc	51.08N	1.18 E
Eaton	44	Ef	39.44N	84.37W
Eatonia	46	Ka	51.13N	109.23W
Eatonton	44	Fi	33.20N	83.23W
Eatonville	46	Dc	46.51N	122.17W
Eau Claire	43	Ic	44.49N	91.31W
Eau-Claire, Lac à l' - ▣	42	Ke	56.20N	74.00W
Eauripik Atoll ▣	57	Fd	6.42N	143.03 E
Eauripik Ridge (EN) ▣	60	Cg	3.00N	142.00 E
Eauze	11	Gk	43.52N	0.06 E
Ebano	48	Jf	22.13N	98.24W
Ebbegebirge ▣	10	De	51.10N	7.45 E
Ebbw Vale	9	Jj	51.47N	3.12W
Ebebiyin	34	He	2.09N	11.20 E
Ebeltoft	8	Dh	56.12N	10.41 E
Ebensburg	44	Ae	40.28N	78.44W
Ebensee	14	Hc	47.48N	13.46 E
Eberbach	10	Ig	49.28N	8.59 E
Eber Gölü ▣	24	Dc	38.38N	31.12 E
Ebersbach	10	Ke	51.01N	14.35 E
Eberswalde	10	Jd	52.50N	13.50 E
Ebetsu	28	Pc	43.07N	141.34 E
Ebino	28	Kh	32.02N	130.47 E
Ebinur Hu ▣	21	Ke	44.55N	82.55 E
Ebla ▣	23	Eb	35.42N	36.50 E
Ebo	36	Ce	11.02S	14.40 E
Ebola ⬅	36	Db	3.20N	20.57 E
Eboli	14	Jd	40.36N	15.04 E
Ebolowa	31	Ih	2.54N	11.09 E
Ebombo	36	Ed	5.42 S	26.07 E
Ebon Atoll ▣	57	Hd	4.38N	168.43 E
Ebre/Ebro ⬅	5	Gg	40.43N	0.54 E
Ebre, Delta de l'-/Ebro,				
Delta del- ▣	13	Md	40.43N	0.54 E
Ebril, Récif- ▣	60	Jd	22.40 S	133.30W
Ebro/Ebre ⬅	5	Gg	40.43N	0.54 E
Ebro, Delta del-/Ebre, Delta				
de l'- ▣	13	Md	40.43N	0.54 E
Ebro, Embalse del- ▣	13	Ia	43.00N	3.58W
Ebschloß ▣	10	Ef	50.58N	8.15 E
Ecaussines	12	Gd	50.34N	4.10 E
Ecbatana ▣	34	Mc	34.48N	48.30 E
Eceabat	15	Ji	40.11N	26.21 E
Echdeiria	32	Ed	27.14N	10.27W
Echegarate, Puerto de- ▣	13	Jb	42.57N	2.14W
Echeng [China]	28	Ci	30.24N	114.52 E
Echeng [China]	27	Kd	36.10N	116.03 E
Echez ⬅	11	Gk	43.28N	0.02 E
Echigo-Sanmyaku ▣	29	Fc	37.30N	139.15 E
Echizen-Misaki ▣	28	Mc	35.59N	135.57 E
Echo Bay	39	Hc	66.04N	118.00W
Echo Seamount (EN) ▣	32	Dc	25.23N	19.25W
Echt	12	Hc	51.06N	5.52 E
Echternach	12	Ie	49.49N	6.25 E
Echuca	59	Ig	36.10S	144.45 E
Echzell	10	Ef	50.23N	8.52 E
Ecija	13	Gg	37.32N	5.05W
Eckernförde	10	Fb	54.28N	9.50 E
Eckerö ▣	7	Ef	60.15N	19.35 E
Eclipse Sound ▣	42	Jb	72.40N	79.30W
Ečmiadzin	16	Gf	40.10N	44.18 E
Ecommoy	11	Gg	47.50N	0.16 E
Ecos	13	Ka	43.00N	1.39 E
Ecouis	12	De	49.19N	1.26 E
Écouves, Forêt d'- ▣	11	Gf	48.32N	0.04 E

Écrin, Barre des- ▣	11	Mj	44.55N	6.22 E
Ecuador ▣	53	If	2.00 S	77.30W
Ecury-sur-Coole	12	Cf	48.54N	4.20 E
Ed	7	Cf	58.54N	11.56 E
Edam-Volendam	12	Hb	52.30N	5.03 E
Edane	8	Ee	59.38N	12.49 E
Eday ▣	9	Kb	59.11N	2.47W
Edchera	32	Ed	27.02N	13.04W
Eddrachillis Bay ▣	9	Hc	58.19N	5.15W
Eddystone Point ▣	59	Jh	41.00 S	148.20 E
Eddystone Rocks ▣	9	Ik	50.15N	4.10W
Eddyville	44	Cg	37.03N	88.04W
Ede [Neth.]	11	Lb	52.03N	5.40 E
Ede [Nig.]	34	Fd	7.44N	4.26 E
Edéa	31	Ih	3.48N	10.08 E
Edefors	35	Gc	13.56N	41.40 E
Edéia	55	Hc	17.18S	49.55W
Edelény	10	Qh	48.18N	20.44 E
Eden [Austl.]	59	Jg	37.04 S	149.54 E
Eden [Tx.-U.S.]	45	Gk	31.13N	99.51W
Edenburg	37	De	29.45 S	25.56 E
Edenderry/Éadan Doire	9	Fh	53.21N	7.03W
Edenkoben	12	Ke	49.17N	8.09 E
Edenton	44	Ig	36.04N	76.39W
Edentown	10	Fe	51.13N	9.27 E
Edersee ⬅	12	Lc	51.11N	9.03 E
Edertal	12	Lc	51.09N	9.09 E
Edewecht	12	Ja	53.08N	7.59 E
Edgar Ranges ▣	59	Ec	18.43 S	123.25 E
Edgartown	44	Le	41.23N	70.31W
Edgecumbe	62	Gb	37.58 S	176.50 E
Edgeley	45	Gc	46.22N	98.43W
Edgell ▣	42	Ld	61.50N	65.00W
Edgeøya ▣	67	Jd	77.45N	22.30 E
Édhessa	15	Fi	40.48N	22.03 E
Edina	45	Id	40.10N	92.10W
Edinburg	43	Gk	26.18N	98.10W
Edinburgh	6	Fd	55.57N	3.15W
Edinburgh, Arrecife- ▣	49	Ff	14.50N	82.39W
Edincik	24	Bb	40.20N	27.51 E
Edingen/Enghien	12	Gd	50.42N	4.02 E
Edirne	24	Bb	41.40N	26.34 E
Edisto Island ▣	44	Gi	32.35N	80.10W
Edisto River ⬅	44	Gi	32.35N	80.24W
Edith, Mount- ▣	46	Jc	46.26N	111.11W
Edith Ronne Land (EN) ▣	66	Qf	78.30 S	61.00W
Edjeleh	32	Id	27.42N	9.53 E
Edjereh ▣	32	Id	23.29N	9.34 E
Édjérir ⬅	34	Fb	18.06N	0.50 E
Edmond	45	Hi	35.39N	97.29W
Edmonds	46	Jc	47.48N	122.22W
Edmonton	39	Hd	53.33N	113.28W
Edmundston	42	Kg	47.22N	68.20W
Edna	45	Hl	28.42N	96.39W
Edremit	23	Cb	39.35N	27.01 E
Edremit, Gulf of- (EN) =				
Edremit Körfezi ▣	24	Bc	39.30N	26.45 E
Edremit Körfezi = Edremit,				
Gulf of- (EN) ▣	24	Bc	39.30N	26.45 E
Edsbro	7	Eg	59.54N	18.29 E
Edsbruk	8	Gf	58.02N	16.28 E
Edsbyn	7	Ec	61.23N	15.49 E
Edson	42	Ff	53.35N	116.26W
Edsvalla	8	Ee	59.26N	13.13 E
Eduardo Castex	56	Ie	35.54 S	64.18W
Eduni, Mount- ▣	42	Ed	64.08N	128.10W
Edward, Lake- ▣	30	Ji	0.25 S	29.30 E
Edward, Lake- (EN) =				
Rutanzige, Lac- ▣	37	Gb	0.25 S	29.30 E
Edwards Creek	59	He	28.21 S	135.51 E
Edwards Plateau ▣	38	If	31.20N	101.00W
Edward VIII Bay ▣	66	Gc	66.55N	57.00 E
Edward VII Peninsula ▣	66	Mf	77.40 S	155.00W
Edzo	42	Fd	62.47N	116.08W
Eeklo	11	Jc	51.11N	3.34 E
Eel River ⬅	43	Cc	40.40N	124.20W
Eem ⬅	12	Hb	52.16N	5.20 E
Eemshaven	12	Ia	53.19N	7.03 E
Eemskanaal ⬅	12	Ia	53.19N	6.57 E
Eenrum	12	Ia	53.23N	6.25 E
Eersel	12	Hc	51.22N	5.19 E
Eesti = Estonskaja SSR	19	Cd	59.00N	26.00 E
Eesti Nõukogude Socialistlik				
Vabarijk/Estonskaja				
SSR — Eesti	19	Cd	59.00N	26.00 E
Eesti NSV → Eesti	19	Cd	59.00N	26.00 E
Efatë, Ile- ▣	57	Hf	17.40 S	168.25 E
Eferding	14	Ib	48.18N	14.01 E
Efes = Ephesus (EN) ▣	15	Kl	37.55N	27.20 E
Effingham	45	Jg	39.07N	88.33W
Eflâni	24	Eb	41.26N	32.57 E
Eforie	15	Le	44.01N	28.38 E
Ega ⬅	13	Kb	42.19N	1.55W
Egadi, Isole- = Egadi Islands				
(EN) ▣	5	Hh	38.00N	12.15 E
Egadi Islands (EN) = Egadi,				
Isole- ▣	5	Hh	38.00N	12.15 E
Egan Range ▣	46	Hg	39.00N	115.00W
Eganville	44	Ic	47.33N	77.06W
Egbe	34	Gd	8.13N	5.31 E
Ege Denizi = Aegean Sea				
(EN) ▣	5	Ih	39.00N	25.00 E
Egedesminde/Ausiait	67	Nc	68.50N	52.45W
Egegik	40	Hf	58.13N	157.22W
Egentliga Finland/Varsinais-				
Suomi ▣	7	Ef	60.40N	22.30 E
Eger	10	Qh	47.54N	20.23 E
Egersund	7	Bd	58.27N	6.01 E
Egerton, Mount- ▣	59	Dd	24.45 S	117.45 E
Egeskov ▣	8	Dj	55.10N	10.30 E
Eggegebirge ▣	10	Ee	51.40N	8.55 E
Eggenfelden	10	Ih	48.24N	12.46 E

Eggenstein Leopoldshafen	12	Ke	49.05N	8.23 E
Eggum	7	Cb	68.19N	13.42 E
Eghezée	12	Gd	5C.36N	4.56 E
Egijn-Gol ⬅	27	Ha	4C.24N	103.36 E
Egletons	11	Ii	4E.24N	2.03 E
Eglinton ▣	42	Fa	75.45N	118.50W
Egmont, Cape- ▣	61	Dg	39.17 S	173.45 E
Egmont, Mount- ▣	62	Fc	39.18 S	174.04 E
Egnazia	14	Lj	40.50N	17.25 E
Eğridir	24	Dc	37.52N	30.51 E
Eğridir Gölü ▣	23	Db	38.02N	30.53 E
Eğrigöz Dağı ▣	15	Mj	39.21N	29.07 E
Egtved	8	Ci	55.37N	9.18 E
Éguas ou Correntina, Rio				
das- ⬅	55	Ja	13.26 S	44.14W
Eguey ▣	30	Ig	16.10N	16.10 E
Egvekinot	22	Tc	63.19N	179.10 E
Egypt (EN) = Mişr ▣	27	Jf	27.00N	30.00 E
Eha Amufu	34	Gd	6.40N	7.46 E
Ehen Hudag → Alxa Youqi	27	Ib	35.35N	132.40 E
Ehime Ken ▣	28	Lh	33.35N	132.40 E
Ehingen	10	Fh	48.17N	9.44 E
Ehrang, Trier-	12	Ie	49.49N	6.41 E
Ehrwald	14	Ec	47.24N	10.55 E
Ei	29	Bf	31.13N	130.30 E
Eiao, Ile- ▣	57	Me	8.00 S	140.40W
Eibar	13	Ja	43.11N	2.28W
Eibergen	12	Ib	52.07N	6.40 E
Eichsfeld ▣	10	Ge	51.25N	10.20 E
Eichstätt	10	Hh	48.53N	11.11 E
Eickelborn, Lippetal-	12	Kc	51.39N	8.13 E
Eide	8	Bd	62.55N	7.26 E
Eider ⬅	10	Eb	54.19N	8.58 E
Eiderstedt ▣	10	Fb	54.22N	8.50 E
Eidet	7	Cd	64.27N	13.37 E
Eidfjord	7	Bf	60.28N	7.05 E
Eidfjorden ▣	8	Bd	60.25N	6.45 E
Eidslandet	8	Ad	60.44N	5.45 E
Eidsvåg	7	Be	62.47N	8.03 E
Eidsvoll	7	Cf	60.19N	11.14 E
Eidsvollfiellet ▣	41	Nc	79.00N	13.00 E
Eierlandse Gat ▣	12	Ga	53.12N	4.52 E
Eifel ▣	10	Cf	50.15N	6.45 E
Eiffel Flats	37	Dc	18.15 S	29.59 E
Eigenbrakel/Braine-l'Alleud	12	Gd	50.41N	4.22 E
Eigerøya ▣	8	Af	58.25N	5.52 E
Eigg ▣	9	Ge	56.54N	6.10W
Eight Degree Channel ▣	21	Ji	8.00N	73.00 E
Eights Coast ▣	66	Pf	73.30 S	96.00W
Eighty Mile Beach ▣	59	Ec	19.45 S	121.00 E
Eigrim, Jabal- ▣	35	Fb	19.22N	35.18 E
Eijsden	12	Hd	50.46N	5.42 E
Eikeren ▣	8	Ce	59.40N	10.00 E
Eikesdalsvatnet ▣	8	Cb	62.35N	8.10 E
ʾEilai	35	Eb	16.33N	30.54 E
Eildon, Lake- ▣	59	Jg	37.10 S	145.50 E
Eilenburg	10	Je	51.28N	12.37 E
Eiler Rasmussen, Kap- ▣	41	Ja	82.40N	20.00W
Eil Malk ▣	64a Ac	7.09N	134.22 E
Eina	8	Dd	60.38N	10.36 E
Einasleigh	59	Ic	18.31 S	144.05 E
Einasleigh River ⬅	59	Ic	17.30 S	142.17 E
Einbeck	10	Fe	51.49N	9.52 E
Eindhoven	11	Lc	51.26N	5.28 E
Einsiedeln	14	Cc	47.08N	8.45 E
Éire/Ireland ▣	6	Fe	53.00N	8.00W
Eiríksjökull ▣	7a Bb	64.46N	20.24W
Eirunepé	53	Jf	6.40 S	69.52W
Eisack/Isarco ⬅	14	Fd	46.47N	11.18 E
Eisacktal/Isarco, Valle- ▣	14	Fd	46.45N	11.35 E
Eisacktal/Valle Isarco ▣	14	Fd	46.45N	11.35 E
Eisenach	10	Gf	50.59N	10.19 E
Eisenberg	10	Hf	50.58N	11.54 E
Eisenberg (Pfalz)	12	Kc	51.15N	8.50 E
Eisenerz	14	Ic	47.33N	14.53 E
Eisenerzer Alpen ▣	14	Ic	47.30N	14.40 E
Eisenhüttenstadt	10	Kd	52.10N	14.42 E
Eisenstadt	14	Kb	47.51N	16.31 E
Eisenwurzen ▣	14	Jc	47.56N	15.02 E
Eišiškės/Ejšiškes	7	Fi	54.14N	25.02 E
Eisleben	10	He	51.31N	11.33 E
Eitorf	12	Jd	50.46N	7.27 E
Eivissa/Ibiza = Iviza (EN) ▣	5	Gh	39.00N	1.25 E
Eje, Sierra del- ▣	13	Fb	42.20N	6.55W
Ejea de los Caballeros	13	Kb	42.08N	1.08W
Ejido	54	Db	8.33N	71.14W
Ejido Insurgentes	38	Ce	25.12N	111.45W
Ejin Horo Qi (Altan Xiret)	27	Ic	39.31N	109.45 E
Ejin Qi	22	Ne	41.50N	100.50 E
Ejšiškes/Eišiškės	7	Fi	54.14N	25.02 E
Ejura	34	Ed	7.23N	1.22W
Ejutla de Crespo	38	Ji	16.34N	96.44W
Ekalaka	46	Md	45.53N	104.33W
Ekecek Dağı ▣	24	Fc	38.39N	34.03 E
Ekenäs/Tammisaari	7	Fg	59.58N	23.26 E
Ekeren, Antwerpen-	12	Gc	51.17N	4.25 E
Eket	34	Ge	4.39N	7.56 E
Eketahuna	62	Fd	40.39 S	175.44 E
Ekhinádhes Nísoi ▣	15	Ek	38.25N	21.02 E
Ekiatapski Hrebet ▣	20	Mc	68.40N	177.50 E
Ekibastuz	19	Ig	51.42N	75.22 E
Ekimčan	20	If	53.07N	133.02 E
Ekoli	36	Dc	0.23 S	24.16 E
Ekoln ▣	8	Fd	59.45N	17.35 E
Ekombe	36	Db	1.16N	21.36 E
Ekonda	20	Fc	65.47N	105.17 E
Eksjö	7	Dh	57.40N	14.57 E
Ekuma ⬅	37	Bc	18.35 S	15.47 E
Ekwan ⬅	42	Jf	53.12N	82.15W
El Aaiún	31	Ic	27.10N	13.12W
El Aargub	32	Cc	20.46N	17.04W
El Aatf ▣	32	Je	23.30N	15.30W
El Abadia	13	Mi	36.23N	1.42 E
El-Abd ⬅	23	Fg	31.09N	34.16 E
El Abiodh Sidi Cheikh	32	Hc	32.53N	0.34 E

El ʾĀçaba ▣	32	Ef	16.30N	12.00W
El ʾĀçaba ▣	30	Fg	16.49N	12.05W
El Adeb Larache	32	Id	27.22N	8.52 E
El Affroun	13	Oh	36.28N	2.37 E
Elafonísi Channel (EN) =				
Elafónisou, Stenón- ▣	15	Fm	36.25N	23.00 E
Elafónisos ▣	15	Fm	36.29N	22.58 E
Elafonísou Stenón- =				
Elafónisi Channel (EN) ▣	15	Fm	36.25N	23.00 E
El Agreb	32	Ic	30.48N	5.30 E
El Aguilar	56	Gb	32.12 S	65.42W
El Álamo	48	Ab	31.34N	116.02W
El Alia	32	Ic	32.42N	5.26 E
El-Amria	13	Ki	35.32N	1.01W
Elan ▣	12	Lc	46.06N	28.04 E
El Andévalo ▣	13	Fg	37.40N	7.00W
El Aouinet	14	Bo	35.52N	7.54 E
El Arahal	13	Gg	37.16N	5.33W
El Aricha	32	Gc	34.13N	1.16W
Elása ▣	15	Jn	35.17N	26.20 E
Elassón	15	Fj	39.54N	22.11 E
Elat	22	Fg	29.33N	34.57 E
Eláti ▣	15	Dk	38.43N	20.39 E
Elato Atoll ▣	57	Fd	7.28N	146.10 E
El Attaf	13	Nh	36.13N	1.40 E
Elâzığ	23	Eb	38.41N	39.14 E
El Azúcar, Presa de- ▣	48	Jd	26.15N	99.00W
Elba	44	Dj	31.25N	86.04W
Elba ▣	5	Hg	42.45N	10.15 E
Elban	20	If	50.05N	136.30 E
El Banco	54	Db	9.01N	73.58W
El Barco de Ávila	13	Gd	40.21N	5.31W
El Barco de Valdeorras	13	Fb	42.25N	6.59W
Elbasani	15	Dh	41.06N	20.05 E
El Baúl	54	Eb	8.57N	68.17W
El Bayadh	32	Hc	33.41N	1.01 E
Elbe (EN) = Labe ⬅	5	Ge	53.50N	9.00 E
Elbe ⬅	5	Ge	53.50N	9.00 E
Elbe-Lübeck-Kanal ⬅	10	Gc	53.50N	10.40 E
Elbert, Mount- ▣	38	If	39.07N	106.27W
Elberton	44	Fh	34.07N	82.52W
Elbe-Seitenkanal ⬅	10	Gd	52.22N	10.34 E
Elbeuf	11	Ge	49.17N	1.00 E
Elbeyli	23	Eb	36.41N	37.26 E
El Bierzo ▣	13	Fb	42.40N	6.50W
Elbistan	24	Gc	38.13N	37.12 E
Elbląg ▣	10	Pb	54.10N	19.25 E
Elbląg, Kanał- ⬅	10	Pc	53.43N	19.53 E
El Bolsón	56	Ff	41.58 S	71.31W
El Bonillo	13	Jf	38.57N	2.32W
Elbow	46	La	51.07N	106.35W
Elbow Cays ▣	49	Gb	23.57N	80.29W
Elbow Lake	45	Hc	46.00N	95.58W
Elbrus ▣	5	Kg	43.21N	42.26 E
Elbsandsteingebirge ▣	10	Kf	50.50N	14.12 E
ʾElbür	35	Hk	4.40N	46.40 E
Elburg	11	Lb	52.26N	5.50 E
El Burgo de Osma	13	Ic	41.35N	3.04W
Elburgon	36	Gc	0.18 S	35.49 E
El Burro	48	Id	29.16N	101.55W
Elburz Mountains (EN) =				
Alborz, Reshteh-ye Kūhhā-				
ye- ▣	21	Hf	36.00N	53.00 E
El Cajon	43	De	32.48N	116.58W
El Callao	54	Fb	7.21N	61.49W
El Calvario	50	Ch	8.59N	67.00W
El Campo	45	Hl	29.12N	96.16W
El Canelo	48	Id	24.19N	100.23W
El Cármen	55	Cd	18.49 S	58.33W
El Carmen de Bolívar	54	Db	9.43N	75.07W
El Casco	48	Ge	25.34N	104.35W
El Castillo	49	Eh	11.01N	84.24W
El Centro	43	De	32.48N	115.34W
El Cerro	54	Fy	17.31 S	61.34W
El Chaparro	50	Dh	9.10N	65.01W
Elche	13	Lf	38.15N	0.42W
Elcho Island ▣	59	Hb	11.55 S	135.45 E
El Cury	54	Ee	39.56 S	68.20W
Elda	13	Lf	38.29N	0.47W
El Desemboque	48	Db	30.30N	112.59W
El Dificil	54	Db	9.51N	74.14W
Eldikan	20	Id	60.38N	135.07 E
El Djouf ▣	30	Gf	21.25N	6.40W
El Doncello	54	Cc	1.43N	75.17W
Eldorado	45	Hk	30.52N	100.36W
Eldorado	56	Jc	26.24 S	54.38W
El Dorado [Ar.-U.S.]	18	Gd	33.13N	92.40W
El Dorado [Ks.-U.S.]	43	Hd	37.49N	96.52W
El Dorado [Mex.]	48	Fe	24.17N	107.31W
El Dorado [Ven.]	54	Fb	6.44N	61.38W
Eldorado Paulista	55	Hg	24.32 S	48.06W
El Dorado Springs	45	Ih	37.52N	94.01W
Eldoret	36	Gb	0.31N	35.17 E
Eldsberga	8	Eh	56.36N	12.59 E
ʾEl Ḍubbo	35	Ec	18.35N	31.20 E
Eldžik	18	De	39.25N	63.01 E
Elefantes, Rio dos- ⬅	37	Ed	24.03 S	32.40 E
El Eglab ▣	32	Gf	26.30N	5.00W
Eléja/Eleja	7	Fh	56.28N	23.41 E
Eleja/Eléja	7	Fh	56.28N	23.41 E
Elektrénai/Elektrenaj	8	Kj	54.46N	24.47 E
Elektrenaj/Elektrénai	8	Kj	54.46N	24.47 E
Elektrostal	19	Ee	55.48N	38.29 E
Elele	34	Gd	5.06N	6.49 E
Elena	15	Ig	42.56N	25.53 E
El Encanto [Bol.]	54	Ce	16.57 S	59.24W
El Encanto [Col.]	54	Cd	1.37 S	73.12W
Elephant Butte Reservoir ▣	45	Cj	33.19N	107.10W
Elephant Island ▣	66	Re	61.10 S	55.14W
Elephant Mountain ▣	45	Bk	30.02N	103.30W
Elesbão Veloso	54	Je	6.13 S	42.08W

El Escorial ▣	13	Hd	40.35N	4.10W
Eleşkirt	24	Jc	39.49N	42.40 E
El Estor	49	Cf	15.32N	89.21W
Eleuthera ▣	38	Lg	25.15N	76.20W
Elevsis	15	Gk	38.02N	23.32 E
Elevtheroúpolis	15	Hi	40.55N	24.15 E
El Fendek	13	Gi	35.34N	5.35W
El Ferrol del Caudillo	13	Da	43.29N	8.14W
El Fud	35	Gd	7.15N	42.51 E
El Galhak	48	Hf	23.50N	103.06W
El Gassi	32	Ic	30.55N	5.50 E
Elgen	20	Kd	62.45N	150.40 E
Elgepiggen ▣	7	Ce	62.10N	11.22 E
El Ghomri	13	Mi	35.41N	0.12 E
Elgi ▣	20	Jd	64.20N	142.05 E
Elgin [Il.-U.S.]	43	Jc	42.02N	88.17W
Elgin [N.D.-U.S.]	45	Fc	46.24N	101.51W
Elgin [Or.-U.S.]	46	Gd	45.34N	117.55W
Elgin [Scot.-U.K.]	9	Jd	57.39N	3.20W
Elginski	20	Jd	64.48N	141.50 E
Elgjaij	20	Gd	62.28N	117.37 E
El Goléa	31	He	30.34N	2.53 E
Elgon, Mont- ▣	30	Kh	1.08N	34.33 E
Elgoran	35	Gd	5.04N	44.22 E
El Grao, Castellón de la				
Plana-	13	Me	39.58N	0.01 E
El Grao, Valencia-	13	Le	39.27N	0.20W
El Guapo	50	Dg	10.09N	65.58W
El Guayabo	49	Ki	8.37N	72.20W
El Hadjar	14	Bn	36.48N	7.45 E
El Hajeb	32	Fc	33.42N	5.22W
El-Ham	32	Qi	35.42N	4.52 E
El Hammam	13	Ji	36.50N	0.15W
ʾEl Hamurre	35	Hd	7.11N	48.55 E
El Hank ▣	30	Gf	24.00N	6.30W
El Harrach, Al Jazā'ir-	13	Ph	36.43N	3.08 E
Elhotovo	16	Nh	43.20N	44.13 E
Elhovo	15	Jg	42.10N	26.34 E
El Huecú	56	Fe	37.37 S	70.36W
Eli	45	Ej	33.57N	103.39W
Éliki, Vallée d'- ▣	34	Gc	14.45N	7.15 E
Elila ⬅	36	Ec	2.43 S	25.53 E
Elila ⬅	30	Ji	2.45 S	25.53 E
Elimäki	8	Ld	60.43N	26.28 E
Elin Pelin	15	Gg	42.40N	23.36 E
Elisejna	15	Gf	43.05N	23.29 E
Elisenvaara	8	Mc	61.19N	29.47 E
Elista	6	Kf	46.16N	44.14 E
Elizabeth [Austl.]	58	Eh	34.45 S	138.39 E
Elizabeth [N.J.-U.S.]	44	Ae	40.40N	74.13W
Elizabeth, Cape- ▣	46	Cc	47.22N	124.22W
Elizabeth City	43	Ld	36.18N	76.14W
Elizabeth Reef ▣	57	Gg	29.55 S	159.05 E
Elizabethton	44	Fg	36.21N	82.13W
Elizabethtown [Ky.-U.S.]	44	Eg	37.42N	85.52W
Elizabethtown [N.C.-U.S.]	44	Hh	34.38N	78.37W
El Jadida ▣	32	Fc	32.54N	8.30W
El Jadida	31	Ge	33.15N	8.30W
El Jicaro	49	Dg	13.43N	86.08W
Elk	10	Sc	53.32N	22.47 E
El Kala	32	Ib	36.54N	8.27 E
El Kantara	32	Ib	35.13N	5.43 E
El-Karimia	13	Nh	36.07N	1.33 E
Elk City [Id.-U.S.]	46	Hd	45.51N	115.29W
Elk City [Ok.-U.S.]	45	Gi	35.25N	99.25W
Elk Grove	46	Fg	38.25N	121.22W
Elk Horn	45	Hf	41.37N	95.26W
El Kelaa des Srarhna	32	Fc	32.03N	7.30W
El Kelaa des Srarhna	32	Fc	32.03N	7.30W
El Kere	35	Gd	5.51N	42.06 E
Elkhart [In.-U.S.]	43	Jc	41.41N	85.58W
Elkhart [Ks.-U.S.]	45	Fh	37.00N	101.54W
El Khatt ▣	32	Ef	19.00N	12.25W
Elkhead Mountains ▣	45	Cf	40.50N	107.05W
El Khnâchich ▣	34	Fa	21.20N	3.45W
Elkhorn River ⬅	45	Hf	41.07N	96.19W
Elkins	44	Hf	38.56N	79.53W
Elk Mountain ▣	46	Lf	41.38N	106.32W
Elko	39	He	40.50N	115.46W
Elk Peak ▣	46	Jc	46.27N	110.46W
Elk River ⬅	44	Dj	38.21N	81.38W
Elk River	45	Jd	45.18N	93.35W
Elku Kalns ▣	8	Kg	57.04N	25.23 E
Elk, Lake- ▣	59	Fe	29.15 S	127.45 E
Ellás = Greece (EN) ▣	6	Ih	39.00N	22.00 E
Ellé ⬅	11	Dg	47.52N	3.32W
Ellef Ringnes ▣	42	Ib	78.30N	104.00W
Ellen, Mount- ▣	46	Hg	38.07N	110.49W
Ellendale	43	Hb	46.06N	98.32W
Ellensburg	46	Dc	46.40N	120.32W
Ellenville	44	Je	41.43N	74.23W
Ellesmere	38	Kb	79.00N	82.00W
Ellesmere, Lake- ▣	63	Ef	43.45 S	172.30 E
Ellice ⬅	42	Hc	68.02N	103.25W
Ellice Islands → Tuvalu ▣	58	Ie	8.00 S	178.00 E
Elliot [Austl.]	59	Gc	17.35 S	133.35 E
Elliot [S.Afr.]	37	Df	31.18 S	27.50 E
Elliot, Mount- ▣	59	Ic	19.29 S	146.58 E
Elliot Lake	42	Jg	46.23N	82.39W
Ellisras	37	Dd	23.40 S	27.46 E
Elliston	58	Dg	33.39 S	134.55 E
Ellön	9	Kd	57.22N	2.05W
Ellmau	14	Gc	47.31N	12.18 E
Ellös	8	Cf	58.11N	11.27 E
Ellsworth [Ks.-U.S.]	45	Gg	38.44N	98.14W
Ellsworth [Me.-U.S.]	44	Mc	44.33N	68.26W
Ellsworth [Nb.-U.S.]	45	Ef	42.04N	102.15W
Ellsworth, Lake- ▣	45	Gi	34.48N	98.20W
Ellsworth Land (EN) ▣	66	Pf	75.30 S	80.00W
Ellsworth Mountains ▣	66	Qf	78.30 S	85.00W
Ellwangen	10	Gh	48.57N	10.08 E

Index Symbols

▣ Independent Nation	▣ Historical or Cultural Region	▣ Pass, Gap
▣ State, Region	▣ Mount, Mountain	▣ Plain, Lowland
▣ District, County	▣ Volcano	▣ Delta
▣ Municipality	▣ Hill	▣ Salt Flat
▣ Colony, Dependency	▣ Mountains, Mountain Range	▣ Valley, Canyon
▣ Continent	▣ Hills, Escarpment	▣ Crater, Cave
▣ Physical Region	▣ Plateau, Upland	▣ Karst Features

▣ Depression	▣ Coast, Beach	▣ Rock, Reef
▣ Polder	▣ Cliff	▣ Islands, Archipelago
▣ Desert, Dunes	▣ Peninsula	▣ Rocks, Reefs
▣ Forest, Woods	▣ Isthmus	▣ Coral Reef
▣ Heath, Steppe	▣ Sandbank	▣ Well, Spring
▣ Oasis	▣ Island	▣ Geyser
▣ Cape, Point	▣ Atoll	▣ River, Stream

▣ Waterfall Rapids	▣ Canal	▣ Lagoon
▣ River Mouth, Estuary	▣ Glacier	▣ Bank
▣ Lake	▣ Ice Shelf, Pack Ice	▣ Seamount
▣ Salt Lake	▣ Ocean	▣ Tablemount
▣ Intermittent Lake	▣ Sea	▣ Ridge
▣ Reservoir	▣ Gulf, Bay	▣ Shelf
▣ Swamp, Pond	▣ Strait, Fjord	▣ Basin

▣ Escarpment, Sea Scarp	▣ Historic Site	▣ Port
▣ Fracture	▣ Ruins	▣ Lighthouse
▣ Trench, Abyss	▣ Wall, Walls	▣ Mine
▣ National Park, Reserve	▣ Church, Abbey	▣ Tunnel
▣ Point of Interest	▣ Temple	▣ Dam, Bridge
▣ Recreation Site	▣ Scientific Station	
▣ Cave, Cavern	▣ Airport	

Index Symbols

[1] Independent Nation	Historical or Cultural Region	Pass, Gap
[2] State, Region	Mount, Mountain	Plain, Lowland
[3] District, County	Volcano	Delta
[4] Municipality	Hill	Salt Flat
[5] Colony, Dependency	Mountains, Mountain Range	Valley, Canyon
Continent	Hills, Escarpment	Crater, Cave
Physical Region	Plateau, Upland	Karst Features

Depression	Coast, Beach	Rock, Reef
Polder	Cliff	Islands, Archipelago
Desert, Dunes	Peninsula	Rocks, Reefs
Forest, Woods	Isthmus	Coral Reef
Heath, Steppe	Sandbank	Well, Spring
Oasis	Island	Geyser
Cape, Point	Atoll	River, Stream

Waterfall Rapids	Canal	Lagoon
River Mouth, Estuary	Glacier	Bank
Lake	Ice Shelf, Pack Ice	Seamount
Salt Lake	Ocean	Tablemount
Intermittent Lake	Sea	Ridge
Reservoir	Gulf, Bay	Shelf
Swamp, Pond	Strait, Fjord	Basin

Escarpment, Sea Scarp	Historic Site	Port
Fracture	Ruins	Lighthouse
Trench, Abyss	Wall, Walls	Mine
National Park, Reserve	Church, Abbey	Tunnel
Point of Interest	Temple	Dam, Bridge
Recreation Site	Scientific Station	
Cave, Cavern	Airport	

Eshowe	37	Ee	28.50S	31.29 E
Eshetehārd	24	Ne	35.44N	50.23 E
Esigodini	37	Dd	20.18S	28.56 E
Esino ⧅	14	Hg	43.39N	13.22 E
Esk ⧅	9	Jg	54.58N	3.04W
Eskifjördur	7a	Cb	65.04N	14.01W
Eskilstuna	7	Dg	59.22N	16.30 E
Eskimo Point	39	Jc	61.07N	94.03W
Eskişehir	22	Ff	39.46N	30.32 E
Esla ⧅	13	Fc	41.29N	6.03W
Eslāmābād	23	Gc	34.11N	46.35 E
Eşler Daği ▲	15	Ml	37.24N	29.43 E
Eslohe (Sauerland)	12	Kc	51.15N	8.10 E
Eslöv	7	Ci	55.50N	13.20 E
Eşme	24	Cc	38.24N	28.59 E
Esmeralda [Braz.]	55	Gi	28.03S	51.12W
Esmeralda [Cuba]	49	Hc	21.51N	78.07W
Esmeralda, Isla- ◈	56	Eg	48.57S	75.25W
Esmeralda Bank (EN) ⊞	65b	Ab	14.57N	145.15 E
Esmeraldas	53	Ie	0.59N	79.42W
Esnagami Lake ⊜	45	Ma	50.21N	86.48W
Esneux	12	Hd	50.32N	5.34 E
Espada, Punta- ►	49	Lg	12.05N	71.07W
Espagnol Point ►	51n	Ba	13.22N	61.09W
Espalion	11	Ij	44.31N	2.46 E
Espalmador, Isla- ◈	13	Nf	38.47N	1.26 E
España=Spain (EN) [1]	6	Fg	40.00N	4.00W
Espanola [N.M.-U.S.]	45	Ch	36.06N	106.02W
Espanola [Ont.-Can.]	44	Gb	46.15N	81.46W
Española, Isla- ◈	54a	Bb	1.25S	89.42W
Espardell, Isla- ◈	13	Nf	38.47N	1.27 E
Esparta	49	Ei	9.59N	84.40W
Espeland	8	Ad	60.23N	5.28 E
Espelkamp	10	Ed	52.25N	8.37 E
Esperance	58	Dh	33.51S	121.53 E
Esperance, Cape- ►	63a	Dc	9.15S	159.43 E
Esperance Bay ◧	59	Ef	33.50S	121.55 E
Esperance Harbour ◧	51k	Ba	14.04N	60.55W
Esperancita	55	Bc	16.55S	60.06W
Esperantina	54	Jd	3.54S	42.14W
Esperanza ⊠	66	Re	63.26S	57.00W
Esperanza [Arg.]	56	Hd	31.27S	60.56W
Esperanza [Mex.]	48	Ed	27.35N	109.56W
Esperanza [P.R.]	51a	Cb	18.06N	65.29W
Esperanza, Sierra la- ⛰	49	Ef	15.40N	85.45W
Espevær	7	Ag	59.36N	5.10 E
Espichel, Cabo- ►	13	Cf	38.25N	9.13W
Espiel	13	Gf	38.12N	5.01W
Espigão Serra do- ⛰	55	Gh	26.55S	50.25W
Espinal [Bol.]	55	Cc	17.13S	58.43W
Espinal [Col.]	54	Dc	4.10N	74.54W
Espinazo del Diablo, Sierra- ⛰	48	Ff	24.00N	106.00W
Espinhaço, Serra do- ⛰	52	Lg	17.30S	43.30W
Espinho	13	Dc	41.01N	8.38W
Espinilho, Serra do- ⛰	55	Ei	28.30S	55.06W
Espinillo	55	Cg	24.58S	58.34W
Espino	50	Dh	8.34N	66.01W
Espinosa	54	Jf	14.56S	42.50W
Espinouse ⛰	11	Ik	43.32N	2.46 E
Espírito Santo [2]	54	Jg	20.00S	40.30W
Espiritu Santo, Bahia del- ◧	48	Ph	19.20N	87.35W
Espíritu Santo, Isla- ◈	48	De	24.30N	110.22W
Espita	48	Og	21.01N	88.19W
Esplanada	54	Kf	11.47S	37.57W
Espoo/Esbo	7	Ff	60.13N	24.40 E
Espoo-Tapiola	8	Kd	60.11N	24.49 E
Esposende	13	Dc	41.32N	8.47W
Espumoso	55	Fi	28.44S	52.51W
Espuña, Sierra de- ⛰	13	Kg	37.52N	1.34W
Espungabera	37	Ed	20.28S	32.46 E
Esquel	53	Ij	42.55S	71.20W
Esquina	56	Id	30.01S	59.32W
Esquinapa de Hidalgo	47	Cd	22.51N	105.48W
Esquipular	49	Cf	14.34N	89.21W
Essandsjøen ⊜	8	Da	63.05N	12.00 E
Essaouira	31	Ge	31.31N	9.46W
Essaouira [3]	32	Fc	31.04N	9.03W
Essen [Bel.]	12	Gc	51.28N	4.28 E
Essen [Ger.]	6	Ge	51.27N	7.01 E
Essen (Oldenburg)	12	Jb	52.42N	7.55 E
Essendon, Mount- ▲	59	Ed	24.59S	120.28 E
Essequibo River ⧅	52	Ke	6.50N	58.30W
Essex	46	Hi	34.42N	115.12W
Essex ▣	9	Nj	51.50N	0.30 E
Essex [3]	9	Mj	51.50N	0.35W
Essex Mountain ▲	46	Ke	42.02N	109.13W
Esslingen am Neckar	10	Fh	48.45N	9.18 E
Esso	20	Ke	55.55N	158.40 E
Essonne ⧅	11	If	48.37N	2.29 E
Essonne [3]	11	If	48.36N	2.20 E
Est [Cam.] [3]	34	He	4.00N	14.00 E
Est	34	Fc	12.00N	1.00 E
Est, Canal de l'- ═	11	Lf	48.45N	5.35 E
Est, Cap- ►	37	Ic	15.16S	50.29 E
Est, Ile de l'- ◈	30	Mm	46.15S	52.05 E
Est, Pointe de l' - ►	42	Lg	49.08N	61.41W
Estaca de Bares, Punta de la- ►	5	Fg	43.46N	7.42W
Estados, Isla de los-= Staten Island (EN) ◈	52	Jk	54.47S	64.15W
Estados Unidos Mexicanos [1]	39	Ig	23.00N	102.00W
Eşţahbān	24	Ph	29.08N	54.04 E
Estaimpuis	12	Fd	50.42N	3.15 E
Estância	54	Kf	11.16S	37.26W
Estancias, Sierra de las- ⛰	13	Jg	37.35N	2.20W
Estanislao del Campo	55	Bg	25.03S	60.06W
Estarreja	13	Dd	40.45N	8.34W
Estats, Pica d'- ▲	11	Hn	42.40N	1.24 E
Estats, Pica d'-/Estats, Pico d'- ▲	11	Hn	42.40N	1.24 E
Estats, Pic d'- ▲	11	Hn	42.40N	1.24 E
Estats, Pico d'- ▲	11	Hn	42.40N	1.24 E
Estats, Pico d'-/Estats, Pica d'- ▲	11	Hn	42.40N	1.24 E
Estcourt	37	De	29.01S	29.52 E
Este	14	Fe	45.14N	11.39 E
Este, Punta- ►	51a	Cb	18.08N	65.16W
Este, Punta del- ►	56	Jd	34.59S	54.57W
Esteban Rams	55	Bi	29.47S	61.29W
Estelí	47	Gf	13.05N	86.23W
Estelí [3]	49	Dg	13.10N	86.20W
Estella	13	Jb	42.40N	2.02W
Estepa	13	Hg	37.18N	4.54W
Estepona	13	Gh	36.26N	5.08W
Estérel ⛰	11	Mk	43.30N	6.50 E
Esternay	12	Ff	48.44N	3.34 E
Esterri d'Aneu/Esterri de Aneu	13	Nb	42.38N	1.08 E
Esterri de Aneu/Esterri d'Aneu	13	Nb	42.38N	1.08 E
Esterwegen	12	Jb	52.59N	7.37 E
Estes Park	45	Df	40.23N	105.31W
Este Sudeste, Cayos del- ❋	47	Hf	12.26N	81.27W
Estevan	42	Hg	49.07N	103.05W
Estherville	45	Ie	43.24N	94.50W
Estissac	11	Jf	48.16N	3.49 E
Eston	46	Ka	51.10N	108.46W
Estonia (EN) ⧗	5	Id	59.00N	26.00 E
Estonia (EN) = Eesti	19	Cd	59.00N	26.00 E
Estonskaja Sovetskaja Socialističeskaja Respublika → Eesti	19	Cd	59.00N	26.00 E
Estonskaja SSR/Eesti Nõukogude Socialistlik Vabarijk → Eesti	19	Cd	59.00N	26.00 E
Estoril	13	Cf	38.42N	9.24W
Estrées-Saint-Denis	12	Ee	49.26N	2.39 E
Estreito	55	Gj	31.50S	51.44W
Estreito, Represa do- ⊡	55	Ie	20.15S	47.09W
Estrêla [Braz.]	55	Gi	29.29S	51.58W
Estrêla [Braz.]	55	Gj	31.15S	21.45W
Estrela, Arroyo- ⧅	55	Df	22.05S	56.25W
Estrela, Serra da- ⛰	55	Fc	16.27S	53.24W
Estrêla, Serra da- ⛰	5	Fg	40.20N	7.38W
Estrêla do Sul	55	Id	18.21S	47.49W
Estrella ▲	13	If	38.28N	3.35W
Estrella, Punta- ►	48	Bb	30.55N	114.40W
Estrema, Serra da- ⛰	55	Jc	16.50S	45.07W
Estremadura ▣	13	Ce	39.15N	9.10W
Estremoz	13	Ef	38.51N	7.35W
Estrondo, Serra do- ⛰	54	Ie	9.00S	48.45W
Estry	12	Bf	48.54N	0.44W
Estuaire [3]	36	Ab	0.10N	10.00 E
Esztergom	10	Oi	47.48N	18.45 E
Etah	41	Ec	78.19N	72.38W
Étain	11	Le	49.13N	5.38 E
Etajima	29	Cd	34.15N	132.29 E
Etalle	12	He	49.41N	5.36 E
Étampes	11	If	48.26N	2.09 E
Étaples	11	Hd	50.31N	1.39 E
Etāwah	25	Fc	26.46N	79.02 E
Ethe, Virton-	12	He	49.35N	5.35 E
Ethel Reefs ✼	63d	Ab	16.56S	177.13 E
Ethiopia (EN)=Itiopya [1]	31	Kh	9.00N	39.00 E
Ethiopian Plateau (EN) ⏏	30	Kg	10.00N	38.10 E
Etive, Loch- ⇋	9	He	56.35N	5.15W
Etna ⧅	8	Dd	60.50N	10.03 E
Etna ⋀	5	Hh	37.50N	14.55 E
Etne	8	Ae	59.40N	5.56 E
Etoile Cay ❋	37b	Bb	5.53S	53.01 E
Etolin Island ◈	40	Me	56.08N	132.26W
Etolin Strait ⇋	40	Fd	60.20N	165.15W
Etomo-Misaki ►	29a	Bb	42.20N	140.55 E
Etorofu Tō/Iturup, Ostrov- ◈	21	Qe	44.54N	147.30 E
Etosha Pan ⊜	30	Ij	18.50S	16.20 E
Etoumbi	36	Bb	0.01N	14.57 E
Etrépagny	12	De	49.18N	1.37 E
Étretat	11	Ge	49.42N	0.12 E
Etropole	15	Gg	42.50N	24.00 E
Etruria	56	Hd	32.56S	63.15W
Etsch/Adige ⧅	5	Hf	45.10N	12.20 E
Ettelbrüch/Ettelbruck	12	Ie	49.51N	6.07 E
Ettelbruck/Ettelbrüch	12	Ie	49.51N	6.07 E
Etten-Leur	12	Gc	51.35N	4.39 E
Ettersberg ▲	10	He	51.03N	11.15 E
Ettlingen	12	Kf	48.57N	8.24 E
Etzna Tixmucuy ⁘	48	Nh	19.35N	90.13W
Eu	11	Hd	50.03N	1.25 E
'Eua Iki ◈	65b	Bc	21.07S	174.59W
Eua Island ◈	61	Gd	21.22S	174.56W
Euboea (EN)=Évvoia ◈	5	Ih	38.30N	24.00 E
Eucla	58	Dh	31.43S	128.52 E
Euclid	44	Ge	41.34N	81.33W
Euclides da Cunha	54	Kf	10.31S	39.01W
Eucumbene, Lake- ⊜	59	Jg	36.05S	148.45 E
Eudora	45	Kj	33.07N	91.16W
Eufaula	44	Ej	31.54N	85.09W
Eufaula Lake ⊜	45	Ii	35.17N	95.31W
Euganei, Colli- ◭	14	Fe	45.19N	11.40 E
Eugene	39	Ge	44.02N	123.05W
Eugenia, Punta- ►	38	Hg	27.50N	115.03W
Eugênio Penzo	55	Ef	22.13S	55.53W
Eugmo ◈	7	Fe	63.49N	22.45 E
Eume ⧅	13	Da	43.25N	8.08W
Eunice [La.-U.S.]	45	Jk	30.30N	92.26W
Eunice [N.M.-U.S.]	45	Ej	32.26N	103.09W
Eupen	11	Md	50.38N	6.02 E
Euphrates (EN)=Al Furāt ⧅	21	Gf	31.00N	47.25 E
Euphrates (EN)=Firat ⧅	21	Gf	31.00N	47.25 E
Eupora	45	Lj	33.32N	89.16W
Eura	7	Ff	61.08N	22.08 E
Eurajoki	8	Ic	61.12N	21.44 E
Eurasia Basin (EN) ∪	67	Ge	87.00N	80.00 E
Eure [3]	11	Ge	49.10N	1.00 E
Eure ⧅	11	He	49.18N	1.12 E
Eure-et-Loir [3]	11	Hf	48.30N	1.30 E
Eureka [Ca.-U.S.]	39	Ge	40.47N	124.09W
Eureka [Ks.-U.S.]	45	Hh	37.49N	96.17W
Eureka [Mt.-U.S.]	46	Hb	48.53N	115.03W
Eureka [Nv.-U.S.]	43	Dd	39.31N	115.58W
Eureka [N.W.T.-Can.]	42	Ia	80.00N	85.59W
Eureka [S.D.-U.S.]	45	Gd	45.46N	99.38W
Eureka [Ut.-U.S.]	46	Ig	39.57N	112.07W
Eureka Sound ⇋	42	Ia	79.00N	87.00W
Europa ◈	30	Lk	22.20S	40.22 E
Europa, Picos de- ⛰	5	Fg	43.12N	4.48W
Europe ■	5	Ie	50.00N	20.00 E
Europoort	11	Jc	51.58N	4.00 E
Euskirchen	10	Cf	50.40N	6.47 E
Eustis	44	Gk	28.51N	81.41W
Eutaw	44	Di	32.50N	87.53W
Eutin	10	Gb	54.08N	10.37 E
Euzkadi/Vascongadas= Basque Provinces (EN) ▣	13	Ja	43.00N	2.30W
Evale	36	Cf	16.33S	15.44 E
Evans, Lac- ⊜	42	Jf	50.50N	77.00W
Evans, Mount- ▲	46	Ic	46.05N	113.07W
Evans Strait ⇋	42	Jd	63.20N	82.00W
Evanston [Il.-U.S.]	45	Me	42.03N	87.42W
Evanston [Wy.-U.S.]	43	Ec	41.16N	110.58 E
Evansville	39	Kf	37.58N	87.35W
Evant	45	Gk	31.29N	98.09W
Evart	44	Ed	43.54N	85.14W
Evaux-les-Bains	11	Ih	46.10N	2.29 E
Evaz	24	Oi	27.46N	53.59 E
Evciler [Tur.]	15	Jj	39.46N	26.46 E
Evciler [Tur.]	15	Mk	38.03N	29.54 E
Evelyn, Mount- ▲	59	Gb	13.36S	132.53 E
Evensk	22	Rc	61.57N	159.14 E
Everard, Lake- ⊜	59	Hf	31.25S	135.05 E
Everard Ranges ⛰	59	Ge	27.05S	132.30 E
Everest, Mount- (EN)= Qomolangma Feng ▲	21	Kg	27.59N	86.56 E
Everest, Mount- (EN)= Saragmatha ▲	21	Kg	27.59N	86.56 E
Everett	43	Cb	47.59N	122.13W
Everett Mountains ⛰	42	Kd	62.45N	67.10W
Evergem	12	Fc	51.07N	3.42 E
Evergem-Sleidinge	12	Fc	51.08N	3.41 E
Everglades City	44	Gm	25.52N	81.23W
Evergreen	44	Dj	31.26N	86.57W
Evertsberg	8	Ec	61.08N	13.57 E
Evesham	9	Li	52.05N	1.56W
Evesham, Vale of- ∨	9	Li	52.05N	1.50W
Evian-les-Bains	11	Mh	46.23N	6.35 E
Evijärvi	7	Fe	63.22N	23.29 E
Evinayong	34	He	1.27N	10.34 E
Évinos ⧅	15	Ek	38.19N	21.32 E
Evje	7	Bg	58.36N	7.51 E
Évora	6	Fh	38.34N	7.54W
Évora [2]	13	Ef	38.35N	7.50W
Evoron	20	If	51.23N	136.23 E
Evowghlī	24	Kc	38.43N	45.13 E
Evre ⧅	11	Eg	47.22N	1.02W
Evrecy	12	Be	49.06N	0.30W
Evrejskaja avtonomnaja respublika	20	Ig	48.30N	132.00 E
Evreux	11	He	49.01N	1.09 E
Evron	11	Ff	48.01N	0.24W
Evrótas ⧅	15	Fm	36.48N	22.41 E
Evry	11	If	48.38N	2.27 E
Évvoia=Euboea (EN) ◈	5	Ih	38.30N	24.00 E
Évvoia, Gulf of- (EN)= Vórios Evvoïkós Kólpos ◧	15	Gk	38.45N	23.10 E
Evzonoi	15	Fh	41.06N	22.33 E
Ewa Beach	65a	Cb	21.19N	158.00W
Ewing Seamount (EN) ⊼	30	Hk	23.20S	8.45 E
Ewo	36	Bc	0.55S	14.49 E
Excelsior Mountain ▲	46	Fg	38.02N	119.18W
Excelsior Mountains ⛰	46	Fg	38.10N	118.30W
Excelsior Springs	45	Ig	39.20N	94.13W
Exe ⧅	9	Jk	50.37N	3.25W
Executive Committee Range ⛰	66	Nf	76.50S	126.00W
Exeter [Eng.-U.K.]	6	Fe	50.43N	3.31W
Exeter [N.H.-U.S.]	44	Ld	42.59N	70.56W
Exeter Sound ⇋	42	Lc	66.10N	62.00W
Exmoor ▲	9	Jj	51.10N	3.45W
Exmouth [Austl.]	59	Cd	21.55S	114.07 E
Exmouth [Eng.-U.K.]	9	Jk	50.37N	3.25W
Exmouth Gulf ◧	57	Cg	22.00S	114.20 E
Exmouth Plateau (EN) ⊓	59	Cc	16.00S	114.00 E
Expedition Range ⛰	59	Jd	24.30S	149.05 E
Explorer Tablemount (EN) ⊓	47	He	16.55N	83.15W
Externsteine ⁘	12	Kc	51.52N	8.55 E
Extertal	12	Lb	52.04N	9.07 E
Extertal-Bösingfeld	12	Lb	52.04N	9.07 E
Extremadura ▣	13	Ge	39.00N	6.00W
Exuma Cays ❋	47	Id	24.00N	76.20W
Exuma Cays ⁂	49	Ia	24.20N	76.40W
Exuma Sound ⇋	47	Id	24.15N	76.00W
Eyasi, Lake- ⊜	30	Ki	3.40S	35.05 E
Eydehavn	8	Cf	58.31N	8.53 E
Eye	12	Db	52.19N	1.09 E
Eyemouth	9	Kf	55.52N	2.06W
Eye Peninsula ⊏	9	Ge	58.13N	6.05W
Eygurande	11	Ii	45.40N	2.28 E
Eyjafjallajökull ▲	7a	Bc	63.38N	19.36W
Ēyl	31	Lh	8.00N	49.51 E
Eymoutiers	11	Hi	45.44N	1.44 E
Eynesil	24	Hb	41.03N	39.08 E
Eyrarbakki	7a	Bc	63.52N	21.09W
Eyre	59	Ff	32.15S	126.18 E
Eyre, Lake- ⧅	57	Eg	28.43S	137.11 E
Eyre Creek ⧅	57	Eg	26.40S	139.00 E
Eyre Mountains ⛰	62	Cf	45.20S	168.20 E
Eyre North, Lake- ⊜	59	He	28.40S	137.10 E
Eyre Peninsula ⊏	57	Ef	34.00S	135.45 E
Eyre South, Lake- ⊜	59	He	29.30S	137.20 E
Eyrieux ⧅	11	Kj	44.48N	4.48 E
Eystrup	12	Lb	52.47N	9.13 E
Eythorne	12	Dc	51.11N	1.17 E
Eyvānakī	24	Oe	35.24N	51.56 E
Ezequiel Ramos Mexia, Embalse- ⊡	56	Ge	39.30S	69.00W
Ezere	8	Jh	56.27N	22.17 E
Ežerelis	8	Jj	54.50N	23.38 E
Ezine	24	Bc	39.47N	26.20 E
Eznas/Jieznas	8	Kj	54.34N	24.17 E
Ežva	17	Ef	61.47N	50.40 E

F

Faaa	65e	Fc	17.33S	149.36W
Faaite Atoll ⊙	61	Lc	16.45S	145.14W
Fabens	45	Ck	31.30N	106.10W
Fåberg	8	Dc	61.10N	10.24 E
Faber Lake ⊜	42	Fd	63.55N	117.15W
Fåborg	7	Ci	55.06N	10.15 E
Fabriano	14	Gg	43.20N	12.54 E
Făcăeni	15	Ke	44.34N	27.54 E
Facatativá	54	Dc	4.49N	74.22W
Facha	33	Cd	29.30N	17.20 E
Fachi	31	Ig	18.06N	11.34 E
Facpi Point ►	64c	Bb	13.20N	144.38 E
Fada	31	Jg	17.14N	21.33 E
Fada N'Gourma	31	Hg	12.04N	0.21 E
Faddeja, Zaliv- ◧	20	Fa	76.30N	107.30 E
Faddejevski, Ostrov- ◈	20	Ja	75.30N	144.00 E
Fadiffolu Atoll ⊙	25a	Ba	5.25N	73.30 E
Fāḑilī	24	Mi	26.58N	49.15 E
Faeara, Pointe- ►	65e	Fc	17.52S	149.11W
Faenza	14	Ff	44.17N	11.53 E
Færœ Bank (EN) ⊞	9	Ea	60.55N	8.40W
Faeroe-Iceland Ridge (EN) ⩙	5	Fc	64.00N	10.00W
Faeroe Islands (EN)= Færøerne/Föroyar ⁂	5	Fc	62.00N	7.00W
Faeroe Islands (EN)= Færøerne/Föroyar [5]	6	Fc	62.00N	7.00W
Faeroe Islands (EN) = Föroyar/Færøerne [5]	6	Fc	62.00N	7.00W
Faeroe Islands (EN)= Föroyar/Færøerne ⁂	5	Fc	62.00N	7.00W
Færøerne/Föroyar=Faeroe Islands (EN) ⁂	5	Fc	62.00N	7.00W
Færøerne/Föroyar=Faeroe Islands (EN) [5]	6	Fc	62.00N	7.00W
Fafa ⧅	35	Bd	7.18N	18.16 E
Fafe	13	Dc	41.27N	8.10W
Fafen ⧅	30	Lh	5.47N	44.11 E
Faga ⧅	34	Fc	13.45N	0.58 E
Fagaloa Bay ◧	65c	Ba	13.54S	171.28W
Fagamalo	65c	Aa	13.25S	172.21W
Făgăraş	15	Hd	45.51N	24.58 E
Făgarasului, Munţii- ⛰	15	Hd	45.35N	25.00 E
Fagataufa Atoll ⊙	57	Ng	22.14S	138.45W
Fågelmara	8	Fh	56.15N	15.57 E
Fagerhult	8	Fg	57.09N	15.40 E
Fagernes	7	Bf	60.59N	9.15 E
Fagersta	7	Df	60.00N	15.47 E
Făget	15	Fd	45.51N	22.11 E
Fagita	26	Jg	1.48S	130.25 E
Fagnano, Lago- ⊜	56	Gh	54.38S	68.00W
Fagne ⧗	11	Kd	50.10N	4.25 E
Faguibine, Lac- ⊜	30	Gg	16.45N	3.54W
Fahliān	24	Ng	30.12N	51.28 E
Fahner Höhe ▲	10	Ge	51.10N	10.45 E
Faial ◈	30	Ee	38.34N	28.42W
Fā'id	24	Eg	30.19N	32.19 E
Faïoa ◈	64h	Bc	13.23S	176.08W
Fairbairn Reservoir ⊡	59	Jd	23.40S	148.00 E
Fairbanks	39	Ec	64.51N	147.43W
Fairborn	44	Ef	39.48N	84.03W
Fairbury	43	Hc	40.08N	97.11W
Fairchild	45	Kd	44.36N	90.58W
Fairfield [Al.-U.S.]	44	Di	33.29N	86.55W
Fairfield [Ca.-U.S.]	46	Dg	38.15N	122.01W
Fairfield [Ia.-U.S.]	45	Kf	40.59N	91.57W
Fairfield [Id.-U.S.]	46	He	43.21N	114.48W
Fairfield [Il.-U.S.]	45	Lg	38.23N	88.22W
Fair Isle ◈	9	Lb	59.30N	1.40W
Fairlie	62	Df	44.06S	170.50 E
Fairmont [Mn.-U.S.]	43	Ic	43.39N	94.28W
Fairmont [W.V.-U.S.]	43	Ld	39.28N	80.08W
Fair Ness ►	42	Kd	63.24N	72.05W
Fairview [Mt.-U.S.]	46	Mc	47.51N	104.03W
Fairview [Ok.-U.S.]	45	Gh	36.16N	98.29W
Fairview Peak ▲	46	De	43.35N	122.39W
Fairweather, Mount- ▲	38	Fd	58.54N	137.32W
Fais Island ◈	57	Fd	9.46N	140.31 E
Faistós ⁘	15	Hn	35.03N	24.48 E
Faith	43	Gb	45.02N	102.02W
Faizābād	25	Gc	26.47N	82.08 E
Fajardo	49	Od	18.20N	65.39W
Fajou, Ilet 'a- ◈	51e	Ab	16.21N	61.35W
Fakahina Atoll ⊙	57	Mf	15.59S	140.08W
Fakaofo Atoll ⊙	57	Je	9.22S	171.14W
Fakarava Atoll ⊙	57	Mf	16.20S	145.37W
Fakaura	29	Fa	40.38N	139.55 E
Fakel	7	Mh	57.40N	53.05 E
Fakenham	12	Cb	52.50N	0.50 E
Fakfak	26	Jg	2.55S	132.18 E
Fakhr	24	Pg	31.25N	54.01 E
Fakse Bugt ◧	8	Ei	55.10N	12.15 E
Faksefjell ▲	8	Ec	61.20N	12.52 E
Fakse Ladeplads	8	Ei	55.15N	12.08 E
Faku	28	Gc	42.30N	123.24 E
Falaba	34	Cd	9.51N	11.19W
Fala-Beguets ◈	64d	Bb	7.21N	151.40 E
Falaise	11	Ff	48.54N	0.12W
Falaise de Tiguidit ◭	34	Gb	16.22N	7.45 E
Falakrón Óros ⛰	5	Gh	41.19N	24.00 E
Falalu ◈	4d	Ba	7.38N	151.41 E
Falam	25	Id	22.55N	93.41 E
Falas ◈	64d	Ba	7.32N	151.46 E
Fălciu	15	Lc	46.18N	28.08 E
Falcón [2]	54	Ea	11.00N	69.50W
Falcon, Cap ►	13	Li	35.46N	0.48W
Falcon, Presa- ⊡	45	Gm	26.37N	99.11W
Falconara Marittima	14	Hg	43.37N	13.24 E
Falcone, Punta- ►	14	Cj	40.58N	8.12 E
Falcon Reservoir ⊡	43	Hf	26.37N	99.11W
Faléa	34	Cc	12.16N	11.15W
Faleallej Pass ⇋	64d	Bb	7.26N	151.34 E
Falealupo	65c	Aa	13.30S	172.48W
Falelima	65c	Aa	13.32S	172.41W
Falémé ⧅	30	Fg	14.46N	12.14W
Falenki	7	Mg	58.23N	51.36 E
Falerum	8	Gf	58.09N	16.13 E
Faleşty	16	Ef	47.35N	27.44 E
Falevai	65c	Ba	13.55S	171.59W
Falfurrias	43	Hf	27.14N	98.09W
Falkenberg	7	Ch	56.54N	12.28 E
Falkensee	10	Jd	52.34N	13.05 E
Falkirk	9	Jf	56.00N	3.48W
Falkland Islands/Malvinas, Islas- [5]	53	Kk	51.45S	59.00W
Falkland Islands/Malvinas, Islas- ⁂	52	Kk	51.45S	59.00W
Falkland Plateau (EN) ⊓	52	Lk	51.00S	50.00W
Falkland Sound ⇋	56	Ih	51.45S	59.25W
Falkonéra ◈	15	Gm	36.50N	23.53 E
Falköping	7	Cg	58.10N	13.31 E
Fallingbostel	10	Fd	52.52N	9.42 E
Fallon [Mt.-U.S.]	46	Mc	46.48N	105.00W
Fallon [Nv.-U.S.]	46	Fg	39.28N	118.47W
Fall River	43	Mc	41.43N	71.08W
Falls City	43	Hc	40.03N	95.36W
Falmouth [Atg.]	51d	Bb	17.01N	61.46W
Falmouth [Eng.-U.K.]	9	Hk	50.08N	5.04W
Falmouth [Jam.]	49	Id	18.30N	77.39W
Falmouth [Ky.-U.S.]	44	Ef	38.40N	84.20W
Falmouth Bay ◧	9	Hk	50.10N	5.05W
Falmouth Harbour ◧	51d	Bb	17.01N	61.46W
Falo ◈	64d	Bb	7.29N	151.53 E
False Bay ◧	30	Il	34.15S	18.35 E
False Pass	40	Gf	54.52N	163.24W
Falset	13	Mc	41.08N	0.49 E
Falso, Cabo- [Dom.Rep.] ►	49	Le	17.47N	71.41W
Falso, Cabo- [Hond.] ►	49	Ff	15.12N	83.20W
Falso, Cabo- [Mex.] ►	47	Cd	22.52N	109.58W
Falso Cabo de Hornos ►	56	Gi	55.43S	68.05W
Falster ◈	7	Ci	54.50N	12.00 E
Falsterbo	8	Ei	55.24N	12.50 E
Falterona ▲	14	Fg	43.52N	11.42 E
Fălticeni	15	Jb	47.27N	26.18 E
Falun	6	Hc	60.36N	15.38 E
Fama ⧅	35	Cb	15.22N	20.34 E
Famagusta (EN)= Gazimağusa	23	Dc	35.07N	33.57 E
Famatina, Nevados de-	56	Gc	29.00S	67.51W
Famenne ⧗	11	Ld	50.15N	5.15 E
Fana	34	Dc	12.45N	6.57W
Fanan ◈	64d	Bb	7.11N	151.59 E
Fanchang	27	Ke	31.00N	118.11 E
Fancy	51n	Ba	13.22N	61.12W
Fandriana	37	Hd	20.13S	47.20 E
Fangak	35	Ed	9.04N	30.53 E
Fangatau Atoll ⊙	57	Mf	15.50S	140.52W
Fangcheng	27	Je	33.09N	113.05 E
Fangliao	27	Lg	22.22N	120.25 E
Fangshan	28	Ce	39.43N	115.58 E
Fangxian	27	Je	32.03N	110.41 E
Fangzheng	27	Mb	45.50N	128.49 E
Fangzi	28	Ef	36.36N	119.08 E
Fanjiatun	28	Hc	43.42N	125.05 E
Fanjing Shan ▲	27	If	27.57N	108.50 E
Fannaråken ▲	8	Bc	61.31N	7.55 E
Fanning → Tabuaeran Atoll ⊙	57	Ld	3.52N	159.20W
Fano	14	Hg	43.50N	13.01 E
Fanø ◈	8	Ci	55.25N	8.25 E
Fanø Bugt ◧	8	Ci	55.25N	8.10 E
Fanshi	28	Be	39.11N	113.16 E
Fan Si Pan ⛰	21	Mg	22.15N	103.50 E
Fan Si Pan ⛰	25	Kd	22.18N	103.46 E
Fanuatapu ◈	65c	Ba	13.59S	171.20W
Fanxian	28	Cg	35.53N	115.29 E
Fāqūs	24	Dg	30.44N	31.48 E
Farab	18	De	39.12N	63.38 E
Faraba	34	Cc	12.52N	11.23W
Faraday ⊠	66	Qe	65.15S	64.15W
Faraday Seamounts (EN) ⊼	5	Df	49.30N	28.30W
Faradje	36	Eb	3.44N	29.43 E
Faradofay	31	Lk	25.01S	46.59 E
Farafangana	37	Hd	22.48S	47.50 E
Farāfirah, Wāḩāt al-= Farafra Oasis (EN) ⚘	30	Jf	27.15N	28.10 E
Farafra Oasis (EN)= Farāfirah, Wāḩāt al- ⚘	30	Jf	27.15N	28.10 E
Farāh ⧅	21	If	31.29N	61.24 E
Farāh	22	If	32.22N	62.07 E
Farāh [3]	23	Jc	33.00N	62.30 E
Far'ah, Wādī al- ⧅	24	Hj	24.02N	38.09 E
Faraḩābād	24	Od	36.47N	53.06 E
Faranah	34	Cc	10.02N	10.44W
Farasan ◈	23	Ff	16.42N	42.00 E
Farasan, Jazā'ir- ⁂	23	Ff	16.48N	41.54 E
Farasān al Kabīr ◈	33	Hf	16.42N	42.00 E
Faraulep Atoll ⊙	57	Fd	8.36N	144.33 E
Farcău, Vîrful- ▲	15	Hb	47.55N	24.27 E
Farciennes	12	Gd	50.26N	4.33 E
Fardes ⧅	13	Jg	37.35N	3.00W
Fare	65e	Db	16.42S	151.01W
Fareham	9	Lk	50.51N	1.10W
Farewell, Cape- ►	57	Ii	40.30S	172.43 E
Farewell Spit ⌓	62	Ed	40.30S	172.50 E
Färgelanda	8	Df	58.34N	11.59 E
Fargo	39	Je	46.52N	96.48W
Faribault	45	Jd	44.18N	93.16W
Faribault, Lac - ⊜	42	Ke	58.00N	72.00W

Index Symbols

- [1] Independent Nation
- [2] State, Region
- [3] District, County
- [4] Municipality
- [5] Colony, Dependency
- ■ Continent
- ⧗ Physical Region
- ▣ Historical or Cultural Region
- ▲ Mount, Mountain
- ⋀ Volcano
- △ Hill
- ⛰ Mountains, Mountain Range
- ◭ Hills, Escarpment
- ⏏ Plateau, Upland
- ⌣ Pass, Gap
- ▁ Plain, Lowland
- ◣ Delta
- ▤ Salt Flat
- ∨ Valley, Canyon
- ◡ Crater, Cave
- ⊛ Karst Features
- ▽ Depression
- ⊔ Polder
- ∴ Desert, Dunes
- ♣ Forest, Woods
- ʬ Heath, Steppe
- ⚘ Oasis
- ► Cape, Point
- ⌒ Coast, Beach
- ▌ Cliff
- ⊏ Peninsula
- ⋈ Isthmus
- ⌓ Sandbank
- ◈ Island
- ⊙ Atoll
- ✳ Rock, Reef
- ⁂ Islands, Archipelago
- ❋ Rocks, Reefs
- ✼ Coral Reef
- ◉ Well, Spring
- ⌶ Geyser
- ⧅ River, Stream
- ⫴ Waterfall Rapids
- ⋎ River Mouth, Estuary
- ⊜ Lake
- ⊝ Salt Lake
- ◻ Intermittent Lake
- ⊡ Reservoir
- ⁓ Swamp, Pond
- ═ Canal
- ❄ Glacier
- ❅ Ice Shelf, Pack Ice
- ≋ Ocean
- ≈ Sea
- ◧ Gulf, Bay
- ⇋ Strait, Fjord
- ◎ Lagoon
- ⊞ Bank
- ⊼ Seamount
- ⊓ Tablemount
- ⩙ Ridge
- ⊥ Shelf
- ∪ Basin
- ⌐ Escarpment, Sea Scarp
- ϟ Fracture
- ⋁ Trench, Abyss
- ♧ National Park, Reserve
- ✪ Point of Interest
- ☗ Recreation Site
- ∩ Cave, Cavern
- ⌂ Historic Site
- ⁘ Ruins
- ▦ Wall, Walls
- ✝ Church, Abbey
- ⏄ Temple
- ⊠ Scientific Station
- ✈ Airport
- ⚓ Port
- ☼ Lighthouse
- ⚒ Mine
- ⋂ Tunnel
- ⫽ Dam, Bridge

Farīd, Qarāt al-	24	Ch	28.43N	28.21 E
Faridpur	25	Hd	23.36N	89.50 E
Färila	7	Df	61.48N	15.51 E
Farilhões, Ilhas-	13	Ce	39.28N	9.34W
Farim	34	Bc	12.29N	15.13W
Farini d'Olmo	14	Df	44.43N	9.34 E
Fāris	24	Ej	24.37N	32.54 E
Fariš	18	Fd	40.33N	66.52 E
Fāris	35	Ia	20.11N	50.56 E
Faris Seamount (EN)	40	Jf	54.30N	147.15W
Färjestaden	7	Dh	56.39N	16.27 E
Farkadhón	15	Fj	39.36N	22.04 E
Farmahīn	24	Me	34.30N	49.41 E
Farmakonísi	15	Kl	37.18N	27.08 E
Farmerville	45	Jj	32.47N	92.24W
Farmington [Me.-U.S.]	44	Lc	44.40N	70.09W
Farmington [Mo.-U.S.]	45	Kh	37.47N	90.25W
Farmington [N.M.-U.S.]	43	Fd	36.44N	108.12W
Farmville	44	Hg	37.17N	78.25W
Färnäs	8	Fc	61.00N	14.38 E
Farnborough	12	Bc	51.16N	0.44W
Farne Deep	9	Mf	55.30N	0.50W
Farne Islands	9	Lf	55.38N	1.38W
Farnham [Eng.-U.K.]	12	Bc	51.12N	0.48W
Farnham [Que.-Can.]	44	Kc	45.17N	72.59W
Farnham, Mount-	46	Ga	50.29N	116.30W
Fårö	7	Eh	57.55N	19.10 E
Faro	34	Hd	9.21N	12.55 E
Faro [2]	13	Dg	37.12N	8.10W
Faro	6	Fh	37.01N	7.56W
Faro, Punta-	49	Jh	11.07N	74.51W
Faro, Sierra del-	13	Eb	42.37N	7.55W
Faro de Avión	13	Db	42.18N	8.16W
Faro de Chantada	13	Eb	42.37N	7.55W
Farofa, Serra da-	55	Gh	28.00S	50.10W
Farosund	8	Hg	57.55N	19.05 E
Fårösund	7	Eh	57.52N	19.03 E
Farquhar, Cape-	59	Cd	23.35S	113.35 E
Farquhar Group	30	Mj	10.10S	51.10 E
Farrar	9	Id	57.27N	4.35W
Farrāshband	24	Oh	28.53N	52.06 E
Farris	8	Ce	59.05N	10.00 E
Farruch, Cabo-	13	Pe	39.47N	3.21 E
Farrukhābād	25	Fc	27.24N	79.34 E
Fārs	21	Hg	29.00N	53.00 E
Fārs [3]	23	Hd	29.00N	53.00 E
Fārsābād	24	Mc	39.30N	48.05 E
Fársala	15	Fj	39.18N	22.23 E
Farshūţ	24	Ei	26.03N	32.09 E
Farsø	8	Ch	56.47N	9.21 E
Farsund	7	Bg	58.05N	6.48 E
Fartak, Ra's-	23	Hf	15.38N	52.15 E
Fartura, Rio-	55	Gc	16.29S	50.33W
Fartura, Serra da- [Braz.]	55	Hf	23.20S	49.25W
Fartura, Serra da- [Braz.]	55	Fh	26.21S	52.52W
Fārūj	24	Rd	37.14N	58.14 E
Farvel, Kap-/ Ūmánarssuaq	67	Nb	59.50N	43.50W
Farwell Island	66	Pf	72.49S	91.10W
Fāryāb [3]	23	Jb	36.00N	65.00 E
Fasā	24	Oh	28.56N	53.42 E
Fasano	14	Lj	40.50N	17.22 E
Fastnet Rock	9	Dj	51.24N	9.35W
Fastov	19	De	50.06N	30.01 E
Fataka Island	57	If	11.55S	170.12 E
Fatala	34	Cc	10.13N	14.00W
Fatehpur	25	Ec	28.01N	74.58 E
Fatež	16	Ic	52.06N	35.52 E
Father Lake	44	Ja	49.24N	75.18W
Fatick	34	Bc	14.20N	16.25W
Fátima	13	De	39.37N	8.39W
Faţīrah, Wādī-	24	Ei	26.39N	32.58 E
Fatsa	24	Gb	40.59N	37.24 E
Fatu Hiva, Ile-	57	Nf	10.28S	138.38W
Fatu Hutu, Ile-	57	Ne	9.00S	138.50W
Fatumanini, Passe-	64h	Ab	13.14S	176.13W
Fatunda	36	Cc	4.08S	17.13 E
Fauabu	63a	Ec	8.34S	160.43 E
Faucigny	11	Mh	46.05N	6.35 E
Faucille, Col de la-	11	Mh	46.22N	6.02 E
Faulkton	45	Gd	45.02N	99.08W
Faulquemont	12	Ie	49.03N	6.36 E
Fauquembergues	12	Ed	50.36N	2.05 E
Făurei	15	Kd	45.04N	27.14 E
Fauro	63a	Cb	6.55S	156.07 E
Fauske	7	Dc	67.15N	15.24 E
Fauville-en-Caux	12	Ce	49.39N	0.35 E
Faux-Lap	37	He	25.32S	45.30 E
Fåvang	8	Dc	61.26N	10.13 E
Favara	14	Hm	37.19N	13.39 E
Faversham	12	Cc	51.19N	0.54 E
Favignana	14	Gm	37.55N	12.19 E
Favignana	14	Gm	37.56N	12.20 E
Favorite	12	Kf	48.49N	8.16 E
Fawley	12	Ad	50.49N	1.21W
Fawn	42	Ie	55.22N	88.20W
Fa'w Qiblī	24	Ei	26.07N	32.24 E
Faxaflói	5	Dc	64.24N	23.00W
Faxinal	55	Gf	23.59S	51.22W
Faya-Largeau	31	Ig	17.55N	19.07 E
Fayaoué	63b	Ce	20.39S	166.32 E
Fayd	24	Ji	27.07N	42.31 E
Fayette [Al.-U.S.]	44	Di	33.42N	87.50W
Fayette [Oh.-U.S.]	44	Ee	41.41N	84.20W
Fayetteville [Ar.-U.S.]	43	Id	36.04N	94.10W
Fayetteville [N.C.-U.S.]	39	Lf	35.03N	78.54W
Fayetteville [Tn.-U.S.]	44	Dh	35.09N	86.35W
Faylakah, Jazīrat-	24	Mh	29.27N	48.20 E
Faysh Khābūr	24	Jd	37.04N	42.23 E
Fayu Island	57	Gd	8.35N	151.22 E
Fazenda de Cima	55	Db	15.56S	56.37W
Fazenda Nova	55	Gc	16.11S	50.48W
Fāzilka	25	Eb	30.24N	74.02 E
Fazrān	24	Mi	26.13N	49.12 E
Fazzān=Fezzan (EN)	33	Bd	25.30N	14.00 E
Fazzān=Fezzan (EN)	30	If	26.00N	14.00 E
Fdérick	31	Ff	22.39N	12.43W
Feale/An Fhéil	9	Di	52.28N	9.40W
Fear, Cape-	43	Le	33.50N	77.58W
Featherston	62	Fd	41.07S	175.19 E
Feathertop, Mount-	59	Jg	36.54S	147.08 E
Fécamp	11	Ge	49.45N	0.22 E
Fecht	11	Nf	48.11N	7.26 E
Federacion	56	Id	31.00S	57.54W
Federal	56	Id	30.55S	58.45W
Federated States of Micronesia [5]	58	Gd	6.30N	152.00 E
Federovka	19	Ge	53.38N	62.42 E
Federovka	17	Gj	53.10N	55.10 E
Federsee	10	Fh	48.05N	9.38 E
Fedje	7	Af	60.47N	4.42 E
Fedorovka	16	Qd	51.16N	52.00 E
Fefan	64d	Bb	7.21N	151.51 E
Fegen	8	Eg	57.11N	13.09 E
Fegen	8	Eg	57.06N	13.02 E
Fehérgyarmat	10	Si	47.59N	22.31 E
Fehmarn	10	Hb	54.30N	11.10 E
Fehmarnbelt	8	Dj	54.35N	11.15 E
Fehrbellin	10	Id	52.48N	12.46 E
Feicheng	28	Df	36.15N	116.46 E
Feidong (Dianbu)	28	Di	31.53N	117.29 E
Fei Huang He	28	Fg	34.15N	120.17 E
Feijó	54	De	8.09S	70.21W
Feilding	61	Eh	40.12S	175.35 E
Feira	36	Ff	15.37S	30.25 E
Feira de Santana	53	Mg	12.15S	38.57W
Feiran Oasis	24	Eh	28.42N	33.38 E
Feistritz	14	Kc	47.01N	16.08 E
Feixi (Shangpaihe)	28	Di	31.42N	117.09 E
Feixian	28	Dg	35.16N	117.59 E
Feixiang	28	Cf	36.32N	114.47 E
Fejão Prêto ou Furtado, Rio-	55	Dc	17.33S	57.23W
Fejér [2]	10	Oi	47.10N	18.35 E
Fejø	8	Dj	54.55N	11.25 E
Feke	24	Fd	37.53N	35.58 E
Fekete-víz	10	Ok	45.47N	18.13 E
Felanitx	13	Pe	39.28N	3.08 E
Feldbach	14	Jd	46.57N	15.53 E
Feldioara	15	Id	45.49N	25.36 E
Feldkirch	14	Dc	47.14N	9.36 E
Feldkirchen	14	Id	46.43N	14.06 E
Feliciano, Arroyo-	55	Cj	31.06S	59.54W
Felidu Atoll	25a	Bb	3.30N	73.30 E
Felipe Carrillo Puerto	47	Ge	19.35N	88.03W
Felix, Cape -	42	Hc	69.55N	97.47W
Felixlândia	55	Jd	18.47S	44.55W
Felixstowe	9	Oj	51.58N	1.20 E
Felletin	11	Ii	45.53N	2.11 E
Feltre	14	Fd	46.01N	11.54 E
Femer Bælt	8	Dj	54.35N	11.15 E
Femø	8	Dj	54.55N	11.35 E
Femund	7	Ce	62.15N	11.50 E
Fena Valley Reservoir	64c	Bb	13.20N	144.45 E
Fener Burnu	24	Hb	41.07N	39.25 E
Fénérive	37	Hc	17.22S	49.25 E
Fenerwa	35	Fc	13.05N	39.01 E
Fénétrange	12	Jf	48.51N	7.01 E
Fengcheng [China]	27	Lc	40.28N	124.01 E
Fengcheng [China]	23	Cj	28.11N	115.47 E
Fengdu	27	If	29.58N	107.39 E
Fenghua	28	Fj	29.40N	121.24 E
Fengjie	27	He	31.06N	104.30 E
Fenglingdu	27	Je	34.40N	110.19 E
Fengnan (Xugezhuang)	28	Ee	39.34N	118.05 E
Fengning (Dagezhen)	28	Dd	41.12N	116.39 E
Fengqing	27	Gg	24.41N	99.53 E
Fengqiu	28	Cg	35.02N	114.24 E
Fengrun	28	Ee	39.50N	118.09 E
Fengshui Shan	27	La	52.15N	123.30 E
Fengtai [China]	28	Dh	32.43N	116.43 E
Fengtai [China]	28	De	39.51N	116.17 E
Fengweiba → Zhenkang	27	Gg	23.54N	99.00 E
Fengxian	28	Dg	34.42N	116.35 E
Fengxian (Nanqiao)	28	Fi	30.55N	121.27 E
Fengxiang	27	Ie	34.32N	107.34 E
Fengxiang → Luobei	27	Nb	47.36N	130.58 E
Fengxin	28	Cj	28.42N	115.23 E
Fengyang	28	Dh	32.53N	117.33 E
Fengzhen	27	Jc	40.28N	113.09 E
Fen He [China]	27	Jd	35.36N	110.42 E
Fen He [China]	28	Ae	38.06N	111.52 E
Feni Islands	57	Ge	4.05S	153.42 E
Fennimore	45	Ke	42.59N	90.39W
Fensfjorden	8	Ad	60.50N	4.50 E
Fenshui Guan	27	Kf	27.56N	117.50 E
Fenton	44	Fd	42.48N	83.42W
Fenua Fu	64h	Ac	13.23S	176.11W
Fenualoa	63c	Bb	10.16S	166.15 E
Fenyang	27	Jd	37.17N	111.45 E
Feodosija	19	Df	45.02N	35.23 E
Fer, Cap de-	32	Ib	37.05N	7.10 E
Fer, Point au-	45	Kl	29.20N	91.21W
Feragen	8	Db	62.30N	11.55 E
Férai	15	Ji	40.54N	26.10 E
Ferdows	23	Ic	34.00N	58.09 E
Fère-Champenoise	11	Jf	48.45N	3.59 E
Fère-en-Tardenois	12	Fe	49.12N	3.31 E
Feren	8	Da	63.34N	11.50 E
Ferentino	14	Hi	41.42N	13.15 E
Ferfer [Eth.]	35	Hd	5.06N	45.09 E
Ferfer [Som.]	35	Hd	5.07N	45.07 E
Fergana	22	Je	40.23N	71.46 E
Fergana	21	Je	40.30N	71.00 E
Ferganskaja Oblast [3]	19	Hg	40.30N	71.20 E
Ferganski Hrebet	19	Hg	41.00N	74.00 E
Fergus Falls	43	Hb	46.17N	96.04W
Ferguson Lake	42	Hc	69.00N	105.00W
Fergusson Island	60	Ei	9.30S	150.40 E
Ferkéssédougou [3]	34	Ed	9.20N	4.55W
Ferkéssédougou	34	Dd	9.36N	5.12W
Ferlo	30	Fg	15.00N	14.00W
Ferlo	30	Fg	15.42N	15.30W
Fermo	14	Hg	43.09N	13.43 E
Fermoselle	13	Fc	41.19N	6.23W
Fermoy/Mainistir Fhear Mai	9	Ei	52.08N	8.16W
Fernandina, Isla-	52	Gf	0.25S	91.30W
Fernandina Beach	44	Gj	30.40N	81.27W
Fernando de Noronha, Ilha-	52	Mf	3.51S	32.25W
Fernando de Noronha, Território de- [2]	54	Ld	3.50S	33.00W
Fernandópolis	56	Kb	20.16S	50.00W
Fernán-Núñez	13	Hg	37.40N	4.43W
Fernelmont	12	Hd	50.35N	5.02 E
Fernie	46	Hb	49.30N	115.03W
Ferrandina	14	Kj	40.29N	16.27 E
Ferrara	14	Ff	44.50N	11.35 E
Ferrat, Cap-	13	Li	35.54N	0.23W
Ferrato, Capo-	14	Dk	39.18N	9.38 E
Ferré	55	Bl	34.08S	61.08W
Ferré, Cap-	51h	Bc	14.28N	60.49W
Ferreira do Alentejo	13	Df	38.03N	8.07W
Ferreñafe	54	Ce	6.38S	79.48W
Ferret, Cap-	11	Ej	44.37N	1.15W
Ferriday	45	Kk	31.38N	91.33W
Ferrières	12	Hd	50.24N	5.36 E
Ferro, Capo-	14	Di	41.09N	9.31 E
Ferro, Rio-	55	Ea	2.27S	54.31W
Ferru, Monte-	14	Cj	40.08N	8.36 E
Ferry, Pointe-	51e	Ab	6.17N	61.49W
Fertilia	14	Cj	40.36N	8.17 E
Fertö → Neusiedler See	10	Mi	47.50N	16.45 E
Fès	31	Ge	34.02N	4.59W
Fès [3]	32	Gc	34.00N	5.00W
Feshi	36	Cd	6.07S	18.10 E
Fessenden	45	Gc	47.39N	99.38W
Festieux	12	Fe	49.31N	3.45 E
Festus	45	Kg	38.13N	90.24W
Feteşti	15	Ke	44.23N	27.50 E
Fethiye	23	Cb	36.37N	29.07 E
Fethiye Körfezi	24	Cd	36.40N	29.00 E
Fetlar	9	Ma	60.37N	0.52W
Fetsund	7	Cg	59.56N	11.10 E
Feuchtwangen	10	Gg	49.10N	10.20 E
Feuilles, Baie aux -	42	Ke	58.55N	69.15W
Feuilles, Rivière aux-	42	Ke	58.46N	70.05W
Feurs	11	Ki	45.45N	4.14 E
Fevik	8	Cf	58.23N	8.42 E
Feyzābād	22	Jf	37.06N	70.34 E
Fezzan (EN)=Fazzān	33	Bd	25.30N	14.00 E
Fezzan (EN)=Fazzān	30	If	26.00N	14.00 E
Fezzane, Emi-	34	Ha	21.42N	14.15 E
Ffestiniog	9	Ji	52.58N	3.55W
Fiambalá	56	Gc	27.41S	67.38W
Fianarantsoa	31	Lk	21.28S	47.05 E
Fianarantsoa [3]	37	Hd	21.30S	47.05 E
Fianga	35	Bd	9.55N	15.09 E
Fiche	35	Fd	9.43N	38.44 E
Fichtelgebirge	5	He	50.00N	12.00 E
Ficksburg	37	De	28.57S	27.50 E
Fidenza	14	Ef	44.52N	10.03 E
Fieni	15	Id	45.08N	25.25 E
Fier	11	Li	45.56N	5.50 E
Fieri	15	Ci	40.43N	19.34 E
Fife [3]	9	Je	56.05N	3.15W
Fife Ness	9	Ke	56.17N	2.36W
Fiffa	34	Dc	11.27N	9.52W
Fifth Cataract (EN)= Khāmis, Ash Shallāl al-	30	Kg	18.23N	33.47 E
Figalo, Cap-	13	Ki	35.35N	1.12W
Figeac	11	Ij	44.36N	2.02 E
Figeholm	8	Gg	57.22N	16.33 E
Figtree	37	Dd	20.22S	28.20 E
Figueira, Baia da-	55	Dc	16.33S	57.25W
Figueira da Foz	13	Dd	40.09N	8.52W
Figueira de Castelo Rodrigo	13	Fd	40.54N	6.58W
Figueras	13	Ob	42.16N	2.58 E
Figueras/Figueres	13	Ob	42.16N	2.58 E
Figueres	13	Ob	42.16N	2.58 E
Figueres/Figueras	13	Ob	42.16N	2.58 E
Figuig [3]	32	Gc	33.00N	2.01W
Figuig	31	Ge	32.06N	1.14W
Fiherenana	37	Gd	23.19S	43.37 E
Fijāj, Shaţţ al-	32	Ic	33.55N	9.10 E
Fiji [1]	58	If	18.00S	178.00 E
Fiji Islands	57	If	18.00S	178.00 E
Fik	35	Gd	8.08N	42.18 E
Filabres, Sierra de los-	13	Jg	37.15N	2.20W
Filabusi	37	Dd	20.32S	29.16 E
Filadélfia	54	Ie	7.21S	47.30W
Filadelfia [C.R.]	49	Eh	10.26N	85.34W
Filadelfia [It.]	14	Kl	38.47N	16.17 E
Filakara	63b	Dc	16.49S	168.24 E
Filákovo	10	Ph	48.16N	19.50 E
Filamana	34	Dc	10.30N	7.57W
Filatova Gora	8	Mg	57.39N	28.21 E
Filchner Ice Shelf	66	Af	79.00S	40.00W
Filey	9	Mg	54.12N	0.17W
Filiaşi	15	Ge	44.33N	23.31 E
Filiátai	15	Dj	39.36N	20.19 E
Filiatrá	15	El	37.09N	21.35 E
Filicudi	14	Il	38.35N	14.35 E
Filingué	34	Fc	14.21N	3.19 E
Filiourí	15	Ii	40.57N	25.20 E
Filippiás	15	Dj	39.12N	20.53 E
Fílippoi	15	Hh	41.02N	24.20 E
Fílippoi = Philippi (EN)	15	Hh	41.02N	24.18 E
Filipstad	7	Dg	59.43N	14.10 E
Fillefjell	8	Cc	61.09N	8.15 E
Filliévres	12	Ed	50.19N	2.10 E
Fillmore	46	Ig	38.58N	112.20W
Fils	10	Fh	48.39N	9.29 E
Filtu	35	Gd	5.06N	40.40 E
Fímaina	15	Jl	37.35N	26.25 E
Fimi	30	Ii	3.01S	16.58 E
Fīn [Iran]	24	Pi	27.38N	55.55 E
Fīn [Iran]	24	Nf	33.57N	51.23 E
Finale Emilia	14	Ff	44.50N	11.17 E
Finale Ligure	14	Cf	44.10N	8.20 E
Findhorn	9	Jd	57.41N	3.37W
Fındıklı	24	Ib	41.17N	41.09 E
Findlay	43	Kc	41.02N	83.40W
Findlay, Mount-	46	Ga	50.04N	116.28W
Findlay Group	42	Ha	77.15N	104.00W
Fineveke	64h	Ab	13.19S	176.12W
Fingoè	37	Ec	15.10S	31.53 E
Finike	24	Dd	36.18N	30.09 E
Finistère [3]	11	Cf	48.20N	4.00W
Finisterre, Cabo de-	5	Fg	42.53N	9.16W
Finisterre Range	59	Ja	5.50S	146.05 E
Finke	58	Eg	25.34S	134.35 E
Finke, Mount-	59	Gf	30.55S	134.02 E
Finke River	57	Eg	27.00S	136.10 E
Finland/Suomi [1]	6	Ic	64.00N	26.00 E
Finland, Gulf of- (EN)= Finski Zaliv	5	Ic	60.00N	27.00 E
Finland, Gulf of- (EN)= Soomenlaht	5	Ic	60.00N	27.00 E
Finland, Gulf of- (EN)= Suomenlahti	5	Ic	60.00N	27.00 E
Finlay	42	Fe	55.59N	123.50W
Finlay Mountains	45	Dk	31.30N	105.35W
Finne	10	He	51.13N	11.19 E
Finngrunden	8	Hc	61.00N	18.19 E
Finnigan, Mount-	59	Jc	15.50S	145.20 E
Finniss, Cape-	59	Gf	33.38S	134.51 E
Finnmark	8	Fc	61.40N	14.45 E
Finnmark [3]	7	Fb	69.50N	24.10 E
Finnmarksvidda	5	Ib	69.30N	24.20 E
Finnøy	8	Ae	59.10N	5.50 E
Finnskogen	8	Ed	60.40N	12.40 E
Finnsnes	7	Eb	69.14N	18.02 E
Finnveden	8	Eh	56.50N	13.40 E
Finote Selam	35	Fc	10.42N	37.12 E
Finschhafen	59	Ja	6.35S	147.50 E
Finse	8	Bd	60.36N	7.30 E
Finski Zaliv=Finland, Gulf of- (EN)	5	Ic	60.00N	27.00 E
Finspång	7	Dg	58.43N	15.47 E
Finstadåa	8	Dc	61.47N	11.10 E
Finsteraarhorn	14	Cd	46.32N	8.08 E
Finsterwalde	10	Je	51.38N	13.43 E
Finström	8	Hd	60.16N	19.50 E
Fiora	14	Fh	42.20N	11.34 E
Fiorenzuola d'Arda	14	Df	44.56N	9.55 E
Firat=Euphrates (EN)	21	Gf	31.00N	47.25 E
Firenze = Florence (EN)	6	Hg	43.46N	11.15 E
Firenzuola	14	Ff	44.07N	11.23 E
Firmat	55	Bk	33.27S	61.29W
Firminópolis	55	Gc	16.40S	50.19W
Firminy	11	Ki	45.23N	4.18 E
Firozābād	25	Fc	27.09N	78.25 E
Firozpur	25	Eb	30.55N	74.36 E
First Cataract (EN)=Aswān, Sadd al-	30	Kf	24.01N	32.52 E
Fīrūzābād	24	Oh	28.50N	52.36 E
Fīrūzābād	24	Pg	31.59N	54.20 E
Fīrūzābād	24	Le	34.09N	46.25 E
Fīrūz Kūh	24	Oe	35.45N	52.47 E
Fischbach	12	Je	49.44N	7.24 E
Fischbacher Alpen	14	Jc	47.25N	15.30 E
Fischland	10	Ib	54.22N	12.25 E
Fish [Nam.]	30	Ik	17.11S	28.08 E
Fish [S.Afr.]	37	Cf	31.14S	20.15 E
Fisher Glacier	66	Ef	73.15S	66.00 E
Fisher Peak	44	Gg	36.33N	80.50W
Fisher Strait	42	Jd	63.00N	84.00W
Fishguard	6	Fe	51.59N	4.59W
Fish River Canyon	37	Be	27.35S	17.35 E
Fiskárdhon	15	Dk	38.28N	20.35 E
Fiskenaes Bank (EN)	41	Gf	63.18N	52.10W
Fiskenæsset	41	Gf	63.10N	50.45W
Fismes	11	Je	49.18N	3.41 E
Fišt, Gora-	19	Dg	43.57N	39.55 E
Fitchburg	44	Ld	42.35N	71.48W
Fitjar	7	Ag	59.55N	5.20 E
Fito, Mount-	65c	Ba	13.55S	171.44W
Fitri, Lac-	35	Bc	12.50N	17.28 E
Fitzcarrald	54	Df	11.49S	71.48W
Fitzgerald [Alta.-Can.]	42	Ge	59.52N	111.40W
Fitzgerald [Ga.-U.S.]	44	Fj	31.43N	83.15W
Fitzroy Crossing	59	Fc	18.11S	125.35 E
Fitzroy River [Austl.]	59	Kc	23.32S	150.52 E
Fitzroy River [Austl.]	57	Df	17.31S	123.35 E
Fitzwilliam Island	44	Gc	45.30N	81.45W
Fiuggi	14	Hi	41.48N	13.13 E
Fiumicino	14	Gi	41.46N	12.14 E
Five Island Harbour	51d	Bb	17.06N	61.54W
Fivizzano	14	Ef	44.14N	10.08 E
Fizi	31	Ji	4.18S	28.57 E
Fizuli	19	Eh	39.35N	47.11 E
Fjærlandsfjorden	8	Bc	61.15N	6.40 E
Fjällbacka	8	Df	58.36N	11.17 E
Fjärås	7	Ch	57.26N	12.09 E
Fjerritslev	8	Cg	57.05N	9.16 E
Fjöllum, Jökulsá á-	7a	Ca	66.02N	16.27W
Fjugesta	8	Fe	59.10N	14.52 E
Flacq	37a	Bb	20.12S	57.43 E
Flade Isblink	41	Kb	81.25N	16.00W
Fladen	8	Dg	57.07N	11.35 E
Fladen	8	Dg	57.10N	11.45 E
Flagler	45	Eg	39.18N	103.04W
Flagstaff	39	Hf	35.12N	111.39W
Flåm	7	Bf	60.50N	7.07 E
Flamborough Head	9	Mg	54.07N	0.04W
Fläming	10	Ie	52.00N	13.00 E
Flaming Gorge Reservoir	46	Kf	41.15N	109.30W
Flamingo	44	Gm	25.09N	80.56W
Flamingo, Teluk-	26	Kh	5.33S	138.00 E
Flanders (EN)=Flandres/ Vlaanderen	5	Ge	51.00N	3.20 E
Flanders (EN)=Flandres/ Vlaanderen	11	Jc	51.00N	3.20 E
Flanders (EN)=Vlaanderen/ Flandres	5	Ge	51.00N	3.20 E
Flanders (EN)=Vlaanderen/ Flandres	11	Jc	51.00N	3.20 E
Flanders Plain (EN) = Flandres, Plaine des-	11	Id	50.40N	2.50 E
Flanders Plain (EN)= Vlamse Vlakte	11	Id	50.40N	2.50 E
Flandreau	45	Hd	44.03N	96.36W
Flandres/Vlaanderen= Flanders (EN)	11	Jc	51.00N	3.20 E
Flandres/Vlaanderen= Flanders (EN)	5	Ge	51.00N	3.20 E
Flandres, Plaine des= Flanders Plain (EN)	11	Id	50.40N	2.50 E
Flannan Isles	9	Fc	58.20N	7.35W
Flåren	8	Fh	57.00N	14.05 E
Flasher	45	Fc	46.27N	101.14W
Fläsjön	7	Dd	64.06N	15.51 E
Flat	40	Hd	62.27N	158.01W
Flatey	7a	Ab	65.22N	22.56W
Flateyri	7a	Aa	66.03N	23.31W
Flathead Lake	43	Eb	47.52N	114.08W
Flathead Range	46	Ib	48.05N	113.28W
Flathead River	46	Hc	47.22N	114.47W
Flat Point	51b	Ab	18.15N	63.05W
Flat River	45	Kh	37.51N	90.31W
Flattery, Cape-	38	Ge	48.23N	124.43W
Flåvatnet	8	Ce	59.20N	8.50 E
Flaxton	45	Eb	48.54N	102.24W
Flaygreen Lake	42	Hf	53.50N	97.20W
Fleckenstein, Château de-	12	Je	49.05N	7.48 E
Fleet	12	Bc	51.17N	0.50W
Fleetwood	9	Jh	53.56N	3.01W
Flekkefjord	7	Bg	58.17N	6.41 E
Flémalle	12	Hd	50.36N	5.29 E
Flemish Bight [Eur.]	11	Dc	51.44N	2.30W
Flemish Bight [U.K.]	9	Pi	52.10N	2.50 E
Flemish Cap (EN)	38	De	47.00N	45.00W
Flemsøya	8	Bb	62.40N	6.20 E
Flen	7	Dg	59.04N	16.35 E
Flensborg Fjord	8	Cj	54.50N	9.45 E
Flensburg	6	Ge	54.47N	9.26 E
Flensburger Förde	8	Cj	54.50N	9.45 E
Flers	11	Ff	48.45N	0.34W
Flesberg	8	Ce	59.51N	9.27 E
Fleurance	11	Gk	43.50N	0.40 E
Fleury-sur-Andelle	12	De	49.22N	1.21 E
Fleuve [3]	34	Cb	16.00N	13.50W
Flevoland	11	Lb	52.25N	5.30 E
Flian	8	Ef	58.27N	13.05 E
Flims	14	Dd	46.50N	9.16 E
Flinders Bay	59	Df	34.25S	115.19 E
Flinders Island	57	Fi	40.00S	148.00 E
Flinders Passage	59	Jc	18.50S	149.00 E
Flinders Ranges	57	Eh	31.25S	138.45 E
Flinders Reefs	57	Ff	17.40S	148.30 E
Flinders River	57	Ff	17.36S	140.36 E
Flin Flon	39	Id	54.56N	101.53W
Flint [Mi.-U.S.]	39	Ke	43.01N	83.41W
Flint [Wales-U.K.]	9	Jh	53.15N	3.07W
Flint Hills	45	Hh	37.20N	96.35W
Flint Island	57	Lf	11.26S	151.48W
Flint River	43	Ke	30.52N	84.38W
Flisa	7	Cf	60.37N	12.04 E
Flisa	8	Ed	60.36N	12.01 E
Flisegga	8	Be	59.50N	7.50 E
Flitwick	12	Bb	52.00N	0.29W
Flix	13	Mc	41.14N	0.33 E
Flixecourt	12	Ed	50.01N	2.05 E
Flize	12	Ge	49.42N	4.46 E
Flobecq/Vloesberg	12	Fc	50.44N	3.44 E
Floby	8	Ef	58.08N	13.20 E
Floda [Swe.]	8	Fd	60.26N	14.49 E
Floda [Swe.]	8	Eg	57.48N	12.22 E
Flood Range	66	Nf	76.03S	134.00W
Flora [Il.-U.S.]	45	Lg	38.40N	88.29W
Flora [Nor.]	7	Af	61.36N	5.00 E
Florac	11	Jj	44.19N	3.36 E
Florala	44	Dj	31.00N	86.20W
Florange	12	Ie	49.20N	6.07 E
Florence [Al.-U.S.]	43	Je	34.49N	87.40W
Florence [Ks.-U.S.]	45	Hg	38.15N	96.56W
Florence [Or.-U.S.]	46	Cd	44.01N	124.07W
Florence [S.C.-U.S.]	43	Le	34.12N	79.44W
Florence (EN) = Firenze	6	Hg	43.46N	11.15 E
Florencia [Arg.]	55	Ci	28.02S	59.15W
Florencia [Col.]	53	Ie	1.36N	75.36W
Florencio Sánchez	55	Dk	33.53S	57.24W
Florennes	12	Gd	50.15N	4.37 E
Florentino Ameghino, Embalse-	56	Gf	43.48S	66.25W
Florenville	11	Le	49.42N	5.18 E
Flores [2]	55	Dk	33.35S	56.50W
Flores	30	De	39.26N	31.13W
Flores [Guat.]	49	Ce	16.56N	89.53W
Flores [Guat.]	47	Ge	16.58N	89.50W
Flores, Arroyo de las-	55	Cl	35.36S	59.01W
Flores, Laut-=Flores Sea (EN)	21	Oj	8.00S	121.00 E
Flores, Pulau-	21	Oj	8.30S	121.00 E
Flores Island	46	Bb	49.20N	126.10W
Flores Sea (EN)=Flores, Laut-	21	Oj	8.00S	121.00 E
Floreşty	16	Ff	47.55N	28.18 E
Floriano	53	Lf	6.47S	43.01W
Florianópolis	53	Lh	27.35S	48.34W
Florida [Braz.]	55	Ei	29.15S	54.36W
Florida [Cuba]	47	Id	21.32N	78.14W
Florida [U.S.] [2]	43	Kf	28.00N	82.00W
Florida [Ur.] [2]	55	Ek	33.50S	55.55W
Florida [Ur.]	56	Id	34.06S	56.13W
Florida, Estrecho de-= Florida, Straits of- (EN)	38	Kg	24.00N	81.00W
Florida, Straits of-	38	Kg	24.00N	81.00W
Florida, Straits of- (EN)= Florida, Estrecho de-	38	Kg	24.00N	81.00W
Florida Bay	44	Gm	25.00N	80.45W
Floridablanca	54	Db	7.04N	73.06W

Index Symbols

- [1] Independent Nation
- [2] State, Region
- [3] District, County
- [4] Municipality
- [5] Colony, Dependency
- Continent
- Physical Region
- Historical or Cultural Region
- Mount, Mountain
- Volcano
- Hill
- Mountains, Mountain Range
- Hills, Escarpment
- Plateau, Upland
- Pass, Gap
- Plain, Lowland
- Delta
- Salt Flat
- Valley, Canyon
- Crater, Cave
- Karst Features
- Depression
- Polder
- Desert, Dunes
- Forest, Woods
- Heath, Steppe
- Oasis
- Cape, Point
- Coast, Beach
- Cliff
- Peninsula
- Isthmus
- Sandbank
- Island
- Atoll
- Rock, Reef
- Islands, Archipelago
- Rocks, Reefs
- Coral Reef
- Well, Spring
- Geyser
- River, Stream
- Waterfall Rapids
- River Mouth, Estuary
- Lake
- Salt Lake
- Intermittent Lake
- Reservoir
- Swamp, Pond
- Canal
- Glacier
- Ice Shelf, Pack Ice
- Ocean
- Sea
- Gulf, Bay
- Strait, Fjord
- Lagoon
- Bank
- Seamount
- Tablemount
- Ridge
- Shelf
- Basin
- Escarpment, Sea Scarp
- Fracture
- Trench, Abyss
- National Park, Reserve
- Point of Interest
- Recreation Site
- Cave, Cavern
- Historic Site
- Ruins
- Wall, Walls
- Church, Abbey
- Temple
- Scientific Station
- Airport
- Port
- Lighthouse
- Mine
- Tunnel
- Dam, Bridge

Index Symbols

[1] Independent Nation	Historical or Cultural Region	Pass, Gap	Depression	Coast, Beach	Rock, Reef	Canal	Lagoon	Escarpment, Sea Scarp	Historic Site	Port
[2] State, Region	Mount, Mountain	Plain, Lowland	Polder	Cliff	Islands, Archipelago	River Mouth, Estuary	Bank	Fracture	Ruins	Lighthouse
[3] District, County	Volcano	Delta	Desert, Dunes	Peninsula	Rocks, Reefs	Lake	Seamount	Trench, Abyss	Wall, Walls	Mine
[4] Municipality	Hill	Salt Flat	Forest, Woods	Isthmus	Coral Reef	Salt Lake	Tablemount	National Park, Reserve	Church, Abbey	Tunnel
[5] Colony, Dependency	Mountains, Mountain Range	Valley, Canyon	Heath, Steppe	Sandbank	Well, Spring	Intermittent Lake	Ridge	Point of Interest	Temple	Dam, Barrage
▣ Continent	Hills, Escarpment	Crater, Cave	Oasis	Island	Geyser	Reservoir	Shelf	Recreation Site	Scientific Station	
▣ Physical Region	Plateau, Upland	Karst Features	Cape, Point	Atoll	River, Stream	Swamp, Pond	Strait, Fjord	Basin	Cave, Cavern	Airport

Friesoythe	10	Dc	53.01N	7.51 E
Frigate Island	51p	Cb	12.25N	61.29W
Friggesund	8	Gc	61.54N	16.32 E
Frignano	14	Ef	44.20N	10.50 E
Frindsbury Reef	63a	Da	5.00S	159.07 E
Frinnaryd	8	Fg	57.56N	14.49 E
Frinton-on-Sea	12	Dc	51.50N	1.15 E
Frio, Cabo-	52	Lh	22.53S	42.00W
Frio, Rio-	49	Eh	11.08N	84.46W
Frio Draw	45	Ei	34.50N	102.08W
Friona	45	Ei	34.38N	102.43W
Frio River	45	Gl	28.30N	98.10W
Frisco Peak	46	Ig	38.31N	113.14W
Frisian Islands (EN)	5	Ge	54.00N	7.00 E
Fristad	8	Eg	57.50N	13.01 E
Fritsla	8	Eg	57.33N	12.47 E
Fritzlar	10	Fe	51.08N	9.17 E
Friuli	14	Gd	46.00N	13.00 E
Friuli-Venezia Giulia [2]	14	Gd	46.00N	13.00 E
Frobisher Bay	38	Mc	62.30N	66.00W
Frobisher Lake	42	Ge	56.20N	108.20W
Froidchapelle	12	Gd	50.09N	4.20 E
Froissy	12	Ee	49.34N	2.13 E
Frolovo	19	Ef	49.45N	43.39 E
Fromberg	46	Kd	45.23N	108.54W
Frombork	10	Pb	54.22N	19.41 E
Frome	9	Kj	51.14N	2.20W
Frome, Lake-	57	Eh	30.50S	139.50 E
Frondenberg	12	Jc	51.28N	7.46 E
Fronteira	13	Ee	39.03N	7.39W
Fronteiras	54	Je	7.05S	40.37W
Frontera	48	Mh	18.32N	92.38W
Frontera, Punta-	48	Mh	18.36N	92.42W
Fronteras	48	Eb	30.56N	109.31W
Frontignan	11	Jk	43.27N	3.45 E
Frontino, Paramo-	54	Cb	6.28N	76.04W
Front Range	38	If	39.45N	105.45W
Front Royal	44	Hf	38.56N	78.13W
Frosinone	14	Hi	41.38N	13.19 E
Frösö	8	Fa	63.11N	14.32 E
Frostburg	44	Hf	39.39N	78.56W
Frost Glacier	66	Ie	67.05S	129.00 E
Frövi	8	Fe	59.28N	15.22 E
Frøya	7	Be	63.43N	8.42 E
Frøysjøen	8	Ac	61.50N	5.05 E
Frozen Strait	42	Jc	65.50N	84.30W
Fruges	11	Id	50.31N	2.08 E
Frunze → Biškek	22	Je	42.54N	74.36 E
Frunze	18	Hd	40.06N	71.45 E
Frunzovka	15	Mb	47.20N	29.37 E
Fruška Gora	15	Cd	45.10N	19.35 E
Frutal	54	Ih	20.02S	48.55W
Frutigen	14	Bd	46.35N	7.40 E
Fry Canyon	46	Jh	37.38N	110.08W
Frýdek Mistek	10	Og	49.41N	18.22 E
Frylinckspan	37	Ce	26.46S	22.28 E
Ftéri	15	Ej	39.09N	21.33 E
Fua'amotu	65b	Ac	21.15S	175.08W
Fua Mulaku Island	25a	Bc	0.15S	73.30 E
Fu'an	27	Kf	27.10N	119.44 E
Fu-chien Sheng → Fujian Sheng = Fukien (EN) [2]	27	Kf	26.00N	118.00 E
Fuchskauten	10	Ef	50.40N	8.05 E
Fuchū [Jap.]	29	Cd	34.34N	133.14 E
Fuchū [Jap.]	29	Fd	35.41N	139.28 E
Fuchun-Jiang	28	Fi	30.15N	120.15 E
Fuchunjiang-Shuiku	28	Ej	29.29N	119.31 E
Fucino, Conca del-	14	Hj	42.01N	13.31 E
Fudai	29	Ga	40.01N	141.52 E
Fuding	27	Lf	27.19N	120.08 E
Fuengirola	13	Hh	36.32N	4.37W
Fuente Alto	56	Fd	33.37S	70.35W
Fuente del Maestre	13	Ff	38.32N	6.27W
Fuente-Obejuna	13	Gf	38.16N	5.25W
Fuentesaúco	13	Gc	41.14N	5.30W
Fuentes de Andalucia	13	Gg	37.28N	5.21W
Fuentes de Cantos	13	Ff	38.15N	6.18W
Fuerte	47	Cc	25.54N	109.22W
Fuerte, Isla-	49	Ii	9.23N	76.11W
Fuerte, Sierra del-	48	Hd	27.30N	102.45W
Fuerte Olimpo	56	Ib	21.02S	57.54W
Fuerteventura	30	Ff	28.20N	14.00W
Fuga	26	Hc	18.52N	121.22 E
Fugong	27	Gf	27.03N	98.57 E
Fugou	28	Cg	34.04N	114.23 E
Fugu	27	Jd	39.02N	111.03 E
Fuguo → Zhanhua	28	Ef	37.42N	118.08 E
Fuhai/Burultokay	27	Eb	47.06N	87.23 E
Fuhayrī, Wādī-	23	Hf	16.04N	52.11 E
Fu He	28	Dj	28.36N	116.04 E
Fuji	28	Og	35.09N	138.38 E
Fujian Sheng (Fu-chien Sheng) = Fukien (EN) [2]	27	Kf	26.00N	118.00 E
Fujieda	29	Fd	34.51N	138.15 E
Fuji-Gawa	29	Fd	35.07N	138.38 E
Fujin	27	Nb	47.15N	132.01 E
Fujinomiya	29	Fd	35.12N	138.38 E
Fujioka	29	Fc	36.15N	139.03 E
Fuji-San	21	Pf	35.26N	138.43 E
Fujisawa	29	Fd	35.21N	139.27 E
Fuji-yoshida	29	Fd	35.29N	138.47 E
Fukagawa	27	Pc	43.43N	142.03 E
Fūkah	24	Bg	31.04N	27.55 E
Fukang	27	Ec	44.10N	87.59 E
Fuka-Shima	29	Be	32.43N	131.56 E
Fukiage	29	Bf	31.30N	130.20 E
Fukien (EN) = Fu-chien Sheng → Fujian Sheng [2]	27	Kf	26.00N	118.00 E
Fukien (EN) = Fujian Sheng (Fu-chien Sheng) [2]	27	Kf	26.00N	118.00 E
Fukuchiyama	28	Mg	35.18N	135.07 E
Fukue	28	Jh	32.41N	128.50 E
Fukueichiao	27	Lf	25.19N	121.34 E
Fukue-Jima	28	Jh	32.41N	128.48 E
Fukui	27	Od	36.04N	136.13 E
Fukui Ken [2]	28	Ng	36.00N	136.20 E
Fukuma	29	Be	33.47N	130.28 E
Fukuoka	22	Pf	33.35N	130.24 E
Fukuoka Ken [2]	28	Kh	33.28N	130.45 E
Fukuroi	29	Ed	34.45N	137.54 E
Fukushima [Jap.]	27	Pd	37.45N	140.28 E
Fukushima [Jap.]	27	Pc	41.29N	140.15 E
Fukushima Ken [2]	28	Pf	37.25N	140.10 E
Fukuyama	27	Ne	34.29N	133.22 E
Fūlādī, Kūh-e-	23	Kc	34.38N	67.32 E
Fūlād Mahalleh	24	Od	36.02N	53.44 E
Fulanga	63d	Cc	19.08S	178.34W
Fulda	5	Ge	51.25N	9.39 E
Fulda	10	Ff	50.33N	9.40 E
Fuliji	28	Dh	33.47N	116.59 E
Fulin → Hanyuan	27	Hf	29.25N	102.12 E
Fuling	27	If	29.40N	107.21 E
Fullerton	45	Hf	41.22N	97.58W
Fulton [Arg.]	55	Cm	37.25S	58.48W
Fulton [Il.-U.S.]	45	Kf	41.52N	90.11W
Fulton [Ky.-U.S.]	44	Cg	36.30N	88.53W
Fulton [Mo.-U.S.]	45	Kg	38.52N	91.57W
Fulton [N.Y.-U.S.]	44	Id	43.20N	76.26W
Fulufjället	8	Ec	61.33N	12.43 E
Fumaiolo	14	Gg	43.47N	12.04 E
Fumay	11	Kd	50.00N	4.42 E
Fumel	11	Gj	44.30N	0.58 E
Funabasi	28	Og	35.42N	139.59 E
Funabiki	29	Gc	37.26N	140.35 E
Funafuti	58	Ie	8.01S	178.00 E
Funafuti Atoll	57	Ie	8.31S	179.08 E
Funagata	29	Gb	38.42N	140.18 E
Funagata-Yama	29	Gb	38.27N	140.37 E
Funakoshi-Wan	29	Hb	39.25N	142.00 E
Funan	28	Ch	32.38N	115.35 E
Funäsdalen	7	Ce	62.32N	12.33 E
Funchal	31	Fe	32.38N	16.54W
Fundación	54	Da	10.29N	74.12W
Fundão	13	Ed	40.08N	7.30W
Fundy, Bay of-	38	Me	45.00N	66.00W
Funeral Peak	46	Gh	36.08N	116.37W
Fungalei	64h	Bb	13.17S	176.07W
Funhalouro	37	Ed	23.05S	34.24 E
Funing [China]	27	Ig	23.39N	105.33 E
Funing [China]	28	Eh	33.48N	119.47 E
Funing [China]	28	Ee	39.56N	119.15 E
Funiu Shan	27	Je	33.40N	112.10 E
Funtua	34	Gc	11.32N	7.19 E
Fuping	28	Ce	38.49N	114.15 E
Fuqing	27	Kf	25.47N	119.24 E
Furancungo	37	Eb	14.54S	33.37 E
Furano	28	Qc	43.21N	142.23 E
Füren	29a	Ca	44.17N	142.25 E
Furenai	29a	Cb	42.43N	142.15 E
Füren-Ko	29a	Db	43.20N	145.20 E
Fürg	24	Ph	28.18N	55.13 E
Fur Jiang	28	Hc	42.37N	125.33 E
Furmanov	7	Jh	57.16N	41.07 E
Furnas, Represa de-	54	Ih	21.20S	45.50W
Furnas, Serra das-	55	Fb	15.45S	53.20W
Furneaux Group	57	Fi	40.10S	148.05 E
Furnes/Veurne	11	Ic	51.04N	2.40 E
Furqlus	24	Ge	34.36N	37.05 E
Furriyānah	32	Ic	34.57N	8.34 E
Fürstenau	12	Jb	52.31N	7.43 E
Fürstenauer Berge	12	Jb	52.35N	7.45 E
Fürstenfeld	14	Kc	47.03N	16.05 E
Fürstenfeldbruck	10	Hh	48.11N	11.15 E
Fürstenlager	12	Ke	49.42N	8.38 E
Fürstenwalde	10	Kd	52.22N	14.04 E
Fürth [Ger.]	10	Gg	49.28N	11.00 E
Fürth [Ger.]	12	Ke	49.39N	8.47 E
Furth im Wald	10	Ig	49.18N	12.51 E
Furubira	29a	Bb	43.16N	140.39 E
Furudal	7	Df	61.10N	15.08 E
Furukawa	27	Pd	38.34N	140.58 E
Furusund	8	He	59.40N	18.55 E
Fury and Hecla Strait	42	Jc	69.55N	84.00W
Fushan [China]	28	Ff	37.30N	121.15 E
Fushan [China]	28	Ag	35.58N	111.51 E
Fushë-Arëzi	15	Dg	42.04N	20.02 E
Fushë-Lura	15	Dh	41.48N	20.13 E
Fu Shui	28	Cj	29.52N	115.26 E
Fushun	22	Oe	41.46N	123.56 E
Fusong	27	Mc	42.20N	127.17 E
Füsselberg	12	Je	49.32N	7.14 E
Füssen	10	Gi	47.34N	10.42 E
Futa, Passo della-	14	Ff	44.05N	11.17 E
Futago-Yama	29	Be	33.35N	131.38 E
Futaoi-Jima	29	Bd	34.06N	130.47 E
Futog	15	Cd	45.15N	19.42 E
Futuna, Ile-	57	Jf	14.17S	178.09W
Fuwah	24	Dg	31.12N	30.33 E
Fuxian (Wafangdian)	27	Ld	39.38N	121.59 E
Fuxian Hu	27	Hg	24.30N	102.55 E
Fuxin	22	Oe	41.59N	121.38 E
Fuxin Monggolzu Zizhixian	28	Fc	42.06N	121.46 E
Fuyang	27	Ke	32.47N	115.46 E
Fuyang He	28	Dg	38.14N	116.05 E
Fuyang Zhan	28	Ch	32.56N	115.53 E
Fuyu [China]	27	Lb	45.10N	124.52 E
Fuyu [China]	27	Lb	47.48N	124.26 E
Fuyuan [China]	27	Lc	42.44N	124.57 E
Fuyuan [China]	27	Nb	48.21N	134.18 E
Fuyuan [China]	27	Hf	25.43N	104.20 E
Fuyun/Koktokay	22	Ke	47.13N	89.39 E
Füzesabony	10	Qi	47.45N	20.25 E
Fuzhou [China]	22	Ng	26.10N	119.20 E
Fuzhou [China]	27	Kf	27.58N	116.20 E
Fuzhou He	28	Fe	39.36N	121.35 E
Fyllas Bank (EN)	41	Gf	64.00N	53.00W
Fyn	8	Di	55.20N	10.30 E
Fyn [2]	8	Di	55.20N	10.30 E
Fyne, Loch-	9	He	56.10N	5.20W
Fyresdal	7	Bg	59.11N	8.06 E
Fyresvatn	8	Ce	59.05N	8.10 E
Fzāra, Gara'et-	14	Bn	36.47N	7.30 E

G

Gaasbeek	12	Gd	50.48N	4.10 E
Gaasterland	12	Hb	52.54N	5.36 E
Gaasterland	12	Hb	52.53N	5.35 E
Gaasterland-Balk	12	Hb	52.54N	5.36 E
Gabaru Reef	64a	Bb	7.53N	134.31 E
Gabas	11	Fk	43.46N	0.42W
Gabba'	35	Id	8.02N	50.08 E
Gabbs	46	Gg	38.52N	117.55W
Gabela	31	Ij	10.52S	14.23 E
Gabel'a (Kutkašen)	16	Oi	40.58N	47.52 E
Gabès, Gulf of-(EN) = Qābis, Khalīj-	30	Ie	34.00N	10.25 E
Gabon	36	Ab	0.25N	9.20 E
Gabon [1]	31	Ii	1.00S	11.45 E
Gaborone	31	Jk	24.40S	25.55 E
Gabras	35	Dc	10.16N	26.14 E
Gabriel Strait	42	Kd	61.50N	65.40W
Gabriel y Galán, Embalse de-	13	Fd	40.15N	6.15W
Gabrovo	15	Ig	42.52N	25.19 E
Gabrovo [2]	15	Ig	42.52N	25.19 E
Gacé	11	Gf	48.48N	0.18 E
Gachsārān	24	Ng	30.12N	50.47 E
Gackle	45	Gc	46.38N	99.09W
Gacko	14	Mg	43.10N	18.32 E
Gadag	25	Fe	15.25N	75.37 E
Gäddede	7	Dd	64.30N	14.09 E
Gadê	27	Ge	34.13N	99.29 E
Gadjač	16	Id	50.22N	34.01 E
Gádor, Sierra de-	13	Jh	36.55N	2.45W
Gadsden	43	Je	34.02N	86.02W
Gadūk, Gardaneh-ye-	24	De	35.55N	52.55 E
Gadzi	35	Be	4.47N	16.42 E
Gael Hamkes Bugt	41	Jd	74.00N	22.00W
Găeşti	15	Ie	44.43N	25.19 E
Gaeta	14	Hi	41.12N	13.35 E
Gaeta, Golfo di-	14	Hi	41.05N	13.30 E
Gaferut Island	57	Fd	9.14N	145.23 E
Gaffney	44	Gh	35.05N	81.39W
Gagan	63a	Ba	5.14S	154.37 E
Gagarin	19	Dd	55.35N	35.01 E
Gagarin	18	Gd	40.40N	68.05 E
Gagévésouva, Pointe-	63b	Ca	13.04S	166.32 E
Gaggenau	12	Kf	48.48N	8.20 E
Gagnef	7	Df	60.35N	15.04 E
Gagnoa	31	Gh	6.08N	5.56W
Gagnoa [3]	34	Dd	6.03N	6.00W
Gagnon	42	Kf	51.55N	68.10W
Gagra	19	Eg	43.17N	40.15 E
Gahkom	24	Ph	28.12N	55.50 E
Gahkom, Kūh-e-	24	Ph	28.10N	55.57 E
Gaíba, Laguna-	55	Dc	17.45S	57.43W
Gail	14	Hd	46.36N	13.53 E
Gaillac	11	Hk	43.54N	1.55 E
Gaillefontaine	12	De	49.39N	1.37 E
Gaillimh/Galway	6	Fe	53.16N	9.03W
Gaillimh/Galway [2]	9	Eh	53.20N	9.00W
Gaillon	12	De	49.10N	1.20 E
Gailtaler Alpen	14	Gd	46.40N	13.00 E
Gaiman	56	Gf	43.17S	65.29W
Găinești	15	Ib	47.25N	25.55 E
Gainesville [Fl.-U.S.]	39	Kg	29.40N	82.20W
Gainesville [Ga.-U.S.]	43	Ke	34.18N	83.50W
Gainesville [Mo.-U.S.]	45	Jh	36.36N	92.26W
Gainesville [Tx.-U.S.]	43	He	33.37N	97.08W
Gainsborough	9	Mh	53.24N	0.46W
Gairdner, Lake-	57	Eh	31.35S	136.00 E
Gairloch	9	Hd	57.43N	5.40W
Gaizina Kalns/Gajzinkalns	8	Kh	56.50N	25.59 E
Gaj	19	Fe	51.31N	58.30 E
Gajny	19	Fc	60.20N	54.15 E
Gajsin	19	Cf	48.50N	29.27 E
Gajvoron	16	Fe	48.22N	29.52 E
Galaasija	18	Ee	39.52N	64.27 E
Gălăbovo	15	Ig	42.08N	25.51 E
Gala Gölü	15	Ji	40.45N	26.12 E
Galaico, Macizo-	13	Eb	42.30N	7.20W
Galán, Cerro-	56	Gc	25.55S	66.52W
Galana	30	Li	3.09S	40.08 E
Galanta	10	Nh	48.12N	17.44 E
Galap	64a	Bb	7.38N	134.39 E
Galápagos, Islas-/Colón, Archipiélago de-= Galapagos Islands (EN)	52	Gf	0.30S	90.30W
Galapagos Fracture Zone (EN)	3	Mi	0.00	100.00W
Galapagos Islands (EN) = Colon, Archipiélago de-/Galápagos, Islas-	52	Gf	0.30S	90.30W
Galapagos Islands (EN) = Galápagos, Islas-/Colón, Archipiélago de-	52	Gf	0.30S	90.30W
Galarza	55	Di	28.03S	56.41W
Galashiels	9	Kf	55.37N	2.49W
Galați [2]	15	Kd	45.38N	27.56 E
Galați	6	If	45.27N	28.03 E
Galatina	14	Mj	40.10N	18.10 E
Galatone	14	Mj	40.09N	18.04 E
Galatzó	13	Oe	39.38N	2.29 E
Galdar	32	Dd	28.09N	15.39W
Galdhøpiggen	7	Bf	61.37N	8.17 E
Galeana [Mex.]	48	Fb	30.07N	107.38W
Galeana [Mex.]	48	Ie	24.50N	100.04W
Galeh Dār	24	Oi	27.36N	52.42 E
Galela	58	Dd	1.50N	127.50 E
Galena [Ak.-U.S.]	40	Hd	64.44N	156.57W
Galena [Il.-U.S.]	45	Ke	42.25N	90.26W
Galeota Point	50	Fg	10.08N	61.59W
Galera, Punta-	56	Fe	39.59S	73.43W
Galera, Rio-	55	Bb	14.25S	60.07W
Galera Point	50	Fg	10.49N	60.55W
Galesburg	43	Ic	40.57N	90.22W
Galga	10	Pi	47.33N	19.43 E
Gal Gaduud [3]	35	Hd	5.00N	47.00 E
Galheirão, Rio-	55	Ja	12.23S	45.05W
Galheiros	55	Ia	13.18S	46.25W
Gali	16	Lh	42.36N	41.42 E
Galič	19	Ed	58.23N	42.21 E
Galič	16	De	49.06N	24.43 E
Galicea Mare	15	Ge	44.06N	23.18 E
Galicia	5	Fg	43.00N	8.00W
Galicia	13	Eb	43.00N	8.00W
Galicia (EN) = Galicija	5	If	49.50N	21.00 E
Galicia (EN) = Galicija [Eur.]	10	Qg	49.50N	21.00 E
Galicia (EN) = Galicja	10	Qg	49.50N	21.00 E
Galicia (EN) = Galicja	5	If	49.50N	21.00 E
Galicija [Eur.] = Galicia (EN)	10	Qg	49.50N	21.00 E
Galicija	10	Jg	49.00N	24.00 E
Galicija = Galicia (EN)	5	If	49.50N	21.00 E
Galicja = Galicia (EN)	5	If	49.50N	21.00 E
Galicja = Galicia (EN)	10	Qg	49.50N	21.00 E
Galilee, Lake-	59	Jd	22.20S	145.55 E
Galimy	20	Kd	62.19N	156.00 E
Galina Point	49	Id	18.24N	76.53W
Galion	44	Fe	40.44N	82.46W
Galion, Baie du-	51h	Bb	14.44N	60.57W
Galiton	14	Cm	37.30N	8.52 E
Galiuro Mountains	46	Jj	32.40N	110.20W
Gālka'yo	31	Lh	6.49N	47.23 E
Galkino	17	Ki	55.40N	62.55 E
Gallarate	14	Ce	45.40N	8.47 E
Gallatin	44	Dg	36.24N	86.27W
Gallatin Range	46	Jd	45.15N	111.05W
Gallatin River	46	Jd	45.56N	111.29W
Galle	22	Ki	6.02N	80.13 E
Gállego	13	Lc	41.39N	0.51W
Gallegos, Río-	52	Jk	51.36S	68.59W
Gallinas, Punta-	52	Id	12.25N	71.40W
Gallinas Peak	45	Di	34.15N	105.45W
Gallipoli	14	Lj	40.03N	17.58 E
Gallipoli Peninsula (EN) = Gelibolu Yarimadası	15	Ji	40.20N	26.30 E
Gallipolis	44	Ff	38.49N	82.14W
Gällivare	6	Ib	67.08N	20.42 E
Galljaaral	18	Fd	40.02N	67.35 E
Gallo	13	Jd	40.48N	2.09W
Gällö	7	De	62.55N	15.14 E
Gallo, Capo-	14	Hl	38.15N	13.19 E
Gallo Mountains	45	Bi	34.00N	108.15W
Galloway	9	If	55.00N	4.25W
Galloway, Mull of-	9	Ig	54.38N	4.50W
Gallup	39	If	35.32N	108.44W
Gallur	13	Kc	41.52N	1.19W
Gallura	14	Dj	41.00N	9.15 E
Galmaarden/Gammerages	12	Fd	50.45N	3.58 E
Galole	36	Hc	1.30S	40.02 E
Galt	44	Gd	43.22N	80.19W
Gal Tardo	35	He	3.37N	45.58 E
Galtasen	8	Eg	57.48N	13.30 E
Galty Mountains/Na Gaibhlte	9	Ei	52.23N	8.11W
Galut	27	Hb	46.43N	100.08 E
Galveston	39	Jg	29.18N	94.48W
Galveston Bay	38	Jg	29.36N	94.57W
Galveston Island	45	Il	29.13N	94.55W
Gálvez	56	Hd	32.02S	61.13W
Galway/Gaillimh [2]	9	Eh	53.20N	9.00W
Galway/Gaillimh	6	Fe	53.16N	9.03W
Galway Bay/Cuan na Gaillimhe	5	Fe	53.10N	9.15W
Gamaches	12	De	49.59N	1.33 E
Gamagōri	29	Ed	34.49N	137.13 E
Gamarra	54	Db	8.19N	73.44W
Gamba [China]	27	Ef	28.17N	88.31 E
Gamba [Gabon]	36	Ac	2.37S	10.00 E
Gambaga	34	Ec	10.32N	0.26W
Gambela	31	Kh	8.15N	34.36 E
Gambell	40	Ed	63.46N	171.46W
Gambia	30	Fg	13.28N	16.34W
Gambia [1]	31	Fg	13.25N	16.00W
Gambie	34	Bc	13.28N	16.34W
Gambier, Iles-= Gambier Islands (EN)	57	Ng	23.09S	134.58W
Gambier Islands (EN) = Gambier, Iles-	57	Ng	23.09S	134.58W
Gambo	35	Ce	4.39N	22.16 E
Gamboma	36	Cc	1.53S	15.51 E
Gamboula	35	Be	4.08N	15.09 E
Gamda → Zamtang	27	He	32.23N	101.05 E
Gamelão	55	Db	15.29S	57.50W
Gamkonora, Gunung-	26	If	1.2[illegible]N	127.31 E
Gamlakarleby/Kokkola	6	Ic	63.50N	23.07 E
Gamla Uppsala	8	Ge	59.54N	17.38 E
Gamleby	7	Dh	57.54N	16.24 E
Gamo Gofa [3]	35	Fd	5.45N	37.20 E
Gamua	64h	Bb	13.15S	176.08W
Gamud	35	Fe	4.05N	38.06 E
Gamvik	7	Ga	71.03N	28.14 E
Ganāne, Webi-= Juba (EN)	30	Lh	0.15S	42.38 E
Gananoque	44	Ic	44.20N	76.10W
Ganāveh	24	Nh	29.32N	50.31 E
Gancedo	55	Bh	27.30S	61.42W
Ganceviči	16	Ec	52.45N	26.29 E
Gand/Gent = Ghent (EN)	11	Jc	51.03N	3.43 E
Ganda	36	Be	12.59S	14.40 E
Gandadiwata, Bulu-	26	Gg	2.42S	119.27 E
Gandajika	36	Dd	6.45S	23.57 E
Gandak	25	Hc	25.39N	85.13 E
Gander	39	Ne	48.57N	54.34W
Ganderkesee	12	Ka	53.04N	8.33 E
Gandesa	13	Mc	41.03N	0.26 E
Gandhinagar	22	Jg	23.21N	72.40 E
Gāndhi Sāgar	25	Fd	24.30N	75.30 E
Gandia	13	Lf	38.58N	0.11W
Gandia-Grao de Gandia	13	Lf	38.59N	0.09W
Gandisê Shan	21	Kf	31.00N	83.00 E
Gandu	54	Kf	13.45S	39.30W
Ganetti	35	Eb	17.58N	31.13 E
Ganga = Ganges (EN)	21	Lg	23.20N	90.30 E
Gangaw	25	Id	22.10N	94.08 E
Gangca (Shaliuhe)	27	Hd	37.30N	100.14 E
Ganges	11	Jk	43.56N	3.42 E
Ganges (EN) = Ganga	21	Lg	23.20N	90.30 E
Ganges, Mouths of the- (EN)	21	Lg	23.20N	90.30 E
Gangi	14	Im	37.48N	4.12 E
Gango	36	Cd	9.48S	5.40 E
Gangtok	22	Kg	27.20N	88.37 E
Gangu	27	Ie	34.45N	105.12 E
Gangziyao	28	Cf	36.17N	114.06 E
Gan He	27	Mb	49.12N	125.14 E
Ganhe	27	La	50.43N	123.00 E
Gani	26	Ig	0.47S	128.13 E
Ganjgah	24	Md	37.42N	48.16 E
Gan Jiang	21	Ng	29.12N	116.00 E
Ganjig → Horqin Zuoyi Houqi	27	Lc	42.57N	122.14 E
Gannan	27	Lb	47.53N	123.26 E
Gannat	11	Jh	46.06N	3.12 E
Gannett Peak	38	Ie	43.10N	109.40W
Gansbaai	37	Bf	34.35S	19.22 E
Gansu Sheng (Kan-su Sheng) = Kansu (EN) [2]	27	Hd	38.00N	102.00 E
Ganta	34	Dd	7.14N	8.59W
Gantang → Taiping	28	Ei	30.18N	118.07 E
Ganyu (Qingkou)	28	Eg	34.50N	119.07 E
Ganzhou	22	Ng	25.49N	114.56 E
Gao [3]	34	Eb	18.15N	[illegible].00W
Gao [Mali]	31	Hg	16.15N	[illegible].01 E
Gao [Niger]	34	Gb	15.25N	[illegible].45 E
Gao'an	27	Kf	28.27N	115.24 E
Gaobeidian → Xincheng	28	Ce	39.20N	115.50 E
Gaocheng	28	Ce	38.02N	114.50 E
Gaolan (Shidongsi)	27	Hd	36.23N	103.55 E
Gaoliangjian → Hongze	27	Ke	33.10N	119.58 E
Gaoligong Shan	27	Gf	25.45N	98.45 E
Gaolou Ling	27	Ig	24.47N	106.48 E
Gaomi	28	Ef	36.23N	119.45 E
Gaoping	27	Jd	35.46N	112.55 E
Gaoqing (Tianzhen)	28	Df	37.10N	117.50 E
Gaotai	27	Gd	39.20N	99.58 E
Gaotingzhen → Daishan	28	Gi	30.15N	122.13 E
Gaoua	34	Ec	10.20N	3.11W
Gaoual	34	Cc	11.45N	13.12W
Gaoyang	28	Ce	38.42N	115.47 E
Gaoyi	28	Cf	37.37N	114.37 E
Gaoyou	28	Eh	32.46N	119.27 E
Gaoyou Hu	27	Ke	32.50N	119.15 E
Gaozhou	27	Jg	21.56N	110.47 E
Gap	11	Mj	44.34N	6.05 E
Gar	27	Ce	32.12N	79.57 E
Gara, Lough-/Loch Ui Ghadra	9	Eh	53.55N	8.30W
Gara'ad	35	Hd	6.54N	49.20 E
Garabato	55	Bi	28.56S	60.09W
Garachiné	49	Hi	8.04N	78.22W
Garachiné, Punta-	49	Hi	8.06N	78.25W
Gara Dragoman	15	Fg	42.55N	22.56 E
Ga'raet el Oubeïra	14	Cn	36.50N	8.23 E
Gara Kostenec	15	Gg	42.18N	23.52 E
Garalo	34	Dc	11.00N	7.26W
Gara Muleta	35	Gd	9.05N	41.43 E
Garanhuns	53	Mf	8.54S	36.29W
Garapan	64b	Ba	15.12N	145.43 E
Garapuava	55	Ic	16.06S	46.33W
Garavuti	18	Gf	37.36N	68.29 E
Garba	35	Cd	9.12N	20.30 E
Garbahārrey	35	Ge	3.20N	42.17 E
Garberville	46	Df	40.06N	123.48W
Gārbosh, Kūh-e-	24	Nf	32.36N	50.04 E
Garça	55	Hf	22.14S	49.37W
Garças, Rio das-	55	Fb	15.54S	52.16W
Garcias	55	Fe	20.34S	52.13W
Gard [3]	11	Jj	44.00N	4.00 E
Gard	11	Kk	43.51N	4.37 E
Garda	14	Ee	45.34N	10.42 E
Garda, Lago di- = Garda, Lake- (EN)	5	Hf	45.35N	10.35 E
Garda, Lake- (EN) = Garda, Lago di-	5	Hf	45.35N	10.35 E
Gardabani	16	Ni	41.29N	45.05 E
Garde, Cap de-	14	Bn	36.58N	7.47 E
Gardelegen	10	Hd	52.32N	11.22 E
Garden City [Ga.-U.S.]	44	Gi	32.06N	81.09W
Garden City [Ks.-U.S.]	43	Gd	37.58N	100.53W
Garden Grove	46	Gj	33.46N	117.57W
Garden Peninsula	44	Dc	45.40N	86.35W
Gardermoen	8	Dd	60.13N	11.06 E
Gardey	55	Cm	37.17S	59.21W
Gardēz	23	Kc	33.37N	69.07 E
Gardiner	46	Jd	45.02N	110.42W
Gardiner Range	59	Fc	19.15S	128.50 E
Gardner → Nikumaroro Atoll	57	Je	4.40S	174.32W
Gardner Pinnacles	57	Kb	25.00N	167.55W
Gardno, Jezioro-	10	Nb	54.43N	17.05 E
Gardone Riviera	14	Ee	45.37N	10.34 E
Gardždai/Gargždaj	7	Ei	55.43N	21.24 E
Gareloi	40a	Cb	51.47N	178.48W
Garessio	14	Cf	44.12N	8.02 E
Garfagnana	14	Ef	44.05N	10.30 E
Gargaliánoi	15	El	37.04N	21.38 E
Gargano	5	Hg	41.50N	16.00 E
Gargano, Testa del-	14	Ki	41.35N	16.12 E
Gargantua, Cape-	44	Eb	47.36N	85.02W
Gargždaj/Gargždai	7	Ei	55.43N	21.24 E
Gari	19	Gd	59.28N	62.25 E
Garibaldi	55	Gi	29.15S	51.32W
Garibaldi, Mount-	46	Db	49.51N	123.01W
Garies	37	Bf	30.30S	18.00 E
Garigliano	14	Hi	41.13N	13.45 E
Garimpo	55	Ed	18.41S	54.50W
Garissa	31	Ki	0.28S	39.38 E

Index Symbols

- [1] Independent Nation
- [2] State, Region
- [3] District, County
- [4] Municipality
- [5] Colony, Dependency
- Continent
- Physical Region
- Historical or Cultural Region
- Mount, Mountain
- Volcano
- Hill
- Mountains, Mountain Range
- Hills, Escarpment
- Plateau, Upland
- Pass, Gap
- Plain, Lowland
- Delta
- Salt Flat
- Valley, Canyon
- Crater, Cave
- Karst Features
- Depression
- Polder
- Desert, Dunes
- Forest, Woods
- Heath, Steppe
- Oasis
- Cape, Point
- Coast, Beach
- Cliff
- Peninsula
- Isthmus
- Sandbank
- Island
- Atoll
- Rock, Reef
- Islands, Archipelago
- Rocks, Reefs
- Coral Reef
- Well, Spring
- Geyser
- River, Stream
- Waterfall Rapids
- River Mouth, Estuary
- Lake
- Salt Lake
- Intermittent Lake
- Reservoir
- Swamp, Pond
- Canal
- Glacier
- Ice Shelf, Pack Ice
- Ocean
- Sea
- Gulf, Bay
- Strait, Fjord
- Lagoon
- Bank
- Seamount
- Tablemount
- Ridge
- Shelf
- Basin
- Escarpment, Sea Scarp
- Fracture
- Trench, Abyss
- National Park, Reserve
- Point of Interest
- Recreation Site
- Cave, Cavern
- Historic Site
- Ruins
- Wall, Walls
- Church, Abbey
- Temple
- Scientific Station
- Airport
- Port
- Lighthouse
- Mine
- Tunnel
- Dam, Bridge

Garkida 34 Hc 10.25N 12.34 E
Garland 45 Hj 32.54N 96.39W
Garlasco 14 Ce 45.12N 8.55 E
Garliava/Garljava 8 Jj 54.46N 23.55 E
Garljava/Garliava 8 Jj 54.46N 23.55 E
Garm 18 He 39.02N 70.18 E
Garmisch-Partenkirchen 10 Hi 47.30N 11.06 E
Garmsar 24 Oe 35.20N 52.13 E
Garnet Bank (EN) 55 Hk 33.05S 49.25W
Garnet Range 46 Ic 46.45N 113.15W
Garnett 45 Ig 38.17N 95.14W
Garonne 5 Ff 45.02N 0.36W
Garonne, Canal latéral à la- 11 Fj 44.34N 0.09W
Garopàba 55 Hi 28.04S 48.40W
Garoua 31 Ih 9.18N 13.24 E
Garoua Boulaï 35 Ad 5.53N 14.33 E
Garoubi 34 Fc 13.07N 2.18 E
Garôwe 31 Lh 8.25N 48.33 E
Garpenberg 8 Gd 60.19N 16.12 E
Garphyttan 8 Fe 59.19N 14.56 E
Garrel 12 Kb 52.57N 8.01 E
Garreru 64a Bc 7.20N 134.33 E
Garri, Kūh-e- 24 Mf 33.59N 48.25 E
Garrigues 11 Kj 44.10N 4.30 E
Garrison 45 Fc 47.40N 101.25W
Garron Point/An Gearran 9 Hf 55.05N 5.58W
Garrovillas 13 Fe 39.43N 6.33W
Garruchos 55 Ei 28.11S 55.39W
Garry 9 Je 56.45N 3.45W
Garry Bay 42 Ic 69.00N 85.10W
Garry Lake 38 Jc 66.00N 100.00W
Garsen 36 Hc 2.16S 40.07 E
Gartar/Qianning 27 He 30.27N 101.29 E
Gartempe 11 Gh 46.47N 0.50 E
Gartog → Markam 27 Gf 29.32N 98.33 E
Garut 26 Eh 7.13S 107.54 E
Garuva 55 Hh 26.01S 48.51W
Garvie Mountains 62 Cf 45.30S 168.50 E
Garwa 25 Gd 24.11N 83.49 E
Garwolin 10 Re 51.54N 21.37 E
Gary 43 Jc 41.36N 87.20W
Garyarsa 27 De 31.40N 80.26 E
Garzê 27 Ge 31.42N 99.58 E
Garzón [Col.] 54 Cc 2.13N 75.38W
Garzón [Ur.] 56 Jd 34.36S 54.33W
Gasan-Kuli 19 Fh 37.29N 53.59 E
Gascogne = Gascony (EN) 11 Gk 43.30N 0.10 E
Gasconade River 45 Kg 38.40N 91.33W
Gascony (EN) = Gascogne 11 Gk 43.30N 0.10 E
Gascoyne Junction 59 De 25.03S 115.12 E
Gascoyne River 57 Cg 24.52S 113.37 E
Gasefjord 41 Je 70.00N 27.30W
Gaseland 41 Jd 70.20N 29.00W
Gash 30 Kg 16.48N 35.51 E
Gas Hu 27 Fd 38.08N 90.45 E
Gashua 31 Ig 12.52N 11.03 E
Gaspar Strait (EN)=Kelasa, Selat- 26 Eg 2.40S 107.15 E
Gaspé 39 Me 48.50N 64.29W
Gaspé, Cap de - 42 Lg 48.45N 64.10W
Gaspé, Péninsule de-= Gaspe Peninsula (EN) 38 Me 48.30N 65.00W
Gaspe Peninsula (EN)= Gaspé, Péninsule de- 38 Me 48.30N 65.00W
Gassan 29 Gb 38.34N 140.01 E
Gassol 34 Hd 8.32N 10.28 E
Gaston, Lake- 44 Ig 36.35N 78.00W
Gastonia 43 Kd 35.16N 81.11W
Gastoúni 15 El 37.51N 21.15 E
Gastre 56 Gf 42.17S 69.14W
Gästrikland 8 Gd 60.30N 16.30 E
Gata, Akrōtērion- 24 Ee 34.34N 33.02 E
Gata, Cabo de- 5 Fh 36.43N 2.12W
Gata, Sierra de- 13 Fd 40.15N 6.45W
Gătaia 15 Ed 45.26N 21.26 E
Gatčina 19 Dd 59.34N 30.09 E
Gate 45 Fh 36.51N 100.01W
Gate City 44 Fg 36.38N 82.37W
Gateshead 9 Lg 54.58N 1.37W
Gateshead 42 Hb 70.35N 100.15W
Gathemo 12 Bf 48.46N 0.58W
Gâtinais 11 If 48.00N 2.20 E
Gâtine, Hauteurs de- 11 Fh 46.38N 0.38W
Gatineau, Rivière- 42 Jg 45.27N 75.42W
Gatlinburg 44 Fh 35.43N 83.31W
Gato, Cumbres del- 48 Fd 27.00N 106.35W
Gattinara 14 Ce 45.37N 8.22 E
Gatún 49 Hi 9.16N 79.55W
Gatún, Lago-=Gatun Lake (EN) 47 Ig 9.12N 79.55W
Gatun Lake (EN)=Gatún, Lago- 47 Ig 9.12N 79.55W
Gatvand 24 Mf 32.15N 48.50 E
Gatwick Airport 12 Bc 51.08N 0.12W
Gaucín 13 Gh 36.31N 5.19W
Gauhati → Guwāhāti 22 Lg 26.11N 91.44 E
Gauiena/Gaujiena 8 Lg 57.25N 26.28 E
Gauja 7 Fh 57.10N 24.16 E
Gaujiena/Gauiena 8 Lg 57.25N 26.28 E
Gaula [Nor.] 8 Da 63.21N 10.14 E
Gaula [Nor.] 8 Ac 61.22N 5.41 E
Gauldalen 8 Db 63.00N 11.00 E
Gauley River 44 Gf 38.10N 81.12W
Gau-Odernheim 12 Ke 49.46N 8.12 E
Gaurdak 19 Gh 37.49N 66.01 E
Gausdal 8 Cc 61.20N 9.55 E
Gausta 7 Bg 59.50N 8.39 E
Gāvbandī 24 Oi 27.12N 53.04 E
Gāvbūs, Kūh-e- 24 Oi 27.10N 54.00 E
Gavdhopoúla 15 Go 34.56N 24.00 E
Gávdhos 5 Ii 34.50N 24.05 E
Gāveh 24 Le 35.00N 46.58 E
Gavere 12 Fd 50.56N 3.40 E
Gavkhūnī, Bāṭlāq-e- 24 Of 32.06N 52.52 E
Gāv Kosh 24 Le 34.00N 48.00 E
Gävle 6 Hc 60.40N 17.10 E
Gävleborg [2] 7 Df 61.30N 16.15 E
Gävlebukten 8 Gd 60.40N 17.20 E
Gavorrano 14 Eh 42.55N 10.54 E
Gavri 8 Lh 56.49N 27.58 E
Gavrilov-Jam 7 Jh 57.19N 39.51 E
Gāw Koshi 23 Id 28.38N 57.12 E
Gawler 59 Hf 34.37S 138.44 E
Gawler Ranges 57 Eh 32.30S 136.00 E
Gaxun Nur 21 Me 42.25N 101.00 E
Gaya [India] 22 Kg 24.47N 85.00 E
Gaya [Niger] 34 Fc 11.53N 3.27 E
Gaya He 28 Jc 42.58N 129.52 E
Gaylord 44 Ec 45.02N 84.40W
Gayndah 59 Ke 25.37S 151.36 E
Gaz 24 Nf 32.48N 51.37 E
Gaza [3] 37 Ed 23.30S 33.00 E
Gaz-Ačak 19 Gg 41.11N 61.27 E
Gazalkent 18 Gd 41.33N 69.46 E
Gazaoua 34 Gc 13.32N 7.55 E
Gazelle, Récif de la- 63b Be 20.11S 165.27 E
Gaziantep 22 Ff 37.05N 37.22 E
Gaziemir 15 Kk 38.19N 27.10 E
Gazimağusa = Famagusta (EN) 23 Dc 35.07N 33.57 E
Gazipaşa 24 Ed 36.17N 32.20 E
Gazli 19 Gg 40.09N 63.23 E
Gbarnga 31 Gh 7.00N 9.29W
Gboko 34 Gd 7.21N 8.58 E
Gbon 34 Dd 9.50N 6.27W
Gdańsk [2] 10 Ob 54.25N 18.40 E
Gdańsk=Danzig (EN) 6 He 54.23N 18.40 E
Gdansk, Gulf of- (EN)= Gdanska, Zatoka- 5 He 54.40N 19.15 E
Gdov 7 Gg 58.47N 27.54 E
Gdynia 6 He 54.32N 18.33 E
Gearhart Mountain 46 Ee 42.30N 120.53W
Gêba 34 Bc 11.58N 15.00W
Gebe, Pulau- 26 Ig 0.05S 129.20 E
Gebze 24 Cb 40.48N 29.25 E
Gecha 35 Fd 7.29N 35.25 E
Geçitkale 25 Ee 35.15N 33.45 E
Gedi 36 Hc 3.18S 40.01 E
Gedinne 12 Ge 49.59N 4.56 E
Gediz 24 Cc 39.02N 29.25 E
Gedo 35 Ge 2.20N 41.20 E
Gedo [3] 35 Ge 3.00N 42.00 E
Gedo 35 Fd 9.00N 37.29 E
Gedser, Sydfalster- 7 Ci 54.35N 11.57 E
Gedser Odde 8 Dj 54.34N 11.59 E
Geel 11 Kc 51.10N 5.00 E
Geelong 58 Fh 38.08S 144.21 E
Geelvink Channel 59 Ce 28.30S 114.10 E
Geer 12 Hd 50.51N 5.42 E
Geeste 12 Jb 52.36N 7.16 E
Geesthacht 10 Gc 53.26N 10.22 E
Gê'gyai 27 De 32.29N 80.52 E
Ge Hu 28 Ei 31.36N 119.51 E
Geidam 34 Hc 12.53N 11.56 E
Geigar 35 Ec 11.59N 32.46 E
Geihoku 29 Cd 34.44N 132.17 E
Geikie 42 He 57.48N 103.46W
Geilo 7 Bf 60.31N 8.12 E
Geiranger 8 Bb 62.06N 7.12 E
Geisenheim 12 Je 49.59N 7.58 E
Geislingen an der Steige 10 Fh 48.37N 9.51 E
Geita 36 Fc 2.52S 32.10 E
Geithus 7 Bg 59.57N 9.59 E
Geiyo-Shotō 29 Cd 34.15N 132.45 E
Gejiu 22 Mg 23.22N 103.14 E
Gel [Sud.] 30 Jh 7.46N 29.36 E
Gel [Sud.] 35 Ed 6.08N 31.17 E
Gela 14 Im 37.04N 14.15 E
Gela, Golfo di- 14 Im 37.05N 14.10 E
Geladi 35 Hd 6.57N 46.25 E
Geldenaken/Jodoigne 12 Gd 50.43N 4.52 E
Gelderland [3] 12 Hb 52.10N 5.50 E
Geldermalsen 12 Hc 51.53N 5.19 E
Geldern 10 Ce 51.31N 6.20 E
Geldrop 12 Hc 51.25N 5.33 E
Geleen 11 Ld 50.58N 5.52 E
Gelembé 15 Kj 39.10N 27.50 E
Gelemso 35 Gd 8.48N 40.32 E
Gelendžik 19 Dg 44.33N 38.06 E
Gelengdeng 35 Bc 10.56N 15.32 E
Gelgaudiškis 8 Ji 55.02N 22.58 E
Gelibolu 24 Bb 40.24N 26.40 E
Gelibolu Yarimadası = Gallipoli Peninsula (EN) 15 Ji 40.20N 26.30 E
Gélise 11 Gj 44.11N 0.17 E
Gellinsör 35 Hd 6.24N 46.46 E
Gelnhausen 10 Ff 50.12N 9.11 E
Gelsenkirchen 10 De 51.31N 7.06 E
Gemena 31 Ih 3.15N 19.46 E
Gemerek 24 Gc 39.11N 36.05 E
Gemert 12 Hc 51.33N 5.41 E
Gemi, Jabal- 35 Ed 9.01N 34.09 E
Gemlik 24 Cb 40.26N 29.09 E
Gemlik Körfezi 24 Cb 40.25N 28.55 E
Gemona del Friuli 14 Hd 46.16N 13.09 E
Gemünden (Felda) 12 Ld 50.42N 9.03 E
Gemünden (Wohra) 12 Kd 50.58N 8.58 E
Gemünden am Main 10 Ff 50.03N 9.42 E
Genale 30 Lh 0.15S 42.38 E
Genç 24 Ic 38.46N 40.35 E
Gendringen 12 Ic 51.52N 6.23 E
Gendringen-Ulft 12 Ic 51.54N 6.24 E
Genemuiden 12 Ib 52.37N 6.02 E
General Acha 56 He 37.23S 64.36W
General Alvear [Arg.] 56 Gd 34.58S 67.42W
General Alvear [Arg.] 56 He 36.03S 60.01W
General Arenales 55 Bl 34.18S 61.18W
General Artigas 55 Dh 26.53S 56.17W
General Belgrano 56 Ie 35.46S 58.30W
General Belgrano Station 66 Af 77.50S 38.00W
General Bernardo O'Higgins 66 Re 63.19S 57.54W
General Bravo 48 Je 25.48N 99.10W
General Cabrera 56 Hd 32.48S 63.52W
General Capdevila 55 Bh 27.26S 61.28W
General Carneiro 55 Gh 26.28S 51.25W
General Carrera, Lago- 52 Ij 46.30S 72.00W
General Cepeda 48 Ie 25.23N 101.27W
General Conesa [Arg.] 55 Dm 36.30S 57.20W
General Conesa [Arg.] 56 Hf 40.06S 64.26W
General Enrique Martinez 55 Fk 33.12S 53.50W
General Galarza 55 Ck 32.43S 59.24W
General Güemes 56 Hb 24.40S 65.00W
General Guide 56 Ie 36.40S 57.46W
General José de San Martin 55 Ch 26.33S 59.21W
General Juan Madariaga 56 Ie 37.00S 57.09W
General La Madrid 56 He 37.16S 61.17W
General Lavalle 56 Ie 36.24S 56.58W
General Manuel Belgrano, Cerro- 52 Jh 29.01S 67.49W
General O'Brien 55 Bl 34.54S 60.45W
General Pico 56 He 35.40S 63.44W
General Pinedo 56 Hc 27.19S 61.17W
General Pinto 55 Bl 34.46S 61.53W
General Pirán 55 Dm 37.16S 57.45W
General Roca 56 Ge 39.02S 67.35W
General Salgado 55 Ge 20.39S 50.22W
General Santos 22 Oi 6.05N 125.10 E
General Sarmiento 55 Cl 34.33S 58.43W
General Terán 48 Je 25.16N 99.41W
General-Toševo 15 Lf 43.42N 28.02 E
General Treviño 48 Jd 26.14N 99.29W
General Trias 48 Fc 28.21N 106.22W
General Vargas 55 Ei 29.42S 54.40W
General Viamonte 55 Bl 35.01S 61.01W
General Villegas 56 He 35.02S 63.01W
Genesee River 44 Id 43.16N 77.36W
Geneseo 44 Id 42.46N 77.49W
Geneva [Al.-U.S.] 44 Ej 31.02N 85.52W
Geneva [Nb.-U.S.] 45 Hf 40.32N 97.36W
Geneva [N.Y.-U.S.] 44 Id 42.53N 76.59W
Geneva (EN) = Genève 6 Gf 46.10N 6.10 E
Geneva, Lake- (EN) = Léman, Lac- 5 Gf 46.25N 6.30 E
Genève [2] 14 Ad 46.10N 6.15 E
Genève = Geneva (EN) 6 Gf 46.10N 6.10 E
Genevois 11 Mh 46.00N 6.10 E
Genhe → Ergun Zuoqi 22 Od 50.47N 121.32 E
Geni 35 Ed 8.31N 33.10 E
Geničesk 19 Df 46.12N 34.48 E
Genil 13 Gg 37.42N 5.19W
Genk 11 Ld 50.58N 5.30 E
Genkai-Nada 29 Ae 33.45N 130.00 E
Gennargentu 5 Gg 40.00N 9.20 E
Gennep 12 Hc 51.42N 5.59 E
Genoa (EN) = Genova 6 Gg 44.25N 8.57 E
Genoa, Gulf of- (EN) = Genova, Golfo di- 5 Gg 44.10N 8.55 E
Genova = Genoa (EN) 6 Gg 44.25N 8.57 E
Genova, Golfo di- = Genoa, Gulf of- (EN) 5 Gg 44.10N 8.55 E
Genova-Nervi 14 Df 44.23N 9.02 E
Genova-Voltri 14 Cf 44.26N 8.45 E
Genovesa, Isla- 54a Ba 0.20N 89.58W
Gent/Gand=Ghent (EN) 11 Jc 51.03N 3.43 E
Gentbrugge, Gent- 12 Fc 51.03N 3.45 E
Gent-Gentbrugge 12 Fc 51.03N 3.45 E
Genthin 10 Id 52.24N 12.10 E
Gent-Sint-Amandsberg 12 Fc 51.04N 3.45 E
Genū, Kūhhā-ye- 23 Id 27.25N 56.09 E
Genyem 26 Lg 2.46S 140.12 E
Genzano di Lucania 14 Kj 40.51N 16.02 E
Genzano di Roma 14 Fi 41.42N 11.41 E
Geographe Bay 57 Ch 33.35S 115.15 E
Geographe Channel 59 Cd 24.40S 113.20 E
Geographical Society Øer 41 Jd 72.40N 22.20W
Geokčaj 16 Oi 40.40N 47.42 E
Geok-Tepe 19 Fh 38.10N 57.58 E
Geomagnetic Pole (1975) (EN) 66 Hf 78.40S 109.33 E
George, Zemlja- 21 Ga 80.30N 49.00 E
George 38 Md 58.30N 66.00W
George 37 Cf 33.58S 22.24 E
George, Lake- [Austl.] 59 Jg 35.05S 149.25 E
George, Lake- [Fl.-U.S.] 44 Gk 29.17N 81.36W
George, Lake- [Ug.] 36 Fc 0.00 30.12 E
George, Lake- [U.S.] 44 Kd 43.35N 73.35W
George Gill Range 59 Gd 24.15S 131.35 E
Georges Bank (EN) 43 Nc 41.15N 67.30W
George Sound 62 Bf 44.50S 167.20 E
George Town [Austl.] 58 Fi 41.06S 146.50 E
George Town [Cay.Is.] 47 He 19.18N 81.23W
George Town [Indon.] 22 Mi 5.25N 100.20 E
George Town [Tx.-U.S.] 45 Hk 30.38N 97.41W
Georgetown [Austl.] 58 Ff 18.18S 143.33 E
Georgetown [Bah.] 49 Jb 23.30N 75.46W
Georgetown [De.-U.S.] 44 Jf 38.42N 75.23W
Georgetown [Gam.] 31 Fg 13.32N 14.46W
Georgetown [Guy.] 53 Ke 6.48N 58.10W
Georgetown [Ky.-U.S.] 44 Ef 38.13N 84.33W
Georgetown [Oh.-U.S.] 44 Ff 38.52N 83.54W
Georgetown [S.C.-U.S.] 43 Le 33.23N 79.18W
Georgetown [St.Hel.] 31 Fi 7.56S 14.25W
Georgetown [St.Vin.] 50 Ff 13.16N 61.08W
George V Coast 66 Je 68.30S 147.30 E
George VI Sound 66 Qf 71.00S 68.00W
George West 45 Gl 28.20N 98.07W
Georgia [2] 43 Ke 32.50N 83.15W
Georgia (EN) 5 Kg 42.00N 44.00 E
Georgia (EN) = Sakartvelo 19 Eg 42.00N 44.00 E
Georgia, Strait of 42 Fg 49.00N 123.20W
Georgia del Sur/South Georgia 66 Ad 54.15S 36.45W
Georgian Bay 38 Ke 45.15N 80.50W
Georgijevka 19 Hg 43.02N 74.43 E
Georgijevka 19 If 49.19N 81.35 E
Georgijevsk 16 Mg 44.09N 43.28 E
Georgina River 57 Eg 23.30S 139.47 E
Georgsmarienhütte 10 Ed 52.16N 8.02 E
Gera 10 Ge 51.08N 10.56 E
Gera 10 If 50.52N 12.05 E
Geraardsbergen/Grammont 12 Fd 50.46N 3.52 E
Gerais, Chapadão dos- 55 Jc 17.40S 45.35W
Geral, Serra- [Braz.] 55 Gi 29.10S 50.15W
Geral, Serra- [Braz.] 52 Kh 26.30S 50.30W
Geral, Serra- [Braz.] 55 Gf 23.54S 50.46W
Geral da Serra, Coxilha- 55 Ej 30.20S 55.15W
Geral de Goiás, Serra- 52 Lg 13.00S 46.15W
Geraldine 62 Df 44.05S 171.15 E
Geral do Paraná, Serra- 55 Ib 14.45S 47.30W
Geraldton [Austl.] 58 Cg 28.46S 114.36 E
Geraldton [Ont.-Can.] 42 Ig 49.44N 86.57W
Gérardmer 11 Mf 48.04N 6.53 E
Gerāsh 24 Pi 27.40N 54.06 E
Gerbiči, Gora- 20 Fc 66.39N 105.02 E
Gerca 15 Ja 48.10N 26.17 E
Gercüş 24 Id 37.34N 41.23 E
Gerecse 10 Oi 47.41N 18.29 E
Gerede 24 Eb 40.52N 32.39 E
Gerede 24 Eb 40.48N 32.12 E
Gerês, Serra do- 13 Ec 41.48N 8.00W
Gereshk 23 Jc 31.48N 64.34 E
Gérgal 13 Jg 37.07N 2.33W
Gering 45 Ef 41.50N 103.40W
Gerlachovský štít 10 Qg 49.12N 20.09 E
Gerlogubi 35 Hd 6.56N 45.03 E
Gerlos 14 Gc 47.14N 12.02 E
Gerlovo 15 Kf 43.03N 27.35 E
German Democratic Republic = Germany 6 Ge 51.00N 10.00 E
Germania 55 Al 34.34S 62.03W
Germania Land 41 Kc 76.50N 20.00W
Germany, Federal Republic of = Germany 6 Ge 51.00N 10.00 E
Germencik 15 Kl 37.51N 27.37 E
Germersheim 12 Ke 49.13N 8.22 E
Germī 23 Hc 33.32N 54.58 E
Germi 24 Mc 39.01N 48.03 E
Germiston 37 De 26.15S 28.05 E
Gernsbach 12 Kf 48.46N 8.19 E
Gernsheim 12 Ke 49.45N 8.29 E
Gero 28 Ng 35.48N 137.14 E
Gerolstein 12 Id 50.13N 6.40 E
Gerona [3] 13 Ob 42.10N 2.40 E
Gerona/Girona 13 Oc 41.59N 2.49 E
Gerpinnes 12 Gd 50.20N 4.31 E
Gers 11 Gj 44.09N 0.39 E
Gers [3] 11 Gk 43.40N 0.30 E
Gersprenz 12 Le 49.59N 9.04 E
Gêrzê 27 De 32.20N 84.04 E
Gerze 24 Fb 41.48N 35.12 E
Gescher 12 Jc 51.57N 7.00 E
Geseke 12 Kc 51.39N 8.31 E
Geser 26 Jg 3.53S 130.54 E
Gesunda 8 Fd 60.54N 14.32 E
Gesunden 8 Fa 63.10N 15.55 E
Geta 7 Ef 60.23N 19.50 E
Getafe 13 Id 40.18N 3.43W
Gete 11 Ld 50.55N 5.08 E
Getinge 7 Ch 56.49N 12.44 E
Gettysburg 45 Gd 45.01N 99.57W
Gettysburg Seamount (EN) 32 Eb 36.32N 11.37W
Getúlio Vargas 55 Fh 27.50S 52.16W
Getz Ice Shelf 66 Nf 74.15S 125.00W
Geul 12 Hd 50.40N 5.43 E
Gévaudan 11 Jj 44.27N 3.30 E
Gevelsberg 12 Jc 51.19N 7.20 E
Gevgelija 15 Fh 41.08N 22.31 E
Gévora 13 Ff 38.53N 6.57W
Gevsjön 8 Ea 63.25N 12.40 E
Gewane 35 Gc 10.10N 40.39 E
Gex 11 Mh 46.20N 6.04 E
Gexianzhuang → Qinghe 28 Cf 37.03N 115.39 E
Geyersberg 10 Fg 49.50N 9.30 E
Geyik Dağı 24 Ed 36.54N 32.10 E
Geyikli 15 Jj 39.48N 26.12 E
Geyser, Banc du- 37 Hb 12.25S 46.25 E
Geysir 5 Dc 64.19N 20.18W
Geyve 24 Db 40.30N 30.18 E
Ghabāri, Darb al- 24 Cj 25.10N 29.50 E
Ghadāmis 31 He 30.08N 9.30 E
Ghadduwah 33 Bd 26.26N 14.18 E
Ghaghara 21 Kg 24.52N 84.55 E
Ghaghe 63a Db 7.23S 158.12 E
Ghallah, Wādī al- 30 Jg 10.25N 27.32 E
Ghamrah, Wādī al- 24 Hj 25.47N 38.45 E
Ghana [1] 31 Gh 8.00N 2.00W
Ghanzi 31 Jk 21.42S 21.38 E
Ghanzi [3] 37 Cd 22.00S 23.00 E
Ghār ad Dimā' 14 Cn 36.27N 8.26 E
Gharaqābād 24 Me 35.06N 49.50 E
Gharbī, Al Hajar al- 24 Qj 24.10N 56.15 E
Gharbīyah, Aş Şahrā' al- = Western Desert (EN) 30 Jf 27.30N 28.00 E
Ghardaïa 31 He 32.29N 3.40 E
Ghārib, Jabal- 33 Fd 28.07N 32.54 E
Gharrāf, Shaţţ al- 24 Kf 32.30N 45.48 E
Gharsah, Shaţţ al- 32 Ic 34.06N 7.50 E
Gharyān 33 Bc 32.10N 13.01 E
Gharyān [3] 33 Bc 30.35N 12.00 E
Ghāt 31 If 24.58N 10.11 E
Ghatere 63a Db 7.58S 159.01 E
Ghaţţī 24 Gg 31.16N 37.31 E
Ghazāl, Bahr al- 35 Ed 9.31N 30.25 E
Ghazal, Bahr el- 30 Ig 13.01N 15.28 E
Ghazal, Bahr el- 35 Bc 14.00N 16.30 E
Ghazaouet 32 Gb 35.06N 1.51W
Ghazipur 25 Gc 25.35N 83.34 E
Ghaznī 22 If 33.33N 68.26 E
Ghaznī [3] 23 Kc 33.00N 68.00 E
Ghent (EN) = Gand/Gent 11 Jc 51.03N 3.43 E
Gheorghe Gheorghiu-Dej → Oneşti 15 Jc 46.12N 26.46 E
Gheorghieni 15 Ic 46.43N 25.37 E
Gheorghiu-Dej → Liski 19 De 51.00N 39.31 E
Gherla 15 Gb 47.02N 23.55 E
Ghidigeni 15 Kc 46.03N 27.30 E
Ghidole (EN)=Gidole 35 Fd 5.37N 37.29 E
Ghilarza 14 Cj 40.07N 8.50 E
Ghimeş, Pasul- 15 Jc 46.33N 26.07 E
Ghisonaccia 11a Ba 42.00N 9.24 E
Ghizunabeana Islands 63a Db 7.33S 158.45 E
Ghowr [3] 23 Jc 34.00N 65.00 E
Ghriss 13 Mi 35.15N 0.10 E
Ghubbat al Qamar 21 Hh 16.00N 52.30 E
Ghudāf, Wādī al- 24 Jf 32.56N 43.30 E
Ghurāb, Jabal al- 24 Hf 34.00N 38.42 E
Ghurayrah 33 Hf 18.37N 42.41 E
Ghūriān 23 Jc 34.21N 61.30 E
Ghurrah, Jabal al- 14 Cn 36.36N 8.23 E
Ghuzayyil, Sabkhat- 33 Dd 29.50N 19.45 E
Giaginskaja 16 Lg 44.47N 40.05 E
Giala, Jabal- 24 Ei 27.20N 32.57 E
Gialo Oasis (EN)=Jālū, Wāhāt- 30 Jf 29.00N 21.20 E
Gialoúsa 24 Fe 35.35N 34.15 E
Gia Nghia 25 Lf 11.59N 107.42 E
Giannutri 14 Fh 42.15N 11.05 E
Giant's Causeway/Clochán an Aifir 9 Gf 55.15N 6.35W
Giarre 14 Jm 37.43N 15.11 E
Gibara 49 Ic 21.07N 76.08W
Gibbon Point 51b Bb 18.14N 63.00W
Gibb River 59 Fc 16.25S 126.25 E
Gibbs Islands 66 Re 61.30S 55.31W
Gibellina 14 Gm 37.47N 12.58 E
Gibeon [3] 37 Bd 25.00S 18.30 E
Gibeon 37 Be 25.09S 17.43 E
Gibostad 7 Db 69.21N 18.00 E
Gibraleón 13 Fg 37.23N 6.58W
Gibraltar 6 Fh 36.11N 5.22W
Gibraltar [5] 6 Fh 36.11N 5.22W
Gibraltar, Estrecho de-= Gibraltar, Strait of- (EN) 5 Fh 35.57N 5.36W
Gibraltar, Strait of- (EN)= Djebel Țāriq, El Bōghāz- 5 Fh 35.57N 5.36W
Gibraltar, Strait of- (EN)= Gibraltar, Estrecho de- 5 Fh 35.57N 5.36W
Gibson Desert 57 Dg 24.30S 126.00 E
Gidami 35 Ed 8.58N 34.40 E
Giddings 45 Hk 30.11N 96.56W
Gidigič 15 Lb 47.04N 28.38 E
Gidole=Ghidole (EN) 35 Fd 5.37N 37.29 E
Gien 11 Ig 47.42N 2.38 E
Giens, Presqu'île de- 11 Mk 43.02N 6.08 E
Gier 11 Ki 45.35N 4.46 E
Gießen 10 Ef 50.35N 8.39 E
Gieten 12 Ia 53.01N 6.48 E
Giethoorn 12 Ib 52.43N 6.07 E
Gifford 42 Jb 70.21N 83.05W
Gifford Seamount (EN) 52 Hi 39.00S 82.00W
Gifhorn 10 Gd 52.29N 10.33 E
Gift Lake 42 Fe 55.49N 115.57W
Gifu 22 Pf 35.25N 136.45 E
Gifu Ken [2] 28 Ng 35.50N 137.00 E
Gigant 16 Lf 46.29N 41.20 E
Giganta, Cerro- 47 Bc 26.07N 111.36W
Giganta, Sierra de la- 47 Bc 26.18N 111.39W
Gigante 54 Cc 2.24N 75.34W
Gigen 15 Hf 43.42N 24.29 E
Gigha 9 Hf 55.41N 5.44W
Giglio 14 Eh 42.20N 10.55 E
Gijón 6 Fg 43.32N 5.40W
Gikongoro 36 Ec 2.30S 29.35 E
Gila Bend 46 Ij 32.57N 112.43W
Gila Bend Mountains 46 Ij 33.10N 113.10W
Gilān [3] 23 Gb 37.00N 49.50 E
Gilān-e-Gharb 24 Ke 34.08N 45.55 E
Gila River 43 Ee 32.43N 114.33W
Gilbert, Mount- 46 Ca 50.51N 124.20W
Gilbert River 59 Ic 16.35S 141.15 E
Gilbert Seamount (EN) 40 If 52.50N 150.10W
Gilbués 54 Ie 9.50S 45.21W
Gilé 37 Fc 16.09S 38.19 E
Giles Meteorological Station 59 Fe 25.02S 128.18 E
Gilford Island 46 Ba 50.45N 126.25W
Gilgandra 59 Jf 31.42S 148.39 E
Gilğau 15 Gb 47.17N 23.43 E
Gilgil 36 Gc 0.30S 36.19 E
Gilgit 25 Ea 35.44N 74.38 E
Gilgit 22 Jf 35.55N 74.18 E
Giliuj 20 Hf 54.17N 127.05 E
Gillam 42 Ie 56.21N 94.43W
Gilleleje 8 Eh 56.07N 12.19 E
Gillen, Lake- 59 Ee 26.10S 124.40 E
Gillenfeld 12 Id 50.07N 6.54 E
Gillette 43 Fc 44.18N 105.30W
Gillian, Lake- 42 Jc 69.30N 75.30W
Gillingham 9 Nj 51.24N 0.33 E
Gilo 35 Ed 8.10N 33.15 E
Gilort 15 Ge 44.36N 23.27 E
Gilroy 46 Eh 37.00N 121.34W
Giluwe, Mount- 60 Ci 6.04S 143.53 E
Gilvān 24 Md 36.47N 49.08 E
Gimån 8 Gb 62.28N 16.20 E
Gimbi 35 Fd 9.10N 35.51 E
Gimie, Mount- 50 Ff 13.52N 61.01W
Gimli 42 Hf 50.39N 97.00W
Gimo 8 Hd 60.11N 18.11 E
Gimolskoje, Ozero- 7 He 63.00N 32.15 E
Gimone 11 Hk 44.00N 1.06 E
Ginda 35 Fb 15.27N 39.06 E
Ginetu 63a Ac 9.30S 152.43 E

Index Symbols

[1] Independent Nation
[2] State, Region
[3] District, County
[4] Municipality
[5] Colony, Dependency
Continent
Physical Region
Historical or Cultural Region
Mount, Mountain
Volcano
Hill
Mountains, Mountain Range
Hills, Escarpment
Plateau, Upland
Pass, Gap
Plain, Lowland
Delta
Salt Flat
Valley, Canyon
Crater, Cave
Karst Features
Depression
Polder
Desert, Dunes
Forest, Woods
Heath, Steppe
Oasis
Cape, Point
Coast, Beach
Cliff
Peninsula
Isthmus
Sandbank
Island
Atoll
Rock, Reef
Islands, Archipelago
Rocks, Reefs
Coral Reef
Well, Spring
Geyser
River, Stream
Waterfall Rapids
River Mouth, Estuary
Lake
Salt Lake
Intermittent Lake
Reservoir
Swamp, Pond
Canal
Glacier
Ice Shelf, Pack Ice
Ocean
Sea
Gulf, Bay
Strait, Fjord
Lagoon
Bank
Seamount
Tablemount
Ridge
Shelf
Basin
Escarpment, Sea Scarp
Fracture
Trench, Abyss
National Park, Reserve
Point of Interest
Recreation Site
Cave, Cavern
Historic Site
Ruins
Wall, Walls
Church, Abbey
Temple
Scientific Station
Airport
Port
Lighthouse
Mine
Tunnel
Dam, Bridge

Gin Gin	59	Kd	25.00 S	151.58 E
Gingin	59	Df	31.21 S	115.42 E
Gingoog	26	Ie	8.50N	125.07 E
Ginir	35	Gd	7.08N	40.43 E
Ginosa	14	Kj	40.35N	16.45 E
Ginowan	29b	Ab	26.17N	127.45 E
Ginzo de Limia	13	Eb	42.03N	7.43W
Giofra Oasis (EN)=Jufrah, Wāḩāt al-	30	If	29.10N	16.00 E
Gioia, Golfo di-	14	Jl	38.30N	15.45 E
Gioia del Colle	14	Kj	40.48N	16.55 E
Gioia Tauro	14	Jl	38.25N	15.54 E
Gion	35	Fd	8.24N	37.55 E
Gióna Óros	15	Fk	38.35N	22.15 E
Giovi, Passo dei-	14	Cf	44.33N	8.57 E
Giraltovce	10	Rg	49.07N	21.31 E
Girardot	54	Dc	4.18N	74.49W
Girdle Ness	9	Kd	57.08N	2.02W
Giresun	23	Ea	40.55N	38.24 E
Giresun Dağları	24	Hb	40.40N	38.10 E
Giri	36	Cb	0.28N	17.59 E
Giridih	25	Hd	24.11N	86.18 E
Giriftu	36	Gb	2.00N	39.45 E
Girne	24	Ee	35.20N	33.19 E
Girón	54	Cd	3.10S	79.09W
Girona/Gerona	13	Oc	41.59N	2.49 E
Gironde [3]	11	Fj	44.55N	0.30W
Gironde	5	Ff	45.35N	1.03W
Gironella	13	Nb	42.02N	1.53 E
Girou	11	Hk	43.46N	1.23 E
Girvan	9	If	55.15N	4.51W
Girvas	7	He	62.31N	33.44 E
Gisborne	58	Ih	38.39 S	178.01 E
Gisenyi	36	Ec	1.42 S	29.15 E
Gislaved	8	Eg	57.18N	13.32 E
Gisors	11	He	49.17N	1.47 E
Gissar	18	Ge	38.31N	68.36 E
Gissarski Hrebet	18	Ge	39.00N	68.40 E
Gistad	8	Ff	58.27N	15.55 E
Gistel	12	Ec	51.10N	2.57 E
Gistral	13	Ea	43.28N	7.35W
Gitarama	36	Ec	2.05 S	29.16 E
Gitega	36	Ec	3.26 S	29.56 E
Gitu	24	Me	35.20N	48.05 E
Giudicarie, Valli-	14	Ed	46.00N	10.40 E
Giulianova	14	Hh	42.45N	13.57 E
Giumalău, Vîrful-	15	Ib	47.26N	25.29 E
Giurgeni	15	Ke	44.35N	27.48 E
Giurgiu	15	If	43.53N	25.58 E
Give	8	Ci	55.51N	9.15 E
Givors	11	Ki	45.35N	4.46 E
Givry-en-Argonne	12	Gf	48.57N	4.53 E
Givry Island	64d	Bb	7.07N	151.53 E
Giwa	34	Gc	11.18N	7.27 E
Giza (EN)=Al Jīzah	31	Ke	30.01N	31.13 E
Gižduvan	19	Gg	40.06N	64.40 E
Gižiga	20	Ld	62.03N	160.30 E
Gižiginskaja Guba	20	Kd	61.10N	158.30 E
Gizo	63a	Cc	8.07 S	156.50 E
Gizo	60	Fi	8.06 S	156.51 E
Giżycko	10	Rb	54.03N	21.47 E
Gjalicës, Mali i-	15	Dg	42.01N	20.28 E
Gjamyš, Gora-	16	Oi	40.20N	46.25 E
Gjandža	6	Kg	40.40N	46.22 E
Gjerstad	8	Cf	58.52N	9.00 E
Gjevilvatn	8	Cb	62.40N	9.25 E
Gjirokastra	15	Di	40.05N	20.10 E
Gjoa Haven	39	Jc	68.38N	95.57W
Gjøvik	6	Hc	60.48N	10.42 E
Gjuhës, Kep i-	15	Ci	40.25N	19.18 E
Glace Bay	42	Lg	46.12N	59.57W
Glacier Bay	40	Le	58.40N	136.00W
Glacier Peak	43	Cb	48.07N	121.07W
Glacier Strait	42	Ja	76.15N	79.00W
Gladbeck	12	Ic	51.34N	6.59 E
Gladenbach	12	Kd	50.46N	8.34 E
Gladewater	45	Ij	32.33N	94.56W
Gladstone [Austl.]	58	Gg	23.51 S	151.16 E
Gladstone [Man.-Can.]	45	Ga	50.15N	98.50W
Gladstone [Mi.-U.S.]	44	Dc	45.51N	87.03W
Gladstone [Mo.-U.S.]	45	Ig	39.13N	94.34W
Glafsfjorden	8	Ee	59.35N	12.35 E
Glåma	5	Hd	59.12N	10.57 E
Gláma	7a	Ab	65.48N	23.00W
Glamis Castle	9	Ke	56.37N	3.00W
Glamoč	23	Ff	44.03N	16.51 E
Glan	7	Dg	58.35N	15.55 E
Glan [Aus.]	14	Id	46.36N	14.25 E
Glan [Ger.]	10	Dg	49.47N	7.43 E
Glan-Münchweiler	12	Je	49.28N	7.26 E
Glarner Alpen	14	Cd	46.55N	9.00 E
Glärnisch	14	Cd	47.00N	9.00 E
Glarus [2]	14	Dd	46.55N	9.05 E
Glarus	14	Dc	47.03N	9.04 E
Glasgow [Ky.-U.S.]	44	Eg	37.00N	85.55W
Glasgow [Mt.-U.S.]	43	Fb	48.12N	106.38W
Glasgow [Scot.-U.K.]	6	Fd	55.53N	4.15W
Glashütte	10	Jf	50.51N	13.47 E
Glass	9	Id	57.25N	4.30W
Glassboro	44	Jf	39.42N	75.07W
Glass Mountains	45	Ek	30.25N	103.15W
Glastonbury	9	Kj	51.09N	2.43W
Glauchau	10	If	50.49N	12.32 E
Glava	8	Ee	59.33N	12.34 E
Glazov	6	Ld	58.09N	52.40 E
Gleann Dá Loch/ Glendalough	9	Gh	53.00N	6.20W
Gledićske Planine	15	Df	43.49N	20.55 E
Gleinalpe	14	Jc	47.10N	15.05 E
Gleisdorf	14	Jc	47.06N	15.43 E
Glen	12	Bb	52.50N	0.07W
Glénan, Iles de-	11	Cg	47.43N	4.00W
Glen Arbor	44	Ec	44.53N	85.58W
Glenavy	62	Df	44.55 S	171.06 E
Glen Canyon	46	Jh	37.05N	111.41W
Glencoe [Mn.-U.S.]	45	Id	44.46N	94.09W
Glencoe [S.Afr.]	37	Ee	28.12 S	30.07 E
Glendale [Az.-U.S.]	43	Ee	33.32N	112.11W
Glendale [Ca.-U.S.]	43	De	34.10N	118.17W
Glendalough/Gleann Dá Loch	9	Gh	53.00N	6.20W
Glendive	43	Gb	47.06N	104.43W
Glendo Reservoir	46	Me	42.31N	104.58W
Glenhope	61	Dh	41.39 S	172.39 E
Glen Innes	58	Gg	29.44 S	151.44 E
Glennallen	40	Jd	62.07N	145.33W
Glenner	14	Dd	46.46N	9.12 E
Glenns Ferry	46	He	42.57N	115.18W
Glenorchy	62	Cf	44.52 S	168.24 E
Glenrock	46	Me	42.52N	105.52W
Glen Rose	45	Hj	32.14N	97.45W
Glenrothes	9	Je	56.12N	3.05W
Glens Falls	44	Kd	43.17N	73.41W
Glenville	44	Gf	38.57N	80.51W
Glenwood [Ia.-U.S.]	45	If	41.03N	95.45W
Glenwood [Mn.-U.S.]	45	Id	45.39N	95.23W
Glenwood Springs	43	Fd	39.32N	107.19W
Glibokaja	15	Ja	48.05N	26.00 E
Glina	14	Ke	45.20N	16.06 E
Glinjany	10	Ug	49.46N	24.33 E
Glittertinden	5	Gc	61.39N	8.33 E
Gliwice	10	Of	50.17N	18.40 E
Globe	43	Ee	33.24 N	110.47 W
Globino	16	He	49.24N	33.18 E
Głogów	10	Me	51.40N	16.05 E
Glomfjord	7	Cc	66.49N	13.58 E
Glommersträsk	7	Ed	65.16N	19.38 E
Glonn	10	Hh	48.11N	11.45 E
Glorieuses, Iles-	30	Lj	11.30 S	47.20 E
Glottof, Mount-	40	Ie	57.30N	153.30W
Gloucester	9	Kj	51.55N	2.15W
Gloucester [Eng.-U.K.]	9	Kj	51.53N	2.14W
Gloucester [Ma.-U.S.]	44	Ld	42.41N	70.39W
Gloucester, Cape-	60	Di	5.27 S	148.25 E
Gloucestershire [3]	9	Lj	51.50N	1.55W
Glover Island	51p	Bb	11.59N	61.47W
Glover's Reef	49	De	16.49N	87.48W
Gloversville	44	Jd	43.03N	74.21W
Głowno	10	Pe	51.58N	19.44 E
Głubczyce	10	Nf	50.13N	17.49 E
Glubokoje	19	Cd	55.08N	27.41 E
Glubokoje	19	Ie	50.06N	82.19 E
Glubokoje, Ozero-	8	Md	60.30N	29.25 E
Głuchołazy	10	Nf	50.20N	17.22 E
Glücksburg	10	Fb	54.50N	9.33 E
Glückstadt	10	Fc	53.47N	9.25 E
Gluhov	19	De	51.43N	33.57 E
Gluša	16	Fc	53.06N	28.52 E
Glyngøre	8	Ch	56.46N	8.52 E
Gmünd [Aus.]	14	Hd	46.54N	13.32 E
Gmünd [Aus.]	14	Ib	48.46N	14.59 E
Gmunden	14	Hc	47.55N	13.48 E
Gnarp	7	De	62.03N	17.16 E
Gnesta	7	Dg	59.03N	17.18 E
Gniben	8	Dh	56.01N	11.18 E
Gniew	10	Oc	53.51N	18.49 E
Gniewkowo	10	Od	52.54N	18.25 E
Gniezno	10	Nd	52.31N	17.37 E
Gnjilane	15	Eg	42.28N	21.29 E
Gnosjö	7	Ch	57.22N	13.44 E
Gnowangerup	59	Df	33.56 S	117.50 E
Goa, Damān and Diu [3]	25	Ee	15.35N	74.00 E
Goageb	37	Be	26.44 S	17.15 E
Goālpāra	25	Ic	26.10N	90.37 E
Goat	63b	Dd	18.42 S	169.17 E
Goat Island	51d	Ba	17.44N	61.51W
Goat Point	51d	Ba	17.44N	61.51W
Goba	31	Kh	7.01N	39.59 E
Gobabis	31	Ik	22.30 S	18.58 E
Gobabis [3]	37	Bd	22.00 S	19.00 E
Göbel	15	Lj	40.00N	28.09 E
Gober	34	Gc	13.48N	6.51 E
Gobernador Gregores	56	Fg	48.46 S	70.15W
Gobernador Ingeniero Valentín Virasoro	56	Ic	28.03 S	56.02W
Gobernador Mansilla	55	Ck	32.33 S	59.22W
Gobi, Pustynja-=Gobi Desert (EN)	21	Me	43.00N	106.00 E
Gobi Altai (EN)=Gobijski Altaj	21	Me	44.00N	102.00 E
Gobi Desert (EN)=Gobi, Pustynja-	21	Me	43.00N	106.00 E
Gobijski Altaj=Gobi Altai (EN)	21	Me	44.00N	102.00 E
Gobō	28	Mh	33.53N	135.10 E
Göçbeyli	15	Kj	39.13N	27.25 E
Goceano	14	Dj	40.30N	9.15 E
Goceano, Catena del-	14	Cj	40.30N	9.00 E
Goce Delčev	15	Gh	41.33N	23.42 E
Goch	10	Ce	51.40N	6.10 E
Gochas	37	Bd	24.55 S	18.55 E
Goczałkowickie, Jezioro-	10	Og	49.53N	18.50 E
Göd	10	Pi	47.42N	19.08 E
Godafoss	7a	Cb	65.41N	17.33W
Godalming	12	Bc	51.11N	0.36W
Godār	24	Qh	29.45N	57.30 E
Godār-e Shah	24	Me	34.45N	48.10 E
Godāvari	21	Kh	17.00N	81.45 E
Godbout, Rivière-	44	Na	49.21N	67.42W
Gode	35	Gd	5.55N	43.40 E
Godeč	15	Gf	43.01N	23.03 E
Godelbukta Breidvika	66	Df	70.15 S	24.15 E
Goderich	44	Gd	43.45N	81.43W
Goderville	12	Ce	49.39N	0.22 E
Godhavn/Qeqertarssuaq	67	Nc	69.20N	53.35W
Godhra	25	Ed	22.45N	73.38 E
Godinlabe	35	Hd	5.54N	46.40 E
Gödöllő	10	Pi	47.36N	19.22 E
Godoy Cruz	56	Gd	32.55 S	68.50W
Gods Lake	42	If	54.40N	94.09W
Gods Lake	42	If	54.40N	94.20W
Gods Mercy, Bay of -	42	Id	63.30N	86.10W
Gods River	42	Ie	56.22N	92.52W
Godthåb/Nûk	67	Nc	64.15N	51.40W
Godthåbfjord	41	Gf	64.20N	51.30W
Godwin Austen (EN)=K2	21	Jf	35.53N	76.30 E
Godwin Austen (EN)=Qogir Feng	21	Jf	35.53N	76.30 E
Goedereede	12	Fc	51.49N	3.58 E
Goéland, Lac au-	42	Jg	49.45N	76.50W
Goélands, Lac aux-	42	Le	55.30N	64.30W
Goële	12	Ee	49.10N	2.40 E
Goelette Island	37b	Bc	10.13 S	51.08 E
Goeree	11	Jc	51.50N	3.55 E
Goes	11	Jc	51.30N	3.54 E
Gogama	42	Jg	47.40N	81.43W
Gō-Gawa	29	Cd	35.01N	132.13 E
Gogebic Range	44	Cb	46.45N	89.25W
Gogland, Ostrov-	7	Gf	60.05N	27.00 E
Gog Magog Hills	12	Cb	52.09N	0.11 E
Gogounou	34	Fc	10.50N	2.50 E
Gogrial	35	Dd	8.32N	28.07 E
Gogu, Vîrful-	15	Fd	45.12N	22.30 E
Gogui	34	Db	15.39N	9.21W
Goğu Karadeniz Dağları	24	Ib	40.40N	40.00 E
Gohelle	12	Ed	50.23N	2.45 E
Goiandira	54	Ig	18.08 S	48.06W
Goianésia	54	Ig	15.19 S	49.04W
Goiânia	53	Lg	16.40 S	49.16W
Goianinha	54	Ke	6.16 S	35.12W
Goiás [2]	54	If	12.00 S	48.00W
Goiás	54	Hg	15.56 S	50.08W
Goiatuba	54	Ig	18.01 S	49.22W
Goikul	64a	Bc	7.22N	134.36 E
Göinge	8	Eh	56.20N	13.50 E
Goio-Erê	56	Jb	24.12 S	53.01W
Goioxim	55	Gg	25.14 S	52.01W
Goirle	12	Hc	51.34N	5.05 E
Góis	13	Dd	40.09N	8.07W
Goito	14	Ee	45.15N	10.40 E
Gojam [3]	35	Fc	10.33N	37.35 E
Gojō	29	Dd	34.21N	135.42 E
Gojōme	29	Gb	39.56N	140.07 E
Gojra	25	Eb	31.09N	72.41 E
Gojthski, Pereval-	16	Kg	44.15N	39.18 E
Gokase-Gawa	29	Be	32.35N	131.42 E
Gokasho-Wan	29	Ed	34.20N	136.40 E
Gökbel Dağı	15	Kl	37.28N	28.00 E
Gökçay	24	Ed	36.36N	33.23 E
Gökçeada	24	Ac	40.10N	25.50 E
Gökçeören	15	Lk	38.35N	28.32 E
Gökçeyazi	15	Kj	39.38N	27.39 E
Gökdere	24	Ed	36.39N	33.35 E
Gökırmak	24	Fb	41.24N	35.08 E
Göksu [Tur.]	24	Fd	36.20N	34.05 E
Göksu [Tur.]	24	Fd	37.37N	35.35 E
Göksu [Tur.]	15	Mi	40.23N	29.58 E
Göksun	24	Gc	38.03N	36.30 E
Gök Tepe	15	Mm	36.53N	29.17 E
Göktepe	15	Ll	37.16N	28.36 E
Gokwe	37	Dc	18.13 S	28.55 E
Gol	7	Bf	60.42N	8.57 E
Golāghāt	25	Ic	26.31N	93.58 E
Golaja Pristan	16	Hf	46.29N	32.31 E
Gołańcz	10	Nd	52.57N	17.18 E
Golconda [Il.-U.S.]	45	Lh	37.22N	88.29W
Golconda [Nv.-U.S.]	46	Gf	40.57N	117.30W
Gölcük	24	Cb	40.44N	29.44 E
Golčův Jeníkov	10	Lg	49.49N	15.30 E
Gołdap	10	Sb	54.19N	22.19 E
Gold Beach	46	Ce	42.25N	124.25W
Gold Coast	58	Gg	27.58 S	153.25 E
Gold Coast	30	Gh	5.20N	1.45W
Golden [B.C.-Can.]	42	Ff	51.18N	116.58W
Golden [Co.-U.S.]	45	Dg	39.46N	105.13W
Golden Bay	62	Ed	40.50 S	172.50 E
Goldendale	40	Ed	45.49N	120.50W
Goldene Aue	10	Ge	51.25N	11.00 E
Golden Gate	46	Dh	37.49N	122.29W
Golden Hinde	42	Eg	49.39N	125.45W
Golden Meadow	45	Kl	29.23N	90.16W
Golden Vale/Machaire na Mumhan	9	Fi	52.30N	8.00W
Goldfield	46	Gh	37.42N	117.14W
Gold River	46	Bb	49.41N	126.08W
Goldsboro	43	Ld	35.23N	77.59W
Goldsworthy	59	Dd	20.20 S	119.30 E
Göle	24	Jb	40.48N	42.36 E
Golegã	13	De	39.24N	8.29W
Goleniów	10	Kc	53.36N	14.50 E
Golešnica	15	Eh	41.42N	21.33 E
Goleta, Cerro-	48	Ih	18.38N	100.04W
Golfito	47	Hg	8.38N	83.11W
Golfo Aranci	14	Dj	41.00N	9.37 E
Gölgeli Dağları	15	Ml	37.15N	29.06 E
Gölhisar	15	Ml	37.08N	29.30 E
Goliad	45	Hl	28.40N	97.23W
Golija [Yugo.]	15	Df	43.19N	20.18 E
Golija [Yugo.]	15	Bf	43.02N	18.47 E
Goljak	15	Eg	42.44N	21.31 E
Goljama Kamčija	15	Kf	43.03N	27.29 E
Goljama Sjutkja	15	Hh	41.54N	24.01 E
Goljamo Konare	15	Hg	42.13N	24.33 E
Goljam Perelik	15	Hh	41.36N	24.34 E
Goljam Persenk	15	Hh	41.49N	24.33 E
Gölköy	24	Gb	40.15N	37.36 E
Gölkük	15	Kj	39.19N	27.59 E
Göllheim	12	Ke	49.35N	8.03 E
Gölmarmara	15	Kk	38.42N	27.56 E
Golmud He	27	Gd	36.54N	95.11 E
Golo	11a	Ba	42.31N	9.32 E
Goloby	10	Ve	51.06N	25.06 E
Gologory	10	Ug	49.35N	24.30 E
Gololcha	35	Gd	8.12N	40.05 E
Golovin	40	Gd	64.33N	163.02W
Golovnin Seamount (EN)	20	Kg	46.50N	157.00 E
Golpāyegān	23	Hc	33.27N	50.18 E
Gölpazarı	24	Db	40.17N	30.19 E
Golšanka	10	Kb	54.00N	26.16 E
Golspie	9	Jd	57.58N	3.58W
Gol Tappeh	24	Kd	36.35N	45.45 E
Golubac	15	Ee	44.39N	21.38 E
Golub-Dobrzyń	10	Pc	53.08N	19.02 E
Golungo Alto	36	Bd	9.08 S	14.47 E
Golyšmanovo	19	Gd	56.23N	68.23 E
Goma	31	Ji	1.37 S	29.12 E
Gómara	13	Jc	41.37N	2.13W
Gombe	31	Ig	10.17N	11.10 E
Gombi	34	Hc	10.10N	12.44 E
Gomel	6	Je	52.25N	31.00 E
Gomelskaja Oblast [3]	19	Ce	52.20N	29.40 E
Gomera	30	Ff	28.06N	17.08W
Gómez Farías	48	Ie	24.57N	101.02W
Gómez Palacio	47	Dc	25.34N	103.30W
Gomo Co	27	Ee	33.45N	85.35 E
Goms	14	Cd	46.25N	8.10 E
Gonābād	23	Ic	34.20N	58.42 E
Gonaïves	47	Je	19.27N	72.43W
Gonam	20	Ie	57.18N	131.20 E
Gonâve, Golfe de la-	47	Je	19.00N	73.30W
Gonâve, Ile de la-	47	Je	18.51N	73.03W
Gonbad-e Qābūs	23	Ib	37.15N	55.09 E
Gonda	25	Gc	27.08N	81.56 E
Gonder [3]	35	Fc	12.00N	38.00 E
Gonder	31	Kg	12.38N	37.27 E
Gondia	25	Gd	21.27N	80.12 E
Gondo	30	Gg	14.20N	3.10W
Gondomar	13	Dc	41.09N	8.32W
Gondwana	21	Kg	23.00N	81.00 E
Gönen	24	Bb	40.06N	27.39 E
Gönen	24	Bb	40.06N	27.36 E
Gonfreville-l'Orcher	12	Ce	49.30N	0.14 E
Gong'ar (Doushi)	27	Je	30.05N	112.12 E
Gongbo gyamda	27	Ff	29.59N	93.25 E
Gonggar	27	Ff	29.17N	90.50 E
Gongga Shan	21	Mg	29.34N	101.53 E
Gonghe	27	Hd	36.21N	100.47 E
Gongliu/Tokkuztara	27	Dc	43.30N	82.15 E
Gongola	30	Ih	9.30N	12.04 E
Gongola [2]	34	Hd	8.40N	11.20 E
Gongpoquan	27	Gc	41.50N	97.00 E
Gongshan	27	Gf	27.39N	98.35 E
Gongxian	27	Kf	26.05N	119.32 E
Gongzian (Xiaoyi)	28	Bg	34.46N	112.57 E
Gongzhuling → Huaide	27	Lc	43.30N	124.52 E
Goñi	55	Dk	33.31 S	56.24W
Goniądz	10	Sc	53.30N	22.45 E
Gonīshān	24	Pd	37.04N	54.06 E
Gonjo	27	Ge	30.52N	98.20 E
Gonohe	29	Ga	40.31N	141.19 E
Go-no-ura	29	Ae	33.45N	129.41 E
Gönuk	24	Ic	39.00N	40.41 E
Gonzales	45	Hl	29.30N	97.27W
Gonzáles, Riacho-	55	Df	22.48 S	57.54W
González	48	Jf	22.50N	98.27W
Goodenough, Cape-	66	Ie	66.16 S	126.10 E
Goodenough Bay	59	Ja	9.55 S	150.00 E
Goodenough Island	60	Ei	9.22 S	150.16 E
Good Hope, Cape of-/Groeie Hoop, Kaap die-	30	Il	34.21 S	18.28 E
Goodhouse	37	Be	28.57 S	18.13 E
Gooding	46	He	42.56N	114.43W
Goodland	43	Gd	39.21N	101.43W
Goodnews Bay	40	Ge	59.07N	161.35W
Goodsir, Mount-	46	Ga	51.12N	116.20W
Good Spirit Lake	46	Na	51.34N	102.40W
Goodwin Sands	12	Dc	51.15N	1.35 E
Goodyear	46	Ij	33.26N	112.21W
Goole	9	Mh	53.42N	0.52W
Goomalling	59	Df	31.19 S	116.49 E
Goondiwindi	58	Gg	28.32 S	150.19 E
Goonyella	59	Jd	21.43 S	147.58 E
Goor	12	Ib	52.14N	6.37 E
Goose Lake	43	Cc	41.57N	120.25W
Goose River	45	Hc	47.23N	96.52W
Gopło, Jezioro-	10	Od	52.35N	18.20 E
Göppingen	10	Fh	48.42N	9.40 E
Góra	10	Me	51.40N	16.33 E
Gora	15	Di	40.40N	20.30 E
Góra Kalwaria	10	Re	51.59N	21.12 E
Gorakhpur	22	Kg	26.45N	83.22 E
Goransko	15	Bf	43.07N	18.50 E
Gorata	15	Ih	41.45N	25.55 E
Goražde	14	Mg	43.40N	18.59 E
Gorda	46	Ei	35.55N	121.27W
Gorda, Cayo	49	Ff	15.55N	82.15W
Gorda, Punta- [Ca.-U.S.]	46	Cf	40.16N	124.20W
Gorda, Punta- [Cuba]	49	Fb	22.24N	82.10W
Gorda, Punta- [Nic.]	49	Ff	14.21N	83.12W
Gördes	15	Lk	38.54N	28.18 E
Gördes	15	Kj	38.46N	27.58 E
Gordil	35	Cd	9.44N	21.35 E
Gordior	24	Ec	39.37N	32.00 E
Gordon [Nb.-U.S.]	45	Ee	42.48N	102.12W
Gordon [Wi.-U.S.]	45	Kc	46.15N	91.47W
Gordon, Lake-	59	Jh	43.05 S	146.05 E
Gordon Horne Peak	46	Fa	51.46N	118.50W
Gordonvale	59	Jc	17.05 S	145.47 E
Goré	35	Bd	7.55N	16.38 E
Gore [Eth.]	35	Fd	8.09N	35.34 E
Gore [N.Z.]	62	Cg	46.06 S	168.56 E
Görele	24	Hb	41.02N	39.00 E
Görenez Dağı	15	Lk	39.00N	28.01 E
Gorenjsko	14	Id	46.20N	14.10 E
Gorey/Guaire	9	Gi	52.40N	6.18W
Gorgān	24	Pd	36.59N	54.05 E
Gorgān	24	Jf	33.21N	43.40 E
Gorgān, Khalīj-e-	24	Od	36.40N	53.50 E
Gorgany	10	Jh	48.30N	24.15 E
Gorgin	24	Ld	36.15N	47.55 E
Gorgol [3]	32	Ef	15.45N	13.00W
Gorgol el Abiod	32	Ef	16.14N	12.58W
Gorgona	14	Dg	43.25N	9.55 E
Gorgona, Isla-	54	Cc	2.59N	78.12W
Gorgora	35	Fc	12.14N	37.17 E
Gorham	44	Lc	44.23N	71.11W
Gori	19	Eg	42.00N	44.02 E
Gorinchem	11	Kc	51.50N	5.00 E
Goring	12	Ac	51.31N	1.08W
Goris	16	Oj	39.31N	46.22 E
Gorizia	14	He	45.57N	13.38 E
Gorj [2]	15	Gd	45.00N	23.20 E
Gorjačegorsk	20	De	55.24N	88.55 E
Gorjači Ključ	16	Kg	44.36N	39.07 E
Gorjanci	14	Je	45.45N	15.20 E
Gorki	16	Gb	54.17N	31.00 E
Gorki → Nižnij Novgorod	6	Kd	57.38N	45.05 E
Gorki	20	Bc	65.05N	65.15 E
Gorkovskoje Vodohranilišče =Gorky Reservoir (EN)	5	Kd	57.00N	43.10 E
Gorkum	10	Hf	50.10N	11.08 E
Gorky Reservoir (EN) = Gorkovskoje Vodohr.	5	Kd	57.00N	43.10 E
Gørlev	8	Di	55.32N	11.14 E
Gorlice	10	Rg	49.40N	21.10 E
Görlitz	10	Ke	51.10N	15.00 E
Gorlovka	6	Jf	48.18N	38.03 E
Gornalunga	14	Jm	37.24N	15.03 E
Gorna Orjahovica	15	If	43.07N	25.41 E
Gornjak	20	Df	51.00N	81.29 E
Gornjak	10	Uf	50.16N	24.13 E
Gornji Milanovac	15	De	44.02N	20.27 E
Gornji Vakuf	23	Fg	43.56N	17.36 E
Gorno-Altajsk	22	Kd	51.58N	85.58 E
Gorno-Badahšanskaja avtonomnaja respublika	19	Hh	38.15N	72.00 E
Gorno-Čujski	20	Ge	57.40N	111.40 E
Gornozavodsk	20	Jg	46.30N	141.55 E
Gornozavodsk	17	Ig	58.25N	58.20 E
Gorny	20	Ih	44.50N	133.56 E
Gorny	16	Pd	51.45N	48.34 E
Gorny	20	If	50.48N	136.26 E
Gornyj Altaj respublika	20	Df	51.00N	87.00 E
Gornyje Ključi	28	Lb	45.15N	133.30 E
Gorochan	35	Fd	9.26N	37.05 E
Gorodec	7	Kh	56.40N	43.30 E
Gorodec	8	Mf	58.30N	29.55 E
Gorodenka	16	De	48.42N	25.32 E
Gorodišče	10	Vc	53.16N	26.03 E
Gorodišče	16	Nc	53.16N	45.42 E
Gorodišče	16	Ge	49.17N	31.27 E
Gorodnica	16	Ed	50.49N	27.22 E
Gorodnja	16	Gd	51.55N	31.31 E
Gorodok	19	Cd	55.26N	29.59 E
Gorodok	16	Ee	49.10N	26.31 E
Gorodok	16	Ce	49.47N	23.39 E
Gorodovikovsk	19	Ef	46.05N	41.59 E
Gorohov	10	Uf	50.28N	24.47 E
Gorohovec	7	Kh	56.12N	42.42 E
Goroka	58	Fe	6.02 S	145.22 E
Gorom-Gorom	34	Ec	14.26N	0.14W
Gorong, Kepulauan-	26	Jg	4.05 S	131.20 E
Gorongosa, Serra da-	37	Ec	18.24 S	34.06 E
Gorontalo	22	Oi	0.33N	123.03 E
Goroual	34	Fc	14.42N	0.53 E
Górowo Iławeckie	10	Qb	54.17N	20.30 E
Gorron	11	Ff	48.25N	0.49W
Goršečnoje	16	Kd	51.33N	38.03 E
Gorski Kotar	14	Ie	45.26N	14.40 E
Gorssel	12	Ib	52.12N	6.13 E
Gort	9	Eh	53.04N	8.50W
Goru, Vîrful-	15	Jd	45.48N	26.25 E
Görükle	15	Li	40.14N	28.50 E
Goryn	19	Ce	52.09N	27.17 E
Gorzów [2]	10	Ld	54.25N	15.15 E
Gorzów Wielkopolski	10	Ld	52.44N	15.15 E
Goschen Strait	59	Kb	10.09 S	150.56 E
Gosen	28	Of	37.44N	139.11 E
Gosford	59	Kf	33.26 S	151.21 E
Goshen	44	Ee	41.35N	85.50W
Goshogawara	28	Pd	40.48N	140.27 E
Gosier	51e	Bb	16.12N	61.30W
Goslar	10	Ge	51.54N	10.26 E
Gospić	14	Jf	44.33N	15.23 E
Gosport	9	Lk	50.48N	1.08W
Gossen	8	Bb	62.50N	6.55 E
Gossi	34	Eb	15.47N	1.18W
Gossinga	35	Dd	8.39N	25.58 E
Gostivar	15	Dh	41.48N	20.54 E
Gostyń	10	Me	51.53N	17.00 E
Gostynin	10	Pd	52.26N	19.29 E
Gota älv	5	Hd	57.42N	11.52 E
Göta Kanal	5	Hd	58.50N	13.58 E
Götaland	5	Hd	57.30N	14.30 E
Götaland	7	Dg	57.30N	14.30 E
Göteborg	6	Hd	57.43N	11.58 E
Göteborg och Bohus [2]	7	Cg	58.30N	11.30 E
Gotel Mountains	30	Ih	7.00N	11.40 E
Gotemba	29	Fd	35.18N	138.56 E
Götene	7	Cg	58.32N	13.29 E
Gotha	10	Gf	50.57N	10.43 E
Gothenburg	45	Ff	40.56N	100.09W
Gothèye	34	Fc	13.52N	1.34 E
Gotland [2]	7	Eh	57.30N	18.30 E
Gotland	5	Hd	57.30N	18.30 E
Gotō-Nada	29	Ae	32.45N	129.30 E
Gotō-Rettō	27	Me	32.50N	129.00 E
Gotowasi	26	If	0.38N	128.26 E
Gotska Sandön	7	Eg	58.25N	19.15 E
Gōtsu	28	Lg	35.00N	132.14 E
Göttingen	10	Fe	51.32N	9.56 E
Gottwaldov → Zlín	10	Ng	49.13N	17.39 E
Goubangzi	28	Fd	41.23N	121.48 E
Gouda	11	Kc	52.01N	4.43 E
Goudiri	34	Cc	14.11N	12.43W
Gouet	11	Df	48.32N	2.45W
Gough Island	30	Gm	40.20 S	10.00W
Gough Lake	46	Ia	52.02N	112.28W
Gouin, Réservoir-	42	Kg	48.35N	74.50W
Goulbin Kaba	34	Gc	13.42N	6.19 E
Goulburn	58	Fh	34.45 S	149.43 E

Index Symbols

- [1] Independent Nation
- [2] State, Region
- [3] District, County
- [4] Municipality
- [5] Colony, Dependency
- Continent
- Physical Region
- Historical or Cultural Region
- Mount, Mountain
- Volcano
- Hill
- Mountains, Mountain Range
- Hills, Escarpment
- Plateau, Upland
- Pass, Gap
- Plain, Lowland
- Delta
- Salt Flat
- Valley, Canyon
- Crater, Cave
- Karst Features
- Depression
- Polder
- Desert, Dunes
- Forest, Woods
- Heath, Steppe
- Oasis
- Cape, Point
- Coast, Beach
- Cliff
- Peninsula
- Isthmus
- Sandbank
- Island
- Atoll
- Rock, Reef
- Islands, Archipelago
- Rocks, Reefs
- Coral Reef
- Well, Spring
- Geyser
- River, Stream
- Waterfall Rapids
- River Mouth, Estuary
- Lake
- Salt Lake
- Intermittent Lake
- Reservoir
- Swamp, Pond
- Canal
- Glacier
- Ice Shelf, Pack Ice
- Ocean
- Sea
- Gulf, Bay
- Strait, Fjord
- Lagoon
- Bank
- Seamount
- Tablemount
- Ridge
- Shelf
- Basin
- Escarpment, Sea Scarp
- Fracture
- Trench, Abyss
- National Park, Reserve
- Point of Interest
- Recreation Site
- Cave, Cavern
- Historic Site
- Ruins
- Wall, Walls
- Church, Abbey
- Temple
- Scientific Station
- Airport
- Port
- Lighthouse
- Mine
- Tunnel
- Dam, Bridge

Goulburn Islands 59 Gb 11.50S 133.30 E
Gould Bay 66 Rf 78.10S 44.00W
Gould Coast 66 Mg 84.30S 150.00W
Goulia 34 Dc 10.01N 7.11W
Goulimine 32 Ed 28.59N 10.04W
Gouménissa 15 Fi 40.57N 22.27 E
Gouna 34 Hd 8.32N 13.34 E
Gounda 35 Cd 9.09N 21.15 E
Goundam 34 Eb 16.24N 3.38W
Goundi 35 Bd 9.22N 17.22 E
Goundoumaria 34 Hc 13.42N 11.10 E
Gounou Gaya 35 Bd 9.38N 15.31 E
Gourara 32 Hd 29.30N 0.40 E
Gouraya 13 Nh 36.34N 1.55 E
Gourcy 34 Ec 13.13N 2.21W
Gourdon 11 Hj 44.44N 1.23 E
Gouré 34 Hc 13.58N 10.18 E
Gourin 11 Cf 48.08N 3.36W
Gourma [Mali] 30 Gg 15.45N 2.00W
Gourma 30 Hg 12.20N 1.30 E
Gourma-Rharous 34 Eb 16.52N 1.55W
Gournay-en-Bray 11 He 49.29N 1.44 E
Gourniá 15 In 35.06N 25.48 E
Gouro 35 Bb 19.40N 19.28 E
Gourrama 32 Gc 32.20N 4.05W
Goussainville 12 Ee 49.01N 2.28 E
Gouyave 51p Bb 12.10N 61.44W
Gouzeaucourt 12 Fd 50.03N 3.07 E
Gouzon 11 Ih 46.11N 2.14 E
Govena, Mys- 20 Le 59.47N 166.02 E
Gove Peninsula 59 Hb 13.02S 136.50 E
Goverla, Gora- 19 Cf 48.10N 24.32 E
Governador Valadares 53 Lg 18.51S 41.56W
Governor's Harbour 47 Ic 25.10N 76.14W
Gowanda 44 Hd 42.28N 78.57W
Gower 9 Ij 51.36N 4.10W
Gowganda 44 Gb 47.38N 80.46W
Goya 53 Kh 29.10S 59.20W
Goyave 51e Ab 16.08N 61.34W
Goyaves, Ilets 'a- 51e Ab 16.10N 61.48W
Goyder River 59 Hb 12.38S 135.05 E
Göynücek 24 Fb 40.24N 35.32 E
Göynük 15 Ni 40.20N 30.05 E
Göynük 24 Db 40.24N 30.47 E
Gozaisho-Yama 29 Ed 35.01N 136.24 E
Goz Arian 35 Bc 14.35N 20.00 E
Goz Beïda 35 Cc 12.13N 21.25 E
Gozha Co 27 De 34.59N 81.06 E
Goz Kerki 35 Bb 15.30N 18.50 E
Gözlü Baba Daği 15 Lk 38.15N 28.28 E
Gozo 5 Hh 36.05N 14.15 E
Graaff-Reinet 37 Cf 32.14S 24.32 E
Graafschap 11 Mb 52.05N 6.30 E
Graben Neudorf 12 Ke 49.10N 8.28 E
Grabia 10 Oe 51.26N 18.56 E
Grabière Point 51g Bb 15.30N 61.29W
Grabowa 10 Mb 54.26N 16.20 E
Gračac 14 Jf 44.18N 15.51 E
Gračanica 14 Mf 44.42N 18.18 E
Gračanica, Manastir- 15 Eg 42.36N 21.12 E
Gracias 49 Cf 14.35N 88.35W
Gracias a Dios 49 Ef 15.20N 84.20W
Gracias a Dios, Cabo 38 Kh 15.00N 83.08W
Graciosa [Azr.] 30 Ee 39.04N 28.00W
Graciosa [Can.Is.] 32 Ed 29.15N 13.30W
Gradačac 14 Mf 44.53N 18.26 E
Gradaús, Serra dos- 52 Kf 8.00S 50.45W
Grado [It.] 14 He 45.40N 13.23 E
Grado [Sp.] 13 Fa 43.23N 6.04W
Grænalon 7a Cb 64.10N 17.24W
Grænlandshaf=Greenland Sea (EN) 67 Ld 77.00N 1.00W
Grafenau 10 Jh 48.51N 13.24 E
Grafham Water 12 Bb 52.19N 0.10W
Grafing bei München 10 Hh 48.03N 11.58 E
Grafschaft Bentheim 12 Jb 52.30N 7.05 E
Grafton [Austl.] 59 Ke 29.41S 152.56 E
Grafton [N.D.-U.S.] 43 Hb 48.25N 97.25W
Grafton [W.V.-U.S.] 44 Hf 39.21N 80.00W
Grafton, Mount- 46 Hg 38.40N 114.45W
Graham 42 Ef 53.40N 132.30W
Graham [N.C.-U.S.] 44 Hg 36.05N 79.25W
Graham [Tx.-U.S.] 45 Gj 33.06N 98.35W
Graham, Mount- 43 Fe 32.42N 109.52W
Graham Land (EN) 66 Qe 66.00S 63.30W
Graham Moore, Cape - 42 Jb 72.51N 76.05W
Grahamstown 31 Jl 33.19S 26.31 E
Grain Coast 30 Gh 5.00N 9.00W
Graisivaudan 11 Li 45.15N 5.50 E
Grajaú 54 Ie 5.49S 46.08W
Grajaú, Rio- 54 Jd 3.41S 44.48W
Grajewo 10 Sc 53.39N 22.27 E
Gram 8 Ci 55.17N 9.04 E
Gramalote 49 Kj 7.54N 72.48W
Gramat 11 Hj 44.47N 1.43 E
Gramat, Causse de- 11 Hj 44.40N 1.50 E
Graminha, Represa da- 55 Ie 21.33S 46.38W
Grammerages/Galmaarden 12 Fd 50.45N 3.58 E
Grammichele 14 Im 37.13N 14.38 E
Grammont/Geraardsbergen 12 Fd 50.46N 3.52 E
Grámmos Óros 15 Di 40.20N 20.45 E
Grampian 9 Kd 57.25N 2.35W
Grampian Mountains 5 Fd 56.45N 4.00W
Gramshi 15 Di 40.52N 20.11 E
Gran 8 Dd 60.22N 10.34 E
Granada [Col.] 54 Dc 3.33N 73.44W
Granada [Nic.] 49 Eh 11.50N 86.00W
Granada [Nic.] 47 Gf 11.56N 85.57W
Granada [Sp.] 13 Ig 37.15N 3.15W
Granada [Sp.] 6 Fh 37.13N 3.41W
Granada, Vega de- 13 Ig 37.15N 4.00W
Gránard/Granard 9 Fh 53.47N 7.30W
Granard/Gránard 9 Fh 53.47N 7.30W
Granby 42 Kg 45.24N 72.43W
Gran Canaria 30 Ff 28.00N 15.36W
Gran Chaco 52 Jh 23.00S 60.00W
Grand Anse Bay 51p Bb 12.02N 61.45W
Grand Bahama 38 Lg 26.40N 78.20W
Grand Ballon 11 Ng 47.55N 7.08 E
Grand Bank 42 Lg 47.06N 55.47W
Grand Banks (EN) 38 Oe 45.00N 50.00W
Grand Bassa 34 Dd 6.10N 9.40W
Grand-Bassam 31 Gh 5.12N 3.44W
Grand Bay 51g Bb 15.14N 61.19W
Grand Bay 51p Cb 12.29N 61.23W
Grand-Béréby 34 De 4.38N 6.55W
Grand-Bourg 50 Fe 15.53N 61.19W
Grand Cache 42 Ff 53.14N 119.00W
Grand Caille Point 51k Ab 13.52N 61.05W
Grandcamp-Maisy 12 Ae 49.23N 1.02W
Grand Canal 9 Gh 53.21N 6.14W
Grand Canal (EN)=Da Yunhe 21 Nf 39.54N 116.44 E
Grand Canyon 43 Ed 36.03N 112.09W
Grand Canyon 38 Hc 36.10N 112.45W
Grand Case 51b Ab 18.06N 63.03W
Grand Cayman 47 He 19.20N 81.15W
Grand Cess 34 De 4.24N 8.13W
Grand Chartreuse 11 Li 45.22N 5.50 E
Grand Colombier 11 Li 45.54N 5.46 E
Grand Coulee 46 Fc 47.56N 119.00W
Grand-Couronne 12 De 49.21N 1.01 E
Grandcourt 12 De 49.55N 1.30 E
Grand Cul de Sac Bay 51k Ab 13.59N 61.02W
Grand Cul-de-Sac Marin 51e Ab 16.20N 61.35W
Grande, Arroyo- 55 Dm 37.32S 57.34W
Grande, Bahía- 52 Jk 50.45S 68.45W
Grande, Boca- 54 Fb 8.45N 60.35W
Grande, Cachoeira- 55 Gb 15.37S 51.48W
Grande, Cerro- 48 If 23.40N 100.40W
Grande, Ciénaga- 49 Ji 9.13N 75.46W
Grande, Corixa- 55 Cc 17.10S 58.20W
Grande, Cuchilla- [Arg.] 55 Cj 31.45S 58.35W
Grande, Cuchilla- [Ur.] 55 Ek 33.15S 55.07W
Grande, Ile- 11 Cf 48.48N 3.35W
Grande, Ilha 54 Jh 23.10S 44.10W
Grande, Rio- [Ven.] 54 Fb 8.39N 60.59W
Grande, Rio- [Braz.] 52 Lg 11.05S 43.09W
Grande, Rio- [N.Amer.] 38 Jg 25.57N 97.09W
Grande, Rio- (EN)=Bravo del Norte, Rio- 38 Jg 25.57N 97.09W
Grande, Rio- o Guapay, Rio- 52 Jg 15.51S 64.39W
Grande, Serra- 52 Lf 6.00S 40.52W
Grande, Sierra- 48 Gc 29.40N 104.55W
Grande-Anse 51e Bb 16.18N 61.04W
Grande Anse 51k Ba 14.01N 60.54W
Grande Briere 11 Dg 47.22N 2.15W
Grande Casse 11 Mi 45.24N 6.50 E
Grande Cayemite 49 Kd 18.37N 73.45W
Grande Comore → Njazidja 30 Lj 11.35S 43.20 E
Grande de Santa Marta, Ciénaga- 49 Jh 10.50N 74.25W
Grande de Santiago, Rio- 38 Ig 21.36N 105.26W
Grande do Gurupa, Ilha- 54 Hd 1.00S 51.30W
Grande Inferior, Cuchilla- 55 Dk 33.50S 56.10W
Grande Kabylie 13 Ph 36.45N 4.00 E
Grande ou Sete Quedas, Ilha- 55 Ef 23.45S 54.03W
Grande Pointe [Guad.] 51b Bc 17.50N 62.50W
Grande Pointe [Guad.] 51e Ac 15.59N 61.38W
Grande Prairie 39 Hd 55.10N 118.48W
Grand Erg de Bilma 30 Ig 18.30N 13.50 E
Grand Erg Occidental 30 He 30.20N 0.01 E
Grand Erg Oriental 30 He 30.00N 7.00 E
Grande Rio- 52 Kh 20.06S 51.04W
Grande Rivière à Goyaves 51e Ab 16.18N 61.37W
Grande Rivière de la Baleine 38 Ld 55.15N 77.45W
Grande Rivière du Nord 49 Kd 19.35N 72.11W
Grande Ronde River 46 Gc 46.05N 116.59W
Grandes, Salinas- 52 Ji 30.05S 65.05W
Grande Sebkha d'Oran 13 Li 35.32N 0.48W
Grandes Rousses 11 Mi 45.06N 6.07 E
Grande-Synthe 12 Ec 51.01N 2.17 E
Grand Etang 51p Bb 12.06N 61.42W
Grande-Terre 50 Fd 16.20N 61.25W
Grande Vigie, Pointe de la- 51e Ba 16.31N 61.28W
Grand Falls [N.B.-Can.] 42 Kg 47.03N 67.44W
Grand Falls [Newf.-Can.] 39 Ne 48.56N 55.40W
Grand Forks [B.C.-Can.] 46 Fb 49.02N 118.27W
Grand Forks [N.D.-U.S.] 39 Je 47.55N 97.03W
Grand Found, Anse du- 51b Bc 17.53N 62.49W
Grand Gedeh 34 Dd 5.45N 8.05W
Grand Haven 44 Dd 43.04N 86.10W
Grand Ilet 51e Ac 15.50N 61.36W
Grand Island 39 Je 40.55N 98.21W
Grand Junction 39 If 39.05N 108.33W
Grand-Lahou 34 Dd 5.08N 5.01W
Grand Lake [La.-U.S.] 45 Kl 29.55N 91.35W
Grand Lake [La.-U.S.] 45 Jl 29.55N 92.47W
Grand Lake [N.B.-Can.] 44 Nc 45.42N 66.05W
Grand Lake [Newf.-Can.] 42 Lg 49.00N 57.20W
Grand Lake [Oh.-U.S.] 44 Ee 40.30N 84.32W
Grand Lake Victoria 44 Ib 47.35N 77.33W
Grand Lieu, Lac de- 11 Eg 47.05N 1.40W
Grand Manan Channel 44 Nc 44.45N 66.52W
Grand Manan Island 42 Kh 44.40N 66.50W
Grand Marais [Mi.-U.S.] 44 Eb 46.40N 85.59W
Grand Marais [Mn.-U.S.] 45 Kc 47.45N 90.20W
Grand-Mère 44 Kb 46.37N 72.41W
Grand Morin 11 If 48.54N 2.50 E
Grândola 13 Df 38.10N 8.34W
Grândola, Serra de- 13 Df 38.06N 8.38W
Grand Passage 63b Ad 18.45S 163.10 E
Grand-Popo 34 Fd 6.17N 1.50 E
Grand Portage 45 Lc 47.58N 89.41W
Grand Prairie 43 He 32.45N 96.59W
Grandpré 12 Ge 49.20N 4.52 E
Grand Rapids [Man.-Can.] 42 Hf 53.10N 99.17W
Grand Rapids [Mi.-U.S.] 39 Ke 42.58N 85.40W
Grand Rapids [Mn.-U.S.] 43 Ib 47.14N 93.31W
Grand Récif Sud 61 Cd 22.38S 167.00 E
Grand River [Mi.-U.S.] 44 Dd 43.04N 86.15W
Grand River [Mo.-U.S.] 45 Jg 39.23N 93.06W
Grand River [Ont.-Can.] 44 Hd 42.51N 79.34W
Grand River [S.D.-U.S.] 45 Fd 45.40N 100.32W
Grand'Rivière 51h Ab 14.52N 61.11W
Grand Roy 51p Bb 12.08N 61.45W
Grand-Sans-Toucher 51e Ab 16.06N 61.41W
Grand Teton 43 Ec 43.44N 110.48W
Grand Traverse Bay 43 Jb 45.02N 85.30W
Grand Turk 49 Lc 21.30N 71.10W
Grand Turk 47 Jd 21.28N 71.09W
Grand Union Canal 12 Bc 51.30N 0.02W
Grand Valley 45 Bg 39.27N 108.03W
Grandview [Man.-Can.] 45 Fa 51.10N 100.45W
Grandview [Mo.-U.S.] 45 Ig 38.53N 94.32W
Grandvilliers 12 De 49.40N 1.56 E
Grand Wash Cliffs 46 Ii 35.45N 113.45W
Grand Wintersberg 11 Ne 43.59N 7.37 E
Granger 46 Ec 46.21N 120.11W
Grängesberg 8 Fd 60.05N 14.59 E
Grangeville 46 Gd 45.56N 116.07W
Gran Guardia 56 Ic 25.52S 58.53W
Granite City 45 Kg 38.42N 90.09W
Granite Falls 45 Id 44.49N 95.33W
Granite Pass 46 Ld 44.38N 107.30W
Granite Peak [Nv.-U.S.] 43 Dc 41.40N 117.35W
Granite Peak [U.S.] 43 Fb 45.10N 109.48W
Granite Range 46 Ff 41.00N 119.35W
Granitola, Punta- 14 Gm 37.34N 12.41 E
Grankulla/Kauniainen 8 Kd 60.13N 24.45 E
Granma 49 Ic 20.30N 77.00W
Gran Malvina, Isla-/West Falkland 52 Kk 51.40S 60.00W
Gran Morelos [Mex.] 48 Eb 30.40N 108.35W
Gran Morelos [Mex.] 48 Fc 28.15N 106.30W
Gränna 8 Ff 58.01N 14.28 E
Granollers/Granollérs 13 Oc 41.37N 2.18 E
Granollérs/Granollers 13 Oc 41.37N 2.18 E
Gran Paradis/Gran Paradiso 14 Be 45.32N 7.16 E
Gran Paradiso/Gran Paradis 14 Be 45.32N 7.16 E
Gran Pilastro/Hochfeiler 14 Fd 46.58N 11.44 E
Gran San Bernardo 14 Be 45.50N 7.10 E
Gran Sasso d'Italia 5 Hg 42.25N 13.40 E
Grant 45 Ff 40.50N 101.56W
Grant, Mount- 46 Fg 38.34N 118.48W
Gran Tarajal 32 Ed 28.12N 14.01W
Grantham 9 Mi 52.54N 0.38W
Grant Island 66 Nf 74.24S 131.20W
Grantown-on-Spey 9 Jd 57.20N 3.38W
Grant Range 46 Hg 38.25N 115.30W
Grants 43 Fd 35.09N 107.52W
Grantsburg 45 Jd 45.47N 92.41W
Grants Pass 43 Cc 42.26N 123.19W
Granville 11 Ef 48.50N 1.36W
Granville Lake 42 He 56.00N 100.20W
Granvin 8 Bd 60.33N 6.43 E
Grao de Gandía, Gandía- 13 Lf 38.59N 0.09W
Grao de Sagunto, Sagunto- 13 Le 39.40N 0.16W
Grappa, Monte- 14 Fe 45.52N 11.48 E
Grappler Bank (EN) 51a Cc 17.48N 65.55W
Graskop 37 Ed 24.58S 30.49 E
Gräsmark 8 Ee 59.57N 12.55 E
Gräsö 7 Ef 60.25N 18.25 E
Grasse 11 Mk 43.40N 6.55 E
Grasset,Lac- 44 Ha 49.58N 78.10W
Grassrange 46 Kc 47.01N 108.48W
Gråsten 7 Bi 54.55N 9.36 E
Grästorp 8 Ef 58.20N 12.40 E
Graubünden 14 Dd 46.35N 9.35 E
Graulhet 11 Hk 43.46N 2.00 E
Graus 13 Mb 42.11N 0.20 E
Grave 12 Hc 51.45N 5.45 E
Grave, Pointe de- 11 Ei 45.34N 1.04W
Gravedona 14 Dd 46.09N 9.18 E
Gravelbourg 42 Gg 49.53N 106.34W
Gravelines 11 Id 50.59N 2.07 E
Gravenhurst 44 Hc 44.55N 79.22W
Gravenor Bay 51d Ba 17.33N 61.45W
Graves 11 Fj 44.35N 0.30W
Gravesend 9 Nj 51.27N 0.24 E
Gravesend-Tilbury 9 Nj 51.28N 0.23 E
Gravina in Puglia 14 Kj 40.49N 16.25 E
Gravone 11a Ab 41.55N 8.47 E
Gray 11 Lg 47.27N 5.35 E
Gray Feather Bank (EN) 60 Df 8.00N 148.40 E
Grayling 44 Ec 44.40N 84.43W
Grays Harbor 46 Cc 46.56N 124.05W
Grayson 44 Ff 38.20N 82.57W
Grays Peak 43 Fd 39.37N 105.45W
Graz 6 Hf 47.04N 15.27 E
Grazalema 13 Gh 36.46N 5.22W
Grdelica 15 Fg 42.54N 22.04 E
Greåker 8 De 59.16N 11.02 E
Great 51p Bb 12.10N 61.38W
Great Artesian Basin 57 Fg 25.00S 143.00 E
Great Astrolabe Reef 63d Bc 18.52S 178.31 E
Great Australian Bight 57 Eh 35.00S 130.00 E
Great Bacolet Point 51p Bb 12.05N 61.37W
Great Bahama Bank (EN) 38 Lg 23.15N 78.00W
Great Bardfield 12 Cc 51.56N 0.29 E
Great Barrier Island 57 Ih 36.10S 175.25 E
Great Barrier Reef 57 Ff 19.10S 149.00 E
Great Basin 38 Hf 40.00N 117.00W
Great Bay 44 Jf 39.30N 74.23W
Great Bear 42 Ed 64.54N 125.35W
Great Bear Lake 38 Hc 66.00N 120.00W
Great Belt (EN)=Store Bælt 5 Hd 55.30N 11.00 E
Great Bend 43 Hd 38.22N 98.46W
Great Blasket/An Blascaod Mór 9 Ci 52.05N 10.32W
Great Britain 5 Fd 54.00N 3.00W
Great Central Lake 46 Cb 49.27N 125.12W
Great Channel 21 Li 6.00N 94.00 E
Great Chesterford 12 Cb 52.04N 0.12 E
Great Dismal Swamp 44 Ig 36.30N 76.30W
Great Dividing Range 57 Fg 25.00S 147.00 E
Great Dunmow 12 Cc 51.53N 0.22 E
Greater Accra 34 Fd 5.45N 0.10 E
Greater Antilles (EN)= Antillas Mayores 38 Lh 20.00N 74.00W
Greater Khingan Range (EN) =Da Hinggan Ling 21 Oe 49.00N 122.00 E
Greater London 9 Mj 51.35N 0.05W
Greater Manchester 9 Kh 53.35N 2.10W
Greater Sunda Islands (EN) 21 Nj 3.52S 111.20 E
Great Exhibition Bay 61 Df 34.40S 173.00 E
Great Exuma Island 47 Id 23.32N 75.50W
Great Falls 39 He 47.30N 111.17W
Great Harbour Cay 44 Im 25.45N 77.52W
Great Inagua 38 Lg 21.02N 73.20W
Great Indian Desert/Thar 21 Ig 27.00N 70.00 E
Great Karasberge (EN)= Groot-Karasberge 30 Ik 27.20S 18.45 E
Great Karroo (EN)=Groot Karoo 30 Jl 33.00S 22.00 E
Great Lake 59 Jh 41.52S 146.45 E
Great Namaland/Groot Namaland 37 Be 26.00S 17.00 E
Great Nicobar 21 Li 7.00N 93.50 E
Great North East Channel 59 Ia 9.30S 143.25 E
Great Ormes Head 9 Jh 53.21N 3.52W
Great Ouse 9 Ni 52.44N 0.23 E
Great Plain of the Koukdjuak 42 Kc 66.25N 72.50W
Great Plains 38 Je 42.00N 100.00W
Great Reef 63c Bb 10.14S 166.02 E
Great Ruaha 30 Ki 7.56S 37.52 E
Great Sacandaga Lake 44 Jd 43.08N 74.10W
Great Sale Cay 44 Hl 27.00N 78.12W
Great Salt Lake 38 He 41.10N 112.30W
Great Salt Lake Desert 43 Ec 40.40N 113.30W
Great Salt Plains Lake 45 Gh 36.44N 98.12W
Great Salt Pond 51c Ab 17.15N 62.38W
Great Sandy Desert [Austl.] 57 Dg 21.30S 125.00 E
Great Sandy Desert [U.S.] 43 Cc 43.35N 120.15W
Great Sea Reef 63d Bb 16.15S 178.33 E
Great Shelford 12 Cb 52.07N 0.08 E
Great Sitkin 40a Cb 52.03N 176.07W
Great Slave Lake 38 Hd 61.30N 114.00W
Great Smoky Mountains 44 Fh 35.35N 83.30W
Great Stour 9 Oj 51.19N 1.15 E
Great Valley [U.S.] 44 Ie 40.15N 76.50W
Great Valley [U.S.] 43 Kd 36.30N 82.00W
Great Victoria Desert 57 Dg 28.30S 127.45 E
Great Yarmouth 9 Oi 52.37N 1.44 E
Grebbestad 7 Cg 58.42N 11.15 E
Grebenka 16 Hd 50.07N 32.25 E
Gréboun, Mont- 34 Gb 20.00N 8.35 E
Greci 15 Ld 45.11N 28.14 E
Gredos, Sierra de- 13 Gd 40.20N 5.05W
Greece (EN)=Ellás 6 Ih 39.00N 22.00 E
Greeley [Co.-U.S.] 43 Gc 40.25N 104.42W
Greeley [Nb.-U.S.] 45 Gf 41.33N 98.32W
Greely Fiord 42 Ja 80.40N 85.00W
Greem-Bell 21 Ia 81.10N 64.00 E
Green 46 De 43.07N 123.28W
Green Bay 43 Jb 45.00N 87.30W
Green Bay 39 Ke 44.30N 88.01W
Greencastle 44 Df 39.38N 86.52W
Green Cay 49 Ia 24.02N 77.11W
Greeneville 44 Fg 36.10N 82.50W
Greenfield [In.-U.S.] 44 Ef 39.47N 85.46W
Greenfield [Ma.-U.S.] 44 Kd 42.36N 72.36W
Greenhorn Mountain 45 Dh 37.57N 105.00W
Green Island 62 Df 45.54S 170.26 E
Green Island [Atg.] 51d Bb 17.03N 61.40W
Green Island [Gren.] 51p Bb 12.14N 61.35W
Green Islands 57 Ge 4.30S 154.10 E
Greenland 51q Ab 13.15N 59.34W
Greenland (EN)=Grønland/ Kalaallit Nunaat 38 Pb 70.00N 40.00W
Greenland (EN)=Grønland/ Kalaallit Nunaat 39 Pb 70.00N 40.00W
Greenland (EN)=Kalaallit Nunaat/Grønland 38 Pb 70.00N 40.00W
Greenland (EN)=Kalaallit Nunaat/Grønland 39 Pb 70.00N 40.00W
Greenland Basin (EN) 3 Gb 77.00N 0.00
Greenland Sea (EN)= Grænlandshaf 67 Ld 77.00N 1.00W
Greenland Sea (EN)= Grønlandshavet 67 Ld 77.00N 1.00W
Green Lookout Mountain 46 Dd 45.52N 122.08W
Green Mountains 38 Le 43.45N 72.45W
Greenock 9 If 55.57N 4.45W
Greenough River 59 Ce 28.51S 114.38 E
Green Peter Lake 46 Dd 44.28N 122.30W
Green River [U.S.] 44 Dg 37.55N 87.30W
Green River [U.S.] 38 If 38.11N 109.53W
Green River [Ut.-U.S.] 43 Ed 38.59N 110.10W
Green River [Wy.-U.S.] 43 Fc 41.32N 109.28W
Green River Lake 44 Eg 37.15N 85.15W
Greensboro 39 Lf 36.04N 79.47W
Greensburg [In.-U.S.] 44 Ef 39.20N 85.29W
Greensburg [Ks.-U.S.] 45 Gh 37.36N 99.18W
Greensburg [La.-U.S.] 45 Kk 30.51N 90.42W
Greenstone Point 9 Hd 57.55N 5.40W
Greenvale 59 Jc 18.55S 145.05 E
Greenville [Al.-U.S.] 44 Dj 31.50N 86.38W
Greenville [Il.-U.S.] 45 Lg 38.53N 89.25W
Greenville [Lbr.] 31 Gh 4.59N 9.02W
Greenville [Me.-U.S.] 44 Mc 45.28N 69.35W
Greenville [Ms.-U.S.] 43 Ie 33.25N 91.05W
Greenville [N.C.-U.S.] 43 Ld 35.37N 77.23W
Greenville [Oh.-U.S.] 44 Ee 40.06N 84.37W
Greenville [Pa.-U.S.] 44 Ge 41.24N 80.24W
Greenville [S.C.-U.S.] 39 Kf 34.51N 82.23W
Greenville [Tx.-U.S.] 43 He 33.08N 96.07W
Greenwich 44 Fe 41.02N 82.32W
Greenwich, London- 9 Mj 51.28N 0.00
Greenwood [Ms.-U.S.] 43 Ie 33.31N 90.11W
Greenwood [S.C.-U.S.] 44 Fh 34.12N 82.10W
Greenwood, Lake- 44 Gh 34.15N 82.00W
Greer 44 Fh 34.55N 82.14W
Greers Ferry Lake 45 Ji 35.30N 92.10W
Greeson, Lake- 45 Ji 34.10N 93.45W
Grefrath 12 Ic 51.18N 6.19 E
Gregoria Pérez de Denis 55 Bi 28.14S 61.32W
Gregorio, Rio- 54 De 6.50S 70.46W
Gregório, Rio- 55 Ha 13.42S 49.58W
Gregory, Lake- 59 He 28.55S 139.00 E
Gregory Lake 59 Fd 20.10S 127.20 E
Gregory Range 57 Ff 19.00S 143.00 E
Gregory River 59 Hc 17.53S 139.17 E
Greifenburg 14 Hd 46.45N 13.11 E
Greifswald 10 Jb 54.06N 13.23 E
Greifswalder Bodden 10 Jb 54.15N 13.35 E
Greifswalder Oie 10 Jb 54.14N 13.55 E
Grein 14 Ib 48.13N 14.51 E
Greiz 10 If 50.39N 12.12 E
Grēko, Akrōtērion- 24 Fe 34.56N 34.05 E
Gremiha 6 Jb 68.03N 39.29 E
Gremjačinsk 17 Hg 58.34N 57.51 E
Grenå 7 Ch 56.25N 10.53 E
Grenada 39 Mh 12.07N 61.40W
Grenada 38 Mh 12.07N 61.40W
Grenada 45 Lj 33.47N 89.55W
Grenada Basin (EN) 47 Lf 13.30N 62.00W
Grenada Lake 45 Lj 33.50N 89.40W
Grenadines 47 Lf 12.40N 61.15W
Grenchen 14 Bc 47.11N 7.25 E
Grenen 5 Hd 57.44N 10.40 E
Grenfell 45 Ea 50.25N 102.56W
Grenoble 6 Gf 45.10N 5.43 E
Grenora 45 Eb 48.37N 103.56W
Grense-Jakobselv 7 Hb 69.47N 30.50 E
Grenville 50 Ff 12.07N 61.37W
Grenville, Cape- 59 Ib 12.00S 143.15 E
Gréoux-les-Bains 11 Lk 43.45N 5.53 E
Gresham 46 Dd 45.30N 122.26W
Gresik 26 Fh 7.09S 112.38 E
Gressoney-la-Trinité 14 Be 45.50N 7.49 E
Gretas Klackar 8 Gc 61.34N 17.50 E
Gretna 45 Kl 29.55N 90.03W
Grevelingen 12 Fc 51.45N 4.00 E
Greven 10 Dd 52.06N 7.37 E
Grevená 15 Ei 40.05N 21.25 E
Grevenbroich 10 Ce 51.05N 6.35 E
Grevenbrück, Lennestadt- 12 Kc 51.08N 8.01 E
Grevenmacher 12 Ie 49.41N 6.27 E
Grevesmühlen 10 Hc 53.52N 11.11 E
Grey 62 De 42.26S 171.11 E
Greybull 46 Kd 44.30N 108.03W
Greybull River 46 Kd 44.28N 108.03W
Grey Islands 42 Lf 50.50N 55.35W
Greymouth 61 Dh 42.27S 171.12 E
Grey Range 57 Fg 27.00S 143.35 E
Greystones/Ná Clocha Liatha 9 Gh 53.09N 6.04W
Greytow 37 Ee 29.07S 30.30 E
Greytown 62 Fd 41.05S 175.28 E
Gribanovski 16 Ld 51.29N 41.58 E
Gribb Bank (EN) 66 Ge 63.00S 90.30 E
Gribës, Mali i- 15 Ci 40.34N 19.34 E
Gribingui 35 Bd 7.00N 19.30 E
Gribingui 35 Bd 8.33N 19.05 E
Griend 12 Ha 53.15N 5.20 E
Griesheim 12 Ke 49.52N 8.33 E
Grieskirchen 14 Hb 48.14N 13.50 E
Griffin 43 Ke 33.15N 84.16W
Griffith 59 Jf 34.17S 146.03 E
Grigoriopol 15 Mb 47.09N 29.13 E
Grijalva 38 Jh 18.36N 92.39W
Grim, Cape- 59 Ih 40.41S 144.41 E
Grimari 35 Cd 5.44N 20.03 E
Grimbergen 12 Gd 50.56N 4.23 E
Grimma 10 Ie 51.14N 12.43 E
Grimmen 10 Jb 54.06N 13.03 E
Grimsby 9 Mh 53.35N 0.05W
Grìmsey 7a Ca 66.33N 18.00W
Grímsstadir 7a Cb 65.39N 16.07W
Grimstad 7 Bg 58.20N 8.36 E
Grímsvotn 7a Cb 64.24N 17.22W
Grindavík 7a Ac 63.50N 22.30W
Grindelwald 14 Cd 46.38N 8.03 E
Grindsted 7 Bi 55.45N 8.56 E
Grinnell 45 Jf 41.45N 92.43W
Grinnel Peninsula 42 Ia 76.40N 95.00W
Grintavec 14 Id 46.22N 14.32 E
Griquatown 37 Ce 28.49S 23.15 E
Grise Fiord 39 Kb 76.10N 83.15W
Gris-Nez, Cap- 11 Hd 50.52N 1.35 E
Grisslehamn 8 Hd 60.06N 18.50 E
Grjazi 19 De 52.29N 39.57 E
Grjazovec 19 Ed 58.53N 40.15 E
Grmeč 14 Kf 44.43N 16.15 E
Grobiņa/Grobinja 7 Eh 56.33N 21.11 E
Grobinja/Grobiņa 7 Eh 56.33N 21.11 E
Groblersdal 37 De 25.15S 29.25 E
Grocka 15 De 44.41N 20.43 E
Grodk/Spremberg 10 Ke 51.33N 14.22 E
Grodków 10 Nf 50.43N 17.22 E
Grodnenskaja Oblast 19 Ce 53.45N 25.10 E
Grodno 6 Ie 53.42N 23.50 E
Grodzisk Mazowiecki 10 Qd 52.07N 20.37 E
Grodzjanka 16 Fc 53.34N 28.48 E
Groeie Hoop, Kaap die-/Good Hope, Cape of- 30 Il 34.21S 18.28 E

Index Symbols

[1] Independent Nation
[2] State, Region
[3] District, County
[4] Municipality
[5] Colony, Dependency
Continent
Physical Region
Historical or Cultural Region
Mount, Mountain
Volcano
Hill
Mountains, Mountain Range
Hills, Escarpment
Plateau, Upland
Pass, Gap
Plain, Lowland
Delta
Salt Flat
Valley, Canyon
Crater, Cave
Karst Features
Depression
Polder
Desert, Dunes
Forest, Woods
Heath, Steppe
Oasis
Cape, Point
Coast, Beach
Cliff
Peninsula
Isthmus
Sandbank
Island
Atoll
Rock, Reef
Islands, Archipelago
Rocks, Reefs
Coral Reef
Well, Spring
Geyser
River, Stream
Waterfall Rapids
River Mouth, Estuary
Lake
Salt Lake
Intermittent Lake
Reservoir
Swamp, Pond
Canal
Glacier
Ice Shelf, Pack Ice
Ocean
Sea
Gulf, Bay
Strait, Fjord
Lagoon
Bank
Seamount
Tablemount
Ridge
Shelf
Basin
Escarpment, Sea Scarp
Fracture
Trench, Abyss
National Park, Reserve
Point of Interest
Recreation Site
Cave, Cavern
Historic Site
Ruins
Wall, Walls
Church, Abbey
Temple
Scientific Station
Airport
Port
Lighthouse
Mine
Tunnel
Dam, Bridge

Groenlo 12 Ib 52.04N 6.39 E
Groesbeek 12 Hc 51.47N 5.56 E
Grofa, Gora- 15 Ha 48.34N 24.03 E
Groix 11 Cg 47.38N 3.28W
Groix, Ile de- 11 Cg 47.38N 3.28W
Grójec 10 Qe 51.52N 20.52 E
Gröll Seamount (EN) 54 Lf 14.00S 32.00W
Gromnik 10 Nf 50.42N 17.07 E
Gronau (Westfalen) 10 Dd 52.12N 7.02 E
Grong 7 Cd 64.30N 12.27 E
Groningen [3] 12 Ia 53.13N 6.33 E
Groningen [Neth.] 6 Ge 53.13N 6.33 E
Groningen [Sur.] 54 Gb 5.48N 55.28W
Groninger-wad 12 Ia 53.27N 6.25 E
Groningerwad 12 Ia 53.25N 6.30 E
Grønland/Kalaallit Nunaat = Greenland (EN) 38 Pb 70.00N 40.00W
Grønland/Kalaallit Nunaat = Greenland (EN) [5] 67 Nd 70.00N 40.00W
Grønlandshavet = Greenland Sea (EN) 67 Ld 77.00N 1.00W
Grønnedal 41 Hf 61.20N 47.45W
Grönskara 8 Fg 57.05N 15.44 E
Groot 30 Jl 33.45S 24.58 E
Groot Baai 51b Ab 18.01N 63.04W
Groote Eylandt 57 Ef 14.00S 136.40 E
Grootfontein 31 Ij 19.32S 18.05 E
Grootfontein [3] 37 Bc 19.00S 19.00 E
Groot-Karasberge = Great Karasberg (EN) 30 Ik 27.20S 18.45 E
Groot Karoo = Great Karroo (EN) 30 Jl 33.00S 22.00 E
Grootlaagte 37 Cd 20.55S 21.27 E
Groot Namaland/Great Namaland 37 Be 26.00S 17.00 E
Grootvloer 37 Ce 30.00S 20.40 E
Gropeni 15 Kd 45.05N 27.54 E
Gros Caps, Pointe des- 51e Bb 16.28N 61.25W
Gros Islet Bay 51k Ba 14.05N 60.58W
Gros Islets 51k Ba 14.05N 60.58W
Gros-Morne 51h Ab 14.43N 61.01W
Gros-Morne 42 Lg 49.00N 57.22W
Grosne 11 Kh 46.42N 4.56 E
Gros Piton 51k Ab 13.49N 61.04W
Große Aa 12 Jb 52.25N 7.23 E
Große Aue 12 Kb 52.30N 8.38 E
Großefehn 12 Ja 53.24N 7.33 E
Große Laaber 10 Ih 48.50N 12.30 E
Großenhain 10 Je 51.17N 13.33 E
Großenkneten 12 Kb 52.57N 8.16 E
Grosse Pointe 51e Bb 16.01N 61.17W
Großer Arber 10 Jg 49.07N 13.07 E
Großer Gleichberg 10 Gf 50.23N 10.35 E
Großer Inselsberg 10 Gf 50.52N 10.28 E
Grosseto 14 Fh 42.46N 11.08 E
Grosseto, Formiche di- 14 Eh 42.40N 10.55 E
Groß-Gerau 10 Eg 49.55N 8.29 E
Großglockner 5 Hf 47.04N 12.42 E
Großräschen 10 Je 51.35N 14.00 E
Groß-Umstadt 12 Ke 49.52N 8.56 E
Großvenediger 14 Gc 47.06N 12.21 E
Grostenquin 12 If 48.59N 6.44 E
Gros Ventre Range 46 Je 43.30N 110.15W
Groswater Bay 38 Nd 54.20N 57.30W
Grøtavær 7 Db 68.58N 16.16 E
Grote Nete 12 Gc 51.07N 4.34 E
Grotli 7 Be 62.01N 7.40 E
Grottaglie 14 Lj 40.32N 17.26 E
Grottammare 14 Hh 42.59N 13.52 E
Groumania 34 Ed 7.55N 4.00W
Groundhog River 44 Ga 49.43N 81.58W
Grouse Creek Mountains 46 If 41.55N 113.50W
Grove Mountains 66 Ff 72.53S 74.53 E
Groves 45 Jl 29.57N 93.55W
Grovfjord 7 Db 68.41N 17.09 E
Grow, Idaarderadeel- 12 Ha 53.06N 5.50 E
Grozny 6 Kg 43.20N 45.42 E
Grubišno Polje 14 Le 45.42N 17.10 E
Grudovo 15 Kg 42.21N 27.10 E
Grudziądz 10 Oc 53.29N 18.45 E
Grumento Nova 14 Jj 40.17N 15.53 E
Grumo Appula 14 Ki 41.01N 16.42 E
Grums 8 Ee 59.21N 13.06 E
Grünau 37 Be 27.47S 18.23 E
Grünberg 12 Kd 50.36N 8.57 E
Gründau 12 Ld 50.14N 9.05 E
Grundy 44 Fg 37.17N 82.06W
Gruñidera 48 Ie 24.15N 101.58W
Grünstadt 12 Ke 49.34N 8.10 E
Grunwald 10 Qc 53.30N 20.05 E
Gruppo di Brenta 14 Ed 46.10N 10.55 E
Gruyère 14 Bd 46.40N 7.10 E
Gruža 15 Df 43.54N 20.47 E
Gruzinskaja Sovetskaja Socialističeskaja Respublika → Sakartvelo 19 Eg 42.00N 44.00 E
Gruzinskaja SSR/ Sakartvelos Sabčata Socialisturi Respublica → Sakartvelo 19 Eg 42.00N 44.00 E
Gruzinskaja SSR → Georgia (EN) 19 Eg 42.00N 44.00 E
Grybów 10 Qg 49.38N 20.56 E
Grycksbo 8 Fd 60.41N 15.28 E
Gryfice 10 Lc 53.56N 15.12 E
Gryfino 10 Kc 53.15N 14.30 E
Grythyttan 8 Fe 59.42N 14.32 E
Grytviken 66 Ad 54.17S 36.31W
Gstaad 14 Bd 46.28N 7.17 E
Guacanayabo, Golfo de- 47 Id 20.28N 77.30W
Guacara 50 Cg 10.14N 67.53W
Guaçu 55 Ef 22.11S 54.31W
Guadaioz 15 Hg 37.50N 4.51W
Guadaira 13 Fg 37.20N 6.01W
Guadalajara [3] 13 Jd 40.50N 2.30W
Guadalajara [Mex.] 39 Ig 20.40N 103.20W
Guadalajara [Sp.] 13 Id 40.38N 3.10W
Guadalbullón 13 Ig 37.59N 3.47W
Guadalcanal 13 Gf 38.06N 5.49W
Guadalcanal Island 57 He 9.32S 160.12 E
Guadalén 13 If 38.05N 3.32W
Guadalentín o Sangonera 13 Kg 37.59N 1.04W
Guadalete 13 Fh 36.35N 6.13W
Guadalfeo 13 Ih 36.43N 3.35W
Guadalimar 13 Ig 37.59N 3.44W
Guadalmena 13 Jf 38.20N 2.55W
Guadalmez 13 Gf 38.46N 5.04W
Guadalope 13 Lc 41.15N 0.03W
Guadalquivir 5 Fh 36.47N 6.22W
Guadalupe [Mex.] 47 Dc 25.41N 100.15W
Guadalupe [Mex.] 48 Hf 22.45N 102.31W
Guadalupe [Mex.] 48 Id 26.12N 101.23W
Guadalupe [Sp.] 13 Ge 39.27N 5.19W
Guadalupe, Isla de- 38 Hg 29.00N 118.16W
Guadalupe, Sierra de- 13 Ge 39.25N 5.25W
Guadalupe Bravos 48 Fb 31.23N 106.07W
Guadalupe Mountains 45 Dj 32.20N 105.00W
Guadalupe Peak 43 Ge 31.50N 104.52W
Guadalupe River 45 Hl 28.30N 96.53W
Guadalupe Victoria, Presa- 48 Gf 23.50N 104.55W
Guadalupe y Calvo 48 Fd 26.06N 106.58W
Guadarrama 13 He 39.53N 4.10W
Guadarrama, Puerto de- 13 Hd 40.43N 4.10W
Guadarrama, Sierra de- 13 Id 40.55N 4.00W
Guadazaón 13 Ke 39.42N 1.36W
Guadeloupe 38 Mh 16.15N 61.35W
Guadeloupe [5] 39 Mh 16.15N 61.35W
Guadeloupe, Canal de la- = Guadeloupe Passage (EN) 47 Le 16.40N 61.50W
Guadeloupe Passage 50 Fd 16.40N 61.50W
Guadeloupe Passage (EN) = Guadeloupe, Canal de la- 47 Le 16.40N 61.50W
Guadiana 5 Fh 37.14N 7.22W
Guadiana, Canal del- 13 Ie 39.20N 3.20W
Guadiana, Ojos del- 13 Ie 39.08N 3.31W
Guadiana Menor 13 Ig 37.56N 3.15W
Guadiaro 13 Gh 36.17N 5.17W
Guadiela 13 Jd 40.22N 2.49W
Guadix 13 Ig 37.18N 3.08W
Guafo, Boca del- 56 Ff 43.40S 74.15W
Guafo, Isla- 56 Ff 43.36S 74.43W
Guaiba 56 Jd 30.06S 51.19W
Guaiba, Rio- 55 Gj 30.15S 51.12W
Guaimaca 49 Df 14.52N 86.51W
Guaimorato, Laguna de- 49 Ef 15.58N 85.55W
Guainía [2] 54 Ec 2.30N 69.00W
Guainía, Rio- 52 Je 2.01N 67.07W
Guaiquinima, Cerro- 54 Fb 5.49N 63.40W
Guaira [3] 55 Dg 25.45S 56.30W
Guaira [Braz.] 56 Jb 24.04S 54.15W
Guaira [Braz.] 55 He 20.19S 48.18W
Guaira Falls (EN) = Sete Quedas, Saltos das- 56 Jb 24.02S 54.16W
Guairas 55 Ja 12.39S 44.16W
Guaire/Gorey 9 Gi 52.40N 6.18W
Guaitecas, Islas- 56 Ff 43.57S 73.50W
Guajaba, Cayo- 49 Ic 21.50N 77.30W
Guajará Mirim 53 Jg 10.48S 65.22W
Guajira, Peninsula de la- 52 Id 12.00N 71.30W
Guajolotes, Sierra del- 48 Ge 26.00N 105.15W
Guakolak, Tanjung- 26 Eh 6.50S 105.14 E
Gualaco 49 Df 15.06N 86.07W
Gualán 49 Cf 15.08N 89.22W
Gualdo Tadino 14 Gg 43.14N 12.47 E
Gualeguay 55 Ck 33.09S 59.20W
Gualeguay, Rio- 55 Ck 33.19S 59.39W
Gualeguaychú 56 Id 33.01S 58.31W
Gualeguaychú, Rio- 55 Ck 33.05S 58.25W
Gualicho, Salina del- 56 Gf 40.24S 65.15W
Guam [5] 58 Fc 13.28N 144.47 E
Guam 57 Fc 13.28N 144.47 E
Guamini 56 He 37.02S 62.25W
Guampi, Sierra de- 54 Eb 6.00N 65.35W
Guamuchil 47 Cc 25.22N 108.22W
Gua Musang 26 Df 4.53N 101.58 E
Gu'an 28 De 39.24N 116.10 E
Guanabacoa 49 Fb 23.07N 82.18W
Guanabara, Baia de- 55 Kf 22.50S 43.10W
Guanacaste [3] 49 Eh 10.30N 85.15W
Guanacaste, Cordillera de- 49 Eh 10.45N 85.05W
Guanacevi 48 Ge 25.56N 105.57W
Guanahacabibes, Golfo de- 49 Eb 22.08N 84.35W
Guanahacabibes, Peninsula de- 49 Ec 21.57N 84.35W
Guana Island 51a Db 18.29N 64.34W
Guanaja 49 Ee 16.27N 85.54W
Guanaja, Isla de- 49 Ee 16.30N 85.55W
Guanajay 49 Fb 22.55N 82.42W
Guanajibo 51a Ab 18.10N 67.09W
Guanajibo, Punta- 51a Ab 18.12N 67.10W
Guanajuato 47 Dd 21.01N 101.15W
Guanajuato [2] 47 Dd 21.00N 101.00W
Guanambi 54 Jf 14.13S 42.47W
Guanare 54 Eb 9.03N 69.45W
Guanare, Rio- 50 Ch 8.13N 67.46W
Guanare Viejo, Rio- 49 Mi 8.19N 68.10W
Guanarito 50 Bh 8.42N 69.12W
Guandacol 56 Gc 29.31S 68.32W
Guandi Shan 27 Jd 38.09N 111.27 E
Guane 47 Hd 22.12N 84.05W
Guangde 27 Ke 30.51N 119.26 E
Guangdong Sheng (Kuang-tung Sheng) = Kwangtung (EN) [2] 27 Jg 23.00N 113.00 E
Guangfeng 28 Ej 28.27N 118.12 E
Guanghua 27 Je 32.18N 111.45 E
Guangji (Wuxue) 27 Kf 29.58N 115.32 E
Guangling 28 Ce 39.46N 114.16 E
Guangmao Shan 27 Hf 26.48N 100.56 E
Guangming Ding 28 Ei 30.09N 118.11 E
Guangnan 27 Ig 24.02N 105.04 E
Guangrao 28 Ef 37.03N 118.25 E
Guangshan 28 Ci 32.02N 114.53 E
Guangshui 28 Ci 31.37N 114.01 E
Guangxi Zhuangzu Zizhiqu (Kuang-hsi-chuang-tsu Tzu-chih-ch'ü) = Kwangsi Chuang (EN) [2] 27 Ig 24.00N 109.00 E
Guangyuan 22 Mf 32.27N 105.55 E
Guangzhou = Canton (EN) 22 Ng 23.07N 113.18 E
Guan He 28 Ch 32.18N 115.44 E
Guánica 51a Bc 17.56N 66.56W
Guanipa, Rio- 50 Eh 9.56N 62.26W
Guannan (Xin'anzhen) 28 Eg 34.04N 119.21 E
Guantánamo [3] 49 Jc 20.10N 75.00W
Guantanamo 39 Lg 20.08N 75.12W
Guantánamo, Bahia de- 49 Jd 20.00N 75.10W
Guantánamo Bay 47 Id 20.00N 75.10W
Guantanamo Bay Naval Station 49 Jd 20.00N 75.08W
Guantao (Nanguantao) 28 Cf 36.33N 115.18 E
Guanting Shuiku 28 Cd 40.13N 115.36 E
Guanxian 22 Mf 31.00N 103.38 E
Guanyun (Dayishan) 28 Eg 34.18N 119.14 E
Guapé 55 Je 20.47S 45.55W
Guapi 54 Cc 2.35N 77.55W
Guápiles 49 Fh 10.13N 83.46W
Guapó 55 Hc 16.51S 49.33W
Guaporé 55 Gi 29.10S 51.54W
Guaporé 56 Jc 28.51S 51.54W
Guaporé, Rio- 52 Jg 11.55S 65.04W
Guaqui 54 Eg 16.35S 68.51W
Guará 55 Gg 25.23S 51.17W
Guara, Sierra de- 13 Lb 42.17N 0.10W
Guarabira 54 Ke 6.51S 35.29W
Guaranda 54 Cd 1.35S 78.59W
Guaraniaçu 56 Jc 25.06S 52.52W
Guarani de Goiás 55 Ia 13.57S 46.28W
Guarapiche, Rio- 50 Eh 9.57N 62.52W
Guarapuava 56 Jc 25.23S 51.27W
Guaraqueçaba 55 Hg 25.17S 48.21W
Guararapes 55 Ge 21.15S 50.38W
Guaratinguetá 55 Jf 22.49S 45.13W
Guaratuba 55 Hg 25.54S 48.34W
Guarayos, Rio- 55 Bb 14.38S 62.11W
Guarda 13 Ed 40.32N 7.16W
Guarda [2] 13 Ed 40.40N 7.10W
Guardafui, Cape-(EN) = 'Asäyr 30 Mg 11.49N 51.15 E
Guardal 13 Jg 37.36N 2.45W
Guarda-Mor 55 Ic 17.47S 47.06W
Guardiagrele 14 Ih 42.11N 14.13 E
Guardian Seamount (EN) 38 Ki 9.32N 87.40W
Guardo 13 Hb 42.47N 4.50W
Guardunha, Serra da- 13 Ed 40.05N 7.31W
Guarei, Rio- 55 Ff 22.40S 53.34W
Guareña 13 Gc 41.29N 5.23W
Guarenas 50 Cg 10.28N 66.37W
Guaribas, Rio- 55 Jc 16.22S 45.03W
Guaribe, Rio- 50 Dh 9.53N 65.11W
Guárico [2] 54 Eb 8.40N 66.35W
Guárico, Embalse del- 50 Ch 9.00N 67.20W
Guarico, Rio- 54 Eb 7.55N 67.23W
Guariquito, Rio- 50 Ci 7.40N 65.18W
Guarita, Rio- 55 Fh 27.11S 53.44W
Guaritico, Caño- 50 Bi 7.52N 68.53W
Guaritire, Rio- 55 Ba 13.43S 60.38W
Guarujá 55 If 24.00S 46.16W
Guarulhos 56 Kb 23.28S 46.32W
Guasave 47 Cc 25.34N 108.27W
Guasdualito 54 Db 7.15N 70.44W
Guasipati 54 Fb 7.28N 61.54W
Guasopa 63a Ac 9.14S 152.55 E
Guastalla 14 Ef 44.55N 10.39 E
Guatemala 39 Jh 14.38N 90.31W
Guatemala [3] 49 Bf 14.40N 90.30W
Guatemala [1] 39 Jh 14.38N 90.31W
Guatemala Basin (EN) 3 Mh 11.00N 95.00W
Guateque [Col.] 54 Db 5.05N 73.30W
Guateque [Col.] 54 Db 5.00N 73.28W
Guatimozin 55 Ak 33.27S 62.27W
Guatisimiña 54 Fc 4.33N 63.57W
Guatraché 56 He 37.40S 63.32W
Guaviare 54 Dc 2.00N 72.00W
Guaviravi 55 Di 29.22S 56.50W
Guaxupé 55 Ie 21.18S 46.42W
Guayabal [Cuba] 49 Ic 20.42N 77.36W
Guayabal [Ven.] 50 Ci 8.00N 67.23W
Guayabero, Rio- 52 Je 4.03N 67.48W
Guayalejo, Rio- 48 Kf 22.13N 97.52W
Guayama 49 Ne 17.59N 66.07W
Guayana, Macizo de la- = Guiana Highlands (EN) 52 Ke 5.00N 60.00W
Guayana Basin (EN) 3 Ci 10.00N 52.00W
Guayaneco, Archipiélago- 56 Eg 47.45S 75.10W
Guayanés, Punta- 51a Cb 18.04N 65.48W
Guayanilla 51a Bb 18.02N 66.47W
Guayanilla, Bahía de- 51a Bc 17.58N 66.45W
Guayape, Rio- 49 Df 14.26N 86.02W
Guayaquil 53 If 2.10S 79.50W
Guayaquil, Golfo de- 52 Hf 3.00S 80.30W
Guaycurú, Rio- 55 Ch 27.19S 58.45W
Guaymas 39 Hg 27.56N 110.54W
Guayquiraró, Rio- 55 Cj 30.10S 58.34W
Guba [Eth.] 35 Fc 11.15N 35.20 E
Guba [Zaire] 36 Ee 10.38S 26.26 E
Guba Dolgaja 19 Fa 70.19N 58.45 E
Gubaha 19 Fd 58.52N 57.36 E
Guban 30 Lg 10.15N 44.26 E
Gubbio 14 Gg 43.21N 12.25 E
Gubdor 17 Hf 60.15N 56.35 E
Guben 10 Ke 51.57N 14.43 E
Gubin 10 Ke 51.56N 14.45 E
Gubio 34 Hc 12.30N 12.47 E
Gubkin 19 De 51.17N 37.33 E
Gúdar, Sierra de- 13 Ld 40.27N 0.42 W
Gudara 19 Hh 38.23N 72.42 E
Gudauta 16 Lh 43.07N 40.37 E
Gudbrandsdalen 7 Bf 61.30N 10.00 E
Gudenå 8 Dh 56.29N 10.13 E
Gudermes 19 Eg 43.22N 46.08 E
Gudivāda 25 Ge 16.27N 80.59 E
Gudiyāttam 25 Ff 12.57N 78.52 E
Gudou Shan 27 Jg 22.12N 112.57 E
Güdül 24 Eb 40.13N 32.15 E
Güdür 25 Ff 14.08N 79.51 E
Gudvangen 8 Bd 60.52N 6.50 E
Guebwiller 11 Ng 47.55N 7.12 E
Guéckédou 34 Cd 8.33N 10.09W
Guelma [3] 32 Ib 36.15N 7.30 E
Guelma 32 Ib 36.28N 7.26 E
Guelph 42 Jh 43.33N 80.15W
Guelta Zemmur 32 Ed 25.08N 12.22W
Guemar 32 Ic 33.29N 6.48 E
Guéméné-Penfao 11 Eg 47.38N 1.50W
Guénange 12 Ie 49.18N 6.11 E
Guéné 34 Fc 11.44N 3.13 E
Guer 11 Dg 47.54N 2.07W
Guéra [3] 35 Bc 11.30N 18.30 E
Guéra 32 De 20.52N 17.03W
Guéra, Massif de- 30 Ig 11.55N 18.12 E
Guérande 11 Dg 47.20N 2.26W
Guerara 32 Hc 32.48N 4.30 E
Guercif 32 Gc 34.14N 3.22W
Guerdjoumane, Djebel- 13 Oh 36.25N 2.51 E
Guere, Rio- 50 Dh 9.50N 65.08W
Guéréda 35 Cc 14.31N 22.05 E
Guéret 11 Hh 46.10N 1.52 E
Guérin-Kouka 34 Fd 9.41N 0.37 E
Guernica y Luno 13 Ja 43.19N 2.41W
Guernsey 9 Kl 49.27N 2.35W
Guerrero [2] 47 De 17.40N 100.00W
Guerrero 48 Ic 28.20N 100.26W
Guessou-Sud 34 Fc 10.03N 2.38 E
Guest Peninsula 66 Mf 76.18S 148.00W
Guge 35 Fd 6.12N 37.30 E
Gügerd, Kūh-e- 24 Oe 34.50N 53.00 E
Guglionesi 14 Ii 41.55N 14.55 E
Guguan Island 57 Fc 17.19N 145.51 E
Guia 55 Db 15.22S 56.14W
Guia Lopes da Laguna 55 Df 21.25S 56.07W
Guiana Highlands (EN) = Guayana, Macizo de la- 52 Ke 5.00N 60.00W
Guiana Island 51d Bb 17.06N 61.44W
Guichi (Chizhou) 27 Ke 30.33N 117.30 E
Guichón 55 Dk 32.21S 57.12W
Guide 27 Hd 36.03N 101.30 E
Guider 34 Hd 9.53N 13.57 E
Guidimaka [3] 32 Ef 15.30N 12.00W
Guidimouni 34 Gc 13.42N 9.30 E
Guiding 27 If 26.33N 107.16 E
Guidong 27 Jf 26.11N 113.58 E
Guiers 11 Li 45.37N 5.37 E
Guiglo 34 Dd 6.33N 7.29W
Guiglo [3] 34 Dd 6.30N 7.40W
Guijá 37 Ed 24.29S 33.00 E
Guija, Lago de- 49 Cf 14.13N 89.34W
Gui Jiang 21 Ng 23.26N 111.18 E
Guijk en Sint Agatha 12 Hc 51.44N 5.52 E
Guijuelo 13 Gd 40.33N 5.40W
Guil 11 Mj 44.40N 6.36 E
Guildford 9 Mj 51.14N 0.35W
Guiler Gol 28 Ga 46.03N 122.06 E
Guilin 22 Ng 25.21N 110.15 E
Guillaume Delisle, Lac- 42 Je 56.25N 76.00W
Guillestre 11 Mj 44.40N 6.39 E
Guilvinec 11 Bg 47.47N 4.17W
Guimarães [Braz.] 54 Jd 2.08S 44.36W
Guimarães [Port.] 13 Dc 41.27N 8.18W
Guimaras 26 Hd 10.35N 122.37 E
Guinchos Cay 49 Hb 22.45N 78.06W
Guinea (EN) = Guinée [1] 31 Fg 11.00N 10.00W
Guinea, Gulf of- 30 Hh 2.00N 2.30 E
Guinea, Gulf of- (EN) = Guinée, Golfe de- 30 Hh 2.00N 2.30 E
Guinea Basin (EN) 3 Di 0.00 5.00W
Guinea-Bissau (EN) = Guiné-Bissau [1] 31 Fg 12.00N 15.00W
Guinea Ecuatorial = Equatorial Guinea (EN) [1] 31 Hh 2.00N 9.00 E
Guinea Rise (EN) 3 Dj 4.00S 0.00
Guiné-Bissau = Guinea-Bissau (EN) [1] 31 Fg 12.00N 15.00W
Guinée = Guinea (EN) [1] 31 Fg 11.00N 10.00W
Guinée, Golfe de- = Guinea, Gulf of- (EN) 30 Hh 2.00N 2.30 E
Guinée Forestière [3] 34 Dd 8.40N 9.50W
Guinée Maritime [3] 34 Cc 10.00N 14.00W
Guines 12 Dd 50.52N 1.52 E
Güines 47 Hd 22.50N 82.02W
Guingamp 11 Cf 48.33N 3.09W
Guinguinéo 34 Bc 14.16N 15.57W
Guines, Purta- 49 Eh 9.54N 85.41W
Guiping 27 Ig 23.23N 110.00 E
Guipúzcoa [3] 13 Ja 43.10N 2.10W
Guir, Hamada du- 30 Ge 31.00N 3.20W
Güira de Melena 49 Fb 22.48N 82.30W
Guiratinga 54 Hg 16.21S 53.45W
Güiria 54 Fa 10.34N 62.18W
Guiscard 12 Fe 49.39N 3.03 E
Guise 11 Je 49.54N 3.38 E
Guitiriz 13 Ea 43.11N 7.54W
Guiuan 26 Id 11.02N 125.43 E
Guixi 27 Kf 28.18N 117.15 E
Guixian 27 Ig 23.10N 109.35 E
Guiyang 22 Mg 26.38N 106.43 E
Guizhou Sheng (Kuei-chou Sheng) = Kweichow (EN) [2] 27 If 27.00N 107.00 E
Gujan-Mestras 11 Ej 44.38N 1.04W
Gujarāt [3] 25 Ed 22.51N 71.30 E
Gujarāt [3] 21 Jg 22.51N 71.30 E
Gujrānwala 22 Jf 32.09N 74.11 E
Gujrāt 25 Eb 32.34N 74.05 E
Gukovo 16 Ke 48.04N 39.53 E
Gulang 27 Hd 37.30N 102.54 E
Gulbarga 22 Jh 17.20N 76.50 E
Gulbene 19 Cd 57.12N 26.49 E
Gulča 19 Hg 40.19N 73.33 E
Gulf 55 Ad 19.08S 62.01W
Gulf Breeze 44 Dj 30.22N 87.07W
Gulf Coastal Plain 38 Jf 31.00N 92.00W
Gulfport 43 Je 30.22N 89.06W
Gulian 27 La 52.56N 122.09 E
Gulin 27 If 28.02N 105.47 E
Gulistan 19 Gg 40.30N 68.45 E
Guliya Shan 27 Lb 49.48N 122.25 E
Gulja 20 Hf 54.43N 121.03 E
Gulja/Yining 27 Dc 43.54N 81.21 E
Guljajpole 16 Jf 47.37N 36.18 E
Gulkana 40 Jd 62.16N 145.23W
Gulkeviči 16 Lg 45.19N 40.44 E
Gull Bay 45 Lb 49.47N 89.02W
Gulleråsen 8 Fc 61.04N 15.11 E
Gullfoss 7a Eb 64.20N 20.08W
Gullkronafjärd 8 Jd 60.05N 22.15 E
Gull Lake 42 Gf 50.08N 108.27W
Gullringen 8 Fg 57.48N 15.42 E
Gull River 45 Lb 49.50N 89.04W
Gullspång 8 Ff 58.59N 14.06 E
Güllü 15 Mk 38.16N 29.07 E
Güllük 24 Bd 37.14N 27.36 E
Gülpinar 15 Jj 39.32N 26.07 E
Gülşehir 24 Fc 38.45N 34.38 E
Gulstav 8 Dj 54.43N 10.41 E
Gulu 31 Kh 2.47N 32.18 E
Guma /Pishan 27 Cd 37.38N 78.19 E
Gumbiri, Jabal- 35 Ee 4.18N 30.57 E
Gumel 34 Gc 12.38N 9.23 E
Gummersbach 10 Da 51.02N 7.33 E
Gummi 34 Gc 12.09N 5.07 E
Gümüşçey 15 Ki 40.17N 27.17 E
Gümüşhacıköy 24 Fb 40.53N 35.14 E
Gümüşhane 24 Ea 40.27N 39.29 E
Gümüşsu 15 Nk 38.14N 30.01 E
Guna 35 Fc 11.44N 38.15 E
Guna 25 Fc 24.19N 77.19 E
Gundagai 59 Jg 35.04S 148.07 E
Gundji 36 Db 2.05N 21.27 E
Gündoğdu 15 Ki 40.15N 27.07 E
Gündoğmuş 24 Ed 36.48N 32.01 E
Güney 15 Mk 38.09N 29.05 E
Güneydoğu Toroslar 21 Gf 38.30N 41.00 E
Gungu 36 Cd 5.44S 19.19 E
Gunma Ken [2] 28 Of 36.20N 139.05 E
Gunnar 42 Ge 59.23N 108.53W
Gunnbjørns Fjeld 67 Mc 68.55N 29.20W
Gunnedah 59 Kf 30.59S 150.15 E
Gunnison 43 Fd 38.33N 106.56W
Gunt 18 Hf 37.30N 71.03 E
Guntakal 25 Fe 15.10N 77.23 E
Guntersville 44 Dh 34.21N 86.18W
Guntersville Lake 44 Dh 34.45N 86.03W
Guntur 22 Kh 16.18N 80.27 E
Gunungapi, Pulau- 26 Ih 6.38S 126.40 E
Gunungsitoli 26 Cf 1.17N 97.37 E
Günz 10 Gh 48.27N 10.16 E
Günzburg 10 Gh 48.27N 10.16 E
Gunzenhausen 10 Gg 49.06N 10.45 E
Guo He 28 Dh 32.58N 117.13 E
Guojiadian 28 Hc 43.20N 124.37 E
Guoyang 28 Dh 33.31N 116.12 E
Guozhen 28 Bj 29.24N 113.09 E
Gurahonț 15 Fc 46.16N 22.21 E
Gura Humorului 15 Ib 47.33N 25.54 E
Gurban Obo 27 Jc 43.06N 112.28 E
Gurbantünggüt Shamo 27 Eb 45.30N 87.30 E
Gurdžaani 16 Ni 41.43N 45.48 E
Güre 15 Mk 38.39N 29.10 E
Gurgei, Jabal- 35 Cc 13.50N 24.19 E
Gurghiului, Munții- 15 Ic 46.41N 25.12 E
Gurgueia, Rio- 52 Lf 6.50S 43.24W
Guri — Raúl Leoni, Represa- 54 Fb 7.30N 63.00W
Gurjev — Atyrau 6 Lf 47.07N 51.56 E
Gurjevsk 20 Df 54.20N 86.00 E
Gurk 14 Id 46.36N 14.31 E
Gurk 14 Id 46.52N 14.18 E
Gurktaler Alpen 14 Hd 46.55N 14.00 E
Guro 37 Ec 17.26S 33.20 E
Gürpınar 24 Jc 38.18N 43.25 E
Gurskoje 20 If 50.20N 138.05 E
Gurskøy 7 Ae 62.15N 5.40 E
Gürsu 15 Mi 40.13N 29.12 E
Gurué 37 Fc 15.28S 36.59 E
Gurumeti 35 Fc 2.05S 33.57 E
Gürün 24 Gc 38.43N 37.17 E
Gurupá 54 Hd 1.25S 51.39W
Gurupi 53 Lg 11.43S 49.04W
Gurupi, Rio- 54 Lf 1.13S 46.06W
Gurupi, Serra do- 54 Id 5.00S 47.30W
Guru Sikhar 25 Ed 24.39N 72.46 E
Gus 7 Ji 55.00N 41.12 E
Gusau 31 Hg 12.10N 6.40 E
Gusev 19 Ce 54.37N 22.12 E
Gushan 28 Ge 39.54N 123.36 E
Gushi 27 Ke 32.02N 115.39 E
Gushikawa 29b Ab 25.21N 127.52 E
Gushk 24 Ph 23.13N 55.52 E
Gus-Hrustalny 7 Ji 55.38N 40.40 E
Gusinaja, Guba- 20 Kb 72.00N 150.00 E
Gusinaja Zemlja, Poluostrov- 19 Fa 71.50N 52.00 E
Gusinje 15 Cg 42.34N 19.50 E
Gusinoozersk 20 Ff 51.17N 106.30 E
Guspini 14 Ck 39.32N 8.37 E
Güssing 14 Kc 47.04N 16.20 E
Gustav Holm, Kap- 41 Ie 66.45N 34.00W
Gustavia 51b Bc 17.54N 62.52W

Index Symbols

[1] Independent Nation
[2] State, Region
[3] District, County
[4] Municipality
[5] Colony, Dependency
Continent
Physical Region
Historical or Cultural Region
Mount, Mountain
Volcano
Hill
Mountains, Mountain Range
Hills, Escarpment
Plateau, Upland
Pass, Gap
Plain, Lowland
Delta
Salt Flat
Valley, Canyon
Crater, Cave
Karst Features
Depression
Polder
Desert, Dunes
Forest, Woods
Heath, Steppe
Oasis
Cape, Point
Coast, Beach
Cliff
Peninsula
Isthmus
Sandbank
Island
Atoll
Rock, Reef
Islands, Archipelago
Rocks, Reefs
Coral Reef
Well, Spring
Geyser
River, Stream
Waterfall Rapids
River Mouth, Estuary
Lake
Salt Lake
Intermittent Lake
Reservoir
Swamp, Pond
Canal
Glacier
Ice Shelf, Pack Ice
Ocean
Sea
Gulf, Bay
Strait, Fjord
Lagoon
Bank
Seamount
Tablemount
Ridge
Shelf
Basin
Escarpment, Sea Scarp
Fracture
Trench, Abyss
National Park, Reserve
Point of Interest
Recreation Site
Cave, Cavern
Historic Site
Ruins
Wall, Walls
Church, Abbey
Temple
Scientific Station
Airport
Port
Lighthouse
Mine
Tunnel
Dam, Bridge

Index Symbols

[1] Independent Nation	⊟ Historical or Cultural Region	⊠ Pass, Gap	⊟ Depression	⊟ Coast, Beach	⊠ Rock, Reef	⊠ Waterfall Rapids	⊟ Canal	⊟ Lagoon	⊠ Escarpment, Sea Scarp	⊟ Historic Site	⊟ Port
[2] State, Region	⌂ Mount, Mountain	⊟ Plain, Lowland	⊟ Polder	⊟ Cliff	⊠ Islands, Archipelago	⊠ River Mouth, Estuary	⊟ Glacier	⊟ Bank	⊟ Fracture	⊟ Ruins	⊟ Lighthouse
[3] District, County	⌂ Volcano	⊟ Delta	⊟ Desert, Dunes	⊠ Peninsula	⊠ Rocks, Reefs	⊟ Lake	⊟ Ice Shelf, Pack Ice	⊟ Seamount	⊟ Trench, Abyss	⊟ Wall, Walls	⊠ Mine
[4] Municipality	⌂ Hill	⊟ Salt Flat	⊟ Forest, Woods	⊟ Isthmus	⊟ Coral Reef	⊟ Salt Lake	⊟ Ocean	⊟ Tablemount	⊟ National Park, Reserve	⊟ Church, Abbey	⊟ Tunnel
[5] Colony, Dependency	⌂ Mountains, Mountain Range	⊟ Valley, Canyon	⊟ Heath, Steppe	⊟ Sandbank	⊟ Well, Spring	⊟ Intermittent Lake	⊟ Sea	⊟ Ridge	⊟ Point of Interest	⊟ Temple	
▪ Continent	⌂ Hills, Escarpment	⊟ Crater, Cave	⊟ Oasis	⊟ Island	⊟ Geyser	⊟ Reservoir	⊟ Gulf, Bay	⊟ Shelf	⊟ Recreation Site	⊟ Scientific Station	
⊠ Physical Region	⊟ Plateau, Upland	⊟ Karst Features	⊟ Cape, Point	⊟ Atoll	⊟ River, Stream	⊟ Swamp, Pond	⊟ Strait, Fjord	⊟ Basin	⊟ Cave, Cavern	⊟ Airport	⊟ Dam, Bridge

Hansen Mountains 66 Ee 68.16S 58.47 E
Hanshan 28 Ei 31.43N 118.07 E
Hanshou 28 Aj 28.55N 111.58 E
Han Shui 21 Nf 30.34N 114.17 E
Hanstholm 8 Cg 57.07N 8.38 E
Han Sum 28 Eb 44.33N 119.58 E
Han-sur-Lesse, Rochefort- 12 Hd 50.08N 5.11 E
Han-sur-Nied 12 If 48.59N 6.26 E
Hantajskoje, Ozero- 20 Ec 68.25N 91.00 E
Hantau 19 Hg 44.13N 73.48 E
Hantengri Feng 27 Dc 42.03N 80.11 E
Hants 9 Lj 51.10N 1.10W
Hanty-Mansijsk 22 Ic 61.00N 69.06 E
Hanty-Mansijski avtonomnyj okrug 19 Hc 62.00N 72.30 E
Hantzsch 42 Kc 67.32N 72.26W
Hanušovice 10 Mf 50.05N 16.55 E
Hanwang 27 He 31.25N 104.13 E
Hanyang 28 Ci 30.34N 114.01 E
Hanyang, Wuhan- 28 Ci 30.33N 114.16 E
Hanyū 29 Fc 36.11N 139.32 E
Hanyuan (Fulin) 27 Hf 29.25N 102.12 E
Hanzhong [China] 22 Mf 32.59N 107.11 E
Hanzhong [China] 27 Ie 33.07N 107.00 E
Hanzhuang 28 Dg 34.38N 117.23 E
Hao Atoll 57 Mf 18.15S 140.54W
Hāora 22 Kg 22.35N 88.20 E
Haoud el Hamra 32 Ic 31.58N 5.59 E
Haoxue 28 Bi 30.02N 112.25 E
Haparanda 7 Fd 65.50N 24.10 E
Hapčeranga 20 Gg 49.42N 112.20 E
Happy Valley-Goose Bay 39 Md 53.19N 60.24W
Hapsu 28 Jd 41.13N 128.51 E
Ḩaql 24 Fh 29.18N 34.57 E
Ḩaql al Barqan 24 Lh 28.55N 47.57 E
Ḩaql al Manāqish 24 Lh 29.02N 47.32 E
Ḩaql as Şābirīyah 24 Lh 29.48N 47.50 E
Hara, Zaliv-/Hara Laht 8 Ke 59.35N 25.30 E
Hara-Ajrag 27 Ib 45.50N 109.20 E
Harabali 19 Ef 47.25N 47.16 E
Ḩaraḑ 23 Ge 24.14N 49.11 E
Haraiki Atoll 57 Mf 17.28S 143.27W
Hara Laht/Hara, Zaliv- 8 Ke 59.35N 25.30 E
Haramachi 28 Pf 37.38N 140.58 E
Haram Dāgh 23 Gb 37.35N 46.43 E
Harami, Pereval- 16 Oh 42.48N 46.12 E
Harand 24 Of 32.34N 52.26 E
Haranui'ia Point 63a Ed 10.21S 161.16 E
Hara Nur 27 Fb 48.05N 93.12 E
Harardēre 35 He 4.32N 47.53 E
Harare 31 Kj 17.50S 31.10 E
Harat 35 Fb 16.05N 39.28 E
Hara-Tas, Krjaž- 20 Fb 72.00N 107.00 E
Haratini 64n Bc 10.28S 160.58W
Ḩarat Zuwayyah 31 Jf 24.14N 21.59 E
Hara-Us-Nur 27 Fb 48.00N 92.10 E
Haraz 35 Bc 13.57N 19.26 E
Harāz 24 Od 36.40N 52.43 E
Harāzah, Jabal- 35 Eb 15.03N 30.27 E
Haraze 35 Cd 9.55N 20.48 E
Harbel 34 Cd 6.16N 10.21W
Harbin 22 Oe 45.45N 126.37 E
Harbor Beach 44 Fd 43.51N 82.39W
Harbour Breton 42 Lg 47.29N 55.50W
Harbour Grace 42 Mg 47.41N 53.15W
Harburg, Hamburg- 10 Fc 53.28N 10.00 E
Harcourt 44 Ob 46.30N 65.15W
Harcuvar Mountains 46 Ii 34.00N 113.30W
Harcyzsk 16 Kf 47.59N 38.11 E
Hardanger 8 Bd 60.20N 6.30 E
Hardangerfjorden 5 Gc 60.10N 6.00 E
Hardangerjøkulen 8 Bd 60.35N 7.25 E
Hardangervidda 7 Bf 60.20N 7.30 E
Hardelot Plage, Neufchâtel Hardelot- 12 Dd 50.38N 1.35 E
Hardenberg 12 Ib 52.34N 6.37 E
Harderwijk 11 Lb 52.21N 5.36 E
Hardin 43 Fb 45.44N 107.37W
Harding 37 Df 30.34S 29.58 E
Hardinsburg 44 Dg 37.47N 86.28W
Härdler 12 Kc 51.06N 8.14 E
Hardoi 25 Gc 27.25N 80.07 E
Hardy, Peninsula- 56 Gi 55.25S 68.30W
Hareid 8 Bb 62.22N 6.02 E
Hareidlandet 7 Ae 62.20N 5.55 E
Hare Indian 42 Ec 66.18N 128.38W
Harelbeke 12 Fd 50.51N 3.18 E
Haren 12 Ia 53.11N 6.38 E
Haren (Ems) 12 Jb 52.47N 7.14 E
Harer 31 Lh 9.18N 42.08 E
Harerge [3] 35 Gd 9.00N 41.30 E
Harēri Mālinwarfā 35 He 4.34N 47.21 E
Harewa 35 Gd 9.54N 41.58 E
Harfleur 12 Ce 49.30N 0.12 E
Harg 8 Hd 60.11N 18.24 E
Hargeysa 31 Lh 9.30N 44.03 E
Harghita [2] 15 Ic 46.25N 25.45 E
Harghita, Munţii- 15 Ic 46.31N 25.33 E
Harghita, Vîrful- 15 Ic 46.27N 25.35 E
Hargla 8 Lg 57.31N 26.25 E
Harhorin 27 Hb 47.13N 102.50 E
Har Hu 38.15N 97.40 E
Ḩarib 23 Gg 14.56N 45.30 E
Haridwār 25 Fc 29.58N 78.10 E
Harihari 62 De 43.09S 170.34 E
Hari Kurk 8 Je 59.00N 22.50 E
Ḩarim 24 Gd 36.12N 36.31 E
Ḩarīm, Jabal al- 24 Qj 25.58N 56.14 E
Harima-Nada 29 Dd 34.30N 134.35 E
Haringey, London- 12 Bc 51.36N 0.06W
Harīrūd 21 If 37.24N 60.38 E
Härjångsfjället 8 Ea 63.01N 12.35 E
Harjavalta 7 Ff 61.19N 22.08 E
Härjedalen 8 Eb 62.20N 13.05 E
Härjehågna 8 Ec 61.44N 12.08 E
Härkan 8 Fa 63.20N 14.55 E
Harkov 6 Je 50.00N 36.15 E
Harkovskaja Oblast [3] 19 Df 49.40N 36.30 E
Harlan [Ia.-U.S.] 45 If 41.39N 95.19W
Harlan [Ky.-U.S.] 44 Fg 36.51N 83.19W
Harlan County Lake 45 Gf 40.04N 99.16W
Harlech Castle 9 Ii 52.52N 4.07W
Harlem 46 Kb 48.32N 108.47W
Harleston 12 Db 52.24N 1.18 E
Harlingen [Neth.] 11 La 53.10N 5.24 E
Harlingen [Tx.-U.S.] 43 Hf 26.11N 97.42W
Harlovka 7 Ib 68.47N 37.20 E
Harlovka 7 Ib 68.47N 37.15 E
Harlow 9 Nj 51.47N 0.08 E
Harlowton 46 Kc 46.26N 109.50W
Harlu 7 Hf 61.51N 30.54 E
Hărman 15 Id 45.43N 25.41 E
Harmancık 24 Cc 39.41N 29.10 E
Harmånger 7 Df 61.56N 17.13 E
Harmanli 15 Ih 41.56N 25.54 E
Harmil 35 Gb 16.30N 40.12 E
Harmony 45 Ke 43.33N 91.59W
Harnai 25 Ee 17.48N 73.06 E
Harney Basin 38 Ge 43.15N 120.40W
Harney Lake 43 Dc 43.14N 119.07W
Harney Peak 43 Gc 44.00N 103.30W
Härnön 6 Gb 62.35N 18.00 E
Härnösand 6 Hc 62.38N 17.56 E
Haro 13 Jb 42.35N 2.51W
Harovsk 19 Ed 59.59N 40.11 E
Harøya 8 Bb 62.45N 6.25 E
Harøyfjorden 8 Bb 62.45N 6.35 E
Harpenden 12 Bc 51.48N 0.21W
Harper [Ks.-U.S.] 45 Gh 37.17N 98.01W
Harper [Lbr.] 31 Gh 4.22N 7.43W
Harper, Mount- 40 Kd 64.14N 143.50W
Harper Pass 62 De 42.44S 171.53 E
Harpline 8 Eh 56.45N 12.43 E
Harqin Qi (Jinshan) 28 Ed 41.57N 118.40 E
Harqin Zuoyi Monggolzu Zizhixian 28 Ed 41.05N 119.40 E
Ḩarrah 23 Hg 14.57N 50.19 E
Ḩarrat al 'Uwayrid 23 Ed 27.00N 37.30 E
Harricana 42 Jf 51.10N 79.47W
Harricana, Rivière- 44 Ha 51.10N 79.45W
Harrington-Harbour 42 Lf 50.26N 59.30W
Harris 9 Gd 57.53N 6.55W
Harris 51c Bc 16.28N 62.10W
Harris, Lake- 44 Gk 28.46N 81.49W
Harris, Sound of- 9 Fd 57.45N 7.08W
Harrisburg 39 Le 40.16N 76.52W
Harrismith 37 De 28.18S 29.03 E
Harrison [Ar.-U.S.] 45 Jh 36.14N 93.07W
Harrison [Mi.-U.S.] 44 Ec 44.01N 84.48W
Harrison [Nb.-U.S.] 45 Ee 42.41N 103.53W
Harrison, Cape- 42 Lf 54.56N 57.55W
Harrison Bay 40 Ib 70.30N 151.30W
Harrisonburg 44 Hf 38.27N 78.54W
Harrison Lake 46 Eb 49.31N 121.59W
Harrison Point 51q Ab 13.18N 59.38W
Harrisonville 45 Ig 38.39N 94.21W
Harrisville [Mi.-U.S.] 44 Fc 44.39N 83.17W
Harrisville [W.V.-U.S.] 44 Gf 39.13N 81.04W
Harrodsburg 44 Eg 37.46N 84.51W
Harrogate 9 Lh 54.00N 1.33W
Harrow, London- 12 Bc 51.36N 0.20W
Harry S. Truman Reservoir 45 Jg 38.00N 93.45W
Har Sai Shan 27 Gd 35.26N 97.41 E
Harsewinkel 12 Kc 51.58N 8.14 E
Harshō 35 Hc 11.17N 47.30 E
Harsim 24 Lf 33.48N 46.50 E
Harsin 24 Le 34.16N 47.35 E
Harstad 7 Db 68.47N 16.30 E
Harsvik 7 Cd 64.03N 10.02 E
Hart 44 Dd 43.42N 86.22W
Hart 42 Dc 65.51N 136.22W
Hartao 28 Gc 42.30N 122.08 E
Hartbees 30 Jk 28.45S 20.33 E
Hartberg 14 Jc 47.17N 15.58 E
Hårteigen 8 Bd 60.12N 7.04 E
Hartford [Ct.-U.S.] 39 Le 41.46N 72.41W
Hartford [Ky.-U.S.] 44 Dg 37.27N 86.55W
Hartford City 44 Ee 40.29N 85.23W
Hartington 45 He 42.37N 97.16W
Hartland 44 Nb 46.18N 67.32W
Hartland Point 9 Ij 51.02N 4.31W
Hartlepool 9 Lg 54.42N 1.11W
Hartmannberge 37 Ac 17.30S 12.23 E
Hartola 7 Gf 61.35N 26.01 E
Harts 28.24S 24.18 E
Hartselle 44 Dh 34.27N 86.56W
Harts Range 59 Gd 23.05S 134.55 E
Hartsville 44 Gh 34.23N 80.04W
Hartwell 44 Fh 34.21N 82.56W
Hartwell Lake 44 Fh 34.30N 82.55W
Harun, Bukit- 26 Gf 4.06N 115.46 E
Haruno 29 Ce 33.30N 133.30 E
Harves Bank (EN) 51c Ac 16.52N 62.35W
Harvey [Austl.] 59 Df 33.05S 115.54 E
Harvey [N.D.-U.S.] 43 Hb 47.47N 99.56W
Harvey Bay 59 Kd 25.30S 153.00 E
Harwich 9 Oj 51.57N 1.17 E
Haryana [3] 25 Fc 29.30N 76.30 E
Harz 5 He 51.45N 10.30 E
Hasaki 29 Gd 35.44N 140.48 E
Hasama 29 Gb 38.42N 141.13 E
Hasan 20 Ih 42.26N 130.39 E
Ḩasanābād [Iran] 24 Ph 28.47N 54.19 E
Ḩasanābād [Iran] 24 Nd 36.28N 50.17 E
Hasan Dağı 24 Db 38.08N 34.12 E
Ḩasan Langī 24 Qi 27.22N 56.52 E
Hasavjurt 16 Oh 43.16N 46.35 E
Hāsbayyā 24 Ff 33.43N 33.52 E
Hasdo 25 Hd 21.44N 82.44 E
Hase 10 Dd 52.41N 7.18 E
Hasekijata 15 Kg 42.08N 27.30 E
Hasenkamp 55 Cj 31.31S 59.51W
Hashimoto 29 Dd 34.19N 135.37 E
Hashtpar 24 Md 37.48N 48.55 E
Hasi Hausert 32 Ee 22.35N 4.18W
Haskell 43 He 33.10N 99.44W
Haskerland 12 Hb 52.58N 5.47 E
Haskerland-Joure 12 Hb 52.58N 5.47 E
Haskovo 15 Ih 41.56N 25.33 E
Haskovo [2] 15 Ih 41.50N 25.55 E
Hasle 8 Fi 55.11N 14.43 E
Haslemere 9 Mj 51.06N 0.43W
Haslev 8 Di 55.20N 11.58 E
Hăşmaşu Mare, Vîrful- 15 Ic 46.30N 25.50 E
Haspengouws Plateau/Hesbaye 11 Ld 50.35N 5.10 E
Haspres 12 Fd 50.15N 3.25 E
Hassa 24 Gd 36.50N 36.29 E
Hassan 25 Ff 13.00N 76.05 E
Hassberge 10 Gf 50.12N 10.29 E
Hassela 7 De 62.07N 16.42 E
Hassel Sound 42 Ha 78.30N 99.00W
Hasselt 11 Ld 50.56N 5.20 E
Hassi Bel Guebbour 32 Id 28.30N 6.41 E
Hassi el Ghella 13 Ki 35.27N 1.03W
Hassi-Mamèche 13 Mi 35.51N 0.04 E
Hassi Messaoud 31 He 31.43N 6.03 E
Hassi R'mel 32 Hc 32.55N 3.16 E
Hassi Serouenout 32 Ie 24.00N 7.50 E
Hässleholm 7 Ch 56.09N 13.46 E
Hasslö 8 Fh 56.05N 15.25 E
Haßloch 12 Ke 49.23N 8.16 E
Hastière 12 Gd 50.13N 4.50 E
Hastière-Hastière par-delà 12 Gd 50.13N 4.50 E
Hastière-par-delà, Hastière- 12 Gd 50.13N 4.50 E
Hastings [Bar.] 51q Ab 13.04N 59.35W
Hastings [Eng.-U.K.] 9 Nk 50.51N 0.36 E
Hastings [Mi.-U.S.] 44 Ed 42.39N 85.17W
Hastings [Mn.-U.S.] 45 Jd 44.44N 92.51W
Hastings [Nb.-U.S.] 43 Hc 40.35N 98.23W
Hastings [N.Z.] 61 Eg 39.38S 176.50 E
Hästveda 8 Eh 56.16N 13.56 E
Hašuri 16 Mi 41.59N 43.33 E
Hasvik 7 Fa 70.29N 22.09 E
Ḩasy al Qaţţār 33 Ec 30. 4N 27.11 E
Ḩasy Hague 33 Bd 26. 7N 10.31 E
Hat'ae-Do 28 Hg 34.23N 125.17 E
Hatanga 22 Mb 71.58N 102.30 E
Hatanga 21 Mb 72.55N 106.00 E
Hatch 45 Cj 32.40N 107.09W
Haţches Creek 59 Hd 20.56S 135.12 E
Haţeg 15 Fd 45.37N 22.57 E
Hatgal 27 Ha 50.26N 100.09 E
Ḩaţībah, Ra's- 23 Ee 21.59N 38.55 E
Ha Tien 25 Kf 10.23N 104.29 E
Ha Tinh 25 Le 18.20N 105.54 E
Hato Mayor 49 Md 18.46N 69.15W
Ḩattá, Jabal- 24 Qj 24.45N 56.04 E
Hattem 12 Ib 52.28N 6.06 E
Hatten 12 Ka 53.08N 8.23 E
Hatteras, Cape- 38 Lf 35.13N 75.32W
Hatteras Inlet 44 Jh 35.00N 75.40W
Hatteras Island 43 Ld 35.25N 75.30W
Hattfjelldal 7 Cd 65.36N 14.00 E
Hattiesburg 43 Je 31.19N 89.16W
Hattingen 12 Jc 51.24N 7.10 E
Hatu Iti, Ile- 61 Ma 8.42S 140.43W
Hatutaa, Ile- 57 Me 7.38S 140.38W
Hatvan 10 Pi 47.40N 19.41 E
Hat Yai 25 Kg 7.01N 100.27 E
Hatyrka 20 Md 62.03N 175.05 E
Hau Bon 25 Lf 13.24N 108.27 E
Haubourdin 12 Ed 50.36N 2.59 E
Hauge 7 Bg 58.21N 6.17 E
Haugesund 6 Gd 59.25N 5.18 E
Hauho 8 Kc 61.10N 24.33 E
Hauhungaroa Range 62 Fc 38.40S 175.35 E
Haukeligrend 7 Bg 59.51N 7.11 E
Haukipudas 7 Fd 65.15N 25.23 E
Haukivesi 5 Ic 62.05N 28.30 E
Haukivuori 8 Lb 62.01N 27.13 E
Hauraha 63a Ed 10.49S 161.57 E
Hauraki Gulf 61 Eg 36.35S 175.00 E
Hauroko, Lake- 62 Bf 45.55S 167.20 E
Hausa 32 Ed 27.06N 11.0 W
Hausruck 14 Hb 48.07N 13.35 E
Haut, Isle au- 44 Mc 44.03N 68.38W
Haut Atlas=High Atlas (EN) 30 Ge 32.00N 6.00W
Haute-Champagne 12 Ge 49.18N 4.15 E
Haute-Corse [3] 11a Aa 42.30N 9.00 E
Haute-Garonne [3] 11 Hk 43.25N 1.30 E
Haute-Guinée [3] 34 Dc 11.30N 10.00W
Haute-Kotto [3] 35 Cd 7.00N 23.00 E
Haute-Loire [3] 11 Ji 45.05N 4.00 E
Haute-Marne [3] 11 Lf 48.05N 5.10 E
Hauterive 44 Ma 49.11N 68.16W
Hautes-Alpes [3] 11 Mj 44.40N 6.30 E
Haute-Sangha [3] 35 Be 4.30N 16.00 E
Haute-Saône [3] 11 Mg 47.40N 6.10 E
Haute-Saône, Plateau de- 11 Lg 47.50N 6.00 E
Haute-Savoie [3] 11 Mi 46.00N 6.20 E
Hautes Fagnes/Hoge Venen 10 Bf 50.30N 6.00 E
Hautes-Pyrénées [3] 11 Gk 43.00N 0.10 E
Haute Vienne [3] 11 Hi 45.50N 1.10 E
Haute Volta→Burkina Faso 31 Gg 13.00N 2.00W
Haut-Mbomou [3] 35 Dd 6.00N 26.00 E
Hautmont 11 Jd 50.15N 3.56 E
Haut-Ogooué [3] 36 Bc 2.00S 14.00 E
Haut Rhin [3] 11 Ng 48.00N 7.20 E
Hauts-Bassins [3] 34 Ec 12.30N 4.30W
Hauts-de-Seine [3] 11 If 48.50N 2.11 E
Hauts-Plateaux 30 He 34.00N 0.01 E
Haut-Zaïre [2] 36 Eb 2.30N 25.30 E
Hauula 65a 21.36N 157.54W
Hauz-Han 18 Cf 37.16N 61.15 E
Hauz-Hanskoje Vodohr. 18 Cf 37.10N 61.20 E
Havana 45 Kf 40.18N 90.04W
Havana (EN)=La Habana 39 Kg 23.08N 82.22W
Havant 9 Mk 50.51N 0.59W
Havast 18 Gd 40.16N 68.51 E
Havasu, Lake- 46 Hi 34.30N 114.20W
Havel 10 Hd 52.53N 11.58 E
Havelange 12 Hd 50.23N 5.14 E
Havelange-Méan 12 Hd 50.22N 5.20 E
Havelberg 10 Id 52.49N 12.05 E
Havelland 10 Id 52.25N 12.45 E
Havelländisches Luch 10 Id 52.40N 12.40 E
Havelock [N.C.-U.S.] 44 Ih 34.53N 76.54W
Havelock [N.Z.] 62 Ed 41.17S 173.46 E
Havelock North 62 Gc 39.40S 176.53 E
Havelte 12 Ib 52.46N 6.16 E
Haverfordwest 9 Ij 51.49N 4.58W
Haverhill [Eng.-U.K.] 9 Ni 52.05N 0.26 E
Haverhill [Ma.-U.S.] 44 Ld 42.47N 71.05W
Havering, London- 12 Cc 51.36N 0.11 E
Havířov 10 Og 49.48N 18.27 E
Havlíčkův Brod 10 Lg 49.36N 15.34 E
Havøysund 7 Fa 71.03N 24.40 E
Havran 24 Bc 39.33N 27.06 E
Havre 39 Ie 48.33N 109.41W
Havre-Saint-Pierre 39 Md 50.15N 63.36W
Havsa 15 Jh 41.33N 26.49 E
Havza 24 Fb 41.05N 35.45 E
Hawaii [2] 58 Kb 24.00N 167.00W
Hawaiian Islands 57 Kb 24.00N 167.00W
Hawaiian Ridge (EN) 3 Kg 24.00N 165.00W
Hawaii Island 57 Lc 19.30N 155.30W
Hawallī 23 Gd 29.19N 48.02 E
Ḩawār 24 Nj 25.40N 50.45 E
Hawarden 62 Ee 42.56S 172.39 E
Ḩawashīyah, Wādī- 24 Eh 28.31N 32.58 E
Ḩawaymī, Sha'īb al- 24 Kg 30.58N 44.15 E
Hawd 30 Lh 7.40N 47.43 E
Ḩawḑ Al Waqf 24 Ei 26.03N 32.22 E
Hawea, Lake- 62 Cf 44.30S 169.20 E
Hawera 61 Dg 39.35S 174.17 E
Hawi 58 Lb 20.14N 155.50W
Hawick 9 Kf 55.25N 2.47W
Ḩawīzah, Hawr al- 24 Lg 31.35N 47.38 E
Hawkdun Range 62 Cf 44.50S 170.00 E
Hawke Bay 61 Eg 39.25S 177.20 E
Hawke Harbour 42 Lf 53.01N 55.50W
Hawker 59 Hf 31.53S 138.25 E
Hawkes, Mount- 66 Rg 83.55S 56.05W
Hawke's Bay [2] 62 Gc 39.30S 176.40 E
Hawkesbury 44 Jc 45.36N 74.37W
Hawkhurst 12 Cc 51.02N 0.30 E
Hawkinsville 44 Fi 32.17N 83.28W
Hawksbill 44 Hf 38.33N 78.23W
Hawk Springs 46 Mf 41.48N 104.09W
Ḩawmat as Sūq 32 Jc 33.53N 10.51 E
Hawng Tuk 25 Jd 20.28N 99.56 E
Ḩawrā' 35 Hb 15.43N 48.18 E
Ḩawrān, Wādī al- 23 Fc 33.58N 42.34 E
Ḩawsh 'Isá 24 Dg 30.55N 30.17 E
Hawthorne 43 Dd 38.32N 118.38W
Hawthorne Mount- 66 Pf 72.10S 98.39W
Haxtun 45 Ef 40.39N 102.38W
Hay 58 Fh 34.30S 144.51 E
Hay 38 Hc 60.51N 115.44W
Hayachine-San 29 Gb 39.34N 141.29 E
Hayakita 29a Bb 42.45N 141.48 E
Hayange 11 Me 49.20N 6.03 E
Hayastan = Armenia (EN) 19 Eg 40.00N 45.00 E
Hayato 29 Bf 31.45N 130.43 E
Haybān 35 Ec 11.13N 30.31 E
Haybān, Jabal- 35 Ec 11.15N 30.31 E
Hayden 46 Jj 33.00N 110.47W
Hayes [Man.-Can.] 42 Ie 57.00N 92.15W
Hayes [N.W.T.-Can.] 42 Hc 67.20N 95.02W
Hayes, Mount- 40 Jd 63.37N 146.43W
Hayes Halvø=Hayes Peninsula (EN) 67 Od 77.40N 64.30W
Hayes Peninsula (EN)=Hayes Halvø 67 Od 77.40N 64.30W
Ḩayl 24 Qj 24.33N 56.06 E
Hayl, Wādī al- 24 He 34.47N 39.18 E
Hayling Island 12 Bd 50.48N 0.58W
Haymana 24 Ec 39.27N 32.30 E
Haymana Platosu 24 Ec 39.25N 32.45 E
Haynin 23 Gf 15.50N 48.18 E
Hayrabolu 24 Bb 41.12N 27.06 E
Ḩayrān 33 Hf 16.02N 42.49 E
Hay River 59 Hd 25.00S 138.00 E
Hay River 39 Hc 60.51N 115.40W
Hayrūt 35 Ib 15.59N 52.09 E
Hays 43 Hd 38.53N 99.20W
Hay Springs 45 Ee 42.41N 102.41W
Haystack Peak 46 Ig 39.50N 113.55W
Hayward [Ca.-U.S.] 46 Dh 37.40N 122.05W
Hayward [Wi.-U.S.] 45 Kc 46.01N 91.29W
Haywards Heath 12 Bc 51.00N 0.06W
Hazar, Wādī- 35 Hb 17.50N 49.07 E
Hazarasp 18 Cd 41.19N 61.08 E
Hazard 44 Fg 37.15N 83.12W
Hazar Gölü 24 Hc 38.30N 39.25 E
Hazāribāgh 25 Hd 23.59N 85.21 E
Hazebrouck 11 Id 50.43N 2.32 E
Hazelton 42 Ee 55.15N 127.40W
Hazen 45 Fc 47.18N 101.38W
Hazen Strait 42 Ga 77.15N 110.00W
Ḩazeva 24 Fg 30.48N 35.15 E
Hazlehurst [Ga.-U.S.] 44 Fj 31.52N 82.36W
Hazlehurst [Ms.-U.S.] 45 Kk 31.52N 90.24W
Hazleton 44 Je 40.58N 76.00W
Hazlett, Lake- 59 Fd 21.30S 128.50 E
Hazrah, Ra's al- 24 Nj 24.22N 51.36 E
Hazro 24 Ic 38.15N 40.47 E
Heacham 12 Cb 52.55N 0.29 E
Headley 12 Bc 51.07N 0.49W
Healdsburg 46 Dg 38.37N 122.52W
Heanor 12 Aa 53.00N 1.18W
Heard Island 30 Dn 53.00S 73.35 E
Hearne 45 Hk 30.53N 96.36W
Hearst 42 Jg 49.41N 83.40W
Heart River 45 Fc 46.47N 100.51W
Heathrow Airport London 12 Bc 51.28N 0.30W
Hebbronville 45 Gm 27.18N 98.41W
Hebei Sheng (Ho-pei Sheng) =Hopeh (EN) [2] 27 Kd 39.00N 116.00 E
Heber City 46 Jf 40.30N 111.25W
Hebi 27 Jd 35.53N 114.09 E
Hebian 27 Jd 38.35N 113.06 E
Hebiji 28 Cf 36.00N 114.08 E
Hebrides 5 Fd 57.00N 6.30W
Hebrides, Sea of the- 9 Ge 57.00N 7.00W
Hebron [N.D.-U.S.] 45 Ec 46.54N 102.03W
Hebron [Newf.-Can.] 42 Le 58.15N 62.35W
Heby 8 Ge 59.56N 16.53 E
Hecate Strait 42 Ef 53.20N 131.00W
Hecelchakán 48 Ng 20.10N 90.08W
Hechi (Jinchengjiang) 27 Ig 24.44N 108.02 E
Hechingen 10 Eh 48.21N 8.59 E
Hechuan 27 Ie 30.07N 106.15 E
Hecla 45 Gd 45.43N 98.09W
Hecla and Griper Bay 42 Ga 76.00N 111.30W
Hecla Island 45 Ha 51.08N 96.45W
Heddalsvatnet 8 Ce 59.30N 9.15 E
Hede 7 Ce 62.25N 13.30 E
Hede → Sheyang 28 Fh 33.47N 120.15 E
Hedemarken 8 Dd 60.50N 11.20 E
Hedemora 7 Df 60.17N 15.59 E
Hedensted 8 Ci 55.46N 9.42 E
Hedesunda 7 Df 60.25N 17.00 E
Hedesunda fjärdarna 8 Gd 60.20N 17.00 E
Hedmark [2] 7 Cf 61.30N 11.45 E
Hedo-Misaki 29b Bb 26.52N 128.16 E
Heemskerk 12 Gb 52.30N 4.42 E
Heemstede 12 Gb 52.21N 4.37 E
Heerenveen 11 Lb 52.57N 5.55 E
Heerhugowaard 12 Gb 52.40N 4.50 E
Heerlen 11 Ld 50.54N 5.59 E
Hefa=Haifa (EN) 22 Ff 32.50N 35.00 E
Hefei 22 Nf 31.47N 117.15 E
Hefeng 27 Jf 29.49N 110.01 E
Hegang 22 Pe 47.20N 130.12 E
Hegau 10 Ei 47.50N 8.45 E
Hegura Jima 27 Od 37.50N 136.55 E
Heide 10 Fb 54.12N 9.06 E
Heidelberg 10 Eg 49.25N 8.42 E
Heidenheim an der Brenz 10 Gh 48.41N 10.09 E
Heidenreichstein 14 Jb 48.52N 15.07 E
Hei-Gawa 29 Gb 39.38N 141.58 E
Heigun-Tō 29 Ce 33.47N 132.15 E
Hei He 27 Hd 38.15N 100.15 E
Heihe → Aihui 22 Od 50.13N 127.26 E
Heilbron 37 De 27.21S 27.58 E
Heilbronn 10 Fg 49.08N 9.13 E
Heiligenblut 14 Gd 47.02N 12.50 E
Heiligenhafen 10 Gb 54.22N 10.59 E
Heiligenhaus 12 Ic 51.19N 6.58 E
Heiligenstadt 10 Ge 51.23N 10.08 E
Heilinzi 28 Ib 44.33N 126.41 E
Heilong Jiang 21 Qd 52.56N 141.10 E
Heilongjiang Sheng (Hei-lung-chiang Sheng)= Heilungkiang (EN) [2] 27 Mb 48.00N 128.00 E
Heiloo 12 Gb 52.36N 4.43 E
Hei-lung-chiang Sheng→Heilongjiang Sheng=Heilungkiang (EN) [2] 27 Mb 48.00N 128.00 E
Heilungkiang (EN)= Heilongjiang Sheng (Hei-lung-chiang Sheng) [2] 27 Mb 48.00N 128.00 E
Heilungkiang (EN)=Hei-lung-chiang Sheng→Heilongjiang Sheng [2] 27 Mb 48.00N 128.00 E
Heimaey 7a c 63.26N 20.17W
Heimbach 12 Id 50.38N 6.29 E
Heimdal 7 Ce 63.21N 10.22 E
Heimsheim 12 Kf 48.48N 8.51 E
Heinävesi 7 Ge 62.26N 28.36 E
Heinola 7 Gf 61.13N 26.02 E
Heinsberg 12 Ic 51.04N 6.05 E
Heishan 28 Gd 41.42N 122.07 E
Heishan Xia 27 Hd 37.18N 104.39 E
Heishui [China] 28 Ec 42.06N 119.22 E
Heishui [China] 27 He 32.03N 103.05 E
Heist, Knokke- 12 Fc 51.21N 3.15 E
Heist-op-den-Berg 12 Gc 51.05N 4.43 E
Hei-Zaki 29 Hb 39.39N 142.00 E
Hejgijaha 17 Pd 65.27N 72.50 E
Hejian 28 De 38.27N 116.05 E
Hejing 27 Ec 42.18N 86.18 E
Hejjaha 17 Kb 63.18N 62.32 E
Hekimhan 24 Gc 38.49N 37.56 E
Hekinan 29 Ed 34.52N 136.58 E
Hekla 5 Ec 64.00N 19.40W
Hekou 28 Ci 31.20N 114.25 E
Hekou → Yanshan 28 Dj 28.18N 117.41 E
Hel 10 Ob 54.37N 18.48 E
Helagsfjället 7 Ce 62.55N 12.27 E
Helan 27 Id 38.35N 106.16 E
Helan Shan 27 Id 39.00N 106.00 E
Helden's Point 51c Ab 17.24N 62.50W
Helena [Ar.-U.S.] 43 Ie 34.32N 90.35W
Helena [Guy.] 54 Gb 6.41N 57.55W
Helena [Mt.-U.S.] 39 He 46.36N 112.01W
Helen Glacier 66 Ge 66.40S 93.55 E
Helen Reef 57 Ed 2.53N 131.47 E
Helensburgh 9 Ie 56.01N 4.44W
Helensville 62 Fb 36.40S 174.27 E
Helgaå 8 Fi 55.53N 14.08 E
Helgasjön 8 Fh 56.55N 14.45 E
Helgeland 7 Cd 66.15N 13.05 E
Helgoland 10 Db 54.12N 7.53 E

Index Symbols

[1] Independent Nation
[2] State, Region
[3] District, County
[4] Municipality
[5] Colony, Dependency
Continent
Physical Region
Historical or Cultural Region
Mount, Mountain
Volcano
Hill
Mountains, Mountain Range
Hills, Escarpment
Plateau, Upland
Pass, Gap
Plain, Lowland
Delta
Salt Flat
Valley, Canyon
Crater, Cave
Karst Features
Depression
Polder
Desert, Dunes
Forest, Woods
Heath, Steppe
Oasis
Cape, Point
Coast, Beach
Cliff
Peninsula
Isthmus
Sandbank
Island
Atoll
Rock, Reef
Islands, Archipelago
Rocks, Reefs
Coral Reef
Well, Spring
Geyser
River, Stream
Waterfall Rapids
River Mouth, Estuary
Lake
Salt Lake
Intermittent Lake
Reservoir
Swamp, Pond
Canal
Glacier
Ice Shelf, Pack Ice
Ocean
Sea
Gulf, Bay
Strait, Fjord
Lagoon
Bank
Seamount
Tablemount
Ridge
Shelf
Basin
Escarpment, Sea Scarp
Fracture
Trench, Abyss
National Park, Reserve
Point of Interest
Recreation Site
Cave, Cavern
Historic Site
Ruins
Wall, Walls
Church, Abbey
Temple
Scientific Station
Airport
Port
Lighthouse
Mine
Tunnel
Dam, Bridge

Index Symbols

[1] Independent Nation
[2] State, Region
[3] District, County
[4] Municipality
[5] Colony, Dependency
[6] Continent
[7] Physical Region

Historical or Cultural Region
Mount, Mountain
Volcano
Hill
Mountains, Mountain Range
Hills, Escarpment
Plateau, Upland

Pass, Gap
Plain, Lowland
Delta
Salt Flat
Valley, Canyon
Crater, Cave
Karst Features

Depression
Polder
Desert, Dunes
Forest, Woods
Heath, Steppe
Oasis
Cape, Point

Coast, Beach
Cliff
Peninsula
Isthmus
Sandbank
Island
Atoll

Rock, Reef
Islands, Archipelago
Rocks, Reefs
Coral Reef
Well, Spring
Geyser
River, Stream

Waterfall Rapids
River Mouth, Estuary
Glacier
Ice Shelf, Pack Ice
Ocean
Sea
Gulf, Bay
Strait, Fjord

Canal
Lagoon
Bank
Fracture
Ridge
Shelf
Basin

Lagoon
Escarpment, Sea Scarp
Trench, Abyss
National Park, Reserve
Point of Interest
Recreation Site
Cave, Cavern

Historic Site
Ruins
Wall, Walls
Church, Abbey
Temple
Scientific Station
Airport

Port
Lighthouse
Mine
Tunnel
Dam, Bridge

Index Symbols

[1] Independent Nation	▲ Historical or Cultural Region	⌣ Pass, Gap
[2] State, Region	▲ Mount, Mountain	⌣ Plain, Lowland
[3] District, County	▲ Volcano	⌣ Delta
[4] Municipality	▲ Hill	⌣ Salt Flat
[5] Colony, Dependency	▲ Mountains, Mountain Range	⌣ Valley, Canyon
■ Continent	▲ Hills, Escarpment	⌣ Crater, Cave
▨ Physical Region	▲ Plateau, Upland	⌣ Karst Features

Depression	Rock, Reef	Waterfall, Rapids	Canal	Lagoon
Polder	Islands, Archipelago	River Mouth, Estuary	Glacier	Bank
Desert, Dunes	Rocks, Reefs	Lake	Ice Shelf, Pack Ice	Fracture
Forest, Woods	Coral Reef	Salt Lake	Ocean	Trench, Abyss
Heath, Steppe	Well, Spring	Intermittent Lake	Sea	Tablemount
Oasis	Geyser	Reservoir	Gulf, Bay	Ridge
Cape, Point	River, Stream	Swamp, Pond	Strait, Ford	Shelf
Coast, Beach				Basin
Cliff				
Peninsula				
Isthmus				
Sandbank				
Island				
Atoll				

National Park, Reserve	Historic Site
Point of Interest	Ruins
Recreation Site	Wall, Walls
Cave, Cavern	Church, Abbey
	Temple
	Scientific Station
	Airport
Port	
Lighthouse	
Mine	
Tunnel	
Dam, Bridge	

Hude (Oldenburg)	12	Ka	53.07N	8.28 E
Huder	27	Lb	49.59N	121.30 E
Hudiksvall	6	Hc	61.44N	17.07 E
Hudson	38	Le	40.42N	74.02W
Hudson [Fl.-U.S.]	44	Fk	28.22N	82.42W
Hudson [N.Y.-U.S.]	44	Kd	42.15N	73.47W
Hudson, Lake-	45	Ih	36.20N	95.05W
Hudson Bay	42	Hf	52.52N	102.23W
Hudson Bay	38	Kd	60.00N	86.00W
Hudson Canyon (EN)	44	Kf	39.27N	72.12W
Hudson Hope	42	Fe	56.02N	121.55W
Hudson Land	41	Jd	73.45N	22.30W
Hudson Mountains	66	Pf	74.32S	99.20W
Hudson Strait	38	Lc	62.30N	72.00W
Hudžirt	27	Hb	47.05N	102.45 E
Hue	22	Mh	16.28N	107.36 E
Huebra	13	Fc	41.02N	6.48W
Huechucuicui, Punta-	56	Ff	41.47S	74.02W
Hueco Montains	45	Dj	32.05N	105.55W
Huedin	15	Gc	46.52N	23.03 E
Huehuetenango [3]	49	Bf	15.40N	91.35W
Huehuetenango	47	Fe	15.20N	91.28W
Huejutla de Reyes	48	Jg	21.08N	98.25W
Huelgoat	11	Cf	48.22N	3.45W
Huelma	13	Ig	37.39N	3.27W
Huelva [3]	13	Fg	37.40N	7.00W
Huelva	6	Fh	37.16N	6.57W
Huelva, Ribera de-	13	Gg	37.27N	6.00W
Huércal Overa	13	Kg	37.23N	1.57W
Huerfano Mountain	45	Bh	36.30N	108.10W
Huertas, Cabo de-	13	Lf	38.21N	0.24W
Huerva	13	Lc	41.39N	0.52W
Huesca	13	Lb	42.08N	0.25W
Huesca [3]	13	Lb	42.10N	0.10W
Huéscar	13	Jg	37.49N	2.32W
Hueso, Sierra del-	48	Gb	30.15N	105.20W
Huesos, Arroyo de los-	55	Cm	36.30S	59.09W
Huetamo de Núñez	48	Ih	18.35N	100.53W
Huete	13	Jd	40.08N	2.41W
Ḩufrat an Naḩās	35	Cd	9.45N	24.19 E
Huftarøy	8	Ad	60.05N	5.15 E
Hugh Butler Lake	45	Ff	40.22N	100.42W
Hughenden	58	Fg	20.51S	144.12 E
Hughes	40	Ic	66.03N	154.16W
Hughes Range	46	Hb	49.55N	115.28W
Hugo	45	Ii	34.01N	95.31W
Huguan	28	Bf	36.05N	113.12 E
Huhur He	28	Fc	43.55N	120.47 E
Hui'an	27	Kf	25.07N	118.47 E
Huiarau Range	62	Gc	38.35S	177.10 E
Huib-Hochplato	37	Be	27.10S	16.50 E
Huichang	27	Kf	25.33N	115.45 E
Huicheng → Shexian	28	Ej	29.53N	118.27 E
Huicholes, Sierra de los-	48	Gf	22.00N	104.00W
Huich'ŏn	27	Mc	40.10N	126.17 E
Huifa He	28	Ic	43.06N	126.53 E
Hui He [China]	27	Kb	48.51N	119.12 E
Hui He [China]	28	Be	39.21N	112.37 E
Huiji He	28	Ch	33.53N	115.37 E
Huila [2]	54	Cc	2.30N	75.45W
Huila [3]	36	Ce	15.00S	15.00 E
Huila, Nevado del-	52	Ie	3.00N	76.00W
Huilai	27	Kg	23.05N	116.18 E
Huili	27	Hf	26.37N	102.19 E
Huimanguillo	48	Mi	17.51N	93.23W
Huimin	27	Kd	37.29N	117.30 E
Huinan (Chaoyang)	28	Ic	42.41N	126.03 E
Huisne	11	Gg	47.59N	0.11 E
Huissen	12	Hc	51.56N	5.55 E
Huiten Nur	27	Fd	35.30N	91.55 E
Huittinen	8	Jc	61.11N	22.42 E
Huivuilay, Isla de-	48	Dd	27.03N	110.01W
Huixian [China]	28	Bg	35.27N	113.47 E
Huixian [China]	27	Ie	33.46N	106.06 E
Huixtla	47	Fe	15.09N	92.28W
Huize	27	Hf	26.28N	103.18 E
Huizen	12	Hb	52.18N	5.16 E
Huizhou	27	Jg	23.02N	114.28 E
Hukou	28	Dj	29.44N	116.14 E
Hu Kou	27	Jd	36.09N	110.20 E
Hŭksan-Chedo	27	Me	34.30N	125.20 E
Hukuntsi	37	Cd	23.59S	21.44 E
Hulan	27	Mb	46.03N	126.36 E
Hulan He	27	Mb	45.54N	126.42 E
Ḩulayfā'	23	Fd	26.00N	40.47 E
Hulett	46	Md	44.41N	104.36W
Hulga	17	Jd	64.15N	60.58 E
Hulin	27	Nb	45.52N	132.58 E
Hulin He	28	Hb	45.19N	124.06 E
Hull	42	Jg	45.26N	75.43W
Hull → Kingston-upon-Hull	6	Fe	53.45N	0.20W
Hull → Orona Atoll	57	Je	4.29S	172.10W
Hull Bay	66	Nf	74.55S	137.40W
Hull Glacier	66	Nf	75.05S	137.15W
Hull Mountain	46	Dg	39.31N	122.59W
Hüls, Krefeld-	12	Ic	51.22N	6.31 E
Hultsfred	7	Dh	57.29N	15.50 E
Huludao	27	Lc	40.44N	120.59 E
Hulun Nur	21	Ne	49.00N	117.30 E
Ḩulwān = Helwān (EN)	33	Fd	29.51N	31.20 E
Hulwāt, Qūr al-	24	Hh	28.49N	38.50 E
Huma [China]	27	Ma	51.44N	126.36 E
Huma [Ton.]	65b	Bc	21.19S	174.56W
Humacao	49	Od	18.09N	65.50W
Huma He	27	Ma	51.42N	126.42 E
Humaitá [Braz.]	53	Jf	7.31S	63.02W
Humaitá [Par.]	56	Ic	27.03S	58.33W
Humansdorp	37	Cf	34.02S	24.46 E
Humbe	36	Bf	16.42S	14.54 E
Humber	5	Fe	53.40N	0.10W
Humberside [3]	9	Mh	53.55N	0.30W
Humbolat River	38	He	40.02N	118.31W
Humboldt	61	Cd	21.53S	166.25 E
Humboldt [Ia.-U.S.]	45	Ie	42.43N	94.13W
Humboldt [Nb.-U.S.]	45	If	40.10N	95.57W
Humboldt [Sask.-Can.]	42	Gf	52.12N	105.07W
Humboldt [Tn.-U.S.]	44	Ch	35.49N	88.55W
Humboldt Gletscher	41	Fc	79.40N	63.45W
Humboldt Range	46	Ff	40.15N	118.10W
Hume, Lake-	59	Jg	36.05S	147.05 E
Humenné	10	Rh	48.56N	21.55 E
Hummelfjell	8	Db	62.27N	11.17 E
Hümmling, Der-	10	Dd	52.52N	7.31 E
Humphreys Peak	38	Hf	35.20N	111.40W
Humppila	7	Ff	60.56N	23.22 E
Humuya, Río-	49	Df	15.13N	87.57W
Hün	31	If	29.07N	15.56 E
Húnaflói	5	Db	65.50N	20.50W
Hunan Sheng (Hu-nan Sheng) [3]	27	Jf	28.00N	112.00 E
Hu-nan Sheng → Hunan Sheng [3]	27	Jf	28.00N	112.00 E
Hunchun	28	Kc	42.52N	130.21 E
Hundested	8	Di	55.58N	11.52 E
Hunedoara [2]	15	Fd	45.45N	22.52 E
Hünfeld	10	Ff	50.40N	9.46 E
Hünfelden	12	Kd	50.19N	8.11 E
Hunga Ha'apai	65b	Ab	20.33S	175.24W
Hungary (EN) = Magyarország [1]	6	Hf	47.00N	20.00 E
Hunga Tonga	65b	Ab	20.32S	175.23W
Hungen	12	Kd	50.28N	8.54 E
Hüngnam	27	Md	39.50N	127.38 E
Hungry Horse Reservoir	46	Ib	48.15N	113.50W
Hun He [China]	28	Be	39.47N	113.15 E
Hun He [China]	28	Gd	40.41N	122.12 E
Hunhedoara	15	Fd	45.45N	22.54 E
Hunish, Rubha-	9	Gd	57.43N	6.20W
Hun Jiang	28	Hd	40.52N	125.42 E
Hunjiang	27	Mc	41.55N	126.27 E
Hunneberg	8	Ef	58.20N	12.27 E
Hunnebostrand	8	Df	58.27N	11.18 E
Hunsrück	10	Cg	49.50N	6.40 E
Hunstanton	9	Ni	52.57N	0.30 E
Hunte	10	Ed	52.30N	8.19 E
Hunter, Ile-	57	Ig	22.24S	172.03 E
Hunter Island	59	Ih	40.30S	144.45 E
Hunter Ridge (EN)	57	Ig	21.30S	174.30 E
Hunter River	59	Kf	32.30S	151.42 E
Hunterville	62	Fc	39.56S	175.34 E
Huntingdon	9	Mi	52.30N	0.10W
Huntingdon [Eng.-U.K.]	9	Mi	52.20N	0.12W
Huntingdon [Pa.-U.S.]	44	He	40.31N	78.02W
Huntingdon [Que.-Can.]	44	Jc	45.05N	74.08W
Huntington [In.-U.S.]	44	Ee	40.53N	85.30W
Huntington [W.V.-U.S.]	43	Kd	38.24N	82.26W
Huntly [N.Z.]	62	Fb	37.33S	175.10 E
Huntly [Scot.-U.K.]	9	Kd	57.27N	2.47W
Huntsville [Al.-U.S.]	39	Kf	34.44N	86.35W
Huntsville [Ont.-Can.]	42	Jg	45.20N	79.13W
Huntsville [Tx.-U.S.]	43	He	30.43N	95.33W
Hunucmá	48	Og	21.01N	89.52W
Hünxe	12	Ic	51.39N	6.47 E
Hunyani	37	Ec	15.37S	30.39 E
Hunyuan	27	Jd	39.38N	113.44 E
Hunza → Baltit	25	Ea	36.20N	74.40 E
Hunze	11	Ma	53.13N	6.40 E
Huocheng (Shuiding)	27	Dc	44.03N	80.49 E
Huojia	28	Bg	35.16N	113.39 E
Huolongmen	27	Mb	49.49N	125.49 E
Huolu	28	Ce	38.05N	114.18 E
Huon, Ile-	57	Hf	18.01S	162.57 E
Huon Gulf	59	Ja	7.10S	147.25 E
Huon Peninsula	60	Di	6.25S	147.30 E
Huonville	59	Jh	43.01S	147.02 E
Huoqin	28	Dh	32.21N	116.17 E
Huoshan	27	Ke	31.19N	116.20 E
Huo Shan [China]	27	Jd	37.00N	111.52 E
Huo Shan [China]	27	Ke	31.06N	116.12 E
Huoxian	27	Jd	36.39N	111.47 E
Hupeh (EN) = Hubei Sheng (Hu-pei Sheng) [2]	27	Je	31.00N	112.00 E
Hu-pei Sheng → Hubei Sheng = Hopeh (EN) [2]	27	Je	31.00N	112.00 E
Hür	24	Qg	30.50N	57.07 E
Hurama → Hongyuan	27	He	32.45N	102.38 E
Huränd	24	Lc	38.40N	47.20 E
Hurd, Cape-	44	Gc	45.13N	81.44W
Hurdalssjøen	8	Dd	60.20N	11.05 E
Hurd Deep = La Grande Trench (EN)	9	Kl	49.40N	3.00W
Hurdiyo	35	Ic	10.32N	51.08 E
Hurepoix	11	If	48.30N	2.10 E
Hure Qi	28	Fc	42.44N	121.44 E
Hurkett	45	Lb	48.50N	88.29W
Hurmuli	20	If	51.01N	136.56 E
Huroizumi	29a	Cb	42.01N	143.07 E
Huron	43	Hc	44.22N	98.13W
Huron, Lake-	38	Ke	44.30N	82.15W
Huron Mountains	44	Db	46.45N	87.45W
Hurricane	46	Ih	37.11N	113.17W
Hurricane Cliffs	46	Ih	37.00N	113.05W
Hurrungane	8	Bc	61.27N	7.51 E
Hursley	12	Ac	51.01N	1.24W
Hurst	45	Hj	32.49N	97.09W
Hurstpierpoint	12	Bd	50.55N	0.10W
Hürth	10	Cf	50.52N	6.52 E
Hurum	8	De	59.35N	10.35 E
Hurunui	62	Ee	42.54S	173.18 E
Hurup	8	Ch	56.45N	8.25 E
Huş	15	Lc	46.41N	28.04 E
Húsavik	7a	Ca	66.03N	17.21W
Hushan → Cixi	28	Fi	30.10N	121.14 E
Huskvarna	8	Fg	57.48N	14.16 E
Huslia	40	Hc	65.42N	156.25W
Husnes	8	Ae	59.52N	5.46 E
Husnesfjorden	8	Ae	59.50N	5.35 E
Hussigny-Godbrange	12	He	49.29N	5.52 E
Hust	16	Ce	48.10N	23.27 E
Hustadvika	8	Ba	63.00N	7.05 E
Husum [Ger.]	10	Fb	54.28N	9.03 E
Husum [Swe.]	7	Ee	63.20N	19.10 E
Hutag	27	Hb	49.23N	102.43 E
Hutchinson [Ks.-U.S.]	43	Hd	38.05N	97.56W
Hutchinson [Mn.-U.S.]	45	Id	44.54N	94.22W
Hutch Mountain	46	Ji	34.47N	111.22W
Hüth	33	Hf	16.14N	43.58 E
Hutou	27	Nb	46.00N	133.36 E
Hutte Sauvage, Lac de la-	42	Ke	55.57N	65.45W
Hutton, Mount-	59	Je	25.51S	148.20 E
Hutubi	27	Ec	44.07N	86.57 E
Hutuiti, Caleta-	65d	Bb	27.07S	109.17W
Hutuo He	28	De	38.14N	116.05 E
Huvhojtun, Gora-	20	Le	57.44N	160.45 E
Huxley, Mount-	62	Cf	44.04S	169.41 E
Huy	10	Ge	51.55N	10.55 E
Huy/Hoei	11	Ld	50.31N	5.14 E
Huzhou → Wuxing	27	Le	30.47N	120.07 E
Hvaler	8	De	59.05N	11.00 E
Hvalynsk	19	Ee	52.30N	48.07 E
Hvammstangi	7a	Bb	65.24N	20.57W
Hvannadalshnúkur	5	Ec	64.01N	16.41W
Hvar	14	Kg	43.07N	16.45 E
Hvar	14	Kg	43.11N	16.27 E
Hvarski kanal	14	Kg	43.15N	16.37 E
Hvatovka	16	Oc	52.21N	46.36 E
Hveragerdi	7a	Bb	64.00N	21.12W
Hveravellir	7a	Bb	64.54N	19.35W
Hvide Sande	8	Ci	55.59N	8.08 E
Hvitá [Ice.]	7a	Bb	64.35N	21.46W
Hvitá [Ice.]	7a	Bb	64.00N	20.58W
Hvittingfoss	8	De	59.29N	10.01 E
Hvojnaja	7	Ig	58.56N	34.31 E
Hwach'on-ni	28	Ie	38.58N	126.02 E
Hwang-Hae = Yellow Sea (EN)	21	Of	36.00N	124.00 E
Hwanghae-Namdo [2]	28	He	38.15N	125.30 E
Hwanghae-Pukto [2]	28	Ie	38.30N	126.25 E
Hwangju	28	He	38.40N	125.45 E
Hyannis [Ma.-U.S.]	44	Le	41.39N	70.17W
Hyannis [Nb.-U.S.]	45	Ff	42.00N	101.44W
Hybo	8	Gc	61.48N	16.12 E
Hyde Park	50	Gi	6.30N	58.16W
Hyderābād [India]	22	Jh	17.23N	78.28 E
Hyderābād [Pak.]	22	Ig	25.22N	68.22 E
Hyères	11	Mk	43.07N	6.07 E
Hyères, Iles d'-	11	Ml	43.00N	6.20 E
Hyesan	27	Mc	41.24N	128.10 E
Hyltebruk	7	Ch	57.00N	13.14 E
Hyndman Peak	46	He	43.50N	114.10W
Hyōgo Ken [2]	28	Mg	34.50N	134.48 E
Hyrov	10	Sg	49.32N	22.48 E
Hyrulä	8	Kd	60.24N	25.02 E
Hyrum	46	Jf	41.38N	111.51W
Hyrynsalmi	7	Gd	64.40N	28.32 E
Hysham	46	Lc	46.18N	107.14W
Hythe [Eng.-U.K.]	12	Ad	50.52N	1.24W
Hythe [Eng.-U.K.]	9	Oj	51.05N	1.05 E
Hyūga	28	Kh	32.25N	131.38 E
Hyūga-Nada	28	Ke	32.25N	131.45 E
Hyvinge/Hyvinkää	7	Ff	60.38N	24.52 E
Hyvinkää/Hyvinge	7	Ff	60.38N	24.52 E
I				
Iaco, Rio-	54	Ee	9.03S	68.35W
Iacobeni	15	Ib	47.26N	25.19 E
Iakora	37	Hd	23.08S	46.38 E
Ialomiţa [2]	15	Ke	44.30N	27.30 E
Ialomiţa	15	Kd	44.42N	27.51 E
Ialomiţei, Balta-	15	Ke	44.30N	28.00 E
Iapó, Rio-	55	Gg	24.30S	50.24W
Iaşi	6	If	47.10N	27.36 E
Iaşi [2]	15	Kb	47.07N	27.39 E
Iba	26	G	15.20N	119.58 E
Ibadan	31	Hh	7.23N	3.54 E
Ibague	53	Ie	4.27N	75.14W
Ibaiti	56	Jb	23.50S	50.10W
Iballja	15	Cg	42.11N	20.00 E
Ibans, Laguna de-	49	Ef	15.53N	84.52W
Ibar	15	Df	43.44N	20.45 E
Ibara	29	Cd	34.36N	133.28 E
Ibaraki	29	Dd	34.49N	135.34 E
Ibaraki Ken [2]	28	Pf	36.25N	140.30 E
Ibaré	55	Ej	30.49S	54.16W
Ibarra	53	Ie	0.21N	78.07W
Ibarreta	56	Ic	25.13S	59.51W
Ibb	22	Gh	13.58N	44.12 E
Ibba	35	De	4.48N	29.06 E
Ibba	35	Dd	7.09N	28.41 E
Ibbenbüren	10	Dd	52.16N	7.44 E
Ibdekkene	34	Fb	18.28N	0.38 E
Ibembo	36	Db	2.38N	23.37 E
Ibenga	36	Cb	2.20N	18.08 E
Iberá, Esteros del-	55	Di	28.05S	57.05W
Iberá, Laguna-	55	Di	28.30S	57.09W
Iberian Basin (EN)	3	De	40.00N	16.00W
Iberian Mountains (EN) = Sistema Ibérico	5	Fg	41.30N	2.30W
Iberian Peninsula (EN) = Peninsula Ibérica	5	Fg	40.00N	4.00W
Iberville, Lac d'-	42	Ke	56.00N	73.10W
Ibestad	7	Db	68.48N	17.08 E
Ibi [Nig.]	34	Gd	8.11N	9.45 E
Ibi [Sp.]	13	Lf	38.38N	0.34W
Ibiá	55	Ig	19.29S	46.32W
Ibiagui	55	Ja	13.03S	44.12W
Ibiai	55	Jc	16.51S	44.55W
Ibibobo	54	Fh	21.35S	62.58W
Ibicarai	54	Kf	14.51S	39.36W
Ibicui, Rio-	52	Kh	29.25S	56.47W
Ibicui da Armada, Rio-	55	Ej	30.16S	54.54W
Ibicuy	55	Ck	33.44S	59.10W
Ibicuy, Rio-	55	Ck	33.48S	59.10W
Ibigawa	29	Ed	35.29N	136.34 E
Ibipetuba	54	Jf	11.00S	44.32W
Ibiraiaras	55	Gi	28.22S	51.39W
Ibirama	55	Hh	27.04S	49.31W
Ibirapuitã, Rio-	55	Ei	29.22S	55.57W
Ibirocai, Arroio-	55	Di	29.26S	56.43W
Ibiruba	55	Fi	28.38S	53.06W
Ibitinga	55	He	21.45S	48.49W
Ibitinga, Reprêsa-	55	He	21.41S	49.05W
Ibity	37	Hd	20.10S	46.58 E
Ibiza	13	Nf	38.54N	1.26 E
Ibiza/Eivissa = Iviza (EN)	5	Gh	39.00N	1.25 E
Iblei, Monti-	14	Im	37.10N	14.55 E
Ibn Hāni', Ra's-	24	Fe	35.35N	35.43 E
Ibn Qawrah	35	Ib	15.43N	50.32 E
Ibo	37	Gb	12.22S	40.36 E
Ibo-Gawa	29	Dd	34.46N	134.35 E
Iboundji, Mont-	36	Bc	1.08S	11.48 E
Ibrā'	23	Ie	22.38N	58.40 E
Ibrah	35	Dc	10.36N	25.20 E
Ibrāhīm, Jabal-	21	Gg	20.27N	41.09 E
Ibresi	7	Li	55.18N	47.05 E
'Ibrī	23	Ie	23.16N	56.32 E
Ibrim	33	Fe	22.39N	32.05 E
Ibshawāy	24	Dh	29.22N	30.41 E
Ibuki-Sanchi	29	Ed	35.35N	136.25 E
Ibuki-Yama	29	Ed	35.25N	136.24 E
Ibusuki	28	Ki	31.16N	130.39 E
Iča	20	Ke	55.28N	155.58 E
Ica [2]	54	Cf	14.20S	75.30W
Ica	53	Ig	14.04S	75.42W
Iça, Rio-	52	Jf	3.07S	67.58W
Icaiché	48	Oh	18.05N	89.10W
Içamaquã, Rio-	55	Ei	28.34S	56.00W
Icana, Rio-	54	Ec	0.26N	67.19W
Icara	55	Hi	28.42S	49.18W
Icaraima	55	Ff	23.23S	53.41W
İçel	23	Db	36.48N	34.38 E
Iceland (EN) = Island	5	Eb	65.00N	18.00W
Iceland Basin (EN)	3	Dc	60.00N	20.00W
Ichalkaranji	25	Ee	16.42N	74.28 E
Ichibusa-Yama	29	Be	32.19N	131.06 E
Ichihara	28	Pg	35.31N	140.05 E
Ichi-Kawa	29	Dd	34.46N	134.43 E
Ichikawa	29	Fd	35.44N	139.55 E
Ichinohe	28	Pd	40.13N	141.17 E
Ichinomiya	28	Ng	35.18N	136.48 E
Ichinoseki	28	Pe	38.55N	141.08 E
Ich'ŏn [N. Kor.]	28	Ie	38.29N	126.53 E
Ich'ŏn [S. Kor.]	28	If	37.17N	127.27 E
Ichtegem	12	Fc	51.06N	3.00 E
Ičigemski Hrebet	20	Ld	63.30N	164.00 E
Ičinskaja Sopka, Vulkan-	21	Rd	55.39N	157.40 E
Ičnja	19	De	50.52N	32.25 E
Icó	54	Ke	6.24S	38.51W
Icy Cape	40	Gb	70.20N	161.52W
Idaarderadeel	12	Ha	53.06N	5.50 E
Idaarderadeel-Grow	12	Ha	53.06N	5.50 E
Idabel	45	Ij	33.54N	94.50W
Idah	34	Gd	7.06N	6.44 E
Idaho [2]	43	Ec	45.00N	115.00W
Idaho Falls	39	He	43.30N	112.02W
Idalia	45	Eg	39.43N	102.14W
Idān	35	Hd	6.03N	49.01 E
Idanha-a-Nova	13	Ee	39.55N	7.14W
Idar-Oberstein	10	Dg	49.42N	7.18 E
Idarwald	12	Je	49.50N	7.13 E
Idel	7	Id	64.08N	34.12 E
Ideles	32	Ie	23.49N	5.55 E
Ider	27	Hb	49.16N	100.41 E
Idfū	33	Fe	24.58N	32.52 E
Idhi Óros	5	Ih	35.15N	24.45 E
Idhra	15	Gl	37.20N	23.30 E
Idhra	15	Gl	37.21N	23.28 E
Idhras, Kólpos-	15	Gl	37.22N	23.22 E
Idice	14	Ff	44.35N	11.49 E
Idil	24	Id	37.21N	41.54 E
Idini	32	Df	17.58N	15.40W
Idiofa	36	Cc	4.59S	19.36 E
Idjil, Kédia d'-	32	Ee	22.38N	12.33W
Idkerberget	8	Fd	60.23N	15.14 E
Idle	9	Mh	53.27N	0.48W
Idlib	23	Eb	35.55N	36.38 E
Idokogo	36	Ab	0.35N	9.19 E
Idolo, Isla del-	48	Kg	21.25N	97.27W
Idre	8	Ec	61.52N	12.43 E
Idrica	8	Mh	56.18N	28.55 E
Idrija	14	Id	46.00N	14.02 E
Idro, Lago d'-	14	Ee	45.47N	10.30 E
Idstein	10	Ef	50.14N	8.16 E
Idževan	16	Ni	40.52N	45.04 E
Iecava	8	Jh	56.40N	23.40 E
Iecava	8	Kh	56.33N	24.11 E
Iepê	55	Gf	22.40S	51.05W
Ieper/Ypres	11	Id	50.51N	2.53 E
Ierápetra	15	In	35.01N	25.45 E
Ierisós	15	Gi	40.24N	23.53 E
Ierisoú, Kólpos-	15	Gi	40.26N	23.55 E
Iernut	15	Hc	46.27N	24.15 E
Ie-Shima	29b	Ab	26.43N	127.47 E
Ieshima-Shotō	29	Dd	34.40N	134.30 E
Iesolo	14	Ge	45.32N	12.38 E
Iezerul, Vîrful-	15	Hd	45.28N	24.57 E
Ifakara	36	Gd	8.08S	36.41 E
Ifaki	34	Gd	7.48N	5.14 E
'Ifāl, Wādī al-	24	Fh	28.07N	35.02 E
Ifalik Atoll	57	Fd	7.15N	144.27 E
Ifanadiana	37	Hd	21.17S	47.35 E
Ife	34	Fd	7.28N	4.34 E
Iferouâne	31	Hg	19.04N	8.24 E
Ifetesene	32	Hd	25.30N	4.33 E
Ifni	32	Ed	29.15N	10.08W
Ifon	34	Gd	6.58N	5.55 E
Iforas, Adrar des-	30	Hg	19.00N	2.00 E
Iga	29	Ed	34.49N	136.12 E
Igal	10	Nj	46.32N	17.57 E
Iganga	36	Fb	0.37N	33.29 E
Igara Paraná, Rio-	54	Dd	2.09N	71.47W
Igarapava	55	Ie	20.03S	47.47W
Igarapé-Açu	54	Id	1.07S	47.37W
Igarapé-Miri	54	Id	1.59S	48.58W
Igarka	22	Kc	67.28N	86.35 E
Igatimi	56	Ib	24.05S	55.30W
Igawa	36	Fd	8.46S	34.23 E
Igbetti	34	Fd	8.45N	4.08 E
Iğdır	24	Kc	39.56N	44.02 E
Iggesund	7	Df	61.38N	17.04 E
Iglesias	14	Ck	39.19N	8.32 E
Iglesiente	14	Ck	39.20N	8.40 E
Igli	32	Gc	30.27N	2.18W
Iglim al Janūbīyah = Southern Region (EN) [2]	35	Dd	6.00N	30.00 E
Iglino	17	Hi	54.50N	56.28 E
Igloolik	39	Kc	69.24N	81.49W
Ignace	42	Ig	49.26N	91.41W
Ignalina	7	Gi	55.22N	26.13 E
Ignatovo	7	If	60.49N	37.48 E
Iğneada	24	Bb	41.50N	27.58 E
Iğneada Burun	15	Lh	41.54N	28.03 E
Igombe	36	Fc	4.25S	31.58 E
Igoumenitsa	15	Dj	39.30N	20.16 E
Igra	19	Fd	57.33N	53.10 E
Igreja, Morro de-	55	Hi	28.08S	49.30W
Igren	16	Ie	48.29N	35.13 E
Igrim	19	Gc	63.12N	64.29 E
Iguaçu, Rio-	52	Kh	25.36S	54.36W
Igualada	13	Nc	41.35N	1.38 E
Iguala de la Independencia	47	Ee	18.21N	99.32W
Iguana, Sierra de la-	48	Id	26.30N	100.15W
Iguape	55	Ig	24.43S	47.33W
Iguariaça, Serra do-	55	Ei	29.03S	55.15W
Iguassu Falls (EN) = Iguazú, Cataratas del-	52	Kh	25.41S	54.26W
Iguatemi	54	If	14.35S	49.02W
Iguatemi, Rio-	55	Ef	23.55S	54.10W
Iguatu	53	Mf	6.22S	39.18W
Iguazú, Cataratas del- = Iguassu Falls (EN)	52	Kh	25.41S	54.26W
Iguéla	36	Ac	1.55S	9.19 E
Iguidi, 'Erg-	30	Gf	27.00N	6.00W
Ihavandiffulu Atoll	25a	Ba	7.00N	72.55 E
Iheya-Jima	29b	Ab	27.03N	127.57 E
Ih-Hajrhan	27	Ib	46.56N	105.56 E
Ihiala	34	Gd	5.51N	6.51 E
Ihirene	32	He	20.28N	4.37 E
Ihnāsiyat al Madīnah	24	Dh	29.05N	30.56 E
Ih-Obo-Ula	27	Gc	44.55N	95.20 E
Ihosy	31	Lk	22.25S	46.07 E
Ihotry, Lac-	37	Gd	21.56S	43.41 E
Ihrhove, Westoverledingen-	12	Ja	53.10N	7.27 E
Ihsaniye	24	Dc	36.55N	34.46 E
Ihtiman	15	Gg	42.26N	23.49 E
Ih-Ula	27	Hb	49.27N	101.27 E
Ii	7	Fd	65.19N	25.27 E
Iida	28	Ng	35.31N	137.50 E
Iide-San	29	Fc	37.52N	139.41 E
Iijoki	7	Fd	65.20N	25.17 E
Iisaku/Isaku	8	Le	59.14N	27.41 E
Iisalmi	7	Ge	63.34N	27.11 E
Iisvesi	8	Lb	62.45N	26.50 E
Iittala	8	Kc	61.04N	24.10 E
Iivaara	7	Gd	65.47N	29.40 E
Iiyama	29	Fc	36.52N	138.20 E
Iizuka	29	Be	33.38N	130.41 E
Ija	20	Fe	55.02N	101.00 E
Ijebu Ode	34	Fd	6.49N	3.56 E
IJmuiden, Velsen-	12	Gb	52.28N	4.35 E
Ijoubbâne, 'Erg-	34	Da	22.30N	6.00W
IJssel	11	Lb	52.30N	6.00 E
IJsselmeer	11	Lb	52.45N	5.25 E
IJsselmuiden	12	Hb	52.34N	5.56 E
IJsselstein	12	Hb	52.01N	5.02 E
Ijui	56	Jc	28.23S	53.55W
Ijuí, Rio-	55	Eh	27.58S	55.20W
Ijüin	29	Bf	31.37N	130.24 E
Ijuizinho, Rio-	55	Ei	28.20S	54.28W
Ijuw	64e	Bb	0.31S	166.57 E
Ijzendijke	12	Fc	51.20N	3.37 E
IJzer	11	Ic	51.09N	2.43 E
Ik	5	Ld	55.55N	52.36 E
Ikaalinen	7	Ff	61.46N	23.03 E
Ikalamavony	37	Hd	21.10S	46.32 E
Ikamatua	62	De	42.17S	171.42 E
Ikaria	15	Jl	37.35N	26.10 E
Ikarion Pélagos	15	Jl	37.30N	26.35 E
Ikast	8	Ch	56.08N	9.10 E
Ikatski Hrebet	20	Gf	54.00N	111.15 E
Ikawa	29	Fd	35.13N	138.14 E
Ikeda [Jap.]	29	Cd	34.01N	133.48 E
Ikeda [Jap.]	27	Pc	42.55N	143.27 E
Ikeda-Ko	29	Bf	31.14N	130.34 E
Ikej	20	Ff	54.12N	100.04 E
Ikeja	34	Fd	6.36N	3.21 E
Ikela	31	Ji	1.11S	23.16 E
Ikelemba	36	Cb	0.07N	18.17 E
Ikerre	34	Gd	7.30N	5.14 E
Ikerssuaq	41	Ie	65.10N	39.45W
Iki	29	Ae	33.45N	129.45 E
Iki-Kaikyō	28	Jh	33.45N	129.50 E
Ikitsuki-Shima	29	Ae	33.25N	129.25 E
Ikizdere	24	Ib	40.47N	40.33 E
Ikom	34	Gd	5.58N	8.42 E
Ikongo	36	Gd	9.04S	36.51 E
Ikopa	37	Hc	16.50S	46.50 E
Ikot Ekpene	34	Gd	5.10N	7.43 E
Ikuno	29	Dd	35.10N	134.48 E
Ikurangi, Mount-	64p	Bb	21.12S	159.45W
Ila	34	Fd	7.40N	4.40 E
Ilaferh	32	He	21.50N	1.20 E
Ilagan	22	Oh	17.10N	121.54 E
Ilām	25	Hc	26.54N	87.56 E
Ilam	23	Gc	33.38N	46.26 E
Ilām	23	Gc	33.00N	47.00 E
Ilan	27	Lg	24.45N	121.44 E
Ilanski	20	Ee	56.10N	96.03 E
Ilaro	34	Fd	6.53N	3.01 E
Iława	10	Pc	53.37N	19.33 E

Index Symbols

- [1] Independent Nation
- [2] State, Region
- [3] District, County
- [4] Municipality
- [5] Colony, Dependency
- Continent
- Physical Region
- Historical or Cultural Region
- Mount, Mountain
- Volcano
- Hill
- Mountains, Mountain Range
- Hills, Escarpment
- Plateau, Upland
- Pass, Gap
- Plain, Lowland
- Delta
- Salt Flat
- Valley, Canyon
- Crater, Cave
- Karst Features
- Depression
- Polder
- Desert, Dunes
- Forest, Woods
- Heath, Steppe
- Oasis
- Cape, Point
- Coast, Beach
- Cliff
- Peninsula
- Isthmus
- Sandbank
- Island
- Atoll
- Rock, Reef
- Islands, Archipelago
- Rocks, Reefs
- Coral Reef
- Well, Spring
- Geyser
- River, Stream
- Waterfall Rapids
- River Mouth, Estuary
- Lake
- Salt Lake
- Intermittent Lake
- Reservoir
- Swamp, Pond
- Canal
- Glacier
- Ice Shelf, Pack Ice
- Ocean
- Sea
- Gulf, Bay
- Strait, Fjord
- Lagoon
- Bank
- Seamount
- Tablemount
- Ridge
- Shelf
- Basin
- Escarpment, Sea Scarp
- Fracture
- Trench, Abyss
- National Park, Reserve
- Point of Interest
- Recreation Site
- Cave, Cavern
- Historic Site
- Ruins
- Wall, Walls
- Church, Abbey
- Temple
- Scientific Station
- Airport
- Port
- Lighthouse
- Mine
- Tunnel
- Dam, Bridge

Index Symbols

[1] Independent Nation
[2] State, Region
[3] District, County
[4] Municipality
[5] Colony, Dependency
[6] Continent
[7] Physical Region

Mount, Mountain
Volcano
Hill
Mountains, Mountain Range
Hills, Escarpment
Plateau, Upland

Historical or Cultural Region

Pass, Gap
Plain, Lowland
Delta
Salt Flat
Valley, Canyon
Crater, Cave
Karst Features

Depression
Polder
Desert, Dunes
Forest, Woods
Heath, Steppe
Oasis
Cape, Point

Coast, Beach
Cliff
Peninsula
Isthmus
Sandbank
Island
Atoll

Rock, Reef
Islands, Archipelago
Rocks, Reefs
Coral Reef
Well, Spring
Geyser
River, Stream

Waterfall, Rapids
River Mouth, Estuary
Lake
Salt Lake
Intermittent Lake
Reservoir
Swamp, Pond

Canal
Glacier
Ice Shelf, Pack Ice
Ocean
Sea
Gulf, Bay
Strait, Fjord

Lagoon
Bank
Seamount
Tablemount
Ridge
Shelf
Basin

Escarpment, Sea Scarp
Trench, Abyss
Fracture
National Park, Reserve
Point of Interest
Recreation Site
Cave, Cavern

Historic Site
Ruins
Wall, Walls
Church, Abbey
Temple
Scientific Station
Airport

Port
Lighthouse
Mine
Tunnel
Dam, Bridge

J

Index Symbols

[1] Independent Nation	[~] Historical or Cultural Region
[2] State, Region	[▲] Mount, Mountain
[3] District, County	[▲] Volcano
[4] Municipality	[▲] Hill
[5] Colony, Dependency	[▲] Mountains, Mountain Range
[6] Continent	[▲] Hills, Escarpment
[7] Physical Region	[▲] Plateau, Upland

[)(] Pass, Gap	[▲] Depression	[▲] Coast, Beach
[▽] Plain, Lowland	[▽] Polder	[◆] Islands, Archipelago
[▽] Delta	[▲] Cliff	[◆] Rocks, Reefs
[▽] Salt Flat	[▲] Peninsula	[◆] Coral Reef
[▽] Valley, Canyon	[▽] Forest, Woods	[▬] Sandbank
[▿] Crater, Cave	[▽] Heath, Steppe	[◆] Island
[▫] Karst Features	[▽] Oasis	[◎] Atoll
	[▼] Cape, Point	[S] River, Stream

[▲] Rock, Reef	[▲] Waterfall Rapids	[▬] Canal
[▲] River Mouth, Estuary	[▲] Glacier	[▬] Bank
[◆] Rocks, Reefs	[▬] Ice Shelf, Pack Ice	[▬] Fracture
[◆] Coral Reef	[▬] Ocean	[▬] Seamount
[▬] Sandbank	[▬] Sea	[▬] Tablemount
[◆] Island	[▬] Gulf, Bay	[▬] Ridge
[◎] Atoll	[▬] Strait, Fjord	[▬] Shelf
[S] River, Stream	[▬] Swamp, Pond	[▬] Basin

[▬] Lagoon	[▬] Escarpment, Sea Scarp	[▬] Historic Site
[▬] Bank	[▬] Trench, Abyss	[▬] Ruins
[▬] Fracture	[▬] National Park, Reserve	[▬] Wall, Walls
[▬] Seamount	[▬] Point of Interest	[▬] Church, Abbey
[▬] Tablemount	[▬] Recreation Site	[▬] Temple
[▬] Ridge	[▬] Scientific Station	[▬] Scientific Station
[▬] Shelf	[▬] Cave, Cavern	[▬] Airport

[▬] Port	
[▬] Lighthouse	
[▬] Mine	
[▬] Tunnel	
[▬] Dam, Bridge	

Jadar [Yugo.]	15	Ce	44.38N	19.16 E
Jaddi, Rās-	25	Cc	25.14N	63.31 E
Jade	10	Ec	53.25N	8.05 E
Jadebusen	10	Ec	53.30N	8.10 E
Jadīd Ra's al Fīl	35	Dc	12.40N	25.43 E
Jadito Wash	46	Ji	35.22N	110.50W
J.A.D. Jensens Nunatakker	41	Hf	62.45N	48.20W
Jädraås	8	Gd	60.51N	16.28 E
Jadransko More=Adriatic Sea (EN)	5	Hg	43.00N	16.00 E
Jadrin	7	Li	55.57N	46.11 E
Jādū	33	Bc	31.57N	12.01 E
Ja'ēl	35	Ic	10.56N	51.09 E
Jaén [3]	13	If	38.00N	3.30W
Jaén	13	Ig	37.46N	3.47W
Jæren	8	Af	58.45N	5.45 E
Jærens rev	8	Af	58.45N	5.29 E
Jaffa, Cape-	59	Hg	36.58S	139.40 E
Jaffna	22	Ji	9.40N	80.00 E
Jafr, Qā' al-	24	Gg	30.17N	36.20 E
Jägala Jõgi	8	Ke	59.28N	25.04 E
Jagdalpur	22	Kh	19.04N	82.02 E
Jagdaqi	27	La	50.26N	124.02 E
Jaghbūb, Wāḩāt al-=Jarabub Oasis (EN)	30	Jf	29.41N	24.43 E
Jagotin	16	Gd	50.17N	31.47 E
Jagst	10	Fg	49.14N	9.11 E
Jaguapitã	55	Gf	23.07S	51.33W
Jaguaquara	54	Kf	13.32S	39.58W
Jaguarão	56	Jd	32.34S	53.23W
Jaguarão, Río-	55	Fk	32.39S	53.12W
Jaguarari	54	Jf	10.16S	40.12W
Jaguari	55	Ei	29.30S	54.41W
Jaguari, Rio- [Braz.]	55	Ei	29.42S	55.07W
Jaguari, Rio- [Braz.]	55	If	22.41S	47.17W
Jaguariaíva	56	Kb	24.15S	49.42W
Jaguaribe	54	Ke	5.53S	38.37W
Jaguaribe, Rio	52	Mf	4.25S	37.45W
Jaguaruana	54	Kd	4.50S	37.47W
Jagüey Grande	49	Gb	22.32N	81.08W
Jahadyjaha	17	Pc	67.03N	72.01 E
Jahām, 'Irq-	24	Li	26.12N	47.00 E
Jahorina	14	Mg	43.42N	18.35 E
Jahrom	23	Hd	28.31N	53.33 E
Jaice	23	Ff	44.21N	17.17 E
Jaicoa, Cordillera-	51a	Ab	18.25N	67.05W
Jaicós	54	Je	7.21S	41.08W
Jailolo	26	If	1.05N	127.30 E
Jailolo, Selat-	26	If	0.05N	129.05 E
Jaina, Isla de-	48	Ng	20.14N	90.40W
Jainca	27	Hd	35.57N	102.00 E
Jaipur	22	Jg	26.55N	75.49 E
Jaisalmer	25	Ec	26.55N	70.54 E
Jaja	20	De	56.12N	86.26 E
Jājarm	24	Qd	36.58N	56.27 E
Jajdúdorog	10	Ri	47.49N	21.30 E
Jajere	34	Hc	11.59N	11.26 E
Jajpan	18	Hd	40.23N	70.50 E
Jajsan	16	Td	50.51N	56.14 E
Jajva	19	Fd	59.20N	57.16 E
Jajva	17	Hg	59.16N	56.42 E
Jakarta	22	Mj	6.10S	106.46 E
Jakobshavn/Ilulissat	67	Nc	69.20N	50.50W
Jakobstad/Pietarsaari	7	Fe	63.40N	22.42 E
Jakoruda	15	Gg	42.02N	23.40 E
Jakupica	15	Eh	41.43N	21.26 E
Jakutsk	22	Oc	62.13N	129.49 E
Jakutskaja ASSR → Saha (Jakutija), respublika	20	Hc	67.00N	130.00 E
Jal	45	Ej	32.07N	103.12W
Jalaid Qi (Inder)	27	Lb	46.41N	122.52 E
Jalājil	24	Kj	25.41N	45.28 E
Jalālābād	23	Lc	34.26N	70.28 E
Jalālah al Baḩrīyah, Jabal al-	24	Eh	29.20N	32.20 E
Jalālah al Qiblīyah, Jabal al-	24	Eh	28.42N	32.22 E
Jalán, Río-	49	Df	15.43N	87.34W
Jalandhar	22	Jf	31.19N	75.34 E
Jalapa [3]	49	Cf	14.35N	89.55W
Jalapa [Guat.]	47	Gf	14.38N	89.59W
Jalapa [Mex.]	48	Mi	17.43N	92.49W
Jalapa [Nic.]	47	Gf	13.55N	86.08W
Jalapa Enriquez	39	Jh	19.32N	96.55W
Jalasjarvi	7	Fe	62.30N	22.45 E
Jales	55	Ge	20.16S	50.33W
Jālgaon	25	Fd	21.01N	75.34 E
Jalhay	12	Hd	50.34N	5.58 E
Jalībah	24	Lg	30.35N	46.32 E
Jalib Shahab	24	Lg	30.23N	46.09 E
Jalingo	34	Hd	8.53N	11.22 E
Jalisco [2]	47	Dd	20.20N	103.40W
Jāliţah=La Galite (EN)	30	He	37.32N	8.56 E
Jāliţah, Canal de-	14	Cm	37.20N	9.00 E
Jallas	13	Cb	42.54N	9.08W
Jālna	25	Fe	19.50N	75.53 E
Jalón	13	Kc	41.47N	1.04W
Jalostotitlán	48	Hg	21.12N	102.28W
Jalpa	48	Hg	21.38N	102.58W
Jalpaiguri	25	Hc	26.31N	88.44 E
Jalpan	48	Jg	21.14N	99.29W
Jalpug, Ozero-	16	Fg	45.25N	28.40 E
Jalta	19	Dg	44.30N	34.10 E
Jaltepec, Río-	48	Li	17.26N	94.59W
Jālū	33	Dd	28.30N	21.05 E
Jālū, Wāḩāt-=Gialo Oasis (EN)	30	Jf	29.00N	21.20 E
Jaluit Atoll	57	Hd	6.00N	169.35 E
Jalūlā'	24	Ke	34.16N	45.10 E
Jalutorovsk	19	Gd	56.40N	66.18 E
Jam [Iran]	24	Pe	35.45N	55.02 E
Jam [Iran]	24	Oi	27.50N	52.22 E
Jama/Jaama	8	Lf	58.59N	27.45 E
Jamaari	30	Ig	12.06N	10.14 E
Jamaica	49	Jc	20.12N	75.09W
Jamaica	38	Lh	18.15N	77.30W
Jamaica [1]	39	Lh	18.15N	77.30W
Jamaica Channel	47	Ie	18.00N	75.30W
Jamaica Channel (EN)= Jamaïque, Canal de-	49	Jd	18.00N	75.30W
Jamaïque, Canal de-= Jamaica Channel (EN)	49	Jd	18.00N	75.30W
Jamal, Poluostrov-=Yamal Peninsula (EN)	21	Ib	70.00N	70.00 E
Jamalo-Neneckij respublika	20	Cc	67.00N	75.00 E
Jamālpur	25	Hd	24.55N	89.56 E
Jamāme	31	Lh	0.04N	42.46 E
Jamantau, Gora-	5	Le	54.15N	58.06 E
Jamanxim, Rio-	52	Kf	4.43S	56.18W
Jamari, Rio-	54	Fe	8.27S	63.30W
Jamarovka	20	Gf	50.38N	110.16 E
Jambi	22	Oj	1.38S	123.42 E
Jambi [3]	26	Dg	1.36S	103.37 E
Jambol [2]	15	Jg	42.15N	26.35 E
Jambol	15	Jg	42.29N	26.30 E
Jambongan, Pulau-	26	Ge	6.41N	117.25 E
Jambuair, Tanjung-	26	Ce	5.16N	97.30 E
Jambusar	25	Ed	22.03N	72.48 E
James Bay	38	Kd	51.00N	80.30W
Jameson Land	41	Jd	70.45N	23.45W
James River [U.S.]	38	Je	42.52N	97.18W
James River [U.S.]	44	Ig	36.56N	76.27W
James Ross	66	Re	64.15S	57.45W
James Ross Strait	42	Hc	69.50N	96.30W
Jamestown [Austl.]	59	Hf	33.12S	138.36 E
Jamestown [N.D.-U.S.]	43	Hb	46.54N	98.42W
Jamestown [N.Y.-U.S.]	43	Lc	42.05N	79.15W
Jamestown [St.Hel.]	31	Gj	15.56S	5.43W
Jamestown Reservoir	45	Gc	47.15N	98.40W
Jamm	8	Mf	58.24N	28.15 E
Jammer Bugt	7	Bh	57.20N	9.30 E
Jammu	22	Jf	32.44N	74.52 E
Jammu and Kashmir [3]	25	Fb	34.00N	76.00 E
Jāmnagar	22	Jg	22.28N	70.04 E
Jamno, Jezioro-	10	Mb	54.15N	16.10 E
Jampol	16	Fe	48.16N	28.17 E
Jämsä	7	Ff	61.52N	25.12 E
Jamsah	24	Ei	27.38N	33.35 E
Jämsänkoski	8	Kc	61.55N	25.11 E
Jamshedpur	22	Kg	22.48N	86.11 E
Jamsk	20	Ke	59.37N	154.10 E
Jämtland [2]	7	De	63.00N	14.40 E
Jämtland	8	Fa	63.25N	14.05 E
Janā	24	Mi	27.22N	49.54 E
Jana	21	Pb	71.31N	136.32 E
Janakpur	25	Hc	26.42N	85.55 E
Janaucu, Ilha-	54	Hc	0.30N	50.10W
Janaul	17	Gh	56.16N	54.59 E
Janda, Laguna de la-	13	Gh	36.15N	5.51W
Jandaia	55	Gc	17.06S	50.07W
Jandaq	24	Pe	34.02N	54.26 E
Jandiatuba, Rio-	54	Ed	3.28S	68.42W
Jandowae	59	Ke	26.47S	151.06 E
Jandula	13	Hf	38.03N	4.06W
Jane Peak	62	Cf	45.20S	168.19 E
Janesville	43	Jc	42.41N	89.01W
Jangada	55	Db	15.14S	56.29W
Jangada, Rio-	55	Db	15.12S	56.24W
Jangao Shan	27	Gf	25.31N	98.08 E
Jange	27	Ie	31.59N	105.28 E
Jangijer	18	Gd	40.18N	68.50 E
Jangijul	19	Gg	41.07N	69.03 E
Jangirabad	18	Ed	40.03N	65.59 E
Jango	55	Ee	20.27S	55.29W
Jangxi Sheng (Chiang-hsi Sheng)=Kiangsi (EN) [2]	27	Kf	28.00N	116.00 E
Jangy-Bazar	18	Hd	41.40N	70.52 E
Janikowo	10	Od	52.45N	18.07 E
Janīn	24	Ff	32.28N	35.18 E
Janisjarvi, Ozero-	7	He	62.00N	31.00 E
Janja	14	Nf	44.40N	19.19 E
Jan Mayen	5	Fa	71.00N	8.30W
Jan Mayen Ridge (EN)	5	Fb	69.00N	8.00W
Jano-Indigirskaja Nizmennost	20	Ib	71.00N	139.30 E
Janos	47	Cb	30.56N	108.08W
Jánoshalma	10	Pj	46.18N	19.20 E
Jánosháza	10	Ni	47.07N	17.10 E
Janów Lubelski	10	Sf	50.43N	22.24 E
Janów Podlaski	10	Td	52.11N	23.11 E
Jansenville	37	Cf	32.56S	24.40 E
Jansha Jang	21	Mg	28.46N	104.38 E
Janski Zaliv	21	Pb	72.00N	136.00 E
Jantarny	8	Hj	54.53N	19.55 E
Jantra	15	If	43.38N	25.34 E
Januária	54	Jg	15.29S	44.22W
Janūbīyah, Aş Şaḩrā' al-= Southern Desert (EN)	30	Jf	24.00N	30.00 E
Janykurgan	19	Gg	43.55N	67.14 E
Janzhang Ansha	27	Ke	9.30N	116.59 E
Japan (EN)	21	Pf	35.00N	135.00 E
Japan (EN)=Nippon [1]	22	Pf	38.00N	137.00 E
Japan, Sea of- (EN)= Japonskoje More	21	Pf	40.00N	134.00 E
Japan, Sea of- (EN)= Nippon Kai	21	Pf	40.00N	134.00 E
Japan, Sea of- (EN)=Tong-Hae	21	Pf	40.00N	134.00 E
Japan Basin (EN)	27	Nc	40.00N	135.00 E
Japan Trench (EN)	3	If	37.00N	143.00 E
Japiim	54	De	7.37S	72.54W
Japonskoje More=Japan, Sea of- (EN)	21	Pf	40.00N	134.00 E
Jäppilä	8	Lb	62.23N	27.26 E
Japtiksale	17	Pb	69.25N	72.29 E
Japurá	54	Ed	1.24S	69.25W
Japurá, Rio-	52	Jf	3.08S	64.46W
Jaqué	49	Hj	7.31N	78.10W
Jaquet, Point-	51g	Ba	15.38N	61.26W
Jaquirana	55	Gi	28.54S	50.23W
Jar	7	Mg	58.17N	52.06 E
Jarabub Oasis (EN)= Jaghbūb, Wāḩāt al-	30	Jf	29.41N	24.43 E
Jarābulus	24	Hd	36.49N	38.01 E
Jaraguá [Braz.]	55	Hb	15.45S	49.20W
Jaraguá [Braz.]	55	Hh	26.29S	49.04W
Jaraguá, Serra do-	55	Hh	26.40S	49.15W
Jaraguari	55	Ee	20.09S	54.25W
Jaraiz de la Vera	13	Gd	40.04N	5.45W
Jarama	13	Id	40.02N	3.39W
Jaramillo	56	Gg	47.11S	67.09W
Jarandilla	13	Gd	40.08N	5.39W
Jaransk	19	Ed	57.18N	47.55 E
Jarānwāla	25	Eb	31.20N	73.26 E
Jarash	24	Ff	32.17N	35.54 E
Jarau, Cêrro do-	55	Dj	30.18S	56.32W
Jarbah	30	Ie	33.48N	10.54 E
Järbo	7	Df	60.43N	16.36 E
Jarcevo	16	Hb	55.05N	32.45 E
Jarcevo	20	Ed	60.15N	90.10 E
Jardāwīyah	24	Jj	25.24N	42.42 E
Jardim	54	Gh	21.28S	56.09W
Jardine River	59	Ib	11.10S	142.30 E
Jardines de la Reina, Archipiélago de los-	47	Id	20.50N	78.55W
Jardinópolis	55	Ie	21.02S	47.46W
Jarega	17	Fe	63.27N	53.31 E
Jaremča	16	De	48.31N	24.33 E
Jarenga	7	Le	62.08N	49.03 E
Jarez de Garcías Salinas	47	Dd	22.39N	103.00W
Järfälla	8	Ge	59.24N	17.50 E
Jargava	15	Lc	46.27N	28.27 E
Jari, Rio-	52	Kf	1.09S	51.54W
Jarīd, Shaţţ al-	30	He	33.42N	8.26 E
Jarīr, Wādī-	24	Jj	25.38N	42.30 E
Jarjīs	32	Jc	33.30N	11.07 E
Jarkovo	17	Mh	57.26N	67.05 E
Jarmah	33	Bd	26.32N	13.04 E
Järna	8	Ge	59.06N	17.34 E
Jarnac	11	Fi	45.41N	0.10W
Järnlunden	8	Ff	58.10N	15.40 E
Jarny	11	Le	49.09N	5.53 E
Jarocin	10	Ne	51.59N	17.31 E
Jaroměř	10	Lf	50.21N	15.55 E
Jaroměřice nad Rokytnou	10	Lg	49.06N	15.54 E
Jaroslavl	6	Jd	57.37N	39.52 E
Jaroslavskaja Oblast [3]	19	Dd	57.45N	39.15 E
Jaroslavski	28	Lb	44.10N	132.13 E
Jarosław	10	Sf	50.02N	22.42 E
Järpen	8	Ea	63.21N	13.29 E
Jarrāḩī	24	Mg	30.44N	48.46 E
Jarroto, Ozero-	17	Dc	67.55N	71.40 E
Jar-Sale	20	Cc	66.50N	70.50 E
Jartai	27	Id	39.45N	105.46 E
Jartai Yanchi	27	Id	39.45N	105.40 E
Jarudej	17	Od	65.50N	71.50 E
Jarud Qi (Lubei)	27	Lc	44.30N	120.55 E
Järva-Jaani/Jarva-Jani	8	Ke	59.00N	25.49 E
Jarva-Jani/Järva-Jaani	8	Ke	59.00N	25.49 E
Jarvakanbdi/Järvakandi	8	Kf	58.45N	24.44 E
Järvakandi/Jarvakanbdi	8	Kf	58.45N	24.44 E
Järvenpää	7	Ff	60.28N	25.06 E
Jarvis Island	57	Ke	0.23S	160.01W
Järvsö	7	Df	61.43N	6.10 E
Jaščera	8	Ne	59.05N	30.00 E
Jaselda	16	Ec	52.07N	26.29 E
Jasień	10	Le	51.46N	5.01 E
Jasikan	34	Fd	7.24N	0.28 E
Jasinja	10	Uh	48.14N	24.31 E
Jasinovataja	16	Je	48.05N	37.57 E
Jasiołka	10	Rg	49.47N	21.30 E
Jasīra	35	He	.57N	45.16 E
Jasīred Mayd	35	Hc	11.12N	47.3 E
Jāsk	23	Id	25.38N	57.46 E
Jaškul	16	Nf	46.17N	45.10 E
Jaškul	16	Nf	46.11N	45.17 E
Jasło	10	Rg	49.45N	21.29 E
Jasmund	10	Jb	54.32N	13.35 E
Jasnogorsk	16	Jb	54.29N	37.42 E
Jasny	19	Fe	51.01N	59.59 E
Jasny	20	Hf	53.18N	128.03 E
Jason Islands	56	Hh	51.00S	61.00W
Jasper [Alta.-Can.]	39	Hd	52.53N	118.05W
Jasper [Al.-U.S.]	43	Je	33.50N	87.17W
Jasper [Fl.-U.S.]	44	Fj	30.31N	82.57W
Jasper [In.-U.S.]	44	Df	38.24N	86.56W
Jasper [Tn.-U.S.]	44	Eh	35.04N	85.38W
Jasper [Tx.-U.S.]	45	Jk	30.55N	94.59W
Jasper Seamount (EN)	38	Gf	30.32N	122.42W
Jaşşān	24	Kf	32.58N	45.53 E
Jastrebarsko	14	Je	45.40N	15.39 E
Jastrowie	10	Mc	53.26N	16.49 E
Jastrzebie Zdrój	10	Og	49.58N	18.34 E
Jászapáti	10	Qi	47.31N	20.09 E
Jászárokszállás	10	Pi	47.38N	19.59 E
Jászberény	10	Pi	47.30N	19.55 E
Jász-Nagykun-Szolnok	10	Qi	47.15N	20.30 E
Jászság	10	Pi	47.25N	20.00 E
Jataí	53	Kg	17.53S	51.43W
Jatapu, Rio-	54	Gd	2.30S	58.17W
Játiva/Xàtiva	13	Lf	38.59N	0.31W
Jatobá, Rio-	55	Ea	12.23S	54.07W
Jaú	56	Kb	22.18S	48.33W
Jaú, Rio-	54	Fd	1.55S	61.25W
Jaua, Cerro-	54	Fc	4.48N	64.26W
Jauaperi, Rio-	52	Jf	1.26S	61.35W
Jauja	54	Cf	11.48S	75.30W
Jaumave	48	Jf	23.25N	99.23W
Jaunanna	8	Lg	57.13N	27.10 E
Jaunelgava/Jaunjelgava	7	Fh	56.37N	25.06 E
Jaunfeld	14	Id	46.35N	14.45 E
Jaungulbene	8	Lh	57.00N	26.42 E
Jaunjelgava/Jaunelgava	7	Fh	56.37N	25.06 E
Jaunpiebalga	8	Lg	57.05N	26.03 E
Jaunpur	25	Gc	25.44N	82.41 E
Jauru	55	Ed	18.35S	54.17W
Jauru, Rio- [Braz.]	54	Hg	18.40S	54.36W
Jauru, Rio- [Braz.]	55	Dc	16.22S	57.36W
Java (EN)=Jawa	21	Mj	7.20S	110.00 E
Javalambre	13	Ld	40.06N	1.00W
Javalambre, Sierra de-	13	Ld	40.05N	1.00W
Javan	18	Ge	38.19N	69.01 E
Javānrūd	24	Le	34.48N	46.30 E
Javari, Rio-	52	If	4.21S	70.02W
Java Sea (EN)=Jawa, Laut-	21	Mj	5.00S	110.00 E
Java Trench (EN)	3	Hk	10.30S	110.00 E
Jávea	13	Mf	38.47N	0.10 E
Javier	13	Kb	42.36N	1.13W
Javor	14	Mf	44.07N	18.59 E
Javorie	10	Ph	48.27N	19.18 E
Javornik	10	Jh	48.10N	13.35 E
Javorníky	10	Og	49.20N	18.20 E
Javorov	16	Cd	50.00N	23.27 E
Javorová skála	10	Kg	49.31N	14.30 E
Jävre	7	Ed	65.09N	21.29 E
Jawa=Java (EN)	21	Mj	7.20S	110.00 E
Jawa, Laut-=Java Sea (EN)	21	Mj	5.00S	110.00 E
Jawa Barat [3]	26	Eh	7.00S	107.00 E
Jawa Tengah [3]	26	Eh	7.30S	110.00 E
Jawa Timur [3]	26	Fh	8.00S	113.00 E
Jawf, Wādī-	33	If	15.50N	45.30 E
Jawor	10	Me	51.03N	16.11 E
Jaworzno	10	Pf	50.13N	19.15 E
Jaya, Puncak-	57	Ee	4.10S	137.00 E
Jayapura	58	Fe	2.32S	140.42 E
Jayawijaya, Pegunungan-	26	Kg	4.30S	139.30 E
Jāyezān	24	Mg	30.50N	49.52 E
Jaypur	25	He	18.51N	82.35 E
Jazāyer va Banāder-e Khalīj-e Fārs va Daryā-ye Omān→ Hormozgān	23	Id	27.30N	56.00 E
Jaz Mūrīān, Hāmūn-e-	23	Id	27.20N	58.55 E
Jazva	17	Hf	60.23N	56.50 E
Jazvān	24	Md	36.58N	48.40 E
Jazykovo	7	Li	54.20N	47.22 E
Jazzīn	24	Ff	33.32N	35.34 E
Jdiouia	13	Mi	35.56N	0.50 E
Jeannetty, Ostrov-	20	Ka	76.45N	158.25 E
Jean-Rabel	49	Kd	19.52N	73.11W
Jebala	13	Gi	35.25N	5.30W
Jebal Bārez, Kūh-e-	23	Id	28.30N	58.20 E
Jebba	34	Fd	9.08N	4.50 E
Jebel	15	Ed	45.33N	21.14 E
Jebha	13	Hi	35.13N	4.40W
Jedincy	16	Ee	48.06N	27.19 E
Jedisa	16	Nh	42.32N	44.14 E
Jędrzejów	10	Qf	50.39N	20.18 E
Jeetze	10	Hc	53.09N	11.04 E
Jefferson	45	Ie	42.01N	94.23W
Jefferson, Mount- [Nv.-U.S.]	43	Dd	38.46N	116.55W
Jefferson, Mount- [Or.-U.S.]	46	Ed	44.40N	121.47W
Jefferson City	39	Jf	38.34N	92.10W
Jefferson River	46	Jd	45.56N	111.30W
Jeffersonville	44	Ef	38.17N	85.44W
Jef-Jef el Kebir	35	Ca	20.30N	21.25 E
Jefremov	19	De	53.11N	38.07 E
Jega	34	Fc	12.13N	4.23 E
Jegersfontein	37	De	29.44S	25.29 E
Jegorjevsk	7	Ji	55.25N	39.07 E
Jegorlyk	16	Lf	46.32N	41.52 E
Jegorlykskaja	16	Lf	46.34N	40.44 E
Jehegnadzor	16	Nj	39.47N	45.18 E
Jeja	16	Kf	46.39N	38.36 E
Jejsk	19	Df	46.40N	38.15 E
Jēkabpils	19	Cd	56.30N	25.59 E
Jekaterinburg (Sverdlovsk)	22	Id	56.51N	60.36 E
Jekaterinburgskaja oblast	19	Gd	59.00N	62.00 E
Jekaterinovka	16	Nc	52.04N	44.30 E
Jelabuga	19	Fd	55.48N	52.05 E
Jelai	26	Fg	2.59S	110.45 E
Jelan	16	Md	50.57N	43.43 E
Jelancy	20	Ff	52.44N	106.27 E
Jelanec	16	Gf	47.42N	31.50 E
Jelcz	10	Ne	51.01N	17.18 E
Jelec	6	Je	52.37N	38.30 E
Jeleckj	17	Lc	67.03N	64.15 E
Jelenia Góra	10	Lf	50.55N	15.46 E
Jelenia Góra [2]	10	Lf	50.55N	15.45 E
Jelgava	19	Cd	56.39N	23.41 E
Jelica	15	Df	43.47N	20.20 E
Jelin vrh	15	Cf	43.02N	19.27 E
Jelizavety, Mys-	5	Qd	54.30N	142.40 E
Jelizovo	16	Fc	53.24N	29.00 E
Jelizovo	20	Kf	53.06N	158.20 E
Jelling	8	Ci	55.45N	9.26 E
Jelnja	16	Hb	54.35N	33.12 E
Jeloguj	20	Dd	63.10N	87.45 E
Jelow Gīr	24	Lf	32.58N	47.48 E
Jeløy	8	De	58.30N	10.40 E
Jelsk	16	Fd	51.49N	29.13 E
Jelva	17	Ee	63.05N	50.50 E
Jemaja, Pulau-	26	Ef	2.55N	105.45 E
Jemanželinsk	19	Ge	54.45N	61.20 E
Jember	26	Fh	8.10S	113.42 E
Jemca	7	Je	63.32N	41.56 E
Jemca	7	Je	63.04N	40.18 E
Jemeppe-sur-Sambre	12	Gd	50.28N	4.40 E
Jeminay	27	Eb	47.28N	85.48 E
Jemnice	10	Lg	49.01N	15.35 E
Jena	10	Hf	50.56N	11.35 E
Jenakijevo	16	Ke	48.12N	38.18 E
Jenašimski Polkan, Gora-	20	Ee	59.50N	92.45 E
Jendyr	17	Mf	61.38N	67.20 E
Jeneponto	26	Gh	5.41S	119.42 E
Jenisej=Yenisey (EN)	21	Kb	71.50N	82.40 E
Jenisejsk	20	Ee	58.27N	92.10 E
Jenisejski Krjaž=Yenisey Ridge (EN)	21	Ld	59.00N	92.30 E
Jenisejski Zaliv=Yenisey Bay (EN)	20	Db	72.00N	81.00 E
Jennersdorf	14	Kd	46.56N	16.08 E
Jennings	45	Jk	30.13N	92.39W
Jenny Lind	42	Hc	68.50N	101.30W
Jenny Point	51g	Bb	15.28N	61.15W
Jensen	46	Kf	40.22N	109.17W
Jens Munk	42	Jc	69.40N	79.40W
Jequié	53	Lg	13.51S	40.05W
Jequitaí	55	Jc	17.15S	44.28W
Jequitaí, Rio	55	Jc	17.04S	44.50W
Jequitinhonha, Rio-	52	Mg	15.51S	38.53W
Jerada	32	Gc	34.19N	2.09W
Jeralijev	19	Fg	43.12N	51.43 E
Jerbogačën	20	Fd	61.15N	107.57 E
Jérémie	47	Je	18.39N	74.08W
Jeremoabo	54	Kf	10.04S	38.21W
Jerer	35	Gd	7.40N	43.48 E
Jerevan	6	Kg	40.11N	44.30 E
Jerez, Punta-	48	Kf	22.54N	97.46W
Jerez de la Frontera	13	Fh	36.41N	6.08W
Jerez de los Caballeros	13	Ff	38.19N	6.46W
Jergeni	5	Kf	47.00N	44.00 E
Jericho	59	Jd	23.36S	146.08 E
Jermak	19	He	52.02N	76.55 E
Jermakovskoje	20	Ef	53.16N	92.24 E
Jermentau	19	He	51.38N	73.10 E
Jermolajevo (Kumertau)	19	Fe	52.46N	55.47 E
Jeroaquara	55	Gb	15.23S	50.25W
Jerofej Pavlovič	20	Hf	53.58N	121.57 E
Jerome	46	He	42.43N	114.31W
Jersa	17	Fc	66.19N	52.32 E
Jersey	9	Kl	49.15N	2.10W
Jersey City	43	Mc	40.44N	74.04W
Jerseyville	45	Kg	39.07N	90.20W
Jeršov	19	Ee	51.20N	48.17 E
Jertarski	17	Lh	56.47N	64.25 E
Jerte	13	Fe	39.58N	6.17W
Jerusalem (EN)= Yerushalayim	22	Ff	31.46N	35.14 E
Jeruslan	16	Od	50.20N	46.25 E
Jervis Bay	59	Kg	35.05S	150.44 E
Jerzu	14	Dk	39.47N	9.31 E
Jesberg	12	Lc	51.00N	9.09 E
Jesenice	14	Jf	44.14N	15.34 E
Jesenice	14	Id	46.27N	14.04 E
Jeseník	10	Nf	50.14N	17.12 E
Jesi	14	Hg	43.31N	13.14 E
Jesil	19	Ge	51.53N	66.24 E
Jeskianhor, Kanal-	18	Fe	39.15N	66.00 E
Jessej	20	Fc	68.29N	102.10 E
Jessentuki	16	Mg	44.03N	42.51 E
Jessheim	7	Cf	60.09N	11.11 E
Jessore	25	Hd	23.10N	89.13 E
Ještěd	10	Kf	50.42N	14.59 E
Jestro, Wabe-	30	Lh	4.11N	42.09 E
Jesup	43	Ke	31.36N	81.53W
Jesús Carranza	48	Li	17.26N	95.02W
Jesús María	56	Hd	30.59S	64.06W
Jesús María, Boca de-	48	Ke	24.29N	97.40W
Jesús María, Río-	48	Gg	21.55N	104.30W
Jetmore	45	Gg	38.03N	99.54W
Jever	10	Dc	53.35N	7.54 E
Jevgenjevka	18	Kc	43.27N	77.40 E
Jevišovka	10	Mh	48.52N	16.36 E
Jevlah	19	Eg	40.35N	47.10 E
Jevnaker	7	Cf	60.15N	10.28 E
Jevpatorija	19	Df	45.12N	33.18 E
Jeyḩūn	24	Pi	27.16N	55.12 E
Jeypore → Jaypur	25	He	18.51N	82.35 E
Jezercës	5	Hg	42.26N	19.49 E
Jezero	14	Lf	44.21N	17.10 E
Jeziorak, Jezioro-	10	Pc	53.50N	19.35 E
Jeziorany	10	Qc	53.58N	20.46 E
Jeziorka	10	Rd	52.10N	21.06 E
Jhang Sadar	25	Eb	31.16N	72.19 E
Jhānsi	22	Jg	25.26N	78.35 E
Jhelum	25	Eb	32.56N	73.44 E
Jhelum	21	Jf	31.12N	72.08 E
Jiaji → Qionghai	27	Jh	19.25N	110.28 E
Jialing Jiang	21	Mg	29.34N	106.35 E
Jiamusi	22	Pe	46.49N	130.21 E
Ji'an [China]	27	Mc	41.03N	126.10 E
Ji'an [China]	22	Ng	27.12N	114.59 E
Jianchang	28	Ed	40.49N	119.46 E
Jianchuan	27	Gf	26.32N	99.53 E
Jiande (Baisha)	27	Kf	29.3 N	119.17 E
Jiang'an	27	If	28.40N	105.07 E
Jiangao Shan	27	Gf	25.3 N	98.08 E
Jiangbiancun	27	Kf	27.13N	115.57 E
Jiangcheng	27	Hg	22.37N	101.48 E
Jiangdu (Xiannümiao)	28	Eh	32.30N	119.33 E
Jianghua (Shuikou)	27	Jg	24.58N	111.56 E
Jiangjin	27	If	29.15N	106.18 E
Jiangle	27	Kf	26.46N	117.29 E
Jiangling (Jingzhou)	27	Je	30.21N	112.10 E
Jiangmen	27	Jg	22.35N	113.02 E
Jiangpu	28	Eh	32.03N	118.37 E
Jiangshan	28	Ej	28.45N	118.37 E
Jiangsu Sheng (Chiang-su Sheng)=Kiangsu (EN) [2]	27	Ke	33.00N	120.00 E
Jiangyou (Zhongba)	27	He	31.48N	104.39 E
Jianhu	28	Eh	33.28N	119.47 E
Jianli	27	Jf	29.50N	112.55 E
Jian'ou	27	Kf	27.08N	118.20 E
Jianping (Yebaishou)	27	Kc	41.55N	119.37 E
Jianshi	27	Ie	30.32N	109.43 E
Jianshui	27	Hg	23.39N	102.46 E
Jianyang	27	Kf	27.23N	118.03 E
Jiaocheng	27	Jd	37.32N	112.09 E
Jiaoding Shan	27	Lc	41.11N	120.01 E
Jiaohe [China]	27	Mc	43.43N	127.20 E
Jiaohe [China]	28	De	38.01N	116.17 E
Jiaolai He [China]	28	Ef	37.07N	119.35 E
Jiaolai He [China]	28	Fc	43.02N	120.48 E
Jiaoliu He	28	Gb	45.21N	122.48 E
Jiaonan (Wanggezhuang)	28	Eg	35.53N	119.58 E

Index Symbols

[1] Independent Nation · [2] State, Region · [3] District, County · [4] Municipality · [5] Colony, Dependency · Continent · Physical Region · Historical or Cultural Region · Mount, Mountain · Volcano · Hill · Mountains, Mountain Range · Hills, Escarpment · Plateau, Upland · Pass, Gap · Plain, Lowland · Delta · Salt Flat · Valley, Canyon · Crater, Cave · Karst Features · Depression · Polder · Desert, Dunes · Forest, Woods · Heath, Steppe · Oasis · Cape, Point · Coast, Beach · Cliff · Peninsula · Isthmus · Sandbank · Island · Atoll · Rock, Reef · Islands, Archipelago · Rocks, Reefs · Coral Reef · Well, Spring · Geyser · River, Stream · Waterfall Rapids · River Mouth, Estuary · Lake · Salt Lake · Intermittent Lake · Reservoir · Swamp, Pond · Canal · Glacier · Ice Shelf, Pack Ice · Ocean · Sea · Gulf, Bay · Strait, Fjord · Lagoon · Bank · Seamount · Tablemount · Ridge · Shelf · Basin · Escarpment, Sea Scarp · Fracture · Trench, Abyss · National Park, Reserve · Point of Interest · Recreation Site · Cave, Cavern · Historic Site · Ruins · Wall, Walls · Church, Abbey · Temple · Scientific Station · Airport · Port · Lighthouse · Mine · Tunnel · Dam, Bridge

Jiaoxian 27 Kd 36.20N 120.00 E
Jiaozhou-Wan 28 Ff 36.10N 120.15 E
Jiaozuo 22 Nf 35.15N 113.18 E
Jiashan 28 Fi 30.51N 120.54 E
Jiashan (Mingguang) 28 Dh 32.47N 118.00 E
Jiashi/Payzawat 27 Cd 39.29N 76.39 E
Jiawang 28 Dg 34.27N 117.26 E
Jiaxian 28 Bh 33.58N 113.13 E
Jiaxing 27 Le 30.44N 120.46 E
Jiayin (Chaoyang) 27 Nb 48.52N 130.21 E
Jiayu 27 Jf 30.00N 113.57 E
Jiayuguan 27 Gd 39.49N 98.18 E
Jibalei 35 Ic 10.07N 50.47 E
Jibão, Serra do- 55 Jb 14.48S 45.15W
Jibiya 34 Gc 13.06N 7.14 E
Jibou 15 Gb 47.16N 23.15 E
Jicarón, Isla- 49 Gj 7.16N 81.47W
Jičín 10 Lf 50.26N 15.22 E
Jiddah 22 Fg 21.29N 39.12 E
Jiddat al Ḩarāsīs 23 Ie 20.05N 56.00 E
Jiehu → Yinan 28 Eg 35.33N 118.27 E
Jieshou 28 Ch 33.17N 115.22 E
Jiesjavrre 7 Fb 69.40N 24.12 E
Jiexiu 27 Jd 37.00N 112.00 E
Jieyang 27 Kg 23.32N 116.25 E
Jieznas/Eznas 8 Kj 54.34N 24.17 E
Jifn, Wādī al- 24 Jj 25.48N 42.15 E
Jiftūn, Jazā'ir- 24 Ei 27.13N 33.56 E
Jīgley 35 He 4.25N 45.22 E
Jiguaní 49 Ic 20.22N 76.26W
Jigüey, Bahía de- 49 Hb 22.08N 78.05W
Jigzhi 27 He 33.28N 101.29 E
Jihlava 10 Mh 48.55N 16.37 E
Jihlava 10 Lg 49.24N 15.34 E
Jihlavské vrchy 10 Lg 49.15N 15.20 E
Jihočeský kraj [3] 10 Kg 49.05N 14.30 E
Jihomoravský kraj [3] 10 Mg 49.10N 16.40 E
Jijel 32 Ib 36.48N 5.46 E
Jijel [3] 32 Ib 36.45N 5.45 E
Jijia 15 Lc 46.54N 28.05 E
Jijiga 35 Gd 9.21N 42.48 E
Jijona 13 Lf 38.32N 0.30W
Jikharrah 33 Dd 29.17N 21.38 E
Jilava 15 Je 44.20N 26.05 E
Jilf al Kabīr, Haḑabat al- 33 Ee 23.30N 26.00 E
Jilib 31 Lh 0.29N 42.47 E
Jilin 27 Mc 43.51N 126.33 E
Jilin Sheng (Chi-lin Sheng) =Kirin (EN) [2] 27 Mc 43.00N 126.00 E
Jiliu He 27 La 52.02N 120.41 E
Jiloca 13 Kc 41.21N 1.39W
Jima=Jimma (EN) 31 Kh 7.39N 36.49 E
Jimāl, Wādī- 24 Fj 24.40N 35.06 E
Jimaní 49 Ld 18.28N 71.51W
Jimbe 36 De 11.05S 24.00 E
Jimbolia 15 Dd 45.48N 20.43 E
Jimena 13 Ig 37.50N 3.28W
Jimena de la Frontera 13 Gh 36.26N 5.27W
Jiménez 47 Dc 27.08N 104.55W
Jiménez del Teul 48 Gf 23.10N 104.05W
Jimma (EN)=Jima 31 Kh 7.39N 36.49 E
Jimo 28 Ff 36.24N 120.27 E
Jimsar 27 Ec 43.59N 89.04 E
Jimulco 48 He 25.20N 103.10W
Jināh 24 Dj 25.20N 30.31 E
Jinan=Tsinan (EN) 22 Nf 36.35N 117.00 E
Jincheng [China] 27 Jd 35.32N 112.53 E
Jincheng [China] 28 Fd 41.12N 121.25 E
Jinchuan /Quqên 27 He 31.02N 102.02 E
Jind 25 Fc 29.19N 76.19 E
Jindřichův Hradec 10 Kg 49.09N 15.00 E
Jinfo Shan 27 If 29.01N 107.14 E
Jing/Jinghe 27 Dc 44.39N 82.50 E
Jing'an 28 Cj 28.51N 115.21 E
Jingbian (Zhangjiapan) 27 Id 37.32N 108.45 E
Jingde 28 Ei 30.18N 118.30 E
Jingdezhen 22 Ng 29.18N 117.18 E
Jingfeng → Hexigten Qi 27 Kc 43.15N 117.31 E
Jinggang Shan 27 Jf 26.42N 114.07 E
Jinggu 27 Hg 23.28N 100.39 E
Jinghai 28 De 38.57N 116.56 E
Jinghe/Jing 27 Dc 44.39N 82.50 E
Jinghong (Yunjinghong) 27 Hg 21.59N 100.48 E
Jinghong Dao 27 Je 9.45N 114.28 E
Jingjiang 28 Fh 32.01N 120.15 E
Jingle 28 Ae 38.22N 111.56 E
Jingmen 27 Je 31.00N 112.11 E
Jingning 27 Id 35.30N 105.45 E
Jingping → Pinglu 28 Be 39.32N 112.14 E
Jingpo Hu 28 Jc 43.50N 128.53 E
Jingshan 28 Bi 31.04N 113.08 E
Jingtai 27 Hd 37.10N 104.08 E
Jingxian [China] 27 If 26.40N 109.37 E
Jingxian [China] 27 Ke 30.41N 118.29 E
Jingxing (Weishui) 28 Ce 38.03N 114.09 E
Jingyu 28 Ic 42.25N 126.48 E
Jingyuan 27 Hd 36.35N 104.40 E
Jingzhi 28 Ef 36.18N 119.22 E
Jingzhou → Jiangling 27 Je 30.21N 112.10 E
Jinhu (Licheng) 28 Eh 33.01N 119.01 E
Jinhua 27 Kf 29.09N 119.38 E
Jining [China] 22 Nf 37.26N 116.36 E
Jining [China] 22 Ne 41.02N 113.07 E
Jinja 31 Kh 0.26N 33.13 E
Jin Jiang 28 Cj 28.23N 115.48 E
Jinkou 28 Ci 30.20N 114.07 E
Jinotega [3] 49 Eg 14.00N 85.25W
Jinotega 47 Gf 13.06N 86.00W
Jinotepe 47 Gf 11.51N 86.12W
Jinping 27 Hg 22.45N 103.15 E
Jinsha 27 If 27.18N 106.16 E
Jinsha → Nantong 28 Fh 32.06N 120.52 E
Jinshan 28 Fi 30.54N 121.09 E
Jinshan → Harqin Qi 28 Ed 41.57N 118.40 E
Jinshi 28 Aj 29.03N 111.52 E
Jinta 27 Gc 40.00N 99.00 E
Jintan 28 Ei 31.45N 119.34 E
Jinxi 27 Lc 40.46N 120.50 E
Jinxian [China] 27 Ld 39.06N 121.44 E
Jinxian [China] 28 Dj 28.21N 116.16 E
Jinxiang 28 Dg 35.04N 116.19 E
Jinyang 27 Hf 27.39N 103.12 E
Jinyun 28 Fj 28.39N 120.05 E
Jinzhai (Meishan) 28 Ci 31.40N 115.52 E
Jinzhou 22 Oe 41.09N 121.08 E
Jinzū-Gawa 29 Ec 36.45N 137.13 E
Jiparaná, Rio- 52 Jf 8.03S 62.52W
Jipijapa 54 Bd 1.22S 80.34W
Jiquilisco 49 Cg 13.19N 88.35W
Jiquilisco, Bahía de- 49 Cg 13.10N 88.28W
Jirjā 33 Fd 26.20N 31.53 E
Jishou 27 If 28.18N 109.43 E
Jishu 28 Ib 44.16N 126.50 E
Jisr ash Shughur 24 Ge 35.48N 36.19 E
Jiu 15 Gd 43.47N 23.48 E
Jiucai Ling 27 Jf 25.33N 111.18 E
Jiucheng → Wucheng 28 Df 37.12N 116.04 E
Jiujiang 22 Ng 29.39N 116.00 E
Jiuling Shan 27 Jf 28.55N 114.50 E
Jiulong/Gyaisi 27 Hf 28.58N 101.33 E
Jiuquan (Suzhou) 22 Lf 39.46N 98.34 E
Jiurongcheng 28 Gf 37.22N 122.33 E
Jiutai 27 Mc 44.10N 125.50 E
Jīwani, Rās- 25 Cc 25.01N 61.44 E
Jixi [China] 28 Ei 30.04N 118.36 E
Jixi [China] 22 Pe 45.15N 130.55 E
Jixian [China] 28 Cg 35.23N 114.04 E
Jixian [China] 28 Cf 37.34N 115.34 E
Jixian [China] 28 Dd 40.03N 117.24 E
Jiyang 28 Df 36.59N 117.11 E
Jiyuan 28 Bg 35.06N 112.35 E
Jiyun He 28 De 39.05N 117.45 E
Jiz, Wādī al- 35 Ib 16.12N 52.14 E
Jīzān 22 Gh 16.54N 42.32 E
Jize 28 Cf 36.54N 114.52 E
Jizera 10 Kf 50.10N 14.43 E
Jizerské Hory 10 Lf 50.50N 15.13 E
Jizl, Wādī al- 24 Hj 25.39N 38.25 E
Jizō-Zaki 28 Lg 35.33N 133.18 E
Jmbe 36 De 10.20S 16.40 E
Jnchengjiang → Hechi 27 Ig 24.44N 108.02 E
Joaçaba 55 Gh 27.10S 51.30W
Joal-Fadiout 34 Bc 14.10N 16.51W
João Câmara 54 Ke 5.32S 35.48W
João Monlevade 55 Kd 19.50S 43.08W
João Pessoa 53 Mf 7.07S 34.52W
João Pinheiro 54 Ig 17.45S 46.10W
Joaquín V. González 56 Hb 25.00S 64.11W
Jobado 49 Ic 20.54N 77.17W
Jódar 13 Ig 37.50N 3.21W
Jodhpur 22 Jg 26.17N 73.02 E
Jodoigne/Geldenaken 12 Gd 50.43N 4.52 E
Joensuu 6 Ic 62.36N 29.46 E
Joerg Plateau 66 Qf 75.00S 69.30W
Joes Hill 64g Bb 1.48N 157.19W
Jōetsu 27 Od 37.06N 138.15 E
Joeuf 12 Ie 49.14N 6.01 E
Jôf di Montasio 14 Hd 46.26N 13.26 E
Joffre, Mount- 46 Ha 50.32N 115.13W
Jogbani 25 Hc 26.25N 87.15 E
Jõgeva/Jygeva 7 Gg 58.46N 26.26 E
Joghatāy 24 Qd 36.36N 57.01 E
Joghatāy, Kūh-e- 24 Qd 36.30N 57.00 E
Jōhana 29 Ec 36.31N 136.54 E
Johannesburg 31 Jk 26.15S 28.00 E
Jōhen 29 Ce 32.57N 132.35 E
John Day 46 Fd 44.25N 118.57W
John Day River 43 Cb 45.44N 120.39W
John H. Kerr Reservoir 44 Hg 36.31N 78.18W
John Martin Reservoir 45 Eg 38.05N 103.02W
John o' Groat's 9 Jc 58.38N 3.05W
Johnson 45 Fh 37.34N 101.45W
Johnson, Pico de- 48 Cc 29.13N 112.07W
Johnson City [Tn.-U.S.] 43 Kd 36.19N 82.21W
Johnson City [Tx.-U.S.] 45 Gk 30.17N 98.25W
Johnsons Crossing 42 Ed 60.29N 133.17W
Johnsons Point 51d Bb 17.02N 61.53W
Johnstone, Lake- 59 Ef 32.20S 120.40 E
Johnstone Strait 46 Ca 50.25N 126.00W
Johnston Island 57 Kc 17.00N 168.30W
Johnston Island [5] 58 Kc 17.00N 168.30W
Johnstown [N.Y.-U.S.] 44 Jd 43.01N 74.22W
Johnstown [Pa.-U.S.] 43 Lc 40.20N 78.56W
Johor Baharu 22 Mi 1.28N 103.45 E
Joia 55 Ei 28.39S 54.08W
Joigny 11 Jg 47.59N 3.24 E
Joinvile 53 Lh 26.18S 48.50W
Joinville 11 Lf 48.27N 5.08 E
Joinville Island 66 Re 63.15S 55.45W
Jokau 35 Ed 8.24N 33.49 E
Jokela 8 Kd 60.33N 24.59 E
Jokelbugten 41 Kc 78.25N 19.00W
Jokioinen 8 Jd 60.49N 23.28 E
Jokkmokk 7 Ec 66.36N 19.51 E
Jøkuleggi 8 Cc 61.03N 8.12 E
Jolfā 24 Kc 38.57N 45.38 E
Joliet 43 Jc 41.32N 88.05W
Joliette 42 Kg 46.01N 73.26W
Jolo 26 He 6.00N 121.00 E
Jolo Group 21 Oi 6.00N 121.09 E
Jølstravatnet 8 Bc 61.30N 6.15 E
Jomala 8 Hd 60.09N 19.58 E
Jombang 26 Fh 7.33S 112.14 E
Jomda 27 Ge 31.37N 98.20 E
Jönåker 8 Gf 58.44N 16.40 E
Jonava/Ionava 7 Fi 55.05N 24.17 E
Jonê 27 He 34.35N 103.32 E
Jones Bank 9 Fl 49.50N 8.00W
Jonesboro [Ar.-U.S.] 43 Id 35.50N 90.42W
Jonesboro [La.-U.S.] 45 Jj 32.15N 92.43W
Jones Mountains 66 Pf 73.32S 94.00W
Jones Sound 38 Kb 76.00N 85.00W
Jonesville 44 Fg 36.41N 83.06W
Jonglei [3] 35 Ed 7.20N 32.00 E
Jonglei 35 Ed 6.50N 31.18 E
Jonglei, Tur'ah-=Jonglei Canal (EN) 35 Ed 9.22N 31.30 E
Jonglei Canal (EN)=Jonglei, Tur'ah- 35 Ed 9.22N 31.30 E
Joniškėlis/Ioniškelis 8 Ki 56.00N 24.14 E
Joniškis/Ioniškis 7 Fh 56.16N 23.37 E
Jönköping 6 Hd 57.47N 14.11 E
Jönköping [2] 7 Dh 57.30N 14.30 E
Jonquière 42 Kg 48.25N 71.15W
Jonuta 48 Mh 18.05N 92.08W
Jonzac 11 Fi 45.27N 0.26W
Joplin 39 Jf 37.06N 94.31W
Jordan 43 Fb 47.19N 106.55W
Jordan 23 Ec 31.46N 35.33 E
Jordan (EN)=Al Urdun [1] 22 Ff 31.00N 36.00 E
Jordan Valley 46 Ge 42.58N 117.03W
Jordão, Rio- 55 Fg 25.46S 52.07W
Jorhāt 22 Lg 26.45N 94.13 E
Jörn 7 Ed 65.04N 20.02 E
Joroinen 7 Ge 62.11N 27.50 E
Jørpeland 7 Bg 59.01N 6.03 E
Jos 31 Hh 9.55N 8.54 E
José A. Guisasola 55 Bn 38.40S 61.05W
José Battle y Ordóñez 55 Ek 33.28S 55.07W
José Bonifácio 55 He 21.03S 49.41W
José de San Martín 56 Ff 44.02S 70.29W
Joselandia 55 Dc 16.32S 56.12W
José Otávio 55 Ej 31.17S 54.07W
José Pedro Varela 55 Ek 33.27S 54.32W
Joseph, Lake- 44 Hc 45.14N 79.45W
Joseph Bonaparte Gulf 57 Df 14.55S 128.15 E
Josephine Seamount (EN) 5 Eh 36.52N 14.20W
Joseph Lake 42 Kf 52.48N 65.17W
Joshimath 25 Fb 30.34N 79.34 E
Joškar-Ola 6 Kd 56.40N 47.55 E
Jos Plateau 30 Hh 10.00N 9.30 E
Josselin 11 Dg 47.57N 2.33W
Jostedalen 8 Bc 61.35N 7.20 E
Jostedalsbreen 7 Bf 61.40N 7.00 E
Jostefonn 8 Bc 61.26N 6.33 E
Jost Van Dyke 51a Db 18.28N 64.45W
Jotunheimen 5 Gc 61.40N 8.20 E
Joubertberge 37 Ac 18.45S 13.55 E
Joué-lès-Tours 11 Gg 47.21N 0.40 E
Jouquara, Rio- 55 Db 15.06S 57.06W
Joure, Haskerland- 12 Hb 52.58N 5.47 E
Joutsa 7 Gf 61.44N 26.07 E
Joutseno 7 Gf 61.06N 28.30 E
Jovan, Deli- 15 Fe 44.15N 22.13 E
Jovellanos 49 Gb 22.48N 81.12W
Joviânia 55 Hc 17.49S 49.30W
Jowhar 31 Lh 2.46N 45.32 E
Jow Kār 24 Me 34.26N 48.42 E
Jowzjān [3] 23 Kb 36.30N 66.00 E
Joya, Laguna de la- 48 Mj 15.55N 93.40W
Jreïda 32 Df 18.19N 16.03W
Jrian Jaya [3] 26 Kg 3.55S 138.00 E
Juan Aldama 47 Dd 24.19N 103.21W
Juana Ramírez, Isla- 48 Kg 21.50N 97.40W
Juan Blanquier 55 Cl 35.46S 59.18W
Juancheng 28 Cg 35.33N 115.30 E
Juan de Fuca, Strait of- 38 Ge 48.20N 124.00W
Juan de Nova, Ile- 30 Lj 17.03S 42.45 E
Juan E. Barra 55 Bm 37.48S 60.29W
Juan Fernández, Archipielago-=Juan Fernández, Islands (EN) 52 Ii 33.00S 80.00W
Juan Fernandez Islands (EN)=Juan Fernández, Archipielago- 52 Ii 33.00S 80.00W
Juan G. Bazán 55 Bg 24.33S 60.50W
Juangriego 50 Eg 11.05N 63.57W
Juanjuy 54 Ce 7.11S 76.45W
Juan L. Lacaze 55 Dl 34.26S 57.27W
Juárez [Arg.] 56 Ie 37.40S 59.48W
Juárez [Mex.] 48 Id 27.37N 100.44W
Juárez, Sierra de- 48 Bb 32.00N 115.50W
Juarzohn 34 Dd 5.20N 8.58W
Juàzeirinho 54 Ke 7.04S 36.35W
Juàzeiro 53 Lf 9.25S 40.30W
Juàzeiro do Norte 53 Mf 7.12S 39.20W
Jūbā 31 Kh 4.51N 31.37 E
Juba (EN)=Ganāne, Webi- 30 Lh 0.15S 42.38 E
Juba, Rio- 55 Db 14.59S 57.44W
Jūbāl, Maḑīq- 24 Ei 27.40N 33.55 E
Jubaland (EN) 30 Lh 1.00N 42.00 E
Jubayl [Eg.] 24 Eh 28.12N 33.38 E
Jubayl [Leb.] 24 Fe 34.07N 35.39 E
Jubayt [Sud.] 35 Fb 18.57N 36.50 E
Jubayt [Sud.] 35 Fa 20.59N 36.18 E
Jubbada Dhexe [3] 35 Ge 1.15N 42.30 E
Jubbada Hoose [3] 35 Gf 0.30S 42.00 E
Jubbah 24 Ih 28.02N 40.56 E
Jubilee Lake 59 Fe 29.10S 126.40 E
Juby, Cap- 30 Ff 27.57N 12.55W
Júcar/Xúquer 5 Fh 39.09N 0.14W
Juçara 55 Gb 15.53S 50.51W
Jucaro 49 Hc 21.37N 78.51W
Jüchen 12 Ic 51.06N 6.30 E
Juchipila 48 Hg 21.25N 103.07W
Juchipila, Río- 48 Hg 21.03N 103.25W
Juchitán de Zaragoza 39 Jh 16.26N 95.01W
Jučjugej 20 Jd 63.20N 142.15 E
Judas, Punta- 49 Ei 9.31N 84.32W
Judayyidat 'Ar'ar 23 Fc 31.22N 41.26 E
Judenburg 14 Ic 47.10N 14.40 E
Juding Shan 27 He 31.30N 104.00 E
Judith Mountains 46 Kc 47.12N 109.15W
Judith River 46 Kc 47.44N 109.38W
Judoma 20 Ie 59.08N 135.03 E
Judomski Hrebet 20 Jd 61.05N 141.30 E
Juegang → Rudong 28 Fh 32.19N 121.11 E
Juelsminde 8 Di 55.43N 10.01 E
Jufrah, Wāḩāt al-=Giofra Oasis (EN) 30 If 29.10N 16.00 E
Jug 5 Kc 60.45N 46.20 E
Jug 17 Hh 57.43N 56.12 E
Jugo Osetija 19 Eg 42.20N 44.05 E
Jugorski poluostrov 17 Kb 69.30N 62.30 E
Jugorski Šar, Proliv- 19 Gb 69.45N 60.35 E
Jugoslavija = Yugoslavia (EN) [1] 6 Hg 44.00N 19.00 E
Jugo-Tala 20 Kc 66.03N 151.05 E
Jugydjan 17 Gf 61.42N 54.58 E
Juhaym 24 Kh 29.36N 45.24 E
Juhnov 16 Ib 54.43N 35.12 E
Juhor 15 Ef 43.50N 21.15 E
Juhoslovenská nížina 10 Ph 48.10N 19.40 E
Juhua Dao 28 Fd 40.32N 120.48 E
Juigalpa 49 Eg 12.05N 85.24W
Juina, Rio- 55 Ca 12.36S 58.57W
Juine 11 If 48.32N 2.23 E
Juininha, Rio- 55 Ca 12.55S 59.13W
Juist 10 Cc 53.40N 7.00 E
Juiz de Fora 53 Lh 21.45S 43.20W
Jujuy [2] 56 Gb 23.00S 66.00W
Jukagirskoje Ploskogorje 20 Kc 66.00N 155.30 E
Jukonda 17 Mg 59.38N 67.20 E
Juksejevo 17 Gg 59.52N 54.16 E
Jula 7 Ke 63.48N 44.44 E
Juldybajevo 17 Hj 52.20N 57.52 E
Julesburg 45 Ef 40.59N 102.16W
Juli 54 Eg 16.13S 69.27W
Juliaca 54 Dg 15.30S 70.08W
Julia Creek 59 Id 20.39S 141.45 E
Julian Alps (EN)=Julijske Alpe 14 Hd 46.20N 13.45 E
Juliana Top 54 Gc 3.41N 56.32W
Julianehåb/Qaqortoq 67 Nc 60.50N 46.10W
Jülich 10 Cf 50.56N 6.22 E
Jülicher Borde 12 Id 50.50N 6.30 E
Julijske Alpe=Julian Alps (EN) 14 Hd 46.20N 13.45 E
Julimes 48 Gc 28.25N 105.27W
Júlio de Castilhos 55 Fi 29.14S 53.41W
Jullundur → Jalandhar 22 Jf 31.19N 75.34 E
Julong/New Kowloon 22 Ng 22.20N 114.09 E
Julu 28 Cf 37.13N 115.02 E
Juma 7 Hd 65.05N 33.13 E
Juma He 28 De 39.31N 116.08 E
Jumet, Charleroi- 11 Kd 50.27N 4.26 E
Jumièges 12 Ce 49.26N 0.49 E
Jumilla 13 Kf 38.29N 1.17W
Jümme 12 Ja 53.13N 7.31 E
Junāgadh 25 Ed 21.31N 70.28 E
Junan (Shizilu) 28 Eg 35.10N 118.50 E
Junaynah, Ra's al- 24 Eh 29.01N 33.58 E
Juncal 48 De 24.50N 111.47W
Juncos 51a Cb 18.13N 65.55W
Junction [Tx.-U.S.] 45 Gk 30.29N 99.46W
Junction [Ut.-U.S.] 46 Ig 38.14N 112.13W
Junction City 43 Hd 39.02N 96.50W
Jundiaí 56 Kb 23.11S 46.52W
Jundiaí do Sul 55 Gf 23.27S 50.17W
Jundūbah 32 Ib 36.30N 8.45 E
Jundūbah [3] 32 Ib 36.28N 8.41 E
Juneau 39 Fd 57.20N 134.27W
Junee 59 Jf 34.52S 147.35 E
Jungar Qi (Shagedu) 27 Jd 39.37N 110.58 E
Jungfrau 14 Bd 46.32N 7.58 E
Junggar Pendi=Dzungarian Basin 21 Ke 45.00N 88.00 E
Junín [2] 54 Df 11.30S 75.00W
Junín [Arg.] 53 Ji 34.35S 60.57W
Junín [Peru] 54 Cf 11.10S 76.00W
Junín, Lago de- 54 Cf 11.02S 76.05W
Junín de los Andes 56 Fe 39.56S 71.05W
Juniville 12 Ge 49.24N 4.23 E
Jūniyah 24 Ff 33.59N 35.38 E
Junjaha 17 Jc 66.25N 62.00 E
Junlian 27 Hf 28.12N 104.34 E
Junsele 7 De 63.41N 16.54 E
Juntura 46 Fe 43.45N 118.05W
Junxian (Danjiang) 27 Je 32.31N 111.32 E
Juodupė 8 Kh 56.03N 25.44 E
Juojärvi 8 Mb 62.45N 28.35 E
Juoksengi 7 Fc 66.34N 23.51 E
Jupiá, Represa de- 56 Jb 20.47S 51.39W
Juquiá 55 Ig 24.19S 47.38W
Juquiá, Rio- 55 Ig 24.22S 47.49W
Juquiá, Serra do- 55 Gg 25.10S 52.00W
Jur 20 Ie 59.48N 137.29 E
Jur 30 Jh 8.39N 29.18 E
Jura [2] 14 Ac 47.25N 6.15 E
Jura 5 Gf 46.45N 6.30 E
Jura [3] 11 Lh 46.50N 5.50 E
Jura 9 Hf 56.00N 5.50W
Jura/Jūra 7 Fi 55.03N 22.10 E
Jūra/Jura 7 Fi 55.03N 22.10 E
Jura, Sound of- 9 Hf 55.55N 5.22W
Juradó 54 Cb 7.07N 77.46W
Juratiški 8 Kj 54.02N 26.00 E
Juraybī'āt 24 Lh 29.50N 46.03 E
Juraybȳ'āt 24 Kh 29.08N 45.30 E
Jurbarkas 7 Fi 55.08N 22.47 E
Jurdī, Wādī- 24 Ei 26.33N 32.44 E
Jurga 20 De 55.42N 84.55 E
Jurgamyš 17 Li 55.25N 64.28 E
Juribej 17 Nb 68.55N 69.05 E
Jurien Bay 59 Cf 30.15S 115.00 E
Jurigue, Rio- 55 Ec 16.29S 54.37W
Jurilovca 15 Le 44.46N 28.52 E
Jurja 7 Lg 59.03N 49.20 E
Jurjaha 17 Gc 66.42N 56.00 E
Jurjevec 7 Kh 57.22N 43.06 E
Jurjev-Polski 7 Jh 56.31N 39.44 E
Jurjuzan 17 Hi 55.43N 56.57 E
Jurjuzan 17 Ii 54.52N 58.28 E
Jurla 17 Gg 59.20N 54.16 E
Jurmala/Jūrmala 19 Cd 56.59N 23.38 E
Jūrmala/Jurmala 19 Cd 56.59N 23.38 E
Jurmo 8 Ie 59.50N 21.35 E
Jurong 28 Ei 31.56N 119.10 E
Juruá 54 Ed 3.27S 66.03W
Juruá, Rio- 52 Jf 2.37S 65.44W
Juruena, Rio- 52 Kf 7.20S 58.03W
Jurumirim, Represa de- 56 Kb 23.20S 49.00W
Juruti 54 Gd 2.09S 56.04W
Jurva 8 Ib 62.41N 21.59 E
Jusan-Kō 29a Bc 41.00N 140.20 E
Jusayrah 24 Nj 25.53N 50.36 E
Jusheng 27 Mb 48.44N 126.37 E
Ju Shui 28 Ci 31.09N 114.52 E
Juškozero 19 Dc 64.45N 32.08 E
Jussarö 8 Je 59.50N 23.35 E
Justo Daract 56 Gd 33.52S 65.11W
Jusva 17 Gg 58.59N 54.57 E
Jutaí 54 Ee 5.11S 68.54W
Jutaí, Rio- 52 Jf 2.43S 66.57W
Jüterbg 10 Je 51.59N 13.05 E
Juti 55 Ef 22.52S 54.37W
Jutiapa [3] 49 Bf 14.10N 89.50W
Jutiapa [Guat.] 47 Gf 14.17N 89.54W
Jutiapa [Hond.] 49 Df 15.46N 86.34W
Juticalpa 47 Gf 14.42N 86.15W
Jutland (EN)=Jylland 5 Gd 56.00N 9.15 E
Juuka 7 Ge 63.14N 29.15 E
Juva 7 Gf 61.54N 27.51 E
Juventud, Isla de la-=Pines, Isle of- (EN) 38 Kg 21.40N 82.50W
Juxian 27 Kd 35.33N 118.45 E
Jūybār 24 Od 36.38N 52.53 E
Juye 28 Dg 35.23N 116.05 E
Jūyom 24 Oh 28.10N 54.02 E
Juža 7 Kh 56.36N 42.01 E
Južnaja Keltma 17 Gf 60.30N 55.40 E
Južna Morava 15 Ef 43.41N 21.24 E
Južni Rodopi 15 Ih 41.15N 25.30 E
Južnoje 20 Jg 46.13N 143.27 E
Južno-Jenisejski 20 Ee 58.48N 94.45 E
Južno-Kurilsk 20 Jh 44.05N 145.52 E
Južno-Sahalinsk 22 Qe 46.58N 142.42 E
Južno-Uralsk 19 Ge 54.26N 61.15 E
Južny, Mys- 20 Ke 57.42N 156.55 E
Južny Bug 5 Jf 46.59N 31.58 E
Južny Ural=Southern Urals (EN) 5 Le 54.00N 58.30 E
Jygeva/Jõgeva 7 Gg 58.46N 26.26 E
Jylland=Jutland (EN) 5 Gd 56.00N 9.15 E
Jylland Bank 8 Bh 56.55N 7.20 E
Jyske Ås 8 Dg 57.15N 10.14 E
Jyväskylä 6 Ic 62.14N 25.44 E

K

K2=Godwin Austen (EN) 21 Jf 35.53N 76.30 E
Ka 34 Fc 11.39N 4.11 E
Kaabong 36 Fb 3.31N 34.09 E
Kaahka 19 Fh 37.21N 59.38 E
Kaala 65a Cb 21.31N 158.09W
Kaala-Gomén 63b Be 20.40S 164.24 E
Kaalualu Bay 65a Fe 18.58N 155.37W
Kaamanen 7 Gb 69.06N 27.12 E
Kaap Kruis 37 Ad 21.46S 13.58 E
Kaap Plateau (EN)= Kaapplato 30 Jk 27.30S 23.45 E
Kaapplato=Kaap Plateau (EN) 30 Jk 27.30S 23.45 E
Kaapprovinsie/Cape Province [2] 37 Cf 32.00S 22.00 E
Kaapstad / Cape Town 31 Il 33.55S 18.22 E
Kaarst 12 Ic 51.15N 6.37 E
Kaarta 34 Cc 14.35N 10.00W
Kaba/Habahe 27 Eb 47.53N 86.12 E
Kabaena, Pulau- 26 Hh 5.15S 121.55 E
Kabah 48 Og 20.07N 89.29W
Kabala 34 Cd 9.35N 11.33W
Kabale 36 Ec 1.15S 29.59 E
Kabalega Falls 36 Fb 2.17N 31.41 E
Kabalo 31 Ji 6.03S 26.55 E
Kabaman 63a Aa 4.38S 152.42 E
Kabambare 36 Ec 4.16S 27.07 E
Kabamet 36 Gb 0.30N 35.45 E
Kabanjahe 26 Cf 3.06N 98.30 E
Kabardino-Balkarskaja respublika 19 Eg 43.30N 43.30 E
Kabare 36 Ec 2.29S 28.48 E
Kabasalan 26 He 7.48N 122.45 E
Kaba-Shima [Jap.] 29 Ae 32.45N 129.00 E
Kaba-Shima [Jap.] 29 Ae 32.34N 129.47 E
Kabba 34 Gd 7.50N 6.04 E
Kåbdalis 7 Ec 66.09N 20.00 E
Kaberamaido 36 Fb 1.45N 33.10 E
Kabetogama Lake 45 Jb 48.28N 92.59W
Kabhegy 10 Ni 47.03N 17.39 E
Kabinakagami Lake 44 Ea 48.58N 84.25W
Kabinda 31 Ji 6.08S 24.29 E
Kabīr, Wādī al- 14 Dn 36.23N 9.52 E
Kabīr Kūh 24 Lf 33.25N 46.45 E
Kabkābīyah 35 Cc 13.39N 24.05 E
Kableškovo 15 Kg 42.39N 27.34 E
Kabna 35 Eb 19.10N 32.41 E
Kabo 35 Bd 7.35N 18.38 E
Kābol 22 If 34.31N 69.12 E
Kābol 23 Kc 34.30N 69.00 E
Kabompo 36 De 13.36S 24.12 E
Kabompo 30 Jj 14.11S 23.11 E
Kabondo Dianda 36 Ed 8.53S 25.40 E
Kabongo 36 Ed 7.19S 25.35 E
Kabou 34 Fd 9.27N 0.49 E
Kabūdiyāh, Ra's- 32 Jb 35.14N 11.10 E
Kabūd Rāhang 24 Me 35.12N 48.44 E
Kābul 21 Jf 33.55N 72.14 E
Kabunda 36 Ee 12.13S 29.23 E

Index Symbols

[1] Independent Nation
[2] State, Region
[3] District, County
[4] Municipality
[5] Colony, Dependency
Continent
Physical Region
Historical or Cultural Region
Mount, Mountain
Volcano
Hill
Mountains, Mountain Range
Hills, Escarpment
Plateau, Upland
Pass, Gap
Plain, Lowland
Delta
Salt Flat
Valley, Canyon
Crater, Cave
Karst Features
Depression
Polder
Desert, Dunes
Forest, Woods
Heath, Steppe
Oasis
Cape, Point
Coast, Beach
Cliff
Peninsula
Isthmus
Sandbank
Island
Atoll
Rock, Reef
Islands, Archipelago
Rocks, Reefs
Coral Reef
Well, Spring
Geyser
River, Stream
Waterfall Rapids
River Mouth, Estuary
Lake
Salt Lake
Intermittent Lake
Reservoir
Swamp, Pond
Canal
Glacier
Ice Shelf, Pack Ice
Ocean
Sea
Gulf, Bay
Strait, Fjord
Lagoon
Bank
Seamount
Tablemount
Ridge
Shelf
Basin
Escarpment, Sea Scarp
Fracture
Trench, Abyss
National Park, Reserve
Point of Interest
Recreation Site
Cave, Cavern
Historic Site
Ruins
Wall, Walls
Church, Abbey
Temple
Scientific Station
Airport
Port
Lighthouse
Mine
Tunnel
Dam, Bridge

Kabunga	36	Ec	1.42S	28.08 E
Kaburuang, Pulau-	26	If	3.48N	126.48 E
Kabwe	31	Jj	14.27S	28.27 E
Kača	16	Hg	44.44N	33.32 E
Kačanik	15	Eg	42.14N	21.15 E
Kačanovo	8	Lg	57.24N	27.53 E
Kačergine	8	Jj	54.53N	23.49 E
Kachchh, Gulf of	21	Ig	22.36N	69.30 E
Kachchh, Rann of	25	Dd	23.51N	70.30 E
Kachia	34	Gd	9.52N	7.57 E
Kachikau	37	Cc	18.09S	24.29 E
Kachin [2]	25	Jc	26.00N	97.30 E
Kachul (Kagul)	19	Cf	45.53N	28.14 E
Kačiry	19	He	53.04N	76.07 E
Kačkanar	19	Fd	58.42N	59.35 E
Kačug	20	Ff	54.00N	105.52 E
Kaczawa	10	Me	51.18N	16.27 E
Kadada	16	Oc	53.09N	46.01 E
Kadaň	10	Jf	50.23N	13.16 E
Kadan Kyun	25	Jf	12.30N	98.22 E
Kadeï	30	Ih	3.31N	16.03 E
Kadijevka	19	Df	48.32N	38.40 E
Kadiköy	24	Bb	40.51N	26.50 E
Kadıköy, İstanbul	15	Mi	40.59N	29.01 E
Kadina	59	Hf	33.58S	137.43 E
Kadınhanı	24	Ec	38.15N	32.14 E
Kadiolo	34	Dc	10.34N	5.45W
Kadiri	25	Ff	14.07N	78.10 E
Kadirli	23	Eb	37.23N	36.05 E
Kadja	35	Cc	12.02N	22.28 E
Kadmat Island	25	Ef	11.14N	72.47 E
Kadnikov	7	Jg	59.30N	40.24 E
Kadoka	45	Fe	43.50N	101.31W
Kaduj	7	Ig	59.14N	37.09 E
Kaduna [2]	34	Gc	11.00N	7.30 E
Kaduna	30	Hh	8.45N	5.48 E
Kaduna	31	Hg	10.31N	7.26 E
Kāduqlī	31	Jg	11.01N	29.43 E
Kadykčan	20	Jd	63.05N	146.58 E
Kadžaran	16	Oj	39.11N	46.10 E
Kadžerom	17	Gd	64.41N	55.54 E
Kadži-Saj	18	Kc	42.08N	77.10 E
Kaech'ŏn	28	He	39.42N	125.53 E
Kaédi	31	Fg	16.08N	13.31W
Kaélé	34	Hc	10.07N	14.27 E
Kaena Point	65a	Cb	21.35N	158.17W
Kaeo	62	Ea	35.06S	173.47 E
Kaesŏng	22	Of	37.58N	126.33 E
Kaesŏng Si [2]	28	Ie	38.05N	126.30 E
Kāf	24	Gg	31.24N	37.29 E
Kafakumba	36	Dd	9.41S	23.44 E
Kafan	19	Eh	39.12N	46.28 E
Kafanchan	34	Gd	9.35N	8.18 E
Kaffrine	34	Bc	14.06N	15.33W
Kafia Kingi	35	Cd	9.16N	24.25 E
Kafiréos, Dhiékplous-	15	Hl	38.00N	24.40 E
Kafirévs, Ákra-	15	Hk	38.10N	24.35 E
Kafr ad Dawwār	24	Dg	31.08N	30.07 E
Kafr ash Shaykh	33	Fc	31.07N	30.56 E
Kafta	35	Fc	13.54N	37.11 E
Kafu	36	Fb	1.39N	32.05 E
Kafue	30	Ef	15.56S	28.55 E
Kafue	31	Jj	15.47S	28.11 E
Kafue Dam	36	Ef	15.45S	28.28 E
Kafue Flats	36	Ef	15.40S	26.25 E
Kafufu	36	Fd	7.12S	31.31 E
Kaga	28	Nf	36.18N	136.18 E
Kaga Bandoro	35	Bd	7.02N	19.13 E
Kagalaska	40a	Cb	51.47N	176.23W
Kagalnik	16	Kf	47.04N	39.18 E
Kagami	29	Be	32.34N	130.40 E
Kagan	19	Gh	39.43N	64.32 E
Kagarlyk	16	Ge	49.53N	30.56 E
Kagawa Ken [2]	28	Mg	34.15N	134.15 E
Kagera	30	Ki	0.57S	31.47 E
Kağızman	24	Jb	40.09N	43.07 E
Kagoshima	22	Pf	31.36N	130.33 E
Kagoshima Bay (EN) = Kagoshima-Wan	28	Ki	31.27N	130.40 E
Kagoshima Ken [2]	28	Ki	31.45N	130.40 E
Kagoshima-Taniyama	29	Bf	31.31N	130.31 E
Kagoshima-Wan = Kagoshima Bay (EN)	28	Ki	31.27N	130.40 E
Kagul → Kachul	19	Cf	45.53N	28.14 E
Kahal Tabelbala	32	Gd	28.45N	2.15W
Kahama	36	Fc	3.50S	32.36 E
Kahemba	31	Ii	7.17S	19.00 E
Kahi	16	Oi	41.23N	46.59 E
Kahiu Point	65a	Eb	21.13N	156.58W
Kahler Asten	10	Ee	51.11N	8.29 E
Kahnūj	24	Qi	27.58N	57.47 E
Kahoku	29	Gb	38.30N	141.20 E
Kahoku-Gata	29	Ec	36.40N	136.40 E
Kahoolawe Island	57	Lb	20.33N	156.35W
Kahouanne, Ilet à-	51e	Ab	16.22N	61.47W
Kahovka	19	Df	46.47N	33.32 E
Kahovskoje Vodohranilišče = Kakhovka Reservoir (EN)	5	Jf	47.25N	34.10 E
Kahramanmaraş	23	Eb	37.36N	36.55 E
Kahrūyeh	24	Ng	31.43N	51.48 E
Kâhta	24	Hd	37.46N	38.36 E
Kahuku	65a	Db	21.41N	157.57W
Kahuku Point	65a	Db	21.43N	157.59W
Kahului	65a	Ec	20.53N	156.27W
Kahului Bay	65a	Ec	20.55N	156.30W
Kahurangi Point	62	Ed	40.46S	172.13 E
Kai, Kepulauan-	57	Ee	5.35S	132.45 E
Kaiama	34	Fd	9.36N	3.57 E
Kaiapoi	62	Ee	43.23S	172.39 E
Kaibab Plateau	46	Ih	36.30N	112.15W
Kai Besar	26	Jh	5.35S	133.00 E
Kaidu He/Karaxabar He	27	Ec	41.55N	86.38 E
Kaieteur Falls	54	Gc	5.10N	59.28W
Kaifeng	22	Nf	34.45N	114.25 E
Kaihua	28	Ej	29.10N	118.24 E
Kai Kecil	26	Jh	5.45S	132.40 E
Kaikohe	62	Ea	35.24S	173.48 E
Kaikoura	61	Dh	42.25S	173.41 E
Kaili	27	If	26.35N	107.59 E
Kailu	27	Lc	43.37N	121.19 E
Kailua [Hi.-U.S.]	65a	Fd	19.39N	155.59W
Kailua [Hi.-U.S.]	65a	Db	21.23N	157.44W
Kaimana	26	Jg	3.39S	133.45 E
Kaimanawa Mountains	62	Fc	39.15S	176.00 E
Kaimon-Dake	29	Bf	31.10N	130.32 E
Kain, Tournai-	12	Fd	50.38N	3.22 E
Kainach	14	Jd	46.54N	15.31 E
Kainan [Jap.]	29	Dd	34.09N	135.12 E
Kainan [Jap.]	29	De	33.36N	134.22 E
Kainantu	60	Di	6.15S	145.53 E
Kainji Dam	34	Fd	9.55N	4.40 E
Kainji Reservoir	34	Fc	10.30N	4.35 E
Kaipara Harbour	62	Fb	36.25S	174.15 E
Kaiparowits Plateau	46	Jh	37.20N	111.15W
Kaiser Franz Josephs Fjord	41	Jd	73.30N	24.00W
Kaisersesch	12	Jd	50.14N	7.09 E
Kaiserslautern	10	Dg	49.27N	7.45 E
Kaiserstuhl	10	Dh	48.06N	7.40 E
Kaishantun	27	Mc	42.43N	129.37 E
Kaišiadorys/Kajšjadoris	7	Fi	54.53N	24.31 E
Kaita	29	Cd	34.20N	132.32 E
Kaitaia	62	Ea	35.07S	173.14 E
Kaitangata	62	Cg	46.17S	169.51 E
Kaithal	25	Fc	29.48N	76.23 E
Kaitong → Tongyu	27	Lc	44.47N	123.05 E
Kaituma River	50	Gh	8.11N	59.41W
Kaiwaka	61	Dg	36.10S	174.26 E
Kaiwi Channel	60	Oc	21.13N	157.30W
Kaixian	27	Ie	31.10N	108.25 E
Kaiyuan [China]	27	Lc	42.33N	124.04 E
Kaiyuan [China]	27	Hg	23.47N	103.15 E
Kaiyuh Mountains	40	Hd	64.00N	158.00W
Kaja	30	Jg	12.02N	22.28 E
Kajaani	6	Ic	64.14N	27.41 E
Kajaapu	26	Dh	5.26S	102.24 E
Kajabbi	58	Fg	20.02S	140.02 E
Kajak	20	Fb	71.30N	103.15 E
Kajang	26	Df	2.59N	101.47 E
Kajdak, Sor-	16	Rg	44.40N	53.30 E
Kajerkan	20	Dc	69.25N	87.30 E
Kajiado	36	Gc	1.51S	36.47 E
Kajiki	29	Bf	31.44N	130.40 E
Kajmakčalan	15	Ei	40.58N	21.48 E
Kajnar	15	Lb	47.50N	28.06 E
Kajo Kaji	35	Ee	3.53N	31.40 E
Kajrakkumskoje Vodohranilišče	18	Hd	40.20N	70.05 E
Kajrakty	19	Hf	48.31N	73.14 E
Kajšjadoris/Kaišiadorys	7	Fi	54.53N	24.31 E
Kajuru	34	Gc	10.19N	7.41 E
Kaka	35	Fd	7.28N	39.06 E
Kākā	35	Ec	10.36N	32.11 E
Kakagi Lake	45	Jb	49.13N	93.52W
Kakamas	37	Ce	28.45S	20.33 E
Kakamega	36	Fb	0.17N	34.45 E
Kakamigahara	29	Ed	35.25N	136.50 E
Kakanj	14	Mf	44.08N	18.05 E
Kaka Point	65a	Ec	20.32N	156.33W
Kakata	34	Cd	6.32N	10.21W
Kake	29	Cd	34.36N	132.19 E
Kakegawa	29	Ed	34.46N	138.00 E
Kakenge	36	Dc	4.51S	21.55 E
Kakeroma-Jima	29b	Ba	28.08N	129.15 E
Kakhovka Reservoir (EN) = Kahovskoje Vodohranilišče	5	Jf	47.25N	34.10 E
Kākī	24	Nh	28.19N	51.34 E
Kākināda	22	Kh	16.56N	82.13 E
Kakisa Lake	42	Fd	60.55N	117.40W
Kakizaki	29	Fc	37.16N	138.22 E
Kaklkan	24	Cd	36.15N	29.24 E
Kakogawa	29	Dd	34.46N	134.51 E
Kakpin	34	Ed	8.39N	3.48W
Kaktovik	40	Kb	70.08N	143.37W
Kakuda	29	Gc	37.58N	140.47 E
Kakuma	36	Fb	3.43N	34.52 E
Kakunodate	28	Pe	39.40N	140.32 E
Kakva	17	Jg	59.37N	60.50 E
Kakya	36	Gc	1.36S	39.02 E
Kalaa	13	Mi	35.35N	0.20 E
Kalaa Khasba	14	Co	35.38N	8.36 E
Kalaallit Nunaat/Grønland = Greenland (EN) [5]	39	Pb	70.00N	40.00W
Kalaallit Nunaat/Grønland = Greenland (EN)	38	Pb	70.00N	40.00W
Kalabahi	26	Hh	8.13S	124.31 E
Kalabáka	15	Ej	39.42N	21.38 E
Kalabera	64b	Ba	15.14N	145.48 E
Kalabo	36	De	14.58S	22.41 E
Kalâbsha	33	Fe	23.33N	32.50 E
Kalač	19	Ee	50.23N	41.01 E
Kalačinsk	19	Hd	55.03N	74.34 E
Kalač-na-Donu	19	Ef	48.43N	43.32 E
Kaladan	25	Id	20.09N	92.57 E
Ka Lae	60	Od	18.55N	155.41W
Kalahari Desert	30	Jk	23.00S	22.00 E
Kalaheo	65a	Bb	21.56N	159.32W
Kalai-Mor	19	Gh	35.37N	62.31 E
Kalaj Humo	18	He	38.25N	70.47 E
Kalajoki	7	Fd	64.15N	23.57 E
Kalakan	20	Ge	55.10N	116.45 E
Kalaldi	34	Hd	6.30N	14.04 E
Kalāleh	24	Pd	37.25N	55.40 E
Kalámai	6	Ih	37.02N	22.07 E
Kalamákion	15	Gl	37.55N	23.43 E
Kalamazoo	43	Jc	42.17N	85.32W
Kalambo Falls	36	Fd	8.36S	31.14 E
Kalamitski Zaliv	16	Hg	45.00N	33.25 E
Kálamos	15	Dk	38.37N	20.55 E
Kalamunda, Perth-	59	Df	31.57S	116.03 E
Kalan	23	Eb	39.07N	39.32 E
Kalanshiyū, Sarīr-	30	Jf	27.00N	21.30 E
Kalao, Pulau-	26	Hh	7.18S	120.58 E
Kalaotoa, Pulau-	26	Hh	7.22S	121.47 E
Kalapana	65a	Gd	19.21N	154.59W
Kalaraš	16	Ff	47.16N	28.16 E
Kälarne	8	Gb	62.59N	16.05 E
Kalarski Hrebet	20	Ge	56.30N	118.50 E
Kalasin [Indon.]	26	Ff	0.12N	114.16 E
Kalasin [Thai.]	25	Ke	16.29N	103.31 E
Kalāt	25	Dc	29.02N	66.35 E
Kalāteh	24	Pd	36.29N	54.10 E
Kalau	65b	Bc	21.28S	174.57W
Kalaupapa	65a	Eb	21.12N	156.59W
Kalaus	16	Ng	45.43N	44.07 E
Kalavárdha	15	Km	36.20N	27.57 E
Kálavrita	15	Fk	38.02N	22.07 E
Kalbā'	24	Qj	25.03N	56.21 E
Kalbīyah, Sabkhat al-	14	Eo	35.51N	10.17 E
Kaldbakur	7a	Ab	65.49N	23.39W
Kaldygajty	16	Re	49.20N	52.38 E
Kale [Tur.]	24	Cd	37.26N	28.51 E
Kale [Tur.]	24	Cd	36.14N	29.59 E
Kalecik	24	Eb	40.06N	33.25 E
Kalehe	36	Ec	2.06S	28.55 E
Kalemie	31	Ji	5.56S	29.12 E
Kāl-e Shur	23	Jb	35.05N	60.59 E
Kalevala	19	Db	65.12N	31.10 E
Kalewa	25	Id	23.12N	94.18 E
Kaleybar	24	Lc	38.47N	47.02 E
Kalgoorlie	58	Dh	30.45S	121.28 E
Kaliakoúdha	15	Ek	38.43N	21.46 E
Kaliakra, Nos-	15	Lf	43.18N	28.30 E
Kalibo	26	Hd	11.43N	122.22 E
Kalí Límni	15	Kn	35.35N	27.08 E
Kalima	31	Ji	2.34S	26.37 E
Kalimantan/Borneo	21	Ni	1.00N	114.00 E
Kalimantan Barat [3]	26	Ff	0.01N	110.30 E
Kalimantan Selatan [3]	26	Gg	2.30S	115.30 E
Kalimantan Tengah [3]	26	Fg	2.00S	113.30 E
Kalimantan Timur [3]	26	Gf	1.30N	116.30 E
Kálimnos	15	Jm	36.57N	26.59 E
Kalinin → Tver'	6	Jd	56.52N	35.55 E
Kalinin	19	Fg	42.07N	59.40 E
Kalininabad-	18	Gf	37.53N	38.57 E
Kaliningrad	6	Ie	54.43N	20.30 E
Kaliningrad	7	Ii	55.55N	37.57 E
Kaliningradskaja oblast	19	Ce	54.45N	21.20 E
Kalinino → Tašir	16	Ni	41.08N	44.14 E
Kalinino	16	Kg	45.05N	38.59 E
Kalininsk	15	Ka	48.07N	27.16 E
Kalininsk	16	Nd	51.30N	44.30 E
Kalinkoviči	19	Ce	52.07N	29.23 E
Kalino	17	Hg	58.15N	57.35 E
Kalinovik	14	Mg	43.31N	18.26 E
Kalinovka	16	Fe	49.29N	28.32 E
Kaliro	36	Fb	0.54N	33.30 E
Kalispell	39	He	48.12N	114.19W
Kalisz [2]	10	Of	51.45N	18.05 E
Kalisz	10	Oe	51.46N	18.06 E
Kalisz Pomorski	10	Lc	53.19N	15.54 E
Kalitva	16	Le	48.10N	40.46 E
Kaliua	36	Fd	5.04S	31.48 E
Kalix	7	Fd	65.51N	23.08 E
Kalixälven	7	Fd	65.47N	23.13 E
Kalja	17	Jf	60.20N	60.01 E
Kaljazin	19	Dd	57.15N	37.55 E
Kalkandere	24	Ib	40.55N	40.28 E
Kalkar	12	Ic	51.44N	6.18 E
Kalkaska	44	Ec	44.44N	85.11W
Kalkfeld	37	Bd	20.53S	16.11 E
Kalkfontein	37	Cd	22.07S	20.54 E
Kalkim	15	Kj	39.48N	27.13 E
Kalkrand	37	Bd	24.03S	17.33 E
Kall	7	Ce	63.28N	13.15 E
Kållands Halvö	8	Ef	58.35N	13.05 E
Kållandsö	8	Ef	58.40N	13.10 E
Kallaste	7	Gg	58.41N	27.08 E
Kallavesi	5	Ic	62.50N	27.45 E
Kalletal	12	Kb	52.08N	8.57 E
Kallhäll	8	Ge	59.27N	17.48 E
Kallídhromon Óros	15	Fk	38.44N	22.34 E
Kallinge	7	Dh	56.14N	15.17 E
Kallonís, Kolpos-	15	Jj	39.07N	26.08 E
Kallsjön	7	Ce	63.35N	13.00 E
Kalmar	6	Hd	56.40N	16.22 E
Kalmar [2]	7	Dh	57.20N	16.00 E
Kalmarsund	7	Dh	56.40N	16.25 E
Kalmit	12	Ke	49.19N	8.05 E
Kalmius	16	Jf	47.03N	37.34 E
Kalmthout	12	Gc	51.23N	4.28 E
Kalmykija, respublika	19	Ef	46.30N	45.30 E
Kalmykovo	16	Qe	49.05N	51.47 E
Kalnciems	8	Jh	56.48N	23.34 E
Kalnik	14	Kd	46.10N	16.30 E
Kalocsa	10	Oj	46.32N	19.00 E
Kalofer	15	Hg	42.37N	24.59 E
Kalohi Channel	65a	Ec	21.00N	156.56W
Kaloko	36	Ed	6.47S	25.47 E
Kalole	36	Ec	3.42S	27.22 E
Kaloli Point	65a	Gd	19.37N	154.57W
Kalomo	36	Ef	17.02S	26.30 E
Kalpa	25	Fb	31.37N	78.10 E
Kalpákion	15	Dj	39.53N	20.35 E
Kalpeni Island	25	Ef	10.05N	73.38 E
Kalpin	27	Cc	40.31N	79.03 E
Kalsūbai	21	Jh	19.36N	73.43 E
Kaltern/Caldaro	14	Fd	46.25N	11.14 E
Kaltungo	34	Hd	9.49N	11.19 E
Kaluga	6	Je	54.31N	36.16 E
Kalulushi	36	Ee	12.50S	28.05 E
Kalumburu Mission	59	Fb	14.13S	126.39 E
Kalundborg	7	Ci	55.41N	11.06 E
Kaluš	19	Cf	49.03N	24.23 E
Kałuszyn	10	Rd	52.13N	21.49 E
Kalužskaja Oblast [3]	19	De	54.20N	35.30 E
Kalvåg	8	Ac	61.46N	4.53 E
Kalvarija	7	Fi	54.27N	23.14 E
Kalya	36	Fd	6.28S	30.03 E
Kalyān	25	Ee	19.15N	73.09 E
Kám	10	Mi	47.06N	16.53 E
Kama	36	Ec	3.32S	27.07 E
Kama	17	Nf	30.27N	69.00 E
Kama	5	Ld	55.45N	52.00 E
Kamae	29	Be	32.48N	131.56 E
Kamaï	35	Ba	21.12N	17.30 E
Kamaing	25	Jc	25.31N	96.44 E
Kamaishi	28	Pe	39.16N	141.53 E
Kamakou	65a	Eb	21.07N	156.52W
Kamakura	29	Fd	35.19N	139.32 E
Kamālia	25	Eb	30.44N	72.39 E
Kamalo	65a	Eb	21.03N	156.53W
Kaman	24	Ec	39.25N	33.45 E
Kamand, Āb-e-	24	Mf	33.28N	49.04 E
Kamanjab	37	Ac	19.35S	14.51 E
Kamanyola	36	Ec	2.46S	29.00 E
Kamaran	23	Ff	15.12N	42.35 E
Kamarang	54	Fb	5.53N	60.35W
Kama Reservoir (EN) = Kamskoje Vodohranilišče	5	Ld	58.50N	56.15 E
Kamaši	19	Gh	38.48N	66.29 E
Kamativi	37	Dc	18.19S	27.03 E
Kambalda	59	Ef	31.10S	121.37 E
Kambalnaja Sopka, Vulkan-	20	Kf	51.17N	156.57 E
Kambara	29	Fd	35.07N	138.36 E
Kambara	63d	Cc	13.57S	178.57W
Kambarka	7	Nh	56.18N	54.14 E
Kambia	34	Cd	9.07N	12.55W
Kambja	8	Lf	58.11N	26.43 E
Kambove	36	Ee	10.52S	26.35 E
Kamčatka	20	Le	56.10N	162.30 E
Kamčatka, Poluostrov- = Kamchatka Peninsula (EN)	21	Rd	56.00N	160.00 E
Kamčatskaja Oblast [3]	20	Kf	54.50N	159.00 E
Kamčatski Zaliv	20	Le	55.30N	163.00 E
Kamchatka Peninsula (EN) = Kamčatka, Poluostrov-	21	Rd	56.00N	160.00 E
Kamčija	15	Kf	43.02N	27.53 E
Kamčijska Plato	15	Kg	42.56N	27.32 E
Kameda [Jap.]	29	Fc	37.52N	139.06 E
Kameda [Jap.]	29a	Bc	41.49N	140.46 E
Kameda-Hantō	29a	Bc	41.45N	141.00 E
Kámeiros	15	Km	36.18N	27.56 E
Kamelik	16	Pc	52.06N	49.30 E
Kamen	12	Jc	51.36N	7.40 E
Kaménai	15	Im	36.25N	25.25 E
Kamende	36	Dd	6.28S	24.33 E
Kamenec	10	Td	52.23N	23.49 E
Kamenec-Podolski	19	Cf	48.39N	26.33 E
Kamenijak, Rt-	14	Hf	44.46N	13.56 E
Kamenka	16	Qd	51.07N	50.20 E
Kamenka	16	Fe	48.03N	28.45 E
Kamenka	16	Kd	50.43N	39.25 E
Kamenka	19	Ee	53.13N	44.03 E
Kamenka	7	Kd	65.54N	44.04 E
Kamenka	28	Nb	44.28N	136.01 E
Kamenka	19	Df	49.03N	32.06 E
Kamenka-Bugskaja	10	Uf	50.01N	24.25 E
Kamenka-Dneprovskaja	16	If	47.29N	34.29 E
Kamen-Kaširski	16	Dd	51.36N	24.59 E
Kamen-na-Obi	20	Df	53.47N	81.20 E
Kamennogorsk	7	Gf	60.59N	29.12 E
Kamennoje, Ozero-	7	Hd	64.30N	30.15 E
Kamennomostski	16	Lg	44.17N	40.12 E
Kamen-Rybolov	28	Kb	44.45N	132.04 E
Kamenskoje	20	Ld	62.30N	166.12 E
Kamensk-Šahtinski	16	Le	48.18N	40.16 E
Kamensk-Uralski	22	Id	56.28N	61.54 E
Kamenz/Kamjenc	10	Ke	51.16N	14.06 E
Kameoka	29	Dd	35.00N	135.35 E
Kameškovo	7	Jh	56.22N	41.01 E
Kamet	25	Fd	30.55N	79.35 E
Kameyama	29	Ed	34.51N	136.27 E
Kami-Agata	29	Ad	34.38N	129.25 E
Kamiah	46	Gc	46.14N	116.02W
Kamicharo	29a	Cb	43.11N	143.52 E
Kamienna	10	Re	51.06N	21.47 E
Kamienna Góra	10	Mf	50.47N	16.01 E
Kamień Pomorski	10	Kc	53.58N	14.46 E
Kamiénsk	10	Pe	51.12N	19.30 E
Kamieskroon	37	Bf	30.09S	17.56 E
Kami-furano	29a	Cb	43.29N	142.27 E
Kamiiso	28	Pd	41.49N	140.39 E
Kamiita	29	Dd	34.08N	134.24 E
Kamiji	36	Dd	6.39S	23.17 E
Kamikawa	29a	Cb	43.50N	142.47 E
Kami-Koshiki-Jima	29	Af	31.50N	129.55 E
Kamina	31	Ji	8.44S	24.59 E
Kaminak Lake	42	Id	62.13N	95.00W
Kaminokuni	29a	Bc	41.43N	140.05 E
Kamino-Shima	29	Ad	34.30N	129.25 E
Kaminoyama	28	Pe	38.09N	140.17 E
Kaminuriak Lake	42	Hd	63.00N	95.45W
Kamioka	28	Nf	36.16N	137.18 E
Kami-shihoro	29a	Cb	43.13N	143.16 E
Kamisunagawa	29a	Bb	43.28N	141.58 E
Kamitsushima	29	Ad	34.39N	129.28 E
Kamituga	36	Ec	3.04S	28.11 E
Kamiyama	29	De	33.58N	134.21 E
Kami-yūbetsu	29a	Ca	44.11N	143.34 E
Kamjenc/Kamenz	10	Ke	51.16N	14.06 E
Kamloops	39	Gd	50.40N	120.20W
Kamloops Plateau	46	Ea	50.10N	120.35W
Kamnik	14	Id	46.14N	14.37 E
Kamo	16	Ni	40.22N	45.05 E
Kamo [Jap.]	29	Fc	37.39N	139.03 E
Kamo [N.Z.]	62	Fa	35.41S	174.17 E
Kamōda-Misaki	29	De	33.50N	134.45 E
Kamogawa	29	Gd	35.06N	140.05 E
Kamp	14	Jb	48.23N	15.48 E
Kampala	31	Kh	0.19N	32.35 E
Kampar	26	Df	4.18N	101.09 E
Kampar	26	Mi	0.32N	103.08 E
Kampen	11	Lb	52.33N	5.54 E
Kampene	36	Ec	3.36S	26.40 E
Kamphaeng Phet	25	Je	16.26N	99.33 E
Kamp-Lintford	12	Ic	51.30N	6.32 E
Kamp'o	28	Jg	35.48N	129.30 E
Kâmpóng Cham	22	Mh	12.00N	105.27 E
Kâmpóng Chhnâng	25	Kf	12.15N	104.40 E
Kâmpóng Saôm	22	Mh	10.38N	103.30 E
Kâmpóng Saôm, Chhâk-	25	Kf	10.50N	103.32 E
Kâmpóng Thum	25	Kf	12.42N	104.54 E
Kâmpôt	25	Kf	10.37N	104.11 E
Kampti	34	Ec	10.08N	3.27W
Kampuchea → Cambodia	22	Mh	13.00N	105.00 E
Kamrau, Teluk-	26	Jg	3.32S	133.37 E
Kamsack	42	Hf	51.34N	101.54W
Kamsar	34	Cc	10.40N	14.36W
Kamskoje Ustje	7	Li	55.14N	49.16 E
Kamskoje Vodohranilišče = Kama Reservoir (EN)	5	Ld	58.50N	56.15 E
Kam Summa	35	Ge	0.21N	42.44 E
Kamuenai	29a	Bb	43.08N	140.26 E
Kamui-Dake	29a	Cb	42.25N	142.52 E
Kamui-Misaki	27	Pc	43.20N	140.20 E
Kámuk, Cerro-	49	Fi	9.17N	83.04W
Kamvoúnia Óri	15	Ei	40.00N	21.52 E
Kāmyārān	24	Le	34.47N	46.56 E
Kamyšin	6	Ke	50.06N	45.24 E
Kamyšlov	19	Gd	56.52N	62.43 E
Kamyšovaja Buhta	16	Hg	44.31N	33.33 E
Kamysty-Ajat	17	Jj	53.01N	61.35 E
Kamyzjak	19	Ef	46.06N	48.05 E
Kan	24	Ne	35.45N	51.16 E
Kan	20	Ee	56.31N	93.47 E
Kana	37	Dc	18.32S	27.24 E
Kanaaupscow	42	Jf	54.01N	76.32W
Kanaaupscow	42	Jf	53.40N	77.08W
Kanab	43	Ed	37.03N	112.32W
Kanab Creek	46	Ih	36.24N	112.38W
Kanaga	40a	Cb	51.45N	177.10W
Kanagawa Ken [2]	28	Og	35.30N	139.10 E
Kanaliasem	26	Dg	1.44S	103.35 E
Kanami-Zaki	29b	Bb	27.53N	128.58 E
Kananga	31	Ji	5.54S	22.25 E
Kanariktok	42	Le	55.03N	60.10W
Kanaš	7	Li	55.31N	47.31 E
Kanathea	63d	Cb	17.16S	179.09W
Kanaya	29	Fd	34.48N	138.07 E
Kanayama	29	Ed	35.39N	137.09 E
Kanazawa	22	Pf	36.34N	136.39 E
Kanbalu	25	Jd	23.12N	95.31 E
Kanbe	25	Je	16.42N	96.01 E
Kanchanaburi	25	Jf	14.02N	99.33 E
Kānchenjunga	21	Kg	27.42N	88.08 E
Kānchipuram	25	Ff	12.50N	79.43 E
Kandalakša	6	Jb	67.09N	32.21 E
Kandalaksha, Gulf of- (EN) = Kandalakšski Zaliv	5	Jb	66.35N	32.45 E
Kandalakšski Zaliv = Kandalaksha, Gulf of- (EN)	5	Jb	66.35N	32.45 E
Kandangan	26	Gg	2.47S	115.16 E
Kándanos	15	Gn	35.20N	23.44 E
Kandava	7	Fh	57.03N	22.46 E
Kandavu Island	57	If	19.00S	178.13 E
Kandavu Passage	63d	Ac	18.45S	178.00 E
Kandel	12	Ke	49.05N	8.12 E
Kandel	10	Eh	48.04N	8.01 E
Kandhelioúsa	15	Jm	36.30N	26.58 E
Kandi	31	Hg	11.08N	2.56 E
Kandıra	24	Db	41.04N	30.09 E
Kandla	25	Ed	23.02N	70.14 E
Kando-Gawa	29	Cd	35.22N	132.40 E
Kandovān, Gardaneh-ye-	24	Nd	36.09N	51.18 E
Kandrian	60	Di	6.13S	149.33 E
Kandry	17	Gi	54.34N	54.10 E
Kandy	22	Ki	7.18N	80.38 E
Kane	44	He	41.40N	78.48W
Kane Bassin	67	Od	79.35N	67.00W
Kaneh	24	Pi	27.04N	54.18 E
Kanem [3]	35	Bc	15.00N	16.00 E
Kanem	30	Ig	14.45N	15.30 E
Kaneohe	60	Oc	21.25N	157.48W
Kaneohe Bay	65a	Db	21.28N	157.48W
Kánestron, Ákra-	15	Gj	39.56N	23.45 E
Kanev	16	Ge	49.42N	31.29 E
Kanevskaja	19	Df	46.06N	38.58 E
Kaneyama	29	Fc	37.27N	139.30 E
Kang	37	Cd	23.44S	22.50 E
Kangaba	34	Dc	11.56N	8.25W
Kangal	24	Gc	39.15N	37.24 E
Kangalassy	20	Hd	62.17N	129.58 E
Kangâmiut	41	Ge	65.39N	53.55W
Kangān [Iran]	24	Oi	27.50N	52.03 E
Kangān [Iran]	24	Qj	25.48N	57.28 E
Kangar	26	De	6.26N	100.12 E
Kangaré	34	Dc	11.37N	8.08W
Kangaroo Island	57	Eh	35.50S	137.05 E
Kangasala	8	Kc	61.28N	24.05 E
Kangasniemi	7	Gf	61.59N	26.38 E
Kangâtsiaq	41	Ge	68.20N	53.18W
Kangāvar	24	Le	34.30N	47.58 E
Kangbao	28	Cd	41.51N	114.37 E
Kangding/Dardo	27	He	30.01N	101.58 E
Kangean, Kepulauan- = Kangean Islands (EN)	26	Gh	6.55S	115.30 E
Kangean, Pulau-	26	Gh	6.54S	115.20 E
Kangean Islands (EN) = Kangean, Kepulauan-	26	Gh	6.55S	115.30 E
Kangeeak Point	42	Lc	68.01N	64.45W
Kangen	30	Kh	6.47N	33.09 E
Kangerdlugssuaq	41	Ie	68.20N	31.40W
Kangetet	36	Gb	1.58N	36.06 E

Index Symbols

[1] Independent Nation
[2] State, Region
[3] District, County
[4] Municipality
[5] Colony, Dependency
Continent
Physical Region
Historical or Cultural Region
Mount, Mountain
Volcano
Hill
Mountains, Mountain Range
Hills, Escarpment
Plateau, Upland
Pass, Gap
Plain, Lowland
Delta
Salt Flat
Valley, Canyon
Crater, Cave
Karst Features
Depression
Polder
Desert, Dunes
Forest, Woods
Heath, Steppe
Oasis
Cape, Point
Coast, Beach
Cliff
Peninsula
Isthmus
Sandbank
Island
Atoll
Rock, Reef
Islands, Archipelago
Rocks, Reefs
Coral Reef
Well, Spring
Geyser
River, Stream
Waterfall Rapids
River Mouth, Estuary
Lake
Salt Lake
Intermittent Lake
Reservoir
Swamp, Pond
Canal
Glacier
Ice Shelf, Pack Ice
Ocean
Sea
Gulf, Bay
Strait, Fjord
Lagoon
Bank
Seamount
Tablemount
Ridge
Shelf
Basin
Escarpment, Sea Scarp
Fracture
Trench, Abyss
National Park, Reserve
Point of Interest
Recreation Site
Cave, Cavern
Historic Site
Ruins
Wall, Walls
Church, Abbey
Temple
Scientific Station
Airport
Port
Lighthouse
Mine
Tunnel
Dam, Bridge

Kanggup'o 28 Id 41.07N 127.31 E
Kanggye 27 Mc 40.58N 126.36 E
Kangi 35 Dd 8.10N 27.39 E
Kangjin 28 Ig 34.38N 126.46 E
Kangiqsualujjuaq 39 Md 58.35N 65.59W
Kangiqsujuaq 42 Kd 61.36N 71.57W
Kangirsuk 39 Lc 60.00N 70.01W
Kangmar 27 Ef 28.32N 89.43 E
Kangnŭng 27 Md 37.44N 128.54 E
Kango 36 Bb 0.09N 10.08 E
Kangondu 36 Gc 1.06S 37.42 E
Kangping 28 Gc 42.45N 123.20 E
Kangrinboqê Feng 27 De 31.04N 81.30 E
Kangto 25 Ic 27.52N 92.30 E
Kangwŏn-Do [N.Kor.] [2] 28 Ie 38.45N 127.35 E
Kangwŏn-Do [S.Kor.] [2] 28 Jf 37.45N 128.15 E
Kani 34 Dd 8.29N 6.36W
Kaniama 36 Dd 7.31S 24.11 E
Kanibadam 18 Hd 40.17N 70.25 E
Kaniet Islands 57 Fe 0.53S 145.30 E
Kanija 15 Lc 46.16N 28.13 E
Kanimeh 18 Ed 40.18N 65.09 E
Kanina 15 Ci 40.26N 19.31 E
Kanin Kamen 17 Bb 68.15N 45.15 E
Kanin Nos 19 Eb 68.39N 43.14 E
Kanin Nos, Mys- 5 Kb 68.39N 43.16 E
Kanin Peninsula (EN)=
Kanin Poluostrov 5 Kb 68.00N 45.00 E
Kanin Poluostrov=Kanin
Peninsula (EN) 5 Kb 68.00N 45.00 E
Kanioumé 34 Eb 15.46N 3.09W
Kanita 29a Bc 41.02N 140.38 E
Kanjiža 15 Dc 46.04N 20.03 E
Kankaanpää 7 Ff 61.48N 22.25 E
Kankakee 43 Jc 41.07N 87.52W
Kankakee River 45 Lf 41.23N 88.16W
Kankalabé 34 Cc 11.00N 12.00W
Kankan 31 Gg 10.23N 9.18W
Kanker 25 Gd 20.17N 81.29 E
Kankesanturai 25 Gg 9.49N 80.02 E
Kankossa 32 Ef 15.55N 11.31W
Kankunski 20 He 57.39N 126.25 E
Kanla 10 Hf 50.48N 11.35 E
Kanmav Kyun 25 Jf 11.40N 98.28 E
Kanmon-Kaikyō 29 Bd 33.56N 130.57 E
Kanmuri-Yama 29 Cd 34.28N 132.05 E
Kannapolis 43 Kd 35.30N 80.37W
Kannone-Jima 28 Jj 28.51N 128.58 E
Kannonkoski 8 Kb 62.58N 25.15 E
Kannus 7 Fe 63.54N 23.54 E
Kano [2] 34 Gc 12.00N 9.00 E
Kano 31 Hg 12.00N 8.31 E
Kanona 36 Fe 13.04S 30.38 E
Kan'onji 28 Lg 34.07N 133.39 E
Kanoya 28 Ki 31.23N 130.51 E
Kanozero, Ozero- 7 Ic 67.00N 34.05 E
Kānpur 22 Kg 26.28N 80.21 E
Kansas 38 Jf 39.07N 94.36W
Kansas [2] 43 Hd 38.45N 98.15W
Kansas City [Ks.-U.S.] 39 Jf 39.07N 94.39W
Kansas City [Mo.-U.S.] 39 Jf 39.05N 94.35W
Kanshi 27 Kg 24.57N 116.52 E
Kansk 22 Ld 56.13N 95.41 E
Kansŏng 28 Je 38.22N 128.28 E
Kansu (EN)=Gansu Sheng
(Kan-su Sheng) [2] 27 Hd 38.00N 102.00 E
Kansu (EN)=Kan-su
Sheng→Gansu Sheng [2] 27 Hd 38.00N 102.00 E
Kan-su Sheng→Gansu
Sheng=Kansu (EN) [2] 27 Hd 38.00N 102.00 E
Kansyat 26 Kg 2.15S 138.51 E
Kant 18 Jc 42.52N 74.50 E
Kantang 25 Jg 7.23N 99.32 E
Kantchari 34 Fc 12.29N 1.31 E
Kanté 34 Fd 9.57N 1.03 E
Kantemirovka 19 Df 49.45N 39.53 E
Kantō-Heiya 29 Fc 36.00N 139.30 E
Kanton Atoll 57 Je 2.50S 171.41W
Kantō-Sanchi 29 Fc 36.00N 138.45 E
Kantubek 18 Bb 45.06N 59.16 E
Kanturk/Ceann Toirc 9 Ei 52.10N 8.55W
Kanuma 29 Fc 36.34N 139.45 E
Kanye 31 Jk 24.58S 25.21 E
Kanyu 37 Cd 20.04S 24.36 E
Kanzenze 36 Ee 10.31S 25.12 E
Kao 65b Aa 19.40S 175.01W
Kaohsiung 22 Og 22.38N 120.17 E
Kaôk Nhêk 25 Lf 13.05N 107.04 E
Kaoko Otavi 37 Ac 18.15S 13.37 E
Kaokoveld [3] 37 Ac 18.00S 13.00 E
Kaokoveld 30 Ij 19.30S 13.30 E
Kaolack 31 Fg 14.09N 16.04W
Kao Neua, Col de- 25 Le 18.23N 105.10 E
Kaouadja 35 Cd 8.00N 23.14 E
Kaouar 34 Hb 19.05N 12.52 E
Kapaa 65a Ba 22.05N 159.19W
Kapanga 31 Ji 8.21S 22.35 E
Kapar 24 Ld 36.32N 47.30 E
Kapčagaj 19 Hg 43.52N 77.03 E
Kapčagajskoje
Vodohranilišče 19 Hg 43.45N 78.00 E
Kapchorwa 36 Fb 1.24N 34.27 E
Kap Dan 41 Ie 65.32N 37.30W
Kapelle 12 Fc 51.39N 3.57 E
Kapellskär 8 He 59.43N 19.04 E
Kapena 36 Ee 10.47S 28.20 E
Kapenguria 36 Gb 1.14N 35.07 E
Kapfenberg 14 Jc 47.26N 15.18 E
Kapidaği Yarimadası 15 Ki 40.28N 27.50 E
Kapiri Mposhi 36 Ee 13.58S 28.41 E
Kāpīsā [3] 23 Kc 34.45N 69.30 E
Kapit 26 Ff 2.01N 112.56 E
Kapiti Island 62 Fd 40.50S 174.55 E
Kapka, Massif du- 35 Cb 15.07N 21.45 E
Kapoeta 31 Kh 4.47N 33.35 E
Kapona 36 Ed 7.11S 29.09 E
Kapos 10 Oj 46.44N 18.29 E
Kaposvár 10 Nj 46.22N 17.48 E
Kapp 8 Dd 60.42N 10.52 E
Kappeln 10 Fb 54.40N 9.56 E
Kapša 7 Hg 59.52N 33.45 E
Kapsan 28 Jd 41.05N 128.18 E
Kapuas [Indon.] 26 Mj 0.25S 109.40 E
Kapuas [Indon.] 26 Fg 3.01S 114.20 E
Kapuas Hulu, Pegunungan-
=Kapuas Mountains (EN)
26 Ff 1.25N 113.15 E
Kapuas Mountains (EN)=
Kapuas Hulu,
Pegunungan 26 Ff 1.25N 113.15 E
Kapugargin 15 Lm 36.40N 28.50 E
Kapušany 10 Rg 49.03N 21.21 E
Kapuskasing 39 Ke 49.25N 82.26W
Kapustin Jar 16 Ne 48.35N 45.45 E
Kapustoje 7 Ic 67.17N 34.12 E
Kaputdžuh, Gora- 16 Oj 39.12N 46.01 E
Kapuvár 10 Ni 47.36N 17.02 E
Kara 17 Lb 69.10N 64.45 E
Kara 34 Fd 9.33N 1.12 E
Kara [3] 34 Fd 9.35N 1.05 E
Kara Ada [Tur.] 15 Km 36.58N 27.28 E
Kara Ada [Tur.] 15 Jk 38.25N 26.20 E
Kara-Balta 19 Hg 42.49N 73.57 E
Karabas 19 Hf 49.30N 73.00 E
Karabaš 17 Ji 55.29N 60.13 E
Karabekaul 19 Gh 38.28N 64.10 E
Karabiga 15 Ki 40.24N 27.18 E
Karabil, Vozvyšennost- 18 Df 36.20N 63.30 E
Kara-Bogaz-Gol 19 Fg 41.01N 52.59 E
Kara-Bogaz-Gol, proliv-
16 Ri 41.04N 52.59 E
Kara-Bogaz-Gol, Zaliv- 5 Lg 41.00N 53.15 E
Karabuk 23 Da 41.12N 32.37 E
Karabulak 18 Lb 44.54N 78.29 E
Karabulak 19 Gg 42.31N 69.47 E
Kara Burun 15 Jj 38.37N 27.58 E
Karaburun [Tur.] 24 Cb 41.21N 28.40 E
Karaburun [Tur.] 24 Bc 38.37N 26.31 E
Karabutak 19 Gf 49.57N 60.08 E
Karacabey 24 Cb 40.13N 28.21 E
Karaca Dağ 24 Hd 37.40N 39.50 E
Karačajevo-Čerkesskaja
respublika 19 Eg 43.45N 41.45 E
Karačajevsk 16 Lh 43.44N 41.58 E
Karacaköy 24 Cb 41.22N 28.30 E
Karacaoğlan 15 Kh 41.32N 27.04 E
Karacasu 24 Cd 37.43N 28.37 E
Karačev 19 De 53.04N 34.59 E
Karāchi 22 Ig 24.52N 67.03 E
Kara Dağ [Tur.] 24 Jd 37.40N 43.42 E
Kara Dağ [Tur.] 24 Ed 37.23N 33.10 E
Karadah 16 Oh 42.29N 46.54 E
Karadeniz=Black Sea (EN)
5 Jg 43.00N 35.00 E
Kara Dong 27 Dd 38.26N 81.50 E
Karagajly 19 Hf 49.20N 75.48 E
Karaganda 22 Je 49.50N 73.10 E
Karagandinskaja Oblast [3] 19 Hf 50.00N 74.00 E
Karaginski, Ostrov- 21 Sd 58.48N 164.05 E
Karaginski Zaliv 21 Sd 58.50N 164.00 E
Kara Gölü 15 Mm 36.42N 29.50 E
Karagoš, Gora- 20 Df 51.44N 89.24 E
Karahalli 15 Mk 38.20N 29.32 E
Karaidelski 17 Hi 55.49N 57.05 E
Kara-Irtyš 21 Ke 47.52N 84.16 E
Karaisali 24 Fd 37.16N 35.03 E
Karaj 24 Ne 35.48N 50.59 E
Karaj 24 Ne 35.07N 51.35 E
Karak, Gora- 19 Gg 44.59N 63.05 E
Kara-Kala 19 Fh 38.28N 56.18 E
Karakalpakstan
respublika 19 Fg 43.30N 59.00 E
Karakax/Moyu 27 Cd 37.17N 79.42 E
Karakax He 27 Dd 38.06N 80.24 E
Karakaya Barajı 24 Hc 38.25N 38.45 E
Karakeçi 24 Hd 37.26N 39.26 E
Karakelong, Pulau- 26 If 4.15N 126.48 E
Karakoçan 24 Ic 38.02N 40.07 E
Karakoin, Ozero- 18 Ga 46.10N 68.40 E
Karakojsu 16 Oh 42.30N 47.05 E
Karakolka 18 Kd 41.29N 77.24 E
Karakoram 21 Jf 34.00N 78.00 E
Karakoram Pass 21 Jf 35.30N 77.50 E
Karakore 35 Gc 10.25N 40.01 E
Karakoro 34 Cc 14.43N 12.03 E
Karakorum Shan 27 Cd 36.00N 76.00 E
Karakorum Shankou 27 Cd 35.30N 77.50 E
Karaköy 24 Ic 39.04N 41.42 E
Kara-Kul 18 Id 41.34N 72.47 E
Karakul, Ozero- 19 Hh 39.05N 73.25 E
Karakumski kanal imeni V.I.
Lenina 19 Gh 37.42N 64.20 E
Karakumy 21 Hf 39.00N 60.00 E
Karakuwisa 37 Bc 18.56S 19.40 E
Karam 20 Fe 55.09N 107.37 E
Karama 26 Gg 2.18S 119.06 E
Karaman 23 Db 37.11N 33.14 E
Karamanli 15 Ml 37.22N 29.47 E
Karamay 22 Ke 45.30N 84.55 E
Karamea 61 Dh 41.15S 172.06 E
Karamea Bight 62 Dd 41.25S 171.50 E
Karamet-Nijaz 19 Gh 37.43N 64.31 E
Karamiran He 27 Dd 37.50N 84.35 E
Karamiran Shankou 27 Ed 36.15N 87.05 E
Karamiševo 7 Gh 57.44N 28.50 E
Karamoja [3] 36 Fb 2.45N 34.15 E
Karamürsel 15 Mi 40.42N 29.36 E
Kara-myk 19 Hh 39.30N 71.51 E
Karamyš 16 Nd 51.18N 45.00 E
Karān 24 Mi 27.43N 49.49 E
Karaova 15 Kl 37.05N 27.40 E
Karapınar 24 Ed 37.43N 33.33 E
Kara-Saki 29 Ad 34.40N 129.29 E
Kara-Sal 16 Mf 47.18N 43.36 E
Karasay 27 Dd 36.48N 83.48 E
Karasburg 31 Ik 28.00S 18.43 E
Kara Sea (EN)=Karskoje
More 67 Hd 76.00N 80.00 E
Karašica 14 Me 45.36N 18.36 E
Karasjok 7 Fb 69.27N 25.30 E
Kara Strait (EN)=Karskije
Vorota, Proliv- 21 Hb 70.30N 58.00 E
Karasu 24 Db 41.04N 30.47 E
Karasu [Tur.] 21 Ff 38.52N 38.48 E
Karasu [Tur.] 24 Ic 38.49N 41.28 E
Karasu [Tur.] 24 Jc 38.32N 43.10 E
Karasu Dağları 24 Ic 39.30N 40.45 E
Karasuk 20 Cf 53.44N 78.08 E
Karasuk 20 Cf 53.35N 77.30 E
Karasuyama 29 Gc 36.39N 140.08 E
Karatá, Laguna- 49 Fg 13.56N 83.30W
Karatal 19 Hf 46.26N 77.10 E
Karataş [Tur.] 24 Fd 36.36N 35.21 E
Karataş [Tur.] 15 Lk 38.34N 28.17 E
Karataş Burun 24 Fb 36.35N 35.22 E
Karatau 19 Hg 43.10N 70.29 E
Karatau, Hrebet- 21 Ie 43.40N 69.00 E
Karatj 7 Ec 66.43N 18.33 E
Karatobe 16 Re 49.42N 53.33 E
Karaton 19 Ff 46.25N 53.34 E
Karatsu 28 Jh 33.26N 130.00 E
Karatsu-Wan 29 Be 33.30N 130.00 E
Kara-Turgaj 21 Ie 48.01N 62.45 E
Karaul 19 Hf 49.00N 79.20 E
Karaul 20 Db 70.10N 83.08 E
Karaulbazar 18 Ee 39.29N 64.47 E
Karaulkala 18 Bc 42.18N 58.41 E
Karáva 15 Ej 39.19N 21.36 E
Karavanke 14 Id 46.25N 14.25 E
Karavastase, Gjiri i- 15 Ci 40.55N 19.30 E
Karavastase, Laguna e- 15 Ci 40.55N 19.30 E
Karávi 15 Gm 36.45N 23.35 E
Karavonisia 15 Jn 35.59N 26.26 E
Karawa 36 Db 3.20N 20.18 E
Karaxabar He/Kaidu He 27 Ec 41.55N 86.38 E
Karažal 19 Hf 47.59N 70.53 E
Karbalā' 22 Gf 32.36N 44.02 E
Karbalā' [3] 24 Jf 32.30N 43.45 E
Kårbole 7 Df 61.59N 15.19 E
Karcag 10 Qi 47.19N 20.56 E
Kardeljevo (Ploče) 14 Lg 43.04N 17.26 E
Kardhámaina 15 Km 36.47N 27.09 E
Kardhámila 15 Jk 38.31N 26.06 E
Kardhiotissa 15 Im 36.38N 25.01 E
Kardhitsa 15 Ej 39.22N 21.55 E
Kärdla/Kjardla 7 Fg 59.01N 22.42 E
Kărdžali 15 Ih 41.39N 25.22 E
Kărdžali [2] 15 Ih 41.30N 25.30 E
Kareha, Jbel- 13 Gi 35.15N 5.30W
Karelia (EN) 5 Jc 64.00N 32.00 E
Karelija, respublika 19 Dc 63.30N 33.30 E
Karema 36 Fd 6.49S 30.26 E
Karen — Kayin 25 Je 17.30N 97.45 E
Karen 25 If 12.51N 92.53 E
Karesuando 7 Fb 68.27N 22.29 E
Karêt 30 Gf 24.00N 7.30W
Kärevere/Kjarevere 8 Lf 58.23N 26.30 E
Kargala 16 Sd 51.59N 55.10 E
Kargapazarı Dağı 24 Ib 40.07N 41.35 E
Kargapolje 17 Li 55.57N 64.27 E
Kargasok 20 De 59.07N 81.01 E
Kargat 20 De 55.10N 80.17 E
Kargı 24 Fb 41.08N 34.30 E
Kargil 25 Fb 34.34N 76.06 E
Kargilik/Yecheng 22 Jf 37.54N 77.26 E
Kargopol 19 Dc 61.32N 38.58 E
Karhula 7 Gf 60.31N 26.57 E
Kari 34 Hc 11.14N 10.34 E
Kariai 6 Ig 40.15N 24.15 E
Kariba 31 Jj 16.30S 28.45 E
Kariba, Lake- 30 Jj 17.00S 28.00 E
Kariba-Dake 29a Ab 42.37N 139.56 E
Kariba Dam 37 Dc 16.30S 28.50 E
Karibib 31 Ik 21.58S 15.51 E
Karibib [3] 37 Bd 22.00S 16.00 E
Kariet-Arkmane 13 Ji 35.06N 2.45W
Karigasniemi 7 Fb 69.24N 25.50 E
Karijärvi 8 Jc 61.35N 22.30 E
Karikachi Tōge 29a Cb 43.10N 142.40 E
Kārikāl 25 Ff 10.55N 79.50 E
Karikari, Cape- 62 Ea 34.47S 173.24 E
Karima (EN)=Kuraymah 31 Kg 18.33N 31.51 E
Karimama 34 Fc 12.04N 3.11 E
Karimata, Kepulauan-=
Karimata Islands (EN) 26 Eg 1.25S 109.05 E
Karimata, Pulau- 26 Eg 1.36S 108.55 E
Karimata, Selat-=Karimata
Strait (EN) 21 Mj 2.05S 108.40 E
Karimata Islands (EN)=
Karimata, Kepulauan- 26 Eg 1.25S 109.05 E
Karimata Strait (EN)=
Karimata, Selat- 21 Mj 2.05S 108.40 E
Karimganj 25 Id 24.42N 92.33 E
Karīmnagar 25 Fe 18.26N 79.09 E
Karimunjawa, Kepulauan-=
Karimunjawa Islands (EN) 26 Fh 5.50S 110.25 E
Karimunjawa Islands (EN)=
Karimunjawa, Kepulauan- 26 Fh 5.50S 110.25 E
Karin [Som.] 35 Hc 10.59N 49.13 E
Karin [Som.] 35 Hc 10.51N 45.45 E
Karis/Karjaa 7 Ff 60.05N 23.40 E
Karisimbi 30 Ji 1.30S 29.27 E
Káristos 15 Hk 38.01N 24.25 E
Karkār 35 Hd 9.57N 49.20 E
Karkaralinsk 19 Hf 49.23N 75.31 E
Karkar Island 57 Fe 4.40S 146.00 E
Karkas, Kūh-e 24 Nf 33.27N 51.48 E
Karkheh 23 Gc 31.31N 47.55 E
Karkinitski zaliv 5 Jf 45.55N 33.00 E
Karkkila/Högfors 7 Ff 60.32N 24.11 E
Karkku 8 Jc 61.25N 23.01 E
Kärkölä 8 Kd 60.55N 25.15 E
Kärla/Kjarla 8 Jf 58.16N 22.05 E
Karlholm 8 Gd 60.31N 17.37 E
Karlik Shan 21 Le 43.00N 94.30 E
Karlino 10 Lb 54.03N 15.51 E
Karliova 24 Ic 39.18N 41.01 E
Karl Marx, Pik- 19 Hh 37.08N 72.29 E
Karl-Marx-Stadt —
Chemnitz 6 He 50.50N 12.55 E
Karlö/Hailuoto 5 Ib 65.02N 24.42 E
Karlobag 14 Jf 44.32N 15.05 E
Karlovac 14 Je 45.29N 15.33 E
Karlovka 16 Ie 49.28N 35.08 E
Karlovo 15 Hg 42.38N 24.48 E
Karlovy Vary 10 If 50.14N 12.52 E
Karlsbad 12 Kf 48.55N 8.35 E
Karlsborg 7 Df 58.32N 14.31 E
Karlshamn 7 Dh 56.10N 14.51 E
Karlskoga 7 Dg 59.20N 14.31 E
Karlskrona 6 Hd 56.10N 15.35 E
Karlsöarna 8 Gg 57.15N 18.00 E
Karlsruhe 10 Eg 49.01N 8.24 E
Karlstad [Mn.-U.S.] 45 Hb 48.35N 96.31W
Karlstad [Swe.] 6 Hd 59.22N 13.30 E
Karluk 40 Ie 57.34N 154.28W
Karmah=Kerma (EN) 35 Eb 19.38N 30.25 E
Karmana 18 Ed 40.09N 65.15 E
Karmøy 7 Ag 59.15N 5.15 E
Karnāli 25 Gc 28.45N 81.16 E
Karnataka (Mysore) [3] 25 Ff 13.30N 76.00 E
Karnobat 15 Jg 42.39N 26.59 E
Kärnten = Carinthia (EN)
[2] 14 Hd 46.45N 14.00 E
Kärnten = Carinthia (EN)
14 Hd 46.45N 14.00 E
Karoi 37 Dc 16.50S 29.40 E
Karonga 31 Ki 9.56S 33.56 E
Karora 35 Fb 17.39N 38.22 E
Káros 15 Im 36.53N 25.39 E
Kárpathos 15 Kn 35.30N 27.14 E
Kárpathos=Karpathos (EN)
5 Ih 35.40N 27.10 E
Karpathos (EN)=
Kárpathos 5 Ih 35.40N 27.10 E
Karpáthou, Stenón- 15 Kn 35.50N 27.30 E
Karpenision 15 Ek 38.55N 21.47 E
Karpinsk 17 Jg 59.45N 60.01 E
Karpuzlu 15 Kl 37.33N 27.50 E
Kars 23 Fa 40.37N 43.05 E
Karsakpaj 19 Gf 47.48N 66.45 E
Kärsämäki 7 Fe 64.00N 25.46 E
Karsava/Kārsava 7 Gh 56.47N 27.42 E
Kārsava/Karsava 7 Gh 56.47N 27.42 E
Karši 22 If 38.53N 65.48 E
Karşiyaka 15 Ki 40.26N 28.00 E
Karsiyaka 15 Kk 38.27N 27.07 E
Karskije Vorota, Proliv-=
Kara Strait (EN) 21 Hb 70.30N 58.00 E
Karskoje More=Kara Sea
(EN) 67 Hd 76.00N 80.00 E
Kars Platosu 24 Jb 40.40N 43.07 E
Karst (EN)=Kras 5 Hf 45.48N 14.00 E
Kårsta 8 He 59.39N 18.14 E
Karstula 7 Fe 62.52N 24.47 E
Kartal 24 Cb 40.53N 29.10 E
Kartaly 19 Ge 53.03N 60.40 E
Kartaly-Ajat 17 Jj 53.01N 61.50 E
Karttula 8 Lb 62.53N 26.58 E
Kartuzy 10 Ob 54.20N 18.12 E
Karumai 29 Ga 40.20N 141.28 E
Karumba 59 Ic 17.29S 140.50 E
Kārūn 21 Gf 30.25N 48.12 E
Karungi 7 Fc 66.03N 23.57 E
Karungu 36 Fc 0.51S 34.09 E
Karunki 7 Fc 66.02N 24.01 E
Karūr 25 Ff 10.57N 78.05 E
Karvia 7 Fe 62.08N 22.34 E
Karviná 10 Og 49.51N 18.32 E
Kārwār 25 Ef 14.48N 74.08 E
Karwendel Gebirge 14 Fc 47.28N 11.20 E
Karymskoje 20 Gf 51.37N 114.21 E
Kas 35 Cc 12.34N 24.14 E
Kaş 24 Cd 36.12N 29.38 E
Kasaba [Tur.] 15 Mm 36.18N 29.44 E
Kasaba [Zam.] 36 Ee 10.44S 29.43 E
Kasado-Shima 29 Be 33.57N 131.50 E
Kasah 16 Mi 40.03N 43.52 E
Kasai 29 Dd 34.56N 134.49 E
Kasai 30 Ii 3.02S 16.57 E
Kasai Occidental [2] 36 Dc 5.00S 21.30 E
Kasai Oriental [2] 36 Dc 3.00S 23.00 E
Kasaji 36 De 10.22S 23.27 E
Kasaku 36 Ec 1.55S 25.50 E
Kasama [Jap.] 29 Gc 36.22N 140.16 E
Kasama [Zam.] 31 Kj 10.13S 31.12 E
Kasan 18 Ee 39.01N 65.35 E
Kasane 31 Jj 17.48S 25.09 E
Kasanga 36 Fd 8.28S 31.09 E
Kasangulu 36 Bc 4.36S 15.10 E
Kasansaj 18 Hd 41.10N 71.32 E
Kasaoka 29 Cd 34.30N 133.29 E
Kāsaragod 25 Ef 12.30N 75.00 E
Kasari 29b Ba 28.27N 129.41 E
Kašary 16 Le 49.02N 41.03 E
Kasatori-Yama 29 Ce 33.33N 132.55 E
Kasba Lake 42 Hd 60.20N 102.10W
Kasba Tatla 32 Fc 32.36N 6.16W
Kaseda 28 Ki 31.25N 130.19 E
Kasempa 36 Ee 13.27S 25.50 E
Kasenga 31 Jj 10.22S 28.37 E
Kasenye 36 Fb 1.24N 30.26 E
Kasese [Ug.] 36 Fb 0.10N 30.05 E
Kasese [Zaire] 36 Ec 1.38S 27.07 E
Kashaf 23 Jb 35.58N 61.07 E
Kāshān 22 Hf 33.59N 51.29 E
Kashi 22 Jf 39.29N 75.58 E
Kashihara 29 Dd 34.31N 135.47 E
Kashima [Jap.] 29 Cd 35.31N 132.59 E
Kashima [Jap.] 29 Gd 35.58N 140.38 E
Kashima [Jap.] 29 Be 33.07N 130.07 E
Kashima-Nada 29 Gc 36.30N 140.45 E
Kashiobwe 36 Ed 9.39S 28.37 E
Kashiwazaki 28 Of 37.25N 138.30 E
Kashkū'īyeh 24 Qh 28.58N 56.37 E
Kāshmar 23 Ib 35.12N 58.27 E
Kashmir 21 Jf 34.00N 76.00 E
Kashmor 25 Dc 28.26N 69.35 E
Kasimov 19 Ee 54.59N 41.28 E
Kašin 19 Dd 57.23N 37.37 E
Kasindi 36 Eb 0.02N 29.43 E
Kašira 7 Ji 54.52N 38.11 E
Kasiruta, Pulau- 26 Ig 0.25S 127.12 E
Kasisty 20 Fb 73.40N 109.45 E
Kaškadarinskaja Oblast [3] 19 Gh 38.50N 66.10 E
Kaškadarja 18 Ee 39.35N 64.38 E
Kaskaskia River 45 Lh 37.59N 89.56W
Kaskelen 19 Hg 43.09N 76.37 E
Kaskö/Kaskinen 7 Ee 62.23N 21.13 E
Kasli 17 Ji 55.53N 60.48 E
Kaslo 46 Gb 49.55N 116.55W
Kasongo 31 Ji 4.27S 26.40 E
Kasongo-Lunda 36 Cd 6.28S 16.49 E
Kásos 15 Jn 35.25N 26.55 E
Kásou, Stenon- 15 Jn 35.25N 26.35 E
Kaspi 16 Ni 41.58N 44.25 E
Kaspičan 15 Kf 43.18N 27.11 E
Kaspijsk 19 Eg 42.57N 47.35 E
Kaspijski 19 Ef 45.25N 47.22 E
Kaspijskoje More=Caspian
Sea (EN) 5 Lg 42.00N 50.30 E
Kasplja 16 Gb 55.24N 30.43 E
Kasr, Ra's- 35 Fb 18.04N 38.33 E
Kassaar/Kassar 8 Jf 58.47N 22.40 E
Kassalā 31 Kg 15.28N 36.24 E
Kassalā [3] 35 Fc 14.40N 35.30 E
Kassándra 15 Gi 40.00N 23.30 E
Kassandra, Gulf of- (EN) =
Kassándras, Kólpos- 15 Gi 40.05N 23.30 E
Kassándras, Ákra- 15 Gj 39.57N 23.21 E
Kassándras, Kólpos- =
Kassandra, Gulf of- (EN)
15 Gi 40.05N 23.30 E
Kassel 10 Fe 51.19N 9.30 E
Kassiópi 15 Cj 39.47N 19.55 E
Kastamonu 23 Da 41.22N 33.47 E
Kastanéai 15 Jh 41.39N 26.28 E
Kastellaun 12 Jd 50.04N 7.27 E
Kastéllion [Grc.] 15 In 35.12N 25.20 E
Kastéllion [Grc.] 15 Gn 35.30N 23.39 E
Kastéllos, Ákra- 15 Kn 35.23N 27.09 E
Kasterlee 12 Gc 51.15N 4.57 E
Kastlösa 8 Gh 56.28N 16.25 E
Kastoria 15 Ei 40.31N 21.16 E
Kastorias, Limni- 15 Ei 40.31N 21.18 E
Kastornoje 16 Kd 51.51N 38.07 E
Kastós 15 Dk 38.35N 20.55 E
Kasuga 29 Be 33.32N 130.27 E
Kasugai 29 Ed 35.14N 136.58 E
Kasulu 36 Fc 4.34S 30.06 E
Kasumbalesa 36 Ee 12.13S 27.48 E
Kasumi 29 Dd 35.38N 134.38 E
Kasumi-ga-Ura 28 Pf 36.00N 140.25 E
Kasumkent 16 Pi 41.42N 48.10 E
Kasungan 26 Fg 1.58S 113.24 E
Kasungu 36 Fe 13.02S 33.29 E
Kasupe 36 Gf 15.10S 35.18 E
Kasūr 25 Eb 31.07N 74.27 E
Kaszuby 10 Ob 54.10N 18.15 E
Kataba 31 Jj 16.05S 25.10 E
Katahdin, Mount- 43 Nb 45.55N 68.55W
Katajsk 17 Kh 56.18N 62.35 E
Katako-Kombe 36 Dc 3.24S 24.25 E
Katanga 36 Ed 10.00S 25.30 E
Katanga 20 Fd 60.10N 102.10 E
Katangli 20 Jf 51.43N 143.16 E
Katanning 59 Df 33.42S 117.33 E
Katav-Ivanovsk 17 Ii 54.47N 58.15 E
Katchall 25 Ig 7.57N 93.22 E
Katchi 32 Ef 17.00N 13.55W
Katende, Chutes de- 36 Dd 6.30S 22.10 E
Katerini 15 Fi 40.16N 22.30 E
Katesh 36 Gc 4.31S 35.23 E
Katete 36 Fe 14.06S 32.05 E
Katha 25 Jd 24.11N 96.21 E
Katherine 58 Ef 14.28S 132.16 E
Katherine River 59 Gb 14.39S 131.42 E
Kāthiāwār 21 Jg 21.58N 70.30 E
Kāthmāndāu =
Kathmandu (EN) 22 Kg 27.43N 85.19 E
Kathmandu (EN) —
Kāthmāndāu 22 Kg 27.43N 85.19 E
Kathua 36 Gc 1.17S 39.03 E
Kati 34 Dc 12.43N 8.05W
Katihār 25 Hc 25.32N 87.35 E
Katiki, Volcán- 65d Bb 27.06S 109.16W
Katima Mulilo 37 Dc 17.28S 24.14 E
Katiola 34 Dd 8.08N 5.06W
Katiola [3] 34 Dd 8.13N 5.02W
Katiu Atoll 61 Mc 16.26S 144.22W
Katla 7a Bc 63.36N 18.58W
Katlabuh, Ozero- 15 Ld 45.25N 29.00 E
Katlanovo 15 Eh 41.54N 21.41 E
Katmai, Mount- 40 Ie 58.17N 154.56W
Káto Akhaia 15 Ek 38.09N 21.33 E
Katofio 36 Ee 11.02S 28.01 E
Katompi 36 Ed 6.11S 26.20 E
Katonga 36 Fb 0.10N 30.40 E
Katon-Karagaj 19 If 49.11N 85.37 E
Káto Ólimbos 15 Fj 39.55N 22.28 E
Katoomba 59 Kf 33.42S 150.18 E
Katopasa, Gunung- 26 Hg 1.14S 121.25 E

Index Symbols

[1] Independent Nation
[2] State, Region
[3] District, County
[4] Municipality
[5] Colony, Dependency
Continent
Physical Region
Historical or Cultural Region
Mount, Mountain
Volcano
Hill
Mountains, Mountain Range
Hills, Escarpment
Plateau, Upland
Pass, Gap
Plain, Lowland
Delta
Salt Flat
Valley, Canyon
Crater, Cave
Karst Features
Depression
Polder
Desert, Dunes
Forest, Woods
Heath, Steppe
Oasis
Cape, Point
Coast, Beach
Cliff
Peninsula
Isthmus
Sandbank
Island
Atoll
Rock, Reef
Islands, Archipelago
Rocks, Reefs
Coral Reef
Well, Spring
Geyser
River, Stream
Waterfall Rapids
River Mouth, Estuary
Lake
Salt Lake
Intermittent Lake
Reservoir
Swamp, Pond
Canal
Glacier
Ice Shelf, Pack Ice
Ocean
Sea
Gulf, Bay
Strait, Fjord
Lagoon
Bank
Seamount
Tablemount
Ridge
Shelf
Basin
Escarpment, Sea Scarp
Fracture
Trench, Abyss
National Park, Reserve
Point of Interest
Recreation Site
Cave, Cavern
Historic Site
Ruins
Wall, Walls
Church, Abbey
Temple
Scientific Station
Airport
Port
Lighthouse
Mine
Tunnel
Dam, Bridge

Katowice [2]	10	Of	50.15N	19.00 E
Katowice	6	He	50.16N	19.00 E
Katrancık Dağı	24	Dd	37.27N	30.25 E
Kātrīnā, Jabal-	30	Kf	28.31N	33.57 E
Katrineholm	7	Dg	59.00N	16.12 E
Katsina	31	Hg	13.00N	7.36 E
Katsina Ala	34	Gd	7.48N	8.52 E
Katsumoto	28	Jh	33.51N	129.42 E
Katsuta	28	Pf	36.24N	140.32 E
Katsuura	28	Pg	35.08N	140.18 E
Katsuyama [Jap.]	28	Nf	36.03N	136.30 E
Katsuyama [Jap.]	29	Cd	35.06N	133.41 E
Kattakurgan	19	Gh	39.55N	66.15 E
Kattavia	15	Kn	35.57N	27.46 E
Kattegat	5	Hd	57.00N	11.00 E
Katthammarsvik	8	Hg	57.26N	18.50 E
Katulo, Lagh-	36	Hb	2.08N	40.56 E
Katumbi	36	Fe	10.49S	33.32 E
Katun	21	Kd	52.25N	85.05 E
Katwijk aan Zee	11	Kb	52.13N	4.24 E
Katwijk aan Zee, Katwijk-	12	Gb	52.12N	4.25 E
Katwijk-Katwijk aan Zee	12	Gb	52.12N	4.25 E
Katzenelnbogen	12	Jd	50.17N	7.57 E
Kau	26	If	1.11N	127.54 E
Kauai Channel	60	Oc	21.45N	158.50W
Kauai Island	57	Lb	22.03N	159.30W
Kaub	12	Jd	50.05N	7.46 E
Kauehi Atoll	61	Lc	15.51S	145.09W
Kaufbeuren	10	Gi	47.53N	10.37 E
Kauhajoki	7	Fe	62.26N	22.11 E
Kauhava	7	Fe	63.06N	23.05 E
Kauiki Head	60	Oc	20.46N	155.59W
Kaukauna	45	Ld	44.17N	88.17W
Kaukauveld	30	Jk	20.00S	21.50 E
Kaukonen	7	Fc	67.29N	24.54 E
Kaukura Atoll	57	Mf	15.45S	146.42W
Kaula Island	57	Kb	21.40N	160.32W
Kaulakahi Channel	65a	Ba	22.02N	159.53W
Kaumalapau	65a	Ec	20.47N	156.59W
Kaunakakai	60	Oc	21.05N	157.02W
Kaunas	6	Ie	54.54N	23.54 E
Kaunasskoje Vodohranilišče /Kauno Marios	8	Kj	54.50N	24.15 E
Kauniainen/Grankulla	8	Kd	60.13N	24.45 E
Kauno Marios/Kaunasskoje Vodohranilišče	8	Kj	54.50N	24.15 E
Kaunos	15	Lm	36.50N	28.35 E
Kaupanger	7	Bf	61.11N	7.14 E
Kau Paulatmada, Gunung-	26	Ig	3.15S	126.09 E
Kaura Namoda	34	Gc	12.36N	6.35 E
Kauriāla Ghāt	25	Gc	28.27N	80.59 E
Kaušany	16	Ff	46.39N	29.25 E
Kaustinen	7	Fe	63.32N	23.42 E
Kautokeino	7	Fb	68.59N	23.08 E
Kavacik	15	Lj	39.40N	28.30 E
Kavadarci	15	Fh	41.26N	22.01 E
Kavaja	15	Ch	41.11N	19.33 E
Kavak [Tur.]	15	Ji	40.36N	26.54 E
Kavak [Tur.]	24	Gb	41.05N	36.03 E
Kavaklidere	15	Ll	37.26N	28.22 E
Kavála	6	Ig	40.56N	24.25 E
Kaválas, Kólpos-	15	Hi	40.52N	24.25 E
Kavalerovo	20	Ih	44.19N	135.05 E
Kavali	25	Ff	14.55N	79.59 E
Kavār	24	Oh	29.11N	52.44 E
Kavaratti	22	Jh	10.33N	72.38 E
Kavaratti Island	25	Ef	10.33N	72.38 E
Kavarna	15	Lf	43.25N	28.20 E
Kavarskas/Kovarskas	8	Ki	55.24N	25.03 E
Kavendou, Mont-	30	Fg	10.41N	12.12W
Kavieng	60	Eh	2.34S	150.48 E
Kavīr, Dasht-e-	21	Hf	34.40N	54.30 E
Kavkaz	16	Jg	45.21N	36.12 E
Kavkaz, Bolšoj-=Caucasus (EN)	5	Kg	42.30N	45.00 E
Kävlinge	8	Ei	55.48N	13.06 E
Kävlingeån	8	Ei	55.47N	13.06 E
Kawa	35	Eb	19.10N	30.39 E
Kawabe	29	Gb	39.39N	140.15 E
Kawachi-nagano	29	Dd	34.27N	135.34 E
Kawagoe	29	Fd	35.55N	139.28 E
Kawaguchi	29	Fd	35.48N	139.42 E
Kawaihae Bay	65a	Fc	20.02N	155.51W
Kawaihoa Point	65a	Ab	21.47N	160.12W
Kawakawa	62	Fa	35.23S	174.04 E
Kawalusu, Pulau-	26	If	4.15N	125.19 E
Kawamata	29	Gc	37.40N	140.36 E
Kawambwa	36	Ed	9.47S	29.05 E
Kawaminami	29	Be	32.12N	131.32 E
Kawamoto	29	Cd	34.59N	132.29 E
Kawanishi	29	Gc	37.59N	140.03 E
Kawanoe	29	Cd	34.01N	133.34 E
Kawartha Lakes	44	Hc	44.32N	78.30W
Kawasaki [Jap.]	29	Gb	38.10N	140.38 E
Kawasaki [Jap.]	28	Og	35.32N	139.43 E
Kawashiri-Misaki	29	Bd	34.26N	130.58 E
Kawauchi	29a	Bc	41.12N	141.00 E
Kawau Island	62	Fb	36.25S	174.50 E
Kawaura	29	Be	32.21N	130.05 E
Kawerau	62	Gc	38.05S	176.42 E
Kawhia	62	Fc	38.04S	174.49 E
Kawich Range	46	Gh	37.40N	116.30W
Kawio, Kepulauan-	26	If	4.30N	125.30 E
Kawkareik	25	Je	16.33N	98.14 E
Kawm Umbū	33	Fe	24.28N	32.57 E
Kawthaung	25	Jg	9.59N	98.33 E
Kaxgar He	21	Jf	39.46N	78.15 E
Kax He	27	Dc	43.37N	81.48 E
Kaya	34	Ec	13.05N	1.05W
Kayah [2]	25	Je	19.15N	97.30 E
Kayak	40	Ke	59.52N	144.30W
Kayali Daği	15	Jj	39.58N	26.38 E
Kayan	21	Ni	2.55N	117.35 E
Kayanga	34	Bc	11.58N	15.00W
Kayangel Islands	57	Ed	8.04N	134.43 E
Kayangel Passage	64a	Ba	8.01N	134.42 E
Kaycee	46	Le	43.43N	106.38W
Kayenta	46	Jh	36.44N	110.17W
Kayes [3]	34	Cc	14.00N	11.00W
Kayes	31	Fg	14.26N	11.27W
Kayin	25	Je	17.30N	97.45 E
Kayoa, Pulau-	26	Ig	0.05S	127.25 E
Kayseri	22	Ff	38.43N	35.30 E
Kayuagung	26	Dg	3.24S	104.50 E
Kayu Ara, Pulau-	26	Ef	1.31N	106.26 E
Kazačje	20	Ib	70.40N	136.13 E
Kazah	16	Ni	41.05N	45.22 E
Kazahskaja Sovetskaja Socialističeskaja Respublika → Kazakhstan	19	Gf	48.00N	68.00 E
Kazahskaja SSR/Kazak Sovettik Socialistik Respublikasy → Kazakhstan	19	Gf	48.00N	68.00 E
Kazahskaja SSR → Kazakhstan	19	Gf	48.00N	68.00 E
Kazahski Melkosopočnik = Kazakh Hills (EN)	21	Je	49.00N	73.00 E
Kazahski Zaliv	16	Rh	42.40N	52.25 E
Kazakh Hills (EN) = Kazahski Melkosopočnik	21	Je	49.00N	73.00 E
Kazakhstan (EN) = Qazaqstan	19	Gf	48.00N	68.00 E
Kazakhstan (EN)	21	Ie	47.00N	65.00 E
Kazaklija	15	Lc	46.05N	28.38 E
Kazak SSR → Qazaqstan	19	Gf	48.00N	68.00 E
Kazalinsk	19	Gf	45.46N	62.07 E
Kazan	6	Kd	55.45N	49.08 E
Kazan	38	Jc	64.02N	95.30W
Kazandžik	19	Fh	39.17N	55.34 E
Kazanka	7	Li	55.48N	49.05 E
Kazanka	16	Hf	47.50N	32.49 E
Kazanlăk	15	Ig	42.37N	25.24 E
Kazan-Rettō/Iō=Volcano Islands (EN)	21	Qg	25.00N	141.00 E
Kazanskoje	19	Gd	55.38N	69.14 E
Kazarman	19	Hg	41.20N	74.02 E
Kazatin	19	Cf	49.43N	28.50 E
Kazbek, Gora-	5	Kg	42.42N	44.31 E
Kaz Daği	23	Cb	39.42N	26.50 E
Kaz Daği	15	Mk	38.35N	29.15 E
Kāzerūn	22	Hg	29.37N	51.38 E
Kažim	17	Ef	60.20N	51.32 E
Kazi-Magomed	16	Pi	40.02N	48.56 E
Kazimierza Wielka	10	Qf	50.16N	20.30 E
Kâzımkarabekir	24	Ed	37.14N	32.59 E
Kazincbarcika	10	Qh	48.15N	20.38 E
Kazinga Channel	36	Ec	0.13S	29.53 E
Kazlų-Rūda/Kazlu-Ruda	8	Jj	54.42N	23.32 E
Kazo	29	Fc	36.08N	139.36 E
Kaztalovka	16	Pe	49.46N	48.44 E
Kazumba	36	Dd	6.25S	22.02 E
Kazuno	28	Pd	40.14N	140.48 E
Kazym	19	Gc	63.54N	65.50 E
Kazyr	20	Ef	53.50N	92.53 E
Kcynia	10	Nd	53.00N	17.30 E
Kdyně	10	Jg	49.24N	13.02 E
Ké	35	Bb	18.32N	17.55 E
Kéa	15	Hl	37.37N	24.20 E
Kéa	15	Hl	37.39N	24.20 E
Keaau	65a	Fd	19.37N	155.03W
Keahole Point	65a	Ed	19.44N	156.04W
Kealaikahiki Channel	65a	Ec	20.37N	156.50W
Kealaikahiki Point	65a	Ec	20.32N	156.42W
Kealakekua Bay	65a	Fd	19.28N	155.56W
Keams Canyon	46	Ji	35.49N	110.12W
Keanae	65a	Ec	20.52N	156.09W
Keanapapa Point	65a	Dc	20.54N	157.04W
Kearney	43	Hc	40.42N	99.05W
Kearns	46	Jf	40.39N	111.59W
Kéas, Stenón-	15	Hl	37.40N	24.12 E
Keats Bank (EN)	57	Id	5.23N	173.28 E
Keb	8	Mg	57.44N	28.38 E
Keban Baraji	24	Hc	38.53N	39.00 E
Kébémer	34	Bb	15.22N	16.27W
Kebir, Oued el-	14	Bn	36.51N	7.57 E
Kebnekaise	5	Hb	67.53N	18.33 E
Kebri Dehar	31	Lh	6.45N	44.17 E
Kebumen	26	Eh	7.40S	109.39 E
Kecel	10	Pj	46.32N	19.16 E
Kechika	42	Ee	59.38N	127.09W
Kecskemét	10	Pj	46.54N	19.42 E
Kėdainiai/Kedajnjaj	7	Fi	55.18N	23.59 E
Kedajnjaj/Kėdainiai	7	Fi	55.18N	23.59 E
Kedgwick	44	Nb	47.39N	67.21W
Kediri	22	Nj	7.49S	112.01 E
Kédougou	34	Cc	12.33N	12.11W
Kedva	17	Fd	64.14N	53.30 E
Kędzierzyn-Koźle	10	Of	50.20N	18.10 E
Keele	42	Fd	64.24N	124.47W
Keele Peak	38	Fc	63.26N	130.19W
Keeling Islands → Cocos Islands	21	Lk	12.10S	96.55 E
Keeling Islands → Cocos Islands [5]	22	Lk	12.10S	96.55 E
Keelung	22	Og	25.08N	121.44 E
Keene	44	Kd	42.55N	72.17W
Keer-Weer, Cape-	59	Ib	13.58S	141.30 E
Keetmanshoop	31	Ik	26.36S	18.08 E
Keetmanshoop [3]	37	Be	26.30S	18.30 E
Keewatin	42	Ig	49.46N	94.34W
Keewatin, District of- [3]	42	Hd	64.00N	96.00W
Kefa [3]	35	Fd	7.00N	36.00 E
Kefallinía=Cephalonia (EN)	5	Ih	38.15N	20.35 E
Kefamenanu	26	Hh	9.27S	124.29 E
Kefar Sava	24	Ff	32.10N	34.54 E
Keffi	34	Gd	8.51N	7.52 E
Keflavík	7a	Ab	64.01N	22.34W
Kegen	19	Hg	42.58N	79.12 E
Kegums	8	Kh	56.41N	24.44 E
Kehdingen	10	Fc	53.45N	9.20 E
Kehl	10	Dh	48.35N	7.49 E
Kehra	7	Fg	59.19N	25.18 E
Keighley	9	Lh	53.52N	1.54W
Keila/Kejla	7	Fg	59.19N	24.27 E
Ķeila Jõgi/Kejla	8	Ke	59.25N	24.15 E
Keimoes	37	Ce	28.41S	21.00 E
Keipel Bank (EN)	59	Le	25.15S	159.30 E
Keïta	34	Gc	14.46N	5.46 E
Kéita, Bahr-	35	Bd	9.14N	18.21 E
Keitele	5	Ic	62.55N	26.00 E
Keith [Austl.]	59	Ig	36.06S	140.21 E
Keith [Scot.-U.K.]	9	Kd	57.32N	2.57W
Keith Arm	42	Fc	65.20N	122.00W
Keiyasi	63d	Ab	17.53S	177.45 E
Kejla/Keila	7	Fg	59.19N	24.27 E
Kejla/Keila Jõgi	8	Ke	59.25N	24.15 E
Kejvy	7	Ic	67.30N	37.45 E
Kekaha	65a	Bb	21.58N	159.43W
Kekerengu	62	Ee	42.00S	174.00 E
Kékes	10	Qi	47.52N	20.01 E
Keklau	64a	Bb	7.35N	134.39 E
Kelafo	35	Gd	5.37N	44.13 E
Kelakam	34	Hc	13.35N	11.44 E
Kela Met	35	Fb	15.50N	38.23 E
Kelan	27	Jd	38.44N	111.34 E
Kelang	22	Mi	3.02N	101.27 E
Kelasa, Selat-=Gaspar Strait (EN)	26	Eg	2.40S	107.15 E
Kelberg	12	Id	50.18N	6.55 E
Këlcyra	15	Di	40.19N	20.11 E
Kelefesia	65b	Bb	20.30S	174.44W
Kelekçi	15	Ml	37.14N	29.28 E
Kelem	35	Fe	4.49N	35.59 E
Keles	15	Mj	39.55N	29.14 E
Keles	18	Gd	41.02N	68.37 E
Kelheim	10	Hh	48.55N	11.52 E
Kelifely, Causse du-	37	Hc	17.15S	45.30 E
Kelifski Uzboj	18	Ef	37.45N	64.40 E
Keli Hāji Ibrāhīm	24	Kd	36.42N	45.00 E
Kelkheim	12	Kd	50.08N	8.27 E
Kelkit	23	Ea	36.32N	40.46 E
Kelkit	24	Hb	40.08N	39.27 E
Kellé	36	Bc	0.06S	14.33 E
Kellerberrin	59	Df	31.38S	117.43 E
Kellerwald	10	Fe	51.03N	9.10 E
Kellett, Cape -	42	Eb	72.57N	125.27W
Kellett Strait	42	Fa	75.50N	117.40W
Kellog	20	Dd	62.27N	86.35 E
Kellogg	43	Db	47.32N	116.07W
Kelloselkä	7	Gc	66.56N	29.00 E
Kells/Ceanannas Mór	9	Gh	53.44N	6.53W
Kelmé/Kelme	7	Fi	55.39N	22.58 E
Kelme/Kelmé	7	Fi	55.39N	22.58 E
Kelmency	15	Ja	48.27N	26.47 E
Kelmis/La Calamine	12	Hd	50.43N	6.00 E
Kélo	35	Bd	9.15N	15.48 E
Kelowna	39	He	49.53N	119.29W
Kelsey	42	He	56.00N	97.00W
Kelsey Bay	42	Ef	50.24N	125.57W
Kelso	46	Dc	46.09N	122.54W
Kelso Bank	59	Ld	24.10S	159.10 E
Kelso Bank (EN)	59	Ld	24.10S	159.30 E
Kel Tepe [Tur.]	24	Eb	41.05N	32.27 E
Kel Tepe [Tur.]	15	Ni	40.39N	30.06 E
Keltie, Mount-	66	Jf	79.15S	159.00 E
Keluang	26	Df	2.02N	103.19 E
Kelvin Seamount (EN)	43	Od	38.50N	64.00W
Kelyeḥēd	35	Hd	4.44N	9.10 E
Kém	19	Dc	64.57N	34.31 E
Kema	7	If	60.19N	37.15 E
Ké Macina	34	Dc	13.57N	5.23W
Kemah	24	Hc	39.36N	39.02 E
Kemaliye	24	Hc	39.16N	38.29 E
Kemalpaşa	24	Cc	40.00N	28.20 E
Kemalpaşa	15	Kk	38.25N	27.26 E
Kembé	35	Ce	4.36N	21.54 E
Kemer [Tur.]	15	Mm	36.23N	30.21 E
Kemer [Tur.]	24	Dd	36.36N	30.34 E
Kemer Baraji	15	Ll	37.30N	28.35 E
Kemeri/Ķemeri	8	Jh	56.56N	23.25 E
Ķemeri/Kemeri	8	Jh	56.56N	23.25 E
Kemerovo	22	Kd	55.20N	86.05 E
Kemerovskaja Oblast [3]	20	De	55.00N	86.00 E
Kemi	6	Ib	65.44N	24.34 E
Kemijärvi	7	Gc	66.40N	27.25 E
Kemijärvi=Kenni, Lake- (EN)	7	Gc	66.36N	27.24 E
Kemijoki	5	Ib	65.47N	24.30 E
Kemiö	8	Jd	60.10N	22.40 E
Kemiö/Kimito	8	Jd	60.10N	22.40 E
Kemlja	7	Ki	54.43N	45.15 E
Kemmerer	46	Jf	41.48N	110.32W
Kémo-Gribingui [3]	35	Bd	6.00N	19.00 E
Kemp, Lake-	45	Gj	33.45N	99.13W
Kempaž	17	Jd	64.03N	61.02 E
Kempele	7	Fd	64.55N	25.30 E
Kempen	12	Ic	51.22N	6.25 E
Kempen/Campine	11	Lc	51.10N	5.20 E
Kempendjaj	20	Gd	62.02N	118.42 E
Kempenich	12	Jd	50.25N	7.08 E
Kemp Land	66	Ee	67.10S	58.00 E
Kemps Bay	49	Ia	24.02N	77.33W
Kempsey	59	Kf	31.05S	152.50 E
Kempston	12	Bb	52.06N	0.29W
Kempt, Lac-	42	Kg	47.25N	74.15W
Kempten	10	Gi	47.43N	10.19 E
Ken	25	Hc	25.46N	80.31 E
Ken, Loch-	9	If	55.02N	4.02W
Kena	7	Je	62.06N	39.05 E
Kenadsa	32	Gc	31.34N	2.26W
Kenai	39	Dc	60.33N	151.15W
Kenai Mountains	40	Ie	60.00N	150.00W
Kenai Peninsula	38	Ed	60.10N	150.00W
Kendal	9	Kg	54.20N	2.45W
Kendall	44	Gm	25.41N	80.19W
Kendall, Cape -	42	Id	63.36N	87.13W
Kendallville	44	Ee	41.27N	85.16W
Kendari	22	Oj	3.57S	122.35 E
Kendawangan	26	Fg	2.32S	110.12 E
Kenema	31	Fh	7.52N	11.12W
Kenge	31	Ii	4.52S	16.59 E
Kengere	36	Ee	11.10S	25.28 E
Keng Tung	25	Jd	21.17N	99.36 E
Kenhardt	37	Ce	29.19S	21.12 E
Kéniéba	34	Cc	12.50N	11.14W
Keningau	26	Ge	5.20N	116.10 E
Kenitra	31	Ge	34.16N	6.36W
Kenitra [3]	32	Fc	34.00N	6.00W
Kenli (Xishuanghe)	28	Ef	37.35N	118.30 E
Kenmare	43	Gb	48.40N	102.05W
Kenmare/Neidín	9	Dj	51.53N	9.35W
Kenmare River/An Ribhéar	9	Dj	51.50N	9.50W
Kennebunk	44	Ld	43.23N	70.33W
Kennedy Peak	25	Id	23.19N	93.46 E
Kennedy Range	59	Cd	24.30S	115.00 E
Kenner	45	Ki	29.59N	90.15W
Kennet	9	Mj	51.28N	0.57W
Kennett	45	Kh	36.14N	90.03W
Kennewick	46	Fc	46.12N	119.07W
Kenni, Lake- (EN) = Kemijärvi	7	Gc	66.36N	27.24 E
Kennington	12	Cc	51.09N	0.53 E
Kenn Reef	57	Gg	21.10S	155.50 E
Kénogami	44	La	48.26N	71.14W
Kénogami, Lac-	44	La	48.21N	71.28W
Kenogami River	42	Jf	51.06N	84.29W
Keno Hill	42	Dd	63.54N	135.18W
Kenora	39	Je	49.47N	94.29W
Kenosha	43	Jc	42.35N	87.49W
Kent	9	Nj	51.10N	0.55 E
Kent [3]	9	Nj	51.20N	0.55 E
Kent [S.L.]	34	Cd	8.10N	13.10W
Kent [Wa.-U.S.]	46	Dc	47.23N	122.14W
Kent, Vale of-	9	Nj	51.10N	0.30 E
Kentau	19	Gg	43.32N	68.33 E
Kent Group	59	Jg	39.30S	147.20 E
Kenton	44	Fe	40.38N	83.38W
Kent Peninsula	42	Gc	68.30N	107.00W
Kentucky [2]	43	Jd	37.30N	85.15W
Kentucky Lake	43	Jd	36.25N	88.05W
Kentucky River	44	Ef	38.41N	85.11W
Kenya [1]	31	Kh	1.00N	38.00 E
Kenya, Mount-/Kirinyaga	30	Ki	0.10S	37.20 E
Keokea	65a	Ec	20.42N	156.21W
Keokuk	43	Ic	40.24N	91.24W
Keonjhargarh	25	Hd	21.38N	85.35 E
Keowee, Lake-	44	Fh	34.55N	82.50W
Kepe	7	Hd	65.09N	32.08 E
Kepi	26	Kh	6.32S	139.19 E
Kępno	10	Ne	51.17N	17.59 E
Kepsut	24	Cc	39.41N	28.09 E
Kerala [3]	25	Ff	11.00N	76.30 E
Kerama-Rettō	29b	Ab	26.10N	127.15 E
Kerang	59	Ig	35.44S	143.55 E
Keratéa	15	Gl	37.48N	23.59 E
Kerava/Kervo	8	Kd	60.24N	25.07 E
Kerč	6	Jf	45.22N	36.27 E
Kerčenski Poluostrov	16	Ig	45.15N	36.00 E
Kerčenski Proliv	5	Jf	45.22N	36.38 E
Kerdhílion Óros	15	Gi	40.47N	23.39 E
Kerema	60	Di	7.58S	145.46 E
Keren	35	Fb	15.47N	38.27 E
Keret, Ozero-	7	Hd	65.50N	32.50 E
Kerewan	34	Bc	13.29N	16.06W
Kerguélen	30	Nm	49.20S	69.30 E
Kerguélen, Iles-	30	Nm	49.15S	69.10 E
Kerguelen Plateau (EN)	3	Go	55.00S	75.00 E
Kericho	36	Gc	0.22S	35.17 E
Keri Kera	35	Ec	12.21N	32.46 E
Kerimäk	8	Mc	61.55N	29.17 E
Kerinci, Gunung-	21	Mj	1.42S	101.16 E
Kerio	30	Kh	2.59N	36.07 E
Keríon	15	Dl	37.40N	20.49 E
Keriya/Yutian	22	Kf	36.52N	81.42 E
Keriya He	27	Dd	38.30N	82.10 E
Keriya Shankou	27	Dd	35.12N	81.44 E
Kerka	10	Mj	46.28N	16.36 E
Kerken	12	Ic	51.27N	6.26 E
Kerkennah Islands (EN)= Qarqannah, Juzur-	30	Ie	34.44N	11.12 E
Kerketevs Óros	15	Jl	37.44N	26.38 E
Kerki	19	Gh	37.50N	65.13 E
Kerkini Óros	15	Fh	41.21N	22.50 E
Kérkira	15	Cj	39.36N	19.55 E
Kérkira=Corfu (EN)	5	Hh	39.40N	19.45 E
Kerkiras, Stenón- = Corfu, Strait of- (EN)	15	Dj	39.35N	20.05 E
Kerkrade	12	Id	50.52N	6.04 E
Kerma (EN)=Karmah	35	Eb	19.38N	30.25 E
Kermadec Islands	57	Jh	30.00S	178.30W
Kermadec Ridge (EN)	57	Jh	30.30S	178.30W
Kermadec Trench (EN)	3	Km	30.00S	177.00W
Kermajarvi	8	Mb	62.30N	28.40 E
Kermān [3]	23	Ic	30.50N	57.50 E
Kermān	22	Hf	30.17N	57.05 E
Kermānshāh→ Bakhtarān	22	Gf	34.19N	47.04 E
Kermānshāhān	24	Pg	31.17N	54.55 E
Kerme	15	Kl	37.02N	28.00 E
Kerme Körfezi	24	Bd	36.50N	28.00 E
Kermit	45	Ek	31.51N	103.06W
Kern River	46	Fi	35.13N	119.17W
Kérouané	34	Dd	9.16N	9.01W
Kerpen	12	Id	50.52N	6.41 E
Kerrobert	42	Gf	51.55N	109.08W
Kerrville	43	He	30.03N	99.08W
Kerry/Ciarraí [2]	9	Di	52.10N	9.30W
Kerry, Mountains of-	9	Dj	51.55N	9.50W
Kertamulya	26	Eg	0.23N	109.09 E
Kerteh	26	Df	4.31N	103.27 E
Kerteminde	8	Di	55.27N	10.40 E
Kerulen (Cherlen)	21	Ne	48.48N	117.00 E
Kervo/Kerava	8	Kd	60.24N	25.07 E
Kerzaz	32	Gd	29.27N	1.25W
Kerženec	7	Kh	56.04N	45.01 E
Kesagami Lake	42	Jf	50.23N	80.10W
Kesälahti	8	Mc	61.54N	29.50 E
Keşan	23	Ca	40.51N	26.37 E
Keşap	24	Hb	40.55N	38.31 E
Kesen'numa	23	Pe	38.54N	141.35 E
Kesen'numa-Wan	29	Gb	38.50N	141.35 E
Keshan	27	Mb	48.04N	125.51 E
Keskastel	12	Jf	48.58N	7.02 E
Keskin	24	Ec	39.41N	33.37 E
Keski-Suomi [2]	7	Fe	62.30N	25.30 E
Kestenga	7	Hd	65.53N	31.45 E
Keswick	9	Jg	54.37N	3.08W
Keszthely	10	Nj	46.46N	17.15 E
Ket	21	Kd	58.55N	81.32 E
Kéta	34	Fd	5.55N	0.59 E
Ketanda	20	Jd	60.38N	141.30 E
Ketapang	22	Mj	1.52S	109.59 E
Ketčenery (Sovetskoje)	19	Ef	47.17N	44.30 E
Ketchikan	39	Fd	55.21N	131.35W
Ketchum	43	Ec	43.41N	114.22W
Ketchum Mountain	45	Fk	31.15N	101.00W
Kete Krachi	34	Ed	7.46N	0.03W
Ketelmeer	12	Hb	52.35N	5.45 E
Ketli, Jbel-	13	Gi	35.22N	5.17W
Ketmen, Hrebet-	18	Lc	43.20N	80.00 E
Kétou	34	Fd	7.22N	2.36 E
Kętrzyn	10	Rb	54.06N	21.23 E
Kettering [Eng.-U.K.]	9	Mi	52.24N	0.44W
Kettering [Oh.-U.S.]	44	Ef	39.41N	84.10W
Kettle River	46	Fb	48.42N	118.07W
Kettle River Range	46	Fb	48.30N	118.40W
Keuka Lake	44	Id	42.27N	77.10W
Keur Massène	32	Df	16.33N	16.14W
Keuruu	7	Fe	62.16N	24.42 E
Keuruunselkä	8	Kb	62.10N	24.40 E
Kevelaer	12	Ic	51.35N	6.15 E
Kew	49	Kc	21.54N	72.02W
Kewanee	43	Jc	41.14N	89.56W
Keweenaw Bay	44	Cb	46.56N	88.23W
Keweenaw Peninsula	43	Jb	47.12N	88.25W
Key, Lough-/Loch Ce	9	Eg	54.00N	8.15W
Keya Paha River	45	Ge	42.54N	99.00W
Keyhole Reservoir	46	Md	44.21N	104.51W
Key Largo	44	Gm	25.04N	80.28W
Keypel Bank (EN)	59	Le	25.15S	159.30 E
Keystone Lake	45	Hh	36.15N	96.25W
Key West	39	Kg	24.33N	81.48W
Kez	7	Mh	57.56N	53.43 E
Kezi	37	Dd	20.55S	28.29 E
Kežma	20	Fe	59.02N	101.09 E
Kežmarok	10	Qg	49.08N	20.25 E
Kgalagadi [3]	37	Ce	25.00S	22.00 E
Kgatleng [3]	37	Dd	24.28S	26.05 E
Kghoti	37	Cd	24.55S	21.59 E
Khabr, Kūh-e-	23	Id	28.50N	56.26 E
Khābūr, Nahr al-	24	Ie	35.08N	40.26 E
Khadari, Wādī al-	35	Dc	10.29N	27.00 E
Khādim, Shūshat al-	24	Bh	28.35N	27.43 E
Khadki (Kirkee)	25	Ee	18.34N	73.52 E
Khadra	13	Mh	36.15N	0.35 E
Khafs Banbān	24	Lj	25.31N	46.27 E
Khairónia	15	Fk	38.30N	22.51 E
Khairpur	25	Dc	27.32N	68.46 E
Khāīz, Kūh-e-	24	Ng	30.27N	50.55 E
Khakhea	37	Cd	24.42S	23.30 E
Khalatse	25	Fb	34.20N	76.49 E
Khalīj-e Fārs=Persian Gulf (EN)	21	Hg	27.00N	51.00 E
Khálki	15	Km	36.13N	27.37 E
Khálki	15	Km	36.14N	27.36 E
Khalkidhiki=Chalcidice (EN)	5	Ig	40.25N	23.25 E
Khalkis	15	Gk	38.28N	23.36 E
Khaluf	23	Ie	20.29N	57.59 E
Khambhāt	25	Ed	22.18N	72.37 E
Khambhāt, Gulf of-	21	Jg	21.00N	72.30 E
Khāmgaon	25	Fd	20.41N	76.34 E
Khamili	15	Jn	35.52N	26.14 E
Khamir	23	Ff	15.59N	43.57 E
Khāmis, Ash Shallāl al-= Fifth Cataract (EN)	30	Kg	18.23N	33.47 E
Khamīs Mushayṭ	23	Ff	18.18N	42.44 E
Khammam	25	Ge	17.15N	80.09 E
Khamseh	24	Md	36.40N	48.50 E
Khan	37	Ad	22.42S	14.54 E
Khān	24	Oj	24.13N	56.20 E
Khānābād	23	Kb	36.41N	69.07 E
Khān al Baghdādi	24	Jf	33.51N	42.33 E
Khān al Hammād	24	Kf	32.19N	44.17 E
Khānaqīn	23	Gc	34.21N	45.22 E
Khān az Zabīb	24	Gg	31.28N	36.06 E
Khandwa	25	Fd	21.50N	76.20 E
Khāneh Sorkh, Gardaneh-ye-	24	Qh	29.49N	56.06 E
Khānewāl	25	Eb	30.18N	71.56 E
Khangai Mountains (EN)= Changajn Nuruu → Hangaj, Hrebet-	21	Le	47.30N	100.00 E
Khangai Mountains (EN)= Hangaj, Hrebet- (Changa Nuruu)	21	Le	47.30N	100.00 E
Khánia	6	Ih	35.31N	24.02 E
Khanion, Kólpos-	15	Gn	35.35N	23.50 E
Khanka, Lake- (EN)=Hanka, Ozero-	21	Pe	45.00N	132.24 E
Khanka Lake (EN)=Xingkai Hu	21	Pe	45.00N	132.24 E
Khānpur	25	Ec	28.39N	70.39 E
Khān Shaykhūn	24	Ge	35.26N	36.38 E
Khan Takhtī	24	Kc	38.09N	44.55 E
Khān Yūnus	24	Fg	31.21N	34.19 E
Khānzīr, Rās-	35	Hc	10.50N	45.50 E

Index Symbols

- [1] Independent Nation
- [2] State, Region
- [3] District, County
- [4] Municipality
- [5] Colony, Dependency
- Continent
- Physical Region
- Historical or Cultural Region
- Mount, Mountain
- Volcano
- Hill
- Mountains, Mountain Range
- Hills, Escarpment
- Plateau, Upland
- Pass, Gap
- Plain, Lowland
- Delta
- Salt Flat
- Valley, Canyon
- Crater, Cave
- Karst Features
- Depression
- Polder
- Desert, Dunes
- Forest, Woods
- Heath, Steppe
- Oasis
- Cape, Point
- Coast, Beach
- Cliff
- Peninsula
- Isthmus
- Sandbank
- Island
- Atoll
- Rock, Reef
- Islands, Archipelago
- Rocks, Reefs
- Coral Reef
- Well, Spring
- Geyser
- River, Stream
- Waterfall Rapids
- River Mouth, Estuary
- Lake
- Salt Lake
- Intermittent Lake
- Reservoir
- Swamp, Pond
- Canal
- Glacier
- Ice Shelf, Pack Ice
- Ocean
- Sea
- Gulf, Bay
- Strait, Fjord
- Lagoon
- Bank
- Seamount
- Tablemount
- Ridge
- Shelf
- Basin
- Escarpment, Sea Scarp
- Fracture
- Trench, Abyss
- National Park, Reserve
- Point of Interest
- Recreation Site
- Cave, Cavern
- Historic Site
- Ruins
- Wall, Walls
- Church, Abbey
- Temple
- Scientific Station
- Airport
- Port
- Lighthouse
- Mine
- Tunnel
- Dam, Bridge

Index Symbols

[1]	Independent Nation	◻	Pass, Gap	◻	Depression	◻	Coast, Beach	◻	Rock, Reef
[2]	State, Region	◻	Plain, Lowland	◻	Polder	◻	Cliff	◻	Islands, Archipelago
[3]	District, County	◻	Delta	◻	Desert, Dunes	◻	Peninsula	◻	Rocks, Reefs
[4]	Municipality	◻	Salt Flat	◻	Forest, Woods	◻	Isthmus	◻	Coral Reef
[5]	Colony, Dependency	◻	Valley, Canyon	◻	Heath, Steppe	◻	Sandbank	◻	Well, Spring
◻	Continent	◻	Crater, Cave	◻	Oasis	◻	Island	◻	Geyser
◻	Physical Region	◻	Karst Features	◻	Cape, Point	◻	Atoll	◻	River, Stream

Symbol	Meaning	Symbol	Meaning	Symbol	Meaning	Symbol	Meaning
◻	Waterfall Rapids	◻	Canal	◻	Lagoon	◻	Escarpment, Sea Scarp
◻	River Mouth, Estuary	◻	Glacier, Ice	◻	Bank	◻	Fracture
◻	Lake	◻	Ice Shelf, Pack Ice	◻	Seamount	◻	Trench, Abyss
◻	Salt Lake	◻	Ocean	◻	Tablemount	◻	National Park, Reserve
◻	Intermittent Lake	◻	Sea	◻	Ridge	◻	Point of Interest
◻	Reservoir	◻	Gulf, Bay	◻	Shelf	◻	Recreation Site
◻	Swamp, Pond	◻	Strait, Fjord	◻	Basin	◻	Cave, Cavern

Symbol	Meaning	Symbol	Meaning
◻	Historic Site	◻	Port
◻	Ruins	◻	Lighthouse
◻	Wall, Walls	◻	Mine
◻	Church, Abbey	◻	Tunnel
◻	Temple	◻	Dam, Barrage
◻	Scientific Station		
◻	Airport		

Index Symbols

Index Symbols

Symbol					
[1] Independent Nation	Historical or Cultural Region	Pass, Gap	Depression	Coast, Beach	Rock, Reef
[2] State, Region	Mount, Mountain	Plain, Lowland	Polder	Islands, Archipelago	Waterfall Rapids
[3] District, County	Volcano	Delta	Cliff	Peninsula	River Mouth, Estuary
[4] Municipality	Hill	Salt Flat	Desert, Dunes	Rocks, Reefs	Ice Shelf, Pack Ice
[5] Colony, Dependency	Mountains, Mountain Range	Valley, Canyon	Forest, Woods	Isthmus	Coral Reef
■ Continent	Hills, Escarpment	Crater, Cave	Heath, Steppe	Sandbank	Well, Spring
▨ Physical Region	Plateau, Upland	Karst Features	Oasis	Island	Geyser
			Cape, Point	Atoll	River, Stream

Canal	Lagoon	Escarpment, Sea Scarp	Historic Site	Port
Glacier	Bank	Fracture	Ruins	Lighthouse
Salt Lake	Seamount	Trench, Abyss	Wall, Walls	Mine
Lake	Ocean	Tablemount	National Park, Reserve	Church, Abbey	Tunnel
Intermittent Lake	Sea	Ridge	Point of Interest	Temple	Dam, Bridge
Reservoir	Gulf, Bay	Shelf	Recreation Site	Scientific Station
Swamp, Pond	Strait, Fjord	Basin	Cave, Cavern	Airport

Krokom 7 De 63.20N 14.28 E
Krolevec 16 Hd 51.32N 33.30 E
Kroměříž 10 Ng 49.18N 17.22 E
Krompachy 10 Qh 48.56N 20.52 E
Kronach 10 Hf 50.14N 11.19 E
Krông Kaôh Kŏng 25 Kf 11.37N 102.59 E
Kronoberg 7 Dh 56.40N 14.40 E
Kronockaja Sopka, Vulkan- 20 Lf 54.47N 160.35 E
Kronocki, Mys- 20 Lf 54.43N 162.07 E
Kronocki Zaliv 20 Lf 54.00N 161.00 E
Kronoki 20 Lf 54.33N 161.14 E
Kronprins Christian Land 41 Jb 80.45N 22.00W
Kronprinsesse Mærtha Kyst 66 Bf 72.00S 7.30W
Kronprins Frederiks Bjerge 41 Ie 67.20N 34.00W
Kronprins Olav Kyst 66 Ee 68.30S 42.30 E
Kronštadt 19 Cc 60.01N 29.44 E
Kroonstad 31 Jk 27.46S 27.12 E
Kropotkin 19 Ef 45.26N 40.34 E
Kropotkin 20 Ge 58.36N 115.27 E
Kroppefjäll 8 Ef 58.40N 12.13 E
Krośniewice 10 Pd 52.16N 19.10 E
Krosno 10 Rg 49.42N 21.46 E
Krosno 10 Rg 49.40N 21.45 E
Krosno Odrzańskie 10 Ld 52.04N 15.05 E
Krossfjorden 8 Ad 60.10N 5.05 E
Krotoszyn 10 Ne 51.42N 17.26 E
Kroviga, Gora- 20 Ed 60.40N 91.30 E
Krško 14 Je 45.58N 15.28 E
Krstača 15 Dg 42.58N 20.08 E
Krugersdorp 31 Jk 26.05S 27.35 E
Krui 26 Dh 5.11S 103.56 E
Kruibeke 12 Gc 50.10N 4.19 E
Kruiningen 12 Gc 51.27N 4.02 E
Kruja 15 Ch 41.30N 19.48 E
Krulevščina 8 Li 55.03N 27.52 E
Krumbach 10 Gh 48.15N 10.22 E
Krumovgrad 15 Ih 41.28N 25.39 E
Krung Thep=Bangkok (EN) 22 Mh 13.45N 100.31 E
Krupanj 15 Ce 44.22N 19.22 E
Krupinica 10 Oh 48.05N 18.54 E
Krupinská vrchovina 10 Ph 48.20N 19.15 E
Kruså 8 Cj 54.50N 9.25 E
Krušedol 15 Cd 45.07N 19.57 E
Kruševac 15 Ef 43.35N 21.20 E
Kruševo 15 Eh 41.22N 21.15 E
Krušné Hory=Ore Mountains (EN) 5 He 50.30N 13.15 E
Krustpils 8 Lh 56.29N 26.00 E
Kruzof 40 Le 57.10N 135.40W
Krym 16 Jg 45.23N 36.36 E
Krym, respublika 19 Dg 45.15N 34.20 E
Krymsk 19 Dg 44.54N 37.57 E
Krymskije Gory=Crimean Mountains (EN) 5 Jg 44.45N 34.30 E
Krymski Poluostrov=Crimea (EN) 5 Jf 45.00N 34.00 E
Krynica 10 Qg 49.25N 20.56 E
Krzemieniucha 10 Sb 54.12N 22.54 E
Krzepice 10 Of 50.58N 18.44 E
Krzna 10 Td 52.08N 23.31 E
Krzywiń 10 Me 51.58N 16.49 E
Krzyż 10 Md 52.53N 16.01 E
Ksar el Boukhari 32 Hb 35.53N 2.45 E
Ksar el Kebir 32 Fc 35.00N 5.59W
Ksar es Srhir 13 Gi 35.51N 5.34W
Ksenjevka 20 Gf 53.34N 118.44 E
Kšenski 16 Jd 51.52N 37.44 E
Ksour, Monts des- 32 Gc 32.45N 0.10W
Kū', Wādī al- 35 Dc 12.12N 25.43 E
Kuai He 28 Dh 33.09N 117.32 E
Kuala Belait 26 Ff 4.35N 114.11 E
Kuala Dungun 26 Df 4.47N 103.26 E
Kuala Kangsar 26 Df 4.46N 100.56 E
Kualakapuas 26 Fg 3.01S 114.21 E
Kuala Kerai 26 De 5.32N 102.12 E
Kualakurun 26 Fg 1.07S 113.53 E
Kualalangsa 26 Cf 4.32N 98.01 E
Kuala Lipis 26 Df 4.11N 102.03 E
Kuala Lumpur 22 Mi 3.10N 101.42 E
Kuala Pilah 26 Df 2.44N 102.15 E
Kuala Rompin 26 Df 2.49N 103.29 E
Kuala Terengganu 22 Mi 5.20N 103.08 E
Kuancheng 28 Ed 40.37N 118.31 E
Kuandang 26 Hf 0.52N 122.55 E
Kuandian 27 Lc 40.45N 124.48 E
Kuang-hsi-chuang-tsu Tzu-chih-ch'ü→Guangxi Zhuangzu Zizhiqu=Kwangsi Chuang (EN) 27 Ig 24.00N 109.00 E
Kuang-tun Sheng→Guangdong Sheng=Kwangtung (EN) 27 Jg 23.00N 113.00 E
Kuantan 26 Df 3.48N 103.20 E
Kuba 19 Eg 41.20N 48.35 E
Kuban 5 Jf 45.20N 37.30 E
Kuba-Shima 29b b 26.10N 127.15 E
Kubaysah 24 Jf 33.35N 42.37 E
Kubbum 35 Cc 11.47N 23.47 E
Kubena 7 Jg 59.37N 39.48 E
Kubenskoje, Ozero- 7 Jg 59.40N 39.30 E
Kubnja 7 Li 55.32N 48.28 E
Kubokawa 28 Lh 33.12N 133.08 E
Kubolta 15 Lb 47.48N 28.03 E
Kubrat 15 Jf 43.48N 26.30 E
Kubumesaai 26 Gf 1.31N 115.06 E
Kučaj 15 Ef 43.53N 21.44 E
Kučevo 15 Ee 44.29N 21.41 E
Kutching 22 Ni 1.33N 110.20 E
Kuchinotsu 29 Be 32.36N 130.12 E
Kuçova (Qyteti Stalin) 15 Ci 40.48N 19.54 E
Küçükçekmece 15 Li 40.59N 28.46 E
Küçükerenköy 24 Ee 35.22N 33.45 E
Küçükkuyu 15 Jj 39.32N 26.36 E
Küçük Menderes 15 Kl 37.57N 27.16 E
Kučurgan 15 Mc 46.35N 29.55 E
Kudaka-Jima 29b Ab 26.10N 127.54 E
Kudamatsu 29 Bd 34.01N 131.53 E
Kudat 26 Ge 6.53N 116.50 E
Kudeb 8 Mg 57.30N 28.16 E
Kudirkos-Naumestis 8 Jj 54.43N 22.49 E
Kudowa-Zdrój 10 Mf 50.27N 16.20 E
Kudremukh 25 Ff 13.08N 75.16 E
Kudus 26 Fh 6.48S 110.50 E
Kudymkar 19 Fd 59.01N 54.37 E
Kuee Ruins 65a Fd 19.12N 155.23W
Kuei-chou Sheng→Guizhou Sheng=Kweichow (EN) 27 If 27.00N 107.00 E
Kufi 24 Cc 38.10N 29.43 E
Kufrah, Wāḩāt al-=Kufra Oasis (EN) 30 Jf 24.10N 23.15 E
Kufra Oasis (EN)=Kufrah, Wāḩāt al- 30 Jf 24.10N 23.15 E
Kufstein 14 Gc 47.35N 12.10 E
Kuganavolok 7 Ie 62.16N 36.55 E
Kugmallit Bay 42 Ek 69.30N 133.20W
Kugojeja 16 Kf 46.33N 39.38 E
Kūh, Ra's al- 23 Id 25.48N 57.19 E
Kuḩaylī 35 Eb 19.29N 32.49 E
Kūhbonān 24 Qg 31.23N 56.19 E
Kūhdasht 24 Lf 33.32N 47.36 E
Kūh-e Būrh 24 Pi 27.22N 54.40 E
Kūh-e Gāvbūs 24 Oi 27.10N 54.00 E
Kūh-e Karkas 24 Nf 33.27N 51.48 E
Kūh-e Kārūn 24 Ng 31.27N 50.18 E
Kūhestak 24 Qi 23.47N 57.02 E
Kūhīn, Gardaneh-ye- 24 Md 33.23N 49.37 E
Kühlungsborn 10 Hb 54.09N 11.43 E
Kuhmo 7 Gd 64.08N 29.31 E
Kuhmoinen 8 Kc 61.34N 25.11 E
Kuhn 41 Kd 74.45N 19.45W
Kūhpāyeh 23 Ic 30.35N 57.15 E
Kūhpāyeh [Iran] 24 Of 32.43N 52.26 E
Kūhpāyeh [Iran] 24 Qg 30.43N 57.30 E
Kūhrān, Kūh-e- 23 Id 26.46N 58.12 E
Kuhtuj 20 Je 59.23N 143.10 E
Kuhva 8 Mg 57.17N 28.17 E
Kuiseb 37 Ad 23.00S 14.33 E
Kuishan Ding 27 Ig 22.32N 109.52 E
Kuito 31 Ij 12.23S 16.56 E
Kuiu 40 Me 57.45N 134.10W
Kuivaniemi 7 Fd 65.35N 25.11 E
Kujang 27 Md 39.52N 126.01 E
Kujawy 10 Od 52.45N 18.30 E
Kujawy 10 Od 52.45N 18.35 E
Kujbyšev → Samara 6 Le 53.12N 50.09 E
Kujbyšev → Bulgar 7 Li 55.01N 49.06 E
Kujbyšev 20 Ce 55.27N 78.29 E
Kujbyševskaja Oblast 19 Fe 53.20N 50.30 E
Kujbyševski 19 Ge 53.15N 66.51 E
Kujbyševski 18 Gf 37.53N 68.44 E
Kujbyševskoje Vodohranilišče=Kuybyshev Reservoir (EN) 5 Ke 53.50N 49.00 E
Kujeda 17 Gh 56.26N 55.35 E
Kujgan 19 Hf 45.22N 74.10 E
Kuji 23 Pd 40.11N 141.46 E
Kuji-Gawa 29 Gc 36.30N 140.37 E
Kujtun 20 Ff 54.21N 101.35 E
Kujūkuri-Hama 29 Gd 35.40N 140.30 E
Kujū-San 28 Kh 33.09N 131.15 E
Kūkalār, Kūh-e- 24 Ng 31.50N 50.53 E
Kukalaya, Río- 49 Fg 13.39N 83.37W
Kukësi 15 Dg 42.05N 20.24 E
Kukkia 8 Kc 61.20N 24.40 E
Kukmor 7 Mh 56.13N 50.52 E
Kükürt Dağı 24 Ib 41.07N 41.27 E
Kula [Bul.] 15 Ff 43.53N 22.31 E
Kula [Tur.] 24 Cc 38.30N 28.40 E
Kula [Yugo.] 15 Cd 45.37N 19.32 E
Kulai 26 Df 1.40N 103.36 E
Kulanak 18 Jd 41.18N 75.34 E
Kulandy 19 Ff 46.08N 59.31 E
Kular 20 Ib 70.32N 134.26 E
Kular, Hrebet- 20 Ic 69.00N 133.30 E
Kulata 15 Gh 41.23N 23.22 E
Kulautuva 8 Jj 54.55N 23.43 E
Kulbus 35 Cc 14.24N 22.31 E
Kuldiga/Kuldīga 19 Cd 56.59N 21.59 E
Kuldīga/Kuldiga 19 Cd 56.59N 21.59 E
Kuldur 20 Ig 49.10N 131.40 E
Kulebaki 7 Ki 55.26N 42.32 E
Kulenjin 24 Me 35.40N 49.30 E
Kulen Vakuf 14 Kf 44.33N 16.06 E
Kulgera 58 Eg 25.50S 133.18 E
Kulikov 10 Ug 49.55N 24.06 E
Kulim 26 De 5.22N 100.34 E
Kuljab 19 Gh 37.55N 69.47 E
Kuljabskaja Oblast 19 Gh 38.00N 69.40 E
Kullaa 8 Jc 61.28N 22.10 E
Kullen 7 Ch 56.18N 12.26 E
Kulmasa 34 Ed 9.35N 2.27W
Kulmbach 10 Hf 50.06N 11.27 E
Kuloj 7 Kf 61.03N 42.30 E
Kuloj 19 Eb 66.00N 43.30 E
Kuloj 7 Kf 61.01N 42.12 E
Kulp 24 Ic 38.30N 41.02 E
Kulsary 19 Ff 46.57N 54.02 E
Kultuk 20 Ff 51.44N 103.42 E
Kulu 20 Jd 62.15N 147.45 E
Kulu [India] 25 Fb 31.58N 77.06 E
Kulu [Tur.] 24 Ec 39.06N 33.05 E
Kulumadau 63a Ac 9.03S 152.43 E
Kulunda 20 Cf 52.35N 78.57 E
Kulundinskaja Step 20 Cf 52.45N 79.00 E
Kulundinskoje, Ozero- 20 Cf 53.00N 79.30 E
Kum 24 Bc 38.38N 27.32 E
Kum, Kūh-e- 24 Oh 29.55N 53.45 E
Kuma 29 Ce 33.39N 132.54 E
Kuma 17 Mg 59.33N 66.40 E
Kuma 7 Hc 66.15N 31.02 E
Kuma 5 Kg 44.56N 47.00 E
Kumagaya 28 Of 36.08N 139.23 E
Kumai [Indon.] 26 Fg 2.44S 111.43 E
Kumai [Indon.] 26 Fg 3.23S 112.33 E
Kumaishi 29a Ab 42.08N 139.59 E
Kumajri (Leninakan) 6 Kg 40.47N 43.50 E
Kumak 16 Vd 51.13N 60.08 E
Kumamoto 22 Pf 32.48N 130.43 E
Kumamoto Ken 28 Kh 32.30N 130.50 E
Kumano 28 Nh 33.54N 136.05 E
Kumano-Gawa 29 De 33.45N 135.59 E
Kumano-Nada 29 Ee 34.00N 136.30 E
Kumanovo 15 Eg 42.08N 21.43 E
Kumara [N.Z.] 62 De 42.38S 171.11 E
Kumara 20 Hf 51.35N 126.45 E
Kumasi 31 Gh 6.41N 1.37W
Kumba 34 Ge 4.38N 9.25 E
Kumbakonam 25 Ff 10.58N 79.23 E
Kumbe 26 Lh 8.21S 140.13 E
Kumbo 34 Hd 6.12N 10.40 E
Kumboro Cape 63a Cb 7.18S 157.32 E
Kŭmch'ŏn 28 Ie 38.10N 126.30 E
Kum-Dag 19 Fh 39.13N 54.40 E
Kumdah 33 Ie 20.23N 45.05 E
Kumertau → Jermolajevo 19 Fe 52.45N 55.47 E
Kumhwa 28 Ie 38.17N 127.28 E
Kumihama 29 Dd 35.36N 134.54 E
Kuminski 19 Gd 58.40N 65.55 E
Kumköy (Kilyos) 15 Mh 41.15N 29.02 E
Kumkuduk 27 Fc 40.15N 91.55 E
Kumkurgan 18 Ff 37.50N 67.35 E
Kumla 7 Dg 59.08N 15.08 E
Kumlinge 8 Id 60.15N 20.45 E
Kumluca 24 Dd 36.22N 30.18 E
Kummerower See 10 Ic 53.49N 12.52 E
Kumo/Kokemäki 7 Ff 61.15N 22.21 E
Kumo-Manyčski Kanal 16 Ng 45.27N 44.38 E
Kumon Taung 21 Lg 26.30N 96.50 E
Kumora 20 Ge 55.56N 111.13 E
Kumru 24 Gb 40.53N 37.17 E
Kumu 36 Eb 3.04N 25.09 E
Kumuh 16 Oh 42.11N 47.07 E
Kumukahi, Cape- 60 Od 19.31N 154.49W
Kumul/Hami 22 Le 42.48N 93.27 E
Kümüx 27 Ec 42.15N 88.10 E
Kumzār 24 Qj 26.20N 56.25 E
Kunashiri-Tō/Kunašir, Ostrov- 21 Qe 44.05N 145.51 E
Kunašir, Ostrov-/Kunashiri-Tō 21 Qe 44.05N 145.51 E
Kunašhirski Proliv=Nemuro Strait (EN) 20 Jh 43.50N 145.30 E
Kunchaung 25 Jd 23.50N 96.35 E
Kunda 7 Gg 59.30N 26.30 E
Kunda Jõgi 8 Le 59.25N 26.27 E
Kundelungu, Monts- 36 Ed 9.30S 28.00 E
Kundiawa 59 Ia 6.00S 145.00 E
Kunduchi 36 Gd 6.40S 39.13 E
Kunduk 15 Md 45.51N 29.38 E
Kunduk → Kogilnik 15 Md 45.51N 29.38 E
Kunduk → Sasyk, Ozero- 16 Fg 45.45N 29.40 E
Kunene 30 Ij 17.20S 11.50 E
Kunene (EN)=Cunene 30 Ij 17.20S 11.50 E
Künes/Xinyuan 27 Dc 43.24N 83.18 E
Künes He 27 Dc 43.32N 82.29 E
Kungälv 7 Ch 57.52N 11.58 E
Kungej-Alatau, Hrebet- 19 Hg 42.50N 77.15 E
Kungmiut 41 Ie 65.50N 36.15W
Kungrad 19 Fg 43.06N 58.54 E
Kungsbacka 7 Ch 57.29N 12.04 E
Kungsbackafjorden 8 Eg 57.25N 12.04 E
Kungshamn 8 Df 58.21N 11.15 E
Kungsör 8 Ge 59.25N 16.05 E
Kungu 36 Cb 2.47N 19.12 E
Kungur 19 Fd 57.25N 56.57 E
Kunhegyes 10 Qi 47.22N 20.38 E
Kunhing 25 Jd 21.18N 98.26 E
Kunigami 29b Bb 26.45N 128.11 E
Kunigami-Misaki 29b Bb 27.26N 128.43 E
Kunimi-Dake 29 Be 32.33N 131.03 E
Kunisaki 29 Be 33.34N 131.45 E
Kunisaki-Hantō 29 Be 33.30N 131.40 E
Kunja 7 Hh 57.09N 31.10 E
Kunja-Urgenč 19 Fg 42.20N 59.12 E
Kunlong 25 Jd 23.25N 98.39 E
Kunlun Guan 27 Ig 23.08N 108.40 E
Kunlun Shan 21 Kf 36.00N 84.00 E
Kunlun Shankou 27 Fd 35.40N 94.08 E
Kunming 22 Mg 25.08N 102.43 E
Kunnui 29a Bb 42.26N 140.10 E
Kunovat 17 Ld 64.59N 65.34 E
Kunsan 27 Md 35.59N 126.43 E
Kunshan 28 Fi 31.22N 120.57 E
Kuntaur 34 Cc 13.40N 14.53W
Kununurra 59 Fc 15.47S 128.44 E
Kunyao 36 Gb 1.47N 35.05 E
Kunyu Shan 28 Ff 37.15N 121.45 E
Künzelsau 10 Fg 49.17N 9.41 E
Kuohijärvi 8 Kc 61.15N 24.55 E
Kuolimo 8 Lc 61.15N 27.35 E
Kuop Atoll 64d Bb 7.03N 151.56 E
Kuopio 7 Ge 63.20N 27.35 E
Kuopio 6 Ic 62.54N 27.40 E
Kuorboaivi 7 Gb 69.41N 27.45 E
Kuortane 8 Jb 62.48N 23.30 E
Kupa 14 Ke 45.28N 16.24 E
Kupang 22 Ok 10.10S 123.35 E
Kupiano 60 Dj 10.10S 148.02 E
Kupičev 10 Uf 50.58N 24.52 E
Kupino 20 Cf 54.22N 77.18 E
Kupiškis 7 Fi 55.49N 25.01 E
Kupjansk 19 Df 49.42N 37.37 E
Kupjansk-Uzlovoj 16 Je 49.39N 37.45 E
Küplü [Tur.] 15 Jh 41.07N 26.21 E
Küplü [Tur.] 15 Mi 40.06N 30.00 E
Kuppenheim 12 Kf 48.50N 8.15 E
Kupreanof 40 Me 56.50N 133.30W
Kuqa 22 Ke 41.43N 82.57 E
Kura 16 Mh 44.05N 44.45 E
Kura 5 Kh 39.20N 49.25 E
Kuragaty 18 Ic 43.55N 73.34 E
Kuragino 20 Ef 53.53N 92.40 E
Kurahashi-Jima 29 Cd 34.08N 132.31 E
Kuraminski Hrebet 18 Hd 40.50N 70.30 E
Kurashiki 28 Lg 34.35N 133.46 E
Kurashiki-Kojima 29 Cd 34.28N 133.48 E
Kurashiki-Tamashima 29 Cd 34.33N 133.40 E
Kura-Take 29 Be 32.27N 130.20 E
Kuraymah=Karima (EN) 31 Kg 18.33N 31.51 E
Kurayoshi 28 Lg 35.28N 133.49 E
Kurbneshi 15 Dh 41.47N 20.05 E
Kurčatov 16 Id 51.41N 35.42 E
Kurdaj 18 Jc 43.18N 74.59 E
Kurdistan 21 Gf 37.00N 44.00 E
Kurdistan 23 Fb 37.00N 44.00 E
Kurdufān 30 Jg 13.00N 30.00 E
Kurdufān al Janūbīyah 35 Dc 11.00N 29.30 E
Kurdufān ash Shamālīyah 35 Dc 14.50N 29.40 E
Kure 28 Lg 34.14N 132.34 E
Küre 24 Eb 41.48N 33.43 E
Kure Island 57 Jb 28.25N 178.25W
Kurejka 21 Kc 66.25N 87.12 E
Kuressaare (Kingissepp) 19 Cd 58.17N 22.29 E
Kurgaldžinski 19 He 50.30N 70.03 E
Kurgan 22 Id 55.26N 65.18 E
Kurganinsk 16 Lg 44.57N 40.35 E
Kurganskaja Oblast 19 Gd 55.00N 65.00 E
Kurgan-Tjube 19 Gh 37.51N 68.46 E
Kurgan-Tjubinskaja Oblast 19 Gh 37.30N 68.30 E
Kuria Island 57 Id 0.14N 173.25 E
Kuria Muria Islands (EN)=Khurīyā Murīyā, Jazā'ir 21 Hh 17.30N 56.00 E
Kuri Bay 59 Ec 15.35S 124.50 E
Kurikka 7 Fe 62.37N 22.25 E
Kurikoma 29 Gb 38.50N 140.59 E
Kurikoma-Yama 29 Gb 38.57N 140.47 E
Kuril Basin (EN) 20 Jg 47.00N 150.00 E
Kuril Islands (EN)=Kurilskije Ostrova 21 Re 46.10N 152.00 E
Kurilo 15 Gg 42.49N 23.21 E
Kurilsk 20 Jg 45.16N 147.58 E
Kurilskije Ostrova=Kuril Islands (EN) 21 Re 46.10N 152.00 E
Kuril Trench (EN) 3 Je 47.00N 155.00 E
Kuring Kuru 37 Bc 17.33S 18.33 E
Kurino 29 Bf 31.57N 130.43 E
Kurinskaja Kosa 16 Pj 39.05N 49.10 E
Kurinwás, Río- 49 Fg 12.49N 83.41W
Kuriyama 29a Bb 43.03N 141.45 E
Kurkhūd, Kūh-e- 24 Qd 37.15N 56.30 E
Kurkosa 16 Pj 39.59N 49.08 E
Kurkūmā, Ra's- 24 Gj 25.51N 36.39 E
Kurkur 24 Ek 23.54N 32.19 E
Kurlovski 7 Ji 55.29N 40.39 E
Kurmuk 35 Ec 10.33N 34.17 E
Kurnool 22 Jh 15.50N 78.03 E
Kurobe 28 Nf 36.51N 137.26 E
Kurobe-Gawa 29 Ec 36.55N 137.24 E
Kurogi 29 Be 33.14N 130.40 E
Kuroishi 28 Pd 40.38N 140.36 E
Kuroiso 28 Pf 36.56N 140.03 E
Kuromatsunai 28 Pc 42.43N 140.20 E
Kurono-Seto 29 Be 32.05N 130.10 E
Kurort Družba 15 Kf 43.12N 28.00 E
Kurort Slănčev brjag 15 Kg 42.40N 27.42 E
Kurort Zlatni pjasăci 15 Lf 43.16N 28.02 E
Kuro-Shima 28 Jh 31.52N 129.58 E
Kurovskoje 7 Ji 55.35N 38.59 E
Kurow 61 Dh 44.44S 170.28 E
Kurów 10 Se 51.25N 22.10 E
Kurpiowska, Puszcza- 10 Rc 53.20N 21.30 E
Kuršėnai/Kuršenaj 19 Cd 56.03N 22.58 E
Kuršenaj/Kuršėnai 19 Cd 56.03N 22.58 E
Kuršiu užuriskis 8 Ii 55.05N 21.00 E
Kursk 6 Je 51.42N 36.12 E
Kurskaja Kosa 7 Ei 55.18N 21.00 E
Kurskaja Oblast 19 De 51.45N 36.15 E
Kurski zaliv 7 Ei 55.05N 21.00 E
Kuršumlija 15 Ef 43.09N 21.16 E
Kurtalan 24 Id 37.57N 41.42 E
Kurtamyš 19 Ge 54.55N 64.27 E
Kurti 31 Kg 18.07N 31.33 E
Kurtistown 65 Fd 19.36N 155.04W
Kuru 18 Kb 44.19N 76.42 E
Kuru 8 Jc 61.52N 23.44 E
Kuru 35 Dd 9.08N 26.57 E
Kurugsile 24 Eb 41.51N 32.43 E
Kuruktag 21 Ec 41.30N 89.00 E
Kuruman 30 Jk 26.56S 20.39 E
Kuruman 31 Jk 27.28S 23.28 E
Kurume 28 Kh 33.19N 130.31 E
Kurunegala 25 Gg 7.29N 80.22 E
Kurur, Jabal- 35 Ea 20.31N 31.32 E
Kuraeme=Courland (EN) 8 Ih 56.50N 22.00 E
Kuraemes Augstiene/Kurzemskaja Vozvyšennost 8 Jh 56.45N 22.15 E
Kurzemskaja Vozvyšennost/Kurzemes Augstiene 8 Jh 56.45N 22.15 E
Kusa 17 Ii 55.20N 59.29 E
Kuşada Körfezi 15 Kl 37.50N 27.08 E
Kuşadası 24 Bd 37.51N 27.15 E
Kusagaki-Guntō 27 Me 31.00N 129.00 E
Kusaie → Kosrae 57 Hd 5.19N 162.59 E
Kusalu/Kuusalu 8 Ke 59.23N 25.25 E
Kusary 16 Pi 41.24N 48.29 E
Kusatsu [Jap.] 29 Fc 36.37N 138.35 E
Kusatsu [Jap.] 29 Dd 35.03N 135.59 E
Kuščevskaja 16 Kf 46.33N 39.37 E
Kušcinski 16 Oi 40.33N 46.06 E
Kusel 12 Je 49.33N 7.24 E
Kuş Gölü 24 Bb 40.10N 27.59 E
Kushida-Gawa 29 Ed 34.36N 136.34 E
Kushikino 28 Ki 31.44N 130.16 E
Kushima 28 Ki 31.29N 131.14 E
Kushimoto 28 Mh 33.28N 135.47 E
Kushiro 22 Qe 42.58N 144.23 E
Kushiro-Gawa 29a Db 42.59N 144.23 E
Kushtia 25 Hd 23.55N 89.07 E
Kuška 18 Dg 35.16N 62.18 E
Kuskokwim 38 Cc 60.17N 162.27W
Kuskokwim Bay 38 Cd 59.45N 162.25W
Kuskokwim Mountains 38 Dc 62.30N 156.00W
Kušmurun 19 Ge 52.27N 64.40 E
Kušmurun, Ozero- 19 Ge 52.40N 64.45 E
Kušnarenkovo 17 Gi 55.06N 55.22 E
Kušnica 16 Ce 48.29N 23.20 E
Kusŏng 27 Md 39.59N 125.16 E
Kussharo Ko 28 Rc 43.35N 144.15 E
Kustanaj 22 Id 53.10N 63.35 E
Kustanajskaja Oblast 19 Ge 53.00N 64.00 E
Kustavi 8 Id 60.30N 21.25 E
Kustavi/Gustavs 8 Id 60.30N 21.25 E
Küstenkanal 10 Dd 52.57N 7.18 E
Kūstī 31 Kg 13.10N 32.40 E
Kustvlakte=Coast Plain (EN) 11 Ic 51.00N 2.40 E
Kusu 29 Be 33.16N 131.09 E
Kušva 19 Fd 58.18N 59.45 E
Kut, Ko- 25 Kf 11.40N 102.35 E
Kūt 'Abdollāh 24 Mg 31.13N 48.39 E
Kutacane 26 Cf 3.30N 97.48 E
Kutahya 23 Cb 39.25N 29.59 E
Kutaisi 6 Kg 42.15N 42.40 E
Kutch, Gulf of- → Kachchh, Gulf of 21 Ig 22.36N 69.30 E
Kutch, Rann of- 25 Ed 24.05N 70.10 E
Kutchan 28 Pc 42.54N 140.45 E
Kutcharo-Ko 29a Ca 45.10N 142.20 E
Kutina 14 Ke 45.29N 16.47 E
Kutkai 25 Jd 23.27N 97.56 E
Kutkašen → Gabel'a 16 Oi 40.58N 47.52 E
Kutná Hora 10 Lg 49.57N 15.16 E
Kutno 10 Pd 52.15N 19.23 E
Kutse, Gora-/Kuutse Mägi 8 Lg 57.58N 26.23 E
Kuttara-Ko 29a Bb 42.30N 141.11 E
Kutu 31 Ii 2.44S 18.09 E
Kutum 35 Cc 14.12N 24.40 E
Küty 10 Nh 48.40N 17.0 E
Kuty 15 Ia 48.13N 25.1 E
Kuujjuaq 39 Md 58.10N 68.30W
Kuujjuarapik 42 Je 55.20N 76.56W
Kuuli-Majak 19 Fg 40.16N 52.45 E
Kuurne 12 Fd 50.51N 3.17 E
Kuusalu/Kusalu 8 Ke 59.23N 25.25 E
Kuusamo 6 Ib 66.00N 29.10 E
Kuusankoski 8 Ld 60.54N 26.38 E
Kuutse Mägi/Kutse, Gora- 8 Lg 57.58N 26.24 E
Kuvandyk 16 Td 51.29N 57.20 E
Kuvdlorssuaq 41 Gd 74.38N 56.40W
Kuvšinovo 7 Ih 57.03N 34.13 E
Kuwait (EN)=Al Kuwayt 22 Gg 29.30N 47.45 E
Kuwait (EN)=Al Kuwayt 22 Gg 29.20N 47.59 E
Kuwana 29 Ed 35.04N 136.39 E
Kuybyshev Reservoir (EN)=Kujbyševskoje Vodohranilišče 5 Ke 53.50N 49.00 E
Küysanjaq 24 Kd 36.05N 44.38 E
Kuytun 27 Dc 44.25N 84.58 E
Kuyucak 15 Ll 37.55N 28.28 E
Kuzey Kibris = North Cyprus 23 Db 35.15N 33.40 E
Kuzneck 19 Ee 53.07N 46.36 E
Kuznecki Alatau 21 Kd 54.45N 88.00 E
Kuznečnoje 8 Mc 61.04N 29.58 E
Kuźnia Raciborska 10 Of 50.11N 18.15 E
Kuzomen 19 Db 66.18N 36.49 E
Kuzovatovo 7 Lj 53.33N 47.41 E
Kuzumaki 29 Ga 40.02N 141.26 E
Kuzuryū-Gawa 29 Ec 36.13N 136.08 E
Kvænangen 7 Ea 70.05N 21.13 E
Kvaløy 7 Eb 69.40N 18.30 E
Kvaløya 7 Fa 70.37N 23.52 E
Kvalsund 7 Fa 70.30N 24.00 E
Kvam 3 Cc 61.40N 9.42 E
Kvareli 16 Ni 41.57N 45.47 E
Kvarkeno 17 Ij 52.05N 59.40 E
Kvarnbergsvattnet 7 Dd 64.36N 14.03 E
Kvarner 14 If 44.45N 14.15 E
Kvarnerić 14 If 44.45N 14.35 E
Kvichak Bay 40 He 58.48N 157.30W
Kvemo-Kedi 16 Oi 41.22N 46.31 E
Kvenna 8 Bd 60.01N 7.56 E
Kvichak 40 He 59.10N 156.40W
Kvikkjokk 7 Dc 66.57N 17.47 E
Kvina 8 Bf 58.17N 6.56 E
Kvinesdal 7 Bg 58.19N 6.57 E
Kvissleby 8 Gb 62.17N 17.21 E
Kviteggia 8 Bb 62.05N 6.40 E
Kviteseid 8 Ce 59.24N 8.30 E
Kvitøya 67 Je 80.08N 32.35 E
Kwa 30 Ii 3.10S 6.11 E
Kwahu Plateau 34 Ed 6.30N 0.30W
Kwailibesi 63a Ec 8.20S 160.40 E
Kwajalein Atoll 57 Hd 9.05N 167.20 E
Kwakoegron 54 Gb 5.15N 55.20W
Kwale [Kenya] 36 Gc 4.11S 39.27 E
Kwale [Nig.] 34 Gd 5.45N 6.25 E
Kwamouth 36 Cc 3.10S 16.12 E
Kwa Mtoro 36 Gd 5.14S 35.26 E
Kwando 36 Df 18.27S 23.32 E
Kwangdae-ri 27 Mc 40.34N 127.33 E
Kwangju 22 Of 35.09N 126.55 E
Kwango 30 Ii 3.14S 17.22 E

Index Symbols

Independent Nation	Historical or Cultural Region	Pass, Gap	Depression	Coast, Beach	Rock, Reef	Waterfall Rapids	Canal	Lagoon	Escarpment, Sea Scarp
State, Region	Mount, Mountain	Plain, Lowland	Polder	Cliff	Islands, Archipelago	River Mouth, Estuary	Glacier	Bank	Fracture
District, County	Volcano	Delta	Desert, Dunes	Peninsula	Rocks, Reefs	Lake	Ice Shelf, Pack Ice	Seamount	Trench, Abyss
Municipality	Hill	Salt Flat	Forest Woods	Isthmus	Coral Reef	Salt Lake	Ocean	Tablemount	National Park, Reserve
Colony, Dependency	Mountains, Mountain Range	Valley, Canyon	Heath, Steppe	Sandbank	Well, Spring	Intermittent Lake	Sea	Ridge	Point of Interest
Continent	Hills, Escarpment	Crater, Cave	Oasis	Island	Geyser	Reservoir	Gulf, Bay	Shelf	Recreation Site
Physical Region	Plateau, Upland	Karst Features	Cape, Point	Atoll	River, Stream	Swamp, Pond	Strait, Fjord	Basin	Cave, Cavern

Historic Site, Ruins, Wall, Walls, Church, Abbey, Temple, Scientific Station, Airport, Port, Lighthouse, Mine, Tunnel, Dam, Bridge

Kwangsi Chuang (EN) = Guangxi Zhuangzu Zizhiqu (Kuang-hsi-chuang-tsu Tzu-chih-ch'ü) [2] 27 Ig 24.00N 109.00 E
Kwangsi Chuang (EN) = Kuang-hsi-chuang-tsu Tzu-chih-ch'ü → Guangxi Zhuangzu Zizhiqu [2] 27 Ig 24.00N 109.00 E
Kwangtung (EN) = Guangdong Sheng (Kuang-tung Sheng) [2] 27 Jg 23.00N 113.00 E
Kwangtung (EN) = Kuang-tun Sheng → Guangdong Sheng [2] 27 Jg 23.00N 113.00 E
Kwanmo-bong 28 Jd 41.42N 129.13 E
Kwara [2] 34 Fd 8.30N 5.00 E
Kweichow (EN) = Guizhou Sheng (Kuei-chou Sheng) [2] 27 If 27.00N 107.00 E
Kweichow (EN) = Kuei-chou Sheng → Guizhou Sheng 27 If 27.00N 107.00 E
Kwekwe 31 Jj 18.55S 29.49 E
Kweneng [3] 37 Cd 24.00S 24.00 E
Kwenge 30 Ii 4.50S 18.44 E
Kwethluk 40 Gd 60.49N 161.27W
Kwidzyn 10 Oc 53.45N 18.56 E
Kwigillingok 40 Ge 59.51N 163.08W
Kwilu 30 Ii 3.22S 17.22 E
Kwisa 10 Le 51.35N 15.25 E
Kwoka, Gunung- 26 Jg 0.31S 132.27 E
Kyabé 31 Ih 9.27N 18.57 E
Kyabram 59 Jg 36.19S 145.03 E
Kyaikkami 25 Je 16.04N 97.34 E
Kyaikto 25 Je 17.18N 97.01 E
Kyaka 36 Fc 1.16S 31.25 E
Kyancutta 58 Eh 33.08S 135.34 E
Kyan-Zaki 29b Ab 26.05N 127.40 E
Kyaukpyu 25 Id 20.51N 92.58 E
Kyaukse 25 Jd 21.36N 96.08 E
Kybartai/Kibartaj 8 Jj 54.38N 22.44 E
Kyeintali 25 Ie 18.00N 94.29 E
Kyelang 25 Fb 32.35N 77.02 E
Kyfhauser 10 He 51.25N 11.10 E
Kyjov 10 Ng 49.01N 17.08 E
Kyle, Lake- 37 Ed 20.12S 31.00 E
Kyle of Lochalsh 9 Hd 57.17N 5.43W
Kyll 10 Cg 49.48N 6.42 E
Kyllburg 12 Id 50.02N 6.35 E
Kymi [2] 7 Gf 61.00N 28.00 E
Kymijoki 8 Ld 60.30N 26.52 E
Kyn 17 Ih 57.52N 58.32 E
Kynnefjäll 8 Df 58.42N 11.41 E
Kynsivesi 8 Lb 62.25N 26.10 E
Kyoga, Lake- 30 Kh 1.30N 33.00 E
Kyōga-Dake 29 Be 33.00N 130.05 E
Kyōga-Misaki 28 Mg 35.45N 135.11 E
Kyonan 29 Fd 35.07N 139.49 E
Kyŏnggi-Do [2] 28 If 37.30N 127.15 E
Kyŏnggi-man 28 Hf 37.25N 126.00 E
Kyŏngju 27 Md 35.50N 129.13 E
Kyŏngsang-Namdo [2] 28 Jg 35.15N 128.30 E
Kyŏngsang-Pukto [2] 28 Jf 36.20N 128.40 E
Kyŏngsŏng 28 Jd 41.40N 129.40 E
Kyōto 22 Pf 35.00N 135.45 E
Kyōto Fu 28 Mg 35.25N 135.15 E
Kypros → Kipros = Cyprus (EN) 23 Db 35.01N 33.00 E
Kyra 20 Gg 49.36N 111.58 E
Kyren 20 Ef 51.41N 102.10 E
Kyrenia 24 Ee 35.20N 33.19 E
Kyrgesara/Kõrgesaare 8 Je 59.00N 22.25 E
Kyrgyz Sovetik Socialistik Respublikasy/Kirgizskaja SSR → Kyrgyzstan 19 Hg 41.30N 75.00 E
Kyrgyzstan 19 Hg 41.30N 75.00 E
Kyritz 10 Id 52.57N 12.24 E
Kyrkheden 8 Ed 60.10N 13.29 E
Kyrksæterora 7 Be 63.17N 9.06 E
Kyrkslätt/Kirkkonummi 8 Kd 60.07N 24.26 E
Kyrö 8 Jd 60.42N 22.45 E
Kyrönjoki 8 Ia 63.14N 21.45 E
Kyrösjärvi 8 Jc 61.45N 23.10 E
Kyröskoski 8 Jc 61.40N 23.11 E
Kyštym 19 Gd 55.42N 60.34 E
Kysucké Nové Mesto 10 Og 49.18N 18.48 E
Kythera (EN) = Kíthira 5 Ih 36.15N 23.00 E
Kythraia 24 Ee 35.15N 33.29 E
Kyuquot Sound 46 Bb 49.55N 127.25W
Kyūshū 21 Pf 32.50N 131.00 E
Kyushu-Palau Ridge (EN) 3 Ih 20.00N 136.00 E
Kyūshū-Sanchi 29 Be 32.40N 131.10 E
Kyyjärvi 7 Fe 63.02N 24.34 E
Kyyvesi 8 Lc 61.55N 27.05 E
Kyzikos 24 Bb 40.28N 27.47 E
Kyzyl 22 Ld 51.42N 94.27 E
Kyzylart, Pereval- 19 Hh 39.22N 73.20 E
Kyzyl-Kija 19 Hg 40.14N 72.12 E
Kyzylkum 21 Ie 42.00N 64.00 E
Kyzylrabot 19 Hh 37.28N 74.45 E
Kyzylsu 18 Gf 37.22N 69.22 E
Kyzylsu 18 He 39.17N 71.25 E
Kyzylžar 19 Gf 48.17N 69.49 E
Kzyl-Orda 22 Ie 44.48N 65.28 E
Kzyl-Ordinskaja Oblast [3] 19 Gf 45.00N 65.00 E
Kzyltu 19 He 53.41N 72.15 E

L

Laa an der Thaya 14 Kb 48.43N 16.23 E
Laakdal 12 Gc 51.05N 4.59 E
La Alberca 13 Fd 40.29N 6.06W
La Alcarria 13 Jd 40.31N 2.45W
La Almunia de Doña Godina 13 Kc 41.29N 1.22W
La Ametlla de Mar 13 Md 40.54N 0.48 E
La Ardilla, Cerro- 48 Hf 22.15N 102.40W
La Armuña 13 Gc 41.05N 5.35W
Laasphe 12 Kd 50.56N 8.24 E
La Asunción 54 Fa 11.02N 63.53W
Laau Point 65a Db 21.06N 157.16W
Laayoune 13 Ni 35.42N 2.00 E
Lab 15 Eg 42.45N 21.01 E
Laba 16 Kg 45.10N 39.40 E
La Babia 48 Hc 28.34N 102.04W
Laba Dağı 15 Kl 37.22N 27.33 E
Labaddey 35 Ge 0.32N 42.45 E
Labadie Bank 9 Ek 50.30N 8.15W
La Banda 56 Hc 27.44S 64.15W
La Bañeza 13 Gb 42.18N 5.54W
La Barca 48 Hg 20.17N 102.34W
Labardén 55 Cm 36.57S 58.06W
La Barge 46 Je 42.16N 110.12W
La Barra, Punta- 49 Lh 11.30N 70.10W
La-Barre-en-Ouche 12 Cf 48.57N 0.40 E
La Baule-Escoublac 11 Dg 47.17N 2.24W
Labbezanga 34 Fc 14.59N 0.43 E
Labe 31 Fg 11.19N 12.17W
Labe = Elbe (EN) 5 Ge 53.50N 9.00 E
La Belle 44 Gl 26.46N 81.26W
Labelle 44 Jb 46.17N 74.45W
La Berzosa 13 Fd 40.35N 6.40W
Labin 14 Ie 45.05N 14.08 E
Labinsk 19 Eg 44.35N 40.44 E
Labis 26 Df 2.23N 103.02 E
La Bisbal/La Bisbal d'Empordà 13 Pc 41.57N 3.03 E
La Bisbal d'Empordà/La Bisbal 13 Pc 41.57N 3.03 E
La Blanca, Laguna- 55 Bj 30.14S 60.38W
Labo 26 Gb 54.24N 10.13 E
Laborec 10 Rh 48.31N 21.54 E
Laborie 51k Bb 13.45N 61.00W
Labota 26 Hg 2.52S 122.10 E
Labouheyre 11 Fj 44.13N 0.55W
Laboulaye 56 Hd 34.07S 63.24W
Labra, Peña- 13 Ha 43.03N 4.26W
Labrador 38 Md 55.00N 70.00W
Labrador, Coast of- 38 Me 56.00N 60.35W
Labrador Basin (EN) 3 Dd 53.00N 48.00W
Labrador City 39 Md 52.57N 66.54W
Labrador Sea 38 Nd 57.00N 53.00W
Labrang → Xiahe 27 Hd 35.18N 102.30 E
Lábrea 53 Jf 7.16S 64.46W
Labrieville 44 Ma 49.19N 69.34W
Labrit 11 Fj 44.06N 0.33W
Labuan, Pulau- 26 Ge 5.19N 115.13 E
Labudalin → Ergun Youqi 27 La 50.16N 120.09 E
Labuha 26 Ig 0.37S 127.29 E
Labuhan 26 Eh 6.22S 105.50 E
Labuhanbajo 26 Gh 8.29S 119.54 E
Labuhanbilik 26 Df 2.31N 100.10 E
Labuk, Teluk- 26 Ge 6.10N 117.50 E
La Bureba 13 Ib 42.36N 3.24W
Labutta 25 Ie 16.09N 94.46 E
Labytnangi 22 Ic 66.39N 66.21 E
Lac [3] 35 Ac 13.30N 14.20 E
Lača, Ozero- 7 Jf 61.20N 38.50 E
La Cadena 48 Ge 25.53N 104.12W
La Calamine/Kelmis 12 Hd 50.43N 6.00 E
La Calandria 55 Cj 30.48S 58.39W
Lac Allard 42 Lf 50.30N 63.30W
La Campiña 13 Hg 37.45N 4.45W
Lacanau 11 Ej 44.59N 1.05W
Lacanau, Étang de- 11 Ej 44.58N 1.07W
Lacanau-Océan 11 Ei 45.00N 1.12W
Lacantún, Rio- 48 Ni 16.36N 90.39W
La-Capelle 11 Je 49.58N 3.55 E
Laćarak 15 Ce 45.00N 19.34 E
La Carlota [Arg.] 56 Hd 33.26S 63.18W
La Carlota [Phil.] 26 Hd 10.25N 122.55 E
La Carlota [Sp.] 13 Hg 37.40N 4.56W
La Carolina 13 If 38.15N 3.37W
Lacaune 11 Ik 43.43N 2.42 E
Lacaune, Monts de- 11 Ik 43.40N 2.36 E
Laccadive Islands → Lakshadweep 21 Jh 11.00N 72.00 E
La Ceiba [Hond.] 39 Kh 15.47N 86.50W
La Ceiba [Ven.] 49 Li 9.28N 71.04W
Lacepede Bay 59 Hg 36.45S 139.45 E
Lacepede Islands 59 Ec 16.50S 122.10 E
La Cerdaña/La Cerdanya 13 Nb 42.24N 1.40 E
La Cerdanya/La Cerdaña 13 Nb 42.24N 1.40 E
Lacey 46 Dc 47.07N 122.49W
Lac Giao → Buon Me Thuot 25 Lf 12.40N 108.03 E
La Chaise-Dieu 11 Ji 45.19N 3.42 E
La Charité-sur-Loire 11 Jg 47.11N 3.01 E
La Châtre 11 Hh 46.35N 1.59 E
La Chaux-de-Fonds 14 Ac 47.06N 6.50 E
Lachay, Punta- 54 Cf 11.18S 77.39W
La China, Sierra- 55 Bm 36.47S 60.34W
Lachine 44 Kc 45.26N 73.40W
Lachlan River 57 Fh 34.21S 143.57 E
La Chorrera [Col.] 54 Dd 0.45S 73.00W
La Chorrera [Pan.] 47 Ig 8.53N 79.47W
Laçi 15 Ch 41.38N 19.43 E
Lačin 16 Oj 39.39N 46.33 E
La Ciotat 11 Lk 43.10N 5.36 E
Łąck 10 Pd 52.28N 19.40 E
Lackawanna 44 Hd 42.49N 78.49W
Lac La Biche 42 Gf 54.46N 111.58W
Lac la Martre 42 Fd 63.21N 117.00W
Lac Mégantic 42 Kg 45.35N 70.53W
La Colina 55 Bm 37.20S 61.32W
La Coloma 49 Fb 22.15N 83.34W
La Colorada 48 Dc 28.41N 110.25W
Lacombe 42 Gf 52.28N 113.44W
Lacon 45 Lf 41.02N 89.24W
La Concepción [Pan.] 49 Fi 8.31N 82.37W
La Concepción [Ven.] 49 Lh 10.48N 71.46W
La Concha 48 Gg 21.46N 105.29W
Laconi 14 Dk 39.51N 9.03 E
Laconia 43 Mc 43.32N 71.29W
Laconia, Gulf of- (EN) = Lakonikós Kólpos 15 Fm 36.35N 22.40 E
La Coronilla 55 Fk 33.44S 53.31W
La Coruña 6 Fg 43.22N 8.23W
La Coruña [3] 13 Da 43.10N 8.25W
La Côte-Saint-André 11 Li 45.23N 5.15 E
La Couronne 11 Gi 45.37N 0.06 E
La Courtine-le-Trucq 11 Ii 45.42N 2.16 E
Lacq 11 Fk 43.25N 0.38W
Lacroix-sur-Meuse 12 Hf 48.58N 5.31 E
La Crosse [Ks.-U.S.] 45 Gg 38.32N 99.18W
La Crosse [Wi.-U.S.] 39 Je 43.49N 91.15W
La Cruz [Arg.] 56 Ic 29.10S 56.38W
La Cruz [C.R.] 49 Eh 11.04N 85.39W
La Cruz [Mex.] 47 Cd 23.55N 106.54W
La Cruz [Ur.] 56 Id 33.56S 56.15W
La Cruz de Río Grande 49 Eg 13.06N 84.10W
La Cruz de Taratara 49 Mh 11.03N 69.44W
La Cuesta 48 Hc 28.45N 102.25W
La Cumbre 56 Hd 30.58S 64.30W
Lac Yora 35 Cb 9.08N 20.35 E
Ladário 55 Dd 19.01S 57.35W
Ladbergen 12 Jb 52.08N 7.45 E
Lądek-Zdrój 10 Mf 50.21N 16.50 E
Ladenburg 12 Ke 49.28N 8.37 E
La Désirade 50 Fd 16.19N 61.03W
La Digue Island 37b Ca 4.21S 55.50 E
Lādik 24 Fb 40.36N 36.45 E
Ladismith 37 Cf 33.30S 21.16 E
Ladispoli 14 Gi 41.56N 12.05 E
Lado, Jabal- 35 Ed 5.06N 31.35 E
Ladoga, Lake- (EN) = Ladožkoje Ozero 5 Jc 61.00N 31.00 E
Ladong 27 Ig 24.49N 109.34 E
La Dorada 54 Db 5.22N 74.42W
Ladožkoje Ozero = Ladoga, Lake (EN) 5 Jc 61.00N 31.00 E
Ladrones, Islas- 49 Fj 7.52N 82.26W
Laduškin 8 Ij 54.35N 20.10 E
Ladva-Vetka 7 If 61.20N 34.29 E
Lady Ann Strait 42 Ja 75.45N 80.00W
Ladybrand 37 De 29.19S 27.25 E
Lady Evelyn Lake 44 Gb 47.20N 80.10W
Lady Newnes Ice Shelf 66 Kf 73.40S 167.30 E
Ladysmith [B.C.-Can.] 46 Db 48.58N 123.49W
Ladysmith [S.Afr.] 31 Jk 28.34S 29.45 E
Ladysmith [Wi.-U.S.] 43 Ib 45.28N 91.07W
Ladyžin 16 Fe 48.40N 29.13 E
Lae 58 Fe 6.43S 147.01 E
Lae Atoll 57 Hd 8.56N 166.14 E
La Eduvigis 55 Ch 26.50S 59.05W
Laem, Khao- 25 Kf 14.19N 101.11 E
Laer [Ger.] 12 Jb 52.04N 7.21 E
Laer [Ger.] 12 Kb 52.06N 8.05 E
Lærdalsøyri 7 Bf 61.06N 7.29 E
La Escala/L'Escala 13 Pb 42.07N 3.08 E
La Esmeralda 54 Ec 3.10N 65.33W
Læsø 7 Bh 57.15N 10.00 E
Læsø Rende 8 Dg 57.15N 10.45 E
La Española = Hispaniola (EN) 38 Lh 19.00N 71.00W
La Esperanza [Bol.] 54 Ff 14.34S 62.10W
La Esperanza [Hond.] 49 Cf 14.20N 88.10W
La Estrada 13 Db 42.41N 8.29W
Lafayette [Al.-U.S.] 44 Ei 32.54N 85.24W
Lafayette [In.-U.S.] 43 Jc 40.25N 86.53W
Lafayette [La.-U.S.] 39 Jf 30.14N 92.01W
La Fère 12 Fe 49.40N 3.22 E
La Ferrière-sur-Risle 12 Cf 48.59N 0.48 E
La Ferté-Bernard 11 Gf 48.11N 0.40 E
La Ferté-Frênel 12 Cf 48.50N 0.30 E
La Ferté-Macé 11 Ff 48.36N 0.22W
La Ferté-Milon 12 Fe 49.10N 3.07 E
La Ferté-Saint-Aubin 11 Hg 47.43N 1.56 E
La Ferté-sous-Jouarre 11 Jf 48.57N 3.08 E
Laffān, Ra's- 24 Nj 25.54N 51.35 E
Lafia 34 Gd 8.29N 8.31 E
Lafiagi 34 Gd 8.52N 5.25 E
La Flèche 11 Fg 47.42N 0.05W
Lafnitz 14 Kd 46.57N 16.16 E
La Foa 63b Be 21.43S 165.49 E
La Follette 44 Eg 36.23N 84.07W
La Fria 49 Ki 8.13N 72.15W
Laft 24 Pi 26.54N 55.46 E
La Fuente de San Esteban 13 Fd 40.48N 6.15W
Laga, Monti della- 14 Hh 42.45N 13.35 E
La Galite (EN) = Jālitah 30 He 37.32N 8.56 E
La Gallareta 55 Bi 29.34S 60.23W
Lagamar 55 Id 18.13S 46.48W
Lagan 8 Eh 56.33N 12.56 E
Lagan 8 Eh 56.55N 13.59 E
Lagan/Abhainn an Lagáin 9 Hg 54.37N 5.53W
Lagarina, Val- 14 Fe 45.50N 11.10 E
La Garita Mountains 45 Ch 38.00N 106.40W
Lagarto 54 Kf 10.54S 37.41W
Lagash 24 Lg 31.27N 46.13 E
Lagawe 26 Hc 16.49N 121.06 E
Lage 12 Kc 51.59N 8.48 E
Lågen 7 Cf 61.08N 10.25 E
Lagh Bogal 36 Gb 0.42N 40.55 E
Laghmān [3] 23 Lb 35.00N 70.15 E
Laghouat 31 He 33.48N 2.53 E
Laghouat [3] 32 Hc 33.30N 3.15 E
La Gloria 49 Ki 8.38N 73.48W
Lagny 11 If 48.52N 2.43 E
Lagoa 13 Dg 37.08N 8.27W
Lagôa 55 Eb 14.08S 55.20W
Lagoa da Prata 55 Je 20.01S 45.33W
Lagoa Vermelha 56 Jc 28.13S 51.32W
Lagodehi 16 Oi 41.50N 46.14 E
La Gomera 49 Bf 14.05N 91.03W
Lagonegro 14 Jj 40.07N 15.46 E
Lagonoy Gulf 26 Hd 13.35N 123.45 E
Lagoon 64n Ab 10.23S 161.05W
Lagos 13 Dg 37.06N 8.40W
Lagos 31 Hh 6.27N 3.23 E
Lágos 15 Ih 41.01N 25.07 E
Lagos [2] 34 Fd 6.30N 3.30 E
Lagos, Baía de- 13 Dg 37.06N 8.39W
Lagosa 36 Ed 5.57S 29.53 E
Lagos de Moreno 47 Dd 21.21N 101.55W
La Grand-Combe 11 Kj 44.13N 4.02 E
La Grande 43 Db 45.20N 118.05W
La Grande Fosse 9 Kl 49.40N 3.00W
La Grande-Motte 11 Kk 43.34N 4.07 E
La Grande Rivière 38 Ld 53.50N 79.00W
La Grande Trench (EN) = Hurd Deep 9 Kl 49.40N 3.00W
La Grange 44 Ef 38.24N 85.23W
Lagrange 44 Ee 41.39N 85.25W
La Grange [Ga.-U.S.] 43 Je 33.02N 85.02W
La Grange [Tx.-U.S.] 45 Hl 29.54N 96.52W
La Gran Sabana 54 Fb 5.30N 61.30W
La Grita 54 Db 8.08N 71.59W
Lagskär 8 He 59.50N 20.00 E
La Guaira 53 Jd 10.36N 66.56W
La Guajira [2] 54 Da 11.30N 72.30W
Lagua Lichan, Puntan- 64b Ba 15.16N 145.50 E
Laguardia 13 Jb 42.33N 2.35W
La Guardia [Sp.] 13 Dc 41.54N 8.53W
La Guardia [Sp.] 13 Ie 39.47N 3.29W
La Guasima 48 Kg 21.06N 97.49W
La Guerche-sur-l'Aubois 11 Ih 46.57N 2.57 E
Laguiole 11 Ij 44.41N 2.51 E
Laguna 56 Kc 28.29S 48.47W
Laguna Alsina 55 Am 36.49S 62.13W
Laguna Beach 46 Gj 33.33N 117.51W
Laguna Blanca 55 Cg 25.08S 58.15W
Laguna de Bay 26 Hd 14.23N 121.15 E
Laguna Limpia 55 Ch 26.29S 59.41W
Laguna Mountains 46 Gj 32.55N 116.25W
Laguna Paiva 56 Hd 31.19S 60.39W
Laguna Superior 47 Fe 16.20N 94.25W
Laguna Veneta 14 Ge 45.25N 12.20 E
Laguna Yema 55 Bg 24.15S 61.15W
Lagunillas [Bol.] 54 Fg 19.38S 63.43W
Lagunillas [Mex.] 48 Ii 17.50N 101.44W
Lagunillas [Ven.] 49 Lh 10.08N 71.16W
Lagunillas [Ven.] 49 Li 8.31N 71.24W
Laha 27 Lb 48.13N 124.36 E
La Habana [3] 49 Fb 22.45N 82.10W
La Habana = Havana (EN) 39 Kg 23.08N 82.22W
Lahad Datu 26 Ge 5.02N 118.19 E
Laham 34 Fc 14.54N 4.25 E
Lahat 26 Dg 3.48S 103.32 E
Lahdenpohja 7 Hf 61.33N 30.13 E
Lahewa 26 Cf 1.24N 97.11 E
Lahij 23 Fg 13.04N 44.53 E
Lāhījān 23 Hb 37.12N 50.01 E
Lahn 10 Df 50.18N 7.37 E
Lahnstein 12 Jd 50.20N 7.29 E
Laholm 7 Ch 56.31N 13.02 E
Laholmsbukten 8 Eh 56.35N 12.50 E
Lahore 22 Jf 31.35N 74.18 E
Lahr 10 Dh 48.20N 7.52 E
Lahti 6 Ic 60.58N 25.40 E
Laï 31 Ih 9.24N 16.18 E
Laiagam 60 Ci 5.31S 143.39 E
Lai'an 28 Eh 32.28N 118.26 E
Lai Chau 25 Kd 22.02N 103.10 E
Laich o'Moray 9 Jd 57.40N 3.30W
Laie 65a Db 21.39N 157.56W
Laifeng 27 If 29.31N 109.23 E
Laighean/Leinster 9 Gh 53.00N 7.00W
L'Aigle 11 Gf 48.45N 0.38 E
Laignes 11 Kg 47.50N 4.22 E
Laihia 7 Fe 62.58N 22.01 E
Lainioälven 7 Fc 67.22N 22.39 E
Lairg 9 Ic 58.01N 4.25W
Lairi 35 Bc 10.49N 17.06 E
Lairi, Batha de- 35 Bc 12.28N 16.45 E
Lais 26 Dg 3.32S 102.03 E
La Isabela 49 Gb 22.57N 80.01W
Laisamis 36 Gb 1.36N 37.48 E
Laiševo 7 Li 55.26N 49.32 E
Laishui 28 Ce 39.23N 115.42 E
Laisvall 7 Dc 66.08N 17.10 E
Laitila 7 Ef 60.53N 21.41 E
Laiwu 28 Df 36.12N 117.40 E
Laiwui 26 Ig 1.22S 127.40 E
Laixi (Shuiji) 28 Ff 36.52N 120.31 E
Laiyang 27 Ld 36.59N 120.39 E
Laiyuan 27 Jd 39.19N 114.43 E
Laizhou Wan 27 Ef 37.30N 119.30 E
Laja 56 Fe 37.16S 72.42W
Laja 17 Hc 66.20N 56.16 E
La Jara 16 He 39.40N 4.55W
Lajeado 55 Gi 29.27S 51.58W
Lajeado, Serra do- 55 Hd 19.08S 49.56W
Lājerd 24 Oe 35.24N 53.04 E
Lajeş [Braz.] 54 Ke 5.41S 36.14W
Lajes [Braz.] 53 Kh 27.48S 50.19W
Lajes do Pico 32 Bb 38.23N 28.16W
Lajosmizse 10 Pi 47.01N 19.33 E
La Junta [Co.-U.S.] 43 Gd 37.59N 103.33W
La Junta [Mex.] 48 Fc 28.28N 107.20W
Lak Bor 36 Hb 1.18N 40.40 E
Lake Cargelligo 59 Jf 33.18S 146.23 E
Lake Charles 39 Jf 30.12N 93.12W
Lake City 43 Ke 30.12N 82.38W
Lake District 9 Jg 54.30N 3.10W
Lake Fork Creek 46 Jf 40.13N 110.07W
Lake Geneva 45 Le 42.36N 88.26W
Lake George 44 Kd 43.25N 73.45W
Lake Grace 59 Df 33.06S 118.28 E
Lake Harbour 42 Kd 62.51N 69.53W
Lake Havasu City 46 Hi 34.27N 114.22W
Lake Itasca 45 Ic 46.51N 95.13W
Lake Jackson 45 Il 29.02N 95.27W
Lake King 59 Df 33.05S 119.40 E
Lakeland 43 Kf 28.03N 81.57W
Lake Louise 46 Ga 51.26N 116.11W
Lakemba 63d Cc 18.13S 178.47W
Lakemba Passage 63d Cb 17.53S 178.32W
Lake Mills 45 Je 43.25N 93.32W
Lake Minchumina 40 Ia 63.53N 152.19W
Lake Murray 60 Ci 6.54S 141.28 E
Lake Oswego 46 Dd 45.26N 122.39W
Lake Placid 44 Kc 44.18N 73.59W
Lake Providence 45 Kj 32.48N 91.11W
Lake Pukaki 62 Df 44.11S 170.08 E
Lake Range 46 Ff 40.15N 119.25W
Lake River 42 Jf 54.28N 82.30W
Lakes Entrance 59 Jg 37.53S 147.59 E
Lakeside 46 If 41.13N 112.57W
Lake Tekapo 62 Df 44.00S 170.29 E
Lakeview 43 Cc 42.11N 120.21W
Lakeville 45 Jd 44.39N 93.14W
Lake Wales 44 Gl 27.55N 81.35W
Lakewood [Co.-U.S.] 45 Dg 39.44N 105.06W
Lakewood [Oh.-U.S.] 44 Ge 41.29N 81.50W
Lake Worth 44 Gl 26.37N 80.03W
Lakhdar, Chergui Kef- 13 Pi 35.57N 3.16 E
Lakhdaria 13 Ph 36.34N 3.35 E
Lâki 15 Hh 41.50N 24.50 E
Lakin 45 Fh 37.58N 101.15W
Lakinsk 7 Jh 56.04N 39.58 E
Lákmos Óros 15 Ej 39.40N 21.07 E
Lakon, Ile- 57 Hf 14.17S 167.30 E
Lakonikós Kólpos = Laconia, Gulf of- (EN) 15 Fm 36.35N 22.40 E
Lakota [3] 34 Dd 5.53N 5.42W
Lakota [I.C.] 34 Dd 5.51N 5.41W
Lakota [N.D.-U.S.] 45 Gb 48.02N 98.21W
Lakselv 7 Fa 70.03N 25.01 E
Lakshadweep = Laccadive Islands 21 Jh 11.00N 72.00 E
Lakshadweep [3] 25 Ef 11.00N 72.00 E
La Laguna 55 Bb 14.30S 61.06W
Lalanna 37 Hd 23.28S 45.05 E
Lalapaşa 15 Jh 41.50N 26.44 E
Lāleh Zār, Kūh-e- 21 Hg 29.24N 56.46 E
La Leonesa 55 Ch 27.03S 58.43W
Lālī 24 Mf 32.21N 49.06 E
Lalibela 35 Fc 12.00N 39.04 E
La Libertad [2] 54 Ce 8.00S 78.30W
La Libertad [ElSal.] 47 Gf 13.29N 89.16W
La Libertad [Guat.] 49 Be 16.47N 90.07W
La Libertad [Guat.] 49 Bf 15.30N 91.50W
La Libertad [Hond.] 49 Df 14.43N 87.36W
La Ligua 56 Fd 32.27S 71.14W
Lalín 13 Db 42.39N 8.07W
La Línea 13 Gh 36.10N 5.19W
Lalitpur 25 Fd 24.41N 78.25 E
Lalla Khedidja 13 Qh 36.27N 4.14 E
Lālmanir Hāt 25 Hc 25.54N 89.27 E
La Loche 42 Ge 56.29N 109.27W
La Loupe 11 Hf 48.28N 1.01 E
La Louvière 11 Kd 50.29N 4.11 E
L'Alpe-d'Huez 11 Mi 45.06N 6.04 E
La Lucila 55 Bj 30.25S 61.01W
Lalzit, Gjiri i- 15 Ch 41.31N 19.29 E
La Machine 11 Jh 46.53N 3.28 E
La Maddalena 14 Di 41.13N 9.24 E
La Maiella 5 Hg 42.05N 14.07 E
La Maladeta/Malditos, Montes- 13 Mb 42.40N 0.50 E
La Malbaie 42 Kg 47.39N 70.10W
La Mancha 5 Fh 39.05N 3.00W
La Manche 5 Fe 50.20N 1.00W
Lamap 61 Cc 16.26S 167.43 E
Lamar 43 Gd 38.05N 102.37W
La Maragatería 13 Fb 42.25N 6.10W
La Marina 13 Lf 38.35N 0.05W
La Marmora 14 Dk 39.59N 9.20 E
La Marque 45 Il 29.22N 94.58W
Lamas 54 Ce 6.25S 76.35W
Lamastre 11 Kj 44.59N 4.35 E
Lamawan 28 Ad 40.05N 111.25 E
Lambach 14 Hb 48.05N 13.53 E
Lamballe 11 Df 48.28N 2.31W
Lambar, Rio- 55 Jd 19.30S 45.00W
Lambaréné 31 Ii 0.42S 10.13 E
Lambari 55 Je 21.58S 45.21W
Lambasa 61 Ec 16.26S 179.24 E
Lambay/Reachrainn 9 Gh 53.29N 6.01W
Lambayeque [2] 54 Ce 6.20S 80.00W
Lambayeque 54 Ce 6.42S 79.55W
Lambert Glacier 66 Ff 71.00S 70.00 E
Lambert Land 41 Jc 79.10N 21.00W
Lamberts Bay 31 Il 32.05S 18.17 E
Lambro 14 De 45.08N 9.32 E
Lambsheim 12 Ke 49.31N 8.17 E
Lambton, Cape- 42 Fb 71.04N 123.08W
Lamé 35 Ad 9.15N 14.32 E
Lame Deer 46 Ld 45.37N 106.40W
Lamego 13 Ec 41.06N 7.49W
Lamentin 51e Ab 16.16N 61.38W
La Mesa 46 Gj 32.46N 117.01W
Lamesa 43 Ge 32.44N 101.57W
La Meta 14 Hj 41.41N 13.56 E
Lamezia Terme 14 Kl 38.59N 16.17 E
Lamia 15 Fk 38.54N 22.26 E
Lamina 55 De 20.34S 56.14W
Lamlam, Mount- 64c Bb 13.20N 144.40 E
Lammermuir Hills 9 Kf 55.52N 2.40W
Lammhult 8 Fg 57.10N 14.35 E
Lammi 7 Ff 61.05N 25.01 E
Lamoil 64d Ba 7.39N 151.41 E
Lamon Bay 21 Oh 14.25N 122.00 E
Lamone 14 Gf 44.29N 12.08 E
Lamoni 45 Jf 40.37N 93.56W
Lamont 44 Fj 30.21N 83.50W
La Montaña 52 If 10.00S 72.50W
La Moraña 13 Hd 40.45N 4.55W
La Mosquitia 49 Ef 15.00N 84.20W
La Mothe-Achard 11 Eh 46.37N 1.40W
Lamotrek Atoll 57 Fd 7.30N 146.20 E

Index Symbols

[1] Independent Nation
[2] State, Region
[3] District, County
[4] Municipality
[5] Colony, Dependency
Continent
Physical Region
Historical or Cultural Region
Mount, Mountain
Volcano
Hill
Mountains, Mountain Range
Hills, Escarpment
Plateau, Upland
Pass, Gap
Plain, Lowland
Delta
Salt Flat
Valley, Canyon
Crater, Cave
Karst Features
Depression
Polder
Desert, Dunes
Forest, Woods
Heath, Steppe
Oasis
Cape, Point
Coast, Beach
Cliff
Peninsula
Isthmus
Sandbank
Island
Atoll
Rock, Reef
Islands, Archipelago
Rocks, Reefs
Coral Reef
Well, Spring
Geyser
River, Stream
Waterfall Rapids
River Mouth, Estuary
Lake
Salt Lake
Intermittent Lake
Reservoir
Swamp, Pond
Canal
Glacier
Ice Shelf, Pack Ice
Ocean
Sea
Gulf, Bay
Strait, Fjord
Lagoon
Bank
Seamount
Tablemount
Ridge
Shelf
Basin
Escarpment, Sea Scarp
Fracture
Trench, Abyss
National Park, Reserve
Point of Interest
Recreation Site
Cave, Cavern
Historic Site
Ruins
Wall, Walls
Church, Abbey
Temple
Scientific Station
Airport
Port
Lighthouse
Mine
Tunnel
Dam, Bridge

Lamotte-Beuvron	11 Ig	47.36N	2.01 E
La Moure	45 Gc	46.21N	98.18W
Lampang	25 Je	18.16N	99.34 E
Lampasas	45 Gk	31.03N	98.12W
Lampazos de Naranjo	48 Id	27.01N	100.31W
Lampedusa	14 Go	35.30N	12.35 E
Lampertheim	10 Eg	49.36N	8.28 E
Lampeter	9 Ii	52.07N	4.05W
Lamphun	25 Je	18.35N	99.00 E
Lampione	14 Go	35.35N	12.20 E
Lampung	26 Dg	5.00 S	105.00 E
Lamu	31 Li	2.16 S	40.54 E
Lamud	54 Ce	6.09 S	77.55W
La Mure	11 Lj	44.54N	5.47 E
Lan	16 Ec	52.09N	27.18 E
Lana	14 Fd	46.37N	11.09 E
Lana, Rio de la-	48 Li	17.49N	95.09W
Lanai	65a Ec	20.50N	156.55W
Lanaihale	65a Ec	20.49N	156.52W
Lanai Island	57 Lb	20.50N	156.55W
Lanaken	12 Hd	50.53N	5.39 E
Lanark	9 Jf	55.41N	3.48W
Lanbi Kyun	25 Jf	10.50N	98.15 E
Lancang (Menglangba)	27 Gg	22.37N	99.57 E
Lancang Jiang = Mekong (EN)	21 Mh	10.15N	105.55 E
Lancashire	9 Kh	53.55N	2.40W
Lancashire Plain	9 Kh	53.40N	2.45W
Lancaster	9 Kh	53.45N	2.50W
Lancaster [Ca.-U.S.]	43 De	34.42N	118.08W
Lancaster [Eng.-U.K.]	9 Kg	54.03N	2.48W
Lancaster [Mo.-U.S.]	45 Jf	40.31N	92.32W
Lancaster [N.H.-U.S.]	44 Lc	44.29N	71.34W
Lancaster [Oh.-U.S.]	44 Ff	39.43N	82.37W
Lancaster [Ont.-Can.]	44 Jc	45.12N	74.30W
Lancaster [Pa.-U.S.]	43 Lc	40.01N	76.19W
Lancaster [S.C.-U.S.]	44 Gh	34.43N	80.47W
Lancaster Sound	38 Kb	74.13N	84.00W
Lançeiro	55 Fe	20.59 S	53.43W
Lancelin	59 Df	31.01 S	115.19 E
Lanciano	14 Ih	42.14N	14.23 E
Lančín	15 Gi	48.31N	24.49 E
Lancun	28 Ff	36.25N	120.11 E
Łańcut	10 Sf	50.05N	22.13 E
Land	8 Cd	60.45N	10.00 E
Ländana	38 Bd	5.15 S	12.10 E
Landau an der Isar	10 Ih	48.41N	12.41 E
Landau in der Pfalz	10 Eg	49.12N	8.07 E
Land Bay	66 Mf	75.25 S	141.45W
Landeck	14 Ec	47.08N	10.34 E
Landen	12 Hd	50.45N	5.05 E
Lander	43 Fc	42.50N	108.44W
Landerneau	11 Bf	48.27N	4.15W
Lander River	59 Gd	20.25 S	132.00 E
Landeryd	8 Gd	57.05N	13.16 E
Landes	11 Fj	44.15N	1.00W
Landes	11 Fj	44.00N	0.50W
Landesbergen	12 Lb	52.34N	9.08 E
Landeta	55 Ak	32.01 S	62.04W
Landete	13 Ke	39.54N	1.22W
Landfallis	25 If	13.40N	93.02 E
Land Glacier	66 Mf	75.40 S	141.45W
Landi Kotal	25 Eb	34.06N	71.09 E
Landless Corner	36 Ee	14.53 S	28.04 E
Landrecies	12 Fd	50.08N	3.42 E
Landsberg am Lech	10 Gh	48.03N	10.52 E
Landsbro	8 Fg	57.22N	14.54 E
Land's End	5 Fe	50.05N	5.44W
Lands End	42 Fa	76.25N	122.45W
Landshut	10 Ih	48.32N	12.09 E
Landskrona	8 Ei	55.52N	12.50 E
Landsort	8 Gf	58.45N	17.50 E
Landsortsdjupet	8 Hf	58.40N	18.30 E
Landusky	46 Kc	47.54N	108.37W
La Neuve-Lyre	12 Cf	48.54N	0.45 E
Lanfeng → Lankao	28 Cg	34.49N	114.48 E
Lang	46 Mb	49.56N	104.23W
La'nga Co	27 De	30.41N	81.17 E
Langádha	15 Gi	40.45N	23.04 E
Langádhia	15 Fl	37.39N	22.03 E
Långan	7 De	63.19N	14.44 E
Langano, Lake-	35 Fd	7.36N	38.43 E
Langao	27 Ie	32.20N	108.53 E
Langara	26 Mg	4.02 S	123.00 E
Langarfoss	7a Cb	65.35N	14.15W
Langasian	26 Ie	8.16N	125.39 E
Langdon	45 Gb	48.46N	98.22W
Langeac	11 Ji	45.06N	3.29 E
Langeais	11 Gg	47.20N	0.24 E
Langeb	35 Fb	17.46N	36.41 E
Langebaan	37 Bf	33.06 S	18.02 E
Langeberg	37 Cf	33.56 S	20.45 E
Langedijk	12 Gb	52.42N	4.48 E
Langeland	7 Ci	55.00N	10.50 E
Langelands Bælt	8 Dj	54.50N	10.55 E
Längelmävesi	8 Kc	61.30N	24.20 E
Langen	12 Ke	49.59N	8.40 E
Langenberg	12 Kc	51.17N	7.38 E
Langenburg	45 Fa	50.50N	101.43W
Langenfeld (Rheinland)	12 Ic	51.06N	6.57 E
Langenhagen	10 Fd	52.27N	9.45 E
Langenselbold	12 Ld	50.11N	9.02 E
Langeoog	10 Dc	53.46N	7.32 E
Langeri	20 Jf	50.08N	143.20 E
Langesund	8 Ce	59.00N	9.45 E
Langesundsfjorden	8 Bb	62.27N	6.12 E
Langevåg	8 Bb	62.27N	6.12 E
Langfang → Anci	27 Kd	39.29N	116.40 E
Långfjället	8 Bb	62.45N	12.20 E
Langfjorden	8 Bb	62.45N	7.30 E
Langhe	14 Mm	38.40N	8.00 E
Langholm	9 Kf	55.09N	3.00W
Langjökull	5 Ec	64.39N	20.00W
Langkawi, Pulau-	26 Ce	6.32N	99.48 E
Langkon	26 Ge	6.32N	116.42 E

Langlade	44 Ja	48.12N	75.57W
Langnau im Emmental	14 Ed	46.56N	7.46 E
Langnoc	11 Jj	44.43N	3.51 E
Langon	11 Fj	44.33N	0.15W
Langörüd	24 Md	37.11N	50.10 E
Langøya	7 Db	68.44N	14.50 E
Langreo	13 Ga	43.18N	5.41W
Langres	11 Lg	47.52N	5.20 E
Langres, Plateau de-	5 Gf	47.41N	5.03 E
Langrune-sur-Mer	12 Be	49.19N	0.22W
Langsa	22 Li	4.28N	97.58 E
Långsele	8 Ga	63.11N	17.04 E
Långshyttan	8 Gd	60.27N	16.01 E
Lang Son	25 Ld	21.50N	106.44 E
Lang Suan	25 Jg	9.55N	99.07 E
Languedoc	5 Gg	44.00N	4.00 E
Languedoc	11 Jj	44.00N	4.00 E
Langueyú, Arroyo-	55 Cm	36.39 S	58.27W
Langwedel	12 Lb	52.58N	9.13 E
Langxi	28 Ei	31.08N	119.11 E
Langzhong	27 Ie	31.40N	106.04 E
Lan Hsu	27 Lg	22.00N	121.30 E
Laniel	44 Hb	47.06N	79.15W
Lanin, Volcán-	52 Ii	39.38 S	71.30W
Lankao	27 Cc	35.12N	79.50 E
Lankao (Lanfeng)	27 Kg	21.00N	116.00 E
Lankao (Lanfeng)	28 Cg	34.49N	114.48 E
Länkipohja	8 Kc	61.44N	24.48 E
Lannemezan	11 Gk	43.08N	0.23 E
Lannemezan, Plateau de-	11 Gk	43.09N	0.27 E
Lannion	11 Cf	48.44N	3.28W
Lannion, Baie de-	11 Cf	48.43N	3.34W
La Noria	56 Bb	20.23 S	69.53W
La Puntilla	42 If	52.13N	87.53W
L'Anse	44 Cb	46.45N	88.27W
Lansdowne House	45 Ke	43.22N	91.13W
Lansing [Ia.-U.S.]	39 Ke	42.43N	84.34W
Lansing [Mi.-U.S.]	7 Fc	66.39N	22.12 E
Lansjärv	10 Qc	53.33N	20.30 E
Lantar	20 Ie	56.05N	137.35 E
Lanta Yai, Ko-	25 Jg	7.35N	99.03 E
Lanteri	55 Ci	29.50 S	59.39W
Lanterne	11 Mg	47.44N	6.03 E
Lanús	55 Ci	34.43 S	58.24W
Lanusei	14 Dk	39.53N	9.32 E
Lanvaux, Landes de-	11 Dg	47.47N	2.36W
Lanxi [China]	28 Ej	29.13N	119.28 E
Lanxi [China]	23 Ha	46.15N	126.16 E
Lanxian (Dongcun)	28 Ae	38.17N	111.38 E
Lanyi He	28 Ae	38.40N	110.53 E
Lanzarote	30 Ff	29.00N	13.40W
Lanzhou	22 Mf	36.03N	103.41 E
Lanzo Torinese	14 Be	45.16N	7.28 E
Lao	14 Jk	39.47N	15.48 E
Laoag	22 Oh	18.12N	120.36 E
Laoang	26 Id	12.34N	125.00 E
Lao Cai	22 Mg	22.30N	103.57 E
Laocheng	28 Hc	42.37N	124.04 E
Laoha He	27 Lc	43.24N	120.39 E
Lao He	28 Cj	29.02N	115.47 E
Laohuanghe Kou	28 Ef	37.39N	119.02 E
Laois	9 Fi	53.00N	7.30W
Laojunmiao → Yumen	22 Lf	39.50N	97.44 E
Laojun Shan	27 Je	33.45N	111.38 E
Lao Ling	28 If	41.24N	126.10 E
Laon	11 Je	49.34N	3.37 E
Laona	45 Ld	45.34N	88.40W
Laonnois	12 Ge	49.35N	3.40 E
La Orchila, Isla-	54 Ea	11.48N	66.10W
La Oroya	53 Ij	11.32 S	75.57W
Laos	22 Mh	18.00N	105.00 E
Laoshan (Licun)	28 Ff	36.10N	120.25 E
Laotougou	28 Jc	42.54N	129.09 E
Laou	13 Gi	35.26N	5.05W
Laoye Ling	28 Kb	44.50N	130.10 E
Lapa	56 Kc	25.45 S	49.42W
Lapai	34 Gd	9.03N	6.43 E
Lapalisse	11 Jh	46.15N	3.38 E
La Palma	30 Ff	28.40N	17.52W
La Palma [El.Sal.]	49 Cf	14.19N	89.11W
La Palma [Pan.]	47 Ig	8.25N	78.09W
La Palma del Condado	13 Fg	37.23N	6.33W
La Paloma	55 El	34.40 S	54.10W
La Pampa	56 Ge	37.00 S	66.00W
La Panne/De Panne	12 Ec	51.06N	2.35 E
La Paragua	54 Fb	6.50 S	63.20W
La Partida, Isla-	48 De	24.30N	110.25W
La Paz	54 Ee	15.00 S	68.00W
La Paz [Arg.]	56 Id	30.45 S	59.39W
La Paz [Arg.]	56 Gd	33.28 S	67.33W
La Paz [Bol.]	53 Jg	16.30 S	68.09W
La Paz [Col.]	49 Kh	10.23N	73.10W
La Paz [Hond.]	49 Cf	14.16N	87.40W
La Paz [Mex.]	39 Hg	24.10N	110.18W
La Paz [Ur.]	55 Dk	34.46 S	56.13W
La Paz [Ur.]	49 Lh	10.41N	72.00W
La Paz, Bahía de-	47 Bd	24.09N	110.25W
La Paz, Llano de-	48 De	24.00N	110.30W
La Paz Centro	49 Dg	12.20N	86.41W
La Pedrera	54 Dd	1.18 S	69.40W
La Peer	44 Fd	43.03N	83.19W
La Pelada	55 Bj	30.52 S	60.59W
La Pérouse, Bahía-	65d Bd	27.04 S	109.18W
La Perouse Strait (EN) = Söya-Kaikyō	21 Qe	45.30N	142.00 E
La Perouse Strait (EN) = Laperuza, Proliv-	21 Qe	45.30N	142.00 E
La Pesca	48 Ke	23.47N	97.47W
La Petite Pierre	12 Jf	48.52N	7.19 E
La Picasa, Laguna-	55 Bj	34.20 S	62.14W
La Piedad Cavadas	48 Ig	20.21N	102.00W
La Pine	46 Ee	43.40N	121.30W
Lapinjärvi/ Lappträsk	8 Ld	60.36N	26.09 E

Lapinlahti	7 Ge	63.22N	27.30 E
La Plaine	51g Bb	5.20N	61.15W
La Plana	13 Ld	0.00N	0.05W
Lapland (EN) = Lappi	5 Ib	66.50N	22.00 E
Lapland (EN) = Lappland	5 Ib	66.50N	22.00 E
La Plant	45 Fd	5.10N	100.38W
La Plata	53 Ki	34.55 S	57.57W
La Pobla de Lillet	13 Nb	42.15N	1.59 E
La Pobla de Segur/Pobla de Segur	13 Mb	42.15N	0.58 E
La Pocatière	44 Lb	47.21N	70.02W
La Porte	44 De	41.36N	86.43W
Lapovo	15 Ee	44.11N	21.06 E
Lappajärvi	7 Fe	63.08N	23.40 E
Lappeenranta/Villmanstrand	6 Ic	61.04N	28.11 E
Lappfjärd/Lapväärtti	7 Fe	62.15N	21.32 E
Lappi	7 Gc	67.40N	26.30 E
Lappi	7 Gc	67.40N	26.30 E
Lappi = Lapland (EN)	5 Ib	66.50N	22.00 E
Lappo/Lapua	7 Fe	62.57N	23.00 E
Lappträsk/Lapinjärvi	8 Ld	60.36N	26.09 E
Lapri	20 He	56.45N	124.59 E
Laprida	56 He	37.33 S	60.49W
Lâpseki	24 Bb	40.20N	26.31 E
Lapta	24 Ee	35.20N	33.10 E
Laptev Sea (EN) = Laptevyh, More-	67 Fd	74.00N	126.00 E
Laptevyh, More- = Laptev Sea (EN)	67 Fd	74.00N	126.00 E
Lapua/Lappo	7 Fa	62.57N	23.00 E
La Puebla	13 Pe	39.46N	3.01 E
La Puebla de Cazalla	13 Gg	37.14N	5.19W
Lapuna	55 Ba	17.19 S	60.28W
La Puntilla	52 Hf	2.11 S	81.01W
La Purisima	48 Cd	26.10N	112.04W
Lâpuş	15 Hc	47.30N	24.01 E
Lâpuş	15 Gc	47.39N	23.54 E
Le Push	46 Cc	47.55N	124.38W
Lapväärtti/Lappfjärd	7 Fe	62.15N	21.32 E
Łapy	10 Sd	52.00N	22.53 E
Laqiyat al Arba'in	35 Da	20.03N	28.02 E
La Quemada	48 If	22.27N	102.45W
La Quiaca	56 Gb	22.06 S	65.37W
L'Aquila	14 Hh	42.22N	13.22 E
Lar	23 Hd	27.41N	54.17 E
Lara	54 Ea	10.10N	69.50W
Larache	32 Fb	35.12N	6.09W
Laragne-Montéglin	11 Lj	44.19N	5.49 E
Lârak	23 Id	26.52N	56.22 E
La Rambla	13 Hg	37.36N	4.44W
Laramie	39 Ie	41.19N	105.36W
Laramie Mountains	43 Fc	42.00N	105.40W
Laramie Peak	46 Me	42.17N	105.27W
Laramie River	46 Me	42.12N	104.32W
Laranjal, Rio-	55 Ff	23.12 S	51.45W
Laranjeiras do Sul	56 Jc	25.25 S	52.25W
Larantuka	26 Hh	8.21 S	122.59 E
Larat	22 Jh	7.09 S	131.46 E
Larat, Pulau-	26 Jh	7.00 S	131.50 E
La Raya	49 Ji	8.20N	74.34W
L'Arba	13 Ph	36.34N	3.05 E
L'Arbaa-Naït-Irathen	13 Qh	36.38N	4.12 E
L'Arbresle	11 Ki	45.49N	4.37 E
Lârbro	7 Eh	57.-7N	18.47 E
Larche, Col de-	11 Mj	44.25N	6.53 E
Larde	37 Fc	16.28 S	39.43 E
Larderello	14 Gg	43.14N	10.53 E
La Réale	11 Fj	44.35N	0.02W
Laredo [Sp.]	13 Ia	43.24N	3.25W
Laredo [Tx.-U.S.]	39 Jg	27.31N	99.30W
Laren	12 Hb	52.16N	5.16 E
Lärestän	27 Fc	27.00N	55.30 E
Larestan	24 Fd	27.00N	55.00 E
Large Island	51p Cb	12.24N	61.30W
Largentière	11 Kj	44.32N	4.18 E
L'Argentière-la-Bessée	11 Mj	44.49N	6.33 E
Largo, Cayo-	49 Gc	21.36N	81.28W
Largs	9 If	55.48N	4.52W
La Ribagorça/Ribagorza	13 Mb	42.15N	0.30 E
La Ribera	13 Kb	42.30N	2.00W
Larimore	45 Hc	47.54N	97.38W
Larino	14 Ii	41.48N	14.54 E
La Rioja	56 Gc	30.00 S	67.00W
La Rioja	13 Jb	42.20N	2.30W
La Rioja	53 Jh	29.25 S	66.40W
Lérisa	6 Ih	39.38N	22.25 E
La Rivière-Thibouville-Nassandres-	12 Ce	49.00N	0.45 E
Las Tunas	49 Ic	21.00N	77.00W
Lârkâna	25 Dc	27.34N	68.13 E
Larmor-Plage	11 Cg	47.42N	3.23W
Larnaka/Lárnax	23 Dc	34.55N	33.38 E
Lárnax/Larnaka	23 Dc	34.55N	33.38 E
Larne/Latharna	9 Hg	54.51N	5.49W
Larned	45 Gg	38.11N	99.06W
La Robla	13 Gb	42.48N	5.37W
La Roche	63b De	21.28 S	168.02 E
La Roche-en-Ardenne	12 Hd	50.11N	5.35 E
La Rochefoucauld	11 Gi	45.44N	0.23 E
La Roche-Guyon	12 De	49.05N	1.38 E
La Rochelle	6 Ff	46.10N	1.09W
La Roche-sur-Yon	11 Fh	46.40N	1.26W
La Roda	13 Je	39.13N	2.09W
La Romana	49 Ke	18.25N	68.58W
La Ronge	42 Gg	55.06N	105.17W
La Ronge, Lac-	33 Id	55.05N	105.00W
La Rosita	29 Ji	25.35N	90.23W
La Rouco	13 Ec	41.56N	7.44W
Larreynaga	49 Mg	12.40N	86.33W
Larrey Point	59 Bc	20.00 S	119.11 E
Larrimah	58 Ef	15.35 S	133.12 E
Larsa	24 Kg	31.16N	45.44 E
Lars Christensen Kyst	68 Fe	69.30 S	68.00 E
Larsen, Mount-	66 Kf	74.51 S	162.12 E
Larsen Ice Shelf	68 Qe	68.30 S	62.30W

Lartijas Padomju Socialistiska Republika →			
Latvija	19 Cd	57.00N	25.00 E
La Rumorosa	48 Aa	32.34N	116.06W
Laruns	11 Fk	43.00N	0.25W
Larvik	7 Cg	59.04N	10.00 E
La Sabana [Arg.]	55 Ch	27.52 S	59.57W
La Sabana [Col.]	54 Ec	2.20N	68.32W
Las Adjuntas, Presa de-	43 Jf	23.55N	98.45W
La Sagra	13 Id	40.05N	4.00W
La Sagra	13 Jg	37.57N	2.34W
La Salle	45 Lf	4.20N	89.06W
La Salle, Pic-	47 Je	18.22N	71.59W
La Sal Mountains	46 Kg	38.30N	109.10W
La Sanabria	13 Fb	42.08N	6.30W
Las Animas	45 Eg	38.04N	103.13W
Lås 'änäd	35 Hd	8.26N	47.24 E
La Sarre	42 Jg	48.48N	79.12W
Las Aves, Islas-	54 Ea	11.58N	67.33W
Las Avispas	55 Bi	29.53 S	61.18W
Las Bardenas	13 Kb	42.10N	1.25W
Las Bonitas	50 Di	7.52N	65.40W
Las Breñas	56 Hc	27.05 S	61.05W
Las Cabezas de San Juan	13 Gh	36.59N	5.56W
Lascahobas	49 Le	18.50N	71.56W
Lascano	55 Ek	33.40 S	54.12W
Las Casitas, Cerro-	47 Bc	23.31N	109.53W
Lascaux, Grotte de-	11 Hi	45.03N	1.11 E
Las Cejas	56 Hc	26.53 S	64.44W
Las Chilcas, Arroyo-	55 Cm	37.16 S	58.26W
Las Choapas	47 Fe	17.55N	94.05W
Las Cinco Villas	13 Kb	42.05N	1.07W
Las Cruces	43 Fe	32.23N	106.29W
Lasdsdere	35 Hc	10.10N	46.01 E
Las Dawa'o	35 Hc	10.22N	49.03 E
La Segarra	13 Nc	41.30N	1.10 E
La Selva	13 Oc	41.40N	2.50 E
La Serena	13 Gf	38.45N	5.30W
La Serena	53 Ih	29.54 S	71.16W
La Seu d'Urgell/Seo de Urgel	13 Nb	42.21N	1.28 E
La-Seyne-sur-Mer	11 Lk	43.36N	5.53 E
Las Flores	56 Je	36.03 S	59.07W
Las Heras	56 Gd	32.51 S	68.49W
Lashkar Gāh	23 If	31.35N	64.21 E
Las Hurdes	13 Fd	40.20N	6.20W
La Sila	5 Hh	39. 5N	16.30 E
Łasin	10 Pc	53.32N	19.05 E
Łask	10 Pe	51.36N	19.07 E
Las Lajas	56 Fe	38.31 S	70.22W
Las Lomitas	56 Hb	24.42 S	60.36W
Las Margaritas	48 Ni	16.19N	91.59W
Las Mariñas	13 Da	43.20N	8.15W
Las Marismas	13 Fg	37.00N	6.15W
Las Mercedes	54 Eb	9.07N	66.24W
Las Mestenas	48 Gc	28.13N	104.35W
Las Minas, Cerro-	47 Cf	14.33N	88.39W
Las Minas, Sierra de-	47 Ge	15.05N	90.00W
Las Mixtecas, Sierra del-	48 Ki	17.45N	97.15W
La Sola, Isla-	54 Fa	11.23N	63.34W
La Solana	13 If	38.53N	3.14W
Lasolo	26 Hg	3.23 S	122.04 E
La Sorcière	51k Bb	13.55N	60.56W
La Souterraine	11 Hh	46.14N	1.29 E
La Spezia	14 Dg	44.07N	9.50 E
Las Piedras	56 Id	34.45 S	56.13W
Las Plumas	52 Jj	43.45N	67.15W
Läs Qoray	35 Hc	11.15N	48.22 E
Las Rosas	55 Bk	32.28 S	61.34W
Lassen Peak	43 Cc	40.25N	121.31W
Lassigny	12 Ee	49.35N	2.51 E
Łaßnitz	14 Kd	46.50N	15.39 E
Łasso	64b Ba	15.02N	145.38 E
Las Tablas	49 Gj	7.46N	80.30W
Last Mountain Lake	45 Gf	51.10N	105.15W
Las Toscas	55 Ci	28.21 S	59.17W
Lastoursville	36 Bc	0.49 S	12.42 E
Lastovo	14 Kh	42.46N	16.55 E
Lastovski kanal	14 Kh	42.45N	16.59 E
Las Tres Virgenes, Volcán-	47 Bc	27.27N	112.34W
Las Varillas	56 Hd	31.52 S	62.43W
Las Vegas [N.M.-U.S.]	43 Fd	35.36N	105.13W
Las Vegas [Nv.-U.S.]	39 Hf	36.11N	115.08W
Las Villuercas	13 Ge	39.30N	5.21W
Łaszczów	10 Tf	50.32N	23.40 E
Lata	65b Da	14.14 S	169.29W
La Tacunga	54 Cd	0.55 S	78.37W
La Tagua	54 Dd	0.03 S	74.40W
Larakia (EN) = Al Lādhiqiyah	22 Fr	35.31N	35.07 E
Latare, Causse du-	11 Jk	43.37N	3.11 E
Late Island	61 Qc	18.48 S	174.39W
Laterza	14 Kj	40.37N	16.48 E
La Teste	11 Ej	44.38N	1.09W
Latgales Augstiene/Latgalskaja vozvyšennost'	6 Ih	56.30N	27.30 E
Latgalskaja Augstiene/Latgales Augstiene	6 Ih	56.30N	27.30 E
Lathen	12 Jb	52.52N	7.19 E
La Tigra	55 Bh	26.55 S	60.34W
Latina	14 Gi	41.28N	12.53 E
Latisana	14 Ge	45.47N	13.00 E
Latium (EN) = Lazio	13 Gh	42.02N	12.23 E
La Toja	13 Db	42.27N	8.50W
La Toma	56 Gd	33.03 S	65.37W

La Tontouta	63b Ce	22.00 S	166.15 E
Latorica	10 Rh	48.23N	21.50 E
La Tortuga, Isla-	54 Ea	10.55N	65.20W
La-Tour-du-Pin	11 Li	45.34N	5.27 E
La Trimouille	11 Hh	46.23N	1.03 E
La Trinidad	49 Dg	12.58N	86.14W
La Trinidad de Orichuna	50 Bi	7.07N	69.45W
La Trinité	50 Fe	14.44N	60.58W
Latronico	14 Kj	40.05N	16.01 E
Lattari, Monti-	14 Ij	40.40N	14.30 E
La Tuque	42 Kg	47.27N	72.47W
Lätür	25 Fe	18.24N	76.35 E
Latvia (EN) = Latvija	19 Cd	57.00N	25.00 E
Latvija = Latvia (EN)	19 Cd	57.00N	25.00 E
Latvijas PSR → Latvija	19 Cd	57.00N	25.00 E
Latvija	19 Cd	57.00N	25.00 E
Latvijskaja Sovetskaja Socialističeskaja Respublika → Latvija	19 Cd	57.00N	25.00 E
Latvijas SSR/Latvijas Padomju Socialistiska Respublika → Latvija	19 Cd	57.00N	25.00 E
Lau	30 Kb	6.56N	30.16 E
Laubach	12 Kd	50.33N	8.59 E
Lauchert	10 Fh	48.05N	9.15 E
Lauchhammer	10 Je	51.30N	13.48 E
Lauenburg	10 Gc	53.22N	10.34 E
Lauf an der Pegnitz	10 Hg	49.31N	11.17 E
Laughlan Islands	63a Ac	9.15 S	153.40 E
Laughlin Peak	45 Dh	36.38N	104.12W
Lau Group	57 Jf	18.20 S	178.30W
Lauhanvuori	8 Jb	62.10N	22.10 E
Laujar de Andarax	13 Jg	36.59N	2.51W
Laukaa	7 Fe	62.25N	25.57 E
Laukuva	8 Ji	55.35N	22.03 E
Laulau, Bahia-	64b Ba	15.08N	145.46 E
Launceston [Austl.]	58 Fi	41.26 S	147.08 E
Launceston [Eng.-U.K.]	9 Ik	50.38N	4.21W
La Unión [Bol.]	55 Bb	15.18 S	61.05W
La Unión [Chile]	56 Ff	40.17 S	73.05W
La Unión [Col.]	54 Cc	1.37N	77.08W
La Unión [El.Sal.]	47 Gf	13.20N	87.51W
La Unión [Mex.]	48 Ii	17.58N	101.49W
La Unión [Peru]	54 Ce	9.46 S	76.48W
La Unión [Sp.]	13 Lg	37.37N	0.52W
La Unión [Ven.]	49 Ni	8.13N	67.46W
Laura	59 Ic	15.35 S	144.28 E
La Urbana	50 Ci	7.08N	66.56W
Laurel [Mo.-U.S.]	43 Fb	45.40N	108.46W
Laurel [Mt.-U.S.]	55 Ej	31.23 S	55.52W
Laureles	49 Hf	39.20N	79.17W
Laurel Hill	44 Hf	39.20N	79.50W
Laurel Mountain	44 Fh	34.30N	82.01W
Laurentian Plateau (EN) = Laurentien, Plateau-	38 Md	50.00N	70.00W
Laurentian Scarp	44 Ic	45.50N	76.15W
Laurentide Scarp	44 Kb	46.38N	73.00W
Laurentien, Plateau- (EN) = Laurentian Plateau (EN)	38 Md	50.00N	70.00W
Lauria	14 Jj	40.02N	15.50 E
Lau Ridge (EN)	3 Kl	25.00 S	179.00 E
Laurie River	42 Ne	56.00N	100.58W
Laurinburg	44 Hh	34.47N	79.27W
Laurium	44 Cb	47.14N	88.26W
Lauro Muller	55 Hl	28.24 S	49.23 E
Lausanne	6 Gf	46.30N	6.40 E
Lausitzer Gebirge	10 Kf	50.48N	14.40 E
Lausitzer Neiße	10 Kd	52.04N	14.46 E
Laut, Pulau-	26 Ef	4.43N	107.59 E
Laut, Pulau-	21 Nj	3.40 S	116.10 E
Lautaret, Col du-	11 Mi	45.02N	6.24 E
Lautém	26 Ih	8.22 S	126.54 E
Lauterbach	10 Ff	50.38N	9.24 E
Lauterbourg	12 Kf	48.59N	8.11 E
Lauterecken	12 Jf	49.39N	7.36 E
Lauthala	63d Cb	16.45 S	179.41W
Laut Kecil, Kepulauan-	26 Gg	4.50 S	115.45 E
Lautoka	61 Ec	17.37 S	177.27 E
Lauvergne Island	64d Cb	7.00 S	152.00 E
Lauwersmeer	12 Ia	53.25N	6.13 E
Lauzerte	11 Hj	44.15N	1.08 E
Lauzon	44 Kb	46.50N	71.10W
Lauzoue	11 Gj	44.03N	0.15 E
Lava	10 Rb	54.37N	21.14 E
Lava, Nosy- [Mad.]	37 Hb	12.49 S	48.41 E
Lava, Nosy- [Mad.]	37 Hb	14.33 S	47.36 E
Lavaca River	45 Hj	29.56N	96.36W
Lava Flow	45 Bi	34.45N	108.20W
Laval	6 Ff	48.04N	0.46W
Lavalle	55 Bi	29.01 S	59.11W
Lavalleja	55 Ek	34.25 S	55.11W
Livän, Jazireh-ye-	23 Hd	26.48N	53.00 E
Lavanggu	63a Ed	11.37 S	160.15 E
Lavapié, Punta-	52 Ii	37.09 S	73.35W
Lävar Meydän	23 Hd	30.20N	54.30 E
Lavassaare	8 Kf	58.29N	24.16 E
Lavaur	11 Hk	43.42N	1.49 E
La Vecilla	13 Gb	42.51N	5.24W
La Vega	47 Je	19.13N	70.31W
La Vela de Coro	49 Mh	11.27N	69.34W
Levelanet	11 Hl	42.56N	1.51 E
Levello	14 Jj	40.34N	15.48 E
La Venta	47 Fe	18.08N	94.03W
La Ventura	12 Gd	50.38N	2.46 E
La Vera	13 Gd	40.05N	5.30W
L'Averdy, Cape-	63a Ba	5.33 S	155.04 E
Laverton	59 Ee	28.38 S	122.25 E
Lavia	8 Jc	61.36N	22.36 E
La Victoria	54 Ea	10.14N	67.20W
La Vila Jojosa/Villajoyosa	13 Lf	38.30N	0.14W
La Vilita, Presa-	48 Hi	18.05N	102.05W
La Viña	54 Ce	6.54 S	79.28W

La Vôge 11 Mf 48.05N 6.05 E
Lavoisier Island 66 Qe 66.12S 66.44W
Lavougba 35 Cd 5.37N 23.19 E
La Voulte-sur-Rhône 11 Kj 44.48N 4.47 E
Lavouras 55 Db 14.59S 56.47W
Lavras 54 Jh 21.14S 45.00W
Lavras do Sul 55 Fj 30.49S 53.55W
Lavrentija 20 Nc 65.33N 171.02W
Lávrion 15 Hl 37.43N 24.03 E
Lavumisa 37 Ee 27.15S 31.55 E
Lawas 26 Gf 4.51N 115.24 E
Lawdar 23 Gg 13.53N 45.52 E
Lawe 12 Ed 50.38N 2.42 E
Lawers, Ben- 9 Ie 56.33N 4.15W
Lawit, Gunong- 26 Ff 1.23N 112.55 E
Lawqah 24 Jh 29.49N 42.45 E
Lawra 34 Ec 10.39N 2.52W
Lawrence [Ks.-U.S.] 43 Hd 38.58N 95.14W
Lawrence [Ma.-U.S.] 43 Mc 42.42N 71.09W
Lawrence [N.Z.] 62 Cf 45.55S 169.42 E
Lawrenceburg [Ky.-U.S.] 44 Ef 38.02N 84.54W
Lawrenceburg [Tn.-U.S.] 44 Dh 35.15N 87.20W
Lawson, Mount- 59 Ja 7.44S 146.37 E
Lawton 39 Jf 34.37N 98.25W
Lawu, Gunung- 21 Nj 7.38S 111.11 E
Lawz, Jabal al- 24 Fh 28.41N 35.18 E
Laxå 7 Dg 58.59N 14.37 E
Lay 11 Eh 46.18N 1.17W
Laylá 23 Ge 22.17N 46.45 E
Layon 11 Fg 47.20N 0.45W
Layou 51g Bb 15.23N 61.26W
Layou 51n Ba 13.12N 61.17W
Laysan Island 57 Jb 25.50N 171.50W
Layton 46 Jf 41.04N 111.58W
La Zarca 48 Ge 25.50N 104.44W
Lazarev 20 Jf 52.13N 141.35 E
Lazarevac 15 De 44.23N 20.16 E
Lázaro Cárdenas, Presa- 48 Ge 25.35N 105.05W
Lazdijai/Lazdijaj 7 Fi 54.13N 23.33 E
Lazdijaj/Lazdijai 7 Fi 54.13N 23.33 E
Lāzeh 24 Oi 26.48N 53.22 E
Lazio = Latium (EN) [2] 14 Gh 42.02N 12.23 E
Lazo 28 Mc 43.25N 134.01 E
Lazovsk 16 Ff 47.38N 28.12 E
Łazy 10 Pf 50.27N 19.26 E
Lea 9 Nj 51.30N 0.01 E
Lead 43 Gc 44.21N 103.46W
Leader 46 Ka 50.53N 109.31W
Lead Hill 45 Jh 37.06N 92.38W
Leadville 43 Fd 39.15N 106.20W
Leaf River 45 Lk 31.00N 88.45W
League City 45 Il 29.31N 95.05W
Leamington 44 Fd 42.03N 82.36W
Leandro N. Alem 55 Bl 34.30S 61.24W
Leane, Lough-/Loch Léin 9 Di 52.05N 9.35W
Le'an Jiang 28 Dj 28.58N 116.41 E
Learmonth 59 Cd 22.13S 114.04 E
Leavenworth [Ks.-U.S.] 45 Ig 39.19N 94.55W
Leavenworth [Wa.-U.S.] 46 Ec 47.36N 120.40W
Łeba 10 Nb 54.47N 17.33 E
Łeba 10 Nb 54.43N 17.25 E
Lebach 12 Ie 49.24N 6.55 E
Lébamba 36 Bc 2.12S 11.30 E
Lebanon [In.-U.S.] 44 De 40.03N 86.28W
Lebanon [Ky.-U.S.] 44 Eg 37.34N 85.15W
Lebanon [Mo.-U.S.] 45 Jh 37.41N 92.40W
Lebanon [N.H.-U.S.] 44 Kd 43.38N 72.15W
Lebanon [Or.-U.S.] 46 Dd 44.32N 122.54W
Lebanon [Pa.-U.S.] 44 Ie 40.21N 76.25W
Lebanon [Tn.-U.S.] 44 Dg 36.12N 86.18W
Lebanon (EN)=Lubnān [1] 22 Ff 33.50N 35.50 E
Lebanon Mountains (EN)= Lubnān, Jabal- 23 Ec 34.00N 36.30 E
Lebap 18 Cd 41.02N 61.54 E
Le Bec-Hellouin 12 Ce 49.14N 0.43 E
Lebedin 19 De 50.36N 34.30 E
Lebediny 20 He 58.25N 125.58 E
Lebedjan 19 De 53.02N 39.07 E
Le Bény-Bocage 12 Bf 48.56N 0.50W
Lebjažje 19 He 51.28N 77.46 E
Lebjažje 17 Mi 55.16N 66.29 E
Le Blanc 11 Hh 46.38N 1.04 E
Lebo 36 Db 4.29N 23.57 E
Lebomboberge 30 Kk 26.15S 32.00 E
Lebombo Mountains 30 Kk 26.15S 32.00 E
Lębork 10 Nb 54.33N 17.44 E
Le Bourget 12 Ef 48.56N 2.25 E
Lebrija 13 Fh 36.55N 6.04W
Łebsko, Jezioro- 10 Nb 54.44N 17.24 E
Lebu 56 Fe 37.37S 73.39W
Le Carbet 51h Ab 14.43N 61.11W
Le Cateau 12 Fd 50.06N 3.33 E
Le Catelet 12 Fd 50.01N 3.15 E
Lecce 6 Hg 40.23N 18.11 E
Lecco 14 De 45.51N 9.23 E
Lech 10 Gh 48.44N 10.56 E
Lech 14 Ec 47.12N 10.09 E
Le Champ du Feu 11 Nf 48.24N 7.15 E
Lechang 27 Jf 25.15N 113.25 E
Le Château-d'Oléron 11 Ei 45.54N 1.12W
Le Chesne 11 Ke 49.31N 4.46 E
Le Cheylard 11 Kj 44.54N 4.25 E
Lechfeld 10 Gh 48.10N 10.50 E
Lechiguiri, Cerro- 48 Li 16.43N 95.30W
Lechtaler Alpen 14 Ec 47.15N 10.30 E
Léconi 36 Bc 1.11S 13.16 E
Léconi 36 Bc 1.35S 14.14 E
Le Cornate 14 Eg 43.10N 10.58 E
Le Coudray-Saint-Germer 12 De 49.25N 1.50 E
Le Creusot 11 Kh 46.48N 4.26 E
Le Croisic 11 Dg 47.18N 2.30W
Le Crotoy 12 Dd 50.13N 1.37 E
Łęczna 10 Se 51.19N 22.52 E
Łęczyca 10 Pd 52.04N 19.13 E
Led 7 Ke 62.20N 43.00 E
Lede 12 Fd 50.57N 3.59 E
Ledesma 13 Gc 41.05N 6.00W
Le Diamant 51h Ac 14.29N 61.02W
Ledjanaja, Gora- 21 Tc 61.45N 171.15 E
Ledjanaja, Gora- 21 Qe 49.28N 142.45 E
Lednik Entuziastov 66 Cf 70.30S 16.00 E
Lednik Mušketova 66 Cf 72.00S 14.00 E
Ledo, Cabo- 36 Bd 9.41S 13.12 E
Ledolom Tajmyrski 66 Ge 66.00S 83.00 E
Le Donjon 11 Jh 46.21N 3.48 E
Le Dorat 11 Hh 46.13N 1.05 E
Lędyczek 10 Mc 53.33N 16.58 E
Lee/An Laoi 9 Ej 51.55N 8.30W
Leech Lake 43 Ib 47.09N 94.23W
Leeds [Al.-U.S.] 44 Di 33.33N 86.33W
Leeds [Eng.-U.K.] 6 Fe 53.50N 1.35W
Leeds [N.D.-U.S.] 45 Gb 48.17N 99.27W
Leek 12 Ia 53.10N 6.24 E
Leer 10 Dc 53.14N 7.26 E
Leer (Ostfriesland) 10 Dc 53.14N 7.26 E
Leerdam 12 Hc 51.53N 5.06 E
Lées 11 Fk 43.38N 0.14W
Leesburg 43 Kf 29.49N 81.53W
Leeste, Weyhe- 12 Kb 52.59N 8.50 E
Leesville 45 Jk 31.08N 93.16W
Leeuwarden 11 La 53.12N 5.46 E
Leeuwarderadeel 12 Ha 53.16N 5.46 E
Leeuwarderadeel-Stiens 12 Ha 53.16N 5.46 E
Leeuwin, Cape- 59 Cf 34.25S 115.00 E
Leeward Islands 47 Le 17.00N 63.00W
Leeward Islands (EN)=Sous le Vent, Iles- 57 Lf 16.38S 151.30W
Léfini 36 Cc 2.57S 16.10 E
Lefka 15 Jh 41.52N 26.16 E
Lefke 24 Ee 35.07N 32.51 E
Lefkoşa/Levkosía = Nicosia (EN) 22 Ff 35.10N 33.22 E
Le François 51h Bb 14.37N 60.54W
Lefroy, Lake- 59 Ef 31.15S 121.40 E
Łęg 10 Rf 50.38N 21.49 E
Leganés 13 Id 40.19N 3.45W
Legazpi 22 Oh 13.09N 123.44 E
Legden 12 Jb 52.02N 7.06 E
Legges Tor 59 Jh 41.32S 147.40 E
Leggett 46 Dg 39.52N 123.43W
Leghorn (EN)=Livorno 6 Hg 43.33N 10.19 E
Legionowo 10 Qd 52.25N 20.56 E
Léglise 12 He 49.48N 5.32 E
Legnago 14 Fe 45.11N 11.18 E
Legnano 14 Ce 45.36N 8.54 E
Legnica [2] 10 Me 51.15N 16.10 E
Legnica 10 Me 51.13N 16.09 E
Le Grand-Quevilly 12 De 49.25N 1.02 E
Le Grand Veymont 11 Lj 44.52N 5.32 E
Le Grau-du-Roi 11 Kk 43.32N 4.08 E
Léguer 11 Cf 48.44N 3.32W
Leh 25 Fb 34.10N 77.35 E
Le Havre 6 Gf 49.30N 0.08 E
Lehi 46 Jf 40.24N 111.51W
Lehmann 55 Bj 31.08S 61.27W
Le Hohneck 11 Nf 48.02N 7.01 E
Le Houlme 12 De 49.31N 1.02 E
Lehrte 10 Fd 52.23N 9.58 E
Lehtimäki 8 Jb 62.47N 23.55 E
Lehua Island 65a Aa 22.01N 160.06W
Lehututu 37 Cd 23.53S 21.49 E
Leibnitz 14 Jd 46.46N 15.32 E
Leibo 27 Hf 28.13N 103.34 E
Leicester 6 Fe 52.38N 1.05W
Leicester 9 Mi 52.40N 1.00W
Leicestershire [3] 9 Mi 52.38N 1.00W
Leichhardt Range 59 Jd 20.40S 147.05 E
Leichhardt River 59 Hc 17.35S 139.48 E
Leiden 11 Kc 52.09N 4.30 E
Leidschendam 12 Gb 52.05N 4.26 E
Leie 11 Jc 51.03N 3.43 E
Leifear/Lifford 9 Fg 54.50N 7.29W
Leigh Creek 58 Eh 30.28S 138.25 E
Leighton Buzzard 12 Bc 51.55N 0.39W
Leigong Shan 27 If 26.23N 108.15 E
Leikanger 7 Ae 62.07N 5.20 E
Leim an Mhadaidh/ Limavady 9 Gf 55.03N 6.57W
Leimen 12 Ke 49.21N 8.41 E
Leimus 49 Ef 14.44N 84.07W
Leine 10 Fd 52.40N 9.40 E
Leinster/Laighean 9 Gh 53.00N 7.00W
Leipzig 6 He 51.18N 12.20 E
Leira 8 Cd 60.58N 9.18 E
Leiria [2] 13 De 39.40N 8.50W
Leiria 13 De 39.45N 8.48W
Leirvik 7 Ag 59.47N 5.30 E
Leisi/Lejsi 8 Jf 58.33N 22.30 E
Leisler, Mount- 59 Fd 23.30S 129.20 E
Leiston 12 Db 52.12N 1.34 E
Leitariegos, Puerto de- 13 Fa 43.00N 6.25W
Leitha 14 Lc 47.52N 17.18 E
Leithagebirge 14 Kc 47.58N 16.40 E
Leitir Ceanainn/Letterkenny 9 Fg 54.57N 7.44W
Leitrim/Liatroim [2] 9 Eg 54.20N 8.20W
Leiva, Cerro- 54 Dc 2.54N 74.48W
Leiyang 27 Jf 26.30N 112.57 E
Leizhou → Haikang 27 Jg 20.56N 110.06 E
Leizhou Bandao 21 Ng 20.40N 110.05 E
Lejasciems 8 Lg 57.08N 26.36 E
Lejsi/Leisi 8 Jf 58.33N 22.30 E
Lek 11 Lc 52.00N 6.00 E
Leka 7 Cd 65.05N 11.37 E
Lékana 36 Cc 2.19S 14.36 E
Leketi, Monts de la- 30 Ii 2.34S 14.17 E
Lekhainá 15 El 37.56N 21.16 E
Lekhal 13 Ph 36.20N 3.51 E
Lekitobi 26 Hg 1.58S 124.33 E
Lekki Lagoon 34 Fd 6.30N 4.07 E
Leknes 7 Cb 68.10N 13.42 E
Łęknica 10 Ke 51.32N 14.48 E
Lékoumou [3] 36 Bc 3.00S 13.50 E
Leksand 7 Df 60.44N 15.01 E
Leksozero, Ozero- 7 He 63.45N 31.00 E
Leksula 26 Ig 3.46S 126.31 E
Leksvik 7 Ce 63.40N 10.37 E
Le Lamentin 50 Fe 14.37N 61.01W
Leland 45 Kj 33.24N 90.54W
Lelång 8 Ee 59.10N 12.10 E
Le Lavandou 11 Mk 43.08N 6.22 E
Lelčicy 16 Fd 51.49N 28.21 E
Leleiwi Point 65a Gd 19.44N 155.00W
Lelepa 63b Dc 17.36S 168.13 E
Leleque 56 Ff 42.23S 71.03W
Leli 63a Ec 8.45S 161.02 E
Leli → Tianlin 27 Ig 24.22N 106.11 E
Lelija 14 Mg 43.26N 18.29 E
Leling 28 Df 37.44N 117.13 E
Léliogat 63b Ce 21.18S 167.35 E
Lelle 7 Fg 58.53N 25.00 E
Le Locle 14 Ac 47.05N 6.45 E
Le Lorrain 51h Ab 14.50N 61.04W
Lelystad 11 Lb 52.31N 5.27 E
Le Madonie 14 Hm 37.50N 14.00 E
Le Maire, Estrecho de- 56 Hh 54.50S 65.00W
Léman, Lac-=Geneva, Lake- (EN) 5 Gf 46.25N 6.30 E
Leman Bank 9 Oh 53.10N 1.58 E
Lemankoa 63a Ba 5.03S 154.34 E
Le Mans 6 Gf 48.00N 0.12 E
Le Marin 51h Bc 14.28N 60.52W
Le Mars 45 He 42.47N 96.10W
Le Mas-d'Azil 11 Hk 43.05N 1.22 E
Lembach 12 Je 49.00N 7.48 E
Lembeck 12 Ic 51.44N 6.59 E
Lemberg 12 Je 49.00N 7.23 E
Lembolovskaja Vozvyšennost 8 Md 60.50N 30.15 E
Lembruch 12 Kb 52.32N 8.21 E
Leme 55 If 22.12S 47.24W
Lemelerberg 12 Ib 52.29N 6.23 E
Lemesós/Limassol 23 Dc 34.40N 33.02 E
Lemgo 10 Ed 52.02N 8.54 E
Lemhi Range 46 Id 44.30N 113.25W
Lemieux Islands 42 Ld 64.00N 64.20W
Lemju 17 He 63.50N 56.57 E
Lemland 8 Id 60.05N 20.10 E
Lemmer, Lemsterland- 12 Hb 52.51N 5.42 E
Lemmon 43 Gb 45.66N 102.10W
Lemmon, Mount- 46 Jj 32.26N 110.47W
Lemnos (EN)=Límnos 5 Ih 39.55N 25.15 E
Le-Molay-Littry 12 Be 49.15N 0.53W
Le-Mont-Saint-Michel 11 Ef 48.38N 1.30W
Le Morne Rouge 51h Ab 14.46N 61.08W
Lemotol Bay 64d Bb 7.21N 151.35 E
Le Moyne, Lac - 42 Ke 57.00N 68.00W
Lempa, Río- 47 Gf 13.14N 88.49W
Lempäälä 8 Jc 61.19N 23.45 E
Lempira [3] 49 Cf 14.20N 88.40W
L'Empordà/Ampurdán 13 Ob 42.12N 2.45 E
Lemro 25 Id 20.25N 93.20 E
Lemsid 32 Ed 26.33N 13.51W
Lemsterland 12 Hb 52.51N 5.42 E
Lemsterland-Lemmer 12 Hb 52.51N 5.42 E
Le Murge 5 Hg 40.50N 16.40 E
Le Muy 11 Mk 43.28N 6.33 E
Lemvig 8 Ch 56.32N 8.18 E
Lemya 17 Jc 66.30N 62.00 E
Lena 21 Ob 72.25N 126.40 E
Lena, Mount- 46 Kf 40.50N 109.27W
Lénakel 63b Dd 19.32S 169.16 E
Lena Mountains (EN) = Prilenskoje Plato 21 Oc 60.45N 125.00 E
Lena Tablemount (EN) 30 Ln 53.00S 45.00 E
Lençóis Paulista 55 Hf 22.36S 48.47W
Lendava 14 Kd 46.34N 16.27 E
Lendery 7 He 63.26N 31.12 E
Lendinara 14 Fe 45.05N 11.36 E
Le Neubourg 12 Ce 49.09N 0.55 E
Lenger 19 Gg 42.10N 69.55 E
Lengerich 10 Dd 52.11N 7.52 E
Lengoué 36 Cb 0.49N 15.47 E
Lengshuijiang 27 Jf 27.41N 111.28 E
Lengua de Vaca, Punta- 56 Fd 30.14S 71.38W
Lengulu 36 Eb 3.15N 26.30 E
Lenhovda 7 Dh 57.00N 15.17 E
Lenina, Pik-=Lenin Peak (EN) 21 Jf 39.19N 73.01 E
Leninabad → Chudžand 22 Ie 40.17N 69.37 E
Leninakan → Kumajri 6 Kg 40.47N 43.50 E
Lenin Canal (EN) = Volgo-Donskoj sudohodny kanal imeni V.I.Lenina 5 Kf 48.40N 43.37 E
Leningrad → Sankt-Peterburg 6 Jc 59.55N 30.15 E
Leningradskaja 16 Kf 46.17N 39.25 E
Leningradskaja Oblast [3] 19 Dd 60.00N 31.40 E
Leningradski 20 Mc 69.17N 178.10 E
Leningradski 19 Hh 38.09N 70.01 E
Lenino 16 Ig 45.17N 35.44 E
Leninogorsk 22 Kd 50.27N 83.32 E
Leninogorsk 19 Fe 54.38N 52.30 E
Lenin Peak (EN)=Lenina, Pik- 21 Jf 39.19N 73.01 E
Leninsk 16 Me 48.42N 45.11 E
Leninsk 18 Bc 42.04N 59.24 E
Leninsk 18 Id 40.40N 72.20 E
Leninski 19 He 52.13N 76.50 E
Leninski 15 Lb 47.50N 28.16 E
Leninski 20 He 58.32N 125.58 E
Leninsk-Kuznecki 22 Kd 54.38N 86.10 E
Leninskoje 19 Ge 54.05N 65.23 E
Leninskoje 7 Lg 58.21N 47.07 E
Leninskoje 20 Ig 47.59N 132.38 E
Leninváros → Tiszaújvaros 10 Ri 47.56N 21.05 E
Lenkoran 6 Kh 38.44N 48.50 E
Lenne 10 De 51.25N 7.30 E
Lenne 12 Jc 51.15N 7.50 E
Lennestadt 12 Kc 51.08N 8.01 E
Lennestadt-Grevenbrück 12 Kc 51.08N 8.01 E
Lennox Hills 9 Ie 56.05N 4.10W
Leno-Angarskoje Plato 20 Fe 55.00N 104.30 E
Lenoir 44 Gh 35.55N 81.32W
Le Nouvion-en-Thiérache 12 Fd 50.01N 3.47 E
Lens 11 Id 50.26N 2.50 E
Lensk 22 Nc 61.00N 114.50 E
Lenti 10 Mi 46.37N 16.33 E
Lentiira 7 Gd 64.21N 29.50 E
Lentini 14 Jm 37.17N 15.01 E
Lentua 7 Gd 64.14N 29.36 E
Lentvaris 8 Kj 54.38N 25.13 E
Léo 34 Ec 11.06N 2.06W
Leoben 14 Jc 47.23N 15.06 E
Léogâne 49 Kd 18.31N 72.38W
Leok 26 Hf 1.11N 121.26 E
Leola 45 Gd 45.43N 98.56W
Leominster 9 Ki 52.14N 2.45W
León 13 Gc 42.00N 6.00W
Léon 11 Ek 43.53N 1.18W
León [Mex.] 39 Ig 21.10N 101.42W
León [Nic.] [3] 49 Dg 12.35N 86.35W
León [Nic.] 39 Kh 12.26N 86.54W
León [Sp.] 6 Fg 42.36N 5.34W
León [Sp.] [3] 13 Gb 42.40N 6.00W
León, Montes de- 13 Fb 42.30N 6.20W
León, Puerto del- 13 Hh 36.50N 4.21W
Leonardville 37 Bd 23.29S 18.49 E
Leonberg 12 Kf 48.48N 9.01 E
Leone, Monte- 14 Cd 46.15N 8.10 E
Leones 55 Ak 32.39S 62.18W
Leonessa 14 Gh 42.34N 12.58 E
Leonforte 14 Im 37.38N 14.23 E
Leōnídhion 15 Fl 37.10N 22.52 E
Leonora 58 Dg 28.53S 121.20 E
Leon River 45 Hk 30.59N 97.24W
Leopold and Astrid Coast 66 Ge 67.10S 84.10 E
Leopoldina 54 Jh 21.32S 42.38W
Leopold McClintock, Cape - 42 Fa 77.38N 116.20W
Leopoldo de Bulhões 55 Hc 16.37S 48.46W
Leopoldsburg 12 Hc 51.07N 5.15 E
Leopoldville → Kinshasa 31 Ii 4.18S 15.18 E
Leovo 16 Ff 46.29N 28.15 E
Lepa 65c Bb 14.01S 171.28W
Le Palais 11 Cg 47.21N 3.09W
Lepar, Pulau- 26 Eg 2.57S 106.50 E
Le Parcq 12 Ed 50.23N 2.06 E
Lepaterique 49 Df 14.02N 87.27W
Lepe 13 Eg 37.15N 7.12W
Lepel 19 Ce 54.53N 28.46 E
Lepenica 15 Ee 44.10N 21.08 E
Le Petit Caux 12 De 49.55N 1.20 E
Le Petit-Couronne 12 De 49.23N 1.01 E
Le Petit-Quevilly 12 De 49.26N 1.02 E
Lephepe 37 Dd 23.22S 25.52 E
Leping 27 Kf 28.59N 117.07 E
Lepini, Monti- 14 Gi 41.35N 13.00 E
Le Plessis-Belleville 12 Ee 49.06N 2.46 E
Le Pont-de-Claix 11 Li 45.07N 5.42 E
Le Portel 12 Dd 50.42N 1.34 E
Leppävesi 8 Kb 62.15N 25.55 E
Leppävirta 8 Lb 62.29N 27.47 E
Le Prêcheur 51h Ab 14.48N 61.14W
Lepsøya 8 Bb 62.35N 6.10 E
Lepsy 18 La 46.18N 78.20 E
Lepsy 19 Hf 46.12N 78.55 E
Leptis Magna 33 Bc 32.38N 14.18 E
Le Puy 11 Ji 45.02N 3.53 E
Leqemt (EN)=Nekemt 31 Kh 9.05N 36.33 E
Le Quesnoy 12 Fd 50.15N 3.38 E
Lercara Friddi 14 Hm 37.45N 13.36 E
Lerchenfeld Glacier 66 Af 77.50S 34.50W
Lere 34 Gc 10.23N 8.35 E
Léré 35 Ad 9.39N 14.13 E
Lérida 54 Dc 0.06N 70.43W
Lérida [3] 13 Nc 42.00N 1.10 E
Lérida/Lleida 13 Mc 41.37N 0.37 E
Lérins, Iles de- 11 Nk 43.31N 7.03 E
Lerma 13 Ib 42.02N 3.45W
Lerma, Río- 48 Hg 20.13N 102.46W
Lermontov 16 Mg 44.06N 42.45 E
Le Robert 51h Bb 14.41N 60.57W
Léros 15 Jl 37.08N 26.50 E
Lerum 7 Ch 57.46N 12.16 E
Lerwick 9 La 60.09N 1.09W
Léry 12 De 49.17N 1.13 E
Les Abrets 11 Li 45.32N 5.35 E
Le Saint-Esprit 51h Bb 14.34N 60.57W
Les Alberes/Albères, Montes- 11 In 42.28N 2.56 E
Les Allobroges 63b Dc 16.47S 168.09 E
Les Andelys 11 He 49.15N 1.25 E
Les Anses-d'Arlets 51h Ac 14.29N 61.05W
Les-Baux-de-Provence 11 Kk 43.45N 4.48 E
Les Borges Blanques/Borjas Blancas 13 Mc 41.31N 0.52 E
Lesbos (EN)=Lésvos 5 Ih 39.10N 26.32 E
L'Escala/La Escala 13 Pb 42.07N 3.08 E
Les Cayes 47 Je 18.12N 73.45W
Les Coëvrons 11 Ff 48.12N 0.10W
Le Serre 14 Kl 38.30N 16.30 E
Les Escoumins 44 Ma 48.25N 69.29W
Les Eyzies-de-Tayac 11 Hj 44.56N 1.01 E
Les Falaises 12 Ce 49.44N 0.21 E
Leshan 27 Hf 29.34N 103.45 E
Les Herbiers 11 Eh 46.52N 1.01W
Lesina, Lago di- 14 Ji 41.55N 15.25 E
Lesja 8 Cb 62.07N 8.52 E
Lesjöfors 7 Dg 59.59N 14.11 E
Leskino 20 Cb 72.25N 79.40 E
Lesko 10 Sg 49.29N 22.21 E
Leskov 66 Ad 56.40S 28.10W
Leskovac 15 Eg 42.59N 21.57 E
Leskoviku 15 Di 40.09N 20.35 E
Les Mangles 51e Ab 16.23N 61.27W
Les Mauges 11 Fg 47.10N 1.00W
Les Minquiers 9 Km 48.58N 2.08W
Les Monédières 11 Hi 45.30N 1.52 E
Les Mureaux 12 Df 49.00N 1.55 E
Lesnaja 10 Vd 52.55N 25.52 E
Lesnaja 16 Cc 52.11N 23.30 E
Lesneven 11 Bf 48.34N 4.19W
Lešnica 15 Ce 44.39N 19.19 E
Lesnoj 19 Gd 57.01N 67.50 E
Lesnoj 19 Fd 59.49N 52.10 E
Lesnoj, Ostrov- 8 Md 60.02N 28.20 E
Lesný 10 If 50.02N 12.37 E
Lesogorski 8 Mc 61.01N 28.51 E
Lesosibirsk 22 Ld 58.15N 92.30 E
Lesotho [1] 31 Jk 29.30S 28.30 E
Lesozavodsk 20 Ig 45.26N 133.25 E
Lesozavodski 7 Hc 66.45N 32.50 E
Lesparre-Médoc 11 Fi 45.18N 0.56W
L'Espérance Rock 57 Jh 31.26S 178.54W
Les Ponts-de-Cé 11 Fg 47.25N 0.31W
Les Posets 13 Mb 42.39N 0.25 E
Les Sables-d'Olonne 11 Eh 46.30N 1.47W
Lessay 11 Ee 49.13N 1.32W
Lesse 11 Kd 50.14N 4.54 E
Lessebo 7 Dh 56.45N 15.16 E
Lessen/Lessines 12 Fd 50.43N 3.50 E
Les Sept Iles 11 Cf 48.53N 3.28W
Lesser Antilles (EN)= Antillas Menores 38 Mh 15.00N 61.00W
Lesser Caucasus (EN)= Maly Kavkaz 5 Kg 41.00N 44.35 E
Lesser Khingan Range (EN)= Xiao Hinggan Ling 21 Oe 48.45N 127.00 E
Lesser Slave Lake 38 Hd 55.25N 115.30W
Lesser Sunda Islands (EN) 21 Oj 9.13S 121.12 E
Lessines/Lessen 12 Fd 50.43N 3.50 E
Lessini 14 Fe 45.41N 11.13 E
Les Tantes 51p Bb 12.19N 61.33W
Les Thilliers-en-Vexin 12 De 49.14N 1.36 E
Les Triagoz 11 Cf 48.53N 3.40W
Les Trois-Ilets 51h Ab 14.33N 61.03W
Lešukonskoje 7 Kd 64.52N 45.40 E
Lésvos=Lesbos (EN) 5 Ih 39.10N 26.32 E
Leszno [2] 10 Me 51.50N 16.35 E
Leszno 10 Me 51.51N 16.35 E
Letälven 8 Fe 59.05N 14.20 E
Le Tanargue 11 Kj 44.37N 4.09 E
Letchworth 12 Bc 51.58N 0.13W
Letea, Ostrovul- 15 Md 45.20N 29.20 E
Le Teil 11 Kj 44.33N 4.41 E
Letenye 10 Mj 46.26N 16.44 E
Lethbridge 39 He 49.42N 110.50W
Lethem 53 Ke 3.20N 59.50W
Le Thillot 11 Mg 47.53N 6.46 E
Leti, Kepulauan-=Leti Islands (EN) 26 Ih 8.13S 127.50 E
Letiahau 30 Jk 21.04S 24.25 E
Leticia 53 Jf 4.09S 69.57W
Leti Islands (EN)=Leti, Kepulauan- 26 Ih 8.13S 127.50 E
Leting 28 Ee 39.25N 118.55 E
Letka 7 Mg 58.59N 50.14 E
Letlhakane 37 Dd 21.25S 25.36 E
Letnerečenski 7 Id 64.19N 34.25 E
Letni Bereg 7 Jd 64.50N 38.20 E
Letohrad 10 Mf 50.03N 16.31 E
Le Touquet-Paris-Plage 11 Hd 50.31N 1.35 E
Letovice 10 Mg 49.33N 16.36 E
Letpadan 25 Je 17.47N 95.45 E
Le Translay 12 De 49.58N 1.41 E
Le Tréport 11 Hd 50.04N 1.22 E
Letsôk-aw Kyun 25 Jf 11.37N 98.15 E
Letterkenny/Leitir = Ceanainn 9 Fg 54.57N 7.44W
Leu 15 Ge 44.11N 24.00 E
Leuca 14 Mk 39.48N 18.21 E
Leucas (EN) = Levkás 15 Dk 38.43N 20.38 E
Leucate 11 Jl 42.55N 3.02 E
Leucate, Étang de- 11 Il 42.51N 3.00 E
Leuk 14 Bd 46.20N 7.38 E
Leukónoikon 24 Ee 35.15N 33.42 E
Leulumoega 65c Ba 13.49S 171.55W
Leuna 10 Ie 51.19N 12.01 E
Leušeny 15 Lc 46.51N 28.11 E
Leuser, Gunung- 21 Li 3.45N 97.11 E
Leutkirch im Allgäu 10 Gi 47.50N 10.02 E
Leuven/Louvain 11 Kd 50.53N 4.42 E
Leuze-en-Hainaut 12 Fd 50.36N 3.36 E
Levádhia 15 Fk 38.26N 22.53 E
Levaja Hetta 20 Cc 65.15N 73.20 E
Levanger 7 Ce 63.45N 11.18 E
Levante, Riviera di- 14 Df 44.15N 9.30 E
Levanzo 14 Gm 38.00N 12.20 E
Levaši 16 Oh 42.27N 47.20 E
Le Vauclin 51h Bb 14.33N 60.51W
Levelland 45 Ej 33.35N 102.23W
Lévêque, Cape- 59 Ec 16.25S 122.55 E
Le Verdon-sur-Mer 11 Ei 45.33N 1.04W
Leverkusen 10 Ce 51.01N 6.59 E
Leverkusen-Opladen 10 De 51.04N 7.01 E
Lévèzou 11 Ij 44.09N 2.53 E
Levice 10 Oh 48.13N 18.37 E
Levico Terme 14 Fd 46.01N 11.18 E
Le Vigan 11 Jk 43.59N 3.36 E
Levin 61 Eh 40.37S 175.17 E
Lévis 42 Kg 46.48N 71.10W
Levisa Fork 44 Ff 38.06N 82.37W
Levítha 15 Jm 37.00N 26.28 E
Levittown 44 Je 40.09N 74.50W
Levká Óri 15 Gn 35.20N 24.00 E
Levkás 15 Dk 38.50N 20.42 E
Levkás = Leucas (EN) 15 Dk 38.43N 20.38 E

Index Symbols

[1] Independent Nation
[2] State, Region
[3] District, County
Municipality
Colony, Dependency
Continent
Physical Region
Historical or Cultural Region
Mount, Mountain
Volcano
Hill
Mountains, Mountain Range
Hills, Escarpment
Plateau, Upland
Pass, Gap
Plain, Lowland
Delta
Salt Flat
Valley, Canyon
Crater, Cave
Karst Features
Depression
Polder
Desert, Dunes
Forest, Woods
Heath, Steppe
Oasis
Cape, Point
Coast, Beach
Cliff
Peninsula
Isthmus
Sandbank
Island
Atoll
Rock, Reef
Islands, Archipelago
Rocks, Reefs
Coral Reef
Well, Spring
Geyser
River, Stream
Waterfall Rapids
River Mouth, Estuary
Lake
Salt Lake
Intermittent Lake
Reservoir
Swamp, Pond
Canal
Glacier
Ice Shelf, Pack Ice
Ocean
Sea
Gulf, Bay
Strait, Fjord
Lagoon
Bank
Seamount
Tablemount
Ridge
Shelf
Basin
Escarpment, Sea Scarp
Fracture
Trench, Abyss
National Park, Reserve
Point of Interest
Recreation Site
Cave, Cavern
Historic Site
Ruins
Wall, Walls
Church, Abbey
Temple
Scientific Station
Airport
Port
Lighthouse
Mine
Tunnel
Dam, Bridge

Levkōsia/Lefkosa=Nicosia (EN) 22 Ff 35.10N 33.22 E
Levoča 10 Qg 49.02N 20.35 E
Levroux 11 Hh 46.59N 1.37 E
Levski 15 If 43.22N 25.08 E
Lev Tolstoj 16 Kc 53.12N 39.28 E
Levuka 63d Bb 17.41S 178.50 E
Levuo/Lévuo 8 Kh 56.02N 24.28 E
Lévuo/Levuo 8 Kh 56.02N 24.28 E
Lewes [De.-U.S.] 44 Jf 38.47N 75.08W
Lewes [Eng.-U.K.] 9 Nk 50.52N 0.01 E
Lewin Brzeski 10 Nf 50.46N 17.37 E
Lewis, Butt of- 9 Gc 58.31N 6.15W
Lewis, Isle of- 5 Fd 58.10N 6.40W
Lewis and Clark Lake 45 He 42.50N 97.45W
Lewisburg 44 Gg 37.49N 80.28W
Lewis Pass 62 Ee 42.24S 172.24 E
Lewis Range 38 He 48.30N 113.15W
Lewis River 46 Dd 45.51N 122.48W
Lewis Smith Lake 44 Dh 34.00N 87.07W
Lewiston [Id.-U.S.] 39 He 46.25N 117.01W
Lewiston [Me.-U.S.] 43 Mc 44.06N 70.13W
Lewistown [Mt.-U.S.] 43 Fb 47.04N 109.26W
Lewistown [Pa.-U.S.] 44 Ie 40.37N 77.36W
Lewisville 45 Jj 33.22N 93.35W
Lexington [Ky.-U.S.] 39 Kf 38.03N 84.30W
Lexington [Nb.-U.S.] 43 Hc 40.47N 99.45W
Lexington [N.C.-U.S.] 44 Gh 35.49N 80.15W
Lexington [Ok.-U.S.] 45 Hi 35.01N 97.20W
Lexington [Va.-U.S.] 44 Hg 37.47N 79.27W
Leygues, Iles- 30 Nm 48.45S 69.30 E
Leyre 11 Ej 44.39N 1.01W
Leysdown-on-Sea 12 Cc 51.23N 0.55 E
Leyte 21 Oh 10.50N 124.50 E
Lez 11 Kj 44.13N 4.43 E
Leżajsk 10 Sf 50.16N 22.24 E
Lézard, Pointe à- 51e Ab 16.08N 61.47W
Lézarde, Rivière- 51h Ab 14.36N 61.01W
Lezha 15 Ch 41.47N 19.39 E
Lézignan-Corbières 11 Ik 43.12N 2.46 E
Lgov 19 De 51.41N 35.17 E
Lhari 27 Fe 30.48N 93.25 E
Lhasa 22 Lg 29.42N 91.07 E
Lhazê 27 Ef 29.13N 87.44 E
Lhazhong 27 Ee 31.28N 86.36 E
Lhokseumawe 26 Ce 5.10N 97.08 E
Lhoksukon 26 Ce 5.03N 97.19 E
L'Hôpital 12 Ie 49.10N 6.44 E
Lhorong 27 Ge 30.45N 95.48 E
L'Hospitalet de l'Infant/Hospitalet del Infante 13 Md 40.59N 0.56 E
Lhozhag 27 Ff 28.18N 90.51 E
Lhünzhub (Poindo) 27 Fe 30.17N 91.20 E
Liádhi 15 Jm 36.55N 26.10 E
Liákoura 15 Fk 38.32N 22.37 E
Liamone 11a Aa 42.04N 8.43 E
Liancheng 27 Kf 25.48N 116.48 E
Liancourt 12 Ee 49.20N 2.28 E
Liane 12 Dd 50.43N 1.36 E
Liangcheng 28 Bd 40.32N 112.28 E
Liangpran, Gunung- 26 Ff 1.04N 114.23 E
Liangshan (Houji) 28 Dg 35.48N 116.07 E
Liangzhou → Wuwei 22 Mf 37.58N 102.48 E
Liangzi Hu 27 Je 30.15N 114.32 E
Lianjiang 27 Jg 21.42N 110.14 E
Lianshui 28 Eh 33.47N 119.16 E
Lianxian 27 Jg 24.48N 112.26 E
Lianyin 27 La 53.26N 123.50 E
Lianyungang 27 Ke 34.38N 119.27 E
Lianyungang (Xinpu) 22 Nf 34.34N 119.15 E
Lianzhou → Hepu 27 Ig 21.40N 109.12 E
Lianzhushan 28 Kb 45.28N 131.45 E
Liaocheng 27 Kd 36.27N 115.58 E
Liaodong Bandao=Liaotung Peninsula (EN) 21 Of 40.00N 122.20 E
Liaodong Wan=Liaotung, Gulf of- (EN) 27 Lc 40.00N 121.30 E
Liao He 21 Oe 40.39N 122.12 E
Liaoning Sheng (Liao-ning Sheng) [2] 27 Lc 41.00N 123.00 E
Liao-ning Sheng → Liaoning Sheng [2] 27 Lc 41.00N 123.00 E
Liaotung, Gulf of- (EN)=Liaodong Wan 27 Lc 40.00N 121.30 E
Liaotung Peninsula (EN)=Liaodong Bandao 21 Of 40.00N 122.20 E
Liaoyang 27 Lc 41.16N 123.10 E
Liaoyuan 22 Oe 42.55N 125.09 E
Liaozhong 28 Gd 41.30N 122.42 E
Liard 38 Gc 61.52N 121.18W
Liard River 42 Ee 59.15N 126.09W
Liat, Pulau- 26 Eg 2.53S 107.05 E
Liatorp 8 Fh 56.40N 14.16 E
Liatroim/Leitrim [2] 9 Eg 54.20N 8.20W
Liban 30 Lh 5.05N 40.05 E
Libano 55 Bm 37.32S 61.18W
Libby 46 Hb 48.23N 115.33W
Libenge 31 Ih 3.39N 18.38 E
Libengé 36 Cb 3.39N 18.38 E
Liberal 43 Gd 37.02N 100.55W
Liberec 10 Lf 50.46N 15.03 E
Liberia 47 Gf 10.38N 85.27W
Liberia [1] 31 Fh 6.00N 10.00W
Libertad [Ur.] 55 Dl 34.38S 56.39W
Libertad [Ven.] 49 Li 8.08N 71.28W
Libertad [Ven.] 54 Eb 8.20N 69.37W
Libertade, Rio- 54 He 9.35S 52.17W
Libertador General Bernardo O'Higgins [2] 56 Fd 33.35S 70.45W
Libertador Gen. San Martín 56 Hb 23.48S 64.48W
Libertador General San Martín, Cumbre del- 52 Jh 24.55S 66.40W
Liberty [Mo.-U.S.] 45 Ig 39.15N 94.25W
Liberty [Tx.-U.S.] 45 Ik 30.03N 94.47W
Lībiyā=Libya (EN) [1] 31 If 27.00N 17.00 E
Lībīyah, Aş Şaḩrā' al-=Libyan Desert (EN) 30 Jf 24.00N 25.00 E
Libo 27 If 25.28N 107.52 E
Libobo, Tanjung- 26 Ig 0.54S 128.28 E
Liboi 36 Hb 0.24N 40.57 E
Libourne 11 Fj 44.55N 0.14W
Libramont-Chevigny 12 He 49.55N 5.23 E
Librazhdi 15 Dh 41.11N 20.19 E
Libreville 31 Hh 0.23N 9.27 E
Libro Point 26 Gd 11.26N 119.29 E
Libya (EN)=Lībiyā [1] 31 If 27.00N 17.00 E
Libyan Desert (EN)=Lībīyah, Aş Şaḩrā' al- 30 Jf 24.00N 25.00 E
Licantén 56 Fe 34.59S 72.00W
Licata 14 Hm 37.06N 13.56 E
Lice 24 Ic 38.28N 40.39 E
Licenciado Matienzo 55 Cm 37.55S 58.54W
Lich 12 Kd 50.31N 8.50 E
Licheng → Jinhu 28 Eh 33.01N 119.01 E
Lichfield 9 Li 52.42N 1.48W
Lichinga 31 Kj 13.20S 35.20 E
Lichtenau 12 Kc 51.37N 8.54 E
Lichtenburg 37 De 26.08S 26.08 E
Lichtenfels 10 Hf 50.09N 11.04 E
Lichtenvoorde 12 Ic 51.59N 6.34 E
Licking River 44 Ef 39.06N 84.30W
Licosa, Punta- 14 Ij 40.15N 14.54 E
Licuare 37 Fc 17.54S 36.49 E
Licun → Laoshan 28 Ff 36.10N 120.25 E
Licungo 37 Fc 17.40S 37.22 E
Lida 19 Ce 53.56N 25.18 E
Lidan 8 Ef 58.31N 13.09 E
Liddel 9 Kf 55.04N 2.57W
Liddon Gulf 42 Gb 75.00N 113.30W
Liden 7 De 62.42N 16.48 E
Lidhoríkion 15 Fk 38.32N 22.12 E
Lidhult 8 Eh 56.50N 13.26 E
Lidingö 7 Eg 59.22N 18.08 E
Lidköping 7 Cg 58.30N 13.10 E
Lido 34 Fc 12.54N 3.44 E
Lido, Venezia- 14 Ge 45.25N 12.22 E
Lido di Ostia 14 Gi 41.44N 12.16 E
Lidzbark 10 Pc 53.17N 19.49 E
Lidzbark Warmiński 10 Qb 54.09N 20.35 E
Lié 11 Df 48.00N 2.40W
Liebenau 12 Lb 52.36N 9.06 E
Liebig, Mount- 59 Gd 23.15S 131.20 E
Liechtenstein [1] 6 Gf 47.10N 9.30 E
Liège [3] 12 Hd 50.30N 5.40 E
Liège/Luik 6 Ge 50.38N 5.34 E
Lieksa 7 He 63.19N 30.01 E
Lielupé 7 Fh 57.03N 23.56 E
Lielvarde/Lielvārde 8 Kh 56.40N 24.49 E
Lielvārde/Lielvarde 8 Kh 56.40N 24.49 E
Lienen 12 Jb 52.09N 7.59 E
Lienz 14 Gd 46.50N 12.47 E
Liepaja/Liepāja 6 Id 56.35N 21.01 E
Liepāja/Liepaja 6 Id 56.35N 21.01 E
Liepajas, Ozero-/Liepājas Ezers 8 Ih 56.35N 20.35 E
Liepājas ezers/Liepaja, Ozero- 8 Ih 56.35N 20.35 E
Liepna 8 Lg 57.16N 27.35 E
Liepupe 8 Kg 57.22N 24.22 E
Lier/Lierre 11 Kc 51.08N 4.34 E
Lierbyen 8 De 59.47N 10.14 E
Lierneux 12 Hd 50.17N 5.48 E
Lierre/Lier 11 Kc 51.08N 4.34 E
Liesborn, Wadersloh- 12 Kc 51.43N 8.16 E
Lieser 10 Dg 49.55N 7.01 E
Liesing 14 Jc 47.20N 15.02 E
Liestal 14 Bc 47.29N 7.44 E
Lieşti 15 Kd 45.37N 27.31 E
Lieto 8 Jd 60.30N 22.27 E
Lietuva = Lithuania (EN) 19 Cd 56.00N 24.00 E
Lietuvos Tarybu Socialistine Respublika/Litovskaja SSR → Lietuva 19 Cd 56.00N 24.00 E
Lietuvos TSR → Lietuva 19 Cd 56.00N 24.00 E
Lietvesi 8 Lc 61.30N 28.00 E
Lieurey 12 Ce 49.14N 0.29 E
Lieuvin 11 Ge 49.10N 0.30 E
Lievestuoreenjärvi 8 Lb 62.20N 26.10 E
Liévin 11 Id 50.25N 2.46 E
Lievre, Rivière du- 44 Jc 45.35N 75.25W
Liezen 14 Ic 47.34N 14.14 E
Lifford/Leifear 9 Fg 54.50N 7.29W
Li Fiord 42 Ia 80.17N 94.35W
Lifjell 8 Ce 59.30N 8.52 E
Lifou, Ile- 57 Hg 20.53S 167.13 E
Lifuka 65b Ba 19.48S 174.21W
Līgatne/Ligatne 8 Kg 57.07N 25.00 E
Ligatne/Līgatne 8 Kg 57.07N 25.00 E
Lighthouse Reef 49 De 17.20N 87.32W
Lignano Sabbiadoro 14 He 45.52N 13.09 E
Lignières 11 Ih 46.45N 2.10 E
Lignon 11 Ki 45.44N 4.08 E
Ligny-en-Barrois 11 Lf 48.41N 5.20 E
Ligonha 37 Fc 16.51S 39.09 E
Ligure, Mar-=Ligurian Sea (EN) 5 Gg 43.30N 9.00 E
Liguria [2] 14 Cf 44.30N 8.50 E
Ligurian Sea (EN)=Ligure, Mar- 5 Gg 43.30N 9.00 E
Lihir Group 57 Ge 3.05S 152.40 E
Lihme 8 Ch 56.36N 8.44 E
Lihoslavl 7 Ih 57.09N 35.29 E
Lihou Reefs and Cays 57 Gf 17.25S 151.40 E
Lihue 60 Oc 21.59N 159.22W
Lihula 7 Fg 58.44N 23.49 E
Liinahamari 7 Hb 69.40N 31.22 E
Lijiang (Dayan) 22 Mg 26.56N 100.15 E
Lijin 28 Ef 37.29N 118.15 E
Lika 14 Jf 44.46N 15.10 E
Lika 14 Jf 44.30N 15.30 E
Likasi 31 Jj 10.59S 26.43 E
Likati 36 Db 2.53N 24.03 E
Likati 36 Db 3.21N 23.53 E
Likėnai/Likenaj 8 Kh 56.11N 24.42 E
Likenaj/Likėnai 8 Kh 56.11N 24.42 E
Likenäs 8 Ed 60.37N 13.02 E
Likhapani 25 Jc 27.19N 95.54 E
Likiep Atoll 57 Hc 9.53N 169.09 E
Likolo 36 Cc 0.43S 19.40 E
Likoma Island 36 Fe 12.04S 34.44 E
Likoto 36 Dc 1.10S 24.45 E
Likouala [3] 36 Cb 2.00N 17.30 E
Likouala 36 Cc 1.13S 16.48 E
Likouala aux Herbes 36 Cc 0.50S 17.11 E
Liku 64k Bb 19.02S 169.47W
L'Ile Rousse 11a Aa 42.38N 8.56 E
Lilibeo, Capo- → Boeo, Capo- 14 Gm 37.34N 12.41 E
Lilienfeld 14 Jb 48.01N 15.38 E
Lilienthal 12 Ka 53.08N 8.55 E
Lilla Edet 7 Cg 58.08N 12.08 E
Lille [Bel.] 12 Gc 51.14N 4.50 E
Lille [Fr.] 6 Ge 50.38N 3.04 E
Lille Bælt=Little Belt (EN) 5 Gd 55.20N 9.45 E
Lillebonne 11 Ge 49.31N 0.33 E
Lille Fiskebanke 8 Bh 56.56N 6.20 E
Lillehammer 7 Cf 61.08N 10.30 E
Lille Hellefiske Bank (EN) 41 Ge 65.05N 54.00W
Lillers 11 Id 50.34N 2.29 E
Lillesand 7 Bg 58.15N 8.24 E
Lillestrøm 8 De 59.57N 11.05 E
Lillhärdal 7 Df 61.51N 14.04 E
Lillie Glacier 66 Kf 70.45S 163.55 E
Lillo 13 Ie 39.43N 3.18W
Lillooet 42 Ff 50.42N 121.56W
Lillooet Range 46 Eb 50.00N 121.45W
Lillooet River 42 Fg 49.45N 122.10W
Lilongwe 31 Kj 13.59S 33.47 E
Liloy 26 He 8.08N 122.40 E
Lim [Afr.] 35 Bd 7.54N 15.46 E
Lim 14 Ng 43.45N 19.13 E
Lima 13 Dc 41.41N 8.50W
Lima [2] 54 Cf 12.00S 76.35W
Lima [Mt.-U.S.] 46 Id 44.38N 112.36W
Lima [Oh.-U.S.] 43 Kc 40.43N 84.06W
Lima [Par.] 55 Df 23.54S 56.20W
Lima [Peru] 53 Ig 12.03S 77.03W
Lima [Swe.] 8 Ed 60.56N 13.21 E
Lima, Pulau-Pulau- 26 Gg 3.03S 107.24 E
Limagne 11 Jh 46.00N 3.20 E
Līmah 24 Qj 25.56N 56.25 E
Liman 16 Og 45.45N 47.14 E
Liman 15 Md 45.42N 29.46 E
Limanskoje 15 Mc 46.38N 29.54 E
Limari, Río- 56 Fd 30.44S 71.43W
Limassol/Lemesós 23 Dc 34.40N 33.02 E
Limavady/Léim an Mhadaidh 9 Gf 55.03N 6.57W
Limay 12 Df 48.59N 1.44 E
Limay, Río- 52 Ji 38.59S 68.00W
Limbara 14 Dj 40.51N 9.10 E
Limbaži 7 Fh 57.31N 24.47 E
Limbé 49 Kd 19.42N 72.24W
Limbe, Blantyre- 36 Gf 15.49S 35.03 E
Limbot 63b Cb 14.12S 167.34 E
Limboto 26 Hf 0.37N 122.57 E
Limbourg 12 Hd 50.37N 5.56 E
Limbourg/Limburg 11 Lc 51.05N 5.40 E
Limburg [Bel.] [3] 12 Hc 51.00N 5.30 E
Limburg [Neth.] [3] 12 Hc 51.14N 5.50 E
Limburg/Limbourg 11 Lc 51.05N 5.40 E
Limburg an der Lahn 10 Ef 50.23N 8.03 E
Limedsforsen 8 Ed 60.54N 13.23 E
Limeira 56 Kb 22.34S 47.24W
Limerick/Luimneach [2] 9 Ei 52.30N 9.00W
Limerick/Luimneach 6 Fe 52.40N 8.38W
Limestone, Haḑabat- 33 Fe 24.50N 32.00 E
Limfjorden 5 Gd 56.55N 9.10 E
Limia 13 Dc 41.41N 8.50W
Limingen 7 Cd 64.47N 13.35 E
Liminka 7 Fd 64.49N 25.29 E
Limmat 14 Cc 47.30N 8.15 E
Limmen Bight 59 Hb 14.45S 135.40 E
Limmen Bight River 59 Hc 15.15S 135.30 E
Límni 15 Gk 38.46N 23.19 E
Límnos=Lemnos (EN) 5 Ih 39.55N 25.15 E
Limoeiro 54 Ke 7.52S 35.27W
Limoges 6 Gf 45.51N 1.15 E
Limogne, Causse de- 11 Hj 44.20N 1.55 E
Limon 43 Gd 39.16N 103.41W
Limón [3] 49 Fi 10.00N 83.15W
Limón [C.R.] 39 Kh 10.00N 83.02W
Limón [Hond.] 49 Ef 15.52N 85.33W
Limone Piemonte 14 Bf 44.12N 7.34 E
Limousin 11 Hi 45.30N 1.50 E
Limousin, Plateau du- 11 Hi 45.50N 1.10 E
Limoux 11 Ik 43.04N 2.14 E
Limpopo 30 Jk 25.12S 33.32 E
Limu Ling 27 Ie 19.02N 109.43 E
Limuru 36 Gc 1.06S 36.39 E
Līnah 24 Jh 28.42N 43.48 E
Lin'an 27 Ke 30.14N 119.39 E
Linapacan 26 Gd 11.27N 119.49 E
Linares [Chile] 53 Ii 35.51S 71.36W
Linares [Mex.] 47 Ed 24.52N 99.34W
Linares [Sp.] 13 If 38.05N 3.38W
Linares Viejo 55 Bf 23.09S 61.46W
Linaro, Capo- 14 Fh 42.02N 11.50 E
Lincang 22 Mg 23.48N 100.04 E
Lincheng 28 Cf 37.25N 114.34 E
Lincheng → Xuecheng 28 Dg 34.48N 117.14 E
Lincoln 9 Mh 53.20N 0.30W
Lincoln [Arg.] 56 Hd 34.52S 61.32W
Lincoln [Eng.-U.K.] 9 Mh 53.14N 0.33W
Lincoln [Il.-U.S.] 45 Lf 40.09N 89.22W
Lincoln [Nb.-U.S.] 39 Je 40.48N 96.42W
Lincoln [N.Z.] 62 Ee 43.38S 172.29 E
Lincoln, Mount- 45 Cg 39.21N 106.07W
Lincoln City 46 Cd 44.59N 124.01W
Lincoln Sea 67 Ne 83.00N 56.00W
Lincolnshire [3] 9 Mh 53.00N 0.10W
Lindashalvøya 8 Ad 60.40N 5.15 E
Lindau 10 Fi 47.33N 9.41 E
Linde [Neth.] 12 Hb 52.49N 5.52 E
Linde 20 Hd 64.59N 124.36 E
Linden [Guy.] 54 Gb 6.00N 58.18W
Linden [Tn.-U.S.] 44 Dh 35.37N 87.50W
Lindenows Fjord 41 Hf 60.25N 43.00W
Linderödsåsen 8 Ei 55.53N 13.56 E
Lindesberg 7 Dg 59.35N 15.15 E
Lindesnes 5 Gd 58.00N 7.02 E
Lindhorst 12 Lb 52.22N 9.17 E
Lindhos 15 Lm 36.06N 28.04 E
Lindi [3] 36 Gd 9.30S 38.20 E
Lindi 31 Ki 10.00S 39.43 E
Lindi 30 Jh 0.33N 25.05 E
Lindis Pass 62 Cf 44.35S 169.39 E
Lindlar 12 Jc 51.01N 7.23 E
Lindome 8 Eg 57.34N 12.05 E
Lindong → Bairin Zuoqi 27 Kc 43.59N 119.22 E
Lindsay [Ca.-U.S.] 46 Fh 36.12N 119.05W
Lindsay [Ont.-Can.] 44 Hc 44.21N 78.44W
Lindsdal 8 Gh 56.44N 16.18 E
Line Islands 57 Le 0.01S 157.00W
Linfen 27 Jd 36.03N 111.32 E
Lingayen 22 Oh 16.01N 120.14 E
Lingayen Gulf 26 Hc 16.15N 120.14 E
Lingbi 28 Dh 33.33N 117.33 E
Lingbo 7 Df 61.03N 16.41 E
Lingchuan 28 Bg 35.46N 113.16 E
Lingen (Ems) 10 Dd 52.31N 7.19 E
Lingfield 12 Bc 51.10N 0.01W
Lingga, Kepulauan-=Lingga Archipelago (EN) 21 Mj 0.02S 104.35 E
Lingga, Pulau- 26 Dg 0.12S 104.35 E
Lingga Archipelago (EN)=Lingga, Kepulauan- 21 Mj 0.02S 104.35 E
Linghed 8 Fd 60.47N 15.51 E
Lingling 27 Jf 26.24N 111.41 E
Lingomo 36 Db 0.38N 21.59 E
Lingqiu 28 Ce 39.26N 114.14 E
Lingshan 27 Ig 22.30N 109.17 E
Lingshan Dao 28 Fg 35.45N 120.10 E
Lingshi 28 Af 36.50N 111.46 E
Lingshou 28 Ce 38.18N 114.22 E
Linguère 31 Fg 15.24N 15.07W
Lingwu 27 Id 38.05N 106.20 E
Lingxian 28 Df 37.20N 116.35 E
Lingyuan 28 Ed 41.15N 119.23 E
Linh, Ngoc- 21 Mh 15.04N 107.59 E
Linhai 27 La 51.36N 124.22 E
Linhai (Taizhou) 27 Lf 28.52N 121.08 E
Linhares 54 Jg 19.25S 40.04W
Linhe 27 Ic 40.49N 107.28 E
Linhuaiguan 28 Dh 32.54N 117.39 E
Linjiang 28 Id 41.49N 126.55 E
Linköping 6 Hd 58.25N 15.37 E
Linkou 27 Nb 45.18N 130.18 E
Linkuva 8 Jh 56.02N 23.58 E
Linlü Shan 28 Bf 36.02N 113.42 E
Linn, Mount- 46 Df 40.03N 122.48W
Linneryd 8 Fh 56.40N 15.07 E
Linnhe, Loch- 9 He 56.37N 5.25W
Linnich 12 Id 50.59N 6.16 E
Linosa 14 Go 35.50N 12.50 E
Linovo 10 Ud 52.28N 24.35 E
Linqing 27 Kd 36.48N 115.49 E
Linqu 28 Ef 36.31N 118.32 E
Linquan 28 Ch 33.04N 115.16 E
Linru 28 Bg 34.10N 112.51 E
Lins 56 Kb 21.40S 49.45W
Linsell 8 Eb 62.09N 13.53 E
Linshu (Xiazhuang) 28 Eg 34.56N 118.38 E
Linslade 12 Bc 51.55N 0.40W
Linta 37 Ge 25.02S 44.05 E
Lintao 27 Hd 35.20N 104.00 E
Linthal 14 Cd 46.55N 9.00 E
Linton [Eng.-U.K.] 12 Cb 52.06N 0.16 E
Linton [N.D.-U.S.] 45 Fc 46.16N 100.14W
Linxi [China] 22 Ne 43.36N 118.02 E
Linxi [China] 28 Ee 39.42N 118.26 E
Linxia 22 Mf 35.28N 102.59 E
Linxian 27 Jd 37.57N 111.00 E
Linxiang 28 Bj 29.29N 113.28 E
Linyi [China] 28 Df 37.11N 116.51 E
Linyi [China]' 27 Kd 35.09N 118.15 E
Linz 6 Hf 48.18N 14.18 E
Linze (Shahezhen) 27 Hd 39.10N 100.21 E
Lion, Golfe du-=Lion, Gulf of- (EN) 5 Gg 43.00N 4.00 E
Lion, Gulf of- (EN)=Lion, Golfe du- 5 Gg 43.00N 4.00 E
Lions Den 37 Ec 17.16S 30.02 E
Lion-sur-Mer 12 Be 49.18N 0.19W
Lioppa 26 Ih 7.40S 126.00 E
Lios Mór/Lismore 9 Fi 52.08N 7.55W
Lios na gCearrbhach/Lisburn 9 Gg 54.31N 6.03W
Lios Tuathail/Listovel 9 Di 52.27N 9.29W
Liouesso 36 Cb 1.02N 15.43 E
Lipa 26 Hd 13.57N 121.10 E
Lipany 10 Qg 49.10N 20.58 E
Lipari 14 Il 38.30N 14.55 E
Lipari 14 Il 38.28N 14.57 E
Lipari Islands (EN)=Eolie o Lipari, Isole- 5 Hh 38.35N 14.55 E
Lipeck 6 Je 52.37N 39.35 E
Lipeckaja Oblast [3] 19 De 52.45N 39.10 E
Lipenská přehradní nádrž 10 Kh 48.45N 14.05 E
Liperi 7 Ge 62.32N 29.22 E
Lipez, Cordillera de- 54 Eh 22.00S 66.45W
Liphook 12 Bc 51.04N 0.48W
Lipkani 15 Ja 48.13N 26.48 E
Lipljan 15 Eg 42.32N 21.08 E
Lipno 10 Pd 52.51N 19.10 E
Lipova 15 Ec 46.05N 21.42 E
Lipovcy 20 Ih 44.15N 131.45 E
Lippborg, Lippetal- 12 Kc 51.40N 8.02 E
Lippe 10 Ce 51.39N 6.38 E
Lipper Bergland 12 Kb 52.05N 8.57 E
Lippetal 12 Kc 51.40N 8.13 E
Lippetal-Eickelborn 12 Kc 51.39N 8.13 E
Lippetal-Lippborg 12 Kc 51.40N 8.02 E
Lippischer Wald 12 Kc 51.56N 8.45 E
Lippstadt 10 Ee 51.40N 8.21 E
Lipsko 10 Re 51.09N 21.39 E
Lipsoí 15 Jl 37.20N 26.45 E
Liptako 30 Hg 14.15N 0.02 E
Liptovský Mikuláš 10 Pg 49.05N 19.38 E
Lira 36 Fb 2.15N 32.54 E
Liranga 36 Cc 0.40S 17.36 E
Liri 14 Hi 41.25N 13.52 E
Liria 13 Le 39.38N 0.36W
Lis 13 De 39.53N 8.58W
Lisa 15 Cf 43.08N 19.42 E
Lisac 15 Eg 42.45N 21.56 E
Lisakovsk 19 Ge 52.33N 62.28 E
Lisala 31 Jh 2.09N 21.31 E
Lisboa [2] 13 Ce 39.00N 9.08W
Lisboa=Lisbon (EN) 6 Fh 38.43N 9.08W
Lisbon 45 Hc 46.27N 97.41W
Lisbon (EN)=Lisboa 6 Fh 38.43N 9.08W
Lisbon Canyon (EN) 13 Cf 38.20N 9.20W
Lisburn/Lios na gCearrbhach 9 Gg 54.31N 6.03W
Lisburne, Cape- 40 Fc 68.52N 166.14W
Liscannor Bay/Bá Thuath Reanna 9 Di 52.55N 9.25W
Lisec 10 Uh 48.48N 24.45 E
Li Shan 28 Ag 35.25N 111.58 E
Lishi 27 Jd 37.29N 111.08 E
Lishu 28 Hc 43.19N 124.20 E
Lishui 27 Kf 28.30N 119.55 E
Lisianski Island 57 Jb 26.02N 174.00W
Lisičansk 19 Df 48.53N 38.28 E
Lisieux 11 Ge 49.09N 0.14 E
Liski (Gheorghiu-Dej) 19 De 51.00N 39.31 E
L'Isle-Adam 12 Ee 49.07N 2.14 E
L'Isle-Jourdain 11 Hk 43.37N 1.05 E
L'Isle sur-la-Sorgue 11 Lk 43.55N 5.03 E
Lismore 58 Gg 28.48S 153.17 E
Lismore/Lios Mór 9 Fi 52.08N 7.55W
Liss 24 Hg 31.14N 38.31 E
Liss 12 Bc 51.02N 0.54W
List 10 Ea 55.01N 8.26 E
Lista 8 Bf 58.0 0N 6.40 E
Listafjorden 8 Bf 58.0 0N 6.35 E
Lister, Mount- 66 Kf 78.04S 162.41 E
Lištica 14 Lg 43.23N 17.39 E
Listovel/Lios Tuathail 9 Di 52.27N 9.29W
Listowel 44 Gd 43.44N 80.57W
Liswarta 10 Pe 51.06N 19.01 E
Lit 8 Fa 63.19N 14.49 E
Litang [China] 27 Ig 23.12N 109.05 E
Litang [China] 27 He 30.02N 100.18 E
Litani Rivier 54 Hc 3.18N 54.06W
Litchfield 45 Id 45.08N 94.31W
Lithgow 58 Gh 33.29S 150.09 E
Lithinon, Ákra- 15 Ho 34.55N 24.44 E
Lithuania (EN) 5 Id 56.00N 24.00 E
Lithuania (EN) = Lietuva 19 Cd 56.00N 24.00 E
Litókhoron 15 Fi 40.06N 22.30 E
Litoměřice 10 Kf 50.32N 14.08 E
Litovel 10 Ng 49.43N 17.05 E
Litovko 20 Ig 49.17N 135.10 E
Litovskaja Sovetskaja Socialističeskaja Respublika → Lietuva 19 Cd 56.00N 24.00 E
Litovskaja SSR/Lietuvos Tarybu Socialistine Respublika → Lietuva 19 Cd 56.00N 24.00 E
Little Abaco Island 47 Ic 26.53N 77.43W
Little Abitibi River 44 Ha 49.29N 79.32W
Little Aden 23 Fg 12.45N 44.52 E
Little America 46 Kf 41.32N 109.47W
Little Andaman 21 Lh 10.45N 92.30 E
Little Bahama Bank (EN) 47 Ic 26.30N 78.00W
Little Barrier Island 62 Fb 36.10S 175.05 E
Little Beaver Creek 45 Ec 46.17N 103.56W
Little Belt (EN)=Lille Bælt 5 Gd 55.20N 9.45 E
Little Belt Mountains 46 Jc 46.45N 110.35W
Little Blue River 45 Hg 39.41N 96.40W
Little Bow River 46 Ib 49.53N 112.29W
Little Carpathians (EN) = Malé Karpaty 10 Nh 48.30N 17.20 E
Little Cayman 47 He 19.41N 80.03W
Little Colorado River 38 Hc 36.11N 111.48W
Little Current 42 Jg 45.58N 81.56W
Little Current 42 Jf 50.57N 84.36W
Little Dry Creek 46 Lc 47.21N 106.22W
Little Exuma Island 49 Jb 23.27N 75.37W
Little Falls 43 Ib 45.59N 94.21W
Littlefield 45 Ej 33.55N 102.20W
Little Fort 46 Ea 51.25N 120.12W
Little Grand Rapids 42 Hf 52.02N 95.25W
Little Halibut Bank 9 Lc 58.20N 1.15W
Littlehampton 12 Bd 50.48N 0.32W
Little Inagua Island 47 Jd 21.30N 73.00W
Little Karroo (EN)=Klein-Karoo 37 Cf 33.42S 21.20 E
Little Missouri 38 Ie 47.30N 102.25W
Little Namaland (EN)=Namakwaland 37 Be 29.00S 17.00 E
Little Nicobar 25 Ig 7.20N 93.40 E
Little Ouse 9 Ni 52.30N 0.22 E
Littleport 12 Cb 52.27N 0.18 E
Little Powder River 46 Md 45.28N 105.20W
Little Quill Lake 46 Ma 51.55N 104.05W
Little River 62 Ee 43.46S 172.47 E
Little Rock 39 Jf 34.44N 92.15W
Little Rocky Mountains 46 Kb 48.00N 108.45W

Index Symbols

[1] Independent Nation
[2] State, Region
[3] District, County
[4] Municipality
[5] Colony, Dependency
Continent
Physical Region
Historical or Cultural Region
Mount, Mountain
Volcano
Hill
Mountains, Mountain Range
Hills, Escarpment
Plateau, Upland
Pass, Gap
Plain, Lowland
Delta
Salt Flat
Valley, Canyon
Crater, Cave
Karst Features
Depression
Polder
Desert, Dunes
Forest, Woods
Heath, Steppe
Oasis
Cape, Point
Coast, Beach
Cliff
Peninsula
Isthmus
Sandbank
Island
Atoll
Rock, Reef
Islands, Archipelago
Rocks, Reefs
Coral Reef
Well, Spring
Geyser
River, Stream
Waterfall Rapids
River Mouth, Estuary
Lake
Salt Lake
Intermittent Lake
Reservoir
Swamp, Pond
Canal
Glacier
Ice Shelf, Pack Ice
Ocean
Sea
Gulf, Bay
Strait, Fjord
Lagoon
Bank
Seamount
Tablemount
Ridge
Shelf
Basin
Escarpment, Sea Scarp
Fracture
Trench, Abyss
National Park, Reserve
Point of Interest
Recreation Site
Cave, Cavern
Historic Site
Ruins
Wall, Walls
Church, Abbey
Temple
Scientific Station
Airport
Port
Lighthouse
Mine
Tunnel
Dam, Bridge

Name	Page	Grid	Lat.	Long.
Little Scarcies	34	Cd	8.51N	13.09W
Little Sioux River	45	Hf	41.49N	96.04W
Little Sitkin	40a	Cb	51.55N	178.30 E
Little Smoky	42	Fe	55.39N	117.37W
Little Snake River	45	Bf	40.27N	108.26W
Littleton [Co.-U.S.]	45	Dg	39.37N	105.01W
Littleton [N.H.-U.S.]	44	Lc	44.18N	71.46W
Little White River [Ont.-Can.]	44	Fb	46.15N	83.00W
Little White River [S.D.-U.S.]	45	Fe	43.44N	100.40W
Littoral [3]	34	He	4.30N	10.00 E
Litvínov	10	Jf	50.36N	13.36 E
Liuba	27	Ie	33.39N	106.53 E
Liuhe	27	Mc	42.16N	125.46 E
Liu He [China]	28	Gd	41.48N	122.43 E
Liu He [China]	28	Ic	42.46N	126.13 E
Liuheng Dao	28	Gj	29.43N	122.08 E
Liujia Xia	27	Hd	35.50N	103.00 E
Liukang Tenggaja, Kepulauan-	26	Gh	6.45S	118.50 E
Liupai → Tian'e	27	If	25.05N	107.12 E
Liupan Shan	27	Id	35.40N	106.15 E
Liuqu He	28	Fd	40.10N	120.15 E
Liuwa Plain	36	De	14.27S	22.25 E
Liuyang	28	Bj	28.09N	113.38 E
Liuzhangzhen → Yuanqu	27	Jd	35.19N	111.44 E
Liuzhou	22	Mg	24.22N	109.20 E
Līvāni/Livány	7	Gh	56.22N	26.12 E
Livanjsko Polje	14	Kg	43.51N	16.50 E
Livany/Līvāni	7	Gh	56.22N	26.12 E
Livarot	12	Ce	49.01N	0.09 E
Livengood	40	Jc	65.32N	148.33W
Livenza	14	Ge	45.35N	12.51 E
Livenzi	15	Ge	44.14N	23.47 E
Live Oak	44	Fj	30.18N	82.59W
Livermore	46	Eh	37.41N	121.46W
Livermore, Mount-	45	Dk	30.37N	104.08W
Liverpool [Eng.-U.K.]	6	Fe	53.25N	2.55W
Liverpool [N.S.-Can.]	42	Lh	44.02N	64.43W
Liverpool, Cape-	42	Jb	73.38N	78.05W
Liverpool Bay [Can.]	42	Ec	70.00N	129.00W
Liverpool Bay [Eng.-U.K.]	9	Jh	53.30N	3.16W
Liverpool Range	59	Kf	31.45S	150.30 E
Liverpool River	59	Gb	12.00S	134.00 E
Livigno	14	Ed	46.32N	10.04 E
Livingston [Guat.]	49	Cf	15.50N	88.45W
Livingston [Mt.-U.S.]	43	Eb	45.40N	110.34W
Livingston [Newf.-Can.]	42	Kf	53.40N	66.10W
Livingston [Tn.-U.S.]	44	Eg	36.23N	85.19W
Livingston [Tx.-U.S.]	45	Ik	30.43N	94.56W
Livingston, Lake-	45	Ik	30.45N	95.15W
Livingstone, Chutes de- = Livingstone Falls (EN)	30	Ii	4.50S	14.30 E
Livingstone Falls (EN) = Livingstone, Chutes de-	30	Ii	4.50S	14.30 E
Livingstone Memorial	36	Fe	12.19S	30.18 E
Livingstone Mountains	36	Fd	9.45S	34.20 E
Livingstonia	36	Fe	10.36S	34.07 E
Livingston Island	66	Qe	62.36S	60.30W
Livno	14	Lg	43.50N	17.01 E
Livny	19	De	52.28N	37.37 E
Livonia	44	Fd	42.25N	83.23W
Livonia (EN)=Livonija	5	Id	58.50N	27.30 E
Livonija=Livonia (EN)	5	Id	58.50N	25.30 E
Livorno=Leghorn (EN)	6	Hg	43.33N	10.19 E
Livradois, Monts du-	11	Ji	45.30N	3.33 E
Livramento do Brumado	54	Jf	13.39S	41.50W
Livron-sur-Drôme	11	Kj	44.46N	4.51 E
Liwale	36	Gd	9.46S	37.56 E
Liwiec	10	Rd	52.35N	21.33 E
Liwonde	36	Gf	15.01S	35.13 E
Lixi	27	Hf	26.21N	102.03 E
Lixian [China]	27	Ie	34.11N	105.02 E
Lixian [China]	27	Jf	29.40N	111.45 E
Lixian [China]	28	Ce	38.29N	115.34 E
Lixin	28	Dh	33.09N	116.12 E
Lixoúrion	15	Dk	38.12N	20.26 E
Liyang	28	Ei	31.26N	119.29 E
Lizard	9	Hl	49.57N	5.13W
Lizard Point	5	Ff	49.56N	5.13W
Lizhu	28	Fj	29.58N	120.26 E
Lizy sur Ourcq	12	Fe	49.01N	3.02 E
Ljady	8	Mf	58.35N	28.55 E
Ljahoviči	16	Ec	53.04N	26.15 E
Ljahovskije Ostrova= Lyakhov Islands (EN)	21	Qb	73.30N	141.00 E
Ljalja	17	Jg	59.10N	61.30 E
Ljamin	17	Of	61.18N	71.45 E
Ljangar	18	Ed	40.23N	65.59 E
Ljangasovo	7	Lg	58.33N	49.29 E
Ljapin	17	Je	63.38N	61.58 E
Ljaskelja	8	Nc	61.39N	31.03 E
Ljaskovec	15	If	43.06N	25.43 E
Ljig	15	De	44.14N	20.15 E
Ljuban	16	Ec	52.48N	27.59 E
Ljuban	7	Hg	59.22N	31.13 E
Ljubar	16	Ee	49.55N	27.44 E
Ljubaščevka	15	Nb	47.50N	30.07 E
Ljubelj	14	Id	46.26N	14.16 E
Ljubercy	19	Dd	55.40N	37.55 E
Ljubešov	10	Ve	51.45N	25.37 E
Ljubim	7	Jg	58.22N	40.41 E
Ljubimec	15	Jh	41.50N	26.05 E
Ljubinje	14	Mh	42.57N	18.06 E
Ljubišnja	15	Cf	43.20N	19.07 E
Ljubljana	6	Hf	46.02N	14.30 E
Ljuboml	16	Cd	51.15N	23.59 E
Ljubotin	16	Ie	49.59N	35.55 E
Ljubovija	15	Ce	44.12N	19.22 E
Ljubuški	14	Lg	43.12N	17.33 E
Ljubytino	7	Hg	58.50N	33.25 E
Ljudinovo	19	De	53.51N	34.28 E
Ljugarn	7	Eh	57.19N	18.42 E
Ljungan	5	Hc	62.19N	17.23 E
Ljungaverk	8	Gb	62.29N	16.03 E
Ljungby	7	Ch	56.50N	13.56 E
Ljungbyholm	8	Gh	56.38N	16.10 E
Ljungdalen	7	Ce	62.51N	12.47 E
Ljungsbro	8	Ff	58.31N	15.30 E
Ljungskile	8	Df	58.14N	11.55 E
Ljusdal	7	Df	61.50N	16.05 E
Ljusnan	5	Hc	61.12N	17.08 E
Ljusne	7	Df	61.13N	17.08 E
Ljusterö	8	He	59.30N	18.35 E
Ljuta	8	Mf	58.33N	28.45 E
Llandilo	9	Jj	51.53N	3.59W
Llandovery	9	Jj	51.59N	3.48W
Llandrindod Wells	9	Ji	52.15N	3.23W
Llandudno	9	Jh	53.19N	3.49W
Llanelli	9	Ij	51.42N	4.10W
Llanes	13	Ha	43.25N	4.45W
Llangefni	9	Ih	53.16N	4.18W
Llangollen	9	Ji	52.58N	3.10W
Llano	45	Gk	30.45N	98.41W
Llano Estacado	38	If	33.30N	102.40W
Llano River	45	Gk	30.35N	98.25W
Llanos	52	Je	5.00N	70.00W
Llanos de Sonora	47	Bc	28.20N	111.00W
Llanquihue, Lago-	56	Ff	41.08S	72.48W
Llata	54	Ce	9.25S	76.47W
Lleida/Lérida	13	Mc	41.37N	0.37 E
Llerena	13	Ff	38.14N	6.01W
Lleyn	9	Ii	52.54N	4.30W
Llica	54	Eg	19.52S	68.16W
Llivia	13	Nb	42.28N	1.59 E
Llobregat	13	Oc	41.19N	2.09 E
Lloret de Mar	13	Oc	41.42N	2.51 E
Llorona, Punta-	49	Fi	8.37N	83.44W
Llorri/Orri, Pic d'-	13	Nb	42.23N	1.12 E
Lloydminster	42	Gf	53.17N	110.00W
Lluchmayor	13	Oe	39.29N	2.54 E
Llullaillaco, Volcán-	52	Jh	24.43S	68.33W
Lo	63b	Ca	13.21S	166.38 E
Loa	46	Jg	38.24N	111.38W
Loa, Rio-	56	Fb	21.26S	70.04W
Loanatit, Pointe-	63b	Dd	19.21S	169.14 E
Loange	30	Ji	4.17S	20.02 E
Loango	36	Bc	4.39S	11.48 E
Loano	14	Cf	44.08N	8.15 E
Loban	7	Mh	56.59N	51.12 E
Lobatse	31	Jk	25.13S	25.41 E
Löbau/Lubij	10	Ke	51.06N	14.40 E
Lobaye	30	Ih	3.41N	18.35 E
Lobaye [3]	35	Be	4.00N	17.40 E
Lobenstein	10	Hf	50.27N	11.39 E
Loberia	56	Ie	38.09S	58.47W
Łobez	10	Lc	53.39N	15.36 E
Lobito	31	Ij	12.22S	13.34 E
Lobo	34	Dd	6.02N	6.47W
Lobos	56	Ie	35.11S	59.06W
Lobos	32	Ed	28.45N	13.49W
Lobos, Cabo-	48	Cc	29.55N	112.45W
Lobos, Cay-	49	Ib	22.24N	77.32W
Lobos, Cayo-	48	Ph	18.22N	87.24W
Lobos, Isla-	48	Dd	27.20N	110.36W
Lobos, Islas de-	48	Kg	21.27N	97.15W
Lobos de Afuera, Islas-	54	Be	6.57S	80.42W
Lobos de Tierra, Isla-	54	Be	6.27S	80.52W
Lobva	19	Gd	59.12N	60.30 E
Łobżonka	10	Nc	53.07N	17.18 E
Locana	14	Be	45.25N	7.27 E
Locarno	14	Cd	46.10N	8.48 E
Loch Aillionn/Allen, Lough-	9	Eg	54.08N	8.08W
Loch Arabhach/Arrow, Lough-	9	Eg	54.05N	8.20W
Lochboisdale	9	Fd	57.09N	7.19W
Loch Cairlinn/Carlingford Lough	9	Gg	54.05N	6.14W
Loch Ce/Key, Lough-	9	Eg	54.00N	8.15W
Loch Coirib/Corrib, Lough	9	Dh	53.05N	9.10W
Loch Con/Conn, Lough-	9	Dg	54.04N	9.20W
Loch Cuan/Strangford Lough	9	Hg	54.26N	5.36W
Loch Deirgeirt/Derg, Lough-	9	Ei	53.00N	8.20W
Lochearnhead	9	Ie	56.23N	4.18W
Loch Éirne Iochtair/Lower Lough Erne	9	Fg	54.30N	7.50W
Loch Éirne Uachtair/Upper Lough Erne	9	Fg	54.20N	7.30W
Lochem	12	Ib	52.10N	6.25 E
Loches	11	Gg	47.08N	1.00 E
Loch Feabhail/Foyle, Lough-	9	Ff	55.05N	7.10W
Loch Garman/Wexford	6	Fe	52.20N	6.27W
Loch Garman/Wexford [2]	9	Gi	52.20N	6.40W
Lochgilphead	9	He	56.03N	5.26W
Loch Hinninn/Ennell, Lough-	9	Fh	53.28N	7.24W
Lochinver	9	Hc	58.09N	5.15W
Loch Lao/Belfast Lough	9	Hg	54.40N	5.50W
Loch Léin/Leane, Lough-	9	Di	52.05N	9.35W
Loch Leven	9	Je	56.13N	3.10W
Loch Long	9	Ie	56.04N	4.50W
Lochmaddy	9	Fd	57.36N	7.10W
Loch Measca/Mask, Lough-	9	Dh	53.35N	9.20W
Lochnagar	9	Je	56.55N	3.10W
Loch nEathach/Neagh, Lough-	5	Fe	54.38N	6.24W
Loch Ness	9	Id	57.15N	4.30W
Łochów	10	Rd	52.32N	21.48 E
Loch Pholl an Phúca/Poulaphuca Reservoir	9	Gh	53.10N	6.30W
Loch Rí/Ree, Lough-	9	Fh	53.35N	8.00W
Lochsa River	46	Hc	46.08N	115.36W
Loch Sileann/Sheelin, Lough-	9	Fh	53.48N	7.20W
Loch Suilí/Swilly, Lough-	9	Ff	55.10N	7.38W
Loch Uí Ghadra/Gara, Lough-	9	Eh	53.55N	8.30W
Lochy	9	He	56.49N	5.06W
Lochy, Loch-	9	Ie	56.55N	4.55W
Lockerbie	9	Jf	55.07N	3.22W
Lockhart	45	Hl	29.53N	97.41W
Lock Haven	44	Ie	41.09N	77.28W
Löcknitz	10	Hc	53.07N	11.16 E
Lockport	44	Hd	43.11N	78.39W
Locminé	11	Dg	47.53N	2.50W
Locri	14	Kl	38.14N	16.16 E
Lod	24	Fg	31.58N	34.54 E
Lodalskåpa	7	Bf	61.47N	7.12 E
Loddon	12	Db	52.32N	1.29 E
Loddon River	59	Ig	36.41S	143.55 E
Lodejnoje Pole	19	Dc	60.44N	33.33 E
Lodève	11	Jk	43.43N	3.19 E
Lodi [Ca.-U.S.]	46	Eg	38.08N	121.16W
Lodi [It.]	14	De	45.19N	9.30 E
Lødingen	7	Db	68.25N	16.00 E
Lodja	31	Ji	3.29S	23.26 E
Lodosa	13	Jb	42.25N	2.05W
Lödöse	8	Ef	58.02N	12.08 E
Lodwar	31	Kh	3.07N	35.36 E
Łódź	6	He	51.46N	19.30 E
Łódź [2]	10	Pe	51.45N	19.30 E
Loei	25	Ke	17.32N	101.34 E
Loeriesfontein	37	Bf	30.56S	19.26 E
Lofanga	65b	Ba	19.50S	174.33W
Loffa	30	Fh	6.36N	11.05W
Loffa [3]	34	Dd	7.45N	10.00W
Lofoten	5	Hb	68.30N	15.00 E
Lofoten Basin (EN)	5	Ga	70.00N	4.00 E
Lofsdalen	8	Eb	62.07N	13.16 E
Loftahammar	8	Gg	57.52N	16.40 E
Loga	34	Fc	13.37N	3.14 E
Logan [N.M.-U.S.]	45	Ei	35.22N	103.25W
Logan [Oh.-U.S.]	44	Ff	39.32N	82.24W
Logan [Ut.-U.S.]	43	Ec	41.44N	111.50W
Logan [W.V.-U.S.]	44	Gg	37.52N	81.58W
Logan, Mount- [Can.]	38	Ec	60.34N	140.24W
Logan, Mount- [Wa.-U.S.]	46	Eb	48.32N	120.57W
Logan Martin Lake	44	Di	33.40N	86.15W
Logan Mountains	42	Ed	61.00N	128.00W
Logansport	44	De	40.45N	86.21W
Loge	30	Ii	7.49S	13.06 E
Logojsk	8	Lj	54.12N	27.57 E
Logone	30	Ig	12.06N	15.02 E
Logone Birni	34	Ic	11.47N	15.06 E
Logone Occidental [3]	35	Bd	8.40N	16.00 E
Logone Occidental	35	Bd	9.07N	16.26 E
Logone Oriental [3]	35	Bd	8.20N	16.30 E
Logone Oriental	35	Bd	9.07N	16.26 E
Logroño [3]	13	Jb	42.15N	2.30W
Logroño [Arg.]	55	Bi	29.30S	61.42W
Logroño [Sp.]	13	Jb	42.28N	2.27W
Logrosán	13	Ge	39.20N	5.29W
Løgstør	7	Bh	56.58N	9.15 E
Logudoro	14	Cj	40.35N	8.40 E
Løgumkloster	8	Ci	55.03N	8.57 E
Lögurinn	7a	Cb	65.15N	14.30W
Lohja/Lojo	7	Ff	60.15N	24.05 E
Lohjanjärvi	8	Jd	60.15N	23.55 E
Lohjanselkä/Lojo åsen	8	Kd	60.15N	24.10 E
Löhme	12	Kc	51.41N	8.42 E
Löhne	10	Ed	52.11N	8.41 E
Lohne	12	Kb	52.40N	8.14 E
Lohra	12	Kd	50.44N	8.38 E
Lohr am Main	10	Ff	49.59N	9.35 E
Lohusuu/Lokusu	8	Lf	58.53N	27.01 E
Lohvica	16	Id	50.22N	33.15 E
Loi, Phou-	25	Kd	20.16N	103.12 E
Loi-Kaw	25	Je	19.41N	97.13 E
Loile	36	Dc	0.52S	20.12 E
Loimaa	7	Ff	60.51N	23.03 E
Loimijoki	8	Jc	61.13N	22.38 E
Loing	11	If	48.23N	2.48 E
Loir	11	Fg	47.33N	0.32W
Loir, Vaux du-	11	Gg	47.45N	0.25 E
Loire [3]	11	Ji	45.30N	4.00 E
Loire	5	Ff	47.16N	2.11W
Loire, Canal latéral à la-	11	Jh	46.29N	3.59 E
Loire, Val de-	11	Hg	47.40N	1.35 E
Loire-Atlantique [3]	11	Eg	47.15N	1.50W
Loiret [3]	11	Ig	47.55N	2.20 E
Loir-et-Cher [3]	11	Hg	47.30N	1.30 E
Loisach	10	Hi	47.56N	11.27 E
Loison	12	He	49.30N	5.17 E
Loja [Ec.]	53	If	4.00S	79.13W
Loja [Sp.]	13	Hg	37.10N	4.09W
Lojo/Lohja	7	Ff	60.15N	24.05 E
Lojo åsen/Lohjanselkä	8	Kd	60.15N	24.10 E
Loka	35	Ee	4.16N	31.01 E
Lokači	10	Uf	50.43N	24.44 E
Lokalahti	8	Id	60.41N	21.28 E
Lokandu	36	Ec	2.31S	25.47 E
Lokantekojärvi	7	Gc	68.56N	27.40 E
Lokbatan	16	Pi	40.21N	49.42 E
Lokčim	17	Ef	61.48N	51.45 E
Løken	8	De	59.48N	11.29 E
Lokeren	11	Jc	51.06N	4.00 E
Lokichar	36	Gb	2.23N	35.39 E
Lokichokio	36	Fb	4.12N	34.21 E
Lokitaung	36	Gb	4.16N	35.45 E
Løkken [Den.]	8	Cg	57.22N	9.43 E
Løkken [Nor.]	7	Be	63.05N	9.36 E
Loknja	7	Hh	56.49N	30.09 E
Loko	34	Gd	8.00N	7.50 E
Lokoja	34	Gd	7.48N	6.44 E
Lokomo	34	Ie	2.41N	15.19 E
Lokoro	36	Cc	1.43S	18.23 E
Lokossa	34	Fd	6.38N	1.43 E
Lokot	16	Ic	52.33N	34.31 E
Lokoti	34	Hd	6.22N	14.20 E
Loksa	7	Fg	59.34N	25.44 E
Loks Land	42	Ld	62.27N	64.30W
Lokuru	63a	Cc	8.35S	157.20 E
Lokusu/Lohusuu	8	Lf	58.53N	27.01 E
Lokwa Kangole	36	Gb	3.32N	35.54 E
Lol	30	Jh	9.13N	28.59 E
Lola	34	Dd	7.48N	8.32W
Lolimi	35	Ee	4.35N	33.59 E
Loliondo	36	Gc	2.03S	35.37 E
Lolland	5	He	54.45N	11.30 E
Lollar	12	Kd	50.38N	8.42 E
Lolo	36	Db	2.13N	23.00 E
Lolo	36	Bc	0.40S	12.28 E
Lolodorf	34	He	3.14N	10.44 E
Lolo Pass	46	Hc	46.40N	114.33W
Loloway	63b	Cb	15.17S	167.58 E
Lom	15	Gf	43.49N	23.14 E
Lom [Afr.]	34	Hd	5.20N	13.24 E
Lom [Bul.]	15	Gf	43.50N	23.15 E
Loma Bonita	48	Lh	18.07N	95.53W
Lomaloma	63d	Cb	17.17S	178.59W
Lomami	30	Jh	0.46N	24.16 E
Loma Mountains	30	Fh	9.10N	11.07W
Lomas de Vallejos	55	Dh	27.44S	57.56W
Loma Verde	55	Cl	35.16S	58.24W
Lomba	36	Df	15.36S	21.32 E
Lombarda, Serra-	54	Hc	2.50N	51.50W
Lombarde, Prealpi-	14	De	46.00N	9.30 E
Lombardia = Lombardy (EN) [2]	14	De	45.40N	9.30 E
Lombardy (EN) = Lombardia [2]	14	De	45.40N	9.30 E
Lomblen, Pulau-	21	Oj	8.25S	123.30 E
Lombok, Pulau-	21	Nj	8.45S	116.30 E
Lombok, Selat-	26	Gh	8.30S	115.50 E
Lomé	31	Hh	6.08N	1.13 E
Lomela	31	Ji	2.18S	23.17 E
Lomela	30	Ji	0.14S	20.42 E
Lomellina	14	Ce	45.15N	8.45 E
Loméméti	63b	Dd	19.30S	169.27 E
Lomié	34	He	3.10N	13.37 E
Lomlom	63c	Bb	10.19S	166.16 E
Lomma	8	Ei	55.41N	13.05 E
Lomme	12	Hd	50.08N	5.10 E
Lommel	11	Lc	51.14N	5.18 E
Lomnica	10	Ug	49.02N	24.47 E
Lomond, Loch-	9	Ie	56.08N	4.38W
Lomonosov	19	Cd	59.55N	29.40 E
Lomonosovski	19	Ge	52.50N	66.28 E
Lomonosov Ridge (EN)	67	De	88.00N	140.00 E
Lomont	11	Mg	47.21N	6.36 E
Lompobatang, Gunung-	26	Gh	5.20S	119.55 E
Lompoc	43	Ce	34.38N	120.27W
Lomsegga	8	Cc	61.49N	8.22 E
Łomża	10	Sc	53.11N	22.05 E
Łomża [2]	10	Sc	53.10N	22.05 E
Lønahorg	8	Bd	60.42N	6.25 E
Loncoche	56	Fe	39.22S	72.38W
Londa	25	Ee	15.28N	74.31 E
Londerzeel	12	Gc	51.01N	4.18 E
Londiani	36	Gc	0.10S	35.36 E
Londinières	12	De	49.50N	1.24 E
London [Eng.-U.K.]	6	Fe	51.30N	0.10W
London [Kir.]	64g	Bb	1.58N	157.29W
London [Ky.-U.S.]	44	Eg	37.08N	84.05W
London [Ont.-Can.]	39	Ke	42.59N	81.14W
London-Barnet	12	Bc	51.39N	0.12W
London-Bexley	12	Cc	51.26N	0.09 E
London Bridge	51p	Bb	12.17N	61.35W
London-Bromley	12	Cc	51.25N	0.01 E
London-Croydon	9	Mj	51.23N	0.07W
Londonderry/Doire	6	Fd	55.00N	7.19W
Londonderry, Cape-	59	Fb	13.45S	126.55 E
London-Ealing	12	Bc	51.30N	0.19W
London-Enfield	12	Bc	51.40N	0.04W
London-Greenwich	9	Mj	51.28N	0.00
London-Haringey	12	Bc	51.36N	0.06W
London-Harrow	12	Bc	51.36N	0.20W
London-Havering	12	Cc	51.36N	0.11 E
London-Hillingdon	12	Bc	51.31N	0.27W
London-Kingston-upon-Thames	9	Mj	51.28N	0.19W
London-Redbridge	12	Cc	51.35N	0.08 E
London-Sutton	12	Bc	51.21N	0.12W
London-Wandsworth	12	Bc	51.27N	0.12W
London-Westminster	12	Bc	51.30N	0.07W
Londrina	53	Kh	23.18S	51.09W
Lone Pine	46	Fh	36.36N	118.04W
Longa	36	Ce	14.41S	18.29 E
Longa [Ang.]	36	Cf	16.25S	19.04 E
Longa [Ang.]	36	Be	10.15S	13.30 E
Longa, Proliv-=De Long Strait (EN)	21	Tb	70.20N	178.00 E
Longá, Rio-	54	Jd	3.09S	41.56W
Long Akah	26	Ff	3.19N	114.47 E
Longarone	14	Gd	46.16N	12.18 E
Longbangun	26	Gf	0.36N	115.11 E
Long Bay [Bar.]	51q	Bb	13.04N	59.29W
Long Bay [S.C.-U.S.]	43	Le	33.35N	78.45W
Long Beach [Ca.-U.S.]	39	Hf	33.46N	118.11W
Long Beach [N.Y.-U.S.]	44	Ke	40.35N	73.40W
Long Beach [Wa.-U.S.]	46	Cc	46.21N	124.03W
Long Branch	43	Mc	40.17N	73.59W
Long Buckby	12	Ab	52.18N	1.04W
Long Cay	49	Jb	22.37N	74.20W
Longchuan	27	Kg	24.10N	115.17 E
Long Creek	46	Nb	49.07N	103.00W
Long Eaton	12	Ab	52.54N	1.16W
Longfeng	28	Ha	46.31N	125.02 E
Longford/An Longfort [2]	9	Fh	53.40N	7.40W
Longford/An Longfort	9	Fh	53.44N	7.47W
Long Forties	9	Nd	57.10N	0.05 E
Long Hu	28	Dj	29.37N	116.12 E
Longhua	28	Dd	41.18N	117.44 E
Longido	36	Gc	2.44S	36.41 E
Long Island [Atg.]	51d	Bb	17.08N	61.45W
Long Island [Bah.]	38	Lg	23.10N	75.10W
Long Island [Can.]	42	Jf	54.50N	79.20W
Long Island [Can.]	44	Nc	44.20N	66.15W
Long Island [Pap.N.Gui.]	57	Fe	5.36S	148.00 E
Long Island [U.S.]	38	Le	40.50N	73.00W
Long Island Sound	44	Ke	41.05N	72.58W
Longjiang	27	Lb	47.20N	123.09 E
Longjuzhai → Danfeng	27	Je	33.44N	110.22 E
Longkou	27	Ld	37.39N	120.20 E
Longlac	42	Ig	49.50N	86.32W
Long Lake [N.D.-U.S.]	45	Fc	46.43N	100.07W
Long Lake [Ont.-Can.]	45	Mb	49.32N	86.45W
Longmalinau	26	Gf	3.30N	116.31 E
Long Men	27	Je	34.40N	110.30 E
Longmont	45	Df	40.10N	105.06W
Longnan	27	Jg	24.54N	114.48 E
Longobucco	14	Kk	39.27N	16.37 E
Longoz	15	Kf	43.02N	27.41 E
Longping → Luodian	27	If	25.26N	106.47 E
Long Point	44	Gd	42.34N	80.15W
Long Point Bay	44	Gd	42.40N	80.14W
Longpujungan	26	Gf	2.34N	115.40 E
Longquan	27	Kf	28.06N	119.05 E
Long Range Mountains	42	Lg	48.00N	58.30W
Longreach	58	Fg	23.26S	144.15 E
Long Sand	12	Dc	51.37N	1.10 E
Longs Peak	38	Ie	40.15N	105.37W
Long Sutton	12	Cb	52.47N	0.08 E
Longtan	28	Eh	32.10N	119.03 E
Longtown	9	Kf	55.01N	2.58W
Longué	11	Fg	47.23N	0.07W
Longueau	12	Ee	49.52N	2.21 E
Longueville-sur-Scie	12	De	49.48N	1.06 E
Longuyon	11	Le	49.26N	5.36 E
Long Valley	46	Ji	34.37N	111.16W
Longview [Tx.-U.S.]	43	Ie	32.30N	94.44W
Longview [Wa.-U.S.]	43	Cb	46.08N	122.57W
Longwu	27	Hg	24.07N	102.18 E
Longwy	11	Le	49.31N	5.46 E
Longxi	27	Hd	35.01N	104.38 E
Longxian	27	Id	35.00N	106.53 E
Longxian → Wengyuan	27	Jg	24.21N	114.13 E
Longxi Shan	27	Kf	26.35N	117.17 E
Long Xuyen	25	Lf	10.23N	105.25 E
Longyan	27	Kf	25.06N	117.01 E
Longyao	28	Cf	37.21N	114.46 E
Longyearbyen	67	Kd	78.13N	15.38 E
Longyou	28	Ej	29.01N	119.10 E
Longzhou	27	Ig	22.23N	106.49 E
Lonigo	14	Fe	45.23N	11.23 E
Löningen	10	Dd	52.44N	7.46 E
Lonja	14	Ke	45.27N	16.41 E
Lonjsko Polje	14	Ke	45.24N	16.42 E
Lönsboda	8	Fh	56.24N	14.19 E
Lons-le-Saunier	11	Lh	46.40N	5.33 E
Lontra, Ribeirão-	55	Fe	21.28S	53.37W
Lookout, Cape- [N.C.-U.S.]	43	Le	34.35N	76.32W
Lookout, Cape- [Or.-U.S.]	46	Dd	45.20N	124.00W
Lookout Mountain	44	Eh	34.40N	85.20W
Lookout Pass	43	Db	47.27N	115.42W
Loolmalasin	36	Gc	3.03S	35.49 E
Loop Head/Ceann Léime	9	Di	52.34N	9.56W
Loosdrechtse Plassen	12	Hb	52.10N	5.08 E
Lop	27	Dd	37.01N	80.16 E
Lopatina, Gora-	21	Qd	50.52N	143.10 E
Lopatino	16	Nc	52.37N	45.47 E
Lopatka, Mys-	21	Rd	50.52N	156.40 E
Lop Buri	25	Kf	14.48N	100.37 E
Lopča	20	He	55.44N	122.45 E
Lopévi	63b	Dc	16.30S	168.21 E
Lopez, Cap-=Lopez, Cape- (EN)	30	Hi	0.37S	8.43 E
Lopez, Cape-(EN)=Lopez, Cap-	30	Hi	0.37S	8.43 E
Lop Nur	21	Le	40.30N	90.30 E
Lopnur/Yuli	27	Ec	41.22N	86.09 E
Lopori	30	Ih	1.14N	19.49 E
Loppersum	12	Ia	53.19N	6.45 E
Lopphavet	7	Ea	70.25N	22.00 E
Loppi	8	Kd	60.43N	24.27 E
Lopud	14	Lh	42.41N	17.57 E
Łopuszno	10	Qf	50.57N	20.15 E
Lora del Rio	13	Gg	37.39N	5.32W
Lorain	43	Kc	41.28N	82.11W
Lorán, Boca-	54	Fb	9.00N	60.45W
Lorca	13	Kg	37.40N	1.42W
Lorch	12	Jd	50.03N	7.49 E
Lord Howe Island	57	Gh	31.35S	159.05 E
Lord Howe Rise (EN)	3	Jm	32.00S	162.00 E
Lord Mayor Bay	42	Ic	69.45N	92.00W
Lordsburg	45	Bj	32.21N	108.43W
Loreley	12	Jd	50.08N	7.43 E
Lorena	55	Jf	22.44S	45.08W
Lorengau	60	Dh	2.01S	147.17 E
Lorestān [3]	23	Gc	33.30N	48.40 E
Loreto [2]	54	Dd	5.00S	75.00W
Loreto [Arg.]	55	Dh	27.46S	57.17W
Loreto [Bol.]	54	Fg	15.13S	64.40W
Loreto [Braz.]	54	Ie	7.05S	45.09W
Loreto [It.]	14	Hg	43.26N	13.36 E
Loreto [Mex.]	48	If	22.16N	101.58W
Loreto [Mex.]	47	Bc	26.01N	111.21W
Loreto [Par.]	56	Ib	23.16S	57.11W
Loreto Aprutino	14	Hh	42.26N	13.59 E
Lorica	54	Cb	9.14N	75.49W
Lorient	6	Ff	47.45N	3.22W
Lőrinci	10	Pi	47.44N	19.41 E
Lorn, Firth of-	9	He	56.20N	5.40W
Lorne	59	Ig	38.33S	143.59 E
Lörrach	10	Di	47.37N	7.40 E
Lorrain, Plateau-	11	Mf	49.00N	6.30 E
Lorrain, Rivière du-	51h	Ab	14.50N	61.03W
Lorraine	11	Lf	49.00N	6.00 E
Lorraine, Plaine-	11	Lf	48.10N	5.50 E
Lorsch	12	Ke	49.39N	8.34 E
Los	7	Df	61.44N	15.10 E
Los, Iles de- = Los Islands (EN)	34	Cd	9.30N	13.48W

Index Symbols

[1] Independent Nation, [2] State, Region, [3] District, County, [4] Municipality, [5] Colony, Dependency, Continent, Physical Region, Historical or Cultural Region, Mount, Mountain, Volcano, Hill, Mountains, Mountain Range, Hills, Escarpment, Plateau, Upland, Pass, Gap, Plain, Lowland, Delta, Salt Flat, Valley, Canyon, Crater, Cave, Karst Features, Depression, Polder, Desert, Dunes, Forest, Woods, Heath, Steppe, Oasis, Cape, Point, Coast, Beach, Cliff, Peninsula, Isthmus, Sandbank, Island, Atoll, Rock, Reef, Islands, Archipelago, Rocks, Reefs, Coral Reef, Well, Spring, Geyser, River, Stream, Waterfall Rapids, River Mouth, Estuary, Lake, Salt Lake, Intermittent Lake, Reservoir, Swamp, Pond, Canal, Glacier, Ice Shelf, Pack Ice, Ocean, Sea, Gulf, Bay, Strait, Fjord, Lagoon, Bank, Seamount, Tablemount, Ridge, Shelf, Basin, Escarpment, Sea Scarp, Fracture, Trench, Abyss, National Park, Reserve, Point of Interest, Recreation Site, Cave, Cavern, Historic Site, Ruins, Wall, Walls, Church, Abbey, Temple, Scientific Station, Airport, Port, Lighthouse, Mine, Tunnel, Dam, Bridge

Los Alamos 39 If 35.53N 106.19W
Los Amates 49 Cf 15.16N 89.06W
Los Amores 55 Ci 28.06S 59.59W
Los Angeles 39 Hf 34.03N 118.15W
Los Ángeles 53 Ii 37.28S 72.21W
Los Angeles Aqueduct 46 Fi 35.22N 118.05W
Losap Atoll 57 Gd 6.54N 152.44 E
Los Banos 46 Eh 37.04N 120.51W
Los Blancos 56 Hb 23.36S 62.36W
Los Charrúas 55 Cj 31.10S 58.11W
Los Chiles 49 Eh 11.02N 84.43W
Los Conquistadores 55 Cj 30.36S 58.28W
Los Frailes, Islas- 50 Eg 11.12N 63.45W
Los Frentones 55 Bh 26.25S 61.25W
Los Gatos 46 Eh 37.14N 121.59W
Losheim 12 Ie 49.31N 6.45 E
Los Hermanos, Islas- 54 Fa 11.45N 64.25W
Łosice 10 Sd 52.14N 22.43 E
Lošinj 14 If 44.35N 14.28 E
Los Islands (EN)=Los, Iles de- 34 Cd 9.30N 13.48W
Los Juries 55 Ai 28.28S 62.06W
Los Lagos 56 Fe 39.51S 72.50W
Los Lagos [2] 56 Ff 41.20S 73.00W
Los Llanos de Aridane 32 Dd 28.39N 17.54W
Los Médanos, Istmo de- 49 Mh 11.35N 69.45W
Los Mochis 39 Ig 25.45N 108.53W
Los Monegros 13 Lc 41.29N 0.03W
Los Monjes, Islas- 54 Da 12.25N 70.55W
Los Navalmorales 13 He 39.43N 4.38W
Loso 36 Ec 1.10S 27.10 E
Los Palacios 49 Fb 22.35N 83.12W
Los Palacios y Villafranca 13 Gg 37.10N 5.56W
Los Pedroches 13 Hf 38.27N 4.45W
Los Pirpintos 55 Ah 26.08S 62.05W
Los Remedios, Río de- 48 Fe 24.41N 106.28W
Los Reyes de Salgado 48 Hh 19.35N 102.29W
Los Roques, Islas- 54 Ea 11.50N 66.45W
Los Roques Basin (EN) 50 Cf 12.20N 67.40W
Los Santos [3] 49 Gj 7.45N 80.30W
Los Santos 49 Gj 7.56N 80.25W
Losser 12 Jb 52.16N 7.01 E
Lossiemouth 9 Jd 57.43N 3.18W
Lossnen 8 Eb 62.30N 12.50 E
Los Taques 49 Lh 11.50N 70.16W
Los Telares 56 Hc 28.59S 63.26W
Los Teques 54 Ea 10.21N 67.02W
Los Testigos, Islas- 54 Fa 11.23N 63.06W
Lost River 46 Ef 41.56N 121.30W
Lost River Range 46 Id 44.10N 113.35W
Lost Trail Pass 43 Eb 45.41N 113.57W
Los Vilos 56 Fd 31.55S 71.31W
Lot 5 Gj 44.18N 0.20 E
Lot [3] 11 Hj 44.30N 1.30 E
Lota 56 Fe 37.05S 73.10W
Lotagipi Swamp 35 Ee 4.36N 34.55 E
Løten 8 Dd 60.49N 11.19 E
Lot-et-Garonne [3] 11 Gj 44.20N 0.30 E
Lothair 37 Ee 26.26S 30.27 E
Lothian [3] 9 Jf 55.55N 3.30W
Lothian 9 Jf 55.55N 3.05W
Loto 36 Dc 2.47S 22.30 E
Lotofaga 65c Ba 13.59S 171.50W
Lotoi 36 Cc 1.35S 18.30 E
Lotru 15 Hd 45.20N 24.16 E
Lotrului, Munţii- 15 Gd 45.30N 23.52 E
Lotta 7 Hb 68.39N 30.20 E
Lottefors 8 Gc 61.25N 16.24 E
Löttorp 8 Gg 57.10N 16.59 E
Lotuke, Jabal- 35 Ee 4.07N 33.48 E
Louang Namtha 25 Kd 20.57N 101.25 E
Louangphrabang 22 Mh 19.52N 102.08 E
Loubomo 31 Ii 4.12S 12.41 E
Loučná 10 Lf 50.06N 15.48 E
Loudéac 11 Df 48.10N 2.45W
Loudima 36 Bc 4.07S 13.04 E
Loudon 44 Eh 35.44N 84.20W
Loudun 11 Gh 47.00N 0.04 E
Loué 11 Fg 48.00N 0.09W
Loue 11 Lg 47.01N 5.27 E
Loufan 28 Ae 38.04N 111.47 E
Louga 34 Bb 15.37N 16.13W
Louga [3] 34 Bb 15.00N 15.30W
Louge 11 Hk 43.27N 1.20 E
Loughborough 9 Li 52.47N 1.11W
Lougheed 42 Ha 77.30N 105.00W
Loughrea/Baile Locha Riach 9 Eh 53.12N 8.34W
Louhans 11 Lh 46.38N 5.13 E
Louhi 19 Db 66.04N 33.01 E
Louisa 44 Ff 38.07N 82.36W
Louiseville 44 Kb 46.16N 72.57W
Louisiade Archipelago 57 Gf 11.00S 153.00 E
Louisiana 45 Kg 39.27N 91.03W
Louisiana [2] 43 Ie 31.15N 92.15W
Louis Trichardt 37 Dd 23.01S 29.43 E
Louisville [Ky.-U.S.] 39 Kf 38.16N 85.45W
Louisville [Ms.-U.S.] 45 Lj 33.07N 89.03W
Louis-XIV, Pointe - 42 Jf 54.50N 79.30W
Loukoléla 36 Cc 1.02S 17.07 E
Loulan Yiji 27 Ec 40.32N 89.50 E
Loulé 13 Dg 37.08N 8.02W
Loum 34 Ge 4.43N 9.44 E
Lount Lake 45 Ia 50.10N 94.20W
Louny 10 Jf 50.22N 13.49 E
Loup City 45 Gf 41.17N 98.58W
Loup River 43 Hc 41.24N 97.19W
Loups Marins, Lacs des - 42 Ke 56.40N 74.00W
Lourdes 11 Fk 43.06N 0.03W
Lourenço Marques→Maputo 31 Kk 25.58S 32.34 E
Lousa, Serra da- 13 Dd 40.04N 8.13W
Loushan Guan 27 If 28.02N 106.51 E
Louštín 10 Jf 50.12N 13.48 E
Louth [Austl.] 59 Jf 30.32S 145.07 E
Louth [Eng.-U.K.] 9 Mh 53.22N 0.01W
Louth/Lú [2] 9 Gh 53.55N 6.30W
Loutrá Aidhipsoú 15 Gk 38.51N 23.03 E
Loutrá Killinis 15 El 37.52N 21.07 E
Loutrákion 15 Fl 37.59N 23.00 E
Louvain/Leuven 11 Kd 50.53N 4.42 E
Louvet Point 51k Bb 13.58N 60.53W
Louviers 11 He 49.13N 1.10 E
Lövånger 7 Ed 64.22N 21.18 E
Lovászi 10 Mj 46.33N 16.34 E
Lovat 5 Jd 58.14N 31.28 E
Lovćen 15 Bg 42.24N 18.49 E
Loveč [2] 15 Hf 43.08N 24.43 E
Loveč 15 Hf 43.08N 24.43 E
Loveland 45 Df 40.24N 105.05W
Lovell 43 Fc 44.50N 108.24W
Lovelock 43 Dc 40.11N 118.28W
Lövenich, Köln- 12 Id 50.57N 6.50 E
Lovenske Gorice 14 Jd 46.40N 16.00 E
Lovere 14 Ee 45.49N 10.04 E
Loviisa 7 Gf 60.27N 26.14 E
Loviisa/Lovisa 7 Gf 60.27N 26.14 E
Loving 45 Dj 32.17N 104.06W
Lovington 43 Ge 33.27N 103.21W
Lovisa 7 Gf 60.27N 26.14 E
Lovisa/Loviisa 7 Gf 60.27N 26.14 E
Lovoi 36 Ed 8.05S 26.40 E
Lovosice 10 Kf 50.31N 14.03 E
Lovozero 7 Ib 68.01N 35.01 E
Lovozero, Ozero- 7 Ic 67.50N 35.10 E
Lövstabruk 8 Gd 60.24N 17.53 E
Lövstabukten 8 Gd 60.35N 17.45 E
Lovua 36 Dd 6.07S 20.35 E
Lovua 36 De 11.31S 23.35 E
Low, Cape - 42 Id 63.06N 85.18W
Lowa 30 Ji 1.24S 25.52 E
Lowell 43 Mc 42.39N 71.18W
Löwenberg in der Mark 10 Jd 52.53N 13.09 E
Lower Arrow Lake 46 Fb 49.40N 118.08W
Lower Austria (EN) = Niederösterreich [2] 14 Jb 48.30N 15.45 E
Lower California (EN) → Baja California 38 Hg 28.00N 112.00W
Lower Hutt 62 Fd 41.13S 174.55 E
Lower Lake 46 Ef 41.15N 120.02W
Lower Lake 46 Dg 38.55N 122.36W
Lower Lough Erne/Loch Éirne Iochtair 9 Fg 54.30N 7.50W
Lower Post 42 Ee 59.55N 128.30W
Lower Red Lake 45 Ic 48.00N 94.50W
Lower Rhine (EN) = Neder-Rijn 11 Mc 51.59N 6.20 E
Lower Saxony (EN)= Niedersachsen [2] 10 Fd 52.00N 10.00 E
Lower Trajan's Wall (EN)= Nižni Trajanov Val 15 Ld 45.45N 28.30 E
Lower Tunguska (EN)= Nižnjaja Tunguska 21 Kc 65.48N 88.04 E
Lowestoft 9 Oi 52.29N 1.45 E
Lowestoft Ness 9 Oi 52.28N 1.44 E
Lowgar [3] 23 Kc 33.50N 69.00 E
Łowicz 10 Pd 52.07N 19.56 E
Lowlands 9 Jf 56.00N 4.00W
Lowrah 21 If 31.33N 66.33 E
Lowshān 24 Md 36.39N 49.32 E
Low Tatra (EN) = Nízke Tatry 10 Ph 48.54N 19.40 E
Lowther 42 Hb 74.35N 97.40W
Lowville 44 Jd 43.47N 75.30W
Loxton [Austl.] 59 If 34.27S 140.35 E
Loxton [S.Afr.] 37 Cf 31.30S 22.22 E
Loyalty Islands (EN)= Loyauté, Iles- 57 Hg 21.00S 167.00 E
Loyauté, Iles-=Loyalty Islands (EN) 57 Hg 21.00S 167.00 E
Loyoro 36 Fb 3.21N 34.17 E
Lozère [3] 11 Jj 44.30N 3.30 E
Lozère, Mont- 11 Jj 44.25N 3.46 E
Loznica 15 Ce 44.32N 19.13 E
Lozovaja 19 Df 48.53N 36.15 E
Lozva 19 Gd 59.36N 62.20 E
Lú/Louth [2] 9 Gh 53.55N 6.30W
Lua 36 Cb 2.46N 18.26 E
Luacano 36 De 11.16S 21.38 E
Luachimo 36 Dd 6.33S 20.59 E
Luaha-Sibuha 26 Cg 0.31S 98.28 E
Luahoko 65b Ba 19.40S 174.24W
Luala 37 Fc 17.57S 36.30 E
Lualaba 29 Jh 0.26N 25.20 E
Luama 36 Ec 4.46S 26.53 E
Lua Makika 65a Ec 20.35N 156.34W
Luampa 36 De 14.32S 24.10 E
Lu'an 27 Ke 31.44N 116.30 E
Luanda 31 Ii 8.50S 13.15 E
Luanda [3] 36 Bd 8.30S 13.20 E
Luando 30 Ij 10.19S 16.40 E
Luang, Khao- 25 Jg 8.31N 99.47 E
Luang, Thale- 25 Kg 7.30N 100.15 E
Luang Chiang Dao, Doi- 25 Je 19.23N 98.54 E
Luanginga 30 Jj 15.11S 22.55 E
Luang Prabang Range 25 Ke 18.30N 101.15 E
Luangue 36 Dc 4.17S 20.01 E
Luangwa 30 Kj 15.36S 30.25 E
Luan He 21 Nf 39.20N 119.10 E
Luaniva 64h Bb 13.16S 176.07W
Luannan (Bencheng) 28 Ee 39.30N 118.42 E
Luanping (Anjiangying) 28 Dd 40.55N 117.19 E
Luanshya 31 Jj 13.08S 28.25 E
Luanxian 27 Kd 39.45N 118.44 E
Luanza 36 Ed 8.40S 28.40 E
Luapula 30 Ji 9.25S 28.33 E
Luapula [3] 36 Ee 10.43S 29.15 E
Luarca 13 Fa 43.32N 6.32W
Luashi 36 De 10.53S 23.37 E
Luba 34 Ge 3.23N 8.40 E
Lubaantum 49 Ce 16.17N 88.58W
Lubaczów 10 Tf 50.10N 23.08 E
Lubaczówka 10 Sf 50.08N 22.35 E
Lubalo 36 Cd 7.22S 19.20 E
Lubalo 36 Cd 9.07S 19.15 E
Lubamba 36 Ed 5.14S 26.02 E
Lubań 10 Le 51.08N 15.18 E
Lubāna/Lubana 8 Lh 56.49N 26.49 E
Lubana/Lubāna 8 Lh 56.49N 26.49 E
Lubanas, Ozero-/Lubānas Ezers 8 Lh 56.40N 27.00 E
Lubānas Ezers/Lubanas, Ozero- 8 Lh 56.40N 27.00 E
Lubang Islands 26 Hd 3.45N 20.15 E
Lubango 31 Ij 4.55S 13.28 E
Lubao 31 Ji 5.22S 25.45 E
Lubartów 10 Se 51.28N 22.46 E
Lubawa 10 Pc 53.30N 19.45 E
Lübbecke 10 Ed 52.18N 8.37 E
Lubbeek 12 Gd 50.53N 4.50 E
Lübben/Lubin 10 Je 51.57N 13.54 E
Lübbenau/Lubnjow 10 Je 51.52N 13.58 E
Lubbock 39 If 33.35N 101.51W
Lübeck 6 He 53.52N 10.42 E
Lübecker Bucht 10 Gb 54.00N 10.55 E
Lübeck-Travemünde 10 Gc 53.57N 10.52 E
Lubefu 36 Dc 4.10S 23.00 E
Lubefu 36 Dc 4.43S 24.25 E
Lubei→Jarud Qi 27 Lc 44.30N 120.55 E
Lubelska, Wyżyna- 10 Sf 51.00N 23.00 E
Lubenec 10 Jf 50.08N 13.20 E
Lubenka 16 Sd 50.28N 54.06 E
Lubero 36 Ec 0.06S 29.06 E
Lubéron, Montagne du- 11 Lk 43.48N 5.22 E
Lubi 36 Dc 4.59S 23.26 E
Lubie, Jezioro- 10 Lc 53.30N 5.50 E
Lubień Kujawski 10 Pd 52.25N 9.10 E
Lubij/Löbau 10 Ke 5 .06N 4.40 E
Lubilash 29 Ji 6.02S 23.45 E
Lubin 10 Me 5 .24N 6.13 E
Lubin/Lübben 10 Je 5 .57N 3.54 E
Lublin 6 Ie 5 .15N 22.35 E
Lublin [2] 10 Se 5 .15N 22.35 E
Lubliniec 10 Of 50.40N 8.41 E
Lubnān=Lebanon (EN) [1] 22 Ff 33.50N 35.50 E
Lubnān, Jabal-=Lebanon Mountains (EN) 23 Ec 34.00N 36.30 E
Lubnjow/Lübbenau 10 Je 51.52N 13.58 E
Lubny 19 De 50.01N 33.00 E
Luboń 10 Md 52.23N 16.54 E
Lubraniec 10 Od 52.33N 18.50 E
Lubsko 10 Ke 51.46N 14.59 E
Lubsza 10 Ke 51.55N 14.45 E
Lubudi 29 Ji 9.13S 25.38 E
Lubudi 36 Ed 9.57S 25.58 E
Lubue 36 Cc 4.10S 19.53 E
Lubuklinggau 26 Dg 3.10S 102.52 E
Lubuksikaping 26 Df 0.08N 100.10 E
Lubumba 36 Ec 3.58S 29.06 E
Lubumbashi 31 Jj 11.40S 27.30 E
Lubuskie, Pojezierze- 10 Ld 52.18N 15.20 E
Lubutu 31 Ji 0.44S 26.35 E
Lucala 36 Bd 6.38S 12.34 E
Lucala 36 Cd 9.16S 15.13 E
Lucania, Mount- 42 Dd 61.01N 140.29W
Lucas 55 Ea 13.05S 55.56W
Lucca 14 Eg 43.50N 10.29 E
Lucea 49 Hd 18.27N 78.10W
Luce Bay 9 Ig 54.47N 4.50W
Lucedale 45 Lk 30.55N 88.35W
Lučegorsk 20 Ig 46.25N 134.20 E
Lucélia 55 Ge 21.44S 51.01W
Lucena [Phil.] 26 Hd 13.56N 121.37 E
Lucena [Sp.] 13 Hg 37.24N 4.29W
Lucena del Cid 13 Ld 40.08N 0.17W
Luc-en-Diois 11 Lj 44.37N 5.27 E
Lučenec 10 Ph 48.20N 19.41 E
Lucera 14 Ji 41.30N 15.20 E
Lucerne (EN) = Luzern 14 Cc 47.05N 8.20 E
Lucerne, Lake- (EN) = Vierwaldstätter-See 14 Cc 47.00N 8.30 E
Lucero 48 Fb 30.49N 106.30W
Lucheng 28 Bf 36.18N 113.15 E
Lucheringo 37 Fb 11.43S 36.15 E
Lucheux 12 Ed 50.12N 2.25 E
Luchico 30 Lj 12.15S 44.25 E
Luchico 36 Cd 6.12S 19.42 E
Lüchow 10 Hd 52.58N 11.09 E
Lüchun 27 Hg 23.02N 102.19 E
Lucipara, Kepulauan- 26 Ih 5.30S 127.33 E
Lucira 36 Be 13.52S 12.32 E
Luck 19 Ce 50.47N 25.20 E
Luckau 10 Je 51.51N 13.43 E
Luckenwalde 10 Jd 52.05N 13.10 E
Lucknow 22 Kg 26.51N 80.55 E
Luçon 11 Eh 46.27N 1.10W
Lucrecia, Cabo- 49 Jc 21.04N 75.37W
Luc-sur-Mer 12 Be 49.13N 0.21W
Lucunga 36 Bd 6.49S 14.35 E
Lucusse 36 De 12.38S 20.51 E
Lüda→Dalian=Dairan (EN) 22 Of 38.55N 121.39 E
Luda Kamčija 15 Kg 43.03N 27.29 E
Ludbreg 14 Kd 46.15N 16.37 E
Lüdenscheid 10 De 51.13N 7.37 E
Lüderitz 31 Ik 26.38S 15.10 E
Lüderitz [3] 37 Be 26.00S 15.00 E
Lüderitz Bay 37 Be 26.35S 15.10 E
Ludhiāna 22 Jf 30.54N 75.51 E
Ludinghausen 10 De 51.46N 7.28 E
Ludington 43 Jc 43.57N 86.27W
Ludlow 9 Ki 52.22N 2.43W
Ludogorije 15 Jf 43.46N 26.56 E
Ludogorsko Plato 15 Kf 43.36N 27.03 E
Luduş 15 Hc 46.29N 24.05 E
Ludvika 7 Df 60.09N 15.11 E
Ludwigsburg 10 Fh 48.54N 9.11 E
Ludwigshafen am Rhein 10 Eg 49.29N 8.27 E
Ludwigslust 10 Hc 53.19N 11.30 E
Ludza 7 Gh 56.32N 27.45 E
Luebo 31 Ji 5.21S 21.25 E
Lueki 36 Ec 3.24S 25.57 E
Lueki 36 Ec 3.22S 25.51 E
Luele 36 Dd 7.55S 20.00 E
Luembé 36 Dd 6.43S 24.11 E
Luembe 36 Dd 6.37S 21.06 E
Luena [Ang.] 36 De 12.31S 22.34 E
Luena [Ang.] 31 Ij 11.48S 19.55 E
Luena [Zaire] 36 Ed 9.27S 25.47 E
Luena [Zam.] 36 Df 15.20S 23.30 E
Luengué 36 Df 16.54S 21.52 E
Luenha 37 Ec 16.24S 33.48 E
Luera Peak 45 Cj 33.47N 107.49W
Lueta 36 Dd 7.04S 21.40 E
Lueyang 27 Ie 33.25N 106.14 E
Lufeng 27 Kg 22.57N 115.41 E
Lufico 36 Bd 6.22S 13.30 E
Lufira 29 Ji 8.16S 26.27 E
Lufira, Chutes de la- 36 Ed 9.50S 27.30 E
Lufkin 43 Ie 31.20N 94.44W
Lug 15 De 44.23N 20.45 E
Luga 19 Cd 59.43N 28.18 E
Luga 19 Cd 58.44N 29.50 E
Lugano 14 Cd 46.00N 8.57 E
Lugano, Lago di- 14 Cd 46.00N 9.00 E
Lugansk = Vorošilovgrad 6 Jf 48.34N 39.20 E
Luganville 58 Hf 15.32S 167.10 E
Lügde 12 Lc 51.57N 9.15 E
Lugela 37 Fc 16.26S 36.39 E
Lugenda 30 Kj 11.26S 38.33 E
Lugnaquillia 5 Fe 52.58N 6.27W
Lugo [3] 13 Eb 43.00N 7.30W
Lugo [It.] 14 Ff 44.25N 11.54 E
Lugo [Sp.] 13 Ea 43.00N 7.34W
Lugoj 15 Ed 45.41N 21.55 E
Lugovoj 19 Hg 42.55N 72.47 E
Lugovoj 19 Gd 59.44N 65.55 E
Lugovski 20 Ge 58.05N 112.55 E
Lugulu 36 Ec 2.17S 26.32 E
Luh 7 Kh 56.14N 42.28 E
Luhe 10 Gc 53.18N 10.11 E
Luhe 28 Eh 32.21N 118.50 E
Luhin Sum 27 Kb 46.41N 118.38 E
Luhit 25 Jc 27.48N 95.28 E
Luhovicy 7 Ji 54.59N 39.02 E
Luhuo 27 He 31.21N 100.40 E
Lui 36 Cd 8.41S 17.56 E
Luia 36 Dd 8.26S 21.45 E
Luiana 36 Df 17.22S 22.59 E
Luiana 30 Jj 17.27S 23.14 E
Luie 36 Cc 4.33S 17.41 E
Luik/Liège 6 Ge 50.38N 5.34 E
Luilaka 30 Ji 0.52S 20.12 E
Luilu 36 Dd 6.22S 23.50 E
Luimneach/Limerick 6 Fe 52.40N 8.38W
Luimneach/Limerick [2] 9 Ei 52.30N 9.00W
Luing 9 He 56.13N 5.39W
Luino 14 Cd 46.00N 8.44 E
Luio 36 De 13.15S 21.39 E
Lui Pătru, Vîrful- 15 Gd 45.30N 23.30 E
Luis Correia 54 Jd 2.53S 41.40W
Luishia 36 Ee 11.13S 27.07 E
Luitpold Coast 66 Af 78.30S 32.00W
Luiza 36 Dd 7.12S 22.25 E
Luján [Arg.] 56 Gd 32.22S 65.57W
Luján [Arg.] 56 Id 34.34S 59.07W
Lujiang 28 Di 31.15N 117.17 E
Lukafu 36 Ee 10.30S 27.33 E
Lukanga Swamp 36 Ee 14.25S 27.45 E
Lukavac 14 Mf 44.33N 18.32 E
Lukengo 36 Ed 5.46S 29.06 E
Lukenie 30 Ii 2.44S 18.09 E
Lukeville 46 Ik 31.57N 112.50W
Lukojanov 19 Ed 55.02N 44.30 E
Lukolela 36 Cc 1.03S 17.12 E
Lukonzolwa 36 Ed 8.47S 28.39 E
Lukov 10 Ue 51.14N 24.25 E
Lukovit 15 Hf 43.12N 24.10 E
Łuków 10 Se 51.56N 22.23 E
Lukuga 30 Ji 5.40S 26.55 E
Lukula 36 Bd 5.23S 12.57 E
Lukulu 36 De 14.23S 23.15 E
Lukusashi 36 Fe 14.38S 30.00 E
Luleå 6 Ib 65.34N 22.10 E
Luleälven 5 Ib 65.35N 22.03 E
Lüleburgaz 23 Ca 41.24N 27.21 E
Lüliang Shan 21 Nf 37.45N 111.25 E
Lulimba 36 Ec 4.42S 28.38 E
Luling 45 Hl 29.41N 97.39W
Lulong 28 Ee 39.53N 118.52 E
Lulonga 36 Cb 0.37N 18.23 E
Lulonga 30 Ih 0.43N 18.23 E
Lulua 30 Ji 5.02S 21.07 E
Lulu Fakahega, Mount- 64h Bb 13.16S 176.10W
Luma 65c Db 14.14S 169.32W
Lumajang 26 Fh 8.08S 113.13 E
Lumajangdong
Co 27 De 34.00N 81.37 E
Lumbala Kaquengue 31 Jj 14.06S 21.25 E
Lumbala N'guimbo 36 De 12.39S 22.32 E
Lumberton 43 Le 34.37N 79.00W
Lumbo 37 Gc 15.00S 40.44 E
Lumbrales 13 Fd 40.56N 6.43W
Lumbres 12 Ed 50.42N 2.08 E
Lumby 46 Fa 50.15N 118.58W
Lumding 25 Ic 25.45N 93.10 E
Lumege 36 De 11.34S 20.48 E
Lumesule 36 Ge 11.14S 38.06 E
Lumi 60 Ch 3.29S 142.03 E
Lummen 12 Hd 50.59N 5.15 E
Lumparland 8 Id 60.10N 20.15 E
Lumphăt 25 Lf 13.30N 106.59 E
Lumsden [N.Z.] 62 Cf 45.44S 168.26 E
Lumsden [Sask.-Can.] 46 Ma 50.34N 104.53W
Lumuna 36 Ec 3.46S 26.24 E
Lumut 26 Df 4.14N 100.38 E
Luna 13 Gb 42.40N 5.49W
Luna, Laguna de- 55 Di 28.06S 56.46W
Lunan Shan 27 Hf 27.00N 102.30 E
Lunayyr, Harrat- 24 Ej 25.10N 37.50 E
Lunca Ilvei 15 Hb 47.22N 24.59 E
Lund 7 Ci 55.42N 13.11 E
Lunda [3] 36 Cd 9.30S 20.00 E
Lundazi 31 Kj 12.19S 33.13 E
Lunde 8 Gb 62.53N 17.51 E
Lundevatn 8 Bf 58.20N 6.35 E
Lundi 30 Kk 21.13S 32.24 E
Lundu 26 Ef 1.40N 109.51 E
Lundy Island 9 Ij 51.10N 4.40W
Lüneburg 10 Gc 53.15N 10.24 E
Lüneburger Heide 10 Gc 53.10N 10.20 E
Lunel 11 Kk 43.41N 4.08 E
Lünen 10 De 51.37N 7.31 E
Lunéville 11 Mf 48.36N 6.30 E
Lunga 30 Jj 14.34S 26.26 E
Lungué-Bungo 37 Jj 28.38S 16.27 E
Lungwebungu 36 De 14.19S 23.14 E
Lūni 25 Ed 24.41N 71.14 E
Lūni 25 Ec 26.00N 73.00 E
Lunigiana 14 Df 44.20N 9.55 E
Luninec 19 Ce 52.16N 26.50 E
Lunino 16 Nc 53.35N 45.14 E
Lunsemfwa 36 Fe 14.54S 30.12 E
Luntai/Bügür 27 Dc 41.46N 84.10 E
Luobei (Fengxiang) 27 Nb 47.36N 130.58 E
Luobuzhuang 27 Ed 39.30N 88.15 E
Luocheng 27 Ig 24.51N 108.53 E
Luodian (Longping) 27 If 25.26N 106.47 E
Luoding 27 Jg 22.43N 111.33 E
Luohe 27 Je 33.30N 114.08 E
Luo He 27 Id 32.18N 109.12 E
Luoma Hu 28 Eg 34.10N 118.12 E
Luonteri 8 Lc 61.35N 27.45 E
Luoping 27 Hg 24.58N 104.19 E
Luopioinen 8 Kc 61.22N 24.40 E
Luoshan 28 Ch 32.13N 114.32 E
Luotian 28 Ci 30.48N 115.23 E
Luoxiao Shan 27 Jf 26.35N 114.00 E
Luoyang 22 Nf 34.41N 112.25 E
Luoyuan 27 Kf 26.31N 119.32 E
Luozi 36 Bc 4.57S 14.08 E
Lupa 36 Fd 8.39S 33.12 E
Lupane 37 Dc 18.56S 27.48 E
Łupawa 10 Nb 54.42N 17.07 E
Lupeni 15 Gd 45.21N 23.14 E
Luperón 49 Ld 19.54N 70.57W
Łupków 10 Sg 49.12N 22.06 E
Luputa 36 Dd 7.10S 23.42 E
Lūq 31 Lh 3.56N 42.32 E
Luqiao 28 Fj 28.39N 120.05 E
Luqu 27 He 34.36N 102.30 E
Luque 56 Ic 25.16S 57.34W
Luquillo 51a Cb 18.22N 65.43W
Luray 44 Hf 38.40N 78.28W
Lure 11 Mg 47.41N 6.30 E
Lure, Montagne de- 11 Lj 44.07N 5.47 E
Luremo 36 Cd 8.30S 17.51 E
Lurgan/An Lorgain 9 Gg 54.28N 6.20W
Lurín 54 Cf 12.17S 76.52W
Lúrio 37 Gb 13.32S 40.30 E
Lúrio 30 Lj 13.31S 40.42 E
Lusaka 31 Jj 15.25S 28.17 E
Lusambo 31 Ji 4.58S 23.27 E
Lusanga 36 Cc 4.44S 18.58 E
Lusangi 36 Ec 4.37S 27.08 E
Lu Shan 27 Kf 29.30N 115.55 E
Lushan [China] 28 Cj 29.33N 115.58 E
Lushan [China] 28 Bh 33.44N 112.54 E
Lushi 27 Je 34.04N 111.02 E
Lushiko 36 Cd 6.12S 19.42 E
Lushnja 15 Ci 40.56N 19.42 E
Lushoto 36 Gc 4.47S 38.17 E
Lu Shui 28 Bj 29.54N 113.39 E
Lushui (Luzhangjie) 27 Gf 26.00N 98.50 E
Lüshun=Port Arthur (EN) 27 Ld 38.50N 121.13 E
Lusignan 11 Gh 46.26N 0.07 E
Lusk 43 Gc 42.46N 104.27W
Lussac-les-Châteaux 11 Gh 46.24N 0.43 E
Lustrafjorden 8 Bc 61.20N 7.20 E
Lūt, Dasht-e-=Lut, Dasht-i- (EN) 21 Hf 33.00N 57.00 E
Lut, Dasht-i- (EN)=Lūt, Dasht-e- 21 Hf 33.00N 57.00 E
Lu Tao 27 Lg 22.35N 121.30 E
Lutembo 36 De 13.28S 21.22 E
Luti 63a Cb 7.14S 157.00 E
Lütjenburg 10 Gb 54.17N 10.35 E
Luton 9 Mj 51.53N 0.25W
Luton Airport 12 Bc 51.50N 0.22W
Lutong 26 Ff 4.28N 114.00 E
Lutshima 36 Cd 5.22S 18.59 E
Lutshima 36 Cd 5.22S 18.59 E
Lutterworth 12 Ab 52.27N 1.12W
Lutuai 36 De 12.40S 20.12 E
Lutugino 16 Ke 48.23N 39.13 E
Lützow-Holmbukta 66 De 69.10S 37.30 E
Lutzputs 37 Ce 28.22S 20.37 E
Luuk 26 He 5.58N 121.18 E
Luverne 45 He 43.39N 96.13W
Luvidjo 36 Ed 6.26S 26.59 E
Luvua 30 Ji 6.46S 26.58 E
Luvuei 36 De 13.06S 21.12 E
Luwegu 30 Ki 8.31S 37.23 E
Luwingu 36 Ee 10.16S 29.54 E
Luwuk 26 Hg 0.56S 122.47 E
Luxembourg [3] 12 He 50.00N 5.30 E
Luxembourg/Luxemburg [1] 6 Gf 49.45N 6.05 E
Luxembourg/Luxemburg 6 Gf 49.45N 6.05 E
Luxemburg/Luxembourg 6 Gf 49.45N 6.05 E
Luxemburg/Luxembourg [1] 6 Gf 49.45N 6.05 E
Luxeuil-les-Bains 11 Mg 47.49N 6.23 E
Luxi 22 Mg 24.34N 103.44 E
Luxi (Mangshi) 27 Gg 24.29N 98.40 E
Luxor (EN)=Al Uqşur 33 Fd 25.41N 32.39 E
Luy 11 Ek 43.39N 1.08W
Luy de Béarn 11 Fk 43.38N 0.47W

Index Symbols

[1] Independent Nation
[2] State, Region
[3] District, County
[4] Municipality
[5] Colony, Dependency
Continent
Physical Region
Historical or Cultural Region
Mount, Mountain
Volcano
Hill
Mountains, Mountain Range
Hills, Escarpment
Plateau, Upland
Pass, Gap
Plain, Lowland
Delta
Salt Flat
Valley, Canyon
Crater, Cave
Karst Features
Depression
Polder
Desert, Dunes
Forest, Woods
Heath, Steppe
Oasis
Cape, Point
Coast, Beach
Cliff
Peninsula
Isthmus
Sandbank
Island
Atoll
Rock, Reef
Islands, Archipelago
Rocks, Reefs
Coral Reef
Well, Spring
Geyser
River, Stream
Waterfall Rapids
River Mouth, Estuary
Lake
Salt Lake
Intermittent Lake
Reservoir
Swamp, Pond
Canal
Glacier
Ice Shelf, Pack Ice
Ocean
Sea
Gulf, Bay
Strait, Fjord
Lagoon
Bank
Seamount
Tablemount
Ridge
Shelf
Basin
Escarpment, Sea Scarp
Fracture
Trench, Abyss
National Park, Reserve
Point of Interest
Recreation Site
Cave, Cavern
Historic Site
Ruins
Wall, Walls
Church, Abbey
Temple
Scientific Station
Airport
Port
Lighthouse
Mine
Tunnel
Dam, Bridge

Luy de France 11 Fk 43.38N 0.47W
Luyi 28 Ch 33.51N 115.28 E
Luz 55 Jd 19.48S 45.41W
Luz, Costa de la- 13 Fh 36.40N 6.20W
Luza 19 Ec 60.39N 47.15 E
Luza 5 Kc 60.40N 46.25 E
Luzarches 12 Ee 49.07N 2.25 E
Luzern [2] 14 Cc 47.05N 8.10 E
Luzern = Lucerne (EN) 14 Cc 47.05N 8.20 E
Luzhai 27 Ig 24.31N 109.46 E
Luzhangjie → Lushui 27 Gf 26.00N 98.50 E
Luzhou 22 Mg 28.55N 105.20 E
Luziânia 54 Ig 16.15S 47.56W
Lužická Nisa 10 Kd 52.04N 14.46 E
Luzilândia 54 Jd 3.28S 42.22W
Lužnice 10 Kg 49.16N 14.25 E
Luzon 21 Oh 16.00N 121.00 E
Luzon Sea 26 Gd 12.30N 119.00 E
Luzon Strait (EN) 21 Og 21.00N 122.00 E
Luz-Saint-Sauveur 11 Gl 42.52N 0.01 E
Lužskaja Guba 8 Me 59.35N 28.25 E
Lužskaja Vozvyšennost 8 Mf 58.15N 28.45 E
Luzy 11 Jh 46.47N 3.58 E
Łużyca 10 Oe 51.33N 18.15 E
Lvov 6 If 49.50N 24.00 E
Lvovskaja Oblast [3] 19 Cf 49.45N 24.00 E
Lwowa 60 Hj 10.44S 165.45 E
Lwówek 10 Md 52.28N 16.10 E
Lwówek Śląski 10 Le 51.07N 15.35 E
Lyakhov Islands (EN) = Ljahovskije Ostrova 21 Qb 73.30N 141.00 E
Lyall, Mount- 62 Bf 45.17S 167.33 E
Lyallpur 22 Jf 31.25N 73.05 E
Lychsele 7 Ed 64.36N 18.40 E
Lycia 15 Mm 36.30N 29.30 E
Lyckeby 8 Fh 56.12N 15.39 E
Lyckebyån 8 Fh 56.11N 15.40 E
Lyčkovo 7 Hh 57.57N 32.24 E
Lydd 9 Nk 50.57N 0.55 E
Lydd Airport 12 Cd 50.58N 0.56 E
Lydenburg 37 Ee 25.10S 30.29 E
Lydia 15 Lk 38.35N 28.30 E
Lygna 8 Bf 58.10N 7.02 E
Lygnern 8 Eg 57.29N 12.20 E
Lyme Bay 9 Kk 50.38N 3.00W
Lyminge 12 Dc 51.07N 1.05 E
Lymington 9 Lk 50.46N 1.33W
Łyna 10 Rb 54.37N 21.14 E
Lynchburg 43 Ld 37.24N 79.09W
Lynd 58 Ff 18.56S 144.30 E
Lynden 46 Db 48.57N 122.27W
Lyndon River 59 Cd 23.29S 114.06 E
Lyngdal 7 Bg 58.08N 7.05 E
Lyngen 7 Eb 69.58N 20.30 E
Lyngør 8 Cf 58.38N 9.10 E
Lyngseidet 7 Eb 69.35N 20.13 E
Lynn 44 Ld 42.28N 70.57W
Lynnaj, Gora- 20 Ld 62.55N 163.58 E
Lynn Canal 40 Le 58.50N 135.15W
Lynn Deeps 12 Cb 52.58N 0.20 E
Lynn Lake 39 Id 56.51N 101.03W
Lyntupy 8 Li 55.02N 26.27 E
Lynx Lake 42 Gd 62.25N 106.20W
Lyon 6 Gf 45.45N 4.51 E
Lyon Inlet 42 Jc 66.20N 83.40W
Lyonnais, Monts du- 11 Ki 45.40N 4.30 E
Lyon River 59 De 25.00S 115.20 E
Lyons [Ga.-U.S.] 44 Fi 32.12N 82.19W
Lyons [Ks.-U.S.] 45 Gg 38.21N 98.12W
Lyons, Forêt de- 12 De 49.25N 1.30 E
Lyons-la-Forêt 12 De 49.24N 1.28 E
Lyra Reef 60 Eh 1.50S 153.35 E
Lys 11 Jc 51.03N 3.43 E
Łysa Góra 11 Nd 52.07N 17.33 E
Lysaja, Gora- 8 Lj 54.12N 27.40 E
Lysá nad Labem 10 Kf 50.12N 14.50 E
Lysefjorden 8 Be 59.00N 6.14 E
Lysekil 7 Cf 58.16N 11.26 E
Lyskovo 19 Ed 56.03N 45.03 E
Lyss 14 Bc 47.04N 7.37 E
Lysva 19 Fd 58.07N 57.47 E
Lytham Saint Anne's 9 Jh 53.45N 3.01W
Lyttelton 62 Ee 43.36S 172.43 E
Lytton 46 Ea 50.14N 121.34W
Lyža 17 Hd 65.42N 56.40 E

M

Ma, Oued el- 32 Fe 24.03N 9.10W
Ma, Song 25 Le 19.45N 105.55 E
Maâdis, Djebel- 13 Qi 35.52N 4.44 E
Maalaea Bay 65a Ec 20.47N 156.29W
Ma'āmīr 24 Mg 30.04N 48.20 E
Ma'ān 23 Ec 30.12N 35.44 E
Ma'ānīyah 24 Jg 30.44N 43.00 E
Maanselkä 5 Ib 68.07N 28.29 E
Maanselka 7 Ge 63.54N 28.30 E
Ma'anshan 27 Ke 31.38N 118.30 E
Maardu 8 Ke 59.28N 24.56 E
Maarianhamina/Mariehamn 7 Ef 60.06N 19.57 E
Ma 'arrat an Nu 'mān 24 Ge 35.38N 36.40 E
Maarssen 12 Hb 52.08N 5.03 E
Maas = Meuse (EN) 5 Ge 51.49N 5.01 E
Maaseik 11 Lc 51.06N 5.48 E
Maaseik-Neeroeteren 12 Hc 51.05N 5.42 E
Maasin 26 Hd 10.08N 124.50 E
Maasmechelen/Mechelen 12 Hd 50.57N 5.40 E
Maassluis 12 Gc 51.55N 4.17 E
Maastricht 11 Ld 50.52N 5.43 E
Maasupa 63a Ec 9.18S 161.15 E
Ma'āzah, Al Haḍabat al- 33 Fd 27.44N 31.44 E
Mabalane 37 Ed 23.38S 32.31 E
Mabaruma 50 Gh 8.12N 59.47W
Mabechi-Gawa 29 Ga 40.31N 141.31 E
Mabella 45 Lb 48.37N 89.58W
Mabel Lake 46 Fa 50.35N 118.44W
Mablethorpe 9 Nh 53.21N 0.15 E
Mabote 37 Ed 22.03S 34.08 E
Ma'būs Yūsuf 31 Jf 25.45N 21.00 E
Maçaão 13 Ee 39.33N 8.00W
McAdam 42 Kg 45.36N 67.20W
Macajaí, Rio- 54 Fc 2.25N 60.50W
McAllen 43 Hf 26.12N 98.15W
Macaloge 37 Fb 12.25S 35.25 E
Mac Alpine Lake 42 Hc 66.40N 102.50W
Macambará 55 Di 29.08S 56.03W
Macamic 44 Ha 48.48N 79.01W
Macamic, Lac- 44 Ha 48.46N 79.00W
Macao (EN) = Aomen/Macau [5] 22 Ng 22.10N 113.33 E
Macao (EN) = Aomen/Macau 27 Jg 22.12N 113.33 E
Macao (EN) = Macau/Aomen [5] 22 Ng 22.10N 113.33 E
Macao (EN) = Macau/Aomen 27 Jg 22.12N 113.33 E
Macapá 53 Ke 0.02N 51.03W
Macará 54 Cd 4.21S 79.56W
Macaracas 49 Gj 7.44N 80.33W
Macareo, Caño- 54 Fb 9.47N 61.36W
McArthur 44 Ff 39.14N 82.29W
Mc Arthur River 59 Hc 15.54S 136.40 E
Maçãs 13 Fc 41.29N 6.39W
Macas 54 Cd 2.18S 78.06W
Macatete, Sierra de- 40 Dd 28.00N 110.05W
Macau 53 Mf 5.07S 36.38W
Macau/Aomen = Macao (EN) 27 Jg 22.12N 113.33 E
Macau/Aomen = Macao (EN) [5] 22 Ng 22.10N 113.33 E
Macaúbas 54 Jf 13.02S 42.42W
Macauley Island 57 Ih 30.13S 178.33W
Macaya, Pic de- 47 Je 18.23N 74.02W
McBeth Fiord 42 Kc 69.43N 69.20W
McCamey 45 Ek 31.08N 102.13W
McCammon 46 Ie 42.39N 112.12W
Mc Carthy 40 Kd 61.26N 142.55W
McCellanville 44 Hi 33.06N 79.28W
MacClenny 44 Fj 30.18N 82.07W
Macclesfield 9 Kh 53.16N 2.07W
Macclesfield Bank (EN) 26 Fc 15.50N 114.20 E
McClintock 42 Ie 57.48N 94.12W
McClintock, Mount- 66 Jg 80.13S 157.26 E
Mc Clintock Channel 38 Ib 71.00N 101.00W
McCluer Gulf (EN) = Berau, Teluk- 26 Jg 2.30S 132.30 E
Mc Clure Strait 38 Hb 74.30N 116.00W
McClusky 45 Fc 47.29N 100.27W
McComb 43 Ie 31.14N 90.27W
McConaughy, Lake- 45 Ff 41.18N 101.46W
McConnelsville 44 Gf 39.39N 81.51W
McCook 43 Gc 40.12N 100.38W
McCormick 44 Fi 33.55N 82.19W
McDame 42 Ee 59.13N 129.14W
McDermitt 46 Gf 41.59N 117.36W
Macdhui, Ben- 9 Jd 57.04N 3.40W
Macdonald, Lake- 59 Fd 23.30S 129.00 E
Mc Donald Islands 30 On 52.59S 72.50 E
McDonald Peak [Ca.-U.S.] 46 Ef 40.58N 120.26W
McDonald Peak [Mt.-U.S.] 46 Ic 47.29N 113.46W
Macdonald Range 46 Hb 49.12N 114.46W
Macdonnell Ranges 57 Eg 23.45S 132.20 E
McDouglas Sound 42 Hd 75.15N 97.30W
Macduff 9 Kd 57.40N 2.29W
Macedo de Cavaleiros 13 Fc 41.32N 6.58W
Macedonia (EN) = Makedhonia 5 Ig 41.00N 23.00 E
Macedonia (EN) = Makedhonia 15 Fh 41.00N 23.00 E
Macedonia (EN) = Makedonija 15 Eh 41.50N 22.00 E
Macedonia (EN) = Makedonija 5 Ig 41.00N 23.00 E
Macedonia (EN) = Makedonija 15 Fh 41.00N 23.00 E
Maceió 53 Mf 9.40S 35.43W
Macenta 34 Dd 8.33N 9.28W
Macerata 14 Hg 43.18N 13.27 E
McGehee 45 Kj 33.38N 91.24W
McGill 46 Hg 39.23N 114.47W
Macgillycuddy's Reeks/Na Cruacha Dubha 9 Di 52.00N 9.50W
McGrath 40 Hd 62.58N 155.38W
MacGregor 45 Gb 49.57N 98.49W
McGregor 45 Jc 46.36N 93.19W
McGregor Lake 46 Ia 50.31N 112.53W
Mc Gregor Range 59 Ie 26.40S 142.45 E
McGuire, Mount- 46 Hd 45.10N 114.36W
Machachi 54 Cd 0.30S 78.34W
Machado 55 Je 21.41S 45.56W
Machagai 56 Hc 26.56S 60.03W
Machaila 37 Ed 22.15S 32.58 E
Machaire na Mumhan/Golden Vale 9 Fi 52.30N 8.00W
Machaire Rátha/Maghera 9 Gg 54.51N 6.40W
Machakos 36 Gc 1.31S 37.16 E
Machala 54 Cd 3.16S 79.58W
Machaneng 37 Dd 23.12S 27.30 E
Machareti 54 Fh 20.49S 63.24W
Machar Marshes 35 Ed 9.20N 33.10 E
Machattie, Lake- 59 Hd 24.50S 139.48 E
Machault 12 Ge 49.21N 4.30 E
Macheke 37 Ec 18.05S 31.51 E
Macheng 27 Je 31.10N 115.00 E
Machias 44 Nc 44.43N 67.28W
Machida 29 Fd 35.32N 139.27 E
Machilipatnam (Bandar) 25 Ge 16.10N 81.08 E
Machiques 54 Da 10.04N 72.34W
Machona, Laguna- 48 Mh 18.20N 93.40W
Machów 10 Rf 50.34N 21.40 E
Machupicchu 53 Ig 13.07S 72.34W
Macia 37 Ef 25.02S 33.06 E
Mc Ilwraith Range 59 Ib 13.45S 143.20 E
Măcin 15 Ld 45.15N 28.09 E
Macina 30 Gg 14.30N 5.00W
McIntosh 45 Fd 45.55N 101.21W
Macintyre River 59 Je 29.25S 148.45 E
Maçka 24 Hb 40.50N 39.38 E
Mackay [Austl.] 58 Fg 21.09S 149.11 E
Mackay [Id.-U.S.] 46 Ie 43.55N 113.37W
Mackay, Lake- 57 Dg 22.30S 129.00 E
McKay Lake 45 Mb 49.35N 86.22W
McKean Atoll 57 Je 3.36S 174.08W
McKeand 42 Kd 63.00N 65.05W
McKeesport 44 He 40.21N 79.52W
Mackenzie 38 Fc 69.15N 134.08W
McKenzie 44 Cg 36.08N 88.31W
Mackenzie, District of- [3] 42 Gd 65.00N 115.00W
Mackenzie Bay [Ant.] 66 Fe 68.20S 71.15 E
Mackenzie Bay [Can.] 38 Fc 69.00N 136.30W
McKenzie Island 42 If 51.05N 93.48W
Mackenzie King 38 Hb 77.45N 111.00W
Mackenzie Mountains 38 Gc 64.00N 130.00W
McKenzie River 46 Dd 44.07N 123.06W
Mackenzie River 59 Jd 24.00S 149.55 E
McKerrow, Lake- 62 Cf 44.30S 168.05 E
Mackinac, Straits of- 43 Kb 45.49N 82.45W
Mackinaw City 44 Ec 45.47N 84.44W
McKinley, Mount- 38 Dc 63.30N 151.00W
McKinley Park 40 Jd 63.44N 148.54W
McKinney 45 Hj 33.12N 96.37W
Mackinnon Road 36 Gc 3.44S 39.03 E
McLaughlin 45 Fd 45.49N 100.49W
McLean 45 Fi 35.14N 100.36W
McLeans Town 44 Il 26.39N 77.59W
Maclean Strait 42 Ha 77.30N 103.10W
Maclear 37 Df 31.02S 28.23 E
Macleay River 59 Kf 30.52S 153.01 E
Mc Leod, Lake- 57 Cg 24.10S 113.35 E
McLeod Bay 42 Gd 62.53N 110.15W
McLeod Lake 42 Ff 54.59N 123.02W
McLoughlin, Mount- 46 De 42.27N 122.19W
McLure 46 Ea 51.03N 120.14W
Macmillan 42 Dd 62.52N 135.55W
McMillan, Lake- 45 Dj 32.40N 104.20W
McMillan Pass 42 Ed 63.00N 130.00W
McMinnville [Or.-U.S.] 46 Dd 45.13N 123.12W
McMinnville [Tn.-U.S.] 44 Eh 35.41N 85.46W
McMurdo 66 Kf 77.51S 166.37 E
McNaughton Lake 42 Ff 52.40N 117.50W
Macomb 45 Kf 40.27N 90.40W
Macomer 14 Cj 40.16N 8.47 E
Macomia 37 Gb 12.15S 40.08 E
Mâcon 11 Kh 46.18N 4.50 E
Macon [Ga.-U.S.] 39 Kf 32.50N 83.38W
Macon [Mo.-U.S.] 45 Jg 39.44N 92.28W
Macon [Ms.-U.S.] 45 Lj 33.07N 88.34W
Macondo 36 De 12.36S 23.43 E
Mâconnais, Monts du- 11 Kh 46.18N 4.45 E
Macorís, Cabo- 49 Ld 19.47N 70.28W
Macouba 51h Ab 14.52N 61.09W
McPherson 43 Hd 38.22N 97.40W
Mc Pherson Range 59 Ke 28.20S 153.00 E
Macquarie 66 Jd 54.30S 158.30 E
Macquarie Harbour 59 Jh 42.20S 145.25 E
Macquarie Ridge (EN) 3 Jo 57.00S 159.00 E
Macquarie River 57 Fh 30.07S 147.24 E
Mac Robertson Land 66 Fe 70.00S 65.00 E
Macroom/Maigh Chromtha 9 Ej 51.54N 8.57W
Macugnaga 14 Be 45.58N 7.58 E
Macujer 54 Dc 0.24N 73.07W
Macuro 50 Fg 10.39N 61.56W
Macusani 54 Df 14.05S 70.26W
Macuspana 48 Mi 17.48N 92.36W
Mačva 15 Ce 44.49N 19.30 E
McVicar Arm 42 Fc 65.10N 120.30W
Ma'dabā 24 Fg 31.43N 35.48 E
Madagali 34 Hc 10.53N 13.38 E
Madagascar 30 Lj 20.00S 47.00 E
Madagascar (EN) = Madagasikara [1] 31 Lj 19.00S 46.00 E
Madagascar Basin (EN) 3 Fl 27.00S 53.00 E
Madagascar Plateau (EN) 3 Fm 30.00S 45.00 E
Madagasikara = Madagascar (EN) [1] 31 Lj 19.00S 46.00 E
Madā'in Ṣāliḥ 24 Gi 26.48N 37.53 E
Madalai 64a Ac 7.20N 134.28 E
Madama 34 Ha 21.58N 13.39 E
Madan 15 Hh 41.30N 24.57 E
Madang 58 Fe 5.13S 145.48 E
Madanīyīn 31 Ie 33.21N 10.30 E
Madanīyīn [3] 32 Jc 33.00N 10.45 E
Madaoua 34 Gc 14.05N 5.58 E
Madara 15 Kf 43.17N 27.06 E
Madara-Shima 29 Ae 33.35N 129.45 E
Madaroumfa 34 Gc 13.18N 7.09 E
Madau 63a Ac 9.00S 152.26 E
Madawaska Highlands 44 He 45.20N 78.15W
Maddalena 14 Di 41.15N 9.25 E
Maddalena, Colle della- 11 Mj 44.25N 6.53 E
Maddaloni 14 Ii 41.02N 14.23 E
Made, Made en Drimmelen- 12 Gc 51.41N 4.48 E
Made en Drimmelen 12 Gc 51.41N 4.48 E
Made en Drimmelen-Made 12 Gc 51.41N 4.48 E
Madeir 35 Dd 7.50N 29.12 E
Madeira [5] 31 Fe 32.40N 16.45W
Madeira 30 Fe 32.44N 17.00W
Madeira, Arquipélago da- = Madeira Islands (EN) 30 Fe 32.40N 16.45W
Madeira, Rio- 52 Kf 3.22S 58.45W
Madeira Islands (EN) = Madeira, Arquipélago da- 30 Fe 32.40N 16.45W
Madeleine, Ile de la- 42 Lg 47.26N 61.44W
Madeleine, Monts de la- 11 Jh 46.03N 3.50 E
Maden 24 Hc 38.23N 39.40 E
Madenassa Veld 30 Jj 19.00N 25.30 E
Madera [Ca.-U.S.] 46 Eh 36.57N 120.03W
Madera [Mex.] 47 Cc 29.12N 108.07W
Mader-Chih 13 Ri 35.26N 5.07 E
Madero, Puerto del- 13 Jc 41.48N 2.05W
Madesimo 14 Dd 46.26N 9.21 E
Madgaon 25 Ee 15.22N 73.49 E
Madhya Pradesh [3] 25 Fd 22.00N 79.00 E
Madimba 36 Cc 4.58S 15.08 E
Madina do Boé 34 Cc 11.45N 14.13W
Madinani 34 Dd 9.37N 6.57W
Madīnat al Abyār 33 Dc 32.11N 20.36 E
Madīnat ash Sha'b 23 Gh 12.50N 44.56 E
Madingo-Kayes 36 Bc 4.10S 12.18 E
Madingou 36 Bc 4.09S 13.34 E
Madirovalo 37 Hc 16.29S 46.30 E
Madison [Fl.-U.S.] 44 Fj 30.28N 83.25W
Madison [In.-U.S.] 44 Ef 38.44N 85.23W
Madison [Mn.-U.S.] 45 Hd 45.01N 96.11W
Madison [S.D.-U.S.] 45 He 44.00N 97.07W
Madison [Wi.-U.S.] 39 Ke 43.05N 89.22W
Madison [W.V.-U.S.] 44 Gf 38.03N 81.50W
Madison Range 46 Jd 45.15N 111.20W
Madison River 46 Jd 45.56N 111.30W
Madisonville 43 Jd 37.20N 87.30W
Madiun 26 Fh 7.37S 111.31 E
Mado Gashi 36 Gb 0.44N 39.10 E
Madoi (Huangheyan) 22 Lf 35.00N 98.56 E
Madon 11 Mf 48.36N 6.06 E
Madona 7 Gh 56.53N 26.20 E
Madra Dağı 15 Kj 39.23N 27.12 E
Madrakah, Ra's al- 23 If 18.59N 57.45 E
Madranbaba Dağı 15 Ll 37.38N 28.12 E
Madras [India] 22 Kh 13.05N 80.17 E
Madras [Or.-U.S.] 43 Ed 44.38N 121.08W
Madre, Laguna- [Mex.] 47 Ed 25.00N 97.40W
Madre, Laguna- [Tx.-U.S.] 43 Hf 27.00N 97.35W
Madre, Sierra- 38 Jh 15.20N 92.20W
Madre de Dios [2] 54 Df 12.00S 70.15W
Madre de Dios 54 Df 12.36S 69.59W
Madre de Dios, Isla- 52 Ik 50.15S 75.05W
Madre de Dios, Río- 52 Jg 10.59S 66.08W
Madre del Sur, Sierra- = Southern Sierra Madre (EN) 38 Jj 17.00N 100.00W
Madre Occidental, Sierra- = Western Sierra Madre (EN) 38 Ig 25.00N 105.00W
Madre Oriental, Sierra- = Eastern Sierra Madre (EN) 38 Jg 22.00N 99.30W
Madrid [3] 13 Id 40.30N 3.40W
Madrid 6 Fg 40.24N 3.41W
Madrid-Aravaca 13 Id 40.27N 3.47W
Madridejos 13 Ie 39.28N 3.32W
Madrid-El Pardo 13 Id 40.32N 3.46W
Madrid-Vallecas 13 Id 40.23N 3.37W
Madrid-Villaverde 13 Id 40.21N 3.42W
Madrigal de las Altas Torres 13 Hc 41.05N 5.00W
Mad River 46 Cf 40.57N 124.07W
Madriz [3] 49 Dg 13.30N 86.30W
Madrona, Sierra- 13 Hf 38.25N 4.10W
Madula 36 Eb 0.28N 25.23 E
Madura, Palau- 21 Nj 7.00S 113.20 E
Madurai 22 Ji 9.56N 78.07 E
Madvār, Kūh-e- 23 Hc 30.36N 54.52 E
Madwīn 33 Cd 28.42N 17.31 E
Madyan 21 Fg 27.40N 35.35 E
Madžalis 16 Oh 42.08N 47.50 E
Maebara 29 Be 33.34N 130.13 E
Maebashi 27 Od 36.23N 139.04 E
Mae Hong Son 25 Je 19.16N 97.56 E
Mæl 8 Ce 59.56N 8.48 E
Mae Nam Khong = Mekong (EN) 21 Mh 10.15N 105.55 E
Maesawa 29 Gb 39.03N 141.07 E
Mae Sot 25 Je 16.40N 98.35 E
Maestra, Sierra- 38 Lh 20.00N 76.45W
Maevatanana 37 Hc 16.56S 46.49 E
Maéwo, Ile- 57 Hf 15.10S 168.10 E
Mafeteng 37 De 29.45S 27.18 E
Mafia Channel 36 Gd 7.50S 39.35 E
Mafia Island 30 Ki 7.50S 39.50 E
Mafikeng 31 Jk 25.53S 25.39 E
Mafra [Braz.] 56 Kc 26.07S 49.49W
Mafra [Port.] 13 Cf 38.56N 9.20W
Magadan 22 Rd 59.34N 150.48 E
Magadanskaja Oblast [3] 20 Kd 62.30N 154.00 E
Magadi 36 Gc 1.54S 36.17 E
Magallanes, Estrecho de- = Magellan, Strait of- (EN) 52 Ik 54.00S 71.00W
Magallanes y Antártica Chilena [2] 56 Fh 51.30S 73.30W
Magangué 54 Db 9.14N 74.46W
Maganik 15 Cg 42.44N 19.16 E
Maganoy 26 He 6.51N 124.31 E
Magaria 34 Gc 12.59N 8.50 E
Magazine Mountain 45 Ji 35.10N 93.38W
Magdagači 20 Hf 53.29N 125.55 E
Magdala 55 Bm 36.06S 61.42W
Magdalena [2] 54 Db 10.00N 74.15W
Magdalena [Arg.] 55 Dl 35.04S 57.32W
Magdalena [Bol.] 54 Ff 13.20S 64.08W
Magdalena [Mex.] 47 Bb 30.38N 110.57W
Magdalena [N.M.-U.S.] 45 Ci 34.07N 107.14W
Magdalena, Bahía- 48 Ce 24.35N 112.00W
Magdalena, Isla- 47 Bd 24.55N 112.15W
Magdalena, Llano de la- 48 Bd 24.30N 111.40W
Magdalena, Río- [Col.] 52 Id 11.06N 74.51W
Magdalena, Río- [Mex.] 48 Cb 30.48N 112.32W
Magda Plateau 42 Jb 72.18N 82.55W
Magdeburg 6 He 52.10N 11.40 E
Magdeburger Börde 10 Hd 52.00N 11.30 E
Magdelaine Cays 57 Gf 16.35S 150.15 E
Magee 45 Lk 31.52N 89.44W
Magee, Island-/Oileán Mhic Aodha 9 Hg 54.50N 5.50W
Magelang 26 Fh 7.28S 110.13 E
Magellan, Strait of- (EN) = Magallanes, Estrecho de- 52 Ik 54.00S 71.00W
Magellan Seamounts (EN) 57 Gc 17.30N 152.00 E
Magenta 14 Ce 45.28N 8.53 E
Magerøya 7 Fa 71.03N 25.45 E
Magetan 26 Fh 7.39S 111.20 E
Maggiorasca 14 Df 44.33N 9.29 E
Maggiore, Lago- 14 Ce 45.55N 8.40 E
Maghāghah 33 Fd 28.39N 30.50 E
Maghama 32 Ef 15.31N 12.50W
Maghera/Machaire Rátha 9 Gg 54.51N 6.40W
Maghnia 32 Gc 34.51N 1.44W
Magic Reservoir 46 He 43.20N 114.18W
Mágina, Sierra- 13 Ig 37.45N 3.30W
Magistralny 20 Fe 56.03N 107.35 E
Maglaj 14 Mf 44.33N 18.06 E
Măglenik 15 Ih 41.20N 25.45 E
Maglie 14 Mj 40.07N 18.18 E
Măgliž 15 Ig 42.36N 25.33 E
Magnetawan River 44 Gc 45.46N 80.37W
Magnetic Island 59 Jc 19.10S 146.50 E
Magnitka 17 Ii 55.21N 59.43 E
Magnitnaja, Gora- 17 Ij 53.10N 59.10 E
Magnitogorsk 6 Le 53.27N 59.04 E
Magnolia 45 Jj 33.16N 93.14W
Magnor 7 Cg 59.57N 12.12 E
Magny-en-Vexin 11 He 49.09N 1.47 E
Mago 20 Jf 53.18N 140.20 E
Magoé 37 Ec 15.48S 31.43 E
Magoebaskloof 37 Ed 23.51S 30.02 E
Magog 44 Kc 45.16N 72.09W
Magosa = Famagusta (EN) 23 Dc 35.07N 33.57 E
Magra [Alg.] 13 Qi 35.29N 4.58 E
Magra [It.] 14 Df 44.03N 9.58 E
Magtá Lahjar 32 Ef 17.50N 13.20W
Maguarinho, Cabo- 54 Id 0.20S 48.20W
Magude 37 Ee 25.02S 32.40 E
Magumeri 34 Hc 12.07N 12.49 E
Magura, Gora- 10 Th 48.50N 23.44 E
Magway 25 Jd 20.00N 95.00 E
Magway 22 Lg 20.09N 94.55 E
Magyarország = Hungary (EN) [1] 6 Hf 47.00N 20.00 E
Mahābād 23 Gb 36.45N 45.53 E
Mahabalipuram 25 Gf 12.37N 80.12 E
Mahabe 37 Hc 17.05S 45.20 E
Mahabo 37 Gd 20.21S 44.39 E
Mahačkala 6 Kg 42.58N 47.30 E
Mahadday Wêyne 35 He 3.00N 45.32 E
Mahādeo Range 25 Ee 17.50N 74.15 E
Mahafaly, Plateau- 37 Gd 24.30S 44.00 E
Mahagi 36 Fb 2.18N 30.59 E
Mahajamba 37 Hc 15.33S 47.08 E
Mahājan 25 Ec 28.47N 73.50 E
Mahajanga 31 Lj 15.17S 46.43 E
Mahajanga [3] 37 Hc 16.30S 47.00 E
Mahajilo 37 Hc 19.42S 45.22 E
Mahakam 21 Nj 0.35S 117.17 E
Mahalapye 37 Dd 23.07S 26.46 E
Mahalevona 37 Hc 15.26S 49.55 E
Mahallāt 24 Nf 33.55N 50.27 E
Mahamid 35 Cb 15.09N 20.25 E
Māhān 24 Qg 30.05N 57.19 E
Mahānadi 21 Kg 20.19N 86.45 E
Mahanoro 37 Hc 19.53S 48.49 E
Mahārāshtra [3] 25 Ee 18.00N 75.00 E
Mahārlū, Daryācheh-ye- 24 Oh 29.25N 52.50 E
Maḥās 35 He 4.24N 46.07 E
Maha Sarakham 25 Ke 16.12N 103.16 E
Mahavavy 37 Hc 15.57S 45.54 E
Mahbés 32 Dd 27.10N 9.50W
Maḥḍah 24 Pj 24.24N 55.59 E
Mahdia 54 Gb 5.16N 59.09W
Mahe 25 Ff 11.42N 75.32 E
Mahébourg 37a Bb 20.24S 57.42 E
Mahé Island 30 Mi 4.40S 55.28 E
Mahendra Giri 25 Ge 18.58N 84.21 E
Mahenge 31 Ki 8.41S 36.43W
Maheno 62 Df 45.10S 170.52 E
Mahesāna 25 Ed 23.36N 72.24 E
Mahi 25 Ed 22.16N 72.58 E
Mahia Peninsula 61 Eg 39.10S 177.55 E
Mahmudābād 24 Lc 39.25N 47.15 E
Mahmūdābād 24 Od 36.38N 52.15 E
Mahmūd-e 'Erāqī 23 Kb 35.01N 69.20 E
Mahmudiye 24 Dc 39.30N 31.00 E
Mahmutşevketpaşa 15 Mh 41.09N 29.11 E
Māhneshān 24 Ld 36.45N 47.38 E
Mahnevo 17 Jg 58.27N 61.42 E
Mahnomen 45 Ic 47.19N 95.59W
Mahón/Mao 13 Qe 39.53N 4.15 E
Mahoré/Mayotte 30 Lj 12.50S 45.10 E
Mahrāt, Jabal- 35 Ib 17.00N 52.00 E
Mahuan Dao 27 Kd 10.50N 115.47 E
Mahua Point 63a Fd 10.28S 162.05 E
Maiana Atoll 57 Id 0.55N 173.00 E
Maïao, Ile- (Tubai-Manu) 57 Lf 17.34S 150.35W
Maicao 54 Da 11.23N 72.15W
Maicasagi, Lac- 44 Ia 49.52N 76.48W
Maîche 11 Mg 47.15N 6.48 E
Maicuru, Rio- 54 Hd 2.10S 54.17W
Maidenhead 12 Bc 51.31N 0.42W
Maidstone 9 Nj 51.17N 0.32 E
Maiduguri 31 Ig 11.51N 13.09 E
Maigh Chromtha/Macroom 9 Ej 51.54N 8.57W
Maigudo 35 Fd 7.26N 37.10 E
Maihara 29 Ed 35.20N 136.18 E
Maikala Range 25 Gd 22.30N 81.30 E
Maiko 36 Eb 0.14N 25.33 E
Maikona 36 Gb 2.56N 37.38 E
Maikoor, Pulau- 26 Jh 6.15S 134.15 E
Main 10 Ef 50.00N 8.18 E
Mainalon Óros 15 Fl 37.40N 22.15 E

Index Symbols

[1] Independent Nation
[2] State, Region
[3] District, County
[4] Municipality
[5] Colony, Dependency
Continent
Physical Region
Historical or Cultural Region
Mount, Mountain
Volcano
Hill
Mountains, Mountain Range
Hills, Escarpment
Plateau, Upland
Pass, Gap
Plain, Lowland
Delta
Salt Flat
Valley, Canyon
Crater, Cave
Karst Features
Depression
Polder
Desert, Dunes
Forest, Woods
Heath, Steppe
Oasis
Cape, Point
Coast, Beach
Cliff
Peninsula
Isthmus
Sandbank
Island
Atoll
Rock, Reef
Islands, Archipelago
Rocks, Reefs
Coral Reef
Well, Spring
Geyser
River, Stream
Waterfall Rapids
River Mouth, Estuary
Lake
Salt Lake
Intermittent Lake
Reservoir
Swamp, Pond
Canal
Glacier
Ice Shelf, Pack Ice
Ocean
Sea
Gulf, Bay
Strait, Fjord
Lagoon
Bank
Seamount
Tablemount
Ridge
Shelf
Basin
Escarpment, Sea Scarp
Fracture
Trench, Abyss
National Park, Reserve
Point of Interest
Recreation Site
Cave, Cavern
Historic Site
Ruins
Wall, Walls
Church, Abbey
Temple
Scientific Station
Airport
Port
Lighthouse
Mine
Tunnel
Dam, Bridge

Index Symbols

[1] Independent Nation	Historical or Cultural Region	Pass, Gap
[2] State, Region	Mount, Mountain	Plain, Lowland
[3] District, County	Volcano	Delta
[4] Municipality	Hill	Desert, Dunes
[5] Colony, Dependency	Mountains, Mountain Range	Salt Flat
Continent	Valley, Canyon	Forest, Woods
Physical Region	Hills, Escarpment	Heath, Steppe
	Plateau, Upland	Crater, Cave
		Karst Features

Depression	Coast, Beach	Rock, Reef
Polder	Cliff	Islands, Archipelago
Peninsula	Rocks, Reefs	
Isthmus	Coral Reef	
Sandbank	Well, Spring	
Island	Intermittent Lake	
Oasis	Geyser	
Cape, Point	River, Stream	
Atoll	Swamp, Pond	

Waterfall Rapids	Canal	Lagoon
River Mouth, Estuary	Glacier	Bank
Lake	Ice Shelf, Pack Ice	Seamount
Salt Lake	Ocean	Tablemount
Reservoir	Sea	Shelf
Gulf, Bay	Strait, Fjord	Basin

Escarpment, Sea Scarp	Historic Site	Port
Fracture	Ruins	Lighthouse
Trench, Abyss	Wall, Walls	Mine
National Park, Reserve	Church, Abbey	Tunnel
Point of Interest	Temple	Dam, Bridge
Recreation Site	Scientific Station	
Cave, Cavern	Airport	

International Map Index

Index Symbols

[1] Independent Nation	Historical or Cultural Region	Pass, Gap	Depression
[2] State, Region	Mount, Mountain	Plain, Lowland	Polder
[3] District, County	Volcano	Delta	Desert, Dunes
[4] Municipality	Hill	Salt Flat	Forest, Woods
[5] Colony, Dependency	Mountains, Mountain Range	Valley, Canyon	Heath, Steppe
Continent	Hills, Escarpment	Crater, Cave	Oasis
Physical Region	Plateau, Upland	Karst Features	Cape, Point

Coast, Beach	Rock, Reef	Waterfall Rapids	Canal
Cliff	Islands, Archipelago	River Mouth, Estuary	Glacier
Peninsula	Rocks, Reefs	Lake	Ice Shelf, Pack Ice
Isthmus	Coral Reef	Salt Lake	Ocean
Sandbank	Well, Spring	Intermittent Lake	Sea
Island	Geyser	Reservoir	Gulf, Bay
Atoll	River, Stream	Swamp, Pond	Strait, Fjord

Lagoon	Escarpment, Sea Scarp	Historic Site	Port
Bank	Fracture	Ruins	Lighthouse
Seamount	Trench, Abyss	Wall, Walls	Mine
Tablemount	National Park, Reserve	Church, Abbey	Tunnel
Ridge	Point of Interest	Temple	Dam, Bridge
Shelf	Recreation Site	Scientific Station	
Basin	Cave, Cavern	Airport	

Name	Page	Grid	Lat.	Long.
Marsá al Uwayjah	33	Cc	30.55N	17.52 E
Marsa Ben Mehidi	13	Ji	35.05N	2.11W
Marsabit	31	Kh	2.20N	37.59 E
Marsala	14	Gm	37.48N	12.26 E
Marsá Sha'b	35	Fa	22.52N	35.47 E
Marsá Umm Ghayj	24	Fj	25.38N	34.30 E
Marsberg	10	Ee	51.27N	8.51 E
Marsciano	14	Gh	42.54N	12.20 E
Marsdiep	12	Gb	52.58N	4.45 E
Marseille=Marseilles (EN)	6	Gg	43.18N	5.24 E
Marseille-en-Beauvaisis	11	He	49.35N	1.57 E
Marseilles (EN)=Marseille	6	Gg	43.18N	5.24 E
Marshall [Ak.-U.S.]	40	Gd	61.52N	162.04W
Marshall [Ar.-U.S.]	45	Ji	35.55N	92.38W
Marshall [Il.-U.S.]	45	Mg	39.23N	87.42W
Marshall [Lbr.]	34	Cd	6.09N	10.23W
Marshall [Mn.-U.S.]	43	Hc	44.27N	95.47W
Marshall [Mo.-U.S.]	45	Jg	39.07N	93.12W
Marshall [Tx.-U.S.]	43	Ie	32.33N	94.23W
Marshall Islands [5]	58	Hd	9.00N	168.00 E
Marshall Islands	57	Hd	9.00N	168.00 E
Marshall River	59	Hd	22.59S	136.59 E
Marshalltown	43	Ic	42.03N	92.54W
Marshfield	45	Kd	44.40N	90.10W
Marsh Harbour	47	Ic	26.33N	77.03W
Mārshinān, Kūh-e-	24	Of	32.53N	52.24 E
Marsh Island	45	Kl	29.35N	91.53W
Marsica	14	Hi	41.55N	13.35 E
Marsico Nuovo	14	Jj	40.25N	15.44 E
Marsjaty	17	Jf	60.05N	60.29 E
Marsland	45	Ee	42.29N	103.16W
Mars-la-Tour	12	He	49.06N	5.54 E
Marson	12	Gf	48.55N	4.32 E
Märsta	8	Ge	59.37N	17.51 E
Marstal	8	Dj	54.51N	10.31 E
Marstrand	8	Dg	57.53N	11.35 E
Marta	14	Fh	42.14N	11.42 E
Martaban	25	Je	16.32N	97.37 E
Martaban, Gulf of- (EN)	21	Lh	16.30N	97.00 E
Martap	34	Hd	6.54N	13.03 E
Martapura [Indon.]	26	Dg	4.19S	104.22 E
Martapura [Indon.]	26	Fg	3.25S	114.51 E
Martelange/Martelingen	12	He	49.50N	5.44 E
Martelingen/Martelange	12	He	49.50N	5.44 E
Martés, Sierra de-	13	Le	39.20N	0.57W
Martha's Vineyard	43	Mc	41.25N	70.40W
Martigny	14	Bd	46.06N	7.05 E
Martigues	11	Lk	43.24N	5.03 E
Martil	13	Gi	35.37N	5.17W
Martim Vaz, Ilhas-	52	Nh	20.30S	28.51W
Martín	13	Lc	41.18N	0.19W
Martin [Czech.]	10	Og	49.04N	18.55 E
Martin [S.D.-U.S.]	43	Gc	43.10N	101.44W
Martin [Tn.-U.S.]	44	Cg	36.21N	88.51W
Martina Franca	14	Lj	40.42N	17.20 E
Martinez de Hoz	55	Bl	35.19S	61.37W
Martínez de la Torre	48	Kg	20.04N	97.03W
Martín García, Isla-	55	Cl	34.11S	58.15W
Martin Hills	66	Pg	82.04S	88.01W
Martinho Campos	55	Jd	19.20S	45.13W
Martinique	38	Mh	14.40N	61.00W
Martinique [5]	39	Mh	14.40N	61.00W
Martinique, Canal de la-= Martinique Passage (EN)	47	Le	15.10N	61.20W
Martinique Passage	50	Fe	15.10N	61.20W
Martinique Passage (EN)= Martinique, Canal de la-	47	Le	15.10N	61.20W
Martin Lake	44	Ei	32.50N	85.55W
Martin Peninsula	66	Of	74.25S	114.10W
Martinsburg	44	If	39.28N	77.59W
Martins Ferry	44	Ge	40.07N	80.45W
Martinsville [In.-U.S.]	44	Df	39.26N	86.25W
Martinsville [Va.-U.S.]	43	Ld	36.43N	79.53W
Marton	62	Fd	40.05S	175.23 E
Martos	13	Ig	37.43N	3.58W
Martre, Lac la-	42	Fd	63.20N	118.00W
Martuk	19	Fe	50.47N	56.31 E
Martuni	16	Ni	40.06N	45.18 E
Maru	34	Gc	12.21N	6.24 E
Marud	25	Ee	18.19N	72.58 E
Marudi	26	Ff	4.11N	114.19 E
Marudu, Teluk-	26	Ge	6.45N	116.55 E
Marugame	29	Cd	34.18N	133.47 E
Maruko	29	Fc	36.19N	138.15 E
Mārūn	24	Mg	31.02N	49.36 E
Marungu, Monts-	30	Ji	7.42S	30.00 E
Maruoka	29	Ec	36.09N	136.16 E
Maruseppu	29a	Ca	44.01N	143.19 E
Marutea Atoll [W.F.]	57	Ng	21.30S	135.34W
Marutea Atoll [W.F.]	57	Mf	17.00S	143.10W
Maruyama-Gawa	29	Dd	35.40N	134.50 E
Marvão	13	Ee	39.24N	7.23W
Marvast	24	Pg	30.30N	54.15 E
Marvast, Kavīr-e-	24	Pg	30.20N	54.25 E
Mårvatn	8	Cd	60.10N	8.15 E
Marv-Dasht	23	Hd	29.50N	52.40 E
Marvejols	11	Jj	44.33N	3.17 E
Marvine, Mount-	46	Jg	38.40N	111.39W
Marx	16	Od	51.42N	46.46 E
Mary	22	If	37.36N	61.50 E
Maryborough [Austl.]	58	Gg	25.32S	152.42 E
Maryborough [Austl.]	59	Ig	37.03S	143.45 E
Marydale	37	Ce	29.23S	22.05 E
Maryjskaja Oblast [3]	19	Gh	37.15N	62.30 E
Maryland [2]	43	Ld	39.00N	76.45W
Maryland [3]	34	De	4.45N	8.00W
Maryport	9	Jg	54.43N	3.30W
Mary River	59	Gb	12.53S	131.38 E
Marysville [Ca.-U.S.]	46	Eg	39.09N	121.35W
Marysville [Ks.-U.S.]	45	Hg	39.51N	96.39W
Marysville [N.B.-Can.]	44	Nc	45.59N	66.35W
Marysville [Oh.-U.S.]	44	Fe	40.13N	83.22W
Marysville [Wa.-U.S.]	46	Db	48.03N	122.11W
Maryville [Mo.-U.S.]	43	Ic	40.21N	94.52W
Maryville [Tn.-U.S.]	44	Fh	35.46N	83.58W
Marzūq	31	If	25.55N	13.55 E
Marzūq, Ḩamādat-	33	Bd	26.00N	12.30 E
Marzuq, Şaḩrā'-	30	If	24.30N	13.00 E
Masachapa	49	Dh	11.47N	86.31W
Masāhīm, Kūh-e-	24	Pg	30.21N	55.20 E
Masai Steppe	30	Ki	4.45S	37.00 E
Masaka	36	Fc	0.20S	31.44 E
Masākin	32	Jb	35.44N	10.35 E
Masalembo, Kepulauan-	26	Fh	5.30S	114.26 E
Masally	19	Eh	39.01N	48.40 E
Masalog, Puntan-	64b	Ba	15.01N	145.41 E
Masan	27	Md	35.11N	128.24 E
Masasi	31	Kj	10.43S	38.48 E
Masaya [3]	49	Dh	12.00N	86.10W
Masaya	47	Gf	11.58N	86.06W
Masbate	21	Oh	12.15N	123.30 E
Masbate	26	Hd	12.10N	123.35 E
Mascara	32	Hb	35.24N	0.08 E
Mascara [3]	32	Hb	35.30N	0.15 E
Mascareignes, Iles-/ Mascarene Islands	30	Mk	21.00S	57.00 E
Mascarene Basin (EN)	3	Fk	15.00S	56.00 E
Mascarene Islands/ Mascareignes, Iles-	30	Mk	21.00S	57.00 E
Mascarene Plateau (EN)	3	Gk	10.00S	60.00 E
Mascota	48	Gg	20.32N	104.49W
Masela, Pulau-	26	Ih	8.09S	129.50 E
Maseru	31	Jk	29.28S	27.29 E
Maşfūţ	24	Qk	24.48N	56.06 E
Mashābih	24	Gj	25.37N	36.32 E
Mashan	28	Kb	45.12N	130.32 E
Mashava	37	Ed	20.02S	30.29 E
Mashhad	22	Hf	36.18N	59.36 E
Mashike	28	Pc	43.51N	141.31 E
Mashiki	29	Be	32.47N	130.50 E
Mashīz	24	Qh	29.56N	56.37 E
Mashkel	21	Ig	28.02N	63.25 E
Mashonaland North [3]	37	Ec	17.00S	31.00 E
Mashonaland South [3]	37	Ec	18.00S	31.00 E
Mashra' ar Raqq	35	Dd	8.25N	29.16 E
Mashū-Ko	29a	Db	43.35N	144.30 E
Masiaca	48	Ed	26.45N	109.18W
Masīlah, Wādī al-	21	Hh	15.10N	51.08 E
Masi-Manimba	36	Cc	4.46S	17.55 E
Masindi	36	Fb	1.42N	31.43 E
Maşīrah, Jazīrat-	21	Hg	20.29N	58.33 E
Maşīrah, Khalīj-	21	Hg	20.15N	57.40 E
Masisi	36	Ec	1.24S	28.49 E
Masjed-Soleymān	23	Gc	31.58N	49.18 E
Mask, Lough-/Loch Measca	9	Dh	53.35N	9.20W
Maskanah	24	Hd	36.01N	38.05 E
Maskelynes, Iles-	63b	Cc	16.32S	167.49 E
Maslovare	14	Lf	44.34N	17.33 E
Masoala, Cap-	30	Mj	15.59S	50.13 E
Masoala, Presqu'île de-	37	Ic	15.40S	50.12 E
Mason	45	Gk	30.45N	99.14W
Mason Bay	62	Bg	46.55S	167.45 E
Mason City	39	Je	43.09N	93.12W
Masovia (EN)= Mazowsze	5	Ie	52.40N	20.20 E
Masparro, Río-	49	Mi	8.04N	69.26W
Masqaţ=Muscat (EN)	22	Hg	23.29N	58.33 E
Massa	14	Ef	44.01N	10.09 E
Massachusetts [2]	43	Mc	42.15N	71.50W
Massachusetts Bay	44	Ld	42.20N	70.50W
Massaciuccoli, Lago di-	14	Eg	43.50N	10.20 E
Massafra	14	Lj	40.35N	17.07 E
Massaguet	35	Bc	12.28N	15.26 E
Massakori	35	Bc	13.00N	15.44 E
Massa Marittima	14	Eg	43.03N	10.53 E
Massangano	36	Bd	9.37S	14.17 E
Massangena	37	Ed	21.32S	32.57 E
Massapê	54	Jd	3.31S	40.19W
Massawa (EN)=Mitsiwa	31	Kg	15.37N	39.39 E
Massena	43	Mc	44.56N	74.57W
Massénya	35	Bc	11.24N	16.10 E
Masset	42	Ef	54.02N	132.09W
Masseube	11	Gk	43.26N	0.35 E
Massey Sound	42	Ia	78.00N	94.00W
Massiac	11	Ji	45.15N	3.13 E
Massiaru	8	Kg	57.52N	24.27 E
Massillon	44	Ge	40.48N	81.32W
Massinga	37	Fd	23.20S	35.22 E
Masson Island	66	Ge	66.08S	96.34 E
Massuma	36	De	14.05S	22.00 E
Mastābah	33	Ge	20.49N	39.26 E
Maštaga	16	Pi	40.32N	49.59 E
Masterton	61	Eh	40.57S	175.39 E
Mastūrah	33	Ge	23.06N	38.50 E
Masuda	27	Ne	34.40N	131.51 E
Māsūleh	24	Md	37.10N	48.59 E
Masurai, Gunung-	26	Dg	2.30S	101.51 E
Masuria (EN)	5	Ie	53.50N	21.30 E
Masurian Lakes (EN)	5	Ie	53.45N	21.45 E
Maşyāf	24	Ge	35.03N	36.21 E
Maszewo	10	Lc	53.29N	15.02 E
Mataabé, Cap-	63b	Cb	15.38S	166.46 E
Matabeleland North [3]	37	Dc	19.00S	27.30 E
Matabeleland South [3]	37	Dd	21.00S	29.30 E
Matachel	13	Ff	38.50N	6.17W
Matachewan	42	Jg	47.56N	80.39W
Matacu	55	Bc	17.21S	61.28W
Matadi	31	Ii	5.49S	13.27 E
Matador	45	Fi	34.01N	100.49W
Matagalpa [3]	49	Eg	13.00N	85.30W
Matagalpa	39	Kh	12.53N	85.57W
Matagami	42	Jg	49.45N	77.35W
Matagami, Lac-	44	Ia	49.54N	77.32W
Mata Gassile	35	Ge	2.30N	42.16 E
Matagorda Bay	45	Hl	28.35N	96.20W
Matagorda Island	43	Hf	28.15N	96.30W
Matagorda Peninsula	45	Hl	28.32N	96.07W
Mataiea	65e	Fc	17.46S	149.25W
Mataiva Atoll	57	Mf	14.53S	148.40W
Mataj	19	Hf	45.51N	78.43 E
Matak, Pulau-	26	Ef	3.18N	106.16 E
Matakana Island	62	Gb	37.35S	176.05 E
Matala	36	Ce	14.43S	15.02 E
Matalaa, Pointe-	64h	Bc	13.20S	76.08W
Matale	25	Gg	7.28N	80.37 E
Mataliele	37	Df	30.24S	28.43 E
Matam	34	Cb	15.40N	13.15W
Matamey	34	Gc	13.26N	8.28 E
Matamoros [Mex.]	47	Dc	25.32N	103.15W
Matamoros [Mex.]	39	Jg	25.53N	97.30W
Matana, Danau-	26	Hg	2.28S	21.20 E
Ma'ţan as Sarra	33	De	21.41N	21.52 E
Matancita	48	De	25.09N	111.59W
Matane	42	Kg	48.51N	67.32W
Matankari	34	Fc	3.46N	4.01 E
Matanza	55	Cl	34.33S	58.35W
Matanzas	39	Kg	23.03N	81.35W
Matanzas [3]	49	Gb	22.40N	81.10W
Matão	55	He	21.35S	48.22W
Matapalo, Cabo-	49	Fi	8.23N	83.19W
Matapan, Cape- (EN)= Tainaron, Akra-	5	Ih	36.23N	22.29 E
Matape, Rio-	48	Dc	28.17N	110.41W
Mata Point	64k	Bb	19.07S	169.50W
Matara	35	Fc	14.35N	39.28 E
Matara	25	Gg	5.56N	80.33 E
Mataram	22	Nj	8.35S	116.07 E
Mataranka	59	Gb	14.56S	133.07 E
Mataró	13	Oc	41.32N	2.27 E
Matarraña/Matarranya	13	Mc	41.14N	0.22 E
Matarranya/Matarraña	13	Mc	41.14N	0.22 E
Mataso	63b	Dc	17.15S	168.25 E
Matatula, Cape-	65c	Cb	14.15S	170.34W
Mataura	62	Cg	46.34S	168.44 E
Mataura	62	Cg	46.12S	168.52 E
Mata-Utu	58	Jf	13.17S	176.08W
Mata-Utu, Baie de-	64h	Bb	13.19S	176.07W
Matavai	61	Gb	13.28S	172.35W
Matavera	64p	Cb	21.13S	159.44W
Mataverj	65d	Ab	27.10S	109.27W
Matawai	62	Gc	38.21S	177.32 E
Matawin, Réservoir-	44	Kb	46.45N	73.50W
Matawin, Rivière-	44	Kb	46.55N	72.55W
Maţāy	24	Dh	28.25N	30.46 E
Maţbakhayn	33	Hf	11.29N	41.48 E
Matca	15	Kd	45.51N	27.32 E
Matemo, Ilha-	37	Gb	12.13S	40.36 E
Matera	14	Kj	40.40N	16.36 E
Matese	14	Ii	41.25N	14.20 E
Mátészalka	10	Si	47.57N	22.20 E
Matfors	7	De	62.21N	17.02 E
Matha	11	Fi	45.52N	0.19W
Mathematicians Seamounts (EN)	47	Be	15.30N	111.00W
Matheson	44	Ga	48.32N	80.28W
Mathis	45	Hl	28.06N	97.50W
Mathrákion	15	Cj	39.46N	19.31 E
Mathura	25	Fc	27.30N	77.41 E
Mati	15	Ch	41.39N	19.34 E
Mati	26	Ie	6.57N	126.13 E
Matias Cardoso	55	Kb	14.52S	43.56W
Matías Romero	47	Ee	16.53N	95.02W
Matícora, Río-	49	Lh	11.01N	[illegible]
Matina	49	Fh	10.05N	83.17W
Matinha	54	Id	3.06S	45.02W
Māţir	32	Ib	37.03N	9.40 E
Matiyure, Río-	50	Ci	7.36N	67.39W
Matkaselkja	8	Nc	61.57N	30.33 E
Mātmāţah	32	Ic	33.33N	9.58 E
Matnog	26	Hd	12.35N	124.05 E
Mato, Cerro-	50	Di	7.15N	65.14W
Mato, Río-	50	Di	7.09N	65.07W
Matočkin Šar, Proliv-	19	Fa	73.30N	54.55 E
Mato Grosso [2]	54	Gf	14.00S	56.00W
Mato Grosso [Braz.]	55	Dd	18.18S	57.20W
Mato Grosso [Braz.]	53	Kg	15.00S	59.57W
Mato Grosso, Planalto do- = Mato Grosso, Plateau of- (EN)	52	Kg	15.30S	56.00W
Mato Grosso, Plateau of- (EN) = Mato Grosso, Planalto do-	52	Kg	15.30S	56.00W
Mato Grosso do Sul [2]	54	Hg	20.00S	55.00W
Matos Costa	55	Gh	26.27S	51.09W
Matosinhos	13	Dc	41.11N	8.42W
Matou	28	Cj	29.50N	115.32 E
Matov → Qiuxian	28	Cf	36.47N	114.30 E
Mátra	5	Hf	47.53N	19.57 E
Maţraḩ	23	Ie	23.29N	58.31 E
Matrei in Osttirol	14	Gc	47.00N	12.32 E
Maţrūḩ	31	Je	31.21N	27.14 E
Matsiatra	37	Hd	21.25S	45.33 E
Matsudo	28	Og	35.48N	139.55 E
Matsue	27	Nd	35.28N	133.04 E
Matsukawa [Jap.]	29	Gc	37.40N	140.28 E
Matsukawa [Jap.]	29	Ed	35.36N	137.53 E
Matsu Liehtao	27	Kf	26.05N	119.56 E
Matsumae	29a	Bc	41.25N	140.07 E
Matsumae-Hantō	29a	Bc	41.40N	140.15 E
Matsumoto	27	Od	36.14N	137.58 E
Matsuo	29	Gb	39.53N	141.02 E
Matsu-Ōminato	29a	Bc	41.15N	141.09 E
Matsusaka	28	Ng	34.34N	136.32 E
Matsushima	29	Gb	38.22N	141.04 E
Matsutō	29	Ec	36.30N	136.33 E
Matsuura	29	Ae	33.22N	129.42 E
Matsuyama	22	Pf	33.50N	132.45 E
Matsuzaki	29	Fd	34.44N	138.45 E
Mattagami Lake	44	Gb	47.57N	81.35W
Mattagami River	42	Jf	50.43N	81.30W
Mattawa	42	Jg	46.19N	78.42W
Matterhorn [Eur.]	14	Be	45.58N	7.39 E
Matterhorn [Nv.-U.S.]	46	Hf	41.49N	115.23W
Matthew, Ile-	57	Ig	22.20S	171.20 E
Matthews Ridge	54	Fb	7.30N	60.10W
Matthew Town	47	Jd	20.57N	73.40W
Maţţī, Sabhat-	35	Ia	23.30N	52.00 E
Mattighofen	14	Hb	48.06N	13.09 E
Mattoon	45	Lg	39.29N	88.22W
Matua, Ostrov-	20	Kg	48.00N	153.10 E
Matucana	54	Cf	11.51S	76.24W
Matuku Island	61	Ec	19.10S	179.46 E
Matundu	36	Db	4.21N	23.40 E
Matundu	36	Gd	8.50S	39.30 E
Maturín	53	Je	9.45N	63.11W
Matvejev Kurgan	16	Kf	47.34N	38.55 E
Maua	37	Fb	13.52S	37.09 E
Maubeuge	11	Jd	50.17N	3.58 E
Ma-ubin	25	Je	16.44N	95.39 E
Maudheimvidda	66	Bf	74.00S	8.00W
Maud Seamount (EN)	66	Ce	65.00S	2.35 E
Maués	54	Gd	3.24S	57.42W
Maués, Rio-	54	Gd	3.22S	57.44W
Mau Escarpment	36	Gc	0.40S	36.02 E
Maug Islands	57	Fb	20.01N	145.13 E
Maui Island	57	Lb	20.45N	156.20W
Mauke Island	57	Lg	20.09S	157.23W
Mau Kyun	25	Jf	12.45N	98.20 E
Mauldre	12	Df	48.59N	1.49 E
Maule [2]	56	Fe	35.45S	72.15W
Mauléon	11	Fh	46.55N	0.45W
Mauléon-Licharre	11	Fk	43.14N	0.53W
Maullín	56	Ff	41.38S	73.37W
Maumee	44	Fe	41.34N	83.39W
Maumere	26	Hh	8.37S	122.14 E
Maun	31	Jj	19.58S	23.26 E
Maun	14	If	44.26N	14.55 E
Mauna Kea	57	Lc	19.50N	155.28W
Maunaloa	65a	Db	21.08N	157.13W
Mauna Loa	65a	Fd	19.28N	155.36W
Maunath	25	Gc	25.40N	82.38 E
Maunawili	65a	Db	21.21N	157.47W
Maunga Roa	64p	Bb	21.13S	159.48W
Maungdaw	25	Id	20.49N	92.22 E
Maunoir, Lac -	42	Fc	67.30N	125.00W
Maupihaa Atoll (Mopelia, Atoll-)	57	Lf	16.50S	153.55W
Maupin	46	Ed	45.11N	121.05W
Maupiti, Ile-	57	Lf	16.27S	152.15W
Maurepas, Lake-	45	Kk	30.15N	90.30W
Maures	11	Mk	43.16N	6.23 E
Mauriac	11	Ii	45.13N	2.20 E
Maurice, Lake-	59	Ge	29.30S	131.00 E
Maurienne	11	Mi	45.13N	6.30 E
Mauritania (EN)= Mūrītānīyā [1]	31	Fg	20.00N	12.00W
Mauriti	54	Ke	7.23S	38.46W
Mauritius	30	Mk	20.17S	57.33 E
Mauritius [1]	31	Mj	18.00S	57.40 E
Mauron	11	Df	48.05N	2.18W
Maurs	11	Ij	44.43N	2.12 E
Mauston	45	Ke	43.48N	90.05W
Mauthausen	14	Ib	48.14N	14.31 E
Mauzé-sur-le-Mignon	11	Fh	46.12N	0.40W
Mavinga	36	Df	15.47S	20.24 E
Mavita	37	Ec	19.32S	33.09 E
Mavrovouni [Grc.]	15	Fj	39.37N	22.47 E
Mavrovouni [Grc.]	15	Gh	41.07N	23.08 E
Mawchi	25	Je	18.49N	97.09 E
Mawei	27	Kf	26.02N	119.30 E
Mawlaik	25	Id	23.38N	94.25 E
Mawlamyine	22	Le	16.30N	97.38 E
Mawqaq	24	Ii	27.25N	41.08 E
Mawr, Wādī-	23	Ff	15.41N	42.42 E
Mawson	66	Fe	67.36S	62.53 E
Mawson Coast	66	Fe	67.40S	63.30 E
Mawson Escarpment	66	Ff	73.05S	68.10 E
Maxcanú	47	Fd	20.35N	90.01W
Maxixe	37	Fd	23.51S	35.21 E
Maxwell Bay	42	Ib	74.32N	89.00W
May, Isle of-	9	Ke	56.10N	2.30W
Maya, Pulau-	26	Eg	1.10S	109.35 E
Mayaguana Island	47	Jd	22.23N	72.57W
Mayaguana Passage	49	Kb	22.32N	73.15W
Mayagüez	47	Ke	18.12N	67.09W
Mayahi	34	Gc	13.58N	7.40 E
Mayama	36	Bc	3.51S	14.54 E
Mayāmey	24	Pd	36.24N	55.42 E
Maya Mountains	47	Ge	16.40N	88.50W
Mayapan	47	Gd	20.33N	89.27W
Mayarí	49	Jc	20.40N	75.41W
Maybell	45	Bf	40.31N	108.05W
Maychew	35	Fc	12.46N	39.34 E
Mayd	35	Hc	10.57N	47.06 E
Maydān	24	Ke	34.55N	45.37 E
Maydena	59	Jh	42.55S	146.30 E
Maydī	23	Ff	16.18N	42.48 E
Mayen	10	Df	50.20N	7.13 E
Mayenne	11	Ff	48.18N	0.37W
Mayenne	11	Fg	47.30N	0.32W
Mayenne [3]	11	Ff	48.05N	0.40W
Mayfa'ah	35	Hc	14.16N	47.35 E
Mayfield	44	Cg	36.44N	88.38W
May Glacier	66	Ie	67.00S	130.00 E
Mayi He	28	Jb	45.52N	128.46 E
Maymyo	25	Jd	22.02N	96.28 E
Maynas	54	Dd	3.00S	75.00W
Mayo	39	Fc	63.35N	135.54W
Mayo/Muigheo [2]	9	Dh	53.50N	9.30W
Mayo, Mountains of-	9	Dg	54.05N	9.30W
Mayo, Río-	48	Ed	26.45N	109.47W
Mayo Darlé	34	Hd	6.30N	11.55 E
Mayo-Kébbi	35	Ad	9.18N	13.33 E
Mayo-Kébbi [3]	35	Bd	10.00N	15.30 E
Mayoko	36	Bc	2.18S	12.49 E
Mayon, Mount-	21	Oh	13.15N	123.41 E
Mayor, Puig-/Major, Puig-	13	Oe	39.48N	2.48 E
Mayor Island	62	Gb	37.15S	176.15 E
Mayor Pablo Lagerenza	56	Ha	19.58S	60.45W
Mayotte [5]	31	Lj	12.50S	45.10 E
Mayotte/Mahoré	30	Lj	12.50S	45.10 E
May Pen	47	Ie	17.58N	77.14W
Mayraira Point	26	Hc	18.39N	120.51 E
Mayran, Laguna de-	48	He	25.45N	102.45W
Mayreau Island	51n	Bb	12.39N	61.23W
May-sur-Orne	12	Be	49.06N	0.22W
Maysville	44	Ff	38.39N	83.46W
Mayumba [Gabon]	31	Ii	3.25S	10.39 E
Mayumba [Zaire]	36	Ed	7.16S	27.03 E
Mayum La	27	Ce	30.35N	82.27 E
Mayville	44	Hd	42.15N	79.32W
Mayyit, Al Baḩr al-=Dead Sea (EN)	21	Ff	31.30N	35.30 E
Mazabuka	36	Ef	15.51S	27.46 E
Mazagão	54	Hd	0.07S	51.17W
Mazamet	11	Ik	43.30N	2.24 E
Māzandarān [3]	23	Hb	36.00N	54.00 E
Māzandarān, Daryā-ye-= Caspian Sea (EN)	5	Lg	42.00N	50.30 E
Mazar	27	Cd	36.27N	77.03 E
Mazara del Vallo	14	Gm	37.39N	12.35 E
Mazār-e Sharīf	22	If	36.42N	67.06 E
Mazarrón, Golfo de-	13	Kg	37.30N	1.18W
Mazartag	27	Dd	38.29N	80.50 E
Mazaruni River	54	Gb	6.25N	58.38W
Mazatenango	47	Ff	14.32N	91.30W
Mazatlán	39	Ig	23.13N	106.25W
Mažeikiai/Mažejkjaj	7	Fh	56.20N	22.22 E
Mažejkjaj/Mážeikiai	7	Fh	56.20N	22.22 E
Mazḩafah, Jabal-	24	Fh	28.48N	34.57 E
Mazḩūr, 'Irq al-	24	Ji	27.25N	43.55 E
Mazinga	51c	Ab	17.29N	62.58W
Mazirbe	8	Jg	57.40N	22.10 E
Mazoe	37	Ec	17.30S	30.58 E
Mazoe	30	Kj	16.32S	33.25 E
Mazomeno	36	Ec	4.55S	27.13 E
Mazong Shan	27	Gc	41.33N	97.10 E
Mazowsze	10	Qd	52.40N	20.20 E
Mazowsze=Masovia (EN)	5	Ie	52.40N	20.20 E
Mazsalaca	8	Kg	57.45N	24.59 E
Mazunga	37	Dd	21.44S	29.52 E
Mazurskie, Pojezierze-	10	Qc	53.40N	21.00 E
Mazzarino	14	Im	37.18N	14.13 E
Mba	63d	Ab	17.32S	177.42 E
Mbabane	31	Kk	26.18S	31.07 E
Mbabo, Tchabal-	34	Hd	7.16N	12.09 E
Mbacké	34	Bc	14.48N	15.55W
Mbaéré	35	Be	3.47N	17.31 E
Mbaïki	31	Ih	3.53N	18.00 E
Mbakaou	34	Hd	6.19N	12.49 E
Mbakaou, Barrage de-	34	Hd	6.25N	13.00 E
Mbala	31	Ki	8.50S	31.22 E
Mbalam	34	He	2.13N	13.49 E
Mbale	31	Kh	1.05N	34.10 E
Mbali	35	Be	4.27N	18.20 E
Mbalmayo	34	He	3.31N	11.30 E
Mbam	30	Ih	4.24N	11.17 E
Mbamba Bay	36	Fe	11.17S	34.46 E
Mbandaka	31	Ih	0.04N	18.16 E
Mbanga	34	Ge	4.30N	9.34 E
Mbanika	63a	Dc	9.05S	159.12 E
M'banza Congo	36	Bd	6.16S	14.15 E
Mbanza-Ngungu	31	Ii	5.35S	14.47 E
Mbarangandu	36	Gd	8.57S	37.24 E
Mbarara	36	Fc	0.36S	30.38 E
Mbari	35	Ce	4.34N	22.43 E
Mbatiki	63d	Bb	17.46S	179.08 E
Mbava	63a	Cb	7.49S	156.37 E
Mbé	34	Hd	7.51N	13.36 E
Mbengga	63d	Bc	18.23S	178.08 E
Mbengwi	34	Hd	6.01N	10.00 E
Mbéré	35	Bd	9.07N	16.26 E
Mbeya	31	Ki	8.54S	33.27 E
Mbeya [3]	36	Fd	8.00S	33.30 E
Mbi	35	Be	4.28N	18.07 E
Mbigou	36	Bc	1.53S	11.56 E
Mbinda	31	Ii	2.07S	12.52 E
Mbinga	36	Ge	10.56S	35.01 E
Mbingué	34	Dc	10.00N	5.54W
Mbini	34	Ge	1.34N	9.37 E
Mbini [3]	34	He	1.30N	10.00 E
Mbini	30	Ih	1.30N	10.30 E
Mboki	35	Dd	5.19N	25.58 E
Mbokonimbeti	63a	Ec	8.57S	160.05 E
Mbomo	36	Bb	0.24N	14.44 E
Mbomou=Bomu (EN) [3]	35	Cd	5.30N	23.30 E
Mbomou=Bomu (EN)	30	Jh	4.08N	22.26 E
Mborokua	63a	Dc	9.02S	158.44 E
Mbour	34	Bc	14.24N	16.58W
Mbout	32	Ef	16.01N	12.35W
Mbozi	36	Fd	9.02S	32.56 E
Mbrés	35	Bd	6.40N	19.48 E
M'Bridge	36	Bd	7.14S	12.52 E
Mbua	63d	Bb	16.48S	178.37 E
Mbuji-Mayi	31	Ji	6.09S	23.33 E
Mbulo	63a	Dc	8.46S	158.21 E
Mbulu	36	Gc	3.51S	35.32 E
Mburucuyá	55	Ci	28.03S	58.14W
Mbutha	63d	Bb	16.39S	179.51 E
Mbuyuni	36	Gd	7.23S	36.32 E
Mbwemburu	36	Gd	9.29S	39.39 E
Mcalester	43	He	34.56N	95.46W
Mcensk	19	De	53.17N	36.32 E
M'Chedallah	13	Qh	36.22N	4.16 E
Mcherrah	32	Gd	27.00N	4.30W
Mchinga	36	Gd	9.44S	39.42 E
Mchinji	36	Fe	13.48S	32.54 E
Mdandu	36	Fd	9.09S	34.42 E
M'Daourouch	14	Bn	36.05N	7.49 E
Mdennah	32	Gd	25.00N	4.50W
Mdiq	13	Gi	35.41N	5.19W
Mead	44	Fa	49.29N	83.50W
Mead, Lake-	43	Ed	36.05N	114.25W
Meade	40	Hb	70.50N	156.25W
Meade	45	Fh	37.17N	100.20W
Meade Peak	46	Je	42.30N	111.15W
Meadow Lake	42	Gf	54.07N	108.20W
Meadville	44	Ge	41.38N	80.10W
Me-akan-Dake	29a	Cb	43.23N	143.59 E
Mealhada	13	Dd	40.22N	8.27W

Index Symbols

- [1] Independent Nation
- [2] State, Region
- [3] District, County
- [4] Municipality
- [5] Colony, Dependency
- Continent
- Physical Region
- Historical or Cultural Region
- Mount, Mountain
- Volcano
- Hill
- Mountains, Mountain Range
- Hills, Escarpment
- Plateau, Upland
- Pass, Gap
- Plain, Lowland
- Delta
- Salt Flat
- Valley, Canyon
- Crater, Cave
- Karst Features
- Depression
- Polder
- Desert, Dunes
- Forest, Woods
- Heath, Steppe
- Oasis
- Cape, Point
- Coast, Beach
- Cliff
- Peninsula
- Isthmus
- Sandbank
- Island
- Atoll
- Rock, Reef
- Islands, Archipelago
- Rocks, Reefs
- Coral Reef
- Well, Spring
- Geyser
- River, Stream
- Waterfall Rapids
- River Mouth, Estuary
- Lake
- Salt Lake
- Intermittent Lake
- Reservoir
- Swamp, Pond
- Canal
- Glacier
- Ice Shelf, Pack Ice
- Ocean
- Sea
- Gulf, Bay
- Strait, Fjord
- Lagoon
- Bank
- Seamount
- Tablemount
- Ridge
- Shelf
- Basin
- Escarpment, Sea Scarp
- Fracture
- Trench, Abyss
- National Park, Reserve
- Point of Interest
- Recreation Site
- Cave, Cavern
- Historic Site
- Ruins
- Wall, Walls
- Church, Abbey
- Temple
- Scientific Station
- Airport
- Port
- Lighthouse
- Mine
- Tunnel
- Dam, Bridge

Mealy Mountains 42 Lf 53.20N 59.30W
Meama 65b Ba 19.45S 174.34W
Méan, Havelange- 12 Hd 50.22N 5.20 E
Meander Reef 26 Ge 8.09N 119.14 E
Meander River 42 Fe 59.02N 117.42W
Meanguera, Isla- 49 Dg 13.12N 87.43W
Mearim, Rio- 52 Lf 3.04S 44.35W
Meath/An Mhí [2] 9 Gh 53.35N 6.40W
Meaux 11 If 48.57N 2.52 E
Mecca (EN)=Makkah 22 Fg 21.27N 39.49 E
Mechara 35 Gd 8.34N 40.28 E
Mechelen/Maasmechelen 12 Hd 50.57N 5.40 E
Mechelen/Malines 11 Kc 51.02N 4.29 E
Mecheraa-Asfa 13 Ni 35.24N 1.03 E
Mecheria 32 Gc 33.33N 0.17W
Mechernich 12 Id 50.36N 6.39 E
Mechongué 55 Cn 38.09S 58.13W
Mecidiye 15 Ji 40.38N 26.32 E
Mecitözü 24 Fb 40.31N 35.19 E
Mecklemburgischer
Höhenrücken 10 Ic 53.40N 12.10 E
Mecklenburg 10 Hc 53.30N 12.00 E
Mecklenburger Bucht 10 Hb 54.20N 11.40 E
Mecklenburger Schweiz 10 Ic 53.45N 12.35 E
Mecoacán, Laguna- 48 Mh 18.20N 93.10W
Meconta 37 Fb 14.59S 39.50 E
Mecsek 10 Oj 46.10N 18.18 E
Mecubúri 37 Gb 14.10S 40.31 E
Mecúfi 37 Gb 13.17S 40.33 E
Mecula 37 Fb 12.05S 37.39 E
Médala 32 Ff 15.30N 5.37W
Medan 22 Li 3.35N 98.40 E
Médanos [Arg.] 56 He 38.50S 62.41W
Médanos [Arg.] 55 Ck 33.24S 59.05W
Medanosa, Punta- 56 Gg 48.06S 65.55W
Mede 14 Ce 45.06N 8.44 E
Médéa 32 Hb 36.16N 2.45 E
Médéa [3] 32 Hb 36.20N 3.25 E
Medebach 12 Kc 51.12N 8.43 E
Medellin 26 Hd 11.08N 123.58 E
Medellín 53 Ie 6.15N 75.35W
Medelpad 8 Gb 62.35N 16.15 E
Medemblik 12 Hb 52.46N 5.06 E
Medenica 10 Tg 49.21N 23.45 E
Mederdra 32 Df 16.54N 15.40W
Medetzız 24 Fd 37.25N 34.40 E
Medford [Or.-U.S.] 39 Ge 42.19N 122.52W
Medford [Wi.-U.S.] 45 Kd 45.09N 90.20W
Medgidia 15 Le 44.15N 28.17 E
Medi 35 Ed 5.06N 30.44 E
Media Luna, Arrecife de la- 49 Ff 15.13N 82.36W
Medianeira 55 Eg 25.17S 54.05W
Mediaş 15 Hc 46.10N 24.21 E
Medical Lake 46 Gc 47.34N 117.41W
Medicine Bow 46 Lf 41.54N 106.12W
Medicine Bow Mountains 46 Lf 41.10N 106.25W
Medicine Butte 46 Jf 41.29N 110.48W
Medicine Hat 39 Hd 50.03N 110.40W
Medicine Lake 46 Mb 48.28N 104.24W
Medicine Lodge 45 Gh 37.17N 98.35W
Međimurje 14 Kd 46.25N 16.30 E
Medina (EN)=Al Madīnah [Sau.Ar.] 22 Fg 24.28N 39.36 E
Medina Az-Zahra 13 Hg 37.52N 4.50W
Medinaceli 13 Jc 41.10N 2.26W
Medina del Campo 13 Hc 41.18N 4.55W
Medina de Rioseco 13 Gc 41.53N 5.02W
Medina-Sidonia 13 Gh 36.27N 5.55W
Medininkai/Medininkaj 8 Kj 54.32N 25.46 E
Medinīpur 25 Hd 22.26N 87.20 E
Medio, Arroyo del- 55 Bk 33.16S 60.15W
Mediterranean Sea (EN)= Akdeniz 5 Hh 35.00N 20.00 E
Mediterranean Sea (EN)= Khatikhon, Yam- 5 Hh 35.00N 20.00 E
Mediterranean Sea (EN)= Méditerranée, Mer- 5 Hh 35.00N 20.00 E
Mediterranean Sea (EN)= Mediterraneo, Mar- 5 Hh 35.00N 20.00 E
Mediterranean Sea (EN)= Mediterráneo, Mar- 5 Hh 35.00N 20.00 E
Mediterranean Sea (EN)= Mesoyéios Thálassa 5 Hh 35.00N 20.00 E
Mediterranean Sea (EN)= Mutawassiṭ, Al Baḥr al- 5 Hh 35.00N 20.00 E
Méditerranée, Mer-= Mediterranean Sea (EN) 5 Hh 35.00N 20.00 E
Mediterráneo, Mar-= Mediterranean Sea (EN) 5 Hh 35.00N 20.00 E
Mediterraneo, Mar-= Mediterranean Sea (EN) 5 Hh 35.00N 20.00 E
Medje 36 Eb 2.25N 27.18 E
Medjerda, Monts de la- 32 Ib 36.35N 8.15 E
Mednogorsk 19 Fe 51.26N 57.40 E
Medny, Ostrov- 20 Lf 54.40N 167.50 E
Médoc 11 Fi 45.00N 1.00W
Mêdog 27 Gf 29.18N 95.27 E
Médouneu 36 Bb 1.01N 10.48 E
Medveđa 15 Eg 42.51N 21.36 E
Medvedica 5 Kf 49.35N 42.41 E
Medvedica 7 Ih 57.05N 37.31 E
Medvednica 14 Je 45.55N 15.58 E
Medvedok 7 Mh 57.24N 50.06 E
Medvenka 16 Jd 51.27N 36.08 E
Medveži, Ostrova-=Bear Islands (EN) 21 Sb 70.52N 161.26 E
Medvežjegorsk 19 Dc 62.56N 34.29 E
Medway 12 Cc 51.23N 0.31 E
Medzilaborce 10 Rg 49.16N 21.55 E
Meekatharra 58 Cg 26.36S 118.29 E
Meeker 45 Cf 40.02N 107.55W
Meerane 10 If 50.51N 12.28 E
Meerbusch 12 Ic 51.16N 6.40 E
Meerut 25 Fc 28.59N 77.42 E
Meeteetse 46 Kd 44.09N 108.52W
Mefarlane, Lake- 59 Hf 32.00S 136.40 E
Mega [Eth.] 31 Kh 4.03N 38.20 E
Mega [Indon.] 26 Jg 0.41S 131.53 E
Mega, Pulau- 26 Dg 4.00S 101.02 E
Megalo 35 Gd 6.52N 40.47 E
Megálon Khorion 15 Km 36.27N 27.21 E
Megalópolis 15 Fl 37.24N 22.08 E
Megálo Sofráno 15 Jm 36.04N 26.25 E
Meganísion 15 Dk 38.38N 20.43 E
Meganom, Mys- 16 Ig 44.48N 35.05 E
Mégara 15 Gk 38.00N 23.21 E
Megève 11 Mi 45.52N 6.37 E
Meghalaya [3] 25 Ic 26.00N 91.00 E
Megid 33 Dd 28.35N 22.10 E
Megion 19 Hc 61.00N 76.15 E
Megiscane, Lac- 44 Ia 48.30N 76.04W
Megri 16 Oj 38.55N 46.15 E
Mehadia 15 Fe 44.54N 22.22 E
Mehaigne 12 Hd 50.32N 5.13 E
Meharry, Mount- 59 Dd 23.00S 118.35 E
Mehdia 13 Ni 35.25N 1.45 E
Mehdīshahr 24 Oe 35.44N 53.22 E
Mehedinţi [2] 15 Fe 44.30N 23.00 E
Mehetia, Ile- 61 Lc 17.52S 148.03W
Mehrabān 24 Lc 38.05N 47.08 E
Mehrān 24 Pi 26.52N 55.24 E
Mehrān 24 Lf 33.07N 46.10 E
Mehrenga 7 Je 63.17N 41.20 E
Mehrīz 24 Pg 31.35N 54.28 E
Mehtar Lām 23 Lc 34.39N 70.10 E
Mehun-sur-Yèvre 11 Ig 47.09N 2.13 E
Meia Meia 36 Gd 5.49S 35.48 E
Meia Ponte, Rio- 54 Ig 18.32S 49.36W
Meiganga 34 Hd 6.31N 14.18 E
Meighen 42 Ha 79.55N 99.00W
Meihekou → Hailong 27 Mc 42.32N 125.37 E
Meiktila 25 Jd 20.52N 95.52 E
Meilü → Wuchuan 27 Jg 21.28N 110.44 E
Meinerzhagen 12 Jc 51.07N 7.39 E
Meiningen 10 Gf 50.33N 10.25 E
Meio, Rio do- 55 Ja 13.20S 44.34W
Meisenheim 12 Je 49.43N 7.40 E
Meishan [China] 27 He 30.05N 103.48 E
Meishan [China] 28 Ei 31.06N 119.43 E
Meishan → Jinzhai 28 Ci 31.40N 115.52 E
Meißen 10 Je 51.09N 13.29 E
Meißner 10 Fe 51.12N 9.50 E
Meitan (Yiquan) 27 If 27.48N 107.32 E
Meixian 27 Kg 24.21N 116.07 E
Meiyukou 28 Bd 40.01N 113.08 E
Méjean, Causse- 11 Jj 44.16N 3.22 E
Mejillones 56 Fb 23.06S 70.27W
Mékambo 36 Bb 1.01N 13.56 E
Mekdela 35 Fc 11.28N 39.20 E
Mekele=Meqele (EN) 31 Kg 13.30N 39.28 E
Mékhé 34 Bb 15.07N 16.38W
Mekherrhane, Sebkha- 30 Hf 26.22N 1.20 E
Meknès [3] 32 Fc 33.00N 5.30W
Meknès 31 Ge 33.54N 5.32W
Mekong (EN)=Lancang Jiang 21 Mh 10.15N 105.55 E
Mekong (EN)=Mae Nam Khong 21 Mh 10.15N 105.55 E
Mekong (EN)=Mékôngk 21 Mh 10.15N 105.55 E
Mekong (EN)=Mènam Khong 21 Mh 10.15N 105.55 E
Mekong Delta (EN) 21 Mi 10.20N 106.40 E
Mekongga, Gunung- 26 Hg 3.35S 121.15 E
Mékôngk=Mekong (EN) 21 Mh 10.15N 105.55 E
Mekoryuk 40 Fd 60.23N 166.12W
Mékrou 34 Fc 12.24N 2.49 E
Mel, Ilha do- 55 Hg 25.31S 48.20W
Melaab 13 Ni 35.43N 1.20 E
Mēladēn 35 Hc 10.25N 49.52 E
Melaka 22 Mi 2.12N 102.15 E
Melaka, Selat-=Malacca, Strait of- (EN) 21 Mi 2.30N 101.20 E
Melamo, Cabo- 30 Lj 14.24S 40.49 E
Melanesia 57 Hf 13.00S 164.00 E
Melanesian Basin (EN) 3 Jj 0.05S 160.35 E
Melawi 26 Ff 0.05N 111.29 E
Melbourne [Ar.-U.S.] 45 Kh 36.04N 91.54W
Melbourne [Austl.] 58 Fh 37.49S 144.58 E
Melbourne [Eng.-U.K.] 12 Ab 52.49N 1.26W
Melbourne [Fl.-U.S.] 43 Kf 28.05N 80.37W
Melbourne-Dandenong 59 Jg 37.59S 145.12 E
Melchor Múzquiz 47 Dc 27.53N 101.31W
Melchor Ocampo 48 Hi 17.59N 102.11W
Meldorf 10 Fb 54.05N 9.05 E
Mele, Capo- 14 Cg 43.57N 8.10 E
Melekeiok 64a Bc 7.29N 134.38 E
Melela 37 Fc 17.04S 38.36 E
Melenci 15 Dd 45.31N 20.19 E
Melenki 19 Ed 55.23N 41.42 E
Meleto Dağı 24 Ic 38.35N 41.32 E
Meleuz 19 Fe 52.58N 55.59 E
Mélèzes, Rivière aux- 42 Ke 57.00N 69.00W
Melfa 14 Hi 41.30N 13.35 E
Melfi [Chad] 35 Bc 11.04N 17.56 E
Melfi [It.] 14 Jj 41.00N 15.39 E
Melfort 42 Hf 52.52N 104.36W
Melgaço 54 Hd 1.47S 50.44W
Melibocus 10 Eg 49.42N 8.40 E
Melilla [5] 31 Ge 35.19N 2.58W
Melincué, Laguna- 55 Bk 33.42S 61.28W
Melipilla 56 Fd 33.42S 71.13W
Melita 45 Fb 49.16N 101.00W
Meliti 15 Ei 40.50N 21.35 E
Melito di Porto Salvo 14 Jm 37.55N 15.47 E
Melito di Porto Salvo, Punta di- 14 Jm 37.57N 15.45 E
Melitopol 6 Jf 46.50N 35.22 E
Melk 14 Jb 48.13N 15.19 E
Mella 14 Ee 45.13N 10.13 E
Mellakou 13 Ni 35.15N 1.14 E
Mellanfryken 8 Ee 59.40N 13.15 E
Melle [Fr.] 11 Fh 46.13N 0.08W
Melle [Ger.] 12 Kb 52.12N 8.21 E
Mellen 45 Kc 46.20N 90.40W
Mellerud 7 Cg 58.42N 12.28 E
Mellish Reef 59 Lc 17.25S 155.50 E
Mellish Seamount (EN) 57 Ia 34.00N 178.15 E
Mellit 35 Dc 14.08N 25.33 E
Mělník 10 Kf 50.21N 14.30 E
Melnik 15 Gh 41.31N 23.24 E
Melo 53 Ki 32.22S 54.11W
Melo, Río- 55 De 21.25S 57.55W
Melrhir, Chott- 30 He 34.20N 6.20 E
Melrose 46 Id 45.38N 112.40W
Melsungen 10 Fe 51.08N 9.33 E
Meltaus 7 Fc 66.54N 25.22 E
Melton Constable 12 Db 52.51N 1.02 E
Melton Mowbray 9 Mi 52.46N 0.53W
Meluco 37 Fb 12.33S 39.37 E
Meluli 37 Fc 16.28S 39.44 E
Melun 11 If 48.32N 2.40 E
Melville 38 Ib 75.15N 110.00W
Melville 46 Na 50.55N 102.48W
Melville, Cape- 59 Ib 14.10S 144.30 E
Melville, Lake- 42 Lf 53.42N 59.30W
Melville Bay 59 Hb 12.05S 136.45 E
Melville Bay (EN)=Melville Bugt 67 Od 75.35N 62.30W
Melville Bugt=Melville Bay (EN) 67 Od 75.35N 62.30W
Melville Hills 42 Fc 69.20N 123.00W
Melville Island 57 Ef 11.40S 131.00 E
Melville Peninsula 38 Kc 68.00N 84.00W
Melville Sound 42 Gc 68.05N 107.30W
Melvin, Lough- 9 Eg 54.25N 8.10W
Mélykút 10 Pj 46.13N 19.23 E
Memaliaj 15 Ci 40.20N 19.58 E
Memambetsu 29a Db 43.55N 144.11 E
Memba, Baía de- 37 Gb 14.11S 40.35 E
Memberamo 26 Kg 1.28S 137.52 E
Memboro 26 Gh 9.22S 119.32 E
Mēmele 8 Kh 56.24N 24.10 E
Memmert 10 Cc 53.39N 6.53 E
Memmingen 10 Gi 47.59N 10.10 E
Mempawan 26 Ef 0.22N 108.58 E
Memphis 33 Fd 29.52N 31.15 E
Memphis [Mo.-U.S.] 45 Jf 40.28N 92.10W
Memphis [Tn.-U.S.] 39 Jf 35.08N 90.03W
Memphis [Tx.-U.S.] 45 Fi 34.44N 100.32W
Memrut Dağı 24 Jc 38.40N 42.12 E
Memuro 28 Qc 42.55N 143.03 E
Memuro-Dake 29a Cb 42.52N 142.45 E
Mena 35 Gd 5.30N 41.06 E
Mena [Ar.-U.S.] 45 Ii 34.35N 94.15W
Mena 19 De 51.33N 32.14 E
Menabe 30 Lk 20.00S 44.40 E
Menai Strait 9 Ih 53.12N 4.12W
Ménaka 31 Hg 15.55N 2.26 E
Mènam Khong=Mekong (EN) 21 Mh 10.15N 105.55 E
Menangalaku 26 Gh 9.36S 119.01 E
Menard 45 Gk 30.55N 99.47W
Menawashei 35 Dc 12.40N 25.01 E
Menčul, Gora- 10 Th 48.16N 23.49 E
Mendala, Puncak- 26 Lg 4.44S 140.20 E
Mendanau, Pulau- 26 Eg 2.51S 107.26 E
Mendanha 55 Kd 18.06S 43.30W
Mende 11 Jj 44.31N 3.30 E
Mendebo 30 Kh 6.50N 39.40 E
Mendelejevsk 7 Mi 55.57N 52.22 E
Menden (Sauerland) 10 De 51.26N 7.48 E
Mendes 13 Mi 35.39N 0.52 E
Méndez 48 Je 25.07N 98.34W
Mendi [Eth.] 35 Fd 9.48N 35.05 E
Mendi [Pap.N.Gui.] 60 Ci 6.10S 143.40 E
Mendig 12 Jd 50.22N 7.16 E
Mendip Hills 9 Kj 51.15N 2.40W
Mendocino 46 Dg 39.19N 123.48W
Mendocino, Cape- 38 Ge 40.25N 124.25W
Mendocino Fracture Zone (EN) 3 Lf 40.00N 145.00W
Mendota [Ca.-U.S.] 46 Eh 36.45N 120.23W
Mendota [Il.-U.S.] 45 Lf 41.33N 89.07W
Mendoza 53 Ji 32.54S 68.50W
Mendoza [2] 56 Gd 34.30S 68.30W
Mené, Landes du- 11 Df 48.15N 2.32W
Mene de Mauroa 49 Lh 10.43N 71.01W
Mene Grande 54 Db 9.49S 70.56W
Menemen 24 Bc 38.36N 27.04 E
Menen/Menin 11 Jd 50.48N 3.07 E
Meneng Point 64e Bb 0.33S 166.57 E
Meneses 55 Dj 30.53S 56.30W
Ménez Hom 11 Bf 48.13N 4.16W
Menfi 14 Gm 37.36N 12.58 E
Mengcheng 27 Ke 33.11N 116.30 E
Mengdingjie 27 Gg 23.31N 99.07 E
Menggala 26 Eg 4.28S 105.17 E
Mengíbar 13 Ig 37.58N 3.48W
Mengjin 28 Bg 34.50N 112.26 E
Mengla 27 Hg 21.30N 101.35 E
Menglangba → Lancang 27 Gg 22.37N 99.57 E
Menglian 27 Gg 22.20N 99.27 E
Mengoun Huizu Zizhixian 28 De 38.04N 117.06 E
Mengyin 28 Dg 35.42N 117.56 E
Mengzi 22 Mg 23.23N 103.34 E
Menihek Lakes 42 Kf 54.00N 66.30W
Menin/Menen 11 Jd 50.48N 3.07 E
Menindee 59 If 32.24S 142.26 E
Menindee Lake 59 If 22.00S 142.23 E
Meningie 59 Hg 35.42S 139.20 E
Menjapa, Gunung- 26 Gf 1.05N 116.05 E
Menno 45 He 43.14N 97.34W
Menoíkion Óros 15 Gh 41.11N 23.48 E
Menominee 44 Dc 45.07N 87.39W
Menongue 31 Ij 14.40S 17.39 E
Menor, Mar- 13 Lg 37.43N 0.48W
Menorca=Minorca (EN) 5 Gg 40.00N 4.00 E
Menor do Araguaia, Braço- ou Javaes 54 He 9.50S 50.12W
Mentana 14 Gh 42.02N 12.38 E
Mentasta Lake 40 Kd 62.55N 143.45W
Mentawai, Kepulauan-= Mentawai Islands (EN) 21 Lj 2.00S 99.30 E
Mentawai, Selat- 21 Lj 2.00S 99.30 E
Mentawai Islands (EN)= Mentawai, Kepulauan- 21 Lj 2.00S 99.30 E
Menton 11 Nk 43.47N 7.30 E
Mentougou 28 De 39.56N 116.02 E
Menyuan 27 Hd 37.30N 101.35 E
Menzelinsk 7 Mi 55.45N 53.09 E
Menzies 59 Ee 29.41S 121.02 E
Menzies, Mount- 66 Ff 73.30S 61.50 E
Meon 12 Ad 50.49N 1.15W
Meoqui 47 Cc 28.17N 105.29W
Meponda 37 Eb 13.25S 34.52 E
Meppel 11 Mb 52.42N 6.11 E
Meppen 10 Dd 52.41N 7.19 E
Meqele(EN)=Mekele 31 Kg 13.30N 39.28 E
Mê Qu 27 He 33.58N 102.10 E
Mequinensa, Pantà de-/ Mequinenza, Embalse de- 13 Lc 41.15N 0.02W
Mequinenza, Embalse de-/ Mequinensa, Pantà de- 13 Lc 41.15N 0.02W
Mera 14 Dd 46.11N 9.25 E
Merabello, Gulf of- (EN) = Merabéllou, Kólpos- 15 In 35.14N 25.47 E
Merabéllou, Kólpos- = Merabello, Gulf of- (EN) 15 In 35.14N 25.47 E
Merak 26 Eh 5.56S 106.00 E
Meråker 7 Ce 63.26N 11.45 E
Méralab 63b Db 14.27S 168.03 E
Meramangye, Lake- 59 Ge 28.25S 132.15 E
Meran / Merano 14 Fd 46.40N 11.09 E
Merano / Meran 14 Fd 46.40N 11.09 E
Meratus, Pegunungan- 26 Gg 2.45S 115.40 E
Merauke 58 Fe 8.28S 140.20 E
Mercadal 13 Qe 39.59N 4.05 E
Mercato Saraceno 14 Gg 43.57N 12.12 E
Merced 43 Cd 37.18N 120.29W
Mercedario, Cerro- 52 Ii 31.59S 70.14W
Mercedes [Arg.] 56 Id 34.39S 59.27W
Mercedes [Arg.] 56 Ic 29.12S 58.05W
Mercedes [Arg.] 53 Ji 33.40S 65.30W
Mercedes [Ur.] 53 Ki 33.16S 58.01W
Merchants Bay 42 Lc 67.10N 62.50W
Merchtem 12 Gd 50.58N 4.14 E
Mercury Islands 62 Fb 36.35S 175.50 E
Mercy, Cape - 42 Ld 64.56N 63.40W
Mercy Bay 42 Fb 74.15N 118.10W
Meredith, Cape- 56 Hh 52.12S 60.38W
Meredith, Lake- 45 Fi 35.36N 101.42W
Meredoua 32 Hd 25.20N 2.05 E
Merefa 19 Df 49.51N 36.00 E
Merelbeke 12 Fd 51.00N 3.45 E
Merenga 20 Kd 61.43N 156.05 E
Mergui 22 Lh 12.26N 98.36 E
Mergui Archipelago 21 Lh 12.00N 98.00 E
Méri 34 Hc 10.47N 14.06 E
Meriç 15 Jh 41.11N 26.25 E
Meriç 24 Bb 40.52N 26.12 E
Mérida [2] 54 Db 8.30N 71.10W
Mérida [Mex.] 39 Kg 20.58N 89.37W
Mérida [Sp.] 13 Ff 38.55N 6.20W
Mérida [Ven.] 53 Ie 8.36N 71.08W
Merida, Cordillera de- 52 Ie 8.40N 71.00W
Meridian 39 Kf 32.22N 88.42W
Mérig 63b Cb 14.19S 167.48 E
Mérignac 11 Fj 44.50N 0.38W
Merikarvia 7 Ef 61.51N 21.30 E
Merín, Laguna- 56 Jd 32.45S 52.50W
Meringur 59 If 34.24S 141.29 E
Merir Island 57 Ed 4.19N 132.19 E
Merizo 64c Bb 13.16N 144.40 E
Merke 18 Ic 42.52N 73.12 E
Merkem, Houthulst- 12 Ed 50.57N 2.51 E
Merkine/Merkiné 8 Kj 54.07N 24.20 E
Merkiné/Merkine 8 Kj 54.07N 24.20 E
Merkis/Merkys 7 Fi 54.10N 24.11 E
Merksem, Antwerpen- 12 Gc 51.15N 4.27 E
Merksplas 12 Gc 51.22N 4.52 E
Merkys/Merkis 7 Fi 54.10N 24.11 E
Meroe 35 Eb 16.56N 33.59 E
Meroe 35 Eb 16.05N 33.55 E
Merouane, Chott- 32 Ic 34.00N 6.02 E
Merredin 59 Df 31.29S 118.16 E
Merrick 9 If 55.08N 4.29W
Merrill 43 Jb 45.11N 89.41W
Merriman 45 Fe 42.55N 101.42W
Merritt 42 Ff 50.07N 120.47W
Merritt Island 43 Kf 28.21N 80.42W
Merritt Reservoir 45 Fe 42.35N 100.55W
Mersa Fatma 35 Gc 14.53N 40.19 E
Mersa Teklay 35 Fb 17.25N 38.45 E
Mersea Island 12 Cc 51.47N 0.57 E
Merseburg 10 He 51.22N 12.00 E
Mers el Kebir 13 Li 35.44N 0.43W
Mersey 9 Kh 53.25N 3.00W
Merseyside [3] 9 Kh 53.30N 3.00W
Mersin → İçel 23 Db 36.48N 34.38 E
Mersing 26 Df 2.26N 103.50 E
Mers-les-Bains 12 Dd 50.04N 1.23 E
Mērsrags/Mersrags 8 Jg 57.19N 23.01 E
Mersrags/Mērsrags 8 Jg 57.19N 23.01 E
Merta 25 Ec 26.39N 74.02 E
Merta Road 25 Ec 26.43N 73.55 E
Mertert 12 Ie 49.42N 6.29 E
Merthyr Tydfil 9 Jj 51.46N 3.23W
Merti 36 Gb 1.04N 38.40 E
Mértola 13 Eg 37.38N 7.40W
Mertule Maryam 35 Fc 10.50N 38.15 E
Mertvy Kultuk, Sor- 16 Rg 45.30N 53.40 E
Mertz Glacier 66 Je 67.40S 144.45 E
Meru 36 Gb 0.03N 37.39 E
Méru 11 Ie 49.14N 2.08 E
Meru, Mount- 36 Gc 3.14S 36.45 E
Merure 55 Fb 15.33S 53.05W
Merville 12 Ed 50.38N 2.38 E
Merzifon 23 Ea 40.53N 35.29 E
Merzig 10 Cg 49.27N 6.38 E
Meša 7 Li 55.34N 49.24 E
Mesa [Az.-U.S.] 39 Hf 33.25N 111.50W
Mesa [Co.-U.S.] 45 Bg 39.14N 108.08W
Mesabi Range 45 Jc 47.30N 92.50W
Mesagne 14 Lj 40.34N 17.48 E
Mescalero 45 Dj 33.09N 105.46W
Meščera=Moscow Basin 5 Kd 55.00N 40.30 E
Meschede 10 Ee 51.21N 8.17 E
Mescit Dağı 24 Ib 40.22N 41.11 E
Meščovsk 16 Ib 54.19N 35.18 E
Mesegon 64d Bb 7.09N 151.55 E
Mesfinto 35 Fc 13.28N 37.23 E
Me-Shima 28 Jh 32.01N 128.25 E
Meshkīnshahr 24 Lc 38.24N 47.40 E
Mesima 14 Jl 38.30N 15.55 E
Mesjagutovo 17 Ii 55.35N 58.20 E
Meskiana 14 Bo 35.38N 7.40 E
Meskiana, Oued- 14 Bo 35.48N 7.53 E
Meslo 35 Fd 6.22N 39.50 E
Mesnil-Val, Criel-sur-Mer- 12 Dd 50.03N 1.20 E
Mesola 14 Gf 44.55N 12.14 E
Mesolóngion 15 Ek 38.22N 21.26 E
Mesopotamia 52 Kh 30.00S 58.00W
Mesopotamia (EN) 23 Fc 34.00N 44.00 E
Mesoyéios Thálassa= Mediterranean Sea (EN) 5 Hh 35.00N 20.00 E
Mesquite [Nv.-U.S.] 46 Hh 36.48N 114.04W
Mesquite [Tx.-U.S.] 45 Hj 32.46N 96.36W
Mesra 13 Mi 35.50N 0.10 E
Messaad 32 Hc 34.10N 3.30 E
Messalo 30 Lj 11.40S 40.46 E
Messará, Órmos- 15 Ho 35.00N 24.40 E
Messina [It.] 6 Hh 38.11N 15.34 E
Messina [S.Afr.] 31 Kk 22.23S 30.00 E
Messina, Strait of- (EN) = Messina, Stretto di- 5 Hh 38.15N 15.35 E
Messina, Stretto di- = Messina, Strait of- (EN) 5 Hh 38.15N 15.35 E
Messíni 15 El 37.15N 21.50 E
Messíni 15 Fl 37.03N 22.01 E
Messiniakós Kólpos 15 Fm 36.45N 22.10 E
Messojaha 20 Cc 67.52N 77.27 E
Mesta 15 Hi 40.51N 24.44 E
Mestecăniş, Pasul- 15 Ib 47.28N 25.20 E
Mesters Vig 41 Jd 72.15N 24.20W
Mestia 16 Mh 43.03N 42.43 E
Mestre, Espigão- 54 If 12.30S 46.00W
Mestre, Venezia- 14 Ge 45.29N 12.14 E
Mesuji 26 Eg 4.08S 105.52 E
Meta [2] 54 Dc 3.30N 73.00W
Meta, Río- 52 Je 6.12N 67.28W
Meta Incognita Peninsula 38 Mc 62.40N 68.00W
Metairie 45 Kl 29.59N 90.09W
Metaliferi, Munţii- 15 Fc 46.10N 22.50 E
Metallifere, Colline- 14 Eg 43.10N 10.55 E
Metán 56 Hc 25.29S 64.57W
Metangula 37 Eb 12.43S 34.49 E
Metaponto 14 Kj 40.20N 16.50 E
Metauro 14 Hg 43.50N 13.03 E
Metautu 65c Ba 13.57S 171.54W
Meteghan 44 Nc 44.11N 66.10W
Metelen 12 Jb 52.09N 7.12 E
Metéora 15 Ej 39.43N 21.40 E
Meteor Seamount (EN) 30 Hm 48.00S 8.30 E
Meteor Trench (EN) 3 Do 55.00S 27.00 E
Méthana 15 Gl 37.35N 23.23 E
Methánon, Khersónisos- 15 Gl 37.36N 23.22 E
Methven 62 De 43.38S 171.38 E
Methwold 12 Cb 52.31N 0.33 E
Metković 14 Lg 43.03N 17.39 E
Metlakatla 40 Me 55.08N 131.35W
Metlika 14 Je 45.39N 15.19 E
Metlili Chaamba 32 Hc 32.16N 3.38 E
Metmárfag 32 Ed 26.26N 13.26W
Metohija 15 Dg 42.40N 20.27 E
Metro 26 Eh 5.05S 105.20 E
Metropolis 45 Lh 37.09N 88.44W
Métsovon 15 Ej 39.46N 21.11 E
Métsovon, Zigós- = Métsovon Pass (EN) 15 Ej 39.47N 21.15 E
Métsovon Pass (EN) = Métsovon, Zigós- 15 Ej 39.47N 21.15 E
Mettet 12 Gd 50.19N 4.40 E
Mettingen 12 Jb 52.19N 7.47 E
Mettlach 12 Ie 49.30N 6.36 E
Mettmann 12 Ic 51.15N 6.58 E
Metu 31 Kh 8.20N 35.38 E
Metuje 10 Lf 50.20N 15.55 E
Metz 6 Gf 49.08N 6.10 E
Metzervisse 12 Ie 49.19N 6.17 E
Meu 11 Ef 48.02N 1.47W
Meulaboh 26 Cf 4.09N 96.08 E
Meulan 12 De 49.01N 1.54 E
Meulebeke 12 Fd 50.57N 3.17 E
Meureudu 26 Ce 5.16N 96.16 E
Meurthe 11 Mf 48.47N 6.09 E
Meurthe-et-Moselle [3] 11 Mf 48.35N 6.10 E
Meuse [3] 11 Lf 49.00N 5.30 E
Meuse 5 Ge 51.49N 5.01 E
Meuse (EN)=Maas 5 Ge 51.49N 5.01 E
Meuse, Côtes de- 11 Le 49.10N 5.30 E
Meuzenti 35 Bb 18.14N 17.06 E
Mexia 45 Hk 31.41N 96.29W
Mexiana, Ilha 54 Ic 0.00 49.35W
Mexicali 39 Hf 32.40N 115.29W
Mexicana, Altiplanicie-= Mexico, Plateau of- (EN) 38 Ig 25.30N 104.00W
Mexican Hat 46 Kh 37.09N 109.52W
Mexicanos, Laguna de los- 48 Fc 28.09N 106.57W
Mexico 45 Kg 39.10N 91.53W
México [1] 39 Ig 23.00N 102.00W

Index Symbols

[1] Independent Nation
[2] State, Region
[3] District, County
[4] Municipality
[5] Colony, Dependency
Continent
Physical Region
Historical or Cultural Region
Mount, Mountain
Volcano
Hill
Mountains, Mountain Range
Hills, Escarpment
Plateau, Upland
Pass, Gap
Plain, Lowland
Delta
Salt Flat
Valley, Canyon
Crater, Cave
Karst Features
Depression
Polder
Desert, Dunes
Forest, Woods
Heath, Steppe
Oasis
Cape, Point
Coast, Beach
Cliff
Peninsula
Isthmus
Sandbank
Island
Atoll
Rock, Reef
Islands, Archipelago
Rocks, Reefs
Coral Reef
Well, Spring
Geyser
River, Stream
Waterfall Rapids
River Mouth, Estuary
Lake
Salt Lake
Intermittent Lake
Reservoir
Swamp, Pond
Canal
Glacier
Ice Shelf, Pack Ice
Ocean
Sea
Gulf, Bay
Strait, Fjord
Lagoon
Bank
Seamount
Tablemount
Ridge
Shelf
Basin
Escarpment, Sea Scarp
Fracture
Trench, Abyss
National Park, Reserve
Point of Interest
Recreation Site
Cave, Cavern
Historic Site
Ruins
Wall, Walls
Church, Abbey
Temple
Scientific Station
Airport
Port
Lighthouse
Mine
Tunnel
Dam, Bridge

Index Symbols

[1] Independent Nation	Historical or Cultural Region	Pass, Gap	Depression	Coast, Beach	Rock, Reef
[2] State, Region	Mount, Mountain	Plain, Lowland	Polder	Cliff	Islands, Archipelago
[3] District, County	Volcano	Delta	Desert, Dunes	Peninsula	Rocks, Reefs
[4] Municipality	Hill	Salt Flat	Forest, Woods	Isthmus	Coral Reef
[5] Colony, Dependency	Mountains, Mountain Range	Valley, Canyon	Heath, Steppe	Sandbank	Well, Spring
■ Continent	Hills, Escarpment	Crater, Cave	Oasis	Island	Geyser
[⊠] Physical Region	Plateau, Upland	Karst Features	Cape, Point	Atoll	River, Stream

Water Basins	Canal	Lagoon	Escarpment, Sea Scarp	Historic Site	Port
River Mouth, Estuary	Glacier	Bank	Ruins	Mine	Lighthouse
Lake	Ice Shelf, Pack Ice	Fracture	Wall, Walls		Tunnel
Salt Lake	Ocean	Seamount	Church, Abbey		Dam, Bridge
Intermittent Lake	Tablemount	Trench, Abyss	National Park, Reserve		
Sea	Ridge	Point of Interest	Temple		
Gulf, Bay	Shelf	Recreation Site	Scientific Station		
Swamp, Pond	Basin	Cave, Cavern	Airport		

Name	Page	Grid	Lat.	Long.
Mitsamiouli	37	Gb	11.23S	43.18 E
Mitsinjo	37	Hc	16.00S	45.52 E
Mitsio, Nosy-	37	Hb	12.54S	48.36 E
Mitsiwa=Massawa (EN)	31	Kg	15.37N	39.39 E
Mitsiwa Channel	35	Fb	15.30N	40.00 E
Mitsuishi	29a	Cb	42.15N	142.33 E
Mitsukaido	29	Fc	36.01N	139.59 E
Mitsuke	29	Fc	37.32N	138.56 E
Mitsushima	29	Ad	34.16N	129.20 E
Mittelfranken	10	Gg	49.20N	10.40 E
Mittelland	14	Bd	46.50N	7.05 E
Mittellandkanal	5	He	52.16N	11.41 E
Mittelmark	10	Jd	52.20N	13.20 E
Mittenwald	10	Hi	47.27N	11.15 E
Mittersheim	12	If	48.52N	6.56 E
Mittersill	14	Gc	47.16N	12.29 E
Mittweida	10	If	50.59N	12.59 E
Mitú	53	Ie	1.08N	70.03W
Mitumba, Monts-=Mitumba Range (EN)	30	Ji	6.00S	29.00 E
Mitumba Range (EN)= Mitumba, Monts-	30	Ji	6.00S	29.00 E
Mituva	8	Jj	55.00N	22.45 E
Mitwaba	36	Ed	8.38S	27.20 E
Mitzic	36	Bb	0.47N	11.34 E
Miura	29	Fd	35.08N	139.37 E
Miura-Hantō	29	Fd	35.15N	139.40 E
Mixco Viejo	49	Bf	14.52N	90.40W
Mixian	28	Bg	34.31N	113.22 E
Mixteco, Río-	48	Jh	18.11N	98.30W
Miya-Gawa	29	Ed	34.32N	136.42 E
Miyagi Ken	28	Pe	38.30N	140.50 E
Miyagusuku-Jima	29b	Ab	26.22N	127.59 E
Miyāh, Wādī al- [Eg.]	24	Ej	25.00N	33.23 E
Miyāh, Wādī al- [Sau. Ar.]	24	Gi	26.06N	36.31 E
Miyāh, Wādī al- [Syr.]	24	He	34.44N	39.57 E
Miyake-Jima	27	Oe	34.05N	139.30 E
Miyako	27	Pd	39.38N	141.57 E
Miyako-Jima	27	Mg	24.45N	125.20 E
Miyakonojō	28	Ki	31.44N	131.04 E
Miyako-Rettō	27	Lg	24.25N	125.00 E
Miyako-Wan	29	Hb	39.40N	142.00 E
Miyama	29	Dd	35.17N	135.34 E
Miyanojō	29	Bf	31.54N	130.27 E
Miyanoura-Dake	28	Ki	30.20N	130.29 E
Miyata	29	Be	33.45N	130.45 E
Miyazaki	27	Ne	31.54N	131.26 E
Miyazaki Ken	28	Kh	32.05N	131.20 E
Miyazu	28	Mg	35.32N	135.11 E
Miyazuka-Yama	29	Fd	34.24N	139.16 E
Miyazu-Wan	29	Dd	35.35N	135.13 E
Miyoshi	28	Lg	34.48N	132.51 E
Miyun	27	Kc	40.22N	116.53 E
Miyun Shuiku	28	Dd	40.31N	116.58 E
Mizan Teferi	35	Fd	6.53N	35.28 E
Mizdah	33	Bc	31.26N	12.59 E
Mizen Head/Carn Ui Néid	5	Fe	51.27N	9.49W
Mizil	15	Je	45.01N	26.27 E
Mizoram	25	Id	23.00N	93.00 E
Mizque	54	Eg	17.56S	65.19W
Mizuho	29	Cd	34.50N	132.29 E
Mizuho	66	Ef	70.43S	40.20 E
Mizunami	29	Ed	35.22N	137.15 E
Mizusawa	28	Pe	39.08N	141.08 E
Mjadel	8	Lj	54.54N	27.03 E
Mjakiševo	8	Mh	56.30N	28.54 E
Mjakit	20	Kd	61.23N	152.10 E
Mjällom	8	Ha	62.59N	18.26 E
Mjaundža	20	Jd	63.02N	147.13 E
Mjölby	7	Dg	58.19N	15.08 E
Mjøndalen	8	De	59.45N	10.01 E
Mjorn	8	Eg	57.54N	12.25 E
Mjøsa	5	Hc	60.40N	11.00 E
Mkoani	36	Gd	5.22S	39.39 E
Mkokotoni	36	Gd	5.52S	39.15 E
Mkushi Bona	36	Ee	13.37S	29.23 E
Mkushi River	36	Fe	13.33S	29.40 E
Mkuze	37	Ee	27.10S	32.00 E
Mladá Boleslav	10	Kf	50.21N	14.54 E
Mladenovac	15	De	44.26N	20.42 E
Mlava	15	Ee	44.45N	21.14 E
Mława	10	Qc	53.06N	20.23 E
Mljet	14	Lh	42.45N	17.30 E
Mljetski kanal	14	Lh	42.48N	17.35 E
Mmadinare	37	Dd	21.53S	27.45 E
Mnichovo Hradiště	10	Kf	50.32N	14.59 E
Mnogoveršinny	20	If	53.55N	139.50 E
Moa	49	Jc	20.40N	74.56W
Moa	34	Cd	6.59N	11.36W
Moa, Pulau-	26	Ih	8.10S	127.56 E
Moab	43	Fd	38.35N	109.33W
Moabi	36	Bc	2.24S	10.59 E
Moala	63d	Bc	18.36S	179.53 E
Moamba	37	Ee	25.36S	32.15 E
Moanda [Gabon]	36	Bc	1.34S	13.11 E
Moanda [Zaire]	36	Bd	5.56S	12.21 E
Moatize	37	Ec	16.10S	33.46 E
Moba	31	Ji	7.03S	29.47 E
Mobara	29	Gd	35.25N	140.17 E
Mobārakeh	24	Nf	32.20N	51.30 E
Mobaye	31	Jh	4.19N	21.11 E
Mobayi-Mbongo	36	Db	4.18N	21.11 E
Mobeka	36	Cb	1.53N	19.46 E
Moberly	43	Id	39.25N	92.26W
Mobile	39	Kf	30.42N	88.05W
Mobile Bay	43	Je	30.25N	88.00W
Mobridge	43	Gb	45.32N	100.26W
Mobuto Sese Seko, Lac-= Albert, Lake- (EN)	30	Kh	1.40N	31.00 E
Moca	49	Ld	19.24N	70.31W
Moçambique= Mozambique (EN)	31	Kj	18.15S	35.00 E
Moçambique= Mozambique (EN)	31	Lk	15.03S	40.45 E
Moçambique, Canal de-= Mozambique Channel (EN)	30	Lk	20.00S	43.00 E
Moçâmedes → Namibe	36	Bf	15.20S	12.30 E
Moçâmedes → Namibe	31	Ij	15.12S	12.10 E
Mocapra, Río-	50	Ci	7.56N	66.46W
Mocha, Isla-	56	Fe	38.22S	73.56W
Moc Hoa	25	Lf	10.46N	105.56 E
Mochudi	37	Dd	24.23S	26.08 E
Mocímboa da Praia	31	Lj	11.20S	40.21 E
Möckeln	8	Fh	56.40N	14.10 E
Mockfjärd	8	Fd	60.30N	14.58 E
Môco, Serra-	30	Ij	12.28S	15.10 E
Mocoa	54	Cc	1.09N	76.38W
Mococa	55	Ie	21.28S	47.01W
Mocovi	55	Ci	28.24S	59.42W
Moctezuma [Mex.]	47	Cc	29.48N	109.42W
Moctezuma [Mex.]	47	If	22.45N	101.05W
Moctezuma [Mex.]	48	Fb	30.12N	106.26W
Moctezuma, Río [Mex.]	48	Ec	29.09N	109.40W
Moctezuma, Río- [Mex.]	48	Jg	21.59N	98.34W
Mocuba	31	Kj	16.51S	36.56 E
Mocubúri	37	Fb	14.39S	38.54 E
Močurica	15	Jg	42.31N	26.32 E
Modane	11	Mi	45.12N	6.40 E
Modderrivier	37	Ce	29.02S	24.37 E
Modena [It.]	14	Ef	44.40N	10.55 E
Modena [Ut.-U.S.]	46	Ih	37.49N	113.55W
Moder	11	Of	48.49N	8.06 E
Modesto	43	Cd	37.39N	120.59W
Modica	14	In	36.52N	14.46 E
Modjamboli	36	Db	2.28N	22.06 E
Modjigo	34	Hb	17.09N	13.12 E
Mödling	14	Kb	48.05N	16.28 E
Modriča	14	Mf	44.58N	18.18 E
Modum	8	Ce	59.55N	10.00 E
Moe	59	Jg	38.10S	146.15 E
Moelv	7	Cf	60.56N	10.42 E
Moen	64d	Bb	7.26N	151.52 E
Moengo	54	Hb	5.37N	54.24W
Moer-jo-Daro	25	Dc	27.19N	68.07 E
Moenkopi Wash	46	Ji	35.54N	111.26W
Moerbeke	12	Fc	51.10N	3.56 E
Moers	10	Ce	51.27N	6.39 E
Moeskroen/Mouscron	11	Jd	50.44N	3.13 E
Moffat	9	Jf	55.20N	3.27W
Moga	36	Ec	2.21S	26.49 E
Mogadishu (EN)= Muqdisho	31	Lh	2.03N	45.22 E
Mogadouro	13	Fc	41.20N	6.43W
Mogadouro, Serra do-	13	Ec	41.19N	6.40W
Mogāl	24	Nd	36.35N	50.35 E
Mogalakwena	37	Dd	22.27S	28.55 E
Mogami	29	Gb	38.45N	140.30 E
Mogami-Gawa	28	Oe	38.54N	139.50 E
Mogami Trench (EN)	29	Fb	39.00N	139.00 E
Mogaung	25	Jc	25.18N	96.56 E
Mogho	35	Ge	4.49N	40.19 E
Mogielnica	10	Qe	51.42N	20.43 E
Mogilev	6	Je	53.56N	30.18 E
Mogilev-Podolski	16	Ee	48.27N	27.48 E
Mogilevskaja Oblast	19	De	53.45N	30.30 E
Mogilno	10	Nd	52.40N	17.58 E
Mogincual	37	Gc	15.34S	40.24 E
Mogoča	22	Nd	53.44N	119.44 E
Mogočin	20	De	57.43N	83.40 E
Mogogh	35	Ed	8.26N	31.19 E
Mogojto	20	Gf	54.25N	110.27 E
Mogojtuj	20	Gf	51.15N	114.58 E
Mogok	25	Jd	22.55N	96.30 E
Mogollon Rim	43	Ee	34.20N	111.00W
Mogotes, Punta-	55	Dn	38.06S	57.33W
Mogotón, Pico-	49	Dg	13.45N	86.23W
Mogreïn	31	Ff	25.13N	11.34W
Mogroum	35	Bc	11.06N	15.25 E
Moguer	13	Fg	37.16N	6.50W
Mogzon	20	Gf	51.42N	111.59 E
Mohács	10	Ok	45.59N	18.42 E
Mohaka	62	Gc	39.07S	177.12 E
Mohaka	62	Gc	39.07S	177.12 E
Mohales Hoek	37	Df	30.15S	27.25 E
Mohall	45	Fb	48.46N	101.31W
Mohammadābād	24	Pg	31.47N	54.27 E
Mohammadia	13	Mi	35.35N	0.04 E
Mohammedia	32	Fc	33.42N	7.24W
Mohanganj	25	Id	24.54N	90.59 E
Mchang-ni	28	If	36.46N	126.08 E
Mohave, Lake-	43	Ed	35.25N	114.38W
Mohawk Mountains	46	Ij	32.25N	113.25W
Mohe	22	Od	53.27N	122.18 E
Moheda	8	Fh	57.00N	14.34 E
Mohéli → Mwali	30	Lj	12.15S	43.45 E
Moher, Cliffs of-/Aillte an Mhothair	9	Di	52.58N	9.27W
Mohican, Cape-	40	Fd	60.12N	167.28W
Mohinora	38	Ig	26.06N	107.04W
Möhnesee	12	Kc	51.29N	8.05 E
Mohns Ridge (EN)	5	Ga	73.00N	5.00 E
Moholm	8	Ff	58.37N	14.02 E
Mohon, Charleville-Mézières-	12	Ge	49.46N	4.43 E
Mohon Peak	46	Ii	34.57N	113.15W
Mohoro	36	Gd	8.08S	39.10 E
Mohotani, Ile-	61	Na	9.59S	138.49W
Mohovaja	20	Kf	53.01N	158.38 E
Moi	8	Bf	58.28N	6.32 E
Moikovac	15	Cg	42.58N	19.35 E
Moimenta da Beira	13	Ed	40.59N	7.37W
Moindou	63b	Be	21.42S	165.41 E
Moinești	15	Jc	46.28N	26.29 E
Moirai	15	Hn	35.03N	24.52 E
Mo i Rana	6	Hb	66.18N	14.08 E
Mõisaküla/Myjzakjula	7	Fg	58.07N	25.10 E
Moisés Ville	55	Bj	30.43S	61.29W
Moisie	47	Kf	50.12N	66.06W
Moisie	42	Kf	50.11N	66.06W
Moissac	11	Hj	44.06N	1.05 E
Moissala	35	Bd	8.21N	17.46 E
Moitaco	50	Dh	8.01N	61.21W
Möja	8	He	59.25N	18.55 E
Mojácar	13	Kg	37.08N	1.51W
Mojada, Sierra-	48	Hd	27.15N	103.45W
Mojana, Caño-	49	Ji	9.02N	74.46W
Mojave	43	Dd	35.03N	118.10W
Mojave Desert	38	Hf	35.00N	117.00W
Mojiguaçu, Rio-	55	He	20.53S	48.10W
Moji Mirim	55	If	22.26S	46.57W
Mojjero	20	Fc	68.44N	103.30 E
Mojo	35	Fd	8.36N	39.09 E
Mojo	35	Gd	8.00N	41.50 E
Mojos, Llanos de-	52	Jg	15.00S	65.00W
Moju, Rio-	54	Id	1.40S	48.25W
Mojynty	19	Hf	47.10N	73.18 E
Mokambo	36	Ee	12.25S	28.21 E
Mokapu Peninsula	65a	Db	21.26N	157.45W
Mokau	62	Fc	38.42S	174.35 E
Mokau	61	Dg	38.41S	174.37 E
Mokhotlong	37	De	29.17S	29.05 E
Mokil Atoll	57	Gd	6.40N	159.47 E
Moklakan	20	Gf	54.48N	118.56 E
Möklinta	8	Gd	60.05N	16.32 E
Mokochu, Khao-	25	Je	15.56N	99.06 E
Mokohinau Islands	62	Fa	35.55S	175.05 E
Mokolo	34	Hc	10.45N	13.48 E
Mokp'o	22	Of	34.47N	126.23 E
Mokra Gora	15	Dg	42.50N	20.25 E
Mokrany	10	Ue	51.48N	24.23 E
Mokrin	15	Dd	45.56N	20.25 E
Mokša	5	Ke	54.44N	41.53 E
Mokwa	34	Gd	9.17N	5.03 E
Mol	11	Lc	51.11N	5.07 E
Mola di Bari	14	Li	41.04N	17.05 E
Molango	48	Jg	20.47N	98.43W
Moláoi	15	Fm	36.48N	22.51 E
Molara	14	Dj	40.50N	9.45 E
Molas, Punta-	48	Pg	20.35N	86.44W
Molat	14	If	44.13N	14.50 E
Molatón	13	Kf	38.59N	1.24W
Moldau (EN)=Vltava	5	He	50.21N	14.30 E
Moldava nad Bodvou	10	Qh	48.37N	21.00 E
Moldavia (EN) = Moldova	15	Jc	46.30N	27.00 E
Moldavia (EN)=Moldova	5	If	46.30N	27.00 E
Moldavia (EN) = Moldova	19	Cf	47.00N	29.00 E
Moldavskaja Sovetskaja Socialističeskaja Respublika → Moldova	19	Cf	47.00N	29.00 E
Moldavskaja SSR/ Respublika Sovetike Sočialiste Moldovenjaske → Moldova	19	Cf	47.00N	29.00 E
Moldavskaja SSR → Moldova	19	Cf	47.00N	29.00 E
Molde	6	Gc	62.44N	7.11 E
Moldefjorden	8	Bb	62.45N	7.05 E
Moldova	19	Cf	47.00N	29.00 E
Moldova	15	Jc	46.54N	26.58 E
Moldova = Moldavia (EN)	15	Jc	46.30N	27.00 E
Moldova = Moldavia (EN)	5	If	46.30N	27.00 E
Moldova Nouă	15	Ee	44.44N	21.41 E
Moldoveanu, Vîrful-	5	If	45.36N	24.44 E
Moldovița	15	Ib	47.41N	25.32 E
Mole	12	Bc	51.24N	0.20W
Moléne, Ile de-	11	Bf	48.24N	4.58W
Molens van Kinderdijk	12	Gc	51.52N	4.40 E
Molepolole	31	Jk	24.25S	25.30 E
Môle Saint-Nicolas	49	Kd	19.47N	73.22W
Moletai/Moletaj	8	Ki	55.13N	25.36 E
Moletaj/Moletai	8	Ki	55.13N	25.36 E
Molfetta	14	Ki	41.12N	16.36 E
Molihong Shan	28	Hc	42.11N	124.43 E
Molina, Parameras de-	13	Jd	40.55N	2.01W
Molina de Aragón	13	Kd	40.51N	1.53W
Molina de Segura	13	Kf	38.03N	1.12W
Moline	45	Kf	41.30N	90.31W
Moliniere Point	51p	Bb	12.05N	61.45W
Molise	14	Ii	41.40N	14.30 E
Molkābād	24	Oe	34.32N	52.35 E
Molkom	8	Ee	59.36N	13.43 E
Möll	14	Hd	46.50N	13.26 E
Moll	55	Cl	35.04S	59.39W
Mollafeneri	15	Mi	40.54N	29.30 E
Mölle	8	Eh	56.17N	12.29 E
Mollendo	53	Ig	17.02S	72.01W
Molliens-Dreuil	12	Ee	49.52N	2.01 E
Mölln	10	Gc	53.38N	10.41 E
Möllösund	8	Df	58.04N	11.28 E
Mölndal	7	Ch	57.39N	12.01 E
Mölnlycke	8	Ef	57.39N	12.09 E
Moločansk	16	If	47.10N	35.36 E
Moločny, Liman-	16	Ig	46.30N	35.20 E
Molócuè	37	Fc	17.03S	38.52 E
Molodečno	19	Ce	54.19N	26.53 E
Molodežnaja	66	Ee	67.40S	45.51 E
Molodi	8	Mf	58.00N	28.52 E
Molodogvardejskoje	19	He	54.07N	70.50 E
Mologa	5	Jd	58.50N	37.11 E
Molokai Island	57	Lb	21.08N	157.00W
Moloma	7	Lg	58.20N	48.28 E
Molong	59	Jf	33.06S	148.52 E
Molopo	30	Jk	28.31S	20.13 E
Moloundou	34	Ie	2.02N	15.13 E
Molteno	37	Df	31.24S	26.22 E
Molu, Pulau-	26	Jh	6.45S	131.33 E
Moluccas (EN)=Maluku, Kepulauan-	57	De	2.00S	128.00 E
Molucca Sea (EN)=Maluku, Laut-	21	Oj	0.05S	125.00 E
Molygino	20	Ee	58.11N	94.45 E
Moma	20	Jc	66.20N	143.06 E
Moma	37	Fc	16.44S	39.14 E
Mombaça	54	Ke	5.45S	39.28W
Mombasa	31	Ki	4.03S	39.40 E
Mombo	36	Gc	4.53S	38.17 E
Momboyo	36	Cc	0.16S	19.00 E
Mombuca, Serra da-	55	Fd	18.15S	52.26W
Momčilgrad	15	Ih	41.32N	25.25 E
Mömling	12	Le	49.50N	9.09 E
Momotombo, Volcán-	49	Dg	12.26N	86.33W
Mompono	36	Db	0.04N	21.48 E
Mompós	54	Db	9.14N	74.27W
Momski Hrebet	20	Jc	66.00N	145.00 E
Mon	25	Je	17.22N	97.20 E
Møn	7	Ci	55.00N	12.20 E
Mona, Canal de la-=Mona Passage (EN)	38	Mh	18.30N	67.45W
Mona, Isla-	47	Ke	18.05N	67.54W
Mona, Punta-	49	Fi	9.38N	82.37W
Monach Islands	9	Fd	57.32N	7.40W
Monaco	6	Gg	43.42N	7.23 E
Monadhliath Mountains	9	Id	57.15N	4.10W
Monagas	54	Fb	9.20N	63.00W
Monaghan/Muineachán	9	Gg	54.10N	7.00W
Monaghan/Muineachán	9	Gg	54.15N	6.58W
Monahans	45	Ek	31.36N	102.54W
Mona Passage (EN)=Mona, Canal de la-	38	Mh	18.30N	67.45W
Monapo	37	Gb	14.55S	40.18 E
Monarch Mountain	42	Ef	51.54N	125.54W
Monashee Mountains	42	Ff	51.00N	118.43W
Monastyrščina	16	Gb	54.19N	31.48 E
Monatélé	34	He	4.16N	11.12 E
Monbetsu [Jap.]	28	Qc	42.28N	142.07 E
Monbetsu [Jap.]	27	Pc	44.21N	143.22 E
Monbetsu-Shokotsu	29a	Ca	44.23N	143.16 E
Moncalieri	14	Be	45.00N	7.41 E
Moncalvo	14	Ce	45.03N	8.16 E
Monção [Braz.]	54	Id	3.30S	45.15W
Monção [Port.]	13	Db	42.05N	8.29W
Moncayo	13	Kc	41.46N	1.50W
Moncayo, Sierra del-	13	Kc	41.45N	1.50W
Mončegorsk	19	Db	67.56N	32.58 E
Mönchengladbach	10	Ce	51.12N	6.26 E
Mönchengladbach-Rheydt	12	Ic	51.10N	6.27 E
Mönchengladbach-Wickrath	12	Ic	51.08N	6.25 E
Mönchgut	10	Jb	54.20N	13.40 E
Monchique	13	Dg	37.19N	8.33W
Monchique, Serra de-	13	Dg	37.19N	8.36W
Monclova	39	Ig	26.54N	101.25W
Moncton	39	Me	46.06N	64.07W
Mondai	55	Fh	27.05S	53.25W
Mondego	13	Dd	40.09N	8.52W
Mondego, Cabo-	13	Dd	40.11N	8.55W
Mondeville	12	Be	49.10N	0.19W
Mondjoko	36	Dc	1.41S	21.12 E
Mondo	35	Bc	13.43N	15.32 E
Mondoñedo	13	Ea	43.26N	7.22W
Mondorf-les-Bains/Bad Mondorf	12	Ie	49.30N	6.17 E
Mondoubleau	11	Gg	47.59N	0.54 E
Mondovì	14	Bf	44.23N	7.49 E
Mondragone	14	Hi	41.07N	13.53 E
Mondy	20	Ff	51.40N	100.59 E
Monemvasia	15	Gm	36.41N	23.03 E
Monessen	44	He	40.09N	79.53W
Monett	45	Jh	36.55N	93.55W
Monfalcone	14	He	45.49N	13.32 E
Monferrato	14	Cf	44.55N	8.05 E
Monforte	13	Ee	39.03N	7.26W
Monforte de Lemos	13	Eb	42.31N	7.30W
Monga	36	Db	4.12N	22.49 E
Mongala	36	Cb	1.53N	19.46 E
Mongalla	35	Ed	5.12N	31.46 E
Mongbwalu	36	Fb	1.57N	30.02 E
Mong Cai	25	Ld	21.32N	107.58 E
Monger, Lake-	59	De	29.15S	117.05 E
Mongga	63a	Cb	7.57S	156.59 E
Monggolküre/Zhaosu	27	Dc	43.10N	81.07 E
Monghyr → Munger	25	Hc	25.23N	86.28 E
Monginevro, Colle del-	11	Mj	44.56N	6.44 E
Mongo	31	Ig	12.11N	18.42 E
Mongo	34	Cd	9.34N	12.11W
Mongol Altajn Nuruu → Mongolski Altaj= Mongolian Altai (EN)	21	Le	46.30N	93.00 E
Mongol Ard-Uls=Mongolia (EN)	22	Me	47.00N	104.00 E
Mongolia (EN)=Mongol Ard-Uls	22	Me	47.00N	104.00 E
Mongolian Altai (EN)= Mongol Altajn Nuruu → Mongolski Altaj	21	Le	46.30N	93.00 E
Mongolian Altai (EN)= Mongolski Altaj (Mongol Altajn Nuruu)	21	Le	46.30N	93.00 E
Mongolski Altaj (Mongol Altajn Nuruu)=Mongolian Altai (EN)	21	Le	46.30N	93.00 E
Mongonu	34	Hc	12.41N	13.36 E
Mongororo	35	Cc	12.01N	22.28 E
Mongoumba	35	Be	3.38N	18.36 E
Möng Pan	25	Jd	20.19N	98.22 E
Mongrove, Punta-	48	Hi	17.56N	102.11W
Mongu	31	Jj	15.17S	23.08 E
Monguel	32	Ef	16.25N	13.08W
Möng Yai	25	Jd	22.25N	98.02 E
Monheim	12	Ic	51.05N	6.53 E
Mönichkirchen	14	Kc	47.30N	16.02 E
Mon Idée, Auvillers-lès-Forges-	12	Ge	49.52N	4.21 E
Monigotes	55	Bj	30.30S	61.39W
Moní Hosíou Louká	15	Fk	38.24N	22.49 E
Monistrol-sur-Loire	11	Ki	45.17N	4.10 E
Monito, Isla-	51a	Ab	18.09N	67.56W
Monitor Peak	46	Gg	38.50N	116.32W
Monitor Range	46	Gg	38.45N	116.40W
Monjolos	55	Jd	18.18S	44.05W
Monkayo	26	Ie	7.50N	126.00 E
Monkey Bay	36	Fe	14.05S	34.55 E
Monkey Point	49	Fg	11.36N	83.39W
Monkey River	49	Ce	16.22N	88.29W
Mońki	10	Sc	53.24N	22.49 E
Monkoto	36	Dc	1.38S	20.39 E
Monmouth [Il.-U.S.]	45	Kf	40.55N	90.39W
Monmouth	9	Kj	51.45N	3.00W
Monmouth [Or.-U.S.]	46	Dd	44.51N	123.14W
Monmouth [Wales-U.K.]	9	Kj	51.50N	2.43W
Monmouth Mountain	46	Da	51.00N	123.47W
Mönne	10	De	51.28N	7.30 E
Monnikendam	12	Hb	52.27N	5.02 E
Monnow	9	Kj	51.48N	2.42W
Mono	63a	Bb	7.20S	155.35 E
Mono	34	Fd	6.45N	1.50 E
Monobe-Gawa	29	Ce	33.32N	133.42 E
Mono Lake	43	Dd	38.00N	119.00W
Monólithos	15	Km	36.07N	27.45 E
Monopoli	14	Lj	40.57N	17.18 E
Monor	10	Pi	47.21N	19.27 E
Monou	35	Cb	16.24N	22.11 E
Monóvar	13	Lf	38.26N	0.50W
Monowai, Lake-	62	Bf	45.55S	167.25 E
Monreal	12	Jd	50.18N	7.10 E
Monreal del Campo	13	Kd	40.47N	1.21W
Monreale	14	Hl	38.05N	13.17 E
Monroe [Ga.-U.S.]	44	Fi	33.47N	83.43W
Monroe [La.-U.S.]	39	Jf	32.33N	92.07W
Monroe [Mi.-U.S.]	44	Fe	41.55N	83.24W
Monroe [N.C.-U.S.]	44	Gh	34.59N	80.33W
Monroe [Or.-U.S.]	46	Dd	44.19N	123.18W
Monroe [Wi.-U.S.]	45	Le	42.36N	89.38W
Monroe, Lake-	44	Df	39.05N	86.25W
Monroe City	45	Kg	39.39N	91.44W
Monroeville	44	Dj	31.31N	87.20W
Monrovia	31	Fh	6.19N	10.48W
Mons/Bergen	11	Jd	50.27N	3.56 E
Monsanto	13	Ed	40.02N	7.07W
Monschau	10	Cf	50.33N	6.15 E
Monselice	14	Fe	45.14N	11.45 E
Monserrate, Isla-	48	De	25.41N	111.05W
Monsheim	12	Ke	49.38N	8.12 E
Møns Klint	8	Ej	54.58N	12.33 E
Mönsterås	7	Dh	57.02N	16.26 E
Montabaur	10	Df	50.26N	7.50 E
Montagna Grande	14	Gm	37.56N	12.44 E
Montagne	11	Jh	46.10N	3.40 E
Montagu	66	Ad	58.25S	26.20W
Montague	40	Je	60.00N	147.30W
Montague, Isla-	48	Bb	31.45N	114.48W
Montaigu	11	Eh	46.59N	1.19W
Montalbán	13	Ld	40.50N	0.48W
Montalbano Ionico	14	Kj	40.17N	16.34 E
Montalcino	14	Fg	43.03N	11.29 E
Montalegre	13	Ec	41.49N	7.48W
Montalto di Castro	14	Fh	42.21N	11.37 E
Montalto Uffugo	14	Kk	39.24N	16.09 E
Montalvânia	55	Jb	14.28S	44.32W
Montana	43	Eb	47.00N	110.00W
Montana	14	Bd	46.18N	7.30 E
Montánchez	13	Fe	39.13N	6.09W
Montánchez, Sierra de-	13	Ge	39.15N	5.55W
Montargis	11	Ig	48.00N	2.45 E
Montataire	12	Ee	49.16N	2.26 E
Montauban [Fr.]	11	Hj	44.01N	1.21 E
Montauban [Fr.]	11	Df	48.12N	2.03W
Montauk Point	44	Le	41.04N	71.52W
Montbard	11	Kg	47.37N	4.20 E
Montbéliard	11	Mg	47.31N	6.48 E
Montblanc	13	Nc	41.22N	1.10 E
Mont Blanc	5	Gf	45.50N	6.52 E
Montbrison	11	Ki	45.36N	4.03 E
Montceau-les-Mines	11	Kh	46.40N	4.22 E
Mont Cenis, Col du-	5	Gf	45.15N	6.54 E
Montchanin	11	Kh	46.45N	4.27 E
Mont Darwin	37	Ec	16.46S	31.35 E
Mont-de-Marsan	11	Fk	43.53N	0.30W
Montdidier	11	Ie	49.39N	2.34 E
Mont Dore	11	Ii	45.34N	2.49 E
Mont-Dore	63b	Cf	22.17S	166.35 E
Monte, Laguna del-	55	Am	37.00S	62.28W
Monteagudo	54	Fg	19.49S	63.59W
Monte Alban	39	Jh	17.02N	96.45W
Monte Alegre	54	Hd	2.01S	54.04W
Monte Alegre, Rio-	55	Gc	17.16S	50.41W
Monte Alegre de Goiás	55	Ia	13.14S	47.10W
Montealegre del Castillo	13	Kf	38.47N	1.19W
Monte Alegre de Minas	55	Hd	18.52S	48.52W
Monte Azul	54	Jg	15.09S	42.53W
Montebello	44	Jc	45.39N	74.56W
Monte Bello Islands	59	Dd	20.25S	115.30 E
Monte Carlo	11	Nk	43.44N	7.25 E
Montecarlo	55	Eh	26.34S	54.47W
Monte Carmelo	55	Id	18.43S	47.29W
Monte Caseros	56	Id	30.15S	57.39W
Montecatini Terme	14	Eg	43.23N	10.45 E
Montecchio Maggiore	14	Fe	45.30N	11.24 E
Monte Comán	56	Gd	34.36S	67.54W
Montecristi	49	Ld	19.52N	71.39W
Montecristo	14	Eh	42.20N	10.20 E
Monte Cristo	55	Bb	14.43S	61.14W
Monte Ermoso	55	Bn	38.55S	61.33W
Monte Escobedo	48	Hf	22.18N	103.35W
Montefalco	14	Gh	42.52N	12.39 E
Montefeltro	14	Gg	43.55N	12.15 E
Montefiascone	14	Gh	42.32N	12.02 E
Montefrio	13	Hg	37.19N	4.01W
Montego Bay	39	Lh	18.30N	77.55W
Monteiro	54	Ke	7.53S	37.07W
Montelíbano	49	Ji	8.02N	75.29W
Montélimar	11	Kj	44.34N	4.45 E
Monte Lindo, Arroyo-	55	Cg	25.28S	59.25W
Monte Lindo, Río-	56	Ib	23.56S	57.12W
Monte Lindo Chico, Riacho-	55	Dg	25.53S	57.53W

Index Symbols

1 Independent Nation
2 State, Region
3 District, County
4 Municipality
5 Colony, Dependency
Continent
Physical Region
Historical or Cultural Region
Mount, Mountain
Volcano
Hill
Mountains, Mountain Range
Hills, Escarpment
Plateau, Upland
Pass, Gap
Plain, Lowland
Delta
Salt Flat
Valley, Canyon
Crater, Cave
Karst Features
Depression
Polder
Desert, Dunes
Forest, Woods
Heath, Steppe
Oasis
Cape, Point
Coast, Beach
Cliff
Peninsula
Isthmus
Sandbank
Island
Atoll
Rock, Reef
Islands, Archipelago
Rocks, Reefs
Coral Reef
Well, Spring
Geyser
River, Stream
Waterfall Rapids
River Mouth, Estuary
Lake
Salt Lake
Intermittent Lake
Reservoir
Swamp, Pond
Canal
Glacier
Ice Shelf, Pack Ice
Ocean
Sea
Gulf, Bay
Strait, Fjord
Lagoon
Bank
Seamount
Tablemount
Ridge
Shelf
Basin
Escarpment, Sea Scarp
Fracture
Trench, Abyss
National Park, Reserve
Point of Interest
Recreation Site
Cave, Cavern
Historic Site
Ruins
Wall, Walls
Church, Abbey
Temple
Scientific Station
Airport
Port
Lighthouse
Mine
Tunnel
Dam, Bridge

Monte Lindo Grande, Riacho- 55 Cg 25.45S 58.06W
Montello [Nv.-U.S.] 46 Hf 41.16N 114.12W
Montello [Wi.-U.S.] 45 Le 43.48N 89.20W
Montemorelos 47 Ec 25.12N 99.49W
Montemor-o-Novo 13 Df 38.39N 8.13W
Montemor-o-Velho 13 Dd 40.10N 8.41W
Montemuro, Serra de- 13 Dc 40.58N 8.01W
Montenegro 56 Jc 29.42S 51.28W
Montenegro (EN) = Crna Gora [2] 15 Cg 42.30N 19.18 E
Montenegro (EN)=Crna Gora 15 Cg 42.30N 19.18 E
Monte Plata 49 Md 18.48N 69.47W
Montepuez 37 Gb 12.32S 40.27 E
Montepuez 37 Fb 13.07S 39.00 E
Montepulciano 14 Fg 43.05N 11.47 E
Monte Quemado 56 Hc 25.48S 62.52W
Monte Real 13 De 39.51N 8.52W
Montereale, Passo di- 14 Hh 42.31N 13.13 E
Montereau-Faut-Yonne 11 If 48.23N 2.57 E
Monterey 43 Cd 36.37N 121.55W
Monterey Bay 43 Cd 36.45N 121.55W
Montería 53 Ie 8.46N 75.53W
Montero 54 Fg 17.20S 63.15W
Monteros 56 Gc 27.10S 65.30W
Monterotondo 14 Gh 42.03N 12.37 E
Monterrey 39 Ig 25.40N 100.19W
Montesano 46 Dc 46.59N 123.36W
Monte San Savino 14 Fg 43.20N 11.43 E
Monte Sant'Angelo 14 Ji 41.42N 15.57 E
Monte Santu, Capo di- 14 Dj 45.05N 9.44 E
Montes Claros 53 Lg 16.43S 43.52W
Montes Claros de Goiás 55 Gb 15.54S 51.13W
Montesilvano 14 Ih 42.31N 14.09 E
Montevarchi 14 Fg 43.31N 11.34 E
Montevideo [2] 55 Dl 34.50S 56.10W
Montevideo [Mn.-U.S.] 45 Id 44.57N 95.43W
Montevideo [Ur.] 53 Ki 34.53S 56.11W
Monte Vista 45 Ch 37.35N 106.09W
Montfaucon 12 He 49.17N 5.08 E
Montfort-l'Amaury 12 Df 48.47N 1.49 E
Montfort-sur-Risle 12 Ce 49.18N 0.40 E
Montgenèvre, Col de- 11 Mj 44.56N 6.44 E
Montgomery 39 Kf 32.23N 86.18W
Montgomery Pass 46 Fh 38.00N 118.20W
Montguyon 11 Fi 45.13N 0.11W
Monthermé 12 Ge 49.53N 4.44 E
Monthey 14 Ad 46.15N 6.56 E
Monthois 12 Ge 49.19N 4.43 E
Monticello [Ar.-U.S.] 45 Kj 33.38N 91.47W
Monticello [Fl.-U.S.] 44 Fj 30.33N 83.52W
Monticello [Ia.-U.S.] 45 Ke 42.15N 91.12W
Monticello [In.-U.S.] 44 De 40.45N 86.46W
Monticello [Ky.-U.S.] 44 Eg 36.50N 84.51W
Monticello [N.Y.-U.S.] 44 Je 41.39N 74.41W
Monticello [Ut.-U.S.] 43 Fd 37.52N 109.21W
Montiel 13 Jf 38.42N 2.52W
Montiel, Campo de- 13 Jf 38.46N 2.44W
Montiel, Cuchilla de- 55 Cj 31.05S 59.10W
Montignac 11 Hi 45.04N 1.10 E
Montigny-le-Roi 11 Lf 48.00N 5.30 E
Montigny-les-Metz 11 Me 49.06N 6.09 E
Montigny-le-Tilleul 12 Gd 50.23N 4.22 E
Montijo [Pan.] 49 Gj 7.59N 81.03W
Montijo [Port.] 13 Df 38.42N 8.58W
Montijo [Sp.] 13 Ff 38.55N 6.37W
Montijo, Golfo de- 49 Gj 7.40N 81.07W
Montilla 13 Hg 37.35N 4.38W
Montividiu 55 Gc 17.24S 51.14W
Montivilliers 11 Ge 49.33N 0.12 E
Mont Joli 42 Kg 48.35N 68.11W
Mont-Laurier 42 Jg 46.33N 75.30W
Mont Louis 44 Oa 49.15N 65.43W
Mont-Louis 11 Il 42.31N 2.07 E
Montluçon 11 Ih 46.20N 2.36 E
Montmagny 42 Kg 46.59N 70.33W
Montmarault 11 Ih 46.19N 2.57 E
Montmédy 11 Le 49.31N 5.22 E
Montmirail 11 Jf 48.52N 3.32 E
Montmorency 12 Ef 49.00N 2.20 E
Montmorillon 11 Gh 46.26N 0.52 E
Montmort-Lucy 12 Ff 48.55N 3.49 E
Monto 59 Kd 24.52S 151.07 E
Montoire-sur-le-Loir 11 Gg 47.45N 0.52 E
Montone 14 Gf 44.24N 12.14 E
Montoro 13 Hf 38.01N 4.23W
Montpelier [Id.-U.S.] 43 Ec 42.19N 111.18W
Montpelier [Vt.-U.S.] 39 Le 44.16N 72.35W
Montpellier 6 Gg 43.36N 3.53 E
Montpon-Ménestérol 11 Gi 45.01N 0.10 E
Montréal 39 Le 45.31N 73.34W
Montreal Lake 42 Gf 54.20N 105.40W
Montreal River 44 Hb 47.08N 79.27W
Montréjeau 11 Gk 43.05N 0.35 E
Montreuil [Fr.] 11 Hd 50.28N 1.46 E
Montreuil [Fr.] 12 Ef 48.52N 2.26 E
Montreuil-l'Argillé 12 Cf 48.56N 0.29 E
Montreux 14 Ad 46.26N 6.55 E
Montrose [Co.-U.S.] 43 Fd 38.29N 107.53W
Montrose [Scot.-U.K.] 9 Ke 56.43N 2.29W
Monts, Pointe des- 44 Na 49.19N 67.23W
Mont-Saint-Aignan 12 De 49.28N 1.05 E
Mont-Saint-Michel, Baie du- 11 Ef 48.40N 1.40W
Montsalvy 11 Ij 44.42N 2.30 E
Montsant, Serra del-/Montsant, Sierra de- 13 Mc 41.17N 0.50 E
Montsant, Sierra de-/Montsant, Serra del- 13 Mc 41.17N 0.50 E
Montsec, Serra del-/Montsech, Sierra del- 13 Mb 42.02N 0.50 E
Montsech, Sierra del-/Montsec, Serra del- 13 Mb 42.02N 0.50 E
Montseny/Pallars, Montsent de- 13 Nb 42.29N 1.02 E
Montseny, Sierra de- 13 Oc 41.48N 2.24 E
Montserrado [3] 34 Cd 6.35N 10.35W
Montserrat [5] 39 Mh 16.45N 62.12W
Montserrat, Monasterio de- 13 Nc 41.35N 1.49 E
Montserrat, Monasterio de-/Montserrat, Monèstir de- 13 Nc 41.35N 1.49 E
Montserrat, Monèstir de- 13 Nc 41.35N 1.49 E
Montserrat, Monèstir de-/Montserrat, Monasterio de- 13 Nc 41.35N 1.49 E
Montuosa, Isla- 49 Fj 7.28N 82.14W
Montville 12 De 49.33N 1.07 E
Monument Peak 46 He 42.07N 114.14W
Monument Valley 46 Jh 36.50N 110.20W
Monveda 36 Db 2.57N 21.27 E
Monviso 5 Gg 44.40N 7.07 E
Monywa 25 Jd 22.07N 95.08 E
Monza 14 De 45.35N 9.16 E
Monze 36 Ef 16.16S 27.29 E
Monzen 29 Ec 37.17N 136.46 E
Monzón 13 Mc 41.55N 0.12 E
Mo'oka 29 Fc 36.27N 139.59 E
Moonbeam 44 Fa 49.25N 82.11W
Moonie 59 Ke 27.40S 150.19 E
Moonie River 59 Je 29.19S 148.43 E
Moonta 59 Hf 34.04S 137.35 E
Moora 58 Ch 30.39S 116.00 E
Moorcroft 46 Md 44.16N 104.57W
Moore 45 Hi 35.20N 97.29W
Moore, Lake- 57 Cg 29.50S 117.35 E
Moorea, Ile- 57 Mf 17.32S 149.50W
Moore's Island 44 Il 26.18N 77.33W
Moorhead 43 Hb 46.53N 96.45W
Moormerland 12 Ja 53.18N 7.26 E
Moormerland-Neermoor 12 Ja 53.18N 7.26 E
Moorreesburg 37 Bf 33.09S 18.40 E
Moosburg an der Isar 10 Hh 48.28N 11.56 E
Moose 38 Kd 50.48N 81.18W
Moosehead Lake 43 Nb 45.40N 69.40W
Moose Jaw 39 Id 50.23N 105.32W
Moose Jaw River 46 Ma 50.34N 105.17W
Moose Lake 45 Jc 46.25N 92.45W
Mooselookmeguntic Lake 44 Lc 44.53N 70.48W
Moose Mountain 45 Eb 49.45N 102.37W
Moose Mountain Creek 45 Eb 49.12N 102.10W
Moosomin 42 Hf 50.09N 101.40W
Moosonee 39 Kd 51.17N 80.39W
Mopeia 37 Fc 17.59S 35.43 E
Mopelia, Atoll- → Maupihaa Atoll 57 Lf 16.50S 153.55W
Mopti 31 Gg 14.30N 4.12W
Mopti [3] 34 Ec 14.40N 4.15W
Moqokorei 35 He 4.04N 46.08 E
Moquegua [2] 54 Dg 16.50S 70.55W
Moquegua 53 Dg 17.12S 70.56W
Mór 10 Oi 47.23N 18.12 E
Mor, Glen- 9 Id 57.10N 4.40W
Mora [Cam.] 34 Hc 11.03N 14.09 E
Mora [Port.] 13 Df 38.56N 8.10W
Mora [Sp.] 13 Ie 39.41N 3.46W
Mora [Swe.] 7 Df 61.00N 14.33 E
Morača 15 Cg 42.16N 19.09 E
Morača, Manastir- 15 Cg 42.46N 19.24 E
Morādābād 22 Jg 28.50N 78.47 E
Morada Nova de Minas 55 Jd 18.25S 45.22W
Móra d'Ebre/Mora de Ebro 13 Mc 41.05N 0.38 E
Mora de Ebro/Móra d'Ebre 13 Mc 41.05N 0.38 E
Mora de Rubielos 13 Ld 40.15N 0.45W
Morafenobe 37 Gc 17.49S 44.55 E
Morąg 10 Pc 53.56N 19.56 E
Mórahalom 10 Pj 46.13N 19.53 E
Moraleda, Canal- 56 Ff 44.30S 73.30W
Moraleja 13 Fd 40.04N 6.39W
Morales [Col.] 49 Ki 8.17N 73.52W
Morales [Guat.] 49 Cf 15.29N 88.49W
Morales, Laguna- 48 Kf 23.35N 97.45W
Moramanga 37 Hc 18.57S 48.11 E
Moran 46 Je 43.50N 110.28W
Morane Atoll 57 Ng 23.10S 137.07W
Morangas, Ribeirão- 55 Fd 19.39S 52.19W
Morant Bay 49 Ie 17.53N 76.25W
Morant Cays 47 Ie 17.24N 75.59W
Morant Point 49 Ie 17.55N 76.10W
Morar, Loch- 9 He 56.58N 5.45W
Morarano 37 Hc 17.46S 48.10 E
Mora River 45 Di 35.44N 104.23W
Moraska, Góra- 10 Md 52.30N 16.52 E
Morat/Murten 14 Bd 46.56N 7.08 E
Morata, Puerto de- 13 Kc 41.29N 1.31W
Moratalla 13 Kf 38.12N 1.53W
Moratuwa 25 Fg 6.46N 79.53 E
Morava 5 Hf 48.10N 16.59 E
Morava=Moravia (EN) 5 Hf 49.30N 17.00 E
Morava=Moravia (EN) 10 Mg 49.30N 17.00 E
Moravia (EN)=Morava 5 Hf 49.30N 17.00 E
Moravia (EN)=Morava 10 Mg 49.30N 17.00 E
Moravian Gate (EN)=Moravská Brána 5 Hf 49.33N 17.42 E
Moravian Upland (EN)=Českomoravská Vrchovina 5 Hf 49.20N 15.30 E
Moravica 15 Df 43.51N 20.05 E
Moravská Brána=Moravian Gate(EN) 5 Hf 49.33N 17.42 E
Moravské Budějovice 10 Lg 49.03N 15.49 E
Morawa 59 De 29.13S 116.00 E
Morawhanna 54 Gb 8.16N 59.45W
Moray Firth 9 Fd 57.50N 3.30W
Morbach 12 Je 49.49N 7.07 E
Morbihan [3] 11 Dg 47.55N 2.50W
Morbihan 11 Dg 47.35N 2.48W
Morbylånga 7 Dh 56.31N 16.23 E
Morcenx 11 Fj 44.02N 0.55W
Mordāb 24 Md 37.26N 49.25 E
Mordaga 27 La 51.14N 120.43 E
Morden 42 Hg 49.11N 98.05W
Mordovo 16 Lc 52.05N 40.46 E
Mordovskaja respublika 19 Ee 54.20N 44.30 E
Möre 8 Fh 56.25N 15.55 E
More, Ben- 9 Ie 56.23N 4.31W
Morea 37 Bd 22.41S 15.54 E
More Assynt, Ben- 9 Ic 53.07N 4.51W
Moreau River 43 Gb 45.18N 100.43W
Morecambe 9 Kg 54.04N 2.53W
Morecambe Bay 9 Kg 54.07N 3.00W
Moree 58 Fg 29.28S 149.51 E
Morehead [Ky.-U.S.] 44 Ff 38.11N 83.25W
Morehead [Pap.N.Gui.] 60 Ci 8.50S 141.57 E
Morehead City 39 Lf 34.43N 76.43W
Moreiz, Gora- 19 Gb 69.30N 62.05 E
Moreju 17 Ib 68.20N 59.45 E
Morelia 39 Ih 19.42N 101.07W
Morella 13 Ld 40.37N 0.06W
Morelos 48 Ic 28.25N 100.53W
Morelos [2] 47 Ee 18.45N 99.00W
Morena, Sierra- 5 Fh 38.00N 5.00W
Moreni 15 Ie 44.59N 25.39 E
Møre og Romsdal [2] 7 Be 62.40N 7.50 E
Moresby 42 Ef 52.45N 131.50W
Moreton Bay 59 Ke 27.20S 153.15 E
Moreton Island 59 Ke 27.10S 153.25 E
Moret-sur-Loing 11 If 48.22N 2.49 E
Moreuil 11 Ie 49.46N 2.29 E
Morez 11 Mh 46.31N 6.02 E
Morezu 15 Hd 45.09N 24.01 E
Mörfelden 12 Ke 49.59N 8.34 E
Morgan City 45 Kl 29.42N 91.12W
Morganfield 44 Dg 37.41N 87.55W
Morganton 44 Gh 35.45N 81.41W
Morgantown [Ky.-U.S.] 44 Dg 37.14N 86.41W
Morgantown [W.V.-U.S.] 44 Hf 39.38N 79.57W
Morges 14 Ad 46.31N 6.30 E
Morghāb 23 Jb 38.18N 61.12 E
Morhange 11 Mf 48.55N 6.38 E
Mori [China] 27 Fc 43.49N 90.11 E
Mori [Jap.] 28 Pc 42.06N 140.35 E
Moriarty 45 Ci 34.59N 106.03W
Morichal Largo, Río- 50 Eh 9.27N 62.25W
Moriguchi 29 Dd 34.44N 135.34 E
Morin Dawa (Nirji) 27 Lb 48.30N 124.28 E
Morioka 22 Qf 39.42N 141.09 E
Moriyoshi 29 Ga 40.07N 140.22 E
Moriyoshi-Yama 29 Gb 39.59N 140.33 E
Morjärv 7 Fc 66.04N 22.43 E
Morki 7 Lh 56.28N 49.00 E
Morko 8 Gf 59.00N 17.40 E
Morkoka 20 Gc 65.03N 115.40 E
Mørkøv 8 Di 55.40N 11.32 E
Morlaix 11 Cf 48.35N 3.50W
Morlanwelz 12 Gd 50.27N 4.14 E
Mörlunda 8 Fg 57.19N 15.51 E
Mormanno 14 Jk 39.53N 15.59 E
Morne-à-l'Eau 50 Fd 16.21N 61.31W
Morne Diablotin 47 Le 15.30N 61.24W
Mornington, Isla- 56 Eg 49.45S 75.23W
Mornington Island 59 Hc 16.35S 139.24 E
Moro 46 Ed 45.29N 120.44W
Morobe 58 Fe 7.45S 147.37 E
Morocco (EN)=Al Maghrib [1] 31 Ge 32.00N 5.50W
Morogoro 31 Ki 6.49S 37.40 E
Morogoro [3] 36 Gd 8.20S 37.00 E
Moro Gulf 26 He 6.51N 123.00 E
Moroleón 48 Ig 20.08N 101.12W
Morombe 31 Lk 21.44S 43.23 E
Morón [Arg.] 55 Cl 34.39S 58.37W
Morón [Cuba] 47 Id 22.06N 78.38W
Morón [Ven.] 54 Ea 10.29N 68.11W
Morona, Río- 54 Cd 4.45S 77.04W
Morondava 31 Lk 20.15S 44.17 E
Morón de la Frontera 13 Gg 37.08N 5.27W
Morones, Sierra- 48 Hg 21.55N 103.05W
Moroni 31 Lj 11.41S 43.16 E
Moron Us He 21 Lf 34.42N 94.50 E
Morotai, Pulau- 57 Dd 2.20N 128.25 E
Moroto 31 Kh 2.32N 34.39 E
Moroviţa 15 Ed 45.16N 21.16 E
Morozov 15 Ig 42.30N 25.10 E
Morozovsk 19 Ef 48.20N 41.50 E
Morpeth 9 Lf 55.10N 1.41W
Morphou → Güzelyurt 24 Ee 35.12N 32.59 E
Morrilton 45 Ji 35.09N 92.45W
Morrinhos 54 Ig 17.44S 49.07W
Morrinsville 62 Fb 37.39S 175.32 E
Morris [Il.-U.S.] 45 Lf 41.22N 88.26W
Morris [Man.-Can.] 42 Hg 49.21N 97.22W
Morris [Mn.-U.S.] 45 Id 45.35N 95.55W
Morris, Mount- 59 Ge 26.09S 131.04 E
Morrisburg 44 Jc 44.54N 75.11W
Morris Jesup, Kap- 67 Me 83.45N 35.50W
Morrison Dennis Cays 49 Ff 14.28N 82.53W
Morristown 44 Fg 36.13N 83.18W
Morrito 49 Eh 11.37N 85.05W
Morro, Punta del- 48 Kh 19.51N 96.27W
Morro Bay 43 Cd 35.22N 120.51W
Morro do Chapéu 54 Jf 11.33S 41.09W
Morrosquillo, Golfo de- 49 Ji 9.35N 75.40W
Morro Vermelho, Serra do- 55 Jc 17.45S 45.20W
Mörrum 8 Fh 56.11N 14.45 E
Morrumbala 37 Fc 17.20S 35.35 E
Morrumbene 37 Fd 23.39S 35.20 E
Mörrumsån 8 Fh 56.09N 14.44 E
Mors 8 Ch 56.50N 8.45 E
Moršansk 19 Ee 53.26N 41.49 E
Morsbach 12 Jd 50.52N 7.45 E
Morsberg 12 Ke 49.43N 8.54 E
Mörsil 7 Ce 63.19N 13.38 E
Mörskom/Myrskylä 8 Kd 60.40N 25.51 E
Morsott 14 Co 35.40N 8.01 E
Mortagne 11 Mf 48.33N 6.27 E
Mortagne-au-Perche 11 Gf 48.31N 0.33 E
Mortagne-sur-Sèvre 11 Fg 47.00N 0.57W
Mortain 11 Ff 48.39N 0.56W
Mortara 14 Ce 45.15N 8.44 E
Mortcha 30 Jg 16.00N 21.10 E
Morteau 11 Mg 47.04N 6.37 E
Morteaux-Couliboeuf 12 Bf 48.56N 0.04W
Morteros 56 Hd 30.42S 62.00W
Mortes, Rio das- 55 Je 21.09S 44.53W
Mortesoro 35 Ec 10.12N 34.09 E
Mortlock Islands 57 Gd 5.27N 153.40 E
Morton 46 Dc 46.33N 122.17W
Mortsel 12 Gc 51.10N 4.28 E
Morumbi 55 Ef 23.46S 54.06W
Morvan 11 Jg 47.05N 4.00 E
Morven 59 Je 26.25S 147.07 E
Morvern 9 He 56.35N 5.50W
Morvi 25 Ed 22.49N 70.50 E
Morwell 58 Fh 38.14S 146.24 E
Morzine 11 Mh 46.11N 6.43 E
Moržovec, Ostrov- 7 Kc 66.45N 42.35 E
Moša 7 Je 62.25N 39.48 E
Mosbach 10 Fg 49.21N 9.09 E
Mosby 8 Bf 58.14N 7.54 E
Moščny, Ostrov- 7 Gg 60.00N 27.50 E
Mosconi 55 Bl 35.44S 60.34W
Moscos Islands 25 Jf 14.00N 97.45 E
Moscow [Id.-U.S.] 43 Db 46.44N 116.59W
Moscow (EN)=Moskva 5 Jd 55.08N 38.50 E
Moscow (EN) = Moskva 6 Jd 55.45N 37.35 E
Moscow Basin (EN) = Meščera 5 Kd 55.00N 40.30 E
Moscow Canal (EN)= Moskvy, kanal imeni- 5 Jd 56.43N 37.08 E
Moscow Upland (EN)= Moskovskaja Vozvyšennost 5 Jd 56.30N 37.30 E
Mosel=Moselle (EN) 5 Ge 50.22N 7.36 E
Moselberge 12 Ie 49.57N 6.56 E
Moselle [3] 11 Me 49.00N 6.30 E
Moselle 5 Ge 50.22N 7.36 E
Moselle (EN)=Mosel 5 Ge 50.22N 7.36 E
Moses Lake 43 Db 47.08N 119.17W
Mosgiel 61 Di 45.53S 170.22 E
Moshi 31 Ki 3.21S 37.20 E
Mosina 10 Md 52.16N 16.51 E
Mosjøen 7 Cd 65.50N 13.12 E
Moskalvo 20 Jf 53.39N 142.37 E
Moskenesøy 7 Cc 67.59N 13.00 E
Moskovskaja Oblast [3] 19 Dd 55.45N 37.45 E
Moskovskaja Vozvyšennost =Moscow Upland (EN) 5 Jd 56.30N 37.30 E
Moskovski 18 Gf 37.40N 69.39 E
Moskva Moscow (EN) 6 Jd 55.45N 37.35 E
Moskva 18 Ee 38.27N 64.24 E
Moskva=Moscow (EN) 5 Jd 55.08N 38.50 E
Moskva, Pik- 18 He 38.55N 71.52 E
Moskvy, kanal imeni-= Moscow Canal (EN) 5 Jd 56.43N 37.08 E
Moslavačka Gora 14 Ke 45.38N 16.42 E
Moso 63b Dc 17.32S 168.15 E
Mosomane 37 Dd 24.01S 26.19 E
Mosoni-Duna 10 Ni 47.44N 17.47 E
Mosonmagyaróvár 10 Ni 47.52N 17.17 E
Mosor 14 Kg 43.30N 16.40 E
Mosquero 45 Ei 35.47N 103.58W
Mosquito, Baie - 42 Jd 60.40N 78.00W
Mosquito Coast (EN)= Mosquitos, Costa de- 38 Kh 13.00N 83.45W
Mosquito, Riacho- 55 Cf 22.12S 57.57W
Mosquitos, Costa de-= Mosquito Coast (EN) 38 Kh 13.00N 83.45W
Mosquitos, Golfo de los- 38 Ki 9.00N 81.20W
Moss 6 Hd 59.26N 10.42 E
Mossaka 36 Cc 1.13S 16.48 E
Mossâmedes 55 Gc 16.07S 50.11W
Mossbank 46 Mb 49.55N 105.59W
Mossburn 61 Ci 45.41S 168.15 E
Mosselbaai 31 Jl 34.11S 22.08 E
Mossendjo 36 Bc 2.57S 12.44 E
Mossman 58 Ff 16.28S 145.22 E
Mossø 8 Ch 56.05N 9.50 E
Mossoró 53 Mf 5.11S 37.20W
Moss Point 45 Lk 30.25N 88.29W
Mossuril 37 Gb 14.58S 40.40 E
Most 10 Jf 50.32N 13.39 E
Mostaganem [3] 32 Hb 35.40N 0.30 E
Mostaganem 31 He 35.56N 0.05 E
Mostar 14 Lg 43.21N 17.49 E
Mostardas 55 Gj 31.06S 50.57W
Mesting, Kap- 41 Hf 63.45N 41.00W
Mostiska 16 Ce 49.48N 23.09 E
Mostiştea 15 Je 44.15N 26.54 E
Most na Soci 14 Hd 46.09N 13.45 E
Mostovskoj 16 Lg 44.22N 40.48 E
Mosty 19 Ce 53.27N 24.33 E
Mosul (EN)=Al Mawşil 22 Gf 36.20N 43.08 E
Møsvatn 7 Bg 59.50N 8.05 E
Mota 63b Ca 13.40S 167.42 E
Mota 35 Fc 11.05N 37.53 E
Motaba 36 Cb 2.03N 18.03 E
Motacusito 55 Bc 17.35S 61.31W
Mota del Marques 13 Gc 41.38N 5.10W
Motagua 38 Kh 15.44N 88.14W
Motajica 14 Le 45.04N 17.40 E
Motala 7 Dg 58.33N 15.03 E
Motala ström 8 Gf 58.38N 16.10 E
Motatán 49 Li 9.24N 70.36W
Motatán, Río- 49 Li 9.32N 71.02W
Motegi 29 Gc 36.32N 140.10 E
Motehuala 47 Dd 23.39N 100.39W
Mothe 63d Cc 18.40S 178.30W
Motherwell 9 Jf 55.48N 4.00W
Motihāri 25 Gc 26.39N 84.55 E
Motilla del Palancar 13 Ke 39.34N 1.53W
Motiti Island 62 Gb 37.40S 176.25 E
Motlav 63b Ca 13.40S 167.40 E
Motobu 29b Ab 26.40N 127.55 E
Motol 10 Vd 52.17N 25.40 E
Motovski Zaliv 7 Hb 69.30N 32.30 E
Motoyoshi 29 Gb 38.48N 141.31 E
Motozintla de Mendoza 48 Mj 15.22N 92.14W
Motril 13 Ih 36.45N 3.31W
Motru 15 Ge 44.33N 23.27 E
Motru 15 Fe 44.48N 23.00 E
Motsuta-Misaki 29a Ab 42.36N 139.49 E
Mott 45 Ec 46.22N 102.20W
Motteville 12 Ce 49.38N 0.51 E
Motu 62 Gb 37.51S 177.35 E
Motueka 62 Ed 41.07S 173.01 E
Motuhora Island 62 Gb 37.50S 177.00 E
Motu-Iti 65d Ac 27.11S 109.27W
Motu-Iti → Tupai Atoll 61 Kc 16.17S 151.50W
Motul 47 Gd 21.06N 89.17W
Motu-Nui 65d Ac 27.12S 109.28W
Motu One Atoll 57 Lf 15.48S 154.33W
Motupae 64n Ac 10.27S 161.02W
Motupena Point 63a Bb 6.32S 155.09 E
Moturiki 63d Bb 17.46S 178.45 E
Motutapu 64p Cb 21.14S 159.43W
Motu Tautara 65d Ab 27.05S 109.26W
Motutunga Atoll 57 Mf 17.06S 144.22W
Moubray Bay 66 Kf 72.11S 170.15 E
Mouchard 11 Lh 46.58N 5.48 E
Mouchoir Bank (EN) 47 Jd 20.57N 70.42W
Mouchoir Passage 49 Lc 21.10N 71.00W
Moudjéria 32 Ef 17.52N 12.20W
Mouila 31 Ii 1.52S 11.01 E
Mouka 35 Cd 7.16N 21.52 E
Moul 34 Hb 15.03N 13.18 E
Mould Bay 39 Hb 76.15N 119.30W
Moule 50 Fd 16.20N 61.21W
Moule à Chique, Cap- 51k Bb 13.43N 60.57W
Moulins 11 Jh 46.34N 3.20 E
Moulmein → Mawlamyine 22 Le 16.30N 97.38 E
Moulouya 30 Ge 35.06N 2.20W
Moult 12 Be 49.07N 0.10W
Moultrie 44 Fj 31.11N 83.47W
Moultrie, Lake- 44 Gi 33.20N 80.05W
Mouly, Pointe de- 63b Ce 20.43S 166.23 E
Moúnda, Ákra- 15 Dk 38.03N 20.47 E
Moundou 31 Ih 8.34N 16.05 E
Moundsville 44 Gf 39.54N 80.44W
Mo'unga'one 65b Ba 19.33S 174.29W
Moungoudou 36 Bc 2.40S 12.41 E
Mountainair 45 Ci 34.31N 106.15W
Mountain Grove 45 Jh 37.08N 92.16W
Mountain Home [Ar.-U.S.] 45 Jh 36.21N 92.23W
Mountain Home [Id.-U.S.] 43 Dc 43.08N 115.41W
Mountain Nile (EN)=Jabal, Baḩr al- 30 Kh 9.30N 30.30 E
Mountain Village 40 Gd 62.05N 163.44W
Mount Airy 44 Gg 36.31N 80.37W
Mount Barker 59 Df 34.38S 117.40 E
Mount Carmel 45 Mf 38.25N 87.46W
Mount Desert Island 44 Mc 44.20N 68.20W
Mount Douglas 58 Fg 21.30S 146.50 E
Mount Eba 59 Hf 30.12S 135.40 E
Mount Forest 44 Gd 43.59N 80.44W
Mount Frere 37 Df 31.00S 28.58 E
Mount Gambier 58 Fh 37.50S 140.46 E
Mount Hagen 60 Ci 5.52S 144.13 E
Mount Hope 59 Hf 34.07S 135.23 E
Mount Isa 58 Eg 20.44S 139.30 E
Mountlake Terrace 46 Dc 47.47N 122.18W
Mount Lebanon 44 Ge 40.23N 80.03W
Mount Lofty Ranges 59 Hg 35.15S 138.50 E
Mount Magnet 58 Cg 28.04S 117.49 E
Mount Maunganui 61 Eg 37.38S 176.12 E
Mount Morgan 59 Kd 23.39S 150.23 E
Mountnorris Bay 59 Gb 11.20S 132.45 E
Mount Peck 46 Ha 50.10N 115.02W
Mount Pleasant [Ia.-U.S.] 45 Kf 40.58N 91.33W
Mount Pleasant [Mi.-U.S.] 44 Ed 43.35N 84.47W
Mount Pleasant [S.C.-U.S.] 44 Hi 32.47N 79.52W
Mount Pleasant [Tx.-U.S.] 45 Ij 33.09N 94.58W
Mount Pleasant [Ut.-U.S.] 46 Jg 39.33N 111.27W
Mount's Bay 9 Hk 50.03N 5.25W
Mount Somers 62 De 43.42S 171.25 E
Mount Sterling [Il.-U.S.] 45 Kg 39.59N 90.45W
Mount Sterling [Ky.-U.S.] 44 Ff 38.04N 83.56W
Mount Vancouver 42 Dd 60.20N 139.41W
Mount Vernon [Al.-U.S.] 44 Cj 31.05N 88.01W
Mount Vernon [Austl.] 59 Dd 24.13S 118.14 E
Mount Vernon [Il.-U.S.] 43 Jd 38.19N 88.55W
Mount Vernon [In.-U.S.] 44 Dg 37.56N 87.54W
Mount Vernon [Ky.-U.S.] 44 Eg 37.21N 84.20W
Mount Vernon [Oh.-U.S.] 44 Fe 40.23N 82.30W
Mount Vernon [Wa.-U.S.] 43 Cb 48.25N 122.20W
Moura [Austl.] 59 Jd 24.35S 150.00 E
Moura [Port.] 13 Ef 38.08N 7.27W
Mourão 13 Ef 38.23N 7.21W
Mourdi 35 Cb 17.50N 22.25 E
Mourdi, Dépression du-= Mourdi Depression (EN) 30 Jg 18.10N 23.00 E
Mourdiah 34 Dc 14.26N 7.31W
Mourdi Depression (EN)= Mourdi, Dépression du- 30 Jg 18.10N 23.00 E
Mourmelon-le-Grand 12 Ge 49.08N 4.22 E
Mourne Mountains/Beanna Boirche 9 Gg 54.10N 6.04W
Mouscron/Moeskroen 11 Jd 50.44N 3.13 E
Moussoro 31 Ig 13.39N 16.29 E
Moustiers-Sainte-Marie 11 Mk 43.51N 6.13 E
Moutier/Münster 14 Bc 47.16N 7.22 E
Moutiers 11 Mi 45.29N 6.32 E
Moutong 26 Hf 0.28N 121.13 E
Mouy 12 Ee 49.19N 2.19 E
Mouydir 30 Hf 25.00N 4.10 E
Mouyondzi 36 Bc 3.58S 13.57 E
Mouzaia 13 Oh 36.28N 2.41 E
Mouzon 12 He 49.36N 5.05 E
Movas 48 Ec 28.10N 109.25W

Index Symbols

[1] Independent Nation
[2] State, Region
[3] District, County
[4] Municipality
[5] Colony, Dependency
Continent
Physical Region
Historical or Cultural Region
Mount, Mountain
Volcano
Hill
Mountains, Mountain Range
Hills, Escarpment
Plateau, Upland
Pass, Gap
Plain, Lowland
Delta
Salt Flat
Valley, Canyon
Crater, Cave
Karst Features
Depression
Polder
Desert, Dunes
Forest, Woods
Heath, Steppe
Oasis
Cape, Point
Coast, Beach
Cliff
Peninsula
Isthmus
Sandbank
Island
Atoll
Rock, Reef
Islands, Archipelago
Rocks, Reefs
Coral Reef
Well, Spring
Geyser
River, Stream
Waterfall Rapids
River Mouth, Estuary
Lake
Salt Lake
Intermittent Lake
Reservoir
Swamp, Pond
Canal
Glacier
Ice Shelf, Pack Ice
Ocean
Sea
Gulf, Bay
Strait, Fjord
Lagoon
Bank
Seamount
Tablemount
Ridge
Shelf
Basin
Escarpment, Sea Scarp
Fracture
Trench, Abyss
National Park, Reserve
Point of Interest
Recreation Site
Cave, Cavern
Historic Site
Ruins
Wall, Walls
Church, Abbey
Temple
Scientific Station
Airport
Port
Lighthouse
Mine
Tunnel
Dam, Bridge

Index Symbols

[1] Independent Nation	Historical or Cultural Region	Pass, Gap
[2] State, Region	Mount, Mountain	Plain, Lowland
[3] District, County	Volcano	Delta
[4] Municipality	Hill	Salt Flat
[5] Colony, Dependency	Mountains, Mountain Range	Valley, Canyon
Continent	Hills, Escarpment	Crater, Cave
Physical Region	Plateau, Upland	Karst Features

Depression	Coast, Beach	Rock, Reef
Polder	Cliff	Islands, Archipelago
Desert, Dunes	Peninsula	Rocks, Reefs
Forest, Woods	Isthmus	Coral Reef
Heath, Steppe	Sandbank	Well, Spring
Oasis	Island	Geyser
Cape, Point	Atoll	River, Stream

Waterfall Rapids	Canal	Lagoon
River Mouth, Estuary	Glacier	Bank
Lake	Ice Shelf, Pack Ice	Seamount
Salt Lake	Ocean	Tablemount
Intermittent Lake	Sea	Ridge
Reservoir	Shelf	Shelf
Swamp, Pond	Gulf, Bay	Basin
	Strait, Fjord	

Escarpment, Sea Scarp	Historic Site
Fracture	Ruins
Trench, Abyss	Wall, Walls
National Park, Reserve	Church, Abbey
Point of Interest	Temple
Recreation Site	Scientific Station
Cave, Cavern	Airport
	Port
	Lighthouse
	Mine
	Tunnel
	Dam, Bridge

Myzeqeja 15 Ci 41.01N 19.36 E
M'Zab 32 Hc 32.35N 3.20 E
Mže 10 Jg 49.46N 13.24 E
Mziha 36 Gd 5.54S 37.47 E
Mzimba 36 Fe 11.54S 33.36 E
Mzuzu 31 Kj 11.27S 33.55 E

N

Naab 10 Ig 49.01N 12.02 E
Naaldwijk 12 Gc 51.59N 4.12 E
Naalehu 65a Fd 19.04N 155.35W
Naantali/Nådendal 7 Ff 60.27N 22.02 E
Naarden 12 Hb 52.18N 5.10 E
Naas/An Nás 9 Gh 53.13N 6.39W
Nabadid 35 Gd 9.38N 43.29 E
Nabão 13 De 39.31N 8.21W
Nabari 29 Ed 34.37N 136.05 E
Naberera 36 Gc 4.12S 38.56 E
Naberežnyje Čelny 6 Ld 55.42N 52.19 E
Nabileque, Rio- 55 De 20.55S 57.49W
Nabire 58 Ee 3.22S 135.29 E
Nabī Shu'ayb, Jabal an- 21 Gh 15.17N 43.59 E
Nabq 24 Fh 28.04N 34.25 E
Nābul 31 Ie 36.27N 10.44 E
Nābul [3] 32 Jb 36.45N 10.45 E
Nābulus 24 Ff 32.13N 35.16 E
Nabusanke 36 Fb 0.01N 32.03 E
Nacala 37 Gb 14.33S 40.40 E
Nacala-a-Velha 31 Lj 14.33S 40.36 E
Nacaome 49 Dg 13.31N 87.30W
Nacaroa 37 Fb 14.23S 39.55 E
Nacereddine 13 Ph 36.08N 3.26 E
Nachikatsuura 29 De 33.39N 135.55 E
Nachingwea 36 Ge 10.23S 38.46 E
Nachi-San 29 De 33.42N 135.51 E
Náchod 10 Mf 50.26N 16.10 E
Nachuge 25 If 10.35N 92.28 E
Nachvak Fiord 42 Le 59.03N 63.45W
Nacka 7 Ee 59.18N 18.10 E
Ná Clocha Liatha/Greystones 9 Gh 53.09N 6.04W
Nacogdoches 45 Ik 31.36N 94.39W
Na Comaraigh/Comeragh Mountains 9 Fi 52.13N 7.35W
Nacori, Sierra- 48 Ec 29.50N 108.50W
Nacozari, Rio- 48 Ec 29.48N 109.42W
Nacozari de Garcia 47 Cb 30.24N 109.39W
Na Cruacha/Blue Stack 9 Eg 54.45N 8.06W
Na Cruacha Dubha/Macgillycuddy's Reeks 9 Di 52.00N 9.50W
Nacunday, Rio- 55 Eh 26.03S 54.45W
Nada → Danxian 27 Ih 19.38N 109.32 E
Nådendal/Naantali 7 Ff 60.27N 22.02 E
Nadiād 25 Ed 22.42N 72.52 E
Nădlac 15 Dc 46.10N 20.45 E
Nador [3] 32 Gb 35.00N 3.00W
Nador 32 Gb 35.11N 2.56W
Nádusa 15 Fi 40.38N 22.04 E
Nadvoicy 19 Dc 63.52N 34.20 E
Nadvornaja 16 De 48.38N 24.34 E
Nadym 22 Jc 65.35N 72.42 E
Naeba-San 29 Fc 36.51N 138.41 E
Nærbø 8 Af 58.40N 5.39 E
Næstved 7 Ci 55.14N 11.46 E
Nafada 34 Hc 11.06N 11.20 E
Näfels 14 Dc 47.06N 9.04 E
Naftah 14 Dn 36.57N 9.04 E
Naftan Rock 64b Bb 14.50N 145.32 E
Naft-e Safid 24 Mg 31.40N 49.17 E
Naft-e-Shāh 24 Kf 33.59N 45.30 E
Naft Khāneh 24 Ke 34.02N 45.28 E
Nafūsah, Jabal- 30 Ie 31.50N 12.00 E
Nāg 25 Dc 27.24N 65.08 E
Naga 22 Oh 13.28N 123.39 E
Nāga, Kreb en- 32 Fe 24.00N 6.00W
Nagagami Lake 44 Ea 49.28N 85.02W
Nagagami River 45 Na 50.25N 84.20W
Nagahama [Jap.] 29 Ed 35.23N 136.16 E
Nagahama [Jap.] 29 Ce 33.36N 132.29 E
Nagai 29 Gb 38.06N 140.02 E
Nagai 40 Ge 55.11N 159.55W
Na Gaibhlte/Galty Mountains 9 Ei 52.23N 8.11W
Nāgāland [3] 25 Ic 26.30N 94.00 E
Nagano 27 Pf 36.39N 138.11 E
Nagano Ken [2] 28 Nf 36.10N 138.00 E
Nagano-Matsushiro 29 Fc 36.34N 138.10 E
Nagano-Shinonoi 29 Fc 36.35N 138.06 E
Nagaoka 27 Od 37.27N 138.51 E
Nāgappattinam 25 Ff 10.46N 79.50 E
Nagara-Gawa 29 Ed 35.02N 136.43 E
Nagarote 49 Dg 12.16N 86.34W
Nagarzê 27 Ff 28.59N 90.28 E
Nagasaki 22 Of 32.47N 129.56 E
Nagasaki-Hantō 29 Ae 32.40N 129.45 E
Nagasaki Ken [2] 28 Jh 33.00N 129.50 E
Naga-Shima 29 Ce 33.50N 132.05 E
Nagashima 29 Ed 34.12N 136.19 E
Nagashima 29 Be 32.10N 130.10 E
Naga-Shima-Kaikyō 29 Be 32.15N 130.10 E
Nagato 28 Kg 34.21N 131.10 E
Nagayo 29 Ae 32.50N 129.52 E
Nāgda 25 Fd 23.27N 75.25 E
Nāgercoil 25 Fg 8.10N 77.26 E
Naghora Point 60 Gj 10.50S 162.24 E
Nagichot 35 Ee 4.16N 33.34 E
Nagi-San 29 Dd 35.10N 134.10 E
Nagiso 29 Ed 35.36N 137.36 E
Nago 27 Mf 26.35N 128.01 E
Nagold 10 Eh 48.52N 8.42 E
Nagorno-Karabakh 19 Eh 39.55N 46.45 E
Nagorny 20 He 55.45N 124.58 E
Nagorny 20 Md 63.10N 179.05 E
Nagorsk 7 Mg 59.21N 50.48 E
Nago-Wan 29b Ab 26.35N 127.55 E
Nagoya 22 Pf 35.10N 136.55 E
Nāgpur 22 Jg 21.09N 79.06 E
Nagqu 22 Lf 31.30N 92.00 E
Nag's Head 51c Ab 17.13N 62.38W
Nagua 49 Md 19.23N 69.50W
Naguabo 51a Cb 18.13N 65.44W
Nagyatád 10 Nj 46.13N 17.22 E
Nagybajom 10 Mj 46.23N 16.31 E
Nagyecsed 10 Si 47.52N 22.24 E
Nagyhalász 10 Rh 48.08N 21.46 E
Nagykálló 10 Ri 47.53N 21.51 E
Nagykanizsa 10 Mj 46.27N 16.59 E
Nagykáta 10 Pi 47.25N 19.45 E
Nagykőrös 10 Pi 47.02N 19.47 E
Nagykunság 10 Qj 46.55N 20.15 E
Nagy-Milic 10 Rh 48.35N 21.28 E
Naha 22 Og 26.13N 127.40 E
Nahanni Butte 42 Fd 61.04N 123.24W
Nahari 29 De 33.25N 134.01 E
Naharyya 24 Ff 33.00N 35.05 E
Nahāvand 23 Gc 34.12N 48.22 E
Nahe 10 Dg 49.58N 7.57 E
Nahičevan 6 Kh 39.13N 45.27 E
Nahičevanskaja respublika 19 Eh 39.15N 45.35 E
Na'hīmābād 24 Qg 30.51N 56.31 E
Nahodka 22 Pe 42.48N 132.52 E
Nahr al 'Āsī=Orontes (EN) 23 Eb 36.02N 35.58 E
Nahr Quassel 13 Oi 35.45N 2.46 E
Nahuala, Laguna- 48 Ji 16.50N 99.40W
Nahuel Huapi, Lago- 56 Ff 40.58S 71.30W
Nahunta 44 Gj 31.12N 81.59W
Naie 29a Bb 43.24N 141.52 E
Naiguatá, Pico- 54 Ea 10.33N 66.46W
Naila 10 Hf 50.19N 11.42 E
Naiman Qi (Daqin Tal) 27 Lc 42.49N 120.38 E
Nain 39 Md 57.00N 61.40W
Nā'īn 24 Of 32.52N 53.05 E
Na'īnābād 24 Pd 36.14N 54.39 E
Nairai 63d Bb 17.49S 179.24 E
Nairn 9 Jd 57.35N 3.53W
Nairobi 31 Ki 1.17S 36.49 E
Nairobi [3] 36 Gc 1.17S 36.50 E
Naissaar/Najssar 8 Ke 59.35N 24.25 E
Naitamba 63d Cb 17.01S 179.17W
Naizishan 28 Ic 43.41N 127.27 E
Najafābād 23 Hc 32.37N 51.21 E
Najd 23 Fe 25.00N 44.30 E
Najd 21 Gg 25.00N 44.30 E
Nájera 13 Jb 42.25N 2.44W
Najerilla 13 Jb 42.31N 2.42W
Naj' Hammādī 33 Fd 26.03N 32.15 E
Najībābād 25 Fc 29.58N 78.10 E
Najin 27 Nc 42.15N 130.18 E
Najō 29 Ec 35.47N 136.12 E
Najrān 33 Hf 17.30N 44.10 E
Najrān 33 Hf 17.30N 44.10 E
Najssar/Naissaar 8 Ke 59.35N 24.25 E
Najstenjarvi 7 He 62.18N 32.42 E
Naju 28 Ig 35.02N 126.43 E
Najzataš, Pereval- 18 If 37.52N 73.46 E
Nakadōri-Jima 28 Jh 32.58N 129.05 E
Nakagawa 29a Ca 44.47N 142.05 E
Naka-Gawa [Jap.] 29 Gc 36.20N 140.36 E
Naka-Gawa [Jap.] 29 De 33.56N 134.42 E
Nakagusuku-Wan 29b Ab 26.15N 127.50 E
Nakahechi 29 De 33.47N 135.29 E
Naka-lō-Jima 60 Cc 24.47N 141.20 E
Naka-Jima 29 Ce 33.58N 132.37 E
Nakajō 28 Oe 38.03N 139.24 E
Naka-Koshiki-Jima 29 Af 31.48N 129.50 E
Nakalele Point 65a Eb 21.02N 156.35W
Nakama 29 Be 33.50N 130.43 E
Nakaminato 29 Gc 36.22N 140.36 E
Nakamura 28 Lh 32.59N 132.56 E
Nakanai Mountains 59 Ka 5.35S 151.10 E
Nakano 29 Fc 36.45N 138.22 E
Naka-no-Dake 29 Fc 37.04N 139.06 E
Nakanojō 29 Fc 36.35N 138.51 E
Naka-no-Shima 28 Lf 36.05N 133.04 E
Naka-no- Shima 27 Mf 29.50N 129.50 E
Nakasato 29a Bc 40.58N 140.26 E
Naka-satsunai 29a Cb 42.42N 143.08 E
Nakashibetsu 28 Rc 43.36N 145.00 E
Nakasongola 36 Fb 1.19N 32.28 E
Nakatonbetsu 29a Ca 44.58N 142.17 E
Nakatsu 28 Kh 33.34N 131.13 E
Nakatsugawa 28 Ng 35.29N 137.30 E
Nakfa 35 Fb 16.40N 38.30 E
Nakhon Pathom 25 Kf 13.49N 100.06 E
Nakhon Phanom 25 Mh 17.22N 104.46 E
Nakhon Ratchasima 22 Mh 14.57N 102.09 E
Nakhon Sawan 22 Mh 15.42N 100.06 E
Nakhon Si Thammarat 22 Li 8.26N 99.58 E
Nakijin 29b Ab 26.42N 127.59 E
Nakina 39 Kd 50.10N 86.42W
Nakkila 8 Ic 61.22N 22.00 E
Nakło nad Notecia 10 Nc 53.08N 17.35 E
Naknek 40 He 58.44N 157.02W
Nakonde 36 Fd 9.19S 32.46 E
Nakskov 7 Ci 54.50N 11.09 E
Näkten 8 Fb 62.50N 14.40 E
Naktong-gang 28 Jg 35.07N 128.57 E
Nakuru 31 Ki 0.20S 35.56 E
Nakusp 46 Ga 50.15N 117.48W
Näl 25 Dc 26.02N 65.29 E
Nalajch → Nalajha 27 Ib 47.45N 107.16 E
Nalajha (Nalajch) 27 Ib 47.45N 107.16 E
Nalčik 6 Kg 43.29N 43.37 E
Nallihan 24 Db 40.11N 31.21 E
Nalón 13 Fa 43.32N 6.04W
Nälüt 31 Ie 31.52N 10.59 E
Nalwasha 36 Gc 0.43S 36.26 E
Na Machaìri/Brandon Head 9 Ci 52.16N 10.15W
Namacurra 37 Fc 17.29S 37.01 E
Namai Bay 64a Bb 7.32N 134.39 E
Namak, Daryācheh-ye- = Namak Lake (EN) 21 Hf 34.45N 51.36 E
Namak Lake (EN)= Namak, Daryācheh-ye- 21 Hf 34.45N 51.36 E
Namakan Lake 45 Jb 48.27N 92.35W
Namak-e Mighān, Kavīr-e- 24 Me 34.13N 49.49 E
Namakia 37 Hc 15.56S 45.48 E
Namakwaland = Little Namamland (EN) 37 Be 29.00S 17.00 E
Namanga 36 Gc 2.33S 36.47 E
Namangan 22 Je 41.00N 71.40 E
Namanganskaja Oblast [3] 19 Hg 41.00N 71.20 E
Namanyere 36 Fd 7.31S 31.03 E
Namapa 37 Fb 13.43S 39.50 E
Namaqua Seamount (EN) 37 Af 31.30S 11.20 E
Namarrói 37 Fc 15.57S 36.51 E
Namasagali 36 Fb 1.01N 32.57 E
Namasale 36 Fb 1.30N 32.37 E
Namatanai 60 Eh 3.40S 152.27 E
Namathu 63d Bb 17.21S 179.26 E
Nambavatu 63d Bb 16.36S 178.55 E
Namber 26 Jg 1.04S 134.49 E
Nambour 59 Ke 26.38S 152.58 E
Nambouwalu 61 Ec 16.59S 178.42 E
Nam Can 25 Kg 8.46N 104.59 E
Namche Bazar 25 Hc 27.49N 86.43 E
Nam Co 21 Lf 30.45N 90.35 E
Namčy 20 Hd 62.35N 129.40 E
Namdalen 7 Cd 64.38N 2.35 E
Nam Dinh 22 Mg 20.25N 106.10 E
Nämdö 8 He 59.10N 8.40 E
Nam Du, Quan Dao- 25 Kg 9.42N 104.22 E
Naměche, Andenne- 12 Hd 50.28N 5.00 E
Namelakl Passage 64a Bc 7.24N 134.38 E
Namen/Namur 11 Kd 50.28N 4.52 E
Namerikawa 29 Ec 36.45N 137.20 E
Náměšt nad Oslavou 10 Mg 49.12N 16.09 E
Nametil 37 Fc 15.43S 39.21 E
Namib Desert/Namibwoestyn 30 Ik 23.00S 15.00 E
Namibia (South West Africa) 31 Ik 22.00S 17.00 E
Namibe 31 Ij 15.12S 12.10 E
Namibe 36 Bf 15.20S 12.30 E
Namie 28 Pf 37.29N 140.59 E
Namin 24 Mc 38.25N 48.30 E
Namioka 29 Ga 40.42N 140.35 E
Namiquipa 48 Fc 29.15N 107.40W
Namiranga 37 Gb 10.33S 40.30 E
Namjagbarwa Feng 21 Lg 29.38N 95.04 E
Namja La 27 Df 29.58N 82.34 E
Namkham 25 Jd 23.50N 97.41 E
Namlea 26 Ig 3.18S 127.06 E
Namling 27 Ef 29.44N 89.05 E
Namnoi, Khao- 25 Jf 10.36N 98.38 E
Namoi River 59 Je 30.00S 148.07 E
Namoluk Island 57 Gd 5.55N 153.08 E
Namonuito Atoll 57 Gd 8.46N 150.02 E
Namorik Atoll 57 Hd 5.36N 168.07 E
Namous 32 Gc 30.28N 0.14W
Nampa 43 Dc 43.34N 116.34W
Nampala 34 Db 15.17N 5.33W
Nam Phan = Cochin China (EN) 21 Mg 11.00N 107.00 E
Nam Phong 25 Ke 16.45N 102.52 E
Nampi 28 De 38.02N 116.42 E
Namp'o 27 Md 38.44N 125.25 E
Nampula [3] 37 Fb 15.00S 39.30 E
Nampula 31 Kj 15.07S 39.15 E
Namsê Shankou 27 Df 29.58N 82.34 E
Namsos 6 Hc 64.30N 11.30 E
Namtu 25 Jd 23.05N 97.24 E
Namu 46 Ba 51.49N 127.52W
Namu Atoll 57 Hd 8.00N 168.10 E
Namuka-I-Lau 63d Cc 18.51S 178.33W
Namúli, Serra- 30 Kj 15.21S 37.00 E
Namuno 37 Fb 13.37S 38.43 E
Namur [3] 12 Gd 50.20N 4.50 E
Namur/Namen 11 Kd 50.28N 4.52 E
Namur-Saint Servais 12 Gd 50.28N 4.50 E
Namuruputh 36 Gb 4.34N 35.57 E
Namur-Wépion 12 Gd 50.25N 4.52 E
Namutoni 37 Bc 18.30S 16.55 E
Namwala 36 Ef 15.45S 26.26 E
Namwŏn 28 Ig 35.24N 127.23 E
Namysłów 10 Ne 51.05N 17.42 E
Nan 21 Mh 15.42N 100.09 E
Nan 25 Ke 18.48N 100.46 E
Nana 35 Bd 5.00N 15.50 E
Nana Barya 35 Bd 7.59N 17.43 E
Nanae 29a Bc 41.53N 140.41 E
Nanaimo 42 Fg 49.10N 123.56W
Nanakuli 65a Cb 21.23N 158.08W
Nana-Mambéré [3] 35 Bd 6.00N 16.00 E
Nanango 59 Ke 26.40S 152.00 E
Nanao 27 Od 37.03N 136.58 E
Nanao-Wan 29 Ec 37.10N 137.00 E
Nanatsu-Shima 29 Ec 37.35N 136.50 E
Nancha 27 Mb 47.08N 129.09 E
Nanchang 22 Ng 28.40N 115.58 E
Nancheng 27 Kf 27.32N 116.36 E
Nanchong 22 Mf 30.47N 106.03 E
Nancowry 25 Ig 7.59N 93.32 E
Nancy 6 Gf 48.41N 6.12 E
Nanda Devi 21 Jf 30.23N 79.59 E
Nandaime 49 Dh 11.46N 86.03W
Nandan [China] 27 Ig 24.59N 107.31 E
Nandan [Jap.] 28 Mg 34.15N 134.43 E
Nandarano → Qingyuan 28 Ce 38.46N 115.29 E
Nanded 22 Jh 19.09N 77.20 E
Nandewar Range 59 Kf 30.40S 151.10 E
Nandi 61 Ec 17.48S 177.25 E
Nandu Jiang 27 Jg 20.04N 110.22 E
Nanduri 63d Bb 16.27S 179.09 E
Nandyāl 25 Fe 15.29N 78.29 E
Nanfen 28 Gd 41.06N 123.45 E
Nanfeng 27 Kf 27.15N 116.30 E
Nanga-Eboko 34 He 4.41N 12.22 E
Nanga Parbat 21 Jf 35.15N 74.36 E
Nangapinoh 26 Fg 0.20S 111.44 E
Nangarhār [3] 23 Lc 34.15N 70.30 E
Nangatayap 26 Fg 1.32S 110.34 E
Nangis 11 If 48.33N 3.00 E
Nangnim-san 28 Id 40.21N 126.55 E
Nangnim-Sanmaek 28 Id 40.30N 127.00 E
Nangong 27 Kd 37.22N 115.23 E
Nangqên 27 Ge 32.15N 96.13 E
Nanguan 28 Af 36.42N 111.41 E
Nanguantao → Guantao 28 Cf 36.33N 115.18 E
Nangweshi 36 Df 16.26S 23.20 E
Nan Hai = South China Sea (EN) 21 Ni 10.00N 113.00 E
Nanhaoqian → Shangyi 28 Bd 41.06N 113.58 E
Nanhe 28 Cf 36.58N 114.41 E
Nanhua 27 Hf 25.16N 101.18 E
Nanhui 28 Fi 31.03N 121.46 E
Nan Hu'san Hu 27 Gd 36.45N 95.45 E
Nanjian 27 Hf 25.05N 100.32 E
Nanjiang 27 Ie 32.22N 106.45 E
Nanjing = Nanking (EN) 22 Nf 31.59N 118.51 E
Nankai Trough (EN) 27 Ne 32.00N 135.00 E
Nanking (EN) = Nanjing 22 Nf 31.59N 118.51 E
Nankoku 28 Lh 33.39N 133.44 E
Nanle 28 Cf 36.06N 115.12 E
Nanling 28 Ei 30.55N 118.19 E
Nan Ling 21 Ng 25.00N 112.00 E
Nanlou Shan 28 Ic 43.24N 126.40 E
Nanma → Yiyuan 28 Ef 36.11N 118.10 E
Nanning 22 Mg 22.50N 108.18 E
Nannup 59 Df 33.59S 115.45 E
Nanortalik 41 Hf 60.32N 45.45W
Nanpan Jiang 27 Ig 24.56N 106.12 E
Nānpāra 25 Gc 27.52N 81.30 E
Nanping [China] 22 Ng 26.42N 118.09 E
Nanping [China] 27 He 33.15N 104.13 E
Nanpu 28 Ee 39.16N 118.12 E
Nanqiao → Fengxian 28 Fi 30.55N 121.27 E
Nansei-Shotō = Ryukyu Islands (EN) 21 Og 26.30N 128.00 E
Nansen Cordillera (EN) 67 Ge 87.00N 90.00 E
Nansen Land 41 Hb 83.20N 46.00W
Nanshan Islands (EN) = Nansha Qundao 21 Ni 9.40N 113.30 E
Nansha Qundao = Nanshan Islands (EN) 21 Ni 9.40N 113.30 E
Nansio 36 Fc 2.08S 33.03 E
Nant 11 Jj 44.01N 3.18 E
Nantais, Lac - 42 Kd 61.00N 73.50W
Nanterre 11 If 48.54N 2.12 E
Nantes 6 Ff 47.13N 1.33W
Nantes à Brest, Can. de- 11 Bf 48.12N 4.06W
Nanteuil-le-Haudouin 12 Ee 49.08N 2.48 E
Nanticoke 44 Je 41.13N 76.00W
Nantō 29 Ed 34.17N 136.29 E
Nantong 27 Le 32.00N 120.52 E
Nantong (Jinsha) 28 Fh 32.06N 120.52 E
Nantou 27 Lg 23.54N 120.51 E
Nantua 11 Lh 46.09N 5.37 E
Nantucket 44 Le 41.17N 70.06W
Nantucket Island 43 Mc 41.16N 70.03W
Nantucket Sound 44 Le 41.30N 70.15W
Nanuku Passage 63d Cb 16.45S 179.15W
Nanuku Reef 63d Cb 16.40S 179.26W
Nanumanga Island 57 Ie 6.18S 176.20 E
Nanumea Atoll 57 Ie 5.43S 176.00 E
Nanuque 54 Jg 17.50S 40.21W
Nanusa, Pulau-Pulau- 26 If 4.42N 127.06 E
Nanwan Shuiku 28 Bh 32.02N 113.57 E
Nanwei Dao = Spratly Islands 26 Fe 8.42N 111.40 E
Nanxian 28 Bj 29.22N 112.25 E
Nanxiang 28 Fi 31.18N 121.17 E
Nanxiong 27 Jf 25.13N 114.18 E
Nanxun 28 Fi 30.53N 120.26 E
Nanyandang Shan 27 Lf 27.37N 120.06 E
Nanyang 22 Nf 32.56N 112.32 E
Nanyang Hu 28 Dg 35.15N 116.39 E
Nanyō 28 Pe 38.03N 140.10 E
Nanyuki 31 Kh 0.01N 37.04 E
Nanzhang 27 Je 31.45N 111.53 E
Nanzhao 27 Je 33.28N 112.29 E
Nao, Cabo de la- 5 Gh 38.44N 0.14 E
Naococane, Lac- 42 Kf 52.50N 70.40W
Naoero/Nauru [1] 58 He 0.31S 166.56 E
Naoetsu 29 Fc 37.11N 138.14 E
Não-me-Toque 55 Fi 28.28S 52.49W
Naours, Souterrains de- 12 Ed 50.05N 2.17 E
Napa 46 Dg 38.18N 122.17W
Napanee 44 Ic 44.15N 76.57W
Napassoq 41 Ge 65.45N 52.38W
Napata 35 Eb 18.29N 31.51 E
Na-Peng 25 Lg 23.10N 98.26 E
Napf 14 Bc 47.01N 7.57 E
Napier 58 Ih 39.33S 176.54 E
Napier, Mount- 59 Fc 17.32S 129.10 E
Napier Mountains 66 Ee 66.30S 53.40 E
Naples [FL-U.S.] 43 Kf 26.03N 81.48W
Naples [Id.-U.S.] 46 Gb 48.34N 116.24W
Naples (EN) = Napoli 6 Hg 40.50N 14.15 E
Naples, Gulf of- (EN) = Napoli, Golfo di- 14 Ij 40.45N 14.10 E
Napo 27 Ig 23.25N 105.49 E
Napo, Río- 52 If 3.20S 72.40W
Napoleon 45 Gc 46.30N 99.46W
Napoli = Naples (EN) 6 Hg 40.50N 14.15 E
Napoli, Golfo di- = Naples, Gulf of- (EN) 14 Ij 40.45N 14.10 E
Napostá 55 An 38.26S 62.15W
Napuka, Ile- 57 Mf 14.12S 141.15W
Naqa 35 Eb 16.13N 33.17 E
Naqadeh 23 Gb 36.57N 45.23 E
Naqsh-e-Rostam 24 Og 30.01N 52.50 E
Nar 9 Ni 52.45N 0.24 E
Nāra 25 Dc 24.07N 69.07 E
Nara [Jap.] 27 Oe 34.41N 135.50 E
Nara [Mali] 34 Db 15.11N 7.15W
Naračenskibani 15 Hh 41.54N 24.45 E
Naracoorte 59 Ig 36.58S 140.44 E
Nara-Ken [2] 28 Mg 34.20N 135.55 E
Naranjo 48 Ee 25.48N 108.31W
Naranjos [Bol.] 55 Cd 18.38S 59.09W
Naranjos [Mex.] 48 Kg 21.21N 97.41W
Narao 29 Ae 32.52N 129.04 E
Narathiwat 25 Kg 6.25N 101.48 E
Nārāyanganj 25 Id 23.37N 90.30 E
Narbonne 11 Ik 43.11N 3.00 E
Narca, Ponta da- 36 Bd 6.07S 12.16 E
Narcea 13 Fa 43.28N 6.06W
Narcondam 25 If 13.15N 94.30 E
Nardò 14 Mj 40.11N 18.02 E
Naré 55 Bj 30.58S 60.28W
Nares Land 41 Hb 82.25N 47.30W
Nares Strait 38 Lb 78.50N 73.00W
Narew 10 Td 52.55N 23.29 E
Narew 10 Qd 52.26N 20.42 E
Narian, Pointe- 63b Be 20.05S 164.00 E
Narin Gol 27 Fd 36.54N 92.51 E
Nariño [2] 54 Cc 1.30N 78.00W
Narita 29 Gd 35.47N 140.18 E
Narjan-Mar 6 Lb 67.39N 53.00 E
Närke 8 Ff 59.05N 15.05 E
Narlı 24 Gd 37.27N 37.09 E
Narmada 21 Jg 21.38N 72.36 E
Narman 24 Ib 40.21N 41.52 E
Närnaul 25 Fc 28.03N 76.06 E
Narni 14 Gh 42.31N 12.31 E
Naroč 8 Lj 54.27N 26.45 E
Naroč 8 Lj 54.57N 26.49 E
Naroč, Ozero- 16 Eb 54.50N 26.45 E
Naroda 17 Jd 64.15N 61.00 E
Narodnaja, Gora- 5 Mb 65.04N 60.09 E
Naro-Fominsk 19 Dd 55.24N 36.43 E
Narok 36 Gc 1.05S 35.52 E
Narovlja 16 Fd 51.48N 29.31 E
Närpes/Närpiö 8 Ib 62.28N 21.20 E
Närpiö/Närpes 8 Ib 62.28N 21.20 E
Narrabri 59 Jf 30.19S 149.47 E
Narrandera 59 Jf 34.45S 146.33 E
Narrogin 59 Df 32.56S 117.10 E
Narromine 59 Jf 32.14S 148.15 E
Narrows, The- 51c Ab 17.12N 62.38W
Narryer, Mount- 59 De 26.30S 116.25 E
Narsimhapur 25 Fd 22.57N 79.12 E
Narssalik 41 Hf 61.42N 49.11W
Narssaq [Grld.] 41 Hf 61.00N 46.00W
Narssaq [Grld.] 41 Gf 64.00N 51.33W
Narssarssuaq 41 Hf 61.10N 45.15W
Narthákion 15 Fj 39.14N 22.22 E
Nartkala 16 Mh 43.32N 43.47 E
Narubis 37 Be 26.56S 18.35 E
Narugo 29 Gb 38.44N 140.43 E
Näruja 15 Jd 45.50N 26.47 E
Naru-Shima 29 Ae 32.50N 128.56 E
Naruto 28 Mg 34.11N 134.37 E
Naruto-Kaikyō 29 Dd 34.15N 134.40 E
Narva 7 Gg 59.29N 28.02 E
Narva 6 Id 59.23N 28.11 E
Narva Jõesuu/Narva-Jyesuu 8 Me 59.21N 28.04 E
Narva-Jyesuu/Narva Jõesuu 8 Me 59.21N 28.04 E
Narva laht 7 Gg 59.30N 27.40 E
Narvik 6 Hb 68.26N 17.25 E
Narvski Zaliv 7 Gg 59.30N 27.40 E
Narvskoje Vodohranilišče 8 Me 59.10N 28.30 E
Narym 20 De 58.58N 81.40 E
Naryn 21 Je 40.54N 71.45 E
Naryn 22 Je 41.26N 75.59 E
Naryncol 19 Ig 42.43N 80.08 E
Narynskaja Oblast [3] 19 Hg 41.20N 75.40 E
Nås 7 Df 60.27N 14.29 E
Na Saillti/Saltee Islands 9 Gi 52.07N 6.36W
Näsåker 7 De 63.23N 16.54 E
Nasarawa 34 Gd 8.32N 7.43 E
Năsăud 15 Hb 47.17N 24.24 E
Nasawa 63b Db 15.12S 168.06 E
Na Sceiri/Skerries 9 Gh 53.35N 6.07W
Nāshik 22 Jg 20.05N 73.48 E
Nash Point 9 Jj 51.24N 3.27W
Nashtārud 24 Nd 36.45N 51.02 E
Nashua 44 Ld 42.44N 71.28W
Nashville [Ar.-U.S.] 45 Jj 33.57N 93.51W
Nashville [Ga.-U.S.] 44 Fj 31.12N 83.15W
Nashville [Il.-U.S.] 45 Lg 38.21N 89.23W
Nashville [In.-U.S.] 44 Df 39.12N 86.15W
Nashville [Tn.-U.S.] 39 Kf 36.09N 86.48W
Nashville Seamount (EN) 38 Nf 35.00N 57.20W
Našice 14 Me 45.30N 18.06 E
Nasielsk 10 Qd 52.36N 20.48 E
Näsijärvi 5 Ic 61.35N 23.40 E
Nāşir 35 Ed 8.36N 33.04 E
Naskaupi 42 Lf 53.47N 60.51W
Nasorolevu 63d Bb 16.38S 179.24 E
Naşr [Eg.] 24 Dg 30.36N 30.23 E
Naşr [Lib.] 33 Dd 28.59N 21.13 E
Naşrābād 24 Cf 32.09N 52.08 E
Nass 42 Ee 55.00N 129.50W
Nassandres 12 Ce 49.07N 0.44 E
Nassandres-La Rivière Thibouville 12 Ce 49.07N 0.44 E
Nassau [Bah.] 39 Lg 25.05N 77.21W
Nassau [Ger.] 12 Jd 50.19N 7.48 E
Nassau, Bahia- 56 Gi 55.25S 67.40W
Nassau Island 57 Kf 11.33S 165.25W
Nassau River 59 Ic 15.58S 141.30 E
Nasser, Birkat- = Nasser, Lake-(EN) 30 Kf 22.40N 32.00 E

Index Symbols

[1] Independent Nation
[2] State, Region
[3] District, County
[4] Municipality
[5] Colony, Dependency
Continent
Physical Region
Historical or Cultural Region
Mount, Mountain
Volcano
Hill
Mountains, Mountain Range
Hills, Escarpment
Plateau, Upland
Pass, Gap
Plain, Lowland
Delta
Salt Flat
Valley, Canyon
Crater, Cave
Karst Features
Depression
Polder
Desert, Dunes
Forest, Woods
Heath, Steppe
Oasis
Cape, Point
Coast, Beach
Cliff
Peninsula
Isthmus
Sandbank
Island
Atoll
Rock, Reef
Islands, Archipelago
Rocks, Reefs
Coral Reef
Well, Spring
Geyser
River, Stream
Waterfall Rapids
River Mouth, Estuary
Lake
Salt Lake
Intermittent Lake
Reservoir
Swamp, Pond
Canal
Glacier
Ice Shelf, Pack Ice
Ocean
Sea
Gulf, Bay
Strait, Fjord
Lagoon
Bank
Seamount
Tablemount
Ridge
Shelf
Basin
Escarpment, Sea Scarp
Fracture
Trench, Abyss
National Park, Reserve
Point of Interest
Recreation Site
Cave, Cavern
Historic Site
Ruins
Wall, Walls
Church, Abbey
Temple
Scientific Station
Airport
Port
Lighthouse
Mine
Tunnel
Dam, Bridge

Nasser, Lake-(EN)=Nasser, Birkat- 30 Kf 22.40N 32.00 E
Nassian 34 Ed 9.24N 4.29W
Nässjö 7 Dh 57.39N 14.41 E
Nassogne 12 Hd 50.08N 5.21 E
Na Staighri Dubha/ Blackstairs Mountains 9 Gi 52.33N 6.49W
Nastapoka Islands 42 Je 56.50N 76.50W
Nastätten 12 Jd 50.12N 7.52 E
Nastola 8 Kd 60.57N 25.56 E
Nasu 29 Gc 37.02N 140.06 E
Nasu-Dake 29 Fc 37.07N 139.58 E
Näsviken 8 Gc 61.45N 16.52 E
Natá 49 Gi 8.20N 80.31W
Nata 30 Jk 20.14S 26.10 E
Nata 37 Dd 20.13S 26.11 E
Natal [2] 37 Ee 29.00S 30.00 E
Natal [B.C.-Can.] 46 Hb 49.44N 114.50W
Natal [Braz.] 53 Mf 5.47S 35.13W
Natal [Indon.] 26 Cf 0.33N 99.07 E
Natal Basin (EN) 3 Fm 30.00S 40.00 E
Natanz 24 Nf 33.31N 51.54 E
Natashquan 42 Lf 50.09N 61.37W
Natashquan 42 Lf 50.11N 61.49W
Natchez 43 Ie 31.34N 91.23W
Natchitoches 43 Ie 31.46N 93.05W
Natewa Bay 63d Bb 16.35S 179.40 E
Nathorsts Land 41 Jd 72.20N 27.00W
Nathula 63d Ab 16.53S 177.25 E
Natitingou 31 Hg 10.19N 1.22 E
Natityāy, Jabal- 33 Fe 23.01N 34.22 E
Natividad, Isla- 48 Bd 27.55N 115.10W
Natividade 54 If 11.43S 47.47W
Natori 28 Pe 38.11N 140.58 E
Natron, Lake- 30 Ki 2.25S 36.00 E
Naṭrūn, Wādī an- 24 Dg 30.25N 30.13 E
Natsudomari-Zaki 29a Bc 41.00N 140.53 E
Nättarö 8 Hf 58.50N 18.10 E
Nättraby 8 Fh 56.12N 15.31 E
Natuna Besar, Pulau- 26 Ef 4.00N 108.15 E
Natuna Islands (EN)= Bunguran, Kepulauan- 21 Mi 2.45N 109.00 E
Naturaliste, Cape- 57 Ch 33.32S 115.01 E
Naturaliste Channel 59 Ce 25.25S 113.00 E
Naturita 45 Bg 38.14N 108.34W
Naturno / Naturns 14 Ed 46.39N 11.00 E
Naturns / Naturno 14 Ed 46.39N 11.00 E
Nau 18 Gd 40.09N 69.22 E
Nau, Cap de la-/Nao, Cabo de la- 5 Gh 38.44N 0.14 E
Naucelle 11 Ij 44.12N 2.21 E
Nauëji-Akmjane/Naujoji-Akmenė 7 Fh 56.21N 22.50 E
Naugo/Nauvo 8 Id 60.10N 21.50 E
Nauhcampatépetl→ Cofre de Perote, Cerro- 48 Kh 19.29N 97.08W
Nauja Bay 42 Kc 68.58N 75.00W
Naujamiestis/Naujamiestis 8 Ki 55.41N 24.09 E
Naujamiestis/Naujamestis 8 Ki 55.41N 24.09 E
Naujoji-Akmenė/Nauëji-Akmjane 7 Fh 56.21N 22.50 E
Naukluft 37 Bd 24.10S 16.10 E
Naumburg [Ger.] 12 Lc 51.15N 9.10 E
Naumburg [Ger.] 10 He 51.09N 11.49 E
Nā'ūr 24 Fg 31.53N 35.50 E
Nauru 57 He 0.31S 166.56 E
Nauru/Naoero [1] 58 He 0.31S 166.56 E
Nauški 20 Ff 50.28N 106.07 E
Nausori 61 Ec 18.02S 178.32 E
Nauta 54 Dd 4.32S 73.33W
Nautanwa 25 Gc 27.26N 83.25 E
Nautla 48 Kg 20.13N 96.47W
Nauvo/Naugo 8 Id 60.10N 21.50 E
Nava 48 Ic 28.25N 100.45W
Navacerrada, Puerto de- 13 Id 40.47N 4.00W
Nava del Rey 13 Gc 41.20N 5.05W
Navahermosa 13 He 39.38N 4.28W
Navajo Mountain 46 Jh 37.02N 110.52W
Navajo Reservoir 45 Ch 36.55N 107.30W
Navalmoral de la Mata 13 Ge 39.54N 5.32W
Navan/An Uaimh 9 Gh 53.39N 6.41W
Navarin, Mys- 21 Tc 62.16N 179.10 E
Navarino, Isla- 52 Jk 55.05S 67.40W
Navarra [3] 13 Kb 42.45N 1.40W
Navarra=Navarre (EN) 13 Kb 43.00N 1.30W
Navarre (EN)=Navarra 13 Kb 43.00N 1.30W
Navarro 55 Cl 35.01S 59.16W
Navarro Mills Lake 45 Hk 31.56N 96.45W
Navašino 7 Ki 55.33N 42.12 E
Navasota 45 Hk 30.23N 96.05W
Navasota River 45 Hk 30.20N 96.09W
Navassa 47 Ie 18.24N 75.01W
Navaste Jõgi/Navesti 8 Kf 58.56N 24.58 E
Nävekvarn 8 Gf 58.38N 16.49 E
Naver 9 Ic 58.30N 4.15W
Navesti/Navaste Jõgi 8 Kf 58.56N 24.58 E
Navia 13 Fa 43.32N 6.43W
Navia 13 Fa 43.33N 6.44W
Navidad, Bahía de- 48 Gh 19.10N 104.45W
Navidad Bank (EN) 49 Mc 20.00N 68.50W
Naviti 63d Ab 17.07S 177.15 E
Navlja 16 Ic 52.42N 34.03 E
Navlja 19 De 52.50N 34.31 E
Năvodari 15 Le 44.19N 28.36 E
Navoi 19 Gg 40.10N 65.15 E
Navoja 47 Cc 27.06N 109.26W
Navolato 48 Fe 24.47N 107.42W
Navoloki 7 Jh 57.28N 41.59 E
Návpaktos 15 Ek 38.24N 21.50 E
Návplion 15 Fl 37.34N 22.48 E
Navrongo 34 Ec 10.54N 1.06W
Navsāri 25 Ed 20.55N 72.55 E
Navtilos 15 Gn 35.57N 23.13 E
Navua 63d Bc 18.13S 178.10 E
Navy Board Inlet 42 Jb 73.30N 81.00W
Nawa 24 Gf 32.53N 36.03 E
Nawābshāh 25 Dc 26.15N 68.25 E
Nawāşīf, Ḩarrat- 33 He 21.20N 42.10 E
Nawş, Ra's- 23 If 17.18N 55.16 E
Náxos 15 Il 37.06N 25.23 E
Naxos 14 Jm 37.49N 15.15 E
Náxos=Naxos (EN) 5 Ih 37.02N 25.35 E
Naxos (EN)=Náxos 5 Ih 37.02N 25.35 E
Nayarit [2] 47 Cd 22.00N 105.00W
Nayarit, Sierra- 47 Dd 22.00N 103.50W
Nayau 63d Cb 17.58S 179.03W
Nāy Band [Iran] 24 Oi 27.23N 52.38 E
Nāy Band [Iran] 24 Qf 32.20N 57.34 E
Nāy Band, Ra's-e- 24 Oi 27.23N 52.34 E
Nayoro 27 Pc 44.21N 142.28 E
Nazaré [Braz.] 54 Kf 13.02S 39.00W
Nazaré [Port.] 13 Ce 39.36N 9.04W
Nazareth (EN)=Nazerat 24 Ff 32.42N 35.18 E
Nazarovo 20 Ee 56.01N 90.36 E
Nazas 48 Ge 25.14N 104.08W
Nazas, Rio- 38 Ig 25.35N 105.00W
Nazca 53 Ig 14.50S 74.55W
Nazca Ridge (EN) 3 Nl 22.00S 82.00W
Naze 27 Mf 28.23N 129.30 E
Nazerat=Nazareth (EN) 24 Ff 32.42N 35.18 E
Nazilli 23 Cb 37.55N 28.21 E
Nazimiye 24 Hc 39.11N 39.50 E
Nazimovo 20 Ee 59.30N 90.58 E
Nazino 20 Cd 60.15N 78.58 E
Nazlū 24 Kd 37.42N 45.16 E
Nazran 16 Nh 43.15N 44.46 E
Nazret 35 Fd 8.34N 39.18 E
Nazwa' 23 Ie 22.54N 57.31 E
Nazym 17 Nf 61.12N 68.57 E
Nazyvajevsk 19 Hd 55.34N 71.21 E
Nbâk 32 Ef 17.15N 14.59W
Nchanga 36 Ee 12.31S 27.52 E
Nchəu 36 Fe 14.49S 34.38 E
Ndala 36 Fc 4.46S 33.16 E
N'delatando 36 Bd 9.18S 14.54 E
Ndali 34 Fd 9.51N 2.43 E
Ndélé 31 Jh 8.24N 20.39 E
Ndélélé 34 He 4.02N 14.56 E
Ndendé 36 Bc 2.23S 11.23 E
Ndindi 36 Bc 3.46S 11.09 E
N'Djamena (Fort-Lamy) 31 Ig 12.07N 15.03 E
Ndola 31 Jj 12.58S 28.38 E
Ndouana, Pointe- 63b Dc 16.35S 168.09 E
Ndrhamcha, Sebkha de- 32 Df 18.45N 15.48W
Nduindui 60 Fi 9.48S 159.58 E
Ndui Ndui 63b Cb 15.24S 167.46 E
Né 11 Fi 45.40N 0.23W
Nea 63c Ab 10.51S 165.47 E
Nea 7 Ce 63.13N 11.02 E
Néa Alikarnassós 15 In 35.20N 25.09 E
Néa Artáki 15 Gk 38.31N 23.38 E
Neagari 29 Ec 36.26N 136.26 E
Neagh, Lough-/Loch nEathach 5 Fe 54.38N 6.24W
Neagră, Marea-=Black Sea (EN) 5 Jg 43.00N 35.00 E
Neah Bay 46 Cb 48.22N 124.37W
Néa Ionía 15 Fj 39.23N 22.56 E
Neajlov 15 Je 44.11N 26.12 E
Neale, Lake- 59 Fd 24.20S 130.00 E
Neamţ [2] 15 Jb 47.00N 26.20 E
Neápolis [Grc.] 15 In 35.15N 25.37 E
Neápolis [Grc.] 15 Ei 40.19N 21.23 E
Neápolis [Grc.] 15 Gm 36.31N 23.04 E
Near Islands 38 Bd 52.40N 173.30W
Neath 9 Jj 51.37N 3.50W
Neath 9 Jj 51.40N 3.48W
Néa Zíkhni 15 Gh 41.02N 23.50 E
Nebaj 47 Bf 15.24N 91.08W
Nebbou 34 Ec 11.18N 1.53W
Nebit-Dag 17 Hf 39.30N 54.22 E
Neblina, Pico da- 52 Je 1.08N 66.10W
Nebo 59 Jd 21.40S 148.39 E
Nebo, Mount- 46 Jg 39.49N 111.46W
Nebolči 7 Hg 59.08N 33.21 E
Nebraska [2] 43 Gc 41.30N 100.00W
Nebraska City 43 Hc 40.41N 95.52W
Nebrodi (Caronie) 14 Im 37.55N 14.35 E
Necedah 45 Kd 44.02N 90.03W
Nechako 42 Ff 53.55N 122.44W
Nechako Reservoir 42 Ef 53.00N 126.10W
Nechar, Djebel- 13 Qi 35.52N 4.59 E
Neches River 45 Jl 29.55N 93.52W
Nechi 49 Ji 8.07N 74.46W
Nechi, Rio- 49 Ji 8.08N 74.46W
Nechako Plateau 42 Ff 53.25N 124.40W
Neckar 10 Eg 49.31N 8.26 E
Neckarsulm 10 Fg 49.11N 9.14 E
Necker Island 57 Kb 23.35N 164.42W
Necochea 53 Ki 38.34S 58.45W
Necy 12 Bf 48.50N 0.07W
Nedeley 35 Bb 15.34N 18.10 E
Nederland 45 Jl 29.58N 93.59W
Nederland=Netherlands (EN) [1] 6 Ge 52.15N 5.30 E
Nederlandse Antillen [5] 50 Ec 18.06N 63.10W
Nederlandse Antillen = Netherlands Antilles (EN) [5] 53 Jd 12.15N 69.00W
Neder-Rijn = Lower Rhine (EN) 11 Mc 51.59N 6.20 E
Nedong 22 Lg 29.14N 91.46 E
Nedstrand 8 Ae 59.21N 5.51 E
Nedstrandefjorden 8 Ae 59.20N 5.50 E
Neede 12 Ib 52.08N 6.37 E
Needham Market 12 Db 52.09N 1.02 E
Needham's Point 51q Ab 13.05N 59.36W
Needles 43 Ee 34.51N 114.37W
Neembucú [3] 55 Dh 27.00S 58.00W
Neenah 45 Ld 44.11N 88.28W
Neepawa 45 Ga 50.13N 99.29W
Neermoor, Moormerland- 12 Ja 53.18N 7.26 E
Neeroeteren, Maaseik- 12 Hc 51.05N 5.42 E
Neerpelt 12 Hc 51.13N 5.25 E
Nefasit 35 Fb 15.18N 39.04 E
Nefedova 19 Hd 58.48N 72.34 E
Né Finn/Nephin 9 Dg 54.01N 9.22W
Neftah 32 Ic 33.52N 7.53 E
Neftečala 16 Pj 39.19N 49.13 E
Neftegorsk 16 Kg 44.22N 39.42 E
Neftegorsk 20 Jf 53.00N 143.00 E
Neftegorsk 19 Fe 52.45N 51.13 E
Neftejugansk 19 Hc 61.05N 72.45 E
Neftekamsk → Nikolo-Berjozovka 19 Fd 56.06N 54.17 E
Neftekumsk 19 Eg 44.43N 44.59 E
Neftjanyje Kamin 16 Qi 40.15N 50.49 E
Negage 36 Cd 7.46S 15.18 E
Negara 26 Fh 8.22S 114.37 E
Negele=Neghelle (EN) 31 Kh 5.20N 39.37 E
Negev Desert (EN)= Hanegev 24 Fg 30.30N 34.55 E
Neghelle (EN)=Negele 31 Kh 5.20N 39.37 E
Negola 36 Be 14.10S 14.30 E
Negomano 37 Fb 11.26S 38.33 E
Negombo 25 Fg 7.13N 79.50 E
Negonego Atoll 57 Mf 18.47S 141.48W
Negotin 15 Fe 44.13N 22.32 E
Negotino 15 Fh 41.29N 22.06 E
Negra, Cordillera- 54 Ce 9.25S 77.40W
Negra, Coxilha- 55 Ej 31.02S 55.45W
Negra, Peña- 13 Fb 42.11N 6.30W
Negra, Ponta- 55 Jf 23.21S 44.36W
Negra, Punta- 52 Hf 6.06S 81.10W
Negra, Serra- 55 Fc 16.30S 52.10W
Negra o de los Difuntos, Laguna- 55 Fl 34.03S 53.40W
Negreira 13 Db 42.54N 8.44W
Negreni 15 He 44.34N 24.36 E
Negreşti 15 Gb 47.52N 23.26 E
Negrine 32 Ic 34.29N 7.31 E
Negrinho, Rio- 55 Ed 19.20S 55.05W
Negro, Cabo- 13 Gi 35.41N 5.17W
Negro, Rio- [Arg.] 55 Ch 27.27S 58.54W
Negro, Rio- [Arg.] 52 Jj 41.02S 62.47W
Negro, Rio- [Bol.] 54 Ff 14.11S 63.07W
Negro, Rio- [Braz.] 54 Gg 19.13S 57.17W
Negro, Rio- [Braz.] 56 Jc 26.01S 50.30W
Negro, Rio- [Par.] 56 Ib 24.23S 57.11W
Negro, Rio- [S.Amer.] 52 Kf 3.08S 59.55W
Negro, Rio- [S.Amer.] 55 Ce 20.11S 58.10W
Negro, Rio- [Ur.] 52 Ki 33.24S 58.22W
Negros 21 Oi 10.00N 123.00 E
Negru, Rîu- 15 Id 45.45N 25.46 E
Negru Vodă 15 Lf 43.49N 28.12 E
Nehajevski 16 Ld 50.27N 41.46 E
Nehalem River 46 Dd 45.40N 123.56W
Nehāvand 24 Me 35.56N 49.31 E
Nehe 27 Lb 48.28N 124.53 E
Nehoiu 15 Jd 45.26N 26.17 E
Néhoué, Baie de- 63b Be 20.21S 164.09 E
Neiba 49 Ld 18.28N 71.25W
Neiba, Bahía de- 49 Ld 18.15N 71.02W
Neidin/Kenmare 9 Dj 51.53N 9.35W
Neige, Crêt de la- 11 Lh 46.16N 5.56 E
Neiges, Piton des- 30 Mk 21.05S 55.29 E
Neijiang 22 Mg 29.38N 104.58 E
Neilton 46 Dc 47.25N 123.52W
Nei-meng-ku Tzu-chih-ch'ü→Nei Monggol Zizhiqu [2] 27 Jc 44.00N 112.00 E
Nei Monggol Gaoyuan 21 Ne 42.00N 111.00 E
Nei Monggol Zizhiqu (Nei-meng-ku Tzu-chih-ch'ü)=Inner Mongolia (EN) [2] 27 Jc 44.00N 112.00 E
Neiqiu 28 Cf 37.17N 114.30 E
Neiva 53 Ie 2.56N 75.18W
Neja 19 Ed 58.19N 43.52 E
Nejanilini Lake 42 He 59.30N 97.50W
Nejdek 10 If 50.19N 12.44 E
Nejo 35 Fd 9.30N 35.32 E
Nejva 17 Kh 57.54N 62.18 E
Nekemt=Leqemt (EN) 31 Kh 9.05N 36.33 E
Neksø 8 Fi 55.04N 15.09 E
Nelemnoje 20 Kc 65.23N 151.08 E
Nelgese 20 Ic 66.40N 136.30 E
Nelichu 35 Ed 6.08N 34.25 E
Nelidovo 20 Dd 56.13N 32.50 E
Neligh 45 Ge 42.08N 98.02W
Neljaty 20 Ge 56.29N 115.50 E
Nelkan 20 Jd 64.15N 143.03 E
Nellore 22 Jh 12.56N 79.08 E
Nelma 20 Ig 47.40N 139.08 E
Nelson [2] 62 Ed 41.45S 172.30 E
Nelson 38 Jd 57.04N 92.30W
Nelson [B.C.-Can.] 42 Fg 49.29N 117.17W
Nelson [N.Z.] 58 Ii 41.16S 173.15 E
Nelson, Cape- [Austl.] 57 Fh 38.26S 141.33 E
Nelson, Cape- [Pap.N.Gui.] 59 Ja 9.00S 149.15 E
Nelson Island 40 Gd 60.35N 164.45W
Nelson's Dockyard 51d Bb 17.00N 61.46W
Nelspruit 31 Kk 25.30S 30.58 E
Néma 31 Gg 16.36N 7.15W
Néma, Dahr- 32 Ff 16.14N 7.30W
Neman 5 Id 55.18N 21.23 E
Neman 7 Fi 55.03N 22.01 E
Nembrala 26 Hi 10.53S 122.50 E
Nemda 7 Kh 57.31N 43.15 E
Neméa 15 Fl 37.49N 22.39 E
Neméa 15 Fl 37.49N 22.40 E
Nëmëçkes, Mali i- 15 Di 40.08N 20.24 E
Nemenčinė 8 Kj 54.50N 25.39 E
Nëmërçkës, Mali i- 15 Di 40.08N 20.24 E
Nemira, Vîrful- 15 Jc 46.15N 26.19 E
Nemirov 10 Tf 50.08N 23.28 E
Nemirov 16 Fe 48.59N 28.50 E
Némiscau 42 Jf 51.30N 77.00W
Nemjuga 7 Kd 65.29N 43.40 E
Nemours 11 If 48.16N 2.42 E
Nemunas 5 Id 55.18N 21.23 E
Nemunėlis 8 Kh 56.24N 24.10 E
Nemuro 27 Qc 43.20N 145.35 E
Nemuro-Hantō 29a Db 43.20N 145.35 E
Nemuro-Kaikyō=Nemuro Strait (EN) 20 Jh 43.50N 145.30 E
Nemuro Strait (EN)= Kunaširski Proliv 20 Jh 43.50N 145.30 E
Nemuro Strait (EN)= Nemuro-Kaikyō 20 Jh 43.50N 145.30 E
Nemuro-Wan 29a Db 43.25N 145.25 E
Nenagh/An tAonach 9 Ei 52.52N 8.12W
Nenana 40 Jd 64.30N 149.00W
Nenana 40 Jd 64.34N 149.07W
Nendo Island 57 Hf 10.40S 165.54 E
Nene 9 Ni 52.48N 0.13 E
Neneckij avtonomnaja respublika 19 Fb 67.30N 54.00 E
Nenjiang 22 Oe 49.10N 125.12 E
Nen Jiang 21 Oe 45.26N 124.39 E
Neo 29 Ed 35.38N 136.37 E
Neodesha 45 Ih 37.25N 95.41W
Néon Karlovásion 15 Jl 37.47N 26.42 E
Neosho 45 Ih 36.52N 94.22W
Neosho River 45 Ih 35.48N 95.18W
Néouvielle, Massif de- 11 Gl 42.51N 0.07 E
Nepal [1] 22 Kg 28.00N 84.00 E
Nepalganj 25 Gc 28.03N 81.37 E
Nephi 43 Ed 39.43N 111.50W
Nephin/Né Finn 9 Dg 54.01N 9.22W
Nepisiguit River 44 Ob 47.37N 65.38W
Nepoko 30 Jh 1.40N 27.01 E
Nepomuk 10 Jg 49.29N 13.34 E
Ner 10 Od 52.10N 18.40 E
Nera [It.] 14 Gh 42.26N 12.24 E
Nera [Rom.] 15 Ee 44.49N 21.22 E
Nérac 11 Gj 44.08N 0.21 E
Neratovice 10 Kf 50.16N 14.31 E
Nerău 15 Dd 45.58N 20.34 E
Nerča 20 Gf 51.54N 116.30 E
Nerčinsk 20 Gf 51.58N 116.35 E
Nerčinski Zavod 20 Gf 51.17N 119.30 E
Nerehta 19 Ed 57.28N 40.34 E
Nereju 15 Jd 45.42N 26.43 E
Nereta 8 Kh 56.12N 25.24 E
Neretva 14 Lg 43.02N 17.27 E
Neretvanski kanal 14 Lg 43.03N 17.11 E
Nerica 17 Fd 65.20N 52.45 E
Neringa 7 Ei 55.24N 21.05 E
Neringa 7 Ei 55.18N 21.00 E
Neringa-Juodkrante/ Neringa-Juodkrantė 8 Ii 55.35N 21.01 E
Neringa-Juodkrantė/ Neringa-Juodkrante 8 Ii 55.35N 21.01 E
Neringa-Nida 8 Ii 55.18N 20.53 E
Neringa-Preila/Neringa-Prejla 8 Ii 55.20N 20.59 E
Neringa-Prejla/Neringa-Preila 8 Ii 55.20N 20.59 E
Neriquinha 36 Df 15.45S 21.33 E
Neris/Njaris 8 Kj 54.55N 25.45 E
Nerja 13 Ih 36.44N 3.52W
Nerjungri 20 He 56.40N 124.47 E
Nerl 7 Jh 56.11N 40.34 E
Nerl 7 Jh 57.07N 37.39 E
Nerpio 13 Jf 38.09N 2.18W
Nerussa 16 Hc 52.33N 33.47 E
Nerva 13 Fg 37.42N 6.32W
Nervi, Genova- 14 Df 44.23N 9.02 E
Nervión 13 Ja 43.14N 2.53W
Nes 8 Cd 60.34N 9.59 E
Nes, Ameland- 12 Ha 53.26N 5.48 E
Nesbyen 7 Bf 60.34N 9.06 E
Nesebăr 15 Kg 42.39N 27.44 E
Nesjøen 8 Db 63.00N 12.00 E
Neskaupstaður 7a Db 65.09N 13.42W
Nesle 12 Ee 49.46N 2.45 E
Nesna 7 Cc 66.12N 13.02 E
Ness City 45 Gg 38.27N 99.54W
Nesterov 7 Fi 54.42N 22.34 E
Nesterov 16 Cd 50.03N 24.00 E
Néstos 15 Hi 40.51N 24.44 E
Nesttun 8 Ad 60.19N 5.20 E
Nesviž 16 Ec 53.13N 26.39 E
Netanya 24 Ff 32.20N 34.51 E
Netcong 44 Je 40.54N 74.43W
Nete 11 Kc 51.10N 4.15 E
Nethe 12 Lc 51.44N 9.23 E
Netherdale 59 Jd 21.08S 148.32 E
Netherlands (EN)= Nederland [1] 6 Ge 52.15N 5.30 E
Netherlands Antilles (EN) = Nederlandse Antillen [5] 53 Jd 12.15N 69.00W
Neto 14 Lk 39.12N 17.09 E
Netphen 12 Kd 50.55N 8.06 E
Nettebach 12 Jd 50.26N 7.28 E
Nettersheim 12 Id 50.30N 6.38 E
Nettetal 12 Ic 51.18N 6.12 E
Nettiling Lake 38 Lc 66.30N 70.40W
Nettuno 14 Gi 41.27N 12.39 E
Netzahualcóyotl, Presa- 48 Mi 17.00N 93.30W
Neubourg, Campagne du- 11 Ge 49.08N 1.00 E
Neubrandenburg 10 Jc 53.34N 13.16 E
Neuburg an der Donau 10 Hh 48.44N 11.11 E
Neuchâtel [2] 14 Ac 47.05N 6.50 E
Neuchâtel/Neuenburg 14 Ad 46.59N 6.56 E
Neuchâtel, Lac de- / Neuenburger See 14 Ad 46.55N 6.55 E
Neuenbürg 12 Kf 48.50N 8.35 E
Neuenburg/Neuchâtel 14 Ad 46.59N 6.56 E
Neuenburger See/ Neuchâtel, Lac de- 14 Ad 46.55N 6.55 E
Neuenhaus 12 Ib 52.30N 6.58 E
Neuenkirchen 12 Jb 52.15N 7.22 E
Neuerburg 12 Id 50.01N 6.18 E
Neufchâteau [Bel.] 11 Le 49.51N 5.26 E
Neufchâteau [Fr.] 11 Lf 48.21N 5.42 E
Neufchâtel-en-Bray 11 He 49.44N 1.27 E
Neufchâtel-Hardelot 12 Dd 50.37N 1.38 E
Neufchâtel Hardelot-Hardelot Plage 12 Dd 50.38N 1.35 E
Neufchâtel-sur-Aisne 12 Ge 49.26N 4.02 E
Neuffossé, Canal de- 12 Ed 50.45N 2.15 E
Neuhaus am Rennweg 10 Hf 50.31N 11.09 E
Neuilly-en-Thelle 12 Ee 49.13N 2.17 E
Neuilly-Saint-Front 12 Fe 49.10N 3.16 E
Neu-Isenburg 12 Kd 50.03N 8.42 E
Neukirchen-Vluyn 12 Ic 51.27N 6.35 E
Neum 14 Lh 42.55N 17.38 E
Neumagen Dhron 12 Ie 49.51N 6.54 E
Neumarkter Sattel 14 Id 47.06N 14.22 E
Neumarkt in der Oberpfalz 10 Hg 49.17N 11.28 E
Neumünster 10 Fb 54.04N 9.59 E
Neunkirchen [Aus.] 14 Kc 47.43N 16.05 E
Neunkirchen [Ger.] 10 Dg 49.21N 7.11 E
Neunkirchen [Ger.] 12 Kd 50.48N 8.00 E
Neunkirchen [Ger.] 12 Jd 50.51N 7.20 E
Neuquén 53 Ji 39.00S 68.05W
Neuquén [2] 56 Ge 39.00S 70.00W
Neuquén, Rio- 52 Ji 38.59S 68.00W
Neurupping 10 Id 52.56N 12.48 E
Neuse River 44 Ih 35.06N 76.30W
Neusiedl am See 14 Kc 47.56N 16.50 E
Neusiedler See (Fertö) 10 Mi 47.50N 16.45 E
Neuß 10 Ce 51.12N 6.42 E
Neustadt (Hessen) 12 Ld 50.51N 9.07 E
Neustadt am Rübenberge 10 Fd 52.30N 9.28 E
Neustadt an der Aisch 10 Gg 49.35N 10.36 E
Neustadt an der Orla 10 Hf 50.44N 11.45 E
Neustadt an der Weinstraße 10 Eg 49.21N 8.09 E
Neustadt bei Couburg 10 Hf 50.19N 11.07 E
Neustadt in Holstein 10 Gb 54.06N 10.49 E
Neustrelitz 10 Jc 53.22N 13.05 E
Neu-Ulm 10 Gh 48.24N 10.01 E
Neuville-les-Dieppe 12 De 49.55N 1.06 E
Neuville-sur-Saône 11 Ki 45.52N 4.51 E
Neuwerk 10 Ec 53.55N 8.30 E
Neuwied 10 Df 50.26N 7.28 E
Neva 5 Jd 59.55N 30.15 E
Nevada [2] 43 Dd 39.00N 117.00W
Nevada [Ia.-U.S.] 45 Je 42.01N 93.27W
Nevada [Mo.-U.S.] 43 Id 37.51N 94.22W
Nevada, Sierra- [Sp.] 5 Fh 37.05N 3.10W
Nevada, Sierra- [U.S.] 38 Hf 38.00N 119.15W
Nevada del Cocuy, Sierra- 52 Ie 6.10N 72.15W
Nevada de Santa Marta, Sierra- 52 Id 10.50N 73.40W
Nevado, Cerro- 52 Ie 3.59N 74.04W
Nevado de Ampato 52 Ig 15.50S 71.52W
Neve, Serra da- 30 Ij 13.52S 13.26 E
Nevel 19 Cd 56.02N 29.55 E
Nevele 12 Fc 51.02N 3.33 E
Nevelsk 20 Jg 46.37N 141.57 E
Neverkino 16 Oc 52.47N 46.48 E
Nevers 11 Jh 46.59N 3.10 E
Nevesinje 14 Mg 43.16N 18.07 E
Nevinnomyssk 19 Eg 44.38N 41.58 E
Nevis 47 Le 17.10N 62.34W
Nevis, Ben- 5 Fd 56.48N 5.01W
Nevis Peak 51c Ab 17.10N 62.34W
Nevjansk 19 Gd 57.32N 60.13 E
Nevşehir 23 Db 38.38N 34.43 E
Nevskoje 28 Lb 45.42N 133.40 E
Newala 36 Ge 10.56S 39.18 E
New Albany [In.-U.S.] 43 Jd 38.18N 85.49W
New Albany [Ms.-U.S.] 45 Li 34.29N 89.00W
New Alresford 12 Ac 51.05N 1.10W
New Amsterdam 53 Ke 6.17N 57.36W
Newark [De.-U.S.] 44 Jf 39.41N 75.45W
Newark [N.J.-U.S.] 43 Mc 40.44N 74.11W
Newark [N.Y.-U.S.] 44 Id 43.03N 77.06W
Newark [Oh.-U.S.] 43 Kc 40.03N 82.25W
Newark-on-Trent 9 Mh 53.05N 0.49W
New Bedford 43 Mc 41.38N 70.56W
New Bern 43 Ld 35.07N 77.03W
Newberry [Mi.-U.S.] 44 Eb 46.21N 85.30W
Newberry [S.C.-U.S.] 44 Gh 34.17N 81.37W
New Braunfels 43 Hf 29.42N 98.08W
New Britain 44 Ke 41.40N 72.47W
New Britain Island 57 Ge 5.40S 151.00 E
New Britain Trench (EN) 60 Ei 6.00S 153.00 E
New Brunswick 44 Je 40.29N 74.27W
New Brunswick [3] 42 Kg 46.30N 66.45W
New Buckenham 12 Db 52.28N 1.05 E
New Buffalo 44 De 41.47N 86.45W
Newburgh 43 Mc 41.30N 74.00W
Newbury 9 Lj 51.25N 1.20W
New Caledonia (EN) = Nouvelle-Calédonie [5] 58 Hg 21.30S 165.30 E
New Caledonia (EN)= Nouvelle-Calédonie 57 Hg 21.30S 165.30 E
New Caledonia Basin (EN) 3 Jm 30.00S 165.00 E
New Carlisle 44 Oa 48.01N 65.20W
New Castile (EN)=Castilla la Nueva 13 Id 40.00N 3.45W
New Castle [In.-U.S.] 44 Ef 39.55N 85.22W
New Castle [Pa.-U.S.] 43 Kc 41.00N 80.22W
Newcastle [Austl.] 58 Gh 32.56S 151.46 E
Newcastle [N.B.-Can.] 42 Kg 47.00N 65.34W
Newcastle [N.Ire.-U.K.] 9 Hg 54.12N 5.54W
Newcastle [S.Afr.] 37 De 27.49S 29.55 E
Newcastle [St.C.N.] 51c Ab 17.13N 62.34W
Newcastle/An Caisleán Nua 9 Hg 54.12N 5.54W
Newcastle Creek 59 Gc 17.20S 133.23 E
Newcastle-under-Lyme 9 Kh 53.00N 2.14W

Index Symbols

[1] Independent Nation
[2] State, Region
[3] District, County
[4] Municipality
[5] Colony, Dependency
Continent
Physical Region

Historical or Cultural Region
Mount, Mountain
Volcano
Hill
Mountains, Mountain Range
Hills, Escarpment
Plateau, Upland

Pass, Gap
Plain, Lowland
Delta
Salt Flat
Valley, Canyon
Crater, Cave
Karst Features

Depression
Polder
Desert, Dunes
Forest, Woods
Heath, Steppe
Oasis
Cape, Point

Coast, Beach
Cliff
Peninsula
Isthmus
Sandbank
Island
Atoll

Rock, Reef
Islands, Archipelago
Rocks, Reefs
Coral Reef
Well, Spring
Geyser
River, Stream

Waterfall Rapids
River Mouth, Estuary
Lake
Salt Lake
Intermittent Lake
Reservoir
Swamp, Pond

Canal
Glacier
Ice Shelf, Pack Ice
Ocean
Sea
Gulf, Bay
Strait, Fjord

Lagoon
Bank
Seamount
Tablemount
Ridge
Shelf
Basin

Escarpment, Sea Scarp
Fracture
Trench, Abyss
National Park, Reserve
Point of Interest
Recreation Site
Cave, Cavern

Historic Site
Ruins
Wall, Walls
Church, Abbey
Temple
Scientific Station
Airport

Port
Lighthouse
Mine
Tunnel
Dam, Bridge

Newcastle-upon-Tyne 6 Fd 54.59N 1.35W
Newcastle Waters 58 Ef 17.24S 133.24 E
Newcastle West/An Caisleán Nua 9 Di 52.27N 9.03W
New Delhi 22 Jg 28.36N 77.12 E
New Denver 46 Ga 50.00N 117.22W
Newell 45 Ed 44.43N 103.25W
Newell, Lake- 46 Ja 50.25N 111.56W
New England 38 Le 44.00N 71.20W
New England Range 57 Gh 30.00S 151.50 E
New England Seamounts (EN) 38 Mf 38.00N 61.00W
Newenham, Cape- 40 Ge 58.37N 162.12W
New Forest 9 Lk 50.55N 1.35W
Newfoundland [3] 42 Lf 52.00N 56.00W
Newfoundland, Island of- 38 Ne 48.30N 56.00W
Newfoundland Basin (EN) 3 De 45.00N 40.00W
New Galloway 9 If 55.05N 4.10W
New Georgia 57 Ge 8.30S 157.20 E
New Georgia Island 60 Fi 8.15S 157.30 E
New Georgia Sound (The Slot) 60 Fi 8.00S 158.10 E
New Glasgow 42 Lg 45.35N 62.39W
New Guinea/Pulau Irian 57 Fe 5.00S 140.00 E
New Guinea Trench (EN) 60 Bg 0.05N 135.50 E
New Hampshire [2] 43 Mc 43.35N 71.40W
New Hampton 45 Je 43.03N 92.19W
New Hanover Island 57 Ge 2.30S 150.15 E
New Harmony 44 Df 38.08N 87.56W
New Haven 39 Le 41.18N 72.56W
Newhaven 9 Nk 50.47N 0.03 E
New Hebrides/Nouvelles Hébrides 57 Hf 16.01S 167.01 E
New Hebrides Trench (EN) 3 Jl 20.00S 168.00 E
New Iberia 43 If 30.00N 91.49W
New Ireland Island 57 Ge 3.20S 152.00 E
New Jersey [2] 43 Mc 40.15N 74.30W
New Kowloon/Julong 22 Ng 22.20N 114.09 E
New Liskeard 42 Jg 47.30N 79.40W
New London 43 Mc 41.21N 72.07W
New Madrid 45 Lh 36.36N 89.32W
Newman 59 Dd 23.15S 119.35 E
Newmarket [Eng.-U.K.] 9 Ni 52.15N 0.25 E
Newmarket [Ont.-Can.] 44 Hc 44.03N 79.28W
New Martinsville 44 Gf 39.39N 80.52W
New Meadows 46 Gd 44.58N 116.32W
New Mexico [2] 43 Fe 34.30N 106.00W
Newnan 44 Ei 33.23N 84.48W
New Norfolk 59 Jh 42.47S 147.03 E
New Orleans 39 Jg 29.58N 90.07W
New Philadelphia 44 Ge 40.30N 81.27W
New Pine Creek 46 Ee 42.01N 120.18W
New-Plymouth 58 Ih 39.04S 174.04 E
Newport [Ar.-U.S.] 45 Ki 35.37N 91.17W
Newport [Eng.-U.K.] 12 Cc 51.59N 0.15 E
Newport [Eng.-U.K.] 9 Lk 50.42N 1.18W
Newport [Fl.-U.S.] 44 Ej 30.14N 84.12W
Newport [Or.-U.S.] 43 Cc 44.38N 124.03W
Newport [R.I.-U.S.] 44 Le 41.30N 71.19W
Newport [Tn.-U.S.] 44 Fh 35.58N 83.11W
Newport [Vt.-U.S.] 44 Kc 44.56N 72.13W
Newport [Wales-U.K.] 9 Kj 51.35N 3.00W
Newport [Wa.-U.S.] 46 Gb 48.11N 117.03W
Newport Beach 43 De 33.37N 117.54W
Newport News 39 Lf 37.04N 76.28W
Newport Pagnell 12 Bb 52.05N 0.43W
New Providence Island 47 Ic 25.02N 77.24W
Newquay 9 Hk 50.25N 5.05W
New Quebec Crater (EN) = Nouveau-Québec, Cratère du- 42 Kd 61.30N 73.55W
New Richmond [Oh.-U.S.] 44 Ef 38.57N 84.16W
New Richmond [Que.-Can.] 44 Oa 48.10N 65.52W
New River [Blz.] 49 Cd 18.22N 88.24W
New River [Guy.] 54 Gc 3.23N 57.36W
New River [U.S.] 44 Ff 38.50N 82.06W
New Rockford 45 Gc 47.41N 99.15W
New Romney 12 Cd 50.59N 0.56 E
New Ross/Ros Mhic Thriúin 9 Gi 52.24N 6.56W
Newry/an t-Iúr 9 Gg 54.11N 6.20W
New Salem 45 Fc 46.51N 101.25W
New Sandy Bay 51n Ba 13.20N 61.08W
New Schwabenland (EN) 66 Cf 72.30S 1.00 E
New Siberia (EN)=Novaja Sibir, Ostrov- 21 Qb 75.00N 149.00 E
New Siberian Islands (EN) =Novosibirskije Ostrova 21 Qb 75.00N 142.00 E
New Smyrna Beach 44 Gk 29.02N 80.56W
New South Wales 59 Jf 33.00S 146.00 E
Newton [Ia.-U.S.] 45 Jf 41.42N 93.03W
Newton [Il.-U.S.] 45 Lg 38.59N 88.10W
Newton [Ks.-U.S.] 43 Hd 38.03N 97.21W
Newton [Ma.-U.S.] 44 Ld 42.21N 71.13W
Newton [Ms.-U.S.] 45 Lj 32.19N 89.10W
Newton [N.J.-U.S.] 44 Je 41.03N 74.45W
Newton Abbot 9 Jk 50.32N 3.36W
Newton Stewart 9 Ig 54.57N 4.29W
Newtontoppen 67 Kd 72.02N 17.30 E
New Town 45 Ec 47.59N 102.30W
Newtown 9 Ji 52.32N 3.19W
Newtownabbey/Baile na Mainistreach 9 Hg 54.42N 5.54W
Newtownards/Baile Nua na hArda 9 Hg 54.36N 5.41W
New Ulm 43 Ic 44.19N 94.28W
New Westminster 42 Fg 49.12N 122.55W
New York 39 Le 40.43N 74.01W
New York [2] 43 Lc 43.00N 75.00W
New York State Barge Canal 44 Hd 43.05N 78.43W
New Zealand [1] 58 Ii 41.00S 174.00 E
New Zealand 57 Ii 41.00S 174.00 E
Nexpa, Río- 48 Hh 18.05N 102.46W
Neyagawa 29 Dd 34.46N 135.36 E
Neyrīz 24 Ph 29.12N 54.19 E
Neyshābūr 23 Ib 36.12N 58.50 E
Nežárka 10 Kg 49.11N 14.43 E
Nežin 19 De 51.02N 31.57 E
Ngabé 36 Cc 3.12S 16.11 E
Ngahere 62 De 42.24S 171.26 E
Ngajangel 64a Ba 8.05N 134.43 E
Ngala 34 Hc 12.20N 14.11 E
Ngaliema, Chutes-=Stanley Falls (EN) 30 Jh 0.30N 25.30 E
Ngamegei Passage 64a Bb 7.44N 134.34 E
Ngami, Lake- 37 Cd 20.37S 22.40 E
Ngamiland [3] 37 Cc 19.09S 22.47 E
Ngamring 27 Ef 29.14N 87.12 E
Ngangala 35 Ee 4.42N 31.55 E
Ngangerabeli Plain 36 Hc 1.30S 40.15 E
Ngangla Ringco 27 De 31.40N 83.00 E
Nganglong Kangri 27 De 32.45N 81.12 E
Nganglong Kangri 21 Kf 32.00N 83.00 E
Ngangzê Co 27 Ee 31.00N 86.55 E
Ngao 25 Je 18.45N 99.59 E
Ngaoundéré 31 Ih 7.19N 13.35 E
Ngapara 62 Df 44.57S 170.45 E
Ngara 36 Fc 2.28S 30.39 E
Ngardmau 64a Bb 7.37N 134.35 E
Ngardmau Bay 64a Bb 7.39N 134.35 E
Ngardololok 64a Ac 7.00N 134.16 E
Ngaregur 64a Bb 7.45N 134.38 E
Ngarekeukl 64a Ac 7.00N 134.14 E
Ngariungs 64a Ba 8.03N 134.43 E
Ngaruangl 64a Ba 8.10N 134.39 E
Ngaruangl Passage 64a Ba 8.07N 134.40 E
Ngaruawahia 62 Fb 37.40S 175.09 E
Ngaruroro 62 Gc 39.34S 176.55 E
Ngatangiia 64p Cb 21.14S 159.43W
Ngatangiia Harbour 64p Cb 21.14S 159.43W
Ngateguil, Point- 64a Bc 7.26N 134.37 E
Ngatik Atoll 57 Gd 5.51N 157.16 E
Ngatpang 64a Bc 7.28N 134.32 E
Ngau Island 63d Bc 18.02S 179.18 E
Ngauruhoe 62 Fc 39.09S 175.38 E
Ngawa/Aba 27 He 32.55N 101.45 E
Ngayu 36 Eb 1.35N 27.13 E
Ngemelis Islands 64a Ac 7.07N 134.15 E
Ngeregong 64a Ac 7.07N 134.22 E
Ngergoi 64a Ac 7.05N 134.17 E
Ngesebus 64a Ac 7.03N 134.16 E
Nggamea 63d Cb 16.46S 179.46W
Nggatokae 63a Dc 8.46S 158.11 E
Nggela Pile 63a Ec 9.08S 160.20 E
Nggela Sule 63a Ec 9.03S 160.12 E
Nggelelevu 63d Cb 16.05S 179.09W
Ngidinga 36 Cd 5.37S 15.17 E
Ngiro, Ewaso- 36 Gb 0.28N 39.55 E
Ngo 36 Cc 2.29S 15.45 E
Ngoangoa 35 Dd 5.58N 25.10 E
Ngobasangel 64a Ac 7.16N 134.20 E
Ngoko 36 Cb 1.40N 16.03 E
Ngola Shankou 27 Gd 35.30N 99.36 E
Ngoma 36 Ef 15.58S 25.56 E
Ngoring Hu 27 Gd 35.00N 97.30 E
Ngorongoro Crater 30 Ki 3.10S 35.35 E
Ngoui 34 Cb 16.09N 13.55W
Ngouna 63b Dc 17.26S 168.21 E
Ngounié [3] 36 Bc 2.00S 11.00 E
Ngounié 36 Bc 0.37S 10.18 E
Ngoura 35 Bc 12.52N 16.27 E
Ngouri 35 Bc 13.38N 15.22 E
Ngourti 34 Hb 15.19N 13.12 E
Ngousouboot, Pointe- 63b Ca 13.58S 167.27 E
Ngudu 36 Fc 2.58S 33.20 E
Nguigmi 31 Ig 14.15N 13.07 E
Ngulu Atoll 57 Ed 8.18N 137.29 E
Nguni 36 Gc 0.50S 38.20 E
Nguru 31 Ig 12.53N 10.28 E
Ngwaketse 37 Cd 24.50S 24.00 E
Nhachengue 37 Fd 22.51S 35.11 E
Nhamundá 54 Gd 2.14S 56.43W
Nhamundá, Rio- 54 Gd 2.12S 56.41W
Nhandeara 55 Ge 20.40S 50.02W
Nhandutiba 55 Jb 14.37S 44.12W
Nharea 36 Ce 11.28S 16.53 E
Nha Trang 22 Mh 12.15N 109.11 E
Nhecolândia 55 Dd 19.16S 57.04W
Nhia 36 Be 10.15S 14.12 E
Nhulunbuy 58 Ef 12.00S 35.58 E
Niafounké 34 Eb 15.56N 4.00W
Niagara Escarpment 44 Gc 44.30N 80.35W
Niagara Falls 33 Le 43.05N 79.04W
Niagara Falls [N.Y.-U.S.] 43 Lc 43.06N 79.02W
Niagara Falls [Ont.-Can.] 42 Jh 43.06N 79.04W
Niagara River 44 Hd 43.15N 79.04W
Niagassola 34 Dc 12.19N 9.07W
Niah 26 Ff 3.52N 113.44 E
Niakaramandougou 34 Dd 8.40N 5.17W
Niamey 31 Hg 13.31N 2.07 E
Niamey [2] 34 Fc 14.00N 2.00 E
Niandan 34 Dc 10.35N 9.45W
Niangara 31 Jh 3.42N 27.52 E
Niangay, Lac- 34 Eb 15.50N 3.00W
Niangoloko 34 Ec 10.17N 4.55W
Nia-Nia 36 Eb 1.24N 27.36 E
Nianzishan 27 Lb 47.31N 122.50 E
Niao Dao 27 Gd 37.20N 99.50 E
Niaoshu Shan 27 He 34.54N 104.04 E
Niari [3] 36 Bc 4.30S 13.00 E
Niari 36 Bc 3.56S 12.12 E
Nias, Palau- 21 Li 1.05N 97.35 E
Niassa [3] 37 Fb 13.00S 36.00 E
Niassa, Lago-=Nyasa, Lake- (EN) 30 Kj 12.00S 34.30 E
Niau, Ile- 57 Mf 16.09S 146.21W
Nibāk 24 Nj 24.24N 50.50 E
Nibe 8 Ch 56.59N 9.38 E
Nica 17 Lh 57.29N 64.33 E
Nīca/Nica 8 Ih 56.25N 20.56 E
Nica/Nīca 8 Ih 56.25N 20.56 E
Nicanor Olivera 55 Cn 38.17S 59.12W
Nicaragua [1] 39 Kh 13.00N 85.00W
Nicaragua, Lago de-=Nicaragua, Lake- (EN) 38 Kh 11.35N 85.25W
Nicaragua, Lake- (EN)=Nicaragua, Lago de- 38 Kh 11.35N 85.25W
Nicastro 14 Kl 38.59N 16.19 E
Nice 6 Gg 43.42N 7.15 E
Niceville 44 Dj 30.31N 86.29W
Nichicum, Lac- 42 Kf 53.08N 70.55W
Nichinan [Jap.] 29 Cd 35.10N 133.16 E
Nichinan [Jap.] 28 Ki 31.36N 131.23 E
Nicholas Channel 49 Gb 23.25N 80.05W
Nicholas Channel (EN)=Nicolás, Canal- 47 Hd 23.25N 80.05W
Nicholasville 44 Eg 37.53N 84.34W
Nicholls Town 49 Ia 25.08N 78.00W
Nicholson Range 59 De 27.15S 116.45 E
Nicholson River 57 Ef 17.31S 139.36 E
Nickerson Ice Shelf 66 Mf 75.45S 145.00W
Nickol Bay 59 Dd 20.40S 116.50 E
Nicobar Islands 21 Li 8.00N 93.30 E
Nicoclí 49 Ii 8.26N 76.48W
Nicolajevka 15 Nb 47.33N 30.41 E
Nicola River 46 Ea 50.25N 121.18W
Nicolás, Canal-=Nicholas Channel (EN) 47 Hd 23.25N 80.05W
Nicolet 44 Kb 46.14N 72.37W
Nicopolis (EN) = Nikópolis 15 Dj 39.00N 20.45 E
Nicosia 14 Im 37.45N 14.24 E
Nicosia (EN)=Lefkosa/Levkōsia 22 Ff 35.10N 33.22 E
Nicosia (EN)=Levkōsia/Lefkosa 22 Ff 35.10N 33.22 E
Nicotera 14 Jl 38.33N 15.56 E
Nicoya 47 Gf 10.09N 85.27W
Nicoya, Golfo de- 47 Hg 9.47N 84.48W
Nicoya, Peninsula de-=Nicoya Peninsula (EN) 38 Ki 10.00N 85.25W
Nicoya Peninsula (EN)=Nicoya, Peninsula de- 38 Ki 10.00N 85.25W
Nicuadala 37 Fc 17.37S 36.50 E
Niculiţel 15 Ld 45.11N 28.29 E
Nida 10 Qf 50.18N 20.52 E
Nidda 12 Ld 50.25N 9.00 E
Nidda 10 Ef 50.06N 8.34 E
Nidder 12 Kd 50.12N 8.47 E
Nideggen 12 Id 50.42N 6.29 E
Nidelva [Nor.] 8 Cf 58.24N 8.48 E
Nidelva [Nor.] 8 Da 63.26N 10.25 E
Nido, Sierra del- 48 Fc 29.30N 106.45W
Nidže 15 Ei 41.00N 21.50 E
Nidzica 10 Qf 50.12N 20.40 E
Nidzica 10 Qc 53.22N 20.26 E
Nidzkie, Jezioro- 10 Rc 53.37N 21.30 E
Niebüll 10 Eb 54.48N 8.50 E
Nied 12 Ie 49.23N 6.40 E
Nieddu 14 Dj 40.44N 9.34 E
Niederbayern 10 Ih 48.35N 12.30 E
Niederbronn-les-Bains 11 Nf 48.58N 7.38 E
Niedere Tauern 14 Hc 47.20N 14.00 E
Niederlausitz 10 Ke 51.40N 14.15 E
Nieder-Olm 12 Ke 49.54N 8.13 E
Niederösterreich = Lower Austria (EN) [2] 14 Jb 48.30N 15.45 E
Niedersachsen=Lower Saxony (EN) [2] 10 Fd 52.00N 10.00 E
Niederwald 10 Df 50.00N 8.00 E
Niederzier 12 Id 50.53N 6.28 E
Niefang 34 He 1.50N 10.14 E
Niegocin, Jezioro- 10 Rb 54.00N 21.50 E
Niel 12 Gc 51.07N 4.20 E
Nielfa, Puerto de- 13 Hf 38.32N 4.23W
Niéllé 34 Dc 10.12N 5.38W
Niellim 35 Bd 9.42N 17.49 E
Niemba 36 Ed 5.57S 28.26 E
Niemba 36 Ed 5.57S 28.26 E
Niemodlin 10 Nf 50.39N 17.37 E
Niéna 34 Dc 11.25N 6.20W
Nienburg (Weser) 10 Fd 52.38N 9.13 E
Niepołomice 10 Qf 50.03N 20.13 E
Niermalak, Pointe- 63b Cb 14.21S 167.24 E
Niers 10 Be 51.43N 5.57 E
Nierstein 12 Ke 49.53N 8.20 E
Niesky/Niska 10 Ke 51.18N 14.49 E
Nieszawa 10 Od 52.50N 18.55 E
Nieuport/Nieuwpoort 11 Ic 51.08N 2.45 E
Nieuw Amsterdam 54 Gb 5.53N 55.05W
Nieuwe-Pekela 12 Ia 53.04N 6.59 E
Nieuweschans 12 Ja 53.11N 7.15 E
Nieuw Milligen, Apeldoorn- 12 Hb 52.14N 5.45 E
Nieuw Nickerie 53 Ke 5.57N 56.59W
Nieuwolda 12 Ia 53.14N 6.59 E
Nieuwoudtville 37 Bf 31.22S 19.06 E
Nieuwpoort/Nieuport 11 Ic 51.08N 2.45 E
Nieuw Weerdinge, Emmen- 12 Jb 52.52N 7.01 E
Nieves 48 He 24.00N 103.01W
Nièvre [3] 11 Jg 47.05N 3.30 E
Nièvre 11 Jh 46.59N 3.10 E
Nigata 28 Lg 34.13N 132.39 E
Niğde 23 Db 37.59N 34.42 E
Nigenān 24 Qe 34.13N 57.09 E
Niger [1] 31 Hg 16.00N 8.00 E
Niger 30 Hh 5.33N 6.33 E
Niger [2] 34 Gd 9.40N 6.00 E
Niger Basin (EN) 30 Gg 15.00N 2.00 E
Niger Delta 30 Hh 4.50N 6.00 E
Nigeria [1] 31 Hh 10.00N 8.00 E
Night Hawk Lake 44 Ga 48.28N 81.00W
Nightingale Island 30 Fi 37.25S 12.28W
Nigrita 15 Gi 40.54N 23.30 E
Nihiru Atoll 57 Mf 16.42S 142.50W
Nihoa Island 57 Kb 23.06N 161.58W
Nihonmatsu 28 Pf 37.35N 140.25 E
Nihuil, Embalse del- 56 Ge 35.05S 68.45W
Niigata 22 Pf 37.55N 139.03 E
Niigata Ken [2] 28 Of 37.30N 138.50 E
Niihama 28 Lh 33.58N 133.16 E
Niihau Island 57 Kb 21.55N 160.10W
Niimi 28 Lg 34.59N 133.28 E
Niisato 29 Gb 39.36N 141.49 E
Niitsu 28 Of 37.48N 139.07 E
Nijar 13 Jh 36.58N 2.12W
Nijkerk 12 Hb 52.14N 5.29 E
Nijlen 12 Gc 51.10N 4.39 E
Nijmegen 11 Lc 51.50N 5.50 E
Nijvel/Nivelles 11 Kd 50.36N 4.20 E
Nijverdal, Hellendoorn- 12 Ib 52.22N 6.27 E
Nikel 19 Db 69.24N 30.13 E
Niki 15 Ei 40.55N 21.25 E
Nikitin Seamount (EN) 21 Kj 3.00S 83.00 E
Nikki 34 Fd 9.56N 3.12 E
Nikkō 29 Fc 36.44N 139.35 E
Nikolajev 16 Ce 49.32N 23.58 E
Nikolajev 6 Jf 46.58N 32.00 E
Nikolajevka 18 Kc 43.37N 77.01 E
Nikolajevo 8 Mf 58.14N 29.32 E
Nikolajevsk 19 Ee 50.02N 45.31 E
Nikolajevskaja Oblast [3] 19 Df 47.20N 32.00 E
Nikolajevski 20 Hf 54.50N 129.25 E
Nikolajevsk-na-Amure 22 Od 53.08N 140.44 E
Nikolo-Berjozovka (Neftekamsk) 19 Fd 56.06N 54.17 E
Nikolsk 19 Ee 53.42N 46.03 E
Nikolsk 19 Ed 59.33N 45.31 E
Nikolski [Ak.-U.S.] 40a Eb 53.15N 168.22W
Nikolski → Saptajev 19 Gf 47.55N 67.33 E
Nikonga 36 Fc 4.40S 31.28 E
Nikopol [Bul.] 15 Hf 43.42N 24.54 E
Nikopol 19 Df 47.35N 34.25 E
Nikópolis = Nicopolis (EN) 15 Dj 39.00N 20.45 E
Nikpey 24 Md 36.50N 48.10 E
Niksar 24 Gb 40.36N 36.58 E
Nikšić 15 Bg 42.46N 18.58 E
Nikumaroro Atoll (Gardner) 57 Je 4.40S 174.32W
Nikunau Island 57 Ie 1.23S 176.26 E
Nīl, Kūh-e- 24 Ng 30.52N 50.49 E
Nīl, Nahr an-=Nile (EN) 30 Ke 30.10N 31.06 E
Nila, Pulau- 26 Ih 6.44S 129.31 E
Nilakka 7 Ge 63.07N 26.33 E
Niland 46 Hj 33.14N 115.31W
Nilandu Atoll 25a Bb 3.00N 72.55 E
Nile [3] 36 Fb 3.00N 31.30 E
Nile (EN)=Nīl, Nahr an- 30 Ke 30.10N 31.06 E
Nile Delta (EN) 30 Ke 31.20N 31.00 E
Nīleh, Kūh-e- 24 Nf 32.59N 50.32 E
Niles 44 De 41.50N 86.15W
Nilka 27 Dc 43.47N 82.20 E
Nīl Kowtal 23 Kc 34.48N 67.22 E
Nilsiä 7 Ge 63.12N 28.05 E
Nilüfer 15 Li 40.18N 28.27 E
Nimba [3] 34 Dd 6.45N 8.45W
Nimba, Monts-=Nimba Mountains (EN) 30 Gh 7.35N 8.28W
Nimba Mountains (EN)=Nimba, Monts- 30 Gh 7.35N 8.28W
Nîmes 6 Gg 43.50N 4.21 E
Nimjad 32 Df 17.25N 15.41W
Nimmitabel 59 Jg 36.31S 149.16 E
Nimpkish River 46 Ba 50.32N 126.59W
Nimrode Glacier 66 Kg 82.27S 161.00 E
Nimrud 24 Jd 36.06N 43.20 E
Nīmrūz [3] 23 Jc 30.30N 62.00 E
Nims 12 Ie 49.51N 6.28 E
Nimule 31 Kh 3.36N 32.03 E
Nimún, Punta- 48 Ng 20.46N 90.25W
Nin 14 Jf 44.14N 15.11 E
Nina 37 Bd 22.57S 18.14 E
Nīnawā [3] 24 Je 35.45N 42.45 E
Nīnawā=Nineveh (EN) 23 Fb 36.22N 43.09 E
Nine Degree Channel 21 Ji 9.00N 73.00 E
Ninetyeast Ridge (EN) 3 Gj 10.00S 90.00 E
Ninety Mile Beach [Austl.] 59 Jg 38.15S 147.25 E
Ninety Mile Beach [N.Z.] 62 Ea 34.45S 173.00 E
Nineveh (EN)=Nīnawā 23 Fb 36.22N 43.09 E
Ning'an 27 Mc 44.22N 129.23 E
Ningbo 22 Og 29.55N 121.28 E
Ningcheng (Tianyi) 27 Kc 41.34N 119.25 E
Ningde 27 Kf 26.44N 119.29 E
Ningdu 27 Kf 26.31N 115.59 E
Ningguo 28 Ei 30.39N 119.00 E
Ninghai 28 Fj 29.19N 121.26 E
Ning-hsia-hui-tsu Tzu-chih-ch'ü → Ningxia Huizu Zizhiqu=Ningsia Hui (EN) [2] 27 Id 37.00N 106.00 E
Ningjin [China] 28 Df 37.39N 116.48 E
Ningjin [China] 28 Cf 37.37N 114.55 E
Ningjing Shan 27 Ge 31.45N 97.15 E
Ninglang 27 Hf 27.17N 100.52 E
Ningling 28 Cg 34.27N 115.18 E
Ningnan 27 Hf 27.05N 102.44 E
Ningqiang 27 Ie 32.48N 106.15 E
Ningsia Hui (EN)=Ning-hsia-hui-tsu Tzu-chih-ch'ü → Ningxia Huizu Zizhiqu [2] 27 Id 37.00N 106.00 E
Ningsia Hui (EN)=Ningxia Huizu Zizhiqu (Ning-hsia-hui-tsu Tzu-chih-ch'ü) [2] 27 Id 37.00N 106.00 E
Ningwu 27 Jd 38.59N 112.14 E
Ningxia Huizu Zizhiqu (Ning-hsia-hui-tsu Tzu-chih-ch'ü)=Ningsia Hui (EN) [2] 27 Id 37.00N 106.00 E
Ningxian 27 Id 35.27N 107.50 E
Ningxiang 28 Bj 28.16N 112.33 E
Ningyang 28 Dg 35.45N 116.48 E
Ningyō-Tōge 29 Cd 35.19N 133.56 E
Ninh Binh 25 Ld 20.15N 105.59 E
Ninh Hoa 25 Lf 12.29N 109.08 E
Ninigo Group 57 Fe 1.15S 144.15 E
Niniva 65b Ba 19.46S 174.38W
Ninnis Glacier 66 Je 68.12S 147.12 E
Ninocminda (Bogdanovka) 16 Mi 41.15N 43.36 E
Ninohe 27 Pc 40.16N 141.18 E
Ninove 12 Fd 50.50N 4.00 E
Nioaque 54 Gh 21.08S 55.48W
Niobrara 38 Je 42.45N 98.00W
Niobrara 45 He 42.25N 98.00W
Nioghalvfjerdsfjorden 41 Kc 79.30N 18.45W
Nioki 36 Cc 2.43S 17.41 E
Niono 34 Dc 14.15N 6.00W
Nioro du Rip 34 Bc 13.45N 15.48W
Nioro du Sahel 31 Gg 15.14N 9.37W
Niort 11 Fh 46.19N 0.28W
Nipawin 42 Hf 53.22N 104.00W
Nipe, Bahia de- 49 Jc 20.47N 75.42W
Nipesotsu-Yama 29a Cb 43.27N 143.02 E
Nipigon 39 Ke 49.01N 88.16W
Nipigon, Lake- 38 Ke 49.50N 88.30W
Nipigon Bay 45 Mb 48.53N 87.50W
Nipissing, Lake- 38 Le 46.17N 80.00W
Nippon=Japan (EN) [1] 22 Pf 38.00N 137.00 E
Nippur 24 Kf 32.10N 45.10 E
Niquelândia 54 If 14.27S 48.27W
Niquero 49 Ic 20.03N 77.35W
Niquitao, Teta de- 49 Li 9.07N 70.30W
Niquivil 56 Gd 30.25S 68.42W
Nīr 24 Lc 38.02N 47.59 E
Nirasaki 29 Fd 35.43N 138.27 E
Nirji → Morin Dawa 27 Lb 48.30N 124.28 E
Nirmal 25 Fe 19.06N 78.21 E
Niš 6 Ig 43.19N 21.54 E
Nisa 13 Ee 39.31N 7.39W
Nīşāb 23 Gg 14.24N 46.38 E
Nisāh, Sha'īb- 24 Lj 24.11N 47.11 E
Nišava 15 Ef 43.22N 21.46 E
Niscemi 14 Im 37.09N 14.23 E
Nishibetsu-Gawa 29a Db 43.23N 145.17 E
Nishikawa 29 Gb 38.26N 140.08 E
Nishiki 29 Bd 34.16N 131.57 E
Nishinomiya 29 Dd 34.43N 135.20 E
Nishino'omote 27 Ne 30.44N 131.00 E
Nishino-Shima 60 Cb 27.30N 140.53 E
Nishi-No-Shima 28 Lf 36.06N 133.00 E
Nishiokoppe 29a Ca 44.20N 142.57 E
Nishi-Sonogi-Hantō 29 Ae 32.55N 129.45 E
Nishiwaki 29 Dd 34.59N 134.58 E
Nisiros 15 Km 36.35N 27.10 E
Niska/Niesky 10 Ke 51.18N 14.49 E
Niška Banja 15 Ff 43.18N 22.01 E
Nisko 10 Sf 50.31N 22.09 E
Nismes, Viroinval- 12 Gd 50.05N 4.33 E
Nisoi Aiyaiou [2] 15 Il 37.40N 25.40 E
Nisporeny 16 Ff 47.06N 28.10 E
Nissan 8 Eh 56.40N 12.51 E
Nissan 63a Ba 4.30S 154.14 E
Nisser 8 Ce 59.10N 8.30 E
Nissum Bredning 8 Ch 56.40N 8.20 E
Nissum Fjord 8 Ch 56.20N 8.15 E
Nita 29 Cd 35.12N 133.00 E
Nitchequon 42 Kf 53.15N 70.44W
Niterói 53 Lh 22.53S 43.07W
Nith 9 Jf 55.00N 3.35W
Nitra 10 Oi 47.46N 18.10 E
Nitra 10 Oh 48.19N 18.05 E
Niuafo'ou Island 57 Jf 15.35S 175.38W
Niuatoputapu Island 57 Jf 15.57S 173.45W
Niue [5] 58 Kf 19.02S 169.55W
Niue Island 57 Kf 19.02S 169.55W
Niu'erhe 27 La 51.30N 121.40 E
Niufu 29a Ca 44.35N 142.35 E
Niulakita Island 57 If 10.45S 179.30 E
Niutaca, Corrente- 55 De 20.42S 57.37W
Niutao Island 57 Ie 6.06S 177.16 E
Niutg, Gunung- 26 Ef 1.00N 109.55 E
Niutoushan 27 Ke 31.00N 119.35 E
Niuzhuang 28 Gd 40.57N 122.30 E
Nivala 7 Fe 63.58N 25.01 E
Nive 11 Ek 43.30N 1.29W
Nivelles/Nijvel 11 Kd 50.36N 4.20 E
Nivernais 11 Jg 47.00N 3.30 E
Nivernais, Canal du- 11 Jg 47.40N 3.40 E
Nivernais, Côtes du- 11 Jg 47.10N 3.30 E
Nivillers 12 Ee 49.28N 2.10 E
Nixon 45 Hl 29.16N 97.46W
Niya/Minfeng 27 Dd 37.04N 82.46 E
Nīyābād 24 Le 35.12N 46.20 E
Nīza 24 Ph 28.25N 55.55 E
Nizāmābad 25 Fe 18.40N 78.07 E
Nižankoviči 10 Sg 49.40N 22.48 E
Nižegorodskaja oblast 19 Ed 56.15N 44.45 E
Nizip 23 Eb 37.01N 37.46 E
Nízke Tatry = Low Tatra (EN) 10 Ph 48.54N 19.40 E
Nízký-Jeseník 10 Ng 49.50N 17.30 E
Nižná 10 Pg 49.19N 19.32 E
Nižneangarsk 22 Md 55.47N 109.33 E
Nižnegorski 16 Ig 45.27N 34.44 E
Nižnejansk 20 Ib 71.24N 136.00 E
Nižnekamsk 19 Fd 55.38N 51.49 E
Nižnekolymsk 20 Lc 68.38N 160.56 E
Nižnetroicki 17 Fi 54.20N 53.41 E
Nižneudinsk 20 Ef 54.54N 99.03 E
Nižnevartovsk 22 Jc 61.00N 77.00 E
Nižni Baskunčak 19 Ef 48.13N 46.50 E
Nižni Bestjah 20 Hd 61.48N 129.55 E
Nižni Casučej 20 Gf 50.27N 115.08 E
Nižnije Serogozy 16 If 46.49N 34.24 E
Nižnij Novgorod (Gorki) 6 Kd 57.38N 45.05 E
Nižni Kuranah 20 He 58.40E 125.48 E
Nižni Lomov 19 Ee 53.32N 43.41 E
Nižni Odes 17 Ge 63.40N 54.52 E

Index Symbols

[1] Independent Nation
[2] State, Region
[3] District, County
[4] Municipality
[5] Colony, Dependency
Continent
Physical Region
Historical or Cultural Region
Mount, Mountain
Volcano
Hill
Mountains, Mountain Range
Hills, Escarpment
Plateau, Upland
Pass, Gap
Plain, Lowland
Delta
Salt Flat
Valley, Canyon
Crater, Cave
Karst Features
Depression
Polder
Desert, Dunes
Forest, Woods
Heath, Steppe
Oasis
Cape, Point
Coast, Beach
Cliff
Peninsula
Isthmus
Sandbank
Island
Atoll
Rock, Reef
Islands, Archipelago
Rocks, Reefs
Coral Reef
Well, Spring
Geyser
River, Stream
Waterfall Rapids
River Mouth, Estuary
Lake
Salt Lake
Intermittent Lake
Reservoir
Swamp, Pond
Canal
Glacier
Ice Shelf, Pack Ice
Ocean
Sea
Gulf, Bay
Strait, Fjord
Lagoon
Bank
Seamount
Tablemount
Ridge
Shelf
Basin
Escarpment, Sea Scarp
Fracture
Trench, Abyss
National Park Reserve
Point of Interest
Recreation Site
Cave, Cavern
Historic Site
Ruins
Wall, Walls
Church, Abbey
Temple
Scientific Station
Airport
Port
Lighthouse
Mine
Tunnel
Dam, Bridge

Nižni Oseredok, Ostrov- 16 Pg 45.45N 48.35 E
Nižni Tagil 6 Ld 57.55N 59.57 E
Nižni Trajanov Val=Lower Trajan's Wall (EN) 15 Ld 45.45N 28.30 E
Nižnjaja Omra 17 Ge 62.46N 55.46 E
Nižnjaja Peša 19 Eb 66.43N 47.36 E
Nižnjaja Pojma 20 Ee 56.08N 97.18 E
Nižnjaja Salda 17 Jg 58.05N 60.48 E
Nižnjaja Tavda 19 Gd 57.40N 66.12 E
Nižnjaja Tojma 7 Ke 62.22N 44.15 E
Nižnjaja Tunguska=Lower Tunguska (EN) 21 Kc 65.48N 88.04 E
Nižnjaja Tura 17 Ig 58.37N 59.49 E
Nižnjaja Zolotica 7 Jd 65.41N 40.13 E
Nižny Pjandž 18 Gf 37.14N 68.35 E
Nizza Monferrato 14 Cf 44.46N 8.21 E
Njajs 17 Je 62.25N 60.47 E
Njamunas 5 Id 55.18N 21.23 E
Njandoma 19 Ec 61.43N 40.12 E
Njaris/Neris 8 Kj 54.55N 25.45 E
Njazepetrovsk 17 Ih 56.03N 59.38 E
Njazidja 30 Lj 11.35S 43.20 E
Njegoš 15 Bg 42.53N 18.45 E
Njinjo 36 Gd 8.48S 38.54 E
Njombe 30 Ki 6.56S 35.06 E
Njombe 31 Ki 9.20S 34.46 E
Njudung 8 Fg 57.25N 14.50 E
Njuja 20 Gd 60.32N 116.25 E
Njuk, Ozero- 7 Hd 64.25N 31.45 E
Njuksenica 7 Kf 60.28N 44.15 E
Njukža 20 He 56.30N 121.40 E
Njunes 7 Eb 68.45N 19.30 E
Njurba 22 Nc 63.17N 118.20 E
Njurundabommen 7 De 62.16N 17.22 E
Njutånger 8 Gc 61.37N 17.03 E
Njuvčim 17 Ef 61.22N 50.42 E
Nkambe 34 Hd 6.38N 10.40 E
Nkawkaw 34 Ed 6.33N 0.46W
Nkayi [Con.] 31 Ii 4.05S 13.18 E
Nkayi [Zimb.] 37 Dc 19.00S 28.54 E
Nkhata Bay 36 Fe 11.36S 34.18 E
Nkongsamba 31 Hh 4.57N 9.56 E
Nkota Kota 31 Kj 12.55S 34.18 E
Nkululu 36 Fd 6.26S 32.49 E
Nkusi 36 Fb 1.07N 30.40 E
Nkwalini 37 Ee 28.45S 31.30 E
'Nmai 25 Jc 25.42N 97.30 E
Nmaki 24 Pg 31.16N 55.29 E
Nnewi 34 Gd 6.01N 6.55 E
Nō 29 Ec 37.05N 137.59 E
Noailles 12 Ee 49.20N 2.12 E
Noākhāli 25 Id 22.49N 91.06 E
Noatak 40 Gc 67.34N 162.59W
Nobel 44 Gc 45.25N 80.06W
Nobeoka 27 Ne 32.35N 131.40 E
Noblesville 44 Ee 40.03N 86.00W
Noboribetsu 28 Pc 42.25N 141.11 E
Noce 14 Fd 46.09N 11.04 E
Nocra 35 Fc 15.40N 39.55 E
Nodaway River 45 Ig 39.54N 94.58W
Noën 27 Hc 43.15N 102.20 E
Noeuf, Ile des- 37b Bb 6.14S 53.03 E
Noeux-les-Mines 12 Ed 50.29N 2.40 E
Nogajskaja Step 16 Ng 44.15N 46.00 E
Nogales [Az.-U.S.] 43 Ee 31.21N 110.55W
Nogales [Mex.] 39 Hf 31.20N 110.56W
Nogaro 11 Fk 43.46N 0.02W
Nogat 10 Pb 54.11N 19.15 E
Nōgata 29 Be 33.44N 130.44 E
Nogent-le-Rotrou 11 Gf 48.19N 0.50 E
Nogent-sur-Marne 12 Ef 48.50N 2.29 E
Nogent-sur-Oise 12 Ee 49.16N 2.28 E
Nogent-sur-Seine 11 Jf 48.29N 3.30 E
Noginsk 20 Ed 64.25N 91.10 E
Noginsk 19 Dd 55.54N 38.28 E
Nogliki 20 Jf 51.45N 143.15 E
Nōgo-Hakusan 29 Ed 35.46N 136.31 E
Nogoyá 56 Id 32.24S 59.48W
Nogoya, Arroyo- 55 Ck 32.55S 59.59W
Nógrád [2] 10 Ph 48.00N 19.35 E
Nogueira, Serra da- 13 Fc 41.42N 6.52W
Noguera Pallaresa 13 Mb 42.15N 0.54 E
Noguera Ribagorçana/Noguera Ribagorzana 13 Mc 41.40N 0.43 E
Noguera Ribagorzana/Noguera Ribagorçana 13 Mc 41.40N 0.43 E
Noh, Laguna- 48 Nh 18.40N 90.20W
Nohain 11 Ig 47.24N 2.55 E
Noheji 28 Pd 40.52N 141.08 E
Nohfelden 12 Je 49.35N 7.09 E
Noidore, Rio- 55 Fb 14.50S 52.34W
Noir, Causse- 11 Jj 44.09N 3.15 E
Noire, Montagne- 11 Ik 43.28N 2.18 E
Noires, Montagnes- 11 Cf 48.09N 3.40W
Noirétable 11 Ji 45.49N 3.46 E
Noirmoutier, Ile de- 11 Dh 46.58N 2.12W
Noirmoutier-en-l'Ile 11 Dg 47.00N 2.15W
Nojima-Zaki 29 Fd 34.54N 139.50 E
Nojiri-Ko 29 Fc 36.49N 138.13 E
Noka 63c Bb 10.40S 166.03 E
Nokaneng 37 Cc 19.40S 22.12 E
Nokia 7 Ff 61.28N 23.30 E
Nok Kundi 25 Cc 28.48N 62.46 E
Nokomis 46 Ma 51.30N 105.00W
Nokou 35 Ac 14.35N 14.47 E
Nokra 35 Fb 15.42N 39.56 E
Nol 8 Eg 57.55N 12.03 E
Nola [C.A.R.] 35 Be 3.32N 16.04 E
Nola [It.] 14 Ij 40.55N 14.33 E
Nolin Lake 44 Dg 37.20N 86.10W
Nolinsk 19 Ed 57.33N 50.00 E
Nomad 58 Fe 6.21S 142.12 E
Noma Omuramba 37 Cc 19.10S 22.16 E
Noma-Zaki 29 Bf 31.25N 130.06 E
Nombre de Dios 48 Gf 23.51N 104.14W
Nome 39 Cc 64.30N 165.24W
Nomeny 12 If 48.54N 6.14 E
Nomo-Saki 29 Ae 32.35N 129.45 E
Nomozaki 29 Ae 32.35N 129.45 E
Nomuka 65b Bb 20.15S 174.48W
Nomuka Group 57 Jg 20.20S 174.45W
Nomuka Iki 65b Bb 20.17S 174.49W
Nomwin Atoll 57 Gd 8.32N 151.47 E
Nonacho Lake 42 Gd 62.40N 109.30W
Nonancourt 12 Df 48.46N 1.12 E
Nonette 12 Ee 49.12N 2.24 E
Nong'an 27 Mc 44.24N 125.08 E
Nong Han 25 Ke 17.21N 103.06 E
Nong Khai 22 Mh 17.52N 102.45 E
Nongoma 37 Ee 27.53S 31.38 E
Nonoava 48 Fd 27.28N 106.44W
Nonouti Atoll 57 Ie 0.40S 174.21 E
Nonsan 28 If 36.12N 127.05 E
Nonsuch Bay 51d Bb 17.03N 61.42W
Nontron 11 Gi 45.32N 0.40 E
Noord-Beveland 12 Fc 51.35N 3.45 E
Noord-Brabant [3] 12 Gc 51.30N 5.00 E
Noord-Holland [3] 12 Gb 52.40N 4.50 E
Noordhollandskanaal 11 Kb 52.55N 4.50 E
Noordoewer 37 Be 28.45S 17.37 E
Noordoostpolder 11 Lb 52.42N 5.45 E
Noordoostpolder 12 Hb 52.42N 5.44 E
Noordoostpolder-Emmeloord 12 Hb 52.42N 5.44 E
Noordwijk aan Zee 11 Kb 52.14N 4.26 E
Noordwijk aan Zee, Noordwijk- 12 Gb 52.14N 4.26 E
Noordwijk-Noordwijk aan Zee 12 Gb 52.14N 4.26 E
Noordzee=North Sea (EN) 5 Gd 55.20N 3.00 E
Noordzeekanaal 11 Kb 52.30N 4.35 E
Noormarkku/Norrmark 8 Ic 61.35N 21.52 E
Noorvik 40 Gc 66.50N 161.12W
Nootka Island 46 Bb 49.32N 126.42W
Nootka Sound 46 Bb 49.33N 126.38W
Nóqui 36 Bd 5.50S 13.27 E
Nora [It.] 14 Dk 39.00N 9.02 E
Nora [Swe.] 7 Dg 59.31N 15.02 E
Noraskog 8 Fe 59.40N 14.50 E
Norberg 8 Fd 60.04N 15.56 E
Norcia 14 Hh 42.48N 13.05 E
Nord 41 Kb 81.45N 17.30W
Nord [Cam.] [3] 34 Hd 9.00N 13.50 E
Nord [Fr.] [3] 11 Jd 50.20N 3.40 E
Nord [Burkina] 34 Ec 13.40N 2.50W
Nord, Canal du- 11 Id 49.57N 2.55 E
Nord, Mer du-=North Sea (EN) 5 Gd 55.20N 3.00 E
Nordausques 12 Ed 50.49N 2.05 E
Nordaustlandet 67 Jd 79.48N 22.24 E
Nordborg 8 Ci 55.03N 9.45 E
Nordby 8 Ci 55.27N 8.25 E
Norddeutsches Tiefland=North German Plain (EN) 5 He 53.00N 11.00 E
Norden 10 Dc 53.36N 7.12 E
Nordenham 10 Ec 53.39N 8.29 E
Nordenskjölda, Ostrova-=Nordenskjöld, Archipelago (EN) 20 Ea 76.50N 96.00 E
Nordenskjöld Archipelago (EN)=Nordenskjölda, Ostrova- 20 Ea 76.50N 96.00 E
Norderney 10 Dc 53.42N 7.10 E
Norderstedt 10 Fc 53.41N 9.58 E
Nordfjord 8 Bc 61.50N 6.15 E
Nordfjord 7 Af 61.55N 5.10 E
Nordfjordeid 7 Af 61.54N 6.00 E
Nordfold 7 Dc 67.46N 15.12 E
Nordfriesische Inseln=North Frisian Islands (EN) 10 Ea 54.50N 8.30 E
Nordfriesland 10 Eb 54.40N 8.55 E
Nordgau 10 Hg 49.15N 11.50 E
Nordgrønland=North Greenland (EN) [2] 41 Gc 79.30N 50.00W
Nordhausen 10 Ge 51.31N 10.48 E
Nordhordland 8 Ad 60.50N 5.50 E
Nordhorn 10 Dd 52.26N 7.05 E
Nord-Jylland [2] 8 Cg 57.15N 10.00 E
Nordkapp [Nor.]=North Cape (EN) 5 Ia 71.11N 25.48 E
Nordkapp [Sval.] 41 Nb 80.31N 20.00 E
Nordkinn 5 Ia 71.08N 27.39 E
Nordkinnhalvøya 7 Ga 70.55N 27.45 E
Nord-Kvaløy 7 Ea 70.10N 19.11 E
Nordland [2] 7 Cc 67.06N 13.20 E
Nördlingen 10 Gh 48.51N 10.30 E
Nordloher Tief 12 Ja 53.10N 7.45 E
Nordmark 8 Fe 59.50N 14.06 E
Nordmøre 8 Ca 63.00N 8.30 E
Nordostrundingen 67 Le 81.30N 11.00W
Nord-Ostsee Kanal=Kiel Canal (EN) 5 Ge 53.53N 9.08 E
Nord-Ouest [3] 34 Hd 6.30N 10.30 E
Nordøyane 8 Bb 62.40N 6.15 E
Nordreisa 7 Eb 69.46N 21.03 E
Nordre Rønner 8 Dg 57.22N 10.56 E
Nordrhein-Westfalen=North Rhine-Westphalia (EN) [2] 10 De 51.30N 7.30 E
Nordsee=North Sea (EN) 5 Gd 55.20N 3.00 E
Nordsjøen=North Sea (EN) 5 Gd 55.20N 3.00 E
Nordskjobotn 7 Eb 69.13N 19.34 E
Nordsøen=North Sea (EN) 5 Gd 55.20N 3.00 E
Nord Strand 10 Eb 54.30N 8.55 E
Nordtiroler Kalkalpen 10 Hi 47.30N 11.30 E
Nord-Trøndelag [2] 7 Cd 64.25N 12.00 E
Nordwestfjord 41 Jd 71.30N 26.30W
Nore/An Fheoir 9 Gi 52.25N 6.58W
Norefjell 8 Cd 60.16N 9.29 E
Norefjorden 8 Cd 60.10N 9.00 E
Norfolk 9 Oi 52.40N 1.05 E
Norfolk [3] 9 Mi 52.45N 0.40W
Norfolk [Nb.-U.S.] 43 Hc 42.02N 97.25W
Norfolk [Va.-U.S.] 39 Lf 36.40N 76.14W
Norfolk Island [5] 58 Hg 29.05S 167.59 E
Norfolk Island 57 Hg 29.05S 167.59 E
Norfolk Ridge (EN) 57 Hg 29.00S 168.00 E
Norfork Lake 45 Jh 36.25N 92.10W
Norg 12 Ia 53.04N 6.32 E
Norge=Norway (EN) [1] 6 Gc 62.00N 10.00 E
Norheimsund 7 Bf 60.22N 6.08 E
Norikura-Dake 29 Ec 36.06N 137.33 E
Norilsk 22 Kc 69.20N 88.06 E
Normal 45 Lf 40.31N 88.59W
Norman 43 Hd 35.15N 97.26W
Norman, Lake- 44 Gh 35.35N 81.00W
Normanby Island 60 Ej 10.00S 151.00 E
Normanby River 59 Ib 14.25S 144.08 E
Normand, Bocage- 11 Ef 49.00N 1.10W
Normandie=Normandy (EN) 11 Gf 49.00N 0.10 E
Normandie=Normandy (EN) 5 Gf 49.00N 0.10 E
Normandie, Collines de-=Normandy Hills (EN) 5 Ff 48.50N 0.40W
Normandin 44 Ka 48.52N 72.30W
Normandy (EN)=Normandie 11 Gf 49.00N 0.10 E
Normandy (EN)=Normandie 5 Gf 49.00N 0.10 E
Normandy Hills (EN)=Normandie, Collines de- 5 Ff 48.50N 0.40W
Norman Island 51a Db 18.20N 64.37W
Norman River 59 Ic 17.28S 140.39 E
Normanton 58 Ff 17.40S 141.05 E
Norman Wells 39 Gc 65.17N 126.51W
Norquinco 56 Ff 41.51S 70.54W
Norra Dellen 8 Gc 61.55N 16.40 E
Norrahammar 8 Fg 57.42N 14.06 E
Norrala 8 Gc 61.22N 16.59 E
Norra Midsjöbanken 8 Gh 56.10N 17.30 E
Norra Ny 7 Cf 60.24N 13.15 E
Norra Storfjället 7 Dd 65.53N 15.14 E
Norrbotten [2] 7 Ec 67.26N 19.35 E
Nørre Åby 8 Ci 55.27N 9.54 E
Nørre Alslev 8 Dj 54.54N 11.54 E
Nørre-Nebel 8 Ci 55.47N 8.18 E
Norrent-Fontes 12 Ed 50.35N 2.24 E
Nørresundby 7 Bh 57.04N 9.55 E
Norrhult 7 Dh 57.08N 15.10 E
Norris Lake 44 Fg 36.20N 83.55W
Norristown 44 Je 40.07N 75.20W
Norrköping 6 Hd 58.36N 16.11 E
Norrland 5 Hc 64.27N 17.20 E
Norrland 7 Dd 65.00N 18.00 E
Norrmark/Noormarkku 8 Ic 61.35N 21.52 E
Norrsundet 8 Gd 60.56N 17.08 E
Norrtälje 7 Eg 59.46N 18.42 E
Norseman 58 Dh 32.12S 121.46 E
Norsewood 62 Gd 40.04S 176.13 E
Norsjö 7 Ed 64.55N 19.29 E
Norsjø 8 Ce 59.20N 9.20 E
Norsk 20 Hf 52.20N 129.59 E
Norske Havet=Norwegian Sea (EN) 5 Gc 70.00N 2.00 E
Norske Øer 41 Kc 79.00N 18.00W
Norsoup 63b Cc 16.04S 167.23 E
Norte, Baía- 55 Hh 27.30S 48.35W
Norte, Cabo- [Braz.] 54 Ic 1.40N 50.00W
Norte, Cabo- [Pas.] 65d Ab 27.03S 109.24W
Norte, Canal do- 54 Hc 0.30N 50.30W
Norte, Punta- 56 Hf 42.04S 63.45W
Norte, Serra do- 54 Gf 11.00S 59.00W
Norte del Cabo San Antonio, Punta- 56 Ie 36.17S 56.47W
Norte de Santander [2] 54 Db 8.00N 73.00W
Nortelândia 54 Gf 14.25S 56.48W
North, Cape- 42 Lg 47.02N 60.25W
North Adams 44 Kd 42.42N 73.02W
Northallerton 9 Lg 54.20N 1.26W
Northam [Austl.] 58 Ch 31.39S 116.40 E
Northam [S.Afr.] 37 Dd 24.58S 27.11 E
North America 38 Jf 40.00N 95.00W
North American Basin (EN) 3 Cf 30.00N 60.00W
Northampton 9 Mi 52.30N 1.00W
Northampton [Austl.] 59 Ce 28.21S 114.37 E
Northampton [Eng.-U.K.] 9 Mi 52.14N 0.54W
Northampton [Ma.-U.S.] 44 Kd 42.19N 72.38W
Northampton Seamounts (EN) 57 Jb 25.20N 172.04W
Northamptonshire [3] 9 Mi 52.25N 0.55W
North Andaman 25 If 13.15N 92.55 E
North Arm 42 Gd 62.00N 114.30W
North Astrolabe Reef 63d Bc 18.39S 178.32 E
North Augusta 44 Gi 33.30N 81.58W
North Aulatsivik 42 Le 59.45N 64.04W
North Australian Basin 3 Hk 14.30S 116.30 E
North Battleford 39 Id 52.47N 108.17W
North Bay 39 Le 46.19N 79.28W
North Belcher Islands 42 Je 56.45N 79.45W
North Berwick 9 Ke 56.04N 2.44W
North Buganda [3] 36 Fb 0.50N 32.10 E
North Caicos 49 Lc 21.56N 71.59W
North Canadian River 43 Hd 35.17N 95.31W
North Cape 57 Ih 34.25S 173.03 E
North Cape (EN)=Nordkapp [Nor.] 5 Ia 71.11N 25.48 E
North Caribou Lake 42 If 52.48N 90.45W
North Carolina [2] 43 Ld 35.30N 80.00W
North Channel 42 Jg 46.02N 82.50W
North Channel/Sruth na Maoile 5 Fd 55.10N 5.40W
Northchapel 12 Bc 51.03N 0.38W
North Charleston 44 Hi 32.53N 80.00W
North Chicago 45 Me 42.20N 87.51W
North Cove 46 Cc 46.47N 124.06W
North Cyprus 22 Ff 35.15N 33.40 E
North Dakota 43 Gb 47.30N 100.15W
North Downs 9 Nj 51.20N 0.10 E
North East 44 Hd 42.13N 79.51W
North-East [3] 37 Dd 21.00S 27.30 E
Northeast Cape 40 Fd 63.18N 168.42W
North-Eastern [3] 36 Hb 1.00N 40.15 E
Northeast Islands 64d Ba 7.36N 151.57 E
Northeast Pacific Basin (EN) 3 Lg 20.00N 140.00W
Northeast Pass 64d Ba 7.30N 151.59 E
North East Point 64g Bb 1.57N 157.16W
Northeast Point [Bah.] 49 Kc 21.18N 72.54W
Northeast Point [Bah.] 49 Kb 22.43N 73.50W
Northeast Providence Channel 47 Ic 25.40N 77.09W
Northeim 10 Fe 51.42N 10.00 E
North Entrance 64a Bb 7.59N 134.37 E
Northern [Ghana] [3] 34 Ed 9.30N 1.00W
Northern [Mwi.] [3] 36 Fe 11.00S 34.00 E
Northern [S.L.] [3] 34 Cd 9.15N 11.45W
Northern [Ug.] [3] 36 Fb 2.45N 32.45 E
Northern [Zam.] [3] 36 Fe 11.00S 31.00 E
Northern Cay 49 De 17.27N 87.28W
Northern Cook Islands 57 Kf 10.00S 161.00W
Northern Dvina (EN)=Severnaja Dvina 5 Kc 64.32N 40.30 E
Northern Guinea 30 Gh 8.30N 1.00W
Northern Indian Lake 42 He 57.20N 97.17W
Northern Ireland [2] 9 Gg 54.40N 6.45W
Northern Mariana Islands [5] 58 Fc 16.00N 145.30 E
Northern Sporades (EN)=Vórioi Sporádhes, Nisoi- 5 Ih 39.15N 23.55 E
Northern Territory 59 Gc 20.00S 134.00 E
Northern Urals (EN)=Severny Ural 5 Lc 62.00N 59.00 E
Northern Uvals (EN)=Severnyje Uvaly 5 Kd 59.30N 49.00 E
Northfield 45 Jd 44.27N 93.09W
North Fiji Basin (EN) 3 Jk 16.00S 174.00 E
North Foreland 9 Oj 51.23N 1.27 E
North Fork Grand River 45 Ed 45.47N 102.16W
North Fork John Day River 46 Fd 44.45N 119.38W
North Fork Moreau River 45 Ed 45.09N 102.50W
North Fork Pass 42 Dd 64.00N 138.00W
North Fork Powder River 46 Le 43.40N 106.30W
North Fork Red 45 Gi 34.25N 99.14W
North Fort Myers 44 Gl 26.40N 81.54W
North Frisian Islands (EN)=Nordfriesische Inseln 10 Ea 54.50N 8.30 E
North German Plain (EN)=Norddeutsches Tiefland 5 He 53.00N 11.00 E
North Greenland (EN)=Nordgrønland [2] 41 Gc 79.30N 50.00W
North Highlands 46 Eg 38.40N 121.23W
North Horr 36 Gb 3.19N 37.04 E
North Island [N.Z.] 57 Ih 39.00S 176.00 E
North Island [Sey.] 37b Bc 10.07S 51.11 E
North Kent 42 Ia 76.40N 90.15W
North Korea (EN)=Chosŏn M.I.K. [1] 22 Oe 40.00N 127.30 E
North Lakhimpur 25 Ic 27.14N 94.07 E
Northland [2] 62 Ea 35.30S 173.40 E
North Las Vegas 46 Hh 36.12N 115.07W
North Lincoln Land 42 Ja 76.15N 80.00W
North Little Rock 43 Ie 34.46N 92.14W
North Loup River 45 Gf 41.17N 98.23W
North Magnetic Pole (1980) 67 Od 77.03N 101.08W
North Malosmadulu Atoll 25a Ba 5.35N 72.55 E
North Mamm Peak 45 Cg 39.23N 107.52W
North Mayreau Channel 51n Bb 12.41N 61.20W
North Miami 44 Gm 25.56N 80.09W
North Minch 5 Fd 58.05N 5.55W
North Palisade 46 Fh 37.10N 118.38W
North Pass [F.S.M.] 64d Ba 7.41N 151.48 E
North Pass [U.S.] 45 Ll 29.10N 89.15W
North Platte 43 Gc 41.08N 100.46W
North Platte 38 Ie 41.15N 100.45W
North Point 64n Ab 10.22S 161.02W
North Point [Bar.] 51q Ab 13.20N 59.36W
North Pole 67 Ge 90.00N 0.00
Northport 44 Di 33.14N 87.35W
North Powder 46 Gd 45.03N 117.55W
North Raccoon River 45 Jf 41.35N 93.31W
North Reef 63a Ee 12.13S 160.04 E
North Rhine-Westphalia (EN)=Nordrhein-Westfalen [2] 10 De 51.30N 7.30 E
North Rim 46 Ih 36.12N 112.03W
North River 42 Ie 58.53N 94.42W
North Rona 9 Hb 59.10N 5.40W
North Ronaldsay 9 Kb 59.25N 2.30W
North Saskatchewan 38 Id 53.15N 105.06W
North Sea 5 Gd 55.20N 3.00 E
North Sea (EN)=Noordzee 5 Gd 55.20N 3.00 E
North Sea (EN)=Nord, Mer du- 5 Gd 55.20N 3.00 E
North Sea (EN)=Nordsee 5 Gd 55.20N 3.00 E
North Sea (EN)=Nordsjøen 5 Gd 55.20N 3.00 E
North Sea (EN)=Nordsøen 5 Gd 55.20N 3.00 E
North Sentinel 25 If 11.33N 92.15 E
North Shoshone Peak 46 Gg 39.10N 117.29W
North Siberian Plain (EN)=Severo-Sibirskaja Niz. 21 Mb 72.00N 104.00 E
North Sound 51d Bb 17.07N 61.45W
North Sound 49 Gd 19.25N 81.26W
North Stradbroke Island 59 Ke 27.35S 153.30 E
North Taranaki Bight 62 Fc 38.50S 174.25 E
North Thompson 42 Ff 50.41N 120.11W
North Tokelau Trough (EN) 3 Kj 3.00S 165.00W
North Tonawanda 44 Hd 43.02N 78.54W
North Trap 62 Bg 47.20S 167.55 E
North Tyne 9 Kg 54.59N 2.08W
North Uist 9 Fd 57.37N 7.22W
Northumberland 9 Kf 55.15N 2.10W
Northumberland [3] 9 Kf 55.15N 2.05W
Northumberland Islands 57 Gg 21.40S 150.00 E
Northumberland Strait 42 Lg 46.00N 63.30W
North Umpqua River 46 De 43.16N 123.27W
North Vancouver 46 Db 49.19N 123.04W
North Walsham 12 Db 52.49N 1.23 E
Northway 40 Kd 62.59N 141.43W
North West Bluff 51c Bc 16.49N 62.12W
North West Cape 57 Cg 21.45S 114.10 E
North-Western [3] 36 Ee 13.00S 25.00 E
Northwest Frontier [3] 25 Eb 33.00N 70.30 E
North West Highlands 5 Fd 57.30N 5.00W
Northwest Pacific Basin (EN) 3 Je 40.00N 155.00 E
North West Point 64g Ab 2.02N 157.30W
Northwest Providence Channel 44 Hl 26.10N 78.20W
Northwest Reef 64a Bb 7.59N 134.33 E
North West River 42 Lf 53.32N 60.09W
Northwest Territories [3] 42 Hc 66.00N 102.00W
Northwich 9 Kh 53.16N 2.32W
North York Moors 9 Mg 54.25N 0.50W
North Yorkshire [3] 9 Lg 54.15N 1.40W
Norton [Ks.-U.S.] 43 Gd 39.50N 100.01W
Norton [Va.-U.S.] 44 Fg 36.56N 82.37W
Norton [Zimb.] 37 Ec 17.53S 30.41 E
Norton Bay 40 Gd 64.45N 161.15W
Norton Sound 38 Cc 64.45N 161.15W
Norvegia, Kapp- 66 Bf 71.25S 12.18W
Norwalk [Ct.-U.S.] 44 Ke 41.07N 73.27W
Norwalk [Oh.-U.S.] 44 Fe 41.14N 82.37W
Norway 44 Dc 45.47N 87.55W
Norway (EN)=Norge [1] 6 Gc 62.00N 10.00 E
Norway Bay 42 Hb 71.00N 104.35W
Norway House 42 Hf 53.58N 97.50W
Norwegian Basin (EN) 3 Dc 68.00N 2.00W
Norwegian Bay 42 Ij 77.45N 90.30W
Norwegian Sea (EN)=Norske Havet 5 Gc 70.00N 2.00 E
Norwegian Trench (EN) 5 Gd 59.00N 4.30 E
Norwich [Ct.-U.S.] 44 Ke 41.32N 72.05W
Norwich [Eng.-U.K.] 6 Ge 52.38N 1.18 E
Norwich [N.Y.-U.S.] 44 Jd 42.33N 75.33W
Norwich Airport 12 Db 52.40N 1.18 E
Norwood 44 Ef 39.10N 84.28W
Nosappu-Misaki 29a Db 43.23N 145.47 E
Noshappu-Misaki 29a Ba 45.27N 141.39 E
Noshiro 27 Pc 40.12N 140.02 E
Nosovaja 19 Fb 68.15N 54.31 E
Nosovka 19 De 50.54N 31.37 E
Nosratābād 23 Id 29.54N 59.59 E
Nossa Senhora das Candeias 54 Kf 12.40S 38.33W
Nossa Senhora do Livramento 55 Db 15.48S 56.22W
Noss Head 9 Jc 58.30N 3.05W
Nossob 30 Jk 26.55S 20.40 E
Nossop 37 Ce 26.55S 20.40 E
Nosy-Be 30 Lj 13.20S 48.15 E
Nosy-Be 31 Lj 13.22S 48.16 E
Nosy-Varika 37 Hd 20.35S 48.30 E
Nota 7 Hb 68.07N 30.10 E
Notch Peak 46 Ig 39.08N 113.24W
Noteć 10 Ld 52.44N 15.26 E
Notecka, Puszcza- 10 Ld 52.45N 16.00 E
Note Kemopla 63c b 10.55S 165.51 E
Notengo, Laguna de- 48 Ji 16.15N 98.10W
Notia Pindhos 15 Ej 39.30N 21.20 E
Nótioi Sporádhes=Dodecanese (EN) 5 Ih 36.00N 27.00 E
Nótios Evvoïkós Kólpos 15 Gk 38.20N 23.50 E
Nötö 8 Ie 60.00N 21.45 E
Noto [It.] 14 Jn 36.53N 15.04 E
Noto [Jap.] 28 Nf 37.18N 137.09 E
Noto, Golfo di- 14 Jn 36.50N 15.10 E
Notodden 7 Bg 59.34N 9.17 E
Noto-Hantō 27 Od 37.20N 137.00 E
Noto-Jima 29 Ec 37.07N 137.00 E
Notoro-Ko 29a Da 44.05N 144.10 E
Notoro-Misaki 29a Da 44.07N 144.15 E
Notranjsko 14 Ie 45.46N 14.26 E
Notre-Dame, Monts- 38 Me 48.00N 69.00W
Notre Dame Bay 42 Mg 49.50N 55.00W
Notre-Dame-de-Courson 12 Cf 48.59N 0.16 E
Notre-Dame-de-Gravenchon 12 Ce 49.29N 0.35 E
Notre Dame-du-Lac 44 Mb 47.38N 68.49W
Notre-Dame-du-Nord 44 Hb 47.36N 79.29W
Notsé 34 Fd 6.59N 1.12 E
Notsuke-Zaki 29a Db 43.34N 145.19 E
Nottawasaga Bay 44 Gc 44.40N 80.30W
Nottaway 38 Ld 51.25N 79.50W
Notterøy 8 De 59.15N 10.25 E
Nottingham 6 Fe 52.58N 1.10W
Nottingham 42 Jd 63.20N 78.00W
Nottingham 9 Mh 53.05N 1.00W
Nottinghamshire [3] 9 Mh 53.10N 0.55W
Nottoway River 44 Ig 36.33N 76.55W
Nottuln 12 Jc 51.56N 7.21 E
Notukeu Creek 46 Lb 49.55N 106.30W
Nouâdhibou 31 Ff 20.54N 17.01W
Nouâdhibou, Dahklet- 32 De 21.00N 16.50W
Nouâdhibou, Râs-=Blanc Cape- (EN) 30 Ff 20.46N 17.03W
Nouakchott 31 Fg 18.07N 15.59W
Nouakchott, District de 32 Df 18.06N 15.57W
Nouamrhar 32 Df 19.22N 16.31W
Nouméa 58 Hg 22.16S 166.26 E
Nouna 34 Ec 12.44N 3.52W
Noupoort 37 Cf 31.10S 24.57 E

Index Symbols

[1] Independent Nation
[2] State, Region
[3] District, County
[4] Municipality
[5] Colony, Dependency
Continent
Physical Region
Historical or Cultural Region
Mount, Mountain
Volcano
Hill
Mountains, Mountain Range
Hills, Escarpment
Plateau, Upland
Pass, Gap
Plain, Lowland
Delta
Salt Flat
Valley, Canyon
Crater, Cave
Karst Features
Depression
Polder
Desert, Dunes
Forest, Woods
Heath, Steppe
Oasis
Cape, Point
Coast, Beach
Cliff
Peninsula
Isthmus
Sandbank
Island
Atoll
Rock, Reef
Islands, Archipelago
Rocks, Reefs
Coral Reef
Well, Spring
Geyser
River, Stream
Waterfall Rapids
River Mouth, Estuary
Lake
Salt Lake
Intermittent Lake
Reservoir
Swamp, Pond
Canal
Glacier
Ice Shelf, Pack Ice
Ocean
Sea
Gulf, Bay
Strait, Fjord
Lagoon
Bank
Seamount
Tablemount
Ridge
Shelf
Basin
Escarpment, Sea Scarp
Fracture
Trench, Abyss
National Park, Reserve
Point of Interest
Recreation Site
Cave, Cavern
Historic Site
Ruins
Wall, Walls
Church, Abbey
Temple
Scientific Station
Airport
Port
Lighthouse
Mine
Tunnel
Dam, Bridge

Nouveau-Comptoir	42	Jf	52.35N	78.40W
Nouveau-Québec, Cratère du- = New Quebec Crater (EN)	42	Kd	61.30N	73.55W
Nouvelle-Calédonie = New Caledonia (EN) [5]	58	Hg	21.30S	165.30 E
Nouvelle-Calédonie=New Caledonia (EN)	57	Hg	21.30S	165.30 E
Nouvelle-France, Cap de -	42	Kd	62.33N	73.35W
Nouvelles Hébrides/New Hebrides	57	Hf	16.01S	167.01 E
Nouvion	12	Dd	50.12N	1.47 E
Nouzonville	11	Ke	49.49N	4.45 E
Novabad	18	He	39.01N	70.09 E
Nová Baňa	10	Oh	48.26N	18.39 E
Nová Bystřice	10	Lg	49.02N	15.06 E
Nova Cruz	54	Ke	6.28S	35.26W
Nova Esperança	55	Ff	23.08S	52.13W
Nova Friburgo	54	Jh	22.16S	42.32W
Nova Gaia	36	Ce	10.05S	17.32 E
Nova Gorica	14	He	45.57N	13.39 E
Nova Gradiška	14	Le	45.16N	17.23 E
Nova Granada	55	He	20.29S	49.19W
Nova Iguaçu	53	Lh	22.45S	43.27W
Novaja Igirma	20	Fe	57.10N	103.55 E
Novaja-Ivanovka	15	Md	45.59N	29.04 E
Novaja Kahovka	16	Hf	46.43N	33.23 E
Novaja Kazanka	16	Pe	48.58N	49.37 E
Novaja Ladoga	7	Hf	60.05N	32.16 E
Novaja Ljalja	19	Gd	59.03N	60.36 E
Novaja Odessa	16	Gf	47.18N	31.47 E
Novaja Sibir, Ostrov-=New Siberia (EN)	21	Qb	75.00N	149.00 E
Novaja Vodolaga	16	Ie	49.45N	35.52 E
Novaja Zemlja=Novaya Zemlya (EN)	21	Hb	74.00N	57.00 E
Nova Lamego	34	Cc	12.17N	14.13W
Nova Lima	54	Jh	19.59S	43.51W
Nova Londrina	55	Ff	22.45S	53.00W
Nova Mambone	37	Fd	20.58S	35.00 E
Nova Olinda do Norte	54	Gd	3.45S	59.03W
Nová Paka	10	Lf	50.29N	15.31 E
Nova Prata	55	Gi	28.47S	51.36W
Novara	14	Ce	45.28N	8.38 E
Nova Roma	55	Ia	13.51S	46.57W
Nova Russas	54	Jd	4.42S	40.34W
Nova Scotia [3]	42	Lh	45.00N	63.00W
Nova Scotia	38	Me	45.00N	63.00W
Nova Sintra	32	Cf	14.54N	24.40W
Nova Sofala	37	Ed	20.10S	34.44 E
Novato	46	Dg	38.06N	122.34W
Nova Varoš	15	Cf	43.28N	19.49 E
Nova Venécia	54	Jg	18.43S	40.24W
Novaya Zemlya (EN)= Novaja Zemlja	21	Hb	74.00N	57.00 E
Nova Zagora	15	Jg	42.29N	26.01 E
Novelda	13	Lf	38.23N	0.46W
Novellara	14	Ef	44.51N	10.44 E
Nové Mesto nad Váhom	10	Nh	48.46N	17.50 E
Nové Zámky	10	Oi	47.59N	18.11 E
Novgorod	6	Jd	58.31N	31.17 E
Novgorodka	8	Mg	57.00N	28.37 E
Novgorod-Severski	19	De	52.01N	33.16 E
Novgorodskaja Oblast [3]	19	Dd	58.20N	32.40 E
Novi Bečej	15	Dd	45.36N	20.08 E
Novigrad	14	He	45.19N	13.34 E
Novigrad	14	Jf	44.11N	15.33 E
Novi Kričim	15	Hg	42.03N	24.28 E
Novi Ligure	14	Cf	44.46N	8.47 E
Novillero	48	Gf	22.21N	105.39W
Novion-Porcien	12	Ge	49.36N	4.25 E
Novi Pazar [Bul.]	15	Kf	43.21N	27.12 E
Novi Pazar [Yugo.]	15	Df	43.08N	20.31 E
Novi Sad	6	Hf	45.15N	19.50 E
Novi Travnik	14	Lf	44.10N	17.39 E
Novi Vinodolski	14	Ie	45.08N	14.47 E
Novoaleksandrovsk	16	Lg	45.24N	41.14 E
Novoaleksejevka	16	Sd	50.08N	55.42 E
Novoaleksejevka	16	If	46.16N	34.39 E
Novoaltajsk	20	Df	53.24N	83.58 E
Novoanninski	19	Ee	50.31N	42.45 E
Novoarhangelsk	16	Ge	48.39N	30.50 E
Novo Aripuanã	54	Fe	5.08S	60.22W
Novoazovsk	16	Kf	47.05N	38.05 E
Novobirjusinski	20	Ee	56.58N	97.55 E
Novobogdanovka	16	If	47.05N	35.18 E
Novočeboksarsk	7	Lh	56.08N	47.29 E
Novočeremšansk	7	Mi	54.23N	50.10 E
Novočerkassk	19	Ef	47.25N	40.03 E
Novodevičje	7	Lj	53.35N	48.51 E
Novograd-Volynski	19	Ce	50.36N	27.36 E
Novogrudok	16	Dc	53.37N	25.50 E
Nôvo Hamburgo	56	Jc	29.41S	51.08W
Novohopërsk	16	Ld	51.06N	41.37 E
Novo Horizonte	55	He	21.28S	49.13W
Novoizborsk	8	Mg	57.43N	28.05 E
Novojenisejsk	20	Ee	58.19N	92.27 E
Novojerudinski	20	Ee	59.47N	93.30 E
Novokačalinsk	20	Ig	45.05N	131.59 E
Novokazalinsk	22	Ie	45.50N	62.10 E
Novokubansk	16	Lg	45.06N	41.01 E
Novokujbyševsk	19	Ee	53.08N	49.58 E
Novokuzneck	22	Kd	53.45N	87.06 E
Novolazarevskaja	66	Cf	70.46S	11.50 E
Novolukoml	7	Gi	54.38N	29.07 E
Novo Mesto	14	Je	45.48N	15.10 E
Novomičurinsk	7	Ji	54.02N	39.48 E
Novomihajlovka	20	Ih	44.17N	133.50 E
Novo Miloševo	15	Dd	45.43N	20.18 E
Novomirgorod	16	Ge	48.45N	31.39 E
Novomoskovsk	6	Je	54.05N	38.13 E
Novomoskovsk	19	Df	48.37N	35.16 E
Novonikolajevski	16	Md	50.55N	42.24 E
Novoorsk	19	Fe	51.24N	58.59 E
Novopokrovskaja	16	Lg	45.56N	40.42 E
Novopolock	19	Cd	55.31N	28.40 E
Novorossijsk	6	Jg	44.45N	37.45 E
Novorybnaja	20	Fb	72.50N	105.45 E
Novoržev	19	Cd	57.02N	29.20 E
Novo-Šahtinsk	19	Df	47.47N	39.54 E
Novoselica	15	Ja	48.13N	26.17 E
Novoselje	8	Mf	58.05N	29.00 E
Novoselki	10	Ud	52.04N	24.25 E
Novoselovo	20	Ef	54.55N	91.00 E
Novosergijevka	19	Fe	52.03N	53.39 E
Novosibirsk	22	Kd	55.02N	82.55 E
Novosibirskaja Oblast [3]	20	Ce	55.30N	80.00 E
Novosibirskije Ostrova= New Siberian Islands (EN)	21	Qb	75.00N	142.00 E
Novosibirskoje Vodohranilišče	20	Df	54.40N	82.35 E
Novosil	16	Jc	52.59N	37.01 E
Novosineglazovski	17	Ji	55.05N	61.25 E
Novosokolniki	19	Dd	56.19N	30.12 E
Novospasskoje	7	Lj	53.09N	47.44 E
Novotroick	19	Fe	51.12N	58.35 E
Novotroickoje	19	Hg	43.39N	73.45 E
Novoukrainka	16	Ge	48.19N	31.32 E
Novouljanovsk	7	Li	54.10N	48.23 E
Novouzensk	19	Ee	50.29N	48.08 E
Novovjatsk	7	Lg	58.31N	49.43 E
Novovolynsk	19	Ce	50.46N	24.09 E
Novovoronežski	16	Kd	51.17N	39.16 E
Novozybkov	19	De	52.32N	32.00 E
Novska	14	Ke	45.20N	16.59 E
Novy Bug	16	Hf	47.43N	32.29 E
Nový Bydžov	10	Lf	50.15N	15.29 E
Novy Jaričev	10	Ug	49.50N	24.21 E
Novyje Aneny	15	Mc	46.53N	29.13 E
Novyje Burasy	16	Oc	52.06N	46.06 E
Nový Jičín	10	Og	49.36N	18.01 E
Novy Oskol	19	De	50.43N	37.54 E
Novy Pogost	8	Li	55.30N	27.32 E
Novy Port	22	Jc	67.40N	72.52 E
Novy Tap	17	Mh	56.55N	67.15 E
Novy Terek	16	Oh	43.37N	47.25 E
Novy Uzen	19	Fg	43.19N	52.55 E
Novy Vasjugan	20	Ce	58.34N	76.29 E
Novy Zaj	7	Mi	55.17N	52.02 E
Nowa Dęba	10	Rf	50.26N	21.46 E
Nowa Huta, Kraków-	10	Qf	50.04N	20.05 E
Nowa Ruda	10	Mf	50.35N	16.31 E
Nowa Sarzyna	10	Sf	50.23N	22.22 E
Nowa Sól	10	Le	51.48N	15.44 E
Now Bandegān	24	Oh	28.52N	53.53 E
Nowbarān	24	Me	35.08N	49.42 E
Nowdesheh	24	Le	35.11N	46.15 E
Nowe	10	Oc	53.40N	18.43 E
Nowe Miasto Lubawskie	10	Pc	53.27N	19.35 E
Nowe Miasto-nad-Pilicą	10	Qe	51.38N	20.35 E
Nowe Warpno	10	Kc	53.44N	14.20 E
Nowfel low Shātow	24	Ne	34.27N	50.55 E
Nowgong	25	Ic	26.21N	92.40 E
Nowogard	10	Lc	53.40N	15.08 E
Nowogród	10	Rc	53.15N	21.53 E
Nowood River	46	Ld	44.17N	107.58W
Nowra	59	Kf	34.53S	150.36 E
Nowshahr	24	Nd	36.39N	51.31 E
Nowy Dwór Gdański	10	Pb	54.13N	19.06 E
Nowy Dwór Mazowiecki	10	Qd	52.26N	20.43 E
Nowy Korczyn	10	Qf	50.20N	20.50 E
Nowy Sącz [2]	10	Qg	49.40N	20.40 E
Nowy Sącz	10	Qg	49.38N	20.42 E
Nowy Targ	10	Qg	49.29N	20.02 E
Nowy Tomyśl	10	Md	52.20N	16.07 E
Noya	13	Db	42.47N	8.53W
Noya/Anoia	13	Nc	41.28N	1.56 E
Noyant	11	Gg	47.31N	0.08 E
Noyon	11	Ie	49.35N	3.00 E
Nozaki-Jima	29	Ae	33.11N	129.08 E
Nozay	11	Eg	47.34N	1.38W
Nsanje	36	Gf	16.55S	35.16 E
Nsawan	34	Ed	5.48N	0.21W
Nschodnia	10	Rf	50.30N	21.18 E
Nsefu	36	Fe	13.03S	32.07 E
Nsukka	34	Gd	6.52N	7.23 E
Ntadembele	36	Cc	2.11S	17.08 E
Ntchisi	36	Fe	13.22S	34.00 E
Ntem	30	Hh	2.10N	9.57 E
Ntoum	36	Ab	0.22N	9.47 E
Ntui	34	He	4.27N	11.38 E
Ntusi	36	Fb	0.03N	31.13 E
Nuageuses, Iles-	30	Nm	48.40S	68.58 E
Nuanetsi	30	Kk	22.40S	31.49 E
Nūbah, Jibāl an-	30	Kg	12.00N	30.45 E
Nubian Desert (EN)= Nūbiyah, Aş Şahrā' an-	30	Kf	20.30N	33.00 E
Nūbiyah, Aş Şahrā' an-= Nubian Desert (EN)	30	Kf	20.30N	33.00 E
Nudha	63a	Ec	9.32S	160.48 E
Nueces Plain	43	Hf	28.30N	99.15W
Nueces River	43	Hf	27.50N	97.30W
Nueltin Lake	38	Jc	60.50N	99.30W
Nü'er He	28	Fd	41.06N	121.09 E
Nueva Asunción [3]	55	Be	21.00S	60.20W
Nueva Ciudad Guerrero	48	Jd	26.35N	99.15W
Nueva Esparta [2]	54	Fa	11.00N	64.00W
Nueva Germania	55	Df	23.54S	56.34W
Nueva Gerona	47	Hd	21.53N	82.48W
Nueva Imperial	56	Fe	38.44S	72.57W
Nueva Italia de Ruiz	48	Hh	19.01N	102.06W
Nueva Ocotepeque	49	Cf	14.24N	89.13W
Nueva Palmira	55	Ck	33.53S	58.25W
Nueva Rosita	39	Ig	27.57N	101.13W
Nueva San Salvador	47	Gf	13.41N	89.17W
Nueva Segovia [3]	49	Dg	13.40N	86.10W
Nueve de Julio	56	He	35.27S	60.52W
Nuevitas	47	Id	21.33N	77.16W
Nuevitas, Bahia de-	49	Ic	21.30N	77.12W
Nuevo, Cayo-	48	Mg	21.51N	92.05W
Nuevo, Golfo-	52	Jj	42.42S	64.36W
Nuevo Berlin	55	Ck	32.59S	58.03W
Nuevo Casas Grandes	39	If	30.25N	107.55W
Nuevo Laredo	39	Jg	27.30N	99.31W
Nuevo León [2]	47	Ec	25.40N	100.00W
Nuevo Mundo, Cerro-	54	Eh	21.55S	66.53W
Nuevo Rocafuerte	54	Cd	0.56S	75.25W
Nugaal [3]	35	Hd	8.30N	48.00 E
Nugālēd, Dēḥ-	30	Lh	7.58N	49.51 E
Nugālēd, Dōḥo-	35	Hd	8.35N	48.35 E
Nûgâtsiaq	41	Gd	71.39N	53.45W
Nugget Point	62	Cg	46.27S	169.49 E
Nûgssuaq	41	Gd	70.30N	51.30W
Nuguria Islands	57	Ge	3.20S	154.45 E
Nuguš	17	Gj	53.05N	56.00 E
Nuhaka	62	Gc	39.02S	77.45 E
Nui Atoll	57	Ie	7.15S	77.10 E
Nuijama	8	Md	60.58N	28.32 E
Nuiqsut	40	Ib	70.20N	51.00W
Nu Jang	21	Lh	16.31N	97.37 E
Nûk/Godthåb	67	Nc	64.15N	51.40W
Nukapu	63c	Ab	10.07S	65.59 E
Nukey Bluff	59	Hf	32.35S	35.40 E
Nukhayb	23	Fc	32.02N	42.15 E
Nukhaylak	31	Jg	9.08N	26.20 E
Nukiki	63a	Cb	6.45S	56.29 E
Nukuaéta	64h	Ac	3.22S	76.11W
Nuku'alofa	58	Jg	21.08S	75.12W
Nukufetau Atoll	57	Ie	8.00S	78.22 E
Nukufotu	64h	Bb	3.11S	76.10W
Nukuhifala	64h	Bb	3.17S	76.05W
Nukuhione	64h	Bb	3.15S	76.06W
Nuku Hiva, Ile-	57	Me	8.54S	40.06W
Nukulaelae Atoll	57	Ie	9.23S	79.52 E
Nukuloa	64h	Bb	3.11S	76.09W
Nukumanu Islands	57	Ge	4.30S	159.30 E
Nukumbasanga	63d	Cb	16.13S	179.15W
Nukunonu Atoll	57	Je	9.10S	171.53W
Nukuoro Atoll	57	Gd	3.51N	154.58 E
Nukus	22	He	42.50N	59.29 E
Nukutapu	64h	Bb	13.13S	176.08W
Nukuteatea	64h	Bb	13.12S	176.08W
Nulato	40	Hd	64.43N	158.06W
Nules	13	Le	39.51N	0.09W
Nullagine	58	Dg	21.53S	120.06 E
Nullagine River	59	Ed	20.43S	120.33 E
Nullarbor	59	Gf	31.26S	130.55 E
Nullarbor Plain	57	Dh	31.00S	129.00 E
Nulu'erhu Shan	27	Kc	41.40N	119.50 E
Numakawa	29a	Ba	45.15N	141.51 E
Numan	34	Hd	9.28N	2.02 E
Numancia [Phil.]	26	Ie	9.52N	125.58 E
Numancia [Sp.]	13	Jc	41.47N	2.30W
Numanohata	29a	Bb	42.40N	141.41 E
Numata [Jap.]	29a	Bb	43.49N	141.55 E
Numata [Jap.]	28	Of	36.38N	139.03 E
Numatinna	35	Dd	7.14N	27.37 E
Numazu	28	Og	35.06N	138.52 E
Nümbrecht	12	Jd	50.54N	7.33 E
Numedal	7	Bf	60.05N	9.05 E
Numena	36	Ee	1 .46S	36.31 E
Número Cinco, Canal-	55	Cm	37.14S	58.06W
Número Doce, Canal-	55	Cm	36.30S	59.08W
Número Dos, Canal-	55	Cm	36.51S	58.03W
Número Nueve, Canal-	55	Cm	36.08S	58.36W
Número Once, Canal-	55	Bm	36.28S	60.01W
Número Quince, Canal-	55	Dl	35.55S	57.45W
Número Uno, Canal-	55	Cm	36.40S	58.35W
Numfoor, Pulau-	26	Jg	1.03S	134.54 E
Nuneaton	9	Li	52.32N	1.28W
Nungarin	59	Df	31.11S	118.06 E
Nungnain Sum	27	Kb	45.45N	118.56 E
Nungo	37	Fb	13.25S	37.46 E
Nunivak	38	Cd	60.00N	166.30W
Nunkirchen, Wadern-	12	Ie	49.32N	6.53 E
Nunn	45	Df	40.45N	104.46W
Nunspeet	12	Hb	52.22N	5.46 E
Nunukan Timur, Pulau-	26	Gf	4.05N	117.40 E
Nuomin He	27	Lb	48.21N	124.32 E
Nuorgam	7	Ga	70.05N	27.51 E
Nuoro	6	Gg	40.19N	9.20 E
Nupani	63c	Ab	10.04S	166.40 E
Nūq	24	Pg	30.55N	56.35 E
Nuqayr	24	Mi	27.48N	48.21 E
Nuqrah	24	Ij	25.34N	41.24 E
Nuqruş, Jabal-	33	Fe	24.49N	34.36 E
Nuquí	54	Cb	5.43N	77.16W
Nūr	24	Od	36.15N	52.20 E
Nūr	24	Pg	31.25N	54.20 E
Nura	19	Gf	48.57N	62.20 E
Nura	21	Id	50.30N	69.59 E
Nūrābād	24	Ng	30.48N	51.27 E
Nuraghe Santu Antine	14	Cj	40.29N	8.45 E
Nurata	19	Gg	40.34N	65.35 E
Nur Dağları	24	Gd	36.45N	36.20 E
Nure	14	De	45.03N	9.49 E
Nurek	19	Gh	38.25N	69.20 E
Nurhak Dağı	23	Eb	38.04N	37.29 E
Nūrī	35	Eb	18.30N	32.02 E
Nurki	20	Ie	56.42N	138.28 E
Nurlat	19	Fe	54.28N	50.48 E
Nurlati	7	Li	55.38N	48.17 E
Nurmes	7	Ge	63.33N	29.07 E
Nurmijärvi	8	Kd	60.28N	24.48 E
Nurmo	8	Jb	62.50N	22.54 E
Nürnberg	6	Hf	49.27N	11.05 E
Nurra	14	Cj	40.45N	8.15 E
Nurri, Mount-	59	Jf	31.42S	146.02 E
Nurugas	37	Bc	19.11S	18.54 E
Nurzec	10	Sd	52.23N	22.28 E
Nusa Tenggara Barat [3]	26	Gh	8.50S	117.30 E
Nusa Tenggara Timur [3]	26	Hh	9.30S	122.00 E
Nusaybin	24	Id	37.03N	41.13 E
Nushagak	40	He	58.57N	158.29W
Nushan	27	Gf	25.00N	99.30 E
Nu-Shima	29	Dd	34.10N	134.50 E
Nutak	42	Le	57.31N	62.00W
Nuttal	25	Dc	28.45N	68.08 E
Nuutele	65c	Bb	14.02S	171.22W
Nuwākot	25	Gc	28.08N	83.53 E
Nuwara	25	Gg	6.58N	80.46 E
Nuwaybi 'al Muzayyinah	33	Fd	28.58N	34.39 E
Nyabing	59	Df	33.32S	118.09 E
Nyagquka/Yajiang	27	He	30.07N	100.58 E
Nyagrong/Xinlong	27	He	30.57N	100.12 E
Nyahanga	36	Fc	2.23S	33.33 E
Nyahua	36	Fc	4.58S	33.34 E
Nyainqêntanglha Feng	27	Fe	30.12N	90.33 E
Nyainqêntanglha Shan	21	Kf	30.10N	90.00 E
Nyakanazi	36	Fc	3.00S	31.15 E
Nyala	31	Jg	12.03N	24.53 E
Nyalam	27	Ef	28.15N	85.55 E
Ny-Ålesund	41	Nc	78.56N	11.57 E
Nyalikungu	36	Fc	3.11S	33.47 E
Nyamandhlovu	37	Dc	19.51S	28.16 E
Nyamapanda	37	Ec	16.55S	32.52 E
Nyamell	35	Dd	9.07N	26.58 E
Nyamtumbo	36	Ge	10.30S	36.06 E
Nyanding	35	Ed	8.40N	32.41 E
Nyanga	30	Ii	2.58S	10.15 E
Nyanga [3]	36	Bc	3.00S	11.00 E
Nyanza [3]	36	Fc	0.30S	34.30 E
Nyanza-Lac	36	Ec	4.21S	29.36 E
Nyasa, Lake- (EN)=Niassa, Lago-	30	Kj	12.00S	34.30 E
Nyaunglebin	25	Je	17.57N	96.44 E
Nyborg	7	Ci	55.19N	10.48 E
Nybro	7	Dh	56.45N	15.54 E
Nyda	17	Pc	66.40N	72.50 E
Nyda	20	Cc	66.36N	72.54 E
Nyeboe Land	41	Gb	81.45N	56.40W
Nyêmo	27	Ff	29.30N	90.07 E
Nyeri	36	Gc	0.25S	36.57 E
Nyerol	35	Ed	8.41N	32.02 E
Ny Friesland	41	Nc	79.30N	17.00 E
Nyhammar	8	Fd	60.17N	14.58 E
Nyhem	8	Fb	62.54N	15.40 E
Nyika	30	Ki	2.37S	38.44 E
Nyika Plateau	30	Kj	10.40S	33.50 E
Nyikog Qu	27	He	30.24N	100.40 E
Nyimba	36	Fe	14.33S	30.48 E
Nyingchi	27	Ff	29.38N	94.23 E
Nyírbátor	10	Si	47.50N	22.08 E
Nyíregyháza	10	Ri	47.57N	21.43 E
Nyiri Desert	36	Gc	2.20S	37.20 E
Nyiro, Mount-	36	Gb	2.08N	36.51 E
Nyírség	10	Ri	47.50N	21.55 E
Nykøbing [Den.]	7	Ci	54.46N	11.53 E
Nykøbing [Den.]	7	Ci	55.55N	11.41 E
Nykøbing [Den.]	8	Ch	56.48N	8.52 E
Nyköping	7	Dg	58.45N	17.00 E
Nyköpingsån	8	Gf	58.45N	17.01 E
Nykroppa	8	Fe	59.38N	14.18 E
Nyland	8	Ga	63.00N	17.46 E
Nylstroom	37	Dd	24.42S	28.20 E
Nymburk	10	Lf	50.11N	15.03 E
Nymphe Bank (EN)	9	Fj	51.30N	7.05W
Nynäshamn	7	Dg	58.54N	17.57 E
Nyngan	58	Fh	31.34S	147.11 E
Nyon	14	Ad	46.23N	6.15 E
Nyong	30	Hh	3.17N	9.54 E
Nyonga	36	Fd	6.43S	32.04 E
Nyons	11	Lj	44.22N	5.08 E
Nýřany	10	Jg	49.43N	13.13 E
Nyrob	17	Hf	60.42N	56.45 E
Nyš	20	Jf	51.30N	142.49 E
Nysa	10	Nf	50.29N	17.20 E
Nysa Kłodzka	10	Nf	50.49N	17.50 E
Nysa Łużycka	10	Kd	52.04N	14.46 E
Nyslott/Savonlinna	7	Gf	61.52N	28.53 E
Nyssa	46	Ge	43.53N	117.00W
Nystad/Uusikaupunki	7	Ef	60.48N	21.25 E
Nysted	8	Dj	54.40N	11.45 E
Nytva	19	Fd	57.56N	55.20 E
Nyūdō-Zaki	28	Od	40.00N	139.35 E
Nyunzu	36	Ed	5.57S	28.01 E
Nyūzen	29	Ec	36.56N	137.30 E
Nzambi	36	Bc	3.38S	11.16 E
Nzara	35	De	4.40N	28.14 E
Nzega	36	Fc	4.13S	33.11 E
Nzérékore	31	Gh	7.45N	8.49W
N'zeto	36	Bd	7.05S	12.50 E
Nzi	30	Gh	5.57N	4.50W
Nzilo, Barrage de-	36	Ee	10.35S	25.30 E
Nzo	34	Dd	6.16N	7.03W
Nzoro	36	Eb	3.18N	29.26 E
Nzwani	30	Lj	12.15S	44.25 E
O				
Oa, Mull of-	9	Gf	55.35N	6.20W
Oahe, Lake-	38	Ie	45.30N	100.25W
Oahu Island	57	Lb	21.30N	158.00W
O-akan-Dake	29a	Db	43.27N	144.10 E
Oakdale [Ca.-U.S.]	46	Eh	37.46N	120.51W
Oakdale [La.-U.S.]	45	Jk	30.49N	92.40W
Oakham	9	Mi	52.40N	0.44W
Oak Harbor	46	Db	48.18N	122.39W
Oak Lake	45	Fb	49.40N	100.45W
Oakland [Ca.-U.S.]	39	Gf	37.47N	122.13W
Oakland [Md.-U.S.]	44	Hf	39.25N	79.24W
Oakley [Id.-U.S.]	46	Ie	42.15N	113.53W
Oakley [Ks.-U.S.]	43	Gd	39.08N	100.51W
Oak Park	45	Mf	41.53N	87.48W
Oak Ridge	43	Kd	36.01N	84.16W
Oakridge	46	De	43.45N	122.28W
Oakville	44	Hd	43.27N	79.41W
Oamaru	61	Di	45.05S	170.59 E
Oancea	15	Ld	45.55N	28.06 E
Oani-Gawa	29	Ga	40.12N	140.16 E
Ōarai	29	Gc	36.18N	140.33 E
Oaro	62	Ee	42.31S	173.30 E
Oasis	46	Hf	41.01N	114.37W
Oasis	32	Hd	26.00N	5.00 E
Oates Coast	66	Jf	70.00S	160.00 E
Oaxaca [2]	47	Ee	17.00N	96.30W
Oaxaca, Sierra Madre de-	48	Ki	17.30N	96.30W
Oaxaca de Juárez	39	Jh	17.03N	96.43W
Ob	21	Ic	66.45N	69.30 E
Oba	42	Jg	48.55N	84.17W
Obala	34	He	4.10N	11.32 E
Obama [Jap.]	28	Mg	35.30N	135.45 E
Obama [Jap.]	29	Be	32.43N	130.13 E
Obama-Wan	29	Dd	35.30N	135.40 E
Oban [N.Z.]	61	Ci	46.52S	168.10 E
Oban [Scot.-U.K.]	9	He	56.25N	5.29W
Obanazawa	28	Pe	38.36N	140.24 E
Obando	53	Je	4.07N	67.45W
Oban Hills	34	Gd	5.30N	8.35 E
Obeliai/Obeljaj	8	Ki	55.58N	25.59 E
Obeljaj/Obeliai	8	Ki	55.58N	25.59 E
Oberá	56	Ic	27.29S	55.08W
Oberbayern	10	Hi	47.50N	11.50 E
Oberderdingen	12	Ke	49.04N	8.48 E
Oberfranken	10	Hf	50.10N	11.30 E
Oberhausen	10	Ce	51.28N	6.51 E
Oberkirchen, Schmallenberg-	12	Kc	51.09N	8.18 E
Oberland [Switz.]	14	Bd	46.35N	7.30 E
Oberland [Switz.]	14	Dd	46.45N	9.05 E
Oberlausitz	10	Ke	51.15N	14.30 E
Oberlin	45	Fg	39.49N	100.32W
Obermoschel	12	Je	49.44N	7.46 E
Obernkirchen	12	Lb	52.16N	9.08 E
Oberösterreich=Upper Austria (EN) [2]	14	Hb	48.15N	14.00 E
Oberpfalz	10	Ig	49.30N	12.10 E
Oberpfälzer Wald= Bohemian Forest (EN)	10	Ig	49.50N	12.30 E
Oberpullendorf	14	Kc	47.30N	16.31 E
Ober-Ramstadt	12	Ke	49.50N	8.45 E
Oberstdorf	10	Gi	47.24N	10.16 E
Oberursel (Taunus)	12	Kd	50.12N	8.35 E
Obervellach	14	Hd	46.56N	13.12 E
Oberwesel	12	Jd	50.06N	7.44 E
Ob Gulf (EN)=Obskaja Guba	21	Jc	69.00N	73.00 E
Obi, Kepulauan-	26	Ig	1.30S	127.45 E
Obi, Pulau-	57	De	1.30S	127.45 E
Obi, Selat-	26	Ig	0.52S	127.33 E
Óbidos [Braz.]	53	Kf	1.55S	55.31W
Óbidos [Port.]	13	Ce	39.22N	9.09W
Obihiro	27	Pc	42.55N	143.12 E
Obilić	15	Eg	42.41N	21.05 E
Obira	29a	Ba	44.01N	141.38 E
Obispos	49	Li	8.36N	70.05W
Obispo Trejo	56	Hd	30.46S	63.25W
Obitočnaja Kosa	16	Jf	46.35N	36.15 E
Oblučje	20	Ig	48.59N	131.05 E
Obninsk	19	Dd	55.05N	36.37 E
Obo	31	Jh	5.24N	26.30 E
Obock	35	Gc	11.57N	43.17 E
Obojan	19	De	51.13N	36.16 E
Obokote	36	Ec	0.52S	26.19 E
Obol	7	Gi	55.24N	29.01 E
Oborniki	10	Md	52.39N	16.51 E
Obouya	36	Cc	0.56S	15.43 E
Obozerski	19	Ec	63.28N	40.20 E
Obra	10	Ld	52.36N	15.28 E
Obrenovac	15	De	44.39N	20.12 E
Obrovac	14	Jf	44.12N	15.41 E
Obrovo	10	Vd	52.27N	25.43 E
Obruchev Rise (EN)	20	Lf	52.30N	166.00 E
Obruk Platosu	24	Ec	38.02N	33.30 E
Obšči Syrt	5	Le	51.50N	51.00 E
Obskaja Guba=Ob Gulf (EN)	21	Jc	69.00N	73.00 E
Ob' Tablemount (EN)	30	Ln	52.30S	42.00 E
Ōbu	29	Ed	35.01N	136.58 E
Obuasi	34	Ed	6.12N	1.40W
Obudu	34	Gd	6.40N	9. 0 E
Obuhov	16	Gd	50.07N	30.37 E
Obva	17	Gg	58.35N	55. 5 E
Obzor	15	Kg	42.49N	27. 3 E
Oca	13	Ib	42.46N	3. 6W
Oca, Montes de-	13	Ib	42.20N	3. 5W
Očakov	19	Df	46.38N	31.33 E
Ocala	43	Kf	29.11N	82.07W
Očamčira	16	Lh	42.46N	41.27 E
Ocampo [Mex.]	48	Hd	27.20N	102.21W
Ocampo [Mex.]	48	Ec	28.11N	108.23W
Ocaña [Col.]	54	Db	8.15N	73.20W
Ocaña [Sp.]	13	Ie	39.56N	3.31W
Occhito, Lago di-	14	Ii	41.35N	14.55 E
Ocean Bight	49	Kc	21.15N	73.15W
Ocean City [Md.-U.S.]	43	Ld	38.20N	75.05W
Ocean City [N.J.-U.S.]	44	Jf	39.16N	74.35W
Ocean Falls	42	Ef	52.21N	127.40W
Oceania	57	Ie	5.00S	175.00 E
Ocean Point	44	Il	26.16N	77.03W
Oceanside	43	De	33.12N	117.23W
Ocean Springs	45	Lk	30.25N	88.50W
Ocejón, Pico-	13	Ic	41.07N	3.15W
Očenyrd, Gora-	17	Mb	68.05N	66.20 E
Očer	19	Fd	57.53N	54.45 E
Ochagavia	13	Kb	42.55N	1.05W
Ochiai	29	Cd	35.02N	133.45 E
Ochi-Gata	29	Ec	36.55N	136.43 E
Ochiishi-Misaki	29a	Db	43.10N	145.2 E
Ochil Hills	9	Je	56.23N	3.3 W
Och'onjang	28	Jd	40.55N	128.5 E
Ocho Rios	49	Id	18.25N	77.0 W
Ochsenfurt	10	Gg	49.39N	10.0 E
Ochtrup	12	Jb	52.13N	7.1 E
Ockelbo	7	Dd	60.53N	16.4 E
Öckerö	8	Dg	57.43N	11.3 E
Ocmulgee River	44	Fj	31.58N	82.3 W
Ocna Mureş	15	Gc	46.23N	23.5 E

Index Symbols

[1] Independent Nation · [2] State, Region · [3] District, County · [4] Municipality · [5] Colony, Dependency · Continent · Physical Region · Historical or Cultural Region · Mount, Mountain · Volcano · Hill · Mountains, Mountain Range · Hills, Escarpment · Plateau, Upland · Pass, Gap · Plain, Lowland · Delta · Salt Flat · Valley, Canyon · Crater, Cave · Karst Features · Depression · Polder · Desert, Dunes · Forest, Woods · Heath, Steppe · Oasis · Cape, Point · Coast, Beach · Cliff · Peninsula · Isthmus · Sandbank · Island · Atoll · Rock, Reef · Islands, Archipelago · Rocks, Reefs · Coral Reef · Well, Spring · Geyser · River, Stream · Waterfall Rapids · River Mouth, Estuary · Lake · Salt Lake · Intermittent Lake · Reservoir · Swamp, Pond · Canal · Glacier · Ice Shelf, Pack Ice · Ocean · Sea · Gulf, Bay · Strait, Fjord · Lagoon · Bank · Seamount · Tablemount · Ridge · Shelf · Basin · Escarpment, Sea Scarp · Fracture · Trench, Abyss · National Park, Reserve · Point of Interest · Recreation Site · Cave, Cavern · Historic Site · Ruins · Wall, Walls · Church, Abbey · Temple · Scientific Station · Airport · Port · Lighthouse · Mine · Tunnel · Dam, Bridge

Ocna Sibiului	15	Hc	45.53N	24.03 E
Ocoa, Bahía de-	49	Ld	18.22N	70.39W
Oconee River	44	Fj	31.58N	82.32W
Oconto	45	Md	44.55N	87.52W
Ocosingo	48	Mi	17.04N	92.15W
Ocotal	49	Dg	13.38N	86.29W
Ocotepeque [3]	49	Cf	14.30N	89.00W
Ocotlán	47	Dd	20.21N	102.46W
Ocotlán de Morelos	48	Ki	16.48N	96.43W
Ocracoke Inlet	44	Ih	35.10N	76.05W
Ocracoke Island	44	Jh	35.09N	75.53W
Ocreza	13	Ee	39.32N	7.50W
Octeville-sur-Mer	12	Ce	49.33N	0.07 E
October Revolution Island (EN)=Oktjabrskoj Revoljuci, Ostrov-	21	Lb	79.30N	97.00 E
Ocú	49	Gj	7.57N	80.47W
Ocumare del Tuy	50	Cg	10.07N	66.46W
Oda [Ghana]	34	Ed	5.55N	0.59W
Oda [Jap.]	29	Ce	33.34N	132.48 E
Ōda	28	Lg	35.11N	132.30 E
Oda, Jabal-	35	Fa	20.21N	36.39 E
Ódáðahraun	7a	Cb	65.09N	17.00W
Ōdai	29	Ed	34.24N	136.24 E
Odaigahara-San	29	Ed	34.11N	136.06 E
Odalen	8	Dd	60.15N	11.40 E
Ōdate	28	Pd	40.16N	140.34 E
Odawara	28	Og	35.15N	139.10 E
Odda	7	Bf	60.04N	6.33 E
Odder	8	Di	55.58N	10.10 E
Odeleite	13	Eg	37.21N	7.27W
Odemira	13	Dg	37.36N	8.38W
Ödemiş	24	Bc	38.13N	27.59 E
Odendaalsrus	37	De	27.48S	26.45 E
Odense	6	Hd	55.24N	10.23 E
Odenthal	12	Jc	51.02N	7.07 E
Odenwald	10	Eg	49.40N	9.00 E
Oder [Eur.]	5	He	53.40N	14.33 E
Oder [Ger.]	10	Ge	51.40N	10.02 E
Oderbruch	10	Kd	52.40N	14.15 E
Oderské vrchy	10	Ng	49.40N	17.45 E
Oderzo	14	Ge	45.47N	12.29 E
Ödeshög	7	Dg	58.14N	14.39 E
Odessa [Tx.-U.S.]	39	If	31.51N	102.22W
Odessa	6	Jf	46.28N	30.44 E
Odessa [Wa.-U.S.]	46	Fc	47.20N	118.41W
Odesskaja Oblast [3]	19	Df	46.45N	30.30 E
Odet	11	Bg	47.52N	4.06W
Odiel	13	Fg	37.10N	6.54W
Odienné	31	Gh	9.30N	7.34W
Odienné [3]	34	Dd	9.45N	7.45W
Odivelas	13	Df	38.12N	8.18W
Ödmården	8	Gc	61.05N	16.40 E
Odobeşti	15	Kd	45.46N	27.03 E
Ödöngk	25	Kf	11.48N	104.45 E
Odoorn	12	Ib	52.51N	6.50 E
Odorheiu Secuiesc	15	Ic	46.18N	25.18 E
Ōdose-Zaki	29a	Bc	40.46N	140.03 E
Odra	5	He	53.40N	14.33 E
Ödwēyne	35	Hd	9.23N	45.04 E
Odžaci	15	Cd	45.31N	19.16 E
Odžak	14	Me	45.01N	18.18 E
Odzi	37	Ec	19.45S	32.24 E
Oeiras	13	Eg	37.38N	7.40W
Oeiras [Braz.]	54	Je	7.01S	42.08W
Oeiras [Port.]	13	Cf	38.41N	9.19W
Oelde	12	Kc	51.49N	8.09 E
Oelerbeek	12	Ib	52.21N	6.38 E
Oelrichs	45	Ee	43.15N	103.10W
Oelsnitz	10	If	50.25N	12.10 E
Oelwein	45	Ke	42.41N	91.55W
Oeno Island	57	Ng	23.56S	130.44W
Oer-Erkenschwick	12	Jc	51.38N	7.15 E
Oeste, Punta-	51a	Ab	18.05N	67.57W
Oeventrop, Arnsberg-	12	Kc	51.24N	8.08 E
Ōe-Yama	29	Dd	35.27N	135.06 E
Of	24	Ib	40.57N	40.16 E
O'Fallon Creek	46	Mc	46.50N	105.09W
Ofanto	14	Ki	41.21N	16.13 E
Ofaqim	24	Fg	31.17N	34.37 E
Offa	34	Fd	8.09N	4.43 E
Offaly/Uíbh Fhailí [2]	9	Fh	53.20N	7.30W
Offenbach am Main	10	Ef	50.06N	8.46 E
Offenbach-Hundheim	12	Je	49.37N	7.33 E
Offenburg	10	Dh	48.29N	7.56 E
Offida	14	Hh	42.56N	13.41 E
Offoué	36	Bc	0.04S	11.44 E
Offranville	12	De	49.52N	1.03 E
Ofidhoúsa	15	Jm	36.33N	26.09 E
Ofolanga	65b	Ba	19.36S	174.27W
Ofu	65c	Db	14.11S	169.42W
Ōfunato	28	Pe	39.04N	141.43 E
Oga	28	Oe	40.43N	141.18 E
Ogachi	29	Gb	39.05N	140.28 E
Ogaden	30	Lh	7.30N	45.00 E
Oga-Hantō	28	Oe	39.55N	139.50 E
Ōgaki	28	Ng	35.21N	136.37 E
Ogallala	43	Gc	41.08N	101.43W
Ogasawara-Shotō=Bonin Islands (EN)	21	Qg	27.00N	142.10 E
Ogawara-Ko	29a	Bc	40.45N	141.20 E
Ogbomosho	31	Hh	8.08N	4.16 E
Ogden	39	He	41.14N	111.58W
Ogdensburg	44	Jc	44.42N	75.31W
Ogeechee River	44	Gj	31.51N	81.06W
Oghāsh	24	Lc	39.10N	46.55 E
Ogi	29	Fc	37.50N	138.16 E
Ogilvie Mountains	42	Dc	65.00N	140.00W
Ogi-no-Sen	29	Dd	35.26N	134.26 E
Oginski Kanal	16	Dc	52.20N	25.55 E
Oglanly	16	Sj	39.50N	54.33 E
Oglethorpe	44	Ei	31.28N	84.04W
Ogliastra	14	Dk	39.55N	9.35 E
Oglio	14	Ee	45.02N	10.39 E
Ognon	11	Lg	47.20N	5.29 E
Ogo	35	Hd	9.48N	45.35 E
Ogoamas, Bulu-	26	Hf	0.40N	120.12 E
Ogodža	20	If	52.48N	132.40 E
Ogoja	34	Gd	6.40N	8.48 E
Ogoki	42	If	51.38N	85.56W
Ogoki	42	If	51.38N	85.55W
Ogoki Reservoir	42	If	51.35N	86.00W
Ogoněk	20	Ie	59.40N	138.01 E
Ogooué	30	Hi	0.49S	9.00 E
Ogooué-Ivindo [3]	36	Bb	0.30N	13.00 E
Ogooué-Lolo [3]	36	Bc	1.00S	13.00 E
Ogooué-Maritime [3]	36	Ac	2.00S	9.30 E
Ogōri [Jap.]	29	Bd	34.06N	131.25 E
Ogōri [Jap.]	29	Be	33.24N	130.34 E
Ogosta	15	Gf	43.45N	23.51 E
Ogražden	15	Fh	41.30N	22.55 E
Ogre	8	Kh	56.42N	24.33 E
Ogre	7	Fh	56.50N	24.39 E
Ogulin	14	Je	45.16N	15.14 E
Ogun [2]	34	Fd	7.00N	3.40 E
Oguni [Jap.]	29	Fb	38.04N	139.45 E
Oguni [Jap.]	29	Be	33.07N	131.04 E
Ogurčinski, Ostrov-	16	Rj	38.55N	53.05 E
Oğuzeli	24	Gd	37.00N	37.30 E
Oha	22	Qd	53.34N	142.56 E
Ohai	62	Bf	45.56S	167.57 E
Ohakune	62	Fc	39.25S	175.25 E
Ohanet	32	Id	28.40N	8.50 E
Ohansk	17	Gh	57.42N	55.25 E
Ōhara	29	Gd	35.15N	140.23 E
Ōhasama	29	Gb	39.28N	141.17 E
Ohata	20	Je	59.20N	143.05 E
Ōhata	28	Pd	41.24N	141.10 E
Ohau, Lake-	62	Cf	44.15S	169.50 E
Ohey	12	Hd	50.26N	5.08 E
O'Higgins, Cabo-	65d	Bb	27.05S	109.15W
Ohio	38	Kf	36.59N	89.08W
Ohio [2]	43	Kc	40.15N	82.45W
Ohm	10	Ef	50.51N	8.48 E
Ohmberge	10	Ge	51.30N	10.28 E
'Ohonua	65b	Bc	21.20S	174.57W
Ohopoho	31	Ij	18.03S	13.45 E
Ohotsk	22	Qd	59.23N	143.18 E
Ohotskoje More=Okhotsk, Sea of- (EN)	21	Qd	53.00N	150.00 E
Ohre	10	Hd	52.18N	11.47 E
Ohře	10	Kf	50.32N	14.08 E
Ohrid	15	Dh	41.07N	20.48 E
Ohrid, Lake- (EN) = Ohridsko Jezero	5	Ig	41.00N	20.45 E
Ohrid, Lake- (EN) = Ohrit, Liqen i-	5	Ig	41.00N	20.45 E
Ohridsko Jezero=Ohrid, Lake- (EN)	5	Ig	41.00N	20.45 E
Öhringen	10	Fg	49.12N	9.30 E
Ohrit, Liqen i- = Ohrid, Lake- (EN)	5	Ig	41.00N	20.45 E
Ohura	62	Fc	38.51S	174.59 E
Oiapoque	54	Hc	3.50N	51.50W
Oich	9	Id	57.10N	4.45W
Oi-Gawa	29	Fd	34.46N	138.17 E
Oil City	44	He	41.26N	79.44W
Oildale	46	Fi	35.25N	119.01W
Oileán Baoi/Dursey	9	Cj	51.36N	10.12W
Oileán Ciarraí/Castleisland	9	Di	52.14N	9.27W
Oileán Coarach/Mutton	9	Di	52.49N	9.31W
Oileán Mhic Aodha/Magee, Island-	9	Hg	54.50N	5.50W
Oinoúsai	15	Jk	38.32N	26.13 E
Oinoúsai, Nisoi-	15	Jk	38.31N	26.14 E
Oirschot	12	Hc	51.30N	5.18 E
Oisans	11	Mi	45.02N	6.02 E
Oise [3]	11	Ie	49.30N	2.30 E
Oise	11	Ie	49.00N	2.04 E
Oise à l'Aisne, Canal de l'-	11	Je	49.36N	3.11 E
Oisemont	12	De	49.57N	1.46 E
Oissel	12	De	49.20N	1.06 E
Oisterwijk	12	Hc	51.35N	5.11 E
Oistins	51q	Ab	13.04N	59.32W
Oistins Bay	51q	Ab	13.03N	59.33W
Ōita	27	Ne	33.14N	131.36 E
Ōita Ken [2]	28	Kh	33.15N	131.20 E
Oiti Óros	15	Fk	38.49N	22.17 E
Oituz, Pasul-	15	Jc	46.03N	26.23 E
Oiwake	29a	Bb	42.52N	141.48 E
Ojat	7	Hf	60.31N	33.05 E
Öje	8	Ed	60.49N	13.51 E
Ojestos de Jalisco	48	Ig	21.50N	101.35W
Ojika-Jima	29	Ae	33.13N	129.03 E
O-Jima	29	Be	34.00N	130.45 E
Ojinaga	47	Dc	29.34N	104.25W
Ojiya	28	Of	37.18N	138.48 E
Ojmjakon	20	Jd	63.28N	142.49 E
Ojocaliente	48	Hf	22.34N	102.15W
Ojo Caliente	48	Fb	30.25N	106.33W
Ojos del Salado, Nevado-	52	Jh	27.06S	68.32W
Ojos Negros	13	Kd	40.44N	1.30W
Ojtal	18	Hg	42.54N	73.21 E
Oka	21	Md	55.00N	102.03 E
Oka	5	Kd	56.20N	43.59 E
Okaba	26	Kh	8.06S	139.42 E
Okahandja [3]	37	Bd	21.30S	17.30 E
Okahandja	31	Ik	21.59S	16.58 E
Okahukura	62	Fc	38.47S	175.14 E
Okaihau	62	Ea	35.19S	173.46 E
Okak Islands	42	Le	57.28N	61.48W
Okanagan Lake	42	Fg	49.55N	119.30W
Okano	36	Bc	0.05S	10.57 E
Okanogan River	43	Db	48.06N	119.43W
Okapa	59	Ja	6.31S	145.32 E
Okāra	25	Eb	30.49N	73.27 E
Okarem	19	Fh	38.07N	54.05 E
Okato	62	Ec	39.12S	173.53 E
Okaukuejo	37	Bc	19.10S	15.54 E
Okavango	30	Jj	18.53N	22.24 E
Okavango [3]	37	Cc	18.00S	21.00 E
Okavango Swamp	30	Jj	19.30S	23.00 E
Ōkawa	29	Be	33.12N	130.23 E
Okaya	28	Of	36.03N	138.03 E
Okayama	22	Pf	34.39N	133.55 E
Okayama Ken [2]	28	Lg	34.50N	133.45 E
Okazaki	28	Ng	34.57N	137.10 E
Okeechobee	44	Gl	27.15N	80.50W
Okeechobee, Lake-	38	Kg	26.55N	80.45W
Okefenokee Swamp	44	Fj	30.42N	82.20W
Okehampton	9	Jk	50.44N	4.00W
Okene	34	Gd	7.33N	6.14 E
Oker	10	Gd	52.30N	10.22 E
Oketo	29a	Cb	43.41N	143.32 E
Okha	25	Dd	22.27N	69.04 E
Ókhi Óros	15	Hk	38.04N	24.28 E
Okhotsk, Sea of- (EN)= Hok-Kai	21	Qd	53.00N	150.00 E
Okhotsk, Sea of- (EN)= Ohotskoje More	21	Qd	53.00N	150.00 E
Okhthonía, Ákra-	15	Hk	38.32N	24.14 E
Oki-Daitō-Jima	27	Ng	24.30N	131.00 E
Okiep	37	Be	29.39S	17.53 E
Okinawa	29b	Ab	26.20N	127.47 E
Okinawa Islands (EN)= Okinawa-Shotō	21	Og	26.40N	128.00 E
Okinawa-Jima	27	Mf	26.40N	128.20 E
Okinawa Ken [2]	29b	Ab	26.31N	127.59 E
Okinawa-Shotō=Okinawa Islands (EN)	21	Og	26.40N	128.00 E
Okinoerabu-Jima	27	Mf	27.20N	128.35 E
Okino-Shima [Jap.]	29	Ce	32.44N	132.33 E
Okino-Shima [Jap.]	29	Bd	34.15N	130.08 E
Okino-Tori-Shima	21	Pg	20.25N	136.00 E
Oki Ridge (EN)	28	Mf	37.00N	135.00 E
Oki-Shotō	27	Nd	36.00N	132.50 E
Okitipupa	34	Fd	6.30N	4.48 E
Oki Trench (EN)	29	Dc	37.00N	135.30 E
Oklahoma [2]	43	Hd	35.30N	98.00W
Oklahoma City	39	Jf	35.28N	97.32W
Okmulgee	45	Ii	35.37N	95.58W
Oknica	15	Ka	48.22N	27.24 E
Oko	35	Fa	22.20N	35.56 E
Okoko	36	Fb	2.06N	33.53 E
Okolo	36	Fb	2.40N	31.09 E
Okolona	44	Ef	38.08N	85.41W
Okondja	36	Bc	0.41S	13.47 E
Okonek	10	Mc	53.33N	16.50 E
Okoppe	28	Qb	44.28N	143.08 E
Okotoks	46	Ia	50.44N	113.59W
Okoyo	36	Cc	1.28S	15.04 E
Okrzeika	10	Re	51.40N	21.30 E
Øksfjord	7	Fa	70.14N	22.22 E
Oksino	17	Fc	67.33N	52.10 E
Okstindane	5	Hb	66.02N	14.10 E
Oktemberjan	16	Ni	40.09N	44.03 E
Oktjabrsk	6	Lf	48.40N	57.11 E
Oktjabrsk	7	Lj	53.13N	48.40 E
Oktjabrski	16	Fc	52.38N	28.54 E
Oktjabrski	17	Kj	52.37N	62.43 E
Oktjabrski	20	Ee	56.05N	99.25 E
Oktjabrski	19	Fe	54.31N	53.28 E
Oktjabrski	17	Hh	56.31N	57.12 E
Oktjabrski	7	Kf	61.05N	43.08 E
Oktjabrski	20	Hf	53.00N	128.42 E
Oktjabrski	20	Kf	52.38N	156.15 E
Oktjabrski	16	Mf	47.56N	43.38 E
Oktjabrskoje	19	Gc	62.28N	66.01 E
Oktjabrskoj Revoljuci, Ostrov-=October Revolution Island (EN)	21	Lb	79.30N	97.00 E
Oku	29b	Bb	26.50N	128.17 E
Ōkuchi	28	Kh	32.04N	130.37 E
Okulovka	7	Hg	58.24N	33.18 E
Okushiri	28	Oc	42.09N	139.29 E
Okushiri-Kaikyō	29a	Ab	42.15N	139.40 E
Okushiri-Tō	27	Oc	42.10N	139.25 E
Okuta	34	Fd	9.13N	3.11 E
Oku Tango-Hantō	29	Dd	35.40N	135.10 E
Okwa	30	Jk	22.26S	22.58 E
Ola	20	Ke	59.37N	151.20 E
Ólafsfjördur	7a	Ba	66.04N	18.39W
Ólafsvík	7a	Ab	64.53N	23.43W
Ola Grande, Punta-	51a	Bc	17.55N	66.08W
Olaine/Olajne	7	Fh	56.49N	23.59 E
Olajne/Olaine	7	Fh	56.49N	23.59 E
Olancha	46	Gh	36.17N	117.59W
Olanchito	49	Df	15.30N	86.35W
Olancho [3]	49	Ef	14.45N	86.00W
Öland	5	Hd	56.45N	16.40 E
Ölands norra udde	8	Gg	57.22N	17.05 E
Ölands södra grund	8	Gh	55.40N	17.25 E
Ölands södra udde	8	Gh	56.11N	16.24 E
Olanga	7	Hc	66.08N	30.38 E
Olathe	45	Ig	38.53N	94.49W
Olavarria	53	Ji	36.53S	60.20W
Oława	10	Nf	50.57N	17.17 E
Olawa	10	Nf	50.57N	17.17 E
Olbernhau	10	Jf	50.40N	13.20 E
Olbia	6	Gg	40.55N	9.31 E
Olbia, Golfo di-	14	Dj	40.55N	9.40 E
Old Bahama Channel	49	Ib	22.30N	78.05W
Old Bahama Channel (EN)= Bahamas, Canal Viejo de-	49	Ib	22.30N	78.05W
Old Castile (EN)=Castilla la Vieja	13	Ic	41.30N	4.00W
Old Crow	39	Fc	67.35N	139.50W
Oldeani	36	Gc	3.21S	35.33 E
Oldebroek	12	Hb	52.26N	5.53 E
Oldenburg	10	Ec	53.10N	8.12 E
Oldenburg in Holstein	10	Gb	54.18N	10.53 E
Oldenzaal	11	Mb	52.19N	6.56 E
Old Faithful Geyser	46	Jd	44.30N	110.45W
Old Fletton	12	Bb	52.34N	0.15W
Oldham	9	Kh	53.33N	2.07W
Old Hickory Lake	44	Dg	36.18N	86.30W
Oldman River	46	Jb	49.56N	111.42W
Old Marsh Bed	59	Gd	20.55S	130.30 E
Old Mkushi	36	Ee	14.22S	29.22 E
Old Road	51d	Bb	17.01N	61.50W
Old Road Town	51c	Ab	17.19N	62.48W
Olds	42	Gf	51.47N	114.06W
Old Town	44	Mc	44.56N	68.39W
Old Wives Lake	46	Ma	50.06N	106.00W
Olean	44	Hd	42.05N	78.26W
Olecko	10	Sb	54.03N	22.30 E
Oleiros	13	Ee	39.55N	7.55W
Olëkma	21	Oc	60.22N	120.42 E
Olëkminsk	22	Oc	60.30N	120.15 E
Olëkminski Stanovik	20	Gf	54.00N	119.00 E
Ølen	7	Ag	59.36N	5.48 E
Olenegorsk	19	Db	68.10N	33.13 E
Olenëk	21	Nb	73.00N	119.55 E
Olenëkski Zaliv	20	Hb	73.10N	121.00 E
Olenica	7	Ic	66.29N	35.19 E
Olenj, Ostrov-	20	Cb	72.25N	77.45 E
Olenty	16	Re	49.45N	52.10 E
Oléron, Ile d'-	5	Ff	45.56N	1.18W
Olesko	10	Ug	49.53N	24.58 E
Oleśnica	10	Ne	51.13N	17.23 E
Olesno	10	Of	50.53N	18.25 E
Olevsk	16	Ed	51.13N	27.41 E
Olga	20	Ih	43.46N	135.21 E
Olga, Mount-	59	Ge	25.19S	130.46 E
Olgastretet	41	Oc	78.30N	24.00 E
Ølgod	8	Ci	55.49N	8.37 E
Olhão	13	Eg	37.02N	7.50W
Olhovatka	16	Kd	50.17N	39.17 E
Oli	34	Fd	9.40N	4.29 E
Oliana	13	Nb	42.04N	1.19 E
Olib	14	If	44.23N	14.47 E
Oliena	14	Dj	40.16N	9.24 E
Olifants [Afr.]	30	Kk	24.03S	32.40 E
Olifants [Nam.]	37	Be	25.30S	19.30 E
Olifantshoek	37	Ce	27.57S	22.42 E
Olimarao Atoll	57	Fd	7.42N	145.53 E
Olimbía	15	El	37.39N	21.38 E
Ólimbos	15	Kn	35.44N	27.13 E
Ólimbos, Óros-=Olympus, Mount- (EN)	5	Ig	40.05N	22.21 E
Ólimbos Óros	15	Jj	39.05N	26.20 E
Olímpia	55	He	20.44S	48.54W
Olinda	54	Le	8.01S	34.51W
Olite	13	Kb	42.29N	1.39W
Oliva [Arg.]	56	Hd	32.03S	63.34W
Oliva [Sp.]	13	Lf	38.55N	0.07W
Oliva, Monasterio de la-	13	Kb	42.20N	1.25W
Oliva de la Frontera	13	Ff	38.16N	6.55W
Oliveira	55	Je	20.41S	44.49W
Oliveira dos Brejinhos	54	Jf	12.19S	42.54W
Olivença	37	Fb	11.46S	35.13 E
Olivenza	13	Ef	38.41N	7.06W
Oliver	46	Fb	49.11N	119.33W
Olivet	11	Hg	47.52N	1.54 E
Olivia	45	Id	44.46N	94.59W
Olja	16	Og	45.47N	47.35 E
Olji Moron He	28	Fb	44.16N	121.42 E
Oljutorski, Mys-	21	Td	59.55N	170.25 E
Oljutorski Zaliv	20	Ld	60.00N	168.00 E
Olkusz	10	Pf	50.17N	19.35 E
Ollan	64d	Bb	7.14N	151.38 E
Ollerton	12	Aa	53.13N	1.01W
Olmedo	13	Hc	41.17N	4.41W
Olmos	54	Ce	5.59S	79.46W
Olney [Eng.-U.K.]	12	Bb	52.09N	0.42W
Olney [Il.-U.S.]	45	Lg	38.44N	88.05W
Olney [Tx.-U.S.]	45	Gj	33.22N	98.45W
Oloči	20	Gf	51.20N	119.53 E
Olofström	7	Dh	56.16N	14.30 E
Oloitokitok	36	Gc	2.56S	37.30 E
Oloj	20	Kc	66.20N	159.29 E
Olojski Hrebet	20	Lc	65.50N	162.30 E
Olombo	36	Cc	1.18S	15.53 E
Olomburi	63a	Ec	8.59S	161.09 E
Olomouc	6	Hf	49.36N	17.16 E
Olona	14	De	45.06N	9.21 E
Olonec	19	Dc	61.01N	32.58 E
Olonešty	15	Mc	46.29N	29.52 E
Olongapo	26	Oh	14.50N	120.16 E
Oloron, Gave d'-	11	Ek	43.33N	1.05W
Oloron-Sainte-Marie	11	Fk	43.12N	0.36W
Olosega	65c	Db	14.11S	169.39W
Olot	13	Ob	42.11N	2.29 E
Olovjannaja	20	Gf	50.56N	115.35 E
Olovo	14	Mf	44.07N	18.35 E
Olpe	10	De	51.02N	7.51 E
Olpoy	63b	Cb	14.52S	166.33 E
Olroyd River	59	Ib	14.10S	141.50 E
Olsberg	12	Kc	51.21N	8.30 E
Olshammar	8	Ff	58.45N	14.48 E
Olst	12	Ib	52.20N	6.08 E
Olsztyn	6	Ie	53.48N	20.29 E
Olsztyn [2]	10	Qc	53.50N	20.30 E
Olsztynek	10	Qc	53.36N	20.17 E
Olt [2]	15	He	44.25N	24.30 E
Olt	5	If	43.43N	24.51 E
Oltedal	8	Bf	58.50N	6.02 E
Olten	14	Bc	47.22N	7.55 E
Olteni	15	Ie	44.11N	25.17 E
Oltenia	15	Ge	44.30N	23.30 E
Oltenița	15	Je	44.05N	26.38 E
Oltet	15	He	44.14N	24.27 E
Oltu	24	Ib	40.33N	41.59 E
Oluanpi	21	Og	21.54N	120.51 E
Olutanga	26	He	7.22N	122.52 E
Olvera	13	Gh	36.56N	5.16W
Olym	16	Kc	52.27N	38.05 E
Olympia	39	Ge	47.03N	122.53W
Olympic Mountains	46	Dc	47.50N	123.45W
Olympus, Mount-	38	Ge	47.48N	123.43W
Olympus, Mount- (EN)= Ólimbos, Óros-	5	Ig	40.05N	22.21 E
Om	20	Cf	54.59N	73.22 E
Ōma	29a	Bc	41.30N	140.55 E
Oma	17	Cc	66.45N	46.20 E
Ōmachi	28	Nf	36.30N	137.52 E
Omae-Zaki	29	Fd	34.36N	138.14 E
Ōmagari	28	Pe	39.27N	140.29 E
Omagh/An Ómaigh	9	Fg	54.36N	7.18W
Omaha	39	Je	41.16N	95.57W
Omak	46	Fb	48.24N	119.31W
Omakau	62	Cf	45.06S	169.36 E
Omak Lake	46	Fb	48.16N	119.23W
Oman (EN)='Umān [1]	22	Hg	21.00N	57.00 E
Oman, Gulf of- (EN)= 'Umān, Khalij-	21	Hg	25.00N	58.00 E
Omarama	61	Ch	44.29S	169.58 E
Omar Gambon	35	He	3.10N	45.47 E
Omaru-Gawa	29	Be	32.07N	131.34 E
Omaruru	37	Bd	21.28S	15.56 E
Omaruru [3]	37	Bd	21.30S	15.00 E
Omatako	37	Bd	21.07S	16.43 E
Omatako, Omuramba-	30	Jj	17.57S	20.25 E
Omate	54	Dg	16.41S	70.59W
Ōma-Zaki	29a	Bc	41.32N	140.55 E
Ombai, Selat-	26	Hh	8.30S	125.00 E
Ombella-Mpoko [3]	35	Bd	5.00N	18.00 E
Omberg	8	Ff	58.20N	14.39 E
Ombo	8	Ae	59.15N	6.00 E
Omboué	36	Ac	1.34S	9.15 E
Ombrone	14	Fh	42.39N	11.01 E
Ombu	27	Ee	31.18N	86.33 E
Omčak	20	Jd	61.38N	147.55 E
Omdurman (EN)=Umm Durmān	31	Kg	15.38N	32.30 E
Ōme	29	Fd	35.47N	139.15 E
Omegna	14	Ce	45.53N	8.24 E
Omeo	59	Jg	37.06S	147.36 E
Ömerköy	15	Lj	39.50N	28.04 E
Ometepe, Isla de-	47	Gf	11.30N	85.35W
Ometepec	47	Ee	16.41N	98.25W
Omhajer	35	Fc	14.19N	36.40 E
Ōmihachiman	29	Ed	35.08N	136.05 E
Omihi	62	Ee	43.01S	172.51 E
Omineca	42	Fe	56.05N	124.05W
Omineca Mountains	42	Ee	56.35N	125.55W
Omiš	14	Kg	43.27N	16.42 E
Ōmi-Shima [Jap.]	29	Bd	34.25N	131.15 E
Ōmi-Shima [Jap.]	29	Cd	34.15N	133.00 E
Omitara	37	Bd	22.18S	18.01 E
Ōmiya	27	Od	35.54N	139.38 E
Ommanney Bay	42	Hb	73.00N	101.00W
Omme Å	8	Ci	55.55N	8.25 E
Ommen	12	Ib	52.31N	6.25 E
Omo	30	Kh	4.32N	36.04 E
Omø	8	Di	55.10N	11.10 E
Omoa, Bahía de-	49	Cf	15.50N	88.10W
Omodeo, Lago-	14	Cj	40.10N	8.55 E
Omoloj	20	Ib	71.08N	132.01 E
Omolon	21	Rc	68.42N	158.36 E
Omolon	20	Lc	65.12N	160.27 E
Omono-Gawa	29	Gb	39.44N	140.04 E
Omont	12	Ge	49.36N	4.44 E
Omoto-Gawa	29	Gb	39.51N	141.58 E
Omsk	22	Jd	55.00N	73.24 E
Omskaja Oblast [3]	19	Hd	56.00N	72.30 E
Omsukčan	20	Kd	62.27N	155.50 E
Omsukčanski Hrebet	20	Kd	63.00N	155.10 E
Ōmu	28	Qb	44.34N	142.58 E
Omu, Vîrful-	15	Id	45.26N	25.25 E
Omulew	10	Rc	53.05N	21.32 E
Ōmura	28	Jh	32.54N	129.57 E
Ōmura-Wan	29	Ae	33.00N	129.50 E
Omurtag	15	Jf	43.06N	26.25 E
Ōmuta	28	Kh	33.02N	130.27 E
Omutinski	19	Gd	56.31N	67.45 E
Omutninsk	19	Fd	58.43N	52.12 E
Oña	13	Ib	42.44N	3.24W
Onagawa	29	Gb	38.26N	141.27 E
Onakayale	37	Bc	17.30S	15.01 E
Onaman Lake	45	Ma	50.00N	87.29W
Onamia	45	Jc	46.04N	93.40W
Onamue	64d	Bb	7.21N	151.31 E
Onaping Lake	44	Gb	46.57N	81.30W
Onatchiway, Lac-	44	La	49.03N	71.03W
Onawa	45	He	42.02N	96.06W
Onch'ŏn	28	He	38.49N	125.13 E
Oncócua	36	Bf	16.40S	13.24 E
Onda	13	Le	39.58N	0.15W
Ondangua	31	Ij	17.55S	16.00 E
Ondárroa	13	Ja	43.19N	2.25W
Ondava	10	Rh	48.27N	21.48 E
Ondo [2]	34	Gd	7.00N	5.10 E
Ondo [Jap.]	29	Cd	34.12N	132.32 E
Ondo [Nig.]	34	Fd	7.06N	4.50 E
Ondor Sum	28	Bc	42.30N	113.00 E
Ondozero, Ozero-	7	He	63.40N	33.15 E
One and Half Degree Channel	21	Ji	1.30N	73.10 E
Oneata	63d	Cc	18.27S	178.29W
Oneata Passage	63d	Cc	18.32S	178.28W
Onega	6	Jc	63.57N	38.05 E
Onega	5	Jc	63.58N	37.55 E
Onega, Lake- (EN)= Onežskoje Ozero	5	Jc	61.30N	35.45 E
Onega Peninsula (EN)= Onežski Poluostrov	5	Jc	64.35N	38.00 E
One Hundred Mile House	42	Ff	51.38N	121.16W
Oneida	44	Jd	43.04N	75.40W
Oneida Lake	44	Jd	43.13N	76.00W
O'Neil	43	Hc	42.27N	98.39W
Ōnejime	29	Bf	31.14N	130.47 E
Onekotan, Ostrov-	21	Re	49.25N	154.45 E
Oneonta [Al.-U.S.]	44	Di	33.57N	86.29W
Oneonta [N.Y.-U.S.]	44	Jd	42.28N	75.04W
Oneroa	64p	Cb	21.15S	159.43W
Onești (Gheorghe Gheorghiu-Dej)	15	Jc	46.12N	26.46 E
Onežskaja guba	5	Jc	64.20N	36.30 E
Onežskoje Ozero=Onega, Lake- (EN)	5	Jc	61.30N	35.45 E
Ongea Levu	63d	Cc	19.08S	178.24W

Index Symbols

- [1] Independent Nation
- [2] State, Region
- [3] District, County
- [4] Municipality
- [5] Colony, Dependency
- Continent
- Physical Region
- Historical or Cultural Region
- Mount, Mountain
- Volcano
- Hill
- Mountains, Mountain Range
- Hills, Escarpment
- Plateau, Upland
- Pass, Gap
- Plain, Lowland
- Delta
- Salt Flat
- Valley, Canyon
- Crater, Cave
- Karst Features
- Depression
- Polder
- Desert, Dunes
- Forest, Woods
- Heath, Steppe
- Oasis
- Cape, Point
- Coast, Beach
- Cliff
- Peninsula
- Isthmus
- Sandbank
- Island
- Atoll
- Rock, Reef
- Islands, Archipelago
- Rocks, Reefs
- Coral Reef
- Well, Spring
- Geyser
- River, Stream
- Waterfall Rapids
- River Mouth, Estuary
- Lake
- Salt Lake
- Intermittent Lake
- Reservoir
- Swamp, Pond
- Canal
- Glacier
- Ice Shelf, Pack Ice
- Ocean
- Sea
- Gulf, Bay
- Strait, Fjord
- Lagoon
- Bank
- Seamount
- Tablemount
- Ridge
- Shelf
- Basin
- Escarpment, Sea Scarp
- Fracture
- Trench, Abyss
- National Park, Reserve
- Point of Interest
- Recreation Site
- Cave, Cavern
- Historic Site
- Ruins
- Wall, Walls
- Church, Abbey
- Temple
- Scientific Station
- Airport
- Port
- Lighthouse
- Mine
- Tunnel
- Dam, Bridge

Ongijn-Gol	27	Hc	44.30N	103.40 E
Ongjin	27	Md	37.56N	125.22 E
Ongniud Qi (Wudan)	27	Kc	42.58N	119.01 E
Ongole	25	Ge	15.30N	80.03 E
Ongon	27	Jb	45.49N	113.08 E
Onhaye	12	Gd	50.15N	4.50 E
Oni	16	Mh	42.35N	43.27 E
Onigajō-Yama	29	Ce	33.07N	132.41 E
Onilany	30	Lk	23.34S	43.45 E
Onishibetsu	29a	Ca	45.21N	142.06 E
Onitsha	31	Hh	6.10N	6.47 E
Ono	29	Dd	34.51N	134.57 E
Ono	63d	Bc	18.54S	178.29 E
Ōno [Jap.]	28	Ng	35.59N	136.29 E
Ōno [Jap.]	29	Cd	34.18N	132.17 E
Onoda	29	Be	33.59N	131.11 E
Ōno-Gawa	29	Be	33.15N	131.43 E
Ōnohara-Jima	29	Fd	34.02N	139.23 E
Onohoj	20	Ff	51.55N	108.01 E
Ono-i-Lau Islands	57	Jg	20.39S	178.42W
Onojō	29	Be	33.34N	130.29 E
Onomichi	28	Lg	34.25N	133.12 E
Onon	21	Nd	51.42N	115.50 E
Onoto	50	Dh	9.36N	65.12W
Onotoa Atoll	57	Ie	1.52S	175.34 E
Ons, Isla de-	13	Db	42.23N	8.56W
Onsala	7	Ch	57.25N	12.01 E
Onseepkans	37	Be	28.45S	19.17 E
Onslow	58	Cg	21.39S	115.06 E
Onslow Bay	43	Le	34.20N	77.20W
On-Take	29	Bf	31.35N	130.39 E
Ontake-San	29	Ed	35.53N	137.29 E
Ontario [3]	42	If	50.00N	86.00W
Ontario [Ca.-U.S.]	46	Gi	34.04N	117.39W
Ontario [Or.-U.S.]	43	Dc	44.02N	116.58W
Ontario, Lake-	38	Le	43.40N	78.00W
Ontario Peninsula	38	Ke	43.50N	81.00W
Onteniente/Ontinyent	13	Lf	38.49N	0.37W
Ontinyent/Onteniente	13	Lf	38.49N	0.37W
Ontojärvi	7	Gd	64.08N	29.09 E
Ontonagon	44	Cb	46.52N	89.19W
Ontong Java Atoll	57	Ge	5.20S	159.30 E
Ō-Numa	29a	Bc	41.59N	140.41 E
Oodnadatta	58	Eg	27.33S	135.28 E
Ooidonk	12	Fc	51.01N	3.35 E
Ookala	65a	Fc	20.01N	155.17W
Ooldea	58	Eh	30.27S	131.50 E
Oologah Lake	45	Ih	36.39N	95.36W
Ooltgensplaat, Oostflakkee-	12	Gc	51.41N	4.21 E
Oostburg	12	Fc	51.20N	3.30 E
Oostelijk Flevoland	12	Hb	52.30N	5.40 E
Oostende/Ostende	11	Ic	51.14N	2.55 E
Oosterhout	11	Kc	51.38N	4.51 E
Oosterschelde=East Schelde (EN)	11	Jc	51.30N	4.00 E
Oosterwolde, Ooststellingwerf-	12	Ha	53.00N	6.18 E
Oosterzele	12	Fd	50.57N	3.48 E
Oostflakkee	12	Gc	51.41N	4.21 E
Oostflakkee-Ooltgensplaat	12	Gc	51.41N	4.21 E
Oostkamp	12	Fc	51.09N	3.14 E
Oost-Souburg, Vlissingen-	12	Fc	51.28N	3.36 E
Ooststellingwerf	12	Ib	53.00N	6.18 E
Ooststellingwerf-Oosterwolde	12	Ha	53.00N	6.18 E
Oost Vieland, Vieland-	12	Ha	53.17N	5.06 E
Oost-Vlaanderen [3]	12	Fc	51.00N	3.40 E
Ootmarsum	12	Ib	52.25N	6.54 E
Opala	36	Dc	0.37S	24.21 E
Opalenica	10	Md	52.19N	16.23 E
Opanake	25	Gg	6.36N	80.37 E
Opari	35	Ee	3.56N	32.03 E
Oparino	7	Lg	59.53N	48.25 E
Opasatika	44	Fa	49.31N	82.58W
Opasatika Lake	44	Fa	49.06N	83.08W
Opasatika River	44	Fa	50.15N	82.25W
Opatija	14	Ie	45.20N	14.19 E
Opatów	10	Rf	50.49N	21.26 E
Opatówka	10	Rf	50.42N	21.50 E
Opava	10	Ng	49.57N	17.54 E
Opava	10	Og	49.51N	18.17 E
Opelika	43	Je	32.39N	85.23W
Opelousas	45	Jk	30.32N	92.05W
Opémisca, Lac-	44	Ja	49.58N	74.57W
Opheim	46	Lb	48.51N	106.24W
Ophir	40	Hd	63.10N	156.31W
Ophthalmia Range	59	Dd	23.15S	119.30 E
Opienge	36	Eb	0.12N	27.30 E
Opihikao	65a	Gd	19.26N	154.53W
Opinaca	42	Jf	52.14N	78.02W
Opiscotéo, Lac-	42	Kf	53.09N	68.10W
Opladen, Leverkusen-	10	De	51.04N	7.01 E
Opobo	34	Ge	4.34N	7.27 E
Opočka	19	Cd	56.42N	28.41 E
Opoczno	10	Qe	51.23N	20.17 E
Opole [2]	10	Nf	50.40N	17.55 E
Opole	10	Nf	50.41N	17.55 E
Opole Lubelskie	10	Re	51.09N	21.58 E
Oporny	19	Ff	46.13N	54.29 E
Opotiki	62	Gc	38.01S	177.17 E
Opp	44	Dj	31.17N	86.22W
Oppa-Wan	29	Gb	38.35N	141.30 E
Oppdal	7	Be	62.36N	9.40 E
Oppenheim	10	Eg	49.51N	8.21 E
Oppland [2]	7	Bf	61.10N	9.40 E
Opportunity	46	Gc	47.39N	117.15W
Opsa	8	Li	55.31N	26.54 E
Opsterland	12	Ia	53.03N	6.04 E
Opsterland-Beetsterzwaag	12	Ia	53.03N	6.04 E
Opua	61	Dg	35.18S	174.07 E
Opunake	62	Ec	39.27S	173.51 E
Oputo	48	Eb	30.03N	109.20W
Oquossoc	44	Lc	45.04N	70.44W
Or	16	Ud	51.12N	58.33 E
Ōra	33	Cd	28.20N	19.35 E
Oradea	6	If	47.04N	21.56 E
Orahovac	15	Dg	42.24N	20.40 E
Orahovica	14	Le	45.32N	17.53 E
Orai	25	Fc	25.59N	79.28 E
Oraibi Wash	46	Ji	35.26N	110.49W
Oran	31	Ge	35.42N	0.38W
Oran [3]	32	Gb	36.00N	0.35W
Orange [Austl.]	58	Fh	33.17S	149.06 E
Orange [Fr.]	11	Kj	44.08N	4.48 E
Orange [Tx.-U.S.]	43	Ie	30.01N	93.44W
Orange [Va.-U.S.]	44	Hf	38.14N	78.07W
Orange/Oranje	30	Ik	28.38N	16.27 E
Orange, Cabo-	52	Ke	4.24N	51.33W
Orangeburg	43	Ke	33.30N	80.52W
Orange Free State/Oranje Vrystaat [2]	37	De	29.00S	26.00 E
Orange Lake	44	Fk	29.25N	82.13W
Orange Park	44	Gj	30.10N	81.42W
Orangeville	44	Gd	43.55N	80.06W
Orange Walk	47	Ge	18.06N	88.33W
Orango	30	Fg	11.05N	16.08W
Oranienburg	10	Jd	52.45N	13.14 E
Oranje/Orange	30	Ik	28.38N	16.27 E
Oranje Gebergte	54	Hc	3.00N	55.00W
Oranjemund	37	Be	28.38S	16.24 E
Oranjestad	54	Da	12.33N	70.06W
Oranje Vrystaat/Orange Free State [2]	37	De	29.00S	26.00 E
Oranžerei	16	Og	45.50N	47.36 E
Orapa	37	Dd	21.16S	25.22 E
Orăştie	15	Gd	45.50N	23.12 E
Orava	10	Pg	49.08N	19.10 E
Oraviţa	15	Ed	45.02N	21.42 E
Orayská Priehradní Nádrž	10	Pg	49.20N	19.35 E
Orb	11	Jk	43.15N	3.18 E
Orba	14	Cf	44.53N	8.37 E
Orba Co	27	De	34.33N	81.06 E
Ørbæk	8	Di	55.16N	10.41 E
Orbec	12	Ce	49.01N	0.25 E
Orbetello	14	Fh	42.27N	11.13 E
Orbetello, Laguna di-	14	Fh	42.25N	11.15 E
Orbigo	13	Gc	41.58N	5.40W
Orbiquet	12	Ce	49.09N	0.14 E
Orbost	59	Jg	37.42S	148.27 E
Örbyhus	8	Gd	60.14N	17.42 E
Orcas Island	46	Db	48.39N	122.55W
Orchej (Orgejev)	19	Cf	47.23N	28.50 E
Orchies	12	Fd	50.28N	3.14 E
Orcia	14	Fh	42.58N	11.21 E
Orco	14	Be	45.10N	7.52 E
Ord, Mount-	59	Fc	17.20S	125.35 E
Órdenes	13	Da	43.04N	8.24W
Ordos Desert (EN)=Mu Us Shamo	21	Mf	38.45N	109.10 E
Ord River	57	Df	15.30S	128.21 E
Ordu	23	Ea	41.00N	37.53 E
Ordubad	16	Oj	38.55N	46.01 E
Ordynskoje	20	Df	54.22N	81.58 E
Ordžonikidze	16	If	47.40N	34.04 E
Ordžonikidze	17	Jj	52.25N	61.45 E
Ordžonikidze Vladikavkaz	6	Kg	43.03N	44.40 E
Ordžonikidzeabad	19	Gh	38.34N	69.02 E
Ore älv	8	Fc	61.08N	14.35 E
Orebić	14	Lh	42.58N	17.11 E
Örebro	6	Hd	59.17N	15.13 E
Örebro [2]	7	Dg	59.30N	15.00 E
Oredež	8	Nf	58.50N	30.13 E
Oregon	44	Fe	41.38N	83.28W
Oregon [2]	43	Cc	44.00N	121.00W
Oregon City	43	Cb	45.21N	122.36W
Oregon Inlet	44	Jh	35.50N	75.35W
Öregrund	8	Hd	60.20N	18.26 E
Orehov	16	If	47.34N	35.47 E
Orehovo-Zujevo	6	Jd	55.49N	38.59 E
Orel	6	Je	52.59N	36.05 E
Orel	16	Ie	48.31N	34.55 E
Orel, Gora-	20	Jf	53.55N	140.01 E
Orellana [Peru]	54	Ce	3.54S	75.04W
Orellana [Peru]	54	Cd	4.40S	78.10W
Orem	43	Ec	40.19N	111.42W
Ore Mountains (EN)=Erzgebirge	5	He	50.30N	13.15 E
Ore Mountains (EN)=Krušné Hory	5	He	50.30N	13.15 E
Ören	24	Bd	37.18N	29.17 E
Orenbel	24	Hb	40.00N	39.10 E
Orenburg	6	Le	51.54N	55.06 E
Orenburgskaja Oblast [3]	19	Fe	52.00N	55.00 E
Örencik	24	Cc	39.16N	29.34 E
Orense [3]	13	Eb	42.10N	7.30W
Orense [Arg.]	56	Ie	38.40S	59.47W
Orense [Sp.]	13	Eb	42.20N	7.51W
Oreón, Dhíavlos-	15	Fk	38.54N	22.55 E
Orepuki	62	Bg	46.17S	167.44 E
Orestiás	15	Jh	41.30N	26.31 E
Øresund	5	Hd	55.50N	12.40 E
Oreti	62	Cg	46.28S	168.17 E
Orewa	62	Fb	36.35S	174.42 E
Orford	12	Db	52.05N	1.32 E
Orford Ness	9	Oi	52.05N	1.34 E
Orgañá/Organyà	13	Nb	42.13N	1.20 E
Organ Needle	45	Cj	32.21N	106.33W
Organyà/Orgañá	13	Nb	42.13N	1.20 E
Orgaz	13	Ie	39.39N	3.54W
Orgejev → Orchej	19	Cf	47.23N	28.50 E
Orgelet	11	Lh	46.31N	5.37 E
Orgon Tal	28	Bc	43.20N	112.40 E
Orgosolo	14	Dj	40.12N	9.21 E
Orgūn	23	Kc	32.57N	69.11 E
Orhaneli	15	Lj	39.54N	29.00 E
Orhaneli/Koca Çay	15	Lj	39.56N	28.32 E
Orhangazi	15	Mi	40.30N	29.18 E
Orhomenós	15	Fk	38.35N	22.54 E
Orhon (Orchon)	21	Md	50.21N	106.05 E
Orhy, Pico de-	13	La	42.59N	1.00W
Oria	13	Ja	43.17N	2.08W
Orichuna, Río-	50	Bi	7.30N	68.13W
Orick	46	Cf	41.17N	124.04W
Oriental	48	Kh	19.22N	97.37W
Oriental, Cordillera-	49	Md	18.55N	69.15W
Oriente	56	He	38.44S	60.37W
Orihuela	13	Lf	38.05N	0.57W
Oriku	15	Ci	40.17N	19.25 E
Óri Lekánis	15	Hh	41.08N	24.33 E
Orillia	42	Jh	44.37N	79.25W
Orimattila	7	Ff	60.48N	25.45 E
Orinoco, Río-	52	Je	8.37N	62.15W
Oripää	8	Jd	60.51N	22.41 E
Orissa [3]	25	Gd	21.00N	84.00 E
Orissaare/Orissare	7	Fg	58.34N	23.05 E
Oristano	14	Ck	39.54N	8.36 E
Oristano, Golfo di-	14	Ck	39.50N	8.30 E
Orituco, Río-	50	Ch	8.45N	67.27W
Orivesi	5	Ic	62.15N	29.25 E
Orivesi	7	Ff	61.41N	24.21 E
Oriximiná	54	Gd	1.45S	55.52W
Orizaba	39	Jh	18.51N	97.06W
Orizaba, Pico de- (Citlaltépetl, Volcán-)	38	Jh	19.01N	97.16W
Orizona	55	Hc	17.03S	48.18W
Orjahovo	15	Gf	43.44N	23.58 E
Ørje	8	De	59.29N	11.39 E
Orjen	15	Bg	42.34N	18.33 E
Orjiva	13	Ih	36.54N	3.25W
Orkanger	7	Be	63.19N	9.52 E
Orkdalen	8	Ca	63.15N	9.50 E
Örkelljunga	8	Eh	56.17N	13.17 E
Orkla	8	Ca	63.18N	9.50 E
Orkney	37	De	27.00S	26.39 E
Orkney [3]	9	Kb	59.00N	3.00W
Orkney Islands	5	Fd	59.00N	3.00W
Orlândia	55	Ie	20.43S	47.53W
Orlando	39	Kg	28.32N	81.23W
Orlando, Capo d'-	14	Il	38.10N	14.45 E
Orlanka	10	Td	52.52N	23.12 E
Orléanais	11	Hf	48.40N	1.20 E
Orléans	6	Gf	47.55N	1.54 E
Orlice	10	Lf	50.12N	15.49 E
Orlické Hory	10	Mf	50.10N	16.30 E
Orlik	20	Ef	52.30N	99.55 E
Orlov (Halturin)	19	Ed	58.35N	48.55 E
Orlovskaja oblast	19	De	52.45N	36.30 E
Orlovski	16	Mf	46.52N	42.06 E
Orlovski, mys-	7	Jc	67.16N	41.18 E
Orly	11	If	48.45N	2.24 E
Ormāra	25	Cc	25.12N	64.38 E
Ormes	12	Ce	49.03N	0.59 E
Ormoc	26	Hd	11.00N	124.37 E
Ormond	62	Gc	38.33S	177.55 E
Ormond Beach	44	Gk	29.17N	81.02W
Ornain	11	Kf	48.46N	4.47 E
Ornans	11	Mg	47.06N	6.09 E
Ornäs	8	Fd	60.31N	5.32 E
Orne [3]	11	Gf	48.40N	0.05 E
Orne [Fr.]	11	Ie	49.17N	6.11 E
Orne [Fr.]	11	Be	49.19N	0.14W
Orne Seamount (EN)	61	Je	27.30S	157.30W
Orneta	10	Qb	54.08N	20.08 E
Ornö	7	Eg	59.05N	18.25 E
Örnsköldsvik	7	Ee	63.18N	18.43 E
Oro	28	Id	40.01N	127.27 E
Oro, Río de-	55	Ch	27.04S	58.34W
Oro, Río del-	48	Ge	25.35N	105.03W
Orocué	54	Dc	4.48N	71.20W
Orodara	34	Ec	10.59N	4.55W
Orofino	46	Gc	46.29N	116.15W
Orogrande	45	Cj	32.23N	106.08W
Orohena, Mont-	65e	Fc	17.31S	149.28W
Oroluk Atoll	57	Gd	7.32N	155.18 E
Orom	36	Fb	3.20N	33.40 E
Oromocto	42	Kg	45.51N	66.29W
Oron	34	Ge	4.50N	8.14 E
Orona Atoll (Hull)	57	Je	4.29S	172.10W
Orongo	65d	Ac	27.10S	109.26W
Oronsay	9	Ge	56.01N	6.14W
Orontes (EN)=Nahr al 'Āsī	23	Eb	36.02N	35.58 E
Oropesa [Sp.]	13	Ge	39.55N	5.10W
Oropesa [Sp.]	13	Ld	40.06N	0.09W
Oroqen Zizhiqi (Alihe)	27	La	50.35N	123.42 E
Oroquieta	26	He	8.29N	123.48 E
Orós	54	Ke	6.15S	38.55W
Orós, Açude-	54	Ke	6.15S	39.05W
Orosei	14	Dj	40.23N	9.42 E
Orosei, Golfo di-	14	Dj	40.15N	9.45 E
Orosháza	10	Qj	46.34N	20.40 E
Oro-Shima	29	Be	33.52N	130.02 E
Oroszlány	10	Oi	47.29N	18.19 E
Orote Peninsula	64c	Bb	13.26N	144.38 E
Orote Point	64c	Bb	13.27N	144.37 E
Orotukan	20	Kd	62.17N	151.50 E
Oroville [Ca.-U.S.]	46	Eg	39.31N	121.33W
Oroville [Wa.-U.S.]	46	Fb	48.56N	119.26W
Orp-Jauche	12	Gd	50.40N	4.57 E
Orqohan	27	Lb	49.36N	123.23 E
Orr	45	Jb	48.03N	92.50W
Orrefors	8	Fh	56.50N	15.45 E
Orri, Pic d'-/Llorri	13	Nb	42.23N	1.12 E
Orša	6	Je	54.30N	30.24 E
Orsa	7	Df	61.07N	14.37 E
Orsasjön	8	Fc	61.05N	14.35 E
Orsay	12	Ef	48.42N	2.11 E
Orsjön	8	Gc	61.35N	16.20 E
Orsk	6	Le	51.12N	58.34 E
Orşova	15	Fe	44.42N	22.25 E
Ørsta	7	Be	62.12N	6.09 E
Örsundsbro	8	Ge	59.44N	17.18 E
Orta, Lago d'-	14	Ce	45.50N	8.25 E
Ortaca	24	Cd	36.49N	28.47 E
Ortakent	15	Kl	37.02N	27.21 E
Ortaklar	15	Kl	37.53N	27.30 E
Orta Nova	14	Ji	41.19N	15.42 E
Orte	14	Gh	42.27N	12.23 E
Ortegal, Cabo-	13	Ea	43.45N	7.53W
Ortenberg	12	Ld	50.21N	9.03 E
Orthez	11	Fk	43.29N	0.46W
Orthon, Río-	54	Ef	10.50S	66.04W
Ortigueira [Braz.]	56	Jb	24.12S	50.55W
Ortigueira [Sp.]	13	Fa	43.34N	6.44W
Ortisei / Sankt Ulrich	14	Fd	46.34N	11.40 E
Ortiz [Mex.]	48	Dc	28.15N	110.43W
Ortiz [Ven.]	50	Ch	9.37N	67.17W
Ortlergruppe/Ortles	14	Ed	46.30N	10.40 E
Ortles/Ortlergruppe	14	Ed	46.30N	10.40 E
Ortolo	11a	Ab	41.30N	8.55 E
Ortona	14	Ih	42.21N	14.24 E
Ortonville	45	Hd	45.19N	96.27W
Orto-Tokoj	18	Kc	42.20N	76.02 E
Örtze	10	Fd	52.40N	9.57 E
Orukuizu	64a	Ac	7.10N	134.17 E
Orūmīyeh	22	Gf	37.33N	45.04 E
Orūmīyeh, Daryācheh-ye-=Urmia, Lake- (EN)	21	Gf	37.40N	45.30 E
Oruro [2]	54	Eg	18.40S	67.30W
Oruro	53	Jg	17.59S	67.09W
Orust	8	Df	58.10N	11.38 E
Orūzgān [3]	23	Kc	33.15N	66.00 E
Orūzgān	23	Kc	32.56N	66.38 E
Orval, Abbaye d'-	12	He	49.38N	5.22 E
Orvault	11	Eg	47.16N	1.37W
Orvieto	14	Gh	42.43N	12.07 E
Orville Escarpment	66	Qf	75.45S	65.30W
Órvilos, Óros-	15	Gh	41.23N	23.36 E
Orwell	12	Dc	51.58N	1.18 E
Orxois	12	Fe	49.08N	3.12 E
Orz	10	Rd	52.50N	21.30 E
Orzinuovi	14	De	45.24N	9.55 E
Orzyc	10	Rd	52.47N	21.13 E
Orzysz	10	Rc	53.49N	21.56 E
Oš	19	Hg	40.32N	72.50 E
Os	7	Ce	62.30N	11.12 E
Osa	19	Fd	57.17N	55.26 E
Oša	8	Lh	56.21N	26.29 E
Osa	10	Oc	53.33N	18.45 E
Osa Península de-	47	Hg	8.35N	83.33W
Osage	45	Je	43.17N	92.49W
Osage River	43	Id	38.35N	91.57W
Osaka	29	Ed	35.57N	137.14 E
Ōsaka	22	Pf	34.40N	135.30 E
Osaka Bay (EN)=Ōsaka-Wan	28	Mg	34.36N	135.27 E
Ōsaka-Fu [2]	28	Mg	34.45N	135.35 E
Osakarovka	19	He	50.32N	72.39 E
Ōsaka-Wan=Osaka Bay (EN)	28	Mg	34.36N	135.27 E
Osăm	15	Hf	43.42N	24.51 E
Osan	28	If	37.09N	127.04 E
Osasco	55	If	23.32S	46.46W
Osat	14	Nf	44.02N	19.20 E
Osawatomie	45	Ig	38.31N	94.57W
Osborne	45	Gg	39.26N	98.42W
Osburger Hochwald	12	Ie	49.40N	6.50 E
Osby	7	Ch	56.22N	13.59 E
Osceola [Ar.-U.S.]	45	Li	35.42N	89.58W
Osceola [Ia.-U.S.]	43	Ic	41.02N	93.46W
Osceola [Mo.-U.S.]	45	Jh	38.03N	93.42W
Oschatz	10	Je	51.18N	13.07 E
Oschersleben	10	Hd	52.02N	11.15 E
Oschiri	14	Dj	40.43N	9.06 E
Osen	7	Cd	64.18N	10.31 E
Osered	16	Ld	50.31N	40.48 E
Osetr	16	Kb	55.00N	38.45 E
Ōse-Zaki	28	Jh	32.38N	128.42 E
Oshamambe	28	Pc	42.30N	140.22 E
Oshawa	42	Jh	43.54N	78.51W
Oshekehia Lake	37	Bc	18.08S	15.45 E
Oshika	29	Gb	38.17N	141.31 E
Oshika-Hantō	28	Pe	38.22N	141.27 E
Oshikango	37	Bc	17.22S	15.55 E
Oshima	29	Ce	33.55N	132.11 E
Ō-Shima [Jap.]	29	De	33.28N	135.50 E
Ō-Shima [Jap.]	29	Ae	33.30N	129.33 E
Ō-Shima [Jap.]	29	Ae	32.34N	128.54 E
Ō-Shima [Jap.]	29	Be	33.54N	130.27 E
Ō-Shima [Jap.]	27	Oe	34.45N	139.30 E
Ōshima [Jap.]	29	Fd	34.44N	139.20 E
Ō-Shima [Jap.]	29	Bf	31.32N	131.25 E
Ō-Shima [Jap.]	29	De	33.38N	134.30 E
Ō-Shima [Jap.]	29	Cd	34.10N	133.05 E
Ōshima [Jap.]	29	Ae	33.04N	129.36 E
Ō-Shima [Jap.]	28	Od	41.30N	139.15 E
Ō-Shima [Jap.]	28	Jh	32.04N	128.26 E
Ōshima-Hantō	28	Pd	41.40N	140.30 E
Ōshima-Kaikyō	29b	Ba	28.10N	129.15 E
Oshkosh [Nb.-U.S.]	45	Ef	41.24N	102.21W
Oshkosh [Wi.-U.S.]	43	Jc	44.01N	88.33W
Oshnavīyeh	24	Kd	37.02N	45.06 E
Oshogbo	31	Hh	7.46N	4.34 E
Oshtorān Kūh	23	Gc	33.20N	49.16 E
Oshtorīnān	24	Me	34.01N	48.38 E
Oshwe	36	Cc	3.24S	19.30 E
Osich'ŏn-ni	28	Jd	41.25N	128.16 E
Osijek	6	Hf	45.33N	18.42 E
Osilo	14	Cj	40.45N	8.40 E
Osimo	14	Hg	43.23N	13.29 E
Osinki	7	Lj	52.52N	49.31 E
Osinniki	20	Df	53.37N	87.31 E
Osipaonica	15	Ee	44.33N	21.04 E
Osipoviči	16	Fc	53.19N	28.40 E
Osječenica	14	Kf	44.29N	16.17 E
Oskaloosa	45	Jf	41.18N	92.39W
Oskarshamn	7	Dh	57.16N	16.26 E
Oskarström	8	Eh	56.48N	12.58 E
Oskélanéo	44	Ja	48.08N	75.05W
Oskino	20	Fd	60.48N	107.58 E
Öskjuvatn	7a	Cb	65.02N	16.45W
Oskol	16	Je	49.06N	37.25 E
Oskū	24	Ld	37.55N	46.06 E
Oslava	10	Mg	49.05N	16.22 E
Ösling	11	Le	49.55N	6.00 E
Osljanka, Gora-	17	Ig	59.10N	58.33 E
Oslo [2]	7	Cg	59.55N	10.45 E
Oslo	6	Hd	59.55N	10.45 E
Oslofjorden	5	Hd	59.20N	10.35 E
Osmānābād	25	Fe	18.10N	76.03 E
Osmancık	24	Fb	40.59N	34.49 E
Osmaneli	15	Ni	40.22N	30.01 E
Osmaniye	23	Eb	37.05N	36.14 E
Osmino	8	Mf	58.54N	29.15 E
Ošmjanskaja Vozvyšennost	8	Kj	54.30N	26.00 E
Ošmjany	16	Db	54.27N	25.57 E
Ösmo	8	Gf	58.59N	17.54 E
Osmussaar/Osmussar	8	Je	59.20N	23.15 E
Osmussar/Osmussaar	8	Je	59.20N	23.15 E
Osnabrück	6	Ge	52.16N	8.03 E
Osning	12	Kb	52.10N	8.05 E
Oso, Sierra del-	48	Gd	26.00N	105.25W
Osobłoga	10	Nf	50.27N	17.58 E
Osogovske Planine	15	Fg	42.10N	22.30 E
Osor	14	If	44.42N	14.24 E
Osório	56	Jc	29.54S	50.16W
Osorno	53	Ij	40.34S	73.09W
Osoyoos	42	Fg	49.02N	119.28W
Osøyra	7	Af	60.11N	5.28 E
Ospino	50	Bh	9.18N	69.27W
Osprey Reef	57	Ff	13.55S	146.40 E
Oss	11	Lc	51.46N	5.31 E
Ossa, Mount-	57	Fi	41.54S	146.01 E
Óssa, Óros-	15	Fj	39.49N	22.40 E
Ossabaw Island	44	Gj	31.47N	81.06W
Ossa de Montiel	13	Jf	38.58N	2.45W
Osse	11	Gj	44.07N	0.17 E
Ossining	44	Ke	41.10N	73.52W
Ossjøen	8	Dc	61.15N	11.55 E
Oškaja Oblast [3]	19	Hg	40.45N	73.20 E
Ossora	20	Le	59.15N	163.02 E
Östanvik	8	Fc	61.10N	15.13 E
Ostaškov	19	Dd	57.09N	33.07 E
Ostbevern	12	Jb	52.03N	7.51 E
Oste	10	Fc	53.33N	9.10 E
Ostende/Oostende	11	Ic	51.14N	2.55 E
Oster	16	Gd	50.55N	30.57 E
Oster	16	Gd	50.53N	30.55 E
Oster	16	Gc	53.47N	31.45 E
Osterburg in der Altmark	10	Hd	52.47N	11.44 E
Österbybruk	8	Gd	60.12N	17.54 E
Österdalälven	7	Df	60.33N	15.08 E
Østerdalen	7	Cf	62.00N	10.40 E
Osterfjorden	8	Ad	60.30N	5.20 E
Österforse	8	Ga	63.09N	17.01 E
Östergarnsholm	8	Hg	57.25N	19.00 E
Östergötland	8	Ff	58.25N	15.35 E
Östergötland [2]	7	Dg	58.25N	15.45 E
Osterholz Scharmbeck	10	Ec	53.14N	8.48 E
Österlen	8	Fi	55.30N	14.10 E
Ostermark/Teuva	7	Ee	62.29N	21.44 E
Osterode am Harz	10	Ge	51.44N	10.11 E
Osterøya	7	Af	60.35N	5.35 E
Österreich = Austria (EN) [1]	6	Hf	47.30N	14.00 E
Östersjön=Baltic Sea (EN)	5	Hd	57.00N	19.00 E
Østersøen=Baltic Sea (EN)	5	Hd	57.00N	19.00 E
Östersund	6	Hc	63.11N	14.39 E
Osterwick, Rosendahl-	12	Jb	52.01N	7.12 E
Østfold [2]	7	Cg	59.20N	11.30 E
Ostfriesische Inseln=East Frisian Islands (EN)	10	Dc	53.45N	7.25 E
Ostfriesland=East Friesland (EN)	10	Dc	53.20N	7.40 E
Østgrønland=East Greenland (EN) [2]	41	Id	72.00N	35.00W
Östhammar	7	Ed	60.16N	18.22 E
Osthofen	12	Ke	49.42N	8.20 E
Östmark	8	Ed	60.17N	12.45 E
Ostrach	10	Fh	48.05N	9.25 E
Östra Silen	8	Ee	59.15N	12.20 E
Ostrava	6	Hf	49.50N	18.17 E
Ostrhauderfehn	12	Ja	53.08N	7.37 E
Ostróda	10	Pc	53.43N	19.59 E
Ostrog	16	Ed	50.19N	26.32 E
Ostrogožsk	19	De	50.52N	39.05 E
Ostrołęka [2]	10	Rc	53.05N	21.35 E
Ostrołęka	10	Rc	53.06N	21.34 E
Ostrošicki Gorodok	8	Lj	54.03N	27.46 E
Ostrov	10	Vd	52.48N	26.01 E
Ostrov [Czech.]	10	If	50.18N	12.57 E
Ostrov [Rom.]	15	Ke	44.07N	27.22 E
Ostrov	19	Cd	57.23N	28.22 E
Ostrov	8	Mf	58.28N	28.44 E
Ostrovec	8	Lj	54.38N	26.06 E
Ostrovicës, Mali i-	15	Di	40.34N	20.27 E
Ostrovskoje	7	Kh	57.50N	42.13 E
Ostrov Zmeiny	16	Gg	45.15N	30.12 E
Ostrowiec Świętokrzyski	10	Rf	50.57N	21.23 E
Ostrów Lubelski	10	Se	51.30N	22.52 E
Ostrów Mazowiecka	10	Rd	52.49N	21.54 E
Ostrów Wielkopolski	10	Ne	51.39N	17.49 E
Ostryna	10	Uc	53.41N	24.37 E
Ostrzeszów	10	Ne	51.25N	17.57 E
Ostsee=Baltic Sea (EN)	5	Hd	57.00N	19.00 E
Oststeirisches Hügelland	14	Jd	47.00N	15.45 E
Osttirol	14	Gd	46.55N	12.30 E
Ostuni	14	Lj	40.44N	17.35 E
Osumi	15	Ci	40.48N	19.52 E
Ōsumi	29	Bf	31.36N	130.59 E
Ōsumi-Hantō	29	Bf	31.15N	130.50 E
Osumi Islands (EN)=Ōsumi-Shotō	21	Pf	30.35N	130.59 E
Ōsumi-Shotō=Osumi Islands (EN)	21	Pf	30.35N	130.59 E
Osuna	13	Gg	37.14N	5.07W
Osveja	8	Mi	55.59N	28.10 E
Osvejskoje, Ozero-	8	Mh	56.00N	28.15 E
Oswego	43	Lc	43.27N	76.31W
Oswestry	9	Ji	52.52N	3.04W

Index Symbols

[1] Independent Nation
[2] State, Region
[3] District, County
[4] Municipality
[5] Colony, Dependency
Continent
Physical Region
Historical or Cultural Region
Mount, Mountain
Volcano
Hill
Mountains, Mountain Range
Hills, Escarpment
Plateau, Upland
Pass, Gap
Plain, Lowland
Delta
Salt Flat
Valley, Canyon
Crater, Cave
Karst Features
Depression
Polder
Desert, Dunes
Forest, Woods
Heath, Steppe
Oasis
Cape, Point
Coast, Beach
Cliff
Peninsula
Isthmus
Sandbank
Island
Atoll
Rock, Reef
Islands, Archipelago
Rocks, Reefs
Coral Reef
Well, Spring
Geyser
River, Stream
Waterfall Rapids
River Mouth, Estuary
Lake
Salt Lake
Intermittent Lake
Reservoir
Swamp, Pond
Canal
Glacier
Ice Shelf, Pack Ice
Ocean
Sea
Gulf, Bay
Strait, Fjord
Lagoon
Bank
Seamount
Tablemount
Ridge
Shelf
Basin
Escarpment, Sea Scarp
Fracture
Trench, Abyss
National Park, Reserve
Point of Interest
Recreation Site
Cave, Cavern
Historic Site
Ruins
Wall, Walls
Church, Abbey
Temple
Scientific Station
Airport
Port
Lighthouse
Mine
Tunnel
Dam, Bridge

Oświęcim 10 Pf 50.03N 19.12 E
Osyka 45 Kk 31.00N 90.28W
Ōta 29 Fc 36.18N 139.22 E
Ota 29 Ec 35.56N 136.03 E
Otago [2] 62 Cf 45.00S 169.10 E
Otago Peninsula 62 Df 45.50S 170.45 E
Ōtake 28 Lg 34.12N 132.13 E
Otakeho 62 Fc 39.33S 174.03 E
Otaki 62 Fd 40.45S 175.08 E
Ōtakime-Yama 29 Gc 37.22N 140.42 E
Otanoshike 29a Db 43.01N 144.16 E
Otar 19 Hg 43.31N 75.12 E
Otaru 27 Pc 43.13N 141.00 E
Otautau 62 Bg 46.09S 168.00 E
Otava 10 Kg 49.26N 14.12 E
Otava 8 Lc 61.39N 27.04 E
Otavi 37 Bc 19.39S 17.20 E
Ōtawara 28 Pf 36.52N 140.02 E
Otelu Roşu 15 Fd 45.32N 22.22 E
Otematata 62 Df 44.37S 170.11 E
Otepää/Otepja 7 Gg 58.03N 26.30 E
Otepää, Vozvyšennost-/ Otepää Kõrgustik 8 Lf 58.00N 26.40 E
Otepää Kõrgustik/Otepää, Vozvyšennost- 8 Lf 58.00N 26.40 E
Otepja/Otepää 7 Gg 58.03N 26.30 E
Oteros 47 Cc 26.55N 108.30W
Othain 12 He 49.31N 5.23 E
Othello 46 Fc 46.50N 119.10W
Othonoi 15 Cj 39.50N 19.25 E
Óthris Óros 15 Fj 39.02N 22.37 E
Oti 30 Hh 7.48N 0.08 E
Otira 62 De 42.51S 171.33 E
Otish, Monts- 38 Md 52.45N 69.15W
Otjikondo 37 Bc 19.50S 15.23 E
Otjimbingwe 37 Bd 22.21S 16.08 E
Otjiwarongo 31 Ik 20.29S 16.36 E
Otjiwarongo [3] 37 Bd 20.30S 17.30 E
Otjosondjou, Omuramba- 30 Ij 19.55S 20.00 E
Otjosondu 37 Bd 21.12S 17.58 E
Otmuchowskie, Jezioro- 10 Nf 50.27N 17.15 E
Otnes 7 Cf 61.46N 11.12 E
Otobe 29a Bc 41.57N 140.08 E
Otočac 14 Jf 44.52N 15.14 E
Otofuke 29a Cb 42.59N 143.10 E
Otofuke-Gawa 29a Cb 42.56N 143.12 E
Otog Qi (Ulan) 27 Id 39.07N 108.00 E
Otoineppu 29a Ca 44.43N 142.16 E
Otok 14 Me 45.09N 18.53 E
Otopeni 15 Je 44.33N 26.04 E
Otorohanga 62 Fc 38.11S 175.12 E
Otorten, Gora- 17 If 61.50N 59.13 E
Ōtoyo 29 Ce 33.46N 133.40 E
Otra 5 Gd 58.09N 8.00 E
Otradnaja 16 Lg 44.23N 41.31 E
Otradnoje, Ozero- 8 Nd 60.50N 30.25 E
Otradny 7 Mj 53.23N 51.24 E
Otranto 14 Mj 40.09N 18.30 E
Otranto, Canale d'-= Otranto, Strait of- (EN) 5 Hg 40.00N 19.00 E
Otranto, Capo d'- 14 Mj 40.06N 18.31 E
Otranto, Strait of- (EN)= Otranto, Canale d'- 5 Hg 40.00N 19.00 E
Otranto, Strait of- (EN)= Otrantos, Kanali i- 15 Bi 40.00N 19.00 E
Otranto, Terra d'- 14 Mj 40.20N 18.15 E
Otrantos, Kanali i-=Otranto, Strait of- (EN) 15 Bi 40.00N 19.00 E
Ötscher 14 Jc 47.51N 15.12 E
Ōtsu 28 Mg 35.00N 135.52 E
Ōtsuchi 28 Pe 39.21N 141.54 E
Ōtsuki [Jap.] 29 Fd 35.36N 138.54 E
Ōtsuki [Jap.] 29 Ce 32.50N 132.41 E
Otta 8 Cc 61.46N 9.31 E
Otta 7 Bf 61.46N 9.32 E
Otta 64d Bb 7.09N 151.54 E
Ottadalen 8 Bc 61.55N 8.00 E
Ottana 14 Dj 40.15N 9.05 E
Otta Pass 64d Bb 7.09N 151.53 E
Ottawa [Il.-U.S.] 45 Lf 41.21N 88.51W
Ottawa [Ks.-U.S.] 43 Hd 38.37N 95.16W
Ottawa [Oh.-U.S.] 44 Ee 41.02N 84.03W
Ottawa [Ont.-Can.] 39 Le 45.25N 75.42W
Ottawa Islands 38 Kd 59.30N 80.10W
Ottawa River 38 Le 45.20N 73.58W
Ottemby 7 Dh 56.16N 16.24 E
Otterberg 12 Je 49.30N 7.46 E
Otter Creek 44 Fk 29.19N 82.48W
Otterndorf 10 Ec 53.48N 8.54 E
Otteroy 8 Bb 62.40N 6.50 E
Otter Rapids 44 Ga 50.15N 81.45W
Otterup 8 Di 55.31N 10.24 E
Ottumwa 43 Ic 41.01N 92.25W
Ottweiler 12 Je 49.23N 7.10 E
Otukpa 34 Gd 7.05N 7.40 E
Otumpa 55 Ah 27.19S 62.13W
Otuquis, Bañados de- 54 Gg 19.20S 58.30W
Otuquis, Rio- 55 Cd 19.41S 58.20W
Oturkpo 34 Gd 7.13N 8.09 E
Otu Tolu Group 65b Bb 20.21S 174.32W
Otuzco 54 Ce 7.54S 78.35W
Otway, Cape- 59 Ig 38.52S 143.31 E
Otwock 10 Rd 52.07N 21.16 E
Otynja 10 Uh 48.40N 24.57 E
Ötz 14 Ec 47.12N 10.54 E
Ötztaler Ache 14 Ec 47.14N 10.50 E
Ötztaler Alpen 10 Gi 46.45N 10.55 E
Ou 25 Kd 20.04N 102.13 E
'O'ua 65b Bb 20.02S 174.41W
Oua 63b Ce 21.14S 167.05 E
Ouachita, Lake- 45 Ji 34.40N 93.25W
Ouachita Mountains 38 Jf 34.40N 94.25W
Ouachita River 43 Ie 31.38N 91.49W
Ouadane 31 Ff 20.57N 11.35W
Ouaddai [3] 35 Cc 13.00N 21.00 E
Ouaddai 30 Jg 13.00N 21.00 E
Ouagadougou 31 Gg 12.22N 1.31W
Ouahigouya 31 Gg 13.35N 2.25W
Ouaka [3] 35 Cd 6.00N 21.00 E
Ouaka 30 Ih 4.59N 19.56 E
Oualata 32 Ff 17.18N 7.00W
Oualata, Dahr- 32 Ff 17.48N 7.24W
Oualidia 32 Fc 32.44N 9.02W
Ouallam 34 Fc 14.19N 2.05 E
Ouallene 32 He 24.35N 1.17 E
Ouanda-Djallé 35 Cd 8.54N 22.48 E
Ouandjia 35 Cd 8.35N 23.12 E
Ouandjia 35 Cd 9.35N 21.43 E
Ouango 35 Ce 4.19N 22.33 E
Ouangolodougou 34 Dd 9.58N 5.09W
Ouanne 11 Ig 47.57N 2.47 E
Ouarane 30 Ff 21.00N 10.00W
Ouargaye 34 Fc 11.32N 0.01 E
Ouargla 31 He 31.57N 5.20 E
Ouargla [3] 32 Id 30.00N 6.30 E
Ouarkziz, Jbel- 30 Gf 28.00N 8.20W
Ouarra 30 Jh 5.05N 24.26 E
Ouarsenis, Djebel- 13 Ni 35.53N 1.38 E
Ouarsenis, Massif de l'- 32 Hb 35.50N 2.05 E
Ouarzazate [3] 32 Fc 31.00N 6.30W
Ouarzazate 32 Fc 30.55N 6.55W
Oubangui 30 Ii 0.30S 17.42 E
Ouborré, Pointe- 63b Dd 18.47S 169.16 E
Ouche, Pays d'- 11 Gf 48.55N 0.45 E
Ouchi 29 Gb 39.27N 140.06 E
Oud Beijerland 12 Gc 51.50N 4.26 E
Oude IJssel 12 Ic 52.00N 6.10 E
Oudenaarde/Audenarde 11 Jd 50.51N 3.36 E
Oudenbosch 12 Gc 51.35N 4.34 E
Oude Rijn 11 Kb 52.05N 4.20 E
Oudon 11 Fg 47.37N 0.42W
Oudtshoorn 31 Jl 33.35S 22.14 E
Oued Ben Tili 32 Fd 25.48N 9.32W
Oued el Abtal 13 Mi 35.27N 0.41 E
Oued Fodda 13 Nh 36.11N 1.32 E
Oued Lili 13 Ni 35.31N 1.16 E
Oued Rhiou 32 Hb 35.58N 0.55 E
Oued-Taria 13 Mi 35.07N 0.05 E
Oued Tlelat 13 Li 35.33N 0.27W
Oued Zem 31 Ge 32.52N 6.34W
Ouégoa 63b Be 20.21S 164.26 E
Ouéllé 34 Ed 7.18N 4.01W
Ouémé 30 Hh 6.29N 2.32 E
Ouémé [3] 34 Fd 7.00N 2.35 E
Ouen 63b Cf 22.26S 166.48 E
Ouenza 32 Ib 35.57N 8.07 E
Ouenza, Djebel- 14 Co 35.57N 8.05 E
Ouessa 34 Ec 11.03N 2.47W
Ouessant, Ile d'- 11 Af 48.28N 5.05W
Ouesso 31 Ih 1.37N 16.04 E
Ouest [3] 34 Hd 5.20N 10.30 E
Ouest, Baie de l'- 64h Ab 13.15S 176.13W
Ouezzane 32 Fc 34.48N 5.36W
Oughter, Lough- 9 Fg 54.00N 7.29W
Ouham [3] 35 Bd 7.00N 18.00 E
Ouham 30 Ih 9.18N 18.14 E
Ouham-Pendé [3] 35 Bd 7.00N 16.00 E
Ouicah 34 Fd 6.22N 2.05 E
Ouistreham 11 Fe 49.17N 0.15W
Ouistreham-Riva Bella 12 Be 49.17N 0.16W
Oujda [3] 32 Gc 33.00N 2.00W
Oujda 31 Ge 34.40N 1.54W
Oujeft 32 Ee 20.02N 13.03W
Oulainen 7 Fd 64.16N 24.57 E
Oulchy-le-Château 12 Fe 49.12N 3.21 E
Ouled Djellal 32 Ic 34.25N 5.04 E
Ouled Naïl, Monts des- 32 Hc 34.40N 3.25 E
Oulou, Bahr- 35 Cd 9.48N 21.32 E
Oulu [2] 7 Gd 65.00N 27.00 E
Oulu/Uleåborg 6 Ib 65.01N 25.30 E
Oulu, Lake- (EN)= Oulujärvi 5 Ic 64.20N 27.15 E
Oulujärvi=Oulu, Lake- (EN) 5 Ic 64.20N 27.15 E
Oulujoki 5 Ib 65.01N 25.25 E
Oum Chalouba 31 Jg 15.48N 20.46 E
Oumé [3] 34 Dd 6.25N 5.30W
Oumé 34 Dd 6.23N 5.25W
Oum el Bouaghi [3] 32 Ib 35.30N 7.10 E
Oum el Bouaghi 32 Ib 35.53N 7.07 E
Oum er Rbia 30 Ge 33.19N 8.20W
Oum Hadjer 35 Bc 13.18N 19.41 E
Oumm ed Droûs Guebli, Sebkhet- 32 Ee 24.03N 11.45W
Oumm ed Droûs Telli, Sebkhet- 32 Ee 24.20N 11.30W
Ounasjoki 5 Ib 66.30N 25.45 E
Oundle 12 Bb 52.29N 0.28W
Ounianga [3] 35 Cb 19.10N 20.30 E
Ounianga Kébir 31 Jg 19.04N 20.29 E
Ountivou 34 Fd 7.21N 1.34 E
Ouolossébougou 34 Dc 12.00N 7.55W
Oupeye 12 Hd 50.42N 5.39 E
Oupu 27 Ma 52.45N 126.00 E
Our 12 Ie 49.53N 6.18 E
Ouray 45 Cg 38.01N 107.40W
Ouray, Mount- 45 Cg 38.25N 106.14W
Ource 11 Kf 48.06N 4.23 E
Ourcq 11 Je 49.01N 3.01 E
Ourcq, Canal de l'- 11 If 48.51N 2.22 E
Ourém 54 Id 1.33S 47.06W
Ouricuri 53 Je 7.35S 40.05W
Ourinhos 53 Lh 22.59S 49.52W
Ouro, Rio do- 55 Ha 13.20S 48.59W
Ouro Fino 55 If 22.17S 46.22W
Ouro Prêto 54 Jh 20.23S 43.30W
Ourthe [Bel.] 11 Ld 50.38N 5.35 E
Ourville-en-Caux 12 Ce 49.44N 0.36 E
Ous 19 Gc 60.55N 61.31 E
Ou-Sanmyaku 28 Pe 39.00N 141.00 E
Ouse [Eng.-U.K.] 9 Nk 50.47N 0.03 E
Ouse [Eng.-U.K.] 9 Mh 53.42N 0.41W
Oust 11 Dg 47.35N 2.06W
Outagouna 34 Fb 15.11N 0.43 E
Outaouais, Rivière- 38 Le 45.20N 73.58W
Outardes, Rivière aux- 42 Kg 49.05N 68.23W
Outat Oulad El Hajj 32 Gc 33.21N 3.42W
Outer Dowsing 9 Oh 53.25N 1.05 E
Outer Hebrides 9 Fd 57.50N 7.32W
Outer Santa Barbara Passage 46 Fj 33.10N 118.30W
Outer Silver Pit 9 Od 54.05N 2.00 E
Outjo 31 Ik 20.08S 16.08 E
Outjo [3] 37 Ac 19.30S 14.30 E
Outlook 46 La 51.30N 107.03W
Outokumpu 7 Ge 62.44N 29.01 E
Outram Mountain 46 Eb 49.19N 121.05W
Outreau 12 Dd 50.42N 1.35 E
Out Skerries 9 Ma 60.30N 0.50W
Outwell 12 Cb 52.37N 0.14 E
Ouvéa, Ile- 57 Hg 20.35S 166.35 E
Ouvèze 11 Kk 43.59N 4.51 E
Ouxian 28 Ej 28.58N 118.53 E
Ouyen 59 Ig 35.04S 142.20 E
Ouyou Bézédinga 34 Hb 16.32N 13.15 E
Ouzera 13 Oh 36.15N 2.51 E
Ovacık [Tur.] 24 Ed 39.11N 33.40 E
Ovacık [Tur.] 24 Hc 39.22N 39.13 E
Ovada 14 Cf 44.38N 8.38 E
Ova Gölü 15 Mm 36.16N 29.22 E
Ovakent 15 Lk 39.06N 28.02 E
Ovalau Island 63d Bb 17.40S 178.48 E
Ovalle 53 Ii 30.36S 71.12W
Oval Peak 46 Eb 48.15N 120.25W
Ovamboland 37 Bc 18.30S 16.00 E
Ovamboland [3] 37 Bc 18.00S 16.00 E
Ovan 36 Bb 0.30N 12.10 E
Ovanåker 7 Df 61.21N 15.54 E
Ovar 13 Dd 40.52N 8.38W
Ovau 63a Cb 6.48S 156.02 E
Ovejas 49 Ji 9.32N 75.14W
Overath 12 Jd 50.57N 7.18 E
Øverbygd 7 Eb 69.01N 19.18 E
Overflakkee 11 Kc 51.45N 4.10 E
Overhalla 7 Cd 64.30N 12.00 E
Overije 12 Gd 50.46N 4.32 E
Overijssel [3] 12 Ib 52.25N 6.30 E
Överkalix 7 Fc 66.19N 22.50 E
Overland Park 45 Ig 38.59N 94.40W
Övermark/Ylimarkku 8 Ib 62.37N 21.28 E
Overpelt 12 Hc 51.12N 5.25 E
Overri 34 Gd 5.29N 7.02 E
Overton 46 Hh 36.33N 114.27W
Övertorneå 7 Fc 66.23N 23.40 E
Överum 8 Gg 57.59N 16.19 E
Ovidiu 15 Le 44.16N 28.34 E
Oviedo [3] 13 Ga 43.20N 6.00W
Oviedo [Dom.Rep.] 49 Le 17.47N 71.22W
Oviedo [Sp.] 6 Fg 43.22N 5.50W
Oviši 8 Ig 57.34N 21.35 E
Ovo, Capo dell'- 14 Lj 40.18N 17.30 E
Øvre Årdal 7 Bf 61.19N 7.48 E
Övre Fryken 8 Ed 60.00N 13.05 E
Övre Soppero 7 Eb 68.05N 21.41 E
Ovruč 19 Ce 51.19N 28.50 E
Ovsjanka 20 Hf 53.32N 126.58 E
Owaka 62 Cg 46.27S 169.40 E
Owando 31 Ii 0.29S 15.55 E
Ōwani 28 Pd 40.31N 140.35 E
Owase 28 Ng 34.04N 136.12 E
Owatonna 43 Ic 44.05N 93.14W
Owego 44 Id 42.06N 76.16W
Owen, Mount- 62 Ed 41.33S 172.32 E
Owendo 36 Ab 0.17N 9.30 E
Owen Falls Dam 36 Fb 0.24N 33.11 E
Owensboro 43 Jd 37.46N 87.07W
Owens Lake 46 Gh 36.25N 117.56W
Owen Sound 42 Jh 44.34N 80.56W
Owens River 46 Gh 36.31N 117.57W
Owen Stanley Range 57 Fe 9.20S 148.00 E
Owl Creek Mountains 46 Ke 43.30N 108.35W
Ownay, Kowtal-e- 23 Kc 34.27N 68.22 E
Owo 34 Gd 7.11N 5.35 E
Owosso 44 Ed 43.00N 84.10W
Owyhee 46 Gf 41.57N 116.06W
Owyhee, Lake- 46 Ge 43.28N 117.20W
Owyhee Mountains 46 Ge 43.00N 116.45W
Owyhee River [U.S.] 46 Ge 43.40N 117.16W
Owyhee River [U.S.] 43 Dc 43.46N 117.02W
Oxberg 8 Fc 61.07N 14.10 E
Oxbow 45 Eb 49.14N 102.11W
Oxelösund 7 Dg 58.40N 17.06 E
Oxford 9 Lj 51.50N 1.30W
Oxford [Eng.-U.K.] 6 Fe 51.46N 1.15W
Oxford [Ms.-U.S.] 45 Li 34.22N 89.32W
Oxford [N.C.-U.S.] 44 Hg 36.19N 78.35W
Oxford [N.Z.] 62 Ee 43.17S 172.11 E
Oxford Lake 42 Hf 54.50N 95.35W
Oxfordshire [3] 9 Lj 51.50N 1.20W
Oxia 15 Ek 38.18N 21.06 E
Oxkutzcab 48 Og 20.18N 89.25W
Oxnard 43 De 34.12N 119.11W
Ox or Slieve Gamph Mountains/Sliabh Gamh 9 Eg 54.10N 8.50W
Oxted 12 Bc 51.14N 0.01W
Oyabe 29 Ec 36.40N 136.52 E
Oyahue 53 Jh 21.08S 68.45W
O-Yama 29 Fd 34.04N 139.31 E
Oyama 28 Of 36.21N 139.50 E
Ōyama 29 Ec 36.35N 137.18 E
Ōyano 29 Be 32.35N 130.27 E
Oyapock, Fleuve- 52 Ke 4.08N 51.40W
Oyem 31 Ih 1.37N 11.35 E
Oyen 46 Ja 51.22N 110.28W
Øyeren 8 De 59.50N 11.14 E
Oykel 9 Id 57.50N 4.25W
Oyo [2] 34 Fd 8.00N 3.50 E
Oyo [Nig.] 34 Fd 7.51N 3.56 E
Oyo [Sud.] 35 Fa 21.55N 36.06 E
Oyodo-Gawa 29 Bf 31.55N 131.28 E
Oyonnax 11 Lh 46.15N 5.40 E
Oyster Bay 59 Jh 42.10S 148.10 E
Øystese 8 Bd 60.23N 6.13 E
Özalp 24 Jc 38.39N 43.59 E
Ozamiz 26 He 8.08N 123.50 E
Ozark 44 Ej 31.28N 85.38W
Ozark Plateau 38 Jf 37.00N 93.00W
Ozark Reservoir 45 Ii 35.25N 94.05W
Ozarks, Lake of the- 43 Id 37.39N 92.50W
Ózd 10 Qh 48.13N 20.18 E
Ozeblin 14 Jf 44.35N 15.53 E
Ozernoj, Zaliv- 20 Le 57.00N 163.20 E
Ozernovski 20 Kf 51.21N 156.32 E
Ozerny 16 Vd 51.08N 60.55 E
Ozersk 8 Ij 54.24N 21.59 E
Ozery 10 Uc 53.38N 24.18 E
Ozery 7 Ji 54.54N 38.32 E
Ožezdy 19 Gf 48.03N 67.09 E
Ozieri 14 Cj 40.35N 9.00 E
Ozinki 19 Ee 51.12N 49.47 E
Ožogina 20 Kc 66.12N 151.05 E
Ozona 43 Ge 30.43N 101.12W
Ozorków 10 Pe 51.58N 19.19 E
Ozouri 36 Ac 0.55S 8.55 E
Ozren 14 Mf 44.37N 18.15 E
Ozren 14 Mg 43.59N 18.30 E
Ozren [Yugo.] 15 Ef 43.36N 21.54 E
Özu [Jap.] 29 Be 32.52N 130.52 E
Özu [Jap.] 28 Lh 33.30N 132.23 E
Ozurgeti (Maharadze) 19 Eg 41.53N 42.01 E

P

Pääjärvi 8 Kb 62.50N 24.45 E
Paama 63b Dc 16.28S 168.13 E
Pa-an → Pha-an 25 Je 16.53N 97.38 E
Paar 10 Hh 48.45N 11.35 E
Paarl 31 Il 33.45S 18.56 E
Paauilo 65a Fc 20.03N 155.22W
Paavola 7 Fd 64.36N 25.12 E
Pabbay 9 Fd 57.47N 7.20W
Pabellón, Ensenada del- 48 Fe 24.27N 107.36W
Pabianice 10 Pe 51.40N 19.22 E
Pābna 25 Hd 24.00N 89.15 E
Pabradé/Pabrade 7 Fi 54.59N 25.50 E
Pabrade/Pabradé 7 Fi 54.59N 25.50 E
Pacaás Novos, Serra dos- 54 Ff 10.50S 64.00W
Pacajá, Rio- 54 Hd 1.56S 50.55W
Pacajus 54 Kd 4.10S 38.28W
Pacaraima, Serra- 52 Je 4.30N 60.40W
Pacasmayo 54 Ce 7.24S 79.34W
Paceco 14 Gm 37.59N 12.33 E
Pachala 35 Ed 7.10N 34.06 E
Pacheco 48 Eb 30.06N 108.21W
Pachino 14 Jn 36.43N 15.05 E
Pachitea, Rio- 54 De 8.46S 74.32W
Pachuca de Soto 47 Ed 20.07N 98.44W
Pacific-Antarctic Ridge (EN) 3 Kp 62.00S 157.00W
Pacific City 46 Dd 45.12N 123.57W
Pacific Grove 46 Eh 36.38N 121.56W
Pacific Islands, Trust Territory of the- 58 Ed 7.30N 134.30 E
Pacífico, Océano- = Pacific Ocean (EN) 3 Ki 5.00N 155.00W
Pacific Ocean 3 Ki 5.00N 155.00W
Pacific Ocean (EN)=Kita-Taiheiyō 60 Ch 22.00N 167.00 E
Pacific Ocean (EN)= Pacífico, Océano- 3 Ki 5.00N 155.00W
Pacific Ocean (EN)= Pacifique, Océan- 3 Ki 5.00N 155.00W
Pacific Ocean (EN)= Taiheiyō 3 Ki 5.00N 155.00W
Pacific Ocean (EN)=Tihi Okean 3 Ki 5.00N 155.00W
Pacific Ranges 42 Ef 50.55N 125.10W
Pacifique, Océan-=Pacific Ocean (EN) 3 Ki 5.00N 155.00W
Packsattel 14 Id 46.58N 14.58 E
Pacui, Rio- 55 Jc 16.46S 45.01W
Pacuneiro, Rio- 55 Fa 13.02S 53.25W
Pacy-sur-Eure 12 De 49.01N 1.23 E
Paczków 10 Mf 50.27N 17.00 E
Padana, Pianura-=Po Valley (EN) 5 Gf 45.20N 10.00 E
Padang 22 Mj 0.57S 100.21 E
Padangsidempuan 26 Cf 1.22N 99.16 E
Padangtikar, Pulau- 26 Eg 0.50S 109.30 E
Padany 7 He 63.19N 33.25 E
Padasjoki 8 Kc 61.21N 25.17 E
Padauiri, Rio- 54 Fd 0.15S 64.05W
Paddle Prairie 42 Fe 58.02N 117.50W
Paderborn 10 Ee 51.43N 8.46 E
Paderborn-Elsen 12 Kc 51.44N 8.41 E
Paderborn-Schloß Neuhaus 12 Kc 51.44N 8.42 E
Padeş, Vîrful- 15 Fd 45.40N 22.20 E
Padilla 54 Fg 19.19S 64.20W
Padina 15 Ke 44.50N 27.07 E
Padornelo, Portillo del- 13 Fb 42.03N 6.50W
Padova = Padua (EN) 14 Fe 45.25N 11.53 E
Padre, Morro do- 55 Ic 16.48S 47.35W
Padre Bernardo 55 Hb 15.21S 48.30W
Padre Island 43 Hf 27.00N 97.15W
Padrón 13 Db 42.44N 8.40W
Padua (EN) = Padova 14 Fe 45.25N 11.53 E
Paducah [Ky.-U.S.] 39 Kf 37.05N 88.36W
Paducah [Tx.-U.S.] 45 Fi 34.01N 100.18W
Padula 14 Jj 40.20N 15.39 E
Paea 65e Fc 17.41S 149.35W
Paegam-san 28 Id 40.35N 126.15 E
Paengnyong-Do 27 Ld 38.00N 124.40 E
Paeroa 61 Eg 37.23S 175.41 E
Paestum 14 Jj 40.25N 15.01 E
Paeu 63c Bb 11.22S 166.50 E
Pafuri 37 Ed 22.26S 31.20 E
Pag 14 Jf 44.27N 15.03 E
Pag 14 If 44.30N 15.00 E
Pagadian 26 He 7.49N 123.25 E
Pagai, Kepulauan-=Pagi Islands (EN) 21 Lj 2.45S 100.00 E
Pagai Selatan 26 Dg 3.00S 100.20 E
Pagai Utara 26 Cg 2.42S 100.07 E
Pagan Island 57 Fc 18.07N 145.46 E
Pagasitikós Kólpos 15 Fj 39.15N 23.00 E
Pagatan 26 Gg 3.36S 115.56 E
Pagat Point 64c Bb 13.30N 144.53 E
Page 46 Jh 36.57N 111.27W
Pagėgiai 8 Ii 55.09N 21.54 E
Paget, Mount- 66 Ad 54.26S 36.33W
Pagi Islands (EN)=Pagai, Kepulauan- 21 Lj 2.45S 100.00 E
Paglia 14 Gh 42.42N 12.11 E
Pago Bay 64c Bb 13.25N 144.48 E
Pagoda Point 21 Lh 15.57N 94.15 E
Pāgodār 24 Qh 28.10N 57.22 E
Pago Pago 58 Jf 14.16S 170.42W
Pago Pago Harbor 65c Cb 14.17S 170.40W
Pago Redondo 55 Ci 29.35S 59.13W
Pagosa Springs 45 Ch 37.16N 107.01W
Pagoua Bay 51g Ba 15.32N 61.17W
Pagwa River 45 Na 50.01N 85.10W
Pahači 20 Ld 60.30N 169.00 E
Pahala 65a Fd 19.12N 155.29W
Pāhara, Laguna- 49 Ff 14.18N 83.15W
Pahiatua 62 Fd 40.27S 175.50 E
Pahkaing Bum 21 Lg 26.00N 95.30 E
Pahoa 65a Gd 19.30N 154.57W
Pahokee 44 Gl 26.49N 80.40W
Pahtakor 18 Fd 40.16N 67.55 E
Pahute Mesa 46 Gh 37.20N 116.40W
Paia 63b Dc 16.35S 168.12 E
Paide/Pajde 7 Fg 58.57N 25.35 E
Paignton 9 Jk 50.28N 3.30W
Päijänne 5 Ic 61.35N 25.30 E
Páikon Óros 15 Fi 40.56N 22.21 E
Paila 48 He 25.39N 102.07W
Pailin 25 Kf 12.51N 102.36 E
Pailitas 49 Ki 8.58N 73.38W
Pailolo Channel 65a Eb 21.05N 156.42W
Paimio/Pemar 8 Jd 60.27N 22.42 E
Paimionjoki 8 Jd 60.25N 22.40 E
Paimpol 11 Cf 48.46N 3.03W
Painan 26 Dg 1.21S 100.34 E
Paine, Mount- 66 Mg 86.46S 147.32W
Painel 55 Gh 27.55S 50.06W
Painesville 44 Ge 41.43N 81.15W
Painted Desert 43 Ed 36.00N 111.20W
Paintsville 44 Fg 37.49N 82.48W
Pais do Vinho 13 Ec 41.15N 7.55W
Paisley 9 If 55.50N 4.26W
Paita 54 Be 5.06S 81.07W
Païta 63b Cf 22.08S 166.22 E
Paiva 13 Dc 41.04N 8.16W
Paj 7 If 61.43N 34.28 E
Pajala 7 Fc 67.12N 23.22 E
Pajares, Puerto de- 13 Ga 43.00N 5.46W
Pajaros, Punta- 48 Ph 19.36N 87.25W
Pajaros Point 51a Db 18.31N 64.18W
Pajatén 54 Ce 7.29S 77.22W
Pajde/Paide 7 Fg 58.57N 25.35 E
Pajęczno 10 Oe 51.09N 19.00 E
Pajer, Gora- 19 Gb 66.40N 64.20 E
Paj-Hoj 5 Mb 69.00N 62.30 E
Pajule 36 Fb 2.58N 32.56 E
Pakanbaru 22 Mi 0.32N 101.27 E
Pakaraima Mountains 54 Fb 4.05N 61.30W
Pakch'on 28 He 39.44N 125.35 E
Pakhiá 15 Im 36.16N 25.50 E
Pakhna 24 Ee 34.46N 32.48 E
Pákhnes 15 Gn 35.18N 23.58 E
Paki 34 Gc 11.30N 8.09 E
Pakima 36 Dc 3.21S 24.06 E
Pakin Atoll 57 Gd 7.04N 157.48 E
Pakistan [1] 22 Ig 30.00N 70.00 E
Pakleni Otoci 14 Kg 43.10N 16.23 E
Pakokku 25 Jd 21.17N 95.06 E
Pakowki Lake 46 Jb 49.22N 110.57W
Pak Phanang 25 Kg 8.21N 100.12 E
Pakrac 14 Le 45.26N 17.12 E
Pakruojis/Pakruojis 7 Fi 55.57N 23.50 E
Pakruojis/Pakruojis 7 Fi 55.57N 23.50 E
Paks 10 Oj 46.38N 18.52 E
Paktiā [3] 23 Kc 33.30N 69.30 E
Pakwach 36 Fb 2.28N 31.30 E
Pakxé 22 Mh 15.07N 105.47 E
Pakxèng 25 Kd 20.10N 102.40 E
Pala 35 Ad 9.22N 14.54 E
Palacca Point 49 Kc 21.15N 73.26W
Palacios [Arg.] 55 Bj 30.43S 61.37W
Palacios [Tx.-U.S.] 45 Hl 28.42N 96.13W
Palafrugell 13 Pc 41.55N 3.10 E
Palagruža 14 Kh 42.24N 16.15 E
Palaiokastritsa 15 Cj 39.40N 19.41 E
Palaiokhóra 15 Gn 35.14N 23.41 E
Palaiseau 12 Ef 48.43N 2.15 E
Palamás 15 Fj 39.28N 22.05 E
Palamós 13 Pc 41.51N 3.08 E
Palamuse/Palamuze 8 Lf 58.39N 26.35 E
Palamut 15 Kk 38.59N 27.41 E
Palamuze/Palamuse 8 Lf 58.39N 26.35 E
Palana 22 Rd 59.07N 159.58 E
Palancia 13 Le 39.40N 0.12W
Palanga 19 Cd 55.57N 21.05 E
Palangkaraya 26 Fg 2.16S 113.56 E
Pālanpur 25 Ed 24.10N 72.26 E

Index Symbols

[1] Independent Nation
[2] State, Region
[3] District, County
[4] Municipality
[5] Colony, Dependency
Continent
Physical Region
Historical or Cultural Region
Mount, Mountain
Volcano
Hill
Mountains, Mountain Range
Hills, Escarpment
Plateau, Upland
Pass, Gap
Plain, Lowland
Delta
Salt Flat
Valley, Canyon
Crater, Cave
Karst Features
Depression
Polder
Desert, Dunes
Forest, Woods
Heath, Steppe
Oasis
Cape, Point
Coast, Beach
Cliff
Peninsula
Isthmus
Sandbank
Island
Atoll
Rock, Reef
Islands, Archipelago
Rocks, Reefs
Coral Reef
Well, Spring
Geyser
River, Stream
Waterfall Rapids
River Mouth, Estuary
Lake
Salt Lake
Intermittent Lake
Reservoir
Swamp, Pond
Canal
Glacier
Ice Shelf, Pack Ice
Ocean
Sea
Gulf, Bay
Strait, Fjord
Lagoon
Bank
Seamount
Tablemount
Ridge
Shelf
Basin
Escarpment, Sea Scarp
Fracture
Trench, Abyss
National Park, Reserve
Point of Interest
Recreation Site
Cave, Cavern
Historic Site
Ruins
Wall, Walls
Church, Abbey
Temple
Scientific Station
Airport
Port
Lighthouse
Mine
Tunnel
Dam, Bridge

Palaoa Point	65a	Ec	20.44N	156.58W
Palapye	31	Jk	22.33S	27.08 E
Palasa	26	Hf	0.29N	120.24 E
Palatka [Fl.-U.S.]	43	Kf	29.39N	81.38W
Palatka	20	Kd	60.05N	151.00 E
Palau (EN) = Belau	58	Ed	7.30N	134.30 E
Palau	58	Ed	7.30N	134.30 E
Palau Islands	57	Ed	7.30N	134.30 E
Palauli	65c	Aa	13.44S	172.16W
Palauli Bay	65c	Aa	13.47S	172.14W
Palau Trench (EN)	60	Af	6.30N	134.30 E
Palavas-les-Flots	11	Jk	43.32N	3.56 E
Palaw	25	Jf	12.58N	98.39 E
Palawan	21	Ni	9.30N	118.30 E
Palawan Passage	26	Gd	10.00N	118.00 E
Palayan	26	Hc	15.33N	121.06 E
Pālayankottai	25	Fg	8.43N	77.44 E
Palazzo, Punta-	11a	Aa	42.22N	8.33 E
Palazzolo Acreide	14	Im	37.04N	14.54 E
Palazzolo sull'Oglio	14	De	45.36N	9.53 E
Paldiski	19	Cd	59.20N	24.06 E
Pale di San Martino	14	Fd	46.14N	11.53 E
Paleleh	26	Hf	1.04N	121.57 E
Palembang	22	Mj	2.55S	104.45 E
Palena	14	Ii	41.59N	14.08 E
Palencia	13	Hb	42.25N	4.30W
Palencia	13	Hb	42.01N	4.32W
Palen Lake	46	Hj	33.46N	115.12W
Palenque	39	Jh	17.30N	92.00W
Palenque [Mex.]	48	Ni	17.31N	91.58W
Palenque [Pan.]	49	Hi	9.13N	79.41W
Palenque, Punta-	49	Ld	18.14N	70.09W
Palermo	6	Hh	38.07N	13.22 E
Palermo, Golfo di-	14	Hl	38.10N	13.25 E
Palestine	43	He	31.46N	95.38W
Palestine (EN)	23	Dc	32.15N	34.47 E
Palestrina	14	Gi	41.50N	12.53 E
Pālghāt	25	Ff	10.47N	76.39 E
Palgrave Point	37	Ad	20.28S	13.16 E
Palhoça	55	Hh	27.38S	48.40W
Pāli	25	Ec	25.46N	73.20 E
Palinuro	14	Jj	40.02N	15.17 E
Palinuro, Capo-	14	Jj	40.02N	15.16 E
Palisades Reservoir	46	Je	43.04N	111.26W
Paliseul	12	He	49.54N	5.08 E
Palivere	8	Jf	59.00N	23.45 E
Palizada	48	Mh	18.15N	92.05W
Paljakka	7	Gd	64.45N	28.07 E
Paljavaam	20	Mc	68.50N	170.50 E
Paljenik	5	Hg	44.15N	17.36 E
Pälkäne	8	Kc	61.20N	24.16 E
Palkino	8	Mg	57.29N	28.10 E
Palk Strait	21	Ji	10.00N	79.45 E
Palla Bianca/Weißkugel	14	Ed	46.48N	10.44 E
Pallars	13	Mb	42.25N	0.55 E
Pallars, Montsent de-/Montseny	13	Nb	42.29N	1.02 E
Pallasovka	19	Ee	50.03N	46.55 E
Pallastunturi	7	Fb	68.06N	24.02 E
Palliser, Cape-	61	Eh	41.37S	175.16 E
Palliser, Iles-	57	Mf	15.30S	146.30W
Palma [Moz.]	37	Gb	10.46S	40.28 E
Palma [Sp.]	6	Gh	39.34N	2.39 E
Palma, Badia de-/Palma, Bahía de-	13	Oe	39.27N	2.35 E
Palma, Bahía de-/Palma, Badia de-	13	Oe	39.27N	2.35 E
Palma, Rio-	54	If	12.33S	47.52W
Palma, Sierra de la-	48	Id	26.00N	101.35W
Palma del Río	13	Gg	37.42N	5.17W
Palma di Montechiaro	14	Hm	37.11N	13.46 E
Palmar, Laguna del-	55	Bi	29.35S	60.42W
Palmar, Río-	49	Lh	10.11N	71.52W
Palmar, Salto-	55	Cg	24.18S	59.18W
Palmares	54	Ke	8.41S	35.36W
Palmares do Sul	55	Gj	30.16S	50.31W
Palmarito	54	Db	7.37N	70.10W
Palmarola	14	Gj	40.55N	12.50 E
Palmar Sur	47	Hg	8.58N	83.29W
Palmas	56	Jc	26.30S	52.00W
Palmas, Cape-	30	Gh	4.22N	7.44W
Palmas, Golfo di-	14	Cl	39.00N	8.30 E
Palmas Bellas	49	Gi	9.14N	80.05W
Palma Soriano	47	Id	20.13N	76.00W
Palm Bay	44	Gk	28.01N	80.35W
Palm Beach	43	Kf	26.42N	80.02W
Palmdale	46	Fi	34.35N	118.07W
Palmeira	55	Gg	25.25S	50.00W
Palmeira das Missões	56	Jc	27.55S	53.17W
Palmeira dos Indios	54	Ke	9.25S	36.37W
Palmeirais	54	Je	5.58S	43.04W
Palmeiras, Rio-	55	Gb	15.25S	51.10W
Palmeiras de Goiás	55	Hc	16.47S	49.53W
Palmeirinhas, Ponta das-	30	Ii	9.05S	13.00 E
Palmela	13	Df	38.34N	8.54W
Palmer	40	Jd	61.36N	149.07W
Palmer Archipelago	66	Qe	64.10S	62.00W
Palmer Land (EN)	66	Qf	71.30S	65.00W
Palmer Station	66	Qe	64.46S	64.05W
Palmerston	62	Df	45.29S	170.43 E
Palmerston Atoll	57	Kf	18.04S	163.10W
Palmerston North	58	Ii	40.28S	175.17 E
Palmetto Point	51d	Ba	17.35N	61.52W
Palmi	14	Jl	38.21N	15.51 E
Palmira [Col.]	53	Ie	3.32N	76.16W
Palmira [Cuba]	49	Gb	22.14N	80.23W
Palm Islands	59	Jc	18.40S	146.30 E
Palmital	55	Fg	24.39S	52.16W
Palmitas	55	Dk	33.27S	57.48W
Palmito	55	Cd	18.53S	58.22W
Palmitos	55	Fh	27.05S	53.08W
Palm Springs	43	De	33.50N	116.33W
Palmyra	23	Ec	34.33N	38.17 E
Palmyra Atoll	57	Kd	5.52N	162.06W
Palo Alto	43	Cd	37.27N	122.09W
Paloh	26	Ef	1.43N	109.18 E
Paloich	35	Ec	10.28N	32.32 E
Palomani, Nevado-	52	Jg	14.38S	69.14W
Palomar Mountain	43	De	33.22N	116.50W
Palomera, Sierra-	13	Kd	40.40N	1.12W
Palopo	22	Oj	3.00S	120.12 E
Palos, Cabo de-	5	Fh	37.38N	0.41W
Palo Santo	55	Cg	25.34S	59.21W
Palotina	55	Fg	24.17S	53.50W
Palouse River	46	Fc	46.35N	118.13W
Palpa	54	Cf	14.32S	75.11W
Palsa	8	Lg	57.23N	26.24 E
Pålsboda	8	Fe	59.04N	15.20 E
Paltamo	7	Gd	64.25N	27.50 E
Palu [Indon.]	22	Nj	0.53S	119.53 E
Palu [Tur.]	24	Hc	38.42N	39.57 E
Palu, Pulau-	26	Hh	8.20S	121.43 E
Pam	63b	Be	20.15S	164.17 E
Pama	34	Fc	11.15N	0.42 E
Påmark/Pomarkku	8	Ic	61.42N	22.00 E
Pambarra	37	Fd	21.56S	35.06 E
Pambeguwa	34	Gc	10.40N	8.17 E
Pamekasan	26	Fh	7.10S	113.28 E
Pamiers	11	Hk	43.07N	1.36 E
Pamir	21	Jf	38.00N	73.00 E
Pamir	19	Hh	37.01N	72.41 E
Pâmiut/Frederikshåb	41	Hf	62.00N	49.45W
Pamlico Sound	43	Ld	35.20N	75.55W
Pampa	43	Gd	35.32N	100.58W
Pampa del Indio	55	Ch	26.02S	59.55W
Pampa del Infierno	55	Bh	26.31S	61.10W
Pampa de los Guanacos	56	Hc	26.14S	61.51W
Pampas	54	Df	12.24S	74.54W
Pampas	52	Ji	35.00S	63.00W
Pampeiro	55	Ej	30.38S	55.16W
Pamplona [Col.]	54	Db	7.23N	72.38W
Pamplona [Sp.]	6	Fg	42.49N	1.38W
Pamukkale	15	Ml	37.47N	29.04 E
Pamukova	15	Ni	40.31N	30.09 E
Pamunkey River	44	Ig	37.32N	76.48W
Pan, Tierra del-	13	Gc	41.50N	6.00W
Pana	36	Bc	1.41S	12.39 E
Panagjurište	15	Hg	42.30N	24.11 E
Panaitan, Pulau-	26	Eh	6.36S	105.12 E
Panaitolikón Óros	15	Ek	38.43N	21.39 E
Panaji (Panjim)	22	Jh	15.29N	73.50 E
Panakhaïkón Óros	15	Ek	38.12N	21.54 E
Panamá	39	Li	9.00N	80.00W
Panamá = Panama (EN)	49	Hi	9.00N	79.00W
Panamá=Panama City (EN)	39	Li	8.58N	79.31W
Panama (EN) = Panamá	49	Hi	9.00N	79.00W
Panamá, Bahía de-	49	Hi	8.50N	79.15W
Panamá, Canal de-= Panama Canal (EN)	47	Ig	9.20N	79.55W
Panamá, Golfo de-= Panama, Gulf of- (EN)	38	Li	8.00N	79.10W
Panama, Gulf of- (EN)= Panamá, Golfo de-	38	Li	8.00N	79.10W
Panama, Isthmus of- (EN)= Panamá, Istmo de-	38	Li	9.20N	79.30W
Panamá, Istmo de-= Panama, Isthmus of- (EN)	38	Li	9.20N	79.30W
Panama Canal (EN)= Panamá, Canal de-	47	Ig	9.20N	79.55W
Panama City [La.-U.S.]	39	Kf	30.10N	85.41W
Panama City (EN)=Panamá	39	Li	8.58N	79.31W
Panamá La Vieja	49	Hi	9.00N	79.29W
Panambi	55	Fi	28.18S	53.30W
Panamint Range	46	Gh	36.30N	117.20W
Panao	54	Ce	9.49S	76.00W
Panarea	14	Jl	38.40N	15.05 E
Panaro	14	Ff	44.55N	11.25 E
Pana Tinai	63a	Ad	11.14S	153.10 E
Pana-Wina	63a	Ad	11.11S	153.01 E
Panay	21	Oh	11.15N	122.30 E
Pancake Range	46	Hg	39.00N	115.45W
Pančevo	15	De	44.52N	20.39 E
Pančičev vrh	15	Df	43.15N	20.45 E
Panciu	15	Kd	45.54N	27.05 E
Pancros	63b	Db	15.58S	168.12 E
Panda	37	Ed	24.03S	34.43 E
Panda ma Tenga	37	Dc	18.32S	25.38 E
Pandan	26	Hd	11.43N	122.06 E
Pan de Azúcar	55	El	34.48S	55.14W
Pandeiros, Ribeirão-	55	Jb	15.42S	44.36W
Pandelis/Pandėlys	8	Kh	56.01N	25.21 E
Pandėlys/Pandelis	8	Kh	56.01N	25.21 E
Pandharpur	25	Fe	17.40N	75.20 E
Pándheon	15	Fi	40.05N	22.20 E
Pāndhurna	25	Fd	21.36N	78.31 E
Pandivere Kõrgustik/ Pandivere Vozvyšennost	8	Le	59.00N	26.15 E
Pandivere Vozvyšennost/ Pandivere Kõrgustik	8	Le	59.00N	26.15 E
Pando	56	Id	34.43S	55.57W
Pando	54	Ef	11.20S	67.40W
Pandokrátor	15	Cj	39.45N	19.52 E
Pandora	49	Fi	9.45N	82.57W
Pandrup	8	Cg	57.14N	9.41 E
Pandu	36	Cb	4.59N	19.16 E
Panevežis/Panevėžys	19	Cd	55.44N	24.22 E
Panevėžys/Panevežis	19	Cd	55.44N	24.22 E
Panfilov	19	Ig	44.08N	80.01 E
Panga	36	Eb	1.51N	26.25 E
Pangai	65b	Ba	19.48S	174.21W
Pangaíon Óros	15	Hi	40.50N	24.05 E
Pangalanes, Canal de-	30	Lk	22.48S	47.50 E
Pangani	36	Gd	5.26S	38.58 E
Pangani or Ruvu	36	Gc	5.26S	38.58 E
Pange	12	Ie	49.05N	6.22 E
Panggoe	58	Ge	7.01S	157.05 E
Pangi	36	Ec	3.11S	26.38 E
Pangkajene	26	Gg	4.50S	119.32 E
Pangkalanberandan	26	Cf	4.01N	98.17 E
Pangkalanbuun	26	Fg	2.41S	111.37 E
Pangkalaseang, Tanjung-	26	Hg	0.42S	123.26 E
Pangkalpinang	26	Eg	2.08S	106.08 E
Pangnirtung	39	Mc	66.08N	65.44W
Pang-Pang	63b	Dc	17.41S	168.32 E
Panguitch	43	Ed	37.49N	112.26W
Panguma	34	Cc	8.24N	11.13W
Pangutaran Group	26	He	6.15N	120.30 E
Panhandle	45	Fi	35.21N	101.23W
Pania Mutombo	36	Dc	5.11S	23.51 E
Paniau	65a	Ab	21.57N	160.05W
Panié, Mont-	61	Bd	20.36S	164.46 E
Pānīpat	25	Fc	29.23N	76.58 E
Paniza, Puerto de-	13	Kc	41.15N	1.20W
Panjang	26	Eh	5.29S	105.18 E
Panjang, Pulau-	26	Ef	2.44N	108.55 E
Panjgūr	25	Cc	26.58N	64.06 E
Panjim → Panaji	22	Jh	15.29N	73.50 E
Panjwīn	24	Ke	35.36N	45.58 E
Pankow, Berlin-	10	Jd	52.34N	13.24 E
Pankshin	34	Gd	9.20N	9.27 E
P'anmunjŏm	28	If	37.57N	126.40 E
Panopah	26	Fg	1.56S	111.11 E
Panorama	56	Jb	21.21S	51.51W
Panshan	28	Gd	41.12N	122.03 E
Panshi	27	Mc	42.56N	126.02 E
Pant	12	Cc	51.53N	0.39 E
Pantanal	52	Kg	18.00S	56.00W
Pantar, Pulau-	26	Hh	8.25S	124.07 E
Pantego	44	Ih	35.34N	76.36W
Pantelleria	14	Fn	36.50N	11.57 E
Pantelleria	5	Hh	36.45N	12.00 E
Pantelleria, Canale di-	14	Fn	36.40N	11.45 E
Pante Makassar	26	Hh	9.12S	124.23 E
Pantoja	54	Cd	0.58S	75.10W
Pánuco	48	Jf	22.03N	98.10W
Pánuco	38	Jg	22.16N	97.47W
Panxian	27	Hf	25.45N	104.39 E
Panyam	34	Gd	9.25N	9.13 E
Panzi	36	Cd	7.13S	17.58 E
Panzós	49	Cf	15.24N	89.40W
Pao, Río- [Ven.]	50	Bh	8.33N	68.01W
Pao, Río- [Ven.]	50	Dh	8.06N	64.17W
Paola [It.]	14	Kk	39.21N	16.03 E
Paola [Ks.-U.S.]	45	Ig	38.35N	94.53W
Paoli	44	Df	38.33N	86.28W
Paopao	65e	Fc	17.30S	149.49W
Paoua	35	Bd	7.15N	16.26 E
Pápa	10	Ni	47.20N	17.28 E
Papa	65a	Fd	19.13N	155.52W
Papaaloa	65a	Fd	19.59N	155.13W
Papagaios	55	Jd	19.32S	44.45W
Papagayo, Golfo del-	47	Gf	10.45N	85.45W
Papaikou	65a	Fd	19.47N	155.06W
Papakura	62	Fb	37.03S	174.57 E
Papaloapan, Río-	48	Lh	18.42N	95.38W
Papanduva	55	Gh	26.25S	50.09W
Papangpanjang	26	Dg	0.27S	100.25 E
Papantla de Olarte	47	Ed	20.27N	97.19W
Papar	26	Ge	5.44N	115.56 E
Paparoa Range	62	De	42.05S	171.35 E
Papa Stour	9	La	60.30N	1.40W
Papa Westray	9	Kb	59.22N	2.54W
Papeete	58	Mf	17.32S	149.34W
Papenburg	10	Dc	53.04N	7.24 E
Papenburg-Aschendorf (Ems)	12	Ja	53.04N	7.22 E
Papenoo	65e	Fc	17.30S	149.25W
Papes Ezers/Papes Ozero	8	Ih	56.15N	20.55 E
Papes Ozero/Papes Ezers	8	Ih	56.15N	20.55 E
Papetoai	65e	Fc	17.30S	149.52W
Papey	7a	Cb	64.36N	14.11W
Paphos/Baf	24	Ee	34.50N	32.35 E
Papija	15	Kg	42.07N	27.51 E
Papíkion Óros	15	Ih	41.15N	25.18 E
Papilė/Papile	8	Jh	56.09N	22.45 E
Papile/Papilė	8	Jh	56.09N	22.45 E
Papillion	45	Hf	41.09N	96.03W
Papua, Gulf of-	57	Fe	8.32S	145.00 E
Papua New Guinea	58	Fe	6.00S	150.00 E
Papua Passage	64p	Bc	21.15S	159.47W
Papuk	14	Le	45.31N	17.39 E
Papun	25	Je	18.04N	97.27 E
Para	7	Ji	54.23N	40.53 E
Pará	54	Hd	4.00S	53.00W
Pará, Rio-	55	Jd	19.13S	45.07W
Para, Rio-	52	Lf	1.30S	48.55W
Parabel	20	De	58.40N	81.30 E
Parabel	20	De	58.43N	81.31 E
Paraburdoo	59	Dd	23.15S	117.45 E
Paracas	54	Cf	13.49S	76.16W
Paracatu	54	Ig	17.13S	46.52W
Paracatu, Rio- [Braz.]	55	Ic	17.30S	46.32W
Paracatu, Rio- [Braz.]	55	Jc	16.30S	45.04W
Paracel Islands (EN)=Xisha Qundao	21	Nh	16.30N	12.15 E
Pārachinār	25	Eb	33.54N	70.06 E
Paraćin	15	Ef	43.52N	21.25 E
Paracuru	54	Kd	3.24S	39.04W
Parada Km 329	55	Ek	32.30S	55.25W
Paradip	25	Hd	20.19N	86.42 E
Paradise [Ca.-U.S.]	46	Eg	39.46N	21.37W
Paradise [Mi.-U.S.]	44	Eb	46.38N	85.03W
Paragould	45	Kh	36.03N	90.29W
Paragua, Río-	54	Fb	6.55N	62.55W
Paraguá, Río-	54	Ff	3.34S	61.53W
Paraguaçu, Rio-	52	Mg	2.45S	38.54W
Paraguaçu Paulista	55	Gf	22.25S	50.34W
Paraguai, Rio	52	Kh	27.18S	58.38W
Paraguaipoa	49	Lh	1.21N	71.57W
Paraguaná, Peninsula de	54	Da	1.55N	70.00W
Paraguarí	55	Dg	26.00S	57.10W
Paraguari	56	Ic	25.38S	57.09W
Paraguay	53	Kh	23.00S	58.00W
Paraguay, Río-	52	Kh	27.18S	58.38W
Paraíba	54	Ke	7.10S	36.30W
Paraíba do Sul, Rio-	52	Lh	21.37S	41.03W
Paraibuna, Represa do-	55	Jf	23.25S	45.35W
Paraibuna, Rio-	55	Jf	23.22S	45.40W
Parainen/Pargas	7	Ff	60.18N	22.18 E
Paraíso [Braz.]	55	Fd	19.03S	52.59W
Paraíso [Mex.]	48	Mh	18.24N	93.14W
Paraíso, Rio-	55	Bb	15.08S	61.52W
Parakou	31	Hh	9.21N	2.37 E
Param	64d	Bb	7.22N	151.48 E
Paramaribo	53	Ke	5.50N	55.10W
Paramera, Sierra de la-	13	Hd	40.30N	4.46W
Paramithiá	15	Dj	39.28N	20.31 E
Paramušir, Ostrov-	21	Rd	50.25N	155.50E
Paraná	53	Ji	31.45S	60.30W
Paraná	56	Jb	24.00S	51.00W
Paraná, Pico-	55	Hg	25.14S	48.48W
Paraná, Rio-	52	Ki	33.43S	59.15W
Paranã, Rio-	52	Lg	12.30S	48.14W
Paraná de las Palmas, Río-	55	Cl	34.18S	58.33W
Paranaguá	53	Lh	25.31S	48.30W
Paraná-Guazú, Río-	55	Ck	34.00S	58.25W
Paranaíba	54	Hg	19.40S	51.11W
Paranaíba, Rio-	52	Kh	20.07S	51.05W
Paranaiguara	55	Gd	18.53S	50.28W
Paranapanema, Rio-	52	Kh	22.40S	53.09W
Paranapiacaba, Serra do-	52	Lh	24.20S	49.00W
Paranapuã-Guaçu, Ponta do-	55	Ig	24.24S	47.00W
Paranavaí	56	Jb	23.04S	52.28W
Parandak	24	Ne	35.21N	50.42 E
Paranéstion	15	Hh	41.16N	24.30 E
Paranhos	55	Ef	23.55S	55.25W
Paraoa Atoll	57	Mf	19.09S	140.43W
Paraopeba	55	Jd	19.18S	44.25W
Paraopeba, Rio-	55	Jd	18.50S	45.11W
Parapara	63b	Ca	13.32S	167.20 E
Paraparaumu	62	Fd	40.55S	175.00 E
Paraspóri	15	Kn	35.54N	27.14 E
Parat	55	Jf	23.13S	44.43W
Paratodos, Serra-	55	Jb	14.40S	44.50W
Paratunka	20	Kf	52.52N	158.12 E
Pārāu, Kūh-e-	24	Le	34.37N	47.05 E
Paraúna	55	Gc	17.02S	50.26W
Paravae	64n	Bc	10.27S	160.58W
Paray-le-Monial	11	Kh	46.27N	4.07 E
Parbati	25	Fc	25.51N	76.36 E
Parbhani	25	Fe	19.16N	76.47 E
Parchim	10	Hc	53.26N	11.51 E
Parczew	10	Se	51.39N	22.54 E
Pardo	55	Cm	36.15S	59.22W
Pardo, Rio- [Braz.]	55	Fi	29.59S	52.23W
Pardo, Rio- [Braz.]	54	Hh	21.46S	52.09W
Pardo, Rio- [Braz.]	55	He	20.10S	48.38W
Pardo, Rio- [Braz.]	55	Hf	22.55S	49.58W
Pardo, Rio- [Braz.]	55	Jb	15.48S	44.48W
Pardo, Rio- [Braz.]	54	Kg	15.39S	38.57W
Pardubice	10	Lf	50.02N	15.45 E
Parea	65e	Eb	16.49S	150.58W
Parecis, Chapada dos-	52	Kg	13.00S	60.00W
Parecis, Rio-	55	Da	12.56S	56.43W
Paredes de Nava	13	Hb	42.09N	4.41W
Parelhas	54	Ke	6.41S	36.39W
Paren	20	Ld	62.28N	163.05 E
Parent	42	Kg	47.55N	74.37W
Parentis-en-Born	11	Ej	44.21N	1.04W
Pareora	62	Df	44.29S	171.13 E
Parepare	22	Nj	4.01S	119.38 E
Párga	15	Dj	39.17N	20.24 E
Pargas/Parainen	7	Ff	60.18N	22.18 E
Pargolovo	8	Nd	60.03N	30.30 E
Parham	51d	Bb	17.05N	61.46W
Parhar	19	Gh	37.31N	69.23 E
Pari, Rio-	55	Db	15.36S	56.08W
Paria, Golfo de-/Paria, Gulf of-	54	Fa	10.20N	62.00W
Paria, Gulf of-/Paria, Golfo de-	54	Fa	10.20N	62.00W
Paria, Peninsula de-	50	Eg	10.40N	62.30W
Pariaguán	54	Fb	8.51N	64.43W
Pariaman	26	Dg	0.38S	100.08 E
Paria River	46	Jh	36.52N	111.36W
Paricutín, Volcán-	48	Hh	19.28N	102.15W
Parida, Isla-	49	Fi	8.07N	82.20W
Pari das Pedras	55	Ja	12.45S	44.47W
Parigi	26	Hg	0.48S	120.10 E
Parika	54	Gb	6.52N	58.25W
Parikkala	7	Gf	61.33N	29.30 E
Parima, Serra-	52	Je	3.00N	64.20W
Parinacota	56	Ga	18.12S	69.16W
Pariñas, Punta-	52	Hf	4.40S	81.20W
Paringul Mare, Vîrful-	15	Gd	45.20N	23.30 E
Parintins	53	Kf	2.36S	56.44W
Paris [Fr.]	6	Gf	43.52N	2.20 E
Paris [Il.-U.S.]	45	Mg	39.36N	87.42W
Paris [Kir.]	64g	Ab	1.56N	157.31W
Paris [Ky.-U.S.]	44	Ef	38.13N	84.14W
Paris [Tn.-U.S.]	44	Cg	36.19N	88.20W
Paris [Tx.-U.S.]	43	He	33.40N	95.33W
Paris Basin (EN)=Parisien, Bassin-	5	Gf	49.00N	2.00 E
Parisien, Bassin-=Paris Basin (EN)	5	Gf	49.00N	2.00 E
Parita	49	Gi	8.00N	80.31W
Parita, Bahía de-	49	Gi	8.08N	80.24W
Parit Buntar	26	De	5.07N	100.30 E
Parkano	7	Fe	62.01N	23.01 E
Parkent	18	Gd	41.18N	69.40 E
Parker	46	Hi	34.09N	114.17W
Parker, Mount-	59	Fc	17.10S	128.20 E
Parkersburg	43	Kd	39.17N	81.33W
Parker Seamount (EN)	40	If	52.35N	151.15W
Parkes	58	Fh	33.08S	148.11 E
Park Falls	45	Kd	45.56N	90.32W
Parkland	46	Dc	47.09N	122.26W
Park Range	43	Fc	40.00N	106.30W
Park Rapids	45	Ic	46.55N	95.04W
Park River	45	Hb	48.24N	97.45W
Park Valley	46	If	41.50N	113.21W
Parma	14	Ef	44.56N	10.26 E
Parma [It.]	6	Hg	44.48N	10.20 E
Parma [Oh.-U.S.]	44	Ge	41.24N	81.44W
Parnaguá	54	Jf	10.13S	44.38W
Parnaíba	53	Lf	2.54S	41.47W
Parnaíba, Rio-	52	Lf	3.00S	41.50W
Parnamirim [Braz.]	54	Ke	8.05S	39.34W
Parnamirim [Braz.]	54	Ke	5.55S	35.15W
Parnarama	54	Je	5.41S	43.06W
Parnassós Óros=Parnassus (EN)	5	Ih	38.30N	22.37 E
Parnassus	62	Ee	42.43S	173.17 E
Parnassus (EN)=Parnassós Óros	5	Ih	38.30N	22.37 E
Párnis Óros	15	Gk	38.10N	23.40 E
Párnon Óros	15	Fl	37.12N	22.38 E
Pärnu/Pjarnu	6	Id	58.24N	24.32 E
Pärnu-Jaagupi/Pjarnu-Jagupi	8	Kf	58.36N	24.25 E
Pärnu Jõgi/Pjarnu	7	Fg	58.23N	24.34 E
Pärnu Laht/Pjarnu, Zaliv-	7	Fg	58.15N	24.25 E
Parola	8	Kc	61.03N	24.22 E
Paroo River	57	Fh	31.28S	143.32 E
Paropamisus/Salseleh-ye Safīd Kūh	21	If	34.30N	63.30 E
Páros	15	Il	37.05N	25.09 E
Páros	15	Il	37.06N	25.12 E
Parowan	46	Ih	37.51N	112.57W
Parpaillon	11	Mj	44.35N	6.40 E
Parque Industrial	55	Jd	19.57S	44.01W
Parral	56	Fe	36.09S	71.50W
Parral, Río-	48	Gd	27.35N	105.25W
Parras, Sierra de-	48	He	25.25N	102.00W
Parras de la Fuente	47	Dc	25.25N	102.11W
Parravicini	55	Dm	36.27S	57.46W
Parrett	9	Jj	51.13N	3.01W
Parrita	49	Ei	9.30N	84.19W
Parry, Cape -	42	Fb	70.12N	124.35W
Parry, Kap- [Grld.]	41	Jd	72.28N	22.00W
Parry, Kap- [Grld.]	41	Ec	77.00N	71.00W
Parry Bay	42	Jc	68.00N	82.00W
Parry Islands	38	Ib	76.00N	110.00W
Parry Peninsula	42	Fc	69.45N	124.35W
Parry Sound	42	Jg	45.21N	80.02W
Parsęta	10	Lb	54.12N	15.33 E
Parsons [Ks.-U.S.]	43	Hd	37.20N	95.16W
Parsons [W.V.-U.S.]	44	Hf	39.06N	79.43W
Parsons Range	59	Hb	13.30S	135.15 E
Partanna	14	Gm	37.43N	12.53 E
Parthenay	11	Fh	46.39N	0.15W
Partille	8	Eg	57.44N	12.07 E
Partinico	14	Hl	38.03N	13.07 E
Partizansk	20	Ih	43.13N	133.05 E
Partizánske	10	Oh	48.38N	18.23 E
Partizanskoje	20	Ee	55.30N	94.30 E
Paru, Rio-	52	Kf	1.33S	52.38W
Paru de Este, Rio-	54	Hc	1.10N	54.40W
Paru de Oeste, Rio-	52	Kf	1.30S	56.00W
Paruru	63a	Ec	9.51S	160.49 E
Parvān	23	Kb	35.15N	69.30 E
Părvomaj	15	Ig	42.06N	25.13 E
Parys	37	De	27.04S	27.16 E
Paša	7	Hf	60.28N	32.55 E
Pasadena [Ca.-U.S.]	39	Hf	34.09N	118.09W
Pasadena [Tx.-U.S.]	45	Il	29.42N	95.13W
Paşaeli Yarimadası	15	Lh	41.20N	28.25 E
Paşalimani Adası	15	Ki	40.28N	27.37 E
Pasangkaju	26	Gg	1.10S	119.20 E
Pāsārgād	24	Og	30.17N	52.55 E
Pasarwajo	26	Hh	5.29S	122.50 E
Pascagoula	43	Je	30.23N	88.31W
Paşcani	15	Jb	47.15N	26.44 E
Pasco	43	Db	46.14N	119.06W
Pasco	54	Cf	10.30S	75.15W
Pascoal	55	Ba	13.38S	61.06W
Pascoal, Monte-	54	Kg	16.54S	39.24W
Pascua, Isla de-/Rapa Nui= Easter Island (EN)	57	Qg	27.07S	109.22W
Pas-de-Calais	11	Id	50.30N	2.20 E
Pas-en-Artois	12	Ed	50.09N	2.30 E
Pasewalk	10	Jc	53.31N	13.59 E
Pasinler	24	Ib	40.00N	41.41 E
Pašino	20	De	55.11N	83.02 E
Pasión, Río de la-	49	Be	16.28N	90.33W
Pasir Mas	26	De	6.02N	102.08 E
Pasirpengarayan	26	Df	0.51N	100.16 E
Pasir Puteh	26	De	5.50N	102.24 E
Påskallavik	8	Gg	57.10N	16.27 E
Paškovski	16	Kg	45.01N	39.05 E
Pasłęk	10	Pb	54.05N	19.39 E
Pasłęka	10	Pb	54.25N	19.50 E
Pašman	14	Jg	43.57N	15.21 E
Pasni	22	Ig	25.13N	63.28 E
Paso de Indios	56	Gf	43.52S	69.06W
Paso del Cerro	55	Ej	31.31S	55.46W
Paso de los Libres	56	Ic	29.43S	57.05W
Paso de los Toros	56	Id	32.49S	56.31W
Paso Tranqueras	55	Ej	31.12S	55.45W
Passamaquoddy Bay	44	Nc	45.06N	66.59W
Passa Três, Serra-	55	Hb	14.40S	49.30W
Passau	10	Jh	48.35N	13.29 E
Passero, Capo-	14	Jn	36.40N	15.10 E
Passo Fundo	53	Kh	28.15S	52.24W
Passo Fundo, Rio-	55	Fh	27.16S	52.42W
Passos	54	Ig	20.43S	46.37W
Pastaza, Río-	52	If	4.50S	76.25W
Pasteur	56	He	35.08S	62.14W
Pasto	53	Ie	1.13N	77.17W
Pastora Peak	46	Kh	36.47N	109.10W
Pastoría, Laguna de-	48	Ki	16.00N	97.40W
Pastos Bons	54	Je	6.36S	44.05W
Pastrana	13	Jd	40.25N	2.55W
Paštrik	15	Dg	42.14N	20.32 E
Pasubio	14	Fe	45.47N	11.10 E
Pasvalis/Pasvalys	7	Fh	56.02N	24.28 E
Pasvalys/Pasvalis	7	Fh	56.02N	24.28 E
Pásztó	10	Pi	47.55N	19.42 E

Index Symbols

- Independent Nation
- State, Region
- District, County
- Municipality
- Colony, Dependency
- Continent
- Physical Region
- Historical or Cultural Region
- Mount, Mountain
- Volcano
- Hill
- Mountains, Mountain Range
- Hills, Escarpment
- Plateau, Upland
- Pass, Gap
- Plain, Lowland
- Delta
- Salt Flat
- Valley, Canyon
- Crater, Cave
- Karst Features
- Depression
- Polder
- Desert, Dunes
- Forest, Woods
- Heath, Steppe
- Oasis
- Cape, Point
- Coast, Beach
- Cliff
- Peninsula
- Isthmus
- Sandbank
- Island
- Atoll
- Rock, Reef
- Islands, Archipelago
- Rocks, Reefs
- Coral Reef
- Well, Spring
- Geyser
- River, Stream
- Waterfall Rapids
- River Mouth, Estuary
- Lake
- Salt Lake
- Intermittent Lake
- Reservoir
- Swamp, Pond
- Canal
- Glacier
- Ice Shelf, Pack Ice
- Ocean
- Sea
- Gulf, Bay
- Strait, Fjord
- Lagoon
- Bank
- Seamount
- Tablemount
- Ridge
- Shelf
- Basin
- Escarpment, Sea Scarp
- Fracture
- Trench, Abyss
- National Park, Reserve
- Point of Interest
- Recreation Site
- Cave, Cavern
- Historic Site
- Ruins
- Wall, Walls
- Church, Abbey
- Temple
- Scientific Station
- Airport
- Port
- Lighthouse
- Mine
- Tunnel
- Dam, Bridge

Index Symbols

[1] Independent Nation — Historical or Cultural Region — Pass, Gap — Depression — Coast, Beach — Rock, Reef — Waterfall Rapids — Canal — Lagoon — Escarpment, Sea Scarp — Historic Site — Port
[2] State, Region — Mount, Mountain — Plain, Lowland — Polder — Cliff — Islands, Archipelago — River Mouth, Estuary — Glacier — Bank — Fracture — Ruins — Lighthouse
[3] District, County — Volcano — Delta — Desert, Dunes — Peninsula — Rocks, Reefs — Lake — Ice Shelf, Pack Ice — Seamount — Trench, Abyss — Church, Abbey — Mine
[4] Municipality — Hill — Salt Flat — Forest, Woods — Isthmus — Coral Reef — Salt Lake — Ocean — Tablemount — National Park, Reserve — Temple — Tunnel
[5] Colony, Dependency — Mountains, Mountain Range — Valley, Canyon — Heath, Steppe — Sandbank — Well, Spring — Intermittent Lake — Sea — Ridge — Point of Interest — Recreation Site — Dam, Bridge
[6] Continent — Hills, Escarpment — Crater, Cave — Oasis — Island — Geyser — Reservoir — Gulf, Bay — Shelf — Scientific Station — Scientific Station
[7] Physical Region — Plateau, Upland — Karst Features — Cape, Point — Atoll — River, Stream — Swamp, Pond — Strait, Fjord — Basin — Cave, Cavern — Airport

Pervari 24 Jd 37.54N 42.36 E
Pervomajsk 19 Ee 54.52N 43.48 E
Pervomajsk 16 Ke 48.36N 38.32 E
Pervomajsk 19 Df 48.03N 30.52 E
Pervomajski 10 Vc 53.52N 25.33 E
Pervomajski 19 Ie 50.15N 81.59 E
Pervomajski 16 Lc 53.18N 40.15 E
Pervomajski 19 Ec 64.26N 40.48 E
Pervomajski 17 Ji 54.52N 61.08 E
Pervomajski 16 Sd 51.34N 54.59 E
Pervomajski 16 Je 49.24N 36.15 E
Pervouralsk 19 Fd 57.00N 60.00 E
Pervy Kurilski Proliv 20 Kf 50.50N 156.50 E
Perwez/Perwijs 12 Gd 50.37N 4.49 E
Perwijs/Perwez 12 Gd 50.37N 4.49 E
Pes 7 Ig 59.10N 35.18 E
Peša 17 Cc 66.50N 47.32 E
Pesaro 14 Gg 43.54N 12.55 E
Pescadores (EN)=Penghu Liehtao 27 Kg 23.30N 119.30 E
Pescadores, Punta- 48 Ef 23.45N 109.45W
Pesčany, Mys- 16 Qh 43.10N 51.18 E
Pesčany, Ostrov 20 Gb 74.20N 115.55 E
Pescara 14 Ih 42.28N 14.13 E
Pescara 6 Hg 42.28N 14.13 E
Pescasseroli 14 Hi 41.48N 13.47 E
Peschici 14 Ki 41.57N 16.01 E
Pescia 14 Eg 43.54N 10.41 E
Pescocostanzo 14 Ii 41.53N 14.04 E
Peshāwar 22 Jf 34.01N 71.33 E
Peshkopia 15 Dh 41.41N 20.26 E
Pesio 14 Bf 44.28N 7.53 E
Peskovka 7 Mg 59.03N 52.22 E
Pesmes 11 Lg 47.17N 5.34 E
Pesočny 8 Nd 60.05N 30.20 E
Peso da Régua 13 Ec 41.10N 7.47W
Pesqueira 54 Ke 8.22S 36.42W
Pesquería, Río- 48 Je 25.54N 99.11W
Pessac 11 Fj 44.48N 0.37W
Pest [2] 10 Pi 47.25N 19.20 E
Pešter 15 Df 43.05N 20.02 E
Peštera 15 Hg 42.02N 24.18 E
Pestovo 19 Dd 58.36N 35.47 E
Petacalco, Bahía de- 47 De 17.57N 102.05W
Petah Tiqwa 24 Ff 32.05N 34.53 E
Petäjävesi 8 Kb 62.15N 25.12 E
Petal 45 Lk 31.21N 89.17W
Petalioí 15 Hl 38.01N 24.17 E
Petalioi, Gulf of- (EN) = Petaliòn, Kólpos- 15 Hk 38.00N 24.05 E
Petaliòn, Kólpos- = Petalioi, Gulf of- (EN) 15 Hk 38.00N 24.05 E
Petaluma 46 Dg 38.14N 122.39W
Pétange/Petingen 12 He 49.33N 5.53 E
Petare 54 Ea 10.29N 66.49W
Petatlán 48 Ii 17.31N 101.16W
Petatlán, Río- 48 Fd 26.09N 107.45W
Petauke 36 Fe 14.15S 31.20 E
Petén 47 Fe 16.15N 89.50W
Petén [3] 49 Be 16.50N 90.00W
Petén Itzá, Lago- 49 Ce 16.59N 89.50W
Petenwell Lake 45 Ld 44.05N 89.45W
Peterborough [Austl.] 59 Hf 32.58S 138.50 E
Peterborough [Eng.-U.K.] 9 Mi 52.35N 0.15W
Peterborough [Ont.-Can.] 42 Jh 44.18N 78 19W
Peterhead 9 Ld 57.30N 1.46W
Peter I, Oy- 66 Pe 68.47S 90.35W
Peter Island 51a Db 18.22N 64.35W
Peterlee 9 Lg 54.46N 1.19W
Petermann Gletscher 41 Fb 80.45N 61.00W
Petermann Ranges 59 Fd 25.00S 129.45 E
Petermanns Bjerg 67 Md 73.10N 28.00W
Peter Pond Lake 42 Ge 55.55N 108.40W
Petersberg 10 He 51.35N 11.57 E
Petersburg [Ak.-U.S.] 40 Me 56.49N 132.57W
Petersburg [In.-U.S.] 44 Df 38.30N 87.16W
Petersburg [Va.-U.S.] 43 Ld 37.14N 77.24W
Petersburg [W.V.-U.S.] 44 Hf 39.01N 79.09W
Petersfield 9 Mk 51.00N 0.56W
Petershagen 12 Kb 52.23N 8.58 E
Peter the Great Bay (EN)= Petra Velikogo, Zaliv- 21 Pe 42.40N 132.00 E
Petilia Policastro 14 Kk 39.07N 16.47 E
Petingen/Pétange 12 He 49.33N 5.53 E
Petit-Bourg 51eAb 16.12N 61.36W
Petit-Canal 51eBb 16.23N 61.29W
Petit Canouan 51nBb 12.47N 61.17W
Petit Cul-de-Sac Marin 51eAb 16.12N 61.33W
Petite Kabylie 13 Rh 36.35N 5.25 E
Petite Rivière de l'Artibonite 49 Kd 19.08N 72.29W
Petites Pyrénées 11 Hk 43.05N 1.10 E
Petite-Terre, Iles de la- 51eBb 16.10N 61.07W
Petit-Goâve 49 Kd 18.26N 72.52W
Petit Martinique Island 51p Ca 12.32N 61.22W
Petit-Mécatina, Rivière du- 42 Lf 50.39N 59.25W
Petit Morin 11 Jf 48.56N 3.07 E
Petit Mustique Island 51nBb 12.51N 61.13W
Petit Nevis Island 51nBb 12.58N 61.15W
Petitot 42 Fd 60.14N 123.29W
Petit Saint-Bernard, Col du- 14 Ae 45.40N 6.55 E
Petit Saint Vincent Island 51nBb 12.33N 61.23W
Petit Savanne 51g Bb 15.15N 61.17W
Petitsikapau Lake 42 Kf 54.40N 66.25W
Petkula 7 Gc 67.40N 26.41 E
Petlalcingo 48 Kh 18.05N 97.54W
Peto 47 Gd 20.08N 88.55W
Petorca 56 Fd 32.15S 71.00W
Petoskey 44 Ec 45.22N 84.57W
Petra 24 Fg 30.19N 35.29 E
Petralia Soprana 14 Im 37.47N 14.06 E
Petra Pervogo, Hrebet- 18 He 39.00N 71.10 E
Petra Velikogo, Zaliv-= Peter the Great Bay (EN) 21 Pe 42.40N 132.00 E
Petre, Point- 44 Id 43.50N 77.09W
Petre Bay 62 Je 43.55S 176.40W
Petrel 66 Re 63.28S 56.17W
Petrela 15 Ch 41.15N 19.51 E
Petrella Tifernina 14 Ii 41.41N 14.42 E
Petrič 15 Gh 41.24N 23.13 E
Pétrie, Récif- 61 Bc 18.30S 164.20 E
Petrikov 16 Fc 52.08N 28.31 E
Petrila 15 Gd 45.27N 23.25 E
Petrinja 14 Ke 45.27N 16.17 E
Petrodvorec 7 Gg 59.53N 29.50 E
Petrólea 54 Db 8.30N 72.35W
Petrolia 44 Fd 42.52N 82.09W
Petrolina 54 Je 9.24S 40.30W
Petrolina de Goiás 55 Hc 16.06S 49.20W
Petronanski prohod 15 Gf 43.08N 23.08 E
Petronell 14 Kb 48.07N 16.51 E
Petropavlovka 20 Ff 50.38N 105.19 E
Petropavlovsk 22 Id 54.54N 69.06 E
Petropavlovsk-Kamčatski 22 Rd 53.01N 158.39 E
Petrópolis 53 Lh 22.31S 43.10W
Petroşani 15 Gd 45.25N 23.22 E
Petrovac [Yugo.] 15 Bg 42.12N 18.57 E
Petrovac [Yugo.] 15 Ee 44.22N 21.25 E
Petrova Gora 14 Je 45.17N 15.47 E
Petrovaradin 15 Cd 45.15N 19.53 E
Petrovka 15 Mc 46.55N 30.40 E
Petrovsk 19 Ee 52.18N 45.23 E
Petrovski Jam 7 Ie 63.18N 35.15 E
Petrovsk-Zabajkalski 22 Md 51.17N 108.50 E
Petrov Val 16 Nd 50.10N 45.12 E
Petrozavodsk 6 Jc 61.47N 34.20 E
Petuhovo 19 Gd 55.06N 67.58 E
Petuški 7 Ji 55.59N 39.28 E
Petworth 12 Bd 50.59N 0.36W
Peuetsagoe, Gunung- 26 Cf 4.55N 96.20 E
Peumo 56 Fd 34.24S 71.10W
Peureulak 26 Cf 4.48N 97.53 E
Pevek 22 Tc 69.42N 170.17 E
Pevensey 12 Cd 50.48N 0.21 E
Pevensey Bay 12 Cd 50.48N 0.22 E
Peza 7 Kd 65.34N 44.33 E
Pézenas 11 Jk 43.27N 3.25 E
Pezinok 10 Nh 48.18N 17.16 E
Pfaffenhofen an der Ilm 10 Hh 48.32N 11.31 E
Pfaffenhoffen 12 Jf 48.51N 7.37 E
Pfalz 12 Je 49.20N 7.57 E
Pfalzel, Trier- 12 Ie 49.46N 6.41 E
Pfälzer Bergland 10 Dg 49.35N 7.30 E
Pfälzer Wald 10 Dg 49.15N 7.50 E
Pfarrkirchen 10 Ih 48.26N 12.52 E
Pfinz 12 Ke 49.11N 8.25 E
Pfinztal 12 Ke 49.02N 8.30 E
Pforzheim an der Enz 10 Eh 48.53N 8.42 E
Pfrimm 12 Ke 49.39N 8.22 E
Pfullendorf 10 Fi 47.55N 9.15 E
Pfunds 14 Ed 46.58N 10.33 E
Pfungstadt 12 Ke 49.48N 8.36 E
Phalaborwa 37 Ed 23.55S 31.13 E
Phalodi 25 Ec 27.08N 72.22 E
Pha-an 25 Je 16.53N 97.38 E
Phangnga 25 Jg 8.28N 98.32 E
Phan Ly Cham 25 Lf 11.13N 108.31 E
Phanom 25 Jg 8.49N 98.50 E
Phan Rang 25 Lf 11.34N 108.59 E
Phan Thiet 25 Lf 10.56N 108.06 E
Pharr 45 Gm 26.12N 98.11W
Phatthalung 25 Kg 7.38N 100.04 E
Phayao 25 Ke 18.07N 100.11 E
Phenix City 43 Je 32.29N 85.01W
Phet Buri 25 Jf 13.06N 99.56 E
Phetchabun, Thiu Khao- 25 Ke 16.20N 100.55 E
Phichit 25 Ke 16.24N 100.21 E
Philadelphia [Ms.-U.S.] 45 Lj 32.46N 89.07W
Philadelphia [Pa.-U.S.] 39 Lf 39.57N 75.07W
Philae 33 Fe 23.35N 32.52 E
Philip 45 Fd 44.02N 101.40W
Philippeville 11 Kd 50.12N 4.33 E
Philippi 44 Gf 39.08N 80.03W
Philippi (EN) = Filippoi 15 Hh 41.02N 24.18 E
Philippi, Lake- 59 Hd 24.20S 139.00 E
Philippi Glacier 66 Ge 66.45S 88.20 E
Philippine Basin (EN) 3 Ih 17.00N 132.00 E
Philippine Islands (EN)= Pilipinas 21 Oh 13.00N 122.00 E
Philippines (EN)=Pilipinas [1] 22 Oh 13.00N 122.00 E
Philippine Sea (EN) 21 Oh 20.00N 130.00 E
Philippine Trench (EN) 3 Ii 9.00N 127.00 E
Philippsburg 12 Ke 49.14N 8.27 E
Philipsburg [Mt.-U.S.] 46 Ic 46.20N 113.08W
Philipsburg [Neth.Ant.] 50 Ec 18.01N 63.04W
Philip Smith Mountains 40 Jc 68.30N 148.00W
Philipstown 37 Cf 30.26S 24.29 E
Phillipsburg 45 Gg 39.45N 99.19W
Philpots 42 Jb 74.55N 80.00W
Phitsanulok 22 Mh 16.49N 100.15 E
Phnom Penh (EN)=Phnum Pénh 22 Mh 11.33N 104.55 E
Phnum Penh=Phnom Penh (EN) 22 Mh 11.33N 104.55 E
Phoenix 39 Hf 33.27N 112.05W
Phoenix → Rawaki Atoll 57 Je 3.43S 170.43W
Phoenix Islands 57 Je 4.00S 172.00W
Phôngsali 25 Kd 21.41N 102.06 E
Phrae 25 Ke 18.07N 100.11 E
Phra Nakhom Si Ayutthaya 22 Mh 14.21N 100.33 E
Phrygia 15 Mk 38.30N 29.50 E
Phu Cuong 25 Lf 10.58N 106.39 E
Phuket 22 Li 7.54N 98.24 E
Phuket, Ko- 21 Li 8.00N 98.20 E
Phulbani 25 Gd 20.28N 84.14 E
Phumĭ Mlu Prey 25 Lf 13.48N 105.16 E
Phumĭ Sâmraông 25 Kf 14.11N 103.31 E
Phu My 25 Lf 14.10N 109.03 E
Phuoc Binh 25 Lf 11.50N 106.58 E
Phu Quoc, Dao- 25 Kf 10.12N 104.00 E
Phu Tho 25 Ld 21.24N 105.13 E
Phu Vinh → Tra Vinh 25 Lg 9.56N 106.20 E
Piaanu Pass 64d Ab 7.20N 151.26 E
Piacenza 14 De 45.01N 9.40 E
Piana degli Albanesi 14 Hm 37.59N 13.17 E
Piana Mwanga 36 Ed 7.40S 28.10 E
Piancó 54 Ke 7.12S 37.57W
Pianguan 27 Jd 39.28N 111.32 E
Pianosa [It.] 14 Jh 42.15N 15.45 E
Pianosa [It.] 14 En 42.35N 10.05 E
Piaseczno 10 Rd 52.05N 21.01 E
Piaski 10 Se 51.08N 22.51 E
Piątek 10 Pd 52.05N 19.28 E
Piatra 15 If 43.49N 25.10 E
Piatra Neamţ 15 Jc 46.55N 26.20 E
Piatra Olt 15 He 44.22N 24.16 E
Piauí [2] 54 Je 7.00S 43.00W
Piauí, Rio- 52 L 6.38S 42.42W
Piave 5 Hf 45.32N 12.44 E
Piaxtla, Punta- 48 F 23.38N 106.50W
Piaxtla, Río- 48 F 23.42N 106.49W
Piazza Armerina 14 Im 37.23N 14.22 E
Pibor 35 Ed 8.26N 33.13 E
Pibor Post 35 Ed 6.43N 33.08 E
Pica 56 Gb 20.30S 69.21W
Picachos, Cerro dos- 43 Bc 29.25N 114.10W
Picardie = Picardy (EN) 11 Je 50.00N 3.30 E
Picardy (EN) = Picardie 11 Je 50.00N 3.30 E
Picayune 45 Lk 30.26N 89.41W
Picentini, Monti- 14 Jj 40.45N 15.10 E
Pichanal 53 Jh 23.20S 64.15W
Pichilemu 56 Fe 34.23S 72.00W
Pichilingue 48 De 24.20N 110.20W
Pichna 10 Oe 51.50N 18.40 E
Pichones, Cayos- 49 Ff 15.45N 82.55W
Pichucalco 48 Mi 17.31N 93.04W
Pickering 9 Mg 54.14N 0.46W
Pickering, Vale of- 9 Mg 54.10N 0.45W
Pickle Lake 42 If 51.29N 90.10W
Pickwick Lake 44 Ch 34.55N 88.10W
Pico 30 Ee 38.28N 28.20W
Picos 53 Lf 7.05S 41.28W
Pico Truncado 56 Gg 46.48S 67.58W
Picquigny 11 Ie 49.57N 2.09 E
Picton 61 Dh 41.18S 174.00 E
Pictou 42 Lg 45.41N 62.43W
Picunda 16 Lh 43.12N 40.21 E
Pidurutalagala 21 Ki 7.00N 80.46 E
Piedecuesta 54 Dd 6.59N 73.03W
Piedimonte Matese 14 Ii 41.20N 14.22 E
Piedmont [Al.-U.S.] 44 Ei 33.55N 85.37W
Piedmont [Mo.-U.S.] 45 Kh 37.09N 90.42W
Piedmont (EN) = Piemonte [2] 14 Be 45.00N 8.00 E
Piedmont Plateau 38 Kf 35.00N 81.00W
Piedra 13 Kc 41.19N 1.48W
Piedra, Monasterio de- 13 Kc 41.10N 1.50W
Piedrabuena 13 He 39.02N 4.10W
Piedrafita, Puerto de- 13 Fb 42.36N 6.57W
Piedrahita 13 Gc 40.28N 5.19W
Piedras 54 Cd 3.38S 79.54W
Piedras, Punta- 56 Ie 35.25S 57.08W
Piedras, Río de las- 54 Ef 12.30S 69.14W
Piedras Negras 39 Ig 28.42N 100.31W
Piedras Negras 49 Be 17.12N 91.15W
Piedra Sola 56 Id 32.04S 56.21W
Piekary Śląskie 10 Of 50.24N 18.58 E
Pieksämäki 7 Ge 62.18N 27.08 E
Pielach 14 Jb 48.15N 15.22 E
Pielavesi 7 Ge 63.14N 26.45 E
Pielinen 5 Ic 63.15N 29.40 E
Piemonte = Piedmont (EN) [2] 14 Be 45.00N 8.00 E
Pieniężno 10 Qb 54.15N 20.08 E
Pieni Salpausselkä 8 Lc 61.10N 27.20 E
Piennes 12 He 49.19N 5.47 E
Pienza 14 Fg 43.04N 11.41 E
Pierce 46 Hc 46.29N 115.48W
Piéria Óri 15 Fi 40.12N 22.07 E
Pierre 39 Ie 44.22N 100.21W
Pierrefitte-sur-Aire 12 Hf 48.54N 5.20 E
Pierrefonds 12 Ee 49.21N 2.59 E
Pierrelatte 11 Kj 44.23N 4.42 E
Pieskehaure 7 Dc 66.57N 16.30 E
Piešt'ány 10 Nh 48.36N 17.50 E
Pietarsaari/Jakobstad 7 Fe 63.40N 22.42 E
Pietermaritzburg 31 Kk 29.37S 30.16 E
Pietersburg 31 Jk 23.54S 29.25 E
Pietraperzia 14 Im 37.25N 14.08 E
Pietrasanta 14 Eg 43.57N 10.14 E
Piet Retief 37 Ee 27.01S 30.50 E
Pietrii, Vîrful- 15 Fd 45.23N 22.40 E
Pietroşani 15 If 43.43N 25.38 E
Pietrosu, Vîrful- [Rom.] 15 Ib 47.08N 25.11 E
Pietrosu, Vîrful- [Rom.] 5 If 47.23N 25.33 E
Pieve di Cadore 14 Gd 46.26N 12.22 E
Pigeon Island 51k Ba 14.06N 60.58W
Pigeon River 45 Lb 43.02N 89.41W
Piggott 45 Kh 36.23N 90.11W
Pigg's Peak 37 Ee 25.58S 31.15 E
Pigs, Bay of- (EN)= Cochinos, Bahía de- 49 Gb 22.07N 81.10W
Pigüé 55 Am 37.37S 62.25W
Pi He 28 Dh 32.26N 116.34 E
Pihkva järv=Pskov, Lake- (EN) 7 Gg 58.00N 28.00 E
Pihlajavesi 7 Gf 61.45N 28.45 E
Pihlava 8 Ic 61.33N 21.36 E
Pihtipudas 7 Fe 63.23N 25.34 E
Piikkiö 8 Jd 60.26N 22.31 E
Piirisaar/Pirissar 8 Lf 58.23N 27.40 E
Pijijiapan 48 Mj 15.42N 93.14W
Pijol, Pico- 49 Df 15.06N 87.35W
Pikalevo 7 Ig 59.32N 34.03 E
Pikangikum 42 If 51.49N 94.00W
Pikelot Island 57 Fd 8.05N 147.38 E
Pikes Peak 43 Fd 38.51N 105.03W
Piketberg 37 Bf 32.54S 18.46 E
Pikiutdleq 41 Hf 64.45N 40.10W
Pikeu 28 Ge 39.24N 122.21 E
Pikounda 36 Cb 0.33N 16.42 E
Piła 10 Mc 53.10N 16.44 E
Piła [2] 10 Mc 53.10N 16.45 E
Pila 55 Cm 36.01S 58.08W
Pila, Sierra de la- 13 Kf 38.16N 1.11W
Pilar [Arg.] 55 Bj 31.27S 61.15W
Pilar [Braz.] 54 Ke 9.36S 35.56W
Pilar [Par.] 56 Ic 26.52S 58.23W
Pilas Group 26 He 6.45N 121.35 E
Pilat, Mont- 11 Ki 45.23N 4.35 E
Pilatus 14 Cd 46.59N 8.20 E
Pilaya, Río- 54 Fh 20.55S 64.04W
Pilcaniyeu 56 Ff 41.08S 70.40W
Pilcomayo, Río- 52 Kh 25.21S 57.42W
Pile, Jezioro- 10 Mc 53.35N 16.30 E
Pili 15 Ej 39.28N 21.37 E
Pīlībhīt 25 Fc 28.38N 79.48 E
Pilica 10 Re 51.52N 21.17 E
Pílion Óros 15 Gj 39.24N 23.05 E
Pilipinas=Philippine Islands (EN) 21 Oh 13.00N 122.00 E
Pilipinas=Philippines (EN) [1] 22 Oh 13.00N 122.00 E
Pilis 10 Oi 47.41N 18.53 E
Pillahuincó, Sierra de- 55 Bn 38.18S 60.45W
Pillar, Cape- 59 Jh 43.15S 148.00 E
Pinna 7 Ki 55.33N 45.55 E
Piñões, Rio- 55 Gc 16.14S 50.54W
Pilões, Serra dos- 55 Ic 17.50S 47.13W
Pilón, Río- 48 Je 25.32N 99.32W
Pilos 15 Em 36.55N 21.42 E
Pilos = Pylos (EN) 15 Em 36.56N 21.40 E
Pilot Peak 46 Hf 41.02N 114.06W
Pilot Rock 46 Fd 45.29N 118.50W
Pilsen (EN)=Plzeň 6 Hf 49.45N 13.24 E
Piltene 7 Eh 57.15N 21.42 E
Pilzno 10 Rg 49.59N 21.17 E
Pim 19 Hc 61.18N 71.57 E
Pimba 59 Hf 31.15S 136.47 E
Pimenteiras 54 Je 6.14S 41.25W
Pimža Jõgi 8 Lg 57.57N 27.59 E
Pina 13 Lc 41.29N 0.32W
Pinacate, Cerro- 48 Cb 31.45N 113.31W
Pinaki Atoll 57 Nf 19.22S 138.44W
Pinamar 55 Dm 37.07S 56.50W
Piñami, Arroyo- 48 Cd 27.44N 113.47W
Pinar 13 Gh 36.46N 5.26W
Pinarbaşi 24 Gc 38.50N 36.30 E
Pinar del Rio 39 Kg 22.25N 83.42W
Pinar del Río [3] 49 Eb 22.35N 83.40W
Pinarello 11a Bb 41.41N 9.22 E
Pinarhisar 15 Kh 41.37N 27.30 E
Pinchbeck 12 Bb 52.48N 0.09W
Pincher Creek 42 Gg 49.30N 113.48W
Pinçon, Mont- 11 Ff 48.58N 0.37W
Pîncota 15 Ec 46.20N 21.42 E
Pindaíba, Ribeirão 55 Gb 14.48S 52.00W
Pindaré, Rio- 54 Jd 3.17S 44.47W
Pindaré-Mirim 54 Id 3.37S 45.21W
Pindaval 55 Dc 17.08S 56.09W
Pindhos Óros=Pindus Mountains (EN) 5 Ih 39.45N 21.30 E
Pindus Mountains (EN)= Pindhos Óros 5 Ih 39.45N 21.30 E
Pine Bluff 43 Ie 34.13N 92.01W
Pine Bluffs 46 Mf 41.11N 104.04W
Pine Creek 59 Gb 13.49S 131.49 E
Pine Falls 42 Hf 50.35N 96.15W
Pinega 19 Ec 64.42N 43.22 E
Pinega 5 Kc 64.08N 41.54 E
Pine Island Glacier 66 Of 75.00S 101.00W
Pineland 45 Jk 31.15N 93.58W
Pine Mountain [Ga.-U.S.] 44 Ei 32.51N 84.47W
Pine Mountain [U.S.] 44 Fg 36.55N 83.20W
Pine Pass 42 Fe 55.50N 122.30W
Pine Point 39 Hc 61.01N 114.15W
Pine Ridge 45 Ee 43.02N 102.33W
Pinerolo 14 Bf 44.53N 7.21 E
Pines, Isle of- (EN)= Juventud, Isla de la- 38 Kg 21.40N 82.50W
Pines, Isle of- (EN)=Pins, Ile des- 57 Hg 22.37S 167.30 E
Pines, Lake O' The 45 Ij 32.46N 94.35W
Pinetown 37 Ee 29.52S 30.46 E
Ping 21 Mh 15.42N 100.09 E
Pingbian 27 Hg 22.56N 103.46 E
Pingchang 27 Ie 31.38N 107.06 E
Pingding 28 Bf 37.48N 113.37 E
Pingdingbu → Guyuan 28 Cd 41.40N 115.41 E
Pingding Shan 27 Mb 46.39N 128.30 E
Pingdingshan 27 Je 33.41N 113.27 E
Pingdu 28 Ef 36.47N 119.57 E
Pingelap Atoll 57 Hd 6.13N 160.42 E
Pingelly 59 Df 32.32S 117.05 E
Pinggu 28 Dd 40.08N 117.07 E
Pingguo 27 Ig 23.21N 107.34 E
Pinghu 28 Fi 30.42N 121.02 E
Pingjiang 28 Bj 28.45N 113.37 E
Pingle 27 Jg 24.43N 110.42 E
Pingli 27 Ie 32.27N 109.21 E
Pingliang 22 Mf 35.32N 106.41 E
Pinglu (Jingping) 28 Be 39.32N 112.14 E
Pingluo 22 Mf 38.56N 106.34 E
Pingma → Tiandong 27 Ig 23.40N 107.09 E
Pingnan 27 Jg 23.38N 110.23 E
Pingouins, Ile des- 30 Mm 46.25S 50.19 E
Pingquan 27 Kc 41.00N 118.36 E
Pingshan 28 Ce 38.21N 114.01 E
Pingshun 28 Bf 36.12N 113.26 E
Pingtan 27 Kf 25.31N 119.48 E
Pingtung 27 Lg 22.40N 120.29 E
Pingüicas, Cerro- 48 Jg 21.10N 99.42W
Pingvallavatn 7a Bb 64.15N 21.09W
Pingvellir 7a Bb 64.17N 21.03W
Pingwu 27 He 32.27N 104.35 E
Pingxiang [China] 27 Ig 22.11N 106.46 E
Pingxiang [China] 27 Jf 27.43N 113.48 E
Pingyang 27 Lf 27.40N 120.30 E
Pingyao 27 Jd 37.12N 112.13 E
Pingyi 28 Dg 35.30N 117.38 E
Pingyin 28 Df 36.17N 116.26 E
Pingyu 28 Ci 32.58N 114.36 E
Pingyuan 28 Df 37.10N 116.25 E
Pinhal 55 If 22.12S 46.45W
Pinhão 55 Gg 25.43S 51.38W
Pinheir Machado 55 Fj 31.34S 53.23W
Pinhel 13 Ed 40.46N 7.04W
Pini, Pulau- 26 Cf 0.08N 98.40 E
Piniós [Grc.] 15 Fj 39.53N 22.44 E
Piniós [Grc.] 15 El 37.48N 21.14 E
Pinipel 63a Ba 4.24S 154.08 E
Pinjug 7 Lf 60.16N 47.54 E
Pinka 10 Mi 47.00N 16.35 E
Pink Mountain 42 Fe 56.06N 122.35W
Pinnaroo 59 Ig 35.16S 140.55 E
Pinneberg 10 Fc 53.39N 9.48 E
Pínnes, Ákra- 15 Hi 40.07N 24.18 E
Pinolosean 26 Hf 0.23N 124.07 E
Pinos 48 If 22.18N 101.34W
Pinos, Mount- 38 Hf 34.50N 119.09W
Pinos-Puente 13 Ig 37.15N 3.45W
Pinrang 26 Gg 3.48S 119.38 E
Pins, Cap des- 63b Ce 21.04S 167.28 E
Pins, Ile des-=Pines, Isle of- (EN) 57 Hg 22.37S 167.30 E
Pins, Pointe aux- 44 Gd 42.15N 81.51W
Pinsk 19 Ce 52.08N 26.06 E
Pinta, Isla- 54a Aa 0.35N 90.44W
Pintas, Sierra de las- 48 Bb 31.40N 115.10W
Pinto [Arg.] 56 Hc 29.09S 62.39W
Pinto [Sp.] 13 Id 40.14N 3.41W
Pintwater Range 46 Hh 36.55N 115.30W
Pio 63a Ed 10.12S 161.42 E
Pioche 46 Hh 37.56N 114.27W
Piombino 14 Eh 42.55N 10.32 E
Piombino, Canale di- 14 Eh 42.55N 10.30 E
Pioneer Mountains 46 Id 45.40N 113.00W
Pioner, Ostrov- 21 Lb 79.50N 92.30 E
Pionerski 19 Gc 61.12N 62.57 E
Pionerski 7 Ei 54.57N 20.13 E
Pionki 10 Re 51.30N 21.27 E
Piorini, Lago- 54 Fd 3.35S 63.15W
Piorini, Rio- 54 Fd 3.23S 63.30W
Piotrków [2] 10 Pe 51.25N 19.40 E
Piotrków Trybunalski 10 Pe 51.25N 19.42 E
Piove di Sacco 14 Ge 45.18N 12.02 E
Pipa Dingzi 27 Mc 43.57N 128.14 E
Pipéri 15 Hj 39.19N 24.21 E
Pipestone 45 Hd 44.01N 96.19W
Pipestone Creek 45 Fb 49.42N 100.45W
Pipi 35 Cd 7.27N 22.48 E
Pipinas 55 Dl 35.32S 57.20W
Pipmouacan, Réservoir - 42 Kg 49.40N 70.20W
Piqan → Shanshan 27 Fc 42.52N 90.10 E
Piqua 44 Ee 40.08N 84.14W
Piqueras, Puerto de- 13 Jb 42.03N 2.32W
Piquiri, Rio- 56 Jb 24.03S 54.14W
Piquiri, Serra do- 55 Fg 24.53S 52.25W
Piracanjuba 55 Hc 17.18S 49.01W
Piracanjuba, Rio- [Braz.] 55 Hd 18.14S 48.48W
Piracanjuba, Rio- [Braz.] 55 Hc 17.18S 48.13W
Piracema 55 Je 20.31S 44.29W
Piracicaba 56 Kb 22.43S 47.38W
Piracicaba, Rio- 55 Hf 22.36S 48.19W
Piraçununga 55 Ie 21.59S 47.25W
Piracuruca 54 Jd 3.56S 41.42W
Piraeus (EN) = Piraiévs 6 Ih 37.57N 23.38 E
Pirai do Sul 55 Hg 24.31S 49.56W
Piraiévs = Piraeus (EN) 6 Ih 37.57N 23.38 E
Piraju 55 Hf 23.12S 49.23W
Pirajuí 55 He 21.59S 49.29W
Piramide, Cerro- 52 Ij 49.01S 73.32W
Piran 14 He 45.32N 13.34 E
Pirané 56 Ic 25.43S 59.06W
Piranhas 55 Gc 16.31S 51.51W
Piranhas, Rio- 55 Gc 16.01S 51.52W
Pīrān Shahr 24 Kd 36.40N 45.05 E
Pirapora 53 Lg 17.21S 44.56W
Pirarajá 56 Jd 33.44S 54.45W
Pirate Well 49 Kb 22.26N 73.04W
Piratini 55 Fj 31.27S 53.06W
Piratini, Rio- 55 Fk 32.01S 52.25W
Piratinim, Rio- 55 Ei 28.06S 55.27W
Pirdop 15 Hg 42.42N 24.11 E
Pirenópolis 55 Hb 15.51S 48.57W
Pires do Rio 54 Ig 17.18S 48.17W
Pírgos 15 El 37.41N 21.27 E
Pirgós 15 Fi 40.38N 22.44 E
Piriápolis 55 El 34.54S 55.17W
Pirin 15 Gh 41.40N 23.30 E
Pirineos=Pyrenees (EN) 5 Gg 42.40N 1.00 E
Pirineus, Serra dos- 55 Hc 16.15S 49.10W
Piripiri 54 Jd 4.16S 41.47W
Pirissar/Piirisaar 8 Lf 58.23N 27.40 E
Píritu 50 Bh 9.23N 69.12W
Píritu, Islas- 50 Dg 10.10N 64.56W
Pirizal 55 Dc 16.16S 56.23W
Pirjatin 16 Hd 50.14N 32.30 E
Pirmasens 10 Dg 49.12N 7.36 E
Pirna 10 Jf 50.58N 13.56 E
Piron 63a Ad 11.20S 153.27 E
Pirón 13 Hc 41.23N 4.31W
Pirot 15 Ff 43.09N 22.36 E
Pirre, Cerro- 49 Ij 7.49N 77.43W
Pirrit Hills 66 Pg 81.17S 85.21W
Pirsagat 16 Pj 39.53N 49.19 E
Pīr Tāj 24 Me 35.45N 48.07 E
Pirttikyla/Pörtom 8 Ib 62.42N 21.37 E
Piru 26 Ig 3.04S 128.12 E
Pis 64d Ba 7.41N 151.46 E
Pisa 14 Eg 43.43N 10.23 E
Pisa 10 Rc 53.15N 21.52 E
Pisagua 56 Fa 19.36S 70.13W

Index Symbols

[1] Independent Nation
[2] State, Region
[3] District, County
[4] Municipality
[5] Colony, Dependency
Continent
Physical Region
Historical or Cultural Region
Mount, Mountain
Volcano
Hill
Mountains, Mountain Range
Hills, Escarpment
Plateau, Upland
Pass, Gap
Plain, Lowland
Delta
Salt Flat
Valley, Canyon
Crater, Cave
Karst Features
Depression
Polder
Desert, Dunes
Forest, Woods
Heath, Steppe
Oasis
Cape, Point
Coast, Beach
Cliff
Peninsula
Isthmus
Sandbank
Island
Atoll
Rock, Reef
Islands, Archipelago
Rocks, Reefs
Coral Reef
Well, Spring
Geyser
River, Stream
Waterfall Rapids
River Mouth, Estuary
Lake
Salt Lake
Intermittent Lake
Reservoir
Swamp, Pond
Canal
Glacier
Ice Shelf, Pack Ice
Ocean
Sea
Gulf, Bay
Strait, Fjord
Lagoon
Bank
Seamount
Tablemount
Ridge
Shelf
Basin
Escarpment, Sea Scarp
Fracture
Trench, Abyss
National Park, Reserve
Point of Interest
Recreation Site
Cave, Cavern
Historic Site
Ruins
Wall, Walls
Church, Abbey
Temple
Scientific Station
Airport
Port
Lighthouse
Mine
Tunnel
Dam, Bridge

Index Symbols

Index Symbols

⊡ Independent Nation	⊠ Historical or Cultural Region	Pass, Gap
⊡ State, Province	◭ Mount, Mountain	Plain, Lowland
⊡ District, County	▲ Volcano	Delta
⊡ Municipality	▲ Hill	Salt Flat
⊡ Colony, Dependency	◭ Mountains, Mountain Range	Valley, Canyon
■ Continent	▲ Hills, Escarpment	Crater, Cave
⊠ Physical Region	◰ Plateau, Upland	Karst Features

Depression	Coast, Beach	Rock, Reef
Polder	Cliff	Islands, Archipelago
Desert, Dunes	Peninsula	Rocks, Reefs
Forest, Woods	Isthmus	Coral Reef
Heath, Steppe	Sandbank	Well, Spring
Oasis	Island	Geyser
Cape, Point	Atoll	River, Stream

Waterfall, Rapids	Canal	Lagoon
River, Mouth, Estuary	Bank	Glacier
Lake	Seamount	Ice Shelf, Pack Ice
Salt Lake	Ocean	Tableland
Intermittent Lake	Sea	Ridge
Reservoir	Shelf	Point of Interest
Swamp, Pond	Gulf, Bay	Recreation Site
	Strait, Fjord	Cave, Cavern
	Basin	

Escarpment, Sea Scarp	Historic Site	Port
Fracture	Ruins	Lighthouse
Trench, Abyss	Wall, Walls	Mine
National Park, Reserve	Church, Abbey	Tunnel
Temple	Temple	Dam, Bridge
Scientific Station	Scientific Station	
Airport	Airport	

Princess Margaret Range	42	Ia	79.00N	88.30W
Princess Royal	42	Ef	52.55N	128.50W
Princeton [B.C.-Can.]	42	Fg	49.27N	120.31W
Princeton [Il.-U.S.]	45	Lf	41.23N	89.28W
Princeton [In.-U.S.]	44	Df	38.21N	87.34W
Princeton [Ky.-U.S.]	44	Dg	37.07N	87.53W
Princeton [Mo.-U.S.]	45	Jf	40.24N	93.35W
Prince William Sound	38	Ec	60.40N	147.00W
Principe	30	Hh	1.37N	7.25 E
Prineville	46	Ed	44.18N	120.51W
Prineville Reservoir	46	Ed	44.08N	120.42W
Prins Christians Sund	41	Hf	60.00N	43.10W
Prinsesse Astrid Kyst	66	Cf	70.45S	12.30 E
Prinsesse Ragnhild Kyst	66	Df	70.15S	27.30 E
Prins Harald Kyst	66	De	69.30S	36.00 E
Prins Karls Forland	41	Nc	78.32N	11.10 E
Prinzapolka	47	Hf	13.24N	83.34W
Prinzapolka, Rio-	49	Fg	13.24N	83.34W
Priora, Mount-	59	Ja	6.51S	145.58 E
Priozersk	19	Dc	61.04N	30.07 E
Pripet Marshes (EN)	5	Ie	52.00N	27.00 E
Pripjat	5	Je	51.21N	30.09 E
Pripoljarny Ural=Subpolar Urals (EN)	5	Lb	65.00N	60.00 E
Prirečny	19	Db	69.02N	30.15 E
Prišib	16	Pj	39.06N	48.38 E
Prislop, Pasul-	15	Hb	47.37N	24.55 E
Pristan-Prževalsk	18	Lc	42.33N	78.18 E
Pristen	16	Jd	51.15N	36.42 E
Priština	15	Eg	42.40N	21.10 E
Pritzwalk	10	Ic	53.09N	12.11 E
Privas	11	Kj	44.44N	4.36 E
Priverno	14	Hi	41.28N	13.11 E
Privolžkaja Vozvyšennost= Volga Hills (EN)	5	Ke	52.00N	46.00 E
Privolžsk	7	Jh	57.27N	41.16 E
Privolžski	16	Od	51.23N	46.02 E
Prizren	15	Dg	42.13N	20.45 E
Prizzi	14	Hm	37.43N	13.26 E
Prjaža	7	Hf	61.43N	33.37 E
Prnjavor	14	Lf	44.52N	17.40 E
Probolinggo	26	Fh	7.45S	113.13 E
Prochowice	10	Me	51.17N	16.22 E
Procida	14	Hj	40.45N	14.00 E
Proctor Reservoir	45	Gj	32.02N	98.32W
Proddatur	25	Ff	14.44N	78.33 E
Profitis Ilias [Grc.]	15	Fm	36.53N	22.22 E
Profitis Ilias [Grc.]	15	Fj	39.50N	22.38 E
Profondeville	12	Gd	50.23N	4.52 E
Progonati	15	Ci	40.13N	19.56 E
Prograničnik	18	Dg	35.43N	63.12 E
Progreso [Mex.]	39	Kg	21.17N	89.40W
Progreso [Mex.]	48	Id	27.28N	101.04W
Progress	20	Hg	49.41N	129.40 E
Prohladny	16	Nh	43.45N	44.01 E
Prohorovka	16	Jd	51.02N	36.42 E
Prokopjevsk	22	Kd	53.53N	86.45 E
Prokuplje	15	Ef	43.15N	21.36 E
Proletari	7	Hg	58.26N	31.43 E
Proletarsk	19	Ef	46.41N	41.44 E
Proletarsk	18	Gd	40.10N	69.31 E
Proletarski	16	Id	50.51N	35.46 E
Proletarskoje Vodohranilišče	16	Mf	46.30N	42.10 E
Proliv Soela/Soela Väin	8	Jf	58.40N	22.30 E
Prome	22	Lh	18.49N	95.13 E
Promissãe, Represa-	56	Kb	21.32S	49.52W
Promissão	55	He	21.32S	49.52W
Promyšlenny	17	Kc	67.35N	63.55 E
Pronja	16	Gc	53.27N	31.03 E
Pronja	16	Lb	54.21N	40.24 E
Pronsfeld	12	Id	50.10N	6.20 E
Prophet	42	Fe	58.46N	122.45W
Propriá	54	Kf	10.13S	36.51W
Propriano	11a	Ab	41.40N	8.54 E
Prorva	16	Rg	45.57N	53.13 E
Proserpine	59	Jd	20.24S	148.34 E
Prosna	10	Nd	52.10N	17.39 E
Prosotsáni	15	Gh	41.11N	23.59 E
Prosperidad	26	Ie	8.34N	125.52 E
Prospihino	20	Ee	58.37N	99.20 E
Prosser	46	Fc	46.12N	119.46W
Prostějov	10	Ng	49.29N	17.07 E
Proszowice	10	Qf	50.12N	20.18 E
Próti	15	El	37.03N	21.33 E
Protoka	16	Jg	45.43N	37.46 E
Protva	7	Ii	54.51N	37.16 E
Provadija	15	Kf	43.11N	27.26 E
Prøven	41	Gd	72.15N	55.40W
Provence	11	Lk	44.00N	6.00 E
Provence	5	Gg	44.00N	6.00 E
Providence [Ky.-U.S.]	44	Dg	37.24N	87.39W
Providence [R.I.-U.S.]	39	Le	41.50N	71.25W
Providence, Cape-	62	Bg	46.01S	166.28 E
Providence Bay	44	Fc	45.44N	82.18W
Providence Island	30	Mi	9.14S	51.02 E
Providencia, Isla de-	47	Hf	13.21N	81.22W
Providenciales	49	Kc	21.49N	72.15W
Providenija	22	Uc	64.23N	173.18W
Provincetown	44	Ld	42.03N	70.11W
Provins	11	Jf	48.33N	3.18 E
Provo	39	He	40.14N	111.39W
Prozor	14	Lg	43.49N	17.37 E
Prudentópolis	55	Gg	25.12S	50.57W
Prudhoe Bay	39	Eb	70.20N	148.25W
Prudnik	10	Nf	50.19N	17.34 E
Prüm	12	Ie	49.49N	6.28 E
Prüm	10	Cf	50.13N	6.25 E
Prune Island	51n	Bb	12.35N	61.24W
Prussia (EN)	10	Pc	53.45N	20.00 E
Pruszcz Gdański	10	Ob	54.16N	18.36 E
Pruszków	10	Qd	52.11N	20.48 E
Prut	5	If	45.28N	28.14 E
Pružany	19	Ce	52.36N	24.28 E
Prvić	14	If	44.54N	14.48 E
Prydz Bay	66	Fe	69.00S	76.00 E
Pryor	45	Ih	36.19N	95.19W
Przasnysz	10	Qc	53.01N	20.55 E
Przedbórz	10	Pe	51.06N	19.53 E
Przemyśl [2]	10	Sg	49.45N	22.45 E
Przemyśl	10	Sg	49.47N	22.47 E
Prževalsk	22	Je	42.29N	78.24 E
Przeworsk	10	Sf	50.05N	22.29 E
Przysucha	10	Qe	51.22N	20.38 E
Psakhná	15	Gk	38.35N	23.38 E
Psará	15	Ik	38.35N	25.37 E
Psathoúra	15	Hj	39.30N	24.11 E
Pščiš	16	Kg	45.03N	39.25 E
Psebaj	16	Lg	44.07N	40.47 E
Psël	5	Jf	49.05N	33.30 E
Psérimos	15	Km	36.56N	27.09 E
Psina	10	Of	50.02N	18.16 E
Pšiš, Gora-	16	Lh	43.24N	41.14 E
Pskem	18	Hd	41.38N	70.01 E
Pskent	18	Gd	40.54N	69.23 E
Pskov	6	Id	57.50N	28.20 E
Pskov, Lake- (EN)=Pihkva järv	7	Gg	58.00N	28.00 E
Pskov, Lake- (EN)= Pskovskoje Ozero	5	Id	58.00N	28.00 E
Pskova	8	Mg	57.47N	28.30 E
Pskovskaja Oblast [3]	19	Cd	57.20N	29.20 E
Pskovskoje Ozero=Pskov, Lake- (EN)	5	Id	58.00N	28.00 E
Psunj	14	Le	45.24N	17.20 E
Ptič	16	Fc	52.09N	28.52 E
Ptolemaïs	15	Ei	40.31N	21.41 E
Ptuj	14	Jd	46.25N	15.52 E
Pua-a, Cape-	65c	Aa	13.26S	172.43W
Puah, Pulau-	26	Hg	0.30S	122.34 E
Puapua	65c	Aa	13.34S	172.09W
Pucallpa	53	If	8.20S	74.30W
Pučež	7	Kh	56.59N	43.11 E
Pucheng [China]	27	Kf	27.55N	118.30 E
Pucheng [China]	27	Id	35.00N	109.38 E
Pucho	36	Cf	17.35S	16.30 E
Pucioasa	15	Id	45.05N	25.25 E
Pučišća	14	Kg	43.21N	16.44 E
Puck	10	Ob	54.44N	18.27 E
Pucka, Zatoka-	10	Ob	54.40N	18.35 E
Pudasjärvi	7	Gd	65.23N	27.00 E
Pudož	19	Dc	61.50N	36.32 E
Pudukkottai	25	Ff	10.23N	78.49 E
Puebla [2]	47	Ee	18.50N	98.00W
Puebla, Sierra de-	48	Kh	19.50N	97.00W
Puebla de Alcocer	13	Gf	38.59N	5.15W
Puebla de Don Fabrique	13	Jg	37.58N	2.26W
Puebla de Guzmán	13	Eg	37.37N	7.15W
Puebla de Sanabria	13	Fb	42.03N	6.38W
Puebla de Trives	13	Eb	42.20N	7.15W
Puebla de Zaragoza	39	Jh	19.03N	98.12W
Pueblo	39	If	38.16N	104.37W
Pueblo Libertador	55	Cj	30.13S	59.23W
Pueblo Nuevo [Mex.]	48	Gf	23.23N	105.23W
Pueblo Nuevo [Ven.]	49	Mh	11.58N	69.55W
Pueblo Nuevo Tiquisate	49	Bf	14.17N	91.22W
Pueblo Viejo, Laguna de-	48	Kf	22.10N	97.55W
Puelches	56	Ge	38.09S	65.55W
Puenteáreas	13	Db	42.11N	8.30W
Puente de la Reina	13	Kb	42.40N	1.49W
Puentedeume	13	Da	43.24N	8.10W
Puente-Genil	13	Hg	37.23N	4.47W
Puentelarrá	13	Ib	42.45N	3.03W
Puec Point	65a	Ab	21.54N	160.04W
Pu'er	27	Hg	23.00N	101.00 E
Puerca, Punta-	51a	Cb	18.15N	65.35W
Puerco, Rio-	45	Ci	34.22N	107.50W
Puerco River	46	Ji	34.52N	110.05W
Puerto Abente	55	Df	22.55S	57.43W
Puerto Acosta	54	Eg	15.32S	69.15W
Puerto Adela	55	Eg	24.33S	54.22W
Puerto Aisén	53	Ij	45.24S	72.42W
Puerto Alegre	54	Ff	13.53S	61.36W
Puerto Ángel	47	Ee	15.40N	96.29W
Puerto Arista	48	Mj	15.56N	93.48W
Puerto Armuelles	47	Hg	8.17N	82.52W
Puerto Asís	54	Cc	0.29N	76.32W
Puerto Ayacucho	53	Je	5.40N	67.35W
Puerto Ayora	54a	Ab	0.45S	90.23W
Puerto Barrios	39	Kh	15.43N	88.36W
Puerto Bermejo	55	Ch	26.56S	58.30W
Puerto Berrío	54	Db	6.30N	74.25W
Puerto Boyacá	54	Db	5.45N	74.29W
Puerto Caballo	55	Ce	20.12S	58.12W
Puerto Cabello	53	Jd	10.28N	68.01W
Puerto Cabezas	47	Hf	14.02N	83.23W
Puerto Carreño	53	Je	6.12N	67.22W
Puerto Casado	56	Ib	20.20S	57.55W
Puerto Colombia	49	Jh	10.59N	74.57W
Puerto Colón	55	Df	23.11S	57.33W
Puerto Constanza	55	Ck	33.50S	59.03W
Puerto Cooper	56	Ib	23.03S	57.43W
Puerto Cortés [C.R.]	49	Fi	8.58N	83.32W
Puerto Cortés [Hond.]	39	Kh	15.48N	87.56W
Puerto Cumarebo	54	Ea	11.29N	69.21W
Puerto de Eten	54	Ce	6.56S	79.52W
Puerto de la Cruz	32	Dd	28.23N	16.33W
Puerto de Lajas, Cerro-	47	Cc	28.59N	107.02W
Puerto del Rosario	32	Ed	28.30N	13.52W
Puerto de Mazarrón	13	Kg	37.34N	1.15W
Puerto de San José	47	Ff	13.55N	90.49W
Puerto Deseado	53	Jj	47.45S	65.55W
Puerto de Sóller	13	Oe	39.48N	2.41 E
Puerto Escondido [Mex.]	47	Ee	15.48N	96.57W
Puerto Escondido [Mex.]	48	De	25.48N	111.20W
Puerto Esperanza [Arg.]	55	Eh	26.01S	54.39W
Puerto Esperanza [Par.]	55	Ce	20.26S	58.06W
Puerto Estrella	49	Lg	12.14N	71.13W
Puerto Fonciere	55	Df	22.29S	57.48W
Puerto Francisco de Orellana	54	Cd	0.27S	76.57W
Puerto Frey	55	Bb	14.42S	61.10W
Puerto Gaitán	54	Dc	4.20N	72.10W
Puerto General Díaz	55	Eg	25.12S	54.32W
Puerto Goya	55	Ci	29.09S	59.20W
Puerto Grether	54	Fg	17.12S	64.21W
Puerto Guarani	55	De	21.18S	57.55W
Puerto Heath	54	Ef	12.30S	68.40W
Puerto Huasco	56	Fc	28.28S	71.14W
Puerto Huitoto	54	Dc	0.18N	74.03W
Puerto Iguazú	56	Jc	25.34S	54.34W
Puerto Indio	55	Eg	24.52S	54.29W
Puerto Ingeniero Ibañez	56	Fg	46.18S	71.56W
Puerto Isabel	55	Dd	18.11S	57.37W
Puerto Jesús	49	Eh	10.07N	85.16W
Puerto Juárez	49	Kg	21.11N	86.49W
Puerto la Concordia	54	Dc	2.38N	72.47W
Puerto la Cruz	53	Jd	10.13N	64.38W
Puerto Leguízamo	53	If	0.12S	74.46W
Puerto Lempira	49	Ff	15.15N	83.46W
Puerto Libertad	47	Bc	29.55N	112.43W
Puerto Limón [Col.]	54	Cc	1.02N	76.32W
Puerto Limón [Col.]	54	Dc	3.23N	73.30W
Puertollano	13	Hf	38.41N	4.07W
Puerto Lopez	47	Jh	4.06N	72.58W
Puerto López	49	Lh	11.56N	71.17W
Puerto Lumbreras	13	Kg	37.34N	1.49W
Puerto Madero	48	Mj	14.44N	92.25W
Puerto Madryn	56	Gf	42.46S	65.03W
Puerto Magdalena	48	Ce	24.35N	112.05W
Puerto Maldonado	53	Jg	12.36S	69.11W
Puerto Marangatú	55	Eg	24.39S	54.21W
Puerto Mayor Otaño	55	Eh	26.19S	54.44W
Puerto Mihanovich	55	De	20.52S	57.59W
Puerto Monte Lindo	55	Df	23.57S	57.12W
Puerto Montt	53	Ij	41.28S	72.57W
Puerto Morelos	48	Pg	20.50N	86.52W
Puerto Mutis	54	Cb	6.14N	77.25W
Puerto Naranjito	55	Eh	26.57S	55.18W
Puerto Nariño	54	Ec	4.56N	67.48W
Puerto Natales	53	Ik	51.44S	72.31W
Puerto Nuevo	55	Ce	20.33S	58.03W
Puerto Nuevo, Punta-	51a	Bb	18.30N	66.21W
Puerto Ordaz	54	Fb	8.22N	62.41W
Puerto Padre	49	Ic	21.12N	76.36W
Puerto Páez	54	Eb	6.13N	67.28W
Puerto Peñasco	47	Bb	31.20N	113.33W
Puerto Piña	49	Hj	7.35N	78.10W
Puerto Pinasco	56	Ib	22.43S	57.50W
Puerto Piritu	50	Dg	10.04N	65.03W
Puerto Plata	47	Je	19.48N	70.41W
Puerto Presidente Stroessner	55	Eg	25.33S	54.39W
Puerto Princesa	22	Ni	9.44N	118.44 E
Puerto Quijarro	55	Dc	17.47S	57.46W
Puerto Real	13	Fh	36.32N	6.11W
Puerto Rico [5]	39	Mh	18.15N	66.30W
Puerto Rico	38	Mh	18.15N	66.30W
Puerto Rico [Arg.]	56	Jc	26.48S	54.59W
Puerto Rico [Bol.]	54	Ef	11.05S	67.38W
Puerto Rico [Col.]	54	Cc	1.54N	75.10W
Puerto Rico Trench (EN)	3	Bg	20.00N	66.00W
Puerto Rondón	54	Db	6.18N	71.06W
Puerto San José	55	Eg	25.32S	54.50W
Puerto Santa Cruz	53	Jk	50.09S	68.30W
Puerto Sastre	56	Ib	22.06S	57.59W
Puerto Siles	54	Ef	12.48S	65.05W
Puerto Suárez	53	Kg	18.57S	57.51W
Puerto Tacurú Pytá	55	Df	23.49S	57.09W
Puerto Tirol	55	Ch	27.23S	59.05W
Puerto Tres Palmas	55	Dg	21.43S	57.58W
Puerto Triunfo	55	Eg	26.45S	55.06W
Puerto Vallarta	47	Cd	20.37N	105.15W
Puerto Varas	56	Ff	41.19S	72.59W
Puerto Victoria	55	Eh	26.20S	54.39W
Puerto Viejo	49	Eh	10.26N	83.59W
Puerto Villamizar	49	Ki	8.19N	72.26W
Puerto Villazón	55	Ba	13.32S	61.57W
Puerto Wilches	54	Db	7.20N	73.54W
Puerto Ybapobó	55	Df	23.42S	57.12W
Pueu	65e	Fc	17.44S	149.13W
Pugačev	19	Ee	52.03N	48.48 E
Puget Sound	46	Dc	48.00N	122.30W
Puglia = Apulia (EN) [2]	14	Ki	41.15N	16.15 E
Pu He	28	Gd	41.21N	122.47 E
Puhja	8	Lf	58.13N	26.17 E
Puigcerdá	13	Nb	42.26N	1.56 E
Puigmal	13	Ob	42.23N	2.07 E
Puir	20	Jf	53.10N	141.25 E
Puisaye, Collines de la-	11	Jg	47.35N	3.18 E
Puisieux	12	Ed	50.07N	2.42 E
Pujehum	34	Cd	7.21N	11.42W
Pujeşti	15	Kc	46.25N	27.29 E
Puji → Wugong	27	Ie	34.15N	108.14 E
Pujiang	28	Ei	29.28N	119.53 E
Pujili	54	Cd	0.57S	78.42W
Puka	15	Cg	42.03N	19.54 E
Pukaki, Lake-	62	Df	44.05S	170.10 E
Pukalani	65a	Ec	20.50N	156.21W
Pukapuka Atoll	57	Kf	10.53S	165.49W
Pukapuka Atoll [W.F.]	57	Nf	14.49S	138.48W
Pukaruha Atoll	57	Nf	18.20S	137.02W
Pukatawagan	42	He	55.44N	101.19W
Pukchin	28	Hd	40.12N	125.45 E
Pukch'ŏng	27	Mc	40.14N	128.19 E
Pukega, Pointe-	64h	Ab	13.17S	176.13W
Pukekohe	62	Fb	37.12S	174.54 E
Pukemiro	62	Fb	37.37S	175.01 E
Pukeuri Junction	62	Df	45.02S	171.02 E
Pukšenga	7	Je	63.36N	41.55 E
Puksoozero	7	Ie	62.38N	40.32 E
Puksubaek-san	28	Id	40.42N	127.15 E
Pula [It.]	14	Ck	39.01N	9.00 E
Pula	14	Hf	44.52N	13.50 E
Pula, Capo di-	14	Dl	38.59N	9.01 E
Pulandian → Xinjin	27	Ld	39.24N	121.59 E
Pulap Atoll	57	Fd	7.39N	149.25 E
Pulaski [Tn.-U.S.]	44	Dh	35.12N	87.02W
Pulaski [Va.-U.S.]	44	Gg	37.03N	80.47W
Pulau	26	Kh	5.50S	138.15 E
Pulau Halura	26	Hi	10.19S	120.11 E
Pulau Irian/New Guinea	57	Fe	5.00S	140.00 E
Pulau Sapudi	26	Fh	7.06S	114.20 E
Puławy	10	Re	51.25N	21.57 E
Pulborough	12	Bd	50.57N	0.31W
Pulheim	12	Ic	51.00N	6.48 E
Pulkau	14	Kb	48.43N	16.21 E
Pulkkila	7	Fd	64.16N	25.52 E
Pullman	43	Db	46.44N	117.10W
Pulo Anna Island	57	Ed	4.40N	131.58 E
Pulog, Mount-	21	Oh	16.36N	120.54 E
Pulpito, Punta-	48	Dd	26.30N	111.30W
Pulsano	14	Lj	40.23N	17.21 E
Pułtusk	10	Rd	52.43N	21.05 E
Pülümür	24	Hc	39.30N	39.54 E
Pulusuk Island	57	Fd	6.42N	149.19 E
Puluwat Atoll	57	Fd	7.22N	149.11 E
Puma Yumco	27	Ff	28.35N	90.20 E
Pumpénai/Pumpenaj	8	Ki	55.53N	24.25 E
Pumpenaj/Pumpénai	8	Ki	55.53N	24.25 E
Pumpkin Creek	46	Mc	46.15N	105.45W
Puná, Isla-	54	Bd	2.50S	80.10W
Punākha	25	Hc	27.37N	89.52 E
Punaluu	65a	Fd	19.08N	155.30W
Punch	25	Eb	33.46N	74.06 E
Punda Milia	37	Ed	22.40S	31.05 E
Pune (Poona)	22	Jh	18.32N	73.52 E
Pünel	24	Md	37.33N	49.07 E
Pungan	18	Hd	40.45N	70.50 E
P'unggi	28	Jf	36.52N	128.32 E
Púngoè	37	Ec	19.50S	34.48 E
P'ungsan	28	Jd	40.40N	128.05 E
Punia	36	Ec	1.28S	26.27 E
Punitaqui	56	Fd	30.50S	71.16W
Punjab [3]	25	Fb	31.00N	76.00 E
Punjab	21	Jf	30.00N	74.00 E
Punjab [3]	25	Eb	30.00N	74.00 E
Punkaharju	8	Mc	61.48N	29.24 E
Punkalaidun	8	Jc	61.07N	23.06 E
Puno	53	Ig	15.50S	70.02W
Puno [2]	54	Ef	15.00S	70.00W
Punta, Cerro de-	47	Ke	18.10N	66.36W
Punta Alta	53	Ji	38.53S	62.04W
Punta Arenas	53	Ik	53.09S	70.55W
Punta Cardón	54	Da	11.38N	70.14W
Punta de Mata	50	Eh	9.43N	63.38W
Punta Gorda [Blz.]	47	Ge	16.07N	88.48W
Punta Gorda [Fl.-U.S.]	44	Fl	26.56N	82.03W
Punta Gorda [Nic.]	49	Fh	11.31N	83.47W
Punta Gorda, Bahía de-	49	Fh	11.15N	83.45W
Punta Gorda, Río-	49	Fh	11.30N	83.47W
Punta Indio	55	Dl	35.16S	57.14W
Punta Prieta	47	Bc	28.58N	114.17W
Puntarenas [3]	49	Ei	9.00N	83.15W
Puntarenas	39	Ki	9.58N	84.50W
Punta Róbalo	49	Fi	9.02N	82.15W
Punto Fijo	54	Da	11.42N	70.13W
Puolanka	7	Gd	64.52N	27.40 E
Puolo Point	65a	Bb	21.54N	159.36W
Puqi	27	Jf	29.43N	113.52 E
Puquio	54	Df	14.42S	74.08W
Purace, Volcán-	54	Cc	2.21N	76.23W
Purari	60	Ci	7.52S	145.10 E
Purcell Mountains	42	Fg	49.55N	116.15W
Purdy Islands	57	Fe	2.53S	146.20 E
Purgatoire River	45	Eg	38.04N	103.10W
Puri	25	He	19.48N	85.51 E
Purificación [3]	47	Ed	23.58N	98.42W
Purikari Neem/Purikarinem	8	Ke	59.36N	25.35 E
Purikarinem/Purikari Neem	8	Ke	59.36N	25.35 E
Purmani/Puurmani	8	Lf	58.30N	26.14 E
Purmerend	11	Kb	52.31N	4.57 E
Purna [India]	25	Fe	19.07N	77.02 E
Purna [India]	25	Fd	21.05N	76.00 E
Purnač	7	Jc	67.00N	40.15 E
Pūrnia	25	Hc	25.47N	87.28 E
Purukcahu	26	Fg	0.35S	114.35 E
Puruliya	25	Hd	23.20N	86.22 E
Puruni River	50	Gi	6.00N	59.12W
Purus, Rio-	52	Jf	3.42S	61.28W
Puruvesi	7	Gf	61.50N	29.25 E
Purwakarta	26	Eh	6.34S	107.26 E
Purwokerto	26	Eh	7.25S	109.14 E
Pusala Dağı	24	Ed	37.12N	32.54 E
Pusan	22	Of	35.06N	129.03 E
Pusan Si [2]	28	Jg	35.10N	129.05 E
Pushi He	28	Hd	40.17N	124.43 E
Puškin	19	Dd	59.43N	30.24 E
Puškino	16	Pj	39.28N	48.33 E
Puškino	16	Od	51.14N	46.59 E
Puškino	7	Ih	56.02N	37.53 E
Puškinskije Gory	8	Mh	56.59N	28.59 E
Pušlahta	7	Id	64.48N	36.33 E
Püspökladány	10	Ri	47.19N	21.07 E
Püssi/Pjussi	8	Le	59.17N	26.57 E
Pusteci	15	Di	40.47N	20.54 E
Pusteria, Val-/Pustertal	14	Gd	46.45N	12.20 E
Pustertal/Pusteria, Val-	14	Gd	46.45N	12.20 E
Pustomyty	10	Tg	49.37N	23.59 E
Pustoška	7	Gh	56.20N	29.22 E
Putao	25	Jc	27.21N	97.24 E
Putaruru	62	Fc	38.03S	175.47 E
Putian	27	Kf	25.32N	119.01 E
Putignano	14	Lj	40.51N	17.07 E
Putila	15	Ip	48.00N	25.07 E
Putivl	16	Hd	51.22N	33.55 E
Putjatin	28	Lc	42.52N	132.25 E
Putla de Guerrero	48	Ki	17.02N	97.56W
Putna	15	Kd	45.34N	27.30 E
Putna	15	Ib	47.52N	25.37 E
Putnok	10	Qh	48.18N	20.26 E
Puto	63a	Ba	5.41S	154.43 E
Putorana, Plato-=Putoran Mountains (EN)	21	Lc	69.00N	95.00 E
Putoran Mountains (EN)= Putorana, Plato-	21	Lc	69.00N	95.00 E
Puttalam	25	Fg	8.02N	79.49 E
Putte	12	Gc	51.04N	4.38 E
Puttelange-aux-Lacs	12	Ie	49.03N	6.56 E
Putten	12	Hb	52.16N	5.35 E
Putten	12	Gc	51.50N	4.15 E
Puttgarden, Burg auf Fehmarn-	10	Hb	54.30N	11.13 E
Püttlingen	12	Ie	49.17N	6.53 E
Putumayo [2]	54	Cc	0.30N	76.00W
Putumayo, Rio-	52	Jf	3.07S	67.58W
Putuo (Shenjiamen)	28	Gj	29.57N	122.18 E
Putussibau	26	Ff	0.50N	112.56 E
Puu Kukui	65a	Ec	20.54N	156.35W
Puulavesi	5	Ic	61.50N	26.40 E
Puumala	7	Gf	61.32N	28.11 E
Puu o Umi	65a	Fc	20.05N	155.42W
Puurmani/Purmani	8	Lf	58.30N	26.14 E
Puurs	12	Gc	51.05N	4.17 E
Puuwai	65a	Ab	21.54N	160.12W
Puyallup	46	Dc	47.11N	122.18W
Puyang	27	Jd	35.41N	115.00 E
Puy-de-Dôme [3]	11	Ii	45.40N	3.00 E
Puy-l'Evêque	11	Hj	44.30N	1.08 E
Puymorens, Col de-	11	Hl	42.34N	1.49 E
Puyo	54	Cd	1.29S	77.58W
Puysegur Point	62	Bg	46.10S	166.37 E
Pwani [3]	36	Gd	7.30S	39.00 E
Pweto	31	Ji	8.28S	28.54 E
Pwllheli	9	Ii	52.53N	4.25W
Pyapon	25	Je	16.17N	95.41 E
Pyhäjärvi	7	Fe	63.40N	25.59 E
Pyhäjärvi [Fin.]	7	Ff	61.00N	22.20 E
Pyhäjärvi [Fin.]	7	Fe	63.35N	25.57 E
Pyhäjärvi [Fin.]	8	Kc	62.45N	25.25 E
Pyhäjärvi [Fin.]	8	Jc	61.30N	23.35 E
Pyhäjoki	7	Fd	64.28N	24.13 E
Pyhäjoki	7	Fd	64.28N	24.14 E
Pyhäntä	7	Gd	64.06N	26.19 E
Pyhäranta	8	Id	60.57N	21.27 E
Pyhäselkä	7	Ge	62.30N	29.40 E
Pyhaselkä	8	Mb	62.26N	29.58 E
Pyhätunturi	7	Gc	67.01N	27.09 E
Pyhävesi	8	Lc	61.25N	26.35 E
Pyhävuori	8	Ib	62.17N	21.38 E
Pyhrnpaß	14	Ic	47.38N	14.18 E
Pyhtää/Pyttis	7	Gf	60.29N	26.32 E
Pyinmana	22	Lh	19.44N	96.13 E
Pylos (EN) = Pílos	15	Em	36.56N	21.40 E
Pyltsamaa/Põltsamaa	8	Lf	58.23N	26.08 E
Pyltsamaa/Põltsamaa	7	Fg	58.39N	25.59 E
Pylva/Põlva	7	Gg	58.04N	27.06 E
Pymatuning Reservoir	44	Ge	41.37N	80.30W
P'yŏngan-Namdo [2]	28	Ie	39.20N	126.00 E
P'yŏngan-Pukto [2]	28	Hd	40.00N	125.15 E
P'yŏnggang	27	Md	38.25N	127.17 E
P'yŏngsan	27	Md	38.20N	126.24 E
P'yongt'aek	28	If	36.59N	127.05 E
P'yŏngyang	22	Of	39.01N	125.45 E
P'yŏngyang Si [2]	28	He	39.04N	125.50 E
Pyramiden	41	Nc	77.54N	16.41 E
Pyramid Lake	43	Dc	40.00N	119.35W
Pyramid Mountains	45	Bj	32.00N	108.30W
Pyrénées=Pyrenees (EN)	5	Gg	42.40N	1.00 E
Pyrenees (EN)=Pirineos	5	Gg	42.40N	1.00 E
Pyrenees (EN)= Pyrénées	5	Gg	42.40N	1.00 E
Pyrenees (EN)=Serralada Pirinenca	5	Gg	42.40N	1.00 E
Pyrénées-Atlantiques [3]	11	Fk	43.15N	0.50W
Pyrénées-Orientales [3]	11	Il	42.30N	2.20 E
Pyrzyce	10	Kc	53.10N	14.55 E
Pyšma	19	Gd	57.08N	66.18 E
Pytalovo	7	Gh	57.06N	27.59 E
Pyttegga	8	Bb	62.13N	7.42 E
Pyttis/Pyhtää	7	Gf	60.29N	26.32 E
Pyu	25	Je	18.29N	96.26 E
Pyzaspea/Pöõsaspea Neem	8	Je	59.15N	23.25 E
Pyzdry	10	Nd	52.11N	17.41 E

Q

Qā', Wādī al-	24	Hi	27.04N	38.34 E
Qābis [3]	32	Ic	33.00N	9.30 E
Qābis	31	Ie	33.53N	10.07 E
Qābis, Khalīj-=Gabès, Gulf of-(EN)	30	Ie	34.00N	10.25 E
Qabr Hūd	35	Hb	16.09N	49.34 E
Qāderābād	24	Og	30.17N	53.16 E
Qādir Karam	24	Ke	35.12N	44.53 E
Qaḑub	23	Hg	12.38N	53.57 E
Qa'emshahr	24	Od	36.30N	52.55 E
Qafşah	31	He	34.25N	8.48 E
Qafşah [3]	32	Ic	34.30N	9.00 E
Qa'fūr	14	Dn	36.20N	9.19 E
Qagan	27	Kb	49.16N	118.04 E
Qagan Moron He	28	Ec	43.13N	119.02 E
Qagan Nur	27	Jc	43.20N	112.58 E
Qagan Nur [China]	28	Bd	41.33N	113.48 E
Qagan Nur [China]	27	Jc	43.25N	114.50 E
Qagan Nur [China]	28	Hb	45.14N	124.17 E
Qagan Nur→Zhengxiangbai Qi	27	Jc	42.16N	114.59 E
Qagan Us→Dulan	22	Lf	36.29N	98.29 E
Qagcheng/Xiangcheng	27	Gf	28.56N	99.46 E
Qahar Youyi Houqi (Bayan Qagan)	28	Bd	41.28N	113.10 E
Qahar Youyi Qianqi (Togrog Ul)	28	Bd	40.46N	113.13 E
Qahar Youyi Zhongqi	28	Bd	41.15N	112.36 E
Qahd, Wādī-	24	Ii	26.13N	40.49 E
Qaidam He	27	Gd	36.48N	95.50 E
Qaidam Pendi=Tsaidam Basin (EN)	27	Fd	37.00N	95.00 E

Index Symbols

- [1] Independent Nation
- [2] State, Region
- [3] District, County
- [5] Municipality
- [5] Colony, Dependency
- Continent
- Physical Region
- Historical or Cultural Region
- Mount, Mountain
- Volcano
- Hill
- Mountains, Mountain Range
- Hills, Escarpment
- Plateau, Upland
- Pass, Gap
- Plain, Lowland
- Delta
- Salt Flat
- Valley, Canyon
- Crater, Cave
- Karst Features
- Depression
- Polder
- Desert, Dunes
- Forest, Woods
- Heath, Steppe
- Oasis
- Cape, Point
- Coast, Beach
- Cliff
- Peninsula
- Isthmus
- Sandbank
- Island
- Atoll
- Rock, Reef
- Islands, Archipelago
- Rocks, Reefs
- Coral Reef
- Well, Spring
- Geyser
- River, Stream
- Waterfall Rapids
- River Mouth, Estuary
- Lake
- Salt Lake
- Intermittent Lake
- Reservoir
- Swamp, Pond
- Canal
- Glacier
- Ice Shelf, Pack Ice
- Ocean
- Sea
- Gulf, Bay
- Strait, Fjord
- Lagoon
- Bank
- Seamount
- Tablemount
- Ridge
- Shelf
- Basin
- Escarpment, Sea Scarp
- Fracture
- Trench, Abyss
- National Park, Reserve
- Point of Interest
- Recreation Site
- Cave, Cavern
- Historic Site
- Ruins
- Wall, Walls
- Church, Abbey
- Temple
- Scientific Station
- Airport
- Port
- Lighthouse
- Mine
- Tunnel
- Dam, Bridge

Name	Page	Grid	Lat.	Long.
Qala'an Naḩl	35	Ec	13.38N	34.57 E
Qalāt	23	Kc	32.07N	66.54 E
Qal'at Abū Ghār	24	Lg	30.25N	46.09 E
Qal'at al Akhḑar	23	Ed	28.06N	37.05 E
Qal 'at al Marqab	24	Fe	35.09N	35.57 E
Qal'at al Mu'azzam	24	Gi	27.45N	37.31 E
Qal'at aş Şanam	14	Co	35.46N	8.21 E
Qal'at Bīshah	22	Gh	20.00N	42.36 E
Qal'at Dīzah	24	Kd	36.11N	45.07 E
Qal'at Şāliḩ	24	Lg	31.31N	47.16 E
Qal'at Sukkar	24	Lg	31.53N	46.56 E
Qal'eh Asgar	24	Qh	29.30N	56.35 E
Qal'eh Kūh	24	Mf	33.00N	49.10 E
Qal'eh Mūreh	24	Pe	35.35N	55.58 E
Qal'eh-ye Now	23	Jc	34.59N	63.08 E
Qal'eh-ye Sahar	24	Mg	31.40N	48.33 E
Qalīb ash Shuyūkh	23	Gd	29.12N	47.55 E
Qallābāt	35	Fc	12.58N	36.09 E
Qalmarz, Godār-e-	24	Qf	33.26N	56.14 E
Qalyūb	24	Dg	30.11N	31.13 E
Qamata	37	Df	31.58S	27.24 E
Qamdo	22	Lf	31.15N	97.12 E
Qamīnis	33	Dc	31.40N	20.01 E
Qamsar	24	Nf	33.45N	51.26 E
Qamūdah	32	Ic	35.00N	9.21 E
Qamūdah [3]	32	Ic	34.50N	9.20 E
Qânâq/Thule	67	Od	77.35N	69.40W
Qandahār [3]	23	Kc	31.00N	65.45 E
Qandahār	22	If	31.35N	65.45 E
Qandala	35	Hc	11.23N	49.53 E
Qangdin Gol	28	Cc	43.27N	115.03 E
Qanţarat al Faḩş	14	Dn	36.23N	9.54 E
Qapqal	27	Dc	43.48N	80.47 E
Qaqortoq/Julianehåb	67	Nc	60.50N	46.10W
Qarā Dāgh	24	Lc	38.48N	47.13 E
Qārah	33	Ed	29.37N	26.30 E
Qarah Būlāq	24	Ke	34.32N	45.12 E
Qarah Dagh	24	Jd	37.00N	43.30 E
Qarah Tappah	24	Ke	34.25N	44.56 E
Qarānqū	24	Ld	37.23N	47.43 E
Qardo	31	Lh	9.30N	49.03 E
Qareh Āghāj	24	Ld	36.46N	48.46 E
Qareh Sū [Iran]	23	Ib	37.00N	56.50 E
Qareh Sū [Iran]	23	Hc	34.52N	51.25 E
Qareh Ẕīā'Od Dīn	24	Kc	38.53N	45.02 E
Qarkilik/Ruoqiang	22	Kf	39.02N	88.00 E
Qarnayn, Jazīrat al-	24	Oj	24.56N	52.52 E
Qarnayt, Jabal-	23	Fe	21.02N	40.22 E
Qarqan/Qiemo	22	Kf	38.08N	85.32 E
Qarqan He	21	Kf	39.30N	88.15 E
Qarqannah, Juzur-= Kerkennah Islands (EN)	30	Ie	34.44N	11.12 E
Qartājannah	14	En	36.51N	10.20 E
Qārūn, Birkat-	33	Fd	29.28N	30.40 E
Qaryat Abū Nujaym	33	Cc	30.35N	15.24 E
Qaryat al Gharab	24	Kg	31.27N	44.48 E
Qaryat al Qaddāḩīyah	33	Cc	31.22N	15.14 E
Qaryat al 'Ulyā	23	Gd	27.33N	47.42 E
Qaryat az Zarrūq	33	Cc	32.22N	15.09 E
Qaryat az Zuwaytīnah	33	Dc	30.58N	20.07 E
Qaşabah, Ra's al-	24	Fh	28.02N	34.38 E
Qaşabāt, Hanshīr al-	14	Dn	36.24N	9.54 E
Qasigiánguit/Christianshåb	41	Ge	68.45N	51.30W
Qaşr al Azraq	24	Gg	31.53N	36.49 E
Qasr Al Hayr	24	Ge	34.23N	37.36 E
Qaşr al Qarahbullī	33	Bc	32.45N	13.43 E
Qaşr 'Amij	24	If	33.30N	41.45 E
Qaşr Bū Hādī	33	Cc	31.03N	16.40 E
Qaşr Burqu'	24	Gf	32.37N	37.58 E
Qasr-e Shīrīn	23	Gc	34.31N	45.35 E
Qaşr Farāfirah	31	Jf	27.15N	28.10 E
Qasr Ḩamān	23	Ge	20.50N	45.50 E
Qaşr Qārūn	24	Dh	29.25N	30.25 E
Qaşş Abū Sa'īd	24	Bi	27.00N	27.35 E
Qatana	24	Gf	33.26N	36.05 E
Qaţar	21	Hg	25.30N	51.15 E
Qaţar [1]	22	Hg	25.30N	51.15 E
Qatlīsh	24	Qd	37.50N	57.19 E
Qaţrānī, Jabal-	24	Dh	29.41N	30.35 E
Qatrūyeh	24	Ph	29.09N	54.43 E
Qattara Depression (EN)= Qaţţārah, Munkhafaḑ al-	30	Je	30.00N	27.30 E
Qawām al Hamzah	24	Kg	31.43N	44.58 E
Qawz Abu Ḑulū'	35	Eb	16.55N	32.30 E
Qawz Rajab	35	Fb	16.04N	35.34 E
Qaysān	35	Ec	10.45N	34.48 E
Qayyārah	24	Je	35.48N	43.17 E
Qazaqstan = Kazakhstan (EN)	19	Gf	48.00N	68.00 E
Qazvīn [Iran]	22	Gf	36.16N	50.00 E
Qazvīn [Iraq]	24	Je	34.21N	42.05 E
Qeqertarssuaq/Godhavn	67	Nc	69.20N	53.35W
Qeshm	24	Qi	26.58N	56.16 E
Qeshm	23	Id	26.45N	55.45 E
Qeydār	24	Md	36.07N	48.35 E
Qeys, Jazīreh-ye-	23	Hd	26.32N	53.58 E
Qezel Owzan	23	Gb	36.45N	49.22 E
Qian'an [China]	28	Ed	40.01N	118.42 E
Qian'an [China]	28	Hb	44.58N	124.01 E
Qianfangzi	28	Ad	40.01N	111.23 E
Qian Gorlos (Quianguozhen)	27	Lb	45.05N	124.52 E
Qian He	28	Dh	32.55N	117.10 E
Qianjiang [China]	27	Ig	23.37N	108.58 E
Qianjiang [China]	28	Bi	30.25N	112.54 E
Qianjiang [China]	27	If	29.30N	108.45 E
Qianning/Gartar	27	He	30.27N	101.29 E
Qian Shan	27	Lc	40.35N	123.00 E
Qiansuo	27	Hf	25.27N	100.41 E
Qianwei	27	Hf	29.08N	103.56 E
Qianxi [China]	27	If	27.03N	106.04 E
Qianxi [China]	28	Ed	40.08N	118.19 E
Qianyang (Anjiang)	27	Jf	27.19N	110.13 E
Qiaojia	27	Hf	27.00N	103.00 E
Qiaowan	27	Gc	40.36N	96.42 E
Qibilī	32	Ic	33.42N	8.58 E
Qichun (Caojiahe)	28	Ci	30.15N	115.26 E
Qidaogou	28	Id	41.31N	126.18 E
Qidong	28	Fi	31.48N	121.39 E
Qiemo/Qarqan	22	Kf	38.08N	85.32 E
Qift	24	Ei	26.00N	32.49 E
Qijiang	27	If	29.00N	106.39 E
Qijiaojing	27	Fc	43.28N	91.36 E
Qike → Xunke	27	Mb	49.34N	128.28 E
Qili → Shitai	28	Di	30.12N	117.28 E
Qilian (Babao)	27	Hd	38.14N	100.15 E
Qilian Shan	27	Gd	39.12N	98.35 E
Qilian Shan	21	Lf	38.30N	100.00 E
Qimantag	27	Fd	37.00N	91.00 E
Qimen	27	Kf	29.57N	117.39 E
Qinā	31	Kf	26.10N	32.43 E
Qinā, Wādī-	24	Ei	26.12N	32.44 E
Qin'an	27	Ie	34.50N	105.35 E
Qingchengzi	28	Gd	40.44N	123.36 E
Qingchuan	27	Ie	32.32N	105.11 E
Qingdao=Tsingtao (EN)	22	Of	36.05N	120.21 E
Qingduizi	28	Fd	41.27N	121.52 E
Qingfeng	28	Cg	35.54N	115.07 E
Qinggang	27	Mb	46.41N	126.03 E
Qinggil/Qinghe	27	Fb	46.43N	90.24 E
Qinghai Hu=Koko Nor (EN)	21	Mf	37.00N	100.20 E
Qinghai Sheng (Ch'ing-hai Sheng)=Tsinghai (EN) [2]	27	Gd	36.00N	96.00 E
Qing He	28	Hc	42.16N	124.10 E
Qinghe/Qinggil	27	Fb	46.43N	90.24 E
Qinghe (Gexianzhuang)	28	Cf	37.03N	115.39 E
Qinghemen	28	Fd	41.45N	121.25 E
Qingjian	27	Jd	37.10N	110.09 E
Qingjiang	22	Nf	33.31N	119.03 E
Qing Jiang	27	Je	30.24N	111.30 E
Qingjiang (Zhangshuzhen)	27	Kf	28.02N	115.31 E
Qingkou → Ganyu	28	Eg	34.50N	119.07 E
Qinglong	28	Ed	40.26N	118.58 E
Qinglong He	28	Ee	39.51N	118.51 E
Qingshan	28	Ci	30.39N	114.27 E
Qingshuihe	27	Jd	39.56N	111.41 E
Qingshui Jiang	27	If	27.11N	109.48 E
Qingtian	27	Lf	28.12N	120.17 E
Qingxian	28	De	38.35N	116.48 E
Qingxu	28	Bf	37.36N	112.21 E
Qingyang [China]	27	Id	36.01N	107.48 E
Qingyang [China]	28	Di	30.38N	117.50 E
Qingyuan	27	Lc	42.06N	124.56 E
Qingyuan (Nandaran)	28	Ce	38.46N	115.29 E
Qingyun (Xiejiaji)	28	Df	37.46N	117.22 E
Qing Zang Gaoyuan=Tibet, Plateau of- (EN)	21	Kf	32.30N	87.00 E
Qin He	28	Bg	35.01N	113.25 E
Qinhuangdao	27	Kg	40.00N	119.32 E
Qin Ling	21	Mf	34.00N	108.00 E
Qinshui	28	Bg	35.41N	112.10 E
Qintong	28	Fh	32.39N	120.06 E
Qinxian	28	Bf	36.46N	112.42 E
Qinyang	28	Bg	35.05N	112.56 E
Qinyuan	28	Bf	36.29N	112.20 E
Qinzhou	27	Ig	22.02N	108.30 E
Qionghai (Jiaji)	27	Jh	19.25N	110.28 E
Qionglai	27	He	30.24N	103.28 E
Qiongzhou Haixia	21	Ng	20.10N	110.15 E
Qipan Guan	27	Ie	32.45N	106.11 E
Qiqihar	22	Oe	47.21N	123.58 E
Qīr	24	Oh	28.29N	53.04 E
Qira	27	Dd	37.02N	80.53 E
Qiryat Gat	24	Fg	31.36N	34.46 E
Qiryat Shemona	24	Ff	33.13N	35.34 E
Qiryat Yam	24	Ff	32.51N	35.04 E
Qishn	23	Hf	15.26N	51.40 E
Qi Shui	28	Ci	30.09N	115.22 E
Qishuyan	28	Fi	31.41N	120.04 E
Qitai	22	Ke	44.01N	89.28 E
Qitaihe	27	Nb	45.49N	130.51 E
Qiuxian (Matou)	28	Cf	36.50N	115.10 E
Qixia	28	Ff	37.18N	120.50 E
Qixian [China]	28	Bf	37.23N	112.21 E
Qixian [China]	28	Cg	34.33N	114.46 E
Qixian (Zhaoge)	28	Cg	35.35N	114.12 E
Qiyang	27	Jf	26.44N	111.50 E
Qizhou	28	Ci	30.04N	115.20 E
Qogir Feng=Godwin Austen (EN)	21	Jf	35.53N	76.30 E
Qog Qi	27	Ic	41.31N	107.00 E
Qog Ul	27	Kc	44.50N	116.19 E
Qohrūd, Kūhhā-ye-	21	Hf	32.40N	53.00 E
Qoltag	27	Ec	42.20N	88.45 E
Qom	22	Hf	34.39N	50.54 E
Qom	24	Ne	34.48N	51.02 E
Qomolangma Feng=Everest, Mount- (EN)	21	Kg	27.59N	86.56 E
Qomrud	24	Ne	34.43N	51.04 E
Qomsheh	23	Hc	32.00N	51.50 E
Qondūz [3]	23	Kb	36.45N	68.30 E
Qondūz	22	If	36.45N	68.51 E
Qondūz	23	Kb	37.00N	68.16 E
Qoqek/Tacheng	22	Ke	46.45N	82.57 E
Qôrnoq	41	Gf	64.30N	51.19W
Qorveh	24	Le	35.10N	47.48 E
Qoşbeh-ye Naşşār	23	Gc	30.02N	48.27 E
Qoţbābād [Iran]	24	Oh	28.39N	53.37 E
Qoţbābād [Iran]	24	Qi	27.46N	56.06 E
Qoţūr	24	Kc	38.28N	44.25 E
Qotūr	24	Kc	38.46N	45.16 E
Quadda	31	Jh	8.04N	22.24 E
Quadros, Lagoa dos-	55	Gi	29.42S	50.05W
Quairading	59	Df	32.01S	117.25 E
Quakenbrück	10	Dd	52.41N	7.57 E
Quanah	45	Gi	34.18N	99.44W
Quanbao Shan	27	Je	34.08N	111.26 E
Quang Ngai	25	Le	15.07N	108.48 E
Quang Tri	25	Le	21.02N	106.29 E
Quan He	28	Ch	32.55N	115.52 E
Quanjiao	28	Eh	32.09N	118.16 E
Quan Long	25	Lg	9.11N	105.08 E
Quanzhou [China]	22	Ng	24.57N	118.35 E
Quanzhou [China]	27	Jf	26.01N	111.04 E
Qu'Appelle River	42	Hf	50.27N	101.19W
Quaraí	56	Id	30.23S	56.27W
Quaraí, Rio-	55	Dj	30.12S	57.36W
Quaregnon	12	Fd	50.26N	3.51 E
Quartu Sant'Elena	14	Dk	39.14N	9.11 E
Quartz Lake	42	Jb	70.57N	80.40W
Quartz Mountain	46	De	43.10N	122.40W
Quartzsite	46	Hj	33.40N	114.13W
Quatre, Isle-	51n	Bb	12.57N	61.15W
Quatsino Sound	46	Aa	50.25N	128.10W
Qūchān	22	Hf	37.06N	58.30 E
Qué	36	Ce	14.43S	15.06 E
Queanbeyan	59	Jg	35.21S	149.14 E
Québec	39	Le	46.49N	71.13W
Québec [3]	42	Kf	54.00N	72.00W
Quebó	55	Db	14.36S	56.04W
Quebra Anzol, Rio-	55	Id	19.09S	47.38W
Quebracho	55	Dj	31.57S	57.57W
Quebradillas	51a	Bb	18.28N	66.56W
Quedas do Iguaçu	55	Fg	25.31S	52.54W
Quedlinburg	10	He	51.47N	11.09 E
Queen, Cape -	42	Jd	64.43N	78.18W
Queen Alexandra Range	66	Jg	84.00S	168.00 E
Queen Bess, Mount -	42	Ff	51.18N	124.33W
Queenborough	12	Cc	51.25N	0.46 E
Queen Charlotte Islands	38	Gd	51.30N	129.00W
Queen Charlotte Sound	42	Ef	51.30N	129.30W
Queen Charlotte Strait	38	Gd	50.40N	127.25W
Queen Elizabeth Islands	38	Ib	79.00N	105.00W
Queen Elizabeth Range	66	Kg	83.20S	162.00 E
Queen Mary Land	66	Ge	69.00S	96.00 E
Queen Maud Gulf	38	Ic	68.25N	102.30W
Queen Maud Land (EN)	66	Cf	72.30S	12.00 E
Queen Maud Range	66	Lg	86.00S	160.00W
Queens Channel [Austl.]	59	Fb	14.45S	129.25 E
Queens Channel [N.W.T.-Can.]	42	Ha	76.11N	96.00W
Queensland	59	Id	22.00S	145.00 E
Queenstown [Austl.]	59	Jh	42.05S	145.33 E
Queenstown [Guy.]	50	Gi	7.12N	58.29W
Queenstown [N.Z.]	62	Cf	45.02S	168.40 E
Queenstown [S.Afr.]	31	Jl	31.52S	26.52 E
Queguay, Cuchilla del-	55	Dj	31.50S	57.30W
Queguay Grande, Río-	55	Ck	32.09S	58.09W
Queich	12	Ke	49.14N	8.23 E
Queimadas	54	Kf	10.58S	39.38W
Queiros	55	Ge	21.49S	50.13W
Quela	36	Cd	9.15S	17.05 E
Quelimane	31	Kj	17.51S	36.52 E
Quemado	45	Bi	34.20N	108.30W
Quemado de Güines	49	Gb	22.48N	80.15W
Quembo	36	De	14.57S	20.22 E
Quemú-Quemú	56	He	36.03S	63.33W
Quepos	49	Ei	9.25N	84.09W
Quequén	56	Ie	38.32S	58.42W
Quequén Grande, Río-	55	Cn	38.34S	58.43W
Quequén Salado, Río-	55	Bn	38.56S	60.31W
Quercy	11	Hj	44.15N	1.15 E
Querétaro [2]	47	Ed	21.00N	99.55W
Querétaro	39	Ig	20.36N	100.23W
Querobabi	48	Db	30.03N	111.01W
Quesada [C.R.]	49	Eh	10.19N	84.26W
Quesada [Sp.]	13	Ig	37.51N	3.04W
Queshan	27	Je	32.42N	114.04 E
Quesnel	42	Ff	52.59N	122.30W
Quesnel Lake	42	Ff	52.32N	121.05W
Questa	45	Dh	36.42N	105.36W
Quetena	54	Eh	22.10S	67.25W
Quetico Lake	45	Kb	48.37N	91.52W
Quetta	22	If	30.12N	67.00 E
Quevas, Cerro-	48	Dc	29.15N	111.20W
Quevedo	54	Cd	1.02S	79.27W
Queyras	11	Mj	44.44N	6.49 E
Quezaltenango	39	Jh	14.50N	91.31W
Quezaltenango [3]	49	Bf	14.45N	91.40W
Quezon	26	Ge	9.14N	117.56 E
Quezon City	22	Oh	14.38N	121.00 E
Qufu	28	Dg	35.35N	116.59 E
Quianguozhen → Qian Gorlos	27	Lb	45.05N	124.52 E
Quianshan	28	Di	30.38N	116.35 E
Quibala	36	Be	10.44S	14.59 E
Quibaxe	36	Bd	8.30S	14.36 E
Quibdó	54	Cb	5.42N	76.39W
Quiberon, Baie de-	11	Dg	47.32N	3.00W
Quiberon, Presqu'île de-	11	Cg	47.30N	3.08W
Quíbor	49	Mi	9.56N	69.37W
Quiché [3]	49	Bf	15.30N	90.55W
Quierschied	12	Je	49.19N	7.03 E
Quiha	35	Fc	13.28N	39.33 E
Quiindy	55	Dh	25.58S	57.16W
Quijarro	55	Cd	19.26S	58.08W
Quilá	48	Fe	24.23N	107.13W
Quilàn, Cabo-	56	Ff	43.16S	74.23W
Quillabamba	54	Df	12.49S	72.43W
Quillacollo	54	Eg	17.26S	66.17W
Quillagua	56	Gb	21.39S	69.33W
Quillan	11	Il	42.52N	2.11 E
Quillebeuf-sur-Seine	12	Ce	49.28N	0.31 E
Quillota	56	Fd	32.53S	71.16W
Quilmes	56	Id	34.44S	58.16W
Quilon	25	Fg	8.53N	76.36 E
Quilpie	59	Ie	26.37S	144.15 E
Quilqué	56	Fd	33.03S	71.27W
Quimarí, Alto de-	49	Ii	8.07N	76.23W
Quimbele	36	Cd	6.30S	16.14 E
Quimilí	56	Hc	27.38S	62.25W
Quimome	55	Ec	17.42S	61.16W
Quimome, Río-	55	Ec	17.36S	61.09W
Quimper	11	Ef	48.00N	4.06W
Quimperlé	11	Eg	47.52N	3.33W
Quinault River	46	Ec	47.23N	124.18W
Quincy [Ca.-U.S.]	46	Eg	39.56N	120.57W
Quincy [Fl.-U.S.]	44	Ej	30.37N	84.32W
Quincy [Il.-U.S.]	43	Id	39.56N	91.23W
Quincy [Ma.-U.S.]	44	Ld	42.15N	71.01W
Quincy [Wa.-U.S.]	46	Fc	47.14N	119.51W
Quindío [2]	54	Cc	4.30N	75.40W
Quingey	11	Lg	47.06N	5.53 E
Quinhagak	40	Ge	59.45N	161.43W
Qui Nhon	22	Mh	13.46N	109.14 E
Quiñihual	55	Bm	37.47S	61.36W
Quiniluban Group	26	Hd	11.27N	120.48 E
Quinn River	46	Ff	40.25N	119.00W
Quiñones	48	De	24.22N	111.25W
Quintanar de la Orden	13	Ie	39.34N	3.03W
Quintana Roo [2]	47	Ge	19.40N	88.30W
Quinze, Lac des-	44	Hb	47.30N	79.00W
Quionga	37	Gb	10.35S	40.33 E
Quipongo	36	Be	14.45S	14.05 E
Quirigua	49	Cf	15.18N	89.07W
Quirihue	56	Fe	36.17S	72.32W
Quirima	36	Ce	10.48S	18.09 E
Quirinópolis	54	Hg	18.32S	50.30W
Quiroga	13	Eb	42.29N	7.16W
Quiros, Cap-	63b	Cb	14.56S	167.01 E
Quisiro	49	Lh	10.53N	71.17W
Quissanga	37	Gb	12.25S	40.29 E
Quissico	37	Ed	24.43S	34.45 E
Quita Sueno Bank	47	Hf	14.20N	81.15W
Quitengues	36	Be	14.06S	14.05 E
Quiterage	37	Gb	11.45S	40.27 E
Quitéria, Rio-	55	Ge	20.16S	51.08W
Quitilipi	55	Bh	26.52S	60.13W
Quitman [Ga.-U.S.]	44	Fj	30.47N	83.33W
Quitman [Ms.-U.S.]	45	Lj	32.03N	88.43W
Quito	53	If	0.13S	78.30W
Quitovac	48	Cb	31.32N	112.42W
Quixadá	54	Kd	4.58S	39.01W
Quixeramobim	54	Ke	5.12S	39.17W
Qujiang	28	Cj	28.14N	115.46 E
Qu Jiang [China]	27	Kf	29.32N	119.31 E
Qu Jiang [China]	27	Ie	30.01N	106.24 E
Qujing	27	Hf	25.31N	103.45 E
Qul'ān, Jazā'ir-	24	Fj	24.22N	35.23 E
Qulansiyah	23	Hg	12.41N	53.29 E
Qulaybiah	32	Jb	36.51N	11.06 E
Qulbān al 'Isāwīyah	24	Gg	30.38N	37.53 E
Qulbān an Nabk al Gharbī	24	Gg	31.15N	37.26 E
Qumar He	21	Lf	34.42N	94.50 E
Qumarlêb	27	Ge	34.35N	95.18 E
Qunayfidhah, Nafūd-	24	Kj	24.45N	45.30 E
Quoi	64d	Ba	7.32N	151.59 E
Quoich	42	Id	63.56N	93.25W
Quorn	59	Hf	32.21S	138.03 E
Quqên/Jinchuan	27	He	31.02N	102.02 E
Quraitu	24	Ke	34.36N	45.30 E
Qurayyāt, Juzur-	32	Jb	35.48N	11.02 E
Qurbah	14	En	36.35N	10.52 E
Qurdūd	35	Dc	10.17N	29.56 E
Qūr Laban	24	Cg	30.23N	28.59 E
Qurunbāliyah	14	En	36.36N	10.30 E
Qūş	33	Fd	25.55N	32.45 E
Quşay'ir	35	Ic	14.55N	50.20 E
Qutdligssat	41	Gd	70.12N	53.00W
Quthing	37	Df	30.24S	27.42 E
Quţū	33	Hf	18.30N	41.04 E
Quwaiz	33	He	20.27N	44.53 E
Quxian	27	Kf	28.54N	118.53 E
Qüxü	27	Ff	29.23N	90.45 E
Quyang	28	Ce	38.37N	114.41 E
Quy Chau	25	Le	19.33N	105.06 E
Quzhou	28	Cf	36.47N	114.56 E
Qyteti Stalin → Kuçova	15	Ci	40.48N	19.54 E

R

Name	Page	Grid	Lat.	Long.
Raab	10	Ni	47.41N	17.38 E
Raahe/Brahestad	7	Fd	64.41N	24.29 E
Rääkkylä	8	Mb	62.19N	29.37 E
Raalte	12	Ib	52.23N	6.17 E
Raamsdonk	12	Gc	51.41N	4.54 E
Raanes Peninsula	42	Ia	78.20N	86.20W
Raasay, Island of-	9	Gd	57.25N	6.04W
Raasay, Sound of-	9	Gd	57.25N	6.05W
Raasiku/Raziku	8	Ke	59.22N	25.11 E
Rab	14	If	44.46N	14.46 E
Rab	14	If	44.45N	14.46 E
Rába	10	Ni	47.41N	17.38 E
Raba	10	Qf	50.09N	20.30 E
Raba	22	Nj	8.27S	118.46 E
Rabable	35	Hc	8.14N	48.18 E
Rabaçal	13	Ec	41.30N	7.12W
Rabat [Malta]	14	Io	35.50N	14.29 E
Rabat [Mor.]	31	Ge	34.02N	6.50W
Rabat-Salé [2]	32	Fc	34.02N	6.50W
Rabaul	58	Ge	4.12S	152.12 E
Rábca	10	Ni	47.41N	17.37 E
Rabenau	12	Kd	50.40N	8.52 E
Rabī', Ash Shallāl ar-= Fourth Cataract (EN)	30	Kg	18.47N	32.03 E
Rabiah	24	Jc	36.47N	42.07 E
Rábida, Monasterio de-	13	Fg	37.12N	6.55W
Rābigh	23	Ee	22.48N	39.02 E
Rabinal	49	Bf	15.06N	90.27W
Rabka	10	Pg	49.36N	19.56 E
Rabočeostrovsk	7	Id	64.59N	34.44 E
Rabyānah, Şaḩrā'-	30	Jf	24.30N	21.00 E
Rabyānah, Wāḩāt al-= Rebiana Oasis (EN)	33	De	24.14N	21.59 E
Răcăciuni	15	Jc	46.20N	26.59 E
Racalmuto	14	Hm	37.24N	13.44 E
Răcăşdia	15	Ee	44.59N	21.38 E
Racconigi	14	Bf	44.46N	7.46 E
Race, Cape-	38	Nb	46.40N	53.10W
Race Point	44	Ld	42.04N	70.14W
Rach Gia	22	Mh	10.01N	105.05 E
Rachid	32	Ef	18.48N	11.41W
Raciąż	10	Qd	52.47N	20.06 E
Racibórz	10	Of	50.06N	18.13 E
Racine	43	Jc	42.43N	87.48W
Ráckeve	10	Oi	47.10N	18.57 E
Racos	15	Ic	46.03N	25.30 E
Råda	8	Ed	60.00N	13.36 E
Radama, Iles-	37	Hb	14.00S	47.47 E
Radan	15	Ef	43.02N	21.30 E
Rădăuţi	15	Ib	47.51N	25.55 E
Radbuza	10	Jg	49.46N	13.24 E
Radeberg	10	Je	51.07N	13.55 E
Radebeul	10	Je	51.06N	13.39 E
Radeče	14	Jd	46.04N	15.11 E
Radehov	10	Uf	50.13N	24.43 E
Radenthein	14	Hd	46.48N	13.43 E
Radevormwald	12	Jc	51.12N	7.22 E
Radew	10	Lb	54.07N	15.50 E
Radford	44	Gg	37.07N	80.34W
Radnevo	15	Ig	42.18N	25.56 E
Radolfzell	10	Ei	47.44N	8.58 E
Radom [2]	10	Re	51.25N	21.10 E
Radom	6	Ie	51.25N	21.10 E
Radomir	15	Fg	42.33N	22.58 E
Radomka	10	Re	51.43N	21.26 E
Radomsko	10	Pe	51.05N	19.25 E
Radomyšl	16	Fd	50.29N	29.14 E
Radomyśl Wielki	10	Rf	50.12N	21.16 E
Radoškoviči	8	Lj	54.12N	27.17 E
Radotín	10	Kg	49.59N	14.22 E
Radovanu	15	Je	44.12N	26.31 E
Radoviš	15	Fh	41.38N	22.28 E
Radøy	8	Ad	60.40N	5.00 E
Radstadt	14	Hc	47.23N	13.27 E
Radun	10	Vb	54.02N	25.07 E
Radunia	10	Ob	54.25N	18.45 E
Raduša	14	Lg	43.52N	17.29 E
Radvaniči	10	Ue	51.59N	24.09 E
Radviliškis	7	Fi	55.50N	23.33 E
Radymno	10	Sg	49.57N	22.48 E
Radziejów	10	Od	52.38N	18.32 E
Radzyń Podlaski	10	Se	51.48N	22.38 E
Rae	42	Fd	62.50N	116.00W
Rāe Bareli	25	Gc	26.13N	81.14 E
Rae Isthmus	42	Ic	66.55N	86.10W
Raesfeld	12	Ic	51.46N	6.51 E
Raeside, Lake-	59	Ee	29.30S	121.50 E
Raetihi	62	Fc	39.26S	175.17 E
Raevavae, Ile-	57	Mg	23.52S	147.40W
Raevski, Groupe-	61	Mc	16.45S	144.14W
Rāf, Jabal-	24	Hh	29.12N	39.48 E
Rafaela	53	Ji	31.17S	61.30W
Rafaï	35	Ce	4.58N	23.56 E
Rafḩā'	23	Fd	29.42N	43.30 E
Rafi	34	Fc	13.28N	4.10 E
Rāfkā	24	Qe	35.55N	57.36 E
Rafsanjān	23	Ic	30.24N	56.01 E
Räfsö/Reposaari	8	Ic	61.37N	21.27 E
Raga	31	Jh	8.28N	25.41 E
Ragay Gulf	26	Hd	13.30N	122.45 E
Ragged Island	49	Jb	22.12N	75.44W
Ragged Island Range	47	Id	22.42N	75.55W
Ragged Point	51q	Bb	13.10N	59.25W
Raglan	62	Fb	37.48S	174.52 E
Raguencau	44	Ma	49.04N	68.32W
Ragusa	14	In	36.55N	14.44 E
Raguva	8	Ki	55.30N	24.45 E
Raha	26	Hg	4.51S	122.43 E
Raḩá, Ḩarrat ar-	24	Gi	27.40N	36.40 E
Rahad al Bardī	35	Cc	11.18N	23.53 E
Rahama	34	Gc	10.25N	8.41 E
Rahaţ, Ḩarrat-	33	He	23.00N	40.05 E
Rahat Dağı	15	Ml	37.08N	29.49 E
Rahden	12	Kb	52.26N	8.37 E
Rāhgāmāti	25	Id	22.38N	92.12 E
Rahīmyār Khan	25	Ec	23.25N	70.18 E
Rahmanovskije Ključi	19	If	49.35N	86.35 E
Rahmet	19	Gf	49.19N	65.16 E
Råholt	8	Dd	60.16N	11.11 E
Rahouia	13	Ni	35.32N	1.01 E
Rahov	16	De	48.02N	24.18 E
Rahrbach, Kirchhundem-	12	Jc	51.02N	7.59 E
Raia	13	Df	39.00N	8.17W
Raiatea, Ile-	57	Lf	16.50S	151.25W
Raices	55	Cj	31.54S	59.16W
Rāichūr	22	Jh	16.12N	77.22 E
Raiganj	25	Hc	25.37N	88.07 E
Raigarh	25	Gd	21.54N	83.24 E
Raijua, Pulau-	26	Hi	10.37S	121.36 E
Rainbow Peak	46	Hd	44.55N	115.17W
Rainier, Mount-	38	Ge	46.52N	121.46W
Rainy Lake	43	Ib	48.42N	93.10W
Rainy River	45	Ib	48.43N	94.29W
Rainy River	45	Ib	48.50N	94.41W
Raipur	22	Kg	21.14N	81.38 E
Raisi, Punta-	14	Hl	38.11N	13.06 E
Raisio/Reso	7	Ff	60.29N	22.11 E
Raita Bank (EN)	60	Mb	25.25N	169.30W
Raja Ampat, Kepulauan-	26	Jg	0.50S	130.25 E
Rājahmundry	22	Kh	16.59N	81.47 E
Rajakoski	7	Gb	68.59N	29.07 E
Rajang	21	Ni	2.07N	111.12 E
Rājapālaiyam	25	Fg	9.27N	77.34 E
Rājasthān [3]	25	Ec	26.00N	74.00 E
Rājasthān Canal	25	Eb	31.10N	75.00 E
Rajbiraj	25	Hc	26.30N	86.50 E
Rajčihinsk	20	Hg	49.43N	129.27 E
Rajevski	17	Gi	54.04N	54.56 E
Rājgarh	25	Fc	28.38N	75.23 E
Rajgródzkie, Jezioro-	10	Sc	53.45N	22.38 E
Rajka	10	Ni	48.00N	17.12 E
Rajkot	22	Jg	22.18N	70.47 E
Raj Nāndgaon	25	Gd	21.06N	81.02 E
Rajony respublikanskogo podčinenija → Čujskaja oblast	19	Hg	42.30N	73.50 E

Index Symbols

- [1] Independent Nation
- [2] State, Region
- [3] District, County
- Municipality
- Colony, Dependency
- Continent
- Physical Region
- Historical or Cultural Region
- Mount, Mountain
- Volcano
- Hill
- Mountains, Mountain Range
- Hills, Escarpment
- Plateau, Upland
- Pass, Gap
- Plain, Lowland
- Delta
- Salt Flat
- Valley, Canyon
- Crater, Cave
- Karst Features
- Depression
- Polder
- Desert, Dunes
- Forest, Woods
- Heath, Steppe
- Oasis
- Cape, Point
- Coast, Beach
- Cliff
- Peninsula
- Isthmus
- Sandbank
- Island
- Atoll
- Rock, Reef
- Islands, Archipelago
- Rocks, Reefs
- Coral Reef
- Well, Spring
- Geyser
- River, Stream
- Waterfall Rapids
- River Mouth, Estuary
- Lake
- Salt Lake
- Intermittent Lake
- Reservoir
- Swamp, Pond
- Canal
- Glacier
- Ice Shelf, Pack Ice
- Ocean
- Sea
- Gulf, Bay
- Strait, Fjord
- Lagoon
- Bank
- Seamount
- Tablemount
- Ridge
- Shelf
- Basin
- Escarpment, Sea Scarp
- Fracture
- Trench, Abyss
- National Park, Reserve
- Point of Interest
- Recreation Site
- Cave, Cavern
- Historic Site
- Ruins
- Wall, Walls
- Church, Abbey
- Temple
- Scientific Station
- Airport
- Port
- Lighthouse
- Mine
- Tunnel
- Dam, Bridge

Index Symbols

[1] Independent Nation	Historical or Cultural Region
[2] State, Region	Mount, Mountain
[3] District, County	Volcano
[4] Municipality	Hill
[5] Colony, Dependency	Mountains, Mountain Range
■ Continent	Hills, Escarpment
[X] Physical Region	Plateau, Upland

Pass, Gap · Plain, Lowland · Delta · Salt Flat · Valley, Canyon · Crater, Cave · Karst Features
Depression · Polder · Desert, Dunes · Forest, Woods · Heath, Steppe · Oasis · Cape, Point
Coast, Beach · Cliff · Peninsula · Isthmus · Sandbank · Island · Atoll
Rock, Reef · Islands, Archipelago · Rocks, Reefs · Coral Reef · Well, Spring · Geyser · River, Stream
Waterfall Rapids · River Mouth, Estuary · Lake · Salt Lake · Intermittent Lake · Reservoir · Swamp, Pond
Canal · Glacier · Ice Shelf, Pack Ice · Ocean · Sea · Gulf, Bay · Strait, Fjord
Lagoon · Bank · Fracture · Seamount · Tablemount · Ridge · Shelf · Basin
Escarpment, Sea Scarp · Trench, Abyss · National Park, Reserve · Point of Interest · Recreation Site · Cave, Cavern
Historic Site · Ruins · Wall, Walls · Church, Abbey · Temple · Scientific Station · Airport
Port · Lighthouse · Mine · Tunnel · Dam, Bridge

Retourne 12 Ge 49.26N 4.02 E
Rétság 10 Pi 47.56N 19.08 E
Rettihovka 28 Lb 44.10N 132.45 E
Retz 14 Jc 48.45N 15.57 E
Retz, Pays de- 11 Eg 47.12N 1.58W
Réunion=Reunion (EN) 30 Mk 21.06S 55.36 E
Réunion=Reunion (EN) [5] 31 Mk 21.06S 55.36 E
Reunion (EN)=Réunion 30 Mk 21.06S 55.36 E
Reunion (EN)=Réunion [5] 31 Mk 21.06S 55.36 E
Reus 13 Nc 41.09N 1.07 E
Reusel 12 Hc 51.22N 5.10 E
Reuss 14 Cc 47.28N 8.14 E
Reut 16 Ff 47.15N 29.09 E
Reutlingen 10 Fh 48.29N 9.13 E
Reutte 14 Ed 47.29N 10.43 E
Revda 17 Ih 56.48N 59.57 E
Revda 7 Ic 67.57N 34.32 E
Revel 11 Hk 43.28N 2.00 E
Revelstoke 42 Ff 50.59N 118.12W
Revermont 11 Lh 46.27N 5.25 E
Revillagigedo 40 Me 55.35N 131.23W
Revillagigedo, Islas- 38 Hh 19.00N 111.30W
Revin 11 Ke 49.56N 4.38 E
Revoljucii, Pik- 18 Ie 38.33N 72.28 E
Revsundssjön 8 Fb 62.50N 15.15 E
Rewa 63d Bc 18.08S 178.33 E
Rewa 25 Gd 24.32N 81.18 E
Rewāri 25 Fc 28.11N 76.37 E
Rex, Mount- 66 Qf 74.54S 75.57W
Rexburg 46 Je 43.49N 111.47W
Rexpoëde 12 Ed 50.56N 2.32 E
Rey 23 Hb 35.35N 51.25 E
Rey, Arroyo del- 55 Ci 29.12S 59.36W
Rey, Isla del- 47 Ig 8.22N 78.55W
Rey, Laguna del- 48 Hd 27.00N 103.25W
Rey Bouba 34 Hd 8.40N 14.11 E
Reyes, Point- 46 Dg 38.00N 123.01W
Reyhanli 24 Gd 36.18N 36.32 E
Reykjalid 7a Cb 65.39N 16.55W
Reykjanes 5 Dc 63.49N 22.43W
Reykjanes Ridge (EN) 3 Dc 62.00N 27.00W
Reykjavik 6 Dc 64.09N 21.57W
Reynolds Range 59 Gd 22.20S 132.50 E
Reynosa 39 Jg 26.07N 98.18W
Reyssouze 11 Kh 46.27N 4.54 E
Rež 17 Kh 57.54N 62.20 E
Rež 17 Jh 57.23N 61.24 E
Rezé 11 Eg 47.12N 1.34W
Rezekne/Rēzekne 6 Id 56.30N 27.19 E
Rēzekne/Rezekne 6 Id 56.30N 27.19 E
Rezelm, Lacul- 15 Le 44.54N 28.57 E
Rezina 16 Ff 47.43N 28.58 E
Reznas, Ozero-/Rēznas Ezers 8 Lh 56.20N 27.30 E
Rēznas Ezers/Reznas, Ozero- 8 Lh 56.20N 27.30 E
Rezovo 15 Lh 41.59N 28.02 E
Rezvān 24 Qi 27.34N 56.06 E
Rezve 15 Lh 41.59N 28.01 E
Rgotina 15 Fe 44.01N 22.17 E
Rhaetian Alps (EN)=Alpi Retiche 14 Dd 46.30N 10.00 E
Rhaetian Alps (EN)= Rätische Alpen 14 Dd 46.30N 10.00 E
Rhallamane 30 Ff 23.15N 10.00W
Rhauderfehn 12 Ja 53.08N 7.34 E
Rhaunen 12 Je 49.51N 7.21 E
Rheda-Wiedenbrück 10 Ee 51.51N 8.18 E
Rheden 12 Ib 52.01N 6.01 E
Rheden-Dieren 12 Ib 52.03N 6.08 E
Rheider Land 12 Ja 53.13N 7.18 E
Rhein 12 Ke 49.52N 8.07 E
Rhein=Rhine (EN) 5 Ge 51.52N 6.02 E
Rheinberg 12 Ic 51.33N 6.36 E
Rheine 10 Dd 52.17N 7.27 E
Rheinfall 14 Cc 47.41N 8.38 E
Rheinfelden 10 Di 47.34N 7.48 E
Rheingaugebirge 12 Jd 50.05N 8.00 E
Rheinisches Schiefergebirge =Rhenish Slate Mountains (EN) 5 Ge 50.25N 7.10 E
Rheinland-Pfalz=Rhineland-Palatinate (EN) [2] 10 Cf 50.00N 7.00 E
Rheinsberg 10 Ic 53.06N 12.53 E
Rheinstetten 12 Kf 48.58N 8.18 E
Rhenen 12 Hc 51.58N 5.35 E
Rhenish Slate Mountains (EN)=Rheinisches Schiefergebirge 5 Ge 50.25N 7.10 E
Rheris 32 Gc 30.41N 4.57W
Rheydt, Mönchengladbach- 12 Ic 51.10N 6.27 E
Rhin=Rhine (EN) 5 Ge 51.52N 6.02 E
Rhine (EN)=Rein 5 Ge 51.52N 6.02 E
Rhine (EN)=Rhein 5 Ge 51.52N 6.02 E
Rhine (EN)=Rhin 5 Ge 51.52N 6.02 E
Rhine (EN)=Rijn 5 Ge 51.52N 6.02 E
Rhine Bank (EN) 56 Ji 50.30S 53.30W
Rhineland-Palatinate (EN)= Rheinland Pfalz [2] 10 Cf 50.00N 7.00 E
Rhinelander 43 Jb 45.38N 89.25W
Rhinluch 10 Id 52.50N 12.50 E
Rhino Camp 36 Fb 2.58N 31.24 E
Rhiou 13 Mi 35.59N 0.53 E
Rhir, Cap- 32 Fc 30.38N 9.54W
Rho 14 De 45.32N 9.02 E
Rhode Island [2] 43 Mc 41.40N 71.30W
Rhode Island Sound 44 Le 41.25N 71.15W
Rhodes (EN) = Ródhos 6 Ih 36.26N 28.13 E
Rhodes (EN) = Ródhos 5 Ih 36.10N 28.00 E
Rhodesia→Zimbabwe [1] 31 Jj 20.00S 30.00 E
Rhodes Peak 46 Hc 46.41N 114.47W
Rhodope Mountains (EN) = Rodopi 5 Ig 41.30N 24.30 E
Rhomara 13 Hi 35.10N 4.57W
Rhön 10 Gf 50.25N 10.05 E
Rhondda 9 Jj 51.40N 3.30W
Rhône 5 Gg 43.20N 4.50 E
Rhône [3] 11 Ki 46.00N 4.30 E
Rhône au Rhin, Canal du- 11 Lg 47.06N 5.19 E
Rhourd el Baguel 32 Ic 31.24N 6.57 E
Rhue 11 Ii 45.23N 2.29 E
Rhum 9 Ge 57.00N 6.20W
Rhyl 9 Jh 53.19N 3.29W
Riaba 34 Ge 3.24N 8.42 E
Riacho de Santana 54 Jf 13.37S 42.57W
Riangnom 35 Ed 5.55N 30.01 E
Riaño 13 Gb 42.58N 5.01W
Riánsares 13 Ie 39.32N 3.18W
Říany 10 Kg 50.00N 14.39 E
Rias Altas 13 Da 43.30N 8.30W
Rias Bajas 13 Db 42.30N 9.00W
Riau [3] 26 Df 1.00N 102.00 E
Riau Archipelago (EN)= Riau, Kepulauan- 21 Mi 1.00N 104.30 E
Riau Kepulauan-=Riau Archipelago (EN) 21 Mi 1.00N 104.30 E
Riaza 13 Ic 41.17N 3.28W
Riaza 13 Ic 41.42N 3.55W
Ribadavia 13 Db 42.17N 8.08W
Ribadeo 13 Ea 43.32N 7.02W
Ribadesella 13 Ga 43.28N 5.04W
Ribagorza/La Ribagorça 13 Mb 42.15N 0.30 E
Ribamar 54 Jd 2.33S 44.03W
Ribas do Rio Pardo 55 Fe 20.27S 53.46W
Ribatejo 13 De 39.15N 8.30W
Ribáuè 37 Fb 14.57S 38.17 E
Ribble 9 Kh 53.44N 2.50W
Ribe 7 Bi 55.21N 8.46 E
Ribe [2] 8 Ci 55.35N 8.45 E
Ribécourt-Dreslincourt 12 Ee 49.31N 2.55 E
Ribeira [Braz.] 55 Hg 24.39S 49.00W
Ribeira [Sp.] 13 Db 42.33N 9.00W
Ribeira, Rio- 55 Ig 24.40S 47.24W
Ribeira Brava 32 Cf 16.37N 24.18W
Ribeira Grande 32 Bf 17.11N 25.04W
Ribeirão Prêto 53 Lh 21.10S 47.48W
Ribeirãozinho 55 Fc 16.22S 52.36W
Ribeiro Gonçalves 54 Ie 7.32S 45.14W
Ribemont 12 Fe 49.48N 3.28 E
Ribera 14 Hm 37.30N 13.16 E
Ribérac 11 Gi 45.15N 0.20 E
Riberalta 53 Jg 10.59S 66.06W
Ribnica 14 Ie 45.44N 14.44 E
Ribnitz-Damgarten 10 Ib 54.15N 12.28 E
Ricardo Flores Magón 48 Fc 29.58N 106.58W
Riccia 14 Ii 41.29N 14.50 E
Riccione 14 Gg 43.59N 12.39 E
Rice Lake 44 Hc 44.08N 78.13W
Rich 32 Gc 32.15N 4.30W
Richan 45 Jb 49.59N 92.49W
Richard Collinson Inlet 42 Gb 72.45N 113.00W
Richards 42 Ec 69.20N 134.35W
Richard's Bay 31 Kk 28.47S 32.06 E
Richardson 45 Hj 32.57N 96.44W
Richardson Mountains 38 Fc 65.00N 135.20W
Richard Toll 34 Bb 16.28N 15.41W
Richât, Guel er- 32 Ee 21.07N 11.24W
Richel 12 Ha 53.18N 5.10 E
Richel Griend 12 Ha 53.18N 5.15 E
Richelieu 11 Gg 47.01N 0.19 E
Richer 45 Hb 49.39N 96.28W
Richey 46 Mc 47.39N 105.04W
Richfield 43 Ed 38.46N 112.05W
Richibucto 44 Ob 46.41N 64.52W
Richland 43 Db 46.17N 119.18W
Richland Center 45 Ke 43.22N 90.21W
Richmond [Austl.] 59 Id 20.44S 143.08 E
Richmond [Ca.-U.S.] 43 Cd 37.57N 122.22W
Richmond [Eng.-U.K.] 9 Lg 54.24N 1.44W
Richmond [In.-U.S.] 43 Kd 39.50N 84.54W
Richmond [Ky.-U.S.] 43 Kd 37.45N 84.18W
Richmond [N.Z.] 62 Ed 41.21S 173.11 E
Richmond [S.Afr.] 37 Cf 31.23S 23.56 E
Richmond [Tx.-U.S.] 45 Il 29.35N 95.46W
Richmond [Va.-U.S.] 39 Lf 37.30N 77.28W
Richmond, Mount- 62 Ed 41.28S 173.24 E
Richmond Hill 44 Hd 43.52N 79.27W
Richmond Peak 51n Ba 13.17N 61.13W
Richthofen, Mount- 45 Df 40.29N 105.57W
Rickmansworth 12 Bc 51.38N 0.28W
Ricobayo, Embalse de- 13 Gc 41.35N 5.50W
Ridā' 33 Hg 14.25N 44.50 E
Ridderkerk 12 Gc 51.52N 4.36 E
Ridgecrest 46 Gi 35.38N 117.36W
Ridgway 44 He 41.25N 78.45W
Riding Mountain 45 Fa 50.55N 100.25W
Riecito, Rio- 50 Bi 6.50N 68.51W
Ried 12 Ke 49.50N 8.25 E
Ried im Innkreis 14 Hb 48.13N 13.30 E
Riedlingen 10 Fh 48.09N 9.28 E
Riemst 12 Hd 50.48N 5.35 E
Ries 10 Gh 48.55N 10.40 E
Riesa 10 Je 51.18N 13.18 E
Riesco, Isla- 56 Fh 53.00S 72.30W
Riesi 14 Im 37.17N 14.05 E
Riet 30 Jk 29.00S 23.53 E
Rietavas/Retavas 8 Ii 55.43N 21.49 E
Rietberg 12 Kc 51.48N 8.26 E
Rietbron 37 Cf 32.54S 23.09 E
Rietfontein [Nam.] 37 Cd 21.58S 20.58 E
Rietfontein [S.Afr.] 37 Ce 26.44S 20.01 E
Rieti 14 Gh 42.24N 12.51 E
Rif 30 Ge 35.00N 4.00W
Rifle 45 Cg 39.32N 107.47W
Rifstangi 5 Eb 66.32N 16.12W
Rift Valley [3] 36 Gb 0.30N 36.00 E
Rift Valley 36 Kh 0.30N 36.00 E
Riga/Rīga 6 Id 56.57N 24.06 E
Rīga/Riga 6 Id 56.57N 24.06 E
Riga, Gulf of- (EN)=Rīgas Jūras Līcis 5 Id 57.30N 23.35 E
Riga, Gulf of- (EN)=Riia Laht 5 Id 57.30N 23.35 E
Riga, Gulf of- (EN)=Rižski Zaliv 5 Id 57.30N 23.35 E
Rigachikum 34 Gc 10.38N 7.28 E
Rīgas Jūras Līcis=Riga, Gulf of- (EN) 5 Id 57.30N 23.35 E
Rīgestān=Registan (EN) 21 If 31.00N 65.00 E
Riggins 46 Gd 45.25N 116.19W
Rigolet 42 Lf 54.10N 58.26W
Rig-Rig 35 Ac 14.16N 14.21 E
Rihand Sagar 25 Hd 24.05N 83.05 E
Riia Laht=Riga, Gulf of- (EN) 5 Id 57.30N 23.35 E
Riihimäki 7 Ff 60.45N 24.46 E
Riiser-Larsen-Halvøya 66 De 68.55S 34.00 E
Riito 48 Ba 32.10N 114.45W
Riječki zaljev = Rijeka, Gulf of- (EN) 14 Ie 45.15N 14.25 E
Rijeka 6 Hf 45.21N 14.24 E
Rijeka, Gulf of- (EN)= Riječki zaljev 14 Ie 45.15N 14.25 E
Rijksmuseum Kröller-Müller 12 Hb 52.06N 5.47 E
Rijn=Rhine (EN) 5 Ge 51.52N 6.02 E
Rijssen 12 Ib 52.18N 6.31 E
Rijswijk 12 Gb 52.03N 4.20 E
Rika 10 Th 48.08N 23.20 E
Rikā, Wādī ar- 33 He 22.25N 44.50 E
Rikubetsu 29a Cb 43.28N 143.43 E
Rikuzentakada 28 Pe 39.01N 141.38 E
Rila 15 Gh 42.08N 23.33 E
Rila 15 Gg 42.08N 23.08 E
Riley 46 Fe 43.32N 119.29W
Riley, Mount- 45 Ck 31.58N 107.05W
Rilski Manastir 15 Gg 42.08N 23.20 E
Rima 30 Hg 13.04N 5.10 E
Rimatara, Ile- 57 Lg 22.38S 152.51W
Rimava 10 Qh 48.15N 20.21 E
Rimavská Şobota 10 Qh 48.23N 20.01 E
Rimbo 7 Eg 59.45N 18.22 E
Rimé 35 Bc 14.02N 18.03 E
Rimforsa 8 Ff 58.08N 15.40 E
Rimini 14 Gf 44.04N 12.34 E
Rimito/Rymättylä 8 Jd 60.25N 21.55 E
Rîmnic 15 Kd 45.32N 27.31 E
Rîmnicu Sărat 15 Kd 45.23N 27.03 E
Rîmnicu Vîlcea 15 Hd 45.06N 24.22 E
Rimouski 39 Me 48.27N 68.32W
Rimše/Rimšė 8 Li 55.30N 26.33 E
Rimšė/Rimše 8 Li 55.30N 26.33 E
Rinbung 27 Ef 29.15N 89.52 E
Rincon 50 Bf 12.14N 68.20W
Rincón 51a Ab 18.21N 67.16W
Rincón, Bahia de- 51a Bc 17.57N 66.19W
Rincón del Bonete, Lago Artificial de- 56 Id 32.45S 56.00W
Rincón de Romos 48 Hf 22.14N 102.18W
Rindal 7 Be 63.03N 9.13 E
Ringe 8 Di 55.14N 10.29 E
Ringebu 8 Dc 61.31N 10.10 E
Ringerike 8 Dd 60.05N 10.15 E
Ringgold Isles 57 Jf 16.15S 179.25W
Ringim 34 Gc 12.09N 9.10 E
Ringkøbing [2] 8 Ch 56.10N 8.45 E
Ringkøbing 7 Bh 56.05N 8.15 E
Ringkøbing Fjord 7 Bi 56.00N 8.15 E
Ringládes 15 Dj 39.25N 20.04 E
Ringsjön 8 Ei 55.50N 13.30 E
Ringsted 7 Ci 55.27N 11.49 E
Ringvassøy 7 Eb 69.55N 19.15 E
Rinia 15 Il 37.25N 25.13 E
Rinjani, Gunung- 26 Gh 8.24S 116.28 E
Rinn Chathóir/Cahore Point 9 Gi 52.34N 6.11W
Rinn Dúain/Hook Head 9 Gi 52.07N 6.55W
Rinteln 10 Fd 52.11N 9.05 E
Rinya 10 Nk 45.57N 17.27 E
Rio Azul 55 Gg 25.43S 50.47W
Riobamba 53 If 1.40S 78.38W
Rio Branco 53 Jf 9.58S 67.48W
Río Branco 55 Fk 32.34S 53.25W
Rio Branco do Sul 55 Hg 25.10S 49.18W
Rio Brilhante 54 Hh 21.48S 54.33W
Río Bueno 56 Ff 40.19S 72.58W
Río Caribe 54 Fa 10.42N 63.07W
Río Chico 50 Dg 10.19N 65.59W
Rio Claro [Braz.] 55 If 22.24S 47.33W
Rio Claro [Trin.] 50 Fg 10.18N 61.11W
Río Colorado 56 He 39.01S 64.05W
Río Cuarto 53 Ji 33.08S 64.20W
Rio de Janeiro 53 Lh 22.54S 43.15W
Rio de Janeiro [2] 54 Jh 22.30S 42.30W
Río de Jesús 49 Gj 7.59N 81.10W
Río de Oro 32 Ee 24.00N 14.00W
Río de Oro 49 Ki 8.57N 73.23W
Río de Oro, Bahía de- 32 De 23.45N 15.50W
Rio do Sul 56 Kc 27.13S 49.39W
Rio Fortuna 55 Hi 28.06S 49.07W
Río Gallegos 53 Jk 51.37S 69.10W
Rio Grande 53 Ki 32.02S 52.05W
Río Grande [Arg.] 56 Gh 53.47S 67.42W
Río Grande [Nic.] 49 Dg 12.59N 86.34W
Río Grande [P.R.] 51a Cb 18.23N 65.50W
Rio Grande City 45 Gm 26.23N 98.49W
Río Grande de Añasco 51a Ab 18.17N 67.10W
Río Grande de Manati 51a Bb 18.29N 66.32W
Río Grande de Matagalpa 47 Hf 12.54N 83.32W
Rio Grande do Norte [2] 54 Ke 5.40S 36.00W
Rio Grande do Sul [2] 56 Jc 30.00S 54.00W
Rio Grande Rise (EN) 3 Cm 31.00S 35.00W
Riohacha 54 Da 11.32N 72.54W
Río Hato 49 Gi 8.23N 80.10W
Río Lagartos 48 Og 21.36N 88.10W
Rio Largo 54 Ke 9.29S 35.51W
Riom 11 Ji 45.54N 3.07 E
Rio Maior 13 De 39.20N 8.56W
Río Mayo 56 Fg 45.41S 70.16W
Riom-ès-Montagnes 11 Ii 45.17N 2.40 E
Rio Miranda 54 Gg 19.25S 57.20W
Río Mulatos 54 Eg 19.42S 66.47W
Ríon 15 Ek 38.18N 21.47 E
Río Negro [Chile] 56 Ff 40.47S 73.14W
Río Negro [Arg.] [2] 56 Gf 40.00S 67.00W
Rio Negro [Braz.] 56 Kc 26.06S 49.48W
Rio Negro [Braz.] 55 Dd 19.33S 56.32W
Río Negro [Ur.] [2] 55 Dk 32.45S 57.20W
Rio Negro, Pantanal do- 54 Gg 18.50S 56.00W
Rionero in Vulture 14 Jj 40.56N 15.40 E
Rioni 16 Lh 42.10N 41.38 E
Rio Novo 55 Dc 16.28S 56.30W
Rio Pardo 56 Jc 29.59S 52.22W
Rio Prêto, Serra do- 55 Gd 18.18S 50.42W
Río San Juan [3] 49 Eh 11.10N 84.30W
Río Segundo 56 Hd 31.40S 63.55W
Riosucio 54 Cb 7.27N 77.07W
Río Tercero 56 Hd 32.11S 64.06W
Rio Tinto 54 Ke 6.48S 35.05W
Rioverde 47 Dd 21.56N 100.01W
Rio Verde 54 Hg 17.43S 50.56W
Rio Verde, Serra do- 55 Fc 17.32S 52.25W
Rio Verde de Mato Grosso 54 Hg 18.56S 54.52W
Rio Verde do Sul 55 Ef 22.54S 55.27W
Rioz 11 Mg 47.25N 6.04 E
Říp 10 Kf 50.24N 14.18 E
Ripanj 15 De 44.38N 20.32 E
Ripley [Eng.-U.K.] 12 Aa 53.02N 1.24W
Ripley [Tn.-U.S.] 44 Ch 35.44N 89.33W
Ripley [W.V.-U.S.] 44 Gf 38.49N 81.44W
Ripoll 13 Ob 42.12N 2.12 E
Ripon 9 Lg 54.08N 1.31W
Riposto 14 Jm 37.44N 15.12 E
Ripple Mountain 46 Gb 49.02N 117.05W
Risan 15 Bg 42.31N 18.42 E
Risaralda [2] 54 Cb 5.00N 75.45W
Risbäck 7 Dd 64.42N 15.32 E
Rīshah, Wādī- 24 Kj 25.33N 44.05 E
Rī Shahr 24 Nh 28.55N 50.50 E
Rishiri 28 Pb 45.11N 141.15 E
Rishiri-Suidō 29a Ba 45.10N 141.30 E
Rishiri-Tō 27 Pb 45.11N 141.15 E
Rishiri-Yama 29a Ba 45.11N 141.15 E
Rīshmūk 24 Ng 31.15N 50.20 E
Rishon LeZiyyon 24 Fg 31.58N 34.48 E
Rising Star 45 Gj 32.06N 98.58W
Risle 11 Ge 49.26N 0.23 E
Risnjak 14 Ie 45.26N 14.37 E
Rîşnov 15 Id 45.35N 25.27 E
Risør 7 Bg 58.43N 9.14 E
Risoux, Mont- 11 Mh 46.36N 6.10 E
Risøyhamn 7 Db 69.00N 15.45 E
Riß 10 Fh 48.17N 9.49 E
Risti 7 Fg 59.03N 24.01 E
Ristiina 8 Lc 61.30N 27.16 E
Ristijärvi 7 Gd 64.30N 28.13 E
Ristna, Mys-/Ristna Neem 8 If 58.55N 21.55 E
Ristna Neem/Ristna, Mys- 8 If 58.55N 21.55 E
Rīsū 24 Qf 33.52N 57.28 E
Ritchie's Archipelago 25 If 12.14N 93.10 E
Ritidian Point 64c Ba 13.39N 144.51 E
Ritscher-Hochland 66 Bf 73.20S 9.30W
Ritter, Mount- 43 Dd 37.42N 119.20W
Ritterhude 12 Ka 53.11N 8.45 E
Rituerto 13 Jc 41.36N 2.22W
Ritzville 46 Fc 47.08N 118.23W
Riva-Bella, Ouistreham- 12 Be 49.17N 0.16W
Rivadavia [Arg.] 56 Hb 24.11S 62.53W
Rivadavia [Arg.] 56 Gd 33.11S 68.28W
Riva del Garda 14 Ee 45.53N 10.50 E
Rivas 39 Kh 11.26N 85.51W
Rivas [3] 49 Eh 11.25N 85.50W
Rive-de-Gier 11 Ki 45.22N 4.37 E
Rivellata, Punta di a- 11a Aa 42.35N 8.40 E
Rivera [2] 55 Ej 31.30S 55.15W
Rivera [Arg.] 56 He 37.12S 63.14W
Rivera [Ur.] 53 Ki 30.54S 55.31W
River Cess 34 Dd 5.27N 9.35W
Riverdale 45 Fc 47.30N 101.22W
Riverina 59 Jg 35.25S 145.30 E
River Inlet 42 Ef 51.41N 127.15W
Rivers [2] 34 Ge 4.50N 6.30 E
Rivers, Lake of the- 46 Mb 49.45N 105.45W
Riversdale [N.Z.] 62 Cf 45.54S 168.44 E
Riversdale [S.Afr.] 37 Cf 34.07S 21.15 E
Riverside 43 De 33.59N 117.22W
Riverton [N.Z.] 62 Bg 46.21S 168.00 E
Riverton [Wy.-U.S.] 43 Fc 43.02N 108.23W
Rivesaltes 11 Il 42.46N 2.52 E
Riviera Beach 44 Ge 26.47N 80.04W
Rivière-à-Pierre 44 Kb 46.58N 72.11W
Rivière-du-Loup 42 Kg 47.50N 69.32W
Rivière-Pilote 51h Bc 14.29N 60.54W
Rivière-Salée 51h Bb 14.32N 60.59W
Rivoli 14 Be 45.04N 7.31 E
Rivungo 36 Df 16.15S 22.00 E
Riwaka 62 Ed 41.05S 173.00 E
Riwoqê 27 Ge 31.13N 96.29 E
Rixensart 12 Gd 50.43N 4.35 E
Riyadh (EN)=Ar Riyāḍ 22 Gg 24.38N 46.43 E
Rize 23 Fa 41.02N 40.31 E
Rize, Gora- 18 Bf 37.48N 58.13 E
Rize Dağları 24 Ib 40.30N 40.50 E
Rizhao 27 Kd 35.27N 119.28 E
Rizokarpásso → Dipkarpas 24 Fe 35.36N 34.23 E
Rižskij Zaliv = Riga, Gulf of- (EN) 5 Id 57.30N 23.35 E
Rizzuto, Capo- 14 Ll 38.53N 17.05 E
Rjabovo 8 Md 60.17N 29.01 E
Rjapina/Räpina 8 Lf 58.03N 27.35 E
Rjazan 6 Je 54.38N 39.44 E
Rjazanovski 7 Ji 55.08N 39.35 E
Rjazanskaja Oblast [3] 19 Ee 54.30N 40.40 E
Rjažsk 6 Ke 53.43N 40.04 E
Rjukan 7 Bg 59.52N 8.34 E
Rjuven 8 Be 59.13N 7.10 E
Rkiz 32 Df 16.50N 15.20W
Røldal 8 Be 59.49N 6.48 E
Roa [Nor.] 8 Dd 60.17N 10.37 E
Roa [Sp.] 13 Ic 41.42N 3.55W
Road Town 47 Le 18.27N 64.37W
Roag, Loch- 9 Gc 58.16N 6.50W
Roan Antelope 36 Ee 13.08S 28.24 E
Roannais 11 Kh 46.05N 4.10 E
Roanne 11 Kh 46.02N 4.04 E
Roanoke 38 Lf 35.56N 76.43W
Roanoke [Al.-U.S.] 44 Ei 33.09N 85.22W
Roanoke [Va.-U.S.] 39 Lf 37.16N 79.57W
Roanoke Rapids 44 Ig 36.28N 77.40W
Roan Plateau 46 Kg 39.35N 108.55W
Roaringwater Bay 9 Dj 51.25N 9.30W
Roatán 49 De 16.18N 86.35W
Roatán, Isla de- 49 De 16.23N 86.30W
Robāţ [Iran] 24 Qd 37.55N 57.42 E
Robāţ [Iran] 24 Pg 30.04N 54.49 E
Robāţ-e-Khān 23 Ic 33.21N 56.02 E
Robāţ-e-Kord 24 Qf 33.45N 56.37 E
Robāţ Karīm 24 Ne 35.28N 51.05 E
Robbie Bank (EN) 61 Fb 11.03S 176.53W
Robe, Mount- 59 If 31.40S 141.20 E
Röbel 10 Ic 53.23N 12.36 E
Robert Lee 45 Fk 31.54N 100.29W
Roberts 55 Bl 35.09S 61.57W
Roberts, Mount- 59 Ke 28.13S 152.28 E
Roberts Creek Mountain 46 Gg 39.52N 116.18W
Robertsfors 7 Ed 64.11N 20.51 E
Robert S. Kerr Lake 45 Ii 35.25N 95.00W
Robertson 37 Bf 33.46S 19.50 E
Robertson Bay 66 Kf 71.25S 170.00 E
Robertson Range 59 Ed 23.10S 121.00 E
Robertsport 34 Cd 6.45N 11.22W
Roberval 42 Kg 48.31N 72.13W
Robi 35 Fd 7.38N 39.52 E
Robinson Crusoe (EN) = Robinson Crusoe, Isla- 52 Ii 33.38S 78.52W
Robinson Crusoe, Isla- = Robinson Crusoe (EN) 52 Ii 33.38S 78.52W
Robinson Range 59 De 25.45S 119.00 E
Robinson River 59 Hc 16.03S 137.16 E
Roboré 53 Kg 18.20S 59.45W
Rob Roy 63a Cb 7.23S 157.36 E
Robson, Mount- 38 Hd 53.07N 119.09W
Robstown 45 Hm 27.27N 97.40W
Roby 45 Fj 32.45N 100.23W
Roca, Cabo da- 5 Fh 38.47N 9.30W
Rocamadour 11 Hj 44.48N 1.38 E
Roca Partida, Isla- 47 Be 19.01N 112.02W
Roca Partida, Punta- 48 Lh 18.42N 95.10W
Rocas, Atol das- 52 Mf 3.52S 33.49W
Roccaraso 14 Ii 41.51N 14.05 E
Ročegda 15 Ec 62.42N 43.23 E
Rocha [2] 55 Fk 34.00S 54.00W
Rocha 56 Jd 34.29S 54.20W
Rochdale 9 Kh 53.38N 2.09W
Rochechouart 11 Gi 45.49N 0.49 E
Rochedo 55 Ed 19.57S 54.52W
Rochefort [Bel.] 11 Ld 50.10N 5.13 E
Rochefort [Fr.] 11 Fi 45.56N 0.59W
Rochefort-Han-sur-Lesse 12 Hd 50.08N 5.11 E
Rochelle 45 Lf 41.56N 89.04W
Rocher River 42 Gd 61.23N 112.45W
Roche's Bluff 51c c 16.42N 62.09W
Rochester [Eng.-U.K.] 9 Nj 51.24N 0.30 E
Rochester [In.-U.S.] 44 De 41.04N 86.13W
Rochester [Mn.-U.S.] 43 Ic 44.02N 92.29W
Rochester [N.H.-U.S.] 44 Ld 43.18N 70.59W
Rochester [N.Y.-U.S.] 39 Le 43.10N 77.36W
Rochlitzer Berg 10 Ie 51.05N 12.48 E
Rocigalgo 13 He 39.35N 4.35W
Rockall 5 Ed 57.35N 13.48W
Rockall Rise (EN) 5 Ed 57.00N 14.00W
Rock Creek Butte 46 Fd 44.49N 118.07W
Rockefeller Plateau 66 Ng 80.00S 135.00W
Rockenhausen 12 Je 49.38N 7.50 E
Rockford 43 Jc 42.17N 89.06W
Rockglen 46 Mb 49.10N 105.57W
Rockhampton 58 Gg 23.23S 150.31 E
Rock Hill 43 Ke 34.55N 81.01W
Rockingham [Austl.] 59 Df 32.17S 115.44 E
Rockingham [N.C.-U.S.] 44 Hh 34.56N 79.46W
Rock Island 43 Ic 41.30N 90.34W
Rockland 43 Nc 44.06N 69.06W
Rocklands Reservoir 59 Ig 37.15S 142.00 E
Rockledge 44 Gk 28.20N 80.43W
Rockneby 8 Gh 56.49N 16.20 E
Rockport 45 Hl 28.01N 97.04W
Rock River 45 Kf 41.29N 90.37W
Rock Sound 44 Im 24.53N 76.09W
Rock Spring 45 Fc 41.35N 109.13W
Rocksprings 45 Fk 30.01N 100.13W
Rockville [In.-U.S.] 44 Df 39.45N 87.15W
Rockville [Md.-U.S.] 44 If 39.05N 77.09W
Rockwood 44 Eh 35.52N 84.41W
Rocky Ford 45 Eg 38.03N 103.43W
Rocky Island Lake 44 Fb 46.56N 83.04W
Rocky Mount 43 Ld 35.56N 77.48W
Rocky Mountain 43 Eb 47.49N 112.49W
Rocky Mountain House 42 Gf 52.22N 114.55W
Rocky Mountains 38 He 48.00N 116.00W
Rocky Point [Blz.] 49 Cd 18.22N 88.06W
Rocky Point [Nam.] 37 Ac 19.01S 12.29 E
Rocroi 12 Ge 49.55N 4.31 E
Rodach 10 Gf 50.08N 10.52 E
Rodalben 12 Je 49.14N 7.38 E
Roda Velha, Rio- 55 Ja 12.27S 45.33W
Rødberg 8 Cd 60.16N 8.58 E
Rødby 8 Dj 54.42N 11.24 E
Rødby Havn, Rødby- 7 Ci 54.39N 11.21 E
Rødby-Rødby Havn 7 Ci 54.39N 11.21 E
Roddickton 42 Lf 50.51N 56.07W
Rødding 8 Ci 55.22N 9.04 E

Index Symbols

[1] Independent Nation
[2] State, Region
[3] District, County
[4] Municipality
[5] Colony, Dependency
Continent
Physical Region
Historical or Cultural Region
Mount, Mountain
Volcano
Hill
Mountains, Mountain Range
Hills, Escarpment
Plateau, Upland
Pass, Gap
Plain, Lowland
Delta
Salt Flat
Valley, Canyon
Crater, Cave
Karst Features
Depression
Polder
Desert, Dunes
Forest, Woods
Heath, Steppe
Oasis
Cape, Point
Coast, Beach
Cliff
Peninsula
Isthmus
Sandbank
Island
Atoll
Rock, Reef
Islands, Archipelago
Rocks, Reefs
Coral Reef
Well, Spring
Geyser
River, Stream
Waterfall Rapids
River Mouth, Estuary
Lake
Salt Lake
Intermittent Lake
Reservoir
Swamp, Pond
Canal
Glacier
Ice Shelf, Pack Ice
Ocean
Sea
Gulf, Bay
Strait, Fjord
Lagoon
Bank
Seamount
Tablemount
Ridge
Shelf
Basin
Escarpment, Sea Scarp
Fracture
Trench, Abyss
National Park, Reserve
Point of Interest
Recreation Site
Cave, Cavern
Historic Site
Ruins
Wall, Walls
Church, Abbey
Temple
Scientific Station
Airport
Port
Lighthouse
Mine
Tunnel
Dam, Bridge

Index Symbols

[1] Independent Nation	⬚ Historical or Cultural Region	⬚ Pass, Gap
[2] State, Region	⬚ Mount, Mountain	⬚ Plain, Lowland
[3] District, County	⬚ Volcano	⬚ Delta
[4] Municipality	⬚ Hill	⬚ Salt Flat
[5] Colony, Dependency	⬚ Mountains, Mountain Range	⬚ Valley, Canyon
■ Continent	⬚ Hills, Escarpment	⬚ Crater, Cave
■ Physical Region	⬚ Plateau, Upland	⬚ Karst Features

⬚ Depression	⬚ Coast, Beach	⬚ Rock, Reef
⬚ Polder	⬚ Cliff	⬚ Islands, Archipelago
⬚ Desert, Dunes	⬚ Peninsula	⬚ Rocks, Reefs
⬚ Forest, Woods	⬚ Isthmus	⬚ Coral Reef
⬚ Heath, Steppe	⬚ Sandbank	⬚ Well, Spring
⬚ Oasis	⬚ Island	⬚ Geyser
⬚ Cape, Point	⬚ Atoll	⬚ River, Stream

⬚ Waterfall Rapids	⬚ Canal	⬚ Lagoon
⬚ River Mouth, Estuary	⬚ Glacier	⬚ Bank
⬚ Lake	⬚ Ice Shelf, Pack Ice	⬚ Seamount
⬚ Salt Lake	⬚ Ocean	⬚ Tablemount
⬚ Intermittent Lake	⬚ Sea	⬚ Ridge
⬚ Reservoir	⬚ Gulf, Bay	⬚ Shelf
⬚ Swamp, Pond	⬚ Strait, Fjord	⬚ Basin

⬚ Escarpment, Sea Scarp	⬚ Historic Site	⬚ Port
⬚ Fracture	⬚ Ruins	⬚ Lighthouse
⬚ Trench, Abyss	⬚ Wall, Walls	⬚ Mine
⬚ National Park, Reserve	⬚ Church, Abbey	⬚ Tunnel
⬚ Point of Interest	⬚ Temple	⬚ Dam, Bridge
⬚ Recreation Site	⬚ Scientific Station	
⬚ Cave, Cavern	⬚ Airport	

Rusken	8	Fg	57.17N	14.20 E
Rusne/Rusné	8	Ii	55.19N	21.16 E
Rusné/Rusne	8	Ii	55.19N	21.16 E
Russel	42	Hb	73.55N	98.35W
Russell [Man. Can.]	42	Hf	50.47N	101.15W
Russell [Ks.-U.S.]	45	Gg	38.54N	98.52W
Russell [N.Z.]	62	Fa	35.16S	174.08 E
Russell Islands	60	Fi	9.04S	159.12 E
Russellville [Al.-U.S.]	44	Dh	34.30N	87.44W
Russellville [Ar.-U.S.]	45	Ji	35.17N	93.08W
Russellville [Ky.-U.S.]	44	Dg	36.51N	86.53W
Russel Range	59	Ef	33.25S	123.30 E
Rüsselsheim	10	Eg	50.00N	8.25 E
Russia (EN) = Rossija	19	Jc	60.00N	100.00 E
Russian River	46	Dg	38.27N	123.08W
Rust	14	Kc	47.48N	16.40 E
Rustavi	19	Eg	41.33N	45.02 E
Rustenburg	37	De	25.37S	27.08 E
Ruston	43	Ie	32.32N	92.38W
Rutaki Passage	64p	Bc	21.15S	159.48W
Rutana	36	Fc	3.55S	30.00 E
Rutanzige, Lac- = Edward, Lake- (EN)	30	Ji	0.25S	29.30 E
Rute	13	Hg	37.19N	4.22W
Ruteng	26	Hh	8.36S	120.27 E
Rutenga	37	Ed	21.15S	30.44 E
Rüthen	12	Kc	51.29N	8.27 E
Rutherfordton	44	Gh	35.22N	81.57W
Ruthin	9	Jh	53.07N	3.18W
Rutland	9	Mi	52.40N	0.40W
Rutland	44	Kd	43.37N	72.59W
Rutland	25	If	11.25N	92.10 E
Rutog	22	Jf	33.29N	79.42 E
Rutshuru	36	Ec	1.11S	29.27 E
Rutter	44	Gb	46.06N	80.40W
Rutul	16	Oi	41.33N	47.29 E
Ruutana	8	Kc	61.31N	24.02 E
Ruvo di Puglia	14	Ki	41.09N	16.29 E
Ruvu	36	Gd	6.48S	38.39 E
Ruvuma [3]	36	Ge	10.30S	35.50 E
Ruvuma	30	Lj	10.29S	40.28 E
Ruvuma (EN) = Rovuma	30	Lj	10.29S	40.28 E
Ruwayshid, Wādī	24	Hf	32.41N	38.04 E
Ruwer	12	Ie	49.47N	6.42 E
Ruya	37	Ec	16.34S	33.12 E
Ruyang	28	Bg	34.10N	112.28 E
Ru'yas, Wādī ar-	33	Cd	27.06N	19.24 E
Ruyigi	36	Fc	3.29S	30.15 E
Ruza	7	Ii	55.39N	36.18 E
Ruzajevka	17	Mj	52.49N	67.01 E
Ruzajevka	19	Ee	54.05N	44.54 E
Ružany	10	Ud	52.48N	24.58 E
Ružomberok	10	Pg	49.05N	19.18 E
Rwanda [1]	31	Ji	2.30S	30.00 E
Ry	8	Ch	56.05N	9.46 E
Ryan	45	Hi	34.01N	97.57W
Rybachi Peninsula (EN) = Rybači, Poluostrov-	5	Jb	69.45N	32.35 E
Rybači	8	Ii	55.09N	20.45 E
Rybači, Poluostrov- = Rybachi Peninsula (EN)	5	Jb	69.45N	32.35 E
Rybačje → Issyk-Kul'	19	Hg	42.28N	76.11 E
Rybinsk	6	Jd	58.03N	38.52 E
Rybinskoje Vodohranilišče = Rybinsk Reservoir (EN)	5	Jd	58.30N	38.25 E
Rybinsk Reservoir (EN) = Rybinskoje Vodohranilišče	5	Jd	58.30N	38.25 E
Rybnica	16	Ff	47.45N	29.01 E
Rybnik	10	Of	50.06N	18.32 E
Rybnoje	19	De	54.46N	39.33 E
Rybnovsk	20	Jf	53.15N	141.55 E
Rychnov nad Kněžnou	10	Mf	50.10N	16.17 E
Rychwał	10	Od	52.05N	18.09 E
Ryd	8	Fh	56.28N	14.41 E
Rydaholm	8	Fh	56.59N	14.16 E
Ryde	12	Ad	50.43N	1.10W
Rye	9	Mg	54.10N	0.45W
Rye	9	Nk	50.57N	0.44 E
Rye Bay	12	Cd	50.55N	0.48 E
Ryegate	46	Kc	46.18N	109.15W
Rye Patch Reservoir	46	Ff	40.38N	118.18W
Ryes	12	Be	49.19N	0.37W
Ryfylke	8	Be	59.30N	6.30 E
Ryki	10	Re	51.39N	21.56 E
Rylsk	19	De	51.36N	34.43 E
Rymanów	10	Rg	49.34N	21.53 E
Rymättylä/Rimito	8	Jd	60.25N	21.55 E
Ryn	10	Rc	53.56N	21.33 E
Ryńskie, Jezioro-	10	Rc	53.53N	21.30 E
Ryōhaku-Sanchi	29	Ec	36.05N	136.45 E
Ryōsō-Yosui	29	Gd	35.22N	140.25 E
Ryōtsu	28	Oe	38.05N	138.26 E
Ryōtsu-Wan	29	Fb	38.10N	138.30 E
Ryō-Zen	29	Gc	37.46N	140.41 E
Rypin	10	Pc	53.05N	19.25 E
Ryškany	16	Ef	47.57N	27.32 E
Ryssby	8	Fh	56.52N	14.10 E
Rytterknægten	8	Fi	55.06N	14.54 E
Ryūgasaki	29	Gd	35.54N	140.10 E
Ryukyu Islands (EN) = Nansei-Shotō	21	Og	26.30N	128.00 E
Ryūkyū-Shotō	27	Mf	25.30N	126.30 E
Ryukyu Trench (EN)	3	Ig	25.45N	128.00 E
Rzepin	10	Kd	52.22N	14.50 E
Rzeszów	6	Ie	50.03N	22.00 E
Rzeszów [2]	10	Rf	50.05N	22.00 E
Ržev	6	Jd	56.16N	34.20 E
S				
Šaa, Gora-	16	Nh	42.39N	44.43 E
Sa'ādatābād [Iran]	24	Ph	28.02N	55.50 E
Sa'ādatābād [Iran]	24	Og	30.08N	52.38 E
Sa'ādatābād [Iran]	24	Og	30.06N	53.08 E
Sääksjarvi	8	Jc	61.24N	22.24 E
Saalbach	12	Ke	49.15N	8.27 E
Saale	10	He	51.57N	11.55 E
Saaler Bodden	10	Ib	54.20N	12.28 E
Saalfeld	10	Hf	50.39N	11.22 E
Saalfelden am Steinernen Meer	14	Gc	47.25N	12.51 E
Saaminki	8	Mc	61.52N	28.50 E
Saâne	12	Ce	49.54N	0.56 E
Saane	14	Bd	46.59N	7.16 E
Saanen	14	Bd	46.30N	7.15 E
Saar	10	Cg	49.42N	6.34 E
Saar-Bergland	12	Ie	49.27N	6.45 E
Saarbrücken	6	Gf	49.14N	7.00 E
Saarbrücken-Dudweiler	12	Je	49.17N	7.02 E
Saarburg	10	Cg	49.36N	6.33 E
Sääre/Sjare	8	Ig	57.57N	21.53 E
Saaremaa/Sarema	5	Id	58.25N	22.30 E
Saarijärvi	7	Fe	62.43N	25.16 E
Saaristomeri	8	Id	60.20N	21.10 E
Saarland [2]	10	Cg	49.20N	7.00 E
Saarlouis	10	Cg	49.19N	6.45 E
Šaartuz	19	Gh	37.16N	68.06 E
Saarwellingen	12	Ie	49.21N	6.49 E
Saas Fee	14	Bd	46.07N	7.55 E
Saatly	16	Pj	39.57N	48.26 E
Saavedra	55	Am	37.45S	62.22W
Sab, Tônlé-	25	Kf	11.34N	104.57 E
Saba	47	Le	17.38N	63.10W
Saba	8	Me	59.05N	29.10 E
Saba Bank (EN)	50	Ed	17.30N	63.30W
Šabac	15	Ce	44.45N	19.43 E
Sabadell	13	Oc	41.33N	2.06 E
Sabae	28	Ng	35.57N	136.11 E
Sabah [2]	26	Ge	5.30N	117.00 E
Sab'ah, Qārat as-	33	Cd	27.20N	17.10 E
Sabak Bernam	26	Df	3.46N	100.59 E
Sabalān, Kūhhā-ye-	21	Gf	38.15N	47.49 E
Sab'ān	24	Ii	27.04N	41.58 E
Sabana, Archipiélago de-	49	Hb	22.30N	79.00W
Sabana de la Mar	49	Md	19.04N	69.23W
Sabanagrande	49	Dg	13.50N	87.15W
Sabanalarga	54	Da	10.38N	74.56W
Sabancuy	48	Nh	18.58N	91.11W
Sabaneta	49	Ld	19.12N	70.58W
Sabaneta, Puntan-	64b	Ba	15.17N	145.49 E
Sabang [Indon.]	26	Gf	0.11N	119.51 E
Sabang [Indon.]	26	Ce	5.55N	95.19 E
Şabanözü	24	Eb	40.29N	33.18 E
Săbăoani	15	Jb	47.01N	26.51 E
Sabarei	36	Gb	4.20N	36.55 E
Sab'Atayn, Ramlat as-	33	If	15.30N	46.10 E
Sabatini, Monti-	14	Gh	42.10N	12.15 E
Sabaudia	14	Hi	41.18N	13.01 E
Sabaudia, Lago di-	14	Hi	41.15N	13.05 E
Şabbāgh, Jabal-	24	Fh	28.12N	34.04 E
Sab 'Bi 'Ār	24	Gf	33.46N	37.41 E
Sabbioneta	14	Ee	45.00N	10.39 E
Sa Bec	25	Lf	10.18N	105.46 E
Sabhā [3]	33	Bd	26.00N	14.00 E
Sabhā	31	If	27.02N	14.26 E
Şabḩā	24	Gf	32.20N	36.30 E
Sābhā, Wāḩāt- = Sebha Oasis (EN)	30	If	27.00N	14.25 E
Sabi	30	Kk	21.00S	35.02 E
Sabidana, Jabal-	35	Fb	18.04N	36.50 E
Sabile	8	Jg	57.05N	22.29 E
Sabina	14	Gh	42.20N	12.45 E
Sabinal	48	Fb	30.57N	107.30W
Sabinal, Peninsula de-	49	Ic	21.40N	77.18W
Sabiñánigo	13	Lb	42.31N	0.22W
Sabinas	47	Dc	27.51N	101.07W
Sabinas, Río-	48	Id	27.37N	100.42W
Sabinas Hidalgo	47	Dc	26.30N	100.10W
Sabine Lake	45	Jl	29.50N	93.50W
Sabine Pass	45	Jl	29.44N	93.52W
Sabine Peninsula	42	Ga	76.25N	109.50W
Sabine River	43	Ie	30.00N	93.45W
Sabini, Monti-	14	Gh	42.15N	12.50 E
Şabir, Jabal-	23	Fg	13.30N	44.03 E
Sabirabad	16	Pj	39.59N	48.29 E
Šabla	15	Lf	43.32N	28.32 E
Sable, Anse de-	51e	b	16.07N	61.34W
Sable, Cape- [Can.]	38	Me	43.25N	65.35W
Sable, Cape- [U.S.]	38	Kg	25.12N	81.05W
Sable, Ile de-	57	Gf	19.15S	159.56 E
Sable Island	38	Ne	43.55N	59.55W
Sablé-sur-Sarthe	11	Fg	47.50N	0.20W
Sablūkah, Ash Shallāl as- = Sixth Cataract (EN)	30	Kg	16.20N	32.42 E
Sabonetau, Serra da-	55	Kb	15.20S	43.50W
Sabonkafi	34	Gc	14.38N	8.45 E
Sabór	13	Ec	41.10N	7.07W
Şabrātah	33	Bc	32.47N	12.29 E
Sabres	11	Fj	44.09N	0.44W
Sabrina Coast	66	He	67.00S	119.30 E
Sabtang	26	Hb	20.19N	121.52 E
Sabunči	16	Pi	40.27N	49.57 E
Şabyā	23	Ff	17.09N	42.37 E
Sabzevār	22	Hf	36.13N	57.42 E
Saca, Vîrful-	15	Ic	46.30N	25.15 E
Sacajawea Peak	43	Db	45.15N	117.17W
Sacalin, Insulă-	15	Me	44.50N	29.39 E
Sacandica	36	Cd	5.58S	15.56 E
Sacatepéquez [3]	49	Bf	14.35N	90.45W
Sacavém	13	Cf	38.46N	9.05W
Sac City	45	Ie	42.25N	95.00W
Sacco	14	Hi	41.31N	13.32 E
Sacedón	13	Jd	40.29N	2.43W
Săcel	15	Hb	47.38N	24.26 E
Săcele	15	Id	45.37N	25.41 E
Sachayoj	55	Bh	26.41S	61.50W
Sačhere	16	Mh	42.20N	43.22 E
Sachigo	42	Ie	55.05N	89.00W
Sachsen = Saxony (EN)	10	Jf	51.00N	13.30 E
Sachsenhagen	12	Lb	52.24N	9.16 E
Sachs Harbour	42	Eb	72.00N	125.08W
Šack	7	Ji	54.04N	41.42 E
Šack	10	Je	51.30N	24.00 E
Sackets Harbor	44	Id	43.57N	76.07W
Saco [Me.-U.S.]	44	Ld	43.29N	70.28W
Saco [Mt.-U.S.]	46	Lb	48.28N	107.21W
Sacramento	38	Gf	38.03N	121.56W
Sacramento [Braz.]	54	Ig	19.53S	47.27W
Sacramento [Ca.-U.S.]	39	Gf	38.35N	121.30W
Sacramento, Pampa del-	54	Ce	8.00S	75.50W
Sacramento Mountains	38	If	33.10N	105.50W
Sacramento Valley	43	Cd	39.15N	122.00W
Sacre ou Timalacia, Rio-	55	Ca	13.55S	58.02W
Săcueni	15	Fb	47.21N	22.06 E
Sacuriuiná ou Ponte de Pedra, Rio-	55	Da	13.58S	57.18W
Sádaba	13	Kb	42.17N	1.16W
Sa'dābād	24	Nh	29.23N	51.07 E
Şa'dah	22	Gh	16.57N	43.44 E
Sada-Misaki	29b	Ce	33.22N	132.01 E
Sada-Misaki-Hantō	29	Ce	33.25N	132.15 E
Sadani	36	Gd	6.03S	38.47 E
Sadao	25	Kg	6.39N	100.31 E
Sadd al 'Ālī	33	Fe	23.54N	32.52 E
Saddle Mountains	46	Fc	46.50N	119.55W
Saddle Peak [India]	25	If	13.09N	93.01 E
Saddle Peak [Mt.-U.S.]	46	Jd	45.57N	110.58W
Sad-e Eskandar	24	Pd	37.10N	55.00 E
Sadiya	25	Jc	27.50N	95.40 E
Sa'dīyah, Hawr as-	24	Lf	32.00N	46.45 E
Sad Kharv	24	Qd	36.19N	57.05 E
Sado	13	Df	38.29N	8.55W
Sado-Kaikyō	29	Fc	37.55N	38.40 E
Sado-Shima	21	Pf	38.00N	38.25 E
Sadowara	29	Be	32.04N	31.26 E
Šadrinsk	19	Gd	56.05N	63.38 E
Saeby	7	Ch	57.20N	10.32 E
Saeh, Teluk-	26	Gh	8.00S	17.30 E
Saengcheon	28	Ie	39.55N	26.34 E
Saerbeck	12	Jb	52.11N	7.33 E
Şafājah	24	Hi	26.30N	39.30 E
Şafājah, Jazīrat-	24	Ei	26.45N	33.59 E
Safané	34	Ec	2.08N	3.13W
Şafāqis = Sfax (EN) [3]	32	Jc	34.30N	10.30 E
Şafāqis = Sfax (EN)	31	Ie	34.44N	10.46 E
Safata Harbour	65c	Bb	4.00S	71.50W
Saffānīyah, Ra's as-	23	Gd	27.59N	48.37 E
Säffle	7	Cg	59.08N	12.56 E
Safford	43	Fe	32.50N	109.43W
Saffron Walden	9	Ni	52.01N	0.15 E
Safi	31	Ge	32.18N	9.14W
Safi [3]	32	Fc	31.55N	9.00W
Safia, Hamâda-	34	Ea	23.10N	4.15W
Şafīābād	24	Qd	36.45N	57.58 E
Safid	23	Hb	37.23N	50.11 E
Safid, Kūh-e	24	Lf	33.55N	47.30 E
Safid Kūh, Salseleh-ye-	23	Jc	34.30N	63.30 E
Safonovo	19	Dd	55.06N	33.14 E
Safonovo	7	Ld	65.41N	47.43 E
Şafrā' al Asyāḩ	24	Ji	25.50N	43.57 E
Şafrā' as Sark	24	Kj	25.25N	44.20 E
Safranbolu	24	Eb	41.15N	32.42 E
Şafwān	24	Lg	30.07N	47.43 E
Saga [Jap.]	27	Ne	33.15N	130.18 E
Saga [Jap.]	29	Ce	33.05N	133.06 E
Saga	19	Fe	50.30N	64.14 E
Saga (Gya'gya)	27	Ef	29.22N	85.15 E
Sagae	29	Gb	38.22N	140.17 E
Sagaing [3]	25	Jd	23.30N	95.30 E
Sagaing	25	Jd	21.52N	95.59 E
Saga Ken [2]	28	Kh	33.15N	130.15 E
Sagamihara	29	Fd	35.34N	139.22 E
Sagami-Nada	29	Fd	35.00N	139.30 E
Sagami-Wan	29	Fd	35.15N	139.20 E
Sagan	35	Fd	4.17N	6.57 E
Šagan	19	He	50.37N	79.15 E
Saganaga Lake	45	Kb	48.14N	90.52W
Saganoseki	29	Be	33.15N	131.53 E
Šagany, Ozero-	15	Md	45.45N	29.55 E
Sāgar [India]	25	Ff	14.10N	75.02 E
Sāgar [India]	22	Jg	23.50N	78.42 E
Sagara	29	Fd	34.40N	138.12 E
Sagaredžo	16	Ni	41.43N	45.16 E
Sagavanirktok	40	Jb	70.20N	148.00W
Sagawa	29	Ce	33.29N	133.16 E
Sage	46	Jf	41.50N	110.56W
Saghād	24	Og	31.12N	52.30 E
Saginaw	43	Kc	43.25N	83.58W
Saginaw Bay	43	Kc	43.50N	83.40W
Sagiz	19	Ff	47.32N	53.45 E
Sagiz	19	Ff	48.12N	54.56 E
Sagiz	16	Rf	47.32N	53.27 E
Saglek Bay	42	Le	58.30N	63.00W
Saglouc → Salluit	39	Lc	62.12N	75.38W
Šagonar	20	Ef	51.32N	92.51 E
Sagone, Golfe de-	11a	Aa	42.06N	8.41 E
Sagres	13	Dg	37.01N	8.56W
Şagu	15	Ec	46.03N	21.17 E
Sagu/Sauvo	8	Jd	60.21N	22.42 E
Saguache	45	Cg	38.05N	106.08W
Sagua de Tánamo	49	Jc	20.35N	75.14W
Sagua la Grande	47	Hd	22.49N	80.05W
Saguenay	38	Me	48.10N	69.45W
Saguia el-Hamra	32	Ed	26.50N	12.00W
Sagunt/Sagunto	13	Le	39.41N	0.16W
Sagunto/Sagunt	13	Le	39.41N	0.16W
Sagunto-Grao de Sagunto	13	Le	39.40N	0.16W
Sa'gya	27	Ef	28.53N	88.10 E
Saha (Jakutija), respublika	20	Hc	67.00N	130.00 E
Sahagún [Col.]	54	Cb	8.57N	75.27W
Sahagún [Sp.]	13	Gb	42.22N	5.02W
Sahalin, Ostrov- = Sakhalin (EN)	21	Qd	51.00N	143.00 E
Sahalinskaja Oblast [3]	20	Jf	50.00N	143.30 E
Sahalinski Zaliv	20	Jf	53.45N	141.30 E
Sahara	30	Hf	21.00N	6.00 E
Saharan Atlas (EN) = Atlas Saharien	30	He	34.00N	2.00 E
Sahāranpur	22	Jg	29.58N	77.23 E
Sahel [3]	34	Ec	14.10N	0.50W
Sahel	30	Gg	15.40N	8.30W
Şahin	15	Jh	41.01N	26.50 E
Sāhiwāl [Pak.]	25	Eb	30.41N	72.57 E
Sāhiwāl [Pak.]	25	Eb	31.58N	72.20 E
Sahlābād	23	Ic	32.10N	59.51 E
Sahneh	24	Le	34.29N	47.41 E
Sahnovščina	16	Ie	49.09N	35.57 E
Sahova Kosa, Mys-	16	Qi	40.13N	50.22 E
Sahrihan	18	Id	40.40N	72.03 E
Šahrisabz	19	Gh	39.03N	66.41 E
Šahristan, Pereval-	18	Ge	39.35N	68.38 E
Šahtersk	20	Jg	49.13N	142.09 E
Šahtersk	16	Ke	48.01N	38.32 E
Šahterski	20	Md	64.46N	177.47 E
Šahtinsk	19	Hf	49.40N	72.37 E
Šahty	19	Ef	47.42N	40.13 E
Sahuaripa	47	Cc	29.03N	109.14W
Sahuayo de Díaz	47	Dd	20.04N	102.43W
Šahunja	19	Ed	57.43N	46.35 E
Saḩūq, Wādī-	24	Jj	25.18N	42.20 E
Šahy	10	Oh	48.05N	18.58 E
Sahyadri/Western Ghats	21	Jh	14.00N	75.00 E
Sai Buri	25	Kg	6.42N	101.37 E
Saïda [3]	32	Hc	33.35N	0.30 E
Saïda	31	He	34.50N	0.09 E
Saïda, Monts de-	13	Mi	35.10N	0.30 E
Sa'īdābād	23	Id	29.28N	55.42 E
Saidaiji	29	Dd	34.39N	134.02 E
Said Bundas	35	Cd	8.35N	24.30 E
Saïdia	13	Ji	35.04N	2.13W
Saidor	60	Di	5.37S	146.28 E
Saidu	25	Eb	34.45N	72.21 E
Saigō	29	Cc	36.13N	133.20 E
Saigon → Ho Chi Minh	22	Mh	10.45N	106.40 E
Saihan Tal → Sonid Youqi	27	Jc	42.45N	112.36 E
Saihan Toroi	27	Hc	41.54N	100.24 E
Saijō	29	Ce	33.55N	133.10 E
Saikai	29	Ae	33.03N	129.44 E
Sai-Kawa	29	Fc	36.37N	138.14 E
Saiki	28	Kh	32.57N	131.54 E
Saiki-Wan	29	Be	33.00N	131.55 E
Sail Rock	51n	Bb	12.37N	61.16W
Saimaa	5	Ic	61.15N	28.15 E
Saimaa Canal (EN) = Sajmenski Kanal	8	Mc	61.05N	28.18 E
Sain Alto	48	Hf	23.35N	103.15W
Sā'īn Dezh	24	Ld	36.40N	46.33 E
Sains-Fichaumont	12	Fe	49.49N	3.42 E
Saint Abb's Head	9	Kf	55.54N	2.09W
Saint-Affrique	11	Ik	43.57N	2.53 E
Saint Agnes Head	9	Hk	50.23N	5.07W
Saint-Agrève	11	Ki	45.01N	4.24 E
Saint Albans [Eng.-U.K.]	9	Mj	51.46N	0.21W
Saint Albans [Vt.-U.S.]	44	Kc	44.49N	73.05W
Saint Albans [W.V.-U.S.]	44	Gf	38.24N	81.53W
Saint Alban's Head	9	Kk	50.34N	2.04W
Saint Albert	42	Gf	53.38N	113.38W
Saint-Amand-les-Eaux	11	Jd	50.26N	3.26 E
Saint-Amand-Mont-Rond	11	Ih	46.43N	2.31 E
Saint-André, Cap-	30	Lj	16.11S	44.27 E
Saint-André, Plaine de-	11	Hf	48.55N	1.10 E
Saint-André-de-Cubzac	11	Fi	45.00N	0.27W
Saint-André-de-l'Eure	12	Df	48.54N	1.17 E
Saint-André-sur-Cailly	12	De	49.33N	1.13 E
Saint Andrews [N.B.-Can.]	44	Nc	45.06N	67.02W
Saint Andrews [Scot.-U.K.]	9	Ke	56.20N	2.48W
Saint Anne	9	Kl	49.40N	2.10W
Saint Ann's Bay	49	Id	18.26N	77.16W
Saint Ann's Head	9	Hj	51.41N	5.10W
Saint Anthony [Id.-U.S.]	46	Je	43.58N	111.41W
Saint Anthony [Newf.-Can.]	42	Lf	51.22N	55.35W
Saint Arnaud	59	Ig	36.37S	143.15 E
Saint-Aubert	44	Lb	47.14N	70.15W
Saint-Aubin-sur-Mer	12	Be	49.20N	0.24W
Saint Augustine	43	Kf	29.51N	81.25W
Saint-Augustin-Saguenay	42	Lf	51.14N	58.39W
Saint Austell	9	Ik	50.20N	4.48W
Saint-Avold	11	Me	49.06N	6.42 E
Saint Barthélemy	47	Le	17.55N	62.50W
Saint-Barthélemy	11	Hl	42.49N	1.45 E
Saint Barthélemy, Canal de-	51b	Bb	18.00N	63.00W
Saint Barthélemy, Kanaal Van-	51b	Bb	18.00N	63.00W
Saint Bees Head	9	Jg	54.32N	3.38W
Saint-Benoit	37a	b	21.02S	55.43 E
Saint-Benoît-sur-Loire	11	Ig	47.49N	2.18 E
Saint-Bonnet	11	Mj	44.41N	6.05 E
Saint-Brévin-les-Pins	11	Dg	47.15N	2.10W
Saint Brides Bay	9	Hj	51.48N	5.15W
Saint-Brieuc	11	Df	48.31N	2.47W
Saint-Brieuc, Baie de-	11	Df	48.38N	2.40W
Saint-Calais	11	Gg	47.55N	0.45 E
Saint-Camille	44	Lb	46.29N	70.12W
Saint Catharines	42	Jh	43.10N	79.15W
Saint Catherine, Monastery of- (EN) = Dayr Kātrīnā	33	Fd	28.31N	33.57 E
Saint Catherine, Mount-	51p	Bb	12.10N	61.40W
Saint Catherines Island	44	Gj	31.38N	81.10W
Saint Catherine's Point	9	Lk	50.34N	1.15W
Saint-Céré	11	Hj	44.52N	1.54 E
Saint-Chamond	11	Ki	45.28N	4.30 E
Saint Charles	43	Id	38.47N	90.29W
Saint-Chély-d'Apcher	11	Jj	44.48N	3.17 E
Saint-Christol, Plateau de-	11	Lj	44.00N	5.50 E
Saint Christopher/Saint Kitts	38	Mh	17.21N	62.48W
Saint Christopher-Nevis [5]	39	Mh	17.21N	62.48W
Saint-Cirq-Lapopie	11	Hj	44.28N	1.40 E
Saint Clair, Lake-	38	Ke	42.25N	82.41W
Saint Clair River	44	Fd	42.37N	82.31W
Saint Clair Shores	44	Fd	42.30N	82.54W
Saint-Clair-sur-l'Elle	12	Ae	49.12N	1.02W
Saint-Claud	11	Gi	45.54N	0.28 E
Saint-Claude [Fr.]	11	Lh	46.23N	5.52 E
Saint Claude	45	Gb	49.40N	98.22W
Saint-Claude [Guad.]	51e	Ab	16.02N	61.42W
Saint Cloud	39	Je	45.33N	94.10W
Saint Croix	47	Le	17.45N	64.45W
Saint Croix Falls	45	Jd	45.24N	92.38W
Saint Croix River	43	Ic	44.45N	92.49W
Saint-Cyr-l'Ecole	12	Ef	48.48N	2.04 E
Saint-Cyr-sur-Loire	11	Gg	47.24N	0.40 E
Saint David Bay	51g	Bb	15.26N	61.15W
Saint David's [Gren.]	51p	Bb	12.04N	61.39W
Saint David's [Wales-U.K.]	9	Hj	51.54N	5.16W
Saint David's Head	9	Hj	51.55N	5.19W
Saint David's Point	51p	Bb	12.01N	61.40W
Saint-Denis [Fr.]	11	If	48.56N	2.22 E
Saint-Denis [May.]	31	Mk	20.52S	55.28 E
Saint-Dié	11	Mf	48.17N	6.57 E
Saint-Dizier	11	Kf	48.38N	4.57 E
Sainte-Adresse	12	Ce	49.30N	0.05 E
Sainte-Anne [Guad.]	51e	Bb	16.14N	61.23W
Sainte-Anne [Mart.]	51h	Bc	14.26N	60.53W
Sainte-Anne-des-Monts	44	Na	49.07N	66.29W
Sainte Baume, Chaîne de la-	11	Lk	43.20N	5.45 E
Sainte-Énimie	11	Jj	44.22N	3.25 E
Sainte Genevieve	45	Kh	37.59N	90.03W
Sainte-Geneviève	12	Ee	49.17N	2.12 E
Saint Elias, Mount-	38	Ec	60.18N	140.55W
Saint Elias Mountains	38	Fc	60.30N	139.30W
Saint-Elie	54	Hc	4.50N	53.17W
Sainte-Livrade-sur-Lot	11	Gj	44.24N	0.36 E
Saint-Eloy-les-Mines	11	Ih	46.09N	2.50 E
Sainte Luce	37	Hd	24.46S	47.12 E
Sainte-Luce	51h	Bc	14.28N	60.56W
Sainte-Lucie, Canal de- = Saint Lucia Channel (EN)	50	Fe	14.09N	60.57W
Sainte-Marcellin	11	Li	45.09N	5.19 E
Sainte-Marie [Guad.]	51e	Ab	16.06N	61.34W
Sainte-Marie [Mart.]	51h	Ab	14.47N	61.00W
Sainte-Marie, Cap- = Sainte-Marie, Cape- (EN)	30	Lk	25.36S	45.08 E
Sainte-Marie, Cape-(EN) = Sainte-Marie, Cap-	30	Lk	25.36S	45.08 E
Sainte-Marie, Ile-	30	Lj	16.50S	49.55 E
Sainte-Marie-aux-Mines	11	Nf	48.15N	7.11 E
Sainte-Maure-de-Touraine	11	Gg	47.06N	0.37 E
Sainte-Maxime	11	Mk	43.18N	6.38 E
Sainte-Menehould	11	Ke	49.05N	4.54 E
Sainte-Rose	51e	Ab	16.20N	61.42W
Sainte-Rose-du-Dégelé	44	Mb	47.33N	68.39W
Sainte Rose du Lac	45	Ga	51.03N	99.32W
Saintes	11	Fi	45.45N	0.38W
Saintes, Canal des-	51e	Ac	15.55N	61.40W
Saintes, Iles des-	50	Fe	15.52N	61.37W
Sainte-Savine	11	Kf	48.18N	4.03 E
Saintes-Maries-de-la-Mer	11	Kk	43.27N	4.26 E
Sainte-Thérèse	44	Kc	45.22N	73.15W
Saint-Étienne	6	Gf	45.26N	4.24 E
Saint-Étienne-du-Rouvray	11	He	49.23N	1.06 E
Sainte Victoire, Montagne-	11	Lk	43.32N	5.39 E
Saint-Félicien	44	Ka	48.39N	72.28W
Saint-Florent	11a	Ba	42.41N	9.18 E
Saint-Florent, Golfe de-	11a	Ba	42.45N	9.16 E
Saint-Florentin	11	Jf	48.00N	3.44 E
Saint-Florent-sur-Cher	11	Ih	46.59N	2.15 E
Saint-Flour	11	Ji	45.02N	3.05 E
Saint Francis	45	Fg	39.46N	101.48W
Saint Francis River	45	Ki	34.38N	90.35W
Saint Francisville	45	Kk	30.47N	91.23W
Saint-François	51e	Bb	16.15N	61.17W
Saint François Island	37b	Bb	7.10S	52.44 E
Saint Francois Mountains	45	Kh	37.30N	90.35W
Saint-Gaudens	11	Gk	43.07N	0.44 E
Saint George	40	Fe	56.35N	169.35W
Saint George [Austl.]	59	Je	28.02S	148.35 E
Saint George [N.B.-Can.]	44	Nc	45.10N	66.48W
Saint George [Ut.-U.S.]	43	Ed	37.06N	113.35W
Saint George, Cape - [Newf.-Can.]	42	Lm	48.28N	59.16W
Saint George, Cape- [Pap.N.Gui.]	60	Eh	4.52S	152.52 E
Saint George, Point-	46	Cf	41.47N	124.15W
Saint George Harbour	44	Nd	43.15N	66.10W
Saint George Island	44	Ek	29.39N	84.55W
Saint George's	39	Mh	12.03N	61.45W
Saint-Georges	44	Lb	46.10N	70.38W
Saint George's Bay	42	Lg	48.20N	59.00W
Saint George's Channel	5	Fe	52.00N	6.00W
Saint George's Channel (EN) = Muir Bhreatan	5	Fe	52.00N	6.00W
Saint-Georges-du-Vièvre	12	Ce	49.15N	0.35 E
Saint-Germain-en-Laye	11	If	48.54N	2.05 E
Saint-Gervais-d'Auvergne	11	Ih	46.02N	2.49 E
Saint-Gervais-les-Bains	11	Mi	45.54N	6.43 E
Saint-Ghislain	12	Fd	50.27N	3.49 E
Saint-Ghislain-Baudour	12	Fd	50.29N	3.49 E
Saint-Gildas, Pointe de-	11	Dg	47.08N	2.15W
Saint-Gilles	11	Kk	43.41N	4.26 E
Saint-Gilles-Croix-de-Vie	11	Eh	46.41N	1.55W
Saint-Girons	11	Hl	42.59N	1.09 E
Saint-Gobain	12	Fe	49.36N	3.23 E
Saint Gotthard Pass (EN) = San Gottardo/Sankt Gotthard	5	Gf	46.30N	8.30 E
Saint Gotthard Pass (EN) = Sankt Gotthard/San Gottardo	5	Gf	46.30N	8.30 E
Saint Govan's Head	9	Ij	51.36N	4.55W
Saint Helena [5]	31	Gj	15.57S	5.42W
Saint Helena	30	Gj	15.57S	5.42W
Saint Helena Bay	30	Il	32.45S	18.05 E
Saint Helena Island	44	Gi	32.30N	80.30W

Index Symbols

- [1] Independent Nation
- [2] State, Region
- [3] District, County
- [4] Municipality
- [5] Colony, Dependency
- Continent
- Physical Region
- Historical or Cultural Region
- Mount, Mountain
- Volcano
- Hill
- Mountains, Mountain Range
- Hills, Escarpment
- Plateau, Upland
- Pass, Gap
- Plain, Lowland
- Delta
- Salt Flat
- Valley, Canyon
- Crater, Cave
- Karst Features
- Depression
- Polder
- Desert, Dunes
- Forest, Woods
- Heath, Steppe
- Oasis
- Cape, Point
- Coast, Beach
- Cliff
- Peninsula
- Isthmus
- Sandbank
- Island
- Atoll
- Rock, Reef
- Islands, Archipelago
- Rocks, Reefs
- Coral Reef
- Well, Spring
- Geyser
- River, Stream
- Waterfall Rapids
- River Mouth, Estuary
- Lake
- Salt Lake
- Intermittent Lake
- Reservoir
- Swamp, Pond
- Canal
- Glacier
- Ice Shelf, Pack Ice
- Ocean
- Sea
- Gulf, Bay
- Strait, Fjord
- Lagoon
- Bank
- Seamount
- Tablemount
- Ridge
- Shelf
- Basin
- Escarpment, Sea Scarp
- Fracture
- Trench, Abyss
- National Park, Reserve
- Point of Interest
- Recreation Site
- Cave, Cavern
- Historic Site
- Ruins
- Wall, Walls
- Church, Abbey
- Temple
- Scientific Station
- Airport
- Port
- Lighthouse
- Mine
- Tunnel
- Dam, Bridge

Index Symbols

[1] Independent Nation	▲ Historical or Cultural Region	⌣ Pass, Gap	Depression	Coast, Beach	Rock, Reef	Waterfall Rapids	Canal	Lagoon
[2] State, Region	▲ Mount, Mountain	⌣ Plain, Lowland	Polder	Cliff	Islands, Archipelago	River Mouth, Estuary	Glacier	Bank
[3] District, County	▲ Volcano	⌣ Delta	Desert, Dunes	Peninsula	Rocks, Reefs	Ice Shelf, Pack Ice	Bank	Seamount
[4] Municipality	▲ Hill	⌣ Salt Flat	Forest, Woods	Isthmus	Coral Reef	Lake	Ocean	Tablemount
[5] Colony, Dependency	▲ Mountains, Mountain Range	⌣ Valley, Canyon	Heath, Steppe	Sandbank	Well, Spring	Salt Lake	Sea	Ridge
[6] Continent	▲ Hills, Escarpment	⌣ Crater, Cave	Oasis	Island	Geyser	Intermittent Lake	Gulf, Bay	Shelf
[7] Physical Region	▲ Plateau, Upland	⌣ Karst Features	Cape, Point	Atoll	River, Stream	Swamp, Pond	Strait, Fjord	Basin

Escarpment, Sea Scarp	Historic Site	Port	
Fracture	Ruins	Lighthouse	
Trench, Abyss	Wall, Walls	Mine	
National Park, Reserve	Church, Abbey	Tunnel	
Point of Interest	Temple	Dam, Bridge	
Recreation Site	Scientific Station		
Cave, Cavern	Airport		

Samch'ŏk 27 Md 37.27N 129.10 E
Samch'ŏnp'o 27 Me 34.55N 128.04 E
Samdi Dağı 24 Kd 37.19N 44.15 E
Samdŏng-ni 28 Ie 39.21N 126.14 E
Samdŭng 28 Ie 38.59N 126.11 E
Same [Indon.] 26 Ih 8.59S 125.40 E
Same [Tan.] 36 Gc 4.04S 37.44 E
Samer 12 Dd 50.38N 1.45 E
Sam Ford Fiord 42 Kb 70.40N 70.35W
Samfya 36 Ee 11.20S 29.32 E
Sámi 15 Dk 38.15N 20.39 E
Sāmī Ghar 23 Kc 31.43N 67.01 E
Samīrah 24 Ji 26.18N 42.05 E
Samisu-Jima 27 Oe 31.40N 140.00 E
Šamkir (Samhor) 16 Oi 40.48N 46.01 E
Şamli 15 Kj 39.48N 27.51 E
Samnah, Jabal- 24 Ei 26.26N 33.34 E
Samoa I Sisifo = Western
Samoa (EN) [1] 58 Jf 13.40S 172.30W
Samoa Islands 57 Jf 14.00S 171.00W
Samobor 14 Je 45.48N 15.43 E
Samojlovka 16 Md 51.10N 43.43 E
Samokov 15 Gg 42.20N 23.33 E
Samolva 8 Lf 58.16N 27.45 E
Sámos 15 Jl 37.45N 26.58 E
Sámos 5 Ih 37.45N 26.48 E
Samosir, Pulau- 26 Cf 2.35N 98.50 E
Samothrace (EN) =
Samothráki 15 Ii 40.27N 25.35 E
Samothráki 15 Ii 40.29N 25.31 E
Samothráki = Samothrace
(EN) 15 Ii 40.27N 25.35 E
Sampacho 56 Hd 33.23S 64.43W
Sampaga 26 Gg 2.19S 119.07 E
Sampit 26 Fg 3.00S 113.03 E
Sampit 22 Nj 2.32S 112.57 E
Sampoku 29 Fb 38.30N 139.30 E
Sampwe 36 Ed 9.20S 27.23 E
Sam Rayburn Reservoir 45 Ik 31.27N 94.37W
Samro, Ozero- 8 Mf 58.55N 28.50 E
Samsjøen 8 Da 63.05N 10.40 E
Samsø 7 Ci 55.50N 10.35 E
Samsø Bælt 8 Di 55.50N 10.45 E
Sam Son 25 Ld 19.44N 105.54 E
Samsun 22 Fe 41.17N 36.20 E
Samsun Dağı 15 Kl 37.40N 27.15 E
Samtredia 16 Mh 42.11N 42.17 E
Samuel, Mount- 59 Gc 19.41S 134.09 E
Samuhú 55 Bh 27.31S 60.24W
Samui, Ko- 21 Li 9.30N 100.00 E
Samur 16 Pi 41.53N 48.32 E
Samur-Apšeronski Kanal 16 Pi 40.35N 49.35 E
Samus 20 De 56.46N 84.44 E
Samut Prakan 25 Kf 13.36N 100.36 E
Samut Sakhon 25 Kf 13.31N 100.15 E
San 31 Gg 13.08N 4.53W
San [Asia] 25 Lf 13.32N 105.57 E
San [Pol.] 10 Rf 50.45N 21.51 E
San'ā' 22 Gh 15.23N 44.12 E
Sana 14 Ke 45.03N 16.23 E
Sanaag [3] 35 Hc 10.10N 47.50 E
Şanabū 24 Di 27.30N 30.47 E
Sanae 66 Bf 70.18S 2.22W
Sanāfir 24 Fi 27.55N 34.42 E
Sanāg 35 Hd 7.45N 48.00 E
Sanaga 30 Hh 3.35N 9.38 E
San Agustín 55 Cn 38.01S 58.21W
San Agustin, Cabo- 48 Bc 28.05N 115.20W
San Agustin, Cape- 26 Ie 6.16N 126.11 E
Sanak Islands 40 Gf 54.25N 162.35W
Sanalona, Presa- 48 Fe 24.53N 107.00W
San Ambrosio, Isla- 56 Ec 26.21S 79.52W
Sanana 26 Ig 2.04S 125.08 E
Sanana, Pulau- 26 Ig 2.12S 125.55 E
Sanandaj 23 Gb 35.19N 47.00 E
San Andreas 46 Eg 38.12N 120.41W
San Andrés [3] 47 Hf 12.35N 81.42W
San Andres, Cerro- 48 Ih 19.48N 100.36W
San Andres, Isla de- 52 Hd 12.32N 81.42W
San Andrés, Laguna de- 48 Kf 22.40N 97.50W
San Andrés de Giles 55 Cl 34.27S 59.27W
San Andrés del Rabanedo 13 Gb 42.37N 5.36W
San Andres Mountains 43 Fe 32.55N 106.45W
San Andres Peak 45 Cj 32.43N 106.30W
San Andrés Tuxtla 47 Ee 18.27N 95.13W
San Andrés y
Providencia [2] 54 Ba 12.30N 81.45W
Sananduva 55 Gh 27.57S 51.48W
San Angelo 43 Ge 31.28N 100.26W
San Antonio [Blz.] 49 Ce 16.30N 89.02W
San Antonio [Chile] 56 Fd 33.35S 71.38W
San Antonio [Tx.-U.S.] 39 Jg 29.28N 98.31W
San Antonio [Ur.] 55 Dj 31.20S 57.45W
San Antonio, Cabo- [Arg.] 52 Ki 36.40S 56.42W
San Antonio, Cabo- [Cuba] 38 Kg 21.52N 84.57W
San Antonio, Cabo de-/Sant
Antoni, Cap- 13 Mf 38.48N 0.12 E
San Antonio, Canal- 55 Aj 31.42S 62.15W
San Antonio, Punta- 48 Bc 29.45N 115.45W
San Antonio, Sierra de- 48 Db 30.00N 110.20W
San Antonio Abad 13 Nf 38.58N 1.18 E
San Antonio Bay 45 Hl 28.20N 96.45W
San Antonio de Caparo 49 Lj 7.35N 71.27W
San Antonio de Cortés 49 Cf 15.05N 88.04W
San Antonio de los Baños 49 Fb 22.53N 82.30W
San Antonio de los Cobres 56 Gb 24.11S 66.21W
San Antonio del Táchira 54 Db 7.50N 72.27W
San Antonio de Tamanaco 50 Ch 9.14N 66.03W
San Antonio Oeste 53 Jj 40.44S 64.57W
San Antonio River 43 Hf 28.30N 96.50W
Sanare 49 Mi 9.45N 69.39W
Sanary-sur-Mer 11 Lk 43.07N 5.48 E
San Augustín 53 Ie 1.53N 76.16W
San Augustine 45 Ik 31.32N 94.07W
Sanāw 35 Ib 17.50N 51.05 E
San Bartolomeo in Galdo 14 Ji 41.24N 15.01 E
San Baudilio de Llobregat/
Sant Boi de Llobregat 13 Oc 41.21N 2.03 E
San Benedetto del Tronto 14 Hh 42.57N 13.53 E
San Benedetto Po 14 Ee 45.02N 10.55 E
San Benedicto, Isla- 47 Be 19.18N 110.49W
San Benito [Guat.] 49 Ce 16.55N 89.54W
San Benito [Tx.-U.S.] 45 Hm 26.08N 97.38W
San Benito, Islas- 48 Bc 28.20N 115.35W
San Benito Abad 49 Ji 8.56N 75.02W
San Benito Mountain 46 Eh 36.22N 120.38W
San Bernardino 39 Hf 34.06N 117.17W
San Bernardino, Passo del-/
Sankt Bernardin Paß 14 Dd 46.30N 9.10 E
San Bernardino
Mountains 46 Gi 34.10N 117.00W
San Bernardino Strait 26 Hd 12.32N 124.10 E
San Bernardo [Arg.] 55 Bh 27.17S 60.42W
San Bernardo [Chile] 56 Fd 33.36S 70.43W
San Bernardo [Mex.] 48 De 25.32N 111.45W
San Bernardo, Islas de- 49 Ji 9.45N 75.50W
San Bernardo, Punta de- 49 Ji 9.42N 75.42W
San Bernardo del Viento 54 Cb 9.22N 75.57W
San Blas [3] 49 Hi 7.50N 81.10W
San Blas [Mex.] 47 Cd 21.31N 105.16W
San Blas [Mex.] 47 Cc 26.05N 108.46W
San Blas [Mex.] 48 Id 27.25N 101.40W
San Blas, Archipiélago de-
49 Hi 9.30N 78.30W
San Blas, Cape- 43 Jf 29.40N 85.22W
San Blas, Cordillera de- 49 Hi 9.18N 79.00W
San Blas, Golfo de- 49 Hi 9.30N 79.00W
San Blas, Punta- 49 Hi 9.34N 78.58W
San Borja 54 Ef 14.49S 66.51W
San Borjas, Sierra de- 48 Cc 28.40N 113.45W
San Buenaventura 48 Id 27.05N 101.32W
Sancai 35 Fc 10.43N 35.40 E
San Carlos [Arg.] 55 Eh 27.45S 55.54W
San Carlos [Chile] 56 Fe 36.25S 71.58W
San Carlos [Mex.] 48 Je 24.35N 98.56W
San Carlos [Mex.] 48 Ic 29.01N 100.51W
San Carlos [Nic.] 49 Eh 11.07N 84.47W
San Carlos [Pan.] 49 Hi 8.29N 79.57W
San Carlos [Par.] 55 Df 22.16S 57.18W
San Carlos [Phil.] 26 Hd 10.30N 123.25 E
San Carlos [Phil.] 26 Hc 15.55N 120.20 E
San Carlos [Ur.] 56 Jd 34.48S 54.55W
San Carlos [Ven.] 54 Eb 9.40N 68.39W
San Carlos, Bahia- 47 Cd 27.55N 112.45W
San Carlos, Mesa de- 48 Bc 29.40N 115.25W
San Carlos, Punta- 48 Cc 28.00N 112.45W
San Carlos, Riacho- 55 Df 22.49S 57.53W
San Carlos, Rio- [C.R.] 49 Eh 10.47N 84.12W
San Carlos, Rio- [Ven.] 50 Bh 9.07N 68.25W
San Carlos de Bariloche 53 Ij 41.08S 71.15W
San Carlos de Bolívar 56 He 36.15S 61.06W
San Carlos de la Ràpita/
Sant Carles de la Ràpita 13 Md 40.37N 0.36 E
San Carlos del Zulia 54 Db 9.01N 71.55W
San Carlos de Río Negro 54 Ec 1.55N 67.04W
San Carlos Reservoir 46 Jj 33.13N 110.24W
San Cataldo [It.] 14 Mj 40.23N 18.18 E
San Cataldo [It.] 14 Hm 37.29N 13.59 E
San Cayetano 55 Cn 38.20S 59.37W
Sancerre 11 Ig 47.20N 2.50 E
Sancerrois, Collines du- 11 Ig 47.20N 2.30 E
Sanchahe 28 Ib 44.59N 126.03 E
Sánchez 49 Md 19.14N 69.36W
Sánchez Magallanes 48 Mh 18.17N 93.59W
San Clemente [Ca.-U.S.] 43 De 33.26N 117.37W
San Clemente [Sp.] 13 Je 39.24N 2.26W
San Clemente del Tuyú 55 Dm 36.22S 56.43W
San Clemente Island 46 Fj 32.55N 118.30W
Sancois 11 Ih 46.50N 2.55 E
San Cosme 55 Ch 27.22S 58.31W
San Cristóbal [Arg.] 56 Hd 30.19S 61.14W
San Cristóbal [Bol.] 55 Ba 13.56S 61.50W
San Cristóbal [Cuba] 49 Fb 22.43N 83.03W
San Cristóbal [Dom.Rep.] 49 Ld 18.25N 70.06W
San Cristóbal [Mex.] 48 Li 17.49N 94.32W
San Cristóbal [Ven.] 53 Ie 7.46N 72.14W
San Cristobal, Baia de- 48 Bd 27.25N 114.40W
San Cristóbal, Isla- 52 Hf 0.50S 89.26W
San Cristóbal de las Casas 47 Fe 16.45N 92.38W
San Cristóbal Island 57 Hf 10.36S 161.45 E
San Cristóbal Verapaz 49 Bf 15.23N 90.24W
Sancti Spíritus 47 Id 21.56N 79.27W
Sancti Spíritus [3] 49 Hb 22.00N 79.30W
Sancy, Puy de- 11 Ii 45.32N 2.50 E
Sand 7 Bg 59.29N 6.15 E
Sand 37 Ed 22.25S 30.05 E
Sanda 29 Dd 34.53N 135.14 E
Sandai 26 Fg 1.15S 110.31 E
Sandakan 22 Ni 5.50N 118.07 E
Sandal, Baie de- 63b Ce 20.49S 167.10 E
Sandal, Ozero- 7 Ie 62.25N 34.10 E
Sandane 7 Bf 61.46N 6.13 E
Sandanski 15 Gh 41.34N 23.17 E
Sandaré 34 Cc 14.42N 10.18W
Sandared 8 Eg 57.43N 12.47 E
Sandarne 8 Gc 61.16N 17.10 E
Sanday 9 Kb 59.15N 2.30W
Sande 8 De 59.36N 10.12 E
Sandefjord 7 Cg 59.08N 10.14 E
Sandégué 34 Ed 7.59N 3.33W
Sandeid 7 Ag 59.33N 5.50 E
Sanders 46 Ki 35.13N 109.20W
Sanderson 43 Ge 30.09N 102.24W
Sandersville 44 Fi 32.59N 82.48W
Sandfontein 37 Bd 22.11S 19.58 E
Sandgate 12 Dc 51.04N 1.09 E
Sandhammaren 8 Fi 55.23N 14.12 E
Sandhamn 8 He 59.17N 18.55 E
Sand Hills 43 Gc 41.45N 102.00W
Sandia 54 Ef 14.17S 69.26W
Sandia Crest 45 Ci 35.13N 106.27W
San Diego [Bol.] 55 Bc 16.04S 60.28W
San Diego [Ca.-U.S.] 39 Hf 32.43N 117.09W
San Diego, Cabo- 52 Jk 54.38S 65.07W
Sandıklı 24 Dc 38.28N 30.17 E
San Dimitri Point 14 In 36.05N 14.05 E
Sand in Taufers / Campo
Tures 14 Fd 46.55N 11.57 E
Sand Lake 45 Ia 50.05N 94.39W
Sand Mountain 44 Dh 34.20N 86.02W
Sandnes 7 Ag 58.51N 5.44 E
Sandnessjøen 7 Cc 66.01N 12.38 E
Sandoa 31 Ji 9.41S 22.52 E
Sandö bank 8 Hf 58.10N 19.15 E
Sandomierska, Kotlina- 10 Rf 50.30N 22.00 E
Sandomierz 10 Rf 50.41N 21.45 E
San Domino 14 Jh 42.05N 15.30 E
Sandoná 54 Cc 1.18N 77.28W
San Donà di Piave 14 Ge 45.38N 12.34 E
Sandoval, Boca de- 48 Ke 24.58N 97.32W
Sandover River 59 Hd 21.43S 136.32 E
Sandoway 25 Ie 18.28N 94.22 E
Sandown 9 Lk 50.39N 1.09W
Sand Point 40 Ge 55.20N 160.30W
Sandpoint 43 Db 48.16N 116.33W
Sandras Dağı 15 Ll 37.04N 28.51 E
Sandray 9 Fe 56.54N 7.25W
Sandspit 42 Ef 53.15N 131.50W
Sand Springs [Mt.-U.S.] 46 Lc 47.09N 107.27W
Sand Springs [Ok.-U.S.] 45 Hh 36.09N 96.07W
Sandstone [Austl.] 59 De 27.59S 119.17 E
Sandstone [Mn.-U.S.] 45 Jc 46.08N 92.52W
Sandu 27 Jf 26.08N 113.16 E
Sandusky [Mi.-U.S.] 44 Fd 43.25N 82.50W
Sandusky [Oh.-U.S.] 43 Kc 41.27N 82.42W
Sandveld 37 Cd 21.20S 20.10 E
Sandvig-Allinge 7 Di 55.15N 14.49 E
Sandvika 8 De 59.54N 10.31 E
Sandviken 7 Df 60.37N 16.46 E
Sandwich 9 Oj 51.17N 1.20 E
Sandwich Bay 42 Lf 53.35N 57.15W
Sandy 12 Bb 52.07N 0.17W
Sandy Cape [Austl.] 59 Ih 41.25S 144.45 E
Sandy Cape [Austl.] 57 Gg 24.40S 153.15 E
Sandy Desert 25 Cc 28.46N 62.30 E
Sandykači 19 Gh 36.32N 62.35 E
Sandy Lake 42 If 53.02N 92.55W
Sandy Lake 42 If 53.02N 93.14W
Sandy Point 44 Il 26.01N 77.24W
Sandy Point Town 50 Ed 17.22N 62.50W
Sandžak 15 Cf 43.10N 20.00 E
Sanem 12 He 49.33N 5.56 E
San Estanislao 56 Ib 24.39S 56.26W
San Esteban 49 Ef 15.17N 85.52W
San Esteban, Bahía de- 48 Ee 25.40N 109.15W
San Esteban, Isla- 48 Cc 28.42N 112.36W
San Esteban de Gormaz 13 Ic 41.35N 3.12W
San Felice Circeo 14 Hi 41.14N 13.05 E
San Felipe [Chile] 56 Fd 32.45S 70.44W
San Felipe [Col.] 54 Ec 1.55N 67.06W
San Felipe [Mex.] 47 Bb 31.00N 114.52W
San Felipe [Mex.] 48 Ig 21.29N 101.13W
San Felipe [Ven.] 54 Ea 10.20N 68.44W
San Felipe, Cayos de- 49 Fc 21.58N 83.30W
San Felipe, Cerro de- 13 Kd 40.24N 1.51W
San Felipe Creek 46 Hj 33.09N 115.46W
San Feliu de Guíxols 13 Pc 41.47N 3.02 E
San Feliu de Llobregat/Sant
Feliu de Llobregat 13 Oc 41.23N 2.03 E
San Felix, Isla- 56 Dc 26.17S 80.05W
San Fermin, Punta- 48 Bb 30.25N 114.40W
San Fernando [Chile] 56 Fd 34.35S 71.00W
San Fernando [Mex.] 48 Bb 29.59N 115.17W
San Fernando [Mex.] 47 Ed 24.51N 98.10W
San Fernando [Phil.] 26 Hc 16.37N 120.19 E
San Fernando [Phil.] 26 Hc 15.01N 120.41 E
San Fernando [Sp.] 13 Fh 36.23N 6.12W
San Fernando [Trin.] 54 Fa 10.17N 61.28W
San Fernando, Río- [Bol.] 55 Cc 17.13S 58.23W
San Fernando, Río- [Mex.]
48 Ke 24.55N 97.40W
San Fernando de Apure 53 Je 7.54N 67.28W
San Fernando de Atabapo 54 Ec 4.03N 67.42W
Sanford [Fl.-U.S.] 43 Kf 28.48N 81.16W
Sanford [Me.-U.S.] 44 Ld 43.26N 70.46W
Sanford [N.C.-U.S.] 44 Hh 35.29N 79.10W
Sanford, Mount- 40 Kd 62.13N 144.09W
San Francisco [Arg.] 56 Hd 31.26S 62.05W
San Francisco [Bol.] 55 Cc 17.42S 58.38W
San Francisco [Ca.-U.S.] 39 Gf 37.48N 122.24W
San Francisco [Pan.] 49 Gi 8.15N 80.58W
San Francisco, Isla- 48 De 24.50N 110.35W
San Francisco Bay 38 Gf 37.43N 122.17W
San Francisco Creek 45 El 29.53N 102.19W
San Francisco de Arriba 48 Hd 26.15N 102.50W
San Francisco de Bellocq 55 Bn 38.42S 60.01W
San Francisco de la Paz 49 Df 14.55N 86.14W
San Francisco del Laishi 55 Ch 26.14S 58.38W
San Francisco del Oro 47 Cc 26.52N 105.51W
San Francisco del Rincón 48 Ig 21.01N 101.51W
San Francisco de Macoris 47 Je 19.18N 70.15W
San Francisco Gotera 49 Cg 13.42N 88.06W
San Francisco Javier 13 Nf 38.42N 1.25 E
San Francisco Mountains 46 Kj 33.45N 109.00W
San Francisco River 46 Kj 32.59N 109.22W
San Fratello 14 Il 38.01N 14.36 E
San Gabriel 55 Di 28.58S 56.12W
San Gabriel, Punta- 48 Cc 28.25N 112.50W
San Gabriel Mountains 46 Gi 34.20N 117.45W
San Gallán, Isla- 54 Cf 13.50S 76.28W
Sangamon River 45 Kf 40.07N 90.20W
Sangar [Iran] 24 Md 37.08N 49.02 E
Sangar 22 Oc 63.55N 127.31 E
Sangatte 12 Dd 50.56N 1.45 E
San Gavino Monreale 14 Ck 39.33N 8.47 E
Sangay, Volcán- 52 If 2.00S 78.20W
Sange 36 Ed 7.02S 28.21 E
Sangeang, Pulau- 26 Gh 8.12S 119.04 E
San Gemini 14 Gh 42.37N 12.33 E
Sanger 46 Fh 36.42N 119.27W
Sangerhausen 10 He 51.28N 11.18 E
San Germán [Cuba] 49 Ic 20.36N 76.08W
San Germán [P.R.] 49 Nd 18.05N 67.03W
Sanggan He 28 Cd 40.24N 115.18 E
Sanggau 26 Ff 0.08N 110.36 E
Sangha 30 Ii 1.13S 16.49 E
Sangha [C.A.R.] [3] 35 Be 3.30N 16.00 E
Sangha [Con.] [3] 36 Cb 2.00N 15.00 E
Sangihe, Kepulauan- =
Sangihe Islands (EN) 21 Oi 3.00N 125.30 E
Sangihe, Pulau- 26 If 3.35N 125.32 E
Sangihe Islands (EN) =
Sangihe, Kepulauan- 21 Oi 3.00N 125.30 E
San Gil 54 Db 6.32N 73.08W
San Gimignano 14 Fg 43.28N 11.02 E
San Giovanni in Fiore 14 Kk 39.15N 16.42 E
San Giovanni in Persiceto 14 Ff 44.38N 11.11 E
San Giovanni Rotondo 14 Ji 41.42N 15.44 E
San Giovanni Valdarno 14 Fg 43.34N 11.32 E
Sangju 28 Jf 36.25N 128.10 E
Sāngli 22 Jh 16.52N 74.34 E
Sangmélima 34 He 2.56N 11.59 E
Sangoli 24 Pd 37.25N 54.35 E
San Gorgonio 38 Hf 34.05N 116.50W
San Gottardo/Sankt
Gotthard = Saint Gotthard
Pass (EN) 5 Gf 46.30N 8.30 E
Sangradouro Grande, Rio-
55 Dc 16.24S 57.10W
Sangre de Cristo
Mountains 38 If 37.30N 105.15W
San Gregorio 55 Al 34.19S 62.02W
Sangre Grande 50 Fg 10.35N 61.07W
Sangri 27 Ff 29.20N 92.15 E
Sangro 14 Ih 42.14N 14.32 E
Sangue, Rio- 54 Gf 11.00S 58.40W
Sangüesa 13 Kb 42.35N 1.17W
Sanguinaires, Iles- 11 Ab 41.53N 8.35 E
San Gustavo 55 Cj 30.41S 59.23W
Sangyuan → Wuqiao 28 Df 37.38N 116.23 E
Sangzhi 27 Jf 29.23N 110.11 E
Sanhe [China] 28 Dd 40.00N 117.01 E
Sanhe [China] 27 La 50.30N 120.04 E
Sanhe-San 29 Cd 35.08N 132.37 E
Sanhezhen 28 Di 31.30N 117.15 E
San Hilario [Arg.] 55 Ch 26.02S 58.39W
San Hilario [Mex.] 48 De 24.22N 110.59W
San Hipolito, Bahia- 48 Cd 26.55N 113.55W
San Ignacio [Arg.] 55 Eh 27.16S 55.32W
San Ignacio [Blz.] 47 Ge 17.10N 89.04W
San Ignacio [Bol.] 54 Ef 14.53S 65.36W
San Ignacio [Bol.] 54 Fg 16.23S 60.59W
San Ignacio [Mex.] 48 Ff 25.55N 106.25W
San Ignacio [Mex.] 47 Bc 27.27N 112.51W
San Ignacio [Par.] 56 Ic 26.52S 57.03W
San Ignacio, Isla de- 48 Ee 25.25N 108.55W
San Ignacio, Laguna- 48 Cd 26.55N 113.15W
San Ildefonso, Cape- 26 Hc 16.02N 121.59 E
San Ildefonso, Cerro- 49 Cf 15.31N 88.17W
San Ildefonso o La Granja 13 Id 40.54N 4.00W
Sanique lie 34 Dd 7.22N 8.43W
San Isidro [Arg.] 56 Id 34.27S 58.30W
San Isidro [Phil.] 26 Hd 11.24N 124.21 E
San Isidro de El General 47 Hg 9.22N 83.42W
Sanīyah 24 If 33.49N 42.43 E
San Jacinto 49 Ji 9.50N 75.07W
San Jacinto Peak 46 Gj 33.49N 116.41W
San Jaime 55 Cj 30.20S 58.19W
San Javier [Arg.] 56 Id 30.35S 59.57W
San Javier [Chile] 56 Fe 35.36S 71.45W
San Javier [Sp.] 13 Lg 37.48N 0.51W
San Javier [Ur.] 55 Ck 32.41S 58.08W
San Javier, Río- 55 Bj 31.30S 60.20W
San Jerónimo Taviche 48 Ki 16.44N 96.35W
Sanjiachang 27 Hg 24.45N 101.53 E
Sanjiaocheng → Haiyan 27 Hd 36.58N 100.50 E
Sanjō 28 Of 37.37N 138.57 E
San Joaquín 54 Ff 13.04S 64.49W
San Joaquín, Río- 54 Ff 13.08S 63.41W
San Joaquín, Sierra de- 55 Eg 24.48S 56.00W
San Joaquin River 46 Eh 36.43N 121.50W
San Joaquin Valley 38 Gf 36.50N 120.10W
San Jon 45 Ei 35.06N 103.20W
San Jorge 56 Hd 31.54S 61.52W
San Jorge, Bahia de- 48 Cb 31.10N 113.15W
San Jorge, Golfe de-/Sant
Jordi, Golf de- 13 Md 40.53N 1.00 E
San Jorge, Golfo- 52 Jj 46.00S 67.00W
San Jorge, Río- 49 Ji 9.07N 74.44W
San Jorge, Serranía- 55 Be 20.21S 60.59W
San Jorge Island 63a Dc 8.27S 159.35 E
San José [2] 55 Dl 34.15S 56.45W
San José [3] 49 Ei 9.40N 84.00W
San José [Arg.] 55 Eh 27.46S 55.47W
San Jose [Ca.-U.S.] 39 Gf 37.20N 121.53W
San José [C.R.] 39 Ki 9.56N 84.05W
San José [Mex.] 48 Dd 27.32N 110.09W
San José [Par.] 55 Dg 25.33S 56.45W
San Jose [Phil.] 26 Hc 15.48N 121.00 E
San Jose [Phil.] 26 Hd 12.21N 121.04 E
San José, Isla- [Mex.] 47 Bc 25.00N 110.38W
San José, Isla- [Pan.] 49 Hi 8.15N 79.07W
San José, Salinas de- 55 Bd 19.07S 60.54W
San José, Serranía de- 55 Bc 17.52S 60.49W
San Jose de Buenavista 26 Hd 10.46N 122.30 E
San José de Chiquitos 54 Fg 17.51S 60.47W
San José de Feliciano 55 Cj 30.23S 58.45W
San José de Gracia 48 Fd 26.08N 107.58W
San José de Guanipa 54 Fb 8.54N 64.09W
San José de Jachal 56 Gd 30.14S 68.45W
San José de las Lajas 49 Fb 22.58N 82.09W
San José del Cabo 47 Cd 23.03N 109.41W
San José del Guaviare 53 Ie 2.35N 72.38W
San José del Rosario 55 Dg 24.12S 56.48W
San José de Mayo 56 Id 34.20S 56.42W
San José de Ocuné 54 Dc 4.15N 70.20W
San José de Tiznados 50 Ch 9.23N 67.33W
San Juan [2] 56 Gd 31.00S 69.00W
San Juan [Arg.] 53 Ji 31.30S 68.30W
San Juán [Bol.] 55 Cc 17.52S 59.59W
San Juán [Bol.] 55 Bd 18.08S 60.08W
San Juan [C.Amer.] 38 Kh 10.56N 83.42W
San Juan [Dom.Rep.] 47 Je 18.48N 71.14W
San Juan [P.R.] 39 Mh 18.28N 66.07W
San Juan [U.S.] 38 Hf 37.18N 110.28W
San Juan, Cabezas de- 51a Cb 18.23N 65.36W
San Juan, Cabo- 30 Hh 1.10N 9.21 E
San Juan, Muela de- 13 Kd 40.26N 1.44W
San Juan, Pico- 47 Hd 21.59N 80.09W
San Juan, Punta- 65d Ab 27.03S 109.22W
San Juan, Río- [Arg.] 56 Gd 32.17S 67.22W
San Juan, Río- [Mex.] 48 Jd 26.10N 99.00W
San Juan, Río- [Mex.] 48 Lh 18.36N 95.40W
San Juan, Río- [Ven.] 50 Eg 10.14N 62.39W
San Juan, Volcán- 48 Gg 21.30N 104.57W
San Juan Bautista [Par.] 56 Ic 26.38S 57.10W
San Juan Bautista [Sp.] 13 Ne 39.05N 1.30 E
San Juan Bautista Tuxtepec 48 Kh 18.06N 96.07W
San Juan de Colón 49 Ki 8.02N 72.16W
San Juan de Guadalupe 48 He 24.38N 102.44W
San Juan del César 49 Kh 10.45N 72.59W
San Juan del Norte 47 Hf 10.55N 83.42W
San Juan de los Cayos 54 Ea 11.10N 68.25W
San Juan de los Lagos 48 Hg 21.15N 102.14W
San Juan de los Morros 54 Ea 9.55N 67.21W
San Juan del Río [Mex.] 48 Jg 20.29N 100.00W
San Juan del Río [Mex.] 48 Ge 24.47N 104.27W
San Juan del Sur 47 Gf 11.15N 85.52W
San Juan de Payara 50 Ci 7.39N 67.36W
San Juanico, Isla- 48 Fg 21.55N 106.40W
San Juanico, Punta- 48 Cd 26.05N 112.15W
San Juan Island 46 Db 48.32N 123.05W
San Juan Mountains 43 Fd 37.35N 107.10W
San Juan Neembucú 55 Dh 26.39S 57.56W
San Juan Nepomuceno
[Col.] 54 Cb 9.57N 75.05W
San Juan Nepomuceno
[Par.] 55 Eh 26.06S 55.58W
San Juan y Martínez 49 Fb 22.16N 83.50W
San Julián 53 Jj 49.19S 67.40W
San Just, Sierra de- 13 Ld 40.46N 0.48W
San Justo 56 Hd 30.47S 60.35W
Sankarani 30 Gg 12.01N 8.19W
Sankt Anton am Arlberg 14 Ec 47.08N 10.16 E
Sankt Augustin 12 Jd 50.47N 7.11 E
Sankt Bernardin Paß/San
Bernardino, Passo del- 14 Dd 46.30N 9.10 E
Sankt Gallen 14 Dc 47.25N 9.25 E
Sankt Gallen [2] 14 Dc 47.20N 9.10 E
Sankt Goar 10 Df 50.09N 7.43 E
Sankt Goarshausen 12 Jd 50.09N 7.44 E
Sankt Gotthard/San
Gottardo = Saint Gotthard
Pass (EN) 5 Gf 46.30N 8.30 E
Sankt Ingbert 10 Dg 49.17N 7.07 E
Sankt Johann im Pongau 14 Hc 47.21N 13.12 E
Sankt Michael im Lungau 14 Hc 47.06N 13.38 E
Sankt Michel/Mikkeli 6 If 61.41N 27.15 E
Sankt Moritz 14 Dd 46.30N 9.52 E
Sankt-Peterburg (Leningrad) 6 Jc 59.55N 30.15 E
Sankt Peter-Ording 10 Eb 54.18N 8.38 E
Sankt Pölten 14 Jb 48.12N 15.38 E
Sankt Ulrich / Ortisei 14 Fd 46.34N 11.40 E
Sankt Veit an der Glan 14 Id 46.46N 14.22 E
Sankt-Vith 11 Md 50.17N 6.08 E
Sankt Wendel 10 Dg 49.28N 7.10 E
Sankt Wolfang im
Salzkammergut 14 Hc 47.44N 13.27 E
Sankuru 30 Ji 4.17S 20.25 E
San Lázaro 56 Ib 22.10S 57.55W
San Lázaro, Cabo- 47 Bd 24.48N 112.19W
San Lazaro, Sierra de- 48 Df 23.25N 110.00W
San Leandro 46 Dh 37.43N 122.09W
Şanlıurfa (Urfa) 23 Eb 37.08N 38.46 E
San Lorenzo 47 Fe 17.44N 94.45W
San Lorenzo [Arg.] 55 Bk 32.45S 60.44W
San Lorenzo [Ec.] 53 Ie 1.17N 78.50W
San Lorenzo [Hond.] 49 Dg 13.25N 87.27W
San Lorenzo, Isla- [Mex.] 48 Cc 28.38N 112.51W
San Lorenzo, Isla- [Peru] 54 Cf 12.05S 77.15W
San Lorenzo, Río- [Mex.] 48 Je 25.07N 98.32W
San Lorenzo, Río- [Mex.] 48 Fe 24.15N 107.24W
San Lorenzo de El Escorial 13 Hd 40.35N 4.09W
San Louis Potosí [2] 47 Dd 22.30N 100.30W
Sanlúcar de Barrameda 13 Fh 36.47N 6.21W
Sanlúcar la Mayor 13 Fg 37.23N 6.12W
San Lucas [Mex.] 48 Gf 22.33N 104.24W
San Lucas [Mex.] 47 Cd 22.53N 109.54W
San Lucas, Cabo- 38 Ig 22.50N 109.55W
San Lucas, Serranía de- 54 Db 8.00N 74.20W
San Lucido 14 Kk 39.18N 16.03 E
San Luis [Arg.] 53 Ji 33.20S 66.20W
San Luis [2] 56 Gd 34.00S 66.00W
San Luis [Bol.] 55 Cc 17.39S 58.42W
San Luis [Cuba] 49 Jc 20.12N 75.51W
San Luis [Guat.] 49 Ce 16.14N 89.27W
San Luis [Mex.] 48 Dc 29.33N 111.05W
San Luis, Isla- 48 Bb 29.58N 114.26W
San Luis, Sierra de- 49 Mh 11.11N 69.42W
San Luis de la Paz 48 Ig 21.18N 100.31W
San Luis del Palmar 55 Ch 27.31S 58.34W
San Luis de Palenque 54 Db 5.25N 71.40W
San Luis Gonzaga, Bahía-
48 Bc 30.00N 114.25W
San Luis Obispo 39 Gf 35.17N 120.40W
San Luis Pass 45 Il 29.05N 95.08W
San Luis Peak 45 Ch 37.59N 106.56W
San Luis Potosí 39 Ig 22.09N 100.59W
San Luis Río Colorado 47 Bb 32.29N 114.48W
San Luis Valley 43 Fd 37.25N 106.00W
Sanluri 14 Ck 39.34N 8.54 E
San Manuel [Arg.] 55 Cm 37.47S 58.50W
San Manuel [Az.-U.S.] 46 Jj 32.36N 110.38W

Index Symbols

[1] Independent Nation
[2] State, Region
[3] District, County
[4] Municipality
[5] Colony, Dependency
Continent
Physical Region
Historical or Cultural Region
Mount, Mountain
Volcano
Hill
Mountains, Mountain Range
Hills, Escarpment
Plateau, Upland
Pass, Gap
Plain, Lowland
Delta
Salt Flat
Valley, Canyon
Crater, Cave
Karst Features
Depression
Polder
Desert, Dunes
Forest, Woods
Heath, Steppe
Oasis
Cape, Point
Coast, Beach
Cliff
Peninsula
Isthmus
Sandbank
Island
Atoll
Rock, Reef
Islands, Archipelago
Rocks, Reefs
Coral Reef
Well, Spring
Geyser
River, Stream
Waterfall Rapids
River Mouth, Estuary
Lake
Salt Lake
Intermittent Lake
Reservoir
Swamp, Pond
Canal
Glacier
Ice Shelf, Pack Ice
Ocean
Sea
Gulf, Bay
Strait, Fjord
Lagoon
Bank
Seamount
Tablemount
Ridge
Shelf
Basin
Escarpment, Sea Scarp
Fracture
Trench, Abyss
National Park, Reserve
Point of Interest
Recreation Site
Cave, Cavern
Historic Site
Ruins
Wall, Walls
Church, Abbey
Temple
Scientific Station
Airport
Port
Lighthouse
Mine
Tunnel
Dam, Bridge

Index Symbols

- Independent Nation
- State, Region
- District, County
- Municipality
- Colony, Dependency
- Continent
- Physical Region
- Historical or Cultural Region
- Mount, Mountain
- Volcano
- Hill
- Mountains, Mountain Range
- Hills, Escarpment
- Plateau, Upland
- Pass, Gap
- Plain, Lowland
- Delta
- Salt Flat
- Valley, Canyon
- Crater, Cave
- Karst Features
- Depression
- Polder
- Cliff
- Peninsula
- Desert, Dunes
- Forest, Woods
- Heath, Steppe
- Oasis
- Cape, Point
- Coast, Beach
- Islands, Archipelago
- Rocks, Reefs
- Isthmus
- Sandbank
- Island
- Atoll
- Rock, Reef
- River Mouth, Estuary
- Lake
- Salt Lake
- Intermittent Lake
- Reservoir
- River, Stream
- Swamp, Pond
- Waterfall Rapids
- Glacier
- Ice Shelf, Pack Ice
- Ocean
- Sea
- Shelf
- Gulf, Bay
- Strait, Fjord
- Canal
- Bank
- Fracture
- Trench, Abyss
- Ridge
- Point of Interest
- Recreation Site
- Cave, Cavern
- Lagoon
- Seamount
- Tablemount
- Scientific Station
- Escarpment, Sea Scarp
- National Park, Reserve
- Church, Abbey
- Temple
- Airport
- Historic Site
- Ruins
- Wall, Walls
- Port
- Lighthouse
- Mine
- Tunnel
- Dam, Bridge
- Well, Spring
- Geyser

Index Symbols

① Independent Nation	⊞ Historical or Cultural Region	⊠ Pass, Gap	⊡ Depression	⌐ Coast, Beach
② State, Region	Mount, Mountain	Plain, Lowland	Polder	Cliff
③ District, County	Volcano	Delta	Desert Dunes	Peninsula
④ Municipality	Hill	Salt Flat	Forest, Woods	Isthmus
⑤ Colony, Dependency	Mountains, Mountain Range	Valley, Canyon	Heath, Steppe	Sandbank
⑥ Continent	Hills, Escarpment	Crater, Cave	Oasis	Island
⑦ Physical Region	Plateau, Upland	Karst Features	Cape, Point	Atoll

Rock, Reef	Waterfall Rapid	Canal	Lagoon	Escarpment, Sea Scarp	Historic Site	Port
Islands, Archipelago	River Mouth, Estuary	Glacier	Bank	Fracture	Ruins	Lighthouse
Rocks, Reefs	Lake	Ice Shelf, Pack Ice	Seamount	Trench, Abyss	Wall, Walls	Mine
Coral Reef	Salt Lake	Ocean	Tableland	National Park, Reserve	Church, Abbey	Tunnel
Well, Spring	Intermittent Lake	Sea	Ridge	Point of Interest	Temple	Dam, Bridge
Geyser	Reservoir	Gulf, Bay	Shelf	Recreation Site	Airport	
River, Stream	Swamp, Pond	Strait, Fjord	Basin	Cave, Cavern	Scientific Station	

Index Symbols

[1] Independent Nation	Pass, Gap	Depression	Coast, Beach	Rock, Reef
[2] State, Region	Mount, Mountain	Polder	Cliff	Islands, Archipelago
[3] District, County	Volcano	Desert, Dunes	Peninsula	Rocks, Reefs
[4] Municipality	Hill	Forest, Woods	Isthmus	Coral Reef
[5] Colony, Dependency	Mountains, Mountain Range	Heath, Steppe	Sandbank	Well, Spring
■ Continent	Hills, Escarpment	Oasis	Island	Geyser
Physical Region	Plateau, Upland	Cape, Point	Atoll	River, Stream

Historical or Cultural Region	Waterfall Rapids	Canal	Lagoon	Escarpment, Sea Scarp	Historic Site	Port
Salt Flat	River Mouth, Estuary	Glacier	Bank	Fracture	Ruins	Lighthouse
Valley, Canyon	Lake	Ice Shelf, Pack Ice	Seamount	Trench, Abyss	Wall, Walls	Mine
Crater, Cave	Salt Lake	Ocean	Tableland	National Park, Reserve	Church, Abbey	Tunnel
Karst Features	Intermittent Lake	Sea	Ridge	Point of Interest	Temple	Dam, Bridge
	Reservoir	Gulf, Bay	Shelf	Recreation Site	Scientific Station	
	Swamp, Pond	Strait, Fjord	Basin	Cave, Cavern	Airport	

Sersou, Plateau du- 13 Ni 35.30N 2.00 E
Sertã 13 De 39.48N 8.06W
Sertão 52 Lg 10.00S 41.00W
Sertãozinho 55 Ie 21.08S 47.59W
Sêrtar 27 He 32.20N 100.20 E
Serti 34 Hd 7.30N 11.22 E
Serua, Pulau- 26 Jh 6.18S 130.01 E
Serui 26 Kg 1.53S 136.14 E
Serule 37 Dd 21.55S 27.19 E
Sérvia 15 Ei 40.11N 22.00 E
Sêrxü 27 Ge 32.56N 98.02 E
Seryítsi 15 Ii 40.00N 25.10 E
Seryševo 20 Hf 51.02N 128.25 E
Sesayap 26 Gf 3.36N 117.15 E
Sese 36 Eb 2.11N 25.47 E
Seseganaga Lake 45 Ka 50.10N 90.15W
Sese Islands 36 Fc 0.20S 32.20 E
Sesfontein 37 Ac 19.07S 13.39 E
Sesheke 36 Df 17.29S 24.18 E
Sesia 14 Ce 45.05N 8.37 E
Sesibi 35 Ea 20.05N 30.31 E
Sesimbra 13 Cf 38.26N 9.06W
Šešma 7 Mi 55.20N 51.12 E
Sesnut 8 Be 59.42N 7.21 E
Sessa Aurunca 14 Hi 41.14N 13.56 E
Ses Salines, Cap de-/Salinas, Cabo de- 13 Pe 39.16N 3.03 E
Sestao 13 Ja 43.18N 3.00W
Sesto Fiorentino 14 Fg 43.50N 11.12 E
Sesto San Giovanni 14 De 45.32N 9.14 E
Sestriere 14 Af 44.57N 6.53 E
Sestri Levante 14 Df 44.16N 9.24 E
Sestroreck 7 Gf 60.06N 29.59 E
Šešupė 7 Fi 55.00N 22.10 E
Šešuvis 8 Ji 55.12N 22.31 E
Sesvenna, Piz- 14 Ed 46.42N 10.25 E
Sesvete 14 Ke 45.50N 16.07 E
Šeta/Šėta 8 Ki 55.14N 24.18 E
Šėta/Šeta 8 Ki 55.14N 24.18 E
Setaka 29 Be 33.09N 130.28 E
Setana 28 Oc 42.26N 139.51 E
Sète 11 Jk 43.24N 3.41 E
Sete de Setembro, Rio- 55 Fa 12.56S 52.51W
Sete Lagoas 54 Jg 19.27S 44.14W
Setenil 13 Gh 36.51N 5.11W
Sete Quedas, Saltos das- = Guaira Falls (EN) 56 Jb 24.02S 54.16W
Setermoen 7 Eb 68.52N 18.28 E
Setesdal 7 Bg 59.05N 7.35 E
Setesdalsheiane 8 Be 59.30N 7.10 E
Seti 25 Gc 28.58N 81.06 E
Sétif [3] 32 Ib 36.05N 5.00 E
Sétif 31 He 36.12N 5.24 E
Seto 29 Ed 35.13N 137.05 E
Setonaikai = Inland Sea (EN) 21 Pf 34.10N 133.00 E
Setouchi 29b Ba 28.08N 129.20 E
Šetpe 19 Fg 44.06N 52.02 E
Settat 32 Fc 33.00N 7.37W
Settat [3] 32 Fc 33.00N 7.30W
Setté Cama 36 Ac 2.32S 9.45 E
Sette-Daban, Hrebet- 20 Id 62.00N 138.00 E
Settle 9 Kg 54.04N 2.16W
Setúbal [2] 13 Df 38.20N 8.30W
Setúbal 6 Fh 38.32N 8.54W
Setúbal, Baía de- 13 Df 38.27N 8.53W
Setúbal o de Guadalupe, Laguna- 55 Bj 31.33S 60.35W
Seudre 11 Ei 45.48N 1.09W
Seugne 11 Fi 45.42N 0.32W
Seui 14 Dk 39.50N 9.19 E
Seuil-d'Argonne 12 Hf 48.58N 5.03 E
Seul, Lac- 38 Jd 50.20N 92.30W
Seulles 12 Be 49.20N 0.27W
Seurre 11 Lg 47.00N 5.09 E
Sevan 19 Eg 40.32N 44.57 E
Sevan, Lake- (EN) = Sevan, Ozero- 5 Kg 40.20N 45.20 E
Sevan, Ozero- = Sevan, Lake- (EN) 5 Kg 40.20N 45.20 E
Sévaré 34 Ec 14.32N 4.06W
Sevastopol 6 Jg 44.36N 33.32 E
Ševčenko → Aktau 22 He 43.35N 51.05 E
Ševčenko, Zaliv- 18 Ca 46.30N 60.15 E
Sevenoaks 9 Nj 51.16N 0.12 E
Sever 13 Ee 39.40N 7.32W
Sévérac-le-Château 11 Jj 44.19N 3.04 E
Severn 9 Kj 51.20N 3.10W
Severn [Can.] 38 Kd 56.02N 87.36W
Severn [U.K.] 9 Kj 51.35N 2.40W
Severnaja Dvina = Northern Dvina (EN) 5 Kc 64.32N 40.30 E
Severnaja Keltma 17 Ff 61.30N 54.00 E
Severnaja Pseašho, Gora- 16 Lh 43.47N 40.30 E
Severnaja Sosva 19 Gc 64.10N 65.28 E
Severnaja Zemlja = Severnaya Zemlya (EN) 21 Lb 79.30N 98.00 E
Severnaya Zemlya (EN) = Severnaja Zemlja 21 Lb 79.30N 98.00 E
Severn Lake 42 If 53.52N 90.58W
Severnoje 16 Rb 54.05N 52.32 E
Severnoje 20 Ce 56.21N 78.23 E
Severny 19 Gb 67.38N 64.06 E
Severnyje Uvaly = Northern Uvals (EN) 5 Kd 59.30N 49.00 E
Severny Kommunar 17 Gg 58.23N 54.02 E
Severny Ledovity Okean = Arctic Ocean (EN) 67 Be 85.00N 170.00 E
Severny Ural = Northern Urals (EN) 5 Lc 62.00N 59.00 E
Severobajkalsk 20 Fe 55.40N 109.25 E
Severočeský kraj [3] 10 Kf 50.35N 14.15 E
Severodoneck 16 Ke 48.57N 38.31 E
Severodvinsk 6 Jc 64.34N 39.50 E
Severo-Jenisejski 20 Ed 60.28N 93.01 E
Severo-Kazahstanskaja Oblast [3] 19 Ge 54.30N 68.00 E
Severo-Krymski Kanal 16 Ig 45.30N 34.35 E
Severo-Kurilsk 22 Rd 50.40N 156.08 E
Severomoravský kraj [3] 10 Ng 49.45N 17.50 E
Severomorsk 19 Db 69.04N 33.24 E
Severo-Osetinskaja respublika 19 Eg 43.00N 44.10 E
Severo-Sibirskaja Nizmennost = North Siberian Plain (EN) 21 Mb 72.00N 104.00 E
Severouralsk 19 Gc 60.09N 60.01 E
Sevier 46 Ig 38.35N 112.14W
Sevier Bridge Reservoir 46 Ig 39.21N 111.57W
Sevier Desert 46 Ig 39.25N 112.50W
Sevier Lake 43 Ed 38.55N 113.09W
Sevier River 43 Ed 39.04N 113.06W
Sevilla [3] 13 Gg 37.30N 5.30W
Sevilla [Col.] 54 Cc 4.16N 75.53W
Sevilla [Sp.] = Seville (EN) 6 Fh 37.23N 5.59W
Sevilla, Isla- 49 Fi 8.14N 82.24W
Seville (EN) = Sevilla [Sp.] 6 Fh 37.23N 5.59W
Sevlijevo 15 If 43.01N 25.06 E
Sèvre Nantaise 11 Eg 47.12N 1.33W
Sèvre Niortaise 11 Eh 46.18N 1.08W
Sevron 11 Lh 46.32N 5.16 E
Sevsk 16 Ic 52.08N 34.30 E
Sewa 34 Cd 7.18N 12.08W
Seward [Ak.-U.S.] 39 Ec 60.06N 149.26W
Seward [Nb.-U.S.] 45 Hf 40.55N 97.06W
Seward Peninsula 38 Cc 65.00N 164.00W
Sewell 56 Fd 34.05S 70.21W
Seyāhkal 24 Md 37.09N 49.52 E
Seybaplaya 48 Nh 19.39N 90.40W
Seybaplaya, Punta- 48 Nh 19.45N 90.42W
Seybouse, Oued- 14 Bn 36.53N 7.46 E
Seychelles [1] 31 Mi 8.00S 55.00 E
Seychelles Islands 30 Mi 4.35S 55.40 E
Seydān 24 Og 30.01N 53.01 E
Seydişehir 24 Dd 37.25N 31.51 E
Seyðisfjörður 6 Eb 65.16N 14.00W
Seyfe Gölü 24 Fc 39.13N 34.23 E
Seyf Ţāleh 24 Le 35.57N 46.19 E
Seyhan 23 Db 36.43N 34.53 E
Seyitgazi 24 Dc 39.27N 30.43 E
Seyitömer 15 Mj 39.34N 29.52 E
Seyla' 35 Gc 11.21N 43.30 E
Seymour [Austl.] 59 Jg 37.02S 145.08 E
Seymour [In.-U.S.] 44 Ef 38.58N 85.53W
Seymour [Mo.-U.S.] 45 Jh 37.09N 92.46W
Seymour [S.Afr.] 37 Df 32.33S 26.46 E
Seymour [Tx.-U.S.] 43 He 33.35N 99.16W
Sezana 14 He 45.42N 13.52 E
Sézanne 11 Jf 48.43N 3.43 E
Sfaktiria 15 Em 36.56N 21.40 E
Sfax (EN) = Şafāqis [3] 32 Jc 34.30N 10.30 E
Sfax (EN) = Şafāqis 31 Ie 34.44N 10.46 E
Sferracavallo, Capo- 14 Dk 39.43N 9.40 E
Sfintu Gheorghe [Rom.] 15 Me 44.53N 29.26 E
Sfintu Gheorghe [Rom.] 15 Id 45.52N 25.47 E
Sfintu Gheorghe, Braţul- 15 Me 44.53N 29.36 E
Sfintu Gheorghe, Ostrovul- 15 Md 45.07N 29.22 E
Sfizef 13 Li 35.14N 0.15W
's-Gravenhage/Den Haag = The Hague (EN) 6 Ge 52.06N 4.18 E
's-Gravenhage-Scheveningen 11 Kb 52.06N 4.18 E
Shaanxi Sheng (Shaan-hsi Sheng) = Shensi (EN) [2] 27 Id 36.00N 109.00 E
Shaba [2] 36 Ed 8.30S 25.00 E
Sha'bah, Wādī ash- 24 Ij 25.59N 41.55 E
Shabeellaha Dhexe [3] 35 He 3.00N 46.00 E
Shabellaha Hoose [3] 35 Ge 2.00N 44.40 E
Shabēlle, Webi- = Shebeli Webi (EN) 30 Lh 0.12S 42.45 E
Shabestar 24 Kc 38.11N 45.42 E
Shabunda 36 Ec 2.42S 27.20 E
Shache/Yarkant 27 Cd 38.24N 77.15 E
Shacheng → Huailai 27 Kc 40.29N 115.30 E
Shackleton Coast 66 Kg 82.00S 162.00 E
Shackleton Glacier 66 Lg 84.35S 176.15W
Shackleton Ice Shelf 66 He 66.00S 101.00 E
Shackleton Range 66 Ag 80.40S 26.00W
Shaddādī 24 Id 36.02N 40.45 E
Shādegān 24 Mg 30.40N 48.38 E
Shadwān, Jazīrat- 33 Fd 27.30N 33.55 E
Shaftesbury 9 Kk 51.01N 2.12W
Shagedu → Jungar Qi 27 Jd 39.37N 110.58 E
Shāghir Bazar 24 Id 36.52N 40.53 E
Shag Rocks 66 Rd 54.26S 36.33W
Shāh'Abbās 24 De 34.44N 52.10 E
Shah Alam 26 Df 3.05N 101.29 E
Shahdol 25 Gd 23.13N 81.18 E
Sha He [China] 28 Ch 33.39N 114.38 E
Sha He [China] 28 Cf 37.09N 114.46 E
Shahezhen → Linze 27 Hd 39.10N 100.21 E
Shah Jahān, Kūh-e- 24 Qd 37.02N 57.54 E
Shahjahānpur 25 Fc 27.53N 79.55 E
Shah Kūh 23 Hb 36.35N 54.31 E
Shahmīrzād 24 Oe 35.47N 53.20 E
Shāhpūr 24 Nh 32.50N 51.45 E
Shāhpūr 24 Nh 29.39N 51.03 E
Shahrak 24 Nd 36.14N 50.40 E
Shahr-e-Bābak 24 Pg 30.10N 55.09 E
Shahr-e Khafr 24 Oh 28.56N 53.14 E
Shahr Kord 23 Hc 32.19N 50.50 E
Shāhrūd 24 Md 37.17N 48.43 E
Shahu, Kūh-e- 24 Le 34.45N 46.30 E
Shāh Zeyd 24 Od 36.13N 52.22 E
Shā'ib al Banāt, Jabal- 30 Kf 26.59N 33.29 E
Sha'īt, Wādī- 24 Ej 24.33N 33.01 E
Shakaga-Dake 29 Be 33.11N 130.53 E
Shakawe 31 Ji 18.23S 21.51 E
Shak Bay (Denham) 59 Ce 25.55S 113.32 E
Shaker Heights 44 Ge 41.29N 81.36W
Shaki 34 Fd 8.40N 3.23 E
Shakotan-Dake 29a Bb 43.16N 140.26 E
Shakotan-Hantō 29a Bb 43.15N 140.30 E
Shakotan-Misaki 29a Bb 43.23N 140.28 E
Shaktoolik 40 Gd 64.20N 161.09W
Shāl 24 Me 35.54N 49.46 E
Shala, Lake- 35 Fd 7.29N 38.32 E
Shalamzār 24 Nf 32.02N 50.49 E
Shalānbōd 35 Ge 1.40N 44.42 E
Shaler Mountains 42 Gb 71.45N 111.00W
Shaliuhe → Gangca 27 Hd 37.30N 100.14 E
Shaluli Shan 21 L[illegible] 30.45N 99.45 E
Shām, Bādiyat ash- = Syrian Desert (EN) 21 F[illegible] 32.00N 40.00 E
Shām, Jabal ash- 21 Hg 23.10N 57.20 E
Shamattawa 42 Ie 55.52N 92.05W
Shambe 35 Ee 7.07N 30.46 E
Shambu 35 Fe 9.33N 37.07 E
Shamīl 24 Q[illegible] 27.30N 56.53 E
Shāmīyah 21 Ff 34.00N 39.59 E
Shammar, Jabal- 21 Gg 27.20N 41.45 E
Shamo, Lake- 35 Fe 5.50N 37.40 E
Shamokin 44 Ie 40.47N 76.34W
Shamrock 45 Fi 35.13N 100.15W
Shams 24 Pg 31.04N 55.02 E
Shamsī 35 Db 19.03N 29.54 E
Shamwa 37 Ec 17.18S 31.34 E
Shan [2] 25 Jc 22.00N 98.00 E
Shandī 31 Kg 16.42N 33.26 E
Shandian He 28 Dc 42.20N 116.20 E
Shandong Bandao = Shantung Peninsula (EN) 21 Of 37.00N 121.00 E
Shandong Sheng (Shan-tung Sheng) = Shantung (EN) [2] 27 Ke 36.00N 119.00 E
Shandūr Pass 25 Ea 36.04N 72.31 E
Shangani 37 Dc 19.42S 29.22 E
Shangani 37 Dc 18.30S 27.11 E
Shangbahe 28 Ci 30.39N 115.06 E
Shangcai 28 Ch 33.16N 114.15 E
Shangcheng 28 Ci 31.49N 115.24 E
Shangdu 27 Jc 41.31N 113.32 E
Shanggao 28 Cj 28.15N 114.55 E
Shanghai 22 Of 31.14N 121.28 E
Shanghai Shi (Shang-hai Shih) [4] 27 Le 31.14N 121.28 E
Shang-hai Shih → Shanghai Shi [4] 27 Le 31.14N 121.28 E
Shanghang 27 Kf 25.04N 116.21 E
Shanghe 28 Df 37.19N 117.09 E
Shanghekou 27 Lc 40.23N 124.51 E
Shangpaihe → Feixi 28 Di 31.42N 117.09 E
Shangqiu (Zhuji) 27 Ke 34.24N 115.37 E
Shangrao 27 Kf 28.29N 117.59 E
Shan Guan 27 Kf 27.28N 117.05 E
Shangxian 27 Ie 33.55N 109.57 E
Shangyi (Nanhaoqian) 28 Bd 41.06N 113.58 E
Shangyu (Baiguan) 28 Fi 30.01N 120.53 E
Shangzhi 27 Mb 45.13N 127.55 E
Shanhaiguan 28 Ed 40.01N 119.45 E
Shanhetun 28 Ib 44.43N 127.14 E
Shan-hsi Sheng → Shanxi Sheng = Shansi (EN) [2] 27 Jd 37.00N 112.00 E
Shanklin 12 Ad 50.37N 1.11W
Shanmatang Ding 27 Jg 24.45N 111.50 E
Shannon 41 Kc 75.20N 18.10W
Shannon 62 Fd 40.33S 175.25 E
Shannon/Aerfort na Sionainne 9 Ei 52.42N 8.57W
Shannon/An tSionainn 5 Fe 52.36N 9.41W
Shannon, Mount- 59 Ie 29.58S 141.30 E
Shannon, Mouth of the- 9 Di 52.30N 9.53W
Shanshan (Piqan) 27 Fc 42.52N 90.10 E
Shansi (EN) = Shan-hsi Sheng → Shanxi Sheng [2] 27 Jd 37.00N 112.00 E
Shansi (EN) = Shanxi Sheng (Shan-hsi Sheng) [2] 27 Jd 37.00N 112.00 E
Shansonggang 28 Ic 42.30N 126.13 E
Shanţah, Ra's- 24 Qi 25.22N 56.26 E
Shantar Islands (EN) = Šantarskije Ostrova 21 Pd 55.00N 137.36 E
Shantou 22 Ng 23.26N 116.42 E
Shantung (EN) = Shandong Sheng (Shan-tung Sheng) [2] 27 Kd 36.00N 119.00 E
Shantung (EN) = Shan-tung Sheng → Shandong Sheng [2] 27 Kd 36.00N 119.00 E
Shantung Peninsula (EN) = Shandong Bandao 21 Of 37.00N 121.00 E
Shan-tung Sheng → Shandong Sheng = Shantung (EN) [2] 27 Kd 36.00N 119.00 E
Shanxian 28 Dg 34.47N 116.05 E
Shanxi Sheng (Shan-hsi Sheng) = Shansi (EN) [2] 27 Jd 37.00N 112.00 E
Shanyin (Daiyue) 28 Be 39.30N 112.48 E
Shanyincheng 28 Be 39.27N 112.56 E
Shaoguan 22 Ng 24.57N 113.34 E
Shaoshan 27 Jf 27.55N 112.32 E
Shaowu 27 Kf 27.21N 117.29 E
Shaoxing 22 Og 30.00N 120.30 E
Shaoyang 22 Ng 27.13N 111.31 E
Shapinsay 9 Kb 59.03N 2.51W
Shaqlāwah 24 Kd 36.23N 44.18 E
Shaqq al Ju'ayfir 35 Db 15.16N 26.00 E
Shaqrā' 23 Gg 13.21N 45.42 E
Shaqū 24 Qi 27.14N 56.22 E
Sharāf 24 Jg 30.37N 43.45 E
Sharafah 35 Dc 12.04N 27.07 E
Sharafkhāneh 24 Kc 38.11N 45.29 E
Sharāh, Jibāl ash- 24 Fg 30.10N 35.30 E
Sharā 'Iwah 24 Oj 25.02N 52.14 E
Shareh 24 Kd 37.38N 44.50 E
Shari 27 Pc 43.55N 144.40 E
Shārī, Buḩayrat- 24 Ke 34.23N 44.07 E
Shari-Dake 29a Db 43.46N 144.43 E
Sharifābād [Iran] 24 Nd 36.12N 50.08 E
Sharifābād [Iran] 24 Ne 35.25N 51.47 E
Shark Bay 57 Cg 25.30S 113.30 E
Sharm ash Shaykh 33 Fd 27.50N 34.16 E
Sharon 44 Ge 41.16N 80.30W
Sharon Springs 45 Fg 38.54N 101.45W
Sharp 9 Fc 58.05N 7.05W
Sharqīyah, Aş Şaḩrā' ash- = Arabian Desert (EN) 30 Kf 28.00N 32.00 E
Sharshar, Jabal- 24 Dk 23.52N 30.20 E
Shary 23 Fd 27.15N 43.27 E
Shashe 37 Dd 21.24S 27.27 E
Shashemene 35 Fd 7.13N 38.36 E
Shashi 22 Nf 30.22N 112.11 E
Shashi 30 Jk 22.12S 29.21 E
Shasta, Mount- 38 Ge 41.20N 122.20W
Shasta Lake 43 Cc 40.50N 122.25W
Shāţi', Wādī ash- 33 Bd 27.10N 13.25 E
Shattuck 45 Gh 36.16N 99.53W
Shaunavon 42 Gg 49.40N 108.25W
Shawan 27 Ec 44.21N 85.37 E
Shawano 45 Ld 44.47N 88.36W
Shawinigan 42 Kg 46.33N 72.45W
Shawnee 43 Hd 35.20N 96.55W
Shawneetown 45 Lh 37.42N 88.08W
Shaw River 59 Dd 20.20S 119.17 E
Shāwshāw, Jabal- 24 Ci 26.03N 28.56 E
Shayang 28 Bi 30.42N 112.34 E
Shaybārā 24 Gj 25.25N 36.51 E
Shaykh Aḩmad 24 Lf 32.53N 46.26 E
Shaykh Fāris 24 Lf 32.05N 47.36 E
Shaykh Sa'd 24 Lf 32.34N 46.17 E
Shaykh 'Uthmān 23 Fg 12.52N 44.59 E
Shebar, Kowtal-e- 23 Kc 34.54N 68.14 E
Shebele, Wabe- = Shebeli Webi (EN) 30 Lh 0.12S 42.45 E
Shebeli Webi (EN) = Shabēlle, Webi- 30 Lh 0.12S 42.45 E
Shebeli Webi (EN) = Shebele, Wabe- 30 Lh 0.12S 42.45 E
Sheberghān 22 If 36.41N 65.45 E
Sheboygan 45 Me 43.46N 87.44W
Shebshi Mountains 30 Ih 8.30N 11.45 E
Shedin Peak 42 Ee 55.50N 127.00W
Sheelin, Lough-/Loch Síleann 9 Fh 53.48N 7.20W
Sheenjek 40 Kc 66.45N 144.33W
Sheep Haven/Cuan na gCaorach 9 Ff 55.10N 7.52W
Sheep Mountain 46 Hj 32.32N 114.14W
Sheep Range 46 Hh 36.45N 115.05W
s'Heerenberg, Bergh- 12 Ic 51.53N 6.16 E
Sheerness 9 Nj 51.27N 0.45 E
Sheffield [Al.-U.S.] 44 Dh 34.46N 87.40W
Sheffield [Eng.-U.K.] 6 Fe 53.23N 1.30W
Sheffield [Tx.-U.S.] 45 Fk 30.43N 101.50W
Shefford 12 Bb 52.02N 0.20W
Shek Hasan 35 Fc 12.04N 35.53 E
Shek Husen 35 Gd 7.45N 40.42 E
Shelburne [N.S.-Can.] 42 Kh 43.46N 65.19W
Shelburne [Ont.-Can.] 44 Gc 44.04N 80.12W
Shelby [Mt.-U.S.] 43 Eb 48.30N 111.51W
Shelby [N.C.-U.S.] 44 Gh 35.17N 81.32W
Shelbyville [Il.-U.S.] 45 Lg 39.24N 88.48W
Shelbyville [In.-U.S.] 44 Ef 39.31N 85.47W
Shelbyville [Tn.-U.S.] 44 Dh 35.29N 86.27W
Shelbyville, Lake- 45 Lg 39.30N 88.40W
Sheldon 45 Ie 43.11N 95.51W
Sheldon Point 40 Gd 63.32N 164.52W
Shelikhov Gulf (EN) = Šelihova, Zaliv- 21 Rc 60.00N 158.00 E
Shelikof Strait 40 Ie 57.30N 155.00W
Shell 46 Ld 44.33N 107.44W
Shellbrook 42 Gf 53.13N 106.24W
Shellharbour 58 Gh 34.35S 150.52 E
Shelter Point 62 Cg 47.06S 168.13 E
Shelton 46 Dc 47.13N 123.06W
Shenandoah 45 If 40.46N 95.22W
Shenandoah Mountain 44 Hf 38.58N 79.00W
Shenandoah Valley 44 Hf 38.45N 78.45W
Shenchi 28 Be 39.05N 112.11 E
Shendam 34 Gd 8.53N 9.32 E
Shending Shan 27 Nb 46.34N 133.27 E
Shenge 34 Cd 7.55N 12.57W
Shëngjini 15 Ch 41.49N 19.35 E
Shengsi (Caiyuanzhen) 28 Gi 30.42N 122.29 E
Shengsi Liedao 27 Le 30.45N 122.40 E
Shengxian 27 Lf 29.35N 120.45 E
Shengze 28 Fi 30.55N 120.39 E
Shenjiamen → Putuo 28 Gj 29.57N 122.18 E
Shenmu 27 Jd 38.52N 110.35 E
Shenqiu (Huaidian) 27 Ke 33.27N 115.05 E
Shensi (EN) = Shaan-hsi Sheng → Shaanxi Sheng [2] 27 Id 36.00N 109.00 E
Shensi (EN) = Shaanxi Sheng (Shaan-hsi Sheng) [2] 27 Id 36.00N 109.00 E
Shenton, Mount- 59 Ee 28.00S 123.22 E
Shenxian 28 Ce 38.01N 115.33 E
Shenyang (Mukden) 22 Oe 41.48N 123.24 E
Shenze 28 Ce 38.11N 115.11 E
Shepherd, Iles- = Shepherd Islands (EN) 63b Dc 16.55S 168.35 E
Shepherd Islands (EN) = Shepherd, Iles- 63b Dc 16.55S 168.35 E
Shepparton 58 Fh 36.23S 145.25 E
Sheppey 9 Nj 51.24N 0.50 E
Shepshed 12 Ab 52.45N 1.17W
Sheqi 28 Bh 33.04N 112.56 E
Sherard, Cape - 42 Jb 74.36N 80.10W
Sherard Osborn Fjord 41 Gb 82.10N 51.30W
Sherborne 9 Kk 50.57N 2.31W
Sherbro Island 30 Fh 7.33N 12.42W
Sherbrooke 39 Le 45.24N 71.54W
Sherda 35 Ba 20.08N 16.45 E
Shere Hill 34 Gd 9.57N 9.03 E
Sheridan [Mt.-U.S.] 46 Id 45.27N 112.12W
Sheridan [Wy.-U.S.] 39 Ie 44.48N 106.58W
Sheridan Lake 45 Eg 38.30N 102.15W
Sheringham 9 Oi 52.57N 1.12 E
Sherman 43 He 33.38N 96.36W
Sherman Station 44 Mc 45.54N 68.26W
Sherridon 42 He 55.07N 101.05W
's-Hertogenbosch, Den Bosch 11 Lc 51.41N 5.19 E
Sherwood Forest 9 Lh 53.10N 1.10W
She Shui 28 Ci 30.52N 114.22 E
Shetland [3] 9 La 60.30N 1.30W
Shetland Islands (Zetland) 5 Fc 60.30N 1.30W
Shewa [3] 35 Fd 9.20N 38.55 E
Shewa Gimira 35 Fd 7.00N 35.50 E
Shexian 28 Bf 36.33N 113.40 E
Shexian (Huicheng) 28 Ej 29.53N 118.27 E
Sheyang (Hede) 28 Fh 33.47N 120.15 E
Sheyenne River 43 Hb 47.05N 96.50W
Shiant Islands 9 Gd 57.54N 6.30W
Shibām 35 Hb 15.56N 48.38 E
Shibamīnah, Wādī 23 Ie 22.12N 55.30 E
Shibata [Jap.] 28 Of 37.57N 139.20 E
Shibata [Jap.] 29 Gb 33.05N 140.50 E
Shibayama-Gata 29 Ec 36.21N 136.23 E
Shibazhan 27 Ma 42.28N 125.20 E
Shibecha 28 Rc 43.17N 144.36 E
Shibetsu [Jap.] 28 Rc 43.40N 145.08 E
Shibetsu [Jap.] 27 Pc 44.10N 142.23 E
Shibetsu-Gawa 29a Db 43.40N 145.06 E
Shibīn al Kawm 33 Fc 30.33N 31.01 E
Shibiutan 29a Ca 44.47N 142.35 E
Shibi-Zan 29 Bf 31.59N 130.22 E
Shīb Kūh 23 Hd 27.20N 52.40 E
Shibukawa 28 Of 36.29N 139.00 E
Shibushi 29 Bf 31.28N 131.07 E
Shibushi-Wan 28 Ki 31.25N 131.12 E
Shichinohe 29 Ga 40.41N 141.10 E
Shichiyo Islands 64d Bb 7.23N 151.40 E
Shidao 27 Ld 36.51N 122.18 E
Shido 29 Dd 34.19N 134.10 E
Shidongsi → Gaolan 27 Hd 36.23N 103.55 E
Shiel, Loch- 9 He 56.50N 5.50W
Shiga Ken [2] 28 Ng 35.15N 136.10 E
Shigu 27 Gf 26.54N 99.44 E
Shi He 28 Ch 32.32N 115.52 E
Shihezi 27 Ec 44.18N 86.02 E
Shiiba 29 Be 32.28N 131.09 E
Shijaku 15 Ch 41.20N 19.34 E
Shijiazhuang 22 Nf 38.00N 114.30 E
Shijiusuo 28 Eg 35.24N 119.32 E
Shika 29 Ec 37.01N 136.46 E
Shikabe 29a Bb 42.02N 140.47 E
Shikārpur 25 Dc 27.57N 68.38 E
Shiki Islands 64d Bb 7.24N 151.53 E
Shikine-Jima 29 Fd 34.19N 139.13 E
Shikoku 21 Pf 33.30N 133.30 E
Shikoku Basin (EN) 27 Oe 30.00N 135.30 E
Shikoku-Sanchi 29 Ce 33.45N 133.35 E
Shilabo 35 Gd 6.05N 44.45 E
Shiliguri 22 Kg 26.42N 88.26 E
Shiliu → Changjiang 27 Ih 19.20N 109.03 E
Shilla 25 Fb 32.24N 78.12 E
Shillong 22 Lg 25.34N 91.53 E
Shimabara 28 Kh 32.47N 130.22 E
Shimabara-Hantō 29 Be 32.45N 130.15 E
Shimabara-Wan 29 Be 32.50N 130.30 E
Shimada 29 Fd 34.49N 138.09 E
Shima-Hantō 29 Ed 34.25N 136.45 E
Shimane-Hantō 29 Cd 35.30N 133.00 E
Shimane Ken [2] 28 Lg 35.00N 132.20 E
Shimanto-Gawa 29 Ce 32.56N 133.00 E
Shimaura-Tō 29 Bd 34.50N 131.50 E
Shimian 27 Hf 29.10N 102.26 E
Shimizu [Jap.] 29a Cb 43.01N 142.51 E
Shimizu [Jap.] 28 Og 35.01N 138.29 E
Shimla 22 Jf 31.06N 77.10 E
Shimoda 28 Og 34.40N 138.57 E
Shimodate 29 Fc 36.19N 139.58 E
Shimoga 22 Jh 13.55N 75.34 E
Shimo-Jima 29 Be 32.25N 130.05 E
Shimokawa 29a Ca 44.18N 142.38 E
Shimokita-Hantō 29a Bc 41.15N 141.05 E
Shimo-Koshiki-Jima 29 Af 31.40N 129.40 E
Shimo la Tewa 36 Gc 3.57S 39.44 E
Shimoni 36 Gc 4.39S 39.23 E
Shimonoseki 27 Ne 33.57N 130.57 E
Shimono-Shima 29 Ad 34.15N 129.15 E
Shimotsu 29 Dd 34.07N 135.08 E
Shimotsuma 29 Fc 36.11N 139.58 E
Shin, Loch- 9 Ic 58.07N 4.32W
Shinano 29 Fc 36.47N 138.10 E
Shinano-Gawa 29 Fc 37.57N 139.04 E
Shināş 24 Qj 24.43N 56.27 E
Shindand 23 Jc 33.18N 62.08 E
Shinga 36 Dc 3.16S 24.38 E
Shingbwiyang 25 Jc 26.41N 96.13 E
Shingū 27 Oe 33.44N 135.59 E
Shingwidzi 37 Ed 23.01S 30.43 E
Shinji 29 Cd 35.24N 132.54 E
Shinji-Ko 28 Lg 35.27N 133.02 E
Shinjō 27 Pd 38.46N 140.18 E
Shinkafe 34 Gc 13.05N 6.31 E
Shinminato 29 Ec 36.47N 137.04 E
Shinnanyō 29 Bd 34.05N 131.45 E
Shinshiro 29 Ed 34.53N 137.30 E
Shintoku 28 Qc 43.12N 142.55 E
Shintotsugawa 29a Bb 43.32N 141.40 E
Shinyanga 31 Ki 3.40S 33.26 E
Shinyanga [3] 36 Fc 3.30S 33.00 E
Shiogama 29 Gb 38.19N 141.01 E
Shiojiri 28 Nf 36.06N 137.58 E
Shiokubi-Misaki 29a Bc 41.43N 140.57 E
Shio-no-Misaki 27 Oe 33.25N 135.45 E
Shipai → Huaining 28 Di 30.25N 116.39 E

Index Symbols

- [1] Independent Nation
- [2] State, Region
- [3] District, County
- [4] Municipality
- [5] Colony, Dependency
- Continent
- Physical Region
- Historical or Cultural Region
- Mount, Mountain
- Volcano
- Hill
- Mountains, Mountain Range
- Hills, Escarpment
- Plateau, Upland
- Pass, Gap
- Plain, Lowland
- Delta
- Salt Flat
- Valley, Canyon
- Crater, Cave
- Karst Features
- Depression
- Polder
- Desert, Dunes
- Forest, Woods
- Heath, Steppe
- Oasis
- Cape, Point
- Coast, Beach
- Cliff
- Peninsula
- Isthmus
- Sandbank
- Island
- Atoll
- Rock, Reef
- Islands, Archipelago
- Rocks, Reefs
- Coral Reef
- Well, Spring
- Geyser
- River, Stream
- Waterfall Rapids
- River Mouth, Estuary
- Lake
- Salt Lake
- Intermittent Lake
- Reservoir
- Swamp, Pond
- Canal
- Glacier
- Ice Shelf, Pack Ice
- Ocean
- Sea
- Gulf, Bay
- Strait, Fjord
- Lagoon
- Bank
- Seamount
- Tablemount
- Ridge
- Shelf
- Basin
- Escarpment, Sea Scarp
- Fracture
- Trench, Abyss
- National Park, Reserve
- Point of Interest
- Recreation Site
- Cave, Cavern
- Historic Site
- Ruins
- Wall, Walls
- Church, Abbey
- Temple
- Scientific Station
- Airport
- Port
- Lighthouse
- Mine
- Tunnel
- Dam, Bridge

Shiping 27 Hg 23.44N 102.28 E
Shipki La 27 Ce 31.49N 78.45 E
Shippegan 42 Lg 47.45N 64.42W
Shiprock 45 Bh 36.47N 108.41W
Shipshaw, Rivière- 44 La 48.30N 71.15W
Shipu 28 Fj 29.17N 121.57 E
Shipugi Shankou 27 Ce 31.49N 78.45 E
Shiquan 27 Ie 33.05N 108.15 E
Shiquanhe 22 Jf 32.24N 79.52 E
Shiquan He 27 Ce 32.28N 79.44 E
Shiragami Dake 29 Ga 40.30N 140.01 E
Shiragami-Misaki 28 Pd 41.25N 140.12 E
Shirahama 29 De 33.40N 135.20 E
Shirakawa [Jap.] 29 Ed 35.36N 137.12 E
Shirakawa [Jap.] 29 Ec 36.17N 136.53 E
Shirakawa [Jap.] 28 Pf 37.07N 140.13 E
Shirane-San [Jap.] 27 Od 36.48N 139.22 E
Shirane-San [Jap.] 29 Fd 35.40N 138.13 E
Shirane-San [Jap.] 29 Fc 36.38N 138.32 E
Shiranuka 28 Rc 42.57N 144.05 E
Shiraoi 28 Pc 42.31N 141.16 E
Shirase Coast 66 Mf 78.30S 156.00W
Shirataka 29 Gb 38.11N 140.06 E
Shirataki 29a Cb 43.53N 143.09 E
Shīrāz 22 Hg 29.36N 52.32 E
Shirbīn 24 Dg 31.11N 31.32 E
Shire 30 Kj 17.42S 35.19 E
Shiren 28 Id 41.54N 126.34 E
Shiretoko-Dake 29a Da 44.15N 145.14 E
Shiretoko-Hantō 29a Da 44.00N 145.00 E
Shiretoko-Misaki 27 Qc 44.21N 145.20 E
Shīrgāh 24 Od 36.17N 52.54 E
Shiribetsu-Gawa 29a Bb 42.52N 140.21 E
Shiriha-Misaki 28 Pd 41.46N 144.45 E
Shirikishinai 29a Bc 41.48N 141.05 E
Shīrīn 24 Qi 27.10N 56.41 E
Shīrīn sū 24 Me 35.29N 48.27 E
Shiriya-Zaki 27 Pc 41.26N 141.28 E
Shīr Kūh 21 Hf 31.37N 54.04 E
Shirley Mountains 46 Le 42.15N 106.30W
Shiroishi 28 Pe 38.00N 140.37 E
Shirone 29 Fc 37.46N 139.00 E
Shirotori 29 Ed 35.53N 136.52 E
Shirouma-Dake 29 Ec 36.45N 137.46 E
Shirshov Ridge (EN) 20 Me 57.30N 171.00 E
Shīrvān 24 Lf 33.33N 46.49 E
Shirwan Mazīn 24 Kd 37.03N 44.10 E
Shishaldin Volcano 38 Cd 54.45N 163.57W
Shishi-Jima 29 Be 32.17N 130.15 E
Shishmaref 40 Fc 66.14N 166.09W
Shishou 27 Jf 29.42N 112.23 E
Shitai (Qili) 28 Di 30.12N 117.28 E
Shitara 29 Ed 35.05N 137.34 E
Shitou Shan 27 Ma 51.02N 125.12 E
Shivwits Plateau 46 Ih 36.10N 113.40W
Shiwa 29 Pe 39.33N 141.35 E
Shiwan Dashan 27 Ig 21.45N 107.35 E
Shiwa Ngandu 36 Fe 11.12S 31.43 E
Shiwpuri 25 Fc 25.26N 77.39 E
Shixian 28 Jc 43.05N 129.46 E
Shiyan 27 Je 32.34N 110.48 E
Shiyang He 27 Hd 39.00N 103.25 E
Shizilu → Junan 28 Eg 35.10N 118.50 E
Shizugawa 29 Gb 38.40N 141.28 E
Shizui 28 Ic 43.03N 126.09 E
Shizuishan (Dawukou) 27 Id 39.03N 106.24 E
Shizukuishi 29 Gb 39.42N 140.59 E
Shizunai 28 Qc 42.20N 142.22 E
Shizunai-Gawa 29a Cb 42.20N 142.22 E
Shizuoka 22 Pf 34.58N 138.23 E
Shizuoka Ken [2] 28 Og 35.00N 138.25 E
Shkodra 6 Hg 42.05N 19.30 E
Shkodrës, Liqen i-=Scutari, Lake- (EN) 5 Hg 42.10N 19.20 E
Shkumbini 15 Ch 41.01N 19.26 E
Shoal Lake 45 Fa 50.26N 100.34W
Shoal Lake 45 Ib 49.32N 95.00W
Shoal Lakes 45 Ha 50.20N 97.40W
Shōbara 28 Lg 34.51N 133.01 E
Shodo-Shima 29 Dd 34.30N 134.15 E
Shō-Gawa 29 Ec 36.47N 137.04 E
Shokanbetsu-Dake 29a Bb 43.43N 141.31 E
Shokotsu-Gawa 29a Ca 44.23N 143.17 E
Sholāpur → Solāpur 22 Jh 17.41N 75.55 E
Shoqān 24 Qd 37.20N 56.58 E
Shoranūr 25 Ff 10.46N 76.17 E
Shoreham-by-Sea 9 Mk 50.49N 0.16W
Shortland Islands 60 Fi 6.55S 155.53 E
Shosambetsu 29a Ba 44.32N 141.46 E
Shoshone 46 He 42.56N 114.24W
Shoshone Mountains 43 Dd 39.15N 117.25W
Shoshone Peak 46 Gh 36.56N 116.16W
Shoshone River 46 Kd 44.52N 108.11W
Shoshong 37 Dd 23.02S 26.31 E
Shoshoni 46 Ke 43.14N 108.07W
Shotor Khūn 25 Jc 34.20N 64.55 E
Shouchang 28 Ej 29.23N 119.12 E
Shouguang 28 Ef 36.53N 118.44 E
Shouxian (Shouyang) 28 Dh 32.35N 116.47 E
Shouyang → Shouxian 28 Dh 32.35N 116.47 E
Shōwa 29 Gb 39.51N 140.03 E
Show Low 46 Ji 34.15N 110.02W
Shqiperia=Albania (EN) [1] 6 Hg 41.00N 20.00 E
Shreveport 39 Jf 32.30N 93.45W
Shrewsbury 9 Ki 52.43N 2.45W
Shuangcheng 27 Mb 45.21N 126.17 E
Shuangjiang 27 Gg 23.27N 99.50 E
Shuangjiang → Tongdao 27 If 26.14N 109.45 E
Shuangliao 27 Lc 43.30N 123.30 E
Shuangyang 27 Mc 43.31N 125.28 E
Shuangyashan 22 Pe 46.37N 131.10 E
Shucheng 28 Di 31.28N 116.57 E
Shufu 27 Cd 39.27N 75.52 E
Shuguri Falls 36 Gd 8.31S 37.23 E
Shu He 28 Eg 34.07N 118.30 E
Shuicheng 27 Hf 26.34N 104.52 E
Shuiding → Huocheng 27 Dc 44.03N 80.49 E
Shuiji → Laixi 28 Ff 36.52N 120.31 E
Shuijiahu → Changfeng 28 Dh 32.29N 117.10 E
Shuikou → Jianghua 27 Jg 24.58N 111.56 E
Shuiye 28 Cf 36.08N 114.06 E
Shuizhai → Xiangcheng 28 Ch 33.27N 114.53 E
Shūl 24 Ng 30.10N 51.38 E
Shulan 27 Mc 44.26N 126.55 E
Shule 27 Cd 39.25N 76.06 E
Shule He 21 Le 40.20N 92.50 E
Shulu (Xinji) 28 Cf 37.56N 115.14 E
Shumagin Islands 40 He 55.07N 159.45W
Shumarinai-Ko 29a Ca 44.20N 142.13 E
Shunayn, Sabkhat- 33 Dc 30.10N 21.00 E
Shungnak 40 Hc 66.53N 157.02W
Shunyi 28 Dd 40.09N 116.38 E
Shuolong 27 Ig 22.51N 106.55 E
Shuoxian 27 Jd 39.18N 112.25 E
Shūr [Iran] 24 Pi 26.59N 55.47 E
Shūr [Iran] 24 Oh 28.12N 52.09 E
Shūr [Iran] 24 Ne 35.09N 51.30 E
Shūr [Iran] 24 Oh 28.33N 53.12 E
Shūr Āb 24 Pg 31.45N 55.15 E
Shurāb 23 Ic 33.07N 55.18 E
Shūsf 23 Jc 31.48N 60.01 E
Shūsh 24 Mf 32.12N 48.17 E
Shushica 15 Ci 40.34N 19.34 E
Shūshtar 23 Gc 32.03N 48.51 E
Shuswap Lake 46 Fa 50.57N 119.15W
Shūt 24 Oe 34.44N 52.53 E
Shuwak 35 Fc 14.23N 35.52 E
Shuyang 28 Ke 34.01N 118.52 E
Shuzenji 29 Fd 34.58N 138.55 E
Shwebo 25 Jd 22.34N 95.42 E
Shwell 25 Jd 23.56N 96.17 E
Shyok 25 Fa 35.13N 75.53 E
Sia 26 Jh 6.49S 134.19 E
Siagne 11 Mk 43.32N 6.57 E
Siāh Band 23 Kc 33.25N 65.21 E
Siāh-Chashmeh 24 Kc 39.04N 44.23 E
Siāh-Kūh 24 Oe 34.38N 52.16 E
Siak 26 Df 1.13N 102.09 E
Sialkot [Pak.] 25 Ea 35.15N 73.17 E
Sialkot [Pak.] 22 Jf 32.30N 74.31 E
Sianów 10 Mb 54.15N 16.16 E
Siantan, Pulau- 26 Ef 3.10N 106.15 E
Siargao 26 Ie 9.53N 126.02 E
Šiaškotan, Ostrov- 21 Re 48.49N 154.06 E
Siátista 15 Ei 40.16N 21.33 E
Siau, Pulau- 26 If 2.42N 125.24 E
Šiauliai/Šjauljaj 6 Id 55.53N 23.19 E
Siavonga 36 Ef 16.32S 28.43 E
Siazan 19 Eg 41.04N 49.06 E
Sibā'ī, Jabal as- 33 Fd 25.43N 34.09 E
Sibaj 19 Fe 52.42N 58.39 E
Sibari 14 Kk 39.45N 16.27 E
Sibasa 37 Ed 22.56S 30.29 E
Šibenik 14 Jg 43.44N 15.53 E
Siberimanua 26 Cg 2.09S 99.34 E
Siberut, Pulau- 21 Lj 1.20S 98.55 E
Siberut, Selat- 26 Cg 0.42S 98.35 E
Sibi 25 Dc 29.33N 67.53 E
Sibigo 26 Cf 2.51N 95.55 E
Sibillini, Monti- 14 Hh 42.55N 13.15 E
Sibircatajaha 17 Lb 69.05N 64.43 E
Sibircevo 20 Ih 44.16N 132.20 E
Sibirjakova, Ostrov- 20 Cb 72.50N 79.00 E
Sibiti 36 Bc 3.41S 13.21 E
Sibiu [2] 15 Hd 45.46N 24.12 E
Sibiu 6 If 45.48N 24.09 E
Sibolga 22 Li 1.45N 98.48 E
Sibsāgar 25 Ic 26.59N 94.38 E
Sibu 22 Ni 2.18N 111.49 E
Sibuguey Bay 26 He 7.30N 122.40 E
Sibut 31 Ih 5.44N 19.05 E
Sibutu Islands 26 Gf 4.45N 119.20 E
Sibutu Passage 26 Gf 4.56N 119.36 E
Sibuyan 26 Hd 12.25N 122.34 E
Sibuyan Sea 26 Hd 12.50N 122.40 E
Siby 34 Dc 12.22N 8.22W
Sibyllenstein 10 Ke 51.12N 14.05 E
Sicani, Monti- 14 Hm 37.40N 13.15 E
Sicasica 54 Eg 17.22S 67.45W
Si Chon 25 Jg 9.00N 99.56 E
Sichuan Pendi 21 Mf 30.01N 105.00 E
Sichuan Sheng (Ssu-ch'uan Sheng)=Szechwan (EN) [2] 27 He 30.00N 103.00 E
Sicilia [2] 14 Im 37.45N 14.15 E
Sicilia = Sicily (EN) 5 Hh 37.30N 14.00 E
Sicilia, Canale di-=Sicily, Strait of- (EN) 5 Hh 37.20N 11.20 E
Sicilia, Mar di- 14 Gn 36.30N 13.00 E
Sicily (EN) = Sicilia 5 Hh 37.30N 14.00 E
Sicily, Strait of- (EN)= Sicilia, Canale di- 5 Hh 37.20N 11.20 E
Sicily, Strait of- (EN)= Tūnis, Canal de- 5 Hh 37.20N 11.20 E
Sico Tinto, Rio- 49 Ef 15.58N 84.58W
Sicuani 53 Ig 14.15S 71.15W
Šid 15 Cd 45.08N 19.14 E
Sidamo [3] 35 Fd 5.48N 38.50 E
Siddipet 25 Fe 18.06N 78.51 E
Side 24 Dd 36.46N 31.22 E
Sidéradougou 34 Ec 10.40N 4.15W
Siderno 14 Kl 38.16N 16.18 E
Siders/Sierre 14 Bd 46.17N 7.32 E
Siderty 14 He 52.32N 74.50 E
Šiderty 19 He 51.40N 74.50 E
Sidheros, Ákra- 15 Jn 35.19N 26.19 E
Sidhirókastron 15 Gh 41.14N 23.23 E
Sīdī 'Abd ar Raḥmān 24 Cg 30.58N 28.44 E
Sidi Aïch 13 Qh 36.37N 4.41 E
Sidi-Akacha 13 Nh 36.28N 1.18 E
Sidi Ali 13 Nh 36.06N 0.25 E
Sīdī'Alī al Makkī, Ra's- 14 Em 37.11N 10.17 E
Sīdī Barrānī 33 Ec 31.36N 25.55 E
Sidi Bel Abbes [3] 32 Gc 34.45N 0.35W
Sidi Bel Abbes 32 Gb 35.12N 0.38W
Sidi Bennour 32 Fc 32.39N 8.26W
Sidi di Daoud 13 Ph 36.51N 3.52 E
Sidi Ifni 31 Ff 29.33N 10.10W
Sidi Kacem 32 Fc 34.13N 5.42W
Sidikalang 26 Cf 2.45N 98.19 E
Sidi Lakhdar 13 Mh 36.10N 0.27 E
Sīdī Zayd, Jabal- 14 En 36.29N 10.20 E
Sidlaw Hills 9 Ke 56.30N 3.00W
Sidmouth 9 Jk 50.41N 3.15W
Sidney [B.C.-Can.] 42 Fg 48.39N 123.24W
Sidney [Mt.-U.S.] 43 Gb 47.43N 104.09W
Sidney [Nb.-U.S.] 43 Gc 41.09N 102.59W
Sidney [Oh.-U.S.] 44 Ee 40.16N 84.10W
Sidney Lanier, Lake- 44 Fh 34.15N 83.57W
Sidobre 11 Ik 43.40N 2.30 E
Sidorovsk 20 Dc 66.35N 82.30 E
Sidra 10 Tc 53.33N 23.30 E
Sidra, Gulf of-(EN)=Surt, Khalīj- 30 Ie 31.30N 18.00 E
Sidrolândia 55 Ee 20.55S 54.58W
Siedlce [2] 10 Sd 52.10N 22.15 E
Siedlce 10 Sd 52.11N 22.16 E
Siedlecka, Wysoczyzna- 10 Sd 52.10N 22.15 E
Sieg [Ger.] 10 Df 50.45N 7.05 E
Sieg [Ger.] 12 Kd 50.55N 8.01 E
Siegburg 10 Df 50.48N 7.12 E
Siegen 10 Ef 50.52N 8.02 E
Siemiatycze 10 Sd 52.26N 22.53 E
Siĕmréab 25 Kf 13.22N 103.51 E
Siena 14 Fg 43.19N 11.21 E
Sieniawa 10 Sf 50.11N 22.36 E
Sienne 11 Ee 49.00N 1.34W
Sieradz 10 Oe 51.36N 18.45 E
Sieradz [2] 10 Oe 51.35N 18.45 E
Sieradzka, Niecka- 10 Oe 51.35N 18.50 E
Sierck-les-Bains 12 Ie 49.26N 6.21 E
Sierpc 10 Pd 52.52N 19.41 E
Sierra Blanca 45 Dk 31.11N 105.21W
Sierra Blanca Peak 45 Dj 33.23N 105.48W
Sierra Colorada 56 Gf 40.35S 67.48W
Sierra Leone [1] 31 Fh 8.30N 11.30W
Sierra Leone Basin (EN) 3 Di 5.00N 17.00W
Sierra Leone Rise (EN) 3 Di 5.30N 21.00W
Sierra Madre 21 Oh 16.20N 122.00 E
Sierra Mojada 47 Dc 27.17N 103.42W
Sierre/Siders 14 Bd 46.17N 7.32 E
Siete Palmas 55 Cg 25.13S 58.20W
Siete Puntas, Rio- 55 Df 23.34S 57.20W
Šieu 15 Hb 47.11N 24.13 E
Sifié 34 Dd 7.59N 6.55W
Sífnos 15 Hm 37.00N 24.40 E
Sig 32 Gb 35.32N 0.11W
Sığacik Körfezi 15 Jk 38.12N 26.45 E
Sigean 11 Ik 43.02N 2.59 E
Sighetu Marmaţiei 15 Gb 47.56N 23.53 E
Sighişoara 15 Hc 46.13N 24.48 E
Sigli 26 Ce 5.23N 95.57 E
Siglufjördur 7a Ba 66.09N 18.55W
Sigmaringen 10 Fh 48.05N 9.13 E
Signal Peak 46 Hj 33.22N 114.03W
Signy Island 66 Re 60.43S 45.38W
Signy-l'Abbaye 12 Ge 49.42N 4.25 E
Signy-le-Petit 12 Ge 49.54N 4.17 E
Sigtuna 7 Dg 59.37N 17.43 E
Siguanea, Ensenada de la- 49 Fc 21.38N 83.05W
Siguatepeque 49 Df 14.32N 87.49W
Sigüenza 13 Jc 41.04N 2.38W
Siguiri 31 Gg 11.25N 9.10W
Sigulda 7 Fh 57.09N 24.53 E
Si He 28 Dg 35.11N 116.42 E
Sihong 28 Eh 33.28N 118.13 E
Sihote-Alin 21 Pe 48.00N 138.00 E
Sihou → Changdao 28 Ff 37.56N 120.42 E
Sihuas 54 Ce 8.34S 77.37W
Siikainen 8 Ic 61.52N 21.50 E
Siilinjärvi 7 Ge 63.02N 27.40 E
Siirt 23 Fb 37.56N 41.57 E
Sijunjung 26 Dg 0.42S 100.58 E
Sikaiana 63a Fc 8.22S 162.45 E
Sikakap 26 Dg 2.46S 100.13 E
Sikanni Chief 42 Fe 58.17N 121.46W
Sīkar 25 Fc 27.37N 75.09 E
Sikasso 31 Gg 11.20N 5.40W
Sikasso [3] 34 Dc 10.55N 7.00W
Sikéa [Grc.] 15 Fm 36.46N 22.56 E
Sikéa [Grc.] 15 Gi 40.33N 23.58 E
Sikeston 43 Jd 36.53N 89.35W
Síkinos 15 Im 36.50N 25.05 E
Sikkim [3] 25 Hc 27.50N 88.30 E
Siklós 10 Ok 45.51N 18.18 E
Sikonge 36 Fd 5.38S 32.46 E
Šikotan, Ostrov/Tō, Shikotan- 20 Jh 43.47N 146.45 E
Siktjah 20 Hc 69.55N 125.10 E
Sil 13 Eb 42.27N 7.43W
Sila Grande 14 Kk 39.20N 16.30 E
Sila Greca 14 Kk 39.30N 16.30 E
Šilale/Šilalė 7 Fi 55.29N 22.12 E
Šilalė/Šilale 7 Fi 55.29N 22.12 E
Silao 48 Ig 20.56N 101.26W
Silaogou 28 Be 39.59N 113.03 E
Sila Piccola 14 Kk 39.05N 16.35 E
Silba 14 If 44.23N 14.42 E
Silchar 25 Id 24.49N 92.48 E
Šilda 16 Ud 51.47N 59.50 E
Sildagapet 8 Ab 62.05N 5.10 E
Sile 14 Ge 45.28N 12.35 E
Şile 24 Cb 41.05N 29.35 E
Šilega 19 Ec 64.03N 44.02 E
Silesia (EN)=Śląsk 10 Me 51.00N 16.45 E
Silesia (EN)=Śląsk 5 He 51.00N 16.45 E
Silet 32 He 22.39N 4.35 E
Silhouette Island 37b Ca 4.29S 55.14 E
Silifke 23 Db 36.22N 33.56 E
Siligir 20 Gc 68.27N 114.50 E
Siling Co 21 Kf 31.50N 89.00 E
Siling Jiao 27 Ke 8.20N 115.27 E
Silisili, Mauga- 65c Aa 13.35S 172.27W
Silistra [2] 15 Kf 44.07N 27.16 E
Silistra 15 Ke 44.07N 27.16 E
Silivri 24 Cb 41.04N 28.15 E
Siljan 7 Df 60.50N 14.45 E
Šilka 20 Gf 51.51N 116.02 E
Šilka 21 Od 53.22N 121.32 E
Silkeborg 7 Bh 56.10N 9.34 E
Sillamäe/Sillamjae 7 Gg 59.24N 27.43 E
Sillamjae/Sillamäe 7 Gg 59.24N 27.43 E
Sillaro 14 Ff 44.34N 11.51 E
Silleiro, Cabo- 13 Db 42.07N 8.54W
Sillé-le-Guillaume 11 Ff 48.12N 0.08W
Sillian 14 Gd 46.45N 12.25 E
Sillil 35 Gc 11.00N 43.26 E
Siloam Springs 45 Ih 36.11N 94.32W
Siloana Plains 36 Df 17.15S 23.10 E
Silovo 19 Ee 54.24N 40.52 E
Silsbee 45 Ik 30.21N 94.11W
Siltou 35 Bb 16.52N 15.43 E
Šilutė/Šilute 19 Cd 55.21N 21.30 E
Šilute/Šilutė 19 Cd 55.21N 21.30 E
Silvan 23 Fb 38.08N 41.01 E
Silvassa 25 Ed 20.20N 73.05 E
Silver Bank (EN) 49 Mc 20.30N 69.45W
Silver Bay 43 Ib 47.17N 91.16W
Silver City 43 Fe 32.46N 108.17W
Silverdalen 8 Fg 57.32N 15.44 E
Silver Lake 46 Ee 43.06N 120.53W
Silver Spring 44 If 39.02N 77.03W
Silver Springs 46 Fg 39.25N 119.13W
Silverthrone Mountain 46 Ba 51.31N 126.06W
Silverton [Co.-U.S.] 45 Ch 37.49N 107.40W
Silverton [Tx.-U.S.] 45 Fi 34.28N 101.19W
Silves [Braz.] 54 Gd 2.54S 58.27W
Silves [Port.] 13 Dg 37.11N 8.26W
Silvi 14 Ih 42.34N 14.06 E
Silvia 54 Cc 2.37N 76.24W
Silviers River 46 Fe 43.22N 118.48W
Silvretta 14 Ed 46.50N 10.15 E
Silyānah [3] 32 Ib 36.00N 9.30 E
Silyānah 32 Ib 36.05N 9.22 E
Silyānah, Wādī- 14 Dn 36.33N 9.25 E
Sim 17 Hi 54.59N 57.41 E
Sim 17 Hi 54.32N 56.30 E
Sim, Cap- 32 Fc 31.23N 9.51W
Simanggang 26 Ff 1.15N 111.26 E
Šimanovsk 20 Hf 52.01N 127.36 E
Simao 27 Hg 22.40N 101.02 E
Simard, Lac- 44 Hb 47.38N 78.40W
Simareh 24 Mf 32.08N 48.03 E
Simav 23 Ca 40.23N 28.31 E
Simav 24 Cc 39.05N 28.59 E
Simav Dağ 15 Lj 39.04N 28.54 E
Simav Gölü 15 Lj 39.09N 28.55 E
Simayama-Jima 29 Ae 32.40N 128.38 E
Simba 36 Db 0.36N 22.55 E
Simbo 36 Fc 4.53S 29.44 E
Simbo 63a Cc 8.18S 156.34 E
Simbruini, Monti- 14 Hj 41.55N 13.15 E
Simcoe 44 Gd 42.50N 80.18W
Simcoe, Lake - 42 Jh 44.27N 79.20W
Simen 35 Fc 13.25N 38.00 E
Simenti 34 Cc 13.00N 13.25W
Simeria 15 Gd 45.51N 23.01 E
Simeto 14 Jm 37.24N 15.06 E
Simeulue, Pulau- 21 Li 2.35N 96.05 E
Simferopol 6 Jf 44.57N 34.06 E
Simhah, Jabal- 23 Hf 17.20N 54.50 E
Simi 15 Km 36.36N 27.50 E
Simi 15 Km 36.35N 27.50 E
Simiti 49 Kj 7.58N 73.58W
Simitli 15 Gh 41.53N 23.06 E
Şimleu Silvaniei 15 Fb 47.14N 22.48 E
Simmental 14 Bd 46.35N 7.25 E
Simmerath 12 Id 50.36N 6.18 E
Simmerbach 12 Je 49.48N 7.31 E
Simmern 10 Dg 49.59N 7.31 E
Simmertal 12 Je 49.48N 7.33 E
Simnas 8 Jj 54.20N 23.45 E
Simo 7 Fd 65.39N 24.55 E
Simojärvi 7 Gc 66.06N 27.03 E
Simojoki 7 Fd 65.37N 25.03 E
Simojovel de Allende 48 Mi 17.12N 92.38W
Simonstown 37 Bf 34.14S 18.26 E
Simpele 7 Gf 61.26N 29.22 E
Simpelejärvi 8 Mc 61.30N 29.25 E
Simplon 14 Bd 46.15N 8.00 E
Simpson Desert 57 Eg 25.00S 137.00 E
Simpson Hill 59 Fe 26.30S 126.30 E
Simpson Peninsula 42 Ic 68.45N 89.10W
Simrishamn 7 Di 55.33N 14.20 E
Simsonbaai 51b Ab 18.02N 63.09W
Simušir, Ostrov- 21 Re 46.58N 152.02 E
Sina 25 Fe 17.22N 75.54 E
Sīnā'=Sinai Peninsula (EN) 30 Kf 29.30N 34.00 E
Sinabang 26 Cf 2.29N 96.23 E
Sinadago 35 Hd 5.22N 46.22 E
Sinai, Mount- (EN)=Mūsa, Jabal- 24 Eh 28.32N 33.59 E
Sinaia 15 Id 45.21N 25.33 E
Sinai Peninsula (EN)= Sīnā' 30 Kf 29.30N 34.00 E
Sinajana 64c Bb 13.28N 144.45W
Sinaloa [2] 47 Cc 25.00N 107.30W
Sinaloa, Llanos de- 47 Cc 25.00N 107.30W
Sinaloa, Río- 48 Ee 25.18N 108.30W
Sinaloā de Leyva 48 Ee 25.50N 108.14W
Sinalunga 14 Fg 43.12N 11.44 E
Sinamaica 54 Da 11.05N 71.51W
Sinan 27 If 27.56N 108.11 E
Sinara 17 Kh 56.17N 62.23 E
Sināwin 33 Bc 31.02N 10.36 E
Sinazongwe 36 Ef 17.15S 27.28 E
Şincai 15 Hc 46.39N 24.23 E
Sincanli 24 Dc 38.45N 30.15 E
Sincé 49 Ji 9.14N 75.06W
Sincelejo 53 Ie 9.18N 75.24W
Sinch'am 28 Jc 42.07N 129.25 E
Sinch'ang 28 Jd 40.07N 128.28 E
Sinch'on 28 He 38.28N 125.27 E
Sinclair, Lake- 44 Fi 33.11N 83.16W
Sind [3] 25 Cc 25.30N 69.00 E
Sind 21 Ig 25.30N 69.00 E
Sindal 8 Dg 57.28N 10.13 E
Sindangbarang 26 Eh 7.27S 107.08 E
Sindara 36 Bc 1.02S 10.40 E
Sindelfingen-Böblingen 10 Fh 48.41N 9.01 E
Sindfeld 12 Kc 51.32N 8.48 E
Sindi 7 Fg 58.24N 24.42 E
Sındırgı 24 Cc 39.14N 28.10 E
Sindirgi Geçidi 15 Lj 39.10N 28.04 E
Sindominic 15 Ic 46.35N 25.47 E
Sindri 25 Hd 23.42N 86.29 E
Sinegorje 20 Kd 62.03N 150.25 E
Sinegorski 16 Le 48.00N 40.53 E
Šine-Ider 27 Gb 48.56N 99.33 E
Sinekli 15 Lh 41.14N 28.12 E
Sinelnikovo 16 Ie 48.18N 35.31 E
Sines 13 Dg 37.57N 8.52W
Sines, Cabo de- 13 Dg 37.57N 8.53W
Sine-Saloum [3] 34 Bc 14.00N 15.50W
Singako 35 Bd 9.50N 19.29 E
Singapore / Singapura 22 Mi 1.17N 103.51 E
Singapore Strait (EN)= Singapura, Selat- 26 Df 1.15N 104.00 E
Singapura / Singapore 22 Mi 1.17N 103.51 E
Singapura, Selat-= Singapore Strait (EN) 26 Df 1.15N 104.00 E
Singaraja 26 Gh 8.07S 115.06 E
Singatoka 63d Ac 18.08S 177.30 E
Sing Buri 25 Kf 14.53N 100.25 E
Singen 10 Ei 47.46N 8.50 E
Sîngeroz Băi 15 Hb 47.22N 24.41 E
Singida [3] 36 Fd 5.30S 34.30 E
Singida 31 Ki 4.49S 34.45 E
Singitic Gulf (EN) = Singitikós Kólpos 15 Gi 40.10N 23.55 E
Singitikós Kólpos = Singitic Gulf (EN) 15 Gi 40.10N 23.55 E
Singkaling Hkamti 25 Jc 26.00N 95.42 E
Singkang 26 Hg 4.08S 120.01 E
Singkawang 26 Ef 0.54N 109.00 E
Singkep, Pulau- 26 Dg 0.30S 104.25 E
Singkil 26 Cf 2.17N 97.49 E
Singleton [Austl.] 59 Kf 32.34S 151.10 E
Singleton [Eng.-U.K.] 12 Bd 50.55N 0.44W
Singleton, Mount- 59 De 29.28S 117.18 E
Singö 8 Hd 60.10N 18.45 E
Siniscola 14 Dj 40.34N 9.41 E
Sini vrăh 15 Ih 41.51N 25.01 E
Sinj 14 Kg 43.42N 16.38 E
Sinjah 35 Ec 13.09N 33.56 E
Sinjai 26 Hh 5.07S 120.15 E
Sinjaja 8 Mg 57.05N 28.33 E
Sinjajevina 15 Cf 43.00N 19.18 E
Sinjār 24 Id 36.19N 41.52 E
Sinjār, Jabal- 24 Id 36.23N 41.52 E
Sinjuža 16 Ge 48.03N 30.50 E
Sinkiang (EN)= Hsin-chiang-wei-wu-erh Tzu-chih-ch'ü → Xinjiang Uygur Zizhiqu [2] 27 Ec 42.00N 86.00 E
Sinkiang (EN)= Xinjiang Uygur Zizhiqu (Hsin-chiang-wei-wu-erh Tzu-chih-ch'ü) [2] 27 Ec 42.00N 86.00 E
Sin-le-Noble 12 Fd 50.22N 3.07 E
Sinmi-Do 28 He 39.33N 124.53 E
Sinn 12 Kd 50.39N 8.20 E
Sinn al Kadhdhāb 33 Fe 23.30N 32.05 E
Sinnamary 54 Hb 5.23N 53.00W
Sinni 14 Kj 40.08N 16.41 E
Sînnicolau Mare 15 Dc 46.05N 20.38 E
Sinnūris 33 Fd 29.25N 30.52 E
Sinnyŏng 28 Jf 36.02N 128.47 E
Sinoe [3] 34 Dd 5.20N 8.40W
Sinoe, Lacul- 15 Le 44.38N 28.53 E
Sinop 23 Ea 41.59N 35.09 E
Sinop Burun 24 Fa 42.02N 35.12 E
Sinp'o 28 Jd 40.02N 128.12 E
Sinsang 28 Ie 39.39N 127.25 E
Sinsheim 10 Eg 49.15N 8.53 E
Sint-Amandsberg, Gent- 12 Fc 51.04N 3.45 E
Sîntana 15 Ec 46.21N 21.30 E
Sint-Andries, Brugge- 12 Fc 51.12N 3.10 E
Sintang 26 Ff 0.04N 111.30 E
Sint Eustatius 47 Le 17.30N 62.59W
Sint-Gillis-Waas 12 Gc 51.13N 4.08 E
Sint Kruis 50 Bf 12.18N 69.08W
Sint Laureins 12 Fc 51.15N 3.31 E
Sint Maarten 50 Ec 18.04N 63.04W
Sint Nicolaas 50 Bf 12.26N 69.55W
Sint Niklaas/ Saint-Nicolas 11 Kc 51.10N 4.08 E
Sint-Oedenrode 12 Hc 51.34N 5.28 E
Sinton 45 Hl 28.02N 97.33W
Sint-Pieters-Leeuw 12 Gd 50.47N 4.14 E
Sintra 13 Cf 38.48N 9.23W
Sint-Truiden/Saint-Trond 11 Ld 50.49N 5.12 E
Sintu 35 Fd 8.12N 36.56 E
Sinú, Río- 49 Ji 9.24N 75.49W
Sinŭiju 22 Oe 40.06N 124.24 E
Sinujif 35 Hd 8.30N 48.59 E
Sinzig 12 Jd 50.33N 7.15 E
Sió 10 Oj 46.23N 18.40 E
Siocon 26 He 7.42N 122.08 E
Siófok 10 Oj 46.54N 18.03 E
Sioma 36 Df 16.40S 23.35 E

Index Symbols

[1] Independent Nation
[2] State, Region
[3] District, County
[4] Municipality
[5] Colony, Dependency
Continent
Physical Region
Historical or Cultural Region
Mount, Mountain
Volcano
Hill
Mountains, Mountain Range
Hills, Escarpment
Plateau, Upland
Pass, Gap
Plain, Lowland
Delta
Salt Flat
Valley, Canyon
Crater, Cave
Karst Features
Depression
Polder
Desert, Dunes
Forest, Woods
Heath, Steppe
Oasis
Cape, Point
Coast, Beach
Cliff
Peninsula
Isthmus
Sandbank
Island
Atoll
Rock, Reef
Islands, Archipelago
Rocks, Reefs
Coral Reef
Well, Spring
Geyser
River, Stream
Waterfall Rapids
River Mouth, Estuary
Lake
Salt Lake
Intermittent Lake
Reservoir
Swamp, Pond
Canal
Glacier
Ice Shelf, Pack Ice
Ocean
Sea
Gulf, Bay
Strait, Fjord
Lagoon
Bank
Seamount
Tablemount
Ridge
Shelf
Basin
Escarpment, Sea Scarp
Fracture
Trench, Abyss
National Park, Reserve
Point of Interest
Recreation Site
Cave, Cavern
Historic Site
Ruins
Wall, Walls
Church, Abbey
Temple
Scientific Station
Airport
Port
Lighthouse
Mine
Tunnel
Dam, Bridge

Sion/Sitten 14 Bd 46.15N 7.20 E
Siorapaluk 41 Ec 77.39N 71.00W
Sioule 11 Jh 46.22N 3.19 E
Sioux City 39 Je 42.30N 96.23W
Sioux Falls 39 Je 43.32N 96.44W
Sioux Lookout 42 If 50.06N 91.55W
Sipalay 26 He 9.45N 122.24 E
Šipan 14 Lh 42.43N 17.54 E
Siparia 50 Fg 10.08N 61.30W
Šipčenski prohod 15 Ig 42.46N 25.19 E
Siping 28 Ge 43.11N 124.24 E
Sipiwesk 42 He 55.27N 97.24W
Sipiwesk Lake 42 He 55.05N 97.35W
Siple, Mount- 66 Nf 73.15S 126.06W
Siple Coast 66 Mg 82.00S 153.00W
Siple Island 66 Nf 73.39S 125.00W
Siple Station 66 Pf 75.55S 83.55W
Sipora, Pulau- 26 Cg 2.12S 99.40 E
Sippola 8 Ld 60.44N 27.00 E
Siqueira Campos 55 Hf 23.42S 49.50W
Siquia, Rio- 49 Eg 12.09N 84.13W
Siquijor 26 He 9.13N 123.31 E
Siquisique 54 Ea 10.34N 69.42W
Šira 20 Ef 54.29N 90.02 E
Sira 8 Be 58.17N 6.24 E
Sira 7 Bg 58.25N 6.38 E
Şīr Abū Nu'Ayr 24 Pj 25.13N 54.13 E
Si Racha 25 Kf 13.10N 100.57 E
Siracusa=Syracuse (EN) 6 Hh 37.04N 15.18 E
Sir Alexander, Mount- 42 Ff 53.56N 120.23W
Sirasso 34 Dd 9.16N 6.06W
Şīrāţ, Jabal- 33 Hf 17.00N 43.50 E
Sirba 34 Fc 13.46N 1.40 E
Şīr Banī Yās 24 Oj 24.19N 52.37 E
Sirdalen 8 Bf 58.50N 6.40 E
Sirdalsvatn 8 Bf 58.35N 6.40 E
Sire [Eth.] 35 Fd 8.58N 37.00 E
Sire [Eth.] 35 Fd 8.16N 39.30 E
Sir Edward Pellew Group 59 Hc 15.40S 136.50 E
Siret 5 If 45.24N 28.01 E
Siret 15 Jb 47.57N 26.04 E
Sirevåg 7 Ag 58.30N 5.47 E
Sīrīk 23 Id 26.29N 57.09 E
Sirik, Tanjong- 26 Ff 2.46N 111.19 E
Sirina 15 Jm 36.21N 26.41 E
Sirino 14 Jj 40.07N 15.50 E
Sirius Seamount (EN) 40 Gf 52.00N 160.50W
Širjajevo 16 Gf 47.24N 30.13 E
Sir James Mac Brian, Mount- 42 Ed 62.08N 127.40W
Sirjān, Kavīr-e- 24 Ph 29.30N 55.30 E
Sirmione 14 Ee 45.29N 10.36 E
Şırnak 24 Jd 37.32N 42.28 E
Širokaja Pad 20 Jf 50.15N 142.11 E
Široki 20 Jd 63.04N 148.01 E
Širokoje 16 Hf 47.38N 33.14 E
Sironcha 25 Fe 18.50N 79.58 E
Siros 15 Hl 37.26N 24.55 E
Sirpsindiği 15 Jh 41.50N 26.29 E
Sirr, Nafūd as- 24 Kj 25.15N 44.45 E
Sirrayn 33 Hf 19.38N 40.36 E
Sirretta Peak 46 Fi 35.59N 118.20W
Sirri, Jazīreh-ye- 24 Pj 25.55N 54.32 E
Sirsa 25 Fc 29.32N 75.01 E
Sir Sandford, Mount- 46 Ga 51.40N 117.52W
Sirte Desert (EN)=As Sidrah 30 Ie 30.30N 17.30 E
Sir Thomas, Mount- 59 Fe 27.11S 129.46 E
Širvintos 7 Fi 55.03N 25.01 E
Sir Wilfrid Laurier, Mount- 42 Ff 52.48N 119.45W
Sisak 14 Ke 45.29N 16.22 E
Si Sa Ket 25 Ke 15.07N 104.19 E
Sisakht 24 Ng 30.47N 51.33 E
Sisal 48 Ng 21.10N 90.02W
Sisante 13 Je 39.25N 2.13W
Sisargas, Islas- 13 Da 43.22N 8.50W
Šišchid-Gol 27 Ga 51.30N 97.10 E
Sishen 37 Ce 27.55S 22.59 E
Sishui 28 Dg 35.40N 117.17 E
Sisian 16 Oj 39.31N 46.03 E
Sisili 34 Ec 10.16N 1.15W
Sisimiut/Holsteinsborg 67 Nc 67.05N 53.45W
Siskiyou Mountains 46 Df 41.55N 123.15W
Sisŏphŏn 25 Kf 13.35N 102.59 E
Sissano 60 Ch 3.00S 142.03 E
Sisseton 45 Hd 45.40N 97.03W
Sissonne 12 Fe 49.34N 3.54 E
Sīstān=Seistan (EN) 21 If 30.30N 62.00 E
Sistema Central 5 Fg 40.30N 5.00W
Sistema Ibérico=Iberian Mountains (EN) 5 Fg 41.30N 2.30W
Sistemas Béticos 5 Fh 37.35N 3.30W
Sisteron 11 Lj 44.12N 5.56 E
Sisters 46 Ed 44.17N 121.33W
Sistranda 7 Be 63.43N 8.50 E
Sitāpur 25 Gc 27.34N 80.41 E
Sitasjaure 7 Dc 68.00N 17.25 E
Siteki 37 Ee 26.27S 31.57 E
Sitges 13 Nc 41.14N 1.49 E
Sithonia 15 Gi 40.05N 23.55 E
Sitia 15 Jn 35.12N 26.07 E
Sitio d'Abadia 55 Ib 14.48S 46.16W
Sitio Nuevo 49 Jh 10.46N 74.43W
Sitka 39 Fd 57.03N 135.14W
Sitkalidak 40 Ie 57.10N 153.14W
Sitna 15 Kb 47.30N 27.10 E
Sitnica 15 Dg 42.53N 20.52 E
Sitona 35 Fc 14.23N 37.22 E
Sitrah [Bhr.] 24 Ni 26.10N 50.40 E
Sitrah [Eg.] 24 Bh 28.42N 26.54 E
Sittard 11 Ld 51.00N 5.53 E
Sittee Point 49 Ce 16.48N 88.15W
Sitten/Sion 14 Bd 46.15N 7.20 E
Sittingbourne 12 Cc 51.20N 0.45 E
Sittoung 25 Je 17.10N 96.58 E
Sittwe (Akyab) 22 Lg 20.09N 92.54 E
Siuna 49 Eg 13.44N 84.46W
Siuslaw River 46 Cd 44.01N 124.08W
Siva 7 Mh 56.49N 53.55 E
Sivac 15 Cd 45.42N 19.23 E
Sivaki 20 Hf 52.38N 126.45 E
Sivas 22 Ff 39.50N 37.03 E
Sivaš, Ozero- 16 Ig 45.50N 34.40 E
Sivasli 15 Mk 38.30N 29.42 E
Šiveluč, Vulkan- 20 Le 56.33N 161.25 E
Sivera, Ozero-/Sivera Ezers 8 Li 55.58N 27.25 E
Sivera Ezers/Sivera, Ozero- 8 Li 55.58N 27.25 E
Siverek 23 Eb 37.45N 39.19 E
Siverski 7 Hg 59.22N 30.02 E
Sivomaskinski 17 Kc 66.40N 62.31 E
Sivrice 24 Hc 38.27N 39.19 E
Sivrihisar 24 Dc 39.27N 31.34 E
Sivry-Rance 12 Gd 50.10N 4.16 E
Sivry Rance-Rance 12 Gd 50.09N 4.16 E
Sivry-sur-Meuse 12 He 49.19N 5.16 E
Siwah 31 Jf 29.12N 25.31 E
Siwah, Wāḩāt-=Siwa Oasis (EN) 30 Jf 29.10N 25.40 E
Siwalik Range 21 Jg 29.00N 80.00 E
Siwān 25 Gc 26.13N 84.22 E
Siwa Oasis (EN)=Siwah, Wāḩāt- 30 Jf 29.10N 25.40 E
Sixaola, Rio- 49 Fi 9.35N 82.34W
Six Cross Road 51q Eb 13.07N 59.28W
Six-Fours-la-Plage 11 Lk 43.06N 5.51 E
Sixian 28 Dh 33.29N 117.53 E
Six Men's Bay 51q Ab 13.16N 59.38W
Sixth Cataract (EN)=Sablūkah, Ash Shallāl as- 30 Kg 16.20N 32.42 E
Siyah-Chaman 24 Ld 37.35N 47.10 E
Siyang (Zhongxing) 28 Eh 33.43N 118.40 E
Siziwang Qi (Ulan Hua) 28 Ad 41.31N 111.41 E
Sjaelland=Zealand (EN) 5 Hd 55.30N 11.45 E
Sjamozero, Ozero- 7 Hf 61.55N 33.15 E
Sjare/Sääre 8 Ig 57.57N 21.53 E
Sjas 7 Hf 60.10N 32.31 E
Sjasstroj 7 Hf 60.09N 32.36 E
Šjašupe 7 Fi 55.00N 22.10 E
Šjauljaj/Šiauliai 6 Id 55.53N 23.19 E
Sjenica 15 Cf 43.16N 20.00 E
Sjnjaja 20 Hd 61.00N 126.57 E
Sjoa 8 Cc 61.41N 9.33 E
Sjöbo 8 Ei 55.38N 13.42 E
Sjøholt 7 Be 62.29N 6.50 E
Sjujutlijka 15 Ig 42.17N 25.55 E
Sjun 17 Gi 55.43N 54.17 E
Sjuøyane 41 Ob 80.43N 20.45 E
Skadarsko Jezero=Scutari, Lake- (EN) 5 Hg 42.10N 19.20 E
Skadovsk 19 Df 46.07N 32.56 E
Skælskør 8 Di 55.15N 11.19 E
Skærbæk 8 Ci 55.09N 8.46 E
Skagatá 7a Ba 66.07N 20.06W
Skagen 7 Ch 57.44N 10.36 E
Skagern 8 Ff 59.00N 14.15 E
Skagerrak 5 Gd 57.45N 9.00 E
Skaget 8 Cc 61.17N 9.12 E
Skagit River 46 Db 48.20N 122.25W
Skagway 39 Fd 59.28N 135.19W
Skaidi 7 Fa 70.26N 24.30 E
Skaland 7 Db 69.27N 17.18 E
Skälderviken 8 Eh 56.20N 12.40 E
Skålevik 8 Bf 58.04N 8.00 E
Skalisty Golec, gora- 20 Ge 56.20N 119.10 E
Skalisty Golec, gora- 20 Ie 55.55N 130.35 E
Skanderborg 7 Bh 56.02N 9.56 E
Skåne 5 Hd 56.00N 13.30 E
Skånevik 8 Ae 59.44N 5.59 E
Skänninge 8 Ff 58.24N 15.05 E
Skanör 8 Ei 55.25N 12.52 E
Skántzoura 15 Hj 39.05N 24.07 E
Skara 7 Cg 58.22N 13.25 E
Skaraborg 7 Cg 58.20N 13.30 E
Skärblacka 8 Ff 58.34N 15.54 E
Skärdu 25 Fa 35.18N 75.37 E
Skärhamn 8 Dg 57.59N 11.33 E
Skarnes 8 Dd 60.15N 11.41 E
Skarsstind 8 Cb 62.03N 8.35 E
Skarsvåg 7 Fa 71.06N 25.56 E
Skarszewy 10 Ob 54.05N 18.27 E
Skarvdalsegga 8 Cb 62.09N 8.03 E
Skaryszew 10 Re 51.19N 21.15 E
Skarżysko-Kamienna 10 Qe 51.08N 20.53 E
Skasøy 8 Ca 63.20N 8.35 E
Skät 15 Gf 43.44N 23.51 E
Skattkärr 8 Ee 59.25N 13.41 E
Skattungbyn 8 Fc 61.12N 14.52 E
Skaudvile/Skaudvilė 7 Fi 55.27N 22.33 E
Skaudvilė/Skaudvile 7 Fi 55.27N 22.33 E
Skaulen 8 Be 59.38N 6.35 E
Skawa 10 Pf 50.02N 19.26 E
Skawina 10 Pg 49.59N 19.49 E
Skee 8 Df 58.56N 11.19 E
Skeena 38 Fd 54.09N 130.02W
Skeena Mountains 42 Ee 56.45N 128.40W
Skegness 9 Nh 53.10N 0.21 E
Skeidararsandur 7a Cc 63.54N 17.14W
Skeldon 54 Gb 5.53N 57.08W
Skeleton Coast 37 Ac 17.50S 12.45 E
Skellefteå 6 Ic 64.46N 20.57 E
Skelleftealven 5 Ic 64.42N 21.06 E
Skelleftehamn 7 Ed 64.41N 21.14 E
Skëndërbeut, Mali i- 15 Ch 41.35N 19.50 E
Skene 8 Eg 57.29N 12.38 E
Skerki Bank (EN) 32 Jb 37.45N 10.50 E
Skerries/Na Sceiri 9 Gh 53.35N 6.07W
Skerryvore 9 Fe 56.20N 7.05W
Skhiza 15 Em 36.44N 21.46 E
Skhoinoúsa 15 Im 36.50N 25.30 E
Ski 7 Cg 59.43N 10.50 E
Skiathos 15 Gj 39.10N 23.28 E
Skiathos 15 Gj 39.10N 23.29 E
Skibbereen/An Sciobairin 9 Dj 51.33N 9.15W
Skibotn 7 Eb 69.24N 20.16 E
Skidel 16 Dc 53.38N 24.17 E
Skien 6 Gd 59.12N 9.36 E
Skierniewice 10 Qe 51.58N 20.08 E
Skierniewice 10 Qe 52.00N 20.10 E
Skiftet/Kihti 8 Id 60.15N 21.05 E
Skikda 31 He 36.52N 6.54 E
Skikda 32 Ib 36.45N 6.50 E
Skillet Fork 45 Lg 38.08N 88.07W
Skillingaryd 8 Fg 57.26N 14.05 E
Skinári, Ákra- 15 Dl 37.56N 20.42 E
Skinnskatteberg 8 Fe 59.50N 15.41 E
Skipton 9 Kh 53.58N 2.01W
Skiptvet 8 De 59.28N 11.11 E
Skiropoúla 15 Hk 38.50N 24.21 E
Skiros 15 Hk 38.54N 24.34 E
Skiros 15 Hk 38.53N 24.32 E
Skive 7 Bh 56.34N 9.02 E
Skive Å 8 Ch 56.34N 9.04 E
Skjærhalden 8 De 59.02N 11.02 E
Skjåk 8 Cc 61.52N 8.22 E
Skjálfandafljót 7a Cb 65.59N 17.38W
Skjeberg 8 De 59.14N 11.12 E
Skjern 7 Bi 55.57N 8.30 E
Skjern Å 7 Bi 55.55N 8.24 E
Skjervøy 7 Ea 70.02N 20.59 E
Skjoldungen 41 Hf 63.20N 41.20W
Sklad 20 Hb 71.52N 123.35 E
Šklov 16 Gb 54.14N 30.18 E
Skobeleva, Pik- 18 Ie 39.51N 72.47 E
Skærfjorden 41 Kc 77.30N 19.10W
Škofja Loka 14 Id 46.10N 14.18 E
Skog 8 Gc 61.10N 16.55 E
Skógafoss 7a Bc 63.32N 19.31W
Skoghall 8 Ee 59.19N 13.26 E
Skogshorn 8 Cd 60.53N 8.42 E
Skokie 45 Me 42.02N 87.45W
Skole 10 Th 48.58N 23.32 E
Skópelos 15 Gj 39.07N 23.44 E
Skópelos 15 Gj 39.10N 23.40 E
Skopi 15 Jn 35.11N 26.02 E
Skopin 7 Jj 53.52N 39.37 E
Skopje 6 Ig 42.00N 21.29 E
Skórcz 10 Oc 53.48N 18.32 E
Skorovatn 7 Cd 64.39N 13.07 E
Skorpa 8 Ac 61.35N 4.50 E
Skørping 8 Ch 56.50N 9.53 E
Skorpiós 15 Dk 38.42N 20.45 E
Škotovo 28 Lc 43.20N 132.21 E
Skotselv 8 Ce 59.51N 9.53 E
Skoura 32 Fc 31.04N 6.43W
Skövde 7 Cg 58.24N 13.50 E
Skovorodino 22 Od 53.59N 123.55 E
Skowhegan 44 Mc 44.46N 69.43W
Skradin 14 Jg 43.49N 15.56 E
Skreia 8 Dd 60.34N 11.04 E
Skreia 8 Dd 60.39N 10.56 E
Skrekken 8 Bd 60.13N 7.49 E
Skridulaupen 8 Bc 61.55N 7.35 E
Skrimkolla 8 Cb 62.23N 9.04 E
Skrīveri/Skriveri 8 Kh 56.37N 25.10 E
Skriveri/Skrīveri 8 Kh 56.37N 25.10 E
Skrunda 7 Eh 56.41N 22.00 E
Skrwa 10 Pd 52.33N 19.32 E
Skudenesfjorden 8 Ae 59.05N 5.20 E
Skudeneshavn 7 Ag 59.09N 5.17 E
Skuodas 7 Eh 56.17N 21.31 E
Skurup 8 Ei 55.28N 13.30 E
Skutskär 8 Gd 60.38N 17.25 E
Skvira 16 Fe 49.44N 29.42 E
Skwierzyna 10 Ld 52.35N 15.30 E
Skye, Island of- 5 Fd 57.15N 6.10W
Slagelse 7 Ci 55.24N 11.22 E
Slagnäs 7 Ed 65.36N 18.10 E
Slamet, Gunung- 21 Mj 7.14S 109.12 E
Slaná 10 Ri 47.56N 21.08 E
Slancy 19 Cd 59.08N 28.02 E
Slaney/An tSláine 9 Gi 52.21N 6.30W
Slănic 15 Id 45.15N 25.56 E
Slănic Moldova 15 Jc 46.12N 26.26 E
Slannik 15 Jf 43.06N 26.13 E
Slano 14 Lh 42.47N 17.54 E
Slaný 10 Kf 50.14N 14.06 E
Śląsk=Silesia (EN) 10 Me 51.00N 16.45 E
Śląsk=Silesia (EN) 5 He 51.00N 16.45 E
Śląska, Wyżyna- 10 Of 50.28N 18.40 E
Slate Islands 45 Mb 48.34N 86.45W
Slatina 15 He 44.26N 24.22 E
Slatina 10 Ph 48.32N 19.10 E
Slaton 45 Fj 33.26N 101.39W
Slave Coast 30 Hh 6.00N 3.30 E
Slave Lake 42 Ge 55.17N 114.46W
Slave River 38 Hc 61.18N 113.39W
Slavgorod 16 Gc 53.27N 31.01 E
Slavgorod 20 Cf 53.03N 78.48 E
Slavičín 10 Ng 49.06N 17.53 E
Slavjanka 20 Ih 42.55N 131.20 E
Slavjanka 15 Gh 41.23N 23.36 E
Slavjansk 6 Jf 48.52N 37.37 E
Slavjansk-na-Kubani 19 Df 45.15N 38.08 E
Slavkoje 10 Th 48.45N 23.31 E
Slavkoviči 8 Mg 57.37N 29.10 E
Slavonia (EN) = Slavonija 5 Hf 45.00N 18.00 E
Slavonia (EN)=Slavonija 14 Le 45.00N 18.00 E
Slavonija=Slavonia (EN) 14 Le 45.00N 18.00 E
Slavonija = Slavonia (EN) 5 Hf 45.00N 18.00 E
Slavonska Požega 14 Le 45.20N 17.41 E
Slavonski Brod 14 Me 45.09N 18.02 E
Slavsk 8 Ii 55.01N 21.37 E
Slavuta 19 Ce 50.18N 26.52 E
Sława 10 Me 51.53N 16.04 E
Sławatycze 10 Te 51.43N 23.30 E
Sławno 10 Mb 54.22N 16.40 E
Slayton 45 Id 44.01N 95.45W
Sleaford 9 Mh 53.00N 0.24W
Slea Head/Ceann Sléibhe 9 Ci 52.06N 10.27W
Sleat, Sound of- 9 Hd 57.10N 5.50W
Sleen 12 Ib 52.47N 6.49 E
Sleeper Islands 42 Je 57.25N 79.50W
Sléibhte Chill Mhantáin/Wicklow Mountains 9 Gh 53.02N 6.24W
Sleidinge, Evergem- 12 Fc 51.08N 3.41 E
Slesin 10 Od 52.23N 18.19 E
Slessor Glacier 66 Af 79.50S 28.30W
Slessor Peak 66 Qe 66.31S 64.58W
Slettefjell 8 Cc 61.13N 8.44 E
Sletterhage 8 Dh 56.06N 10.31 E
Ślęża 10 Me 51.10N 16.58 E
Ślęża 10 Mf 50.52N 16.45 E
Sliabh Bearnach/Slieve Bernagh 9 Ei 52.50N 8.35W
Sliabh Bladhma/Slieve Bloom 9 Fh 53.10N 7.35W
Sliabh Eachtai/Slieve Aughty 9 Eh 53.10N 8.30W
Sliabh Gamh/Ox or Slieve Gamph Mountains 9 Eg 54.10N 8.50W
Sliabh Mis/Slieve Mish 9 Di 52.10N 9.50W
Sliabh Speirin/Sperrin Mountains 9 Fg 54.50N 7.05W
Slidell 45 Lk 30.17N 89.47W
Slide Mountain 44 Jd 42.00N 74.23W
Slidre 8 Cc 61.10N 9.00 E
Sliedrecht 12 Gc 51.50N 4.46 E
Slieve Aughty/Sliabh Eachtai 9 Eh 53.10N 8.30W
Slieve Bernagh/Sliabh Bearnach 9 Ei 52.50N 8.35W
Slieve Bloom/Sliabh Bladhma 9 Fh 53.10N 7.35W
Slievefelim Mountains 9 Ei 52.45N 8.15W
Slieve Mish/Sliabh Mis 9 Di 52.10N 9.50W
Sligeach/Sligo 9 Eg 54.10N 8.40W
Sligeach/Sligo 6 Fe 54.17N 8.28W
Sligo/Sligeach 9 Eg 54.10N 8.40W
Sligo/Sligeach 6 Fe 54.17N 8.28W
Sligo Bay/Cuan Shligigh 9 Eg 54.20N 8.40W
Slinge 12 Ib 52.08N 6.31 E
Slingebeek 12 Ic 51.59N 6.18 E
Slite 8 Hg 57.43N 18.48 E
Sliven 15 Jg 42.40N 26.19 E
Sliven 15 Jg 42.40N 26.19 E
Slivnica 15 Gg 42.51N 23.02 E
Sljudjanka 20 Ff 51.38N 103.40 E
Slobodka 15 Mb 47.54N 29.12 E
Slobodskoj 19 Fd 58.47N 50.12 E
Slobodzeja 16 Ff 46.43N 29.43 E
Slobozia [Rom.] 15 Ke 44.34N 27.22 E
Slobozia [Rom.] 15 Ie 44.30N 25.11 E
Slochteren 12 Ia 53.12N 6.50 E
Slocum Mountain 46 Gi 35.18N 117.13W
Slonim 19 Ce 53.05N 25.18 E
Sloten 12 Hb 52.54N 5.40 E
Slotermeer 12 Hb 52.55N 5.40 E
Slough 9 Mj 51.31N 0.36W
Slovakia (EN) = Slovenská Republika 6 Hf 48.00N 17.00 E
Slovakia (EN) = Slovensko 5 Hf 48.45N 19.30 E
Slovečna 16 Fd 51.41N 29.42 E
Slovenia (EN) = Slovenija 5 Hf 46.00N 15.00 E
Slovenia (EN) = Slovenija 14 Id 46.00N 15.00 E
Slovenia (EN) = Slovenija 14 Id 46.00N 15.00 E
Slovenija=Slovenia (EN) 14 Id 46.00N 15.00 E
Slovenija = Slovenia (EN) 14 Id 46.00N 15.00 E
Slovenija = Slovenia (EN) 5 Hf 46.00N 15.00 E
Slovenska Bistrica 14 Jd 46.24N 15.34 E
Slovenská Republika = Slovakia (EN) 6 Hf 48.00N 17.00 E
Slovenske Gorice 14 Jd 46.35N 15.55 E
Slovenské rudohorie 10 Ph 48.45N 20.00 E
Slovenský kras 10 Qh 48.35N 20.40 E
Słubice 10 Kd 52.20N 14.35 E
Sluč 16 Ec 52.08N 27.32 E
Sluč 16 Ed 51.37N 26.38 E
Sluck 19 Ce 53.02N 27.31 E
Slunj 14 Je 45.07N 15.35 E
Słupca 10 Nd 52.19N 17.52 E
Słupia 10 Mb 54.35N 16.50 E
Słupsk 10 Nb 54.28N 17.01 E
Słupsk 10 Mb 54.30N 17.00 E
Slyne Head/Ceann Gólaim 9 Ch 53.24N 10.13W
Småland 7 Dh 57.20N 15.05 E
Smålandsfarvandet 8 Di 55.06N 11.20 E
Smålandsstenar 8 Eg 57.10N 13.24 E
Smalininkai/Smalininkaj 8 Ji 55.01N 22.32 E
Smalininkaj/Smalininkai 8 Ji 55.01N 22.32 E
Smallingerland-Drachten 11 Ma 53.06N 6.05 E
Smallwood Reservoir 38 Md 54.00N 64.30W
Smederevo 15 De 44.39N 20.56 E
Smederevska Palanka 15 De 44.22N 20.58 E
Smedjebacken 7 Df 60.08N 15.25 E
Smela 19 Df 49.13N 31.53 E
Smidovič 20 Ig 48.36N 133.50 E
Šmidta, Mys- 20 Nc 68.45N 178.40W
Šmidta, Ostrov- 21 La 81.08N 90.48 E
Šmidta, Poluostrov- 20 Jf 54.15N 142.40 E
Śmigiel 10 Md 52.01N 16.32 E
Smilde 12 Ib 52.56N 6.28 E
Smiltene 7 Fh 57.28N 25.56 E
Smirnovo 17 Ni 54.31N 69.28 E
Smirnyh 20 Jg 49.45N 142.53 E
Smith 55 Bl 35.30S 61.36W
Smith Arm 42 Fc 66.15N 124.00W
Smith Bay [Ak.-U.S.] 40 Ib 70.51N 154.25W
Smith Bay [Can.] 42 Ja 77.15N 79.00W
Smith Center 45 Gg 39.47N 98.47W
Smithers 42 Ef 54.47N 127.10W
Smithfield [S.Afr.] 37 Df 30.09S 26.30 E
Smithfield [Ut.-U.S.] 46 Jf 41.50N 111.50W
Smith Knoll 9 Pi 52.50N 2.10 E
Smith Mountain Lake 44 Hg 37.10N 79.40W
Smith Peak 46 Gb 48.50N 116.39W
Smith River 46 Jc 47.25N 111.29W
Smiths Falls 42 Jh 44.54N 76.01W
Smith Sound 46 Ba 51.18N 127.48W
Smithton 58 Fi 40.51S 145.07 E
Smjadovo 15 Kf 43.04N 27.01 E
Smjörfjoll 7a Cb 65.35N 14.46W
Smögen 8 Df 58.21N 11.13 E
Smoke Creek Desert 46 Ff 40.30N 119.40W
Smokey Dome 46 He 43.29N 114.56W
Smoky Bay 59 Gf 32.20S 133.45 E
Smoky Cape 59 Kf 30.56S 153.05 E
Smoky Falls 42 Jf 50.03N 82.10W
Smoky Hill 38 Jf 39.03N 96.48W
Smoky Hills 45 Gg 39.15N 99.00W
Smoky River 42 Fe 56.11N 117.19W
Smøla 7 Be 63.25N 8.00 E
Smolensk 6 Je 54.47N 32.03 E
Smolenskaja Oblast 19 De 55.00N 33.00 E
Smolenskaja Vozvyšennost=Smolensk Upland (EN) 5 Je 54.40N 33.00 E
Smolensk Upland (EN)=Smolenskaja Vozvyšennost 5 Je 54.40N 33.00 E
Smolevići 16 Fb 54.03N 28.02 E
Smolianica 10 Ud 52.40N 24.40 E
Smólikas Óros 5 Ig 40.06N 20.55 E
Smoljan 15 Hh 41.35N 24.41 E
Smoljan 15 Hh 41.40N 24.40 E
Smooth Rock Falls 44 Ga 49.20N 81.39W
Smorgon 19 Ce 54.31N 26.23 E
Smørstabbren 8 Cc 61.32N 8.06 E
Smrdeš 15 Fh 41.34N 22.28 E
Smygehamn 8 Ei 55.21N 13.22 E
Smygehuk 8 Ei 55.21N 13.23 E
Smyley, Cape- 66 Qf 72.00S 78.50W
Smyrna 44 Ei 33.53N 84.31W
Smyrna (EN)=İzmir 22 Ef 38.25N 27.09 E
Smyšljajevka 7 Mj 53.17N 50.24 E
Smythe, Mount- 38 Gd 57.50N 124.59W
Snacke Point 51b Bb 18.17N 62.58W
Snæfell 7a Cb 64.48N 15.34W
Snaefell 9 Ig 54.16N 4.27W
Snæfellsjökull 7a Ab 64.49N 23.46W
Snag 42 Dd 62.23N 140.22W
Snake Bay Settlement 59 Gb 11.25S 130.40 E
Snake Range 46 Hg 39.00N 114.15W
Snake River [Can.] 42 Ec 65.57N 134.13W
Snake River [U.S.] 38 He 46.12N 119.02W
Snake River Plain 43 Ec 42.45N 114.30W
Snare 42 Fd 63.15N 116.08W
Snares Islands 61 Ci 48.00S 166.35 E
Snarumselva 8 Cc 59.57N 9.58 E
Snåsa 7 Cd 64.15N 12.22 E
Sneek 11 La 53.02N 5.40 E
Snekermeer 11 La 52.59N 5.40 E
Snežnaja, Gora- 20 Lc 65.18N 165.30 E
Snežnik 14 Ie 45.26N 14.36 E
Snežnogorsk 20 Dc 68.15N 87.35 E
Šnežnoje 16 Kf 47.59N 38.50 E
Śniardwy, Jezioro- 10 Rc 53.46N 21.44 E
Śnieżka 5 He 50.45N 15.43 E
Śnieżnik 10 Mf 50.12N 16.50 E
Snigirevka 16 Hf 47.04N 32.45 E
Snillfjord 8 Ca 63.24N 9.30 E
Snina 10 Sh 48.59N 22.08 E
Snizort, Loch- 9 Gd 57.30N 6.25W
Snjatyn 16 De 48.29N 25.34 E
Snøhetta 5 Gc 62.20N 9.17 E
Snohomish 46 Dc 47.55N 122.06W
Snønuten 8 Be 59.31N 6.54 E
Snøonipa 8 Bc 61.42N 6.41 E
Snota 8 Cb 62.51N 9.06 E
Snov 16 Gd 51.32N 31.33 E
Snowbird Lake 42 Hd 60.40N 102.50W
Snowdon 5 Fe 53.04N 4.05W
Snowdonia 9 Jh 53.05N 3.55W
Snowdrift 42 Gd 62.23N 110.47W
Snowflake 46 Ji 34.30N 110.05W
Snow Hill 44 Jf 38.11N 75.24W
Snow Lake 42 Hf 54.53N 100.02W
Snow Mountain 43 Cd 39.23N 122.46W
Snowshoe Peak 46 Hb 48.13N 115.41W
Snowville 46 If 41.58N 112.43W
Snowy Mountain [B.C.-Can.] 46 Fb 49.02N 119.57W
Snowy Mountain [N.Y.-U.S.] 44 Jd 43.42N 74.23W
Snowy Mountains 59 Jg 36.30S 148.20 E
Snowy River 59 Jg 37.48S 148.32 E
Snudy, Ozero- 8 Li 55.40N 27.15 E
Snug Corner 49 Kb 22.32N 73.53W
Snuŏl 25 Lf 12.04N 106.26 E
Snyder 43 Ge 32.44N 100.55W
Soalala 37 Hc 16.07S 45.21 E
Soalara 37 Gd 23.35S 43.44 E
Soanierana-Ivongo 37 Hc 16.54S 49.34 E
Soar 12 Ab 52.52N 1.17W
Şoarş 15 Hd 45.56N 24.55 E
Soavinandriana 37 Hc 19.10S 46.43 E
Sob 17 Mc 66.20N 66.02 E

Index Symbols

Independent Nation
State, Region
District, County
Municipality
Colony, Dependency
Continent
Physical Region
Historical or Cultural Region
Mount, Mountain
Volcano
Hill
Mountains, Mountain Range
Hills, Escarpment
Plateau, Upland
Pass, Gap
Plain, Lowland
Delta
Salt Flat
Valley, Canyon
Crater, Cave
Karst Features
Depression
Polder
Desert, Dunes
Forest, Woods
Heath, Steppe
Oasis
Cape, Point
Coast, Beach
Cliff
Peninsula
Isthmus
Sandbank
Island
Atoll
Rock, Reef
Islands, Archipelago
Rocks, Reefs
Coral Reef
Well, Spring
Geyser
River, Stream
Waterfall Rapids
River Mouth, Estuary
Lake
Salt Lake
Intermittent Lake
Reservoir
Swamp, Pond
Canal
Glacier
Ice Shelf, Pack Ice
Ocean
Sea
Gulf, Bay
Strait, Fjord
Lagoon
Bank
Seamount
Tablemount
Ridge
Shelf
Basin
Escarpment, Sea Scarp
Fracture
Trench, Abyss
National Park, Reserve
Point of Interest
Recreation Site
Cave, Cavern
Historic Site
Ruins
Wall, Walls
Church, Abbey
Temple
Scientific Station
Airport
Port
Lighthouse
Mine
Tunnel
Dam, Bridge

Sob 16 Fe 48.41N 29.17 E
Soba 34 Gc 10.59N 8.04 E
Sobaek-Sanmaek 28 Jf 36.00N 128.00 E
Sobat (EN)=Sawbā 30 Kh 9.45N 31.45 E
Sobernheim 12 Je 49.48N 7.39 E
Soběslav 10 Kg 49.16N 14.44 E
Sōbetsu 29a Bb 42.33N 140.51 E
Sobinka 7 Jh 56.01N 40.07 E
Sobolevo 16 Qd 51.59N 51.48 E
Sobolevo 20 Kf 54.17N 156.00 E
Sobolew 10 Re 51.41N 21.40 E
Sobo-San 29 Be 32.47N 131.21 E
Sobradinho 55 Fi 29.24S 53.03W
Sobral 53 Lf 3.42S 40.21W
Sobrarbe 13 Mb 42.20N 0.05 E
Soca 55 El 34.41S 55.41W
Soča=Isonzo (EN) 14 He 45.43N 13.33 E
Sochaczew 10 Qd 52.14N 20.14 E
Soči 6 Jg 43.35N 39.45 E
Société, Iles de la-=Society Islands (EN) 57 Lf 17.00S 150.00W
Society Islands (EN)= Société, Iles de la- 57 Lf 17.00S 150.00W
Socompa, Paso- 52 Jh 24.27S 68.18W
Socorro [Col.] 54 Db 6.27N 73.16W
Socorro [N.M.-U.S.] 43 Fe 34.04N 106.54W
Socotra (EN) = Suquṭrá 21 Hh 12.30N 54.00 E
Soc Trang 25 Lg 9.36N 105.58 E
Socuéllamos 13 Je 39.17N 2.48W
Soda Lake 46 Gi 35.08N 116.04W
Sodankylä 7 Gc 67.25N 26.36 E
Soda Springs 46 Je 42.39N 111.36W
Söderåsen 8 Eh 56.04N 13.05 E
Söderfors 7 Df 60.23N 17.14 E
Söderhamn 7 Df 61.18N 17.03 E
Söderköping 8 Gf 58.29N 16.18 E
Södermanland 8 Ge 59.10N 16.50 E
Södermanland [2] 7 Dg 59.15N 16.40 E
Söderslätt 8 Ei 55.30N 13.15 E
Södertälje 7 Dg 59.12N 17.37 E
Södertörn 8 Ge 59.05N 18.00 E
Sodo 35 Fd 6.51N 37.45 E
Södra Dellen 8 Gc 61.50N 16.45 E
Södra Gloppet 8 Ia 63.05N 21.00 E
Södra Kvarken 8 Hd 60.20N 19.08 E
Södra-Midsjöbanken 8 Gi 55.40N 17.20 E
Södra Vi 8 Fg 57.45N 15.48 E
Soe 26 Hh 9.52S 124.17 E
Soekmekaar 37 Dd 23.28S 29.58 E
Soela, proliv-/Soela Väin 8 Jf 58.40N 22.30 E
Soela Väin/Soela, proliv- 8 Jf 58.40N 22.30 E
Soest [Ger.] 10 Ee 51.35N 8.07 E
Soest [Neth.] 12 Hb 52.10N 5.20 E
Soeste 12 Ja 53.10N 7.44 E
Soester Borde 12 Kc 51.38N 8.03 E
Soestwetering 12 Ib 51.30N 6.09 E
Sofádhes 15 Fj 39.20N 22.06 E
Sofala [3] 37 Ec 19.30S 34.40 E
Sofala, Baia de- 30 Kk 20.11S 34.45 E
Sofia 15 Hc 15.27S 47.23 E
Sofia [Bul.] [2] 15 Gg 42.43N 23.25 E
Sofia [Grc.] [2] 15 Gg 42.41N 23.19 E
Sofia (EN)=Sofija 6 Ig 42.41N 23.19 E
Sofija=Sofia (EN) 6 Ig 42.41N 23.19 E
Sofijsk 20 If 52.20N 134.01 E
Sofporog 19 Db 65.48N 31.28 E
Sofrána, Nisídhes- 15 Jm 36.04N 26.24 E
Sōfu-Gan 27 Pf 29.50N 140.20 E
Sogamoso 54 Db 5.43N 72.56W
Soganlı 24 Eb 41.11N 32.38 E
Sogara, Lake- 36 Fd 5.15S 31.00 E
Sogda 20 If 50.24N 132.18 E
Sögel 10 Dd 52.51N 7.31 E
Sogeri 60 Di 9.10S 147.32 E
Sogn 8 Ac 61.05N 5.55 E
Sogndalsfjøra 8 Bc 61.14N 7.06 E
Søgne 8 Bf 58.05N 7.49 E
Sognefjell 8 Bc 61.35N 7.55 E
Sognefjorden 5 Gc 61.05N 5.10 E
Sognesjøen 8 Ac 61.05N 5.00 E
Sogn og Fjordane [2] 7 Bf 61.30N 6.50 E
Sogod 26 Hd 10.23N 124.59 E
Sogo Nur 27 Hc 42.20N 101.20 E
Sogoža 7 Jg 58.30N 39.06 E
Söğüt 15 Nj 40.00N 30.11 E
Söğütalan 15 Li 40.03N 28.34 E
Söğüt Gölü 24 Cd 37.03N 29.53 E
Sog Xian 27 Fe 31.51N 93.42 E
Soh 18 He 39.57N 71.08 E
Sohag (EN)=Sawhāj 31 Kf 26.33N 31.42 E
Sohano 60 Ei 5.29S 154.41 E
Sohŭksan-Do 28 Hg 34.04N 125.07 E
Soignies/Zinnik 11 Kd 50.35N 4.04 E
Soini 8 Kb 62.52N 24.13 E
Soisalo 8 Mb 62.40N 28.10 E
Soissonnais, Plateau du- 11 Je 49.15N 3.10 E
Soissons 11 Je 49.22N 3.20 E
Sōja 29 Cd 34.40N 133.44 E
Sojana 7 Kd 65.53N 43.30 E
Sojma 7 Ec 67.00N 51.00 E
Šojna 17 Bc 67.52N 44.08 E
Sŏjosŏn-man=Korea Bay (EN) 21 Of 39.15N 125.00 E
Sojuznoje 16 Vd 50.50N 60.10 E
Sok 19 Fe 53.25N 50.10 E
Sokal 16 Dd 50.29N 24.17 E
Šokalskogo, Proliv- 20 Ea 79.00N 100.00 E
Sokch'o 27 Md 38.12N 128.36 E
Söke 23 Cb 37.45N 27.24 E
Sokele 36 Dd 9.55S 24.36 E
Sokirjany 16 Ee 48.28N 27.25 E
Sokna 7 Bf 60.14N 9.54 E
Soko Banja 15 Ef 43.39N 21.53 E
Sokodé 31 Hh 8.59N 1.08 E
Sokol 19 Ed 59.29N 40.13 E
Sokol 15 Ce 44.18N 19.25 E
Sokółka 10 Tc 53.25N 23.31 E
Sokolo 34 Dc 14.44N 6.07W
Sokolov 10 If 50.11N 12.38 E
Sokołów Podlaski 10 Sd 52.25N 22.15 E
Sokone 34 Bc 13.53N 16.22W
Sokosti 7 Gb 68.20N 28.01 E
Sokoto 30 Hg 11.24N 4.07 E
Sokoto [2] 34 Gc 12.20N 5.20 E
Sokoto 31 Hg 13.04N 5.15 E
Sokourala 34 Dd 9.13N 8.05W
Sōl 35 Hd 9.20N 49.25 E
Sōl 35 Hd 9.40N 48.30 E
Sol, Costa del- 13 Ih 36.46N 3.55W
Sol, Pico do- 55 Ke 20.07S 43.28W
Sola 10 Pf 50.04N 19.13 E
Sola 63b Ca 13.53S 167.33 E
Solai 36 Gb 0.02N 36.09 E
Solakrossen 8 Af 58.53N 5.36 E
Solander Island 61 Ci 46.35S 166.50 E
Solanet 55 Cm 36.51S 58.31W
Solāpur 22 Jh 17.41N 75.55 E
Solbad Hall in Tirol 14 Fc 47.17N 11.31 E
Solcy 19 Dd 58.09N 30.20 E
Sölder 14 Ed 46.58N 11.00 E
Soldier Point 51d Bb 17.02N 61.41W
Soldotna 40 Id 60.29N 151.04W
Solec Kujawski 10 Oc 53.06N 18.14 E
Soledad [Arg.] 55 Bj 30.37S 60.55W
Soledad [Ca.-U.S.] 46 Eh 36.26N 121.19W
Soledad [Col.] 54 Da 10.55N 74.46W
Soledad [Ven.] 54 Fb 8.10N 63.34W
Soledad, Boca de- 48 Ce 25.17N 112.09W
Soledad, Isla-/East Falkland 52 Kk 51.45S 58.50W
Soledade 56 Jc 28.50S 52.30W
Sølen 8 Dc 61.55N 11.30 E
Sølensjøen 8 Dc 61.55N 11.35 E
Solentiname, Archipiélago de- 49 Fh 11.10N 85.00W
Solenzara 11a Bb 41.51N 9.24 E
Solesmes 12 Fd 50.11N 3.30 E
Solferino 14 Ee 45.23N 10.34 E
Solgen 8 Fg 57.33N 15.07 E
Solgne 12 Ie 48.58N 6.18 E
Soligalič 7 Kg 59.07N 42.13 E
Soligorsk 19 Ce 52.49N 27.31 E
Solihull 9 Li 52.25N 1.45W
Solikamsk 19 Fd 59.39N 56.47 E
Sol-Ileck 6 Le 51.12N 55.03 E
Solimán, Punta- 48 Ph 19.50N 87.27W
Solimoes→Amazonas, Rio-=Amazon (EN) 52 Lf 0.10S 49.00W
Solingen 10 De 51.11N 7.05 E
Solińskie, Jezioro- 10 Sg 49.22N 22.30 E
Solis, Presa- 48 Ig 20.05N 100.36W
Sollebrunn 8 Ef 58.07N 12.32 E
Sollefteå 7 De 63.10N 17.16 E
Sollentuna 8 Ge 59.28N 17.54 E
Söller 13 Oe 39.46N 2.42 E
Sollerön 8 Fd 60.55N 14.37 E
Solling 10 Fe 51.45N 9.35 E
Solms 12 Kd 50.46N 9.36 E
Solna 8 He 59.22N 18.01 E
Solnečnogorsk 7 Ih 56.10N 37.00 E
Solnečny 20 Id 60.10N 137.35 E
Sologne 11 Hg 47.50N 2.00 E
Sologne Bourbonnaise 11 Jh 46.40N 3.30 E
Solok 26 Dg 0.48S 100.39 E
Sololá [3] 49 Bf 14.40N 91.15W
Sololá 49 Bf 14.40N 91.11W
Solomon Islands [1] 58 Ge 8.00S 159.00 E
Solomon Islands 57 Ge 8.00S 159.00 E
Solomon Islands (British Solomon Islands) [1] 58 Ge 8.00S 159.00 E
Solomon River 43 Hd 38.54N 97.22W
Solomon Sea 57 Ge 8.00S 155.00 E
Solon Springs 45 Kc 46.22N 91.48W
Solør 8 Dd 60.30N 11.55 E
Solor, Kepulauan- 26 Hh 8.25S 123.30 E
Solothurn 14 Bc 47.15N 7.30 E
Solothurn [2] 14 Bc 47.20N 7.40 E
Solotvin 10 Uh 48.38N 24.31 E
Soloveckije Ostrova 7 Id 65.05N 35.45 E
Solovjevka 8 Nd 60.44N 30.20 E
Solovjevsk 20 Hf 54.15N 124.30 E
Solovjevsk 20 Gg 49.54N 115.43 E
Solöz 15 Mi 40.23N 29.25 E
Solre-le-Château 12 Gd 50.10N 4.05 E
Solsona 13 Nc 41.59N 1.31 E
Solt 10 Oj 46.48N 19.00 E
Solta 14 Kg 43.23N 16.17 E
Soltānābād [Iran] 24 Mg 31.03N 49.42 E
Soltānābād [Iran] 24 Rd 36.23N 58.02 E
Soltānī, Khowr-e- 24 Nh 29.00N 50.50 E
Soltānīyeh 24 Md 36.26N 48.48 E
Soltau 10 Fd 52.59N 9.50 E
Soltvadkert 10 Pj 46.35N 19.23 E
Solvang 46 Ei 34.36N 120.08W
Sölvesborg 7 Dh 56.03N 14.33 E
Solvyčegodsk 7 Lf 61.21N 46.52 E
Solway Firth 9 Jg 54.50N 3.35W
Solwezi 31 Jj 12.11S 26.24 E
Sōma 28 Pf 37.48N 140.57 E
Soma 24 Bc 39.10N 27.36 E
Somain 12 Fd 50.22N 3.17 E
Somalia (EN)= Soomaaliya [1] 31 Lh 10.00N 49.00 E
Somali Basin (EN) 3 Fi 0.00 52.00 E
Sombo 36 Dd 8.42S 20.57 E
Sombor 15 Cd 45.46N 19.07 E
Sombrerete 47 Dd 23.38N 103.39W
Sombrero 47 Le 18.36N 63.26W
Sombrero Channel 25 Ig 7.41N 93.35 E
Sombrio 55 Hi 29.07S 49.40W
Sombrio, Lagoa do- 55 Hi 29.12S 49.42W
Somcuţa Mare 15 Gb 47.31N 23.28 E
Someren 12 Hc 51.23N 5.43 E
Somero 8 Jd 60.37N 23.32 E
Somerset 38 Jb 73.30N 93.30W
Somerset [3] 9 Jk 51.10N 3.10W
Somerset 9 Kj 51.00N 3.00W
Somerset [Austl.] 59 Ib 10.35S 142.15 E
Somerset [Ky.-U.S.] 43 Kd 37.05N 84.36W
Somerset [Pa.-U.S.] 44 He 40.02N 79.05W
Somerset East 37 Df 32.42S 25.35 E
Somerton 46 Hj 32.36N 114.43W
Somerville Lake 45 Hk 30.18N 96.40W
Someş 15 Fa 48.07N 22.20 E
Someşu Mare 15 Gb 47.39N 23.55 E
Someşu Mic 15 Gb 47.39N 23.55 E
Somme [3] 11 Id 49.55N 2.30 E
Somme 11 Hd 50.11N 1.39 E
Somme, Baie de- 12 Dd 50.14N 1.33 E
Somme, Bassurelle de la- 12 Dd 50.15N 1.10 E
Somme, Canal de la- 11 He 50.11N 1.39 E
Somme-Leuze 12 Hd 50.20N 5.22 E
Somme-Leuze-Hogne 12 Hd 50.15N 5.17 E
Sommen 7 Dh 58.00N 15.15 E
Sommen 8 Ff 58.08N 14.58 E
Sommepy-Tahure 12 Ge 49.15N 4.33 E
Sömmerda 10 He 51.09N 11.06 E
Somogy [2] 10 Nj 46.25N 17.35 E
Somontano 13 Lc 42.02N 0.20W
Somosierra, Puerto de- 13 Ic 41.09N 3.35W
Somosomo Strait 63d Bb 16.47S 179.58 E
Somotillo 49 Dg 13.02N 86.53W
Somoto 47 Gf 13.28N 86.35W
Somovo 16 Kd 51.45N 39.25 E
Sompolno 10 Od 52.24N 18.31 E
Somport, Puerto de- 13 Lb 42.48N 0.31W
Son 21 Kg 25.50N 84.55 E
Sona 10 Qd 52.33N 20.35 E
Soná 49 Gi 8.01N 81.19W
Sonaguera 49 Df 15.38N 86.20W
Sonári, Ákra- 15 Lm 36.27N 28.13 E
Sŏnch'on 28 He 39.48N 124.55 E
Søndeled 7 Bg 58.46N 9.05 E
Sønderborg 7 Bi 54.55N 9.47 E
Sønder-Jylland [2] 8 Ci 55.00N 9.00 E
Sønder-Omme 8 Ci 55.50N 8.54 E
Sondershausen 10 Ge 51.22N 10.52 E
Søndre Strømfjord 67 Nc 66.59N 50.40W
Søndre Strømfjord 41 Ge 66.10N 53.10W
Søndre Upernavik 41 Gd 72.10N 55.38W
Sondrio 14 Dd 46.10N 9.52 E
Sonepat 25 Fc 28.59N 77.01 E
Song 34 Hd 9.50N 12.37 E
Songa 8 Be 59.47N 7.43 E
Songavatn 8 Be 59.50N 7.35 E
Song Cau 25 Lf 13.27N 109.13 E
Songe 8 Cf 58.41N 9.01 E
Songea 31 Kj 10.41S 35.39 E
Songeons 12 De 49.33N 1.52 E
Songhua Hu 28 Ic 43.30N 126.51 E
Songhua Jiang=Sungari (EN) 21 Pe 47.42N 132.30 E
Songjiang 27 Le 31.01N 121.14 E
Songjiang → Antu 28 Jc 42.33N 128.20 E
Songjianghe 28 Ic 42.10N 127.30 E
Sŏngjin→Kimch'aek 27 Mc 40.41N 129.12 E
Songjŏng 28 Ig 35.08N 126.48 E
Songkhla 21 Mi 7.13N 100.34 E
Songling 27 Lb 48.02N 121.08 E
Songnim 28 He 38.44N 125.38 E
Songo [Ang.] 36 Bd 7.21S 14.50 E
Songo [Moz.] 37 Ec 15.33S 32.48 E
Songololo 36 Bd 5.42S 14.02 E
Songpan (Sungqu) 27 He 32.37N 103.34 E
Songsa-dong 28 Hd 39.49N 124.49 E
Song Shan 27 Je 34.31N 113.00 E
Songshuzhen 28 Ic 42.01N 127.09 E
Songueur 13 Ni 35.11N 1.30 E
Songxian 28 Bg 34.12N 112.09 E
Songzi (Xinjiangkou) 28 Ai 30.10N 116.46 E
Sonid Youqi (Saihan Tal) 27 Jc 42.45N 112.36 E
Sonid Zuoqi (Mandalt) 27 Kc 43.50N 116.45 E
Sonkari 8 Lb 62.50N 26.35 E
Sonkël, Ozero- 18 Jd 41.50N 75.10 E
Sonkovo 7 Ih 57.47N 37.09 E
Son La 22 Mg 21.19N 103.54 E
Sonmiāni Bay 25 Dc 25.15N 66.30 E
Sonneberg 10 Hf 50.21N 11.10 E
Sono, Rio do- [Braz.] 55 Jc 17.02S 45.32W
Sono, Rio do- [Braz.] 54 Ie 9.00S 48.11W
Sonobe 29 Dd 35.07N 135.28 E
Sonoita 47 Bb 31.51N 112.50W
Sonoma Peak 46 Gf 40.52N 117.36W
Sonora [2] 47 Bc 29.20N 110.40W
Sonora 47 Bc 28.48N 111.49W
Sonora [Ca.-U.S.] 46 Eh 37.59N 120.23W
Sonora [Tx.-U.S.] 45 Fk 30.34N 100.39W
Sonqor 24 Le 34.47N 47.36 E
Sonsbeck 12 Ic 51.37N 6.22 E
Sonsonate 47 Gf 13.43N 89.44W
Sonsorol Islands 57 Ed 5.20N 132.13 E
Sonthofen 10 Gi 47.31N 10.17 E
Sontra 10 Fe 51.04N 9.56 E
Soomaaliya=Somalia (EN) [1] 31 Lh 10.00N 49.00 E
Soomenlaht=Finland, Gulf of- (EN) 5 Ic 60.00N 27.00 E
Soonwald 12 Je 49.56N 7.35 E
Sørværøy 7 Cc 67.38N 12.40 E
Sopi, Tanjung- 26 If 2.39N 128.34 E
Sopo 35 Dd 8.51N 26.11 E
Sopockin 10 Tc 53.50N 23.42 E
Sopot [Bul.] 15 Hg 42.39N 24.45 E
Sopot [Pol.] 10 Ob 54.28N 18.34 E
Sopron 10 Mi 47.41N 16.36 E
Sopur 25 Eb 34.18N 74.28 E
Sor 13 De 39.00N 8.17W
Sora 14 Hi 41.43N 13.37 E
Sorachi-Gawa 29a Bb 43.32N 141.52 E
Soråker 8 Gb 62.31N 17.30 E
Sorak-san 27 Md 38.07N 128.28 E
Sorano 14 Fh 42.41N 11.43 E
Soratteld 12 Kc 51.40N 8.55 E
Sorbas 13 Jg 37.07N 2.07W
Sorbe 13 Id 40.51N 3.08W
Sörberget 8 Gb 62.31N 17.22 E
Sore 11 Fj 44.19N 0.35W
Sorel 42 Kg 46.03N 73.07W
Sorell, Cape- 59 Jh 42.10S 145.10 E
Soresina 14 De 45.17N 9.51 E
Sorezaru Point 63a Cb 7.37S 156.38 E
Sørfjorden 8 Bd 60.25N 6.40 E
Sørfold 7 Dc 67.28N 15.28 E
Sorgues 11 Kj 44.00N 4.52 E
Sorgun 24 Fc 39.50N 35.19 E
Soria [3] 13 Jc 41.40N 2.40W
Soria 13 Jc 41.46N 2.28W
Soriano [2] 55 Dk 33.30S 57.45W
Sørkapp 67 Kd 76.28N 16.36 E
Sorkh, Godār-e- 24 Pf 33.05N 55.05 E
Sorkh, Kūh-e- 24 Pf 33.05N 55.05 E
Sorkheh 24 Oe 35.28N 53.13 E
Sorø 8 Di 55.26N 11.34 E
Sorocaba 53 Lh 23.29S 47.27W
Soroči Gory 7 Li 55.24N 49.55 E
Soročinsk 19 Fe 52.26N 53.10 E
Soroka 16 Fe 48.07N 28.16 E
Sorol Atoll 57 Fd 8.08N 140.23 E
Sorong 58 Ee 0.53S 131.15 E
Soroti 31 Kh 1.43N 33.37 E
Sørøya 5 Ia 70.36N 22.46 E
Sørøyane 8 Ab 62.20N 5.45 E
Sorraia 13 Df 38.56N 8.53W
Sørreisa 7 Eb 69.09N 18.10 E
Sorrentina, Penisola- 14 Ij 40.35N 14.30 E
Sorrento 14 Ij 40.37N 14.22 E
Sør Rondane 66 Df 72.00S 25.00 E
Sorsatunturi 7 Gc 67.24N 29.38 E
Sorsavesi 8 Lb 62.30N 27.35 E
Sorsele 7 Dd 65.32N 17.30 E
Sorsk 20 Ef 54.00N 90.20 E
Sorso 14 Cj 40.48N 8.34 E
Sorsogon 26 Hd 12.58N 124.00 E
Sort 13 Nb 42.24N 1.08 E
Šortandi 19 He 51.42N 71.05 E
Sortavala 19 Dc 61.44N 30.41 E
Sortland 7 Db 68.42N 15.24 E
Sør-Trøndelag [2] 7 Ce 63.00N 10.40 E
Sorum 17 Ne 63.50N 68.05 E
Sørumsand 8 De 59.58N 11.15 E
Šoša 7 Ih 56.33N 36.09 E
Sŏsan 28 If 36.47N 126.27 E
Sösdala 8 Eh 56.02N 13.40 E
Sos del Rey Católico 13 Kb 42.30N 1.13W
Sosna 16 Kc 52.42N 38.55 E
Sosnogorsk 6 Lc 63.37N 53.51 E
Sosnovka 16 Lc 53.14N 41.22 E
Sosnovka 7 Mh 56.18N 51.17 E
Sosnovka 7 Jc 66.31N 40.33 E
Sosnovka 16 Dd 50.15N 24.13 E
Sosnovo 8 Nd 60.31N 30.29 E
Sosnovo-Ozerskoje 20 Gf 52.31N 111.35 E
Sosnovy Bor 8 Me 59.48N 29.10 E
Sosnowiec 10 Pf 50.18N 19.08 E
Sospel 11 Nk 43.53N 7.27 E
Šostka 19 De 51.52N 33.31 E
Sosumav 37 Hb 13.03S 48.54 E
Sosva 19 Gd 59.32N 62.20 E
Sosva 19 Gc 63.40N 62.02 E
Sosva 19 Gd 59.10N 61.50 E
Sotavento [3] 32 Cf 14.40N 23.25W
Sotavento, Islas de- = Windward Islands (EN) 52 Jd 11.10N 67.00W
Sotik 36 Gc 0.41S 35.07 E
Sotkamo 7 Gd 64.08N 28.25 E
Soto la Marina 48 Jf 23.48N 98.13W
Soto la Marina, Rio- 48 Kf 23.45N 97.45W
Sotonera, Embalse de la- 13 Lb 42.05N 0.48W
Sotouboua 34 Fd 8.34N 0.59 E
Sotra 8 Ad 60.20N 5.05 E
Sotsudaka-Zaki 29b Ba 28.15N 129.10 E
Sottern 8 Fe 59.05N 15.30 E
Sotteville-lès-Rouen 11 He 49.25N 1.06 E
Sottrum 12 La 53.07N 9.14 E
Sottunga 8 Id 60.10N 20.40 E
Sotuf, Adrar- 32 De 21.42N 15.36W
Sotuta 48 Og 20.36N 89.01W
Souanké 36 Bb 2.05N 14.03 E
Soubré 34 Dd 5.47N 6.36W
Soubré [3] 34 Dd 5.47N 6.38W
Soúdha 15 Hn 35.29N 24.04 E
Souf 30 He 33.25N 6.50 E
Soufflenheim 12 Jf 48.50N 7.58 E
Souflion 15 Jh 41.12N 26.18 E
Soufrière 50 Ff 13.52N 61.04W
Soufrière [Guad.] 47 Le 16.03N 61.40W
Soufrière [St.Vin.] 47 Lf 13.21N 61.11W
Soufrière Bay 51g Bb 15.13N 61.22W
Soufrière Hills 51c Bc 16.43N 62.10W
Souillac 11 Hj 44.54N 1.29 E
Souilly 11 Le 49.01N 5.17 E
Souk Ahras 32 Ib 36.17N 7.57 E
Souk el Arba du Rharb 32 Fc 34.41N 5.59W
Sŏul=Seoul (EN) 22 Of 37.34N 127.00 E
Soulac-sur-Mer 11 Ei 45.30N 1.06W
Sŏul Si [2] 28 If 37.35N 127.00 E
Soultz-sous-Forêts 12 Jf 48.56N 7.53 E
Soumagne 12 Hd 50.37N 5.45 E
Soummam 13 Rh 36.44N 5.04 E
Sounding Creek 46 Ja 52.06N 110.28W
Soúnion 15 Hl 37.39N 24.02 E
Soúnion, Ákra- 15 Hl 37.39N 24.01 E
Sources, Mont aux- 30 Jk 28.46S 28.52 E
Soure [Braz.] 54 Id 0.44S 48.31W
Soure [Port.] 13 Dd 40.03N 8.38W
Sour el Ghozlane 32 Hb 36.09N 3.41 E
Souris 42 Hg 49.38N 100.15W
Souris 38 Je 49.39N 99.34W
Sous 32 Fc 30.22N 9.37W
Sous 32 Fc 30.25N 9.30W
Sousa 53 Mf 6.45S 38.14W
Sousel 13 Ef 38.57N 7.40W
Sous le Vent, Iles-= Leeward Islands (EN) 57 Lf 16.38S 151.30W
Sousse (EN)=Sūsah [3] 32 Jb 35.45N 10.30 E
Sousse (EN)=Sūsah [Tun.] 31 Ie 35.49N 10.38 E
Sout 37 Cf 33.03S 23.29 E
South Africa / Suid Africa [1] 31 Jl 30.00S 26.00 E
South Alligator River 59 Gb 12.15S 132.24 E
Southam 12 Ab 52.15N 1.23W
South America (EN) 52 Jg 15.00S 60.00W
Southampton 38 Kc 64.20N 84.40W
Southampton [Eng.-U.K.] 6 Fe 50.55N 1.25W
Southampton [N.Y.-U.S.] 44 Ke 40.54N 72.23W
Southampton, Cape- 42 Jd 62.08N 83.44W
Southampton Airport 12 Ad 50.55N 1.23W
Southampton Water 12 Ad 50.52N 1.20W
South Andaman 25 If 11.45N 92.45 E
Southard, Cape- 66 Ie 66.33S 122.04 E
South Auckland-Bay of Plenty [2] 62 Fb 38.00S 176.00 E
South Aulatsivik 42 Le 56.47N 61.30W
South Australia [2] 59 Ge 30.00S 135.00 E
South Australian Basin (EN) 3 Im 40.00S 128.00 E
Southaven 45 Li 35.00N 90.00W
South Baldy 45 Cj 33.59N 107.11W
South Bay 42 Jd 64.00N 83.25W
South Bend 43 Jc 41.41N 86.15W
South Benfleet 12 Cc 51.32N 0.33 E
Southborough 12 Cc 51.09N 0.15 E
South Boston 44 Hg 36.42N 78.58W
Southbridge 62 Ee 43.48S 172.15 E
South Buganda [3] 36 Fc 0.30S 32.00 E
South Caicos 49 Lc 21.31N 71.30W
South Carolina [2] 43 Ke 34.00N 81.00W
South China Basin (EN) 3 Hh 15.00N 115.00 E
South China Sea (EN)=Bien Dong 21 Ni 10.00N 113.00 E
South China Sea (EN)=Cina Selatan, Laut- 21 Ni 10.00N 113.00 E
South China Sea (EN)=Nan Hai 21 Ni 10.00N 113.00 E
South Dakota [2] 43 Gc 44.15N 100.00W
South Downs 9 Mk 50.55N 0.25W
South-East [3] 37 De 25.00S 25.45 E
South East Cape 57 Fi 43.39S 146.50 E
Southeast Indian Ridge (EN) 3 Ho 50.00S 110.00 E
Southeast Pacific Basin (EN) 3 Mp 60.00S 115.00W
South East Point [Austl.] 57 Fh 39.00S 146.20 E
South East Point [Kir.] 64g Bb 1.40N 157.10W
Southend 42 He 56.20N 103.14W
Southend-on-Sea 9 Nj 51.33N 0.43 E
Southern [Mwi.] [3] 36 Gf 15.30S 35.00 E
Southern [S.L.] [3] 34 Cd 7.40N 12.15W
Southern [Ug.] [3] 36 Fc 0.30S 30.30 E
Southern [Zam.] [3] 36 Ef 16.00S 27.00 E
Southern Alps 57 Ii 43.30S 170.35 E
Southern Cook Island 57 Lg 20.00S 159.00W
Southern Cross 58 Ch 31.13S 119.19 E
Southern Desert (EN)= Janūbīyah, Aş Şaḩrā' al- 30 Jf 24.00N 30.00 E
Southern Ghats 25 Ff 10.00N 76.50 E
Southern Gilbert Islands 60 Jh 1.30S 175.30 E
Southern Indian Lake 38 Jd 57.10N 98.40W
Southern Pines 44 Hh 35.11N 79.24W
Southern Region (EN)= Iqlīm al Janūbīyah [2] 35 Dd 6.00N 30.00 E
Southern Sierra Madre (EN) =Madre del Sur, Sierra- 38 Jj 17.00N 100.00W
Southern Uplands 5 Fd 55.30N 3.30W
Southern Urals (EN)=Južny Ural 5 Le 54.00N 58.30 E
Southern Yemen (EN)→ Yemen, People's Democratic Republic of- (EN) [1] 22 Gh 14.00N 46.00 E
South Esk 9 Ke 56.43N 2.28W
South Fiji Basin (EN) 3 Jl 26.00S 175.00 E
South Foreland 9 Oj 51.09N 1.23 E
South Fork 46 Ge 42.26N 116.53W
South Fork Flathead River 46 Ib 48.07N 113.45W
South Fork Grand River 45 Ed 45.43N 102.17W
South Fork Kern River 46 Fi 35.40N 118.27W
South Fork Moreau River 45 Ed 45.09N 102.50W
South Fork Powder River 46 Le 43.40N 106.30W
South Fork Republican River 45 Ff 40.03N 101.31W
South Georgia/Georgia del Sur, Islas- 66 Ad 54.15S 36.45W
South Glamorgan [3] 9 Jj 51.30N 3.15W
South Haven 44 Dd 42.24N 86.16W
South Honshu Ridge (EN) 3 Ig 24.00N 142.00 E
South Horr 36 Gb 2.06N 36.55 E
South Indian Basin (EN) 3 Ho 60.00S 120.00 E
South Island [F.S.M.] 64d Bc 6.59N 151.59 E
South Island [Kenya] 36 Gb 2.38N 36.36 E
South Island [N.Z.] 57 Ii 44.00S 171.00 E
South Island [Sey.] 37b Ab 9.26S 46.23 E
South Island [Sey.] 37b Bc 10.10S 51.10 E

Index Symbols

[1] Independent Nation
[2] State, Region
[3] District, County
[4] Municipality
[5] Colony, Dependency
Continent
Physical Region
Historical or Cultural Region
Mount, Mountain
Volcano
Hill
Mountains, Mountain Range
Hills, Escarpment
Plateau, Upland
Pass, Gap
Plain, Lowland
Delta
Salt Flat
Valley, Canyon
Crater, Cave
Karst Features
Depression
Polder
Desert, Dunes
Forest, Woods
Heath, Steppe
Oasis
Cape, Point
Coast, Beach
Cliff
Peninsula
Isthmus
Sandbank
Island
Atoll
Rock, Reef
Islands, Archipelago
Rocks, Reefs
Coral Reef
Well, Spring
Geyser
River, Stream
Waterfall Rapids
River Mouth, Estuary
Lake
Salt Lake
Intermittent Lake
Reservoir
Swamp, Pond
Canal
Glacier
Ice Shelf, Pack Ice
Ocean
Sea
Gulf, Bay
Strait, Fjord
Lagoon
Bank
Seamount
Tablemount
Ridge
Shelf
Basin
Escarpment, Sea Scarp
Fracture
Trench, Abyss
National Park, Reserve
Point of Interest
Recreation Site
Cave, Cavern
Historic Site
Ruins
Wall, Walls
Church, Abbey
Temple
Scientific Station
Airport
Port
Lighthouse
Mine
Tunnel
Dam, Bridge

South Korea (EN)=Taehan-Min' guk [1] 22 Of 38.00N 127.30 E
South Lake Tahoe 46 Eg 38.57N 120.01W
Southland [2] 62 Bf 45.45S 168.00 E
South Loup River 45 Gf 41.04N 98.40W
South Lueti 36 Df 16.14S 23.12 E
South Magnetic Pole (1980) 66 Ie 65.08S 139.03 E
South Malosmadulu Atoll 25a Ba 5.10N 72.58 E
South Mountain 46 Ge 42.44N 116.54W
South Nahanni 42 Fd 61.03N 123.22W
South Negril Point 47 Ie 18.16N 78.22W
South Orkney Islands 66 Re 60.35S 45.30W
South Pass 38 Ie 42.22N 108.55W
South Pass [F.S.M.] 64d Bb 7.14N 151.48 E
South Pass [U.S.] 45 Ll 28.55N 89.20W
South Platte 38 Ie 41.07N 100.42W
South Point 51q Ab 13.02N 59.31W
South Pole 66 Bg 90.00S 0.00
South Porcupine 44 Ga 48.28N 81.13W
Southport [Eng.-U.K.] 9 Jh 53.39N 3.01W
Southport [N.C.-U.S.] 44 Hi 33.55N 78.01W
South Reef 63a Ee 13.00S 160.32 E
South Ronaldsay 9 Kc 58.46N 2.50W
South Rukuru 36 Fe 10.44S 34.14 E
South Saint Paul 45 Jd 44.52N 93.02W
South Sandwich Islands 66 Ad 56.00S 26.30W
South Sandwich Trench (EN) 3 Do 56.30S 25.00W
South Saskatchewan River 38 Id 53.15N 105.05W
South Shetland Islands 66 Re 62.00S 58.00W
South Shields 9 Lg 55.00N 1.25W
South Sioux City 45 He 42.28N 96.24W
South Sister 46 Ed 44.12N 121.45W
South Taranaki Bight 62 Fc 39.40S 174.15 E
South Trap 62 Bg 47.30S 167.55 E
South Tyne 9 Kg 54.59N 2.08W
South Uist 9 Fd 57.15N 7.24W
South Umpqua River 46 De 43.20N 123.25W
Southwell 12 Ba 53.04N 0.57W
South Wellesley Islands 59 Hc 17.05S 139.25 E
South West Africa → Namibia [1] 31 Ik 22.00S 17.00 E
Southwest Cape 57 Hi 47.17S 167.27 E
South West Cape 59 Jh 43.34S 146.02 E
Southwest Cape 51a Dc 17.42N 64.53W
Southwest Indian Ridge (EN) 3 Fm 32.00S 55.00 E
Southwest Miramichi River 44 Ob 46.50N 65.45W
Southwest Pacific Basin (EN) 3 Km 40.00S 150.00W
Southwest Pass 45 Ll 29.00N 89.20W
Southwest Point 49 Jb 22.10N 74.10W
South West Point 64g Ab 1.52N 157.33W
South West Point 51p Cb 12.27N 61.30W
Southwold 9 Oi 52.20N 1.40 E
South Yorkshire [3] 9 Lh 53.30N 1.25W
Soutpansberg 37 Dd 22.58S 29.50 E
Soverato 14 Kl 38.41N 16.33 E
Sovetabad 18 Gd 40.14N 69.42 E
Sovetsk 19 Ed 57.36N 48.58 E
Sovetsk 19 Cd 55.05N 21.52 E
Sovetskaja Gavan 22 Qe 48.58N 140.18 E
Sovetski 7 Lh 56.47N 48.30 E
Sovetski 8 Md 60.29N 28.40 E
Sovetski 19 Gc 61.20N 63.29 E
Şowghān 24 Qh 28.20N 56.54 E
Sowie, Góry- 10 Mf 50.38N 16.30 E
Sōya 29a Ba 45.28N 141.53 E
Sōya-Kaikyō=La Perouse Strait (EN) 21 Qe 45.30N 142.00 E
Sōya-Misaki 27 Pb 45.31N 141.56 E
Soyatita 48 Fe 25.45N 107.22W
Soyo 36 Bd 6.05S 12.20 E
Sož 5 Je 51.57N 30.48 E
Sozopol 15 Kg 42.25N 27.42 E
Spa 11 Ld 50.29N 5.52 E
Spain (EN)=España [1] 6 Fg 40.00N 4.00W
Špakovskoje 16 Lg 45.06N 42.00 E
Spalding 9 Mi 52.47N 0.10W
Spanish Fork 46 Jf 40.07N 111.39W
Spanish Peak 46 Fd 44.24N 119.46W
Spanish Point 51d Ba 17.33N 61.44W
Spanish Sahara (EN) → Western Sahara (EN) [5] 31 Ff 24.30N 13.00W
Spanish Town [B.V.I.] 51a Db 18.27N 64.26W
Spanish Town [Jam.] 47 Ie 17.59N 76.57W
Sparbu 7 Ce 63.55N 11.28 E
Spargi, Isola- 14 Di 41.15N 9.20 E
Sparks 43 Dd 39.32N 119.45W
Sparreholm 8 Ge 59.04N 16.49 E
Sparta [Il.-U.S.] 45 Lg 38.07N 89.42W
Sparta [N.C.-U.S.] 44 Gg 36.30N 81.07W
Sparta [Tn.-U.S.] 44 Eh 35.56N 85.29W
Sparta [Wi.-U.S.] 45 Ke 43.57N 90.47W
Sparta (EN) = Spárti 15 Fl 37.05N 22.26 E
Spartanburg 43 Ke 34.57N 81.55W
Spartel, Cap- 30 Ge 35.48N 5.56W
Spárti = Sparta (EN) 15 Fl 37.05N 22.26 E
Spartivento, Capo- [It.] 14 Cl 38.53N 8.50 E
Spartivento, Capo- [It.] 5 Hh 37.55N 16.04 E
Spas-Demensk 16 Ib 54.24N 34.01 E
Spas-Klepiki 7 Ji 55.10N 40.13 E
Spassk-Rjazanski 7 Ji 54.27N 40.22 E
Spátha, Ákra- = Spatha, Cape- (EN) 15 Gn 35.42N 23.44 E
Spatha, Cape- (EN) = Spátha, Ákra- 15 Gn 35.42N 23.44 E
Spearfish 43 Gc 44.30N 103.52W
Spearman 45 Fh 36.12N 101.12W
Speedway 44 Df 39.47N 86.15W
Speicher 12 Ie 49.56N 6.38 E
Speightstown 50 Gf 13.15N 59.39W
Speke Gulf 36 Fc 2.20S 33.15 E
Spello 14 Gh 42.59N 12.40 E
Spenard 40 Jd 61.11N 149.55W
Spence Bay 39 Jc 69.32N 93.31W
Spencer [Ia.-U.S.] 43 Hc 43.09N 95.09W
Spencer [In.-U.S.] 44 Df 39.17N 86.46W
Spencer [Nb.-U.S.] 45 Ge 42.53N 98.42W
Spencer [W.V.-U.S.] 44 Gf 38.48N 81.22W
Spencer, Cape- 59 Hg 35.18S 136.53 E
Spencer Gulf 57 Eh 34.00S 137.00 E
Spenge 12 Kb 52.08N 8.29 E
Spenser Mountains 62 Ee 42.10S 172.35 E
Sperillen 8 Dd 60.30N 10.05 E
Sperkhiós 15 Fk 38.52N 22.34 E
Sperlonga 14 Hi 41.15N 13.26 E
Sperone, Capo- 14 Cl 38.55N 8.25 E
Sperrin Mountains/Sliabh Speirín 9 Fg 54.50N 7.05W
Spessart 10 Fg 49.55N 9.30 E
Spétsai 15 Gl 37.16N 23.09 E
Spétsai 15 Gl 37.16N 23.08 E
Spey 9 Jd 57.40N 3.06W
Spey Bay 9 Jd 57.40N 3.05W
Speyer 10 Eg 49.19N 8.26 E
Speyer-bach 12 Ke 49.19N 8.27 E
Speyside 50 Fg 11.18N 60.32W
Spezzano Albanese 14 Kk 39.40N 16.19 E
Spicer Islands 42 Jc 68.10N 79.00W
Spiekeroog 10 Dc 53.46N 7.42 E
Spiez 14 Bd 46.41N 7.42 E
Spijkenisse 12 Gc 51.51N 4.21 E
Spilimbergo 14 Gd 46.07N 12.54 E
Spilion 15 Hn 35.13N 24.32 E
Spilsby 12 Ca 53.11N 0.06 E
Spina 14 Gf 44.42N 12.08 E
Spinazzola 14 Kj 40.58N 16.05 E
Spincourt 12 He 49.20N 5.40 E
Spirit River 42 Fe 55.47N 118.50W
Spirovo 7 Ih 57.27N 35.01 E
Spiš 10 Qg 49.05N 20.30 E
Spišská Nová Ves 10 Qh 48.57N 20.34 E
Spitak 16 Ni 40.49N 44.14 E
Spitsbergen 67 Kd 78.00N 19.00 E
Spitsbergen 67 Kd 78.45N 16.00 E
Spittal an der Drau 14 Hd 46.48N 13.30 E
Spitzbergen Bank (EN) 41 Oc 76.00N 23.00 E
Spjelkavik 7 Be 62.28N 6.23 E
Split 6 Hg 43.31N 16.26 E
Split Lake 42 He 56.10N 96.10W
Spluga, Passo dello- 14 Dd 46.29N 9.20 E
Splügenpaß 14 Dd 46.29N 9.20 E
Spógi/Špogi 8 Lh 56.02N 26.52 E
Špogi/Spógi 8 Lh 56.02N 26.52 E
Spokane 39 He 47.40N 117.23W
Spokane, Mount- 46 Gc 47.55N 117.07W
Spokane River 46 Fc 47.44N 118.20W
Špola 19 Df 49.01N 31.24 E
Spoleto 14 Gh 42.44N 12.44 E
Spooner 45 Kd 45.50N 91.53W
Spoon River 45 Kf 40.18N 90.04W
Sporovo 10 Vd 52.25N 25.27 E
Spotsylvania 44 If 38.12N 77.35W
Sprague 46 Gc 47.18N 117.59W
Sprague River 46 Ee 42.34N 121.51W
Spratly (EN) → Nanwei Dao 26 Fe 8.42N 111.40 E
Spray 46 Fd 44.50N 119.48W
Spreewald 10 Je 51.55N 14.00 E
Spremberg/Grodk 10 Ke 51.33N 14.22 E
Sprengisandur 7a Bb 64.40N 18.07W
Springbok 31 Ik 29.43S 17.15 E
Spring Creek 45 Fd 45.45N 100.18W
Springdale 45 Ih 36.11N 94.08W
Springe 10 Fd 52.13N 9.33 E
Springer 45 Dh 36.22N 104.36W
Springer, Mount- 44 Ja 49.48N 74.51W
Springerville 46 Ki 34.08N 109.17W
Springfield [Co.-U.S.] 45 Eh 37.24N 102.37W
Springfield [Il.-U.S.] 39 Kf 39.47N 89.40W
Springfield [Ma.-U.S.] 43 Mc 42.07N 72.36W
Springfield [Mn.-U.S.] 45 Id 44.14N 94.59W
Springfield [Mo.-U.S.] 39 Jf 37.14N 93.17W
Springfield [N.Z.] 62 De 43.20S 171.56 E
Springfield [Oh.-U.S.] 43 Kd 39.55N 83.48W
Springfield [Or.-U.S.] 43 Cc 44.03N 123.01W
Springfield [S.D.-U.S.] 45 He 42.49N 97.54W
Springfield [Tn.-U.S.] 44 Dg 36.31N 86.52W
Springfontein 37 Df 30.19S 25.36 E
Spring Garden 54 Gb 6.59N 58.31W
Spring Hall 51q Ab 13.19N 59.36W
Springhill [La.-U.S.] 45 Jj 33.00N 93.28W
Springhill [N.S.-Can.] 42 Lg 45.39N 64.03W
Spring Mountains 46 Hh 36.10N 115.40W
Springs 37 De 26.13S 28.25 E
Springsure 59 Jd 24.07S 148.05 E
Spring Valley 46 Hg 39.10N 114.30W
Spring Valley 45 Je 43.41N 92.23W
Springville 46 Jf 40.10N 111.37W
Spruce Knob 33 Lf 38.42N 79.32W
Spruce Mountain [Az.-U.S.] 46 Ii 34.28N 112.24W
Spruce Mountain [Nv.-U.S.] 46 Hf 40.33N 114.49W
Spulico, Capo- 14 Kk 39.58N 16.38 E
Spurn Head 9 Nh 53.34N 0.07 E
Squamish 42 Fg 49.42N 123.09W
Squillace 14 Kl 38.47N 16.31 E
Squillace, Golfo di- 14 Kl 38.45N 16.50 E
Squinzano 14 Mj 40.26N 18.02 E
Srbica 15 Dg 42.45N 20.47 E
Srbija=Serbia (EN) 15 Df 44.00N 21.00 E
Srbija = Serbia (EN) [2] 15 Df 44.00N 21.00 E
Srbija = Serbia (EN) 5 Ig 43.00N 21.00 E
Srbobran 15 Cd 45.33N 19.48 E
Srê Âmběl 25 Kf 11.07N 103.46 E
Sredinny Hrebet 21 Rd 56.00N 158.00 E
Sredna Gora 15 Hg 42.30N 25.00 E
Srednekolymsk 20 Kc 67.27N 153.41 E
Srednerusskaja Vozvyšennost=Central Russian Uplands (EN) 5 Je 52.00N 38.00 E
Srednesatyginski Tuman, Ozero- 17 Lg 59.45N 65.25 E
Srednesibirskoje Ploskogorje =Central Siberian Uplands (EN) 21 Mc 65.00N 105.00 E
Sredni Kujto, Ozero- 7 Hd 65.05N 31.30 E
Sredni Ural=Central Urals (EN) 5 Ld 58.00N 59.00 E
Sredni Urgal 20 If 51.13N 132.58 E
Sredni Verecki, Pereval- 16 Ce 48.49N 23.07 E
Srednjaja Ahtuba 16 Ne 48.43N 44.52 E
Srednjaja Olëkma 20 He 55.26N 120.40 E
Śrem 10 Nd 52.08N 17.01 E
Sremska Mitrovica 15 Ce 44.58N 19.37 E
Sremski Karlovci 15 Cd 45.12N 19.56 E
Sretensk 22 Nd 52.15N 117.43 E
Sri Gangānagar 25 Ec 29.55N 73.53 E
Sri Jayawardenepura 25 Gg 6.54N 80.02 E
Srijem 15 Cd 45.00N 19.40 E
Srīkākulam 25 Ge 18.18N 83.54 E
Srī Lanka (Ceylon) [1] 22 Ki 7.40N 80.50 E
Srīnagar 22 Jf 34.05N 74.49 E
Srivardhan 25 Ee 18.02N 73.01 E
Środa Śląska 10 Me 51.10N 16.36 E
Środa Wielkopolska 10 Nd 52.14N 17.17 E
Srpska Crnja 15 Dd 45.43N 20.42 E
Sruth na Maoile/North Channel 5 Fd 55.10N 5.40W
Ssu-ch'uan Sheng → Sichuan Sheng = Szechwan (EN) [2] 27 He 30.00N 103.00 E
Staaten River 59 Ic 16.24S 141.17 E
Stabroek 12 Gc 51.20N 4.22 E
Stack Skerry 9 Ib 59.02N 4.30W
Stade 10 Fc 53.36N 9.29 E
Staden 12 Fd 50.59N 3.01 E
Stadhavet 8 Ab 62.15N 5.05 E
Städjan 8 Ec 61.58N 12.52 E
Stadlandet 8 Ab 62.05N 5.20 E
Stadskanaal 11 Ma 53.00N 6.55 E
Stadskanaal-Musselkanaal 12 Jb 52.56N 7.02 E
Stadthagen 12 Lb 52.19N 9.12 E
Stadtkyll 12 Id 50.21N 6.32 E
Stadtlohn 12 Ic 51.59N 6.56 E
Stadtoldendorf 10 Fe 51.54N 9.39 E
Staffa 9 Ge 56.25N 6.10W
Staffanstorp 8 Ei 55.38N 13.13 E
Staffelsee 10 Hi 47.42N 11.10 E
Staffora 14 De 45.04N 9.01 E
Stafford 9 Li 52.50N 2.00W
Stafford 9 Ki 52.48N 2.07W
Staffordshire [3] 9 Li 52.55N 2.00W
Staicele/Stajcele 8 Kg 57.44N 24.39 E
Stainach 14 Ic 47.32N 4.06 E
Staines 12 Bc 51.26N 0.31W
Stakčin 10 Sg 49.00N 22.13 E
Stalać 15 Ef 43.40N 21.25 E
Stalham 12 Db 52.46N 1.31 E
Stalingrad → Volgograd 6 Kf 48.44N 44.25 E
Ställdalen 8 Fe 59.56N 14.56 E
Stalowa Wola 10 Sf 50.35N 22.02 E
Stamberger See 10 Ii 47.55N 2.20 E
Stamford [Ct.-U.S.] 44 Ke 41.03N 73.32W
Stamford [Eng.-U.K.] 9 Mi 52.39N 0.29W
Stamford [Tx.-U.S.] 45 Gj 32.57N 99.48W
Stamford, Lake- 45 Gj 33.05N 99.35W
Stampriet 37 Bd 24.20S 18.28 E
Stamsund 7 Cb 68.08N 13.51 E
Stanberry 45 If 40.13N 94.35W
Stancija Jakkabag 18 Fe 38.59N 66.42 E
Stancija-Karakul 19 Gh 39.30N 63.50 E
Standerton 37 De 26.58S 29.07 E
Standish 44 Fd 44.00N 83.57W
Stanford 46 Jc 47.09N 110.13W
Stånga 8 Hg 57.17N 18.28 E
Stångån 8 Ff 58.27N 15.37 E
Stange 8 Dd 60.43N 11.11 E
Stanger 37 Ee 29.27S 31.14 E
Stanke Dimitrov 15 Gg 42.16N 23.07 E
Stanley [Austl.] 59 Jh 40.46S 145.18 E
Stanley [Falk. Is.] 53 Kk 51.42S 57.51W
Stanley [N.D.-U.S.] 45 Eb 48.19N 102.23W
Stanley Falls (EN)= Ngaliema, Chutes- 30 Jh 0.30N 25.30 E
Stann Creek 49 Ce 16.50N 88.30W
Stanovoje Nagorje= Stanovoy Upland (EN) 21 Nd 56.00N 114.00 E
Stanovoj Hrebet=Stanovoy Range (EN) 21 Od 56.20N 126.00 E
Stanovoy Upland (EN)= Stanovoje Nagorje 21 Nd 56.00N 114.00 E
Stans 14 Cd 46.58N 8.22 E
Stansted Airport 12 Cc 51.54N 0.13 E
Stansted Mountfitchet 12 Cc 51.54N 0.12 E
Stanthorpe 59 Ke 28.39S 151.57 E
Stanton Banks 9 Fe 56.15N 7.50W
Staphorst 12 Ib 52.38N 6.14 E
Staples 45 Ic 46.21N 94.48W
Stapleton 45 Ff 41.29N 100.31W
Stąporków 10 Qe 51.09N 20.34 E
Starachowice 10 Re 51.03N 21.04 E
Staraja Majna 7 Li 54.36N 48.59 E
Staraja Russa 19 Dd 57.59N 31.23 E
Staraja-Vyževka 10 Ue 51.27N 24.34 E
Stará L'ubovňa 10 Qg 49.18N 20.42 E
Stara Moravica 15 Cd 45.52N 19.28 E
Stara Pazova 15 De 44.59N 20.10 E
Stara Planina = Balkan Mountains (EN) 5 Ig 43.15N 25.00 E
Stara Zagora [2] 15 Ig 42.25N 25.38 E
Stara Zagora 6 Ig 42.25N 25.38 E
Starbuck Island 57 Le 5.37S 155.53W
Staretina 14 Kf 44.02N 16.43 E
Stargard Szczeciński 10 Lc 53.20N 15.02 E
Stari Begejski kanal 15 Dd 45.29N 20.25 E
Starica 7 Ih 56.30N 34.56 E
Starigrad 14 Kg 43.11N 16.36 E
Stari Vlah 15 Df 43.23N 20.10 E
Starke 44 Fk 29.57N 82.07W
Starkville 45 Lj 33.28N 88.48W
Starnberg 10 Hh 48.00N 11.21 E
Starobelsk 19 Df 49.15N 38.58 E
Starodub 19 De 52.35N 32.46 E
Starogard Gdański 10 Oc 53.59N 18.33 E
Starokonstantinov 16 Ee 49.43N 27.13 E
Starominskaja 19 Df 46.31N 39.06 E
Staroščerbinovskaja 16 Kf 46.37N 38.42 E
Starosubhangulovo 17 Hj 53.06N 57.20 E
Starotimoškino 7 Lj 53.43N 47.32 E
Start Point 9 Jk 50.13N 3.38W
Staryje Dorogi 16 Fc 53.02N 28.17 E
Stary Krym 16 Ig 45.02N 35.05 E
Stary Oskol 19 De 51.18N 37.51 E
Stary Sambor 16 Ce 49.29N 23.01 E
Stary Terek 16 Og 44.01N 47.24 E
Staßfurt 10 He 51.52N 11.35 E
Staszów 10 Rf 50.34N 21.10 E
State College 44 Ie 40.48N 77.52W
Staten Island (EN)= Estados, Isla de los- 52 Jk 54.47S 64.15W
Statesboro 44 Gi 32.27N 81.47W
Statesville 44 Gh 35.47N 80.53W
Stathelle 8 Ce 59.03N 9.41 E
Stathmós Krioneríou 15 Ek 38.20N 21.35 E
Statland 7 Cd 64.30N 11.08 E
Staunton 43 Ld 38.10N 79.05W
Stavanger 6 Gd 58.58N 5.45 E
Stavelot 12 Hd 50.23N 5.56 E
Staveren 11 Lb 52.53N 5.22 E
Stavern 8 Df 59.00N 10.02 E
Stavnoje 10 Sh 48.59N 22.45 E
Stavropol 6 Kf 45.02N 41.59 E
Stavropolskaja Vozvyšennost 16 Mg 45.10N 43.00 E
Stavropolski Kraj [3] 19 Eg 45.00N 43.15 E
Stavrós [Grc.] 15 Fj 39.19N 22.14 E
Stavrós [Grc.] 15 Gi 40.40N 23.42 E
Stavroúpolis 15 Hh 41.12N 24.42 E
Stawell 59 Ig 37.04S 142.46 E
Stawiski 10 Sc 53.23N 22.09 E
Stawiszyn 10 Oe 51.55N 18.07 E
Stayton 46 Dd 44.48N 122.48W
Steamboat Springs 43 Fc 40.29N 106.50W
Stebnik 10 Tg 49.14N 23.34 E
Stedingen 12 Ka 53.10N 8.30 E
Steele 45 Gc 46.51N 99.55W
Steelpoort 37 Ed 24.48S 30.12 E
Steenbergen 12 Gc 51.35N 4.19 E
Steen River 42 Fe 59.38N 117.06W
Steensby Inlet 42 Jb 70.10N 78.25W
Steenstrups Gletscher 41 Gc 75.15N 57.30W
Steenvoorde 12 Ed 50.48N 2.35 E
Steenwijk 11 Mb 52.47N 6.08 E
Ştefăneşti 15 Kb 47.48N 27.12 E
Stefanie Lake- (EN)=Chew Bahir 30 Kh 4.38N 36.50 E
Stefansson 42 Gb 73.30N 105.30W
Ştefleşti, Vîrful- 15 Gd 45.32N 23.48 E
Stege 8 Ej 54.59N 12.18 E
Steiermark = Styria (EN) 14 Ic 47.15N 15.00 E
Steiermark = Styria (EN) [2] 14 Ic 47.15N 15.00 E
Steigerwald 10 Gg 49.40N 10.20 E
Steilrandberge 37 Ac 17.53S 13.20 E
Steinach 14 Fc 47.05N 11.28 E
Steinbach 42 Hg 49.32N 96.41W
Steinen, Rio- 54 Hf 12.05S 53.46W
Steinfeld (Oldenburg) 12 Kb 52.36N 8.13 E
Steinfort/Steinfurt 12 He 49.40N 5.55 E
Steinfurt 10 Dd 52.09N 7.20 E
Steinfurt/Steinfort 12 He 49.40N 5.55 E
Steinfurt-Borghorst 12 Jb 52.08N 7.25 E
Steinhagen 12 Kb 52.01N 8.24 E
Steinhausen 37 Bd 21.49S 18.20 E
Steinheim 12 Lc 51.51N 9.06 E
Steinhuder Meer 10 Fd 52.28N 9.19 E
Steinkjer 7 Cd 64.01N 11.30 E
Steinkopf 37 Be 29.18S 17.43 E
Steinshamn 8 Bb 62.47N 6.29 E
Steinsøy 7 Ac 61.00N 4.30 E
Steirisch-Niederösterreichische Kalkalpen 14 Jc 47.45N 15.30 E
Stekene 12 Gc 51.12N 4.02 E
Stekolny 20 Ke 60.00N 150.50 E
Stella 37 Ce 26.33S 24.53 E
Stellenbosch 37 Bf 33.58S 18.50 E
Stello 11a Ba 42.47N 9.25 E
Stelvio, Passo dello-/Stilfer Joch 14 Ed 46.32N 10.27 E
Stemwede 12 Kb 52.26N 8.26 E
Stenay 11 Le 49.29N 5.11 E
Stendal 10 Hd 52.36N 11.51 E
Stende 8 Jg 57.10N 22.28 E
Stende 8 Ig 57.40N 21.57 E
Stenhouse Bay 59 Hg 35.17S 136.56 E
Stenstorp 8 Ef 58.16N 13.43 E
Stenungsund 7 Cg 58.05N 11.49 E
Stepanakert 6 Kh 39.49N 46.44 E
Stepanavan 16 Ni 40.59N 44.20 E
Stephens, Cape- 62 Ed 40.42S 173.57 E
Stephens, Mount- 66 Rg 83.23S 51.27W
Stephens Passage 40 Me 57.50N 133.50W
Stephenville [Newf.-Can.] 42 Lg 48.33N 58.35W
Stephenville [Tx.-U.S.] 45 Gj 32.13N 98.12W
Steps Point 65c Cb 14.22S 170.45W
Sterea Ellás kai Évvoia [2] 15 Hk 38.20N 24.30 E
Sterkstroom 37 Df 31.32S 26.32 E
Sterlibaševo 17 Gj 53.28N 55.15 E
Sterling [Co.-U.S.] 43 Gc 40.37N 103.13W
Sterling [Il.-U.S.] 45 Lf 41.48N 89.42W
Sterling City 45 Fk 31.50N 100.59W
Sterlitamak 6 Le 53.37N 55.58 E
Šternberk 10 Ng 49.44N 17.19 E
Sterzing / Vipiteno 14 Fd 46.54N 11.26 E
Stettin (EN)=Szczecin 6 He 53.24N 14.32 E
Stettiner Haff 10 Kc 53.46N 14.14 E
Stettler 42 Gf 52.19N 112.43W
Steubenville 43 Kc 40.22N 80.39W
Stevenage 9 Mj 51.54N 0.11W
Stevenson Entrance 40 Ie 57.45N 152.20W
Stevens Point 43 Jc 44.31N 89.34W
Stewart 42 Dd 63.18N 139.24W
Stewart 42 Ee 55.56N 129.59W
Stewart Crossing 42 Dd 63.19N 136.33W
Stewart Island 57 Hi 47.00S 167.50 E
Stewart Islands 57 He 8.20S 162.40 E
Steyerberg 12 Lb 52.34N 9.02 E
Steyning 12 Bd 50.53N 0.20W
Steynsburg 37 Df 31.15S 25.49 E
Steyr 14 Ib 48.02N 14.25 E
Steyr 14 Ib 48.03N 14.25 E
Štiavnické vrchy 10 Oh 48.15N 18.50 E
Stidia 13 Li 35.50N 0.05W
Stiene 8 Kg 57.19N 24.28 E
Stiens, Leeuwarderadeel- 12 Ha 53.16N 5.46 E
Stigliano 14 Kj 40.24N 16.14 E
St. Ignace 43 Kb 45.52N 84.43W
Stigtomta 8 Gf 58.48N 16.47 E
Stikine 38 Fd 56.40N 132.30W
Stikine Ranges 42 Ee 57.35N 131.00W
Stilfer Joch/Stelvio, Passo dello- 14 Ed 46.32N 10.27 E
Stilfontein 37 De 26.50S 26.50 E
Stilis 15 Fk 38.55N 22.37 E
Stillwater [Mn.-U.S.] 45 Jd 45.04N 92.49W
Stillwater [Ok.-U.S.] 43 Hd 36.07N 97.04W
Stillwater Range 46 Fg 39.50N 118.15W
Stilo 14 Kl 38.29N 16.28 E
Stilo, Punta- 14 Kl 38.27N 16.35 E
Štimlje 15 Eg 42.26N 21.03 E
Stînişoarei, Munţii- 15 Ib 47.20N 26.00 E
Stinnett 45 Fi 35.50N 101.27W
Štip 15 Fh 41.44N 22.12 E
Stirling 9 Je 56.07N 3.57W
Stirling Range 59 Df 34.25S 117.50 E
Stjernøya 7 Fa 70.18N 22.45 E
Stjørdalshalsen 7 Ce 63.28N 10.44 E
Stobi 15 Eh 41.33N 21.59 E
Stobrawa 10 Nf 50.50N 17.32 E
Stocka 8 Gc 61.54N 17.20 E
Stockach 10 Fi 47.51N 9.01 E
Stockbridge 12 Ac 51.06N 1.29W
Stockerau 14 Kb 48.23N 16.13 E
Stockholm [2] 7 Dg 59.20N 18.00 E
Stockholm 6 Hd 59.20N 18.03 E
Stockport 9 Kh 53.25N 2.10W
Stocks Seamount (EN) 52 Mg 12.15S 32.00W
Stockton [Ca.-U.S.] 39 Gf 37.57N 121.17W
Stockton [Mo.-U.S.] 45 Jh 37.42N 93.48W
Stockton Lake 45 Jh 37.40N 93.45W
Stockton-on-Tees 9 Lg 54.34N 1.19W
Stockton Plateau 43 Ge 30.30N 102.30W
Stoczek Łukowski 10 Re 51.58N 21.58 E
Stöde 7 De 62.25N 16.35 E
Stoěng Trêng 25 Lf 13.31N 105.58 E
Stoer, Point of- 9 Hc 58.20N 5.25W
Stogovo 15 Dh 41.29N 20.39 E
Stohod 10 Ve 51.52N 25.44 E
Stoholm 8 Ch 56.29N 9.10 E
Stoj, Gora- 16 Ce 48.39N 23.15 E
Stojba 22 Pd 52.49N 131.43 E
Stoke-on-Trent 9 Kh 53.00N 2.10W
Stokksnes 7a Cb 64.14N 14.58W
Stokmarknes 7 Db 68.34N 14.55 E
Stol 15 Fe 44.11N 22.09 E
Stolac 14 Lg 43.05N 17.58 E
Stolbcy 16 Ec 53.31N 26.43 E
Stolberg 10 Cf 50.46N 6.14 E
Stolbovoj, Ostrov- 20 Ib 74.05N 136.00 E
Stolin 16 Ed 51.57N 26.52 E
Stolzenau 12 Lb 52.31N 9.04 E
Ston 14 Lh 42.50N 17.42 E
Stone 9 Ki 52.54N 2.10W
Stonehaven 9 Ke 56.58N 2.13W
Stonehenge 9 Lj 51.11N 1.49W
Stonehenge 59 Id 24.22S 143.17 E
Stoner 45 Bh 37.37N 108.18W
Stonewall 45 Ha 50.09N 97.21W
Stony 40 Hd 61.45N 156.35W
Stony Rapids 42 Ge 59.16N 105.50W
Stony River 40 Hd 61.47N 156.41W
Stony Stratford 12 Bb 52.03N 0.51W
Stony Tunguska (EN)= Podkamennaja Tunguska 21 Lc 61.36N 90.18 E
Stör 10 Fc 53.50N 9.25 E
Storå 8 Ch 56.19N 8.19 E
Storå 8 Fe 59.43N 15.08 E
Storå/Isojoki 7 Ee 62.07N 21.58 E
Stora Gla 8 Ee 59.30N 12.30 E
Stora Le 8 De 59.05N 11.55 E
Stora Lulevatten 7 Ec 67.08N 19.20 E
Storavan 7 Ed 65.42N 18.12 E
Storby 8 Hd 60.13N 19.34 E
Stord 7 Ag 59.55N 5.25 E
Storða 7 Ee 62.07N 21.58 E
Stordal 8 Bb 62.23N 7.01 E

Index Symbols

[1] Independent Nation
[2] State, Region
[3] District, County
[4] Municipality
[5] Colony, Dependency
Continent
Physical Region
Historical or Cultural Region
Mount, Mountain
Volcano
Hill
Mountains, Mountain Range
Hills, Escarpment
Plateau, Upland
Pass, Gap
Plain, Lowland
Delta
Salt Flat
Valley, Canyon
Crater, Cave
Karst Features
Depression
Polder
Desert, Dunes
Forest, Woods
Heath, Steppe
Oasis
Cape, Point
Coast, Beach
Cliff
Peninsula
Isthmus
Sandbank
Island
Atoll
Rock, Reef
Islands, Archipelago
Rocks, Reefs
Coral Reef
Well, Spring
Geyser
River, Stream
Waterfall Rapids
River Mouth, Estuary
Lake
Salt Lake
Intermittent Lake
Reservoir
Swamp, Pond
Canal
Glacier
Ice Shelf, Pack Ice
Ocean
Sea
Gulf, Bay
Strait, Fjord
Lagoon
Bank
Seamount
Tablemount
Ridge
Shelf
Basin
Escarpment Sea Scarp
Fracture
Trench, Abyss
National Park, Reserve
Point of Interest
Recreation Site
Cave, Cavern
Historic Site
Ruins
Wall, Walls
Church, Abbey
Temple
Scientific Station
Airport
Port
Lighthouse
Mine
Tunnel
Dam, Bridge

Store Bælt=Great Belt (EN) 5 Hd 55.30N 11.00 E
Storebro 8 Fg 57.35N 15.51 E
Storefiskbank 9 Qe 56.50N 4.00 E
Store Heddinge 8 Ei 55.19N 12.25 E
Store Hellefiske Bank (EN) 41 Ge 67.30N 55.00W
Store Koldewey 41 Kc 76.20N 18.30W
Store Kvien 8 Dc 61.34N 10.33 E
Støren 7 Ce 63.02N 10.18 E
Store Nupsfonn 8 Be 59.54N 7.08 E
Store Sølnkletten 8 Dc 61.59N 10.18 E
Storfjorden [Nor.] 8 Bb 62.25N 6.30 E
Storfjorden [Sval.] 41 Nc 77.30N 20.00 E
Storfors 8 Fe 59.32N 14.16 E
Storis Passage 42 Hc 67.40N 98.30W
Storkerson Bay 42 Fb 73.00N 124.00W
Storkerson Peninsula 42 Gb 73.00N 106.30W
Storlien 7 Ce 63.19N 12.06 E
Stormarn 10 Gc 53.45N 10.20 E
Storm Bay 59 Jh 43.10S 147.30 E
Storm Lake 43 Hc 42.39N 95.13W
Stornoway 9 Gc 58.12N 6.23W
Storøya 41 Ob 80.08N 27.50 E
Storožinec 16 De 48.10N 25.46 E
Storsjøen [Nor.] 8 Dd 60.25N 11.40 E
Storsjøen [Nor.] 8 Dd 61.35N 11.15 E
Storsjön [Swe.] 8 Gd 60.35N 16.45 E
Storsjön [Swe.] 5 Hc 63.15N 14.20 E
Storsteinfjellet 7 Db 68.14N 17.52 E
Storstrøm [2] 8 Dj 55.00N 11.50 E
Storstrømmen 41 Jc 77.20N 23.00W
Storsudret 8 Hh 57.00N 18.15 E
Storuman 7 Dd 65.14N 16.54 E
Storuman 6 Hb 65.06N 17.06 E
Storvätteshågna 8 Eb 62.07N 12.27 E
Storvigelen 8 Eb 62.32N 12.04 E
Storvik 8 Gd 60.35N 16.32 E
Storvreta 8 Ge 59.58N 17.42 E
Stöttingfjället 7 Dd 64.38N 17.44 E
Stoughton 46 Nb 49.41N 103.03W
Stour [Eng.-U.K.] 9 Lk 50.43N 1.46W
Stour [Eng.-U.K.] 9 Oj 51.52N 1.16 E
Stourbridge 9 Ki 52.27N 2.09W
Støvring 8 Ch 56.53N 9.51 E
Stowmarket 12 Cb 52.11N 0.59 E
Strabane/An Srath Bán 9 Fg 54.49N 7.27W
Stradella 14 De 45.05N 9.18 E
Straelen 12 Ic 51.27N 6.16 E
Strakonice 10 Jg 49.16N 13.55 E
Straldža 15 Jg 42.36N 26.41 E
Stralsund 6 He 54.18N 13.06 E
Strand 37 Bf 34.06S 18.50 E
Stranda 7 Be 62.19N 6.54 E
Strand Bay 42 Ia 79.00N 94.00W
Strangford Lough/Loch Cuan 9 Hg 54.26N 5.36W
Strängnäs 8 Ge 59.23N 17.02 E
Stranraer 9 Hg 54.54N 5.02W
Strasbourg [Fr.] 6 Gf 48.35N 7.45 E
Strasbourg [Sask.-Can.] 46 Ma 51.04N 104.57W
Strašeny 16 Ff 47.06N 28.34 E
Straßwalchen 14 Hc 47.59N 13.15 E
Stratford [N.Z.] 62 Fc 39.21S 174.17 E
Stratford [Ont.-Can.] 44 Gd 43.22N 80.57W
Stratford [Tx.-U.S.] 45 Eh 36.20N 102.04W
Stratford-upon-Avon 9 Li 52.12N 1.41W
Strathclyde [3] 9 If 55.50N 4.50W
Strathgordon 59 Jh 42.54S 146.10 E
Strathmore 9 Je 56.40N 3.05W
Strathmore 46 Ia 51.03N 113.23W
Strathroy 44 Gd 42.57N 81.38W
Strathy Point 9 Ic 58.35N 4.01W
Straubenhardt 12 Kf 48.50N 8.34 E
Straubing 10 Ih 48.53N 12.34 E
Straumnes 7a Aa 66.26N 23.08W
Straumsjøen 7 Db 68.41N 14.30 E
Strausberg 10 Jd 52.35N 13.53 E
Strawberry Mountain 46 Fd 44.19N 118.43W
Strawberry River 46 Jf 40.10N 110.24W
Straža 15 Fg 42.15N 22.14 E
Stražica 15 If 43.14N 25.58 E
Strážiště 10 Kg 49.32N 14.58 E
Strážovské vrchy 10 Oh 48.55N 18.30 E
Streaky Bay 59 Gf 32.48S 134.13 E
Streaky Bay 59 Gf 32.35S 134.10 E
Streator 45 Lf 41.07N 88.50W
Středočeská pahorkatina 10 Kg 49.30N 14.15 E
Středočeský kraj [3] 10 Kg 49.55N 14.30 E
Středoslovenský kraj [3] 10 Ph 48.50N 19.10 E
Strehaia 15 Ge 44.37N 23.12 E
Strei 15 Gd 45.51N 23.03 E
Střela 10 Jg 49.54N 13.32 E
Strelasund 10 Jb 54.20N 13.05 E
Strelka 20 Ee 58.03N 93.05 E
Strelna 7 Jc 66.04N 38.39 E
Strenči 7 Fh 57.39N 25.38 E
Stresa 14 Ce 45.53N 8.32 E
Streževoj 20 Cd 60.42N 77.35 E
Stříbro 10 Ig 49.46N 13.00 E
Strickland River 59 Ia 6.00S 142.05 E
Strîmbeni 15 He 44.28N 24.58 E
Strimón 15 Gi 40.47N 23.51 E
Strimonikós Kólpos 15 Gi 40.40N 23.50 E
Strjama 15 Hg 42.10N 24.56 E
Strofádhes, Nisoi- 15 Dl 37.15N 21.00 E
Ströhen, Wagenfeld- 12 Kb 52.32N 8.39 E
Stromberg 12 Je 49.57N 7.46 E
Stromboli 14 Jl 38.45N 15.15 E
Strömfors/Ruotsinpyhtää 8 Ld 60.32N 26.27 E
Stromness 9 Jc 58.57N 3.18W
Strömsbro 8 Gd 60.42N 17.10 E
Strömsbruk 7 Dc 61.53N 17.19 E
Strömsnäsbruk 8 Eh 56.33N 13.43 E
Strömstad 7 Cf 58.56N 11.10 E
Strömsund 7 De 63.51N 15.35 E
Strongili 15 Hm 36.58N 24.55 E
Stròngoli 14 Lk 39.16N 17.03 E
Stronsay 9 Kb 59.08N 2.38W
Stropkov 10 Rg 49.12N 21.40 E
Stroud 9 Kj 51.45N 2.12W
Struer 7 Bh 56.29N 8.37 E
Struga 15 Dh 41.11N 20.41 E
Strugi-Krasnyje 7 Gg 58.17N 29.08 E
Strule 9 Fg 54.40N 7.20W
Struma 5 Ig 40.47N 23.51 E
Strumble Head 9 Hi 52.02N 5.04W
Strumica 15 Fh 41.26N 22.39 E
Stry 16 De 49.24N 24.13 E
Stry 19 Cf 49.14N 23.49 E
Strydenburg 37 Ce 29.58S 23.40 E
Stryn 7 Bf 61.55N 6.47 E
Strynsvatn 8 Bc 61.55N 7.05 E
Strzegom 10 Mf 50.57N 16.21 E
Strzegomka 10 Me 51.08N 16.50 E
Strzelce Krajeńskie 10 Ld 52.53N 15.32 E
Strzelce Opolskie 10 Of 50.31N 18.19 E
Strzelin 10 Nf 50.47N 17.03 E
Strzelno 10 Od 52.38N 18.11 E
Strzyżów 10 Rg 49.52N 21.47 E
Stuart 40 Gd 63.35N 162.30W
Stuart, Mount- 46 Ec 47.29N 120.54W
Stuart Bluff Range 59 Gd 22.45S 132.15 E
Stuart Lake 42 Ff 54.33N 124.35W
Stuart Range 59 Ge 29.10S 134.55 E
Stubaier Alpen 14 Fc 47.10N 11.05 E
Stubbekøbing 8 Ej 54.43N 12.03 E
Stubbenkammer 10 Jb 54.35N 13.40 E
Stubbs Bay 51n Ba 13.08N 61.10W
Štubik 15 Fe 44.18N 22.21 E
Studenica, Manastir- 15 Df 43.28N 20.37 E
Studholme Junction 62 Df 44.44S 171.08 E
Stugun 7 De 63.10N 15.36 E
Stuhr 12 Ka 53.02N 8.45 E
Stupino 7 Ji 54.57N 38.03 E
Stura di Demonte 14 Bf 44.40N 7.53 E
Stura di Lanzo 14 Be 45.06N 7.44 E
Sturge Island 66 Ke 67.27S 164.18 E
Sturgeon Bay 45 Md 44.50N 87.23W
Sturgeon Falls 42 Jg 46.22N 79.55W
Sturgeon Lake 45 Kb 50.00N 90.45W
Sturgis [Mi.-U.S.] 44 Ee 41.48N 85.25W
Sturgis [S.D.-U.S.] 45 Ed 44.25N 103.31W
Sturkö 8 Fh 56.05N 15.40 E
Sturt Creek 59 Fd 20.08S 127.24 E
Sturt Desert 59 Ie 28.30S 141.00 E
Stutterheim 37 Df 32.33S 27.28 E
Stuttgart [Ar.-U.S.] 45 Ki 34.30N 91.33W
Stuttgart [Ger.] 6 Gf 48.46N 9.11 E
Stviga 16 Ec 52.04N 27.55 E
Stykkishólmur 7a Ab 65.04N 22.44W
Styr 19 Ce 52.07N 26.35 E
Styria (EN) = Steiermark 14 Ic 47.15N 15.00 E
Styria (EN) = Steiermark [2] 14 Ic 47.15N 15.00 E
Styrsö 8 Dg 57.37N 11.46 E
Suafa Point 63a Ec 8.19S 160.41 E
Suai 26 Ih 9.21S 125.17 E
Suakin Archipelago (EN) = Sawākin, Jazā'ir- 30 Kg 19.07N 37.20 E
Suao 27 Lg 24.36N 121.51 E
Suardi 55 Bj 30.32S 61.58W
Suavanao 60 Fi 7.34S 158.44 E
Subačius/Subačjus 8 Ki 55.44N 24.53 E
Subačjus/Subačius 8 Ki 55.44N 24.53 E
Subang 26 Eh 6.34S 107.45 E
Subansiri 25 Jc 26.48N 93.49 E
Subao Ding 27 Jf 27.10N 110.18 E
Šubarkuduk 19 Ff 49.09N 56.31 E
Šubarši 16 Te 48.38N 57.12 E
Subate 8 Lh 56.01N 26.04 E
Subay', 'Urūq- 33 He 22.15N 43.05 E
Subaytilah 32 Ib 35.14N 9.08 E
Subbético, Sistema- 13 Jf 38.30N 2.30W
Subei (Dangchengwan) 27 Fd 39.36N 94.58 E
Subi, Pulau- 26 Ef 2.55N 108.50 E
Subiaco 14 Hi 41.55N 13.06 E
Sublette 45 Fh 37.29N 100.50W
Submeseta Norte 5 Fg 42.20N 4.50W
Submeseta Sur 5 Fh 39.30N 3.30W
Subotica 15 Cc 46.06N 19.40 E
Subpolar Urals (EN) = Pripoljarny Ural 5 Lb 65.00N 60.00 E
Subugo 36 Gc 1.40S 35.49 E
Suceava 15 Jb 47.32N 26.32 E
Suceava [2] 15 Ib 47.40N 25.45 E
Suceava 15 Jb 47.38N 26.15 E
Sucha Beskidzka 10 Pg 49.44N 19.36 E
Sühbaatar → Suhe-Bator 22 Md 50.15N 106.12 E
Suchedniów 10 Qe 51.03N 20.51 E
Suchiapa, Rio- 48 Mi 16.36N 93.01W
Suchitepéquez [3] 49 Bf 14.25N 91.20W
Sucia, Bahia- 51a Ac 17.57N 67.10W
Sucio, Rio- 49 Ij 7.27N 77.07W
Suck/An tSuca 9 Eh 53.16N 8.03W
Suckling, Mount- 59 Ja 9.45S 148.55 E
Sucre [Bol.] 53 Jg 19.02S 65.17W
Sucre [Col.] [2] 54 Db 9.00N 75.00W
Sucre [Col.] 54 Db 8.50N 74.43W
Sucre [Ven.] [2] 54 Fa 10.25N 63.30W
Suçuarana, Serra da- 55 Jb 14.25S 45.00W
Sucunduri, Rio- 54 Ge 5.30S 59.40W
Sućuraj 14 Lg 43.08N 17.12 E
Sucuriú, Rio- 54 Hh 20.47S 51.38W
Sud, Canal du- 49 Kd 18.40N 73.05W
Sud, Massif du- 49 Kd 18.25N 73.55W
Suda 7 Ig 59.11N 37.33 E
Suda 7 Ig 59.12N 37.30 E
Sudak 19 Dg 44.50N 34.59 E
Sudan 30 Jg 11.30N 15.00 E
Sudan (EN) = As Sūdān [1] 31 Jg 15.00N 30.00 E
Sudbury [Eng.-U.K.] 9 Ni 52.02N 0.44 E
Sudbury [Ont.-Can.] 39 Ke 46.30N 81.00W
Suddie 50 Gi 7.07N 58.29W
Sude 10 Gc 53.22N 10.45 E
Sudeten (EN) 5 He 50.30N 16.00 E
Sudirman, Pegunungan- 26 Kg 4.12S 137.00 E
Sudočje, Ozero- 18 Bc 43.25N 58.30 E
Sudogda 7 Ji 55.59N 40.50 E
Sudost 16 Hc 52.19N 33.24 E
Sud-Ouest [Cam.] [3] 34 Gd 5.20N 9.20 E
Sud-Ouest [U.V.] [3] 34 Ec 10.30N 3.15W
Sudovaja Višnja 10 Tg 49.43N 23.26 E
Südradde 12 Jb 52.41N 7.34 E
Südtirol / Trentino-Alto Adige [2] 14 Fd 46.30N 11.20 E
Sudža 16 Id 51.13N 35.16 E
Sue 30 Jh 7.41N 28.03 E
Sueca 13 Le 39.12N 0.19W
Suess Land 41 Jd 72.45N 26.00W
Suez (EN) = As Suways 31 Kf 29.58N 32.33 E
Suez, Gulf of-(EN) = Suways, Khalīj as- 30 Kf 28.10N 33.27 E
Suez Canal (EN) = Suways, Qanāt as- 30 Ke 29.55N 32.33 E
Suffolk 9 Ni 52.25N 1.00 E
Suffolk 43 Ld 36.44N 76.37W
Suffolk [3] 9 Li 52.10N 1.05W
Sufiān 24 Kc 38.17N 45.59 E
Sugana, Val- 14 Fd 46.00N 11.40 E
Suga-no-Sen 29 Dd 35.22N 134.31 E
Sugar Island 44 Eb 46.25N 84.12W
Sugarloaf Mountain 44 Lc 45.01N 70.22W
Suğla Gölü 24 Ed 37.20N 32.02 E
Sugoj 20 Kd 64.15N 154.29 E
Suguta 36 Gb 2.03N 36.33 E
Suha 15 Ke 44.08N 27.36 E
Suhai Hu 27 Fd 38.55N 94.05 E
Şuḩār 23 Ie 24.22N 56.45 E
Suhe-Bator (Sūchbaatar) 22 Md 50.15N 106.12 E
Suhiniči 16 Ib 54.06N 35.20 E
Suhl 10 Gf 50.36N 10.42 E
Suhodolskoje, Ozero- 8 Nd 60.35N 30.30 E
Suhoj Log 17 Kh 56.55N 62.01 E
Suhona 5 Kc 60.46N 46.24 E
Suhr 14 Cc 47.25N 8.04 E
Suhumi 6 Kg 43.01N 41.02 E
Suhurlui 15 Kd 45.25N 27.35 E
Suiá-Missu, Rio- 54 Hf 11.13S 53.15W
Suibara 29 Fc 37.50N 139.12 E
Suichang 27 Kf 28.34N 119.15 E
Suid Africa / South Africa [1] 31 Jl 30.00S 26.00 E
Suide 27 Jd 37.28N 110.15 E
Suifen He 28 Kc 43.20N 131.49 E
Suifenhe 27 Nc 44.25N 131.09 E
Sui He 28 Eh 33.29N 118.06 E
Suihua 27 Mb 46.38N 126.57 E
Suijiang 27 Hf 28.37N 104.00 E
Suileng 27 Mb 47.17N 127.08 E
Suining [China] 27 Ie 30.30N 105.34 E
Suining [China] 28 Dh 33.54N 117.56 E
Suipacha 55 Cl 34.45S 59.41W
Suiping 28 Bh 33.09N 113.59 E
Suippe 11 Je 49.25N 3.57 E
Suippes 11 Ke 49.08N 4.32 E
Suir/An tSiúir 9 Gi 52.15N 7.00W
Suisse / Svizra / Svizzera / Schweiz = Switzerland (EN) [1] 6 Gf 46.00N 8.30 E
Suisse Normande 12 Bf 48.53N 0.50W
Suita 29 Dd 34.45N 135.32 E
Suixi 28 Dh 33.55N 116.47 E
Suixian [China] 28 Cg 34.25N 115.04 E
Suixian [China] 27 Je 31.44N 113.25 E
Suiyang 28 Kb 44.26N 130.53 E
Suizhong 27 Lc 40.21N 120.20 E
Suj 27 Ic 42.12N 108.01 E
Šuja 7 If 61.54N 34.15 E
Šuja 7 If 61.59N 34.15 E
Šuja 19 Ed 56.52N 41.23 E
Sujer 17 Li 55.59N 65.47 E
Suji → Haixing 28 De 38.10N 117.29 E
Sujstamo 8 Nc 61.49N 31.05 E
Sukabumi 26 Eh 6.55S 106.56 E
Sukadana 26 Eg 1.15S 109.57 E
Sukagawa 28 Pf 37.17N 140.23 E
Sukaja 26 Fg 7.27S 108.12 E
Sukeva 7 Ge 63.54N 27.26 E
Sukhothai 25 Je 17.01N 99.49 E
Suki 35 Ec 13.23N 33.58 E
Sukkertoppen/Manitsoq 41 Ge 65.25N 53.00W
Sukkozero 19 Dc 63.09N 32.23 E
Sukkur 22 Ig 27.42N 68.52 E
Sukon 26 Hg 0.56S 123.10 E
Sukses 37 Bd 21.01S 16.52 E
Suksun 17 Hh 57.07N 57.24 E
Sukumo 28 Ne 32.56N 132.44 E
Sukumo-Wan 29 Ce 32.55N 132.40 E
Sul, Baía- 55 Hh 27.40S 48.35W
Sul, Canal do- 54 Id 0.10S 49.30W
Sula [Nor.] 7 Af 61.10N 4.55 E
Sula [Nor.] 8 Bb 62.25N 6.10 E
Sula 7 Ld 64.41N 47.46 E
Sula 17 Fc 67.16N 52.07 E
Sula 16 He 49.40N 32.43 E
Sula, Kepulauan- = Sulu Islands (EN) 57 De 1.52S 125.22 E
Sulaimāniya 23 Gb 35.33N 45.26 E
Sülaimaniya [3] 24 Ke 35.40N 45.30 E
Sulaimān Range 21 Jf 30.30N 70.10 E
Sulak 16 Oh 43.17N 47.34 E
Sulak 19 Eg 43.17N 47.34 E
Sula Sgeir 9 Gb 59.05N 6.10W
Sulawesi/Celebes 21 Oj 2.00S 121.10 E
Sulawesi, Laut- = Celebes Sea (EN) 21 Oj 3.00N 122.00 E
Sulawesi Selatan [3] 26 Gg 4.00S 120.00 E
Sulawesi Tengah [3] 26 Hg 1.00S 121.00 E
Sulawesi Tenggara [3] 26 Hg 4.00S 122.30 E
Sulawesi Utara [3] 26 Hf 1.00N 123.00 E
Sulaymān 14 En 36.42N 10.30 E
Sulb 35 Ea 20.26N 30.20 E
Sulcis 14 Ck 39.05N 8.40 E
Suldalsvatn 8 Be 59.35N 6.45 E
Süldeh 24 Od 36.34N 52.01 E
Sulechów 10 Ld 52.06N 15.37 E
Sulęcin 10 Ld 52.26N 15.08 E
Suleja 17 Ii 55.11N 58.50 E
Sulejów 10 Pe 51.22N 19.53 E
Süleoğlu 15 Jh 41.46N 26.55 E
Sule Skerry 9 Ib 59.10N 4.10W
Sulima 34 Cd 6.58N 11.35W
Sulina 15 Md 45.09N 29.40 E
Sulina, Braţul- 15 Md 45.09N 29.41 E
Sulingen 10 Ed 52.41N 8.48 E
Sulitjelma 7 Dc 67.09N 16.03 E
Sulitjelma 7 Dc 67.08N 16.24 E
Suljukta 19 Gh 39.56N 69.37 E
Sulkava 7 Gf 61.47N 28.23 E
Sullana 53 Hf 4.53S 80.42W
Süller 15 Mk 38.09N 29.29 E
Sullivan [In.-U.S.] 44 Df 39.06N 87.24W
Sullivan [Mo.-U.S.] 45 Kg 38.13N 91.10W
Sullivan Lake 46 Ja 52.00N 112.00W
Sully-sur-Loire 11 Ig 47.46N 2.22 E
Sulmona 14 Hh 42.03N 13.55 E
Sulphur [La.-U.S.] 45 Jk 30.14N 93.23W
Sulphur [Ok.-U.S.] 45 Hi 34.31N 96.58W
Sulphur Creek 45 Ed 44.46N 102.25W
Sulphur River 45 Jj 33.07N 93.52W
Sulphur Springs 45 Ij 33.08N 95.36W
Sulphur Springs Draw 45 Fj 32.12N 101.36W
Sultandağı 24 Dc 38.32N 31.14 E
Sultan Dağları 24 Dc 38.20N 31.20 E
Sultanhanı 24 Ec 38.15N 33.33 E
Sultanhisar 15 Ll 37.53N 28.10 E
Sultānpur 25 Gc 26.16N 82.04 E
Sulu Archipelago 21 Oi 6.00N 121.00 E
Sulu Basin (EN) 26 Ge 8.00N 121.30 E
Sulu Islands (EN) = Sula, Kepulauan- 57 De 1.52S 125.22 E
Suluova 24 Fb 40.47N 35.42 E
Sulūq 33 Dc 31.40N 20.15 E
Sulu Sea 21 Ni 9.00N 120.00 E
Sulz am Neckar 10 Eh 48.21N 8.37 E
Sulzbach (Saar) 12 Je 49.18N 7.04 E
Sulzbach-Rosenberg 10 Hg 49.30N 11.45 E
Sulzberger Bay 66 Mf 77.00S 152.00W
Šumadija 15 De 44.20N 20.40 E
Sumalata 26 Hf 0.59N 122.30 E
Sumāmus 24 Nd 36.50N 50.30 E
Šumanaj 18 Bc 42.37N 58.55 E
Sumatera = Sumatra (EN) 21 Mj 0.01N 102.00 E
Sumatera Barat [3] 26 Dg 1.00S 100.30 E
Sumatera Selatan [3] 26 Dg 3.30S 104.00 E
Sumatera Utara [3] 26 Cf 2.00N 99.00 E
Sumatra (EN) = Sumatera 21 Mj 0.01N 102.00 E
Šumava = Bohemian Forest (EN) 5 Hf 49.00N 13.30 E
Sumayr 33 Hf 17.47N 41.26 E
Sumba, Pulau- 21 Nj 10.00S 120.00 E
Sumba, Selat- = Sumba Strait (EN) 26 Hh 9.05S 120.00 E
Sumbar 16 Jj 38.00N 55.15 E
Sumba Strait (EN) = Sumba, Selat- 26 Hh 9.05S 120.00 E
Sumbawa, Pulau- 21 Nj 8.40S 118.00 E
Sumbawa Besar 26 Gh 8.30S 117.26 E
Sumbawanga 36 Fd 7.58S 31.37 E
Sumber 27 Ib 46.21N 108.20 E
Sumbi Point 63a Cb 7.19S 157.04 E
Sumbu 36 Fd 8.31S 30.29 E
Sumburgh Head 9 Lb 59.51N 1.16W
Sumedang 26 Eh 6.52S 107.55 E
Šūme'eh Sarā 24 Md 37.18N 49.19 E
Sümeg 10 Nj 46.59N 17.17 E
Šumen 15 Jf 43.16N 26.55 E
Šumen [2] 15 Jf 43.20N 27.00 E
Sumenep 26 Fh 7.01S 113.52 E
Šumerlja 6 Kd 55.30N 46.26 E
Sumgait 16 Pi 40.37N 49.37 E
Sumgait 6 Kg 40.33N 49.40 E
Sumidouro, Rio- 55 Da 13.28S 56.39W
Šumiha 19 Gd 55.14N 63.19 E
Sumkino 19 Gd 58.09N 68.21 E
Summer, Lake- [N.M.-U.S.] 45 Di 34.38N 104.26W
Summer, Lake- [N.Z.] 62 Ee 42.40S 172.15 E
Summer Lake 46 Ee 42.50N 120.45W
Summerland 46 Fb 49.39N 119.33W
Summerside 42 Lg 46.24N 63.47W
Summersville 44 Gf 38.17N 80.52W
Summerville 44 Eh 34.29N 85.21W
Summit Lake 42 Fe 54.17N 122.38W
Summit Mountain 46 Gg 39.23N 116.28W
Summit Peak 45 Ch 37.21N 106.42W
Sumoto 29 Dd 34.20N 134.54 E
Šumperk 10 Mg 49.58N 16.59 E
Sumprabum 25 Jc 26.33N 97.34 E
Sumsar 18 Hd 41.13N 71.23 E
Sumskaja Oblast [3] 19 De 51.00N 34.15 E
Šumšu, Ostrov- 20 Kf 50.45N 156.20 E
Sumter 43 Ke 33.55N 80.20W
Sumuşţā al Waqf 24 Dh 28.55N 30.51 E
Sumy 6 Je 50.54N 34.48 E
Suna 7 Mh 57.53N 50.07 E
Suna 7 Ie 62.08N 34.12 E
Sunagawa 28 Pc 43.29N 141.55 E
Šunak, Gora- 19 Hf 47.05N 72.35 E
Sunan 28 He 39.15N 125.40 E
Sunan (Hongwansi) 27 Gd 38.59N 99.25 E
Sunart, Loch- 9 He 56.45N 5.45W
Sunaysilah 24 Ie 35.35N 41.53 E
Sunburst 46 Jb 48.53N 111.55W
Sunbury 44 Ie 40.52N 76.47W
Sunchales 56 Hd 30.56S 61.34W
Suncho Corral 56 Hc 27.56S 63.27W
Sunch'ŏn [N. Kor.] 27 Me 34.57N 127.29 E
Sunch'ŏn [S. Kor.] 27 Md 39.25N 125.56 E
Sun City 46 Ij 33.36N 112.17W
Suncun → Xinwen 27 Kd 35.49N 117.38 E
Sunda, Selat- = Sunda Strait (EN) 21 Mj 6.00S 105.45 E
Sundance 46 Md 44.24N 104.23W
Sundarbans 25 Hd 22.00N 89.00 E
Sundargarh 25 Gd 22.07N 84.02 E
Sunda Strait (EN) = Sunda, Selat- 21 Mj 6.00S 105.45 E
Sunday Strait 59 Ec 16.20S 123.15 E
Sundborn 8 Fd 60.39N 15.46 E
Sundbron 8 Ha 63.01N 18.11 E
Sundbyberg 8 Ge 59.22N 17.58 E
Sunde 7 Ag 59.50N 5.43 E
Sunderland 9 Lg 54.55N 1.23W
Sundern (Sauerland) 12 Kc 51.20N 8.00 E
Sundgau 11 Ng 47.40N 7.15 E
Sündiken Dağları 24 Dc 39.55N 31.00 E
Sundridge 44 Hc 45.46N 79.24W
Sundsvall 6 Hc 62.23N 17.18 E
Sundsvallsbukten 8 Gb 62.20N 17.35 E
Sunflower, Mount- 45 Eg 39.04N 102.01W
Sungaidareh 26 Dg 0.58S 101.30 E
Sungaigerong 26 Dg 2.59S 104.52 E
Sungaiguntung 26 Df 0.18N 103.37 E
Sungai Kolok 25 Kg 6.02N 101.58 E
Sungai Lembing 26 Df 3.55N 103.02 E
Sungailiat 26 Eg 1.51S 106.08 E
Sungaipenuh 26 Dg 2.05S 101.23 E
Sungai Petani 26 De 5.39N 100.30 E
Sungai Siput 26 Df 4.49N 101.04 E
Sungari (EN) = Songhua Jiang 21 Pe 47.42N 132.30 E
Sungqu → Songpan 27 He 32.37N 103.34 E
Sungurlu 24 Fb 40.10N 34.23 E
Sunharon Roads 64b Bb 14.57N 145.36 E
Suning 28 Ce 38.25N 115.50 E
Sunja 14 Ke 45.21N 16.33 E
Sunjiapuzi 28 Ic 42.02N 126.34 E
Sunkar, Gora- 18 Ib 44.12N 73.55 E
Sun Kosi 25 Hc 26.55N 87.09 E
Sunnadalsøra 7 Be 62.40N 8.33 E
Sunnan 7 Cd 64.04N 11.38 E
Sunndalen 8 Cb 62.40N 8.45 E
Sunndalsfjorden 8 Cb 62.45N 8.25 E
Sunne 7 Cg 59.50N 13.09 E
Sunnerbo 8 Eh 56.45N 13.50 E
Sunnersta 8 Ge 59.48N 17.39 E
Sunnfjord 8 Ac 61.25N 5.20 E
Sunnhordland 8 Ae 59.55N 6.00 E
Sunnmøre 8 Bb 62.20N 6.40 E
Sunnyside 46 Fc 46.20N 120.00W
Sunnyvale 46 Dh 37.23N 122.01W
Su-no-Zaki 29 Fd 34.58N 139.45 E
Sun River 46 Jc 47.30N 111.25W
Sunsas, Serrania de- 55 Cc 17.57S 59.35W
Suntar 20 Gd 62.04N 117.40 E
Suntar-Hajata, Hrebet- = Suntar-Khayata Range (EN) 21 Qc 62.00N 143.00 E
Suntar-Khayata Range (EN) = Suntar-Hajata, Hrebet- 21 Qc 62.00N 143.00 E
Suntaži 8 Kh 56.49N 24.57 E
Sun Valley 43 Ec 43.42N 114.21W
Sunwu 27 Mb 49.27N 127.19 E
Sunyani 31 Gh 7.20N 2.20W
Sunža 16 Oh 43.26N 46.08 E
Suojarvi 19 Dc 62.04N 32.21 E
Suokonmäki 8 Kb 62.47N 24.30 E
Suolahti 7 Fe 62.34N 25.52 E
Suomenlahti = Finland, Gulf of- (EN) 5 Ic 60.00N 27.00 E
Suomenniemi 8 Lc 61.19N 27.27 E
Suomenselkä 5 Ic 62.50N 25.00 E
Suomi/Finland [1] 6 Ic 64.00N 26.00 E
Suomussalmi 7 Gd 64.54N 29.00 E
Suō-Nada 29 Be 33.50N 131.30 E
Suonenjoki 7 Ge 62.37N 27.08 E
Suontee 8 Lc 61.40N 26.35 E
Suordah 20 Ic 66.43N 132.04 E
Suozhen → Huantai 28 Ef 36.57N 118.05 E
Supamo, Rio- 50 Fi 6.48N 61.50W
Superior [Az.-U.S.] 46 Jj 33.18N 110.06W
Superior [Mt.-U.S.] 46 Hc 47.12N 114.53W
Superior [Nb.-U.S.] 45 Gf 40.01N 98.04W
Superior [Wi.-U.S.] 39 Je 46.44N 92.05W
Superior, Lake- 38 Ke 48.00N 88.00W
Suphan Buri 25 Kf 14.29N 100.10 E
Süphan Dağı 23 Fb 38.54N 42.48 E
Supiori, Pulau- 26 Kg 0.45S 135.30 E
Supoj 16 Ge 49.38N 31.50 E
Support Force Glacier 66 Rg 83.05S 47.30W
Supraśl 10 Tc 53.13N 23.20 E
Supraśl 10 Sc 53.12N 22.55 E
Sup'ung 27 Lc 40.27N 124.57 E
Sup'ung-chosuji 28 Hd 40.30N 125.05 E
Suq ash Shuyūkh 24 Lg 30.53N 46.28 E
Suqian 27 Ke 33.55N 118.13 E
Sūq Suwayq 24 Hj 24.23N 38.27 E
Suquţrā = Socotra (EN) 21 Hh 12.30N 54.00 E
Şūr 22 Hg 22.31N 59.30 E
Şūr 23 Ec 33.16N 35.11 E
Sur, Cabo- 65d Ac 27.12S 109.26W
Sur, Point- 46 Eh 36.18N 121.54W
Sura 16 Nc 53.53N 45.44 E
Sura 5 Kd 56.06N 46.00 E
Šurab 18 Hd 40.03N 70.33 E
Surabaya 22 Nj 7.15S 112.45 E

Index Symbols

[1] Independent Nation
[2] State, Region
[3] District, County
[4] Municipality
[5] Colony, Dependency
Continent
Physical Region
Historical or Cultural Region
Mount, Mountain
Volcano
Hill
Mountains, Mountain Range
Hills, Escarpment
Plateau, Upland
Pass, Gap
Plain, Lowland
Delta
Salt Flat
Valley, Canyon
Crater, Cave
Karst Features
Depression
Polder
Desert, Dunes
Forest, Woods
Heath, Steppe
Oasis
Cape, Point
Coast, Beach
Cliff
Peninsula
Isthmus
Sandbank
Island
Atoll
Rock, Reef
Islands, Archipelago
Rocks, Reefs
Coral Reef
Well, Spring
Geyser
River, Stream
Waterfall Rapids
River Mouth, Estuary
Lake
Salt Lake
Intermittent Lake
Reservoir
Swamp, Pond
Canal
Glacier
Ice Shelf, Pack Ice
Ocean
Sea
Gulf, Bay
Strait, Fjord
Lagoon
Bank
Seamount
Tablemount
Ridge
Shelf
Basin
Escarpment, Sea Scarp
Fracture
Trench, Abyss
National Park, Reserve
Point of Interest
Recreation Site
Cave, Cavern
Historic Site
Ruins
Wall, Walls
Church, Abbey
Temple
Scientific Station
Airport
Port
Lighthouse
Mine
Tunnel
Dam, Bridge

Name	Page	Grid	Lat.	Long.
Surahammar	8	Ge	59.43N	16.13 E
Sūrak	23	Id	25.43N	58.48 E
Surakarta	22	Nj	7.35S	110.50 E
Şūrān	24	Ge	35.17N	36.45 E
Šurany	10	Oh	48.06N	18.11 E
Surar	35	Gd	7.29N	40.54 E
Surat	22	Jg	21.10N	72.50 E
Surat Thani	22	Li	9.06N	99.20 E
Suraž	7	Hi	55.26N	30.43 E
Suraž	19	De	53.02N	32.29 E
Surčin	15	De	44.47N	20.17 E
Sur del Cabo San Antonio, Punta-	56	Ie	36.52S	56.40W
Surduc	15	Gb	47.15N	23.21 E
Sûre	10	Cg	49.44N	6.31 E
Surendranagar	25	Ed	22.42N	71.41 E
Surgères	11	Fh	46.06N	0.45W
Surgut	22	Jc	61.14N	73.20 E
Surgutiha	20	Dd	63.47N	87.20 E
Surhandarinskaja Oblast [3]	19	Gh	38.00N	67.30 E
Surhandarja	18	Ff	37.14N	67.20 E
Surhob	19	Hh	38.54N	70.04 E
Surigao	26	Ie	9.45N	125.30 E
Surin	25	Kf	14.53N	103.30 E
Suriname [1]	53	Ke	4.00N	56.00W
Suripá, Rio-	49	Mj	7.47N	69.53W
Sūrīyah=Syria (EN) [1]	22	Ff	35.00N	38.00 E
Sürmaq	24	Og	31.03N	52.48 E
Surmelin	12	Fe	49.04N	3.31 E
Sürmene	24	Ib	40.55N	40.07 E
Surna	8	Cb	62.59N	8.40 E
Surnadalsøra	8	Cb	62.59N	8.39 E
Surovikino	19	Ef	48.36N	42.54 E
Surovo	20	Fe	55.39N	105.36 E
Sur-Pakri/Suur-Pakri	8	Je	59.50N	23.45 E
Surprise, Ile-	63b	Ad	18.32S	163.02 E
Surprise, Lac-	44	Ja	49.20N	74.57W
Surrey [3]	9	Mj	51.25N	0.30W
Surrey	9	Mj	51.20N	0.05W
Sursee	14	Cc	47.10N	8.07 E
Sursk	16	Nc	53.04N	45.42 E
Surskoje	7	Li	54.31N	46.44 E
Surt	31	Ie	31.13N	16.35 E
Surt, Khalīj-=Sidra, Gulf of-(EN)	30	Ie	31.30N	18.00 E
Surte	8	Eg	57.49N	12.01 E
Surtsey	7a	Bc	63.20N	20.38W
Sürüç	24	Hd	36.58N	38.24 E
Surud Ad	30	Lg	10.42N	47.09 E
Suruga-Wan	28	Og	34.55N	138.35 E
Surulangun	26	Dg	2.37S	102.45 E
Survey Pass	40	Ic	67.52N	154.10W
Sur-Vjajn/Suur Väin	8	Jf	58.30N	23.20 E
Surwold	12	Jb	52.57N	7.31 E
Susā	8	Di	55.11N	11.46 E
Šuša	16	Oj	39.43N	46.44 E
Susa [It.]	14	Be	45.08N	7.03 E
Susa [Jap.]	29	Bd	34.37N	131.36 E
Susa, Val di-	14	Be	45.10N	7.10 E
Sušac	14	Kh	42.46N	16.30 E
Sūsah [Lib.]	33	Dc	32.54N	21.58 E
Sūsah [Tun.]=Sousse (EN)	31	Ie	35.49N	10.38 E
Sūsah=Sousse (EN) [3]	32	Jb	35.45N	10.30 E
Susak	14	If	44.31N	14.18 E
Susaki	27	Ne	33.22N	133.17 E
Susami	29	De	33.33N	135.29 E
Susamyr	18	Ic	42.09N	73.59 E
Susanville	43	Cc	40.25N	120.39W
Suşehri	24	Hb	40.11N	38.06 E
Suseja	8	Kh	56.23N	25.00 E
Šušenskoje	20	Ef	53.19N	92.01 E
Sušice	10	Jg	49.14N	13.30 E
Susitna	40	Id	61.16N	150.30W
Suslonger	7	Lh	56.18N	48.12 E
Susoh	26	Cf	3.43N	96.50 E
Susong	28	Di	30.10N	116.06 E
Suspiro	55	Ej	30.38S	54.22W
Suspiro del Moro, Puerto del-	13	Ig	37.08N	3.40W
Susquehanna River	43	Ld	39.33N	76.05W
Susques	56	Gb	23.25S	66.29W
Sussex	9	Mk	50.55N	0.30W
Sussex	44	Oc	45.43N	65.31W
Sussex, Vale of-	9	Mk	51.00N	0.15W
Susubona	63a	Dc	8.19S	159.27 E
Susuman	22	Qc	62.47N	148.10 E
Susurluk	24	Cc	39.54N	28.10 E
Susuzmüsellim	15	Kh	41.06N	27.03 E
Šušvė	8	Ji	55.08N	23.53 E
Susz	10	Pc	53.44N	19.20 E
Suţeşti	15	Kd	45.13N	27.26 E
Sutherland	37	Cf	32.24S	20.40 E
Sutherland Falls	62	Bf	44.48S	167.44 E
Sutherlin	46	De	43.25N	123.19W
Sutla	14	Je	45.51N	15.41 E
Sutlej	21	Jg	29.23N	71.02 E
Sutton	44	Gf	38.41N	80.43W
Sutton, London-	12	Bc	51.21N	0.12W
Sutton Bridge	12	Cb	52.46N	0.11 E
Sutton in Ashfield	12	Aa	53.07N	1.16W
Sutton Scotney	12	Ac	51.09N	1.20W
Suttor River	59	Jd	21.25S	147.45 E
Suttsu	28	Pc	42.48N	140.14 E
Sütüler	24	Dd	37.30N	30.59 E
Sutwik	40	He	56.34N	157.05W
Su'uholo	63a	Ec	9.46S	161.58 E
Suunduk	16	Ud	51.46N	58.46 E
Suure-Jaani	7	Fg	58.31N	25.29 E
Suur-Pakri/Sur-Pakri	8	Je	59.50N	23.45 E
Suur Väin/Sur-Vjajn	8	Jf	58.30N	23.20 E
Suva	58	If	18.08S	178.25 E
Suvadiva Atoll	21	Ji	0.30N	73.13 E
Suva Gora	15	Eh	41.51N	21.03 E
Suva Planina	15	Ff	43.08N	22.13 E
Suvasvesi	7	Ge	62.40N	28.10 E
Suvorov	16	Jb	54.08N	36.32 E
Suvorovo	15	Mc	46.33N	29.35 E
Suvorovo	15	Ld	45.35N	29.00 E
Suvorovskaja	16	Mg	44.10N	42.38 E
Suwa	28	Of	36.02N	138.08 E
Suwa-Ko	29	Fc	36.03N	138.05 E
Suwałki	10	Sb	54.07N	22.56 E
Suwałki [2]	10	Sb	54.05N	22.55 E
Suwalskie, Pojezierze-	10	Sb	54.15N	23.00 E
Suwannee River	44	Fk	29.18N	83.09W
Suwanose-Jima	27	Mf	29.40N	129.45 E
Suwarrow Atoll	57	Kf	13.15S	163.05W
Suwayqiyah, Hawr as-	24	Lf	32.40N	46.03 E
Suways, Khalīj as-=Suez, Gulf of-(EN)	30	Kf	28.10N	33.27 E
Suways, Qanāt as-=Suez Canal (EN)	30	Ke	29.55N	32.33 E
Suwŏn	27	Md	37.16N	127.01 E
Suxian	27	Ke	33.36N	116.58 E
Suzaka	29	Fc	36.39N	138.18 E
Suzdal	7	Jh	56.28N	40.27 E
Suzhou	22	Of	31.16N	120.37 E
Suzhou/Jiuquan	22	Lf	39.46N	98.34 E
Suzi He	28	Hd	41.56N	124.20 E
Suzu	27	Od	37.25N	137.17 E
Suzuka	29	Ed	34.51N	136.35 E
Suzuka-Sanmyaku	29	Ed	35.10N	136.20 E
Suzu-Misaki	28	Nf	37.28N	137.20 E
Suzun	20	Df	53.47N	82.19 E
Suzzara	14	Ef	45.00N	10.45 E
Sværholthalvøya	7	Ga	70.30N	26.05 E
Svågan	8	Gc	61.54N	16.33 E
Svalbard [5]	67	Kd	78.00N	20.00 E
Svaljava	16	Ce	48.32N	22.59 E
Svalöv	8	Ei	55.55N	13.06 E
Svaneholm	8	Ee	59.11N	12.33 E
Svaneke	7	Di	55.08N	15.09 E
Svängsta	8	Fh	56.16N	14.46 E
Svanøy	8	Ac	61.30N	5.05 E
Svapa	16	Id	51.44N	34.59 E
Svappavaara	7	Ec	67.39N	21.04 E
Svärdsjö	8	Fd	60.45N	15.55 E
Svartå	8	Fe	59.08N	14.31 E
Svartälven	8	Fe	59.20N	14.35 E
Svartån [Swe.]	8	Fe	59.17N	15.15 E
Svartån [Swe.]	8	Ff	58.28N	15.33 E
Svartån [Swe.]	8	Ge	59.37N	16.33 E
Svartenhuk Halvø=Svartenhuk Peninsula (EN)	41	Gd	71.30N	55.20W
Svartenhuk Peninsula (EN)=Svartenhuk Halvø	41	Gd	71.30N	55.20W
Svartisen	7	Cc	66.38N	13.58 E
Svatoj Nos, Mys-	20	Jb	72.45N	140.45 E
Svatovo	19	Df	49.24N	38.13 E
Svay Riĕng	25	Lf	11.05N	105.48 E
Sveabreen	66	Cf	72.08S	1.53 E
Sveagruva	41	Nc	78.39N	16.25 E
Svealand	7	Dd	60.30N	15.30 E
Svealand	5	Hc	60.30N	15.30 E
Svedala	8	Ei	55.30N	13.14 E
Sveg	7	De	62.02N	14.21 E
Švėkšna	8	Ii	55.32N	21.30 E
Svelgen	7	Af	61.45N	5.18 E
Svelvik	8	De	59.37N	10.24 E
Švenčeneljaj/Švenčionėliai	7	Gi	55.09N	26.02 E
Švenčėnis/Švenčionys	7	Gi	55.07N	26.12 E
Švenčionėliai/Švenčeneljaj	7	Gi	55.09N	26.02 E
Švenčionys/Švenčėnis	7	Gi	55.07N	26.12 E
Svendborg	7	Ci	55.03N	10.37 E
Svendsen Peninsula	42	Ja	77.50N	84.00W
Svenljunga	7	Ch	57.30N	13.07 E
Svenska högarna	8	He	59.35N	19.35 E
Svenskøya	41	Oc	78.43N	26.30 E
Svenstavik	7	De	62.46N	14.27 E
Šventoji/Šventoj	8	Ih	56.04N	20.59 E
Šventoj/Šventoji	8	Ih	56.04N	20.59 E
Sverdlovsk → Jekaterinburg	22	Id	56.51N	60.36 E
Sverdrup, Ostrov-	20	Cb	74.30N	79.35 E
Sverdrup Channel	42	Ha	80.00N	96.30W
Sverdrup Islands	38	Jb	79.00N	98.00W
Sverige=Sweden (EN) [1]	6	Hc	62.00N	15.00 E
Svetac	14	Jg	43.02N	15.45 E
Svēte/Svete	8	Jh	56.40N	23.38 E
Svete/Svēte	8	Jh	56.40N	23.38 E
Sveti Naum	15	Di	40.55N	20.45 E
Sveti Nikola, Prohod-	15	Ff	43.27N	22.36 E
Sveti Nikole	15	Eh	41.52N	21.57 E
Sveti Stefan	15	Bg	42.16N	18.54 E
Svetlaja	19	Ig	46.31N	138.18 E
Svetli	20	Ge	58.34N	116.00 E
Svetlogorsk	19	Ce	52.38N	29.42 E
Svetlogorsk	8	Ij	54.55N	20.08 E
Svetlograd	19	Ef	45.19N	42.40 E
Svetlovodsk	16	He	49.02N	33.15 E
Svetly	19	Ge	50.51N	60.53 E
Svetly	7	Ei	54.41N	20.08 E
Svetly Jar	16	Ne	48.29N	44.46 E
Svetogorsk	7	Gf	61.07N	28.58 E
Svetozarevo	15	Ef	43.59N	21.15 E
Sviča	10	Ug	49.04N	24.06 E
Svid	7	Jf	61.13N	38.45 E
Svidnik	10	Rg	49.18N	21.35 E
Svidnik	16	Kg	49.23N	14.58 E
Svijaga	19	Ed	55.39N	48.28 E
Svilaja	14	Kg	43.50N	16.26 E
Svilengrad	15	Jh	41.46N	26.12 E
Svincovy Rudnik	18	Ff	37.52N	66.28 E
Svinecea Mare, Vîrful-	15	Fe	44.48N	22.09 E
Svir	5	Jc	60.30N	32.48 E
Svir	8	Lj	54.50N	26.34 E
Svirica	7	Hf	60.30N	32.54 E
Svirsk	20	Ff	53.04N	103.18 E
Svisloč	16	Fc	53.27N	28.59 E
Svisloč	16	Dc	53.03N	24.07 E
Svištov	15	If	43.37N	25.20 E
Svit	10	Qg	49.03N	20.12 E
Svitava	10	Mg	49.11N	16.38 E
Svitavy	10	Mg	49.46N	16.27 E
Svizra / Svizzera / Schweiz / Suisse = Switzerland (EN) [1]	6	Gf	46.00N	8.30 E
Svizzera / Schweiz / Suisse / Svizra = Switzerland (EN) [1]	6	Gf	46.00N	8.30 E
Svjatoj Nos, Mys-	5	Jb	68.10N	39.43 E
Svobodny	22	Od	51.24N	128.07 E
Svoge	15	Gg	42.58N	23.21 E
Svolvær	7	Db	68.14N	14.34 E
Svratka	10	Mh	49.52N	16.38 E
Svrljig	15	Ff	43.25N	22.08 E
Svulrya	8	Ed	60.25N	12.24 E
Svytaya Anna Trough (EN)	67	He	80.00N	70.00 E
Swabia (EN)=Schwaben	10	Gh	48.20N	10.30 E
Swabian-Bavarian Plateau (EN)=Schwäbisch-Bayerisches Alpenvorland	5	Hf	48.15N	10.30 E
Swabian Jura (EN)=Schwäbische Alb	5	Gf	48.25N	9.30 E
Swaffham	12	Cb	52.39N	0.41 E
Swain Reefs	57	Gg	21.40S	152.15 E
Swains Atoll	57	Jf	11.03S	171.05W
Swainsboro	44	Fi	32.36N	82.20W
Swakop	37	Ad	22.41S	14.31 E
Swakopmund [3]	37	Ad	22.30S	15.00 E
Swakopmund	31	Ik	22.41S	14.34 E
Swale	9	Lg	54.06N	1.20W
Swalmen	12	Ic	51.14N	6.02 E
Swanage	9	Lk	50.37N	1.58W
Swan Hill	59	Ig	35.21S	143.34 E
Swan Range	46	Ic	47.50N	113.40W
Swan River	42	Hf	52.06N	101.16W
Swansboro	44	Ih	34.36N	77.07W
Swansea [Austl.]	59	Jh	42.08S	148.04 E
Swansea [Wales-U.K.]	6	Fe	51.38N	3.57W
Swansea Bay	9	Jj	51.35N	3.52W
Swans Island	44	Mc	44.10N	68.25W
Swanson Lake	45	Ff	40.09N	101.06W
Swan Valley	46	Je	43.28N	111.20W
Swartberge	30	Jl	33.23S	21.48 E
Swarzędz	10	Nd	52.26N	17.05 E
Swastika	44	Ga	48.07N	80.12W
Swaziland [1]	31	Kk	26.30S	31.10 E
Sweden (EN)=Sverige [1]	6	Hc	62.00N	15.00 E
Swedru	34	Ed	5.32N	0.42W
Sweet Grass Hills	46	Jb	48.55N	111.30W
Sweet Home	46	Dd	44.24N	122.44W
Sweetwater	43	Ge	32.28N	100.25W
Sweetwater River	43	Fc	42.31N	107.02W
Swellendam	37	Cf	34.02S	20.26 E
Świder	10	Rd	52.08N	21.12 E
Świdnica	10	Mf	50.51N	16.29 E
Świdnik	10	Se	51.14N	22.41 E
Świdwin	10	Lc	53.47N	15.47 E
Świebodzin	10	Ld	52.15N	15.32 E
Świecie	10	Oc	53.25N	18.28 E
Świętej Anny, Góra-	10	Of	50.28N	18.13 E
Świętokrzyskie, Góry-	10	Qf	50.55N	21.00 E
Swift Current	42	Gf	50.17N	107.50W
Swift Current Creek	46	La	50.40N	107.44W
Swift River	42	Ed	60.05N	131.11W
Swilly, Lough-/Loch Suili	9	Ff	55.10N	7.33W
Swinburne, Cape -	42	Hb	71.14N	98.33W
Swindon	9	Lj	51.34N	1.47W
Swinford/Béal Átha na Muice	9	Eh	53.57N	8.57W
Świnoujście	10	Kc	53.53N	14.14 E
Swischenahner Meer	12	Ka	53.12N	8.01 E
Swisttal	12	Id	50.44N	6.54 E
Switzerland (EN) = Schweiz / Suisse / Svizra / Svizzera [1]	6	Gf	46.00N	8.30 E
Switzerland (EN) = Suisse / Svizra / Svizzera / Schweiz [1]	6	Gf	46.00N	8.30 E
Switzerland (EN) = Svizra / Svizzera / Schweiz / Suisse [1]	6	Gf	46.00N	8.30 E
Switzerland (EN) = Svizzera / Schweiz / Suisse / Svizra [1]	6	Gf	46.00N	8.30 E
Syčevka	16	Ib	55.51N	34.15 E
Syców	10	Ne	51.19N	17.43 E
Sydfalster-Gedser	7	Ci	54.35N	11.57 E
Sydkap Ice Cap	42	Ja	75.30N	85.00W
Sydney [Austl.]	58	Gh	33.52S	151.13 E
Sydney [N.S.-Can.]	39	Me	46.09N	60.11W
Sydney → Manra Atoll	57	Je	4.27S	171.15W
Sydney-Campbelltown	59	Kf	34.04S	150.49 E
Sydney Lake	45	Ia	50.40N	94.24W
Sydney Mines	42	Lg	46.14N	60.12W
Sydney-Penrith	59	Kf	33.45S	150.42 E
Syktyvkar	6	Lc	61.40N	50.46 E
Sylacauga	44	Di	33.10N	86.15W
Sylane	7	Ce	63.02N	2.13 E
Sylarna	7	Ce	63.02N	2.13 E
Sylhet	25	Id	24.54N	91.52 E
Sylling	8	De	59.54N	0.17 E
Sylt	10	Eb	54.55N	8.20 E
Sylva	17	Hh	57.40N	56.57 E
Sylvania	44	Gi	32.45N	81.38W
Sylvania Tablemount (EN)	60	Ge	11.58N	165.00 E
Sylvan Pass	43	Ec	44.28N	110.08W
Sylvester	44	Fj	31.32N	83.49W
Sylvester, Lake-	59	Hc	19.50S	135.50 E
Sym	20	Ed	60.15N	90.02 E
Syndassko	20	Fb	73.14N	108.05 E
Synja	17	Ld	65.12N	64.45 E
Synnfjell	8	Cc	61.05N	9.45 E
Syowa	66	De	69.00S	39.35 E
Syracuse [Ks.-U.S.]	45	Fh	37.59N	101.45W
Syracuse [N.Y.-U.S.]	39	Le	43.03N	76.09W
Syracuse (EN)=Siracusa	6	Hh	37.04N	15.18 E
Syrdarinskaja Oblast [3]	19	Gg	40.30N	68.40 E
Syrdarja	19	Gg	40.52N	68.38 E
Syrdarja=Syr Darya (EN)	21	Ie	46.03N	61.00 E
Syr Darya (EN)=Syrdarja	21	Ie	46.03N	61.00 E
Syria (EN)	21	Ff	35.00N	38.00 E
Syria (EN)=Sūrīyah [1]	22	Ff	35.00N	38.00 E
Syriam	25	Je	16.46N	96.15 E
Syrian Desert- (EN)=Shām, Bādiyat ash-	21	Ff	32.00N	40.00 E
Syrkovoje, Ozero-	17	Lf	60.40N	65.00 E
Syrski	16	Kc	52.36N	39.28 E
Sysert	17	Jh	56.31N	60.49 E
Sysmä	7	Ff	61.30N	25.41 E
Sysola	19	Fc	61.42N	50.58 E
Sysslebäck	8	Ed	60.44N	12.52 E
Sysulp, Gora-	15	Ha	48.29N	24.17 E
Syverma, Plato-	21	Lc	67.00N	99.00 E
Syzran	6	Ke	53.09N	48.27 E
Szabolcs-Szatmár-Bereg	10	Sh	48.00N	22.10 E
Szamocin	10	Nc	53.02N	17.08 E
Szamos	15	Fa	48.07N	22.20 E
Szamotuły	10	Md	52.37N	16.35 E
Szarvas	10	Qj	46.52N	20.33 E
Szczawnica Krościenko	10	Qg	49.26N	20.30 E
Szczebrzeszyn	10	Sf	50.42N	22.59 E
Szczecin [2]	10	Kc	52.35N	14.30 E
Szczecin=Stettin (EN)	6	He	53.24N	14.32 E
Szczecinek	10	Mc	53.43N	16.42 E
Szczeciński, Zalew-	10	Kc	53.46N	14.14 E
Szczekociny	10	Pf	50.38N	19.50 E
Szczerców	10	Pe	51.18N	19.09 E
Szczucin	10	Rf	50.18N	21.04 E
Szczuczyn	10	Sc	53.34N	22.18 E
Szczytno	10	Qc	53.34N	21.00 E
Szechwan (EN)=Sichuan Sheng (Ssu-ch'uan Sheng) [2]	27	He	30.00N	103.00 E
Szechwan (EN)=Ssu-ch'uan Sheng → Sichuan Sheng [2]	27	He	30.00N	103.00 E
Szécsény	10	Ph	48.05N	19.31 E
Szeged	6	If	46.15N	20.10 E
Szeged [2]	10	Qj	46.16N	20.08 E
Szeghalom	10	Ri	47.02N	21.10 E
Székesfehérvár	6	Hf	47.12N	18.25 E
Szekszárd	10	Oj	46.21N	18.43 E
Szendrő	10	Qh	48.24N	20.44 E
Szentendre	10	Pi	47.40N	19.05 E
Szentes	10	Qj	46.39N	20.16 E
Szentgotthárd	10	Mj	46.57N	16.17 E
Szerencs	10	Rh	48.10N	21.12 E
Szeskie Wzgórza	10	Sb	54.14N	22.22 E
Szigetvár	10	Nj	46.03N	17.48 E
Szkwa	10	Rc	53.10N	21.45 E
Szlichtyngowa	10	Me	51.43N	16.15 E
Szob	10	Oi	47.49N	18.52 E
Szolnok	10	Qi	47.11N	20.12 E
Szolnok → Jász-Nagykun-Szolnok	10	Qi	47.15N	20.30 E
Szombathely	10	Mi	47.14N	16.37 E
Szprotawa	10	Le	51.34N	15.33 E
Sztum	10	Pc	53.56N	19.01 E
Szubin	10	Nc	53.00N	17.44 E
Szydłów	10	Rf	50.35N	21.01 E
Szydłowiec	10	Qe	51.14N	20.51 E

T

Name	Page	Grid	Lat.	Long.
Taakoka	64p	Cc	21.15S	159.43W
Taalintendas/Dalsbruk	8	Jd	60.02N	22.31 E
Taavetti	8	Ld	60.55N	27.34 E
Tab	10	Oj	46.44N	18.02 E
Tabaca	56	Hb	23.16S	64.15W
Ţābah	24	Ji	27.02N	42.08 E
Tabaqan	24	He	35.52N	38.34 E
Tabar Islands	57	Ge	2.50S	152.00 E
Ţabarqah	32	Ib	36.57N	8.45 E
Ţabas	24	Qf	33.36N	56.54 E
Tabasará, Serranía de-	49	Gi	8.33N	81.40W
Tabasco [2]	47	Fe	18.00N	92.40W
Tabasco y Campeche, Llanos de-	47	Fe	18.15N	91.00W
Tabašino	7	Lh	56.59N	47.43 E
Tābask, Kūh-e-	24	Nh	29.52N	51.49 E
Tabay	55	Ci	28.18S	58.17W
Tabelbala	32	Gd	29.24N	3.15W
Taber	42	Gg	49.47N	112.08W
Taberg	8	Fg	57.41N	14.05 E
Taberg	8	Fg	57.41N	14.05 E
Tabernacle	51c	Ab	17.23N	62.46W
Tabernas	13	Jg	37.03N	2.23W
Tabernes de Valldigna	13	Le	39.04N	0.16W
Tabiteuea Atoll	57	Ie	1.20S	174.50 E
Tabla	34	Fc	13.46N	3.01 E
Tablas	26	Hd	12.24N	122.02 E
Tablas Strait	26	Hd	12.40N	121.48 E
Tablat	13	Ph	36.25N	3.19 E
Tablazo, Bahía del-	49	Lh	10.52N	71.35W
Table Cape	62	Gc	39.06S	178.00 E
Table Rock Lake	45	Jh	36.35N	93.30W
Tabocas	55	Jb	14.39S	45.28W
Taboco, Rio-	55	Ed	19.53S	55.58W
Tabola	16	Pg	45.53N	48.20 E
Tábor	10	Kg	49.25N	14.41 E
Tabora	31	Ki	5.01S	32.48 E
Tabora [3]	36	Fd	5.20S	32.30 E
Tabory	17	Lg	58.31N	64.33 E
Tabou	31	Gh	4.25N	7.21W
Tabrīz	22	Gf	38.05N	46.18 E
Tábua	13	Dd	40.21N	8.02W
Tabuaeran Atoll (Fanning)	57	Ld	3.52N	159.20W
Tabūk	22	Fg	28.23N	36.35 E
Tabuk	26	Hc	17.24N	121.25 E
Ţaburbah	14	Dn	36.50N	9.50 E
Tabursuq	14	Dn	36.28N	9.15 E
Tabursuq, Monts de-	14	Dn	36.25N	9.05 E
Tabusintac	44	Ob	47.24N	65.02W
Tabwemasana	63b	Cb	15.22S	166.45 E
Täby	7	Eg	59.30N	18.03 E
Tacámbaro de Codallos	48	Ih	19.14N	101.28W
Tacarcuna, Cerro-	49	Ij	8.05N	77.17W
Tacarigua, Laguna de-	50	Dg	10.15N	65.50W
Tacheng/Qoqek	22	Ke	46.45N	82.57 E
Tachibana-Wan	29	Be	32.45N	130.05 E
Tachichilte, Isla de-	48	Ee	24.59N	108.04W
Tachikawa [Jap.]	29	Fd	35.42N	139.23 E
Tachikawa [Jap.]	29	Fb	38.48N	139.58 E
Táchira [2]	54	Db	7.50N	72.05W
Tachiumet	33	Bd	26.19N	10.03 E
Tachov	10	Ig	49.48N	12.40 E
Tachungnya	64b	Bb	14.58N	145.36 E
Tacinski	16	Le	48.13N	41.17 E
Tacir	15	Mi	40.32N	29.44 E
Tacloban	22	Oh	11.15N	125.00 E
Tacna	53	Ig	18.01S	70.15W
Tacna [2]	54	Dg	17.40S	70.20W
Tacoma	39	Ge	47.15N	122.27W
Tacotalpa, Río-	48	Mi	17.50N	92.52W
Tacuaral	55	Cd	18.59S	58.07W
Tacuarembó [2]	55	Ek	32.10S	55.30W
Tacuarembó, Río-	55	Ek	32.25S	55.29W
Tacuarí, Río-	55	Fk	32.46S	53.18W
Tacuati	55	Df	23.27S	56.35W
Tadami	29	Fc	37.21N	139.17 E
Tadarimana, Rio-	55	Ec	16.29S	54.31W
Tademaït, Plateau du-	30	Hf	28.30N	2.15 E
Tadine	63b	Ce	21.33S	167.53 E
Tadjeraout	32	He	21.17N	1.20 E
Tadjetaret	32	Ie	22.00N	7.30 E
Tadjourah	35	Gc	11.45N	42.54 E
Tadjourah, Golfe de-	35	Gc	11.45N	43.00 E
Tadoule Lake	42	He	58.35N	98.20W
Tadoussac	44	Ma	48.09N	69.43W
Tadžikskaja Sovetskaja Socialističeskaja Respublika → Tajikistan	19	Hh	39.00N	71.00 E
Tadžikskaja SSR/Respublikai Soveth Socialisti Todžikiston → Tajikistan	19	Hh	39.00N	71.00 E
Tadžikskaya SSR → Tajikistan	19	Hh	39.00N	71.00 E
T'aebaek-Sanmaek	21	Of	37.40N	128.50 E
Taechon	28	If	36.21N	126.36 E
T'aech'on	28	He	39.55N	125.30 E
Taedong-gang	28	He	38.42N	125.15 E
Taegu	22	Of	35.52N	128.36 E
Taeha-dong	28	Kf	37.31N	130.48 E
Taehan-Haehyŏp=Korea Strait (EN)	21	Of	34.40N	129.00 E
Taehan-Min'guk=South Korea (EN) [1]	22	Of	38.00N	127.30 E
Taehuksan-Do	28	Hg	34.40N	125.25 E
Taejŏn	22	Of	36.20N	127.26 E
Tafahi Island	57	Jf	15.52S	173.55W
Tafalla	13	Kb	42.31N	1.40W
Tafassasset	30	If	21.56N	10.12 E
Tafassasset, Ténéré du-	34	Ha	21.20N	11.00 E
Taff	9	Jj	51.27N	3.09W
Tafilalt	32	Gc	31.18N	4.18W
Tafiré	34	Dd	9.04N	5.10W
Tafí Viejo	56	Gc	26.44S	65.16W
Taflan	24	Gb	41.25N	36.09 E
Tafna	13	Ki	35.18N	1.28W
Tafraout	32	Fd	29.43N	9.00W
Tafresh	24	Ne	34.41N	50.01 E
Taft	24	Pg	31.45N	54.14 E
Taftān, Kuh-e-	21	Ig	28.36N	61.06 E
Taftanāz	24	Ge	35.59N	36.47 E
Taga	65c	Aa	13.46S	172.28W
Taga Dzong	25	Hc	27.04N	89.53 E
Tagajō	29	Gb	38.18N	140.58 E
Tagama	30	Hg	15.50N	8.12 E
Taganrog	6	Jf	47.12N	38.56 E
Taganrogski Zaliv	16	Kf	46.50N	38.25 E
Tagant [3]	32	Ef	18.30N	10.30W
Tagant	30	Fg	17.31N	12.07W
Tagarev, Gora-	18	Ae	38.19N	57.18 E
Tagawa	29	Be	33.39N	130.48 E
Tagbilaran	26	He	9.39N	123.51 E
Tageru, Jabal-	35	Db	16.25N	27.10 E
Taggia	14	Bg	43.52N	7.51 E
Taghit	32	Gc	30.55N	2.02W
Tagil	17	Kg	58.33N	62.30 E
Tagish Lake	42	Ed	60.00N	134.00W
Tagliamento	14	He	45.38N	13.06 E
Taglio di Po	14	Ge	45.00N	12.12 E
Tagomago, Isla de-	13	Ne	39.02N	1.39 E
Tagounit	32	Fd	29.58N	5.35W
Tagpochau, Ogso-	64b	Ba	15.11N	145.45 E
Tāgrīfat	33	Cd	29.12N	17.21 E
Taguatinga	54	If	12.25S	46.26W
Taguersimet	32	De	24.09N	15.07W
Tagula	63a	Ad	11.20S	153.00 E
Tagula Island	57	Gf	11.30S	153.30 E
Tagum	26	Ie	7.21N	125.50 E
Tagus (EN)=Tajo	5	Fh	38.40N	9.24W
Tagus (EN)=Tejo	5	Fh	38.40N	9.24W
Tah	32	Ed	27.37N	12.50W
Tahaa, Ile-	61	Kc	16.38S	151.30W
Tahakopa	62	Cg	46.31S	169.23 E
Tahan, Gunong-	21	Mi	4.39N	102.14 E
Tahanea Atoll	57	Mf	16.52S	144.45W

Index Symbols

[1] Independent Nation; [2] State, Region; [3] District, County; [4] Municipality; [5] Colony, Dependency; Continent; Physical Region; Historical or Cultural Region; Mount, Mountain; Volcano; Hill; Mountains, Mountain Range; Hills, Escarpment; Plateau, Upland; Pass, Gap; Plain, Lowland; Delta; Salt Flat; Valley, Canyon; Crater, Cave; Karst Features; Depression; Polder; Desert, Dunes; Forest, Woods; Heath, Steppe; Oasis; Cape, Point; Coast, Beach; Cliff; Peninsula; Isthmus; Sandbank; Island; Atoll; Rock, Reef; Islands, Archipelago; Rocks, Reefs; Coral Reef; Well, Spring; Geyser; River, Stream; Waterfall Rapids; River Mouth, Estuary; Lake; Salt Lake; Intermittent Lake; Reservoir; Swamp, Pond; Canal; Glacier; Ice Shelf, Pack Ice; Ocean; Sea; Gulf, Bay; Strait, Fjord; Lagoon; Bank; Seamount; Tablemount; Ridge; Shelf; Basin; Escarpment, Sea Scarp; Fracture; Trench, Abyss; National Park, Reserve; Point of Interest; Recreation Site; Cave, Cavern; Historic Site; Ruins; Wall, Walls; Church, Abbey; Temple; Scientific Station; Airport; Fort; Lighthouse; Mine; Tunnel; Dam, Bridge

Tahat	30	Hf	23.18N	5.32 E
Tahe	27	La	52.22N	124.48 E
Ţāherī	24	Oi	27.42N	52.21 E
Tahgong, Puntan-	64b	Ba	15.06N	145.39 E
Tahiataš	18	Bc	42.20N	59.33 E
Tahifet	32	Ie	22.56N	5.59 E
Tahir Geçidi	24	Jc	39.52N	42.20 E
Tahiti, Ile-	57	Mf	17.37S	149.27W
Tahkuna Neem/Takuna, Mys-	8	Je	59.05N	22.30 E
Tahlequah	45	Ii	35.55N	94.58W
Tahoe, Lake-	46	Fg	38.54N	120.00W
Tahoua [2]	34	Gb	16.00N	5.30 E
Tahoua	31	Hg	14.54N	5.16 E
Ţahţā	33	Fd	26.46N	31.28 E
Tahta-Bazar	18	Dg	35.55N	62.55 E
Tahtabrod	19	Ge	52.40N	67.35 E
Tahtakarača Pereval	18	Fe	39.17N	66.55 E
Tahtaköprü	15	Mj	39.57N	29.39 E
Tahtakupyr	19	Gg	43.01N	60.22 E
Tahtali Dağları	24	Gc	38.46N	36.47 E
Tahtamygda	20	Hf	54.09N	123.38 E
Tahuata, Ile-	57	Ne	9.57S	139.05W
Tahulandang, Pulau-	26	If	2.20N	125.25 E
Tahuna	26	If	3.37N	125.29 E
Taï	34	Dd	5.52N	7.27W
Tai'an [China]	28	Gd	41.24N	122.27 E
Tai'an [China]	27	Kd	36.09N	117.05 E
Taiarapu, Presqu'île de-	65e	Fc	17.47S	149.14W
Taibai Shan	27	Ie	33.57N	107.40 E
Taibilla, Canal del-	13	Kg	37.43N	1.22W
Taibilla, Sierra de-	13	Jf	38.10N	2.10W
Taibus Qi (Baochang)	27	Kc	41.55N	115.22 E
Taicang	28	Fi	31.26N	121.06 E
Taichung	22	Og	24.09N	120.41 E
Taieri	62	Dg	46.03S	170.12 E
Taiga	20	De	56.04N	85.37 E
Taigonos Peninsula (EN)= Tajgonos, Poluostrov-	20	Ld	61.35N	161.00 E
Taigu	28	Bf	37.26N	112.33 E
Taihang Shan	21	Nf	37.00N	114.00 E
Taihape	62	Fc	39.41S	175.48 E
Taihe [China]	28	Ch	33.11N	115.38 E
Taihe [China]	27	Jf	26.50N	114.52 E
Taiheiyō=Pacific Ocean (EN)	3	Ki	5.00N	155.00W
Tai Hu	21	Of	31.15N	120.10 E
Taihu	27	Ke	30.26N	116.10 E
Taikang	27	Je	34.00N	114.56 E
Taiki	29a	Cb	42.30N	143.16 E
Tailai	27	Lb	46.24N	123.26 E
Tailles, Plateau des-	12	Hd	50.15N	5.45 E
Taim	55	Fk	32.30S	52.35W
Tain	9	Id	57.48N	4.04W
Tainan	22	Og	23.00N	120.11 E
Taínaron, Ákra-=Matapan, Cape- (EN)	5	Ih	36.23N	22.29 E
Taiof	63a	Ba	5.31S	154.39 E
Taipei	22	Og	25.03N	121.30 E
Taiping	26	Df	4.51N	100.44 E
Taiping (Gantang)	28	Ei	30.18N	118.07 E
Taipingchuan	28	Gb	44.24N	123.11 E
Taiping Dao	27	Jd	10.15N	113.42 E
Taiping Ling	27	Lb	47.36N	120.12 E
Tairadate	29a	Bc	41.09N	140.38 E
Tairadate-Kaikyō	29a	Bc	41.10N	140.40 E
Taisei	29a	Ab	42.14N	139.49 E
Taisetsu-Zan	21	Qe	43.40N	142.48 E
Taisha	29	Cd	35.24N	132.40 E
Taishaku-San	29	Fc	36.58N	139.28 E
Tai Shan	21	Nf	36.30N	117.20 E
Taishō	29	Ce	33.12N	132.57 E
Taitao Peninsula (EN) = Taitao, Península de-	52	Ij	46.30S	74.25W
Taitung	27	Lg	22.45N	121.09 E
Taiwa	29	Gb	38.26N	140.52 E
Taiwan [1]	22	Og	23.30N	121.00 E
Taiwan Haixia = Taiwan Strait (EN)	21	Ng	24.00N	119.00 E
Taixian	28	Fh	32.31N	120.08 E
Taixing	28	Fh	32.10N	120.00 E
Taiyang Shan	27	Ie	33.37N	106.26 E
Taiyetos Óros-	15	Fl	37.06N	22.18 E
Taiyuan	22	Nf	37.50N	112.37 E
Taiyue Shan	28	Bf	36.48N	112.00 E
Taizhou	28	Eh	32.29N	119.55 E
Taizhou → Linhai	27	Lf	28.52N	121.08 E
Taizhou Wan	28	Fj	28.40N	121.37 E
Taizi He	28	Gd	41.00N	122.23 E
Ta'izz	22	Gh	13.38N	44.02 E
Tājābād	24	Pg	30.02N	54.24 E
Tajarḩī	33	Be	24.21N	14.28 E
Tajgonos, Mys-	20	Ld	60.35N	160.10 E
Tajgonos, Poluostrov-= Taigonos Peninsula (EN)	20	Ld	61.35N	161.00 E
Tajikistan (EN) = Tojikiston	19	Hh	39.00N	71.00 E
Tajima	28	Of	37.12N	139.46 E
Tajimi	29	Ed	35.19N	137.08 E
Tājirwīn	14	Co	35.54N	8.33 E
Tajito	48	Cb	30.58N	112.18W
Tajmba	20	Ed	60.22N	98.50 E
Tajmyr	20	Ea	76.05N	98.55 E
Tajmyr, Ozero-	21	Mb	74.30N	102.30 E
Tajmyr, Poluostrov-= Taymyr Peninsula (EN)	21	Mb	76.00N	104.00 E
Tajmyra	21	Lb	76.00N	99.40 E
Tajmyrlur	20	Hb	72.30N	121.39 E
Tajo=Tagus (EN)	5	Fh	38.40N	9.24W
Tajo-Segura, Canal de Trasvase-	13	Je	39.30N	2.05W
Tajrīsh	23	Hb	38.48N	51.25 E
Tajšet	22	Ld	55.57N	98.00 E
Tajumulco, Volcán-	38	Jh	15.02N	91.54W
Tajuña	13	Id	40.07N	3.35W
Tak	25	Je	16.52N	99.08 E
Taka Atoll	3	Ii	4.00N	146.45 E
Takāb	24	Ld	36.24N	47.07 E
Takaba	36	Hb	3.27N	40.14 E
Takahagi	28	Pf	36.42N	140.41 E
Takahama	29	Dd	35.29N	135.33 E
Takahara-Gawa	29	Ec	36.27N	137.15 E
Takaharu	29	Bf	31.55N	130.59 E
Takahashi	28	Lg	34.47N	133.37 E
Takahashi-Gawa	29	Cd	34.32N	133.42 E
Takahata	29	Gc	38.00N	140.12 E
Takahe, Mount-	66	Of	76.17S	112.05W
Takaka	62	Ed	40.51S	172.48 E
Takakuma-Yama	29	Bf	31.28N	130.49 E
Takalar	26	Gh	5.28S	119.24 E
Takalous	32	Ie	23.25N	7.02 E
Takamatsu	27	Ne	34.21N	134.03 E
Takamori	29	Be	32.48N	131.08 E
Takanabe	29	Be	32.08N	131.31 E
Takanawa-Hantō	29	Ce	34.00N	132.55 E
Takanawa-San	29	Ce	33.57N	132.50 E
Takanosu	29	Ga	40.14N	140.22 E
Takaoka [Jap.]	28	Nf	36.45N	137.01 E
Takaoka [Jap.]	29	Bf	31.57N	131.17 E
Takapoto Atoll	61	Lb	15.00S	148.10W
Takapuna	62	Fb	36.48S	174.47 E
Takara-Jima	27	Mf	29.10N	129.05 E
Takarazuka	29	Dd	34.49N	135.21 E
Takaroa Atoll	61	Mb	14.28S	144.58W
Takasaki	28	Of	36.20N	139.01 E
Taka-Shima [Jap.]	29	Be	32.40N	131.50 E
Taka-Shima [Jap.]	29	Af	31.26N	129.45 E
Takatshwane	37	Cd	22.36S	21.55 E
Takatsu-Gawa	29	Bd	34.42N	131.49 E
Takatsuki	28	Mg	34.51N	135.37 E
Takayama	28	Nf	36.08N	137.15 E
Takebe	29	Cd	34.53N	133.54 E
Takefu	28	Ng	35.54N	136.10 E
Takehara	29	Cd	34.21N	132.54 E
Takeo	29	Ae	33.12N	130.00 E
Tåkern	8	Ff	58.20N	14.50 E
Take-Shima	28	Kf	37.22N	131.58 E
Tākestān	23	Gb	36.05N	49.14 E
Taketa	29	Be	32.58N	131.24 E
Takêv	25	Kf	10.59N	104.47 E
Takhādīd	24	Kh	29.59N	44.30 E
Takhār [3]	23	Kb	36.30N	69.30 E
Takhmaret	13	Mi	35.06N	0.41 E
Takht-e Soleimān	24	Nd	36.20N	51.00 E
Taki [Jap.]	29	Cd	35.16N	132.38 E
Taki [Pap.N.Gui.]	63a	Bb	6.29S	155.50 E
Takijuq Lake	42	Gc	66.05N	113.00W
Takikawa	28	Pc	43.33N	141.54 E
Takingeun	26	Cf	4.38N	96.50 E
Takinoue	29a	Ca	44.13N	143.03 E
Takko	29	Ga	40.20N	141.09 E
Takla Lake	42	Ee	55.30N	126.00W
Takla Landing	42	Ee	55.29N	125.58W
Takla Makan (EN)= Taklimakan Shamo	21	Kf	39.00N	83.00 E
Takob	18	Ge	38.51N	69.00 E
Tako-Bana	29	Cd	35.35N	133.05 E
Takolokouzet, Massif de-	34	Gb	18.40N	9.30 E
Taksimo (Muhoršibir)	20	Ff	51.01N	107.50 E
Taku	29	Be	33.19N	130.06 E
Takua Pa	25	Jg	8.52N	98.21 E
Takum	34	Gd	7.16N	9.59 E
Takuma	29	Cd	34.14N	133.40 E
Takume Atoll	57	Mf	15.49S	142.12W
Takuna, Mys-/Tahkuna Neem	8	Je	59.05N	22.30 E
Takutea Island	57	Lf	19.49S	158.18W
Tala	48	Hg	20.40N	103.42W
Tālah	32	Ib	35.35N	8.40 E
Talaimmannar	25	Fg	9.05N	79.44 E
Talāīyeh	24	Kd	37.50N	45.00 E
Talaja	20	Kd	61.03N	152.30 E
Talak	30	Hg	18.20N	6.00 E
Talamanca, Cordillera de-	49	Fi	9.30N	83.40W
Talara	53	Hf	4.35S	81.25W
Talas	19	Hg	42.29N	72.14 E
Talas	18	Ic	44.05N	70.20 E
Talasea	59	Ka	5.20S	150.05 E
Talasskaja oblast	18	Ic	42.25N	72.15 E
Talasski Alatau, hrebet-	18	Hc	42.10N	72.00 E
Talata Mafara	34	Gc	12.34N	6.04 E
Talaud, Kepulauan-=Talaud Islands (EN)	21	Oi	4.20N	126.50 E
Talaud Islands (EN)= Talaud, Kepulauan-	21	Oi	4.20N	126.50 E
Talavera, Isla-	55	Dh	27.32S	56.26W
Talavera de la Reina	13	He	39.57N	4.50W
Talawdī	35	Ec	10.38N	30.23 E
Talbot Inlet	42	Ja	77.55N	77.35W
Talca	53	Ii	35.26S	71.40W
Talcahuano	53	Ii	36.43S	73.07W
Tālcher	25	Hd	20.57N	85.13 E
Taldom	7	Ih	56.45N	37.32 E
Taldy-Kurgan	22	Je	44.59N	78.23 E
Taldy-Kurganskaja Oblast [3]	19	Hf	44.00N	78.00 E
Taleḩ	35	Hd	9.09N	48.26 E
Tal-e Khosravī	24	Ng	30.47N	51.29 E
Talence	11	Fj	44.49N	0.36W
Ţalesh, Kūhhā-Ye-	24	Md	37.35N	48.38 E
Talgar	19	Hg	43.18N	77.13 E
Taliabu, Pulau-	26	Hg	1.48S	124.48 E
Talica	19	Gd	57.01N	63.43 E
Talimardžan	19	Gh	38.21N	65.31 E
Tali Post	35	Ed	5.54N	30.47 E
Talisajan	22	Ni	1.37N	118.11 E
Taliwang	26	Gh	8.44S	116.52 E
Talkeetna	40	Id	62.20N	150.07W
Talkeetna Mountains	40	Jd	62.10N	148.15W
Talkheh	24	Kd	37.40N	45.46 E
Talladega	44	Di	33.26N	86.06W
Tall 'Afar	23	Fb	36.22N	42.27 E
Tallah	24	Dh	28.05N	30.44 E
Tallahassee	39	Kf	30.25N	84.16W
Tallahatchie River	45	Kj	33.33N	90.10W
Tall al Abyaḑ	24	Hd	36.41N	38.57 E
Tallapoosa River	44	Di	32.30N	86.16W
Tallard	11	Mj	44.28N	6.03 E
Tällberg	8	Fd	60.49N	15.00 E
Tall Birāk at Taḩtānī	24	Id	36.38N	41.05 E
Tallinn	6	Id	59.25N	24.45 E
Tall Kayf	24	Jd	36.29N	43.08 E
Tall Kūshik	24	Jd	36.48N	42.04 E
Tallulah	45	Kj	32.25N	91.11W
Tălmaciu	15	Hd	45.39N	24.16 E
Talmenka	20	Df	53.51N	83.45 E
Talmest	32	Fc	31.09N	9.00W
Talnah	20	Dc	69.30N	88.15 E
Talnoje	16	Ge	48.53N	30.42 E
Talo	30	Kg	10.44N	37.55 E
Talofofo	64c	Bb	13.20N	144.46 E
Talon	20	Je	59.48N	148.50 E
Tāloqān	23	Kb	36.44N	69.33 E
Talovaja	16	Ld	51.06N	40.48 E
Talpa de Allende	48	Gg	20.23N	104.51W
Talsi	7	Fh	57.17N	22.37 E
Taltal	53	Ih	25.24S	70.29W
Taltson	42	Gd	61.24N	112.45W
Taluk	26	Dg	0.32S	101.35 E
Talvik	7	Fa	70.03N	22.58 E
Talwār	24	Md	36.00N	48.00 E
Tama	35	Cc	14.45N	22.25 E
Tamaghzah	32	Ic	34.23N	7.57 E
Tamala	16	Mc	52.33N	43.18 E
Tamalameque	49	Ki	8.52N	73.38W
Tamale	31	Gh	9.24N	0.50W
Tamames	13	Fd	40.39N	6.06W
Tamana	29	Be	32.55N	130.33 E
Tamanaco, Río-	50	Dh	9.25N	65.23W
Tamana Island	57	Ie	2.29S	175.59 E
Tamano	28	Lg	34.30N	133.56 E
Tamanoura	29	Ae	32.38N	128.37 E
Tamanrasset	30	Hf	22.03N	0.10 E
Tamanrasset	31	Hf	22.47N	5.31 E
Tamanrasset [3]	32	Ie	23.00N	5.30 E
Tamar	9	Ik	50.22N	4.10W
Tamara	15	Cg	42.27N	19.33 E
Támara	54	Db	5.50N	72.10W
Tamarit de Llitera/Tamarite de Litera	13	Mc	41.52N	0.26 E
Tamarite de Litera/Tamarit de Llitera	13	Mc	41.52N	0.26 E
Tamarro	14	Ii	41.09N	14.50 E
Tamarugal, Pampa del-	56	Gb	21.00S	69.25W
Tamási	10	Oj	46.38N	18.17 E
Tamassoumit	32	Ef	18.35N	12.39W
Tamaulipas [2]	47	Ed	24.00N	98.45W
Tamaulipas, Llanos de-	47	Ed	25.00N	98.25W
Tamaulipas, Sierra de-	48	Jf	23.30N	98.30W
Tamayama	29	Gb	39.50N	141.11 E
Tamazula de Gordiano	48	Hh	19.38N	103.15W
Tamazunchale	47	Ed	21.16N	98.47W
Tambach	36	Gb	0.36N	35.31 E
Tambacounda	31	Fg	13.12N	15.48W
Tambara	37	Ec	16.44S	34.15 E
Tambelan, Kepulauan-= Tambelan Islands (EN)	26	Ef	1.00N	107.30 E
Tambelan, Pulau-	26	Ef	0.58N	107.34 E
Tambelan Islands (EN)= Tambelan, Kepulauan-	26	Ef	1.00N	107.30 E
Tambo	59	Jd	24.53S	146.15 E
Tambohorano	37	Gc	17.29S	43.58 E
Tambora, Gunung-	26	Gh	8.14S	117.55 E
Tambores	55	Dj	31.52S	56.16W
Tambov	6	Ke	52.43N	41.27 E
Tambovskaja Oblast [3]	19	Ee	52.45N	41.40 E
Tambre	13	Db	42.49N	8.53W
Tambunan	26	Ge	5.40N	116.22 E
Tambura	31	Jh	5.36N	27.28 E
Tamchaket	32	Ef	17.20N	10.40W
Tame	54	Db	6.27N	71.45W
Tâmega	13	Dc	41.05N	8.21W
Támega	13	Dc	41.05N	8.21W
Tamel Aike	56	Fg	48.19S	70.58W
Tamesi	47	Ed	22.13N	97.52W
Tamesnar	30	Hg	18.25N	3.33 E
Tamgak, Monts-	30	Hg	19.11N	8.42 E
Tamgue, Massif du-	30	Fg	12.00N	12.18W
Tamiahua	48	Kg	21.16N	97.27W
Tamiahua, Laguna de-	47	Ed	21.35N	97.35W
Tamianglajang	26	Gg	2.07S	115.10 E
Tamil Nādu [3]	25	Ff	11.00N	78.00 E
Tamiš	15	De	44.51N	20.39 E
Tamise/Temse	12	Gc	51.08N	4.13 E
Tamitatoala, Rio-	54	Hf	11.56S	53.36W
Ţāmiyah	24	Dh	29.29N	30.58 E
Tam Ky	25	Le	15.34N	108.29 E
Tammela	8	Jd	60.48N	23.46 E
Tammerfors/Tampere	6	Ic	61.30N	23.45 E
Tammisaari/Ekenäs	7	Fg	59.58N	23.26 E
Tämnaren	8	Gd	60.10N	17.20 E
Tamnava	15	De	44.25N	20.05 E
Tamou	34	Fc	12.45N	2.11 E
Tampa	39	Kg	27.57N	82.27W
Tampa Bay	43	Kf	27.45N	82.35W
Tampake-Misaki	29a	Bb	43.43N	141.20 E
Tampere/Tammerfors	6	Ic	61.30N	23.45 E
Tampico	39	Jg	22.13N	97.51W
Tampin	26	Df	2.28N	102.14 E
Tamri	32	Fc	30.43N	9.50 E
Tamsag-Bulak	27	Kb	47.14N	117.21 E
Tamsalu	7	Gg	59.10N	26.07 E
Tamsweg	14	Hc	47.08N	13.48 E
Tamu	25	Id	24.13N	94.19 E
Tamuín	48	Jg	21.59N	98.45W
Tamuín	47	Ed	22.00N	98.44W
Tamuín, Río-	48	Jg	21.47N	98.28W
Tamworth [Austl.]	58	Gh	31.05S	150.55 E
Tamworth [Eng.-U.K.]	9	Li	52.39N	1.40W
Tamyang	28	Ig	35.19N	126.59 E
Tana [Eur.]	5	Ia	70.28N	28.18 E
Tana [Kenya]	30	Li	2.32S	40.31 E
Tana, Lake-	30	Kg	12.00N	37.20 E
Tanabe	28	Mh	33.42N	135.44 E
Tana bru	7	Ga	70.16N	28.10 E
Tanacross	40	Kd	63.23N	143.21W
Tanafjorden	7	Ga	70.54N	28.40 E
Tanaga	40a	Cb	51.50N	178.00W
Tanagro	14	Jj	40.38N	15.14 E
Tanagura	29	Gc	37.02N	140.23 E
Tanahbala, Pulau-	26	Cg	0.25S	98.25 E
Tanahgrogot	26	Gg	1.55S	116.12 E
Tanahjampea, Pulau-	26	Hh	7.05S	120.42 E
Tanahmasa, Pulau-	26	Cg	0.12S	98.27 E
Tanah Merah	26	De	5.48N	102.09 E
Tanahmerah	26	Lh	6.05S	140.17 E
Tanakpur	25	Gc	29.05N	80.07 E
Tanalyk	17	Ij	51.46N	58.45 E
Tanami	59	Fc	19.59S	129.43 E
Tanami Desert	57	Eg	20.00S	132.00 E
Tan An	25	Lf	10.32N	106.25 E
Tanana	40	Ic	65.10N	152.05W
Tanana	38	Dc	65.09N	151.55W
Tanapag	64b	Ba	15.14N	145.45 E
Tanapag, Puetton-	64b	Ba	15.14N	145.44 E
Tanāqīb, Ra's at-	24	Mi	27.50N	48.53 E
Tanaro	14	Ce	45.01N	8.47 E
Tanba-Sanchi	29	Dd	35.15N	135.35 E
Tancheng	28	Eg	34.37N	118.20 E
Tanch'ŏn	27	Mc	40.25N	128.57 E
Tancitaro, Pico de-	47	De	19.26N	102.18W
Tanda	34	Ed	7.48N	3.10W
Tanda, Lac-	34	Eb	15.45N	4.42W
Tandag	26	Ie	9.04N	126.12 E
Tandaltī	35	Ec	13.01N	31.52 E
Tăndărei	15	Ke	44.39N	27.40 E
Tandijungbalai	26	Cf	2.58N	99.48 E
Tandil	53	Ki	37.20S	59.05W
Tandil, Sierras del-	55	Cm	37.24S	59.06W
Tandjilé [3]	35	Bd	9.30N	16.30 E
Tando Ādam	25	Dc	25.46N	68.40 E
Tandsjöborg	7	Df	61.42N	14.43 E
Tanḑubāyah	35	Db	18.40N	28.37 E
Taneatua	62	Gc	38.04S	177.00 E
Tane-Ga-Shima	27	Ne	30.40N	131.00 E
Taneichi	29	Ga	40.24N	141.43 E
Tan Emellel	32	Id	27.28N	9.45 E
Tanew	10	Sf	50.27N	22.16 E
Tanezrouft	30	Gf	24.00N	0.45W
Tanezzuft	33	Bd	25.51N	10.19 E
Tanf, Jabal at-	24	Hf	33.30N	38.42 E
Tanga [3]	36	Gd	5.30S	38.00 E
Tanga	31	Ki	5.04S	39.06 E
Tangail	25	Hd	24.15N	89.55 E
Tanga Islands	57	Ge	3.30S	153.15 E
Tangalla	25	Gg	6.01N	80.48 E
Tanganyika [2]	36	Fd	6.00S	35.00 E
Tanganyika, Lac-= Tanganyika, Lake- (EN)	30	Ji	6.00S	29.30 E
Tanganyika, Lake-	30	Ji	6.00S	29.30 E
Tanganyika, Lake- (EN)= Tanganyika, Lac-	30	Ji	6.00S	29.30 E
Tangará	54	Ke	6.11S	35.49W
Tangarare	63a	Dc	9.35S	159.39 E
Tangdan → Dongchuan	27	Hf	26.07N	103.05 E
Tāngehgol	24	Pd	37.25N	55.50 E
Tanger=Tangier (EN) [3]	32	Fb	35.45N	5.45W
Tanger=Tangier (EN)	31	Ge	35.48N	5.48W
Tangerang	26	Eh	6.11S	106.37 E
Tangermünde	10	Hd	52.33N	11.57 E
Tanggu	27	Kd	39.00N	117.36 E
Tanggula Shan (Dangla Shan)	21	Lf	33.00N	92.00 E
Tanggula Shankou	27	Fe	32.42N	92.27 E
Tanggulashanqu/Tuotuohe	22	Lf	34.15N	92.29 E
Tang He	28	Bh	32.10N	112.20 E
Tanghe	27	Je	32.37N	112.57 E
Tangier (EN)=Tanger	31	Ge	35.48N	5.48W
Tang La	21	Kg	28.00N	89.15 E
Tango	29	Dd	35.44N	135.05 E
Tangra Yumco	21	Kf	31.00N	86.25 E
Tangshan	22	Nf	39.35N	118.09 E
Tanguiéta	34	Fc	10.37N	1.16 E
Tanguro, Rio-	55	Fa	12.36S	52.56W
Tangxian	28	Ce	38.46N	114.58 E
Tangyin	28	Cg	35.54N	114.21 E
Tangyuan	27	Mb	46.45N	129.53 E
Tanhoj	20	Ff	51.33N	105.07 E
Tanhuijo, Arrecife-	48	Kg	21.07N	97.17W
Taniantaweng Shan	27	Ge	30.00N	98.00 E
Tanimbar, Kepulauan-= Tanimbar Islands (EN)	57	Ee	7.30S	131.30 E
Tanimbar Islands (EN)= Tanimbar, Kepulauan-	57	Ee	7.30S	131.30 E
Tanintharyi	25	Jf	13.00N	99.00 E
Tanjung [Indon.]	26	Gg	2.11S	115.23 E
Tanjung [Indon.]	26	Dg	1.23S	103.58 E
Tanjungpandan	26	Eg	2.45S	107.39 E
Tanjungpinang	26	Df	0.55N	104.27 E
Tanjungredep	26	Gf	2.09N	117.29 E
Tanjungselor	26	Gf	2.51N	117.22 E
Tankenberg	12	Ib	52.21N	6.58 E
Tanna, Ile-	57	Hf	19.30S	169.20 E
Tännäs	7	Ce	62.27N	12.40 E
Tanner, Mount-	46	Fb	49.40N	118.34W
Tannis Bugt	8	Dg	57.40N	10.15 E
Tannu-Ola	21	Ld	51.00N	94.00 E
Tano	34	Ed	5.07N	2.56W
Tanout	31	Hg	14.58N	8.53 E
Ţanţā	31	Ke	30.47N	31.00 E
Tan Tan	32	Ed	28.30N	11.02W
Tan-Tan [3]	32	Ed	28.30N	11.00W
Tan Tan Plage	32	Ed	28.26N	11.15W
Tantoyuca	48	Jg	21.21N	98.14W
Tanum	7	Cg	58.43N	11.20 E
Tanzania [1]	31	Ki	6.00S	35.00 E
Tao, Ko-	25	Jf	10.05N	99.52 E
Tao'an (Taonan)	27	Lb	45.20N	122.46 E
Tao'er He	21	Oe	45.42N	124.05 E
Taoghe	37	Cd	20.37S	22.35 E
Tao He	27	Hd	35.50N	103.20 E
Taojiang	28	Bj	28.33N	112.05 E
Taonan → Tao'an	27	Lb	45.20N	122.46 E
Taongi Atoll	57	Hc	14.37N	168.58 E
Taormina	14	Jm	37.51N	15.17 E
Taos	43	Fd	36.24N	105.24W
Taoudenni	31	Gf	22.42N,	3.56W
Taougrite	13	Mh	36.15N	0.55 E
Taounate	32	Gc	34.33N	4.39W
Taounate [3]	32	Gc	34.04N	4.06W
Taoura	14	Cn	36.10N	8.02 E
Taourirt	32	Gc	34.25N	2.54W
Taouz	32	Gc	31.00N	4.00W
Taoyuan	27	Lg	25.00N	121.18 E
Tapa	19	Cd	59.15N	25.59 E
Tapachula	39	Jh	14.54N	92.17W
Tapaga, Cape-	65c	Bb	14.01S	171.23W
Tapah	26	Df	4.11N	101.16 E
Tapajera	55	Fi	28.09S	52.01W
Tapajós, Rio-	52	Kf	2.24S	54.41W
Tapaktuan	26	Cf	3.16N	97.11 E
Tapalqué	55	Bm	36.21S	60.01W
Tapan	26	Dg	2.10S	101.04 E
Tapanahoni Rivier	54	Hc	4.22N	54.27W
Tapanlieh	27	Lg	21.58N	120.47 E
Tapanui	62	Cf	45.57S	169.16 E
Tapauá	54	Fe	5.45S	64.23W
Tapauá, Rio-	52	Jf	5.40S	64.21W
Tapenagá, Río-	55	Ci	28.04S	59.10W
Taperas	55	Bc	17.54S	60.23W
Tapes	56	Jd	30.40S	51.23W
Tapes, Serra do-	55	Fj	30.25S	51.55W
Tapeta	34	Dd	6.29N	8.51W
Taphan Hin	25	Ke	16.12N	100.26 E
Tapili	36	Eb	3.25N	27.40 E
Tapini	60	Di	8.19S	146.59 E
Tapiola, Espoo-	8	Kd	60.11N	24.49 E
Tapiraí	55	Id	19.52S	46.01W
Tapirapuã	55	Db	14.51S	57.45W
Tapolca	10	Nj	46.53N	17.26 E
Tappahannock	44	Ig	37.55N	76.54W
Tappi-Zaki	28	Pd	41.18N	140.22 E
Tappu	29a	Ba	44.04N	141.52 E
Tapsuj	17	Je	62.20N	61.30 E
Tāpti	21	Jg	21.06N	72.41 E
Tapul Group	26	He	5.30N	121.00 E
Tapurucuara	54	Ed	0.24S	65.02W
Taputapu, Cape-	65c	Cb	14.19S	170.50W
Tāqbostān	24	Le	34.30N	46.58 E
Ţaqţaq	24	Ke	35.53N	44.35 E
Taquara	56	Jc	29.39S	50.47W
Taquaral, Serra do-	55	Fb	15.42S	52.30W
Taquarí	55	Fc	17.50S	53.17W
Taquari, Pantanal de-	54	Gg	18.10S	56.30W
Taquari, Rio- [Braz.]	55	Gi	29.56S	51.44W
Taquari, Rio- [Braz.]	55	Hf	23.16S	49.12W
Taquari, Rio- [Braz.]	52	Kg	19.15S	57.17W
Taquari, Serra do-	55	Fd	18.18S	53.49W
Taquaritinga	55	He	21.24S	48.30W
Taquarituba	55	Hf	23.31S	49.15W
Taquaruçu, Rio-	55	Fe	21.35S	52.08W
Tar	18	Id	40.38N	73.26 E
Tara	15	Cf	43.55N	19.25 E
Tara	9	Gh	53.34N	6.35W
Tara [Austl.]	59	Ke	27.17S	150.28 E
Tara [Jap.]	29	Be	33.02N	130.11 E
Tara	20	Ce	56.40N	74.50 E
Tara	19	Hd	56.54N	74.22 E
Tara [Yugo.]	15	Bf	43.21N	18.51 E
Taraba	34	Hd	8.34N	10.15 E
Tarabuco	54	Fg	19.10S	64.57W
Ţarābulus=Tripoli (EN) [3]	33	Bc	32.40N	13.15 E
Ţarābulus [Leb.]=Tripoli (EN)	23	Ec	34.26N	35.51 E
Ţarābulus [Lib.]=Tripoli (EN)	31	Ie	32.54N	13.11 E
Ţarābulus=Tripolitania (EN)	30	Ie	31.00N	14.00 E
Ţarābulus=Tripolitania (EN)	33	Bc	30.00N	15.00 E
Taradale	62	Gc	39.32S	176.51 E
Tarāghin	33	Bd	25.59N	14.26 E
Tarahumara, Sierra-	47	Cc	28.26N	106.50W
Tarakan	22	Ni	3.18N	117.38 E
Tarakan, Pulau-	26	Gf	3.21N	117.36 E
Taraklija	16	Fg	45.57N	28.41 E
Tarama Jima	27	Lg	24.40N	124.40 E
Taran, Mys-	7	Ei	54.57N	19.59 E
Taranaki [2]	62	Fc	39.10S	174.40 E
Tarancón	13	Jd	40.01N	3.00W
Taranga Island	62	Fa	36.00S	174.45 E
Taransay	9	Fd	57.55N	7.10W
Taranto	6	Hg	40.28N	17.14 E
Taranto, Golfo di- = Taranto, Gulf of- (EN)	5	Hg	40.10N	17.20 E
Taranto, Gulf of- (EN) = Taranto, Golfo di-	5	Hg	40.10N	17.20 E
Tarapacá [2]	56	Ga	20.00S	69.20W
Tarapacá	56	Ga	19.55S	69.31W
Tarapaina	63a	Ec	9.23S	161.24 E
Tarapoto	54	Ce	6.30S	76.25W
Taraquá	54	Ec	0.06N	68.28W
Tarara	63a	Bb	6.02S	155.24 E
Tarare	11	Ki	45.54N	4.26 E
Tararua Range	62	Fd	40.40S	175.25 E
Taraščа	16	Ge	49.34N	30.31 E
Tarascon	11	Kk	43.48N	4.40 E
Tarascon-sur-Ariège	11	Hl	42.51N	1.36 E
Tarat	32	Id	26.08N	9.21 E
Tarata	54	Dg	17.27S	70.02W

Index Symbols

- [1] Independent Nation
- [2] State, Region
- [3] District, County
- [4] Municipality
- [5] Colony, Dependency
- Continent
- Physical Region
- Historical or Cultural Region
- Mount, Mountain
- Volcano
- Hill
- Mountains, Mountain Range
- Hills, Escarpment
- Plateau, Upland
- Pass, Gap
- Plain, Lowland
- Delta
- Salt Flat
- Valley, Canyon
- Crater, Cave
- Karst Features
- Depression
- Polder
- Desert, Dunes
- Forest, Woods
- Heath, Steppe
- Oasis
- Cape, Point
- Coast, Beach
- Cliff
- Peninsula
- Isthmus
- Sandbank
- Island
- Atoll
- Rock, Reef
- Islands, Archipelago
- Rocks, Reefs
- Coral Reef
- Well, Spring
- Geyser
- River, Stream
- Waterfall Rapids
- River Mouth, Estuary
- Lake
- Salt Lake
- Intermittent Lake
- Reservoir
- Swamp, Pond
- Canal
- Glacier
- Ice Shelf, Pack Ice
- Ocean
- Sea
- Gulf, Bay
- Strait, Fjord
- Lagoon
- Bank
- Seamount
- Tablemount
- Ridge
- Shelf
- Basin
- Escarpment, Sea Scarp
- Fracture
- Trench, Abyss
- National Park, Reserve
- Point of Interest
- Recreation Site
- Cave, Cavern
- Historic Site
- Ruins
- Wall, Walls
- Church, Abbey
- Temple
- Scientific Station
- Airport
- Port
- Lighthouse
- Mine
- Tunnel
- Dam, Bridge

Tarauacá 54 De 8.10S 70.46W
Tarauacá, Rio 52 Jf 6.42S 69.48W
Taravao 65eFc 17.44S 149.19W
Taravao, Baie de- 65eFc 17.43S 149.17W
Taravo 11a Ab 41.42N 8.48 E
Tarawa Atoll 57 Id 1.25N 173.00 E
Tarawera 62 Gc 39.02S 176.35 E
Tarazi 24 Mg 31.05N 48.18 E
Tarazona 13 Kc 41.54N 1.44W
Tarazona de la Mancha 13 Ke 39.15N 1.55W
Tarbagataj, Hrebet 21 Ke 47.10N 83.00 E
Tarbagatay Shan 27 Db 47.10N 83.00 E
Tarbat Ness 9 Jd 57.50N 3.40W
Tarbert [Scot.-U.K.] 9 Gd 57.54N 6.49W
Tarbert [Scot.-U.K.] 9 Hf 55.52N 5.26W
Tarbes 11 Gk 43.14N 0.05 E
Tarboro 44 Ih 35.54N 77.32W
Tarcăului, Munţii- 15 Jc 46.45N 26.20 E
Tarcoola 59 Gf 30.41S 134.33 E
Tardenois 12 Fe 49.12N 3.40 E
Tardienta 13 Lc 41.59N 0.32W
Tardoire 11 Gi 45.52N 0.14 E
Tardoki-Jani, Gora- 20 Ig 48.50N 137.55 E
Taree 58 Gh 31.54S 152.28 E
Taremert-n-Akli 32 Id 25.53N 5.18 E
Tarentaise 11 Mi 45.30N 6.30 E
Ţarfā', Ra's aţ- 33 Hf 17.02N 42.22 E
Ţarfā', Wādī aţ- 24 Dh 28.38N 30.43 E
Ţarfah, Jazīrat aţ- 33 Hg 14.37N 42.55 E
Tarfaya 31 Ff 27.57N 12.55W
Targa 13 Qi 35.41N 4.09 E
Târgovişki prohod 15 Jf 43.12N 26.30 E
Târgovište 15 Jf 43.15N 26.34 E
Târgovište [2] 15 Jf 43.15N 26.34 E
Tarhankut, Mys- 16 Hg 45.21N 32.30 E
Tarhăus, Vîrful- 15 Jc 46.38N 26.10 E
Tarhūnah 33 Bc 32.26N 13.38 E
Tarhūnī, Jabal at- 33 De 22.12N 22.25 E
Táriba 49 Kj 7.49N 72.13W
Tarif 23 He 24.01N 53.45 E
Tarifa 13 Gh 36.01N 5.36W
Tarifa, Punta de- 13 Ih 36.00N 5.37W
Tarija 53 Jh 21.31S 64.45W
Tarija [2] 54 Fh 21.30S 64.00W
Tarik 64d Bb 7.21N 151.47 E
Tariku 26 Kg 2.55S 138.26 E
Tarīm [Yem.] 23 Gf 16.03N 49.00 E
Tarīm [Sau.Ar.] 24 Fi 27.54N 35.24 E
Tarim Basin (EN) = Tarim Pendi 21 Ke 41.00N 84.00 E
Tarime 36 Fc 1.21S 34.22 E
Tarim He 21 Ke 41.05N 86.40 E
Tarim Pendi=Tarim Basin (EN) 21 Ke 41.00N 84.00 E
Tarin Kowt 23 Kc 32.52N 65.38 E
Taritatu 26 Kg 2.54S 138.27 E
Tarjalan 27 Hb 49.38N 101.59 E
Tarjannevesi 8 Kb 62.10N 24.05 E
Tarjat 27 Gb 48.10N 99.40 E
Tarka, Vallée de- 34 Gc 14.30N 6.30 E
Tarkastad 37 Df 32.00S 26.16 E
Tarkio 45 If 40.27N 95.23W
Tarko-Sale 20 Cd 64.55N 78.05 E
Tarkwa 34 Ed 5.18N 1.59W
Tarlac 22 Oh 15.29N 120.35 E
Tarm 8 Ci 55.55N 8.32 E
Tarma 54 Cf 11.25S 75.42W
Tarn 11 Hj 44.06N 1.02 E
Tarn [3] 11 Hk 43.50N 2.00 E
Tarna 10 Pi 47.31N 19.59 E
Tärnaby 7 Dd 65.43N 15.16 E
Tarn-et-Garonne [3] 11 Hj 44.00N 1.10 E
Tarnica 10 Sg 49.06N 22.47 E
Tarnobrzeg 10 Rf 50.35N 21.41 E
Tarnobrzeg [2] 10 Rf 50.35N 21.40 E
Tarnogród 10 Sf 50.23N 22.45 E
Tarnos 11 Ek 43.32N 1.28W
Tarnów 6 Ie 50.01N 21.00 E
Tarnów [2] 10 Qf 50.00N 21.00 E
Tarnowskie Góry 10 Of 50.27N 18.52 E
Tärnsjö 8 Gd 60.09N 16.56 E
Taro 14 Ef 45.00N 10.15 E
Taron 63a Aa 4.28S 153.04 E
Taroom 58 Fg 25.39S 149.49 E
Taroudant 32 Fc 30.29N 8.52W
Tarpon Springs 44 Fk 28.09N 82.45W
Tarquinia 14 Fh 42.15N 11.45 E
Tarra, Rio- 49 Ki 9.04N 72.27W
Tarrafal 32 Cf 15.17N 23.46W
Tarragona 6 Gg 41.07N 1.15 E
Tarragona [3] 13 Mc 41.10N 1.00 E
Tarraleah 59 Jh 42.10S 146.30 E
Tarrant 44 Di 33.38N 86.46W
Tarrasa 13 Oc 41.34N 2.01 E
Tàrrega 13 Nc 41.39N 1.09 E
Tarsus 23 Db 36.55N 34.53 E
Tart 27 Fd 37.07N 92.57 E
Tartagal 56 Hb 22.32S 63.49W
Tartaro 14 Fe 45.02N 11.30 E
Tartas 11 Fk 43.50N 0.48W
Tartas 20 Ce 55.37N 76.44 E
Tartu 6 Id 58.23N 26.45 E
Tartūs 23 Ec 34.53N 35.53 E
Tarumae-Yama 29a Bb 42.41N 141.23 E
Tarumizu 28 Ki 31.29N 130.42 E
Tarusa 16 Jb 54.43N 37.11 E
Tārūt 24 Ni 26.34N 50.04 E
Tarutau, Ko- 25 Jg 6.35N 99.40 E
Tarutino 16 Ff 46.12N 29.09 E
Tarutung 26 Cf 2.01N 98.58 E
Tarvisio 14 Hd 46.30N 13.35 E
Tarvo 55 Bb 15.06S 60.34W
Tarvo, Rio- 55 Bb 14.47S 61.03W
Tasajera, Sierra- 48 Gc 29.35N 105.35W
Tašanta 20 Dg 49.43N 89.11 E
Tasaral, Ostrov- 18 Ja 46.15N 74.05 E
Tašauz 19 Fg 41.52N 59.59 E
Tašauzskaja Oblast [3] 19 Fg 41.00N 58.40 E
Tasāwah 33 Bd 25.59N 13.29 E
Tasbuget 19 Gg 44.48N 65.38 E
Tasejeva 20 Ee 58.06N 94.01 E
Taseko Lake 46 Da 51.15N 123.35W
Tasendjanet 32 Hd 25.40N 0.59 E
Tashk, Daryācheh-ye- 23 Hd 29.45N 53.35 E
Tasikmalaya 22 Mj 7.20S 108.12 E
Tåsinge 8 Di 55.00N 10.36 E
Tašir (Kalinino) 16 Ni 41.08N 44.14 E
Tasiussaq 41 Gd 73.18N 56.00W
Taskan 20 Kd 62.58N 150.20 E
Taškent 22 Ie 41.20N 69.18 E
Taškentskaja Oblast [3] 19 Gg 41.20N 69.40 E
Taškepri 19 Gh 36.17N 62.38 E
Taškeprinskoje, Vodohranilišče- 18 Df 36.15N 62.40 E
Tasker 34 Hb 15.04N 10.42 E
Taşköprü 24 Fb 41.30N 34.14 E
Taš-Kumyr 19 Hg 41.20N 72.14 E
Taşlıçay 24 Jc 39.38N 43.23 E
Tasman, Mount- 62 De 43.34S 170.09 E
Tasman Basin (EN) 3 Jn 43.00S 158.00 E
Tasman Bay 61 Dh 41.10S 173.15 E
Tasmania 59 Jh 43.00S 147.00 E
Tasmania 57 Fi 43.00S 147.00 E
Tasman Peninsula 59 Jh 43.05S 147.50 E
Tasman Plateau (EN) 3 In 48.00S 148.00 E
Tasman Sea 57 Hh 40.00S 163.00 E
Tăşnad 15 Fb 47.29N 22.35 E
Taşova 24 Gb 40.46N 36.20 E
Tassah, Wādī- 14 Cn 36.35N 8.54 E
Tassara 34 Gb 16.01N 5.39 E
Taštagol 20 Df 52.47N 88.00 E
Tåstrup 8 Ei 55.39N 12.19 E
Tastūr 14 Dn 36.33N 9.27 E
Tasty-Taldy 19 Ge 50.47N 66.31 E
Ţasūj 24 Kc 38.19N 45.21 E
Taşucu 24 Ed 36.19N 33.53 E
Tata [3] 32 Fd 29.40N 8.00W
Tata [Hun.] 10 Oi 47.39N 18.19 E
Tata [Mor.] 32 Fd 29.45N 7.59W
Tataba 26 Hg 1.18S 122.49 E
Tatabánya 10 Oi 47.34N 18.25 E
Tatakoto Atoll 57 Nf 17.20S 138.23W
Tata Mailau 26 Ih 8.55S 125.30 E
Tatarbunary 16 Fg 45.49N 29.35 E
Tatarsk 22 Jd 55.13N 75.58 E
Tatarstan, respublika 19 Fd 55.20N 50.50 E
Tatar Strait (EN)=Tatarski Proliv 21 Qd 50.00N 141.15 E
Tatau 26 Ff 2.53N 112.51 E
Taţāwīn 32 Jc 32.56N 10.27 E
Tateyama 28 Og 34.59N 139.52 E
Tathlina Lake 42 Fd 60.30N 117.30W
Tathlith 23 Ff 19.32N 43.30 E
Tatiščevo 16 Nd 51.40N 45.35 E
Tatla Lake 46 Ca 51.58N 124.25W
Tatla Lake 46 Ca 51.55N 124.36W
Tatlow, Mount- 46 Da 51.23N 123.52W
Tatnam, Cape- 42 Ie 57.16N 91.00W
Tatra Mountains (EN) 5 Hf 49.15N 20.00 E
Tatsuno [Jap.] 29 Dd 34.52N 134.33 E
Tatsuno [Jap.] 29 Ed 35.58N 137.58 E
Tatsuruhama 29 Ec 37.04N 136.53 E
Tatta 25 Dd 24.45N 67.55 E
Tatuí 55 If 23.21S 47.51W
Tatum 45 Ej 33.16N 103.19W
Tatvan 23 Fb 38.30N 42.16 E
Tau 8 Ae 59.04N 5.54 E
Tau [Am.Sam.] 65c Db 14.15S 169.30W
Tau [Ton.] 65b Bc 21.01S 175.00W
Tauá 54 Je 6.01S 40.26W
Taubaté 53 Lh 23.02S 45.33W
Tauberbischofsheim 10 Fg 49.37N 9.40 E
Taučik 19 Fg 44.15N 51.20 E
Tauere Atoll 57 Mf 17.22S 141.30W
Tauern 5 Hf 47.15N 13.15 E
Taufstein 10 Ff 50.31N 9.14 E
Tauhunu 64n Ac 10.25S 161.03W
Tauhunu 64n Ac 10.25S 161.03W
Taujsk 20 Je 59.46N 149.20 E
Taujskaja Guba 20 Je 59.15N 150.00 E
Taukum 18 Jb 44.50N 75.30 E
Taumako 63c Ba 9.57S 167.13 E
Taumarunui 62 Fc 38.52S 175.15 E
Taum Sauk Mountain 45 Kh 37.34N 90.44W
Taunay 55 De 20.18S 56.05W
Taung 37 Ce 27.33S 24.47 E
Taungdwingyi 25 Jd 20.01N 95.33 E
Taunggyi 25 Jd 20.47N 97.02 E
Taungthonlon 25 Jd 24.58N 95.48 E
Taungup 25 Ie 18.51N 94.14 E
Taunton [Eng.-U.K.] 9 Jj 51.01N 3.06W
Taunton [Ma.-U.S.] 44 Le 41.54N 71.06W
Taunus 10 Ef 50.10N 8.15 E
Taunusstein 12 Kd 50.08N 8.10 E
Taupo 61 Eg 38.41S 176.05 E
Taupo, Lake- 61 Eg 38.50S 175.55 E
Tauragė/Tauragé 7 Fi 55.16N 22.19 E
Tauragé/Tauragė 7 Fi 55.16N 22.19 E
Tauranga 58 Ih 37.42S 176.10 E
Taurianova 14 Kl 38.21N 16.01 E
Taurion 11 Hi 45.53N 1.24 E
Taurisano 14 Mk 39.57N 18.13 E
Tauroa Point 62 Ea 35.10S 173.04 E
Taurus Mountains (EN)= Toros Dağları 21 Ff 37.00N 33.00 E
Tauste 13 Kc 41.55N 1.15W
Tauu Islands 57 Ge 4.45S 157.00 E
Tauz 19 Eg 41.01N 45.35 E
Tavālesh, Kūhhā-Ye- 24 Mc 38.42N 48.18 E
Tavas [Tur.] 24 Dc 39.54N 30.03 E
Tavas [Tur.] 24 Cd 37.34N 29.04 E
Tavas Ovasi 15 Ll 37.30N 28.55 E
Tavastehus/Hämeenlinna 7 Ff 61.00N 24.27 E
Tavau/Davos 14 Dd 46.47N 9.50 E
Tavda 19 Gd 58.03N 65.15 E
Tavda 21 Id 57.47N 67.16 E
Tavendroua 63b Cc 16.21S 167.22 E
Taveta 36 Gc 3.24S 37.41 E
Taveuni Island 61 Fc 16.51S 179.58W
Taviano 14 Mk 39.59N 18.05 E
Tavignano 11a Ba 42.06N 9.33 E
Tavira 13 Eg 37.07N 7.39W
Tavistock 9 Ik 50.33N 4.08W
Tavolara 14 Dj 40.55N 9.40 E
Tavoliere 14 Ji 41.35N 15.25 E
Tavolžan 19 He 52.44N 77.30 E
Tavoy → Dawei 22 Lh 14.05N 98.12 E
Tavričanka 28 Kc 43.20N 131.52 E
Tavropoú, Tekhniti Límni- 15 Ej 39.15N 21.40 E
Tavşan Adalari 15 Jj 39.55N 26.05 E
Tavşanlı 24 Cc 39.35N 29.30 E
Tavua 61 Ec 17.27S 177.51 E
Taw 9 Ij 51.04N 4.11W
Tawakoni, Lake- 45 Ij 32.55N 96.00W
Tawas City 43 Kc 44.16N 83.31W
Tawau 22 Ni 4.15N 117.54 E
Tawfīqīyah 35 Ed 9.26N 31.37 E
Ţawīlah, Juzur- 24 Ei 27.35N 33.48 E
Tawitawi Group 26 He 5.10N 120.15 E
Ţawkar 31 Kg 18.26N 37.44 E
Ţāwūq 24 Ke 35.08N 44.27 E
Tawūq Chāy 24 Ke 34.35N 44.31 E
Ţāwurghā', Sabkhat- 33 Cc 31.10N 15.15 E
Tawzar 32 Ic 33.55N 8.08 E
Taxco de Alarcón 48 Jh 18.33N 99.36W
Taxkorgan 27 Cd 37.47N 75.14 E
Tay 9 Je 56.30N 3.30W
Tay, Firth of- 9 Ke 56.28N 3.00W
Tay, Loch- 9 Ie 56.30N 4.10W
Tayandu, Kepulauan- 26 Jh 5.30S 132.15 E
Tayègle 35 Ge 4.02N 44.36 E
Taylor [Nb.-U.S.] 45 Gf 41.46N 99.23W
Taylor [Tx.-U.S.] 43 He 30.34N 97.25W
Taylor, Mount- 43 Fd 35.14N 107.37W
Taylorville 45 Lg 39.33N 89.18W
Taymā' 23 Ed 27.38N 38.29 E
Taymyr Peninsula (EN)= Tajmyr, Poluostrov- 21 Mb 76.00N 104.00 E
Tay Ninh 25 Lf 11.18N 106.06 E
Tayside [3] 9 Je 56.30N 3.40W
Taytay 26 Gd 10.49N 119.31 E
Taza [3] 32 Gc 34.00N 4.00W
Taza [Mor.] 31 Ge 34.13N 4.01W
Taza 20 Gf 54.55N 111.05 E
Tāzah Khurmātū 24 Ke 35.13N 44.20 E
Tazawa-Ko 29 Gb 39.43N 140.40 E
Tazawako 29 Gb 39.42N 140.44 E
Tazenakht 32 Fc 30.35N 7.12W
Tazerbo Oasis (EN)= Tāzirbū, Wāḩāt al- 30 Jf 25.45N 21.00 E
Tazewell [Tn.-U.S.] 44 Fg 36.27N 83.34W
Tazewell [Va.-U.S.] 44 Gg 37.07N 81.34W
Tāzīāzet 32 De 20.55N 15.40W
Tazin Lake 42 Ge 59.48N 109.05W
Tāzirbū, Wāḩāt al-=Tazerbo Oasis (EN) 30 Jf 25.45N 21.00 E
Tazlău 15 Jc 46.16N 26.47 E
Tazmalt 13 Qh 36.43N 4.08 E
Tazouikert 34 Ea 21.46N 1.13W
Tazovskaja Guba 17 Qb 69.05N 76.00 E
Tazovski 20 Cc 67.28N 78.42 E
Tazrouk 32 Ie 23.27N 6.14 E
Tazumal 49 Cg 14.00N 89.40W
Tbilisi 6 Kg 41.43N 44.49 E
Tchad=Chad (EN) 31 Ig 15.00N 19.00 E
Tchad, Lac-=Chad, Lake-(EN) 30 Ig 13.20N 14.00 E
Tchamba [Cam.] 34 Hd 8.37N 12.48 E
Tchamba [Togo] 34 Fd 9.02N 1.25 E
Tchibanga 36 Bc 2.51S 11.02 E
Tchien 34 Dd 6.04N 8.08W
Tchigaï, Plateau du- 30 If 21.30N 14.50 E
Tchin Tabaraden 34 Gb 15.58N 5.50 E
Tcholliré 34 Hd 8.24N 14.10 E
Tczew 10 Ob 54.06N 18.47 E
Tea, Rio- 54 Ed 0.30S 65.09W
Teaca 15 Hc 46.55N 24.31 E
Teacapán 48 Gf 22.33N 105.45W
Teaiti Point 64p Bb 21.11S 159.47W
Te Anau 62 Bf 45.25S 167.43 E
Te Anau, Lake- 61 Ci 45.15S 167.45 E
Teano 14 Ii 41.15N 14.04 E
Teapa 48 Mi 17.33N 92.57W
Te Araroa 61 Eg 37.38S 178.22 E
Te Aroha 62 Fb 37.32S 175.42 E
Tea Tree 59 Gd 22.11S 133.17 E
Te Atu Kura 64p Bb 21.14S 159.45W
Te Awamutu 62 Fc 38.00S 175.19 E
Teberda 16 Lh 43.28N 41.43 E
Tébessa 31 He 35.24N 8.07 E
Tébessa [3] 32 Ic 35.00N 8.45 E
Tébessa, Oued- 14 Bo 35.48N 7.53 E
Tebicuary, Rio- [Par.] 55 Ch 26.36S 58.16W
Tebicuary, Rio- [Par.] 55 Dh 26.26S 58.51W
Tebingtinggi [Indon.] 26 Dg 3.36S 103.05 E
Tebingtinggi [Indon.] 26 Cf 3.20N 99.09 E
Tebulosmta, Gora- 16 Nh 42.33N 45.16 E
Teča 17 Kh 56.17N 61.59 E
Tecate 47 Ab 32.34N 116.38W
Tecer Dağları 24 Gc 39.27N 37.11 E
Techirghiol 15 Le 44.03N 28.36 E
Tecka 56 Ff 43.29S 70.48W
Tecklenburg 12 Jb 52.13N 7.50 E
Tecomán 47 De 18.55N 103.53W
Tecomate, Laguna- 48 Ji 16.45N 99.25W
Tecoripa 48 Ec 28.37N 109.57W
Tecpan de Galeana 47 De 17.15N 100.41W
Tecuala 47 Cd 22.23N 105.27W
Tecuci 15 Kd 45.52N 27.25 E
Tedegra 35 Ba 20.46N 15.34 E
Tedori-Gawa 29 Ec 36.29N 136.28 E
Tedžen 21 If 37.24N 60.38 E
Tedženstroj 19 Gh 36.54N 60.53 E
Teeli 20 Ef 50.57N 90.18 E
Teenuse Jõgi/Tenuze 7 Jf 58.44N 23.58 E
Tees 9 Lg 54.34N 1.16W
Tees Bay 9 Lg 54.35N 1.05W
Teesside → Middlesbrough 6 Fe 54.35N 1.14W
Tefé 53 Jf 3.22S 64.42W
Tefé, Rio- 54 Fd 3.35S 64.47W
Tefedest 32 Ie 24.40N 5.30 E
Tefenni 24 Cd 37.18N 29.47 E
Tegal 22 Mj 6.52S 109.08 E
Tegea (EN) = Teyéa 15 Fl 37.27N 22.25 E
Tegelen 12 Ic 51.20N 6.08 E
Tegernsee 10 Hi 47.43N 11.46 E
Tegina 34 Gc 10.04N 6.11 E
Tégoua 63b Ca 13.15S 166.37 E
Tegucigalpa 39 Kh 14.06N 87.13W
Teguidda I-n-Tessoum 34 Gb 17.26N 6.39 E
Teguldet 20 De 57.20N 88.20 E
Tehachapi 46 Fi 35.08N 118.27W
Tehachapi Mountains 46 Fi 34.56N 118.40W
Tehamiyam 35 Fb 18.20N 36.32 E
Te Hapua 61 Df 34.30S 172.55 E
Tehaupoo 65eFc 17.49S 149.18W
Tehek Lake 42 Hd 64.55N 95.30W
Téhini 34 Ed 9.36N 3.40W
Tehi-n-Isser 32 Ie 24.48N 8.08 E
Tehoru 26 Ig 3.23S 129.30 E
Tehrān 22 Hf 35.40N 51.26 E
Tehrān→ Markazi [3] 23 Hb 35.30N 51.30 E
Tehuacán 47 Ee 18.27N 97.23W
Tehuantepec 47 Ee 16.20N 95.14W
Tehuantepec, Golfo de-= Tehuantepec, Gulf of- (EN) 38 Jh 16.00N 94.50W
Tehuantepec, Gulf of- (EN) =Tehuantepec, Golfo de- 38 Jh 16.00N 94.50W
Tehuantepec, Isthmus of- (EN)=Tehuantepec, Istmo de- 38 Jh 17.00N 94.30W
Tehuantepec, Istmo de-= Tehuantepec, Isthmus of- (EN) 38 Jh 17.00N 94.30W
Tehuantepec Ridge (EN) 47 Ef 13.30N 98.00W
Tehuata Atoll 57 Mf 16.50S 141.55W
Teiga Plateau 35 Db 15.38N 25.40 E
Teignmouth 9 Jk 50.33N 3.30W
Teili/Delet 8 Id 60.15N 20.35 E
Teith 9 Ie 56.14N 4.20W
Teiuş 15 Gc 46.12N 23.41 E
Teixeira Pinto 34 Bc 12.04N 16.02W
Teja 20 Ed 60.27N 92.38 E
Tejkovo 19 Ed 56.50N 40.34 E
Tejo=Tagus (EN) 5 Fh 38.40N 9.24W
Teju 25 Jc 27.55N 96.10 E
Te Kaha 62 Gb 37.44S 177.41 E
Te Kao 62 Ea 34.39S 172.58 E
Tekapo, Lake- 62 De 43.50S 170.30 E
Te Karaka 62 Gc 38.28S 177.52 E
Tekax 48 Og 20.12N 89.17W
Teke 15 Mh 41.04N 29.39 E
Teke 15 Jh 41.21N 26.57 E
Teke Burun [Tur.] 15 Ji 40.02N 26.10 E
Teke Burun [Tur.] 15 Jk 38.05N 26.36 E
Tekeli 19 Hg 44.48N 78.57 E
Tekes 27 Dc 43.10N 81.43 E
Tekes He 27 Dc 43.35N 82.30 E
Tekeze 35 Fc 14.20N 35.50 E
Tekija 15 Fe 44.41N 22.25 E
Tekiliktag 27 Dd 36.35N 80.20 E
Tekirdağ 23 Ca 40.59N 27.31 E
Tekman 24 Ic 39.38N 41.31 E
Te Kopuru 62 Eb 36.02S 173.55 E
Te Kou 64p Bb 21.14S 159.46W
Tekouiat 32 He 22.20N 2.30 E
Tekro 35 Cb 19.34N 20.57 E
Te Kuiti 62 Fc 38.20S 175.10 E
Tela 47 Ge 15.44N 87.27W
Telagh 32 Gc 34.47N 0.34W
Telatai 34 Fb 16.31N 1.30 E
Telavåg 7 Af 60.16N 4.49 E
Telavi 19 Eg 41.55N 45.29 E
Tel Aviv-Yafo 22 Ff 32.04N 34.46 E
Telč 10 Lg 49.11N 15.27 E
Telchac Puerto 48 Og 21.21N 89.16W
Telciu 15 Hb 47.26N 24.24 E
Tele 36 Db 2.48N 23.54 E
Teleac 15 Hc 46.41N 24.48 E
Teleckoje Ozero 20 Df 51.30N 87.45 E
Telefomin 60 Ci 5.08S 141.31 E
Telegraph Creek 42 Ee 57.54N 131.09W
Telekitonga 65b Bb 20.24S 174.32W
Telekivavau'u 65b Bb 20.19S 174.32W
Telêmaco Borba 55 Gg 24.23S 50.28W
Telemark [2] 7 Bg 59.30N 8.40 E
Telemark 8 Ce 59.30N 8.45 E
Telén 56 Ge 36.16S 65.30W
Telen 26 Gf 0.26N 116.42 E
Teleneşty 15 Lb 47.30N 28.16 E
Teleno 13 Fb 42.21N 6.23W
Teleorman 15 If 43.52N 25.26 E
Teleorman [2] 15 If 44.10N 25.15 E
Telertheba, Djebel- 32 Ie 24.10N 6.51 E
Telescope Peak 46 Gh 36.10N 117.05W
Telescope Point 51p Bb 12.08N 61.36W
Telese 14 Ii 41.13N 14.32 E
Teles Pires, Rio- = São Manuel, Rio- 52 Kf 7.21S 58.03W
Telfān, Hadjer- 35 Bc 12.05N 18.57 E
Telford 9 Ki 52.40N 2.30W
Telgte 12 Jc 51.59N 7.47 E
Télimélé 34 Cc 10.54N 13.02W
Teljo, Jabal- 35 Dc 14.42N 25.56 E
Tell al Ubaid 24 Lg 30.59N 46.01 E
Tellaro 14 Jn 36.50N 15.06 E
Tell Atlas (EN)=Atlas Tellien 30 He 36.00N 2.00 E
Tell City 44 Dg 37.57N 86.46W
Teller 40 Fc 65.16N 166.22W
Telok Anson 26 Df 4.02N 101.01 E
Teloloapan 48 Jh 18.21N 99.51W
Telposiz, Gora- 5 Lc 63.54N 59.10 E
Telsen 56 Gf 42.24S 66.57W
Telšiai/Telšjaj 19 Cd 55.59N 22.17 E
Telšjaj/Telšiai 19 Cd 55.59N 22.17 E
Teltow 10 Jd 52.24N 13.16 E
Telukbetung 22 Mj 5.27S 105.16 E
Telukbutun 25 Ef 4.13N 108.12 E
Telukdalem 26 Cf 0.34N 97.49 E
Têma 31 Gh 5.37N 0.01W
Temacine 32 Ic 33.01N 6.01 E
Te Manga 64p Bb 21.13S 159.45W
Tematangi Atoll 57 Mg 21.41S 140.40W
Tembenči 20 Ed 64.36N 99.58 E
Témbi 15 Fj 39.53N 22.35 E
Tembilahan 26 Dg 0.19S 103.09 E
Temblador 50 Eh 8.59N 62.44W
Tembleque 13 Ie 39.42N 3.30W
Temblor Range 46 Fi 35.30N 119.55W
Tembo 36 Cd 7.42S 17.17 E
Tembo, Chutes- 30 Ii 8.50S 15.20 E
Tembo, Mont- 36 Bb 1.50N 12.00 E
Tembué 37 Eb 14.51S 32.50 E
Teme 9 Ki 52.09N 2.18W
Temerin 15 Cd 45.25N 19.53 E
Temerloh 26 Df 3.27N 102.25 E
Teminabuan 26 Jg 1.26S 132.01 E
Temir 19 Ff 49.08N 57.09 E
Temir 16 Te 48.31N 57.29 E
Temirlanovka 18 Gc 42.36N 69.17 E
Temirtau 22 Jd 50.05N 72.56 E
Témiscaming 44 Hb 46.44N 79.06W
Témiscouata, Lac- 44 Mb 47.40N 68.50W
Temki 35 Bc 11.29N 18.13 E
Temnikov 7 Ki 54.40N 43.13 E
Temo 14 Cj 40.17N 8.28 E
Temoe, Ile- 57 Ng 23.20S 134.29W
Temores 48 Ed 27.13N 108.15W
Tempe 46 Jj 33.25N 111.56W
Tempio Pausania 14 Dj 40.54N 9.06 E
Temple 43 He 31.06N 97.21W
Templeman, Mount- 46 Ga 50.43N 117.14W
Templemore/An Teampall Mór 9 Fi 52.48N 7.50W
Templin 10 Jc 53.07N 13.30 E
Tempoal, Rio- 48 Jg 21.47N 98.27W
Tempué 36 Ce 13.27S 18.53 E
Temrjuk 16 Jg 45.15N 37.23 E
Temse/Tamise 12 Gc 51.08N 4.13 E
Temuco 53 Ii 38.44S 72.36W
Temuka 62 Df 44.15S 171.16 E
Tena 54 Cd 0.59S 77.48W
Tenacatita, Bahia de- 48 Gh 19.10N 104.50W
Tenala/Tenhola 8 Jd 60.04N 23.18 E
Tenāli 25 Ge 16.15N 80.35 E
Tenancingo de Degollado 48 Jh 18.58N 99.36W
Tenasserim 25 Jf 12.05N 99.01 E
Tenasserim 25 Jf 12.24N 98.37 E
Tenasserim 21 Lh 12.35N 97.52 E
Tenby 9 Ij 51.41N 4.43W
Tence 11 Ki 45.07N 4.17 E
Tench Island 60 Eh 1.38S 150.42 E
Tenda, Col di- 14 Bf 44.09N 7.34 E
Tendaho 35 Gc 11.38N 41.00 E
Tende 11 Nj 44.05N 7.36 E
Tende, Col de- 14 Bf 44.09N 7.34 E
Ten Degree Channel 21 Lh 10.00N 92.30 E
Tendō 29 Gb 38.22N 140.22 E
Tendrara 32 Gc 33.03N 2.00W
Tendre, Mont- 14 Ad 46.36N 6.19 E
Tendrovskaja Kosa 16 Gf 46.15N 31.45 E
Ténenkou 34 Ec 14.28N 4.55W
Tenente Lira, Rio- 55 Db 15.56S 57.39W
Ténéré 30 Ig 17.35N 10.55 E
Ténéré, 'Erg du- 34 Hb 17.35N 10.55 E
Tenerife 30 Ff 28.19N 16.34W
Ténès 32 Hb 36.31N 1.18 E
Ténès, Cap- 13 Nh 36.33N 1.21 E
Teng 25 Je 19.52N 97.45 E
Tengah, Kepulauan- 26 Gh 7.30S 117.30 E
Tengchong 27 Gg 24.59N 98.32 E
Te Nggano, Lake- 60 Gj 11.45S 160.25 E
Tenggarong 26 Gg 0.24S 116.58 E
Tengger Shamo 21 Mf 38.00N 104.10 E
Tengiz, Ozero- 21 Id 50.25N 69.00 E
Tengréla 34 Dc 10.29N 6.24W
Tengréla [3] 34 Dc 10.27N 6.25W
Tengxian [China] 27 Jg 23.18N 110.49 E
Tengxian [China] 28 Dg 35.07N 117.10 E
Tenhola/Tenala 8 Jd 60.04N 23.18 E
Teniente General Rosendo M. Fraga 55 Af 23.45S 62.09W
Tenkāsi 25 Fg 8.58N 77.18 E
Tenke 36 Ee 10.33S 26.08 E
Tenkeli 20 Jb 70.01N 140.55 E
Tenkodogo 34 Ec 11.47N 0.22W
Tenna 14 Hg 43.14N 13.47 E
Tennant Creek 58 Ef 19.40S 134.10 E
Tennessee 38 Kf 37.04N 88.33W
Tennessee [2] 43 Jd 35.50N 85.30W
Tenneville 12 Hd 50.06N 5.32 E
Tenojoki 7 Ga 70.28N 28.18 E
Tenom 26 Ge 5.08N 115.57 E
Tenosique de Pino Suárez 47 Fe 17.29N 91.26W
Tenri 29 Dd 34.36N 135.49 E
Tenryū 29 Ed 34.52N 137.47 E
Tenryū-Gawa 28 Ng 34.35N 137.48 E
Tensift 32 Fc 32.02N 9.21W
Ten Sleep 46 Ld 44.02N 107.27W
Tenterden 12 Cc 51.03N 0.42 E

Index Symbols

[1] Independent Nation
[2] State, Region
[3] District, County
[4] Municipality
[5] Colony, Dependency
Continent
Physical Region
Historical or Cultural Region
Mount, Mountain
Volcano
Hill
Mountains, Mountain Range
Hills, Escarpment
Plateau, Upland
Pass, Gap
Plain, Lowland
Delta
Salt Flat
Valley, Canyon
Crater, Cave
Karst Features
Depression
Polder
Desert, Dunes
Forest, Woods
Heath, Steppe
Oasis
Cape, Point
Coast, Beach
Cliff
Peninsula
Isthmus
Sandbank
Island
Atoll
Rock, Reef
Islands, Archipelago
Rocks, Reefs
Coral Reef
Well, Spring
Geyser
River, Stream
Waterfall Rapids
River Mouth, Estuary
Lake
Salt Lake
Intermittent Lake
Reservoir
Swamp, Pond
Canal
Glacier
Ice Shelf, Pack Ice
Ocean
Sea
Gulf, Bay
Strait, Fjord
Lagoon
Bank
Seamount
Tablemount
Ridge
Shelf
Basin
Escarpment, Sea Scarp
Fracture
Trench, Abyss
National Park, Reserve
Point of Interest
Recreation Site
Cave, Cavern
Historic Site
Ruins
Wall, Walls
Church, Abbey
Temple
Scientific Station
Airport
Port
Lighthouse
Mine
Tunnel
Dam, Bridge

Tenterfield	59	Ke	29.03S	152.01 E
Tenuku	25	Ge	81.40N	16.45 E
Tenuze/Teenuse Jõgi	7	Jf	58.44N	23.58 E
Ten-Zan	29	Be	33.20N	130.08 E
Teocaltiche	48	Hg	21.26N	102.35W
Teodelina	55	Bl	34.11S	61.32W
Teodoro Sampaio	55	Ff	22.31S	52.10W
Teófilo Otoni	53	Lg	17.51S	41.30W
Teotepec, Cerro-	38	Ih	16.50N	100.50W
Teotihuacan	47	Ee	19.44N	98.50W
Teotilán del Camino	48	Kh	18.08N	97.05W
Tepa [Indon.]	26	Ih	7.52S	129.31 E
Tepa [W.F.]	64h	Bb	13.19S	176.09W
Te Pae Roa Ngake o Tuko	64n	Bb	10.23S	161.00W
Tepako, Pointe-	64h	Bb	13.16S	176.08W
Tepalcatepec, Río-	48	Ih	18.35N	101.59W
Tepa Point	64k	Bb	19.07S	169.56W
Tepatitlán de Morelos	48	Hg	20.49N	102.44W
Tepehuanes	47	Cc	25.21N	105.44W
Tepehuanes, Río-	48	Ge	25.11N	105.26W
Tepehuanes, Sierra de-	47	Cc	25.00N	105.40W
Tepelena	15	Di	40.18N	20.01 E
Tepi	35	Fd	7.03N	35.30 E
Tepic	39	Ig	21.30N	104.54W
Teplá	10	Ig	49.59N	12.52 E
Teplá	10	If	50.14N	12.52 E
Teplice	10	Jf	50.39N	13.50 E
Tepoca, Bahía de-	48	Cb	30.15N	112.50W
Tepopa, Cabo-	48	Cc	29.20N	112.25W
Te Puka	64n	Ac	10.26S	161.02W
Te Puke	62	Gb	37.47S	176.20 E
Tequepa, Bahía de-	48	Ii	17.17N	101.05W
Tequila	48	Hg	20.54N	103.47W
Tequisquiapan	48	Jg	20.31N	99.52W
Ter	13	Pb	42.01N	3.12 E
Téra	31	Hg	14.01N	0.45 E
Tera [Port.]	13	Df	38.56N	8.03W
Tera [Sp.]	13	Gc	41.54N	5.44W
Teradomari	29	Fc	37.38N	138.45 E
Terai	21	Kg	26.30N	85.15 E
Teraina Island (Washington)	57	Kd	4.43N	160.24W
Terakeka	35	Ed	5.26N	31.45 E
Teramo	14	Hh	42.39N	13.42 E
Terampa	26	Ef	3.14N	106.14 E
Ter Apel, Vlagtwedde-	12	Jb	52.52N	7.06 E
Terborg, Wisch-	12	Ic	51.55N	6.22 E
Tercan	24	Ic	39.47N	40.24 E
Terceira	30	Ee	38.43N	27.13W
Tercero, Río-	56	Hd	32.55S	62.19W
Terebovlja	16	De	49.18N	25.42 E
Terehovka	28	Kc	43.38N	131.55 E
Terek	16	Nh	43.29N	44.08 E
Terek	5	Kg	43.44N	47.30 E
Térékolé	34	Cb	15.07N	10.53W
Terek-Saj	18	Hd	41.29N	71.13 E
Terenos	55	Ee	20.26S	54.50W
Teresa Cristina	55	Gg	24.48S	51.07W
Teresina	53	Lf	5.05S	42.49W
Teresinha	54	Hc	0.58N	52.02W
Tereška	16	Od	51.50N	46.45 E
Terespol	10	Td	52.05N	23.36 E
Teressa	25	Ig	8.15N	93.10 E
Teresva	16	Cf	47.59N	23.15 E
Terevaka, Cerro-	65d	Ab	27.05S	109.23W
Tergnier	11	Je	49.39N	3.18 E
Terhazza	34	Ea	23.36N	4.56W
Teriberka	7	Ib	69.10N	35.10 E
Teriberka	7	Ib	69.09N	35.08 E
Terlingua Creek	45	El	29.10N	103.36W
Termas de Río Hondo	56	Hc	27.29S	64.52W
Terme	24	Gb	41.12N	36.59 E
Termez	22	If	37.14N	67.16 E
Termini Imerese	14	Hm	37.59N	13.42 E
Termini Imerese, Golfo di-	14	Hl	38.00N	13.45 E
Terminillo	14	Hh	42.28N	13.01 E
Términos, Laguna de-	47	Fe	18.37N	91.33W
Termit, Massif de-	34	Hb	16.15N	11.17 E
Termit-Kaoboul	34	Hb	15.43N	11.37 E
Termoli	14	Ii	42.00N	15.00 E
Termonde/Dendermonde	12	Gc	51.02N	4.07 E
Ternaard, Westdongeradeel-	12	Ha	53.23N	5.58 E
Ternate	25	If	0.48N	127.24 E
Ternej	20	Ig	45.05N	136.35 E
Terneuzen	11	Jc	51.20N	3.50 E
Terni	14	Gh	42.34N	12.37 E
Ternitz	14	Kc	47.43N	16.02 E
Ternois	12	Ed	50.25N	2.19 E
Ternopol	6	If	49.34N	25.38 E
Ternopolskaja Oblast [3]	19	Cf	49.20N	25.35 E
Terpenija, Mys-	20	Jg	48.38N	144.40 E
Terpenija, Zaliv-	21	Qe	49.00N	143.30 E
Terrace	42	Ef	54.31N	128.35W
Terrace Bay	45	Mb	48.47N	87.09W
Terracina	14	Hi	41.17N	13.15 E
Terra de Basto	13	Ec	41.25N	8.00W
Terra Firma	37	Ce	25.36S	23.24 E
Terråk	7	Cd	65.05N	12.25 E
Terralba	14	Ck	39.43N	8.39 E
Terra Rica	55	Ff	22.43S	52.38W
Terrebonne Bay	45	Kl	29.09N	90.35W
Terre-de-Bas	51e	Ac	15.51N	61.39W
Terre-de-Haut	51e	Ac	15.58N	61.35W
Terre Froides	11	Li	45.30N	5.30 E
Terre Haute	43	Jd	39.28N	87.24W
Terrell	45	Hj	32.44N	96.17W
Terre Plaine	11	Jg	47.25N	4.00 E
Terril	13	Gh	37.00N	5.11W
Territoire de Belfort [3]	11	Mg	47.45N	7.00 E
Terruca	13	Fc	41.45N	6.25W
Terry	46	Mc	46.47N	105.19W
Tersa	16	Nd	50.46N	44.42 E
Terschelling	12	Ha	53.21N	5.13 E
Terschelling	11	La	53.24N	5.20 E
Terschelling-West-Terschelling	12	Ha	53.21N	5.13 E
Tersef	35	Bc	12.55N	16.49 E
Terskej-Alatau, Hrebet-	19	Hg	42.10N	78.45 E
Terski Bereg	7	Jc	66.10N	39.30 E
Tersko-Kumski Kanal	16	Ng	44.47N	44.37 E
Terter (Mir-Bašir)	16	Oi	40.19N	46.58 E
Teruel	13	Kd	40.21N	1.06W
Teruel [3]	13	Ld	40.40N	0.40W
Tervakoski	8	Kd	60.48N	24.37 E
Tervel	15	Kf	43.45N	27.24 E
Tervo	8	Lb	62.57N	26.45 E
Tervola	7	Fc	66.05N	24.48 E
Tes	27	Fa	50.27N	93.30 E
Teša	7	Ki	55.38N	42.10 E
Tesalia	54	Cc	2.29N	75.44W
Tesaret	32	Hd	25.40N	2.43 E
Tesdrero, Cerro-	48	Hf	22.47N	103.04W
Teseney	35	Fb	15.07N	36.40 E
Teshekpuk Lake	40	Ib	70.35N	153.30W
Teshikaga	28	Rc	43.29N	144.28 E
Teshio	28	Pb	44.53N	141.44 E
Teshio-Dake	28	Qc	43.58N	142.50 E
Teshio-Gawa	28	Pb	44.53N	141.44 E
Teshio-Sanchi	29a	Ba	44.20N	142.00 E
Tesijn → Tesijn Gol	21	Ld	50.28N	93.04 E
Tesijn Gol (Tesijn)	21	Ld	50.28N	93.04 E
Teslić	14	Lf	44.37N	17.52 E
Teslin	42	Ed	61.34N	134.50W
Teslin	42	Ed	60.09N	132.45W
Teslin Lake	42	Ed	60.00N	132.30W
Teslui	15	He	44.09N	24.29 E
Tesocoma	48	Ed	27.41N	109.16W
Tesouras, Rio-	55	Gb	14.36S	50.51W
Tesouro	55	Fc	16.04S	53.34W
Tessala, Monts du-	13	Li	35.15N	0.45W
Tessalit	31	Hf	20.14N	0.59 E
Tessaoua	34	Gc	13.45N	7.59 E
Tessenderlo	12	Hc	51.04N	5.05 E
Test	9	Lk	50.55N	1.29W
Test, Tizi n'-	32	Fc	30.50N	8.20W
Testa, Capo-	14	Di	41.14N	9.08 E
Têt	11	Jl	42.44N	3.02 E
Tetari, Cerro-	49	Ki	9.59N	72.55W
Tetas, Punta-	56	Fc	23.31S	70.38W
Tete	31	Kj	16.10S	33.36 E
Tete [3]	37	Ec	15.30S	33.00 E
Te Teko	62	Gc	38.02S	176.48 E
Tetepare Island	63a	Cc	8.45S	157.35 E
Téterchen	12	Ie	49.14N	6.34 E
Tetere	63a	Ec	9.25S	160.15 E
Teterev	16	Gd	51.01N	30.08 E
Teterow	10	Ic	53.47N	12.34 E
Teteven	15	Hg	42.55N	24.16 E
Tetiaroa Atoll	57	Mf	17.05S	149.32W
Tetijev	16	Fe	49.23N	29.41 E
Tetjuši	7	Li	54.57N	48.49 E
Teton Peak	46	Ic	47.55N	112.48W
Teton Range	46	Je	43.50N	110.55W
Teton River	46	Jc	47.56N	110.31W
Téfouan	31	Ge	35.34N	5.22W
Tétouan [3]	32	Fb	35.35N	5.30W
Tetovo	15	Dg	42.01N	20.59 E
Tetri-Ckaro	16	Ni	41.33N	44.27 E
Teuco, Río-	55	Bg	25.38S	60.12W
Teufelskopf	12	Ie	49.36N	6.49 E
Teulada	14	Cl	38.58N	8.46 E
Teulada, Capo-	5	Gh	38.52N	8.38 E
Téul de Gonzales Ortega	48	Hg	21.28N	103.29W
Teun, Pulau-	26	Ih	6.59S	129.08 E
Teupasenti	49	Df	14.13N	86.42W
Teuquito, Río-	55	Bg	24.22S	61.09W
Teuri-Tō	29a	Ba	44.25N	141.20 E
Teutoburger Wald	10	Ee	52.10N	8.15 E
Teuva/Östermark	7	Ee	62.29N	21.44 E
Teuz	15	Ec	46.39N	21.33 E
Tevai	63c	Bb	11.37S	166.55 E
Tevaïtoa	65e	Db	16.46S	151.28W
Tevere = Tiber (EN)	5	Hg	41.44N	12.14 E
Teverya	24	Ff	32.47N	35.32 E
Teviot	9	Kf	55.36N	2.26W
Tevli	10	Ud	52.19N	24.23 E
Tevriz	19	Hd	57.34N	72.24 E
Tevšruleh	27	Hb	47.25N	101.55 E
Te Waewae Bay	62	Bg	46.15S	167.30 E
Tewkesbury	9	Kj	51.59N	2.09W
Têwo (Dêngkagoin)	27	He	34.03N	103.21 E
Texada Island	46	Cb	49.40N	124.24W
Texarkana [Ar.-U.S.]	43	Ie	33.26N	94.02W
Texarkana [Tx.-U.S.]	39	Jf	33.26N	94.03W
Texas	59	Ke	28.51S	151.11 E
Texas [2]	43	He	31.30N	99.00W
Texas City	43	If	29.23N	94.54W
Texcoco	48	Jh	19.31N	98.53W
Texel	12	Ga	53.03N	4.47 E
Texel	11	Ka	53.05N	4.45 E
Texel-De Koog	12	Ga	53.07N	4.46 E
Texel-Den Burg	12	Ga	53.03N	4.47 E
Texoma, Lake-	43	He	33.55N	96.37W
Teyéa = Tegea (EN)	15	Fl	37.27N	22.25 E
Teza	7	Jh	56.32N	41.57 E
Teze-Jel	19	Gh	37.55N	60.22 E
Teziutlán	47	Ee	19.49N	97.21W
Tezpur	25	Ic	26.38N	92.48 E
Tha-anne	42	Id	60.31N	94.37W
Thabana Ntlenyana	30	Jk	29.30S	29.15 E
Thabazimbi	37	Dd	24.41S	27.21 E
Thai, Ao- = Thailand, Gulf of- (EN)	21	Mh	10.00N	102.00 E
Thai Binh	25	Ld	20.27N	106.20 E
Thailand (EN) = Muang Thai [1]	22	Mh	15.00N	100.00 E
Thailand, Gulf of- (EN) = Thai, Ao-	21	Mh	10.00N	102.00 E
Thai Nguyen	25	Ld	21.36N	105.50 E
Thal	25	Eb	31.30N	71.40 E
Thālith, Ash Shallāl ath- = Third Cataract (EN)	30	Kg	19.49N	30.19 E
Thamad Bū Ḩashīshah	33	Cd	25.50N	18.05 E
Thamarīd	35	Ib	17.39N	54.02 E
Thame	12	Bc	51.45N	0.59W
Thames	61	Eg	37.08S	175.33 E
Thames	5	Ge	51.28N	0.43 E
Thames River	44	Fd	42.19N	82.28W
Thamūd	23	Gf	17.15N	49.54 E
Thāna	22	Jh	19.12N	72.58 E
Thandaung	25	Je	19.04N	96.41 E
Thanh Hoa	22	Mh	19.48N	105.46 E
Thanh Pho Ho Chi Minh (Saigon)	22	Mh	10.45N	106.40 E
Thanjāvūr	25	Ff	10.48N	79.08 E
Thanlwin = Salween (EN)	21	Lg	16.31N	97.37 E
Thann	11	Ng	47.49N	7.05 E
Thaon-les-Vosges	11	Mf	48.15N	6.25 E
Thap Sakae	25	Jf	11.14N	99.31 E
Thar/Great Indian Desert	21	Ig	27.00N	70.00 E
Thargomindah	59	Ie	28.00S	143.49 E
Tharrawaddy	25	Je	17.39N	95.48 E
Tharros	14	Ck	39.54N	8.28 E
Tharthār, Baḩr ath-	23	Fc	33.59N	43.12 E
Tharthār, Wādī ath-	23	Fc	33.59N	43.12 E
Thasi Gang Dzong	25	Ic	27.19N	91.34 E
Thásos	5	Ig	40.49N	24.42 E
Thásos	15	Hi	40.47N	24.43 E
Thásou, Dhiavlos-	15	Hi	40.49N	24.42 E
Thathlīth, Wādī-	33	He	20.25N	44.55 E
Thau, Bassin de-	11	Jk	43.23N	3.36 E
Thaxted	12	Cc	51.57N	0.22 E
Thaya	10	Mh	48.37N	16.56 E
Thayetchaung	25	Jf	13.52N	98.16 E
Thayetmyo	25	Je	19.19N	95.11 E
Thaywthadangyi Kyun	25	Jf	12.20N	98.00 E
The Alberga River	59	He	27.06S	135.33 E
The Aldermen Islands	62	Gb	37.00S	176.05 E
Thebai = Thebes (EN)	33	Fd	25.43N	32.35 E
Thebes (EN) = Thebai	33	Fd	25.43N	32.35 E
Thebes (EN) = Thívai	15	Gk	38.19N	23.19 E
The Black Sugarloaf	59	Kf	31.20S	151.33 E
The Borders	9	Kf	55.35N	2.50W
The Bottom	50	Ed	17.38N	63.15W
The Broads	9	Oi	52.40N	1.30 E
The Cheviot	9	Kf	55.28N	2.09W
The Cheviot Hills	9	Kf	55.30N	2.10W
The Crane	51q	Bb	13.06N	59.26W
The Dalles	43	Cb	45.36N	121.10W
Thedford	43	Gc	41.59N	100.35W
The Entrance	59	Kf	33.21S	151.30 E
The Everglades	43	Kf	26.00N	81.00W
The Fens	9	Mi	5.24N	0.02W
The Gap	46	Jh	36.25N	111.30W
The Granites	59	Gd	20.35S	130.21 E
The Hague (EN) = Den Haag /'s-Gravenhage	6	Ge	52.06N	4.18 E
The Little Minch	9	Gd	57.35N	6.55W
Thelle	12	De	49.23N	1.51 E
Thelon	38	Jc	64.16N	96.05W
The Macumba River	57	Eg	27.45S	136.50 E
The Merse	9	Kf	55.50N	2.10W
The Naze	12	Dc	51.42N	1.47 E
The Neales River	59	He	28.08S	136.47 E
The Needles	9	Lk	50.39N	1.34W
Theniet el Had	13	Oi	35.32N	2.01 E
Theodore	59	Kd	24.57S	150.05 E
Theológos	15	Hi	40.40N	24.42 E
The Pas	39	Id	53.50N	101.15W
The Pillories	51n	Bb	12.54N	61.12W
Thérain	11	Ie	49.15N	2.27 E
Thermaïkós Kólpos = Salonika, Gulf of- (EN)	5	Ig	40.20N	22.45 E
Thermopílai = Thermopylae (EN)	15	Fk	38.48N	22.32 E
Thermopolis	43	Fc	43.39N	108.13W
Thermopylae (EN) = Thermopílai	15	Fk	38.48N	22.32 E
Thérouanne	12	Ed	50.38N	2.15 E
The Round Mountain	59	Kf	30.27S	152.16 E
The Sandlings	9	Oi	52.10N	1.30 E
Thesiger Bay	42	Fb	71.30N	124.00W
The Slot → New Georgia Sound	60	Fi	8.00S	158.10 E
The Solent Spithead	9	Lk	50.46N	1.20W
Thessalia [2]	15	Fj	39.30N	22.10 E
Thessalia = Thessaly (EN)	5	Ih	39.30N	22.10 E
Thessalía = Thessaly (EN)	15	Fj	39.30N	22.10 E
Thessalon	44	Fb	46.15N	83.34W
Thessaloníki = Salonika (EN)	6	Ig	40.38N	22.56 E
Thessaly (EN) = Thessalía	15	Fj	39.30N	22.10 E
Thessaly (EN) = Thessalía	5	Ih	39.30N	22.10 E
The Stevenson River	59	He	27.06S	135.33 E
Thet	12	Cb	52.24N	0.45 E
Thetford	9	Ni	52.25N	0.45 E
Thetford Mines	44	Lb	46.05N	71.18W
The Twins	62	Ed	41.14S	172.40 E
Theux	12	Hd	50.33N	5.49 E
The Valley	47	Le	18.03N	63.04W
The Warburton River	59	He	27.55S	137.28 E
The Wash	5	Ge	52.55N	0.15 E
The Weald	9	Nj	51.05N	0.05 E
The Witties	49	Ff	14.10N	82.45W
The Wolds	9	Mh	53.20N	0.10W
Thiaucourt-Regniéville	12	Hf	48.57N	5.52 E
Thiberville	12	Ce	49.08N	0.27 E
Thibodaux	45	Kl	29.48N	90.49W
Thief River Falls	43	Hb	48.07N	96.10W
Thiel Mountains	66	Pg	85.15S	91.00W
Thiene	14	Fe	45.42N	11.29 E
Thiérache, Collines de la-	11	Je	49.48N	3.55 E
Thiers	11	Ji	45.51N	3.34 E
Thiès	31	Fg	14.48N	16.56W
Thiès [3]	34	Bc	14.45N	16.50W
Thiesi	14	Cj	40.31N	8.43 E
Thika	36	Gc	1.03S	37.05 E
Thikombia	61	Fc	15.44S	179.55W
Thimerais	11	Hf	48.40N	1.20 E
Thimphu	22	Kg	27.28N	89.39 E
Thio	61	Cd	21.37S	166.14 E
Thionville	11	Me	49.22N	6.10 E
Thiou	34	Ec	13.48N	2.40W
Thira	15	Im	36.25N	25.26 E
Thíra = Thira (EN)	15	Im	36.24N	25.26 E
Thira (EN) = Thíra	15	Im	36.24N	25.26 E
Thirasía	15	Im	36.25N	25.20 E
Third Cataract (EN) = Thālith, Ash Shallāl ath-	30	Kg	19.49N	30.19 E
Thirsk	9	Lg	54.14N	1.20W
Thisted	7	Bh	56.57N	8.42 E
Thithia	63d	Cb	17.45S	179.18W
Thiu Khao Phetchabun	25	Ke	16.20N	100.55 E
Thívai = Thebes (EN)	15	Gk	38.19N	23.19 E
Thiviers	11	Gi	45.25N	0.55 E
Thlewiaza	42	Id	60.28N	94.42W
Thoa	42	Gd	60.31N	109.45W
Tho Chu, Dao-	25	Kg	9.00N	103.50 E
Thoen	25	Je	17.41N	99.14 E
Tholen	12	Gc	51.32N	4.13 E
Tholen	11	Kc	51.35N	4.05 E
Tholey	12	Je	49.29N	7.04 E
Thomasset, Rocher-	57	Nf	10.21S	138.25W
Thomaston	44	Ei	32.54N	84.20W
Thomasville [Al.-U.S.]	44	Dj	32.18N	87.47W
Thomasville [Ga.-U.S.]	43	Ke	30.50N	83.59W
Thomasville [N.C.-U.S.]	44	Gh	35.53N	80.05W
Thompson	42	He	55.45N	97.45W
Thompson Falls	46	Hc	47.36N	115.21W
Thompson River	45	Jg	39.45N	93.36W
Thompson Sound	62	Bf	45.10S	167.00 E
Thomsen	42	Fb	73.40N	119.30W
Thomson	44	Fi	33.28N	82.30W
Thomson River	59	Ie	25.11S	142.53 E
Thomson's Falls	36	Gb	0.02N	36.22 E
Thon	12	Fe	49.53N	3.55 E
Thon Buri	22	Mh	13.43N	100.24 E
Thong Pha Phum	25	Jf	14.44N	98.38 E
Thongwa	25	Je	16.46N	96.32 E
Thonon-les-Bains	11	Mh	46.22N	6.29 E
Thoreau	45	Bi	35.24N	108.13W
Thornaby-on-Tees	9	Lg	54.34N	1.18W
Thornbury	61	Ci	46.17S	168.06 E
Thorney	12	Bb	52.37N	0.06W
Thornhill	9	Jf	55.18N	3.40W
Thorshavn	6	Fc	62.01N	6.46W
Thouars	11	Fh	46.58N	0.13W
Thouet	11	Fg	47.17N	0.06W
Thrace (EN) = Thráki	15	Jh	41.20N	26.45 E
Thrace (EN) = Thráki	5	Ig	41.20N	26.45 E
Thrace (EN) = Trakya	15	Jh	41.20N	26.45 E
Thrace (EN) = Trakya	5	Ig	41.20N	26.45 E
Thráki [2]	15	Ih	41.10N	25.30 E
Thráki = Thrace (EN)	5	Ig	41.20N	26.45 E
Thráki = Thrace (EN)	15	Jh	41.20N	26.45 E
Thrakikón Pélagos	15	Hi	40.30N	25.00 E
Thrapston	12	Bb	52.24N	0.32W
Three Forks	43	Eb	45.54N	111.33W
Three Kings Islands	57	Ih	34.10S	172.10 E
Three Kings Trough (EN)	3	Jm	32.00S	170.30 E
Three Points, Cape-	30	Gh	4.45N	2.06W
Three Rivers	44	Ee	41.57N	85.38W
Three Sisters Islands	63a	Ed	10.10S	161.57 E
Throckmorton	45	Gj	33.11N	99.11W
Throssel, Lake-	59	Ee	27.25S	124.15 E
Thua	36	Gc	1.17S	40.00 E
Thuin	11	Kd	50.20N	4.17 E
Thule	66	Ad	59.27S	27.19W
Thule/Qânâq	67	Od	77.35N	69.40W
Thule, Mount -	42	Jb	73.00N	78.27W
Thun	14	Bd	46.45N	7.40 E
Thunder Bay	39	Ke	48.23N	89.15W
Thunder Bay [Mi.-U.S.]	44	Fc	45.04N	83.25W
Thunder Bay [Ont.-Can.]	45	Lb	48.24N	89.00W
Thunder Butte	45	Fd	45.19N	101.53W
Thuner See	14	Bd	46.40N	7.45 E
Thung Song	25	Jg	8.11N	99.41 E
Thur	14	Cc	47.36N	8.35 E
Thurgau [2]	14	Dc	47.40N	9.10 E
Thüringen	10	Gf	50.40N	11.00 E
Thüringer Wald = Thuringian Forest (EN)	5	He	50.30N	11.00 E
Thuringian Forest (EN) = Thüringer Wald	5	He	50.30N	11.00 E
Thurles/Durlas	9	Fi	52.41N	7.49W
Thurrock	9	Nj	51.28N	0.20 E
Thursday Island	59	Ib	10.35S	142.13 E
Thurso	6	Fd	58.35N	3.32W
Thurso	9	Jc	58.35N	3.30W
Thurston Island	66	Pf	72.06S	99.00W
Thury-Harcourt	12	Bf	48.59N	0.29W
Thusis/Tusaun	14	Dd	46.42N	9.26 E
Thuwayrāt, Nafūd ath-	24	Kj	26.00N	44.50 E
Thuy Phong	25	Lf	11.14N	108.43 E
Thwaites Iceberg Tongue	66	Of	74.00S	108.30W
Thy	8	Ch	57.00N	8.30 E
Thyborøn	8	Ch	56.42N	8.13 E
Tianbaoshan	28	Jc	42.57N	128.57 E
Tianchang	27	Ke	32.37N	119.00 E
Tiandong (Pingma)	27	Ig	23.40N	107.09 E
Tian'e (Liupai)	27	If	25.05N	107.12 E
Tianguá	54	Jd	3.44S	40.59W
Tianjin = Tientsin (EN)	22	Nf	39.08N	117.12 E
Tianjin Shi (T'ien-chin Shih) [4]	27	Kd	39.08N	117.12 E
Tianjun (Xinyuan)	22	Lf	37.18N	99.15 E
Tianlin (Leli)	27	Ig	24.22N	106.11 E
Tian Ling	28	Kb	44.24N	130.10 E
Tianmen	27	Je	30.40N	113.10 E
Tianmu Shan	28	Ei	30.31N	119.36 E
Tianmu Xi	28	Ej	29.59N	119.24 E
Tianqiaoling	27	Mc	43.35N	129.35 E
Tian Shan	21	Ke	42.00N	80.01 E
Tianshan → Ar Horqin Qi	27	Lc	43.55N	120.05 E
Tianshifu	27	Lc	41.15N	124.20 E
Tianshui	22	Mf	34.35N	105.43 E
Tiantai	28	Fj	29.08N	121.00 E
Tianwangsi	28	Ei	31.45N	119.12 E
Tianyi → Ningcheng	27	Kc	41.34N	119.25 E
Tianzhen	28	Cd	40.24N	114.05 E
Tianzhen → Gaoqing	28	Df	37.10N	117.50 E
Tianzhuangtai	28	Gd	40.49N	122.06 E
Tiaraju	55	Ej	30.15S	54.23W
Tiarei	65e	Fc	17.32S	149.20W
Tiaret [3]	32	Hc	34.50N	1.30 E
Tiaret	31	He	35.20N	1.14 E
Tiaret, Monts de-	13	Ni	35.26N	1.15 E
Tiassalé	34	Ed	5.54N	4.50W
Tiavea	65c	Ba	13.57S	171.24W
Ţīb, Ra's Aţ- = Bon, Cape- (EN)	30	Ie	37.05N	11.03 E
Tibaji	55	Gg	24.30S	50.24W
Tibaji, Rio-	55	Gf	22.47S	51.01W
Tibasti, Sarīr-	30	If	24.00N	17.00 E
Tibati	31	Ih	6.28N	12.38 E
Tiber (EN) = Tevere	5	Hg	41.44N	12.14 E
Tiberina, Val-	14	Gg	43.30N	12.10 E
Tibesti	30	If	21.30N	17.30 E
Tibet (EN) = Xizang Zizhiqu (Hsi-tsang Tzu-chih-ch'ü) [2]	27	Ee	32.00N	90.00 E
Tibet, Plateau of- (EN) = Qing Zang Gaoyuan	21	Kf	32.30N	87.00 E
Tibidabo	13	Oc	41.25N	2.07 E
Tibni	24	He	35.35N	30.49 E
Tibro	8	Ff	58.26N	14.10 E
Tibú	49	Ki	8.40N	72.42W
Tibugà, Golfo de-	54	Cb	5.45N	77.20W
Tiburón, Capo-	49	Ii	8.42N	77.21W
Tiburon, Isla-	47	Bc	29.00N	112.25W
Ticao	26	Hd	12.31N	123.42 E
Tice	44	Gl	26.41N	81.49W
Tichá Orlice	10	Mf	50.09N	16.05 E
Tîchît	31	Gg	18.26N	9.31W
Tîchît, Dahr-	32	Ff	18.30N	9.25W
Tichka, Tizi n'-	32	Fc	31.17N	7.21W
Tichla	32	Ee	21.36N	14.58W
Ticino [2]	14	Cd	46.20N	9.00 E
Ticino	14	De	45.09N	9.14 E
Ticul	47	Gd	20.24N	89.32W
Tidaholm	7	Cg	58.11N	13.57 E
Tidan	8	Ef	58.42N	13.48 E
Tiddim	25	Id	23.22N	93.40 E
Tidikelt, Plaine du-	30	Hf	27.00N	1.30 E
Tidirhine	32	Gc	34.51N	4.31W
Tidjikja	31	Fg	18.32N	11.27W
Tidore	26	If	0.40N	127.26 E
Tidra, Ile-	30	Fg	19.44N	16.24W
Tiebissou	34	Dd	7.10N	5.13W
Tiechang	28	Id	41.40N	126.12 E
Tiel	11	Lc	51.54N	5.25 E
Tieli	27	Mb	47.04N	128.02 E
Tieling	28	Gc	42.18N	123.51 E
Tielt	11	Jc	51.00N	3.20 E
Tienba	34	Dd	8.30N	7.10W
T'ien-chin Shih → Tianjin Shi [4]	27	Kd	39.08N	117.12 E
Tienen/Tirlemont	12	Gd	50.48N	4.57 E
Tiengemeten	12	Gc	51.45N	5.20 E
Tientsin (EN) = Tianjin	22	Nf	39.08N	117.12 E
Tieroko, Tarso-	35	Ba	20.45N	17.52 E
Tierp	7	Df	60.20N	17.30 E
Tierra Amarilla [Chile]	56	Fc	27.29S	70.17W
Tierra Amarilla [N.M.-U.S.]	45	Ch	36.42N	106.33W
Tierra Blanca	47	Ee	18.27N	96.21W
Tierra Colorada	48	Ji	17.10N	99.35W
Tierra del Fuego [2]	56	Gh	54.00S	67.00W
Tierra del Fuego (EN) = Tierra del Fuego, Isla Grande de-	52	Jk	54.00S	69.00W
Tierra del Fuego, Isla Grande de- = Tierra del Fuego (EN)	52	Jk	54.00S	69.00W
Tierralta	54	Cb	8.10N	76.04W
Tiétar	13	Fe	39.50N	6.01W
Tietê, Rio-	52	Kh	20.40S	51.35W
Tietjerksteradeel	12	Ia	53.12N	6.00 E
Tietjerksteradeel-Bergum	12	Hb	52.17N	5.58 E
Tifariti	32	Ed	26.09N	10.33W
Tiffany Mountain	46	Fb	48.40N	119.56W
Tiffin	44	Fe	41.07N	83.11W
Tifton	43	Ke	31.27N	83.31W
Tiga	63b	Ce	21.08S	167.49 E
Tigalda	40a	Fb	54.05N	165.05W
Tigăneşti	15	If	43.54N	25.22 E
Tighennif	13	Mi	35.25N	0.15 E
Tigil	20	Ke	57.57N	158.20 E
Tigil	20	Ke	57.48N	158.40 E
Tignère	34	Hd	7.22N	12.39 E
Tigray [3]	35	Fc	14.00N	39.00 E
Tigre	48	Hh	19.53N	102.59W
Tigre, Cerro del-	48	Jf	23.03N	99.16W
Tigre, Río- [S.Amer.]	52	If	4.30S	74.10W
Tigre, Río- [Ven.]	50	Eh	9.20N	62.30W
Tigris (EN) = Dicle	21	Gf	31.00N	47.25 E
Tigris (EN) = Dijlah	21	Gf	31.00N	47.25 E
Tigrovy Hvost, Mys-	18	Bc	43.57N	58.45 E
Tiguent	32	Df	17.15N	16.00W
Tiguentourine	32	Id	27.43N	9.33 E
Tigui	35	Bb	18.38N	18.47 E
Tigzirt	13	Qh	36.54N	4.07 E
Tīh, Jabal at-	33	Fd	29.35N	34.00 E
Tīh, Şaḩrā' at- = At Tih Desert (EN)	33	Fc	30.05N	34.00 E
Tihāmat	23	Ff	18.30N	41.30 E
Tihāmat Ash Shām	33	Hf	19.15N	41.10 E

Index Symbols

[1] Independent Nation	Historical or Cultural Region	Pass, Gap	Depression	Coast, Beach	Rock, Reef	Waterfall Rapids	Canal	Lagoon	Escarpment, Sea Scarp	Historic Site	Port
[2] State, Region	Mount, Mountain	Plain, Lowland	Polder	Cliff	Islands, Archipelago	River Mouth, Estuary	Glacier	Bank	Fracture	Ruins	Lighthouse
[3] District, County	Volcano	Delta	Desert, Dunes	Peninsula	Rocks, Reefs	Lake	Ice Shelf, Pack Ice	Seamount	Trench, Abyss	Wall, Walls	Mine
[4] Municipality	Hill	Salt Flat	Forest, Woods	Isthmus	Coral Reef	Salt Lake	Ocean	Tablemount	National Park, Reserve	Church, Abbey	Tunnel
[5] Colony, Dependency	Mountains, Mountain Range	Valley, Canyon	Heath, Steppe	Sandbank	Well, Spring	Intermittent Lake	Sea	Ridge	Point of Interest	Temple	Dam, Bridge
Continent	Hills, Escarpment	Crater, Cave	Oasis	Island	Geyser	Reservoir	Gulf, Bay	Shelf	Recreation Site	Scientific Station	
Physical Region	Plateau, Upland	Karst Features	Cape, Point	Atoll	River, Stream	Swamp, Pond	Strait, Fjord	Basin	Cave, Cavern	Airport	

Tihāmat 'Asīr	33	Hf	17.30N	42.20 E
Tihi Okean=Pacific Ocean (EN)	3	Ki	5.00N	155.00W
Tihoreck	6	Kf	45.51N	40.09 E
Tihuţa, Pasul-	15	Hb	47.15N	25.00 E
Tihvin	19	Dd	59.38N	33.31 E
Tiirismaa	8	Kc	61.01N	25.31 E
Tiji	33	Bc	32.01N	11.22 E
Tijirīt	32	Ee	20.30N	15.00W
Tijuana	39	Hf	32.32N	117.01W
Tijucas	55	Hh	27.14S	48.38W
Tijucas, Baía do-	55	Hh	27.15S	48.31W
Tijucas, Rio-	55	Hh	27.15S	48.38W
Tijucas, Serra do-	55	Hh	27.16S	49.10W
Tijucas do Sul	55	Hg	25.56S	49.10W
Tijuco, Rio-	55	Gd	18.40S	50.05W
Tikal	39	Kh	17.20N	89.39W
Tikanlik	27	Ec	40.42N	87.38 E
Tikchik Lakes	40	Hd	60.07N	158.35W
Tikehau Atoll	61	Lb	15.00S	148.10W
Tikei, Ile-	61	Mb	14.58S	144.32W
Tikitiki	62	Hb	37.47S	178.25 E
Tikkakoski	8	Kb	62.24N	25.38 E
Tikkurila	8	Kd	60.18N	25.03 E
Tiko	34	Ge	4.05N	9.22 E
Tikopia Island	57	Hf	12.19S	168.49 E
Tikrīt	23	Fc	34.36N	43.42 E
Tikšeozero, Ozero-	7	Hc	66.15N	31.45 E
Tiksi	22	Ob	71.36N	128.48 E
Tiladummati Atoll	25a	Ba	6.50N	73.05 E
Tilamuta	26	Hf	0.30N	122.20 E
Tilburg	11	Lc	51.34N	5.05 E
Tilbury, Gravesend-	9	Nj	51.28N	0.23 E
Tilcara	56	Gb	23.34S	65.22W
Til-Châtel	11	Lg	47.31N	5.10 E
Tileagd	15	Fb	47.04N	22.12 E
Tilemsès	34	Fb	15.37N	4.44 E
Tilemsi, Vallée du-	30	Hg	19.00N	0.02 E
Tilia	32	Gd	27.22N	0.02W
Tiličiki	20	Ld	60.20N	166.03 E
Tiligul	16	Gf	47.07N	30.57 E
Tiligulski Liman	16	Gf	46.50N	31.10 E
Till	9	Kf	55.41N	2.12W
Tillabéry	34	Fc	14.13N	1.27 E
Tillamook	46	Dd	45.27N	123.51W
Tillamook Bay	46	Dd	45.30N	123.53W
Tillanchong	25	Ig	8.30N	93.37 E
Tillberga	8	Ge	59.41N	16.37 E
Tille	11	Lg	47.07N	5.21 E
Tillia	34	Fb	16.08N	4.47 E
Tillières-sur-Avre	12	Df	48.46N	1.04 E
Tillingham	12	Cd	50.58N	0.44 E
Tillsonburg	44	Gd	42.51N	80.44W
Tilly-sur-Seulles	12	Be	49.11N	0.37W
Tiloa	34	Fb	15.04N	2.03 E
Tílos	15	Km	36.25N	27.25 E
Tilpa	59	If	30.57S	144.24 E
Tim	16	Jd	51.37N	37.11 E
Tim	16	Jc	52.15N	37.22 E
Ţimā	33	Fd	26.54N	31.26 E
Timagami	44	Gb	47.00N	80.05W
Timagami, Lake -	42	Jg	46.57N	80.05W
Timane, Río-	55	Be	20.16S	60.08W
Timan Ridge (EN)= Timanski Krjaž	5	Lc	65.00N	51.00 E
Timanski Bereg	17	Eb	68.20N	51.45 E
Timanski Krjaž=Timan Ridge (EN)	5	Lc	65.00N	51.00 E
Timaru	58	Ii	44.24S	171.15 E
Timaševsk	19	Df	45.35N	38.58 E
Timbalier Bay	45	Kl	29.10N	90.20W
Timbalier Island	45	Kl	29.04N	90.28W
Timbaúba	54	Ke	7.31S	35.19W
Timbédra	32	Ff	16.14N	8.10W
Timbó	55	Hh	26.50S	49.18W
Timbuktu (EN)= Tombouctou	31	Gg	16.46N	2.59W
Timedouine, Ras-	13	Qh	36.28N	4.09 E
Timétrine	34	Eb	19.20N	0.42W
Timétrine	34	Eb	19.27N	0.26W
Tímfi Óros	15	Dj	39.57N	20.50 E
Timfristós	15	Ek	38.57N	21.49 E
Timia	34	Gb	18.04N	8.40 E
Timimoun	31	Hf	29.15N	0.15 E
Timimoun, Sebkha de-	32	Hd	29.00N	0.05 E
Timiris, Cap—	32	Df	19.23N	16.32W
Timirjazevo	19	Ge	53.45N	66.33 E
Timiş	15	De	44.51N	20.39 E
Timiş [2]	15	Ed	45.38N	21.13 E
Timiskaming, Lake-	44	Hb	47.35N	79.35W
Timişoara	6	If	45.45N	21.13 E
Ti-m-Merhsoï	34	Gb	18.00N	5.40 E
Timmins	39	Ke	48.28N	81.20W
Timmoudi	32	Gd	29.19N	1.08W
Timms Hill	45	Kd	45.27N	90.11W
Timok	15	Fe	44.13N	22.40 E
Timon	54	Je	5.06S	42.49W
Timor, Laut-=Timor Sea (EN)	57	Df	11.00S	128.00 E
Timor, Pulau-	21	Oj	8.50S	126.00 E
Timor Sea (EN)=Timor, Laut-	57	Df	11.00S	128.00 E
Timor Timur [3]	26	Ih	8.35S	126.00 E
Timor Trough (EN)	3	Ij	9.50S	126.00 E
Timote	56	He	35.21S	62.14W
Timotes	54	Db	8.59N	70.44W
Timpton	20	He	58.43N	127.12 E
Timrå	7	De	62.29N	17.18 E
Tims Ford Lake	44	Dh	35.15N	86.10W
Tīn, Ra's at-	33	Dc	32.37N	23.08 E
Tinaca Point	21	Oi	5.33N	125.20 E
Tinaco	50	Bh	9.42N	68.26W
Tinakula	63c	Ab	10.24S	165.47 E
Ti-n-Alkoum	32	Je	24.34N	10.11 E
Ti-n-Amzi [Alg.]	32	He	20.32N	4.37 E
Ti-n-Amzi [Niger]	34	Fb	17.54N	4.32 E
Tinaquillo	50	Bh	9.55N	68.18W
Tinchebray	12	Bf	48.46N	0.44W
Tindalo	35	Ed	5.39N	31.03 E
Tindari	14	Jl	38.10N	15.04 E
Tindila	34	Dc	10.16N	8.15W
Tindouf	31	Gf	27.42N	8.09W
Tindouf, Hamada de-	32	Fc	27.45N	8.25W
Tindouf, Sebkha de-	32	Fc	27.45N	7.35W
Tinée	11	Nk	43.55N	7.11 E
Tineo	13	Fa	43.20N	6.25W
Ti-n-Essako	34	Fb	18.27N	2.29 E
Tin Fouye	32	Id	28.15N	7.45 E
Tinghert, Ḩamādat-	30	Hf	28.50N	10.00 E
Tinglev	8	Cj	54.56N	9.15 E
Tingmiarmiut	41	Hf	62.25N	42.15W
Tingo Maria	54	Ce	9.10S	76.00W
Tingri (Xêgar)	27	Ef	28.41N	87.00 E
Tingsryd	7	Dh	56.32N	14.59 E
Tingstäde	8	Hg	57.44N	18.36 E
Tingvoll	7	Be	62.54N	8.12 E
Tinian Channel	64b	Bb	14.54N	145.37 E
Tinian Island	57	Fc	15.00N	145.38 E
Tini Wells	35	Cb	15.02N	22.48 E
Tinkisso	34	Dc	11.21N	9.10W
Tinnelva	8	Ce	59.34N	9.15 E
Tinniswood, Mount-	46	Da	50.19N	123.50W
Tinnoset	8	Ce	59.43N	9.02 E
Tinnsjo	8	Ce	59.54N	8.55 E
Tinogasta	56	Gc	28.04S	67.34W
Tinos	15	Il	37.35N	25.10 E
Tinos	15	Il	37.32N	25.10 E
Tínou, Stenón-	15	Il	37.38N	25.10 E
Tinrhert, Hamada de-	30	Hf	28.50N	10.00 E
Tinrhir	32	Fc	31.31N	5.32W
Tinsukia	25	Jc	27.30N	95.22 E
Tintagel Head	9	Ik	50.41N	4.46W
Tintamarre, Ile-	51b	Bb	18.07N	63.00W
Ti-n-Tarabine	32	Ie	21.16N	7.24 E
Tîntăreni	15	Ge	44.36N	23.29 E
Tintina	56	Hc	27.02S	62.43W
Tinto	13	Fg	37.12N	6.55W
Ti-n-toumma	30	Ig	16.04N	12.40 E
Tinwald	62	De	43.55S	171.43 E
Ti-n-Zaouâtene	31	Hg	19.56N	2.55 E
Tiobraid Árann/Tipperary	9	Ei	52.29N	8.10W
Tiobraid Árann/Tipperary [2]	9	Ei	52.40N	8.20W
Tioga	45	Eb	48.24N	102.56W
Tioman, Pulau-	26	Df	2.48N	104.11 E
Tione di Trento	14	Ed	46.02N	10.43 E
Tioro, Selat-=Tioro, Strait (EN)	26	Hg	4.40S	122.20 E
Tioro Strait (EN)=Tioro, Selat-	26	Hg	4.40S	122.20 E
Tiøtta	7	Cd	65.50N	12.24 E
Tiouilit	32	Df	18.52N	16.10W
Tipasa	13	Oh	36.35N	2.27 E
Tipitapa	47	Gf	12.12N	86.06W
Tipperary/Tiobraid Árann	9	Ei	52.29N	8.10W
Tipperary/Tiobraid Árann [2]	9	Ei	52.40N	8.20W
Tipton, Mount-	46	Hi	35.32N	114.12W
Tip Top Mountain	45	Nb	48.16N	85.59W
Tiptree	12	Cc	51.49N	0.45 E
Tiracambu, Serra do-	54	Id	3.15S	46.30W
Tirahart	32	He	23.45N	2.30 E
Tirān	24	Nf	32.42N	51.09 E
Tirān, Maḑīq-	24	Fi	27.55N	34.28 E
Tirana	6	Hg	41.20N	19.50 E
Tirania	32	Ie	23.08N	9.01 E
Tirano	14	Ed	46.13N	10.10 E
Tiraspol	19	Cf	46.50N	29.37 E
Tirat Karmel	24	Ff	32.46N	34.58 E
Tire	23	Cb	38.04N	27.45 E
Tirebolu	24	Hb	41.00N	38.50 E
Tiree	9	Ge	56.31N	6.49W
Tiree, Passage of-	9	Ge	56.30N	6.30W
Tîrgovişte	15	Ie	44.56N	25.27 E
Tîrgu Bujor	15	Kd	45.52N	27.54 E
Tîrgu Cărbuneşti	15	Ge	44.57N	23.31 E
Tîrgu Frumos	15	Jb	47.12N	27.00 E
Tîrgu Jiu	15	Gd	45.03N	23.17 E
Tîrgu Lăpuş	15	Gb	47.27N	23.52 E
Tîrgu Mureş	6	If	46.33N	24.34 E
Tîrgu Neamţ	15	Jb	47.12N	26.22 E
Tîrgu Ocna	15	Jc	46.17N	26.37 E
Tîrgu Secuiesc	15	Jd	46.00N	26.08 E
Ţîrguşor	15	Le	44.27N	28.25 E
Tirich Mir	21	Jf	36.15N	71.50 E
Tirins	15	Fl	37.36N	22.48 E
Tiririca, Serra da-	55	Ic	17.06S	47.06W
Tiris	30	Ff	23.10N	13.30W
Tiris Zemmour [3]	32	Fe	24.00N	10.00W
Tirlemont/Tienen	12	Gd	50.48N	4.57 E
Tirljanski	17	Ii	54.12N	58.33 E
Tîrnava Mare	15	Gc	46.09N	23.42 E
Tîrnava Mică	15	Gc	46.11N	23.55 E
Tîrnăveni	15	Hc	46.20N	24.17 E
Tirnavos	15	Fj	39.45N	22.17 E
Tiro	34	Cd	9.45N	10.39W
Tirol/Tirolo=Tyrol (EN)	14	Fd	47.00N	11.20 E
Tirol=Tyrol (EN) [2]	14	Fc	47.10N	11.25 E
Tirolo/Tirol=Tyrol (EN)	14	Fd	47.00N	11.20 E
Tiros	55	Jd	19.00S	45.58W
Tirreno, Mar-=Tyrrhenian Sea (EN)	5	Hh	40.00N	12.00 E
Tirschenreuth	10	Ig	49.53N	12.21 E
Tirso	14	Ck	39.53N	8.32 E
Tirstrup	8	Dh	56.18N	10.42 E
Tirua Point	62	Fc	38.23S	174.38 E
Tiruchchirappalli	22	Jh	10.49N	78.41 E
Tiruliai/Tiruliaj	8	Ji	55.44N	23.18 E
Tiruliaj/Tiruliai	8	Ji	55.44N	23.18 E
Tirunelveli	22	Ji	8.44N	77.42 E
Tirupati	25	Ff	13.39N	79.25 E
Tirza	8	Lg	57.09N	26.37 E
Tisa=Tisza (EN)	5	If	45.15N	20.17 E
Tis Ābay	35	Fc	11.20N	37.40 E
Tisdale	42	Hf	52.51N	104.04W
Tisnaren	8	Ff	58.55N	15.55 E
Tisovec	10	Ph	48.42N	19.57 E
Tissemsilt	32	Hb	35.36N	1.49 E
Tissø	8	Di	55.35N	11.20 E
Tisza	5	If	45.15N	20.17 E
Tisza (EN)=Tisa	5	If	45.15N	20.17 E
Tiszaföldvár	10	Qj	46.59N	20.15 E
Tiszafüred	10	Qi	47.37N	20.46 E
Tiszakécske	10	Qj	46.56N	20.06 E
Tiszántúl	10	Qj	47.00N	21.00 E
Tiszaújváros (Leninváros)	10	Ri	47.56N	21.05 E
Tiszavasvári	10	Ri	47.58N	21.21 E
Titao	34	Ec	13.46N	2.04W
Titarísios	15	Fj	39.47N	22.23 E
Tit-Ary	20	Hb	71.55N	127.01 E
Titicaca, Lago-	52	Jg	15.50S	69.20W
Titikaveka	64p	Bc	21.15S	159.45W
Titlagarh	25	Gd	20.18N	83.09 E
Titlis	14	Cd	46.47N	8.26 E
Titograd → Podgorica	6	Hg	42.26N	19.16 E
Titova Korenica	14	Jf	44.45N	15.42 E
Titovo Užice → Užice	15	Cf	43.52N	19.51 E
Titov Veles	15	Eh	41.42N	21.48 E
Titov vrh	15	Dh	41.58N	20.50 E
Titran	7	Be	63.40N	8.18 E
Titteri	13	Pi	35.59N	3.15 E
Titule	36	Eb	3.17N	25.32 E
Titusville [Fl.-U.S.]	43	Kf	28.37N	80.49W
Titusville [Pa.-U.S.]	44	He	41.37N	79.42W
Tituvenaj/Tytuvėnai	8	Ji	55.33N	23.09 E
Tiva	36	Gc	2.20S	39.55 E
Tivaouane	34	Bc	14.57N	16.49W
Tiveden	8	Ff	58.45N	14.40 E
Tiverton	9	Jk	50.55N	3.29W
Tivoli [Gren.]	51p	Bb	12.10N	61.37W
Tivoli [It.]	14	Gi	41.58N	12.48 E
Ţiwāl	35	Cc	10.22N	22.43 E
Tiwi	36	Gc	4.14S	39.35 E
Tiyo	35	Gc	14.41N	40.57 E
Tizatlán	48	Jh	19.21N	98.15W
Tizimín	47	Gd	21.09N	88.09W
Tizi Ouzou [3]	32	Hb	36.35N	4.05 E
Tizi Ouzou	32	Hb	36.42N	4.03 E
Tiznados, Río-	50	Ch	8.16N	67.47W
Tiznit	32	Fd	29.43N	9.43W
Tiznit [3]	32	Fd	29.07N	9.04W
Tjačev	10	Th	48.02N	23.36 E
Tjanšan	27	Dc	42.00N	80.01 E
Tjasmin	16	He	49.03N	32.50 E
Tjeggelvas	7	Dc	66.35N	17.40 E
Tjeukemeer	11	Lb	52.54N	5.50 E
Tjøme	8	De	59.10N	10.25 E
Tjorn	8	Df	58.00N	11.38 E
Tjub-Karagan, Mys-	16	Qg	44.38N	50.20 E
Tjubuk	17	Jh	56.03N	60.58 E
Tjuhtet	20	De	56.32N	89.29 E
Tjukalinsk	19	Hd	55.52N	72.12 E
Tjuleni, Ostrov-	16	Og	44.30N	47.30 E
Tjuleni, Ostrova-	16	Qg	44.55N	50.10 E
Tjulgan	19	Fe	52.22N	56.12 E
Tjumen	22	Id	57.09N	65.32 E
Tjumenskaja Oblast [3]	19	Gd	57.00N	69.00 E
Tjung	20	Hd	63.42N	121.30 E
Tjup	18	Lc	42.44N	78.20 E
Tjuri/Türi	7	Fg	58.50N	25.27 E
Tjust	8	Gg	57.50N	16.15 E
Tjuters Maly, Ostrov-	8	Le	59.45N	26.53 E
Tjuzašu, Pereval-	18	Ic	42.19N	73.50 E
Tkibuli	16	Mh	42.19N	42.59 E
Tkvarčeli	19	Eg	42.52N	41.40 E
Tlacolula	48	Ki	16.57N	96.29W
Tlacotalpan	48	Lh	18.37N	95.40W
Tlahualilo, Sierra del-	48	Hd	26.30N	103.20W
Tlalnepantla	48	Jh	19.33N	99.12W
Tlapa de Comonfort	48	Ji	17.33N	98.33W
Tlapaneco, Río-	48	Jh	18.00N	98.48W
Tlaquepaque	48	Hg	20.39N	103.19W
Tlaxcala [2]	47	Ee	19.25N	98.10W
Tlaxcala	47	Ee	19.19N	98.14W
Tlemcen	32	Gc	34.52N	1.19W
Tlemcen [3]	32	Gc	34.45N	1.30W
Tleń	10	Oc	53.38N	18.20 E
Tleta Rissana	13	Gi	35.14N	5.59W
Tletat ed Douaïr	13	Oi	35.59N	2.55 E
Tljarata	16	Oh	42.06N	46.22 E
Tlumač	10	Vh	48.46N	25.06 E
Tłuszcz	10	Rd	52.26N	21.26 E
Tmassah	33	Cd	26.22N	15.48 E
Tō, Shikotan-/Šikotan, Ostrov-	20	Jh	43.47N	146.45 E
Toaca, Vîrful-	15	Ic	46.55N	25.59 E
Toagel Mlungui	64a	Ab	7.32N	134.28 E
Toamasina	31	Lj	18.10S	49.24 E
Toamasina [3]	37	Hc	18.00S	48.40 E
Toau Atoll	61	Lc	15.55S	146.00W
Toay	56	He	36.40S	64.21W
Toba	28	Ng	34.29N	136.51 E
Toba, Danau-=Toba, Lake- (EN)	26	Li	2.35N	98.50 E
Tobago	52	Jd	11.15N	60.40W
Tobago Basin (EN)	50	Ff	12.30N	60.30W
Tobago Cays	51n	Bb	12.39N	61.22W
Toba Kākar Range	25	Db	31.15N	68.00 E
Tobarra	13	Kf	38.35N	1.41W
Tobe	29	Ce	33.44N	132.47 E
Tobejuba, Isla-	50	Fh	9.20N	61.52W
Tobelo	26	If	1.25N	127.31 E
Tobermory [Ont.-Can.]	44	Gc	45.15N	81.40W
Tobermory [Scot.-U.K.]	9	Ge	56.37N	6.05W
Tōbetsu	29a	Bb	43.14N	141.29 E
Tobi Island	57	Ed	3.00N	131.10 E
Tobin, Kap-	41	Jd	70.30N	21.30W
Tobin, Mount-	46	Gf	40.22N	117.32W
Tobin Lake [Austl.]	59	Fd	21.45S	125.50 E
Tobin Lake [Sask.-Can.]	42	Hf	53.40N	103.20W
Tobi-Shima	29	Fb	39.12N	139.32 E
Toblach / Dobbiaco	14	Gd	46.44N	12.14 E
Toboali	26	Eg	3.00S	106.30 E
Tobol	19	Ge	52.40N	62.39 E
Tobol	21	Id	58.10N	68.12 E
Tobolsk	22	Id	58.12N	68.16 E
Tobruk (EN)=Ţubruq	31	Je	32.05N	23.59 E
Tobseda	19	Fb	68.36N	52.20 E
Tocantinópolis	53	Lf	6.20S	47.25W
Tocantins	54	If	10.30S	48.00W
Tocantins, Rio-	52	Lf	1.45S	49.10W
Tocantinzinho, Rio-	55	Ha	13.57S	48.20W
Toccoa	44	Fh	34.35N	83.19W
Toce	14	Ce	45.56N	8.29 E
Tochigi	29	Fc	36.23N	139.44 E
Tochigi Ken [2]	28	Of	36.50N	139.50 E
Tochio	29	Fc	37.29N	138.58 E
Töcksfors	8	De	59.31N	11.50 E
Toco	50	Fg	10.50N	60.57W
Tocoa	49	Df	15.41N	86.03W
Toconao	56	Gb	23.11S	68.01W
Tocopilla	53	Ih	22.05S	70.12W
Tocumen	49	Hi	9.05N	79.23W
Tocuyo, Río-	49	Mh	11.03N	68.20W
Todd Mountain	44	Nb	46.32N	66.43W
Todi	14	Gh	42.47N	12.24 E
Tödi	14	Cd	46.49N	8.55 E
Todo-ga-Saki	27	Pd	39.33N	142.05 E
Todos os Santos, Baía de-	52	Mg	12.48S	38.38W
Todos Santos	47	Bd	23.27N	110.13W
Todos Santos, Bahía-	48	Ab	31.48N	116.42W
Tofino	42	Eg	49.09N	125.54W
Tofte	8	De	59.33N	10.34 E
Toftlund	8	Ci	55.11N	9.04 E
Tofua Island	61	Fc	19.45S	175.05W
Toga	63b	Ca	13.26S	166.41 E
Tōgane	29	Gd	35.33N	140.21 E
Tog Ḑarōr	35	Hc	10.25N	50.00 E
Togdere	35	Hd	9.01N	47.07 E
Tog-Dheer [3]	35	Hd	9.50N	45.50 E
Togi	29	Ec	37.08N	136.43 E
Togiak	40	Ge	59.04N	160.24W
Togian Islands (EN)= Togian, Kepulauan-	26	Hg	0.20S	122.00 E
Togliatti	6	Ke	53.31N	49.26 E
Togni	35	Fb	13.05N	35.10 E
Togo [1]	31	Hh	8.00N	1.10 E
Togrog Ul → Qahar Youyi Qianqi	28	Bd	40.46N	113.13 E
Togtoh	27	Jc	40.17N	111.15 E
Togučin	20	De	55.16N	84.33 E
Toguzak	17	Ki	54.05N	62.48 E
Toğwotee Pass	43	Ec	43.45N	110.04W
Tohen	35	Ic	11.44N	51.15 E
Tohma	24	Hc	38.31N	38.25 E
Tohmajärvi	7	He	62.11N	30.23 E
Tohopekaliga, Lake-	44	Gk	28.12N	81.23W
Toi	29	Fd	34.54N	138.47 E
Toijala	7	Ff	61.10N	23.52 E
Toi-Misaki	28	Ki	31.26N	131.19 E
Toisvesi	8	Jb	62.20N	23.45 E
Tojikiston = Tajikistan (EN)	19	Hh	39.00N	71.00 E
Tōjō	29	Cd	34.53N	133.16 E
Tojtepa	18	Gd	41.03N	69.22 E
Tok	10	Jg	49.43N	13.50 E
Tok	16	Rc	52.46N	52.22 E
Tok	40	Kd	63.20N	142.59W
Tokachi-Dake	29a	Cb	43.25N	142.41 E
Tokachi-Gawa	29a	Cb	42.41N	143.37 E
Tokachi-Heiya	29a	Cb	43.00N	143.20 E
Tokachimitsumata	29a	Cb	43.31N	143.07 E
Tōkai [Jap.]	29	Gc	36.27N	140.34 E
Tōkai [Jap.]	29	Ed	35.01N	136.51 E
Tokaj	16	Ld	51.18N	41.04 E
Tokaj	10	Rh	48.07N	21.25 E
Tōkamachi	28	Of	37.08N	138.46 E
Tokanui	62	Cg	46.34S	168.57 E
Tokara Islands (EN)= Tokara-Rettō	21	Og	29.35N	129.45 E
Tokara-Kaikyō	28	Ki	30.10N	130.15 E
Tokara-Rettō=Tokara Islands (EN)	21	Og	29.35N	129.45 E
Tokashiki-Jima	29b	Ab	26.13N	127.21 E
Tokat	23	Ea	40.19N	36.34 E
Tŏkch'ŏn	28	Ie	39.45N	126.15 E
Tok-Do	28	Kf	37.22N	131.58 E
Tokelau [5]	58	Je	9.00S	171.46W
Tokelau/Union Islands	57	Je	9.00S	171.45W
Toki	29	Ed	35.22N	137.11 E
Tokke	8	Ce	59.30N	9.15 E
Tokke	8	Be	59.27N	7.58 E
Tokkuztara/Gongliu	27	Dc	43.30N	82.15 E
Tokmak	19	Hg	42.49N	75.19 E
Tokmak	19	Df	47.13N	35.43 E
Tokomaru Bay	61	Eg	38.08S	178.20 E
Tokoname	29	Ed	34.53N	136.49 E
Tokoro	29a	Da	44.08N	144.03 E
Tokoroa	61	Eg	38.13S	175.52 E
Tokoro-Gawa	29a	Da	44.08N	144.04 E
Toksovo	8	Nd	60.10N	30.42 E
Toksu/Xinhe	27	Dc	41.34N	82.38 E
Toksun	27	Ec	42.47N	88.38 E
Toktogul	19	Hg	41.50N	73.01 E
Toktogulskoje Vodohranilišče	18	Id	41.45N	73.00 E
Tokuji	29	Bd	34.11N	131.39 E
Tokulu	65b	Bb	20.06S	174.48W
Toku-no-Shima	27	Mf	27.45N	128.50 E
Tokunoshima	29b	Bb	27.45N	129.00 E
Tokur	20	If	53.09N	132.50 E
Tokushima	27	Ne	34.04N	134.34 E
Tokushima Ken [2]	28	Mh	33.50N	134.10 E
Tokuyama [Jap.]	29	Ed	35.43N	136.27 E
Tokuyama [Jap.]	28	Kg	34.03N	131.49 E
Tokwe	37	Ed	20.09S	31.54 E
Tōkyō	22	Pf	35.40N	139.46 E
Tokyo Bay (EN)=Tōkyō-Wan	28	Og	35.38N	139.57 E
Tōkyō To [2]	28	Og	35.40N	139.20 E
Tōkyō-Wan=Tokyo Bay (EN)	28	Og	35.38N	139.57 E
Tola	21	Me	48.57N	104.48 E
Tolaga Bay	62	Hc	38.22S	178.18 E
Tolbazy	17	Gi	54.02N	55.59 E
Tolbuhin [2]	15	Kf	43.34N	27.50 E
Tolbuhin → Dobrič	15	Kf	43.34N	27.50 E
Toledo	13	Ie	39.50N	4.00W
Toledo [Blz.]	49	Ce	16.25N	88.50W
Toledo [Braz.]	56	Jb	24.44S	53.45W
Toledo [Oh.-U.S.]	39	Ke	41.39N	83.32W
Toledo [Phil.]	26	Hd	10.23N	123.38 E
Toledo [Sp.]	6	Fh	39.52N	4.01W
Toledo, Montes de-	13	He	39.35N	4.20W
Toledo Bend Reservoir	43	Ie	31.30N	93.45W
Tolentino	14	Hg	43.12N	13.17 E
Tolfa	14	Fh	42.09N	11.56 E
Tolfa, Monti della-	14	Fh	42.10N	11.55 E
Tolga	7	Ce	62.25N	11.00 E
Toli	27	Db	45.57N	83.37 E
Toliara	37	Gd	22.00S	44.00 E
Toliara	31	Lk	23.21S	43.39 E
Tolima [2]	54	Cc	3.45N	75.15W
Tolima, Nevado del-	52	Ie	4.40N	75.19W
Toling → Zanda	27	Ce	31.28N	79.50 E
Tolitoli	26	Hf	1.02N	120.49 E
Toll	64d	Bb	7.22N	151.37 E
Tollarp	8	Ei	55.56N	13.59 E
Tollja, Zaliv-	20	Ea	76.40N	100.00 E
Tolmačevo	8	Mf	58.48N	30.01 E
Tolmezzo	14	Hd	46.24N	13.01 E
Tolmin	14	Hd	46.11N	13.44 E
Tolna	10	Oj	46.26N	18.47 E
Tolna [2]	10	Oj	46.30N	18.35 E
Tolo	36	Cc	2.56S	18.34 E
Tolo, Gulf of- (EN)=Tolo, Teluk-	21	Oj	2.00S	122.30 E
Tolo, Teluk-=Tolo, Gulf of- (EN)	21	Oj	2.00S	122.30 E
Toločin	7	Gi	54.25N	29.41 E
Tolosa	13	Ja	43.08N	2.04W
Tolstoj, Mys-	5	Fd	59.10N	155.05 E
Toltén	56	Fe	39.13S	73.14W
Tolú	54	Cb	9.32N	75.34W
Toluca, Nevado de-	38	Jh	19.08N	99.44W
Toluca de Lerdo	39	Jh	19.17N	99.40W
Tom	21	Kd	56.50N	84.27 E
Toma	34	Ec	12.46N	2.53W
Tomah	45	Ke	43.59N	90.30W
Tomakomai	27	Pc	42.38N	141.36 E
Tomamae	29a	Ba	44.18N	141.39 E
Tomanivi	63d	Bb	17.37S	178.01 E
Tomar	13	De	39.36N	8.25W
Tómaros	15	Dj	39.32N	20.45 E
Tomaševka	16	Cd	51.33N	23.40 E
Tomás Young	55	Ai	28.36S	62.11W
Tomaszów Lubelski	10	Tf	50.28N	23.25 E
Tomaszów Mazowiecki	10	Qe	51.32N	20.01 E
Tomatlán	48	Gh	19.56N	105.15W
Tombador, Serra dos-	54	Gf	12.00S	57.40W
Tombigbee River	43	Je	31.04N	87.58W
Tomboco	36	Bd	6.45S	13.18 E
Tombouctou=Timbuktu (EN)	31	Gg	16.46N	2.59W
Tombstone	46	Jj	31.43N	110.04W
Tombua	31	Ij	15.48S	11.52 E
Tomé	56	Fe	36.37S	72.57W
Tomé-Açu	54	Id	2.25S	48.09W
Tomelilla	7	Ci	55.33N	13.57 E
Tomelloso	13	Ie	39.10N	3.01W
Tomichi Creek	45	Cg	38.31N	106.58W
Tomie	29	Ae	32.37N	128.46 E
Tomini, Gulf of- (EN)= Tomini, Teluk-	21	Oj	0.20S	121.00 E
Tomini, Teluk-=Tomini, Gulf of- (EN)	21	Oj	0.20S	121.00 E
Tominian	34	Ec	13.17N	4.35W
Tomioka [Jap.]	29	Gc	37.20N	140.59 E
Tomioka [Jap.]	29	Fc	36.15N	138.52 E
Tomkinson Ranges	59	Fe	26.10S	129.05 E
Tomma	7	Cc	66.15N	12.48 E
Tomo, Río-	54	Eb	5.20N	67.48W
Tomochic	48	Fc	28.20N	107.51W
Tomorit, Mali i-	15	Di	40.40N	20.09 E
Tomotu Neo	63c	Ab	10.41S	165.47 E
Tomotu Noi	63c	Bb	10.50S	166.02 E
Tompa	10	Pj	46.12N	19.33 E
Tompe	26	Gg	0.12S	119.48 E
Tompo	20	Id	62.50N	134.47 E
Tompo	20	Id	64.00N	136.00 E
Tom Price	59	Dd	22.40S	117.55 E
Tomsk	22	Kd	56.30N	84.58 E
Tomskaja Oblast [3]	20	De	58.20N	81.30 E
Tomtabacken	8	Fg	57.30N	14.28 E
Tomur Feng	21	Ke	42.02N	80.05 E
Tom White, Mount-	40	Kd	60.40N	143.40W
Tonaki-Shima	29b	Ab	26.21N	127.09 E
Tonalá	47	Fe	16.04N	93.45W
Tonale, Passo del-	14	Ed	46.16N	10.35 E
Tonami	29	Ec	36.38N	136.57 E
Tonara	14	Dj	40.02N	9.10 E
Tonasket	46	Fb	48.42N	119.26W
Tonb-e Bozorg	24	Pi	26.15N	55.03 E
Tonbetsu-Gawa	29a	Ca	45.08N	142.23 E
Tonbridge	9	Nj	51.12N	0.16 E
Tondano	26	Hf	1.19N	124.54 E
Tondela	13	Dd	40.31N	8.05W
Tønder	7	Bi	54.56N	8.54 E
Tone-Gawa	29	Gd	35.44N	140.51 E
Tonekābon	23	Hb	36.53N	50.56 E
Toney	66	Of	75.48S	115.48W
Tonga [1]	58	Jf	20.00S	175.00W
Tonga	35	Ed	9.28N	31.03 E

Index Symbols

[1] Independent Nation
[2] State, Region
[3] District, County
[4] Municipality
[5] Colony, Dependency
Continent
Physical Region
Historical or Cultural Region
Mount, Mountain
Volcano
Hill
Mountains, Mountain Range
Hills, Escarpment
Plateau, Upland
Pass, Gap
Plain, Lowland
Delta
Salt Flat
Valley, Canyon
Crater, Cave
Karst Features
Depression
Polder
Desert, Dunes
Forest, Woods
Heath, Steppe
Oasis
Cape, Point
Coast, Beach
Cliff
Peninsula
Isthmus
Sandbank
Island
Atoll
Rock, Reef
Islands, Archipelago
Rocks, Reefs
Coral Reef
Well, Spring
Geyser
River, Stream
Waterfall Rapids
River Mouth, Estuary
Lake
Salt Lake
Intermittent Lake
Reservoir
Swamp, Pond
Canal
Glacier
Ice Shelf, Pack Ice
Ocean
Sea
Gulf, Bay
Strait, Fjord
Lagoon
Bank
Seamount
Tablemount
Ridge
Shelf
Basin
Escarpment, Sea Scarp
Fracture
Trench, Abyss
National Park, Reserve
Point of Interest
Recreation Site
Cave, Cavern
Historic Site
Ruins
Wall, Walls
Church, Abbey
Temple
Scientific Station
Airport
Port
Lighthouse
Mine
Tunnel
Dam, Bridge

Tongaat	37	Ee	29.37S	31.03 E
Tonga Islands	57	Jf	20.00S	175.00W
Tonga Ridge (EN)	57	Jg	21.00S	175.00W
Tongariki	63b	Dc	17.01S	168.37 E
Tongatapu Group	57	Jg	21.10S	175.10W
Tongatapu Island	61	Fd	21.10S	175.10W
Tonga Trench (EN)	3	Kl	20.00S	173.00W
Tongbai	28	Bh	32.21N	113.24 E
Tongbai Shan	27	Je	32.20N	113.14 E
Tongcheng [China]	28	Bj	29.15N	113.49 E
Tongcheng [China]	28	Di	31.04N	116.56 E
Tongcheng → Dong'e	28	Df	36.19N	116.14 E
Tongchuan	27	Id	35.10N	109.03 E
Tongdao (Shuangjiang)	27	If	26.14N	109.45 E
Tongde	27	Hd	35.29N	100.32 E
Tongeren/Tongres	11	Ld	50.47N	5.28 E
Tonggu	28	Cj	28.33N	114.21 E
Tongguzbasti	27	Dd	38.23N	82.00 E
Tonggu Zhang	27	Kg	24.12N	116.22 E
Tong-Hae=Japan, Sea of- (EN)	21	Pf	40.00N	134.00 E
Tonghai	22	Mg	24.15N	102.45 E
Tonghe	27	Mb	46.01N	128.42 E
Tonghua	22	Oe	41.43N	125.55 E
Tongjiang	27	Nb	47.39N	132.30 E
Tongjosŏn-man	21	Of	39.30N	128.00 E
Tongliao	22	Oe	43.37N	122.15 E
Tongling	27	Ke	30.49N	117.47 E
Tonglu	28	Ej	29.48N	119.39 E
Tongmun'gŏ-ri	27	Mc	40.58N	127.08 E
Tongoa	63b	Dc	16.54S	168.33 E
Tongoy	56	Fd	30.15S	71.30W
Tongren [China]	27	If	27.45N	109.09 E
Tongren [China]	27	Hd	35.40N	102.07 E
Tongres/Tongeren	11	Ld	50.47N	5.28 E
Tongsa Dzong	25	Ic	27.31N	90.30 E
Tongshan	28	Cj	29.36N	114.30 E
Tongta	25	Jd	21.20N	99.16 E
Tongtian He/Zhi Qu	21	Lf	33.26N	96.36 E
Tongue	9	Ic	58.28N	4.25W
Tongue of the Ocean	49	Ia	24.12N	77.10W
Tongue River	43	Fb	46.24N	105.52W
Tongxian	27	Kd	39.52N	116.38 E
Tongxin	27	Id	36.59N	105.50 E
Tongxu	28	Cg	34.29N	114.27 E
Tongyu (Kaitong)	27	Lc	44.47N	123.05 E
Tongyu Yunhe	28	Eg	34.46N	119.51 E
Tongzi	27	If	28.09N	106.50 E
Tonichi	48	Ec	28.35N	109.34W
Tönisvorst	12	Ic	51.19N	6.28 E
Tonj	35	Dd	7.17N	28.45 E
Tonj	30	Jh	7.31N	29.25 E
Tonk	25	Fc	26.10N	75.47 E
Tonkin (EN)=Bac-Phan	21	Mg	22.00N	105.00 E
Tonkin, Gulf of- (EN)= Beibu Wan	21	Mh	20.00N	108.00 E
Tonkin, Gulf of- (EN)=Vinh Bac Phan	21	Mh	20.00N	108.00 E
Tônlé Sab, Bœng-=Tonle Sap (EN)	21	Mh	13.00N	104.00 E
Tonle Sap (EN)=Tônlé Sab, Bœng-	21	Mh	13.00N	104.00 E
Tonnay-Charente	11	Fi	45.57N	0.54W
Tonneins	11	Gj	44.23N	0.19 E
Tönning	10	Eb	54.19N	8.57 E
Tōno	28	Pe	39.19N	141.32 E
Tonopah	43	Dd	38.04N	117.14W
Tonoshō	29	Dd	34.29N	134.11 E
Tonosí	49	Gj	7.24N	80.27W
Tønsberg	7	Cg	59.17N	10.25 E
Tonstad	7	Bg	58.40N	6.43 E
Tonumeia	65b	Bb	20.28S	174.46W
Tonya	24	Hb	40.53N	39.16 E
Tooele	43	Ec	40.32N	112.18W
Toora-Hem	20	Ef	52.28N	96.22 E
Tootsi	8	Kf	58.34N	24.43 E
Toowoomba	58	Gg	27.33S	151.57 E
Topalu	15	Le	44.33N	28.03 E
Topa Taung	25	Jd	21.08N	95.12 E
Topeka	39	Jf	39.03N	95.41W
Topki	20	De	55.18N	85.40 E
Topko, Gora-	20	Ie	57.00N	137.23 E
Topľa	10	Rh	48.45N	21.45 E
Toplet	15	Fe	44.48N	22.24 E
Toplica	15	Ef	43.13N	21.51 E
Toplița	15	Ic	46.55N	25.20 E
Topola	15	De	44.16N	20.42 E
Topoľčany	10	Oh	48.34N	18.10 E
Topolnica	15	Hg	42.11N	24.18 E
Topolobampo	47	Cc	25.36N	109.03W
Topolobampo, Bahía de-	48	Ee	25.30N	109.05W
Topolog	15	Hd	44.56N	24.16 E
Topolovgrad	15	Jg	42.05N	26.20 E
Topozero, Ozero-	5	Jb	65.40N	32.00 E
Toppenish	46	Ec	46.23N	120.19W
Toprakkale	24	Gd	37.06N	36.07 E
Top Springs	59	Gc	16.38S	131.50 E
Toquepala	54	Eg	17.38S	69.56W
Tor	35	Ed	7.51N	33.36 E
Tora	64d	Ba	7.39N	151.53 E
Toraigh/Tory Island	9	Ef	55.16N	8.13W
Tora Island Pass	64d	Ba	7.39N	151.53 E
Toråker	8	Gd	60.31N	16.29 E
Torbalı	24	Bc	38.10N	27.21 E
Torbat-e Heydarīyeh	22	Hf	35.16N	59.13 E
Torbat-e Jam	23	Jb	35.14N	60.36 E
Torbay	9	Jk	50.28N	3.30W
Torbert, Mount-	40	Id	61.25N	152.24W
Torch Lake	44	Ec	45.00N	85.19W
Torčin	10	Vf	50.44N	25.05 E
Tordesillas	13	Hc	41.30N	5.00W
Tordino	14	Hh	42.44N	13.59 E
Töre	7	Fd	65.54N	22.39 E
Töreboda	7	Dg	58.43N	14.08 E
Torekov	8	Eh	56.26N	12.37 E
Torenberg	11	Lb	52.15N	5.55 E
Torez	16	Kf	47.59N	38.41 E
Torgau	10	Ie	51.34N	13.00 E
Torgelow	10	Kc	53.38N	14.01 E
Torgun	16	Od	50.10N	46.20 E
Torhamn	8	Fh	56.05N	15.50 E
Torhout	11	Jc	51.04N	3.06 E
Toribulu	26	Hg	0.19S	120.01 E
Torigni-sur-Vire	12	Be	49.05N	0.59W
Torii-Tōge	29	Ed	35.59N	137.49 E
Tori-Jima	29b	Ab	26.35N	126.50 E
Torino = Turin (EN)	6	Gf	45.03N	7.40 E
Toriparu	55	Fc	16.20S	53.55W
Tori-Shima [Jap.]	27	Pe	30.25N	140.15 E
Tori-Shima [Jap.]	29b	Bb	27.52N	128.14 E
Torit	35	Ee	4.24N	32.34 E
Torixoreu	54	Hg	16.15S	52.26W
Torkovči	7	Hg	58.53N	30.20 E
Törmänen	7	Gb	68.36N	27.29 E
Tormes	13	Fc	41.18N	6.29W
Tornado Mountain	46	Hb	49.58N	114.39W
Tornavacas, Puerto de-	13	Gd	40.16N	5.37W
Torneå/Tornio	7	Fd	65.51N	24.08 E
Torneälven	5	Ib	65.48N	24.08 E
Torneträsk	7	Eb	68.22N	19.06 E
Torngat Mountains	38	Md	59.00N	64.00W
Tornio/Torneå	7	Fd	65.51N	24.08 E
Tornionjoki	5	Ib	65.48N	24.08 E
Tornquist	55	An	38.06S	62.14W
Toro	13	Gc	41.31N	5.24W
Toro	8	Gf	58.50N	17.50 E
Toro, Cerro del-	52	Jh	29.08S	69.48W
Toro, Isla del-	48	Kg	21.35N	97.32W
Toro, Monte-	13	Qe	39.59N	4.07 E
Toroiaga, Vîrful-	15	Hb	47.44N	24.43 E
Torokina	63a	Bb	6.14S	155.03 E
Tōro-Ko	29a	Db	43.08N	144.30 E
Törökszentmiklós	10	Qi	47.11N	20.25 E
Torola, Río-	49	Cg	13.52N	88.30W
Toronto	39	Le	43.39N	79.23W
Toropec	19	Dd	56.31N	31.39 E
Tororo	36	Fb	0.41N	34.11 E
Toros Dağları=Taurus Mountains (EN)	21	Ff	37.00N	33.00 E
Torquato Severo	55	Ej	31.02S	54.11W
Torquay	9	Jk	50.29N	3.29W
Torrá, Cerro-	52	Ie	4.38N	76.15W
Torrance	46	Fj	33.50N	118.19W
Torre Annunziata	14	Ij	40.45N	14.27 E
Torreblanca	13	Md	40.13N	0.12 E
Torrecilla	13	Hh	36.41N	5.00W
Torrecilla en Cameros	13	Jb	42.16N	2.37W
Torre del Greco	14	Ij	40.47N	14.22 E
Torre del Mar	13	Hh	36.44N	4.06W
Torredembarra	13	Nc	41.09N	1.24 E
Torre de Moncorvo	13	Ec	41.10N	7.03W
Torre de' Passeri	14	Hh	42.14N	13.56 E
Torredonjimeno	13	Ig	37.46N	3.57W
Torrejón de Ardoz	13	Id	40.27N	3.29W
Torrelaguna	13	Id	40.50N	3.32W
Torrelavega	13	Ha	43.21N	4.03W
Torre Miró, Puerto de-	13	Ld	40.42N	0.05W
Torremolinos	13	Hh	36.37N	4.30W
Torrens, Lake-	57	Eh	31.00S	137.50 E
Torrens Creek	59	Jd	20.46S	145.02 E
Torrent de l'Horta/Torrente	13	Le	39.26N	0.28W
Torrente/Torrent de l'Horta	13	Le	39.26N	0.28W
Torrenueva	13	If	38.38N	3.22W
Torreón	39	Ig	25.33N	103.26W
Torre-Pacheco	13	Lg	37.44N	0.57W
Torre Pellice	14	Bf	44.49N	7.13 E
Torres	64d	Ab	7.19N	151.27 E
Tôrres	56	Kc	29.21S	49.44W
Torres, Iles-=Torres Islands (EN)	57	Hf	13.15S	166.37 E
Torres Islands (EN)=Torrès, Iles-	57	Hf	13.15S	166.37 E
Torres Novas	13	De	39.29N	8.32W
Torres Strait	57	Ff	10.25S	142.10 E
Torres Vedras	13	Ce	39.06N	9.16W
Torrevieja	13	Lg	37.59N	0.41W
Torridon, Loch-	9	Hd	57.35N	5.50W
Torriglia	14	Df	44.31N	9.10 E
Torrijos	13	He	39.59N	4.17W
Torrington [Ct.-U.S.]	44	Ke	41.48N	73.08W
Torrington [Wy.-U.S.]	43	Gc	42.04N	104.11W
Torroella de Montgrí	13	Pb	42.02N	3.08 E
Torröjen	7	Cf	63.55N	12.56 E
Torrox	13	Ih	36.46N	3.58W
Torsås	7	Dh	56.24N	16.00 E
Torsby	7	Cf	60.08N	13.00 E
Torshälla	8	Ge	59.25N	16.28 E
Torsken	7	Db	69.20N	17.06 E
Torsö	7	Cg	58.50N	13.50 E
Torto	14	Hm	37.58N	13.46 E
Tortola	47	Le	18.27N	64.36W
Tortoli	14	Dk	39.55N	9.39 E
Tortona	14	Cf	44.54N	8.52 E
Tortorici	14	Il	38.02N	14.49 E
Tortosa	13	Md	40.48N	0.31 E
Tortosa, Cabo de-/Tortosa, Cap de-	13	Md	40.43N	0.55 E
Tortosa, Cap de-/Tortosa, Cabo de-	13	Md	40.43N	0.55 E
Tortue, Ile de la-	47	Jd	20.04N	72.49W
Tortuga, Isla-	48	Dd	27.26N	111.55W
Tortum	24	Ib	40.19N	41.35 E
Torud	24	Pe	35.26N	55.07 E
Torugart, Pereval-	21	Je	40.32N	75.24 E
Torul	24	Hb	40.35N	39.18 E
Toruń	10	Oc	53.00N	18.35 E
Toruń	10	Oc	53.02N	18.35 E
Torunos	49	Li	8.30N	70.04W
Toruńska, Kotlina-	10	Oc	53.00N	18.30 E
Torup	7	Ch	56.58N	13.05 E
Tõrva/Tyrva	7	Fg	58.01N	25.59 E
Tory Island/Toraigh	9	Ef	55.16N	8.13W
Torysa	10	Rh	48.39N	21.21 E
Toržok	19	Dd	57.03N	35.01 E
Tosa	28	Lh	33.29N	133.25 E
Tosas, Puerto de-/Toses, Port de-	13	Ob	42.20N	2.01 E
Tosashimizu	28	Lh	32.46N	132.57 E
Tosa-Wan	28	Lh	33.25N	133.35 E
Tosa-yamada	29	Ce	33.36N	133.40 E
Toscana = Tuscany (EN) [2]	14	Eg	43.25N	11.00 E
Toses, Port de-/Tosas, Puerto de-	13	Ob	42.20N	2.01 E
Toshibetsu-Gawa [Jap.]	29a	Cb	42.54N	143.25 E
Toshibetsu-Gawa [Jap.]	29a	Ab	42.25N	139.48 E
Tōshi-Jima	29	Ed	34.31N	136.52 E
To-Shima	29	Fd	34.31N	139.17 E
Tosno	7	Hg	59.34N	30.50 E
Toson-Cengel	27	Gb	48.47N	98.15 E
Toson Hu	27	Gd	37.08N	96.52 E
Töss	14	Cc	47.33N	8.33 E
Tossa de Mar	13	Oc	41.43N	2.56 E
Tostado	56	Hc	29.14S	61.46W
Tõstamaa/Tystama	8	Jf	58.17N	23.52 E
Tosu	29	Be	33.22N	130.30 E
Tosya	24	Fb	41.01N	34.02 E
Totak	8	Be	59.40N	7.55 E
Totana	13	Kg	37.46N	1.30W
Toten	8	Dd	60.40N	10.50 E
Toteng	37	Cd	20.23S	22.59 E
Tôtes	12	He	49.41N	1.03 E
Totes Gebirge	14	Hc	47.42N	13.55 E
Tótias	35	Ge	3.57N	43.58 E
Totland	12	Ad	50.40N	1.32W
Totma	19	Ed	60.00N	42.45 E
Totness	54	Gb	5.53N	56.19W
Toto	36	Bd	7.10S	14.25 E
Totonicapán [3]	49	Bf	15.00N	91.20W
Totonicapán	47	Ff	14.55N	91.22W
Totora	54	Eg	17.42S	65.09W
Totoras	55	Bk	32.35S	61.11W
Totota	34	Dd	6.49N	9.56W
Totoya	63d	Cc	18.57S	179.50W
Totten Glacier	66	He	66.45S	116.10 E
Totton	12	Ad	50.55N	1.29W
Tottori	27	Nd	35.30N	134.14 E
Tottori Ken [2]	28	Lg	35.25N	133.50 E
Tou, Motu-	64p	Bb	21.11S	159.48W
Touâjil	32	Ee	21.45N	12.35W
Touat	30	Gf	27.40N	0.01W
Touba [3]	34	Dd	8.15N	7.45W
Touba	34	Dd	8.17N	7.41W
Toubkal, Jebel-	30	Ge	31.03N	7.55W
Touch	11	Hk	43.38N	1.24 E
Toucy	11	Jg	47.44N	3.18 E
Tougan	34	Ec	13.04N	3.04W
Touggourt	31	He	33.06N	6.04 E
Tougué	34	Cc	11.27N	11.41W
Touho	63b	Be	20.47S	165.14 E
Touil	32	Hb	35.33N	2.36 E
Touîl	13	Oi	35.33N	2.36 E
Toukoto	34	Dc	13.28N	9.52W
Toul	11	Lf	48.41N	5.54 E
Toulépleu	34	Dd	6.35N	8.25W
Toulon	6	Gg	43.07N	5.56 E
Toulouse	6	Gg	43.36N	1.26 E
Toulumne River	46	Eh	37.36N	121.10W
Toumodi	34	Dd	6.33N	5.01W
Tounassine, Hamada-	32	Fd	28.36N	5.10W
Toungo	34	Hd	8.07N	12.03 E
Toungoo	22	Lh	18.56N	96.26 E
Touques	12	Ge	49.22N	0.06 E
Toura	35	Bc	10.30N	15.19 E
Touraine	11	Hg	47.12N	1.30 E
Touraine, Val de-	11	Hg	47.20N	1.30 E
Tourcoing	11	Jd	50.43N	3.09 E
Touriñan, Cabo de-	13	Ca	43.03N	9.18W
Tourine	32	Ee	22.00N	12.15W
Tournai/Doornik	11	Jd	50.36N	3.23 E
Tournai-Kain	12	Fd	50.38N	3.22 E
Tournon	11	Ki	45.04N	4.50 E
Tournus	11	Kh	46.34N	4.54 E
Touros	54	Ke	5.12S	35.28W
Tours	6	Gf	47.23N	0.41 E
Tourteron	12	Ge	49.32N	4.39 E
Toury	11	Hf	48.12N	1.56 E
Touside, Pic-	35	Ba	21.02N	16.25 E
Toussoro	35	Cd	9.02N	23.55 E
Toutouba	63b	Cb	15.34S	167.16 E
Touwsrivier	37	Cf	33.20S	20.00 E
Toužim	10	If	50.04N	12.59 E
Tovar	49	Li	8.20N	71.46W
Tovarkovski	16	Kc	53.43N	38.13 E
Tovdalselva	8	Cf	58.12N	8.06 E
Tove	12	Bb	52.04N	0.50W
Tōwa	29	Gb	39.23N	141.15 E
Towada	28	Pd	40.35N	141.13 E
Towada-Kō	29	Ga	40.28N	140.55 E
Towanda	44	Ie	41.46N	76.27W
Tower	45	Jc	47.48N	92.17W
Towner	45	Fb	48.21N	100.25W
Townsend	46	Jc	46.19N	111.31W
Townshend, Cape-	59	Kd	22.15S	150.30 E
Townsville	58	Ff	19.16S	146.48 E
Towot	35	Ed	6.12N	34.25 E
Towson	44	If	39.24N	76.36W
Towuti, Danau-	26	Hg	2.45S	121.32 E
Toxkan He	27	Dc	41.08N	80.11 E
Tōya	29a	Bb	42.39N	140.48 E
Toyah Creek	45	Ek	31.18N	103.27W
Tōya-Ko	28	Pc	42.33N	140.50 E
Toyama	22	Pf	36.41N	137.13 E
Toyama Ken [2]	28	Nf	36.40N	137.10 E
Toyama Trench (EN)	29	Ec	38.00N	138.00 E
Toyama-Wan	28	Nf	37.00N	137.15 E
Tōyō	28	Mh	33.22N	134.18 E
Toyohashi	27	Oe	34.46N	137.23 E
Toyokoro	29a	Cb	42.48N	143.28 E
Toyonaka	29	Dd	34.47N	135.28 E
Toyo'oka	27	Od	35.33N	137.54 E
Toyosaka	29	Fc	37.55N	139.12 E
Toyota	28	Ng	35.05N	137.09 E
Toyotama	29	Ad	34.27N	129.19 E
Toyotomi	29a	Ba	45.08N	141.47 E
Toyoura	29	Bd	34.10N	130.55 E
Trabancos	13	Gc	41.27N	5.11W
Traben Trabach	12	Je	49.57N	7.07 E
Trabzon	22	Fe	40.59N	39.43 E
Traer	45	Je	42.12N	92.28W
Trafalgar, Cabo-	13	Fh	36.11N	6.02W
Tragacete	13	Kd	40.21N	1.51W
Traiguén	56	Fe	38.15S	72.41W
Trail	39	He	49.06N	117.43W
Traill	41	Jd	72.45N	24.00W
Trairas, Rio-	55	Hb	14.07S	48.31W
Trairi	54	Kd	3.17S	39.15W
Traisen	14	Jb	48.22N	15.46 E
Trakai/Trakaj	7	Fi	54.38N	24.57 E
Trakaj/Trakai	7	Fi	54.38N	24.57 E
Trakt	17	Ee	62.44N	51.11 E
Trakya = Thrace (EN)	15	Jh	41.20N	26.45 E
Trakya = Thrace (EN)	5	Ig	41.20N	26.45 E
Tralee/Trá Lí	9	Di	52.16N	9.42W
Tralee Bay/Bá Thrá Lí	9	Di	52.15N	9.59W
Trá Lí/Tralee	9	Di	52.16N	9.42W
Trá Mhór/Tramore	9	Fi	52.10N	7.10W
Tramore/Trá Mhór	9	Fi	52.10N	7.10W
Tramping Lake	46	Ka	52.10N	108.48W
Trăn	15	Fg	42.50N	22.39 E
Tranås	7	Dg	58.03N	14.59 E
Trancoso	13	Ed	40.47N	7.21W
Tranebjerg	8	Di	55.50N	10.36 E
Tranemo	8	Eg	57.29N	13.21 E
Trang	22	Li	7.33N	99.36 E
Trani	14	Ki	41.17N	16.25 E
Transantarctic Mountains (EN)	66	Lg	85.00S	175.00W
Transcaucasia (EN)	5	Kg	41.00N	45.00 E
Transilvania = Transylvania (EN)	15	Hc	46.30N	25.00 E
Transilvania = Transylvania (EN)	5	If	46.30N	25.00 E
Transkei	30	Jl	31.30S	29.00 E
Transkei	37	Df	32.45S	28.30 E
Transtrand	8	Ec	61.05N	13.19 E
Transtrandsfjällen	8	Ec	61.15N	12.58 E
Transvaal [2]	37	Dd	25.00S	30.00 E
Transylvania (EN) = Transilvania	15	Hc	46.30N	25.00 E
Transylvania (EN) = Transilvania	5	If	46.30N	25.00 E
Transylvanian Alps (EN)= Carpații Meridionali	5	If	45.30N	24.15 E
Trants Bay	51c	Bc	16.46N	62.09W
Trapani	6	Hh	38.01N	12.29 E
Trapper Peak	46	Hd	45.54N	114.18W
Trappes	12	Ef	48.47N	2.01 E
Traralgon	59	Jg	38.12S	146.32 E
Trarza [3]	32	Ef	18.00N	15.00W
Trarza	30	Fg	17.20N	14.40W
Trașcăului, Munții-	15	Gc	46.23N	23.33 E
Trasimeno, Lago-	14	Gg	43.10N	12.05 E
Träslövsläge	8	Eg	57.04N	12.16 E
Trás os Montes e Alto Douro	13	Ec	41.30N	7.15W
Trat	25	Kf	12.13N	102.16 E
Traun	14	Ib	48.13N	14.14 E
Traun	14	Ib	48.16N	14.22 E
Traunsee	14	Hc	47.52N	13.48 E
Traunstein	10	Ii	47.53N	12.39 E
Trave	10	Gc	53.54N	10.50 E
Travemünde, Lübeck-	10	Gc	53.57N	10.52 E
Travers, Mount-	61	Dh	42.01S	172.44 E
Traverse, Lake-	45	Hd	45.43N	96.40W
Traverse City	43	Jc	44.46N	85.37W
Traverse Islands	66	Ad	56.36S	27.43W
Travers Reservoir	46	Ia	50.14N	112.51W
Tra Vinh	25	Lg	9.56N	106.20 E
Travis, Lake-	45	Hk	30.27N	98.00W
Travnik	23	Ff	44.14N	17.40 E
Travo	11a	Bb	41.54N	9.24 E
Trbovlje	14	Jd	46.10N	15.03 E
Treasurers	63c	Ba	9.53S	167.09 E
Treasury Islands	63a	Bb	7.22S	155.37 E
Trebbia	14	De	45.04N	9.41 E
Třebíč	10	Lg	49.13N	15.53 E
Trebinje	14	Mh	42.43N	18.21 E
Trebisacce	14	Kk	39.52N	16.32 E
Trebišnjica	14	Lg	43.01N	17.47 E
Trebišov	10	Rh	48.40N	21.43 E
Treblinka	10	Sd	52.40N	22.03 E
Trebnje	14	Je	45.54N	15.01 E
Třeboň	10	Kg	49.01N	14.48 E
Třeboňska pánev	10	Kg	49.00N	14.50 E
Trégorrois	11	Cf	48.45N	3.15W
Tregrosse Islets	57	Gf	17.40S	150.45 E
Tréguier	11	Cf	48.47N	3.14W
Treherne	45	Gb	49.38N	98.41W
Treignac	11	Hi	45.32N	1.48 E
Treinta y Tres [2]	55	Ek	33.00S	54.15W
Treinta y Tres	56	Jd	33.14S	54.23W
Treis-Karden	12	Jd	50.11N	7.17 E
Trélazé	11	Fg	47.27N	0.28W
Trelew	56	Gf	43.15S	65.18W
Trelleborg	6	Hd	55.22N	13.10 E
Trélon	12	Gd	50.04N	4.06 E
Tremadoc Bay	9	Ii	52.40N	4.10W
Tremblant, Mount-	38	Le	46.15N	74.34W
Tremiti, Isole-=Tremiti Islands (EN)	5	Hg	42.10N	15.30 E
Tremiti Islands (EN)= Tremiti, Isole-	5	Hg	42.10N	15.30 E
Tremonton	46	If	41.43N	112.10W
Tremp	13	Mb	42.10N	0.54 E
Třemšín	10	Jg	49.33N	13.48 E
Trenche, Rivière-	44	Kb	47.35N	72.58W
Trenčín	10	Oh	48.54N	18.04 E
Trenque Lauquen	56	He	35.58S	62.42W
Trent	9	Mh	53.42N	0.41W
Trent, Vale of-	9	Li	52.45N	1.50W
Trentino-Alto Adige / Südtirol [2]	14	Fd	46.30N	11.20 E
Trento	14	Fd	46.04N	11.08 E
Trenton [Mo.-U.S.]	45	Jf	40.05N	93.37W
Trenton [N.J.-U.S.]	39	Le	40.13N	74.45W
Trenton [Ont.-Can.]	44	Ic	44.06N	77.35W
Tréon	12	Df	48.41N	1.20 E
Trepassey	42	Mg	46.44N	53.22W
Tres Arboles [Ur.]	56	Id	32.24S	56.43W
Tres Arroyos	53	Ji	38.22S	60.15W
Tres Bocas	55	Ck	32.44S	59.45W
Tres Caraçöes	54	Ih	21.42S	45.16W
Tres Cruces, Cerro-	48	Mj	15.28N	92.24W
Três de Maio	55	Eh	27.47S	54.14W
Tres Esquinas	54	Cc	0.43N	75.15W
Tres Isletas	55	Bh	26.21S	60.26W
Treska	15	Eh	41.59N	21.19 E
Treskavica	14	Mg	43.35N	18.24 E
Três Lagoas	53	Kh	20.48S	51.43W
Três Marias, Represa-	54	Ig	18.15S	45.15W
Tres Montes, Peninsula-	56	Eg	46.50S	75.30W
Três Passos	56	Jc	27.27S	53.56W
Tres Picos, Cerro- [Arg.]	52	Ji	38.09S	61.57W
Tres Picos, Cerro- [Mex.]	48	Li	16.36N	94.13W
Três Pontas	55	Je	21.22S	45.31W
Tres Puntas, Cabo- [Arg.]	52	Jj	47.06S	65.53W
Tres Puntas, Cabo- [Guat.]	49	Cf	15.58N	88.37W
Três Ranchos	55	Id	18.22S	47.47W
Três Rios	55	Kf	22.07S	43.12W
Třešť	10	Lg	49.18N	15.28 E
Tres Valles	48	Kh	18.15N	96.08W
Tres Zapotes	47	Ee	18.28N	95.24W
Tretten	7	Cf	61.19N	10.19 E
Treuer Range	59	Gd	22.15S	130.50 E
Treungen	8	Ce	59.02N	8.33 E
Trêve, Lac la-	44	Ja	49.58N	75.31W
Trevi	14	Gh	42.52N	12.45 E
Trévières	12	Be	49.19N	0.54W
Treviglio	14	De	45.31N	9.35 E
Trevinca, Peña-	13	Fb	42.15N	6.46W
Treviño	13	Jb	42.44N	2.45W
Treviso	14	Ge	45.40N	12.15 E
Trevose Head	9	Hk	50.33N	5.01W
Trgovište	15	Fg	42.21N	22.06 E
Triánda	15	Lm	36.24N	28.10 E
Triangle	37	Ed	21.02S	31.28 E
Triángulos, Arrecifes-	48	Mg	20.57N	92.16W
Triánisia	15	Jm	36.18N	26.45 E
Tribeč	10	Oh	48.27N	18.15 E
Tribune	45	Fg	38.28N	101.45W
Tricarico	14	Kj	40.37N	16.09 E
Tricase	14	Mk	39.56N	18.22 E
Trichūr	25	Ff	10.31N	76.13 E
Tri City	46	De	43.02N	123.15W
Trie-Château	12	De	49.17N	1.50 E
Triel-sur-Seine	12	Ef	48.59N	2.01 E
Trier	10	Cg	49.45N	6.38 E
Trier-Ehrang	12	Ie	49.49N	6.41 E
Trier-Pfalzel	12	Ie	49.46N	6.41 E
Trieste	6	Hf	45.40N	13.46 E
Trieste, Golfo di-	14	He	45.40N	13.30 E
Trieux	11	Cf	48.50N	3.03W
Trifels	12	Je	49.11N	7.59 E
Triglav	5	Hf	46.23N	13.50 E
Trigno	14	Ih	42.04N	14.48 E
Tríkala	15	Ej	39.33N	21.46 E
Trikhonís, Límni-	15	Ek	38.34N	21.30 E
Trikomo → Yeniboğaziçi	24	Ee	35.17N	33.52 E
Trikomon → Yeniboğaziçi	24	Ee	35.17N	33.52 E
Trikora, Puncak-	26	Kg	4.15S	138.45 E
Trilport	12	Ef	48.57N	2.57 E
Trim/Baile Átha Troim	9	Gh	53.34N	6.47W
Trincheras	48	Gc	28.55N	104.18W
Trincomalee	22	Ki	8.34N	81.14 E
Trindade	54	Ig	16.40S	49.30W
Trindade, Ilha da-	52	Nh	20.31S	29.19W
Třinec	10	Og	49.41N	18.42 E
Tring	12	Bc	51.47N	0.39W
Tringia	15	Ej	39.38N	21.25 E
Trinidad	52	Jd	10.30N	61.15W
Trinidad [Bol.]	53	Jg	14.47S	64.47W
Trinidad [Ca.-U.S.]	46	Cf	41.07N	124.07W
Trinidad [Co.-U.S.]	39	If	37.10N	104.31W
Trinidad [Cuba]	47	Id	21.48N	79.59W
Trinidad [Mex.]	48	Ec	28.25N	109.06W
Trinidad [Ur.]	56	Id	33.32S	56.54W
Trinidad, Golfo-	56	Eg	49.55S	75.25W
Trinidad, Isla-	55	Bn	39.08S	61.58W
Trinidad, Laguna-	55	Be	20.21S	61.35W
Trinidad and Tobago [1]	53	Jd	11.00N	61.00W
Trinidade Spur (EN)	3	Cl	21.00S	35.00W
Trinitapoli	14	Ki	41.21N	16.05 E
Trinity	45	Ik	30.57N	95.22W
Trinity	38	Jg	29.47N	94.42W
Trinity Bay [Austl.]	59	Jc	16.25S	145.35 E
Trinity Bay [Can.]	42	Mg	48.15N	53.10W
Trinity Islands	40	Ie	56.33N	154.25W
Trinity Range	46	Ff	40.20N	118.45W
Trinity River	46	Df	41.11N	123.42W
Trinkitat	35	Fb	18.41N	37.43 E
Trino	14	Ce	45.12N	8.18 E
Trionto	14	Kk	39.37N	16.45 E
Trionto, Capo-	14	Kk	39.37N	16.45 E
Triora	14	Bf	43.59N	7.46 E
Tripoli (EN)=Țarābulus [3]	33	Bc	32.40N	13.15 E
Tripoli (EN)=Țarābulus [Leb.]	23	Ec	34.26N	35.51 E
Tripoli (EN)=Țarābulus [Lib.]	31	Ie	32.54N	13.11 E
Tripolis	15	Fl	37.31N	22.22 E
Tripolitania (EN)= Țarābulus	30	Ie	31.00N	14.00 E
Tripolitania (EN)= Țarābulus	33	Bc	30.00N	15.00 E

Index Symbols

[1] Independent Nation
[2] State, Region
[3] District, County
[4] Municipality
[5] Colony, Dependency
Continent
Physical Region
Historical or Cultural Region
Mount, Mountain
Volcano
Hill
Mountains, Mountain Range
Hills, Escarpment
Plateau, Upland
Pass, Gap
Plain, Lowland
Delta
Salt Flat
Valley, Canyon
Crater, Cave
Karst Features
Depression
Polder
Desert, Dunes
Forest, Woods
Heath, Steppe
Oasis
Cape, Point
Coast, Beach
Cliff
Peninsula
Isthmus
Sandbank
Island
Atoll
Rock, Reef
Islands, Archipelago
Rocks, Reefs
Coral Reef
Well, Spring
Geyser
River, Stream
Waterfall Rapids
River Mouth, Estuary
Lake
Salt Lake
Intermittent Lake
Reservoir
Swamp, Pond
Canal
Glacier
Ice Shelf, Pack Ice
Ocean
Sea
Gulf, Bay
Strait, Fjord
Lagoon
Bank
Seamount
Tablemount
Ridge
Shelf
Basin
Escarpment, Sea Scarp
Fracture
Trench, Abyss
National Park, Reserve
Point of Interest
Recreation Site
Cave, Cavern
Historic Site
Ruins
Wall, Walls
Church, Abbey
Temple
Scientific Station
Airport
Port
Lighthouse
Mine
Tunnel
Dam, Bridge

Index Symbols

[1] Independent Nation — ⊞ Historical or Cultural Region — ⌐ Pass, Gap — ⌐ Depression — ⌐ Coast Beach — ⌐ Rock, Reef — ⌐ Waterfall Rapids — ⌐ Canal — ⌐ Lagoon — ⌐ Escarpment, Sea Scarp — ⌐ Historic Site — ⌐ Port

[2] State, Region — ⌐ Mount, Mountain — ⌐ Plain, Lowland — ⌐ Polder — ⌐ Cliff — ⌐ Islands, Archipelago — ⌐ River Mouth, Estuary — ⌐ Glacier — ⌐ Bank — ⌐ Trench, Abyss — ⌐ Ruins — ⌐ Lighthouse

[3] District, County — ⌐ Volcano — ⌐ Delta — ⌐ Desert, Dunes — ⌐ Peninsula — ⌐ Rocks, Reefs — ⌐ Lake — ⌐ Ice Shelf, Pack Ice — ⌐ Seamount — ⌐ National Park, Reserve — ⌐ Church, Abbey — ⌐ Mine

[4] Municipality — ⌐ Hill — ⌐ Salt Flat — ⌐ Forest, Woods — ⌐ Isthmus — ⌐ Coral Reef — ⌐ Salt Lake — ⌐ Ocean — ⌐ Tablemount — ⌐ Point of Interest — ⌐ Temple — ⌐ Wall, Walls

[5] Colony, Dependency — ⌐ Mountains, Mountain Range — ⌐ Valley, Canyon — ⌐ Heath, Steppe — ⌐ Sandbank — ⌐ Well, Spring — ⌐ Intermittent Lake — ⌐ Sea — ⌐ Ridge — ⌐ Recreation Site — ⌐ Scientific Station — ⌐ Tunnel

■ Continent — ⌐ Hills, Escárpment — ⌐ Crater, Cave — ⌐ Oasis — ⌐ Island — ⌐ Geyser — ⌐ Reservoir — ⌐ Gulf, Bay — ⌐ Shelf — ⌐ Cave, Cavern — ⌐ Airport — ⌐ Dam, Bridge

⌐ Physical Region — ⌐ Plateau, Upland — ⌐ Karst Features — ⌐ Cape, Point — ⌐ Atoll — ⌐ River, Stream — ⌐ Swamp, Pond — ⌐ Strait, Fjord — ⌐ Basin

Tuy Hoa 25 Lf 13.05N 109.18 E
Tüyserkān 24 Me 34.33N 48.27 E
Tuz, Lake- (EN)=Tuz Gölü 21 Ff 38.45N 33.25 E
Tuzkan, Ozero- 18 Fd 40.35N 67.30 E
Tūz Khurmātū 23 Fc 34.53N 44.38 E
Tuzla 14 Mf 44.33N 18.41 E
Tuzlov 16 Lf 47.23N 40.08 E
Tuzluca 24 Jb 40.03N 43.39 E
Tuzly 15 Nd 45.56N 30.05 E
Tvååker 8 Eg 57.03N 12.24 E
Tvărdica 15 Ig 42.42N 25.54 E
Tvedestrand 7 Bg 58.37N 8.55 E
Tver' (Kalinin) 6 Jd 56.52N 35.55 E
Tver'skaja oblast 19 Dd 57.20N 34.40 E
Tweed 9 Lf 55.46N 2.00W
Tweedsmuir Hills 9 Jf 55.30N 3.22W
Tweerivier 37 Be 25.35S 19.37 E
Twello, Voorst- 12 Ib 52.14N 6.07 E
Twente 11 Mb 52.17N 6.40 E
Twentekanaal 12 Ib 52.13N 6.53 E
Twilight Cove 59 Ff 32.20S 126.00 E
Twin Buttes Reservoir 45 Fk 31.20N 100.35W
Twin Falls 39 He 42.34N 114.28W
Twin Islands 42 Jf 53.50N 80.00W
Twin Peaks 46 Hd 44.35N 114.29W
Twisp 46 Eb 48.22N 120.07W
Twiste 12 Lc 51.29N 9.09 E
Twistringen 10 Ed 52.48N 8.39 E
Two Butte Creek 45 Eg 38.02N 102.08W
Two Harbors 45 Kc 47.01N 91.40W
Two Rivers 45 Md 44.09N 87.34W
Two Thumb Range 62 De 43.45S 170.40 E
Tychy 10 Of 50.09N 18.59 E
Tyczyn 10 Sg 49.58N 22.02 E
Tydal 7 Ce 63.04N 11.34 E
Tygda 20 Hf 53.07N 126.20 E
Tyin 8 Cc 61.15N 8.15 E
Tyin 8 Cc 61.14N 8.14 E
Tyler 43 He 32.21N 95.18W
Tylertown 45 Kk 31.07N 90.09W
Tylösand 8 Eh 56.39N 12.44 E
Tylöskog 8 Ff 58.40N 15.10 E
Tym 20 De 59.30N 80.07 E
Tymovskoje 20 Jf 50.50N 142.41 E
Tympákion 15 Hn 35.06N 24.45 E
Tynda 22 Od 53.07N 126.20 E
Tyne 9 Lf 55.01N 1.26W
Tyne and Wear 9 Lg 55.00N 1.35W
Tynemouth 9 Lf 55.01N 1.24W
Týn nad Vltavou 10 Kg 49.14N 14.26 E
Tynset 7 Ce 62.17N 10.47 E
Tyra, Cayos- 49 Fg 12.50N 83.20W
Tyrifjorden 8 De 60.05N 10.10 E
Tyringe 8 Eh 56.10N 13.35 E
Tyrma 20 If 50.01N 132.10 E
Tyrnyauz 16 Mh 43.23N 42.56 E
Tyrol (EN)=Tirol 14 Fc 47.10N 11.25 E
Tyrol (EN)=Tirol/Tirolo 14 Fd 47.00N 11.20 E
Tyrol (EN)=Tirolo/Tirol 14 Fd 47.00N 11.20 E
Tyrone 44 He 40.41N 78.15W
Tyrrell, Lake- 59 Ig 35.20S 142.50 E
Tyrrel Lake 42 Gd 63.05N 105.30W
Tyrrhenian Basin (EN) 5 Hh 40.00N 13.00 E
Tyrrhenian Sea (EN)= Tirreno, Mar- 5 Hh 40.00N 12.00 E
Tyrva/Tõrva 7 Fg 58.01N 25.59 E
Tyrvää 8 Jc 61.21N 22.53 E
Tysmenica 10 Uh 48.49N 24.56 E
Tyśmienica 10 Se 51.33N 22.30 E
Tysnesøy 7 Af 60.00N 5.35 E
Tysse 8 Ad 60.22N 5.45 E
Tyssedal 8 Bd 60.07N 6.34 E
Tystama/Tõstamaa 8 Jf 58.17N 23.52 E
Tystberga 8 Gf 58.52N 17.15 E
Tyszowce 10 Tf 50.36N 23.41 E
Tytuvénai/Tituvenaj 8 Ji 55.33N 23.09 E
Tywyn 9 Ii 52.35N 4.05W
Tzanconeja, Río- 48 Ni 16.51N 91.47W
Tzaneen 37 Ed 23.50S 30.09 E
Tzintzuntzan 48 Ih 19.38N 101.34W
Tzucacab 48 Og 20.04N 89.05W

U

Uaboe 64e Ab 0.31S 166.54 E
Uacurizal, Ilha do- 55 Dc 16.25S 56.05W
Ua Huka, Ile- 57 Ne 8.54S 139.33W
Uanukuhahaki 65b Ba 19.58S 174.29W
Ua Pou, Ile- 57 Me 9.23S 140.03W
Uaroo 59 Dd 23.00S 115.10 E
Uatumã, Rio- 52 Kf 2.26S 57.37W
Uaupés 53 Jf 0.08S 67.05W
Uaupés, Rio- 52 Je 0.02N 67.16W
Uaxactún 47 Ge 17.25N 89.29W
Ub 15 De 44.27N 20.05 E
Ubá 54 Jh 21.07S 42.56W
Übach-Palenberg [Ger.] 10 Cf 50.56N 6.05 E
Ubagan 19 Ge 54.23N 64.40 E
Ubaila 24 If 33.06N 40.15 E
Ubaitaba 54 Kf 14.18S 39.20W
Ubajay 55 Cj 31.47S 58.18W
Ubangi 30 Ii 0.30S 17.42 E
Ubatuba 55 Jf 23.26S 45.04W
Ubay 26 Hd 10.03N 124.28 E
Ubaye 11 Mj 44.28N 6.18 E
Ubayyiḍ, Wādī al- 23 Fc 32.34N 43.48 E
Ube 28 Kh 33.56N 131.15 E
Ubeda 13 If 38.01N 3.22W
Ubekendt Ejland 41 Gd 71.10N 53.45W
Uberaba 53 Lg 19.45S 47.55W
Uberaba, Lagoa- 55 Dc 17.30S 57.45W
Uberlândia 53 Lg 18.56S 48.18W
Überlingen 10 Fi 47.46N 9.10 E
Ubiaja 34 Gd 6.39N 6.23 E
Ubiña, Peña- 13 Ga 43.01N 5.57W
Ubiratã 55 Fg 24.32S 52.56W
Ubon Ratchathani 22 Mh 15.15N 104.54 E
Ubort 16 Fc 52.06N 28.30 E
Ubrique 13 Gh 36.41N 5.27W
Ubsu-Nur (Uvs nuur) 21 Ld 50.20N 92.45 E
Ubundu 31 Ji 0.21S 25.29 E
Učaly 19 Fe 54.20N 59.31 E
Učami 20 Ed 63.50N 96.39 E
Učaral 19 If 46.08N 80.52 E
Ucayali, Rio- 52 If 4.30S 73.30W
Uccle/Ukkel 12 Gd 50.48N 4.19 E
Üçdoruk Tepe 24 Ib 40.45N 41.05 E
Ucero 13 Ic 41.31N 3.04W
Uchiko 29 Ce 33.34N 132.38 E
Uchi Lake 45 Ja 51.05N 92.35W
Uchinomi 29 Dd 34.30N 134.19 E
Uchinoura 29 Bf 31.16N 131.05 E
Uchiura-Wan 28 Pc 42.18N 140.35 E
Uchte 10 Ed 52.30N 8.55 E
Učka 14 Ie 45.17N 14.12 E
Uckange 12 Ie 49.18N 6.09 E
Uckermark 10 Jc 53.10N 13.35 E
Uckfield 12 Cd 50.58N 0.06 E
Učkuduk 19 Gg 42.10N 63.30 E
Učkurgan 18 Id 41.01N 72.04 E
Ucrainskaja Sovetskaja Socialističeskaja Respublika → Ukrayina 19 Df 49.00N 32.00 E
Ucross 46 Ld 44.33N 106.31W
Ucua 36 Bd 8.40S 14.12 E
Učur 21 Pd 58.48N 130.35 E
Uda 21 Pd 54.42N 135.14 E
Uda 20 Ff 51.45N 107.25 E
Uda 20 Ee 56.05N 99.34 E
Udačny 20 Gc 66.25N 112.20 E
Udaipur 22 Jg 24.35N 73.41 E
Udaj 16 Hd 50.05N 33.07 E
Udaquiola 55 Cm 36.34S 58.31W
Udbina 14 Jf 44.32N 15.46 E
Uddevalla 7 Cg 58.21N 11.55 E
Uddjaure 5 Hb 65.58N 17.50 E
Uden 12 Hc 51.40N 5.37 E
Udgīr 25 Fe 18.23N 77.07 E
Udhampur 25 Fb 32.56N 75.08 E
Udimski 7 Kf 61.09N 45.52 E
Udine 14 Hd 46.03N 13.14 E
Udipi 25 Ef 13.21N 74.45 E
Udmurtskaja respublika 19 Fd 57.20N 52.50 E
Udoha 8 Mg 57.58N 29.50 E
Udomlja 7 Ih 57.56N 35.02 E
Udone-Jima 29 Fd 34.28N 139.17 E
Udon Thani 25 Ke 17.25N 102.48 E
Udot 64d Bb 7.23N 151.43 E
Udskaja Guba 21 Pd 55.00N 136.00 E
Udskoje 20 If 54.36N 134.30 E
Udy 16 Je 49.47N 36.35 E
Udžary 16 Oi 40.31N 47.40 E
Udzungwa Range 36 Gd 8.05S 35.50 E
Uebonti 26 Hg 0.55S 121.38 E
Uecker 10 Kc 53.45N 14.04 E
Ueckermünde 10 Kc 53.44N 14.03 E
Ueda 27 Od 36.24N 138.16 E
Uele 30 Jh 4.09N 22.26 E
Uelen 20 Oc 66.13N 169.48W
Uelzen 10 Gd 52.58N 10.34 E
Ueno 29 Ed 34.46N 136.06 E
Uere 30 Jh 3.42N 25.24 E
Ufa 5 Le 54.40N 56.00 E
Ufa 6 Le 54.44N 55.56 E
Uftjuga 7 Lf 61.28N 46.12 E
Ugab 30 Ik 21.12S 13.38 E
Ugale/Ugāle 8 Ig 57.19N 21.52 E
Ugāle/Ugale 8 Ig 57.19N 21.52 E
Ugalla 36 Fd 5.08S 30.42 E
Uganda 31 Kh 1.00N 32.00 E
Ugărčin 15 Hf 43.06N 24.25 E
Ugashik 40 He 57.32N 157.25W
Ughelli 34 Gd 5.30N 5.59 E
Ugijar 13 Ih 36.57N 3.03W
Uglegorsk 20 Jg 49.05N 142.06 E
Uglekamensk 20 Ih 43.18N 133.08 E
Ugleuralski 17 Hg 58.59N 57.38 E
Uglič 19 Dd 57.33N 38.23 E
Ugljan 14 Jf 44.05N 15.10 E
Uglovoje 28 Lc 43.20N 132.06 E
Ugnev 10 Tf 50.20N 23.45 E
Ugo 29 Gb 39.13N 140.23 E
Ugolnyje Kopi 20 Md 64.42N 177.50 E
Ugoma 36 Ec 4.55S 26.50 E
Ugra 19 De 54.30N 36.07 E
Ugtal-Cajdam 27 Ib 48.25N 105.30 E
Uh 10 Rh 48.33N 22.00 E
Uherské Hradiště 10 Ng 49.04N 17.27 E
Úhlava 10 Jg 49.45N 13.23 E
Uhlenhorst 37 Bd 23.45S 17.55 E
Uhta 6 Lc 63.33N 53.40 E
Uibh Fhaili/Offaly 9 Fh 53.20N 7.30W
Uig 9 Gd 57.30N 6.20W
Uige 31 Ii 7.35S 15.04 E
Uige 36 Cd 7.00S 15.30 E
'Uiha 65b Ba 19.54S 174.25W
Uijec 64d Bb 7.10N 151.57 E
Ŭijŏngbu 28 If 37.44N 127.02 E
Uiju 28 Hd 40.12N 124.32 E
Uil 19 Ff 48.36N 52.30 E
Uil 19 Ff 49.04N 54.42 E
Uilpata, Gora- 16 Mh 42.47N 43.44 E
Uinta Mountains 43 Ec 40.45N 110.05W
Uinta River 46 Kf 40.14N 109.51W
Uis 37 Ad 21.08S 14.49 E
Ŭisŏng 28 Jf 36.21N 128.42 E
Uitenhage 31 Jl 33.40S 25.28 E
Uithoorn 12 Gb 52.14N 4.52 E
Uithuizen 12 Ia 53.25N 6.42 E
Uithuizerwad 12 Ia 53.30N 6.40 E
Ujae Atoll 57 Hd 9.05N 165.40 E
Ūjān 24 Og 30.45N 52.05 E
Ujandina 20 Jc 68.23N 145.50 E
Ujar 20 Ee 55.48N 94.20 E
Ujarrás 49 Fi 9.50N 83.40W
Ujedinenija, Ostrov- 20 Da 77.30N 82.30 E
Ujelang Atoll 57 Hd 9.49N 160.55 E
Újfehértó 10 Ri 47.48N 21.41 E
Uji 29 Dd 34.53N 135.47 E
Uji 19 Ge 54.20N 63.58 E
Uji-Guntō 28 Ji 31.10N 129.28 E
Ujiie 29 Fc 36.41N 139.57 E
Ujiji 31 Ji 4.55S 29.41 E
Ujjain 22 Jg 23.11N 75.46 E
Ujunglamuru 26 Gg 4.40S 119.58 E
Ujung Pandang (Makasar) 22 Nj 5.07S 119.24 E
Uk 20 Ee 55.04N 98.52 E
Ukata 34 Gc 10.50N 5.50 E
Ukeng, Bukit- 26 Gf 1.45N 115.08 E
Ukerewe Island 36 Fc 2.03S 33.00 E
Uke-Shima 29b Ba 28.02N 129.15 E
Ukhayḍir 24 Jf 32.26N 43.36 E
Ukiah [Ca.-U.S.] 43 Cd 39.09N 123.13W
Ukiah [Or.-U.S.] 46 Fd 45.08N 118.56W
Uki Ni Masi 63a Ed 10.15S 161.44 E
Ukkel/Uccle 12 Gd 50.48N 4.19 E
Ukmerge/Ukmergė 7 Fi 55.14N 24.47 E
Ukmergė/Ukmerge 7 Fi 55.14N 24.47 E
Ukraine (EN) 5 Jf 49.00N 32.00 E
Ukraine (EN) = Ukrayina 19 Df 49.00N 32.00 E
Ukrainskaja SSR/Ukrainska Radyanska Socialistična Respublika → Ukrayina 19 Df 49.00N 32.00 E
Ukrainska Radyanska Socialistična Respublika/ Ukrainskaja SSR → Ukrayina 19 Df 49.00N 32.00 E
Ukrayina = Ukraine (EN) 19 Df 49.00N 32.00 E
Ukrina 14 Le 45.05N 17.56 E
Uku-Jima 29 Ae 33.16N 129.07 E
Ula 24 Cd 37.05N 28.26 E
Ulah Lake 45 Hh 36.58N 96.10W
Ulaidh/Ulster 9 Gg 54.30N 7.00W
Ulalu 64d Bb 7.25N 151.40 E
Ulan (Xiligou) 27 Gd 36.55N 98.16 E
Ulan → Otog Qi 27 Id 39.07N 108.00 E
Ulanbaatar → Ulan-Bator 22 Me 47.55N 106.53 E
Ulan-Badrah 28 Ac 43.58N 110.37 E
Ulan-Bator (Ulaanbaatar) 22 Me 47.55N 106.53 E
Ulanbel 19 Hg 44.49N 71.10 E
Ulan-Burgasy, Hrebet- 20 Ff 52.30N 108.30 E
Ulangom 22 Le 49.58N 92.02 E
Ulanhad/Chifeng 27 Kc 42.16N 118.57 E
Ulan Hol 19 Ef 45.27N 46.46 E
Ulan Hot/Horqin Youyi Qianqi 22 Oe 46.04N 122.00 E
Ulan Hua → Siziwang Qi 28 Ad 41.31N 111.41 E
Ulan-Hus 27 Eb 49.02N 89.23 E
Ulanów 10 Sf 50.30N 22.16 E
Ulansuhai Nur 27 Ic 40.56N 108.49 E
Ulan-Tajga 27 Ga 50.45N 98.30 E
Ulan-Ude 22 Md 51.50N 107.37 E
Ulan Ul Hu 27 Fe 34.45N 90.25 E
Ulas 24 Gc 39.27N 37.03 E
Ulawa Island 60 Gi 9.46S 161.57 E
Ulbeja 20 Je 59.20N 144.25 E
Ulchin 28 Jf 36.59N 129.24 E
Ulcinj 15 Ch 41.56N 19.13 E
Uleåborg/Oulu 6 Ib 65.01N 25.30 E
Ulefoss 7 Bg 59.17N 9.16 E
Ulegej 22 Ke 48.56N 89.57 E
Ulety 20 Gf 51.22N 112.30 E
Uleza 15 Ch 41.40N 19.53 E
Ulfborg 8 Ch 56.16N 8.20 E
Ulflingen/Troisvierges 12 Hd 50.07N 6.00 E
Ulft, Gendringen- 12 Ic 51.54N 6.24 E
Ulgain Gol 27 Kb 45.31N 117.50 E
Ulhāsnagar 25 Ee 19.10N 73.07 E
Uliastai → Dong Ujimqin Qi 27 Kc 45.31N 116.58 E
Uliga 58 Id 7.09N 171.13 E
Ulindi 30 Ji 1.40S 25.52 E
Ulithi Atoll 57 Ed 9.58N 139.40 E
Ulja 20 Je 58.48N 141.40 E
Uljanovka 8 Ne 59.37N 30.55 E
Uljanovka 16 Ge 48.20N 30.13 E
Uljanovsk 6 Ke 54.20N 48.24 E
Uljanovskaja Oblast 19 Ee 54.00N 48.00 E
Uljanovski 19 He 50.05N 73.45 E
Uljasutaj 22 Le 47.45N 96.49 E
Ulkan 20 Fe 55.55N 107.55 E
Ulla 13 Db 42.39N 8.44W
Ullapool 9 Hd 57.54N 5.10W
Ullared 7 Ch 57.08N 12.43 E
Ulldecona 13 Md 40.36N 0.27 E
Ullsfjorden 7 Eb 69.58N 20.00 E
Ullswater 9 Kg 54.34N 2.54W
Ullŭng-Do 28 Kf 37.29N 130.52 E
Ullvettern 8 Fe 59.25N 14.15 E
Ulm 10 Fh 48.25N 10.00 E
Ulmen 12 Id 50.13N 6.59 E
Ulmeni 15 Jd 45.04N 26.39 E
Ulmu 15 Je 44.16N 26.55 E
Ulongwé 37 Eb 14.43S 34.21 E
Ulricehamn 7 Ch 57.47N 13.25 E
Ulrichstein 12 Ld 50.35N 9.12 E
Ulrum 12 Ia 53.22N 6.20 E
Ulrum-Zoutkamp 12 Ia 53.20N 6.18 E
Ulsan 27 Md 35.33N 129.19 E
Ulsteinvik 7 Ae 62.20N 5.53 E
Ulster 10 Ff 50.51N 9.59 E
Ulster/Ulaidh 9 Gg 54.30N 7.00W
Ulster Canal 9 Gg 54.27N 6.40W
Ulu 35 Ec 10.43N 33.29 E
Ulu/Uulu 8 Kf 58.13N 24.29 E
Ulúa, Río- 47 Ge 15.56N 87.43W
Ulubat Gölü 24 Cb 40.10N 28.35 E
Ulubey 24 Cc 38.09N 29.33 E
Uludağ 23 Ca 40.04N 29.13 E
Uludere 24 Jd 37.27N 42.51 E
Ulugqat/Wuqia 27 Cd 39.40N 75.07 E
Ulukışla 24 Fd 37.33N 34.30 E
Ulungur He 21 Ke 46.58N 87.28 E
Ulungur Hu 27 Eb 47.20N 87.10 E
Ulus 24 Eb 41.35N 32.39 E
Ulus Dağ 15 Lj 39.18N 28.24 E
Ulva 9 Ge 56.28N 6.12W
Ulverston 9 Jg 54.12N 3.06W
Ulverstone 59 Jh 41.09S 146.10 E
Ulvik 8 Bd 60.34N 6.54 E
Ulvön 8 Ha 63.05N 18.40 E
Ulysses 45 Fh 37.35N 101.22W
Ulytau 19 Gf 48.35N 67.05 E
Ulytau, Gora- 19 Gf 48.45N 67.00 E
Uly-Žilanšik 19 Gf 48.51N 63.47 E
Uma 27 La 52.36N 120.38 E
Umag 14 He 45.25N 13.32 E
Umala 54 Eg 17.24S 67.58W
Umán 48 Og 20.53N 89.45W
Uman 64d Bb 7.18N 151.53 E
Uman 19 Df 48.47N 30.09 E
'Umān 21 Hg 22.10N 58.00 E
'Umān=Oman (EN) 22 Hg 21.00N 57.00 E
'Umān, Khalīj-=Oman, Gulf of- (EN) 21 Hg 25.00N 58.00 E
Umanak 41 Gd 70.36N 52.15W
Ūmánarssuaq/Farvel, Kap- 67 Nb 59.50N 43.50W
Umatac 64c Bb 13.18N 144.40 E
Umba 19 Db 66.41N 34.17 E
Umbelasha 35 Cd 9.51N 24.50 E
Umbertide 14 Gg 43.18N 12.20 E
Umberto de Campos 54 Jd 2.37S 43.27W
Umboi Island 57 Fe 5.36S 148.00 E
Umbozero, Ozero- 7 Ic 67.45N 34.20 E
Umbria 14 Gh 43.00N 12.30 E
Ume 37 Dc 17.15S 28.20 E
Umeå 6 Ic 63.50N 20.15 E
Umeälven 5 Ic 63.47N 20.16 E
Umm al Arānib 33 Bd 26.08N 14.45 E
Umm al Hayf, Wādī- 23 Hf 18.37N 53.59 E
Umm al Jamaājim 24 Ki 26.59N 45.19 E
Umm al Qaywayn 23 Id 25.35N 55.34 E
Ummanz 10 Jb 54.30N 13.10 E
Umm ar Rizam 33 Dc 32.32N 23.00 E
Umm as Samīm 23 Ie 21.30N 56.45 E
Umm Bāb 24 Nj 25.12N 50.48 E
Umm Bel 35 Dc 13.32N 28.04 E
Umm Buru 35 Cb 15.01N 23.36 E
Umm Dhibbān 35 Dc 14.14N 29.37 E
Umm Durmān=Omdurman (EN) 31 Kg 15.38N 32.30 E
Umm Inderaba 35 Eb 15.12N 31.54 E
Umm Kaddādah 35 Dc 13.36N 26.42 E
Umm Lajj 23 Ed 25.04N 37.13 E
Umm Naqqāt, Jabal- 24 Fj 25.30N 34.14 E
Umm Qam'ul 24 Pj 24.47N 54.42 E
Umm Ruwābah 31 Kg 12.54N 31.13 E
Umm Sayyālah 35 Ec 14.25N 31.00 E
Umm Urūmah 24 Gj 25.46N 36.33 E
Umnak 38 Cd 58.25N 168.10W
Umne-Gobi 27 Fb 49.06N 91.43 E
Umpqua River 46 Ce 43.42N 124.03W
Umpulu 36 Ce 12.42S 17.40 E
Umsini, Gunung- 26 Jg 1.35S 133.30 E
Umtata 31 Jl 31.35S 28.47 E
Umuarama 56 Jb 23.45S 53.20W
Umurbey 15 Ji 40.14N 26.36 E
Umvukwes 37 Ec 17.01S 30.52 E
Umvuma 37 Ec 19.19S 30.35 E
Umzingwani 37 Dd 22.12S 29.56 E
Una 14 Ke 45.16N 16.55 E
Unabetsu-Dake 29a Db 43.52N 144.51 E
Unac 14 Kf 44.29N 16.08 E
Unai 54 Ig 16.23S 46.53W
Unalakleet 40 Gd 63.53N 160.47W
Unalaska 38 Cd 53.45N 166.45W
Unare, Río- 50 Dg 10.06N 65.12W
Unauna, Pulau- 26 Hg 0.10S 121.35 E
'Unayzah [Jor.] 24 Fg 30.29N 35.48 E
'Unayzah [Sau. Ar.] 22 Gg 26.06N 43.56 E
Uncia 54 Eg 18.27S 66.37W
Uncompahgre Peak 43 Fd 38.04N 107.28W
Uncompahgre Plateau 45 Bg 38.30N 108.25W
Unden 8 Ff 58.45N 14.25 E
Underberg 37 De 29.50S 29.22 E
Under-Han 22 Ne 47.19N 110.39 E
Undjuljung 20 Hc 66.20N 124.40 E
Undu Point 63d Cb 16.08S 179.57W
Undva Neem/Kiprarenukk, Mys- 8 If 58.25N 21.45 E
Uneča 16 Hc 52.50N 32.44 E
'Ung, Jabal al- 14 Dn 36.45N 9.35 E
Unga 40 Ge 55.15N 160.45W
Ungava, Péninsule d'-= Ungava Peninsula (EN) 38 Lc 60.00N 74.00W
Ungava Bay 38 Md 59.30N 67.30W
Ungava Peninsula (EN)= Ungava, Péninsule d'- 38 Lc 60.00N 74.00W
Ungen' 16 Ef 47.13N 27.50 E
Unggi 28 Kc 42.21N 130.23 E
Ungureni 15 Jb 47.53N 26.47 E
Ungwatiri 35 Fb 16.55N 36.05 E
União 54 Jd 4.35S 42.52W
União da Vitória 56 Jc 26.13S 51.05W
União dos Palmares 54 Ke 9.10S 36.02W
Uničov 10 Ng 49.49N 17.07 E
Uniejów 10 Oe 51.58N 18.49 E
Unije 14 If 44.38N 14.15 E
Unimak 38 Cd 54.50N 164.00W
Unimak Pass 40 Gf 54.35N 164.43W
Unini, Rio- 54 Fd 1.41S 61.30W
Union [Mo.-U.S.] 45 Kg 38.27N 91.00W
Union [S.C.-U.S.] 44 Gh 34.42N 81.37W
Union City 44 Cg 36.26N 89.03W
Uniondale 37 Cf 33.40S 23.08 E
Unión de Reyes 49 Gb 22.48N 81.32W
Unión de Tula 48 Gh 19.58N 104.16W
Union Island 50 Ff 12.36N 61.26W
Union Islands/Tokelau 57 Je 9.00S 171.45W
Union Seamount (EN) 42 Eg 49.35N 132.45W
Union Springs 44 Ei 32.09N 85.49W
Uniontown 44 Hf 39.54N 79.44W
Unionville 45 Jf 40.29N 93.01W
United Arab Emirates (EN) =Al Imārāt al 'Arabīyah al Muttaḥidah 22 Hg 24.00N 54.00 E
United Arab Republic (EN) → Egypt (EN) 31 Jf 27.00N 30.00 E
United Kingdom 6 Fe 54.00N 2.00W
United Kingdom of Great Britain and Northern Ireland 6 Fe 54.00N 2.00W
United States 39 Jf 38.00N 97.00W
United States of America 39 Jf 38.00N 97.00W
Unity [Or.-U.S.] 46 Fd 44.29N 118.13W
Unity [Sask.-Can.] 42 Gf 52.27N 109.10W
Universales, Montes- 13 Kd 40.18N 1.33W
University City 45 Kg 38.39N 90.19W
Unna 10 De 51.32N 7.41 E
Unnāb, Wādī al- 24 Gg 30.11N 36.39 E
Unnukka 8 Lb 62.25N 27.55 E
Unst 5 Fc 60.45N 0.55W
Unstrut 10 He 51.10N 11.48 E
Unterfranken 10 Fg 50.00N 10.00 E
Unterwalden-Nidwalden 14 Cd 46.55N 8.30 E
Unterwalden-Obwalden 14 Cd 46.50N 8.20 E
Unuli Horog 27 Fd 35.12N 91.58 E
Ünye 23 Ea 41.08N 37.17 E
Unža 5 Kd 57.20N 43.08 E
Unzen-Dake 29 Be 32.45N 130.17 E
Uoleva 65b Ba 19.51S 174.24W
Uozu 28 Nf 36.48N 137.24 E
Úpa 10 Lf 50.22N 15.54 E
Upata 54 Fb 8.01N 62.24W
Upemba, Lac- 36 Ed 8.36S 26.26 E
Upernavik 41 Gd 72.20N 56.00W
Upin 26 Ig 2.56S 129.11 E
Upington 31 Jk 28.25S 21.15 E
Upland 12 Kc 51.18N 8.42 E
Upolu Island 57 Jf 13.55S 171.45W
Upolu Point 60 Oc 20.16N 155.52W
Upper 34 Ec 10.30N 1.30W
Upper Arlington 44 Fe 40.01N 83.03W
Upper Arrow Lake 46 Ga 50.30N 117.55W
Upper Austria (EN) = Oberösterreich 14 Hb 48.15N 14.00 E
Upper Hutt 62 Fd 41.07S 175.04 E
Upper Klamath Lake 43 Cc 42.23N 122.00W
Upper Lake 46 Ef 41.44N 120.08W
Upper Lough Erne/Loch Éirne Uachtair 9 Fg 54.20N 7.30W
Upper Red Lake 45 Ib 48.10N 94.40W
Upper Sandusky 44 Fe 40.48N 83.17W
Upper Sheik 35 Hd 9.57N 45.09 E
Upper Thames Valley 9 Lj 51.40N 1.40W
Upper Trajan's Wall (EN)= Verhni Traijanov Val 15 Lc 46.40N 29.00 E
Upper Volta→ Burkina Faso 31 Gg 13.00N 2.00W
Uppingham 12 Bb 52.35N 0.43W
Uppland 8 Gd 60.00N 17.50 E
Upplands Väsby 8 Ge 59.31N 17.54 E
Uppsala 7 Df 60.00N 17.45 E
Uppsala 6 Hd 59.52N 17.38 E
Upsala 45 Kb 49.02N 90.29W
Upshi 25 Fb 33.50N 77.49 E
Upton 46 Md 44.06N 104.38W
Uqbān 33 Hf 15.30N 42.23 E
'Uqlat aş Şuqūr 24 Jj 25.53N 42.15 E
Uqturpan/Wuski 27 Cc 41.10N 79.16 E
Ur 23 Gc 30.58N 46.06 E
Urabá, Golfo de- 54 Cb 8.25N 77.00W
Uracoa 50 Eh 9.00N 62.21W
Uracoa, Río- 50 Eh 9.08N 62.20W
Uradarja 18 Fe 38.51N 66.02 E
Urad Qianqi 27 Ic 40.49N 108.37 E
Urad Zhonghou Lianheqi (Haliut) 27 Ic 41.34N 108.32 E
Uraga-Suido 29 Fd 35.15N 139.45 E
Ura-Guba 7 Hb 69.18N 32.48 E
Urahoro 29a Cb 42.48N 143.38 E
Urahoro-Gawa 29a Cb 42.44N 143.40 E
Uraj 19 Gc 60.08N 64.40 E
Urakawa 28 Qc 42.09N 142.47 E
Ural 5 Lf 47.00N 51.48 E
Ural Mountains (EN)= Uralskije Gory 5 Ld 57.00N 60.00 E
Uralsk 6 Le 51.14N 51.22 E
Uralskaja Oblast 19 Ff 49.45N 51.00 E
Uralskije Gory=Ural Mountains (EN) 5 Ld 57.00N 60.00 E
Urambo 36 Fd 5.04S 32.03 E
Uranium City 39 Id 59.34N 108.36W
Uraricoera 54 Fc 3.27N 60.59W
Uraricoera, Rio- 52 Je 3.02N 60.30W
Ura-Tjube 19 Gh 39.53N 69.01 E
Urawa 28 Og 35.51N 139.39 E
'Uray'irah 24 Mj 25.57N 48.53 E
Urayq, Nafūd al- 24 Jj 25.17N 42.25 E
Urbana [Il.-U.S.] 45 Lf 40.07N 88.12W
Urbana [Oh.-U.S.] 44 Fe 40.06N 83.45W
Urbandale 45 Jf 41.38N 93.48W
Urbania 14 Gg 43.40N 12.31 E

Index Symbols

Independent Nation
State, Region
District, County
Municipality
Colony, Dependency
Continent
Physical Region
Historical or Cultural Region
Mount, Mountain
Volcano
Hill
Mountains, Mountain Range
Hills, Escarpment
Plateau, Upland
Pass, Gap
Plain, Lowland
Delta
Salt Flat
Valley, Canyon
Crater, Cave
Karst Features
Depression
Polder
Desert, Dunes
Forest, Woods
Heath, Steppe
Oasis
Cape, Point
Coast, Beach
Cliff
Peninsula
Isthmus
Sandbank
Island
Atoll
Rock, Reef
Islands, Archipelago
Rocks, Reefs
Coral Reef
Well, Spring
Geyser
River, Stream
Waterfall Rapids
River Mouth, Estuary
Lake
Salt Lake
Intermittent Lake
Reservoir
Swamp, Pond
Canal
Glacier
Ice Shelf, Pack Ice
Ocean
Sea
Gulf, Bay
Strait, Fjord
Lagoon
Bank
Seamount
Tablemount
Ridge
Shelf
Basin
Escarpment, Sea Scarp
Fracture
Trench, Abyss
National Park, Reserve
Point of Interest
Recreation Site
Cave, Cavern
Historic Site
Ruins
Wall, Walls
Church, Abbey
Temple
Scientific Station
Airport
Port
Lighthouse
Mine
Tunnel
Dam, Bridge

Urbano Santos 54 Jd 3.12S 43.23W
Urbino 14 Gg 43.43N 12.38 E
Urbino, Étang d'- 11a Ba 42.02N 9.28 E
Urbión, Picos de- 13 Jb 42.01N 2.52W
Urcel 12 Fe 49.30N 3.33 E
Urcos 54 Df 13.42S 71.38W
Urdinarrain 55 Ck 32.41S 58.53W
Urdoma 7 Lf 61.47N 48.29 E
Urdžar 19 If 47.05N 81.37 E
Ure 9 Lg 54.01N 1.12W
Uré 49 Jj 7.46N 75.31W
Uren 19 Ed 57.29N 45.48 E
Urenui 62 Fc 39.00S 174.23 E
Ures 47 Bc 29.26N 110.24W
Ureshino 29 Ab 33.06N 129.59 E
'Urf, Jabal al- 24 Ei 27.49N 32.55 E
Urfa → Şanlıurfa 23 Eb 37.08N 38.46 E
Urfa Platosu 24 Hd 37.10N 38.50 E
Urgal 20 If 51.00N 132.50 E
Urgel, Llanos de- 13 Lc 41.25N 0.36W
Urgel, Llanos de-/Urgell, Pla d'- 13 Lc 41.25N 0.36W
Urgell, Pla d'- 13 Lc 41.25N 0.36W
Urgell, Pla d'-/Urgel, Llanos de- 13 Lc 41.25N 0.36W
Urgen 28 Ab 44.45N 110.40 E
Urgenč 22 Ie 41.33N 60.38 E
Ürgüp 24 Fc 38.38N 35.56 E
Urgut 19 Gh 39.23N 67.14 E
Uri 25 Eb 34.05N 74.02 E
Uri [2] 14 Cd 46.40N 8.30 E
Uribia 54 Da 11.42N 72.17W
Uricki 19 Ge 53.19N 65.34 E
Urique, Río- 48 Fd 26.29N 107.58W
Urjala 8 Jc 61.05N 23.32 E
Urjupinsk 19 Ee 50.48N 42.02 E
Urk 11 Lb 52.39N 5.36 E
Urkan 20 Hf 53.27N 126.56 E
Urla 24 Bc 38.18N 26.46 E
Urlaţi 15 Je 44.59N 26.14 E
Urluk 20 Ff 50.03N 107.55 E
Urmi 20 Ig 48.43N 134.16 E
Urmia, Lake- (EN) = Orumıyeh, Daryācheh-ye 21 Gf 37.40N 45.30 E
Uromi 34 Gd 6.42N 6.20 E
Uroševac 15 Eg 42.22N 21.10 E
Urshult 8 Fh 56.32N 14.47 E
Ursus 10 Qd 52.12N 20.53 E
Urtazym 17 Ij 52.15N 58.50 E
Urtigueira, Serra da- 55 Gg 24.15S 51.00W
Uru, Rio- 55 Hb 15.24S 49.36W
Uruaçu 54 If 14.30S 49.10W
Uruana 55 Hb 15.30S 49.41W
Uruapan del Progreso 47 De 19.25N 101.58W
Uruará, Rio- 54 Hd 2.00S 53.38W
Urubamba, Río- 52 Ig 10.43S 73.48W
Urubici 55 Hi 28.02S 49.37W
Urubú, Cachoeira do- 55 Ha 12.52S 48.13W
Urucará 54 Gd 2.32S 57.45W
Uruçui 54 Je 7.14S 44.33W
Urucuia, Rio- [Braz.] 55 Ib 15.38S 46.10W
Urucuia, Rio- [Braz.] 55 Jc 16.08S 45.05W
Urucum, Serra do- 55 Dd 19.13S 57.33W
Urucurituba 54 Gd 2.41S 57.40W
Uruguai, Rio- 52 Ki 34.12S 58.18W
Uruguaiana 53 Kh 29.45S 57.05W
Uruguay [1] 53 Ki 33.00S 56.00W
Uruguay, Río- 52 Ki 34.12S 58.18W
Urukthapel 64a Ac 7.15N 134.24 E
Urumbaba Dağı 15 Lj 38.25N 28.49 E
Ürümqi 22 Ke 43.48N 87.35 E
Urup 16 Lg 44.59N 41.10 E
Urup, Ostrov- 21 Qe 46.00N 150.00 E
Uruša 20 Hf 54.03N 122.55 E
Urussu 7 Mi 54.38N 53.24 E
Uruwira 36 Fd 6.27S 31.21 E
Urville, Cape D'- (EN) = Perkam, Tanjung- 26 Kg 1.28S 137.54 E
Uryū 29a Bb 43.39N 141.51 E
Uryū-Gawa 29a Bb 43.40N 141.54 E
Urziceni 15 Je 44.43N 26.38 E
Uržum 19 Fd 57.10N 50.01 E
Usa 29 Be 33.31N 131.22 E
Usa 16 Nc 53.02N 45.18 E
Usa 5 Lb 65.57N 56.55 E
Uşak 23 Cb 38.41N 29.25 E
Usakos 37 Bd 22.01S 15.32 E
Ušakovo 20 Hf 51.54N 126.35 E
Ušakovskoje 20 Nb 71.00N 178.35W
Usambara Mountains 30 Ki 4.45S 38.30 E
Usarp Mountains 66 Jf 71.10S 160.00 E
Usas Escarpment 66 Nf 76.00S 125.00W
Ušba, Gora- 16 Mh 43.06N 42.40 E
Usborne, Mount- 56 Ih 51.42S 58.50W
Ušće 15 Df 43.29N 20.38 E
Usedom 10 Jb 54.00N 14.00 E
Useldange 12 He 49.46N 5.59 E
'Ushayrah [Sau. Ar.] 33 He 21.46N 40.38 E
'Ushayrah [Sau. Ar.] 24 Kj 25.35N 45.46 E
Ushibuka 29 Be 32.13N 130.01 E
Ushikubi-Misaki 29a Bc 41.08N 140.48 E
Ushimado 29 Dd 34.37N 134.09 E
'Ushsh, Wādī al- 24 Fd 27.18N 42.15 E
Ushuaia 53 Jk 54.47S 68.20W
Usingen 12 Kd 50.20N 8.32 E
Usinsk 19 Fb 65.57N 57.29 E
Üsküdar 24 Cb 41.01N 29.03 E
Üsküp 15 Kh 41.44N 27.24 E
Uslar 10 Fe 51.40N 9.39 E
Úslava 10 Jg 49.54N 13.32 E
Usman 16 Kd 51.54N 39.20 E
Usman 19 De 52.00N 39.43 E
Usmas, Ozero-/Usmas Ezers 8 Ig 57.13N 22.00 E
Usmas Ezers/Usmas, Ozero- 8 Ig 57.13N 22.00 E
Usogorsk 19 Ec 63.28N 48.35 E
Usoke 36 Fd 5.06S 32.20 E
Usolje 19 Fd 59.25N 56.41 E
Usolje-Sibirskoje 20 Ff 52.47N 103.38 E
Usora 14 Mf 44.43N 18.04 E
Ussel 11 Ii 45.33N 2.09 E
Ussuri 21 Pe 48.28N 135.02 E
Ussurijsk 22 Pe 43.48N 131.59 E
Usta 7 Kh 56.53N 45.28 E
Ust-Barguzin 20 Ff 53.27N 108.59 E
Ust-Bolšereck 20 Kf 52.40N 156.18 E
Ust-Cilma 19 Fb 65.27N 52.06 E
Ust-Čorna 10 Uh 48.17N 24.02 E
Ust-Donecki 16 Lf 47.39N 40.55 E
Ust-Džeguta 16 Mg 44.05N 42.01 E
Uster 14 Cc 47.20N 8.43 E
Ustevatn 8 Bd 60.30N 8.00 E
Ust-Hajrjuzovo 20 Ke 57.04N 156.50 E
Ustica 5 Hh 38.40N 13.10 E
Ustica 14 Hl 38.42N 13.11 E
Ust-Ilimsk 22 Md 58.03N 102.43 E
Ustilug 10 Uf 50.50N 24.09 E
Ústí nad Labem 10 Kf 50.40N 14.02 E
Ústí nad Orlicí 10 Mg 49.58N 16.24 E
Ustinov → Iževsk 6 Ld 56.51N 53.14 E
Ust-Išim 19 Hd 57.44N 71.10 E
Ust-Judoma 20 Ie 59.10N 135.02 E
Ustjurt, Plato 21 He 43.00N 56.00 E
Ustjužna 7 Ig 58.53N 36.28 E
Ustka 10 Mb 54.35N 16.50 E
Ust-Kamčatsk 22 Sd 56.15N 162.30 E
Ust-Kamenogorsk 22 Ke 49.58N 82.38 E
Ust-Kan 20 Df 50.57N 84.55 E
Ust-Kara 19 Gb 69.15N 64.59 E
Ust-Karsk 20 Gf 52.41N 118.45 E
Ust-Katav 17 Ii 54.56N 58.10 E
Ust-Kujga 22 Pc 70.00N 135.36 E
Ust-Kut 22 Md 56.46N 105.40 E
Ust-Labinsk 19 Df 45.13N 39.40 E
Ust-Luga 7 Gg 59.39N 28.15 E
Ust-Maya 22 Pc 60.25N 134.32 E
Ust-Muja 20 Ge 56.28N 115.30 E
Ust-Nera 22 Qc 64.34N 143.12 E
Ust-Njukža 20 He 56.30N 121.48 E
Uštobe 19 Hf 45.13N 77.59 E
Ust-Olenëk 20 Gb 72.58N 119.42 E
Ust-Omčug 20 Jd 61.05N 149.30 E
Ust-Ordynski 20 Ff 52.48N 104.45 E
Ust-Ordynski Burjatski avtonomnyj okrug 20 Ff 53.30N 104.00 E
Ustovo 15 Hh 41.34N 24.47 E
Ust-Pinega 7 Jd 64.10N 41.58 E
Ust-Pit 20 Ee 58.59N 92.00 E
Ust-Port 20 Dc 69.45N 84.25 E
Ust-Požva 17 Hg 59.05N 56.05 E
Ustrzyki Dolne 10 Sg 49.26N 22.37 E
Ust-Sobolevka 20 Ig 46.10N 137.59 E
Ust-Šonoša 7 Jf 61.11N 41.20 E
Ust-Uda 20 Ff 54.10N 103.03 E
Ust-Ujskoje 17 Ki 54.15N 63.57 E
Ust-Umalta 20 If 51.42N 133.18 E
Ustupo 49 Ii 9.08N 77.56W
Usú 22 Ke 44.27N 84.37 E
Usui-Tōge 29 Fc 36.22N 138.38 E
Usuki 28 Kh 33.08N 131.49 E
Usuki-Wan 29 Be 33.10N 131.50 E
Usulután 49 Cg 13.21N 88.27W
Usumacinta 38 Jh 18.22N 92.40W
Ušumun 20 Hf 52.46N 126.37 E
Usu-San 29a Bb 42.32N 140.49 E
Usva 17 Hg 58.40N 57.35 E
Usva 17 Hg 58.17N 57.47 E
Utah [2] 43 Ed 39.30N 111.30W
Utah Lake 43 Ec 40.13N 111.49W
Utajärvi 7 Gd 64.45N 26.23 E
Utashinai 29a Cb 43.31N 142.03 E
Utata 20 Ff 50.51N 102.45 E
Ute Creek 45 Ei 35.21N 103.50W
Utembo 30 Jj 17.06S 22.01 E
Utena 7 Fi 55.29N 25.40 E
Ute Reservoir 45 Ei 35.21N 103.31W
Utete 36 Gd 7.59S 38.47 E
Uthai Thani 25 Ke 15.20N 100.02 E
Utiariti 55 Ca 13.02S 58.17W
Utica 43 Lc 43.06N 75.15W
Utiel 13 Ke 39.34N 1.12W
Utiel, Sierra de- 13 Ke 39.36N 1.08W
Utila 49 De 16.06N 86.54W
Utila, Isla de- 49 De 16.06N 86.56W
Utique 14 Em 37.04N 10.04 E
Utirik Atoll 57 Hc 11.15N 169.48 E
Utlängan 8 Fh 56.00N 15.45 E
Utljukski Liman 16 If 46.20N 35.15 E
Uto 23 Kh 32.40N 130.41 E
Utö [Fin.] 8 Ie 59.45N 21.25 E
Utö [Swe.] 7 Eg 58.55N 18.15 E
Utoro 29a Da 44.06N 144.58 E
Utrata 10 Qd 52.13N 20.15 E
Utrecht [3] 12 Hb 52.05N 5.08 E
Utrecht [Neth.] 6 Ge 52.05N 5.08 E
Utrecht [S.Afr.] 37 Ee 27.28S 30.20 E
Utrera 13 Gg 37.11N 5.47W
Utsira 8 Ae 59.20N 4.55 E
Utsjoki 7 Gb 69.53N 27.00 E
Utsunomiya 22 Pf 36.33N 139.52 E
Uttaradit 25 Ke 17.38N 100.06 E
Uttar Pradesh [3] 25 Fc 28.00N 80.00 E
Utuado 49 Nd 18.16N 66.42W
Utukok 40 Gb 70.04N 162.18W
Utuloa 64h Ab 13.16S 176.11W
Utupua Island 57 Hf 11.20S 166.36 E
Uturoa 65e Db 16.44S 151.26W
Utva 16 Rd 51.29N 52.40 E
Uudenmaa [2] 7 Ff 60.30N 25.00 E
Uukuniemi 8 Nc 61.47N 30.01 E
Uulu/Ulu 8 Kf 58.13N 24.29 E
Uusikaupunki/Nystad 7 Ef 60.48N 21.25 E
Uusimaa 8 Kd 60.30N 25.00 E
Uva 19 Fd 56.58N 52.14 E
Uvac 15 Cf 43.36N 19.30 E
Uvalde 43 Hf 29.13N 99.47W
Uvarovo 19 Ee 52.00N 42.15 E
Uvdal 8 Cd 60.20N 8.30 E
Uvéa, Ile- 57 Jf 13.18S 176.10W
Uvelka 17 Ji 54.05N 61.35 E
Uvelski 17 Ji 54.26N 61.27 E
Uvildy, Ozero- 17 Ji 55.35N 60.30 E
Uvinza 36 Fd 5.06S 30.22 E
Uvira 31 Ji 3.24S 29.08 E
Uvs nuur → Ubsu-Nur 21 Ld 50.20N 92.45 E
Uwa 29 Ce 33.21N 132.30 E
Uwajima 27 Ne 33.13N 132.34 E
Uwajima-Wan 29 Ce 33.15N 132.30 E
Uwa-Kai 29 Ce 33.20N 132.15 E
Uwayl 35 Dd 8.46N 27.24 E
'Uwaynāt, Jabal al- = Uweinat, Gebel- (EN) 30 Jf 21.54N 24.58 E
'Uwaynat Wannīn 33 Bd 28.05N 12.59 E
Uweinat, Gebel- (EN) = 'Uwaynāt, Jabal al- 30 Jf 21.54N 24.58 E
Uwekuli 26 Hg 1.25S 121.06 E
Uwi, Pulau- 26 Ef 1.05N 107.24 E
Uxin Qi (Dabqig) 27 Id 38.27N 109.08 E
Uxmal 39 Kg 20.20N 89.46W
Uyo 34 Gd 5.07N 7.57 E
Uyuni 53 Jh 20.28S 66.50W
Uyuni, Salar de- 52 Jh 20.20S 67.42W
Už [Eur.] 10 Rh 48.33N 22.00 E
Už 16 Gd 51.15N 30.12 E
Uzbekistan (EN) = Ŭzbekiston 19 Gg 41.00N 64.00 E
Uzbekiston Sovet Socialistik Respublikasy/Uzbekskaja SSR → Ŭzbekiston 19 Gg 41.00N 64.00 E
Uzbekskaja Sovetkaja Socialističeskaja Respublika → Ŭzbekiston 19 Gg 41.00N 64.00 E
Uzbekskaja SSR/Uzbekiston Sovet Socialistik Respublikasy → Ŭzbekiston 19 Gg 41.00N 64.00 E
Ŭzbekiston = Uzbekistan (EN) 19 Gg 41.00N 64.00 E
Uzbel Shankou 27 Bd 38.42N 73.48 E
Uzen 19 Fg 43.22N 52.50 E
Uzerche 11 Hi 45.25N 1.34 E
Uzès 11 Kj 44.01N 4.25 E
Uzgen 18 Id 40.44N 73.21 E
Užgorod 19 Cf 48.37N 22.22 E
Užice (Titovo Užice) 15 Cf 43.52N 19.51 E
Uzin 16 Ge 49.52N 30.27 E
Uzlovaja 16 Kb 54.01N 38.12 E
Uzlovoje 10 Sh 48.23N 22.27 E
Užokski, pereval- 16 Ce 49.02N 22.58 E
Uzümlü 15 Mm 36.44N 29.14 E
Uzun Ada 15 Jk 38.28N 26.42 E
Uzunagač 18 Kc 43.08N 76.20 E
Uzunagač 18 Kc 43.36N 76.19 E
Uzunköprü 24 Bb 41.16N 26.41 E
Užur 20 De 55.20N 90.00 E
Užventis 8 Ji 55.44N 22.37 E
Uzynkair, Mys- 18 Bb 45.47N 59.20 E

V

Vääksy 8 Kc 61.11N 25.33 E
Vaal 30 Jk 29.24S 23.38 E
Vaala 7 Gd 64.34N 26.50 E
Vaals 12 Id 50.46N 6.01 E
Vaalwater 37 Dd 24.20S 28.03 E
Vaasa [2] 7 Fe 63.12N 23.00 E
Vaasa/Vasa 6 Ic 63.06N 21.36 E
Vaassen, Epe- 12 Hb 52.17N 5.58 E
Vabalninkas 8 Ki 55.58N 24.49 E
Vác 10 Pi 47.47N 19.08 E
Vacacaí, Rio- 55 Fi 29.55S 53.06W
Vacaria 56 Jc 28.30S 50.56W
Vacaria, Rio- 55 Fe 21.55S 53.59W
Vacaville 46 Eg 38.21N 121.59W
Vaccarès, Étang de- 11 Kk 43.32N 4.34 E
Vache, Ile à- 49 Kd 18.04N 73.38W
Väddö 8 Hd 60.00N 18.50 E
Vadehavet 8 Ci 55.15N 8.40 E
Vădeni 15 Kd 45.22N 27.56 E
Vadheim 8 Ac 61.13N 5.49 E
Vadodara 22 Jg 22.18N 73.12 E
Vado Ligure 14 Cf 44.17N 8.27 E
Vadsø 6 Ia 70.05N 29.46 E
Vadstena 7 Dg 58.27N 14.54 E
Vaduz 6 Gf 47.08N 9.30 E
Værlandet 8 Ac 61.20N 4.45 E
Vaga 5 Kc 62.48N 42.56 E
Vagaj 17 Mh 56.28N 67.18 E
Vagaj 17 Nh 57.55N 69.01 E
Vågåmo 7 Bf 61.53N 9.06 E
Vaganjski vrh 14 Jf 44.21N 15.30 E
Vågåvatn 8 Cc 61.50N 9.50 E
Vaggeryd 7 Dh 57.30N 14.07 E
Vaghena 63a Cb 7.25S 157.43 E
Vagil 17 Kg 59.45N 62.40 E
Vagis, Gora- 20 Jf 52.20N 142.15 E
Vagnhärad 8 Gf 58.57N 17.31 E
Vågsøy 8 Ac 62.00N 5.05 E
Váh 10 Ni 47.55N 18.00 E
Vah 21 Jc 60.45N 76.45 E
Vahitahi Atoll 57 Nf 18.44S 138.52W
Vahruši 7 Mg 58.43N 50.02 E
Vahš 18 Gf 37.43N 68.49 E
Vahsel Bay → Herzog-Ernst-Bucht 66 Af 77.48S 34.39W
Vahtan 7 Lh 57.59N 46.42 E
Vaïaau 65e Db 16.52S 151.28W
Vaigat 41 Gd 70.30N 54.00W
Vaihingen an der Enz 12 Kf 48.56N 8.58 E
Vaihú 65d Ab 27.10S 109.23W
Väike-Maarja/Vjaike-Maarja 8 Le 59.04N 26.12 E
Väike-Pakri/Vjajke-Pakri 8 Je 59.50N 23.50 E
Väike Väin/Vjajke-Vjajn 8 Jf 58.30N 23.10 E
Vailala 64h Bb 13.13S 176.09W
Vailala, Pointe- 64h Ab 13.13S 176.10W
Vaileka 63d Bb 17.23S 178.09 E
Vailheu, Récif- 37 Gb 11.48S 43.04 E
Vailly-sur-Aisne 12 Fe 49.25N 3.31 E
Vainikkala 8 Md 60.52N 28.18 E
Vainode/Vajnëde 8 Ih 56.26N 21.45 E
Vairaatea Atoll 57 Nf 19.19S 139.20W
Vaison-la-Romaine 11 Lj 44.14N 5.04 E
Vaïtape 65e Db 16.31S 151.45W
Vaïtoare 65e Db 16.41S 151.28W
Vaitupu Island 57 Ie 7.28S 178.41 E
Vajgač, Ostrov- 5 La 70.00N 59.30 E
Vajnëde/Vainode 8 Ih 56.26N 21.45 E
Vakaga [3] 35 Cd 10.00N 23.30 E
Vakfıkebir 24 Hb 41.03N 39.20 E
Vaksdal 8 Ad 60.29N 5.44 E
Val 20 Jf 52.19N 143.09 E
Vala 7 Mh 56.59N 51.16 E
Valaam 7 Hf 61.24N 30.59 E
Valaam, Ostrov- 8 Nc 61.20N 31.05 E
Valahia = Walachia (EN) 15 He 44.00N 25.00 E
Valahia = Walachia (EN) 5 Ig 44.00N 25.00 E
Valais [2] 14 Bd 46.15N 7.30 E
Valamares, Mali i- 15 Di 40.47N 20.28 E
Valamaz 7 Mh 57.36N 52.14 E
Valandovo 15 Fh 41.19N 22.34 E
Valašské Meziříčí 10 Ng 49.29N 17.58 E
Valáxa 15 Hk 38.49N 24.29 E
Vålberg 8 Ee 59.24N 13.12 E
Valburg 12 Hc 51.55N 5.49 E
Valcabra 13 Jg 37.30N 2.43W
Vălcedrăm 15 Gf 43.42N 23.27 E
Valcheta 56 Gf 40.42S 66.09W
Valdagno 14 Fe 45.39N 11.18 E
Valdahon 11 Mg 47.09N 6.21 E
Valdai Hills (EN) = Valdajskaja Vozvyšennost 5 Jd 57.00N 33.30 E
Valdaj 19 Dd 57.59N 33.14 E
Valdajskaja Vozvyšennost = Valdai Hills (EN) 5 Jd 57.00N 33.30 E
Valdarno 14 Fg 43.45N 11.15 E
Valdavia 13 Hb 42.24N 4.16W
Valdecañas, Embalse de- 13 Ge 39.45N 5.30W
Valdeganga 13 Ke 39.09N 1.40W
Val-de-Marne [3] 11 If 43.47N 2.29 E
Valdemārpils/Valdemarpils 7 Fh 57.24N 22.39 E
Valdemarpils/Valdemārpils 7 Fh 57.24N 22.39 E
Valdemarsvik 7 Dg 58.12N 16.32 E
Valdepeñas 13 If 38.46N 3.23W
Valderaduey 13 Gc 41.31N 5.42W
Valderas 13 Gb 42.05N 5.27W
Valderrama, Cienaga de- 49 Ki 8.56N 72.10W
Valderrobres/Vall-de-roures 13 Ld 40.53N 0.09W
Valdés, Peninsula- 52 Jj 42.30S 64.00W
Valdez 39 Ec 61.07N 146.16W
Val d'Isère 11 Mi 45.27N 6.59 E
Valdivia 53 Ii 39.48S 73.14W
Valdivia Seamount (EN) 30 Hk 25.20S 6.15 E
Valdobbiadene 14 Fe 45.54N 12.00 E
Val-d'Oise [3] 11 Ie 49.10N 2.10 E
Val-d'Or 39 Le 48.07N 77.47W
Valdosta 39 Kf 30.50N 83.17W
Valdres 8 Cc 60.55N 9.10 E
Vale 16 Mi 41.36N 42.51 E
Vale [Or.-U.S.] 46 Gd 44.01N 117.15W
Valea lerii 15 Gc 46.39N 23.21 E
Valea lui Mihai 15 Fb 47.31N 22.09 E
Valea Vişeului 15 Hb 47.51N 24.10 E
Valença [Braz.] 55 Kf 22.15S 43.43W
Valença [Braz.] 54 Kf 13.22S 39.05W
Valença do Minho 13 Db 42.02N 8.38W
Valença do Piaui 54 Je 6.24S 41.45W
Valençay 11 Hg 47.09N 1.34 E
Valence [Fr.] 11 Gj 44.06N 0.55 E
Valence [Fr.] 11 Kj 44.56N 4.54 E
Valencia 6 Fh 39.28N 0.22W
Valencia [3] 13 Le 39.20N 0.50W
Valencia 13 Le 39.30N 0.40W
València/Valencia 6 Fh 39.28N 0.22W
Valencia/València 6 Fh 39.28N 0.22W
València, Golf de-/Valencia, Golfo de- 5 Fh 39.30N 0.00
Valencia, Golfo de-/València, Golf de- 5 Fh 39.30N 0.00
Valencia, Lago de- 50 Cg 10.11N 67.45W
Valencia de Alcántara 13 Ee 39.25N 7.14W
Valencia de Don Juan 13 Gb 42.18N 5.31W
Valencia-El Grao 13 Le 39.27N 0.20W
Valenciennes 11 Jd 50.21N 3.32 E
Vălenii de Munte 15 Jd 45.11N 26.02 E
Valentia/Dairbhre 9 Cj 51.55N 10.20W
Valentin 28 Mc 43.07N 134.19 E
Valentine 43 Gc 42.52N 100.33W
Valenza 14 Ce 45.01N 8.38 E
Våler 7 Cf 60.40N 11.50 E
Valera 54 Db 9.19N 70.37W
Valerie Seamount (EN) 57 Ki 42.00S 163.30W
Valga 19 Cd 57.49N 26.05 E
Valge Jõgi 8 Ke 59.32N 25.36 E
Valhalla Mountains 46 Gb 49.45N 117.48W
Valiente, Peninsula- 49 Gi 9.05N 81.51W
Valier 46 Ib 48.18N 112.15W
Valinco, Golfe de- 11a Ab 41.40N 8.49 E
Valjevo 15 Ce 44.16N 19.53 E
Valka 7 Gh 57.47N 26.01 E
Valkeakoski 7 Ff 61.16N 24.02 E
Valkeala 8 Ld 60.57N 26.48 E
Valkenswaard 12 Hc 51.21N 5.28 E
Valkininkai/Valkininkaj 8 Kj 54.18N 25.55 E
Valkininkaj/Valkininkai 8 Kj 54.18N 25.55 E
Valko/Valkom 8 Ld 60.25N 26.15 E
Valkom/Valko 8 Ld 60.25N 26.15 E
Valkumej 20 Mc 69.41N 170.30 E
Valladolid [3] 13 Hc 41.35N 4.40W
Valladolid [Mex.] 47 Gd 20.41N 88.12W
Valladolid [Sp.] 6 Fg 41.39N 4.43W
Valldal 8 Bb 62.20N 7.21 E
Vall-de-Roures/Valderrobres 13 Ld 40.53N 0.09W
Vall de Uxó 13 Le 39.49N 0.14W
Valle [2] 54 Cc 3.40N 76.30W
Valle [3] 49 Dg 13.30N 87.35W
Valle 7 Bg 59.12N 7.32 E
Vallecas, Madrid- 13 Id 40.23N 3.37W
Valle d'Aosta / Vallée d'Aoste [2] 14 Be 45.45N 7.15 E
Valle de Cabuerniga 13 Ha 43.14N 4.18W
Valle de Guanape 50 Dh 9.54N 65.41W
Valle dei Templi 14 Hm 37.18N 13.35 E
Valle de la Pascua 54 Eb 9.13N 66.00W
Valle de Santiago 48 Ig 20.23N 101.12W
Valle de Topia 48 Fe 25.13N 106.25W
Valle de Zaragoza 48 Gd 27.28N 105.49W
Valledupar 54 Da 10.28N 73.15W
Vallée d'Aoste / Valle d'Aosta [2] 14 Be 45.45N 7.15 E
Vallée Jonction 44 Lb 46.23N 70.55W
Valle Hermoso 48 Ke 25.39N 97.52W
Vallejera, Puerto de- 13 Gd 40.30N 5.42W
Vallejo 43 Cd 38.07N 122.14W
Vallejo, Sierra de- 48 Gg 20.55N 105.20W
Valle Nacional 48 Ki 17.47N 96.19W
Vallenar 53 Ih 28.35S 70.46W
Vallentuna 8 He 59.32N 18.05 E
Valles/El Valles 13 Oc 41.35N 2.15 E
Valles de los Daidos 13 Hd 40.39N 4.09W
Valletta 6 Hh 35.54N 14.31 E
Valley City 43 Hb 46.55N 97.59W
Valley Falls 46 Ee 42.31N 120.15W
Valleyfield 42 Kg 45.15N 74.08W
Valley Station 44 Ef 38.06N 85.52W
Valleyview 42 Fe 55.02N 117.08W
Vallgrund 7 Ee 63.12N 21.14 E
Vallhagar 8 Hg 57.20N 18.10 E
Vallimanca 55 Bm 36.21S 61.02W
Vallimanca, Arroyo- 55 Bl 35.40S 60.02W
Vallo della Lucania 14 Jj 40.14N 15.16 E
Valloires, Abbaye de- 12 Dd 50.20N 1.47 E
Vallorbe 14 Ad 46.43N 6.23 E
Valls 13 Nc 41.17N 1.15 E
Valls d'Andorra → Andorra [1] 6 Gg 42.30N 1.30 E
Vallsta 8 Gc 61.32N 16.22 E
Vallvik 8 Gc 61.11N 17.11 E
Valmaseda 13 Ia 43.12N 3.12W
Valmiera 19 Cd 57.32N 25.29 E
Valmont 12 Ce 49.44N 0.31 E
Valnera 13 Ia 43.10N 3.45W
Valognes 11 Ee 49.31N 1.28W
Valois, Plaine du- 11 Ie 49.10N 2.45 E
Valoria la Buena 13 Hc 41.48N 4.32W
Valpaços 13 Ec 41.36N 7.19W
Valparaiso 44 De 41.28N 87.03W
Valparaíso [Braz.] 55 Ge 21.13S 50.51W
Valparaíso [Chile] 53 Ii 33.02S 71.38W
Valparaíso [Mex.] 48 Hf 22.46N 103.34W
Valpovo 14 Me 45.39N 18.25 E
Valréas 11 Kj 44.23N 4.59 E
Vals 30 Jk 27.23S 26.31 E
Vals, Tanjung- 26 Kh 8.26S 137.38 E
Valsjöbyn 7 Dd 64.04N 14.08 E
Valtellina 14 Dd 46.10N 9.55 E
Valtimo 7 Ge 63.40N 28.48 E
Váltou, Óri- 15 Ej 39.10N 21.20 E
Valujki 19 De 50.12N 38.08 E
Valul-Lui Traian 15 Le 44.15N 28.30 E
Valverde 32 Dd 27.48N 17.55W
Valverde de Júcar 13 Je 39.43N 2.12W
Valverde del Camino 13 Fg 37.34N 6.45W
Valverde del Fresno 13 Ff 40.13N 6.52W
Vamdrup 8 Ci 55.25N 9.17 E
Våmhus 7 Df 61.08N 14.28 E
Vamizi, Ilha- 37 Gb 11.02S 40.40 E
Vammala 7 Ff 61.20N 22.54 E
Vámos 15 Hn 35.25N 24.12 E
Van 23 Fb 38.28N 43.20 E
Van, Lake- (EN) = Van Gölü 21 Gf 38.33N 42.46 E
Vanajanselkä 7 Ff 61.09N 24.15 E
Vanak 24 Ng 31.41N 50.52 E
Vanak 24 Ng 31.32N 51.19 E
Vanån 8 Fd 60.31N 14.14 E
Vanault-les-Dames 12 Gf 48.51N 4.46 E
Vanavana Atoll 57 Ng 20.47S 139.09W
Vanavara 20 Fd 60.22N 102.16 E
Van Buren [Ar.-U.S.] 45 Ii 35.26N 94.21W
Van Buren [Me.-U.S.] 44 Nb 47.09N 67.56W
Vanč 18 He 38.23N 71.29 E
Vanceburg 44 Ff 38.36N 83.19W
Vancouver [B.C.-Can.] 39 Ge 49.16N 123.07W
Vancouver [Wa.-U.S.] 43 Cb 45.39N 122.40W
Vancouver Island 38 Ge 49.45N 126.00W
Vandalia [Il.-U.S.] 45 Lg 38.58N 89.06W
Vandalia [Oh.-U.S.] 44 Ef 39.53N 84.12W
Vanderbijl Park 37 De 26.42S 27.54 E
Vanderhoof 42 Ff 54.0 N 124.01W
Vanderlin Island 59 Hc 15.45S 137.00 E
Van Diemen, Cape- 59 Gb 11.10S 130.25 E
Van Diemen Gulf 59 Gb 11.50S 132.00 E
Vandmtor, Ozero- 17 Le 62.15N 65.45 E
Vändra/Vjandra 7 Fg 58.40N 25.01 E
Vänern 5 Hd 58.55N 13.30 E
Vänersborg 7 Cg 58.22N 12.19 E

Index Symbols

[1] Independent Nation
[2] State, Region
[3] District, County
[4] Municipality
[5] Colony, Dependency
Continent
Physical Region
Historical or Cultural Region
Mount, Mountain
Volcano
Hill
Mountains, Mountain Range
Hills, Escarpment
Plateau, Upland
Pass, Gap
Plain, Lowland
Delta
Salt Flat
Valley, Canyon
Crater, Cave
Karst Features
Depression
Polder
Desert, Dunes
Forest, Woods
Heath, Steppe
Oasis
Cape, Point
Coast, Beach
Cliff
Peninsula
Isthmus
Sandbank
Island
Atoll
Rock, Reef
Islands, Archipelago
Rocks, Reefs
Coral Reef
Well, Spring
Geyser
River, Stream
Waterfall Rapids
River Mouth, Estuary
Lake
Salt Lake
Intermittent Lake
Reservoir
Swamp, Pond
Canal
Glacier
Ice Shelf, Pack Ice
Ocean
Sea
Gulf, Bay
Strait, Fjord
Lagoon
Bank
Seamount
Tablemount
Ridge
Shelf
Basin
Escarpment, Sea Scarp
Fracture
Trench, Abyss
National Park, Reserve
Point of Interest
Recreation Site
Cave, Cavern
Historic Site
Ruins
Wall, Walls
Church, Abbey
Temple
Scientific Station
Airport
Port
Lighthouse
Mine
Tunnel
Dam, Bridge

Vang 8 Cc 61.08N 8.35 E
Vangaindrano 37 Hd 23.23S 47.33 E
Van Gölü=Van, Lake- (EN) 21 Gf 38.33N 42.46 E
Vangunu Island 57 Ge 8.40S 158.05 E
Van Horn 43 Ge 31.03N 104.50W
Vanick, Rio- 55 Fa 13.06S 52.52W
Vanier 42 Ha 76.00N 103.50W
Vanikolo 63c Bb 11.37S 166.58 E
Vanikolo Islands 57 Hf 11.37S 167.03 E
Vanimo 60 Ch 2.40S 141.18 E
Vanino 20 Jg 49.11N 140.19 E
Vankavesi 8 Jc 61.50N 23.50 E
Vanna 7 Ea 70.09N 19.51 E
Vännäs 7 Ee 63.55N 19.45 E
Vanne 11 Jf 48.12N 3.16 E
Vannes 11 Dg 47.40N 2.45W
Van Ninh 25 Lf 12.42N 109.14 E
Vannsjø 8 De 59.25N 10.50 E
Vanoise, Massif de la- 11 Mi 45.20N 6.40 E
Vanona Lava, Ile- 57 Hf 14.00S 167.30 E
Van Phong, Vung- 25 Lf 12.33N 109.18 E
Van Rees, Pegunungan- 26 Kg 2.35S 138.15 E
Vanrhynsdorp 37 Bf 31.36S 18.44 E
Vansbro 7 Df 60.31N 14.13 E
Vanse 8 Bf 58.07N 6.42 E
Vansittart 42 Jc 65.50N 84.00W
Vantaa 8 Kd 60.13N 24.59 E
Vänte Litets grund 8 Hb 62.35N 18.12 E
Vanua Levu 57 If 17.28S 177.03 E
Vanua Mbalavu 61 Fc 17.14S 178.57W
Vanuatu 58 Hf 16.00S 167.00 E
Vanua Vatu 63d Cc 18.22S 179.16W
Van Wert 44 Ee 40.53N 84.36W
Van Wyksviei 37 Cf 30.18S 21.49 E
Vanzylsrus 37 Ce 26.52S 22.04 E
Vao 63b Cf 22.40S 167.29 E
Vao, Nosy- 37 Gc 17.30S 43.45 E
Vão das Almas 55 Ia 13.42S 47.27W
Vapnjarka 16 Fe 48.32N 28.46 E
Var 11 Mk 43.30N 6.20 E
Var 11 Nk 43.39N 7.12 E
Vara 14 Df 44.09N 9.53 E
Vara 8 Ef 58.16N 12.57 E
Varaita 14 Bf 44.49N 7.36 E
Varakļāni/Varakljany 7 Gh 56.36N 26.48 E
Varakljany/Varakļāni 7 Gh 56.36N 26.48 E
Varaldsøy 8 Ad 60.10N 6.00 E
Varalé 34 Ed 9.40N 3.17W
Varallo 14 Ce 45.49N 8.15 E
Varāmīn 24 Ne 35.20N 51.39 E
Vārānasi (Benares) 22 Kg 25.20N 83.00 E
Varangerfjorden 5 Ia 70.00N 30.00 E
Varangerhalvøya=Varanger Peninsula (EN) 5 Ia 70.25N 29.30 E
Varanger Peninsula (EN)= Varangerhalvøya 5 Ia 70.25N 29.30 E
Varano, Lago di- 14 Ji 41.53N 15.45 E
Varāvī 24 Oi 27.25N 53.06 E
Varaždin 14 Kd 46.18N 16.20 E
Varazze 14 Cf 44.22N 8.34 E
Varberg 7 Ch 57.06N 12.15 E
Vardak 23 Kc 34.15N 68.00 E
Vardar 5 Ig 40.35N 22.50 E
Varde 7 Bi 55.38N 8.29 E
Varde Å 8 Ci 55.35N 8.20 E
Vardhoúsia Óri 15 Fk 38.40N 22.10 E
Vårdo 8 Id 60.15N 20.20 E
Vardø 7 Ha 70.22N 31.06 E
Varel 10 Ec 53.24N 8.08 E
Varėna/Varena 7 Fi 54.15N 24.39 E
Varena/Varėna 7 Fi 54.15N 24.39 E
Värend 8 Fh 56.45N 14.55 E
Varengeville-sur-Mer 12 Ce 49.55N 0.59 E
Varenikovskaja 16 Jg 45.06N 37.37 E
Varenne 11 Ff 48.24N 0.39W
Varennes-en-Argonne 12 He 49.14N 5.02 E
Varennes-sur-Allier 11 Jh 46.19N 3.24 E
Vareš 14 Mf 44.10N 18.20 E
Varese 14 Ce 45.48N 8.50 E
Varese, Lago di- 14 Ce 45.50N 8.45 E
Vårgårda 8 Ef 58.02N 12.48 E
Vargaši 19 Gd 55.23N 65.48 E
Vargem Grande 54 Jd 3.33S 43.56W
Varginha 54 Ih 21.33S 45.26W
Vargön 8 Ef 58.21N 12.22 E
Varhaug 8 Af 58.37N 5.39 E
Varjão 55 Hc 17.03S 49.37W
Varkaus 6 Ic 62.19N 27.55 E
Värmdö 8 He 59.20N 18.35 E
Värmeln 8 Ee 59.30N 12.55 E
Värmland 8 Ee 59.50N 13.05 E
Värmland 7 Cg 59.45N 13.15 E
Värmlandsnäs 8 Ee 59.00N 13.10 E
Varna 15 Kf 43.10N 27.35 E
Varna [Bul.] 6 Ig 43.13N 27.55 E
Varna 17 Jj 53.24N 60.58 E
Värnamo 7 Dh 57.11N 14.02 E
Varnenski Zaliv 15 Kf 43.11N 27.56 E
Varniai/Varnjaj 8 Ji 55.44N 22.17 E
Varnjaj/Varniai 8 Ji 55.44N 22.17 E
Varnsdorf 10 Kf 50.54N 14.38 E
Várpalota 10 Oi 47.12N 18.08 E
Văršec 15 Gf 43.12N 23.17 E
Varsinais-Suomi/Egentliga Finland 8 Jd 60.40N 22.30 E
Värska 8 Lg 57.58N 27.38 E
Vartašen 16 Oi 41.05N 47.29 E
Varto 24 Ic 39.10N 41.28 E
Vartofta 8 Ef 58.06N 13.38 E
Värtsilä 8 Nb 62.15N 30.40 E
Varzaneh 24 Of 32.25N 52.39 E
Varzaqān 24 Lc 38.31N 46.39 E
Varzarīn, Kūh-e- 23 Gc 33.24N 46.48 E
Várzea, Rio da- 55 Fh 27.13S 53.19W
Várzea da Palma 55 Jc 17.36S 44.44W
Varzea Grande 54 Gg 15.39S 56.08W
Varzelândia 55 Jb 15.42S 44.02W
Varzi 14 Df 44.49N 9.12 E
Varzuga 7 Ic 66.17N 36.50 E
Varzy 11 Jg 47.22N 3.23 E
Vas 10 Mi 47.10N 16.45 E
Vasa/Vaasa 6 Ic 63.06N 21.36 E
Vasai (Bassein) 25 Ee 19.21N 72.48 E
Vasalemma/Vazalemma 8 Ke 59.15N 24.11 E
Vásárosnamény 10 Sh 48.08N 22.19 E
Vascão 13 Eg 37.31N 7.31W
Vaşcău 15 Fc 46.28N 22.28 E
Vascoeuil 12 De 49.27N 1.23 E
Vascongadas/Euzkadi= Basque Provinces (EN) 13 Ja 43.00N 2.30W
Vascos, Montes- 13 Jb 42.50N 2.10W
Vasgūn 24 Qe 34.55N 56.30 E
Vasilevići 16 Fc 52.14N 29.47 E
Vasiliká 15 Gi 40.28N 23.08 E
Vasiljevka 16 If 47.23N 35.18 E
Vasilkov 19 De 50.12N 30.22 E
Vasilkovka 16 Je 48.13N 36.03 E
Vasiss 19 Hd 57.30N 74.55 E
Vasjugan 20 De 59.10N 80.50 E
Vasjuganje 21 Jd 58.00N 77.00 E
Vaška 19 Ec 64.53N 45.47 E
Vaškovcy 15 Ia 48.16N 25.34 E
Vaslui 15 Kc 46.38N 27.44 E
Vaslui 15 Kc 46.37N 27.44 E
Vaslui 15 Kc 46.41N 27.43 E
Väsman 8 Fd 60.11N 15.04 E
Vassako 35 Bd 8.36N 19.07 E
Vassdalsegga 7 Bg 59.46N 7.07 E
Vassy 12 Bf 48.51N 0.40W
Västerås 6 Hd 59.37N 16.33 E
Västerbotten 7 Dd 64.58N 17.28 E
Västerdalälven 7 Df 60.33N 15.08 E
Västergötland 8 Eg 58.00N 13.05 E
Västerhaninge 8 He 59.07N 18.06 E
Västernorrland 7 De 63.00N 17.30 E
Västervik 7 Dh 57.45N 16.38 E
Västmanland 8 Fe 59.40N 15.15 E
Västmanland 7 Dg 59.45N 16.20 E
Vasto 14 Ih 42.07N 14.42 E
Västra Silen 8 Ee 59.15N 12.10 E
Vasvár 10 Mi 47.03N 16.48 E
Vatan 11 Hg 47.04N 1.49 E
Vatersay 9 Fe 56.53N 7.28W
Vatican City (EN) = Città del Vaticano 6 Hg 41.54N 12.27 E
Vaticano, Capo- 14 Jl 38.37N 15.50 E
Vatilau 63a Ec 8.53S 160.01 E
Vatnajökull 5 Ec 64.24N 16.48W
Vatneyri 7a Ab 65.35N 24.00W
Vatoa Island 57 Jf 19.50S 178.13W
Vatomandry 37 Hc 19.20S 48.59 E
Vatra Dornei 15 Ib 47.21N 25.22 E
Vättern 5 Hd 58.25N 14.35 E
Vatu-i-Ra Channel 63d Bb 17.24S 178.29 E
Vatulele 63d Ac 18.33S 177.38 E
Vatutino 16 Ge 49.02N 31.09 E
Vatu Vara 61 Fc 17.26S 179.32W
Vaubecourt 12 Hf 48.56N 5.07 E
Vauclin, Pointe du- 51h Bb 14.34N 60.50W
Vaucluse 11 Lj 44.00N 5.10 E
Vaucluse, Montagne du- 11 Lk 44.32N 5.11 E
Vaucouleurs 11 Lf 48.36N 5.40 E
Vaud 14 Ad 46.35N 6.30 E
Vaudemont, Butte de- 11 Lf 48.25N 6.00 E
Vaughn 43 Fe 34.36N 105.13W
Vaupés 54 Dc 1.00N 71.00W
Vaupés, Río- 52 Je 0.02N 67.16W
Vauvilliers 63b Ce 21.09S 167.35 E
Vaux 12 Ge 49.31N 4.17 E
Vaux-le-Vicomte 11 If 48.34N 2.43 E
Vavatenina 37 Hc 17.26S 49.22 E
Vava'u Group 57 Jf 18.40S 174.00W
Vava'u Island 61 Gc 18.36S 174.00W
Vavoua 34 Dd 7.23N 6.29W
Vavuniya 25 Gg 8.45N 80.30 E
Vaxholm 8 He 59.24N 18.20 E
Växjö 6 Hd 56.53N 14.49 E
Vaza-Barris, Rio- 54 Kf 11.10S 37.10W
Vazalemma/Vasalemma 8 Ke 59.15N 24.11 E
Vazante 54 Ig 18.00S 46.54W
Vazuza 16 Ia 56.10N 34.35 E
Vding Skovhøj 8 Ch 56.01N 9.48 E
Veadeiros, Chapada dos- 54 If 14.05S 47.28W
Vecht 10 Cd 52.35N 6.05 E
Vechta 10 Ed 52.43N 8.17 E
Vechte 10 Cd 52.35N 6.05 E
Vecpiebalga 8 Kh 56.57N 25.50 E
Vecsés 10 Pi 47.24N 19.17 E
Vedavågen 8 Ae 59.19N 5.12 E
Veddige 8 Eg 57.16N 12.19 E
Vedea 15 He 44.47N 24.37 E
Vedea 15 Ie 43.59N 25.59 E
Vedeno 16 Oh 42.57N 46.05 E
Vedia 55 Bl 34.30S 61.32W
Vedrá Isla- 13 Nf 38.52N 1.12 E
Veendam 11 Ma 53.06N 6.58 E
Veenendaal 12 Hb 52.02N 5.35 E
Veere 12 Fc 51.33N 3.40 E
Vega 7 Cd 65.39N 11.50 E
Vega 45 Ei 35.15N 102.26W
Vega Baja 51a Bb 18.25N 66.23W
Veganj 14 Kg 43.50N 16.45 E
Vegår 8 Cf 58.48N 8.47 E
Vegårshei 8 Cf 58.46N 8.48 E
Veghel 12 Hc 51.37N 5.32 E
Veglie 14 Lj 40.20N 17.58 E
Vegorrítis, Límni- 15 Ei 40.45N 21.48 E
Vègre 11 Fg 47.51N 0.14W
Vegreville 42 Gf 53.30N 112.03W
Vehmersalmi 8 Mb 62.46N 28.02 E
Vehnemoor 12 Ka 53.04N 8.02 E
Veinge 8 Eh 56.34N 13.05 E
Veinticinco de Mayo [Arg.] 56 He 35.26S 60.10W
Veinticinco de Mayo [Ur.] 55 Dl 34.12S 56.22W
Veio 14 Gh 42.02N 12.23 E
Veisiejai/Vejsejaj 8 Jj 54.03N 23.46 E
Vejen 7 Bi 55.29N 9.09 E
Vejer de la Frontera 13 Gh 36.15N 5.58W
Vejle 8 Ci 55.45N 9.20 E
Vejle 7 Bi 55.42N 9.32 E
Vejsejaj/Veisiejai 8 Jj 54.03N 23.46 E
Vel 7 Kf 61.06N 42.10 E
Vela, Cabo de la- 49 Kg 12.13N 72.11W
Vela Luka 14 Kh 42.58N 16.44 E
Velas 32 Bb 38.41N 28.13W
Velas, Cabo- 49 Eh 10.22N 85.53W
Velásquez 55 El 34.02S 54.17W
Velay, Plateaux du- 11 Ji 45.10N 3.50 E
Velaz 55 Ch 26.42S 58.40W
Velbăždski prohod 15 Fg 42.14N 22.28 E
Velbert 10 De 51.20N 7.02 E
Velddrif 37 Bf 32.47S 18.10 E
Velden am Wörthersee 14 Id 46.37N 14.03 E
Veldhoven 12 Hc 51.24N 5.24 E
Velebit 5 Hg 44.17N 15.12 E
Velebitski kanal 14 If 44.45N 14.50 E
Veleka 15 Kg 42.04N 27.58 E
Velencei-tó 10 Oi 47.13N 18.36 E
Velenje 14 Jd 46.22N 15.07 E
Velestínon 15 Fj 39.23N 22.45 E
Veleta 13 Ig 37.04N 3.22W
Velež 14 Lg 43.20N 18.00 E
Vélez Blanco 13 Jg 37.41N 2.05W
Vélez de La Gomera, Peñón de- 13 Hi 35.11N 4.54W
Vélez-Málaga 13 Hh 36.47N 4.06W
Vélez Rubio 13 Jg 37.39N 2.04W
Velhas, Rio das- 52 Lg 17.13S 44.49W
Velika Gorica 14 Ke 45.44N 16.04 E
Velikaja 20 Md 64.35N 176.03 E
Velikaja-Gluša 10 Ve 51.49N 25.11 E
Velikaja Guba 7 Ie 62.17N 35.06 E
Velikaja Kema 20 Ig 45.29N 137.08 E
Velikaja Lepetiha 16 Hf 47.09N 33.59 E
Velikaja Mihajlovka 16 Ff 47.04N 29.52 E
Velika Kapela 14 Je 45.13N 15.02 E
Velika Kladuša 14 Je 45.11N 15.49 E
Velika Morava 15 Ee 44.43N 21.03 E
Velika Plana 15 Ee 44.20N 21.05 E
Veliki Berezny 10 Sh 48.54N 22.30 E
Veliki Byčkov 10 Ui 47.58N 24.04 E
Veliki Drvenik 14 Kg 43.27N 16.09 E
Veliki Jastrebac 15 Ef 43.24N 21.26 E
Velikije Luki 6 Jd 56.20N 30.32 E
Velikije Mosty 10 Uf 50.10N 24.12 E
Veliki kanal 15 Bd 45.52N 18.52 E
Veliki Ljuben 10 Tg 49.37N 23.45 E
Veliki Trnovac 15 Eg 42.29N 21.45 E
Veliki Ustjug 6 Kc 60.46N 46.20 E
Velikodolinskoje 15 Nc 46.20N 30.29 E
Veliko Gradište 15 Ee 44.46N 21.32 E
Veliko Tărnovo 15 If 43.04N 25.39 E
Veliko Tărnovo 6 Ig 43.04N 25.39 E
Velikovisočnoje 19 Fb 67.16N 52.01 E
Veli Lošinj 14 If 44.31N 14.31 E
Vélingara 34 Cc 13.09N 14.07W
Velingrad 15 Gg 42.01N 24.00 E
Velino 14 Hh 42.09N 13.23 E
Velino 14 Gh 42.33N 12.43 E
Velíž 16 Gb 55.36N 31.12 E
Veľká Fatra 10 Ph 49.00N 19.05 E
Velké Meziříčí 10 Lg 49.21N 16.00 E
Veľký Krtíš 10 Ph 48.13N 19.20 E
Veľký Meder (Čalovo) 10 Ni 47.52N 17.47 E
Vella Lavella Island 57 Ge 7.45S 156.40 E
Velletri 14 Gi 41.41N 12.47 E
Vellinge 8 Ei 55.28N 13.01 E
Vellore 22 Jh 14.26N 79.58 E
Velmerstot 10 Ee 51.50N 9.00 E
Velmo 20 Ed 61.43N 92.25 E
Velopoúla 15 Gm 36.55N 23.28 E
Vels 17 If 60.45N 58.45 E
Velsen-IJmuiden [Neth.] 11 Kb 52.27N 4.39 E
Velsk 19 Ec 61.05N 42.05 E
Veluwe 11 Lb 52.20N 5.50 E
Veluwemeer 12 Hb 52.23N 5.40 E
Velva 45 Fb 48.04N 100.56W
Velvendós 15 Fi 40.15N 22.04 E
Veman 8 Fb 62.02N 14.16 E
Vema Seamount (EN) 30 Hl 31.38S 8.19 E
Vemdalen 8 Eb 62.27N 13.52 E
Ven 8 Ei 55.55N 12.40 E
Venable Ice Shelf 66 Pf 73.03S 87.20W
Venado 48 If 22.56N 101.05W
Venado, Cerro- 50 Ei 6.17N 62.45W
Venado Tuerto 56 Hd 33.45S 61.58W
Venafro 14 Ii 41.29N 14.02 E
Venamo, Río- 50 Fi 6.43N 61.07W
Vence 11 Nk 43.43N 7.07 E
Venceslau Brás 55 Hf 23.51S 49.48W
Venda 37 Ed 22.35S 30.45 E
Venda Nova 54 Jg 19.45S 43.50W
Vendas Novas 13 Df 38.41N 8.27W
Vendée 11 Eh 46.40N 1.20W
Vendée 11 Hh 46.40N 1.10 E
Vendée 11 Fh 46.19N 0.58W
Vendéen, Bocage- 11 Eh 46.50N 1.20W
Vendéenne, Plaine- 11 Eh 46.40N 1.20W
Vendel 8 Gd 60.10N 17.36 E
Vendeuvre-sur-Barse 11 Kf 48.14N 4.29 E
Vendôme 11 Hg 47.48N 1.04 E
Vendrell/El Vendrell 13 Nc 41.13N 1.32 E
Vendsyssel 8 Cg 57.20N 10.00 E
Venetia (EN) = Veneto 14 Fe 45.30N 12.00 E
Venétiko [Grc.] 15 Jk 38.08N 26.01 E
Venétiko [Grc.] 15 Em 36.42N 21.53 E
Veneto = Venetia (EN) 14 Fe 45.30N 12.00 E
Venev 16 Kb 54.22N 38.18 E
Venezia = Venice (EN) 6 Hf 45.27N 12.21 E
Venezia, Golfo di- = Venice, Gulf of- (EN) 5 Hf 45.15N 13.00 E
Venezia-Lido 14 Ge 45.25N 12.22 E
Venezia-Marghera 14 Ge 45.28N 12.44 E
Venezia-Mestre 14 Ge 45.29N 12.14 E
Venezuela 53 Je 8.00N 65.00W
Venezuela, Golfo de- = Venezuela, Gulf of- (EN) 52 Id 11.30N 71.00W
Venezuela, Gulf of- (EN) = Venezuela, Golfo de- 52 Id 11.30N 71.00W
Venezuelan Basin (EN) 38 Mh 15.00N 68.00W
Vengerovo 20 Ce 55.41N 76.55 E
Veniaminof, Mount- 40 He 56.13N 159.18W
Venice 44 Fl 27.06N 82.27W
Venice (EN) = Venezia 6 Hf 45.27N 12.21 E
Venice, Gulf of- (EN) = Venezia, Golfo di- 5 Hf 45.15N 13.00 E
Vénissieux 11 Ki 45.41N 4.53 E
Venjan 8 Ed 60.57N 13.55 E
Venjansjön 8 Ed 60.55N 14.00 E
Venlo 11 Mc 51.24N 6.10 E
Venlock River 59 Ib 12.15S 142.00 E
Vennesla 7 Bg 58.17N 7.59 E
Venosa 14 Jj 40.58N 15.49 E
Venosta, Val-/ Vintschgau 14 Ed 46.40N 10.35 E
Venraij 11 Lc 51.32N 5.59 E
Vent, Canal du-=Windward Passage (EN) 49 Lh 20.00N 73.50W
Vent, Iles du-=Windward Islands (EN) 57 Mf 17.30S 149.30W
Venta 7 Eh 57.23N 21.32 E
Venta de Baños 13 Hc 41.55N 4.30W
Ventana, Cerro- 48 Fe 24.15N 106.20W
Ventersdorp 37 De 26.17S 26.48 E
Venterstad 37 Df 30.47S 25.48 E
Venticinco de Diciembre 55 Dg 24.42S 56.33W
Ventimiglia 14 Bg 43.47N 7.36 E
Ventnor 12 Ad 50.36N 1.11W
Ventotene 14 Hj 40.45N 13.25 E
Ventoux, Mont- 11 Lj 44.10N 5.17 E
Ventspils 19 Cd 57.24N 21.33 E
Ventuari, Río- 52 Je 3.58N 67.02W
Ventura 43 De 34.17N 119.18W
Vénus, Pointe- 65e Fc 17.29S 149.29W
Venus Bay 59 Jg 38.40S 145.45 E
Venustiano Carranza 48 Mi 16.21N 92.33W
Venustiano Carranza, Presa- 48 Id 27.30N 100.40W
Ver 12 Bc 51.31N 0.27W
Vera [Arg.] 56 Hc 29.28S 60.13W
Vera [Sp.] 13 Kg 37.15N 1.52W
Verá, Laguna- 55 Dh 26.05S 57.39W
Veracruz 47 Ee 19.20N 96.40W
Veracruz Llave 39 Jh 19.12N 96.08W
Veraguas 49 Gj 8.30N 81.00W
Verāval 25 Ed 20.54N 70.22 E
Vera y Pintado 55 Bj 30.09S 60.21W
Verbania 14 Ce 45.56N 8.33 E
Verbovski 7 Ji 55.29N 41.59 E
Vercelli 14 Ce 45.19N 8.25 E
Vercors 11 Lj 44.57N 5.25 E
Verdalsøra 7 Ce 63.48N 11.29 E
Verde, Cape- 49 Jb 22.50N 74.52W
Verde, Cay- 49 Jb 22.02N 75.12W
Verde, Costa- 13 Ga 43.40N 5.40W
Verde, Río- 52 Kh 23.09S 57.37W
Verde, Rio- [Braz.] 54 Hh 21.12S 51.53W
Verde, Rio- [Braz.] 55 Hb 15.07S 48.40W
Verde, Rio- [Braz.] 55 Hd 19.50S 49.45W
Verde, Rio- [Braz.] 55 Ge 21.12S 51.53W
Verde, Rio- [Braz.] 55 Gd 18.01S 50.14W
Verde, Rio- [Braz.] 55 Je 21.27S 45.40W
Verde, Rio- [Braz.] 55 Ca 13.33S 58.01W
Verde, Rio- [Braz.] 54 Gf 11.54S 55.50W
Verde, Rio- [Braz.] 54 Hg 19.11S 50.44W
Verde, Río- [Mex.] 48 Jg 21.37N 99.15W
Verde, Río- [Mex.] 48 Hg 20.42N 103.14W
Verde, Rio- [S.Amer.] 55 Ba 13.59S 60.20W
Verde Grande, Rio- 55 Kb 14.35S 43.53W
Verden (Aller) 10 Fd 52.55N 9.14 E
Verde River 43 Ee 33.33N 111.40W
Verdigris River 45 Ii 35.48N 95.18W
Verdinho, Rio- 55 Gc 17.29S 50.27W
Verdon 11 Lk 43.43N 5.46 E
Verdun [Fr.] 11 Le 49.10N 5.23 E
Verdun [Que.-Can.] 44 Kc 45.28N 73.34W
Verdura 14 Hm 37.28N 13.12 E
Vereeniging 37 De 26.38S 27.57 E
Vereščagino 19 Fd 58.05N 54.40 E
Verga, Cap- 34 Cc 10.12N 14.27W
Vergara [Arg.] 55 Dl 35.23S 57.48W
Vergara [Sp.] 13 Ja 43.07N 2.25W
Vergara [Ur.] 55 Fk 32.56S 53.57W
Vergato 14 Ff 44.17N 11.07 E
Verhnedneprovsk 16 Ie 48.39N 34.21 E
Verhnedneprovski 16 Hb 55.01N 33.21 E
Verhnedvinsk 7 Gi 55.46N 27.59 E
Verhneimbatsk 20 Dd 63.02N 88.00 E
Verhne-Karabahski Kanal 16 Oj 39.44N 47.57 E
Verhnespasskoje 7 Kg 58.45N 45.28 E
Verhnetulomski 7 Hb 68.38N 31.48 E
Verhnetulomskoje Vodohranilišče 7 Hb 68.35N 31.00 E
Verhneuralsk 17 Ij 53.53N 59.13 E
Verhneviljujsk 20 Hd 63.20N 120.25 E
Verhni At-Urjah 20 Kd 62.38N 150.03 E
Verhni Avzjan 17 Hj 53.32N 57.33 E
Verhni Kujto, Ozero- 7 Hd 65.00N 30.40 E
Verhni Most 8 Mg 57.29N 29.00 E
Verhni Tagil 17 Jh 57.22N 60.01 E
Verhni Trajanov Val=Upper Trajan's Wall (EN) 15 Lc 46.40N 29.00 E
Verhni Ufalej 19 Gd 56.04N 60.14 E
Verhnjaja Inta 17 Jd 65.59N 60.29 E
Verhnjaja Pyšma 17 Jh 56.59N 60.37 E
Verhnjaja Salda 17 Jg 58.02N 60.33 E
Verhnjaja Tojma 19 Ec 62.13N 45.01 E
Verhnjaja Tura 17 Ig 58.22N 59.49 E
Verhnj Uslon 7 Li 55.47N 48.58 E
Verhnoje Sinevidnoje 10 Tg 49.02N 23.36 E
Verhojansk 22 Pc 67.35N 133.27 E
Verhojanski Hrebet= Verhoyansk Mountains (EN) 21 Oc 67.00N 129.00 E
Verhoturje 17 Jg 58.52N 60.48 E
Verhovcevo 16 Ie 48.31N 34.12 E
Verhovina 15 Ha 48.08N 24.48 E
Verhovje 16 Jc 52.49N 37.14 E
Verhoyansk Mountains (EN)= Verhojanski Hrebet 21 Oc 67.00N 129.00 E
Verín 13 Ec 41.56N 7.26W
Veriora 8 Lg 58.00N 27.21 E
Veríssimo, Rio- 55 Hd 18.23S 48.20W
Veríssimo, Serra do- 55 Hd 19.33S 48.25W
Verl 12 Kc 51.53N 8.31 E
Vermand 12 Fe 49.52N 3.09 E
Vermeille, Côte- 11 Jl 42.30N 3.20 E
Vermelho, Rio- [Braz.] 55 Ib 14.26S 46.26W
Vermelho, Rio- [Braz.] 55 Ed 19.36S 55.58W
Vermelho, Rio- [Braz.] 55 Gb 14.54S 51.06W
Vermenton 11 Jg 47.40N 3.44 E
Vermilion Bay 42 Ig 49.51N 93.24W
Vermilion Cliffs 46 Ih 37.10N 112.35W
Vermilion Lake 45 Jc 47.53N 92.25W
Vermilion River 44 Gb 46.16N 81.41W
Vermillion 45 He 42.47N 96.56W
Vermillion River 45 He 42.44N 96.53W
Vermillon, Rivière- 44 Kb 47.38N 72.59W
Vérmion Óros 15 Ei 40.30N 22.00 E
Vermont 43 Mc 43.50N 72.45W
Vernal 43 Fc 40.27N 109.32W
Verneuil-sur-Avre 11 Gf 48.44N 0.56 E
Vernhi Barskunčak 16 Oe 48.14N 46.42 E
Vernon [B.C.-Can.] 42 Ff 50.16N 119.16W
Vernon [Fr.] 11 He 49.05N 1.29 E
Vernon [Tx.-U.S.] 43 He 34.09N 99.17W
Vérnon Óros 15 Ei 40.39N 21.22 E
Vernou 51e Ab 16.11N 61.39W
Verny 12 Ie 49.01N 6.12 E
Vero 13 Mb 42.00N 0.10 E
Vero Beach 43 Kf 27.38N 80.24W
Véroia 15 Fi 40.31N 22.12 E
Verona 6 Hf 45.27N 11.00 E
Verónica 56 Ie 35.22S 57.20W
Versailles [Fr.] 11 If 48.48N 2.08 E
Versailles [In.-U.S.] 44 Ef 39.04N 85.15W
Versilia 14 Eg 43.55N 10.15 E
Veršino-Darasunski 20 Gf 52.18N 115.32 E
Veršino-Šahtaminski 20 Gf 51.16N 117.55 E
Versmold 12 Kb 52.03N 8.09 E
Verson 12 Be 49.09N 0.27W
Vert, Cap-=Vert, Cape- (EN) 30 Fg 14.43N 17.30W
Vert, Cape- (EN)=Vert, Cap- 30 Fg 14.43N 17.30W
Vertentes, Serra das- 55 Je 20.56S 44.00W
Vértes 10 Oi 47.25N 18.20 E
Vertientes 49 Hc 21.16N 78.09W
Vertískos Óros 15 Gi 40.50N 23.19 E
Verviers 11 Ld 50.36N 5.52 E
Vervins 12 Fe 49.50N 3.54 E
Vesanto 8 Lb 62.56N 26.25 E
Vescovato 11a Ba 42.29N 9.26 E
Vesder/Vesdre 12 Hd 50.37N 5.37 E
Vesdre/Vesder 12 Hd 50.37N 5.37 E
Veselí nad Lužnici 10 Kg 49.11N 14.43 E
Veselovskoje Vodohranilišče 16 Lf 47.00N 41.15 E
Vešenskaja 19 Ef 49.38N 41.46 E
Vesgre 12 Df 48.53N 1.28 E
Vesijarvi 8 Kc 61.05N 25.30 E
Vesjegonsk 7 Ig 58.41N 37.16 E
Veškajma 7 Li 54.03N 47.08 E
Vesle 11 Je 49.23N 3.28 E
Vesljana 17 Gf 60.20N 54.03 E
Vesoul 11 Mg 47.38N 6.10 E
Vessigebro 8 Eh 56.59N 12.39 E
Vest-Agder 7 Bg 58.30N 7.10 E
Vestbygd 7 Bg 58.06N 6.35 E
Vesterålen 5 Hb 68.45N 15.00 E
Vesterøhavn 8 Dg 57.18N 10.56 E
Vestfjorden 5 Hb 68.35N 14.30 E
Vestfold 7 Cg 59.15N 10.10 E
Vestfonna 41 Oc 79.58N 20.15 E
Vestgrønland = West Greenland (EN) 41 He 69.00N 49.30W
Véstia 55 Ge 20.23S 51.25W
Vestmannæyjar 7a Bc 63.26N 20.16W
Vestnes 8 Bb 62.38N 7.06 E
Vestre Jakobselv 7 Ga 70.07N 29.25 E
Vestsjælland 8 Di 55.30N 11.30 E
Vestvågøy 7 Cb 68.15N 13.50 E
Vésubie 11 Nk 43.52N 7.12 E
Vesuvio = Vesuvius (EN) 5 Hg 40.49N 14.26 E
Vesuvius (EN) = Vesuvio 5 Hg 40.49N 14.26 E
Veszprém 10 Ni 47.10N 17.40 E
Veszprém 10 Ni 47.06N 17.55 E
Vésztő 10 Rj 46.55N 21.16 E
Vétaoundé, Ile- 57 Hf 13.15S 167.38 E
Vetauua 63d Ca 15.57S 179.24W
Vétê, Pointe- 63b Ca 13.27S 166.41 E
Vetka 16 Gc 52.34N 31.13 E
Vetlanda 7 Dh 57.26N 15.04 E
Vetljanka 7 Mj 52.52N 51.09 E
Vetluga 5 Kd 56.18N 46.24 E
Vetluga 7 Kh 57.52N 45.46 E

Index Symbols

- Independent Nation
- State, Region
- District, County
- Municipality
- Colony, Dependency
- Continent
- Physical Region
- Historical or Cultural Region
- Mount, Mountain
- Volcano
- Hill
- Mountains, Mountain Range
- Hills, Escarpment
- Plateau, Upland
- Pass, Gap
- Plain, Lowland
- Delta
- Salt Flat
- Valley, Canyon
- Crater, Cave
- Karst Features
- Depression
- Polder
- Desert, Dunes
- Forest, Woods
- Heath, Steppe
- Oasis
- Cape, Point
- Coast, Beach
- Cliff
- Peninsula
- Isthmus
- Sandbank
- Island
- Atoll
- Rock, Reef
- Islands, Archipelago
- Rocks, Reefs
- Coral Reef
- Well, Spring
- Geyser
- River, Stream
- Waterfall Rapids
- River Mouth, Estuary
- Lake
- Salt Lake
- Intermittent Lake
- Reservoir
- Swamp, Pond
- Canal
- Glacier
- Ice Shelf, Pack Ice
- Ocean
- Sea
- Gulf, Bay
- Strait, Fjord
- Lagoon
- Bank
- Seamount
- Tablemount
- Ridge
- Shelf
- Basin
- Escarpment, Sea Scarp
- Fracture
- Trench, Abyss
- National Park, Reserve
- Point of Interest
- Recreation Site
- Cave, Cavern
- Historic Site
- Ruins
- Wall, Walls
- Church, Abbey
- Temple
- Scientific Station
- Airport
- Port
- Lighthouse
- Mine
- Tunnel
- Dam, Bridge

Index Symbols

[1] Independent Nation	Historical or Cultural Region	Pass, Gap	Depression
[2] State, Region	Mount, Mountain	Plain, Lowland	Polder
[3] District, County	Volcano	Delta	Desert, Dunes
[4] Municipality	Hill	Salt Flat	Forest, Woods
[5] Colony, Dependency	Mountains, Mountain Range	Valley, Canyon	Heath, Steppe
Continent	Hills, Escarpment	Crater, Cave	Oasis
Physical Region	Plateau, Upland	Karst Features	Cape, Point

Coast, Beach	Rock, Reef	Waterfall Rapids	Canal
Cliff	Islands, Archipelago	River Mouth, Estuary	Glacier
Peninsula	Rocks, Reefs	Lake	Bank
Isthmus	Coral Reef	Salt Lake	Ice Shelf, Pack Ice
Sandbank	Well, Spring	Intermittent Lake	Ocean
Island	Geyser	Reservoir	Sea
Atoll	River, Stream	Swamp, Pond	Gulf, Bay

Lagoon	Escarpment, Sea Scarp	Historic Site	Port
Seamount	Fracture	Ruins	Lighthouse
Tablemount	Trench, Abyss	Wall, Walls	Mine
Ridge	National Park, Reserve	Church, Abbey	Tunnel
Shelf	Point of Interest	Temple	Dam, Bridge
Basin	Recreation Site	Scientific Station	
Strait, Fjord	Cave, Cavern	Airport	

Name	Map	Grid	Lat.	Long.
Vittangi	7	Ec	67.41N	21.39 E
Vitteaux	11	Kg	47.24N	4.32 E
Vittel	11	Lf	48.12N	5.57 E
Vittinge	8	Ge	59.54N	17.04 E
Vittoria	14	In	36.57N	14.32 E
Vittorio Veneto	14	Ge	45.59N	12.18 E
Vityaz Depth (EN)	3	Je	44.00N	151.00 E
Vityaz I Depth (EN)	3	Ih	11.20N	141.30 E
Vityaz II Depth (EN)	3	Kl	23.27S	175.00W
Vityaz III Depth (EN)	3	Km	32.00S	178.00W
Vityaz Seamount (EN)	57	Jc	13.30N	173.15W
Vityaz Trench (EN)	3	Jj	10.00S	170.00 E
Vivarais, Monts du-	11	Ki	44.55N	4.15 E
Vivarais, Plateaux du-	11	Kj	44.50N	4.45 E
Viver	13	Le	39.55N	0.36W
Vivero	13	Ea	43.40N	7.35W
Viverone, Lago di-	14	Ce	45.25N	8.05 E
Vivi	20	Ed	63.52N	97.50 E
Vivian	45	Jj	32.53N	93.59W
Viviers	11	Kj	44.29N	4.41 E
Vivo	37	Dd	23.03S	29.17 E
Vivoratá	55	Dm	37.40S	57.39W
Vivorillo, Cayos-	49	Ff	15.50N	83.18W
Viwa	63d	Ab	17.08S	176.56 E
Vizcaíno, Desierto de-	47	Bc	27.40N	114.40W
Vizcaíno, Sierra-	48	Bd	27.20N	114.00W
Vizcaya [3]	13	Ja	43.15N	2.55W
Vizcaya, Golfo de-	5	Fg	44.00N	4.00W
Vize	15	Kh	41.34N	27.45 E
Vize, Ostrov	21	Jb	79.30N	77.00 E
Vizianagaram	25	Ge	18.07N	83.25 E
Vizille	11	Li	45.05N	5.46 E
Vizinga	19	Fc	61.05N	50.10 E
Viziru	15	Kd	45.00N	27.42 E
Vižnica	16	De	48.14N	25.12 E
Vizzini	14	Im	37.10N	14.45 E
Vjaike-Maarja/Väike-Maarja	8	Le	59.04N	26.12 E
Vjajke-Pakri/Väike-Pakri	8	Je	59.50N	23.50 E
Vjajke-Vjajn/Väik Vain	8	Jf	58.30N	23.10 E
Vjalje, Ozero-	8	Ne	59.00N	30.20 E
Vjalozero, Ozero-	7	Ic	66.50N	35.10 E
Vjandra/Vändra	7	Fg	58.40N	25.01 E
Vjartsilja	7	He	62.10N	30.48 E
Vjatka	5	Ld	55.36N	51.30 E
Vjatskije Poljany	19	Fd	56.14N	51.04 E
Vjatski Uval	7	Lg	58.00N	49.45 E
Vjazemski	20	Ig	47.31N	134.45 E
Vjazma	6	Jd	55.13N	34.18 E
Vjazniki	7	Kh	56.15N	42.12 E
Vjeio, Río-	49	Dg	12.17N	86.54W
Vjosa	15	Ci	40.37N	19.20 E
Vlaamse Banken	12	Ec	51.15N	2.30 E
Vlaanderen/Flandres=Flanders (EN)	11	Jc	51.00N	3.20 E
Vlaardingen	11	Kc	51.54N	4.21 E
Vlădeasa, Vîrful-	15	Fc	46.45N	22.48 E
Vlădeni	15	Kb	47.25N	27.20 E
Vladičin Han	15	Fg	42.43N	22.04 E
Vladikavkaz (Ordžonikidze)	6	Kg	43.03N	44.40 E
Vladimir	6	Kd	56.10N	40.25 E
Vladimirskaja Oblast [3]	19	Ed	56.00N	40.40 E
Vladimirski Tupik	16	Hb	55.42N	33.18 E
Vladimir-Volynski	19	Ce	50.51N	24.22 E
Vladivostok	22	Pe	43.10N	131.56 E
Vlad Ţepeş	15	Ke	44.21N	27.05 E
Vlagtwedde	12	Ja	53.02N	7.08 E
Vlagtwedde-Ter Apel	12	Jb	52.52N	7.06 E
Vlahina	15	Fi	41.54N	22.52 E
Vlăhiţa	15	Ic	46.21N	25.31 E
Vlamse Vlakte=Flanders Plain (EN)	11	Id	50.40N	2.50 E
Vlasenica	14	Mf	44.11N	18.57 E
Vlašic [Yugo.]	14	Lf	44.19N	17.40 E
Vlašim	10	Kg	49.42N	14.54 E
Vlasotince	15	Fg	42.58N	22.08 E
Vlasovo	20	Ib	70.40N	134.35 E
Vlieland	11	Ka	53.15N	5.00 E
Vlieland	12	Ha	53.17N	5.06 E
Vlieland-Oost Vlieland	12	Ha	53.17N	5.06 E
Vliestroom	12	Ha	53.17N	5.10 E
Vlissingen	11	Jc	51.26N	3.35 E
Vlissingen-Oost-Souburg	12	Fc	51.28N	3.36 E
Vloesberg/Flobecq	12	Fd	50.44N	3.44 E
Vlora	6	Hg	40.27N	19.30 E
Vlorës, Gjiri i-	15	Ci	40.25N	19.25 E
Vlotho	12	Kb	52.10N	8.51 E
Vltava=Moldau (EN)	5	He	50.21N	14.30 E
Vöcklabruck	14	Hb	48.01N	13.39 E
Vodice	14	Jg	43.46N	15.47 E
Vodla	7	If	61.49N	36.00 E
Vodlozero, Ozero-	7	Ie	62.20N	37.00 E
Vodňany	10	Kg	49.09N	14.11 E
Vodnjan	14	Hf	44.57N	13.51 E
Vodny	17	Fe	63.32N	53.20 E
Voerde (Niederrhein)	10	Ce	51.35N	6.41 E
Voeren/Fouron	12	Hd	50.45N	5.48 E
Vogel Peak	34	Hd	8.24N	11.47 E
Vogelsberg	10	Ff	50.30N	9.15 E
Voghera	14	Df	44.59N	9.01 E
Vogtland	10	If	50.30N	12.05 E
Voh	63b	Be	20.58S	164.42 E
Võhandu Jõgi/Vyhandu	8	Lf	58.03N	27.40 E
Vohémar	37	Ib	13.22S	50.00 E
Vohipeno	37	Hd	22.20S	47.52 E
Vöhl	12	Kc	51.12N	8.56 E
Vohma	7	Lg	58.45N	46.36 E
Vohma	19	Ed	58.58N	46.45 E
Voi	31	Ki	3.23S	38.34 E
Voikoski	8	Lc	61.16N	26.48 E
Voinjama	31	Gh	8.25N	9.45W
Vóïon Óros	15	Ei	40.15N	21.03 E
Voire	11	Kf	48.27N	4.25 E
Voiron	11	Li	45.22N	5.35 E
Voitsberg	14	Jc	47.02N	15.09 E
Voïviïs, Límni-	15	Fj	39.32N	22.45 E
Vojens	8	Ci	55.15N	9.19 E
Vojkar	17	Ld	65.38N	64.40 E
Vojmsjön	7	Dd	65.00N	16.24 E
Vojnić	14	Je	45.19N	15.42 E
Vojnilov	10	Ug	49.04N	24.33 E
Vojvodina [3]	15	Cd	45.00N	20.00 E
Voj-Vož	19	Fc	62.56N	54.59 E
Voknavolok	7	Hd	64.57N	30.31 E
Vokré, Hosséré-	30	Ih	8.21N	13.15 E
Volary	10	Jh	48.55N	13.54 E
Volcán	49	Fi	8.46N	82.38W
Volcanica, Cordillera-	38	Ih	18.00N	101.00W
Volcano	65a	Fd	19.26N	155.20W
Volcano Islands (EN)=Iō/Kazan-Rettō	21	Qg	25.00N	141.00 E
Volcano Islands (EN)=Kazan-Rettō/Iō	21	Qg	25.00N	141.00 E
Volcán Rana Roi	65d	Ab	27.05S	109.23W
Volčansk	17	Jg	59.59N	60.04 E
Volčansk	16	Jd	50.16N	37.01 E
Volčiha	20	Df	52.02N	80.23 E
Volda	7	Be	62.09N	6.06 E
Voldafjorden	8	Ab	62.10N	6.00 E
Volga	5	Kf	45.55N	47.52 E
Volga	7	Jh	57.57N	38.25 E
Volga-Baltic Canal (EN)=Volgo-Baltijski vodny put imeni V. I. Lenina	5	Jd	59.58N	37.10 E
Volga Delta (EN)	5	Kf	46.30N	47.00 E
Volga Hills (EN)=Privolžkaja Vozvyšennost	5	Ke	52.00N	46.00 E
Volgo-Baltijski vodny put imeni V.I. Lenina=Volga-Baltic Canal (EN)	5	Jd	59.58N	37.10 E
Volgodonsk	19	Ef	47.33N	42.08 E
Volgo-Donskoj sudohodny kanal imeni V. I. Lenina=Lenin Canal (EN)	5	Kf	48.40N	43.37 E
Volgograd (Stalingrad)	6	Kf	48.44N	44.25 E
Volgograd Reservoir (EN)=Volgogradskoje Vodohranilišče	5	Kf	49.20N	45.00 E
Volgogradskaja Oblast [3]	19	Ef	49.30N	44.30 E
Volgogradskoje Vodohranilišče=Volgograd Reservoir (EN)	5	Kf	49.20N	45.00 E
Volhov	5	Jc	60.08N	32.20 E
Volhov	6	Jd	59.55N	32.20 E
Volhynia	5	Ie	51.00N	25.00 E
Volissós	15	Ik	38.29N	25.55 E
Volja	17	Je	63.11N	61.16 E
Volka	10	Vd	52.43N	25.43 E
Völkermarkt	14	Id	46.39N	14.38 E
Völklingen	10	Cg	49.15N	6.51 E
Volkmarsen	12	Lc	51.24N	9.07 E
Volkovysk	16	Dc	53.10N	24.31 E
Volkovysskaja Vozvyšennost	10	Kc	53.10N	24.30 E
Volksrust	37	De	27.24S	29.53 E
Vollenhove	12	Hb	52.40N	5.57 E
Vollsjö	8	Ei	55.42N	13.46 E
Volme	12	Jc	51.24N	7.27 E
Volmunster	12	Je	49.07N	7.21 E
Volna, Gora-	20	Kd	63.30N	154.57 E
Volnjansk	16	If	47.54N	35.29 E
Volnovaha	16	Jf	47.37N	37.36 E
Voločajevka 2-ja	20	Ig	48.36N	134.36 E
Voločisk	16	Ee	49.31N	26.13 E
Volodarsk	7	Kh	56.14N	43.13 E
Volodarski	16	Pf	46.26N	48.31 E
Volodarskoje	19	Ge	53.18N	68.08 E
Vologda	6	Jd	59.12N	39.55 E
Vologodskaja Oblast [3]	19	Ed	60.00N	41.00 E
Volokolamsk	7	Ih	56.03N	35.58 E
Volokonovka	16	Jd	50.29N	37.52 E
Vólos	6	Ih	39.22N	22.57 E
Vološka	7	Jf	61.42N	39.15 E
Vološka	7	Jf	61.21N	40.03 E
Volosovo	7	Gg	59.28N	29.31 E
Volovec	10	Jh	48.42N	23.17 E
Volovo	16	Kc	53.35N	38.01 E
Voložin	16	Eb	54.06N	26.32 E
Volquart Boons Kyst	41	Jd	70.20N	24.20W
Volsini, Monti-	14	Fh	42.40N	11.55 E
Volsk	19	Ee	52.02N	47.23 E
Volta	30	Hh	5.46N	0.41 E
Volta [3]	34	Fd	7.00N	0.30 E
Volta Blanche=White Volta (EN)	30	Gh	8.38N	0.59W
Volta Lake	30	Hh	7.30N	0.15 E
Volta Noire=Black Volta (EN)	30	Gh	8.38N	1.30W
Volta Noire=Black Volta (EN) [3]	34	Ec	12.30N	4.00W
Volta Redonda	53	Lh	22.32S	44.07W
Volta Rouge=Red Volta (EN)	30	Gh	10.34N	0.30W
Volterra	14	Eg	43.24N	10.51 E
Voltoya	13	Hc	41.13N	4.31W
Voltri, Genova-	14	Cf	44.26N	8.45 E
Volturino	14	Jj	40.25N	15.48 E
Volturno	14	Hi	41.01N	13.55 E
Volubilis	32	Fc	34.04N	5.33W
Vólvi, Límni-	15	Gi	40.41N	23.28 E
Volynskaja Grjada	10	Ue	51.05N	25.00 E
Volynskaja Oblast [3]	19	Ce	51.10N	25.00 E
Volynskaja Vozvyšennost	16	Dd	50.30N	25.00 E
Volžsk	19	Ed	55.55N	48.19 E
Volžski	6	Kf	48.48N	44.44 E
Volžski	7	Mj	53.28N	50.08 E
Voma	63d	Bc	18.00S	178.08 E
Vomano	14	Ih	42.39N	14.02 E
Vonavona	63a	Cc	8.12S	157.05 E
Vondrozo	37	Hd	22.47S	47.17 E
Von Frank Mountain	40	Id	63.33N	154.20W
Vónitsa	15	Dk	38.55N	20.53 E
Vonne	11	Gh	46.25N	0.15 E
Võnnu/Vynnu	8	Lf	58.15N	27.10 E
Voorne	12	Gc	51.52N	4.05 E
Voorschoten	12	Gb	52.08N	4.28 E
Voorst	12	Ib	52.10N	6.09 E
Voorst-Twello	12	Ib	52.14N	6.07 E
Vop	16	Hb	54.56N	32.44 E
Vopnafjördur	7a	Cb	65.45N	14.50W
Vora	15	Ch	41.23N	19.40 E
Vörå/Vöyri	8	Ja	63.09N	22.15 E
Vorarlberg [2]	14	Dc	47.15N	9.50 E
Vóras Óros	15	Ei	41.00N	21.50 E
Vorau	14	Jc	47.24N	15.53 E
Vorden	12	Ib	52.06N	6.20 E
Vorderrhein	14	Dd	46.49N	9.26 E
Vordingborg	7	Ci	55.01N	11.55 E
Voreifel	12	Jd	50.10N	7.00 E
Vorga Šor	17	Kc	67.35N	63.40 E
Voría Píndhos	15	Dj	40.20N	20.55 E
Vórioi Sporádhes, Nísoi-=Northern Sporades (EN)	5	Ih	39.15N	23.55 E
Vórios Evvoïkós Kólpos=Évvoia, Gulf of- (EN)	15	Gk	38.45N	23.10 E
Vorkuta	6	Mb	67.27N	63.58 E
Vorma	7	Cf	60.09N	11.27 E
Vormsi	8	Je	59.02N	23.05 E
Vormsi	7	Fg	59.00N	23.15 E
Vorniceni	15	Jb	47.59N	26.40 E
Vorogovo	20	Dd	60.58N	89.28 E
Vorona	16	Md	51.22N	42.03 E
Voroncovo	20	Db	71.40N	83.40 E
Voroncovo	8	Mg	57.15N	28.49 E
Voronež	6	Je	51.40N	39.10 E
Voronež	16	Kd	51.31N	39.05 E
Voronežskaja Oblast [3]	19	Ee	51.00N	40.15 E
Voronin Trough (EN)	67	Ge	80.00N	85.00 E
Voronja	7	Ib	69.09N	35.47 E
Voronovo	8	Kj	54.09N	25.19 E
Voropajevo	8	Li	55.07N	27.19 E
Vorošilovgrad → Lugansk	6	Jf	48.34N	39.20 E
Vorošilovgradskaja Oblast [3]	19	Df	49.00N	39.10 E
Vorotan	16	Oj	39.15N	46.43 E
Vorotynec	7	Kh	56.02N	45.52 E
Vorožba	16	Id	51.10N	34.11 E
Vorskla	16	Ie	48.52N	34.05 E
Vorsma	7	Ki	55.53N	43.17 E
Võrts Järv/Vyrtsjarv, Ozero-	7	Gg	58.15N	26.05 E
Võru/Vyru	19	Cd	57.52N	27.05 E
Voruh	18	He	39.52N	70.35 E
Vosges	5	Gf	48.30N	7.10 E
Vosges [3]	11	Mf	48.10N	6.20 E
Voskresensk	7	Ji	55.22N	38.42 E
Voskresenskoje	7	Kh	56.51N	45.27 E
Voss	8	Bd	60.40N	6.30 E
Vossa	8	Ad	60.39N	5.42 E
Vossevangen	7	Bd	60.39N	6.26 E
Vostočno-Kazahstanskaja Oblast [3]	19	If	49.00N	84.00 E
Vostočno-Kounradski	19	Hf	46.58N	75.07 E
Vostočno Sibirskoje More=East Siberian Sea (EN)	67	Cd	74.00N	166.00 E
Vostočny	20	Jg	48.19N	142.40 E
Vostočny	17	Jg	58.48N	61.52 E
Vostočny, Hrebet-	20	Lf	55.00N	160.30 E
Vostočny Sajan=Eastern Sayans (EN)	21	Ld	53.00N	97.00 E
Vostok	66	Hf	78.28S	106.48 E
Vostok Island	57	Lf	10.06S	152.23W
Vostrecovo	20	Ig	45.56N	134.59 E
Vošu/Vyzu	8	Ke	59.30N	25.50 E
Votkinsk	19	Fd	57.05N	53.59 E
Votkinskoje Vodohranilišče = Votkinsk Reservoir (EN)	5	Ld	57.30N	55.10 E
Votkinsk Reservoir (EN) = Votkinskoje Vodohranilišče	5	Ld	57.30N	55.10 E
Votuporanga	55	He	20.24S	49.59W
Vouga	13	Dd	40.41N	8.40W
Vouillé	11	Gh	46.38N	0.10 E
Voulgára	15	Ej	39.06N	21.54 E
Vouliagméni	15	Gl	37.49N	23.47 E
Voúrinos Óros	15	Ei	40.11N	21.40 E
Voúxa, Ákra-	15	Gn	35.38N	23.36 E
Vouziers	11	Ke	49.24N	4.42 E
Voves	11	Hf	48.16N	1.38 E
Vovodo	35	Cd	5.40N	24.21 E
Voxna	8	Fc	61.21N	15.34 E
Voxnan	8	Gc	61.17N	16.26 E
Voyeykov Ice Shelf	66	Ie	66.20S	124.38 E
Vöyri/Vörå	8	Ja	63.09N	22.15 E
Vože, Ozero-	7	Jf	60.35N	39.05 E
Vožega	7	Jf	60.33N	39.13 E
Vožega	7	Jf	60.30N	40.12 E
Voznesenje	7	If	61.01N	35.27 E
Voznesensk	19	Df	47.35N	31.20 E
Vozroždenija, Ostrov-	18	Bb	45.05N	59.15 E
Vraca [2]	15	Gf	43.12N	23.33 E
Vraca	15	Dh	41.54N	20.45 E
Vraca	15	Gf	43.12N	23.33 E
Vradijevka	16	Gf	47.51N	30.34 E
Vrakhiónas	15	Dl	37.48N	20.45 E
Vran	14	Lg	43.39N	17.27 E
Vrancea [2]	15	Jd	45.50N	26.42 E
Vranica	14	Lg	43.57N	17.44 E
Vranje	15	Eg	42.33N	21.54 E
Vranov nad Topľou	10	Rh	48.54N	21.41 E
Vrăška čuka, Prohod-	15	Ff	43.50N	22.23 E
Vratnica	15	Eg	42.08N	21.07 E
Vratnik, prohod-	15	Jg	42.49N	26.10 E
Vrbas	14	Le	45.07N	17.31 E
Vrbas	15	Cd	45.34N	19.39 E
Vrbno pod Pradědem	10	Nf	50.08N	17.23 E
Vrbovsko	14	Je	45.22N	15.05 E
Vrchlabí	10	Lf	50.38N	15.37 E
Vrede	37	De	27.30S	29.06 E
Vreden	12	Ib	52.02N	6.50 E
Vredenburg	37	Bf	32.54S	17.59 E
Vredendal	37	Bf	31.41S	18.35 E
Vresse, Vresse-sur-Semois-	12	Ge	49.52N	4.56 E
Vresse-sur-Semois	12	Ge	49.52N	4.56 E
Vresse-sur-Semois-Vresse	12	Ge	49.52N	4.56 E
Vretstorp	8	Fe	59.02N	14.52 E
Vrhnika	14	Ie	45.58N	14.18 E
Vries	12	Ia	53.05N	6.36 E
Vriezenveen	12	Ib	52.26N	6.36 E
Vrigstad	8	Fg	57.21N	14.28 E
Vron	12	Dd	50.19N	1.45 E
Vršac	15	Ed	45.07N	21.18 E
Vryburg	31	Jk	26.55S	24.45 E
Vryheid	37	Ee	27.52S	30.38 E
Vsetín	10	Ng	49.21N	18.00 E
Vsevidof, Mount-	40a	Eb	53.07N	168.43W
Vsevoložsk	7	Hf	60.04N	30.41 E
Vstrečny	20	Lc	68.00N	165.58 E
Vtačnik	10	Oh	48.42N	18.37 E
Vuanggava	63d	Cc	18.52S	178.54W
Vučitrn	15	Dg	42.49N	20.58 E
Vučjak	15	Fh	41.28N	22.20 E
Vuka	14	Me	45.21N	19.00 E
Vukovar	14	Me	45.21N	19.00 E
Vuktyl	19	Fc	63.50N	57.25 E
Vulavu	63a	Dc	8.31S	159.48 E
Vulcan	15	Gd	45.23N	23.16 E
Vulcan, Vîrful-	15	Fc	46.14N	22.58 E
Vulcano	14	Il	38.25N	15.00 E
Vulkanešty	16	Fg	45.38N	28.27 E
Vulture	14	Jj	40.57N	15.38 E
Vung Tau	25	Lf	10.21N	107.04 E
Vunindawa	63d	Bb	17.49S	178.19 E
Vunisea Station	61	Ec	19.03S	178.09 E
Vuohijarvi	8	Lc	61.10N	26.40 E
Vuoksa	8	Nd	60.35N	30.42 E
Vuoksa, ozero-	8	Mc	61.00N	30.00 E
Vuoksa, ozero-	8	Md	60.38N	29.55 E
Vuollerim	7	Ec	66.25E	20.36 E
Vuosjärvi	8	Ka	63.00N	25.30 E
Vuotso	7	Gb	68.06N	27.08 E
Vuranimala	63a	Ec	9.05S	160.51 E
Vyborg	6	Ic	60.42N	28.45 E
Vyčegda	5	Kc	61.18N	46.36 E
Vyčegodski	7	Lf	61.17N	46.48 E
Vychodočeský kraj [3]	10	Lf	50.10N	16.00 E
Východoslovenska nížina	10	Rh	48.35N	21.50 E
Východoslovenský kraj [3]	10	Rg	49.00N	21.15 E
Vyg	7	Ie	63.17N	35.17 E
Vygoda	15	Nc	46.38N	30.24 E
Vygoda	10	Uh	48.52N	24.01 E
Vygozero, Ozero-	5	Jc	63.35N	34.45 E
Vyhandu/Võhandu Jõgi	8	Lf	58.03N	27.40 E
Vyja	7	Le	62.57N	46.42 E
Vyksa	19	Ed	55.20N	42.12 E
Vym	19	Fc	62.13N	50.25 E
Vynnu/Võnnu	8	Lf	58.15N	27.10 E
Vyrica	19	Dd	59.24N	30.19 E
Vyrnwy	9	Ki	52.45N	2.50W
Vyrtsjarv, Ozero-/Võrts Järv	7	Gg	58.15N	26.05 E
Vyru/Võru	19	Cd	57.52N	27.05 E
Vyša	16	Mb	54.03N	42.06 E
Vyšgorod	16	Gd	50.38N	30.29 E
Vyšgorodok	8	Mh	56.55N	28.05 E
Vyškov	10	Mg	49.17N	17.00 E
Vyškovsk, pereval	10	Th	48.38N	23.45 E
Vyšni Voloček	19	Dd	57.37N	34.32 E
Vysock	7	Gf	60.36N	28.36 E
Vysoké Tatry=High Tatra (EN)	10	Pg	49.10N	20.00 E
Vysokogorny	20	If	50.07N	139.10 E
Vysokogorsk	28	Mb	44.23N	135.23 E
Vysokoje	10	Td	52.22N	23.26 E
Vysokovsk	7	Ih	56.21N	36.29 E
Vyšši Brod	10	Kh	48.37N	14.18 E
Vytebet	16	Ic	53.53N	35.38 E
Vytegra	19	Dc	61.01N	36.28 E
Vyvenka	20	Ld	60.10N	165.20 E
Vyzu/Vošu	8	Ke	59.30N	25.50 E
Vzmorje	20	Jg	47.45N	142.30 E

W

Name	Map	Grid	Lat.	Long.
Wa	34	Ec	10.03N	2.29W
Waal	11	Kc	51.55N	4.30 E
Waalre	12	Hc	51.23N	5.27 E
Waalwijk	12	Hc	51.41N	5.04 E
Waar, Meos-	26	Jg	2.05S	134.23 E
Waardgronden	12	Ha	53.12N	5.05 E
Waarschoot	12	Fc	51.09N	3.36 E
Wabana	42	Mg	47.38N	52.57W
Wabao, Cap-	63b	Ce	21.36S	167.51 E
Wabasca	42	Ge	56.00N	113.53W
Wabasca	42	Fe	58.21N	115.20W
Wabash	38	Kf	37.46N	88.02W
Wabash	44	Ee	40.48N	85.49W
Wabasha	45	Jd	44.23N	92.02W
Wabash River	45	Lh	37.46N	88.02W
Wabowden	42	Hf	54.55N	98.38W
Wąbrzeźno	10	Oc	53.17N	18.57 E
Wabu Hu	27	Ke	32.20N	116.55 E
Wachau	14	Jb	48.20N	15.25 E
Wachile	35	Fe	4.33N	39.03 E
Wachusett Seamount (EN)	57	Lh	32.00S	151.20W
Waco	39	Jf	31.55N	97.08W
Waconda Lake	45	Gg	39.30N	98.30W
Wadayama	29	Dd	35.20N	134.51 E
Wad Bandah	35	Dc	13.06N	27.57 E
Waddān	33	Cd	29.10N	16.08 E
Waddān, Jabal-	33	Cd	29.20N	16.20 E
Waddeneilanden=West Frisian Islands (EN)	11	Ka	53.30N	5.00 E
Waddenzee	12	Ha	53.20N	5.30 E
Waddington, Mount-	38	Gd	51.23N	125.15W
Wadena	45	Ic	46.26N	95.08W
Wadern	12	Ie	49.32N	6.53 E
Wadern-Nunkirchen	12	Ie	49.32N	6.53 E
Wadersloh	12	Kc	51.44N	8.15 E
Wadersloh-Liesborn	12	Kc	51.43N	8.16 E
Wadesboro	44	Gh	34.58N	80.04W
Wadhams	46	Ba	51.30N	127.31W
Wādī Bīshah	23	Fe	21.24N	43.26 E
Wādī Fajr	23	Ec	30.17N	38.18 E
Wādī Ḩalfā'	31	Kf	21.56N	31.20 E
Wādī Jimāl, Jazīrat-	24	Fj	24.40N	35.10 E
Wādī Mūsá	24	Fg	30.19N	35.29 E
Wādī Shiḩan	35	Ib	18.10N	52.57 E
Wad Madanī	31	Kg	14.24N	33.32 E
Wad Nimr	35	Ec	14.32N	32.08 E
Wadowice	10	Pg	49.53N	19.30 E
Wadsworth	46	Fg	39.38N	119.17W
Wafangdian → Fuxian	27	Ld	39.38N	121.59 E
Wafrah	23	Gd	28.25N	47.56 E
Waga-Gawa	29	Gb	39.18N	141.07 E
Wagenfeld	12	Kb	52.33N	8.35 E
Wagenfeld-Ströhen	12	Kb	52.32N	8.39 E
Wageningen	12	Hc	51.57N	5.41 E
Wagēr, Qar-	35	Hc	10.01N	45.30 E
Wager Bay	38	Kc	65.26N	88.40W
Wagga Wagga	58	Fh	35.07S	147.22 E
Waghäusel	12	Ke	49.15N	8.30 E
Wagin	58	Ch	33.18S	117.21 E
Waginger See	10	Ii	47.58N	12.50 E
Wagoner	45	Ii	35.58N	95.22W
Wagon Mound	45	Dh	36.01N	104.42W
Wagontire Mountain	46	Fe	43.21N	119.53W
Wagrien	10	Gb	54.15N	10.45 E
Wągrowiec	10	Nd	52.49N	17.11 E
Wah	25	Eb	33.48N	72.42 E
Waha	31	If	28.10N	19.57 E
Wahai	26	Ig	2.48S	129.30 E
Wahiawa	60	Oc	21.30N	158.02W
Wahoo	45	Hf	41.13N	96.37W
Wahpeton	43	Hb	46.16N	96.36W
Waialeale, Mount-	65a	Ba	22.04N	159.30W
Waialua	65a	Cb	21.35N	158.08W
Waianae	65a	Cb	21.27N	158.12W
Waiau	62	Ee	42.47S	173.22 E
Waiau	61	Dh	42.39S	173.03 E
Waiblingen	10	Fh	48.50N	9.18 E
Waibstadt	12	Ke	49.18N	8.56 E
Waidhofen an der Thaya	14	Jb	48.49N	15.17 E
Waidhofen an der Ybbs	14	Ic	47.58N	14.46 E
Waigame	26	Ig	1.50S	129.49 E
Waigeo, Pulau-	57	Ee	0.14S	130.45 E
Waihi	62	Fb	37.24S	175.50 E
Waihou	62	Fb	37.10S	175.33 E
Waikabubak	26	Gh	9.38S	119.25 E
Waikare, Lake-	62	Fb	37.25S	175.10 E
Waikaremoana, Lake-	61	Eg	38.45S	177.05 E
Waikato	62	Fb	37.23S	174.43 E
Waikawa	62	Cg	46.38S	169.08 E
Waikouaiti	62	Df	45.36S	170.41 E
Wailangilala	63d	Cb	16.45S	179.06W
Wailua	65a	Ba	22.03N	159.20W
Wailuku	60	Oc	20.53N	156.30W
Waimamaku	62	Ea	35.34S	173.29 E
Waimanalo Beach	65a	Db	21.20N	157.42W
Waimangaroa	62	Dd	41.43S	171.46 E
Waimate	62	Df	44.45S	171.03 E
Waimea	65a	Fc	20.02N	155.40W
Waimes	12	Id	50.25N	6.07 E
Wainfleet All Saints	12	Ca	53.06N	0.15 E
Wainganga	21	Jh	19.36N	79.48 E
Waingapu	26	Hh	9.39S	120.16 E
Waini Point	50	Gh	8.24N	59.49W
Waini River	50	Gh	8.24N	59.51W
Wainwright [Ak.-U.S.]	40	Gb	70.38N	160.01W
Wainwright [Alta.-Can.]	42	Gf	52.49N	110.52W
Waiouru	61	Eg	39.29S	175.40 E
Waipahu	65a	Cb	21.23N	158.01W
Waipara	62	Ee	43.03S	172.45 E
Waipawa	62	Gc	39.56S	176.35 E
Waipiro	62	Hc	38.02S	178.20 E
Waipu	62	Fa	35.59S	174.26 E
Waipukurau	62	Gd	40.00S	176.33 E
Wairakei	62	Gc	38.37S	176.05 E
Wairarapa, Lake-	62	Fd	41.15S	175.15 E
Wairau	62	Fd	41.31S	174.03 E
Wairoa	61	Eg	39.03S	177.26 E
Wairoa	62	Fb	36.11S	174.02 E
Waitaki	62	Df	44.56S	171.09 E
Waitangi	61	Fh	43.56S	176.34W
Waitara	61	Dg	39.00S	174.14 E
Waitati	62	Df	45.45S	170.34 E
Waitemata	62	Fb	36.50S	174.40 E
Waitotara	62	Fc	39.48S	174.44 E
Waiuku	62	Fb	37.15S	174.44 E
Waiwerang	26	Hh	8.23S	123.09 E
Waiyevo	63d	Fc	16.48S	179.59W
Wājid	35	Ge	3.50N	43.14 E
Wajima	28	Nf	37.24N	136.54 E
Wajir	31	Ih	1.42N	40.04 E
Waka [Eth.]	35	Fd	7.09N	37.19 E
Waka [Zaire]	36	Db	1.01N	20.13 E
Wakamatsu-Shima	29	Ae	32.54N	129.00 E
Wakasa-Wan	27	Od	35.45N	135.40 E
Wakatipu, Lake-	61	Ci	45.05S	168.35 E
Wakaya	63d	Bb	17.37S	179.00 E
Wakayama	22	Pf	34.13N	135.11 E
Wakayama Ken [2]	28	Mh	33.55N	135.20 E
Wake	29	Dd	34.48N	134.08 E
Wa Keeney	45	Gg	39.01N	99.53W
Wakefield [Eng.-U.K.]	9	Lh	53.42N	1.29W
Wakefield [N.Z.]	62	Ed	41.24S	173.03 E

Index Symbols

[1] Independent Nation
[2] State, Region
[3] District, County
[4] Municipality
[5] Colony, Dependency
Continent
Physical Region

Historical or Cultural Region
Mount, Mountain
Volcano
Hill
Mountains, Mountain Range
Hills, Escarpment
Plateau, Upland

Pass, Gap
Plain, Lowland
Delta
Salt Flat
Valley, Canyon
Crater, Cave
Karst Features

Depression
Polder
Desert, Dunes
Forest, Woods
Heath, Steppe
Oasis
Cape, Point

Coast, Beach
Cliff
Peninsula
Isthmus
Sandbank
Island
Atoll

Rock, Reef
Islands, Archipelago
Rocks, Reefs
Coral Reef
Well, Spring
Geyser
River, Stream

Waterfall Rapids
River Mouth, Estuary
Lake
Salt Lake
Intermittent Lake
Reservoir
Swamp, Pond

Canal
Glacier
Ice Shelf, Pack Ice
Ocean
Sea
Gulf, Bay
Strait, Fjord

Lagoon
Bank
Seamount
Tablemount
Ridge
Shelf
Basin

Escarpment, Sea Scarp
Fracture
Trench, Abyss
National Park, Reserve
Point of Interest
Recreation Site
Cave, Cavern

Historic Site
Ruins
Wall, Walls
Church, Abbey
Temple
Scientific Station
Airport

Port
Lighthouse
Mine
Tunnel
Dam, Bridge

Wake Island [5]	58	Jd	19.18N	166.36W
Wake Island	57	Hc	19.18N	166.36 E
Wakkanai	22	Qe	45.25N	141.40 E
Wakunai	63a	Ba	5.52S	155.13 E
Wakuya	29	Gb	38.33N	141.05 E
Wala	36	Fd	5.46S	32.04 E
Walachia (EN) = Valahia	5	Ig	44.00N	25.00 E
Walachia (EN) = Valahia	15	He	44.00N	25.00 E
Wałbrzych [2]	10	Mf	50.45N	16.15 E
Wałbrzych	6	He	50.46N	16.17 E
Walchensee	10	Hi	47.35N	11.20 E
Walcheren	11	Jc	51.33N	3.35 E
Walcott, Lake-	46	Ie	42.40N	113.23W
Walcourt	12	Gd	50.15N	4.25 E
Walcourt-Fraire	12	Gd	50.16N	4.30 E
Wałcz	10	Mc	53.17N	16.28 E
Waldböckelheim	12	Je	49.49N	7.43 E
Waldbröl	10	Df	50.53N	7.37 E
Waldeck	12	Kc	51.17N	8.50 E
Waldeck	12	Lc	51.12N	9.05 E
Waldems	12	Kd	50.15N	8.18 E
Walden	45	Cf	40.44N	106.17W
Waldfischbach-Burgalben	12	Je	49.17N	7.40 E
Waldkirchen	10	Jh	48.44N	13.36 E
Waldkraiburg	10	Ih	48.12N	12.25 E
Wald-Michelbach	12	Ke	49.34N	8.49 E
Waldnaab	10	Ig	49.35N	12.07 E
Waldorf	44	If	38.37N	76.54W
Waldrach	12	Ie	49.45N	6.45 E
Waldron	45	Ii	34.54N	94.05W
Waldshut	10	Ei	47.37N	8.13 E
Waldviertel	14	Jb	48.30N	15.30 E
Waleabahi, Pulau-	26	Hg	0.15S	122.20 E
Wales	40	Fc	65.36N	168.05W
Wales	42	Ic	67.50N	86.40W
Wales	5	Fe	52.30N	3.30W
Wales [2]	9	Ji	52.30N	3.30W
Walewale	34	Ec	10.21N	0.48W
Walferdange	12	Ie	49.39N	6.08 E
Walgett	58	Fh	30.01S	148.07 E
Walgreen Coast	66	Of	75.15S	105.00W
Walhalla	45	Hb	48.55N	97.55W
Walikale	36	Ec	1.25S	28.03 E
Walker	45	Ic	47.06N	94.35W
Walker Lake	43	Dd	38.40N	118.43W
Walkerston	59	Jd	21.10S	149.10 E
Wall	45	Ed	44.01N	102.14W
Wallace	46	Hc	47.28N	115.56W
Wallaceburg	44	Fd	42.36N	82.23W
Wallangarra	59	Ke	28.56S	151.56 E
Wallaroo	59	Hf	33.56S	137.38 E
Wallary Island	59	Ic	15.05S	141.50 E
Wallasey	9	Jh	53.26N	3.03W
Walla Walla	43	Db	46.08N	118.20W
Walldorf	12	Ke	49.20N	8.39 E
Wallenhorst	12	Kb	52.21N	8.01 E
Wallibu	51n	Ba	13.19N	61.15W
Wallingford	12	Ac	51.36N	1.08W
Wallis, Iles-=Wallis Islands (EN)	57	Jf	13.18S	176.10W
Wallis and Futuna (EN)= Wallis-et-Futuna, Iles- [5]	58	Jf	14.00S	177.00W
Walliser Alpen/Alpes Valaisannes	14	Bd	46.10N	7.30 E
Wallis-et-Futuna, Iles- = Wallis and Futuna (EN) [5]	58	Jf	14.00S	177.00W
Wallis Islands (EN)=Wallis, Iles-	57	Jf	13.18S	176.10W
Wallowa	46	Gd	45.34N	117.32W
Wallowa Mountains	46	Gd	45.10N	117.30W
Walmer	12	Dc	51.12N	1.24 E
Walney, Isle of-	9	Jg	54.07N	3.15W
Walnut Ridge	43	Id	36.04N	90.57W
Walpole, Ile-	57	Hg	22.37S	168.57 E
Walrus Islands	40	Ge	58.45N	160.20W
Walsall	9	Li	52.35N	1.58W
Walsenburg	43	Gd	37.37N	104.47W
Walsrode	10	Fd	52.52N	9.35 E
Walterboro	44	Gi	32.54N	80.39W
Walter F. George Lake	44	Ej	31.49N	85.08W
Walter Lake	43	Dd	38.44N	118.43W
Walters	45	Gi	34.22N	98.19W
Waltershausen	10	Gf	50.54N	10.34 E
Waltham	44	Ic	45.58N	76.57W
Walton-on-the-Naze	12	Dc	51.51N	1.17 E
Waltrop	12	Jc	51.38N	7.24 E
Walvisbaai/Walvis Bay [3]	37	Ad	23.00S	14.30 E
Walvisbaai=Walvis Bay (EN)	31	Ik	22.59S	14.31 E
Walvisbaai=Walvis Bay (EN) [5]	31	Ik	22.59S	14.31 E
Walvisbaai=Walvis Bay (EN)	30	Ik	22.57S	14.30 E
Walvis Bay/Walvisbaai [3]	37	Ad	23.00S	14.30 E
Walvis Bay (EN)= Walvisbaai	30	Ik	22.57S	14.30 E
Walvis Bay (EN)= Walvisbaai [5]	31	Ik	22.59S	14.31 E
Walvis Bay (EN)= Walvisbaai	31	Ik	22.59S	14.31 E
Walvis Ridge (EN)	3	El	28.00S	3.00 E
Wamba	30	Ii	3.56S	17.12 E
Wamba [Kenya]	36	Gb	0.59N	37.19 E
Wamba [Nig.]	34	Gd	8.56N	8.36 E
Wamba [Zaire]	36	Eb	2.09N	28.00 E
Wamena	26	Kg	4.00S	138.57 E
Wami	30	Ki	6.08S	38.49 E
Wampusirpi	49	Ef	15.15N	84.37W
Wamsutter	46	Lf	41.40N	107.58W
Wan	26	Kh	8.23S	137.56 E
Wana	25	Db	32.17N	69.35 E
Wanaka	58	Hi	44.42S	169.08 E
Wanaka, Lake-	62	Cf	44.30S	169.10 E
Wan'an	27	Jf	26.32N	114.48 E
Wanapiri	26	Kg	4.33S	135.59 E
Wanapitei Lake	44	Gb	46.45N	80.45W
Wandel Hav=Wandel Sea (EN)	41	Gb	83.00N	15.00W
Wandel Sea (EN)=Wandel Hav	41	Gb	83.00N	15.00W
Wandsworth, London-	12	Bc	51.27N	0.12W
Wanganui	62	Fc	39.58S	175.00 E
Wanganui	61	Eg	39.56S	175.02 E
Wangaratta	59	Jg	36.22S	146.20 E
Wangcun [China]	28	Df	36.41N	117.42 E
Wangcun [China]	27	Jd	39.58N	112.53 E
Wangda/Zogang	27	Gf	29.37N	97.58 E
Wangdu	28	Ce	38.43N	115.09 E
Wangen in Allgäu	10	Fi	47.41N	9.50 E
Wangerooge	10	Dc	53.46N	7.55 E
Wanggameti, Gunung-	26	Hi	10.07S	120.14 E
Wanggezhuang → Jiaonan	28	Eg	35.53N	119.58 E
Wangiwangi, Pulau-	26	Hh	5.20S	123.35 E
Wangjiang	28	Di	30.08N	116.41 E
Wangkui	27	Mb	46.50N	126.29 E
Wangpan Yang	21	Of	30.33N	121.26 E
Wangping	27	Mc	43.18N	129.46 E
Wangying → Huaiyin	28	Eh	33.35N	119.02 E
Wani, Laguna-	49	Ff	14.50N	83.25W
Wanie-Rukula	36	Eb	0.14N	25.34 E
Wanitsuka-Yama	29	Bf	31.45N	131.17 E
Wanlewëyn	35	Ge	2.35N	44.55 E
Wan Namton	25	Jd	22.03N	99.33 E
Wannian (Chenying)	28	Dj	28.42N	117.04 E
Wanning	27	Jh	18.59N	110.24 E
Wanquan	28	Cd	40.52N	114.44 E
Wansbeck	9	Lf	55.10N	1.34W
Wan Shui	28	Di	30.30N	117.31 E
Wanxian	22	Mf	30.48N	108.21 E
Wanyuan	27	Ie	32.03N	108.04 E
Wanzai	28	Cj	28.06N	114.27 E
Wanzhi → Wuhu	28	Ei	31.21N	118.23 E
Wapato	46	Ec	46.27N	120.25W
Wapiti	46	Kd	44.28N	109.28W
Wapiti	42	Fe	55.08N	118.19W
Wapsipinicon River	45	Kf	41.44N	90.20W
Waqooyi Galbeed [3]	35	Gc	10.00N	44.00 E
Warangal	22	Jh	18.18N	79.35 E
Waratah Bay	59	Jg	38.50S	146.05 E
Warburg	10	Fe	51.30N	9.10 E
Warburger Borde	12	Lc	51.35N	9.12 E
Warburg-Scherfede	12	Lc	51.32N	9.02 E
Warburton Bay	42	Gd	63.50N	111.30W
Warburton Mission	59	Fe	26.10S	126.35 E
Warburton Range	59	Fe	26.10S	126.40 E
Ward	62	Fd	41.50S	174.08 E
Warden	37	De	27.56S	29.00 E
Wardenburg	12	Ka	53.04N	8.12 E
Wardha	25	Fd	20.45N	78.37 E
Ward Hunt Strait	59	Ja	9.25S	149.55 E
Ware [B.C.-Can.]	42	Ee	57.27N	125.38W
Ware [Eng.-U.K.]	12	Bc	51.49N	0.01W
Waregem	12	Fd	50.53N	3.25 E
Waremme/Borgworm	11	Lc	50.42N	5.15 E
Waren [Ger.]	10	Ic	53.31N	12.41 E
Waren [Indon.]	58	Ee	2.16S	136.20 E
Warendorf	10	De	51.57N	7.59 E
Warin Chamrap	25	Ke	15.14N	104.52 E
Warka	10	Re	51.47N	21.10 E
Warkworth	62	Fb	36.24S	174.40 E
Warmbad [3]	37	Be	28.00S	18.30 E
Warmbad [Nam.]	37	Be	28.29S	18.41 E
Warmbad [S.Afr.]	37	Dd	24.53S	28.17 E
Warming Land	41	Gb	81.50N	52.45W
Warmington	12	Ab	52.08N	1.24W
Warminster	9	Kj	51.13N	2.12W
Warm Springs [Nv.-U.S.]	43	Gg	38.13N	116.20W
Warm Springs [Or.-U.S.]	46	Ed	44.46N	121.16W
Warnemünde, Rostock-	10	Ib	54.10N	12.05 E
Warner, Mount-	46	Db	51.03N	123.12W
Warner Mountains	43	Cc	41.40N	120.20W
Warner Peak	46	Fe	42.27N	119.44W
Warner Robins	43	Ke	32.37N	83.36W
Warner Valley	46	Fe	42.30N	119.55W
Warnes	54	Fg	17.30S	63.10W
Warnow	10	Ib	54.06N	12.09 E
Waroona	59	Df	32.50S	115.55 E
Warragul	59	Jg	38.10S	145.56 E
Warrego Range	59	Je	25.00S	145.45 E
Warrego River	57	Fh	30.24S	145.21 E
Warren [Ar.-U.S.]	45	Jj	33.38N	92.05W
Warren [Mi.-U.S.]	44	Fd	42.28N	83.01W
Warren [Mn.-U.S.]	45	Hb	48.12N	96.46W
Warren [Oh.-U.S.]	44	Kc	41.15N	80.49W
Warren [Pa.-U.S.]	44	He	41.52N	79.09W
Warrenpoint/An Pointe	9	Gg	54.06N	6.15W
Warrensburg	45	Jg	38.46N	93.44W
Warrenton	37	Ce	28.09S	24.47 E
Warri	34	Gd	5.31N	5.45 E
Warrington [Eng.-U.K.]	9	Kh	53.24N	2.37W
Warrington [Fl.-U.S.]	44	Dj	30.23N	87.16W
Warrior Reefs	59	Ia	9.35S	143.10 E
Warrnambool	58	Fh	38.23S	142.29 E
Warroad	43	Hb	48.54N	95.19W
Warrumbungle Range	59	Jf	31.30S	149.40 E
Warsaw [In.-U.S.]	44	Ee	41.14N	85.51W
Warsaw [Mo.-U.S.]	45	Jg	38.15N	93.23W
Warsaw [N.Y.-U.S.]	44	Hd	42.45N	78.07W
Warsaw (EN)=Warszawa	6	Ie	52.15N	21.00 E
Warshikh	35	He	2.18N	45.48 E
Warstein	12	Kc	51.27N	8.22 E
Warstein-Belecke	12	Kc	51.29N	8.20 E
Warszawa [2]	10	Qd	52.15N	21.00 E
Warszawa=Warsaw (EN)	6	Ie	52.15N	21.00 E
Warta	5	He	52.35N	14.39 E
Waru	26	Jg	3.24S	130.40 E
Warwick	59	Ke	28.13S	152.02 E
Warwick	9	Li	52.25N	1.30W
Warwick [Eng.-U.K.]	9	Li	52.17N	1.34W
Warwick [R.I.-U.S.]	44	Le	41.42N	71.23W
Warwickshire [3]	9	Li	52.10N	1.35W
Wasagu	34	Gc	11.22N	5.48 E
Wasatch Range	38	He	41.15N	111.30W
Wascana Creek	46	Ma	50.40N	104.55W
Wasco	46	F	35.36N	119.20W
Waseca	45	Jd	44.05N	93.30W
Washburn	45	Fc	47.17N	101.02W
Washess Bay	64g	Ab	1.49N	157.31W
Wāshim	25	Fd	20.10N	76.58 E
Washington [2]	43	Cb	47.30N	120.30W
Washington [D.C.-U.S.]	39	Lf	38.54N	77.01W
Washington [Eng.-U.K.]	9	Lg	54.54N	1.31W
Washington [Ga.-U.S.]	44	Fi	33.44N	82.44W
Washington [Ia.-U.S.]	45	Kf	41.18N	91.42W
Washington [In.-U.S.]	44	Df	38.40N	87.10W
Washington [N.C.-U.S.]	44	Ih	35.33N	77.03W
Washington [Pa.-U.S.]	44	Ge	40.11N	80.16W
Washington → Teraina Island	57	Kd	4.43N	160.24W
Washington, Mount-	38	Le	44.15N	71.15W
Washington Court House	44	Ff	39.32N	83.29W
Washington Island	45	Md	45.23N	86.55W
Washington Land	41	Fb	80.15N	65.00W
Washita River	45	Hi	34.12N	96.50W
Washtucna	46	Fc	46.45N	118.19W
Wasile	26	If	1.04N	127.59 E
Wasilków	10	Tc	53.12N	23.12 E
Wasior	26	Jg	2.43S	134.30 E
Wāsiţ [3]	24	Lf	32.35N	46.00 E
Waskaganish	39	Lc	51.25N	78.45W
Wąsosz	10	Me	51.34N	16.42 E
Waspán	47	Hf	14.44N	83.58W
Wassamu	29a	Ca	44.02N	142.24 E
Wassenaar	12	Gb	52.09N	4.24 E
Wassenberg	12	Ic	51.06N	6.09 E
Wasserburg am Inn	10	Ih	48.04N	12.14 E
Wasserkuppe	10	Ff	50.30N	9.56 E
Wassigny	12	Fd	50.01N	3.36 E
Wassuk Range	46	Fg	38.40N	118.50W
Wassy	11	Kf	48.30N	4.57 E
Waswanipi, Lac-	44	Ia	49.32N	76.29W
Watampone	22	Oj	4.32S	120.20 E
Watansoppeng	26	Gg	4.21S	119.53 E
Watari	29	Gb	38.02N	140.51 E
Waterbeach	12	Cb	52.16N	0.12 E
Waterberg	37	Bd	20.25S	17.15 E
Waterbury	43	Mc	41.33N	73.02W
Water Cays	49	Ib	23.40N	77.45W
Wateree Pond	44	Gh	34.25N	80.50W
Waterford/Port Láirge	6	Fe	52.15N	7.06W
Waterford/Port Láirge [2]	9	Fi	52.10N	7.40W
Waterford Harbour/Cuan Phort Láirge	9	Gi	52.10N	6.57W
Wateringues	11	Ic	51.00N	2.30 E
Waterloo [Bel.]	11	Kd	50.43N	4.24 E
Waterloo [Ia.-U.S.]	43	Ic	42.30N	92.20W
Waterloo [Il.-U.S.]	45	Kg	38.20N	90.09W
Waterlooville	12	Ad	50.52N	1.01W
Watersmeet	44	Cb	46.16N	89.11W
Watertown [N.Y.-U.S.]	43	Lc	43.57N	75.56W
Watertown [S.D.-U.S.]	43	Hc	44.54N	97.07W
Watertown [Wi.-U.S.]	45	Le	43.12N	88.43W
Waterville	43	Nc	44.33N	69.38W
Watford	9	Mj	51.40N	0.25W
Watford City	45	Ec	47.48N	103.17W
Wa'th	35	Ed	8.10N	32.07 E
Watheroo	59	Df	30.17S	116.04 E
Watīr, Wādī-	24	Fh	29.01N	34.40 E
Watkins Glen	44	Id	42.23N	76.53W
Watling → San Salvador	47	Jd	24.02N	74.28W
Watlington	12	Ac	51.38N	1.00W
Watonga	45	Gi	35.51N	98.25W
Watou, Poperinge-	12	Ed	50.51N	2.37 E
Watrous	42	Gf	51.40N	105.28W
Watsa	31	Jh	3.03N	29.32 E
Watseka	45	Mf	40.47N	87.44W
Watsi [C.R.]	49	Fi	9.37N	82.52W
Watsi [Zaire]	36	Dc	0.19S	21.04 E
Watsi Kengo	36	Dc	0.48S	20.33 E
Watson Lake	39	Gc	60.07N	128.48W
Watsonville	46	Eh	36.55N	121.45W
Watt, Morne-	51g	Bb	15.19N	61.19W
Watton	12	Cb	52.34N	0.50 E
Watts Bar Lake	44	Eh	35.48N	84.39W
Wattwil	14	Dc	47.18N	9.05 E
Watubela, Kepulauan-	26	Jg	4.35S	131.40 E
Wau	59	Ja	7.20S	146.45 E
Waubay Lake	45	Hd	45.25N	97.25W
Wauchope	59	Kf	31.27S	152.44 E
Wauchula	44	Gl	27.33N	81.49W
Waucoba Mountain	46	Fh	37.00N	118.01W
Waukara, Gunung-	26	Gg	1.15S	119.42 E
Waukarlycarly, Lake-	59	Ed	21.25S	121.50 E
Waukegan	43	Jc	42.22N	87.50W
Waukesha	45	Le	43.01N	88.14W
Waupaca	45	Ld	44.21N	89.05W
Wausau	43	Jc	44.59N	89.39W
Wauseon	44	Ee	41.33N	84.09W
Wauwatosa	45	Me	43.03N	88.00W
Wave Hill	59	Gc	17.29S	130.57 E
Waveney	9	Di	52.28N	1.45 E
Waver/Wavre	11	Kd	50.43N	4.37 E
Waverly [Ia.-U.S.]	45	Je	42.44N	92.29W
Waverly [Oh.-U.S.]	44	Ff	39.07N	82.59W
Waverly [Tn.-U.S.]	44	Dg	36.05N	87.48W
Waves	44	Jh	35.37N	75.29W
Wavre/Waver	11	Kd	50.43N	4.37 E
Wāw	31	Jh	7.42N	28.00 E
Wawa [Nig.]	34	Fd	9.55N	4.27 E
Wawa [Ont.-Can.]	42	Jg	47.59N	84.47W
Wawa, Río-	49	Fg	13.53N	83.28W
Wāw al Kabīr	31	If	25.20N	16.43 E
Wāw an Nāmūs	33	Ce	24.55N	19.45 E
Wāw Nahr	35	Dd	7.03N	27.13 E
Wawo	26	Hg	3.41S	121.02 E
Wawotobi	26	Hg	3.51S	122.06 E
Waxahachie	45	Hj	32.24N	96.51W
Waxweiler	12	Id	50.06N	6.22 E
Waxxari	27	Ed	38.37N	87.22 E
Way, Lake-	59	Ee	26.50S	120.20 E
Waya	63d	Ab	17.18S	177.08 E
Wayabula	26	If	2.17N	128.12 E
Wayan	46	Je	43.00N	111.22W
Waycross	43	Ke	31.13N	82.21W
Wayne [Nb.-U.S.]	45	He	42.14N	97.01W
Wayne [W.V.-U.S.]	44	Ff	38.14N	82.27W
Waynesboro [Ga.-U.S.]	44	Fi	33.06N	82.01W
Waynesboro [Ms.-U.S.]	45	Lk	31.40N	88.39W
Waynesboro [Pa.-U.S.]	44	If	39.45N	77.36W
Waynesboro [Va.-U.S.]	44	Hf	38.04N	78.54W
Waynesville [Mo.-U.S.]	45	Jh	37.50N	92.12W
Waynesville [N.C.-U.S.]	44	Fh	35.29N	83.00W
Waynoka	45	Gh	36.35N	98.53W
Waziers	12	Fd	50.23N	3.07 E
Wda	10	Oc	53.25N	18.29 E
Wdzydze, Jezioro-	10	Nc	54.00N	17.50 E
Wé	61	Cd	20.55S	167.16 E
We, Pulau-	26	Ce	5.51N	95.18 E
Wear	9	Lg	54.55N	1.22W
Weatherford [Ok.-U.S.]	45	Gi	35.32N	98.42W
Weatherford [Tx.-U.S.]	43	He	32.46N	97.48W
Weaverville	46	Df	40.44N	122.56W
Weber	62	Gd	40.24S	176.20 E
Webster	45	Hd	45.20N	97.31W
Webster City	45	Je	42.28N	93.49W
Webster Springs	44	Gf	38.29N	80.25W
Weda	26	If	0.21N	127.52 E
Weda, Teluk-	26	If	0.20N	128.00 E
Weddell Island	56	Hh	51.50S	61.00W
Weddel Sea (EN)	66	Rf	72.00S	45.00W
Wedel	10	Fc	53.35N	9.41 E
Wedgeport	44	Od	43.44N	65.59W
Wedza	37	Ec	18.35S	31.35 E
Weed	46	Df	41.25N	122.27W
Weener	10	Dc	53.10N	7.21 E
Weerdinge, Emmen-	12	Ib	52.49N	6.57 E
Weert	11	Lc	51.15N	5.43 E
Weesp	12	Hb	52.18N	5.02 E
Wegberg	12	Ic	51.09N	6.16 E
Węgliniec	10	Le	51.17N	15.13 E
Węgorzewo	10	Rb	54.14N	21.44 E
Węgrów	10	Sd	52.25N	22.01 E
Wehni	35	Fc	12.40N	36.42 E
Weichang (Zhuizishan)	28	Kc	41.55N	117.45 E
Weida	10	If	50.46N	12.04 E
Weiden in der Oberpfalz	10	Ig	49.41N	12.10 E
Weifang	22	Nf	36.43N	119.06 E
Weihai	27	Ld	37.27N	122.02 E
Weihe	28	Jb	44.55N	128.23 E
Wei He	21	Nf	34.36N	110.10 E
Weilburg	10	Ef	50.29N	8.15 E
Weilerbach	12	Je	49.29N	7.38 E
Weilerswist	12	Id	50.46N	6.50 E
Weilheim in Oberbayern	10	Hi	47.50N	11.09 E
Weilmünster	12	Kd	50.26N	8.21 E
Weimar [Ger.]	12	Kd	50.46N	8.43 E
Weimar [Ger.]	10	Hf	50.59N	11.19 E
Weinan	27	Ie	34.30N	109.34 E
Weingarten	10	Fi	47.48N	9.38 E
Weinheim	10	Eg	49.33N	8.40 E
Weining	27	Hf	26.46N	104.18 E
Weinsberger Wald	14	Ib	48.25N	15.00 E
Weinstraße	12	Ke	49.20N	8.05 E
Weinviertel	14	Kb	48.35N	16.30 E
Weipa	58	Ff	12.41S	141.52 E
Weirton	44	Ge	40.24N	80.37W
Weiser	46	Gd	44.15N	116.58W
Weiser River	46	Gd	44.15N	116.59W
Weishan Hu	27	Ke	34.35N	117.15 E
Weishi	28	Cg	34.25N	114.10 E
Weishui → Jingxing	28	Ce	38.03N	114.09 E
Weiße Elster	10	He	51.26N	11.57 E
Weißenberg	12	Je	49.15N	7.49 E
Weißenburg in Bayern	10	Gg	49.02N	10.59 E
Weißenfels	10	He	51.12N	11.58 E
Weißer Main	10	Hf	50.05N	11.24 E
Weißerstein	12	Id	50.24N	6.22 E
Weißkugel/Palla Bianca	14	Ed	46.48N	10.44 E
Weiss Lake	44	Eh	34.15N	85.35W
Weißwasser/Běła Woda	10	Ke	51.31N	14.38 E
Weitra	14	Ib	48.42N	14.53 E
Weixi	27	Gf	27.13N	99.19 E
Weixian	28	Cf	36.59N	115.15 E
Weixin (Zhaxi)	27	If	27.46N	105.04 E
Weiz	14	Jc	47.13N	15.37 E
Wejherowo	10	Ob	54.37N	18.15 E
Welbourn Hill	58	Eg	27.21S	134.06 E
Welch	44	Gg	37.26N	81.36W
Weldiya	35	Fc	11.48N	39.35 E
Weld Range	59	De	26.55S	117.25 E
Welega [3]	35	Fd	8.38N	35.40 E
Welel	35	Ed	8.56N	34.52 E
Weligama	25	Gg	5.58N	80.25 E
Welkenraedt	12	Hd	50.39N	5.58 E
Welker Seamount (EN)	40	Ke	55.07N	140.20W
Welkite	35	Fd	8.17N	37.49 E
Welkom	31	Jk	27.59S	26.45 E
Welland	42	Jh	42.59N	79.15W
Welland	9	Ni	52.53N	0.02 E
Welland Canal	44	Hd	43.14N	79.13W
Wellesley Islands	57	Ef	16.45S	139.30 E
Wellin	12	Hd	50.05N	5.07 E
Wellingborough	9	Mi	52.19N	0.42W
Wellington [2]	62	Fd	40.10S	175.30 E
Wellington [Austl.]	59	Jf	32.33S	148.57 E
Wellington [Eng.-U.K.]	9	Jk	50.59N	3.14W
Wellington [Ks.-U.S.]	45	Hh	37.16N	97.24W
Wellington [Nv.-U.S.]	46	Fg	38.45N	119.22W
Wellington [N.Z.]	58	Ii	41.17S	174.46 E
Wellington, Isla-	52	Ij	49.20S	74.40W
Wellington, Lake-	59	Jg	38.10S	147.15 E
Wellington Channel	42	Ia	75.10N	93.00W
Wells [Eng.-U.K.]	9	Kj	51.13N	2.39W
Wells [Nv.-U.S.]	43	Dc	41.07N	115.01W
Wells, Lake-	59	Ee	26.45S	123.15 E
Wells, Mount-	59	Fc	17.26S	127.14 E
Wellsboro	44	Ie	41.45N	77.18W
Wellsford	62	Fb	36.18S	174.31 E
Wells-next-the-Sea	9	Ni	52.58N	0.51 E
Wellton	46	Hj	32.40N	114.08W
Welmel	35	Gd	5.35N	40.55 E
Wełna	10	Md	52.36N	16.50 E
Welo [3]	35	Fc	12.00N	40.00 E
Wels	14	Ib	48.10N	14.02 E
Welshpool	9	Ji	52.40N	3.09W
Welver	12	Jc	51.37N	7.58 E
Welwitschia	37	Ad	20.21S	14.57 E
Welwyn Garden City	9	Mj	51.48N	0.13W
Wema	36	Dc	0.26S	21.38 E
Wemding	10	Gh	48.52N	10.43 E
Wen'an	28	De	38.52N	116.30 E
Wenatchee	43	Cb	47.25N	120.19W
Wenatchee Mountains	46	Ec	47.20N	120.45W
Wenchang	27	Jh	19.43N	110.44 E
Wenchi	34	Ed	7.44N	2.06W
Wenchit	35	Fc	10.03N	38.35 E
Wenden	12	Jd	50.58N	7.52 E
Wendeng	27	Ld	37.10N	122.01 E
Wendland	10	Gc	53.10N	11.00 E
Wendo	35	Fd	6.37N	38.25 E
Wengyuan (Longxian)	27	Jg	24.21N	114.13 E
Wen He	28	Ef	37.06N	119.29 E
Wenling	27	Lf	28.23N	121.22 E
Wenquan	27	Fe	33.15N	91.55 E
Wenquan/Arixang	27	Dc	44.59N	81.04 E
Wenshan	27	Hg	23.22N	104.23 E
Wenshui	28	Bf	37.26N	112.01 E
Wensu	27	Dc	41.15N	80.14 E
Wensum	12	Db	52.37N	1.22 E
Wentworth	59	If	34.07S	141.55 E
Wenxian	27	He	32.52N	104.40 E
Wenzhou	22	Og	27.57N	120.38 E
Wenzhu	27	Jf	27.00N	114.00 E
Wepener	37	De	29.46S	27.00 E
Wépion, Namur-	12	Gd	50.25N	4.52 E
Werda	37	Ce	25.16S	23.17 E
Werder	31	Lh	7.00N	45.21 E
Werder	10	Jc	53.40N	13.25 E
Werdohl	12	Jc	51.16N	7.46 E
Were Ilu	35	Fc	10.38N	39.23 E
Werkendam	12	Gc	51.49N	4.55 E
Werl	12	Jc	51.33N	7.55 E
Werlte	12	Jb	52.51N	7.41 E
Wermelskirchen	12	Jc	51.09N	7.13 E
Werne	12	Jc	51.40N	7.38 E
Wernigerode	10	Ge	51.50N	10.47 E
Werra	5	Ge	51.26N	9.39 E
Werribee	59	Ig	37.54S	144.40 E
Werris Creek	59	Kf	31.21S	150.39 E
Werse	12	Jb	52.02N	7.41 E
Wertach	10	Gh	48.24N	10.53 E
Wertheim	10	Fg	49.45N	9.31 E
Wesel	10	Ce	51.40N	6.37 E
Weser	5	Ge	53.32N	8.34 E
Weserbergland	10	Fe	51.55N	9.30 E
Wesergebirge	10	Fd	52.15N	9.10 E
Weslaco	45	Gm	26.09N	98.01W
Wesley	51g	Ba	15.34N	61.19W
Wesleyville	42	Mg	49.09N	53.34W
Wessel, Cape-	59	Hb	11.00S	136.45 E
Wesseling	12	Id	50.50N	6.59 E
Wessel Islands	57	Ef	12.00S	136.45 E
Wessington Springs	45	Gd	44.05N	98.34W
West Allis	45	Me	43.01N	88.00W
West Baines River	59	Gc	15.26S	130.08 E
West Bay	45	Ll	29.00N	89.30W
West Bend	45	Le	43.25N	88.11W
West Bengal [3]	25	Hd	24.00N	88.00 E
West Berlin (EN) = Berlin	6	He	52.31N	13.24 E
West Branch	44	Ec	44.17N	84.14W
West Bridgford	12	Ab	52.55N	1.07W
West Bromwich	9	Li	52.31N	1.59W
Westbrook	44	Ld	43.41N	70.21W
West Burra	9	La	60.05N	1.10W
West Caicos	49	Kc	21.47N	72.17W
West Cape	57	Hi	45.55S	166.26 E
West Caroline Basin (EN)	3	Ii	4.00N	138.00 E
West Carpathians (EN)= Západné Karpaty	10	Og	49.30N	19.00 E
West Des Moines	45	Jf	41.35N	93.43W
Westdongeradeel	12	Ha	53.23N	5.58 E
Westdongeradeel-Holwerd	12	Ha	53.22N	5.54 E
Westdongeradeel-Ternaard	12	Ha	53.23N	5.58 E
Westeinderplassen	12	Gb	52.15N	4.30 E
West Elk Mountains	45	Cg	38.40N	107.15W
West End	44	Hl	26.41N	78.58W
Westende, Middelkerke-	12	Ec	51.10N	2.46 E
West End Village	51b	Aa	18.11N	63.09W
West Entrance	64a	Ba	7.57N	134.30 E
Westerbork	12	Ib	52.51N	6.36 E
Westerburg	12	Je	50.34N	7.59 E
Westerland	10	Eb	54.54N	8.18 E
Westerlo	12	Gc	51.05N	4.55 E
Western [Ghana] [3]	34	Ec	5.30N	2.30W
Western [Kenya] [3]	36	Fb	0.30N	34.35 E
Western [S.L.] [3]	34	Cd	8.20N	13.00W
Western [Ug.] [3]	36	Fb	1.00N	31.00 E
Western [Zam.] [3]	36	Df	15.00S	24.00 E
Western Australia [2]	59	Ec	25.00S	122.00 E
Western Desert (EN)= Gharbīyah, Aş Şaḩrā' Al-	30	Jf	27.30N	28.00 E
Western Dvina (EN)= Zapadnaja Dvina	5	Id	57.04N	24.03 E
Western Entrance	63a	Bb	6.55S	155.40 E
Western Ghats/Sahyadri	21	Jh	14.00N	75.00 E
Western Isles [3]	9	Fd	57.40N	7.10W
Western Port	59	Jg	38.25S	145.10 E
Western River	42	Gc	66.22N	107.15W
Western Sahara (EN) [5]	31	Ff	24.30N	13.00W

Index Symbols

- [1] Independent Nation
- [2] State, Region
- [3] District, County
- [4] Municipality
- [5] Colony, Dependency
- Continent
- Physical Region
- Historical or Cultural Region
- Mount, Mountain
- Volcano
- Hill
- Mountains, Mountain Range
- Hills, Escarpment
- Plateau, Upland
- Pass, Gap
- Plain, Lowland
- Delta
- Salt Flat
- Valley, Canyon
- Crater, Cave
- Karst Features
- Depression
- Polder
- Desert, Dunes
- Forest, Woods
- Heath, Steppe
- Oasis
- Cape, Point
- Coast, Beach
- Cliff
- Peninsula
- Isthmus
- Sandbank
- Island
- Atoll
- Rock, Reef
- Islands, Archipelago
- Rocks, Reefs
- Coral Reef
- Well, Spring
- Geyser
- River, Stream
- Waterfall Rapids
- River Mouth Estuary
- Lake
- Salt Lake
- Intermittent Lake
- Reservoir
- Swamp, Pond
- Canal
- Glacier
- Ice Shelf, Pack Ice
- Ocean
- Sea
- Gulf, Bay
- Strait, Fjord
- Lagoon
- Bank
- Seamount
- Tablemount
- Ridge
- Shelf
- Basin
- Escarpment, Sea Scarp
- Fracture
- Trench, Abyss
- National Park, Reserve
- Point of Interest
- Recreation Site
- Cave, Cavern
- Historic Site
- Ruins
- Wall, Walls
- Church, Abbey
- Temple
- Scientific Station
- Airport
- Port
- Lighthouse
- Mine
- Tunnel
- Dam, Bridge

Index Symbols

- [1] Independent Nation
- [2] State, Region
- [3] District, County
- [4] Municipality
- [5] Colony, Dependency
- [R] Continent
- [R] Physical Region
- Historical or Cultural Region
- Mount, Mountain
- Volcano
- Hill
- Mountains, Mountain Range
- Hills, Escarpment
- Plateau, Upland
- Pass, Gap
- Plain, Lowland
- Delta
- Salt Flat
- Valley, Canyon
- Crater, Cave
- Karst Features
- Depression
- Polder
- Desert, Dunes
- Forest, Woods
- Heath, Steppe
- Oasis
- Cape, Point*
- Coast, Beach
- Cliff
- Peninsula
- Isthmus
- Sandbank
- Island
- Atoll
- Rock, Reef
- Islands, Archipelago
- Rocks, Reefs
- Coral Reef
- Well, Spring
- Geyser
- River, Stream
- Waterfall Rapids
- River Mouth, Estuary
- Lake
- Salt Lake
- Intermittent Lake
- Reservoir
- Swamp, Pond
- Canal
- Glacier
- Ice Shelf, Pack Ice
- Ocean
- Sea
- Ridge
- Gulf, Bay
- Strait, Fjord
- Lagoon
- Bank
- Seamount
- Tablemount
- Shelf
- Basin
- Escarpment, Sea Scarp
- Fracture
- Trench, Abyss
- National Park, Reserve
- Point of Interest
- Recreation Site
- Cave, Cavern
- Historic Site
- Ruins
- Church, Abbey
- Temple
- Scientific Station
- Airport
- Port
- Lighthouse
- Mine
- Tunnel
- Dam, Bridge

Wolseley	42	Hf	50.25N	103.19W
Wolstenholme, Cap -	42	Jd	62.34N	77.30W
Wolstenholme Fjord	41	Ec	76.40N	69.45W
Wolsztyn	10	Md	52.08N	16.06 E
Wolvega, Weststellingwerf-	12	Ib	52.53N	6.00 E
Wolverhampton	9	Ki	52.36N	2.08W
Wolverton	9	Mi	52.04N	0.50W
Wŏnju	27	Md	37.21N	127.58 E
Wŏnsan	22	Of	39.10N	127.26 E
Wonseradeel	12	Ha	53.06N	5.28 E
Wonseradeel-Witmarsum	12	Ha	53.06N	5.28 E
Wonthaggi	59	Jg	38.36S	145.35 E
Woodall Mountain	45	Li	34.45N	88.11W
Woodbridge	9	Oi	52.06N	1.19 E
Woodbridge Bay	51g	Bb	15.19N	61.25W
Woodhall Spa	12	Ba	53.09N	0.13W
Woodland [Ca.-U.S.]	46	Eg	38.41N	121.46W
Woodland [Wa.-U.S.]	46	Dd	45.54N	122.45W
Woodlark Island	57	Ge	9.05S	152.50 E
Wood Mountain	46	Lb	49.14N	106.20W
Woodridge	45	Hb	49.17N	96.09W
Wood River	46	Lb	50.08N	106.10W
Wood River Lakes	40	He	59.30N	158.45W
Woodroffe, Mount-	59	Ge	26.20S	131.45 E
Woods, Lake-	59	Gc	17.50S	133.30 E
Woods, Lake of the-	38	Je	49.15N	94.45W
Woods Hole	44	Le	41.31N	70.40W
Woodside	46	Jg	39.21N	110.18W
Woodstock [Eng.-U.K.]	9	Lj	51.52N	1.21W
Woodstock [N.B.-Can.]	42	Kg	46.09N	67.34W
Woodstock [Ont.-Can.]	44	Gd	43.08N	80.45W
Woodstock [Vt.-U.S.]	44	Kd	43.37N	72.31W
Woodville [Ms.-U.S.]	45	Kk	31.01N	91.18W
Woodville [N.Z.]	62	Fd	40.20S	175.52 E
Woodville [Tx.-U.S.]	45	Ik	30.46N	94.25W
Woodward	43	Hd	36.26N	99.24W
Wooler	9	Kf	55.33N	2.01W
Woomera	59	Hf	31.11S	137.10 E
Wooramel River	59	Ce	25.47S	114.10 E
Wooster	44	Ge	40.46N	81.57W
Worcester	9	Ki	52.15N	2.10W
Worcester [Eng.-U.K.]	9	Ki	52.11N	2.13W
Worcester [Ma.-U.S.]	43	Mc	42.16N	71.48W
Worcester [S.Afr.]	31	Il	33.39S	19.27 E
Worcester Range	66	Jf	78.50S	161.00 E
Wörgl	14	Gc	47.29N	12.04 E
Workai, Pulau-	26	Jh	6.40S	134.40 E
Workington	9	Jg	54.39N	3.33W
Worksop	9	Lh	53.18N	1.07W
Workum	12	Hb	52.59N	5.27 E
Worland	43	Fc	44.01N	107.57W
Wormer	12	Gb	52.30N	4.52 E
Wormhout	12	Ed	50.53N	2.28 E
Worms	10	Eg	49.38N	8.21 E
Worms Head	9	Ij	51.34N	4.20W
Wörrstadt	12	Ke	49.50N	8.06 E
Wörth am Rhein	12	Ke	49.03N	8.16 E
Wörther-See	14	Id	46.37N	14.10 E
Worthing	9	Mk	50.48N	0.23W
Worthington	43	Hc	43.37N	95.36W
Wosi	26	Ig	0.11S	127.58 E
Wotho Atoll	57	Hc	10.06N	165.59 E
Wotje Atoll	57	Id	9.27N	170.02 E
Woudenberg	12	Hb	52.05N	5.25 E
Wounnioné, Pointe-	63b	Db	14.54S	168.02 E
Wounta, Laguna de-	49	Fg	13.38N	83.34W
Wour	35	Ba	21.21N	15.57 E
Wousi	63b	Cb	15.22S	166.39 E
Wowoni, Pulau-	26	Hg	4.08S	123.06 E
Woy Woy	59	Kf	33.30S	151.20 E
Wrangel, Ostrov-=Wrangel				
Island (EN)	21	Tb	71.00N	179.30 E
Wrangel Island (EN)=				
Wrangel, Ostrov-	21	Tb	71.00N	179.30 E
Wrangell	39	Fd	56.28N	132.23W
Wrangell, Cape-	40a	Ab	52.50N	172.26 E
Wrangell Mountains	38	Ec	62.00N	143.00W
Wrath, Cape-	5	Fd	58.37N	5.01W
Wray	43	Gc	40.05N	102.13W
Wreake	12	Ab	52.41N	1.05W
Wreck Reef	57	Gg	22.15S	155.10 E
Wrecks, Bay of-	64g	Bb	1.52N	157.17W
Wrexham	9	Kh	53.03N	3.00W
Wright Island	66	Of	74.03S	116.45W
Wright Patman Lake	45	Ij	33.16N	94.14W
Wrightson, Mount-	46	Jk	31.42N	110.50W
Wrigley	42	Fd	63.19N	123.38W
Wrigley Gulf	66	Nf	74.00S	129.00W
Wrocław [2]	10	Me	51.05N	17.00 E
Wrocław=Breslau (EN)	6	He	51.06N	17.00 E
Wronki	10	Md	52.43N	16.23 E
Wrotham	12	Cc	51.18N	0.19 E
Wroxham	12	Db	52.42N	1.24 E
Września	10	Nd	52.20N	17.34 E
Wschowa	10	Me	51.48N	16.19 E
Wu'an	28	Cf	36.42N	114.12 E
Wuchale	35	Fc	11.31N	39.37 E
Wuchang	28	Ib	44.55N	127.11 E
Wuchang, Wuhan-	28	Ci	30.32N	114.18 E
Wucheng (Jiucheng)	28	Df	37.12N	116.04 E
Wuchiu Hsu	27	Kg	25.00N	119.27 E
Wuchuan	28	Ad	41.08N	111.25 E
Wuchuan (Duru)	27	If	28.28N	107.57 E
Wuchuan (Meilü)	27	Jg	21.28N	110.44 E
Wuda	27	Id	39.30N	106.33 E
Wudan → Ongniud Qi	27	Kc	42.58N	119.01 E
Wudao	27	Ld	39.28N	121.30 E
Wudaoliang	27	Fd	35.15N	93.14 E
Wudi	28	Df	37.44N	117.36 E
Wudil	34	Gc	11.49N	8.51 E
Wuding	27	Hf	25.36N	102.27 E
Wudu	27	He	33.24N	105.00 E
Wugang	27	Jf	26.48N	110.32 E
Wugong (Puji)	27	Ie	34.15N	108.14 E
Wuhai	27	Id	39.32N	106.55 E
Wuhan	22	Nf	30.30N	114.20 E
Wuhan-Hankou	28	Ci	30.35N	114.16 E
Wuhan-Hanyang	28	Ci	30.33N	114.13 E
Wuhan- Wuchang	28	Ci	30.32N	114.13 E
Wuhe	27	Ke	33.08N	117.51 E
Wuhu	22	Nf	31.18N	118.27 E
Wuhu (Wanzhi)	28	Ei	31.21N	118.23 E
Wujia He	27	Ic	40.56N	108.52 E
Wu Jiang	28	Mi	29.43N	107.24 E
Wujiang	28	Fi	31.09N	120.38 E
Wukari	31	Hh	7.51N	9.47 E
Wukro	35	Fc	13.48N	39.37 E
Wular	25	Eb	34.30N	74.30 E
Wulff Land	41	Hb	82.19N	50.00W
Wulian (Hongning)	28	Eg	35.45N	119.13 E
Wuliang Shan	27	Hg	24.00N	101.00 E
Wuliaru, Pulau-	26	Jh	7.27S	131.04 E
Wuling Shan	21	Mg	28.20N	110.00 E
Wulongbei	28	Hd	40.15N	124.16 E
Wulongji → Huaibin	28	Ci	32.27N	115.23 E
Wulur	26	Ih	7.09S	128.39 E
Wum	34	Hd	6.23N	10.04 E
Wumei Shan	28	Cj	28.47N	114.50 E
Wümme	12	Ka	53.10N	8.40 E
Wuning	28	Cj	29.17N	115.05 E
Wünnenberg	12	Kc	51.31N	8.42 E
Wünnenberg-Haaren	12	Kc	51.34N	8.44 E
Wunnummin Lake	42	If	52.55N	89.10W
Wun Rog	35	Dd	9.00N	28.21 E
Wunstorf	10	Fd	52.26N	9.25 E
Wuntho	25	Jd	23.54N	95.41 E
Wupper	10	Ce	51.05N	7.30 E
Wuppertal	10	De	51.16N	7.11 E
Wuqi	27	Id	36.57N	108.15 E
Wuqia/Uluqqat	27	Cd	39.40N	75.07 E
Wuqiao (Sangyuan)	28	Df	37.38N	116.23 E
Wuqing (Yangcun)	28	De	39.23N	117.04 E
Würm	12	Kf	48.53N	8.42 E
Wurno	34	Gc	13.18N	5.26 E
Würselen	12	Id	50.49N	6.08 E
Würzburg	6	Gf	49.48N	9.56 E
Wurzen	10	Ie	51.22N	12.44 E
Wu Shan	27	Ie	31.00N	110.00 E
Wushaoling	27	Hd	37.15N	102.50 E
Wuski/Uqturpan	27	Cc	41.10N	79.16 E
Wusong	28	Fi	31.23N	121.29 E
Wüst Seamount (EN)	30	Gl	34.00S	3.40W
Wusuli Jiang	27	Ob	48.28N	135.02 E
Wutach	10	Ei	47.37N	8.15 E
Wutai [China]	28	Be	38.43N	113.14 E
Wutai [China]	27	Dc	44.38N	82.06 E
Wutai Shan	27	Jd	39.04N	113.28 E
Wuustwezel	12	Gc	51.23N	4.36 E
Wuvulu Island	57	Fe	1.43S	142.50 E
Wuwei	28	Di	31.17N	117.54 E
Wuwei (Liangzhou)	22	Mf	37.58N	102.48 E
Wuxi [China]	27	Of	31.32N	120.18 E
Wuxi [China]	27	Ie	31.27N	109.34 E
Wu Xia	27	Je	31.02N	110.10 E
Wuxiang (Duancun)	28	Bf	36.50N	112.51 E
Wuxing (Huzhou)	27	Le	30.47N	120.07 E
Wuxue → Guangji	27	Kf	29.58N	115.32 E
Wuyang [China]	28	Bh	33.26N	113.35 E
Wuyang [China]	28	Jd	36.29N	113.07 E
Wuyang → Zhenyuan	27	If	27.05N	108.25 E
Wuyi [China]	28	Cf	37.49N	115.54 E
Wuyi [China]	28	Ej	28.54N	119.50 E
Wuyiling	27	Mb	48.37N	129.20 E
Wuyi Shan	21	Ng	27.00N	117.00 E
Wuyuan [China]	22	Me	41.08N	108.17 E
Wuyuan [China]	28	Dj	29.15N	117.52 E
Wuyuanzhen → Haiyan	28	Fi	30.31N	120.56 E
Wuzhai	28	Ae	38.54N	111.49 E
Wuzhen	28	Ai	31.42N	112.00 E
Wuzhi Shan [China]	28	Ed	40.31N	118.02 E
Wuzhi Shan [China]	27	Ih	18.54N	109.40 E
Wuzhong	27	Id	38.00N	106.10 E
Wuzhou	22	Ng	23.32N	111.21 E
Wyalkatchem	59	Df	31.10S	117.22 E
Wyandotte	44	Fd	42.12N	83.10W
Wyandra	59	Je	27.15S	145.59 E
Wye	9	Kj	51.37N	2.39W
Wye	12	Cc	51.11N	0.56 E
Wyemandoo, Mount-	59	De	28.31S	118.32 E
Wyk auf Föhr	10	Eb	54.42N	8.34 E
Wylie, Lake-	44	Gh	35.07N	81.02W
Wymondham	9	Oi	52.34N	1.07 E
Wyndham [Austl.]	58	Df	15.28S	128.06 E
Wyndham [N.Z.]	62	Cg	46.20S	168.51 E
Wyndmere	45	Hc	46.16N	97.08W
Wynne	45	Ki	35.14N	90.47W
Wynniatt Bay	42	Gb	72.50N	111.00W
Wynyard [Austl.]	59	Jh	40.59S	145.41 E
Wynyard [Sask.-Can.]	42	Hf	51.47N	104.10W
Wyoming	44	Ed	42.54N	85.42W
Wyoming [2]	43	Fc	43.00N	107.30W
Wyoming Peak	43	Ec	42.36N	110.37W
Wyśmierzyce	10	Qe	51.38N	20.49 E
Wysoka	10	Nc	53.11N	17.05 E
Wysokie Mazowieckie	10	Sd	52.56N	22.32 E
Wyszków	10	Rd	52.36N	21.28 E
Wyszogród	10	Qd	52.23N	20.11 E
Wytheville	44	Gg	36.57N	81.07W
Wyville Thomson Ridge (EN)				
	9	Fa	60.10N	8.00W
Wyvis, Ben-	9	Id	57.42N	4.30W

X

Xaintrie	11	Ii	45.00N	2.10 E
Xainza	27	Ee	30.50N	88.37 E
Xaitongmoin	27	Ef	29.26N	88.08 E
Xai-Xai	31	Kk	25.04S	33.39 E
Xamba → Hanggin Houqi	27	Ic	40.59N	107.07 E
Xam Nua	25	Kd	20.25N	104.02 E
Xangongo	31	Ij	16.46S	14.59 E
Xang Qu	27	Ef	29.22N	89.09 E
Xanten	10	Ce	51.40N	6.27 E
Xánthi	15	Hh	41.08N	24.53 E
Xanthos	24	Cd	36.20N	29.20 E
Xanxerê	56	Jc	26.53S	52.23W
Xapuri	54	Ef	10.39S	68.31W
Xar Hudag	27	Jc	45.06N	114.30 E
Xar Moron	28	Ac	42.37N	111.02 E
Xar Moron He	27	Lc	43.24N	120.39 E
Xarrama	13	Df	38.14N	8.20W
Xàtiva/Játiva	13	Lf	38.59N	0.31W
Xau, Lake-	37	Cd	21.15S	24.44 E
Xavantes, Represa de-	55	Hf	23.20S	49.35W
Xavantina	55	Fe	21.15S	52.48W
Xayar	27	Dc	41.15N	82.50 E
Xebert	28	Fc	44.00N	122.00 E
Xêgar → Tingri	27	Ef	28.41N	87.00 E
Xenia	44	Ff	39.41N	83.56W
Xiabin Ansha	27	Ke	9.48N	116.38 E
Xiachengzi	28	Kb	44.41N	130.26 E
Xiacun → Rushan	28	Ff	36.55N	121.30 E
Xiaguan	27	Hf	25.32N	100.12 E
Xiahe (Labrang)	27	He	35.18N	102.30 E
Xiajin	28	Cf	36.57N	116.00 E
Xiamen	22	Ng	24.32N	118.06 E
Xi'an	22	Mf	34.15N	108.50 E
Xianfeng	27	If	29.41N	109.09 E
Xiangcheng	28	Bh	33.51N	113.29 E
Xiangcheng/Qagchêng	27	Gf	28.56N	99.46 E
Xiangcheng (Shuizhai)	28	Ch	33.27N	114.53 E
Xiangfan	22	Nf	32.03N	112.05 E
Xianggang/Hong Kong [5]	22	Ng	22.15N	114.10 E
Xianghua Ling	27	Jf	25.25N	112.32 E
Xianghuang Qi (Xin Bulag)	27	Jc	42.12N	113.59 E
Xiang Jang	21	Ng	29.26N	113.08 E
Xiangkhoang	25	Ke	19.20N	103.22 E
Xiangkhoang, Plateau de-				
	25	Ke	19.30N	103.10 E
Xiangquan He	27	Ce	32.05N	79.20 E
Xiangshan (Dancheng)	27	Lf	29.29N	121.52 E
Xiangshan Gang	28	Fj	29.35N	121.38 E
Xiangtan	22	Ng	27.54N	112.55 E
Xiangtang	28	Cj	28.26N	115.59 E
Xiangyin	28	Bj	28.41N	112.53 E
Xiangyuan	28	Bf	36.32N	113.02 E
Xianju	27	Lf	28.50N	120.42 E
Xianning	28	Cj	29.52N	114.17 E
Xiannümiao → Jiangdu	28	Eh	32.30N	119.33 E
Xiantaozhen → Mianyang	28	Bi	30.22N	113.27 E
Xianxia Ling	27	Kf	28.24N	118.40 E
Xianxian	28	De	38.12N	116.07 E
Xianyang	27	Ie	34.26N	108.40 E
Xiaobole Shan	27	La	51.46N	124.09 E
Xiao'ergou	27	Lb	49.10N	123.43 E
Xiaogan	27	Je	30.52N	113.58 E
Xiao He	28	Bf	37.38N	112.24 E
Xiao Hinggan Ling=Lesser				
Khingan Range (EN)	21	Oe	48.45N	127.00 E
Xiaoling He	28	Fd	40.55N	121.12 E
Xiaoluan He	28	Dd	41.36N	117.05 E
Xiaoqing He	28	Ef	37.19N	118.59 E
Xiaowutai Shan	28	Ce	39.57N	114.59 E
Xiaoxian	28	Dg	34.11N	116.56 E
Xiaoyi	28	Af	37.07N	111.48 E
Xiaoyi → Gongxian	28	Bg	34.46N	112.57 E
Xiapu	27	Kf	26.57N	119.59 E
Xiawa	28	Fc	42.36N	120.33 E
Xiayi	28	Dg	34.14N	116.07 E
Xiazhuang → Linshu	28	Eg	34.56N	118.38 E
Xicalango, Punta-	48	Nh	19.41N	92.00W
Xichang	22	Mg	27.52N	102.15 E
Xicheng → Yangyuan	28	Cd	40.08N	114.10 E
Xicoténcatl	48	Jf	23.00N	98.56W
Xicotepec de Juárez	48	Kg	20.17N	97.57W
Xiejiaji → Qingyun	28	Df	37.46N	117.22 E
Xifei He	28	Dh	32.38N	116.39 E
Xifeng	28	Hc	42.45N	124.44 E
Xifengzhen	27	Id	35.40N	107.42 E
Xigazê	22	Kg	29.15N	88.52 E
Xi He [China]	27	Hc	42.23N	101.03 E
Xi He [China]	28	Dj	29.38N	116.53 E
Xiheying	28	Ce	39.53N	114.42 E
Xihua	28	Ch	33.48N	114.31 E
Xi Jang	21	Ng	23.05N	114.23 E
Xiji [China]	27	Id	35.52N	105.35 E
Xiji [China]	28	Ia	46.09N	127.08 E
Xi Jiang	27	Jg	23.05N	114.23 E
Xijir,Ulan Hu	27	Fd	35.12N	90.13 E
Xikouzi	27	La	52.58N	120.29 E
Xiligou → Ulan	27	Gd	36.55N	98.16 E
Xilin	27	Ig	24.30N	105.05 E
Xilin Gol	28	Dc	43.55N	116.05 E
Xilin Hot → Abagnar Qi	22	Ne	43.58N	116.08 E
Xilitla	48	Jg	21.20N	98.58W
Xilókastron	15	Fk	38.05N	22.38 E
Ximiao	27	Hc	41.04N	100.14 E
Xin'an	28	Bg	34.43N	112.09 E
Xin'anjiang	28	Ei	29.27N	119.15 E
Xin'anjiang Shuiku	27	Kf	29.25N	119.05 E
Xin'anzhen → Guannan	28	Eg	34.04N	119.21 E
Xin'anzhen → Xinyi	27	Ke	34.17N	118.14 E
Xin Barag Youqi				
(Altan-Emel)	27	Kb	48.41N	116.47 E
Xin Barag Zuoqi (Amgalang)	27	Kb	48.13N	118.14 E
Xinbin	28	Hd	41.44N	125.02 E
Xin Bulag → Xianghuang Qi	27	Jc	42.12N	113.59 E
Xincai	27	Je	32.40N	114.57 E
Xinchang	28	Fj	29.30N	120.54 E
Xincheng [China]	28	Bf	37.57N	112.33 E
Xincheng [China]	27	Ig	24.04N	108.39 E
Xincheng [China]	27	Id	38.33N	106.10 E
Xincheng (Gaobeidian)	28	Ce	39.20N	115.50 E
Xindi → Honghu	28	Bj	29.50N	113.28 E
Xing'an → Ankang	22	Mf	32.37N	109.03 E
Xingcheng	28	Fd	40.38N	120.43 E
Xingguo	27	Kf	26.22N	115.21 E
Xinghai	27	Gd	35.45N	99.59 E
Xinghe	27	Jc	40.52N	113.56 E
Xinghua	28	Eh	32.56N	119.49 E
Xingkai Hu=Khanka Lake				
(EN)	21	Pe	45.00N	132.24 E
Xinglong	28	Dc	40.25N	117.31 E
Xinglongzhen	28	Ia	46.26N	127.03 E
Xingren	27	If	25.26N	105.08 E
Xingtai	22	Nf	37.00N	114.30 E
Xingtang	28	Ce	38.26N	114.33 E
Xingu, Rio-	52	Kf	1.30S	51.53W
Xingxingxia	27	Gc	41.47N	95.07 E
Xingyang	28	Bg	34.47N	113.21 E
Xinryi				
(Huangcaoba)	27	Hf	25.03N	104.55 E
Xingzi	28	Dj	29.28N	116.03 E
Xinhe	28	Cf	37.32N	115.14 E
Xinhe/Toksu	27	Dc	41.34N	82.38 E
Xin Hot → Abag Qi	27	Jc	44.01N	114.59 E
Xinhuai He	28	Fg	34.23N	120.05 E
Xinhui → Aohan Qi	28	Ec	42.18N	119.53 E
Xining	22	Mf	36.37N	101.46 E
Xinji → Shulu	28	Cf	37.56N	115.14 E
Xinjian	28	Cj	28.41N	115.50 E
Xin Jiang	28	Dj	28.37N	116.40 E
Xinjiangkou → Songzi	28	Ai	30.10N	116.46 E
Xinjiang Uygur Zizhiqu				
(Hsin-chiang-wei-wu-erh				
Tzu-chih-ch'ü)=Sinkiang				
(EN) [2]	27	Ec	42.00N	86.00 E
Xinjin	27	He	30.25N	103.46 E
Xinjin				
(Pulandian)	27	Ld	39.24N	121.59 E
Xinkai He	28	Gc	43.36N	122.31 E
Xinle	28	Ce	38.15N	114.40 E
Xinlin	28	Ec	43.58N	118.03 E
Xinlitun [China]	27	Ma	50.58N	126.39 E
Xinlitun [China]	28	Gc	42.01N	122.11 E
Xinlong/Nyagrong	27	He	30.57N	100.12 E
Xinmin	28	Gc	42.00N	122.50 E
Xinpu → Lianyungang	22	Nf	34.34N	119.15 E
Xinqing	27	Mb	48.15N	129.31 E
Xintai	28	Dg	35.54N	117.44 E
Xinwen (Suncun)	27	Kd	35.49N	117.38 E
Xinxian [China]	27	Jd	38.24N	112.43 E
Xinxian [China]	28	Ci	31.42N	114.50 E
Xinxiang	22	Nf	35.17N	113.50 E
Xinyang	27	Je	32.05N	114.07 E
Xinye	28	Bh	32.30N	112.22 E
Xinyi				
(Xin'anzhen)	27	Ke	34.17N	118.14 E
Xinyi He	28	Eg	34.29N	119.49 E
Xinyuan/Künes	27	Dc	43.24N	83.18 E
Xinyuan → Tianjun	22	Lf	37.18N	99.15 E
Xinzhan	28	Ic	43.52N	127.20 E
Xin Zhen → Hanggin Qi	27	Id	39.54N	108.55 E
Xinzheng	28	Bg	34.25N	113.46 E
Xinzhou	28	Ci	30.51N	114.49 E
Xioashan	28	Fi	30.10N	120.16 E
Xiong Xian	28	De	38.59N	116.06 E
Xionyuecheng	28	Gd	40.12N	122.08 E
Xiping [China]	28	Ej	28.27N	119.29 E
Xiping [China]	28	Bh	33.22N	114.00 E
Xisha Qundao=Paracel				
Islands (EN)	21	Nh	16.30N	112.15 E
Xishuangbanna	27	Gg	22.15N	100.00 E
Xishuanghe → Kenli	28	Ef	37.35N	118.30 E
Xishui	28	Ci	30.28N	115.15 E
Xitianmu Shan	27	Ke	30.21N	119.25 E
Xiuanzi → Chongli	28	Cd	40.57N	115.12 E
Xi Ujimqin Qi				
(Bayan Ul Hot)	27	Kc	44.31N	117.33 E
Xiuning	28	Ej	29.47N	118.11 E
Xiushan	27	If	28.29N	108.58 E
Xiu Shui	28	Cj	29.13N	116.00 E
Xiushui	27	Jf	29.02N	114.33 E
Xiuwu	28	Bg	35.13N	113.27 E
Xiuyan	27	Lc	40.18N	123.10 E
Xiwanzi → Chongli	28	Cf	36.50N	115.10 E
Xixabangma Feng	27	Ef	28.21N	85.47 E
Xixian	28	Ch	32.21N	114.43 E
Xixiang	27	Ie	32.58N	107.45 E
Xiyang	28	Bf	37.38N	113.41 E
Xizang Zizhiqu (Hsi-tsang				
Tzu-chih-ch'ü)=Tibet (EN)				
[2]	27	Ee	32.00N	90.00 E
Xizhong Dao	28	Fe	39.25N	121.18 E
Xi Taijnar Hu	27	Fd	37.15N	93.30 E
Xochicalco	48	Jh	18.45N	99.20W
Xochimilco	48	Jh	19.16N	99.06W
Xorkol	27	Fd	39.04N	91.05 E
Xpujil	48	Oh	18.35N	89.25W
Xuancheng	28	Ei	30.56N	118.44 E
Xuande Qundao	26	Fc	17.08N	111.30 E
Xuan'en	27	Ie	30.02N	109.30 E
Xuanhan	27	Ie	31.23N	107.39 E
Xuanhua	27	Kc	40.39N	115.05 E
Xuanwei	27	Hf	26.19N	104.05 E
Xuchang	22	Nf	34.00N	113.58 E
Xuecheng				
(Lincheng)	28	Dg	34.38N	117.14 E
Xuefeng Shan	27	Jf	27.35N	110.50 E
Xue Shan	27	Gf	27.30N	99.55 E
Xugezhuang → Fengnan	28	Ee	39.34N	118.05 E
Xugou	28	Eg	34.37N	119.08 E
Xugui	27	Gd	35.45N	96.08 E
Xuguit Qi (Yakeshi)	27	Lb	49.16N	120.41 E
Xümatang	27	Ge	33.57N	97.00 E
Xun Jiang	23	Hf	23.28N	111.18 E
Xunke (Qike)	27	Mb	49.34N	128.28 E
Xunwu	27	Kg	24.59N	115.33 E
Xunxian	28	Cg	35.40N	114.33 E
Xupu	27	Jf	27.54N	110.35 E
Xúquer/Júcar	5	Fh	39.09N	0.14W
Xushui	28	Ce	39.02N	115.40 E
Xuwen	27	Jg	20.22N	110.10 E
Xuyi	27	Ke	32.58N	118.33 E
Xuyong (Yongning)	27	If	28.13N	105.26 E
Xuzhou	22	Nf	34.12N	117.13 E

Y

Ya'an	22	Mg	30.00N	102.57 E
Yabassi	34	Ge	4.28N	9.58 E
Yabe	29	Be	32.42N	130.59 E
Yabebyry	55	Dh	27.24S	57.11W
Yabelo	35	Fe	4.53N	38.07 E
Yablonovy Range (EN)=				
Jablonovy Hrebet	21	Nd	53.30N	115.00 E
Yabrai Shan	27	Hc	40.00N	103.10 E
Yabrīn	35	Ha	23.15N	48.59 E
Yabrūd	24	Gf	33.58N	36.40 E
Yabucoa	51a	Cb	18.03N	65.53W
Yabuli	27	Mc	44.56N	128.37 E
Yabulu	59	Jc	19.00S	146.40 E
Yacaré Cururú, Cuchilla-	55	Dj	30.30S	56.33W
Yacaré Norte, Riacho-	55	Cf	22.43S	58.14W
Yacaré Sur, Riacho-	55	Cf	22.43S	58.14W
Yachats	46	Cd	44.20N	124.03W
Yacuma, Río-	54	Ef	13.38S	65.23W
Yacyretá, Isla-	55	Dh	27.25S	56.30W
Yadé, Massif du-	35	Bd	7.00N	15.30 E
Yādgīr	25	Fe	16.46N	77.08 E
Yadong/Chomo	27	Ef	27.38N	89.03 E
Yae-Dake	29b	Ab	26.38N	127.56 E
Yaeyama-Rettō	27	Lg	24.20N	124.00 E
Yafran	33	Bc	32.04N	12.31 E
Yağcilar	15	Lj	39.25N	28.23 E
Yagishiri-Tō	29a	Ba	44.26N	141.25 E
Yagoua	34	Ic	10.20N	15.14 E
Yagradagzê Shan	27	Gd	35.09N	95.39 E
Yaguajay	49	Hb	22.19N	79.14W
Yaguari	55	Ej	31.31S	54.58W
Yaguari, Arroyo-	55	Di	29.44S	57.37W
Yahalica de Gonzáles Gallo	48	Hg	21.08N	102.51W
Yahuma	36	Db	1.06N	23.10 E
Yaita	29	Fc	36.50N	139.55 E
Yaizu	29	Fd	34.51N	138.19 E
Yajiang/Nyagquka	27	He	30.07N	100.58 E
Yakacik	24	Ed	36.05N	32.45 E
Yake-Dake	29	Ec	36.14N	137.35 E
Yakeishi-Dake	29	Gb	39.10N	140.50 E
Yakeshi → Xuguit Qi	27	Lb	49.16N	120.41 E
Yake-Yama	29	Gb	39.58N	140.48 E
Yakima	39	Ge	46.36N	120.31W
Yakima River	46	Fc	46.15N	119.02W
Yako	34	Ec	12.58N	2.16W
Yakumo	27	Pc	42.15N	140.16 E
Yaku-Shima	27	Ne	30.20N	130.30 E
Yakutat	40	Le	59.33N	139.44W
Yakutat Bay	40	Ke	59.45N	140.45W
Yala	25	Kg	6.32N	101.19 E
Yalahán, Laguna de-	48	Pg	21.30N	87.15W
Yalcubul, Punta-	48	Og	21.35N	88.35W
Yale Point	46	Kh	36.25N	109.48W
Yalewa Kalou	63d	Ab	16.40S	177.46 E
Yalgoo	59	De	28.20S	116.41 E
Yalikavak	15	Kl	37.06N	27.18 E
Yaliköy	15	Lh	41.29N	28.17 E
Yalinga	35	Cd	6.31N	23.13 E
Yaloké	35	Bd	5.19N	17.05 E
Yalong Jiang	21	Mg	26.37N	101.48 E
Yalova	24	Cb	40.39N	29.15 E
Yalu Jiang	21	Of	39.55N	124.20 E
Yalvaç	24	Dc	38.17N	31.11 E
Yām, Ramlat-	33	If	17.42N	45.09 E
Yamada [Jap.]	28	Pe	39.28N	141.57 E
Yamada [Jap.]	29	Be	33.33N	130.45 E
Yamada-Wan	29	Hb	39.30N	142.00 E
Yamaga	29	Be	33.01N	130.41 E
Yamagata	27	Pd	38.15N	140.15 E
Yamagata Ken [2]	28	Pe	38.30N	140.00 E
Yamagawa	29	Bf	31.12N	130.39 E
Yamaguchi	27	Ne	34.10N	131.29 E
Yamaguchi Ken [2]	28	Kh	34.10N	131.30 E
Yamakuni	29	Be	33.24N	131.02 E
Yamal Peninsula (EN)=				
Jamal, Poluostrov-	21	Ib	70.00N	70.00 E
Yamamoto	29	Ga	40.06N	140.03 E
Yamanaka	29	Ec	36.15N	136.22 E
Yamanashi Ken [2]	28	Og	35.30N	138.45 E
Yamashiro	29	Ce	33.57N	133.43 E
Yamato Rise (EN)	28	Me	39.30N	134.30 E
Yamatsuri	29	Gc	36.53N	140.25 E
Yamazaki	29	Dd	35.00N	134.33 E
Yambi, Mesa de-	54	Dc	1.30N	71.20W
Yambio	31	Jh	4.34N	28.23 E
Yambo	35	Fd	8.25N	36.00 E
Yambu Head	51n	Ba	13.03N	61.09W
Yambuya	36	Db	1.16N	24.33 E
Yame	29	Be	33.13N	130.34 E
Yamethin	25	Jd	20.26N	96.09 E
Yamma Yamma, Lake-	59	Ie	26.20S	141.25 E
Yamoto	29	Gb	38.25N	141.13 E
Yamoussoukro	34	Dd	6.49N	5.17W
Yampa River	43	Fc	40.32N	108.59W
Yampi Sound	59	Ec	16.15S	123.40 E
Yamuna	21	Kg	25.30N	81.53 E
Yamunanagar	25	Fb	30.08N	76.59 E
Yamzho Yumco	27	Ff	29.00N	90.40 E
Yanagawa	29	Be	33.10N	130.24 E
Yanahara	29	Dd	34.57N	134.05 E
Yanahuanca	54	Cf	10.30S	76.30W
Yanai	29	Ce	33.56N	132.07 E
Yanam	25	Ge	16.51N	82.15 E
Yan'an	22	Mf	36.36N	109.32 E
Yanaoca	54	Df	14.13S	71.26W
Yanbian	27	Hf	26.51N	101.32 E
Yanbu'	23	Ee	24.05N	38.03 E
Yanchang	27	Jd	36.39N	110.03 E
Yancheng [China]	28	Bh	33.35N	114.00 E
Yancheng [China]	27	Le	33.16N	120.10 E
Yanchi	27	Id	37.47N	107.24 E
Yandé	63b	Ae	20.03S	163.48 E
Yandina	63a	Dc	9.07S	159.13 E
Yandja	36	Cc	1.41S	17.43 E

Index Symbols

- [1] Independent Nation
- [2] State, Region
- [3] District, County
- [4] Municipality
- [5] Colony, Dependency
- Continent
- Physical Region
- Historical or Cultural Region
- Mount, Mountain
- Volcano
- Hill
- Mountains, Mountain Range
- Hills, Escarpment
- Plateau, Upland
- Pass, Gap
- Plain, Lowland
- Delta
- Salt Flat
- Valley, Canyon
- Crater, Cave
- Karst Features
- Depression
- Folder
- Desert, Dunes
- Forest, Woods
- Heath, Steppe
- Oasis
- Cape, Point
- Coast, Beach
- Cliff
- Peninsula
- Isthmus
- Sandbank
- Island
- Atoll
- Rock, Reef
- Islands, Archipelago
- Rocks, Reefs
- Coral Reef
- Well, Spring
- Geyser
- River, Stream
- Waterfall Rapids
- River Mouth Estuary
- Lake
- Salt Lake
- Intermittent Lake
- Reservoir
- Swamp, Pond
- Canal
- Glacier
- Ice Shelf, Pack Ice
- Ocean
- Sea
- Gulf, Bay
- Strait, Fjord
- Lagoon
- Bank
- Seamount
- Tablemount
- Ridge
- Shelf
- Basin
- Escarpment, Sea Scarp
- Fracture
- Trench, Abyss
- National Park, Reserve
- Point of Interest
- Recreation Site
- Cave, Cavern
- Historic Site
- Ruins
- Wall, Walls
- Church, Abbey
- Temple
- Scientific Station
- Airport
- Fort
- Lighthouse
- Mine
- Tunnel
- Dam, Bridge

Yandua 🖭	63d Bb 16.49 S 178.18 E	Yayladağı	24 Ge 35.56N 36.01 E	Yichang
Yanfolila	34 Dc 11.11N 8.08W	Yazd	22 Hf 31.53N 54.25 E	Yicheng [China]

Yandua 🖭 63d Bb 16.49 S 178.18 E
Yanfolila 34 Dc 11.11N 8.08W
Yangalia 35 Cd 6.58N 21.01 E
Yangambi 31 Jh 0.47N 24.28 E
Yangcheng 28 Bg 35.32N 112.36 E
Yangchun 27 Jg 22.11N 111.48 E
Yangdŏg-ŭp 28 Ie 39.13N 126.39 E
Yangganga 🖭 63d Bb 16.35 S 178.35 E
Yanggang-Do [2] 28 Jd 41.15N 128.00 E
Yanggao 27 Jc 40.21N 113.47 E
Yanggeta 🖭 63d Ab 17.01 S 177.20 E
Yanggu 28 Cf 36.08N 115.48 E
Yang He 🔌 28 Cd 40.24N 115.18 E
Yangi 15 Mm 36.55N 29.01 E
Yangjiang 27 Jg 21.59N 111.59 E
Yangjiazhangzi 28 Fd 40.48N 120.30 E
Yangon = Rangoon (EN) 22 Lh 16.47N 96.10 E
Yangor 64e Ab 0.32 S 166.54 E
Yangqu (Huangzhai) 28 Be 38.05N 112.37 E
Yangquan 27 Jd 37.49N 113.34 E
Yangquanqu 27 Jd 37.04N 111.30 E
Yangshuo 27 Jg 24.46N 110.28 E
Yang Sin, Chu- ▲ 25 Lf 12.24N 108.26 E
Yangtze Kiang → Chang
Jiang 21 Of 31.48N 121.10 E
Yangxian 27 Ie 33.20N 107.35 E
Yangxin [China] 28 Df 37.39N 117.34 E
Yangxin [China] 27 Kf 29.50N 115.11 E
Yangyuan (Xicheng) 28 Cd 40.08N 114.10 E
Yangzhou 27 Ke 32.20N 119.25 E
Yanhe (Heping) 27 If 28.31N 108.28 E
Yanji 27 Mc 42.56N 129.30 E
Yanjin 28 Cg 35.09N 114.11 E
Yankton 43 Hc 42.53N 97.23W
Yanling 28 Cg 34.07N 114.11 E
Yanqi 22 Ke 42.04N 86.34 E
Yanqing 28 Cd 40.28N 115.57 E
Yan Shan ▲ 21 Ne 40.18N 117.36 E
Yanshan [China] 28 De 38.03N 117.12 E
Yanshan [China] 27 Hg 23.38N 104.24 E
Yanshan (Hekou) 28 Dj 28.18N 117.41 E
Yanshou 28 Mb 45.28N 128.19 E
Yanshi 28 Bg 34.44N 112.47 E
Yantai 22 Of 37.28N 121.24 E
Yanutha 🖭 63d Ac 16.14 S 178.00 E
Yanweigang 28 Eg 34.28N 119.46 E
Yanyuan 27 Hf 27.26N 101.32 E
Yanzhou 27 Kd 35.33N 116.49 E
Yao [Chad] 35 Bc 12.51N 17.34 E
Yao [Jap.] 29 Dd 34.38N 135.36 E
Yaodu → Dongzhi 28 Di 30.06N 117.01 E
Yaoundé 31 Ih 3.52N 11.31 E
Yapei 34 Gd 9.10N 1.10W
Yapen, Pulau- 🖭 57 Ee 1.45 S 136.15 E
Yapen, Selat- 26 Kg 1.30 S 136.10 E
Yapeyú 55 Di 29.28 S 56.49W
Yap Islands ◻ 57 Ed 9.32N 138.08 E
Yaprakli 24 Eb 40.46N 33.47 E
Yapu 25 Jf 14.51N 98.03 E
Yaqian → Yuexi 28 Di 30.51N 116.22 E
Yaque del Norte, Rio- 🔌 49 Ld 19.51N 71.41W
Yaque del Sur, Rio- 🔌 49 Ld 18.17N 71.06W
Yaqueling 28 Ai 30.40N 111.36 E
Yaqui 38 Hg 27.37N 110.39W
Yaracuy [5] 54 Ea 10.20N 68.45W
Yaraka 58 Fg 24.53 S 144.04 E
Yaralıgöz ▲ 24 Fb 41.45N 34.10 E
Yare 🔌 9 Oi 52.35N 1.44 E
Yari, Rio- 🔌 52 If 0.23 S 72.16W
Yariga-Take ▲ 29 Ec 36.20N 137.39 E
Yarim 23 Fg 14.21N 44.22 E
Yaritagua 54 Ea 10.05N 69.08W
Yarkant/Shache 27 Cd 38.24N 77.15 E
Yarkant He 🔌 21 Ke 40.28N 80.52 E
Yarlung Zangbo Jiang 🔌 21 Lg 24.02N 90.59 E
Yarmouth [Eng.-U.K.] 12 Ad 50.41N 1.30W
Yarmouth [N.S.-Can.] 39 Me 43.50N 66.07W
Yarram 59 Jg 38.33 S 146.41 E
Yarumal 54 Cb 6.58N 75.25W
Yasawa 🖭 63d Ab 16.47 S 177.31 E
Yasawa Group ◻ 57 If 17.00 S 177.23 E
Yashi 34 Gc 12.22N 7.55 E
Ya-Shima 29 Ce 33.45N 132.10 E
Yashima 29 Gb 39.09N 140.10 E
Yashiro-Jima 🖭 29 Ce 33.55N 132.15 E
Yasothon 25 Ke 15.46N 104.12 E
Yass 59 Jf 34.50 S 148.55 E
Yassiören 15 Lh 41.18N 28.35 E
Yasugi 29 Cd 35.26N 133.15 E
Yäsüj 23 Hc 30.45N 51.33 E
Yasun Burnu 🖭 24 Gb 41.09N 37.41 E
Yatağan 24 Cf 37.20N 28.09 E
Yatate Tõge 🖭 29 Ga 40.26N 140.37 E
Yatate-Yama ▲ 29 Ad 34.12N 129.14 E
Yatenga [1] 34 Ec 13.48N 2.10W
Yaté-Village 61 Cd 22.09 S 166.57 E
Yathata 🖭 63d Cb 17.15 S 179.32W
Yathkyed Lake 🔌 42 Hd 62.40N 98.00W
Yatolema 36 Db 0.21N 24.33 E
Yatou → Rongcheng 28 Gf 37.10N 122.25 E
Yatsu-ga-Take ▲ 29 Fd 35.59N 138.23 E
Yatsushiro 32 Me 32.30N 130.36 E
Yatsushiro-Kai 🔌 28 Be 32.20N 130.25 E
Yatta Plateau ▲ 36 Gc 2.00 S 38.00 E
Yauco 49 Nd 18.02N 66.51W
Yauri 54 Df 14.47 S 71.29W
Yauyos 54 Cf 12.24 S 75.57W
Yavari, Rio- 🔌 54 Dd 4.21 S 70.02W
Yavi, Cerro- ▲ 54 Eb 5.32N 65.59W
Yaviza 49 Ii 8.11N 77.41W
Yawatahama 28 Lh 33.27N 132.24 E
Yaxchilán 🖭 47 Fe 16.54N 90.58W
Yaxian (Sanya) 21 Mh 18.27N 109.28 E
Yayalı 24 Fc 38.05N 35.25 E

Yayladağı 24 Ge 35.56N 36.01 E
Yazd 22 Hf 31.53N 54.25 E
Yazd [3] 23 Hc 31.30N 54.30 E
Yazoo City 45 Kj 32.51N 90.28W
Yazoo River 🔌 45 Kj 32.22N 91.00W
Ybbs 🔌 14 Jb 48.10N 15.06 E
Ybbs an der Donau 14 Jc 48.10N 15.05 E
Ydre ◻ 8 Fg 57.52N 15.15 E
Ydstebøhamn 8 Ae 59.03N 5.25 E
Ye 22 Lh 15.15N 97.51 E
Yebaishou → Jianping 27 Kc 41.55N 119.37 E
Yebbi Bou 35 Ba 20.58N 18.04 E
Yébigé 35 Ba 22.04N 17.49 E
Yecheng/Kargilik 22 Jf 37.54N 77.26 E
Yech'ŏn 28 Jf 36.39N 128.27 E
Yecla 13 Kf 38.37N 1.07W
Yécora 47 Cc 28.20N 108.58W
Yêd 35 Ge 4.48N 43.02 E
Yedi Burun 🖭 15 Mm 36.23N 29.05 E
Yedseram 34 Hc 12.16N 14.09 E
Yegros 55 Dh 26.24 S 56.25W
Yeguas 🔌 13 Hf 38.02N 4.15W
Yeha 🖭 35 Fc 14.21N 39.05 E
Yei 35 Ee 4.05N 30.40 E
Yei 🔌 35 Ee 4.40N 30.30 E
Yeji [China] 28 Ci 31.51N 115.55 E
Yeji [Ghana] 34 Ed 8.13N 0.39W
Yekepa 34 Dd 7.35N 8.32W
Yelgu 35 Ec 10.01N 32.31 E
Yélimané 34 Cb 15.07N 10.36W
Yell 5 Fc 60.35N 1.05W
Yellice Dağı ▲ 15 Mj 39.23N 29.57 E
Yellowhead Pass 🖭 42 Ff 52.50N 117.55W
Yellowknife 🔌 42 Gd 62.23N 114.20W
Yellowknife 39 Hc 62.27N 114.21W
Yellow River (EN) = Huang
He 🔌 21 Nf 37.32N 118.19 E
Yellow Sea (EN) = Huang
Hai 🖭 21 Of 36.00N 124.00 E
Yellow Sea (EN) = Hwang-
Hae 🖭 21 Of 36.00N 124.00 E
Yellowstone 🔌 38 Ie 47.58N 103.59W
Yellowstone Lake 🔌 38 He 44.25N 110.22W
Yellowstone National
Park 46 Jd 44.58N 110.42W
Yell Sound 🔌 9 La 60.33N 1.15W
Yeltes 🔌 13 Fd 40.56N 6.31W
Yelwa [Nig.] 34 Gd 8.51N 9.37 E
Yelwa [Nig.] 34 Gd 10.50N -4.44 E
Yemen (EN) = Al Yaman 35 Gh 15.00N 44.00 E
Yemen, People's Democratic
Republic of- (EN)
→ Al Yaman 22 Gh 15.00N 44.00 E
Yenagoa 34 Ge 4.55N 6.16 E
Yenangyaung 25 Id 20.28N 94.53 E
Yen Bay 25 Kd 21.42N 104.52 E
Yendi 34 Ed 9.26N 0.01W
Yenge 🔌 36 Dc 0.55 S 20.40 E
Yengisar 27 Cd 38.56N 76.09 E
Yengo 36 Cb 0.22N 15.29 E
Yeniboğaziçi 24 Ee 35.17N 33.52 E
Yenice [Tur.] 15 Kj 39.55N 27.18 E
Yenice [Tur.] 24 Fd 41.00N 35.03 E
Yeni Erenköy 24 Fe 35.35N 34.15 E
Yenifoça 15 Jk 38.44N 26.51 E
Yenihisar 15 Kl 37.22N 27.15 E
Yenimahalle 24 Ec 39.56N 32.52 E
Yenipazar 15 Ll 37.48N 28.12 E
Yenişehir 24 Cb 40.16N 29.39 E
Yenisey (EN) = Jenisej 🔌 21 Kb 71.50N 82.40 E
Yenisey Bay (EN) =
Jenisejskij Zaliv ◻ 20 Db 72.00N 81.00 E
Yenisey Ridge (EN) =
Jenisejskij Krjaž ▲ 21 Ld 59.00N 92.30 E
Yennâdhion 15 Km 36.01N 27.56 E
Yeo, Lake- 🔌 59 Ee 28.05 S 124.25 E
Yeovil 9 Kk 50.57N 2.39W
Yepes 13 Ie 39.54N 3.38W
Yeppoon 59 Kd 23.08 S 150.45 E
Yerákion 15 Fm 37.00N 22.42 E
Yerbabuena 48 Hf 23.00N 103.30W
Yerer 35 Gd 7.32N 42.05 E
Yerington 46 Ng 38.59N 119.10W
Yerkesik 24 Ll 37.07N 28.17 E
Yerköy 24 Fc 39.38N 34.29 E
Yerlisu 15 Ji 40.46N 26.39 E
Yermak Plateau (EN) ▲ 41 Mb 82.00N 6.00 E
Yeroham 24 Pj 31.00N 34.55 E
Yerres 🔌 11 Hf 48.43N 2.27 E
Yerupaja, Nevado- ▲ 52 Ig 10.16 S 76.54W
Yerushalayim = Jerusalem
(EN) 22 Ff 31.46N 35.14 E
Yerville 12 Ce 49.40N 0.54 E
Yerwa 34 Hc 11.31N 12.53 E
Yesa, Embalse de- 🔌 13 Kb 42.36N 1.09W
Yeşan 28 If 36.41N 126.51 E
Yeşilhisar 24 Fc 38.21N 35.06 E
Yeşilırmak 🔌 23 Ea 41.24N 36.35 E
Yeşilköy 24 Cb 40.57N 29.49 E
Yeşilova 15 Ml 37.30N 29.46 E
Yeşilyurt 15 Ll 37.31N 28.17 E
Yeso 55 Cj 30.56 S 59.28W
Yeste 13 Jf 38.22N 2.18W
Yetti 🔌 35 Gf 26.10N 7.50W
Ye-u 25 Jd 22.46N 95.26 E
Yeu, Île d'- ◻ 11 Dh 46.43N 2.20W
Yexian [China] 28 Bf 37.11N 119.58 E
Yexian [China] 55 Dh 33.38N 113.21 E
Yguazú, Rio- 🔌 55 Eg 25.20 S 55.00W
Yhú 55 Eg 25.00 S 55.59W
Yi, Rio- 🔌 55 Eg 24.59 S 55.59W
Yiali 🖭 55 Dk 33.07 S 57.56W
Yi'an 15 Km 36.40N 27.05 E

Yichang 22 Nf 30.42N 111.22 E
Yicheng [China] 28 Ag 35.44N 111.43 E
Yicheng [China] 28 Bi 31.42N 112.16 E
Yichuan 27 Jd 36.00N 110.06 E
Yichun [China] 27 Jf 27.47N 114.25 E
Yichun [China] 27 Mb 47.41N 128.55 E
Yıdılzeli 24 Gc 39.52N 36.38 E
Yidu [China] 28 Je 30.23N 111.28 E
Yidu [China] 27 Kd 36.41N 118.29 E
Yidun (Dagxoi) 27 Ee 30.25N 99.28 E
Yifag 35 Fc 12.02N 37.41 E
Yifeng 28 Cj 28.25N 114.47 E
Yiğılca 24 Db 40.53N 31.27 E
Yigo 64c Ba 13.32N 144.53W
Yi He [China] 🔌 28 Eg 34.07N 118.15 E
Yi He [China] 🔌 28 Ea 34.41N 112.33 E
Yilan 27 Mb 46.18N 129.33 E
Yılıng 23 Ea 40.08N 36.56 E
Yiliang 27 Hg 24.59N 103.08 E
Yimianpo 28 Jb 45.04N 128.03 E
Yimin He 🔌 28 Kb 49.15N 119.42 E
Yinan (Jiehu) 28 Eg 35.33N 118.27 E
Yinchuan 22 Mf 38.28N 106.19 E
Yindarlgooda, Lake- 🔌 59 Ef 30.45 S 121.55 E
Yingcheng [China] 28 Mb 44.C8N 125.54 E
Yingcheng [China] 28 Bi 30.57N 113.33 E
Yingde 27 Jg 24.13N 113.24 E
Ying He 🔌 28 Ke 32.30N 116.31 E
Yingjiang 27 Gg 24.45N 97.58 E
Yingjin He 🔌 28 Ec 42.20N 119.19 E
Yingkou 22 Oe 40.40N 122.12 E
Yingkou (Dashiqiao) 28 Gd 40.39N 122.31 E
Yingshan 27 Ci 30.45N 115.40 E
Yingshang 28 Dh 32.38N 116.16 E
Yingshouyingzi 28 Dd 40.33N 117.37 E
Yingtan 28 Dj 28.13N 117.00 E
Yingxian 28 Be 39.33N 113.10 E
Ying zhan/Victoria 22 Ng 22.17N 114.09 E
Yining/Gulja 27 Dc 43.54N 81.21 E
Yinma He 🔌 28 Hb 44.50N 125.45 E
Yinqing Qunjiao 🖭 26 Fe 8.55N 112.35 E
Yin Shan ▲ 21 Me 41.30N 109.00 E
Yi'ong Zangbo 🔌 27 Gf 29.56N 95.10 E
Yioúra 🖭 15 Hj 39.24N 24.10 E
Yipinglang 27 Hf 25.13N 101.55 E
Yiquan → Meitan 27 If 27.48N 107.32 E
Yirga Alem 35 Fd 6.44N 38.24 E
Yirol 35 Ed 6.33N 30.30 E
Yirshi 27 Kb 47.17N 119.55 E
Yishui 28 Eg 35.47N 118.38 E
Yisra'el = Israel (EN) [1] 22 Ff 31.30N 35.00 E
Yithion 15 Fm 36.45N 22.34 E
Yitong 28 Hc 43.20N 125.17 E
Yitong He 🔌 28 Hb 44.45N 125.40 E
Yitulihe 22 La 50.41N 121.33 E
Yiwu 28 Fj 29.19N 120.04 E
Yiwu/Aratürük 27 Fc 43.15N 94.35 E
Yixian [China] 28 Ce 39.21N 115.30 E
Yixian [China] 28 Dj 29.56N 117.56 E
Yixian [China] 28 Fd 41.33N 121.14 E
Yixing 28 Ei 31.21N 119.48 E
Yixun He 🔌 28 Dd 41.00N 117.41 E
Yiyang [China] 27 Jf 28.41N 112.20 E
Yiyang [China] 28 Dj 28.24N 117.24 E
Yiyang [China] 28 Bg 34.30N 112.10 E
Yiyuan (Nanma) 28 Ef 36.11N 118.10 E
Yizheng 28 Eh 32.16N 119.10 E
Yläne 8 Jd 60.53N 22.25 E
Ylikitka 🔌 8 Gc 66.08N 28.30 E
Yli-Li 7 Fd 65.22N 25.50 E
Ylimarkku/Övermark 8 Ib 62.37N 21.28 E
Ylistaro 7 Fe 62.57N 22.31 E
Ylitornio 7 Fc 66.18N 23.40 E
Yliveska 7 Fd 64.05N 24.33 E
Ylöjärvi 8 Jc 61.33N 23.36 E
Ymers 🖭 41 Jd 73.20N 25.00W
Yngaren 🔌 8 Gf 53.50N 16.35 E
Yngen 🔌 8 Gf 59.45N 14.20 E
Ynykćanski 20 Id 60.08N 137.47 E
Yoboki 35 Gc 11.28N 42.06 E
Yobuko 29 Ae 33.33N 129.54 E
Yodo-Gawa 🔌 29 Dd 34.41N 135.25 E
Yogan, Cerro- ▲ 52 Jk 54.38 S 69.29W
Yogoum 35 Bb 17.27N 19.31 E
Yoğuntaş 15 Kh 41.50N 27.04 E
Yogyakarta 22 Nj 7.48 S 110.22 E
Yoichi 28 Pc 43.12N 140.41 E
Yojoa, Lago de- 🔌 49 Df 14.50N 88.00W
Yōju 28 If 37.18N 127.38 E
Yokadouma 31 Ih 3.31N 15.03 E
Yōkaichi 29 Ed 35.07N 136.11 E
Yōkaichiba 29 Gd 35.40N 140.28 E
Yokkaichi 28 Ng 34.58N 136.37 E
Yoko 34 Hd 5.32N 12.19 E
Yokoate-Jima 🖭 28 Kk 29.00N 129.00 E
Yokohama 22 Pf 35.27N 139.39 E
Yokosuka 28 Og 35.18N 139.40 E
Yokote 28 Ph 39.18N 140.34 E
Yola 31 Ih 9.12N 12.29 E
Yolania, Serranias de- ▲ 49 Fh 11.40N 84.20W
Yolombo 36 Dc 1.32 S 23.15 E
Yom 🔌 25 Ke 15.52N 100.16 E
Yōmju 28 He 39.50N 124.33 E
Yomou 34 Dd 7.34N 9.16W
Yomra 23 Ea 40.58N 39.54 E
Yon 🔌 11 Eh 46.30N 1.18W
Yonago 64c Lg 35.28N 133.20 E
Yōnan 28 If 37.55N 126.05 E
Yoneshiro-Gawa 🔌 29 Ga 40.13N 140.00 E
Yonezawa 28 Pf 37.55N 140.07 E
Yong 🔌 34 Ne 14.54N 13.12 E
Yong [2] 27 Mc 41.15N 129.30 E
Yong'an 27 Kf 25.58N 117.29 E

Yongchang 27 Hd 38.17N 102.07 E
Yongcheng 28 Dh 33.56N 116.21 E
Yongch'on 28 Jg 35.59N 127.59 E
Yongchuan 27 If 29.22N 105.59 E
Yongding 27 Kf 24.43N 116.29 E
Yongding He 🔌 28 Kd 39.20N 117.04 E
Yŏngdŏk 28 Jf 36.24N 129.22 E
Yŏngdong 28 If 36.10N 127.47 E
Yonghung 28 Ie 39.33N 127.14 E
Yongji (Kouqian) 28 Hc 30.25N 99.28 E
Yongjing 28 Ic 43.40N 126.30 E
Yŏngju 27 Hd 36.00N 103.17 E
Yongkang 28 Md 36.49N 128.37 E
Yongle Qundao ◻ 27 Lf 28.51N 120.05 E
Yongnian 🖭 26 Fc 16.35N 111.40 E
Yongnian (Linmingguan) 28 Cf 36.47N 114.30 E
Yongqing 28 De 39.19N 116.29 E
Yŏngsanp'o 18 If 35.00N 126.43 E
Yongsheng 27 Hf 26.41N 100.45 E
Yongshu Jiao 🖭 26 Fe 9.35N 112.50 E
Yŏngwŏl 28 Jf 37.11N 128.28 E
Yongxiu (Tujiabu) 27 Kf 29.05N 115.49 E
Yonibana 34 Cd 8.26N 12.14W
Yonkers 44 Ke 40.56N 73.54W
Yonne [3] 11 Jg 47.55N 3.45 E
Yonne 🔌 11 If 48.23N 2.58 E
Yopal 54 Db 5.21N 72.23W
Yopurga 27 Cd 39.15N 76.45 E
York 9 Lg 54.10N 1.30W
York [Al.-U.S.] 44 Ci 32.29N 88.18W
York [Austl.] 59 Df 31.53 S 116.46 E
York [Eng.-U.K.] 9 Lh 53.58N 1.05W
York [Nb.-U.S.] 45 Hf 40.52N 97.36W
York [Pa.-U.S.] 43 Ld 39.57N 76.44W
York, Cape- 🖭 57 Fe 10.40 S 142.30 E
York, Vale of- 🔌 9 Lg 54.10N 1.20W
Yorke Peninsula 🖭 59 Hf 35.00 S 137.30 E
Yorkshire Dales 🖭 9 Kg 54.15N 2.10W
Yorkshire Wolds 🖭 9 Mh 54.00N 0.40W
York Sound 🔌 59 Fb 14.50 S 125.05 E
Yorkton 39 Id 51.13N 102.28W
Yorktown 44 Ig 37.14N 76.32W
Yoro [3] 3 Df 15.15N 87.15W
Yoro 🔌 27 Pd 37.55N 140.07 E
Yoron-Jima 🖭 29b Bb 27.03N 128.26 E
Yoro-Shima 🖭 29b Ba 28.02N 129.10 E
Yorosso 34 Ec 12.21N 4.47W
Yorubaland Plateau ▲ 34 Gd 8.00N 4.30 E
Yörük 24 Hb 36.49N 38.23 E
Yosemite National Park 43 Md 35.28N 119.33W
Yosemite Rock 🖭 52 Hi 31.58 S 83.15W
Yoshida [Jap.] 29 Ce 33.16N 132.32 E
Yoshida [Jap.] 29 Cd 34.40N 132.42 E
Yoshii 29 Ae 33.18N 129.40 E
Yoshii-Gawa 🔌 29 Dd 34.36N 134.02 E
Yoshino-Gawa 🔌 29 Dd 34.05N 134.36 E
Yōsu 27 Me 34.44N 127.44 E
Yotaú 54 Fg 16.03 S 63.03W
Yōtei-Zan ▲ 29a Bc 42.49N 140.47 E
Yotvata 24 Fh 29.53N 35.03 E
Youghal/Eochaill 9 Fj 51.57N 7.50W
Youghal Harbour/Cuan
Eochaille ◻ 9 Fj 51.52N 7.50W
You Jiang 🔌 21 Mg 22.50N 108.06 E
Youllemmedene 🖭 30 Ng 16.00N 1.00 E
Young [Austl.] 59 Jf 34.19 S 148.18 E
Young [Ur.] 55 Dk 32.41 S 57.38W
Young, Cape- 🖭 62 Je 43.42 S 176.37W
Younghusband Peninsula 🖭 59 Hg 36.00 S 139.30 E
Youngs Rock 🖭 64q Ab 25.03 S 130.06W
Youngstown 43 Kc 41.05N 80.40W
Youshashan 38 Df 38.04N 90.53 E
Youssoufia 30 Db 32.15N 8.32W
Youyang 27 If 28.49N 108.45 E
Yozgat 23 Db 39.50N 34.48 E
Ypacaraí 56 Ic 25.23 S 57.16W
Ypacarai, Laguna- 🔌 55 Dg 25.17 S 57.20W
Ypané, Rio- 🔌 55 Df 23.29 S 57.19W
Ypé Jhú 55 Ef 23.54 S 55.20W
Ypoá, Lago- 🔌 55 Dg 25.48 S 57.28W
Yport 12 Ce 49.44N 0.19 E
Ypres/Ieper 11 Id 50.51N 2.53 E
Yreka 43 Cc 41.44N 122.43W
Yser 🔌 11 Ic 51.09N 2.43 E
Yssingeaux 11 Kk 45.08N 4.07 E
Ystad 7 Ci 55.25N 13.49 E
Ythan 🔌 9 Mj 57.20N 2.00W
Ytre Arna 8 Ad 60.28N 5.26 E
Ytre Sula 🖭 8 Ac 61.05N 4.40 E
Ytterhogdal 8 Fb 62.11N 14.56 E
Ytterlännäs 7 De 63.01N 17.41 E
Yttermalung 8 Ed 60.35N 13.50 E
Ytyk-Kjuēl 20 Id 62.28N 133.25 E
Yu 'Alliq, Jabal- ▲ 24 Eg 30.13N 33.31 E
Yuan'an 28 Ai 31.04N 111.39 E
Yuanbaoshan 28 Ec 42.19N 119.19 E
Yuanbao Shan ▲ 27 If 25.24N 109.11 E
Yuan Jiang [Asia] = Red
River (EN) 🔌 21 Mg 20.17N 106.34 E
Yuanjiang [China] 28 Bj 28.50N 112.23 E
Yuanjiang [China] 27 Hg 23.22N 102.26 E
Yuan Jiang [China] 🔌 28 Bj 28.58N 111.49 E
Yuanling 28 Bj 28.26N 110.22 E
Yuanmou 27 Hf 25.45N 101.54 E
Yuanping 28 Jd 38.43N 112.42 E
Yuanqu (Liuzhangzhen) 28 Bg 35.19N 111.44 E
Yuanshi 28 Cf 37.45N 114.30 E
Yuba City 43 Dd 39.08N 121.37W
Yūbari 28 Pc 43.04N 141.59 E
Yūbari-Dake ▲ 29a Cb 43.06N 142.35 E
Yūbari-Gawa 🔌 29a Bb 43.08N 141.35 E
Yūbari-Sanchi ▲ 29a Cb 43.10N 142.15 E

Yuba River 🔌 46 Eg 39.07N 121.36W
Yubdo 35 Fd 8.58N 35.27 E
Yūbetsu 28 Qb 43.13N 144.05 E
Yūbetsu-Gawa 🔌 29a Ca 44.14N 143.37 E
Yucatán [2] 47 Gd 20.50N 89.00W
Yucatán, Canal de- =
Yucatan Channel (EN) 🖭 38 Kg 21.45N 85.45W
Yucatán, Península de- =
Yucatan Peninsula (EN) 🖭 38 Kh 19.30N 89.00W
Yucatan Basin (EN) 🖭 47 Ge 20.00N 84.00W
Yucatan, Canal de- (EN) =
Yucatán, Canal de- 🖭 38 Kg 21.45N 85.45W
Yucatan Peninsula (EN) =
Yucatán, Península de- 🖭 38 Kh 19.30N 89.00W
Yucheng 28 Df 36.56N 116.38 E
Yuci 27 Jd 37.41N 112.49 E
Yucuyácua, Cerro- ▲ 47 Ee 17.07N 97.40W
Yuda 29 Gb 39.19N 140.48 E
Yudi Shan ▲ 21 Lb 52.17N 121.52 E
Yueliang Pao 🔌 28 Gb 45.44N 123.51 E
Yueqing 27 Lf 28.08N 120.58 E
Yuexi 27 Hf 28.37N 102.36 E
Yuexi (Yaqian) 28 Di 30.51N 116.22 E
Yueyang 27 Jf 29.18N 113.12 E
Yufu-Dake ▲ 29 Be 33.17N 131.23 E
Yugan 27 Kf 29.12N 116.39 E
Yugoslavia (EN) =
Jugoslavija [1] 6 Hg 44.00N 19.00 E
Yu He 🔌 28 Be 39.51N 113.26 E
Yuhuang Ding ▲ 28 Df 36.20N 117.01 E
Yuki [Jap.] 29 Cd 34.29N 132.16 E
Yuki [Zaire] 36 Cc 3.55 S 19.25 E
Yukon 45 Hi 35.31N 97.44W
Yukon 🔌 38 Cc 62.33N 163.59W
Yukon Flats 🔌 40 Jc 66.35N 146.00W
Yukon Plateau 🔌 38 Fc 61.30N 135.40W
Yukon Territory [3] 42 Dd 63.00N 136.00W
Yüksekova 24 Kd 37.19N 44.10 E
Yukuhashi 29 Be 33.44N 130.58 E
Yule River 🔌 59 Dd 20.41 S 118.17 E
Yuli/Iopnur 27 Ec 41.22N 86.09 E
Yulin [China] 22 Mf 38.14N 109.48 E
Yulin [China] 21 Mh 17.50N 109.30 E
Yuling Guan 28 Df 36.04N 118.53 E
Yulin Jiao 🖭 21 Mh 17.50N 109.30 E
Yulongxue Shan ▲ 27 Hf 27.09N 100.12 E
Yuma [Az.-U.S.] 39 Hf 32.43N 114.37W
Yuma [Co.-U.S.] 45 Ef 40.08N 102.43W
Yuma, Bahia de- 🔌 49 Md 18.21N 68.35W
Yumare 50 Bg 10.37N 68.41W
Yumari, Cerro- ▲ 54 Ec 4.27N 66.50W
Yumbe 36 Fb 3.28N 31.15 E
Yumbi [Zaire] 36 Cc 1.14 S 26.14 E
Yumbi [Zaire] 36 Cc 1.53 S 16.32 E
Yumen (Laojunmiao) 22 Lf 39.50N 97.44 E
Yumenkou 28 Jd 35.42N 110.37 E
Yumenzhen 27 Gc 40.17N 97.12 E
Yumin 24 Fd 36.49N 35.45 E
Yumurtalik 27 Me 34.44N 127.44 E
Yuna, Rio- 🔌 49 Md 19.12N 69.37W
Yunaska 🖭 40a Db 52.40N 170.50W
Yuncheng [China] 22 Nf 35.02N 111.00 E
Yuncheng [China] 28 Cg 35.35N 115.56 E
Yungas 52 Jg 16.20 S 66.45W
Yungay 56 Fe 37.07 S 72.01W
Yungui Gaoyuan 🔌 21 Mg 26.00N 105.00 E
Yunjinghong → Jinghong 27 Hg 21.59N 100.48 E
Yunkai Dashan ▲ 21 Mg 22.00N 111.00 E
Yunlin 27 Lg 23.43N 120.33 E
Yun Ling ▲ 27 Gf 27.00N 99.30 E
Yunmeng 28 Bi 31.01N 113.45 E
Yunnan Sheng (Yün-nan
Sheng) [2] 21 Mg 25.00N 102.00 E
Yün-nan Sheng → Yunnan
Sheng 21 Mg 25.00N 102.00 E
Yunomae 29 Be 32.15N 130.57 E
Yunotsu 28 Cd 35.05N 132.21 E
Yun Shui 🔌 28 Bi 30.43N 113.57 E
Yunxian 27 Je 32.50N 110.50 E
Yunxiao 27 Kg 24.05N 117.18 E
Yunyang 28 Ai 31.00N 108.55 E
Yunzhong Shan ▲ 27 Jd 38.50N 112.27 E
Yuquan 28 Ib 45.27N 127.08 E
Yuqing 27 If 27.14N 107.52 E
Yura 54 Ci 28.53 S 58.02W
Yura 54 Dg 16.12 S 71.42W
Yura-Gawa 🔌 29 Dd 35.31N 135.17 E
Yurimaguas 53 If 5.54 S 76.05W
Yuriria 48 Ig 20.12N 101.09W
Yururi, Rio- 🔌 50 Fi 6.44N 61.40W
Yurungkax He 🔌 27 Dd 38.05N 80.20 E
Yuscarán 49 Dg 13.55N 86.51W
Yushan 27 Kf 28.40N 118.16 E
Yu Shan ▲ 27 Kf 27.40N 116.05 E
Yushe 28 Be 37.04N 112.58 E
Yushu 21 Lf 33.00N 97.00 E
Yushutun 21 Lb 47.06N 123.41 E
Yūsuf, Baḥr- 🔌 24 Dh 29.19N 30.50 E
Yusufeli 24 Ib 40.50N 41.33 E
Yutai (Guting) 28 Dg 35.00N 116.40 E
Yutian/Keriya 27 Dd 36.52N 81.42 E
Yutian 28 De 39.53N 117.45 E
Yuty 54 Ci 26.32 S 56.18W
Yuwan-Dake ▲ 29b Ba 28.18N 129.19 E
Yuxi 27 Hg 24.27N 102.34 E
Yuxian [China] 27 Jd 39.49N 114.35 E
Yuxian [China] 28 Be 38.03N 113.28 E
Yuxian [China] 28 Bg 34.09N 113.29 E
Yuxikou 28 Ei 31.35N 118.25 E
Yuyao 28 Fi 30.04N 121.10 E
Yuya-Wan 🔌 29 Bd 34.20N 130.55 E
Yuza 29 Fb 39.01N 139.53 E
Yuzawa [Jap.] 28 Pe 39.10N 140.30 E

Index Symbols

[1] Independent Nation	Historical or Cultural Region	Pass, Gap	Depression	Coast, Beach	Rock, Reef	Waterfall Rapids
[2] State, Region	Mount, Mountain	Plain, Lowland	Polder	Cliff	Islands, Archipelago	River Mouth, Estuary
[3] District, County	Volcano	Delta	Desert, Dunes	Peninsula	Rocks, Reefs	Lake
[4] Municipality	Hill	Salt Flat	Forest, Woods	Isthmus	Coral Reef	Salt Lake
[5] Colony, Dependency	Mountains, Mountain Range	Valley, Canyon	Heath, Steppe	Sandbank	Well, Spring	Intermittent Lake
■ Continent	Hills, Escarpment	Crater, Cave	Oasis	Island	Geyser	Reservoir
◆ Physical Region	Plateau, Upland	Karst Features	Cape, Point	Atoll	River, Stream	Swamp, Pond

Canal	Lagoon	Escarpment, Sea Scarp	Historic Site	Port
Glacier	Bank	Fracture	Ruins	Lighthouse
Ice Shelf, Pack Ice	Seamount	Trench, Abyss	Wall, Walls	Mine
Ocean	Tablemount	National Park, Reserve	Church, Abbey	Tunnel
Sea	Ridge	Point of Interest	Temple	Dam, Bridge
Gulf, Bay	Shelf	Recreation Site	Scientific Station	
Strait, Fjord	Basin	Cave, Cavern	Airport	